METRO-GOLDWYN-MAYER FILM CO.

CINEMA INTERNATIONAL CORPORATION

1982

INTERNATIONAL

MOTION PICTURE

ALMANAC

Editor: RICHARD GERTNER
Associate Editor: WILLIAM PAY

Quigley Publishing Company, Inc.
New York • **London**
(212) 247-3100 **(0268 42824)**

HOLLYWOOD **LONDON**

ervices
to the
international
motion picture
and television
industries

Foreword

The American motion picture industry remains
as hardy and volatile as ever. 1981 began badly;
grosses were down; then came the summer and
the industry not only recovered but set all-time
records in revenues and ticket sales. This 53rd
edition of the International Motion Picture
Almanac—with its thousands of listings extensively updated—is dedicated to the continued
resilience of a great industry.

—RICHARD GERTNER

INTERNATIONAL
MOTION PICTURE ALMANAC
For 1982
ISSN: 0074-7084
ISBN: 0-900610-26-3

PRINTED IN THE UNITED STATES OF AMERICA

Table of

Contents

ALPHABETICAL INDEX OF SUBJECTS

WARNER BROS.

A WARNER COMMUNICATIONS COMPANY

I

J

K

L

It's Better
At Burbank

M

United Artists

N

O

P

22A

T

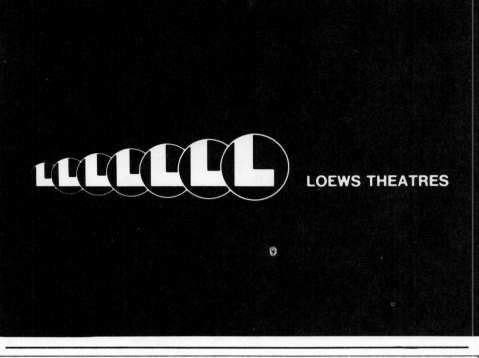

LOEWS THEATRES

UNITED ARTISTS THEATRE CIRCUIT, INC.

•

UNITED FILM
DISTRIBUTION COMPANY

•

ARISTA FILMS INC.

Film — TV & Video Sales Worldwide

**Serving Distributors throughout the World
with the finest Independent American
Motion Pictures.**

LOUIS GEORGE, *President*

NIKI GEORGE, *Treasurer*

MAX ROMAN,
Director/European Operations

IN LOS ANGELES
16027 Ventura Blvd.
Encino, California 91436
Telephone: (213) 907-7660
Cable "Airifilm"

IN LONDON
Berkeley Mansions, 64 Seymour Street
London W1 H 5AF
Telephone: (01) 723-8444
Telex: 912881 CWUK TX ROMAN

Y

Z

STATISTICS

Motion Picture Industry

EXHIBITION

THEATRE GROSSES, 1941–1980:

U.S. Box Office Receipts in Relation to Personal Consumption Expenditures

SOURCES: U.S. Dept. of Commerce, Office of Business Economics, National Income Division and the Motion Picture Association of America. (Latest revisions included.)

	1941	1942	1943	1944	1945	1946	1947	1948	1949	1950
Admissions to U.S. motion picture theatres (millions $)	809	1,022	1,275	1,341	1,450	1,692	1,594	1,506	1,451	1,376
Percentage of total U.S. personal consumption expenditures (%)	1.00	1.15	1.28	1.24	1.21	1.18	0.99	0.87	0.82	0.72
Percentage of total U.S. recreation expenditures (%)	19.08	21.85	25.70	24.73	23.62	19.81	17.23	15.54	14.50	12.34
Percentage of total U.S. spectator amusement expenditures (%)	81.31	84.88	87.63	85.80	84.60	81.90	79.58	78.52	77.51	77.26

	1951	1952	1953	1954	1955	1956	1957	1958	1959	1960
Admissions to U.S. motion picture theatres (millions $)	1,310	1,246	1,187	1,228	1,326	1,394	1,126	992	958	951
Percentage of total U.S. personal consumption expenditures (%)	0.64	0.58	0.52	0.52	0.52	0.52	0.40	0.34	0.31	0.29
Percentage of total U.S. recreation expenditures (%)	11.33	10.30	9.33	9.39	9.42	9.31	7.34	6.27	5.51	5.20
Percentage of total U.S. spectator amusement expenditures (%)	76.34	75.29	73.96	73.44	73.63	73.41	68.04	64.50	60.98	59.22

	1961	1962	1963	1964	1965	1966	1967	1968	1969	1970
Admissions to U.S. motion picture theatres (million $)	921	903	904	913	927	964	989	1,045	1,099	1,162
Percentage of total U.S. personal consumption expenditures (%)	0.27	0.25	0.24	0.23	0.21	0.23	0.22	0.20	0.19	0.19
Percentage of total U.S. recreation expenditures (%)	4.72	4.41	4.07	3.71	3.51	3.34	3.20	3.11	2.98	2.86
Percentage of total U.S. spectator amusement expenditures (%)	56.68	54.86	53.43	51.81	51.19	50.13	48.79	46.71	48.59	48.00

	1971	1972	1973	1974	1975	1976	1977	1978	1979	1980
Admissions to U.S. motion picture theatres (millions $)	1,170	1,644	1,524	1,909	2,115	2,036	2,372	2,643	2,821	2,748
Percentage of total U.S. personal consumption expenditures (%)	0.18	0.22	0.20	0.28	0.26	0.27	0.56	0.54	—	—
Percentage of total U.S. recreation expenditures (%)	2.74	3.03	3.50	4.10	3.84	4.12	—	—	—	—
Percentage of total U.S. spectator amusement expenditures (%)	47.74	47.01	50.77	53.99	51.81	53.36	34.8	35.8	—	—

NUMBER OF THEATRES:

There are about 16,965 theatres regularly exhibiting motion pictures in the U.S. according to Commerce Dept. estimates. Of these some 13,329 are indoor theatres and 3,636 drive-ins.

The average number of seats in indoor theatres in the U.S. today is 500, compared with about 750 in 1950. About 10 per cent of indoor theatres are multiplex units, and 80 per cent of these have two screens. The remaining 20 per cent range from three to seven screens per theatre. (Total number of screens is estimated at 17,590 in 1981.)

The total number of drive-ins in the U.S. decreased in the mid-1970s, due mainly to rising land costs and stricter zoning regulations. The average drive-in capacity is estimated at 550 cars. A list of drive-in theatres operating in the U.S., along with their owners and car capacities, appears in a special section in this book.

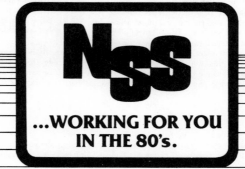

ATTENDANCE:

Total theatre admissions at U.S. theatres in 1980 were approximately 1,021,500,000, down from 1,120,900,000 in 1979.

A survey prepared by the Opinion Research Corporation of Princeton, New Jersey, for the Motion Picture Association of America in 1980 analyzed the motion picture audience according to age and frequency of attendance. It showed:

The 25 to 39 age group—currently at its highest attendance level in 11 years—is expented to provide 50,000,000 moviegoers by 1980, a jump of 10,000,000. That number will represent 36 per cent of the projected total of 140,000,000 moviegoers anticipated by the end of the 1980s decade.

The 25-to-39 moviegoers currently pay for 28 per cent of all admissions, third highest mark since 1969, and account for 34 per cent of all movie patrons, the largest such representation in 11 years.

The survey further forecasts that attendance during the 1990s will be significantly bolstered by continuing proliferation of "non-family households." With a 40 per cent increase in such households, the survey sees a beneficial fallout for exhibition, since 53 per cent of single people are classified as frequent or occasional moviegoers.

Double income families are viewed as another source of increasing theatre patronage since 42 percent of women are now in the labor force.

ADMISSION PRICES:

Average admission price in 1980 was $2.69, up from $2.517 for 1979.

A survey of the American Chamber of Commerce Researchers Association showed that New York City charges the highest average price for theatre tickets at downtown houses. This is $5.00, although in such cities as Hartford, Conn., Miami and Minneapolis, the figure is $4.00.

AUDIENCE PREFERENCES:

Some 60 per cent of U.S. moviegoers go to a neighborhood theatre. 65 per cent prefer single features to double bills. 80 per cent consider the subject matter of a film important in deciding what to see. 30 per cent consider the stars important in deciding what to see. 70 per cent prefer American films to foreign films. 83 per cent prefer color to black-and-white films. 39 per cent of moviegoers are influenced by movie critics. 47 per cent of drive-in admissions are from the suburban market. 87.5 per cent of moviegoers are aware of the MPAA ratings. 74 percent of the movie audience is under 30 years of age, and only 7 per cent is 50 and over.

Motion picture theatres do their biggest business on Saturdays with Friday second and Sunday third. Mondays through Thursdays are about equal. Best month of the year is July with August second and January third. The worst month is May.

HOW THE RECREATION DOLLAR IS DIVIDED:

The recreation dollar of the U.S. public is spent on a widely diversified front from books and magazines to pleasure aircraft. The following table shows the position of motion picture admissions in relation to this spending. (Data from the Department of Commerce).

	1976	1977	1978	1979
	Millions of Dollars			
Recreation	**72,499**	**79,782**	**89,313**	**99,051**
Books and maps	3,866	4,586	5,505	6,183
Magazines, newspapers, and sheet music	6,054	6,653	7,427	8,129
Nondurable toys and sport supplies	9,342	10,063	11,304	12,832
Wheel goods, durable toys, sports equipment, boats, and pleasure aircraft	10,769	12,171	13,905	15,699
Radio and television receivers, records, and musical instruments	15,631	16,960	18,654	20,324
Radio and television repair	2,415	2,668	2,925	3,253
Flowers, seeds, and potted plants	3,442	3,543	4,156	4,454
Admissions to specified spectator amusements	4,076	4,997	5,450	5,931
Motion picture theaters	1,742	2,376	2,442	2,562
Legitimate theaters and opera, and entertainments of nonprofit institutions (except athletic)	777	868	1,064	1,230
Spectator sports	1,557	1,753	1,944	2,139
Clubs and fraternal organizations except insurance	1,746	1,811	1,922	2,078
Commercial participant amusements	4,027	4,414	4,898	5,455
Parimutuel net receipts	1,669	1,712	1,722	1,762
Other	9,462	10,204	11,445	12,951

PRODUCTION

NUMBER OF FILMS:

Ten member companies of the Motion Picture Association of America distributed 171 features in the U.S. during 1980—137 new films and 34 reissues. In the decade of the 1960s the average number of new films per year was about 163; in the 1950s it was 373 and in the 1940s, 445. In addition, during 1980, some 13 independent distributing companies released 65 new pictures and 9 reissues.

PRODUCTION COSTS:

According to industry estimates, the average feature production cost of the major U.S. companies increased many times since the beginning of World War II. In 1941, average cost per feature was $400,000. In 1949, this had risen to more than $1,000,000. The average negative cost of theatrical film in 1972 was $1,890,000. In 1974 it was more than $2,500,000 and in 1976, $4,000,000. In 1978 it jumped to $5,000,000. In 1980 it was placed at $8,500,000 and 1981 at $10,000,000.

HOW THE PRODUCTION DOLLAR IS DIVIDED:

The average production budget is divided as follows:

Story Costs	5%
Production and direction costs	5
Sets and other physical properties	35
Stars and cast	20
Studio overhead	20
Income taxes	5
Contingency fund	10

EMPLOYMENT:

The average number of full and part-time employees in the industry in 1979 was 221,000, up from the 213,000 in 1978 and the 210,000 of 1977. The average number of full and part-time employees was 205,000 in 1976; 204,000 in 1975; 203,000 in 1974; 204,000 in 1973; 199,000 in 1972; 201,000 in 1971; 210,000 in 1970; 202,000 in 1969; 194,000 in 1968; 193,000 in 1967; 187,000 in 1966; 181,000 in 1965; 176,000 in 1964; 175,000 in 1963; 174,000 in 1962; 183,000 in 1961; 192,000 in 1960; and 184,000 in 1959.

Wages and salaries in 1929 were $308,000,000 and $339,000,000 in 1939. By 1942, payroll had risen to $410,000,000 and in 1943 to $459,000,000. In 1944, it was $509,000,000; in 1945, $552,000,000; in 1946, $679,000,000; in 1947, $649,000,000; in 1948, $655,000,000; in 1949, $659,000,000; in 1950, $651,000,000; in 1951, .$668,000,000; in 1952, $684,000,000; in 1953, $678,000,000; in 1956, $800,000,000; in 1957, $795,000,000; in 1958, $756,000,000; in 1959, $789,000,000; in 1960, $754,000,000; in 1961, $833,000,000; in 1962, $805,000,000; in 1963, $806,000,000; in 1964, $864,000,000; in 1965, $967,000,000; in 1966, $1,039,000,000; in 1967, $1,100,000,000; in 1968, $1,172,000,000; in 1969, $1,278,000,000; in 1970, $1,274,000,000; in 1971, $1,277,000,000; in 1972, $1,343,000,000; in 1973, $1,429,000,000; in 1974, $1,575,000,000; in 1975, $1,662,000,000, in 1976, $1,887,000,000; in 1977, $2,133,000,000; in 1978, $2,449,000,000; in 1979, $2,878,000,000.

INDUSTRY FILM RATING SYSTEM:

On November 1, 1968, member companies of the Motion Picture Association put into effect a voluntary film program will all pictures released after that date to carry one of four identifying rating symbols on all prints, trailers, advertising and at theatre box offices. The four categories were originally "G" for general audiences; "M" for adults and mature young people, on which parental discretion is advised; "R" for attendance restricted to persons over 16, unless accompanied by parent or adult guardian and "X" pictures to which no one under 16 is to be admitted. On March 1, 1970, the "M" rating was changed to "GP" (all ages admitted—parental guidance) and later this was changed to "PG." (For further details see text of the rules and regulations of the Classification and Rating Administration elsewhere in this book.)

THE GREAT HUNDRED

THIS is a list of outstanding motion pictures down through the years. It includes notable money-making attractions of their day as well as those films which have found a permanent place in motion picture tradition for creative reasons.

ALL ABOUT EVE (20th Century-Fox) Darryl F. Zanuck, prod.; Joseph L. Mankiewicz, dir.; Bette Davis, Anne Baxter, George Sanders; 1950.

ALL QUIET ON THE WESTERN FRONT (Universal) Lewis Milestone, dir.; Lew Ayres,; 1930.

AROUND THE WORLD IN 80 DAYS (United Artists) Michael Todd, prod.; Michael Anderson, dir.; David Niven, Cantinflas: 1956.

BEN-HUR (MGM) Sam Zimbalist, prod.; William Wyler, dir.; Charlton Heston, Jack Hawkins, Haya Harareet; Special (1959).

BEN HUR (MGM) Fred Niblo, dir.; Ramon Novarro, Francis X. Bushman, May McAvoy; 1927.

BEST YEARS OF OUR LIVES, THE (RKO Radio) Samuel Goldwyn, prod.; William Wyler, dir.; Myrna Loy, Fredric March, Dana Andrews; 1946.

BIG PARADE, THE (MGM) King Vidor, dir.; John Gilbert, Renee Adoree; 1927.

BIRTH OF A NATION, THE (D.W. Griffith) D.W. Griffith, prod. and dir.; Lillian Gish, Mae Marsh, Robert Harron, Wallace Reid, Henry B. Walthall, Miriam Cooper; 1915.

BRIDGE ON THE RIVER KWAI, THE (Columbia) Sam Spiegel, prod.; David Lean, dir.; William Holden, Alec Guinness; 1958.

BROKEN BLOSSOMS (D.W. Griffith) D.W. Griffith, prod. and dir.; Lillian Gish, Donald Crisp, Richard Barthelmess; 1919.

BUTCH CASSIDY AND THE SUNDANCE KID (20th Century-Fox) John Foreman, prod.; George Roy Hill, dir.; Paul Newman, Robert Redford, Katherine Ross; 1969.

CABARET (Allied Artists) Cy Feuer, prod.; Bob Fosse, dir.; Liza Minnelli, Michael York; 1972.

CABINET OF DR. CALIGARI, THE (UFA) Decla-Bioskop, prod.; Robert Wiene, dir.; Werner Krauss, Conrad Veidt; 1919.

CAMILLE (MGM) Irving G. Thalberg, prod.; George Cukor, dir.; Greta Garbo, Robert Taylor, Lionel Barrymore; 1937.

CASABLANCA (W.B.) Hal B. Wallis, prod.; Michael Curtiz, dir.; Humphrey Bogart, Ingrid Bergman, Paul Henreid; 1943.

CHILDREN OF PARADISE (Pathe) Marcel Carne, dir.; Alrletty, Jean-Louis Barrault, Pierre Brasseur; 1945.

CITIZEN KANE (RKO Radio) Orson Welles, prod. and dir.; Orson Welles, Joseph Cotton; 1941.

CITY LIGHTS (U.A.) Charles Chaplin, prod. and dir.; Charles Chaplin, Virginia Cherrill; 1931.

COVERED WAGON, THE (Famous Players-Lasky Corp.) James Cruze, dir.; J. Warren Kerrigan, Lois Wilson, Alan Hale; 1924.

DOCTOR ZHIVAGO (MGM) Carlo Ponti, prod.; David Lean, dir.; Omar Sharif, Julie Christie; 1966.

EXORCIST, THE (W.B.) William Peter Blatty, prod.; William Friedkin, dir.; Ellen Burstyn, Max von Sydow, Lee J. Cobb; 1973.

42nd STREET (W.B.) Lloyd Bacon, dir.; Ginger Rogers, Dick Powell, George Brent, Ruby Keeler; 1933.

FOUR HORSEMEN OF THE APOCALYPSE, THE (Metro) Rex Ingram, dir.; Rudolph Valentino, Alice Terry; 1921.

FRANKENSTEIN (Universal) James Whale, dir; Colin Clive, Boris Karloff, Mae Clarke; 1931.

GIANT (W.B.) Henry Ginsberg, George Stevens, prods.; George Stevens, dir.; Rock Hudson, Elizabeth Taylor, James Dean; 1956.

GODFATHER, THE (Paramount) Albert S. Ruddy, prod.; Francis Ford Coppola, dir.; Marlon Brando, Al Pacino, James Caan; 1972.

GOING MY WAY (Paramount) Leo McCarey, prod. and dir.; Bing Crosby, Barry Fitzgerald, Frank McHugh, Rise Stevens; 1944.

GONE WITH THE WIND (MGM) David O. Selznick, prod.; Victor Fleming and George Cukor (started), Sam Wood (finished), dir.; Clark Gable, Vivien Leigh. Leslie Howard, Olivia De Havilland; 1939.

GOODBYE MR. CHIPS (MGM) Victor Saville, prod.; Sam Wood, dir.; Robert Donat, Greer Garson; 1939.

GRADUATE, THE (Avco Embassy) Lawrence Turman, prod.; Mike Nichols, dir.; Dustin Hoffman, Anne Bancroft, Katharine Ross. 1967.

GRAND HOTEL (MGM) Edmund Goulding, dir.; Greta Garbo, John and Lionel Barrymore, Joan Crawford, Wallace Beery. 1932.

GRAPES OF WRATH, THE (20th-Century-Fox) Nunnally Johnson, assoc. prod.; John Ford, dir.; Henry Fonda, Jane Darwell; 1940.

GREAT EXPECTATIONS (Cineguild-Universal-International) Ronald Neame, prod.; David Lean, dir.; John Mills, Jean Simmons, Valerie Hobson; 1947.

GREAT TRAIN ROBBERY, THE (Edison) Edwin S. Porter, dir.; G. M. ("Bronco Billy") Anderson, George Barnes, Marie Murphy; 1903.

GREATEST SHOW ON EARTH, THE (Paramount) Cecil B. DeMille, prod. and dir.; Betty Hutton, Cornel Wilde, James Stewart; 1952.

HELL'S ANGELS (U.A.) Howard Hughes, prod.; Ben Lyon, Jean Harlow; 1930.

HENRY V (Two Cities-U.A.) Laurence Olivier, prod. and dir.; Laurence Olivier; 1945.

HOW THE WEST WAS WON (MGM-Cinerama) Bernard Smith, prod.; John Ford, Henry Hathaway, George Marshall, directors; James Stewart, Gregory Peck, 1962.

HUNCHBACK OF NOTRE DAME, THE (Universal) Wallace Worsley, dir.; Lon Chaney, Patsy Ruth Miller, Ernest Torrance; 1923.

INTOLERANCE (Griffith) D. W. Griffith, prod. and dir.; Lillian Gish, Mae Marsh; 1916.

IT HAPPENED ONE NIGHT (Columbia) Frank Capra, dir.; Clark Gable, Claudette Colbert; 1934.

JAWS (Universal) Richard D. Zanuck and David Brown, prods.; Steven Spielberg, dir.; Roy Scheider, Robert Shaw, Richard Dreyfuss; 1975.

JAZZ SINGER, THE (W.B.) Alan Crosland, dir.; Al Jolson, Eugenie Besserer, May McAvoy, Warner Oland; 1927.

KING KONG (RKO) Ernest B. Schoedsack, Merrian C. Cooper, prod. and dir.; Fay Wray, Robert Armstrong, Bruce Cabot; 1933.

KING OF KINGS, THE (Paramount) Cecil B. deMille, prod. and dir.; H. B. Warner, Rudolph Schildkraut, Joseph Schildkraut, May Robson; 1927.

L'AVVENTURA (Janus) Luciano Perugia, prod.; Michelangelo Antonioni, dir.; Gabriele Farzetti, Monica Vitti, Lea Massari; 1960.

LAST LAUGH, THE (Universal) UFA, prod.; F. W. Murnau, dir.; Emil Jannings; 1925.

LAST TANGO IN PARIS (U.A.) Alberto Grimaldi, prod.; Bernardo Bertolucci, dir.; Marlon Brando; 1973.

LAWRENCE OF ARABIA (Columbia) Sam Spiegel, prod.; David Lean, dir.; Peter O'Toole, Sir Alec Guinness, Anthony Quinn; 1962.

LOVE STORY (Paramount) Howard G. Minsky, prod.; Arthur Hiller, dir.; Ali MacGraw, Ryan O'Neal, Ray Milland; 1971.

LOST WEEKEND (Paramount) Charles Brackett, prod.; Billy Wilder, dir.; Ray Milland, Jane Wyman, Howard Da Silva; 1945.

A MAN FOR ALL SEASONS (Columbia) Fred Zinnemann, prod. and dir.; Paul Scofield, Wendy Hiller, Orson Welles; 1966.

MERRY WIDOW, THE (MGM) Erich Von Stroheim, dir.; Mae Murray. John Gilbert; 1925.

MR. SMITH GOES TO WASHINGTON (Columbia) Frank Capra, prod. and dir.; James Stewart, Jean Arthur, Claude Rains; 1939.

MRS. MINIVER (MGM) Sidney Franklin, prod.; William Wyler, dir.; Greer Garson, Walter Pidgeon; 1942.

MUTINY ON THE BOUNTY (MGM) Irving Thalberg, prod.; Frank Lloyd, dir.; Charles Laughton, Clark Gable; 1935.

MY FAIR LADY (W.B.) Jack L. Warner, prod.; George Cukor, dir.; Rex Harrison, Audrey Hepburn; 1964.

NANOOK OF THE NORTH (Revillon Freres-Pathe Exchange, Inc.) Produced by Robert Flaherty; 1922.

NAUGHTY MARIETTA (MGM) Hunt Stomberg, prod.; W. S. Van Dyke, dir.; Jeanette MacDonald, Nelson Eddy; 1935.

NIGHT AT THE OPERA, A (MGM) Irving G. Thalberg, prod.; Sam Wood, dir.; Groucho, Harpo & Chico Marx, Margaret Dumont; 1935.

OPEN CITY (Excelsa) Roberto Rossellini, prod. and dir.; Aldo Fabrizzi, Anna Magnani; 1945.

PHANTOM OF THE OPERA, THE (Universal) Rupert Julian, dir.; Lon Chaney, Mary Philbin; 1925.

PLACE IN THE SUN, A (Paramount) George Stevens, prod. and dir.; Montgomery Clift, Elizabeth Taylor, Shelley Winters; 1951.

PRIVATE LIFE OF HENRY VIII, THE (U.A.) London Films, prod.; Alexander Korda, dir.; Charles Laughton, Robert Donat; 1933.

QUEEN ELIZABETH (Famous Players) Louis Mercanton, Sarah Bernhardt, Lou Tellegen; 1912.

QUO VADIS? (Kleine) Cines, prod.; Enrico Guazzani, dir.; G. Serena, Amleto Novelli; 1912.

REBECCA (U.A.) David O. Selznick, prod.; Alfred Hitchcock, dir.; Laurence Olivier, Joan Fontaine; 1940.

RED SHOES, THE (J. Arthur Rank-Eagle Lion) Michael Powell and Emeric Pressburger, prod. and dir.; Anton Walbrook, Moira Shearer; 1949.

ROBE, THE (20th Century-Fox) Frank Ross, prod; Henry Koster, dir.; Jean Simmons, Richard Burton, Victor Mature; 1953.

SAN FRANCISCO (MGM) W. S. Van Dyke, prod. and dir.; Clark Gable, Spencer Tracy, Jeanette MacDonald; 1936.

SCARFACE (U.A.) Howard Hughes, prod.; Howard Hawks, dir.; Paul Muni, Ann Dvorak, George Raft; 1932.

SERGEANT YORK (B.) Jesse L. Lasky and Hal B. Wallis, prod.; Howard Hawks, dir.; Gary Cooper, Walter Brennan; 1941.

SHEIK, THE (Paramount) George Melford, prod. and dir.; Rudolph Valentino, Agnes Ayres; 1921.

SHOULDER ARMS (First National) Charles Chaplin, prod.; Charles Chaplin, Syd Chaplin, Edna Purviance; 1918.

SHOW BOAT (MGM) Arthur Freed, prod.; Ben Feiner, Jr., assoc. prod.; George Sidney, dir.; Kathryn Grayson, Ava Gardner, Howard Keel, Joe E. Brown; 1951.

SINGIN' IN THE RAIN (MGM) Arthur Freed, prod.; Gene Kelly and Stanley Donen, dir.; Gene Kelly, Debbie Reynolds; 1952.

SNOW WHITE AND THE SEVEN DWARFS (RKO) Walt Disney, prod.; David Hand, supervising dir.; 1937.

SOUND OF MUSIC, THE (Todd-AO-Fox) Robert Wise, prod. and dir.; Julie Andrews, Christopher Plummer; 1965.

SOUTH PACIFIC (Todd-AO-Fox) Buddy Adler, prod.; Joshua Logan, dir.; Rossano Brazzi, Mitzi Gaynor; 1958.

SPOILERS, THE (Selig) Col. Wm. N. Selig, prod.; Colin Campbell, dir.; William Farnum, Tom Santschi; 1914.

STAGECOACH (U.A.) Walter Wanger, prod.; John Ford, dir.; Claire Trevor, John Wayne; 1939.

STAR WARS (20th Century-Fox) Gary Kurtz, prod.; George Lucas, dir.; Alec Guinness, Carrie Fisher; 1977.

STELLA DALLAS (U.A.) Samuel Goldwyn, prod.; Henry King, dir.; Ronald Colman, Belle Bennett; 1925.

STING, THE (Universal) Tony Bill and Michael and Julia Phillips, prod.; George Roy Hill, dir.; Paul Newman, Robert Redford; 1973.

STORY OF LOUIS PASTEUR, THE (W.B.) William Dieterle, dir.; Paul Muni, Josephine Hutchinson, Anita Louise; 1935.

SUNRISE (Fox) Winfield Sheehan, prod.; F. W. Murnau, dir.; George O'Brien, Janet Gaynor; 1927.

SUNSET BOULEVARD (Paramount) Billy Wilder, dir.; Gloria Swanson, William Holden, Erich Von Stroheim; 1950.

TEN COMMANDMENTS, THE (DeMille-Paramount) Cecil B. DeMille, prod. and dir.; Charlton Heston, Anne Baxter, Yul Brynner; 1956.

THIS IS CINERAMA (Cinerama) Lowell Thomas, Merian C. Cooper, prod.; 1952.

TILLIE'S PUNCTURED ROMANCE (Alco) Keystone prod.; Mack Sennett, dir.; Marie Dressler, Fatty Arbuckle, Charles Chaplin, Mabel Normand; 1914.

TOL'ABLE DAVID (First National) Inspiration pictures, Inc., prod.; Henry King, dir.; Richard Barthelmess; 1921.

TOM JONES (U.A.) Tony Richardson, prod. and dir.; Albert Finney, Hugh Griffith, Susannah York; 1963.

TOP HAT (RKO Radio) Pandro S. Berman, prod.; Mark Sandrich, dir.; Fred Astaire, Ginger Rogers; 1935.

2001: A SPACE ODYSSEY (MGM) Stanley Kubrick, prod. and dir.; Keir Dullea, Gary Lockwood, William Sylvester; 1968.

VARIETY (Paramount) UFA, prod.; E. A. DuPont, dir.; Emil Jannings, Lya de Putti; 1926.

WAY DOWN EAST (U.A.) D. W. Griffith, prod. and dir.; Richard Barthelmess, Lillian Gish; 1920.

WEST SIDE STORY (U.A.) Robert Wise prod.; Robert Wise and Jerome Robbins, directors; Natalie Wood, Richard Beymer; 1961.

WHAT PRICE GLORY? (Fox) Raoul Walsh, dir.; Victor McLaglen, Edmund Lowe; 1926.

WUTHERING HEIGHTS (U.A.) Samuel Goldwyn, prod.; William Wyler, dir.; Merle Oberon, Laurence Olivier; 1939.

THE HISTORY OF OSCAR

OSCAR, the golden symbol of fame conferred by the Academy of Motion Picture Arts and Sciences, in its present form, has reached full maturity. Long since his first appearance on the scene of glory in Hollywood, his birth, origins and history have become confused in tradition and much elaborated myth.

Oft beset by perplexed inquiries in the years between, Motion Picture Almanac set about research for the purpose of presenting for the industry the truth about Oscar.

Oscar was nameless when he came into the world as an award symbol the year the Academy was founded, 1927, and he remained so for four years, known then just as "the statuette."

The idea for a statuette originated at a meeting of the first board of governors of the Academy. Cedric Gibbons, then executive art director for Metro-Goldwyn-Mayer, after hearing discussions of certificates, scrolls, medals and plaques, urged that the awards should be represented by a figure of dignity and individual character which recipients would be proud to display. While he talked he sketched a figure and design. It was Oscar's first picture. The drawing was adopted and sent for execution in the round to George Stanley, a Los Angeles sculptor. From his hands came the Oscar who has been growing in fame ever since.

THE golden figure was still without a name that day in 1931 when Mrs. Margaret Herrick, former executive secretary of the Academy, reported for her first day's work as librarian. A copy of the statuette stood on an executive's desk and she was formally introduced to it as the foremost member of the organization.

She regarded it a moment. "He reminds me," she observed, "of my Uncle Oscar."

Nearby sat a newspaper columnist and the next day his syndicated copy contained the line "Employees have affectionately dubbed their famous statuette 'Oscar'." From that day on he has been Oscar.

The Academy's Oscar is ten inches high, weighs seven pounds, his insides being bronze and his exterior gold plate. He costs about a hundred dollars.

ON MAY 6, 1929, first year awards were presented—for achievements of 1927–28—eleven "Oscars" were presented by the Academy. Since that day the number of statuettes given the annual "choice few" has increased. During the intervening years a total of several hundred golden knights have gone to persons contributing "best achievements" in motion pictures.

The trophy is fully protected by copyright and is produced by only one manufacturer, licensed by the Academy. Use of the statuette or reproduction of it in any manner is prohibited, without written permission of the Academy.

ACADEMY AWARD WINNERS OF 1980

The Academy of Motion Picture Arts and Sciences was founded in May, 1927, in Hollywood with 36 charter members, including production executives and cinema luminaries. Its aims included a determination to raise the standards of production educationally, culturally and scientifically.

In the years since its inception this non-subsidized organization has grown to embrace 12 principal branches of film making. Through these branches almost 2,000 active motion picture members have been gathered from the acting field, the cinematograph group, the executive branch, the film editors division, the music group, the writers, the directors, the sound division, the art directors, the short subject and the public relations fields.

Voting for the Academy Awards of Merit is done by the entire membership with each of the 12 branches creating its own procedure and conducting individual nominations in the manner best suited to its special requirements. The final nominating ballot from each branch is limited to a maximum of five entrants. After nominations have been closed the Academy holds screenings of the nominated films in order that eligible voters can review them. A final ballot is then prepared and sent to the Academy membership. These ballots are marked and returned to Price Waterhouse and Company, certified public accountants, who prepare the tabulation. The names of the winners are announced only at the annual Academy Awards presentation ceremonies.

Awards of the Academy of Motion Picture Arts and Sciences for 1980, made March 30, 1981, were as follows:

BEST PICTURE
"Ordinary People," A Wildwood Enterprises Production, Paramount. Ronald L. Schwary, producer.

BEST FOREIGN-LANGUAGE FILM
"Moscow Does Not Believe In Tears," A Mosfilm Studio Production (U.S.S.R.)

BEST DIRECTOR
Robert Redford for "Ordinary People."

BEST ACTOR
Robert De Niro in "Raging Bull," a Robert Chartoff-Irwin Winkler production. United Artists.

BEST ACTRESS
Sissy Spacek in "Coal Miner's Daughter," a Bernard Schwartz-Universal Pictures production. Universal.

BEST SUPPORTING ACTOR
Timothy Hutton in "Ordinary People."

BEST SUPPORTING ACTRESS
Mary Steenburgen in "Melvin and Howard," a Linson-Phillips-Demme-Universal Pictures production, Universal.

BEST CINEMATOGRAPHY
Geoffrey Unsworth (deceased) and Ghislain Cloquet for "Tess," a Renn-Burrill coproduction, with the participation of the Societe Francaise de Production (S.F.F.), Columbia.

BEST FILM EDITING
Thelma Schoonmaker for "Raging Bull."

BEST ART DIRECTION
Pierre Guffroy, production designer, Jack Stephens, art director, for "Tess."

BEST COSTUME DESIGN
Anthony Powell for "Tess."

BEST DOCUMENTARY FEATURE
"From Mao To Mozart: Isaac Stern In China," The Hopewell Foundation. Murray Lerner, producer.

BEST DOCUMENTARY SHORT SUBJECT
"Karl Hess: Toward Liberty," Halle/Ladue Inc., Peter W. Ladue, Roland Halle, producers.

BEST ORIGINAL SCORE
Michael Gore for "Fame," a Metro-Goldwyn-Mayer production. MGM.

BEST ORIGINAL SONG
"Fame," from "Fame." Music by Michael Gore; lyrics by Dean Pitchford.

BEST SHORT SUBJECTS—ANIMATED
"The Fly," Pannonia Film, Budapest. Ference Rofusz, producer.

BEST SHORT SUBJECTS—LIVE
"The Dollar Bottom," Rocking Horse Films Ltd., Paramount. Lloyd Phillips, producer.

BEST SOUND
"The Empire Strikes Back," a Lucasfilm Ltd. production, 20th Century-Fox. Bill Varney, Steve Maslow, Gregg Landaker, Peter Sutton.

BEST SCREENPLAY WRITTEN DIRECTLY FOR THE SCREEN
"Melvin and Howard," screenplay by Bo Goldman.

BEST SCREENPLAY BASED ON MATERIAL FROM ANOTHER MEDIUM
"Ordinary People," screenplay by Alvin Sargent, based on a novel by Judith Guest.

HONORARY AWARDS
HENRY FONDA "the consummate actor, in recognition of his brilliant accomplishments and enduring contribution to the art of motion pictures."

SCIENTIFIC OR TECHNICAL AWARDS

ACADEMY AWARD OF MERIT (STATUETTE)
Lindwood G. Dunn, Cecil D. Love, Edward Furter and Acme Tool and Manufacturing Co., for concept, engineering and development of Acme-Dunn Optical Printer for motion picture special effects.

SCIENTIFIC & ENGINEERING AWARD (PLAQUES)
Jean-Marie Lavalou, Alain Masseron and David Samuelson of Samuelson Alga Cinema S.A. and Samuelson Film Service Ltd., for engineering and development of the Louma Camera Crane and remote-control system for motion picture production.

Edward B. Krause of Filmline Corp. for the engineering and manufacture of the microdemand drive for continuous motion picture film processors.

Ross Taylor for concept and development of a system of air guns for propelling objects used in special effects motion picture production.

Bernhard Kuhl and Werner Block of OSRAM GmbH, for progressive engineering and manufacture of the OSRAM HMI light source for motion picture color photography.

David A. Grafton for optical design and engineering of a telecentric anamorphic lens for motion picture optical effects prints.

TECHNICAL ACHIEVEMENT AWARD (CERTIFICATE)
Carter Equipment Co. for development of a continuous contact, total immersion, additive color motion picture printer.

Hollywood Film Co. for development of a continuous contact, total immersion, additive color motion picture printer.

Andre DeBrie S.A. for development of a continuous contact, total immersion, additive color motion picture printer.

Charles Vaughn and Eugene Nottingham of Cinetron Computer Systems Inc., for development of a versatile general purpose computer system for animation and optical effects motion picture photography.

John W. Lang, Walter Hrastnik and Charles J. Watson of Bell & Howell Co. for development and manufacture of a modular continuous contact motion picture film printer.

Worth Biard of La Vezzi Machine Works for the advanced design and manufacture of a film sprocket for motion picture projectors.

Peter A. Regla and Dan Slater of Elicon, for development of a follow focus system for motion picture optical printers and animation stands.

MEDAL OF COMMENDATION
Fred Hynes.

SPECIAL ACHIEVEMENT AWARD FOR VISUAL EFFECTS
"The Empire Strikes Back," Brian Johnson, Richard Edlund, Dennis Muren, Bruce Nicholson.

PRINCIPAL WINNERS OF ACADEMY AWARDS, 1928—79

Productions, players and directors named for superior merit by the Academy of Motion Picture Arts and Sciences, from inception of the awards through 1979.

Feature Pictures—Wings, *Best Production*, Paramount, 1927–28; Sunrise, *artistic quality of production*, Fox, 1927–28; The Broadway Melody, MGM, 1928–29; All Quiet on the Western Front, Universal, 1929–30; Cimarron, RKO, 1930–31; Grand Hotel, MGM, 1931–32; Cavalcade, Fox, 1932–33; It Happened One Night, Columbia, 1934; Mutiny on the Bounty, MGM, 1935; The Great Ziegfeld, MGM, 1936; The Life of Emile Zola, Warner Bros., 1937; You Can't Take It With You, Columbia, 1938; Gone With The Wind, Selznick-MGM, Rebecca, Selznick-United Artists, 1940; How Green Was My Valley, 20th Century-Fox, 1941; Mrs. Miniver, MGM, 1942; Casablanca, Warner Bros., 1943; Going My Way, Paramount, 1944; The Lost Weekend, Paramount, 1945; The Best Years of Our Lives, Goldwyn-RKO, 1946; Gentleman's Agreement, 20th Century-Fox, 1947; Hamlet, J. Arthur Rank-Two Cities-Universal-International (British), 1948; All the King's Men, Robert Rossen-Columbia, 1949; All About Eve, 20th Century-Fox, 1950; An American In Paris, MGM, 1951; The Greatest Show on Earth, Cecil B. DeMille-Paramount, 1952; From Here to Eternity, Columbia, 1953; On the Waterfront, Horizon Picture-Columbia, 1954; Marty, Hecht-Lancaster-United Artists, 1955; Around the World in 80 Days, Michael Todd, United Artists, 1956; The Bridge on the River Kwai, Sam Spiegel, Columbia, 1957; Gigi, Arthur Freed, MGM, 1958; Ben-Hur, Sam Zimbalist, MGM, 1959; The Apartment, Billy Wilder, United Artists, 1960; West Side Story, Robert Wise, United Artists, 1961; Laurence of Arabia, Sam Spiegel, Columbia, 1962; Tom Jones, Tony Richardson United Artists-Lopert, 1963; My Fair Lady, Jack L. Warner, Warner Bros., 1964; The Sound of Music, Robert Wise, 20th Century-Fox, 1965; A Man For All Seasons, Fred Zinnemann, Columbia, 1966; In the Heat of the Night, United Artists, 1967; Oliver, Columbia, 1968; Midnight Cowboy, United Artists, 1969; Patton, 20th Century-Fox, 1970; The French Connection, 20th Century-Fox, 1971; The Godfather, Paramount, 1972; The Sting, Universal, 1973; The Godfather, Part II, Paramount, 1974; One Flew Over the Cuckoo's Nest, United Artists, 1975; Rocky, United Artists, 1976; Annie Hall, United Artists, 1977; The Deer Hunter, Universal, 1977; Kramer vs. Kramer, Columbia, 1979.

Best Performance by an Actor—Emil Jannings, The Way of All Flesh and The Last Command, Paramount, 1927–28; Warner Baxter, In Old Arizona, Fox, 1928–29; George Arliss, Disraeli, Warner Bros., 1929–30; Lionel Barrymore, A Free Soul, MGM, 1930–31; Fredric March, Dr. Jekyll and Mr. Hyde, Paramount and Wallace Beery, The Champ, MGM, 1931–32; Charles Laughton, The Private Life of Henry VIII, London Films-United Artists (British), 1932–33; Clark Gable, It Happened One Night, Columbia, 1934; Victor McLaglen, The Informer, RKO, 1935; Paul Muni, The Story of Louis Pasteur, Warner Bros., 1936; Spencer Tracy, Captains Courageous, MGM, 1937; Spencer Tracy, Boys Town, MGM, 1938; Robert Donat, Goodbye, Mr. Chips, MGM (British), 1939; James Stewart, The Philadelphia Story, MGM, 1940; Gary Cooper, Sergeant York, Warner Bros., 1941; James Cagney, Yankee Doodle Dandy, Warner Bros., 1942; Paul Lukas, Watch on the Rhine, Warner Bros., 1943; Bing Crosby, Going My Way, Paramount, 1944; Ray Milland, The Lost Weekend, Paramount, 1945; Fredric March, The Best Years of Our Lives, Goldwyn-RKO, 1946; Ronald Colman, A Double Life, Kanin Productions-U-1, 1947; Laurence Olivier, Hamlet, J. Arthur Rank-Two Cities-Universal-International (British), 1948; Broderick Crawford, All the King's Men, Robert Rossen-Columbia, 1949; Jose Ferrer, Cyrano de Bergerac, Stanley Kramer-United Artists, 1950; Humphrey Bogart, The African Queen, Horizon Enterprises-United Artists, 1951; Gary Cooper, High Noon, Stanley Kramer Productions-United Artists, 1952; William Holden, Stalag 17, Paramount, 1953; Marlon Brando, On the Waterfront, Horizon Pictures-Columbia, 1954; Ernest Borgnine, Marty, Hecht-Lancaster-United Artists, 1955; Yul Brynner, The King and I, 20th Century-Fox, 1956; Alec Guinness, The Bridge on the River Kwai, Columbia, 1957; David Niven, Separate Tables, UA, 1958; Charlton Heston, Ben-Hur, MGM, 1959; Burt Lancaster, Elmer Gantry, United Artists, 1960; Maximillian Schell, Judgment at Nuremberg, United Artists, 1961; Gregory Peck, To Kill A Mockingbird, Universal-International, 1962; Sidney Poitier, Lilies of the Field, United Artists, 1963; Rex Harrison, My Fair Lady, Warner Bros., 1964; Lee Marvin, Cat Ballou, Columbia, 1965; Paul Scofield, A Man For

All Seasons, Columbia, 1966; Rod Steiger, In the Heat of the Night, United Artists, 1967; Cliff Robertson, Charly, Cinerama, 1968; John Wayne, True Grit, Paramount, 1969; George C. Scott, Patton, 20th Century-Fox, 1970; Gene Hackman, The French Connection, 20th Century-Fox, 1971; Marlon Brando, The Godfather, Paramount, 1972; Jack Lemmon, Save The Tiger, Paramount, 1973; Art Carney, Harry and Tonto, 20th Century-Fox, 1974; Jack Nicholson, One Flew Over the Cuckoo's Nest, United Artists, 1975; Peter Finch, Network, MGM, 1976; Richard Dreyfuss, The Goodbye Girl, Warner Bros/MGM, 1977; Jon Voight, Coming Home, 1978; Dustin Hoffman, Kramer vs. Kramer, 1979.

Best Performance by an Actress—Janet Gaynor, Seventh Heaven, Street Angel and Sunrise, Fox, 1927–28; Mary Pickford, Coquette, United Artists, 1928–29; Norma Shearer, The Divorcee, MGM, 1929–30; Marie Dressler, Min and Bill, MGM, 1930–31; Helen Hayes, The Sin of Madelon Claudet, MGM, 1931–32; Katharine Hepburn, Morning Glory, RKO, 1932–33; Claudette Colbert, It Happened One Night, Columbia, 1934; Bette Davis, Dangerous, Warner Bros., 1935; Luise Rainer, The Great Ziegfeld, MGM, 1936; Luise Rainer, The Good Earth, MGM, 1937; Bette Davis, Jezebel, Warner Bros., 1938; Vivien Leigh, Gone With the Wind, Selznick-MGM, 1939; Ginger Rogers, Kitty Foyle, RKO, 1940; Joan Fontaine, Suspicion, RKO, 1941; Greer Garson, Mrs. Miniver, MGM, 1942; Jennifer Jones, The Song of Bernadette, 20th Century-Fox, 1943; Ingrid Bergman, Gaslight, MGM, 1944; Joan Crawford, Mildred Pierce, Warner Bros., 1945; Olivia deHavilland, To Each His Own, Paramount, 1946; Loretta Young, The Farmer's Daughter, RKO, 1947; Jane Wyman, Johnny Belinda, Warner Bros., 1948; Olivia deHavilland, The Heiress, Paramount, 1949; Judy Holiday, Born Yesterday, Columbia, 1950; Vivien Leigh, A Streetcar Named Desire, Charles K. Feldman-Warner Bros., 1951; Shirley Booth, Come Back Little Sheba, Hal Wallis-Paramount, 1952; Audrey Hepburn, Roman Holiday, Paramount, 1953; Grace Kelly, The Country Girl, Paramount, 1954; Anna Magnani, The Rose Tattoo, Hal Wallis-Paramount, 1955; Ingrid Bergman, Anastasia, 20th Century-Fox, 1956; Joanne Woodward, The Three Faces of Eve, 20th Century-Fox, 1957; Susan Hayward, I Want to Live! UA, 1958; Simone Signoret, Room At The Top, Cont. Distr., 1959; Elizabeth Taylor, Butterfield 8, M-G-M, 1960; Sophia Loren, Two Women, Embassy Pictures, 1961; Anne Bancroft, The Miracle Worker, United Artists, 1962; Patricia Neal, Hud, Paramount, 1963; Julie Andrews, Mary Poppins, Buena Vista, 1964; Julie Christie, Darling, Embassy, 1965; Elizabeth Taylor, Who's Afraid of Virginia Woolf?, Warner Bros.-Seven Arts, 1966; Katharine Hepburn, Guess Who's Coming to Dinner, Columbia, 1967; Tie Between Katharine Hepburn, The Lion in Winter, Avco Embassy and Barbra Streisand, Funny Girl, Columbia, 1968; Maggie Smith, The Prime of Miss Jean Brodie, 20th Century-Fox, 1969; Glenda Jackson, Women In Love, United Artists, 1970; Jane Fonda, Klute, Warner Bros., 1971; Liza Minnelli, Cabaret, Allied Artists, 1972; Glenda Jackson, A Touch of Class, Avco-Embassy, 1973; Ellen Burstyn, Alice Doesn't Live Here Anymore, Warner-Bros., 1974; Louise Fletcher, One Flew Over the Cuckoo's Nest, United Artists, 1975; Faye Dunaway, Network, MGM, 1976; Diane Keaton, Annie Hall, United Artists, 1977; Jane Fonda, Coming Home, 1978; Sally Field, Norma Rae, 1979.

Best Performance by an Actor in a Supporting Role—Walter Brennan, Come and Get It, Goldwyn-United Artists, 1936; Joseph Schildkraut, the Life of Emile Zola, Warner Bros., 1937; Walter Brennan, Kentucky, 20th Century-Fox, 1938; Thomas Mitchell, Stagecoach, Wanger-United Artists, 1939; Walter Brennan, The Westerner, Goldwyn-United Artists, 1940; Donald Crisp, How Green Was My Valley, 20th Century-Fox, 1941; Van Heflin, Johnny Eager, MGM, 1942; Charles Coburn, The More the Merrier, Columbia, 1943; Barry Fitzgerald, Going My Way, Paramount, 1944; James Dunn, A Tree Grows in Brooklyn, 20th Century-Fox, 1945; Harold Russell, The Best Years of Our Lives, Goldwyn-RKO, 1946; Edmund Gwenn, Miracle on 34th Street, 20th Century-Fox, 1947; Walter Huston, Treasure of Sierra Madre, Warner Bros., 1948; Dean Jagger, Twelve O'Clock High, 20th Century-Fox, 1949; George Sanders, All About Eve, 20th Century-Fox, 1950; Karl Malden, A Streetcar Named Desire, Charles K. Feldman-Warner Bros., 1951; Anthony Quinn, Viva Zapata, 20th Century-Fox, 1952; Frank Sinatra, From Here to Eternity, Columbia, 1953; Edmond O'Brien, The Barefoot Contessa, Figaro-United Artists, 1954; Jack Lemmon, Mister Roberts, Orange Production-Warner Bros., 1955; Anthony Quinn, Lust for Life, MGM, 1956; Red Buttons, Sayonara, Warner Bros., 1957; Burl Ives, The Big Country, UA, 1958; Hugh Griffith, Ben-Hur, MGM, 1959; Peter Ustinov, Spartacus, Universal, 1960; George Chakiris, West Side Story, United Artists, 1961; Ed Begley, Sweet Bird of Youth, MGM, 1962; Melvyn Douglas, Hud, Paramount, 1963; Peter Ustinov, Topkapi, United Artists, 1964; Martin Balsam, A Thousand Clowns, United Artists, 1965; Walter Matthau, The Fortune Cookie, United Artists, 1966; George Kennedy, Cool Hand Luke, Warner Bros.-Seven Arts, 1967; Jack Albertson, The Subject Was Roses, MGM, 1968; Gig Young, They Shoot Horses, Don't They, Cinerama, 1969; John Mills, Ryan's Daughter, MGM 1970; Ben Johnson, The Last Picture Show, Columbia, 1971; Joel Grey, Cabaret, Allied Artists, 1972; John Houseman, The Paper

Chase, 20th-Fox, 1973; Robert de Niro, The Godfather, Part II, Paramount, 1974; George Burns, The Sunshine Boys, MGM, 1975; Jason Robards, All The President's Men, Warner Bros., 1976.; Jason Robards, Julia, 20th Century-Fox, 1977; Christopher Walken, The Deer Hunter, 1978; Melvyn Douglas, Being There, 1979.

Best Performance by an Actress in a Supporting Role—Gale Sondergaard, Anthony Adverse, Warner Bros., 1936; Alice Brady, In Old Chicago, 20th Century-Fox, 1937; Fay Bainter, Jezebel, Warner Bros., 1938; Hattie McDaniel, Gone With the Wind, Selznick-MGM, 1939; Jane Darwell, The Grapes of Wrath, 20th Century-Fox, 1940; Mary Astor, The Great Lie, Warner Bros., 1941; Teresa Wright, Mrs. Miniver, MGM, 1942; Katina Paxinou, For Whom the Bell Tolls, Paramount, 1943; Ethel Barrymore, None But the Lonely Heart, RKO, 1944; Anne Revere, National Velvet, MGM, 1945; Anne Baxter, The Razor's Edge, 20th Century-Fox, 1946; Celeste Holm, Gentleman's Agreement, 20th Century-Fox, 1947; Claire Trevor, Key Largo, Warner Bros., 1948; Mercedes McCambridge, All the King's Men, Robert Rossen-Columbia, 1949; Josephine Hull, Harvey, Universal-International, 1950; Kim Hunter, A Streetcar Named Desire, Charles K. Feldman-Warner Bros., 1951; Gloria Grahame, The Bad and the Beautiful, MGM, 1952; Donna Reed, From Here to Eternity, Columbia, 1953; Eva Marie Saint, On the Waterfront, Horizon Pictures-Columbia, 1954; Jo Van Fleet, East of Eden, Warner Bros., 1955; Dorothy Malone, Written on the Wind, Universal-International, 1956; Miyoshi Umeki, Sayonara, Warner Bros., 1957; Wendy Hiller, Separate Tables, UA, 1958; Shelley Winters, The Diary of Anne Frank, Fox, 1959; Shirley Jones, Elmer Gantry, United Artists, 1960; Rita Moreno, West Side Story, United Artists, 1961; Patty Duke, The Miracle Worker, United Artists, 1962; Margaret Rutherford, The V.I.P.'s MGM, 1963; Lila Kedrova, Zorba the Greek, International Classics, 1964; Shelley Winters, A Patch of Blue, MGM, 1965; Sandy Dennis, Who's Afraid of Virginia Woolf?, Warner Bros.-Seven Arts, 1966; Estelle Parsons, Bonnie and Clyde, Warner Bros.-Seven Arts, 1967; Ruth Gordon, Rosemary's Baby, Paramount, 1968; Goldie Hawn, Cactus Flower, Columbia, 1969; Helen Hayes, Airport, Universal, 1970; Cloris Leachman, The Last Picture Show, Columbia, 1971; Eileen Heckart, Butterflies Are Free, Columbia, 1972; Tatum O'Neal, Paper Moon, Paramount, 1973; Ingrid Bergman, Murder on the Orient Express, Paramount, 1974; Lee Grant, Shampoo, Columbia, 1975; Beatric Straight, Network, MGM, 1976; Vanessa Redgrave, Julia, 20th Century-Fox, 1977; Maggie Smith, California Suite, 1978; Meryl Streep, Kramer vs. Kramer, 1979.

Best Achievement in Directing—Frank Borzage, Seventh Heaven, Fox, 1927–28; Lewis Milestone, comedy direction, Two Arabian Knights, United Artists, 1927–28; Frank Lloyd, The Divine Lady, First National, 1928–29; Lewis Milestone, All Quiet on the Western Front, Universal, 1929–30; Norman Taurog, Skippy, Paramount, 1930–31; Frank Borzage, Bad Girl, Fox, 1931–32; Frank Lloyd, Cavalcade, Fox, 1932–33; Frank Capra, It Happened One Night, Columbia, 1934; John Ford, The Informer, RKO, 1935; Frank Capra, Mr. Deeds Goes to Town, Columbia, 1936; Leo McCarey, The Awful Truth, Columbia, 1937; Frank Capra, You Can't Take It With You, Columbia, 1938; Victor Fleming, Gone With the Wind, Selznick-MGM, 1939; John Ford, The Grapes of Wrath, 20th Century-Fox, 1940; John Ford, How Green Was My Valley, 20th Century-Fox, 1941; William Wyler, Mrs. Miniver, MGM, 1942; Michael Curtiz, Casablanca, Warner Bros., 1943; Leo McCarey, Going My Way, Paramount, 1944; Billy Wilder, The Lost Weekend, Paramount, 1945; William Wyler, The Best Years of Our Lives, Goldwyn-RKO, 1946; Elia Kazan, Gentleman's Agreement, 20th Century-Fox, 1947; John Huston, Treasure of Sierra Madre, Warner Bros., 1948; Joseph L. Mankiewicz, A Letter to Three Wives, 20th Century-Fox, 1949; Joseph L. Mankiewicz, All About Eve, 20th Century-Fox, 1950; George Stevens, A Place in the Sun, Paramount, 1951; John Ford, The Quiet Man, Argosy Pictures Corp.-Republic, 1952; Fred Zinneman, From Here to Eternity, Columbia, 1953; Elia Kazan, On the Waterfront, Horizon Pictures-Columbia, 1954; Delbert Mann, Marty, Hecht-Lancaster-United Artists, 1955; George Stevens, Giant, Giant Productions, Warner Bros., 1956; David Lean, The Bridge on the River Kwai, Columbia, 1957; Vincente Minelli, Gigi, MGM, 1958; William Wyler, Ben-Hur, MGM, 1959; Billy Wilder, The Apartment, United Artists, 1960; Robert Wise and Jerome Robbins, West Side Story, United Artists, 1961; David Lean, Lawrence of Arabia, Columbia, 1962; Tony Richardson, Tom Jones, United Artists-Lopert, 1963; George Cukor, My Fair Lady, Warner Bros., 1964; Robert Wise, The Sound of Music, 20th Century-Fox, 1965; Fred Zinnemann, A Man For All Seasons, Columbia, 1966; Mike Nichols, The Graduate, Embassy, 1967; Carol Reed, Oliver!, Columbia, 1968; Franklin J. Schaffner, Patton, 20th Century-Fox, 1970; William Friedkin, The French Connection, 20th Century-Fox, 1971; Bob Fosse, Cabaret, Allied Artists, 1972; George Roy Hill, The Sting, Universal, 1973; Francis Ford Coppola, The Godfather, Part II, Paramount, 1974; Milos Forman, One Flew Over the Cuckoo's Nest, United Artists, 1975; John Avildsen, Rocky, United Artists, 1976; Woody Allen, Annie Hall, United Artists, 1977; Michael Cimino, The Deer Hunter, Universal, 1978; Robert Benton, Kramer vs. Kramer, 1979.

QP MONEY-MAKING STARS OF 1980

In the 1980 annual poll of circuit and independent exhibitors in the United States, conducted by Quigley Publications, these stars were voted the Top Ten:

Burt Reynolds .... First
Robert Redford .... Second
Clint Eastwood .... Third
Jane Fonda .... Fourth
Dustin Hoffman .... Fifth
John Travolta .... Sixth
Sally Field .... Seventh
Sissy Spacek .... Eighth
Barbra Streisand .... Ninth
Steve Martin .... Tenth

Winners in the preceding 48 Money-Making Stars Polls were:

1979: (1) Burt Reynolds; (2) Clint Eastwood; (3) Jane Fonda; (4) Woody Allen; (5) Barbra Streisand; (6) Sylvester Stallone; (7) John Travolta; (8) Jill Clayburgh; (9) Roger Moore; (10) Mel Brooks.

1978: (1) Burt Reynolds; (2) John Travolta; (3) Richard Dreyfuss; (4) Warren Beatty; (5) Clint Eastwood; (6) Woody Allen; (7) Diane Keaton; (8) Jane Fonda; (9) Peter Sellers; (10) Barbra Streisand.

1977: (1) Sylvester Stallone; (2) Barbra Streisand; (3) Clint Eastwood; (4) Burt Reynolds; (5) Robert Redford; (6) Woody Allen; (7) Mel Brooks; (8) Al Pacino; (9) Diane Keaton; (10) Robert De Niro.

1976: (1) Robert Redford, (2) Jack Nicholson, (3) Dustin Hoffman, (4) Clint Eastwood, (5) Mel Brooks, (6) Burt Reynolds, (7) Al Pacino, (8) Tatum O'Neal, (9) Woody Allen, (10) Charles Bronson.

1975: (1) Robert Redford, (2) Barbra Streisand, (3) Al Pacino, (4) Charles Bronson, (5) Paul Newman, (6) Clint Eastwood, (7) Burt Reynolds, (8) Woody Allen, (9) Steve McQueen, (10) Gene Hackman.

1974: (1) Robert Redford, (2) Clint Eastwood, (3) Paul Newman, (4) Barbra Streisand, (5) Steve McQueen, (6) Burt Reynolds, (7) Charles Bronson, (8) Jack Nicholson, (9) Al Pacino, (10) John Wayne.

1973: (1) Clint Eastwood, (2) Ryan O'Neal, (3) Steve McQueen, (4) Burt Reynolds, (5) Robert Redford, (6) Barbra Streisand, (7) Paul Newman, (8) Charles Bronson, (9) John Wayne, (10) Marlon Brando.

1972: (1) Clint Eastwood, (2) George C. Scott, (3) Gene Hackman, (4) John Wayne, (5) Barbra Streisand, (6) Marlon Brando, (7) Paul Newman, (8) Steve McQueen, (9) Dustin Hoffman, (10) Goldie Hawn.

1971: (1) John Wayne, (2) Clint Eastwood, (3) Paul Newman, (4) Steve McQueen, (5) George C. Scott, (6) Dustin Hoffman, (7) Walter Matthau (8) Ali MacGraw, (9) Sean Connery, (10) Lee Marvin.

1970: (1) Paul Newman, (2) Clint Eastwood, (3) Steve McQueen, (4) John Wayne, (5) Elliott Gould, (6) Dustin Hoffman, (7) Lee Marvin, (8) Jack Lemmon, (9) Barbra Streisand, (10) Walter Matthau.

1969: (1) Paul Newman, (2) John Wayne, (3) Steve McQueen, (4) Dustin Hoffman, (5) Clint Eastwood, (6) Sidney Poitier, (7) Lee Marvin, (8) Jack Lemmon, (9) Katharine Hepburn, (10) Barbra Streisand.

1968: (1) Sidney Poitier, (2) Paul Newman, (3) Julie Andrews, (4) John Wayne, (5) Clint Eastwood, (6) Dean Martin, (7) Steve McQueen, (8) Jack Lemmon, (9) Lee Marvin, (10) Elizabeth Taylor.

1967: (1) Julie Andrews, (2) Lee Marvin, (3) Paul Newman, (4) Dean Martin, (5) Sean Connery, (6) Elizabeth Taylor, (7) Sidney Poitier, (8) John Wayne, (9) Richard Burton, (10) Steve McQueen.

1966: (1) Julie Andrews, (2) Sean Connery, (3) Elizabeth Taylor, (4) Jack Lemmon, (5) Richard Burton, (6) Cary Grant, (7) John Wayne, (8) Doris Day, (9) Paul Nweman, (10) Elvis Presley.

1965: (1) Sean Connery, (2) John Wayne, (3) Doris Day, (4) Julie Andrews, (5) Jack Lemmon, (6) Elvis Presley, (7) Cary Grant, (8) James Stewart, (9) Elizabeth Taylor, (10) Richard Burton.

1964: (1) Doris Day, (2) Jack Lemmon, (3) Rock Hudson, (4) John Wayne, (5) Cary Grant, (6) Elvis Presley, (7) Shirley MacLaine, (8) Ann-Margaret, (9) Paul Newman, (10) Richard Burton.

1963: (1) Doris Day, (2) John Wayne, (3) Rock Hudson, (4) Jack Lemmon, (5) Cary Grant, (6) Elizabeth Taylor, (7) Elvis Presley, (8) Sandra Dee, (9) Paul Newman, (10) Jerry Lewis.

1962: (1) Doris Day, (2) Rock Hudson, (3) Cary Grant, (4) John Wayne, (5) Elvis Presley, (6) Elizabeth Taylor, (7) Jerry Lewis, (8) Frank Sinatra, (9) Sandra Dee, (10) Burt Lancaster.

1961: (1) Elizabeth Taylor, (2) Rock Hudson, (3) Doris Day, (4) John Wayne, (5) Cary Grant, (6) Sandra Dee, (7) Jerry Lewis, (8) William Holden, (9) Tony Curtis, (10) Elvis Presley.

1960: (1) Doris Day, (2) Rock Hudson, (3) Cary Grant, (4) Elizabeth Taylor, (5) Debbie Reynolds, (6) Tony Curtis, (7) Sandra Dee, (8) Frank Sinatra, (9) Jack Lemmon, (10) John Wayne.

1959: (1) Rock Hudson, (2) Cary Grant, (3) James Stewart, (4) Doris Day, (5) Debbie Reynolds, (6) Glenn Ford, (7) Frank Sinatra, (8) John Wayne, (9) Jerry Lewis, (10) Susan Hayward.

1958: (1) Glenn Ford, (2) Elizabeth Taylor, (3) Jerry Lewis, (4) Marlon Brando, (5) Rock Hudson, (6) William Holden, (7) Brigitte Bardot, (8) Yul Brynner, (9) James Stewart, (10) Frank Sinatra.

1957: (1) Rock Hudson, (2) John Wayne, (3) Pat Boone, (4) Elvis Presley, (5) Frank Sinatra, (6) Gary Cooper, (7) William Holden, (8) James Stewart, (9) Jerry Lewis, (10) Yul Brynner.

1956: (1) William Holden, (2) John Wayne, (3) James Stewart, (4) Burt Lancaster, (5) Glenn Ford, (6) Dean Martin & Jerry Lewis, (7) Gary Cooper, (8) Marilyn Monroe, (9) Kim Novak, (10) Frank Sinatra.

1955: (1) James Stewart, (2) Grace Kelly, (3) John Wayne, (4) William Holden, (5) Gary Cooper, (6) Marlon Brando, (7) Dean Martin & Jerry Lewis, (8) Humphrey Bogart, (9) June Allyson, (10) Clark Gable.

1954: (1) John Wayne, (2) Martin & Lewis, (3) Gary Cooper, (4) James Stewart, (5) Marilyn Monroe, (6) Alan Ladd, (7) William Holden, (8) Bing Crosby, (9) Jane Wyman, (10) Marlon Brando.

1953: (1) Gary Cooper, (2) Martin & Lewis, (3) John Wayne, (4) Alan Ladd, (5) Bing Crosby, (6) Marilyn Monroe, (7) James Stewart, (8) Bob Hope, (9) Susan Hayward, (10) Randolph Scott.

1952: (1) Martin & Lewis, (2) Gary Cooper, (3) John Wayne, (4) Bing Crosby, (5) Bob Hope, (6) James Stewart, (7) Doris Day, (8) Gregory Peck, (9) Susan Hayward, (10) Randolph Scott.

1951: (1) John Wayne, (2) Martin & Lewis, (3) Betty Grable, (4) Abbott & Costello, (5) Bing Crosby, (6) Bob Hope, (7) Randolph Scott, (8) Gary Cooper, (9) Doris Day, (10) Spencer Tracy.

1950: (1) John Wayne, (2) Bob Hope, (3) Bing Crosby, (4) Betty Grable, (5) James Stewart, (6) Abbott and Costello, (7) Clifton Webb, (8) Esther Williams, (9) Spencer Tracy, (10) Randolph Scott.

1949: (1) Bob Hope, (2) Bing Crosby, (3) Abbott & Costello, (4) John Wayne, (5) Gary Cooper, (6) Cary Grant, (7) Betty Grable, (8) Esther Williams, (9) Humphrey Bogart, (10) Clark Gable.

1948: (1) Bing Crosby, (2) Betty Grable, (3) Abbott & Costello, (4) Gary Cooper, (5) Bob Hope, (6) Humphrey Bogart, (7) Clark Gable, (8) Cary Grant, (9) Spencer Tracy, (10) Ingrid Bergman.

1947: (1) Bing Crosby, (2) Betty Grable, (3) Ingrid Bergman, (4) Gary Cooper, (5) Humphrey Bogart, (6) Bob Hope, (7) Clark Gable, (8) Gregory Peck, (9) Claudette Colbert, (10) Alan Ladd.

1946: (1) Bing Crosby, (2) Ingrid Bergman, (3) Van Johnson, (4) Gary Cooper, (5) Bob Hope, (6) Humphrey Bogart, (7) Greer Garson, (8) Margaret O'Brien, (9) Betty Grable, (10) Roy Rogers.

1945: (1) Bing Crosby, (2) Van Johnson, (3) Greer Garson, (4) Betty Grable, (5) Spencer Tracy, (6) Humphrey Bogart, Gary Cooper, (7) Bob Hope, (8) Judy Garland, (9) Margaret O'Brien, (10) Roy Rogers.

1944: (1) Bing Crosby, (2) Gary Cooper, (3) Bob Hope, (4) Betty Grable, (5) Spencer Tracy, (6) Greer Garson, (7) Humphrey Bogart, (8) Abbott & Costello, (9) Cary Grant, (10) Bette Davis.

1943: (1) Betty Grable, (2) Bob Hope, (3) Abbott & Costello, (4) Bing Crosby, (5) Gary Cooper, (6) Greer Garson, (7) Humphrey Bogart, (8) James Cagney, (9) Mickey Rooney, (10) Clark Gable.

1942: (1) Abbott & Costello, (2) Clark Gable, (3) Gary Cooper, (4) Mickey Rooney, (5) Bob Hope, (6) James Cagney, (7) Gene Autry, (8) Betty Grable, (9) Greer Garson, (10) Spencer Tracy.

1941: (1) Mickey Rooney, (2) Clark Gable, (3) Abbott & Costello, (4) Bob Hope, (5) Spencer Tracy, (6) Gene Autry, (7) Gary Cooper, (8) Bette Davis, (9) James Cagney, (10) Judy Garland.

1940: (1) Mickey Rooney, (2) Spencer Tracy, (3) Clark Gable, (4) Gene Autry, (5) Tyrone Power, (6) James Cagney, (7) Bing Crosby, (8) Wallace Beery, (9) Bette Davis, (10) Judy Garland.

1939: Mickey Rooney, (2) Tyrone Power, (3) Spencer Tracy, (4) Clark Gable, (5) Shirley Temple, (6) Bette Davis, (7) Alice Faye, (8) Errol Flynn, (9) James Cagney, (10) Sonja Henie.

1938: (1) Shirley Temple, (2) Clark Gable, (3) Sonja Henie, (4) Mickey Rooney, (5) Spencer Tracy, (6) Robert Taylor, (7) Myrna Loy, (8) Jane Withers, (9) Alice Faye, (10) Tyrone Power.

1937: (1) Shirley Temple, (2) Clark Gable, (3) Robert Taylor, (4) Bing Crosby, (5) William Powell, (6) Jane Withers, (7) Fred Astaire and Ginger Rogers, (8) Sonja Henie, (9) Gary Cooper, (10) Myrna Loy.

1936: (1) Shirley Temple, (2) Clark Gable, (3) Fred Astaire and Ginger Rogers, (4) Robert Taylor, (5) Joe E. Brown, (6) Dick Powell, (7) Joan Crawford, (8) Claudette Colbert, (9) Jeanette MacDonald, (10) Gary Cooper.

1935: (1) Shirley Temple, (2) Will Rogers, (3) Clark Gable, (4) Fred Astaire and Ginger Rogers, (5) Joan Crawford, (6) Claudette Colbert, (7) Dick Powell, (8) Wallace Beery, (9) Joe E. Brown, (10) James Cagney.

1934: (1) Will Rogers, (2) Clark Cable, (3) Janet Gaynor, (4) Wallace Beery, (5) Mae West, (6) Joan Crawford, (7) Bing Crosby, (8) Shirley Temple, (9) Marie Dressler, (10) Norma Shearer.

1933: (1) Marie Dressler, (2) Will Rogers, (3) Janet Gaynor, (4) Eddie Cantor, (5) Wallace Beery, (6) Jean Harlow, (7) Clark Gable, (8) Mae West, (9) Norma Shearer, (10) Joan Crawford.

1932: (1) Marie Dressler, (2) Janet Gaynor, (3) Joan Crawford, (4) Charles Farrell, (5) Greta Garbo, (6) Norma Shearer, (7) Wallace Beery, (8) Clark Gable, (9) Will Rogers, (10) Joe E. Brown.

STARS OF TOMORROW

In the Quigley Publications Poll for 1980–81 the following were selected the "Stars of Tomorrow":

Timothy Hutton	First
Debra Winter	Second
Cathy Moriarty	Third
Dennis Quaid	Fourth
Diana Scarwid	Fifth
William Hurt	Sixth
Michael Biehn	Seventh
Miles O'Keefe	Eighth
Peter Gallagher	Ninth
Martin Hewitt	Tenth

Winners of the previous 39 polls are as follows:

1979: (1) Bo Derek; (2) Dennis Christopher; (3) Treat Williams; (4) Michael O'Keefe; (5) Lisa Eichhorn; (6) Sigourney Weaver; (7) Chris Makepeace; (8) Ricky Schroder; (9) Karen Allen; (10) Marry Steenburgen.

1978: (1) Christopher Reeve, (2) John Beluchi, (3) Brad Davis, (4) Amy Irving, (5) John Savage, (6) Brooke Adams, (7) Gary Busey, (8) Brooke Shields, (9) Harry Hamlin, (10) Tim Matheson.

1977: (1) John Travolta, (2) Karen Lynn Gorney, (3) Michael Ontkean, (4) Mark Hamill, (5) Harrison Ford, (6) Carrie Fisher, (7) Kathleen Quinlan, (8) Peter Firth, (9) Richard Gere, (10) Melinda Dillon.

1976: (1) Sylvester Stallone, (2) Talia Shire, (3) Jessica Lange, (4) Sissy Spacek, (5) Robby Benson, (6) Sam Elliott, (7) Margaux Hemingway (8) Susan Sarandon, (9) Ellen Greene, (10) Lenny Baker.

1975: (1) Stockard Channing, (2) Bo Svenson, (3) Susan Blakely, (4) William Atherton, (5) Brad Dourif, (6) Perry King, (7) Bo Hopkins, (8) Conny Van Dyke, (9) Ronee Blakley, (10) Paul Le Mat.

1974: (1) Valerie Perrine, (2) Richard Dreyfuss, (3) Randy Quaid, (4) Deborah Raffin, (5) Joseph Bottoms, (6) Ron Howard, (7) Sam Waterston, (8) Linda Blair, (9) Keith Carradine, (10) Steven Warner.

1973: (1) Diana Ross, (2) Michael Moriarty, (3) Marsha Mason, (4) Joe Don Baker, (5) Jeannie Berlin, (6) Candy Clark, (7) Robert De Niro, (8) Jan-Michael Vincent, (9) Roy Scheider, (10) Tatum O'Neal.

1972: (1) Al Pacino, (2) Edward Albert, (3) Jeff Bridges, (4) Joel Grey, (5) Sandy Duncan, (6) Timothy Bottoms, (7) Madeline Kahn, (8) Cybill Shepherd, (9) Malcolm McDowell, (10) Ron O'Neal.

1971: (1) Jennifer O'Neill, (2) Karen Black, (3) Gary Grimes, (4) Sally Kellerman, (5) Arthur Garfunkel, (6) Bruce Davison, (7) Richard Roundtree, (8) Deborah Winters, (9) Jane Alexander, (10) Rosalind Cash.

1970: (1) Donald Sutherland, (2) Liza Minelli, (3) Goldie Hawn, (4) Jack Nicholson, (5) Genevieve Bujold, (6) Dyan Cannon, (7) Marlo Thomas, (8) Beau Bridges, (9) Sharon Farrell, (10) Peter Boyle.

1969: (1) Jon Voight, (2) Kim Darby, (3) Glenn Campbell, (4) Richard Benjamin, (5) Mark Lester, (6) Olivia Hussey, (7) Leonard Whiting, (8) Ali McGraw, (9) Barbara Hershey, (10) Alan Alda.

1968: (1) Dustin Hoffman, (2) Katharine Ross, (3) Katharine Houghton, (4) Estelle Parsons, (5) Judy Geeson, (6) Robert Drivas, (7) Robert Blake, (8) Jim Brown, (9) Gayle Hunnicut, (10) Carol White.

1967: (1) Lynn Redgrave, (2) Faye Dunaway, (3) James Caan, (4) John Phillip Law, (5) Michele Lee, (6) Michael Sarrazin, (7) Sharon Tate, (8) Michael York, (9) Hywel Bennett, (10) David Hemmings.

1966: (1) Elizabeth Hartman, (2) George Segal, (3) Alan Arkin, (4) Raquel Welch, (5) Geraldine Chaplin, (6) Guy Stockwell, (7) Robert Redford, (8) Beverly Adams, (9) Sandy Dennis, (10) Chad Everett.

1965: (1) Rosemary Forsyth, (2) Michael Anderson, Jr., (3) Michael Caine, (4) Michael Parks, (5) Mary Ann Mobley, (6) Jocelyn Lane, (7) Mia Farrow, (8) Julie Christie, (9) Richard Johnson, (10) Senta Berger.

1964: (1) Elke Sommer, (2) Annette Funicello, (3) Susannah York, (4) Elizabeth Ashley, (5) Stefanie Powers, (6) Harve Presnell, (7) Dean Jones, (8) Keir Dullea, (9) Nancy Sinatra, (10) Joey Heatherton.

1963: (1) George Chakiris, (2) Peter Fonda, (3) Stella Stevens, (4) Diane McBain, (5) Pamela Tiffin, (6) Pat Wayne, (7) Dorothy Provine, (8) Barbara Eden, (9) Ursula Andress, (10) Tony Bill.

1962: (1) Bobby Darin, (2) Ann Margaret, (3) Richard Beymer, (4) Suzanne Pleshette, (5) Capucine, (6) George Peppard, (7) James MacArthur, (8) Peter Falk, (9) Michael Callan, (10) Yvette Mimieux.

1961: Hayley Mills, (2) Nancy Kwan, (3) Horst Buchholz, (4) Carol Lynley, (5) Delores Hart, (6) Paula Prentiss, (7) Jim Hutton, (8) Juliet Prowse, (9) Connie Stevens, (10) Warren Beatty.

1960: (1) Jane Fonda, (2) Stephen Boyd, (3) John Gavin, (4) Susan

Kohner, (5) Troy Donahue, (6) Angie Dickinson, (7) Tuesday Weld, (8) Fabian, (9) James Darren, (10) George Hamilton.

1959: (1) Sandra Dee, (2) Rickey Nelson, (3) James Garner, (4) Curt Jurgens, (5) Lee Remick, (6) John Saxon, (7) Sidney Poitier, (8) Ernie Kovacs, (9) Kathryn Grant, (10) Carolyn Jones.

1958: (1) Joanne Woodward, (2) Red Buttons, (3) Diane Varsi, (4) Andy Griffith, (5) Anthony Franciosa, (6) Hope Lange, (7) Brigitte Bardot, (8) Burl Ives, (9) Mickey Shaughnessy, (10) Russ Tamblyn.

1957: (1) Anthony Perkins, (2) Sophia Loren, (3) Jayne Mansfield, (4) Don Murray, (5) Carroll Baker, (6) Martha Hyer, (7) Elvis Presley, (8) Anita Ekberg, (9) Paul Newman, (10) John Kerr.

1956: (1) Rod Steiger, (2) Jeffrey Hunter, (3) Natalie Wood, (4) Dana Wynter, (5) Tim Hovey, (6) Yul Brynner, (7) George Nader, (8) Joan Collins, (9) Sheree North, (10) Sal Mineo.

1955: (1) Jack Lemmon, (2) Tab Hunter, (3) Dorothy Malone, (4) Kim Novak, (5) Ernest Borgnine, (6) James Dean, (7) Anne Francis, (8) Richard Egan, (9) Eva Marie Saint, (10) Russ Tamblyn.

1954: (1) Audrey Hepburn, (2) Maggie McNamara, (3) Grace Kelly, (4) Richard Burton, (5) Pat Crowley, (6) Guy Madison, (7) Suzan Ball, (8) Elaine Stewart, (9) Aldo Ray, (10) Cameron Mitchell.

1953: (1) Janet Leigh, (2) Gloria Grahame, (3) Tony Curtis, (4) Terry Moore, (5) Rosemary Clooney, (6) Julie Adams, (7) Robert Wagner, (8) Scott Brady, (9) Pier Angeli, (10) Jack Palance.

1952: (1) Marilyn Monroe, (2) Debbie Reynolds, (3) Marge & Gower Champion, (4) Mitzi Gaynor, (5) Kim Hunter, (6) Rock Hudson, (7) Audie Murphy, (8) David Wayne, (9) Forrest Tucker, (10) Danny Thomas.

1951: (1) Howard Keel, (2) Thelma Ritter, (3) Shelley Winters, (4) Frank Lovejoy, (5) Debra Paget, (6) David Brian, (7) Piper Laurie, (8) Gene Nelson, (9) Dale Robertson, (10) Corinne Calvet.

1950: (1) Dean Martin and Jerry Lewis, (2) William Holden, (3) Arlene Dahl, (4) Ruth Roman, (5) Vera-Ellen, (6) John Lund, (7) William Lundigan, (8) Dean Jagger, (9) Joanne Dru, (10) James Whitmore.

1949: (1) Montgomery Clift, (2) Kirk Douglas, (3) Betty Garrett, (4) Paul Douglas, (5) Howard Duff, (6) Pedro Armendariz, (7) Dean Stockwell, (8) Wanda Hendrix, (9) Wendell Corey, (10) Barbara Bel Geddes.

1948: (1) Jane Powell, (2) Cyd Charisse, (3) Ann Blyth, (4) Celeste Holm, (5) Robert Ryan, (6) Angela Lansbury, (7) Jean Peters, (8) Mona Freeman, (9) Eleanor Parker, (10) Doris Day.

1947: (1) Evelyn Keyes, (2) Billy De Wolfe, (3) Peter Lawford, (4) Janis Paige, (5) Elizabeth Taylor, (6) Claude Jarmon, Jr., (7) Janet Blair, (8) Macdonald Carey, (9) Gail Russell, (10) Richard Conte.

1946: (1) Joan Leslie, (2) Butch Jenkins, (3) Zachary Scott, (4) Don De Fore, (5) Mark Stevens, (6) Eve Arden, (7) Lizabeth Scott, (8) Dan Duryea, (9) Yvonne De Carlo, (10) Robert Mitchum.

1945: (1) Dane Clark, (2) Jeanne Crain, (3) Keenan Wynn, (4) Peggy Ann Garner, (5) Cornel Wilde, (6) Tom Drake, (7) Lon McCallister, (8) Diana Lynn, (9) Marilyn Maxwell, (10) William Eythe.

1944: (1) Sonny Tufts, (2) James Craig, (3) Gloria DeHaven, (4) Roddy McDowall, (5) June Allyson, (6) Barry Fitzgerald, (7) Marsha Hunt, (8) Sydney Greenstreet, (9) Turhan Bey, (10) Helmut Dantine.

1943: (1) William Bendix, (2) Philip Dorn, (3) Susan Peters, (4) Donald O'Connor, (5) Anne Baxter, (6) Van Johnson, (7) Gene Kelly, (8) Diana Barrymore, (9) Gig Young, (10) Alexis Smith.

1942: (1) Van Heflin, (2) Eddie Bracken, (3) Jane Wyman, (4) John Carroll, (5) Alan Ladd, (6) Lynn Bari, (7) Nancy Kelly, (8) Donna Reed, (9) Betty Hutton, (10) Teresa Wright.

1941: (1) Laraine Day, (2) Rita Hayworth, (3) Ruth Hussey, (4) Robert Preston, (5) Ronald Reagan, (6) John Payne, (7) Jeffrey Lynn, (8) Ann Rutherford, (9) Dennis Morgan, (10) Jackie Cooper.

TOP-GROSSING FILMS

Top-grossing attractions in the United States, as selected by Quigley Publications, for the last five years follow:

1980: Airplane, Paramount—Jon Davison, producer; All That Jazz, 20th Century-Fox—Daniel Melnick; The Black Hole, Buena Vista—Ron Miller; The Black Stallion, United Artists—Fred Roos and Tom Sternberg; The Blue Lagoon, Columbia—Randal Kleiser and Richard Franklin; The Blues Brothers, Universal—Bernie Brillstein and Robert K. Weiss; Brubaker, 20th-Fox—Ron Silverman; Caddyshack, Warner Bros.—Douglas Kenney; Chapter Two, Columbia—Ray Stark; Cheech and Chong's Next Movie, Universal—Howard Brown; Coal Miner's Daughter, Universal—Bernard Schwartz; Dressed To Kill, Filmways—George Litto; The Electric Horseman, Columbia—Ray Stark; The Empire Strikes Back, 20th-Fox—Gary Kurtz; Friday the 13th, Paramount—Sean Cunningham; The Jerk, Universal—William E. McEuen and David V. Picker; Kramer vs. Kramer, Columbia—Stanley R. Jaffe; Little Darlings, Paramount—Stephen J. Friedman; 1941, Universal—Buzz Feitshans; Private Benjamin, Warner Bros.—Nancy Meyers, Charles Shyer and Harvey Miller; The Rose, 20th-Fox—Marvin Worth and Aaron Russo; The Shining, Warner Bros.—Stanley Kubrick; Smokey and the Bandit

II, Universal—Hank Moonjean; Star Trek—The Motion Picture, Paramount—Gene Roddenberry; Stir Crazy, Columbia—Hannah Weinstein; Urban Cowboy, Paramount—Robert Evans and Irving Azoff.

1979: Alien, 20th Century-Fox—Gordon Carroll, David Giler and Walter Hill, producers; The Amityville Horror, American-International—Ronald Saland and Elliot Gresinger; Apocalypse Now, United Artists—Francis Coppola; California Suite, Columbia—Ray Stark; The China Syndrome, Columbia—Michael Douglas; The Deer Hunter, Universal—John Peverall; Escape from Alcatraz, Paramount—Robert Daley; Every Which Way But Loose, Warner Bros.—Robert Daley; The In-Laws, Warner Bros.—Arthur Hiller and William Sackheim; Love at First Bite, American-International—Joel Freeman; The Main Event, Warner Bros.—Jon Peters and Barbra Streisand; Meatballs, Paramount—Dan Goldberg; Manhattan, United Artists—Charles H. Joffe; Moonraker, United Artists—Albert Broccoli; The Muppet Movie, Associated Film Distribution—Jim Henson; Rocky II, United Artists—Robert Chartoff and Irwin Winkler; Star Trek, Paramount—Gene Roddenberry; Starting Over, Paramount—Alan J. Pakula and James L. Brooks; Superman, Warner Bros.—Pierre Spengler; "10," Warner Bros.—Blake Edwards and Tony Adams.

1978: Capricorn One, Warner Bros.—Paul Lazarus, producer; The Cheap Detective, Columbia—Ray Stark; Close Encounters of the Third Kind, Columbia—Michael and Julia Phillips; Coma, MGM/United Artists—Martin Erlichman; The End, United Artists—A. Lawrence Gordon; Foul Play, Paramount—Thomas L. Miller and Edward K. Milkis; The Fury, 20th Century-Fox—Frank Yablans; The Gauntlet, Warner Bros.—Robert Daley; Grease, Paramount—Robert Stigwood and Allan Carr; The Goodbye Girl, MGM/Warner Bros.—Ray Stark; Heaven Can Wait, Paramount—Warren Beatty; High Anxiety, 20th Century-Fox—Mel Brooks; Hooper, Warner Bros.—Hank Moonjean; Hot Lead, Cold Feet, Buena Vista—Ron Miller and Charles Hibler; House Calls, Universal—Alex Winitsky and Arlene Sellers; Jaws 2, Universal—Richard Zanuck and David Brown; Julia, 20th Century-Fox—Richard Roth; Midnight Express, Columbia—Alan Marshall and David Putnam; National Lampoon's Animal House, Universal—Matty Simmons and Ivan Reitman; Omen II: Damien, 20th Century-Fox—Harvey Bernhard; The One and Only, Paramount—Steve Gordon and David V. Picker; Pete's Dragon, Buena Vista—Ron Miller and Jerome Courtland; Revenge of the Pink Panther, United Artists—Blake Edwards; Saturday Night Fever, Paramount—Robert Stigwood; Sgt. Pepper's Lonely Hearts Club, Universal—Robert Stigwood; Star Wars, 20th Century-Fox—Gary Kurtz; Superman, Warner Bros.—Pierre Spengler; The Turning Point, 20th Century-Fox—Herbert Ross and Arthur Laurents; An Unmarried Woman, 20th Century-Fox—Paul Mazursky and Tony Ray; Up in Smoke, Paramount—Lou Adler and Lou Lombardo.

1977: Airport '77, Universal—William Frye, producer; Annie Hall, United Artists—Charles H. Joffe; The Bad News Bears in Breaking Training, Paramount—Leonard Goldberg; Black Sunday, Paramount—Robert Evans; A Bridge Too Far, United Artists—Joseph E. Levine and Richard P. Levine; Close Encounters of the Third Kind, Columbia—Michael and Julia Phillips; The Deep, Columbia—Peter Guber; The Enforcer, Warner Bros.—Robert Daley; Exorcist II: The Heretic, Warner Bros.—John Boorman and Richard Lederer; Freaky Friday, Buena Vista—Ron Miller; Fun with Dick and Jane, Columbia—Peter Bart and Max Palevsky; Herbie Goes to Monte Carlo, Buena Vista—Ron Miller; In Search of Noah's Ark, Sunn Classic—Charles L. Sellier, Jr.; King Kong, Paramount—Dino De Laurentiis; Network, MGM—Howard Gottfried; Oh, God!, Warner Bros.—Jerry Weintraub; One on One, Warner Bros.—Martin Hornstein; The Other Side of Midnight, 20th Century-Fox—Frank Yablans; The Pink Panther Strikes Again, United Artists—Blake Edwards; The Rescuers, Buena Vista—Wolfgang Reitherman; Rocky, United Artists—Robert Chartoff and Irwin Winkler; The Shaggy D.A., Buena Vista—Bill Anderson; Silver Streak, 20th Century-Fox—Thomas L. Miller and Edward K. Milkis; Slap Shot, Universal—Robert J. Wunsch and Stephen Friedman; Smokey and the Bandit, Universal—Mort Engelberg; The Spy Who Loved Me, United Artists—Albert R. Broccoli; A Star Is Born, Warner Bros.—Jon Peters; Star Wars, 20th Century-Fox—Gary Kurtz.

1976: Adventures of Sherlock Holmes' Younger Brother, 20th Century-Fox—Richard A. Roth, producer; All the President's Men, Warner Bros.—Walter Coblenz; The Bad News Bears, Paramount—Stanley R. Jaffe; Barry Lyndon, Warner Bros.—Stanley Kubrick; Blazing Saddles, Warner Bros.—Michael Hertzberg; Dog Day Afternoon, Warner Bros.—Martin Bregman and Martin Elfand; The Exorcist, Warner Bros.—William Peter Blatty; Gus, Buena Vista—Ron Miller; Hustle, Paramount—Robert Aldrich; Jaws, Universal—Richard D. Zanuck and David Brown; Logan's Run, MGM—Saul David; Lucky Lady, 20th Century-Fox—Michael Gruskoff; Marathon Man, Paramount—Robert Evans and Sidney Beckerman; Midway, Universal—Walter Mirisch; Murder by Death, Columbia—Ray Stark; No Deposit, No Return, Buena Vista—Ron Miller; Ode to Billy Joe, Warner Bros.—Max Baer and Roger Camras; The Omen, 20th Century-Fox—Mace Neufeld; One Flew Over the Cuckoo's Nest, United Artists—Saul Zentz and Michael Douglas; The Other Side of the Mountain, Universal—Edward S. Feldman; Outlaw Josey Wales, Warner Bros.—Robert Daley; Silent Movie, 20th Century-Fox—Michael Hertzberg; Taxi Driver, Columbia, Michael Phillips and Julia Phillips.

1975: The Apple Dumpling Gang, Buena Vista—Bill Anderson; Benji, Mulberry—Joe Camp; Escape to Witch Mountain, Buena Vista—Jerome Courtland; Freebie and the Bean, Warner Bros.—Richard Rush; Funny Lady, Columbia—Ray Stark; The Godfather, Part II, Paramount—Francis Ford Coppola; The Great Waldo Pepper, Universal—George Roy Hill; The Island at the Top of the World, Buena Vista—Winston Hibler; Jaws, Universal—Richard D. Zanuck and David Brown; Lenny, United Artists—Marvin Worth; The Man with the Golden Gun, United Artists—Albert R. Broccoli and Harry Saltzman; Mandingo, Paramount—Dino de Laurentiis; Murder on the Orient Express, Paramount—John Brabourne and Richard Goodwin; The Other Side of the Mountain, Universal—Edward S. Feldman; Part II, Walking Tall, American International—Charles A. Pratt; The Return of the Pink Panther, United Artists—Blake Edwards; Shampoo, Columbia—Warren Beatty; Three Days of the Condor, Paramount—Stanley Schneider; Tommy, Columbia—Robert Stigwood and Ken Russell; The Towering Inferno, 20th Century-Fox—Irwin Allen; W. W. and the Dixie Dancekings, 20th Century-Fox—Stanley Canter; Young Frankenstein, 20th Century-Fox—Michael Gruskoff.

DIRECTORS GUILD OF AMERICA AWARDS 1966 TO 1979

(formerly Screen Directors Guild Awards)

1980: Film Director's Award: ROBERT REDFORD, Ordinary People; Television Awards—Comedy Series: NOAM PITLIK, Fog episode of Barney Miller; Dramatic Series: ROGER YOUNG, Lou episode of Lou Grant; Musical/Variety: DWIGHT HEMION, IBM Presents Baryshinkov on Broadway; Actuality (recording live): DON MISCHER, The Kennedy Center Honors; Special: JERRY LONDON, Shogun; Documentaries: (tie) PERRY MILLER ADATO, Picasso: A Painter's Diary; and ALFRED R. KELMAN, Body Beautiful segment of The Body Human.

1979: Film Director's Award: ROBERT BENTON, Kramer Vs. Kramer; Television Awards—Comedy Series: CHARLES S. DUBIN, Period of Adjustment episode of MASH; Dramatic Series: ROGER YOUNG, Cop segment of Lou Grant; Musical/Variety: TONY CHARMOLI, John Denver—The Muppets; News Specials/Sports: DON MISCHER, The Kennedy Center Honors; Documentaries: ALFRED R. KELMAN, The Magic Sense chapter of the Body Human; Specials: MICHAEL MANN, The Jericho Mile; Commercials: (directors judged by two or more examples of their work): ROBERT LIEBERMAN, Mary Ryan for McDonald's and Mary Lou for R.C. Cola.

1978: Film Director's Award: MICHAEL CIMINO, The Deer Hunter; Television Awards—Comedy Series: PAUL BOGART, California, Here We Are, All in the Family; Dramatic Series: GENE REYNOLDS, Prisoner, Lous Grant; Musical/Variety: MERRILL BROCKWAY, Choreography by Balanchine, Part 3; News Specials/Sports: DON MISCHER, The Kennedy Center Honors; Documentaries: JOHN KORTY, Who Are the Debolts?; Specials: MARVIN CHOMSKY, Holocaust.

1977: Film Director's Award: WOODY ALLEN, Annie Hall. Television Awards—Comedy Series: PAUL BOGART, Edith's 50th Birthday, All in the Family; Dramatic Series: JOHN ERMAN, Show #2—2nd Hour (Roots); Musical/Variety: ART FISHER, Neil Diamond: Glad You're Here With Me Tonight (Special); News Specials/Sports: RAY LOCKHART, A Day with President Carter; Documentaries: PERRY MILLER ADATO, Georgia O'Keefe (Special); Specials: DANIEL PETRIE, Eleanor and Franklin—The White House Years.

1976: Film Director's Award: JOHN G. AVILDSEN, Rocky, Television Awards—Specials: DANIELL PETRIE, Eleanor and Franklin; Comedy Series: ROBERT ALDA, Dear Sigmond, episode of MASH; Dramatic Series: GLENN JORDAN, Rites of Friendship; Musical Variety: TONY CHARMOLI, Shirley MacLaine's Gypsy in My Soul; Documentary-News Special: ARTHUR BLOOM, Democratic & Republican Conventions.

1975: Film Director's Award: MILOS FORMAN, One Flew Over the Cuckoo's Nest. Television Director's Award: SAM O'STEEN, Queen of the Stardust Ballroom.

1974: Film Director's Award: FRANCIS FORD COPPOLA, The Godfather, Part II, Television Director's Award: JOHN KORTY, The Autobiography of Miss Jane Pittman.

1973: Film Director's Award: GEORGE ROY HILL, The Sting. Television Director's Award: JOSEPH SARGENT, The Marcus Nelson Murders.

1972: Film Directors Award: FRANCIS FORD COPPOLA, The Godfather; Television Director's Award: LAMONT JOHNSON, That Certain Summer.

1971: Film Director's Award: WILLIAM FRIEDKIN, The French Connection; Television Director's Award: (Special) BUZZ KULICK, Brian's Song.

1970: Film Director's Award: FRANKLIN SCHAFFNER, Patton; Television Director's Award: LAMONT JOHNSON, My Sweet Charlie; D. W. Griffith Award: None presented.

1969: *Film Director's Award:* JOHN SCHLESINGER, Midnight Cowboy; *Television Director's Award:* FIELDER COOK, "Teacher, Teacher," *D. W. Griffith Award:* FRED ZINNEMANN.

1968: *Film Director's Award:* ANTHONY HARVEY, The Lion in Winter; *Television Director's Award:* GEORGE SCHAEFER; *D. W. Griffith Award:* ALFRED HITCHCOCK.

1967: *Film Director's Award:* MIKE NICHOLS, The Graduate; *Television Director's Award:* GEORGE SCHAEFER.

1966: *Film Director's Award:* FRED ZINNEMANN, A Man for All Seasons; *Television Director's Award:* ALEX SEGAL.

INTERNATIONAL FILM FESTIVALS

Listed alphabetically by country. Exact dates vary from year to year but months indicated are generally the same. Those marked with an asterisk are recognized by the International Federation of Film Producers Association.

AUSTRALIA
* Adelaide (May-June)
* Sydney (June)
Melbourne (June)

AUSTRIA
* Vienna—Humor in Film (March)
Vienna—MDT-Audiovisual (June)

BELGIUM
Brussels DIDACTA Audiovisual (June)
Brussels—Belgian Festival and Market (October)

BULGARIA
Varna (June)

CANADA
Montreal—Environment (June)
Stratford (September)
Ottawa (October)

COLOMBIA
Cartagena Film Festival (March)

CZECHOSLOVAKIA
Prague Television Festival (June)
* Karlovy Vary (July)
Brno Film and TV Market (October)

EAST GERMANY
Leipzig (November)

ENGLAND
London Film Festival (November-December)

FINLAND
Tampere Film Festival (February)

FRANCE
Cannes MIDEM Music Market (January)
Rheims Sport Films (March-April)
Cannes MIP-TV Video Market (April)
Beaune Histoical Films (May)
* Cannes Film Festival (May)
Grenoble Shorts (June-July)
Cannes VIDCOM (visual communications) (September)
Ouistreham (environmental) (September)

GREECE
* Thessaloniki International (June)

IRAN
Teheran (November-December)

IRELAND
* Cork (June)

ITALY
Bergamo at San Remo (March)
MIFED (film and TV market) at Milan (April)
Trento (mountain films) (April-May)
Asolo (art and painting)
Alghero (June)
Fermo and Porto S. Giorgio (marine) (June)
* Trieste (science fiction) (July)
Taormina Festival of Nations (July)
Venice (August)
Lucca (animation) (October-November)
* San Sebastian (September)
Sorrento (Canadian) (September)
Pessaro (new cinema) (September)
Prix Italia (TV) at Florence (September)
MIFED TV Market at Milan (October)
ORVIETO (folk art and artisans) (October)
Lucca (animation) (October-November)
Porretta Temer (November)
Festival dei Popoli at Florence (December)

MONTE CARLO
Monte Carlo TV Festival (February)

POLAND
* Cracow (shorts) (June)

SCOTLAND
Edinburgh (August-September)

SPAIN
* Valladolid (human values) (April-May)
Fijon (children's) (June)
San Sebastian (September)
* Sitges (horror) (September-October)
* Barcelona (color) (October-November)
Barcelona (November)

SWITZERLAND
Montreux TV Festival (April-May)
Geneva Telecom (May)

44A

* Locarno (August)
Montreux (new form) (August)
* Nyon (shorts) (October)

TAIWAN
Taipei (Asian) (June)

UNITED STATES
* New York Animation Festival (January)
American Film Market (Los Angeles—March)
* Los Angeles International Film Exposition
(Filmex) (March)
Philadelphia (May)
* New York Film Festival (September-October)
* San Francisco (October)
Chicago (November)

U.S.S.R.
* Tashkent (Afro-Asian) (May)

VIRGIN ISLANDS
International Film Festival

WEST GERMANY
* Oberhausen (shorts) (April)
* Berlin (June-July)
Munich (Youth Prize—TV) (June)
Cologne Photokina (September-October)
Oberhausen Sports Festival (October)

YUGOSLAVIA
Belgrade Film Festival (February)
Belgrade (science and technology) (April)
* Zagreb (animation) (June)
Pula (national) (July)

INDEX OF ADVERTISERS

Who's Who

In MOTION PICTURES and TELEVISION

A

AARON, ROY H.: Executive. Attorney in L.A. law firm of Pacht, Ross, Warne, Bernhard & Sears. Joined Plitt Companies in 1978 as snr. v.p. & gen. counsel. In 1980 named pres. & chief operating officer of Plitt Theatres, Inc. and related Plitt companies.

ABARBANEL, SAM X.: Producer, writer, publicist. b. Jersey City, N.J. Mar. 27, 1914. e. Cornell U & U. of Illinois, B.S. 1935. Newspaperman Chicago before joining N.Y. exploitation dept. Republic, then to studio as ass't publicity director. World War II in Europe with 103rd Div. After war independent publicist and producer. Co-prod. Argyle Secrets, 1948. Co-wrote orig. s.p., co-produced U.A.'s Prehistoric Women, 1950. Exec. Prod. U.A.'s Golden Mistress. In 1963 to Spain as associate prod. MGM's Gunfighters of Casa Grande, and Son of Gunfighter. Formed own co. in Spain, 1966. Produced Narco Men. Co-authored, prod. Last Day of War. Orig. & co-s.p. Avco's Summertime Killer, 1972.

ABEL, WALTER: Actor, b. St. Paul, Minn.; e. Amer. Acad. Dram. Art, N.Y. Role in touring co. of N.Y. prod. "Come Out of the Kitchen," then stock, vaudeville; stage mgr. touring cos. Minnie Maddern Fiske & others; on Broadway in "A Square Peg," "Long Watch"; m.p. sound debut in "Three Musketeers" 1935.
PICTURES INCLUDE: Witness Chair, Racket Busters; Arise, My Love; Holiday Inn, Star Spangled Rhythm, 13 Rue Madeleine, Kid from Brooklyn, Hal Roach Comedy Carnival, So This Is Love, Island in the Sky, Night People, Indian Fighter, The Steel Jungle, Bernadine, Raintree County, Handle with Care, Mirage.

ABELES, ARTHUR: Chairman, Filmartketeers, Ltd. b. 1914. Educated Duke University, Columbia University, U.S. 1939–1941: general manager, West Indies, Warner. 1941: assistant general manager, Brazil, Universal. 1942–5: general manager, Uruguay, Warner. 1945–7: supervisor, Argentina, Chile, Uruguay, Paraguay, Warner. 1948–68: Managing director, Warner Bros. Pictures, Warner Theatre, Warner Bros. Production; Director Henderson Film Laboratories; Vice-president Warner Bros. International Cor.; in charge of Europe, the Near East and North Africa. 1968–70: Managing director, Universal Pictures Ltd. Vice-president Universal International in charge of U.K., Continent and Middle East. 1970–7: Co-chairman, Cinema International Corporation. 1978: Chairman, Filmarketeers, Ltd.

ABEND, SHELDON: Executive. b. New York, N.Y. June 13, 1929. Maritime Labor-Rel. Negotiator, 1954–56; chmn, Maritime Union, 1954–56; head, exec. dir. Research Co. rep. estates decreased authors, est. 1957. indep. literary negotiator, C&C Films, A.A.P., RKO General Inc., David O. Selznick, 1959–65; pres. American Play Co. Inc., Century Play Co. Inc., 1961–72; est. Million Dollar Movie Play Library, 1962; pres. American Literary Consultants est. 1965; exec. v.p. Chantec Enterprises Inc., 1965; Literary prod. consultant Zane Grey Corp. Inc. 1969–72. Marketing Literary Consultant for Damon Runyon Estate. Copyright analyst and literary rights negotiator, United Artists Corp. Founder and chrm. of Guild for Author's Heirs, 1970–72, Literary negotiator and prod. consultant for Robert Fryer, 1972. Founder of the Copyright Royalty Co. for Authors Heirs, 1974; copyright consultant for Films Inc. 1975; literary agent for Bway. play, Chicago, 1975. Owner of 53 classic RKO motion pictures for the non-theatrical markets. Distributed by Films, Inc. Revived publishing of Damon Runyon stories in quality paperback in conjunction with Runyon-Winchell cancer fund. Published six mystery stories written by Cornell Woolrich—all of which were produced by Alfred Hitchcock for TV & motion pictures, 1976. 1978—assoc.

prod. of film, Why Would I Lie?; Originator of Million Dollar Movie Book Theatre and Million Dollar Movie Sound Track Co., 1980; assoc. prod. of Bdwy. revival, Shanghai Gesture, 1981.

ABRAHAMS, GARY: Executive. e. Univ. of Arizona (BA); in 1968 joined Paramount TV as asst. to v.p.; 1974–75, asst. to prod., The Movies; 1971–78, assoc. dir., Los Angeles Intl. Film Exposition (Filmex); 1978, joined Marble Arch Productions, as exec. asst. to pres.; named dir. of corporate relations & merchandising, 1979; project coordinator, Los Angeles Film Center, 1981.

ABRAHAMS, MORT: Producer. b. New York, N.Y., March 26, 1916; e. NYU, A.B., 1936; Columbia U., M.A., 1940. Prod. shorts, documentaries, Paul Falkenberg Prod., N.Y., 1940–42; Columbia Pictures, 1942–48; TV prod., Rockhill Radio, N.Y., 1950; film consultant, Bank of America, N.Y. 1951; TV prod. George F. Foley, 1952–53; TV prod., Music Corp. of America, 1953; v.p. in charge of East Coast TV prod., 1956; exec. prod. Producers Showcase, NBC-TV, June 1956–57; Suspicion, 1958; dir. programming, prod., NTA, 1958–1960; exec. prod. Cooga Mooga Prod. Inc., 1960–1961. Producer: Target, The Corruptors 1961, Route 66, 1962–63; writer T.V. Shows, 1963–64; prod., Kraft Suspense Theatre, 1965; prod., Man from U.N.C.L.E., 1965–66; Executive Vice-President, AJAC Prod. 1966. Assoc. prod. "Doctor Doolittle," "Planet of the Apes," "Goodbye, Mr. Chips." Prod., "The Chairman." Assoc. producer & writer, "Beneath the Planet of the Apes;" 1969, Vice President in charge of production, Rastar Prods.: 1971–74 exec. prod. American Film Theatre & v.p. Ely Landay Org. in chg. West Coast exec. prod. on Luther, Homecoming, Man in the Glass Booth; 1975-exec. chg. prod., Transworld Entertainment; 1977–78, exec. prod., The Greek Tycoon, Hopscotch, exec. prod.; 1980; exec. in chg. prod., The Chosen, Beatlemania, 1981.

ACKERMAN, BETTYE: Actress. b. Cottageville, S.C., Feb. 28, 1928. e. Columbia Univ., 1948–52. Taught dancing 1950–54.
PLAYS INCLUDE: No Count Boy (1954), Tartuffe (1956), Sophocles' Antigone, and "Oedipus at Colonus" (1956). The Merchant of Venice (1971).
PICTURES INCLUDE: Face of Fire (1959), Companions in Nightmare, Rascal.
TV: Alcoa Premiere, Hitchcock, Perry Mason, Breaking Point, Dr. Maggie Graham on Ben Casey series for five yrs., Hope-Chrysler Theatre, Bonanza, FBI Story, Mannix, Ironsides, "Medical Center," regular on "Bracken's World," Colombo, Sixth Sense, Heat of Anger, Return to Peyton Place, (6 months 1972) Rookies, Barnaby Jones, Police Story, Gunsmoke, Harry O, Streets of San Francisco, S.W.A.T.
LP RECORDS: Salome & School for Scandal.

ACKERMAN, HARRY S.: Executive. b. Albany, N.Y., Nov. 17, 1912. e. Dartmouth Coll. Began as writer, actor, producer. Joined Young & Rubicam adv. agcy. 1936; became v.p. of program operations, 1946. Exec. prod. CBS, 1948. Dir. of network programs—Hollywood, June, 1948; v.p. charge network radio programs, 1950; v.p. chge. network TV programs CBS-TV, Hollywood, June, 1951; exec. dir. spec. progs. CBS network, 1956; formed independent company 1957; v.p. and exec. prod. Screen Gems Inc., 1958–1973; pres. Harry Ackerman Prods. nat'l. pres., Academy TV Arts and Sciences, two terms; now v.p. in chg. TV, Capitol Pictures.

ACKLAND, JOSS: Actor. b. London, England, Feb. 29, 1928. Member of old Vic; toured Russia and U.S. with them. Over 400 TV appearances.
PICTURES INCLUDE: Seven Days to Noon, Royal Flash, Crescendo, The House That Dripped Blood, Villain, England Made Me, The Black Windmill, Great Expectations, The Greek Tycoon, Someone is Killing the Great Chefs of Europe, Saint Jack, The Apple, Rough Cut.

1

ADAM, KEN: Art dir. b. Berlin, Germany, 1921. e. St. Pauls School, London, and London Univ., student of architecture. 6 years war service as RAF pilot. Ent. m.p. ind. as draughtsman 1947. Art dir. Around the World in 80 Days, Trials of Oscar Wilde, Dr. No, Sodom and Gomorrah, Dr. Strangelove, Goldfinger, Thunderball, Ipcress File, You Only Live Twice, Funeral in Berlin, Chitty Chitty Bang Bang, Goodbye Mr. Chips, The Owl and the Pussycat, Diamonds Are Forever, Sleuth, The Last of Sheila, Barry Lyndon, Salon Kitty, 7% Solution, The Spy Who Loved Me, Moonraker.

ADAMS, BROOKE: Actress. b. New York City. e. High School of Performing Arts; Institute of American Ballet; Lee Strasberg. Made professional debut at age of six in Finian's Rainbow. Worked steadily in summer stock and TV until age 18. After hiatus resumed acting career.
PICTURES INCLUDE: Car Wash, Days of Heaven, Invasion of the Body Snatchers, Cuba, a Man, a Woman and a Bank.
TELEVISION: James Dean: Portrait of a Friend, The Last of the Belles, The Lords of Flatbush, The Daughters of Joshua Cabe, Murder on Flight 502, The Bob Newhart Show, Police Woman.

ADAMS, EDIE: Actress, singer. r.n. Edith Adams Kovacs. b. Kingston, Pa., April 16, 1931. e. Juilliard School of Music, Columbia School of Drama.
STAGE: Wonderful Town, 1952–54; Lil Abner, 1956–57.
TV: The Chevy Show, 1958: Take a Good Look, 1960–61; Here's Edie, 1962–63.
PICTURES INCLUDE: The Apartment, Mad, Mad, Mad, Mad World, Call Me Bwana, Under the Yum, Yum Tree, Love With A Proper Stranger, Lover Come Back, The Best Man, Maid in Paris, The Honey Pot, Up in Smoke.

ADAMS, GERALD DRAYSON: Writer. b. Winnipeg, Manitoba; e. Oxford University. Export exec. 1925–30; literary agt. 1931–45. Member: Screen Writers' Guild.
PICTURES INCLUDE: (jt. orig. screen story) Magnificent Rogue, (jt. s.p.) Plunderers, (s.p.) Gallant Legion, (jt. s.p.) Big Steal; collab. story, Dead Reckoning; Orig. s.p. Battle of Apache Pass, Son of Ali Baba, Flaming Feather, Flame of Araby; collab. s.p. Lady from Texas, Steel Town, Untamed, Frontier; story, collab. s.p., Duel at Silver Creek; st., s.p., Princess of the Nile, Three Young Texans, Gambler from Natchez; st., Wings of the Hawk, Between Midnight and Dawn; st., adapt., Taza Son of Cochise; collab. s.p. story, Gambler from Natchez, Chief Crazy Horse, s.p. Golden Horde; adapt. s.p. Prince Who Was a Thief; orig. s.p., Sea Hornet; s.p., Three Bad Sisters; orig., s.p., Duel on the Mississippi; orig. Black Sleep, s.p., War Drums; story, collab. s.p., Gun Brothers; story, Affair in Reno; story, s.p., Frontier Rangers; story, s.p., Gold, Glory & Custer; orig. story, collab. s.p. Kissin Cousins. Orig. s.p. Harem Scarem.
TV: Maverick, G.E. Theatre, Northwest Passage, Broken Arrow, Cheyenne, 77 Sunset Strip.

ADAMS, JULIE: Actress. r.n. Betty May Adams. b. Waterloo, La., Oct. 17, 1928; e. Jr. Coll., Little Rock, Ark., m. Ray Danton, Actor; Coll. dramatic; m.p. debut in Red Hot and Blue, Bright Victory; as Betty Adams in: The Dalton Gang, Marshal of Heldorado, West of the Brazos; since in Hollywood Story, Finders Keepers, Bend of the River, Treasure of Lost Canyon, Horizons West, Lawless Breed, Mississippi Gambler, Man from the Alamo, Wings of the Hawk, Star of Tomorrow, 1953.
PICTURES INCLUDE: Tickle Me, The Last Movie, MCQ, The Wild McCullochs, Killer Force, The Fifth Floor.
TV: Go Ask Alice.

ADDAMS, DAWN: Actress. b. Felixstowe, Suffolk, England, Sept. 21, 1930. e. Royal Acad. of Drama, London. Acted in rep. in Europe & on English stage; to Hollywood 1950.
PICTURES INCLUDE: Night into Morning, Singin' in the Rain, Hour of 13, Plymouth Adventure, Young Bess, Unknown Man, Moon is Blue, The Robe, Riders to the Stars, Return to Treasure Island, Khyber Patrol, Mizar, The Bed, Treasure of Rommel, London Calling North Pole, King in New York, The Silent Enemy, Secret Professional, Long Distance, The Two Faces of Dr. Jekyll, Follow That Man, The Liars, Lessons In Love, Come Fly With Me, The Black Tulip, Ballad in Blue, Vampire Lovers, Zeta One, The Vault of Horror.
PLAYS: London: Peter Pan, The Coming Out Party, The Wild Duck.
TV: The Saint, Danger Man, Romans and Friends, Emergency Ward 10, Dept. S. International Lawyer, Star Maidens.

ADDISON, JOHN: Composer. b. West Chobham (Surrey) Eng., March 16, 1920; e. Wellington and Royal Coll. of Music. Entered m.p. ind. in 1948, Professor, Royal College of Music.
PICTURES INCLUDE: (Music scores) The Honey Pot, Torn Curtain, A Fine Madness, I Was Happy Here, The Loved One, Guns At Batasi, The Uncle, Girl With Green Eyes, Tom Jones, The Loneliness of the Long Distance Runner, A Taste of Honey, The Charge of the Light Brigade, Smashing Time, Start The Revolution Without Me, Country Dance (in U.S., Brotherly Love), Forbush and the Penguins, Sleuth, Luther, Dead Cert, Ride A Wild Pony, Seven-Per-Cent Solution, Swashbuckler, Joseph Andrews, A Bridge Too Far, The Pilot, High Point.
BALLETS INCLUDE: Carte Blanche (at Sadler Wells and Edinburgh Festival).
PLAYS INCLUDE: The Entertainer, The Chairs, Luther, Midsummer Nights Dream, The Broken Heart, The Workhouse Donkey, Hamlet, Semi-Detached, The Seagull, Saint Joan of the Stockyards, Listen to the Mockingbird, Cranks (revue), Antony & Cleopatra, I Claudius, Twelfth Night, Bloomsbury.
TV: Sambo and the Snow Mountains, Detective, Hamlet, The Search for Ulysses, Way of the World, Back of Beyond, Black Beauty, The Bastard, Deadly Price of Paradise, Centennial, Pearl, Love's Savage Fury, Like Normal People, The French Atlantic Affair.
STAGE MUSICALS: The Amazons, Popkiss.

ADELMAN, JOSEPH A.: Executive. b. Winnipeg, Manitoba, Canada, Dec. 27, 1933. e. New York University, B.A., 1954; Harvard Law School, J.D., 1957, graduated cum laude, Attorney, United Artists Corp., New York, 1958; named west coast counsel, Hollywood, 1964; named executive assistant to the vice-president in charge of production 1968; named vice-president, west coast business and legal affairs, 1972; named executive vice-president, Association of Motion Pictures and Television Producers, 1977. Admitted to New York, California and U.S. Supreme Court bars; member, Phi Beta Kappa; American Bar Association; Los Angeles Copyright Society; Academy of Motion Picture Arts and Sciences; legislative liaison committee, Motion Picture Association of America; board of directors, AMPTP, 1969–   ; board of trustees, Theatre Authority, 1970–   .

ADLER, BOB: Actor, r.n. Robert Fick Adler. b. Hoboken, N.J., Mar. 24, 1906. Ranch Foreman, polo player, horse trainer, riding instructor; horseman in D. W. Griffiths "America" 1924, and others; in many Westerns since; member 20th-Fox Stock Co. from 1944.
PICTURES INCLUDE: My Darling Clementine, Smoky, Captain from Castile, Green Grass of Wyoming, Yellow Sky, Broken Arrow, Two Flags West, Lure of the Wilderness, Inferno, Hell and High Water, Prince Valiant, Broken Lance, Violent Saturday, Untamed, The Tall Men, Bottom of the Bottle, Proud Ones, The Silver Ship, Valerie, Fury at Showdown, Yellow Sky, Rope Law, Untamed, Rios Conchos, Whiskey Renegades, Stagecoach, Bandalero, The Undefeated.
TV: Flicka, Broken Arrow, Have Gun Will Travel, Cheyenne, Laramie, Rawhide, Bonanza, Daniel Boone, Gunsmoke, Batman, Judd, Big Valley, Lancer, Outcasts, Land of the Giants, Medical Center.

ADLER, LUTHER: Actor. b. New York City, 1903. On stage: Saigon, Loves of Carmen, Wake of the Red Witch.
PICTURES INCLUDE: House of Strangers, D.O.A., South Sea Sinner, Under My Skin, Kiss Tomorrow Goodbye, M. Magic Face, Desert Fox, Hoodlum Empire, Tall Texan, Miami Story, Girl in the Red Velvet Swing, Crashout, Hot Blood, Crazy Joe, Murph the Surf.

ADRIAN, IRIS: Actress, r.n. Iris Adrian Hostetter. b. Los Angeles, May 29, 1913; p. prof. Dancer, on stage N.Y. and abroad in "Follies of 1931"; m.p. debut in MGM two-reel color films.
PICTURES INCLUDE: Smart Woman, Out of the Storm, Paleface, Sky Dragon, There's a Girl in My Heart, Tough Assignment, Once a Thief, Always Leave Them Laughing, Stop That Cab, My Favorite Spy, Highway Magnet, Fast & The Furious, Crime Wave, Devil's Harbor, Carnival Rock, The Buccaneer, Blue Hawaii, The Errand Boy, Fate is the Hunter, That Darn Cat, The Odd Couple, The Love Bug.

AFTON, RICHARD LORD: Actor, director, producer, writer, sen. prod/dir. BBC Television since 1947. Prod. over 1200 shows on TV and many stage, film productions. Resigned BBC Oct. 1965 to form Freelance Co. Former man. dir. Ardmore Studios, Ireland. TV Columnist, London Evening News.

AGAR, JOHN: Actor. b. Chicago, Ill., Jan 31, 1921. In service World War II. Has appeared in Fort Apache, Adventure in Baltimore.
PICTURES INCLUDE: I Married a Communist, Sands of Iwo Jima, She Wore a Yellow Ribbon, Breakthrough, Magic Carpet, Along the Great Divide, Woman of the North Country, Man of Conflict, Bait, Rocket Man, Shield for Murder, Golden Mistress, Revenge of the Creature, Hold Back Tomorrow, Tarantula, Star in the Dust, Joe Butterfly, St. Valentine's Day Massacre, Waco, Johnny Reno, Women of the Prehistoric Planet.

AHERNE, BRIAN: Actor. b. Worcestershire, Eng., May 2, 1902; e. Malvern Coll., U. London 1920. In Brit. m.p. since 1924; on stage in London, on Broadway in Barretts of Wimpole Street, Lucrece, Romeo and Juliet, St. Joan, Othello, French Touch, The Constant Wife, She Stoops to Conquer, Quad-

rille, Escapade, On Tour, My Fair Lady, Dear Liar. LL.D (Hon., Baylor Univ., Texas).
PICTURES INCLUDE: Song of Songs, Constant Nymph, What Every Woman Knows, Beloved Enemy, I Live My Life, What a Woman, Hired Wife, Skylark, Man Who Lost Himself, The Great Garrick, Captain Fury, Smiling Through Juarez, My Son My Son, My Sister Eileen, Forever and a Day, Smart Woman, The Locket, I Confess, Titanic, Prince Valiant, Bullet Is Waiting, The Swan, The Best of Everything, Lancelot & Guinevere, The Waltz King, Rosie.
AUTHOR: A Proper Job, A Dreadful Man.

AIMEE, ANOUK: Actress. b. April 27, 1934. Paris, France. r.n. Francoise Dreyfus. Studied, Bauer-Therond dramatic school, Paris. Debut: 1946. La Maison Sous La Mer.
FILMS INCLUDE: Les Amants De Verone. The Golden Salamander, Le Rideau Cramoisi, Nuit D'Orage, La Bergere et Le Ramoneur (Cartoon), Mauvais Rencontres, Nina, Stresemann, Tous Peuvent Me Tuer, Pot Bouille, Modigliani of Montparnasse, Le Tete Contres Les Murs, Les Dragueurs, La Dolce Vita, Le Farceur, Lola, Les Amours De Paris L'Imprevu, 8½, Sodom and Gomorrah, La Fuga, A Man and a Woman, Un Soir, Un Train, The Appointment, The Model Shop, Justine, The Mandarians.

AKINS, CLAUDE: Actor. b. May 25, Nelson, Ga. e. Northwestern Univ. Worked as salesman in Indiana before joining Barter Theatre for season. Came to New York; appeared in The Rose Tattoo. Spent several seasons with touring cos.
PICTURES INCLUDE: From Here to Eternity, The Caine Mutiny, Skyjacked, Flap, Devil's Brigade, Inherit the Wind, The Great Bank Robbery.
TV: Police Story, Cannon, McCloud, Marcus Welby, M.D., Mannix, The Streets of San Francisco, Movin' On, The Rhinemann Exchange.

AKTER, MAHMOOD ALI KHAN: Producer-Distributor-Exhibitor: b. Hyderabad Deccan, India, Apr. 12, 1926. Graduate of Arts. Formerly with Columbia Films of Pakistan Ltd., gen. mgr.; Hussein & Co. controlling film dist. of United Artists Corp., Selznick Intl., London Films, Pathe Overseas. Participant foreign leaders prog. of Intl. Educational Exchange Service of U.S.A. State Dept.; mgr., Paramount Films of Pakistan, Ltd., 1959–64; mgr. dir., General Film Distributors, Lahore. Chm., Motion Picture Importer's Group, Lahore, Mgr. dir., Pak Boor Corp.

ALBECK, ANDY: Executive. Pres. & chief exec. officer, United Artists Corp. b. U.S.S.R., Sept. 25, 1921. Industry career began in 1939 with Columbia Pictures Intl. Corp. 1947, Central Motion Picture Exchange. 1949, Eagle Lion Classics, Inc. Joined UA in 1951 in intl. dept., functioning in the area of operations. After filling a number of key posts, named asst. treas. in 1970. In 1972 became v.p. of UA and its subsidiary, UA Broadcasting, Inc. 1973, appt. pres. of UA Broadcasting and in 1976 named snr. v.p—operations. Named UA Corp. pres & chief exec. officer in 1978. Retired, 1981.

ALBERGHETTI, ANNA MARIA: Singer, actress. b. Pesaro, Italy, May 15, 1936; d. Daniele Alberghetti, cellist. Concert debut in 1948 in Pesaro, then toured Italy, Scandinavia, Spain; Am. debut Carnegie Hall, 1950, sang with N.Y. Philharmonic Society, Phila. Symphony, on television. Screen debut in The Medium, 1950; then Here Comes Groom, Stars Are Singing, Last Command, 10,000 Bedrooms, Cinderfella. Star: Carnival. Broadway stage. Winner Antoinette Perry (Tony) Award for best actress.
TV: Toast of the Town, Cavalcade of Stars, Arthur Murray Show, Bob Hope, Eddie Fisher, Red Skelton, Dinah Shore, Desilu Playhouse, G.E. Theatre, Chevy Show, Dupont Show, Voice of Firestone, Colgate Hour, Climax, Loretta Young, Ford Jubilee, Perry Como.

ALBERT, EDDIE: Actor. r.n. Eddie Albert Heimberger. b. Rock Island, Ill. Apr. 22, 1908, e. U. Minn., Radio NBC.
BROADWAY: Brother Rat, Say Darling, The Music Man, Room Service, The Boys from Syracuse, Seven Year Itch.
PICTURES INCLUDE: Brother Rat, Four Wives, Angel from Texas, Dispatch from Reuter's, Rendezvous With Annie, Perfect Marriage, Smash-Up, The Story of a Woman, Time Out of Mind, Hit Parade of 1947, Dude Goes West, You Gotta Stay Happy, Fuller Brush Girl, You're in the Navy Now, Carrie, Meet Me After the Show, Actors and Sin, Roman Holiday, Girl Rush, I'll Cry Tomorrow, Oklahoma Attack, Teahouse of the August Moon, Orders to Kill, Gun Runners, Roots of Heaven, The Young Doctors, The Longest Day, Captain Newman, The Heartbreak Kid, Miracle of the White Stallions, Seven Women, McQ, The Take, The Longest Yard, Escape to Witch Mountain, The Devil's Rain, Hustle, Birch Interval, Foolin' Around, Yesterday, The Concorde-Airport 79, The Border, Ladyfingers, How to Beat the High Cost of Living, Take This Job and Shove It.
TV: Green Acres, Switch!, The Yeagers, Benjamin Franklin, The Borrowers, Killer Bees, Nutcracker, Anything Goes, Crash, The Word, Evening in Byzantium, Pirates Key, Living in Paradise.

ALBERT, EDWARD: b. Los Angeles, Feb. 20, 1951. e. UCLA. Son of actor Eddie Albert and actress Margo. Was prod. asst. on Patton in Spain. Has appeared with father on radio and TV shows. Is photographer and has exhibited work in L.A.
PICTURES INCLUDE: Butterflies Are Free (debut), Forty Carats, Midway, The Domino Principle, The Greek Tycoon, When Time Ran Out.

ALBERTSON, JACK: Actor. b. Malden, Mass.
PICTURES INCLUDE: The George Raft Story, Convicts Four, The Harder They Fall, Never Steal Anything Small, Man of A Thousand Faces, Miracle on 34th Street, Teacher's Pet, Lover Come Back, Monkey on My Back, Kissin' Cousins, Days of Wine and Roses, Period of Adjustment, Roustabout, How to Murder Your Wife, The Subject Was Roses, Justine, Willie Wonka & the Chocolate Factory, Rabbit Run, Dead & Buried.
BROADWAY: Meet the People, Make Mine Manhattan, Tickets, Please, High Time, Top Banana, High Button Shoes, Strip For Action, Allah Be Praised, The Lady Says Yes, Showboat, The Red Mill, The Subject Was Roses (won Tony Award for performance).
OPERA: The Cradle Will Rock.
TV: Ensign O'Toole, The Thin Man, Jack Benny Show, Red Skelton Show, Playhouse 90, Dick Van Dyke, I Love Lucy, Joey Bishop, The Defenders, Chico and The Man, Grandpa Goes to Washington.

ALBRIGHT, LOLA: Actress. b. Akron, Ohio, July 20, 1925; e. Studied piano 12 years. Switchboard operator and stenographer NBC; stenographer with WHAM and bit player; photographers' model. screen debut in "The Pirate" 1948.
PICTURES INCLUDE: Easter Parade, Girl from Jones Beach, Tulsa, Champion, Good Humor Man, Bodyhold, When You're Smiling, Sierra Passage, Killer That Stalked New York, Arctic Flight, Silver Whip, Treasure of Ruby Hills, Magnificent Matador, Beauty on Parade, Tender Trap, A Cold Wind in August, Kid Galahad, Lord Love a Duck, Where Were You When the Lights Went Out?, The Impossible Years, The Money Jungle.

ALDA, ALAN: Actor. b. New York City, Jan. 28, 1936. e. Fordham. f. Robert Alda. Studied at Cleveland Playhouse; performed with Second City, then on TV in That Was The Week That Was; Broadway credits include The Owl and The Pussycat, Purlie Victorious, Fair Game For Lovers (Theatre World Award), The Apple Tree (Tony Award nomination).
PICTURES INCLUDE: Gone Are The Days, The Moonshine War, Jenny, The Mephisto Waltz, Paper Lion, To Kill a Clown, Same Time Next Year, California Suite, The Seduction of Joe Tynan (also dir.), The Four Seasons (actor, dir., s.p.).
TV: M*A*S*H, The Glass House.

ALDA, ROBERT: Actor. r.n. Alphonso D'Abruzo; b. New York City, Feb. 26, 1914. e. New York U. Architectural draftsman, then in radio, dramatic stock. Signed by Warners 1943.
PICTURES INCLUDE: Cinderella Jones, Rhapsody in Blue, Cloak and Dagger, Man I Love, Nora Prentiss, Hollywood Varieties, Mr. Universe, Two Gals and A Guy.
N.Y. STAGE: in Guys and Dolls 1950–52; Harbor Lights 1955; What Makes Sammy Run? 1963–64; My Daughter, Your Son, 1969; Front Page, 1970.
OTHER FILMS: April Showers, Homicide, Beast With 5 Fingers, Force of Impulse, The Devil's Hand, Beautiful But Dangerous, Muskateers of the Sea, Revenge of the Barbarians, Cleopatra's Daughter, A Soldier and One Half, Imitation of Life, I Will . . . I Will . . . For Now, Bittersweet Love.

ALDON, MARI: Actress. b. Toronto, Canada, Nov. 17; e. Central High, Toronto. A.T.C.L. of Trinity College, London, England: With Canadian ballet six yrs.; nat'l co. of Streetcar Named Desire; sang on radio; m.p. debut in Distant Drums; since in The Tanks Are Coming, This Woman Is Dangerous, Tangier Incident, Barefoot Contessa, Race for Life, Summertime.

ALDRICH, ROBERT: Director. b. Cranston, R.I. 1918. e. U. of Va. Started as prod. clerk, RKO; then script clerk, asst. dir., prod. mgr., assoc. prod., dir. TV shows: The Doctor, China Smith.
PICTURES INCLUDE: Big Leaguer, World for Ransom, Apache, Vera Cruz, Kiss Me Deadly, Big Knife, Autumn Leaves, Attack!, Ten Seconds to Hell, Angry Hills, Last Sunset, What Ever Happened to Baby Jane?, 4 for Texas, Hush, Hush, Sweet Charlotte, Flight of the Phoenix, Dirty Dozen, The Legend of Lylah Clare, The Killing of Sister George, Too Late the Hero, The Grissom Gang, The Emperor of the North, Hustle, The Longest Yard, Twilight's Last Gleaming, The Choirboys, The Frisco Kid, All the Marbles.

ALEXANDER, JANE: Actress. b. Boston, Oct. 28, 1939. e. Sarah Lawrence Coll., Univ. Edinburgh. Stage career includes appearances on Bdwy., at Arena Stage, Washington, and Shakespeare Festival at Stamford, Conn.

3

PICTURES: The Great White Hope, A Gunfight, The New Centurions, All the President's Men, The Betsy.
TELEVISION: Welcome Home, Johny Bristol, Miracle on 34th St., Death Be Not Proud, Eleanor and Franklin, Eleanor and Franklin: The White House Years.

ALEXANDER, JOHN: Actor. b. Newport, Ky. On N.Y. stage Arsenic and Old Lace (1943), Ondine (1954).
PICTURES INCLUDE: Jolson Story, New Orleans, Cass Timberlane, Fancy Pants, Sleeping City, Night Has Thousand Eyes, Summer Holiday, Winchester '73, Model and the Marriage Broker, Marrying Kind, Untamed Frontier, A Tree Grows in Brooklyn, Junior Miss Broadway: Kiss the Boys Goodbye, Born Yesterday, Never Too Late, Visit to a Small Planet, Teahouse of the August Moon.

ALGAR, JAMES: Prod.-writer-director. b. Modesto, Calif. June 11, 1912. e. Stanford U.; B.A., M.A. Journalism. Entire career since 1934. Walt Disney Prods. Animator: Snow White; Director: Fantasia, Bambi, Wind in the Willows, Ichabod & Mr. Toad.
DOCUMENTARIES: war. health. True-Life Adventures: Seal Island, The Living Desert, Vanishing Prairie, The African Lion, Secrets of Life.
FEATURE CREDITS: Ten Who Dared, The Incredible Journey, Gnome-Mobile, White Wilderness, Rascal, The Legend of Lobo, The Jungle Cat, Run, Cougar, Run.
TELEVISION CREDITS: Producer: Run Light Buck, Run, The Not So Lonely Lighthouse Keeper, One Day on Beetle Rock, Wild Heart, Along the Oregon Trail, The Best Doggoned Dog in the World, One Day at Teton Marsh, Solomon, the Sea Turtle, Manado the Wolverine, Wild Geese Calling, Two Against the Arctic, Bayou Bay, Secrets of the Pond, Boy Who Talked to Badgers, Big Sky Man. Wrote and co-produced Great Moments with Mr. Lincoln; New York World's Fair; Circarama, America the Beautiful, Circle Vision 1958 Brussels World's Fair; Disneyland, Hall of Presidents, Disney World, Florida.
Shares in nine Oscars.

ALIN, MORRIS: Editor, writer, publicist, lyricist. e. College of the City of New York came into the M.P. industry, auditor of Hunchback of Notre Dame, roadshow oper., 1924; asst. sls. prom. mgr. Universal, 1926–27; slsmn., Universal, 1927; assoc. editor. The Distributor, MGM publication, 1927; editor, 1928–33; writer, publicist, MGM Studio, 1933–34; writer, publicist, Hollywood, New York, 1935–38; rej. Universal. 1938, editor, Progress: (Univ. publication); Twice winner of award, International Competition on Industrial Journalism; Senior publicist and Progress editor, Universal, 1961–67; editor Enterprise Press, 1968; member, executive Enterprise Press 1973; American Guild of Authors and Composers, American Society of Composers, Authors and Publishers, National Academy of Popular Music, and Motion Picture Pioneers.

ALLAN, TED. b. Clifton, Ariz., Comm. artist, actor SAG 1945, cameraman; photo training at Technicolor, Consolidated, MGM labs.; portrait photog., MGM, 20th-Century Fox, Selznick; created own film studio, 1952, prod. M.P. features, TV series, & pilots; Dir. of photog. 1956; 2 yr. contract Sinatra Enter.; 9 yrs. head CBS Cam. Dept. Hollywood; 3 yrs. 20th Cen. Fox, Pub-Stills & Featurettes for Von Ryan's Express, Fantastic Voyage, Sand Pebbles, Dr. Doolittle, The Detective, Lady in Cement, Tora, Tora, Tora. Featurettes for Universal: Seven Per Cent Solution, Hindenburg, Rollercoaster, Two Minute Warning, Gray Lady Down, The Promise Dracula.

ALLAND, WILLIAM: Producer. b. Delmar, Del., March 4, 1916. e. Baltimore. Acted in semi-professional groups; with Orson Welles' Mercury Theatre as actor, stage mgr.; asst. prod. Mercury Theatre radio series; ac., dialogue dir.; Citizen Kane; act., Macbeth; U.S. Air Force, World War II; then radio writer; prod., Universal, 1952.
PICTURES INCLUDE: The Raiders, Flesh and Fury, Stand At Apache River, It Came From Outer Space, Creature From The Black Lagoon, Johnny Dark, This Island Earth, Dawn At Socorro, Four Guns To The Border, Chief Crazy Horse, Revenge Of The Creature, Tarantula, Creature Walks Among Us, Gun for a Coward, Land Unknown, Deadly Mantis, Mole People, Raw Wind in Eden, The Lady Takes a Flyer, As Young As We Are; Paramount, The Party Crashers, Colsus of New York, The Space Children; Allied Artists, Look In Any Window, The Lively Set.

ALLEN, DAYTON: Performer. b. New York, N.Y., Sept. 24, 1919. e. Mt. Vernon H.S. Motion picture road shows, 1936–40; disc jockey, WINS, N.Y., 1940–41; writer, vaudeville comedy bits, 1941–45; then radio comic, puppeteer and voices; TV since 1948; film commercials; shows include Oaky Doky, Bonny Maid Varieties, Howdy Doody, Jack Barry's Winky Dink, Abe Lincoln in Illinois, The Circle of Chalk, The Steve Allen Show.

ALLEN, DEDE: Film Editor. b. 1924. Once a messenger at Columbia Pictures, moved to editing dept., then to commercials and features.
PICTURES INCLUDE: Odds Against Tomorrow (1959),

America, America, Bonnie and Clyde, Rachel Rachel, Alice's Restaurant, Little Big Man, Serpico, Dog Day Afternoon.

ALLEN, HERB: Producer. b. San Francisco, Calif., Dec. 24, 1913. e. U. of San Francisco, Pasadena Playhouse. Radio actor, anncr., Los Angeles, San Francisco; m.c., packager. Meet the Champ, children's TV show; asso. prod., Bob Crosby Show; prod., Johnny Carson Show. CBS-TV.

ALLEN, IRVING: Dir., Prod. b. Poland, Nov. 24, 1905; e. Georgetown U., Ph.B. 1926. Film ed. Universal, Paramount, Republic 1929–40; shorts dir. RKO & Warner 1941–42; Academy Award 1942 for ed. short subject "Forty Boys and a Song"; U.S. Signal Corps officer 1942–45; debut as dir. "Strange Voyage" 1945; Academy Award 1947, prod. "Climbing the Matterhorn," best two-reel short. Exec. prod., Warwick Films.
PICTURES INCLUDE: Avalanche, Strange Voyage, High Conquest, 16 Fathoms Deep, Man on the Eiffel Tower, New Mexico, Slaughter Trail, (prod.): Paratrooper, Hell Below Zero, The Black Knight, Prize of Gold, Cockleshell Heroes, Safari, Zarak, Pickup Alley, Fire Down Below, High Flight, No Time to Die, The Man Inside, Bandit of Zhobe, Idol on Parade, Adamson of Africa, Jazz Boat, In the Nick, Let's Get Married, The Trials of Oscar Wilde, The Hellions, The Long Ships, Ghengis Khan, The Silencers, Murderers Row, the Ambushers, Hammerhead, The Wrecking Crew, The Desperados, Run Wild, Run Free, Cromwell, Eyewitness, The Story of a Racehorse.

ALLEN, IRWIN: Producer. b. New York, N.Y. e. Columbia U., CCNY, journalism & adv. ed., Key Magazine, Hollywood; radio prod. dir., daily Hollywood program, 11 yrs.; radio & literary dir., own agency; then M.P. prod.
PICTURES INCLUDE: Double Dynamite, Girl in Every Port (co-prod.); assoc., prod., Where Danger Lives; prod., Dangerous Mission, The Animal World; prod., co-writer, director, The Story of Mankind; prod., writer, director, Sea Around Us (Academy Award), prod., co-writer, The Big Circus; prod., co-writer, director, The Lost World, Voyage to the Bottom of the Sea, Five Weeks in a Balloon; prod., director action sequences, The Poseidon Adventure, The Towering Inferno. 1978; The Swarm (prod.-dir.); Beyond the Poseidon Adventure (prod.-dir.); When Time Ran Out (prod.).
TV): Creator-prod., Voyage to the Bottom of the Sea, Lost in Space, Land of the Giant, The Time Tunnel, Adventures of the Queen, Swiss Family Robinson, Flood, Fire, The Return of Captain Nemo, Hanging by a Thread, Cave-In, Night the Bridge Fell Down, Memory of Eva Ryker. Producer: Code Red.

ALLEN, KAREN: Actress. b. Carrollton, Ill. e. George Washington Univ., Univ. of Maryland. Auditioned for theatrical company in Washington, D.C. and won a role in Saint, touring with it for 7 months. Spent several years with Washington Theatre Laboratory Co. Moved to N.Y., acting in student films at NYU and studying acting with Lee Strasberg at Theatre Institute. Major film debut in National Lampoon's Animal House in 1978.
PICTURES: Manhattan, The Wanderers, Cruising, A Small Circle of Friends, Raiders of the Lost Ark.
TELEVISION: Circle of Children, Part II.

ALLEN, LEWIS: Director. b. Shropshire, England, Dec. 25, 1905; e. Tettenhall Coll., Staffs, Eng. Exec. in chg. of N.Y. & London prod. for Gilbert Miller; actor & stage dir. N.Y. & England; dir. (N.Y.) Laburnum Grove, Amazing Doctor Clitterhouse, Ladies & Gentlemen; (London) The Women, studied m.p. prod. at Paramount 2 yrs.; apptd. dir. with debut of "The Uninvited" 1943.
PICTURES INCLUDE: Appointment With Danger, Suddenly, Another Time Another Place, The Lorelei.

ALLEN, MEL: TV commentator b. Birmingham, Ala., Feb. 14, 1913. e. U. Alabama, A.B. 1932, U. Alabama Law School LL.B. 1936. Started as sportscaster in Birmingham, while in law school; speech instructor in U. Ala. 1935–37; to N.Y. 1937, as staff announcer CBS to 1943; served in U.S. Army, World War II in infantry until the war ended, then before discharge was transferred to work on NBC Army Hour; sportscasting throughout U.S., joined N.Y. Yankees, 1946, concurrently narrating many shorts incl. How to Make a Yankee, appearing on radio & video and in Babe Ruth Story; sports commentator Fox Movietonews; voted best sportscaster in Motion Picture Daily-Fame radio. TV polls; Monitor, NBC; NCAA TV College Football, NBC; World Series (1938–1964), CBS-NBC; Rose Bowl (1951–1962), NBC; Sports Broadcasters Hall Of Fame.

ALLEN, NANCY: Actress. b. New York City, June 24.
PICTURES: The Last Victim, The Last Detail, Carrie, I Wanna Hold Your Hand, Home Movies, 1941, Dressed to Kill, Blow Out.

ALLEN, REX: Actor. b. Wilcox, Ariz., Dec. 31, 1922; e. Wilcox H.S. 1939. Vaudeville & radio actor; WLS, Chicago, 5 yrs.; was rodeo star appearing in shows through USA.
PICTURES INCLUDE: Arizona Cowboy, Hills of Oklahoma, Under Mexicali Stars, Thunder in God's Country,

Rodeo King & The Senorita, I Dream of Jeanie, Last Musketeer, South Pacific Trail, Old Overland Trail, Down Laredo Way, Phantom Stallion, For the Love of Mike, Tomboy and the Champ; narr., Walt Disney.

TV: Perry Como Special; commercials, Wonderful World of Color (NBC) Frontier Doctor.

RECORDINGS: Crying in The Chapel, Don't Go Near the Indians, Warner Bros. Records. 1966 Radio Man of the Year; 1966 Cowboy Hall of Fame.

ALLEN, ROBERT: Actor. e. Dartmouth Coll. Began film career in 1926.

PICTURES INCLUDE: Love Me Forever, Party Wire, Winter Carnival, Crime and Punishment, Pride of the Marines, Black Room Mystery, Death Flies East, Air Hawks, Bob Allen Ranger Series, Craig's Wife, Awful Truth, Lady of Secrets, Keep Smiling, Meet the Girls, Everybody's Baby, The City, Winner Take All, Fire-Away, Pie In The Sky.

PLAYS INCLUDE: Blessed Event, Popsy, Kiss Them for Me, Show Boat, I Killed the Count, Auntie Mame, A Few Wild Oats, Time Out for Ginger.

TV: Kraft, Armstrong Theatre, Philco, The Web, Suspense, Ethel & Albert, Danger, Lux Playhouse, Pulitzer Prize Playhouse, Lamp Unto My Feet.

ALLEN, STEVE: Performer. b. New York, N.Y., Dec. 26, 1921. U.S. Army 1942; radio shows, Los Angeles; TV, N.Y., 1950; shows include: What's My Line, Steve Allen Show, Tonight, I've Got a Secret, Meeting of Minds, Laughback.

PICTURES INCLUDE: Down Memory Lane, Warning Shot, I'll Get By, Benny Goodman Story, College Confidential.

COMPOSER: This Could Be the Start of Something Big, Pretend You Don't See Her, South Rampart St. Parade, Picnic, Houseboat, On the Beach, Sleeping Beauty, Bell, Book and Candle, Gravy Waltz, Impossible.

AUTHOR: Fourteen For Tonight, Steve Allen's Bop Fables, The Funny Men, Wry On the Rocks, The Girls on the Tenth Floor, The Question Man, Mark It and Strike It, Not All of Your Laughter, Not All of Your Tears, Letter to a Conservative, The Ground is Our Table, Bigger Than a Breadbox, A Flash of Swallows, The Wake, Princess Snip-Snip and the Puppykittens, Curses, Schmock-Schmock!, Meeting of Minds, Ripoff, Meeting of Minds-Second Series, Rip-off, Explaining China, The Funny People.

ALLEN, WOODY: Actor, Director, Writer. r.n. Allen Stewart Konigsberg. b. New York City, 1935. Began writing comedy at age 17, contributing to various magazine and top TV comedy shows.

STAGE: Author of Play It Again, Sam; Don't Drink The Water.

PICTURES INCLUDE: What's New Pussycat? (story, screenplay, actor); Casino Royale (actor); What's Up Tiger Lily? (dubbed scr., act.); Take the Money and Run (co-story, co-scr., dir., act.); Bananas (scr., dir., act.); Everything You Always Wanted to Know About Sex* But Were Afraid to Ask (scr., dir., act.); Sleeper, (scr., dir., act.); Love and Death (s.p., act.), The Front (act.), Annie Hall (co. s.p., dir., act.), Interiors (s.p.-dir.), Manhattan (co.-s.p., dir., act.), Stardust Memories (s.p., dir., act.)

ALLISON, FRAN: Performer. b. LaPorte City, Iowa; m. Archie Levington; e. Coe College, Cedar Rapids; sch. teacher, Iowa; started radio career as songstress Iowa Sta., 1934; starred in numerous programs, Chicago, 1937; Aunt Fanny of Breakfast Club; Fran of Kukla, Fran and Ollie on TV since 1947. Numerous commercials, daily TV variety show, 1958; Fac. mem., Careers Acad. Milwaukee.

ALLYSON, JUNE: Actress. r.n. Ella Geisman. b. Westchester, N.Y., Oct. 7, 1917. Started as chorus girl in school; m.p. debut in Best Foot Forward (1943). Voted one of ten best money-making stars in m.p. Herald-Fame poll, 1955.

BROADWAY INCLUDES: Best Foot Forward, 40 Carats, National Company, No No Nanette.

PICTURES INCLUDE: Girl Grazy, Thousands Cheer, Meet the people, Two Girls and a Sailor, Secret Heart, Reformer and Redhead, Right Cross, Too Young to Kiss, Girl in White, Battle Circus, Remains to be Seen, The Stratton Story, Little Women, Executive Suite, Glenn Miller Story, Woman's World, Strategic Air Command, The Strike, McConnell Story, You Can't Run Away From It, Opposite Sex, Interlude, My Man Godfrey, Stranger In My Arms, They Only Kill Their Masters, That's Entertainment!

TV: The June Allyson Show, Movie-of-the-Week: See the Man Run, 20th Century Follies.

ALMOND, PAUL: Producer-Director-Writer. b. Montreal, Canada, April 26, 1931; e. McGill U., Balliol Coll. Oxford. 1954–66 produced and directed over a hundred television dramas in Toronto, London, N.Y., and Hollywood; prod., dir., s.p., Isabel 1968, Act of the Heart 1970; Etrog (dir.; best Canadian feature); Journey 1972.

ALTERMAN, JOSEPH GEORGE: Executive. b. New Haven, Conn., Dec. 17, 1919. e. Wesleyan Univ., B.A., 1942; Institute for Organization Management, Yale Univ. 1957–59; exec. assist., SoundScriber Corp., 1945–48; district mgr., Industrial Luncheon Service, 1948–55; asst. secretary and admin. Secretary, Theatre Owners of America, 1955; Exec. dir. and vice pres., Natl. Assn. of Theatre Owners, 1966; Exec. v.p. COMPO., 1970.

ALTMAN, ROBERT: Director, writer, producer. b. Kansas City, Mo., Feb. 20; e. U. of Mo. Worked as Director for Dean Story; dir., Countdown, That Cold Day in the Park, M.A.S.H.; s.p. and dir., McCabe & Mrs. Miller, Brewster McCloud, Images, The Long Goodbye, Thieves Like Us, California Split, Nashville, Buffalo Bill and the Indians, The Late Show (prod.) Welcome to L.A. (prod.), Three Women (prod., dir., s.p.); A Wedding (prod., dir.); Remember My Name (prod.); Quintet (prod., dir.); A Perfect Couple (prod., dir.); Rich Kids (prod.); Health (prod., dir., s.p.), Popeye (dir.)

TV: Wrote, prod. and dir., Roaring Twenties, Bonanza, Bus Stop, Combat, Kraft Theatre and pilots for The Gallant Men and The Long Hot Summer.

ALTON, JOHN: Cinematographer. b. Oct. 5, 1901, Hungary. Laboratory technician, MGM 1924; Paramount cameraman 1928; sent to Paris, France, chg. camera dept., 1931; installed studios for Lumiton & Sono Film (South America); writer, photographer & dir. many Spanish pictures; returned to U.S. 1937, cinematographer Hollywood; served in U.S. Signal Corps as Capt., World War II. Books include: Painting With Light, Photography and Lighting in General; received Sintonia Medal for best photography in Argentina, 1937. Academy Award best color photog. American in Paris ballet, 1951.

PICTURES INCLUDE: Witness to Murder, Big Combo, Catered Affair. Member: ASC, AMPAS.

ALVIN, JOHN: Actor. r.n. John Alvin Hoffstadt; b. Chicago, Oct. 24, 1917; e. Pasadena (Calif.) Playhouse. On radio Chicago & Detroit; on N.Y. stage "Leaning on Letty," "Life of the Party," Screen debut 1944 in "Destination Tokyo."

PICTURES INCLUDE: Missing Women, Two Guys from Texas, Bold Frontiersman, Train to Alcatraz, Shanghai Chest, Carrie, April In Paris, Torpedo Alley.

ALWYN, WILLIAM: Composer. b. Northampton, England, 1905; e. Royal Academy of Music. Held Collard Fellowship in Music, Worshipful Company of Musicians, 1937–40. From 1936 author incidental music many British films.

PICTURES INCLUDE: Odd Man Out, Fallen Idol, I'll Never Forget You, Crimson Pirate, Magic Box, The Card (The Promoter), Mandy, Master of Ballantrae, Personal Affair, Million Pound Note (Man with a Million), Malta Story, The Seekers (Land of Fury), Bedevilled, Svengali, Cure for Love, Safari, Ship That Died of Shame, Manuela, I Accuse, Silent Enemy, Swiss Family Robinson, In Search of The Castaways, Life For Ruth, The Running Man.

AMATEAU, ROD: Director. b. New York, N.Y., Dec. 20, 1927. Staff writer, CBS radio; stage mgr., Lux Radio Theatre; U.S. Army, 1941; junior writer, 20th Century-Fox; then test dir., second unit dir.; TV dir., numerous shows including Schlitz Playhouse of Stars, Four Star Playhouse, General Electric Theatre, Private Secretary, Dennis Day Show, Lassie, Ray Milland Show, Bob Cummings Show, dir. & prod. Burns & Allen Show, Dobie Gillis.

PICTURES INCLUDE: The Statue, Where Does It Hurt?, The Wilby Conspiracy, Drive-In.

AMECHE, DON: Actor. b. Kenosha, Wis., 1908; e. Columbia Coll., U. Wisconsin. In stock; on radio; m.p. debut 1936. In television from 1951; on Broadway in Silk Stockings, 1955; International Show Time.

PICTURES INCLUDE: Sins of Man, Ladies in Love, Ramona, You Can't Have Everything, Alexander's Ragtime Band, Swanee River, Four Sons, That Night in Rio, Kiss the Boys Goodbye, So Goes My Love, That's My Man, Sleep My Love, Slightly French, A Fever in the Blood, Ring Around the World, Picture Mommy Dead, Suppose They Gave a War & Nobody Came, The Boatniks.

AMES, LEON: Actor. r.n. Leon Wycoff. b. Portland, Ind., Jan. 20, 1903. Aviator; with Champlin Players, Lansford, Pa., in stock and on stage; plays include: Tobacco Road, Male Animal, Land Is Bright; m.p. debut in "Murders in the Rue Morgue," 1932; owner & vice-pres. Studio City Ford Co.

PICTURES INCLUDE: Meet Me in St. Louis, Thirty Seconds Over Tokyo, Yolanda and the Thief, Merton of the Movies, On an Island With You, Velvet Touch, Date With Judy, Battleground, Ambush, Big Hangover, Little Women, Dial 1119, Happy Years, Alias a Gentleman, Watch the Birdie, Cattle Drive, On Moonlight Bay, It's a Big Country, Angel Face, By the Light of the Silvery Moon, Let's Do It Again, Sabre Jet, Peyton Place, From the Terrace, Absent Minded Professor, Son of Flubber, Misadventures of Merlin Jones, The Monkey's Uncle, On a Clear Day You Can See Forever, Tora! Tora! Tora!.

Under contract CBS TV; Life with Father, Father of the Bride, Mr. Ed.

AMES, LOUIS B.: Executive. b. St. Louis, Mo. Aug. 9, 1918; e. Washington U., St. Louis; m. Jetti Preminger; began as music consultant and staff director of musical programs for NBC; music dir. 1948, WPIX; 1951 apptd. program mgr., WPIX; assoc. prod., Today, NBC TV, 1954; feature editor

Home, 1957; Adm.-prod. NBC Opera, 1958; dir. cultural prog. N.Y. World's Fair, 1960–63; dir. RCA Pavillion, N.Y. World's Fair, 1963–65; 1966 dir., Nighttime, TV; 1969, dir. of Programming N.W. Ayer & Sons, Inc. 1973 Mgr. Station Services, Television Information Office. NYC.

AMFITHEATROF, DANIELE: Composer, conductor. b. St. Petersburg, Russia, Oct. 29, 1901. e. Royal Conserv. Music, Rome (D. Mus.). Guest conductor symphony orchs. Paris, Rome, Budapest, Vienna, etc.; assoc. conductor Minneapolis Symphony, 1937–38; guest conductor Boston Symphony, 1938.
PICTURES INCLUDE: (Composer scores) Lassie, Come Home, Beginning or the End, Song of the South, O.S.S., I'll Be Seeing You, Ivy, Senator Was Indiscreet, Letter from an Unknown Woman, Another Part of the Forest, An Act of Murder, Somewhere in the City, Fan, House of Strangers, Sand, Storm Warning, Bird of Paradise, Tomorrow is Another Day, Angels in the Outfield, Desert Fox, Scandal at Scourie, Devil's Canyon, Naked Jungle, Human Desire, Day of Triumph, Trial, Last Hunt, The Mountain, Unholy Wife, Spanish Affair, From Hell to Texas, Heller in Pink Tights, Edge of Eternity, Major Dundee.

AMSTERDAM, MOREY: Prod., Writer, Composer, Musician, Actor. b. Chicago, Ill., Dec. 14, 1914. e. U. of Calif., Berkeley. Boy soprano. Radio KPO, 1922; night-club performer, Chicago, 1929; comedian, singer, musician. Rube Wolf Orchestra; comedian, Optimistic Doughnut Program, 1930; writer, vaudeville; comedian, writer, Al Pearce Gang, 1932; writer, MGM, 1937; co-writer, radio shows; m.p. Columbia, Universal; writer, performer, USO Shows, 1942–43; owner, performer, the Playgoers-club; v.p. American International Pictures.
TV: Stop Me If You've Heard This One, Broadway Open House, Morey Amsterdam Silver Swan Show, Dick Van Dyke Show. Exec. Star-prod. Can You Top This.
PICTURES INCLUDE: Don't Worry . . . We'll Think of a Title, Machine Gun Kelly, Murder, Inc.
SONGS: Rum and Coca Cola, Why Oh Why Did I Ever Leave Wyoming, Yak A Puk, etc.

AMYES, JULIAN: TV producer. b. Cambridge, England, Aug. 9, 1917. e. Cambridge Univ. Early career, stage-producer, actor, film-actor, 1946–51; ent. TV 1951 as drama producer.
PRODUCTIONS INCLUDE: Dial M for Murder, The Deep Blue Sea, The Liberators, The Small Victory, Fifty-Fifty, The Troubled Air; dir., A Hill in Korea, Miracle in Soho. TV series, The Third Man, Maigret; 1959 Granada TV; Head of Drama, Granada TV, 1961; hd. progs., Granada TV, 1963–68. Dir. Granada TV, 1968.

ANDERSON, DAPHNE: Actress. b. London, Eng., April 27, 1922; e. Kensington High School. Stage debut in pantomime chorus 1937; screen debut in Trottie True 1948.
PICTURES INCLUDE: Cloudburst, Beggar's opera, Hobson's Choice, A Kid for Two Farthings, The Prince and the Showgirl, No Time for Tears, Snowball, Stork Talk, Captain Clegg, The Launching, I Want What I Want.
TV: Silas Marner (Serial), Gideon's Way (Serial), Dr. Finlay's Casebook, Happy Family, The Imposter, The Harry Worth Show, The Whitehall Worrier, The Suede Jacket, Casanova, Haunted Series, Thirty Minute Theatre, Justice is a Woman, Paul Temple, Today, 2 Cars.

ANDERSON, EDDIE ("ROCHESTER"): Actor b. Oakland, Calif., Sept. 18, 1905. Vaud.; night clubs; featured Jack Benny radio program.
PICTURES INCLUDE: Transient Lady, Three Men on a Horse, Jezebel, You Can't Take It With You, Thanks for the Memory, Gone With the Wind, Tales of Manhattan, Cabin in the Sky, Broadway Rhythm, I Love a Bandleader, The Show-Off.

ANDERSON, GERRY: Hon. F.B.K.S., Producer, b. London, 1929. Ent. ind. 1946. Chmn./man. dir. Gerry Anderson Productions, Ltd. Over 320 pictures produced for TV worldwide. 1978 Prod. The Male Chauvinist Pig!

ANDERSON, HENRY: Executive. b. New York City; e. N.Y.U., B.S. 1910. In construction work; joined E.I. duPont de Nemours & Co. (Del.); mgr. insurance dept. Paramount 1924; chmn. of many comms. on theat. engineering, construction, operation, protection, projection; mem. Advisory comm. N.Y. State Labor Dept. 1944–48; chmn. insurance comm. MPAA; author of articles on insurance.

ANDERSON, JUDITH: Actress. b. Adelaide, Australia, Feb. 10, 1898. Stage debut (Sydney) in "Royal Divorce" 1915; on New York stage & in stock 1918; toured 1920; m.p. debut in "Blood Money" 1933. Entertained U.S. Armed Forces overseas, World War II; received Donaldson Award 1948, New York Critics Award 1948, American Academy of Arts & Sciences Award for Best Speech 1948. N.Y. stage, 1952, In the Summer House, 1953.
PLAYS INCLUDE: Dear Brutus, Cobra, Dove, Strange Interlude, Old Maid, Mourning Becomes Electra, Macbeth, Medea.
PICTURES INCLUDE: King's Row, Rebecca, Laura, Spector of the Rose, Diary of a Chambermaid, Strange

Love of Martha Ivers, Red House, And Then There Were None, Tycoon, Pursued, Salome, Come of Age, Cinderfella, Cat on a Hot Tin Roof, A Man Called Horse.

ANDERSON, LINDSAY: director (cinema & theatre) and writer. b. Bangalore, India, 1923. e. Cheltenham College and Wadham College, Oxford (classical scholar). Ent. Ind. 1948 as writer-director in charge industrial film prod., also contributing editor independent film quarterly Sequence. Principal doc. films; O. Dreamland, Thursdays Children (collab. s.p. & dir.) Guy Brenton: Hollywood Short Subject Award, 1954, Three Installations, Pleasure Garden, Wakefield Express, Every Day Except Christmas (Venice Grand Prix, 1957), March to Aldermaston. Founder mem. Free Cinema group. National Film Theatre 1956/9. Recent Doc.: The Singing Lesson (Documentary Studio, Warsaw).
TV INCLUDES: Five episodes Robin Hood series, commercials, 1959–75. 1978 Dir. The Old Crowd.
PLAYS INCLUDE: The Long and the Short and the Tall, Billy Liar, The Fire Raisers, Diary of a Madman, Sergeant Musgraves Dance, The Cherry Orchard, Inadmissible Evidence (At Contemporary Theatre, Warsaw), In Celebration, The Contractor Home, The Changing Room, Artistic director, Royal Court theatre 1969–70. Associate, 1970–76. The Farm, Life Class, What the Butler Saw, The Sea Gull, The Bed Before Yesterday 1977 The Kingfisher, 1978 Alice's Boys, 1980, Early Days.
PICTURES INCLUDE: The Sporting Life, 1963; The White Bus, 1966; If . . . , 1968; O Lucky Man!, 1973, In Celebration, 1975.

ANDERSON, MELISSA SUE: Actress. b. Berkeley, CA, Sept. 26, 1962. Took up acting at suggestion of a dancing teacher. Did series of commercials; guest role in episode of Brady bunch; episode of Shaft. Gained fame as Mary Ingalls on Little House on the Prairie series.
TELEVISION: Very Good Friends, James at 15, The Loneliest Runner.

ANDERSON, MICHAEL: Director. b. London, England, 1920; e. France, Germany, Spain. Ent. m.p. industry as actor, 1936; asst. dir., unit manager on such films as In Which We Serve, Pygmalion, French Without Tears; Army service 1942–46; Co-dir., Private Angelo, 1949; since dir. Waterfront, Hell Is Sold Out, Night Was Our Friend, Will Any Gentleman?, The Dam Busters, 1984, Around the World in 80 Days, Yangtse Incident (Battle Hell), Chase A Crooked Shadow, Shake Hands with the Devil, The Wreck of the Mary Deare, All the Fine Young Cannibals, The Naked Edge, Flight From Ashiya, Monsieur Cognac, Operation Crossbow, The Quiller Memorandum, Shoes of the Fisherman, Pope Joan, Dr. Savage, Conduct Unbecoming, Logan's Run, Orca, Dominique, The Martian Chronicles.

ANDERSON, MICHAEL, JR.: Actor. b. London, 1943. son of dir. Michael Anderson. ent. films as child actor, 1954.
TV: Queen's Champion, Ivanhoe, The Monroes.
PICTURES INCLUDE: Tiger Bay, the Moonraker, The Sundowners, Reach For Glory, In Search of The Castaways, Play It Cool, Greatest Story Ever Told, Dear Heart, Major Dundee, The Glory Days, The Sons of Katie Elder, Logan's Run, The Martin Chronicles.

ANDERSON, RICHARD: Actor. b. Long Branch, N.J., Aug. 8, 1926. U.S. Army, World War II. Began acting career in summer theatre in Santa Barbara and Laguna Playhouse where spotted by MGM executives who signed him to six-yr. contract. Appeared in 26 films for MGM before leaving studio.
PICTURES INCLUDE: 12 O'Clock High, The People Against O'Hara, The Story of Three Loves, Escape from Fort Bravo, Forbidden Planet, The Long Hot Summer, Compulsion, Seconds, Paths of Glory, Tora! Tora! Tora!, Along Came a Spider, Macho Callahan, Doctors' Wives, Play It as It Lays, The Honkers, Stone, Redneck America.
TV: Bus Stop, Perry Mason, 12 O'Clock High (all regular), Ironside, The Big Valley, Mannix, My Friend Tony, The Mod Squad, Land of the Giants, The FBI, Gunsmoke. Series: The Six Million Dollar Man, The Bionic Woman.

ANDERSON, ROLAND: Art director. In 1933 collab. with Hans Dreier on "This Day and Age," Par. Since then collaborated in art direction on many productions, including Lives of a Bengal Lancer, Hands Across the Table, Give Us This Night, Till We Meet Again, The Buccaneer, Union Pacific, North West Mounted Police, Love Thy Neighbor, The Crystal Ball, Story of Dr. Wassel, Road to Utopia, Let's Dance, Branded, Carried, Son of Paleface, Just For You, Here Come the Girls, White Christmas, Country Girl, We're No Angels, Court Jester.

ANDERSON, SYLVIA: Producer/Writer. Sylvia Anderson Productions Ltd. (Pinewood Studios). b. London. e. London Univ. Entered m.p. ind. 1960.
TV: Thunderbirds; U.F.O.; Space: 1999.
PICTURES INCLUDE: Doppelganger; Thunderbird 6; Thunderbirds Are Go.

ANDERSON, WILLIAM H.: Producer; Member of Bd. of Dir. Walt Disney Productions. b. Utah, October 12, 1911. e.

Compton College. Firestone Rubber Co.; Universal Credit Co.; Walt Disney Prods. 35 years.

PICTURES INCLUDE: Old Yeller, Swiss Family Robinson, Happiest Millionaire, The Computer Wore Tennis Shoes, Barefoot Executive, $1,000,000 Duck, Superdad, Strongest Man In The World, Apple Dumpling Gang, Treasure of Matecumbe, Shaggy D.A.

TV: Zorro Series 1958–1959 (20 half-hour segments); 1959–1960 (38 half-hour segments), Wonderful World of Disney: Zorro, Texas John Slaughter, Daniel Boone, The Swamp Fox, Pop Warner Football (1960–1961), Johnny Shiloh, Mooncussers, 1962–1963; Bristle Face, The Scarecrow of Romney Marsh (1963–1964); The Legend of Young Dick Turpin (1965–1966); Willie and the Yank (1966–1967); A Boy Called Nuthin', The Young Loner (1967–1968); The Wacky Zoo of Morgan City (1970–1971); The Mystery of Dracula's Castle (1972–1973); The Bull From the Sky, co-producer; 1975–1976; Great Sleeping Bear Sled Dog Race, co-producer (1976–1977).

ANDERSSON, BIBI: Actress. b. Stockholm, 1935. e. Royal Dramatic Theatre School.

PICTURES INCLUDE: (for director, Ingmar Bergman) Smiles of a Summer Night, 1955; The Seventh Seal, Wild Strawberries, Brink of Life, The Magician, The Devil's Eye, Not to Mention All these Women, Persona; other films: My Sister, My Love Le Vio A Passion, Black Palm Trees, Story of a Woman, Duel at Diablo, The Kremlin Letter, The Passion of Anna, I Never Promised You a Rose Garden, Quintet.

ANDES, KEITH: Actor. b. Ocean City, N.J., July 12, 1920. e. Temple U., Oxford. Radio work; on Broadway in Winged Victory, Kiss Me Kate, Maggie.

PICTURES INCLUDE: Farmer's Daughter, Clash By Night, Blackbeard the Pirate, Split Second, Life at Stake, Second Greatest Sex, Away All Boats, Pillars of the Sky, Back from Eternity, Damn Citizen, Surrender, Hells Bloody Devils.

TV: This Man Dawson, Glynis.

BROADWAY: Wildcat.

ANDRESS, URSULA: Actress. b. Berne, Switzerland, 1936. M.p. Hollywood, 1955.

PICTURES INCLUDE: Dr. No, Four For Texas, Fun in Acapulco, Toys For Christmas, She, Tenth Victim, What's New Pussycat?, Chinese Adventures in China, Casino Royale, The Southern Star, Perfect Friday, The Red Sun, Scaramouche, Clash of the Titans.

ANDREWS, DANA: Actor. b. Collins, Miss., Jan. 1, 1912: e. Sam Houston Coll.; Pasadena Community Playhouse. Account with Gulf Refining Co., 1930; chief accountant Tobins, Inc., 1931; acted with Pasadena Playhouse 3 yrs.; m.p. debut in "The Westerner" 1939; Vice Pres., Screen Actor's Guild, 1962–63, Pres. 1964–66.

PICTURES INCLUDE: Best Years of Our Lives, Iron Curtain, Foolish Heart, Forbidden Street Bway play, Two for the See-Saw, Laura, Edge of Doom, Where Sidewalk Ends, Sealed Cargo, The Frogmen, I Want You, Assignment—Paris, Elephant Walk, Duel in the Jungle, Three Hours to Kill, Smoke Signal, Strange Lady in Town, While the City Sleeps, Commanche, Beyond a Reasonable Doubt, Spring Reunion, Night of the Demon, Zero Hour, Enchanted Island, The Fear Makers, The Crowded Sky, Madison Avenue, The Satan Bug, Crack in the World, In Harm's Way, Battle of the Bulge, Devil's Brigade, The Loved One, Innocent Bystander, The Last Tycoon, Airport, 1975, Born Again.

TV: Alas Babylon; G.E., The Playoff; Barbara Stanwyck; Dupont, Mutiny; 4 Star, Crazy Sunday; Checkmate, Alcoa, The Boy Who Wasn't Wanted; Twilight Zone, No Time Like The Past; Dick Powell, Last of the Big Spenders; Alcoa, The Town That Died, Bob Hope Chrysler, A Wind of Hurricane Force, Bright Promise (movie), Shadow in the Streets, One Small Step Forward (series), The Right Hand Man (Playhouse 90) Ike (ABC movie).

DINNER THEATRE: The Marriage-Go-Round; The Best of Friends, Angel Street, The Gang's All Here, Any Wednesday, A Man for All Seasons.

ANDREWS, EAMONN: C.B.E. Announcer and commentator. b. Dublin, Ireland, Dec. 19, 1922. e. Irish Christian Brothers (Dublin), Radio, vaudeville and legit. stage experience in Dublin; TV with BBC 1950; quiz master on several programs, sports com., columnist, author, playwright; Founder, chairman, Irish Television Authority; ABC-TV, 1964–67; Eamonn Andrews Show, and World of Sport, Thames TV's daily, Today, This Is Your Life, Time For Business.

ANDREWS, EDWARD: Actor. b. Griffin, Ga., Oct. 9. e. Univ. of Virginia. Broadway debut, How Beautiful With Shoes, 1935; So Proudly We Hail, Of Mice and Men, The Time of Your Life, They Knew What They Wanted, I Am a Camera, Come Back Little Sheba, A Visit to a Small Planet, The Gazebo.

TV: co-star, Broadside; co-star, Mr. Terrific. Universal pilot; Thriller, U.S. Steel, Kraft Theatre, Studio One, Alfred Hitchcock, Gunsmoke, 11th Hour, Kildare, Bonanza, etc.

PICTURES INCLUDE: Birds Do It, The Thrill of It All, Advise and Consent, The Young Doctors, The Absent-

Minded Professor, The Young Savages, Elmer Gantry, Those Wilder Years, The Tattered Dress, Tea and Sympathy, The Phoenix City Story, The Glass Bottom Boat, Charley and the Angel.

ANDREWS, HARRY: CBE, Actor. b. Tonbridge, Kent, England, 1911. First stage appearance, Liverpool, 1933. London stage 1935, "Worse Things Happen at Sea," to U.S., 1936, "Hamlet." Army Service 1939–45. Screen debut 1952, The Red Beret.

PICTURES INCLUDE: The Black Knight, The Man Who Loved Redheads, A Hill in Korea, Alexander the Great, Moby Dick, Ice Cold in Alex, Devil's Disciple, Solomon and Sheba, In the Nick, Circle of Deception, Cleopatra, The Best of Enemies, Reach For Glory, The Inspector, Barrabas, 55 Days at Peking, The Snout, The System, The Hill, The Agony and the Ecstasy, The Sands of the Kalahari, The Deadly Affair, A Dandy in Aspic, The Charge of the Light Brigade, The Night They Raided Minsky's, The Seagull, A Nice Girl Like Me, Too Late the Hero, The Gaunt Woman, Country Dance (in U.S. Brotherly Love), Entertaining Mr. Sloane, Wuthering Heights, I Want What I Want, Nicholas and Alexandra, The Nightcomers, The Ruling Class, Man of La Mancha, Theatre of Blood, The Mackintosh Man, Man at the Top, The Skyriders, The Bluebird, The Passover Plot, The Prince and The Pauper, Equus, Superman, The Medusa Touch, The Big Sleep, Death on the Nile, SOS Titanic.

TV: Affair of Honour, Clayhanger, Two Gentle People, Leo Tolstoy.

ANDREWS, JULIE: Actress, Singer. b. Walton-on-Thames. Eng., 1935 debut, Eng. Starlight Roof Revue; pantomime of Cinderella.

PLAYS: The Boy Friend, My Fair Lady, Camelot.

PICTURES INCLUDE: Mary Poppins, The Americanization of Emily, The Sound of Music, Hawaii, Torn Curtain, Thoroughly Modern Millie, Star!, Darling Lili, The Tamarind Seed, "10," "S.O.B.," Victor/Victoria.

TV: High Tor, Julie and Carol at Carnegie Hall, The Andy Williams Show, The Julie Andrews Show, An Evening with Julie Andrews and Harry Belafonte, The World of Walt Disney, Julie and Carol at Lincoln Center, Julie Andrews Hour (ABC Television series 1972–73); Julie on Sesame Street, 1973; Julie Andrews' Christmas Special, 1973; Julie and Dick in Covent Garden, 1974; Julie Andrews and Jackie Gleason Together, 1974; Julie Andrews—My Favorite Things, 1975.

AUTHOR: Mandy, Last of the Really Great Whangdoodles, 1973.

ANGEL, HEATHER: Actress. b. Oxford, England, Feb. 9, 1909; e. Wycombe Abbey School. On stage 1926–30; British m.p. debut in "City of Song" 1939; U.S. m.p. debut in "Pilgrimage" 1932.

PICTURES INCLUDE: Hound of the Baskervilles, After Office Hours, Berkeley Square, Charlie Chan's Greatest Case, Orient Express, Springtime for Henry, Informer, Three Musketeers, Last of the Mohicans, Bulldog Drummond series, Pride and Prejudice, That Hamilton Woman, Suspicion, Lifeboat, In the Meantime Darling, Saxon Charm, Alice in Wonderland, Peter Pan.

TV: Family Affair.

ANGERS, AVRIL: Actress, comedienne, singer. b. Liverpool, Eng., April 18; Stage debut at age of 14; screen debut in 1947 in Lucky Mascot.

PICTURES INCLUDE: Miss Pilgrim's Progress, Don't Blame the Stork, Women Without Men, Green Man, Devils of Darkness, Be My Guest, Three Bites of the Apple, The Family Way, Two a Penny, The Best House in London, Staircase, There's a Girl in My Soup, Forbush and the Penguins, Gollocks (1973), Confessions of a Driving Instructor, Dangerous Davies.

TV: How Do You View, Friends and Neighbors, Dear Dotty, Holiday Town, Charlie Fainsbarn Show, Arthur Askey Show, All Aboard, The Gold Hunter, Bob Monkhouse Show, Before The Fringe, Hudd, Coronation Street, Dick Emery Show, Dad's Army, Bright Boffins, The More We Are Together, The Millionairess, Liver Birds, Looks Familiar, No Appointment Necessary, The Songwriters, All Creatures Great and Small, Coronation Concert.

PLAYS INCLUDE: The Mating Game; Musical, Cockie; Murder at the Vicarage, Little Me, Norman, Is That You?, Blithe Spirit.

ANHALT, EDNA: Associate producer, writer. b. New York, N.Y., Apr. 10, 1914; e. Kathryn Gibbs Sch., 1932; U. doc. films; prod. mgr., Rockefeller Found. films.

PICTURES INCLUDE: (Orig. story, collab., assoc. prod., s.p.) Strange Voyage, Avalanche, Younger Brothers, Return of Frontiersman, Embraceable You, Sierra, The Sniper, My Six Convicts, Eight Iron Men, Member of the Wedding, Three Lives, The Big Kill, Not as a Stranger, Pride and the Passion, Girls, Girls, Girls, Decision at Delphi.

Academy Award, orig. story collab., Panic in the Streets.

Member: Acad. of M.P. Arts & Sciences; S.W.G.

7

ANHALT, EDWARD: Writer. b. New York, N.Y. Academy Award. orig. story collab., Panic in the Streets.
PICTURES INCLUDE: The Young Savages, Academy Award, screenplay, Becket, In Enemy Country, Boeing-Boeing, The Young Lions, Day of the Guns, Not As a Stranger, Madwoman of Chaillot, Member of the Wedding, Boston Strangler, Jeremiah Johnson, Q B VII (TV), Luther, Escape to Athena.

ANKERS, EVELYN: Actress. b. Valparaiso, Chile (English parents); e. Latymer and Godolphyn School, Royal Academy Dramatic Art (London); wife of Richard Denning. In British pictures and stage, then on stage New York (in ("Ladies in Retirement") (West End, London) Bats in The Belfry.
PICTURES INCLUDE: Black Beauty, Queen of Burlesque, Wolf Man, Ghost of Frankenstein, Frozen Ghost, All By Myself, Texan Meets Calamity Jane, Parole, Inc., Tarzan's Magic Fountain, No Greater Love.
TV: TV shows, Mr. & Mrs. North, Ford Theatre, Screen Directors Playhouse, Star and the Story, 20th Century-Fox Hour, Cheyenne, etc.

ANN-MARGRET: Actress, singer. b. Stockholm, Sweden, April 28, 1941. e. grad., New Trier High School, Winnetka, Ill., attended Northwestern University. Radio shows, toured with band; worked with George Burns, Sahara, Las Vegas. TV debut, Jack Benny Show, April, 1961.
PICTURES INCLUDE: debut, Pocketful of Miracles, State Fair, Bye, Bye Birdie, Viva Las Vegas, Kitten With a Whip, Bus Riley's Back in Town, Once A Thief, Cincinnati Kid, The Pleasure Seekers, Made in Paris, The Tiger and the Pussycat, C. C. & Company, Carnal Knowledge, RPM, The Outside Man, The Train Robbers, Tommy, The Last Remake of Beau Geste, Joseph Andrews, The Cheap Detective, Magic, The Villain, Middle Age Crazy, Lookin' To Get Out.

ANNAKIN, KENNETH: Director, writer. b. Yorkshire, England. Graduated through Experimental Theatre and Documentary. Films incl: Across The Bridge, Swiss Family Robinson, Very Important Person, The Longest Day, The Fast Lady, The Informers, Those Magnificent Men In Their Flying Machines, Battle Of The Bulge, The Long Duel, Monte Carlo Or Bust, Call Of The Wild, Paper Tiger, The Fifth Musketeer, The Pirate.

ANSARA, MICHAEL: Actor. b. Lowell, Mass., April 15, 1927. e. Pasadena Playhouse. Served in U.S. Army; then summer stock, little theatre, road shows.
PICTURES INCLUDE: The Robe, Julius Caesar, Sign of the Pagan, Bengal Brigade, Soldiers Three, Only the Valiant, New Orleans Uncensored, Diane, Lone Ranger, Sol Madrid, Daring Game, The Bears And I, Mohammad, Messenger of God, The Manitou.
TV: Broken Arrow, Law of the Plainsman, Westerner.

ANSPACH, SUSAN: Actress. b. New York City. e. Catholic University (Washington, D.C.) After school returned to N.Y. and in 3 years had performed in 11 off-Bdwy. and moved to Los Angeles and entered films.
PICTURES INCLUDE: Five Easy Pieces, The Landlord, Play It Again Sam, Blume in Love, The Big Fix, Running, The Devil and Max Devlin, Gas.

ANTHONY, TONY: Actor-producer. b. Clarksburg, West Virginia. e. Carnegie Tech.
PICTURES INCLUDE: Force of Impulse, Pity Me Not, The Wounds of Hunger, A Stranger in Town, The Stranger Returns, A Stranger in Japan, Come Together, Blindman, Pete Pearl and the Pole, Let's Talk About Men, Get Mean, The Boy Who Owned a Melephant.

ANTONIONI, MICHELANGELO: Director. b. Ferrara, Italy, Sept. 29, 1913. e. Bologna University. Film critic on local paper, then script writer and asst. director. First films as a director were documentaries, including: Gente del Po (1947) and N.U. First feature Love Story, 1950; since The Lady Without Camelias, Love in a City, I Vinti, The Friend, The City, L'Avventura, The Night, The Eclipse, The Red Desert, Blow-Up, Zabriskie Point, The Passenger.

ANTONY, SCOTT: Actor. b. Gosforth, Newcastle-upon-Tyne, England. e. Leeds Univ. Rec'd scholarship at Royal Academy of Dramatic Art. Ken Russell found him there and gave him role in Savage Messiah (1972). Has done much TV work in Britain.
PICTURES INCLUDE: Savage Messiah, The Mutations, Dead Cert.

ANZARUT, RAYMOND: Executive producer. b. Lebanon, 1912. e. French Lyceum, Alexandria, Egypt and Paris. Entered film industry 1941 on Jeannie. Subsequently worked on The Day Will Dawn, Talk About Jacqueline, Secret Mission, On Approval. Prod. asst. on They Met in the Dark. Prod. mgr. Flight from Folly. Prod. mgr. in Egypt on Caesar and Cleopatra in 1945. With Marcel Hellman as prod. mgr. on Meet Me at Dawn. Prod. mgr. Swiss location, Scott of the Antarctic; prod. mgr. of Wessex Film Productions Ltd. on Esther Waters, Once a Jolly Swagman, All Over the Town, Mr. Prohack, The Wooden Horse, Gen. prod. mgr. on The Grand Design (six technicolor two-

reelers on European Recovery for E.C.A.). Appointed gen. mgr. of Wessex 1950. Appointed prod. & admin. head, E.C.A. Motion Picture Section, Paris, 1952. Then with Coronado (Sea Devils), Carol Reed 1–1 British Lion (Man Between), Watergate-British Lion (An Inspector Calls) 1953. British Lion-London Films (The Man Who Loved Redheads), David Lean-Lopert Films Inc. (Summer Madness) 1954, London Films (Storm Over the Nile) 1955, Sailor Beware 1955, Dry Rot 1956, Esther Costello 1956–57. Assoc. prod. on The Silent Enemy 1957, Room at the Top, 1958, Our Man in Havana, 1959, 1960; prod. sup. Mysterious Island (Charles Schneer 1–1 Columbia), 1961; Lolita, 1962; The War Lover, Lord Jim. Reconnaissance of South-East Asia, setting up and filming in Hong Kong and Cambodia. Decorated by Prince Sihanouk of Cambodia; prod. sup., Scene Nun, Take One. Assoc. prod. The Hill, 1966–67; The Dirty Dozen. Exec. prod. for Warner Bros. Seven Arts Prods. Ltd. London, May 1967–Sept. 1969 when Company was taken over by Kinney. Re-joined Ken Hyman in Nov., 1969 (Inter-Hemisphere Productions Ltd.) as prod. exec., 71/72 preparing projects for Universal Pictures Ltd. 1972 with Kenneth Hyman reverted to indep. prod. and helped prepare Emperor of the North Pole, in London. Organized and supervised all London filming for Gaumont International (Paris). Le Silencieux. 1973: preparing the Heights of Aervos for Inter-Hemisphere Productions. Organized and supervised Eng. loc. for La Gifle. Rejoined Inter-Hemisphere Prod., 1975–76.

APFEL, EDWIN R.: Executive. b. New York, N.Y., Jan. 2, 1934. e. Franklin and Marshall College, B.A., 1955. copywriter and account executive, Donahue and Coe, 1955–60; adv. publicity dept., Metro-Goldwyn-Mayer, 1960–62; dir. of adv. and creative services, MGM, Verve Records, 1962–63; dir. of adv., Embassy Pictures 1963–65; Advertising Writer, Consultant, 1965.

APPELBOOM, MAX: Producer. b. Amsterdam, Holland, March 7, 1924. e. art schools in Holland, Belgium and France. Started in the motion picture business in 1946 with J. Arthur Rank, then to RKO Radio Pictures. Worked from 1953–56 in Hollywood as writer, director and producer. Returned in 1956 to his home base, Amsterdam. Now pres. Max Appelboom Productions Inc. and Appletree Filmproductions Inc.
PICTURES INCLUDE: Floris, Monkey Business, Will O' The Wisp, Water For Waterland, The Bearboat, Gangrene, The Buggy Man and The New Adventures of Heidi.

APTED, MICHAEL: DIRECTOR. Broke into show business at Granada TV in England in early 1960s as trainee, researcher, and finally director. By 1965 was producer-director for local programs and current affairs; then staff drama dir. for TV series, plays and serials. In late 1960s left Granada to free-lance.
PICTURES: Triple Echo, Stardust, The Squeeze, Agatha, Coal Miner's Daughter, Continental Divide.
TELEVISION: Poor Girl, High Kampf, Highway Robbery, Kisses at 50, The Collection (won Intl. Emmy Award for last).

ARBEID, BEN: Producer. b. London, England, 1924. Ent. m.p. ind. 1947. Prod. man./executive some 20 features, TV series, 1961–1964 prod. The Barber of Stamford Hill, Private Potter, The Children of the Damned, Murder Most Foul, Murder Ahoy, The Alphabet Murders, 1966; The Jokers, 1967; Assignment K.; 1968: Exec. prod., Before Winter Comes; 1969; Hoffman; 1972; The Hireling, Grand Prix—Cannes 1973; 1977 The Water Babies; 1978 The Eagles Wing.

ARCHAINBAUD, GEORGE: Director. b. Paris, France, e. Paris U.; film director since 1915; in U.S. dir. World Films, later Selznick Pictures, RKO, Paramount, etc. Many Hopalong Cassidys, Gene Autrys for Col.; Lone Ranger, Gene Autry, Range Rider, Anne Oakley, Screen Gem, etc., film series for TV.

ARCHER, ANNE: Actress. Daughter of actress Marjorie Lord and actor John Archer. Married Terry Jastrow, actor and TV network sports producer-director.
PICTURES: The All-American Boy, Honkers, Cancel My Reservation, Trackdown, Lifeguard, Paradise Alley, Hero at Large, Green Ice.
TELEVISION: The Pirate (mini-series), The Blue Knight, Seventh Avenue.

ARCHER, JOHN: Actor. r.n. Ralph Bowman, b. Osceola, Neb., May 8, 1915; e. U. So. Calif. Won Jesse L. Lasky "Gateway to Hollywood" talent quest; m.p. debut in "Flaming Frontiers" 1938"; on N.Y. stage also.
PICTURES INCLUDE: White Heat, After Nightfall, Destination Moon, Big Trees, Yank in Indo-China, Sound Off, Rodeo, Sea Tiger, The Stars Are Singing, Dragon's Gold, No Man's Woman, Emergency Hospital.

ARCHER, ROBERT V.: Executive. Joined Paramount Pictures in 1967 as adm. asst. to v.p. of facilities and TV prod. In 1975 named dir. of studio admin. 1977 promoted to dir. of studio operations and admin., responsible for prod. servicing and admin. depts. of studio.

ARCHERD, ARMY: Columnist-TV Commentator. rn. Armand Archerd, b. N.Y., Jan. 13. e. UCLA Grad. '41, US Naval Academy Post Graduate School, 1943. Started as usher at Criterion Theatre, N.Y., while in high school. After grad. UCLA, worked at Paramount studios before entering Navy, Lt., joined AP Hollywood bureau 1945, Herald-Express, Daily Variety as columnist, 1953. M.C. Hollywood premieres and Academy Awards. President, founder Hollywood Press Club, awards from Masquers, L.A. Press Club, Hollywood Foreign Press Club, and "Newsman of the Year" award from Publicists Guild, 1970; "Movie Game" TV Series; People's Choice, co-host.

ARCHIBALD, JAMES: (M.B.E., OSr.J., J.P., M.A., Hon. F.T.C.L., F.R.S.A.). Producer, writer, b. 1920. e. Westminster School, Merten College, Oxford. With Rank Organization 1950–57, later J. Walter Thompson Co. Currently chairman James Archibald & Associates Ltd. Chmn. Nat. Mus. Counc. of G.B. Prod. writer credits incl.: Some People, The King's Breakfast, The Launching, The Scheme, Overture and Beginners, The More Man Understands, Breakthrough, Town Nurse Country Nurse, Soldier '67, Opus, Speaking of Britain, In Search of Opportunity, 16 shorts for British Pavilion Expo '67, Music! The Violin, The Threadmakers, Dialogue, Ambience, Island of Rainbows, For the Community, Enigma Variations, Shapes of The Future, The Engineer is a Woman, Magic Ride, The Science of Farming, Sweet Thames, 15 short color films for British Pavilion, Expo '70, Heuga, Images, International Company, Hovertrain, Talking of Science, What Did You Learn at School Today?, Richness and Complexity, Danger from Fire, 1000th Chance, Time for Thought?, Barriers, It's All Man Made, A Child's World, No Turning Back, Rehearsal, Cement, Birdstrike, A New Beginning, Sugar, Attitudes, Festival, Sea Symphony, Music in Scotland, The Single Team, To Sustain Life, Figures, Royal Doolton, Electronics of Film, Stock Exchange.

ARDEN, EVE: Actress. r.n. Eunice Quedens. b. Mill Valley, Calif., 1912. Appeared with Alcazar stock co., Bandbox Repertory Theatre; Broadway debut in "Ziegfeld Follies of 1936" also in "Ziegfeld Follies of 1938" and Let's Face It, Night and Day, Cover Girl, Voice of the Turtle, Goodbye, My Fancy, We're Not Married, Our Miss Brooks, Anatomy of a Murder, Dark at the Top of the Stairs, Sergeant Deadhead, The Strongest Man in the World, Grease.
   TV: Our Miss Brooks, The Eve Arden Show, The Mothers-in-Law.
   STAGE: Mame, Hello Dolly, Butterflies Are Free.

ARDEN, MARY: Actress. b. Litchfield, Mich., Dec. 9, 1910. e. Northwestern U., Anne Wolters School of Speech & Drama. Appeared in stock; radio, March of Time, Lux.
   PICTURES INCLUDE: Jealousy, Youth Aflame, Missing Corps, Father Take a Wife, Best Years of Our Lives.
   TV: Playhouse 90, Climax, Studio One.

ARKIN, ALAN: Actor-Director, b. New York City, March 26, 1934. e. Los Angeles City College, Los Angeles State College, Bennington (Vt.) College. Member folk singing group The Tarriers; off-Broadway, Second City, Man Out Loud, From the Second City; Broadway, Enter Laughing, Luv. Dir. Little Murders, White House Murders.
   PICTURES INCLUDE: The Russians Are Coming, The Russians Are Coming, Wait Until Dark, The Heart is a Lonely Hunter, Popi, Catch 22, Deadhead Miles, Last of the Red Hot Lovers, Freebie and the Bean, Rafferty and the Gold Dust Twins. Director: Little Murders, Hearts of the West, 7½ Per Cent Solution, The In-Laws, Simon, Chu Chu and the Philly Flash.

ARKOFF, SAMUEL Z.: Producer, Motion Picture Executive. Chairman & President of the Samuel Z. Arkoff Company (formed 1980) and Arkoff Int'l. Pictures (formed 1981). b. Fort Dodge, Ia., June 12, 1918. e. U. of Colorado, U. of Iowa & Loyola U. Law School. m. Hilda Rusoff. USAF Cryptographer World War II. Co-founder American Releasing, 1954, and American International Pictures, 1955. President and Chairman of the Board American International Pictures until 1979. Named with partner James H. Nicholson as Producers of the Year in 1963 by Allied States Association of Motion Picture Theatre Owners and in 1964 as Master Showmen of the Decade by the Theatre Owners of America. Also named Producers of the Year at the Show-A-Rama VIII, and in 1966 and 1967 voted among top ten producers in exhibitor ratings by the independent theatre owners. In Rome in 1970 honored by President of the Republic of Italy with decree naming him a Commendatore of the Order of Merit. In 1971 he and Nicholson named Pioneers of the Year by the Foundation of the Motion Picture Pioneers, Inc. Since appointment in 1973, has served as International Ambassador of Variety Clubs International. Appointed Member of the Board of Trustees of Loyola Marymount Univ., Los Angeles, in 1979.
   PRODUCTION CREDITS: On more than 200 pictures including Amityville Horror, Dressed to Kill, How to Beat the High Cost of Living, The Earthling, Love at First Bite, Meteor, California Dreaming, Force Ten from Navarone, The

House of Usher, Pit and the Pendulum, Tales of Terror, Master of The World, Premature Burial, Panic in the Year Zero, The Raven, Beach Party, Haunted Palace, Comedy of Terrors, Bikini Beach, Masque of the Red Death, Muscle Beach Party, Pajama Party, Tomb of Ligeia, Wild Angels, Devil's Angels, The Trip, Three in the Attic, Wild in the Streets, The Oblong Box, Scream and Scream Again, Murders in the Rue Morgue, Cry of the Banshee, Bloody Mama, Wuthering Heights, Dr. Phibes, Frogs, Blacula, Dillinger, Heavy Traffic, Hennessy, Cooley High, Food of the Gods, Futureworld, Great Scout and Cathouse Thursday, Land that Time Forgot, People That Time Forgot, At The Earth's Core, Island of Dr. Moreau, and A Winning Season.

ARLEDGE, ROONE: Executive. b. Forest Hills, N.Y. e. Columbia Univ. Entered industry with Dumont Network in 1952; joined U.S. Army, 1953, serving at Aberdeen Proving Ground in Maryland, where produced and directed radio programs. Joined NBC in 1954 where held various production positions. Joined NBC in 1954 where held various production positions. In 1960 went to ABC TV; 1964, named v.p. in chg. of ABC Sports. Created ABC's Wide World of Sports in April, 1961. Named pres. of ABC Sports in 1968; pres. of ABC News and Sports, 1977. Holds four George Foster Peabody Awards for sports reporting; 19 Emmy awards.

ARLEN, HAROLD: Composer, b. Buffalo, N.Y., Feb. 15, 1905. Started as pianist, singer, arranger for popular orchestras; songs include: Stormy Weather, I've Got the World On a String, Let's Fall in Love, Blues in the Night, Accentuate the Positive.
   BROADWAY: You Said It, Earl Carroll's Vanities, Americana, Life Begins at 8:40, Bloomer Girl, Hooray for What, House of Flowers, Jamaica, etc.
   PICTURES INCLUDE: Strike Me Pink, Let's Fall in Love, Wizard of Oz (Academy Award, 1939, for best song, Over the Rainbow), A Day at the Circus, Star-Spangled Rhythm, Love Affair, Sky's the Limit, Here Come the Waves, Cabin in the Sky, Country Girl, Gay Purr-ee, I Could Go On Singin

ARLING, ARTHUR E.: Cinematographer. b. Missouri, Sept. 2, 1906; e. N.Y. Institute of Photography. Entered m.p. Fox studio 1927 as asst. cameraman, 2nd cameraman 1931; operative cameraman on "Gone With the Wind" which won the Academy Award for technicolor photography 1939. Lt. Comdr. U.S.N.R., World War II; received Academy Award as dir. of Photography on "The Yearling" 1946. Member: Amer. Soc. of Cinematographers.
   PICTURES INCLUDE: Homestretch, Captain from Castile, Mother Was a Freshman, You're My Everything, Wabash Avenue, My Blue Heaven, Call Me Mister, Belles on their Toes, The Glass Slipper, Three for the Show, Love Me or Leave Me, I'll Cry Tomorrow, Ransom, Great American Pastime, Tammy & the Bachelor, Pay the Devil, Story of Ruth, Pillow Talk, Lover Come Back, Notorious Landlady, Boys Night Out, My Six Loves.

ARMOUR, REGINALD: Foreign dist., prod. b. Chicago, Ill., Nov. 28, 1905; e. Edinburgh, Scotland. Exec. RCA Victor Co. to 1933; estab. exch. India, Burma, Ceylon RKO Radio; Far East gen. mgr.; European gen. mgr. (Paris) 1937; exec. asst. to pres. RKO 1941; asst. gen. mgr. RKO studios 1942; British & European rep. Walt Disney Prod. 1942; financial field (N.Y.) 1943; exec. vice-pres. Richard Condon, Inc. 1944; with overseas br. OWI 1945; foreign rep. Columbia Internatl. Corp. (N.Y.) 1945–49; joined Republic Pictures Internatl. Corp. 1949; apptd. v.p., 1950; supvr., Europe & Near East for Republic 1952, exec. v.p. Republic Pictures International (Great Britain) and man. dir. Republic Prod. (Gt. Brit.) Ltd.; exec. v.p. Republic Pictures International Corp., 1955; pres., The Dorsey Corp., 1960; Vice Chmn., The Dorsey Corp., 1964; pres., SOS Photo-Cine-Optics, Inc., 1965; pres. F&B/Ceco of Calif. Inc., 1967; pres. Instant Protection Systems, Inc., 1971. Exec. V.P. and Treas. The Quedo Corporation and International Producers Services, Inc. 1973.; 1974, V.P. & Treas., Dyna-Soar, Inc.; 1977, exec. v.p. & treas., Two Feathers Prods.

ARMSTRONG, GORDON: Executive, b. East Orange, N.J., Nov. 26, 1937. e. Arizona State Univ., graduate studies at N.Y.U. Entered ind. as newspaper contact for MGM (1960–63); with Allan, Foster, Ingersoll and Weber 1963–70 as acct. exec.; joined 20th Century-Fox in 1970 as nat. pub. dir. In 1975 appt. dir. of adv.-pub.-promo. for Dino De Laurentiis Corp. In 1978, became vice pres., worldwide marketing for the company; 1980, named v.p., adv.-pub.-prom., Universal Pictures.

ARNALL, ELLIS GIBBS: Lawyer, Exec. b. Newnan, Ga. Mar. 20, 1907; e. Mercer U.; U. of South, A.B. 1928, D.C.L. 1947; U. of Georgia LL.B. 1931; Atlanta Law School, LL.D. 1947; Piedmont Coll., LL.D. 1943; Bryant Coll., LL.D. 1948. Georgia state representative from Coweta County, 1936–38; asst. Attorney-General (Ga.) 1938–42; Attorney-General (Ga.) 1942–43; Governor of Ga. 1943–47; pres. Dixie Life Insurance Co.; pres., Columbus National Life Insurance Co. senior mem. law firm Arnall, Golden & Gregory; pres. Georgia State Jr. Chamber of Commerce 1939; trustee U.

9

of South; author of "The Shore Dimly Seen" 1946. "What The People Want" 1948; member U.S. Natl. Com. on UNESCO; member U.S. delegation to 4th annual conference UNESCO, Paris, France, 1949. Member: SIMPP (Pres. 1948); 1952 on leave as dir. Office of Price Stabilization, Washington; back to SIMPP, Sept. 1952; pres. Ind. Film Prod. Export Corp., 1953; member bd. of dir., exec. comm., COMPO, numerous honorary societies, mem. exec. com., U.S. Nat. Comm. for UNESCO, 1964–65, trustee, Mercer Univ. 1964–68; chair. bd. Coastal States Life Insurance Co., chair. bd. National Association of Life Companies. Member Academy Motion Picture Arts & Sciences; vice chm., Sun Life of America Group, Inc.

ARNAZ, DESI: Actor, b. Santiago, Cuba, Mar. 2, 1917. e. Colegio Dolores, Jesuit Prep School, Santiago; at the age of 17 was the vocalist with a band at Miami Beach, Fla.; later with own rhumba band; played in N.Y. night clubs; on stage in "Too Many Girls" m.p. debut in "Too Many Girls" 1940; served as Staff Sgt. U.S. Army Medical Corps 3 years; musical dir. Bob Hope show 1946–47. Indep. prod.-owner, Corona Breeding Farm.
PICTURES INCLUDE: Father Takes a Wife, Four Jacks and a Jill, Navy Comes Through, Bataan, Cuban Pete, Long Long Trailer, Holiday in Havana; (actor-prod.) Forever Darling.
TV: (Actor-exec. prod.) I Love Lucy TV films, The Lucille Ball-Desi Arnaz Show; Pres. Desilu Productions, Inc., 1962; Pres. Desi Arnaz Prod. Inc., 1965; Prod. The Mothers-in-Law.

ARNAZ, JR., DESI: Actor-Singer, b. Jan. 19, 1953. Son of Lucille Ball and Desi Arnaz. Began appearing on I Love Lucy show on TV in infancy and on various Lucy shows since. Gained fame as rock singer and musician with the Dino, Desi and Billy group. Film debut in Red Sky at Morning in 1972.
PICTURES INCLUDE: Red Sky at Morning, Marco, She Lives (tv), A Wedding.

ARNAUD, LEO: Composer, arranger, conductor. b. Lyons, France, July 24, 1904. e. Ormesson Music Acad., Ph.D. Faculty mem. & symph. cond., Ormesson Music Acad., 1922–27; mus. dir. & arr. in France & England, 1927–30; Fred Waring Orch., U.S., 1931–35; arr., vocal coach, comp., mus. dir., MGM, 1936–44; U.S. Armed Forces, 1945 dir. many orch. including; L.A. Concert Band, American Legion Band, Hollywood String Orch., Beverly Hills, Symph. Orch.; free-lance mus. dir., comp., arr. since 1945.
PICTURES INCLUDE: One Touch of Venus, Easter Parade, Date With Judy, Three Little Words, Lovely to Look At, Stars & Stripes Forever, Rose Marie, Seven Brides for Seven Brothers.

ARNE, PETER: Actor. b. British Malaya, 1922. Screen debut England 1955 in Timeslip. Under contract to Associated British Picture Corporation since 1956.
PICTURES INCLUDE: Murder Anonymous, Cockelshell Heroes, Tarzan and the Lost Safari, High Tide at Noon, The Moonraker, Intent to Kill, Danger Within, Conspiracy of Hearts, Scent of Mystery, Sands of the Desert, Hellfire Club, The Story of David, Treasure of Monte Cristo, Pirates of Blood River, Ice Cold in Alex, The Victors, Black Torment, The Girl in the Headlines, Strangers Meeting, The Sandwich Man, The Dambusters, The Purple Plain, Khartouri, Battle Beneath the Earth, Chitty Chitty Bang Bang, The Oblong Box, When Eight Bells Toll, House of Evil, Straw Dogs, Nobody Ordered Love, Antony and Cleopatra, Return of the Pink Panther, Providence, Agatha, Pentious Passage.
TV: The Saint, Danger Man, Crane, series. The Mask of Janus, The Spies, Baron, Man in the Suitcase, Gulliver's Travels, The Champion, Night Conspirators, Hereward The Wake, The Avengers, Father Tiger, The Third Man, This Way for Murder, Vendetta, Poor Charley, Departments, The Champions, The Survivors, The Trigaree Affair, All Out for Kangaroo Valley, Special Branch, The Shattered Eye, Take 3 Girls, The Stallion, Rivals of Sherlock Holmes, Softly Softly, Task Force, The Fox, A Place in Europe, The Ventures Quiller, The Expert, Tycoon.

ARNELL, PETER: Producer. b. Bridgeport, Conn., e. U. of Mich., A.B. Pub. dir., prog. dir., WJLS, Beckley, W.Va.; m.c. & disc jockey, WPEN, Philadelphia; actor, announcer, N.Y.; creator of Rate Your Mate, Name's the Same; creator & prod. of Wheel of Fortune, Balance Your Budget, I'll Buy That, Take a Guess, What's in a Word? prod. Chance of Romance, Take a Good Look, Celebrity Talent Scouts, Face the Facts, Talent Scouts, Take My Word, Ernie Kovacs' Take a Good Look.

ARNESS, JAMES: Actor. b. Minneapolis, Minn., May 26, 1923. e. Beloit College. Served in U.S. Army; worked in advertising, real estate; m.p. debut in Farmer's Daughter.
PICTURES INCLUDE: Battleground, Hell Gate, Man from Texas, People Against O'Hara, Iron Man, The Thing, Big Jim McLain, Horizon's West, Lone Hand, Island in the Sky, Veils of Bagdad, Hondo, Her Twelve Men, Them, Many Rivers to Cross, Flame of the Islands, Sea Chase.
TV SHOWS: Gunsmoke, How the West Was Won.

ARNOLD, DANNY: Writer, actor. r.n. Arnold Rothman; b. New York, N.Y., Jan. 23, 1925. Appeared in summer stock, night clubs, vaudeville; entered m.p. ind. as sound effects ed., Columbia, 1944–46; then legit., night clubs, vaudeville, 1946–50. Appeared in m.p., Breakthrough, Inside the Walls of Folsom Prison, Sailor Beware, Jumping Jacks, Scared Stiff, Stars Are Singing; featured on Martin and Lewis TV show 2 yrs., and wrote their Comedy Hours to 1953.
PICTURES INCLUDE: collab. s.p., story, The Caddy; collab. s.p., Desert Sands: story, s.p., Fort Yuma, story, s.p. Rebel in Town; s.p., Outside the Law. Writer-TV, Tennessee Ernie Ford Show.

ARNOLD, EDDY: Singer. Radio performer, Nashville, Tenn.; recording star since 1946; records include That's How Much I Love You, Anytime; star of Eddy Arnold Show, ABC-TV.

ARNOLD, JACK: Producer, Director. b. New Haven, Conn., Oct. 14, 1916; e. Ohio State U., Amer. Acad. of Dramatic Arts. Actor on B'way, Brit. m.p.; U.S. Air Force, 1942–45; prod. 25 documentary films for State Dept., Army & private industry including With These Hands; dir., 1952.
PICTURES INCLUDE: The Mouse That Roared, Bachelor in Paradise, Global Affair, The Incredible Shrinking Man, It Came From Outer Space, The Creature from the Black Lagoon, Girls in The Night, Revenge of The Creature, The Tattered Dress, Glass Web, Man in The Shadow, Man From Bitter Ridge; dir. story; Tarantula, Red Sundown, Decision at Durango, Outside The Law, Pay The Devil, No Name On The Bullet, The Lady Takes A Flyer, The Lively Set, High School Confidential. Producer, Universal 1956; dir., Black Eye, 1974, Swiss Conspiracy, 1975.

ARNOUL, FRANCOISE: Actress. r.n. Francoise Gautsch. b. Algeria, 1931. Studied acting in Paris; m.p. debut in 1949.
PICTURES INCLUDE: Companions of the Night, Sheep Has Five Legs, The Bed, Inside a Girl's Dormitory, Tempest in the Flesh, Only the French Can (French CanCan).

ARNOW, MAXWELL: Executive. b. New York; married; e. graduate New York University school of law. Manager New York office Leo Morrison, Inc.; then talent executive for Warner Brothers in east from Jan. 1, 1932. Coast casting director, August, 1932, July, 1937. Then executive capacity to 1938; production executive, Selznick-International, "Gone With the Wind"; production executive Walter Wanger Production, 1939–1940; talent exec. Columbia Pictures, 1941–56; v.p., Hecht-Lancaster Org., 1956; talent exec., Columbia Pictures, 1958–61; exec. v.p. Artists & Production Associates, Inc., 1962.

ARNOW, TED J.: Executive. b. Brooklyn, N.Y. e. St. Johns Univ. Washington and Lee Univ. Served as dir. of recreation for 262nd General Hospital in Panama. Veteran of over 40 yrs. in amusement industry. Is v.p. for adv., pub., & promo, for Loew's Theatres. Member: Motion Picture Pioneers, Variety Clubs, Will Rogers Hospital; former pres. of AMPA (Assoc. M.P. Advertisers).

ARTHUR, ART: Prod. writ. exec. b. Toronto, Can., July 24, 1911. e. Jarvis Collegiate Inst. M. Jessica Pepper. Broadway columnist, Brooklyn Daily Eagle; news mgr. Toronto Star News Service; newspaperman on various dailies; pub. rel. in 1936, entered m.p. ind. as writer 1937; U.S. Army 1943–46; wrote script for "Seeds of Destiny" which won 1947 Academy Award for documentary; & AAF films incl. "Air Pattern-Pacific" Member: Writers Guild of America (exec. bd. mem. 3 times), Prod. Guild of America, Nat. Academy of TV Arts & Science, AMPAS, Pub. Rel. Society of America, Pub. Guild, exec. staff C. B. DeMille, former exec. secy. Hollywood M.P. Ind. Council, exec. staff, Ivan Tors Films. Former member, exec. bd. COMPO; former Executive Coordinator, Film and Television Coordinating Committee.
PICTURES INCLUDE: Sun Valley Serenade; (collab. s.p.) Tight Shoes, Riding High, Everything Happens at Night, Fabulous Dorseys, Montana Mike, Northwest Stampede, Song of India, Clarence The Cross-Eyed Lion, Zebra in The Kitchen, Around the World Under the Sea, Birds Do It, The Daring Game, Hello Down There; co-prod., collab. story Battle Taxi, co-prod., writ. Rhino, Flipper's New Adventure; writer, TV., Sea Hunt, Ripcord, Beachcomber, Man and The Challenge, Flipper, Aquanauts, Daktari, Gentle Ben.

ARTHUR, BEATRICE: Actress. b. New York City, May 13. e. Franklin Institute of Sciences & Art. m. Gene Saks. Studied with Erwin Piscator at New School for Social Research; first stage role as Lysistrata; professional stage debut in Dog Beneath the Skin, 1947, followed by Gas, Yerma, No Exit, Six Characters in Search of an Author, The Owl and the Pussycat, etc.; stock appearances include Personal Appearance, Candlelight, Love or Money, The Voice of the Turtle; recent N.Y. stage includes Ullysses in Nighttown, Chic, Mame (Tony award), Fiddler on the Roof.
PICTURES INCLUDE: That Kind of Woman, Lovers and Other Strangers, Mame, History of the World—Part I.
TV: Numerous guest appearances; Maude.

ARTHUR, EDWARD B.: Executive. b. New York City, Sept. 30, 1915. e. San Jose State Coll.; Los Angeles Jr. Coll. Engaged in operation management, purchasing of films etc. in Calif., N.Y., Missouri, Illinois; served in armored div. World War II, 1st Lt., at close of war Special Service unit (Germany) in chg. of distribution of films to service units; resumed his post as gen. mgr. Arthur Enterprises, Inc. which he had joined in 1935; named pres. St. Louis Amusement Co., 1946. Member: Variety Club.

ARTHUR, JEAN: Actress b. New York City, Oct. 17, 1908. On stage; minor roles. m.p. debut as lead in "Warming Up" 1928.
PICTURES INCLUDE: Canary Murder Case, Mysterious Dr. Fu Manchu, Whirlpool, Mr. Deeds Goes to Town, You Can't Take It With You, Too Many Husbands, Talk of the Town, Lady Takes a Chance, Impatient Years, Foreign Affair, Shane.
N.Y. STAGE: Peter Pan, 1950.
TV: The Jean Arthur Show.

ARTHUR, ROBERT: Actor, r.n. Robert Arthaud. b. Aberdeen, Wash., June 18; e. U. Washington (U.S. Navy training program). Won H.S. radio announcing contest; prof. announcer & disc jockey; m.p. debut in "Roughly Speaking" 1945.
PICTURES INCLUDE: Nora Prentiss, Sweetheart of Sigma Chi, Devil on Wheels, Mother Wore Tights, 12 O'Clock High, September Affair, Air Cadet, Big Carnival, On the Loose, Belles on Their Toes, Just For You, The Ring, Young Bess, Take the High Ground, Return from the Sea, Top of the World, Desperadoes Are in Town, The System, Green Grass of Wyoming, Switchblade, Hellcats of the Navy, Young and Wild, Yellow Sky, Mother is a Freshman.

ARTHUR, ROBERT: Producer, b. New York City, Nov. 1, 1909; e. Southwestern U., U. Southern Calif. Oil operator 1929–36; joined MGM as writer 1937. Served in the United States Army 1942–5.
PICTURES INCLUDE: (prod.) Buck Private Come Home, For the Love of Mary, Mexican Hayride, Abbott and Costello in Foreign Legion, Louisa, Wistful Widow of Wagon Gap, Abbott & Costello Meet Frankenstein, Francis, Golden Horde, Starlift, Story of Will Rogers, The Big Heat, The Black Shield of Falworth, Ricochet Romance, The Long Gray Line, Francis in the Haunted House, Day of Fury, Pillars of the Sky, Kelly and Me, Mr. Cory, Midnight Story, Man of a Thousand Faces, A Time to Love and a Time to Die, The Perfect Furlough, Operation Petticoat, The Great Impostor, Come September, Lover, Come Back, The Spiral Road, That Touch of Mink, For Love or Money, The Brass Bottle, Captain Newman, M.D., Bedtime Story, Father Goose, Shenandoah, Blindfold, A Man Could Get Killed, Hellfighters, Sweet Charity.

ASH, RENE: Publicist. b. Brussels, Belgium, March 14, 1939; e. U. of Omaha. Member of AMPA trustee since 1967; member of the Publicists Guild since 1968; Eastern Vice President of Pub Guild since 1973; Author of The Film Editor in Motion Pictures & Television; employed with I.A.T.S.E. 1968–1979, prior to which was assoc. editor, Greater Amusements; various articles published in foreign film magazines; editor-in-chief, Backstage; 1979–80; est. R.L. Ash, Inc., entertainment consultants.

ASHBY, HAL: Director. b. Ogden, Utah. e. Utah State Univ. Began career as film editor. Worked with Norman Jewison on The Cincinnati Kid, The Russians Are Coming, The Russians Are Coming, In the Heat of the Night (AA) and also as assoc. prod on The Thomas Crown Affair and Gaily, Gaily, Directing debut, The Landlord, 1970.
PICTURES INCLUDE: Harold and Maude, The Last Detail, Shampoo, Bound for Glory, Coming Home, Second Hand Hearts, Lookin' To Get Out.

ASHER, IRVING: Production executive. b. San Francisco, Sept. 16, 1903; m. Laura La Plante; began career in pictures in 1919; 1931–38 managing dir. of Warner Bros. First National Prod. in England, 1938; assoc. prod. London Films, exec. prod. Columbia British. In 1945 pres. Rainbow Prods. Exec. in charge TV prod., TCF Television Production, sales head, 1958.
PICTURES INCLUDE: Prison Without Bars, The Four Feathers, Billy the Kid, Blossoms in the Dust, Mr. and Mrs. North, Nazi Agent, The War Against Mrs. Hadley, Here Comes the Groom, Turning Point, The Stars Are Singing, Elephant Walk.

ASHER, JACK: Producer, dir. of photography. b. London, 1916. Ent. m.p. ind. 1930 as asst. cameraman for Gainsborough camera operator 1935; 1940 returned to Gainsborough as camera operator; dir., photography Gainsborough 1961. Many films since; 1961 Co. prod. with brother Robert, She'll Have to Go; dir. of photo., Scarlett Blade, Stitch in Time; dir., photo., The Intelligence Men, dir. photog., The Early Bird, 1965.

ASHER, JANE: Actress. Born London, England, 1946. She has acted in many films and TV plays. Films: Greengage Summer, Masque Of The Red Death, Alfie, Deep End, Henry The Eighth and His Six Wives, etc.

ASHERSON, RENEE: Actress. b. London, Eng., e. Gerrards Cross, Eng. On the stage in rep. Birmingham. London screen debut 1944 in Henry V.
PICTURES INCLUDE: Way to the Stars, Once a Jolly Swagman, Small Black Room, Cure for Love, Pool of London, Malta Story, Red Dress, The Day the Earth Caught Fire.
TV: The Red Dress, The Man Who Could Find Things, At Home, Door of Opportunity. Balance of Her Mind, Life With Father, Black Limelight, The Long Memory, The Simple Truth, The Whole Truth, A Love Story, A Quiet Halfhour, Clayhanger, Jubilee, Quiet as a Nun, Disraeli, Flesh and Blood, Good-bye Dollins.

ASHLEY, ELIZABETH: Actress. b. 1939. Success on stage in 1960 with role in Take Her, She's Mine, winning Tony Award. Next starred in Barefoot in the Park.
PICTURES INCLUDE: The Carpetbaggers, Ship of Fools, The Third Day, The Marriage of a Young Stockbroker, Paperback Hero, Golden Needles, Rancho DeLuxe, 92 in the Shade, Great Scout and Cathouse Thursday, Coma, Windows, Captured.

ASHLEY, JOHN: Actor. r.n. John Atchley. b. Kansas City, Mo., Dec. 25, 1934; e. Oklahoma State U., BA 1956. Career started in Tulsa Little Theatre, 1956; screen debut, 1957, Dragstrip Girl; later: Motorcycle Gang, Suicide Battalion.
TV: Men of Annapolis, Sheriff of Cochise, Frontier Doctor; Matinee Theatre, Jefferson Drum.

ASHLEY, TED: executive b. Brooklyn, N.Y. Aug. 3, 1922. e. City College of N.Y. School of Business Administration. 1937–1939. With William Morris Agency, agent. 1939–1946; formed Ted Ashley Associates, 1946; pres. Ashley Famous Agency, 1954; director and chairman of executive committee of Warner Communications Inc., 1967 to 1974; chairman of bd. and chief exec. officer, Warner Bros. 1969–76.

ASKEY, ARTHUR: Actor. b. Liverpool, Eng., June 6, 1900. e. Liverpool Inst. Experience in concert parties, vaudeville, revues, musical comedy, pantomime; starred in several films including Charley's Aunt, Ghost Train, The Love Match, Ramsbottom Rides Again, and in BBC series. Many command performances.
PICTURES INCLUDE: Make Mine A Million, Friends and Neighbors.

ASNER, EDWARD: Actor. b. Nov. 15, Kansas City, Kans. e. Univ. of Chicago, where affiliated with campus acting group. Served two years with U.S. Army in France. Returned to Chicago to join Playwright's Theatre Club. Moved to N.Y.C.; Broadway debut in Face of a Hero. Appeared off-Broadway, in stock, and with American Shakespeare Festival. In 1961 moved to Hollywood to become active in films and TV.
PICTURES INCLUDE: Peter Gunn, The Slender Thread, The Satan Bug, Kid Galahad, The Wrestler, Fort Apache, The Bronx.
TELEVISION: Medical Center, Name of the Game, Mod Squad, Ironside, The Mary Tyler Moore Show (regular), Hey, I'm Alive (telefilm), Rich Man, Poor Man, Roots, Lou Grant.

ASSEYEV, TAMARA: Producer. Began career as asst. to Roger Corman, working on 8 films withhim. In 1967 started to produce films independently. In 1972 met Alex (Alexandra) Rose and later began co-producing films with her, starting with Drive-In, released by Columbia.
PICTURES INCLUDE: The Wild Racers, Paddy, The Arousers, The History of Atlantic Records, Co-produced with Ms. Rose: Drive-In, I Wanna Hold Your Hand, Big Wednesday, Norma Rae.

ASTAIRE, FRED: Dancer, actor, b. Omaha, Neb. May 10, 1900; e. at home; sister: Adele Astaire, dancer. Brother-sister dance team formed 1907; vaudeville debut 1908; Broadway shows include, Over the Top, Passing Show of 1918, Apple Blossoms, For Goodness Sakes, Lady Be Good, Smiles, Funny Face, Gay Divorcee, Bandwagon; team dissolved 1932; m.p. debut in Dancing Lady 1933; voted Money-Making Star in Motion Picture Herald-Fame Polls 1935–36–37; served with U.S.O. overseas World War II.
PICTURES INCLUDE: Flying Down to Rio, Gay Divorcee, Roberta, Top Hat, Swing Time, Carefree, Story of Vernon and Irene Castle, Holiday Inn, Sky's the Limit, Ziegfeld Follies, Blue Skies, Easter Parade, Special Academy Award for "raising standards of all musicals," 1949. TV specials. Won 9 Emmy Awards, 1958 (An Evening with Fred Astaire) 1959, Another Eve, with Fred Astaire; 1960 Astaire Time; Alcoa Premiere, 1962, Barkleys of Broadway, Let's Dance, Three Little Words, Royal Wedding, Belle of New York, Band Wagon, Daddy Long Legs, Funny Face, Silk Stockings, On the Beach, The Pleasure of His Company, Notorious Landlady, Finians Rainbow, 1967, Midas Run, 1968. The Towering Inferno, 1974, That's Entertainment, Part Two, 1976, The Purple Taxi, Ghost Story.

TV: Fred Astaire Show, 1968, It Takes A Thief, A Family Upside Down, Man in the Santa Claus Suit.

ASTIN, JOHN: Actor. b. Baltimore, Md., March 30, 1930. e. Washington and Jefferson College, Washington Drama School, Johns Hopkins U., grad. B.A., U. of Minnesota Graduate School; first prof. job., off broadway, Threepenny Opera; Broadway debut, Major Barbara; dir., co-prod., A Sleep of Prisoners, Phoenix Theatre; during 1955–59, did voices in cartoons, commercials; I'm Dickens . . . He's Fenster, as Harry Dickens, The Adams Family.
STAGE SHOWS INCLUDE: The Cave Dwellers, Ulysses in Nighttown, Tall Story.
PICTURES INCLUDE: West Side Story, That Touch of Mink, Candy, Viva, Max!, Bunny O'Hare, Get to Know Your Rabbi, Every Little Crook and Nanny, Freaky Friday.

ASTOR, MARY: Actress. r.n. Lucille V. Langhanke; b. May 3, 1906; e. Kenwood-Loring School (Chicago). Beauty contest winner 1920; m.p. debut in "Beggar's Maid" 1920; radio m.c. 2½ yrs.; on stage in: Among the Married, Tonight at 8:30, Male Animal.
PICTURES INCLUDE: (silent Don Juan, Bright Shawl, Beau Brummel; (sound) Lost Squadron, Jennie Gerhardt, Easy to Love, Man With Two Faces, Listen Darling, Dodsworth, Maltese Falcon, Across the Pacific, Meet Me in St. Louis, Fiesta, Cynthia, Cass Timberlane, Desert Fury, Act of Violence, Little Women, Any Number Can Play, Kiss Before Dying, Return to Peyton Place, Youngblood Hawke, Hush, Hush Sweet Charlotte.

ATHERTON, WILLIAM: b. New Haven, Conn., 1949. While in high school became youngest member of Long Wharf Theatre Co. Given scholarship to Pasadena Playhouse; then switched to Carnegie Tech School of Drama in 1965. In college years toured with USO prods. in Europe and in stock and industrial shows. Came to N.Y. where first prof. job was in nat'l. co. of Little Murders.
PICTURES INCLUDE: The New Centurions, The Sugarland Express, The Day of the Locust, The Hindenburg, Looking for Mr. Goodbar.
PLAYS: The House of Blue Leaves, The Basic Training of Pavlo Hummel, The Sign in Sidney Brustein's Window.

ATTENBOROUGH DAVID: Broadcaster. b. London, May 8, 1926; e. Wyggeston School, Leicester; Clare College, Cambridge, early career, editor in educational publishing house, ent. BBC-TC Sept. 1952. Prod. Zoo Quest series, Travellers Tales, Adventure and other prog., travel, Eastward with Attenborough, The Tribal Eye, Life on Earth, exploration natural History and anthropology. Controller BBC-2, 1965–68; Dir. of Prog. BBC-TV, 1969–72.

ATTENBOROUGH, RICHARD: Actor, producer, director. b. Cambridge, Eng., Aug. 29, 1923; m. 1945 Sheila Beryl Grant Sim. Wyggeston Grammar School, Leicester. Leverhulme Scholarship to Royal Academy of Dramatic Art, 1941 (Bancroft Medal). First stage appearance Ah Wilderness, 1941. London debut in Awake and Sing, 1942. First film appearance in In Which We Serve, 1942. Appeared in The Little Foxes, Piccadilly Theatre, 1942; Brighton Rock, Garrick Theatre 1943. Joined R.A.F. 1943; seconded to R.A.F Film Unit, 1944, and appeared in Journey Together; demobilised, 1946. Returned to stage, Jan. 1949, in The Way Back (Home of the Brave), to Dorothy, A Son, 1950; Sweet Madness, 1952; The Mousetrap, 1952–54; Double Image, 1956–1957; The Rape of the Belt, 1957–1958.
PICTURES INCLUDE: School for Secrets (Secret Flight), The Man Within (The Smugglers), Dancing with Crime, Brighton Rock (Young Scarface), London Belongs to Me (Dulcimer Street), The Guinea Pig, The Lost People, Boys in Brown, Morning Departure (Operation Disaster), Hell is Sold Out, The Magic Box, Gift Horse (Glory at Sea), Father's Doing Fine, Eight O'Clock Walk, The Ship That Died of Shame, Private's Progress, The Baby and the Battleship, Brothers-in-Law, The Scamp, Dunkirk, The Man Upstairs, Sea of Sand, Danger Within, I'm All Right Jack, Jetstorm, S.O.S. Pacific; 1959 formed Beaver Films with Bryan Forbes and appeared in and co-produced The Angry Silence; formed Allied Film Makers and appeared in their first film The League of Gentlemen; produced Whistle Down The Wind, appeared in Only Two Can Play, All Night Long, The Dock Brief (Trial & Error); produced The L-Shaped Room, appeared in The Great Escape, appeared in and produced Seance on a Wet Afternoon; appeared in The Third Secret, 1963; Guns at Batasi, 1964; The Flight of the Phoenix, 1965; The Sand Pebbles 1965–66; Dr. Dolittle, 1966; The Bliss of Mrs. Blossom, Only When I Larf, 1968. Prod. and dir.: Oh! What a Lovely War, 1968. Appeared in The Last Grenade, A Severed Head, Loot, and made guest appearances in The Magic Christian and David Copperfield, 1969, 10 Rillington Place, 1970, Young Winston, 1972 appeared in Rosebud, Ten Little Indians, Brannigan. Conduct Unbecoming 1974, directed A Bridge Too Far, 1976. Appeared in The Chess Players, 1977; dir. Magic, 1978, actor, The Human Factor, 1978.

ATTERBURY, MALCOLM: Actor. b. Philadelphia, Pa., Feb. 20, 1907, e. Hill School, Pa. Radio editor, Phila. Ledger; prog.

mgr., gen. mgr., performer, Phila. Ledger radio station, WHAT, 7 yrs.; concert, vaudeville, Schubert musicals, 7 yrs.; Tamarack Playhouse, 5 yrs.; owned, oper., Albany Playhouse, 6 yrs.; conducted thea. seminars, Skidmore, R.P.I., College of St. Rose.
TV: Hallmark Hall of Fame, Lux Video Thea., Playhouse 90, Studio One, G.E. Theatre, Cheyenne, Perry Mason, Gunsmoke, 77 Sunset Strip, Alfred Hitchcock Presents, Route 66, The Defenders, The Untouchables, Dr. Kildare, Profiles In Courage, Fugitive, FBI, Hazel, Bonanza, Voyage to the Bottom of the Sea, Judd.
PICTURES INCLUDE: Dragnet, Storm Center, Crime in the Streets, Reprisal, Crime of Passion, Toward the Unknown, No Time for Sergeants, Rio Bravo, North by Northwest, Wild River, From the Terrace, Summer and Smoke, Advise and Consent, The Birds, The Chase, Hawaii.
BROADWAY: One Flew Over the Cuckoo's Nest.

ATTWOOLL, HUGH: Assoc. Producer. b. 1914. Ent. films 1928.
PICTURES INCLUDE: The Castaways, The Horse Without A Head, Three Lives or Thomasina, Dr. Syn, The Moonspinners, The Legend of Young Dick Turpin, The Fighting Prince of Donegal, Only When I Larf, Guns in the Heather, David Copperfield, Kidnapped, Diamonds on Wheels, Persecution, One of our Dinosaurs Is Missing, Escape From The Dark, Harness Fever, Candleshoe, The Spaceman and King Arthur, Watcher in the Woods, The London Connection.

ATWATER, GLADYS: Writer. Has written many m.p. scripts; member of writing team with Robert Bren since 1939; v.p. Bremex, Inc., writings include: (collab. orig.) Man Who Found Himself: (collab. orig. story) Argentine Nights, First Yank into Tokyo, in Old California; (collab. s.p.) Criminal Lawyer, Crashing Hollywood, This Marriage Business, Crime Ring; (collab. story) El Paso, Tag for Murder, Blood on the Shrine, Legacy in Nylons, Aztec Dagger, Female Menagerie. Collab. story, s.p., Great Sioux Uprising, Siege at Red River; collab. s.p. Overland Pacific; collab. stor. Naked Alibi, Treasure of Pancho Villa; TV: Lone Wolf in Mexico, Stolen Train, Casey Jones series, Winds of the Four Seasons, collab. s.p.; collab. s.p. orig. story The Hawaiians.

AUBREY, JAMES T., JR.: Executive. b. La Salle, Ill., Dec. 14, 1918. e. Princeton U., 1941, m. Phyllis Thaxter, U.S. Air Force, 1941–45; salesman, Street and Smith, Conde Nast Pub., 1946–47; account exec. KNX, Los Angeles, 1948; account exec., KNXT, 1951; sales mgr., then gen. mgr., KNXT and CTPN, 1952. Man. network prog., Hollywood CBS-TV, 1956; V.P. programs and talent, ABC-TV 1957; v.-p. CBS. 1958; exec. v.p. CBS-TV, 1959; pres. CBS-TV, 1959.
PICTURES INCLUDE: Futureworld (prod.).

AUDRAN, STEPHANE: Actress. b. France, 1938. Ex-wife of French star Jean-Louis Trintignant; now married to director Claude Chabrol.
PICTURES INCLUDE: Les Cousins (debut under direction of Chabrol), The Champagne Murders, Les Biches, La Femme Infidele, The Beast Must Die, The Lady in the Car, Le Boucher, Without Apparent Motive, Dead Pigeon on Beethoven Street, The Discreet Charm of the Bourgeoisie, The Devil's Advocate, The Blackbird (American film debut), Silver Bears, Blood Relatives.

AUERBACH, NORBERT T.: President & Chief Executive Officer, United Artists Corp. b. Vienna, 1923. Educated in U.S. and served with U.S. Army Intelligence in Europe during World War II. Joined m.p. business in 1946 after graduation from U.C.L.A. (business admin.). First asst. dir. at Service Studios in Calif. Moved to N.Y. to join domestic sales dept. of Film Classics. Left for position with Columbia Pictures in foreign dept. In 1950 assigned to Paris office, where remained for over decade, except for 18 mos. in Portugal as mgr. Returned to Paris in 1953 and filled number of exec. sis. positions for Columbia, ultimately rising to continental mgr. 1961, left Columbia to produce films in France. Resumed career in dist., this time at Paris office of United Artists, becoming continental mgr. In 1966 returned to production to make The Thief of Paris. 1967, joined Seven Arts Prods. heading theatrical and TV sis. operations in Paris. When Seven Arts acquired Warner Bros., he became continental sls. mgr. for Warners in Paris. 1968, set up European prod. and dist. org. for CBS Cinema Center Films, operating from London. 1972, moved to L.A. as v.p., foreign mgr. for CCF. Returned to London in 1973 to be consultant in prod. and dist. Rejoined UA in 1977 as sls. mgr. for Europe and the Middle East. Named snr. v.p. & foreign mgr. in 1978. Named pres. & COO, Jan. 1981; pres., CEO, Feb. 1981.

AUMONT, JEAN PIERRE: Actor. b. Paris, 1913. e. Conservatoire of Drama. Roles French stage and films. U.S. pictures: Assignment in Brittany, Cross of Lorraine. In 1943 enlisted Free French Army.
PICTURES INCLUDE: Heartbeat, Siren of Atlantis, Affairs of a Rogue, Wicked City, Lili, Life Begins Tomorrow, Gay Adventure, Charge of the Lancers, Hilda Crane, Enemy

General, The Devil at 4 O'Clock, Castle Keep, Cauldron of Blood, Day for Night, Mahogany, Catherine & Co.
STAGE: Tovarich, Incident at Vichy, Carnival, Camino Real.

AURELIUS, GEORGE M.: Executive. b. Grasston, Minn., Sept. 16, 1911; e. U. of Minnesota. Ent. m.p. ind. 1927 as usher Finkelstein & Ruben, St. Paul; asst. mgr. 1929–30; to Warner Theatres, New York 1931; man. Moss' Broadway; Minnesota Amusement Co. 1932–41; city mgr. Publix-Rickards-Nace. Paramount-Nace Theatres, Tucson, Ariz. 1941–46; city mgr. Paramount-Nace, Phoenix, Ariz. 1946–49; V.P. ABC Theas. of Arizona, Inc. 1949–67; pres. ABC North Central Theatres, Inc., 1967–1972; V.P. ABC Intermountain Theatres, Inc., V.P. ABC Theatres of California, Inc. 1972–1974; Mgmt. Consulting and ShoWest Convention & Trade Show since 1975, named exec. dir., 1979.

AURTHUR, ROBERT ALAN: Writer-producer. b. New York, N.Y., June 10, 1922. e. Univ. of Pennsylvania, BA, 1942. U.S. Marine Corps., 1942–46; author: History of the Third Marine Division, Inf. Journal Press, 1946; short story writer, The New Yorker, Harpers, Esquire, Sat. Eve. Post, etc., 1946–50; novel: The Glorification of Al Toolum; Rinehart, 1951; partner, Circle Records, 1947–50; freelance TV dramatist, 1951–58, vice-pres., Talent Associates-Paramount Ltd., 1961; pres., Edgewater Prods. Monthly column "Hanging Out" Esquire Magazine 1972, NYU School of Arts, Instructor screenplay writing, 1975; Delegate to Moscow Film Festival, International Writers Guild Symposium, Leningrad, 1975.
TV INCLUDES: script ed., Philco Playhouse, Mr. Peepers, assoc. prod., Philco Playhouse, then prod.; prod., Sunday Showcase, NBC, Years of Decision, pilots: Inside Danny Baker, The Laughmakers, ABC. Head of new prog. dev. United Artists-TV, 1963–4.
PICTURES INCLUDE: screenwriter. Warlock, The Mountain Is Young; writer, co-prod., Edge of the City; s.p. Lilith, s.p. Grand Prix, For the Love of Ivy, s.p. and dir. The Lost Man, Indians (s.p.), Ending (s.p.).
BROADWAY: Author, A Very Special Baby, Kwamina, Carry Me Back to Morningside Heights.

AUSTIN, BUD: Executive. r.n. Harold M. b. New York, N.Y. e. Univ. of North Carolina, New York U., Pres. Austin Productions 1971; U.S. Army 1942–46; pres., Donna Hale Corp. 1948; pres., Lindley Corp. 1949; nat'l sis. mgr. Official Films, 1950–53; vice-pres., Telefilm Ent., 1954; vice-pres, NTA, 1955; pres. Austin Television Prods. Inc., 1956; exec. vice-pres., Goodson-Todman Prods., 1956; exec. vice-pres., Filmways, Inc., 1965; 1973, Vice President Creative Services and Marketing Paramount Pictures Corp. Executive Producer, Elaine May film "Mikey and Nicky," Executive Producer and Creator "Take Five" for CBS-TV; 1973–1976, exec. v.p., Paramount TV; pres., Bud Austin Productions 1979, prod., Perfect Gentlemen; exec. prod., Whew (TV game show).

AUSTIN, EMERY M.: Executive. b. Dallas, Texas, Oct. 5, 1911. e. Central H.S., 1929. Usher with Ralph Talbot theatres, Tulsa, 1928; then doorman, chief usher, house mgr.; mgr. & asst. gen. mgr.; MGM, New Orleans, 1941; Atlanta, 1942; New York 1953; asst. dir. of advtg.-publicity-exploitation. RXET. Feb., 1969. Now pres., Bali-Hai Marine Services, Inc., Miami, Fla.

AUSTIN, JOHN: Producer. b. Australia, 1923; Asst. Dir. of Entertainment for American Red Cross, 1942–45; assoc. West Coast rep. of Rodgers & Hammerstein, 1945–47; with Ministry of Info., Gov't of India, 1947–48; prod. TV films in Europe, 1949; shows include Intrigue, International Rendezvous, International Affair; prod. film, Lasca.

AUSTIN, RAY: Director-Writer-Producer. b. London, England, Dec. 5, 1932. Has written, produced and directed many TV series, specials and movies.
TELEVISION: Director of series: Avengers, The Champions, Department S, Randall & Hopkirk, Ugliest Girl in Town, Journey into the Unknown, etc. Writer: Randall & Hopkirk, Department S. Producer-Director: The Perfumed Garden. Director: It's the Only Way To Go, Virgin Witches, Fun and Games, Space 1999, New Avengers, Hawaii Five-O, Sword of Justice, Webb, Barnaby Jones, Hardy Boys, Wonder Woman, Salvage, B.G. and the Bears, Hart to Hart, The Yeagers, Man Called Sloane, From Here to Eternity, Bad Cast, Westworld. Director-Writer: Black Beauty.
PICTURES: House of the Living Dead.

AUSTRIAN, RALPH BROOKE: Executive. b. New York City, April 29, 1898. Asst. sound dir. Paramount-Publix Lasky Corp. 1928–29; in chg. retail dist. Westinghouse Elec. & Mfg. Co. 1930–32; gen. sales mgr. Koster Radio Corp. 1932; same Emerson Radio & Phono. Corp. 1933–34; asst. v.p. RCA Mfg. Co. 1935–42; WPB Planning Com. 1942–43; exec. v.p. RKO Television Corp. 1943–44, pres. 1945–47; to Foote, Cone and Belding in chg. TV 1948; org. TV consultant service to adv. agencies, theatres, TV stations & m.p. cos. 1949; assoc. N. P. Rathvon & Co., exec. v.p. Multi-Deck Corp. of America; senior associate, Pereira & Luckman, architect-engineers; v.p. Paco, Inc.; west coast

mgr., Allen B. DuMont Labs., Inc., SLS. Man. Ling Electronics, Inc.; Financial Consultant. Dir. Marketing of TV sta. KPLM. Member: SMPTE (fellow), m.p. Pioneers, IRE (senior mem.).

AUTANT-LARA, CLAUDE: Director. Began career as scenic designer for French films in early 1920's; then asst. director; first solo venture experimental film, 1923; in Hollywood, 1930–32. dir. Parlor Bedroom and Bath, Incomplete Athlete.
PICTURES INCLUDE: Devil in the Flesh, Seven Deadly Sins (seq.), Red Inn, Oh Amelia, Game of Love, Red and the Black.

AUTEN, H. WILLIAM; Executive. b. Cardiff, Wales, Mar. 7, 1921; e. Neville House, Eastbourne; U. Coll. School of London. With sales dept., Warner Bros. (London) 1939; served as Major on Brit. Army Staff 1939–47, including custodianship of UFA, GMBH 1945–46; European & Near Eastern mgr. United Artists 1948; asst. foreign mgr. Eagle Lion Films, Inc. (N.Y.) 1948–49; founder & pres. Benagoss Productions, Inc. June, 1949, to produce and finance pictures; org. Ballentine Pict., 1951.

AUTRY, GENE: Actor. b. Tioga, Tex., Sept. 29, 1907. Railroad telegrapher at Sapulpa, Okla., 1925; became radio singer and recording artist (Columbia Records) 1928; screen debut 1934 at Mascot Pictures (later became Republic) as screen's first singing cowboy. Voted top money making Western star 1937–42, and in top Western stars 1936, 1946–54; first Western star to be in top ten money makers from 1938 to 1942. Served in U.S.A.A.F. as flight officer, 1942–45; on USO tour overseas 3 mos.; immediately thereafter resumed radio career with formed sponsor, the Wm. Wrigley Co., formed Gene Autry Productions, Inc.; star of Madison Square Garden Rodeo first in 1940; composed & recorded song "Here Comes Santa Claus"; owner radio & TV stations, and California Angels ball team.

AVAKIAN, ARAM: Director. b. N.Y.C. Was still photographer and editor before becoming director with The End of the Road.
PICTURES INCLUDE: Cops and Robbers, 11 Harrowhouse.

AVALON, FRANKIE: Entertainer. r.n. Francis Thomas Avalone. b. Phila., Sept. 18, 1940; e. South Phila. High. Trumpet Prodigy age 9 yrs.; Recording contract, Chancellor Records, 1957; Gold Record, Venus, 1959; Gold Album, Swingin' on a Rainbow, 1959; Night Clubs.
TV: Ed Sullivan, Perry Como, Pat Boone, Arthur Murray. Dick Clark Shows, Milton Berle, Golden Circle Spectacular; Dinah Shore Show, Steve Allen Show.
PICTURES INCLUDE: Guns of the Timberland, The Alamo, Voyage to the Bottom of the Sea, Sail a Crooked Ship, Panic in the Year Zero, Bikini Beach, Beach Blanket Bingo, Jet Set, I'll Take Sweden, Sgt. Deadhead, The Take, Grease.

AVEDON, DOE: Actress. b. Old Westbury, N.Y. Bookkeeper; then actress.
BROADWAY: Young and the Fair, My Name is Aquilon.
PICTURES INCLUDE: High and the Mighty, Deep In My Heart, The Boss.
TV: Big Town.

AVILDSEN, JOHN G.: Director-Cinematographer-Editor. b. Chicago. e. N.Y. Univ. After service in Army made film with friend, Greenwich Village Story. Then joined ad agency to write and produce film commercials. Entered m.p. industry as ass't. cameraman on Below the Hill, followed with prod. mgr. job on Italian film made in U.S. Then made first theatrical short, Smiles. Arthur Penn hired him as prod. mgr. on Mickey One. Produced, photographed and edited a short, Light, Sound, Diffuse. Returned to industry to make films for ad agencies before resuming theatrical career.
PICTURES INCLUDE: Turn on to Love (1st feature, dir., photo.), Out of It (dir., photo.), Sweet Dreams (dir., photo, editor), Guess What We Learned in School Today? (dir., photo editor), Joe (dir., photo.), Cry Uncle (dir., photo., editor), Save The Tiger (dir.), W.W. and the Dixie Dancekings (dir., editor), The President's Women, Rocky (dir.); Slow Dancing in the Big City (dir., editor, operator), The Formula (dir.), Neighbors (dir.).

AXELROD, GEORGE: Playwright, writer, prod., dir. b. New York, N.Y., June 9, 1922, stage mgr., actor, summer stock, 1940–41; radio writer, 1941–52; writer, novels: Beggar's Choice, Blackmailer; co-writer, night club musical: All About Love, 1951.
BROADWAY: The Seven Year Itch, Will Success Spoil Rock Hunter?, Visit to a Small Planet, Once More With Feeling, Goodbye Charlie.
PICTURES INCLUDE: Phfft, The Seven Year Itch, Bus Stop, Breakfast at Tiffany's, The Manchurian Candidate, Paris When It Sizzles, How to Murder Your Wife, Lord Love a Duck, The Secret Life of an American Wife (prod., s.p.).

AXELROD, JONATHAN: Writer. b. N.Y.C. July 9, 1948. Stepson of writer George Axelrod. Started as on-set "gofer" before writing screen plays.
PICTURES INCLUDE: The Dirty Movie, Every Little Crook and Nanny.

AYRES, GERALD: Producer. e. Yale Univ., where had four plays produced. Became Broadway play doctor and then joined Columbia Pictures as freelance reader. Named story editor; exec. ass't. to v.p. Mike Frankovich; then v.p. in chg. creative affairs in Hollywood. Left in 1970 to become independent. Formed Acrobat Films.
PICTURES INCLUDE: Cisco Pike, The Last Detail.

AYRES, LEW: Actor. b. Minneapolis, Minn., Dec. 28, 1908. Toured Mexico with own orchestra; played with Henry Halstead's Orchestra; screen debut in The Sophomore, "The Kiss" 1929; served as medical corpsman & asst. chaplain World War II.
PICTURES INCLUDE: All Quiet on the Western Front, Common Clay, Doorway to Hell, Okay America, State Fair, Dr. Kildare series; (dir.) Hearts of Bondage, Dark Mirror, Unfaithful, Johnny Belinda, The Capture, New Mexico, No Escape, Donovan's Brain, The Carpetbaggers, Advise and Consent, Altars to the East (dir-nar. star-prod.), Last Generation, 1971, Biscuit Eater, The Man, Battle for the Planet of the Apes, Damien-Omen II, Battlestar Galactica.

AZZATO, ANTHONY: Executive: b. New York City, Oct. 7, 1912. e. Fordham Univ., City Col. of New York; production supervisor, film editor, director, documentary and comm. films, 1938–48; Sound Masters, Inc.; U.S. Army Signal Corps, 1942–46; film editor, Paramount, 1932–42; appt'd director of film programs, WPIX, 1948; also film program consultant, KLAC, Los Angeles; dir. of station relations, National Telefilm Assoc. 1956, v.p., Swan & Mason Adv., 1961; v.p., Sales, Teledynamics Corp.; v.p. Teledynamics Corp.

B

BABCOCK, DWIGHT V.: Writer. b. Ida Grove, Ia., Feb. 19, 1909. e. Modesto Jr. Coll. Author short stories, novelist. First Screenplay at Universal, 1943. 26 screen credits since at various studios. TV, free lance, includes 100 produced teleplays; co-author, Chautauqua.

BACALL, LAUREN: Actress. b. New York City, Sept. 16, 1924; e. American Acad. Dram. Arts. m. late Humphrey Bogart, actor. Fashion model; on stage, plays include: Johnny Two-by-Four, Franklin Street; m.p. debut in "To Have and Have Not" 1944.
BROADWAY: Cactus Flower, Goodbye Charlie, Applause (Tony Award, Best Actress in musical), Woman of the Year.
PICTURES INCLUDE: Big Sleep, Confidential Agent, Dark Passage, Key Largo, Young Man with a Horn, Bright Leaf, How to Marry a Millionaire, Woman's World, Cobweb, Blood Alley, Written on the Wind, Designing Woman, Flame Over India, Shock Treatment, Gift of Love, Sex and the Single Girl, Harper, Murder on the Orient Express, The Shootist, The Fan.
TV: Applause

BACH, STEVEN K.: Production Executive. b. Pocatello, Idaho, April 29, 1940. e. Northwestern Univ. (B.A., 1961; M.A., 1962); Univ. of So. Calif. (cinema, 1966); Universite de Paris (Sorbonne), 1960. Was public school teacher, Winnetka, Ill, 1961–65. Story editor for Mark Taper Forum, 1968; story editor, Katzka-Berne Productions, 1968–70. Joined Palomar Pictures as head of creative affairs in 1970; left to become v.p., Pantheon Pictures 1974–78. Sr. v.p., worldwide production, for United Artists Corp to May, 1981. Formed Lester (Richard)/Bach Prods., 1981.
PICTURES: Worked on Kelly's Heroes, Sleuth, The Heartbreak Kid, The Parallax View, The Taking of Pelham One-Two-Three. Producer of Mr. Billion and Butch and Sundance: The Early Days, both for 20th-Fox. Co-producer of Bdwy. play, Same Time Next Year.

BACK, LEON B.: Exhibitor. b. Philadelphia, Pa., Oct. 23, 1912; e. Johns Hopkins U., B.E., 1932; U. of Baltimore, LL.B., 1933. Entered m.p. ind. as mgr. for Rome Theatres, Inc., Baltimore, Md., 1934; booker, asst. buyer, 1936; asst. to gen. mgr., 1939; U.S. Navy, 1944–46; v.p., gen. mgr., Rome Theatres, 1946; Allied MPTO of Md. 1952–55; nat'l dir. Allied States, 1952–55; nat'l secy. 1954, Pres. NATO of Maryland 1969–80, Pres. USO Council, Greater Baltimore 1969–75; Chairman board of trustees, Employees Benefit Trust for Health & Welfare Council of Central Maryland, 1970–79.

BACKUS, JIM: Actor. b. Cleveland, Ohio, Feb. 25, 1913; e. Amer. Acad. of Dram. Arts. Began in stock & vaudeville; radio announcer; radio actor on Ilum On stage in Hitch

Your Wagon; m.p. debut in Easy Living, Abner, Alan Young show & own shows
PICTURES INCLUDE: Half Angel, His Kind of Woman, Bright Victory, Hollywood Story, Man With a Cloak, Iron Man, Here Come the Nelsons, I'll See You in My Dreams, Deadline, U.S.A., Androcles and the Lion, Don't Bother to Knock, Pat and Mike, Above and Beyond, I Love Melvin, Angel Face, Geraldine, Human Jungle, Francis in the Navy, Rebel Without a Cause, Square Jungle, Meet Me in Las Vegas, The Wonderful World of the Brothers Grimm, Critics Choice, Six Loves, Boys' Night Out, The Horizontal Lieutenant, Zotz!, Hello Down There, Pete's Dragon.
TV: I Married Joan, Gilligan's Island.
RECORDINGS: Delicious, Cave Man.
BOOKS: Rocks On the Roof, Back to Backus, What Are You Doing After the Orgy.

BADDELEY, HERMIONE: Actress. b. Shropshire, Eng., Nov. 13, 1908; e. privately and at Margaret Morris School of Dancing. Stage debut in La Boite A Joujou at Court theatre, 1918; screen debut in Brighton Rock, 1947; many TV, radio, nightclub appearances.
BROADWAY: The Milk Train Doesn't Stop Here Anymore, Canterbury Tales.
PICTURES INCLUDE: Passport to Pimlico, Quartet, Christmas Carol, Pickwick Papers, Mr. Prohack, Belles of St. Trinians, Room at the Top, Jetstream, Expresso Bongo, Let's Get Married, Midnight Lace, Rag Doll, Mary Poppins, The Unsinkable Molly Brown.
TV: Richard of Bordeaux, Drink Doggie Drink, The Gambler, Airmail from Cyprus, The Castaway, Maude.

BADHAM, JOHN: Director. b. England. Raised in Alabama; schooled at Yale, where acquired 2 degrees. Landed first job in Universal Studio mailroom; later was Universal Tour guide and assoc. prod. to Steven Spielberg. Made film trailers. Started directing movies for TV which led to theatrical debut with The Bingo Long & Travelling All-Stars and Motor Kings.
PICTURES: Saturday Night Fever, Dracula, Whose Life Is It Anyway?
TELEVISION: The Law, Isn't It Shocking?, etc.

BAER, JOHN G.: Executive—Engineer. b. New York City, May 8, 1934. e. Univ. of Tenn. at Chattanooga (B.S., physics, 1955). Joined Bausch and Lomb, Inc., as optical and mechanical engineer, 1957–67; director of research and development, 20th Century-Fox, New York, 1967–72; sales/engineering, Century Projector Corp., named pres. & chief exec. officer, Jan. 1, 1975.
MEMBER: Optical Society of America; Society of American Magicians; Intl. Brotherhood of Magicians; Magic Circle (London); 25–30 Club (honorary). Fellow of SMPTE and dir. Theatre Equip. Assn. Chm., PH-22 (motion picture) American Natl. Standards Institute U.S. delegate to Intl. Standards Organization. Elected mayor West Windsor Township, N.J., 1977.

BAILEY, JOSEPH W.: Attorney, producer. b. Columbia City, Ind., Dec. 13, 1910; e. U. of Chicago, PHB, 1928–31, U. of Chicago Law School., J.D., 1931–34. Practicing atty. at law, Chicago, Oct., 1934–June, 1940; with Louis G. Cowan to Apr. 1942; U.S. Navy, 1942–46; v.p. & treas., Louis G. Cowan, 1946–49; mgr., radio-TV dept., Grey Adv. Agency, 1949; exec. prod., Robert Montgomery Show & mgr., John Gibbs literary & talent agency, 1950–1957; Prod. v.p. Ziv-United Artists, Inc. 1957–61. Resigned June 1961 to become partner in firm, Bronstein, Van Veen & Bailey; in practice of law specializing in allied field of TV, motion pictures and the theatre.

BAILEY, PEARL: Entertainer. b. Newport News, Va., March 29, 1918; e. Philadelphia and Washington, D.C. Career started when 15 years old, winner of amateur stage contest; toured mining towns of Pennsylvania as dancer; dancer and singer in vaudeville with Noble Sissle's band; stage acting debut in St. Louis Woman (won Donaldson Award, best newcomer of 1946); many night club appearances and TV shows; screen debut 1947, Variety Girl.
PLAYS INCLUDE: Arms and the Girl, Bless You All, House of Flowers, Hello Dolly.
PICTURES INCLUDE: Carmen Jones, Isn't It Romantic, That Certain Feeling, St. Louis Blues, Porgy and Bess, All the Fine Young Cannibals, The Landlord, Last Generation, Norman, Is That You?

BAILEY, ROBIN: Actor. b. Hucknall (Nottingham) Eng., Oct. 5, 1919. e. Henry Mellish School, Nottingham.
STAGE: Barrets of Wimpole Street, Theatre Royal, Nottingham, 1938; Screen debut, School for Secrets, 1946.
PICTURES INCLUDE: Private Angelo, Portrait of Clare, His Excellency, Gift Horse, Folly to be Wise, Single Handed, Sailor of the King, The Young Lovers, For Better or Worse, Catch Us If You Can, The Whisperers, Spy With A Cold Nose, You Only Live Twice, The Eliminator, Blind Terror, Down by the Riverside, Nightmare Rally, The Four Feathers.
TV: Olive Latimer's Husband, Seven Deadly Sins, The Power Game, Public Eye, Person To Person, Troubleshooters, Armchair Theatre, Split Level, The Newcomers,

Discharge of Trooper Lusby, Brett, Owen M.D., Solidarity, General Hospital, Murder Must Advertise, Vienna 1900, Justice, The Pallisers, The Couch, Way of the World, Upstairs, Downstairs, Walk with Destiny, North and South, A Legacy, I Didn't Know You Cared, Punch Review, Play for Today, The Velvet Glove, Crown Court, Took and Co., The Good Companions

BAKER, CARROLL: Actress. b. Johnstown, Pa., May 28; e. schools there and St. Petersburg (Fla.) Junior Coll. Career started as dancer in night clubs. Actors' Studio N.Y. Stage debut: Escapade, Then, All Summer Long; screen debut; Easy to Love.
PICTURES INCLUDE: Giant. Starred in Baby Doll, But Not for Me, The Miracle, Bridge to the Sun, Something Wild, How the West Was Won, The Carpetbaggers, Station Six Sahara, Sylvia, Cheyenne Autumn, Mister Moses, Harlow, The Sweet Body of Deborah, Paranoia, Andy Warhol's Bad, Watcher in the Woods.

BAKER, DON: Theatre Executive. b. St. Louis, Mo., Dec. 16, 1931. e. St. Louis Univ. V.P., adv.-prom., Loews Theatres, New York. Member NATO nat'l. chm. adv. comm., 1972–present; mem. bd. of dir., Will Rogers Hospital, 1974.

BAKER, GEORGE: Actor. b. Varna, Bulgaria, April 1, 1931, e. Lancing College, Sussex. Stage debut Deal Repertory Theatre, 1946. Film debut The Intruder, 1953.
PICTURES INCLUDE: Dam Busters, Ship That Died Of Shame, Woman For Joe, Extra Day, Feminine Touch, A Hill In Korea, No Time for Tears, These Dangerous Years, Tread Softly Stranger, Lancelot and Guinivere, Curse of the Fly, Mister Ten Per Cent, Goodbye Mr. Chips, Justine, The Executioner, On Her Majesty's Secret Service, A Warm December, The Fire Fighters, The Spy Who Loved Me, Thirtynine Steps, A Nightingale Sang in Berkeley Square.
TV FILM: Fan Show, Ron Raudell's programme 1956, Guinea Pig, Death of a Salesman, The Last Troubadour, The Square Ring, Nick of the River, Mary Stuart, Probation Officers, Far Away Music, It Happened Like This, Boule de Suif, Maigret, Zero One, Rupert Henzau, Miss Memory, Any Other Business, The Navigators, Common Ground, Alice, The Queen and Jackson, The Big Man Coughed and Died, Up and Down, Call My Bluff, The Baron, St. Patrick, Love Life, Seven Deadly Virtues, The Prisoner, The Sex Games, Z Cars, Paul Temple, Candida, Fenn Street, Man Outside, The Persuaders, Main Chance, Ministry of Fear, Voyage in the Dark, Dial M for Murder, Zodiac, The Survivors, I, Claudius, Print Out, Goodbye, Darling.

BAKER, J. EDWIN: Executive. b. Detroit, Mich., June 27, 1914. e. St. John's Coll. m. Marjorie R. Baker, actress. In 1935 produced Asylum of Horrors, stage show featuring the Frankenstein Monster (in person), which is still playing dates after 40 years. Known professionally as Dr. Silkini. In 1960 organized Intl. Artists Pictures, of which he is pres., to produce films.
PICTURES INCLUDE: Phycoscope, Magic Land of Mother Goose, Santa Visits Mother Goose Land, Vampire's Coffin, Teenage Tramp, Aztec Mummy.

BAKER, JOE DON: Actor. b. Texas. Began career on N.Y. stage, impressing critics in Marathon 33 and Blues for Mr. Charlie. Film debut, Cool Hand Luke, 1967.
PICTURES INCLUDE: Guns of the Magnificent Seven, Adam at Six A.M., The Wild Rovers, Welcome Home, Soldier Boys, Junior Bonner, Walking Tall, Charley Varrick, The Outfit, Golden Needles, Mitchell, Framed.

BAKER, LESLIE F.: Executive. b. London 1903. dir. Michael Balcon Productions Ltd., Associated Talking Pictures Ltd., E.M.I. British Film Distributors Ltd., Santor Film Productions Ltd. Ent. film ind. with Gainsborough, 1924. Part. in Baker, Todman and Co., Chartered Accountants 1930–1933; Ass. Gen. Mgr. of Prod. Gainsborough and Gaumont-British, 1933–1935; dir. sec. and gen. prod. mgr. New World Pictures, 1935–1937; dir. sec. gen. prod. mgr. and assoc. prod. Twentieth Century Productions Ltd., 1937–1943; in 1943 joined Ealing Studios Ltd. and assoc. co. as sec., later, as dir. 1961–77, chmn., man. dir., London Film Productions Ltd. Man. dir., Kew Ferry Management (Films) Ltd.

BAKER, ROBERT S.: Producer. b. London, 1916; e. Tenterden Hall; Ent. m.p. ind., 1938 as assistant dir.; war service, later Army Film Unit as combat cameraman; dir., Tribune Productions, Bamore Film Productions.
PICTURES INCLUDE: Crossplot, Sea of Sand, Hellfire Club, Treasure of Monte Cristo, Jack The Ripper.
TV: The Persuaders series, The Saint series, Gideon C.I.D. "Return of the Saint."

BAKER, ROY: Prod.-Dir. b. London; e. Lycee Corneille, Rouen; City of London School. Asst. dir. with Gainsborough 1934–40; served in Army 1940–46.
PICTURES INCLUDE: Operation Disaster, Don't Bother to Knock, Inferno, One That Got Away, A Night to Remember, The Singer Not the Song, Flame in the Streets, Quartermass and the Pit, The Anniversary, Vampire Lovers,

Dr. Jekyll and Mr. Hyde, Asylum (Paris Grand Prize), Seven Golden Vampires.
TV: The Human Jungle, The Saint, Gideon's Way, The Baron, The Avengers, The Champions, Department S., The Persuaders, Danger UXB, Minder.

BALABAN, A. J.: Theatre executive. b. Chicago, Apr. 18, 1889. In 1907 entered m.p. exhibition as operator of M.s. Nickelodeon Kedzie Theatre, Chicago; owned Movie Inn, restaurant with booths named for stars 1915; co-founder Balaban & Katz 1917; upon affiliation of B & K with Paramount named dir. of entertainment, then vice-pres.; abroad 9 yrs., returned to U.S. as circuit exhibitor 1935; gen. mgr. Roxy Theatre, N.Y., 1942; res. Jan 1, 1952, now consultant for 3 years; holds interest in Esquire, Carnegie theat., Chicago, with Harry and Elmer, brothers. Member: M.P. Pioneers, Jewish Theatrical Guild, French-American Club.

BALABAN, ELMER: President H. & E. Balaban Corp., Chicago, Ill. e. U of Pa., 1931. With Paramount Publix 1931; Balaban & Katz, 1933; then H. & E. Balaban Corp. Pres., Plains Television; interest in WTVO, Rockford, Ill.; interest in WHNB, Hartford, Conn. and numerous cable-TV systems.

BALABAN, HARRY: Executive. b. Chicago, Ill., July 23, 1903; e. U. of Illinois, 1925. With First Nat'l Pictures 1925–26; joined Balaban & Katz 1926–30; co-founder & Chairman of Board H. and E. Balaban Corp., 1932.

BALIN, INA: b. Bklyn, N.Y. e. Forest Hills High; Part time drama, psychology courses. N.Y. Univ. Comm. model, salesgirl, receptionist. Prof. debut, Perry Como Show. Off-Bway, summer stock, Compulsion, Majority of One. N.Y. Stage. Film debut, The Black Orchid. TV and Broadway. Toured Europe 1961. Int'l Star of Tomorrow. Hollywood Foreign Press Golden Globe Award.
PICTURES INCLUDE: From the Terrace, Young Doctors, The Comancheros, The Greatest Story Ever Told, The Patsy, Charro!, The Projectionist.
TV: American Heritage, Stoney Burke, Adventures in Paradise, Kraft Theatre, The Lieutenant, Bonanza, The Loner, Voyage to the Bottom of the Sea, Run for Your Life.

BALL, LUCILLE: Actress. b. Jamestown, N.Y., Aug. 6. e. Chautaqua Inst. Music; John Murray Anderson Dram. School, p. Desiree Ball, concert pianist. Hattie Carnegie model, stage debut in "Rio Rita"; on Broadway in "Hey Diddle, Diddle," "Dream Girl," "Wildcat;" m.p. debut in "Roman Scandals" 1933; entertained in Hollywood Canteen World War II; Voted most promising star in Motion Picture Daily's TV poll, 1951; best performer, 1952; best comedy team, 1954; best comedienne 1952, 54–55, 57; pres. Desilu Prod., Inc.; exec. prod., The Lucy Show; pres. Lucille Ball Prods., 1967.
PICTURES INCLUDE: Roberts, Stage Door, Big Street, Du Barry Was a Lady, Easy to Wed, Ziegfeld Follies, Lured, Sorrowful Jones, Easy Living, Miss Grant Takes Richmond, Fuller Brush Girl, Fancy Pants, Magic Carpet, Long Long Trailer, Forever Darling, Facts of Life, Critics Choice, Yours, Mine and Ours, Mame.
TV: I Love Lucy, The Lucy Show, Here's Lucy.

BALLARD, LUCIEN: Cinematographer. b. Miami, Okla., May 6, 1908; e. U. Okla., U. Pa. Started with Paramount as asst. cinematographer & cutter; since operative cinematographer.
PICTURES INCLUDE: Will Penny, The Party, How Sweet It Is!, The Wild Bunch, True Grit, The Ballad of Cable Hogue.

BALSAM, MARTIN: Actor. b. Nov. 4, 1919, N.Y.
PICTURES INCLUDE: On the Waterfront, 1954. Twelve Angry Men, Time Limit, Marjorie Morningstar, Al Capone, Middle of the Night, Psycho, Ada, Breakfast at Tiffany's, Cape Fear, Who's Been Sleeping in My Bed?, The Carpetbaggers, Youngblood Hawke, Seven Days in May, Harlow, The Bedford Incident, A Thousand Clowns, After the Fox, Hombre, 2001: A Space Odyssey, Trilogy, Catch 22, The Anderson Tapes, The Stone Killer, Summer Wishes, Winter Dreams, The Taking of Pelham 1,2,3, Murder on the Orient Express, Mitchell, All The President's Men, Two-Minute Warning, The Sentinel, Silver Bears, Cuba.

BALTER, ALLAN: Executive. b. Detroit, Mich., August 28, 1925. e. Univ. of Michigan, B.A. Asst. casting dept., 20th Century-Fox Film Corp. 1950–53; mgr., Encino theatre, 1953–54; asst. casting dept., MGM Studios, 1954–55; editor, Action mag., 20th Century-Fox house-organ 1955–56; trade planter, 20th Century-Fox publicity, 1956–57; unit publicist, Bryna Prods. (UA) 1957–58; unit publicist, 20th Century-Fox, 1958–62; dir. of pub., adv., Daystar Prods.

BANCROFT, ANNE: Actress. r.n. Anne Italiano; b. N.Y.C., Sep. 17, 1931; e. American Academy of Dramatic Arts. Acting debut on TV, Studio One; many TV shows; film debut, Don't Bother to Knock.
PICTURES INCLUDE: Tonight We Sing, Treasure of the Golden Condor, Kid from Left Field, Demitrius and the Gladiators, Gorilla at Large, The Raid, Life in the Balance,

New York Confidential, The Brass Ring, Naked Street, Last Frontier, Girl in the Black Stockings, Restless Breed, The Miracle Worker, The Pumpkin Eater (1964), Slender Thread, The Graduate (1967), Young Winston (1972), The Prisoner of Second Avenue, The Hindenburg, The Turning Point, Fatso (also dir. & s.p.), The Elephant Man.
PLAYS: Two For the Seasaw, The Miracle Worker, Mother Courage, The Devils, A Cry of Players.

BAND, ALBERT: Producer-director. b. Paris, France, May 7, 1924; e. Lyceum Louis le Grand, won French-English Literature Prize 1938; entered film industry as cutter Pathe Lab.; prod. ass't to John Huston at MGM; first screen credit adaptation Red Badge of Courage novel; first direction. The Young Guns, Allied Artists; formed Maxim Productions, Inc., Sept. 1956; prod.-dir. Killer on the Wall for United Artists. 1958 prod.-dir. Face of Fire; 1962 dir. The Avenger; 1963 dir. Grand Canyon Massacre; 1965 prod.-dir. The Tramplers; 1966 prod. The Hellbenders and then formed Albert Hand Prod. in Rome.
PICTURES INCLUDE: A Minute to Pray, A Second to Die, Little Cigars, Dracula's Dog, She Came to the Valley.

BANNEN, IAN: Actor. b. Airdrie, Scotland, 1928. Early career Shakespeare Memorial Theatre, Stratford-on-Avon.
STAGE: A View From the Bridge, The Iceman Cometh, Long Days Journey Into Night, Sergeant Musgrave's Dance. Royal Shakespeare Thea. Co. 1961–62. The Iceman Cometh, 1974. Hedda Gabler, 1977.
PICTURES INCLUDE: Carlton-Browne of the F.O., Man in Cocked Hat, Macbeth, Station Six Sahara, Mister Moses, The Hill, Rotten To the Core, Flight of the Phoenix, Sailor From Gibraltar, Penelope, Lock Up Your Daughters, Too Late the Hero, The Deserter, Jane Eyre, Fright, The Offence, The Macintosh Man, The Driver's Seat, The Voyage, Bite the Bullet, Sweeney, Darkness Into Darkness, Inglorious Bastards, Watcher in the Woods, Eye of the Needle.
TV: Johnny Belinda, Tinker, Tailor, Soldier, Spy, Cousin Phillis.

BANNER, BOB: Producer-director. b. Ennis, Tex., Aug. 15, 1921; e. Southern Methodist Univ., B.A., 1939–43, Northwestern Univ., M.A., 1946–48. U.S. Naval Reserve 1943–46; faculty, Northwestern Univ., 1948–50; staff dir., NBC-TV in Chicago, 1949–50; dir., Garroway at Large, 1949–50; prod. & dir., Fred Waring Show, 1950–53; dir. Omnibus. Metropolitan Opera Prod., 1953; Nothing But the Best (prod. dir.) NBC, 1953; Omnibus, CBS, 1953–54; Dave Garroway Show, NBC, 1953–54; (prod. dir.); Dinah Shore Show, 1954–57; exec. prod. Garry Moore Show; exec. prod. Candid Camera TV show; exec. prod., Carnegie Hall Salutes Jack Benny, 1961; exec. prod., Julie & Carol at Carnegie Hall, 1962; exec. prod., Carol & Co., 1963; Jimmy Dean Show, 1963–66; Calamity Jane, Once Upon A Mattress, '64; The Entertainers, '65; Carol × 2, '66; Kraft Summer Music Hall, '66, 1966 Carol & Co., Ice Follies, Carol Burnett Show, 1969, Peggy Fleming at Madison Square Garden, 1967; John Davidson at Notre Dame, Here's Peggy Fleming, 1971; Peggy Fleming at Sun Valley, The American West of John Ford, 1971; Love! Love! Love!—Hallmark Hall of Fame, 1972; To Europe With Love, 1972.
PICTURES INCLUDE: Warning Shot (for TV), My Sweet Charlie, Mongo's Back in Town, 1971.
TELEVISION: Movies of the week: The Last Survivors, Journey From Darkness. Special: Peggy Fleming Visits the Soviet Union. Game Show: Almost Anything Goes. Specials: Perry Como's Lake Tahoe Holiday '75, Perry Como's Christmas In Mexico '75, Perry Como's Hawaiian Holiday '76, Perry Como's Spring In New Orleans '76. Daily Variety Series: Don Ho Show '76; Perry Como Las Vegas Style '76, Perry Como's Christmas in Austria '76, Jr. Almost Anything Goes '76, All-Star Anything Goes '77, Peggy Fleming and Holiday on Ice at Madison Square Garden '76; Julie Andrews, One Step Into Spring '78; Leapin Lizards It's Liberace '78; Perry Como's Easter By The Sea '78.

BANTAU, J. W.: Consulting electrical engineer and purchasing agent; b. Argyle, Tex. Jan. 23, 1904. e. Rice Institute; with public utilities, U.S. Navy and Paramount Public Corp. National General Corp., now theatre consultant.

BAR, JACQUES JEAN LOUIS: Executive. Producer. b. Chateauroux, France, Sept. 12, 1921; e. Lycees Lakanal and Saint Louis, France. Formed Cinema-Theatre d'Avallon, 1944; Cite-Films S.A., 1947; Spira in assoc. with MGM, 1961; first Hollywood film, co-prod. Scratch A Thief, 1964; prod. 43 pictures in France, Spain, Italy, Switzerland, Japan and Brazil, 1948–64.
PICTURES INCLUDE: Where the Hot Wind Blows, Bridge to the Sun, Rififfi in Tokyo, A Very Private Affair, Swordsmen of Siena, Monkey in Winter, The Turfist, Any Number Can Win, The Day and the Hour, Joy House, Guns for San Sebastian.

BARAGREY, JOHN: Actor. b. April 15, 1919; e. U. of Alabama, 1939.
PICTURES INCLUDE: Loves of Carmen, Shockproof, Pardners, The Fugitive Kind.

BROADWAY: The Enchanted, Royal Family, Richard III, The Devils, The Grass Harp, Murderous Angels.
TV: Studio One, Suspense, Television Playhouse, Danger, Kraft Theatre, You Are There, U.S. Steel Hour, Robert Montgomery Playhouse, Omnibus, Climax, Hitchcock Presents, G.E. Theatre, Suspicion, Schlitz Playhouse, Playhouse 90, Cimarron City, American Heritage, The Defenders.

BARBER, ARNOLD: Executive. b. London, England. Career in m.p. ind. started with RKO. Subsequently with AB-Pathe following war service until appointment with Warner-Pathe Dist. which led him through sales exec. positions until he headed company. Formed Sotia-Barber Distributors Ltd. in 1970. Now man. dir. Barber Intl. Films, Ltd.

BARBERA, JOSEPH R.: Executive. b. N.Y.C. e. N.Y. Univ., American Institute of Banking. After schooling joined Irving Trust Co. in N.Y.C.; started submitting cartoon drawings to leading magazines' selling one to Collier's. Left banking to seek career in cartooning. Joined Van Buren Associates as sketch artist, later going to work in animation dept. of MGM Studios. At MGM met William Hanna, who became his lifelong business associate. Made first animated short together in 1938, starting the famous Tom & Jerry series which they produced for 20 years. Left MGM in 1957 to form Hanna-Barbera Productions to make cartoons for TV. Series have included Yogi Bear, Huckleberry Hound, The Flintstones. Hanna-Barbera became a subsidiary of Taft Bdg. Co. in 1968 with both men operating studio under long-term agreements with Taft. Barbera is pres. until 1980. Company entered theatrical production with Charlotte's Web in 1973.

BARBOUR, ALAN G.: Writer, editor, publisher. b. Oakland, Calif., July 25, 1933. ed. e. Rutgers University, m. Catherine Jean Barbour, actress, teacher, American Academy of Dramatic Arts. U.S. Army, worked as computer programmer. Formed Screen Facts Press in 1963, Screen Facts Magazine. Compiled, edited: The Serials of Republic, The Serials of Columbia, Great Serial Ads, The B Western, Serial Showcase, Hit the Saddle, The Wonderful World of B-Films, Days of Thrills and Adventure, Serial Quarterly, Serial Pictorial, Karloff—A Pictorial History, Errol Flynn—A Pictorial Biography, A Pictorial History of the Serial, A Thousand and One Delights, Cliffhanger, The Old-Time Radio Quiz Book.

BARBOUR, MALCOLM: Executive. b. London, England, May 3, 1934; e. Radley College, Oxford, England, Columbia Coll. At N.B.C. was press info. asst., 1958–59; asst. magazine ed., 1959–62; assoc. mag. ed., 1962–64; sr. mag. ed., 1964–65; mgr. of magazine pub., National Broadcasting Company, 1965–67; pub. mgr., Buena Vista, 1967–68; Eastern story ed., Walt Disney Prod., 1968–69; dir. of adv. & pub. relations, Buena Vista, 1969.

BARDOT, BRIGITTE: Actress. b. Paris, France, 1934. Model.
PICTURES INCLUDE: Le Trou Normand, Un Acte D'Amour, Helen of Troy, Le Fils De Caroline Cherie, Les Grandes Moneuvres, Doctor at Sea, En Effeuillant La Marguerite, The Bride Is Much Too Beautiful, Moonlight Jewelers, La Femme et Le Pantin, Will You Dance With Me, Manina, La Fille Sans Voiles, Si Versailles M'Etait Conte, Trahi, Futures Vedettes, La Lumiere D'En Face, Une Sacre Gamine, And God Created Woman, Le Parisienne, En Cas De Malheur, Love Is My Profession, Babette Goes to War, La Verite Contempt, A Very Private Affair, Two Weeks in September, Viva Maria, Shalako, Spirits of the Dead, Les Femmes.

BARE, RICHARD L.: Producer, director. b. Turlock, Calif. Dir. or Warner: Smart Girls Don't Talk, Flaxy Martin, This Side of The Law, House Across The Street, Return of Frontiersman; SDG Best Dir. TV award, 1959; author, The Film Director (Macmillan), 1971.
TV: 77 Sunset Strip, Maverick, 1956, So This is Hollywood (1955-NBC), The Islanders (1960), Dangerous Robin (1961), This Rebel Breed, Twilight Zone, Bus Stop (1962), Adventures in Paradise, The Virginian (1963), Kraft Theatre, Run For Your Life, Green Acres Series (186 episodes-1969), Farraday and Son, 1974; Westwind (NBC) 1976.
PICTURES INCLUDE: Wrote, directed and produced Wicked, Wicked, MGM, 1973.

BAREN, HARVEY M.: Executive. b. New York City, Nov. 25, 1931. e. N.Y. State U. Served in U.S. Army, 1952–54; United Artists Corp., 1954–59 (contract dept., print dept., booker—N.Y. branch); asst. to general mgr., Magna Pictures Corp., 1959–61; road show mgr., national sales coordinator, 20th Century-Fox, 1961–71; asst. general sales manager, Allied Artists Pictures, 1971–79. Since 1980 pres. of Summit Film Distributors.

BARI, LYNN: Actress. r.n. Marjorie Bitzer; b. Roanoke, Va., 1917. First screen appearance as dancing girl in Dancing Lady (MGM). Became Fox contract player 1934.
PICTURES INCLUDE: Shock, Margie, Home Sweet Homicide, Nocturne, Amazing Mr. X, Kid from Cleveland, I'd Climb Highest Mountain, On the Loose, Sunny Side of

the Street, Has Anybody Seen My Gal, I Dream of Jeanie, Francis Joins the Wacs, A&C Meet the Keystone Kops, Women of Pitcairn Island, Damn Citizen, Trauma.

BARING, AUBREY: Producer. b. London, Eng., May 3, 1912. e. Eton & Cambridge. Ent. m.p. ind., 1935. Served in R.A.F. 1939–45, Squadron Leader, D.F.C.
PICTURES INCLUDE: Cairo Road, So Little Time. South of Algiers (Golden-Mask), Appointment in London. They Who Dare, Abominable Snowman, The Key, Cone of Silence, Wrong Arm of the Law.

BARKER, NORMAN: Executive. b. Toronto, Canada. Ent. m.p. industry as artist-copy writer, Famous Players Canadian Corp. Ltd., 1934; Presently advg. & pub. rel. Famous Players.

BARKER, ROBERT WILLIAM: TV Host. b. Darrington, Wash., Dec. 12. e. Springfield Central H.S., Drury Coll. News writer, announcer, disc jockey KTTS until 1949. News editor, staff announcer, Station WWPG; wife, Dorothy Jo. Emcee Truth or Consequences, 1956. Pres. Bob Barker Prod., Inc., M.C. Miss USA Pageant, CBS-TV, since 1967, M.C. Miss Universe Pageant, CBS-TV since 1967, M.C. Rose Parade, since 1970. Prod.-M. C. Pillsbury Bakeoff, since 1970 CBS. Prod. Lucky Pair, syndicated, M.C., Price Is Right-CBS, 1972; Narrator, 500 Festival Parade, Indianapolis since 1969.

BARKETT, STEVE: Actor-Director-Producer-Film Editor. b. Jan. 1, 1950, Oklahoma City, Okla. Exhibited and scored over 52 feature length classic silent films prior to coming to Los Angeles in 1970. Executive in several nontheatrical releasing companies including Independent Film Associates. Established the Nautilus Film Company in 1978.
PICTURES INCLUDE: Actor: The Egyptians are Coming, Corpsegrinders, Cruise Missile. Films as Actor, Director, Producer: The Movie People, Night Caller, The Aftermath.

BARNES, BILL: Motion Picture Executive b. Wilson, N.C., Jan. 28. e. Univ. of N.C., Chapel Hill, BA. Radio, TV, Motion Pictures. NBC-TV Stations Relations Dept., 1958–1959; prod. asst. to Broadway producers Bloomgarden and Shumlin, 1960–61; casting dir. and story ed. for Otto Preminger 1962–1969; motion picture agent with IFA in 1970 and merged into Intl. Creative Management; joined Producer Circle Co., Jan. 1979 as v.p., creative affairs.

BARNETT, GABRIEL: Graduate U.S.C. 1925 with B.L.L., publisher of theatre programs and commercial film advertising. Established in 1938. Creator of the Barnett theatre clock. Now engaged in producing intermission music for motion picture theatres.

BARR, ANTHONY: Producer, director, actor. r.n. Morris Yaffe. b. St. Louis, Mo., March 14, 1921. e. Washington Univ., B.S. 1942. Actor, asst. stage mgr., 1944–46; stage mgr., Katherine Dunham Dancers, 1946–47; teacher, actor, dir. in chg., Film Actors' Workshop, Professional Theatre Workshop, Hollywood; v.p. current prime time series, ABC-TV; director, current dramatic programming, CBS-TV.
BROADWAY: Jacobowsky and the Colonel, Winters' Tale, Embezzled Heaven.
PICTURES INCLUDE: (actor) People Against O'Hara, Border Incident, The Hollywood Story, The Mozart Story, (co-prod.) Dame With A Halo.
TV: (dir.) Art Linkletter's Houseparty, About Faces (ABC-TV), (assoc. dir.) Climax, Shower of Stars, (prod.) Climax, Summer Studio One, (assoc. prod. CBS-TV) Climax, Playhouse 90, Pursuit, G.E. Theatre, The Law and Mr. Jones, Four-Star.

BARR, PATRICK: Actor. b. Akola, India, Feb. 13, 1908. e. Radley and Trinity College, Oxford, as engineer; stage debut in Miss Black's Son, 1933; appeared in Young Madame Conti, Music Box, N.Y., 1937; entered m.p. 1939; winner "Daily Mail" award, outstanding TV actor, 1954 and 1957; Royal Shakespeare Company, 1970.
PICTURES INCLUDE: Brain Machine, Duel in the Jungle, Dam Busters, It's Never Too Late, The Valiant, The Longest Day, Ring of Spies.
TV: Flag Fall, Count-Down at Woomera, Quiet Game of Cards, Galileo, A Beast with Two Backs, The Vortex, The Pueblo Affair.

BARRETT, JAMES LEE: Screen writer, producer. b. Charlotte, N.C., Nov. 19, 1929. e. Anderson Jr. College, Furman Univ., Penn State Univ., Art Students League. U.S. Marine Corps.
PICTURES INCLUDE: The D.I. (Marine Corps Combat Correspondents Award), The Greatest Story Ever Told, The Truth About Spring, Shenandoah, The Green Berets, Bandolero, The Undefeated, tick . . . tick . . . tick, The Cheyenne Social Club, Fools' Parade, something big, Smokey and the Bandit.
STAGE: Shenandoah (Tony Award) best musical book, 1974–75; Theatre Club annual award.
TV: The Awakening Land, Parts I and II (Certificate of Commendation, American Women in Radio and Television), Stubby Pringles' Christmas (Humanitas Nomination), The Day Christ Died, Belle Starr, Angels Gates.

BARRETT, RONA: News Correspondent e. N.Y. Univ. (communications major) created the column, Rona Barrett's Young Hollywood, which led to featured column in 1960 in Motion Picture Magazine and a nationally syndicated column distributed to 125 newspapers by the North American Newspaper Alliance. Turned to TV; initial appearances on ABC Owned Stations in 5 cities, providing two-minute reports for local newscasts. This resulted in a network morning program, co-hosted by Joanna Barnes, called Dateline Hollywood. In 1969 she created first daily syndicated TV news segment for Metromedia. Now Art & Entertainment editor for Good Morning, America.

BARRIE, GEORGE: Executive. b. Brooklyn, N.Y. Feb. 9, 1918. e. N.Y.U. Left school to embark on business career, beginning with soda fountain concessions in drugstores. Played in dance band and later became booker for bands. Turned to beauty products, forming co. Caryl Richards. In 1963 acquired Faberge, merging it with own firm. Entered leisure time field with records, books, films and TV.
PICTURES INCLUDE: A Touch of Class, Night Watch, Welcome to Arrow Beach, Book of Numbers, Hang-Up, Miracles Still Happen, Hugo the Hippo, Whiffs, Thieves.

BARRIE, MONA: Actress. b. London, England, Dec. 18, 1909. On stage Australia, England (Hay Fever, Bitter Sweet Autumn Crocus, others). From 1933 on screen.
PICTURES INCLUDE: Devil's Mask, Just Before Dawn, Secret of the Whistler, I Cover Big Town, Cass Timberlane, When a Girl's Beautiful, The First Time, Strange Fascination.

BARRON, ARTHUR RAY: Executive. b. Mt. Lake, Minn., July 12, 1934. e. San Diego State College, 1956–60; B.S. Accounting. Certified public acc't, Calif. 1960. Lybrond, Rans Bros. and Montgomery, 1960–63; Desilu Productions, Inc., 1963–67; v.p. finance and administration, Paramount Television, 1967–70 v.p. Finance, Paramount Pictures Corp., 1970; senior v.p. finance and administration, 1971; exec. v.p., finance & admin., 1974; exec. v.p. 1980.

BARRON, WINSTON (Win): Sales executive, newsreel editor. b. Toronto, Ont., Canada; e. Toronto U. Started in radio; announcer, studio mgr., mgr. various stations; later freelance sports & newscaster; radio prod.; actor in Canadian m.p.; dir. Lux Radio Theatre (England) 1937–39; with Ortus Film Co. 1940; chg. Canadian sales prom. Paramount Pictures 1941; commentator & assoc. ed. Canadian Paramount News 1943; mgr. Canadian Public Relations Paramount 1944; ed. Canadian Paramount News since 1945; dir., pub. rel., sp. events, International Air Show; TV announcer and commentator. Variety Club, Toronto Press Club, Aviation Writers Ass'n; CIAS Scholarship Comm.; York Flying Club, chmn., Film Advertising Circle, Public Relations Society, Goodfellowship Club, Theatres Branch, Ontario Government; now dir. of promotion, O'Keefe Centre for the Performing Arts in Toronto, Canada. Received city of Toronto Award of Merit.

BARRY, DONALD (Red): Actor, r.n. Donald Barry de Acosta; b. Houston, Tex.; e. Tex. Sch. Mines. In 1936 in "Night Waitress" (RKO Radio), thereafter to 1939 in number of feature pictures, including "The Woman I Love," "Sinners in Paradise," "The Crowd Roars." From 1939 in Westerns, attaining wide popularity as Republic Western star. Entertained troops overseas. Voted one of first ten Money-Making Western Stars in Motion Picture Herald-Fame Polls 1942, 1943, 1944.
PICTURES INCLUDE: Jesse James' Women, Untamed Heiress, Twinkle in God's Eye, I'll Cry Tomorrow, Seven Men From Now, Shalako, The Shakiest Gun in the West, Orca, The Swarm.

BARRY, GENE: Actor. r.n. Eugene Klass; b. New York, N.Y., June 14, 1921; e. New Utrecht H.S., Bklyn. Appeared in little & summer theatre.
BROADWAY: Rosalinda, Catherine Was Great, Happy Is Larry, Bless You All.
PICTURES INCLUDE: Atomic City, Girls of Pleasure Island, War of the Worlds, Those Redheads from Seattle, Alaska Seas, Red Garters, Naked Alibi, Soldier of Fortune, Purple Mask, Houston Story, Back from Eternity, China Gate, 27th Day, Maroc 7.
TV: Bat Masterson, Burke's Law, The Name of the Game.

BARRY, JACK: Executive, performer. b. Lindenhurst, N.Y., March 20, 1918; e. U. of Pa. Prod. & mc. of Juvenile Jury, Life Begins at 80, Winky Dink & You, Oh! Baby, The Big Surprise, Twenty-one, Tic Tac Dough; pres., WGMA, Hollywood, Fla.; prod Paramount TV Corp.

BARRY, JOHN: Composer, arranger, conductor. b. York, England, 1933. Artist and prod., CBS Records; TV: Elizabeth Taylor in London, Sophia Loren in Rome.
PICTURES INCLUDE: Beat Girl, Never Let Go, The Amorous Prawn, From Russia With Love, Seance On a Wet Afternoon, Zulu, Goldfinger, The Ipcress File, The Knack, King Rat, Born Free, Thunderball, The Chase, The Wrong Box, The Quiller Memorandum, The Whisperers, Deadfall, Petulia, You Only Live Twice, The Lion in Winter, Midnight

Cowboy, The Appointment, The Tamarind Seed, The Dove, The Day of the Locust, Robin and Marian, King Kong, The Deep, The Betsy, Moonraker, The Black Hole, Somewhere in Time.

BARRY, MICHAEL: Executive. b. May 15, 1910. Theatre & film dir., TV as BBC prod., 1938; during war in Royal Marines; rejoined TV as writer, prod., 1946; wrote and prod. Promise of Tomorrow, Passionate, Pilgrim, Shout Aloud Salvation; head of TV Drama Dept. June 1951. Awarded O.B.E. June, 1956. Programme Controller Telefis Eireann, Sept. 1961.

BARRYMORE, JOHN BLYTH, JR.; Actor. b. Beverly Hills, Calif., June 4, 1932. e. St. John's Military Acad., various public and private schools; p. late John Barrymore, Delores Costello (Mrs. John Vruwink). Debut in The Sundowners; many TV appearances.
PICTURES INCLUDE: High Lonesome, Big Night, Thunderbirds, While the City Sleeps, Shadow on the Window, War of The Zombies, Never Love A Stranger, The Night They Killed Rasputin, High School Confidential.

BART, PETER: Executive. e. Swarthmore College and The London School of Economics. Served eight years as correspondent for The New York Times and wrote for such magazines as Harper's, The Atlantic Saturday Review, etc. Joined Paramount Pictures in 1965. Named exec. ass't. to Robert Evans, exec. in charge of world-wide production. Appointed v.p. prod. Resigned post in 1973 to develop and produce own films for Para. Appointed pres. Lorimar Films, 1978. Resigned, 1979, to be independent producer
PICTURES INCLUDE: Islands in the Stream, Fun with Dick and Jane (both co-prod.).

BARTHOLOMEW, FREDDIE: Actor. b. London, Eng., Mar. 28, 1924. Stage debut 1927; m.p. debut U.S. in "David Copperfield" 1935.
PICTURES INCLUDE: Anna Karenina, Lloyds of London, Little Lord Fauntleroy, Devil Is a Sissy, Lord Jeff, Captains Courageous, Kidnapped, Swiss Family Robinson, Naval Academy, Yank at Eton, Junior Army, The Town Went Wild, St. Benny the Dip.

BARTLETT, HALL: Producer, Director, Writer. b. Kansas City, Mo., Nov. 27, 1922; e. Yale U., B.A. 1942. U.S. Naval Reserve 1942–47; formed Hall Bartlett Productions, 1952; prod. Navajo (winner of 27 nat'l awards & Festival of Brit. Award at Edinburgh); prod., s.p. Crazy-legs (winner of 9 nat'l awards, including Parents Mag. Gold Medal); prod., dir., s.p. Unchained (winner of Parents Mag. Gold Medal, Brotherhd. award of Nat. Con. of Christians and Jews); theme song, Unchained Melody, most pop. song of '55; prod., dir., s.p. Durango; prod. dir. s.p. Zero Hour, All the Young Men, Sol Madrid, photog., prod., Changes, prod. dir. Winner of the Sans Sebastian Festival. The Sandpit Generals, prod., dir., writer; winner of Grand Prize of VII International Film Festival of Moscow. Producer, director Jonathan Livingston Seagull; Producer, director, Cleo Laine Special, Zubin Mehta Special, and producer, director, The Children of Sanchez.

BARTON, CHARLES: Director, b. near San Francisco, Calif., May 25, 1902. In stock, vaudeville; then on screen in two comedies. Became "prop" boy for James Cruze, then William Wellman, including work on "Wings." Appt. asst. dir. Wellman Company; later dir. at Paramount; also directing TV films.
PICTURES INCLUDE: Men in Her Diary, Beautiful Cheat, Wagon Wheels, Vanishing Pioneer, Nevada Notorious Gentleman, Wistful Widow of Wagon Gap, Noose Hangs High, Abbott and Costello Meet Frankenstein, Mexican Hayride, Africa Screams, Abbott and Costello Meet the Killer, Free for All Double Crossbones, The Milkman, Ma and Pa Kettle at the Fair.
TV: McHales Navy, Hazel, Amos & Andy, Oh Susana, Dennis the Menace, Petti Coat Junction, Family Affair.

BARUCH, ANDRE: Announcer, commentator. b. Paris, France. e. Pratt Institute, Brooklyn, N.Y.; Columbia U.; Beaux Arts. Commercials for American Character, BC Headache Powder, Transogram Helene Curtis, Drajel, Lorillard; Prod. dir. for national sales conventions; TV, film prod. Helizer, Waring & Wayne, Inc.

BARUCH, RALPH M.: Executive. b. Paris, France, Aug. 5, 1923. e. The Sorbonne, Administrative aide, SESAC, Inc. 1944–48; account exec., DuMont Television Network, 1948–52; Eastern sales mgr., Consolidated Television Films, 1953–54; account exec., CBS Films, 1954; account supervisor, 1957; dir. international sales, 1959; v.p., CBS Enterprises, 1961–70; pres., Viacom Enterprises, 1971; pres., Viacom International, 1979; named chm. & chief exec. officer, Viacom International; gov., International Radio & Television Society; chmn., Rewrite Committee (Communications Act), NCTA; former member of the board of directors and former chmn., Pay Cable Committee, NCTA; gov. (New York), former chmn. of activities committee and former chmn. of forum program committee, International Council of the National Academy of Television Arts & Sciences.

BARWOOD, HAL: Writer-Producer. e. Univ. of S. Calif. School of Cinema. Writes scripts in collaboration with Matthew Robbins, Barwood branching out into producing with Corvette Summer in 1978.
PICTURES INCLUDE: Scripts, all with Robbins: The Sugarland Express, The Bingo Long Traveling All-Stars and Motor Kings, Corvette Summer (also prod.), Dragonslayer (also prod.).

BASCH, BUDDY: Publicist-promoter-producer-writer. b. South Orange, N.J., June 28, 1922. e. Columbia Univ. Began career as "Youngest Radio Editor in U.S." at 15, since written for national mags, syndicates, wire services, and newspapers. Edited and published "Top Hit Club News"-7 years. Joined Donahue and Coe 1940 on m.p. accounts, U.S. Army in Europe 1942–45. 1945 until 1967: own publicity and promotion office, working on m.p. company accounts and stars such as Burl Ives, Dinah Shore, Tony Martin, Danny Kaye, Peter Lorre, Tony Bennett, Gloria De Haven, McGuire Sisters, Rhonda Fleming, Sammy Davis, Jr., Anna Maria Alberghetti, Polly Bergen, Meyer Davis, The Beatles, Glenn Miller and Tommy Dorsey Orchestras. Produced many shows for radio, TV and stage in New York, Newark, Chicago, Hartford. Asst. to publisher, The Brooklyn Eagle 1962. Formed syndicate Buddy Basch Synd., 1965, 1966 formed Buddy Basch Feature Syndicate, formed BSB Creative Communications Unltd. in 1976, handling personal communications projects in all media, while continuing doing freelance writing on show bus, and travel subjects and general subject for N.Y. Daily News, A.P., Travel Holiday, Frontier Magazine, Kaleidoscope, True, United Features, Gannett Westchester-Rockland Newspapers, Bergen (N.J.) Record, Argosy, N.A.N.A., Womens' New Service, Today Magazine, Christian Science Monitor.

BASEHART, RICHARD: Actor. b. Zanesville, Ohio, Aug. 31, 1914. News reporter while in h.s.; surveying crew radio announcer, ward politician; with Hedgerow Theatre 5 yrs.; on N.Y. stage; won N.Y. Critics Award for "Hasty Heart"; plays include: Counter Attack, Land of Fame, Othello, etc.; m.p. debut in "Cry Wolf" 1945; summer stock.
PICTURES INCLUDE: Repeat Performance, He Walked By Night, Reign of Terror, Roseanna McCoy, Tension, House on Telegraph Hill, Fourteen Hours, Decision Before Dawn, Fixed Bayonets, Titanic, Good Die Young, Stranger's Hand, Canyon Crossroads, Moby Dick, La Strada, Five Branded Women, Hitler, Four Days In November, The Satan Bug, And Millions Must Die, The Island of Dr. Moreau, The Great Georgia Bank Hoax, Being There.

BASS, SAUL: Director-Producer. b. New York City May 8, 1920. e. Arts Students League. Pres. of, Saul Bass/Herb Yoger & Assoc. Has directed short films, m.p. titles/prologues/epilogues, TV show openings, TV commercials. Directorial feature debut in 1974 with Phase IV.
PICTURES INCLUDE: (shorts), The Searching Eye, From Here to There, Why Man Creates; Notes on the Popular Art, The Solar Film, Bass on Titles, (titles) Carmen Jones, The Man With The Golden Arm, Anatomy of a Murder, Vertigo, Psycho, Around the World in 80 Days, West Side Story, That's Entertainment II.

BATCHELOR, JOY: Director. b. Watford (Eng), May 12, 1914. e. Grammar School & Art School. Early career, illustrator & Designer. Entered m.p. in 1935 & is connected with the production of over 500 cartoon films. Co-director, co-prod., collab. s.p., Animal Farm, first British full length color feature cartoon; dir. Dam the Delta, The Colombo Plan, The Commonwealth, Ruddigore, The Five, Wotdot, Contact, Ass and the Stick. Christmas Feast, Carry in Milkmaids.

BATES, ALAN: Actor. b. Allestree, Derbyshire England, Feb. 17, 1934.
TV APPEARANCES: The Thug, A Memory of Two Mondays, The Jukebox, The Square Ring, The Wind and the Rain, Look Back in Anger, Three on a Gasring, Duel for Love, A Hero for Our Time, Plaintiff & Defendant, Two Sundays, The Collection, The Mayor of Casterbridge.
STAGE: On London and New York stage. The Caretaker, Long Days Journey Into Night, Poor Richard, In Celebration, Hamlet, Butley, The Taming of the Shrew, Life Class, Otherwise Engaged, The Seagull, Stage Struck.
PICTURES INCLUDE: The Entertainer, Whistle Down the Wind, A Kind of Loving, The Caretaker, Nothing But the Best, Zorba The Greek, Georgy Girl, King of Hearts, Three Sisters, Far From the Madding Crowd, The Fixer, Women in Love, Joe Egg, The Go Between, Impossible Object, Butley, In Celebration, Royal Flash, An Unmarried Woman, The Shout, Rose, Nijinsky, Quartet.

BATTY, PETER: Producer, director, writer. b. Sunderland, England, 1931. e. Bede Grammar School and Queen's College, Oxford. Feature-writer both sides Atlantic 1954–58. Joined BBC TV 1958 dir. short films. Edited Tonight programme 1963–4. Exec. prod. ATV 1964–68. Awarded Grand Prix for doc. at 1965 Venice and Leipzig festivals. Official entries 1970 and 1971 San Francisco and Melbourne festivals. Own company since 1968 prod. TV specials, series, commercials.

TV PRODUCTIONS INCLUDE: The Quiet Revolution, The Big Freeze, The Katanga Affair, Sons of the Navy Man, The Fall and Rise of the House of Krupp, The Road to Suez, The Suez Affair, Battle for the Desert, Vietnam Fly-In, The Plutocrats, The Aristocrats, Battle for Cassino, Battle for the Bulge, Birth of the Bomb, Search for the Super, Operation Barbarossa, Farouk: Last of the Pharaohs, Superspy, Spy Extraordinary, Sunderland's Pride and Passion, A Rothschild and His Red Gold, The World of Television, The Story of Wine, The Rise and Rise of Laura Ashley, The Gospel According to Saint Michael, Battle for Warsaw, Battle for Dien Bien Phu, Nuclear Nightmares. Contributed 6 episodes to Emmy-winning WORLD AT WAR series.

BAUM, MARTIN: Executive. b. New York, N.Y. March 2, 1924; president, ABC Pictures; previously partner Baum & Newborn Theatrical Agency; head of West Coast office General Artists Corp.; head of m.p. dept., Ashley Famous Agency; President of Martin Baum Agency; sr. exec. v.p. Creative Management Associations; president Optimus Productions, Inc., producing Bring Me the Head of Alfredo Garcia, The Wilby Conspiracy, and The Killer Elite. Partners with Michael Ovitz, Steven Roth, Michael Rosenfeld, Ron Meyer, Rowland Perkins, Bill Haber in Creative Artists Agency, Inc.

BAUM, MAURICE: Executive. b. Chesterfield, Eng., April, 1912; e. Manchester Central High School. Ent. m.p. ind. in Manchester, 1925; to Ireland, 1936; pres. Theatre and Cinema Assn. 1945 & 1964–65; Nat'l Films Ltd., National Tele-Films Ltd., National TV; pres. Irish Cinema Trade Benevolent Fund; also man. dir. National Film Distributors, Ltd.

BAUMSTONE, HAROLD: Executive. b. New York City, June 27, 1911; e. U. No. Carolina, B.A. 1932; prod. & distrib. of short subjects; pres., Institutional Cinema Inc., National 16mm Film Exchange, now representing Columbia Pictures, Warner Bros., American International and ind. prod. Exclusive distributor for 16mm markets for foreign films.

BAXTER, ANNE: Actress. b. Michigan City, Ind., May 7, 1923; granddaughter of Frank Lloyd Wright, architect; e. Theodora Ervine School of Drama; with Mme. Maria Ouspenskaya 3 yrs. Stage debut in "Seen But Not Heard" 1935; in summer stock on Cape Cod; in N.Y. in "Madam Capet" 1938; film debut in Twenty Mule Team" 1940.
PICTURE INCLUDE: Great Profile, Charley's Aunt, Swamp Water, Magnificent Ambersons, North Star, The Razor's Edge, All About Eve, Follow the Sun, Outcasts of Poker Flat, O. Henry's Full House, My Wife's Best Friend, I Confess, Blue Gardenia, The Carnival Story, Bedeviled, One Desire, The Spoilers, The Come On, Three Violent People, Chase a Crooked Shadow, Summer of the Seventeenth Doll, Cimarron, The Ten Commandments, The Tall Women, The Late Liz.
STAGE: Applause (1972), Noel Coward in Two Keys (1974).
TV: The Moneychangers, East of Eden.
BOOK: Intermission, 1976.

BAXTER, BILLY: Executive. b. N.Y.C., Feb. 8, 1926. e. Holy Cross, 1948. Mgr., Ambassador Brokerage Group, Albany, 1957–58; Bill Doll & Co., 1959–63; organ., prod., radio show, Earl Wilson Celebrity Column, 1962; prod. Bwy show, Mandingo, with Franchot Tone, 1962; dir. of promotion, spec. events, Rumrill Ad Agency, 1963–64; dir. of promotion, exploitation, Landau Co., 1964–65; dir. of adv. and pub., Rizzoli Co., 1965; resigned, Rizzoli, 1966. Consultant on special events to the Philip Morris Corp. and American Express. Coproducer on movies Love and Anarchy, Daughters-Daughters, Outrageous, One Man, Dawn of the Dead. Produced Diary of the Cannes Film Festival with Rex Reed, 1980.

BAXTER, KEITH: Actor. b. April 29, 1933, Monmouthshire, South Wales. e. Wales, entered Royal Academy of Dramatic Arts in 1951. 1952–55 in national service; returned to RADA. Did years of repertory work in Dublin, Croydon, Chichester, London's West End, and New York. Biggest stage hit in Sleuth, both London and N.Y.
PICTURES INCLUDE: The Barretts of Wimpole Street, Peeping Tom, Chimese at Midnight, With Love in Mind, Ash Wednesday.
TELEVISION: For Tea on Sunday, Hold My Hand Soldier, Saint Joan.

BAXTER, STANLEY: Actor. b. Glasgow, Scotland, 1928. e. Hillhead High School, Glasgow. Principal comedian in Howard & Wyndham pantomimes. Summer revues. Televised regularly on BBC-TV, and also frequent broadcaster. M.P. debut 1955 in Geordie.
STAGE: On the Brighter Side, 1961, Chase Me Comrade, in Australia, 1965; Cinderella. 1966–68, What the Butler Saw; 1969; Phil The Fluter, 1969–70. Mother Goose Pantomime seasons 1970/71, 71/72, 72/73, 73/74. Jack & The Beanstalk, 75/76/77/78. Cinderella 77/80.
PICTURES INCLUDE: Very Important Person, Crooks Anonymous, The Fast Lady, Father Came Too Joey Boy.
TV: Baxter on (Series) 1964; The Confidence Course

1965, The World of Stanley Baxter, 1966; Stanley Baxter Show, 1967, Stanley Baxter Show, 1968, 1971, Time for Baxter, 1972, The Stanley Baxter Big Picture Show, 1973. The Stanley Baxter Moving Picture Show, 1974. Part III, 1975. "Stanley Baxter's Christmas Box," 1976. Bing Crosby's Merrie Olde Christmas, 1977. Stanley Baxter's Greatest Hits, 1977. Baxter on Television, 1979.

BEAL, JOHN: Actor, r.n. J. Alexander Bliedung. b. Joplin, Mo., Aug. 13, 1909; e. Wharton School, Pa. U. On Broadway in: Another Language, She Loves Me Not, Petrified Forest, etc.; m.p. debut in "Another Language" 1933; serves in U.S.A.A.F World War II.
PICTURES INCLUDE: Little Minister, Les Miserables, We Who Are About to Die, Man Who Found Himself, Arkansas Traveler, Cat and the Canary, Great Commandment, Doctors Don't Tell, Atlantic Convoy, Edge of Darkness; Stand By, All Networks, Key Witness, Madame X, Double Wedding, Beg, Borrow or Steal, Port of Seven Seas, Alimony, Song of Surrender, Chicago Deadline, My Six Convicts, Remains to Be Seen, The Vampire, The Sound and the Fury, That Night, Ten Who Dared.

BEATTY, NED: Actor. Worked at Barter Theatre in Virginia for seven years, appearing in over 70 plays. First N.Y. performance in The Great White Hope.
PICTURES: Deliverance (debut), Nashville, W.W. and the Dixie Dance Kings, Exorcist II: The Heretic, Network, The Great Georgia Bank Hoax, Superman, Promises in the Dark, Hopscotch, The Incredible Shrinking Woman, Superman II.

BEATTY, ROBERT: Actor. b. Hamilton, Ont., Canada, Oct. 19, 1909. e. U. Toronto. London stage debut: Idiot's Delight, 1938. On screen first in Suspected Persons, 1942.
PICTURES INCLUDE: San Demetrio London, It Happened One Sunday, Appointment with Crime, Odd Man Out, Green Fingers, Against the Wind, Another Shore, Portrait from Life, Her Favorite Husband, Captain Horatio Hornblower, Calling Bulldog Drummond, Magic Box, Wings of Danger, The Gentle Gunman, The Oracle, The Net (Project M. 7), Man on the Tightrope, Broken Horseshoe, The Square Ring, Albert RN (Break to Freedom), Loves of Three Women, Out of the Clouds, Portrait of Alison (Postmark for Danger), Tarzan and the Lost Safari, Something of Value, Time Lock, The Shakedown, The Amorous Prawn, Stanley Kubrick's 2001, Where Eagles Dare, Sitting Target, Pope Joan, The Pink Panther Strikes Again, Golden Rendezvous.
TV: Weekly guide, Saturday Night Out, Dial 999 series, The Human Jungle (Series), Court Martial Series, Time Lock, Man at the Top, The Venturers, Thriller, Jesus of Nazareth, Blake's Seven, Park Ranger, The Martian Chronicles, Walk with Destiny, Suez, The Rose, Medallion.

BEATTY, WARREN: Actor. b. Richmond, Va., March 30, 1938. e. Northwestern U.; small roles on television; Compulsion, winter stock. North Jersey Playhouse; Broadway debut, A Loss of Roses.
PICTURES INCLUDE: Splendor in the Grass, The Roman Spring of Mrs. Stone, All Fall Down, Lilith, Mickey One, Promise Her Anything, Kaleidoscope; prod. & starred in Bonnie and Clyde, The Only Game in Town, McCabe and Mrs. Miller, Dollars, The Parallax View, Shampoo (producer, co-author, star), The Fortune, Heaven Can Wait (star, co-prod., co-dir., co-s.p.), Reds (star, prod., dir.).

BEAUMONT, HUGH: Actor. b. Lawrence, Kan., Feb. 16, 1909. e. U. of Chattanooga; U.S.C.
PICTURES INCLUDE: Michael Shayne series, PRC; Blue Dahlia, Guilt of Janet Ames, Counterfeiters, Last Outpost, Lost Continent, Phone Call from a Stranger, Wild Stallion, Night Without Sleep, The Mississippi Gambler, Hell's Horizon.

BECK, ALEXANDER J.: Executive. b. Ung. Brod, Czechoslovakia, Nov. 5, 1922. e. Charles Univ. Prague, NYU. Owns many features and westerns for foreign distribution and library of 500 shorts. Importer and exporter; Pres., chairman of bd. Alexander Beck Films, 1955; formed Albex Films and A.B. Enterprises, 1959; formed & pres., Beckman Film Corp., 1960; formed Alexander Beck Productions, 1964. Sept. '69 formed Screencom Int'l Corp.

BECK, JACKSON: Actor-announcer-narrator. b. N.Y.C. TV and radio commercials, children's records, comm. & industrial films & shows; Narrator.

BECK, JOHN: Actor. b. Chicago. Acted with mid-western theatre groups; had basic training in scores of TV series. Theatrical debut in Three in the Attic.
PICTURES INCLUDE: Three in the Attic, Mrs. Pollifax Spy, Lawman, Pat Garrett and Billy the Kid, Sleeper, Deadly Honeymoon, Rollerball, Paperback Hero, The Big Bus, Audrey Rose, The Other Side of Midnight.
TV: Guest star roles on Bonanza, Mannix, Hawaii Five-0, etc.

BECK, MICHAEL: Actor. b. Memphis, TN. e. Millsap College on football scholarship (quarterback). Became active in college theatre. In 1971 went to London, England to attend Central School of Speech and Drama; studied 3 years, following which toured England with repertory companies for 2 years. Returned to U.S.; cast as lead in independent film, Madman (shot in Israel in 1977).

PICTURES: Madman, The Warriors, Xanadu.

TELEVISION: Holocaust, Mayflower: The Pilgrim Adventure, Alcatraz: The Rock and Clarence Carnes.

BECK, MYER P.: Sales, prod. rep. b. Meriden, Conn.; e. N.Y.U. School of Journalism. Newspaperman; publicist; publicity dir. United Artists; eastern mgr. Russell Birdwell Associates; formed own sls. prod. rep. office 1945, repr. Albert R. Broccoli; Jerome Hellman Productions, Stanley Kramer Pictures Corp., Harry Saltzman.

BECKER, VIOLA S.: Executive; r.n. Mrs. George J. Waas, b. New York, N.Y.; e. Columbia Univ.; organ V. S. Becker Productions, 1946, and V. S. Becker Adv. Svce.; AFRA International, Inc., Am. Women in International Radio & TV Society, Inc., Advertising Women of New York. Now free lance advertising consultant.

BEERY, NOAH, JR.: Actor. b. New York City, Aug. 10, 1916; son of Noah Beery, screen actor; e. Urban and Harvard Mil. Acad. Travelled with parents in stock company. Appeared as child in Mark of Zorro 1920.

PICTURES INCLUDE: Father and Son, Road Back, Only Angels Have Wings, Doolins of Oklahoma, Davy Crockett, Indian Scout, Last Outpost, Savage Horde, Rocketship XM, Two Flags West, Tropic Zone, Cimarron Kid, Wagons West, Story of Will Rogers, Wings of the Hawk, War Arrow, The Yellow Tomahawk, Black Dakotas, White Feather, Jubal, Fastest Gun Alive, Journey to Shiloh, Heaven With A Gun, Walking Tall, The Spikes Gang.

BEGELMAN, DAVID: President and Chief Operating Officer, Metro-Goldwyn-Mayer Film Co.; member of board of directors and member of executive committee. Independent Producer. President of Columbia Pictures; sr. exec. v.p., Columbia Pictures Industries, and member of board of directors, 1973 to 1978. Career in entertainment industry began with Music Corp. of America in N.Y. Resigned in 1960 as v.p. in charge of special projects to establish Creative Management Associates (talent agency) with Freddie Fields. CMA acquired General Artists Corp. in 1968 with Begelman as vice chairman of board of directors and member of exec. comm. Resigned to join Columbia.

BEICH, ALBERT: Writer. b. Bloomington, Ill., June 25, 1919. e. McGill U. Radio writer.

PICTURES INCLUDE: You Can't Beat the Law, Girls in Chains, Gangs of the Waterfront, Gay Blades, Bridge Goes Wild, Key to the City, Yellow Cab Man, The Milkman, Lieutenant Wore Skirts.

BEJTMAN, VINCENT: Executive. b. Poland. Started career producing entertainment films in native land. Came to U.S. during war. Named pres. of PIC Films, Inc., financed by Polish govt.-in-exile in London and the British Information Center. Company produced over 30 films depicting Poland participation in World War II. Formed Cine Classics Films, Inc., specializing in import of foreign films for U.S. market, including Rules of the Game, Zero De Conduit, etc. Produced documentaries (The Great Betrayal, Last Days of Warsaw.) Co-produced Naked Amazon. Now pres. of Vee Bee Productions, Inc. and involved in American-European co-production.

BELAFONTE, HARRY: Actor, singer. b. New York City, March 1, 1927. Professional debut; Royal Roost nightclub, N.Y., Village Vanguard, 1950. Broadway debut: John Murray Anderson's Almanac, 1953.

SHOWS INCLUDE: Three for Tonight, A Night With-Belafonte.

PICTURES INCLUDE: Bright Road, Carmen Jones, Island In The Sun, Odds Against Tomorrow, The World, The Flesh & The Devil, The Angel Levine, Buck and the Preacher, Uptown Saturday Night (prod., star).

BELFER, HAL B.: Exec. Producer-Director-Choreographer. b. Los Angeles, Feb. 16. e. Univ of So. Calif. (cinematography); Univ. of Calif. (writing). Head of choreography dept. at 20th Century-Fox. Head of choreography dept. at Universal Studios. Dir. of entertainment, in Las Vegas, Riviera and Flamingo Hotels. Choreog.; musical shows for Mexico City, Aruba, Puerto Rico, Montreal, Las Vegas. Dir., TV commercials and industrials. H. R. Pufnstuf TV series. Theatricals: Over 150 features. Producer-Director-Choreographer, Premore, Inc. Develop TV specials and sitcom, tape and film. Exec. prod., Once Upon a Tour and Dora's World, Rose on Broadway, Secret Sleuth, Inn by the Side of the Road, Imagine That!. Special staging "Tony The Pony" Series and prod., segment of What a Way to Run a Railroad; TV specials. Talent development programs, Universal Studios, 20th Century-Fox. Personal management and show packager.

BEL GEDDES, BARBARA: Actress. r.n. Barbara Geddes Lewis. b. New York City, Oct. 31, 1922; p. Norman Bel Geddes,

scenic designer. Stage debut in "Out of the Frying Pan"; toured USO camps in "Junior Miss" 1941; screen debut in "The Long Night" 1946; Star of Tomorrow, 1949. N.Y. Stage: The Moon is Blue, Cat on a Hot Tin Roof, Mary, Mary, Everything in the Garden.

PICTURES INCLUDE: I Remember Mama, Blood on the Moon, Caught, Panic in Streets, Fourteen Hours, The Five Pennies, Five Branded Women, By Love Possessed, Summertree, The Todd Killings.

BELL, TOM: Actor. b. Liverpool, England, 1932. Early career in repertory and on West End stage. First TV appearance in Promenade.

TV: No Trams to Lime Street, Love On the Dole, A Night Out, Cul de Sac, The Seekers, Long Distance Blue, The Virginian. Film debut 1960 in Payroll.

PICTURES INCLUDE: The Kitchen, H.M.S. Defiant, Prize of Arms, L-Shaped Room, Rebels Against the Light, Ballad in Blue, He Who Rides a Tiger, In Enemy Country, The Long Days Dying, Lock Up Your Daughters.

BELLAMY, EARL: Prod. Dir. b. Minneapolis, Minn., March 11, 1917. e. L.A. City Coll. Universal Studios; latest m.p.: Fluffy, Gun Point, Munsters Go Home.

TV: Bachelor Father, Wells Fargo, Lone Ranger, Alcoa Premiere, Arrest and Trial, The Virginian, The Crusaders, Schlitz Playhouse, Heinz, Rawhide, The Donna Reed Show, Andy Griffith Show, Wagon Train, now president, The Bellamy Productions Co., Laramie, Laredo, I Spy, Mod Squad, Medical Center.

BELLAMY, RALPH: Actor. b. Chicago, Ill., June 17, 1905. Stock and repertory, 1922–30; pres. Actors Equity, 1952; council, Lambs, 1952; TV includes major live and film dramatic shows, voted many TV awards.

BROADWAY: Town Boy, Roadside, Tomorrow the World, State of the Union, Detective Story.

PICTURES INCLUDE: Great Impersonation, Lady on a Train, Guest in the House, Delightfully Dangerous, Court Martial of Billy Mitchell, Sunrise at Campobello, The Professionals, Rosemary's Baby, Oh, God!

BELLFORT, JOSEPH: b. New York. e. New York U., B'klyn Law Sch. Joined RKO Service Corp., Feb., 1930; trans. to RKO Radio Pictures, legal dept., May 1942; joined RKO Fgn. dept., Oct., 1944; handled Far Eastern division, Dec. 1946; then asst. to European gen. mgr.; gen. European mgr., 1949–1958; gen. sales mgr. National Screen Service, 1959; home office sup., Europe & Near East, 20th Century Fox, 1963; home office intl. mgr., 20th Century-Fox, 1966. Ass't v.p. and foreign mgr. 20th Cent.-Fox, 1967; vice president 20th Century-Fox, Int. Corp. & Inter-America, Inc. 1968; named sr. v.p., 1975. Resigned from Fox, 1977, to become v.p., m.p. Export Assn. of America in New York.

BELMONDO, JEAN-PAUL: Actor. b. Neuilly-sur-Seine, France, April 9, 1933. e. private drama school of Raymond Girard, and the Conservatoire d'Art Dramatique. Formed a theater group with Annie Girardot and Guy Bedos.

THEATRE INCLUDE: Jean Marais' production of Caesar and Cleopatra, Treasure Party. Oscar, 1958.

PICTURES INCLUDE: A Pied, A Cheval et En Voiture (By Foot, Horse and Car), Look Pretty and Shut Up, Drole de Dimanche, Les Tricheurs, Les Copains du Dimanche, Charlotte et Son Jules, A Double Tour, Breathless, Classe Tous Risques, Moderato Cantabile, La Francasie et l'Amour, Les Distractions, Mademoiselle Ange, La Novice, Two Women, La Viaccia, Une Femme Est Une Femme, Leon Morin, Pretre, Les Amours Celebres, Un Singe en Hiver, Le Doulos, L'Aine des Ferchaux, La Mer A Boire, Banana Peel, That Man From Rio, Cent Mille Dollars au Soleil, Echappement Libre, La Chasse a l'Homme, Dieu a Choisi Paris, Weekend a Zuydcoote, 100,000 Dollars au Soleil, Par Un Beau Matin d'Ete, Up to His Ears, Is Paris Burning?, The Thief of Paris, Tender Scoundrel, Pierrot le Fou, The Brain, Love Is a Funny Thing, Mississippi Mermaid, Borsalino, Inheritor, Stavisky, Fear Over the City.

BELUSHI, JOHN: Actor. b. Chicago, Jan. 24. Member of Second City improvisational group. Appeared in National Lampoon prod. of Lemmings on Broadway; directed one of the shows when it went on tour. Wrote, acted in and directed National Lampoon Radio Hour. Affiliation continued with The National Lampoon Show off-Bdwy., in which he performed and served as writer-director. Gained fame on NBC's Saturday Night Live.

PICTURES: Goin' South, Old Boyfriends, National Lampoon's Animal House, 1941, The Blues Brothers, Continental Divide, Neighbors.

TELEVISION: Richard Pryor Special, Beach Boys Special, All You Need is Cash, etc.

BENDHEIM, III, SAM: Executive. b. Richmond, Va., June 15, 1935. e. Washington & Lee Univ. Joined Neighborhood Theatre, Inc., 1958 as exec. trainee. Was dir. of adv. (1960–63); bd. member, ass't treas. (1962); ass't to gen. mgr. (1963–67) v.p. (1967). Bd. mem., ass't sec., treas., Prince Edward Amusement Corp. Member of NATO of Va. bd.;

former vice-pres. NATO of Virginia, now pres.; Neighborhood Booking & Buying Service.

BENDICK, ROBERT: b. New York City, Feb. 8, 1917; e. New York U., White School Photography; U.S. Airforce, World War II. Documentary and still cameraman before joining CBS Television as cameraman and dir., 1940; rejoined CBS Television as dir. special events, 1946; promoted dir. news & special events; acting program dir. 1947; res. Oct. '51. Collab. with Jeanne Bendick on Making the Movies, Electronics for Young People, Television Works Like This, Filming Works Like This, 1971; Prod. Peabody Awardwinning U.N. show. The U.N. in Action; v.p., Cinerama Prod., co-prod. This Is Cinerama; co-dir., Cinerama Holiday; prod. Dave Garroway Show Today, prod., Wide Wide World 1955–56, NBC prod. dir. C. V. Whitney Pict., June, 1956; Merian C. Cooper Ent., 1957; prod. NBC, 1958. Prod.; Garroway Today Show, Bob Hope 25 Yrs. of Life Show, 1961; Bell Telephone Threshold Science Series, Groucho Marx, Merrily We Roll Along, US Steel Opening New York World's Fair, 1964. Prod. First Look Series 1965 (Ohio St. Award); prod. & dir. American Sportsman, ABC; prod., pilot, Great American Dream Machine (NET) Emmy Award, 1971 and 1972; 1975, Co-exec. prod., Dick Cavett—Feeling Good. pres. Bendick Assoc. Inc.; prod. of education audio-visual systems, Bd. of Governors, N.Y. Academy of TV Arts and Sciences. 1976, co-author with Jeanne Bendick, TV Reporting. Consultant, Warner Qube Cable Co.; 1978, produced/directed, Fight for Food (PBS). Program consultant to Times-Miror Cable Co., L.A. Produced segment ABC 20/20.

BENEDEK, LASLO: Director. b. Budapest, Hungary, Mar. 5, 1907; e. U. Vienna; Psycho-Analytic Clinic. Writer & photographer while in coll.; cameraman Budapest; first asst. cameraman several studios; cameraman UFA & Terra; film cutter; cutter & asst. prod. to Joe Pasternak; to Paris as cutter, then Engl dial. on "Antonia''; writer (England) 2 yrs.; montage dir. MGM 1937; writer (Mexico); assoc. prod. (Hollywood) on musicals; contract dir. MGM; Stanley Kramer Co., Col.; 1976–80, Chairman of Graduate Film Program, New York University.
PICTURES INCLUDE: Kissing Bandit, Port of New York, Death of a Salesman, Storm Over Tibet, Wild One, Bengal Brigade; Sons, Mothers and a General, Affair in Havana, Moment of Danger, Recours en Grace, Namu, The Killer Whale, A Daring Game, The Night Visitor.
TV: 4 Star Playhouse, Dupont Theatre, Stage 7, Loretta Young Show, Telephone Time, Perry Mason, Naked City, Untouchables, Outer Limits.
STAGE: Belial, Twelfth Night.

BENEDICT, DIRK: Actor. b. Helena, Mont. r.n. Dirk Niewoehner. e. Whitman College, Walla Walla, Wash. Enrolled in John Fernald Academy of Dramatic Arts, Rochester, Mich., after which had season with Seattle Repertory Theatre; other in summer stock at Ann Arbor, Mich. Broadway debut, 1970, Abelard and Heloise. Film debut, Georgia, Georgia, 1972.
PICTURES INCLUDE: Ssssss, W, Battlestar Galactica, Scavenger Hunt.
TELEVISION: Hawaii Five-O (one episode), Chopper One (series), Battlestar Galactica.

BENJAMIN, RICHARD: Actor. b. New York, N.Y., May 22, 1939; e. Northwestern U. Plays: Central Park productions of The Taming of the Shrew, As You Like It; toured in Tchin Tchin, A Thousand Clowns, Barefoot in the Park, The Odd Couple. Broadway debut in Star Spangled Girl, 1966. Directed London productions of Barefoot in the Park. TV series, He and She, with wife Paula Prentiss, 1967.
PICTURES INCLUDE: Goodbye, Columbus, Catch 22, Diary of a Mad Housewife, The Marriage of a Young Stockbroker, The Steagle, Portnoy's Complaint, The Last of Sheila, Westworld, The Sunshine Boys, Love at First Bite, Scavenger Hunt, The Last Married Couple in America, How to Beat the High Cost of Living, First Family.

BENNET, SPENCER G.: Director. b. Brooklyn, N.Y., Jan. 5, 1893. e. Manual Training H.S., Brooklyn, N.Y.; played stunt and thrill parts; asst. dir., Pathe; prod., dir., from 1925–64. Retired.
CREDITS INCLUDE: Play Ball (serial), The Green Archer (serial), Snowed in (serial), The Fighting Marine (serial) and many other serials and westerns. Submarine Seahawk, Atomic Submarine, Bounty Killer, Requiem For a Gunfighter.

BENNETT, BRUCE: Actor. r.n. Herman Brix. b. Tacoma, Wash.; e. U. Washington.
PICTURES INCLUDE: My Son is Guilty, Lone Wolf Keeps a Date, Atlantic Convoy, Sabotage, Underground Agent, More the Merrier, Sahara, Man I Love, Stolen Life, Nora Prentiss, Cheyenne, Treasure of Sierra Madre, Dark Passage, Smart Girls Don't Talk, Second Face, Great Missouri Raid, Last Outpost, Angels in the Outfield, Sudden Fear, Dream Wife, Dragonfly Squadron, Robbers Roost, Big Tip off, Hidden Guns, Bottom of the Bottle, Strategic Air Command.

BENNETT, CHARLES: Writer, director. b. Shoreham, England. British Army. Contract, Universal, 1937; wrote British Ministry of Information, WW II; dir. s.p. over 50 TV shows, including Cavalcade of America, Schlitz Playhouse, The Christophers, Four Star.
PLAYS INCLUDE: Blackmail, The Last Hour, Sensation, The Danger Line, Page From a Diary, The Return, After Midnight.
PICTURES INCLUDE: Blackmail, The 39 Steps, Secret Agent, The Man Who Knew Too Much (orig.), Sabotage, The Girl Was Young, Balalaika, The Young in Heart, Foreign Correspondent, Reap the Wild Wind, Joan of Paris, They Dare Not Love, The Story of Dr. Wassell, Unconquered, Ivy, Sign of the Ram, Kind Lady, The Green Glove, Dangerous Assignment, Madness of the Heart (dir.), The Big Circus, The Lost World, Voyage to the Bottom of the Sea, Five Weeks in a Balloon.

BENNETT, HARVE: Producer. r.n. Harve Fischman. b. Chicago, Ill., Aug. 17, 1930. e. U.C.L.A. Quiz Kids radio show, 5 yrs.; newspaper columnist, drama critic; freelance writer; Assoc. prod., CBS-TV; free-lance TV writer; prod. of special events. CBS-TV; dir., Television film commercials; program exec., ABC, vice pres., programs west coast—ABC-TV; prod.-writer, Mod Squad. Creator-writer, The Young Rebels, Screen Gems; exec. prod., Six Million Dollar Man, Bionic Woman, Rich Man, Poor Man, Universal Studios; Pres., Bennett-Katleman. Productions at Columbia Studios, and exec. prod. on American Girls series (CBS), From Here to Eternity (NBC), Salvage I (ABC).

BENNETT, JILL: Actress. b. Penang (Federated Malay Straits), Dec. 24, 1931. Stage debut at Stratford-on-Avon, 1948; screen debut 1952 in Moulin Rouge.
PICTURES INCLUDE: Hell Below Zero, The Criminal, Extra-Day, Lust for Life, The Skull, The Nanny, Charge of Light Brigade, Inadmissible Evidence, I Want What I Want, Quilp, Full Circle.
TV: The Heiress, Trilby, Jealousy, A Midsummer Night's Dream, The Three Sisters, Glimpse of the Sea, Return to the Sea, The Book Bag (Somerset Maugham Series), It's Only Us, The Parachute, Hotel in Amsterdam, Speaking of Murder, Intent to Murder, Jill and Jack, Almost A Vision, Hello Lola, The Old Crowd.

BENNETT, JOAN. Actress. b. Palisades, N.J., Feb. 27, 1910; e. St. Margaret's Boarding School, Waterbury, Conn.; L'Ermitage, Versailles, France; member of famous Bennett acting family; m. Walter Wanger, prod. On stage with father, Richard Bennett in "Jarnegan'' 1929; vice-pres. & treas. Diana Prods. 1945.
PICTURES INCLUDE: Three Live Ghosts, Disraeli, Moby Dick, Little Women, Pursuit of Happiness, Mississippi, Woman in the Window, Secret Beyond the Door, Man Who Reclaimed His Head, Hollow Triumph, Scar, Reckless Moment, For Heaven's Sake, Father of Bride, Father's Little Dividend, The Guy Who Came Back, Highway, Dragnet, We're No Angels, There's Always Tomorrow, Navy Wife, Desire in the Dust, Suspiria.
TV: Starring in ABC Dark Shadows.

BENSON, HUGH: Executive. b. New York. Sept. 7, 1917. e. New York public schools. Six yrs. infantry, then Air Force. Three yrs. European Theatre of War, As master sergeant, Air Force, two yrs., non com in chg. of soldier units under, prod.-dir., Joshua Logan. Joined Blaine-Thompson Advertising Agency as dir. of public relations; assist. to producers, Ed Sullivan and Marlo Lewis, Ed Sullivan Show, 1947–50; dir. television, public relations, Roy Dunstine Agency, 1951; hd. of radio, television promotion, publicity dept., Warner Bros., June, 1955; appointed assist. to Steve Trilling, vice-pres. and exec. associate of Jack L. Warner, 1956; exec. asst. to William T. Orr, Warner v.p. in chg. of production, 1956; prod., United Artists, 1963; exec. asst. to William T. Orr, Warner Bros., 1964–65. Exec., Prod., Screen Gems, 1966, prod.; Cinema Center Films, 1969–71, prod., MGM, 1972; appointed exec. prod., MGM Television, 1972. 1975 indep. prod. On staff Col.-tv, 1975, pilots and long form.
PICTURES: Nightmare Honeymoon (prod.), Logan's Run (assoc. prod.), Billy Jack Goes to Washington (prod.).
TELEVISION: Contract On Cherry St. (prod.) Child Stealers, Goldie and the Boxer, A Fire in the Sky, Confessions of a Lady Cop, The Dream Merchants, Goldie and the Box Go to Hollywood, Goliath Waits.

BENSON, LEON: Producer-Director. b. Cincinnati, Ohio, Nov. 9. e. New York schools, University of Cincinnati. Advertising Dept. Paramount, 1938, head of Trailer Dept., 1940. U.S. Army Air Corps, 1942–46, Major, First head of TV Dept. L.A. office of J. Walter Thompson Co., 1946–51. Head of Story Dept. Ziv TV, 1951; prod. and dir. West Point, 1955–56; Sea Hunt, 1956–60; Ripcord, 1960–62. Prod.-Dir. Flipper TV series, 1963–64. Under contract, Universal 1965–66, prod.-dir. episodes, Kraft Suspense Theatre, The Virginian, dir. episodes, Chrysler Theatre, Laredo. Prod. Tarzan TV series, 1966. Under contract, NBC Prods., 1967–70, as staff dir. Bonanza, High Chaparral. Prod. theatrical feature, Chosen Survivors, 1973. Also dir. Owen Marshall, Counsellor at Law, Mission Impossible, The Eleventh Hour, Ben Casey, Wild Wild West, Rat Patrol, The Lieutenant, Outer Limits, The Loner, Empire.

BENSON, ROBBY: Actor. b. Dallas, 1957. Father, Jerry Segal, is writer, and mother, Ann Nelson, veteran of Dallas stage and natl. summer stock. Robby appeared on Broadway in The King and I at age five. Also worked 6 mos. in soap opera, Search for Tomorrow. Big break in feature films in Jeremy. Co-wrote screenplay of One on One (1977) with father and starred in film.
PICTURES INCLUDE: Jeremy, Jory, The Godfather—Part II, Ode to Billy Joe, Lucky Lady, One on One, The End, Ice Castles, Walk Proud, Die Laughing (also prod., co-s.p.), Tribute.
TV: The Death of Richie, Remember When, Virginia Hill, All the Kind Strangers, Death Be Not Proud.
STAGE: Zelda, The Rothschilds.

BENTLEY, JOHN: Actor. b. Warwickshire, Eng. Dec. 2, 1916. e. King Edward's Grammar Sch., Birmingham. Radio debut, 1933; Alexandra & Birmingham Rep. Cos. in 1934; stage debut in New Faces, London, 1940; m.p. debut in Hills of Donegal, 1946.
PICTURES INCLUDE: Calling Paul Temple, Paul Temple's Triumph, Happiest Days of Your Life, Torment, She Shall Have Murder, Salute the Toff, Hammer the Toff, Woman's Angle, Lost Hours, Tread Softly, Black Orchid, Paul Temple Returns, River Beat, Double Exposure, Scarlet Spear, Golden Ivory, The Flaw, Profile, Last Appointment, Confession, Deadliest Sin, Flight from Vienna, Strangehold, Blind Man's Bluff, Dial 999, Way Out, Escape in the Sun, Istanbul, Submarine Seahawk, The Singer Not the Song, Mary Had a Little, The Sinister Man, An Helligen Wassern, The Fur Collar, The Shadow of Treason.
TV: Strictly Personal, African Patrol, Crossroads, Armchair Theatre, Any Other Business, Misfire, Time Out of Mind.

BENTON, ROBERT: Writer-Director. b. Waxahachie, Texas, 1932. e. Univ. of Texas (B.A.); Was art director at Esquire Magazine where he met David Newman, a writer-editor, and formed writing partnership. All writing credits shared with Newman. Benton made directorial debut with Bad Company (1972).
PICTURES INCLUDE: Bonnie and Clyde, There Was a Crooked Man, What's Up, Doc?, Bad Company (also directed) The Late Show (written and directed solo), Superman (with Mario Puzo and Tom Mankiewicz), Money's Tight, Bad Company (also dir., solo), Superman (co.-s.p.); Kramer vs. Kramer (dir. s.p.); Stab (dir., s.p.).
STAGE: It's a Bird . . . It's a Plane . . . It's Superman (libretto), Oh! Calcutta (one sketch).

BERCUTT MAX: Executive. b. Omaha, Neb., Oct. 14, 1910. e. U. of Southern California, 1933. Pres., Paris-American Guide Services, Paris, France; publicist David O. Selznick Prod.; U.S. Navy officer World War II; Warner Bros. field rep.; assistant to exec. vice-pres.; director of publicity, Warner Bros. Seven Arts Studio; resigned, September, 1969. Formed Max Bercutt Co., Jan. 1970.

BERENGER, TOM: Actor. b. Chicago. e. Univ. of Missouri (drama dept.) Acted in regional theatres and off Bdwy. Plays include The Rose Tattoo, Electra, Streetcar Named Desire, End as a Man.
PICTURES: Looking for Mr. Goodbar, In Praise of Older Women, Butch and Sundance: The Early Days.
TELEVISION: One Life to Live (series), Johnny We Hardly Knew Ye.

BERG HARVEY M.: Executive. b. Portland, Oregon, June 9, 1943. e. BS and MBA from UCLA. 1969 Arthur Young & Co., leaving as audit manager/computer audit specialist. 1974 Warner Bros., Inc. as studio controller serving both Warner Bros. and The Burbank Studios. 1976 The Burbank Studio as exec. asst. to the pres. and member of exec. comm. 1977 dir., of studio services and secty. of exec. comm.

BERGEN, CANDICE: Actress. b. Beverly Hills, Calif., May 9, 1946. e. U. of Pennsylvania. Modeled during college; m.p. debut, The Group, 1965; free lance photo-journalist.
PICTURES INCLUDE: The Group, The Sand Pebbles, The Day the Fish Came Out, Live for Life, The Magus, The Adventurers, Getting Straight, Soldier Blue, Carnal Knowledge, The Hunting Party, T. R. Baskin, 11 Harrowhouse, Bite the Bullet, The Wind and the Lion, The Domino Principle, A Night Full of Rain, Olivers' Story, Starting Over, Rich and Famous.

BERGEN, POLLY: Singer, actress. b. Knoxville, Tenn., July 14, 1930. e. Compton Jr. Coll., Calif. Prof. debut radio at 14; in light opera, summer stock; sang with orchestra and appeared in night clubs; Columbia recording star; Emmy Award, best actress, 1957–58; pres. The Polly Bergen Co.; on stage, John Murray Anderson's Almanac, Champagne Complex, First Impressions.
TV: G.E. Theatre, Schlitz Playhouse, Playhouse 90, Studio One, Perry Como, Ed Sullivan Show, To Tell the Truth,

Polly Bergen Show, Bob Hope Show, Bell Telephone, Wonderful World of Entertainment, Dinah Shore Show, NBC, CBS specials, Dean Martin Show, Andy Williams Show, Red Skelton Show, Mike Douglas Show.

BERGER, BENJAMIN N.: Executive. b. Poland, Mar. 5, 1896. Pres. Berger Amusement Co.; won decision in Fed. Court against payment to ASCAP for theatre seat tax.

BERGER, HELMUT: Actor. b. Salzburg, e. Feldkirk College and Univ. of Perugia. First film, small role in Luchino Visconti's The Witches (Le Streghe) in 1966.
PICTURES INCLUDE: The Young Tigers, The Damned, Do You Know What Stalin Did To Women?, The Garden of the Finzi-Continis, Dorian Gray, A Butterfly with Bloody Wings, The Greedy Ones, The Strange Love Affair, Ludwig, Ash Wednesday, Conversation Piece, The Romantic Englishwoman, Orders to Kill, Madame Kitty, Merry-Go-Round.

BERGER, RICHARD L.: Executive. e. UCLA. In 1964 joined acct. dept., 20th Century-Fox; promoted to exec. position in Fox-TV. Was dir. of programming, then v.p. of programs. Appt. asst. v.p., prod. 20th-Fox. Left in 1975 to join CBS-TV as v.p. dramatic development. Returned to 20th-Fox in 1977 as v.p., domestic prod., 20th Century-Fox Pictures.

BERGERAC, JACQUES: Actor. b. Biarritz, France. Career includes Five Minutes With Jacques Bergerac on radio; in the theatre, on tour in Once More With Feeling; on most major network TV shows.
PICTURES INCLUDE: Twist of Fate, The Time is Now, Strange Intruder, Come Away With Me, Les Girls, Gigi, Man and His Past, Thunder in the Sun, Hypnotic Eye, A Sunday in Summer, Fear No More, Achiles, A Global Affair, Taffy and the Jungle Hunter, The Emergency Operation, Lady Chaplin, The Last Party, One Plus One.

BERGMAN, INGMAR: Writer-director. b. Uppsala, Sweden, July 14, 1918. e. Stockhom U. Directed university play prods.; wrote & dir. Death of Punch, 1940; first theatrical success, dir., Macbeth, 1940; writer-director, Svensk Film-industri, 1942-present; first s.p., Frenzy, 1943; first directorial assignment, Crisis, 1946; chief prod., Civic Malmo, 1956–60.
PICTURES INCLUDE: Kris, 1946 Det Regnar Pa Var Karlek, Skepp Till Indialand, Night is My Future, Port of Call, The Devil's Wanton, Three Strange Loves, Till Gladje, Summer Interlude (Illicit Interlude), High Tension, Bris (soap ads), Secrets of Women, Monika, The Naked Light, A Lesson in Love, Dreams, Smiles of a Summer Night, Sista Parei Ut, The Seventh Seal, Wild Strawberries, Brink of Life, The Magician, The Virgin Spring, The Devil's Eye, Through a Glass Darkly, Winter Light, The Silence, All These Women, Persona, Hour of the Wolf, Shame, The Passion of Anna, Cries and Whispers, Scenes from a Marriage, Face to Face, The Serpent's Egg, Autumn Sonata, Life of the Marionettes.

BERGMAN, INGRID: Actress. b. Sweden, 1917; e. Lyceum for Flickor, Royal Dram. Theatre School. In Swedish m.p.; U.S. motion picture debut in Intermezzo, 1939; Academy Award best actress, Gaslight, 1944; voted one of ten best money making stars, Motion Picture Herald-Fame Poll, 1946–48; British TV, Hedda Gabler.
PICTURES INCLUDE: Adam Had Four Sons, Rage in Heaven, Dr. Jekyll and Mr. Hyde, En Enda Natt, Casablanca, For Whom the Bell Tolls, Notorious, Saratoga Trunk, Spellbound, Bells of St. Mary's, Arch of Triumph, Joan of Arc, Under Capricorn, Stromboli, Greatest Love, Strangers, Fear, Anastasia, Paris Does Strange Things, Indiscreet, The Inn of the Sixth Happiness, Goodbye Again, The Visit, The Yellow Rolls Royce, Cactus Flower, A Walk in the Spring Rain, From The Mixed-Up Files of Mrs. Basil E. Frankweiler, Murder on the Orient Express, A Matter of Time, Autumn Sonata.
STAGE: Captain Bassbound's Conversion (1972), More Stately Mansions.
TV: 24 Hours in the Life of a Woman.

BERGMANN, TED: Executive; b. Brooklyn, N.Y., Sept. 12, 1920. e. Gov. Dummer Acad. and Amherst Col.; joined NBC 1941; 1942–46 Captain, U.S. Army in pub. rel. div. of SHAEF; awarded Bronze Star Medal for combat reporting; returned to NBC 1946 international div.; 1947, acc't exec. DuMont TV Network; 1951 appt. dir. of sales of DuMont TV Network; named gen. mgr., 1953; managing dir. of broadcast div. DuMont, 1954–56; v.p. McCann-Erickson, 1956–57; pres. Parkson Adv. Agency, Inc., 1957–60; v.p. adv. Revlon Inc. 1960–62.
Member of Bd. Dir. NAB, 1954–56; V.P. Radio-TV Exec. Society; Bd. of Gov. 1957–62, Academy TV Arts & Sciences, 1959–61. President, Charter Producers Corp., 1962.

BERLE, MILTON: Actor. r.n. Milton Berlinger; b. New York City, July 12, 1908; e. Professional Children's Sch., N.Y. in vaudeville; on N.Y. stage (Ziegfeld Follies 1936, Life Begins at 8:40, etc.): night clubs; concurrently on radio & screen.
TV: Star of own NBC show; Texaco Star Theatre, 1948–54, Kraft Music Hall TV Show, 1958–59, Jackpot Bowling,

1960–61, Doyle Against the House, Dick Powell Show, 1961, Chrysler TV special, 1962, The Milton Berle Show, 1966.
PICTURES INCLUDE: Tall, Dark and Handsome, Sun Valley Serenade, Over My Dead Body, Margin for Error, Always Leave Them Laughing, Let's Make Love, It's a Mad Mad Mad World, The Happening, Who's Minding the Mint, Where Angels Go . . . Trouble Follows, Can Hieronymus Merkin Ever Forget Mercy Humppe and Find True Happiness?, Lepke.

BERLIN, IRVING: Composer. r.n. Israel Baline. b. Russia, May 11, 1888. To New York, 1893. As youth, singing waiter in N.Y.; early began writing songs. One of first successes, Alexander's Ragtime Band. Entered music pub.; member Waterson, Berlin & Snyder. W.W I, sgt. inf. U.S. Army. Composer many indiv. and stage musical songs. In 1937 wrote songs for screen prod. Top Hat (RKO); in 1942 prod. stage musical This Is the Army for U.S. Army Fund; in 1943 assoc. with Warner Bros. in prod. film version. Member: Lambs, Friars (N.Y.); pres. Irving Berlin Music Corp., music pub.
PICTURES INCLUDE: Follow the Fleet, On the Avenue, Carefree, Alexander's Ragtime Band, Second Fiddle, Holiday Inn, Blue Skies, Easter Parade, Annie Get Your Gun, Call me Madam, White Christmas, There's No Business Like Show Business.

BERLINGER, WARREN: Actor, b. Brooklyn, N.Y., Aug. 31, 1937. e. Col. Univ.
STAGE: Annie Get Your Gun, The Happy Time, Bernardine, Take A Giant Step, Anniversary Waltz, Roomful of Roses, Blue Denim, Come Blow Your Horn, How To Succeed in Business Without Really Trying, (London) Who's Happy Now?, California Suite, 77–78 tour.
PICTURES INCLUDE: Teenage Rebel, Three Brave Men, Blue Denim, Because They're Young, Platinum High School, The Wackiest Ship in the Army, All Hands on Deck, Billie, Spinout, Thunder Alley, Lepke, The Four Deuces, I Will . . . I Will . . . For Now, Harry and Walter Go to New York, The Shaggy D.A., The Magician of Dublin, The Cannonball Run.
TV: Secret Storm (serial), Alcoa, Goodyear, Armstrong, Matinee Theatre, Joey Bishop Show, The London Palladium, Kilroy, Billie, Bracken's World, The Funny Side (NBC 1971–72); Touch of Grace, (ABC-TV 1972–73); The Most Wanted Woman.

BERMAN, CHARLES. U.K. & European dir. of operations, the Saul Zaentz Production Co. Previously dep. man. dir. and dir., pub./adv./exploit., United Artists, London. Joined Odeon 1946 as trainee mgr.; later as publicity man with Hammer Theatrical Enterprises. Transferred to Exclusive Films pub. dept., before joining UA 1953. From pub. asst. promoted press officer. Later asst. pub. dir.; appt. dir. of pub./exploit. 1963; appt. to board, 1969.

BERMAN, MONTY: producer/cinematographer. b. London, England.
PICTURES INCLUDE: Voice of Merill, Tiger by the Tail, Blood of the Vampire, The Trollenberg Terror, Sea of Sand, Jack The Ripper, Flesh and the Fiends, The Siege of Sidney Street, Hellfire Club, Treasure of Monte Cristo, What a Carve Up.
TV: The Saint, Gideon's Way, The Baron, The Champions, Department S. Randall & Hopkirk (Deceased), Jason King, The Adventurer, Secret of Storm Mountain.

BERMAN, MONTY, M.: Film and theatrical costumier. b. London, England, 1912. Personally costumed films and shows since 1931. Squad Leader RAF 1940–45; Bomber Command, M.B.E. Since war has costumed major films and shows and numerous TV prod.
PICTURES INCLUDE: Doctor Zhivago, Tom Jones, Longest Day, My Fair Lady, Oliver, Cromwell, Patton, The Devils, Fiddler on the Roof, A Bridge Too Far, The Other Side of Midnight, Julia, The Seven Per Cent Solution, The Slipper And The Rose, A Little Night Music, Star Wars, Superman.

BERMAN, PANDRO S.: Producer. b. Pittsburgh, Pa. Mar. 28, 1905. Son of late Harry M. Berman, gen. mgr. Universal, FBO. Asst. dir. film ed., FBO; film & title ed. Columbia Studios; chief film ed. RKO, later asst. to William Le Baron & David Selznick; became prod. 1931 (RKO). A Champion of Champions Producers in Fame ratings. Joined MGM 1940.
PICTURES INCLUDE: What Price Hollywood, Symphony of Six Million, Bachelor Mother, The Gay Divorcee, Of Human Bondage, Morning Glory, Roberta, Alice Adams, Top Hat, Winterset, Stage Door, Vivacious Lady, Gunga Din, Hunchback of Notre Dame, Ziegfeld Girl, Honky Tonk, Seventh Cross, National Velvet, Dragon Seed, Portrait of Dorian Grey, Love Affair, Undercurrent, Sea of Grass, Three Musketeers, Madame Bovary, Father of the Bride, Father's Little Dividend, Prisoner of Zenda, Ivanhoe, All the Brothers Were Valiant, Knights of the Round Table, Long, Long Trailer, Blackboard Jungle, Bhowani Junction, Something of Value, Tea and Sympathy, Brothers Karamazov, Reluc-

tant Debutante, Butterfield 8, Sweet Bird of Youth, The Prize, A Patch of Blue, Justine, Move.

BERNARD, JUDD: Writer-producer. b. Chicago, Ill., stage, The World of Carl Sandberg.
PICTURES INCLUDE: Double Trouble, Point Blank, Blue, Fade In, Negatives, The Ma Who Had Power Over Women, Deep End, Glad All Over, and Now For Something Completely Different, The Marsailles Contract, Inside Out, The Class of Miss MacMichael.

BERNARD, MARVIN A.: Executive. b. New York City, Oct. 1, 1934. e. N.Y.U. Associated with Rapid Film Technique, Inc.; 1949–63: developed technological advances in film preservation, responsible for public underwriting; 1964–69; real estate sales & investments in Bahamas, then with Tishman Realty (commercial leasing div.); v.p. and operating head of International Film Treat 1970–1973; authored film damaged control chart, a critical analysis of film care and repair—1971; 1973-elected to and for inclusion in 1973–74 edition of Who's Who, because of his expertise in the field of motion picture film rejuvenation; for more than two decades; founded Filmlife Inc. with latest mechanical and technical advancement in field of film rejuvenation; 1973–75 bd. chrmn. and chief operating officer of Filmlife Inc., motion picture film rejuvenation company. Feb. 1975 elected President in addition to remaining bd. chairman.

BERNHARD, HARVEY: Producer. b. Seattle, Wash., March 5, 1924. e. Stanford Univ. In real estate in Seattle, 1947–50; started live lounge entertainment at the Last Frontier Hotel, Las Vegas, 1950. Partner with Sandy Howard, 1958–60; v.p. in chg. prod., David L. Wolper Prods., dividing time between TV and feature films, 1961–68; with MPC, v.p., chg. prod., 1968–70. Now pres. of Harvey Bernhard Ent., Inc.
PICTURES INCLUDE: The Mack (1973), The Omen (1976), Damien—Omen II (1978), The Final Conflict (1981), The Beast Within (1981).

BERNS, SEYMOUR: Director. Started as dir. CBS radio, 1946; radio shows include Art Linkletter's House Party, Double or Nothing, Hollywood Barn Dance, Free for All; joined CBS-TV network 1952; v.p. National General TV Productions, 1969; National pres. TV Academy, 1969–70; Chairman of the Board 1970–71; pres. The Valjon Prod. Co. 1971.
TV: Art Linkletter's House Party, Meet Millie, Red Skelton Show, Shower of Stars, My Friend Irma, Ford Star Jubilee, Edsel Show, Jack Benny Show, Gunsmoke, Lineup.

BERNSTEIN, Baron cr 1969 (Life Peer) of Leigh; Sidney Lewis Bernstein LLd; Chairman; Granada Group Limited in 1974–79. Pres. since 1979. (Granada Television, Granada Publishing, Granada Theatres, Granada TV Rental, Granada Motorway Services, Novello & Co). b. 30 Jan. 1899. A founder, Film Society, 1924. Films Adviser, Min. of Inf. 1940–45; Liason, British Embassy, Washington 1942; Chief, Film Section SHAEF 1943–45. Lecturer on Film and International Affairs, New York Univ. and Yale. Governor, Sevenoaks School. Member, Resources for Learning Committee, Nuffield Foundation. Address: 36 Golden Square, London, W1.

BERNSTEIN, BOB: Executive. Began public relations career 1952 at DuMont TV Network, followed by 2 yrs. as press agent for Liberace. With Billboard Magazine as review editor 3 yrs. Joined Westinghouse Bdg. Co. as p.r. director 1959. In 1963 named p.r. director for Triangle Publications, serving in various capacities to 1971. Joined Viacom Intl. as director of information services. In 1975 formed own co., March Five Inc., p.r. and promotion firm.

BERNSTEIN, ELMER: Composer-conductor. b. New York, N.Y. Apr. 4, 1922. Scholarship, Juilliard. e. Walden School, New York U., U.S. Army Air Force radio unit. After war 3 yrs. recitals, musical shows, United Nations radio dept; pres., Young Musicians Found.; 1st v.p. Academy of Motion Picture Arts & Sciences; co-chairman music branch. Music dir. Valley Symphony. Recording: United Artists. More than 90 major films. Pres. of Composers & Lyricists Guild of America past 5 years.
PICTURES INCLUDE: The Ten Commandments, Man With the Golden Arm, The Great Escape, To Kill a Mockingbird (received ten Academy Award nominations and Oscar, 1967), The Carpetbaggers, The Magnificent Seven, Birdman of Alcatraz, Walk on the Wild Side, Hallelujah Trail, The Reward, Seven Women, Cast A Giant Shadow, Hawaii, Thoroughly Modern Millie, True Grit, Cahill, U.S. Marshall, McQ., Gold, The Trial of Billy Jack, Report to the Commissioner, From Noon Till Three, Sarah, The Shootist, Bloodbrothers, Meatballs, Airplane!, Going Ape.
TV: Hollywood: The Golden Years (special), The Race for Space; Parts I & II (special), D-Day (special), The Making of the President—1960 (special), won Emmy Award), Hollywood and the Stars (special), Voyage of the Brigantine Yankee (special), Crucification of Jesus (special), Julia series, Owen Marshall series, Ellery Queen series, Serpico series.

BERNSTEIN, RICHARD: b. Rochester, N.Y., Aug. 8, 1922; e. Los Angeles City Coll. Radio prod., writer, dir. created shows Food for Fun, Mr. Celebrity. Press agent personalities and indep. co. 1951. M.P. prod. exec. 1951–54. Producing debut Walk The Dark Street, Prod. exec. Milner Bros. 1955. The Phantom from 10,000 Leagues. Coauthored, wrote screen play and ass't prod. From Hell It Came. Formed Viscount Films with Richard B. Duckett and George W. Waters, 1957; prod., co-author Tank Battalion; prod., co-author Speed Crazy; wrote Jail Break; prod. co-author, Why Must I Die?, prod. and story, Atlantic Attack, Woman By Night; prod., s.p. Terrified, prod., The Gun Hawk, 1968, co-author s.p., Treasure of Kota Twai, Max Orloff Productions; 1969 s.p., Laughter in Hell, Palisades Productions; 1970; s.p., The Wild Wild Wild West and Fast and Furious; presenter, the Challenges, 2nd place winner San Sebastian, Transworld Film Enterprises release; screen plays, Backlash, William Productions; prod.; wrote story, screen play for The Dirt Gang; Creator TV Series, "Bureau of Missing Persons." Co-producer of Women of the World, Major Films Inc. Writer, producer, director, Ripoff; Original screen story, Win, Place and Steal, feature. Writer, Producer, TV series, My Mother . . . The Maid, Colebern Productions; pres.; Pacific Global Film Enterprises.

BERNSTEIN, WALTER: Director-Writer. b. New York City. e. Dartmouth. Wrote for New Yorker Magazine; in World War II was roving correspondent for Yank Magazine. Returned to New Yorker after war. Wrote TV scripts; published book Keep Your Head Down (collection of articles).
PICTURES INCLUDE: Writer: The Molly McGuires, The Money Trap, Fail Safe, Paris Blues, Heller in Pink Tights, Semi-Tough, The Front, An Almost Perfect Affair, Yanks, Little Miss Marker. Director: Little Miss Marker (debut).

BERRY, JOHN: Director. b. N.Y.C., 1917. Directed films in Hollywood mid and late '40s; went abroad during McCarthy era in U.S. where worked in French film industry. Later went to London to do stage work, acting as well as directing. Returned to U.S. to do stage work; returned to Hollywood to do TV.
PICTURES INCLUDE: Cross My Heart, From This Day Forward, Miss Susie Slagle's, Casbah, Tension, He Ran All the Way, Ca Va Barder, The Great Lover, Je Suis un Sentimental, Tamango, On Que Mambo, Maya, Thieves.
TV: One Drink at a Time, Farewell Party, Mr. Broadway, etc.

BERTOLUCCI, BERNARDO: Director-Writer. b. Parma, Italy, March 16, 1941. e. Rome University. Son of Attilio Bertolucci poet and film critic. First worked in films at age of 20 as asst. dir. to Pier Paolo Pasolini on latter's first film, Accattone; in 1962 made debut film, The Grim Reaper, from script by Pasolini.
PICTURES INCLUDE: Before the Revolution, Partner, Love and Rage (one episode: Agony). The Spider's Stratagem, 1900, Luna.

BEST, BARBARA: Publicist. b. San Diego, Calif., Dec. 2, 1921. e. U.S.C., A.B. 1943. Pub., 20th Century-Fox, 1943–49; reporter, San Diego Journal, 1950 Stanley Kramer Co. 1950–53; own agency, Barbara Best & Associates, 1953–66; 1966 exec. v.p. Jay Bernstein Public rel.; Freeman and Best, 1967–74; Barbara Best Inc. current.

BEST, JAMES: Actor. b. Corydon, Ind., July 26, 1926. Magazine model; on stage; in European roadshow cast of "My Sister Eileen"; served as M.P. with U.S.A.A.F., World War II; m.p. debut in Comanche Territory, 1949.
PICTURES INCLUDE: Winchester 73, Air Cadet, Cimarron Kid, Steel Town, Ma & Pa Kettle At the Fair, Francis Goes to West Point, Seminole, The President's Lady, City of Bad Men, Column South, Riders to the Stars, The Raid, Caine Mutiny, Return from the Sea, The Left-Handed Gun, They Rode West, Seven Angry Men, Come Next Spring, Baby, The Rack, Sounder, Ode to Billy Joe.

BETHUNE, ZINA: Acress, dancer, singer. B. New York, 1950. B'way: Most Happy Fella, Nutcracker. New York City Ballet (Balanchine), Zina Bethune & Company Dance Theater.
PICTURES: Sunrise At Campobello, Who's That Knocking At My Door. National Tours: Sweet Charity, Carnival, Oklahoma, Damn Yankees, Member of the Wedding, The Owl & The Pussycat.
TV: The Nurses, Lancer, Cains Hundred, Naked City, Route 66, Little Women, Judy Garland Show, Jackie Gleason Show, Gunsmoke, Dr. Kildare, Emergency, Planet of The Apes, Police Story, Chips, Hardy Boys.

BETTGER, LYLE: Actor. b. Philadelphia, Pa., Feb. 13, 1915; m. Mary Rolfe, actress; e. Haverford School, Phila., Amer. Acad. Dramatic Art, N.Y.C. Started in summer stock; in road cos. of Brother Rat, Man Who Came to Dinner.
STAGE: John Loves Mary, Love Life, Eve of St. Mark.
PICTURES INCLUDE: No Man of Her Own, Union Station, First Legion, Greatest Show on Earth, Sea Chase, Gunfight at OK Corral, Johnny Reno, Nevada Smith, Return of The Gunfighter, The Hawaiians, Carnival Story, The Seven Minutes.
TV: Court of Last Resort, Grand Jury, Hawaii 5-0, Police Story.

BETTINSON, RALPH: Writer. b. London, Eng., Apr. 18, 1908; e. Radley Coll. Film ed. London Films, Korda (Paris), Brit. Paramount; prod. Sound City Films; writer Gaumont & Paramount Brit.; with Republic Pictures, Hollywood 1935; spec. supvr. Monogram Brit. Prod. 1937–42; prod. of training films & documentaries U.S. Army 1943–6; writer Eagle-Lion 1947–8; contract writer Columbia Pictures 1949; (orig. story) Rogues of Sherwood Forest; adapt. Mask of the Avenger; collab. s.p., asst. prod., 1948.

BEVILLE, HUGH M., Jr.: Executive; b. April 18, 1908; e. Syracuse U.; to NBC 1930 statistician, Chief Statistician; Research mgr., dir., research; U.S. Army 1942–46; dir. of research and planning for NBC, v.p., planning and research, 1956; v.p., Planning, 1964; Consultant, 1968; Professor Business Admin., Southampton College, 1968. Exec. dir., Broadcast Rating Council, 1971.

BEY, TURHAN: Actor. b. Vienna, Austria, March 30. Made U.S. m.p. debut in 1941.
PICTURES INCLUDE: Footsteps in the Dark, Burma Convoy, Bombay Clipper, Drums of the Congo, Destination Unknown, White Savage, Dragon Seed, Arabian Nights, Bowery to Broadway, Night in Paradise, Out of the Blue, Amazing Mr. X, Parole, Inc., Adventures of Casanova, Song of India, Prisoners of the Casbah, Stolen Identity.

BEYMER, RICHARD: Actor, r.n. George Richard Beymer, Jr., b. Avoca, Iowa, Feb. 21, 1939. e. N. Hollywood H. S., Actors Studio. Performer, KTLA, Sandy Dreams, Fantastic Studios, Inc., 1949, Playhouse 90.
PICTURES INCLUDE: Indiscretion of an American Wife, So Big, Johnny Tremaine, The Diary of Anne Frank, High Time, West Side Story, Bachelor Flat, Five Finger Exercise, Hemingway's Adventures of a Young Man, The Longest Day, The Stripper.

BIBAS, FRANK PERCY: Executive. b. New York City, 1917; e. Brown & Columbia Universities; Capt., Army Air Corps, World War II. Entered m.p. ind. adv. dept., Donahue & Coe; later pub. dept. American Display, thence to dist. dept., National Screen Service. In 1945 joined Casanave-Artlee Pictures Inc.; apptd. vice-pres. in charge of sales 1946 (dist. Selznick reissues in U.S.); vice-pres. Casanave Pictures, Inc. & Sixteen M.M. Pictures Inc., from 1949 mgr. m.p. dept., McCann-Erickson ad agency; joined Roland Reed TV Inc., v.p., prod., 1955. Prod-dir. with Hal Roach Studios, 1957. 1961 to present N.Y.C. partner, Bibas-Redford Inc. Production Co. 1962 won Academy Award for "Project Hope," documentary. Member: S.M.P.T.E., Acad. of TV Arts and Sciences, Directors Guild of America.

BICK, JERRY: Producer. b. New York City. e. Columbia Univ., Sorbonne. m. actress Louise Fletcher. Taught English at Univ. of Ga. and was radio sports announcer in Savannah, Ga., before entering firm industry in pub. dept. of MGM, N.Y. Opened own literary agency in Hollywood representing film, TV writers. Began career as producer in London; debut film, Michael Kohlhaas (1969), made in Czechoslovakia.
PICTURES INCLUDE: The Long Goodbye, Thieves Like Us, Russian Roulette.

BIEN, WALTER H.: Producer. b. San Francisco, April 16, 1923; e. UCLA, 1944. Entered m.p. ind. as film editor, MGM, 1943, Monogram, 1946; Eagle Lion, 1948; formed TV production company 1950, prod. live shows in L.A. area; Universal TV comm. dept., 1954; Warner Bros., to start comm. & ind. div., 1960; exec. prod. in chg. TV comm. & ind. films div., prod. Bell System Science Series; pres., SIB Productions, Inc., SIB-Tower 12.

BILBY, KENNETH W.: Executive. b. Salt Lake City, Utah, Oct. 7, 1918. e. Columbia U., U. of Ariz., B.A. With N.Y. Herald-Tribune, 47–50; author, New Star in the Near East, 1950; pub. rel. rep. to RCA Victor, Camden, New Jersey, 1950–54; exec. v.p. National Broadcasting Co., N.Y., 1954–60; v.p. public affairs, RCA, 1960–62, exec. v.p., 1962–75; exec. v.p., corporate affairs, 1976–present.

BILIMORIA, N. M.: Distributor. b. Oct. 7, 1922. Partner in M. B. Bilimoria & Son, Bombay; dir. Dominion Films (P) Ltd. Bombay; Modern Films Private Ltd., Bombay; Partner, Bilimoria & Lalji, Calcutta; Distributors Combine, Bombay; Bilimoria & Chhotubhai, Delhi; Moti Talkies, Delhi; Agent: Union Carbide India Ltd., Calcutta and Union Carbide International Co., N.Y.

BILL, TONY: Actor-Producer. b. San Diego, Ca. e. Notre Dame. Began career in films in 1963 acting in Come Blow Your Horn. In 1971 founded Bill/Phillips Prods. with Julia and Michael Phillips. Left in 1973 to be independent.
PICTURES INCLUDE: Actor: You're a Big Boy Now, Castle Keep, Shampoo, Heartbeat. Co-producer: Deadhead Miles, Steelyard Blues, The Sting. Prod.: Hearts of the West, Harry and Walter Go to New York, Boulevard Nights

(exec. prod.); Going in Style (co-prod.). Director: My Bodyguard.

BILLITTERI, SALVATORE: Executive. b. Belleville, N.J., March 21, 1921. e. Fordham U.; U.S. Air Force, 1943–45; ent. m.p. ind., doorman in N.Y. theatre, 1939; theatre mgr., 1947; film slsman, Casolaro Film Distributing Co., 1947–51; co-owner many foreign films; film editor, I.F.E., 1951; head of editing, prod. dept., Titra Sound Corp., 1956; head of east coast production, American International Pictures, 1961; dir. Post Prod., 1970; named v.p. 1974, sr. v.p. of Filmways Pictures, 1980.

BILSON, GEORGE: Prod., dir., writer. b. Leeds, Eng. e. C.C.N.Y. dir. advertising, W.B., 1927–32; West Coast adv. mgr. Warner Bros. Chg. of prod. of trailers 1932–37; prod., Universal 1938; exec. producer-writer short subjects RKO Studio, 1943–53. Freelance TV writer.

BINNS, EDWARD: Actor. b. Penn. Broadway debut in Command Decision, 1947. Has since appeared in TV, theatre, m.p. and commercial voice-overs.
PICTURES INCLUDE: Fail-Safe, Twelve Angry Men, Compulsion, Patton, The Americanization of Emily, Judgment at Nuremburg, Lovin' Molly, Night Moves, Oliver's Story.
TV: Kraft Theatre, Studio One, Danger, Brenner (series), The Defenders, The Nurses, It Takes a Thief (series).
STAGE: Detective Story, Caligula, The Caine Mutiny Court Martial, A Touch of the Poet.

BIONDI, GUY: Executive. b. Newark, N.J. e. Oklahoma Univ. Entered m.p. career on roadshow of Henry V, UA; Universal pub. staff, 1952; Mike Todd Company, 1956; Harold Mirisch Co., o., 1960; v.p. Walter Reade-Sterling, 1964; AFT, 1972; v.p. adv. & pub. Gamma III.

BIRCH, WILLIAM: Cinematographer. b. Chicago, Ill., Mar. 1, 1918. Asst., Movietonews, 1937–40; army signal corp, 1940–44; head of midwestern bureau, did camera, NBC News & Document.; established own service; estab. William Birch & Assoc. Inc.
Won two Emmys, cameraman of the yr., Nat. Headliners Award.

BIRMINGHAM, PAUL A.: Executive. b. Burbank, Calif., Feb. 12, 1937. e. University of Calif., Univ. of South. Calif.; sr., v.p., studio operations and admin., Paramount Pictures.

BIRNEY, DAVID: Actor. b. Washington, D.C., April 23. e. Dartmouth, UCLA. m. actress Meredith Baxter Birney. Following college and the Army went to N.Y. where appeared in Lincoln Center prod. of Summertree. Appeared for two yrs. on TV daytime series, Love is a Many Splendored Thing, doing other stage roles in same period.
PICTURES INCLUDE: Trial by Combat, Oh, God, Book II.
TV: Bridget Loves Bernie (series), Police Story (segments), The Adams Chronicles, Serpico (series).

BIROC, JOSEPH F.: Cinematographer. b. New York, N.Y., Feb. 12, 1903. e. Emerson H.S., Union City, N.J.
PICTURES INCLUDE: Bwana Devil, Glass Wall, Tall Texan, Vice Squad, Donovan's Brain, Appointment in Honduras, Down Three Dark Streets, Lone Wolf, T-Men in Action, Man Behind the Badge, Dear Phoebe, Nightmare, Tension at Table Rock, Attack, Black Whip, Run of the Arrow, Ride Back, Garment Jungle, China Gate, Ice Palace, FBI Story, 13 Ghosts, Home Before Dark, Operation Eichmann, Devil at 4 O'clock, Gold of the Seven Saints, Reprieve, Opium Eaters, Hitler, Sail a Crooked Ship, Bye Bye Birdie, Toys in the Attic, Promises-Promises, Under the Yum-Yum Tree, Viva Las Vegas, Kitten With a Whip, Ride the Wild Surf, Renegade Posse, Gunfight at Commanche Pass, Hush . . . Hush Sweet Charlotte, I Saw What You Did, Flight of the Phoenix, The Russians are Coming, The Russians are Coming, The Swinger, Warning Shot, Enter Laughing, Who is Minding the Mint, Garden of Cucumbers, The Killing of Sister George, What Ever Happened to Aunt Alice?, Too Late the Hero, Mrs. Polifax Spy, Escape from the Planet of the Apes, The Organization, The Grissom Gang, Cahill, U.S. Marshall, The Longest Yard, The Towering Inferno, Hustle, The Duchess And The Dirtwater Fox, The Choirboys, Beyond the Poseidon Adventure, Airplane!, Hammet, All the Marbles.
TV: Four Star Theatre, Readers Digest, Superman, Richard Diamond, Alcoa Theatre, Grindl, Solo, Ghost Breakers, Take Her She's Mine, Heaven Help Us, Hardy Boys, Brian's Song, Gidget Gets Married, Ghost Story, Thursdays Game, Lonely Hearts "555," Family Upside Down, S.S.T. Death Flight, Little Women, Scruples, The Gambler.
TV PILOTS: Wonder Woman, Honky Tonk, The Moneychangers, Washington, D.C., Clone Master.

BISHOP, JULIE: Actress. b. Denver, Colo., Aug. 30, 1917. e. Westlake, Kenwood, Schools for Girls (Former screen name Jacqueline Wells); m.p. debut 1941.
PICTURES INCLUDE: Nurse's Secret, International Squadron, Steel Against the Sky, Lady Gangster, Busses

Roar, Cinderella Jones, Murder in the Music Hall, Idea Girl, Strange Conquest, Last of the Redmen, High Tide, Deputy Marshal, Threat, Sands of Iwo Jima, Westward the Women, Sabre Jet, High and the Mighty, Headline Hunters.

BISSET, JACQUELINE: Actress. b. Weybridge, England, September 13, 1944. e. French Lycee, London. After photographic modeling made film debut in The Knack.
PICTURES INCLUDE: Two For The Road, The Sweet Ride, The Detective, Bullitt, The First Time, Airport, The Grasshopper, The Mephisto Waltz, Believe in Me, Stand Up and Be Counted, The Thief Who Came to Dinner, Murder on the Orient Express, End of the Game, The Spiral Staircase, St. Ives, Sunday Woman, The Deep, The Greek Tycoon, Who Is Killing the Great Chefs of Europe?, When Time Ran Out, Rich and Famous.

BIXBY, BILL: Actor. b. San Francisco, Calif., Jan. 22. e. Univ. of Calif., Berkeley. Worked in indust. films. Gen. Motors, Chrysler.
TV: Dobie Gillis, Danny Thomas Show, Joey Bishop Show, Andy Griffith Show, My Favorite Martian, Eddie's Father, The Hulk.
STAGE: Fantasticks (nat'l company), Under the Yum Yum Tree.
PICTURES INCLUDE: Lonely Are the Brave, Irma La Douce, Yum Yum Tree, Ride Beyond Vengeance, This Way Out Please.

BLACK, ALEXANDER F.: Publicist. b. New Rochelle, N.Y., Dec. 27, 1918. B.A. Brown U., 1940. Joined Universal 1941. U.S. Navy 1942–45, Lt. Sr. Grade. Rejoined Universal 1946 serving in various capacities in Foreign Department, becoming Director of Foreign Publicity for Universal International Films, Inc. in 1967; 1974, named exec. in chg. intl. promotion for MCA-TV.

BLACK, KAREN: Actress. b. Park Ridge, Ill., 1943. e. Northwestern Univ. Left school for New York to join the Hecscher House, where she appeared in several Shakespearean plays. In 1965 starred in Playroom, which ran only 1 mth. but won her a nom. as best actress of season by N.Y. drama critics. Made m.p. debut in 1966 in You're a Big Boy Now.
PICTURES INCLUDE: Easy Rider, Five Easy Pieces, Drive, He Said, A Gunfight, Born To Win, Portnoy's Complaint, The Pyx, Rhinoceros, The Outfit, The Great Gatsby, Airport 1975, Law and Disorder, Day of the Locust, Nashville, Family Plot, Crime and Passion, Burnt Offerings, Capricorn One, Because He's My Friend, In Praise of Older Women, The Rip-off, Greed, Danny Travis.
STAGE: Happily Never After, Keep It in the Family.

BLACK, STANLEY: Composer, conductor, musical director. Resident Conductor, BBC, 1944–52. Musical Director 105 feature films and Pathe Newsreel music: Music dir. Associated British Film Studios 1958–64. Guest Conductor Royal Philharmonic Orchestra and London Symphony Orchestra; many overseas conducting engagements including (1977) Boston Pops and Winnipeg Symphony. Associated Conductor Osaka Philharmonic Orchestra. Exclusive recording contract with Decca Record Co. since 1944.
PICTURES INCLUDE: Crossplot, The Long, The Short and The Tall, Rattle of a Simple Man, The Young Ones, Hell is a City, Top Secret, etc., 1977 Valentino.

BLACK, THEODORE R.: Attorney, b. New Jersey, Aug. 11, 1906; e. Harvard, B.A. 1927, LL.B., 1930 (Sigma Alpha Mu Frat.). Formerly General Counsel, bd. member, Republic Pictures Corp. Member: Nat'l Panel of Arbitrators, American Arbit. Assn., Bd. N.Y. Ethical Culture Society.

BLACKMAN, HONOR: Actress. b. London, Eng. Stage debut. The Gleam 1946. Screen debut, Fame Is the Spur.
TV: African Patrol, The Witness, Four Just Men, Probation Officer series, Top Secret, Ghost Squad, Invisible Man, The Saint, The Avengers series.
PICTURES INCLUDE: Quartet, Daughter of Darkness, A Boy A Girl and a Bike, Diamond City, Conspirator, So Long at the Fair, Set a Murderer, Green Grow the Rushes, Come Die My Love, Rainbow Jacket, Outsiders, Delavine Affair, Three Musketeers, Breakaway, Homecoming, Suspended Alibi, Dangerous Drugs, A Night to Remember, The Square Peg, A Matter of Who, Present Laughter, The Recount, Serena, Jason & The Golden Fleece, Goldfinger, The Secret of My Success, Moment to Moment, Life at the Top, A Twist of Sand, Shalako, Struggle for Rome, Twinky, The Last Grenade, The Virgin and the Gypsy, Fright, Something Big, Out Damned Spot, Ragtime, Summer, Cat and the Canary.

BLAINE, VIVIAN: Actress. r.n. Vivian S. Stapleton. b. Newark, N.J., Nov. 21, 1924; e. South Side H.S., Newark. Singer with various bands in New Jersey 1937–39, thereafter night clubs; 20th-Fox contract 1942. Personal appearance on Great Britain stage from 1947; co-starred Guys and Dolls N.Y. stage and London stage; Hatful of Rain, N.Y. stage; Guys and Dolls film 1955.

Member: Academy of M.P. Arts & Sciences, A.F.R.A., Equity, S.A.G., A.G.V.A.
PICTURES INCLUDE: He Married His Boss, Thru Different Eyes, Greenwich Village, Something for the Boys, Nob Hill, State Fair, Three Little Girls in Blue, If I'm Lucky, Skirts Ahoy, Public Pigeon No. 1.

BLAIR, BETSY: Actress. r.n. Betsy Boger. b. New York, N.Y., Dec. 11.
BROADWAY: Beautiful People, Richard II, actress in little theatre groups.
PICTURES INCLUDE: Another Part of the Forest, Kind Lady, Othello, Marty, Halliday Brand, A Delicate Balance.
TV: Appearances on U.S. Steel Hour, Ford Theatre, Philco, Kraft.

BLAIR, JANET: Actress. b. Blair, Pa., April 23, 1921. With Hal Kemp's Orchestra; on tour South Pacific play, 1950–52.
PICTURES INCLUDE: Three Girls About Town, Blondie Goes to College, Two Yanks in Trinidad, Burn Witch Burn, Broadway, My Sister Eileen, Something to Shout About, Once Upon a Time, Tars and Spars, Gallant Journey, Fabulous Dorseys, I Love Trouble, Black Arrow, Fuller Brush Man, Public Pigeon No. 1, Boys Night Out, The One and Only, Genuine, Original Family Band.

BLAIR, LARRY: Actor. r.n. Larry Bess. b. Newark, N.J., June 27, 1935; f. Herman Bess, NYC radio executive. e. public and private schools, Newark and Asbury Park, N.J. Worked as lifeguard. Began in showbusiness, age 13 as D.J. and actor in NYC; 1954–55, production assistant, WABC-TV, NYC; 1955–62, associate director and director, WNEW-TV, NYC; 1962–71, D.J., newscaster with WFIL, Phila., WIIC (Hartford), WHN, WMCA, NYC. 1971 to present, commercial spokesman, narrator and actor in educational and industrial films and videotapes.

BLAIR, LINDA: Actress. b. St. Louis, Jan. 22, 1959. Model and actress on TV commercials before going into films.
PICTURES: The Sporting Club, The Way We Live Now, The Exorcist, Airport '75, Sweet Hostage, Exorcist II: The Heretic.
TELEVISION: Born Innocent, Sarah T.—Portrait of a Teenage Alcoholic, Victory at Entebbe.

BLAKE, AMANDA: Actress. r.n. Beverly Louise Neill; b. Buffalo, N.Y., Feb. 20. Telephone operator; in m.p. 1950.
PICTURES INCLUDE: Battleground, Stars in My Crown, Counterspy Meets Scotland Yard, Scarlet Angel, Cattle Town, Lili, Sabre Jet, Miss Robin Crusoe, About Mrs. Leslie, Adventures of Hajji Baba, Star Is Born, Glass Slipper, High Society.
TV: Double Exposure; Schlitz Playhouse, General Electric Theater, Four Star Playhouse, Cavalcade of America, Lux Video Playhouse, My Favorite Husband, Professional Father, The Red Skelton Show, Climax, Gunsmoke.

BLAKE, DAVID M.: Producers' Representative. b. Trincomalee, Ceylon, April 19, 1948. Ent. m.p. ind. 1968 British Lion Films, London. Lion Int'l. Films, O'Seas Division. Appointed 1970 U.S. representative. New York. British Lion Films, Shepperton Studios, Lion TV.

BLAKE, ROBERT: Actor. b. Nutley, N.J., Sept. 18, 1938. m. actress Sondra Kerry. Started as Hollywood stunt man in Rumble on the Docks and The Tijuana Story. First acting job was in the Gallery Theater in Hatful of Rain.
PICTURES INCLUDE: Town Without Pity, Pt-109, The Greatest Story Ever Told, The Connection, This Property is Condemned, In Cold Blood, Tell Them Willie Boy is Here, Corky, Electra-Glide in Blue, Busting, Second Hand Hearts.
TV: Baretta.

BLAKELY, SUSAN: Actress. b. Germany, where father was stationed in Army. Studied at Univ. of Texas. m. writer Todd Merer. Became top magazine and TV commercial model in N.Y. Film acting debut in Savages.
PICTURES INCLUDE: The Lords of Flatbush, The Way We Were, The Towering Inferno, Report to the Commissioner, Shampoo, Capone, The Concorde—Airport '79.
TELEVISION: Rich Man, Poor Man, Secrets (film).

BLALOCK, RICHARD: Orchestra leader-composer. b. Delano, Calif.: e. Public Schools—Simi and Ventura, Calif., Composed score, Hobart Donavan feature, History in Blue, 1960. Wrote music for singers Nick Lucas, Geo. Wallace. Appearances with band: Highlands Inn, Carmel, Calif., Santa Barbara Biltmore Hotel, Los Posas Country Club, Saticoy Country Club, La Cumbre Country Club, Glendale Civic Auditorium, Mira Mar Hotel; Latest comp., The Flea.

BLANC, MEL: Executive, voice specialist. r.n. Melvin Jerome Blanc. b. San Francisco, Calif., May 30, 1908. e. Lincoln H.S., Portland, Ore., 1918–21. musician, NBC Radio, San Francisco, 1928; orchestra conductor, Orpheum theatre, Portland, Ore., 1931; free lance, violin, tuba, bass player, 1925–30; voices on Warner Bros. Cartoons, Bugs Bunny, Porky Pig, Daffy Duck, etc. since 1937; running characters, Jack Benny Show, Radio & TV since 1940.
In radio: Point Sublime, 1942–44; Judy Canova Show,

1940–48; Burns and Allen; Jack Carson Show; Abbott and Costello; Dagwood and Blondie; Al Pierce Show, 1938–50; Chairman of the Board, Blanc Communications Corp., 1960–63.
TV: The Bugs Bunny Show, The Porky Pig Show, The Munsters, Flintstones, Speed Buggy Animated Show (Hanna Barbera).

BLANCO, RICHARD M.: Executive, b. Brooklyn, N.Y., e. electrical engineering, Wentworth Institute. J.C., 1925–27; bus. admin., Univ. of Calif., 1939–40; U.S. Govt. College, 1942. Superv. Technicolor Corp., 1931–56; organ. and oper. Consumer Products, Kodachrome film process., Technicolor, 1956–62; dir. of MP Govt. and theatr. sales, N.Y. and Washington, D.C. 1963–65; gen. mgr. of Technicolor Florida photo. operations at Kennedy Space Center., prod. document and educ. films for NASA, 1965; VP of TV division, Technicolor Corp. of America; 1967 elected corporate v.p. Technicolor, Inc.; 1971 pres., Technicolor Graphic Services, Inc.; 1974, elected chm. of bd. of Technicolor Graphic Services; 1977, elected to board of directors of Technicolor Inc.

BLANE, RALPH: Composer. b. Broken Arrow, Okla., July 26, 1914. e. Northwestern U. Started as singer, then vocal arranger for Broadway shows; appeared on NBC radio. Formed partnership with Hugh Martin, wrote Best Foot Forward; m.p. composer since 1939.
PICTURES INCLUDE: Best Foot Forward, Meet Me in St. Louis, My Dream Is Yours, One Sunday Afternoon, My Blue Heaven, Friendly Islands, Skirts Ahoy, French Line, Athena, Girl Rush, The Girl Most Likely, Who is Sylvia?, Ziegfeld Follies, Broadway Rhythm, Abbott and Costello in Hollywood, Easy to Wed.
TV: The Great Quillow. 1961; same in color for NBC, 1963.
BROADWAY: Three Wishes for Janie, Tattered Tom, Something About Anne, Don't Flash Tonight.

BLANK, EDWARD L.: Critic. b. Pittsburgh, Pa. e. Duquesne University, Pittsburgh, Pa. Started working at Pittsburgh Press, 1967. Radio-TV critic, 1969–72. Became Drama Editor, 1972.

BLANK, MYRON: Circuit executive. b. Des Moines, Ia. Aug. 30, 1911; son of A. H. Blank, circuit operator; e. U. Mich. On leaving coll. joined father in operation Tri-States and Central States circuits. On leave 1943–46 in U.S. Navy, officer in charge visual educ. Now pres. Central States Theatre Corp.; pres. TOA, 1955; chmn. bd. TOA Inc. 1956–57; exec. chm. of NATO. Pres. of Greater Des Moines Comm.; treas., Iowa Methodist Medical Center; board, Iowa Des Moines Natl. Bank.; pres., Iowa Phoenix Corp., recipient of Brotherhood Award of National Conference of Christians & Jews; board, Simpson College.

BLANKFORT, MICHAEL: Writer. b. New York City, Dec. 10, 1907. e. U. Pa., B.A.; Princeton U., M.A. On faculty Bowdoin Coll., 1929–30; Princeton U., 1931–33; New Jersey State Prison psychiatrist, 1933. Writer, prod., dir., stage plays, 1933–36; novelist magazine contrib., U.S.M.C., 1942–45. Member exec. bd. Screen Writers Guild, 1939–40; 1962–66, secy-treas.; 1963–65, president, Writers Guild 1967–69; Nat. Chm. 1971–1973; Gov. Acad. of Motion Picture Arts & Sciences, 1969; v.p. 1971–73, 1976–77, 1978–80.
PICTURES INCLUDE: Blind Alley, Texas, Adam Had Four Sons, An Act of Murder, Broken Arrow, Halls of Montezuma, Untamed, The Vintage, The Plainsman, See How They Run, The Other Man, Lydia Bailey, The Juggler, My Six Convicts, Tribute to a Bad Man, The Caine Mutiny, A Fire in the Sky.

BLATTNER, GERRY: Producer. b. Liverpool, 1913. Ent. industry 1928. Blattner Studios, Boreham Wood. Studies include Berlin Research Labs, 1930. Studio mgr., British National Studios, 1936. Gen. mgr., British Lion Studios, Isleworth and Shepperton studios. Joined board of Warner Bros. First National Prods., 1946–67. Was exec. in charge of Warner Bros. European Prods. Started own indep. prod. co. in Nov. 1967.
PICTURES INCLUDE: The Crimson Pirate, Helen of Troy, The Nun's Story, Indiscreet, The Sundowners.

BLATTY, WILLIAM PETER: Writer-Producer. Novelist who wrote John Goldfarb, Please Come Home (filmed) and Twinkle, Twinkle, Killer Kane before biggest success with The Exorcist, which became a 55-week best-selling book. He wrote s.p. and functioned as prod. on film version.
PICTURES INCLUDE: A Shot in the Dark (s.p.), What Did You Do in the War, Daddy? (s.p.), The Great Bank Robbery, Darling Lilli (co. s.p.), The Exorcist (s.p., prod.), The Ninth Configuration (s.p., prod. dir.).

BLAU, MARTIN: Executive. b. N.Y.C., June 6, 1924. e. Ohio U., 1948. Employed on newspapers in Ohio, Tex., W.Va., Pub. dept., Columbia Pictures, 1951; asst. pub. mgr. 1959; pub. mgr., Columbia Internat'l, 1961; admin. asst. to v.p. of adv. & pub. Columbia Pictures, 1966. Dir. adv. and publicity, Columbia Pictures International, 1970; v.p., 1971.

BLAUSTEIN, JULIAN: Producer. b. New York City, May 30, 1913. e. Harvard 1933. Ent. m.p. ind. as reader for Universal 1935; asst. story ed. 1935–36; story ed. 1936–38; in chg. story dept. Music Corp. of America 1938–39; story ed. Paramount 1939–41; Signal Corps Photo. Center 1941–46; edit. supervisor of Selznick 1946–48; to 20th-Fox as prod. 1949; apptd. exec. prod. 20th Cent.-Fox, 1951 to Dec. 1952.
    PICTURES INCLUDE: Broken Arrow, Mister 880, Half Angel, Just One More Chance, Take Care of My Little Girl, Day the Earth Stood Still, Outcasts, Don't Bother to Knock, Desiree, The Racers, Storm Center, Cowboy, Bell Book and Candle, The Wreck of The Mary Deare, Two Loves, The Four Horsemen of the Apocalypse, Khartoum.

BLEES, ROBERT: Writer-Producer. Phi Beta Kappa, Dartmouth. Time and Life Magazines. Exec. boards of Writers Guild, Producers Guild.
    PICTURES INCLUDE: Magnificent Obsession, Autumn Leaves, Dr. Phibes Rises Again, Glass Web.
    TV: Producer of Combat!, Bonanza, Bus Stop, Kraft Theater. Writer also of Alfred Hitchcock, Cannon, Barnaby Jones, Harry O, Columbo, Flamingo Road, Magnum.

BLEIER, EDWARD: Executive. b. N.Y., N.Y., October 16, 1929. e. Syracuse University, 1951, C.C.N.Y. Graduate Courses. Reporter: Syracuse Herald Journal, Long Island Daily Press 1947–50. Sportscaster: WNEW, N.Y.; WSYR, Syracuse, 1947–50. American Broadcasting Company, 1952–57; 1959–68. Vice President in charge of Public Relations & Planning (Marketing, Advertising, Publicity), Broadcast Div. Vice President in chg. of daytime Programming & Sales, ABC-TV Network; vice pres./gen. mgr. sales, ABC-TV Network; Account Executive, ABC-TV Network & WABC-TV. Vice Pres. Radio-Television-Film, Tex McCrary, Inc. 1959; Program Service Manager, DuMont Televison Network, 1951; Trustee, New York Chapter, Natl. Academy of TV Arts & Sciences; Director, Int'l Academy TV Arts & Sciences; Steering Committee, Aspen Institute Broadcaster's Conference.
    Board Member: IRTS; Overseas Press Club; exec. v.p., Warner Bros Television, New York (a Warner Communications company).

BLENDER, LEON PHILIP: Executive. b. Kansas City, Mo., Feb. 15, 1920; e. Kansas State Co., 1941. 20th Century-Fox Dist. Co., 1947–51; Kranz-Levin pictures, 1951–56. gen. sls. mgr. American International Film Dist. Co., 1956–57; v.p. 1960; American Intl. Pictures, senior v.p., sales dist., later exec. v.p. sales and distribution; 1979, exec. v.p. sales & distribution, Film Ventures Intl.

BLOCH, ROBERT: Writer. b. Chicago, Ill., April 5, 1917; novelist short-story writer; 47 published books, incl. Psycho, Yours Truly, Jack the Ripper, etc.; wrote radio series, Stay Tuned for Terror, adapting own stories; national pres., Mystery Writers of Amer. (1970–71); entered films, 1960.
    PICTURES INCLUDE: The Couch, Cabinet of Caligari, Straitjacket, The Night-Walker, The Psychopath, The Deadly Bees, (collab.) Torture Garden, The House That Dripped Blood, Asylum 1. (Films adapted from published work). Psycho, The Skull.
    TV: Features: The Cat Creature, The Dead Don't Die.

BLOCK, WILLARD: Executive. b. New York, N.Y., March 18, 1930. e. Columbia College, Columbia University Law School, 1952. Counter-Intelligence Corps., U.S. Army, 1952–54, account exec., Plus Marketing, Inc. 1954–55; joined sales staff, NBC Television Network, 1955–57; sales staff, CBS Enterprises, Inc., 1957; international sales mgr, 1960; dir., international sales, 1965; v.p., 1967; v.p., Viacom Enterprises, 1971; pres., 1972; v.p. MCA-TV, 1973; v.p., gen. mgr., Taft, H-B International, Inc.; pres., Willard Block, Ltd.; 1979, named pres., Viacom Enterprises.

BLOOM, CLAIRE: Actress. b. London, Eng., Feb. 15, 1931; e. Badminton School (U.S.A.). Stage debut at Playhouse, Oxford, Sept., 1947; Old Vic seasons, etc.; screen debut in Limelight, 1951.
    PICTURES INCLUDE: Innocents in Paris, Limelight, The Man Between, Richard III, Alexander the Great, The Brothers Karamazov, Look Back in Anger, The Royal Game, The Wonderful World of the Brothers Grimm, The Chapman Report, The Haunting, Alta Infidelita, Il Maestro di Vigeuono, The Outrage, The Spy Who Came In From the Cold, Charley, The Illustrated Man, Three Into Two Won't Go, A Severed Head, Red Sky at Morning, A Doll's House, Islands In the Stream, Clash of the Titans.
    TV: Misalliance, (Playhouse 90), Anna Karenina, Wuthering Heights, Ivanov, Wessex Tales, An Imaginative Woman, A Legacy, In Praise of Love, The Orestaia, Henry VIII, Brideshead Revisited.

BLOOM, VERNA: Actress. b. Lynn, Mass. e. Boston Univ. Studied drama at Uta Hagen-Herbert Berghof School. Performed with small theatre groups all over country; then started repertory theatre in Denver. Appeared on Broadway in Marat/Sade (played Charlotte Corday). Film debut, Medium Cool, 1969.

PICTURES INCLUDE: The Hired Hand, High Plains Drifter, Badge 373, National Lampoon's Animal House.

BLOOM, WILLIAM: Producer. b. New York, N.Y., Feb. 28, 1915. e. U. of Pa., BA, 1935. Story dept., Columbia, N.Y., 1936; U.S. Army Signal Corps, 1941–45; asst. to Ender Bohem, Columbia, Hollywood; then prod. and asst. to B. B. Kahane, 1947–51; asst. to Julian Blaustein, Fox, 1951; prod., 1952.
    PICTURES INCLUDE: Glory Brigade, Inferno, On the Threshold of Space.

BLOWITZ, JOHN S.: President, Blowitz & Canton Co. Inc. Held publicist position with United Artists, Cinema Center Films, Universal Pictures. Handled publicity-promotion for Stanley Kramer Productions on Oklahoma Crude. Coordinated promotional activities on Mame for Warner Bros. In 1974 joined Columbia Pictures as worldwide director of promotion and publicity. Formed John Blowitz Public Relations in 1975. Merged with Arthur Canton to form Blowitz & Canton Co. Inc. in April, 1976. Member of Academy of Motion Picture Arts and Sciences and Film Information Council, exec. dir., Variety Clubs Intl.

BLUHDORN, CHARLES G.: Executive. e. CCNY in 1945. After U.S. Air Force resumed studies at CCNY and Columbia while employed in commodity and export-import business. Became pres. coffee co. in 1949; 1956 acquired interest in Michigan Bumper Co. which firm became nucleus of Gulf & Western Industries in 1958. Chairman & chief exec. officer, Gulf & Western Industries, Inc., chair. Famous Players, Ltd., char., exec. comm, Madison Square Garden Corp.

BLUM, HARRY N.: Executive. b. Cleveland, Oh., Oct. 3, 1932. e. Univ. of Mich. (BBA, LLB). Was attorney in Ohio, toy & hobby industry executive, management consultant, and venture capital and investment manager before entering industry. Now heads The Blum Group.
    PICTURES: Executive Action (assoc. prod.); The Land That Time Forgot (assoc. prod.); At the Earth's Core (exec. prod.); Drive-In, (assoc. prod.) Diamonds (exec. prod.); The Bluebird (assoc. prod.); Obsession (co-prod.); Skateboard (prod.); The Magician of Lublin (exec. prod.).

BLUMENFELD, JOSEPH: Exhibitor. b. New York City, Jan. 14, 1901; owns and operates Blumenfeld Theatres, founded by father in 1917; hdqts., San Francisco, Calif., active real estate, shopping centers, bowling alleys, etc.

BLUMENSTOCK, SID: Ad. exec. New York City. Publicity dir. Warner Bros. Atlantic City theatres 1934–38; joined 20th Fox adv. dept. 1938; asst. exploitation mgr. 1944–49; advertising mgr. Paramount 1949; asst. nat'l. dir. adv. pub., exploit, 1951–58; MPH Coord. 1959 Academy telecast; v.p. Embassy Pictures, 1959; v.p. Chas. Schlaifer Agency, Hollywood, October, 1959–62; v.p. Safranski Prod., Inc.; adv. dir., Embassy Pictures, 1964–67; Walter Reade Org., 1967–70; Levitt-Pickman Film Corp., adv. dir., 1971–72.

BLUMOFE, ROBERT F.: Producer. b. New York, N.Y. e. Columbia Coll., A.B., Columbia U. Sch. of Law. J.D.; v.p., West Coast oper., U.A., 1953–66; independent prod., pres. RFB Enterprises, Inc; American Film Institute, director, AFI-West, Sept. 1, 1977 to date.

BLYTH, ANN: Actress. b. Mt. Kisco, N.Y., Aug. 16, 1928; e. New Wayburn's Dramatic School. On radio in childhood; with San Carlos Opera Co. 3 years; Broadway debut in "Watch on the Rhine"; on tour.
    PICTURES INCLUDE: Chip Off the Old Block, Merry Monahans, Brute Force, Swell Guy, Mr. Peabody and the Mermaid, Woman's Vengeance, Mildred Pierce, Free for All, Top o' the Morning, Our Very Own, Great Caruso, Katie Did It, Thunder on the Hill, I'll Never Forget You, Golden Horde, One Minute to Zero, World in His Arms, Sally and Saint Anne, All the Brothers Were Valiant, Rose Marie, The Student Prince, King's Thief, Kismet, Buster Keaton Story, Jazz Age, Slander, The Helen Morgan Story.

BOASBERG, CHARLES: Sales executive. b. Buffalo, N.Y., Aug. 20, 1906; e. Cornell U., A.B. 1927. MGM special repr. 1927; RKO salesman, Buffalo 1930; br. mgr. Buffalo 1937; dist. mgr., Cleveland 1940; Metropolitan dist. mgr., N.Y.C. 1944; apptd. north south div. mgr. 1947. Named gen. sales mgr., dir., RKO Pict., Oct., 1952; v.p., gen. mgr. Dist. Corp. of America, 1954–55; joined Paramount, 1955, in chg. world wide sales of the Ten Commandments, gen. sls. mgr., pres. Warner Bros. Dist. Corp., Jan. 1958. Res., July, 1961; domestic gen. sls. mgr. & v.p., Paramount Film Dist. Corp., 1962; pres., Paramount Film Dist. Corp., 1963, and V.P. Paramount Pictures, Inc. 1967; v.p. National General Corporation, 1968; pres., Nat'l Gen'l Pictures Corp., 1969. In 1974 formed Boasberg/Goldstein, consultants to film producers, now Charles Boasberg, Inc.

BODE, RALF: Cinematographer. b. Berlin, Germany. Attended Yale where was actor with drama school and acquired degree in directing. Received on-job training teaching combat photography and making films for Army at Ft. Monmouth. First professional job in films was gaffer on Harry, followed by long association with director John G.

Avildsen, for whom served as gaffer and lighting designer on Guess What We Learned in School Today, Joe, and Cry Uncle. Later served as dir. of photography for Avildsen on Inaugural Ball and as East Coast dir. phot. for Rocky.
PICTURES: Saturday Night Fever, Slow Dancing in the Big City.
TELEVISION: PBS Theatre in America, working as lighting designer and dir. of photo. Also many TV commercials.

BOEHM, SYDNEY: Writer. b. Philadelphia, Pa., Apr. 4, 1908; Lehigh U., 1925–29. m. Ellen Kasputis. Reporter, N.Y. Journal-American & I.N.S., 1930–45.
PICTURES INCLUDE: Union Station, Big Heat, Atomic City, Six Bridges to Cross, The Raid, Rogue Cop, The Savage, Violent Saturday, Hell on Frisco Bay, Tall Men, Bottom of the Bottle, Revolt of Mamie Stover, Woman Obsessed, Seven Thieves, Sylvia, Rough Night in Jericho.

BOETTICHER, BUDD: Producer, director, writer. r.n. Oscar Boetticher, Jr. b. Chicago, Ill., July 29, 1918. e. Ohio State U. bull fighter; then technical dir., "Blood and Sand," 1941; asst. dir., Hal Roach studios and Columbia 1941–44; became feature director at Columbia in 1944; dir. Eagle Lion, 1946; dir., Universal; independ. prod., 1954.
PICTURES INCLUDE: Behind Locked Doors, Assigned to Danger, Black Midnight, Killer Shark, Wolf Hunters, Bullfighter and the Lady, Cimarron Kid, Bronco Busters, Red Ball Express, Horizons West, City Beneath the Sea, Seminole, Man from the Alamo, Wings of the Hawk, East of Sumatra, Magnificent Matador, Killer Is Loose, Seven Men From Now, Decision at Sundown, The Tall T, Buchanan Rides Alone, Ride Lonesome Westbound, The Rise and Fall of Legs Diamond, Comanche Station, The Carlos Arruza Story.

BOFFETY, JEAN: Cinematographer. Born in France.
PICTURES INCLUDE: Act of the Heart, Journey, Les Choses De La Vie, Cesar and Rosalie, Thieves Like Us.

BOGARDE, DIRK: Actor. b. Hampstead, London, Eng., March 28, 1921. e. Allen Glens College, Glasgow & University College, London. Started theatrical career with Amersham Repertory Co., then London stage; in Army in World War II; screen debut in Esther Waters Films. Top ten British star, 1953–54, 1956–64; number one British moneymaking star 1955, 1957, 1958, 1959; Variety Club Award—Best Performance 1961–64. British Academy Award, Darling, 1966.
PICTURES INCLUDE: Quartet, Once a Jolly Swagman, Mr. Prohack, Blue Lamp, Five Angles on Murder, Gentle Gunman, So Long at the Fair, Blackmailed, Woman in Question, Hunted (Stranger in Between), Penny Princess, Desperate Moment, They Who Dare, The Sleeping Tiger, Doctor in the House, For Better or Worse, The Sea Shall Not Have Them, Simba, Doctor at Sea, Appointment in London, Cast a Dark Shadow, Doctor At Large, Spanish Gardener, Ill Met by Moonlight, Campbell's Kingdom, A Tale of Two Cities, The Wind Cannot Read, The Doctor's Dilemma, Libel, The Angel Wore Red, Song Without End, The Singer Not The Song, Victim, H.M.S. Defiant, The Password Is Courage, I Could Go on Singing, The Mind Benders, The Servant (British Academy Award 1964), Hot Enough for June, Doctor Distress, The High Bright Sun, King and Country, Darling . . ., Modesty Blaise, Accident, Our Mother's House, Sebastion, The Fixer, Justine, Oh What a Lovely War, The Damned, Death in Venice, Le Serpent, The Night Porter, Permission to Kill, Providence, A Bridge Too Far, Despair.
TV: (USA) The Little Moon of Alban, Hallmark, 1964. Blythe Spirit, Hallmark, 1966, Upon This Rock.

BOGART, NEIL: Executive. Pres. of Casablanca Record and Film Works. Began as pop singer and moved into record prod. and promo. First associated with Cameo/Parkway Records Co. in New York; then pres. of Buddah Records, which he and partners formed in 1966. Formed Casablanca in 1974; company has had 29 Gold and 3 Platinum albums. Expanded into films in 1978 as exec. prod. of Thank God It's Friday.

BOGART, PAUL: Director. b. New York, N.Y. Nov. 21, 1919.
FILMS INCLUDE: Marlowe, Halls of Anger, Skin Game, Class of '44, Mr. Ricco.
TV: (Specials) Ages of Man, Mark Twain Tonight, The Final War of Ollie Winter, Dear Friends, Secrets, The House Without a Christmas Tree, Look Homeward Angel, The Country Girl, Double Solitaire, The Thanksgiving Treasure, Tell Me Where it Hurts, The Adams Chronicles.

BOGDANOVICH, PETER: Director, producer, writer, actor. b. Kingston, N.Y., July 30, 1939 e. Collegiate School, Stella Adler Theatre School, N.Y. 1954–58. Stage debut, N.Y. Shakespeare Festival, Amer. Shakespeare Festival, others, 1955–58. Off-Bway: dir.-co.prod. The Big Knife, 1959, Camino Real, Ten Little Indians, Rocket to the Moon, 1961, dir.-prod. Once in a Lifetime, 1964. Film critic and feature writer, general publications. Monographs for Museum of Modern Art Film Library on Orson Welles, Alfred Hitchcock, Howard Hawks, 1961–63. Books: John Ford,

(U. of Calif. Press), Fritz Lang in America (Praeger), 1969; Allan Dwan—The Last Pioneer (Praeger), 1971; Pieces of Time (Arbor House), 1973. Second-unit dir.-writer, The Wild Angels (Roger Corman-Amer. International), 1966. Dir.-prod.-writer-actor Targets (Saticoy Prod.-Paramount), 1968. Dir.-writer, The Last Picture Show (BBS Prods. Col.) 1971, dir.-writer, Directed by John Ford (AFL-Calif. Arts Comm.), 1971; dir.-prod.-writer What's Up, Doc?, (Saticoy Prod.-WB), 1972; dir.-prod. Paper Moon (Saticoy Prod.-Directors Company-Para.), 1973; dir.-prod. Daisy Miller (Copa De Oro Prod. Directors Company-Para.), 1974; dir.-prod.-writer At Long Last Love (Copa De Oro Prod.-20th Century-Fox), 1975; dir.-writer Nickelodeon (Chartoff-Winkler Prod.-Col.), 1976; dir.-writer, Saint Jack (Copa de Oro-Orio-New World), 1979; dir., writer, They All Laughed, 1981.

BOHEM, ENDRE: Producer, writer. b. Hungary, e. U. Vienna. Exec. Asst. to E. Mannix, MGM and Harry Cohn, Columbia. Prod. shorts series: Passing Parade, Nostradamus, What do You Think, Crime Does Not Pay, Tell Tale Heart.
PICTURES INCLUDE: Night Has a 1000 Eyes, The Redhead and the Cowboy, Alias Nick Beal, Streets of Laredo, Postal Inspector, Wonder of Women, Thirst, House With a 1000 Candles, Two Wise Maids, Little Orphan Annie, Lord Jeff, Crime of the Century, Twin Stars, Bengazi.
TV: Revlon Mirror, Ford Theatre, Rawhide.

BOLGER, RAY: Actor, dancer. b. Dorchester, Mass., Jan. 10, 1906; e. O'Brien Dancing School, Boston. Bank clerk; vacuum salesman; accountant & student Russakoff's Ballet School; with insurance co.; stage debut with Bob Ott's Musical Comedy repertory touring New England; in dance team Sanford & Bolger; prod. two-reel M.P. Toured South Pacific with USO, World War II; m.p. debut in "Great Ziegfeld" 1936; Own TV show, ABC, 1954–55.
SHOWS INCLUDE: Passing Show of 1926, Heads Up, Scandals of 1931, Life Begins at 8:40, On Your Toes, By Jupiter; N.Y. stage, Three to Make Ready, Where's Charley?, All American, Come Summer.
PICTURES INCLUDE: Rosalie, Wizard of Oz, Sunny, Four Jacks and a Jill, Look for the Silver Lining, Make Mine Laughs, Where's Charley?, April in Paris, Babes in Toyland, The Runner Stumble.

BOLOGNA, JOSEPH: Actor-Writer. m. actress-writer Renee Taylor. b. Brooklyn, N.Y. e. Brown Univ., Providence, R.I. Service in Marine Corps and on discharge joined ad agency, becoming director-producer of TV commercials. Collaborated with wife on short film, 2, shown at 1966 N.Y. Film Festival. Together they wrote Lovers and Other Strangers, Bdwy. play, in which both also acted. Wrote s.p. for film version. Both wrote and starred in Made for Each Other, and created and wrote TV series, Calucci's Dept.
PICTURES INCLUDE: Lovers and Other Strangers (co.-s.p.), Made for Each Other (co.-s.p., star), Cops and Robbers (actor), Mixed Company (actor), The Big Bus (actor), Chapter Two (actor).
TV: Calucci's Dept. (co.-s.p.), Honor Thy Father (movie—actor).

BOLT, ROBERT: Writer, b. Sale, England, 1924. Ent. m.p. ind. 1961.
PICTURES INCLUDE: Lawrence of Arabia, Dr. Zhivago, A Man For All Seasons (play and film), Ryan's Daughter, Dir. own s.p. Lady Caroline Lamb.

BOND, ANSON: Producer, writer. b. Cleveland, Ohio, Mar. 21, 1914; p. Charles Anson Bond, founder, Bond Clothing Co. & Bond Stores, Inc. e. Yale Prep. & pre-legal, Stuyvesant Sch., Warrenton, Va. Washington corr., 30 Ohio newspapers, 1930–33; asst. to pres., C.W. Hord Co., N.Y. 1933–36; apprenticeship in m.p. prod. 1936–39; dir., prod., writer. U.S. armed forces, 1940–45; head pub. firm, Bond-Charteris, prod. radio program. The Saint; publ. Craig Rice Crime Digest & Movie Mystery Magazine.
PICTURES INCLUDE: The Judge, Not Wanted, Vicious Years, (co-prod.) Journey Into Light, Japanese War Bride, China Venture.

BOND, DEREK: Actor, Scriptwriter. b. Glasgow, Jan. 26, 1920; e. Haberdasher' Askes School, London. Stage debut in "As Husbands Go" 1937; served in Grenadier Guards H.M. Forces 1939–46, awarded Military Cross; m.p. debut in "Captive Heart" 1946; author of Unscheduled Stop, Two Young Samaritans, Ask Father Christmas, Packdrill, Double Strung, Order to Kill, The Riverdale Dam, Sentence Deferred, The Mavroletty Fund. Many TV appearances.
PICTURES INCLUDE: Nicholas Nickleby, Joanna Godden, Uncle Silas, Scott of the Antarctic, Marry Me, Poets Pub, Weaker Sex, Broken Journey, Christopher Columbus, Tony Draws a Horse, Quiet Woman, Hour of Thirteen, Distant Trumpet, Love's A Luxury, Trouble in Store, Svengali, High Terrace, Stormy Crossing, Rogues Yarn, Gideon's Day, The Hand, Saturday Night Out, Wonderful Life, Press For Time, When Eight Bells Toll, Intimate Reflections.

BONET, NAI: Actress—Producer. Worked in entertainment field since age of 13, including opera, films, TV, stage, night clubs and records.
PICTURES: Actress: The Soul Hustlers, The Seventh Veil, Fairy Tales, The Soul of Nigger Charlie, The Spy with the Cold Nose, John Goldfarb Please Come Home, etc. Wrote and starred in Nocturna and Hoodlums.
TELEVISION: Johnny Carson Show, Merv Griffin Show, Joe Franklyn Show, Beverly Hillbillies, Tom Snyder Show.

BONO, SONNY: Singer-Actor-Director-Writer. b. Detroit, Mich. Feb. 16. r.n. Salvatore Bono. Started writing songs at age 16; entered record business with Specialty Records as apprentice prod. Became ass't. to Phil Spector, rock music prod. and did background singing. Has recorded albums with former wife Cher and made two feature films, and formed nightclub act with her. CBS comedy-variety series began as summer show in 1971 and made regular later that year.
PICTURES INCLUDE: Good Times, Chastity (prod., s.p.), Escape to Athena.
TELEVISION: Sonny & Cher Comedy Hour, Sonny Comedy Revue.

BOOKMAN, ROBERT: Executive. b. Los Angeles. e. University of California, Yale Law School. Motion picture literary agent, IFA 1972–74, ICM 1974–79. 1979 joined ABC Motion Pictures as v.p., worldwide production.

BOONE, JR., ASHLEY A.: Executive. b. 1939. e. Brandeis Univ. Started career at United Artists in adv./pub.; later with Cinema Center films; adm. asst., Motown Records; assoc. prod. for Sidney Poitier's E&R Productions. Joined 20th-Fox in 1972 in sls. dept.; advanced to sr. sls. & mktg. positions in feature film operation. In 1979 appt. pres. of 20th-Fox Distribution & Marketing.

BOONE, PAT: Singer. b. Jacksonville, Fla., June 1, 1934. e. David LipsComb College, No. Texas State Coll., grad. magna cum laude, Columbia U. Winner of Ted Mack's TV show; joined Arthur Godfrey TV show, 1955. m.p. debut in Bernadine. Most promising new male star, M.P.D.-Fame Poll 1957.
AUTHOR: Twixt Twelve and Twenty, and Between You & Me and the Gatepost. One of top ten moneymaking stars M.P. Herald-Fame Poll, 1957; wrote book, The Real Christmas.
RECORDINGS: Ain't That a Shame, I Almost Lost My Mind, Friendly Persuasion, Love Letters in the Sand, April Love, Tutti Frutti, Speedy Gonzalez, Days of Wine & Roses, Moody River.
PICTURES INCLUDE: Bernadine, April Love, Mardi Gras, Journey to the Center of the Earth, All Hands on Deck, State Fair, The Main Attraction, The Yellow Canary, The Horror of It All, The Perils of Pauline, The Cross and the Switchblade.

BOORMAN, JOHN: Producer, director. b. London, England. Wrote film criticism at age of 17 for British publications; served in National Service in Army; joined independent Television News as film editor; prod. documentaries for Southern Television; joined BBC, headed BBC Documentary Film Unit.
PICTURES INCLUDE: Catch Us If You Can, Point Blank, Hell In the Pacific, Leo The Last, Deliverance, Zardoz, Exorcist II: The Heretic, Excalibur (prod., dir., s.p.).

BOOTH, JAMES: Actor, Scriptwriter. b. Croydon, England, 1931. Early career with R.A.D.A., Old Vic and Theatre Workshop; on West End stage: Fings Aint Wot They Used To Be. Subsequently: King Lear, Comedy of Errors, A Thousand Clowns, The Fire Raisers, The Entertainer, The Recruiting Officer, Travesties, The Tempest.
PICTURES INCLUDE: Trials of Oscar Wilde, Sparrows Can't Sing, The Hellions, French Dressing, Zulu, 90 Degrees in the Shade, Secret of My Success, Bliss of Mrs. Blossom, Boomerang, The Man Who Had Power Over Women, Darker Than Amber (1969), Macho Callaghan (1970), Revenge, Percy's Progress, Brannigan, Robbery, Penny Gold, Airport 77.
TV: The Ruffians, The Great Gold Bullion Robbery, Stray Cats and Empty Bottles, Them.

BOOTH, SHIRLEY: Actress. b. New York, N.Y., Aug. 20, 1907. Joined Poli Stock Co., Hartford, Conn., at 12; Broadway debut in Hell's Bells, 1925; on radio in Duffy's Tavern; m.p. debut in Come Back Little Sheba (Academy Award, Best Actress, 1952).
PLAYS: After Such Pleasures, 3 Men on a Horse, Philadelphia Story, My Sister Eileen, Tomorrow the World, Goodbye My Fancy, Come Back Little Sheba, A Tree Grows in Brooklyn, Time of the Cuckoo, The Desk Set, Look to the Lillies, Miss Isobel, Juno, Colettes Second String, Glass Menagerie.
PICTURES INCLUDE: About Mrs. Leslie, Hot Spell, The Matchmaker.
TV: Perle Mesta Story, Hazel, A Touch of Grace.

BORCHERS, CORNELL: Actress. b. Heydekrug, Germany, March 16; e. Gottingen U. Berlin actors school, m. Dr. Anton Schelkopf.
PICTURES INCLUDE: (German) Martina, Das ewige Spiel, Haus des Lebens, Schule fur Ehegluck; (English) Big Lift, Divided Heart, Oasis, Never Say Goodbye, Istanbul, Alone Together.

BORGE, VICTOR: Comedian, pianist. b. Copenhagen, Denmark, Jan. 3. Child prodigy at age 10. Later became humorous concert artist. Wrote and starred in musical plays and films in Denmark. Fled Nazis in 1941, came to America. Appeared on Bing Crosby radio show. Concert and nightclub tours. TV variety shows. One-man Broadway show. Comedy in Music, 1953, three-year run. Second edition in 1964. World tour. One-man TV show.

BORGNINE, ERNEST: Actor. b. Hamden, Conn., Jan. 24, 1918. e. Randall School of Dramatic Art, Hartford. Served in U.S. Navy; then little theatre work, stock companies; on Broadway in Harvey, Mrs. McThing; many TV appearances; m.p. debut in Whistle at Eaton Falls.
PICTURES INCLUDE: The Mob, China Corsair, From Here to Eternity, Demetrius & the Gladiators, Johnny Guitar, Vera Cruz, Bad Day at Black Rock, Marty (Acad. Award best actor 1955), Run for Cover, Violent Saturday, Last Command, Square Jungle, Catered Affair, Jubal, Best Things in Life are Free, Three Brave Men, Pay or Die, Go Naked in the World, Rabbit Trap, 10 Years a Counterspy, Summer of the Seventeenth Doll, Barabbas, Chuka, The Dirty Dozen, The Wild Bunch, The Adventurers, Suppose They Gave a War and Nobody Came?, A Bullet for Sandoval, Bunny, O'Hare, Hannie Caulder, The Revengers, Legend of Lylah Clare, The Poseidon Adventure, The Emperor of the North, Law and Disorder, The Devil's Rain, Hustle, Shoot, The Greatest, Crossed Swords, Convoy, The Black Hole, When Time Ran Out, Escape from New York, Deadly Blessing.
TV: Philco Playhouse, General Electric Theater, Wagon Train, Laramie, Zane Grey Theater, Alcoa Premiere, McHale's Navy.

BORNSTEIN, ALLEN: Executive. b. Bronx, N.Y. e. CCNY. Entered m.p. career 1957 as asst. branch cashier, 20th Century Fox; booker, Buena Vista, 1962; N.Y. branch mgr., Cinerama, 1968; natl. dir. branch operations, Gamma III.

BORODINSKY, SAMUEL: Executive. b. Brooklyn, NY, Oct. 25, 1941. e. Industrial School of Arts & Photography. Expert in film care and rejuvenation. Now exec. v.p., Filmtreat International Corp. Previously with Modern Film Corp. (technician) and Comprehensive Filmtreat, Inc. & International Filmtreat (service manager).

BOSLEY, TOM: Actor. b. Chicago, Oct. 1, 1927. e. DePaul Univ. Had roles on radio in Chicago and in stock productions before moving to New York. Appeared off-Bdwy and on road before signed to play lead in Fiorello! for George Abbott on Bdwy. First actor to win Tony, Drama Critics, ANTA and Newspaper Guild awards in one season for that role. Has since done many plays, movies and TV appearances.
PICTURES: Love with the Proper Stranger, The World of Henry Orient, Divorce, American Style, Yours, Mine & Ours, The Secret War of Harry Frigg, Mixed Company, Gus.
TELEVISION Series: Debbie Reynolds Show, Sandy Duncan Show, Happy Days, Movies: The Girl Who Came Gift Wrapped, Death Cruise, The Night the Martians Landed, Love Boat. Specials: Testimony of Two Men, The Bastard.

BOSTICK, ROBERT L.: b. Waynesboro, Georgia, Oct. 25, 1909. e. Georgia Tech, Atlanta (ME, Eng.) 1932. Started with National Theatre Supply, Atlanta, salesman, Memphis, 1933; br. mgr. 1937; br. mgr. Dallas, 1942; Vice Pres., Southern Division Mgr., 1952; retired 1968. Chief Barker Variety Club Tent 20, Memphis 1950–51. Since 1957, has served as International Rep., International Ambassador-at-Large, and International Vice Pres. for Variety Clubs International. Since 1968, owner & operator of theatres in Memphis and Charlotte areas.

BOSUSTOW, NICK: Producer. b. Los Angeles, Calif., March 28, 1940. e. Menlo College, Calif. Administration. MCA, International sales, 1963. Pres., Stephen Bosustow Productions, 1967; pres., ASIFA-West; Academy Award '70 best short, Is it always right to be right?; 1973 Academy Award nomination, The Legend of John Henry. The Incredible Book Escape, Misunderstood Monsters, A Tale of Four Wishes (TV specials). 1977, pres., Bosustow Entertainment, Inc.

BOSUSTOW, TEE: Producer-Director-Editor. b. Hollywood, Calif., Feb. 18, 1938. e. UCLA Cinema in Westwood, La Sorbonne, Paris.
PICTURES INCLUDE: Beware of Thin Ice, Big Boys Don't Cry, Avati and the Mezzotint. Edited short, Is It Always Right to Be Right? (AA, 1971).

TELEVISION: About a Week (community affairs series; Emmy award).

BOTTOMS, JOSEPH: Actor. b. Santa Barbara, Calif. April 22, 1954. Did plays in jr. high school in Santa Barbara and then with community theatre. Made m.p. debut in The Dove (1974).
   PICTURES: Crime and Passion, King of the Mountain.
   TV: Owen Marshall, Winesburg, Ohio.

BOTTOMS, TIMOTHY: Actor. b. Santa Barbara, Calif., Aug. 30, 1951. Early interest in acting; was member of S.B. Madrigal Society, touring Europe in 1967. Sang and danced in West Side Story local prod.
   PICTURES INCLUDE: Johnny Got His Gun (debut), The Last Picture Show, Love and Pain, The Paper Chase, The White Dawn, The Crazy World of Julius Vrooch, Seven Men at Daybreak, A Small Town in Texas, Rollercoaster, The Other Side of the Mountain: Part II, Hurricane.

BOUDOURIS, A: Executive. b. Toledo, Ohio, Jan. 31, 1918. e. U. of Toledo, 1945–47. USN, radio-radar, 1941–45; carrier pilot. Service, installation, projection equip., 1934–36; Strong Electric, 1936–41; Pres., Theatre Equip. Co., 1945–65; Theatre Operating Co., since 1947; pres. Eprad, Inc., 1949, bd. chmn., 1980. Member (ex-chm.) of NATO's Technical Advisory Comm., Pres. NATO of Ohio, NATO representative on American National Standards Committee; now Vice Pres. NATO. Chairman, NATO Statistical Committee; Member, Projection Practices and Sound Comm. of SMPTE; NATO Representative International Standards Organization (Geneva); Member National Electrical Code Committee Panel #15. Recipient, SMPTE Fellowship Award, 1980.

BOULTING, JOHN: Producer, director, writer. b. Bray, Buckinghamshire, England, Nov. 21, 1913. With brother, Roy, formed Charter Film Productions in 1937. Produced 1938/40; Consider Your Verdict, Trunk Crime, Inquest, Pastor Hall. Went into RAF 1940. Seconded RAF Film Unit, directed several documentaries and Journey Together feature. Post-war: Prod. Fame is the Spur; The Guinea Pig; Seagulls over Sorrento; Josephine and Men; Brothers in Law; dir. Brighton Rock, Seven Days to Noon, The Magic Box, Lucky Jim (Edinburgh Festival 1957); dir. co-author s.p. Private's Progress, 1955; prod. Carlton-Browne of the FO, 1958; dir. co-author s.p. I'm All Right Jack, 1959; produced The Risk, and The French Mistress, 1960; co-author s.p. dir. Heavens Above, 1962; prod. The Family Way, 1966; There's a Girl in My Soup, 1970; Soft Beds, Hard Battles, 1974. Dir. 1958–72, Man. Dir. 1966–72, Consultant, 1972, British Lion Films Ltd. Former Chm., Local Radio Assoc.

BOULTING, ROY: Producer, director. b. Bray, Buckinghamshire, England, Nov. 21, 1913. e. McGill U., Montreal. Capt., Brit. Army, World War II. Dir. Charter Film, Charter Film Prod. Ltd., London; dir. British Lion Films, Ltd., 1958.
   PICTURES INCLUDE: Inquest, Trunk Crime, Pastor Hall, Thunder Rock, Desert Victory, Burma Victory, Fame is the Spur, Brighton Rock, Guinea Pig, Seven Days to Noon, Lucky Jim, High Treason, Singlehanded (Sailor of the King), Seagulls Over Sorrento (Crest of the Wave), Josephine and Men, Private's Progress, Run for the Sun, Brothers in Law, Happy Is the Bride, Carlton-Browne of the F.O., I'm All Right Jack, The Risk, The French Mistress, Heavens Above! Rotten to the Core, The Family Way, Twisted Nerve, There's a Girl in My Soup, Soft Beds, Hard Battles, 1977, co-author with Leo Marks of play, Favourites, Danny Travis, 1978; The Last Word, 1979.

BOWER, DALLAS: Producer, director. b. London, 1907. Ent. film prod. 1927; film ed., writer, dir., prod. with BBC-TV 1936. Commissioned in Royal Corps of Signals, 1939; supvr. film prod. Ministry of Inf., Films Div. 1942; prod. official and comm. documentaries; author, Plan for Cinema, 1936.
   PICTURES AND TV INCLUDE: Aida, Tristan & Isolde, Master Peter's Puppet Show, Cinderella, Julius Caesar, The Tempest, The Taming of the Shrew, The Silver Box, The Mock Emperor, The Emperor Jones, Rope, Path of Glory, Victory Over Space, Henry V. Alice in Wonderland, Second Mrs. Tanquery, Fire One, Doorway to Suspicion, Adventures of Sir Lancelot. In prep. for T.V., The Ring, The Trojans.

BOWERS, WILLIAM: Writer, producer. b. Las Cruces, New Mexico, Jan. 17, 1916; e. U. Mo. Playwright (Where Do We Go From Here, Back to Eden). Reporter, feature writer, N.Y. World-Telegram: then N.E.A. Hollywood corresp.; later radio scripts (Helen Hayes Theat., etc.). Began screen writing 1942 with collab. s.p. My Favorite Spy.
   PICTURES INCLUDE: Alias Jesse James, Imitation General, The Law and Jake Wade, The Sheepman, My Man Godfrey, The Best Things in Life, Tight Spot, Split Second, The Gunfighter, The Web, Support Your Local Sheriff.

BOX, BETTY: OBE. Producer. b. Beckenham, Kent. Assisted Sydney Box in prod. 200 propaganda films in World War II. Assoc. prod. Upturned Glass.
   PRODUCTIONS INCLUDE: Dear Murderer, When the Bough Breaks, Miranda, Blind Goddess, Huggett Family series. It's Not Cricket, Marry Me, Don't Ever Leave Me, So Long At the Fair, The Clouded Yellow, Appointment With Venus (Island Rescue). Venetian Bird (The Assassin), A Day to Remember, Doctor in the House, Mad About Men, Doctor at Sea, The Iron Petticoat, Checkpoint, Doctor at Large, Campbell's Kingdom, A Tale of Two Cities, The Wind Cannot Read, The 39 Steps, Upstairs and Downstairs, Conspiracy of Hearts, Doctor in Love, No Love for Johnnie, No, My Darling Daughter, A Pair of Briefs, The Wild and the Willing, Doctor in Distress, Hot Enough for June (Agent 8¾), The High Bright Sun, (McGuire Go Home), Doctor in Clover, Deadlier Than the Male, Nobody Runs Forever, The High Commissioner, Some Girls Do, Doctor in Trouble, Percy, The Love Ban, Percy's Progress.

BOYARS, ALBERT: Executive. b. N.Y.C. Aug. 11, 1924: e. N.Y.U.: U.S. Navy, 1941–45. David O. Alber Assoc., 1945–51: Greater N.Y. Fund, Robert S. Taplinger Assoc., Michael Myerberg Prod., 1951–54: pub. rel. dir., Transfilm-Caravel Inc., and parent co. Buckeye Corp., 1954–63: director spec. projects in adv-pub-exploit. M-G-M, 1963–64; dir. of adv. & pub. Trans-Lux Corp., 1964, v.p. of adv. and pub. rel., Trans Lux, 1972, v.p. special projects, Trans-Lux, 1974; v.p. chg. Trans-Lux Multimedia Corp., 1976. Under his aegis are the attractions New York Experience & Space Works.

BOYER, PHIL: TV Executive. b. Portland, Oreg. e. Sacramento State Univ. Began broadcasting career as 12-year-old in Portland, establishing nation's first youth radio facility—a 5-watt facility in the basement of his home. At 16 began working at KPDQ, Portland; two years later joined KPTV, Portland, as announcer. In 1960 joined KEZI-TV, Eugene, Oreg., heading prod. and prog. depts. In 1965 named staff prod.-dir. for KCRA, TV, Sacramento, Calif., becoming prod. mgr. in 1967 and prog. mgr. in 1969. In 1972 joined KNBC-TV, Los Angeles, as prog. dir. In 1974 named v.p., programming, of ABC Owned Television Stations; 1977, v.p.-gen. mgr., WLS-TV, Chicago; 1979, v.p.-gen. mgr. of WABC-TV, New York.

BOYETT, ROBERT: Producer. e. Duke University (B.A.) and Col. Univ. (Master's in mkt.). Began career in media and mkt. research at Grey Advertising, Inc. Was program development consultant for PBS. In 1973 joined ABC as dir. of prime time series TV, East Coast. In 1975 named ABC TV v.p. & asst. to v.p. programs for West Coast. In 1977 joined Paramount Pictures in newly created position of v.p., exec. asst. to pres. & chief operating officer. 1979, formed Miller-Milkis—Boyett Productions to produce for Paramount Television.

BOYLE PETER: Actor. b. Philadelphia, e. LaSalle College. Was monk in Christian Bros. order before leaving in early 60's to come to N.Y. Acted in off-Broadway shows and joined The Second City in Chicago. Also did TV commercials.
   PICTURES INCLUDE: Joe (debut), T.R. Baskin, The Candidate, Steelyard Blues, Slither, The Friends of Eddie Coyle, Kid Blue, Crazy Joe, Young Frankenstein, Swashbuckler, F.I.S.T., Brinks' Job, Hardcore, Beyond the Poseidon Adventure, Where the Buffalo Roam, In God We Trust, Outland.

BOYLE, WILLIAM NEAL (Billy): Producer. b. London, England; e. Rothschild Grammar School. Ent. m.p. 1927 with British International Pictures on set design & construction. Subsequently con. manager, first asst. Dir., Pro. & Loc.; several American and British Cos.; Produced 17 pictures for Republic Pictures International; Productions Controller, Dudley Pictures International-Hollywood; United Artists. Paramount Pictures. dir., W.N.B. Prods., 1966. Incorporated Films and W.N.B. Prods., 1970, W.N.B. World Locations, 1971, TV series.
   PICTURES INCLUDE: Demi Paradise, Tawny Pipit, Good Time Girl, Man Within, Quartet, Trio, Encore, So Long at The Fair. Highly Dangerous, Holiday Camp, Easy Money, Lady of Vengeance, High Hell, African Story (World locations, 1978).

BRABOURNE, THE LORD: Producer. b. London, Nov. 9, 1924.
   PRODUCTIONS INCLUDE: Harry Black, Sink the Bismarck, H.M.S. Defiant, Othello, The Mikado, Up the Junction, Romeo and Juliet, Dance of Death, Tales of Beatrix Potter, Murder on the Orient Express, Death On The Nile, Stories from a Flying Trunk, The Mirror Crack'd.

BRACKEN, EDDIE: Actor. b. New York City, Feb. 7, 1920: e. Prof. Children's School for Actors, N.Y.C.; m. Connie Nickerson, actress. Vaudeville & night club singer: stage debut in "Lottery" 1930; m.p. debut in "Life with Henry" 1940.
   PLAYS: Lady Refuses, Iron Men, So Proudly We Hail, Brother Rat, What A Life, Too Many Girls, Seven Year Itch, Shinbone Alley, Teahouse of the August Moon, You Know I Can't Hear You when The Water's Running, The Odd Couple, Never Too Late, Sunshine Boys, Hotline to Heaven, Hello, Dolly.
   PICTURES INCLUDE: Fleet's In, Happy Go Lucky, Sweater Girl, Star Spangled Rhythm, Young and Willing, Hail the Conquering Hero, Miracle of Morgan's Creek, Girl

From Jones Beach, Summer Stock, Two Tickets to Broadway, About Face, We're Not Married, Slight Case of Larceny.

TV: Masquerade Party, NBC.

BRADEN, WILLIAM: Executive/Producer. b. Alberta, Canada, 1939. e. Vancouver, British Columbia. Began career as stuntman in Hollywood, later working in all aspects of industry for 22 years. Worked for Elliott Kastner as prod. executive with offices at Paramount and with Jeffrey Bloom, of Feature Films, Inc., as prod. and v.p. in chg. of prod. before forming own co., Dunatai Corp., for film and t.v. prod.

PICTURES: Pyramid (assoc. prod., prod. supv.), Russian Roulette (prod. exec.), 92 in the Shade (prod. exec.), Breakheart Pass (prod. exec.), Dogpound Shuffle (asst. dir., prod. supv.); He Wants Her Back (prod.); Goldengirl (prod. exec.); Running Scared (prod.); Death Valley (asst. dir.); The Seduction (prod. exec.).

TELEVISION: Requiem for a Planet (series, prod./creator); Nothing Great is Easy (special, exec. prod.); King of the Channel (special, exec. prod.); I Believe (special, prod.); If My People . . . (special, prod.), Jude (pilot, prod.); America: Life in the Family (dir./prod.) Also various Movies of the Week for networks.

BRADFORD, PETER: Producer and Director. b. Bradford Abbas, 1919. e. Bryanston School, Reimann School of Art and Cinematography, 1941–44 Head of Photo. Dept. Naval Intelligence, Oxford, and concurrently lecturer in photography and cinematography at School of Art and Technology, Oxford. 1944–48 Film Director with Paul Rotha Productions and Films of Fact Ltd. 1948–57 Associated British-Pathe. 1957–59 Film Prod., with Ogilvy & Mather advertising agents; prod., World Wide Pictures, 1960–81. Now freelance.

BRADLEY, BILL: Performer, r.n. William M. Silbert. b. Jan. 1, 1921, Detroit, Mich.; e. Univ. of Detroit, So. Methodist; Disc jockey, m.c., many radio-TV shows, Detroit; panelist, Songs for Sale, CBS-TV, 1952; emcee, Bill Silbert Show, Let's Go Bowling WABD-DuMont TV, 1952–53; Bill Silbert Show. WMGM radio; announcer, Red Buttons Show, NBC-TV; Philco Phonorama Time, Mutual; m.c., National Radio Fan Club, NBC; Magazine of the Air, Mutual, KLAC Hollywood, Bill Bradley Show; KTLA, Hollywood, M.C. Crime Story, Greet the People, Ad Lib, Hollywood Diary. Sales mgr., KLOS, Los Angeles.

PICTURES INCLUDE: Bundle of Joy, Thunderjets, The Alligator People, Young Jesse James, Lost Missile, Breakfast at Tiffanys, Return to Peyton Place, Looking for Love.

TV: Bronco, 77 Sunset Strip, Hawaiian Eye, Sugarfoot, Combat, Adventures in Paradise, Police Station, Michael Shayne, Roaring 20's, The Outlaws, Breaking Point, The Fugitive, Bill Dana Show, My Living Doll, Joey Bishop Show, Ben Casey, Bing Crosby Show. Many commercials, Mannix, Wild Wild West, Name of the Game.

BRADY, FRANK L.: Theatre Executive. b. Columbus, Ga., Jan. 11, 1914. Former pres., Martin Theatres.

BRADY, SCOTT: Actor. r.n. Jerry Tierney; b. Brooklyn, N.Y., Sept. 13, 1924; b. Lawrence Tierney, actor; e. Bliss-Hayden Dram. School, Beverly Hills, Calif. Served in U.S. Navy, won light-heavyweight boxing championship of naval base, discharged 1945. First starring role Born to Fight, Star of Tomorrow, 1953.

PICTURES INCLUDE: Canon City, He Walked By Night, In This Corner, Port of New York, Undertow, Kansas Raiders, Undercover Girl, Model and the Marriage Broker, Bronco Buster, Montana Belle, Untamed Frontier, Yankee Buccaneer, Bloodhounds of Broadway, Perilous Journey, El Alamein, White Fire, Johnny Guitar, Law vs. Billy the Kid, Gentlemen Marry Brunettes, Vanishing American, They Were So Young, Terror at Midnight, Mohawk, Maverick Queen, Fort Utah, Arizona Bushwackers, Dollars, The Loners, Wicked, Wicked. The China Syndrome.

BRAMBELL, WILFRID: Actor. b. Dublin, Ireland, 1912. Early career as reporter. Gate and Abbey Theatres, Dublin. Repertory, variety, pantomime, tours, etc.

STAGE: Blind Man's Bluff (1953), Stop It, Whoever You Are (1961), first Steptoe and Son.

TV: The Importance of Being Earnest, Canterbury Tales.

PICTURES INCLUDE: Dry Rot, Serious Charge, The Long Hot Summer, What a Whopper, The Castaways, Crooks in Cloisters, The Small World of Sammy Lee, Fast Lady, Thomasina, Hard Day's Night, Call Me a Spy, Steptoe and Son.

BRAND, NEVILLE: Actor. b. Kewanee, Ill., Aug. 13, 1921. e. high sch., Kewanee. U.S. Army, 10 yrs to 1946; studied acting in N.Y.: M.P. debut in D.O.A.

PICTURES INCLUDE: Halls of Montezuma, Only the Valiant, The Mob, Flame of Araby, Stalag 17, Charge at Feather River, Man Crazy, Gun Fury, Riot in Cell Block 11, Long Gun, Prince Valiant, Return from the Sea, Fury at Gunsight Pass, The Prodigal, Return of Jack Slade, Bobby Ware Is Missing, Mohawk, Raw Edge, The Adven-

tures of Huckleberry Finn, The Desperadoes, Three Guns for Texas, Birdman of Alcatraz, That Darn Cat, Scalawag, Cahill, U.S. Marshall, The Deadly Trackers, Psychic Killer.

TV: Laredo, The Captain and the Kings.

BRANDO, JOCELYN: Actress. b. San Francisco, Calif. e. Lake Forest Coll.; m.p. debut in The Big Heat; on B'way in Mr. Roberts, Desire Under the Elms, Golden State.

PICTURES INCLUDE: China Venture, Ten Wanted Men.

BRANDO, MARLON: Actor. b. Omaha, Neb., April 3, 1924. e. Shattuck Military Acad., Faribault, Minn. Studied Dramatic Workshop, New York; played stock Sayville, Long Island, m.p. screen debut: The New state debut: I Remember Mama, then Truckline Cafe, Candida, A Flag is Born, Street Car Named Desire.

PICTURES INCLUDE: Streetcar Named Desire, Viva Zapata, Julius Caesar, Wild One, On the Waterfront (Acad. Award best actor, 1954). One of top ten Money-Making Stars, M.P. Herald-Fame poll, 1954–55. Guys and Dolls, Teahouse of the August Moon, Sayonara, The Young Lions, Mutiny on the Bounty, One-Eyed Jacks, The Ugly American, Bedtime Story, The Saboteur, Code Name, Morituri, The Fugitive Kind, The Chase, Appaloosa, The Countess From Hong Kong, Reflections in A Golden Eye, Night of the Following Day, Candy, Burn!, The Nightcomers, The Godfather, Last Tango in Paris, The Missouri Breaks, Superman, The Formula.

BRANDT, JANET: Actress. b. New York City. Acting debut at 6 years old with Yiddish Theater. Over 100 stage appearances in New York where she studied with Martha Graham and with Michael Chekov. Lectured on Shakespeare at the Strasberg Institute in L.A.

PICTURES INCLUDE: Actress: Cold Wind in August, Kotch, Mad Adventures of Rabbi Jacob, Sheila Levine, Semi-Tough, Dialogue Director: Battle of the Bulge, El Cid, Phaedre, View from the Bridge, King of Kings, etc.

TV: Actress: Odd Couple, Mannix, Lou Grant, etc.

BRANDT, RICHARD PAUL: Executive. b. New York, N.Y., Dec. 6, 1927; e. Yale U., chief exec. off. & bd. chm. Trans Lux Corp.; bd. chm., Brandt Theatres; dir., American Book-Stratford Press, Inc.; dir., Harris Creatline Corp.; member President's Advisory Council, National Association of Theatre Owners; member, bd. of trustees & chm. of exec. committee, American Film Institute; member, bd. of dirs., Presidential Realty Corp.; Bd. of Dir.: American Theatre Wing; trustee, Museum of Holography.

BRANDY, HOWARD: Executive. b. Brooklyn, N.Y., 1929. e. Emory Univ. Served with Marine Corps in Korean War. Worked as N.Y. press agent; in 1956 went with NBC. Was columnist for Hollywood Reporter in Las Vegas then went back into publicity as acct. exec. for Rogers and Cowan. Started own business; clients included Frankie Avalon, Fabian, Monkees, Fifth Dimension, Johnny Cash, etc. Joined Commonwealth United in London working for co. 5 yrs. before it folded. Entered film prod.

PICTURES INCLUDE: Blood from the Mummy's Tomb, The Take.

BRANNUM, HUGH: Performer. b. Sandwich, Ill., 1910. Musician, photographer, TV writer, artist; with Fred Waring's Pennsylvanians, 1940–55; writer, Waring TV show, 3 yrs.; children's songs; TV show, Captain Kangaroo.

BRANSON, WALTER E.: Western division sales manager, RKO Pictures Corp. e. U. of Nebraska. Booker for Pathe, Omaha, 1922–24; then salesman in South Dakota; city salesman, br. mgr., Omaha, 1925–27; br. mgr.; Des Moines, 1927–28; St. Louis, 1928–29; to Pathe h.o. as western sales mgr.; br. mgr. Chicago, 1931; midwest dist. mgr., 1932; Midwest dist. mgr., 1932–41; Western sales mgr., 1941–51, asst. gen. sales mgr., 1952; gen. mgr. foreign operations, RKO-Radio Pictures, February, 1954; gen. sales mgr., Aug., 1954; v.p. in charge of world-wide distribution 1955; exec. asst. to pres., National Screen Service, 1960; v.p. distrib., National Screen Service, 1963; v.p. in charge of prod., National Screen Service, 1966.

BRASLOFF, STANLEY H.: Producer, director. b. Philadelphia, Pa., July 23, 1930. In U.S. Army was entertainment dir., Heidelberg military post, 1948–50; prod., dir. & acted for various little theatre & summer stock groups, 1950–60; created, wrote, co-prod., dir. & starred in "Time For Teens" TV show (Chicago); formed VCS Pictures Ltd., prod. & dir. "Two Girls for a Madman," 1967; formed SHB Productions, Inc., prod. "Nightmare at Ghost Beach," 1968; wrote, co-prod, & dir. "Toys Are Not for Children," 1971.

BRAUDY, SUSAN: Executive. e. Bryn Mawr College; taught writing at Brooklyn College (1974). 1970–72, editor and writer at Newsweek; same posts at Ms. Magazine, 1973–78. Worked in 1978 for producer Alberto Grimaldi. Has published numerous articles in New York Magazine, New Journal (Yale), The Atlantic, Village Voice, etc. In 1981 appt. Warner Bros. v.p., east coast production. 1981, novel, Who Killed Sal Mineo?, published.

31

BRAUER, LE ROY: Executive. b. Cincinnati, Ohio, Sept. 30, 1902, e. Col. U. Salesman, Cincinnati Standard Film Service, 1919. Universal, 1921–46, as salesman, branch mgr., Supvsr., China, Japan; br. mgr. New Orleans, other cities, then sales mgr., Europe, Middle East and India. Columbia Pictures, Intl. Corp. 1949–1951. Man. dir. Australia, 1951; chmn. bd., Exotic TV Film Distribs. Pty. Ltd.

BRAUNAGEL, JACK D.: Exhibitor. b. San Francisco, Calif., Jan. 4, 1912; e. U. of Utah, 1929. Entered m.p. ind. as usher, Paramount-Publix, San Francisco, 1927; Des Moines, Ia., 1929; asst. mgr. in Ogden and Salt Lake City, Utah 1930; mgr., Ogden, 1932; mgr., Boise, Ida., 1935; city mgr., Logan, Utah, 1936; city mgr., Provo, Utah, 1937; dist. mgr., Intermountain Theatres, 1939–43; U.S. Army, 1943–46; supervisor, Northio Theatres, Cincinnati, 1946; film buyer, supervisor, Durwood Theatres, Kansas City, 1947; gen. mgr. drive-ins, Commonwealth Theatres, 1948–54; asst. to pres., in charge of theatre oper., United Theatres, No. Little Rock, 1955; exec. bd., TOA, 1953–55; formed Jay D. Bee Circuit, No. Little Rock, 1958; mem. bd. Motion Picture Investors, Inc.; pres., Money Investors, Inc., 1964; pres., Helene Theatres, Inc.

BRAUNSTEIN, GEORGE GREGORY: Producer. b. New York City, May 23, 1947. e. Culver Military Academy, Univ. of CA (b.a. biology, chemistry—1970). Father is Jacques Braunstein (Screen Televideo Prods. At War with the Army, Young Lions, etc.). 1971, co-founder of The Crystal Jukebox—record productions, music management, music publishing co. Produced 12 hit albums for Decca Records of England and London Records, U.S.A. Entered m.p. production in 1975–76 producing Train Ride to Hollywood for Taylor-Laughlin Co. 1979–80, produced Fade to Black for American Cinema Corp. Now pres. of Solar Survival Film Corp.

BRAVERMAN, CHARLES: Producer-Director. b. Los Angeles, Calif., March 3, 1944; e. L.A. City Coll., U. of S. Cal. (BA); m. Kendall Carly Browne, actress. Child actor, 1950–57. Two time Emmy winner.
TV: An American Time Capsule, The Smothers Brothers Racing Team Special, How to Stay Alive, David Hartman . . . Birth and Babies, Breathe a Sigh of Relief, The Television Newsman, Getting Married, The Making of a Live TV Show, Televisionland, Nixon: Checkers to Watergate, Braverman's Condensed Cream of Beatles, Two Cops, Peanuts to the Presidency: The Jimmy Carter Campaign; The Making of Beatlemania, Willie Nelson Plays Lake Tahoe, Tony Bennett Sings, What's Up, America?, The Big Laff Off, Engelbert at the MGM Grand, Oscar's First 50 Years, Frankie Valli Show, The Sixties.
PICTURES: Dillinger, Soylent Green, Same Time Next Year (all montages, titles), Can't Stop the Music (titles).

BRAVERMAN, MILLICENT: Adv. agency-pub. relations agency president (Braverman-Mirisch Inc.) KFAC AM & FM, syndicated radio Los Angeles commentator on books, literary critic, publishing specialist. b. New York City, B-M. Inc. founded 1963 to date. West coast consultant for number of NYC publisher accounts, general advertising, print and broadcast media nationally.

BRAY, PAUL, JR.: e. Rensselaer Polytechnic Institute. Experienced airline transport pilot and instrument flight instructor. Writer and director specializing in motion picture scripts and productions on all phases aviation, engineering and electronic from theoretical to practical industrial personnel training, and for Armed Forces and Vocational-Technical school instruction.

BRAZZI, ROSSANO: Actor. b. Bologna, Italy, 1916. e. U. of Florence. Started career on Italian stage; has appeared in numerous Italian pictures.
PICTURES INCLUDE: (U.S.) Little Women, Three Coins in the Fountain, Barefoot Contessa, Summertime, South Pacific, Light in the Piazza, The Battle of Villa Fiorita, Rome Adventure, Dark Purpose, The Christmas That Almost Wasn't, The Bobo, Woman Times Seven, Krakatoa, East of Java, The Adventurers, Psychout for Murder, The Great Waltz, The Final Conflict.

BREACHER, HAROLD: Executive. b. June 17, 1910. e. University of Calif. at L.A., B.A.; Univ. of Southern Calif., LL.B.; Univ. of South Calif., JD. Attorney at Law, 7 years. Bergerman-Breacher Motion Picture Agency, part owner. William Morris Agency, exec. agent; Famous Arts Agency, head Television Dept.; Ashley-Famous Agency, exec. packaging agent; United Artists Pictures Corp., head of sales & distribution United Kingdom, Europe, Middle East and Africa (TV); director, sales, U.K., Europe, Middle East & South Africa, Warner Bros. Television.

BRECHER, IRVING: Writer. b. New York City, Jan. 17, 1914. Yonkers Herald reporter; network programs writer for Milton Berle, Willie Howard, Al Jolson, etc., m.p. writer since 1937.
PICTURES INCLUDE: (collab. s.p.) Shadow of the Thin Man, Best Foot Forward, Meet Me in St. Louis; (collab. adapt.) Summer Holiday: (s.p.) Go West, At the Circus,

Du Barry Was a Lady, Yolanda and the Thief, Life of Riley, Somebody Loves Me, Cry for Happy, Bye Bye Birdie, Sail a Crooked Ship.
TV: The Peoples Choice, The Life of Riley.

BREGMAN, MARTIN: Motion Picture Producer.
PICTURES INCLUDE: Serpico, Dog Day Afternoon, The Next Man, The Seduction of Joe Tynan, S*H*E, Simon, The Four Seasons.

BREN, ROBERT J.: Producer, writer. b. Guanajuato, Mex. Film writing debut with "Looking for Trouble" 1934; in U.S. Signal Corps, World War II, also co-ordinator Inter-American Affairs as m.p. program office head, N.Y.C. & Wash. D.C.
PICTURES INCLUDE: This Marriage Business, Crime Ring, Parents on Trial, American Empire, Underground Agent, Charter Pilot, In Old California, Gay Senorita, Five Little Peppers and How They Grew, prod. First Yank into Tokyo, assoc. prod. El Paso, Overland Pacific; Naked Alibi, Treasure of Pancho Villa, The Great Sioux Uprising, Siege at Red River, Without Orders, Maltrata (O.S., S.P., producer) for Bremex Corp.; Mexico; Cajeme (O.S., S.P., producer) for Bremex, S.A., Mexico.
TV: Lone Wolf in Mexico, Stolen Train, Casey Jones series. Formed Bremex, indep. picture co., 1963; collab. s.p., Winds of the Four Seasons; collab. s.p., orig. story, The Hawaiians, 1967. Wrote & collaborated on Blood On the Shrine, Legacy in Nylons, Aztec Dagger, Female Menagerie, Tag for Murder.

BRENNAN, EILEEN: Actress. b. Los Angeles. Daughter of silent film actress Jean Manahan. e. Georgetown Univ. American Academy of Dramatic Arts (N.Y.). Big break came with lead in off-Bdwy. musical, Little Mary Sunshine.
PICTURES INCLUDE: Divorce, American Style, The Last Picture Show, Scarecrow, The Sting, Daisy Miller, At Long Last Love, Hustle, Murder by Death, The Cheap Detective, Private Benjamin.
STAGE: The Miracle Worker (tour), Hello, Dolly! (Bdwy.), and revivals of The King and I, Guys and Dolls, Camelot, Bells Are Ringing, etc. Did one-woman revue, An Evening with Eileen Brennan.

BRENNER, JOSEPH: Executive. b. Brooklyn, N.Y., Oct. 27, 1918; e. Brooklyn Coll. Started as usher, 1935, becoming mgr., Rogers Theatre, 1936; salesman, Eagle Lion Films, 1946; Screen Guild Prods., 1948; sales mgr., Ellis Films, 1949; formed Joseph Brenner Associates, 1953.

BREWER, ROY M.: b. Cairo, Neb., Aug. 9, 1909. Was projectionist 1925; chief projectionist, Capitol Theatre, Grand Island, Neb. 1927–39; pres. Nebraska State Fed. of Labor 1933; active in Nebraska labor movement in this period; NRA labor compliance officer for Nebraska 1934–35; campaigned for U.S. Senator George W. Norris in chg. campaign hdqts. 1936; re-elected pres. Nebraska State Federation of Labor 1937; covered legislature for Federation 1939, 1941, 1943; chief, plant & community facilities service War Prod. Bd. Washington 1943–45; apptd. specl. internl. rep. LATSE 1945; then made internl. rep. in Hollywood, rep. Richard F. Walsh, LATSE pres.; exec. ass't Steve Broidy, Allied Artists president, October, 1953; mgr. of br. oper., 1955; apptd. admin. sls. asst. to Edward Morey, vice-pres., Allied Artists, 1962; mgr. prod. dev., 1965. Member: Hollywood AFL Film Council, M.P. Ind. Council, M.P. Alliance, Pres, Pern Char. Committee 1965 Studio mgr. and prod. rep. for West Coast.

BRIAN, DAVID: Actor. b. New York City, Aug. 5, 1914; e. C.C.N.Y. Doorman; chorus boy stage debut in New Moon.
STAGE: You Said It, Bittersweet, Princess Charming, Let 'Em Eat Cake, Crazy Quilt, Beat the Band, Candle in the Wind. By Jupiter and night club singer & dancer; in vandeville; m.c. in South American night club; served as instructor in U.S. Coast Guard 1942–45; m.p. debut 1949, in Flamingo Road.
PICTURES INCLUDE: Intruder in the Dust, Beyond the Forest, Breakthrough, Damned Don't Cry, Inside Straight, Forth Worth, Inside Walls of Folsom Prison, This Woman is Dangerous, Springfield Rifle, Million Dollar Mermaid, Ambush at Tomahawk Gap, Perilous Journey, Dawn at Socorro, High and the Mighty, Timberjack, Fury at Gunsight Pass, The Rabbit Trap, The Seven Minutes.
TV: Mr. District Attorney.

BRICKNER, ROY: Executive. b. New York City, January 3, 1904. Advertising copywriting, sales promotion New York, Baltimore. Started motion picture career 1931 MGM film editing dept.; transferred advertising & trailer production, 1938; 1945 joined Warner Bros.; in 1955 appointed head Warner trailer and main title dept.

BRIDGES, BEAU: Actor. b. Hollywood, Calif., Dec. 19, 1941. f. Lloyd Bridges; e. U.C.L.A., U. of Hawaii. After several feature film bit parts and more than 80 TV credits, made screen feature debut in The Incident.
PICTURES INCLUDE: For Love of Ivy, Gaily, Gaily, The Landlord, Adam's Woman, The Christian Licorice Store, Hammersmith Is Out, Child's Play, Your Three Minutes

Are Up, Lovin' Molly, The Other Side of the Mountain, Dragonfly, Swashbuckler, Two Minute Warning, Greased Lightning, Norma Rae, The Runner Stumbles, Honky Tonk Freeway.

TV: Ensign O'Toole, Sea Hunt, Ben Casey, Dr. Kildare, Mr. Novak, Combat, Eleventh Hour.

BRIDGES, JAMES: Actor-Writer-Director. b. Paris, Ark., Appeared as an actor in 50 TV shows and five feature films. Has written 16 plays and is published in New Theatre for Now, 18 hour Hitchcock Shows and one Great Adventure, Go Down Moses. Worked as writer on 14 features. As director, worked in New York, Edinburgh Festival, Mark Taper and Ahmanson in LA.

PICTURES INCLUDE: The Appaloosa (A.P.), Forbin Project, (s.p.), The Baby Maker (s.p. dir.), The Paper Chase (s.p., dir.); September 30, 1955 (s.p., dir.); The China Syndrome (dir., co-s.p.); Urban Cowboy (co-s.p., dir.).

BRIDGES, JEFF: Actor. b. Los Angeles, 1951. Made acting debut at eight in the TV Sea Hunt series of his father, Lloyd Bridges. Acted also in Lloyd Bridges Show. At 14 toured New England with father in stock production Anniversary Waltz. Studied acting with Uta Hagen in New York. Brother of actor Beau Bridges.

PICTURES: The Last Picture Show, Fat City, Bad Company, Lolly Madonna (XXX), The Last American Hero, The Iceman Cometh, Thunderbolt and Lightfoot, Rancho Deluxe, Hearts of the West, Stay Hungry, King Kong, Somebody Killed Her Husband, Winter Kills, Heaven's Gate, Cutter and Bone.

BRIDGES, LLOYD: Actor. b. San Leandro, California, January 15, 1913. Went into stock from college dramatics.

PICTURES INCLUDE: Miss Susie Slagle's, Abilene Town, Canyon Passage, Ramrod, Trouble with Women, Hideout, Calamity Jane and Sam Bass, Trapped, Rocketship X M, Try and Get Me, Colt .45, Three Steps North, Whistle at Eaton Falls, Last of the Comanches, High Noon, Plymouth Adventure, Tall Texan, Kid from Left Field, City of Bad Men, Limping Man, Pride of the Blue Grass, Deadly Game, Apache Woman, Wichita, Wetbacks, The Rainmaker, Daring Game. The Goddess, The Happy Ending, Silent Night, Lonely Night, Airplane!

TELEVISION: Sea Hunt, The Loner, Movieola.

BRIEN, LIGE: Executive. b. Pittsburgh, Pa., Mar. 23; e. U. Pittsburgh, B.A. Asst. theatre mgr. 1937; theatre mgr. (Pa.); winner of many prizes for publicity, exploitation, grosses; winner of M.P. Herald Bronze Grand Award 1939, Silver Award 1944 & War Showmanship Award; press-book ed. PRC Pictures 1945, appt'd exploitation mgr., 1946; since exploit. mgr. Eagle Lion Classics; to U.A. as dir., spcl. events, April, 1951. Pres. AMPA, 153–54; asst. exploitation mgr., 20th Fox, 1960; nat'l dir. mdsg., Paramount Pictures, 1961–65; Expl. Dir., Seven Arts Pictures. (Warner Bros.). Now exploitation liaison between Hollywood studio and New York offices.

BRIGHT, RICHARD S.: Executive. b. New Rochelle, N.Y., Feb. 28, 1936. e. Hotchkiss School (1953–54); Wharton School of Finance, Univ. of Penna. (1954–58). With U.S. Army Finance Corp., 1959–60. Was corporate exec. prior to founding in 1973 Persky-Bright Organization, private investment group to finance films. Now bd. chm., Persky-Bright Productions, Inc.; adjunct professor at Columbia Univ. School of Fine Arts.

PICTURES: Last Detail, Golden Voyage of Sinbad, For Pete's Sake, California Split, The Man Who Would Be King, Funny Lady, The Front, and Equus. Financing/production services for: Hard Times, Taxi Driver, Missouri Breaks, Bound for Glory, Sinbad and the Eye of the Tiger, Hair.

TELEVISION: The President's Mistress (co-prod.), a CBS TV feature.

STAGE: A History of the American Film (1978).

BRIGHTMAN, HOMER H.: Writer b. Port Townsend, Washington. e. at the Washington State Nautical School-ship. Apprentice at 14, spent 10 years at sea as 2nd and 3rd officer; claims dept., Dollar Steamship Lines Shanghai, Hong Kong, Singapore: Academy Award for short Lend a Paw 1939; assoc. Walt Disney Prod. 13 years; created It's A Dog's Life, TV show; animated cartoon shorts for MGM, Walter Lantz, U.P.A.

PICTURES INCLUDE: Saludos Amigos, Three Caballeros, Make Mine Music, Fun and Fancy Free, Melody Time, Cinderella. Writer (collab.) TV shorts.

BRINKLEY, DAVID: TV News Correspondent. b. Wilmington, N.C., July 10, 1920. Started writing for hometown newspaper; attended Univ. of N.C., Vanderbilt University. Joined United Press before entering Army, World War II. After discharge in 1943 jointed NBC News in Washington as White House corr. Co-chm. for many years with late Chet Huntley on NBC Nightly News. Now delivers personal reports (David Brinkley's Journal) on same program.

BRISKIN, MORT: Producer-Writer. b. Oak Park, Ill. e. Univ. of So. Calif. Attended Harvard and Northwestern law schools,

being admitted to the Bar at 20. Practiced law before entering m.p. industry in management with such stars as Mickey Rooney. Turned to production and also wrote screenplays for 16 of his 29 films. Created nine TV series and was prod. or exec. prod. of some 1,350 TV segments, of which he wrote more than 300.

PICTURES INCLUDE: The River, The Magic Face, No Time for Flowers, The Second Woman, Quicksand, The Big Wheel, The Jackie Robinson Story, Ben, Williard, Walking Tall, Framed.

TV: Sheriff of Cochise, U.S. Marshal, The Texan, Grand Jury, The Walter Winchell File, Official Detective, Whirlybirds.

BRISSON, FREDERICK: producer; b. Copenhagen, Denmark, Mar. 17, 1913; s. of Carl Brisson, the stage and film actor, and his wife Cleo; e. Rossall College, England; m. the late Rosalind Russell. Formerly a successful actor's agent with offices in London, Paris and Hollywood; was asst. mgr. at London Hippodrome for The Merry Widow, Adelphi, London, Oct. 1937, co-produced Transatlantic Rhythm; came to America in 1939 and engaged in artists' representation and film production; first Broadway production was at the St. James, May, 1954, when he co-produced The Pajama Game; has since produced or co-produced Damn Yankees, 1955; New Girl in Town, 1957; The Pleasure of His Company, The Gazebo, 1958; Five Finger Exercise, 1959; Under the Yum-Yum Tree, 1960; The Caretaker, First Love, 1961; The Time of the Barracudas, 1963; Alfie, 1964; Generation, 1965; The Flip Side, 1968; Coco, 1969; Twigs, 1971; Jumpers, 1974; So Long, 174th Street, 1976; Mixed Couples, 1980; entered film production in England in 1937 with Two Hearts in Three-Quarters Time, and subsequently co-produced Prince of Arcadia and, 1938, produced Moonlight Sonata; entered Hollywood Film production in 1948 when he founded Independent Artists Pictures and produced The Velvet Touch; has subsequently produced Never Wave at a Wac, The Pajama Game, Damn Yankees, Five Finger Exercise, Under the Yum-Yum Tree, Generation, Mrs. Pollifax—Spy, etc.; served in the Air Force during the war as a Lt. Col. and was awarded the US Legion of Merit and the King Christian X Medal of Denmark. Since 1979 co-chm., Rosalind Russell Medical Research Center for Arthritis.

BRITTON, TONY: Actor, b. Birmingham, England, 1924; e. Thornbury Grammar School, Glos. Early career as clerk and in repertory; TV debut, 1952, The Six Proud Walkers (serial), m.p. debut, 1955 in Loser Takes All.

PLAYS INCLUDE: The Guv'nor, Romeo and Juliet, The Scarlet Pimpernel, The Other Man, The Dashing White Sergeant, Importance of Being Earnest, An Ideal Husband, School for Scandal, A Dream of Treason, That Lady, The Private Lives of Edward Whiteley, Affairs of State, The Night of The Ball, Gigi, The Seagull, Henry IV Part 1, Kill Two Birds, Cactus Flower, A Woman of No Importance, The Boston Story, Lady Frederick, My Fair Lady, Move Over Mrs. Markham, No No Nanette, Dame of Sark, The Chairman.

PICTURES INCLUDE: Birthday Present, Behind the Mask, Operation Amsterdam, The Heart of a Man, The Rough and the Smooth, The Risk, The Horsemasters, Stork Talk, The Break, There's a Girl in My Soup, Forbush and The Penguins, Sunday Bloody Sunday, Night Watch, The Day of the Jackal.

TV: Melissa series, Father Dear Father series, The Man Who Understood Women, Ooh La La, Call My Bluff, The Nearly Man.

BROCCOLI, ALBERT: Producer. b. New York City, April 5, 1909, e. C.C.N.Y. Agriculturist in early years; entered m.p. ind. as asst. director, 20th Century-Fox, 1938; exec. prod., Warwick Films.

PRODUCTIONS INCLUDE: Red Beret (Paratrooper), Hell Below Zero, Black Knight, Prize of Gold, Cockleshell Heroes, Safari, Zarak, Pickup Alley, Fire Down Below, Odongo, High Flight, No Time to Die, The Man Inside, Idle on Parade, Adamson of Africa, Bandit of Zhobe, Jazz Boat, In the Nick, Let's Get Married, The Trials of Oscar Wilde, Johnny Nobody, Carolina, Dr. No, Call Me Bwana, From Russia With Love, Goldfinger, Thunderball, You Only Live Twice, Chitty Chitty Bang Bang, On Her Majesty's Secret Service, Diamonds Are Forever, Live and Let Die, The Man With The Golden Gun, The Spy Who Loved Me.

BRODERICK, JAMES: Actor. b. Charlestown, N.Y., March 7. Bdwy. debut after years of study and stock in musical, Maggie. Has appeared in many plays, both on Bdwy. and the road.

PICTURES: Alice's Restaurant, The Group, The Taking of Pelham One Two Three, Dog Day Afternoon.

TELEVISION: Series; Brenner, Family. Specials: The Iceman Cometh, The Children of Innocence, John Brown.

BRODKIN, HERBERT: Producer. b. New York, N.Y., Nov. 9, 1912. e. Michigan U., Yale Drama School, U.S. Army, World War II; then scenery designer, prod. mgr., dir., summer stock; designer, dir., prod. mgr., Broadway theatres; prod.

exec., Paramount, Universal; prod., designer, Charlie Wild Private Detective, CBS-TV; prod., ABC, 1951.

TV: Album, TV Hour, Motorola TV Hour, Center Stage, Elgin Hour, Goodyear Playhouse, Alcoa Hour, Sebastian.

BRODNEY, OSCAR: Writer, Producer. b. Boston, Mass., e. Boston U., LLB, 1927; Harvard, LLM, 1928. Atty., Mass. Bar, 1928–35.

PICTURES INCLUDE: She Wrote the Book, If You Knew Susie, Are You With It?, For the Love of Mary, Mexican Hayride, Arctic Manhunt, Yes Sire, That's My Baby, Double Crossbone, Gal Who Took the West, South Sea Sinner, Comanche Territory, Harvey; story, Frenchie, Francis Goes to the Races, Little Egypt, Francis Covers the Big Town, Willie & Joe Back at the Front, Scarlet Angel, Francis Goes to West Point, Walking My Baby Back Home, Sign of the Pagan, Glenn Miller Story, Black Shield of Falworth, Captain Lightfoot, The Spoilers, Purple Mask, Lady Godiva, Day of Fury, Star in the Dust, Tammy and the Bachelor, When Hell Broke Loose, Bobbikins, Tammy Tell Me True, The Right Approach, All Hands on Deck, Tammy and the Doctor, The Brass Bottle, I'd Rather Be Rich.

BRODSHAUG, MELVIN: Producer. b. Davenport, N.D., May 22, 1900; e. No. Dakota State University, B.S., 1923; Litt.D. 1958 Chicago U., M.A. 1927, Columbia U., Ph.D. 1931; Supt. of Schools, Arnegard, N.D. 1923–28; research assoc. Erpi Classroom Films 1930; apptd. dir. research Encyclopaedia Britannica Films, Inc., apptd. vice-pres. 1945, in chg. of product development; apptd. member bd. dir. 1951, Dean of Boston U. Sch. of Public Relations & Communications, 1954–62, dir., Boston U film library, 1962–65. Prof. and consultant, Norfolk State Coll., Va., 1965–70; independent educational film producer 1970.

BRODSKY, JACK: Producer. b. Brooklyn, N.Y. e. George Washington High School. Writer for N.Y. Times; joined 20th-Fox publicity in N.Y. in 1956. Left in 1961 to head national ad-pub for Filmways. Joined Rastar Productions to work on "Funny Girl"; later named v.p. in charge of prod. In 1976 named v.p. in chg. film prod. prom., Rogers & Cowan; 1978, Columbia Pictures v.p., adv., pub., promo.; 1979, named exec. v.p. of Michael Douglas' Big Stick Productions.

PICTURES INCLUDE: Little Murders, Everything You Always Wanted To Know About Sex (exec. prod.), Summer Wishes, Winter Dreams.

AUTHOR: The Cleopatra Papers, with Nat Weiss.

BROIDY, STEVE: Executive. b. Malden, Mass., June 14, 1905. e. Boston U. Sales exec. Franklin Film Co., N.Y., 1935, Universal, 1926–1930; Warner Bros. 1931–1933; joined Monogram (original corporate name of Allied Artists) 1933 as sales mgr., in 1940 elected to bd. of dir., in 1945, elected v.p. in charge of oper.; Nov. 1945 pres. to 1964; pres., Motion Pictures Intl., 1965. MPI name changed to Associated Film Enterprises.

BROKAW, NORMAN R.: Executive. b. April 21, 1927, New York City. Joined William Morris Agency as trainee, in 1943, junior agent, 1948; sr. agent, company exec. in m.p. and TV, 1951; 1974, v.p., William Morris Agency, World Wide all areas. 1981, named exec. v.p. of member of board, William Morris Agency, worldwide. Member Academy of TV Arts & Sciences, Academy M.P. Arts & Sciences. Member bd. of dir. of Cedars-Sinai Medical Center, Los Angeles; pres., The Betty Ford Cancer Center. Clients include President and Mrs. Gerald R. Ford.

BROKAW, TOM: TV Host–Anchorman. e. Univ. of So. Dakota. Joined KMTV, NBC affiliate in Omaha, in 1962; 1965, joined WSB-TV, Atlanta. Worked in L.A. bureau of NBC News, anchored local news shows for KNBC, NBC station (1966–73). In 1973 named NBC News' White House correspondent; was anchorman of NBC Saturday Night News. Named host of Today Show in August, 1976.

BROLIN, JAMES: Actor. b. Los Angeles, July 10, 1942. e. UCLA. Debut in Bus Stop (TV series); named Most Promising Actor of 1970 by Fame and Photoplay magazines.

PICTURES INCLUDE: Take Her She's Mine, Goodbye, Charlie, Von Ryan's Express, Morituri, Our Man Flint, The Boston Strangler, Skyjacked, West World, Gable and Lombard, The Car, Capricorn One, The Amityville Horror.

TV: The Monroes, Marcus Welby, M.D. (Emmy award), Short Walk to Daylight, Class of '63.

BROMFIELD, JOHN: Actor. r.n. Farron Bromfield; b. South Bend, Ind., June 11, 1922; e. St. Mary's College. College football star. Served in U. S. Navy, medical discharge; worked as tuna fisherman. Film debut in Harpoon, 1948; under contract to Hal Wallis.

PICTURES INCLUDE: Sorry Wrong Number, Harpoon, Rope of Sand, Hold That Line, Flat Top, Easy to Love, Ring of Fear, Black Dakotas, Revenge of the Creature, Big Bluff, Three Bad Sisters, Manfish, Crime Against Joe, Quincannon Frontier Scout, Hot Cars.

BROMHEAD, MICHAEL: Executive. b. London, England, May 30, 1942. e. Charterhouse and St. John's College, Cambridge, RAF pilot during war, Ent. m.p. ind. 1947, with Eagle-Lion; resigned, 1950. Appt. overseas man. Independent Film Dist.; dir. One World Film Dist. 1953; dir. Lion International Films, 1955; New York rep. Lion International, 1958; pres., Lion International Films, Inc., 1959; general manager Lion International Films, 1962; dir. London Independent Producers, Ltd.; man. dir., Alliance Intl. Film Distribs., Ltd., 1966. Dir. EMI Film Dist., 1970. Dir., gen. mgr., 1971; appt. dir. overseas dist., 1975; dir., EMI Film Theatre Corp., man. dir., EMI Film Dist. Overseas Ltd., 1979.

BROMHEAD, RALPH S. (M.V.O., F.C.A.): b. Ealing, Dec. 22, 1906; e. St. Bees, Cumberland, 1927–29; theatre controller Gaumont-Brit. & P.C.T. Ltd.; 1929–34, asst. gen. mgr. Associated British Cinemas Ltd., Managing dir. Regent Circuit Ltd.; 1934–39, dir. and gen. mgr. County Cinemas Ltd. & Entertainments Investment Corporation; 1928, Chartered Accountant; 1939–45, Royal Artillery; 1945–50, dir. & controller of export Eagle Lion; 1950 to date, dir. Romulus Films, Remus Films, etc. and later British & American Film Holdings; 1950 dir. of administration Better Business Drive; 1934, Council C.T.B.F.; 1956–69, Chairman M.V.O.; 1969 to date Trustee C.T.B.F. 1971, Appointed M.V.O.

BRON, ELEANOR: Actress. Started career in Establishment Club, London, and on American tour. Leading lady on British TV show Not So Much A Programme, More a Way of Life.

PICTURES INCLUDE: Help, Alfie, Two For The Road, Bedazzled, Women in Love, The Millstone.

THEATRE: The Doctor's Dilemma, Howard's End, The Prime of Miss Jean Brodie.

BRONDFIELD, JEROME: b. Cleveland, O., Dec. 9, 1913; e. Ohio State U., 1936. Reporter, ed. on Columbus Dispatch, Cleveland News, Scripps-Howard NEA Svce., I.N.S., A.P.; story ed., script head, RKO Pathe, Oct., 1944; writer, dir. & supvr. of many doc. shorts incl. This is America series; TV writer; short story writer; collab. s.p., Below the Sahara; s.p., Louisiana Territory; doc. film writer; now Sports Editor, Scholastic Magazines, Inc. Author, Woody Hayes, The 100-Yard War, Knute Rockne, The Man & the Legend.

BRONSON, CHARLES: Actor. b. Penn., 1920. m. Jill Ireland, actress. Worked as a coal miner. Starred on his own TV series, Meet McGraw.

PICTURES INCLUDE: Red Skies of Montana, Pat and Mike, House of Wax, Drumbeat, Vera Cruz, Jubel, Lonely Are the Brave, Machine Gun Kelly, Never So Few, A Thunder of Drums, The Magnificent Seven, The Great Escape, The Sandpiper, The Battle of the Bulge, Pancho Villa, The Dirty Dozen, This Property is Condemned, Once Upon a Time in the West, Goodbye, Friend, Rider in the Rain, You Can't Win 'Em All, Someone Behind the Door, Red Sun, Chato's Land, The Mechanic, The Valachi Papers, The Stone Killer, Mr. Majestyk, Death Wish, Breakout, Hard Times, Breakheart Pass, From Noon Till Three, St. Ives, The White Buffalo, Telefon, Borderline, Cabolbanco, Death Hunt.

BRONSTON, SAMUEL: Producer. b. Russia; e. Sorbonne, Paris. Film distributor, Paris; prod. exec. Columbia Studios, Hollywood; Martin Eden, City Without Men, Producer, Columbia Pictures; resigned to form Samuel Bronston Pict., Inc.; exec. prod. Jack London, A Walk in the Sun. Color documentaries produced first time in Vatican; prod. John Paul Jones 1959; Received U.S. Navy Meritorious Pub. Serv. Citation; pres. Samuel Bronston Productions; 1960 prod. King of Kings, El Cid; 1962, 55 Days at Peking; 1963. The Fall of the Roman Empire; prod. Circus World, 1964, Condor Award, Society for Pan American Culture—for El Cid, 1962 (Award shared with Stanford University), The Hollywood Foreign Press Association Golden Globe for the achievement of his outstanding production of El Cid, 1962, Italian Order of Merit with Medal of Commendatore. Grand Cross of Merit by the Equestrian Order of the Knights of the Holy Sepulchre. (The highest honor of the Catholic Church); The Encomienda of the Order of the Great Cross of Isabel la Catolica. President Samuel Bronston Studios, Madrid, Spain.

BROOKE, PETER R.: Writer. b. Berlin, Germany, April 12, 1929. e. Germany, Switzerland, England. With Warner Bros., 1944–46, mail room, pub. dept., then asst. casting dir.; contract writer, Robert Riskin Prod., Paramount; then free lance; radio writer many shows; TV writer for Teevee Prod., Celebrity Playhouse, Science Fiction Theatre; staff writer, Universal Pictures; left Universal to join Excelsior under new banner of Warbrook Inc. as writer-producer.

PICTURES INCLUDE: Basketball Fix, Sweet Violence orig., Outside the Law.

TV: Sea Hunt, 77 Sunset Strip, Sugar Foot, The Fugitive, Six Million Dollar Man.

BROOKING, DOROTHEA: TV producer. b. Slough, Bucks, Eng., Dec. 7, 1916. e. St. George's School, Windsor. Stage trained at Old Vic Theatre; TV as prod. BBC children's programmes 1950; from July 1972 freelance producer, actress.

PRODUCTIONS INCLUDE: Railway Children, Secret Garden, Great Expectations, The Viaduct, Thursday's Child, Kizzy, The Phoenix and the Carpet.

BROOKS, DICK: Executive. b. New York, N.Y., e. U. of Georgia, grad. 1951; reporter, Atlanta (Ga.) Journal, 1951; sports ed., Gainesville Times, 1952; war correspondent, Pacific Stars & Stripes, 1952–54; entered m.p. industry, 1957 as staff writer, 20th Century-Fox pub. dept; N.Y. press rep., Embassy Picts., 1959; N.Y. press rep., 20th Century Fox, 1960; nat'l publ. dir., Seven Arts Productions, 1962; Paramount pub. mgr., 1965; nat'l pub. dir., 20th-Fox, 1967; adv.-pub. dir., Rastar Prods., 1970; formed Dick Brooks Organization, independent p.r. and prod. co., 1972. In 1977 joined Rogers & Cowan as dir. of mktg., film division. In 1978 named Warner Bros. pub. dir.; 1980, formed Dick Brooks Unlimited, p.r. & m.p. prod. co.

BROOKS, JOSEPH: Producer-Director-Writer-Composer-Conductor. Well-known for composing music for TV commercials before turning to producing, directing, writing and scoring theatrical feature, You Light Up My Life, in 1977. Winner of 21 Clio Awards (made by adv. industry); created music for 100 commercials. Has also composed for theatrical films.
PICTURES INCLUDE: Scores: The Garden of the Finzi Continis, Marjoe, Jeremy, The Lords of Flatbush. Produced, directed, wrote, and composed, arranged and conducted music for You Light Up My Life. Produced, directed, wrote, starred in and composed music for If Ever I See You Again.

BROOKS, MEL: Writer-Director-Actor. b. Brooklyn, 1926. m. actress Anne Bancroft. As child did impressions and was amateur drummer and pianist. First appearance as actor in Golden Boy in Redbank, N.J. Was also director and social director in the Catskills. Became writer for Sid Caesar on TV's Broadway Review and Your Show of Shows, writing for latter for decade. Teamed with Carl Reiner for comedy record album, 2000 Year Old Man and The 2000 and 13 Year Old Man.
PICTURES INCLUDE: The Critic (short, s.p.-narrator), The Producers, The Twelve Chairs, Blazing Saddles, Young Frankenstein, Silent Movie, High Anxiety (prod., dir., s.p.). History of the World—Part I (prod., dir., s.p., actor, composer).
TV: Get Smart (writer), When Things Were Rotten (creator).
STAGE: Shinbone Alley, All-American (books for musicals).

BROOKS, RICHARD: Writer, director. b. Philadelphia, May 18, 1912; e. Temple Univ.; Radio writer, narrator and commentator, NBC. Author of several short stories. Novels, Brick Fox Hole, Boiling Point, The Producer.
PICTURES INCLUDE: Swell Guy, Brute Force, To the Victor, Crossfire, Key Largo, Mystery Street, Storm Warning, Deadline U.S.A., Battle Circus, Take The High Ground, Flame and the Flesh, Last Time I Saw Paris, Blackboard Jungle, Last Hunt, Catered Affair, Something of Value, The Brothers Karamazov, Cat on A Hot Tin Roof, Elmer Gantry (Academy Award for s.p. 1961); Sweet Bird of Youth, writer, Lord Jim, The Professionals, In Cold Blood, The Happy Ending, Dollars, Bite the Bullet, Looking for Mr. Goodbar.

BROOKS, THOR L.: Director. b. Stockholm, Sweden. Studied m.p. photographer at Reinman School, Berlin, dramatics & dir. in Paris & Stockholm; dir. 36 films in Europe, 1936–41; U.S. Air Force, 1942–46; dir., commercial films, 1947–49; staff dir., KLAC-TV; dir., assoc. prod., TV film series supervisor, I Search for Adventure, 1955; dir. Medi; prod. docum. feature, Kwaheri.
PICTURES INCLUDE: Legion of the Doomed, Arson for Hire.
TV: 7 League Boots, Sweet Success; dir., Devils Disciple.

BROUMAS, JOHN G.: Exec. b. Youngstown, O. Oct. 12, 1917, e. Youngstown, O. Usher, Altoona Publix Theatres, 1933, usher to asst. mgr., Warner Thea. 1934–39; mgr. Grand 1939–40; mgr. Orpheum 1940–41. WW-II active, Officer Chemical Corps, past Commander 453rd Chem. Grp. (Reserve); Member Reserve Officers Assoc.; Gen. mgr. Pitts & Roth Theatres 1946–54; President, Broumas Theatres; bd. govnrs., Variety Club, Tent No. 11, 1959–73; Wash., first asst. chief barker, 1964 & 1971; chief barker, 1965–1966, 1972 V.P.T.O.A. 1965; V.P. NATO, 1969; past bd. chmn. Maryland Theatre Owners; bd. of directors of NATO of Va., Md., D.C.; pres., Broumas Theatre Service; pres., Showcase Theatres; pres., Capital Plaza Corp.; mem. bd. Foundation of Religious Action (FRASCO). Mem. Nat'l Immigration Comm. Founder of John G. Broumas Scholarship for Drama at Youngstown State Univ.; past pres. & Board Chairman Maryland Theatre Owners; v.p. & bd. of dir.—Virginia Theatre Owners; bd. of dir. NATO of D.C.; pres. B.C. Theatres; Sponsor of Andre G. Broumas Memorial Award—West Point; pres., McLean Theatre Corp.; member, Motion Picture Pioneers; sponsor, Broumas Scholastic and Athletic Scholarship for AHEPA Wash. D.C. area; director, McLean Bank McLean, Va.; honorary member, West

Point Class 1954; Director, Exchange, Ltd., Wash., D.C.; President, University III Cinema Corp.; Secretary-Treasurer, Tenley Circle Twin Theatre Corp.; President, Cinema Mgt. Corp; Director: Motion Picture Pioneers; Advisory Council: Will Rogers Memorial Hospital; Chief Barker: Washington, D. C. Variety Club, Tent #11, 1978–79 and bd. chmn., 1980.

BROWN, CLARENCE: Director. b. Clinton, Mass., May 10, 1890; e. U. Tenn. Aviator, U.S. Army, World War I. Engineer, automobile industry; formed Brown Motor Co., Birmingham, Ala. To Hollywood 1915 as asst. to dir. Maurice Tourneur for whom he directed his first picutre. The Great Redeemer. Joined MGM 1924. Launched Greta Garbo as star in Flesh and the Devil; other pictures with Garbo are Woman of Affairs, Anna Christie, Romance, Inspiration, Anna Karenina, Conquest.
PICTURES INCLUDE: The Eagle, Kiki, Night Flight, Sadie McKee, Ah, Wilderness!, Wife vs. Secretary, The Gorgeous Hussy, Of Human Hearts, Idiot's Delight, Edison the Man, The Human Comedy, White Cliffs of Dover, National Velvet, Letty Lynton, Possessed, Trail of '98, The Rains Came, The Human Comedy, Song of Love, Intruder in the Dust, To Please a Lady, Angels in the Outfield, When in Rome, The Yearling, Plymouth Adventure, The Secret Garden, Never Let Me Go.

BROWN, DAVID: Executive and Producer. b. New York, N.Y., July 28, 1916; e. Stanford U., A.B., 1936; Columbia U. (school of Journalism), M.S., 1937. Apprentice reporter, copy-editing, San Francisco News & Wall St. Journal, 1936; night ed. asst. drama critic, Fairchild Publications, N.Y., 1937–39; edit. dir. Milk Research Council, N.Y., 1939–40; assoc. ed., Street & Smith Publ., N.Y., 1940–43; assoc. ed., exec. ed., then ed.-in-chief, Liberty Mag., N.Y., 1943–49; edit. dir., nat'l editorial campaign, Amer. Medical Assn. 1949; assoc. ed., man. ed., Cosmopolitan Mag., N.Y., 1949–52; contrib. stories & articles to many nat'l mags.; man. ed., story dept., 20th-Fox, L.A., Jan., 1952; story ed. & head of scenario dept., May, 1953–56; appt'd. member of exec. staff of Darryl F. Zanuck, 1956; mem. of exec. staff, 20th-Fox studios, and exec. studio story editor, 1956–1960; Prod. 20th-Fox Studios, Sept. 1960–62; Editorial v.p. New American Library of World Literature, Inc., 1963–64; exec. story opers., 20th Century-Fox, 1964–67; v.p. dir. of story operations, 1967; exec. vice-pres., creative operations and members, Board of Directors, 1969–71. Exec. v.p., member board of directors Warner Bros. 1971–1972; partner and director, The Zanuck/Brown Co., 1972; mbr., bd. of trustees, American Film Institute, 1972–80.
FILMS INCLUDE: The Sugarland Express, The Black Windmill, Ssssssss, The Eiger Sanction, The Sting, MacArthur, Jaws, Jaws 2, The Island, Neighbors.

BROWN, GEORGE: Producer. b. London, Eng., e. Latymer Upper Sch., Colegio Franco, Barcelona. C.O., RAF Film Unit (overseas), World War II. Asst. dir., Ealing and others.
PICTURES INCLUDE: Fire Over England, Farewell Again, Vessel of Wrath, Jamaica Inn, 49th Parallel, Journey Together, School for Secrets, Vice Versa, Sleeping Car to Trieste, Chiltern Hundreds, Hotel Sahara, Made in Heaven, Desperate Moment, The Seekers (Land of Fury), Jacqueline, Dangerous Exile, Rooney, Tommy the Toreador, The Boy Who Stole A Million, Double Bunk, Murder at The Gallop, Ladies Who Do, Murder She Said, Village of Daughters, Kill or Cure, Guns of Batasi, The Trap, Finders Keepers, Ghost of a Chance, Up in the Air, Fanfare Films Ltd., Eyeline Films, Parallel Prods. Hoverbug, Assault, Revenge, All Coppers Are . . . , Innocent Bystanders, Penny Gold, Open Season.

BROWN, HAROLD: Executive. Pres., International Picture Show Co. since Dec., 1980. Previously pres., American International TV; v.p. & bd. mbr., American International Pictures (now Filmways).

BROWN, HARRY: Writer. b. Portland, Me., April 30, 1917. e. Harvard. With The New Yorker 1940; U.S. Army 1941–45.
PICTURES INCLUDE: (collab:) True Glory 1945, Walk in the Sun 1945; The Other Love, Arch of Triumph 1947; Wake of Red Witch, Man on Eiffel Tower, Sands of Iwo Jima (s.p.), Kiss Tomorrow Goodbye, Only the Valiant, Bugles in Afternoon, Place in the Sun (orig. story;) Academy Award collab., Apache Drums, The Sniper, Eight Iron Men, All the Brothers Were Valiant, Many Rivers to Cross, Virgin Queen, D-Day The Sixth of June, Between Heaven and Hell, Ocean's 11, El Dorado.

BROWN, HENRY: Executive. b. New York, N.Y., Feb. 18, 1899; e. C.C.N.Y., 1920; Columbia University, 1923. pres., Lakewood Amusement Corp.; pres., Atlas TV Corp.; pres. Capt. Zero Prods., Inc.

BROWN, HIMAN: M.P. Producer & director. b. N.Y.C. July 21, 1910; e. C.C.N.Y., St. Lawrence Univ. Radio & TV package prod. since 1927 include: Inner Sanctum, Thin Man, Bulldog Drummond, Dick Tracy, Terry and the Pirates, Joyce Jordan MD, Grand Central Station, CBS Radio Mystery Theatre, pres. Production Center, Inc.

PICTURES INCLUDE: That Night, Violators, The Stars Salute, The Price of Silence, The Road Ahead.

BROWN, HOWARD C.: Executive. b. Newport, N.H., Aug. 15, 1901. e. Boston U. Assoc. with Technicolor Motion Picture Corp., before org. Colorart Pictures, 1926. Merged with Synchrotone Pictures & Kennedy Pictures, 1929, forming Colorart Synchrotone Corp. In 1930 org. Brown-Nagel Productions. Since 1933 has produced numerous shorts. Sales mgr., Cinecolor, 1936–37; pres. Howard C. Brown Co. 1937–1938. Sales mgr., Trimble Laboratories, Inc. 1947; formed Howard C. Brown Productions 1948, to release for United Artists. Prod. Kangaroo Kid; prod. Mating Urge, inter-nations, documentary; 1969, Film Exporter.

BROWN, JIM: Actor. b. St. Simons Island, Feb. 17, 1936. e. Manhasset H.S., Syracuse U. For nine years played football with the Cleveland Browns; in 1964 won Hickock Belt as Professional Athlete of the year; founder, Black Economic Union.

PICTURES INCLUDE: Rio Conchos, The Dirty Dozen, Ice Station Zebra, The Split, Riot, Dark Of The Sun, 100 Rifles, Kenner, Tick . . . Tick . . . Tick, The Grasshopper, Slaughter, Slaughter's Big Rip-Off, I Escaped from Devil's Island, The Slams, Three the Hard Way, Take a Hard Ride.

BROWN, TOM: Actor. b. New York City, Jan. 6, 1913; son of Harry Brown, actor-producer, and Marie Francis, actress; e. N.Y. Prof. Children's School. On radio, then dram. stage (Neighbors, Many a Slip, Pardon My Glove, etc.). Screen debut in A Lady Lies, 1929.

PICTURES INCLUDE: Buck Privates Come Home, Duke of Chicago, Operation Haylift, Fireman Save My Child.

TV: General Hospital.

BROWN, WILLIAM: Executive. b. Ayr, Scotland, June 24, 1929. e. Ayr Academy, University of Edinburgh, where graduated Bachelor of Commerce 1950. Served to Lieutenant, Royal Artillery, 1950–52. Sales mgr. for Scotland Television Ltd. in London, England, 1958 to 1961, sales director 1961 to 1963. Deputy mng. dir. of Scottish Television Ltd. at Glasgow 1963–66, mng. dir. in 1966. Deputy chm. and mng.-dir. of STV from 1974. Director, independent TV Publications, London, England, 1968. On board of directors for Scottish National Orchestra, 1973. Member of Independent TV Companies Association, and chairman of same 1978–80. Holds C.B.E. honor from British Royalty.

BROWN, WILLIAM H., JR: Director, concert mgr.; Juilliard School of Music, 1946; TV prod., Young and Rubicam, 1948; dir., Life with Father, Climax, CBS-TV, 1954, Studio One 1955; prod. Paramount Television, 1958; Exec. prod., Shirley Temple Show, NBC, 1960; TV prod., Norman, Craig and Kummel, 1962; Compton, 1963; Post-Keyes-Gardner, 1965; Free lance, 1967.

BROWN, WILLET HENRY: Executive. Assist. gen. mgr., Don Lee, Inc., 1932–33; exec. v.p. Don Lee Broadcasting System, Hollywood, 1938–48; pres. Don Lee Broadcasting System, 1949–58; consultant, R.K.O. General Inc.: pres. Don Lee, Inc. pres. Laurie Leasing Corp.: pres. Pacific States Invest. Corp.: pres. Hillcrest Motor Company: pres., KGB INC, KGB-AM and KGB-FM, San Diego, Calif.: pres. bd. and dir. of KXOA, Inc., KXOA, AM and KXOA-FM, Sacramento, Calif.

BROWNE, ROSCOE LEE: Actor, director, writer. b. Woodbury, N.J. e. Lincoln University, Pa. Post graduate studies in comparative literature and French at Middlebury College, Vermont, and Columbia U., N.Y. Taught French and lit. at Lincoln U. until 1952. National sales rep. for Schenley Import Corp. 1946–56; he was one of the United States' international track stars and a member of ten A.A.U. teams. He was twice American champion in the 1000-yard indoor competition, twice all-American and, in 1951 in Paris, ran the fastest 800 meters in the world for that year. Professional acting debut, 1956, in Julius Caesar at the N.Y. Shakespeare Festival; published poet and short story writer.

BROADWAY: The Ballad of the Sad Cafe, The Cool World, General Seeger, Tiger, Tiger Burning Bright!, The Old Glory. Star and dir. A Hand is On The Gate; off Broadway; The Blacks, Aria da Capo.

PICTURES INCLUDE: The Comedians, Uptight, The Liberation of L.B. Jones, The Cowboys, World's Greatest Athlete, Superfly T.N.T., Logan's Run, Twilight's Last Gleaming, The Fifth Door.

BROWNING, KIRK: TV Director; b. N.Y.C., Mar. 28, 1921; e. Brooks School, Andover, Mass., Avon Old Farms, Avon, Conn., and Cornell U.; 1940, reporter to News-Tribune in Waco, Texas; with American Field Service, 1942–45; adv. copywriter for Franklin Spier, 1945–48; became floor manager NBC-TV 1949; app'ty asst. dir. NBC-TV Opera Theatre in 1951 directing NBC Opera Theatre, TV Recital Hall, and Toscanini Simulcasts.

BRUCE, BRENDA: Actress. b. Manchester, England, 1922. e. privately. London stage debut, 1066 And All That; On screen 1944; Millions Like Us; TV Best Actress Award 1962.

PICTURES INCLUDE: Night Boat to Dublin, I see a Dark Stranger, They Came To A City, Carnival, Piccadilly Incident, While The Sun Shines, When The Bough Breaks, My Brother's Keeper, Don't Ever Leave Me, The Final Test, Law and Disorder, Behind the Mask, Peeping Tom, Nightmare, The Uncle.

BROADWAY: Gently Does it (1953), This Year Next Year, Happy Days, Woman In A Dressing Gown, Victor Eh!, Merry Wives of Windsor, The Revenger's Tragedy, Little Murders, Winters Tale, Pericles, Twelfth Night, Hamlet.

TV Appearances: Mary Britton series, Nearer to Heaven, Wrong Side of the Park, The Lodger, The Monkey And the Mohawk, Love Story, A Piece of Resistance, Give the Clown His Supper, Knock on Any Door, The Browning Version, Death of a Teddy Bear, Softly, Softly, The Girl, Happy, Family at War, Budgie.

BRUCE, GEORGE: Writer. b. Danville, Pa., Sept. 15, 1898; e. priv. Aviator, 1919–27; then free lance writer; mag. pub. From 1937 sole author or collab. s.p.

PICTURES INCLUDE: She's No Lady, The Crowd Roars, Navy Blue and Gold, Duke of West Point, King of the Turf, South of Pago Pago, Man in Iron Mask, Son of Monte Cristo, Corsican Brothers, Two Years Before the Mast, Miss Annie Rooney, Fiesta, Killer McCoy, Walk A Crooked Mile, Rogues of Sherwood Forest, Lorna Doone, Valentino, The Brigand, Kansas City, Confidential, Fury in Paradise, Solomon and Sheba.

BRUCKHEIMER, JERRY: Producer. Was adv. agency exec. in TV commercials before becoming producer of films.

PICTURES: Assoc. Prod.: Culpepper Cattle Company, Rafferty and the Gold Dust Twins. Producer: Farewell My Lovely, March or Die, Defiance, American Gigolo, Thief.

BRUCKNER, SIDNEY THOMAS: Executive. b. New York City, May 28, 1914; e. C.C.N.Y., B.B.A. 1931; Columbia U., post-graduate study 1931–32. Textile Buyer (partner) 1931–35; joined Columbia Pictures Intern. Corp. as home office rep., covered all countries south of U.S. 1935–38 and 1940–42, covered Europe with hdqtrs in England and Paris 1938–40; apptd. prod. supervisor (Mexican prod.) 1943; res. 1950; ind. prod., 1950, of Mexican films, American TV films; pres. Prod. Espada S.A.; technical advisor, Garden of Evil, Tall Men; prod. 19 TV shows, Capt. David Grief. Spanish/English dubbing of features, TV films, commercials. Mem. Prod. Guild (Mexico), Variety Club (Mexico), American Club, Am. Soc.

BRUNING, RICHARD R.: Executive. b. Kansas City, MO. e. Yale University, Harvard Business School. Asst. treas. Transamerica Corp., parent corp. of United Artists, from 1972. In 1979 named treas. of UA. 1980, named v.p. and treas. of UA Corp.

BRUSKI, NATALIO: Writer, Journalist, Buenos Aires. b. Buenos Aires, B.A. Argentina, Aug. 9, 1906; p. non-professionals; e. high school graduate; married; Had commercial career before entering m.p. ind. In 1932, mgr. Coliseo Theatre. In 1933, mgr. Govena Theatre. In 1934, film critic. La Pelicula, show business professional organ. In 1939; founded own trade paper, Cine-Prensa, since 1951, publicity mgr. for Columbia Pictures. Buenos Aires corresp., M.P. Herald since 1931.

BRUSSEAU, WILLIAM E.: Executive. b. Detroit, Mich. June 6, 1926. e. Engineering, Lawrence Institute of Technology, 1942–44; theatre arts UCLA, 1948; m.p. prod., USC, 1948–50. Joined staff engaged in producing documentaries; prod. films, science, industry, medical profession and the military. gen. doc., TV in Europe, Africa, Middle East, Far East, Latin America, U.S.; formed & pres. Westminster Films, 1950.

PICTURES INCLUDE: Mr. Texas, orig. story, A Cry in the Night, Skidrow, Stop Gap. The Glass Mountain, Dream of Paradise, Flamingo Feather, Shackleton.

BRYAN, DORA: Actress. b. Southport (Lancashire), Eng. e. Council School. Stage debut 1935. Screen debut Fallen Idol, 1948.

PICTURES INCLUDE: No Room at the Inn, Once Upon a Dream, Blue Lamp, Cure for Love, Now Barabas, The Ringer, Women of Twilight, The Quiet Woman, The Intruder, You Know What Sailors Are, Mad About Men, See How They Run, Cockleshell Heroes, Child in the House, Green Man, Carry on Sergeant, Operation Bullshine, Desert Mice, The Night We Got the Bird, A Taste of Honey.

TV: Dora Bryan Show.

STAGE: Hello Dolly, 1966.

BRYNNER, YUL: Actor. b. Sakhalin Island, July 11, Started singing in night clubs in Paris with gypsy groups at age of 13; then joined Cirque d'Hiver as trapeze artist; joined repertory company of Theatre des Maturins, Paris; made American stage debut in Twelfth Night; TV director for CBS.

BROADWAY: Lute Song, Dark Eyes. The King and I (Donaldson award, Antoinette Perry Award, Critics Circle Award.)

PICTURES INCLUDE: Port of New York, King and I (Academy award, 1956, best actor), Ten Commandments,

Anastasia, The Journey, Solomon and Sheba, Once More, With Feeling, The Magnificent Seven, Taras Bulba, Escape to Zahrain, Kings of the Sun, The Saboteur, Code Name, Morituri, Invitation To A Gunfighter, Return of the Seven, Triple Cross, The Double Man, The Long Duel, The Battle of Neretva, The Magic Christian, File of the Golden Goose, Madwoman of Chaillot, Romance of a Horsethief, Light at the Edge of the World, Fuzz, Westworld, Futureworld.
TV: Anna and the King of Siam.

BUCHHOLZ, HORST: Actor. b. 1933. e. High School. In radio and stage plays. Film debut. Marianne (French) 1955.
PICTURES INCLUDE: Himmel Ohne Sterne (No Star in the Sky), Robinson Must Not Die, Mon Petit, The Confessions of Felix Krull, Tiger Bay, Fanny One, Two, Three, Nine Hours to Rama, The Empty Canvas, The Great Waltz, Cervantes.
TV: Raid on Entebbe.

BUCK, JULES: Producer. b. St. Louis, Mo., July 30, 1917. Asst. to prod., The Killers; assoc. prod., Brute Force, Naked City, We Were Strangers; prod., Love Nest, Fixed Bayonets, Treasure of the Golden Condor, O.S.S., TV series; prod., The Day They Robbed the Bank of England, Great Catherine; formed Keep Films with Peter O'Toole. Co-prod., Under Milkwood. Prod., The Ruling Class. Exec. Prod., Man Friday. Prod., The Great Scout and Cathouse Thursday.

BUCKNER, ROBERT H.: Producer, writer b. Crewe Va., May 28, 1906; e. U. Va.: Edinburgh (Scotland) U. Newspaper corresp. New York World. 1926–27 in England: instructor, Belgian Mil. Acad. 1927–28: with Alfred A. Knopf, Inc., Doubleday, Doran, N.Y., pub., 1928–33; corresp. in Russia, Scandinavia, 1933–35; contrib. fiction, Amer. & Brit. mags., 1926–36. Author & collab. many s.p.
PICTURES INCLUDE: Gold Is Where You Find It, Jezebel, Dodge City, Virginia City, Knute Rockne, Santa Fe Trail, Dive Bomber, Yankee Doodle Dandy, Desert Song. In 1943 prod. Gentleman Jim, Mission to Moscow, Desert Song. A Champion of Champion Producer in Fame ratings. (See Index). The Gang's All Here, Cheyenne, Life With Father, prod. Rogue's Regiment. Sword in the Desert; Free For All, Deported, Bright Victory, The Man Behind the Gun, Safari.

BUJOLD, GENEVIEVE: Actress. b. Montreal, July 1, 1942. e. Montreal Conservatory of Drama. m. TV Director Paul Almond. Worked in a Montreal cinema as an usherette; American TV debut: St. Joan.
STAGE: The Barber of Seville, A Midsummer Night's Dream, A House . . . A Day.
PICTURES INCLUDE: La Guerre est Finie, La Fleur de L'Age, Entre La Mer et L'eau Douce, King of Hearts, The Thief, Isabel, Anne of The Thousand Days, The Act of the Heart, The Journey, Earthquake, Swashbuckler, Obsession, Alex and the Gypsy, Another Man, Another Chance, Coma, Murder by Decree, The Last Flight of Noah's Ark.
TV: Anthony and Cleopatra.

BUNDY, FRANK: Producer. b. Hanwell, England. Jan. 12, 1908. Entered m.p. industry with Herbert Wilcox Productions, London: from 1925–29 successively asst. Brit. Natl. Pictures. Ltd.: Brit. Int. Pictures, Ltd.: Brit. Instruct. Films, Ltd.; G.B. Pictures Corp.; Imperator Films Ltd.: joined Brit. Council as prod. on propaganda films 1939: apptd. assoc. prod. Sydney Box Productions, Ltd., Jan. 1946; apptd. personal asst. Sydney Box Aug. 1946; apptd., prod. Gainsborough Pictures 1947; Dir. Screen Audiences Ltd.; 1955; Man. dir., Wallace Prods. Mercurio D'Oro Award Venice, 1960.
PICTURES INCLUDE: Steel, Easy Money, Christopher Columbus, Diamond City: Daybreak, Stone Into Steel, Fair Oriana, Caught in the Net, Master of Venus, Count Down to Danger, for children's Film Foundation.

BUNUEL, LUIS: Director. b. 1900, Calanda, Spain. Jesuit education. Dir. first performance of Falla's puppet opera, El Retablo de maese Pedro. Founded one of the first European film clubs in 1920. After taking a degree in philosophy and letters, worked as assistant dir. to Jean Epstein on Mauprat and The Fall of the House of Usher. 1927, Assist. dir. La Sirene des Tropiques; 1928, Un Chien Andalou. 1930, L'Age D'or. Spanish films: 1932, Land Without Bread, Exec. prod.; Don Quentin el Amargao, La Hija de Juan Simon, Quien me Quiere a Mi?, Centinela!, Centinela! Alerta! 1939 & 42 worked on American propaganda films. Dir. in Mexico: 1947 Gran Casino; 1949, El Gran Calavera; 1950, Los Olvidalos (The Young and the Damned), Susana; 1951, Daughter of Deceit, Woman Without Love, Ascent to Heaven; 1952, El Bruto, The Adventures of Robinson Crusoe, El; 1953, Wuthering Heights, Illusion Travels By Streetcar; 1954, El Rio Y La Muerte; 1955. The Criminal Life of Archibaldo De La Cruz; 1956, La Mort en Ce Jerdin; 1958, Nazarin; 1959, La fievre monte a El Pao; 1960, The Young One; 1961, Viridana; 1962, The Exterminating Angel; 1965, Diary of Chambermaid, Simon of the Desert; 1967. Belle de Jour; 1969, The Milky Way, Tristana, The Discreet Charm of the Bourgeoisie, Le Fantome de la Liberte.

BUONO, VICTOR: Actor. b. San Diego, Calif. 1939. Studied English and drama at Vallanova and acted at Old Globe Theatre, San Diego.
PICTURES INCLUDE: Whatever Happened to Baby Jane?, Four for Texas, The Strangler, Robin and the Seven Hoods, Hush, Hush . . . Sweet Charlotte, The Greatest Story Ever Told, Young Dillinger, The Silencers, Who's Minding the Mint?, The Wrath of God, Arnold.

BURGER, HENRY: Executive. b. Pittsburgh, Pa., Mar. 26, 1915. Asst. mgr. and mgr., various theatres in Pittsburgh and W.Va.; asst. ad. pub. mgr., Pittsburgh Zone Warner Bros. Theatres, 1942; ad., pub. mgr., 1948; district mgr., Stanley Warner Theatres, Erie district, 1951; district mgr., Pittsburgh City Theaters, zone ad. pub. mgr., 1953; Zone mgr., Stanley-Warner Midwest-Zone Theatres, 1962; nat. adv. pub. dir., Stanley Warner Theatres, 1965; zone manager, 1967.

BURKE, ALFRED, Actor. b. London, England, 1918. Ent. films 154.
PICTURES INCLUDE: The Angry Silence, Moment of Danger, The Man Inside, The Man Upstairs, No Time To Die, Law and Disorder, Yangtse Incident, Interpol, Bitter Victory.
TV: The Crucible, Mock Auction, Parole, No Gun, No Guilt, The Big Knife, Parnell, The Strong Are Lonely, Home Of The Brave, The Birthday Party, The Watching Eye, Public Eye series.

BURKE, PAUL: Actor. b. New Orleans, La., July 21, 1926, e. Prep Schools, N.O., Pasadena Playhouse.
TV: Five Fingers, Harbor Master, Noah's Ark, Naked City, Playhouse 90, Studio One, Medic, Frontier, Men in Space, Man and the Challenge, Target, M-Squad, Black Saddle, Philip Marlowe, Mantin Kane, Line Up, Dragnet, Man Without a Gun, Tightrope, Panic, Highway Patrol, Men of Annapolis, Flight, Naked City, 12 O'Clock High.
PICTURES INCLUDE: Once You Kiss a Stranger, Daddy's Gone A-Hunting, Valley of the Dolls.

BURKS, J. COOPER: Executive. b. Pilot Point, Texas, April 26, 1919. e. Oklahoma City University Oklahoma City Law School, American Institute of Banking (Special Finance Courses), U.S. Navy Schools at Wesleyan College, Middletown, Conn. University of North Carolina, Chapel Hill, N.C., Virginia Polytechnic Institute, Blacksburg, Va. Military: Commander USNR-Ret. WWII PT Boats, North Atlantic then as Naval Aviator—latter part WWII and Korean War. Business experience: Prior to theatre business, was in banking & construction business. Formed present company March, 1970. Now president at chairman of the board of AATI (American Automated Theatres, Inc.) in Oklahoma City. Military Affairs Committee, Chamber of Commerce, Life Member-Navy League.

BURLINSON, JOHN J. JR.: Executive. b. New York, N.Y., Dec. 26, 1930. e. Collegiate Sch. N.Y., Fordham U.; dir. promotion and adv., Henry Regnery Co. (book publishers). 1960; sls. mgr. Regnery, 1962; N.Y. rep., US Press Association, 1963; v.p., Quigley Publishing Co., N.Y., 1964. Ad Dir. Better Theatres Theatre vending; adv. mgr. Motion Picture Daily, 1966; National Screen Service Corp. 1970, dir. inter-corporate promotion. 1972; dir. of admin., National Theatre Supply; 1974, gen. mgr., NTS; 1977, v.p. & gen. mgr., EPRAD, Inc.; 1980, named pres., EPRAD: Elected exec. dir. & treasurer of TESMA in 1967. Co-director NATO/NAC/TESMA Trade Show; secr. & dir., M.P. Pioneers, 1970; hon. dir. TESMA, 1971; member SMPTE, Variety Club. 1972; Vice President Equipment Assoc.; 1974; bd. mem. TEA and Conference chm.; Chm. annual NY Variety Golf Tournament 1972–75; vice chairman, Motion Picture Div., Catholic Charities of NY, 1972–75.

BURNETT, CAROL: Actress-comedienne-singer; b. San Antonio, Apr. 26, 1936; Jody and Louise (Creighton) Burnett; e. Hollywood H.S., UCLA. m. Joseph Hamilton, 1963; children-Carrie Louise, Judy Ann, Erin Kate. Introduced comedy song, I Made a Fool of Myself Over John Foster Dulles, 1957; Broadway debut in Once Upon a Mattress, 1959; regular performer Garry Moore TV show, 1959–62; appeared several CBS-TV spls., 1962–63, Broadway play Fade Out-Fade In, 1964, play Plaza Suite, 1970, film Pete 'n Tillie, 1972, musical play I Do, I Do, 1973; Same Time Next Year, 1977; Film Front Page, club engagements Harrah's Club, The Sands, Caesar's Palace; star Carol Burnett Show, CBS-TV. CBS-TV Spec. "6 Rooms Riv Vu" 74; "Twigs" The Grass Is Always Greener, Friendly Fire, The Tenth Month. 75. Films: The Front Page, A Wedding (best actress, San Sebastian Film Festival), Health, The Four Seasons, Chu Chu and the Philly Flash. Recipient outstanding comedienne award Am. Guild Variety Artists, 5 times; 5 Emmy awards for outstanding variety performance Acad. TV Arts and Scis., TV Guide award for outstanding female performer 1961, 62, 63; Peabody award, 1963; Golden Globe award for outstanding comedienne of year Fgn. Press Assn.; Woman of Year award Acad. TV Arts and Scis. One of the world's 20 most admired women voted in poll conducted by George Gallup (1977). First Annual National

Television Critics Award for Outstanding Performance, 1977.

BURNETT, W. R.: Writer. b. Springfield, Ohio, Nov. 25, 1899; e. Miami Mil. Inst., Ohio State U. Novelist (Little Caesar, Dark Hazard, Iron Man). Author of collab. s.p. including Scarface, Heart of a City, Whole Town's Talking, Dr. Socrates, High Sierra, Wake Island, This Gun for Hire, Yellow Sky, Belle Starr's Daughter, Asphalt Jungle, Vendetta, Iron Man, I Died a Thousand Times, The Racket, Dangerous Mission, Captain Lightfoot, Illegal.

BURNS, GEORGE: Actor. r.n. Nathan Birnbaum; b. New York City. In vaudeville as singer in children's quartet, later as roller skater, then comedian; formed team Burns & (Gracie) Allen 1925; m. partner 1926. Team many years on Keith and Orpheum vaudeville circuits, then on screen in Paramount short subjects, on radio in England; in 1930 began long career Amer. radio. Feature picture debut 1932 in The Big Broadcast.
PICTURES INCLUDE: International House, Love in Bloom, College Swing, Honolulu, Two Girls and A Sailor, The Sunshine Boys, Oh, God, Just You and Me, Kid, Oh, God! Book II.
TV: Co-star Burns & Allen show, CBS-TV.

BURR, RAYMOND: Actor. b. New Westminister, B.C., Canada, May 21, 1917; e. Stanford U., U of Calif., Columbia U, U of Chungking. Forestry svce.: appeared on stage in many countries in Night Must Fall, Mandarin, Crazy with the Heat, Duke in Darkness; dir., Pasdena Community Playhouse, 1943; on radio.
PICTURES INCLUDE: Pitfall, Raw Deal, Key to the City, His Kind of Woman, Place in the Sun, New Mexico, Meet Danny Wilson, Mara Maru, Horizons West, Blue Gardenia, Fort Algiers, Casanova's Big Night, Gorilla at Large, Khyber Patrol, Rear Window, Passion, They Were So Young, You're Never Too Young, A Man Alone, Count Three and Pray, Please Murder Me, Godzilla King of the Monsters, Great Day in the Morning, Secret of Treasure Mountain, Cry in the Night, P.J.
TV: Perry Mason series, CBS-TV, 1957. Ironside series, CBS, 1970, Centennial (1978).

BURRELL-DAVIS, Derek: Freelance producer, director with own company "B.D. Productions": b. York 1918 entered m.p 1946 with J. Arthur Rank Org. 1950 joined B.B.C. T.V. as stage manager then producer. 1951 producer North Region. 1955 returned London, senior producer then executive producer. 1970 editor in charge B.B.C. T.V. O.B. entertainment progs. 1971 Head of Network Production Centre Manchester. 1977 left B.B.C. to freelance. Reponsible for wide range of television productions covering sport, features and entertainment in U.K. and Europe.
PRODUCTIONS INCLUDE: Continental, Russian and British Circuses, State Dance Groups, The Bolshoi Ballet. Satellite Work Hook-Up programmes. The Beatles, It's a Knock-Out, Gala Variety, etc. Currently producer "3-2-1" (network) series for Y.T.V.

BURRILL, TIMOTHY: Producer, executive. b. North Wales, 1931. e. Eton College, Sorbonne Univ., Paris, Grenadier Guards 2 yrs., then London Shipping Co. Ent. m.p. ind. as resident prod. mgr. Samaritan Films Ltd., working on shorts, commercials, documentaries, 1954. Ass't dir. on feature films: The Criminal, The Valiant Years (TV series), On the Fiddle, Reach for Glory, War Lover. Prod. mgr.: The Cracksman, Night Must Fall, Lord Jim, Yellow Rolls Royce, The Heroes of Telemark. Resident producer with World Film Services, 1968–1969: Privilege, Oedipus The King, 1969–1970: A Severed Head, Three Sisters. 1970 produced two films on pop music for Anglo-EMI. 1971 assoc. prod., Macbeth. 1972 first production administrator National Film School in U.K. 1973 Prod. Alpha Beta. 1974 Post production administrator The Three Musketeers. 1974: Prod. TV Special The Canterville Ghost; 1975: asst. prod., That Lucky Touch; 1976: UK Administrator, The Prince and the Pauper; 1977: North American production controller, Superman; 1974/80: Council Member of BAFTA. Produced Polanski's Tess. 1979–80, man. dir., Allied Stars Council mbr., BAFTA, 1974–80. V. chmn. film, 79–80.

BURROWS, JOHN, H.: Producer. b. Brooklyn, N.Y., September 4, 1924. e. Yale, New York U. Law with interruption for service. U.S. Navy, World War II, lieut., son of George D. Burrows, vice-president Allied Artists, started film career as salesman for AA later joining studio; ass. prod. Lindsley Parsons Productions.

BURRUD, BILL: Exec. b. Los Angeles, Calif., Jan. 12, 1925. e. U. of Southern Calif., B.S.; Harvard Bus. School, ent. ind. as child actor; U.S. Navy, W.W. II; formed Bill Burrud Prods., 1952.
TV: Animal World, World of the Sea, Safari to Adventure, Challenging Sea, Secret World of Reptiles, Vanishing Africa, The Great American Wilderness, Predators of the Sea, Creatures of the Amazon, The Amazing Apes, The Amazing World.

BURSTYN, ELLEN: Actress. b. Detroit, 1932. Majored in art; was fashion model in Texas when 18. Moved to Montreal as dancer; then N.Y. to do TV commercials, appearing for a year on the Jackie Gleason show. In 1957 turned to dramatics and won lead in show, Fair Game. Then went to Hollywood to do TV and films. Returned to N.Y. to study acting with Lee Strasberg; worked in TV serial, The Doctors.
PICTURES INCLUDE: For Those Who Think Young, Goodbye, Charlie, Tropic of Cancer, Alex in Wonderland, The Last Picture Show, The King of Marvin Gardens, The Exorcist, Harry and Tonto, Alice Doesn't Live Here Anymore, Providence, A Dream of Passion, Same Time Next Year, Resurrection, Silence of the North.

BURTON, BERNARD: Producer. Started as film ed.; prod. "Vagabond Lady" 1935.
PICTURES INCLUDE: She Gets Her Man, Fighting Youth, Invisible Ray, Showboat, When Love is Young, One Hundred Men and a Girl, You're a Sweetheart, Midnight Intruder, Little Tough Guy, Three Smart Girls Grow Up, Spring Parade, Moonlight in Havana, Get Help to Love, Gentleman Joe Palooka, Fighting Mad, Smart Woman, Underworld Story, Cry Danger, The Highwayman, Triple Cross, Beast from 20,000 Fathoms.

BURTON, LeVAR: Actor. b. Landstuhl, Germany, Feb. 16, 1957. e. Univ. of So. Calif. Signed to play role of Kunta Kinte in TV series, Roots, while still in school. Appears frequently on public TV, hosts children's show, Bebop, (PBC).
PICTURES: Looking for Mr. Goodbar, The Hunter.
TELEVISION: Roots, Billy: Portrait of a Street Kid, Battered, The Ron LeFlore Story, Dummy.

BURTON, MARGARET: Actress, opera singer. b. Keighley, Eng., March 18, 1924. Leading opera roles at Sadler's Wells, London, in La Belle Helene, La Vie Parisienne, and Bluebeard. M.p. debut, 1962, in The Comedy Man. Numerous broadcasts and TV appearances in England and the U.S. London stage debut in Mother Goose, Palladium, 1954–55. Broadway debut in Time Gentlemen Please, 1961–62.
STAGE: (London) Twenty Minutes South, Romance in Candlelight, The Three Caskets, Annie, Mandrake, Oliver! (1978–80).
TV: The Gold Old Days, The Quick One, Harpers West One, The Plane Makers, Z-Cars, A Variety of Reg Varney, The Harry Secombe Show, Free As a Bird, Orson Welles Great Mysteries, Pygmalion Smith, South Riding, The Tomorrow People, The Last of the Summer Wine, Angels, Send in the Girls (1978), Sally Ann (1979), Coronation Street (1980).

BURTON, RICHARD: Actor. r.n. Richard Jenkins; b. Pontrhydyfen, So. Wales, Nov. 10, 1925. e. Oxford. Actor, legit. stage, England, Lady Is Not for Burning, Monserrat; actor, Bway, legit. stage, The Legend of Lovers; 8 yrs. on radio BBC, London.
PICTURES INCLUDE: The Last Days of Dolwyn, Now Barrabas, Waterfront, The Woman with No Name; with Old Vic; appeared in Henry V, Othello, Troilus and Cressida, Iago; Time Remembered, 1957–8, New York; Camelot, 1960–61, N.Y.U.S. film debut, My Cousin Rachel, Star of Tomorrow, The Desert Rats, The Robe, Prince of Players, Alexander The Great, Rains of Ranchipur, Seawife, Bitter Victory, Look Back in Anger, The Bramble Bush, Cleopatra, The V.I.P.'s, Becket, Night of the Iguana, The Sandpiper, The Spy Who Came in From the Cold, Who's Afraid of Virginia Woolf?; The Taming of The Shrew, Dr. Faustus, The Comedians, Candy, Boom, Where Eagles Dare, Staircase, Anne of the Thousand Days, Hammersmith is Out, The Assassination of Trotsky, Bluebeard, Massacre in Rome, The Klansman, The Voyage, Exorcist II: The Heretic, Equus, The Medusa Touch, The Wild Geese, Absolution, Sgt. Steiner II, Tristan & Iseult, Circle of Two.
TV: His and Hers (movie), Brief Encounter.
PLAYS: Camelot, Hamlet, Othello, The Tempest, Henry V, Equus

BUSCH, NIVEN: Writer. b. New York City, N.Y., Apr. 26, 1903; e. Princeton U.; p. Briton Niven Busch, former v-p Lewis J. Selznick Enterprises; Exec. prod., Samuel Goldwyn Productions; m. Phyllis Cooper, 1936; children: Peter, Briton, Terence, Mary Kelly, Joseph, Nicholas, and Eliza. m. Carmencita Baker, 1956. div. 1969, m. Suzanne de Sanz 1973. Assoc. ed. Time mag., 1923–31; assoc. ed. & contrib. New Yorker, 1927–31; numerous articles, many national magazines. Regents professor, Univ. of Calif. 1971–78. Special lectures on film.
AUTHOR: Books: Twenty One Americans, Carrington Incident, Duel in the Sun, They Dream of Home, Day of the Conquerors, The Furies, The Hate Merchant, The Actor, California Street, The San Franciscans, The Gentlemen from California, The Takeover, No Place for a Hero, Continent's Edge.
PICTURES INCLUDE: The Crowd Roars, In Old Chicago, The Westerner, The Postman Always Rings Twice, Duel in the Sun, Till the End of Time, Pursued, Moss Rose; prod., The Capture, Distant Drums, Man from the Alamo, Moonlighter, Treasure of Pancho Villa, Moss Rose, He

Was Her Man, The Angels Wash Their Face, Big Shakedown, Little Miss Pinkerton, Regents Professor, Univ. of Cal., Irvine, 1971–75. San Diego, 1974; Lecturer Berkeley, 1977.

BUTLER, DAWS: Actor (Voice), r.n. Charles Dawson Butler. b. Toledo, Nov. 16, 1916. With Time for Beany, 1948–53. Host (voice) of Off to See the Wizard TV program. From 1953 to present, various cartoon voices, including: Yogi Bear, Huckleberry Hound, Quick Draw McGraw, Loopie DeLoop, Chilly Willy, Peter Potamus, Mr. Jinx.

BUTTERFIELD, ELIZABETH: Production Manager. b. London, England e. London. Extensive theatrical experience as stage manager for The Old Vic Company (Michael Benthall, Tyrone Guthrie) and Donald Wolfit Company. Emigrated to Canada in 1957. Television experience includes: Quentin Durgens M.P. and Whiteoaks Of Jaina for C.B.C., Seaway, Ind.
    PICTURES INCLUDE: A Fan's Notes, Warner Bros. 1971; Sunday In The Country, Quadrant, 1973; It Seemed Like A Good Idea At The Time, Quadrant, 1975; Find the Lady, Quadrant, 1976; Running, Buena Vista, 1978; Middle Age Crazy, Torment, 1979.

BUTTOLPH, DAVID: Music director.
    PICTURES INCLUDE: Phantom of Rue Morgue, Secret of the Incas, Bounty Hunter, Long John Silver, Jump Into Hell, Target Zero, Lone Ranger, Steel Jungle, Santiago, Burning Hills, Cry in the Night.

BUTTONS, RED: Performer. r.n. Aaron Chwatt; b. N.Y.C., Feb. 5, 1919. Singer at the age of 13; comic, Minsky's. U.S. Army, 1943; in Army and film version of Winged Victory.
    TV: Vickie, Wine, Women and Song, Barefoot Boy With Cheek, Hold It. Many TV appearances; star of Red Buttons Show CBS-TV, 1953; Best Comedian award 1953; NBC-TV, 1954; on screen in Sayonara (Academy Award best actor in supporting role 1957).
    PICTURES INCLUDE: Imitation General, The Big Circus, Five Weeks in a Balloon, Harlow, They Shoot Horses Don't They, Who Killed Mary What's 'er name?, The Poseidon Adventure, Gable and Lombard, Viva, Knievel!, Movie Movie, When Time Ran Out.

BUTTS, R. DALE: Composer. b. Lamasco, Ky., March 12, 1910; e. Louisville Conservatory of Music. Started in vaudeville at 16, later playing, arranging for dance bands; staff arranger, pianist, radio stations; to Republic Pictures, 1944.
    PICTURES INCLUDE: The Plunderers, Too Late for Tears, House by the River, Sea Hornet, The Outcast, Geraldine, Shanghai Story, Hell's Outpost, Santa Fe Passage, Fighting Chance, No Man's Woman, Headline Hunter's, Lay That Rifle Down, Double Jeopardy, City of Shadows, Terror at Midnight, Stranger at My Door, Dakota Incident.

BUXBAUM, JAMES M.: Executive, producer, writer. b. Jamaica N.Y., March 8. e. Harvard, B.A., 1949, Columbia Law School, LL.B., 1955, spec. studies, The Hague Acad., Netherlands, 1953. Story ed. ZIV, Ivan Tors' Sea Hunt series, then assoc. prod., ZIV-CBS, Ivan Tors' Aquanauts series, story ed., 1957–60. Attorney, Wm. Morris Agency, 1962–63. Joined Ivan Tors Films, Inc. as v.p., prod. and wrote many episodes of Flipper series, 1964; exec. v.p. Ivan Tors Miami Studios, 1967–69; exec. v.p. Ivan Tors Films, Inc. 1968–69. Gen. mgr. Amer. Film Institute Center, Beverly Hills, 1969. Member: State Bar of Calif., Amer. Bar Assoc. Exec. in charge of prod. for Island of the Lost.

BUZZELL, EDWARD: Actor, director. b. Brooklyn, N.Y., Nov. 13, 1907. Musical comedy star prior to directorial debut 1932.
    PICTURES INCLUDE: Best Foot Forward, Youngest Profession, Keep Your Powder Dry, Three Wise Fools, Song of Thin Man, Neptune's Daughter, At the Circus, Woman of Distinction, Emergency Wedding, Easy to Wed, Confidentially Connie, Ain't Misbehavin', My Favorite Husband.

BUZZI, RUTH: Actress. b. Wequetequak, CT, July 24, 1939. e. Pasadena Playhouse. Launched TV career on Garry Moore Show as comedy partner of Dom DeLuise. Created character Gladys Ormphby with Artie Johnson on TV's Laugh-In.
    PICTURES: Freaky Friday, The Apple Dumpling Gang Rides Again, The Villain, Chu Chu and the Philly Flash, Easter Sunday.
    TELEVISION: The Entertainers, The Donny & Marie Show (semi-regular), Rowan & Martin's Laugh-In, The Dean Martin Show, The Dean Martin Roasts, The Tonight Show, Kroft's Superstars, Rhoda (recurring role), Gladys and Tyrone (cartoon show, partial creator and voice of character) etc.
    STAGE: Sweet Charity (Broadway), The Ruth Buzzi Show (Las Vegas), Pasadena Playhouse Theatre, and summer stock.
    AWARDS: 4 Grammy nominations; Golden Globe winner, AGVA Variety Artist of the Year, 1977, Rhode Island Hall of Fame, Presidential Commendation for outstanding artist in the field of entertainment, 1980.

BYGRAVES, MAX: Comedian, actor. b. London, Eng., October 16, 1922. e. St. Joseph's R.C. School, Rotherhithe. After RAF service, touring revues and London stage, M.P. debut 1949 in Skimpy in The Navy. TV debut in 1953, with own show.
    TV: Roamin Holiday series.
    PICTURES INCLUDE: Tom Brown's Schooldays, Charlie Moon, A Cry from the Streets, Boobikins, Spare the Rod, Autobiograph "I Wanna Tell you A Story" Pub. 1976.
    NOVEL: The Milkman's on His Way, pub. 1977.

BYRD, CARUTH C.: Production Executive. b. Dallas, Texas, March 25, 1942. Multi-millionaire businessman, chm. of Caruth C. Byrd Enterprises, Inc., who entered entertainment industry forming Communications Network Inc. in 1972, producer of TV commercials. Was principal investor in film Santee (1972) and in 1973 formed Caruth C. Byrd Prods. to make theatrical features.
    PICTURES INCLUDE: Allan and Murph the Surf, The Monkeys of Bandapur (both exec. prod.).

BYRD, JOHN: Writer, director, producer. Entered m.p. industry 1934 via scenario dept. Rock Studios, Elstree; visited Hollywood to study requirements of U.S. market, 1939; 1940–45 B.B.C. War Correspondent, 1945–46 Riverside Studios, 1947–8 British National Studios.
    PICTURES INCLUDE: Murder in Reverse, World Owes Me a Living, Waltz Time. 1949 formed own org. prod. bus. TV films. Prod. films in South Africa, Uganda, Kenya, Portugal and Mexico. Filming Durgapur Steelworks project, India, 1961; Steel Strides Ahead. Concerning Colour, Design for Tall Building, Jungle to Steel Town, Steelworks in Action, 1962–4; Dryer Felt Loom, Bridging the Highways, 1965; Filming in Afghanistan, 1966; Filming in South Africa, 1967; Built from Top, 1968; Building With Steel and Plastics, 1969; The Desert Will Yield, 1970; Long Sea Outfall, One Steelworks, One Contract, Highweld Process. 1971: Go-Con Process, Mechanical Handling, 1972. Undersea Tunnel to Hong Kong. 1973: Contract 1306—Zambia, Bridge Across the Avon; 1974 filming for British Steel Corp.
    OTHER PICTURES: Murder in Reverse, World Owes Me a Living, Waltz Time. 1974–5 Anchor Project for British Steel Corporation. 1976–77 Filming in Mexico AHMSA Steelworks project. 1977, More Steel for Mexico; 1978, Filming in South Africa; 1979, Filming in South Africa; 1980, Filming in France & Spain.

BYRNES, EDWARD: Actor. b. New York, N.Y., July 30, 1933. e. Harren H.S.; prof. debut, Joe E. Brown's Circus Show; appeared on stage in Tea and Sympathy.
    PICTURES INCLUDE: Periscope, Marjorie Morningstar, Secret Invasion, Wicked, Wicked.
    TV: Matinee Theatre, Crossroads, Jim Bowie, Wire Service, Navy Log, Oh Susanna!, 77 Sunset Strip.

BRYON, CHARLES ANTHONY: Producer. b. Constantinople, December 15, 1919. e. University of Paris, Harvard; Army Air Force 1942–1947. With UNESCO in Paris; NBC-International produced and wrote foreign programs for Dept. of State; public relations ECA mission to France. Film industry 1952 as director of public relations, research, Louis de Rochemont Associates, European prod. Cinerama Holiday; Dragon Prod., 1959, pres., exec. prod. of: The Silken Affair, Chase a Crooked Shadow, etc.

BYRON, KATHLEEN: Actress. b. London, England, Jan. 11, 1922; e. London U., Old Vic. Co. student 1942. Screen debut in Young Mr. Pitt 1943.
    PICTURES INCLUDE: Silver Fleet, Black Narcissus, Matter of Life and Death, Small Back Room, Madness of the Heart, Reluctant Widow, Prelude to Fame, Scarlet Thread, Tom Brown's Schooldays, Four Days, Hell Is Sold Out, I'll Never Forget You, Gambler and the Lady, Young Bess, Night of the Silvery Moon, Profile, Secret Venture, Hand in Hand, Night of the Eagle, Hammerhead, Wolfshead, Private Road, Twins of Evil, Craze, Abdication, One of Our Dinosaurs Is Missing.
    TV: The Lonely World of Harry Braintree, All My Own Work, Emergency Ward 10, Probation Officer, Design for Murder, Sergeant Cork, Oxbridge 2000, The Navigators, The Worker; Hereward the Wake, Breaking Point, Vendetta, Play To Win, Who is Sylvia, Portrait of a Lady, Callan, You're Wrecking My Marriage, Take Three Girls, The Confession of Mariona Evans, Paul Temple, The Worker, The Moonstone, The Challengers, The Golden Bowl, The Edwardians, The New Life, Menace, The Rivals of Sherlock Holmes, The Brontes, On Call, Edward VII, Sutherland's Law, Crown Court, Anne of Avonlea, Heidi, Notorious Woman, General Hospital, North & South, Angelo, Within these Walls, Jubilee, Z Cars, Tales from the Supernatural, Secret Army, An Englishman's Castle, The Professionals, Forty Weeks, Emmerdale Farm, Blake Seven.

BYRON, WARD: TV Prod.-writer-dir. b. N.Y.C., June 2, 1910. e. New York. Orchestra leader, 1929–32; radio prod., writer, 1932–39. Ent. TV as asst. to prog. dir. of ABC; writer & producer of Paul Whiteman show in 1950; app'td exec. prod. of ABC-TV in 1950. Exec. prod., Canadian TV, Young & Rubicam, 1955–57. Freelance writer prod., TV Specials

& film series, v.p. gen, mgr. Trans-Nat'l Communications O'way Recording Studios; 1970, v.p. & sec. International Coproductions, motion picture distributors.

BYRUM, JOHN: Writer—Director. b. Winnetka, Ill., March 14, 1947. e. N.Y. Univ. Film School. First job as "go-fer" on industrial films and cutting dailies for underground filmmakers. Went to England where wrote 1st s.p., Comeback. From 1970–73 was in N.Y.C: writing and re-writing scripts for low-budget films.
PICTURES INCLUDE: Mahogany (s.p.), Inserts (s.p., dir.), Harry and Walter Go to New York (story, s.p.), Heart Beat (s.p. dir.), Sphinx (s.p.).

C

CAAN, JAMES: Actor. b. New York, N.Y., March 26, 1939; e. Hofstra Coll.: Appeared off-Broadway in La Ronde, 1961.
PICTURES INCLUDE: Lady in a Cage, The Glory Guys, Red Line 7000, Eldorado, Games, Journey to Shiloh, Submarine XQ/⅛, Rain People, Rabbit, Run, Brian's Song (TV), The Godfather, Slither, Cinderella Liberty, Freebie and the Bean, The Gambler, Godfather II, Funny Lady, Rollerball, The Killer Elite, Harry and Walter Go To New York, Silent Movie, A Bridge Too Far, Another Man, Another Chance, Comes a Horseman, Chapter Two, Hide in Plain Sight (also dir.), Thief.

CACOYANNIS, MICHAEL: Producer, director, writer. b. Cyprus, June 11, 1922. Studied law in London, admitted to bar at age 21. Became a producer of BBC's wartime Greek programs while attending dramatic school. After acting on the stage in England, left in 1952 for Greece, where he made his first film, Windfall in Athens, with his own original script. While directing Greek classical plays, he continued making films.
PICTURES INCLUDE: Stella, The Girl in Black, A Matter of Dignity, Our Last Spring, The Wastrel, Electra, Zorba the Greek, The Day the Fish Came Out, The Trojan Women.

CADELL, JEAN: Actress. b. Edinburgh, Scotland, Sept. 13, 1884; e. Edinburgh & Paris. Early prof. stage appearances on tour in Gt. Brit., beginning in London 1906 (The Inspector General); with Sir George Alexander's Co. in Eng.; later numerous London, N.Y. prods.
PICTURES INCLUDE: Madeleine, Reluctant Widow, No Place for Jennifer, Obsessed, Whisky Galore, Meet Mr. Lucifer, Little Hut, The Surgeon's Knife, Rockets Galore, Upstairs and Downstairs, A Taste of Money, V.I.P.
TV: Whiteoakes, Arsenic and Old Lace, Doomsday for Dyson, Mary Rose, Eustace Diamonds (serial).

CAESAR, IRVING: Author, composer, publisher. b. New York, N.Y., July 4, 1895, e. C.C.N.Y. Abroad with Henry Ford on Peace Ship, World War I; songwriter since then, several songs with George Gershwin, songwriter for stage, screen and radio, including Swanee, Tea for Two, Sometimes I'm Happy, I want to Be Happy, Lady Play Your Mandolin, Songs of Safety, Songs of Friendship, Songs of Health and Pledge of Allegiance to the Flag.

CAESAR, SID: Performer. b. Yonkers, N.Y. Sept. 8, 1922. Musician. Joined Coast Guard in 1942. Appeared in "Tars and Spars." Signed for Broadway Revue by Max Liebman, 1949. Star of Your Show of Shows on NBC-TV 1950–54; star of Caesar's Hour, 1954–1957; voted best comedian (tied) in M.P. Daily's TV poll, 1951. Best Comedian, 1952; Best Comedy Team (with Imogene Coca), 1953; 5 Emmy Awards 1957; Sylvania Award, 1958. Sid Caesar Invites You, 1958; Formed Shelbrick Corp., TV, 1959; TV series, As Caesar Sees It, 1962; Bway Play: Little Me, 1962–64; The Sid Caesar Show, 1963–64.
PICTURES INCLUDE: It's a Mad, Mad, Mad, Mad World, The Spirit is Willing, The Busy Body, Guide for the Married Man, Ten from Your Show of Shows, Airport 1975, Silent Movie, Grease, The Cheap Detective, History of the World—Part I.

CAGNEY, JAMES: Actor. b. New York City, July 1, 1904; e. Columbia U. In vaudeville 1924 and later; on dramatic stage ("Outside Looking In," "Women Go On Forever," etc.). On screen from 1931. Pres. Screen Actors Guild 1942–43. Voted one of best ten Money-Making Stars in Motion Pictures Herald-Fame Poll 1935, 39, 40, 41, 42, 43. Academy Award, 1942 (Yankee Doodle Dandy).
PICTURES INCLUDE: Doorway to Hell, Steel Highway, Crowd Roars, Jimmy the Gent, A Midsummer Night's Dream, Angels With Dirty Faces, Each Dawn I Die, The Strawberry Blonde, Yankee Doodle Dandy, Johnny Come Lately, Blood on the Sun, 13 Rue Madeleine, Time of Your Life, White Heat, The West Point Story, Come Fill the Cup, Starlift, What Price Glory? A Lion is in the Streets, Run for Cover, Love Me Or Leave Me, Mr. Roberts, Seven Little Foys, Tribute to a Bad Man, These Wilder Years, Man of a Thousand Faces; dir., Short Cut to Hell, Shake Hands

with the Devil, The Gallant Hours, One, Two, Three, Ragtime.

CAGNEY, JEANNE: Actress. b. New York City, Mar. 25, e. Hunter College, sister of James Cagney. m. Jack Morrison.
THEATRE: Broadway: I'll Take The High Road, A Place of Our Own, Streets Are Guarded, The Iceman Cometh, La Jolla, Marriage Go Round, World of Carl Sandburg, The Just.
PICTURES INCLUDE: All Women Have Secrets, Golden Gloves, Queen of the Mob, Yankee Doodle Dandy, Time of Your Life, Don't Bother to Knock, Quicksand, A Lion is in the Streets, Kentucky Rifle, Man of A Thousand Faces, Town Tamer.
TV FILMS: Big Hello, Legal Tender, Hill, Number One, Trial at Tara, Mr. and Mrs. North, Big Town, TV Readers Digest, Wild Bill Hickok.
LIVE TV: Jack Benny Show, This Is Your Life, Lux Video, Stairway to Stardom, Pantomime Quiz, Wild Bill Hickok, Pstter Potter Platter Panel, A Capture, Red Skelton Show, Fashion Commentator on Queen for a Day.

CAGNEY, WILLIAM J.: Producer. b. New York; brother of James Cagney, actor. e. City Coll., N.Y. (law student). Adv. rep., Fairchild Publications. From 1933 on screen in Ace of Aces, Lost in the Stratosphere, Stolen Harmony, etc. Became talent agent, Hollywood, then in 1940 joined Warner Bros. as assoc. prod. (The Strawberry Blonde), The Bride Came C.O.D., Captains of the Clouds, Yankee Doodle Dandy, etc.). In 1942 org. (with James C.) Cagney Prods.: pres. Cagney Prod.
PICTURES INCLUDE: Blood on the Sun, Johnny Come Lately, Time of Your Life, Kiss Tomorrow Goodbye, Only the Valiant, Bugles in the Afternoon, A Lion Is in the Streets.

CAHN, SAMMY: Lyricist, Producer. b. New York, N.Y. June 18, 1913; e. Seward Park H.S. Org. dance band with Saul Chaplin; collab. song writer for shows. m.p.
PLAYS INCLUDE: High Button Shoes, Skyscraper, Walking Happy, many songs, 30 Acad. Award Nominations, Four Oscars for 3 Coins in Fountain, All The Way, High Hopes, and Call Me Irresponsible! Only TV Emmy ever given a song "Love & Marriage" From the TV award winning "Our Town".
PICTURES INCLUDE: Anchors Aweigh, 3 Coins in Fountain, Romance on High Seas, Some Came Running, Robin & Seven Hoods, The Tender Trap, Pocketfull of Miracles, Thoroughly Modern Millie. 1972, inducted into Songwriters' Hall of Fame.

CAIN, SUGAR: Actress. r.n. Constance McCain. b. Jerome, Ariz., Mar. 13. e. Univ. Washington, B.A., radio-drama; Colo. Woman's Col., A.A. journalism; Columbia Univ., grad. TV. MP. Reg. on radio serials. Hopalong Cassidy, Clyde Beatty Show, Night club act, Mexico; appeared TV, Hollywood & N.Y. Plays include: nat. tours, Pajama Tops, In One Bed, Idiots Delight, Streetcar Named Desire, The Rainmaker, Dead End, Druid Circle.
PICTURES INCLUDE: Breakstone Affair, Life with Edmer, I've Been Here Before, Monster from 20,000 Fathoms, Dalton Women, I Shot Billy the Kid, Hostle Country, Dalton Gang, Africa Screams; Sporting Club, Apple Man, Klute, Panic in Needle Park, The French Connection, Effect of Gamma Rays, Summer Wishes, Winter Dreams; Dir.-writer, m.p. short, Rama.

CAINE, MICHAEL: Actor. b. London, Eng., 1933.
TV: The Compartment, The Playmates, Hobson's Choice, Funny Noises With Their Mouths, The Way With Reggie, Luck of the Draw, Hamlet, The Other Man.
PICTURES INCLUDE: Zulu, Ipcress File, Alfie, The Wrong Box, Gambit, Funeral in Berlin, Hurry Sundown, Billion Dollar Brain, Deadfall, The Magus, Play Dirty, Italian Job, The Battle of Britain, Too Late the Hero, Get Carter, Kidnapped, Zee and Company, Pulp, Sleuth, The Black Windmill, The Destructors, The Wilby Conspiracy, Peepers, The Romantic Englishwoman, The Man Who Would Be King, Harry and Walter Go to New York, The Eagle Has Landed, A Bridge Too Far, The Silver Bears, The Swarm, Ashanti, California Suite, Beyond the Poseidon Adventure, The Island, Dressed to Kill, The Hand, Victory.

CALHOUN, RORY: Actor. r.n. Francis Timothy Durgin. b. Los Angeles, Calif., Aug. 8, 1923. e. Santa Cruz H.S. Worked as logger, miner, cowpuncher, for firefighter; m.p. debut in Something for the Boys, 1944.
PICTURES INCLUDE: Sunday Dinner for a Soldier, Nob Hill, Great John L, Red House, Adventure Island, That Hagen Girl, Sand, Massacre River, Ticket to Tomahawk, County Fair, I'd Climb the Highest Mountain, Rogue River, Meet Me After the Show, With a Song in My Heart, Way of a Gaucho, The Silver Whip, Powder River, How to Marry a Millionaire, River of No Return, Yellow Tomahawk, Bullet Is Waiting, Dawn at Socorro, Four Guns to the Border, The Looters, Ain't Misbehavin', Shotgun, Domino and Actor; actor, Treasure of Pancho Villa, The Spoilers, Red Sundown, Raw Edge, Flight to Hongkong, Utah Blaine,

Big Caper, Finger On the Trigger, Young Fury, Black Spurs, Adventures of Marco Polo, Colossus of Rhodes.
TV: The Texans.

CALL, CHARLES W.: Exec. b. New York, N.Y., Century Theatres, 1933; chief usher; asst. mgr.; student mgr.; mgr., 1937–42; U.S. Army Air Force, 1942–46; mgr., various theatres, Century Circuit, 1946–50; field rep., L.I. theatres; adv. & publ. exec., home office, 1957–63; asst. v.p., 1963–78; Joined United Artists as mgr. co-op adv., 1979.

CALLAN, MICHAEL: Actor, singer, dancer. b. Philadelphia, Pa. Singer, dancer, Philadelphia night clubs; to New York in musicals, including The Boy Friend and West Side Story; dancer Copacabana; in short-run plays, Las Vegas: 5 month run starred in That Certain Girl. Guest starred on major dramatic TV shows and Occasional Wife (series, star).
PICTURES INCLUDE: debut, They Came to Cordura, The Flying Fontaines, Because They're Young, Pepe, Mysterious Island, Gidget Goes Hawaiian, 13 West Street, Bon Voyage, The Interns, The Victors, The "New" Interns, Cat Ballou, Frasier, The Sensuous Lion, Lepke, The Photographer, The Cat and The Canary (1977), Record City (1977); The Donner Party (1978).
TELEVISION: Blind Ambition, Scruples.

CALLEY, JOHN: executive. b. New Jersey, 1930. Dir. of night time programming, dir. programming sales, NBC, 1951–57; prod. exec. and TV prod. Henry Jaffe Enterprises, 1957; v.p. in charge of Radio and Television, Ted Bates Advertising Agency, 1958; joined Filmways, Inc., 1960; exec. v.p. and prod. to 1969; exec. v.p. chg. world-wide prod. Warner Bros.; Pres., W.B. from Jan. 6, 1975; vice chm. bd., 1977.
PICTURES INCLUDE: Wheeler Dealer, The Americanization of Emily, Topkapi, The Cincinnati Kid, Loved One, Don't Make Waves, Ice Station Zebra, Catch-22.

CALLOW, EVERETT C.: Publicist. b. Perth Amboy, N.J. e. St. John's Coll. On ed. staff N.Y. World; service staff chief Paramount Thea., N.Y., 1926; mgr. Keith & Albee Theas., Phila., 1928; mgr. Stanley Theatre, Phila., 1929–31; dist. theatre mgr. various dists. in N.J., Pa. & Del.; apptd. dir. of adv. & publicity Warner Bros., Phila. zone, 1939; winner Quigley Silver Award, 1940; Lt. Col. U.S.M.C., 1943; returned to Warner post after war; 1950–51, internat'l dir. adv., pub., Cinerama, Feb., 1954. Member: American Legion Variety Post 713 (past commdr.); Military Order of Foreign Wars of U.S.; Adv. pub. dir., National Screen Service, 1965; VP in charge of adv. and pub. sales. TV, Foreign; pres. United Screen Arts, Inc. 1966; world wide dist. and adv. and production. Presently consultant.

CALVERT, PHYLLIS: Actress. b. London, England, Feb. 18, 1917. e. Margaret Morris Sch. Dancing, London; m. Peter Murray Hill, actor. On stage at 10 as dancer; later in provincial repertory; London debut 1939 in "A Woman's Privilege." Screen debut 1939 in "They Came By Night"; voted one of Britain's ten best money-making stars in Motion Picture Herald-Fame Poll 1945–46.
PICTURES INCLUDE: Kipps, Young Mr. Pitt, Uncensored, Fanny by Gaslight, 2,000 Women, Madonna of the Seven Moons, They Were Sisters, Men of Two Worlds, Magic Bow, Root of All Evil, Time Out of Mind, Broken Journey, My Own True Love, Golden Madonna, Man of Evil, Appointment with Danger, Woman With No Name, Mr. Denning Drives North, Mandy, The Net, Its Never Too Late, Child in the House, Indiscreet, Twisted Nerve, Oh! What a Lovely War, The Walking Stick.
TV: Little Women (series), Good Wives, Mrs. Dot, Parnell, You'll Know Me By The Stars in My Eyes, Love Story, The Kindness of Mrs. Radcliffe, Kate (series), Owen M.D.

CALVET, CORINNE: Actress. r.n. Corinne Dibos. b. Paris, France, April 30; e. U. of Paris School of Fine Arts; French stage and radio. Screen debut in France; La Part de L'Ombre, Nous Ne Sommes Pas Maries, Petrus. American screen debut: Rope of Sand.
PICTURES INCLUDE: When Willie Comes Marching Home, My Friend Irma Goes West, Quebec, On the Riviera, Peking Express, Thunder in the East, Sailor Beware, What Price Glory? Powder River, Flight to Tangier, The Far Country, So This Is Paris, Bluebeard's Ten Honeymoons, Adventures of a Young Man, Pound.

CAMERON, JOANNA: Actress—Director. b. Sept. 20, Aspen, Colo. r.n. Patricia Cameron, e. Univ. of Calif., Sorbonne. Pasadena Playhouse, 1968. Guinness Record: Most network programmed TV commercials. Prod., dir., documentary, Razor Sharp, 1981.
PICTURES INCLUDE: How To Commit Marriage (debut), P.S., I Love You, Pretty Maids All in a Row.
TV: Features: The All-American Beauty Contest, It Couldn't Happen to a Nicer Guy, High Risk. Other: The Survivors, Love American Style, Danial Boone, Mission Impossible, The Partners, Search, Medical Center, Isis, Name of the Game, The Bold Ones, Marcus Welby, Petrocelli, Columbo, Switch, Bob Hope Special, Bob Hope 25th NBC Anniversary Special, Westwind, MacMillian, Spider-

man, Swan Song, Johnny Carson, numerous commercials. Director: Various commercials, CBS Preview Special, closed circuit program host U.S.N., all TV equipped ships—actress and director.

CAMERON, ROD: Actor, r.n. Rod Cox; b. Calgary, Alberta, Canada, Dec. 7, 1912.
PICTURES INCLUDE: Christmas in July, Quarterback, North West Mounted Police, Monster and the Girl, Henry Aldrich for President, True to the Army, Wake Island; Salome Where She Danced; Swing Out Sister; Panhandle, Belle Starr's Daughter, Plunderers, Strike It Rich, Brimstone, Dakota Lil, Cavalry Scout, Short Grass, Stage to Tucson, O! Susanna, Fort Osage, Sea Hornet, Wagons West, Woman of the North Country, The Jungle, Ride the Man Down, San Antone, Steel Lady, Southwest Passage, Hell's Outpost, Santa Fe Passage, Fighting Chance, Headline Hunters, Double Jeopardy, Zex, The Bounty Killer, Evel Knievel, Psychic Killer.

CAMPAGNOLA, GINO: Executive. Joined Paramount Pictures in 1975; held various sales positions, including v.p., sls. admin. In 1980 named v.p., asst. sls. mgr.

CAMPBELL, GLEN: Actor, singer. b. Delight, Ark., April 22. After forming local band became guitarist in Hollywood; records won two Grammy awards, 1967.
PICTURES INCLUDE: True Grit, Norwood.

CAMPBELL, MAE E.: Actress. b. March 19, St. Louis, Mo. Studied with the Actors Studio and Lee Strasberg.
PICTURES INCLUDE: The Old Boyfriends; two industrial films for the Veterans Administration Hospital.

CAMPBELL, ROBERT MAURICE: Producer, director. b. Detroit, Mich., Feb. 16, 1922. e. Mich. Conservatory of Music. Detroit Inst. of Musical Arts, American Theatre Wing. Featured player. assoc. dir., Detroit stage prod.; numerous radio appearances; pub. relations, U.S. Coast Guard, World War II; since 1946 dir., off-Broadway shows; dir.-prod., Springer Pictures, Inc.; TV show: All-Star News; exec., Visual Transcriptions, Inc.; prod. Jazz Dance (Robert J. Flaherty Award, Edinburgh Film Festival Merit Award); co-author, prod. designer, See No Evil.

CAMPBELL, WILLIAM: Actor. b. Newark, N.J.; e. Feagin School of Drama Appeared in summer stock. B'way plays; m.p. debut in The Breaking Point; then in People Against O'Hara, Holiday for Sinners, Battle Circus, Code Two, Big Leaguer, Escape from Fort Bravo, High and the Mighty, Man Without a Star, Cell 2455 Death Row, Battle Cry, Running Wild, Backlash, Pretty Maids All in a Row, Black Gunn.

CANALE, GIANNA MARIA: Actress. b. Reggio Calabria, Italy, Sept. 12, e. Florence. Debut in Mysterious Knight.
PICTURES INCLUDE: Kiss of a Dead Woman, Count Orgolino, Son of D'Artagnan, Go for Broke, Adventure in Algiers, Eternal Chain, Theodora Slave Empress, Madame DuBarry, The Whole Truth.

CANBY, VINCENT: Journalist-Critic. b. Chicago, July 27, 1924. e. Dartmouth Coll. Navy officer during World War II. Worked on newspapers in Paris and Chicago. Joined Quigley Publications in 1951 in editorial posts on Motion Picture Herald. Reporter for Weekly Variety 1959–1965. Joined New York Times film news staff, 1965; named film ritic, 1969.

CANFIELD, ALYCE: Writer. b. Los Angeles. e. U. of Calif. Magazine writer; author Mervyn LeRoy book It Takes More Than Talent; in collab. with Howard Duff original story for Models, Inc.; story Journey Into Fire, Assignment for Murder; s.p. for latter in collab. with Jerry Jerome; creator, exec. prod. Ziv TV series, Underground, USA.

CANNON, DYAN: Actress. b. Tacoma, Wash. January 4, 1937. e. U. of Washington. Studied with Sanford Meisner. Modelled.
TV: Playhouse 90, Diane's Adventure.
BROADWAY: The Fun Couple, Ninety-Day Mistress.
ROAD TOUR: How to Succeed in Business Without Really Trying.
PICTURES INCLUDE: Bob and Carol and Ted and Alice (Academy Award nomination), Doctors' Wives, The Anderson Tapes, The Love Machine, The Burglars, Such Good Friends, Shamus, The Last of Sheila, Child Under a Leaf, Heaven Can Wait, Revenge of the Pink Panther, Coast To Coast, Honeysuckle Rose, Deathtrap.

CANNON, JUDY: Actress. b. Santa Fe, N.M., June 16, 1938. e. Santa Monica City College, 1957; teenage Adrian model, 1954–56; toured as band singer, Orlo Wagner Orchestra, 1957; appeared in: The Little Hut, Girls of Summer, Made in Japan, Los Angeles Little Theatre, 1959–61; midwest musical comedy tour group, 1962; m.p. debut, Lullaby, 1963; Critics Choice, '63; A Comedy Tale of Fanny Hill, 1964.
TV: Smothers Bros. Show, Man From U.N.C.L.E., Chrysler Theatre, Run For Your Life, The Road West, My Three Sons, Death Valley Days.
PICTURES INCLUDE: More, 1970.

CANNON, WILLIAM: Writer, Producer, Director. b. Toledo, Ohio, Feb. 11, 1937. e. Columbia Coll., B.A., 1959, M.B.A., 1962. Dir. Off-B'way, Death of a Salesman, Pirates of Penzance, 1960. Wrote, prod., dir., Square Root of Zero, Locarno and San Francisco Film Festivals, 1963–65; Distrib., Doran Enterprises, Ltd; author, Skidoo, (Par-Otto Preminger), 1968, Brewster McCloud, (MGM), 1970; HEX (20th Century Fox) 1974; Author, Novel, The Veteran (E.P. Dutton) 1974.

CANOVA, JUDY: Actress, singer. b. Jacksonville, Fla., Nov. 20, 1916; p. Joe and Henrietta Canova. In Ziegfield Follies, "Calling All Stars," and with Paul Whiteman on the air; 10 yrs., Judy Canova Show, NBC Radio.
PICTURES INCLUDE: Going Highbrow, Artists and Models, Thrill of a Lifetime, Scatterbrain, Singin' In the Corn, Honeychile, Oklahoma Annie, Wac from Walla Walla, Untamed Heiress, Carolina Cannonball, Lay That Rifle Down, Cannonball.
TV: The Adventures of Huckleberry Finn, Party Line, Alfred Hitchcock, Pistols 'n Petticoats, Love American Style, Paramount TV, 1973; Joy Commercial, Proctor, Gamble, 1974; Policewoman, 1974. Recent: Dinah Shore Show, Mike Douglas Show, I'm a Big Girl Now (1980 series), Love Boat, Mother's Day Special (1981).

CANTON, ARTHUR H.: Executive, Blowitz & Canton Co. Inc. b. New York. e. N.Y. University, Columbia University, Capt. USAF. Pres., Canton-Weiner Films, indep. foreign films importers, 1947; MGM Pictures, eastern div. publicity manager, executive liaison, advertising-publicity, Independent Productions; public relations executive, v.p.; pres., Blowitz, Thomas & Canton Inc., 1964; pres., Arthur H. Canton Co. Inc.; prod. exec., Warner Bros., 1968–70; advertising-publicity v.p., Columbia Pictures, 1971; executive v.p. of advertising and publicity, Billy Jack Productions, 1974–76. Co-founder of Blowitz & Canton Co. Inc., 1976, chairman of the board. Member Academy of Motion Picture Arts and Sciences, Variety Clubs International, Film Information Council; Friars Club.

CANUTT, YAKIMA: Director. b. Colfax, Wash., Nov. 29, 1895. World's Champion All-around Rodeo, 1917–24. From 1924 in pictures; stunt man, double, asst. dir.; dir. Republic Pictures, Hollywood, 1944.
PICTURES INCLUDE: Angel and the Badmen, Oklahoma Badlands, Carson City Raiders, Sons of Adventure, G-Men Never Forget, Dangers of the Canadian Mounted, Adventures of Frank and Jesse James, Lawless Rider.

CAPLAN, HARRY: Executive. b. New Haven, Conn., June 2, 1908. e. UCLA, Southwestern U.; mem. King Brothers dance team on stage, Orpheum and Loew's Circuit; 1930, joined Paramount as property master, became unit production mgr., did directorial assignments; 1960, assoc. producer UA Love is a Ball; 1962, joined Filmways as exec. prod. mgr.; 1964–7, Unit prod. mgr. 20th Century-Fox; 1967, joined National General Productions as exec. prod. mgr.

CAPRA, FRANK: Producer, Director. b. Palermo, Sicily, Italy, May 19, 1897; e. Manual Arts H.S.; Calif. Inst. of Tech., B.Sc., 1918 dir., The Strong Man, Long Pants, Platinum Blonde, American Madness, Bitter Tea of General Yen, Lady for a Day, Broadway Bill, It Happened One Night, 1934; Mr. Deeds Goes to Town, 1936; You Can't Take It With You, 1938, Lost Horizon, Mr. Smith Goes to Washington, Meet John Doe, Arsenic and Old Lace, It's a Wonderful Life, State of the Union, Riding High, Here Comes the Groom, A Hole in the Head, Pocketful of Miracles; prod., dir., Why We Fight Series, U.S. Army; pres. Academy of Motion Picture Arts and Sciences, 1935–39; pres., Directors Guild of America, 1938–40, 1959. 1964 Prod. & Dir. Rendezvous in Space.

CAPRA, JR., FRANK: Executive. Son of famed director Frank Capra. Served in various creative capacities on TV series (Zane Grey Theatre, Gunsmoke, The Rifleman, etc.). Associate producer on theatrical films (Planet of the Apes, Play It Again Sam, Marooned, etc). Joined Avco Embassy Pictures in March, 1981, as v.p., worldwide production. In July, 1981, became pres. of A-E.
PICTURES: Producer: Born Again, The Black Marble, An Eye for an Eye.

CAPUCINE: Actress. r.n. Germaine Lefebvre. b. Toulon, France, January 6. e. attended schools at Saumur, France, B.A. Photographer's model, Paris. Came to N.Y. to model. Signed contract, Famous Artists.
PICTURES INCLUDE: debut, Song Without End, North To Alaska, Walk On the Wild Side, The Lion, The 7th Dawn, What's New Pussycat?, The Honey Pot, Fraulein Doktor, Fellini's Satyricon, Red Sun, Arabian Adventure.

CAPUTO, GEORGE: Executive. b. Genoa, Italy, Oct. 24, 1916. e. Lycee de Nice (France) 1930, Sorbonne, Paris, 1934. Partner, gen. mgr., Caputo & Co., Colombia, S.A.; pres., Master Films Dist., Inc., 1950; pres., Fiesta Tele-Cinema, S.A.; pres. International Sound Studios Inc.; pres., Fall River Investments S.A.; acquired Latin America and South America rights in perpetuity to full RKO package feature films library, 1961.

CARDIFF, JACK: Director. b. Yarmouth, England, September 18, 1914. Early career as child actor, later cinematographer on Stairway to Heaven, Black Narcissus, Red Shoes, Scott of the Antarctic, Black Rose, Under Capricorn, Pandora and the Flying Dutchman, African Queen, Magic Box, The Brave One, War and Peace, The Vikings; started as dir. 1958.
PICTURES INCLUDE: Intent to Kill, Beyond This Place, Scent of Mystery, Sons and Lovers, Fanny, My Geisha, The Lion, The Long Ships, Young Cassidy, The Liquidator, Dark of the Sun, The Girl on the Motorcycle, Penny Gold, The Mutations, Ride A Wild Pony, The Prince and The Pauper, Behind the Iron Mask, Death on the Nile, The Dogs of War (Cinematographer).

CARDINALE, CLAUDIA: Actress. b. Italy, 1939.
PICTURES INCLUDE: Persons Unknown, 1958; Upstairs and Downstairs, Il Bell' Antonio, Rocco and His Brothers, Cartouche, The Leopard, Eight and a Half, The Pink Panther, Circus World, Of A Thousand Delights, Blindfold, Last Command, The Professionals, Don't Make Waves, The Queens, The Red Tent, Conversation Piece, Escape to Athena, Immortal Bachelor.

CAREY, HARRY JR.: Actor. b. Saugus, Calif., May 16, e. Newhall, Cal., public school, Black Fox Military Acad., Hollywood; m. Marilyn Fix. two children, Steven and Melinda; Summer stock, Skowhegan, Me., with father; page boy, NBC, New York; U.S. Navy 1941–46; Screen debut: Pursued, then Red River, Moonrise.
PICTURES INCLUDE: Three Godfathers, She Wore a Yellow Ribbon, Wagonmaster, Rio Grande, Copper Canyon, Warpath, Wild Blue Yonder, Monkey Business, San Antone, Island in the Sky, Gentlemen Prefer Blondes, Beneath the 12-Mile Reef, Silver Lode, The Outcast, Long Gray Line, Mister Roberts, House of Bamboo, Great Locomotive Chase, The Undefeated Big Jake, Something Big, One More Train To Rob.

CAREY, JOYCE: Actress. b. London, England, p. Lillian Braithwaite, actress. e. Florence Ettinger Dramatic School, London. Stage debut in Mr. Wu 1916; in many plays, England & U.S.; writings include: Sweet Aloes, Thing Apart, under pseud. Jay Mallory; m.p. debut in In Which We Serve.
PICTURES INCLUDE: Brief Encounter, Blithe Spirit, October Man, Astonished Heart, Dulcimer Street, The Chiltern Hundreds, Cry the Beloved Country, Street Corner (Both Sides of the Law), End of the Affair, Loser Takes All.
TV PLAYS: Full House, The Farmer's Wife, The Family First, Before the Party, Not Many Mansions, Silas Marner, Sergeant Cork, Sally, Tarnish On a Golden Boy, Wings of The Dove, The Secret Agent, The Chink in the Wall.
TV: Mr. Samson, A Question of Fact, Frolic Wind, No Escape, The Carrington Case, The Bristol Case, Greyfriars Bobby, Barchester Towers, Maggie, No Hiding Place, The Flemish Shop (Maigret), Take the Plunge, The Scissors, The Case of the Self-Made Man, Quite Nice, Gideon's Way, Danger Man, Eyes of Annie Jones, A Family and a Fortune, The Cocktail Party, The Ideal Husband, Howard's End, A Nice Girl Like Me, The Avengers, Father Dear Father, The Shopper, The Last Witness, At the Villa Pandora, The Coffee Lace, Barbara's I, The Cedar Tree, Wedding, Only a Scream Away, Edward VI.
STAGE: Heirs and Graces, Maigret and the Lady, Sergeant Cork, Dear Octopus, The Old Ladies, Trelawny, A Ghost on Tiptoe.

CAREY, MACDONALD: Actor. b. Sioux City, Iowa, March 15, 1913; e. Phillip Exeter Acad., U. Wis., U. Iowa. On stage (stock); in radio serials. On B'way in Anniversary Waltz; m.p. debut in 1942.
PICTURES INCLUDE: Dr. Broadway, Take a Letter Darling, Wake Island, Suddenly It's Spring, Variety Girl, Dream Girl, Hazzard, Streets of Laredo, Song of Surrender, South Sea Sinner, Copper Canyon, Great Missouri Raid, Mystery Submarine, Excuse My Dust, Meet Me After the Show, Let's Make It Legal, Cave of the Outlaws, My Wife's Best Friend, Count the Hours, Outlaw Territory, Fire Over Africa, Stranger At My Door, American Gigolo.
TV: Days of our Lives, Roots.

CAREY, PHIL: Actor. b. Hackensack, N.J., July 15, 1925; e. Mohawk U., U. of Miami, U.S. Marines; New England stock; m.p. debut in Operation Pacific.
PICTURES INCLUDE: Inside the Walls of Folsom Prison, This Woman Is Dangerous, Springfield Rifle, Calamity Jane, Gun Fury, The Nebraskan, Massacre Canyon, Outlaw Stallion, They Rode West, Pushover, The Long Gray Line, Wyoming Renegades, Mister Roberts, Count Three and Pray, Three Stripes in the Sun, The Time Traveler, Once You Kiss a Stranger, Three Guns for Texas, The Seven Minutes. TV: Laredo.

CARLIDGE, WILLIAM: Executive. b. Fenton, Eng., May 2, 1910. e. Grafton Boys' School. Entered m.p. ind. in 1930 as mgr. Ilford Hippodrome; circuit mgr. Union Cinemas, 1935; supervisor for Northern Ireland. Associated British Cinemas Ltd., 1947; first regional controller for Northern Region, personal asst. to man. dir. 1949; gen. man. Associated British Cinemas Ltd. 1951; dir. 1955; asst. man. dir. 1959; Board of Associated British Picture Corp., 1964, now known as EMI Film and Theatre Corp.

CARLILE, TOM: Publicist-Writer, b. Lindsay, Okla., June 9. e. Los Angeles City College (A.A., Journ.), Fresno State College (B.A.) U.C.L.A. (grad work); So. Calif. PR rep. Time, Inc., 1941; correspondent, Life Mag., 1942–43; movie editor, Life Mag., 1944–45; pres. Picture Surveys, Inc., 1945–47; western ed. director, Dell Publishing Co., 1947–49; western ed. PIC Magazine and freelance writer, 1950–54; Pub., Public Affairs Dept., CBS Television, 1954–55; ed. and publisher, Weekend Outdoor News, 1955–56; Sr. pub., Warner Bros. (Giant, The D.I. and Old Man and the Sea), 1956–1957; manager, Advertising Associates, Inc., San Diego, 1958–59; unit. pub., The Alamo, 1959; studio pub. manager, Samuel Bronston Productions, Madrid, (King of Kings and El Cid), 1960–61; pub. dir., Eon Productions Ltd., London (Call Me Bwana, From Russia With Love, Goldfinger, Thunderball, You Only Live Twice) 1962–67; Creative supervisor, European pub., Paramount Pictures, 1967–68; pub. dir., The Adventurers, 1968; ad-pub. dir., Dino De Laurentiis Studios, Rome, 1968–1971; pub. supervisor, Man of La Mancha, 1971–72; U.S. pub., Diamonds Are Forever and Live and Let Die, 1973–74; pub. dir., Algonquin Productions Ltd., London (Rollerball) 1975–76; U.S. pub., A Bridge Too Far, 1977; spec. projects, United Artists, 1977–78; pub. supervisor, Bloodline, Paramount 1978–79. Has written numerous magazine articles and fact books on motion picture subjects.

CARLINO, LEWIS JOHN: Writer. b. N.Y.C., Jan. 1, 1932. e. USC. Early interest in theatre, specializing in writing 1-act plays. Winner of Obie award (off-Bdwy. play). Won Rockefeller Grant for Theatre, the Int'l. Playwriting Competition from British Drama League, Huntington Hartford Fellowship.
PICTURES INCLUDE: Seconds, The Brotherhood, The Fox (co-s.p.), The Mechanic, The Sailor Who Fell from the Sea (s.p., dir.), I Never Promised You a Rose Garden (co. s.p.), The Ace (s.p., dir.), Resurrection (s.p.)
PLAYS: Cages, Telemachus Clay, The Exercise, Double Talk, Objective Case, Used Car for Sale, Junk Yard.

CARLISLE, ROBERT: Producer. b. Los Angeles, Calif., Sept. 19, 1906. Cutter, Metro; Universal; John Stahl; Columbia; film ed. in chf. Columbia; prod. short subjects with Jerry Fairbanks including: Popular Science, Unusual Occupations, Speaking of Animals (two Academy of M.P. Arts & Sciences awards); prod. industrials for Dupont, Union Pacific RR; trophy at Italy's Cortina Sports Film Festival for ski film, 1957; prod. and dir. films on world affairs for Dept. of Defense; prod. Wondsel, Carlisle & Dunphy, Inc., 1957.

CARLTON, RICHARD: Executive. b. New York City, Feb. 9, 1919. e. Columbia U., Pace Inst. Columbia Pictures 1935–41; U.S. Army 1941–45; National Screen Serv. 1945–51, head of agency sales div. of Sterling Television 1951–53; v.p. of Sterling Television, 1954; eastern sales mgr., U.M. & M. TV Corp. 1955; v.p. in charge of sales, Trans-Lux Television Corp., 1956; exec. vice-pres., Television Affiliates Corp., 1961; v.p., Trans-Lux T.V Corp.; exec. v.p. Trans-Lux Television Corp., 1966. Pres., Schnur Appel, TV, Inc. 1970; Deputy Director, American Film Institute, 1973.

CARMICHAEL, HOAGY: Composer, actor. b. Bloomington, Ind., Nov. 22, 1899; e. Indiana U., LL.B., 1926. Composer song hits including: Star Dust. Member: Bel Air Club, Kappa Sigma.
PICTURES INCLUDE: To Have and Have Not, Johnny Angel, Canyon Passage, Best Years of Our Lives, Night Song, Young Man With a Horn, Johnny Holiday, Belles on Their Toes, Las Vegas Story, Timberjack. Academy Award, best song in Cool, Cool, Cool Evening from Here Comes The Groom, 1951.
TV: Laramie, also commercials.

CARMICHAEL, IAN: Actor. b. Hull, England, June 18, 1920. e. Scarborough College, Bromsgrove School, Stage debut; R.U.R. 1939. Film debut: Bond Street, one of the top ten British money making stars M.P.H.—Fame Poll 1957, 1958.
TV: New Faces, Twice Upon a Time, Passing Show, Tell Her The Truth, Lady Luck, Give My Regards to Leicester Square, Jill Darling, Don't Look Now, Regency Room, Globe Revue, Off the Record, Here and Now, The Girl at the Next Table, Gilt and Gingerbread, The Importance of being Earnest, Simon and Laura, 90 Years On, The World of Wooster, The Last of the Big Spenders, The Coward Revue, Odd Man In, Bachelor Father, Lord Peter Wimsey, Alma Master, Comedy Tonight, Song by Song, Country Calendar.
PICTURES INCLUDE: Trottie True, Mr. Prohack, Time Gentlemen Please, Meet Mr. Lucifer, Betrayed, Coldits Story, Storm Over the Nile, Simon and Laura, Private's Progress, Brothers in Law, Lucky Jim, Happy Is the Bride, The Big Money, Right, Left and Center, I'm Alright Jack, School for Scoundrels, Light Up the Sky, Double Bunk, The Amorous Prawn, Hide and Seek, Heavens Above,

Smashing Time, The Magnificent Seven, Deadly Sins, From Beyond the Grave, The Lady Vanishes.

CARNEY, ART: Performer. b. Mt. Vernon, N.Y., Nov. 4, 1918. Many radio shows. U.S. Army, 1944–45; performer, Jackie Gleason's Honeymooners.
TV: Studio One, Kraft, Omnibus, Chevy Show, Playhouse 90, Dupont Show of the Month—"Harvey," Sid Caesar Show, Alfred Hitchcock Presents—"Safety for the Witness," Art Carney Meets Peter and the Wolf, "Playhouse 90—"Fabulous Irishman," "Charley's Aunt," "Velvet Alley," "Art Carney Meets the Sorcerer's Apprentice," The Sid Caesar-Art Carney Show, Our Town, Very Important People, Man in the Dog Suit, Call Me Back, Batman, Carol Burnett Show, Jonathan Winters Show, Tonight Show.
PICTURES INCLUDE: Harry and Tonto, W. W. and the Dixie Dancekings, Won Ton Ton, The Late Show, Take This Job and Shove It.
STAGE: The Rope Dancers, Take Her She's Mine, (Bdwy.), The Odd Couple (Bdwy.), Lovers (Bdwy.), The Prisoner of Second Avenue (Bdwy.), Sunburn, Going in Style, Defiance, Roadie.

CARNEY, FRED: Producer, director. b. Brooklyn, N.Y., June 10, 1914; e. Mt. Vernon H.S., 1932. Actor on B'way & summer stock; prod. mgr. for radio show, Truth or Consequences; asst. to prod.-dir of Kraft TV Theatre, 3 yrs.; dir., Kraft, Pond's Show; creator-prod., Medical Horizons; dir., Lux Video Theatre; prod. commercials at Cunningham & Walsh. Assoc. Prod. Everybody's Talking for ABC-TV; Assoc. Prod. 40th Acad. Award show, ABC-TV. Ass't. exec. dir., Hollywood chpt., Nat'l. Acad. TV Arts & Sciences; currently acting in feature films and TV.

CARNOW, HOWARD N.: Executive. b. Brooklyn, N.Y., Sept. 25, 1912. e. Brooklyn College, 1929–35. Pub., Columbia Pictures, 1929–33; ad. mgr., Radio Attractions Inc., 1935–36; ad. & pub mgr., Brandt Theatres, Subway Circuit, 1937–38; Warner Bros., 1939–44; U.S. Navy, 1944–46; Warner Bros., 1946; ad. mgr., United Artists, 1966. Retired 1977.

CARON, LESLIE: Dancer, actress. b. Paris, France. July 1, 1931. e. Covent of Assumption, Paris; Nat'l Conservatory of Dance, Paris. Did solo bit parts, then starred joined Ballet des Champs Elysees. In 1950, signed MGM lead film role in An American in Paris; since in Man with a Cloak, Glory Alley, Story of Three Loves, Lili, Glass Slipper, Daddy Long Legs, Gaby, Gigi, The Doctor's Dilemma, The Man Who Understood Women, The Subterraneans, Fanny, Guns of Darkness, The L Shaped Room, Father Goose, Promise Her Anything, A Very Special Favor, Is Paris Burning, Head of the Family, The Beginners, Madron, Chandler, Purple Night, Valentino.

CARPENTER, CARLETON: Actor. b. Bennington, Vt., July 10; e. Bennington H.S.; Northwestern U. (summer scholarship). Began career with magic act, clubs, camps, hospitals, New Eng.; then toured with carnival; first N.Y. stage appearance in Bright Boy.
STAGE: Career Angel, Three To Make Ready, The Magic Touch, The Big People, Art of Dust, John Murray Anderson's Almanac. Appeared night clubs; radio; as model magazines, TV debut, Campus HoopLa show. Screen debut Lost Boundaries (also wrote song for film, I Wouldn't Mind).
PICTURES INCLUDE: Summer Stock, Father of the Bride, Two Weeks With Love, Whistle at Eaton Falls, Fearless Fagan, Sky Full of Moon, Take the High Ground, Some of My Best Friends Are . . .

CARPENTER, JOHN: Director-Writer. b. Carthage, NY, Jan. 16, 1948. e. USC. Married to Adrienne Barbeau. At USC became involved in film short, Resurrection of Bronco Billy, which won Oscar as best live-action short of 1970. Also at USC began directing what ultimately became Dark Star, science fiction film that launched his career.
PICTURES: Assault on Precinct 13, Halloween (also music), Eyes of Laura Mars (s.p. only), The Fog (also music), Escape from New York (also music).

CARPENTER, ROBERT L.: Executive. b. March 20, 1927, Memphis, Tenn. Joined Universal Pictures in 1949 as booker in Memphis exchange; promoted to salesman there in 1952 and branch mgr. in 1958. In 1963 named Los Angeles branch manager. In Dec., 1971 moved to New York to become asst. to general sales mgr. Named gen. sls. mgr. on April 16, 1973, replacing Henry H. Martin when latter became pres. of Universal.

CARR, ARNOLD: Publicist. b. Chicago, Ill., Aug. 9, 1931. e. Univ. of Missouri. Began public relations handling tour with Dimitri Mitropoulos, U.S. State Depart.; Columbia Broadcasting System; pub. dir., KABC-TV; Screen Gems; pub. rel. dir., Hanna-Barbera Prod.; formed own firm, 1962; partnered with Richard Carter 1964; resumed business under own name, Arnold Carr Public Relations.

CARR, ALAN: Producer—Personal Manager. b. Highland Park, Ill. e. Lake Forest College, Northwestern Univ. First venture in show business as one of creators of Playboy Penthouse TV series. Produced plays at Civic Theatre, Chicago. Asst.

to Nicholas Ray on King of Kings shot in Madrid. Became talent scout, launching Marlo Thomas in play, Sunday in New York, on West Coast. Other clients have included Ann-Margret, Peter Sellers, Nancy Walker, Marvin Hamlisch, Stockard Channing, Melina Mercouri, Franke Valli, etc. Served as creative consultant to Robert Stigwood Organisation in marketing and promotion of movie, Tommy. Presented Survive! with Stigwood.
PICTURES: Producer: The First Time, C.C. and Company, Grease (co-prod.), Can't Stop the Music (co-prod., co. s.p.).

CARR, MARTIN: Producer-Director-Writer b. N.Y.C. Jan 20, 1932. e. Williams Coll. Worked for all three networks.
TELEVISION: For CBS produced, wrote and directed CBS Reports: Hunger in America, The Search for Ulysses, Gauguin in Tahiti, Five Faces of Tokyo, Dublin Through Different Eyes. For NBC produced, wrote and directed NBC White Paper: Migrant, NBC White Paper: This Child Is Rated X. Also directed drama, dance, music, opera specials and daytime serial for CBS-TV. ABC Close-Up. The Culture Thieves. PRS Global Paper: Waging Peace, ABC News 20/20.
AWARDS: Winner of 4 Emmys; 3 Peabody awards; 2 Du-Pont Col. Journalism awards; Robert F. Kennedy award; Sidney Hillman award; Writers Guild Award.

CARR, THOMAS: Director; b. Philadelphia, Pa., July 4, 1907. On screen at 2½ yrs. for Lubin Co., Phil.; starred in Little Britches at 5 yrs., actor on stage, radio & screen until 1937; then became dialogue clerk, Republic Studios, advancing to script; asst. assoc. prod.; assoc. prod. 1944; dir. 1945. Pictures include many westerns, Bobby Ware is Missing.

CARRADINE, DAVID: Actor. b. Hollywood, Oct. 8, 1940. f. John Carradine. e. San Francisco State. Began career in local repetory; first TV on Armstrong Circle Theatre and East Side, West Side; later TV includes Shane series and Kung Fu; N.Y. stage in The Deputy, Royal Hunt of The Sun.
PICTURES INCLUDE: Taggart, Bus Riley's Back in Town, Too Many Thieves, The Violent Ones, Heaven With a Gun, Young Billy Young, The Good Guys and the Bad Guys, Gallery of Horrors, The McMasters, Macho Callahan, A Gunfight, McCabe & Mrs. Miller, Boxcar Bertha, Death Race 2000, Bound for Glory, The Serpent's Egg, Gray Lady Down, The Long Riders, Cloud Dancer.

CARRADINE, JOHN: Actor. b. New York City, Feb. 5, 1908. On stage in Shakespearian roles. A Funny Thing Happened on My Way to the Forum. On screen from 1936.
PICTURES INCLUDE: Fallen Angel, House of Dracula, Captain Kidd, Face of Marble, House of Frankenstein, It's in the Bag, Private Affairs of Bel Ami, C-Man, Cassanova's Big Night, Thunder Pass, Johnny Guitar, The Egyptian, Stranger on Horseback, Hidden Guns, Court Jester, Desert Sands, The Kentuckian, Dark Venture, Black Sheep, The Good Guys and the Bad Guys, Boxcar Bertha, Everything You Always Wanted to Know About Sex*, The Shootist, The Last Tycoon, The Sentinel, Zorro, The Gay Blade.

CARRADINE, KEITH: Actor. b. San Mateo, Calif. Aug. 8 Son of actor John Carradine, brother of David. e. Colorado State Univ. Got first break in rock opera "Hair." Screen debut in A Gunfight (1971).
PICTURES INCLUDE: McCabe and Mrs. Miller, Idaho Transfer, Emperor of the North, Thieves Like Us, Nashville, Lumiere, Welcome to L.A., The Duellists, Pretty Baby, Old Boyfriends, An Almost Perfect Affair, The Long Riders, Southern Comfort.

CARRERAS, SIR JAMES M.B.E.: Chairman and chief executive. Hammer Film Productions Ltd. 1946–1973. Special advisor to the EMI group of companies; director, Studio Film Laboratories Ltd.; chairman, Variety International Executive board; deputy chairman, Royal Naval Film Corporation; deputy chairman, Police Dependents Trust; cochairman, Friends of the Duke of Edinburgh's Award Scheme; director, National Screen Service; trustee, Young Volunteer Force Foundation; chairman, Sobell Variety Islington Trust; vice-president, London Federation of Boys' Clubs; member of the board, Services Kinema Corporation; member of the council, Cinema and Television Benevolent Fund.

CARROLL, CARROLL: Writer, producer, b. New York, N.Y. m.p. critic, feature writer, N.Y. Sunday World; free lance writer, nat'l mags: head writer & edit. supvr., J. Walter Thompson, N.Y. 1932–36; Coast, 1936–46; v.p., writer, prod., Ward Wheelock Co., West Coast, 1946–53. CBS, NBC, JWT, East Coast 1957–67. Now based in Hollywood.
SHOWS INCLUDE: (radio) Bing Crosby, Al Johnson, Rudy Vallee, Eddie Cantor, Burns & Allen, Joe Penner, Kraft Music Hall, Edgar Bergen, Frank Sinatra, Bob Crosby, Corliss Archer, Double or Nothing. Club 15; (TV) head writer, Bob Crosby Show; CBS-TV creative staff, 1953–55; General Electric Hour; Young & Rubicam TV, 1955; NBC-TV creative staff, 1956–57; ed. dept., J. Walter Thompson Co., 1957–67. Writer, prod., Chase & Sanborn Anniv. Radio Show with Edgar Bergen, 1964; C & S 101. Anniv. Show with Fred Allen, 1965; 1966 NBC 40th Anniv. Show. Free-

lance writer and adv. consultant, 1967–77. Book Reviewer for Variety and Columnist, "And Now a Word from . . ." in Variety.
AUTHOR: "None of Your Business or My Life with J. Walter Thompson," 1970. "My Life With . . ." 1978. Co-author with Henny Youngman, "Take My Wife . . . Please!" Editorial consultant "Liberace." Editorial Consultant "Mike Douglas, My Story," Co-author with Ed McMahon, "Here's Ed." Co-author with Bob Hope: "I Never Left Home", "So This is Peace," Author, Carroll's First Book of Proverbs.

CARROLL, GORDON: Producer. b. Balt. Md., Feb. 2, 1928. e. Princeton U. Advtg. exec., Foote, Cone & Belding, 1954–58; Ent. industry, Seven Arts Prods., 1958–61; Staff Prod., Columbia Pictures, 1962; V.P., Jalem Prods., 1966–1969; Independent Producer to present.
PICTURES INCLUDE: How to Murder Your Wife, Luv, Cool Hand Luke, The April Fools, Pat Garrett and Billy the Kid, Alien.

CARROLL, LAURIE: Singer, actress. b. Cambridge, Mass., April 15, 1935. e. U.S.C. Actress in little theatre group, Los Angeles; on Broadway in Plain and Fancy.
TV: You Are There, Damon Runyon Theatre, Shower of Stars; feature singer, Johnny Carson Show, CBS-TV.

CARROLL, MADELEINE: Actress. b. West Bromwich, England, Feb. 26, 1906; e. Birmingham U., B.A. Taught school. Given leading role in Brit. "Guns of Loos" 1929; thereafter in many Brit. & U.S. (from 1934).
PICTURES INCLUDE: Young Woodley, Madame Guillotine, I Was a Spy, Thirty-Nine Steps, Case Against Mrs. Ames, General Died at Dawn, Lloyds of London, Prisoner of Zenda, Cafe Society, Convoy, Lady in Distress, My Favorite Blonde. From 1942, prominent in USO Fund and War Bond drives, soldier shows.

CARROLL PAT: Performer. b. Shreveport, La., May 5, 1927. e. Immaculate Heart College, LA.; Catholic University, Wash., D.C. Joined U.S. Army in capacity of "civilian actress technician." Night club entertainer in N.Y., 1949.
TV: Red Buttons, George Gobel, Jimmy Durante and Mickey Rooney; Caesar's Hour, 1956. Bdwy.
STAGE: Catch a Star.

CARSON, JEANNIE: Actress. b. Yorkshire, England. Amer. Citizen, 1966, in musicals Ace of Clubs, Love from Judy; Ent. Motion Pictures in 1954 in As Long as They're Happy; Alligator Named Daisy, Mad Little Island.
TV: Best Foot Forward, Little Women, Berkeley Square, The Rivals, Frank Sinatra Show, Own TV Series, Hey Jeannie and Jeannie Carson Show. Toured in Sound of Music, Camelot, 110 in the Shade. Under contract to Decca.

ARSON, JOHNNY: Comedian. b. Corning, Ia., Oct. 23, 1925. e. U. of Neb. U.S. Navy service; with station KFAB, Lincoln, Neb.; WOW radio-TV, Omaha, 1948; announcer, KNXT, Los Angeles, 1950; then program, Carson's Cellar; quizmaster, Earn Your Vacation, 1954; writer for Red Skelton; star of Johnny Carson Show, CBS-TV; Who Do You Trust, ABC-TV; The Tonight Show Starring Johnny Carson, NBC-TV.

CARSON, ROBERT: Writer. Served in U.S. Armed Forces 1942–45.
WRITINGS: Western Union, Tuttles of Tahiti, Desperadoes, Bedside Manner, Perilous Holiday, Reformer and the Redhead, The Groom Wore Spurs, Just For You, Men With Wings, Light That Failed, Beau Geste, Bundle of Joy, Action of the Tiger, You Gotta Stay Happy.

CARSTENSEN, VERN: Exec. b. Clinton, Ia., May 24, 1914. e. U. of Iowa, 1933–38.
RADIO: announcer, 1936–38, WSUI, Iowa City, WOC, Davenport, WHBF, Rock Island, CBS, Chicago; prog. dir., sls. prom., KROS, Clinton, 1939–42; U.S. Army, 1942–46, Armed Forces Radio Network, No. Africa, orig. Mobile Radio Station, Italy, Armed Forces Radio Service Hdqtrs., Hollywood, OIC overseas liaison; prod. mgr., Mayfair Transcription Co., 1946–51; exec. asst., Alan Ladd Enterprises Inc., 1951–58; assoc. prod., exec. coord., Jaquar Prods., 1958–61; v.p., sec., Eagle Animation Corp.; sec.-treas., Juggernaut Prods. Inc., 1962–64; exec. v.p. Dale Robertson Assoc., 1963; exec. v.p., United Screen Arts Inc. 1964–66; exec. v.p. Juggernaut, Inc. 1966–68, v.p. Entertainment Associates, Inc. 1968–70; v.p Tommy Walker Productions 1970–1973; pres. Center Features, Inc. 1973–1976; 1977–1978, exec. v.p., Justin & Assoc. Inc.; 1979–81, v.p. Great Rollerworks Corp.

CARTER, JACK: Actor, r.n., Jack Chakrin. b. New York, June 24, 1923. e. Brooklyn College, Feagin Sch. of Dram. Arts. Worked as comm. artist for adv. agencies. Debut Broadway in Call Me Mister, 1947; starred in TV Jack Carter Show. Seen on most major variety, dram. programs, incl. Ed Sullivan Show. Emmy nom. 1962 for Dr. Kildare seg. Played most major nightclubs. App. Broadway in Top Banana; Mr. Wonderful.
PICTURES INCLUDE: The Horizontal Lieutenant, Viva

Las Vegas, The Extraordinary Seaman, The Resurrection of Zachary Wheeler.

CARTER, LYNDA: Actress. b. Phoenix, Ariz., July 24. e. Arizona State Univ. Wrote songs and sang professionally in Arizona from age of 15; later toured for 4 yrs. with rock 'n' roll band. Won beauty contests in Ariz. and became Miss World-USA in 1973. Dramatic training with Stella Adler and Charles Conrad.
TELEVISION: The New Adventures of Wonder Woman.

CARTER, MAURICE: Art director/designer. b. London, England, 1913. Grad. of The Royal Society of Art Masters. Early career as interior decoration designer. Ent. m.p. ind. 1934/5 Islington Studios, became art dir. 1938. Involved in development back projection. Has art dir. or designed over eighty features includ. Man in Grey, Becket, The Battle of Britain, Anne of the Thousand Days, Innocent Bystanders, The Land that Time Forgot, At The Earth's Core, The People That Time Forgot, The Great Train Robbery. Specializes in period subject and special effect. Three times nominated for American Academy awards and twice for British Film Academy awards. Founder of Guild of Film Art Directors.

CARTER, TRACY: Actress. r.n. Tracy Olsen. b. Los Angeles Calif., Feb. 16, 1940. e. Hollywood Sch. of Drama, 1957-58; Pasadena Playhouse, 1958-61. Pianist, 15 years, Los Angeles Conservatory.
TV: Have Gun Will Travel, Ripcord, 77 Sunset Strip, Fred McMurray Show, The Deputy, June Allyson Show, Michael Shayne, Betty Hutton Show, Divorce Court, Kraft Suspense Theatre, Bonanza, Beauty Fair.
PLAYS: Desperate Hours, Look Back in Anger, Puss 'n Boots, The Thousand Dollar Mule, Taming of the Shrew, Richard III.
PICTURES INCLUDE: The Couch, Boy on the Run, Terrified, Dust Is My Tomorrow, Sweet Hell, I'll Love You Forever, Johnny Reno, Waco, Red Tomahawk, Journey to the Center of Time.

CARTIER, RUDOLPH: TV producer, director. b. Vienna, Austria, April 17, 1908. Stage designer, journalist, writer, film dir. and prod.; entered m.p. industry 1929. Joined BBC-TV drama dept., 1952; senior producer-director, 1953.
PICTURES INCLUDE: L'Aigion, Quartermass Experiment, Wuthering Heights, That Lady, Such Men Are Dangerous, Rebecca, Liebelei, Captain Banner, Nineteen Eighty-Four, The Creature, Moment of Truth, Midsummer Fire, Thunder Rock, Quartermass II, Devil's General, White Falcon, Maverling Affair, Arrow to the Heart, Fugitive, Cold Light, Saint of Bleecker Street, Dark Victory, Clive of India, Queen and the Rebels, Salome, Mother Courage, A Tale of Two Cities, Midsummer Night's Dream, Quatermass and the Pit, Tobias and the Angel, Roshomon, Adventure Story, Anna Karenina, Cross of Iron, Golden Fleece, The Liars, Carmen, Dr. Korczak and the Children, Sword of Vengeance, Aspern Papers, Anna Christie, Stalingrad, Respectable Prostitute, Lady of the Camellias, Midnight Men, July Plot, Wings of the Dove, Ironhand, Joel Brand Story, Gordon of Khartoum, Lee Oswald-Assassin, The Survivors, Level Seven, Firebrand, The Burning Bush, The Fanatics, The Rebel, Conversation at Night, An Ideal Husband, Rembrandt, The Bear, The Year of the Crow, The Proposal, Lady Windermere's Fan (1972), The Deep Blue Sea, Fall of Eagles (1974), Loyalties (1976).
TV: Winslow Boy, Gaslight, Sacrifice to the Wind, The Patriot, A Night Out, Death Has Many Faces, Attorney-General, The Consul, Aspern Papers, That Lady, Corinth House, The Savages, Alibi for James, Mr. Pickwick, The Spanish Civil War, In the Name of Conscience.

CASE, NELSON: Announcer. b. Long Beach, Calif. e. William and Mary Coll. Joined NBC, San Francisco, 1931, announcer, NBC, New York, 1934; freelance 1939; U.S. Navy, 1942-45; Lowell Thomas Show, 1946; TV announcer-host.
SHOWS: Pulitzer Prize Playhouse, Robert Montgomery Presents, Jackie Gleason Show, Omnibus, Red Buttons Show, Masquerade Party, Wide Wide World.

CASELLI, LAMAR: Director. b. San Francisco, Calif., June 16, 1921. e. U. of Wash.; U. of Calif. at L.A.; B.A., 1946; M.A. Telecommunications UCLA 1971; Pilot-Air Corps, 1943-45, legit actor & stage mgr., 1947-50; stg. mgr., assoc. dir. and dir., CBS-TV and NBC-TV, 1950-56; C.C. medical and industrial TV, 1955-63; staff dir., CBS-TV, The Last Word, Lamp Unto My Feet, Look Up and Live, 1957-58; F.L. dir., G.E. College Bowl, CBS-TV. NBC-TV, 1959-64; dir. Alumni Fun CBS-TV, 1964; 1965 Insight CBS-TV; Morning Star, serial NBC-TV; 1966 Young Marrieds, serial ABC-TV; 1967-present, prof., Loyola Univ., 1969, dir. film TV, Death Valley Days; 1970-71, also 1976-77 dir., General Hospital (ABC-TV serial), dir., This is the Life, synd. series, 1975-79.

CASSAVETES, JOHN: Director, Actor. b. New York, N.Y., Dec. 9, 1929. e. Colgate College, N.Y. Acad. of Dramatic Arts. m. Gena Rowlands. Actor in stock co.; asst. stage mgr. for Broadway play Fifth Season; many TV credits including Omnibus, Elgin Playhouse.
PICTURES INCLUDE: Taxi, Night Holds Terror, Crime

in the Streets, Edge of the City, Fever Tree, Shadows (dir.), Too Late Blues (dir., s.p.), A Child is Waiting (dir.), Faces, Husbands (actor, s.p., dir.), Minnie & Moskowitz (s.p., dir.), Devil's Angels, The Dirty Dozen, Rosemary's Baby, Machine Gun McCann, Woman Under The Influence, (dir.), Mikey and Nicky, Killing of a Chinese Bookie (dir., s.p.); Two Minute Warning (actor); Opening Night, 1977 (s.p., dir.), The Fury (actor) 1978. Brass target (actor) 1978, Gloria (s.p., dir.), Whose Life Is It Anyway? (actor).

CASSEL, JEAN-PIERRE: Actor. b. Paris, Oct. 27, 1932. Began as dancer, attracting attention of Gene Kelly in Left Bank nightspot, who gave him film work. Appeared in plays before becoming established as leading French screen star.
PICTURES INCLUDE: Games of Love, The Gay Deceiver, Five Day Lover, The Vanishing Corporal, The Male Companion, A Woman Passed By, Is Paris Burning?, Those Magnificent Men in Their Flying Machines, The Killing Game, Oh! What a Lovely War, The Bear and The Doll, The Rupture, The Boat on the Grass, Baxter!, The Discreet Charm of the Bourgeoisie, The Three Musketeers, Le Mouton Enrage, Murder on the Orient Express, Who Is Killing the Great Chefs of Europe?

CASSIDY, SHAUN: Actor/Singer/Composer. b. Los Angeles, Sept. 27. One of 3 sons of Shirley Jones and late Jack Cassidy. e. Bev. Hills high school. Began recording in 1976 and toured Europe and Australia, appearing on numerous TV shows. Has had several hit records.
TELEVISION: Hardy Boys Mysteries, numerous specials, talk shows.
PICTURES: Born of Water (debut for Ameri. Film Inst.).

CASTELL, ANTONIO: Executive. b. Havana, Cuba, Dec. 9, 1911; e. U. of Havana; publicity dir., Cuba, 1937; motion picture exhibitor, 1937-48; distributor, Cooperative Cinematografica; owner dir., Alex and Atlas Films, up to 1961; distributor, Spanish pictures for the Americas.

CASTELLANO, RICHARD S.: Actor, Producer. b. New York City, September 4, 1933. e. Commerce H.S., Columbia U. Before acting career was owner of construction company and employed as construction consultant.
THEATRE: 1963: New Yiddish Theatre; 1965-66: starred off-Broadway in A View From The Bridge; 1966: on Broadway in The Investigation and That Summer That Fall; 1967: Stratford Shakespeare Company Festival; 1968: Milk Downstairs, Why I Went Crazy. Also on Broadway in Sheep On The Runway and Lovers and Other Strangers (Tony nomination).
PICTURES: A Fine Madness, Lovers and Other Strangers (Academy nomination, The Godfather.)
TELEVISION: NYPD, The Super, Incident on a Dark Street, Honor Thy Father.

CASTLE, WALTER H.: Cinematographer. b. Santa Ana, Calif., May 19, 1905. Engaged continuously in photographic work for 27 years with Fox Film Corp. and 20th Century-Fox Film Corp., as director of photography; Walt Disney Prod., TV, Hardy Boys, American Dairy Story, Spin, Mickey Mouse Club, Our Friend the Atom, Saga of Andy Burnett; spec. effects for Trapeze.

CATES, GILBERT: Director-Producer. b. New York City, June 6, 1934. e. Syracuse Univ. Began TV career as guide at NBC studios in N.Y., working way up to prod. and dir. of game shows (Camouflage, Haggis Baggis, Mother's Day, etc.). Created Hootenanny and packaged and directed many TV specials.
PICTURES INCLUDE: The Painting (short), Rings Around the World, I Never Sang for My Father, Summer Wishes, Winter Dreams (dir. only) One Summer Love, Dragonfly (prod.-dir.), 1975; The Promise, 1978, The Last Married Couple in America, 1980; Oh, God! Oh, God!—Book II, 1980.
TELEVISION: International Showtime (1963-65 exec. prod.-dir.), Electric Showcase Specials ('65, dir.-prod.), To All My Friends on Shore ('72-dir.-prod.), The Affair ('73-dir.), After the Fall ('74-dir.-prod.), Johnny, We Hardly Knew Ye, (1976-prod.-dir.), The Kid from Nowhere (1981-prod.).
STAGE: Director: Tricks of the Trade, Voices, The Price (Long Wharf Theatre). Producer: Solitaire/Double Solitaire, The Chinese and Mr. Fish, I Never Sang for My Father, You Know I Can't Hear You When the Water's Running.

CAULFIELD, JOAN: Actress. b. Orange, N.J., June 1; e. Columbia U. Harry Conover model 1942-3; on stage 1943-4; screen debut in "Miss Susie Slagle's" 1945.
PICTURES INCLUDE: Dear Ruth, Variety Girl, Unsuspected, Sainted Sisters, Larceny, Pretty Girl, Lady Said No, Rains of Ranchipur, Buckskin.
TV: Sally, My Favorite Husband, CBS.

CAVALCANTI, ALBERTO: Director. b. Rio de Janeiro, Brazil. Feb. 6, 1897; e. Geneva Fine Arts School (architecture). Began in m.p. as art dir., Paris; then dir., later prod. many pictures Paris. To London as head of GPO Film Unit (later Crown Unit).
PICTURES INCLUDE: North Sea, First Days, Squadron

992, Men of the Lightship, Foreman Went to France, Halfway House, Went the Day Well, Champagne Charlie, Dead of Night, Nicholas Nickleby, They Made Me a Fugitive, First Gentleman, For Them That Trespass, & features in Brazil, One Man and The Cinema, Parts I and II.
STAGE: Blood Wedding, Fuente-Ovejuna.
TV: Thus Spake Theodor Herzl, Les Empailles, La Visite de la Vieille Dame.

CAVETT, DICK: Actor-Writer. b. Kearny, Nebr., 1937. e. Yale Univ. Acted in TV dramas and Army training films. Was writer for Jack Paar, and his successors on the Tonight Show and had comedy writing assignments with Merv Griffin, Jerry Lewis, Johnny Carson. In 1967 wrote for self and appeared in night clubs. On TV starred in Where It's At (special on ABC Stage 67) and What's In (special). Began daytime series for ABC-TV in 1968, three-weekly series summer of 1969. Current program: The Dick Cavett Show.

CHABROL, CLAUDE: Director. b. 1930. One of the first directors involved in the French New Wave.
PICTURES INCLUDE: Le Beau Serge, The Cousins, Leda, Les Bonnes Femmes, Les Godelureaux, The Third Lover, Seven Capital Sins, Ophelia, Landru, Le Tigre Aime la Chair Fraiche, Marie-Chantal Contre le Docteur Kah, Le Tigre Se Parfume a la Dunamite, Paris vu par . . . Chabrol, La Ligne de Demarcation, The Champagne Murders, The Route to Corinth, Les Biches, Le Femme Infidele, This Man Must Die, Le Boucher, La Rapture, Ten Days' Wonder, Just Before Nightfall, Dr. Popaul, Les Noces Rouges, Nada.

CHAFFEY, DON: Director. b. Hastings, England, 1917. Trained as artist; secured work in art dept. of Gainsborough Studios in early 40s. Eventually moved to Gaumont British International where directed first film, a documentary on dogfish.
PICTURES INCLUDE: Time Is My Enemy, The Girl in the Picture, The Flesh is Weak, A Question of Adultery, The Man Upstairs, Danger Within, Dentist in the Chair, Greyfriars Bobby, Nearly a Nasty Accident, A Matter of Who, The Prince and the Pauper, Jason and the Argonauts, A Jolly Bad Fellow, One Million Years B.C., The Viking Queen, A Twist of Sand, Creature the World Forgot, The Three Lives of Thomasina, The Horse Without a Head, Ride a Wild Pony.

CHAIKIN, WILLIAM E.: Executive. b. Cleveland, Ohio, April 7, 1919. e. Ohio State Univ. (BS, journalism; MS political science). Was newspaper reporter and columnist for paper in Ohio, Indiana and Florida before joining 20th-Fox pub. dept. in 1945. And in pub. depts. of Republic and Eagle Lion Films. Later pres., Chaikin-Perret, p.r. firm. Became v.p. and treas. of Standard Capital, investment banking firm, where financed and supervised prod. of over 60 films. In 1963 named pres. and bd. chm. of Charter Title Insurance Co. in Los Angeles. Is member of the Board of Mariners Savings and Loan. Is mem. of bd. of Mariners Financial Corp., financial holding co. diversified building firm. From 1968–74 was v.p. in chg. of West Coast operations of Avco Embassy Pictures Corp. and asst. to James R. Kerr, pres. of Avco Corp. in July, 1974, assumed presidency of Avco Embassy Pictures Corp to 1980.

CHAKERES, MICHAEL H.: Executive b. Ohio, Ky. Graduate of Wittenberg University; pres. and chm. of bd. of Chakeres Theatres of Ohio and Kentucky. U.S. Army AF 1942–45. Bd. of Dir.: National NATO, NATO of Ohio, Will Rogers Memorial Fund, Motion Picture Pioneers, Society National Bank, Wittenberg University, Mercy Medical Center. Member: Variety Club, Masonic Lodge, I.O.O.F. Order of AHEPA, Ohio Heart Ass'n.

CHAKIRIS, GEORGE: Actor. b. Norwood, Ohio, Sept. 16, 1934. Entered m.p. industry as a dancer in There's No Business Like Show Business and Brigadoon; academy award for West Side Story. Starred in the Young Girls of Rocheford, The Big Cube.

CHALMERS, PATRICK: b. Aberdeenshire, Scotland, 1940. e. Fettes College, Edinburgh, Aberdeen School of Agriculture, and Durham University. Joined BBC in 1973 as radio producer, and became television producer, 1975. Senior producer at Aberdeen 1970, helping with launch of Radio Aberdeen. Has won awards for films at Berlin Film Festival. Head of Television, BBC Scotland, 1978.

CHAMBERLAIN, RICHARD: Actor. b. Los Angeles, 1935. Became TV star in Dr. Kildare series (1961–65). Theatrical film debut in 1962. A Thunder of Drums.
PICTURES INCLUDE: Twilight of Honor, Joy in the Morning, Petulia, The Madwoman of Chaillot, Julius Caesar, The Music Lovers, Lady Caroline Lamb, The Three Musketeers, The Towering Inferno, The Slipper and the Rose, The Last Wave, The Swarm.
TV: Hamlet (1970), F. Scott Fitzgerald and the Last of the Belles, The Count of Monte Cristo, Centennial, Shogun.

CHAMBERS, EVERETT: Producer, director. b. Montrose, Calif., Aug. 19, 1926. e. New School For Soc. Res., Dramatic Workshop, NYC. Entered industry as actor; worked with

Fred Coe as casting dir. and dir., NBC, 1952–57; prod., dir. Run Across the River, indep. feature and The Kiss, short nominated for Acad. Award, 1958; prod. Johnny Staccato, MCA, 1959; prod., Tess of the Storm Country, 20th-Fox.
TV: Target: The Corrupters, Dick Powell Theater, Saints and Sinners (pilot), The New Lloyd Bridges Show, numerous pilots; prod., dir., co-author with Don Gordon, The Lollipop Cover, Chicago Film Fest. awards, Best Film, Best Actor, 365 episodes Peyton Place, prod. writer for Nightslaves-ABC Movie of the Week, exec. prod. Monty Nash, prod. staff producer ABC TV; produced movies of the week, Moon of the Wolf, Trouble Comes to Town, The Great American Beauty Contest, Can Ellen Be Saved?, The Girl Must Live, They Only Come Out at Night. Currently prod. of Columbo.

CHAMPION, JOHN C.: Director, producer, writer. b. Denver, Col., Oct. 13, 1923; e. Stanford U., Wittenberg Coll.; p. Lee R. Champion, Supreme Court Judge. Col. Entered m.p. in Fiesta; did some radio work; in stock at MGM briefly; co-pilot Western Air Lines, Inc., 1943; served in U.S. Army Air Forces, air transport command pilot 1943–45; public relations officer AAF; writer & prod. for Allied Artists; v.p. prod. Commander Films Corp.: press. Champion Pictures, Inc.; prod., MGM, Warner, Para., Universal. Member: SAG, SWG, SIMPP, SPG; TV Academy, Prod. Writer, MIRISCH-U.A.: prod. TV Laramie series; created McHales Navy; author, novel, The Hawks of Noon, 1965; National Cowboy, Hall of Fame Award, 1976.
PICTURES INCLUDE: Panhandle, Stampede, Hellgate, Dragonfly Squadron, Shotgun, Allied Artists; Zero Hour, Paramount; The Texican, Columbia; Attack on the Iron Coast, Submarine X-1, The Last Escape, Mirisch-United Artists; Brother of the Wind, Sun International, dir-prod-writer, Mustang Country, Universal.

CHAMPION, MARGE: Dancer, actress. b. Los Angeles, Calif., Sept. 2. e. Los Angeles public schools; p. Ernest Belcher, ballet master; m. Gower Champion, dancer, actor. In Blossom Time, Student Prince for Los Angeles Civic Opera; Dark of the Moon. Beggar's Holiday in N.Y. Made debut with husband as dancing team, played many night clubs; m.p. Debut in Mr. Music; then signed by MGM; Fame Star of Tomorrow, 1952; on B'way in 3 for Tonight, 1955; toured, invitation to A March 1962.
PICTURES INCLUDE: Show Boat, Lovely to Look At, Everything I Have Is Yours, Give a Girl a Break, Three for the Show, Jupiter's Darling, The Swimmer, The Party, The Cockeyed Cowboys of Calico County.
TV: GE Theatre, Chevy Show, Telephone Hour, etc.

CHANCELLOR, JOHN: TV Anchorman and News Reporter. b. Chicago, 1927. e. Univ. of Ill. Following military service joined Chicago Sun-Times (1948) and after two years moved to NBC News as Midwest corr. In 1948 assigned to Vienna bureau. Subsequently reported from London; was chief of Moscow bureau before appt. as host of Today program for one year (1961). Left NBC 1965–67 to become dir. of Voice of America. In recent yrs. anchorman for special coverage of moon landings, political conventions, inaugurations etc. Now anchorman, principal reporter on NBC Nightly News and writes and delivers daily series on NBC Radio, The Chancellor Report.

CHANDLER, CHICK: Actor. b. Kingston, N.Y.
STAGE: Great Magoo, Best Man, Harvey, Our Town, Dinner at Eight, Star Dust, Show Boat, Maytime, Roberta, Firefly.
MUSICAL COMEDY: Pajama Game, Damn Yankees, Brigadoon. On screen from 1934.
PICTURES INCLUDE: Blood Money, Big Shot, Alexander's Ragtime Band, Mother Wore Tights, Battle Cry, Mad Mad Mad World, Lost Continent and over 100 more.
TV: Soldiers of Fortune, One Happy Family, Freelance major TV shows.

CHANNING, CAROL: Actress. b. Seattle, Jan. 31, 1923. e. Bennington Col. Long career on Broadway and road; most notably in Gentlemen Prefer Blondes, Lend an Ear, and Hello, Dolly!
PICTURES: First Traveling Saleslady, Thoroughly Modern Millie, Skidoo.
TELEVISION: Svengali and the Blonde, Three Men on a Horse, Crescendo; many guest appearances.

CHANNING, STOCKARD: Actress. b. New York City. Has performed in some 25 plays as well as small roles in two Hollywood films, leading to the starring role in the ABC Movie-of-the-Week, The Girl Most Likely To.
PICTURES INCLUDE: The Fortune, The Big Bus, Sweet Revenge, Grease, The Cheap Detective, The Fish That Saved Pittsburgh.

CHAPIN, SLOCUM: Executive. b. Quincy, Mass. May 12, 1913; e. Dartmouth College, 1936. With Broadcast Builders, Hanover, N.H.; sales prom., World Broadcasting System; sales exec., WOC, Davenport, Ia.; sales mgr., WKBN, Youngstown, O.; gen. mgr., WSTC, Stamford, Conn.; network sales staff, ABC, 1942–48; east. TV sales mgr., ABC, 1948–51; v.p. in charge of owned TV stations, ABC, 1951; sales vice pres., ABC-TV, 1954; V.P. client relations, 1957; v.p. sls., Western division 1959; v.p. sls. National division, 1963; v.p. exec. relations, 1964.

CHAPLIN, CHARLES S.: Executive. b. Toronto, Ont., Canada, June 24, 1911. Studied Law. Entered m.p. ind. 1930 as office boy with United Artists; then office mgr. booker, St. John, N.B., 1933; br. mgr. 1935; to Montreal in same capacity, 1941; named Canadian gen. mgr., June 11, 1945; resigned January 1962. Vice-pres. Canadian sls. mgr., Seven Arts Prod., 1962. Member: B'nai Brith, Toronto Bd. of Trade, various charitable org., many trade assns., pres. Canadian M.P. Dist. Assn., Chmn. m.p. section Com. Chest, chmn. publ rel comm. & past-chmn., M.P. Industry Council.

CHAPLIN, GERALDINE: Actress. b. Santa Monica, CA., 1944. Daughter of Charles Chaplin. Starred in over 20 European productions, including seven with Spain's leading filmmaker, Carlos Saura.
PICTURES INCLUDE: Doctor Zhivago, Stranger in the House, I Killed Rasputin, The Hawaiians, Zero Population Growth, Innocent Bystanders, The Three Musketeers, Nashville, Buffalo Bill and the Indians, Welcome to L.A., Roseland, Remember My Name, The Mirror Crack'd.

CHAPLIN, SAUL: Musical director and producer. b. Brooklyn, N.Y., Feb. 19, 1912. e. NYU 1929–34. Wrote vaude. material, 1933–36; songwriter Vitaphone Corp.; other, 1934–40; Columbia, 1940–48; MGM, from 1948; songs include: Bei Mir Bist Du Schoen, Shoe Shine Boy, Anniversary Song.
PICTURES INCLUDE: Acad. Award, collab. best scoring of mus., American in Paris, 1951, 7 Brides for 7 Brothers, 1954; West Side Story, 1961; mus. dir., Lovely to Look At, Give A Girl a Break, Kiss Me Kate, Jupiter's Darling; mus. supvr. Interrupted Melody, High Society; assoc. prod. Les Girls; music assoc. prod. Merry Andrew; assoc. prod. Can-Can, West Side Story, The Sound of Music; prod. Star, 1968; assoc. prod., The Man of La Mancha, 1972; co-prod. That's Entertainment, Part Two.

CHAPMAN, MICHAEL: Cinematographer. b. New York. Early career in N.Y. area working on documentaries before becoming camera operator for cinematographer Gordon Willis on The Godfather.
PICTURES: The Last Detail, White Dawn, Taxi Driver, The Front, The Next Man, Fingers, The Last Waltz, Invasion of the Body Snatchers.

CHAPMAN, TEDWELL: Playwright, journalist. b. Chicago, Ill., April 12, 1917. e. De Paul University, Layola University, Columnist, Hollywood Feature Syndicate, editor, Tailwagger Magazine, Hoja de Lunes (weekly, Malaga, Spain).
CREDITS: Abroad With Two Yanks (collab. orig. story & s.p.), The Fabulous Suzanne (collab. orig. s.p), The Flanagan Boy (collab. s.p.), Drop In Anytime (orig. s.p.), Forever Is a Long Time (TV, orig. story & s.p.), The Crowded Bed (TV, orig. s.p.), Twice Upon a Time (Stage), The Intriguing Stranger (Stage), Bedlam (Stage), The Shame of Cain (Stage, book & lyrics), South of Granada (Stage, book & lyrics).

CHARI, V.K.N.: Public relations counsel & Publicity advisor. b. Salem, 1913. Till 1956 publicity & pub. relations officer, Gemini Studios, Madras. Presently film publicity adviser to film studios and film producers. Editor: Advertiser's Vademecum, Indian Advertising Year Book, An Economic Guide to India, The Languages of India. Refer-india, etc. Hon. Genl. Secretary. The Indian Council of Public Affairs, Madras. Journalist & news correspondent, B44 First Mainroad Sastrinagar, Madras 20.

CHARISSE, CYD: Dancer, actress. r.n. Tula Ellice Finklea. b. Amarillo, Tex., Mar. 8, 1923. m. Tony Martin, singer; e. Hollywood Prof. School. Toured U.S. & Europe with Ballet Russe; screen debut in "Something to Shout About," 1943. Elected Star of Tomorrow 1948.
PICTURES INCLUDE: Mission to Moscow, Three Wise Fools, Till the Clouds Roll By, On an Island with You, Words and Music, Kissing Bandit, Tension, East Side, West Side, Mark of the Renegade, Wild North, Singin' in the Rain, Sombrero, Band Wagon, Easy to Love, Brigadoon, Deep in My Heart, It's Always Fair Weather, Meet Me in Las Vegas, Silk Stockings, Black Tights, Two Weeks in Another Town, The Silencers, Maroc 7.

CHARLES, MARIA: Actress. b. London, England, Sept. 22, 1929. Trained at Royal Academy of Dramatic Art. London Stage Debut 1946 in Pick Up Girl. Subseq.
STAGE (London): Women of Twilight, The Boy Friend, Divorce Me, Darling!, Enter A Free Man, They Don't Grow on Trees, Winnie the Pooh, Jack the Ripper, The Matchmaker, Measure for Measure, Annie (1979–80).
PICTURES INCLUDE: Folly To Be Wise, The Deadly Affair, Eye of the Devil, Great Expectations, The Return of the Pink Panther, Cuba.
TELEVISION: The Likes of 'Er, The Moon and the Yellow River, Down Our Street, Easter Passion, Nicholas Nickleby, The Voice of the Turtle, The Fourth Wall, The Good Old

Days, Turn Out the Lights, Angel Pavement, The Ugliest Girl in Town, Other Peoples Houses, Rogues Gallery, The Prince and the Pauper, Crown Court, Barmitzvah Boy, Secret Army, Agony.

CHARPENTIER, GASTON L. G.: Producer, director. b. London 1912. Early career: dramatic school, theatre and film actor, author short stories, asst. dir. Ent. m.p. industry as prod. man., writer, dir. scriptwriter, 1932; prod. for Strand Films Ltd., National Studios, ABPC., Denham; with Rank Organ. 4½ years; exec. prod. and man. dir., Impact Production Ltd., 1957. At present MGM Studios, Boreham Woods.

CHARTERIS, LESLIE: Writer, producer. b. Singapore, 1907; e. Cambridge, Eng. Novelist; creator The Saint, protagonist of mystery novels and series of pictures based on them prod. by RKO from 1938 and by Julian Lesser from 1952.

CHARTOFF, ROBERT: Producer. b. N.Y.C. e. Union College (A.B.), Col. Univ. (LLB). Met Irvin Winkler through mutual client at William Morris Agency (N.M.) and established Chartoff-Winkler Prods. All films co-produced with Winkler.
PICTURES INCLUDE: Double Trouble, Point Blank, The Split, They Shoot Horses, Don't They?, The Strawberry Statement, Leo The Last, Believe in Me, The Gang That Couldn't Shoot Straight, The New Centurions, Up the Sandbox, The Mechanic, Busting, The Gambler, SPYs, Breakout, Nickelodeon, New York, New York, Valentino, Rocky, Comes a Horseman, Uncle Joe Shannon, Rocky II, Raging Bull, True Confessions.

CHASE, BRANDON: Producer-Director. President MPA Feature Films, Inc.; newscaster-news director NBC-TV 1952–57. Executive director Mardi Gras Productions, Inc. and member of Board of Directors. Now pres., Group I Films, Ltd., and V.I. Prods., Ltd.
PICTURES INCLUDE: The Dead One, The Sinner and the Slave Girl, Bourbon Street Shadows, Verdict Homicide, Face of Fire, Four for the Morgue, Mission To Hell, The Wanton, Harlow, Girl In Trouble, Threesome, Wild Cargo, The Depraved, Alice in Wonderland, The Models, Sensuous 3, The Four of Us, Against All Odds, The Giant Spider Invasion, House of 1,000 Pleasures, The Rogue, Eyes of Dr. Chaney, Alligator, Crash!, Take All of Me, The Teasers, The Psychic, UFOs Are Real, The Actresses.
TELEVISION: Wild Cargo (series prod.-dir.); This Strange and Wondrous World (prod.-dir.).

CHASE, CHEVY: Actor. b. New York City, Oct. 8. e. Bard College. Teamed with Kenny Shapiro and Lane Sarasohn while still in school to collaborate on material for underground TV, which ultimately became off-Broadway show and later movie called Groove Tube. Co-wrote and starred in Saturday Night Live on TV, winning 2 Emmys for outstanding continuing or single performance by a supporting actor in variety and music and as writer for show. Has exclusive contract as performer with NBC. Feature film debut in Foul Play in 1978.
PICTURES: Caddyshack, Seems Like Old Times, Under the Rainbow.

CHASE, STANLEY: Producer. b. Brooklyn, N.Y., May 3. e. NYU (B.A.); Columbia (post-grad.). M. actress/artist Dorothy Rice. Began career as assoc. prod. of TV show Star Time; story dept., CBS-TV; then produced plays off-Bdwy. and on Bdwy., winner Tony and Obie awards for Threepenny Opera. Joined ABC-TV as dir. in chg. programming; exec. consultant, Metromedia Producers Org.; prod. & exec., Alan Landsburg Productions. Formed Stanley Chase Productions, Inc. in 1975, which heads as pres.
PICTURES INCLUDE: To Hell with Heroes, Colossus: The Forbin Project; High-Ballin' (exec. prod.); Fish Hawk (exec. prod.).
TELEVISION: Inside Danny Baker (pilot); Al Capp special (prod., writer); Happily Ever After (pilot; prod., writer); Bob Hope Presents the Chrysler Theatre series; Jigsaw (pilot); Fear on Trial (Emmy nomination); Courage of Kavik (exec. prod.); An American Christmas Carol.
STAGE: Producer of following plays: Threepenny Opera, The Potting Shed, The Cave Dwellers, A Moon for the Misbegotten, Free and Easy.

CHASEMAN, JOEL: Executive. b. Albany, N.Y., Feb. 18, 1926. e. Cornell. Entered broadcasting in 1943 as engineer and announcer at New York State radio stations. Worked at WAAM—TV, Baltimore, from 1948 to 1955 as announcer, director, news director and public service producer; later as advertising and promotion mgr. 1955–57, returned to radio as air personality for WITH, Baltimore; returned to WAAM as asst. gen. mgr. & dir. of natl sls. Named program mgr. in 1957. 1960, moved to N.Y. for Group W as natl. radio program mgr. 1961 named v.p. & gen. mgr. Moved to Los Angeles in 1962 as exec. prod. of The Steve Allen Show; returned to Group W, 1964 as v.p. & gen. mgr. of WINS. Named pres. of Group W Radio, 1967; 1970, made snr. v.p., programming & production. Later named pres. of Group W Television. 1973, moved to Washington to assume presidency of Post-Newsweek Stations, Inc.

CHASMAN, DAVID: Executive. b. N.Y., Sept. 28, 1925. e. School of Industrial Art, 1940–43; Academie De La Grande-Chaumiere, 1949–50. Monroe Greenthal Co., Inc. 1950–53; Grey Advertising Agency, Inc., 1953–60. Free lance consultant to industry 1950–60; worked on pictures for UA, 20th-Fox, Columbia, Samuel Goldwyn, City Film; Adv. mgr. United Artists, 1960; exec. dir. adv., United Artists, 1962; exec. production, United Artists, London, 1964; v.p. in prod. United Artists, 1969; v.p. of west coast operations, U.A. 1970; Senior Vice President in charge of Production, U.A. 1972; President, Convivium Productions Inc., 1974.

CHATELAIN, DIDIER: Production Executive. b. Jan. 24, Paris, France. Educated Paris and Polytechnic, London. Degree in Business Administration, Marketing & Advertising. Entered industry in 1970 joining Herman Cohen Productions in London and Hollywood, starting with the advertising & promotion of Crooks and Coronets, 1971; Trog, 1972, Today We Kill . . . Tomorrow We Die!, 1973; The Strangers Gundown, 1974. Assistant Producer, Craze, 1974.

CHAUDHRI, AMIN QAMAR: Director, Cinematographer-Editor. b. Punjab, India, April 18, 1938; e. Hampstead Polytechnic, London, City U., N.Y. President, Artscope Ltd., 1967.
PICTURES INCLUDE: Direction, Kashish, Sweet Vengeance, Khajuraho, Eternal, Vice Girl, Urvasi, Konarak, Black Rodeo, The Land of Buddha, Love Generation, Woman's Urge.
CINEMATOGRAPHY: Right On, Sweet Vengeance, The Hopefuls, The Wicked Die Slow, The Love Statute, Vice Girls, Ltd., Who Says I Can't Ride a Rainbow, Black Rodeo, Medium is the Message, Death of a Dunbar Girl, Kashish.

CHER: Singer-Actress. b. El Centro, Calif. May 20, 1946. r.n. Cherilyn Sarkisian. Began singing with then husband Sonny Bono in 1965; first hit record, I Got You Babe, sold 3 million. Made two films and then debuted nightclub musical-comedy act in 1969. CBS comedy-variety series started as summer show in 1971; became regular following December.
PICTURES INCLUDE: Good Times, Chastity.
TELEVISION: Sonny & Cher Comedy Hour, Cher.

CHERMAK, CY: Producer-Writer. b. Bayonne, N.J., Sept. 20, 1929. e. Brooklyn College; Ithaca College.
TELEVISION: Produced Ironsides, The Virginian, The New Doctors, Amy Prentiss, Night Stalkers, Barbary Coast, CHIPS. TV movie: Murder at the World Series.

CHERTOK, HARVEY: Executive. b. New York, N.Y., Oct. 29, 1932. e. N.Y.U., grad. school, bus. admin. Merchandising mgr., National Telefilm Assocs., Jan. 1956–Aug. 1959; supv., adv., United Artists Associated, Aug. 1959–March 1961; dir., adv., sls. prom., publicity, Seven Arts Associated Corp., 1961–1968; prod., 7 Surprizes, 1964; 1968 TV v.p. advertising-publicity, Warner-7 Arts, co.-prod., The Great Charlie Chan (TV spec.) 1968, co-author Quotations from Charlie Chan (Golden Press) 1968; Pres. The Children's Movie of the Month, Inc., 1969–71; marketing consultant, United Artists Television, 1972–73; V.P.-special-projects, The American Film Theatre, Inc. 1973–75; v.p. adv., sls. prom., pub. for Time-Life Television, 1975; named v.p., adv./promo, Time Life-tv, 1978–81.

CHERTOK, JACK: Producer. b. Atlanta, Ga., July 13. Began career as script clerk, MGM; later asst. cameraman, asst. dir., head of music dept., short subjects prod. Feature prod. MGM 1939–42 ("The Penalty," "Joe Smith, American," "Kid Glove Killer," "The Omaha Trail," "Eyes in the Night," etc.). In July, 1942, apptd. Hollywood prod. chief, Co-Ord. Inter-Amer. Affairs, serving concurrently with regular studio work. Left MGM 1942 and prod. for Warner Bros. to late 1944; pres.: Produced The Corn is Green and Northern Pursuit for Warner Bros. Pres. Jack Chertok TV, Inc.

CHESTER, HAL E.: Producer. b. Brooklyn, N.Y., Mar. 6, 1921. On N.Y. stage; film debut in "Crime School" 1937, followed by "Little Tough Guy" series. "Juvenile Court"; personal appearance tour of U.S and Canada 1941–44; entered m.p. production 1944, doing a series of musical shorts. Member: IMPPA. Prod. Joe Palooka series beginning with "Joe Palooka Champ" 1946, released via Monogram, Smart Woman; v.p. in chge. prod., Mutual Films Corp., 1951.
PICTURES INCLUDE: Joe Palooka In The Squared Circle, Underworld Story, The Highwayman, Triple Cross, Models, Beast from 20,000 Fathoms, Crashout, Bold and The Brave, The Weapon, The Haunted, School for Scoundrels, Two-Headed Spy, His and Hers, Hide and Seek, The Comedy Man, The Double Man, The Secret War of Harry Frigg.

CHETWYND, LIONEL: Executive, writer. b. London, England, 1940. Emigrated to Canada, 1948. B.A. (Economics, Sir George Williams Univ. Montreal), B.C.L.-McGill University, Montreal. Graduate Work-Law—Trinity College, Oxford. Admitted to Bar—Province of Quebec, 1968. C.B.C.—TV-Public Affairs and Talks, 1961–1965. CTV Network 1965–67. Controller commercial TV and film rights, Expo '67. Freelance writer and consultant 1961–68. Joined Columbia Pictures Intern. New York July 1968, transferred to Co-lumbia Pictures Corp. Ltd., London, Sept. 1968. Asst. man. dir. January 1969. Asst. man. dir. Columbia-Warner UK, 1971. Story and book for musical Maybe That's Your Problem, 1971–1973: s.p., Apprenticeship of Duddy Kravitz; The Guest Room (TV).

CHIKADA, TADASHI: Executive. b. Japan Nov. 20, 1919. e. Tokyo Foreign Language Univ. 1940–6 with Showa Tsusho in Japan and China; 1947–50 Izumi Sangyo, transferring to Nihon Eiga Shizai (Japan Movie Equipment Co.) which later became Toshiba Photo Phone Co.; appt. director and gen. mgr. of Trade Div. in 1972, and in 1974 director in charge of trade.

CHILTON, T.E.: Executive. b. Kent, England, 1929. Ent. m.p. ind. 1951 with J.F. Brockliss. 1953 Simplex Apro. 1955. Rank Precision Industries, then various appointments in equipment industry in Rank Organisation becoming Asst. Man. Dir. 1968, Man. Dir. 1971. Appt. man. dir. Rank Leisure Service 1973. Appt. chairman Rank Leisure Services, Rank Hotels, Rank Advertising Films, Rank Film Distributors, Pinewood Studios, 1976, dir. Rank Organisation 1976.

CHIN, ELIZABETH MAE: Executive. b. New York, N.Y. Nov. 2, 1938. e. George Washington H.S. 1956; C.C.N.Y., Business Administration 1960; Internal Auditor 1960; International trade and entrepreneur of international dairy franchise 1968. Entered motion picture industry in 1974 as agent for independent film distribution in theatrical and television. Presently, executive of Far East Enterprises, and Emcee World Associates, Inc. and Bergen Intl. Corp.

CHING, WILLIAM: Actor. b. St. Louis, Mo., Oct. 2, 1913. e. Spring Hills Coll. Radio Singer; on Broadway in Allegro.
PICTURES INCLUDE: Pat and Mike, Never Wave at a Wac, Give a Girl a Break, Scared Stiff, The Moonlighter, Tall Man Riding, Magnificent Matador.
TV: featured actor, Our Miss Brooks; NBC-TV.

CHINICH, JESSE: Executive. b. Hoboken, N.J., Dec. 17, 1921; e. N.Y.U. Law S., L.L.B. 1938. Lawyer with Hovell, Clarkson and Klupt, 1938–41; U.S. Army, 1941–46; joined Paramount Theatres as film buyer, 1946–51; circuit supervisor, Rugoff & Becker, NYC, 1951–53 western div. sales mgr.; Buena Vista Film Dist., Co., 1953–61; Ass't gen. sales mgr. coordinator Cinema V Dist.; ass't sales mgr., Allied Artists; sales executive, special projects, Warner Bros. Dist. Corp. Now Publisher of weekly newsletters.

CHISSELL, NOBLE (KID): Actor. b. Indianapolis, Ind., Feb. 16, 1910; e. City Coll. of L.A., U.S. Merchant Marine, prof. boxer, prison officer, U.S. Navy Middleweight Boxing Champ 1932, World Marathon Dance Champion 1928, Champ Walkathoner 1934–35. Chairman/m.c. world famed Cauliflower Alley Club, co-ed boxing/wrestling group, since 1968. Middleweight Senior Olympic Skill Boxing Champ 1974–78 m.c. Burbank Easter Parade 1979–80. Nostalgic Movie/Boxing columnist, Hollywood Independent; Boxing columnist, Official Boxing Record; Master of Ceremonies, Film Welfare League benefit Show, 1980.
STAGE: Cafe Frisco, All the Kings Men, J. Silverheel's Indian Pageant, Love in Upper Sandusky, Lower Depths, Meet the World, Twelfth Night.
PICTURES INCLUDE: Abe Lincoln in Illinois, Home in Indiana, Dillinger, Grand Canyon, Young At Heart, Guys and Dolls, Big Chase, Friendly Persuasion, Bonnie and Clyde, More Dead Than Alive, Hell Cats, Big Foot, They Shoot Horses, Don't They?, Mule Feathers, The Clones, Ex-Champ, Jealousy, The Leather-pusher, Song of Arizona, The Polygamist, The Traveling Executioner, Three in The Saddle, Arizona Mission, El Salvaje, Pistol Packing Mama, The Rebel Breed, etc.
TV: Marshall of Gunsight Pass, Colgate Comedy Hour, Life of Riley, It's a Great Life, Dragnet, Playhouse 90, Climax, People's Court, Gunsmoke, Gallagher-Disney Series, High Chaparral, To Tell the Truth, Dating Game, 20 Bob Hope Comedy Specials. Also, Minsky Follies 1975, Hollywood.

CHIVERS, ALAN: Executive. b. 1918. Joined BBC (Radio) 1946 transferred to Television Outside Broadcasts 1948 as prod.; moved to Independent Television 1959. Returned to BBC as Exec. Prod. special projects television outside broadcasts from 1969.

CHODOROV, EDWARD: Writer, dir. b. New York City, April 17, 1914. e. Brown U. Writer, dir., plays; Writer, prod., films.
PLAYS INCLUDE: Wonder Boy, Kind Lady, Cue for Passion, Those Endearing Young Charms, Decision, Common Ground, The Spa, Signor Chicago, Oh Men Oh Women, M. Lautrec, Erskine, Listen to the Mocking Bird, etc. Writer-prod. Warners, 20th, Col., MGM. Wrote Billy Rose Show ABC; writer dir., prod. Sam Spiegel, Horizon Pictures, 1961–63; Writer-prod.-dir. A.C.E. Prods. (London) 1964; Columbia, 1965; 20th-Fox, 1966–67; writer-producer, Warner-7 Arts, 1968, 1969; writer-dir., Dowling, Whitehead, Stevens, 1971–72; Cheryl Crawford Prods., 1973, Universal, 1974–75; Theatre Guild 1976; The Lecturer, California State University 1977–78; the Sorbonne 1979. Play commissioned

by Roger Stevens-Robert Whitehead, A Very Important Man Is Dead.

CHOMSKY, MARVIN J.: Director. b. Bronx, N.Y. Started in theatre business at early age as art dir. with such TV credits as U.S. Steel Hour, Playhouse 90, Studio One, etc. Later worked with Herb Brodkin who advanced him to assoc. prod. with such TV shows as The Doctors and The Nurses. Brought to Hollywood in 1965 as assoc. prod. for Talent Associates, producing series of TV pilots. First theatrical film, Maya, for King Bros.
PICTURES INCLUDE: Evel Knievel, Murph the Surf, Mackintosh and T.J.
TV: The Wild, Wild West, Gunsmoke, Star Trek, Then Came Bronson, and many Movies of the Week, Victory at Entebbe, Roots.

CHONG, TOMMY: Singer-Actor-Writer. b. Edmonton, Atla., Canada. Was guitar player with various Canadian rhythm and blues combinations, teamed with Richard Marin (Cheech) in improvisational group. Has made comedy recordings.
PICTURES: Cheech and Chong's Up in Smoke, Cheech and Chong's Next Movie, Cheech and Chong's Nice Dreams.

CHOOLUCK, LEON: Producer-Director. b. New York, March 19, 1920; e. CCNY, 1938. Production, distribution, editing with Consolidated Film Industries 1936–40; Army Pictorial Service as news photographer 1941–45; Indep. as ass. dir. and prod. mgr. 1946–56; prod. for Regal Films and Orbit Pro., 1957–58; dir. Highway Patrol, 1958. Various occupations on stage 1947–58; prod. mgr., Daystar Prods., ABC-TV series, Stoney Burke; prod. mgr., assoc. prod., Daystar Prods., 1962–63; prod. supv., Encyclopedia Britannica Films, in Spain, 1964; prod. supv., U.S. Pictures, Battle of the Bulge; loc. mgr., Three F Prods., assoc. prod. I Spy, TV Series, 1965–67. Vice Pres. Fouad Said Cinemobile Systems, 1969–70. Pres., The Society (film prod. org.).
PICTURES INCLUDE: Hell on Devil's Island, Plunder Road, Murder by Contract, City of Fear, The Fearmakers, Day of the Outlaw, Bramble Bush, Rise and Fall of Legs Diamond, Studs Lonigan, Three Blonds in His Life, El Cid, The Outer Limits, Midas Run, The Grissom Gang, Kotch, Payday, 1971; Three the Hard Way-'73–74; Take a Ride-'74–75, Apocalypse Now, Loving Couples.
TELEVISION: Prod. supvr. 1974–76; NBC (2 hr.) Specials, Strange Homecoming, Michener's Dynasty, Judge Horton and the Scottsboro Boys, Pearl, A Rumor of War, Murder in Texas.

CHOW, RAYMOND: Producer. b. Hong Kong. e. St. John's University, Shanghai. Worked as journalist for Hong Kong Standard; then joined the U.S. Information Agency, establishing its Chinese radio station which broadcast to the Chinese mainland. In late 1950s joined Shaw Brothers as head of their publicity operations. In next 12 years became right-hand man of Run Run Shaw and head of production. In 1971 formed The Golden Harvest Group to produce Chinese-language films in Hong Kong. Two kung-fu films featuring Bruce Lee put Harvest into intl. market. Started English-language films in 1977, beginning with The Amsterdam Kill and The Boys in Company C.

CHRISMAN, H. ED: Executive. b. Nashville, Tenn., Sept. 6, 1914. e. Vanderbilt Univ., 1932. Sales, br. mgr., Dun and Bradstreet, 1935–50; v.p. and sales mgr., Cretors and Co., Popcorn Machine manufacturer, Chicago and Nashville, 1950–66; purchased Shoemaker Popcorn Co., Murray, Ky.; incorporated bus. as Chrisman Popcorn Co., processors and packers of Rocket popcorn; regional v.p. & comm. chmn, National Assc. of Concessionaires.

CHRISTIAN, LINDA: Actress. r.n. Blanca Rosa Welter. b. Tampico, Mex., Nov. 13, 1924, e. Mexico, Venezuela, Palestine, So. Africa, Holland, Italy; attended medical school in Palestine; Worked for British Censorship Bureau in Palestine; asst. to plastic surgeon; screen debut in Holiday in Mexico.
PICTURES INCLUDE: Green Dolphin Street, Tarzan and the Mermaids, The Happy Time, Battle Zone, Slave of Babylon, Athena, Thunderstorm.

CHRISTIANSEN, ROBERT W.: Producer. B. Porterville, CA. e. Bakersfield College. Spent 3 years in Marine Corps. Worked on Hollywood Reporter in circulation and advertising. Joined Cinema Center Films; prod. asst. on Monte Walsh and Hail Hero. Co-produced first feature in 1970, Adam at Six A.M., with Rick Rosenberg, with whom co-produced all credits listed.
PICTURES INCLUDE: Adam at Six A.M., Hide in Plain Sight.
TV: Features: Suddenly Single, The Glass House, A Brand New Life, The Man Who Could Talk to Kids, The Autobiography of Miss Jane Pittman, I Love You . . . Goodbye, Queen of the Stardust Ballroom, Born Innocent, A Death in Canaan, Strangers.

CHRISTIE, HOWARD J: Producer. b. San Francisco, Calif., Sept. 16, 1912. e. Berkeley, U. of Calif. Entered m.p. ind. following graduation from coll. in 1934, as actor; asst. dir. 1936–40;

assoc. prod., 1942–44, Deanna Durbin pictures. Member: Screen Directors Guild, Screen Producers Guild, Delta Tau Delta, vice pres., Reeve M.C.A. Inc., 1961.
PICTURES INCLUDE: Lady on a Train, Because of Him I'll Be Yours, A & C Meet the Invisible Man, Golden Horde, Comin' Round the Mountain, Lost in Alaska, Against All Flags, Yankee Buccaneer, Seminole, Lone Hand, A & C Go To Mars, A & C Meet Dr. Jekyll and Mr. Hyde, Back to God's Country, Yankee Pasha, A & C Meet Keystone Kops, Smoke Signal, The Looters, Purple Mask, A & C Meet the Mummy, Price of Fear, Congi Crossing, Showdown at Abilene, Toy Tiger, Away All Boats, I've Lived Before, Wagon Train, The Raiders, Sword of Ali Baba, Senes, Laredo, Ride to Hangman's Tree, Journey to Shiloh, Nobody's Perfect, A Man Called Gannon.
TV: The Virginian.

CHRISTIE, JULIE: Actress. b. Chukua, Assam, India, July 14, 1941. e. Year in France followed by Drama School in England. TV debut in A for Andromeda. Birmingham Rep.; Royal Shakespeare Co.; East European and American tour, Starred (NY) in Uncle Vanya.
PICTURES INCLUDE: Fast Lady, Billy Liar, Young Cassidy, Darling, Dr. Zhivago, Farenheit 451, Far From the Madding Crowd, Petulia, In Search of Gregory, The Go-Between, McCabe and Mrs. Miller, Don't Look Now, Shampoo, The Demon Seed, Heaven Can Wait.

CHRISTINE, VIRGINIA: Actress. b. Stanton, Iowa, March 5. e. UCLA Los Angeles, Calif.; has appeared in more than 400 motion pictures and television productions.
PICTURES INCLUDE: Mission to Moscow, Counter Attack, The Killers, Cover Up, The Men, Cyrano De Bergerac, Cobweb, High Noon, Not as a Stranger, Spirit of St. Louis, Three Brave Men, Judgment in Nuremberg, The Prize, Four For Texas, A Rage to Live, Guess Who's Coming to Dinner, Hail Hero, Daughter of the Mind.
TV: Dragnet, Abbot & Costello, Dangerous Assignment, Racket Squad, Superman, Schlitz Playhouse, Four Star Playhouse, The Whistler, Code 3, Ford Theatre, You Are There, Stage 7, Passport to Danger, Soldier of Fortune, Heinz Show, Anthology, Four Star Playhouse, Cavalcade of America, Alfred Hitchcock Presents, Father Knows Best, Crusader, Kellogg, Front Row Center, The Twisted Road, Matinee, Private Secretary, Fort Laramie, Big Town, Science Fiction, Frontier Detective, Lone Ranger, Jim Bowie, Wire Service, Whirlybirds, Gunsmoke, Las Vegas Story, Trackdown, The Thin Man, San Francisco Beat, Stranger In Town, T Men, Casey Jones, Climax, Mickey Spillane, The Millionaire, Behind Closed Doors, Target, Peter Gunn, Zane Grey Theatre, Wyatt Earp, Secret Mission, The Donna Reed Show, Wanted Dead Or Alive, Buckskin, Loretta Young Show, Starperformance, Rescue 8, Steve Canyon, State Trooper, Twilight Zone, General Electric Theatre, How to Marry A Millionaire, Rifle Man, June Allyson Show, Rawhide, M Squad, Coronado 9, Man From Black Hawk, Grand Jury, Riverboat, 77 Sunset Strip, Happy, The Thriller, Lawless Years, The Untouchables, Death Valley Days, Verdict Is Yours, Deputy, Perry Mason, Wagon Train, Mr. Ed, Maverick, The Shirley Temple Show, Asphalt Jungle, Harrigan and Son, Tales of Wells Fargo, Bronco, Line Of Duty, The New Breed, Going My Way, Stoney Burke, Bonanza, The Eleventh Hour, Ben Casey, The Virginian, The Fugitive, Day In Court, Hazel, Singing Nun, Billy The Kid, The Big Valley, The FBI, Laredo, A Man Called Shenandoah, Jericho, Judd for the Defense, The Invaders, Lancer, Nanny And The Professor.
STAGE: Hedda Gabler, Mary, Queen of Scots, Miss Julie, Desdemona.

CHRISTOPHER, JORDAN: Actor, musician. b. Youngstown, Ohio, 1941. e. Kent State U. Led rock 'n' roll group, "The Wild Ones." Broadway debut, Black Comedy, 1967.
PICTURES INCLUDE: Return of the Seven, The Fat Spy, The Tree, Pigeons.

CHURCHILL, SARAH: Actress. b. Oct. 7, 1916, Admiralty House, London. p. Winston Churchill. e. England and France. At 17 attended ballet school. Made first appearance in chorus of C.B. Cochrane's Follow the Sun, in London; and continued in theatre. Women's Auxiliary Air Force, World War II. In 1945, returned to professional life: two Italian films, When In Rome and Daniele Cortis. Also on stage, London, The Barretts of Wimpole Street. A personal appearance in America with J. Arthur Rank's All Over the Town brought her a Theatre Guild contract for touring with The Philadelphia Story, after which she danced for MGM in The Royal Wedding. Has appeared on Broadway in Gramercy Ghost, and for two years actress, hostess Hallmark's Hall of Fame, TV.

CIANNELLI, LEWIS E: Associate Producer. b. New York, Jan. 12, 1923 Univ. of Calif., 1941, Leland Stanford Univ.-AB 1947. Meschini Institute, Rome, 1950. World War II 1942–46. Acct. exec. adv. firm 1947–48. Actor: TV and motion pictures, 1948–50. Exec. asst. Industrie Cinematografiche Sociali, 1950, Director of Foreign Sls. I.C.S. and on board of A.N.I.C.A. 1953. Production exec. Lux Film, Rome 1953.

Head of Production Republic Pictures, Italy 1954–55; assoc. prod. The Best of the Post; assoc. prod., exec. asst. Ponti & Girosi, That Kind of Woman; Heller in Pink Tights, assoc. prod. NBC-TV; Ford Startime, Chevy Special Mexico, Rivak The Barbarian, The Americans, Outlaws.
PLAYS: OK Nero! Twin Trouble, The Bed.

CILENTO, DIANE: Actress. b. Queensland, Australia, 1934. e. Toowoomba. Went to New York and finished schooling and then American Acad. of Dramatic Art; first theatre job at 16; toured U.S. with Barter Co.; returned to London and joined Royal Acad. of Dramatic Art; several small parts and later repertory at Manchester's Library Theatre.
PICTURES INCLUDE: Angel Who Pawned Her Harp, Passing Stranger, Passage Home, Woman for Joe, Admirable Crichton, Truth About Women, Jet Storm, The Full Treatment, The Naked Edge, The Breaking Point, Once Upon A Tractor for UN, Hombre.
THEATRE: N.Y. stage: Tiger at the Gates, I Thank a Fool, The Third Secret, Tom Jones, The Rattle of a Simple Man, The Agony and the Ecstay, Hombre, Once Upon a Tractor, Negatives, The Four Seasons, The Bonne Soup, Heartbreak House. (NY), the Big Knife, Orpheus, Altona, Castle in Sweden, Naked, Marys, I've Seen You Cut Lemons.
TV: La Bell France (series), Court Martial, Blackmail, Dial M for Murder, Rogues Gallery, Rain, Lysistrata.

CIMINO, MICHAEL: Writer-Director. b. 1943. Protege of Clint Eastwood, who signed him to do s.p. for Magnum Force and then to write and direct Thunderbolt and Lightfoot, in both of which Eastwood starred.
PICTURES: The Deer Hunter, Heavens' Gate.

CIPES, ARIANNE ULMER: Executive. b. New York City, July 25, 1937. Daughter of film director Edgar G. Ulmer. e. Royal Academy of Dramatic Arts, London, University of London; actress, then production and dubbing, Paris; CDC, Rome; Titra, New York; 1975–77, v.p., Best International Films (international film distributor), Los Angeles; 1977 co-founder and v.p./sales & services of Producers Sales Organization.

CIPES, J.H.: Executive. b. N.Y., Dec. 14. e. Cornell U. 1960–66, Independent Producer-Packager-Distributor European features for U.S. TV sales; 1967, Producer Columbia Pictures Hollywood; 1968, Producer 20th Century-Fox TV; 1970, Producer Four Star TV; 1971, Marketing Executive, Technicolor, Inc.; 1973, Vice President, Marketing Technicolor, Inc.

CLAGETT, MANNING (TIM): Executive. b. Washington, D.C., Aug. 22, 1913. e. U. of Southern Calif.; U. of Calif., Los Angeles; Geo. Wash. U. Correspondent for Washington Herald, Washington Times-Herald 1937–41; Washington Star, 1941–48. Joined U.S. merchant marine 1943–44; corr., Washington Post 1945–46; own news bureau 1946–48. Assoc. Director of information, Motion Picture Assoc. of America, Washington, 1948–1958; dir. pub. rel. MPAA, 1953; dir. State Leg. Service, MPAA, 1956; v.p., 1961; special consultant, 1970.

CLARK, CANDY: Actress. b. Oklahoma. Was successful model in N.Y. before landing role in Fat City, 1972. Continues to model between films.
PICTURES INCLUDE: Fat City, American Graffiti, The Man Who Fell To Earth, Citizens Band, The Big Steep, When You Comin' Back, Red Ryder, More American Graffiti.

CLARK, DANE: Actor. b. New York City, Feb. 18, 1915; e. Cornell U., Johns Hopkins U. In radio series 2 yrs.; on N.Y. stage (Of Mice and Men, Dead End, etc.).
PICTURES INCLUDE: Glass Key, Sunday Punch, Pride of the Yankees, Tennessee Johnson, Action in the North Atlantic, Destination Tokyo, Very Thought of You, Hollywood Canteen, God Is My Co-Pilot, Her Kind of Man, That Way With Women, Deep Valley, Embraceable You, Moonrise, Whiplash, Without Honor, Backfire, Barricade, Never Trust a Gambler, Fort Defiance, Highly Dangerous, Gambler and the Lady, Go Man Go, Blackout, Paid to Kill, Thunder Pass, Port of Hell, Toughest Man Alive.
TV: No Exit, The Closing Door, Wire Service, Bold Venture (series).

CLARK, DICK: Performer. b. Mt. Vernon, N.Y. Nov. 30, 1929. Syracuse Univ. graduated 1951, summer announcer WRUN, Utica 1949, staff announcer WOLF, Syracuse 1950. After graduation 1951, took regular job with WOLF. Rejoined WRUN, Utica, then joined WKTV, Utica. Announcer WFIL Philadelphia 1952. Host of American Bandstand ABC-TV nationwide, the Dick Clark Beechnut Show, Dick Clark's World of Talent, The Object Is, Missing Links, Record Years, Years of Rock. Producer of TV shows, Where The Action Is, Swinging Country, Happening, Get It Together, Shebang, Record Years, Years of Rock. Author of Your Happiest Years, Random House . . . 1959, Author of Rock, Roll & Remember, T.Y. Crowell, 1976 and To Goof or Not to Goof, Bernard Geis, 1963. Formed Dick Clark Productions 1956 . . . Business engaged in motion picture production: Because They're Young, The Young Doctors, Psychout, The

Savage Seven, Killers Three, Elvis, the Movie. In-person concert division, marketing and communications division, cable TV programing department and radio division. Executive Producer of Dick Clark's Rockin' New Year's Eve, American Music Awards, Academy of Country Music Award, and other TV specials. 1978: Dick Clark's Live Wednesday. Produced TV Movies: Elvis, Man in the Santa Claus Suit.

CLARK, GREYDON: Producer-Director-Writer. b. Niles, MI, Feb. 7, 1943. e. Western Michigan Univ. (B.A., theatre arts, 1963). Heads own company, World Amusement Corp., Sherman Oaks, CA.
PICTURES: Writer: Satan's Sadists, Psychic Killer. Director-Writer: Mothers, Fathers, & Lovers, Bad Bunch. Producer-Writer-Director: Hi-Riders, Angel's Brigade, The Warning.

CLARK, JOHN L.: Executive. b. Owenton, Ky., Sep. 13, 1907; e. Univ. of Tenn. Talent scout, Brunswick Phono. Co.; mgr., WLW, Cincinnati; formed Transamerican Broad. & Tele. Corp. with Warner Bros.; prod. 50 TV films, 1941–44; created & prod. many radio & TV programs; pres. & sole owner, Transamerican.

CLARK, JOHN R., JR.: Executive. b. Owensburg, Ind., Aug. 18, 1915. e. Columbia U., 1930–34; Columbia Teachers Coll., 1934–35; U. of Calif., 1935–36. Employed in manufacturing plant, Technicolor Corp., 1936–38; research dept., administrative asst., 1938–46; civilian, Office of Scientific Research and Development, 1944; asst. to pres., Technicolor Corp., 1946; exec. v.p., 1955; pres., gen. mgr. Technicolor companies, 1960; dir., Technicolor, Inc., and Technicolor Corp. Fellow member: SMPTE.

CLARK, KENNETH: Journalist, executive. b. Dekalb, Ill., Aug. 1, 1899; e. U. Ill. Washington & foreign corresp. United Press, Internatl. News Service, Universal Service. Joined M.P. Prod. & Dist. Amer., 1936. Leave of absence 1942 to join U.S. Army; Maj., Lt. Col. and Col.; Returned to MPAA, Nov., 1945; v.p., 1953; exec. v.p., MPAA, 1962; v.p., MPEAA, 1953.

CLARK, PETULA: Actress and vocalist. b. Ewell, Surry, England, Nov. 15, 1932.
PICTURES INCLUDE: The Huggets, Dance Hall, White Corridors, The Card, Made in Heaven, Gay Dog, Runaway Bus, That Man Opposite, Finian's Rainbow, Goodbye Mr. Chips.

CLARK, ROBERT: Executive. b. Paisley, Renfrewshire, Scotland, July 26, 1905; e. Glasgow Univ. M.A., LL.B. Member of English bar 1929; joined m.p. industry at Elstree Studios, 1929; mem. bd. dir. Associated British Picture Corp., Aug., 1945; exec. dir. of prod. at Elstree Studios, 1948. Pres. Brit. Film Prod. Assn., 1953–55, 62–65; chmn. Nat. Film Thea. Appeal Comm., 1957; deputy chmn., Associated British Picture Corp. Ltd., Nov. 1964 & chief exec. ABP Ltd. Oct. 1966.

CLARK, SAMUEL H.: Exhibitor. b. Boston, Mass., Jan. 10, 1914. Owner, Music Suppliers, Boston, Mass.; founded Music Suppliers of New England, 1945; pres., ABC-Paramount Records Inc., 1955–65; v.p., head thea. operations, American Broadcasting-Paramount Theatres, Inc., Jan. 1965; dir., May, 1965.

CLARK, SUSAN: Actress. b. Canada. Trained at Royal Academy of Dramatic Arts in London. Made m.p. debut in Banning, 1967.
PICTURES INCLUDE: Coogan's Bluff, Madigan, Colossus: The Forbin Project, Tell Them Willie Boy Is Here, Skullduggery, Skin Game, Valdez Is Coming, Showdown, The Midnight Man, Night Moves, Airport 1975, The Apple Dumpling Gang, The North Avenue Irregulars, Murder by Decree, City on Fire, Promises in the Dark.

CLARKE, CHARLES G.: Cinematographer. b. Potter Valley, Cal., Mar. 19, 1899. Started in film laboratory for D. W. Griffith and others, then on camera for Natl. Film Co. in 1919. Cinematographer ever since for Famous Players, Wm. Fox, MGM, under contract to 20th Cent.-Fox, 1937–61.
PICTURES INCLUDE: Barbarian and Geisha, The Hunters, Sound and Fury, These Thousand Hills, A Private Affair, Holiday for Lovers, Return to Peyton Place.
TV: Arnie.

CLAYBURGH, JILL: Actress. Appeared on Broadway in Jumpers, Pippin, The Rothschilds, etc.
PICTURES INCLUDE: Portnoy's Complaint, The Thief Who Came To Dinner, Terminal Man, Gable and Lombard, Silver Streak, Semi-Tough, An Unmarried Woman, Starting Over, Luna, It's My Turn, First Monday in October.
TV: Griffin and Phoenix.

CLAYTON, JACK: Producer, director. b. 1921. Ent. m.p. 1935 as asst. dir. for London Films, Fox, Warner. Served H.M. Forces 1940–46. prod. man. Ideal Husband; assoc. prod. Queen of Spades, Flesh and Blood, Moulin Rouge, Beat the Devil, The Good Die Young, I am a Camera; prod. dir. Bespoke Overcoat, 1955, Venice Festival prize-winning film; prod. Sailors Beware, Dry Rot, Three Men in a Boat; dir.

Room at the Top, The Innocents, The Pumpkin Eater; prod.-dir., Our Mother's House, 1967; The Great Gatsby, 1974.

CLAYTON, JAN: Actress, singer. b Tularosa, N.M. Numerous motion picture roles; on Broadway in Showboat, Carousel; TV series, Lassie, CBS.

CLEARY, CHIP: Pub. Relations. b. New Bedford, Mass., Jan. 20, 1910; e. Amherst, 1929–31. Reporter, New Bedford Times, Standard-Times; legis. reporter, U.P., Pa., pub. rel., Wash., D.C.; feat. writer, I.N.S.; ed. writer, Phoenix Gazette; man. ed., Hollywood Reporter, 1936–40; Hollywood ed. consultant, Time, Inc., 1938–42; U.S. Army, 1942–45; ad., pub. dir., Mark Hellinger Prod., 1945–46; asst. ad., pub. dir., Liberty Films, 1946–47; mag. dept. head, Columbia Pictures, 1947; org. pub. rel. firm, Cleary-Strauss & Irwin, 1949; pres. since 1959, Chip Cleary Co.

CLEMENS, BRIAN. Writer, producer, director. b. Croydon, England, 1931. Early career in advertising then wrote BBC TV play. Later TV filmed series as writer, script editor and features. Script editor "Danger Man"; Won Edgar Allen Poe Award for Best TV Thriller of 1962 (Scene of the Crime for U.S. Steel Hour). Various plays for Armchair Theatre; ATV Drama 70; Love Story. Writer and Producer of The Avengers (two Emmy nominations for Best Production 1967 and 1968), Winner two Edgar Allen Poe Awards, Cinema Fantastique Award for best Screenplay.
PICTURES INCLUDE: The Tell-Tale Heart, Station Six-Sahara, The Peking Medallion, And Soon The Darkness, The Major, and When The Wind Blows, See No Evil, Dr. Jekyll and Sister Hyde, Golden Voyage of Sinbad, Watcher in the Woods, Stiff.
TV: Wrote and prod.: The New Avengers, The Professionals, Escapade (in US for Quinn Martin).

CLIFT, DENISON: Author and director. b. May 2, 1893; e. Stanford U. Editor, Overland Monthly and other publications; publicity expert, San Francisco, 1917. Scenario writer and dir. for Fox, Paramount, MGM; dir. Honor Among Men, Ports of Call, This Freedom, A Bill of Divorcement, Paradise, The Mystery of the Mary Celeste, etc. Dir. for British International, Ideal Films, Gainsborough Pictures and Hammer Prod., London. Author of novels, Guns of Galt, Man About Town, The Mighty Thing, I Belong to You. Author of the New York plays, The Woman Disputed, Scotland Yard; and London plays, The Moon Is Red and Gentle Rain.

CLORE, LEON: Producer. Co-prod. Conquest Of Everest. Virgin Island. exec. prod. Time Without Pity; Prod. Sunday By The Sea, Bow Bells, Every Day Except Christmas, We Are the Lambeth Boys, Dispute, I Want to Go to School, Morgan, A Suitable Case for Treatment, All Neat in Black Stockings.

CLORK, HARRY: Writer. r.n. Clarke; b. Galveston, Tex. e. St. Paul's Academy, Garden City, Long Island, N.Y. Was husband of late Nora Bayes, writer of her stage material; author several stage plays (Smiling Faces, The Milky Way, See My Lawyer) (collab., filmed in 1936 by Paramount); adapt. many plays for Shubert stage enterprises; radio writer. From 1935 writer many s.p. & adapt.
PICTURES INCLUDE: Thrill of Brazil, Mighty McGurk, Sainted Sisters, Painting the Clouds with Sunshine, Tea for Two, Ma and Pa Kettle at Waikiki, The Prisoner.
TV: Beulah, Life of Riley.

CLOVER, DAVID: Actor. b. November 10.
TELEVISION INCLUDES: Policewoman, Police Story, McLaren's Raiders; Kate McShane; One Day At A Time; Delphi Bureau; On The Rocks; The Dick Cavett Special.

CLUG, A. STEPHEN: Executive. b. New York City, Apr. 2, 1929. e. Colgate Univ., Columbia Law School. Was special agent, U.S. Army Counter Intelligence Corps, Far East Command, 1951–4. Started with industry as branch mgr., Paramount Films of Indonesia, 1954; mgr. dir., Paramount Films of India, Ltd., supervising India, Burma, Pakistan, Persian Gulf, 1955–57; Far East supvr. for special handling, The Ten Commandments, 1957–8; co-ordinator world-wide program theatrical re-releases, Paramount Intl., 1958–9; mgr., dir., Paramount Films of Brasil, 1959–65; v.p. & exec. prod., Gold Dolphin Prods., Inc., N.Y., 1965–69; gen. mgr. & supvr. Central America/Caribbean areas, MGM Intl. Inc., Panama, 1969–71; gen. mgr., MGM Puerto Rico/supvr. Caribbean area/MGM Cinemas, 1971–3; dir. sls. & asst. continental supvr. for Europe, UK, Middle East, MGM Intl., Inc. 1973–79; now v.p./sls.mgr., MGM Intl., headquartered in Paris.

CLYDE, THOMAS: Producer. b. Battle, England, Ent. m.p. ind. 1949. After writ. dir. documentaries, with Ivan Foxwell as prod. mgr. The Intruder, Coldits Story; 1956 to Douglas Fairbanks, Ltd., prod. The Hostage, 1957 for own Company, Cavalcade Films, Ltd. Chase a Crooked Shadow; Moment of Danger, Follow That Horse, Guns of Darkness, Work Is a Four Letter Word.

CLYNE, LIONEL: Executive. b. London, Eng., 1908. Entered m.p. ind. 1934 as sales representative theatre catering.

1942 Granada Circuit. Joined Pathe 1943. 1950: gen. sales mgr., Republic International (G.B.), Inc.; dir. Rep. Prod. (G.B.) Ltd., 1953; joined Columbia, 1957; man. dir. Regent Film & TV Prod. Ltd.; Sherwood Picture House Co. Ltd., 1959.

COBE, SANDY: Executive, Producer-Distributor. b. New York City, N.Y., Nov. 30, 1928. e. Tulane Univ. (B. of A., fine arts). U.S. Army WW II & Korea, combat photographer; Loews Theatre Corp., theatre mgr., N.Y. Daily News, photographer; WPIX-TV, cinematographer; Artmark Pictures, N.Y., produced 11 features. Pepsicola, v.p., Pepco Special events, in charge of N.Y.'s World's Fair operations and promotion. General Studios, exec. v.p., distribution; First Cinema Releasing Corp., pres. formed Sandy Cobe Productions, Inc., producer, packager, European features for U.S. theatrical & television. Pres., Intercontinental Releasing Corporation, domestic and foreign distribution of theatrical features. Golden Image Motion Picture Corp., bd. chm.
MEMBER: Masons (Scottish-Rite 32nd), Shrine, Variety Clubs Tent 25, Academy of Television Arts and Sciences. Special commendations from: California State Senate, Los Angeles City Counsel, California State Assembly and County of Los Angeles.

COBE, SHARYON REIS: Executive. b. Honolulu, Hawaii. e. Univ. of Hawaii. Dancer Fitzgerald, & Sample, N.Y. United Air Lines, N.Y.; v.p.; story editor, Gotham Publishing N.Y.; v.p., distribution-foreign sales, World Wide Film Distributors, L.A.; current v.p., foreign sales-finance, Intercontinental Releasing Corp., L.A.

COBURN, JAMES: Actor. b. Laurel, Neb., Aug. 31, 1928. e. Los Angeles City College, where he studied drama. Served in U.S. Army. First acting role in coast production of Billy Budd. Later to New York, where he worked on TV commercials, then in teleplays on Studio One, GE Theatre, Robert Montgomery Presents. Summer stock in Detroit before returning to Hollywood. First film, 1959, was Ride Lonesome.
PICTURES INCLUDE: Foes of the Fugitive, The Magnificent Seven, Hell Is for Heroes, The Great Escape, Charade, The Americanization of Emily, The Loved One, Major Dundee, A High Wind in Jamaica, Our Man Flint, What Did You Do in the War, Daddy?, Dead Heat on a Merry-Go-Round, In Like Flint, Waterhole No. 3, Candy, Hard Contract, The Last of the Mobile Hot Shots, The Carey Treatment, The Honkers, Duck, You Sucker, The Last of Sheila, Harry in Your Pocket, A Reason to Live, A Reason to Die, The Internecine Project, Bite the Bullet, Hard Times, Sky Riders, The Last Hard Men, Midway, Cross of Iron, Firepower, The Big Bullet, Loving Couples, Looker.

COCA, IMOGENE: Actress. b. Philadelphia; p. the late Joe Coca, orchestra leader, and Sadie Brady, retired vaudevillian. At 11, debut tap dancer in New York vaudeville; solo dancer Broadway musicals; as comedienne, in New Faces of 1934; with husband, Bob Burton, in Straw Hat Revue in 1939, and others through 1942. New York night clubs, Cafe Society and Le Ruban Bleu, New York; Palmer House, Chicago; Park Plaza, St. Louis. 1949 to TV via Broadway Revue, evolved routines with Sid Caesar, Your Show of Shows, 1950–54. NBC-TV; Imogene Coca Show, 1954, 1955; Sid Caesar invites you, 1958, Glinda.
PICTURES INCLUDE: Under the Yum Yum Tree.

COCCHI, JOHN: Writer-Critic. b. Brooklyn, N.Y., June 19, 1939. e. Fort Hamilton High School, 1957; Brooklyn College, AAS, 1961. U.S. Army, 1963–65. Puritan Film Labs, manager, 1967–9. Independent-International Pictures, biographer-researcher, 1969. Boxoffice Magazine, critic, reporter, columnist, 1970. Co-author: The American Movies Reference Book (Prentice-Hall). Contributor: Screen Facts, Film Fan Monthly. Actor in: The Diabolical Dr. Ongo, Thick as Thieves, Captain Celluloid VS. the Film Pirates. Worked on dubbing: Dirtymouth, 1970. Author, The Westerns, a Movie Quiz Book. Contributor to various books on films.

COCHRAN, RON: Producer, writer, narrator. b. Saskatchewan, Canada, Sept. 20, 1912. e. Parsons College U. of Fla. Newscaster for radio stations in Rock Island, Ill., Des Moines, St. Louis; special agent, FBI 1942–45; then returned to radio as news dir., dir. of news WCOP Boston 1945–51; joined CBS-TV news staff, 1951, in Washington; newscaster, Late News Show; news roundups, CBS radio; moderator, Capitol Cloakroom, Where Do You Stand, Man of the Week; CBS news staff, N.Y., 1954; newscaster. The Late News; moderator, Youth Takes a Stand, One O'clock Report, CBS-TV; In Person, CBS-Radio; News, ABC-TV, 1962; Ron Cochran With the News 1967; Pres., Ron Cochran Enterprises Inc., producer and syndicator or radio and television.

COCO, JAMES: b. Bronx, N.Y., Mar. 21, 1929. Became stage mgr. of touring children's theatre while still in teens. Was character actor in summer stock and off-Bdwy. prods. before appearing on Bdwy. in Man of La Mancha and The Last of the Red Hot Lovers.
PICTURES INCLUDE: A New Leaf, The Strawberry

Statement, Tell Me That You Love Me, Junie Moon, Such Good Friends, Man of La Mancha, The Wild Party, Murder by Death, The Cheap Detective, Scavenger Hunt, Wholly Moses, Only When I Laugh.
TELEVISION: Marcus Welby, M.D, The Flip Wilson Show, The Trouble With People, VD Blues, Calucci's Dept.

COE, RICHARD L.: Newspaper editor and critic. b. New York, N.Y., Nov. 8, 1916; e. George Washington U. Joined Washington Post as asst. dramatic ed. & radio ed., 1937; Stars & Stripes, 1942–46; dramatic & film ed., Washington Post and Times Herald, 1946–69. Drama Critic, The Washington Post 1946. Film and theater commentator, NBC-WRC-TV 1969–75.

COEN, GUIDO: Producer and Executive. Prod. series pictures for Fortress Films and Kenilworth Films.
PICTURES INCLUDE: One Jump Ahead, Golden Link, The Hornet's Nest, Behind the Headlines, Murder Reported, There's Always a Thursday, Date with Disaster, The End of the Line, The Man Without A Body, Woman Eater, Kill Her Gently, Naked Fury, Operation Cupid, Strictly Confidential, Dangerous Afternoon, Jungle Street, Strongroom, Penthouse, Baby Love, One Brief Summer, Burke and Hare, Au Pair Girls, Intimate Games, Twickenham Studios.

COHEN, CHARLES: Executive. b. Brooklyn, N.Y., Sept. 15, 1912; e. Brooklyn Coll. Pub. dept., MGM, 1931; U-I, 1948–50; 20th-Fox, 1950; assoc. adv. mgr.; eastern asst. adv & pub. mgr. Allied Artists, 1955; home off. pub. mgr. Warner Bros., 1957. Eastern adv. mgr. 1958; eastern adv., pub. mgr., 1960; Exec. ass't to adv. director, 1960; expl. dir., Embassy Pictures, 1961; nat. adv. & pub. dir., Cinema V Dist., 1964; Adv. & Pub. dir., Sigma III, 1968; adv., pub. mgr., The Cannon Group, 1970, v.p., adv.-pub. rel. 1971; Adv.-Pub. Dir., U.A. Eastern Theatres, 1973–77.

COHEN, ELLIS A.: Executive, Producer-Writer. b. Baltimore, Md. Sept. 15, 1945. e. Balt. Jr. Coll. (A.A.), Univ. of So. Carolina (B.S.). 1980, pres. Ellis A. Cohen Prods., 1978, Director of TV Network Boxing Events, Don King Productions, Inc., NYC 1978, Account Exec., Solters & Roskin P.R. L.A. 1977, Exec. Prod., Henry Jaffe Enterprises, Inc., 1974–76 dir., worldwide pub./adv., William Morris Agency. 1963, talent coordinator, Cerebral Palsy Telethon, WBAL-TV, Baltimore; 1964, p.r. asst. Campbell-Ewald Adv. Agency, L.A.; 1966, and mgr., Hochschild Kohn Dept. Stores, Baltimore; 1968, asst. dir., p.r. entertainment, talent booking for Club Venus Night Club, Baltimore; 1968, created-edited The Forum Oracle, national entertainment mag. 1969–72, dir., p.r., Jewish Community Center of Baltimore; 1970, leave of absence to work as corr. in Israel, Denmark & London; 1972, dir., p.r. & adv., The Camera Mart, New York; 1972–74 creator & editor-in-chief, TV/New York Magazine, nationwide TV mag.; Producer, New York Area Emmy Awards Telecast (1973 & 1974), WOR-TV (Co-Prod.), chm., exec. prod. of TV Academy Celebrity drop-in luncheon series; 1972, talent coordinator Bob Hope's Celebrity Flood Relief Telethon. Member: Writers Guild of America, Producers Guild of America, Friars Club, Amer. Newspaper Guild, Intl. Press Corp., Israeli Press Corp., National Academy of TV Arts & Sciences, Academy of Television Arts & Sciences, Screen Actors Guild. Mayor Beame's Committee In The Public Interest for NYC; executive producer, 1976 Democratic National Convention Gala.
TV: Aunt Mary (Dec. 1979), a Hallmark Hall of Fame, 2-hr. special, CBS-TV starring Jean Stapleton (Exec Prod-Story By); New York Area Emmy Awards. Telecast; January 1973 WOR-TV (co.-prod.) and January 1974, WOR-TV (co.-prod.).
FILM: Slob Sisters (prod.).

COHEN, HERMAN: Producer, writer. b. Detroit, Mich. Age 12, usher, Detroit, Dexter theatre; chief of service, Detroit, Fox theatre; mgr., booker, Dexter Theatres; military service; house mgr., Fox theatre; sales mgr. Columbia Pictures, Detroit; prod., Realart, Jack Broder Productions, Hollywood; formed own prod. Co., 1953; owner, Fox and Cinderella Theatres, Detroit; prod. pictures for Columbia and Warner Bros.
PICTURES INCLUDE: River Beat, Magnificent Roughnecks, The Brass Legend, Target Earth, Crime of Passion, Horrors of the Black Museum, I was a Teenage Werewolf, I Was a Teenage Frankenstein, Blood of Dracula, How to Make a Monster, Konga, Headless Ghost, Black Zoo, A Study in Terror, Berserk, Crooks and Coronets, TROG, Craze.

COHEN, IRWIN R.: Exhibition Executive. b. Baltimore, Md., Sept. 4, 1924. Attended Massanutten Academy, Woodstock, Va., Member of alumni board of directors; attended University of Baltimore, bachelor of laws, 1948. Admitted to Maryland bar, 1948; member law firm Cohen & Dackman since 1952. In exhibition 1938 to date. Founded R/C Theatres 1966, chief exec. officer 1966 to date. Member of Variety Club, Tent #11, Member of Board of Directors NATO of Maryland, past pres. NATO of Virginia 1975–77, past chmn. board NATO of Virginia 1977–79. Member of exec. comm. and member of board of directors National

NATO. One of the founders, co-atny., and vice-chmn. of Key Federal Savings & Loan Association 1961 to date.

COHEN, MILTON E.: Distributor. b. Chicago, Ill., e. University of Illinois. Entered motion picture industry as salesman. United Artists, Chicago, 1925–29; Columbia, Chicago, 1929–31; salesman, Detroit, 1931–38; sales mgr., RKO, Detroit, 1938; branch mgr., 1943; Eastern-Central dist. mgr., 1946; Eastern sales mgr., Eagle Lion Classics, 1948; genl. sales mgr., 1951; western & southern sales mgr., United Artist, 1951; Eastern & Southern sales mgr., 1952; supervisor, sales, Around The World In 80 Days, 1958; Eastern Canadian sales mgr., 1959; national dir., Roadshow Sales, 1961; retired. United Artists, 1969; exec. v.p. in charge of theatrical distrib. for Trans Globe Films, Inc., 1971.

COHEN, NATHAN: Executive. b. London, Eng., Dec. 23, 1905. Entered m.p. ind. as exhibitor 1930; into production and distribution 1942. Director: EMI Films Ltd.

COHEN, ROB: Producer. Formerly exec. v.p. in chg of m.p. and TV for Motown. Started as dir. of m.p. for TV at 20th Century-Fox. Joined Motown at age of 24 to produce films. Now heads own production co.
PICTURES INCLUDE: Mahogany, Bingo, Long and the Traveling All-Stars, Scott Joplin, Almost Summer, Thank God It's Friday, The Wiz, A Small Circle of Friends (dir.).

COHN, ROBERT: Producer. b. Avon, N.J, Sept. 6, 1920; e. U. Michigan, B.A., '41; p. Jack Cohn. Joined Columbia as asst. dir. In World War II, as Signal Corps film cutter. Air Corps Training Lab. unit mgr., combat aerial m.p. camera man with 13th A.A.F. Awarded: DFC, Air Medal & 3 clusters, Purple Heart. Assoc. prod. "Lone Wolf In London" 1947; prod. "Adventures in Silverado" 1948, all Col. Headed Robert Cohn prod. unit at Columbia, pres. International Cinema Guild. Columbia European prod.: exec. Columbia Studios. Hollywood: formed Robert Cohn Prod.
PICTURES INCLUDE: Black Eagle, Rusty Leads the Way, Palomino, Kazan, Killer That Stalked New York, The Barefoot Mailman, Mission Over Korea, The Interns, The New Interns, The Young Americans.

COLBERT, CLAUDETTE: Actress: r.n. Claudette Chauchoin. b. Paris, Sept. 13, 1907. e. public schools, Paris, New York; Art Students League (N.Y.). On N.Y. stage (debut, Wild Wescotts; following Marionette Man, We've Got to Have Money, Cat Came Back, Kiss in a Taxi, Ghost Train, The Barker, Dynamo, etc.). First screen role in Love O' Mike (silent); thereafter featured and starred in many period. Academy Award best actress, 1934 (It Happened One Night, Columbia); voted one of ten best Money Making Stars in Fame Poll, 1935, 36, 47.
PICTURES INCLUDE: Cleopatra, I Cover the Waterfront, No Time for Love, Practically Yours, Since You Went Away, So Proudly We Hail, Guest Wife, Tomorrow is Forever, The Egg and I, Sleep My Love, Family Honeymoon, Bride for Sale, Three Came Home, The Secret Fury, Thunder on the Hill, Let's Make It Legal, Outpost in Malaya, Daughters of Destiny, Texas Lady, Parrish.
BROADWAY: Marriage Go Round, Irregular Verb to Love.

COLBY, ETHEL: Drama critic and m.p. amuse. ed. b. N.Y.C., Sept. 15, 1908; e. N.Y.C. Vaudeville, operettas.
RADIO: Programs include B'way Busybody, Miss Hollywood.
TV: Programs include Personality Spotlight, Here and There in N.Y., Curtain Call, Mad About Music, B'way Matinee.
BROADCAST: for Army & Navy during war; drama critic and film editor-critic, Journal of Commerce; treas., New York Drama Critics Circle, N.Y. Drama Desk. Member: Women's Broadcasters of America, Newspaper Womens Club.

COLE, GEORGE: Actor. b. London, Eng., Apr. 22, 1925. e. Secondary Sch. Surrey. Stage debut in White Horse Inn, 1939; m.p. debut in Cottage to Let, 1941.
PICTURES INCLUDE: Henry V, Quartet, My Brother's Keeper, Laughter in Paradise, Scrooge, Lady Godiva Rides Again, Who Goes There (Passionate Sentry), Morning Departure (Operation Disaster), Top Secret (Mr. Potts Goes to Moscow), Happy Family, Will Any Gentleman, Apes of the Rock, The Intruder, Happy Ever After (Tonight's the Night), Our Girl Friday (Adventures of Sadie), Belles of St. Trinian's, Prize of Gold, Where There's a Will, Constant Husband, Quentin Durward, The Weapon, It's a Wonderful Life, Green Man, Bridal Path, Too Many Crooks, Blue Murder at St. Trinians, Don't Panic Chaps, Dr. Syn, One Way Pendulum, Legend of Young Dick Turpin, The Great St. Trinian's Train Robbery, Cleopatra, The Green Shoes, Vampire Lovers, Fright, The Bluebird.
TV: Life of Bliss, A Man of Our Times, Don't Forget To Write, The Good Life, Minder.

COLE, SIDNEY: Prod., dir., writer. b. London, England, 1908; e. Westminster City Sch.; London U., BSc. Began at Stoll Studios 1930; then various feature and documentary studios. Dir. Roads Across Britain. Spanish ABC. Behind the Spanish Lines. Ed. Gaslight. Mr. Pimpernel Smith, San

Demetrio, London, Nine Men, etc.; tech. adviser First of the Few; writer and assoc. prod. They Came to a City, Return of the Vikings; assoc. prod. Dead of Night, Loves of Joanna Godden, Against the Wind, Scott of the Antarctic, The Magnet, Man in the White Suit, Train of Events (co-dir.); Operation Swallow (Eng. adapt.); The Angel Who Pawned Her Harp (writer-prod.); s.p.; North Sea Bus. Assoc. prod. Escapade; prod. Sword of Sherwood Forest; prod. s.p. The Kitchen; prod. We Are The Engineers, One in Five.
TV: prod. Adventures of Robin Hood, The Buccaneers, Sword of Freedom, The Four Just Men, Danger Man (Secret Agent), Man In A Suitcase, Adventures of Black Beauty, Dick Turpin.

COLEMAN, NANCY: Actress. b. Everett, Wash. e. U. Wash. In radio serials; on New York stage (with Gertrude Lawrence, in Theatre Guild productions, etc.). Desperate Hours, 1955; m.p. debut, 1941, Rep. Co. tour of Europe and So. Am.
PICTURES INCLUDE: Kings Row, Dangerously They Live, Gay Sisters, Desperate Journey, Edge of Darkness, In Our Time, Devotion, Violence, Mourning Becomes Electra, That Man from Tangier, Slaves.
TV: Valiant Lady Producers Showcase. Am. Theatre Guild.

COLER, JOEL H.: Executive. b. Bronx, N.Y., 1931. e. Syracuse University (B.A., journalism). Married and has two daughters. Worked as adv. asst. NBC; acct. exec. Grey advertising. Joined 20th Century-Fox 1964 as adv. coordinator Fox Intl.; 1967, named intl. adv./pub. mgr. 1974, named dir., intl. adv./pub.

COLLERAN, BILL: Producer-Director. b. April 16; story department 20th Century-Fox 1945–46; Director Louis de Rochemont 1946–50; stage mgr. NBC 1951; Assoc. Dir. The Hit Parade 1952–53; Dir. The Hit Parade, various TV specs. 1954–56; Dir. Cinerama Windjammer 1956; TV Specs. Bing Crosby, Frank Sinatra, Debbie Reynolds 1957–60; various TV Specs. 1960–65, Exec. Prod. Judy Garland Show, Dean Martin Show, 1965–66; Dir. Richard Burton's "Hamlet" film, Prod. "Popendipity" ABC-TV spec. various other TV specs. 1967–70; 1971–77 Various TV specials and series; 1978–79, prod., dir., writer for Hill-Eubanks Group.

COLLIN, REGINALD: Producer/director. Trained at the Old Vic Theatre School as actor. Directed in repertory, also pantomimes and summer shows. Entered television 1958. Producer ITV's First Arts Programme Tempo. Producer of Callan, Mystery And Imagination, Special Branch, Napoleon And Love. 1975: Producer/director two Armchair Cinemas, also documentary on the Royal Shakespeare Theatre. Board member IBA's Repertory Theatre Trainee Director Scheme. 1976; Vice-Chairman of The British Academy of Film and Television Arts. Chairman of the Awards Committee. 1977: Appt. first dir. of BAFTA.

COLLINS, HAL: Writer, assoc. prod. b. New York, N.Y., Nov. 1, 1920. e. Bklyn. Technical H.S., James Monroe H.S., 1932–35.
PICTURES: Monogram, Columbia, 1945–48.
TV: Texaco Star Theatre, Red Buttons Shows, Celeste Holmes Shows, Milton Berle Shows, Kraft Shows, Jackpot Bowling, Share Boomtown Shows, Andy Williams Shows, Bob Hope Shows, Ed Sullivan Shows.
RADIO: Hearns Kiddie Radio Revue, Eddie Cantor Shows, Milton Berle Shows, Rudy Vallee Shows, Duffy's Tavern, Take It or Leave It, Zeke Manners Radio Shows.

COLLINS, JOAN: Actress. b. London, Eng., May 23. e. Francis Holland School (London). Made stage debut in A Dolls House, Arts Theatre 1946. Screen debut in I Believe in You, 1952. TV appearances.
PICTURES INCLUDE: I Believe in You, Judgment Deferred, Decameron Nights, Cosh Boy, The Square Ring, Turn the Key Softly, Our Girl Friday (Adventures of Sadie), The Good Die Young, Land of the Pharaohs, Virgin Queen, Girl in the Red Velvet Swing, Opposite Sex, Sea Wife, Island in the Sun, Wayward Bus, Stopover Tokyo, The Bravados, Rally Round the Flag Boys, Seven Thieves, Esther and the King, Warning Shot, Can Hieronymus Merkin Ever Forget Mercy Humpe and Find True Happiness?, The Executioner, Tales from the Crypt, The Bawdy Adventures of Tom Jones, Empire of the Ants, The Big Sleep, Sunburn.

COLLINS, NORMAN: Executive. b. Beaconsfield, Bucks, Eng., Oct. 3, 1907. e. William Ellis Sch., Hampstead, London. Oxford University Press, 1926–29; asst. literary ed. London News Chronicle, 1929–33; deputy-chmn. Victor Gollancz, publishers, 1939–41; joined BBC as controller Light Program, 1946 & later dir. BBC Overseas Services; TV as controller BBC service, 1947; Dep. chmn. Associated-Tele-Vision Corp. Ltd., Dir., Independent Television News Ltd., 1971–73. Chmn. Independent TV Companies Assoc. Ltd. 1960, Chmn., Central School of Speech and Drama. Gen. commiss. of taxes 1967. Dir. English Stage Soc. Governor, Sadler's Wells Foundation. Author numerous works.

COLLINS, PAT: Performer. r.n. Patricia Colinaka Allan. b. Detroit, Mich., May 7, 1935. e. U. of Ill., 1953. District mgr., Yardley Created Prods., Chicago; played in various nightclubs, Chicago, Miami, Las Vegas, etc.
PICTURE: Experiment in Nightmares.
TV (1963–65): Steven Allen, Bill Dana Show, No Time for Sergeants, Mike Douglas, Art Linkletter, Honey West.

COLLINS, STEPHEN: Actor. b. Hastings-on-Hudson, N.Y., 1948. Appeared off-Bdwy. in Joseph Papp production before acquiring role on Bdwy. in The Ritz.
PICTURES: All the President's Men, Between the Lines, The Promise, Star Trek, Fedora, Loving Couples.
TELEVISION: The Waltons, Barnaby Jones.

COLVILLE, JOHN: Producer, Director. Started in theatre. Worked in all departments before becoming Film Editor on Features, Documentaries, and Television Series for both BBC/ITV. Extensive experience in Greece, Singapore, Spain, Switzerland—now establishing new Unit, Studios, and Producing films in Nigeria.

COMDEN, BETTY: Writer. b. Brooklyn, N.Y., May 3; e. NYU. Nightclub performer, 1939–44; all writing in collab. with Adolph Green; writer book, sketches & lyrics for many Bway. shows including: On the Town, Billion Dollar Baby, Two On the Aisle, Wonderful Town, Peter Pan, Fade Out . . . Fade In.
PICTURES INCLUDE: Good News, On the Town, Barkleys of Broadway, Singin' in the Rain, Band Wagon, It's Always Fair Weather, What a Way to Go, Bells Are Ringing, Auntie Mame, Say Darling.
BROADWAY: Lyrics with Adolph Green—Do Re Mi. Collab. writing, Adolph Green, A Party; worked on Bells Are Ringing; book, lyrics, Subways Are For Sleeping; Show, Hallelujah, Baby! Book for show Applause. Tony Awards for: Wonderful Town, Hallelujah Baby, Applause.

COMO, PERRY: Singer. b. Canonsburg, Penn., May 18; p. Pietro and Lucille Travaglini Como; e. Canonsburg local schools. Barber at 15; joined Carlone Band, then Ted Weems in 1936; CBS sustaining show; played many night clubs, records for Victor. Screen debut, Something for the Boys, 20th Century Fox.
PICTURES INCLUDE: Doll Face, If I'm Lucky.
TV: Perry Como show. NBC-TV. Best Male vocalist M.P. Daily, TV poll, 1952–55; radio poll, 1954. Best Male vocalist M.P. Daily, TV Poll, 1956: best TV performer M.P.D.—Fame poll 1957. Interfaith Award, 1953; Emmy, Peabody, Christopher Awards, 1955–56; Knight Commander and Lady Com. (Mrs. Como) of Equestrian Order of Holy Sepulchre of Jerusalem; personality of the yr., Variety Club, 1956. Perry Como Kraft Music Hall, NBC-TV.

COMPTON, JOYCE: Actress. b. Lexington, Ky.; e. Tulsa U. Screen debut in Ankles Preferred.
PICTURES INCLUDE: If I Had a Million, Luxury Liner, Only Yesterday, Affairs of a Gentleman, Christmas in Connecticut, Danger Signal, Hitchhike to Happiness, Charlie Chan of Alcatraz, Exposed, Incident, Grand Canyon, Jet Pilot.

CONAWAY, JEFF: Actor. b. New York City, Oct. 5, 1950. Started in show business at the age of 10 when he appeared in Bdwy. production, All the Way Home. Later toured in Critics Choice before turning to fashion modeling. Toured with musical group, 3½, as lead singer and guitarist. Entered theatre arts program at N.Y. Univ. Film debut at 19 in Jennifer on My Mind.
PICTURES: The Eagle Has Landed, Pete's Dragon, I Never Promised You a Rose Garden, Grease.
TELEVISION: The Mary Tyler Moore Show, Happy Days, Movin' On, Barnaby Jones, Kojak. TV movies: Having Babies and Delta County, U.S.A.
SERIES: Taxi.

CONDON, CHRIS J.: Producer-Director-Motion Equipment Designer. b. Chicago, Dec. 7, 1922. e. Davidson Institute, USC, U.S. Air Force 1943–46. Founded Century Precision Optics, 1948. Designed Athenar telephoto lenses, Century Super wide-angle lenses and Duplikins. Co-founded StereoVision International, Inc. 1969 specializing in films produced in new 3-D process.
FILMS PRODUCED: The Wild Ride, The Surfer, Girls, Airline, The New Dimensions. Member SMPTE. Lecturer and consultant on motion picture optics and 3-D motoion picture technology.

CONLEY, DICK: Executive. r.n. Richard Glen. b. La Cygne, Kansas, Feb. 7, 1920. e. Lamar Union H.S., Lamar, Colorado. Atlas Theatre Corp., Denver, 1938–43; merchandising specialist, National General Corp., 1944–62; district mgr., Kansas City-St. Louis area, 1962–68; area superv. Kansas City-Omaha-Des Moines-St. Louis area; pres., Petite Amusement Corp., Kansas City.

CONN, ROBERT A.: Executive. b. Philadelphia, Pa., Jan. 16, 1926; e. Lehigh U. 1944; U. of Pa., 1948. 1st Lt. Army Security Agency, 1944–46, 1951–52; furniture dist., Philadelphia, 1948–51; band & act. dept., MCA, 1952–53; dir.

of adv. & prom. Official Films N.Y. 1954; head of Official Films Philadelphia sales office serving Pennsylvania, Baltimore, Washington, Cleveland and Detroit, 1956. Eastern Reg. Sls. Mgr. Flamingo Films, 1957; acct. exec. Dunnan and Jeffrey, Inc., June, 1961; v.p., Dunnan and Jeffrey, Jan. 1962; pres., adv. mgr., Suburban Knitwear Co., 1963; exec. v.p. Rogal Travel Service, 1964–68. 1968–78, pres. RAC Travel, Inc., Jenkintown, Pa. and pres. Royal Palm Travel, Inc. Palm Beach, Florida, 1978; Rosenbluth Travel Service, 1979.

CONNELLY, PAUL V.: Executive. b. Boston, Mass., June 11, 1923. e. Boston Coll., MA, 1951, B.S.B.A.; 1949; Fordham Univ., 1951–54; Asst. professor of Economics, Manhattan Coll., 1950–54; treas., America Corp. (formerly Chespeake Industries), 1957–59; treas., dir., Pathe-America Dist. Co. Inc., Sutton Pictures Co.; vice-pres., dir., Pathe Labs., Inc.; pres., dir., Pathe-DeLuxe of Canada, Ltd. 1959–65; pres. International Business Relations, 1965–67; v.p., treas., dir. Movielab, Inc., 1968; v.p.—finance, Tele-Tape Corp., 1970.

CONNERY, SEAN: Actor. b. Edinburgh, Scotland, Aug. 25, 1930. Stage debut South Pacific, 1953.
TV: Requiem for a Heavyweight, Anna Christie, Boy With the Meataxe, Women in Love, The Crucible, Riders to the Sea, Colombe, Adventure Story, Anna Karenina, Macbeth (Canadian TV).
PICTURES INCLUDE: The Longest Day, Dr. No, From Russia With Love, Marnie, Woman of Straw, Goldfinger, The Hill, Thunderball, A Fine Madness, You Only Live Twice, Shalako, The Molly Maguires, The Red Tent, The Anderson Tapes, Diamonds Are Forever, The Offence, Zardoz, Ransom, Murder on the Orient Express. The Wind and The Lion, The Man Who Would Be King, Robin and Marian. The Next Man, A Bridge Too Far, The Great Train Robbery, Meteor, Cuba, Outland.
Prod. dir., The Bowler and the Bonnet (film doc.), I've Seen You Cut Lemons (London stage). Director of Tantallon Films Ltd. (First production: Something Like the Truth).

CONNOR, KENNETH: Actor. b. London, England. Ent. m.p. industry 1949 in The Lady Killers.
TV: Ted Ray Show, Show Called Fred, Charlie Farnabarn's Show, Alfred Marks Time, As You Like It, Dickie Valentine Show, Black and White Minstrel, Anne Shelton, Hi Summer, series Don't Say A Word, Room at the Bottom, On the Houses, Frankie Howard Reveals All.
PICTURES INCLUDE: Carry on Sergeant, Carry on Nurse, Carry on Constable, Watch Your Stern, Carry on Regardless, Nearly a Nasty Accident, What a Carve Up, Call Me a Cab, Carry on Cleo, Captain Nemo, Carry On Up The Jungle, Carry On Matron, Carry On Abroad, Carry on England, Carry on Emanuelle.

CONNORS, CHUCK: Actor. r.n. Kevin Joseph Connors. b. Brooklyn, N.Y., April 10, 1924; e. Adelphi Acad., Seton Hall Coll., U.S. Army 3 yrs., then prof. baseball player.
TV: Dennis Day Show, Four Star Playhouse, Star and the Story, Reader's Digest, Gunsmoke, West Point, Rifleman series, Roots.
PICTURES INCLUDE: Pat and Mike, Code Two, Trouble Along the Way, South Sea Women, Dragonfly Squadron, Naked Alibi, Human Jungle, Target Zero, Three Stripes in the Sun, Good Morning Miss Dove, Hold Back the Night, Hot Rod Girl, Tomahawk Trail, Walk the Dark Street, Geronimo, Kill Them All and Come Back Alive, Capt. Nemo and the Underwater City, Profane Comedy, The Deserter, Support Your Local Gunfighter, Soylent Green, 99 and 44/100ths½ Dead.

CONNORS, MIKE: Actor. b. Fresno, Cal., Aug. 15, 1925. r.n. Krekor Ohanian. e. UCLA. Film debut in Sudden Fear; other pictures include Sky Commando, Day of Triumph, Flesh and Spur, Seed of Violence, Harlow, Good Neighbor Sam, Where Love Has Gone.
TV: Tightrope, Mannix (Golden Globe award).

CONRAD, ROBERT: Actor, singer. r.n. Conrad Robert Falk; b. Chicago, Ill., March 1, 1935; e. public schools, Northwestern U.; prof. debut, nightclub singer. Formed Robert Conrad Production, 1966.
TV: Lawman, Maverick, 77 Sunset Strip, Hawaiian Eye (series), Wild Wild West (series), Baa, Baa, Black Sheep (series), Centennial (mini-series), A Man Called Sloane (series).
PICTURES: Thundering Jets, Palm Springs Weekend, Young Dillinger, Murph the Surf, Sudden Death, The Women in Red.

CONRAD, WILLIAM: Actor, Producer, Director. b. Louisville, Ky., Sept. 27. e. Fullerton College. Announcer-writer-director for L.A. radio station KMPC before becoming WW II fighter pilot in 1943; returned to radio drama as original Matt Dillon of Gunsmoke Series; m.p. debut in The Killers, 1946; later acting credits include 30, Body and Soul, Sorry, Wrong Number, East Side, West Side, The Naked Jungle; TV credits include This Man Dawson, Klondike (produced and directed), 77 Sunset Strip (producer), True (directed 35 episodes); as m.p. producer for Warner Bros. credits

include: Two On a Guillotine, Brainstorm, An American Dream, A Covenant With Death, First To Fight, The Cool Ones, The Assignment.
RECENT TV: Acting credits include The Brotherhood of the Bell, The D.A., Conspiracy to Kill, O'Hara, U.S. Treasury, Cannon (series).

CONROY, THOMAS: Exec. r.n. Coleman Thomas Conroy. b. Camden, N.J., Nov. 3, 1924; e. Yale U., hd. prof. camera dept., Bell and Howell Inc., New York, 1951; hd. camera dept., Cinerama Inc., 1952–55; National Theatres Inc., 1955; hd. camera dept., Cinemiracle; v.p. prod., prod. supv., Cinerama, Inc. 1960. Developed Cinerama single-lens system; v.p., production, Shannon Prod., Inc., 1967.
PICTURES INCLUDE: This Is Cinerama, Cinerama Holiday, Seven Wonders of the World, Windjammer, The Wonderful World of The Brothers Grimm, How the West Was Won, The Best of Cinerama, The Golden Head.

CONTE, JOHN: Actor, singer. b. Palmer, Mass.; e. Lincoln h.s., Los Angeles. Actor, Pasadena Playhouse; radio anncr., m.c.; Armed Forces World War II.
THEATRE: On Broadway in Windy City, Allegro, Carousel, Arms and the Girl.
TV: John Conte's Little Show, Max Liebman Spectaculars and dramatic shows, host and star of NBC Matinee Theatre; TV Hour of Stars; Mantovani Welcomes You.
PICTURES INCLUDE: Debut in Man With the Golden Arm, The Carpetbaggers.
Pres. KMIR-TV, Channel 36, Desert Empire Television Corp., Palm Springs.

CONTI, BILL: Composer. b. Providence, Rhode Island, 1943. Studied piano at age 7, forming first band at age 15. e. Juilliard School of Music. Toured Italy with jazz trio where scored first film, Candidate for a Killing. Returned to U.S. to be music supvr. on Blume in Love. for Paul Mazursky.
PICTURES: Harry and Tonto, Rocky, Handle with Care, F.I.S.T., Slow Dancing in the Big City, The Big Fix, Uncle Joe Shannon, An Unmarried Woman, Hurricane, Paradise Alley, Rocky II, Golden Girl, A Man, A Woman, and A Bank, Gloria, Private Benjamin, For Your Eyes Only, Carbon Copy.
TELEVISION: Kill Me If You Can.

CONVERSE, FRANK: Actor. b. St. Louis, Mo., May 22, 1938. e. Carnegie Tech. Early training on stage in New York. Active in repertory theatres. Two seasons with Amer. Shakespeare Fest.
PICTURES INCLUDE: Hurry Sundown, Hour of the Gun.
TV: Mod Squad, Medical Center, The Bold Ones, N.Y.P.D. (series) Coronet Blue (series), The Guest Room, Movin' On, The Widowing of Mrs. Holyrod. Movies: The Rowdyman, Shadow of a Gunman, Tattered Web, Dr. Cook's Garden.
STAGE: The Seagull, Death of a Salesman, Night of the Iguana, A Man for All Seasons, The House of Blue Leaves, First One Asleep Whistle, Arturo Ui.

CONWAY, GARY: Actor. b. Boston, 1938. r.n. Gareth Carmody, e. UCLA. As college senior was chosen for title role in Teen-Age Frankenstein. After graduating served in military at Ford Ord, CA. In 1960 began contract with Warner Bros., doing bits for films and TV. Has also appeared on stage.
PICTURES INCLUDE: The Guns of Texas, Once is not Enough, The Farmer (also prod.).
TV: Burke's Law.

CONWAY, KEVIN: Actor. Gained reputation on N.Y. stage, winning Obie for performance in When You Comin Back, Red Ryder? Also on and off Broadway in such plays as One Flew Over the Cuckoo's Nest, Of Mice and Men, Moonchildren, The Plough and the Stars, etc.
PICTURES INCLUDE: Slaughterhouse Five, Shamus, Portnoy's Complaint, F.I.S.T.
TV: Johnny We Hardly Knew You, The Deadliest Season.

CONWAY, TIM: Actor. b. Dec. 15, 1933, Willoughby, Ohio. e. Bowling Green State Univ. After 2 yrs. Army service joined KWY-TV in Cleveland as writer-director and occasional performer. Comedienne Rose Marie discovered him and arranged audition for The Steve Allen Show on which he became regular. In 1962 signed for McHale's Navy, series. Also has done night club appearances.
PICTURES INCLUDE: McHale's Navy, The World's Greatest Athlete, The Apple Dumpling Gang, Gus, The Shaggy D.A.
TV: The Steve Allen Show, The Gary Moore Show, McHale's Navy, guest appearances on Hollywood Palace and shows starring Carol Burnett, Red Skelton, Danny Kaye, Dean Martin, Cher, Doris Day, etc.

CONWAY, SHIRL: Actress. r.n., Shirl Conway Larson; b. Franklinville, New York, June 13, 1916; e. U. of Michigan, 1934–38. Singer, comedian, nightclubs.
PLAYS: Gentlemen Prefer Blondes, Plain and Fancy.
TV: The Doctors and The Nurses.

COOGAN, JACKIE: Actor. b. Los Angeles, Calif., Oct. 26, 1914; e. Villanova Coll.
PICTURES INCLUDE: Debut in The Kid at 4. Peck's Bad

Boy, My Boy Trouble, Daddy, Oliver Twist, Circus Days, Long Live the King, Boy of Flanders, Rag Man, Old Clothes, Johnny Get Your Gun, Bugle Call, Buttons, Tom Sawyer, Huckleberry Finn, Home on the Range, College Swing, Million Dollar Legs, Sky Patrol, Kilroy Was Here, French Leave, Skipalong Rosenbloom, Outlaw Women, Lost Women, Proud Ones, Marlowe.

COOK, ELISHA, JR.: Actor. b. San Francisco, December 26, 1907; e. St. Albans, Chicago boarding school. Joined Frank Bacon in "Lightnin', " at the age of 14.
THEATRE: Appeared with Ethel Barrymore in "Kingdom of God," in "Henry, Behave," "Many a Slip," "Three Cornered Moon," in London in "Coquette." Played in vaudeville and summer stock companies. Appeared in "Chrysalis," then "Ah, Wilderness," Theatre Guild success. Signed by Par. in 1936: Two in a Crowd, U; Pigskin Parade, etc.
PICTURES INCLUDE: Up in Arms, Cassanova Brown, Cinderella Jones, Dillinger, The Big Sleep, The Long Night, Don't Bother to Knock, I the Jury, Shane, Thunder Over the Plains, Drum Beat, Outlaw's Daughter, Timberjack, Indian Fighter, The Killing, Voodoo Island, Rosemary's Baby, Welcome to Hard Times, Blacula, The Great Northfield, Minnesota Raid, Emperor of the North, Electra-Glide in Blue, the Outfit, The Black Bird, The Champ, Parny.

COOK, FIELDER: Prod., dir. b. Atlanta, Ga., Mar. 9, 1923. e. Washington & Lee U., BA, 1947; U. of Birmingham, Eng., post grad., 1948. Doctor of Fine Arts (Hon) (1973) (W&L). USNR, 1944; 7th Amphibious Force, 1944–45, J. Walter Thompson Co., 1947–48.
TV: Asst. prod-dir., Kraft Television Theatre; dir., Believe It or Not; dir., Lux Video Theatre; prod.-dir. (owner, Unit Four Prod. Co.) Kaiser Aluminum Hour, 1956–57; freelance, 1952–56; Alcoa-Goodyear Hour, Studio One, Theatre Guild on The Air (U.S. Steel), Playhouse 90; prod.-dir., Amer. Jewish Comm.'s Destiny Tot; prod.-dir., The Fifty Minute Hour, Focus, 1962; formed Eden Prods. to prod.: DuPont Show of the Week, The Directors Company dramas; TV pilots; Ben Casey, The Eleventh Hour, Going My Way, Mr. Roberts, The Waltons, Beacon Hill.
PICTURES INCLUDE: Patterns, Home Is the Hero, A Big Hand for the Little Lady, How to Save a Marriage and Ruin Your Life, Prudence and the Pill, Eagle In a Cage, From the Mixed Up Files of Mrs. Basil E. Frankweiler.
PLAY: A Cook For Mr. General.
AWARDS: Various for (after 1956): Patterns, Project Immortality; Big Deal in Laredo; Teacher, Teacher; Ben Casey Pilot; The Price; Brigadoon; Judge Horton And The Scottsboro Boys; The Homecoming.

COOK, KWENAM DAVID: Exec. b. Seoul, Korea, Mar. 16, 1922. e. Waseda U., Tokyo, Japan. ROK national assemblyman (Congress) 1959–61. Pres. Korean Gymnastic Assoc. 1967–70. Chairman: Century Co., Ltd., Seoul, producers, distributors, exhibitors, and importers of films. Honorary consul general for Peru.

COOK, ZALE EDWARD: Executive. b. Corpus Christi, TX., June 29, 1942. e. Del Mar Jr. College, Corpus Christi; Texas A&L; Univ. of Maryland; Univ. of Hawaii. Partner in Corpus Christi Egg Co., 1961–72. U.S. Army, 1966–70. Formed Cinema Southwest, Inc. in April, 1972, acquiring 1st theatre in April, 1973, in Murray, Ky. Opened 1st theatre in Texas in Feb., 1974. Cinema Southwest currently owns and manages 28 screens, all in Texas; has 6 screens under construction (3 in New Mexico). Theatres previously owned in Kentucky, Indiana and Arkansas have been sold.

COOKE, ALISTAIR: Journalist and Broadcaster. b. Eng., Nov. 20, 1908; e. Jesus Coll., Cambridge; Yale; Harvard. Film crit. of BBC 1934–37. London corr. NBC 1936–37. BBC commentator in U.S. since 1937. Chief Amer. corr., Manchester Guardian, 1948–72; English narrator, The March of Time, 1938–39; v.o. narrator, Sorrowful Jones, 1948; narrator, Three Faces of Eve, 1957; narrator, Hitler, 1973; Peabody award winner for International reporting, 1952; author, Douglas Fairbanks, Garbo & The Night Watchmen. A Generation on Trial, One Man's America, Christmas Eve, The Vintage Mencken, etc.; m.c. Omnibus, TV show, 1952–61; narrator, Three Faces of Eve, 1957, m.c. prod. U.N.'s International Zone, Emmy Award, 1958. Talk About America; writer & narrator, America: A Personal History of The United States, TV series BBC, NBC, PBS, for which 5 Emmy Awards, 1973; Franklin Medal, Royal Society of Arts, 1973; Knighted, KBE, 1973; America (book) 1973; Six Men, 1977, The Americans, 1979; Above London, 1980.

COOPER, BEN: Actor. b. Hartford, Conn., Sept. 30. e. Columbia U. On stage in Life with Father, Theatre; numerous radio, TV appearances.
PICTURES INCLUDE: Woman They Almost Lynched, A Perilous Journey, Sea of Lost Ships, Flight Nurse, Fortune Hunter, Johnny Guitar, Hell's Outpost, Eternal Sea, Last Command, Fighting Chance, Headline Hunters, Rose Tattoo, Rebel in Town, Chartroose Caboose, Red Tomahawk,

The Fastest Gun Alive, One More Train to Rob, Support Your Local Gunfighter.

COOPER, EDWARD: Exec. b. New York, Oct. 21, 1903; e. Montana State Univ., 1928; Washington Coll. of Law, 1936. Reporter, city ed. papers in Montana, Colorado, Wash., D.C.; Chief of Staff, Senate Interstate Commerce Com., investigating communications, domestic and intern'l, 1939–41; U.S. Navy officer, 1942–45. Returned to previous post, handling radio broadcast, TV, m.p. matters, 1946–50; staff dir., Senate Democratic Policy com., 1951–52.
Member: Masons (Scottish Rite-32nd), Army & Navy Club, Armed Forces Communications Assn.; Joined MPAA 1952 as director national legislative dept., v.p. since 1967. Member advisory council of Endowment and Res. Found., Montana State U., 1966.

COOPER, HAL: Director and Performer. b. Feb. 22, 1923; N.Y.C.; e. U. of Mich.; m. Marta Salcido; child actor in various radio prog. since 1932; featured Bob Emery's Rainbow House, Mutual, 1936–46; asst. dir. Dock St. Theatre, Charleston, S.C., 1946–48.
TV: Your Sch. Reporter, TV Baby Sitter, The Magic Cottage as writer and producer; dir., Valiant Lady, Search for Tomorrow, Portia Faces Life, CBS-TV; dir., assoc. prod. Kitty Foyle, NBC-TV; prod. dir. Indictment, Para. TV; assoc. prod. dir. The Happy Time, Para. TV; prod. dir. For Better or Worse, CBS-TV; dir., The Clear Horizon, CBS-TV; Assoc., prod., dir., Surprise Package, CBS-TV; dir., Dick Van Dyke Show; prod., dir., The Art Linkletter Show, The Object Is. Dir.: Death Valley Days, I Dream of Jeannie, That Girl, I Spy, Hazel, Gidget, Gilligan's Island, NYPD, Mayberry, Courtship of Eddie's Father, My World and Welcome to It, The Odd Couple, Mary Tyler Moore, All in the Family. Exec. prod., dir. Maude, 1972–78.

COOPER, JACKIE: Actor-Director-Producer. b. Los Angeles, Sept. 15, 1922. Began theatrical career at age of 3 as m.p. actor; was member of Our Gang comedies. First starring role in 1930 in Skippy. Worked at every major studio, always with star billing. At 20 enlisted in Navy. After three-yr. tour of duty went to N.Y. to work in live TV. Appeared on Broadway stage in Mr. Roberts and on natl. tour and in London. Directed as well as acted in live and filmed TV. Served as v.p. in chg. of TV prod., for Screen Gems, from 1964 to 1969, when resigned to return to acting, directing, producing.
PICTURES INCLUDE: Actor—Movietone Follies, Sunny Side Up, Skippy, Sooky, The Champ, When a Fellow Needs a Friend, Lumpy, Lost, The Bowery, Treasure Island, O'Shaughnessy's Boy, The Devil Is a Sissy, Gangster's Boy, Seventeen, Gallant Sons, Her First Beau, Syncopation, Stork Bites Man, Kilroy Was Here, Everything's Ducky, The Love Machine, Chosen Survivors, Superman, Superman II. Director: Stand Up And Be Counted.
TELEVISION: People's Choice (directed 71 segments; also starred); Hennesy (dir. 91 segments; also starred) 1975 series: Mobile Two (star).

COOPER, TOMMY: Comedian. b. Caerphilly, Wales, 1921. TV debut, 1947; stage debut, 1948. First starring TV series, It's Magic, 1952; London Palladium debut, 1952; U.S.A. cabaret debut, Las Vegas, 1954; Royal Variety Performances.
TV: Coopers Capers, Life With Tommy, all principal London cabarets; Ed Sullivan, USA; Sunday Night at the London Palladium. Cooperama series, 1966; Life with Cooper, 1967–68 and 1969–70.
STAGE: Paris By Night, Blue Magic, and pantomimes, London Palladium, 1971.
PICTURES INCLUDE: The Cool Mikado, The Plank.

COOPERMAN, ALVIN: Producer. b. Brooklyn, N.Y., July 24, 1923; e. NYU, 1939–43. Started career with Lee & J. J. Shubert, 1939–51; color team, dev. color TV for FCC approval, 1953; prod. first color TV shows with mobile unit, 1954; developed & prod. first Wide Wide World, June 1955; mgr. program sls., NBC Network, 1955; exec. prod. Producers Showcase, Dodsworth, Rosalinda, 1956; prod. Jack and the Beanstalk, Festival of Music, 1957; dir. prog. NBC-TV, Apr. 1957; joined HJ Enterprises as prod. NBC-TV, The Shirley Temple Storybook, 1957; exec. prod. Screen Gems, 1958; prod. Du Pont Show, 1959; exec. prod. Roncom Prod. 1960; Prod., Untouchables, 1961–63; exec. dir., Shubert Thea. Ent. 1963; v.p., special programs, NBC, 1967–68; exec. v.p., Madison Square Garden Center, 1968–1972 Exec. Vice President Madison Square Garden Center, Inc.; Present-Chairman of the Board Athena Communications Corporation.

COOTE, BERNARD: Producer, exec., ent. m.p. industry 1945. Denham Studios; 1951, joined Group 3, Ltd.; 1953, studio manager, Beaconsfield Studios; 1955, gen. man.; 1957, dir. prod. Ivanhoe TV series; 1958, prod. Violent Moment, dir. Shepperton TV Productions, Ltd.; Assoc. prod. TV series, The Third Man, Samson of the Circus, Voyage of Discovery; 1960–63, mgr. Shell Intntl. documentary film unit; 1963–65, dir. documentary films in Africa; 1965–67, freelance feature prod., Europe and Middle East; 1967–present, U.K. prod. supervisor, United Artists.

COPPOLA, FRANCIS FORD: Writer-Producer-Director. b. Detroit, April 7, 1939. e. Hofstra Univ. (BA 1958); UCLA (1958–68, masters cinema). Heads own production facility, American Zoetrope, San Francisco.
PICTURES INCLUDE: Director: Dementia 13, You're a Big Boy Now, Finian's Rainbow, The Rain People. Writer: Patton, This Property is Condemned, Reflections in a Golden Eye, The Rain People, Is Paris Burning?, The Great Gatsby. Writer-Producer-Director: The Conversation, The Godfather, The Godfather, Part II; Apocalypse, Now. Producer: American Graffiti, THX 1138. Executive Producer: The Black Stallion, Hammett. Director-co-writer: One from the Heart.
TV: The People (movie of the week).

CORBETT, HARRY H.: Actor. b. Rangoon, 1925. Ent. m.p. ind. 1955.
PICTURES INCLUDE: Floods of Fear, The Big Day, Cover Girl Killer, The Unstoppable Man, Marriage of Convenience, Shakedown, Sammy Going South, What A Crazy World, Ladies Who Do, The Bargee, Rattle of a Simple Man, Joey Boy, Carry on Screaming, Crooks and Coronets.
TV: Song in a Strange Land, Thunder on the Snow, Steptoe and Son, Mr. Aitch.

CORD, ALEX: Actor. b. Floral Park, L.I., Aug. 3, 1931. r.n. Alexander Viespi. Early career in rodeo; left to become actor. Studied at Shakespeare Academy (Stratford, Conn.) and Actor's Studio (N.Y.). Spent two yrs. in summer stock; in 1961 went on tour with Stratford Shakespeare Co. Made m.p. debut in Synanon, 1965.
PICTURES INCLUDE: Stagecoach, The Scorpio Letters, The Prodigal Gun, The Brotherhood, Stiletto, The Dead Are Alive, Chosen Survivors, Sidewinder One, Grayeagle.
TELEVISION: Guest in many series; Genesis II (tf).

COREY, JEFF: Actor. b. New York City, Aug. 10, 1914; e. Feagin Sch. of Dram. Art. On stage in Leslie Howard prod. of Hamlet, 1936; Life and Death of an American, 1938. Screen debut 1940 in All That Money Can Buy, In The Matter of J. Robert Oppenheimer and Hamlet-Mark Taper Forum, L.A. King Lear, Beverly Music Center '73.
PICTURES INCLUDE: Syncopation, The Killers, Ramrod, Joan of Arc, Roughshod, Black Shadows, Bagdad, Outriders, Singing Guns, Seconds, In Cold Blood, Golden Bullet, Boston Strangler, True Grit, Butch Cassidy and The Sundance Kid, Beneath the Planet of the Apes, Getting Straight, Little Big Man, They Call Me Mister Tibbs, Clear and Present Danger, High Flying Lowe, Catlow, Something Evil, Premonition, Shine, Rooster, Oh, God! Butch and Sundance: The Early Days, Up River.
TV: The Untouchables, The Beachcomber, The Balcony, Yellow Canary, Lady in A Cage, Outer Limits, Channing, The Doctors and The Nurses, Perry Mason, Gomer Pyle, Wild, Wild West, Run for Your Life, Bonanza, Iron Horse, Judd for Defense, Garrisons Gorillas, Gunsmoke, Hawaii Five O, Star Trek, dir. The Psychiatrist, Night Gallery, Alias Smith and Jones, Sixth Sense, Hawkins, Owen Marshall, Police Story, Bob Newhart Show, Six Million Dollar Man, Doctors Hospital, Starsky and Hutch, Land of the Free (film), Kojak, McCloud, Captains Courageous (Bell Tel. Hr.), Bionic Woman, Barney Miller, One Day At a Time, The Pirate, Lou Grant.

CORMAN, GENE: Producer. b. Detroit, Mich. e9 Stanford Univ. Went to work for MCA as agent; left to produce his first feature film, Hot Car Girl. Partner with brother Roger in Corman Company and New World Distributors.
PICTURES INCLUDE: Attack of the Giant Leaches, Not of This Earth, Blood and Steel, Valley of the Redwoods, Purple Reef, Beast from Haunted Cave, Cat Burglar, Tobruk, You Can't Win 'Em All, The Intruder, Von Richthofen and Brown, I Escaped from Devil's Island, Secret Invasion, Vigilante Force, F.I.S.T. (exec. prod.), The Big Red One.

CORMAN, ROGER WILLIAM: Executive-Director, Producer, Writer, Distributor. b. Detroit, Michigan, April 5, 1926. e. Stanford U. 1947; Oxford U., England 1950; U.S. Navy 1944; 20th Century-Fox, production department, 1948, story analyst 1948–49; Literary agent, 1951–52; story, s.p., assoc.-prod. Highway Dragnet. Formed Roger Corman Prod. and Filmgroup. Produced over 200 feature films and directed over 60 of them. Formed production-releasing company, organization, New World Pictures, Inc., 1970.
PICTURES INCLUDE: Five Guns West, 1953, House of Usher, Little Shop of Horrors, 1961; Pit and the Pendulum, The Intruder, Masque of the Red Death, Tomb of Ligeia, The Secret Invasion, The Wild Angels, The Trip, Bloody Mama, Von Richtofen and Brown, Gasss, St. Valentine's Day Massacre, Box Car Bertha, Big Bad Mama, Death Race 2000, Eat My Dust, Capone, Jackson County Jail, Fighting Mad, Thunder & Lightning, Grand Theft Auto, I Never Promised You A Rosegarden, Deathsport, Avalanche.

CORNFIELD, HUBERT: Director-Writer-Producer. b. Istanbul, Turkey. e. University of Pennsylvania. Actors' Studio, 1952–54. Story analyst Allied Artists 1954. Directed first picture 1955. Lives in Paris since 1964.
PICTURES INCLUDE: Sudden Danger, Lure of the Swamp, Plunder Road, The Third Voice, Pressure Point, The Night of the Following Day.

CORRADINE, TOM J.: Producer, distributor. b. Chicago, Ill., Nov. 14, 1924. e. parochial schools; theatre mgr., booker, 1944; ent. TV ind. as film dir., CBS, west coast, 1949; formed Associate Co., 1952; assoc. prod., TV, Wild Bill Hickock, Judge Roy Bean, Rendezvous with Adventure; formed Artists Productions, Inc., 1963. Dir. west coast operations Republic Film Corp., 1965. Reactivated co. of artists to prod. TV commercials and specials, 1968. V.P. charge of production and V.P. national sales, TVNATIONAL Releasing Corp., 1977; 1978, formed Videobrary Inc. to produce and distribute pre-recorded video tapes for the home consumer.
PICTURES INCLUDE: The Big Tipoff, Night Freight, Port of Hell, Highway Dragnet, Kroma.

CORRI, ADRIENNE: Actress. b. Glasgow, Scotland, Nov. 13, 1933. Ent. Royal Acad. of Dramatic Art at 13; parts in several stageplays including The Human Touch; m.p. debut in The River.
PICTURES INCLUDE: Quo Vadis, The Kidnappers, A Clockwork Orange, Lease of Life, Make Me An Offer, Feminine Touch, The Big Chance, Corridors of Blood, Doctor of Seven Dials, The Rough and the Smooth, Hellfire Club, The Tell-Tale Heart, Dynamite Jack, Doctor Zhivago, Epilogue to Capricorn, Rosebud. Numerous TV appearances.

CORT, ROBERT W.: Executive. e. Univ. of Pennsylvania (Phi Beta Kappa). Has worked primarily in marketing/advertising. Joined Columbia Pictures as v.p., 1976; elevated to v.p., adv./pub./promo. Named exec. v.p. of mktg. for 20th-Fox, 1980.

CORTESA, VALENTINA: Actress. b. Milan, Italy, Jan. 1, 1925. Started career at 15 in Rome. Screen debut: La Cens Delle Beffe, 1941; brought to Hollywood by 20th Century-Fox, following picture, A Yank in Rome; experience on dramatic stage in variety of roles inc. Shakespeare, O'Neill, Shaw.
PICTURES INCLUDE: Cagliostro, Glass Mountain, House on Telegraph Hill, Thieves' Highway, Les Miserables, Secret People, Barefoot Contessa, Shadow of the Eagle, Magic Fire, The Legend of Lylah Clare, Juliet of the Spirits, Day for Night, When Time Ran Out.

CORTEZ, STANLEY: Dir. Photography. b. New York City, br. Ricardo Cortez, actor; e. N.Y.U. Began working with portrait photographers (Steichen, Pirie MacDonald, Bachrach, etc.), N.Y. Entered film industry on Paramount Pictures; to Hollywood as camera asst. and later second cameraman, various studios; pioneer in use of montage; Signal Corps World War II, Yalta, Quebec, etc. Received Film Critics of Amer. award for work on Magnificent Ambersons. Under personal contract to David O. Selznick, Orson Welles, Walter Wanger, David Wolper. Contributor Encyclopedia Britannica.
PICTURES INCLUDE: Man on the Eiffel Tower, Shark River, (A.A. nominee) Since You Went Away, (A.A. nominee), Bad Lands of Dakota, Magnificent Ambersons, Eagle Squadron, Powers Girl, Since You Went Away, Smash Up, Flesh and Fantasy, Captain Kidd, Secret Beyond the Door, Fort Defiance, Riders to the Stars, Black Tuesday, Night of the Hunter, Man from Del Rio, Three Faces of Eve, Top Secret Affair, Angry Red Planet, Dinosaurus, Back Street, Shock Corridor, Nightmare in the Sun, The Naked Kiss, Blue, The Bridge of Remagen, The Date, Another Man, Another Chance. Special sequences on Damien, Omen II, Day the World Ended, Le Bon Vivant.

CORWIN, BRUCE CONRAD: Exhibitor. b. June 11, 1940, Los Angeles, Calif.; e. Wesleyan U.; Pres., Metropolitan Theatres Corp.; chmn., Will Rogers Hospital area ind. campaigns; exec. v.p., Variety Boys Club; chmn., Education Task Force; bd. member, Coro Foundation; Board of Trustees American Film Institute; Board of Trustees U.C.L.A. Foundation.

CORWIN, NORMAN: Writer, producer, director. b. Boston, Mass., May 3, 1910. Sports ed. Greenfield, Mass. Daily Recorder, 1926–29; radio ed., news commentator, Springfield Republican & Daily News, 1929–36; prog. dir., CBS, 1938. Bok Medal "for distinguished services to radio," 1942; Peabody Medal, 1942; awarded grant by Amer. Acad. of Arts & Letters, 1942; Page One Award, 1944; Distinguished Merit Award, Nat'l Conf. of Christians & Jews, 1945; Unity Award, Interracial Film & Radio Guild, 1945; Wendell Willkie One World Flight Award, 1946; Met. Opera Award for modern opera in collab. Bernard Rogers, 1946; first award, Res. Comm. of U.N., 1950; Radio & TV first award, Nat'l Conf. of Christians & Jews, 1951; Honor Medal of Freedom Foundation for TV show, Between Americans, 1951; ent., Radio Hall of Fame, 1962. Hon. doctorate Columbia Col. of Comms., 1967; Valentine Davies Award, WGA, 1972; author of Thirteen by Corwin, More by Corwin,

Untitled & Other Plays; The Plot to Overthrow Christmas, Dog in the Sky, Overkill and Megalove, Prayer for the 70s. Holes in a Stained Glass Window; lectured at various colleges; taught courses U.C.L.A., U.S.C., San Diego State U., regents lecturer, UC at Santa Barbara; Chairman, Creative Writing, USC-Isomata; U. of Alberta, U. of So. Col., Witswatersrand U., Rand Afrikaans U., So. Africa, Cantatas, The Golden Door, 55; Yes Speak Out Yes (commissioned by UN, 1968)

STAGE PLAYS: The Rivalry, The World of Carl Sandburg, The Hyphen, Overkill and Megalove, Cervantes. Together Tonight: Jefferson, Hamilton and Burr.

PICTURES INCLUDE: Once Upon a Time, Blue Veil, The Grand Design, Scandal in Scourie, Lust for Life, The Story of Ruth.

TV: Inside the Movie Kingdom, The FDR series, The Plot to Overthrow Christmas, Norman Corwin Presents (for Westinghouse), The Court Martial of General Yamashita, Network at 50 (CBS). Critic, monthly media column, Westways Magazine, Corwin on Media.

Chmn. Doc. Award Com., Motion Picture Academy 1965–80; elected to bd. of governors, 1980. Chm., writers' exec. comm., M.P. Academy; co-chmn. scholarship com., m.p. Academy; member, Film Advisory Bd.; L.A. County Museum; Norman Corwin Presents series; member, bd. of trustees, Advisory Board, Filmex, member, board of directors, WGA.

COSBY, BILL: Actor, comedian. b. Philadelphia, Pa., July 12, 1938. e. Temple U.; served in United States Navy Medical Corps. Started as night club entertainer. Has appeared many times on TV variety shows, in numerous one-nighters across the country, and concert tours.

TV: Emmy Award 1966, 1967, 1968: Best Actor in Dramatic Series—"I Spy," NBC-TV. Emmy Award, 1969; The First Bill Cosby Special, I Spy, The Bill Cosby Special, The Second Bill Cosby Special, The Bill Cosby Show, Fat Albert, Fat Albert and the Cosby Kids.

COMEDY ALBUMS: Bill Cosby Is A Very Funny Fellow . . . Right!; I Started Out As a Child; Why Is There Air?; Wonderfulness; Revenge; To Russell, My Brother, Whom I Slept With; 200 MPH; It's True, It's True; 8:15, 12:15.

SINGING ALBUMS: Silverthroat, Hooray for the Salvation Army Band. Grammy Award, 1964, 1965, 1966, 1967, 1969: Best Comedy Album.

RADIO: The Bill Cosby Radio Program.

PICTURES INCLUDE: Man and Boy, Uptown Saturday Night, Let's Do It Again, Mother, Jugs, and Speed, A Piece of the Action, California Suite, The Devil and Max Devlin.

COSLOW, SAM: Producer, song writer. b. New York City, Dec. 27, 1905. Writer popular songs, many for screen prod. (Cocktails for Two, Just One More Chance, Sing You Sinners, etc.). In 1941 formed RCM Prod., Inc., with James Roosevelt. Apptd. Paramount prod. 1944. Academy Award (with Jerry Bresler), best two-reel short, 1943 (Heavenly Music). In 1945 joined Mary Pickford Prods. as prod.

PICTURES INCLUDE: Out of This World, Copacabana, Dreaming Out Loud.

COSELL, HOWARD: Sports Commentator. b. Winston-Salem, N.C., 1920. Studied law and practiced. Broadcasting career began in 1953 when hired to host program on which N.Y. area Little Leaguers were introduced to baseball stars. In 1956 ABC hired him for ten five-minute sports shows on weekends. He dropped legal work to concentrate on sports reporting. Has had wide variety of roles in TV: commentator on ABC Monday Night Football, Monday Night Baseball, and various sports specials. Has hosted the Howard Cosell Sports Magazine for 4 yrs. and hosts 14 shows each week on American Contemporary Radio Network. Has guested on numerous prime-time TV shows.

PICTURES: Bananas, Sleeper, The World's Greatest Athlete.

COSMATOS, GEORGE P.: Director-Producer-Writer. b. Jan. 4, 1941. e. London Univ. Asst. dir., Exodus and Zorba the Greek.

PICTURES: Restless (co-prod., s.p., dir.); Massacre in Rome (co-s.p., dir.); The Cassandra Crossing (co-s.p., dir.); Escape to Athena (co-s.p., dir.).

COSTA-GAVRAS, HENRI: Director. b. Athens, Greece, 1933. e. Studied at the Sorbonne. Worked as second, then first assistant to Marcel Ophuls, Rene Calir, and Rene Clement, on Banana Peel, All the Gold in the World, The Thieves, 1964; dir. and wrote s.p. The Sleeping Car Murders. Second film Un Homme De Trop won prize at the Moscow Festival, 1966. Dir. and collab. s.p. Z (won Acad. Award, Best Foreign Lang. Film). L'Aveu (The Vow), State of Siege, Special Section.

COTES, PETER: F.R.S.A. Producer, dir., writer. Began early career as actor; stage debut Henry V, London 1926; debut as stage producer, 1942; founded Peter Cotes prods. 1946 and Peter Cotes Players 1948, prod., dir. numerous plays; prod. dir. for BBC: Same Sky, The Mask, Shadow of the Vine, Infinite Shoeblack, The Road, What the Public Wants; exec. prod., dir. Associated-Rediffusion, 1956; Sup. prod.

TV series, London Playhouse. Dir. Woman in a Dressing Gown, Ashes in the Wind, Hungry God. Co. dir., Waterfront; dir., Young and the Guilty, The Right Person Publications; No, Star Nonsense, Little Fellow (Charles Chaplin), A Handbook for the Amateur Theatre, George Robey. Head prod. Channel 7, Melbourne, Australia 1961. dir. doc., Australian Snowy Mountains; setting, dir., plays London, Broadway, 1962–63; TV consultant, McCann-Erickson (London); prod., dir.

TV: The Offence, Winter in Ischia, Also stage prods. in London. Assoc. prod., The World of Wooster, TV series for BBC, Prod. & Dir. West End Theatre, among others: Impossible Years, Staring At the Sun, Janie Jackson, West End Revival, The Old Ladies; wrote TV Omnibus program, gave R.S.A. theatre lectures. Devised-directed, Down With All Parties, Look, No Hands, My Brother, Willie, Lecturing, writing series of radio portraits; working on auto-biography. Publications: The Trial of Elvira Barney, Circus, The Man Called Mitch. 1978: Music Hall Tragedies, Charlie Chaplin Merryn Peake (radio), The Diminutive One.

COTTEN, JOSEPH: Actor. b. Petersburg, Va., 1905. In stock and on New York Stage, 1930–40, including Accent on Youth, Philadelphia Story; also Orson Welles' Federal Theatres productions and Mercury Theatre of the Air.

STAGE: Sabrina Fair, Once More With Feeling, Prescription: Murder, Calculated Risk.

TV: narrator, Hollywood and the Stars, own show.

PICTURES INCLUDE: Citizen Kane, Lydia, Magnificent Ambersons, Journey Into Fear, Shadow of a Doubt, Hers to Hold, Temptation, The Last Sunset, Two Flags West, September Affair, Walk Softly, Stranger, Half Angel, Peking Express, Man With a Cloak, The Untamed Frontier, The Steel Trap, Niagara, Blueprint for Murder, Special Delivery, Bottom of the Bottle, Killer Is Loose, Halliday Brand, From the Earth to the Moon, The Angel Wore Red, The Great Sioux Massacre, The Oscar, The Hellbenders, The Tramplers, The Money Trap, They Also Killed, The White Comanche, Petulia, The Grasshopper, The Abominable Dr. Phibes, Soylent Green, A Delicate Balance, Twilight's Last Gleaming, Airport '77, Caravans, Heaven's Gate.

COTY, HENRI ROLAND: Executive. b. Neuilly-sur-Seine, France, Feb. 13, 1922. e. Lycee Descartes, Tours, France. Baccalaureat, 1939–40, St. Jean DePassy, WWII Buchmaster Underground network; arrested 1942, deported to Dachau, Dora, Manthauson; Bergen-Belsen concentration camps; liberated, 1945. Sales mgr., Coty Perfume Co., 1946–55; found own company, s.a. Coty & Co., promotion, publicity, public relations, printing, now TV program prod.

COURTENAY, TOM: Actor. b. Hull, England, 1937; e. University Coll., London, Royal Academy of Dramatic Art, 1960–61; Old Vic. Ent. TV 1961 in Private Potter and The Lads; I Heard the Owl Call My Name (U.S.).

STAGE: Billy Liar, Andorra, Hamlet, She Stoops to Conquer, Otherwise Engaged (N.Y. debut).

PICTURES INCLUDE: Loneliness of the Long Distance Runner, Private Potter, Billy Liar, King and Country, Operation Crossbow, King Rat, Dr. Zhivago, Night of the Generals, The Day the Fish Came Out, A Dandy in Aspic, Otley, One Day in the Life of Ivan Denisovich.

COURTLAND, JEROME: Actor-Producer-Director. Began career in 40s as actor, then turned to directing and producing.

PICTURES INCLUDE: Actor: Kiss and Tell, Man from Colorado, Battleground, The Barefoot Mailman, The Bamboo Prison, Tonka, Black Spurs. Director: Run, Cougar, Run, Diamonds on Wheels. Producer: Escape to Witch Mountain, Ride a Wild Pony, Return from Witch Mountain.

TV: Actor: The Saga of Andy Burnett, Tonka. Director: Hog Wild (also co-prod.), Harness Fever.

COWAN, THEODORE: Executive. b. Letchworth, Eng. e. Parmiters School. Entered m.p. ind., J. Arthur Rank Productions, pub. div., asst. dir. pub. & adv., 1960. Formed own pr. & publ. Co., 1962.

COWAN, WARREN J.: Publicist. b. New York, Mar. 13. e. Townsend Harris H.S., U.C.L.A., graduated 1941. Entered public relations, 1941 with Alan Gordon & Associates; three yrs. Air Force; to Henry C. Rogers office; became partner, 1949 and changed name to Rogers & Cowan, Public Relations Advisor, Rogers & Cowan, Inc., 1960; pres., Rogers & Cowan, Inc., 1964-present.

CRABBE, (LARRY) BUSTER: Actor. r.n. Clarence Linden C.; b. Oakland, Calif.; e. U. So. Calif. Spent boyhood Hawaii; expert swimmer. In 1933 on screen in King of the Jungle; thereafter in many adventure pictures, serials and others.

PICTURES INCLUDE: The Sweetheart of Sigma Chi, Wanderer of the Wasteland, Desert Gold, various Flash Gordon & Billy the Kid, Gunfighters of Abilene.

TV: The Foreign Legion.

CRAIG, MICHAEL: Actor. b. India. 1929. At 16 joined Merchant Navy. 1949 returned to England and made stage debut in repertory. M.P. debut as crowd artist 1950.

PICTURES INCLUDE: Malta Story, The Love Lottery, Passage Home, The Black Tent, Yield to the Night, Eyewitness, House of Secrets, High Tide At Noon, Sea of Sand, Sapphire, Upstairs and Downstairs, The Angry Silence, Cone of Silence, Doctor In Love, The Mysterious Island, Payroll, No My Darling Daughter, A Pair of Briefs. Under contract Rank Organisation. A Life for Ruth, The Iron Maiden, Captive City, Summer Flight, Of a Thousand Delights, Life at the Top, Modesty Blaise, Star, A Town Called Hell, Ride a Wild Pony.

CRAIG, STANLEY HERBERT: Executive. Began career with Co-operative Films, Melbourne, Australia, 1914; Paramount, 1917; asst. mgr. Melbourne, 1921; br. mgr., Adelaide, 1923; gen. mgr., New Zealand, 1928–67; Pres. M.P. Distributors Assn. of New Zealand, 1938–55; chmn., 1963–64; mem. Cinematograph Films Licensing Authority, 1968–70.

CRAIN, JEANNE: Actress. b. Barstow, Calif., May 25, 1925. Model; crowned Miss Long Beach of 1941: Camera Girl of 1942.
   PICTURES INCLUDE: Home in Indiana, In the Meantime Darling, Winged Victory, State Fair, Leave Her to Heaven, Margie, Centennial Summer, You Were Meant for Me, Apartment for Peggy, Letter to Three Wives, Pinky, Cheaper by the Dozen, Take Care of My Little Girl, People Will Talk, Model and the Marriage Broker, Belles on Their Toes, O. Henry's Full House, City of Bad Men, Dangerous Crossing, Vicki, Duel in the Jungle, Man Without a Star, Second Greatest Sex, Gentlemen Marry Brunettes, Fastest Gun Alive, Tattered Dress, The Joker, Guns of the Timberland, Skyjacked.

CRAMER, WM. DOUGLAS: Executive. b. Aug. 22, 1931. e. Northwestern U., Sorbonne, Cincinnati U., B.A.; Columbia U.M.F.A., M. Joyce Haber, columnist. Taught at Carnegie Inst. of Tech., 1954–55; Production asst. Radio City Music Hall 1950–51; MGM Script Dept. 1952; Manag. Dir. Cincinnati Summer Playhouse 1953–54. TV supvr. Procter and Gamble 1956–59; Broadcast supvr. Ogilvy, Benson and Mather, Adv. 1959–62; V-P Program Dev. ABC-TV 1962–66; V-P Program Dev. 20 Cent.-Fox TV 1966; Exec. v.p. in chg. of production, Paramount Television, 1968.
   PLAYS: Love is a Smoke, Whose Baby Are You, Call of Duty.

CRAWFORD, BRODERICK: Actor. b. Philadelphia, Dec. 9, 1911; p. Helen Broderick and Lester Crawford, prof.
   PICTURES INCLUDE: Submarine D-1, Ambush, Undercover Doctor, Real Glory, Eternally Yours, I Can't Give You Anything But Love Baby, Slightly Honorable, When the Daltons Rode, Butch Minds the Baby, Broadway, Sin Town, Night Unto Night, Flame, Anna Lucasta, All the King's Men, Born Yesterday, The Mob, Lone Star, Scandal Sheet, Last of the Comanches, Stop You're Killing Me, Last Posse, Night People, Human Desire, Down 3 Dark Streets, New York Confidential, Big House, Not As a Stranger, Fastest Gun Alive, Between Heaven and Hell, The Oscar, Gregorio and His Angels, The Texican, Hell's Bloody Devils, The Private Files of J. Edgar Hoover.
   TV: Highway Patrol (series), The Interns (CBS).

CRAWFORD, MICHAEL: Actor. b. Salisbury, England, 1942. Early career as boy actor in children's films and sound radio.
   TV: Still Life, Destiny, Byron, Move After Checkmate, Three Barrelled Shotgun, Home Sweet Honeycomb, Some mothers do 'ave 'em, Chalk and Cheese.
   PICTURES INCLUDE: Two Left Feet, The War Lover, Two Living, One Dead, The Knack, A Funny Thing Happened On The Way to the Forum, The Jokers, How I Won the War, Hello, Dolly!, The Games, Hello and Goodbye, The Adventures of Alice in Wonderland.
   STAGE: Come Blow Your Horn, Traveling Light, The Anniversary, Black Comedy (N.Y.), No Sex Please We're British, Billy, Same Time Next Year, Flowers for Algernon.

CRENNA, RICHARD: Actor. b. L.A., Calif., Nov. 30, 1927. e. Belmont H.S., U. of Southern Calif.
   RADIO: Boy Scout Jambouree, A Date With Judy, The Great Gildersleeve, Johnny Dollar, Our Miss Brooks.
   TV: Our Miss Brooks, The Real McCoys, Slattery's People, All's Fair.
   PICTURES INCLUDE: Pride of St. Louis, It Grows on Trees, Red Skies Over Montana, John Goldfarb, Please Come Home, Pendick Enterprises, The Sand Pebbles, Star, Marooned, The Deserter, Doctor's Wives, Red Sky at Morning, A Man Called Noon, Catlow, Dirty Money, Death Ship.

CRICHTON, CHARLES: Director. b. Wallasey, Aug. 6, 1910; e. Oundle & Oxford. Collab. dir. Dead of Night.
   PICTURES INCLUDE: Painted Boats, Hue and Cry, Against the Wind, Another Shore, Dance Hall, Lavender Hill Mob, Hunted (Stranger in Between), Titfield Thunderbolt, The Love Lottery, Divided Heart, Man in the Sky, Floods of Fear, Battle of the Sexes, The Third Secret, He Who Rides a Tiger.
   TV: The Wild Duck, Danger Man, The Avengers, Man in a Suitcase, The Strange Report, Shirley's World, Black

Beauty, The Protectors, Space 1999, Return of the Saint, Dick Turpin 1 & 2 Series.

CRICHTON, MICHAEL: Writer-Director. Entered Harvard Medical School in 1965; while there completed first novel, Easy God, under pseudonym, John Lange. Has written 15 books under four different names, including A Case of Need (filmed as The Carey Treatment) and The Andromeda Strain (first book to appear under his own name). Did post-graduate work at Salk Institute in La Jolla. Also wrote novels Dealing and The Terminal Man, both filmed.
   PICTURES INCLUDE: Westworld (s.p., dir.), Coma (s.p., dir.), The Great Train Robbery (s.p., dir.), Looker (s.p., dir.).
   TELEVISION: Pursuit (Movie of Week), dir.; script by Robert Dozier based on Crichton's book, Binary.

CRIST, JUDITH: Journalist-Critic. b. N.Y.C. e. Hunter College, Columbia Univ. (School of Journalism). Joined New York Herald Tribune, serving as reporter, arts editor, assoc. drama critic, film critic. Continued as film critic for New York World Journal Tribune, NBC-TV Today Show, New York, Saturday Review, New York Post. Now regular film critic for TV Guide, Saturday Review. 50 Plus, Medical/Mrs. Teaches at Col. Grad. School of Journ.
   AUTHOR: The Private Eye, the Cowboy and the Very Naked Girl, Judith Crist's TV Guide to the Movies.

CRISTALDI, FRANCO: Producer. b. Turin, Italy, Oct. 3, 1924. Owner, prod. Vides Cinematografica; President of Italian Producer's Union.
   PICTURES INCLUDE: White Nights, The Strawman, The Challenge, Big Deal On Madonna Street, Kapo, The Dauphins, Salvatore Giuliano, The Assassin, Divorce Italian Style, The Organizer, Bebo's Girl, Seduced and Abandoned, Time of Indifference, Sandra, A Rose for Every-One, China Is Near, A Quiet Couple, The Red Tent.

CRITCHFIELD, EDWARD: Producer. B. Cleveland, Ohio, Jan. 9, 1919. e. Glenville H.S., 1937. Gen. insurance broker; real estate mortgage financing; motion picture financier, Delta Diamond Productions; then joined Bernfeld Publications Inc., as vice-pres.; assoc. prod. Terrified.

CRON, JOHN B.: Executive. b. Mt. Vernon, New York, June 11, 1923. e. Princeton U.: Exec. vice-pres., Robert Lawrence Productions; managing dir., Screen Gems (Europe); sales dir., N.B.C. Film Division; vice-pres., sales dir. SIB Productions.

CRONKITE, WALTER: Correspondent. b. St. Joseph, Mo., Nov. 4, 1916; e. Univ. of Texas. Reporter: radio reporter; U.P. Correspondent. Joined CBS as Washington news correspondent, 1950; many TV shows including You Are There, Twentieth Century, Eyewitness to History: CBS Reports: 21st Century, past nat'l pres. & mem. bd. Trustees, Acad. TV Arts & Sciences. Managing Editor of CBS Evening News since 1963.

CRONYN, HUME: Actor, writer, director. b. London, Ontario, Canada, July 18, 1911; e. Ridley Coll.; U. of McGill; Amer. Acad. of Dramatic Art; m. Jessica Tandy, actress. m.p. acting debut in Shadow of a Doubt.
   STAGE: (Actor N.Y. plays) High Tor, Escape This Night, Three Men on a Horse, Boy Meets Girl, Three Sisters, Mr. Big, The Survivors; dir. plays Now I Lay Me Down to Sleep, Hilda Crane, Madam Will You Walk. N.Y. stage, The Fourposter, 1951–53; Madam Will You Walk, 1953–54; The Honeys, A Day by the Sea, 1955; The Man in The Dog Suit, 1957; Directed The Egghead, 1957; Directed and toured with his wife, Miss Tandy, in Triple Play, 1958–59; Big Fish, Little Fish, 1961; also in London, 1962; The Miser, 1963; The Three Sisters, 1963; Hamlet, 1964; The Physicists, 1964; Produced Slow Dance on The Killing Ground, 1964; Appeared at the White House; Hear America Speaking 1965; Richard III, 1965; Revival The Miser, 1965; A Delicate Balance, 1966 and tour, 1967; The Miser, 1968; Hadrian VII tour, 1969–70; Caine Mutiny Court Martial, 1971; Promenade All 1972–73; Krapp's Last Tape, Happy Days, Act Without Words I, 1972; Coward In Two Keys, 1974, Concert recital Many Faces Of Love 1974; National tour, Noel Coward in Two Keys, 1975, Merchant of Venice and A Midsummer Night's Dream, at Stratford Festival Theatre, Canada 1976. 1976; Many Faces of Love limited tour 1975–76 and at Theatre London, Ontario, Canada '76 as well as for CBC, Canada, 1977; Appeared in The Gin Game, Long Wharf Thea., New Haven, Conn. June, 1977. Co-produced with Mike Nichols and also appeared in The Gin Game, The Golden Theatre, N.Y.C. 1977–78. Toured U.S., Toronto, London, U.S.S.R., 1978
   TV: The Marriage, and other network dramatic shows, 1957.
   PICTURES INCLUDE: Cross of Lorraine, Lifeboat, Seventh Cross, Main Street, After Dark, The Sailor Takes a Wife, A Letter for Evie, The Green Years, Brute Force, Bride Goes Wild, Postman Always Rings Twice, Top O' the Morning, People Will Talk, Crowded Paradise, Sunrise at Campobello, Cleopatra, Gaily, Gaily, The Arrangement,

There Was a Crooked Man, Conrack, Parallax View, Honky Tonk Freeway, Roll-over, Garp.

CROSBY, BOB: Band leader, actor; r.n. George Robert C.; b. Spokane, Wash., Aug. 23, 1913; e. Gonzaga U. Began as singer; later featured vocalist Jimmie & Tommy Dorsey band. Org. own band (Bobcats); appeared with orch. on screen in Let's Make Music, 1940.
PICTURES INCLUDE: Sis Hopkins, Reveille with Beverly, Thousands Cheer, Presenting Lily Mars, See Here Private Hargrove; Meet Miss Bobby Socks, Kansas City Kitty, My Gal Loves Music, Pardon My Rhythm, Singing Sheriff, Two Tickets to Broadway.
TV: Bob Crosby Show.

CROSBY, KATHRYN: Actress. r.n. Kathryn Grandstaff. b. Houston, Tex., Nov. 25, 1933. e. University of Texas, U.C.L.A. m. Bing Crosby.
CREDITS: Forever Female, Rear Window, Living It Up, Arrowhead, Cassandra's Big Night, Unchained, Cell 2455 Death Row, Tight Spot, Five Against the House, Reprisal, Guns of Fort Petticoat, Phoenix City Story, Wild Party, Mister Cory, Night the World Exploded, Brothers Rico, Operation Mad Ball, The Big Circus, Bob Hope Chrysler Theatre (TV), Bing Crosby Christmas Specials (TV), Suspense Theatre (TV), Ben Casey (TV), The Kathryn Crosby Show KPIX-TV-San Francisco.

CROSS, PERRY: Performer. b. Brooklyn, N.Y., Feb. 26. e. R.I. State Coll. At various clubs; to NBC, 1947. Guest relations staff, then TV production supervisor, coordinator, unit mgr.
TV: Ernie Kovacs Show, Henie Ice Spectacular, Ruggles of Red Gap, Tonight, Jack Paar Show, Today, TV network programs, night time.

CROUSE, LINDSAY: Actress. b. New York City. Daughter of playwright Russel Crouse. e. Radcliffe. Began career as modern and jazz dancer; is also flutist and pianist. Has worked in films, theatre and TV.
PICTURES INCLUDE: All the President's Men, Slap Shot, Between the Lines.
TV: Eleanor and Franklin, The Tenth Level.

CROWN, ALFRED W.: Executive. b. New York City, Sept. 30, 1913. e. Columbia U. To South America for MGM 1933–35; foreign mgr. Grand Natl. Pictures, 1935–38; coordinator of Inter-American Affairs, 1939–40; served in U.S. Army, 1940–42; with Chas. Feldman, Hollywood 1942–43; Film Classics, 1943–45; world-wide sales mgr. for Goldwyn; vice-pres., Samuel Goldwyn Prod., Inc., 1950; v.p., foreign sales mgr., RKO Pictures, Oct. 1952; pres. Moulin Prod., Inc., Jan. 1954; v.p., Allied Artists; indep. prod. Motion Pictures; TV packager; prod., B'way play: The Deputy; prod., electronovision, Hamlet with Richard Burton. Film Prod. Midsummer Night's Dream, Columbia; Prod. Last Summer, Allied Artists; Taking Off, Universal, 1975—senior vice pres., Penthouse Films.

CROYDON, JOHN: Consult. & Rep. Film Finances, Ltd. b. London, England, Nov. 3, 1907. Entered industry 1931.
CREDITS INCLUDE: Foreman Went to France, Goose Steps Out, Champagne Charlie, Dead of Night, Nicholas Nickleby, One Wild Oat, White Corridors, Tarzan and the Lost Safari, The Entertainer, First Man Into Space, The Projected Man, High Wind in Jamaica.

CRUEA, EDMOND D.: Executive. b. Jersey City, N.J., June 3, 1918. Joined Grand National Pictures, Los Angeles, 1935; Monogram Pictures, 1938–41 (L.A. & Seattle); U.S. Army Signal Corps, 1942–46; Monogram Pictures, Seattle, 1946–48; branch mgr., 1948–49; branch mgr. Allied Artists, 1950–65 (Seattle, Portland, San Francisco); Western Division Mgr., 1965–66; v.p., sales, 1970; v.p., gen. sls. mgr., 1970–71; v.p., Western Division, 1971; dir. of distribution for Abkco Films div. of Abkco Industries, Inc., 1971–73; pres. of Royal Dist. Corp., 1974; pres., Esco Film Corp., 1975; joined Film Ventures Intl. in 1976 as exec. v.p., succeeding to pres. and chief operating officer in August, 1976. Resigned Sept. 1977 to form Fil-Mark Inc.

CRYSTAL, BILLY: Actor. b. Long Island, NY, Mar. 14. Father, Jack, produced jazz concerts; family owned Commodore jazz record label. e. Marshall Univ., New York Univ. Worked with Alumni Theatre Group at Nassau Community College. Later teamed with two friends (billed as 3's Company) and toured coffee houses and colleges. Became stand-up comedian on own, appearing on TV.
PICTURES INCLUDE: Rabbit Test.
TELEVISION: Tonight Show, Dinah, Mike Douglas Show, That Was the Year That Was, All in the Family, Love Boat, Soap. Movies: Death Flight, Breaking Up Is Hard to Do.

CUKOR, GEORGE: Director. b. N.Y.C. Began on Broadway stage. Some noted plays were The Constant Wife, The Cardboard Lover, The Furies, Great Gatsby. Stage dir. & mgr. Charles Frohman Co.; with Lyceum Theatre Co. 1920–8. Rochester, N.Y.
PICTURES INCLUDE: dial. All Quiet on the Western Front, River of Romance, Grumpy, Virtuous Sin, Royal Family, Bill of Divorcement, Sylvia Scarlett, Tarnished Lady, Girls About Town, One Hour with You, Little Women, Dinner at Eight, David Copperfield, Romeo and Juliet, Holiday, Philadelphia Story, Two-Faced Woman, Keeper of the Flame, Winged Victory, Camille, Gaslight, Double Life, Edward, My Son; Adam's Rib, A Life of Her Own, Born Yesterday, Model and Marriage Broker, The Marrying Kind, Pat and Mike, The Actress, It Should Happen to You, A Star Is Born, Bhowani Junction, Wild is the Wind, Les Girls, Heller in Pink Tights, Song Without End, Let's Make Love, The Chapman Report, My Fair Lady, Justine, Travels with My Aunt, The Blue Bird, Rich and Famous.
TV: Love Among the Ruins, The Corn Is Green.

CULLEN, BILL: Performer. b. Pittsburgh, Pa., Feb. 18, 1920; U. of Pittsburgh, B.A. Asst. disc jockey; announcer, KDKA, Pittsburgh; sportcaster; staff announcer. CBS radio, 1943; then m.c., panel member; shows include: m.c. Three on a Match, To Tell the Truth, Winning Streak, 25,000 Pyramid; Love Experts.

CULLEN, JAMES V.: Executive. b. San Francisco, Dec. 29, 1938; e. City College of S.F. Sales mgr., M.P.I. Toys, Los Angeles, 1963–65; entered film industry 1965 with 20th-Fox in S.F. exchange as ass't. field man; Named Southwest ad-pub. mgr. for Fox 1966 and Western Division ad-pub mgr. 1968. Appointed Fox director of exploitation 1971; then nat'l. dir. field adv. & pro.; Joined Sandy Howard Prods., v.p. creative affairs, 1974. Produced The Devils' Rain, 1975.

CULP, ROBERT: Actor, Writer, Director. b. Berkeley, Cal., Aug. 16, 1930. e. Stockton, College of the Pacific, Washington U., San Francisco State; to N.Y. to study with Herbert Berghof; starred in off B'way prod. He Who Gets Slapped. Best Actor of the Year in an off B'way Play; motion picture debut, 1962; P.T. 109; television guest appearances in Rawhide, Wagon Train, Bob Hope Presents the Chrysler Theatre; wrote and acted in Rifleman, Cain's Hundred, The Dick Powell Show.
PLAYS: The Prescott Proposals, He Who Gets Slapped, A Clearing in the Woods.
TV: Trackdown, I Spy.
PICTURES INCLUDE: PT 109, Sammy, The Way Out Seal, The Raiders, Sunday in New York, Rhino, The Hanged Man, Bob & Carol & Ted & Alice, The Grove, Hannie Caulder, Hickey and Boggs, Sky Riders, Great Scout and Cathouse, Thursday.

CULVER, ROLAND: Actor. b. London, England, Aug. 31, 1900; e. Highgate Coll.; Royal Acad. of Dram. Arts, London. On London stage (Old Bachelor, Average Man, Fortune, French Without Tears, Five Finger Exercise, Hay Fever.
TV: Spread of the Eagle, The Caesars, The Letter, The Yellow Rolls-Royce.
PICTURES INCLUDE: 77 Park Lane, Love on Wheels, Accused, French Without Tears, Folly to Be Wise, Holly & the Ivy, True and the Brave (Betrayed), Man Who Loved Redheads, Teckman Mystery, Ship that Died of Shame, An Alligator Named Daisy, Touch and Go, Safari, The Hypnotist, My Friend Charles, The Rise and Rise of Michael Rimmer, Fragment of Fear, The Magic Christian, Thunderball, A Man Could Get Killed, To Each His Own, Down to Earth, Emperor Waltz, Singapore, Isn't it Romantic, The Great Lovers.

CUMMINGS, BOB: Godson of Orville Wright. Actor, dir. b. Joplin, Mo., June 9, 1910; e. Drury Coll., Carnegie Inst. Tech.; American Academy of Dramatic Arts; on dram. & musical stage, also radio.
TV: Bob Cummings Show; My Hero, Twelve Angry Men (Emmy, 1954).
PICTURES INCLUDE: Three Smart Girls Grow Up, Spring Parade, Saboteur, Heaven Only Knows, So Red the Rose, Kings Row, Flesh and Fantasy, Princess O'Rourke, You Came Along, Reign of Terror, The Accused, Free for All, Tell It to the Judge, Paid in Full, Petty Girl, For Heaven's Sake, Barefoot Mailman, The Lost Moment, Free and Easy, First Time, Marry Me Again, Lucky Me, Dial M for Murder, How to Be Very Very Popular, My Geisha, Beach Party, The Carpetbaggers, What A Way to Go, Stage Coach, Promise Her Anything, Gidget Grows Up, The Great American Beauty Contest, (TV). Has toured Dinner Theater Circuit since '73 and established new attendence records in 16 theaters playing Never Too Late, Marriage Go Round, No Hard Feelings, Harvey, Fun and Games.

CUMMINGS, CONSTANCE: Actress. b. Seattle, Wash., May 15, 1910; p. D.V. Halverstadt, attorney, and Kate Cummings, concert soprano; m. Benn Levy, English playwright. Was chorus girl in The Little Show and also appeared in June Moon.
PICTURES INCLUDE: Behind the Mask, Washington Merry-Go-Round, Broadway Through a Keyhole, Channel Crossing, Glamour, Doomed Cargo, Busman's Honeymoon, This England, The Outsider, The Foreman Went to France, Somewhere in France, Blithe Spirit, Into the Blue, The Scream, John and Julie, The Intimate Stranger, Battle of the Sexes, A Boy 10 Feet Tall.

TV: Touch of the Sun, Clutterbuck, The Last Tycoon, Ruth, Late Summer.

CUMMINGS, IRVING, JR.: Writer, producer.
PICTURES INCLUDE: Yesterday's Heroes, Lone Star Ranger, He Hired the Boss, Sign of the Ram, It's Only Money, Where Danger Lives, Double Dynamite, Girl in Every Port, Edward Small Productions, 1953–54, Television Programs of America, Fury.

CUMMINGS, JACK: Producer. b. New Brunswick, Canada. Started at MGM as office boy. Later worked as script boy, assistant director, director, producer of short subjects. Became producer of feature pictures. In 1934 produced The Winning Ticket.
PICTURES INCLUDE: Bathing Beauty, I Dood It, Broadway Melody, Girl from Rectors, Romance of Rosy Ridge, Neptunes Daughter, Two Weeks with Love, Three Little Words, Excuse My Dust, Texas Carnival, Lovely to Look At, Fiesta, Stratton Story, Sombrero, Give a Girl a Break, Kiss Me Kate, Seven Brides for Seven Brothers, Last Time I Saw Paris, Many Rivers to Cross, Interrupted Melody, Teahouse of the August Moon, Can Can, Bachelor Flat, Viva, Las Vegas.

CUMMINGS, SANDY: Executive. r.n. Sanford Cummings. b. Oct. 31, 1913. e. University of Southern Calif. Child actor; Broadway. Summer stock, 1935; asst. prod., Paramount; assist. to Walter Wanger, 1936; started Hollywood office of Benton & Bowles, 1937; major, army, 1939–46; Head American Forces Network, Germany; prod. Columbia, 1946; ABC Coordinator, Walt Disney Studios, 1954; manager, TV Net Programs, Western Div. ABC, 1957; dir. TV Net Prog., 1958; V.P. & Dir. of pgms., Western Div., 1958–62; prod. specials, STV, 1964; prod., 20th Fox Television, 1965–66; NBC Broadcast Standards; 1969 mgr., live night-time and special programs, NBC.

CUMMINS, DWIGHT W.: Writer. b. San Francisco, Cal., Feb. 20, 1901; e. U. Calif., L.A., B.A. '26. m. Dorothy Yost, writer. Tech. dir. & prod. asst. Film Booking Office studio, 1926–27. Began writing scripts 1927. Ed. & story asst. various major producers 1932–38. Instructor in Cinematog., U. So. Calif., 1938–42. Member Phi Gamma Delta.
PICTURES INCLUDE: Naughty but Nice, None but the Brave, The River, Thunderhead, Smoky, The Strawberry Roan, The Saginaw Trail.
TV: Gene Autry, Range Rider; TV writer for Roy Rogers, 1955–60; TV free lance.

CUMMINS, PEGGY: Actress. b. Prestatyn, North Wales, Dec. 18, 1926. e. Alexandra School, Dublin, Gate Theatre, Dublin. Starred in Let's Pretend on London Stage 1938. Made Dr. O'Dowd WB, Eng., 1939. In 1942: Salute John Citizen; Welcome Mr. Washington; On London stage in Junior Miss, Alice in Wonderland, Peter Pan. From 1946 Hollywood, starred in Late George Apley.
PICTURES INCLUDE: Moss Rose, Green Grass of Wyoming, Escape, That Dangerous Age, Gun Crazy, My Daughter Joy, Returned to Eng. 1950. Who Goes There (Passionate Sentry), Street Corner (Both Sides of the Law), Meet Mr. Lucifer, Always a Bride, Love Lottery, To Dorothy a Son, Cash on Delivery, March Hare, Carry on Admiral, Night of the Demon, Hell Drivers, The Captain's Table, Your Money or Your Wife, Dentist in the Chair, In the Doghouse.
TV: The Human Jungle, Looks Familiar.

CUNNINGHAM, SEAN S.: Producer-Director. b. New York City, 1949. e. B.A. Franklin & Marshall, MFA Stanford Univ. Worked briefly as actor, moving into stage-managing. Became producer of Mineola Theatre (Long Island, NY) and took several productions to Broadway. Formed Sean S. Cunningham Films, Ltd., 1971. Produced commercials, industrial film, documentaries, features.
PICTURES: Together (prod.-dir.), Last House on the Left (prod.); The Case of the Full Moon Murders (prod.); Here Come the Tigers (prod.-dir.); Kick (prod.-dir.); Friday the 13th (prod.-dir.).

CURTIN, JOHN P.: Distributor. b. Pittsfield, Mass., Nov. 24, 1915; e. Williams Coll., 1938; B.A. Columbia U. Graduate School, 1939. Eastern div. man., Republic; v.p., Color Service Corp.; sls. mgr. Guffanti Film Lab., Inc.
MEMBER: Montclair Golf Club, Alpha Delta Phi Fraternity, Dir., Seaboard Corp.

CURTIS, DAN: Producer-Director. b. Bridgeport, Conn., Aug. 12. e. Univ. of Bridgeport; Syracuse Univ. (BA, 1950). Was sales exec. for NBC and MCA before forming own company, Dan Curitis Productions, now heads. Producer/owner of CBS Golf Classic (1963–73).
PICTURES INCLUDE: House of Dark Shadows, Night of Dark Shadows (features for MGM, prod.-dir.), Burnt Offerings (prod., dir., co-s.p.).
TV: Producer: Dark Shadows (ABC serial, 1966–71), and following movies: The Night Stalker, Frankenstein, The Picture of Dorian Gray. Producer-Director of movies: The Night Strangler, The Norliss Tapes, The Turn of the Screw, Dracula, The Scream of the Wolf, Purvis.

CURTIS, KEN: Actor. b. Lamar, Colo., July 2, 1916. e. Colorado Coll. Success as songwriter for college prod. steered him to musical career in Hollywood. Sang with several groups, including Sons of the Pioneers, Tommy Dorsey Orchestra, Shep Fields band. In infantry and anti-aircraft unit in World War II. Signed by Columbia Pictures for series of westerns with "Big Boy" Williams in 1945.
PICTURES INCLUDE: The Searchers, The Alamo, The Quiet Man, Cheyenne Autumn, How the West Was Won, The Killer Shrews, The Giant Gila Monster, My Dog, Buddy.
TV: Ripcord, Perry Mason, Rawhide, Have Gun, Will Travel, Gunsmoke (joined later series as Festus Haggin in 1963).

CURTIS, TONY: Actor. r.n. Bernard Schwartz. b. New York, N.Y., June 3, 1925; e. Seward Park H. Sch. In U.S. Navy, amateur dramatics, NYC, started Empire Players Theatre, Newark, N.J., with Dramatic Workshop, Cherry Lane Theatre, Jr. Drama Workshop of Walt Whitman School; first prod. work with Stanley Woolf Players; m.p. debut in Criss-Cross; signed with U-I Star of Tomorrow, 1953.
PICTURES INCLUDE: City Across the River, Johnny Stool Pigeon, Francis, Sierra, I Was a Shoplifter, Winchester 73, Kansas Raiders, Prince Who Was a Thief, Flesh and Fury, Son of Ali Baba, No Room for the Groom, Houdini, All American, Forbidden, Beachhead, Johnny Dark, Black Shield of Falworth, 6 Bridges to Cross, So This is Paris, Purple Mask, Square Jungle, Rawhide Years, Trapeze, Mister Cory, Midnight Story, Sweet Smell of Success, Some Like It Hot, Spartacus, Operation Petticoat, Who Was That Lady?, The Rat Race, The Defiant Ones, Perfect Furlough, The Great Impostor, The Outsider, Taras Bulba, 40 Pounds of Trouble, Paris When It Sizzles, The List of Adrian Messenger, Captain Newman, M.D., Wild and Wonderful, Sex and the Single Girl, Goodbye, Charlie, The Great Race, Boeing-Boeing, Arrivederci, Baby!, Not With My Wife, You Don't!, Don't Make Waves, On My Way to The Crusades I Met a Girl Who—; The Boston Strangler; Those Daring Young Men in Their Jaunty Jalopies, Suppose They Gave a War and Nobody Came; You Can't Win 'Em All, Lepke, The Last Tycoon, The Manitou, Bad News Bears Go To Japan, The Mirror Crack'd.
TV: The Persuaders, The Second Girl on the Right (movie), Vegas (series).

CUSACK, CYRIL: Actor. b. Durban, S. Africa, Nov. 26, 1910. e. Newbridge, Co. Kildare; University College, Dublin, Eire. LL.D (Honoris Causa-National University of Ireland). Stage debut: Candida, Abbey Theatre, 1932. Screen debut: Odd Man Out, 1945.
PICTURES INCLUDE: Esther Waters, Escape, The Blue Lagoon, Once a Jolly Swagman, All Over the Town, Small Back Room, The Elusive Pimpernel, Soldiers Three, Blue Veil, Secret of Convict Lake, Gone to Earth (Wild Heart), Saadia, Passage Home, Man in the Road, Man Who Never Was, March Hare, Jacqueline, Spanish Gardner, Ill Met By Moonlight, Rising of the Moon, Miracle in Soho, Shake Hands with the Devil, Floods of Fear, Gideon's Day, A Terrible Beauty, Johnny Nobody, The Waltz of the Toreadors, I Thank a Fool, 80,000 Suspects, Passport to Oblivion, The Spy Who Came In From The Cold, Fahrenheit 451, Taming of the Shrew, I Was Happy Here, Oedipus Rex, Galileo, King Lear, Country Dance, David Copperfield, Harold and Maude, Sacco Vanzetti, La La Polizia Ringrazia, The Day of the Jackal, Juggernaut, Homecoming, Gallileo, Tristan and Iseult, True Confessions.
TV: The Dumms, The Moon and Sixpence, What Every Woman Knows, The Enchanted, The Power and The Glory, The Chairs, Don Juan in Hell, The Lotus Eater, Krapp's Last Tape, Murder in the Cathedral, Six Characters in Search of An Author, The Big Toe, Workhouse Ward, In the Train, Purgatory, The Moon in the Yellow River, Passage to India, Deirdre, The Tower, Dial M for Murder, St. Francis, The Physicists, Trial of Marshal Petain, In the Bosom of the Country, Uncle Vanya, A Time of Wolves and Tigers, Them, Clochemerle, The Golden Bowl, The Reunion, I Stand Well With All Parties, Catholics, Crystal & Fox, Jesus of Nazareth, The Plough and The Stars, You Never Can Tell, The Hitchhiker.

CUSHING, PETER: Actor. b. Kenley, Surrey, Eng., May 26, 1913. e. Purley Secondary Sch. Stage debut with Worthington Repertory Co.
TV: Asmodee, Anastasia, 1984, Gaslight, Home at Seven, Tovarich, Beau Brummell, Epitaph for a Spy, Pride and Prejudice, The Moment of Truth, Uncle Harry, Eden End, Rookery Nook, The Creature, The Browning Version, Winslow Boy, Peace With Terror, Julius Caesar (Cassius), Monica. Daily Mail TV award actor, 1953–54; Guild of TV award, 1955; News Chronicle T.V. Top Ten award, 1956, The Plan, Caves of Steel, Sherlock Holmes series, 1968, Morecambe & Wise Show, Wild-life Spectacular, The Zoo Gang, Orson Welles Great Mysteries, Space 1999, The New Avengers, The Great Houdini, A Land Looking West.
PICTURES INCLUDE: Vigil in the Night, Moulin Rouge, Hamlet, Black Knight, End of the Affair, Alexander the Great, Magic Fire, Time Without Pity, Curse of Frankenstein,

Abominable Snowman, Dracula, John Paul Jones, The Hound of the Baskervilles, Violent Playground, The Mummy, Suspect, The Flesh and the Friends, The Revenge of Frankenstein, Cone of Silence, Brides of Dracula, Sword of Sherwood Forest, The Naked Edge, Cash on Demand, The Devil's Agent, Captain Clegg, Fury at Smuggler's Bay, Hell-Fire Club, The Man Who Finally Died, The Evil of Frankenstein, The Gorgon, Dr. Terror's House of Horrors, She, The Skull, Dr. Who and the Daleks, The Frightened Island, Daleks Invade Earth, Frankenstein Created Woman, Torture Garden, Some May Live, The Night of the Big Heat, Corruption, Death's Head Moth, Frankenstein Must Be Destroyed, Doctors Wear Scarlet, The Vampire Lovers, Scream and Scream Again, House That Dripped Blood, I Monster, Twins of Evil, Tales from the Crypt, Dracula Today, Fear in the Night, Horror Express, The Creeping Flesh, Asylum, Nothing But the Night, Bride of Fengriffen, Frankenstein and the Monster from Hell, The Satanic Rites of Dracula, The Revenge of Dr. Death, From Beyond the Grave, The Beast Must Die, Dracula and the Legend of the Seven Golden Vampires, Shatter, Tender Dracula, The Ghoul, Legend of the Werewolf, The Devil's People, Death Corps, Trial by Combat, At The Earth's Core, Star Wars, Battleflag, The Uncanny, Hitler's Son, Touch of the Sun, Arabian Adventure.

D

DAFF, ALFRED EDWARD: Executive. b. Melbourne, Australia, Aug. 18, 1902. e. McDonald's Private Coll., Melbourne. Office boy Progressive Films, night asst. projectionist Moonee Ponds Theatre 6 mos., then in chg. of dispatch, adv. & accessory depts., booker & in chg. of shipping, repairing, adv. & accessory depts. Cooperative Films; joined Universal Mar., 1920 booker & suburban salesman 2 yrs., asst. mgr., then mgr. of Victoria & Tasmania; apptd. managing dir. of Japanese subsidiaries, 1935; Far Eastern supvr., 1938; also of Far and Middle East, 1940; to N.Y.C., 1942; apptd. foreign supvr. 1943; Universal Internatl Films, Inc., 1944; pres. same co., 1950; v.p. dir. world sales, Universal Pictures Co., since 1951. Named dir. Universal, May, 1952; exec. v.p., July, 1952; res. 1958; consultant motion pictures, TV.

DAHL, ARLENE: b. Aug. 11, 1928, Mpls., Minn., USA Actress-writer; Designer. e. Mpls. Bus. Coll.; Univ. of Minn., summers 1941–44; Mpls. Coll. of Music. m. (1) Fernando Lamas, 1954, 1 s, Lorenzo Lamas b. 1958, (2) Christian R. Holmes III, 1960, 1 d, Carole Christine b. 1961 (3) Rounseville W. Schaum, 1969, 1 s. Sonny b. 1970. Acting career begun at age 8, playing heroine of children's adventure serials on radio, Broadway stage debut in Mr. Strauss Goes to Boston, 1946; other Broadway starring roles include: Cyrano de Bergerac; Applause; other starring roles onstage in major US cities include: The King and I, One Touch of Venus, Pal Joey, Bell Book and Candle, The Camel Bell, Lilliom, Marriage Go Round, Blythe Spirit; 28 film appearances include: debut in My Wild Irish Rose (Warner Bros., (1947), Three Little Words, Desert Legion, Here Come the Girls, Sangaree, Woman's World, Journey to the Center of the Earth, Kisses for My President. Num. TV appearances include: Series of 65 films for ABC-TV—Arlene Dahl's Beauty Spot, 1965; Hostess, CBS Model of the Year Show, 1969, Arlene Dahl's Starscope, 1980. Appts: Internationally syndicated beauty columnist, Chgo. Tribune-N.Y. News Syndicate, 1951–71; Sleepwear Designer, A.N. Saab & Co., 1952–57; Nat. Beauty Advisor, Sears Roebuck & Co., 1970–75; v.p. Kenyon & Eckhart, pres., Women's World Div., Kenyon-Eckhart, 1967–72, Fashion Consultant, O.M.A. 1975–1978, Int'l. Director of S.M.E.I, 1973–76, Pres., Dahlia Parfums Inc., 1975, pres., Dahlia Prods., 1978–, Publs: Always Ask a Man, 1965 (6th ed.), Your Beautyscope (series of 12), 1969, Secrets of Hair Care, 1971, Your Beautyscope (series of 12) 1977–1978. Profl. Assns. include: Screen Actors Guild, Actors Equity, Am. Fedn. of TV & Radio Artists, International Platform, Inc., Acad. of Motion Picture Arts and Sciences. Honrs. include: 8 Motion Picture Laurel Awards, 1948–63; Hds. of Fame Award, 1971, Woman of Year, N.Y. Adv. Council, 1969.

DALES, L. JOHN: Executive. b. Santa Monica, Calif., Feb. 24, 1907; e. Stanford U., B.A., 1929; J.D., 1932. Practiced law 1932–37; v.p. Calif. Labor Federation, Nat'l exec. sec. Screen Actor's Guild, 1937–1972. Retired.

DALEY, ROBERT: Producer. Began career in TV; later joined Clint Eastwood's Maplasco Co.
PICTURES INCLUDE: Dirty Harry, Magnum Force (both exec. prod.), Thunderbolt and Lightfoot (prod.), The Enforcer (prod.), The Gauntlet (prod.), Every Which Way But Loose (prod.), Escape from Alcatrez (exec. prod.)., Any Which Way You Can (exec. prod.).

TV: The Untouchables, Ben Casey, The FBI, 12 O'Clock High, The Invaders, etc.

DALY, JOHN: Chm., Hemdale Group Ltd. b. London, England, 1937. After working in journalism joined Royal Navy. On leaving Service after three years, trained as underwriter with an Assurance Company. In 1966 became David Hemmings manager and in 1967 formed the Hemdale Company. Subsequently, in 1968, Hemdale obtained public status and produced features including The Passage, Sunburn, Cattle Annie and Little Britches, High Risk, Going Ape and Carbon Copy (exec. prod.).

DAMON, MARK: Executive. b. Chicago, April 22, 1933. e. University of California at Los Angeles, B.A. Literature, M.A. Business Administration. Actor: 1958 under contract to 20th Century Fox, 1960 winner Golden Globe Award—Newcomer of the Year; early career includes The Fall of The House of Usher, The Longest Day; 1961 moved to Italy, stayed 16 years appearing in leading roles in 50 films; 1973 co-producer of The Arena with Roger Corman; 1974 head of foreign department for PAC, a leading film distributor in Italy; 1976 returned to the U.S.A. as executive producer of The Choirboys and in charge of its foreign distribution; 1977 founder and pres. of Producers Sales Organization, international distribution organization.

DAMONE, VIC: Singer, actor. r.n. Vito Farinola. b. Brooklyn, N.Y., June 12. e. Lafayette H. Sch., B'klyn. Winner Arthur Godfrey talent show, 1945; then night clubs, radio, theatres, hotels. m.p. debut in Rich, Young and Pretty; U.S. Army, 1951–53.
PICTURES INCLUDE: The Strip, Athena, Deep in My Heart, Hit the Deck, Kismet, Hell to Eternity.
TV: Vic Damone Show, 1958. Lively Ones, 1962.

D'ANGELO, BEVERLY: Actress. b. Columbia, Ohio. Studied visual arts and was exchange student in Italy before working as cartoonist for Hanna-Barbera Studios in Hollywood. Toured Canada's coffeehouse circuit as singer and appeared with rock band called Elephant. Joined Charlotte Town Festival Company. Bdwy. debut in rock musical, Rockabye Hamlet. Film debut in The Sentinel.
PICTURES: Annie Hall, First Love, Every Which Way But Loose, Hair, Coal Miner's Daughter.

DANHEISER, MELVIN B.: Executive. Held positions at RKO Radio Pictures and National Telefilm Associates before joining United Artists in 1961 in intl. div.'s sls. dept. Since served in various capacities—asst. intl. sls. mgr. for Europe, Middle East, and English-speaking mkts. overseas. 1978 promoted to exec. asst. to foreign mgr. Appt. v.p. of UA in 1979; 1981, named exec. asst. to Norbert T. Auerbach, pres. & chief operating officer for UA.

DANIEL, SEAN: Executive. b. 1952. e. California Inst. of Arts film school. Was journalist for Village Voice before starting m.p. career as documentary filmmaker and asst. dir. for New World Pictures. In 1976 joined Universal Pictures as prod. exec.; 1979, named v.p.

DANIELEWSKI, TAD: Director-Writer. b. Poland. Studied Royal Academy of Dramatic Art, London; Ohio University; State Univ. of Iowa. At Johns Hopkins Univ. won national award for research in prod. and dir. methods for TV. Produced and directed a series of dramatic shows on WAAM-TV in cooperation with NBC-TV, 1953–54.
PICTURES INCLUDE: Imperial Woman (co-writer), No Exit (dir.), The Guide (writer-dir.), Spain (writer-dir.), Copernicus (writer-dir. of English version).
TELEVISION: Omnibus, Wide Wide World, Eddie Fisher Show, Matinee Theatre, Robert Montgomery Presents, etc.
STAGE: Artistic director New York Repertory Theatre; directed Man with a Load of Mischief (London), A Desert Incident (Bdwy.), Brouhaha (off-Bdwy.), etc.

DANIELS, HAROLD: Director, producer, writer. b. Buffalo, N.Y. e. Carnegie Tech Drama Dept. B.A., U. of Pittsburgh, PHG.
STAGE: Director in Pittsburgh for Prof. Stage Guild Co., N.Y., Rhode Island and Boston Repertoire. Directed over 50 plays.
PICTURES INCLUDE: Joined MGM in 1940, directed shorts and won award from M.P. Council; joined David Selznick as director 1943–45; produced, directed and wrote Prince of Peace, won spec. award for dir., directed Woman from Tangier, Sword of Venus, Port Sinister, Roadblock, Daughter of the West Classics, Terror in the Haunted House, Date With Death, My World Dies Screaming, Bayou, Poor White Trash, Ten Girls Ago; directed, Night of the Beast, House of Black Death, Annabelle Lee, 1968–69, Moonfire, 1969–70. Pigmy, 1971.
TV: directed over 200 half-hour and hour films including My Hero, Readers Digest, Fury, Colt 45, Jilley Queen, Jim Backus Theatre, G.E. Theatre, etc. Wrote many original screenplays for both films and TV. The Phantom, On Guard, Death Valley Days, Hannibal Cobb.

DANIELS, WILLIAM: Actor. b. Brooklyn. e. Northwestern University. Stage debut in Life with Father. Brought to national

attention by role in A Thousand Clowns in original Bdwy. play and film version.
PICTURES: Marlowe, The Parallax View, Two for the Road, Black Sunday, Oh God, Sunburn, The Blue Lagoon.
TELEVISION: The Adams Chronicle, A Case of Rape, Blind Ambition, The Nancy Walker Show, Captain Nice.
STAGE: On a Clear Day You Can See Forever, 1776, Dear Me, the Sky Is Falling, A Little Night Music, etc.

DANIELSON, DALE H.: Exhibitor, Operator, Dream, Sky-Vu Drive-In theatres, Russell, Kan.; past pres., Kansas-Missouri Theatre Assn.

DANISCHEWSKY, J.: Producer-Director. b. London, England, 1940. Chelsea Art School, 1957. Ent. m.p. ind. 1959 as asst. dir. 1967; Prod. dir. Avalanche, 1968. Prod., Run Wild, Run Free.

DANNER, BLYTHE: Actress. b. Philadelphia. e. Bard College. m. writer-producer Bruce Paltrow. Appeared in repertory cos. in U.S. before Lincoln Center (N.Y.) productions of Cyrano de Bergerac, Summertree, and The Miser (Theatre World Award for last).
PICTURES INCLUDE: 1776, To Kill a Clown, Lovin' Molly, Hearts of the West, Futureworld, The Ace.
TV: Dr. Cook's Garden, To Confuse the Angel, George M, To Be Young, Gifted and Black, The Scarecrow, Adam's Rib (series), F. Scott Fitzgerald and The Last of the Belles, Eccentricities of a Nightingale.

DANSON, HAROLD L.: Executive. b. New York, N.Y., Nov. 15, 1905. e. Brooklyn Polytechnic Institute, 1926. Feature ed., Brooklyn Eagle, 1927; press rep., Shubert Theatrical Co., asst. city ed., Newark Star-Eagle, 1928; dir. of adv. pub., RCA Photophone, 1929–30; asst. nat'l adv. mgr., RKO, 1930–32; exploit. mgr., studio adv. dir., asst. nat'l adv. dir., head of feature prod., Paramount, 1932–44; account exec., 20th Century-Fox, 1944–46; nat. adv. dir., Eagle Lion, 1946–49; v.p., gen. sales mgr., Adler Communications Labs., 1951–54; dir. of adv., pub., TV National Screen Service Corp., 1955; acct. exec. ZIV TV Programs, 1956; Nat'l Telefilm Assoc. program sales, 1959; nat'l sales mgr., syndication Independent Television Corp., 1961–68; consultant 1969.

DANTINE, HELMUT: Actor, Director, Executive b. Vienna. e. Europe; UCLA, Calif. Member: Pasadena Community Players, then on screen in International Squadron, 1941. V.p. Joseph M. Schenck Ent. 1959; pres., Hand Enterprises, Inc., 1963; pres., N.M. Schenck Enterprises, Inc., 1970.
PICTURES INCLUDE: Mrs. Miniver, Casablanca, Edge of Darkness, Northern Pursuit, Mission to Moscow, Passage to Marseille, Hotel Berlin, Escape in the Desert, Shadow of a Woman, Whispering City, Guerilla Girl, Call Me Madam, Alexander the Great, War and Peace, The Story of Mankind, Hell on Devil's Island, Fraulein, Tempest, Operation Crossbow, Dir. Thundering Jets; 1974: Bring Me the Head of Alfredo Garcia (exec. prod., actor); 1975; The Wilby Conspiracy (exec. prod., actor); 1975: The Killer Elite (exec. prod., actor); Tarzan (exec. prod.).

DANTON, RAY: Actor. b. New York, N.Y., Sept. 19, 1931. e. Horace Mann School, Carnegie Tech. m. Julie Adams. Radio actor on many programs; summer stock; London prod. of Mr. Roberts; U.S. Army, 1951–53; then TV actor numerous programs. Became dir. in 1976 with Psychic Killer (also co-s.p.).
PICTURES INCLUDE: Chief Crazy Horse, The Looters, The Spoilers, I'll Cry Tomorrow, Outside the Law, The Night Runner, Onionhead, Too Much Too Soon, Ice Palace, Legs Diamond, Tarawa Beachhead, Majority of One, The George Raft Story, Fever In The Blood, Portrait of a Mobster, The Chapman Report, The Longest Day, Sandokan, FBI Code 98, New York Calling Superdrago.

D'ANTONI, PHILIP: Producer-Director. b. NYC, Feb. 19, 1929. e. Fordham Univ. Has degree in business admn. Joined CBS in mailroom, advanced into prod., sales development, prog. analysis, mkt. rsrch. Became indep. radio-TV repr. in 1954 for two years; then joined Mutual Broadcasting as sales manager; later, exec. v.p. Resigned in 1962 to form own prod. co. Made theatrical film debut with Bullitt as producer; directing debut with The Seven Ups. Heads Phil D'Antoni Prods.
PICTURES INCLUDE: Producer: Bullitt, The French Connection. Prod.-Dir.: The Seven Ups.
TELEVISION: Elizabeth Taylor in London, Sophia Loren in Rome, Melina Mercouri in Greece, Jack Jones Special, This Proud Land, and two movies: Mr. Inside/Mr. Outside, The Connection.

DANZ, FREDERIC A.: Executive. b. Seattle, Wash., Feb. 28, 1918. Is president of Sterling Recreation Organization Co., Seattle; member, Foundation of M.P. Pioneers; v.p., Variety Club Intl.

DANZA, TONY: Actor. b. Brooklyn, NY, Apr. 21. e. Univ. of Dubuque. Professional boxer before tested for role in TV pilot (Fast Lane Blues) which he won. Back to New York

and fighting until called to coast to appear as Tony Banta in Taxi series.
PICTURES: Hollywood Knights.

DARBY, KIM: Actress. r.n. Derby Zerby. b. July 8, 1948, Hollywood, Calif. e. Swanson's Ranch School, Van Nuys High School. Studied at the Desilu Workshop in Hollywood. Professional debut on the Mr. Novak TV series.
TV: Eleventh Hour, Gunsmoke, Flesh and Blood (special).
PICTURES INCLUDE: Bus Riley's Back in Town, True Grit, Generation, Norwood, The Strawberry Statement, The Grissom Gang, The One and Only

DARK, JOHN: Producer. Films include, as associate: Light Up the Sky, Lost Innocence, The 7th Dawn, Casino Royale. Production exec., Paramount Pictures, exec. producer: Half a Sixpence, There's a Girl in My Soup. Produced: Wind of Change, Bachelor of Arts, Land That Time Forgot, At the Earth's Core, People That Time Forgot, Warlords of Atlantis, Arabian Adventure.

DARLEY, DICK: Director, Producer network TV series and specials. Over 180 TV film shows; over 1,370 TV live/tape shows. Numerous pilots and commercials. Credits in U.S.A. and 27 foreign countries include drama, musical-variety, comedy, sports and documentary.

DARNBOROUGH, ANTONY: Producer, director. b. London, Eng., ent. m.p. ind. 1944.
PICTURES INCLUDE: Seventh Veil, Years Between, Daybreak, Girl in a Million, Upturned Glass, When the Bough Breaks, Dear Murderer, The Calendar, My Brother's Keeper, The Girl in the Painting, Helter Skelter, Once Upon a Dream, Traveller's Joy, Boys in Brown, The Astonished Heart, So Long at the Fair, Quartet, Trio, Highly Dangerous, Encore, The Net (Project M. 7), Personal Affair, To Paris With Love, Baby and the Battleship.
TV: Also made many TV and documentary films for own co. and in assoc. with NSS.

DARREN, JAMES: Actor. b. Philadelphia, Pa., June 8, 1936. Studied with Stella Adler group. Hollywood debut: Rumble on the Docks.
PICTURES INCLUDE: The Brothers Rico, Guns of Navarone, Gidget Goes Hawaiian, The Lively Set, 633 Squadron, Venus in Furs.

DARRIEUX, DANIELLE: Actress. b. Bordeaux, France, May 1, 1917. e. Lycee LaTour; Conservatoire de Musique.
PICTURES INCLUDE: La Crise Est Finis, Mayerling, Club des Femmes, Abus de Confiance, Counsel for Romance, Mademoiselle Ma Mere, Katia, Orders from Tokyo, Oh Amelia, Rage of Paris, Rich Young and Pretty, 5 Fingers, La Ronde, Le Plaisir, Earrings of Madame De, Alexander the Great, Adorable Creatures, A Friend of the Family, Loss of Innocence.
THEATRE: Coco.

DARTIGUE, JOHN: Executive. b. Port-au-Prince, Haiti, Sept. 12, 1940. e. Brandeis Univ. (B.A.), 1961), Columbia Univ. (M.A., 1965). United Artists: named director of worldwide pub. in 1975; appointed executive assistant to the senior vice president for advertising and publicity in 1977; named v.p. adv.-pub., 1978. Joined Warner Bros. in 1978 as project executive. Named sr. exec. asst. to the exec. v.p. of worldwide adv./pub., Jan., 1980; v.p. & exec. asst., July 1980.

DARTNALL, GARY: Exec. b. Whitchurch, Eng., May 9, 1937. e. Kings Coll., Taunton. Overseas Div., Associated British Pathe; Eur. rep., 1958–60; Middle & Far East rep., Lion International Films; Amer. rep., 1962; pres., Lion International Inc., 1963; Amer. rep., Alliance International Films Distributors, Ltd., and London Independent Producers, Ltd.; pres., Alliance International Films Corp. & Dartnall Films Ltd., 1966; managing dir., Overseas Division, Walter Reade Organization, 1969. pres., EMI Film Distributors, Inc., 1971; vice chairman, EMI Television Programs, Inc., 1976; pres., EMI Videograms, Inc., 1979; pres., VHD Programs, Inc. & VHD Disc Mfg. Co., 1980.

DA SILVA, HOWARD: Actor. b. Cleveland, Ohio, May 4, 1909; e. Carnegie Inst. Tech. With Civic Repertory Theatre, Theatre Union, Group Theatre & Mercury Theatre.
PLAYS: Master Builder, Alice in Wonderland, Three Sisters, Alison's House, Liliom, Doll's House, Sailors of Cattaro, Waiting for Lefty, Golden Boy, Cradle Will Rock, Abe Lincoln in Illinois, Oklahoma, 1776; m. p. debut in "I'm Still Alive," 1940.
PICTURES INCLUDE: Abe Lincoln in Illinois, Sea Wolf, Nine Lives Are Not Enough, Big Shot, Omaha Trail, Tonight We Raid Calais, Lost Weekend, Duffy's Tavern, Unconquered, Blaze of Noon, They Live By Night. Tripoli, Underworld Story, Three Husbands, Wyoming Mail, Fourteen Hours, M. David and Lisa, 1776, The Great Gatsby.
BROADWAY STAGE: 1776.

DASILVA, RAUL: Creative consultant, writer, director, producer, b. New York City. June 12, 1933. e. Adelphi U., B.A. 1958, elected to Academy of Distinction Adelphi Alumni Assoc. 1978. Specializes in script evaluation, rework of script, art and graphic look. Exp. Corporate AV dir., exec. prod. adv.

agencies; indep. writer, producer, dir., univ. lecturer (business aspects of film prod. writing).

PUBLICATIONS: The World of Animation (Eastman Kodak Co. Rochester, 1979); The Business of Filmmaking (Eastman Kodak Co., Rochester, 1978); SOUND; Magnetic recording for Motion Pictures (Eastman Kodak Co., Rochester, 1977); Wrote articles for American Cinematographer, Filmmakers Monthly, Today's Film Maker Millimeter. ProFilm; Filmmaker's Monthly.

PICTURES: Fear No Evil (creative consultant)

TV: Nat Hurst, M.D.; The Strangest Voyage (dir., prod)

AWARDS: Numerous national & international for films, 6 in 1975–76 for The Strangest Voyage, (Coleridge and his masterpiece). The Ancient Mariner with Sir Michael Redgrave.

DA SILVA, RAY: Director and designer of animated films, animator, illustrator, character designer. b. New York City, July 13, 1934. e. School of Visual Arts, NYC, also instructor there. Specializes in animation direction, character design. Numerous national and international TV spots for the advertising industry.

PICTURES: Raggedy Ann & Andy; Heavy Metal.

TELEVISION: The Strangest Voyage, Noah's Animals, The Little Brown Burro, Ichabod Crane.

DASSIN, JULES: Director. b. Middletown, Conn. Actor on dramatic stage several years; radio writer. Joined MGM, 1940, as dir. short subjects; later dir. features.

PICTURES INCLUDE: Canterville Ghost, Brute Force, Naked City, Thieves' Highway, Night and the City, Rififi, He Who Must Die, Never On Sunday, Phaedra, 10:30 p.m. Summer, Promise At Dawn, Uptight, A Dream of Passion.

PLAYS: Ilya, Darling, 1967.

DAUPHIN, CLAUDE: Actor. b. Corbeil, France, Aug. 19. e. Lycee de Grand, Paris. In French & Allied armies, 1940–45; org. French stock co.; screen debut in Deported; B'way stage debut in Happy Time.

PICTURES INCLUDE: Casque D'or, April in Paris, L'enentaile (Naughty Martine), Little Boy Lost, Phantom of the Rue Morgue, Le Plaisir, Innocents in Paris, Two for the Road, Hard Contract, Madwoman of Chaillot, Rosebud, Madame Rosa.

DAVEE, LAWRENCE W.: Engineer. b. Foxcroft, Me., March 28, 1900; e. U. Me., B.S. (elec. eng.). Research eng. Bell Telephone Lab.; Fox Case Corp.; studio mgr. Fox Hearst Corp.; Bronx Studio. Elec. Research Prods., Inc.; Century Projector Corp., N.Y.; engineer & sales mgr.; pres. 1959. Member: 25–30 Club (Honorary). Lifemember, N.Y. State Projectionists.

DAVENPORT, NIGEL: Actor. b. Cambridge, England, May 23, 1928. e. Trinity Coll., Oxford. Began acting after stint in British military at 18 years. First 10 years of professional career in theatre. Majority of screen work in British films in 1950s and 60s.

PICTURES INCLUDE: Peeping Tom, A High Wind in Jamaica, A Man for All Seasons, Royal Hunt of the Sun, No Blade of Grass, Villain, Mary, Queen of Scots, Island of Dr. Moreau, Zulu Dawn, Nighthawks.

DAVID, SAUL: Producer. b. Springfield, Mass., June 27, 1921. e. Classical High School, Springfield, Mass., Rhode Island School of Design. Started in radio, newspaper work and as editorial director for Bantam Books. Worked for Columbia Pictures, 1960–62; Warner Bros., 1962–63; 20th Century-Fox, 1963–67, and Universal, 1968–69; Executive story editor at MGM, 1972.

PICTURES INCLUDE: Produced Von Ryan's Express, Our Man Flint, Fantastic Voyage, In Like Flint, Skullduggery, Logan's Run.

DAVIDSON, JOHN: Actor-Singer. b. Pittsburgh, Penna., Dec. 13, 1941. e. Denison Univ. In numerous school stage prods. before coming to N.Y. where won co-star role with Bert Lahr in Bdwy. show, Foxy. Signed as regular on The Entertainers with Carol Burnett.

PICTURES INCLUDE: The Happiest Millionaire, The Concorde—Airport '79.

TELEVISION: The Fantasticks, USA, The FBI, The Interns, Owen Marshall, Kraft Summer Music Hall (own variety series), The Tonight Show, The Girl with Something Extra, The John Davidson Talk Show (1980).

DAVIDSON, MARTIN: Director. Acted in and directed off-Bdwy. plays, wrote material for Sid Caesar, worked as agent with N.Y. offices of Int'l. Famous Artists.

PICTURES: The Lords of Flatbush, Almost Summer, Hero at Large.

DAVIES, JACK: Screen writer. b. London 1913. Ent. m.p. ind. 1932 as screen writer with B.I.P. Collab. number of films. Also coll. on Convict 99 before joining Daily Sketch as film critic 1938. Served with R.A.F. 1940–5. Became columnist Daily Graphic and film critic Sunday Graphic 1948. Wrote orig. story and s.p. Trouble in the Air, Helter-Skelter.

PICTURES INCLUDE: Dance Band, Heart's Desire, Radio Parade, One in a Million, Mimi, The Tenth Man. Laughter

in Paradise, Top Secret, Curtain Up, Happy Ever After, Doctor at Sea, An Alligator Named Daisy, High Flight, Up in the World, True as a Turtle, The Square Peg, Don't Panic Chaps, Follow a Star, It Started in Naples, The Bulldog Breed, Very Important Person, Crooks Anonymous, On The Beat, The Fast Lady, A Stitch In Time, Father Came Too, Those Magnificent Men In Their Flying Machines, The Early Bird, Doctor in Clover, Gambit, Doctor in Trouble, Monte Carlo or Bust, Paper Tiger, Le Hold-Up, ffolkes.

DAVIES, JOHN W. (O.B.E.): Executive. b. London, Eng., 1908. Originally shipbroker; entered m.p. ind., 1931; man. dir., Davies Cinemas, Ltd. and British Cinematograph Theatres, Ltd.; R.A.F. 1939–45, awarded U.S. Legion of Merit; chmn. London & Home Counties Branch, C.E.A. 1948; apptd. mem., Cinematograph Films Council, Dept. of Trade, 1951–76; v.p. C.E.A., 1952; pres. 1953; dir., FIDO, 1962.

DAVIES, PAUL: Executive. b. Toronto, Canada, M.A. Columbia Univ. Service with RCAF. Prod. Your Man Everywhere, many documentaries; Isle of Rainbow, Kansanshe, African Heritage, etc. Originator and pilot prod. Jazz in Europe, Man About the House. Manager of Malachite Films, NBC reporter and cameraman, bureau chief for Visnews, Israel 1980: Jerusalem Capital Studios.

DAVIES, WILLIAM C.: Director. b. Auburn, N.Y., June 17, 1932. e. Auburn Community Coll., School of Radio Technique. Radio & T.V. announcer & narrator, then cameraman & editor. Formed Virgo Productions, 1965.

PICTURES INCLUDE: Legend of Horror, Orgy of the Dead, The Seekers, Day the Adults Died, Pink Garter Gang, Night at the Feast, Laughter in Hell, The Crimson Cult, Submarine X-1.

DAVIS, ALFRED: Exhibitor. b. Brighton, England, Aug. 19, 1899. e. University College Sch., London. In Brit. Army 1914 before entering m.p. ind. as dir. & booking mgr. Davis Pavillion circuit; later same position GaumontBritish, New Era Pictures. Chr. London & Home Counties Branch, C.E.A., 1937, 1953, 1955. Dep. asst. dir., War Office Army Kinematograph, World War II; v.p. CEA; 1959–60; pres. CEA, 1960–61.

DAVIS, ARTHUR: Executive. b. New York, N.Y., Dec. 28, 1927. e. N.Y. Univ. Began as exhibitor in U.S.; founded Arthur Davis Organization in Tokyo, Japan, in 1963, representing European and American films for sales to Japanese TV and motion picture industry. 1979, released two documentaries, Brutes and Savages, The Art of Killing.

DAVIS, BETTE: Actress. b. Lowell, Mass., April 5, 1908; e. Cushing Academy; Mariarden School of Dancing; John Murray Anderson Dram. School. Stage debut in "Broadway" (Rochester, N.Y.); with Provincetown & Cape Players; on Broadway in: Broken Dishes, Solid South; m.p. debut in "Man Who played God" 1932; won Academy Award twice: best actress 1935, in Dangerous and 1938, in Jezebel; voted one of the 10 best Money-Making Stars in Motion Picture Herald-Fame Poll 1939; 40, 41, 44; founder & pres. Hollywood Canteen 1942; pres. AMPAS 1940. Received American Film Institute Life Achievement Award, 1977; 1979, Emmy for performance in Strangers.

PICTURES INCLUDE: Of Human Bondage, Fog Over Frisco, Sisters, Dark Victory, Juarez, Old Maid, Private Lives of Elizabeth and Essex, All This and Heaven Too, Letter, Now Voyager, Corn Is Green, Little Foxes, Deception, Winter Meeting, N.Y. stage, Night of the Iguana, Sandburg, June Bride, Beyond the Forest, All About Eve, Payment on Demand, Another Man's Poison, Phone Call From a Stranger, The Star, Virgin Queen, Catered Affair, Storm Center, John Paul Jones, The Scapegoat, A Pocketful of Miracles, What Ever Happened To Baby Jane, Dead Ringer, Empty Canvas, Where Love Has Gone, Hush . . . Hush Sweet Charlotte, The Nanny, The Anniversary, Connecting Rooms, Bunny O'Hare, Madame Sin (TV in U.S.), Scientific Card Game, Burnt Offerings, Return from Witch Mountain, Death on the Nile, Watcher in the Woods.

TV: The Disappearance of Aimee, Laugh-In, The Dark Secret of Harvest Home, Strangers, The Story of a Mother and Daughter, White Mama, Skyward, Family Reunion.

DAVIS, BRAD: Actor. b. Florida. Won music talent contest at 17; moved to Atlanta and acted in theatres before settling in New York, N.Y. stage debut in Crystal and Fox; did several off-Bdwy. plays. Appeared in TV soap opera, How to Survive a Marriage, for 10 months.

PICTURES: Midnight Express, A Small Circle of Friends.

TELEVISION: Walt Whitman, Sybil, Roots, A Rumor of War, The Greatest Man in the World.

DAVIS, FRANK I.: Executive. b. Poolesville, Md. Feb. 18, 1919. e. U. of Md., AB, 1941; Harvard Law School, LL.B., 1948; law firm, Donovan, Leisure, Newton, Lombard and Irvine, 1948–50; v.p., gen. counsel, Vanguard Films, 1951; v.p., gen. counsel, Selznick Releasing Org., 1951–53; pres., The Selznick Company, 1953–55; v.p., Famous Artists Corp., 1956–62; v.p. George Stevens Productions Inc., 1962–65; exec. prod., The Greatest Story Ever Told; v.p. in charge of m.p. affairs, Seven Arts, 1966; exec. in chg. talent and exec. asst. to v.p. in chg. prod., MGM, 1967; dir. m.p. business affairs, MGM, 1970; v.p., business affairs, MGM, 1972.

DAVIS, GEORGE W.: Art director, b. Kokomo, Ind., Apr. 17, 1914. e. U. Southern California.
PICTURES INCLUDE: The Robe, The Diary of Anne Frank, Love Is A Many Splendored Thing, All About Eve, David and Bathsheba, Americanization of Emily, Unsinkable Molly Brown, Funny Face, Cimarron, Period of Adjustment, Mutiny on the Bounty, Twilight of Honor, How The West Was Won, Patch of Blue, The Wonderful World of the Bros. Grimm, Mr. Buddwing, The Shoes of the Fisherman, etc. Including 200 feature films and 2000 TV segments.

DAVIS, JORDAN P.: Executive. b. N.Y., N.Y., October 29, 1933. e. Lehigh University, 1954; Columbia University Law School, 1958. Attorney for five years. Director of Business Affairs, ABC TV Network, 1963–67. NBC TV Network 1967–69. Director of Talent and Program Admin. v.p. Warner Bros. Television, 1969–1972. Executive, The Sy Fischer Company, 1972–1973. Executive in charge of production, Four D. Productions, Inc.; The Mimus Corp., The Triseme Corporation to present.

DAVIS, LUTHER. Writer, producer. b. N.Y., Aug. 29, 1921. e. Yale Univ., WWII major U.S. Air Corps.; B'way play 1945. Kiss Them for Me. Ent. m.p. 1946. Solo s.p., The Hucksters, B.F.'s Daughter, Black Hand, A Lion Is in the Streets, The Gift of Love, Holiday for Lovers, The Wonders of Aladdin; Across 110th St.; collab. book B'way musical Kismet, collab. s.p.; author, prod., Lady In A Cage; s.p. Across 110th St. Prod. and wrote book for Bdwy musical, Timbuktu!, 1978–79.
TV: Wrote, prod., Kraft Suspense Theatre and several pilots for series (Run for Your Life, The Silent Force, etc.). Wrote, prod. Arsenic and Old Lace (TV special). Wrote teleplays for MOW's Daughter of the Mind, The Old Man Who Cried Wolf, Colombo, etc.

DAVIS, MAC: Singer-Songwriter-Actor. b. Lubbock, TX, Jan. 21, 1942. e. Emory Univ., Ga. State Coll. Employed as ditch digger, service station attendant, laborer, probation officer and record company salesman before gaining fame as entertainer-singer in 1969. Recording artist and composer of many popular songs.
PICTURES: North Dallas Forty, Cheaper To Keep Her.

DAVIS, MARTIN S.: Executive. b. New York City. e. City Coll., N.Y.; New York Univ. U.S. Army, 1943–46; joined Saml. Goldwyn Prod., Inc., 1946; Allied Artists, 1955; Paramount Pictures, 1958. Dir. adv., pub. expl. 1960; vice-pres., 1963; exec. v.p., 1966; exec. comm. & bd. of dir. Member of Bd., Gulf & Western, 1967. Exec. v.p. Gulf and Western, member exec. comm.

DAVIS, SIR JOHN: Executive. b. London, Eng., 1906; e. City of London Sch.; fellow Inst. of Chartered Secretaries and Administrators. Secy. to various ind. gps.; entered m.p. ind. as acct.-secy. to Odeon Theatres, Ltd., 1938; joint man. dir., 1941; man. dir., 1948; deputy chmn. 1951–62; chmn. and chief exec. The Rank Organisation Ltd. 1962–74; chmn. 1974–77; pres. 1977– . Dir. of Eagle Star Insurance Co. Ltd., Jt.-Pres. Rank Xerox Ltd., Chairman, Children's Film Foundation, National Centre of Films for Children, Trustee, Westminster Abbey Trust and Chairman, fund raising committee, Westminster Abbey Appeal 1973. Knighted June, 1971; Hon. D. Tech. (Loughborough) 1975; Knight Commander of the Order of St. John. Commandeur de l'Ordre de la Couronne (Belgium) 1974.

DAVIS, OSSIE: Actor-Writer-Director. b. Cogdell, Ga., Dec. 18, 1917. e. Howard Univ., Washington, D.C. m. actress Ruby Dee. Studied acting in N.Y. with Rose McLendon Players, leading to Broadway debut in 1946 in Jeb. For 11 years thereafter was one of most well-known blacks on Broadway stage (Anna Lucasta, Jamaica, A Raisin in the Sun, etc.) Wrote and starred in Purlie Victorious, repeating role for film version.
PICTURES INCLUDE: Actor: The Joe Louis Story, Fourteen Hours, Shock Treatment, No Way Out, The Cardinal, The Hill, Man Called Adam, The Scalphunters, Sam Whiskey, Let's Do It Again. Director: Cotton Comes to Harlem, Black Girl, Gordon's War, Countdown at Kusini (also star).
TELEVISION: Author: East Side/West Side, The Eleventh Hour. Acted in many top dramatic series.

DAVIS, ROGER H.: Attorney. b. June 19, 1923, Chicago. e. U. Calif.-Berkeley, 1951, A.B., LL.B. Private law practice, partner, Loeb and Loeb, Los Angeles, 1951–1961; atty., William Morris Agency, head of west coast legal, literary and M.P. depts., exec./admin., asst. sec. WMA, Inc., 1969–present, made v.p., 1974. exec. v.p. & bd. member, 1980.

DAVIS, SAMMY, JR.: Entertainer. b. New York City, Dec. 8, 1925. Father: Sammy Davis, Sr., entertainer. Professional debut at age 2, Gibson Theatre, in act with father and uncle, Will Mastin; singer, dancer, comedian, vocal and acting impressions; song writer; recording artist; starred

in Mr. Wonderful, & Golden Boy on B'way; in many major TV shows.
PICTURES INCLUDE: Anna Lucasta, Porgy & Bess, Ocean's 11, Robin and the Seven Hoods, Salt and Pepper, A Man Called Adam, Sweet Charity, One More Time, The Cannonball Run.

DAVIDSON, BRUCE: Actor. b. Philadelphia. e. Penn State, New York University. debut, Lincoln Center Repertory.
PICTURES INCLUDE: Last Summer, The Strawberry Statement, Willard, Been Down So Long It Looks Like Up To Me, The Jerusalem File, Ulzana's Raid, Mame, Mother, Jugs, and Speed, Short Eyes, Brass Target.

DAWBER, PAM: Actress-Singer. b. Detroit, Mich. e. Farmington High School, Oakland Community College. Travelled nationally to trade shows to introduce new auto model; also began working in commercials. In 1971 came to N.Y.C.; hired as model, also doing commercials. First professional performance as singer in Sweet Adeleine at Goodspeed Opera House, East Haddam, Conn. Signed by Robert Altman to appear in theatrical film, A Wedding. On TV in comedy special, Sister Terri. Plays Mindy in Mork and Mindy.

DAWSON, ANTHONY: Actor-producer. b. Edinburgh, Scot., Oct. 18, 1916. e. Bryanstone School, Dorset, Eng., Royal Academy of Dramatic Art. Jockey, trainer, 1939–43; British Army.
PICTURES INCLUDE: Queen of Spades, Way to Stars, Beware of Pity, School for Secrets, Long Dark Hall, Valley of the Eagles, Haunted Strangler, Curse of the Werewolf, That Lady, Action of the Tiger, Tiger Bay, Dial M for Murder, Death Rides a Horse, Dr. No, Midnight Lace, Red Sun, Battle of Neretva.
TV: USA. '51–'62. US Steel Hour, Hitchcock Presents, Philco TV Playhouse, Lux, Montgomery Presents, Studio One, Hallmark.
WRITER: The Deserter, The Snorkel, The Papoose Sitter, Oil, Break Point, 1976. Formed Arengo Prod. (Italy).

DAY, DORIS: Singer, actress. r. n. Doris Kappelhoff. b. Cincinnati, Ohio, Apr. 3, 1924. e. dancing, singing. Toured as dancer; radio and band singer; screen debut in Romance on the High Seas, 1948. Voted one of Top Ten Money-Making Stars in Motion Picture Herald-Fame poll, 1951–52. Best female vocalist. M. P. Daily radio poll, 1952.
PICTURES INCLUDE: Young Man With a Horn, Tea for Two, Storm Warning, West Point Story, Lullaby of Broadway, On Moonlight Bay, I'll See You in My Dreams, Starlift, Winning Team, April in Paris, By The Light of the Silvery Moon, Calamity Jane, Lucky Me, Young at Heart, Love Me or Leave Me, Man Who Knew Too Much, Julie, Pajama Game, Teacher's Pet, Pillow Talk, Please Don't Eat the Daisies, Midnight Lace, Lover, Come Back, That Touch of Mink, Jumbo, Thrill of It All, Move Over, Darling, Do Not Disturb, Send Me No Flowers, Glass Bottom Boat, Caprice, The Ballad of Josie, Where Were You When the Lights Went Out, With Six You Get Eggrolls.
TV: The Doris Day Show 1968–73.

DAY, LARAINE: Actress. r.n. Laraine Johnson. b. Roosevelt, Utah, Oct. 13, 1920. In school dramatics; with Players Guild, Long Beach, Calif.; toured in church prod. Conflict; Professionally on stage in Lost Horizon, The Women, Time of the Cukoo, Angel Street; m.p. debut in Border G-Men 1938.
PICTURES INCLUDE: Story of Dr. Wassell, Those Endearing Young Charms, Locket, Tycoon, My Son, My Son, Foreign Correspondent, Woman on Pier 13, Without Honor, High and the Mighty, Mr. Lucky, Toy Tiger, Three for Jamie Dawn, The Third Voice, Yank on The Burma Road, The Bad Man, Fingers at The Window, Bride By Mistake, My Dear Secretary.
RECENT ACTIVITIES: mem bd., Te Arohanui Maori Co., New Zealand, Share, Inc.
TV: Climax, Playhouse 90, Alfred Hitchcock, Wagon Train, Let Freedom Ring, Name of the Game, FBI, Sixth Sense, Medical Center, Murder on Flight #504 (ABC Movie), Fantasy Island, Love Boat, Lou Grant.

DAY, ROBERT: Director. b. London, England, September 11, 1922. Ent. m.p. ind. 1938 in camera dept. Warners' Teddington Studios.
PICTURES INCLUDE: The Green Man, Grip of the Strangler, First Man into Space, Life in Emergency War 10, Bobbikins, Two-Way Stretch, Tarzan The Magnificent, The Rebel, Operation Snatch, Tarzan's Three Challenges, She, Tarzan, 1966, Tarzan and the Great River.
TV: Robin Hood, O.S.S., Rendezvous, Danger Man, The Avengers.

DAYTON, LYMAN D.: Producer. b. Salt Lake City, Aug. 17, 1941. m. Elizabeth Doty Dayton. e. Brigham Young Univ. After college worked in film lab at MGM, 1967–68; joined Screen Gems and General DeLuxe, 1968–69; became indep. prod. 1969. Heads Doty-Dayton Productions.
PICTURES INCLUDE: Where the Red Fern Grows, Seven Alone, Against A Crooked Sky, Pony Express Rider, Baker's Hawk, Young Rivals, Powder Keg.

DEAN, EDDIE: Actor. r.n. Edgar D. Glosup. b. Posey, Texas; married. From 1930–33 in radio throughout middle west; 1934 National Barn Dance, Station WLS; 1935 on CBS & NBC with same program. Featured male singer on TV KTLA Western Varieties 1944–55. Came to Hollywood in 1936; since then has starred in many westerns. Featured performer in western series for PRC in 1945. Voted one of the ten best money making Western Stars in Motion Picture Herald-Fame Poll 1936–47; recording artists, personal appearances, rodeos, fairs, etc.; 1966 V.P. Academy of Country & Western Music; 1967–68 on Bd. of Dir. of Academy of Western Music, Calif. Winner, Pioneer Award of Academy of Country Music, 1978.

DEAN, JIMMY: Performer. b. Plainview, Tex., Aug. 10, 1928. Joined armed forces, 1946–49; first appeared in various clubs in Wash., 1949; then app. on Town and Country Jamboree; toured Caribbean and Europe with his troupe.
SONGS: Comp. of following songs: Bummin' Around, Freight Train Blues, Glad Rags, Little, Mr. Blues, I Found Out, Big Bad John, PT-109, Little Black Book, This Ole House.
TV: Sunday Night at the Palladium (London), The Jimmy Dean Show.

DEAN, MERRILL C.: Executive. b. May 24, 1941. e. UCLA (bus. admin.). 1967–68, involved with Walt Disney Productions, starting in m.p. distribution internationally with Buena Vista Intl., concentrating on Latin America. Later involved with world-wide publications and gen. mgr. of direct mktg. Was v.p., Walt Disney Records Music Division, four years. 1978–present, pres. of Televisa Intl. Marketing Group, Inc., and pres. of Televicine Intl. Distribution Corp., whose activities are principally involved with dist. of films to the Hispanic mkt. in U.S. & Puerto Rico.

DE BROCA, PHILIPPE: Director. b. 1933. French director.
PICTURES INCLUDE: Les Jeux de l'Amour, L'Amant, de Cinq Jours, Cartouche, That Man from Rio, Un Monsieur de Compagnie, Tribulations, Chinoise en Chine, King of Hearts, Devil By the Tail, Give Her the Moon, Louise.

DECAE, HENRI: Cinematographer b. France, 1915. Career spans 30 years and 60 films.
PICTURES INCLUDE: Le Silence de la Mer, Les Enfants Terribles, Creve-Coeur, Bob le Flambeur, Lift to the Scaffold, Le Beau Serge, A Double Tour, Les Quatre Cents Coup, Les Cousins, Plein Soleil, Les Bonnes Femmes, Leon Morin, Priest, Sundays and Cybele, Dragees au Poivre, Viva Maria, Weekend at Dunkirk, Night of the Generals, La Voleur, The Comedians, Castle Keep, The Sicilian Clan, The Light at the Edge of the World, Bobby Deerfield, The Island.

De CAESAR, GABRIEL: Producer. b. New York, Nov. 15, 1928. e. L.A. City College, 1952. Dir.-mgr. Little Theatre, L.A. Group, 3 yrs.; actor, 6 years; acting member Catholic Coll. Thea., Santa Monica Thea. Group, Pilgrimage Play Thea. Group, 3 yrs., producer: Three Wishes for Jamie, Bullfight; assoc. prod., asst. prod., Viscount Films, Inc. 1957–59; dir., N.A.B.E.T.; acted: Unexpected, TV series; ABC-TV series; producer, TV pilots, 1958; asst. prod., pictures: Tank Battalian, Speed Crazy, 1959; assoc. prod., Why Must I Die?

DE CAMP ROSEMARY: Actress. b. Prescott Ariz., 1913.
TV: Robert Cummings Show, That Girl, Life of Riley (with Jackie Gleason); Death Valley Days; Partridge Family; Love American Style, Police Story, Rockford Files, Days of Our Lives, Misadventures of Sheriff Lobo, Love Boat, Blind Ambition, B.J. & the Bear.
PICTURES INCLUDE: Cheers for Miss Bishop, Hold Back the Dawn, Jungle Book, Yankee Doodle Dandy, Eyes in the Night, Pride of the Marines, Look for the Silver Lining, Story of Seabiscuit, Big Hangover, Scandal Sheet, On Moonlight Bay, Treasure of Los Canyon, By the Light of the Silvery Moon, Main Street to Broadway, So This Is Love, Many Rivers to Cross, Strategic Air Command, Saturday the 14th.

DE CAPRIO, AL: Producer-director. e. Brooklyn Tech., NYU. Started as radio engineer, cameraman, tech. dir., prod. & dir. CBS; dir. Sgt. Bilko, Car 54 Where Are You?, Musical specials for ABC, CBS, NBC; v.p. exec. prod. dir., MPO Videotronics, Pres. World Wide Videotape.

DE CARLO, YVONNE: Actress. b. Vancouver, B.C., Sept. 1, 1924; e. Vancouver School of Drama, Fauchon & Marco, Hollywood; specialty dancing at Florentine Gardens, Earl Carroll's; m.p. debut in This Gun for Hire 1942.
PICTURES INCLUDE: Harvard Here I Come, Youth on Parade, Road to Morocco, Story of Dr. Wassell, Salome, Where She Danced; Frontier Gal, Brute Force, Song of Scheherazade, Black Bart, Casbah, River Lady, Criss Cross, Gal Who Took the West, Calamity Jane and Sam Bass, Buccaneer's Girl, Tomahawk, Hotel Sahara, Silver City, Scarlet Angel, San Francisco Story. Hurricane Smith, Sombrero, Sea Devils, Fort Algiers, Border River, Captain's Paradise, Passion, Tonight's the Night, Shotgun, Magic Fire, Flame of the Islands, Ten Commandments, Raw Edge,

Death of a Scoundrel, Band of Angels, Timbuktu, Law of the Lawless, Hostile Guns, The Power, McClintock.
BROADWAY STAGE: Follies.

DE CORDOVA, FREDERICK: Director. b. New York City, Oct. 27, 1910; e. Northwestern U., B.S. '31. Gen. stage dir. Shubert enterprises, N.Y., 1938–41; same for Alfred Bloomingdale Prods., N.Y., and prod. Louisville (Ky.) Amphitheatre 1942–43; m.p. dir.
PICTURES INCLUDE: (dial. dir.) San Antonio, Janie, Between Two Worlds; (dir.) Too Young to Know, Her Kind of Man, That Way with Women, Always Together, Wallflower, For the Love of Mary, Countess of Monte Cristo, Illegal Entry, Girl Who Took the West, Buccaneer's Girl, Peggy, Desert Hawk, Bedtime for Bonzo, Katie Did It, Little Egypt, Finders Keepers, Here Come the Nelsons, Yankee Buccaneer, Bonzo Goes to College, Column South.
Under contract CBS-TV, prod., dir. Burns and Allen, 1955–56; prod., December Bride, 1954–55; prod. and dir., Mr. Adams and Eve, prod. dir. December Bride; prod. dir. George Gobel Show; prod. dir., Jack Benny Program, 1960–63; dir., program planning, Screen Gems, 1964; prod. dir., Smothers Bros. Show, 1965–66; 1965 dir. I'll Take Sweden and Frankie & Johnny; 1966–70 dir. My Three Sons; 1971–1981, prod., Tonight Show.

DECUIR, JOHN: Art Dir. Prod. Des. b. San Francisco Universal 1938–49; Mark Hellinger Prods., 1946. 20th Fox 1949. Nominated for Acad. Award 11 times.
PICTURES INCLUDE: The Naked City, Snows of Kilimanjaro, My Cousin Rachel, Call Me Madam, Three Coins in the Fountain, There's No Business Like Show Business, Daddy Long Legs, The King and I (A.A., Art Dir.), Island in the Sun, South Pacific, The Big Fisherman, A Certain Smile, Cleopatra (A.A.: Prod. Des.), The Agony and the Ecstasy, The Honey Pot, Zefferelli's Taming of The Shrew, Dr. Faustus, Hello, Dolly! (A.A.: Prod. Des.), On A Clear Day You Can See Forever, The Great White Hope, Once Is Not Enough, That's Entertainment, Too!, The Other Side of Midnight, Ziegfeld: The Man and his Women, Love and Bullets, Charlie.

DEE, RUBY: Actress. b. Cleveland, Oct. 27, 1924. m., Ossie Davis. e. Hunter Coll. Stage appearances include Jeb, Raisin in the Sun, Purlie Victorious, Wedding Band, etc.
PICTURES INCLUDE: Jackie Robinson Story, Take a Giant Step, St. Louis Blues, Raisin in the Sun, Purlie Victorious, Buck and the Preacher.

DEE, SANDRA: Actress. b. Bayonne, N.J., April 23, 1942. Modeled, Harry Conover and Huntington Hartford Agencies, N.Y., 1954–56; signed long term exclusive contract, U-I, 1957.
PICTURES INCLUDE: Until They Sail, The Restless Years, Stranger in My Arms, The Reluctant Debutante, Gidget, The Wild and the Innocent, Imitation of Life, Summer Place, Portrait in Black, Romanoff and Juliet, Come September, Tammy Tell Me True, If a Man Answers, Tammy and the Doctor, Take Her, She Is Mine, I'd Rather Be Rich, That Funny Feeling, Doctor You've Got to Be Kidding!, Rosie, The Dunwich Horror.

DEELEY, MICHAEL: Chief Exec. EMI Film Inc. and Int. Head of Worldwide EMI Film Prod. and Dist. 1978. b. London, England, 1932. Ent. m.p. ind. 1951 and TV, 1967, as alt. dir. Harlech Television Ltd. Film editor, 1951–58. MCA-TV 1958–61, later with Woodfall as prod. and assoc. prod. Proc. One Way Pendulum. Assoc. prod. The Knack, The White Bus, Ride of the Valkyrie, Prod. Robbery, The Italian Job. Executive prod. Long Days Dying, Where's Jack, Sleep Is Lovely, Murphy's War, Convoy, The Deer Hunter (AA), Great Western Investments Ltd.; 1972; Great Western Festivals Ltd.; 1973, man. dir. British Lion Films Ltd. 1975, purchased BLF, Ltd. Appt. Jnt. man. dir. EMI Films Ltd., 1977; pres., EMI Films, 1978.

DE GRUNWALD, DIMITRI: Producer. Managing director Script Development Ltd. de Grunwald Films Ltd. and Films include: That Lucky Touch, The Millionairess, Shalako, Stranger in the House, The McMasters, Murphy's War, The Virgin and the Gypsy, Time for Loving, Perfect Friday.

DE HAVILLAND, OLIVIA: Actress b. Tokyo, Japan, July 1, 1916. e. California schools and Notre Dame Convent, Belmont. Acting debut, Max Reinhardt's stage prod., Midsummer Night's Dream; film debut in m.p. version, 1935; won Academy Award twice, best actress performance in To Each His Own, 1946, and The Heiress, 1949; N.Y. Film Critics award twice, 1948–49; Women's Natl. Press Club Award, 1949; Look award, best perf. 3 times, 1941-48-49.
PICTURES INCLUDE: Anthony Adverse, Gone With the Wind, Strawberry Blonde, Hold Back the Dawn, Princess O'Rourke, Dark Mirror, Snake Pit, My Cousin Rachel, Not as a Stranger, Ambassador's Daughter, Proud Rebel, Libel, Light in the Piazza, The Adventurers, Pope Joan, Airport '77, The Swarm.
STAGE: Romeo and Juliet, 1951; U.S. tour Candida, 1951–52, N.Y., 1952; A Gift of Time, Bdwy. 1962.
TV: Noon Wine for Stage 67.

DEIN, EDWARD: Director-Writer. b. Chicago, Ill.
PICTURES INCLUDE: dir., s.p. Shack Out on 101, Seven Guns to Sin, Curse of the Undead, Calypso Joe, I Trust My Wife, Hard Yellow, Come Die My Love (Spain), The Naked Sword (Mexico), Gaby (Brazil); story s.p. The Fighting Guardsman, Calling Dr. Death, The Gallant Blade, Leopard Man, All this and More, 13 French Street, Hang Me High; dir., prod., wrote, Capito, in Italy.
TV: Lawless Years, Hawaiian Eye, Bronco, Philip Marlowe, Not for Hire, Wild, Wild West series.

DE LANE LEA, JACQUES: Executive. b. Nice, France, 1931. Early career as prod. shorts, second features; later prod. sup. features. Ent. m.p. ind. 1952, prod. own films. Became man. dir. De Lane Lea Ltd., after death his father 1964. Also dir. Delmore Film Productions Ltd., Mole-Richardson (England) Ltd., Humphries Holdings, Ltd., Int'l Library Service Ltd., CTS Ltd.

DELANNOY, JEAN: Director. b. Noisy-le-Dec, France, Jan. 12, 1908; e. Universite de Paris, Lycee Montaigne, Lycee Louis le Grand, La Sorbonne; actor, 1927–29; film edit., 1929–37; dir., 1937–52.
PICTURES INCLUDE: Black Diamond, The Eternal Return, Symphonie Pastorale, The Chips Are Down, Souvenir, The Secret of Mayerling, Savage Triangle, Moment of Truth, Daughter of Destiny, The Bed.

DE LAURENTIIS, DINO: Producer. b. Torre Annunziata, Italy, Aug. 8, 1919. Took part in Rome Experimental Film Center; dir., prod.
PICTURES INCLUDE: The Bandit Mussolino, Bitter Rice, Girls Marked Danger, Side Street Story, She Wolf (La Lupa), Lure of the Sila, Attila Scourge of God, Europe 51, Anna, War and Peace, Gold of Naples, Ulysses, Mambo, The Great War, La Strada, Nights of Cabiria, The Tempest, Barabbas, The Best of Enemies, Il Mafioso, The Trial of Verona, The Bible, The Hills Run Red, The Stranger, Barbarella, L'Odissea, Anzio, The Valachi Papers, The Stone Killer, Crazy Joe, Serpico, Death Wish, Mandingo, Three Days of the Condor, Lipstick, Face to Face, Buffalo Bill & The Indians, The Shootist, Drum, King Kong, Orca, The Serpent's Egg, The Brinks Job, King of the Gypsies, Hurricane, Flash Gordon.

DE LA VARRE, ANDRE, JR.: Producer-Director. b. Vienna, Austria, Oct. 26, 1934. Prod. "Grand Tour" Travelogues; producer of promotion films for KLM, Swissair, tourist offices, recent productions: Bicentennial films for State of Virginia, City of Charleston, NY State; winner, Atlanta Film Festival, Sunset Travel Film Festival; Burton Holmes Travelogue subjects; V-P-R Educational Films; producer, director, lecturer, narrator.

DEL VALLE, JOHN: Publicist. b. San Francisco, Calif., Mar. 23, 1904; e. U. California. Adv., edit. staff various newspapers including asst. drama ed. S.F. Call-Bulletin, L.A. Mirror; adv.-publicity dir. San Francisco Fox Theatre 1933–36; publicist, Paramount Studio, 1936–42; dir. pub., adv. Arnold Prod. 1946; Chaplin Studios, 1947; Nat Holt Prod., 1948–52; Editor, TV Family mag., N.Y., 1952–53; adv. pub. dir. Century Films, 1954; pub. rel. Academy M.P. Arts & Sciences, 1965; publicist, various U.A. indep. film prod., 1955–56; unit publicist, Para., 1956; TC-F 1957–62, Para., 1962–63; Universal, 1964–65; Mirisch Corp.—UA Filming, "Hawaii," 1965; pub. rel. and editor, Atomics Int'l div. North American Rockwell, 1966–71; present, free-lance writer; res. Santa Barbara.

DEL BELSO, RICHARD: Executive. e. New York Univ. (1965). Began career in adv./research dept. at Benton & Bowles. Served as research dept. group head for Kenyon and Eckhart; group head for Gruden/Appell/Haley Research Co. (now known as A/H/F Marketing Research, Inc.) Two years as assoc. dir. of mktg., research for Grey Advertising (N.Y.). Joined MCA/Universal in 1977 as assoc. dir., mktg. research. In 1980 named v.p. & dir. of mktg. research for Warner Bros.

DELERUE, GEORGES: Composer-Conductor. b. Roubaix, France, 1924. Studied with Busser and Milhaud at Paris Cons. Was conductor for RTF (Radio-TV Francais).
PICTURES INCLUDE: Hiroshima Mon Amour, King of Hearts, Shoot the Pianist, Jules and Jim, Silken Skin, The Pumpkin Eater, Viva Maria, The 25th Hour, Interlude, The Day of the Jackal, The Day of the Dolphin, A Little Romance.

DELFONT, BERNARD LORD: Chief Executive EMI, Division of Tharn-EMI, Ltd. b. Tokmak, Russia, September 5, 1909. e. London, England. Dir. more than 30 companies incl. Forte's Trust Houses, chairman Grade and Delfont Organization. Presents entertainment at London's Talk of the Town. Ent. theatrical management 1941. Since presented over 250 shows in London; pantomimes in provinces and seaside resorts; presented annual Royal Variety Performance. Controls New London and Prince of Wales Theatres in London's West End. 1969: Chief Barker (Pres.) Variety Club of Great Britain; Companion of the Grand Order of Water Rats, President of Entertainment. Artistes' Benevolent Fund, member of Saints and Sinners organisation.

DELMAINE, BARRY: Writer, director. b. London. Began motion picture career as extra. Later roles in comedies; then asst. dir. for Gloria Swanson prod. in England. From 1936–39 wrote sketches, lyrics London stage musicals; radio scripts. In 1939 apptd. chief scenarist Gaumont-British Instructional. In 1941 dir. films for Brit. Ministry of Information; 1942–43 scenarist, Brit. War Office mi. training films. In 1944 author & dir. Here We Come Gathering, J. Arthur Rank experimental film for child audiences. In 1946 joined Film Producers Guild, writer, dir.; 1949–50, dir. Concord Productions, Ltd., freelance writer films, radio, TV; s.p. Heir Conditioned; dir. ind. films, Concord Prod. Ltd., ass't dir. Advance Films; The Great Game, Les Parent Terrible (Eng. version), Is Your Honeymoon Really Necessary? Unit dir. Don't Blame the Stork; Unit dir., loc. mgr. Douglas Fairbanks Ltd.; prod. mgr. 1955; prod. man. Chase a Crooked Shadow, Ice Cold in Alex, Jetstream; prod. sup. The Night We Dropped a Clanger. Prod. Sup., Nothing Barred; prod. man., The Hellions; prod. The Golden Rabbit; prog. sup., Man of The World, Sentimental Agent, assoc. prod., Danger Man (secret agent) series. Assoc. prod. Man in the Suitcase series; Assoc. prod., Strange Report series; assoc. prod. Mr. Jerico feature. TV series: assoc. prod. The Firechasers; prod. Shirley's World; assoc. prod. The Adventurers. Assoc. Prod. Three For All. Currently: Free lance Writer and Prod. Consultant.

DELON, ALAIN: Actor. b. Sceaux, France, Nov. 8, 1935. Discovered by Yves Allgret. Served in French Navy as a Marine. Worked as cafe waiter, heavy-load carrier.
PICTURES INCLUDE: When a Woman Gets Involved, Be Beautiful, and Keep Quiet, Plein Soleil and Quelle Joie de Vivre, Rocco and His Brothers, L'Eclipse, The Leopard, The Big Crab, The Black Tulip, The Felines, The Yellow Rolls Royce, The Killers of San Francisco, The Centurions, Is Paris Burning?, Texas, Here We Come, The Adventures, Extraordinary Stories, Le Samourai, Diaboliquement Votre, The Motorcycle, Goodbye Friend, The Swimming Pool, Jeff, The Sicilian Clan, Borsalino, Red Sun, Assassination of Trotsky, Scorpio, Dirty Money, Mr. Klein, The Concord-Airport '79.

DEL RIO, DOLORES: Actress. r.n. Dolores Ansunsolo; b. Durango, Mexico, Aug. 3, 1905; e. St. Joseph's Conv., Mexico, D.F.; studied voice Madrid & Paris. Screen debut in Joanna, 1925.
PICTURES INCLUDE: What Price Glory?, Resurrection, Ramona, Evangeline, Flying Down to Rio, Wonder Bar, Madame DuBarry, Accused, The Devil's Playground, Journey Into Fear, Portrait of Maria, The Fugitive, More Than a Miracle, Cheyenne Autumn.

DeLUISE, DOM: Comedian-Actor. b. Brooklyn, Aug. 1. e. Tufts Coll. Spent two seasons with Cleveland Playhouse. Launched TV career on The Garry Moore Show with character, Dominick the Great, a bumbling magician.
PICTURES INCLUDE: Fail Safe, The Busybody, The Glass Bottom Boat, 12 Chairs, Who Is Harry Kellerman?, Every Little Crook and Nanny, The Adventures of Sherlock Holmes' Smarter Brother, Silent Movie, The World's Greatest Lover, The End, The Cheap Detective, The Last Married Couple in America, Fatso, Wholly Moses, Smokey and the Bandit II, History of the World—Part I, The Cannonball Run.
TV: The Entertainers, The Dean Martin Summer Show, Dom DeLuise Variety Show, The Barrum-Bump Show, The Dean Martin Show, The Tonight Show, Lotsa Luck.
STAGE: The Student Gypsy, Last of the Red Hot Lovers, Here's Love.

DEL VALLE, JAIME: Producer. b. Los Angeles, Calif., Jan. 19, 1910. e. Stanford U. Motion Pictures 1932 as writer. Since then writer, director, producer in motion pictures, radio and television with exception of four years USAAF. Currently Metro-Goldwyn-Mayer.

DEMAREST, WILLIAM: Actor. b. St. Paul, Minn., Feb. 27, 1892. Began theat. career 1897 with brothers Reuben & George in vaudeville; later also stock, carnival acts, occasionally professional boxer; played Palace, N.Y., 1917; on Broadway in: Sketch Book, Vanities; talent agent one yr.; m.p. debut in Fingerprints, 1926. Starred in first released talking picture (a short), 1927, A Night in Coffee Dans.
PICTURES INCLUDE: Diamond Jim, Wedding Present, Love on the Run, Mr. Smith Goes to Washington, Pardon My Sarong, Hail the Conquering Hero, Miracle of Morgan's Creek, Duffy's Tavern, Perils of Pauline, Jolson Story, Miracles Can Happen, Red, Hot and Blue, The First Legion, When Willie Comes Marching Home, Riding High, Jolson Sings Again, Never a Dull Moment, Excuse My Dust, The Strip, Blazing Forest, The Lady Wants Mink, Dangerous When Wet, Here Come the Girls, Escape from Fort Bravo, Yellow Mountain, Far Horizons, Jupiter's Darling, Private War of Major Benson, Hell on Frisco Bay, Lucy Gallant, Rawhide Years, Son of Flubber, It's a Mad, Mad, Mad, World.
TV: My 3 Sons.

DEMBY, EMANUEL H.: Producer, writer. b. New York, N.Y., Dec. 12, 1919. e. C.C.N.Y., New School. Chung Ang University (Ph.D.). Pioneered new programs for radio, 1936–47; story dept., Universal Pictures, 1937; writer, Gangbusters, Crime of the Week, Thrill of the Week (NBC, CBS); TV shows; What's Playing, 1950–52; Hollywood to Broadway, currently in TV syndication, How To Be a Cowboy; The Shadow; prod., theatrical features, filmed commercials; pub. rel. consultant. Author: My Forty Year Fight for Korea; Indonesia; King of The Hill; Hot Tip on Wall St.; prod. Cavalcade of Music (TV); The World in Space (TV, theatrical); The Edge of Violence (stage); Man Into Space; Year III-Space Age (TV); The Communications Gap, The Creative Consumer, (P.R. films). Book: Who's Alienated, Youth or Society? Research Consultant, NBC TV News; consultant, Radio Advertising Bureau, Smash, Crash, Pow! (feature).

DEMME, JONATHAN: Director-Writer. b. Rockville Center, N.Y., 1944. e. Univ. of Florida. First job in industry as usher; was film critic for college paper, The Florida Alligator. Did publicity work for United Artists, Avco Embassy, Pathe Contemporary Films; wrote for trade publication, Film Daily, 1966–68. Moved to England in 1969; served as musical co-ordinator on Irving Allen's EyeWitness in 1970. In 1972 produced and co-wrote first film, Angels, Hard As they Come.
PICTURES: Hot Box (prod., co-writer); Caged Heat (writer-dir.); Crazy Mama (writer-dir.); Fighting Mad (writer-dir.); Citizen's Band (dir.), Last Embrace (dir.), Melvin and Howard (dir.).

DEMOSS, LYLE: Executive. b. Anthony, Kansas, Sept. 14, 1907; e. York Coll. and U. of Nebraska School of Music; 1925. KGBZ in York, Nebr.; 1928. KFAB in Lincoln, Nebr.; in 1932 became Prog. Mgr. of KFAB-KFOR; held same position for WOW from 1936 to 1946; asst. gen. mgr. Meredith WOW, 1946–59. Allen & Reynolds v.p. radio-TV dept. Omaha Advertising Club, Variety Club Canvasman, past pres. Omaha Ad. Club. Radio KLNG, 1965–67; freelance TV; Elected to Nebr. Broadcasters Hall of Fame—1972; KYNN-community relations director.

DENCH, JUDI: O.B.E. Actress. b. York, England, 1934. Studied for stage at Central School of Speech and Drama. Theatre debut Old Vic, 1961.
TELEVISION: Major Barbara, Pink String and Sealing Wax, Talking to a Stranger, The Funambulists, Age of Kings, Jackanory, Hilda Lessways, Luther, Neighbours, Parade's End, Marching Song, On Approval, Days to Come, Emilie, The Comedy of Errors, Macbeth (both RSC productions), Langrishe Go Down, On Giant's Shoulders, Love in a Cold Climate, Village Wooing.
PICTURES: He Who Rides a Tiger, Study in Terror, Four in the Morning, A Midsummer Night's Dream (RSC Production), The Third Secret, Dead Cert.

DENEAU, SIDNEY G.: Sales executive. Head film buyer Fabian Theatres; U.S. Army 1942–46; gen. mgr. Schine Theatres 1947; v.p.; gen. sales mgr., Selznick Releasing Orgn., 1949; 1956; v.p. asst. gen. sls. mgr., Para. Film Dist., 1958; exec. v.p., Rugoff Theatres, 1964. Resigned, September, 1969 to engage in own theatre consultant business.

DENEUVE, CATHERINE: Actress. b. 1945. r.n. Catherine Dorleac. Sister was the late Francoise Dorleac.
PICTURES INCLUDE: The Doors Slam, Vice and Virtue, Satan Leads the Dance, Umbrellas of Cherbourg, (received the French Film Academy's best actress award); Repulsion, Le Chant du Monde, La Vie de Chateau, Les Creatures, The Young Girls of Rochefort, Belle de Jour, Benjamin, Manon 70, Mayerling, La Chamade, April Fools, Mississippi Mermaid, Tristana, It Only Happens to Others, Dirty Money, Hustle, March or Die.

DENHAM, MAURICE: Actor. b. Beckenham, Kent, Eng., Dec. 23, 1909. e. Tonbridge School. Started theatrical career with repertory com. 1934. Served in World War II and since demobilization played in numerous plays, films & radio shows.
PICTURES INCLUDE: Blanche Fury, London Belongs To Me, It's Not Cricket, Traveller's Joy, Landfall, Spider and the Fly, No Highway in the Sky, The Net, Time Bomb, Street Corner (Both Sides of the Law), Million Pound Note (Man With a Million), Eight O'Clock Walk, Purple Plain, Simon and Laura, 23 Paces to Baker Street, Checkpoint, Carrington V.C. (Court Martial), Doctor at Sea, Night of the Demon, Man With a Dog, Barnacle Bill, The Captain's Table, Our Man in Havana, Sink the Bismark, Two-Way Stretch, Greengage Summer, Invasion, Quartette, The Mark, HMS Defiant.
TV: appearances include: Uncle Harry, Day of the Monkey, Miss Mabel, Angel Pavement, The Paraguayan Harp, The Wild Bird, Soldier Soldier, Changing Values, Maigret, The Assassins, Saturday Spectacular, Vanishing Act, A Chance in Life, Virtue, Somerset Maugham, Three of A Kind, Sapper, Pig In The Middle, Their Obedient Servants, Long Past Glory, Devil in The Wind, Any Other Business, The Retired Colourman, Sherlock Holmes (series), Black-

mail, Knock on Any Door, Danger Man, Dr. Finley's Casebook, How To Get Rid of Your Husband, Talking to A Stranger, A Slight Ache, From Chekhov With Love, Home Sweet Honeycomb, St. Joan, Julius Caesar, Golden Days, Marshall Petain, The Lotus Eaters, Fall of Eagles, Carnforth Practice. The Unofficial Rose, Omnibus, Balzac, Loves Labour Lost, Angels, Huggy Bear, The Portrait, The Crumbles Murder, A Chink In The Wall, Porridge, For God's Sake, Bosch, Marie Curie, Upchat Line, Secret Army, My Son, My Son, Edward and Mrs. Simpson, Gate of Eden, Potting Shed, Double Dealer.
OTHER PICTURES: The Very Edge, Paranoiac, The Set Up, Penang, The Kings Breakfast, Downfall, Hysteria, The Uncle, Operation Crossbow, Legend of Dick Turpin, The Alphabet Murders, The Night Callers, The Nanny, Those Magnificent Men in Their Flying Machines, Heroes of Telemark, After the Fox, The Torture Garden, The Long Duel, The Eliminator, Danger Route, Attack on the Iron Coast, The Best House in London, Negatives, The Midas Run, Some Girls Do, The Touch of Love, The Virgin and the Gypsy, Bloody Sunday, Countess Dracula, Nicholas and Alexandra, The Day of the Jackal, Luther, Shout at the Devil, Julia, The Recluse.

DE NIRO, ROBERT: Actor. b. New York City, 1945. Studied acting with Stella Adler and Lee Strasberg. In off-Broadway productions and touring shows.
PICTURES INCLUDE: The Wedding Party, Jennifer on My Mind, Bloody Mama, Born To Win, The Gang That Couldn't Shoot Straight, Bang the Drum Slowly, Mean Streets, Godfather II, Taxi Driver, 1900, The Last Tycoon, New York, New York, The Deer Hunter, Raging Bull, True Confessions.

DENISON, MICHAEL: Actor. b. Doncaster, York, Eng., Nov. 1, 1915; e. Harrow & Magdalen Coll., Oxford and Webber Douglas Sch.; m. Dulcie Gray, prof. Served overseas, Capt. Intelligence Corps, 1940–46. On stage first, 1938, Charlie's Aunt. Screen debut 1940, Tilly of Bloomsbury.
THEATRE: Ever Since Paradise, Rain on the Just, Queen Elizabeth Slept Here, Fourposter, Dragon's Mouth, Bad Samaritan; Shakespeare Season Stratford-on-Avon; Edinburgh Festival. Meet Me By Moonlight, Let Them Eat Cake, Candida, Heartbreak House, My Fair Lady (Australia), Where Angels Fear to Tread, Hostile Witness, An Ideal Husband, On Approval, Happy Family, No. 10, Out of the Question, Trio, The Wild Duck, The Clandestine Marriage, The Dragon Variation, At the End of the Day, The Sack Race, Peter Pan, The Black Mikado, The First Mrs. Fraser, The Earl and the Pussycat, Robert and Elizabeth, The Cabinet Minister, Old Vic Season: Twelfth Night, Lady's Not for Burning, Ivanov, Bedroom Farce.
PICTURES INCLUDE: Hungry Hill, My Brother Jonathan, The Blind Goddess, The Glass Mountain, Landfall, The Franchise Affair, Angels One Five, Tall Headlines, Importance of Being Earnest, There Was a Young Lady, Contraband Spain, The Truth About Women, Faces in the Dark.
TV: Boyd QC Series, Funeral Games, Unexpectedly Vacant, Tale of Piccadilly. 1973: The Twelve Pound Look, The Provincial Lady, Subject: This Is Your Life, 1977, Bedroom Farce.

DENNIS, SANDY: Actress. b. Hastings, Nebraska, April 27. m. Gerry Mulligan. Joined the Lincoln Community Theatre group. Made her professional acting debut in summer stock at London, N.H. Studied with Herbert Berghof, N.Y. Understudy for N.Y. prod. Dark at the Top of the Stairs. Broadway debut in Any Wednesday (Antoinette Perry Award), then A Thousand Clowns (Tony Award for best supporting actress).
PICTURES INCLUDE: Who's Afraid of Virginia Wolf? (won an Academy Award as best supporting actress), Up the Down Staircase, Sweet November, The Fox, Thank You All Very Much, That Cold Day in the Park, The Out-of-Towners, Nasty Habits, The Four Seasons.

DE NORMAND, GEORGE: Actor, director. b. New York, N.Y., Sept. 22. Actor many westerns & TV series; dir., TV series, Man of Tomorrow. Member: SAG, SEG, NSTP.

DE PALMA, BRIAN: Director. b. Newark, N.J., 1940. e. Columbia Univ. (B.A.) and Sarah Lawrence (M.A.). While in college made series of shorts, including Wotan's Wake, winner of Rosenthal Foundation Award for best film made by American under 25. Also judged most popular film of Midwest Film Festival (1963); later shown at San Francisco Film Festival.
PICTURES INCLUDE: The Wedding Party, Murder A La Mod, Greetings, Hi Mom, Dinoysus in '69, Get To Know Your Rabbit, Sisters, Phantom of the Paradise, Obsession, Carrie, The Fury, Home Movies, Dressed to Kill, Blow Out.

DEPARDIEU, GERARD: Actor. b. Chateauroux, France, Dec. 27, 1948. Studied acting at Theatre National Populaire in Paris. Made film debut at 16 in short by Roger Leenhardt (Le Beatnik et Le Minet). Acted in feature film by Agnes Varda which was never finished.
PICTURES INCLUDE: Going Places, Stavisky, 1900, Get

Your Handkerchiefs, LouLou, The Last Metro, Mon Oncle d'Amerique.

DEPEW, RICHARD H.: Executive. b. New York, N.Y., Jan. 16, 1925. e. Princeton U. U.S. Navy; American Broadcasting Co., 1947; television director, 1950; assistant, eastern TV network program director, 1953; mgr. of TV network program oper., 1954–57; Cunningham & Walsh; Radio & TV acct. supv. & programming coordinator, 1961–65 v. & dir. of TV programming; 1965 Broadcast supr., Ogilvy and Mather; 1967, v.p. dir. TV program Fuller & Smith & Ross. V.P. Media and Programming 1969, FS&R.; 1973, Director of Corporate Underwriting Department WNET/13, Educational Broadcasting Corp. 1977 Management Supervisor, J. Walter Thompson, N.Y.C.; 1978, v.p., Account Director, 1980, Marstella, Inc., mgt. supvr.

DEREK, BO: Actress. r.n. Cathleen Collins. Discovered by John Derek, actor turned film producer, who changed her first name to Bo, now married to him. Film debut in "10" in 1979.
PICTURES: Change of Seasons, Tarzan, the Ape Man.

DERN, BRUCE: Actor. b. Chicago, Ill., 1937. e. University of Pennsylvania. Studied acting with Gordon Phillips, member, Actor's Studio, 1959 after N.Y. debut in Shadow of a Gunman.
CREDITS: The Trip, The Wild Angels, Hush, Hush, Sweet Charlotte, Support Your Local Sheriff, Thumbtripping, Drive, He Said; They Shoot Horses, Don't They?; The Cowboys, Silent Running, Sweet Bird of Youth (Stage), Orpheus Descending (Stage), The King of Marvin Gardens, The Laughing Policeman, The Great Gatsby, Smile, Posse, Family Plot, Won Ton Ton, Black Sunday, Coming Home, The Driver, Middle Age Crazy.

DE ROCHEMONT, RICHARD: Producer. b. Chelsea, Mass.; e. Cambridge (Mass.) Latin Sch.; Harvard U., B.A. On ed. staffs Boston Daily Advertiser, Pathe News (newsreel), N.Y. American, N.Y. Sun. Joined March of Time News; ed. Paris edition 1931–34. Joined March of Time 1934; European mgr.; man. dir. March of Time, Ltd., England, to 1940 (1939–40, 1944–45 accredited Amer. war corresp., France). In 1941 prod. Story of the Vatican for RKO Radio; in 1942 man. ed. March of Time; prod. 1943–51; prod. A Chance to Live, March of Time short (Academy Award, 1949;) prod. The Golden Twenties, 1950; Modern Arms and Free Men, 1951; World Assembly of Youth, 1952, feature documentaries. Prod. TV series, Mr. Lincoln for Ford Foundation; v.p., TV prod., J. Walter Thompson ad agency, New York, 1953–55; pres., Vavin Inc., 1955. Contrib. to Time, Life, Readers Digest, American Mercury, etc. Clubs: Harvard, Williams, Coffee House, Sky, Explorers, Overseas Press (bd. gov. 1943–55, 1961–1963). France Forever (pres. 1943–44), Paris-American (pres. 1963–66). Decorations: Chevalier du Merite Agricole (1938); officer French Legion of Honor (1945); officer, Order of Merite Touristique (1959); officer, Merite Agricole (1959).; order of National Merit (commander) France, 1979.

DE SANTIS, GIUSEPPE: Director. b. Italy, 1917. Film publicists; asst. dir.
PICTURES INCLUDE: Tragic Hunt, Bitter Rice, Under the Olive Tree, Rome 11 O'Clock, A Husband for Anna Zaccheo, Days of Love.

DE SCHAAP, PHILIP: Dutch correspondent, Quigley Publications, N.Y. b. Amsterdam, Holland, May 26, 1911. Entered m.p. ind. 1934 as publicity mgr., MGM br. office, Amsterdam; in 1936 corresp. for Quigley Publications. Also in 1937 exploitation mgr., RKO Radio Pictures, Amsterdam; to Paris 1938 as spec. publicity repr. in Paris and Brussels, RKO; in 1939 org. own co. for exploitation and publicity; non-active 1940–45; on Oct. 1, 1945 estab. Phidesa Publiciteitsbureau voor de Filmbranche.

DESMOND, JOHNNY: Performer; r.n. Giovanni Alfredo De Simone; b. Nov. 14, 1923, Detroit, Mich.; began singing in Detroit, 1932; organ. Bob-O-Links which were hired by Bob Crosby 1939; enlisted, Army Air Corps and transferred to Glenn Miller Air Corps band; sang over Armed Forces network; TV singer, Don McNeill's Breakfast Club Show, 1949–51. Songs for Sale, 1951–52, Jackie Gleason Show, 1952; Ed Sullivan, 1952; Coral Records, TV shows, radio.
BROADWAY: Funny Girl.

DE TITTA, ARTHUR A.: Newsreel editor. b. North Bergen, N.J., July 9, 1904. Began work 1916 in employ newspaper in Union City, N.J.; joined Fox Film Corp., N.Y. office & lab. staff; later became asst. & second cameraman, performing in that capacity numerous pictures Fox and other produs. (The Mountain Woman, When Knighthood Was in Flower, The Royale Girl, East Side, West Side, Untamed, etc.). In 1928 joined Movietonews, Inc.; Wash. (D.C.) suprv. to 1938; asst. Europ. supvr. to 1940; Pacific Coast supvr. to 1943. Commis. Lt. USNR, assigned to M.P. Sect., 1943; ret. 1944. Appt. news ed. Movietonews; west coast superv., 1951–63; pub. rel., prod., documentaries; West Coast Bureau mgr. for foreign editions of Movietone News, now retired.

DE TOTH, ANDRE: Writer-Director-Producer. b. Hungary. Dr.-writer European films, 1931–39; U.S. assoc. Alexander Korda prod., 1940; dir. Columbia, 1943; assoc. David Selznick, 1943; assoc. Hunt Stromberg-UA, 1944–45; staff dir., Enterprise 1946–47; dir., 20th-Fox, 1948–49; collab. story, The Gunfighter; dir., Columbia & Warner Bros., 1951; contract dir., Warner Bros., 1952; U.A. Columbia, W.B., 1953–55; Palladiums U.A., Denmark, 1956; Col. U.A. 1957; Columbia, 1960; assoc., Sam Spiegel, Horizon Pictures, Columbia, 1962; Harry Saltzman, Lowndes Prod., U.A., 1966–68; National General, 1969–70.
PICTURES INCLUDE: Passport to Suez, None Shall Escape, Since You Went Away, Pitfall, Springfield Rifle, Thunder Over the Plains, House of Wax, Bounty Hunter, Tanganyika, Indian Fighter, Monkey on My Back, Two-Headed Spy, Man on a String, Morgan, The Pirate, The Mongols, Gold for the Caesars, Billion Dollar Brain, Play Dirty, El Condor.

DEUTSCH, ARMAND S.: Producer. b. Chicago, Ill., Jan. 25, 1913. e. U. of Chicago, 1935; B.A. Producer, MGM.
PICTURES INCLUDE: Ambush, Right Cross, Magnificent Yankee, Three Guys Named Mike, Kind Lady, Girl in White, Carbine Williams, Girl Who Had Everything, Green Fire, Slander.

DEUTSCH, DAVID: Producer-Writer. b. Birmingham, England, January 10, 1926. e. in Birmingham and Queen Mary College, London Univ. Ent. m.p. ind. apprentice at Gainsborough Pictures, Ltd.; 1949; asst. Sydney Box, 1954; J. Arthur Rank asst. to prod. 1955 Lost; assoc. prod. High Tide at Noon, The One That Got Away, Floods of Fear; prod. Blind Date; Anglo Amalgamated Film Dist. Ltd., as exec. in chrg. prod., 1960. Prod., Play It Cool, 1962, Nothing But the Best. 1963: Domino Prods. Ltd., Catch Us If You Can, 1965; Interlude, 1967; Lock Up Your Daughter, 1968. A Day in the Death of Joe Egg, 1970. Co-prod. The Day of the Jackal, 1972; s.p., The Blue Train, The Jacaranda Tree.

DEUTSCH, HELEN: Writer. b. New York, N.Y. e. Barnard Coll., B.A. Author: The Provincetown.
PICTURES INCLUDE: Seventh Cross, National Velvet, King Solomon's Mines, Golden Earrings, Kim, Plymouth Adventure, Lili, The Glass Slipper, I'll Cry Tomorrow, Forever Darling.
TV: Jack and the Beanstalk, NBC Gen. Motors 50th Anniv. Show, 1957; book of Broadway musical, Carnival, 1961.

DEVANE, WILLIAM: Actor. b. New York City. Appeared in some 15 productions with N.Y. Shakespeare Festival and off-Bdwy. shows before heading for California and films and TV. Has own theatre, Actors for Themselves, in Los Angeles. Has also directed plays.
PICTURES: Rolling Thunder, Marathon Man, Yanks, Honky Tonk Freeway.
TELEVISION: The Missiles of October, Fear on Trial, From Here to Eternity (series).

DE VITO, DANNY: Actor. b. Neptune, NJ, Nov. 17. e. Academy of Dramatic Arts, Manhattan. Produced two short motion pictures with associate Rhea Perlman), The Sound Sleeper and Minestrone (latter on grant from American Film Institute). Acted off Broadway in The Man with the Flower in His Mouth, Shrinking Bride, etc.
PICTURES: One Flew Over the Cuckoo's Nest, Goin' South.
TELEVISION: Taxi (series), Valentine (movie).

DEWHURST, COLLEEN: Actress. b. Montreal, Canada, June 3, 1926. Gained fame as stage actress, appearing in, among others, Mourning Becomes Electra, All Over, A Moon for the Misbegotten, More Stately Mansions, All the Way Home, The Ballad of the Sad Cafe, etc.
PICTURES: The Nun's Story, A Fine Madness, McQ, The Cowboys, The Last Run, Annie Hall, Ice Castles, When a Stranger Calls, Tribute.
TELEVISION: The Price, The Crucible, The Hands of Cormac Joyce, Jacob and Joseph, Studs Lonigan, The Kitty O'Neill Story, And Baby Makes Six, etc.

DEWITT, JOYCE: Actress. b. Wheeling, W. Va., April 23. e. Ball State Univ. (B.A.), theatre. Performed in summer stock musical comedies (Damn Yankee, Li'l Abner, etc.). Worked at Indianapolis dinner theatres, directing, staging and starring in musical revues.
TELEVISION: Baretta, The Tony Randall Show, Most Wanted, Risko, Three's Company. Movie: With This Ring.

DEY, SUSAN: Actress. b. Pekin, Ill. Began modeling at 15 for magazines. Has been frequent guest star on TV series: The Rookies, S.W.A.T., Hawaii Five-O, Born Free, Petrocelli, etc.
PICTURES INCLUDE: First Love, Looker.
TV: Movies: Terror on the Beach, Cage without a Key.

DEZEL, ALBERT: Exhibitor. b. Russia, May 21, 1900; e. Chicago Acad. Fine Arts; also Art Inst. & Crane Coll., Chicago. Art work, theatre publicity, exploitation & Middle West. Org. Albert Dezel Roadshows, exploitation films, 1926; in 1945 owner, operator, Film Classics Franchise, Detroit, Cleveland, Cincinnati; in 1946 acquired rights in same territory for Screen Guild Products; operator, operator, Avon Art Theatre, South Bend; Cinema, Hamilton Theatre, Indianapolis; Guild Theatres, Detroit.

DIAMANT, LINCOLN: Executive. b. New York City, Jan. 25, 1923. e. Columbia College, AB cum Laude 1943; cofounder, Columbia University Radio Station. Advertising mgr., World Publ. Co.; writer-prod., CBS; prod.-dir., Blue Network (NBC); prom. dir., Book Find Club; creative dir., Ben Sackheim; group hd., McCann-Erickson; copy chief, DKG; Sr. TV prod., Ogilvy & Mather; TV prod. super., Grey Adv; founder, pres., Spots Alive, Inc., broadcast advertising consultants, 1969; author, The Broadcast Communications Dictionary, Anatomy of a Television Commercial, Television's Classic Commercials, contrib., to Effective Advertising, to Messages and Meaning; member, Broadcast Pioneers, Acad. TV Arts & Sciences; v.p. Broadcast Advertising Producer's Society of America. Adjunct faculty member, Pace College, Hofstra University. Fellow, Royal Society of Arts. President, Teatown Lake Reservation of Brooklyn Botanic Garden.

DIAMOND, BERNARD: Theatre Executive. b. Chicago, Jan. 24, 1918. e. Univ. of Indiana, Univ. of Minnesota. Except for military service was with Schine Theatre chain from 1940 to 1963, working up from ass't. mgr., booker, buyer, dir. of personnel to gen. mgr. Then joined Loews Theatres; now exec. v.p.

DIAMOND, I.A.L.: Writer. b. Unghani, Roumania, June 27, 1920. r.n. Isidore Diamond. e. Col Univ. Came to US when 9 yrs. old. Hired as Junior writer by Paramount in 1941. Usually collaborates on scripts with other writers, particularly in recent years with Billy Wilder.
PICTURES INCLUDE: (All co-written except where indicated by (s) for solo) Murder in the Blue Room, Never Say Goodbye, Two Guys from Milwaukee, Two Guys from Texas, Always Together, The Girl from Jones Beach (s), It's a Great Feeling (s), Love Nest (s), Let's Make It Legal, Monkey Business, Something for the Birds, That Certain Feeling, Love in the Afternoon, Merry Andrew, Some Like It Hot, The Apartment, One, Two, Three, Irma La Douce, Kiss Me, Stupid, The Fortune Cookie, Cactus Flower (s), The Private Life of Sherlock Holmes, Forty Carats (s), Avantil, The Front Page, Fedora.

DICKINSON, ANGIE: Actress. b. Kulm, N.D. Sept. 30, 1936. e. Parochial Schools, Heart Coll., Glendale Coll., secretarial course. m. Burt Bacharach. Won a beauty contest.
PICTURES INCLUDE: Sins of Rachel Cade, Rio Bravo, Bramble Bush, Ocean's 11, Jessica, Capt. Newman, M.D., The Killers, The Art of Love, The Chase, The Last Challenge, Point Blank, Sam Whiskey, Young Billy Young, Pretty Maids All in a Row, The Outside Man, Dressed to Kill, Charlie Chan and the Curse of the Dragon Queen, Death Hunt.

DICKINSON, DESMOND: Dir., photog. b. Surrey, May 25, 1902. e. privately. Entered m.p. indust. old Clarendon Film Co., 1919; 1922 camera asst. Stoll. Film Co.; with various motion picture cos. since.
PICTURES INCLUDE: Hamlet, Rocking Horse Winner, The Woman in Question, The Browning Version, Encore, Importance of Being Earnest, The Net, Man Between, Carrington V.C., Gentlemen Marry Brunettes, Black Tent, Fire Down Below, Action of the Tiger, Orders to Kill, Intent to Kill, Horrors of the Black Museum, Moment of Danger, City of Death, Foxhole in Cairo, Kongo, Hands of Orlac, Mary Had a Little, The Frightened City, The Devils Daffodil, Two & Two Make Six, Cairo, Sparrows Can't Sing, Murder Most Foul, Murder Ahoy, Alphabet Murders, A Study in Terror, Berserk, Decline and Fall, Baby Love, Crooks and Coronets, Trog, Incense for the Damned, The Fiend, Burke and Hore, Nobody Ordered Love, Who Slew Auntie Roo?, Tower of Evil, The Man From Nowhere.

DICKINSON, GLEN JR.: Executive. b. Brookfield, Mo., May 29, 1914. e. Pembroke County Day, Kansas U.; officer, U.S. Navy; chm., Dickinson Operating Co., Inc.; chm., Dickinson Inc.; chm., Glenwood Manor, Inc.

DICKINSON, ROBERT PRESTON: Actor. b. Newhall, W. Va.; Dec. 24, 1924. e. Va. Polytechnic Inst. & State University, B.S., 1947; N.Y. Univ., U. Calif., American Academy of Dramatic Arts, Pasadena, Ca. Private schools. U.S. Army Signal, Infantry Corp, W.W. II U.S. chemical-aerospace films, 10 yrs., prof. chemical engineer-writer; legit. stage plays include: Murder in the Red Barn; Career; The Ponder Heart. M.p. include: The Brain Eaters; Her Conversion. Elected member Int'l. Platform Ass'n.
TV: The Rank & File (Playhouse 90 series, CBS).

DICKINSON, THOROLD: C.B.E. 1973. Prof. Emeritus of Film. b. Bristol, England, Nov. 16, 1903. e. Clifton Coll., Bristol; Oxford U. Entered m.p. ind. 1925 as asst. dir.; from 1927–36 film ed., prod. supvr. Midshipman Easy; from 1936–41 dir. (High Command, Spanish A.B.C., Arsenal Stadium Mystery, Gaslight, Prime Minister, Next of Kin, M.O.I. short subjects, etc.). From 1941–45 Army Kine Service. Since 1945 dir. Men of Two Worlds, Queen of Spades; A.B.P.C. 1949–50; dir., collab. s.p., Secret People; 1952–53 chmn.

British Film Acad.; dir., collab. story & s.p., Hill 24 Doesn't Answer; 1956–60 in chge. U.N. Film Services, N.Y.; Slade School of Fine Arts, Univ. Coll., London, Eng.; Film Dept. 1967–71; Prof. of Film U. of London. Ph.D. (London U.). 1973–6 Hon. Consultant. Council of National Academic Awards. 1976 D. Univ (Surrey). Visiting Prof. of Film (Surrey U.) until 1977.
PUBLICATIONS: A Discovery of Cinema, Soviet Cinema (with Catherine de la Roche).

DIEBOLD, JEROME C.: Executive. b. Madison, Wis., May 30, 1909. e. U. of Wis. in economics and law; photographer and teacher, Univ. of Wisc.; visual education, 1933–43; served in U.S. Navy as Lt. Commdr., 1943–46; producer and director of Navy training motion pictures; head, Training Film Branch, 1945–46; asst. prod. mgr., Wilding Inc., 1946–48; assist. to the pres. Wilding Inc. 1948–53; executive producer, 1954–63; dir. of prod., Enclop. Brit. Films, 1963–65; pres., Diebold Film Prod., 1965, Life Fellow SMPTE.

DIEHL, WALTER F.: Executive. International President, I.A.T.S.E. b. Revere, Mass., April 13, 1907. e. Northeastern Univ., Boston Catholic Labor Guild School. Became projectionist in Boston in 1927 and member of Boston Moving Picture Machine Operators Local 182 in 1933. After several years of service on the executive board became business agent in 1946 and held that post until 1953, when he resigned to accept an appointment as an International Representative, handling assignments throughout New England until 1957, when was appointed assistant international president. In 1952 made a member of the Minimum Wage Commission for the amusement industry in the state of Massachusetts. Also served several years on the executive board of the Boston Central Labor Union and as Labor Representative on the Suffolk County March of Dimes. IATSE pres. since March, 1974.

DIENER, JOAN: Actress. b. Cleveland, Ohio, Feb. 24. e. Sarah Lawrence College.
THEATRE: Plays: H.M.S. Pinafore, Cleveland Playhouse 1947; Broadway debut, Small Wonder, 1948; Season in the Sun, 1950; Kismet, 1953, also London production, 1955. Road tours, The Ziegfeld Follies, 1956; At the Grand, 1958; La Belle, 1962. Man of the La Mancha, 1965. New York, Los Angeles and London productions, Cry For Us All.

DIETRICH, MARLENE: Actress. r.n. Maria Magdalene von Losch. b. Berlin, Germany, Dec. 27, 1904; e. pvt. sch., Weimar; Musical Acad., Berlin; m. Rudolph Sieber; d. Maria Riva, actress. Stage training, Max Reinhardt's Sch. of Drama; debut in Viennese version of play, Broadway; then mus. com.
PICTURES INCLUDE: In German film, Blue Angel; in Hollywood: Morocco, Dishonored, Blonde Venus, Shanghai Express, Scarlet Empress, Song of Songs, Desire, Angel, Garden of Allah, Knight Without Armour, Destry Rides Again, Seven Sinners, Flame of New Orleans, Manpower, Pittsburgh, The Spoilers; with Army overseas (USO), 1942–45. Golden Earrings, Martin Roumagnac (French), Foreign Affair, Stage Fright, No Highway in the Sky, Rancho Notorious, Witness for the Prosecution, Judgment at Nuremberg.

DIFFRING, ANTON: Actor. b. Koblenz, Germany. Early career Academy of Drama, Berlin. Acted in Canada and U.S. before ent. m.p. ind. in Britain, 1951.
PICTURES INCLUDE: I Am a Camera, Seven Thunders, House of Secrets, Albert RN, Circus of Horrors, The Man Who Could Cheat Death, A Question of Adultery, Lady of Vengeance, The Traitor, The Crooked Sky, The Sea Shall Not Have Them, The Colditz Story, The Black Tent, Enter Inspector Duval, Incident at Midnight. 1963/65 working in Germany, The Heroes of Telemark, The Blue Max, Farenheit 451, The Double Man, Counterpoint, Where Eagles Dare, Michael Kohlhaas, Horse Dealer, Uccidete Rommel, Piggies, Zeppelin, L'Iguana della lingua del Fuoco, Sutjeska, Corringa, Assassination of Little Sister, Dead Pigeon on Beethoven St., Der Stoff aus dem die Traume sind, The Day the Clown Cried, Das Schicksal ist der Jager, Tony Arzenta, The Beast Must Die, Shatter, Swiss Conspiracy, Vanessa, Operation Daybreak, Potato Fritz, Valentino, Les Indiens sont encore loin, L'Imprecateur, Waldrausch, Anna Ferroli, Das Einhorn, Return to Munich, Arsene Lupen, Escape to Victory, Tristan und Isolde.
TV: The Last Hours, A Small Revolution, Wedding Day, The One Who Came Back, The Man in Half Moon Street, The Queen and the Rebels, The Cold Light, The Magnificent Egoist, The One Who Got Away, Autumn Crocus, The Fourposter, Dear Charles, Cross of Iron, One Step Beyond, Ghost Squad, Dr. Korczak and His Children, Dixon of Dock Green, The Joel Brandt Story, Firebrand, Scobie in September, The Trouble Shooters, The Million Pound Note, Strange Report, Kommissar, A Place in the Sun, Die Krise, Assignment Vienna, Liebe 74, Yoster, Kiss Me and Die, Die Himmlischen Tochter, Car along the Pass, MM Le Mutant, Flambards, Plutoniumaler Alte.

DILLER, BARRY: Executive. Joined ABC in April, 1966, as asst. to v.p. in chg. programming. In March, 1968, made exec. asst. to v.p. in chg. programming and dir. of feature films. In May, 1969, named v.p., feature films and program development, east coast. In Feb., 1971, made v.p., Feature Films and Circle Entertainment, a unit of ABC Entertainment, responsible for selecting, producing and scheduling The Tuesday Movie of the Week, The Wednesday Movie of the Week, and Circle Film original features for airing on ABC-TV, as well as for acquisition and scheduling of theatrical features for telecasting on ABC Sunday Night Movie and ABC Monday Night Movie. On May 30, 1973, named v.p. in chg. of prime time TV for ABC Entertainment. In 1974 joined Paramount Pictures as bd. chm. and chief exec. officer.

DILLER, PHYLLIS: Comedienne. b. Lima, O., July 17, 1917. e. Sherwood Music School, 1935–37; Bluffton College, O., 1938–39.
PICTURES INCLUDE: Boy, Did I Get A Wrong Number! 1966; Mad Monster Party, 1967; Eight on the Lam, 1967; Did You Hear the One About the Traveling Saleslady, 1967; The Private Navy of Serg. O'Farrell, 1967; The Adding Machine.
TV: Series, The Phyllis Diller Show, ABC 1966–67; The Beautiful Phyllis Diller Show (NBC) 1968. Guest spots on major shows here and abroad.
BOOKS: Phyllis Diller's Housekeeping Hints, 1968, Phyllis Diller's Marriage Manual, Phyllis Diller's The Complete Mother.
RECORDS: Verve and Columbia.
BROADWAY: Hello, Dolly!
CONCERTS: A dozen annual piano concerts with symphony orchestras.

DILLMAN, BRADFORD: Actor. b. San Francisco, Calif., April 14, 1930. e. Yale, 1951.
PICTURES INCLUDE: A Certain Smile, In Love and War, Compulsion, Crack in the Mirror, Circle of Deception, Sanctuary, Francis of Assisi, A Rage to Live, Sergeant Ryker, Bridge at Remagen, Jigsaw, Suppose They Gave a War and Nobody Came, Mastermind, Brother John, The Mephisto Waltz, Escape from the Planet of the Apes, The Way We Were, The Iceman Cometh, Chosen Survivors, 99 and 44/100ths ½ Dead, Gold Bug, A Black Ribbon for Deborah, One Away, The Enforcer, Amsterdam Kill, The Lincoln Conspiracy, The Swarm, Love and Bullets, Piranha, Guyana-Crime of the Century, Running Scared.

DILLON, MELINDA: Actress. Launched career on Broadway in original company of Who's Afraid of Virginia Woolf? Screen debut with bit in The April Fools (1969).
PICTURES INCLUDE: Bound for Glory, Slap Shot, Close Encounters of the Third Kind, F.I.S.T.

DILLOW, JEAN CARMEN: Producer, writer, actress, director. Began as baby star at age 5 on stage, screen. Film work in England, Germany, Switzerland, Mexico, Italy. Playwriting with George S. Kaufman; screenplay-writing with Andrew Solt. Wrote and produced with John Croydon, London producer. Wrote produced, directed and starred in The Pawn, filmed in Italy, Vienna, Warner Bros. TV feature. Author, Morning Angel, Boy Doll; Latest play to music for London, in which she stars, There is No Other Prince But Aly. Completed scripts Spirit-Doll. The Resurrection, for Pinewood Studios, London. Features in production, The Lavender Mule From Leningrad and Little Yakov's Visions, Norway. See Carmen Productions under Corporations. 1979, non-fiction books on phenomena: Do You Hear the Voices? and The Kidnapping of Aldo Moro. Wrote TV show, Portrait of Zsa Zsa.

DIMMOCK, PETER: CVO, OBE. Vice President-managing Director ABC Sports Worldwide Enterprises Ltd. b. Dec. 6, 1920. e. Dulwich Coll. & in France, R.A.F. pilot & Staff Officer during war. TV as prod. & commentator BBC Outside Broadcasts Dept., 1946. Prod. more than 500 TV relays including telecast from Windsor Castle of King George VI's funeral, 1952. Coronation telecast Westminster Abbey; State Opening Parliament. Commentator, introduced BBC-TV weekly Sportsview, 1954–64. Head of BBC-TV Outside Broadcasts 1954–72. Head of BBC Enterprises 1973, v.p. ABC Cos., Inc., 1977. Fellow Royal TV Society.

DIPSON, WILLIAM D.: Circuit executive. b. U.S.A., July 24, 1916; e. Phillips Exeter Acad., 1933; Dartmouth Coll., 1937, A.B.; Harvard Law School. Currently pres., Dipson Theatres, Inc.; Army 1940–45. Member: Variety Club of Buffalo, chief barker, 1948.

DISNEY, ROY E. Prod.-dir.-writer, cameraman, film editor. b. January 10, 1930, Los Angeles; e. Pomona College, Calif. 1951 started as page, NBC-TV. Asst. film editor "Dragnet" TV series. 1952–78, Walt Disney Prods., Burbank, Calif., various capacities; now pres. Roy E. Disney Prods.; bd. chm., Shamrock Bldg. Co., bd. dir., Walt Disney.
PICTURES INCLUDE: Perri, Mysteries of the Deep, Pacific High.
TV: Walt Disney's Wonderful World of Color; The Hound

That Thought He Was A Raccoon, Sancho, The Homing Steer, The Silver Fox and Sam Davenport, Wonders of the Water World, Legend of Two Gypsy Dogs, Adventure in Wildwood Heart. Also, The Postponed Wedding, (Zorro series), (Wonder World of Color); An Otter in the Family, My Family Is A Menagerie, Legend of El Blanco, Pancho, The Fastest Paw In The West, The Owl That Didn't Give A Hoot, Varda the Peregrine Falcon, Cristobalito, The Calypso Colt, Three Without Fear, Hamad and the Pirates, Chango, Guardian of the Mayan Treasure, Nosey, the Sweetest Skunk in the World, Mustang!, Call It Courage, Ringo, the Refugee Raccoon, Shokee, the Everglades Panther, Deacon, the High-Noon Dog, Wise One, Whale's Tooth, Track of African Bongo, Dorsey, the Mail-Carrying Dog.

DMYTRYK, EDWARD: Director. b. Grand Forks, B.C., Canada, Sept. 4, 1908. Entered employ Paramount 1923, working after school. Film editor 1930–1939; dir. from 1939.
PICTURES INCLUDE: Murder My Sweet, Back to Bataan, Cornered Crossfire, So Well Remembered, Till the End of Time, Give Us This Day, Mutiny, The Sniper, Eight Iron Men, The Juggler, Caine Mutiny, Broken Lance, End of the Affair, Left Hand of God, Soldier of Fortune, The Young Lions, Where Love Has Gone, Mirage, Alvarez Kelly, Anzio, Bluebeard.

DODD, WILFRID E.: Executive. b. Hamburg, Germany, March 19, 1923. e. Institut Fisher, Montreux (Switzerland), Downside College, Bath (England), Royal Military College, Sandhurst (England). In the '50s formed the Canadian Investing Banking firm: Oswald Drinkwater & Graham Ltd., Vice Pres. and partner. Pres. Allied Artists International Corp., 1964. President of Allied Artists Productions, Inc., 1969. Formed Cinepix Inc., Canadian dist. firm, 1963.

DOLLINGER, IRVING: Exhibitor. Columbia Amusement Co. b. N.Y.C., Sept. 20, 1905; e. U. of Pennsylvania. Stanley-Fabian mgr., 1926. Then with Warner Theatres in New Jersey. Owner and operator of theatre since 1929. Past pres. Allied Theat. Owners of N.J. Pres., Assoc. Theats. of N.J., booking org. 1938–44; v.p. & buyer, Independent Theatre Service Eastern regional v.p. Allied States Assoc., 1949–54; treas., Nat'l Allied, 1955–56; partner, Triangle Theatre Service, 1957; chief barker, N.Y. Tent 35, Variety Club, 1966.

DONAHUE, PHIL: Television Personality. b. 1936. Started daytime talk show in Dayton, Ohio, 1967. Originally called The Phil Donahue Show. Syndicated show, Host, Donahue, now in 165 outlets in U.S. Home base: WGN—TV, Chicago, an independent station. In 1979 a mini-version of show became 3-times-a-week segment on NBC's Today Show. Winner of 2 Emmys.

DONAHUE, TROY: Actor. r.n. Merle Johnson, Jr. b. New York City, Jan. 17, 1937. e. Bayport H.S., N.Y. Military Acad. Directed, wrote, acted in school plays. Journalism, Columbia Univ.; Summer stock, Bucks County Playhouse, Sayville Playhouse; contract, Warner Brothers, 1959.
PICTURES INCLUDE: A Summer Place, The Crowded Sky, Parrish, Susan Slade, Palm Springs Weekend, Rome Adventure, A Distant Trumpet, My Blood Runs Cold, Come Spy With Me, Sweet Savior, Godfather, Part II.
TV: Surfside 6, Hawaiian Eye.

DONALD, JAMES: Actor. b. Aberdeen, Scotland, May 18, 1917; e. Rossall School, McGill U., Edinburgh U. Stage debut: The Scarlet Pimpernel, 1936; screen debut: The Missing Million, 1940.
PICTURES INCLUDE: In Which We Serve, The Way Ahead, Broken Journey, The Small Voice, Trottie True (The Gay Lady), White Corridors, Brandy for the Parson, The Gift Horse, The Pickwick Papers, Lust for Life, Bridge on the River Kwai, The Vikings, Third Man on the Mountain, The Great Escape, King Rat, Cast a Giant Shadow, The Jokers, Epitaph For a Spy, The Royal Hunt of the Sun, David Copperfield, Conduct Unbecoming, The Big Sleep.
THEATRE & TV: Numerous U.S. and Br. TV and stage appearances.

DONCASTER, CARYL: TV writer, prod. b. Liverpool, Eng., Sept. 28, 1923. e. London U. (B.A. Honors). Educational film & film strip prod.; TV as BBC Talks producer in 1948; docum. writer & prod., 1950.
PRODUCTIONS: Made by Hand series, Report on Gambling, Report on Women, Born with the Century, The Rising Twenties, The Declining Years, Make Me an Offer, Pattern of Marriage, Children in Trust, Return to Living, New Canadians, Those Who Dare. Writer, dir., Canadian Venture, 1955; joined Associated Rediffusion, prod., Big City, This Week, People Are Talking, Secret Mission, Mantrap, Boyd Q.C., Outlook, Look In on London, Northern Journey, Members Mail, The Unwanted; head, Assoc. Rediffusion features; free lance TV writer-prod.; writ., dir., School at Sea, Supermarket; Lecturer in prod., Thomson TV; Four Men of India. Prod. BBC TV, Report on Immigrant School Children, on Nurses, 1966; TV experiments in Sierra Leone, 1966. 1968 Nigerian TV; 1969 Documentaries in Mexico, Peru, Java, Zambia, Baffin Island, India.

DONEN, STANLEY: Prod dir. b. Columbia, S.C., April 13; p. Mortie and Helen Donen; e. local public, high schools, U. of South Carolina.

PICTURES INCLUDE: Royal Wedding; Singin' in the Rain; It's Always Fair Weather, Deep in My Heart, Seven Brides for Seven Brothers, On the Town, Funny Face, Pajama Game, Kiss Them for Me, Indiscreet, Damn Yankees, Once More With Feeling, The Grass Is Greener, Charade, Arabesque, Two for the Road, Bedazzled, Staircase, The Little Prince, Lucky Lady, Movie, Movie.

DONIGER, WALTER: Writer, dir. prod. b. New York City. e. Valley Forge Military Academy, Duke University, Harvard Graduate Business School. Entered m.p. business as writer later writer-prod-dir. Wrote documentaries in Army Air Forces M.P. Unit in World War II.

PICTURES INCLUDE: Rope of Sand; Desperate Search, Cease Fire, Safe At Home, House of Women, Duffy of San Quentin, Along the Great Divide, Tokyo Joe, Alaska Seas, Steel Cage, Steel Jungle, Hold Back the Night, Guns of Fort Petticoat, Shannon (pilot) and Movies of Week.

TELEVISION: Delvecchio, Mad Bull, Switch, Moving On, Baa, Baa, Blacksheep, McCloud, The Man and the City, Sarge, Owen Marshall, Peyton Place (200 episodes), Mr. Novak, The Greatest Show On Earth, Travels of Jaimie McPheeters, Outlaws, Hong Kong, Checkmate, Bat Masterson, The Web, Bold Venture, Tombstone Territory, Maverick, Rough Riders, Captain Grief, Lockup, Dick Powell, The Survivors. Bracken's World, Bold Ones, Kung Fu, Barnaby Jones, Marcus Welby, Lucas Tanner.

DONLAN, YOLANDE: Actress. b. Jersey City, June 2; e. Immaculate Heart Convent, Hollywood, Calif. English stage debut in Born Yesterday at the Garrick Theatre (London) 1947; screen debut in Miss Pilgrim's Progress 1950.

PICTURES INCLUDE: To Dorothy a Son, The Body Said No, Traveller's Joy, Mr. Drake's Duck, Penny Princess, They Can't Hang Me, Expresso Bongo, Jigsaw, 80,000 Suspects, The Adventurers, Seven Nights in Japan.

DONNELL, JEFF: Actress. b. South Windham, Me., July 10, 1921. r.n. Jean Donnell, e. Leland Powers Sch. of Theat., Yale Sch. Dram. On stage Farragut Playhouse, Rye Beach, N.H., before screen debut 1942. Summer stock, N.Y., Fla., Ohio, Wash., Calif.

PICTURES INCLUDE: Sweet Smell of Success, My Man Godfrey, Gidget Goes Hawaiian, Gidget Goes to Rome, Fran Maidin, Stand Up and Be Counted.

TV: George Gobel Show, U.S. Steel Hour, Play of the Week, June Allyson, Ann Southern Shows.

DONNELLY, RALPH E.: Executive. b. Lynbrook, New York, Jan. 20, 1932. e. Bellmore (L.I.) Public School; W.C. Mepman High School (1949). Worked for Variety (publication) as writer, 1950; Long Island Press as daily columnist, 1951; joined Associated Independent Theatres, 1953, as gen. mgr.; later film buyer; in 1973 left to become independent buyer and booker for Creative Films; film buyer and v.p., RKO/Stanley Warner Theatres, 1976–79; now v.p. & gen. mgr. for Cinema Ltd. circuit in New York.

DONNENFELD, BERNARD: Exec. b. New York, N.Y. Oct. 28, 1926. e. New York U., LL.B. Admitted to New York, Cal. Bar. Spvsr., corp. affrs., legal dept., Paramount Pictures Corp., New York, 1957–61; exec. asst., asst. secy. corp., Hollywood Studio, 1961–64; asst. to pres., asst. secy. corp., New York, 1964–65; assoc. hd. stud. activities, asst. secy. corp., Hollywood Studio, 1965, v.p. in charge of World Wide Production, Administration, Paramount, 1965–69. Pres. The Filmakers Group, 1970.

DONNER, CLIVE: Director. b. London, Eng. Ent. m.p. ind. 1942.

PICTURES INCLUDE: The Card, Meet Me Tonight, Genevieve, Million Pound Note, Purple Plain, I Am a Camera, The Secret Place, Heart of a Child, Marriage of Convenience, Some People, The Caretaker, Nothing But the Best, What's New Pussy Cat, Luv, Here We Go Round The Mulberry Bush, Alfred the Great, Vampira, Spectre, Rogue Male, Three Hostages, She Fell Among Thieves, The Thief of Baghdad, The Nude Bomb, Carlie Chan and the Curse of the Dragon Queen.

TV: Danger Man, Sir Francis Drake, Mighty and Mystical, British Institutions, Tempo.

DONNER, RICHARD: Director. b. New York City. Began career as actor off-Bdwy. Worked with director Martin Ritt on TV production of Maugham's Of Human Bondage. Moved to California 1958, directing commercials, industrial films and documentaries. First TV drama: Wanted: Dead or Alive (Steve McQueen series).

TELEVISION: Many Movies of the Week; episodes of Kojak, Bronk, etc.; Portrait of a Teen-Age Alcoholic.

PICTURES INCLUDE: The Omen, Superman, The Final Conflict, exec. prod.

DONOHUE, JACK: Director. b. New York City, Nov. 3, 1914. Entered show business as dancer in Ziegfeld Follies; later danced in and directed dances for numerous productions on Broadway and London stage. Dance dir. Fox, Pana., MGM.

PICTURES INCLUDE: Close Up, Yellow Cab Man, Watch the Birdie, Calamity Jane, Lucky Me, Babes in Toyland, Marriage on the Rocks, Assault on a Queen.

THEATRE: Top Banana, Mr. Wonderful.

TV: Frank Sinatra, Dean Martin, Red Skelton, George Gobel, Ed Wynn shows, The Lucy Show, The Jim Nabors Show, Chico and the Man.

DONOVAN, HENRY B.: Executive. producer. b. Boston, Mass. Entered m.p. ind. for RKO Pathe Studios 1932; asst. cameraman, head of property dept., special effects dept., unit mgr.; asst. dir., prod. mgr.; worked on over 300 pictures for many studios; dept. head Sherman Prod. 10 yrs., U.S. Army Signal Corps, as head of dept. of California studios prod. training m.p.; pres. Telemount Pictures, Inc. Prod., dir., writer for Cowboy G Men (TV series).

PICTURES INCLUDE: Hopalong Cassidy Features, Gone with the Wind, Becky Sharp, dir. Our Flag; Magic Lady (live-action TV show); Magic Lady (13 one-reel featurettes), others. Prod. writer, Cowboy G. Men (39 films), TV, 1952–54; Law in Action; Frontier Lawyer; Safe Crackers.

TV: programming, financing, distribution. Global Scope; International TV; Dist., Financing, programming; sls. consultant, Internat'l TV & motion pictures. Cable TV & distribution & program development, collector of movie memorabilia.

DOOLEY, PAUL: Actor. Began career on N.Y. stage in Threepenny Opera. Later member of Second City. Bdwy. credits include The Odd Couple, Adaptation/Next, The White House Murder Case, Hold Me, etc. Co-creator and writer for The Electric Company on PBS. Owns co. called All Over Creation, which produces original industrial films and shows and has created over 1,000 radio commercials.

PICTURES: What's So Bad About Feeling Good?, Slap Shot, Gravy Train, Death Wish, The Out-of-Towners, A Wedding, A Perfect Couple, Rich Kids, Breaking Away, Popeye.

DORAISWAMY, V.: Executive, publicist. b. Trichur, India, 1912. Nat'l Council of YMCA's for India, Burma & Ceylon, 1928; dist. secy., Rotary Inter'l, India, Burma & Ceylon, 1935–42; secy., RCA Photophone Equip., Bombay, 1942; later sales admin. Ed. & Compiler, Asian Film Directory & Who's Who; Film Technician and Theatreman's Diary. India-Ceylon representative, Motion Picture Herald & Motion Picture Daily; Secretary, Cinematographic Suppliers Association of India, Post Box No. 311A, Bombay-1.

DORFMAN, IRVIN S.: Executive. b. New York, Sept. 3, 1924. e. Yale University, 1945 B.A. Following three years in U.S. Navy, joined Dorfman Associates, press rep. organ. handling film, and TV personalities. Handled pub. and promotion for more than 100 B'way shows and worked for 20th Cen.-Fox and U.A. Also produced off-B'way "The Lion in Love." Top ranking amateur tennis star, 1950; pres., Surrogate Releasing and Dandrea Releasing.

DORFMAN, ROBERT S.: Executive. b. New York, N.Y. March 23, 1930. e. CCNY. Newspaper and magazine contact, exploit. mgr. publicity and asst. adv. and publ. dir., Walt Disney Prod. and Buena Vista 1948–64. Joined Seven Arts in 1964 as national promotion dir.; appointed adv. dir. 1966; app'ted nat'l adv. dir. Warner Bros. 1967; Eastern adv.-pub. dir., 1970. Joined 20th Century-Fox as eastern pub. dir., 1980.

DORS, DIANA: Actress. b. Swindon, Wilshire, Oct. 23, 1931; e. Colville House, Swindon; studied at London Acad. of Music and Dramatic Art; first screen role in The Shop at Sly Corner at 14; contract work with J. Arthur Rank Organization at 15.

PICTURES INCLUDE: Lady Godiva Rides Again, The Weak and the Wicked, Is Your Honeymoon Really Necessary, A Kid for Two Farthings, Value for Money, An Alligator Called Daisy, As Long as They're Happy, Yield to the Night (Blonde Sinner), I Married a Woman, Unholy Wife, Long Haul, Tread Softly Stranger, Passport to Shame, Room 43, Love Specialist, Ladies May, On the Double, Mrs. Gibbon's Boys, West Eleven, Allez France, Circus of Blood, Baby Love.

TV: The Innocent.

DORTORT, DAVID: Executive Producer. b. New York, Oct. 23, 1916. e. City Coll. of N.Y. Served U.S. Army, 1943–46. Novelist and short story writer, 1943–49. Also TV writer. Now pres. of Xanadu Prods. and Aurora Enterprises, Inc., Pres. TV branch, WGA, West, 1954–55; TV-radio branch, 1955–57; v.p. PGA, 1967; pres. 1968. Chairman of The Caucus for Producers, Writers and Directors, 1973–75. Pres., PGA, 1980; campaign director, Permanent Charities Comm., 1980–81; chm., Interguild Council 1980–81.

AUTHOR: Novels include Burial of the Fruit and The Post of Honor.

PICTURES INCLUDE: The Lusty Men, Reprisal, The Big Land, Cry in the Night, Clash by Night.

TV: Creator, of Bonanza TV series; High Chaparral, The Chisholms.

71

DOUGHERTY, MARION: Executive. Gained fame as casting director. Acted as co-executive producer on Smile (1975). In 1977 named v.p. in chg. talent for Paramount Pictures. In 1979 joined Warner Bros. v.p. in chg. talent to work with production dept. and producers and directors.

DOUGLAS, GORDON: Director. b. New York, New York. Actor. Hal Roach stock company; writer; callab. Topper series, Housekeeper's Daughter; dir., 30 Our Gang shorts.
PICTURES INCLUDE: Saps at Sea, Broadway Limited, Devil with Hitler, First Yank into Tokyo, San Quentin, If You Knew Suzie, Black Arrow, Walk a Crooked Mile, Doolins of Oklahoma, Mr. Soft Touch, The Nevadan, Between Midnight and Dawn, Kiss Tomorrow Goodbye, Great Missouri Raid, Only the Valient, I Was a Communist for the FBI, Come Fill the Cup, Mara Maru, Iron Mistress, She's Back on Broadway, So This Is Love, The Charge at Feather River, Them, Young at Heart, McConnell Story, Sincerely Yours, Santiago, The Big Land, Bombers B-52, Fort Dobbs, Yellowstone Kelly, Rachel Cade, Gold of 7 Saints, Follow That Dream, Call Me Bwana, Rio Conchos, Robin and the Seven Hoods, Sylvia, Harlow, Stagecoach, Way Way Out, In Like Flint, Chuka, Tony Rome, The Detective, Lady in Cement, Barquero, They Call Me Mr. Tibbs, Slaughter's Big Rip Off, Nevada Smith (MOW), Viva Knieval.

DOUGLAS, KIRK: Actor, Producer, Director. b. Amsterdam, N.Y. Dec. 9, 1918; e. St. Lawrence U; B.A. Stage debut in New York: Spring Again; others: The Sisters, Kiss and Tell; U.S. Navy during World War II; resumed stage work in Trio; did radio soap operas. Signed by Hal B. Wallis from The Wind is Ninety, B'way show, 1945. Screen debut: The Strange Love of Martha Ivers. *President of The Bryna Company. Recipient of U.S. Freedom Medal, 1981.
TV: Mousey, 1974; The Money Changers, 1976.
PICTURES INCLUDE: Out of the Past, I Walk Alone, Mourning Becomes Electra, The Walls of Jericho, Letter to Three Wives, Champion, Young Man With a Horn, The Glass Managerie, Big Carnival, Along the Great Divide, Detective Story, Big Trees, Big Sky, Bad and the Beautiful, Story of Three Loves, The Juggler, Art of Love, Ulysses, Man Without a Star, 20,000 Leagues Under the Sea, The Racers, Indian Fighter, Lust for Life, Top Secret Affair, Gunfight at the OK Corral, Paths of Glory, The Vikings, Last Train from Gun Hill, The Devil's Disciple, Spartacus, Town Without Pity, Lonely Are the Brave, Two Weeks in Another Town, List of Adrian Messenger, For Love or Money, Seven Days in May, In Harms Way, Cast a Giant Shadow, The Way West, The War Wagon, Heroes of Telemark, A Lovely Way to Die, The Brotherhood, The Arrangement, There Was a Crooked Man, A Gunfight, Light at the Edge of the World, Catch Me a Spy, A Man to Respect. Producer: Indian Fighter, The Vikings, Spartacus, Lonely Are The Brave, List of Adrian Messenger, Seven Days in May, The Brotherhood, Summertree, (prod.) Scalawag; (prod., dir., act.) Once Is Not Enough, Posse (prod., dir., act.) The Chosen, The Fury, Home Movies, The Villain, Saturn III, The Final Countdown, The Man from Snowy River.

DOUGLAS, MICHAEL: Actor. b. N. Brunswick, N.J., Sept. 25. f. Kirk Douglas. e. Black Fox Military Academy, Choate, U. of Cal. Worked as asst. director on Lonely Are The Brave, Heroes of Telemark, Cast A Giant Shadow; after TV debut in The Experiment, appeared off-Broadway in City Scene, Pinkville; m.p. debut in Hail Hero, followed by Adam at 6 A.M., Summertree, Napoleon and Samantha, Coma, China Syndrome (also prod.). Co-prod., One Flew Over the Cuckoo's Nest; Running (actor). It's My Turn (actor).
TV: The FBI, Medical Center, When Michael Calls, Streets of San Francisco (series).

DOUGLAS, MIKE: TV host, commentator. r.n. Michael Delaney Dowd, Jr. b. Chicago, 1925. Started career singing with bands in and around Chicago. In 1950 became featured singer with Kay Kyser's band, staying four years. In 1953 became host of WGN-TV's Hi Ladies in Chicago; also featured on WMAQ-TV, Chicago, as singer and host. Moved to Hollywood in late '50s, working as piano bar singer. In 1961 hired as host for new show on station KYW-TV in Cleveland, owned by Westinghouse Bdg. Co., featuring celebrity guests. This became the Mike Douglas Show which was later nationally syndicated and moved base of operations to Philadelphia. Presently is seen in about 130 U.S. outlets and 15 in Canada.

DOUGLAS, VALERIE: Executive. b. Hollywood, CA, Dec. 3. e. UCLA (Journalism). Uncle was actor Elmo Lincoln (first Tarzan). 1945–46, publicist, Vic Shapiro Public Relations; 1946–49, sub-agent, Manning O'Connor Agency; 1949–51, TV coordinator, Bing Crosby Enterprises, Fireside Theatre Series; 1951–52, publicist, RKO Studios; 1952–59, personal mgr., Richard Burton, v.p. & dir. Denham Films, Ltd., London; 1959–61, pub. coordinator, Hecht-Lancaster-Hill; 1961–64, dir. of pub. relations, IPAR Productions, France; 1964–67, v.p., Illustra Films, West Coast branch; 1967–75, asst. dir. pub., United Artists Corp., West

Coast; 1975–78, exec. v.p., Guttman & Pam Public Relations; 1978, formed Suvarie, Inc., m.p. representation, of which is pres., Personal manager, Richard Burton.

DOURIF, BRAD: Actor. b. Huntington, WV. Stage actor before films and TV.
PICTURES INCLUDE: Split, W.W. and the Dixie Dancekings, One Flew Over the Cuckoo's Nest, Group Portrait with Lady, Eyes of Laura Mars, Wise Blood, Heaven's Gate, Ragtime.
TELEVISION: Mound Builders, The Gardeners's Son, Studs Lonigan, Guyana Tragedy—The Story of Jim Jones.

DOWN, LESLEY-ANN: Actress. b. London, England, March 17, 1954. At age of 10 modeled for TV and film commercials, leading to roles in features. At 14 appeared in All the Right Noises (debut).
PICTURES: Pope Joan, Scalawag, Brannigan, The Pink Panther Strikes Again, The Betsy, A Little Night Music, The Great Train Robbery, Hanover Street, Sphinx.
TELEVISION: Upstairs, Downstairs (series), Heartbreak House, The One and Only Phyllis Dixey (film).
STAGE: Great Expectations, Hamlet, etc.

DOWNS, HUGH: Broadcaster. b. Akron, Ohio, Feb. 14, 1921. e. Bluffton Coll., 1938. Wayne Univ. 1941. Col. Univ., NYC, 1955; Supervisor of Science Programming, NBC's Science Dept. one yr.; science consultant for Westinghouse Labs., Ford Foundation, etc.; chm. of bd., Raylin Prods., Inc. Today, Chairman, U.S. Committee for UNICEF. Pres. National Space Institute.
TV: Hawkins Falls, Kukla Fran & Ollie, Short Story Playhouse, American Inventory, Home, Sid Caesar Show, Tonight (Jack Paar Show), Concentration, Today. Host: ABC-TV 20/20 Program, Host: Over-Easy-PBS Network.
RADIO: NBC's Monitor.

DOWSON, GRAHAM R.: Dep. Chief Exec. Rank Organization, 1972–75. Chrm. Erskine House Investments Ltd., Cambridge Communication Ltd., Nimslo Ltd., Pincus Vidler-Arthur Fitzgerald Ltd., 1979. Dir. Carron Company (Holdings) Ltd. b. Southend England, 1923. e. City of London School and Ecole Alpina, Switzerland. 1941; commissioned in RAF serving as pilot with RAF and US Navy. 1946; joined United States Steel Corp. as salesman. 1952; returned to England joining A.C. Nielsen Co., appt. dir. 1954. Council Mem. Incorp. Soc. British Advertisers; Cinema and Television Benevolent Fund. Fellow Inst. Directors and Inst. of Marketing. Mem. Industrial Advertising Assoc. and European Soc. for Opinion Survey and Market Survey. Chrm. British Section European League Economic Co-operation, June 1972. Past pres. of Appeals for National Playing Fields Assoc. Member Carlton Club St. James's, United Service and Royal Aero, vice commodore Royal London Yacht Club, Royal Cork Yacht Club and Royal Air Force Yacht Club. Royal Southern Yacht Club.

DOYLE, KEVIN: Executive. b. Sydney, Aust., June 21, 1933. e. N. Sydney Tech. HS, Aust. Jr. exec., asst. adv. & pub. div., 20th Century-Fox, Aust., 1947–59; adv. & pub. dir., Columbia Pictures Aust., 1960–66; international ad/pub. mgr.; Columbia Pictures Int'l, N.Y. 1966; intl. pub./promo. mgr., 1980.

DRAKE, CHARLES: Actor. r.n. Charles Ruppert; b. New York City, Oct. 2, 1914; e. Nicholas Coll. 1937. With Electric Boat Co., Groton, Conn.; adv. salesman; in little theatres; in m.p. as an actor.
PICTURES INCLUDE: I Wanted Wings, Man Who Came to Dinner, Now, Voyager, Air Force, Mr. Skefflington, Whistle Stop, Pretender, You Came Along, Tender Years, Bowie Knife, Comanche Territory, Air Cadet, Winchester '73, Harvey, Little Egypt, You Never Can Tell, Treasure of Lost Canyon, Red Ball Express, Bonzo Goes to College, Gunsmoke, Lone Hand, It Came from Outer Space, War Arrow, Glenn Miller Story, Tobor the Great, Four Guns to the Border, Female on the Beach, All That Heaven Allows, Price of Fear, The Arrangement.

DRAKE, CHARLIE: Actor, comedian, scriptwriter. b. London, England. Ent. TV in Nuffield Centre Show, 1950. Two years children's television followed by Askey Show, Star Time, Benny Hill Show, Fast and Loose. Two-and-a-half years children's television programme, Mick and Montmorency. Own BBC show 1958–9; signed film contract with Associated British studios, 1959–61.
TV: Charlie Drake Show, BBC TV, 1965; TV show, The Worker, Meet Peters & Lee 1976.
PICTURES INCLUDE: Sands of the Desert, Petticoat Pirates, The Cracksman, Mr. Ten Per Cent, Professor Poppers Problems 1975.

DRAKE, DONA: Actress. r.n. Rita Nevella; b. Mexico City.
PICTURES INCLUDE: Louisiana Purchase, Road to Morocco, Star Spangled Rhythm, So This is New York, Another Part of the Forest, Beyond the Forest, Valentino, Bandits of Corsica, Kansas City Confidential, Son of Belle Starr, Princess of the Nile.

DREIFUSS, ARTHUR: Producer-director-writer. b. Frankfurt on Main. e. Univ. of Frankfurt on Main, Germany, Conservatory of Music, Columbia University; choreographer, producer; many U. lectures; legit. producer: Allure, Baby Pompadour; producer many night club shows; associate producer Fanchon & Marco, Hollywood; dir. over 50 features, many musical shorts for Columbia, RKO, Universal, Allied Artists, Ind. to 1952; director Paul Muni debut Screen Gems-Ford Theatre, TV 1953; prod-director Secret File, U.S.A. Official Films; TV 1954–54; prod-dir: features Secret File and Assignment Abroad, Anglo-Amalgamated, London, 1956; dir: The Last Blitzkrieg; Life Begins at Seventeen; Juke Box Rythm, Columbia 1958–59; writer-director Brendan Behan's The Quare Fello British-Lion-Bryanston, London, 1961–62; director: Riot on Sunset Strip, AIP; The Love-Ins, For Singles Only, Columbia; The Young Runaways, A Time to Sing, MGM, 1963 to 1968; assoc. producer Angel, Angel, Down We Go, AIP, 1969; executive producer New Age Productions, 1970 to 1972; executive producer The Peter Hurkos Show, CBS; writer Owl Hill; Dolls behind Walls, 1973, director, Wildlife in Crisis, Viacom TV series 1975. Assoc. prod. Chennault China Tiger (Genson Prods.), 1978; assoc. video editor Creative Editing, Inc., 1979–80.

DREW, ELLEN: Actress. Previously known as Terry Ray. b. Kansas City, Mo. Nov. 23, 1915. Played on stage. Appeared in many pictures for major companies. In 1940: Women Without Names, Buck Benny Rides Again, Christmas in July, Texas Rangers Ride Again, Par. Many others.

DREXLER, ELIAS J.: Executive. b. New York City, Dec. 24, 1911. e. Columbia University, Columbia Law School, L.L.B. 1936. Special agent. Div. of Investigations, U.S. Dept. of Interior, 1937–40; dir., Preclusive operations, 1944–45; dir., Surlluettgterty Div., Foreign Economic Admin; exec., National Screen Service, 1945–56; general counsel and nat. sales mgr. AGFA-Gavaert; 1956–65; nat. sales mgr. and exclusive U.S. and Mexican dist. of motion picture products manufactured by Fuji Photo Film Co., Ltd., Tokyo, Japan, 1965-present.

DREYFUSS, RICHARD: Actor. b. Brooklyn, N.Y., 1949. e. Beverly Hills High. Prof. career began at Gallery Theatre (L.A.) in In Mama's House. Has also acted off-Bdwy. and on Bdwy.
PICTURES INCLUDE: Hello Down There, The Young Runaways, American Graffiti, The Apprenticeship of Duddy Kravitz, Jaws, Inserts, Close Encounters of the Third Kind, The Goodbye Girl, The Big Fix (also co-prod.) The Competition, Whose Life Is It Anyway?
TV: The Big Valley, Room 222, Judd For the Defense, Mod Squad, The Bold Ones.
STAGE: Journey to the Day, Incident at Vichy, People Need People, Enemy, Enemy, Line, Whose Little Boy Are You, But Seriously, Major Barbara, The Time of Your Life.

DRU, JOANNE: Actress. r.n. Joanne La Cock; b. Logan, W. Virginia, Jan. 31, 1923. John Robert Powers model: on stage as showgirl in Hold on to Your Hats; a Samba Siren at Ritz Carlton & Paramount; with theatrical group under Batami Schneider. Hollywood: m.p. debut in Abie's Irish Rose, 1946.
PICTURES INCLUDE: Red River, She Wore a Yellow Ribbon, All the King's Men, Wagonmaster, Vengeance Valley, 711 Ocean Drive, Mr. Belvedere Rings the Bell, Siege at Red River, Outlaw Territory, Southwest Passage, Three Ring Circus, Day of Triumph, Hell on Frisco Bay, Sincerely Yours, The Warriors.

DRURY, JAMES: Actor. b. N.Y.C. ed. N.Y. Univ. Acting debut at age 8 in Biblical play for children at Greenwich Settlement Playhouse. Performed on stage while youngster. Signed by MGM in 1955, working one day in each of seven movies that year, including Blackboard Jungle. Then got two-year contract at 20th-Fox. Gained fame as hero of TV series, The Virginian, which had nine-year run.
PICTURES INCLUDE: Love Me Tender, Bernardine.
TELEVISION: The Virginian, The Devil and Miss Sarah (movie of week), Firehouse (series).

DRURY, WESTON, JR.: Freelance casting director. b. Leeds, England, April 1916. Ent. m.p. ind. 1933. Rank Organization 1946–71; I.T.C. Ltd. 74–76. TV series include Return of the Saint, TV series 1977–78, Danger U. X. B. Minder; Masada, The Acts of Peter and Paul.

DRUXMAN, MICHAEL B.: Publicist, producer. b. Seattle, Wash., Feb. 23, 1941. e. Univ. of Washington. m.p. exec. v.p., Seattle Civic Playhouse, 1962–63; founder, exec. dir., Actor's Theatre, Seattle; formed public relations firm, Michael B. Druxman and Associates.
CREDITS: Genesis (wrote, prod., dir.); produced and directed plays in the Los Angeles area—A Shot in the Dark, A Thousand Clowns.

DUBBINS, DON: Actor. b. Brooklyn, N.Y., June 28. Appeared in stock company of Mr. Roberts, also Tea and Sympathy. Many television shows including Ed Sullivan show.
PICTURES INCLUDE: From Here to Eternity, Caine Mutiny, Tribute to a Bad Man, These Wilder Years, The D.I., Gunfight in Abilene, The Illustrated Man.

DUBENS, STANLEY: Writer-Producer. b. London, England, 1920. e. St. Paul's School, s. of Harry Dubens, Royal Corps Signals 1939–1945. From 1946, agent and theatrical productions. Ent. film production 1963. Currently making commercials, Doc., Film and video.
THEATRE: prod. incl. Sweet and Low, And No Birds Sing, The Train for Venice, The Man Who Let it Rain, The Hands of Eurydice, I Want to See Mioussov, Sign Here Please.
PICTURE INCLUDE: Tperation Snatch, Live Now Pay Later, The World Ten Times Over, Modesty Blaise, Marble Heroes, Matchgirls, Archie's Caper. 1975 formed with Roger Moss, The Original Electric Picture Company, making commercials, doc., video, AV presentations.

DUBIN, JOSEPH S.: Attorney, Los Angeles, Calif.: Chief Studio Counsel, Universal Pictures, Calif., 1950–1970; Member, U.S. State Department International Copyright Panel, Panel of Consultants on General Revision of Copyright Law, Panel of Neighboring Rights; Chairman, Copyright Subsection, ABA (1956); Member of Council, Patent Trademark and COLTIGT ABA (1957–61); Past Chairman, Committee on Related Rights, ABA; Past Chairman, Committee on Program for Revision of Copyright Law, ABA (1961–1969); Past Chairman, Committee on International Copyrights, AIPPI; Past Chairman, Committee on Copyright Law, APLA (1964–1969); Member, Board of Managers, APLA (1969–1972); President, Los Angeles Copyright Society (1964–65).
AUTHOR: Copyright Relations Between Nations; Copyright—Duration of Protection; Copyright—Formalities; Moral Rights and Protection for U.S. Works; Copyright Aspects of Sound Recordings; Universal Copyright Convention; Motion Picture Recordings; Universal Copyright Convention; Motion Picture Rights—U.S. and International; An Exclusive Federal System for All Works; Neighboring Rights; The New French Copyright Law of 1957; Wartime Extensions of Copyright in Europe; International Developments in Copyrights; Copyright Relations with the Soviet Bloc and Less Industrialized Nations; The New German Copyright Law of 1965; Copyright Duration. Waiver of the exercise of the Droit Moral.

DUDELHEIM, HANS R.: Producer—Director—Editor. Began film career in Germany after World War II. Hired by U.S. Army Signal Corps as photographer, being sent to Far East Command. Came to New York, where joined ABC-TV as film editor. Beginning with hard news, moved to documentaries, editing many films. In 1981 established Cinema Arts Associates, Inc. as film society; 1966 expanded into indep. m.p. prod. co., of which he is pres.

DUDELSON, STANLEY E.: Executive. b. Cleveland, O., July 12, 1924. Regnl. sales mgr., Hygo-Unity; natl. sales mgr. Screen Gems; producer's rep., Selma Ent., Italian Intl. Uni-Export Films of Rome, AIP; first vice pres., American Intl. Television, Inc. Now with New Line Dist. Corp., pres., New Line Intl. Releasing.

DUFF, HOWARD: Actor. Bremerton, Wash. Nov. 24, 1917: e. Reportory Playhouse, Seattle. With KOMO radio station 1935; served with U.S. Army 1941–5; entered m.p. 1947. Radio's original Sam Spade.
PICTURES INCLUDE: Brute Force, Naked City, All My Sons, Calamity Jane and Sam Bass, Illegal Entry, Johnny Stoolpigeon, Woman in Hiding, Shakedown, Lady from Texas, Models Inc., Spaceways, Roar of the Crowd, Jennifer, Tanganyika, Private Hell 36, Women's Prison, Yellow Mountain, Flame of the Islands, Broken Star, Sierra Stranger, Blackjack Ketchum Desperado, While the City Sleeps, Boy's Night Out, Syria Against Babylon, Panic in the City, The Late Show, A Wedding, Kramer vs. Kramer, Oh, God! Book II.
TV: Mr. Adams and Eve, Dante, Felony Squad; Movies of the Week: The D.A. and The Heist.

DUFFY, JAMES E.: Executive. b. Decatur, Ill. e. Beloit College. Radio announcer, then reporter; joined publicity dept., ABC in 1949; named director of adv. & Promo., then account exec. for Central division of ABC Radio Network; director of sales ABC Radio, 1957; central division account exec., ABC Television Network, 1955: natl. director of Sales, ABC Radio central division, 1960; vice president, ABC Radio Network, 1961; exec. v.p. & natl. director of sales, 1962; vice president in charge of sales, ABC Television Network, 1963; president, ABC Television Network, 1970.

DUFFY, PATRICK: Actor. b. Townsend, Mont., March 17. e. Univ. of Washington. Became actor-in-residence in state of Washington, where performed with various statefunded groups. Acted off-Bdwy. Taught mime and movement classes in summer camp in Seattle. Moved to L.A. and began TV acting career.
TELEVISION: Movies: The Stranger Who Looks Like Me, Hurricane. Series: Man from Atlantis (star), Switch (guest), Dallas (star).

DUKE, PATTY: Actress. b. New York, N.Y., Dec. 14, 1947. e. Quintano School for Young Professionals.

THEATRE: The Miracle Worker, Isle of Children.
PICTURES INCLUDE: The Miracle Worker, Valley of the Dolls, Billie, My Sweet Charlie, Me, Natalie, The Swarm.
TV: Armstrong Circle Theatre, The Prince and the Pauper, Wuthering Heights, United States Steel Hour, Meet Me in St. Louis, Swiss Family Robinson, The Power and the Glory; now star, The Patty Duke Show.

DULLEA, KEIR: Actor. b. Cleveland, Ohio, May 30, 1936. e. San Francisco State College, Sanford Meisner's Neighborhood Playhouse. Worked as ice cream vendor, carpenter with a construction co. Acted as resident juvenile at the Totem Pole Playhouse in Pa. N.Y. theatre debut in the revue Sticks and Stones, 1956; appeared in stock co. prods. at the Berkshire Playhouse and Philadelphia's Hedgerow Theatre, 1959, off-Broadway debut in Season of Choice, 1969, Butterflies Are Free.
TV: All Summer Long.
PICTURES INCLUDE: The Hoodlum Priest, David and Lisa (Best Actor Award, San Francisco Intern'l Film Festival), The Thin Red Line, Mail Order Bride, The Naked Hours, Madame X, Bunny Lake Is Missing, The Fox, 2001: A Space Odyssey, de Sade, Pope Joan, Paul and Michelle, The Paperback Hero, Silent Night, Evil Night, Leopard in the Snow.

DUNAWAY, FAYE: Actress. b. Bascom, Fla., Jan. 14, 1941. e. Texas, Arkansas, Utah, Germany, University of Fla., Awarded a Fulbright scholarship in Theatre. Boston U. of Fine Applied Arts. Appeared on N.Y. stage in: A Man For All Seasons, After the Fall (with Lincoln Center Repertory Co., three years), Hogan's Goat.
PICTURES INCLUDE: The Happening, Bonnie and Clyde, Hurry Sundown, The Thomas Crown Affair, The Extraordinary Seaman, A Place for Lovers, The Arrangement, Puzzle of a Downfall Child, Little Big Man, Doc, Oklahoma Crude, The Three Musketeers, Chinatown, The Towering Inferno, The Four Musketeers, Three Days of the Condor, Network, Voyage of the Damned, Eyes of Laura Mars, The Champ, The First Deadly Sin, Mommie Dearest.
TV: The Disappearance of Aimee, Evita.

DUNCAN, SANDY: Actress. b. Henderson, Tex., Feb. 20, 1946. e. Len Morris Col.
STAGE: Ceremony of Innocence, Your Own Thing, Canterbury Tales, etc.
PICTURES INCLUDE: $1,000,000 Duck, Star Spangled Girl, The Cat From Outer Space.
TV: The Sandy Duncan Show, Roots.

DUNING, GEORGE: Composer, Conductor, Arranger. b. Richmond, Ind., Feb. 25; e. Cincinnati Conservatory of Music; University of Cincinnati. Musical director; music scores for many m.p. including: Jolson Sings Again, Eddy Duchin Story, From Here to Eternity, Picnic, World of Susie Wong, Devil at 4 O'Clock, Toys in the Attic, Any Wednesday, The Man with Bogart's Face. TV: No Time for Sergeants, Wendy and Me, The Farmer's Daughter, Big Valley, The Long Hot Summer, The Second Hundred Years, Star Trek, Mannix, Then Came Bronson; music dir. Aaron Spelling Prods., 1970–71, Bobby Sherman Show, "Movies" of Week—NBC, CBS, ABC. OPT. Board of directors, ASCAP.

DUNLAP, RICHARD D.: Producer, director. b. Pomona, Calif., Jan. 30, 1923; e. Yale U., B.A., 1944; M.F.A., 1948. U.S. Navy 1943–46; Instructor, English dept., Yale U., 1947–48; Prod.-dir., Kraft TV Theatre, 3 years; Dir., Assoc. Prod., Omnibus, 3 seasons; Dir., 25 half-hr. Dramatic Film Shows. Frank Sinatra Specials, Prod.-Dir., 10 Academy Award Shows, 4 Emmy Award Shows.

DUNNE, DOMINICK: Producer. Began career as stage manager at NBC-TV; then produced shows for CBS Studio One. Later exec. prod. at 20th-Fox TV, v.p. at Four Star.
PICTURES INCLUDE: Boys in the Band (exec. prod.), The Panic in Needle Park, Play It As It Lays, Ash Wednesday.

DUNNE, IRENE: Actress. b. Louisville, Ky., Dec. 20. e. Loretta Academy in St. Louis, Mo.; Chicago Coll. of Music (D.M., 1945), N.Y.; one child, Mary Frances. Screen debut 1931.
THEATRE: Stage prods. include Sweetheart Time, The City Chap, Show Boat.
PICTURES INCLUDE: Cimarron, Consolation Marriage, Back Street, Silver Cord, Ann Vickers, The Age of Innocence, Sweet Adeline, Roberta, The Magnificent Obsession, Showboat, The Awful Truth, Invitation to Happiness, My Favorite Wife, Penny Serenade, Lady in a Jam, A Guy Named Joe, The White Cliffs, Together Again, Over 21, Anna and the King of Siam, Life With Father, I Remember Mama, Never A Dull Moment, The Mudlark, It Grows on Trees, Love Affair, Theodora Goes Wild.

DUNNE, PHILIP: Writer-prod. dir. b. N.Y.C., Feb. 11, 1908; p. Finley P. and Margaret Abbott Dunne; e. Harvard Univ.; m. Amanda Duff.
PICTURES INCLUDE: How Green Was My Valley, Stanley and Livingstone, The Rains Came, Johnnie Apollo, Son of Fury, Suez, Lancer Spy, The Last of the Mohicans, The Count of Monte Cristo, The Late George Apley, Forever Amber, The Ghost and Mrs. Muir, Escape, Luck of the

Irish, Pinky, David and Bathsheba, Anne of the Indies, Lydia Bailey, Way of a Gaucho, Demetrius and the Gladiators, The Egyptian, Prince of Players, View from Pompey's Head, Hilda Crane, Three Brave Men, Ten North Frederick, In Love and War, Blue Denim, Wild In The Country, Lisa, Blindfold, The Agony and the Ecstasy.
PUBLICATIONS: Mr. Dooley Remembers, Atlantic-Little Brown. Take Two (McGraw Hill, 1980).

DUNNING, JOHN: Film editor. b. Los Angeles, Calif., May 5, 1916; e. U.C.L.A., A.B., 1939. With MGM since 1935; U.S. Armed Forces, 1942–45.
PICTURES INCLUDE: Cass Timberlane, Homecoming, Julia Misbehaves, Battleground, Show Boat, Julius Caesar, Take the High Ground, Rhapsody, Last Time I Saw Paris, Tender Trap, Interrupted Melody, The Swan, Brothers Karamazov, Raintree County, Cimarron, Ben-Hur (Academy Award).
Post prod. supervisor, MGM, Inc.

DUNNOCK, MILDRED: Actress. b. Baltimore, Md., Jan. 25,; e. Goucher Co., Baltimore. Teacher, Brearly Sch., N.Y.; acted in summer stock.
THEATRE: Prof. B'way debut, Corn Is Green; since in Richard III, Vicki, Lute Song, Another Part of the Forest, Cat on a Hot Tin Roof, The Chinese, Colette.
PICTURES INCLUDE: Corn Is Green, Kiss of Death, I Want You, Death of a Salesman, Viva Zapata, Girl in White, The Jazz Singer, Bad for Each Other, Hansel & Gretel (voice), Trouble with Harry, Love Me Tender, Sweet Bird of Youth, Whatever Happened to Aunt Alice?, Dragonfly.
TV: Death of a Salesman.

DUPONT, ADLEY: Actress. r.n. Adley Stoltz. b. New York City, Aug. 7, 1946. e. Geller School of Theatre, Film Industry Workshop, Desilu School.
PICTURES INCLUDE: Movie Star, The Golden Poodle.

DURBRIDGE, FRANCIS: Writer. b. Hull, England, Nov. 25, 1912. e. Birmingham University. Early career, radio playwright and novelist; entered TV 1946.
TV PLAYS AND SERIALS INCLUDE: Broken Horseshoe, Operation Diplomat, Teckman Biography, Portrait of Alison, My Friend Charles, A Time of Day, The Scarf, The Other Man, The Desperate People, Bat Out of Hell, The Passenger, The Dool.
TV: The World of Tim Frazier, Melissa.
PICTURES INCLUDE: The Teckman Mystery, The Vicious Circle.
THEATRE: London stage play: Suddenly At Home, The Gentle Hook, Murder With Love.
RADIO PLAYS: Paul Temple plays, La Boutique.

DURNING, CHARLES: Actor. Many stage credits on Broadway (That Championship Season, The Happiness Cage, etc.).
PICTURES: Harry and Walter Go to New York, Twilight's Last Gleaming, The Choirboys, Breakheart Pass, The Hindenburg, Enemy of the People, The Sting, Dog Day Afternoon, The Fury, The Greek Tycoon, Tilt, The Muppet Movie, North Dallas Forty, Starting Over, When a Stranger Calls, The Final Countdown.
TELEVISION: Captains and the Kings, The Rivalry, The Dancing Bear, The Copy and the Kid (1975 series), Queen of the Stardust Ballroom, Studs Lonigan.

DURSTON, DAVID E.: Writer-Director. b. Newcastle, Pa., Sept. 10, 1925. e. Evanston Township H.S. Served as TV-Radio director, Lynn Baker Adv. Agency, 1952–57; assoc. producer, Your Hit Parade, 1957–58. Acting credits include Winged Victory (B'way, film), Young Man's Fancy (B'way); TV writing credits include Tales of Tomorrow, Navy Log.
PICTURES: Felicia, Love Statue, Reflections, Blue Sextet (also edited), I Drink Your Blood, Stigma.

DURWOOD, RICHARD M.: Executive. b. Kansas City, MO., Aug. 18, 1929. e. Brown Univ. (A.B.). Pres. Crown Cinema Corp. Member: Motion Picture Assn. of Kansas City (pres.); United Motion Picture Assn. (pres. 1972–73); Young NATO (chm., 1968–69); National NATO bd., Past Chief Barker, Tent #8; exec. comm., National NATO.

DURWOOD, STANLEY H.: President, American Multi-Cinema, Inc.; BS Harvard College (Varsity Football, Varsity Wrestling); Air Force navigator 3 years; six children. Member: Harvard Club of Kansas City; Harvard Club of New York; Rotary, Chamber of Commerce (board of directors); Downtown, Inc. (board of directors), United Motion Picture Assoc. of America, Variety Club International. Board of Directors and major stockholder First National Charter Corp. (23 bank holding company), Kansas City, Mo.

DUTFIELD, RAY: Executive. Early career as chief accountant to in Hawker Siddeley Group. Ent. m.p. ind. 1957, as exec. accountant with Rank Film Laboratories, gen. man., 1967; Appt. to board of dir., 1969; Appt. man. dir., 1970. Appt. man. dir., Rank Leisure Services, 1976 and vice-chmn., Rank Film Labortories. 1979 January appt. chmn. and chief executive officer, Technicolor Limited, and v.p., Technicolor Cinema Systems, Hollywood, Fellow Member of Inst.

Chartered Accounts, SMPTE, BKSTS, Member Institute of Directors, Institute of Marketing.

DUVALL, ROBERT: Actor. b. San Diego, Calif., 1931.
PICTURES INCLUDE: To Kill a Mockingbird, Captain Newman, M.D., The Chase, Countdown, The Detective, Bullitt, True Grit, The Rain People, M*A*S*H*, The Revolutionary, THX-1138, The Godfather, Tomorrow, The Great Northfield, Minn. Raid, Joe Kidd, Lady Ice, Badge 373, The Outfit, The Conversation, Godfather, Part II, Breakout, The Killer Elite, 7½ Per Cent Solution, Network, The Eagle Has Landed, The Greatest, The Betsy, True Confessions, Pursuit.

DUVALL, SHELLEY: Actress. b. Houston, TX, 1949.
PICTURES INCLUDE: Brewster McCloud, McCabe and Mrs. Miller, Thieves Like Us, Nashville, Three Women, Annie Hall, The Shining, Popeye.

DWAN, ALLAN: Director. b. Toronto, Ont. Canada, April 3, 1885; e. Notre Dame, Ind.; m. First film work writing and selling a scenario to Essanay. With American Film Co., San Diego, Cal., as scenarist, scenario ed. and dir. for three years. Dir. for Selznick, Goldwyn, Triangle, C. K. Young Prod., Louise Glaum Prod., then organized own co. Later connected with Associated Exhibitors, American Releasing Corp., UA, Douglas Fairbanks' pictures, Robin Hood, and Par., switching in 1926 to Fox, and later to FN. In 1941; prod.-dir. Look Who's Laughing, RKO; director Rise and Shine, 20th-Fox. In 1942; Prod. and dir. Here We Go Again; dir. Friendly Enemies, Up in Mabel's Room, Around the World, Abroad with Two Yanks, Brewster's Millions.
PICTURES INCLUDE: Northwest Outpost, Driftwood, Montana Belle, Calendar Girl, Inside Story, Sands of Iwo Jima, Surrender, Belle Le Grand, Wild Blue Yonder, I Dream of Jeanie, Woman They Almost Lynched, Flight Nurse, Silver Lode, Passion, Cattle Queen of Montana, Escape to Burma, Pearl of the South Pacific, Tennessee's Partner, Slightly Scarlet, Hold Back the Night, Restless Breed, River's Edge.

E

EADES, WILFRID: Director, producer, writer. b. England, 1920. Early career studying civil engineering. Ent. m.p. ind. as camera asst. 1939; asst. dir. prod. man., 2nd unit dir. since 1950.
PICTURES INCLUDE: No Place for Jennifer, The Last Holiday, Yellow Balloon, Moby Dick, Tarzan and the Lost Safari, You Can't Escape, The Small Hotel, The Moonraker, Gorgo.
TV: The Man in Half Moon Street, Portrait in Black, Wolf Pack, The Franchise Affair, I Can Destroy the Sun, Please Murder Me, Soundings, The Dangerous Word, To Ride a Tiger, The Angry Flower, Other People's Houses, The Upstart, Each Wind That Blows, The Intruder, Harriet, Then We Fail, Exits and Entrances, A Sickening Thud, Deadline Midnight, Echo Two Four, Tales of Mystery, No Hiding Place, The Pursuers, The Danny Thomas Show in Europe, TV Script adaptations: The Man in Half Moon Street, Portrait In Black, Wolf Pack, The Franchise Affair, Each Wind That Blows.
1963: exec. prod., Zenith Film Prod. Ltd.; 1964: prod. sup., Light Out of Darkness, 2nd unit dir., Operation Crossbow. 1965–68; gen. man., Ardmore Studios, Ireland. 1966: assoc. prod. Ulysses. 1968–69: Prod., The Violent Enemy; 1969 2nd unit dir. The Kremlin Letter. 1970–71: Exec. in chg. of prod., Interservice Mediterranean Ltd.; Britannia Studios, Inc., Ltd. 1972: prod. controller. Pictures at an Exhibition for CIP Ltd. 1973–75 Story and Prod. Adviser, Star Services (Isle of Man) Ltd., 1976 Chief Exec. Eurofilm Advisers Ltd.

EASTWOOD, CLINT: b. San Francisco, Calif., May 31. e. Oakland Technical High School, Los Angeles City College. Worked as a lumberjack in Oregon before being drafted into the Army. Starred in TV series Rawhide, for seven and a half years. Formed Malpaso Productions, 1969.
PICTURES INCLUDE: A Fistful of Dollars, For a Few Dollars More, The Witches, The Good The Bad and The Ugly, Paint Your Wagon, Hang 'Em High, Coogan's Bluff, Where Eagles Dare, Kelly's Heroes, Two Mules For Sister Sara, Beguiled, Play Misty For Me (dir. and star); Magnum Force, Breezy (dir.); Thunderbolt & Lightfoot; The Eiger Sanction, The Outlaw Josey Wales, The Enforcer, The Gauntlet (dir., star), Every Which Way But Loose, Escape from Alcatraz, Bronco Billy (dir., star), Any Which Way You Can.

EBERSON, DREW: Architect. Stamford, Conn; b. Hamilton, Ohio, Feb. 29, 1904; e. Northwestern, Military and Naval Academy; University of Pennsylvania, Architect U.S.A. and England. WB production, Burbank. In 1931–38: Director,

Coronet Pictures. Then theatre architect practicing throughout U.S.A. in 1942: Colonel, Corps of Engineers.

EBSEN, BUDDY: Actor. b. Belleville, Ill., April 2, 1908. r.n. Christian Ebsen, Jr. e. Univ. of Fla., Rollins College. Won first Broadway role as dancer in Ziegfeld's Whoopee in 1928. Sister, Vilma, became dancing partner and they played nightclubs and did road tours. Went to Hollywood and appeared in many musicials as single. Later became dramatic actor and appeared on TV.
PICTURES INCLUDE: Broadway Melody of 1936, Captain January, Banjo on My Knee, Four Girls in White, My Lucky Star, Thunder in God's Country, Red Garters, Davy Crockett, Attack, Breakfast at Tiffany's, Mail Order Bride, The Family Band.
TELEVISION: Hawaii Five-O, Gunsmoke, The Beverly Hillbillies, Davy Crockett, Barnaby Jones.
STAGE: Take Her, She's Mine, Our Town.

EBY, GEORGE W.: Executive. b. Pittsburgh, Pa., Jan. 2, 1914. e. Carnegie Tech.: Penna. State U., BA 1934. pres., Ice Capades, Inc., 1963–78, chm., Jan. 1, 1979; Int. Chief Barker Variety Clubs, 1958–60.

ECKERT, JOHN M.: Co-Producer, Assoc. Producer. b. Chatham, Ontario, Canada, 1948.
PICTURES INCLUDE: Middle Age Crazy, 1979 (co-prod.), Running, 1978 (co-prod.), Power Play, 1977 (assoc. prod.), The Clown Murders, 1975 (Associate Prod.) As Prod. Man/Assist. Dir.; Second Wind, 1975, Sudden Fury, 1974. First assist. dir. Rituals, Find the Lady, It Seemed Like a Good Idea at the Time, Lions for Breakfast. Second unit asst. dir., Silver Streak. Second asst. dir., Equus, Black Christmas. Various TV dramas and series.

EDELE, DURAND (BUD) J.: Executive e. St. Louis U., Washington U. Reportorial staff, St. Louis Globe Democrat, 1934–35; booking dept., Paramount, 1935; booker & salesman, Warner Bros., 1936–41; branch & dist. mgr., Film Classics, 1946; branch mgr., United Artists, 1952–60; managed various divisions, United Artists, 1960–63; gen. sales mgr., v.p., Avco Embassy Pictures Corp., 1964, gen. sales mgr., Venture Dist. Inc., 1976; Consultant, RCMC 1976–78.

EDWARDS, BLAKE: Writer-director-producer. b. Tulsa, Okla., July 26, 1922. e. Beverly Hills High. Coast Guard during war.
RADIO: Johnny Dollar. Line-Up; writer-creator: Richard Diamond.
TV: creator: Dante's Inferno, Peter Gunn, Mr. Lucky.
PICTURES INCLUDE: Panhandle, Stampede, Sound Off, Bring Your Smile Along, All Ashore, Crusin' Down the River, Rainbow Round My Shoulder, He Laughed Last, Drive a Crooked Road, My Sister Eileen, Mr. Cory, This Happy Feeling, The Perfect Furlough, Operation Mad Ball, Notorious Landlady, Operation Petticoat, High Time, Breakfast at Tiffany's, Experiment in Terror, Days of Wine and Roses, Soldier in the Rain, The Pink Panther, Shot in the Dark, The Great Race, What Did You Do in the War, Daddy, Gunn, Darling Lili, The Party, The Wild Rovers, Carey Treatment, The Tamarind Seed (dir. s.p.) The Return of the Pink Panther (prod., dir., co-s.p.), The Pink Panther Strikes Again (prod., dir., co-s.p.), Revenge of the Pink Panther (prod., dir., co-s.p.); "10" (co-prod., dir., s.p.), "S.O.B." (co-prod., dir., Victor/Victoria (co-prod., dir., s.p.).

EDWARDS, DOUGLAS: News Correspondent. b. Ada, Okla, July 14, 1917. Became radio reporter in Troy, Ala., at 15 yrs. e. Univ. of Ala., Emory Univ., Univ. of Ga. News reporter for WAGF, Dothan, Ala.; ass't. news editor for Atlanta Journal and its station, WSB. Transferred to WXYZ, Detroit, returning to WSB as ass't news editor 2 yrs. later. Joined CBS Radio News staff, 1942, appearing on Report to the Nation, and The World Today. Chief of CBS News Paris Bureau. First major newsman to make transition to TV, 1947. Anchorman on CBS Afternoon News and Douglas Edwards with the News for 15 years on CBS-TV. Presently on CBS Mid-Day News with Douglas Edwards.

EDWARDS, JAMES H.: Executive. President, Storey Theatres, Inc. b. Cedartown, GA, Aug. 14, 1927. e. Georgia State. U.S. Navy, 1948–50. With Ga. Theatre Co., 1950–1952; Storey Theatres, 1952–present. Pres., NATO of Ga; formerly pres., Variety Club of Atlanta. Director at large, Nat'l. NATO. Director, numerous theatre cos.

EDWARDS, VINCE: Actor. b. New York City, July 9, 1928. e. Ohio State U., Univ. of Hawaii, Amer. Acad. of Dram. Arts. N.Y. stage. High Button Shoes.
TV APPEARANCES INCLUDE: Studio One, Philco, Kraft, Ben Casey, The Untouchables, General Electric Theatre, Hitchcock, The Deputy, Firehouse (movie), The Rhinemann Exchange.
PICTURES INCLUDE: Sailor Beware, Hiawatha, Rogue Cop, Night Holds Terror, Serenade, The Killing, Hit and Run, The Scavengers, The Three Faces of Eve, City of Fear, Murder by Contract, The Victors, Devil's Brigade, The Desperados, Las Vegas, Los Angeles.

EGAN, RICHARD: Actor. b. San Francisco, Calif., July 29, 1923. e. U. of San Francisco, B.A.; Stanford U., M.A.; U.S. Army, 1942–46; then taught public speaking; several TV appearances.
PICTURES INCLUDE: Damned Don't Cry, Undercover Girl, Bright Victory, One Minute to Zero, Devil Makes Three, Blackbeard the Pirate, Split Second, Demetrius and the Gladiators, Wicked Woman, Gog, Khyber Pass, Underwater, Untamed. Violent Saturday, View from Pompey's Head, Seven Cities of Gold, Revolt of Mamie Stover, Love Me Tender, Tension At Table Rock, These Thousand Hills, A Summer Place, Pollyanna, Esther and the King, The Lion of Sparta, Valley of Mystery, The Big Cube.

EGGAR, SAMANTHA: Actress. b. London, Eng., 1940.
PICTURES INCLUDE: The Wild and the Willing, Dr. Crippen, Doctor in Distress, Psyche 59, The Collector, Walk, Don't Run, Return From the Ashes, Doctor Dolittle, Molly Maguires, The Lady in the Car, Walking Stick, The Grove, Light at the Edge of the World, 7½ Solution, Why Shoot the Teacher, Blood City, The Uncanny.
TV INCLUDES: Anna and the King (CBS), Man of Destiny, Double Indemnity, The Hope Diamond, Columbo, Baretta, The Hemingway Play, Love Story, Kojak, McMillan & Wife, Streets of San Francisco, Starsky and Hutch.

EICHHORN, LISA: Actress. b. Reading, Pa. Went to England for literature studies at Oxford. Studied at RADA. Made film debut in Yanks (1979).
PICTURES: The Europeans, Why Would I Lie?, Cutter and Bone.

EISNER, MICHAEL D.: Executive. b. New York City, 1942. e. Denison Univ., (B.A.). Started career with programming dept. of CBS TV network. Joined ABC in 1966 as asst. to v.p. & natl program director. Two years later named manager of specials and talent. Dec., 1968 became dir. of program development—east coast. In March, 1971 named v.p., daytime programming, ABC-TV. In June, 1975 made v.p., program planning and development. In May, 1976 named sr. v.p., prime time production and development, ABC Entertainment. In Nov., 1976, left ABC to join Paramount Pictures as pres. & chief operating officer.

EKBERG, ANITA: Actress. b. Malmoe, Sweden, Sept. 29, 1931. Started career as a model.
PICTURES INCLUDE: Man in the Vault, Blood Alley, Artists and Models, War and Peace, Back from Eternity, Zarak, Pickup Alley, Sheba and the Gladiator, Sign of the Gladiator, La Dolce Vita, Boccaccio '70, The Alphabet Murder, The Cobra, Fellini's Clowns.

EKLAND, BRITT: Actress. b. Stockholm, Sweden, 1942.
TV: England: A Cold Peace. U.S.A.: Trials of O'Brien, McCloud, Six Million Dollar Man.
PICTURES INCLUDE: After the Fox, Double Man, Bobo, Night They Raided Minsky's, At Any Price, Stiletto, Cannibals, Tintomara, Percy, Carter, Night Hair Child, Endless Night, Baxter, Asylum, Wickerman, Ultimate Thrill, Man With Golden Gun, Royal Flash, Cassanova and Company, Slaves, King Soloman's Treasures.

ELAM, JACK: Actor. b. Miami, AZ, Nov. 13, 1916. e. Santa Monica Jr. College, Modesto Jr. College. Worked in Los Angeles as bookkeeper and theatre mgr.; served in Navy in World War II. Introduction to show business was as bookkeeper for Sam Goldwyn. Later worked as controller for other film producers. Given first acting job by producer George Templeton in 1948; has since appeared in over 100 films.
PICTURES: Rawhide, Kansas City Confidential, The Moonlighter, Vera Cruz, Moonfleet, Kiss Me Deadly, Gunfight at the OK Corral, Baby Face Nelson, Edge of Eternity, The Comancheros, The Rare Breed, The Way West, Firecreek, Once Upon a Time in the West, Support Your Local Sheriff, Rio Lobo, Support Your Local Gunfighter, Dirty Dingus Magee, The Cannonball Run, etc.
TELEVISION: The Texas Wheelers, The Dakotas, Temple Houston, Gunsmoke, Struck by Lightning, etc.

ELFAND, MARTIN: Executive. Was talent agent for ten years with top agencies; joined Artists Entertainment Complex in 1972. First film project as producer: Kansas City Bomber, first venture of AEC, of which he was snr. v.p. In 1977 joined Warner Bros. as production chief. 1980, produced It's My Turn.

ELG, TAINA: Actress, dancer. b. Helsinki, Finland, March 9. e. Helsinki. Sadler's Wells Ballet. Toured with Marquis de Cuevas Ballet; m.p. debut in The Prodigal.
PICTURES INCLUDE: Diane, Gaby, Les Girls, Imitation General, The 39 Steps.

ELIAS, HAL: Executive. b. Bklyn., N.Y. Dec. 23. Publicity dir., State Theatre, Denver; western exploitation mgr., MGM; adv. dept., pub. dept., MGM, Culver City studios; Head, MGM cartoon studio (Tom and Jerry); UPA Pictures, Inc., vice-pres. studio mgr.: Hollywood Museum; bd. dir., Academy of Motion Picture Arts & Sciences, 30 years; treasurer, AMPAS 1976–1979.

ELIZONDO, HECTOR: Actor. b. N.Y.C. m. actress Carolee Campbell. Studied with Ballet Arts Co. of Carnegie Hall and Actors Studio. Many stage credits in N.Y. and Boston.
PICTURES INCLUDE: Pocket Money, Born to Win, Deadhead Miles, Stand Up and Be Counted, One Across, Two Down, The Taking of Pelham One Two Three, Report to the Commissioner.
STAGE: Mr. Roberts, Island in Infinity, Madonna of the Orchard, Drums in the Night, The Prisoner of Second Avenue, Dance of Death, Steambath, The Great White Hope.
TV: The Impatient Heart (tf), Kojack, the Jackie Gleason Show, All in the Family.

ELKINS, SAUL: Producer. b. New York City, June 22, 1907; e. C.C.N.Y., B.S. 1927. Radio writer, dir., prod. 1930–2; dir., prod. stock co. touring Latin America 1932–4; writer Fox Films, 20th Century-Fox; writer RKO, Columbia 1937–42; writer, dial-dir., dir. Warner Bros. 1943–7; prod. Warner Bros. since 1947. Member: AMPAS, Screen Writer's Guild. Presently: exec. prod., Comprenetics, Inc.
PICTURES INCLUDE: Younger Brothers, One Last Fling, Homicide, House Across the Street, Flaxy Martin, Barricade, Return of the Frontiersmen, This Side of the Law, Colt 45, Sugarfoot, Raton Pass, The Big Punch, Smart Girls Don't Talk, Embraceable You.

ELLIOTT, DENHOLM: Actor. b. London, Eng., May 31, 1922; e. Malvern College. Screen debut in Dear Mr. Proback, 1948; films include: The Sound Barrier, The Holly and the Ivy, The Ringer, The Cruel Sea, Heart of the Matter, They Who Dare, Man Who Loved Redheads, Lease of Life, Night My Number Came Up, Pacific Destiny, Scent of Mystery; TV appearances; Stage: Write Me A Murder, N.Y., Seagull, N.Y., 1964.
PICTURES INCLUDE: Nothing But the Best, Station Six Sahara, King Rat, You Must Be Joking, The High Bright Sun, Alfie, Here We Go Round The Mulberry Bush, The Night They Raided Minskys, The Seagull, Too Late the Hero, The Rise and Rise of Michael Rimmer, A Doll's House, The Apprenticeship of Duddy Kravitz, Robin & Marion, To The Devil A Daughter, Russian Roulette, Voyage of the Damned, The Boys from Brazil, St. Jacques, Zulu Dawn, A Game for Vultures, Cuba, Illusions, Saint Jack, Bad Timing, Sunday Lovers.

ELLIOTT, LANG: Producer-Director. b. Los Angeles, CA, Oct. 18, 1949. Given first job in films by his uncle, the late actor William Elliott (known as Wild Bill Elliott). Worked as actor from early years; employed by, among others, the McGowan Brothers. Turned to film production; co-founded distribution co., The International Picture Show Company, serving as exec. v.p. in chg. of financing, production & distribution. Under banner of TriStar Pictures, Inc. also finances productions.
PICTURES: Produced Ride the Hot Wind, Where Time Began, The Farmer, The Billion Dollar Hobo, They Went That-a-Way & That-a-Way, The Prize Fighter. Produced and directed the Private Eyes.
TELEVISION: Produced Experiment in Love (special).

ELLSWORTH, JAMES: Producer. b. Deltaville, Virginia, March 12, 1927. e. U.C.L.A., 1949. Pro. baseball player.
TV SERIES: Champions of Sports.
PICTURES INCLUDE: Naked Fury, Marine, Life Story of Lt. General Lewis B. (Chesty) Fuller, Door to Door Maniac (Five Minutes to Live.)

ELMES, GUY: Writer. b. London, Eng., July 22, 1920; e. Aberdeen U. Painter and writer for radio after War Service (1939–45) in Royal Navy.
PICTURES INCLUDE: The Planter's Wife, The Flanagan Boy, Counterspy, Bang! You're Dead, Across the Bridge, Nor the Moon by Night, Wheel of Fate, Stranger's Hand, Serious Charge, Hello London, The Lady Takes a Gun, Joseph and His Brothers, Hannibal, The Blue Countess, Pontius Pilate, A Face in the Rain, The Captive City, Stranglehold, Flames Over India, El Greco, Submarine X, The Heroes, The Night Visitor, s.p.

ELSON, NORMAN: Executive. b. New York City, July 5, 1907; e. U. of Maryland. Contact clerk for Columbia; accessory mgr. N.Y. Columbia Exchange; district mgr. film buyer & gen. mgr. Brandt Theatres; gen. mgr. Trans-Lux Theatre Circuit, then apptd. vice-pres. 1950. Guild Enterprises, Inc., circuit pres. operating nine theatres in New York City.

EMANUEL, DAVID: Executive. b. New York, N.Y., Dec. 14, 1910; e. grad. Coll. 1932; ent. m.p. ind., slsman., Classic Pictures, 1948; formed, pres., sls. mgr., Phoenix Films, 1951; formed, pres., gen. sls. mgr., Governor Films Inc.; Pres. Gen. sls. mgr. Phase One Films, Inc.

ENDERS, ROBERT: Producer, Writer. Began in television, being responsible for 64 hrs. of live programming weekly for industry and govt. as pres. of Robert J. Enders, Inc. In 1961 turned to theatrical prod. and writing.
PICTURES INCLUDE: A Thunder of Drums (prod.), The Maltese Bippy (prod.), How Do I Love Thee (prod.), Zig Zag (story), Voices (prod., s.p.), The Maids, (s.p.), Winter

Rates (exec. prod.), Conduct Unbecoming (s.p.), Hedda (prod.), Nasty Habits (prod., s.p.).
TV: The Best of the Post (prod. of series), Ben Franklin, High Noon (prod., special). Co-prod. of Acad. Award Show, 1968.

ENDFIELD, CY: Producer, director, writer. b. Nov. 1914. Ent. m.p. ind. 1942; credits include: Joe Palooka series. Argyle Secrets, Underworld Story, Sound of Fury, Limping Man, Impulse, The Secret Child in the House, shorts for MGM; dir., Hell Drivers, Sea Fury.
PICTURES INCLUDE: dir., Jet Storm, Mysterious Island, Hide and Seek; dir., co-prod., co-scripted, Zulu, Sands of the Kalahari. Dir. De Sade.

ENGELBERG, MORT: Producer. b. Memphis, TN. e. Univ. of Illinois; Univ. of Missouri. Taught journalism; worked as reporter for UPI, AP. Worked for US government, including USIA, Peace Corps., Office of Economic Opportunity; President's Task Force on War on Poverty. Left government service in 1967 to become film unit publicist, working on three films in Europe: Dirty Dozen, Far From the Madding Crowd, The Comedians. Returned to US; appt. pub. mgr. for United Artists. Sent to Hollywood as asst. to Herb Jaffe, UA head of west coast production, which post he assumed when Jaffe left. Left to join with independent producer, Ray Stark.
PICTURES: Smokey and the Bandit, Hot Stuff, The Villain, The Hunter.

ENGLUND, GEORGE H.: Producer-Director. b. Washington, D.C., June 22, 1926. Producer, Paramount, Pennebaker Prods.; prod., MGM; prod.-dir., Universal.
PICTURES INCLUDE: The World the Flesh and the Devil, The Ugly American, Signpost to Murder, Snow Job.

ENGLUND, KEN: Writer. b. Chicago, Ill., May 6, 1914. e. Lane Tech., Chicago. Started career as magazine writer; then vaudeville routines, comedy radio shows. B'way revues and musicals. Twice elec. pres. screen branch Writers Guild of America, West; then pres. of WGAW. Member national council.
TV SHOWS INCLUDE: Jackie Gleason Show, Dear Phoebe, Ray Milland Show, Loretta Young Show, several spectaculars. Prod.-writer CBS-TV staff 1957; Sonja Henie Spect. London, 1958; 20th Fox and Warner Bros. TV Films, My Three Sons; sev. teleplays, Bewitched, 1965, That Girl!, Dr. Joyce Brothers (head writer for series).
PICTURES INCLUDE: Big Broadcast of 1938, Artists and Models Abroad, Good Girls Go to Paris, Slightly Honorable, Doctor Takes a Wife, No No Nanette, This Thing Called Love, There's That Woman Again, Nothing But the Truth, Springtime in the Rockies, Sweet Rosie O'Grady, Here Comes the Waves, Secret Life of Walter Mitty, Androcles and the Lion, Good Sam, A Millionaire for Christy, The Caddy, Never Wave at a Wac, Vagabond King, The Wicked Dreams of Paula Schultz, Surviving the Savage Sea.
AUTHOR: Tour D'Amour, Larks in a Casserole; B'way musical in work, and literary projects. Co-author (with George Marshall) The Ghosts in Emily's Trunk.

EPSTEIN, MEL: Producing. b. Dayton, O., Mar. 25, 1910, e. Ohio State U. Adv. & edit. depts. on newspapers; entered m.p. ind. as player in 1931; then asst. dir., unit prod. mgr., second unit & shorts dir.; U.S. Army Signal Corps (1st Lt.); apptd Para. prod., 1946. Now retired.
PICTURES INCLUDE: Whispering Smith, Hazard, Copper Canyon, Dear Brat, Branded, The Savage, Alaska Seas, Secret of the Incas.
TV: Broken Arrow, Men into Space, The Islanders, Asphalt Jungle, Rawhide, Long Hot Summer, The Monroes, Custer TV, Lancer TV Pilot, unit mgr. Lancer TV series, Medical Center, TV series.

ERDMAN, RICHARD: Actor-director. b. Enid, Okla., June 1, 1925, e. Hollywood High Sch.
PICTURES INCLUDE: Janie, Objective Burma, Time of Your Life, Four Days Leave, The Men, Cry Danger, Jumping Jacks, Happy Time, The Stooge, Stalag 17, The Power and the Prize, Saddle the Wind, Namu, The Killer Whale. Features directed: Bleep, The Brothers O'Toole.
TV: Ray Bolger Show, Perry Mason, Police Story, Tab Hunter Show, Alice, Bionic Woman, One Day at a Time, Playhouse of Stars, Twilight Zone, The Lucy Show, Lou Grant.
DIRECTED: The Dick Van Dyke Show, Mooch (special).

ERICKSON, CORYDON: Actor-Singer. b. New York, Dec. 26, 1944.
TV SHOWS: Robert Montgomery Presents, Goodyear, Lux Video Theater, Starstage, Omnibus, U.S. Steel, The Naked City, Phil Silvers Show, Ingrid Bergman Spectacular, True Story, The Defenders, Model.
Special for the United Nations, Declaration of Human Rights, The Children of Strangers, V.O. Paramount Pictures, Slide Films, Transcriptions, Records, Radio comm., comm. live and on film; Girls in the Night, It Should Happen To You, Man Against Crime, Norby, Radio, The Bible, etc.

ERIKSON, LAUNCELOT: Actor-singer. b. New York, Sept. 6, 1949. Industrial films, Stanley Neal Prod., Faith for Today, Gifts, Take My Name, Odds Against Tomorrow, dubbing for Carosello Napolitano; Commercials; Transcriptions, Radio comm. & dramas. Model.
TV LIVE: Studio One, Omnibus, U.S. Steel, Du Pont Show of the Month.

ERIKSON, LEIF: Actor. b. Alameda, Calif., Oct. 27, 1911; e. Glenn Taylor Mil. Acad., Calif. U., L.A., studied singing. With Ted Fio Rito orch., San Francisco, then Max Reinhardt's stage prod., A Midsummer Night's Dream; next joined Olsen & Johnson, comedy team. Screen debut in Wanderer of the Wasteland, 1935. On Bway, in Tea & Sympathy, 1953–55.
PICTURES INCLUDE: Sorry, Wrong Number, Miss Tatlock's Millions, Joan of Arc, Snake Pit, Stella, Three Secrets, Dallas, Tall Target, Show Boat, Reunion in Reno, Cimarron Kid, With A Song in My Heart, Sailor Beware, Carbine Williams, My Wife's Best Friend, A & C Meet Captain Kidd, Never Wave at a Wac, Trouble Along the Way, Perilous Journey, Paris Model, On the Waterfront, Star in the Dust, Fastest Gun Alive, Tea and Sympathy, The Vintage, Man and Boy, Twilight's Last Gleaming.
TV: High Chapparal.

ERICSON, JOHN: Actor. b. Dusseldorf, Germany, Sept. 25, 1926. e. American Acad. of Dramatic Arts. Appeared in summer stock; m.p. debut, Teresa, 1951, then Stalag 17 on Broadway.
PICTURES INCLUDE: Rhapsody, Student Prince, Green Fire, Bad Day at Black Rock, Return of Jack Slade, Pretty Boy Floyd, Bedknobs and Broomsticks.
TV: Honey West.

ESBIN, JERRY: Executive. Joined Paramount Pictures in 1975 as mgr. of branch operations; later named v.p., asst. sls. mgr. In 1980 named v.p., gen. sls. mgr. 1981, snr. v.p., domestic sls. & mktg.

ESMOND, CARL: Actor. b. Vienna, Austria, June 14, 1906; e. U. Vienna. On stage Vienna, Berlin, London, etc. (Shakespeare, Shaw, German modern classicals. On screen in Brit. prod. including Blossom Time, Even Song, Invitation to the Waltz. To U.S. in 1938.
PICTURES INCLUDE: The Catman of Paris, Smash-Up, Story of a Woman, Slave Girl, Walk a Crooked Mile, Mystery Submarine, World In His Arms, Agent for H.A.R.M., Morituri.

ESSENFELD, BARRY: Executive. b. Bronx, N.Y., Feb. 16, 1936. e. De Witt Clinton, N.Y.U. Acct., American Broadcasting Company, 1957–62; division controller, International Paper Co., 1962–67; group controller & division exec., New England Industries, 1968–70; Controller & asst. secty., Allied Artists Pictures Corp., 1970–73; named asst. treas. & dir. admin., Sept. 1973; gen. sls. mgr. 1979.

ESSERT, GARY: Executive. b. Oakland, Calif., Oct. 15, 1938. e. UCLA. Entered the entertainment field through motion picture exhibition; managed theatres in San Francisco and Los Angeles; has created advertising art campaigns for major motion picture studios and main titles for feature films; acts regularly as technical consultant for professional motion picture presentation installations, including Kennedy Center for the Performing Arts, Lincoln Center film theatre, Juilliard School of Music, American Zoetrope; Coordinated and supervised the design and planning of UCLA Motion Picture Center (Melnitz Hall), 1964–1967. Co-owned and operated a multi-media dance/concert hall in Hollywood known as The Kaleidoscope; technical coordinator for the American Film Institute's Center for Advanced Film Studies (Greystone) in Beverly Hills, 1968–1970, designing and outfitting complete facilities. Produced The Movies, a two-part, four-hour compilation documentary on the history of American motion pictures, telecast nationally on ABC-TV in March, 1975. Co-founded (1971) and currently director of the Los Angeles International Film Exposition (Filmex).

ESSEX, DAVID: Actor-singer. B. Plaistow, London, Eng. July 23, 1947. e. Shipman Sch., Custom House. Started as a singer-drummer in East London band. 1967: Joined touring Repertory Co. in "The Fantasticks," "Oh, Kay," etc. 1970: West End debut in "Ten Years Hard," 1972: Jesus Christ in Godspell, Che in Evita; Phonogram recording artist.
TV: appearances include: Top of the Pops, Own Specials, BBC series. Appearances on TV: France, Japan, Germany, Spain, Denmark, Australia.
PICTURES INCLUDE: Assault, All Coppers Are . . . , Recent pictures: That'll Be the Day, Stardust, Silver Dreaam Racer.
U.S. TV: Merv Griffin, Johnny Carson, Dinah Shore, American Bandstand, Midnight Special, Grammy Awards, Salute To The Beetles, Don Kirshners Rock Concert, A.M. America, Phil Everle in Session.

ESSEX, FRANCIS: Prod. b. Essex, Eng., 1929. Began career in films and theatre, including The Bells of St. Martin's, London, 1952; prod. BBC first anniversary program, 1954–60; prod. Associated TeleVision Ltd., London, 1960; prod.

Six of One (stage musical), London, 1964; controller programs, Scottish Television Ltd., Glasgow, 1955.

TV: Saturday Spectacular, Sunday Night at London Palladium, The Eartha Kitt Show, Anthony Newley Show, Mainly Millicent (tv series). 1969 Rejoined ATV as Prod. Controller, elected to Board of Dir. 1974. Appt. Dir. Prod. 1976.

ESSEX, HARRY J.: Writer. b. New York City, N.Y. e. St. John's Univ., Brooklyn, B.A. With Dept. Welfare, author play Something for Nothing, on New York stage, followed by Stronger than Brass. Wrote orig. story, Man Made Monster, for Universal. During World War II in U.S. Army Signal Corps; scenarist, training films on combat methods, censorship. Since release has written orig. s.p. Boston Blackie and the Law, Dangerous Business, (s.p.) Desperate Bodyguard, He Walked by Night, Dragnet, Killer That Stalked New York, Wyoming Mail, The Fat Man, Undercover Girl, Las Vegas Story, Models, Inc., Kansas City Confidential, The 49th Man, It Came From Outer Space; s.p., dir., I the Jury; s.p. Creature from the Black Lagoon; collab. s.p., story, Southwest Passage; adapt., Devil's Canyon; s.p., dir., Mad at the World; collab. s.p., Teen-age Crime Wave, Raw Edge; story, s.p. Lonely Man; play. One for the Dame; collab., Sons of Katie Elder, Man and Boy, s.p. & dir. Octman, s.p., dir., prod. The Cremators, The Amigos, story and SP Metro, release 1973. Collaboration with Oscar Saul, Chrysalis, in preparation from a story by Ray Bradbury.

TV: Untouchables (various series). The Racers, Alcoa Hour, Westinghouse, Desilu; story consultant and head writer: Target, The Corruptors, The Dick Powell Show, Bewitched, I Dream of Jeannie, Kraft Suspense Theatres.

NOVELIST: I Put My Right Foot In, Little Brown. Stage prod., Fatty, B'way, Sept., 1976; Man and Boy, (Dell) 1971, Marina, Playboy Press, 1981.

PLAYS: Something for Nothing; Neighborhood Affair; One for the Dame; Fatty; Current production, stage: Twilight, When the Bough Breaks.

ETKES, RAPHAEL: Executive. Joined MCA in 1961; named v.p. of Universal Pictures in 1973. Appt. v.p. of MCA, Inc. in 1978; named sr. v.p., Universal Pictures, 1979; 1980, named pres. chief exec. off., AIP; 1981, joined United Artists as snr. v.p.—Worldwide Prod.

ETTINGER, EDWIN D.: Publicist. b. New York City. 1921. Entered m.p. ind. as office boy, MGM; pub. rel. and publ. for industrial, comm. clients, 1946–52; joined Ettinger Co., pub. rel., 1952; pub. rel. dir., Disneyland Inc., 1955; marketing dir., Disneyland, 1955–65; v.p., M.C.A. Enterprises, Inc., 1955.

ETTLINGER, JOHN A.: Prod.-dir., distributor. b. Chicago, Ill., Oct. 14, 1924. e. Peddie Inst., Cheshire Acad., Signal Corps Photog. Center, 1942–45; with Paramount Theatres Corp., 1945–47; dir., KTLA, Paramount TV Prod., Inc., Los Angeles, 1948–50; radio-TV prod., Nat C. Goldstone Agency, 1950–53; pres. Medallion TV Enterprises, Inc.; TV prod., View the Clue, Greenwich Village, High Road to Danger, Medallion cartoons; Sur Demande, Star Route, Las Vegas Fights, Celebrity Billiards; Pres., KUDO-FM, Las Vegas.

EVANS, BARRY: Director. b. Guildford, England, 1943. Trained Central School. Repertory: Barrow, Nottingham, Chester, Royal Court, Nat. Theatre, Hampstead Th. Club, Chips with Everything, London and B'way. Young Vic. Theatre Clwyd Mold.

TV: Redcap, Undermined, The Baron, The Class, Armchair Theatre, Love Story, Doctor at Large, Short Story, Crossroads, Mind Your Language.

PICTURES INCLUDE: The White Bus, Here We Go 'Round the Mulberry Bush, Alfred the Great, Die Screaming, Marriane, The Adventures of a Taxi-Driver, Under the Doctor.

EVANS, CLIFFORD: Actor, director, writer. b. Cardiff, February 17, 1912; e. Royal Acad. Dram. Art, London.

STAGE: London debut 1930 in The Witch; later also on tour; N.Y. debut 1934 in The Distaff Side; other appearances include many Shakespearean prods., Gallows Glorious, Cul-de-Sac, Ghosts, The Emperor of the World, The Doctor's Dilemma, The Judge's Story, The Marquise.

PICTURES INCLUDE: The Mutiny of the Elsinore, Mademoiselle Docteur, The Proud Valley, Fingers, Love on the Dole, The Foreman Went to France, The Flemish Farm. Served H.M. Forces during World War II, The Silver Darlings, While I Live, Twenty Question Murder Mystery, A Run for Your Money, Escape Route, Valley of Song, Stryker of the Yard, Passport to Treason, Violent Playground, At the Stroke of Nine, SOS Pacific, The Curse of the Werewolf, Kiss of the Vampire, The Long Ships, Twist of Sand, One Brief Summer.

TV: The Accused, The Red Dress, White Hunter series, The Hour of the Rat, Treason, The Quiet Man, Roman Gestures, Man With a Feather In His Hat, Madras House, Traitor At the Gate, 12th Hour, Dr. Finlay's Casebook, Woman Beware Women, The Local Boy, Old Man's Fancy, Lime Street, Power Game series, The Avengers, Treason, War and Peace, The Prisoners, Who's For Tennis?, The Saint, Randall and Hopkirk, Codename. 1973: Co-producer

series The Inheritors, Memories of Xmas (ABC Am.), Strife, Land of Ice Cream, Childs Play, 1974. The Kilvert Diaries, 1977; Dylan, 1978; Coal's Prayer, 1979.

EVANS, GENE: Actor. b. Holbrook, Ariz., July 11, 1924; e. Colton H.S. Started career in summer stock, Penthouse Theatre, Altadena, Calif. Screen debut: Under Colorado Skies, 1947.

PICTURES INCLUDE: Crisscross, Larceny, Berlin Express, Assigned to Danger, Mother Was a Freshman, Sugarfoot, Armored Car Robbery, Steel Helmet, I was an American Spy, Force of Arms, Jet Pilot, Fixed Bayonets, Mutiny, Park Row, Thunderbirds, Donovan's Brain, Golden Blade, Hell & High Water, Long Wait, Cattle Queen of Montana, Wyoming Renegades, Crashout, Helen Morgan Story, Bravados, Sad Sack, The Hangman, Operation Petticoat, Support Your Local Sheriff, War Wagon, Nevada Smith, Young and Wild, Ballad of Cable Hogue, There Was a Crooked Man, Support Your Local Gunfighter, Camper John, Walking Tall, People Toys, Pat Garrett & Billy The Kid, Magic of Lassie.

TELEVISION: Matt Helm (series), Spencer's Pilots (series); Kate Bliss & Ticker Tape Kid Fire.

EVANS, JEROME M.: Executive. b. N.Y., Jan. 6, 1923. e. Univ. of Pa., B.S.; N.Y. Univ., M.B.A.; Ph.D.; Exec. in Charge Eastern Advertising & Publicity, Universal Pictures; Lecturer in Economics and Marketing, Bernard Baruch College; Graduate School of Business, City University of New York; Nat'l. Panel American Arbitration Assn.

EVANS, JULIUS: Writer, producer. e. N.Y.U., B.S.

THEATRE: Dir. B'way prods., Searching for the Sun, Dream Child; prod. and dir. summer stock. Later Assoc. Administrator So. Calif. Fed Theatre Project; organized Caravan Theatre Circuit, N.Y. Eastern play editor, Samuel Goldwyn, 1937; Test dir. in charge of new talent at RKO, 1938–40; assoc. prod. to Jesse L. Lasky on Adventures of Mark Twain, Sergeant York, Rhapsody in Blue. Signal Corps, U.S. Army, became chief of training films branch, 1942–46. Story ed., Sol Lesser Prod.; Ziv-TV Prod.; wrote screenplay for Sword of the Avenger; wrote for Mayor of the Town Series and The Phantom. Wrote and prod. ind. doc. films, including Achievement in Hong Kong (Edinburgh Film Festival); TV journalist with wife in personal interview series Topic for British Foreign Office. Partner in Chelsea International Films (Goldwyn Studios), s.p. & Assoc. prod.: Rain for a Dusty Summer, v.p., World View Prod. Co-Prod. The Challenge (A Tribute to Modern Art).

EVANS, MAURICE: Actor. b. Dorchester, Eng., June 3, 1901. On the stage since 1926.

THEATRE: London theatrical, career included Justice, Loyalties, Diversion, Journey's End, The Man I Killed, The Queen Bee. The Swan, See Ourselves, The Heart Line and starred for one season at the Old Vic; to U.S. 1935 and appeared in Romeo and Juliet, St. Helena, Richard II, Hamlet (Entirety), Henry IV (Part I), Twelfth Night, Macbeth, 1942; after War returned to Broadway, 1945 and appeared in G.I., Hamlet, Man and Superman, The Devil's Disciple, The Wild Duck, Dial 'M' For Murder, The Apple Cart, Heartbreak House, Tenderloin, The Aspern Papers, Shakespeare Revisited, A Program for Two Players.

PICTURES INCLUDE: Kind Lady, Androcles and the Lion, Gilbert and Sullivan, Macbeth, Warlord, Planet of The Apes, Rosemary's Baby, The Body Stealers.

Prod. Teahouse of the August Moon. No Time for Sergeants, N.Y. stage.

TV SHOWS: Hamlet, Richard II, Macbeth, Devil's Disciple, Taming of the Shrew, Man and Superman, The Tempest, St. John, series of 7 plays for Hallmark, NBC; G.E. Theatre (Caesar & Cleopatra), Theatre Guild, etc., Gen. Motors Motorama, Bewitched.

EVANS, RAY: Songwriter. b. Salamanca, N.Y., Feb. 4, 1915. e. Wharton School of Pa. U. Musician on cruise ships, radio writer spec. material. Hellzapoppin', Sons o' Fun.

SONGS INCLUDE: To Each His Own, Golden Earrings, Buttons and Bows (Academy Award, 1948), Mona Lisa (Academy Award, 1950), Whatever Will Be Will Be (Academy Award, 1956), A Thousand Violins, I'll Always Love You, Dreamsville, Love Song From Houseboat, Tammy, Silver Bells, Dear Heart, Angel, Never Let Me Go, Almost In Your Arms, As I Love You, In the Arms of Love, Wish Me a Rainbow.

PICTURES INCLUDE: Paleface, Sorrowful Jones, Fancy Pants, My Friend Irma, Capt. Carey U.S.A., Off Limits, Here Come the Girls, Red Garters, Man Who Knew Too Much, Stars Are Singing, Tammy, Houseboat, Blue Angel, A Private's Affair, All Hands on Deck, Dear Heart, The Third Day, What Did You Do In The War Daddy?, This Property Is Condemned.

BROADWAY MUSICAL: Oh Captain! Let It Ride!, Sugar Babies.

TV THEMES: Bonanza, Mr. Ed, Mr. Lucky, To Rome With Love.

EVANS, ROBERT: Producer. b. N.Y.C., June 29, 1930. Made appearance on radio as actor at age 11; went on to appear in more than 300 radio programs on major networks. Also appeared on TV in its early days. At 20 joined brother, Charles, and Joseph Picone, as partner in firm of Evans-Picone, Inc. In 1957 signed by Universal to play Irving Thalberg in The Man of a Thousand Faces after recommendation by Norma Shearer, Thalberg's widow. (See credits below for other acting assignments.) Turned to production and signed as independent by 20th Century-Fox. In August, 1966, joined Paramount Pictures as head of prod., a post he held ten years. Resigned to become indep. prod. again; has exclusive contract with Para.

PICTURES INCLUDE: Actor: The Sun Also Rises, The Fiend Who Walked the West, The Best of Everything. Independent Producer: Chinatown, Marathon Man, Black Sunday, Players, Urban Cowboy, Popeye.

EVANS, SY: Exec. r.n. Seymour H. Evans. b. New York, N.Y., March 14. e. Columbia U., B.A., 1941. U.S.A.F., 1941–46. Field prom. rep., Universal Pictures, 1946; asst. dir. adv., pub. & exploit., Schine Circuit, 1951; hd. dept., 1960; gen. mgr., 1963–65; dir. adv., pub. & prom., General Cinema Corp., 1965; named v.p., pub. and p.r., 1976.

EVERETT, CHAD: Actor. b. South Bend, Ind., June 11, 1936. r.n. Ray Canton. e. Wayne State Univ., Detroit. Signed by William T. Orr, head of TV prod. for Warner Bros. to 3-year contract. Appeared in many TV series as well as films. Next became contract player at MGM.

PICTURES INCLUDE: Claudelle Inglish, The Chapman Report, The Singing Nun, The Last Challenge, Made in Paris, Johnny Tiger, Return of the Gunfighter, The Impossible Years.

TELEVISION: Hawaiian Eye, 77 Sunset Strip, Surfside Six, Lawman, Bronco, The Dakotas, The Lieutenant, Re-digo, Route 66, Ironside, Medical Center.

EVERSON, WILLIAM K.: Writer. b. Yeovil, Eng., April 8, 1929. Pub. dir., Renown Pictures Corp., Ltd., London, 1944; film critic; m.p. journalist; in armed forces, 1947–49; thea. mgr., pub. & booking consultant, Monseigneur News Theatres, London, 1949; pub. dir., Allied Artists Inc. Corp., 1951; prod., writer Paul Killiam Org., 1956. Writer-editor-researcher on TV series "Movie Museum" and "Silents Please," also on TV specials and theatrical features "Hollywood the Golden Years," "The Valentino Legend," "The Love Goddesses" and "The Great Director."

AUTHOR: Several books on movie history, including "The Western," "The Bad Guys," "The American Movie," "The Films of Laurel & Hardy," "The Art of W. C. Fields," "Hal Roach," "The Detective in Film," "Classics of the Horror Film," "Claudette Colbert."

Lecturer, archival consultant, American Film Institute representative. Film History instructor at New York University, The New School and The School of Visual Arts, all in New York. Also, Harvard Univ.

EWELL, TOM: Actor. r.n. Yewell Tompkins. b. Owensboro, Ky., April 29. e. U. of Wisconsin. Active in coll. dramatics; salesman at Macy's. Stage debut, New York: They Shall Not Die, 1934; thereafter many unsuccessful plays. U.S. Navy 1942–46.

THEATRE: Returned to stage in John Loves Mary; Small Wonder; on road in Stage Door, Tobacco Road, Roberta, Key Largo; on Broadway in Seven-Year Itch, Tunnel of Love.

RADIO: Many programs.

PICTURES INCLUDE: Adam's Rib, Mr. Music, A Life of Her Own, American Guerilla in the Philippines, Up Front, Finders Keepers, Lost in Alaska, Willie & Joe Back at the Front, Seven-Year Itch, Lieutenant Wore Skirts, Girl Can't Help It, Tender Is the Night, State Fair, Suppose They Gave A War and Nobody Came?, To Find a Man, They Only Kill Their Masters, The Great Gatsby.

F

FABRAY, NANETTE: Actress. b. San Diego, Calif., Oct. 27, 1920. d. Raoul Fabares and Lillian (McGovern) Fabares; student Los Angeles City College. m. David Tebet 1947 (div. July, 1951); m. 2d Ranald MacDougall 1957, deceased Dec. 11, 1973. One son, Jamie. First prof. stage appearance at age of three and a half in vaudeville as Baby Nan. Leading lady in Charlie Chan series. Member of the cast, radio, Showboat. 1938, won two-year scholarship to Max Reinhardt school in Hollywood, and starred in his Calif. productions of The Miracle, Six Characters in Search of an Author, and Servant With Two Masters.

PICTURES INCLUDE: Elizabeth and Essex, A Child is Born, The Happy Ending, Cockeyed Cowboys, The Band-wagon.

TV: Own TV Series, Yes, Yes Nanette 1961–62. Also starred on shows with every major TV star. Two years on Caesar's Hour.

BROADWAY SHOWS: Meet the People, By Jupiter, Jackpot, May Dear Public, Let's Face It, Bloomer Girl, Arms

and the Girl, High Button Shoes, Make A Wish, Love Life, Mr. President, No Hard Feelings.

AWARDS: High Button Shoes 1948, two Donaldson Awards for best performance in a musical and best supporting performance; Love Life 1947, the Tony Awards best musical actress of the year; Three Emmy Awards for Caesars Hour as best comedienne, 1955, 1956, best supporting actress 1955; Woman of the Year, 1955, Radio and TV Editors of America; Hollywood Women's Press Club, 1960; Honorary Mayor of Pacific Palisades 1967–68; One of Ten Best Dressed Women in America, Fashion Academy Award, 1950.

FABRIZI, ALDO: Actor. b. Rome, Italy. Stage actor to 1942.

PICTURES INCLUDE: Go Ahead, Passengers, Square of Rome, Open City, My Son, the Professor, To Live in Peace, Christmas at Camp 119, Emigrants, Welcome, Reverend, First Communion (Father's Dilemma), Flowers of St. Francis, Mishappy Family, Thieves and Cops, Times Gone By, Lucky Five, Too Young for Love, Voice of Silence.

FACTOR, ALAN JAY: Producer-Director. b. Chicago, Ill. Dec. 25, 1925; e. Northwestern Univ. & Goodman Theatre. Former actor under name Alan Frost. Broadway: Richard III, Pick Up Girl, E=MC2, Battle For Heaven (ANTA).

PICTURES INCLUDE: Portrait of Jennie, All Hands On Deck, Double Lift, The Braineaters, The Right Approach, Female Jungle, Producer, Screen Gems, Metromedia, Columbia Broadcasting System. Currently President, Bedford Productions. Recent TV credits: Bewitched, (Director), Something Evil, Let Me Live Unseen

FADIMAN, CLIFTON: Performer. e. Columbia Univ. Contributor to magazines since 1924. Asst. ed. Simon & Schuster, 1927–29, ed. 1929–35. Book ed. The New Yorker, 1933–43. Mc. on Information Please radio program 1938–48; TV, 1952; Judge, Book of the Month Club, since 1945; Mc. This Is Show Business, TV; author, Party of One; Any Number Can Play; Enter Conversing; The Lifetime Reading Plan; editor, American Treasury, 50 years; m.c., Conversation, 1954; m.c., Quiz Kids, 1956; Metropolitan Opera Roving Reporter, 1955–60; m.c., Alumni Fun, 1964; bd. of editors, Encyclopaedia Britannica; Edit. consultant Encyclopaedia Britannica Educational Corp.; Editorial Board, CRICKET: The Magazine for Children, Co-author, The Joys of Wine, 1975. Co-author, The Wine Buyers Guide, 1977; Co-author, Empty Pages: A Search for Writing Competence in School and Society, 1979.

FAICHNEY, JAMES B.: Producer-Director-Writer-Consultant. b. Yonkers, N.Y. Pathe News; RKO Pathe, film editor, writer, director; U.S. Army WW II, chief motion picture security censorship; Soundmasters; James B. Faichney Prod.; U.S. Dept. of State—USIA; Freelance producer, director, writer for CBS Films, ABC-CBS-NBC News, U.S. Army, National Foundation, Communications Four, Cul-Crieff Associates. Consultant to the U.S. Atomic Energy Commission, U.S. Air Force, Committee for Free Asia, etc.

PICTURES INCLUDE: The Most Rewarding Law, The Third Pillar, Air Power, Dead Man's Voice, Dawn of a New Day, Kampong Sentesa.

TV: Air Power, Twentieth Century, 21st Century, David Brinkley's Journal, NBC White Paper, ABC Close-up, The Great Conventions (the Republicans, the Democrats), Viet Cong, The Green Scene, The Revolutionaries, The Will for Peace, A Better World, 1945, The Diplomat, The General.

AWARDS: George Foster Peabody, Sylvania. Billboard and United States Air Force exceptional service awards; two ATVAS nominations for best documentary program and series.

FAIN, SAMMY: Composer. b. New York. e. Public and high schools. Self taught on piano. Commenced career in Tin Pan Alley as teenage staff pianist-composer for leading music publishers, then in vaudeville. Recording contract at Harmony Records (Columbia); featured solo performer on many New York radio stations. Joined ASCAP, 1926. Wrote first song hit, "Let a Smile Be Your Umbrella." Lyrics by Irving Kahal, 1927.

STAGE: Scores for Hellzapoppin, Son's of Fun, George White's Scandals, Ed Wynn's Boys & Girls Together, Flahooley, Christine & others.

PICTURES INCLUDE: Scores & Songs—Big Pond, Young Man of Manhattan, Footlight Parade, Sweet Music, Harold Teen, New Faces of '37, Geo. White's Scandals, Call Me Mister, Alice in Wonderland, Peter Pan, Jazz Singer, Weekend at the Waldorf, Anchors Aweigh, Imitation of Life, Mardi Gras, Calamity Jane, April Love, Marjorie Morningstar, Certain Smile, Love is a Many Splendored Thing, Tender is the Night, Made in Paris, The Stepmother and many others.

SONGS: Let a Smile Be Your Umbrella, Wedding Bells Are Breaking Up That Old Gang of Mine, When I Take My Sugar to Tea, You Brought a New Kind of Love to Me, Was That the Human Thing to Do, By A Waterfall, Are You Having Any fun, I'm Late, I Can Dream Can't I, That Old Feeling, I'll Be Seeing You, Dear Hearts and Gentle People, April Love, A Certain Smile, A Very Precious Love, Tender

Is the Night, Secret Love, Love Is a Many Splendored Thing, many others. Elected to Songwriters' Hall of Fame.

CITATIONS: Oscar awards for Secret Love and Love is a Many Splendored Thing, plus eight Acad. Oscar nominations: International awards—Diploma Di Benemerenza most coveted honor by the Hall of Artists in Nice, France, and Augasto Messinesse Gold Award from Messina, Italy. Also two Laurel Awards.

FAIRBANKS, DOUGLAS, JR.: Actor, prod. Bus. exec. b. N.Y. Dec. 9, 1909; son of late Douglas Fairbanks. e. Pasadena (Calif.) Polytech. Sch.; Harvard Mil. Acad., Los Angeles; Bovee and Collegiate Sch., N.Y.; also Paris, London. Began as screen actor 1923 in Stephen Steps Out; thereafter in more than 75 pictures. Stage from 1927 in U.S., U.K. (Young Woodley, Saturday's Children, etc.); 1934 in Manchester, England (The Winding Journey), London (Moonlight in Silver), 1968–1977 My Fair Lady, The Secretary Bird, Present Laughter (U.S.), The Pleasure of His Company (U.S., U.K., Ireland, Australia and Hong Kong), Out on a Limb. Since sound in both British & U.S. prods.; formed own co. 1935, prod. & starring, The Amateur Gentleman, etc. U.S. Navy, 1941; Silver Star Combat Legion of Merit; K.B.E., D.S.C., Legion of Honor, Croix de Guerre, etc. 1949. Entered TV film prod., 1952.

PICTURES INCLUDE: (since sound): Dawn Patrol, Little Caesar, Outward Bound, Union Depot, Captured, Catherine the Great, Accused, The Prisoner of Zenda, Having Wonderful Time, Gunga Din, Morning Glory, Angels Over Broadway, The Corsican Brothers, The Exile, Sinbad the Sailor, That Lady in Ermine, Joy of Living, Fighting O'Flynn, State Secret; prod. Another Man's Poison; Chase Crooked Shadow, Ghost Story.

TV: prod. Douglas Fairbanks Presents, etc.

FAIRBANKS, JERRY: Exec. prod. b. San Francisco, Calif.; cameraman, 1924–29; prod., shorts, Universal, 1929–34; prod., Popular Science, Unusual Occupations, Speaking of Animals Series, Para., 1935–49; Winner two Acad. Awards; set up film div., NBC, 1948; formed, NBC Newsreel, 1949; devel. Zoomar Lens; formed Jerry Fairbanks Prods., 1950.

TV: Front Page Detective, Crusader Rabbit, Hollywood Theatre; owner, Jerry Fairbanks Productions.

PICTURES INCLUDE: Lost Wilderness, Down Liberty Road, With This Ring, Counterattack, Collision Course, Land of the Sea, Brink of Disaster, The Legend of Amaluk, North of The Yukon, Damage Report, Seven Lies South, The Boundless Seas.

FAIRCHILD, WILLIAM: Director, screenwriter, playwright. b. Cornwall, England. e. Royal Naval College, Dartmouth. Early career Royal Navy.

PICTURES INCLUDE: Screenplays: Morning Departure, Outcast of the Islands, The Gift Horse, The Net, Newspaper Story, Malta Story, The Seekers, Passage Home, Value For Money, Star!, Embassy, The Darwin Adventure, Dir.: John and Julie, The Extra Day, The Silent Enemy.

SCREENPLAYS AND TV PLAYS INCLUDE: The Man With the Gun, No Man's Land, The Signal, Four Just Men, Some Other Love, Cunningham 5101, The Break, The Zoo Gang, Lady with a Past.

STAGE: Sound of Murder, Breaking Point, Poor Horace, The Pay-Off, The Flight of The Bumble B, The Paternal Optimist.

BOOKS: A Matter of Duty, The Swiss Arrangement.

FALK, PETER: Actor. b. New York City, Sept. 16, 1927.

THEATRE: Off-Broadway: The Iceman Cometh, Comic Strip, Purple Dust, Bonds of Interest, The Lady's Not For Burning, Saint Joan, Diary of a Scoundrel. On Broadway: Saint Joan, The Passion of Josef D., The Prisoner of Second Avenue.

TV: Studio One, Kraft Theatre, Alcoa Theatre, N.T.A. Play of the Week, Armstrong Circle Theatre, Omnibus, Robert Montgomery Presents, Brenner, Deadline, Kraft Mystery Theatre, Rendezvous, Sunday Showcase, The Untouchables, N.B.C.'s Sacco—Vanzetti Story, Dick Powell Show—The Price of Tomatoes, Danny Kay Show, Edie Adams Show, Bob Hope Chrysler Hour, Columbo (1971).

PICTURES INCLUDE: Murder, Pocketful of Miracles, The Balcony, Robin and the Seven Hoods, Mad, Mad, Mad World, Italiano Brava Gente, Luv, Castle Keep, Anzio, Husbands, Machine Gun McCann, Mikey and Nicky, Murder by Death, The Cheap Detective, Brinks' Job, The In-Laws, All the Marbles.

FANTOZZI, TONY: Theatrical Agent. b. May 1, 1933. New Britain, Conn. William Morris Agency.

FARBER, BART: Executive. Joined United Artists Corp. in early 1960s when UA acquired ZIV TV Programs. Served as v.p. United Artists Television and United Artists Broadcasting. In 1971 named v.p. in charge of legal affairs of the cos. In January 1978, named snr. v.p.—TV, video and special markets; now indep. consultant, TV, Pay TV, home video.

FARENTINO, JAMES: b. Brooklyn, N.Y., Feb. 24, 1938. m. Michele Lee, actress, singer. e. American Academy of Dramatic Arts.

THEATRE: Appeared in Broadway prod. of Night of the Iguana. A Streetcar Named Desire (revival, 1973).

TV INCLUDES: Naked City, daytime soap operas, Laredo, Route 66, The Alfred Hitchcock Hour, Ben Casey, Twelve O'Clock High, Death of a Salesman.

PICTURES INCLUDE: The Pad (And How to Use It) (Golden Globe Award, 1966), The Ride of Hangman's Tree, Banning Rosie!, The Story of A Woman, The Final Countdown, Dead & Buried.

FARR, DEREK: Actor. b. London, England, Feb. 7, 1912; e. St. Michael's, Uckfield & Cranbrooke, Lieut. Royal Artillery World War II. Stage debut, "Gate Revue." On screen 1940.

PICTURES INCLUDE: Outsider, Spellbound, Bond Street, Murder Without Crime, Young Wives' Tale, Reluctant Heroes, Double Confession, Bang! You're Dead, Dam Busters, Front Page Story, Eight O'Clock Walk, Man in the Road, Town on Trial, Doctor At Large, Vicious Circle, The Truth About Women, Attempt to Kill, 30 Is a Dangerous Age, Cynthia, Pope Joan.

TV: Murder Mistaken, Escapade, Two Dozen Red Roses, Deadline Midnight, Faraway Music, Zero One, The Saint, The Human Jungle, series. 1963–64; acting in Australia: The Projected Man, in England, 1956–66. 1966: Dixon of Dock Green 1967; Inspector Rose; Adam Adamant, Owen MD, The Visitors, Crossroads. Garrick Theatre, 1967–68. Strand Theatre, 1969. Treasure Island Tour for Mermaid, 1970–71.

FARR, FELICIA: Actress. b. Westchester, N.Y., Oct. 4. e. Penn State College. m. Jack Lemmon. Stage debut: Picnic (Players Ring Theatre).

PICTURES INCLUDE: Timetable, Jubal, Reprisal, First Texan, Last Wagon, 3:10 to Yuma, Hell Bent For Leather, Kiss Me Stupid, Kotch, Charley Varrick.

FARRAR, DAVID: Actor. b. Forest Gate, Essex, England.

PICTURES INCLUDE: Black Narcissus, Frieda, Mr. Perrin & Mr. Traill, Small Back Room, Diamond City, Gone to Earth. One of top ten British money makers Motion Picture Herald-Fame poll, Cage of Gold, Night Without Stars, The Golden Horde, Obsessed, Wild Heart, Duel in the Jungle, Black Shield of Falworth, Lilacs in the Spring, Escape to Burma, Sea Chase, Pearl of the South Pacific, Lost, Woman and the Hunter, I Accuse, Son of Robin Hood, John Paul Jones, Watusi, Solomon and Sheba, Best Girl, Middle of Nowhere, The 300 Spartans, Beat Girl.

TV: Dick Powell Show.

FARRELL, CHARLES: Actor. b. Dublin, Eire, Aug. 6, 1906. m. Babbie McManus. First stage appearance as a child with Detroit (Mich.) stock co., 1912; London debut at the Coliseum, May, 1921, in The Crown Diamond. Since in many Brit. stage prods.

THEATRE: (Brit. stage) The Nervous Wreck, Derby Day, The Bowery Touch, Get a Load of This, My Sister Eileen, Carissima, Detective Story, Wise Guys, Remains to Be Seen, Never Too Late, Harvey with James Stewart 1975.

PICTURES: Began screen career 1912, Vitagraph. Later in many British films including Jack's the Boy, Meet Sexton Blake, The Way to the Stars, Don Chicago, This Man Is Mine, Black Michael, They Made Me a Fugitive, Boys in Brown, Night and the City, The Turners of Prospect Road, The Crimson Pirate, Madame Louise, There Was a Lady, Miss Robin Hood, Far and Wide, See How They Run, Hornet's Nest, Round the Bend, My Infallible Uncle, Morning Call, Sheriff of Fractured Jaw, Best of All, Operation Cupid, No Hiding Place, Too Young to Love, Too Hot to Handle, Humanite, Moonlight, Girl Hunters, The Unkind Philanthropist, Chimes at Midnight, Man of Atlas, Golden Silence, Mr. Sebastian; Generalissimo, 1966–67. Crossplot, Oh, What a Lovely War, From a Bird's Eye View, Vampire Lovers, Doctor Phibes, Countess Dracula, The Common Error, Scoop, Rudolph Valentino, 1976.

TV: Many appearances, including BBC-TV series, Hans Christian Andersen series in London; Look Out series, TV films. Dir. English Dialogue 13 TV Films in Italy; Hon.-treas. British Actors Equity 1949–75.

FARRELL, CHARLES: Actor. b. Onset Bay, Mass., Aug. 9, 1901; e. Boston U. Entered m.p. ind. in silent films.

PICTURES INCLUDE: Seventh Heaven, Street Angel, Lucky Star, Sunny Side Up, Wild Girl, Big Shakedown, Moonlight Sonata, Just Around the Corner, Tailspin. U.S.Navy, 1942–45; mayor of Palm Springs since 1947.

TV: My Little Margie; The Charles Farrell Show.

FARRELL, HENRY: Author of novels and screenplays

SCREENPLAYS INCLUDE: Whatever Happened to Baby Jane? Hush . . . Hush, Sweet Charlotte, and What's the Matter with Helen?

TV: How Awful About Allan, The House That Would Not Die.

FARREN, JACK: Prod.-Writer. b. New York City; e. B.A., NYU. Theatre: prod., Take a Giant Step, Lorenzo 1967, Robert

Anderson's You Know I Can't Hear You When the Water's Running; 1968, The Education of Hyman Kaplan.
PICTURES INCLUDE: Silent Night, Lonely Night; Fuzz.
TV: Goodson-Todman Productions; NBC, CBS.

FARROW, MIA: Actress. b. Los Angeles, Feb. 9. e. Marymount, Los Angeles, Cygnet House, London. Bway. debut. The Importance of Being Earnest, 1963. Screen debut: Guns at Batasi.
PICTURES INCLUDE: Guns at Batasi, A Dandy in Aspic, Rosemary's Baby, John and Mary, Secret Ceremony, See No Evil, The Public Eye. The Great Gatsby, Full Circle, A Wedding, Death on the Nile, Hurricane.
TV: Peyton Place, Johnny Belinda.
THEATRE: Mary Rose (London).

FASS, M. MONROE: Theatre Broker. b. New York City, Feb. 26, 1901. e. City College of N.Y. (M.E. degree, engineering). Entered real estate business in 1925, making first deal with Marcus Loew for land on which Paradise Theatre, Bronx, N.Y., was built. Thereafter made theatre deals (sale or lease of land or building) in most major cities in the U.S. and in major shopping centers. Member: Real Estate Board of N.Y.; Natl. Institute of Real Estate Brokers, Natl. Assoc. of Real Estate Board; Amer. Society of Real Estate Appraisers, Natl. Assoc. of Theatre Owners.

FAWCETT, FARRAH: Actress. b. Corpus Christi, Texas, Feb. 2. e. Univ. of Texas. m. Actor Lee Majors. Picked as one of the Ten Most Beautiful Girls while a freshman; went to Hollywood and signed by Screen Gems. Did films, TV shows, and made over 100 TV commercials.
PICTURES INCLUDE: Love Is a Funny Thing. Myra Breckenridge, Logan's Run, Somebody Killed Her Husband, Sunburn, Saturn III, The Cannonball Run.
TV: Owen Marshall, Counselor at Law, The Six Million Dollar Man. The Feminist and the Fuzz (movie), Charlie's Angels (regular).

FAY, PATRICK J.: Director, producer. b. June 7. e. Carnegie Tech; Dumont TV Network, 10 years. Director of over 100 Army training films.
TV: Bishop Sheen, Broadway to Hollywood, Manhattan Spotlight, Life is Worth Living, Front Row Center, Ilona Massey Show, Alec Templeton Show, Maggi McNellis Show, Key to Missing Persons, Kids and Company; co-prod., dir., Confession; dir., TV film series, Confession; dir. IBM Industrials, IBM World Trade, Europe Industrial, The Big Picture.
AUTHOR: Melba, The Toast of Pithole, The Last Family Portrait in Oil, Coal Oil Johnny, French Kate, The Water's Fine, No Pardon in Heaven.
FILMS: Director for RCA, General Electric H.G. Peters Company, Bransby Films.

FAYLEN, FRANK: Actor.
PICTURES INCLUDE: Address Unknown, The Angels Sing, The Lost Weekend, You Came Along, Road to Rio, The Centerville Ghost, Cooper Canyon, Whispering Smith, Detective Story, Blood on the Moon, Sniper, The Lusty Men, 99 River Street, Red Garters, Lone Gun, Riot in Cellblock 11, The Looters, McConnell Story, Away All Boats, Return of Custer, Gunfight at the OK Corral, Death of a Nobody, Fluffy, The Monkey's Uncle, Funny Girl.
TV: The Dobie Gillis Show, That Girl, Tell Tale Gun, Joe & Lillian, Quincy.

FAZALBHOY, M.A.: Executive. b. Bombay, India, 1902. equip. mfg., mgr., dir., Photophone Ltd.; dir. several business houses.
Member of Rotary. International Business Men's Convention in America, 1944. Development Panel of Manufacture of Cinema & Studio Equipment of Government of India.

FEHR, RUDI: Executive. b. Berlin, Germany; m. Maris Wrixon actress. Started career with Tobis-Klangfilm, Berlin. Joined Warner Bros. editorial department, 1936. Became producer, 1952; promoted to executive, 1956; Post Production Exec. Warner Bros.; WB title changed to dir. of editorial & post-prod. operations. Now retired; is consultant to industry.

FEINBERG, MILTON: Executive. b. Milwaukee, Wis. e. Univ. of Minn., school of Bus. Admin. Salesman, 20th Century-Fox, Des Moines, 1942–44; branch mgr., National Screen Service, Des Moines, 1945–57; branch mgr., in Chicago, superv. Chicago, Milwaukee, Des Moines exchange territories, National Screen Service, 1958–65; gen. sales mgr., NSS, 1966; v.p. & gen. sls. mgr. 1967; May, 1974, sr. v.p., N.S.S.

FEINSTEIN, HARRY: Exhibitor. b. Pittsburgh, Pa., Aug. 22, 1906; e. U. of Pittsburgh. Dept. store exec. prior to entering m.p. ind. 1930, as asst. mgr. Embassy Theatre, East Orange, N.J.; mgr. Warner theatres, Newark & Pittsburgh, asst. to various zone mgrs.; apptd. zone mgr. Warner New Eng. Theatres, hdqts. New Haven, Conn., 1951. Apptd. zone mgr., Stanley Warner, Pittsburgh, May, 1960.

FEITSHANS, BUZZ: Executive. Worked for 10 years at American-International as supvr. of prod., jobs including film editing

and supervision of editing and dubbing. Bowed as producer on Dillinger (1973). In 1975 formed A-Team Productions with John Milius.
PICTURES INCLUDE: Big Wednesday (prod.), Hardcore (prod.), 1941 (prod.), Extreme Prejudice (exec. prod.).

FELD, FRITZ: Actor. b. Berlin, Germany, Oct. 15, 1900. e. U. Berlin; Max Reinhardt Sch. of Drama, Berlin. Actor, prod. asst. dir. for Reinhardt in Berlin 7 yrs.; on screen 1918 in The Golem, Ufa. Since found variously assoc. U.S. m.p. prod., as writer, director, actor: has appeared in more than 410 pictures. 1971; nat'l bd. dir., Screen Actors Guild. 1968 chairman of the "American National Committee," Southern California Chapter. 1976 chairman Hollywood Museum Project committee—Screen Actors Guild, 20th Century-Fox Film Corp. staged A Tribute To Fritz Feld-60 Years In The Movies and the Los Angeles City named a theater in Brentwood The Fritz Feld Community Theatre. In April 1979 Feld was elected honorary Mayor of Brentwood by the Chamber of Commerce.
TV: Dangerous Assignment, Racket Squad, Mr. & Mrs. North, Jimmy Durante Show, Jack Paar, Thin Man, Chevy Show, Red Skelton, Milton Berle, Colonel Flack, Accused, Peter Gunn, General Electric Thea., Kraft Music Hall, Danny Thomas, Bachelor Father, Commercials. Adventures in Paradise, Follow the Sun, The Donna Reed Show, Valentine Day, No Time for Sergeants, The Farmer's Daughter, The Bing Crosby Show, Batman, Lost in Space, The Man From U.N.C.L.E., Laredo, Please Don't Eat the Daisies, Girl From U.N.C.L.E., The Smothers Bros., The Wild, Wild, West, Bewitched, Donald O'Conner Show, The Beverly Hillbillies, Land of the Giants, Arnie, Love, American Style, The Merv Griffin Show, Movie of the Week, The New Bill Cosby Show, The Julie Andrews Hour, Fire House, The Odd Couple, The Night Couple, The Night Stalker, Only With Married Men, The Mike Douglas Show, The Tonight Show, Tabitha, The Hardy Boys, Flying High, Over Easy, Hizzonner, NBC's Sunday Show, General Hospital, Heidi, Supertrain.
STAGE: The Miracle, Once More With Feeling, Would Be Gentleman, Midsummer Night's Dream, Arsenic and Old Lace.
PICTURES INCLUDE: Wives and Lovers, Promises, Promises, Who's Minding the Store?, Four for Texas, The Patsy, Harlow, Made in Paris, Three on a Couch, Way . . . Way Out, The Comic, Hello, Dolly!, The Computer Wore Tennis Shoes, The Phynx, Which Way to the Front? Hebie Rides Again, The Strongest Man in the World, Only With Married Men, Hoyd Axton's Country Western Rock 'Roll Show, The Sunshine Boys, Won Ton Ton, The Dog Who Saved Hollywood, Broadway Rose, Mel Brooks' Silent Movie, Pennsylvania Lynch, Freaky Friday, The World's Greatest Lover, Herbie Goes Bananas, Mel Brook's History of the World.

FELDKAMP, FRED: Producer. b. Newark, N.J., Mar. 2, 1914. Reporter, writer, editor many publications; writer, chair., edit. bd. March of Time, motion picture release, 1947–51; adapted Crusade in Europe for TV: Crusade in the Pacific for TV: produced Operation Manhunt, Silken Affair. Executive prod. Triple Cross.
Co-author with wife, Phyllis—The Good Life—Or What's Left of It. New book: Not Everybody's Europe.

FELDMAN, EDWARD S.: Producer. b. New York, Sept. 5, 1929. e. Michigan State Univ. Trade press contact, newspaper and mag. contact, 20th Century Fox, 1950; dir. info. services, Dover Air Force Base. 1954–56; publicity coordinator, The World of Suzie Wong, Para., 1959; joined Embassy, dir. of publicity, 1969; vice pres. in chg., adv. & pub., Seven Arts Prods., 1962; v.p. exec. asst. to head prod. Warner-7 Arts Prods., 1967, pres., m.p. dept., Filmways, 1970; exec. prod., What's the Matter With Helen?, 1971, exec. prod. Fuzz, 1972, Save the Tiger, 1972; prod. The Other Side of the Mountain, 1974; prod. Two-Minute Warning, 1976; exec. prod. 21 Hours At Munich, 1976; prod., King, 1977. Formed Edward S. Feldman Co., 1978. Co-prod. The Last Married Couple in America; Valentine (exec. prod.), 1980, 300 Miles for Stephanie (exec. prod.).

FELDMAN, MARTY: Actor-Writer-Director. b. England, 1933. Started as comic on TV in Britain (Every Home Should Have One, Marty, etc.). Appeared in theatrical films for Mel Brooks before co-writing and directing and starring in The Last Remake of Beau Geste in 1976.
PICTURES INCLUDE: The Bed-Sitting Room, Young Frankenstein, The Adventures of Sherlock Holmes' Smarter Brother, Silent Movie, The Last Remake of Beau Geste, In God We Trust (co. s.p., dir., act.).

FELDMAN, PHIL: Producer. b. Boston, Mass. Jan. 22, 1922. e. Harvard, 1943; Georgetown U., 1946; Harvard Law School, 1949, Harvard Business School, 1947. First Lieutenant, U.S. Army, 1943–46. Owner, Wholesale and retail dry goods firm, 1946–49. Law practice, 1950–51. Legal counsel Famous Artists Corp. 1951–53. Assoc. Dir. of Business Affairs CBS, 1953; Dir. of Business Affairs CBS, 1954–57. V.P. Talent & Contract Properties CBS, 1957–60. Exec. v.p. Broadcast Management, 1960–62. Head Business Relations

20th-Century Fox, 1962. V.P. 7 Arts Assoc. Corp. 1962–66 Pres., Phil Feldman Prods., Inc., 1967. Pres., First Artists, 1969; 1980, joined Rastar Films as exec. v.p.
PICTURES INCLUDE: You're a Big Boy Now, The Wild Bunch, The Ballad of Cable Hogue.

FELL, NORMAN: Actor. b. Philadelphia, March 24. e. Temple Univ. Studied acting with Stella Adler. Member, Actors Studio. Professional debut at Circle-in-the-Square Theatre in N.Y. in Bonds of Interest.
Summer stock; appearances on TV; moved to Hollywood in 1958 to begin theatrical film career.
PICTURES: The Graduate, Pork Chop Hill, Oceans 11, Rat Race, Inherit the Wind, Bullitt, If It's Tuesday, This Must Be Belgium, Catch 22, The End.
TELEVISION: Over 150 live plays from New York and some 200 shows filmed in Hollywood. Series: Dan August, 87th Precinct, Joe and Mable, Tom Ewell Show, Needles and Pins, Three's Company, The Ropers. Mini-Series: Rich Man, Poor Man, Roots: The Next Generation.

FELLERMAN, MAX: Theatre executive. b. New York City, June 5, 1899. Entered m.p. ind. with Pathe Films in 1916, becoming salesman in 1918; resigned from RKO Distributing Co. to join RKO Theatre Co. 1932; joined United Paramount Theatres 1944 in theatre administration: to Lopert Films; v.p., gen. mgr., March, 1954–59; MGM, 1959–61, v.p. dir. film industry affairs, Inflight Motion Pictures, 1961–74. Now m.p. consultant.

FELLINI, FEDERICO: Director. b. Rimini, Italy. Jan. 8, 1920. Cartoonist, caricaturist; then m.p. dir., writer, actor; s.p.; actor.
PICTURES INCLUDE: The Miracle, Open City, Paisa, Variety Lights, White Sheik, I Vitelloni, The Matrimonial Agency (Love in the City), Il Bidone, The Wastrels, La Strada, The Swindlers, La Dolce Vita, Boccaccio '70, "8½", The Nights of Cabiria, Juliet of the Spirits, Spirits of the Dead, Fellini Satyricon, The Clowns, Fellini's Rome, Amarcord, Casanova, City of Women.

FELLMAN, DANIEL R.: Executive. b. Cleveland, Ohio, March 14, 1943. e. Rider College (BS, 1964). Joined Paramount N.Y. 1964; later sales mgr. Washington DC, Dallas. Next branch mgr. Cleveland; then Chicago. In 1969 joined Loews Theatres as film buyer. In 1971 joined Cinema National Theatres, division of Carrols Development Corp., as v.p./chief film buyer. In 1973 named v.p./dir., Cinema National Theatres. Joined Warner Bros. in 1978 as eastern sales mgr. 1979 named v.p./ass't. gen. sales mgr. Elected to: board directors NATO, 1975–76. Assistant Chief Barker Variety Club, Tent 35 NY 1976. President Variety Club Tent 35, 1977–78. 1980 Chairman Will Rogers Raffle Committee. v.p., bd. member, Variety Club Tent 25.

FELLMAN, NAT D.: Executive. b. New York, N.Y., Feb. 19, 1910. 1928. Started as office boy, Warner Bros. Pictures, 1928; transferred to Warner Bros. Theatres, asst. to chief booker; handled pool, partnership operations; head buyer, booker for Ohio zone, 1941; asst. to chief film buyer in New York, 1943; apptd. chief film buyer, 1952; exec. asst. to v.-p. and gen. mgr., Stanley Warner Theatres, 1955; asst. gen. mgr., Stanley Warner Theatres, 1962; acting gen. mgr. Stanley Warner Theatres, July, 1964; Stanley Warner Theatres, v.p. and gen. mgr., 1965; v.p., NGC Theatre Corp. and division mgr. Fox Eastern Theatres, 1968; v.p. National General Corp., and pres., National General Theatres, 1969; 1974, formed Exhibitor Relations Co., operations consultant; vice pres., Variety Clubs International; NATO, Chrm., presidents' advisory comm.

FENADY, ANDREW J.: Producer-writer. b. Toledo, Ohio, Oct. 4, 1928. e. Univ. of Toledo, 1946–50. Radio-prod.-actorwriter, WTOD; Actor, Summer Stock, 1948–51; National Classic Theatre, 1950–51; writer-prod., Confidential File, TV, 1954–56; joined Screen Gems as indep. prod. with own company, Fenady Associates, 1962.
PICTURES INCLUDE: Stakeout on Dope Street, The Young Captives, Ride Beyond Vengeance, Chisum, Terror in the Wax Museum, Arnold.
TV: The Rebel, Branded series, Hondo, Mission: Impossible.

FENNELLY, VINCENT M.: Producer. b. Brooklyn, July 6, 1920. e. Holy Cross, 1938–42. U.S. Navy, 1942–46; salesman, Monogram, Des Moines, 1947; entered prod. field, 1949; indep. prod. for Monogram, 1950; Ent. TV field,.1957; prod. Transwestern Films, Inc., Frontier Pictures, Silvermine Productions Co., Allied Artists; Malcolm Enterprises, Hilgarde Enter.
PICTURES INCLUDE: Kansas Territory, Wagons West, Fargo, Marksman, Star of Texas, Topeka, Texas Bad Man, Bitter Creek, The Desperado, Seven Angry Men, Dial Red O, Bobby Ware Is Missing, At Gunpoint, Crime in the Streets, Last of the Badmen.
TV: Four Star Films, Alcoa-Goodyear, Trackdown, Wanted Dead or Alive, David Niven Show, Richard Diamond, Stagecoach West, The Dick Powell Theatre, Target,

The Corruptors, Rawhide; A Man Called Shenandoah, MGM.

FENNEMAN, GEORGE: M.C., Announcer. b. Peking, China, Nov. 10.; e. San Francisco State Univ.
CREDITS INCLUDE: Groucho Marx Show You Bet Your Life, M.C. Host: Surprise Package, Funny Funny Films, Talk About Pictures, On Campus, Donny & Marie, Spokesman for Home Savings & Loan Assoc.

FERGUSON, HELEN: Public rel., career counsel. b. Decatur, Ill., July 23. e. Chicago Academy of Fine Arts. Film debut at 13, Essanay Studio, with Vitagraph, Lasky, Goldwyn, etc.; stage debut in Alias the Deacon, 1927.
THEATRE: New Brooms, Lomardi Ltd., This Thing Called Love, Intimate Strangers.
Freelance film work for many companies; retired from acting, 1930; entered pub. & pub. rel., 1933.
TV Panelist, RSVP, 1949–50.
Author: Loretta Young's The Things I Had to Learn, 1961. Bobbs-Merrill, other professional biographies.

FERGUSON, ROBERT S.: Executive. b. New York, N.Y., May 8, 1915. e. N.Y.U., BS, 1936. Started in newspaper field, Scripps Howard, 1936–37; m.p. ind., 1938 with Warner Bros. Pictures; Columbia Pictures, 1940; asst. dir. of adv. & pub., 1950; dir. adv., exploitation & pub., 1957; pres. Screen Publicists Guild, 1946; V.P. World-Wide Adv. & Pub. Columbia, 1963; V.P. Corporate Relations, Columbia Pictures Industries, 1974; V.P. Marketing—The American Film Theatre, 1974; V.P. and mgr., Entertainment Division—Rosenfeld, Sirowitz and Lawson Advertising, 1975; Director Marketing—Horizon Pictures, 1976; pres. Cinema Think Tank 1977–; instructor, Adelphi University, 1978. Rejoined Columbia Pictures Industries as consultant to pres., 1979.

FERRER, JOSE: Producer, director, actor. b. Santurce, Puerto Rico, Jan. 8, 1912; e. Princeton U.; Director and actor, New York stage, prior to screen career; dir. stage play, Strange Fruit; New York stage; Twentieth Century, 1951; dir., prod. Stalag 17, N.Y. stage, 1951; prod. and dir., The Chase; prod., dir., act., The Shrike, N.Y. stage, 1952; dir. My Three Angels.
PICTURES INCLUDE: Joan of Arc, Whirlpool, Crisis, Cyrano de Bergerac, Anything Can Happen, Moulin Rouge, Miss Sadie Thompson, Caine Mutiny, Deep in My Heart, The Shrike, Cockleshell Heroes, Great Man, I Accuse, State Fair; Lawrence of Arabia, Stop Train 349 From Berlin, Enter Laughing, Voyage of the Damned, The Sentinel, The Swarm, Fedora.

FERRER, MEL: Producer, director, actor. b. Elberon, N.J., Aug. 25, 1917; e. Princeton U. During coll. and early career spent summers at Cape Cod Playhouse, Dennis, Mass.; then writer in Mexico, authored juvenile book, Tito's Hats; later ed. Stephen Daye Press, Vt. Left publishing upon reaching leading-man status at Dennis; first two Broadway appearances, dancing roles, You'll Never Know, Everywhere I Roam; others. Kind Lady, Cue For Passion; then to radio, serving apprenticeship in small towns; prod.-dir., NBC; dir. Land of the Free, The Hit Parade, and Hildegarde program. Entered m.p. ind., 1945, when signed by Columbia, dial. dir.: The Girl of the Limberlost; later, returned to Broadway, leading role, Strange Fruit; signed by David Selznick as producer-actor, on loan to John Ford as prod. asst. on The Fugitive; then to RKO for Vendetta. Acted in Lost Boundaries, Born to be Bad, Ondine on Bway., 1954.
PICTURES INCLUDE: The Secret Fury, The Brave Bulls, Rancho Notorious, Scaramouche, Lili, Knights of the Round Table, Saada, War and Peace, Paris Does Strange Things, The Vintage, The World, The Flesh, and the Devil, Blood and Roses, El Greco; prod., Wait Until Dark, "W."

FERRI, ROGER: Executive. b. Providence, R.I. Sports ed. Providence News, Springfield, Mass. Union; others; feature writer, Boston Post (co-author, Life of Gen. Pershing); Detroit Free Press; New York World, Press repr., Shubert Attractions, Comstock, Elliott & Gest, John Cort; agent, Sells-Floto and Forepaugh circuses; adv. pub. dir. Emery Circuit, R.I.; Nathanson Amusements, New England; on staff, Exhibitors' Trade Review, M.P. World, Variety, M.P. News; adv. pub. mgr., Chadwick Pictures; 1924, dist. expl. rep., Fox Film Corp., Cleveland, Cincinnati, Detroit, Indianapolis, Chicago; 1925, Home Office executive, 1926–62, sales promotions director, publisher-editor 20th Century-Fox Dynamo, 1963, adv. pub. dir., National Screen Service Corp.

FETZER, JOHN E.: Executive. b. Decatur, Ind., March 25, 1901. e. Purdue Univ., U. of Mich. A.B., Andrews U. Hon. LL.D., West. Mich. Univ. 1958; chairman, owner Fetzer Broadcasting Co., Kalamazoo, Mich.; chmn., owner Detroit Baseball Club; pres., owner Fetzer Communications, Inc., Kalamazoo; chairman, dir., Cornhusker TV Corp.; Ch. Wolverine Cablevision; Mem., former bd. dir., Amer. Nat'l Bank and Trust Co., former mem. Bd. of Trustees, Kalamazoo College. Radio research Europe, 1925; asst. dir., U.S. Censorship in charge of radio. 1944–46; served as war corr. in ETO, 1945; spl. assignment radio, TV, newspaper mission to Europe and Middle East, 1952. chmn., TV code review bd., NARTB, 1952–55. Fellow, Royal Society of Arts, London; mem., Acad. of Polit. Science. Clubs: Park, Kalamazoo Country, (Kalamazoo); Park and Television Execs. Soc. (Assoc.); Broadcast Pioneers, N.Y.C.

FIELD, DAVID M.: Executive. b. Kansas City, MO. e. Princeton University. Worked as reporter on city desk at Hartford (Conn.) Courant. In 1968 with NBC News in N.Y.C. and Washington, D.C. Entered film school at U.S.C. (L.A.) after which joined Columbia Pictures as west coast story editor. In 1973 went to ABC-TV Network as mgr., movies of the week. 1975, moved to 20th-Fox as v.p., creative afffairs. Joined United Artists in 1978; named snr. v.p.—west coast production. Left in 1980 to become 20th-Fox exec. v.p. in chg. of worldwide production.

FIELD, SALLY: Actress. b. Pasadena, Calif., 1946. Gained stardom lead of TV series, Gidget, 1965, followed by The Flying Nun, 1967–68. Theatrical film debut in The Way West (1967).
PICTURES INCLUDE: Stay Hungry, Smokey and the Bandit, Heroes, The End, Hooper, Norma Rae, Beyond the Poseidon Adventure, Smokey and the Bandit II, Back Roads, Absence of Malice.
TV: Home for the Holidays, The Girl with Something Extra, Sybil.

FIELD, SHIRLEY ANNE: Actress. b. London. Ent. films after repertory experience 1955. Under contract to Ealing-M.G.M. 1958.
THEATRE: The Lily White Boys, Kennedys Children, Fire.
PICTURES INCLUDE: Saturday Night and Sunday Morning, The Man in the Moon, War Lover, Lunch Hour, Kings of the Sun, Doctor in Clover, Alfie, Hell is Empty.
TV: Risking It.

FIELD, VIRGINIA: Actress. r.n. Margaret Cynthia Field. b. London; e. England, Paris, Vienna. On N.Y. stage in Victoria Regina & others. On screen from 1934.
PICTURES INCLUDE: The Lady is Willing, Little Lord Fauntleroy, Ladies in Love, Lloyds of London, Singapore Woman, Atlantic Convoy, The Crystal Ball, Christmas Eve, Repeat Performance, Ladies Man, Dial 1119, Weekend With Father, Veils of Bagdad.
THEATRE: The Doughgirls.

FIELDS, FREDDIE: Executive. b. Ferndale, N.Y. July 12, 1923. Vice-pres., member of bd. of directors, MCA-TV, MCA Canada Ltd., MCA Corp.; mem., Pres. Club, Wash., D.C.; pres., Freddie Fields Associates Ltd., 1961 Pres., Kam Ent., Ltd.; v.p. F/B Prod., Inc., pres., chief exec. officer Creative Management Assoc. Ltd. Agency, Chicago, Las Vegas, Miami, Paris, Los Angeles, N.Y., London, Rome, 1962. Exclusive agent of Henry Fonda, Phil Silvers, Joanne Woodward, Paul Newman, Peter Sellers, Barbara Streisand, Steve McQueen, Ali MacGraw, Woody Allen, Robert Redford, Ryan O'Neal, Liza Minnelli and others. Dir. Chelsea Nat'l Bank, N.Y., Polly Bergen Co., First Consolidated Corp. In 1975 resigned post with CMA (now International Creative Mgt.) but continues as consultant. Presently producing for Paramount Pictures. 1977: Looking for Mr. Goodbar. 1980: Wholly Moses. 1981: Victory.

FINBERG, JACK GERALD: Writer technician. b. London, England. Asst. to exec. prod., story dept., British National Studios; Offic. shorthand writer, Royal Courts of Justice and Central Criminal court; hon. sec., Film Studios Club; personal asst. to Sam Spiegel; verbatim report., nuclear weapons, testing and disarmament conferences, UN; asst. prod., ABC TV; two feature writing credits; six major, 18 second feature film adaptations; Film/TV prod., Australia.

FINCH, JON: Actor. b. England, 1941. Came to acting via backstage activities, working for five years as stage manager in repertory theatres all over Britain.
PICTURES INCLUDE: MacBeth, Sunday, Bloody Sunday, Frenzy, Lady Caroline Lamb, The Final Program, Une Femme Fidele, The Man of the Green Cross, Battleflag, Death on the Nile.

FINE, HARRY: Producer. e. St. Andrew's College and Dublin Univ.
FILMS INCLUDE: Up The Junction, The Liquidator, The Penthouse, Long Days Dying, Vampire Lovers, Fright, Twins of Evil, Too Far To Go, Quadrophenia, McVicar.
T.V. FILM SERIES: Sir Francis Drake, Man of The World, The Sentimental Agent.

FINESHRIBER, WILLIAM H., JR.: Executive. b. Davenport, Ia. Nov. 4, 1909; e. Princeton U., B.A., 1931. Pub., CBS, 1931–34; mgr. Carnegie Hall, N.Y., 1934–37; script writer, dir., music comm., dir. of music dept., CBS, 1937–40; dir. of short wave programs, CBS, 1940–43; gen. mgr. CBS program dept. 1943–49; v.p. in charge of programs MBS, 1949–51; exec. v.p. & dir., MBS, 1951–53; v.p. & gen. mgr. of networks, NBC, 1953–54; v.p. in charge of Radio Network, NBC, 1955; v.p., Television Programs of America, 1956; director International operations, Screen Gems, 1957; v.p., Motion Picture Assoc. of America and Motion Picture Ex-

port Assoc. of America, 1960; bd. of dir., NARTB; exec. comm., bd. of dir., R.A.B.; v.p Radio Pioneers.

FINKELSTEIN, HERMAN: Attorney. b. Torrington, Conn., Jan. 9, 1903; e. Clark U., A.B.: Yale Law School, LL.B., member of Conn., Pa. & N.Y., U.S. Sup. Ct. bar; American Law Institute; director, ASCAP Nathan Burkan Memorial Competition; Mem.; State Dept. Panel on intl. Copyright; U.S. National Commission for UNESCO 1957–62; Consultant to U.S. Delegation, Inter-Amer. Conf. of Copyright Exports, Wash., D.C., 1946; Mem. U.S. Delegation, Intergovernmental Conference on Universal Copyright Convention Geneva (1952), Berne Convention-Stockholm Revision Conf. 1967, Paris Revision Conf. 1971, Communication Satellite Conf. 1973, past pres., Copyright Soc. U.S.A., past pres., Exec. Bureau, CISAC; past pres., SCRIBES.
AUTHOR: Numerous articles on copyright.

FINNEY, ALBERT: Actor. b. Salford, England, May 9, 1936. Studied for stage at R.A.D.A. making his West End debut 1958 in The Party. Appeared at Stratford-on-Avon 1959 season playing title role in Coriolanus, etc. 1960; On West End stage in The Lily White Boys and Billy Liar, Luther; New York, 1963, Luther. National Theatre 1965; Much Ado About Nothing, Armstrong's Last Goodnight, Love for Love, Miss Julie, Black Comedy, A Flea in Her Ear; Broadway, Joe Egg; London Stage, Alpha Beta, Krapp's Last Tape, Cromwell, Chez Nous, Hamlet, Tamburlaine, Uncle Vanya, Present Laughter. National Theatre: The Country Wife, The Cherry Orchard, Macbeth 1978.
PICTURES INCLUDE: The Entertainer, Saturday Night and Sunday Morning, Tom Jones, Night Must Fall, Two for the Road, Charlie Bubbles, Scrooge, Gumshoe, Alpha Beta, Murder on the Orient Express, Wolfen, Loophole, Looker.

FINEY, EDWARD: Producer. b. New York City; e. C.C.N.Y. Began as engineer, Western Electric. Then property man, Johnny Hines, C.C. Burr comedies. To MGM as press sheet ed.; sales promotion mgr., Pathe; asst. adv. dir. UA; story ed. and adv. dir., Mon-Rep., prod. & adv. dir., Grand Natl.; then prod. Monogram, many westerns. In 1941 org. Edward Finney Prod. Discovered Tex Ritter and made his first 40 features. Prod. & dir. Silver Stallion, Code of the Redman, Queen of the Amazons, etc. Clubs: Masquers. ex. pres. Catholic Press Council, Board Member Permanent Charities, M.P. Acad. of Arts and Sciences Dramatic Guild; pres., Indep. M.P. Prod. Assn. Film chrm. Catholic Press Council.
PICTURES INCLUDE: Corregidor, Golden Stallion, Call of the Forest, Hi Diddle Diddle, Primitive Passion, Mormon Battalion, This Is Pippin (TV); Seven Wonders, Baron Munchausen, Enchanted Years, Buffalo Bill in Tomahawk Territory, Slash of the Knife, Gun Girls, Journey to Freedom, London After Dark, Dark Road, Halfway to Hell, The Prairie, Secret Tower, Barrels Away, Things That Make America Great, (TV); Spring Affair, Dragons Across Asia, The Madcaps, The Happy Clown, The Great Dogtown Robbery.
TV: Pilots for Law and the People and the Circle Kids. Now preparing Small Crossing, Dog House Blues and The Italian.

FIRTH, PETER: Actor. b. Bradford, Yorkshire, Oct. 27, 1953. Selected to appear in local TV children's show where casting director spotted him and got him role in series, The Flaxton Boys. Moved to London and worked in TV, first in children's show, later on dramas for BBC. Big break came in 1973 when signed for Equus at National Theatre, London, which role repeated for film.
PICTURES: Joseph Andrews, Aces High, Equus, When You Comin Back, Red Ryder.
STAGE: Equus, Romeo and Juliet, Spring Awakening.

FISCHER, JOSEPH A.: Executive. e. Syracuse Univ.; As CPA was mgr. with Price Waterhouse & Co. Joined Columbia Pictures in 1967 as comptroller; In 1972 made v.p. In 1973 named financial v.p.-treas. of Col. Pictures Industries; 1976, sr. v.p. & chief financial officer; 1979, exec. v.p. Mem. American Inst. of CPA's and N.Y Society of CPA's.

FISHER, AL: Executive. b. Brooklyn, N.Y. Entered m.p. industry as office boy, Fox Metropolitan Theatres; U.S. Army Provost Marshal General's Office, 1942–46; Universal Pictures, mgr., Park Avenue Theatre, N.Y & Copley Plaza Theatre, Boston, 1946; Eagle Lion Film Co., mgr., Red Shoe's Bijou Theatre, N.Y., 1947; Stanley Kramer Prods., exploitation, Cyrano de Bergerac, 1951; press agent, 1951; prod., Bway show, Daphine, 1952; joined United Artists Corporation, 1952, named dir. of exploitation; now freelancing as producer's repr.

FISHER, CARRIE: b. Beverly Hills, CA, Oct. 21, 1956. e. London Central School of Speech & Drama. Daughter of Debbie Reynolds and Eddie Fisher. On Broadway in revival of Irene and Censored Scenes from King Kong.
PICTURES: Shampoo, Star Wars, Mr. Mike's Mondo Video, The Empire STrikes Back, The Blues Brothers, Under the Rainbow.

FISHER, EDDIE: Singer. b. Philadelphia, Pa., Aug. 10, 1928. Band, nightclub, hotel singer; discovered by Eddie Cantor, 1949; U.S. Army, 1951–53; many hit records include: Wish You Were Here, Lady of Spain; radio & TV shows, NBC. PICTURES INCLUDE: Butterfield 8.

FISHER, FRANK H.: Executive. b. Toronto, Ont., Canada, May 16, 1907. e. Hillhurst public sch., Calgary, Alberta, 1912–19; Crescent Hghts. Collegiate Institute, Calgary, 1919–23. Bank of Toronto, 1923–26. Cashier, booker, Educational Films, 1926–32; br. mgr., Empire Universal Films, Calgary, 1932–34; office mgr., Toronto, 1935; br. mgr., Montreal, 1938; br. mgr. Toronto, 1939; asst. gen. mgr. 1939–45; chief buyer, then western div. mgr., Odeon Theatres, 1945–47; dir., vice-pres. gen. mgr., Rank Film Distr., 1947–54; apptd., vice-pres. & gen. mgr.; Odeon Theatres of Canada, 1954. In 1973 joined Canadian Theatre Group Ltd. as Toronto rep. and v.p.-asst. to pres. Past Pres., Canadian Picture Pioneers; past pres., Canadian Motion Picture Industry Council; past pres., Rotary Club of Toronto; past pres., Convention and Tourist Bur. of Metro Toronto; dir. Health League of Canada and Ontario Crippled Children's Society; retired May, 1972; chairman of board of Governors O'Keefe Centre for the performing arts Toronto; director of Y.E.S. (Youth Employment Service.)

FISZ, BENJAMIN: Producer. b. Warsaw, Poland, Nov. 4, 1922. Formed in assoc. Golden Era Films, 1954. Later Aqua Films Ltd., 1957 as ind. prod. for Rank Org. and formed S. Benjamin Fisz Prod. Ltd., 1963 formed Benton Film Prod. Ltd. in assoc. with Anthony Mann. 1967 Spitfire Prods. with Harry Saltzman. 1969 Benmar Prods. Incorporated into Scotia Investments Ltd. Formed Scotia Intl. under name group for dist. Dir., Scotia-Barber. 1972: Formed Scotia Int. (Film Sales.) Jointly formed Scotia Deutschland and International Film Theatre Ltd.
PICTURES INCLUDE: Capri, The Secret, Child in the House, Hell Drivers, Sea Fury, On the Fiddle, The Heroes of Telemark, The Battle of Britain, A Town Called Bastard, Aces High, A Nightingale Sang in Berkeley Square, Philby.

FITELSON, H. WILLIAM: Attorney, counsel to Fitelson, Lasky and Aslan, law firm, New York City, specializing in the field of communications (publishing, motion pictures, theatre, television, radio); born New York City Jan. 21, 1905; educated Columbia University (extension), New York Law School; newspaper and editorial work, librarian and tutor New York Law School, Story Department Tiffany-Stahl Productions 1929, counsel Tiffany-Stahl Productions 1929–1932, United States counsel to British and foreign motion picture and theatrical producers, counsel to The Theatre Guild and numerous members motion picture industry, theatre industry, newspaper and publishing, television and radio interests, managing director Theatre Guild Television and radio divisions, including U.S. Steel Hour. Non-legal consultant on communications projects to Allen & Co., and Columbia Pictures Industries.

FITZGERALD, GERALDINE: Actress. b. Dublin, Eire, Nov. 24, 1914; e. Dublin Art Sch. On stage Gate theat., Dublin; then in number of Brit. screen prod. including Turn of the Tide, Mill on the Floss. On N.Y. stage in Heartbreak House. In U.S. screen prod. from 1939 Wuthering Heights. Pictures (U.S.) include Dark Victory, Till We Meet Again, Flight from Destiny, Gay Sisters, Ladies Courageous, Watch on the Rhine, Wilson, The Strange Affair of Uncle Harry, Three Strangers, Nobody Lives Forever, So Evil My Love, Obsessed, Ten North Frederick, The Pawnbroker, Rachel, Rachel, Believe in Me, The Last American Hero, Harry and Tonto, Echoes of a Summer, Arthur.
STAGE: A Long Day's Journey Into Night (1971).
TV: The Best of Everything.

FITZGERALD, PEGEEN: Commentator, executive. b. Norcatur, Kans., Nov. 24. e. Coll. of St. Theresa, Winona, Minn.; LL.D. (hon.) Seton Hall U. m. Ed Fitzgerald. Sales prom. adv. in retail field; magazine editor; originator (with husband) of husband and wife radio-TV conversation; radio-TV commentator, WOR, N.Y.; pres. Vivisection Investigation League; founder, Crusade for the Abolition of Cruelty; president Millennium Guild; co-author of Cast of Characters, author of Meatless Cooking pub. by Prentice-Hall.

FITZGERALD, ROBERT: Actor-writer. b. San Francisco, Calif., Nov. 28, 1925. e. Hollywood H.S.; Univ. of Calif, 1949. John Golden Award, 1945; Erskine Johnson Award, 1948; pioneered Late Show on TV Midnite Shack, CBS, 1951; prod., Peter Lind Hayes Review, 1953; Actor: Verdict is Yours, CBS-TV, 1960; prod., Japanese Plan, Hotel Bunker, The Big Trip (Docu.), In The Looking Glass (Short), Spook Tours Europe (Docu.), Funnyman (Short), The Welt Story (Docu.); prod. dir., Whoever He Was?, short; The Southern Gentleman, short; The World is Three Drinks Behind, docu.; Bradley For President, (doc.), Gunga Din Massey (short); 1967 prod. The Bogart Years; 1968 London Girl, Bogie Revisited. Prod. I Love You Rick Leland, 1968; John Garfield Story.

FITZPATRICK, JAMES A.: Producer. b. Shelton, Conn. February 26, 1902; e. Yale and American Academy of Dramatic Arts; m. Lesley Champlin. Newspaper field and stage. Writing, directing and producing since 1925. Pioneer producer and originator of off-stage voice for FitzPatrick Traveltalks and others through his own company. Distributes through MGM, Paramount, Warner Bros.; in 1944 org. own prod. co., Fitz-Patrick Pictures, Hollywood, Calif.

FIX, PAUL: Actor. b. Dobbs Ferry, N.Y., March 13, 1902. Toured with stock companies in the eastern states, also in numerous stage productions in the twenties and thirties on the west coast. In motion pictures since 1922.
PICTURES INCLUDE: High and the Mighty, Giant, Bad Seed, To Kill a Mockingbird, Pat Garret and Billy the Kid, 1973.
TV: Numerous prods., five yrs. as Marshall Micah on The Rifleman, Zabreskie Point.

FLAKS, STEPHEN: Executive. b. Jan. 1, 1941, New York. e. City College of New York, B.B.A. Early career as an investment banker & stock broker for various companies, including First Hanover, First Devonshire, 1962–69. Founded Flaks-Zaslow in 1969. Entered motion picture industry in 1974 in capacity of production financing. Established VideoVision, Inc., in 1978.

FLATTERY, THOMAS L.: Executive-Lawyer b. Detroit, Mich., Nov. 14, 1922. e. U.S.M.A., West Point, B.S., 1944–47; U.C.L.A., LL.B., 1952–55; U.S.C., LL.M, 1955–65. Gen'l counsel and asst. sec'y, McCulloch Corp., Calif. 1957–64; sec'y and corporate counsel, Technicolor, Inc., 1964–70; Vice President, Secretary & General Counsel, Amcord, Inc (formerly American Cement Corporation) 1970–72; Vice President, Secretary & General Counsel, Schick Incorporated, 1972–1975; counsel asst. secretary, C.F. Braun & Co., 1975–1976; sr. vice pres., secretary & general counsel Automation Industries, Inc. since 1976 to present.

FLAXMAN, JOHN P.: Producer. b. New York City, March 3, 1934. e. Dartmouth Univ. B.A. 1956; 1st Lt. U.S. Army, 1956–58. Ent. m.p. industry in executive training program, Columbia Pictures Corp., 1958–1963; exec. story consultant, Profiles in Courage, 1964–65; head of Eastern Literary Dept., Universal Pictures, 1965; writer's agent, William Morris Agency, 1966; partner with Harold Prince in Media Productions, Inc. 1967; pro. m.p. Something for Everyone. Founded Flaxman Film Corp., 1975. Prod. Jacob Two-Two Meets the Hooded Fang, 1976. President-Tricorn Productions 1977; pres. Filmworks Capital Corp., 1979–present: Becker/Flaxman & Associates, 1979–present.

FLEISCHER, RICHARD O.: Director. b. Brooklyn, N.Y., Dec. 8, 1916; e. Brown U., B.A.; Yale U., M.F.A. Stage dir.; joined RKO Pathe 1942.
PICTURES INCLUDE: Flicker Flashbacks, This is America, Design for Death, Child of Divorce, Banjo, So This Is New York, Bodyguard, Follow Me Quietly, The Clay Pigeon, Narrow Margin, The Happy Time, Arena, 20,000 Leagues Under the Sea, Violent Saturday, Girl in the Red Velvet Swing, Bandido, Between Heaven and Hell, The Vikings, These Thousand Hills, Compulsion, Crack in the Mirror, The Big Gamble, Barabbas, Fantastic Voyage, Doctor Dolittle, Boston Strangler, Tora! Tora! Tora!, Ten Rillington Place, The Last Run, See No Evil, The New Centurions, Soylent Green, The Don is Dead, The Spikes Gang, Mister Majestyk, Mandingo, The Incredible Sarah, Crossed Swords, Ashante, The Jazz Singer, Tough Enough.

FLEMING, JANET BLAIR: Executive. b. Ottawa, Canada, November 29, 1944. e. Bachelor Arts Degree, Carlton University, Ottawa, Canada; Special asst. to Canada's Federal Minister of Transport 1967–1972; 1973–77, asst. to Sandy Howard—business affairs; 1977, co-founder and v.p./sales & admin. of Producers Sales organization.

FLEMING, RHONDA: Actress. r.n. Marilyn Louis. b. Los Angeles, Aug. 10. b. Harold and Effie Graham Lewis, prof.; e. Beverly Hills High School. Calif. Screen debut: Spellbound. L.A. Civic Light Opera in Kismet revival; 1976. Broadway debut in 1973: Revival of The Women.
PICTURES INCLUDE: Spiral Staircase, Adventure Island, Out of the Past; singing debut: A Connecticut Yankee in King Arthur's Court, The Last Outpost, Cry Danger, The Redhead and the Cowboy, The Great Lover, Crosswinds, Little Egypt, Hong Kong, Golden Hawk, Tropic Zone, Pony Express, Serpent of the Nile, Inferno, Those Redheads from Seattle, Jivaro, Yankee Pasha, Tennessee's Partner, While the City Sleeps, Killer Is Loose, Slightly Scarlet, Odongo, Queen of Babylon, Gunfight at the OK Corral, Buster Keaton Story, Gun Glory, Home Before Dark, Alias Jesse James, The Big Circus, The Crowded Sky, Instant Love, The American Wife, Won Ton Ton, The Dog Who Saved Hollywood, The Nude Bomb.

FLEMYNG, ROBERT: Actor. b. Jan. 3, 1912, Liverpool, Eng. e. Halleybury Coll. Stage debut: Rope 1931. Screen debut: Head Over Heels 1937.
PICTURES INCLUDE: Bond Street, The Guinea Pig, The Conspirators, The Blue Lamp, Blackmailed, The Magic

Box, The Holly and the Ivy, Cast a Dark Shadow, Man Who Never Was, Funny Face, Let's Be Happy, Windom's Way, Blind Date, A Touch of Larceny, Radtus (Italian), The King's Breakfast, The Deadly Affair, The Spy with the Cold Nose, The Quiller Memorandum, Deathhead Avenger, OH! What a Lovely War, Battle of Britain, Cause for Alarm, Young Winston, The Darwin Adventure, Travels with my Aunt, Golden Rendezvous, The Medosa Touch, The Four Feathers, The Thirtynine Steps.

TV: appearances in England, U.S. inc.: Rainy Day, Playhouse 90, Wuthering Heights, Browning Version, After the Party, Boyd Q.C., They Made History, Somerset Maugham Show, Woman in White, The Datchet Diamonds, Probation Officer, Family Solicitor (series), Man of the World, Zero One, Compact, (serial), Day By the Sea, The Living Room, Hawks and Doves, Vanity Fair, The Inside Man, The Doctor's Dilemma, The Persuaders, Major Lavender, Public Eye, Florence Nightingale, Edward VIII, Spy Trap, The Venturers' Loyalties, The Avengers, Crown Court, Enemy at the Door, Rebecca, Edward and Mrs. Simpson.

FLETCHER, LOUISE: Actress. Came to Hollywood at age 21; studied with Jeff Corey. Worked on TV shows (including Playhouse 90). Gave up career to be housewife for 10 yrs.; returned to work in 1973.
PICTURES INCLUDE: Thieves Like Us, One Flew Over the Cuckoo's Nest, Exorcist II: The Heretic, The Cheap Detective, Natural Enemies.

FLEXER, DAVID: Executive. b. Mt. Plasant, Tenn., June 29, 1909; e. Wallace U. School, 1926; Vanderbilt U., 1930; m. Eleanor Handmacher, concert pianist. Was adv. rep. on national magazines, 1930–32; joined United Artists 1932–33; entered exhib. 1933, head of Flexer Theatres, operating in Tenn. and Miss.; The Albany Corp.; Theatre Real Estate Corp.; v.p. Impossible Pictures, Inc., producers of cartoons currently distrib. by Republic; constructed first drive-in theatres in Minneapolis, and St. Louis, 1947; pres., Flexer Theatres of Tenn., Inc., Flexer Theatres of Miss., Inc., The Albany Corp. Pres., Inflight Motion Pictures.

FLINN, JOHN C.: Publicist. b. Yonkers, N.Y. May 4, 1917; p. late John C. Flinn, pioneer m.p. executive; e. U. of Calif. In pub. dept. David O. Selznick, 1936–39; unit publicist, then head planner, Warner, 1936–46; joined Monogram as asst. to nat'l adv. & pub. head & pub. mgr. Aug. 5, 1946; apptd. nat'l dir. of pub. & adv. of Allied Artists Pictures Corp., March, 1951, appt'd studio dir. adv. & pub., Columbia, March, 1959; v.p., Jim Mahoney & Associates (pub. rel. firm) in 1971. Joined MGM West Coast publicity department as publicity coordinator, January, 1973; Rejoined Columbia Pictures in Feb., 1974 as studio pub. dir.; 1979, promoted to dir. industry relations.

FLOREA, JOHN: Producer-Director. b. Alliance, O., May 28, 1916. Served as photo journalist with Life magazine, 1940–50; assoc. editor Colliers magazine, 1950–53. Prod.-dir.
TV: Sea Hunt TV series, 1957–60; also dir. TV shows Bonanza, The Virginian, Honey West, Daktari, Gentle Ben, Cowboy in Africa. Prod.-dir. of film Islands of the Lost. With Ivon Tors Films. Nominated as one of the top 10 directors in America by DGA for 1968 Mission Impossible episode. Dir. several Ironsides episodes.
PICTURES INCLUDE: A Time to Every Purpose.

FLYNN, JOHN: Director-Writer. Began career as trainee script supvr. for dir. Robert Wise. Soon working as ass't. dir. on MGM-TV shows. Made dir. debut with The Sergeant, 1969.
PICTURES INCLUDE: The Jerusalem File (dir.), The Outfit (s.p., dir.), Rolling Thunder (dir.); Defiance (dir.).

FOCH, NINA: Actress. b. Leyden, Holland, April 20, 1924; daughter of Consuelo Flowerton, actress, & Dirk Foch, symphony orch. conductor. Many stage, radio, television appearances. Prof. Univ. South. Calif, 1966–67; 1978–80, senior faculty, American Film Institute, 1974–77; Board of Governors, Hollywood Acad. Television Arts & Sciences, 1976–77; Exec. Comm. Foreign Film Award, Acad. Motion Picture Arts & Sciences, 1970–.
PICTURES INCLUDE: Nine Girls, Song to Remember, My Name is Julia Ross, An American in Paris, Scaramouche, Young Man in Hurry, Undercover Man, Sombrero, Fast Company, Executive Suite, Four Guns to the Border, Ten Commandments, Illegal, You're Never Too Young, Cry of the Werewolf, Escape in the Fog, I Love A Mystery, Johnny Allegro, Johnny O'Clock, Prison Ship, Return of the Vampire, Shadows In The Night, The Dark Past, The Guilt of Janet Ames, Three Brave Men, Spartacus, Cash McCall, Such Good Friends, Salty, Mahogany, Jennifer.

FOGARTY, JACK V.: Executive-Writer. b. Los Angeles, Calif. e. UCLA. hd. travel dept., MGM, 1960–62; exec. prod. mgr., Cinerama, Inc., 1962–64; assoc. prod., The Best of Cinerama, 1963; co-creator, The Boilermakers, CBS-TV, 1964; own p.r. firm, 1965; pres., AstroScope, Inc., 1969; named chm. bd., chief exec. off., 1974.
TV: (writer) The Rookies, SWAT, D'Angelo Superstar, Charlie's Angels, Most Wanted, Barnaby Jones, A Man Called Sloane, others. Story Editor, Charlie's Angels; exec.

story editor, A Man Called Sloane. exec. story editor, Most Wanted, exec. story consultant, Sheriff Lobo.

FOGELSON, ANDREW: Executive. b. New Rochelle, N.Y., August 5, 1942. e. Union College (1960–64). First entered m.p. industry in 1968 with Warner Bros., starting as copywriter and soon made exec. asst. to v.p. of adv.-pub. In 1973 appt. v.p., marketing services. Joined Columbia Pictures in Dec. 1973, as v.p. in chg. world-wide adv.-pub. In 1977 went to Warner Bros. as exec. v.p. in chg. worldwide adv.-pub, 1979, left to become pres. of Rastor Prods. Resigned 1981 to become indep. producer.

FOGELSON, DAVID: b. Netcong, N.J., Mar. 15, 1903; e. New York U. (Sch. of Commerce), B.C.S., '23; Fordham U., LL.B. '26. Trustee Joe & Emily Lowe Fund, CPA, (N.Y.).

FOLEY, GEORGE F.: TV. m.p. prod., lawyer. b. Grantwood, N.J., March 26, 1919; e. Fordham U., 1941. Attorney, N.Y.; dir. of pub. rel., Newell-Emmett Co., 1946–48; dir. radio & TV Newell-Emmett Co., 1948–49; Cecil & Presbrey, 1949–50; prod. package shows including Tales of Tomorrow, Gallup Poll, Herman Hickman, etc.
PICTURES INCLUDE: Public Enemy No. 1, Frankenstein's Daughter, Missile to the Moon, Leave Me Alone, The Vulture, Importer of films: La Dolce Vita, Last Year at Marienbad, Rocco and His Brothers.
Counsel, CBS-EVR, Believe It Or Not, Inc., Crosby Enterprizes.

FOLSEY, GEORGE: Cameraman.
PICTURES INCLUDE: Reunion in Vienna, Storm at Daybreak, Stage Mother, Going Hollywood, MGM, Men in White, Operator 13, MGM. In 1935, Reckless, I Live My Life, The Great Ziegfeld. The Gorgeous Hussy, MGM; Hearts Divided, Meet Me in St. Louis, Mr. Imperium, Law and Lady, Lovely to Look At, Million Dollar Mermaid, All The Brothers Were Valiant, Executive Suite, Seven Brides for Seven Brothers, Deep in My Heart, The Cobweb, Fastest Gun Alive, House of Numbers, Imitation General, Cash McCall, Glass Houses.

FONDA, HENRY: Actor. b. Grand Island, Neb., May 16, 1905; e. Minn. U. With Community Playhouse (Omaha), then Cape Playhouse (Dennis, Mass.), also other theat. groups & tourist cos.; later with N.Y. Theatre Guild as extra & understudy.
STAGE: New Faces, The Swan, The Farmer Takes a Wife; extended N.Y. run in Mr. Roberts, 1949–50; Point of No Return, 1952; Caine Mutiny, Court Martial, 1953, Gift of Time, Generation, Our Town, The Time of Your Life, Two For The Seasaw, Silent Night, Lonely Night, Critics Choice. U.S. Navy, WW II. Screen debut in Farmer Takes a Wife, 1935; Clarence Darrow, 1974–75, First Monday in October, The Oldest Living Graduate (1980), Showdown at the Adobe Hotel (1981).
PICTURES INCLUDE: Jesse James, Young Mr. Lincoln, Drums Along the Mohawk, Grapes of Wrath, Male Animal, Immortal Sergeant, Ox-Bow Incident, My Darling Clementine, Daisy Kenyon, Long Night, The Fugitive, Fort Apache, On Our Merry Way, Mister Roberts, War and Peace, Wrong Man, 12 Angry Men, Warlock, Advise and Consent, Spencer's Mountain, Fail-Safe, The Rounders, The Best Man, Battle of the Bulge, A Big Hand for the Little Lady, Welcome to Hard Times, Firecreek, Yours, Mine, and Ours, Madigan, Once Upon a Time in the West, Boston Strangler, Too Late the Hero, There Was a Crooked Man, Cheyenne Social Club, Sometimes a Great Notion, Ash Wednesday, The Serpent, The Last Days of Mussolini, My Name is Nobody, Midway, Great Smokey Roadblock, Rollercoaster, Tentacles, The Swarm, Fedora, Meteor, Battle of Mareth, Wanda Nevada, City on Fire, On Golden Pond.
TV: Films: The Red Pony, Clarence Darrow, Home to Stay, AFI Henry Fonda Life Achievement Award; Roots 2, Gideon's Trumpet, Oldest Living Graduate.

FONDA, JANE: Actress. b. New York City, Dec. 21, 1937. p. Henry Fonda. e. Emma Willard School, Troy, N.Y. active in dramatics. Vassar. Appeared with father. Summer stock production. The Country Girl, Omaha, Neb. Studied painting, languages, Paris. Art Students League, N.Y. Appeared in The Male Animal, Dennis, Mass. Modeled, appeared on covers, Esquire, Vogue, The Ladies Home Journal, Glamour, and McCall's, 1959.
PICTURES INCLUDE: Tall Story (debut), Walk on the Wild Side, The Chapman Report, Period of Adjustment, In the Cool of The Day, Sunday in New York, The Love Cage, La Ronde, Cat Ballou, The Chase, La Curee, Any Wednesday, The Game Is Over, Hurry Sundown, Barefoot in the Park, Barbarella, Spirits of The Dead, They Shoot Horses, Don't They? (Acad. Award nom.), Klute, Steelyard Blues, F.T.A., A Doll's House, The Bluebird, Fun with Dick and Jane, Julia, Coming Home, Comes a Horseman, California Suite, The China Syndrome, The Electric Horseman, Nine To Five, Roll-Over, On Golden Pond.
STAGE: There Was A Little Girl, Invitation to a March, The Fun Couple, Strange Interlude.

FONDA, PETER: Actor. b. 1939. Son of Henry Fonda. Brother of Jane Fonda.

PICTURES INCLUDE: Tammy and the Doctor, The Victors, Lilith, The Wild Angels, Easy Rider, The Last Movie, The Hired Hand (also dir.), Two People, Dirty Mary Crazy Larry, Open Season, Race with the Devil, 91 In The Shade, Killer Force, Futureworld, Outlaw Blues, High Ballin!, UWanda Nevada (also dir.).

FONTAINE, JOAN: Actress. b. Tokyo, Oct. 22, 1917; e. art, privately; sister of Olivia de Haviland, actress; on B'way in Tea and Sympathy; m.p. debut in "Quality Street" 1937; won Academy Award best performance, 1941, for "Suspicion."

PICTURES INCLUDE: Women, Rebecca, Man Who Found Himself, You Can't Beat Love, Music for Madame, Blond Cheat, Gunga Din, This Above All, Jane Eyre, Frenchman's Creek, Affairs of Susan, Emperor Waltz, Kiss the Blood Off My Hands, You Gotta Stay Happy, Letter from an Unknown Woman, Duke of West Point, Ivy, Born to Be Bad, Something to Live For, September Affair, Darling How Could You?, Ivanhoe, Decameron Nights, Flight to Tangier, The Bigamist, Casanova's Big Night, Island in the Sun, Until We Sail, A Certain Smile, Tender Is the Night, The Devil's Own.

FORBES, BRYAN: Actor, writer, producer, director. Former head of prod., man. dir., Associated British Prods. (EMI). b. Stratford (London) July 22, 1926. Stage debut, The Corn is Green (London), 1942; screen debut, The Small Back Room 1948.

PICTURES INCLUDE: All Over the Town, The Wooden Horse, Dear Mr. Prohack, Appointment in London, Sea Devils, Wheel of Fate, Million Pound Note (Man with a Million), An Inspector Calls, Colditz Story, Passage Home, Extra Day, It's Great to be Young, Satellite in the Sky, Quartermass 11, Cockleshell Heroes, Black Tent, House of Secrets, Baby and the Battleship, I was Monty's Double, A Piece of Cake, Man in the Moon, Whistle Down The Wind, League of Gentlemen, Only Two Can Play, The L-Shaped Room, Of Human Bondage, Station Six Sahara, Seance on a Wet Afternoon, King Rat, The Wrong Box, The Whisperers, Deadfall, The Madwoman of Chaillot, The Go-Between (executive producer), The Railway Children (exec. prod.) Tales of Beatrix Potter (exec. prod.) The Raging Moon (US title; Long Ago Tomorrow). Also: I Caught Acting Like the Measles (produced/directed for television), Goodbye Norma Jean and Other Things, The Stepford Wives (dir.), The Slipper & The Rose, International Velvet, Sunday Lovers, Jessie, Hopscotch (s.p.).

TV: The Breadwinner, French Without Tears, Johnnie was a Hero, The Gift, The Road, The Heiress. Theatre: Flarepath, Fighters Calling, Gathering Storm, September Tide, The Holly and the Ivy, Tobias and the Angel, A Touch of Fear, Three Way Switch.

PUBLICATIONS: Truth Lies Sleeping (short stories) 1951; Distant Laughter (novel) 1972; Notes For a Life (Autobiog.) 1973/4. The Slipper & The Rose (Book of Film) 1975/6. Ned's Girl, 1977, International Velvet 1978 (novel); Familiar Strangers (novel), 1979 (US Title "Stranger"), That Despicable Race, 1980.

FORBES, GORDON B.: Executive. b. New York, New York. e. Yale University Drama Dept. Republic Studio-1945 Budget and Cost Control Dept.; 1950 asst. to production mgr.; 1952 head of production operations; 1954–1958 UPM Batjack Productions, production manager RKO-El Dorado Pictures (Cuba); 1959–1976 v.p. Universal TV, production operations mgr.; 1977 executive assistant to the pres. of The Burbank Studios and member of the executive committee. In 1979 named v.p. of studio productions for Paramount Pictures.

FORD, GLENN: Actor. r.n. Gwylin Ford; b. Quebec, Canada, May 1, 1916. m. Eleanor Powell, actress. On stage in western co. "Children's Hour" 1935; on Broadway in: Broom for a Bride, Soliloquy; served in U.S. Marine Corps 1942–45; m.p. debut in Heaven With a Barbed Wire Fence 1940.

PICTURES INCLUDE: Men Without Souls, Lady in Question, So Ends Our Night, Desperadoes, Stolen Life, Gilda, Framed, Mating of Millie, Return of October, Loves of Carmen, Mr. Soft Touch, Man from Colorado, Undercover Man, Lust for Gold, Doctor and the Girl, Flying Missile, The Redhead and the Cowboy, Follow the Sun, The Secret of Convict Lake, Green Glove, Young Man With Ideas, Affair in Trinidad, Man from the Alamo, Terror on a Train, Plunder of the Sun, Big Heat, Appointment in Honduras, Human Desire, The Americano, Violent Men, Blackboard Jungle, Interrupted Melody, Trial, Ransom, Fastest Gun Alive, Jubal, Teahouse of the August Moon, Don't Go Near the Water, Cowboy, The Sheepman, Imitation General, Torpedo Run, It Started with a Kiss, The Gazebo, Cimarron, Cry for Happy, The Four Horsemen of the Apocalypse, Experiment in Terror, Love Is a Ball, The Courtship of Eddie's Father, The Rounders, The Money Trap, Fate Is the Hunter, Dear Heart, The Last Challenge, Heaven With a Gun, Smith! The Day of the Evil Gun, A Time for Killing, Midway, Superman, Happy Birthday To Me.

TV: The Brotherhood of Ty Bell (movie); Cade's Country (series); Jarret; The Holvak Family.

FORD, HARRISON: Actor. b. Chicago, July 13, 1942. e. Ripon Coll.

PICTURES: Dead Heat on a Merry-Go-Round, Luv, Getting Straight, The Long Ride Home, Journey to Shiloh, Zabriskie Point, The Conversation, American Graffiti, Star Wars, Heroes, Force 10 from Navarone, Hanover Street, Apocalypse Now, The Frisco Kid, The Empire Strikes Back, Raiders of the Lost Ark.

TELEVISION: Dynasty, Trial of Lt. Calley, The Possessed.

FORD, TENNESSEE ERNIE: Singer. r.n. Ernest J. Ford, b. Bristol, Tenn., Feb. 13, 1919. e. Cincinnati Conserv. of Music. Radio anncr., 1939–41; U.S. Air Force, 1942–45; radio anncr., San Bernardino, Calif.; hillbilly disc jockey, Pasadena; Capital Recording Star.

TV: own TV shows, NBC; guest appearances on I Love Lucy, Red Skelton Show, Perry Como Show, George Gobel Show; own show, Tennessee Ford Show, ABC.

RECORDS INCLUDE: 16 Tons, etc.

FORD, TONY: Executive. b. August 6, 1925, New York City. e. St. Johns Univ. In U.S. Navy World War II; in life insurance business, 1946–48. Agent with MCA 1949–53. TV indep. prod., specials for Timex, Ringling Bros. Circus, Pontiac Victor Borge. Re-entered agency business, General Artists Corp., v.p., TV dept. Headed own agency, Tony Ford Mgt., Inc., which was acquired by William Morris Agency. Headed creative services division WMA representing producers, directors, writers specializing in the packaging of TV series and specials, left Morris Agency Jan. 1, 1977; now pres. of Tony Ford Productions, affiliated with Universal Studios.

FOREMAN, CARL (C.B.E.): Writer, prod., dir., b. Chicago, July 23, 1914. e. U. of Ill., Northwestern U., Crane Coll., John Marshall Law Sch.; m. In circus & carnival exploit.; then freelance writer, newspaper pub. rel., radio U.S. Army Signal Corps. World War II; former Executive producer, Managing director, Open Road Films, Ltd., England. Pres., Writer's Guild of Great Britain, 1968–75.

PICTURES INCLUDE: So This Is New York, Champion, Young Man With a Horn, Home of the Brave, The Men (Robert Metzger Award Screen Writers Guild), Cyrano de Bergerac, High Noon, The Key, The Bridge over the River Kwai, The Mouse that Roared, The Guns of Navarone, The Victors, Born Free, MacKenna's Gold, Otley, The Virgin Soldiers, Living Free, Young Winston, When Time Ran Out.

FOREMAN, JOHN: Producer. b. Idaho Falls, Idaho. Cofounder of CMA Agency. Resigned Jan., 1968, to form production co. with Paul Newman: Newman-Foreman Company.

PICTURES INCLUDE: Winning, Butch Cassidy and the Sundance Kid, WUSA (co-prod.), Puzzle of a Downfall Child, They Might Be Giants, Sometimes a Great Notion, Pocket Money, The Effect of Gamma Rays on Man-in-the-Moon Marigolds (exec. prod.), The Mackintosh Man, The Man Who Would Be King, Bobby Deerfield, The Great Train Robbery.

FORMAN, SIR DENIS, O.B.E., M.A.: Executive. b. Moffat, Dumfriesshire, Scot., Oct. 13, 1917. e. Loretto School, Musselburgh, Pembroke College, Cambridge. Served in Argyll & Sutherland Highlanders, World War II. Entered film business May, 1946, production staff Central Office of Information, 1947; Chief Production Officer C.O.I. 1948; appointed dir. of the British Film Institute, 1949; joined Granada Television Ltd., 1955. Jnt. Mng. Dir., 1965 chm., British Film Institute, Bd. of Gov., 1971–73. Chmn. Granada T.V. 1975. Chmn. Novello & Co. 1972. Fellow, British Acad. Film & TV Arts, 1976.

FORMAN, MILOS: Director. b. Czechoslovakia, 1932. Trained as writer at Czech Film School and as director at Laterna Magika. Won Int'l. attention with first film, Black Peter, 1963. Emigrated to U.S. after collapse of Dubcek Govt. in Czech.

PICTURES INCLUDE: The Loves of a Blonde, Fireman's Ball, Taking Off, Visions of Eight (segment) One Flew Over the Cuckoo's Nest, Hair, Ragtime.

FORREST, FREDERIC: Actor. Began career off-Broadway in Futz, Massachusetts Trust and Tom Paine, all with La Mama Troupe under direction of Tom O'Horgan. Moved to Hollywood in 1970. Made film debut in When The Legends Die in 1972.

PICTURES INCLUDE: The Don is Dead, The Conversation, The Gravy Train, Permission to Kill, The Missouri Breaks, It Lives Again, Apocalypse Now, The Rose, One from the Heart.

FORREST, STEVE: Actor. b. Huntsville, Texas, Sept. 29. e. UCLA, 1950. Acted at La Jolla Playhouse; appeared on radio, TV; m.p. debut in Geisha Girl.

PICTURES INCLUDE: Bad and the Beautiful, Battle Circus, The Clown, Band Wagon, Dream Wife, So Big, Take the High Ground, Phantom of the Rue Morgue, Prisoner of War, Rogue Cop, Bedeviled, It Happened to Jane, Heller in Pink Tights, Five Branded Women, Flaming Star, The Second Time Around, Rascal, The Wild Country, The Late Liz, North Dallas Forty.

FORRESTER, LARRY: Writer. b. Glasgow, Scotland, 1924. Ent. TV industry with his wife Pauline as Special investigators on audience participation shows. Later scripting for TV.
SERIES INCLUDE: Ivanhoe, William Tell, Flying Doctor, International Detective, Interpol Calling, Knight Errant, No Hiding Place, The Golden Girl, Sir Francis Drake, Top Secret, Ghost Squad, This Man Craig, Danger Man, Espionage, The Saint.
PICTURES INCLUDE: Hercules and the Princess of Troy; Tora! Tora! Tora!
BOOKS INCLUDE: Battle of the April Storm, A Girl Called Fathom, Fly for Your Life, Skymen, Diamond Beach.

FORSTER, ROBERT: Actor. b. Rochester, N.Y., July 13, 1941. e. Heidelberg College, Alfred University, Rochester U., B.S.
THEATRE: Plays, Mrs. Dally, 1965. Summer tour, A Streetcar Named Desire, 1967.
PICTURES INCLUDE: Reflections in a Golden Eye, Medium Cool, Justine, Journey Through Rosebud, The Don is Dead, The Black Hole.

FORSYTHE, JOHN: Actor. b. Penn's Grove, N.J., Jan. 29, 1918.
STAGE CREDITS: Mr. Roberts, All My Sons, Yellow Jack, Teahouse of the August Moon, and others.
TV: Started in 1947; appeared on Studio One, Kraft Theatre, Robert Montgomery Presents, and others. Bachelor Father series; To Rome with Love series.
PICTURES INCLUDE: Captive City, It Happens Every Thursday, The Glass Web, Escape from Fort Bravo, Trouble With Harry, Ambassador's Daughter, Everything But the Truth, Kitten With a Whip, Madame X, in Cold Blood, The Happy Ending, Topaz, And Justice for All.

FORTE, FABIAN: Singer, Actor. b. Philadelphia, Feb. 6, 1940. e. South Philadelphia high sch. At 14, discovered by Marcucci and DeAngelis, voice teacher. Chancellor Records; signed contract. Studied with Carlo Menotti.
RECORDS INCLUDE: Turn Me Loose, This Friendly World, The Fabulous Fabian (Gold album), Foggy Foggy Dew (High Time).
PICTURES INCLUDE: Hound Dog Man, High Tim, North to Alaska, Love in a Goldfish Bowl, Mr. Hobbs Takes a Vacation, Ride the Wild Surf, Dear Brigette, Longest Day, 10 Little Indians, Fireball 500, Thunder Alley, Five Weeks in a Balloon, Devil's Eight, The Longest Day, A Bullet for Pretty Boy, Little Laura and Big John.

FOSSE, BOB: Director, Choreographer, Actor. b. Chicago, 1927. Began dancing at age of 9 and made first professional appearance at 13. After service with U.S. Navy in World War II toured with Mary Ann Miles in Call Me Mister. Signed by MGM in 1953 and acted in three films. First big Broadway success as choreographer of Pajama Game in 1955.
PICTURES INCLUDE: Actor: Give a Girl A Break, The Affairs of Dobie Gillis, Kiss Me Kate, The Little Prince. Choreographer: My Sister Eileen. Director-Choreographer: Sweet Charity, Cabaret. Director: Lenny. All That Jazz (also co. s.p.)
BROADWAY: Choreographer: Pajama Game, Damn Yankees, Redhead, Little Me, New Girl in Town, How To Succeed in Business Without Really Trying, Sweet Charity, Pippin, Chicago. Director: Redhead, Little Me, Sweet Charity, Pippin, Chicago, Dancin'.

FOSTER, DAVID: Producer. b. New York City, Nov. 25, 1929. e. Dorsey H.S., U. of Southern California (School of Journalism). U.S. Army, 1952–54; entered public relations field in 1952 with Rogers, Cowan & Brenner; Jim Mahoney, 1956; Allen, Foster, Ingersoll & Weber, 1958; left field in 1968 to enter independent m.p. production.
PICTURES INCLUDES: Co-produced (with Mitchell Brower) McCabe and Mrs. Miller, The Getaway, The Nickel Ride (exec. prod.), The Drowning Pool (co-prod.), The Legacy.

FOSTER, JODIE: Actress. b. Los Angeles. Acting debut on Mayberry, R.F.D. TV series. Followed with many TV appearances, from series to Movies-of-the-Week.
PICTURES INCLUDE: Napoleon and Samantha, Menace of the Mountain, One Little Indian, Tom Sawyer, Kansas City Bomber, Taxi Driver, Echoes of a Summer, Bugsy Malone, Freaky Friday, The Little Girl Who Lives Down the Lane, Candleshoe, Foxes, Carny.
TV: The Courtship of Eddie's Father (regular), My Three Sons (regular), Paper Moon (regular), Smile, Jenny, You're Dead (movie), Rookie of the Year (movie).

FOSTER, JULIA: Actress. b. 1944, in Lewes, Sussex, England. First acted with the Brighton Repertory Company, then two years with the Worthing, Harrogate and Richmond companies. 1956, TV debut as Ann Carson in Emergency Ward 10.

PICTURES INCLUDE: Term of Trial, The Loneliness of the Long Distance Runner, The Small World of Sammy Lee, The System, The Bargee, One Way Pendulum, Alfie, Half A Sixpence.
TV: A Cosy Little Arrangement, The Planemakers, Love Story, Taxi, Consequences, They Throw It At You, Crime & Punishment, The Image.
STAGE: No. 1 tour of The Country Wife; 1969, What the Butler Saw.

FOSTER KEMP, CECIL R.: (M.B.E.) Assoc. prod. and prod. supervisor. b. Shanghai. e. Brighton College.
PICTURES INCLUDE: Paris Holiday, Interpol, Tarzan and the Lost Safari. Around the World in Eighty Days. Front Page Story, Appointment in London, South of Algiers, Under Capricorn, Scott of the Antarctic, Untamed, John Paul Jones, King of Kings, Offbeat, El Cid, Fifty Five Days at Peking, The Fall of the Roman Empire. William The Conqueror. Girl on the Motorcycle, Arthur! Arthur!, I Saw Him Die, Ferdinand and Isabella, Wild Violets.

FOSTER, MAURICE DAVID: Prod.-Wrt. e. St. Paul's Ent. m.p. ind. 1943 as asst. to gen. man. and prod. sup. Easling Studios. From 1950–61, prod. sup. and dir. Film Finances, 1961–63, dir. and gen. man. MGM British Studios.
PICTURES INCLUDE: The Jokers (Universal), Assignment K (Columbia).

FOWLER, HARRY: Actor. b. Lambeth Walk (London). Stage debut, Nothing Up My Sleeve (London) 1950; Screen debut, 1941.
PICTURES INCLUDE: Demi-Paradise, Don't Take It to Heart, Champaigne Charlie, Painted Boats, Hue and Cry, Now Barabbas, The Dark Man, She Shall Have Murder, The Scarlet Thread, High Treason, The Last Page, I Believe in You, Pickwick Papers, Top of the Form, Angels One Five, Conflict of Wings (Fuss Over Feathers), A Day to Remember, Blue Peter, Home and Away, Booby Trap, Town on Trial, Lucky Jim, Birthday Present, Idle on Parade, Don't Panic Chaps, Heart of a Man, Crooks Anonymous, The Longest Day, Lawrence of Arabia, Flight From Singapore, The Golliwog, Ladies Who Do, Clash By Night, The Nanny, Life At the Top, Start the Revolution Without Me, The Prince & The Pauper.
TV: Stalingrad, I Remember the Battle, Gideon's Way, That's For Me, Our Man At St. Mark's, Dixon of Dock Green, Dr. Finlay's Case Book, I Was There, Cruffs Dog Show, The Londoners, Jackanory, Get This, Movie Quiz, Get This series, Going a Bundle. Ask a Silly Answer, London Scene, Flockton Flyer, Sun Trap, The Little World of Don Camillo.

FOWLEY, DOUGLAS: Actor. b. New York City, May 30, 1911; e. St. Francis Xavier's Mil. Acad., N.Y. In stock; operated dramatic sch. N.Y.; on screen in bit parts. From 1934 in regular roles. Has appeared in many pictures.
PICTURES INCLUDE: Battleground, Just Once, This Woman Is Dangerous, Singin' in the Rain, Man Behind the Gun, Slight Case of Larceny, Naked Jungle, Casanova's Big Night, Lone Gun, High & Mighty, Three Ring Circus, Texas Lady, Broken Star, Girl Rush, Bandido, Nightmare in the Sun.

FOX, EDWARD: Actor. b. England, 1937. Comes from theatrical family; father was agent for leading London actors; brother is actor James Fox.
PICTURES INCLUDE: The Mind Benders, The Long Duel, Morgan, The Naked Runner, The Jokers, I'll Never Forget What's 'Is Name, The Battle of Britain, Oh! What a Lovely War, Skullduggery, A Doll's House, Galileo, The Squeeze, A Bridge Too Far, The Duellists, The Big Sleep, Force 10 from Navarone, The Mirror Crack'd.

FOX, JAMES: Actor. b. London, England, 1939. Ent. films as child actor in 1950 in The Magnet and Mrs. Minniver.
TV APPEARANCES INCLUDE: The Door, Espionage.
PICTURES INCLUDE: The Loneliness of the Long-Distance Runner, Tamahine, The Servant, Those Magnificent Men in Their Flying Machines, King Rat, The Chase, Thoroughly Modern Millie, Arabella, Duffy, Loves of Isadora, Performance.

FOXWELL, IVAN: Producer. b. Feb. 22, 1914, London, Eng. Entered m.p. ind. 1933 as technician with British & Dominions Film Corp., subsequently with Paramount British & London Films; Assoc. with Curtis Bernhardt in Paris 1937 becoming producer & collaborating on story, s.p. of Carefour, Le Train pur Venise, Sarajevo, others. In World War II with BEF and AEF 1939–46. Returned to British films 1947 as producer, co-author screen adapt., No Room at the Inn; prod., collab. s.p., Guilt Is My Shadow; prod., Twenty-Four Hours of a Woman's Life; co-author s.p. and prod. The Intruder, The Colditz Story (TV series adapt. 1972), Manuela, A Touch of Larceny, Tiara Tahiti, The Quiller Memorandum; s.p. and prod. Decline and Fall. Director, Foxwell Film Prods. Ltd.

FOXWORTH, ROBERT: Actor. b. Houston, Tx. e. Mellon Univ. Began acting at age 10 at Houston Alley Theatre and stayed with stage part-time while completing formal education.

Returned to theatre on full-time basis after graduation from Mellon. Made TV debut in Sadbird, 1969.
TELEVISION: The Storefront Lawyers (series), Mrs. Sundance, Hogan's Goat.
PICTURES: Treasure of Matecumbe (debut), The Astral Factor, Airport '77, Damien-Omen II, The Black Marble.
STAGE: P.S., Your Cat Is Dead.

FOXX, RED: Actor, Performer. b. St. Louis, Mo., Dec. 9, 1922. Began career by running away from home to join a washboard band at age 13; first nightclub appearances as a single, then with Slappy White from 1951 to 1956; 50 record albums in last 17 years.
TV: Sanford and Son.
PICTURE: Norman, Is That You?

FRAKER, WILLIAM A.: Cinematographer—Director. b. Los Angeles, 1923. Graduate USC Film School. Worked as operator with Conrad Hall; moved to TV before feature films.
PICTURES: Cinematographer: Games, The Fox, President's Analyst, Fade In, Rosemary's Baby, Bullitt, Paint Your Wagon, Dusty and Sweets McGee, Day of the Dolphin, Rancho Deluxe, The Killer Inside Me, Aloha, Bobby and Rose, Gator, Close Encounters of the Third Kind, Looking for Mr. Goodbar, Heaven Can Wait, Odd Boyfriends, 1941. Director: Monte Walsh, Reflection of Fear, Bette Midler's Divine Madness, The Legend of the Lone Ranger.
TELEVISION: Stony Burke, Outer Limits, Ozzie and Harriet, Daktari.

FRAMER, WALT: TV Producer. b. Pittsburgh, Pa., Apr. 7, 1908; e. Univ. of Pittsburgh. Former theatre magr.; news commentator, KDKA, Pitts.; sidewalk interviewer of Radio Swaps; creator-prod. Strike It Rich, The Big Payoff, Million Dollar Family, Futures Unlimited, Penny-a-Mile, Lady Luck, For Love or Money, Man on the Beat, It's in the Cards, Meet the People, Make It Big, The Fashion News Reel, Make Your Move, Holiday for Two, Take A Letter. Your Great Escape, Run For the Money, Heartline U.S.A., Look For Tomorrow, What's It Worth?

FRANCIOSA, ANTHONY: Actor. b. New York City, Oct. 25, 1928. e. High School there. First stage part in Y.W.C.A. play; joined Off-Broadway stage group; stock at Lake Tahoe, Calif., Chicago and Boston.
THEATRE: N.Y. stage in End As a Man, The Wedding Breakfast; lead in A Hatful of Rain.
PICTURES INCLUDE: A Face in the Crowd, This Could Be The Night, A Hatful of Rain, Wild Is the Wind, The Long Hot Summer, The Naked Maja, Career Story, On Page One, Go Naked in the World, Period of Adjustment, The Swinger, Fathom, A Man Called Gannon, The Sweet Ride, Rio Conchos, In Enemy Country, Across 110th Street, The Drowning Pool, Firepower.
TV: Valentine's Day, The Name of the Game, Search, Matt Helm.

FRANCIS, ANNE: Actress b. Ossining, N.Y., Sept. 16. Child model; radio TV shows as child & adult; on B'way in Lady in the Dark.
PICTURES INCLUDE: Summer Holiday, So Young So Bad, Whistle at Eaton Falls, Lydia Bailey, Elopement, Dream Boat, Lion is in the Streets, Rocket Man, Susan Slept Here, Rogue Cop, Bad Day at Black Rock, Battle Cry, Blackboard Jungle, Scarlet Coat, Forbidden Planet, The Rack, Great American Pastime, Don't Go Near the Water, Crowded Sky, Girl of the Night, Satan Bug, Brainstorm, Hook, Line, and Sinker, More Dead Than Alive, The Impasse, The Love God, Funny Girl, Born Again.

FRANCIS, ARLENE: Actress. r.n. Arlene Kazanjian; b. Boston, Mass. e. Convent of Mount St. Vincent Academy, Riverdale, N.Y.; Finch Finishing School, Theatre Guild School, N.Y.; m. Martin Gabel, actor.
STAGE: All That Glitters, Doughgirls, The Overtons, Once More With Feeling, Tchin-Tchin, Beekman Place, Mrs. Dally, Dinner at Eight, Kind Sin, Lion in Winter, Pal Joey, Who Killed Santa Claus?, Gigi.
TV: Regular panelist What's My Line, WCBS-TV; Home, Arlene Francis Show, NBC-TV; Talent Patrol, etc.
RADIO: Arlene Francis Show, Emphasis, Monitor.
PICTURES INCLUDE: All My Sons, One, Two, Three, The Thrill of It All.

FRANCIS, CONNIE: Singer. r.n. Constance Franconero. b. Newark, N.J., Dec. 12, 1938. Appeared, Star Time since 12 years old; won Arthur Godfrey's Talent Scout Show, 12 years old.
GOLD RECORDS: Who's Sorry Now, My Happiness. Numerous vocalist awards: All Major TV shows.
PICTURES INCLUDE: Where the Boys Are, Follow the Boys, Looking For Love.

FRANCIS, FREDDIE: Producer-Director-Cameraman. b. London, 1917. Joined Gaumont British Studios as apprentice to stills photographer; then clapper boy at B.I.P. Studios, Elstree; camera asst. at British Dominion. After World War II returned to Shepperton Studios to work for Korda and with Powell and Pressburger as cameraman.

PICTURES INCLUDE: Cameraman: Moby Dick (second unit photo., special effects), Room at the Top, Saturday Night and Sunday Morning, Sons and Lovers (Oscar), The Innocents, The Elephant Man. Director: Paranoiac, Vengeance, Evil of Frankenstein, Nightmare, Hysteria, Dr. Terror's House of Horrors, The Skull, Traitor's Gate, The Psychopath, The Deadly Bees, They Came from Beyond Space, Torture Garden, Dracula Has Risen from the Grave, Girly, Trog, Tales from the Crypt, The Creeping Flesh, Tales That Witness Madness, The Ghoul, Legend of The Werewolf.

FRANCIS, KEVIN: Producer. b. London, England, 1947, 1967–1970 Production mgr., assoc. producer 1970–1972. Produced It's Life, Passport, Trouble With Canada: 1972 Founder Tybum Productions Limited: 1973 Produced Persecution: 1974 Produced The Ghoul and Legend of the Werewolf, 1975 Founder Tyburn Prods. Inc. 1976 Prod. Film Techniques Educ. Course for BFI. 1977–81 Exec. Prod. the Satanists, Master of the Shell, Courier.

FRANCISCUS, JAMES: Actor. b. Clayton, Mo., 1934; e. Taft Prep, Yale U.
PICTURES INCLUDE: Four Boys And A Gun, I Passed For White, The Outsiders, The Miracle of the White Stallions, Youngblood Hawke, The Valley of Gwangi, Marooned, Beneath the Planet of the Apes, The Cat O' Nine Tails, The Greek Tycoon, City on Fire, When Time Ran Out.
TV: Naked City, Mr. Novak, Longstreet (TV film feature), The 500 Pound Jerk (TV feature).

FRANK, MELVIN: Writer, producer, director. In 1942: collaborated on story, My Favorite Blonde, Par. In June, 1942: appointed consultant in the radio branch of the War Department, working under Lt. Col. E. M. Kirby. In 1942 collab. s.p. Happy-Go-Lucky, Thank Your Lucky Stars; collab. Star Spangled Rhythm, (collab. s.p.) And the Angels Sing, Monsieur Beaucaire, Road to Utopia, Duffy's Tavern, The Return of October, It Had To Be You.
PICTURES INCLUDE: Mr. Blandings Builds His Dream House, Southern Yankee, The Redhead and the Reformer, Strictly Dishonorable, Callaway Went Thataway, Above and Beyond, Knock on Wood, White Christmas, Court Jester, That Certain Feeling, Li'l Abner, A Funny Thing Happened on the Way to the Forum, The Facts of Life, The Road to Hong Kong, Strange Bedfellows, Buona Sera, Mrs. Campbell, A Touch of Class, The Prisoner of Second Avenue, The Duchess and the Dirtwater Fox, Lost and Found.

FRANKEL, DANIEL: Executive. b. New York City, Aug. 21, 1903; e. U. Mich., U. Berlin (Germany). Gen. mgr.; Films Erka, Paris, 1925–1930. Ran Theatre des Champs Elysees, 1928–1929. Produced two French pictures. Returned to New York and joined Pathe 1930; dir. foreign dept., later of all sales to 1941; resigned to engage in prod. unit org. Vicepres. & exec. dir., Four Continents Films, 1945; with U.A. in Europe 1953–56; ret. U.S. & org., pres., Zenith Int'l Film Corp., 1956, distr., Lovers, 400 Blows, Hiroshima, Mon Amour, etc. Governor IFIDA.

FRANKENHEIMER, JOHN: Director. B. Malba, N.Y. e. Williams College. Actor, dir., summer stock: radio-TV actor, dir., Washington, D.C.; then joined CBS network.
TV: Mama, You Are There, Danger, Climax, Studio One, Playhouse 90, Du Pont Show of the Month; Ford Startime, Sunday Showcase.
PICTURES INCLUDE: The Young Stranger, The Young Savages, Birdman of Alcatraz, All Fall Down, The Manchurian Candidate, Seven Days in May, The Train, Seconds, Grand Prix, The Extraordinary Seaman, The Fixer, The Gypsy Moths, I Walk the Line, Horsemen, The Impossible Object, The Iceman Cometh, 99 and 44/100½ Dead, French Connection II, Black Sunday.

FRANKLIN, MICHAEL HAROLD: Executive. b. Los Angeles, Dec. 25, 1923. e. Univ. of Cal. (A.B.), Univ. So. Cal. (LL.B.). Admitted to Cal. bar, 1951; pvt. practice in L.A. 1951–52; atty. CBS, 1952–54; atty. Paramount Pictures, 1954–58; exec. dir. Writers Guild Am. West, Inc. 1958–1978; national exec. dir., Directors Guild of America 1978– . Mem. Am. Civil Liberties Union, Los Angeles Copywright Soc., Order of Coif.

FRANKLIN, PAMELA: Actress. b. Tokyo, Japan. Feb. 4, 1950. Attended, Elmshurst Ballet School, Camberley, Surrey.
PICTURES INCLUDE: The Innocents, The Lion, Flipper's New Adventure, The Prime of Miss Jean Brodie, The Night of the Following Day, And Soon the Darkness, The Legend of Hell House, Food of the Gods.

FRANKLYN, ARTHUR R.: b. N.Y.C. July 19, 1928. Child actor with Life With Father, Farewell Tour and Just Because. New York stage 1941–44. Featured skater, Ice Frolic Latin American tour, 1948–49; star and prod. ice revues at Havana Coliseum, 1949–50; served with U.S. Marines, Korea 1950–51; prod. dir., Los Angeles Ice Palace, 1951–56; exploitation and special events, Fox West Coast Theatres, 1956–59; Lippert Theatres, 1960; purchased Amador Chain of Central California Theatres. Pres. U.S. Bowling Photographers, Inc.; 1960–65 Dist. Mgr. Theatre Amuse Co., Tarzana, Calif.; Mgr. Florida State Theas., Dist. mgr. Arlo Enterprises.

FRANKOVICH M. J.: Executive. b. Bisbee, Arizona, Sept. 29, 1910. e. U.C.L.A., B.A. Ent. Radio 1934 as producer, commentator; began writing screenplays for Universal, 1938; Republic Pictures, 1940–49 (except for period war service U.S. Army); to Europe 1949 to make Fugitive Lady, Lucky Nick Kane, Thief of Venice etc.; England 1952. prod., Decameron Nights, Malaga, Footsteps in the Fog, Joe Macbeth; apptd. man. dir. Columbia Pictures Corp. Ltd., in U.K. and Eire Aug. 1955; elected vice-pres., Columbia Pictures International Corp., Dec. 1955; head Col. Pictures Int. Prod., 1958; vice-pres., Col. Pics. Corp., 1959. Appt. Chrmn., Columbia Pics. Corp. Ltd., 1959. Variety Club Crew Member; chief barker, Tent 36 Variety Club, 1957. dir., BLC Films; chmn., Screen Gems Ltd.; first v.p. chge world prod., Columbia; resigned July, 1967 to return to independent production. Long Term Deal, 1969, rel. through Columbia.

PICTURES INCLUDE: Bob & Carol & Ted & Alice, Marooned, Cactus Flower, The Looking Glass War, Doctors' Wives, There's A Girl in My Soup, The Love Machine, Dollars, Butterflies Are Free, Stand Up and Be Counted, 40 Carats, A Report to the Commissioner, From Noon Till Three, The Shootist.

FRANZ, ARTHUR: Actor. b. Perth Amboy, N.J. Feb. 29, 1920; e. Blue Ridge Coll., Md. U.S. Air Force. Radio, TV shows.
THEATRE: Streetcar Named Desire, Second Threshold.
PICTURES INCLUDE: Jungle Patrol, Roseanna McCoy, Red Light, Doctor and the Girl, Sands of Iwo Jima, Strictly Dishonorable, Submarine Command, Member of the Wedding, Flight Nurse, Bad for Each Other, Eddie Cantor Story, Caine Mutiny, Steel Cage, Battle Taxi, New Orleans Uncensored, Bobby Ware Is Missing, Atomic Submarine, The Human Factor.

FRASER, SIR ROBERT: TV executive. b. Adelaide, South Australia, Sept. 26, 1904; e. Melbourne and London Universities; OBE, 1944 controller of production, Ministry of Information, 1945; director-general, Central Office of Information, 1946–54; director-general, Independent Television Authority, 1954–70; Hon. Fellow, London School of Economics, 1965; chmn., Independent TV news, 1971–74.

FRASER, RONALD: Actor. b. Ashton-under-Lyne, England, 1930. Ent. films and TV, 1954.
TV: Lonesome Road, Sealed With A Loving Kiss, Stray Cats and Empty Bottles, John Bulls Other Island, Captain Rubian, And the Walls Came Tumbling Down, Sword of Honour, The Corn Is Green, The Brahmin Widow.
PICTURES INCLUDE: There Was a Crooked Man, The Long & the Short and the Tall, The Best of Enemies, The Hellions, The Pot Carriers, The Punch and Judy Men, Private Potter, Crooks in Cloisters, Table Bay, The Beauty Jungle, Code 7, Victim 5, Flight of the Phoenix, The Whisperers, Fathom, Sinful Davey.

FRAWLEY, JAMES: Director. b. Houston, Texas. Studied drama at Carnegie Tech and Actors Studio, where later taught and ran the directors unit. Was charter member of comedy group, The Premise; has acted in plays on and off Bdwy. Won Emmy Award for Monkees series, where staged two musical numbers a week for two seasons.
PICTURES: Kid Blue, The Big Bus, The Muppet Movie.
TELEVISION: Columbo, Delancy Street, Capra, etc.

FRAZER, AUSTIN: Prod. consultant. b. London, England. Early career, designer and writer. Fellow SIAD. Writer's Guild Award 1967, Dante's Inferno.

FRAZIER, CLIFF: Director, actor. b. Detroit, Mich., Aug. 27, 1934; e. Wayne State U., Harold Clurman. Exec. dir., The Community Film Workshop Council; was co-founder & artistic dir.: Stables Theatre, Detroit, 1960–63; Concept East Theatre, Detroit, 1962–64; co-produced and acted in Study in Color, 1964–65; assoc. dir., Theatre of Latin America, N.Y.C., 1968; dir. of drama, Mobilization for Youth, N.Y.C., 1966–68; East Coast dir. of rsch., Brooks Foundation, Sta. Barbara, 1966–68.
TV ACTING INCLUDES: Today, Tell It Like It Is, NYPD. The Nurses, The Negro Experimental Theatre, Othello.
THEATRE: Stage repertories: Washington Theatre Club, Irish Hills Rep., Will-O-Way Playhouse.
Co-author, Discovery in Drama and book critic, Catholic Reporter, 1969.

FRAZIER, SHEILA E.: Actress. b. Bronx, N.Y., Nov. 13, 1948. e. Englewood, N.J. Was exec. sect'y. and high-fashion model. Steered to acting career by friend Richard Roundtree. Studied drama with N.Y. Negro Ensemble Co. and New Federal Theatre, N.Y.
PICTURES INCLUDE: Super Fly (debut), Superfly T.N.T., The Super Cops.

FREDERIC, MARC: Producer. b. New York, Apr. 25, 1916. e. Washington & Lee Univ. Capt. U.S. Air Force. Prod., dist.

"Little Theatre" 1948, 104 episodes. First to make deal through AFTRA for kinescope release of live shows for dist. Tales of Tomorrow series. Org., Marc Frederic Prods., Inc.
PICTURES INCLUDE: Giant of the Unknown, She Demon, Missile to the Moon, Frankenstein's Daughter, Girl in Room 13, Career Girl, Festival Girl.

FREDERICKSON, H. GRAY, JR.: Producer. b. Oklahoma City, Okla., July 31, 1937. e. U. of Lausanne, Switzerland, 1958–9; U. of Okla. B.A., 1960. m. Victoria Schmidlapp. Worked one yr. with Panero, Weidlinger & Salvatori Engineering Co., Rome, Italy. In 1978 named v.p. for prod. of Lorimar Films.
PICTURES INCLUDE: Candy, Inspector Sterling, Gospel 70, An Italian in America, The Man Who Wouldn't Die, The Good, Bad & Ugly, Intrigue in Suez, How to Learn to Love Women, God's Own Country, Wedding March, An American Wife, Natika, Echo in the Village, Little Fauss & Big Halsey, Making It, The Godfather, The Godfather, Part II, Hit (exec. prod.), Apocalypse Now (co.-prod.).

FREEMAN, EVERETT: Writer. b. New York City. Contrib. Sat. Eve. Post. From 1942 writer for screen.
PICTURES INCLUDE: George Washington Slept Here, Princess and the Pirate, It Happened on Fifth Ave., Secret Life of Walter Mitty, Too Young to Kiss, Lady Takes a Sailor, Jim Thorpe—All American, Pretty Baby, Million Dollar Mermaid, Destination Gobi, Kelly and Me, My Man Godfrey, Marjorie Morningstar, Sunday In New York, The Glass Bottom Boat, Where Were You When the Lights Went Out, The Maltese Bippy, How Do I Love Thee, ZigZag.
TV: Prod. Bachelor Father series.

FREEMAN, JOEL: Producer. b. Newark, N.J., June 12, 1922. e. Upsala Coll. Obtained job as messenger at MGM studios in 1941; promoted to short subjects dep., then prod. planning dept. In Air Force 1942–46. Became assist. dir. at RKO and David O. Selznick Organization. In 1948 returned to MGM as asst. dir; later assoc. prod. In 1956 entered indep. field as prod. supvr. on films and TV series. In 1960 to Warner Bros., working on Sunrise at Campobello and The Music Man. Worked in N.Y. for CBS, returning to Calif. in 1965 to be assoc. prod. at Warners. Named studio prod. exec; assigned to prod. contract when Seven Arts bought co. Also produced for 20th-Fox and MGM. Now heads Joel Freeman Productions. Most recent credit: It's a Wonderful Life, exec. prod. for Universal-ABC.

FREEMAN, SIR N. BERNARD: (C.B.E.) Executive. b. Sydney, Sept. 1, 1896; e. public schools, Xavier College, Melbourne; established MGM throughout Australia, New Zealand, man. dir., chmn., retired 1967. European War, 1914–18.
Member: Admin. Comm. of Brit. Centre, 1944–46. Chairman: Anzac House Appeal 1945, Anzac House Trust 1946, Miss Australia Quest, 1948–49. N.S.W. Comm. for World Refugee Year, 1960. Nat'l Chmn., UNICEF, 1953; pres. Rotary Club of Sydney, 1960–61; Created C.B.E. (Civil) 1946; chmn., Motion Picture Distributors' Association of Australia, 1939–41, '63 Deputy Chairman, Council of International House, University of Sydney.

FREGONESE, HUGO: Director. b. Argentina. e. Buenos Aires College, Buenos Aires U. Prior to entering m.p. ind., newspaperman, Buenos Aires; ed. All Sports, in cattle ind., Azul; arrived New York City, for study at Columbia U.; to Los Angeles, as tech. adv.; back to Buenos Aires, 1938; made shorts in Argentina, cutter; asst. dir.; co-dir., Pampa Barbara; dir. Where Words Fail; signed by Hollywood, when MGM bought releasing rights; dir. Hardly A Criminal, Argentina; to Universal-International, 1949. Stanley Kramer Prod., 1951.
PICTURES INCLUDE: One Way Street, Saddle Tramp, Apache Drums, Mark of the Renegade, My Six Convicts, Untamed Frontier, Blowing Wild, Decameron Nights, Man in the Attic, The Raid, Black Tuesday, Thunders, Harry Black and the Tiger, I Girovadei, Marco Polo, Moneta, Sperzzata (Italy), Shatterhand (Germany), The Tramps, Broken Coin, Savage Pampas (Spain).

FRENCH, HAROLD: Film and stage director. b. London, England, April 23, 1900. Popular London player in revue musical comedy, etc., 1930–35. Started directing 1936. Cavalier of the Streets, at Pinewood. Since: The House of the Arrow, Dead Men Are Dangerous, Jeannie, Unpublished Story, The Day Will Dawn. Directed stage plays: Youth at the Helm, Design for Living, No Time for Comedy, French Without Tears. In 1942: Secret Mission, Helm-General Film: The Avengers, Par. In 1944 dir. Mr. Emmanuel.
PICTURES INCLUDE: English Without Tears, Quiet Weekend, My Brother Jonathan, The Blind Goddess, Quartet, Adam & Evelyn, The Dancing Years, Trio, Hour of Thirteen, Encore, Isn't Life Wonderful, Rob Roy, Man Who Watched Trains Go By (Paris Express), Man Who Loved Redheads.

FRENKE, EUGENE: Producer. m. Anna Sten.
PICTURES INCLUDE: Life Returns, Two Who Dared, Three Russians Girls, Let's Live a Little, Lady in Iron Mask, Miss Robin Crusoe, Heaven Knows, Mr. Allison, Barbarian and the Geisha, The Last Sunset, Royal Hunt of the Sun.

FRESCO, ROBERT M.: Writer. b. Burbank, Calif., Oct. 18, 1928. e. Los Angeles City Coll. Newspaperman. Los Angeles, 1946–47; U.S. Army, 1948–49; staff writer, Hakim Prod., 1950–51; various screenplays, 1951–56.
PICTURES INCLUDE: Tarantula, They Came to Destroy the Earth, Monolith.
TV: Scripts for Science Fiction Theatre, Highway Patrol.

FREULICH, HENRY: Cinematographer. b. New York City, April 14, 1906. Four years with Universal as assistant camera-man and still man. Seven years with First National as still man and second cameraman. Five years with Columbia as second cameraman; then with Columbia as director of photography.

FRIEDKIN, JOHN: Executive. Entered industry in New York as publicist for Columbia Pictures; spent eight years at Young & Rubicam adv. agency. Formed Sumner & Friedkin with Gabe Sumner as partner; left to join Rogers & Cowan, where named v.p. In 1967 resigned to join 20th-Fox, mov-ing to California in 1972 when home offices were trans-ferred. Appointed Fox v.p. worldwide publ. & promo. In 1979 joined Warner Bros. as v.p.—adv. pub. for intl. div.

FRIEDKIN, WILLIAM: Director. b. Chicago, Ill., 1939. Joined NBC-TV, 1957, worked for National Education TV, did TV documentaries before feature films.
PICTURES INCLUDE: Good Times, The Night They Raided Minsky's, The Birthday Party, The Boys in the Band, The French Connection. (Academy Award, best picture, dir. 1971), The Exorcist, Sorcerer (prod.-dir.), Cruising (dir.-s.p.).

FRIEDMAN, ARNOLD J.: Executive b. New York, N.Y. Entered m.p. industry as exploiteer for Columbia Pictures Corp. 1957–60; advng dept. United Artists Corp. 1960–62; adv. mgr., Embassy Pictures Corp. and later director of adv., publ., prom. for Embassy Pictures Television, 1962–67; pres. Arnold Friedman's Company, 1967–70; dir. of ad./pub./promo for Metromedia Producers Corp., 1970–72; creative dir., ITC, 1973–76; vice pres. of ad./pub./promo for Cinema Shares International Television Ltd., 1976, present.

FRIEDMAN, DAVID F.: Executive. b. Birmingham, Ala., Dec. 24, 1923. e. Cornell Univ. With U.S. Army Signal Corps, 1944–46. With Paramount Pictures as booker office man-ager 1946–50; circus press agent, 1950–51; Para. publ. agent, 1952–55; partner, Modern Film Distributors, 1956–60; partner, Sonney Amusement, 1960–64. Formed Enter-tainment Ventures, Inc. in 1965, of which he is pres. Pro-duced a total of 53 features between 1958 and 1981.

FRIEDMAN, JOSEPH: Executive. b. New York, N.Y. e. City Coll. of N.Y., 1940–42; N.Y. Univ., 1946–47. U.S. Navy 3 yrs. Asst. to nat'l dir. field exploitation, Warner Bros. Pictures, 1946–58; nat'l exploitation mgr., Paramount Pictures, 1958–60; exec. asst. to dir. of adv., publicity & exploitation, Para., 1961; dir. adv. & pub., Paramount 1964; a v.p., Para., 1966; v.p. in charge of Marketing, 1968; v.p., adv., and p.r., Avco Embassy Pictures, 1969; v.p., p.r. American Film Theatre, 1973; v.p., adv. and p.r., ITC, motion picture div., 1976, pres., Joseph Friedman Marketing and Advertising, Inc., 1977. Exec. dir. New Jersey M.P. & T.V. Commission, 1978; v.p. worldwide adv./pub./promo., Edie & Ely Landau, Inc., 1980.

FRIEDMAN, MARTIN: Executive. b. New York City, Oct. 9. Warner 1928 sls. and contract dept.; booking sales, Cleve-land 1939–42; U.S. Marine Corps, production unit; 1945 joined A. W. Schwalberg at Artists Producers, when com-pany was dissolved in 1946 then joined Liberty Films as ass't. to E. K. (Ted) O'Shea. Liberty was taken over by Paramount Pictures; remained with Paramount in their sales division until 1957 at which time joined American Broadcasting-Paramount Theatres as their producers representative. Production was stopped, then Friedman assigned to the theatre division in 1960; v.p., gen. mgr., ABC Theas. of Penn. Inc., ABC Theas. of N.Y., Inc., New England Theas., Inc.; pres., Countrywide Theaters, 1970. In 1973 formed own corp., Martin Films, Inc., of which is pres. Co. buys and distributes indep. product.

FRIEDMAN, ROBERT L.: Executive. b. Bronx, N.Y., March 1, 1930. e. DeWitt Clinton High School. Started as radio an-nouncer and disc jockey with Armed Forces Radio Ser-vice in Europe and U.S. v.p., marketing, United Artists Corp.; now pres. domestic distribution, Columbia Pic-tures.
MEMBER: M.P. Associated Foundation, Phila., pres. 2 yrs.; Variety Club (on board) M.P. Pioneers; (on board) area chm. and N.Y. participation in Will Rogers Hospital Foundation, American Film Institute, Academy of M.P. Arts & Sciences.

FRIEDMAN, SEYMOUR MARK: Director. b. Detroit, Mich., Aug. 17, 1917; e. Magdalene Coll., Cambridge, B.S., 1936; St. Mary's Hospital Medical School, London. Entered m.p. ind. as asst. film ed. 1937; 2nd asst. dir. 1938; 1st asst. dir. 1939, on budget pictures; entered U.S. Army 1942; returned to ind. 1946; dir. Columbia Pictures 1947. Mem-ber: Screen Directors Guild; Vice president & executive production for Columbia Pictures Television, division of Columbia Pictures Industries, since 1955.
PICTURES INCLUDE: To the Ends of the Earth, Rusty's Birthday, Prison Warden, Her First Romance, Rookie Fire-man, Son of Dr. Jekyll, Loan Shark, Flame of Calcutta, I'll Get You, Saint's Girl Friday, Hyber Patrol, African Man-hunt, Secret of Treasure Mountain.

FRIEDMAN, STEPHEN: Writer-Producer. e. Univ. of Penn., Harvard Law School. Worked as lawyer for Columbia Pic-tures and Ashley-Famous Agency. Formed and heads Kings Road Productions.
PICTURES INCLUDE: The Last Picture Show (prod.), Lovin' Molly (prod.-s.p.), Slap Shot (prod.), Bloodbrothers (prod.) Fast Break (prod.), Hero at Large (prod.); Little Darlings (prod.).

FRIEND, PHILIP: Actor. b. Horsham, Sussex, England, Feb. 20, 1915; e. Bradfield Coll.; m. Eileen Erskine, prof.
THEATRE: With musical comedy tour 1935; at Drury Lane Theatre 1936; Broadway debut in "French Wihout Tears" 1937; plays include: Pink Strings and Sealing Wax, First Gentlemen, Hide Out, 1969; Dictator's Slippers, The Ladder, 1970. Blindsight, Forgotten Factor, 1970.
Brit. m.p. debut in "Midas Touch" 1939; on Brit. radio; served in Brit. Army 3 yrs. World War II; made training m.p. for Brit. govt.
PICTURES INCLUDE: My Own True Love, In Which We Serve, Next of Kin, Great Day, Enchantment, Sword in the Desert, Buccaneer's Girl, The Highwayman, Thunder on the Hill, Desperate Moment, Background (Edge of Di-vorce), The Diamond, The Betrayal, Son of Robin Hood, Web of Suspicion, The Solitary Child, Stranglehold, The Fur Collar, Manutara.
TV: Rendezvous, Invisible Man series, The Third Man Series, Z Cars, Freewheelers, Short Story, Dial M for Mur-der, Moody & Peg, Suez.

FRIES, CHARLES W.: Executive. b. Cincinnati, Ohio. Ohio State U., B.S.; exec.-prod., Ziv Television; v.p., prod., Screen Gems; v.p., prod., Columbia Pictures; exec. v.p., prod. and exec. prod., Metromedia Prod. Corp., 1970–74; pres., exec. prod., Alpine Prods. and Charles Fries Prods. 1974 to date. Nat'l treas., TV Academy; pres., Alliance TV Film Producers; exec. comm., MPPA. Chm., Comm. of Pro-ducers, Writers and Directors, board of governors and exec. comm. of Academy of TV Arts and Sciences.

FRISCH, LARRY: Producer, Director, Writer. b. Indianapolis, Ind., Dec. 27, 1929; e. Univ. of So. California, 1947–49; Columbia Univ., 1951–54. Prof. child actor, Radio 1944–47; writer/dir. with Caravel Films, NYC, 1950; Assist. dir.; Exodus, El Cid (Spain); Pro., Dir.; Writer, Tel Aviv Taxi, 1956 (Israel), Pillar of Fire 1962 (Israel), Casablan, 1963 (Greece).
TV: Dir., Story of a Teenage Drug Addict, Power of Pot Roast, Beyond Three Doors, Destination Vietnam, Bus to Sinai (NBC-TV), Biafra Eye-Witness (UPI-TV); Metromedia TV News, overseas correspondent 1969–71; prod., Mira-cle of Survival (TV special), An American Family In China, 1971.

FROBE, GERT: Actor. b. Zwickau, Germany, 1912. Began act-ing career in 1935 in German films and theatrical produc-tions. In post-war period there became street comedian; later worked in more than 70 German and French films, usually as villain.
PICTURES: Those Magnificent Men in Their Flying Ma-chines, Is Paris Burning?, The Three Penny Opera, He Who Must Die, Those Daring Young Men in Their Jaunty Jalopies, Chitty Chitty Bang-Bang, Goldfinger, Bloodline.

FRONTIERE, DOMINIC: Executive. b. New Haven, Conn., June 17, 1931. e. Yale School of Music. Studied composing, arranging and conducting; concert accordionist, World's Champion Accordionist, 1943; An Hour with Dominic Frontiere, WNHC-TV, New Haven, 3 years, 1947; exec. vice-pres., musical dir., Daystar Prods. Composer or arranger over 75 films.
PICTURES INCLUDE: Giant, Gentlemen Prefer Blondes, Let's Make Love, High Noon, Meet Me in Las Vegas, 10,000 Bedrooms, Hit the Deck; composer-conductor; Marriage-Go-Round, The Right Approach, One Foot in Hell, Hero's Island, Popi, Barquero, Chisum, A For Alpha.
TV: Composer-conductor: The New Breed, Stoney Burke, Bankamericard commercials (Venice Film Festival Award Best Use of Original Classical Music for filmed TV com-mercials), Outerlimits, Branded, Iron Horse, Rat Patrol, Flying Nun, The Invaders, Name of the Game, That Girl, Twelve O'Clock High, Zig Zag, The Young Rebel, The Im-mortal, Jean C. Killy, Fugitive, The Love War.

FROST, DAVID: Performer. b. Tenterdon, England, April 7, 1939; e. Cambridge U. Writer, co-creator, co-star, That Was The Week That Was, 1962–63; star of The David Frost Show, nationally syndicated; honors include 2 Emmy Awards, Golden Rose of Montreux Award, TV Personality of the Year, Guild of TV Producers Award, Order of the British Empire.
AUTHOR: The Americans; co-author, The English.

FRUCHTMAN, MILTON A.: Producer, director. b. New York, N.Y. e. Columbia U.
TV: High Adventure Series, CBS, Every Man's Dream, ABC, Verdict for Tomorrow, NBC Spectaculars, Assignment Southeast Asia, It Happened in Naples; Son of Sulan, worked for Columbia and independent producers in various production capacities, set up first worldwide TV network, Eichmann Trial, Capital Cities Broadcasting, The Makebelievers, Odyssey Prods.; received Peabody Emmy, and Gabriel awards.

FRYE, WILLIAM: Producer. Was agency exec. before beginning prod. career as associate prod. of Four Star Playhouse in assoc. with late Dick Powell, David Niven and Charles Boyer. Later joined Revue Prods., which became Universal TV; he produced General Electric Theatre and other series. Has produced many Movie of the Week entries for ABC-TV.
PICTURES INCLUDE: The Trouble with Angels, Where Angels Go, Trouble Follows, Airport 1975, Airport 1977.

FUCHS, LEO L.: Indep. prod. b. Vienna, June 14, 1929; moved to U.S., 1939; ed. Vienna and New York; U.S. Army cameraman 1951–3; int'l mag. photographer until entered motion pictures as producer with Universal in Hollywood in 1961.
PICTURES INCLUDE: Gambit, A Fine Pair; Jo (French version of The Gazebo).

FUEST, ROBERT: Director. Early career as painter, graphic designer. Ent. TV industry as designer with ABC-TV, 1958. 1962: directing doc., commercials. 1966: Wrote and dir. Just Like A Woman, 1967–68; dir. 7 episodes of The Avengers, 1969: dir. And Soon The Darkness, 1970: dir. Wuthering Heights, Doctor Phibes. 1972: wrote and dir. Doctor Phibes Rises Again. 1973: wrote, designed and dir. The Final Programme. 1975: The Devils Rain.

FULLER, JACK DUBOSE: Exhib. b. Columbia, S.C. March 7, 1921. U. of So. Carolina, B.S. Palmetto Theatre Co. 1936–1942; U.S. Navy, 1942–45; theatre mgr. Wilby-Kincey Service Corp., 1945–47; booker, 1947–1951; partner Irvin-Fuller Theatres, operate 24 theatres No. & So. Carolina, since 1951; Pres., Theatre Owners of N.C. and S.C. 1957: Dir. NATO since 1956.

FULLER, SAMUEL: Director, writer, producer. Copy boy, N.Y. Journal; reporter, rewrite man, N.Y. Graphic, N.Y. Journal, San Diego Sun; journeyman reporter many papers. Author of novel The Dark Page; many orig. s.p.; in U.S. Army, 16th Inf. 1st U.S. Inf. Div. 1942–45; s.p., dir., I Shot Jesse James, Baron of Arizona; prod., dir., also screen play author of The Steel Helmet; dir., Fixed Bayonets; s.p., dir., prod., Park Row; s.p., dir., Pickup On South Street; s.p., dir., Hell and High Water, House of Bamboo; prod. dir., s.p. Run of the Arrow, China Gate, Forty Guns, Verboten, The Crimson Kimono, Underworld U.S.A., Merrill's Marauders, (collab. s.p., dir.), s.p., dir., prod. Shock Corridor, s.p. prod., dir., The Naked Kiss; s.p. dir., Dead Pigeon on Beethoven Street. s.p. dir., The Big Red One; co-s.p., dir., White Dog.
AUTHOR: Novel, Crown of India. Novel; 144 Piccadilly Street; Dead Pigeon on Beethoven Street; The Rifle; The Big Red One.

FUNT, ALLEN: Producer—Performer. b. New York City, 1914. Best known as producer and creator of Candid Camera series which originated on radio in 1947 as Candid Microphone which inspired theatrical film shorts. TV version began in 1948 as Candid Mike, changed in 1949 to Candid Camera which played off and on until 1960 when became regular series on CBS, lasting until 1967. Revived briefly in early '70s in new format; then syndicated as The New Candid Camera. Funt produced and starred in film, What Do You Say to a Naked Lady?

FURBER, PERCIVAL E.: b. Paris, France, May 16, 1906; e. Hotchkiss School, Princeton '27; chm. emeritus div., Trans-Lux Corp.; dir., Tampax, Inc., Fedders Corp. & Fedders Fin. Corp.

FURIE, SIDNEY J.: Director, writer, producer. b. Toronto, Canada, 1933. Ent. TV and films 1954. Canadian features include: Dangerous Age, A Cool Sound from Hell. Also dir. many Hudson Bay TV series. To England 1960. Films since include Dr. Blood's Coffin, During One Night, Brewster's Millions, The Young Ones, The Boys. 1961 appt. exec. dir. Galaworldfilm Productions, Ltd.
PICTURES INCLUDE: The Leather Boys, Wonderful Life, The Incress File, The Appaloosa, The Naked Runner, The Lawyer, Little Fauss and Big Halsy, Lady Sings the Blues,

Hit!, Sheila Levine, Gable and Lombard, The Boys in Company C.

FURNEAUX, YVONNE: Actress. English. b. France. e. St. Paul's London and Oxford Univ. Student at R.A.D.A.
PICTURES INCLUDE: (In England:) Master of Ballantrae, Beggar's Opera, Dark Avenger, House of the Arrow, Lisbon, Repulsion (1965). (Films in Italy:) Le Amiche, Dolce Vita, Via Margutta, A Noi Place Freddo, I Lancieri Neri, Semiramide, Helen of Troy, Le Ultime Sette Ore, I Quattro Tassisti, Caccia all'Uomo, The Man Who Never Was. In France: Le Comte de Monte Cristo, Le Meurtrier. In Germany: Dr. Mabuse, The Champagne Murder.
TV: Children's hour for Rex Tucker. Tigress on the Hearth, Hereward the Wake. TV Films: Danger Man, The Baron. The Survivors (TV series).
STAGE: Bristol Old Vic.

FURNESS, BETTY: Actress—TV Correspondent. b. New York City, 1916. Stage and screen actress in the '40s; TV commercial spokeswoman in '50s' leading consumer advocate in '70s. Host on both local TV and radio shows in New York (At Your Beck and Call, Ask Betty Furness, etc.). Named President Johnson's asst. for consumer affairs in 1967. 1970, head of New York State's consumer protection board. Joined WNBC-TV in 1970 as consumer reporter and occasional contributor to network news specials and Today Shows.

FURSE, RUSSELL L.: Executive. b. Humansville, Mo., Jan. 27, 1908. e. Colorado Teachers College, Greely, Colo. Film. dir., prod. Warner Bros., Hal Roach: Prod. vice pres. Televisions Programs, Inc. Executive prod., ABC Television, Hollywood. Gen. mgr. network prog. dept., CBS Television: dir; prog. oper.; KEY T Santa Barbara. Gen. mgr. CHEK TV Victoria, B.C. Santa Barbara; exec. v.p. Santa Maria Telecasting Corp. Co-founder Academy of Televisions Arts & Sciences. Chmn. of board, Communications Foundation, pres. Tri-County Public Service Corporation, pres. KBBY-KBBQ Radio Oxnard, member Affiliated Producers Work Shop, Board of Directors Affiliates University of California Santa Barbara, Managing director, Riviera Park Research & Communications Center; pres. & chief exec. off., California Video Communications.

G

GABOR, ZSA ZSA: Actress. r.n. Sari Gabor; b. Hungary, Feb. 6, 1923. e. Budapest, Lausanne, Switzerland; Stage debut in Europe.
PICTURE INCLUDE: Lovely to Look At, We're Not Married, The Story of Three Loves, Lili, Moulin Rouge, Three Ring Circus, Death of a Scoundrel, Girl in the Kremlin, For The First Time, Boys' Night Out, Picture Mommy Dead, Jack of Diamonds.

GAFFNEY, ROBERT: Prod.-dir. b. New York, Oct. 8, 1931. e. Iona College, 1949–51. Staff, Louis de Rochemont mer; prod., Rooftops of New York, in assoc. with Robert Associates, prod. staff, Cinerama Holiday, Man on a String; camera technical consultant, Cinemiracle prod., Windjam-McCarty, 1960; prod. industrial films, Seneca Prods., prod., Light Fantastic; prod., Troublemaker; assoc. prod., Harvey Middleman Fireman; dir., Frankenstein Meets the Space Monster.

GAGE, EDWIN: Executive. b. Deal, N.J., July 20, 1915; e. U. of Pennsylvania, 1938; Admin. v.p. & treas., secy., Walter Reade-Sterling, Inc., resigned, 1966; TV dist. & real estate oper. in Oakhurst, N.J.

GAINES, JAMES M.: Executive. b. Saxe, Va., May 8, 1911; m. Associated with Major Bowes Amateur Hour; former manager of WNBC-WNBT, New York; vice-president of NBC and director of NBC owned and operated stations; Pres., gen. mgr. Southland Industries, Inc. (WOAI, WOAI-TV), v.p. Blanco Oil Co.

GAITHER, GANT: Producer, writer. b. Hopkinsville, Kentucky, Aug. 1. e. Royal Academy, London, Yale U.; build Miami Beach Playhouse, 1940–42; stage mgr., The Army Air Forces, 1942–43; asst. dir., George Cukor, 1944; Pacific theatre operations, W.W. II, Winged Pigeons' assoc. prod., Beverly Hills, Broadway; prod., Craig's Wife, The First Mrs. Fraser, The Shop At Sly Corner, Gayden, Alexander, Seventh Heaven; wrote: The Long Street, The Swan, Princess of Monaco; exec. prod., Paramount Pictures, 1960–61.
PICTURES INCLUDE: My Six Loves.
TV: Simon Says, for Qualis Productions.

GALANTE, M. CHRISTINA: Executive. b. Tucson, AZ, Aug. 30, 1942. e. U. of Arizona, New School for Social Research (NYC). Started career as child model in 1948. Entered film career as stunt double in 1955 working in dozens of major films made in Arizona. 1962–66, feature vocalist with big bands for USO tours and major night clubs. 1967–70, spokeswoman and actress in TV commercials and feature films. 1970–74, television commercials producer. 1974–77, film coordinator for mayor's office, City of New York, coordinating and supervising all m.p. and television filming in City. 1977 named special consultant to California Motion Picture Council. 1980, named to Council by Governor Edmund G. Brown and elected it's Chairman. 1980, named to Los Angeles Film Commission by Mayor Tom Bradley, currently on executive board. Professional photographer and writer, former President of Women in Film, Sponsor, Women in the Performing Arts Coalition, Member of the Board, Inter Agency Council on Child Abuse and Neglect.

GALE, BOB: Writer-Producer. b. St. Louis, 1952. e. USC School of Cinema. Joined with friend Robert Zemeckis to write screenplays, starting with episode for TV series, McCloud. Also co-wrote s.p. for The Nightstalker series. Turned to feature films, co-writing with Zemeckis script for I Wanna Hold Your Hand, on which Gale also acted as associate producer.
PICTURES: 1941 (s.p.).

GALE, GEORGE: Executive. e. Sorbonne U., Paris, France. Feature editor, Budapest Ed., U.S. Army Pictorial Service, Astoria, N.Y., 1944–45; shorts editor, MGM; Hal Roach Studios, as super, film ed.; ed. Oriental-Internat'l films; ed. The River, winner of Int. Award in Venice, 1951; free lance features editory, 1951–54; ed. Disney Studios, films and TV, Disneyland, 1955–65 asst. prod. to Ivan Tors; assoc. prod. Daktari; prod. exec. Cowboy in Africa. assoc. prod. Jambo; assoc. prod., From Africa With love; post prod. exec. "Primus" Metromedia. 1971–1976, American National Enterprises, Inc., vice-president in charge of production. Producer and director. Supervised the production of approximately 30 features for television syndication. Producer-director of: UFO: Fact or Fiction, Animals Are the Craziest People, Mysteries From Beyond Earth (theatrical feature). Formed George Gale Productions, Inc. in 1976. Wrote story and produced feature, Escape from Angola, in South Africa; prod. for American National Ent., Mysteries from Beyond the Triangle, The Force on Thunder Mountain, Mysteries of the Mind, Anne of the Seven Seas, Lure of the Blue Planet, Quest of Courage. Produced for own co.: Neptune's Squad (TV pilot).

GANIS, SIDNEY M.: Publicist. b. New York, Jan. 8, 1940. e. Brooklyn College. Staff writer, newspaper and wire service contact, 20th Century-Fox 1961–62; radio, TV contact and special projects, Columbia Pictures 1963–64. Joined Seven Arts Prod. 1965 as publicity mgr; 1967, appt. prod. publicity mgr. Warner-7 Arts, Ass't prod. There Was a Crooked Man, 1969. Studio Publicity dir., Cinema Center Films, 1970. Director of Ad-Pub for "Mame", Warner Bros., 1973; Director of Advertising, Warner Bros., 1974; named WB v.p., worldwide adv. & pub., 1977; 1979, exec. v.p., Lucasfilm, Ltd..

GARBO, GRETA: Actress. r.n. Greta Gustafson. b. Stockholm, Sept. 18, 1906; e. Stockholm. Stage career as a dancer in Sweden. Hollywood screen career started 1926 with Torrent. Voted one of the ten best Money-Making Stars in Motion Picture Herald-Fame Poll 1932. Spec. Academy Award, 1954.
PICTURES INCLUDE: Temptress, Flesh and the Devil, Love, Divine Woman, Mysterious Lady, Single Standard, Wild Orchids, Woman of Affairs, Kiss, Anna Christie, Susan Lennox, Her Fall and Rise, Romance, Mata Hari, Grand Hotel, Queen Christina, Anna Karenina, Camille, Conquest, Ninotchka, Two-Faced Woman.

GARDENIA, VINCENT: Actor. b. Naples, Italy, Jan. 7, 1923. f. was actor and singer who brought Vincent to U.S. at age 2, formed theatrical co. in which Vincent took part. Vincent served in U.S. Army, World War II, and after landed first English-speaking role in summer stock prod. of Burlesque. Made off-Bdwy. debut in The Man with the Golden Arm; first Bdwy. role in The Visit (1958) with the Lunts.
PICTURES INCLUDE: Cop Haters, Cold Turkey, Little Murders, Hickey and Boggs, Bang the Drum Slowly, Luciano, The Manchu Eagle, Death Wish, The Front Page, Heaven Can Wait, Firepower, Home Movies, The Last Flight of Noah's Ark.
TV: All in the Family.
STAGE: Machinal, Passing Through from Exotic Places, The Prisoner of Second Avenue.

GARDNER, ARTHUR: Producer. b. Marinette, Wis.
PICTURES INCLUDE: Without Warning, Vice Squad, Down Three Dark Streets, Geronimo, The Glory Guys, Clambake, Scalphunters, Sam Whiskey, Underground, McKenzie Break, The Honkers, Hunting Party, Kansas City Bomber, White Lighting, McQ, Brannigan, Gator, Rally.
TV: Rifleman, Robert Taylor's Detectives, Law of The Plainsman, The Big Valley.

GARDNER, AVA: Actress. b. Smithfield, N.C., Dec. 24, 1922. e. Atlantic Christian Coll.

PICTURES INCLUDE: We Were Dancing, Joe Smith, American, Lost Angel, Three Men in White, Maisie Goes to Reno, Whistle Stop, The Killers, The Hucksters, Singapore, One Touch of Venus, The Bribe, Great Sinner, East Side, West Side, Show Boat, Pandora and the Flying Dutchman, Lone Star, Snows of Kilimanjaro, Ride Vaquero, Mogambo, Knights of the Round Table, Barefoot Contessa, Bhowani Junction, Little Hut, The Naked Maja, On The Beach, The Fair Bride, 55 Days at Peking, Night of the Iguana, The Bible, Mayerling, Life and Times of Judge Roy Bean, The Devil's Widow, Earthquake, The Bluebird, Permission to Kill, The Cassandra Crossing, The Sentinel, City on Fire.

GARFIELD, WARREN: Writer, publicist. b. Nov. 18, 1936. e. UCLA, Loyola Of Los Angeles School of Law. Story analyst, assistant to dir., Hecht-Hill-Lancaster, 1948–58; casting dir. Assist., assist. film editor, Columbia Pictures, films, featurettes, trailers, TV spots, Paramount Pictures, 1966–68; creative film services, Walt Disney Productions, 1968–present. Member: Academy of Motion Picture, Arts & Sciences.
CREDITS: A Stranger in Town (wrote s.p.), Cat Ballou, Wild and Wonderful, Flight From Ashiya, Taras Bulba (as assist. to Harold Hecht); The High Chaparral (wrote, TV).

GARFINKLE, LOUIS: Writer-Director-Producer. b. Seattle, Wash., February 11, 1928. e. U. of Calif., U. of Washington, U. of So. Calif. Writer KOMO, Seattle, 1945; Executive Research, Inc., 1948; Writer, educ. doc. screenplays, Emerson Films, EBF. 1948–50; s.p. You Can Beat the A-bomb (RKO), 1950; Writer-dir. training films, info. films, Signal Photo, 1950–53; Copy, Weinberg Adv., 1953; Head of Doc. Research in TV, U. of Calif., Berkeley, 1954–55; staff, Sheilah Graham Show, 1955; story and s.p. The Young Guns (AA), formed Maxim Prod. Inc. with Albert Band, 1956; story, s.p. and co-producer I Bury the Living (UA), 1957 (Killer on the Wall); s.p. and co-producer Face of Fire (AA), 1958; Writer, 712 teleplays for Day in Court, Morning Court, Accused for Selmur—ABC-TV, 1959–66; Co-writer-creator Direct Line pilot, Selmur, 1960; Story and t.p. June Allyson Show, Threat of Evil, 1960; s.p. in collab. The Hellbenders (Embassy) 1967; story and t.p. Death Valley Days, Crullers At Sundown, 1967; story, Death Valley Days, Captain Dick Mine, 1967; s.p. in collab. A Minute to Pray A Second to Die (ABC-Cinerama) 1968; story, s.p. and co-producer The Love Doctors (Sigma III) 1969; story, s.p. and director Beautiful People, (I.P.C.) 1970; s.p. (collab.) The Models, 1971; head writer, No. 3 Peanut Place (pilot), 1972; story & s.p. (collab.) The Doberman Gang, (Dimension) 1971; story & s.p. (collab.) Little Cigars (AIP) 1973; The Deerhunter (U-EMI) 1978, (story collab.).

GARFUNKEL, ART: Actor-Singer-Composer. b. New York City, 1942. e. Columbia Univ. Began singing at age 4. Long partnership with Paul Simon began in grade school at 13 (Queens); first big success in 1965 with hit single, Sound of Silence. Partnership dissolved in 1970. Film debut in Catch 22 (1969).
PICTURES: Carnal Knowledge, Bad Timing/A Sensual Obsession.

GARLAND, BEVERLY: Actress. b. Santa Cruz, Calif., Oct. 17, 1930. e. Glendale College, 1945–47.
TV: starred, Decoy, Bing Crosby; Twilight Zone, Dr. Kildare, Medic, Emmy Nomination, 1954; My Three Sons; M.P. The Mad Room, Where the Red Fern Grows, Airport, 1975, Roller Boogie, It's My Turn.

GARLAND, P. HARVEY: Theatre Executive. b. Jacksonville, Fla., Apr. 4, 1919. e. Univ. of Fla. Entire career with same co., joining Fla. State Theatres in 1935 as usher, advancing to doorman, ass't., mgr., mgr., film booker, buyer, v.p. and then president. Named v.p. ABC Theatres; now pres.

GARNER, JAMES: Actor. b. Norman, Okla., April 7, 1928; e. High School there, then joined Merchant Marine, U.S. Army ser. in Korean War. Prod. Paul Gregory suggested acting career. Studied drama at N.Y. Berghof School. Toured with road companies; Warner Bros. studio contract followed with screen debut in Toward the Unknown.
PICTURES INCLUDE: Shoot-out at Medicine Bend, Darby's Rangers, Sayonara, Up Periscope, Cash McCall, The Children's Hour, The Great Escape. Thrill of It All, Move Over Darling, The Americanization of Emily, 36 Hours, The Art of Love, Mister Buddwing, Duel at Diablo, Grand Prix, Hour of the Gun, Support Your Local Sheriff, Marlowe, Support Your Local Gunfighter, Skin Game, They Only Kill Their Masters, One Little Indian, Hawaiian Cowboy, Health, The Fan, Victor/Victoria.
TV: Cheyenne, Maverick, Rockford Files.

GARNER, PEGGY ANN: Actress. b. Canton, Ohio, Feb. 8, 1932. John Powers child model. Screen debut 1938 in Little Miss

Thoroughbred; Acad. Award most promising juvenile of the yr. 1945.
PICTURES INCLUDE: In Name Only, Blondie Brings Up Baby, Abe Lincoln in Illinois, Eagle Squadron, The Pied Piper, Jane Eyre, Keys of the Kingdom, Tree Grows in Brooklyn, Nob Hill, Junior Miss, Home Sweet Homicide, Daisy Kenyon, Thunder in the Valley, Sign of the Ram, Bomba, The Jungle Boy, Teresa, Black Widow, The Cat.
TV: Studio One, Lux Playhouse, Schlitz Playhouse, Best of Broadway, etc.

GARRETT, BETTY: Singer, actress. b. St. Joseph, Mo., May 23. e. scholarships; Annie Wright Seminary, Tacoma, Wash., Neighborhood Playhouse, N.Y.C. Sang in night clubs, hotels, Broadway shows (1942–46); won Donaldson award for best musical comedy performance of 1946, Spoon River Anthology.
PICTURES INCLUDE: (Screen debut) The Big City 1947, Star of Tomorrow, '49; Words and Music, Neptune's Daughter, On The Town, My Sister Eileen, Shadow on the Window.
TV: Laverne and Shirley.

GARRISON, PAUL: Writer, producer, director. Adv. photog. in N.Y., Hollywood; production of TV films since 1948; dir. first series of half hour TV pictures made, Cases of Eddie Drake; dir., writer for more than 100 TV film shows; currently in chge. of TV Workshop, Hollywood.

GARROWAY, DAVE: Performer. b. Schenectady, N.Y., July 13. e. Washington Univ., St. Louis. U.S. Navy, 1942–45; star of Garroway at Large, NBC-TV, 1948–51 and Today Show, 1952–61; Dave Garroway Show, NBC-TV, Oct. 1953–54; NBC radio; Friday with Garroway, 1954–56; Monitor, 1955–61; NBC-TV, Wide Wide World, 1955–58; Exploring the Universe, NET, 1962–63; Bd. of Gov. N.A.T.A.S., 1968–69. Dave Garroway Show (syndication) Boston, 1969–70; Los Angeles, 1970–71.

GARSON, GREER: Actress. b. County Down, Northern Ireland; e. London U., B.A. cum laude; Grenoble U.
THEATRE: Stage debut Birmingham (England) Rep. theat. 1932 in Street Scene; London debut 1935 in Golden Arrow; continued London stage to 1938 (Vintage Wine, Mademoiselle, Accent on Youth, Page From a Diary, Old Music, etc.).
Screen debut 1939 in Goodbye, Mr. Chips. Academy Award best performance by actress, 1942 (Mrs. Miniver, MGM). Voted one of the ten best Money-Making Stars in Motion Picture Herald-Fame Poll 1942–46 inclusive. Photoplay Mag. Gold Medal 1944–45.
PICTURES INCLUDE: Pride and Prejudice, Blossoms in the Dust, When Ladies Meet, Mrs. Miniver, Random Harvest, Mme. Curie, Mrs. Parkington, Valley of Decision, Adventure, Desire Me, Julia Misbehaves, That Forsythe Woman, The Miniver Story, The Law and the Lady, Scandal at Scourie, Julius Caesar, Her Twelve Men, Strange Lady in Town, Sunrise at Campobella, The Singing Nun, The Happiest Millionaire.

GASSMAN, VITTORIO: Actor. b. Genoa, Italy, Sept. 1, 1922; e. Academy of Dramatic Art, Rome. Stage actor, 1943; m.p. debut, 1946.
PICTURES INCLUDE: Daniele Cortis, Mysterious Rider, Bitter Rice, Lure of Sila, The Outlaws, Anna, Streets of Sorrow; to U.S., Cry of the Hunted, Sombrero, The Glass Wall, Rhapsody, Girls Marked Danger, Mambo, War and Peace, World's Most Beautiful Woman, Tempest, The Love Specialist, The Great War, Let's Talk About Women, Il Successo, The Tiger, Woman Times Seven, Ghosts—Italian Style, Scent of a Woman, Viva Italia!, A Wedding, Quintet, Immortal Bachelor, The Nude Bomb.

GAVIN, JOHN: Actor. b. Los Angeles, Calif., April 8. e. St. John's Military Acad., Villanova Prep at Ojai, Stanford Univ.. Naval service: air intelligence officer. Married to actress Constance Towers, 1974. Four children. pres. Screen Actors Guild. Broadway Stage debut: Seesaw, 1973. Named U.S. Ambassador to Mexico, 1981.
PICTURES INCLUDE: A Time to Love and a Time to Die, Imitation of Life, Spartacus, A Breath of Scandal, Romanoff and Juliet, Tammy, Tell Me True, Back Street, Thoroughly Modern Millie, Mad Woman of Chaillot, Psycho, Midnight Lace.

GAYLARD, JAMES W., III: Exhibitor b. Knoxville, Tenn., Sept. 18, 1943. e. Henderson H.S., Troy, Ala., 1961. Troy State Univ. 1965 BS Mathematics Ent. industry, managed theatres, Troy Drive-In Theatres, Inc. 1966.

GAYLE, PETER: Producer, writer, actor. b. New York City. American Academy of Dramatic Arts; New York School of Theatre Arts. Formed Peter Gayle Productions; v.p. television, Screen Gems–Columbia Pictures v.p., MGM Studios; v.p., m.p. development, United Artists.
PICTURES INCLUDE: Without Each Other (winner of Cannes Film Festival), The Gang; Never Too Young To Rock; Black Cobra; Shoot; The Boy Who Owned A Melephant (winner of the Venice Film Festival); Intercept, Scenes from a Murder.

TV: (Specials) Producer, writer, The World of Brigette Bardot, The Goldie Hawn Special, The Rolling Stones in Concert, The Janis Joplin Special, Hollywood: The Magic Kingdom, On Location With.
TV: (Series) The Young Revels (ABC-TV), The Protectors (ABC-TV), Spindletop (Universal Studios).

GAYNOR, MITZI: Actress. b. Chicago, Ill., e. Powers Professional H.S., Hollywood. Studied ballet since age four; was in L.A. Light Opera prod. Roberta.
OPERA: Fortune Teller, Song of Norway, Louisiana Purchase, Naughty Marietta, Great Waltz.
PICTURES INCLUDE: My Blue Heaven, Take Care of My Little Girl, Golden Girl, The I Don't Care Girl, We're Not Married, Bloodhounds of Broadway, There's No Business Like Show Business, Anything Goes, Birds and the Bees, The Joker, Les Girls, South Pacific, Surprise Package, Happy Anniversary, For Love or Money.

GAZZARA, BEN: Actor. b. N.Y.C., 1930. Won scholarship to study with Erwin Piscator; joined Actor's Studio, where students improvised a play, End As a Man, which then was performed on Broadway with him in lead. Screen debut (1957) in film version of that play retitled The Strange One.
PICTURES INCLUDE: Anatomy of a Murder, The Passionate Thief, The Young Doctors, Convicts Four, Conquered City, A Rage To Live, The Bridge at Remagen, Husbands, Capone, Killing of a Chinese Bookie, Voyage of the Damned, Bloodline, They All Laughed.
TV: Arrest and Trial, Run for Your Life, etc.
STAGE: Cat on a Hot Tin Roof, A Hatful of Rain, Hughie, etc.

GEBHARDT, FRED: Prod.-writer, exhibitor. b. Vienna, Austria, Mar. 16, 1925. e. Schotten Gymnasium, Vienna. U.C.L.A., 1939. Usher Boyd Theatre, Bethlehem, Pa.; Mgr., Rivoli Thea. L.A., 1944; 18 yrs. mgr. many theatres. Fox West Coast, then Fine Arts Theatre. Writer, prod.: 12 To the Moon, The Phantom Planet; prod., Assignment Outer Space, Operation M; s.p.: 12 to The Moon, All But Glory, The Starmaker, Phantom Planet, Shed No Blood, Fortress in Heaven, Eternal Woman.
BOOKS: Mental Disarmament, All But Glory, Starmaker, Shed No Blood, The Last of the Templars.
Pres., Four Crown Prods., Inc.; recipient of Medal of Americanism, D.A.R., 1963; Honorary Lifetime Member, P.T.A., Young Man of The Year Award, 1956, 24 Showmanship Awards; Mem. Acad. M.P. Arts and Sciences, Ind. M.P. Prod. Assoc.

GEDDES, HENRY: Executive producer and chief executive Children's Film Foundation since 1964; President, International Centre Films for Children, Mem. Governing Body Prix Jeunesse. b. Dover, England, 1912; e. Dulwich College, Polytechnic School of Kinematography. Early career Hudson's Bay Company, N. Canada 1928–32. 1934–39 freelance asst. dir., prod. man. 1939–46. Served in Royal Artillery. 1946–52 Gen. Prod. Man. Crown Film Unit. 1953–63 freelance prod./dir.
ORIG. S. P. INCLUDE: Seal Island, Ali and the Camel, Last Rhino, Magnificent 6½.

GEESON, JUDY: Actress. b. Arundel, Sussex, England, Sept. 10, 1948. e. Corona Stage School. Began professional career on British TV, 1960.
PICTURES INCLUDE: To Sir With Love, Circus of Blood, Here We Go Round the Mulberry Bush, Hammerhead, Three into Two Won't Go; Two Gentlemen Sharing, The Executioner. 10 Rillington Place, Brannigan, The Eagle Has Landed.
TV: Dance of Death, Lady Windermere's Fan, Room with a View, The Skin Game, Star Maidens, Poldark, She.
THEATRE: Othello, Titus Andronicus, Two Gentlemen of Verona, Section Nine, An Ideal Husband.

GENOCK, TED: Newsreel Editor. r.n. Edouard Paul Genock. b. Paris, France, Mar. 7, 1907; e. Chelsea Polytechnic London U. (BS), Columbia (MA). Initiated prod. and pictorial news, Egypt. From 1930–39 covered Ethiopia, Iraq, Iran, India, Malaya, Netherlands Indies, Australia as newsreel war correspondent. British Paramount News. Apptd. assignment editor, Paramount News (N.Y.C.), 1942. Tech. dir., Neighbor to North (1948), Cassino to Korea (1950) for Parat.; dev. 22-second high-speed processing machine for TV film recording, now inc. in Parat. theatre TV system. Ed. in chief, Telenews Prod., Inc., 1952; Television, Eastman Kodak adv. dept., 1954. Fellow: Soc. M.P. & TV Engineers. Member, Dir. American TV Commercials Festival, 1962; dir. TV adv. Eastman-Kodak; chmn. Assn. Nat'l Advertisers Television Committee, 1969; Director Media Development Film & TV, Mercer County College, N.J., 1972.

GEORGE, GEORGE LOUIS: Director. b. Moscow, Russia, July 31, 1907. e. U. Paris (law). Began as cutter, later asst. dir., French prods. To Hollywood 1935 as corresp. French pubs. Re-entered prod. 1939 as asst. dir. & prod. French version of The Four Hundred Million; in similar capacity numerous French versions of Hollywood prods. thereafter. In

1942 asst. prod. Our Russian Front. Became assoc. Natl. Film Board of Canada in prod. war information films; also dir. The Labor Front for World in Action series. In 1944 dir. University Town for Co-ord. Inter-Amer. Affairs; 1946–49 dir. 16 films for Signal Corps Photo. Center, Astoria, L.I., incl. Acad. Award Winner Toward Independence. In 1949 dir. in TV, also Women of Tomorrow, WB. 1950, dir. in Israel for Palestine Films; dir., prod., TV & documentary films, 1950–55; exec. secr., Screen Directors International Guild, 1956–63; admin., SDIG Trust Fund, 1963–67; member, Natl. Bd. Directors Guild of America 1966–69; since 1966, member Eastern Directors Council, DGA; pres. Film & TV Book Club, Inc. 1967–69. Currently free-lancing.

GEORGE, GEORGE W.: Writer/Producer. b. New York, N.Y., Feb. 8, 1920. e. Williams College; U.S. Navy, 1941–44; screen writer since 1948. President, SAGA PRODUCTIONS. N.Y.C. based, Industrial Video/film company.
PICTURES INCLUDE: Bodyguard, The Nevadan, Woman on Pier 13, Peggy Mystery Submarine, Red Mountain Experiment, Alcatraz, Fight Town, Smoke Signal, Desert Sands, Uranium Boom, Halliday Brand, Doc, The James Story, The Two Little Bears.
PRODUCER STAGE: Dylan, Any Wednesday, Ben Franklin in Paris, The Great Indoors, Happily Never After, Night Watch, Via Galaetica, Bedroom Force.
PRODUCER PICTURES: A Matter of Innocence, Twisted Nerve, Hello-Goodbye, Night Watch, Rich Kids, My Dinner with Andre.
TV: Climax, Screen Gems, Loretta Young Show, The Rifleman, Peter Gunn, The Real McCoys, Adventures in Paradise, Hong Kong, Follow The Sun.

GEORGE, LOUIS: Executive. Pres. & chief operating officer, Arista Films, Inc. b. Karavas, Kyrenia, Cyprus, June 7, 1935. e. Kyrenia Business Academy, Cyprus (honored 1951). Emigrated to U.S. in 1952. After brief stint in Foreign Exchange Dept. of City National Bank New York, served in U.S. Army, 1953–55. Entered industry in 1956 as theatre manager with Loew's Theatres in N.Y. metro area, managing Metropolitan, Triboro, New Rochelle, between 1958–66. In 1966 joined MGM as dir. of intl. theatre dept. In 1969 promoted to dir. of world-wide non-theatrical sales. From 1972 to 1974 served as regional dir. of MGM Far East operations. In 1974 left MGM to establish Arista Films, Inc., handling foreign sales of independently produced U.S. films.

GEORGE, SUSAN: Actress. b. England. Studied at London's Corona Stage School, appearing in The Sound of Music at 12 on London stage. Has appeared in many TV programs.
PICTURES INCLUDE: Billion Dollar Brain, Up the Junction, Spring and Port Wine, The Strange Affair, Lola, Straw Dogs, The Looking Glass War, Sunny and Jed, Dirty Mary Crazy Larry, Mandingo, A Small Town in Texas.

GERAGHTY, MAURICE: Writer, director, producer. b. Rushville, Ind., Sept. 29, 1908; e. Princeton. Western story suprv. Republic 3 yrs; prod Falcon series, China Sky, Action In Arabia at RKO; Flash Gordon (feature and serial).
PICTURES INCLUDE: Red Canyon, Dakota Lil, Calamity Jane and Sam Bass, Tomahawk, Sword of Monte Cristo, Rose of Cimarron, Mohawk, Love Me Tender (Elvis Presley), Tall In The Saddle (John Wayne), Gene Autry and Roy Rogers series, Hopalong Cassidy series, Mesquiteers series (John Wayne) Darby O'Gill And The Little People.
TV: Created Cheyenne series, Warner Bros, Virginian, Bonanza, Daniel Boone, 87th Precinct, Thriller, 21 Beacon Street, Cavalcade of America, Panic, Whiplash (Australia) The Addams Family, Annie Oakley, Gene Autry series, Champion series, No Warning, Flight, Jane Wyman Theater, Laramie, Lassie (Emmy and Peabody Awards).

GERALD, HELEN: Actress. b. New York City, Aug. 13. e. U. of Southern Calif. 1948. Stage: Italian Teatro D'Arte, Les Miserables, The Civil Death, Feudalism.
PICTURES INCLUDE: The Gay Cavalier, The Trap, Tarzan nd the Leopard Woman, Cigarette Girl, Meet Miss Bobby Socks, G.I. War Brides, Gentleman's Agreement, A Bell For Adano, Tomorrow is Forever, Janie, Grand Prix, The Sandpiper, Make Mine Mink, Best of Everything.
TV: Robert Montgomery Presents, Frontiers of Faith, Valiant Lady, Kraft Theatre, Gangbusters, Adventures of the Falcon, Schlitz Playhouse of Stars, This Is the Answer, Man from UNCLE, Run for Your Life, Perry Mason.

GERARD, LILLIAN: Publicist-Writer, Publicity, Rialto Theatre, 1936; publicity-adv. Filmarte Theatre, 1938, Gerard Associates, 1938–47; V.P. and managing dir. of Paris Theatre, 1948–62; publicity-adv. dir., Rugoff Theatres, 1962. Film consultant to Times Films, Lopert Films, Landau Co., 1962–65. Exec. secy. to the National Soc. of Film Critics, 1966–68. Adjunct Professor, Film, 1968–1970, Columbia Univ., School of the Arts, Special Projects Co-ordinator, Museum of Modern Art, 1968–80. Contributor to American Film. Published by American Film Institute. Now associated with Philip Gerard in Gerard Associates.

GERARD, PHILIP R.: Executive. b. New York City, Aug. 23, 1913. e. C.C.N.Y., B.B.A. 1935; Columbia U.; Publicity dir. Mayer-Burstyn 1936–9; Gerard Associates, 1939–41; in public relations U.S. War Dept. 1942–4; with MGM 1944–8; with Universal Pictures since 1948; Eastern pub. mgr., 1950–59; Eastern ad. and pub. dir., Dec. 1959; N.Y. Production Exec., 1968–76. As of Jan. 1, 1977 formed Gerard Associates, film consultants on marketing, production and acquisitions; Film Consultant to The Jewish Film Archives, Jerusalem, International Board of American Friends of Hebrew University; and American Arbitration Association.

GERAY, STEVEN: Actor. b. Uzhored, Czechoslovakia, Nov. 10, 1904. Member Hungarian Natl. Theat.
THEATRE: Stage roles (abroad) include Tulip Time, Let's Go Gay, Silver Swan, etc.
PICTURES INCLUDE: Appeared in 40 European films. Hollywood career started 1941 with Man at Large; Cornered, The Unfaithful, I Love Trouble, Mr. District Attorney, House on Telegraph Hill, Little Egypt, Lady Possessed, Big Sky, Affair in Trinidad, O. Henry's Full House, Night Without Sleep, Tonight We Sing, Call Me Madam, Gentlemen Prefer Blondes, French Line, Knock on Wood, Paris Playboys, Tobor the Great, New York Confidential, A Bullet for Joey, Daddy Long Legs, Artista and Models, Birds and the Bees, Attack, Ship of Fools, Jesse James Meets Frankenstein's Daughter, The Swinger.

GERBER, DAVID: Executive. b. Brooklyn, N.Y. e. Univ. of Pacific. m actress Laraine Stephens. Joined Batten, Barton, Durstine and Osborn ad agency in N.Y. as TV supvr. Left to become senior v.p. of TV at General Artists Corp. In Jan., 1956, named v.p. in chg. sales at 20th-Fox TV where sold and packaged over 50 prime-time series and specials. Entered indep. prod. with The Ghost and Mrs. Muir, followed by Nanny and the Professor. In 1970 was exec. prod. of The Double Deckers, children's series made in England. In 1971 was exec. prod. of Cade's County (CBS). In 1972 he joined Columbia Pictures Television as an independent producer and in 1974 was named executive vice president worldwide production for CPT. In 1976 he returned to independent production and has been the executive producer on such programs as Police Story, Police Woman, The Lindbergh Kidnapping Case, Joe Forrester, The Quest and Gibbsville. For Police Story he received an Emmy award for best dramatic series.

GERBER, MICHAEL H.: Executive. b. New York City, Feb. 6, 1944. e. St. Johns Univ. (BA, '69); St. Johns Univ. School of Law (Juris Doctor, '69). Atty. for Screen Gems, 1969–71; asst. secy. & asst. to gen. counsel, Columbia Pictures Industries, 1971–74; corporate counsel and secretary, Allied Artists Pictures, 1974, v.p. Corporate affairs, Allied Artists, 1978; Parther, Talmodge, Pritzler, & Gerber.

GERE, RICHARD: Actor. e. Univ. of Massachusetts. Started acting in college; later joined Provincetown Playhouse and Seattle Repertory Theatre. Composed music for productions of these groups. Appeared on Broadway in Grease, Soon, Habeas Corpus, and Bent and in London in Taming of the Shrew with Young Vic.
PICTURES INCLUDE: Report to the Commissioner, Baby Blue Marine, Looking for Mr. Goodbar, Days of Heaven, Bloodbrothers, Yanks, American Gigolo.
TV: Kojak, Strike (movie).

GERETY, T. MICHAEL: Executive. b. Rockville Center, N.Y., Oct. 30, 1942. U.S., Navy, 1961–64. Started industry career in Chicago with MGM as regional adv/pub. repr.; transferred to Atlanta in same capacity, 1966 and then to Dallas, 1967–70. Joined Durwood Theatres in Dallas in 1971 as div. operations mgr. In 1972 returned to MGM as south west div. dir. adv./pub. in Dallas. Moved to MGM Studios in 1973 as asst. natl. adv. coordinator. In 1974 joined American International as dir. of cooperative adv./exploit. In 1976 named exec. dir. of adv./pub. for AIP (now Filmways Pictures). In 1980 joined the Milton I. Moritz Co., film marketing firm, as v.p. Member: Variety Clubs Int'l., Academy of MP. Arts & Sciences.

GERSHENSON, JOSEPH: Musician. b. Russia, Jan. 12, 1904; e. N.Y. public sch.; Pace Inst., N.Y.; studied music priv. Conductor orch. B.F. Keith Theats. 1920–28; asst. genl. music dir. RKO Theats., 1928–33. Joined Universal Pictures 1933; assoc. prod. & music dir. of shorts in 1939; assoc. prod. (under name of Joseph G. Sanford) of features from 1940; in 1941 apptd. exec. prod.; head of music dept. Universal International.
PICTURES INCLUDE: Glenn Miller Story, Magnificent Obsession, So This Is Paris, Man Without a Star, Foxfire, Benny Goodman Story, All That Heaven Allows. There's Always Tomorrow, Spoilers, Never Say Goodbye, Battle Hymn, Away All Boats, Written on the Wind, My Man Godfrey, Man of a Thousand Faces, Never Steal Anything Small, Imitation of Life, This Earth Is Mine, Pillow Talk, Operation Petticoat, Back Street, Come September, Lover Come Back, Spiral Road, Freud, Captain Newman, Father Goose, Send Me No Flowers, I'd Rather Be Rich, Warlord, Madame X,

Shenandoah, Blindfold, Thoroughly Modern Millie, Sweet Charity.

GERSHWIN, IRA: Music lyricist. b. New York City, Dec. 6, 1896. e. Coll. City of New York; Pulitzer Prize, 1932; brother of late George Gershwin. Began writing songs when 22.

FILMS INCLUDE: 1931 Delicious, Fox; 1937 Shall We Dance, RKO; 1937 Damsel in Distress, RKO; 1938 The Goldwyn Follies, Goldwyn; 1943 Rhapsody in Blue, Warner Bros.; Cover Girl, Where Do We Go From Here? The Shocking Miss Pilgrim, The Barkleys of Broadway, An American in Paris, Give the Girl A Break, A Star is Born, The Country Girl, Kiss Me Stupid.

AUTHOR: Lyrics on Several Occasions, 1959.

GERTNER, RICHARD: Editor. b. Tampa, Florida, Nov. 1; e. Rollins College, B.A., 1949, Columbia U., M.A., 1950; editor, Hoffman Publications, 1950–52; editorial asst., Better Theatres, 1952; news editor, Motion Picture Daily, 1956; managing editor, Motion Picture Daily, 1962; managing editor, Motion Picture Herald, 1963; editor, Better Theatres, 1963; executive editor, Motion Picture Herald, 1964; editor, Motion Picture Herald, 1966; editor, Motion Picture Almanac and TV Almanac, 1970. Managing editor Motion Picture Daily, Oct. 1970; Editor, Motion Picture Daily, 1971; Editor-in-chief, Quigley Publications, Nov., 1971.

GERTZ, IRVING: Composer, musical director. b. Providence, R.I., May 19, 1915; e. Providence Coll. of Music, 1934–37. Assoc. with Providence Symph. Orch., comp. choral works for Catholic Choral Soc.; music dept., Columbia, 1939–41; U.S. Army, 1941–46; then comp. arranger, mus. dir. for many cos. incl. Columbia, U-I, NBC.

PICTURES INCLUDE: Bandits of Corsica, Gun Belt, Long Wait, The Fiercest Heart, First Travelling Saleslady, Fluffy, Nobody's Perfect, Marines, Let's Go! It Came From Outer Space, The Man From Bitter Ridge, Posse From Hell, The Creature Walks Among Us, The Incredible Shrinking Man, Hell Bent For Leather, Seven Ways From Sundown, Francis Joins the WACS, Raw Edge, East of Sumatra, A Day of Fury, To Hell and Back, Cult of the Cobra, Plunder Road, Top Gun, Tombstone Express, The Alligator People, Khyber Patrol, The Wizard of Baghdad.

Record album (Dot Records) Leaves of Grass; published works for mixed voices; Fluffy, feature, Universal. Marines, Let's Go! feature, 20th Century Fox Serenata for String Quartet, Divertimento for String Orchestra, Tableau for Orchestra.

TV: Orig. theme & scores for TV: America, The Golden Voyage, Across the Seven Seas, The Legend of Jesse James, Daniel Boone, Voyage to the Bottom of the Sea, Peyton Place, Land of the Giants, Lancer, Medical Center.

GETTY, J. RONALD: Producer. b. -Berlin, Germany, Dec. 19, 1929. e. Zurich U., Heidelberg U., U. of Southern California. Prior to entering m.p. industry was oil executive, Tidewater Oil Co., mgn. dir. Veedol GmbH, 1955; Getty Oil, Hamburg, 1954–61; pres. & chm. of bd., Veedol Petroleum Int'l, Switzerland, 1961–69; dir., Huiles Veedol France, 1961–69. President & Chm. of bd., Getty Picture Corp.; pres. & chm., Getty Labs, Inc.; dir., Home Theatre Network.

PICTURES: Flare Up, Zeppelin, Shelia.

GIANNINI, GIANCARLO: Actor. b. Spezia, Italy, Aug. 1, 1942. Acquired degree in electronics but immediately after school enrolled at Academy for Drama in Rome. Cast by Franco Zeffirelli as Romeo at age of 20. Subsequently appeared in a play also directed by Zeffirelli, Two Plus Two No Longer Make Four, written by Lina Wertmuller.

PICTURES INCLUDE: Love and Anarchy, The Seduction of Mimi, Swept Away by an Unusual Destiny in the Blue Sea of August, Seven Beauties . . . That's What They Call Him, How Funny Can Sex Be?, A Night Full of Rain, The Innocent, Immortal Bachelor.

GIBSON, HENRY: Actor. b. Germantown, PA, Sept. 21, 1935. e. Catholic Univ. Amer. Appeared as child actor with stock companies, 1943–57; Bwdy. debut in My Mother, My Father and Me, 1962. Many appearances on stage since and in films and TV.

PICTURES INCLUDE: The Long Goodbye, Charlotte's Web, Nashville, The Last Remake of Beau Geste.

TELEVISION: Laugh-In co-star.

GIELGUD, SIR JOHN: Actor. b. London, England, Apr. 14, 1904; e. Westminster Sch., Lady Benson's Sch. (dram.), London; Royal Acad. Dram. Art. Knighted, 1953.

THEATRE: Began stage career in Shakespearean roles; on London stage also in the Constant Nymph, The Good Companions, Dear Octopus, The Importance of Being Earnest, Dear Brutus, etc., various Shakespearean seasons, London & N.Y.

PICTURES INCLUDE: On screen 1932 in Brit. prod. Insult; later (1936) films The Good Companions, Secret Agent (Warner-Brit.); The Prime Minister, Other films: Julius Caesar, Richard III. Around the World in 80 Days, Barretts of Wimpole Street, Becket. The Loved One, Chimes At

Night, St. Joan, Sebastian, The Assignment, Charge of the Light Brigade, The Shoes of the Fisherman, Oh, What a Lovely War, Eagle in a Cage, Lost Horizon, 11 Harrowhouse, Gold, Murder on the Orient Express, Providence, Portrait of the Artists as a Young Man, Joseph Andrews, Murder by Decree, The Human Factor, The Elephant Man, The Formula, Sphinx, Lion of the Desert, Arthur.

TV: A Day by the Sea, The Browning Version (U.S.A.), The Rehearsal, Great Acting, Ages of Man, Mayfly and the Frog, Cherry Orchard, Ivanov, From Chekhov With Love, St. Joan, Good King Charles' Golden Days, Conversation at Night, Hassan, Deliver Us From Evil, Heartbreak House.

GIFFORD, ALAN: Actor. b. Boston, Mass., March 11, 1911. Early career in Group Theatres and summer stock. Served with SHAEF as Col. U.S. Army during World War II. To England 1951 for Love of Four Colonels. Since extensive appearances films and television and stage roles.

PICTURES INCLUDE: The Iron Petticoat, Time Lock, The Flying Scot, Paris Holiday, Screaming Mimi, Onionhead, Table in the Corner, Mouse That Roared, Too Young to Love, I Aim at the Stars, The Royal Game, No Kidding, The Road to Hong Kong, Town Without Pity, Devil Poll, One Spy Too Many, Drop Dead Darling, Only When I Larf, 2001, A Space Odyssey, Isadora, Legend of Nigger Charlie, Phase IV.

TV PLAYS INCLUDE: High Tension, No Deadly Medicine, Ernie Barger is 50, My Lost Saints, Philadelphia Story, Flight For Martin Wheeler, Man on the Mountain Top, Woman of Fifty, The Executioners, Means To an End, A Quiet Game of Cards, Winter Journey, The Velvet Cage, Marching Song, Saint Series, Sentimental Agent, The Monster, Espionage Series; stage: License to Murder, Danger Man series, The Ambassadors, The Champions, Troubleshooters, Champion House, Randall and Hopkirk (Deceased), The Male Animal, Softly, Softly, The Name of the Game, As the World Turns, Edge of Night, Somerset, Duchess of Duke Street, Crossroads series.

GIL, DAVID: Producer. b. Tel Aviv, Israel, Jan. 24, 1930; e. U. of Jerusalem; m. Joan Andre. After commission in Israeli Army worked for Israeli Embassy, Paris, 1950–52; Israeli film ind., 1953–55; prod. educational films, 1955–61; headed Gilart Productions, 1962–68; foreign sales dir.. Commonwealth United, 1968; prod. Guess What We Learned in School Today, Joe, A Journey Through Rosebud, A Change in the Wind.

GILBERT, ARTHUR N.: Producer. b. Oct. 17, 1920, Detroit; Lt., U.S.M.C., 1941–45; ed. Univ. of Chicago, 1946; Special Agent, FBI, 1946–53; world sales dir., Gen. Motors, Cadillac Div., 1953–59; investments in mot. pictures and hotel chains, 1959–1964; exec. prod., Mondo Hollywood, 1965; exec. prod. Jeannie-Wife Child, 1966; assoc. prod., The Golden Breed, 1967; commissioned rank of Colonel U.S.M.C., 1968.

PICTURES INCLUDE: The Glory Stompers, Fire Grass, Cycle Savages, Bigfoot, Incredible Transplant.

GILBERT, BRUCE: Producer. e. University of Calif. Pursued film interests at Berkeley's Pacific Film Archive; in summer involved in production in film dept. of San Francisco State Univ. Founded progressive pre-school in Bay Area. Became story editor in feature film division of Cine-Ar tists; involved in several projects, including Aloha, Bobby and Rose. Partnered with Jane Fonda and IPC Films, Inc.

PICTURES: Coming Home (assoc. prod.); The China Syndrome (exec. prod.).

GILBERT, LEWIS: Writer, director, actor. b. London, England, Mar. 6, 1920. In RAF, World War II. Screen debut 1932; asst. dir. (1930–39) with London Films, Assoc. British; Mayflower, RKO-Radio; from 1939–44 attached U.S. Air Corps Film Unit (asst. dir., "Target for Today"). In 1944 joined G.B.I. as writer and dir. In 1948, Gainsborough Pictures as writer, dir., 1949; Argyle Prod. 1950; under contract Nettlefold Films, Ltd. as dir.

PICTURES INCLUDE: Under One Roof, I Want to Get Married, Haunting Melody, Once a Sinner, Scarlet Thread, There Is Another Sun, Time Gentlemen Please, Emergency Call, Cosh Boy, Johnny on the Run, Albert R.N., The Good Die Young, The Sea Shall Not Have Them, Reach for the Sky, Cast a Dark Shadow, The Admirable Crichton, Carve Her Name with Pride, A Cry from the Street, Ferry to Hong Kong, Sink the Bismarck, Light Up the Sky, The Greengage Summer, H.M.S. Defiant, The Patriots, Spare the Rod, The Seventh Dawn, You Only Live Twice, The Adventurers, Friends, Paul & Michelle, Operation Daybreak, Seven Nights in Japan, The Spy Who Loved Me. 1978–79: Dir. Moonraker.

GILBERT, MELISSA: Actress. b. Los Angeles, May 8, 1964. Made debut at age of 3 in TV commercial. Comes from show business family: father, late comedian Paul Gilbert; mother, former dancer-actress Barbara Crane.

TELEVISION: Gunsmoke, Emergency, Tenafly, The Hanna-Barbera Happy Hour, Christmas Miracle in Caufield U.S.A., Love Boat, Little House on the Prairie (regular).

GILFORD, JACK: Actor. Made first stage appearances in amateur night performances as stand-up comic. Wrote own material, specializing in imitations. First theatrical role in 1952 in The World of Sholem Aleichem, which he repeated in TV special based on play.
PICTURES INCLUDE: They Might Be Giants, Catch-22, Save the Tiger, Harry and Walter Go to New York, Wholly Moses.
STAGE: The Diary of Anne Frank, Romanoff and Juliet, Once Upon a Mattress, Cabaret, No, No, Nanette.

GILKISON, ANTHONY: Producer. b. York, England, June 3, 1913. e. Stowe School. Assistant dir. and prod. mgr. European and British companies, 1932–38; film director Rayant Pictures, 1938; executive producer, managing director Rayant Pictures, 1945; chmn. Rayant Television, Ltd.; founded Anthony Gilkison Associates, International Motion Picture and Television Consultants, 1963. 1976, Chmn. Anthony Gilkison Assoc. (Holdings) Ltd.

GILLASPY, RICHARD M.: Producer, director. b. St. Louis, Mo., Dec. 10, 1927; joined NBC in New York as exec. trainee, 1947; headed Marine Corps Radio, 1952–54; rejoined NBC-TV as stage mgr., became prod. dir.; won Emmy Award, 1960, for Nixon-Khrushchev debate; pres., Seven League Productions, 1961–63, owner, Radio Station WIII, Homestead, Fla., 1963–67; freelance prod.-dir., 1967–70; v.p. of Ivan Tors Studios, N. Miami, 1970–1972; pres. RMG Productions, 1972.

GILLIAT, LESLIE: Producer. b. New Malden, England, 1917. e. Epson College. Ent. m.p. ind. 1935.
PICTURES INCLUDE: Only Two Can Play, The Amorous Prawn, Joey Boy, The Great St. Trinians Train Robbery, A Dandy in Aspic, The Virgin Soldiers, The Buttercup Chain, Endless Night, Priest of Love (prod. supvr.).

GILLIAT, SIDNEY: Writer, producer, director of many British films. b. Cheshire, Eng., 1968.

GILLIN, DONALD T.: Executive. b. Council Bluffs, Iowa, June 17, 1914. e. Univ. of Minn., bus. adm., 1929–32; sls., Warner Bros., 1932–39; World War II; home office sup., Warner Bros., 1946–48; sls. exec., Universal, 1948–50; v.p., gen. sls. mgr., mgr., Sol Lesser, 1950–59; establ., Donald T. Gillin Inc., producers' rep., 1960. Muchnic-Gillin Internat'l, Inc., 1961; Producers' Representatives, Inc., 1967.

GILLING, JOHN: Writer, producer, director. b. 1912. Started in show business in U.S., 1930. Ent. Brit. m.p. ind. 1933 as asst. dir. B.I.P., Gainsborough, Gaumont. Served in R.N.V.R. during war. Has written 56 s.p. inc. 29 orig., all prod. since 1946; dir. 26 pictures.
PICTURES INCLUDE: Interpol, The Man Inside, Odongo, High Flight, The Flesh and the Fields, The Challenge, Fury at Smugglers Bay, The Pirates of Blood River, The Shadow of the Cat, Blood River, Scarlet Blade, Brigand of Kandahar, Plague of the Zombies, The Reptile, The Night Caller.
TV: Written and dir. TV films.

GILLIS, ANNE: Actress. r.n. Alma Mable O'Connor. b. Little Rock, Arkansas, Feb. 12, 1927. Screen debut 1936 in The Garden of Allah; thereafter in number child roles.
PICTURES INCLUDE: King of Hockey, Off to the Races, The Californian, The Adventures of Tom Sawyer, Peck's Bad Boy with the Circus, Little Orphan Annie, Edison the Man, All This and Heaven Too, Janie; A Wave, a Wac, a Marine; The Cheaters, Gay Blades, Big Town After Dark.

GIMBEL, ROGER: Producer. Began television production career as copy and creative chief of RCA Victor TV, then became assoc. prod. of the Tonight Show for NBC. Subsequently named head of program development of NBC daytime programming; later became producer of the 90-minute NBC Tonight Specials, including The Jack Paar Show and the Ernie Kovacs Show. Became prod. and copackager of the Glen Campbell Goodtime Hour for CBS, 1969; vice pres. in charge of production for Tomorrow Entertainment, 1971. Produced 15 major movies for television including The Autobiography of Miss Jane Pittman, Born Innocent, Birds of Prey, Brand New Life, Gargoyles, Glass House, In This House of Brede (General Electric Theatre), I heard the Owl Call My Name (G.E. Theatre), I Love You, Good-Bye, Larry (G.E. Theatre), Miles to Go (G.E. Theatre), Queen of the Stardust Ballroom, Tell Me Where It Hurts (G.E. Theatre) Things in Their Season (G.E. Theatre), War of the Children (Emmy award, Outstanding Single Program, Drama or Comedy). Formed his own production company, Roger Gimbel's Tomorrow Enterprises, Inc., 1975; produced two-hour CBS special, Minstrel Man. Became U.S. pres. of EMI-TV, 1976. Received special personal Emmy as exec. prod. of War of the Children, 1975.

GINGOLD, DAN: Freelance Executive Producer, Producer, Director. Credits include all types live and film prod. Specialist in Special Events and Documentary. Awards include Emmy, Ohio State, Northwestern, Ed Murrow, Assoc. Press, San Francisco State.

GINGOLD, HERMIONE: Actress. b. London, England, 1897. Appeared with Old Vic and at Shakespeare at Stratford on Avon and in Paris before coming to America and Bdwy.
PICTURES: Gigi, Naked Edge, Music Man, Gay Paree, Harvey Middleman—Fireman, I'd Rather Be Rich, Promise Her Anything, Rocket to the Moon.
TELEVISION: Ed Sullivan Show, Omnibus, Matinee Theatre, Jack Paar, Alfred Hitchcock Presents, Merv Griffin Show, Mike Douglas Show, etc.

GINNA, ROBERT EMMETT, JR.: Producer. writer. b. New York City, Dec. 3, 1925. e. U. of Rochester, Harvard, M.A. Lt. j.g. U.S. Navy Amphibious Forces, W.W. II. Journalist, editor, Life, Scientific American, Horizon, 1950–61; contributor many other magazines, particularly on stage and screen. Worked as writer, director, producer or associate producer, Public Affairs TV, Wisdom series, FDR series, Specials. 1955–58, 1961–63; v.p., Sextant, Inc., 1961–64; dir. Sextant Films, Ltd.; co-prod., Young Cassidy, 1964; founder and pres., Windward Productions, Inc., 1965; founder and mgr. dir., Windward Film Productions, Ltd., 1965.

GINSBERG, SIDNEY: Executive. b. New York City, Oct. 26, 1920; e. City Coll., 1938; entered m.p. ind., as asst. mgr., Loew's Theatres; joined Trans-Lux, 1943, as thea. mgr.; film booker; helped form Trans-Lux Distributing Corp., 1956; asst. to pres., Trans-Lux Dist. Corp.; asst. vice-pres., Trans-Lux Picture, Distributing and TV Corp., 1961, V.P. Trans-Lux Dist. Corp., 1967, V.P. in charge of world wide sales, 1969. Haven International Pictures, Inc., Haven Intern'l 1970; IFIDA gov., 1970, v.p. sales, Scotia International Films, Inc., 1971; exec. v.p., Scotia American Prods; 1977, pres., Rob-Rich Films Inc.; 1979, exec. v.p., A Major Studio, Inc.; 1980, exec. v.p., The Health and Entertainment Corp. of America.

GINSBURG, LEWIS S.: Distrib., Import., prob. b. New York, May 16, 1914. e. City Coll., N.Y., 1931–32. Columbia Univ., 1932–33. Ent. film industry, tabulating dept., United Artists, Sept. 1932; sls. contract dept. 1933; asst. to eastern district mgr., 1938; slsmn., New Haven exch., 1939. Army, 1943. Ret. to U.S., then formed first buying & booking service in Connecticut, 1945–55; in chg., New England Screen Guild Exchanges, 1955; TV film distr., 1955; Formed & org. International Film Assoc., Vid-EX Film Distr. Corp., 1961. Prod., TV half-hour series; vice-pres. in chg., dist., Desilu Film Dist. C., 1962; organized Carl Releasing Co., x963; Walter Reade-Sterling Inc., 1964–65; formed L.G. Films Corp.; contract and playdate mgr., 20th Fox, 1965–68. Cinerama Releasing Corp. Adm. Ass't to sales mgr., 1968–69; 20th Cent.-Fox. Nat'l sales coordinator, 1969–present. 1970, 20th Century-Fox, Asst. to the Sales Mgr. 1971, Transnational Pictures Corp., v.p. in chg. of dist., pres., Stellar IV Film Corp., 1972.

GIRARDOT, ANNIE: Actress. Studied nursing. Studied acting at the Paris Conservatory, made her acting debut with the Comedie Francaise. Has acted on the French stage and in reviews in the Latin Quarter.
PICTURES INCLUDE: Rocco and His Brothers, The Organizer, Les Galoise Bleues, Live For Life, Trois Chambres A Manhattan (Best Actress Award at the Venice Film Festival), Story of A Woman, Love Is A Funny Thing, The Slap, No Time for Breakfast.

GISH, LILLIAN: Actress. b. Springfield, Ohio, Oct. 14, 1899; sister of Dorothy G., actress. At 5 appeared in In Convict's Stripes, at Rising Sun, Ohio; following year danced in Sarah Bernhardt prod. in N.Y. In 1913 appeared with Mary Pickford in A Good Little Devil, N.Y. Began screen career 1912 with Biograph, beginning there assn. with D. W. Griffith, dir., which culminated in such films as The Birth of a Nation, Intolerance, Hearts of the World, The Great Love, Broken Blossoms, Way Down East and Orphans of the Storm. Continued in films: White Sister, Romola, The Wind, La Boheme, Scarlet Letter. From 1930 on N.Y. stage in number orig. prods. & classics Uncle Vanya, Camille, 9 Pine Street, Within the Gates, Hamlet, Star Wagon, Old Maid, Dear Octopus, Life With Father, Mr. Sycamore, The Marquise, Legend of Leonora, Crime and Punishment, Miss Mable, Curious Savage, A Passage to India, Too True to be Good; Romeo and Juliet, Stratford Shakespeare Theatre, 1965. 1969–71, one woman int'l. concert tour, Lillian Gish and the Movies. Received honorary Oscar, 1971. International touring with illustrated lecture on the art of film and TV, 1974. Lecture tour on Queen Elizabeth 2, 1975.
PICTURES INCLUDE: One Romantic Night, His Double Life, Commandos Strike at Dawn, Duel in the Sun, Miss Susie Slagle's, Portrait of Jenny, Follow Me Boys!, Night of the Hunter, 1954; The Cobweb, 1955; The Unforgiven, Orders to Kill; Warning Shot, The Comedians, A Wedding (her 100th film).
PLAYS: Theatre Guild play The Trip to Bountiful, 1954; Chalk Garden, 1956; Phoenix Theatre, N.Y., The Family Reunion; in Berlin, Ger., Portrait of a Madonna, Wreck of the 5:25, Uncle Vanya, 1973. All The Way Home, 1960;

Anya, 1965; I Never Sang For My Father, 1968; A Musical Jubilee, 1976.

TV: I Mrs. Bibbs, Sound and the Fury, Day Lincoln Was Shot, Mornings at Seven, The Grass Harp, Grandma T.N.T., Mr. Novak, Alfred Hitchcock Hour, Breaking Point, The Defenders, The Silent Years (hostess). Twin Detectives—(ABC Movie-of-the-Week), 1976.

AUTHOR: The Movies, Mr. Griffith and Me, published by Prentice-Hall, 1969; Dorothy and Lillian Gish published by Charles Scribner, October, 1973.

GITHENS, W. FRENCH: Executive. b. New York City, April 30, 1906; e. Columbia U. in 1928 secy. Amer. embassy Madrid. Entered m.p. ind. 1929 as member ed. staff Movietonews, editing program Embassy Newsreel theat., N.Y.; asst. ed. Pathe News 1933. On 1934 org. Newsreel Theats. (Embassy theat., Broadway, N.Y. & others), becoming pres. & dir. Org. Sound Masters 1937 to prod. industrial & educational films. Lt. Comdr., U.S.N.R. Bureau Aeronautics World War II; com. U.S.N.R.; pres. National Educational Films, Inc.; on bd. of Viterama & Cinerama Corps. developers of 3-dimensional projection system, 1950. Mayor of Bernardsville, N.J., 2 terms; prod., Movietime Digest; prod., V.P. and dir. Steel Properties, N.Y.C.

GLASER, PAUL MICHAEL: Actor. b. Cambridge, Mass., March 25. e. Tulane Univ., Boston Univ. (M.A.). Did five seasons in summer stock before starting career in New York City, making stage debut in rock version of Hamlet in 1968. Appeared in numerous off-Bdwy. plays and got early TV training as regular in daytime series, Love of Life and Love Is a Many Splendored Thing.

PICTURES INCLUDE: Fiddler on the Roof, Butterflies Are Free.

TV: Kojak, Toma, The Streets of San Francisco, The Rockford Files, The Sixth Sense, The Waltons. Movies: Trapped Beneath the Sea, The Great Houdini. Series: Starsky & Hutch.

GLASER, SIDNEY: Exec. adv., prod. b. New York, N.Y., July 12, 1912. e. CCNY, b. Eng., 1936; NYU, m. Eng., 1942; office boy, adv. dept., Metro-Goldwyn-Mayer, 1929; prod. asst. 1934; prod. mgr., 1957; adv. prod. mgr., 1972; gen. adv. exec.

GLASS, GEORGE: Producer, publicist. b. Los Angeles, Calif., Aug. 19, 1910. e. L.A. schools. Reporter, sports writer L.A. Herald, Record; news commentator, special events broadcaster L.A. Examiner; joined Selznick publ. dept., 1936; West Coast dir. adv. for United Artists 1941; dir. pub. and adv. Samuel Goldwyn 1944. In 1945 special consultant to ind. prod. cos. In 1947 joined Stanley Kramer as partner and v.p. Stanley Kramer Co.; assoc. prod. The Men, Cyrano de Bergerac, Death of a Salesman. In 1954 dissolved Kramer partnership, exec. staff, Hecht-Lancaster, 1956; org. with Walter Seltzer, Glass-Seltzer Co.; joined Pennebaker, Inc. as exec. prod., v.p.; co-prod. Shake Hands With the Devil; exec. prod. One-Eyed Jacks. Co-prod., The Naked Edge, Paris Blues, 1960–61. Prod., Universal-International, 1963; assoc. prod., The Day Custer Fell, 20th Century-Fox, 1964. Rejoined Stanley Kramer as v.p.-assoc. prod. 1967. Assoc. Prod. Guess Who's Coming to Dinner, 1968. Assoc. prod. The Secret of Santa Vittoria, 1969; Assoc. prod. R.P.M., 1970; assoc. prod., Bless the Beasts and Children, 1971. Now consultant for production and p.r.

GLAZIER, SIDNEY: Producer. b. Philadelphia, May 29, 1918. Managed movie and legitimate theatres in Pennsylvania and Ohio. Air Force captain during World War II. Became v.p. of Washington Federal Savings and Loan Bank in Miami. Org. and became exec. dir. of Eleanor Roosevelt Cancer Foundation. Prod. network TV public service programs. First m.p. The Eleanor Roosevelt Story won Academy Award, 1966. Pres. of U-M Film Distributors, 1969.

PICTURES INCLUDE: The Producers, Take the Money and Run, The Gamblers, Quackser Fortune Has a Cousin in the Bronx, The 12 Chairs, Glen and Panda, The Night Visitor, The Only Way.

GLEASON, JACKIE: Performer. b. Brooklyn, N.Y., Feb. 26, 1916. Started as amateur entertainer, clubs, WB pact, appeared in Navy Blues, All Through the Night, Larceny, Inc., Orchestra Wives, Springtime in the Rockies; returned to Broadway appearing on the stage and summer stock.

BWY. STAGE: Take Me Along, 1959–60 (Tony Award).

TV: Started as lead in The Life of Riley; then star and m.c. Cavalcade of Stars on the Du Mont network; The Honeymooners; Jackie Gleason Show, CBS-TV network. Best comedian, Fame poll, 1953; best comedy show, 1954.

PICTURES INCLUDE: The Hustler, Requiem For a Heavyweight, Gigot, Papa's Delicate Condition, Soldier in the Rain, Ski-doo; How to Commit a Marriage, Don't Drink the Water, How Do I Love Thee?, The Late Show, Smokey and the Bandit, Smokey and the Bandit II.

GLEASON, KEOGH: Set decorator. b. Minneapolis, Minn., April 14, e. U. of Minn. Vaudeville, 1929–30; interior decorator, portrait painter, 1932–34; set decorator, MGM, 1936; Acad.

Award, An American in Paris, 1951; Bad and the Beautiful, 1952. Somebody Up There Likes Me, 1956; Gigi, 1958; Nominations, Story of Three Loves, 1953; Brigadoon, 1954; Lust for Life, 1956.

PICTURES INCLUDE: Father of the Bride, Fathers Little Dividend, The Trailer, Cob Web, Kismet, Tea and Sympathy, For Me and My Gal, Bells are Ringing, Four Horsemen of the Apocalypse, Two Weeks in Another Town, Goodbye Charlie, Courtship of Eddie's Father, The Sandpiper, Point Blank, Legend of Lylah Clare, There was a Crooked Man.

TV: Richard Boone Rep. Theatre, Twilight Zone.

GLENN, CHARLES OWEN: Executive. b. Binghamton, N.Y., March 27, 1938; e. Syracuse U., (BA), U. of Pa. Asst. to dir. of adv., 20th Cent. Fox, 1966–67; asst. adv. mgr., Paramount, 1967–68; acct. spvsr. & exec., MGM record & m.p. div., 1968–69; nat'l adv. mgr., Paramount, 1969–70; nat'l. dir. of adv., Paramount, 1970–71; v.p. adv.-pub.-prom., 1971–73; v.p. marketing, 1974; v.p. prod. mktg., 1975; joined American Intl. Pictures as v.p. in chg. of adv./creative affairs, 1979. 1980, when Filmways took AIP over he was named their v.p. in chg. worldwide adv./pub./promo.

GLICK, HYMAN J.: Executive. b. Russia, Dec. 15, 1904; e. N.Y.U., B.C.S., '26, C.P.A. (N.Y.); with public accounting firm, N.Y., 1923–29; own public accounting Business, 1929–32. Became assoc. m.p. ind. as member comptrollers' com., repr. Republic; 1932–36, tax & financial counsel Mascot Pictures Corp. Joined Republic 1936 as comptroller; apptd. asst. secy.-asst. treas. Jan., 1945.

Member: B'nai Brith Lodge 1325; YMCA, State Soc. of Certified Public Accountants, Am. Inst. of Accountants. Resigned Republic, 1959; CPA (Calif.), member, Calif. Soc. of CPA; sec'y-treas., Own Accounting and Tax Practice.

GLICKMAN, JOEL: Producer. b. Los Angeles, July 29, 1930. e. UCLA (film dep't.). Was actor and director for LA little theatre groups and writer-director for industrial films. Early TV work on series, documentaries and commercials. Directed videotaping of off-Broadway shows. Was production assoc. on film, Wedding and Babies, 1958. Was assoc. prod. and prod. mgr. on films (Terror in the City, The Balcony, All the Way Home, For Love of Ivy, Hamlet (Richard Burton, assoc. director), Dion Brothers, Last Summer and TV (East Side, West Side, Mr. Broadway), N.Y.P.D., Love Song of Barney Kempinski, Among the Paths To Eden. Member Motion Picture Academy & D.G.A. Has own co.: Selznick/Glickman Productions.

PICTURES INCLUDE: Brother John, Buck and the Preacher, Trial of the Catonsville Nine (exec. prod.), Night Terror (NBC-TV movie), Angel on Horseback (CBS-TV movie), Kennedy-Hoffa War (NBC-TV miniseries).

GLUCK, NORMAN E.: Executive. b. Racine, Wisc., Apr. 17, 1914. Worked for RKO Theaters, Albany dist., 1932–34; Skouras Theatres, 1935–46; U.S. Army; oper. Park Ave. Theatre, N.Y., 1947–48; United World Films (Univ. subsid.), 1949; v.p. and dir., head Universal Pictures TV dept.; dir. corp. oper., Screen Gems, 1959–60; Universal Pictures, 1960; Asst. to gen. sales mgr. Now retired.

GLUCKSMAN, ERNEST D.: Producer, director, writer. b. Vienna, Austria, March 21. Broadway musicals, summer stock, vaudeville, night clubs. Legit: Odd Couple. Consultant to Commissioner of Cultural Affairs, City of New York.

PICTURES INCLUDE: The Nutty Professor, The Errand Boy, The Patsy, Rock-A-Bye-Baby, Bell Boy, Cinderfella, Geisha Boy.

TV: Here Come the Stars, Can You Top This, Colgate Comedy Hour, Saturday Night Revue. Specials: Timex All-Star Swing Festival; Dr. Jekyll and Mr. Hyde, Bobby Sherman, Fifth Dimension, Bobby Darin, Sonny & Cher, George Kirby, Kenny Rogers and The First Edition, Charles Aznavour & Liza Minnelli; game show What's the Good Word?; series Story Theatre.

GOATMAN, ALAN H.: Consultant, Entered m.p. industry 1934. Officer of the Venerable Order of St. John of Jerusalem. Fellow Society of Company and Commercial Accountants. Memb. Brit. Computer Soc. Fellow Brit. Inst. Management; member Inst. Data Processing; Management Dir. Gen. Man. E.M.I. Films Ltd. and E.M.I. Film Distributors Overseas Ltd. Dir. E.M.I. Pathe Ltd., Anglo-E.M.I. Productions Ltd. Databank Computing Services Ltd., Columbia-EMI-Warner Dist. Ltd.

GODARD, JEAN-LUC: Writer-Director. b. Paris, France, Dec. 3, 1930.

PICTURES INCLUDE: A Bout de Souffle, Une Femme Est Une Femme, Vivre Sa Vie, Le Petie Soldat, Les Carabiniera, Bande a Part, Une Femme Marlee, A Little Godard; Pierrot Le Fou, Made in USA, Weekend, Tout va Bien.

GODBOLD, GEOFF: Executive. b. London, England, 1935. Ent. ind. 1959. Specialized in supply of location requirements for film and TV prods. Formed Prop Workshops Ltd., co-promoted Television Recordings Ltd. Man. dir. Facilities

(Screen & Television) Ltd. Dir. TV Recordings, Investments, Ltd.; Centrepoint Screen Prod. Ltd.; Tape Commercials, Ltd. Council Mem. Film and TV Contractors Assoc. Dir. Lancair Export Services Ltd.; 1968 Freelance production buyer, Screen Gems and Tigon. 1969. Feature Prod. Rep. Film Div. N.A.T.T.K.E.

PICTURES INCLUDE: Dubious Patriot, Every Home Should Have One, Melody, Up Pompeii. Morocco location, Young Winston. The Asphyx, Our Miss Fred, Death of a Snow Queen, Man in the Iron Mask.

GODDARD, PAULETTE: Actress. b. Great Neck, N.Y., June 3, 1911. On N.Y. stage in Rio Rita; then member of Hal Roach Studios stock co. In 1936 opposite Charles Chaplin in Modern Times.

PICTURES INCLUDE: The Young in Heart, The Women, North West Mounted Police, The Great Dictator, Hold Back the Dawn, Reap the Wild Wind, Star Spangled Rhythm, I Love a Soldier, So Proudly We Hail, Standing Room Only, Duffy's Tavern, Kitty, Unconquered, An Ideal Husband, Hazard, On Our Merry Way, Bride of Vengeance, Anna Lucasta, Babes in Bagdad, Vice Squad, Paris Model, Sins of Jezebel, Charge of the Lancers, Unholy Four, Time of Indifference.

GODFREY, ARTHUR: Performer. b. New York City, Aug. 31, now 54th year in show business—actor, writer, narrator, entertainer.

CLUBS: New York Yacht, Explorers, Quiet Birdmen. Calif. Yacht, Sky, Illustrators.

PICTURES INCLUDE: The Glass Bottom Boat, Where Angels Go . . . Trouble Follows, Four for Texas, The Great Georgia Bank Hoax.

GODWIN, FRANK: Producer, Director. Joined Gainsborough Pictures 1943, subsequently exec. with Rank Organization; asst. to exec. prod. Earl St. John.

PICTURES INCLUDE: Woman in a Dressing Gown, No Trees in the Street, Operation Bullshine, Don't Bother to Knock, The Small World of Sammy Lee, Danny the Dragon, Headline Hunters, Demons of the Mind, The Boy With Two Heads, The Firefighters, Sky Pirates, Sammy's Super T-Shirt, Electric Eskimo, The Boy Who Never Was.

GOLD, MELVIN: Executive. b. Chicago, Ill., Sept. 3, 1909. In 1930 joined MGM, Chicago, as assistant office manager. To Reinheimer Circuit 1932 to operate theatres Hammond, Indiana; in 1940 organized own advertising agency, Sales, Inc., mgr.; mgr. Vogue Theatre, Hollywood, Calif., 1943. Joined National Screen Service 1943 as editor Mister Showman; Feb., 1945 named director of advtsng. and publicity; assumed east coast film prod. and TV, Sept., 1948 to May, 1954. Formed Mel Gold Productions, Inc., June 1954.

Member Publicity Club of N.Y.; Associated Motion Picture Advertisers; founded National Television Film Council in 1948, elected Honorary Lifetime President, 1955. Partner Melmon Productions; Melvin L. Gold Enterprises, 1958; pres., Mesal Prods., Inc., 1961; wrote s.p., Not For Love, 1961; pres., Associated Motion Picture Advertisers, 1963–64–65–66; gen. sls. mgr., National Screen Service, 1963. Pres., Melvin L. Gold Enterprises, Inc., 1966. Pres., Manhattan Sound Studios, 1967, v.p. in chg. m.p. div., National Showmanship Services, 1968; 1971, Pres. East Side Productions; Pres. Melvin L. Gold Enterprises. Motion picture consultant, Philip Morris, Inc., 1976–present. Operations director, Benson & Hedges 100, Film classics, 1976–79. Wrote s.p., The Sheriff is a Lady, 1979.

GOLDBERG, BERNARD: Executive. b. Bronx, N.Y., Aug. 25, 1932. e. Queens College (B.A.). Co-owner, Golden Theatre Mgt. Corp.; named vice pres. 1973.

GOLDBERG, FRED: Publicist. b. N.Y.C., Aug. 26, 1921. e. Pace College, School of Marketing and Advertising. expl., Paramount, 1946; asst. expl. mgr., trade paper contact, syndicate contact, N.Y. newspaper contact promotion mgr., 1946–52; ass't publ. mgr., RKO, 1952; national publ. mgr., IFE, 1953; v.p. Norton and Condon, pub.; 1953; returned to IFE Sept., 1954, as nat'l pub. mgr.; head of N.Y. office, Arthur Jacobs, then Blowitz-Maskel, 1956; exec. asst. to dir. pub., adv., United Artists Corp., 1958; exec. dir., adv., pub., exploitation, United Artists Corp., 1961; named vice pres., 1962, senior vice president, 1972, Senior Vice President, Director of Marketing, 1977. Left in 1978 to be consultant with Piener, Hauser & Bates Agency. In 1979 joined Columbia Pictures as snr. v.p. in chg. adv./pub. Left in 1981 to form new company.

GOLDBERG, LEON: Executive. b. Providence, R.I., Aug. 29, 1900; e. A.B., Brown U., 1921; M.B.A. Harvard Graduate School of Business Administration, 1923. Assoc. with Goldman, Sachs, investment bankers, from September, 1923 to April, 1934. In April, 1934 became treasurer of Keith-Albee-Orpheum Corp. In December, 1941, became treasurer of RKO and RKO Radio Pictures, Inc. Resigned October, 1943, to become studio mgr., RKO Studios, Hollywood; elected vice-pres., 1946; elected fin'l. v.p., treas., Universal-International 1950; res. Oct., 1953; to United

Artists as financial v.p., treas., November 1953–67, dir., National Screen Service Corp. 1969.

GOLDBERG, LEONARD: Executive. b. Brooklyn. e. Wharton School, Univ. of PA. Began career in ABC-TV research dept.; moved to NBC-TV research div.; 1961 joined Batten. Barton, Durstine & Osborn ad agency in chg. of daytime TV shows and overall bdcst. coordinator. In 1963 rejoined ABC-TV as mgr. of program devel. In 1966 named VP in chg of network TV programming. Resigned in 1969 to join Screen Gems as VP in chg. of prod. Left for partnership with Aaron Spelling in Spelling/Goldberg Prods. Goldberg is now producing TV and theatrical films under own banner, Mandy Prods. 1981: co-prod., All Night Long.

GOLDEN, HERBERT L.: b. Philadelphia, Feb. 12. e. Temple U., 1936, B.S. Reporter, rewrite man. asst. city ed., Philadelphia Record, 1933–38; joined Variety, 1938; on leave of absence, 1942–43, when asst. to John Hay Whitney and Francis Alstock, directors, M.P. Division, Coordinator of Inter-American Affairs (U.S.); commissioned in U.S. Navy, 1943, served on destroyer to 1946; then returned to Variety. M.p. ed. Consultant on motion pictures, Good Housekeeping magazine, McGraw-Hill Publications, American Yearbook. Ent. Ind. Div. Bankers Trust Co., N.Y.C., 1952; named v.p. 1954–56; treas., Children's Asthma Research Institute, 1956; v.p. & mem. of bd. United Artists Corp., 1958; member of board, MPAA, 1959; pres., Lexington Int., Inc. investments, 1962; mem. bd., chmn. exec. com., Perfect Photo Inc., 1962; 1965 sect. & mem. bd. Century Broadcasting Group; chmn. G & G Thea. Corp.; pres. Diversifax Corp., 1966; consult. Pathe Lab, 1967; Mem. bd. Childhood Prod. Inc., 1967. Member bd. Music Makers Group, Inc., 1962. Mem. bd. Cinecom Corp., 1968; pres., Vere/Swiss Corp., 1977; mem. bd., Coral Reef Publications, Inc., 1977. Returned to Bankers Trust, 1979, to head its Media Group (service to film and TV industries).

GOLDEN, JEROME B.: Executive. b. New York, N.Y., Nov. 26, 1917. e. St. Lawrence Univ., LL.B., 1942. Member legal dept., Paramount Pictures, Inc., 1942–50; United Paramount Theatres, Inc., 1950–53; American Broadcasting Companies, Inc., 1953; secy., ABC, 1958; vice-pres., ABC, 1959.

GOLDEN, NATHAN D.: Director, Scientific, M.P. Photographic Products Division, Business-Defense Services Adm., Dept. of Commerce, Washington. b. Bellaire, O., July 4, 1895. e. Emerson Inst. (Washington, D.C.); Columbus U. & Washington Coll. of Law, LL.B., J.D. American University. Wounded during World War I, serving in the U.S. Infantry. In 1926 entered Bureau of Foreign & Domestic Commerce as asst. chief; chief of section, 1933; chief, m.p. div., 1937. Has written numerous articles on world m.p. market developments. Motion Picture Consultant to the Golden Gate International Exposition, 1939. Awarded first Gold Medal for outstanding contribution field of m.p. projection, by Projection Advisory Council, 1930. Fellow, Soc. of M.P. Engineers; Chief Barker, 1947, Variety Club of Washington, D.C.; Int'l Heart Chmn., Variety Clubs International. Headed mission to Europe for the Joint Chiefs of Staff 1945 to obtain technical data on Agfa Color Film for which rec. War Dept. Certificate of Appreciation. Dept. of Commerce Silver Medal Award for meritorious service for the m.p. ind. Feb., 1954; Chevalier French Legion of Honor, 1956. Awarded Order of Merit, First Class, from Federal Republic of Germany, Oct. 2, 1961; presented with Medaille de Vermeil by Society for the Encouragement of Progress, Paris, France, Nov. 19, 1961; Decorated by French Photographic Industry with their "Gold Medallion" at Photokima in September 1976; retired from Dept. of Commerce, 1963; practicing Law, Washington, D.C.

GOLDENSON, LEONARD H.: Executive. b. Scottsdale, Pennsylvania, December 7, 1905; e. Harvard College, B.A., Harvard Law School, LL.B. Practiced law, New York; counsel in reorg. Paramount theats. in New England, 1933–37; in 1937 apptd. asst. to vice-pres. Paramount in charge theat. operations; became head of theat. operations, 1938; elected pres. Paramount Theat. Service Corp., vice-pres. Paramount Pictures, Inc., 1938; dir. Paramount Pictures, 1942 (also pres. various Paramount theat. subsids., see Paramount circuits in Theatre Circuits section). Pres., chief exec. off. and director United Paramount Theatres, Inc., 1950, and of American Broadcasting-Paramount Theatres, Inc., 1953, result of merger of ABC and United Paramount Theatres, Inc.; name changed to American Broadcasting Companies, Inc. 1965; Chairman of the Board and Chief Executive Officer; of American Broadcasting Companies, Inc. since January 17, 1972; mem., board chm. of United Cerebral Palsy Assns.; trustee, John F. Kennedy Center for the Performing Arts; dir., Daughters of Jacob Geriatric Center; mem., International Radio and Television Society; Founder Member of Hollywood Museum; Trustee of Children's Cancer Research Foundation of the Children's Medical Center, Boston, Mass.; Director of Allied Stores Corporation; Trustee of Highway Users Federation for Safety and Mobility; Member of National Academy of Television Arts and Sciences; Member of Uptown Advisory Committee of Bankers Trust Company; Graduate Director of The Advertising Council, Inc.; Associate Trustee and Member of Advisory Council for the Performing Arts of University of Pennsylvania; Member of Broadcast Pioneers; Member of Inter Lochen Arts Academy-National Advisory Board; Member of Motion Picture Pioneers; Member of National Citizens' Advisory Committee on Vocational Rehabilitation; Member of United Negro College Fund-National Corporations Committee; Director of World Rehabilitation Fund, Inc.

GOLDFARB, HOWARD: Executive. b. New York City, Sept. 19, 1941. e. Wharton School of Business. Joined Columbia Pictures as exec. trainee; 1964–69 mgn. dir., U.A., central America; 1969–70, supervisor of sales, Buena Vista Intl.; 1972–75, pres. H.C. Entertainment Ltd.; 1975–76, dir. of dist., CIC, London; v.p.; intl. operations, NTA; 1978–79, v.p., intl. sls., Dino de Laurentiis pres., Goldfarb Distributors, since 1979.

GOLDIN, BERNARD: Executive. Began career with Universal Pictures as branch mgr. in number of territories. Named Philadelphia mgr. for United Artists; 1977–81, Midwestern div. mgr. for Columbia Pictures. Returned to UA, 1981, as v.p. & asst. gen. sls. mgr.

GOLDING, DAVID: Executive. b. New York City, U. of Wisc., B.A. Now operating public relations consultancy in London, David Golding and Associates Ltd. Formerly Universal advertising and publicity representative in UK. During war, mg. ed. Mediterranean edition, The Stars and Stripes. Also pub. dir. Samuel Goldwyn, 20th-Fox, Hecht-Hill-Lancaster, Otto Preminger.

GOLDMAN, EDMUND: Executive-Producer. b. Shanghai, China, Nov. 12, 1906. e. in Shanghai and San Francisco. Entered ind. as asst. mgr., for Universal in Shanghai, 1935–36; named mgr. Columbia Pictures' Philippine office, 1937. In 1951 named Far East. supvr. for Columbia, headquartering in Tokyo. From 1953 to present indep. m.p. dist., specializing in foreign marketing, representing indep. producers and distributors. Now chm. of bd. for Manson International.
PICTURES: Surrender Hell (prod.), The Quick and the Dead (exec. prod.).

GOLDMAN, LES: Executive. b. New York, N.Y., July 2, 1913. e. N.Y. Univ., Magna Cum Laude, 1933. Prod. supv., MGM, Tom & Jerry cartoons; prod. supv., animated commercials, industrials, theatrical & TV films; produced educational & public affairs films, Information Films, Inc. Commercial prod., Tempo, Academy and Transfilm, Inc.; prod., combat & staff reports, Army Pictorial Service; org. teacher-training & instruction curriculum, APS School, London; cinema dept., USC est. animation curriculum, 1960 & taught courses first yrs., USC prog.; officer, Storyboard, Inc., 1955–56; org., Quartet Films, Inc., 1956–63; prod.: The Hangman; prod. mgr., SIB-TOWER 12, Animation Studio Hollywood; hd., prod., MGM Animation-Visual Arts Div.: Tom and Jerry Cartoons, animated short subjects; co-prod., The Dot and the Line, MGM; Prod. The Phantom Tollbooth, MGM: Prod. exec. Dr. Seuss' How the Grinch Stole Christmas; Off to See the Wizard; exec. prod.: FILM/SENSE, live action and animation film for industry, TV, and special applications; prod. Breakthrough for IBM Corp. Pres. & exec. prod. Film Sense, Inc. (a Media Creations, Ltd. Co.), prod. Mr. and Mrs. for IBM Corp.; prod. Apres le Silence. prod. On Your Mark, dir. of prod. Bonanza Films: The Cosmic Bicycle, Director/Producer Cinetics: The Curious Fish, The Adventures of Menachem/Mendl, The Perfectly Fair, The Romantic Revolutionaries. President: International Tournee of Animation. In production: Beyond the Milky Way.

GOLDMAN, MARVIN: Executive. b. New York City. e. Fordham & Univ. of Miami. Served in U.S. Navy in WW II, leaving with rank of Lt. commander. In 1947 went to Washington, D.C. to work for K-B Theatres; with present partner, Fred Burka, purchased the chain of five theatres. Circuit now operates 28 theatres in the D.C., Maryland, Virginia area. (Partnership now includes Goldman's son, Ronald, and Burka's son, David.) Goldman also involved with son in indep. film prod. co., which has completed 6 features and planning more. Active in theatre organizations for many years; named pres. of National NATO in 1976. Former pres. of Metropolitan, Washington, D.C. area chapter of NATO and now bd. chmn. Past chief barker of Variety Club of Washington. Named exhibitor of year by IFIDA in 1966.

GOLDMAN, MICHAEL F.: Executive. b. Manila, Philippines, Sept. 28, 1939. e. UCLA (B.S. in acct.), 1962). C.P.A. certificate issued June, 1972. Owner and sole proprietor, Taurus Film Co. of Hollywood. In 1962 incorporated Manson Distributing Corp. as specialist in exporting indep. American feature films. Presently owner and pres. of Manson International, succeeding company to Manson Distributing Corp. Co-founder and chief financial officer of American Film Marketing Association. Sponsor of First

American Film Market in Los Angeles 1981. Produced Jessi's Girls, 1975.

GOLDMAN, WILLIAM: Writer. b. Chicago, 1931. e. Oberlin College (B.A.), Columbia Univ. (M.A.). Novels include The Temple of Gold, Soldier in the Rain (filmed), No Way to Treat a Lady (filmed), Father's Day, The Princess Bride, Marathon Man (filmed), Magic (filmed), Tinsel, etc.
PICTURES INCLUDE: Harper, Butch Cassidy and the Sundance Kid, The Great Waldo Pepper, Marathon Man (based on own book), All the President's Men, A Bridge Too Far, Magic (based on own book).

GOLDSMITH, JERRY: Composer. b. Los Angeles, 1930. e. L.A. City College. Studied piano with Jacob Gimpel and music composition, harmony, theory with Mario Casteinuovo Tedesco. Taught music; went with CBS radio first with own show (Romance) and then moved on to others (Suspense). Began scoring for TV, including Climax, Playhouse 90, Studio One, Gunsmoke, etc.
PICTURES INCLUDE: Black Patch (debut), Freud, Lilies of the Field, The Stripper, The Prize, Seven Days in May, In Harm's Way, Von Ryan's Express, A Patch of Blue, Our Man Flint, Stagecoach, The Blue Max, Seconds, Sand Pebbles, In Like Flint, Patton, Papillon, The Reincarnation of Peter Proud, The Cassandra Crossing, Islands in the Stream, MacArthur, Coma, Damien-Omen II, The Boys from Brazil, The Great Train Robbery, Alien, Players, Star Trek, The Final Conflict, Outland.

GOLDSMITH, MARTIN M.: Writer. b. New York, N.Y., Nov. 6, 1913. Bush pilot.
AUTHOR: Novels include: Double Jeopardy, Detour, Shadows at Noon, Miraculous Fish of Domingo Gonzales.
PICTURES INCLUDE: Detour, Blind Spot, Narrow Margin, Mission Over Korea, Overland Pacific, Hell's Island.

GOLDSTEIN, DAVID M.: Producer's rep. b. Cairo, Egypt, 1973. Ent. industry 1958 with Eros Films Ltd. Then to Sweden as owner/director Swedish International Motion Pictures. Opened up Savant Films, 1965, conducting all import and export from London specializing Scandinavian, Benelux Distribution, 1969; vice pres. in charge world sales, Counselor Films Ltd.

GOLDSTEIN, MILTON: Executive. b. N.Y.C., Aug. 1, 1926. e. N.Y.U., 1949. In exec. capac., Paramount; foreign sales coord., "The Ten Commandments," "Psycho"; v.p. foreign sales, Samuel Bronston org.; asst. to Pres., Paramount Int'l., special prods., 1964; Foreign sales mgr., 1966; v.p., world wide sales, 1967, Cinerama; Sr. v.p. Cinema Center Films, 1969; pres., Cinema Center Films, 1971; v.p. Theatrical Mktg. & Sales, Metromedia Producers Corp., 1973; in March, 1974, formed Boasberg-Goldstein, Inc., consultants in prod. and dist. of m.p.; 1975, named exec. vice pres., Avco Embassy Pictures; 1978, named exec. v.p. & chief operating officer, Melvin Simon Prods. 1980, named pres.

GOLDSTONE, JAMES: Director. b. Los Angeles, Calif. June 8, 1931. e. Dartmouth College, BA, Bennington College, MA. Film Editor from 1950. Writer, story editor from 1957. Director, TV, from 1958, including pilots of Star Trek, Ironside, The Senator, etc., A Clear and Present Danger, (Emmy nomination); Eric, Virgin Islands Int'l. Film Festival Gold Medal, Journey From Darkness, Christopher Award. Feature director since 1967, Studs Lonigan, 6 hr. miniseries, 1978, Kent State, 1980.
PICTURES INCLUDE: Jigsaw, Man Called Gannon, Winning, Brother John, Red Sky at Morning, The Gang That Couldn't Shoot Straight, They Only Kill Their Masters, Swashbuckler, Rollercoaster, When Time Ran Out.

GOLDSTONE, RICHARD: Producer. b. New York City, July 14, 1912. e. University of Cal., Los Angeles, B.A., '33. Capt., Army Air Forces, office of Motion Picture Services, World War II. Adv. exec. Entered m.p. ind. 1934 as writer, MGM; in 1935 asst. head short subjects dept.; in 1939 assoc. prod. short subjects; apptd. prod. mgr.; MGM short subjects dept., co-holder 3 Academy Awards short subjects, 1942. Prod. The Set-Up, (RKO), 1948, won Int'l Critics Grand Prix, Cannes, 1949. v.p. Dudley Pict. Corp.; v.p., Goldcoast Productions, Inc.
PICTURES INCLUDE: The Outriders, Yellow Cab Man, Dial 1119, Inside Straight, The Tall Target, Talk About a Stranger, Devil Makes Three, Terror on the Train, Tabor the Great, The Big Search, East of Kilimanjaro, South Seas Adventures; No Man Is an Island, Rage, The Sergeant, The Babymaker.
TV: Prod. Adventures in Paradise, Combat, Peyton Place, We Ask, Why Not? (doc.)

GOLDWURM, JEAN: Executive. b. Bucharest, Rumania, Feb. 21, 1893. e. Univ. of Vienna. Owner, Little Carnegie and World theatres, New York; pres. Times Film Corp. officer French Legion of Honor; commander Italian Order of Merit, Commander French Order of Arts and Letters.

GOLDWYN, SAMUEL, JR.: Producer, director. b. Los Angeles, Calif., Sept. 7, 1926; e. U. of Va. U.S. Army, 1944; following

war writer, assoc. prod., J. Arthur Rank Org.; prod. Gathering Storm on London stage; returned to U.S., 1948; assoc. prod., Universal; recalled to Army service, 1951; prod., dir., Army documentary films including Alliance for Peace (Edinburgh Film Festival prize); prod. TV shows, Adventure series for CBS, 1952–53; prod. TV series, The Unexpected, 1954; pres., The Samuel Goldwyn Company.
PICTURES INCLUDE: Man With the Gun, The Sharkfighters, The Proud Rebel, The Adventures of Huckleberry Finn, The Young Lovers, Cotton Comes to Harlem, Come Back Charleston Blue.

GOLLINGS, FRANKLIN: Producer, writer, director. b. Llandudno, Wales. Ent. m.p. ind. 1936. Film prod. adviser to the Admiralty, 1945–8. Shorts pro. Rayant Pictures, 1948–52. Unit man. Mogambo. First asst. The Maggie. S.p. The Sitting Duck. Prod. man. Bhowani Junction. Exec. prod. Associated-Rediffusion. Writ. 2nd unit dir. assoc. prod. Yangtse Incident, 1960. Writ. Tempt Not the Stars, The Stirling Moss Story, 1961; Writ. Force 136 and The Stone; writer, dir., The Changing Face, 1963; dir., Woman; res., writer, The Story of Yang-Kwei-Fei; writer, prod., Jason and the Argonauts, 1964; writer, dir., Mystery Horse, A Price for Dorothy, The Big Design, 1965; Writer Dictionary of 1001 Famous People, Great Moments in Amer. History. S.P. dir. prod. Connecting rooms. Formed Four Cities Int. Corp., 1968; program of Internat'l co-prods., 1969. Research and Script High Risk (based on The Junkie Priest), 1970. Prod., dir. High Risk. Dir. The Todd Dossier.

GONZALEZ-GONZALEZ, PEDRO: Actor. b. Aguilares, Tex., Dec. 21, 1926. Comedian in San Antonio Mexican theatres.
PICTURES INCLUDE: Wing of the Hawk, Ring of Fear, Ricochet Romance, High and the Mighty, Strange Lady in Town, Bengazi, I Died a Thousand Times, Bottom of the Bottle, Gun the Man Down, Wetbacks, The Love Bug, Hellfighters, Support Your Local Gunfighter.
TV: O'Henry Stories, Felix, the Fourth, Hostile Guns.

GOOD, CHUCK: Executive. b. 1922. Joined Buena Vista in 1957 in Chicago office; progressed from salesman to branch manager and then district manager. Later moved to Burbank as domestic sales manager in 1975; 1978, named v.p. & general sales manager; 1980, appointed pres., BV Distribution Co.

GOODFRIED, ROBERT: Publicity executive. b. New York City, Apr. 8. Entered motion picture industry with Skouras Theats. Corp.; management & adv.; in 1943 joined United Artists as asst. exploitation dir. In July 1945 named pub. dir., PRC Studios, Hollywood. Then mem. pub. staff, Eagle-Lion Studios; adv., pub. rel. dir. Metropolitan Theatres, Los Angeles; rejoined UA field force, 1951; chge. of expl., prom., Paramount Studios, 1952; pub. mgr., 1958; pub. mgr. Columbia Studio, 1958; studio publicity div., Paramount Studio, 1963. Appt. v.p. in chg. of studio publicity, 1971; exec. consultant to West coast pub. dept., 1980.

GOODMAN, ABE I.: Advertising executive. b. New York City. Entered Motion Picture Industry with Universal Pictures, N.Y.; later in foreign dept. Engaged in theat. circuit exploitation then joined Fox Film Corp. as adv. dir.

GOODMAN, GENE: Executive. Joined United Artists as salesman in 1954; promoted to branch mgr., Atlanta (1958–61). Served successively as branch mgr., New Orleans (1961–68); southern regional mgr. (1968–70); and southern div. mgr., (1970–78), New Orleans. Moved to N.Y. in 1978 to become asst. gen. sls. mgr. Promoted to v.p. & gen. sls. mgr. in 1980. Later in year named snr. v.p. for domestic sls.

GOODMAN, JOHN B.: Art director. b. Denver, Colo., Aug. 15, 1901. Studied architecture. Joined Famous Players Lasky 1920–27; later Pathe, RKO Radio, Warner; Paramount, 1932–39; Frank Lloyd Prods., 1940–41; Universal as superv. art dir. Academy Award (with Alexander Golitzen), art direction, color picture, 1943 (Phantom of the Opera, Universal), Rainbow Prod., Nuys Theatre Corp., Arfan Prods., 1949–50; Nat Holt Pictures, 1950; Paramount 1953–58; MGM, 1959–62; Republic Prods., 1962; CBS Studio Center, 1963–66; M-G-M, 1967. Semi-retired. 1968. Retired, 1969.

GOODMAN, JULIAN: Executive. b. Glasgow, Ky., May 1, 1922. e. B.A. Western Kentucky Univ; B.A. Geo. Washington Univ; Office mgr., Comb. Prod. & Resources, 1943–1945. History at NBC: news writer, WRC, NBC owned station in Washington, D.C., 1945; Washington ed., News of the World, NBC Radio network; mgr. of news and special events, NBC-TV, 1951; dir. of news and public affairs, NBC News Div., 1959; v.p., NBC News, 1961; exec. v.p., 1965; sr. exec. v.p., Operations, Jan. 1, 1966; pres., NBC, April 1, 1966. Mem. bd. of dirs., NBC, 1966; chief executive officer, Jan. 1, 1970; elected director of RCA Corporation, Jan. 1, 1972; chmn., chief exec. off., NBC, April, 1, 1974; chmn., Jan. 5, 1977.

GOODMAN, MORT: Advertising-public relations executive. b. Cleveland, O., Oct. 17, 1910. e. Western Reserve U. With sports dept. Cleveland News 1928–9; joined pub. dept. Warner Bros. Theatres (Ohio), 1930; transferred to Hollywood as pub. dir. for Pacific Coast zone, 1937; pub. dir. Republic Studios, 1946; res. 1952, apptd. v.-p. Stodel Adv. Agcy., formed Mort Goodman Adv., 1953; formed Goodman Org., advertising agency, pub. rel., 1955. Currently pres., Goodman Nemoy and Partners, adv.-p.r. firm started 1977. In 1980 became adv. & p.r. consultant for m.p. industry.

GOODSON, MARK: TV producer; b. Sacramento, Jan. 24, 1915; s. Abraham Ellis and Fannie (Gross) G.; A.B., U. Cal., 1937. Announcer, newscaster, dir. Radio Sta. KFRC, San Francisco, 1938–41; radio announcer, dir., N.Y.C. 1941–43; producer—Appointment with Life, ABC, 1943; dir. Portia Faces Life, Young & Rubicam, advt. agy., 1944; radio dir. U.S. Treasury War Bond Drive, 1944–45; formed Goodson-Todman Prodns., 1946, originated radio shows Winner Take All, 1946, Stop the Music, 1947, Hit the Jackpot, 1947–49. Creator of TV game programs What's My Line, It's News To Me, The Name's the Same, I've Got a Secret, Two For The Money, To Tell the Truth, The Price Is Right, Password, Match Game, Family Feud, and others; TV film series, The Web, The Rebel, Richard Boone Theater, Branded. 1st v.p. Capitol City Pub. Co.; v.p. New Eng. Newspapers, Inc.; dir. City Center Music and Drama, Mem. American Film Institute. Recipient nat. television award Great Britain, 1951; Emmy award Acad. TV Arts and Scis., 1951, 52; Sylvania award. Pres. N.Y. Acad. TV Arts and Sci. 1957–58. Phi Beta Kappa.

GOODWIN, BERNARD: Executive and lawyer. b. New York, N.Y., Dec. 19, 1907. e. N.Y.U., Harvard Law School; with Paramount Pictures Corporation 1934–1957, vice president, general manager, director, Paramount music publishing subsidiaries, Famous Music Corporation and Paramount Music Corporation, executive producer Paramount short subjects, vice-president, director Paramount Television Productions, Inc.; secretary, director Allen B. DuMont Laboratories, Inc., 1938–1955; president, director Metropolitan Broadcasting Corporation, 1955–1959; director, ASCAP, since 1951.

GOODWIN, RICHARD: Producer. b. Bombay, India, Sept. 13, 1934. e. Rugby. Entered film world by chance: while waiting to go to Cambridge Univ. took temporary job as tea boy at studio which led to 20-year-long association with producer Lord Brabourne. First worked as asst. on Seven Thunders, of which Brabourne was assoc. prod. Named location manager for Brabourne's company, Mershal Productions; promoted to prod. mgr. Named assoc. prod. for Brabourne's British Home Entertainment Productions in 1960 (now defunct).
PICTURES: Prod. Mgr.: The Sheriff of Fractured Jaw, Carve Her Name with Pride, The Grass Is Greener, Sink the Bismarck, HMS Defiant. Prod.: The Tales of Beatrix Potter. Co-Prod.: Murder on the Orient Express, Death on the Nile, The Mirror Crack'd.

GOODWIN, RONALD: Composer, arranger, conductor. b. Plymouth, England. Early career: arranger for BBC dance orchestra; mus. dir. Parlophone Records; orchestra leader for radio, TV and records. Fut. m.p. ind., 1958. Many major film scores. Guest cond. R.P.O., B.S.O., Toronto Symph. Orch. New Zealand Symphony Orch., Sydney Symphony Orch.
PICTURES INCLUDE: The Trials of Oscar Wilde, 633 Squadron, Those Magnificent Men in Their Flying Machines, The Trap, Where Eagles Dare, Monte Carlo or Bust, Battle of Britain, The Executioner, The Selfish Giant, Frenzy (1972), Diamonds on Wheels, The Little Mermaid, The Happy Prince, One of Our Dinosaurs Is Missing, Escape From the Dark, Born to Run, Beauty and the Beast, Candleshoe, Force Ten from Navarone, Spaceman and King Arthur.

GORDON, ALEX: Producer. b. London, Eng., Sept. 8, 1922; ed. Canford Coll., Dorset, 1939. Writer, m.p. fan magazines, 1939–41; British Army, 1942–45; pub. dir. Renown Pictures Corp., 1946–47; P.R. and pub. rep. for Gene Autry, 1948–1953; v.p. and prod. Golden State Productions, 1954–58; prod. Alex Gordon Prods., 1958–66; producer Twentieth Century-Fox Television.
PICTURES INCLUDE: Lawless Rider, Bride of the Monster, Apache Woman, Day the World Ended, Oklahoma Woman, Girls in Prison, The She-Creature, Runaway Daughters, Shake Rattle and Rock, Flesh and the Spur, Voodoo Woman, Dragstrip Girl, Motorcycle Gang, Jet Attack, Submarine Seahawk, Atomic Submarine, The Underwater City, The Bounty Killer, Requiem for a Gunfighter.
TV: Movie of the Year, Golden Century, Great Moments in Motion Pictures.

GORDON, BERT I: Producer-director-writer. b. Kenosha, Wis., U. of Wisconsin, grad.
PICTURES INCLUDE: Beginning of the End, The Amaz-

ing Colossal Man, the Fantastic Puppet People, The Colossal Beast, The Cyclops, The Spider, Tormented, Boy and The Pirates, The Magic Sword, Village of the Giants, Picture Mommy Dead, How to Succeed With the Opposite Sex, Necromancy, Geronimo, The Mad Bomber, The Police Connection, The Food of the Gods, Empire of the Ants, The Coming.

GORDON, GALE: Actor. r.n. Charles T. Aldrich, Jr. b. New York City, Feb. 2, 1906. Stage debut in the Dancers; m.p. debut in The Pilgrimage Play, 1929.
PICTURES INCLUDE: Rally Round the Flag Boys, All in a Night's Work, Don't Give Up the Ship, Visit to a Small Planet, All Hands on Deck, Speedway.
TV: My Favorite Husband, Our Miss Brooks, The Brothers, Dennis The Menace, The Lucy Show, Here's Lucy.

GORDON, JACK: Executive. b. Brooklyn, N.Y., Mar. 13, 1929. e. UCLA. Father is Mack Gordon, songwriter. Started in industry as TV production asst. in 1949. Served in U.S. Infantry, Korea, 1951–52. Joined MGM in 1953; named dir. of non-threatrical div., 1956; v.p., MGM Intl., 1972. Appointed exec. v.p., MGM, Intl. 1979.
Member: ASCAP, Motion Picture Pioneers, Academy of Motion Picture Arts & Sciences.

GORDON, LAWRENCE: Producer. b. Yazoo, Miss., March 25, 1936. e. Tulane Univ. First show business venture with TV producer Aaron Spelling on Burke's Law series, 1964. Joined ABC-TV as head of west coast talent development 1965, left to become v.p. of Screen Gems (now Columbia Pictures TV) where worked on developing new projects. Joined American Intl. Pictures as v.p. in chg. of worldwide production. Resigned to form his own company, Lawrence Gordon Productions, Inc.
PICTURES: Hard Times, Rolling Thunder, The Driver, The End, Hooper, Warriors, Xanadu, Paternity.

GORDON, MICHAEL: Director. b. Balimore, Md., Sept., 1909; e. Johns Hopkins Univ., B.A.; Yale, M.F.A. Stage experience as technician, stage mgr., actor, stage dir. (Stevedore, Golden Boy, Home of the Brave, Anna Christie, One Bright Day); m.p. debut: dial. dir. Columbia on over 20 films; dir. in 1942. Professor of Theater Arts, UCLA.
PICTURES INCLUDE: Boston Blackie Goes Hollywood, Underground Agent, One Dangerous Night, The Crime Doctor, The Web, Another Part of the Forest, An Act of Murder, The Lady Gambles, Woman in Hiding, Cyrano de Bergerac, I Can Get It for You Wholesale, The Secret of Convict Lake, Any Way the Wind Blows, Pillow Talk, Portrait in Black, Boy's Night Out, For Love or Money, Move Over Darling, Texas Across the River, A Very Special Favor, The Impossible Years, How Do I Love Thee?
PLAYS: Deadfall, The Lovers, Tender Trap, Male Animal, His & Hers, Champagne Complex, Home of the Brave, etc.

GORDON, RICHARD: Producer. b. London, Eng., Dec. 31, 1925; e. U. of London, 1943. Served in Brit. Royal Navy, 1944–46; ed. & writer on fan magazines & repr. independent American cos. 1946, with publicity dept. Assoc. Brit. Pathe 1947; org. export-import business for independent, British and American product; formed Gordon Films, Inc., 1949; formed Amalgamated prod., 1956; formed Grenadier Films, Ltd. 1971.
PICTURES INCLUDE: The Counterfeit Plan, The Haunted Strangler, Fiend Without a Face, The Secret Man, First Man into Space, Corridors of Blood, Devil Doll, Curse of Simba, The Projected Man, Naked Evil, Island of Terror; Tales of the Bizarre, Tower of Evil, Horror Hospital, The Cat and the Canary, Inseminoid.

GORDON, RUTH: Actress. b. Wollaston, Mass., Oct. 30, 1896; e. Amer. Acad. Dram. Art; m. Garson Kanin, producer, director. First stage appearance with Maude Adams in Peter Pan, 1915. Mem. Screen Actor's Guild, Academy of Motion Picture Arts and Sciences. Author of Book, Myself Among Others, 1971; My Side, 1976 (autobiography).
STAGE: The Doll's House, Serena Blandish, Ethan Frome, Here Today, Seventeen, Clarence, The First Year, Three Cornered Moon, The Violet, Hotel Universe, Saturday's Children, The Three Sisters, Over Twenty-One, The Leading Lady, The Matchmaker (London, Berlin), The Smile of the World, The Good Soup, A Time to Laugh (London), My Mother, My Father and Me, A Very Rich Woman (playwright and star), Fair and Warmer, The Loves of Cass McGuire, Dreyfus in Rehearsal, Mrs. Warren's Profession.
PICTURES INCLUDE: Abe Lincoln in Illinois, Two Faced Woman, Dr. Ehrlich's Magic Bullet, Action in the North Atlantic, Edge of Darkness, Inside Daisy-Clover, Lord Love a Duck, Whatever Happened to Aunt Alice?, Rosemary's Baby (Academy Award for Best Supporting Actress), Where's Poppa?, Harold and Maude, The Big Bus, Every Which Way But Loose, Boardwalk, Scavenger Hunt, My Bodyguard, Any Which Way You Can, Jimmy the Kid.
TV: The American Dream, Blithe Spirit, The Prince of Central Park.
AUTHOR: Plays: Over Twenty-One, Years Ago, The Leading Lady. Screenplays: A Double Life (with Garson

Kanin), Adam's Rib, with Garson Kanin, The Marrying Kind, Pat and Mike Contbr. to Reader's Digest, Forum Magazine, Atlantic Monthly, McCalls, Ladies Home Journal.

GORDY, BERRY: Executive. Was working on auto assembly line in Detroit when decided to launch record co., Motown. In 1961 wrote song, Shop Around; recording by Smokey Robinson made it his first million dollar record. Expanded into music publishing, personal mgt., recording studios, film and TV, also backing stage shows. Now bd. chm., Motown Industries.
PICTURES INCLUDE: Lady Sings the Blues (prod.), Mahogany (dir.).

GORING, MARIUS: Actor. b. Newport, Isle of Wight. e. Cambridge & Universities of Frankfurt-on-Main, Munich, Vienna, Paris. Early career with Old Vic; stage debut 1927, Jean Sterling Rackinlay's Children's Matinees.
PICTURES INCLUDE: Rembrandt, UA-London Films. Dead Men Tell No Tales, Flying 55 Admiral Films, Consider Your Verdict, Spy in Black, Pastor Hall, The Case of the Fightened Lady, Br. Lion. 1940–46 serving with H.M. Forces & Foreign Office. In 1942, The Big Blockade, The Night Raider. In 1944, Lilli Marlene. Others: Stairway to Heaven, Night Boat to Dublin, Take My Life, Red Shoes, Mr. Perrin and Mr. Traill, Odette, Pandora and the Flying Dutchman, Circle of Danger, Highly Dangerous, So Little Time, The Man Who Watched Trains Go By, Rough Shoot, The Barefoot Contessa, Break in the Circle, Quentin Durward, III Met By Moonlight, The Moonraker, Family Doctor, Angry Hills, Whirlpool, Treasure of St. Teresa, Monty's Double, Beyond the Curtain, Desert Mice, The Inspector, Girl On a Motorcycle, Subterfuge.
TV: Numerous appearances, Sleeping Dog, Man In a Suitcase, Scarlet Pimpernel, The Expert.

GORMAN, KENNETH F.: TV Executive. Career in communications started at NBC on corporate staff. Joined NBC radio division then NBC Enterprises, program syndication arm. Joined CBS radio division, 1967; later CBS Broadcast Group. Career with Viacom International began at spin-off in 1971; named controller, 1974; v.p., finance, 1978; snr. v.p., January, 1979. In April 1979 named pres. of Viacom Entertainment Group, consisting of Viacom Enterprises and Showtime.

GOROG, LASZLO: Writer. b. Hungary, Sept. 30, 1903. e. U. of Sciences, Budapest. Playwright, short story writer, asst. editor, Budapest, 1928–39.
PICTURES INCLUDE: Tales of Manhattan, The Affairs of Susan, She Wouldn't Say Yes, The Land Unknown, for U-I.
TV: 4 Star, Dupont, The Roaring Twenties, 77 Sunset Strip, Maverick, etc.

GORTNER, MARJOE: Actor—Producer. Was child evangelist, whose career as such was basis for documentary film, Marjoe (AA). Acted in films and TV; turned producer in 1978 for When You Comin' Back, Red Ryder.
PICTURES: Bobbie Joe and the Outlaw, The Food of the Gods, Viva Knievel, Sidewinder One, Earthquake, When You Comin' Back, Red Ryder.
TELEVISON: Films: The Marcus-Nelson Murders, The Gun and the Pulpit, Pray for the Wildcats. Guest appearances on Police Story, Mayday: 40,900 Feet, etc.

GOTTLIEB, ALEX: Producer, writer. b. Dec. 21, 1906; e. U. of Wisconsin. Pub. Dir. Paramount theatre, New York; adv. mgr. United Artists, Columbia 1930–37; prod., W.B., Universal, RKO, 1941–50; then ind. prod. Member, ASCAP, WGA, Dramatists Guild, Academy of Motion Picture Arts and Sciences, Sigma Delta Chi, Pi Lambda Phi.
TV: writer, prod., Dear Phoebe, The Gale Storm Show, The Tab Hunter Show, Bob Hope Chrysler Theatre, Donna Reed Show, The Smothers Brothers Show, ABC Movie of the Week.
PICTURES INCLUDE: I'll Take Sweden, Frankie and Johnny, Arizona Ranger, The Pigeon, Blue Gardenia, Macao, Susan Slept Here, Hollywood Canteen.
AUTHOR OF B'WAY PLAYS: Wake Up Darling, Separate Rooms, Susan Slept Here, Stud, Your Place or Mine?, Divorce Me, Darling; Marcus, Farkus and O'Brien.
ONE-ACT PLAYS: Published in Best Short Plays of 1969, Best Short Plays of 1976.

GOTTLIEB, MARTIN: Executive. b. New York, April 16, 1903. Entered m.p. ind. 1919 with Louis Meyer, m.p. Title Studio, New York. Nine years with Consolidated Film Industry (Craftmen Lab.). Chief cameraman and business manager of 19th St. plant. Leave of absence, 1921 and 1925. Photog. m. p. in Mexico and Hollywood. Helped organize Meyer-Rieger Lab. Became secretary 1930. In 1932 organized Welgot Trailer Service. Partnership with C.L. Welsh, liquidated, 1959; C&G Film Effects, Inc. 1959–65, partner; secy., treas. with Hugo A. Casolaro; secy., treas., dir., Colodzin Productions Inc., 1965; pres., Celebrity In'l Films; v.p. Zodiak International Prod. Inc. of Canada; Pres. Wellmax Film Corp.; Pres. Celebrity Holdings, Inc. Semi-retired since 1965. Associated with Globe Picture Corp., 1968 to present.

GOTTLIEB, STAN: Actor, Film Distributor. b. N.Y.C. April 22, 1917. e. N.Y.U., Col. Univ. Has acted in films, theatrical, stage and TV since 1970. Gen. mgr. for Impact Films, Inc. 1966–72. Gen. Mgr., Mammoth Films (1973–76).
PICTURES INCLUDE: Actor: Putney Swope, You Gotta Walk It Like You Talk It, The Owl and the Pussycat, Pound, The Anderson Tapes, Cold Turkey, Slaughterhouse Five, Black Fantasy, Greaser's Palace, Compliments to the World. TV: Actor: Sticks & Bones, Hot L Baltimore, The Jeffersons.
STAGE: Steambath.

GOTTSCHALK, ROBERT: Executive. b. Chicago, Ill., March 12, 1918. e. Carleton College. B.A., 1939. Short subject prod., 1940–49; org. R.E.G., Inc., camera equipment, 1949; pres., 1949–53; pres., Panavision, Inc., 1953.

GOULD, ELLIOTT: Actor. b. Brooklyn, N.Y., August 29, 1938. Broadway debut in Rumple.
STAGE: Say Darling, Irma La Douce, I Can Get It For You Wholesale, On the Town (London), Fantasticks (tour), Drat the Cat, Little Murders, Luv (tour), A Way of Life.
TV: Once Upon A Mattress. Formed, with prod. Jack Brodsky, independent m.p. co.
PICTURES INCLUDE: The Night They Raided Minsky's, Bob & Carol & Ted & Alice, M*A*S*H*, Getting Straight, Move, Little Murders, The Touch, I Love My Wife, The Long Goodbye, Busting, S*P*Y*S/*, California Split, Who?, Nashville, (guest), Whiffs, I Will . . . I Will . . . For Now, Harry and Walter Go to New York, A Bridge Too Far, Capricorn One, Matilda, Escape to Athena, The Last Flight of Noah's Ark, The Devil and Max Devlin, Dirty Tricks.

GOULD, JAMES F.: Exec. Radio City Music Hall. b. Plymouth, Eng., Sept. 30, 1908; e. City of London Coll., C.P.A., N.Y.; asst. cashier, Dakin Bros. Ltd., London; came to USA, joined Radio Keith Orpheum Corp., acct. dept.; 1930; joined opening staff, Radio City Music Hall, Nov. 1932; asst. treas.; 1942; treas., 1948; vice-pres., 1957; exec. v.p., 1964; pres., 1966, member Board of Directors Rockefeller Center Inc. Retired Feb., 1973.

GOULD, JON J.: Executive. e. New England College, Harvard Graduate Program in Publishing. In 1977 joined Straight Arrow Publishers as east coast sales mgr. for publications, Rolling Stone and Outside. In 1978 left for post at Paramount Pictures in m.p. div. as dir. of mktg. admin. for mktg. group. 1979, appt. exec. asst. to Frank G. Mancuso, then exec. v.p., dist. & mktg. In 1980 named v.p., corporate communications, for Paramount.

GOULD, JOSEPH: Executive. b. New York, N.Y. Jan. 30, 1915. e. B.A., New York U., 1935; M.S., Pulitzer School of Journ., Columbia U., 1936. Adv. dept., United Artists, 1939–46; Universal, 1947–48; asst. adv. mgr. 20th Century-Fox. 1949–52; adv. consultant, Joseph Burstyn. Louis De Rochemont Assoc., I.F.E. Releasing Corp. 1953–55; adv. mgr. United Artists, 1955–60; adv. mgr. Paramount Pictures, 1960–62; David Singer Associates, 1962–64; partner, Konheim Gould & Ackerman, 1968–1974; principal, Joseph Gould Associates, 1974–1977; creative services director, WIXT-TV, Syracuse, 1978.

GOULET, ROBERT: Singer, actor. b. Lawrence, Mass., Nov. 26, 1933. e. attended school, Edmonton; scholarship, Royal Conservatory of Music. Sang in choirs, appeared with numerous orchestras; disk jockey, CKUA, Edmonton; pub. rel., The Merrick Co.
STAGE: Camelot, The Happy Time.
TV: The Ed Sullivan Show, Garry Moore, The Enchanted Nutcracker, Omnibus, The Broadway of Lerner and Loewe, Rainbow of Stars, Judy Garland Show, Bob Hope Show, The Bell Telephone Hour; England: Granada—TV special, Jack Benny; Dean Martin; Andy Williams; Jack Paar; Red Skelton; Hollywood Palace; Patty Duke Show, Star of Robert Goulet Show, Blue Light series for ABC-TV, Brigadoon & Carousel for ABC-TV. Kiss Me Kate.
PICTURES INCLUDE: Honeymoon Hotel, I'd Rather Be Rich, I Deal in Danger, Underground.
RECORDS: Always You, Two of Us, Sincerely Yours, The Wonderful World of Love, Robert Goulet in Person, This Christmas I Spend With You, Manhattan Tower, Without You, My Love Forgive Me, Travelling On, Robert Goulet on Tour, Robert Goulet on Broadway, Robert Goulet on Broadway II, Camelot, Happy Time.

GOWDY, CURT: Sportscaster. b. Green River, Wyoming, 1919. Basketball star at U. of Wyoming. All-Conference member; graduated U. of Wyoming. 1942; officer in U.S. Air Force WWII, then became sportscaster. Voted Sportscaster of the Year, 1967, Nat'l Assn. of Sportwriters Broadcasters. Best Sportscaster, FAME, 1967. Sports staff at NBC; American Sportsman, ABC. Won Peabody Award, 1975. Host of The Way It Was on PSS.

GRADE, LORD: Chmn & Man. dir., Incorporated Television Co. Ltd. Chmn. Associated TeleVision Corporation Ltd. Created Life Peer 1976.

GRADUS, BEN: Producer-Director-Writer. b. N.Y.C. e. Brooklyn Coll. Is principal in Directors Group Motion Pictures, Inc. Positions held include v.p. Filmways, Inc.; prod.-dir. for Screen Gems. Specialist in educational and doc. films; also has done feature, children's comedy TV shows and series, Decision: The Conflicts of Harry S. Truman. Author, Directing the Television Commercial.
CREDITS INCLUDE: Dawn over Ecuador, Gentlemen of the Jury, To Save Your Life, Lifewatch Six, Ford Around the World, Art Heritage, A Girl from Puerto Rico, Span of Life, Crowded Paradise.

GRADY, BILLY, Jr.: Producer. b. Brooklyn, July 4, 1917. Entered m.p. ind. as asst. film ed., MGM, 1934; film ed. MGM, 1938; asst. to Arthur Freed, 1940; U.S. Air Force four years; then joined Frank Capra as asst.; thereafter to U-I as assoc. prod., Ma and Pa Kettle series; Arctic Manhunt, Hollywood Story; then to MGM prod., Cry of the Hunted, Code Two, Gypsy Colt; CBS-TV prod. That's My Boy.

GRAF, BILLY: Executive. b. 1945. Entered industry 1965. Was asst. dir.; unit/location mgr./production mgr. for American, British and European compies. Now v.p., Legion Films, Inc., Beverly Hills.
PICTURES: Alfie, A Man for All Seasons, Billion Dollar Brain, Scrooge, Run Wild Run Free, The Best House in London, Chitty Chitty Bang Bang, Galaxina, Khartoum, You Only Live Twice, Women in Love, Song of Norway, Prudence and the Pill, Hammerhead, Underground Aces.
TELEVISION: Secret Agent, The Saint, "Q" Branch, Private Eye Public Ear, The Avengers, Department "S", The Dave Cash Radio Show.

GRAF, WILLIAN N.: Executive. b. New York City. Entered industry in 1934. 1937–42, exec. secty./asst. to Mark Hellinger at Warner Bros. & 20th-Fox. 1942–45, writer of armed forces training films. 1946–50, exec. secty./asst. to Harry Cohn, pres., Columbia Pictures; 1951, prod. asst. to Jack Fier, prod. head, Columbia. 1952–65, Amer. repr. for British productions, Columbia Pictures; 1965–66, exec. asst. to J.J. Frankovich, Columbia Pictures, London; 1965–66, v.p., Columbia Pictures Intl., London; 1969–70, indep. prod., Cinema Center Films; 1980–present, v.p. in chg. of prod., Legion Films, Inc., Beverly Hills
PICTURES: (Producer): The Red Beret, A Man for All Seasons, Sinful Davey, The African Elephant.

GRAFF, RICHARD: Executive. b. Milwaukee, Wisc., Nov. 9, 1924; e. U. of Illinois; served U.S. Air Force, 1942–46; 1946 joined Universal Pictures in Chicago as film booker; later salesman, then sales mgr., in 1956 became Universal branch mgr. in Detroit, served until return to Chicago as branch mgr. in 1961. 1963 became asst. to gen. sales mgr. in New York for Universal Pictures. 1964 went to National General Corp. in Los Angeles as asst. to exec. v.p. Became asst. v.p. of National General Corp. in 1965. 1967 became v.p. and gen. sales mgr. of National General Pictures and formed company. Became exec. v.p. of National General Pictures 1968 in charge of worldwide sales and marketing. 1968 became v.p. of parent National General Corp. v.p. and gen. Sales Mgr., American International Pictures, December, 1971; pres., Cine Artists Pictures, 1975; pres., The Richard Graff Co., 1977.

GRAFF, ROBERT D.: Producer. b. New York City 1919. Early career 1951–60 with National Broadcasting Co. and consultant to m.p. and t.v. orgs. in Iran, Venezuela, U.S.A. Formed Sextant Inc., 1960. Sextant Films Ltd., 1963.
PICTURES INCLUDE: Young Cassidy.

GRAHAM, RODERICK: b. Edinburgh, Scotland, 1934. e. Royal High School, Edinburgh, and Edinburgh University. Directed TV drama in Scotland and London, and was senior producer of Z Cars series. Won Emmy awards as producer of The Sextet and Elizabeth R. Deputised for Head of Serials, Drama, at BBC Television Centre, London. Since 1959 actively associated with BBC work in drama, both radio and television. Appointed head of drama, television, Scotland, June 1976.

GRAHAME, GLORIA: Actress. r.n. Gloria Grahame Hallward. b. Los Angeles, Calif., Nov. 28, 1929. In numerous stage plays; screen debut in Blonde Fever, 1944, Academy Award, best supporting actress, The Bad and the Beautiful, 1952; Star of Tomorrow, 1953.
PICTURES INCLUDE: It Happened in Brooklyn, Crossfire, Merton of the Movies, Roughshod, Woman's Secret, The Greatest Show on Earth, Sudden Fear, The Glass Wall, Man On a Tight Rope, The Big Heat, The Good Die Young, Human Desire, Naked Alibi, Not as a Stranger, The Cobweb, Man Who Never Was, Oklahoma!, Blood and Lace, Ride Out for Revenge, The Todd Killings, Head Over Heels.

GRANET, BERT: Producer, writer. b. New York City, July 10, 1910; e. Yale U., Sch. Fine Arts (47 Workshop). From 1936 author s.p. orig. & adapt. numerous pictures. Exec. prod., Universal, 1967–69.

PICTURES INCLUDE: Quick Money, The Affairs of Annabel, Mr. Doodle Kicks Off, Laddie, A Girl a Guy and a Gob, My Favorite Wife, Bride by Mistake, Sing Your Way Home, Those Endearing Young Charms, Do You Love Me?, The Marrying Kind, Berlin Express, The Torch, Scarface.

TV: Desilu (1957–1961), Twilight Zone, The Mob, The Untouchables Pilot, Scarface Mob; Loretta Young Show (1955–56), Walter Winchell File 1956–57, Lucille Ball-Desi Arnaz Show 1957–60, Westinghouse Desilu Playhouse, The Great Adventure.

GRANGER, FARLEY: Actor. b. San Jose, Calif., July 1, 1925; e. Hollywood. School prior to m.p. career; screen debut in North Star 1943; in U.S. Armed Forces 1944–6.

PICTURES INCLUDE: They Live By Night, Rope, Enchantment, Roseanna McCoy, Side Street, Our Very Own, Edge of Doom, Strangers on a Train, Behave Yourself, I Want You, O. Henry's Full House, Hans Christian Andersen, Story of Three Loves, Small Town Girl, Summer Hurricane, Brass Ring, Naked Street, Girl in the Red Velvet Swing, Arrow Smith, The Heiress, The Prisoner of Zenda, Senso, The Serpent, A Man Called Noon, Those Days in the Sun, The Chief of Homicide, The Painter and the Red Head, Call Me Trinity, The Syndicate, Arnold, A Crime for a Crime.

TV: Playhouse of Stars, U.S. Steel Hour, Producer's Showcase, Climax, Ford Theatre, Playhouse 90, 20th Century Fox Hour, Robert Montgomery Presents, Arthur Murray Dance Party, Wagon Train, Masquerade Party, Kojak, 6 Million Dollar Man, Ellery Queen, 5 Lives of Jenny Dolan, Widow, National Repeitory Co., One Life To Live.

GRANGER, STEWART: Actor. r.n. James Stewart. b. May 6, 1913; e. medicine; Webber-Douglas Sch. of Acting, London. m. Jean Simmons, actress. In Brit. Army, World War II. On stage from 1935, Hull Repertory theat.; Birmingham Repertory; Malvery Festivals (1936–37); Old Vic Co. Screen debut 1940 in So This Is Voted one of Brit. top ten money-making stars in M.P. Herald-Fame Poll, 1945, 1946, 1947, 1949.

PICTURES INCLUDE: Convoy, Secret Mission, Thursday's Child, Man in Grey, The Lamp Still Burns, Fanny by Gaslight, Love Story, Waterloo-Road, Madonna of the Seven Moons, Caesar and Cleopatra, Caravan, Magic Bow, Captain Boycott, Blanche Fury, Saraband for Dead Lovers, Woman Hater, Adam and Evalyn, King Solomon's Mines, Soldiers Three, Light Touch, Wild North, Scaramouche, Prisoner of Zenda, Salome, Young Bess, All the Brothers Were Valiant, Beau Brummell, Green Fire, Moonfleet, Deadlock, Bhowani Junction, Last Hunt, Footsteps in the Fog, The Little Hut, Gun Glory, The Secret Invasion, Flaming Frontier, The Trygon Factor, The Last Safari, The Wild Geese.

GRANT, CARY: Actor. r.n. Archibald Alexander Leach. b. Bristol, England, Jan. 18, 1904. On dram. stage in England, then to U.S. and appeared with St. Louis (Mo.) Municipal Opera Co. a season. Screen debut 1932 in Paramount prod. This is the Night. Voted one of the ten best Money-Making Stars in M.P. Herald-Fame Poll 1944, 1949.

PICTURES INCLUDE: Gambling Ship, Alice in Wonderland, Sylvia Scarlett, Suzy, Holiday, Gunga Din, The Philadelphia Story, The Howards of Virginia, Penny Serenade, Suspicion, Once Upon a Honeymoon, Mr. Lucky, Destination Tokyo, Once Upon a Time, None But the Lonely Heart, Arsenic and Old Lace, Bachelor and the Bobby Soxer, The Bishop's Wife, Every Girl Should Be Married, Mr. Blandings Builds His Dream House, I Was a Male War Bride, Crisis, People Will Talk, Room for One More, Monkey Business, Dream Wife, To Catch A Thief, The Pride and the Passion, An Affair to Remember, Kiss Them for Me, Houseboat, North by Northwest, Operation Petticoat, The Grass is Greener, That Touch of Mink, Charade, Father Goose, Walk Don't Run.

GRANT, LEE: Actress. At 4 was member of Metropolitan Opera Company; played princess in L'Orocolo. Member of the American Ballet at 11. e. Juilliard School of Music, studied voice, violin and dance. At 18 with road co. Oklahoma as understudy. Acting debut: Joy To The World.

THEATRE: acted in a series of one-acters at ANTA with Henry Fonda. 1949, played shoplifter in The Detective Story (won Critics Circle Award); Lo and Behold, A Hole in he Head, Wedding Breakfast; road co. Two for the Seesaw, The Captains and the Kings; toured with Electra, Silk Stockings, St. Joan, Arms and the Man, The Maids (Obie Award), Prisoner of Second Avenue.

TV: Studio One, The Kraft Theatre, Slattery's People, The Fugitive, Ben Casey, The Nurses, The Defenders, East Side/West Side, Peyton Place (Emmy Award, Best Supporting Player, 1966), Bob Hope Show (Emmy nom.), The Love Song of Bernard Kempenski, BBC's The Respectful Prostitute, The Neon Ceilings (Emmy Award), Fay (series), The Spell (movie).

PICTURES INCLUDE: The Detective Story, Terror in the Streets, Affair of the Skin, The Balcony, Divorce American

Style, Valley of the Dolls, In the Heat of the Night, Buona Sera, Mrs. Campbell, The Big Bounce, Marooned, The Landlord, There Was a Crooked Man, Plaza Suite, Portnoy's Complaint, Shampoo, Voyage of the Damned, Airport '77, When You Comin' Back, Red Ryder, Charlie Chan and the Curse of the Dragon Queen.

GRASGREEN, MARTIN: Executive. B. New York City, July 1, 1925. Entered m.p. ind. Jan., 1944, Columbia Pictures h.o. in contract dept. Promoted to travelling auditor April, 1946. Appt. office mgr. Omaha branch Dec., 1948; salesman Omaha, Dec., 1950. Transferred to Indianapolis, 1952, as city salesman; transferred to Cleveland as sales mgr., 1953. Left Columbia in 1960 to become 20th-Fox branch mgr. in Cleveland. Transferred to Philadelphia in 1965 as branch mgr.; transferred to N.Y. in 1967 as Eastern dist. mgr. Resigned in 1970 to form Paragon Pictures, prod.-dist. co. In Jan., 1975, formed Lanir Releasing Corp., representing producers for U.S. and Latin American sales and dist. of films in U.S., Canada.

GRASSHOFF, ALEX: Writer, producer, director. b. Boston, Mass. e. Tufts Coll., and U. of Southern Calif., 3 Academy Award nominations for feature documentaries; 1974, Journey to the Outer Limits; 1966, Really Big Family; 1968, Young Americans won Oscar; Future Shock; 1973 Cannes Film Festival. T.V. Series (Dir.): The Rockford Files, Chips, Foul Play, Harper Valley, Toma. Worked in Berlin, Paris, Rome.

GRAVES, PETER: Actor. b. London, Oct. 21, 1911: e. Harrow. With Knight, Frank & Rutley, then Lloyds prior to theat. career. First stage appearance 1934 in Charles B. Cochran's Streamline.

THEATRE: Novello musicals at Drury Lane; repertory at Windsor, Old Chelsea, The Merry Widow, The Sound of Music, Private Lives. Recent: The Reluctant Peer, The Last of Mrs. Cheyney, Dear Charles, An Ideal Husband (S. Africa), A Boston Story (tour), His, Hers, and Theirs, The Great Waltz, No Sex Please We're British.

PICTURES INCLUDE: Mrs. Fitzherbert, Spring in Park Lane, Spring in Mayfair, Lady With a Lamp, Encore, Derby Day (Four Against Fate), Lilacs in the Spring (Let's Make Up), Admirable Crichton, Alfie, The Wrong Box, The Jokers, I'll Never Forget What's Is Name, How I Won the War, Assassination Bureau, The Adventurers, The Slipper and the Rose, Airplane!.

TV: Those Wonderful Snows, Chelsea at 9, One O'Clock Show, Lunch Box, 2 Cars, Dickie Henderson Show, Ivor Novello Series, East Lynne, Ninety Years On, The Sleeping Doe, The Frobisher Game, The Jazz Age series, Kate series, Crown Court, Softly, Softly, 10 from the 20s. Quiller, Duchess of Duke Street.

GRAVES, PETER: Actor. b. Minneapolis, Minn., March 18, 1936, brother, James Arness, e. U. of Minn. Played with bands, radio announcer, while at school; U.S. Air Force 2 yrs.; summer stock appearances; m.p. debut in Rogue River.

PICTURES INCLUDE: Fort Defiance, Stalag 17, East of Sumatra, Beneath the 12-Mile Reef, The Raid, Black Tuesday, Wichita, Long Gray Line, Night of the Hunter, Naked Street, Fort Yuma, Court Martial of Billy Mitchell, The Ballad of Josie, Sergeant Ryker, The Five Man Army, Sidecar Racers, Airplane!.

TV: Fury, 1955–58, Mission Impossible, 1967–1973.

GRAY, BARRY: Composer-arranger, Musical Dir. B. Blackburn, England. 1949–59, Accompaniest-arranger for Dame Vera Lynn 1956–75, musical dir. for AP Films Ltd. Century 21 ATV productions, and composed, arranged and directed original music for TV series: Four Feather Falls, Supercar, Fireball XL5, Stingray, Thunderbirds, Joe 90, Captain Scarlet, The Secret Service, UFO, Space 1999, and feature films: Thunderbirds are Go!, Thunderbird Six, Doppelganger, Journey to the Far Side of the Sun.

GRAY, COLLEEN: Actress. r.n. Doris Jensen. b. Staplehurst, Neb., Oct. 23, 1922; e. Hamline U., B.A. summa cum laude, 1943, Actor's Lab.; m. William C. Bidlack. Member: Nat'l Collegiate Players, Kappa Phi, a Capella choir, little theatres, 1943–4; screen debut State Fair, 1945.

PICTURES INCLUDE: Kiss of Death, Nightmare Alley, Fury at Furnace Creek, Red River, Sleeping City, Riding High, Father Is a Bachelor, Models Inc., Kansas City Confidential, Sabre Jet, Arrow in the Dust, The Fake, The Vanquished, Las Vegas Shakedown, Twinkle in God's Eye, Tennessee's Partner, The Killing, Wild Dakotas, Death of a Scoundrel, Frontier Gambler, Black Whip, Star in the Dust, The Vampires, Hell's Five Hours, Copper Sky, Johnny Rocco, The Leech Woman, The Phantom Planet, Town Tamer, P.J., The Late Liz.

TV: Day of Our Lives, NBC-TV, 1966–67. Family Affair, Ironside, Bonanza, Judd for the Defense, Name of the Game, Bright Promise, The FBI, The Bold Ones, World Premiere, Mannix, Sixth Sense, McCloud, The Best Place To Be.

GRAY, DULCIE: Actress b. Malaya, Nov. 20; e. Webber Douglas Sch., London Stage debut 1939, Aberdeen, Hay Fever,

Author: Love Affair (play), 18 detective novels, book of short stories. 8 radio plays; co-author with husband Michael Denison, An Actor and His World.

STAGE: 37 plays including Little Foxes, Brighton Rock, Dear Ruth, Rain on the Just, Candida, An Ideal Husband, Where Angels Fear to Tread, Heartbreak House, On Approval, Happy Family, We, Out of the Question, Village Wooing, Wild Duck, At The End of the Day, The Pay Off, A Murder Has Been Announced, Bedroom Farce.

PICTURES INCLUDE: Two Thousand Women, A Man About the House, Mine Own Executioner, My Brother Jonathan, The Glass Mountain, They Were Sisters Wanted for Murder, The Franchise Affair, Angels One Five, There Was a Young Lady, A Man Could Get Killed.

TV: Milestones, The Will, Crime Passionel, Art and Opportunity, Fish in the Family, The Governess, What the Public Wants, Lesson in Love, The Happy McBaines, Winter Cruise, The Letter, Tribute to Maugham, Virtue, Beautiful Forever, East Lynne, Unexpectedly Vacant, The Importance of Being Earnest, This Is Your Life, Crown Court, Making Faces, Read all about it, The Voysey Inheritance.

GRAY, GORDON: Broadcast Management Consultant. b. Albert Lea, Minn., Nov. 16, 1905; e. U. of Missouri. Entered broadcasting ind. 1932, v.p., gen. mgr., WOR, WOR TV; pres. WKTV, Utica, N.Y., KAUZ, Wichita Falls, Tex. Founded Central N.Y. Cable, Utica, N.Y. Board of Governors, WFTV, Orlando, Fla. and management consultant, presently.

GRAY, VERNON: Actor b. Saskatoon, Canada, e. Elk Point. Early career engineering plant; repertory Canada and America; studied Irving School of the Theatre; in Britain for more repertory; London stage, Stalag 17; screen debut: A Day to Remember.

PICTURES INCLUDE: To Paris With Love, Now and Forever, Barretts of Wimpole Street.

GRAYSON, KATHRYN: Actress. r.n. Zelma Hedrick; b. Winston-Salem, N.C. Feb. 9, 1923. e. St. Louis schools. Singer. Screen debut; Andy Hardy's Private Secretary, 1940; The Vanishing Virginian, Rio Rita, Seven Sweethearts, Thousands Cheer; achieved stardom in Anchors Aweigh, 1945.

PICTURES INCLUDE: Ziegfeld Follies of 1946, Two Sisters from Boston, Showboat, That Midnight Kiss, Grounds For Marriage, The Toast of New Orleans, The Kissing Bandit, Lovely To Look At, Desert Song, So This Is Love, Kiss Me Kate, Vagabond King.

TV: GE Theatre, Emmy Nomination, 1960; Die Fledermaus, ABC, '66.

STAGE: Debut in N.Y. and tour, Camelot, 1963; Rosalinda, Merry Widow, Kiss Me Kate, Showboat, (N.Y. and U.S. tour).

GREEN, ADOLPH: Writer. b. New York, N.Y., Dec. 2. Wrote book, sketches & lyrics for many Broadway shows including: On the Town, Billion Dollar Baby, Two on the Aisle, Wonderful Town, Peter Pan (Mary Martin), Bells Are Ringing, Applause (Tony Award).

PICTURES INCLUDE: Good News, On the Town, Barkleys of Broadway, Take Me Out to the Ball Game, Singin' in the Rain, Band Wagon, It's Always Fair Weather, Auntie Mame; all in collab. with Betty Comden.

GREEN, GUY: Director. b. Somerset, Eng. 1913. Joined Film Advertising Co. as projectionist & camera asst. 1933; camera asst., Elstree Studios (BIP) 1935; started as camera operator on films including One of Our Aircraft Is Missing, In Which We Serve, This Happy Breed. 1944: Director of Photography; Dir of Allied Film Makers Ltd.

PICTURES INCLUDE: The Way Ahead, Great Expectations, Oliver Twist, Captain Horatio Hornblower, I Am A Camera, River Beat, Tears For Simon, House of Secrets, Sea of Sand, The Angry Silence, The Mark, Light In The Piazza, Diamond Head, A Patch of Blue, Pretty Polly, A Matter of Innocence, The Magus, A Walk in the Spring Rain, Luther, Once Is Not Enough, The Devil's Advocate.

GREEN, JANET: Actress, screen writer. b. Hertfordshire, England, 1914. Early career as actress; Wrote first play, 1945; Ent. m.p. ind. 1947, wrote orig. s.p., The Clouded Yellow; further orig. s.p. incl. The Good Beginning, Lost Eye Witness, The Long Arm (in coll.), The Fever Tree, Saphire, Cast a Dark Shadow, Midnight Lace, Gathering of Eagles, Ashenden, Victim, Life for Ruth, Christobel; Show Me A Murderer, Walk in the Shadow, Seven Women, The Golden Keel, It Happened in Havana, My Turn Now, Gutsy, The Sweetest Voice in the World (USA).

GREEN, JOHN: Music director-conductor-composer-pianist. b. New York City, Oct. 10, 1908; e. Horace Mann School, Harvard U., 1928, A.B. Entered m.p. industry as rehearsal pianist. Paramount Astoria, N.Y.; composer-conductor 1930–32. Conductor, Paramount-Publix Theatres, 1930–33. Name band leader, 1933–40. Made numerous shorts, appeared on many TC commercial radio programs. Composer of songs: Coquette, I'm Yours, Out of Nowhere, I Cover the Waterfront, Song of Raintree County, Body and Soul, Easy Come, Easy Go, I Wanna Be Loved etc.; also symphonic works performed by major orchestra U.S. and

abroad; Symphony, Mine Eyes Have Seen, 1977 Joined MGM, composer-conductor, 1942–46; Univ. Internat'l. 1947; returned to MGM for Easter Parade (Acad. Award, scoring of musical); Warner 1948–49. Inspector General (Golden Globe Award 1949, best score of year). Apptd. gen. music dir. and exec-in-chg-of-music MGM 1949; produced shorts series MGM Concert Hall (Acad. Award, best one real short 1953); Acad. Award, best scoring of musical, American in Paris 1951; composed score Raintree County (Acad. Nom. 1957): left MGM to freelance 1958. Prod. Desilu 1958–59. Comp. many original scores. V.p., Academy M.P. Arts and Sciences, 1953–55; chmn. Music Br. several terms: Acad. Life Member; prod. Acad.'s first Award Show TV, 1953. Acad. Award, best scoring of musical, West Side Story, 1961, nominated for Acad. Award, 14 times. Other films incl. High Society, Bye Bye Birdie, The Great Caruso, etc. Music dir. film, Oliver, won Acad. Award, 1968. Assoc. prod. They Shoot Horses, Don't They? (Acad. Award nomination, best music score). Pres. Screen Comp. Assoc., U.S.A. 1966–1972; Member Bd of Governors Performing Arts Council L.A. Music Center, 1965–1971; Chmn. bd. Emeritus, Young Musicians Foundation since 1965. Pres., Young Musicians Foundation 1973–1977; Since 1949, guest conductor, many U.S. orchestras; 1980–24th season Hollywood Bowl; co-chairman, music branch and v.p., Academy of Motion Picture Arts and Sciences, 1973–77.

GREEN, JOSEPH: Executive. b. Warsaw, Poland, Apr. 23, 1905. e. high school, prep school. Industry, legitimate theatre prod. Foreign film dist. since 1933; headed Green Film Co., Warsaw, Poland; head of Sphinx Film Dist. Co., N.Y., until 1940. Co-owner, Art Theatre Circuit, N.Y., 1940–52; pres., Globe Dist. Co. of Foreign Films; formed President Films, Inc., 1954, now Globe Pictures, Inc.

GREEN, MICHAEL L.: Executive. Eng. m.p. ind. United Artists 1934 terminating 1948, as Sales sup. Cont. Europe and Near East. Man. dir. Michael Green Enterprises Ltd., Nitrev Entertainments, Ltd. Chm., Entertainment Film Dist. Ltd.

GREEN, NATHANIEL CHARLES: Executive (Retired) b. Spokane, Wash. Feb. 16, 1903. e. Pleasant Prairie School until 14 yrs. of age; ent. banking bus., Spokane & Eastern Trust Co., until 1921; came to Calif., became associated Bank of America. Br. bank mgr., 26 yrs. of age, youngest in the U.S. at the time; became vice-pres., 1941; Jan. 1960 became v.p., and senior pub rel. officer between bank and m.p. and TV industry.

GREENBERG, BERRY: Executive. b. Shanghai, China, June 1, 1912. e. Shanghai Public School London Chamber of Commerce. MGM International Dept., Gen. Mgr. 15 yrs. from 1933, in Far East Branches. Joint rep. and dir. for Far East sales for Walt Disney Productions, Samuel Goldwyn Prods. Warner Bros. Pictures Int'l, div. sales mgr. for Far East, Australia and New Zealand, theatrical and TV. Vice pres. in chg. of all foreign TV sales and admin. and supervisor theatrical sales Australia and New Zealand, Warner Bros. Int'l Corp. (Sunset Int'l). Vice pres. foreign TV admin. and sales, Warner Bros-7 Arts. Vice pres. International sales and admin., Warner Bros. Television; vice-pres. International sales and admin., 1970 to June 30, 1977. Retired 1977.

GREENE, CLARENCE: Producer, writer. b. New York City. e. St. John's Univ. (L.L.B.); author of play Need a Lawyer. Formed Greene-Rouse Prods. with Russell Rouse; Acad. Oscar co-orig. story Pillow Talk. Acad. award nom. co-orig. s.p. The Well. Two Writers Guild nominations. Writers Guild award outstanding teleplay, One Day in the Life of Ivan Denisovitch.

PICTURES INCLUDE: Prod., collab. s.p. The Town Went Wild, D.O.A., The Well, The Thief, Wicked Woman, New York Confidential, A House Is Not a Home, The Oscar. Prod. Unidentified Flying Objects, The Gun Runners, Fastest Gun Alive, Thunder in the Sun, The Caper of the Golden Bulls. Collab. prod., writer TV series Tightrope.

GREENE, DAVID: Director, Writer. Early career as actor. To U.S. with Shakespeare company early 1950's; remained direct TV in Canada, New York and Hollywood.

TV: The Defenders. Emmy Awds. The People Next Door, Rich Man, Poor Man, Roots. Recent: Friendly Fire.

PICTURES INCLUDE: The Shuttered Room, Sebastian, The Strange Affair, I Start Counting, Madame Sin, Godspell, Count of Monte Cristo, Gray Lady Down, Hard Country.

GREENE, LORNE: Actor. b. Ottawa, Can., Feb. 12, 1915. e. Queene's University, where began acting and directing plays. Entered radio and became chief announcer for Canadian Broadcasting Corp. and chief news broadcaster. Following World War II service returned to Canadian radio. Came to N.Y. and appeared in TV production and Broadway plays. Went to Hollywood for films and gained biggest fame as Ben Cartwright in Bonanza series started in Sept., 1959.

PICTURES INCLUDE: The Silver Chalice, Autumn Leaves,

The Gift of Love, The Buccaneer, etc. 1974: Earthquake. 1975: Tidal Wave.
TV: Destiny of a Spy, The Harness (films), Lorne Greene's American West, Christmas Special with UNs Children's Chorus, Lewis and Clark Expedition, Big Cats, Little Cats, Wonderful World of Horses, Swing Out Sweet Land, Andy Williams Show, Johnny Cash Show, Sonny and Cher Show, Celebration, The Barnum & Bailey NBC-TV Special, Roots, Battlestar Galactica, The Bastard.

GREENFIELD, IRVING H.: b. Nov. 15, 1902; e. Brooklyn Law School. Formerly president, Cinema Lodge, B'nai B'rith. Former sec'y, attorney, Metro-Goldwyn-Mayer, Inc. and Key chairman M.P. Amusement Div. of U.J.A. Federation. Engaged in law practice: Greenfield, Lipsky, and Bress.

GREENFIELD, LEO: Executive, b. N. Y. C., Education: St. John's Univ, college Arts & Sciences; v.p., gen. sales mgr. Buena Vista, 1965; Columbia road show sales mgr. 1966; v.p.-gen. sales mgr., Cinerama Rel. Corp. 1966; v.p-gen. sales mgr., Warners, 1969; sr. v.p. worldwide distribution, MGM 1975; v.p. distribution & marketing, Marble Arch Productions, 1978; sr. v.p., mkt. & dist. (domestic) Associated Film Distribution, 1979.

GREENWOOD, JACK: Producer. b. 1919.
PICTURES INCLUDE: Horrors of the Black Museum, Concrete Jungle, Invasion, Act of Murder, We Shall See, Face of A Stranger.
Also prod. Scotland Yard, The Scales of Justice and the Edgar Wallace series, Avengers series, 1967–68.
TV: From a Bird's Eye View, TV series with Sheldon Leonard 1969.

GREENWOOD, JOAN: Actress. b. Chelsea, London, Eng. e. St. Catherines, Bramley, Surrey, Royal Academy Dramatic Art. Stage debut: Le Malade Imaginaire, London; in other London plays & repertory.
PICTURES INCLUDE: The Gentle Sex, They Knew Mr. Knight, Latin Quarter, Girl In a Million, The Man Within, The October Man, The White Unicorn, Saraband for Dead Lovers, Bad Lord Byron, Whiskey Galore, Kind Hearts & Coronets, Train of Events, Flesh & Blood, Young Wives' Tale, Mr. Peek-A-Boo, Man in the White Suit, Importance of Being Earnest, Father Brown (The Detective), Knave of Hearts (Lovers, Happy Lovers), Moonfleet, Stage Struck, Mysterious Island Pawn, The Amorous Pawn, Tom Jones, The Moonshiners, Boy Stroke Girl, Water Babies, The Uneasy, Hound of the Baskervilles.
THEATRE: N.Y. Stage, Confidential Clerk 1954, Those That Play the Clowns. London Stage, Moon & the Chimney, Bell Book and Candle, Doll's House, Grass is Greener, Hedda Gabler, Irregular Verb to Love, Au Pair, Chalk Garden, Eden End, In Praise of Love.
TV: Doll's House, Confidential Clerk, King and Mrs. Candle, Man and Superman, Fat of the Land, Good King Charles, Golden Days, Love is the Flame, Love Among the Artists, Wainwright's Law.

GREER, JANE: Actress. b. Washington, D.C., Sept. 9, 1924. Orchestra singer; photograph as WAC on Life Magazine cover won screen debut in Pan-Americana 1945.
PICTURES INCLUDE: They Won't Believe Me, Out of the Past, Station West, Big Steal, You're in the Navy Now, The Company She Keeps, You For Me, Prisoner of Zenda, Desperate Search, The Clown, Down Among the Sheltering Palms, Run for the Sun, Man of a Thousand Faces, Where Love Has Gone, Billie, The Outfit.

GREFE, WILLIAM: Director, Producer, Writer. b. Miami, Fla., May 17. Pres., Film Artists Corp., Miami.
PICTURES INCLUDE: Naked Zoo, The Hooked Generation, Racing Fever, The Checkered Flag, Wild Rebels, Devil's Sisters, Death Curse of Tartu, Sting of Death, Beatrice, Caribbean Adventure, Electric Shades of Grey, V, Stanley, The Godmothers. Impulse, Live and Let Die, Mako, Whiskey Mountain.
AUTHOR: Writer, Daytona, Jo-Ann, Film Financing.

GREGORY, DAVID: Writer. b. Nashville, Tenn. e. U. of Pittsburgh, Carnegie Tech.
Writer of sketches and lyrics for Broadway shows including Hot Mikado, Ziegfeld Follies, Fools Rush In, Star and Garter, Make Mine Manhattan; night club and special material for Andrews Sisters, Bob Crosby, Betty Garrett, others.
RADIO: Writer for shows including Bob Crosby, Kraft Music Hall, Fred Allen, Doris Day, Double or Nothing, Corliss Archer.
TV: Colgate Comedy Hour, Saturday Night Revue, Hollywood Music Hall, Milton Berle Show, Frank Sinatra Show, Frankie Laine Show, Jackie Gleason's Honeymooners, Johnny Carson Show.

GREGORY, JOHN R.: Executive, producer, writer. b. Bklyn, N.Y., Nov. 19, 1918. e. Grover Cleveland H.S., 1935, New Institute of M.P. & Telev; Sls., adv. dept. Fotoshop, Inc., N.Y., 1938–42; Spec. Serv., Photo. instructor, chief projectionist, supv., war dept. theatres, U.S. Army, 1942–46; sls. mgr., J.L. Galef & Son, N.Y. 1948–49; gen. mgr., Cam-

era Corner Co., 1949–58; pres., City Film Center, Inc. 1957; exec. v.p., Talent Guild of New York, Inc., 1958; pres., Teleview Prods., Inc., 1961; executive producer, City Film Productions, 1970. Executive post-production supervisor, Jerry Liotta Films, 1977.
AUTHOR: many articles in nat'l publications dealing with m.p. practices and techniques; tech. editor, "Better Movie-Making" Magazine, 1962; editor, pub., National Directory of Movie-Making Information, 1963; assoc. ed., Photographic Product News, 1964; contrib. editor, U.S. Camera. M.P. columnist, contributing ed. Travel and Camera magazine, 1969; Advisory panelist, Photo-methods (NY), 1975. Consultant, Photographic Guidance Council, 1957, assoc. Society of M.P. & Television-Engineers, 1952.

GRESHLER, ABNER J.: Producer. b. New York City. e. Fordham U., St. John's School of Law. Prior to entering m.p. ind., prod. shows for resort hotels; mgd., booked artists for vaudeville, hotels, cafes. Now pres., York Pictures Corp.; Abner J. Greshler Prod., Inc. Executive prod. At War with the Army, 1951; Hundred Hour Hunt, Yesterday and Today, 1953; Johnny and the Gaucho, 1955; prog. consultant, NBC; coord. of prog. development dept., NTA; pres., R.G. Prod., Ltd. Pres. Damond Artists Ltd.; dir. Yesterday and Today, The Fugitive, Odd Couple; v.p.; Astron Prod Ltd.

GREY, JOEL: Actor-Singer. b. Cleveland, 1932. e. Alexander Hamilton High, L.A. Acting debut at 10 years in On Borrowed Time at Cleveland Playhouse. Extensive nightclub appearances before returning to theatres and TV.
PICTURES INCLUDE: About Face, Calypso Heat Wave, Come September, Cabaret, Man on a Swing, Buffalo Bill and the Indians, 7 percent Solution.
TV: Maverick, December Bride, Jack and the Beanstalk (special), Ironside, Night Gallery, The Burt Bacharach Show, The Tom Jones Show, The Englebert Humperdinck Show, George M! (special), The Carol Burnett Show, The Julie Andrews Hour.
STAGE: Come Blow Your Horn, Stop the World—I Want to Get Off, Half a Sixpence, Harry, Noon and Night, West Side Story, Finian's Rainbow, Tom Sawyer, Mardi Gras, Littlest Revue, Cabaret, George M!

GREY, VIRGINIA: Actress. b. Los Angeles, Calif., March 22, 1923. Screen career started 1935 with She Gets Her Man.
PICTURES INCLUDE: Who Killed Doc Robbin, Bullfighter and the Lady, Highway 301, Slaughter Trail, Desert Pursuit, Perilous Journey, Forty-Niners, Target Earth, Eternal Sea, Last Command, Rose Tattoo, All That Heaven Allows, Tammy Tell Me True, Bachelor In Paradise, Back Street, Madame X, Rosie, Airport.

GRIFFIN, MERV: Singer, M.C. b. San Mateo, Calif., July 6, 1925. e. Univ. of San Francisco and Stanford. w. Julann Wright. The Merv Griffin Show, KFRC-Radio, 1945–48; vocalist, Freddy Martin's orch., 1948–52; Contract, Warner Bros., 1952–54. co-starred, So This Is Love, The Boy From Oklahoma; CBS-TV, toured Niteclubs, 1954–55; Prod. Finians Rainbow, City Center, N.Y.C., 1955; Vocalist, CBS-TV, Morning Show, and Robt. Q. Lewis Show, 1956; M.C., Look Up And Live, CBS-TV, Going Places, ABC-TV, 1957, Merv. Griffin Show, 1958, Play Your Hunch, 1960; M.C., Keep Talking, ABC-TV, 1960; Merv. Griffin Show, NBC-TV, 1962; Word for Word, NBC-TV, 1963; Merv. Griffin Show, Westinghouse Broadcasting, 1965; pres., Griffin Prods.

GRIFFITH, ANDY: Actor. b. Mount Airy, N.C., June 1, 1926. e. U. of North Carolina.
THEATRE: Broadway stage: No Time for Sergeants, Destry Rides Again.
TV: The Andy Griffith Show, Andy of Mayberry, No Time for Sergeants, The Headmaster (series), Go Ask Alice (movie). Salvage I.
PICTURES INCLUDE: A Face in the Crowd, No Time for Sergeants, Onionhead, The Second Time Around, Angel in My Pocket, Hearts of the West.

GRILLO, BASIL F.: Executive. b. Angel's Camp, Calif., Oct. 8, 1910. e. A.B., Univ. of Calif., Berkeley. Certified public accountant, exec. vice-pres., dir., Bing Crosby Ent., Inc., 1948–57; bus. mgr., Bing Crosby, 1945; co-organizer, dir., 3rd pres. & treas. Alliance of T.V. Film Producers, 1950–54; exec. prod., BCE, Inc., shows incl. Fireside Thea., Rebound, Royal Playhouse, The Chimps; dir., KCOP, Inc. 1957–60; dir. KFOX, Inc., 1958–62; pres., dir., Bing Crosby Prods., 1955–69; dir., Seven Leagues Ent., Inc., 1958; dir. Electrovision Prods., 1970, chief exec. off., Bing Crosby Enterprises.

GRIMALDI, ALBERTO: Producer. b. Naples, 1927. Studied law, serving as counsel for Italian film companies, before turning to production with Italian westerns starring Clint Eastwood and Lee Van Cleef. Is pres. of P.E.A. (Produzioni Europee Associate, S.A.S).
PICTURES INCLUDE: For a Few Dollars More, The Good, the Bad and the Ugly, Three Steps in Delerium, Satyricon, Burn!, The Decameron, The Canterbury Tales, 1001 Nights,

Salo, or the 100 Days of Sodom, Bawdy Tales, Man of La Mancha, Last Tango in Paris, Avanti, Fellini's Casanova, 1900, The True Story of General Custer.

GRIMES, GARY: Actor. b. San Francisco, 1955. Family moved to L.A. when he was nine. Made film debut at 15 yrs. in Summer of '42, 1971. Voted Star of Tomorrow in QP poll, 1971.
PICTURES INCLUDE: The Culpepper Cattle Company, Cahill, United States Marshall, Class of '44, The Spikes Gang, Gus.

GRINBERG, SHERMAN: Executive. b. Los Angeles, June 29, 1927; e. grad., Woodbury School of Business, 1950; accountant, 20th Century-Fox Studios, 1950; agent, 20th Century-Fox, rep. stock footage film libraries, 1953; formed Sherman Grinberg Film Libraries, Inc., 1958; agent, Columbia Studios, 1959; ABC News, 1963; MBM, 1970; 20th Century-Fox, 1971; pres., chmn. of bd., Sherman Grinberg Film Libraries, Inc.; co-prod., with David L. Wolper, Biography, 1961; pres., chmn. of bd., Filmrite Associates, Inc., 1963-64; pres., chmn of bd., American Color Laboratories, Inc.; pres., Brilliant Music, Inc.; TV, prod., Battle Line series; prod., Survival series. Partner, Flaum-Grinberg Prod. Bogart Special. Exec., prod. Untamed World, 1969. with exec. prod., Whatever Happened To, Explorers, 1971; producer of Adventures in Life Pilot, 1972; 1975, created feature film digests for airline usage; pres., Classic Film Digest, Inc. Distributor, Bogart & Hollywood—the Selznick Years. 1976, Exec. prod. for KABC-TV & synd; 1980, prod. for Landsbury Prods., ABC-TV, No Safe Place.

GRIPPO, JAN: Producer. b. Beacon, N.Y., Dec. 15, 1906; e. Eastman Coll., 1925; N.Y. Sch. of Design; m. Flo Browne. From 1926-28 cartoonist New York Herald-Tribune Syndicate; com. artist, caricaturist for Shubert shows, cartoonist national magazines; agent in Hollywood, 1940-49; prod. since 1945. Produced 23 Bowery Boys features for Monogram; assoc. producer Edward Small on Valentino for Columbia, 1950; prod. Bowery Battalion, Ghost Chasers, Let's Go Navy for Monogram, 1951.
MEMBER: Soc. American Magicians.

GRIZZARD, GEORGE: Actor. b. Roanoke Rapids, N.C., 1928. Debut on Broadway in The Desperate Hours. Has been member of APA repertory company and Tyrone Guthrie resident company in Minneapolis. Broadway plays include The Disenchanted, The Country Girl, The Royal Family, Who's Afraid of Virginia Woolf, California Suite, etc.
PICTURES: From the Terrace, Advise and Consent, Warning Shot, Happy Birthday, Wanda June, Comes a Horseman.

GRODIN, CHARLES: Actor-Director. e. Univ. of Miami. Studied acting with Uta Hagen and Lee Strasberg; began directing career in New York 1965 in New York as asst. to Gene Saks. Has appeared in some 75 plays all over country and has been quest of major network TV shows. Has also written scripts produced plays.
PICTURES INCLUDE: Actor: Rosemary's Baby, Catch-22, The Heartbreak Kid, 11 Harrowhouse, Thieves, King Kong, Heaven Can Wait, Real Life, Sunburn, It's My Turn, Seems Like Old Times, The Incredible Shrinking Woman, Great Muppet Caper.
TV: Candid Camera (writer, dir.); Simon and Garfunkel Special (writer, dir.); Acts of Love and Other Comedies (dir.); Paradise (prod., dir.).

GROESSE, PAUL: Art director, MGM Studios, Culver City, Calif. b. Hungary, Feb 28, 1906; e. Northwestern U., 1928; Yale U. (BFA), 1930. Architectural practice, Chicago, 1930-31; designer, Century of Progress exposition, Chicago, 1931-34.
PICTURES INCLUDE: The Firefly, The Great Waltz, Pride and Prejudice, Madame Curie, Human Comedy, Thirty Seconds Over Tokyo, The Yearling, Little Women, Annie Get Your Gun, King Solomon's Mines, The Merry Widow, Rhapsody, Catered Affair.
MEMBER: M.P. Ind. Council; Soc. of M.P. Art Directors.

GROSS, JERRY: Executive, producer, writer, director. e. N.Y. pub. schools, night sch.
PICTURES INCLUDE: Girl on a Chain Gang, Teen Age Mother and Female Animal.
Pres., Jerry Gross Productions, 1962; Pres., Cinemation Industries, Inc., 1964-75. Pres., Jerry Gross Org., 1979.

GROSS, KENNETH H.: Executive. e. New School for Social Research, Univ. of London. Conducted film seminars at New School and active in several indep. film projects. Published film criticism in various journals and magazines. Joined ABC Entertainment Oct. 1971. Named supvr. of feature films for ABC-TV. Appt. mgr. of feature films, Jan. 1974. Promoted in Nov, 1975 to program executive, ABC Entertainment Prime Time/West Coast. Moved to L.A. offices, Nov. 1976, promoted to exec. producer, movies for TV, ABC Ent.; 1978, with literary agency F.C.A. as partner in Los Angeles; 1979 producer for Lorimar; currently with Intl. Creative Mgt.

GROSSBERG, JACK: Producer/Executive. b. Brooklyn, N.Y., June 5, 1927.
FEATURES PRODUCED: Requiem for a Heavyweight, Pretty Poison, The Producers, Take The Money and Run, Don't Drink the Water, They Might Be Giants, Bananas, Everything You Always Wanted to Know About Sex.

GROSSMAN, ERNIE: Exec. b. N.Y.C., Sept. 19, 1924. Still dept., pressbook edit., asst. field mgr., Warner Bros., 1940-58; Studio publicist, 1958-60; exploitation, promo. mgr. field dept., 1960-64; nat'l mgr., pub., exploit., promo.; 1964-67 exec. co-ord. advt., pub. & promo., Warner-7 Arts, 1967; WB nat'l supv. ad.-pub., 1970. exec. assist. to Richard Lederer, 1971-72; 1973 nat'l dir. of Pub. & Promotion, Warner Bros. Inc.; 1977, natl. dir. of adv.-pub.; 1980, natl. dir. promo.

GROSZ, PAUL: Art Director. b. New York, N.Y. e. Cooper Union, 1928-30; Pratt, 1930-32; National Academy. Ent. m.p. ind. as artist-apprentice, Universal Pictures, 1929; art, adv., Warner Bros., Paramount, Buchanan Ad Agency, Monroe Greenthal Agency, Roxy Theatre; 20th Century-Fox, 1948-62; art dir. United Artists, 1962 to date, art director.

GRUEN, ROBERT: Executive. b. New York, N.Y., Apr. 2, 1913. e. Carnegie Mellon University, B.A. Stage designer, 1934-35; designer, 20th-Fox, 1936; prod. exec., National Screen Service Corp., 1936; head, Robert Gruen Associates, ind. design org., 1940; nat. pres. Industrial Designers Institute, 1954-55; dir. and v.p., National Screen Service Corp. since 1951; senior v.p. 1975-1978; mkt. consultant, 1978-; dir., 1978-; design & mkt. consultant, 1978-.

GRUENBERG, AXEL: Producer, director. b. Riga, Latvia, Aug. 17, 1902. e. U. of Ill., A.B., 1925. High sch. teacher 1930-36; dir. WWJ Detroit 1934-39; prod. dir., NBC Chicago, 1949-40; freelance dir. many radio shows, N.Y., 1940-43; dir., writer, 1944-50, incl. This Is Your Life, N.Y.; TV films: Stars Over Hollywood, General Electric, etc.; prod., This Is Your Life, TV, 1952. Now freelance writer.

GRUENBERG, JERRY: Executive. b. Minneapolis, Minn., June 7, 1927. e. U. of Minn. United Artists, Minneapolis, 1952; m.p. exhibitor 1952-67; v.p Sigma III Corp. 1965-67. division mgr., 20th Century-Fox, 1967-71; Senior V.P., general sales mgr., Allied Artists Pictures, 1971-79. Now pres., Blossom Pictures, Inc. Member of Variety Club, Friars Club. Director of Will Rogers Memorial Fund.

GRUENBERG, LEONARD S.: Executive. b. Minneapolis, Minn., Sept. 10, 1913. e. Minnesota U. Began as salesman Republic pictures (Minneapolis), 1935; with RKO in same capacity, 1936; promoted to city sales mgr., (St. Louis), 1937, then branch mgr. (Salt Lake City), 1941; later that year apptd. Rocky Mt. Dist. Mgr. (hqts., Denver, Colo.); 1946 Metropolitan, div. mgr.; v.p. NTA, v.p Cinemiracle Prods.; Pres., Chmn. of bd., Sigma III Corp., 1962. Chmn. of bd., Filmways, 1967. Chmn. of bd. Gamma III Dist. Co. & Chmn of bd. and Pres. Gamma III Group Ltd., 1976. Member variety Club, Sigma Alpha Mu Fraternity; Lieut. Civil Air Patrol, Lieut. Comdr., U.S.N.R.

GRUSIN, DAVID: Composer-Conductor-Performer. Directed music for the Andy Williams Show on TV for 7 yrs in the 1960s, where met Norman Lear and Bud Yorkin, producers of the series. They signed him to score their first feature film, Divorce, American Style.
PICTURES INCLUDE: Winning, The Heart Is a Lonely Hunter, Tell Them Willie Boy Is Here, The Front, Murder by Death, The Yakuza, Three Days of the Condor, Bobby Deerfield, And Justice for All, My Bodyguard.

GUARDINO, HARRY: Actor. b. Brooklyn, N.Y., Dec. 23, 1925. e. Haaren H.S.
THEATRE: B'way: End As A Man, A Hatful of Rain, Anyone Can Whistle, One More River, Natural Affection, The Rose Tattoo (revival), Seven Descents of Myrtle.
TV: Studio One, Playhouse 90, The Alcoa Theatre, Naked City, Dr. Kildare, The Untouchables, The Dick Powell Show, The Reporter, The New Perry Mason.
PICTURES INCLUDE: Pork Chop Hill, The Five Pennies, Houseboat, The Pigeon That Took Rome, Treasure of San Grennaro, Madigan, Lovers and Other Strangers, Red Sky at Morning, Dirty Harry, They Only Kill Their Masters, St. Ives, The Enforcer, Rollercoaster, Matilda, Any Which Way You Can.

GUARINI, ALFREDO: Producer. b. Genoa, Italy, May 23, 1901; m. Isa Miranda, prof.; p. Maria and Ettore Guarini. e. U. of Commerce, Genoa. In 1930, executive of various film companies in Italy, France and Germany; represented in Italy, the Consortium Emelka and Bavaria Films Co. In 1939; writer, Adventure in Diamonds, Par. in 1940: prod. Without Heaven (Rome, Italy) Academy Award for Walls of Malapaga, best foreign film, 1950.

GUBER, PETER: Producer. e. Syracuse Univ. (B.A.); Univ. at Florence (Italy), (S.S.P.); N.Y.U. School of Law (Juris Doctor, L.L.M.). Recruited by Columbia Pictures as exec. asst. in 1968 while pursuing MBA degree at N.Y.U. Graduate School of Business Adm. With Col. seven yrs. in key prod.

exec. capacities, serving last three as exec. v.p. in chg. of worldwide prod. Formed own company, Peter Guber's Filmworks, which in 1976 was merged with Casablanca Records to become Casablanca Record and Filmworks. He was chm of bd. of co. now called PolyGram, of which he is co.-mgr. dir.
PICTURES INCLUDE: The Deep (first under own banner), Midnight Express (6 Golden Globes, 2 Oscars).

GUEST, VAL: Writer, dir., prod. b. London, England, 1911; e. England and America. Journalist with Hollywood Reporter, Zit's Los Angeles Examiner and Walter Winchell.
PICTURES INCLUDE: Murder at the Windmill, Miss Pilgrim's Progress, The Body Said No, Mr. Drake's Duck, Happy Go Lovely, Another Man's Poison, Penny Princess, The Runaway Bus, Life With the Lyons, Dance Little Lady, Men of Sherwood Forest, Lyons in Paris, Break in the Circle, It's A Great Life, Quatermass Experiment, They Can't Hang Me, The Weapon, The Abominable Snowman, Carry on Admiral, It's a Wonderful World, Camp on Blood Island, Up the Creek, Further Up the Creek, Life is a Circus, Yesterday's Enemy, Expresso Bongo, Hell Is a City, Full Treatment, The Day the Earth Caught Fire, Jigsaw, 80,000 Suspects, The Beauty Jungle, Where the Spies Are, Casino Royale, Assignment K, When Dinosaurs Ruled the Earth, Tomorrow, The Persuaders, Au Pair, Girls, The Adventurers, Confessions of a Window Cleaner, Killer Force, Diamond Mercenaries. TV. Space 1999, The Shillingbury Blowers, The Band Played On, Sherlock Holmes & Dr. Watson.

GUFFEY, BURNETT: Cinematographer. b. Del Rio, Tenn., May 26, 1905. e. Etowah, Tenn., H.S. Asst. cameraman, William Fox Co., 1923–27; operative cameraman, 1928; dir. of photography, Columbia, 1943.
PICTURES INCLUDE: The Informer, Foreign Correspondent, Cover Girl, Gallant Journey, All the King's Men, From Here to Eternity (Acad. Award, best black and white photography, 1953), Human Desire, Violent Men, Harder They Fall, Good Neighbor Sam, Mad Woman of Chaillot, Halls of Anger, Bonnie and Clyde (AA, 1967), The Steogle, The Great White Hope.

GUILLAUME, ROBERT: Actor. b. St. Louis. Nov. 30. e. St. Louis Univ., Washington, Univ. Studied voice; acting career debut in Carousel. Has appeared in many Bdwy. plays and musicals.
TELEVISION: Dinah, Mel and Susan Together, Rich Little's Washington Follies, Jim Nabors, All in the Family, Sanford and Son, The Jeffersons, Marcus Welby, M.D., Soap, Benson.

GUILLERMIN, JOHN: Director. b. London, England, Nov. 11, 1925. e. City of London School, Cambridge Univ. RAF pilot prior to entering film industry.
PICTURES INCLUDE: Waltz of the Toreadors, Guns at Batasi, Rapture, The Blue Max, P.J., House of Cards, Bridge at Remagen, El Condor, Skyjacked, Shaft in Africa, The Towering Inferno, King Kong, Death on the Nile.

GUINNESS, SIR ALEC: Actor. b. London, Eng., April 2, 1914. e. Pembroke Lodge, Southbourne & Roborough School, Eastbourne. created C.B.E. 1955; Knighted 1959. Stage debut: London, 1934. Theatre appearances in London, New York & Continent. Special AA (1979) foir services to film.
PICTURES INCLUDE: Kind Hearts & Coronets, Run For Your Money, Last Holiday, The Mudlark, Lavender Hill Mob (Academy Nomination), The Man in the White Suit, The Card (The Promoter), Malta Story, Captain's Paradise, Father Brown (The Detective), To Paris With Love, The Prisoner, The Ladykillers, The Swan, The Bridge On the River Kwai (Academy Award 1957, best actor); The Horse's Mouth (Academy Nomination for s.p.), The Scapegoat, Our Man in Havana, Tunes of Glory, A Majority of One, H.M.S. Defiant, Lawrence of Arabia, Dr. Zhivago, The Comedians, Cromwell, Scrooge, Brother Sun and Sister Moon, Hitler: The Last Ten Days, Murder by Death, Star Wars (Academy Nomination), The Empire Strikes Back.
TV: The Wicked Scheme of Jehel Deeks (National Academy Nomination), Twelfth Night, Conversation at Night, Solo, E.E. Cummings, Little Gidding, The Gift of Friendship, Caesar & Cleopatra, Tinker, Tailor, Soldier, Spy (7-part series).

GULAGER, CLU: Actor. Father, John Gualger, cowboy entertainer. e. Baylor Univ. Starred at school in original play, A Different Drummer, where spotted by prod. of TV's Omnibus; invited to New York to recreate role on TV.
PICTURES INCLUDE: The Last Picture Show, Winning, The Other Side of Midnight, Touched by Love, etc.
TELEVISION: The Virginian, San Francisco International, Glass House, Ski Lift to Death, etc.

GUNN, MOSES: Actor. b. St. Louis. e. Tenn. State Univ. Taught speech and drama at Grambling College. Came to N.Y. and first cast in off-Bdwy. prod. of Genet's The Blacks. Later joined Negro Ensemble Company.
PICTURES INCLUDE: WUSA, The Great White Hope,

The Wild Rovers, Shaft, Shaft's Big Score, Eagle in a Cake, Hot Rock, Amazing Grace, The Iceman Cometh, Rollerball, Aaron Loves Angela, Ragtime.
STAGE: In White America, Day of Absence, Song of the Lusitanian Bogey, Summer of the 17th Doll, Daddy Goodness, Harvest, Titus Andronicus, Measure for Measure, Romeo and Juliet, The Tempest, As You Like It, Macbeth, Othello, A Hand Is on the Gate.
TELEVISION: Mr. Carter's Army, The Borgia Stick, Of Mice and Men, Haunts of the Very Rich, Hawaii Five-O, The FBI, Kung Fu, If You Give a Dance, You Gotta Pay the Band, The Cowboys, Roots.

GUNSBERG, SHELDON: Executive. b. Jersey City, N.J., Aug. 10, 1920; e. St. Peters Coll., N.J. State Normal, N.Y. Univ. With Night of Stars, Madison Sq. Garden, 1942; for. pub., 20th-Fox 1942; United Artists, 1945–47; Universal, roadshows. Rank product, asst. adv., pub. dir., 1947–54; v. pres., Walter Reade Theatres; exec. v.p. & dir., Walter Reade Org. 1962; Made chief operating officer, 1971; president, and Chief Executive Officer, 1973.

GUNZBURG, M.L.: President, Natural Vision Corporation. b. Denver, Colo. e. UCLA; Columbia U. Newspaper man, columnist, Los Angeles Times, New York Times; radio writer, screen writer many m.p. cos.
Developed 3-D process, Natural Vision; contract Polaroid Corp. for 3-D, 1953.

GURIAN, PAUL R.: Executive. b. New Haven, CT., Oct. 18, 1946. e. Lake Forest Coll., Univ. of Vienna, N.Y. Univ. Started producing films in 1971 with Cats and Dogs, a dramatic short which won prizes at Chicago Int. Film Fest and Edinburgh Fest. In 1977 formed Gurian Entertainment Corp., to acquire film properties for production.
PICTURES INCLUDE: The Garden Party (PBS program), Profile Ricardo Alegria (short), Bernice Bobs Her Hair (shown at 1977 N.Y. Film Festival); Cutter and Bone (United Artists, distributor).

GUYETT, HAROLD P.: Executive. b. Woodbine, Iowa, Nov. 21, 1920. e. K.C. School of Watchmaking and Jewelry; 1938–41; ass't mgr. Golden State Theaters, San Francisco; 1946–9; ass't mgr. Fox Midwest Theatres, Kansas City, Mo.; 1950–64, managed var. Fox Midwest Theatres, Kansas City, Mo.; 1964–5, Booker Fox Midwest Theatres, Kansas City, Mo.; 1965–6, Film buyer and booker Fox Midwest Theatres, St. Louis, Mo.; 1966, transferred to Fox Eastern Theatres, NYC; 1966–67, ass't div. mgr. Fox Eastern Theatres; 1968–1972; dist. mgr. Fox Eastern Theatres, div. National General Corp.; 1974, resigned and moved to Des Moines as film buyer and booker Davis Theatres, Inc., and heading B&I Booking Agency, Des Moines; Inc., and heading B&I Booking Agency, Des Moines; 1975, resigned from Davis Theatres. At present president and film buyer Guy-Con Enterprises, Shawnee Mission, Kansas.

GWYNNE, ANNE: Actress. r.n. Marguerite Gwynne Trice. b. Waco, Tex., Dec. 10, 1918. e. San Antonio High School, Stephens Coll.
THEATRE: Stage Door, Inside Story, The Colonel's Lady.
PICTURES INCLUDE: Charlie McCarthy, Detective; Framed, Unexpected Father, Honeymoon Deferred, Fear, Ghost Goes Wild, Glass Alibi, Dick Tracy Meets Gruesome, Panhandle, Enchanted Valley, Blazing Sun, Call of Klondike, Breakdown, Teenage Monster.

H

HABEEB, TONY G.: Executive. b. San Francisco, Calif., Oct. 26, 1927. e. San Francisco City College, 1945–47, Univ. of Calif., 1947–49, Lincoln Univ. Law School, LLB, 1949–53. TV Editor, San Francisco Chronicle, 1949–54; Information Specialist, U.S. Army, 1954–56; managing editor; Torrance Press, 1956–57; CBS-TV Network Press information Division, 1957–61; ass't dir. promo. and pub., Screen Gems, 1961–63; dir. promo. and pub., Screen Gems, 1963–67; world-wide dir. advertising, pub. and promo., Paramount Television; 1967–70. v.p., adv. and publicity, Metromedia Producers Corp. 1970–1974. v.p. adv. and publicity, Irwin Allen Productions, 1974–present. President, Publicist Guild of America.

HABER, JOYCE: Writer, syndicated Hollywood columnist. r.n. Mrs. Joyce Haber Cramer. b. Dec. 28, 1932, New York, N.Y. e. Brearley School, N.Y.C., class of '48; Bryn Mawr College, 1949–50, Cum Laude List; Barnard College, B.A., 1953.
Researcher, Time magazine, 1953–63; Hollywood Reporter, L.A. Bureau Time, 1963–66; Columnist, Los Angeles Times, 1966 to 1975; contributing editor, Los Angeles Magazine, 1977—
Published "Caroline's Doll Book," illus. by R. Taylor, 1962. freelance writing: Esquire, Herald Tribune's New

York Magazine, Harper's Bazaar, New York Magazine, Town and Country. Published "The Users," a novel, 1976.

HACK, SHELLEY: Actress. b. Connecticut, July 6. e. Smith College. Made modeling debut at 14 on cover of Glamour Magazine. Gained fame as Revlon's Charlie Girl on TV commercials.
PICTURES: Annie Hall, If Ever I See You Again.
TELEVISION: Death Car, Charlie's Angels.

HACKER, CHARLES R.: Executive. b. Milwaukee, Oct. 8. e. Univ. Wisconsin. Thea. mgr., Fox Wisc. Amuse. Corp., 1940; served in U.S.A.F., 1943–5; rejoined Fox Wisconsin Amusement Corp.; joined Standard Theatres Management Corp. 1947, on special assignments; apptd. district mgr. of Milwaukee & Waukesha theatres 1948; joined Radio City Music Hall Corp. as administrative asst. July, 1948; mgr. of oper., 1952; asst. to the pres., Feb. 1957. Award: Quigley Silver Grand Award for Showmanship, 1947; v.p., Radio City Music Hall Corp., 1964; appointed executive vice president and chief operating officer, February 1, 1973.

HACKETT, BUDDY: Actor, comedian. b. Brooklyn. Prof. debut, Borscht Circuit.
TV: Stanley series, Bud and Lou (movie).
THEATRE: B'way, Lunatics and Lovers, I Had A Ball.
PICTURES INCLUDE: God's Little Acre, All Hands on Deck, The Music Man, Everything's Ducky, It's a Mad, Mad, Mad, Mad World, Muscle Beach Party.

HACKETT, JOAN: Actress. b. N.Y.C. 1942. Made stage debut on Bdwy. in A Clearing the Woods which lead to other N.Y. plays. TV debut on Ellery Queen, followed by many other shows. Film debut in The Group (1966).
PICTURES INCLUDE: Will Penny, Support Your Local Sheriff, Assignment to Kill, The Rivals, The Last of Sheila, Mackintosh and T. J., Treasure of Matecumbe, One Trick Pony, Only When I Laugh.
THEATRE: Laurette, She Didn't Say Yes, etc.
TV: Young Doctor Malone, The Defenders, Alfred Hitchcock Show, Ben Casey, The Nurses, Dr. Kildare, The Twilight Zone, The Young Country (movie), etc.

HACKMAN, GENE: Actor. b. San Bernardino, Calif., 1930. First major broadway role in Any Wednesday. Other stage productions include: Poor Richard, Children from their Games, A Rainy Day in Newark, The Natural Look. Formed own production co., Chelly Ltd.
TV: CBS Playhouse's My Father, My Mother, The F.B.I., The Invaders, The Iron Horse, etc.
PICTURES INCLUDE: Lilith, Bonnie and Clyde (Acad. Award nom. for Best Supporting Actor), First to Fight, Out by the Country Club, Hawaii, Riot, The Split, The Gypsy Moths, Downhill Racer, Marooned, I Never Sang for My Father, Doctor's Wives, Cisco Pike, The French Connection (Acad. Award best actor, 1971), Prime Cut, The Poseidon Adventure, Scarecrow, The Conversation, Zandy's Bride, Young Frankenstein, Night Moves, Bite the Bullet, French Connection II, Lucky Lady, The Domino Principle, A Bridge Too Far, March or Die, Superman, All Night Long, Superman II.

HADLOCK, CHANNING M.: Mktg. TV exec. b. Mason City, Iowa. e. Duke Univ., Univ. of North Carolina. Newspaperman, Durham, N.C. Herald, war corr.; Yank; NBC, Hollywood; television prod.-writer, Cunningham & Walsh Adv.; v.p. account supr. Chirug & Cairns Adv.; v.p. Marketing Innovations; dir. mktg. Paramount Pictures; mktg. svcs, Ogilvy & Mather; mktg, Time Life Books.

HAGEL, ROBERT K.: Executive. b. Salmon, Idaho, Aug. 7, 1940. e. Univ. of Idaho, UCLA. Became TV production exec. for The Johnny Cash Show, The Ugliest Girl in Town and Three for Tahiti. Later joined Screen Gems as dir. of budgets, controls; promoted to ass't. prod. mgr. Named v.p. of Columbia Pictures in facilities and operations div. Appointed gen. mgr., chief operations exec. of newly-formed corp., The Burbank Studios, Inc., Dec. 1971.

HAGMAN, LARRY: Actor. b. Fort Worth, TX, Sept. 21. Son of actress Mary Martin. e. Bard College. First stage experience with Marg Jones Theatre in the Round in Dallas. Appeared in N.Y. in Taming of the Shrew; two years with London production of South Pacific. 1952–56 was in London with US Air Force where produced and directed show for servicemen. Returned to N.Y. for plays on and off Bdwy. Starred in daytime serial, Edge of Night, for over 2 years.
PICTURES: Fail Safe, Ensign Pulver and the Captain, The Cavern, Stardust, 3 in the Cellar, Mother, Jugs and Speed, Harry and Tonto, The Eagle Has Landed, Superman, etc.
TELEVISION: Series: I Dream of Jeannie, The Good Life, Here We Go Again, Dalllas. Movies: The President's Mistress, Last of the Good Guys, Battered.

HAHN, HERBERT R.: Executive. b. Boston, Mass., June 12, 1924. e. Harvard Coll, 1941–43, 1946–47, BA, Harvard Bus. School, 1947–49, M.B.A. Theatre exec., United Paramount Theatres, Inc., 1949–53; dir. of public & stockholder re-

lations, American Broadcasting Companies, Inc., vice-pres., investor relations, 1959.

HALAS, JOHN: Director. b. Budapest, Apr. 16, 1912; e. Hungary & Paris. Entered m.p. ind. 1928; prod. over 500 documentary, educational shorts & cartoons.
PICTURES INCLUDE: Animal Farm, The Owl and the Pussycat (3-D), History of the Cinema, Animal Vegetable and Mineral, The Candlemaker; anim. seq., The First 99, The Energy Picture, Habatales, A Christmas Visitor, Hamilton Cartoon series, Automania 2000, Is There Intelligent Life On Earth, Midsummer Nightmare, Hoffnung Cartoon Series, Dodo, The Kid From Outer Space (series), Ruddigore, The Question, Children and Cars, Parkinson's Law, Tomfoolery Show, Max and Moritz series, Ten for Survival, Autobahn.

HALE, ALAN, JR.: Actor. Son late Alan Hale, actor.
PICTURES INCLUDE: Short Grass, The Gunfighter, West Point Story, At Sword's Point, Wait Till the Sun Shines Nellie, Big Trees, Lady in the Iron Mask, Springfield Rifle, Man Behind the Gun, Capt. John Smith & Pocahontas, Iron Glove, Silver Lode, Rogue Cop, Young at Heart, Many Rivers to Cross, Destry, A Man Alone, Sea Chase, Indian Fighter, Killer Is Loose, Up Periscope, Advance to the Rear, Hang 'Em High, The True Story of Jesse James.
TV: The Lucy Show, Hazel, Wagon Train, Cheyenne, Maverick, Route 66, Jack Benny Show, Biff Baker, U.S.A. (series), Casey Jones (series), Gilligan's Island (series).

HALE, BARBARA: Actress. b. DeKalb, Ill., April 18, 1922; e. Chicago Acad. Fine Arts. Beauty contest winner, Little Theatre actress. Screen debut, 1943: Higher and Higher.
PICTURES INCLUDE: Belle of the Yukon, Goin' to Town, Boy with Green Hair, Window, Jolson Sings Again, And Baby Makes Three, Emergency Wedding, Jackpot, Lorna Doone, First Time, Last of the Comanches, Seminole, Lone Hand, Lion Is in the Streets, Unchained, Far Horizons, Houston Story, Buckskin.

HALE, MONTE: Actor. b. San Angelo, Texas, June 8, 1919. Night clubs and theatres, radio singer. Under contract to Republic Pictures, 1942–50.
PICTURES INCLUDE: Home on the Range, Timber Trail, Prince of the Plains, Bandits of the Badlands, Pioneer Marshal, The Old Frontier, Giant, The Chase.
TV: Gunsmoke, Honey West, Circus Boy, Wild Bill Hickok.

HALEY, JR., JACK: Executive. Sr. v.p. at Wolper Productions before joining MGM. Named dir. of creative affairs. Produced, wrote and directed That's Entertainment! (1974). Left Nov., 1974, to join 20th Century-Fox as pres. of TV Div. and v.p., TV for 20th-Fox Film Corp. Winner of 2 Peabody Awards, best prod. at Int'l. TV Festival at Monte Carlo and 3 Silver Lion Awards at Venice Film Festival. Won Emmy for best dir. in music or variety shows for Movin' on with Nancy. Directed M.P. Academy Awards Show in 1970; prod. it in 1974.

HALL, CONRAD: Cinematographer. b. Tahiti, 1926. Worked as camera operator with Robert Surtees, Ted McCord, Ernest Haller; moved to TV as director of photography before feature films.
PICTURES INCLUDE: Wild Seed, The Sabateur—Code Name Morituri, Harper, The Professionals, Rogue's Gallery, Incubus, Divorce, American Style, In Cold Blood, Cool Hand Luke, Hell in the Pacific, Butch Cassidy and the Sundance Kid, Tell Them Willie Boy Is Here, The Happy Ending, Fat City, Electra-Glide in Blue, The Day of the Locust, Smile, Marathon Man.

HALL, HUNTZ: Actor. In 1937 appeared in stage and screen production Dead End.
PICTURES INCLUDE: Crime School, Angels with Dirty Faces, They Made Me a Criminal, Hell's Kitchen, Muggs Rides Again, Live Wires, A Walk in the Sun, Jinx Money, Smuggler's Cove, Fighting Fools, Blues Busters, Bowery Battalion, Ghost Chasers, Crazy Over Horses, Let's Go Navy, Here Come the Marines, Hold That Line, Feudin' Fools, No Holds Barred, Private Eyes, Paris Playboys, Bowery Boys Meet the Monsters, Clipped Wings, Jungle Gents, Bowery to Bagdad, High Society, Spy Chasers, Jail Busters, Dig That Uranium, Up in Smoke, Second Fiddle to a Steel Guitar, Gentle Giant.
TV: The Teddy Bears (series).

HALL, KEN G.: Producer, director. b. Sydney, Australia, Feb. 22, 1901. Reporter. Joined pub. dept., Union Theats., Sydney; adv. mgr. 1920. In 1922 adv. mgr. FN (Asia) Ltd. Became adv. mgr. & pub. dir., State theat., Sydney, 1928; then asst. to managing dir., Union Theats. In 1931 gen. mgr. & dir., Cinesound Prods., Ltd.
PICTURES INCLUDE: (dir.) On Our Selection, Squatter's Daughter, Tall Timbers, Lovers and Luggers, Mr. Chedworth Steps Out, Vengeance of the Deep, Pacific Adventure.

HALPERN, NATHAN L.: Executive. b. Sioux City, Ia., Oct. 22, 1914; e. U. of South. Calif. 1936, B.A.; Harvard Law School 1939, L.L.B. With general counsel's office, U.S. Securities

& Exchange Commission, 1939–41; exec. asst. to dir., Civilian Supply, U.S. War Prod. Board, 1941–43; naval officer, Psychological Warfare Div., Supreme Headquarters, Allied Expeditionary Force, 1943–45; exec. asst. to dir., U.S. Information Service, Paris, 1945; ast. to pres., Columbia Broadcasting System, 1945–49; 1949–present; pres., TNT Communications, Inc.

HAMILL, MARK: Actor. Started in TV, including General Hospital (serial) and the Texas Wheelers (series). Film debut in Star Wars.
PICTURES INCLUDE: Star Wars, Corvette Summer, The Empire Strikes Back, The Night the Lights Went Out in Georgia.
TV: Sarah T: Portrait of A Teenage Alcoholic, The F.B.I., Owen Marshall, Room 222, The Partridge Family.

HAMILL, PETE: Journalist-Writer. b. Brooklyn. Worked as ad designer, NBC page boy and sheetmetal worker before joining staff of New York Post. In 1962 won Mike Berger Award of Col. Univ. Graduate School of Journalism for N.Y.'s worst slum. Received citation from Newspaper Reporters' Assn. for series on NY Police Dept. Made s.p. writing debut with Doc, 1971.
PICTURES INCLUDE: Doc, Death at an Early Age, Badge 373, Report from Engine Co. 82.
BOOKS: A Killing for Christ (novel), Irrational Ravings (collection of N.Y. Post columns), The Seventeenth Christmas (novel).

HAMILTON, GEORGE: Actor. b. Memphis, Tenn. Aug. 12, 1939. e. grammar, Hawthorne, Calf.; military sch., Gulfport, Miss., N.Y. Hackley Prep Sch., Florida, Palm Beach H.S. Won Best Actor Award for the State of Florida, high sch. contest.
TV: Rin Tin Tin, The Donna Reed Show, prod., The Veil, Roots.
PICTURES INCLUDE: Crime and Punishment, USA (debut), Home from the Hill, All The Fine Young Cannibals, Angel Baby, Where the Boys Are, By Love Possessed, A Thunder of Drums, Light in the Piazza, Two Weeks in Another Town, The Victors, Your Cheatin' Heart, Viva Maria, That Man George, Doctor, You've Got to Be Kidding!, The Long Ride Home, Jack of Diamonds, A Time for Killing, The Power, Evel Knievel, The Man Who Loved Cat Dancing, Once is Not Enough, Love at First Bite (also exec. prod.), Zorro, the Gay Blade (also co-prod.).

HAMILTON, GUY: Director. b. Paris, Sept. 1922. Ent. m.p. industry 1939 as apprentice at Victorine Studio, Nice; Royal Navy, 1940–45, in England asst. dir., Fallen Idol, Third Man, Outcast of the Islands, African Queen.
PICTURES INCLUDE: The Ringer, The Intruder, An Inspector Calls, Colditz Story, Manuela, The Devil's Disciple, A Touch of Larceny, The Best of Enemies, The Party's Over, Man In the Middle, Goldfinger, Funeral in Berlin, Battle of Britain, Diamonds Are Forever, Live and Let Die, The Man with the Golden Gun, Force Ten From Navarone, The Mirror Crack'd.

HAMILTON, MARGARET: Actress. b. Dec. 9, 1902. Kindergarten teacher; joined Cleveland Playhouse group. Played in Another Language on Broadway in 1932 and same role in screen version (1933), Wizard of Oz.
PICTURES INCLUDE: Driftwood, Bungalow 13, Sun Comes Up, Beautiful Blond from Bashful Bend, Riding High, Wabash Avenue, Great Plane Robbery, Brewster McCloud, Anderson Tapes.

HAMLIN, HARRY: Actor. b. California. e. Univ. of Calif., Yale (graduate 1974 in theatre, psychology). Joined American Conservatory Theatre (San Francisco) for two years' study before joining as professional actor. Screen debut in Movie, Movie (1979).
PICTURES INCLUDE: King of the Mountain, Clash of the Titans, Making Love.
TELEVISION: Studs Lonigan (mini-series).

HAMLISCH, MARVIN: Composer. b. New York City. Winner of Tony Award for score of Broadway show, A Chorus Line.
PICTURES INCLUDE: The Way We Were (Oscars for original score and song), The Sting (Oscar for adaptation), The Spy Who Loved Me, Starting Over, Ordinary People, The Fan.

HAMMOND, PETER: Actor, writer, dir. b. London, Eng., Nov. 15, 1923. e. Harrow School of Art. Stage debut: Landslide, Westminster Theatre. Screen debut: Holiday Camp.
PICTURES INCLUDE: The Huggetts, Helter Skelter, Fools Rush in, The Reluctant Widow, Fly Away Peter, The Adventurers, Operation Disaster; Come Back, Peter; Little Lambs Eat Ivy, Its Never Too Late, The Unknown, Morning Departure, Confession, dir.: Spring and Port Wine.
TV: William Tell, Robin Hood, The Buccaneers series. 1959–61. writ., dir. TV plays. TV dir. credits: Avengers, 4 Armchair Theatres, Theatre 625, BBC classic serials Count of Monte Cristo, Three Musketeers, Hereward the Wake, Treasure Island, Lord Raingo, Cold Comfort Farm, The White Rabbit, Out of the Unknown, Follyfoot; Lukes Kingdom, Time to Think, Franklin's Farm, Sea Song, Shades

of Greene, Our Mutual Friend, The House that Jack Built, The King of the Castle, The Black Knight, Kilvert's Army, Turgenev's Liza, Wuthering Heights, Funnyman, Little World of Don Camillo.

HAMPSHIRE, SUSAN: Actress. b. London, Eng., 1941.
STAGE: Expresso Bongo, Follow That Girl, Fairy Tales of New York, Ginger Man, Past Imperfect, She Stoops to Conquer, On Approval, The Sleeping Prince, A Doll's House, Taming of the Shrew, Peter Pan, Romeo & Jeanette, As You Like it, Miss Julie, The Circle, Arms and the Man, Man and Superman, Tribades, An Audience Called Edward, The Crucifer of Blood, Night and Day.
TV: Andromeda, The Forsyte Saga, Vanity Fair, Katy, The First Churchills; An Ideal Husband, The Lady is a Liar, The Improbable Mr. Clayville, musical version of Dr. Jekyll and Mr. Hyde, The Pallisers.
PICTURES INCLUDE: The Three Lives of Thomasina, Night Must Fall, Wonderful Life, Paris Au Mois d'Aout, The Fighting Prince of Donegal, The Trygon Factor, Monte Carlo or Bust, Rogan, David Copperfield, A Room in Paris, Living Free, Time for Loving, Malpertius, Baffled, Neither the Sea nor the Sand, Roses and Green Peppers, David the King, Bang.

HANCOCK, JOHN: Director. b. Kansas City, Mo., Feb. 12, 1939. e. Harvard. Was musician and theatre director before turning to films. Nominated for AA for short, Sticky My Fingers, Fleet My Feet.
PICTURES INCLUDE: Let's Scare Jessica to Death, Bang the Drum Slowly, Baby Blue Marine, California Dreaming.

HAND, BETHLYN J.: Executive. b. Alton, Illinois. e. University of Texas. Entered motion picture industry in 1966 as administrative assistant to president of Motion Picture Association of America, Inc. In 1975 became associate director of Code of advertising of MPAA. In 1976 became director of Code for advertising; v.p.—west coast activities, board of directors, SPCA, Los Angeles.

HANDEL, LEO A.: Producer. Organized a film research bureau, New York, 1941; dir. audience research, MGM, 1942–51; organized Meteor Prod., 1951; organized Leo A. Handel Prod., for TV films, 1953; author, Hollywood Looks at Its Audience, also TV plays; pres., Handel Film Corp.; prod. TV series including Everyday Adventures, Magic of the Atom. Exec. prod. & v.p., Four Crown Prods., Inc., exec. prod., Phantom Planet, 1961; prod.-writer-dir., feature film, The Case of Patty Smith, 1961; Americana Series, 1963; book, A Dog Named Duke, 1965. TV specials, Age of the Atom, 1966; Sweden-Vikings Now Style, 1968, Benjamin Franklin, 1969; The Mexican American Heritage and Destiny, 1970, The American Indian, 1971, Police Dog (TV special), 1972; Art in America, 10 half-hour films, 1981.

HANNA, LEE: Executive. e. Univ. of Colo., N.Y. City Coll., Long Island Univ. Joined CBS as news writer, 1954, later becoming producer-writer. Left in 1958 to write speeches and make documentaries for Gov. Averell Harriman, Gov. George Leader, Se. Harrison Williams. Ass't. dir., WNEW News, Dec. 1959; later dir. of news to 1964 when rejoined CBS News ass't. gen. mgr. Named dir. of news, WCBS-TV, N.Y., 1966. Joined NBC News, Aug., 1972, as gen. mgr., news, NBC TV stations. Appt. v.p., news, NBC TV, March, 1973.

HANNA, WILLIAM: Executive. b. Melrose, N.M. Studied engineering and journalism. Joined firm in Calif. as structural engineer; turned to cartooning with Leon Schlessinger's company in Hollywood. In 1937 hired by MGM as director and story man in cartoon dept. There met Joseph R. Barbera and created famous cartoon series Tom & Jerry, continuing to produce it from 1938 to 1957. Left MGM in 1957 to form Hanna-Barbera Productions to make cartoons for TV. Series have included Yogi Bear, Huckleberry Hound, The Flintstones, Hanna-Barbera became a subsidiary of Taft Bdg. Co. in 1968 with both men operating studio under long-term agreements with Taft. Hanna is senior v.p. of Hanna-Barbera Productions. Company entered theatrical production with Charlotte's Web in 1973.

HANNEMANN, WALTER A.: Film editor. b. Atlanta, G., May 2; U.S.C., the Class of 1935. Editorial training, RKO 1936–40; edit. supvr., Universal, 1941–42; consultant 1970–75 national educational media.
PICTURES INCLUDE: Interval, The Revengers, Dream of Kings, Guns of the Magnificent Seven, East of Java, Pay or Die, Al Capone, Hell's Five Hours, Armoured Command, Only the Valiant, Time of Your Life, Kiss Tomorrow Goodbye, Blood on the Sun, Guest in the House, Texas Masquerade, Cannon for Cardoba, El Condor, Maurie, Lost in the Stars, Mad Mad Movie Making, Big Mo, Two Minute Warning, (Oscar nominee) The Peter Hill Puzzle, Smokey and the Bandit, Other Side of the Mountain—Part II, The Visitor, The Villain, Return of Maxwell Smart.
TV: Death Valley Days, Reader's Digest, Rosemary Clooney Show, The New Breed, The Fugitive, Twelve O'Clock High, The Invaders, Hawaii Five-O, Streets of San Francisco, Cannon, Barnaby Jones, Caribe.

HANSON, JOHN: Independent Film-maker. Aegis Productions Ltd. b. St. Leonards-on-Sea, England. Early career: studio porter, designer, ecologist and actor. Docs incl: Days of Our Youth (John Irwin dir.) won 1st prize Mexico Olympics film festival.
PICTURES INCLUDE: Secrets, Shh!, The Dilessi Affair.

HANSON, PETER: Actor. b. Oakland, Calif.; p. Sydney and Lee Hansen; e. Cranbrook Acad. of Arts, Mich.; U. of Mich., 1940–41. Studied acting at Pasadena Playhouse, Calif., 1946, following war service as marine fighter pilot. Campagne, Arsenic and Old Lace, This Happy Breed; m.p. debut in Branded.
PICTURES INCLUDE: Molly, Something to Live For, When Worlds Collide, Passage West, Darling How Could You, The Savage, Violent Men, Proud and Profane, Harlow.

HARARI, ROBERT: Writer. Served in U.S. Armed Forces, 1942–45.
PICTURES INCLUDE: Music for Madame, Hitting a New High, Daytime Wife, Ice Capades, Everything Happens at Night, Sun Valley Serenade, Larceny With Music, Foreign Affair, Millionaire for Christy, story, Three Steps North.
TV: Haunted Honeymoon, Death Takes A Pass, It Happened in a Pawnshop.

HARBACH, WILLIAM O.: Producer. b. Yonkers, N.Y., Oct. 12, 1919; p. Otto Harbach, lyricist, author; e. Brown U. U.S. Coast Guard, 1940–45; actor, MGM, 1945–47; broadcast co-ordinator. NBC, 1947–49; stage mgr., 1949–50; dir., NBC, 1950–53; prod., Tonight, 1954; prod. Steve Allen Show, 1960–61 prod., dir., Bing Crosby shows; prod., Milton Berle Special, 1962; prod., Hollywood Palace Shows, 1963–69.; co-produced Julie Andrews Show, 1972–73. Emmy for Shirley MacLaine's Gypsy In My Soul, 1976.

HARDIMAN, JAMES W: Publicist. b. Brighton, England 1926. Director Advtg. & Pub., Rank Organization of Canada & Odeon Canada, 1947–56. Asst. dir. ad & pub, National Theatres, 1956–58. Dir. radio & TV promotion, Walt Disney, 1959–60. Dir. pub, Screen Gems Hollywood, 1960–64. Dir. press infmtn, CBS TV Network, Hollywood, 1964–67. Studio dir. promtn. & pub, Screen Gems, Hollywood, 1967–70. VP Yuni public rels, Tokyo and v.p. and resident director, Sijohn o Enterprises, Japan, 1970–75. Dir. pub, (entertainment) Rogers & Cowan, Beverly Hills, 1975–77. President, Suhosky & Hardiman Public Rels, 1977 to date. 1968 named Hollywood Showman of the Year by the Publicists Guild.

HARDING, ANN: Actress. r.n. Dorothy Walton Gatley. b. Fort Sam Houston, Tex., August. 17, 1904. Provincetown Players, stock, Broadway Stage: Trial of Mary Dugan, Screen: Paris Bound, Holiday, Animal Kingdom, Peter Ibbetson, others.
PICTURES INCLUDE: Mission to Moscow, The North Star, Cinderella Jones, Nine Girls, Janie, Those Endearing Young Charms, It Happened on Fifth Avenue, Christmas Eve, The Magnificent Yankee, Unknown Man, Man in the Gray Flannel Suit.

HARGREAVES, JOHN: Executive. Joined Gainsborough Pictures 1945. Transferred to Denham Studios 1946 and later Pinewood Studios. Joined Allied Film Makers 1960, then Salamander Film Productions as Bryan Forbes' financial controller and Asst. Prod. 1965. Joined EMI Film Prods. Ltd. as Asst. Man. Dir. and prod. controller May 1969–May 1972. Produced Don Quixote (with Rudolf Nureyer, in Australia), 1973. Asst. Prod. The Slipper & The Rose 1975, Man. Dir; Cinderella Promotions Ltd; 1978: assoc. prod., International Velvet. Orion repr., 1979, The Awakening; post prod. exec., Fiendish Plot of Dr. Fu Manchu, 1980.

HARINGTON, JOY: Producer. b. London, Eng., Feb. 22, 1914. e. private school, Kate Rorke Dram. School. 6 years in English theatre; New York theatre and radio; Hollywood Studios. Since 1971, freelance writer, producer and actress.
PICTURES INCLUDE: Our Hearts Were Young and Gay, Gaslight, National Velvet, Salome Where She Danced, Tony Draws A Horse.
TV: Treasure Island, Holly and the Ivy, Bridesman Danger, Midsummer Night's Dream, Beauty andThe Beast, Billy Bunter of Greyfriars, Heidi, Heidi Grows Up, Clementine, Vice Versa, Robin Hood, Kidnapped, Jesus of Nazareth, Little Women, Jo's Boys, Paul of Tarsus, Hurricane, The Chen-Lab. Mystery serials. Prod. Fothergale Co. Ltd., Law and Life, Make the Best of Yourself.
AUTHOR: Jesus of Nazareth, Paul of Tarsus, TV Script Pollyanna, Radio Play, Play It By Ear.

HARMON, MARK: Actor. b. Burbank, CA, Sept. 2. Son of actress Elyse Knox and football star Tom Harmon.
PICTURES: Beyond the Poseidon Adventure; Comes a Horseman.
TELEVISION: Series: Sam, Laverene & Shirley, Nancy Drew, Police Story, Adam-12, 240-Robert. Movies: Eleanor and Franklin: The White House Years, Little Moe, Getting Married.

HARMON, TOM: Performer. b. Rensselaer, Ind., Sept. 28, 1919; e. U. of Mich., B.S., 1941; m. Elyse Knox, actress. All American football player, 1939–40; U.S. Air Corps, 1941–46; sports dir., WJR, Detroit, 1941; KFI, Los Angeles, 1947; broadcaster, many football, baseball games; sports dir., Columbia Pacific Radio Network, 1948–61; Tom Harmon Sports Show (ABC) 1961–70; Golden West Broadcasters (Channel 5, Hollywood), 1970; 1974—Hughes Television Network—sports dir.; 1976—Editor-Publisher—Tom Harmon's Football Today. (weekly national football paper).

HARNELL, STEWART D.: Executive. b. New York City, Aug. 18, 1938. e. Univ. of Miami, UCLA, New School of Social Research, Entertainer with Youth on Parade in Coral Gables, 1948–55, performing for handicapped children, Variety Club, etc. Singer, dancer, musician. Had own bands, Teen Aces & Rhythm Rascals, 1950–56; performed on Cactus Jim TV show and Wood & Ivory, 1959–61, WTVJ. Miami. Catskills, Sand Lake, N.Y., 1954–55. Joined National Screen Service as exec. trainee in 1960 in Chicago; worked as booker & salesman. Transferred to N.Y. home office, 1963; worked in special trailer production. Promoted to asst. gen. sls. mgr., 1964–66; New Orleans branch mgr., 1966–67; Atlanta division mgr., 1967–80. Formed own independent distribution co., 1970—Harnell Independent Productions. Resumed post as gen. sls. mgr. of NSS, New York, 1977–78; resigned to become pres. of Cinema Concepts, Inc. in 1978 to present. Pres. of Variety Club of Atlanta, Tent 21, 1972, 1976, 1979.

HARPER, JOE: Theatre Executive. b. Dallas, Texas, Aug. 11, 1941. e. El Centro Coll., Dallas; Ga. State Univ. Was in public relations, N.Y.C., 1961–65 when joined Academy Theatres, Dallas. In 1968–69, with American Multi-Cinema, Dallas. In 1969 joined R. C. Cobb Theatre, Atlanta. Now v.p. in chg. booking, buying, Member: Democratic Executive Committee, Officer Ruritan International Active in Scouting and Little League sports.

HARPER, KENNETH: Producer. Formerly an agent with MCA, became an indep. prod. 1955.
PICTURES INCLUDE: Yield to the Night, Action of the Tiger, The Passionate Summer. Formed Elstree Film Distributors, 1961. Since prod. Go to Blazes, The Young Ones, Summer Holiday, French Dressing, Wonderful Life, Prudence and the Pill, 1966; Virgin and the Gypsy, 1970.

HARPER, RICHARD A.: TV Executive. b. Johnstown, Pa. e. Univ. of So. Calif. 1939; Columbia Univ. 1943 (MA); Harvard Grad. School of Bus. Admin. 1945; National City Bank of New York in Japan, China, Malaya, India and Burma 1939–42; Lt. Cmd. USNR 1942–45; MGM-New York, ass't to gen. sales mgr., circuit sales mgr. 1945–1956; director world-wide syndication MGM-TV 1956–63; gen. sales mgr. Samuel Goldwyn Prod's. 1963–64; Warner Bros.-Seven Arts v.p.-administration 1964–71; Twentieth Century-Fox Television, v.p. World-Wide syndication 1971; sr. v.p., 20th-Fox Intl. TV, 1980.

HARPER, VALERIE: Actress. b. Aug. 22, Suffern, N.Y. m. actor-writer Dick Schaal. Started as dancer in stage shows at Radio City Music Hall. First professional acting in summer stock in Conn. Appeared on Bdwy. in Take Me Along, Wildcat, Subways Are for Sleeping. Won 3 Emmys for best performance in supporting role in comedy for portrayal of Rhoda on The Mary Tyler Moore Show.
PICTURES INCLUDE: Freebie and the Bean, Chapter Two, The Last Married Couple in America.
TV: The Mary Tyler Moore Show, Rhoda.

HARPER, WILLIAM A.: Producer. b. Port Jervis, N.Y., Sept. 3, 1915; e. Univ. So. Calif. (BS), 1936. Founder member Delta Kappa Alpha frat (cinematography), U.S.C.; started in m.p. ind. in pub.; later asst. dir., prod. mgr., director; In WW II Major, USMC. Organized Marine Corps Photo Service, then in chg. Marine Corps Photo activities Pacific Ocean Areas. End of war organized Reliance Film Co., Inc., eng. in prod., dist., early TV prod. Recalled active duty for Korean War, headed USMC Photo Service. Co-prod. with Navy (Adm. John Ford) feat. documentary, This is Korea; govt. liaison with March of Time, Crusade in Pacific and with NBC US Navy Victory at Sea; prod. dir., writer, Loucks & Norling Studios, 1952; free lance writer-director 1953–55; with Fred Feldkamp Prods. 1955–56; in Europe 1956–58. Assoc. prod. The Silken Affair (RKO) 1956; Producer, The Stranding in Holland 1957; prod. advisor The Last Blitzkreig (Col.). Europe, (1958); producer, The Stone, 1962; Managing Director, St. James Productions Ltd., (England) and Pres. American-European Film Service (Paris).

HARRINGTON, CURTIS: Director, writer. b. Los Angeles, Calif., Sept. 17; e. U. Southern Calif., B.A. Exec. assts. to Jerry Wald, 1955–61 Associate Producer at 20th Cent. Fox.
PICTURES INCLUDE: Hound Dog Man, Return to Peyton Place, The Stripper, Night Tide and Queen of Blood, released by A.I.P. For Universal, What's the Matter with Helen? (UA) 1971, Gingerbread House, The Killing Kind.

HARRINGTON, PAT (JR): Actor. b. e. Fordham U. Served USAF as 1st Lt., 1952–54. Time salesman for NBC, 1954–58. Some

150 TV appearances on Jack Paar, Steve Allen and Danny Thomas TV shows, 1958–61; nightclub appearances, 1960–63. TV and films, 1963 to present. Television Series include: Mr. Deeds Goes to Town, Owen Marshall, and One Day at a Time.
PICTURES INCLUDE: The Wheeler Dealers, Move Over Darling, Easy Come, Easy Go, The President's Analyst, 2000 Years Later, The Candidate.

HARRIS, BARBARA: Actress. b. Evanston, Ill.; e. Wright Junior College (Chicago), Goodman School of the Theatre and U. of Chicago. Joined acting troop, The Compass, and came to N.Y. where first role was in Oh, Dad, Poor Dad, Mamma's Hung You in the Closet and I'm Feeling So Sad, repeating in m.p.
PLAYS: On a Clear Day You Can See Forever, The Apple Tree.
PICTURES INCLUDE: Thousand Clowns, Who Is Harry Kellerman?, The War Between Men and Women, Mixed Company, Nashville, Family Plot, Movie Movie, The North Avenue Irregulars, The Seduction of Joe Tynan.

HARRIS, EDWARD M.: Exhibitor. b. Holdenville, Okla., Aug. 21, 1916. e. Tulsa U. Theatre mgr. in Neosho, Mo., since 1933; now mgr., co-owner, Gardner Theatres there. Member: Kans.-Mo. Theatre Assn. (pres. 1954–56).

HARRIS, JAMES B.: Prod. Dir. b. New York City, Aug. 3, 1928; e. Julliard School. U.S. film export, 1947; Realart Pictures, 1948; formed Flamingo Films, 1949; formed Harris-Kubrick Productions, 1954. Producer of The Killing, Paths of Glory, Lolita; formed James B. Harris Prods., Inc., 1963; prod., dir., The Bedford Incident, 1965; produced, directed & wrote screenplay, Some Call It Loving, 1973; prod., Telefon, 1977; Fast-Walking, 1981 (prod., dir., s.p.).

HARRIS, JOHN H.: Circuit executive. b. Pittsburgh, Pa., July 9, 1898; fr. John Harris, founder of first all-film theatre, coined name Nickelodeon; e. Georgetown U., LL.B. Born in show business, managed theatres in summer as relief manager while going to school; 1917 on first definite assignment, 1922 as mgr. Strand Theat., Youngstown, Ohio; in 1923, mgr. Harris theat., McKeesport, Pa. On death of father, Senator J. P. Harris, 1926, became gen. mgr. of all Harris Theats. in Pittsburgh office. In 1930 sold Harris Theats. to RKO and Warner Bros., becoming asst. to gen. mgr., Warner Bros. Theats., N.Y., then zone mgr., Pittsburgh. In 1935 on expiration of Warner contract, assumed control of new theats., comprising Harris circuit; later pres. and gen. mgr. Harris Amusement Cos., Pittsburgh. Also pres., Arena Managers, Inc.; Pres. Prod. Ice Capades, Inc.; Ice Cycles, Int.; H. Harris Assoc.; Penna. Promotions; Arena Promotions; John Harris Assoc.; Harris & Harris (insurance); F. J. Harris Real Estate; Founder and international Big Boss of Variety Clubs International for Life.

HARRIS, JULIE: Designer. b. London, England. e. Chelsea Arts School. Entered industry in 1945 designing for Gainsborough Studios. First film, Holiday Camp.
PICTURES INCLUDE: Greengage Summer, Naked Edge, The War Lover, Fast Lady, Chalk Garden, Psyche 59, A Hard Day's Night, Darling, Help, The Wrong Box, Casino Royale, Deadfall, Prudence and the Pill, Decline and Fall, Goodbye Mr. Chips, Sherlock Holmes, Follow Me!, Live and Let Die, Rollerball, Slipper and The Rose, Dracula.
TV: Laura (with Lee Radziwill), Candleshoe, The Sailor's Return, Lost and Found.

HARRIS, JULIE: Actress. b. Grosse Pointe, Mich., Dec. 2, 1925; e. Yale Drama Sch. m.p. debut in Member of the Wedding.
PICTURES INCLUDE: East of Eden, I Am a Camera, The Trouble with Women, The Haunting, Harper, Reflection in a Golden Eye, The Poacher's Daughter, You're a Big Boy Now, The Split, The People Next Door, The Hiding Place, Voyage of the Damned, The Bell Jar.
B'WAY PLAYS: Sundown Beach, Playboy of the Western World, Macbeth, Young and the Fair, Magnolia Alley, Monserrat, Member of the Wedding, I Am a Camera, Colombe, The Lark, And Miss Reardon Drinks a Little, The Last of Mrs. Lincoln (Tony Award).
TV: Little Moon of Alban, Johnny Belinda, A Doll's House, Ethan Frome, The Good Fairy, The Lark, He Who Gets Slapped, The Heiress, Victoria Regina, Pygmalion, Anastasia, The Holy Terror, The Power and The Glory.

HARRIS, PHIL: Orchestra leader. b. Linton, Ind., June 24, 1906; husband of Alice Faye, actress. In 1933: with orchestra in Melody Cruise. In 1936: Vitaphone short prod. In 1937: Turn Off the Moon. In 1939: Man About Town. In 1940: Buck Benny Rides Again, Dreaming Out Loud.
PICTURES INCLUDE: I Love a Bandleader, Wabash Avenue, Wild Blue Yonder, Starlift, High and the Mighty, Anything Goes, Good-Bye My Lady. Co-starred with Alice Faye in weekly radio show; many TV appearances.

HARRIS, RICHARD: Actor. b. Limerick, Ireland, Oct. 1, 1930.
PICTURES INCLUDE: Alive and Kicking, Shake Hands With the Devil, The Long, The Short and The Tall, Guns of Navarone, Mutiny on the Bounty, This Sporting Life, The Red Desert (Italy), Major Dundee, The Heroes of Telemark, The Bible, Hawaii, Camelot, The Molly Maguires, A Man Called Horse, Cromwell, Bloomfield (actor & dir.), Man in the Wilderness, The Snow Goose, The Deadly Trackers, Gulliver, 99 and 44/100% Dead, Juggernaut, Echoes of a Summer, Robin and Marian, Return of the Man Called Horse, The Cassandra Crossing, Orca, Golden Rendezvous, The Wild Geese, The Ravagers, The Number, Game for Vultures, High Point, Your Ticket is No Longer Valid.

HARRIS, ROBERT: Executive. Senior v.p., Universal TV, with responsibility of supervising Universal programming on CBS network. In 1981 named pres. of Universal TV.

HARRIS, ROSEMARY: Actress. b. Ashby, Suffolk, 1930; e. India and England. Early career, nursing; studied Royal Acad. of Dramatic Art, 1951–52.
PLAYS INCLUDE: Climate of Eden (New York), Seven Year Itch, Confidential Clerk (Paris Festival), and with Bristol Old Vic, The Crucible, Much Ado About Nothing, Merchant of Venice.
Screen debut in Beau Brummell, The Shiralee, TV, Cradle of Willow, Othello, The Prince and the Pauper, The Tale of Two Cities, Dial M for Murder, etc. On stage, at Old Vic, 1955–56; U.S. tour, 1956–57; U.S. stage, 1959–63.
TV: Profiles in Courage, A Dickens Chronicle, Athens Where the Theatre Began; Blithe Spirit.
Chichester Festivals 1962 and 63; Nat'l Theatre 1963–64; You Can't Take It With You, 1965; The Lion in Winter, 1966, (U.S. Stage): 1967, APA Repertory Co., A Lion in Winter.
PICTURES INCLUDE: Camelot, The Boys from Brazil.

HARRISON, JOAN: Writer, producer. b. Guildford, Surrey, England; e. U. Sorbonne; Oxford U., B. A. Began screen career in England as asst. & writer with Alfred Hitchcock, dir. To U.S. 1939 to write s.p. Rebecca.
PICTURES INCLUDE: Foreign Correspondent, Suspicion, Saboteur, Phantom Lady, Dark Waters, The Strange Affair of Uncle Harry, Ride A Pink Horse, Circle of Danger, Eye Witness.
Prod. Alfred Hitchcock Presents, TV.

HARRISON, KATHLEEN: Actress. b. Lancashire, Eng., Trained at R.A.D.A.
PLAYS: Night Must Fall, Corn Is Green, Flare Path, Winslow Boy, Flowers for the Living, The Silver Box, Waters of the Moon, All for Mary, Nude With Violin, How Say You, Watch It Sailor, The Chances, Norman, Collapse of Stout Party, Mrs. Puffin, Harvey, She Stoops to Conquer (1972).
PICTURES INCLUDE: Bank Holiday, A Girl Must Live, Night Must Fall, In Which We Serve, Major Barbara, Holiday Camp, Bond Street, Oliver Twist, Winslow Boy, Trio, Magic Box, Waterfront, Here Comes the Huggetts, Vote for Huggett, Huggetts Abroad, Scrooge, The Happy Family, Pickwick Papers, Turn the Key Softly, Lilacs in the Spring, Where There's a Will, Cast a Dark Shadow, All for Mary, It's a Great Life, Big Money, Home and Away, Seven Thunders, A Cry From the Streets, Alive and Kicking, Mrs. Gibbons Boys, Fast Lady, West Eleven, Lock Up Your Daughters, Our Mutual Friend.
TV: Mrs. Thursday, series, Waters of the Moon, High Finance, Dixon of Dock Green, Spring & Autumn, VXB.

HARRISON, REX: Actor. b. Derry House, Huyton, Lancashire, England, Mar. 5, 1908; m. Rachel Roberts. In the RAF, World War II. Stage debut 1924 in "Thirty Minutes in a Street," Liverpool Repertory theatre, England; later on British tour ("Charley's Aunt," "Alibi," etc.) London debut 1930 in "Getting George Married." To New York, 1936, in "Sweet Aloes."
PLAYS INCLUDE: London, repertory, tour. New York stage: Anne of a Thousand Days, Henry VIII, 1948; Cocktail Party, London, 1950; Bell, Book & Candle, New York, 1951; Venus Observed, Love of 4 Colonels, N.Y.; Bell, Book & Candle, London.
PICTURES INCLUDE: Began screen career, 1929. Films include Men Are Not Gods, Storm in a Teacup, School for Husbands, Over the Moon, The Citadel, Ten Days in Paris, Sidewalks of London, Night Train, Major Barbara, Blithe Spirit. Voted one of top ten British money-making stars in Motion Picture Herald-Fame Poll, 1945–46. To Hollywood, 1946. I Live in Grosvenor Square, The Rake's Progress, Anna and the King of Siam, The Ghost and Mrs. Muir, Foxes of Harrow, Escape, Unfaithfully Yours, The Long Dark Hall, The Four Poster, King Richard & the Crusaders, Constant Husband, The Reluctant Debutante, Midnight Lace, Once a Thief, Cleopatra, My Fair Lady, The Yellow Rolls-Royce, The Agony and the Ecstasy, The Honey Pot, Dr. Doolittle, A Flea In Her Ear, Staircase, The Prince and the Pauper.
BROADWAY STAGE: in My Fair Lady, 1956–57; B'way stage in The Fighting Cock, 1959–60; London, My Fair Lady, 1958–59; Platinov, London, 1960; 1961, August for The People. Both Seasons at Royal Court Theatre, London. nom. best actor for Cleopatra; acad. award, 1965, My Fair Lady; New York Film Critics Award, 1965; Golden

Globe, 1965; David di Donatello award, 1965; Top ten world box office star, 1966.

HARROLD, KATHRYN: Actress. b. Tazewell, VA. e. Mills College. Studied acting at Neighborhood Playhouse in N.Y.; also with Uta Hagen. Appeared in off-off-Bdwy. plays for year; then joined experimental theatre group, Section Ten, touring East, performing and teaching at Connecticut College and New York univ. Cast in TV daytime serial, The Doctors.
PICTURES: Nightwing (debut), The Hunter, Modern Romance.
TELEVISION: Movies: Son-Rise, a Miracle of Love, Vampire, Bogie. Series: Starsky and Hutch.

HARRYHAUSEN, RAY: Producer, Writer, Special Effects Expert. b. L.A. e. L.A. City Coll. While at coll. made 16mm animated film, Evolution, which got him job as model animator for George Pal's Puppetoons in early '40s. Served in U.S. Signal Corps; then made series of filmed fairy tales with animated puppets for schools and churches. In 1946 worked on Mighty Joe Young as ass't. to Willis O'Brien. Designed and created special visual effects for The Beast from 20,000 Fathoms; then began evolving own model animation system called Dynarama. In 1952 joined forces with prod. Charles H. Schneer, using new process for first time in It Came from Beneath the Sea. Subsequently made many films with Schneer in Dynarama.
PICTURES INCLUDE: Twenty Million Miles to Earth, The Three Worlds of Gulliver, Jason and the Argonauts, The First Men in the Moon, One Million Years B.C., The Valley of Gwangi, The Golden Voyage of Sinbad, Sinbad and the Eye of the Tiger, Clash of the Titans (co. prod., special effects).

HART, HARVEY: Director. b. Canada, 1928. Began career on TV in native country then went to Hollywood.
PICTURES INCLUDE: Bus Riley's Back in Town, Sullivan's Empire, The Sweet Ride, Fortune and Men's Eyes.

HARTFORD, K.: Executive. b. New York, July 5, 1922. Graduate Univ. Cincinnati, Los Angeles City college. Active in Film Financing, co-production, packaging. Executive of Hartford Industries, Latin American Development & Investment Co., Western International. Has offices in 8 countries.

HARTMAN, DAVID: Actor. b. Pawtucket, R.I., May 19. e. Duke Univ. Was 2nd lt. in Air Force; entered Amer. Acad. of Dramatic Arts in N.Y. Appeared in off-Bdwy. musicals and summer stock; Bdwy. debut in Hello, Dolly!
PICTURES INCLUDE: The Island at the Top of the World.
TV: World Premiere: I Love a Mystery, Nobody's Perfect, Ballad of Josie. Series: The Virginian, The Bold Ones, Lucas Tanner, Good Morning, America.

HARTMAN, ELIZABETH: Actress. b. Youngstown, O., December, 1943. e. Carnegie Tech.
PICTURES INCLUDE: Patch of Blue, The Group, You're a Big Boy Now, The Fixer, The Beguiled, Walking Tall.

HARTMAN, PAUL: Actor, dancer, comedian. e. U. of Calif.; pr. Ferris Hartman. In show business since a child; toured West Coast with own vaude. act; toured Asia & Europe; worked in supper clubs.
BROADWAY: Red Hot & Blue, You Never Know, Of Thee I Sing, Angel in the Wings, Tickets Please, Ballyhoo, Topnotchers, Keep 'Em Laughing, All for Love, Showboat, The Pajama Game, Drink to Me Only, What A Killing, A Funny Thing Happened on the Way to the Forum.
PICTURES INCLUDE: 45 Fathers, Sunny, Higher & Higher, Man on a Tightrope, Inherit the Wind, The Thrill of It All, Soldiers in the Rain, Those Calloways, How To Succeed in Business Without Really Trying, The Reluctant Astronaut, Luv.
TV: Our Town, Petrified Forest, 12 Angry Men, Good Old Charlie Faye, Alfred Hitchcock, Ben Casey, The Defenders, Have Gun, Will Travel, Mary Martin Easter Show, Hazel, Ozzie & Harriet, Chrysler Thea., Pride of the Family, Andy Griffith Show, Petticoat Junction, Mayberry RFD, The Hartmans At Home.
AWARDS: Tony Award, Comedian of the Year; Donaldson Award, Best Comedian on Broadway; Newspaper Guild Page One Award, Best Night Club Act; Lambs Club Award, contribution to Amer. Theatre; Daily Mirror Night Club Award; Critics Award for Best Comedian in Musical; Variety Poll Award, 1947–48.

HARTZ, JIM: TV Newsman and Panelist. b. Feb. 3, 1940, Tulsa, Okla. Pre-med student at University of Tulsa, where worked in spare time as reporter for radio station KRMG. In 1963 left studies for career as newsman and joined KOTV in Tulsa. In 1964 moved to NBC News in New York, acting as reporter and anchorman. In 1974 became co-host of Today Show, joined Barbara Walter.

HARVEY, ANTHONY: Director. b. London, Eng., June 3, 1931. Royal Academy of Dramatic Arts; two yrs. as actor. Ent. m.p. ind. 1949 with Crown Film Unit.
PICTURES INCLUDE: Private's Progress, Brothers-in-

Law, Man in the Cocked Hat, Carlton Brown of the F.O., I'm Alright Jack, The Angry Silence, The Millionairess, Lolita, The L-Shaped Room, Dr. Strangelove, Spy Who Came In From the Cold, The Whisperers, Directed Dutchman; Dir. The Lion in Winter, They Might Be Giants, Eagles' Wing, Players, The Abdication, The Glass Menagerie, Richard's Things.
TV: The Disappearance of Aimee.

HARVEY, WALTER F.W.: Cinematographer, director. b. London, England, Feb. 9, 1903; e. Germany. In 1921 with Anfa Laboratory, Germany; then to Decla-Bioscope, Neubabelsberg in 1922; until 1928 with UFA and subsidiaries as asst. to such photographers as Carl Hoffman, Carl Freund, Franz Planer, Carl Hoesch, F.A. Wagner, etc. To England as asst. to Charles Rosher, Dupont Prods., Elstree, 1928; m.p. photographer 1930; dir.-photog. G.B. on Ministry of Inf. War Office & Admiralty Training m.p., 1941; children's m.p., 1946; dir. of photography Exclusive Films Ltd.
PICTURES INCLUDE: Crime at Blossoms, Badgers Green, Dark Street, Cloudbust, Case for P.C. 49, Death of An Angel, Whispering Smith Hits London, Last Page, Wings of Danger, Stolen Face, Lady in the Fog, Gambler and the Lady, Flannagan Boy, Noose for a Lady, Saint Returns, Blood Orange, Thirty-six Hours, House on the Lake, Face the Music, Murder by Proxy, Life with the Lyons, Five Days, The Stranger, Third Party Risk, Mask of Dust, Men of Sherwood Forest, Lyons in Paris, Glass Cage, Break in the Circle, Quartermass Experiment, Prison Story, You Pay Your Money, West of Suez, Morning Call, Kill Her Gently, Spy in the Sky, Broth of a Boy, Naked Fury, Trouble with Eve, The Hand, Jackpot, The Man Who Couldn't Walk, Operation Cupid, Strictly Confidentially, Transatlantic, Stranger in Town, Part Time Wife, The Twisted Tape, Jungle Street, Out of The Fog, Murder In Eden, Three Spare Wives, Spanish Sword, Danger By My Side, Night of The Prowler, Echo of Diana, Shadow of Fear, The HiJackers, Beware of the Dog, Boy With a Flute, The Runaways Delayed Flight, Scales of Justice series.
TV: The Cheaters, Richard the Lionheart, The Saint, Gideon's Way, The Baron, The Champions, The Saint, The Avengers, commercials and documentaries.

HARWOOD, RONALD: Writer. b. Cape Town, South Africa, 1934. To England to study acting at RADA, 1951.
TV: The Barber of Stamford Hill, Private Potter, Take a Fellow Like Me, The Lads, Convalescence, Guests of Honor, The Paris Trip, New Assistant, The Guests. Adapted several of the Tales of the Unexpected.
PICTURES INCLUDE: Barber of Stamford Hill, Private Potter (written with Casper Wrede), subsequently High Wind in Jamaica, Eye Witness, One Day in the Life of Ivan Denisovich, Operation Daybreak.

HASKIN, BYRON: Director. e. U. Calif., Berkeley. Cartoonist, San Francisco Daily News; later adv. man., traveling & photog. industrial pictures. Entered m.p. ind. as cameraman Pathe; Internatl. Newsreel; then asst. dir., Selznick, 1920; later asst. cameraman, Marshall Neilan, Sidney Franklin, Raoul Walsh; in 1923 first cameraman, Holubar; then made own prods. To Warner, filming John Barrymore pictures.
PICTURES INCLUDE: Ginsborg the Great, The Siren.
Dir.: Too Late for Tears, Man-Haters of Kumson, Treasure Island, Warpath, Tarzan's Peril, Silver City, Denver and Rio Grande, War of the Worlds, His Majesty O'Keefe, Naked Jungle, Long John Silver, Conquest of Space, The Power.

HASSANEIN, SALAH M.: Executive. b. Suez, Egypt, e. British School, Alexandria, Egypt, Nat'l Bank of Egypt, Cairo, 1939–42. Asst. division mgr. Middle East, 20th-Fox, Cairo, Egypt, 1942–44; U.S. armed forces, 1945–47; usher, asst. mgr., Rivoli Theatre, N.Y., 1947–48. Film buyer, booker, oper. v.p. U.A. Eastern Theas., 1948–59; pres. 1960; exec. v.p. U.A. Theatre Circuit, Inc. 1960; pres. Todd-AO Corp., 1963.

HASTINGS, DON: Performer; b. Apr. 1, 1934, Bklyn., N.Y., e. Professional Children's Sch.; on B'way in Life With Father, I Remember Mama, Summer and Smoke, etc.; on various radio shows, video ranger on Capt. Video since 1949, also occasional TV guest appearances.

HATFIELD, BOBBY: Performer. b. Beaver Dam, Wis., Aug. 10, 1940. e. Long Beach State Coll. Mem., Righteous Bros. recording team.
TV: Shindig, The Danny Kaye Show, Ed Sullivan Show.
PICTURES INCLUDE: Beach Ball, Swingin' Summer.

HATFIELD, HURD: Actor. b. New York City; e. Morristown prep, Horace Mann; Riverdale Acad.; Columbia U., Chekhov Drama School, Devonshire, Eng., on dramatic stage, Lower Depths, Twelfth Night, Cricket on the Hearth, King Lear, then Screen debut Dragon Seed, The Picture of Dorian Gray, 1943–44.
PICTURES INCLUDE: The Unsuspected, Joan of Arc, Destination Murder, Tarzan & Slave Girl, Left-Handed Gun, Mickey One, Harlow, Von Richtofen and Brown.
N.Y. stage 1952, Venus Observed. TV appearances.

HATFIELD, TED: Executive. b. Wilton Junction, Iowa, Aug. 26, 1936. e. Hot Springs, Ark., U.S. Army-NCO Academy (1954). Entered industry as usher, ABC Paramount Theatre, Hot Springs, Ark (1949) continuously employed by ABC Theatres as doorman, ass't manager, manager, city manager (1949–1967). Joined MGM Studios as assistant exploitation director (1967) assistant national advertising coordinator (1970) national advertising coordinator (1971).
MEMBER: Variety Club; Motion Picture Pioneers; past v.p., Louisiana Jr. Chamber of Commerce; Past pres. Ark.-La.-Miss. Advertising Club; Great Western Boy Scout Council of L.A.

HATHAWAY, HENRY: Director. b. Sacramento, Calif., Mar. 13, 1898. Child star with American Film Co., 1908; property boy Universal, 1914–17; juvenile roles; gunnery instructor in U.S. Army, 1918–19; with Morris Audit Co.; property man for Frank Lloyd, 1921; to India with Paul Bern; dir. Westerns for Paramount, then features.
PICTURES INCLUDE: Come On, Marines, Trail of the Lonesome Pine; Go West, Young Man; Souls at Sea, Spawn of the North, Johnny Apollo, Ten Gentlemen from West Point, House on 92nd Street, Nob Hill, The Dark Corner, 13 Rue Madeleine, Kiss of Death, Call Northside 777, Down to Sea in Ships, The Black Rose, You're in the Navy Now, Fourteen Hours, Rawhide, Desert Fox, Diplomatic Courier; seq., O. Henry's Full House; Niagara, White Witch Doctor, Prince Valiant, Garden of Evil, The Racers, Bottom of the Bottle, 23 Paces to Baker Street, Legend of the Lost, Woman Obsessed, North to Alaska, Circus World, The Sons of Katie Elder; prod., dir., Nevada Smith, True Grit, Raid on Rommel, Hangup.

HAUER, RUTGER: Actor. b. Breukelen, Netherlands, Jan. 23, 1944. Stage actor in Amsterdam for six years. Motion picture debut in Turkish Delight, 1975.
PICTURES INCLUDE: The Wilby Conspiracy, Keetje Tippl'e, Max Havelaar, Soldier of Orange, Pastorale 1943, Femme Entre Chien et Loup, Mysteries, Nighthawks.

HAVELOCK-ALLAN, SIR ANTHONY: Baronet; film producer, born Durham County, England; e. Charterhouse, Switzerland; 1924–1929 Artists and Recording Manager, Brunswick Grammophone Co. London & Vox AG. Berlin; 1930 Advertising Dept. "Evening Standard"; 1930–1933 presented Cabaret-Ciro's Club, London; 1933 entered Films as Casting Director and Producer's Assistant; 1935–1937 produced 23 Quota Films for Paramount; 1938–1940 produced for Pinebrook Ltd. and Two Cities Films; 1941 Associate producer to Noel Coward; 1942 with David Lean and Ronald Neame formed Cineguild; 1942–1947 Producer, associate Producer or in charge of production for Cineguild; 1949 formed Constellation Films, independent company producing for Rank Org. and British Lion; from 1948–1951 Member of the Cinematographic Films Council and the National Film Production Council; also Member of Home Department's Committee on Employment of Children in Entertainment; 1952 Chairman of the British Film Academy; 1958 formed with John Brabourne and Daniel Angel British Home Entertainment; 1962 and 1963 Chairman of the Council of the Society of Film and Television Arts (B.A.F.T.A.); Member of National Film Archive Committee; from 1958–1965 a Governor of the British Film Institute and Chairman of the Institute's Production Committee; 1970 Member of the U.S. Academy of Motion Pictures Arts & Sciences.
PICTURES INCLUDE: This Man Is News, This Man in Paris, Lambeth Walk, Unpublished Story, From the Four Corners (documentary produced and directed), Brief Encounter (shared Academy script nomination), Great Expectations (shared Academy script nomination), Take My Life, Blanche Fury, Shadow of the Eagle, Never Take No for an Answer, Young Lovers, (director Anthony Asquith), Orders to Kill, (director Anthony Asquith), Brendon Behan's The Quare Fellow, An Evening with The Royal Ballet (directed two ballets); (for Television only): National Theatre's "Uncle Vanya"; Olivier's "Othello," Zeffirelli's "Romeo and Juliet," David Lean's "Ryan's Daughter."

HAVOC, JUNE: Actress. r.n. Hovick. b. Seattle, Washington. Sister of Gypsy Rose Lee, actress. Made film bow when two in Hal Roach prod. Danced with Anna Pavlova troupe, then entered vaudeville in own act. Later, joined Municipal Opera Company, St. Louis, and appeared in Shubert shows. To Hollywood, 1942.
PICTURES INCLUDE: Hello Frisco, Hello; No Time for Love, Sweet and Low Down, Brewster's Millions, Intrigue, Gentleman's Agreement; Red, Hot and Blue; Chicago Deadline, Once a Thief, Follow the Sun, Lady Possessed, Can't Stop the Music.
PLAYS: Pal Joey, Sadie Thompson, Mexican Hayride, Dunnigan's Daughter, Dream Girl, Affairs of State, The Ryan Girl, The Infernal Machine, The Beaux Strategem.
American Shakespeare Festival, Stratford, 1958; The Skin of Our Teeth, Tour for U.S. Dept. of St., 1961; wrote Marathon 33.
TV: Anna Christie, The Bear, Cakes and Ale, Daisy Mayme, The Untouchables; co-owner, Willy.

HAWN, GOLDIE: Actress. b. Washington, D.C., November 21, 1945; was a professional dancer and made TV debut dancing on an Andy Griffith Special; TV acting debut, "Good Morning World" followed by "Laugh-In." Screen debut: Catus Flower.
PICTURES INCLUDE: There's A Girl In My Soup, Dollars, Butterflies Are Free, The Sugarland Express, The Girl from Petrovka, Shampoo, The Duchess and the Dirtwater Fox, Foul Play, Private Benjamin (also prod.), Seems Like Old Times.

HAYDEN, STERLING: Actor. b. Montclair, N.J.; e. Browne and Nichols School, Cambridge, Mass. In 1937: cruised around world as mate. In 1939: captain of the "Aries" owned by Warner Buxton.
PICTURES INCLUDE: Virginia, Bahama Passage, Blaze of Noon, El Paso, Manhandled, The Asphalt Jungle, Flaming Feather, Journey Into Light, Denver and Rio Grande, Golden Hawk, Hellgate, Flat Top, The Star, Take Me to Town, So Big, Crime Wave, Arrow in the Dust, Prince Valiant, Johnny Guitar, Naked Alibi, Suddenly, Battle Taxi, Timberjack, Eternal Sea, Last Command, Shotgun, Top Gun, The Killing, Hard Contract, The Godfather, The Long Goodbye, King of the Gypsies, Winter Kills, Nine to Five, Gas.

HAYDN, RICHARD: Director, actor. In 1941: Charley's Aunt. In 1942: Are Husbands Necessary?, Thunder Birds. In 1943: Forever and a Day.
PICTURES INCLUDE: The Beginning or the End, Ball of Fire, Sitting Pretty, The Lost World, Five Weeks in a Balloon, Clarence the Crosseyed Lion, Bullwhip Griffin, And Then There Were None, Adventure, The Green Years, Cluny Brown, The Late George Apley, Foxes of Harrow, Singapore, Forever Amber, (dir. actor) Miss Tatlock's Millions; (dir.) Mr. Music, Dear Wife, Merry Widow, You Belong to Me, Never Let Me Go, Money from Home, Her Twelve Men, Jupiter's Darling, Toy Tiger, Please Don't Eat the Daisies, Mutiny On The Bounty, Sound of Music, retired in 1965.

HAYES, HELEN: Actress, r.n. Helen H. Brown. b. Wash., D.C., Oct. 10, 1901; e. Sacred Heart Convent, Wash.; wife of Charles MacArthur, writer. Started film career in 1931.
PLAYS INCLUDE: What Every Woman Knows, Coquette, Petticoat Influence, The Good Fairy, Mary of Scotland, Victoria Regina, Harriet, Happy Birthday, Wisteria Trees, Mrs. McThing, Skin of Our Teeth, Glass Menagerie, The Show Off, Front Page (revivals).
PICTURES INCLUDE: Arrowsmith, The White Sister, Another Language, Night Flight, A Farewell to Arms, Academy Award 1931–32 (The Sin of Madelon Claudet), My Son, John, Main Street to Broadway, Anastasia, Airport (AA, 1970), Herbie Rides Again, One of Our Dinosaurs Is Missing, Candleshoe.
TV: Twelve Pound Look, Mary of Scotland, Dear Brutus, Skin of Our Teeth, Christmas Tie, Drugstore on a Sunday Afternoon, Omnibus.

HAYES, JOHN MICHAEL: Writer. b. Worcester, Mass., May 11, 1919; e. University of Massachusetts, 1941.
PICTURES INCLUDE: Red Ball Express, Thunder Bay, Torch Song, War Arrow, Rear Window, To Catch a Thief, Trouble with Harry, It's A Dog's Life, Man Who Knew Too Much, The Matchmaker, Peyton Place, But Not for Me, Butterfield 8, The Children's Hour, Where Love Has Gone, The Chalk Garden, Judith, Nevada Smith.

HAYES, PETER LIND: Actor: m. Mary Healy, prof.
PICTURES INCLUDE: Million Dollar Legs, All Women Have Secrets, These Glamour Girls, Seventeen, Dancing on a Dime, Playmates, Seven Days Leave.
Was radio singer, actor, vaudeville, night clubs. Producer, Grace Hayes Lodge Review: on TV show with Mary Healy; 5000 Fingers of Dr. T. Recent films: Once You Kiss A Stranger.

HAYES, RICHARD: Film censor. b. Bruree, Co. Limerick, Ireland; e. Catholic U. Medical Sch., Dublin, 1908; D. Litt. (Honoris Causa), Natl. U. Ireland, 1940. Practised prof. of medicine & surgery until 1940. In Irish Insurrection, 1916; member of Dail Eireann (Irish Parliament) 1918–23 Dir. Abbey Theat., Dublin. M.R.I.A. Author various books (Ireland and Irishmen in the French Revolution, Irish Swordsmen of France, The Last Invasion of Ireland, Old Irish Links with France). In 1940 apptd. Film Censor for Eire.

HAYS, ROBERT: Actor. b. Bethesda, MD, July 24. e. Grossmont College, San Diego State. Left school to join Old Globe Theatre for five years. Cast in ABC series, Harry O.
PICTURES: Airplane, Take This Job and Shove It!
TELEVISION: Series: Love Boat, Laverne & Shirley, Most Wanted, Wonder Woman, Angie. Movie: California Gold Rush. Mini-series: Will Rogers: Champion of the People.

HAYTER, JAMES: Actor. b. Lanoula, India, April 23, 1907; e. Dollar Acad.; Scotland; Royal Acad. Dram. Art, London. In Royal Armored Corps, World War II. On prof. stage from 1925, tour. repertory; London debut 1936 in The Composite Man. Screen debut, 1936.

PICTURES INCLUDE: Morning Departure (Operation Disaster), Trio, Robin Hood, Crimson Pirate, Pickwick Papers, Great Game, Will Any Gentleman, Always a Bride, A Day to Remember, Beau Brummell, For Better For Worse, Land of the Pharaohs, Touch and Go, Port Afrique, Keep It Clean, Seven Waves Away (Abandon Ship), Sail Into Danger, The Heart Within, The Captain's Table, The Boy on the Bridge, The 39 Steps, Carry On Admiral, Go To Blazes, Out of The Fog, Stranger in the House, Oliver, A Challenge to Robin Hood, Song of Norway, David Copperfield, Cause for Alarm, Horror of Frankenstein, Burke & Hane, The Loving Game.

STAGE: My Fair Lady 1959–66, A Woman of No Importance, Oh Clarence, Yellow Sands, Pride and Prejudice, Pygmalion, 1966; A Woman of No Importance, 1967; The Duel, 1968; Forget Me Not Lane, 1971; The Grouse Moor, 1973; There Goes The Bride, 1976; Babes In The Wood, 1974; Gaslight, Rain, She Stoops To Conquer, 1977; Crime & Punishment, 1978.

T.V. SERIES: Huntingtower, The Moonstone, Last Chronicles of Barsett, The Flaxman Boys, The Onedin Line, For the Love of Ada, Doctor at Large, Dr. Finlay's Casebook, Old Newsom, Under The Same Sun, Are You Being Served.

HAYWARD, LOUIS: Actor. b. Johannesburg, So. Africa, March 19. On English stage in Dracula, Vinegar Tree, Another Language, Conversation Piece. The Ringer; to N.Y., 1935; won N.Y. Critics Award in first show, Point Valaine; m.p. debut in Self-Made Lady. U.S. Marines, W.W. II; owner Assoc. Film Artists.

PICTURES INCLUDE: Flame Within, Anthony Adverse, Duke of West Point, Man in the Iron Mask, My Son, My Son, Son of Monte Cristo, And Then There Were None, Ruthless, Black Arrow, Walk a Crooked Mile; Road Show, Camelot, Pirates of Capri, Fortunes of Captain Blood, Lady and the Bandit, Son of Dr. Jekyll, Lady in the Iron Mask; Captain Pirate, The Saint's Girl Friday, Duffy of San Quentin, Royal African Rifles, Search for Bridey Murphy, The Christmas Kid, Chuka.

TV: The Lone Wolf series, Climax, Studio One, Schlitz Playhouse, Pursuers, The Survivors.

HAYWORTH, RITA: Actress. r.n. Margarita Cansino; b. New York City, Oct. 17, 1919; e. private schools. Danced at Foreign Club in Tiajuana, Mexico, then at Agua Caliente. Started screen career 1935 with Dante's Inferno. Formed prod. co. with Dick Haymes, Crystal Bay Prods., 1955.

PICTURES INCLUDE: Meet Nero Wolfe, Who Killed Gail Preston?, There's Always a Woman, Convicted, The Lone Wolf, Spy Hunt, Gilda, Cover Girl, Tonight and Every Night, Down to Earth, Lady from Shanghai, Loves of Carmen, Affair in Trinidad, Salome, Miss Sadie Thompson, Fire Down Below, Pal Joey, Separate Tables, They Came to Cordura, Story on Page One, The Happy Thieves, Circus World, Money Trap, The Poppy Is Also a Flower, The Naked Zoo, Road to Salina, The Wrath of God.

HAZEN, JOSEPH H.: Attorney b. Kingston, N.Y., May 23, 1898; e. George Washington U. & Law School. Formerly assoc. as member of firm, Thomas and Friedman. In 1939 member ind. com. in discussions with Commerce Dept. Member com. which negotiated consent decree. Member ind. Committee of Six, lawyers to study and reorganize ind. activities. Mem. War Activities Committee. In 1944 resigned as v.p. and dir., Warner Bros. to join Hal Wallis Prods. as pres., 1944–48; pres. Wallis-Hazen, Inc., Tillco. dissolved, June 1953; photoplay prod., Hal B. Wallis, Paramount Pictures Corp., since 1953. Dir. USO Camps, Inc., M.P.A.A.

HEAD, EDITH: Chief designer. Universal. b. Los Angeles, Calif., October 28. e. Univ. of Calif., A.B.; Stanford Univ., M.A.; Otis Art School and Chouinard Art Sch., L.A. Taught French, Spanish and Art, Hollywood Sch. for Girls and Bishops Sch. at La Jolla, Calif.

PICTURES INCLUDE: The Heiress (Acad. Award B&W, 1949), All About Eve (Acad. Award B&W, 1950), Samson and Delilah (Acad. Award Tech., 1950), A Place In The Sun (Acad. Award B&W, 1951), The Greatest Show On Earth, Carrie, Roman Holiday (Acad. Award B&W, 1953), Sabrina (Acad. Award B&W, 1954), The Rose Tattoo, To Catch A Thief, The Ten Commandments, The Proud and Profane, Funny Face, The Facts of Life (Acad. Award B&W, 1969), Pepe, Pocketful of Miracles, Tell Them Willie Boy Is Here, Airport, Butch Cassidy and The Sundance Kid, The Sting. (Acad. Award 1973) Author of The Dress Doctor and How to Dress for Success; 1967, with Universal Studios.

HEALEY, MYRON: Actor, writer, dialogue director. b. Petaluma, Calif., e. East Central State Teachers Coll., Okla.; bombardier, navigator, World War II.

PICTURES INCLUDE: Monsoon, Son of Belle Starr, The Longhorn, African Manhunt, Gang Busters, Man from Bitter Ridge, Cattle Queen of Montana, Rage at Dawn, Shoot Out at Medicine Bend.

Writer on several s.p.; TV shows. Stars in numerous live and filmed TV shows.

HEALY, JOHN T.: Executive. e. Brooklyn Coll. Taught economics and was associated with Lehigh Valley Industries and General Food Corp. before joining ABC, Inc. in 1970 as assoc. dir. of corp. planning. Named dir. of planning and develop. June, 1972. Elected v.p., planning and admin. of ABC Leisure Group, March, 1974; elected vice pres. of corporate planning, Feb., 1976.

HEARD, JOHN: Actor. b. 1947. Married, actress Margot Kidder. Career began at Organic Theatre, starring in Chicago & N.Y. productions of Warp. Other stage roles include Streamers, G.R. Point, Othello.

PICTURES INCLUDE: Between the Lines, On the Yard, Head Over Heels, Heartbeat, Cutter and Bone.

TELEVISION: The Scarlet Letter.

HEARD, PAUL F.: Producer. b. Olivia, Minn., Oct. 14, 1913; e. Lawrence Coll., 1929–31; U. of Minn., 1933–35. Production supvr., Visual Ed. Dept., U. of Minn., 1938–40; dir. of films, Methodist Church Hdqts., N.Y., 1940–42; Orientation Film Officer, Bureau of Personnel, U.S. Navy, Washington, 1942–45; nat'l exec. dir. Protestant Film Comm., N.Y., 1945–50; dir. of films. Broadcasting & Film Comm., Nat'l Council of Churches of Christ in U.S., 1950–52; pres., Paul F. Heard, Inc., m.p. & TV prod. co., 1952–63.

PICTURES INCLUDE: Kenji Comes Home, The Broken Mask, For Every Child, Hong Kong Affair, What's Your Trouble.

HECHT, HAROLD: Producer. b. New York City, June 1, 1907. New York stage, asst. late Richard Boleslavsky, dance dir. Screen: dance dir. Horsefeathers, She Done Him Wrong, Bottoms Up, many others; literary agt. Org. Norma Prod. with Burt Lancaster, 1947, and later other prod. companies now known as Hecht-Hill-Lancaster Companies.

PICTURES INCLUDE: The Flame and the Arrow, Ten Tall Men, First Time, Crimson Pirate, His Majesty O'Keefe, Apache, Vera Cruz, Marty (Academy Award, best picture, 1955), The Kentuckian, Trapeze, The Bachelor Party, Sweet Smell of Success, Run Silent Run Deep, Separate Tables, The Devil's Disciple, The Unforgiven, The Young Savages, Bird Man of Alcatraz, Taras Bulba, Wild and Wonderful, Flight From Ashiya, Cat Ballou, The Way West.

HECKART, EILEEN: Actress. b. Columbia, Ohio. e. Ohio State U., American Theatre Wing. m. Jack Yankee.

BROADWAY: Bad Seed, View from the Bridge.

TV: Kraft, Suspense, Philco Playhouse, The Web (CBS Playhouse). m.p. debut in Miracle in the Rain.

AWARDS: Daniel Blum and Outer Circle (Picnic), Foreign Press, and Donaldson, Oscar nom. and Film Daily Citation, (Bad Seed), TV Sylvania for the Haven, Variety Poll of N.Y. and Drama Critics (Dark at The Top of the Stairs); Emmy, (Save Me a Place at Forest Lawn).

PICTURES INCLUDE: Somebody Up There Likes Me, Bus Stop, Hot Spell, Heller in Pink Tights, My Six Loves, Up the Down Staircase, No Way to Treat a Lady, Butterflies Are Free, Zandy's Bride, The Hiding Place, Burnt Offerings.

STAGE: Bad Seed, Family Affair, Pal Joey, Invitation to a March, Everybody Loves Opal, Dark at the Top of the Stairs, And Things That Go Bump in the Night, You Know I Can't Hear You When the Water's Running, Too True to Be Good, Butterflies Are Free.

HEDRICK, A. EARL: Art director. b. Los Angeles, Calif., March 2, 1896; e. U. So. Calif. (Sch. Archit.), Beaux Art Sch. Design. Began as architect. Joined Paramount 1930, as art dir., 1933.

PICTURES INCLUDE: So Proudly We Hail, Wake Island, Lost Weekend, Cocoanut Grove, The Forest Rangers, Road to Rio, Fancy Pants, Mr. Music, Union Station, Great Lover, Here Comes the Groom, Detective Story, Somebody Loves Me, About Mrs. Leslie, Strategic Air Command, Far Horizons, You're Never Too Young, Proud and Profane, Teacher's Pet, But Not for Me, Michael O'Hare IV, Jory

TV: Bonanza series, The High Chaparral.

HEDWIG, GORDON W.: President, Nu-Art Films, Inc. b. Jersey City, N.J., April 27, 1913; p. William K. and Elsa Hedwig; e. Newtown high school, Rensselaer Polytechnic Inst., Lt., Signal Corp. World War II. Part-time work film lab., 1927–33; salesman, 1933–35. Started 16 mm. distribution in 1935 as Nu-Art Film Co., an individual enterprise and incorporated as Nu-Art Films, Inc., 1937. President NuArt Films, Inc., org. Telecast Films, Inc., org. in 1947 for TV film distribution. Sec. Theatre-on-films, Inc. Now active in all corporations, in TV & non theatrical.

HEFFNER, RICHARD D.: Executive. b. Aug. 5, 1925. e. Columbia Univ. Instrumental in acquisition of Channel 13 (WNET) as New York's educational tv station; served as its first general manager. Previously had produced and moderated Man of the Year, The Open Mind, etc. for commercial tv. Served as dir. of public affairs programs for WNBC-TV in N.Y. Was also dir. of special projects for CBS TV Network and editorial consultant to CBS, Inc. Editorial Board. Was radio newsman for ABC. Taught history at Univ. of Calif. at Berkeley, Sarah Lawrence College, Columbia Univ.

and New School for Social Research, N.Y. Served as American specialist in communications for U.S. Dept. of State in Japan, Soviet Union, Germany, Yugoslavia, Israel, etc. Now produces and moderates The Open Mind on Channel 11 (WPIX) in New York. Is Univ. Prof. of Communications and Public Policy at Rutgers University. In July, 1974 appt. chm. of MPAA Rating Board.

HEFFRON, RICHARD T.: Director.
PICTURES INCLUDE: Fillmore, Newman's Law, Trackdown, Futureworld, Outlaw Blues.
TV: The Morning After, Dick Van Dyke Special, I Will Fight No More Forever, Toma (pilot), Rockford Files (pilot).

HEIDER, FREDERICK: Producer. b. Milwaukee, Wis., April 9, 1917. e. Notre Dame U., Goodman Theatre, Chicago. Actor in Globe Theatre, Orson Welles' Mercury Theatre.
TV: Chesterfield Supper Club, Sammy Kaye's So You Want to Lead a Band, Frankie Carle Show, Jo Stafford Show, prod., writer, Paul Whitman Goodyear Revue, Billy Daniels Show, Martha Wright Show, Earl Wrightson Show, Club Seven, Mindy Carson Show; prod., ABC, Ted Mack Family Hour, Dr. I.Q., Miss America Pageant, Bishop Sheen's Life Is Worth Living, Voice of Firestone, Music for a Summer Night. Music for a Spring Night, The Bell Telephone Hour. (Warner Bros. TV) publisher, Television Quarterly, National Academy of Television Arts and Sciences. Presently syndicated columnist, Desert Post, Palm Desert, CA.

HEINECKE, RUTH C.: executive. b. New York, N.Y. Treas., Breitkopf & Hartel, Inc., N.Y., and treas., Breitkopf Pub., Inc. N.Y., 1914–26; v.p., Assoc. Music Pub., Inc., N.Y., 1927–29; treas., SESAC Inc. 1930.

HELLER, FRANKLIN: Producer-director. b. Dover, N.J.; Carnegie Inst. of Tech., B.A., 1934. Actor, 1934–36; stage mgr., Sam Harris-Max Gordon Prods., 1936–44; exec. prod., USO shows N.Y., 1944–45; prod. & dir., Paramount, 1945–47; dir., summer stock, 1947–48; prod. & dir., CBS TV, 1949–54; exec., prod. and dir. Goodson-Todman Prods., 1954–69; exec. prod. Protocol Prods., 1969–72 Literary Representative 1972. Dirs. Guild of America, Nat'l bd. 1965–77; Treas. 1965–69; Sec. 1970–73; Chr. Publications 1966–76.
TV SHOWS: What's My Line?, Beat the Clock, The Front Page, The Web, Danger, To Tell the Truth, I've Got a Secret.

HELLER, HUGH: Executive. b. Fargo, N.D. e. San Jose State Coll. Prod.-agent, for MCA; asst. exec. prod., George Gobel Show; prog. consultant to CBS, other networks; winner of IBA and AAW awards since 1963; clients incl.: Hamm's Beer, Folger's Coffee, Dial Soap, Signal Oil, Bargermeister Beer; pres., Heller Ferguson and Heller Corp.

HELLER, PAUL M.: Producer. b. N.Y.C. Sept. 25, 1927. e. Hunter Coll., Drexel Inst. of Technology. President, Sequoia Pictures, Inc. Studied engineering until entry into U.S. Army as member of security agency, special branch of signal corps. Left Army and went into fine arts and theatre. Worked as set designer (Westport, East Hampton, Palm Beach) and in live TV and then on theatrical films. Debut as film producer, David and Lisa (1963). From 1964 to 1969 was president of MPO Pictures Inc. Joined Warner Bros. as prod. exec., 1970. In 1972 founded Sequoia Pictures, Inc. with Fred Weintraub. Now pres. of Paul Heller Prods. Inc.
PICTURES INCLUDE: David & Lisa, The Eavesdropper, Secret Ceremony, Enter the Dragon, Truck Turner, Golden Needles, Dirty Knight's Work, Outlaw Blues, The Pack, The Promise, First Monday in October.

HELLER, WILSON B.: Publicist. b. Omaha, Neb., Aug. 1, 1893; e. U. of Mo., 1914. Free-lance pub. 1922 to 1945 maintaining own office, L.A.; clients, mainly m.p. and radio players, some prod. cos. Was long sec'y & treas. of Wampas; permanent secy., Pioneer Publicists; mgr. owner of College Survey Bureau since 1912; club and college lectures and Commencement addressing; publ., author, Annual, College Fraternities & Sororities Comparisons office; 1574 S. Hayworth, L.A. Calif. 90035. Retired 1970.

HELLMAN, JEROME: Producer. b. New York City. e. N.Y.U. Joined ad dept. of New York Times then went to William Morris Agency as apprentice. Made Asst. in TV dept. Worked as agent for Jaffe Agency. After hiatus in Europe joined Ashley-Steiner Agency (later IFA) where clients included Franklin Schaffner, Sidney Lumet, George Roy Hill, John Frankenheimer. Functioned as TV prod., including Kaiser Aluminum Hour. Left to form own agency, Ziegler, Hellman and Ross. Switched to feature prod. with The World of Henry Orient in 1964.
PICTURES INCLUDE: A Fine Madness, Midnight Cowboy (AA), The Day of the Locust, Coming Home, Promises in the Dark (also dir.).

HELLMAN, LILLIAN: Playwright. b. New Orleans, La.; e. New York U., Columbia. Hon. Degrees: M.A., Tufts College, 1950; LL.D., Wheaton College, 1962; LL.D., Rutgers, 1963; Brandeis, 1965; Mt. Holyoke, 1966; L.L.D. Yale University, 1974;

Smith College, 1974; New York University, 1974; Franklin and Marshall College, 1975; Columbia Univ., 1976. With Horace Liveright, Inc. (N.Y. pubs.) 1924–25; theat. playreader. 1927–30; book reviewer, 1925–28. Author: The Children's Hour, The Little Foxes, Watch on the Rhine, The Searching Wind, Another Part of the Forest, Autumn Garden, Toys In the Attic; adapt., The Lark, Montserrat, Candide, My Mother, My Father and Me. Member: Dramatists Guild, Academy of Arts & Letters, Am. Acad. of Arts & Sciences. Started film career 1935 (collab.) The Dark Angel. American Academy of Arts & Letters, Awarded Gold Medal for Drama from Institute of Arts & Letters, 1964; Awarded Brandeis U. Medal of Achievement, 1961. An Unfinished Woman, memoir, 1969, Winner of National Book Award, "The Collected Plays," 1972; "Pentimento," 1973; Scoundrel Time, 1976.
PICTURES INCLUDE: (s.p. based on The Children's Hour), These Three; (s.p.) Dead End, The Little Foxes, The North Star, The Searching Wind, The Children's Hour, The Chase (s.p.).

HELLMAN, MARCEL: Producer. b. Bucharest, Rumania. e. Commercial U., Berlin. Entered m.p. Ind. 1924 as managing dir. & prod., Nero Film A.G., Berlin (And Let It Be Light with Conrad Veidt). Later to England as prod. various Brit. cos.
PICTURES INCLUDE: Since 1936, The Amateur Gentleman, Accused, When Thief Meets Thief, Crime Over London, Double Crime in the Maginot Line (English version), Jeannie, Talk About Jacqueline, Secret Mission, They Met in the Dark, Wanted for Murder, Meet Me At Dawn, This Was a Woman, Happy Go Lovely, Duel in the Jungle, Let's Be Happy, North West Frontier, The Amorous Adventures of Moll Flanders. Exec. prod. Eng. version Mayerling.

HELPMANN, ROBERT SIR: CBE., Actor-dancer, producer, choreographer. b. Mount Gambier, Australia, April 9, 1909; e. Prince Alfred's Coll., Adelaide, Aus.; studied dancing under Laurent Novikoff. Solo dancer, 1923, Theatre Royal, Adelaide. London debut, 1931, at Sadler's Wells. Appeared on screen, 1942 in One of Our Aircraft Is Missing.
PICTURES INCLUDE: Henry V, Caravan, The Red Shoes, Tales of Hoffmann, Iron Petticoat, Big Money, The Quiller Memorandum, 55 Days at Peking, Chitty Chitty Bang Bang, Alice's Adventures in Wonderland, Don Quixote, The Mango Tree, Patrick.
London & N.Y. stage in Caesar and Cleopatra, Anthony and Cleopatra, The Millionaires, TV, U.S. and England; Old Vic Australian tour, 1955; Old Vic London, 1956–57, Nude with Violin, Royal Ballet, 1958–59; Australian tour. Prod.: The Sleeping Beauty, Paris 1960; The Ghost Sonata, BBC TV play, 1962; awarded CBE 1965; Australian of the Year, 1966; co-artistic dir. of Australian Ballet, 1965–1976. Knighted, 1968.

HELPRIN, MORRIS: Executive. b. Paterson, N.J., Dec. 20, 1904; p. Henrietta Helprin; e. Columbia. Assistant film critic, New York Times. General newspaper experience. Publicity, Par. L.I. Studio. Special writer, Samuel Goldwyn, Hollywood. Publicity, Fox Films. Publicity manager, UA. Joined Alexander Korda. In July, 1942 apptd. by Samuel Goldwyn as adv. & pub. repr. in the east. Asst. Chief Overseas M.P. Div. OWI; 1943, Spec. Film Mission OWI. In 1946 rejoined Alexander Korda; pres. London Film Prod. Inc. (America); v.p. Tricolore Films, Inc.; g.m. British Lion Film Corp. Ltd. U.S. rep. all Korda film interests.

HEMMINGS, DAVID: Actor, director. b. Guildford, England, 1941. Early career in opera. Ent. m.p. ind. 1956.
THEATRE: Dylan Thomas in Adventures in the Skin Trade.
TV: Auto Stop, The Big Toe, Out of the Unknown.
PICTURES INCLUDE: Some People, Two Left Feet, The System, The Eye of the Devil, Blow Up, Camelot, Charge of the Light Brigade, Only When I Larf, Barbarella, The Best House in London, Alfred The Great, The Walking Stick, Fragment of Fear, Unman Wittering and Zigo, Voices, Juggernaut, Crossed Swords. Directed: Running Scared, The 14, Quilp, Profundo Rosso, Islands In The Stream, The Squeeze, Murder by Decree.

HENDERSON, DICKIE: Entertainer, actor. Son of late Dick Henderson. Began career in 1933 as child actor in film Cavalcade. Since starred in London West End plays and musicals; variety and revue London Palladium; seven appearances in The Royal Variety Show; cabaret seasons at Savoy, London: and Talk of the Town, as well as New York, Las Vegas, Monaco, Hong Kong, Australia, Kenya, South Africa, Toronto. On TV starred in his own show for 12 years doing 120 shows; guested in every major British show; has done 50 TV shows in USA for Ed Sullivan, Jack Paar etc. London, Palladium, one-man show in UK. 1978: Series for ATV, 'I'm Dickie—That's Show Business.'

HENDERSON, DONALD A.: Executive. b. Melrose, Mass., March 19, 1903. e. Mass. Inst. Technology (1925). From 1925–35 in buying dept. Halsey-Stuart Co.; 1935–45, industrial dept., Lehman Bros. Joined 20th Century-Fox as treasurer and financial dir., later named treasurer and secretary. 1962 elected financial vice-pres., dir., 1968–71 Financial Consultant and Dir. former dir. Gen. Public Utilities Corp. and P. Lorillard Co.; trustee Athens College, Greece.

HENDERSON, MARCIA: Actress. b. Seattle, Wash., Dec. 11, 1934. e. Univ. of Arizona. Appeared in stock in west; m.p. debut in Delicate Delinquent, 1957.
PICTURES INCLUDE: Short Cut to Hell, I Married a Monster from Outer Space, G.I. Blues, Guns of Wyoming, Town Tamers, Dear Phoebe.
Many TV appearances.

HENDERSON, SKITCH: Mus. dir. r.n. Lyle Henderson, b. Birmingham, England. e. U. of Calif.
TV: Steve Allen Show, Tonight Show.

HENDRICKS, BILL L.: Owner/Director Bill Hendricks Films; writer, prod. dir. of documentaries & shorts and TV commercials. b. Grand Prairie, Texas, May 3; e. St. John's College. Formerly Warner Bros. Studio Publicity Director; special asst. to Jack Warner; and Director WB Cartoon Studios. Winner first Quigley Grand Award; mgr., Friendship Train & Merci Train. Author "Encyclopedia of Exploitation" with Howard Waugh, "Showmanship in Advertising" with Montgomery Orr; writer, prod., A Force in Readiness, (Academy Award). The John Glenn Story; The FBI, Seapower, The Land We Love, A Free People, Top Story, A World of Pleasure, Red Nightmare, Star Spangled Revue, This is Eucom, An American Legend, Scenes to Remember, Freedom and You, Jobs, Wonderful World of Warner, Global Marine; Football Safety; An American Partnership, Free Enterprise, Today's Demand, Tomorrow's Challenge, That's Us in the USA, A Special Day.

HENDRY, IAN: Actor. b. Ipswich, Eng., 1931.
TV: Probation Officer, Beyond the Horizon, Afternoon of a Nymph, Ben Spray, A Suitable Case for Treatment, The Avengers, Joy, Police Surgeon, Lotus Eaters.
PICTURES INCLUDE: In the Nick, Live Now, Pay Later, The Girl in The Headlines, This is my Street, The Beauty Jungle, The Hill, The Southern Star, The Internecine File, Get Carter, The Assassin, The Birch, Theatre of Blood.

HENKIN, HOWARD, H.: Executive writer, producer, director. b. New York, Sept. 13, 1926. e. U. of Delaware, 1944. U.S. Army, 1944–46, TV dept., Newell Emmett Agency, 1947–48; gen. mgr., TelePrompter, 1950–54; eastern sales mgr., Shamus Culhane Prod. 1955–57; Academy Pictures 1957–58; pres. HFH Productions, 1958; pres., Henkin Prods. Inc. & Henkin-Faillace Prods. Inc., 1962–1968; ch. of bd., Trio Prods., Inc., 1968; pres., Dot Enterprises, Ltd., 1981.

HENNING, LINDAY KAY: Actress, singer. b. Toluca Lake, Calif. Sept. 16, 1944. e. San Fernando Valley State College, Stage Theatre work in Carousel, Brigadoon, Best Foot Forward, Gidget, Rebel Without a Cause, Bus Stop, Sound of Music, Generation, Enter Laughing, High Button Shoes.
PICTURES INCLUDE: Bye Bye Birdie.
TV: Mr. Ed, Dobie Gillis, P.J., Petticoat Junction

HENNING, PAUL: TV producer-writer. b. Independence, Mo., Sept. 16, 1911. e. Kansas City School of Law. grad. 1932. Radio singer and disc jockey. Also acted, ran sound effects, sang, wrote scripts. To Chicago 1937–38, to write Fibber McGee and Molly. w. Don Quinn. To Hollywood as writer for Rudy Vallee, 1939. Wrote scripts for Burns and Allen 10 years, including transition radio to TV. In 1953 wrote, produced live and film shows for Dennis Day. Created, wrote, produced Bob Cummings Show, 1954–59. Wrote Beverly Hillbillies, 1962 to date. Created, prod. wrote Petticoat Junction. Exec. prod. Green Acres series. Wrote motion pictures, Lover Come Back, Bedtime Story.

HENREID, PAUL: Actor, director. b. Trieste, Italy, 1908; son of Baron Carl von Henreid. e. Maria Therese Acad. Inst. Graphic Arts, Vienna. With book pub. taking night courses at Konservatorium, dramatic arts school in Vienna. In Max Reinhardt's Vienna Theat., then in Austrian films. On dramatic stage and in films among them Jersey Lily and Victoria Regina, London. Arrived in N.Y. 1940 for stage play Flight to the West. In Brit. film Night Train. In 1980 awarded Austrian Cross of Honor, 1st Class, for Science and Arts.
PICTURES INCLUDE: Joan of Paris, Now Voyager, Casablanca, Of Human Bondage, Song of Love, In Our Time, Devotion, Deception, Between Two Worlds, The Spanish Main, Conspirators, Rope of Sand, Last of the Buccaneers, Pardon My French, So Young—So Bad, Stolen face, Man in Hiding, Pirates of Tripoli; actor, dir., prod. For Men Only. Actor, dir., Acapulco, Ten Thousand Bedrooms, etc. Dir. of TV films for Revue Productions, Warner, Desilu, 4-Star, CBS, Screen Gems, Universal, 20th Century-Fox Studios, Actor; Holiday for Lovers, Never So Few, The Four Horsemen of The Apocalypse, The Great Spy Mission; dir., Live Fast Die Young, Take Five From Five, Deadringer, Blues For Lovers, actor. The Madwoman of Chaillot, Colors of Love, Exorcist II: The Heretic; dir., Bracken's World, dir., The Man and the City, 1972–73, "Don Juan in Hell" on major theatrical tour in the U.S. and Canada for 6 months.
TV: Film: Any Number Can Kill.

HENRY, BUCK: Actor, writer. e. Dartmouth College. Acted in Life with Father, tour, 1948; Fortress of Glass, Circle in the Square; Bernardine, Bwy; 1952–54, U.S. Army; No Time for Sergeants, Nat'l. Co.; The Premise, improvis. theatre, off-Bwy; TV's The Steve Allen Show, writer, performer; That Was the Week That Was, writer, performer.
TV: Garry Moore Show; Steve Allen Show; Get Smart, co-creator with Mel Brooks, story editor; producer of Captain Nice series, pilot for NBC-TV.
PICTURES INCLUDE: The Troublemaker; The Graduate, 1966 for Laurance Turman, (producer); Catch 22 (author & actor); Taking Off, Candy, The Owl and the Pussycat, What's Up, Doc?, The Day of the Dolphin (s.p.), The Man Who Fell to Earth, Heaven Can Wait (actor, co-s.p.), Gloria, First Family (s.p., dir., act.).

HENRY, FRED: Producer. b. L.A., Calif., May 30, USC Journalism and business administration; CBS-LA radio station KNX newscaster, writer; news, spec. events dir., KMPC-LA. Co-News commentator, CBS, Let's Talk Over the News; Served, U.S.N. Office of Naval Intelligence, Radio Relations Officer on Staff of Supreme Allied Commander, C-B-I Theatre, Admiral Lord Louis Mountbatten; officer, chg. short-wave broadcasting, AFRS, S.F., 1945; appointed news, spec. events dir., KLAC, Don Fedderson; prg. dir. asst. gen. mgr., prg. dir. combined radio-tv operations, KLAC; res. KLAC, Jan. 1954, as vice-pres., exec. prod., Don Fedderson Prod.; supv. prod.: The Millionaire, Do You Trust Your Wife, Betty White Show, Date With Angels, Liberace, Life with Elizabeth, Who Do You Trust; My Three Sons, 1960; Family Affair, 1966; To Rome With Love, 1969; Henry Fonda Show, 1970.

HENSON, JIM: Producer-Director-Writer. b. Greenville, Miss., Sept. 24, 1936. e. Univ. of Maryland. Early TV work with Washington station, appearing with puppets he built called The Muppets. Did commercials in Washington area, followed by bookings on Today, Tonight shows and Ed Sullivan Show. Followed with Sesame Street, The Muppet Show, and series of TV specials he produced and/or directed. Heads own production company, Henson Associates. First theatrical feature: The Muppet Movie, 1979. 1981: Great Muppet Capor.

HEPBURN, AUDREY: Actress. b. Brussels, May 4, 1929. Appeared in London plays; screen debut in Laughter in Paradise; on B'way in Gigi, Ondine; Star of Tomorrow, 1954.
PICTURES INCLUDE: One Wild Oat, Young Wives' Tales, Lavender Hill Mob, Secret People, Roman Holiday (Academy Award, best actress, 1953), Sabrina, War and Peace, Funny Face, Love in the Afternoon, Green Mansions, The Nun's Story, The Unforgiven, Breakfast at Tiffanys, Paris When it Sizzles, Charade, My Fair Lady; Two for the Road, Wait Until Dark, Robin and Marian, Bloodline, They All Laughed.
TV: Producers Showcase, Mayerling, 1957.

HEPBURN, KATHARINE: Actress. b. Hartford, Conn., Nov. 8, 1909. On stage in Death Takes a Holiday, Warrior's Husband, The Lake, Philadelphia Story, (film version 1940), As You Like It, Millionairess. Started screen career 1933 with A Bill of Divorcement; then Christopher Strong and won Academy Award same year for Morning Glory. On stage 1956 in Merchant of Venice, Taming of the Shrew, Measure for Measure, Coco.
PICTURES INCLUDE: Little Women, Spitfire, The Little Minister, Alice Adams, Sylvia Scarlett, Mary of Scotland, A Woman Rebels, Quality Street, Stage Door, Bringing Up Baby, Holiday, Woman of the Year, Keeper of the Flame, Dragon Seed, Without Love, Song of Love, State of the Union, Adam's Rib, Sea of Grass, African Queen, Pat and Mike, Summertime, Iron Petticoat, The Rainmaker, Desk Set, Suddenly Last Summer, Long Day's Journey Into Night, Guess Who's Coming to Dinner, Lion in Winter, The Madwoman of Chaillot, The Trojan Women, A Delicate Balance, Rooster Cogburn, Olly, Olly, Oxen Free, On Golden Pond.
TV: The Glass Menagerie, Love Among the Ruins.

HERALD, PETER: Executive. UCLA, BA. Supervisory production mgr., Columbia Pictures.
PICTURES INCLUDE: assoc. prod. Almost Angels, Magnificent Rebel, Miracle of the White Stallions, Waltz King, Emil and the Detectives, The Young Loner, prod. supr. There Was a Crooked Man, Soldier Blue; co-prod., Ballerina, assoc. prod. The Great Waltz, Assignment: Vienna, Crazy World of Julius Vrooder, Foul Play, Nightwing. Also: W.W. and the Dixie Dancekings, Mandingo, W.C. Fields and Me, Alex and the Gypsy, Silver Streak, Fire Sale, Star Wars.

HERBERT, HOLMES: Actor. b. Mansfield, Nottinghamshire, England, July 3, 1882; e. Rugby, England, First appearance on stage 1890, London; later with John Sanger circus, Robys Minstrels. F.R. Benson Co., in English provinces; also in many London prods.; on Amer. stage with Charles Frohman Co. Began m.p. career in The Terror 1928.
PICTURES INCLUDE: Gentlemen Prefer Blondes, Sporting Age, Madame X, The Kiss, Untamed, Dr. Jekyll

and Mr. Hyde (1931), The House of Rothschild, Captain Blood, Lloyds of London, Lancer Spy, British Intelligence, This Above All, Sherlock Holmes in Washington, The Verdict, The Swordsman, Singapore, The Brigand.

HERBUVEAUX, JULES: Executive. b. Utica, N.Y., October 2, 1897; e., Culver Military Academy, McGill U., Montreal; m. Jeannette McNulty. Professional musician, 1919–21; orchestra dir., 1921–32; orchestra dir. NBC, 1927–32. asst. prod. mgr., 1932–38; program mgr., central div., 1938–47; mgr. television, 1948–53; ass't gen. man., 1953, gen. mgr., 1954; v.p. and gen. mgr., 1955, v.p. Central Div.; Merchants and Manufacturers (Chicago); retired, NBC, 1962; communications consultant for Zenith Radio Corp., Chicago; retired Jan., 1972.

HERDER, W. ED: Producer. b. New York City. Univ. of Miami (BBA). Pres. and chm. of bd., Worldfilm Corp. Financial investor in many m.p. and t.v. prods.
PICTURES INCLUDE: Force of Impulse, Without Each Other, Black Cobra, Shoot, Never Too Young to Rock, The Liberian Move.
TELEVISION: Hollywood, The Magic Kingdom.

HERFEL, CHRIS.: Executive. b. Bklyn, N.Y., Sept. 5, 1927. e. Univ. of Delaware, 1944–45; N.Y. Univ., 1949. Studio mgr., prod., exec. prod., Transfilm-Carnvel, Inc., 1957–61; Asst. dir., MPO-TV, 1957; studio mgr., assoc. prod., ATV-Films, 1956–57; Asst. dir., dir., Army Pictorial Centre, 1950–56; v.p. chg. of prod. Wylde Films, Inc.

HERMAN, LEONARD WOOD: Editor, assoc. prod. b. Springfield, Ohio, Jan. 16, 1913. Managed theat. circuits, Iowa, Nebraska, 1931–36. With Universal in mailing, casting, projection, library cutting depts., 1938–42; in 1943 film ed. In 1945 to Monogram in same capacity.
PICTURES INCLUDE: Great Alaskan Mystery, Raiders of Ghost City, Mystery of the River Boat, Jungle Queen, The Master Key, Shanghai Cobra, Suspense, Swing Parade, Charlie Chan in Mexico, Vacation Days, and Louisiana (edit.), Ginger, Rocky (assoc. prod.); (ed.) Big Timber, Jack Slade.

HERMAN, NORMAN: Producer-Director. b. Newark, N.J. e. Rutgers Univ., N.Y. Univ. Was accountant in California; in 1955 switched to film ind., joining American Int'l Pictures. Headed AIP math. dept. 4 years, incl. prod., post-prod., labor negotiations, supervising story dept., etc. Now pres. of Zide-Herman Co., Inc.
PICTURES INCLUDE: All producer in some capacity except where noted as also directing and/or writing: Sierra Stranger, Tokyo After Dark (dir.), Hot Rod Girl, Hot Rod Rumble, Crime Beneath Seas, Look in any Window, Mondy Teeno (dir., co-s.p.), Glory Stompers, Three in the Attic, Bloody Mama, Pretty Boy Floyd, Dunwich, Three in the Cellar, Angle Unchained, Bunny O'Hare, Psych-Out, Killers Three, Frogs, Blacula, Legend of Hell House, Dirty Mary Crazy Larry.
TELEVISION: Writer: Robert Taylor Detectives, Iron Horse, Invaders, Adam 12, Lancer. Director-Producer: Hannibal Cobb, You Are the Judge.

HERMAN, PINKY: Journalist, songwriter. b. N.Y.C., Dec. 23, 1905; e. N.Y.U. Song writer; member, ASCAP. Counsel member, S.P.A.; writer, M.P. News, 1930; 1934; charter member, Songwriters Protective Assoc.; writer, M.P. Daily, 1935–43; columnist, Radio Daily, 1943–50; TV columnist for M.P. Daily. Retired, 1973.
SONGS INCLUDE: (collab.) Face the Sun, All Around the Town, Boom Ta Ra Ra, It Must Be LUV, Piano Teacher Song, Manhattan Merry Go Round, Lucky, I'm Still in Love With You, Havin' A Wonderful Time, Where Can You Be, Seven Days a Week, Texas Lullaby, Lighthouse in the Harbor, I'm Cuckoo Over You, It's a Coincidence, If I Had a Million Dollars, Masquerade of Love, Mademoiselle Hortensia, Come Back to Me My Love, Someday When Shadows Fall, Myrtle the Turtle & Flip the Frog, Cowboy Isn't Speaking to His Horse, Gotta Horse That Loves to Rhumba, Girl on My Grandfather's Shaving Mug, Definition Song, Got a Gal in a Town Way Out West, Sing Something Irish, Little Sweetheart of the Mountains, Make a Million, Music Sets Me Free, She's the Daughter of the Sweetheart of Sigma Chi, Who Wants Love, Good-Lookin' It's Good Lookin' at You, Carib Gold, What Makes the Rainbow, Right Across de Ribber, Shadows in the Moonlight, Bible My Mother Left to Me, Poor Little Doll, Little Bit O'Rhythmn in the Best of Us, Lovely Lady, When a Girl's In Love, Never Leave A Lady When She Loves You, Without You, That's The Way to Live, It's Time to Sing, Acapulco (By The Sea), Councilman; The Lambs.

HERSHEY, BARBARA: Actress. e. Hollywood H.S.; Screen debut in With Six You Get Eggroll.
PICTURES INCLUDE: Last Summer, The Liberation of Lord Byron Jones, The Baby Maker, The Pursuit of Happiness, Boxcar Bertha, Vrooder's Hooch, Diamonds, The Last Hard Men, The Stunt Man, Take This Job and Shove It.
TV: Gidget, The Monroes, The Farmer's Daughter, Run For Your Life, The Invaders, Daniel Boone, CBS Playhouse, Chrysler Theatre.

HERSKOVITZ, ARTHUR M.: Executive. b. Mukden, China. Nov. 28, 1920. e. CCNY, 1939. Joined RKO, scenario dept., 1939. U.S. Army, 1942–46; appt. mgr., RKO Radio Pictures of Peru, 1955; RKO Pict. Peru, 1958; Warner Bros., Peru, 1958–64; MGM, Panama, 1965–67; MGM rep. in Japan, 1968; Far East supvr., 1970; Joined National General Pictures, 1973 as foreign sls. mgr. In 1974 appt. dir. of sls., JAD Films Int'l.; named v.p., 1978; pres., 1979.

HERTZ, WILLIAM: Executive. Began theatre career in 1939; 1946 joined Fox West Coast Theatres; theatre mgr., booking dept.; 1965 appointed Los Angeles first-run district mgr.; promoted to Pacific Coast Division Mgr., National General Corp., 1967; v.p. Southern Pacific Div. Mgr., National General Theatres, Inc. 1971. Now with Mann Theatres as dir. of theatre operations.

HESSLER, GORDON: Producer, director. b. Berlin, Germany. e. Reading U., England; dir., vice pres., Fordel Films, Inc., 1950–58; dir., St. John's Story (Edinborough Film Festival), March of Medicine Series, Dr. Albert Lasker Award; story edit., Alfred Hitchcock Presents 1960–62; assoc. prod., dir., Alfred Hitchcock Hour, 1962; prod., Alfred Hitchcock Hour; prod., dir., Universal TV 1964–66.
PICTURES INCLUDE: The Woman Who Wouldn't Die, The Last Shot You Hear, The Oblong Box, Scream and Scream Again, Cry of the Banshee, Murders of the Rue Morgue, Sinbad's Golden Voyage, Medusa, Next Week Rio, Puzzle, Starlock.
TV: Alfred Hitchcock Presents, 1960–62; Alfred Hitchcock Hour, 1962–65; Run For Your Life, Convoy, Bob Hope Chrysler Show, 1964–66; ABC Suspense Movies of the Week, ABC Movies of the Week, 1973. Lucas Tanner, Night Stalker, Amy Prentis, Switch, 1974; Kung Fu, Sara, Hawaii Five O, 1975–76; Blue Knight; Wonder Woman.
Pilots: Tender Warriors, Chips, Thief.

HESTON, CHARLTON: Actor. b. Evanston, Ill., Oct. 4, 1924; e. Northwestern U. School of Speech, Radio, stage, TV experience. Following coll. served 8 yrs. 11th Air Force, Aleutians. After war, co-acted (leads) and dir. with wife, Thomas Wolfe Memorial Theatre, Asheville, N.C. in State of the Union, Glass Menagerie; member, Katharine Cornell's Co., during first year on Broadway; Anthony and Cleopatra, other Bway. plays, Leaf and Bogh, Cockadoodle Doo; Studio One (TV): Macbeth, Taming of the Shrew, Of Human Bondage, Julius Caesar, etc.
PICTURES INCLUDE: Dark City, Greatest Show on Earth, The Savage, Ruby Gentry, President's Lady, Pony Express, Arrowhead, Bad for Each Other, Naked Jungle, Secret of the Incas, Far Horizons, Lucy Gallant, Private War of Major Benson, Ten Commandments, The Maverick, Ben-Hur, Wreck of the Mary Deare, El Cid, The Pigeon That Took Rome, 55 Days at Peking, Major Dundee, The Agony & The Ecstasy, The War Lord, The Greatest Story Ever Told, Khartoum, The Battle Horns, Planet of the Apes, Beneath the Planet of the Apes, The Omega Man, Anthony and Cleopatra, (star & dir.), Skyjacked, Soylent Green, The Three Musketeers, Airport 1975, Earthquake, The Four Musketeers, The Last Hard Men, Midway, Two Minute Warning, The Prince and the Pauper (Crossed Swords), Gray Lady Down, The Awakening.

HETZEL, RALPH D.: Executive. b. Corvallis, Ore., August 18, 1912; e. Penn. State Univ. (A.B.), 1933; University of London, 1935–36; Private secy. to Gov. Pinchot of Pa. 1933–35; did research & study, 1936–39; exec. secty. natl. hdqts., CIO, 1937–40; economic dir., 1938–40; in service, 1942–45. Consultant on labor, Natl. Selective Service hdqts., 1942; manpower consultant War Prod. Bd., 1942–43; dept. vice chmn., manpower requirements, W.P.B., 1943–45; acting vice-chmn., 1945; dir. Office of Labor Requirements, Civilian Prod. Admin., 1945–46; asst. to Secy. of Commerce, U.S. Dept. of Comm., 1946–48; asst. to secty. & dir. Office of Program Planning, 1948–51; asst. admin., Economic Stabilization Agency, 1951; exec. v.p. Motion Picture Association, MP Export Assn., 1951–71, Past president, International Federation of Film Producers Assns.; member of Board of Trustees, California Institute of the Arts and of Penn State University; member of Film Advisory Committee of Museum of Modern Art, and of Advisory Council of Edward R. Murrow Center of Public Diplomacy at Tufts University. Dean, College of Fine and Professional Arts, Professor of Art, Kent State University, 1971–76; provost and vice president, academic affairs, California Institute of the Arts 1976–80; faculty member, 1976–.

HEYER, JOHN: Producer, director. b. Devenport, Australia, 1916. e. Scotch College, Melbourne. Dir., s.p., Native Earth, Journey of a Nation, The Valley Is Ours, Back of Beyond (Venice Grand Prix, 1954) Forerunner. Prod. for Allied Works Council, Film advisor to Prime Minister's Propaganda Comm., World War II; collab., s.p., dir., The Overlanders, 1945; prod., Australian Nat'l. Film Board, 1945–48; prod., Shell Film Unit Aust., 1948–1956; Appt'd. by Government, exec. of New South Wales Film Council, several yrs. pres., Federation of Film Societies, Sydney Film Society; v.p., Scientific Film Soc., Governor, Australian

Film Institute; many Int. film awards; exec. prod. films & TV Shell Inter'l., London, 1957–67.

HEYWARD, LOUIS M.: Writer, prod., exec. b. New York, N.Y., June 29, 1920. e. NYU, Brooklyn Law School. Sr. ed., Press Assoc. Div., AP; formed Radio Transcript Div.; Radio writer: CBS Garry Moore Show, Ernie Kovacs Show; co-owner, Heyward-Wilkes Industrial Film Co.; prod., Warner Bros.; s.p., Pajama Party. TV: Dick Clark Show, Pete and Gladys Show; dir. TV prog. dev., 20th Century Fox; dev. of live progs., MCA-TV Ltd.; dir. m.p. & TV dev., American International Pictures.

HEYWOOD, ANNE: Actress. m. Raymond Stross.
PICTURES INCLUDE: Checkpoint, Doctor at Large, Dangerous Exile, The Depraved, Violent Playground, Floods of Fear, Heart of a Man, Upstairs and Downstairs, A Terrible Beauty, Carthage in Flames, Petticoat Pirates, Stork Talk, Over My Dead Body, The Very Edge, 90 Degrees In The Shade, The Fox, A Run On Gold, The Most Dangerous Man in the World, The Nun of Monza, I Want What I Want, And Presumed Dead.

HICKMAN, DARRYL: Actor. b. Hollywood, July 28, 1933. Started screen career 1938 with The Starmaker. Now with CBS as exec. prod., daytime programming.
PICTURES INCLUDE: Grapes of Wrath, Young People, Jackass Mail, Northwest Rangers, Keeper of the Flame, And Now Tomorrow, Salty O'Rourke, Captain Eddie, Kiss and Tell, Leave Her to Heaven, Black Gold, Happy Years, Submarine Command, Destination Gobi, Island in the Sky, Sea of Lost Ships, Southwest Passage, The Human Comedy, Men of Boystown, Fighting Father Dunn, Tea and Sympathy.

HIFT, FRED: Executive. b. Vienna, 1924. e. Vienna, London and Chicago. Early career reporter Chicago Sun and radio work with CBS News, New York. 1946 joined Boxoffice magazine; 1947 Quigley Publications; 1950 Variety. 1960 began career as publicist on Exodus. 1961 dir. pub., The Longest Day for Darryl Zanuck. 1962 joined Fox in Paris as ad-pub. dir. for Europe. 1964 became dir. European prod. pub. with headquarters London. Formed own pub., p.r. Co., Fred Hift Associates, 1970. 1979, joined Columbia Pictures as dir. of eastern ad-pub operations in N.Y.; 1980, to United Artists as intl. adv./pub. v.p.

HIGGINS, COLIN: Writer-Director. e. Sanford Univ., Sorbonne, UCLA (masters in film). Co-wrote The Ik for Peter Brook's International Center of Theatrical Research; brought to U.S. in 1977 where toured college campuses. Wrote s.p. for Harold and Maude and Silver Streak before turning to directing with Foul Play (also s.p.).
PICTURES: Nine to Five (co. s.p., dir.).

HILFORD, LAWRENCE B.: Executive. b. New York City. e. Yale University; Harvard Business School. Held exec. positions with Columbia Pictures Industries, as v.p. & gen. mgr. of Screen Gems Intl.; named exec. v.p., SGI; v.p. & gen. mgr., Cassette Division of Columbia Pictures. Pres. of Cartridge Rental Network. Pres. Viacom Enterprises Division. Served as exec. v.p. & dir. of Viacom Intl. Inc. In 1979 named snr. v.p. of Columbia Pictures Industries to develop new markets in area of video cassettes and discs.

HILL, ARTHUR: Actor. b. Saskatchewan, Canada, 1922. e. U. of British Columbia. Moved to England in 1948, spending ten years in varied stage & screen pursuits; starred on Broadway in Who's Afraid of Virginia Woolf? (Tony Award), later in More Stately Mansions; film debut in Miss Pilgrim's Progress; other British work includes The Body Said No, Raising A Riot, The Deep Blue Sea.
PICTURES INCLUDE: The Young Doctors, The Ugly American, In the Cool of the Day, Moment to Moment, Harper, Petulia, Don't Let the Angels Fall, The Chairman, The Pursuit of Happiness, Rabbit Run, The Andromeda Strain, The Killer Elite, Future World, A Bridge Too Far, A Little Romance, The Champ, Dirty Tricks, Making Love.
TV: Owen Marshall, Counselor-At-Law, Death Be Not Proud, Churchill and the Generals.

HILL, BENJAMIN (BENNY): TV performer. b. Southampton, England, Jan. 21, 1925. TV debut 1952; since many TV appearances including Showcase, Benny Hill Show; Midsummer Night's Dream, 1964; winner Daily Mail Award TV personality of the year 1954; m.p. debut, Who Done It, 1955; Light Up the Sky, 1960; Those Magnificent Men in Their Flying Machines, 1965; Chitty Chitty Bang Bang.

HILL, GEORGE ROY: Director. b. Minneapolis. e. Yale and Trinity College in Dublin. Started as actor, Irish theatres and U.S. Shakespeare repertory company, also off-Broadway. Served as Marine pilot in World War II and again in Korean War. Wrote TV play, My Brother's Keeper, for Kraft Theatre, later rose to director with show. TV assignments included A Night to Remember, The Helen Morgan Story, Judgment at Nuremberg. Directed first Broadway play in 1957, Look Homeward Angel, followed by The Gang's All Here, Greenwillow. First film, Period of Adjustment, 1962.
PICTURES INCLUDE: Toys in the Attic, The World of Henry Orient, Hawaii, Thoroughly Modern Millie, Butch

Cassidy and the Sundance Kid, Slaughterhouse Five, The Sting, The Great Waldo Pepper, Slap Shot, A Little Romance.

HILL, TERENCE: Actor. b. Venice. r.n. Mario Girotti. First attracted attention as actor in Visconti's The Leopard (1963). Gained fame in European-made westerns.
PICTURES INCLUDE: God Forgives, I Don't, Boot Hill, Ace High, Barbagia, Anger of the Wind, They Call Me Trinity, Trinity Is Still My Name, My Name Is Nobody, Mr. Billion, March or Die.

HILL, WALTER: Writer. b. Long Beach, Calif. Jan. 10, 1942. e. Michigan State Univ. Was construction and oilfield worker before writing screenplays.
PICTURES INCLUDE: Hickey & Boggs, The Getaway, The Thief Who Came to Dinner, The Mackintosh Man, The Drowning Pool, Hard Times (also dir.). The Driver (s.p., dir.). The Warriors (s.p., dir.), Alien (co-prod.); The Long Riders (dir.); Southern Comfort (dir., co-s.p.).

HILLER, ARTHUR: Director. b. Edmonton, Alberta, Can., Nov. 22, 1923. e. Univs. of Alberta, Toronto, Brit. Columbia.
TV: Matinee Theatre, Playhouse 90, Climax, Alfred Hitchcock Presents, Gunsmoke, Ben Casey, Rte. 66, Naked City, The Dick Powell Show.
PICTURES INCLUDE: The Careless Years, Bryne Prods., Americanization of Emily, Tobruk, The Tiger Makes Out, Popi, The Out-of-Towners, Love Story, Plaza Suite, The Hospital, Man of La Mancha, The Man in the Glass Booth, W. C. Fields and Me, Silver Streak, Nightwing, Making Love.

HILLER, WENDY: (DBE, 1975, OBE, 1971). Actress. b. Bramhall, Cheshire, England, Aug. 15, 1912. e. Winceby House Sch., Bexhill. On stage 1930, Manchester Repertory Theatre, England; then on British tour. London debut 1935 in "Love On the Dole"; to N.Y., same role 1936. m.p. debut in "Lancashire Luck," 1937.
PLAYS: First Gentleman, Cradle Song, Tess of the D'Urbervilles, Heiress, Ann Veronica, Waters of the Moon, Night of the Ball, Old Vic Theatre, Wings of the Dove, Sacred Flame, Battle of Shrivings, Crown Matrimonial, John Gabriel Borkman, Waters of the Moon (revival).
PICTURES INCLUDE: Pygmalion, Major Barbara, I Know Where I'm Going, Outcast of the Islands, Single Handed (Sailor of the King), Something of Value, Uncle George, Separate Tables, Sons and Lovers, Toys in the Attic, Man For All Seasons, David Copperfield, Murder on the Orient Express, Voyage of The Damned, The Elephant Man.

HILLIER, ERWIN: Director of Photography-Producer. e. Academia of Arts, Berlin.
PICTURES INCLUDE: I Know Where I am Going, Private Angelo, Interrupted Journey, October Man, Canterbury Tale, Shadow of the Eagle, Chase A Crooked Shadow, Happy Go Lovely, Where's Charley, Will Any Gentleman, House of the Arrow, Isn't Life Wonderful, Duel in the Jungle, Dam Busters, Now and Forever, The Mark of the Hawk, Let's Be Happy, Naked Earth, Shake Hands with the Devil, The Long and the Short and the Tall, School for Scoundrels, The Naked Edge, A Matter of Who, Sammy Going South, The Great Spy Mission, Sands of Kalahari, The Eyes of the Devil, Berlin Memorandum, The Valley Time Forgot, The Shoes of the Fisherman; preparing for production: Anna Pavlova, Eliza Lynch, The Lost City, Shaka Zulu, African Adventure, El Dorado by Alistair Maclean, Los Vagabundos, Uganda Queen.

HILTON, MARS: Actor. b. New York City, Nov. 6, 1951. Since age 3 has appeared on TV and five films in Europe and U.S. Title role, The Pawn, for Seven Arts—Frank Sollento. Speaks Italian; dubbing Pawn and other films at Fono-Roma Studios, Rome.

HINDIN, PHILIP: Executive. b. London, England, 1916; prod., stage dir., m.p. casting, 1937–39; Wielands Ltd. prod., revues, Far East; mgr. dir., Maurice Winnick Org.
TV: Password, Play Your Hunch, Call My Bluff, 20 Questions, He Said; She Said, Watchword, G.O. Water Rats, Goodson-Todman Prods., Chuchin Chow, Hit the Deck, Gentlemen Prefer Blondes, The Hanging Man, Funny Girl, Rumanian State Dance Co., Where Did That Come From, Beat the Clock, The Merry Widow, Bayerische Rundfunk Munich, Belgische Radio en Televisie, Radio Telefis Eireann, Dansk Radio and Television, What's My Line, Music Bingo, Was Bin Ich, The Sunshine Boys, What's The Origin?, 1000 Pd. Pyramid Show: Take My Word.

HINGLE, PAT: Actor. b. 1923.
THEATRE: Man for All Seasons (Oherbein College, Ohio); The Price, Macbeth (American Shakespeare Festival).
RADIO: Voice of America.
PICTURES INCLUDE: On the Waterfront, The Strange One, No Down Payment, Splendor in the Grass, The Ugly American, Sol Madrid, Hang Em High, Jigsaw, Norwood, Bloody Mama, WUSA, Corporal Crocker, The Carey Treatment, One Little Indian, The Super Cops, The Gauntlet, When You Comin' Back, Red Ryder, Norma Rae.

HINKLE, ROBERT: Actor-Prod.-Dir. b. Brownfield, Texas, July 25, 1930; e. Brownfield High School. Joined Rodeo Cow-

boys Association, 1948 and rodeoed professionally until 1953 when began acting career in Outlaw Treasure.
PICTURES INCLUDE: The First Texan, Dakota Incident, Gun the Man Down, The Oklahoman, First Traveling Saleslady, No Place to Land, Under Fire, Speed Crazy, The Gunfight at Dodge City, Broken Land, Law in Silver City, Ole Rex (award for Family Entertainment), Born Hunter, Trauma, Something Can Be Done, Mr. Chat, Stuntman, Jumping Frog Jubilee, Mr. Chat-Mexico Safari, Oregon Today, California Today, Alabama Today, Ride Trail, Virginia City Cent., Texas Today, Texas Long Horns, Kentucky Thoroughbred Racing, Produced & Directed Country Music, Guns of a Stranger.
TV: Test Pilot, Dial 111, Juvenile Squad, X13 Vertijet, Giant, Opposite Sex, All the Fine Young Cannibals, Hollywood Jamboree, Color Me Lucky, Cellist Extraordinary. Pres. Hinkle Pictures, Inc.

HIRD, THORA: Actress. b. Morecambe (Lancs), Eng., May 28, 1914. e. The Nelson School, Morecambe.
PICTURES INCLUDE: (Screen debut, 1940) The Black Sheep of Whitehall; Street Corner, Turn the Key Softly, Personal Affair, The Great Game, Storks Don't Talk, Shop Soiled, For Better or Worse; Love Match, One Good Turn, Quatermass Experiment, Simon and Laura, Lost, Sailor Beware, Home and Away, Good Companions, The Entertainer, A Kind of Loving, Term of Trial, Bitter Harvest, Rattle of A Simple Man, Some Will, Some Won't, The Nightcomers.
TV: The Winslow Boy, The Bachelor, What Happens to Love, The Witching Hour, So Many Children, The Queen Came By, Albert Hope, All Things Bright and Beautiful, Say Nothing, Meet the Wife, Who's A Good Boy Then? I AM! Dixon of Dock Green, Romeo & Juliet, The First Lady, Ours Is a Nice House, The Foxtrot, Seasons, She Stoops to Conquer, Villa Maroc, When We Are Married, The Loving Memory, Flesh and Blood, Your Songs of Praise Choice.

HIRSCH, JUDD: Actor. b. New York City, March 15. e. City College of N.Y. Studied physics but turned to acting; first job in 1962 when performed with stock co. in Colorado. Returned to N.Y. to work on stage and since has also done films and TV.
PICTURES INCLUDE: Serpico, Ordinary People.
TV: Medical Story, Delvecchio. Movies: Fear on Trial, Valentino, The Law, The Keegans, Taxi.

HIRSCHFIELD, ALAN J.: Executive. e., University of Oklahoma (BA); Harvard Business School (MBP). Presently vice-chm., chief operating officer, 20th Century-Fox. V.P., Allen & Co., 1959–66; Financial v.p. & dir. Warner/7 Arts, 1967–68; v.p. & dir., American Diversified Enterprises, 1969–73; pres. & chief exec. officer, Columbia Pictures Industries, 1973–78; consultant, Warner Communications, 1979.
Trustee: Cancer Research Institute. Director: Film Society of Lincoln Center, Motion Picture Association of America, N.Y. State Motion Picture and Television Advisory Board, Straight Arrow Publishing Co., John B. Coleman Co.

HIRSCHMAN, HERBERT: Prod.-dir. b. N.Y.C.; e. Univ. of Michigan, B.A., Yale Univ. Drama School, M.F.A. Story dept. RKO & Paramount; Prod. & dir. summer stock; B'way stage mgr., production manager, TV since 1948. Awards: Peabody (dir., Mr. I-Magination), Robert E. Sherwood (dir., PH 90, "Made in Japan"), TV Guide (prod. Perry Mason); 2 Christophers, dir., London Stage. A Thousand Clowns; prod., m.p. features, Scalplock, Halls of Anger, They Call Me Mister Tibbs.
TV: Dir. Omnibus, Starlight Theatre, Mr. I-Magination, Steve Allen Show, Celebrity Time, What's My Line, Beat the Clock, Inside USA, Love Paul & Mary Ford, The Nurses, The Defenders, For the People, Iron Horse, Felony Squad, Hawaii 5-O, Waltons, prod. and dir., The Web, Alcoa Hour, Goodyear Playhouse, Studio One, Playhouse 90, Perry Mason, Hong Kong, Dr. Kildare, Twilight Zone, Espionage, Wackiest Ship in the Army; Men from Shiloh, Young Lawyers, Bold Ones (The Doctors), GE Theatre: Tell Me Where It Hurts, Larry, Things In Their Season, Miles to Go Before I Sleep; MOW's: Returning Home, Eric, The Zoo Gang, The Amazing Howard Hughes, The Greatest Thing that Almost Happened, The President's Mistress, Human Feelings, Flesh and Blood, And Baby Makes Six: Exec. prod. Iron Horse, Planet of the Apes, The Scarlet Letter, Sophia.

HIRSHAN, LEONARD: Theatrical Agent. b. Dec. 27, 1927, New York City. e. NYU. Joined William Morris Agency as agent trainee, New York, 1951. Agent legit theatre & TV dept. 1952–1954. Sr. exec. agent M.P. dept., California office, 1955.

HIRSHBERG, JACK: Publicist. b. Montreal, Canada, July 17, 1917; e. Sir George Williams Univ., Montreal. Did pub., Montreal Symph. Orch. Canadian Broad. Co.; Hollywood staff rep. Toronto Star, Montreal Star, 1939. Paramount Pictures pub., 1940; in U.S. Navy, 1941–45. Returned to Paramount; pub., expl. rep. Perlberg-Seaton Prod., Frank Ross, Mirisch Co., publicist for C. B. DeMille; 1963 p.b. dir. for Geo. Stevens, Greatest Story Ever Told, 1964; in-

dep. prod., corp. pub. rel. publicist, APJAC Prod. Dr. Doolittle, Planet of the Apes, 1966–67; dir. of publicity, APJAC Prod., 1969; v.p., APJAC Prod., 1971.

HIRT, AL: Musician. b. New Orleans, La., Nov. 7, 1922. e. Cincinnati Conservatory of Music. Military service four years. Played with Tommy and Jimmy Dorsey bands, Ray McKinley and Horace Heidt; appeared, Dunes Hotel, Harrah's Club, Basin Street East, Cloisters, Palmer House, Eden Roc Hotel, Greek Theatre. European tour concerts. Inaugural Ball, President John F. Kennedy, Jan., 1961.
TV: Dinah Shore Show, Jack Paar Show, Ed Sullivan, NBC Special Home For the Holidays, Bell Telephone Hour Rainbow of Stars, Andy Williams Show, Tonight Show, Today Show, Perry Como Show, Lively Ones, Jerry Lewis Show.
PICTURES INCLUDE: World By Night, Rome Adventure.
RECORDINGS: RCA: The Greatest Horn in the World, Al—He's the King—Hirt, Horn-A-Plenty, Al Hirt at the Mardi Gras, Trumpet & Strings, Our Man in New Orleans, Honey In The Horn, Beauty And The Beard, Pop Goes the Trumpet, Boston Pops.

HITT, J. T.: Executive. b. Spearman, Texas, Dec. 16, 1922. e. Grad., Gentry, Ark. H.S., 1940. Farming and ranching. Ent. motion picture industry 1947; Pres., Independent Theatre Owners of Arkansas, 1961–63; chmn. bd., 1964; sec.-treas., Tri-States Theatre Owners, mem. bd., Theatre Owners of America; pres. Tri-State T.O. Ark., Tenn. & Miss., 1965–66.

HIX, AL: Publicist. b. N.Y., Feb. 19, 1918. e. U.S.C., B.A., Phi Beta Kappa, 1949. Pubrel, Ephebian Soc. L.A., 1937–40; U.S. Army Signal Corps, 1941–49; edit.-prod. office, Time mag., & editor Underwriters Report, L.A., 1948–52; unit publicist Europe, & Paris col., Hlywd Rpt, 1952–54; senior publicist, 20th-Fox, 1954–56; since then film publicist in Europe, Asia, Africa & Mid-East (60-plus films) except for publ. "The Rain People," WB, 1968, and publicity for Academy Awards in L.A., 1971.

HOARE, VICTOR J.: Executive. Entered m.p. ind. with United Artists 1931; Dir., British Lion Films, 1961; man. dir., BLC Films, 1962; dep. chmn., BLC Films, 1965; man. dir. British Lion Films, 1965; v.p. in chg. of Continental Europe, Columbia International, in Paris, 1966; v.p., theatres, C.I.C., 1974.

HOBBES, HALLIWELL: Actor. b. Stratford-on-Avon, England, November 16, 1877. First appearance on stage in Glasgow, 1898. First sound picture with Jeanne Eagels in Jealousy, then Grumpy.
PICTURES INCLUDE: Dr. Jekyll and Mr. Hyde, Should Ladies Behave? Captured, Lady for a Day, Mandalay, The Key, Sherlock Holmes Faces Death, The Invisible Man's Revenge, Gaslight, Mr. Skeffington, Casanova Brown, If Winter Comes, You Gotta Stay Happy, You Can't Take It With You, Here Comes Mr. Jordan, Black Arrow, That Forsythe Woman, Life of Pasteur, Miracle in the Rain.

HOBIN, BILL: TV prod. dir.; r.n. Charles W. Hobin; b. Nov. 12, 1923, Evanston, Ill.; e. U. of So. Calif.; prod. mgr., Coronet Instructional Films, Glenview, Ill.; dir., Garroway at Large, Wayne King Show from Chic., 1949–51; dir., Assignment Manhunt, 1952; Nothing But the Best, 1953; Les Paul and Mary Ford, 1953; Your Show of Shows, 1951–54; assoc. prod. dir. Fred Waring Show, Andy Williams Show, Pat Boone, Timex All-Star Jazz Show. dir. Your Hit Parade. Prod.-dir. The Golden Circle, 1959; The Bell Telephone Hour, 1959–60; The American Cowboy, 1960; Sing Along with Mitch, 1960–63; dir., Judy Garland Show, 1963; prod., dir., Victor Borge at Carnegie Hall, 1964; dir., m.p. Chrysler Show-Go-Round, N.Y. World's Fair. 1964. Dir.: Meredith Wilson Special, 1964; Jack Jones on the Move Special, 1966; Red Skelton Hour, 1964–68; prod.; Red Skelton Hour, 1968–70; prod. and dir. The Bill Cosby Special I, 1968; prod., dir., The Tim Conway Comedy Hour, 1970–71; prod., dir. The CBS Newcomers series, 1972; dir. An Evening With My Three Sons special, prod., dir. Michel Legrand Special; prod., dir. Fred Astaire special; director, Maude, 1972; director, A Touch of Grace, 1972–73; 1974, prod.-dir. credits: Dinah, Won't You Please Come Home! (NBC Special); Bobby Goldsboro Show (syn) Your Hit Parade (CBS), prod.-dir. Flip Wilson Special, Dionne Warwick Special, Wayne Newton Special, all 1975; 1976—dir., Welcome (Back), Kotter, Prod.-dir., Monty Hall's Variety Special. Dir. Bert Convy Show; 1976 Director, George Burns Special; McLean Stevenson Show, 1976–78, Director, Three's Company. Producer-director Bob Hope Specials, (1978–79) (NBC); director Celebrity Challenge of the Sexes, 1979 (CBS).

HOBLEY, McDONALD: b. Port Stanley, Falkland Islands; e. South America; Brighton Coll. Early career in repertory cos. tours, etc.; entered TV in 1946 as TV announcer; won Nat'l TV Award for Personality of the Year, 1953–54; resigned from BBC, 1956; now free-lance.
PICTURES INCLUDE: Checkpoint, The Entertainer.

TV: Holiday Town Parade, The Dave King Show, Tell the Truth, The Tommy Steele Show, Close-up.

HOCK, MORT: Executive. b. New York, N.Y., June 24, 1929. United States Army, 1951–53. Blaine-Thompson Agency; A. E. Warner Bros., 1945; David Merrick B'way Prod., 1958; asst. adv. mgr., Paramount Pictures Corp., 1960; adv. mgr., United Artists Corp., 1962; dir. adv., United Artists Corp., July 1964; adv. dir., Para., 1965; v.p. advertising and public relations, Paramount Pict. Corp., 1968–71; pres., Atina Enterprises, Inc. 1971; v.p., marketing, Rastar Prods., 1973; exec. v.p., Charles Schlaifer & Co., 1974.

HODDER-WILLIAMS, CHRISTOPHER: Writer. b. 1927. e. Eton. Military Service, 1944–48; early career as entertainer, property man, songwriter, prof. novelist, writer, 1957.
AUTHOR: The Cummings Report, Chain Reaction, Final Approach, Turbulence, The Higher They Fly. Novels: 1964, The Main Experiment; 1967, The Egg-Shaped Thing; 1968, Fistful of Digits, 98.4, Panic O'Clock, Coward's Paradise, The Prayer Machine.
TV: (Writer) The Ship That Couldn't Stop, The Higher They Fly.

HOFF, J. ROBERT: Executive. b. Chicago, Ill., Mar. 6, 1909; e. U. of Illinois, A.B. 1930; John Marshall Law School, J.D. 1934. With law firm of Hoff & Collis, Chic. 1934–41; Lt. Comdr. U.S.N.R. 1941–45; sales mgr. Ballantyne Co. 1945–55; pres., 1957–61; exec. v.p., Ballantyne Instr. and Elec. Inc., subsid. ABC Consol., 1962; ABC Consol. Sub., Ogden Corp., 1967 (repurchased and renamed Ballantyne of Omaha, Inc.); bd. chm., Ballantyne of Omaha, 1970–1978, retired. Now protecting law in Omaha.
MEMBER: TESMA (dir. 1947–49; vice-pres., 1949–1951; pres. 1951–53); SMPTE, Variety Club, Life member, Variety Int'l., 1973. (Chief Barker, 1954–56; Internat'l repr., 1955–57–59). Elected board member Theatre Equip. & Supply Mfrs. Assn., member board dir. Will Rogers Memorial Hospital; honorary life member TEA, 1975.

HOFFMAN, DUSTIN: b. Los Angeles, Calif., Aug. 8, 1937. m. Anne Byrne. e. Los Angeles Conservatory of Music, Santa Monica College, Pasadena Playhouse, 1958. Worked as an attendant at a psychiatric institution, a demonstrator in Macy's toy dept., and a waiter. First stage role in Yes Is For A Very Young Man, at Sarah Lawrence College. Acted in summer stock, television and dir. at community theatre. Broadway and Off Broadway plays include: 1964, Harry, Noon and Night (American Place Theatre); 1966, Journey of the Fifth Horse (APT, won Obie Award); Eh? (won Vernon Rice & Theatre World Award); Jimmy Shine. Asst. Dir.: A View From The Bridge. Dir. (1974): All Over Town
TV: Journey of the Fifth Horse, The Star Wagons.
PICTURES INCLUDE: Madigan's Millions, The Graduate (Acad. Award nom.); Midnight Cowboy (Acad. Award nom.); John and Mary, Little Big Man, Who Is Harry Kellerman?, Straw Dogs, Alfredo, Papillon, Lenny (Acad. Award nom), All the President's Men, Marathon Man, Straight Time, Agatha, Kramer vs. Kramer (AA).

HOFFMAN, HERMAN: Wrt. Dir. b. Montgomery, Ala., e. Baltimore City Coll., U.S. Navy.
FEATURE DIRECTING: The Bar Sinister, Great American Pastime, The Invisible Boy, The Battle of Gettysburg.
FEATURE WRITING: Attack on the Iron Coast, Guns of the Magnificent Seven, Escapeline, Reluctant Heroes (Movie-of-Week), The Icemen.
TV DIRECTING: Alcoa Premiere, Untouchables, Bonanza, Virginians, M-Squad, The Nurses, Room 222, Run Joe Run, Monster Squad, The Phantom Rebel.

HOFFMAN, JOSEPH: Writer. b. New York City, Newspaperman, radio writer, magazine writer. TV prod. for Screen Gems, Warner Bros., Four Star. Now TV and screen free lance writer.
PICTURES INCLUDE: China Sky, Don't Trust Your Husband, Gung-Ho, And Baby Makes Three, Weekend with Father, Duel at Silver Creek, At Sword's Point, Has Anybody Seen My Gal?, Against All Flags, No Room For the Groom, Lone Hand, Yankee Pasha, Rails into Laramie, Tall Man Riding, Chicago Syndicate, Live A Little, How to Make Love and Like It, Sex and the Single Girl.

HOGARTH, JOHN M.: Executive. b. Hampstead, London, England. 1931. Ent. m.p. ind. 1947 in domestic distri. div. British Lion; appt. indep. circuits man., 1958. Appt. prod. rep. in charge UK dist. Britannia Film. Bryanston Films, Pax Films, 1962. Joined Sydney Box group, 1964 as gen. man. and dir. Monarch Film Corp. Exec. prod. various films. Formed Crispin Film Distribs. 1969. Apptd., man. dir. London Screen Dists. Ltd. 1970. Dir. of U.K. Dist. EMI Film Dist. 1975–77. Man. Dir. Enterprise Pictures Ltd. 1977.

HOHL, ARTHUR: Actor. b. Pittsburgh, Pa., May 21, 1889. e. Leland Stanford U., Wsh. Sq. Players (later Theatre Guild). On dramatic stage in White Cargo, Mary Dugan, etc. Made screen debut 1933. More than 100 films.
PICTURES INCLUDE: The Whole Town's Talking, Eight Bells, The Unknown Woman, Woman on the Town, The Eve of St. Mark, Salome, Where She Danced, Love Letters, It Happened on Fifth Avenue, Monsieur Verdoux, Down to Sea in Ships.

HOLBROOK, HAL: Actor. b. Cleveland, O., Feb. 17, 1925. Gained fame as impersonator of Mark Twain on stage.
PICTURES INCLUDE: The Group, Wild in the Streets, They Only Kill Their Masters, Magnum Force, The Girl rom Petrovka. All the President's Men, Midway, Julia, Capricorn One, Natural Enemies, The Fog.

HOLDEN, GLORIA: Actress. b. London, Eng. Sept. 5, 1911. e. Amer. Acad. of Dramatic Arts. Church soloist and singer, artists' & clothes model; mgr. Elizabeth Arden salon, Southhampton, L.I.; stage and radio roles, lead in As Husbands Go, Theatre Guild road tour. Began screen career 1937.
PICTURES INCLUDE: Life of Emile Zola, The Girl of Limberlost, Dracula's Daughter, Test Pilot, Girls' School, Behind the Rising Sun, The Hucksters, Kiss for Corliss, Dream Wife, Music by Duchin.
TV: Lux Theatre, Hallmark Theatre.

HOLDEN, WILLIAM: Actor. b. O'Fallon, Ill., April 17, 1918; e. South Pasadena junior coll.; husband of Brenda Marshall, actress. Began screen career 1939. Voted one of ten best Money-Making Stars, M.P. Herald-Fame poll, 1954, 1955, 1957.
PICTURES INCLUDE: Golden Boy, Invisible Stripes, Those Were the Days, Our Town, Arizona, I Wanted Wings, Texas, The Remarkable Andrew, The Fleet's In, Meet the Stewarts, Young and Willing, Dear Ruth, Rachel and the Stranger, Apartment for Peggy, The Dark Past, Dear Wife, Miss Grant Takes Richmond, Union Station, Sunset Boulevard, Born Yesterday, Submarine Command, Force of Arms, Turning Point, Boots Malone, Stalag 17 (Academy Award, best actor, 1953), Moon Is Blue, Forever Female, Escape from Fort Bravo, Executive Suite, Sabrina, Bridges at Toko-Ri, Country Girl, Love Is a Many-Splendored Thing, Picnic, Proud and Profane, Toward the Unknown, Bridge on the River Kwai, The Horse Soldiers, World of Susie Wong, Counterfeit Traitor, Satan Never Sleeps, The Lion, The Longest Day, Paris When It Sizzles, The 7th Dawn, Alvarez Kelley, Casino Royale, Devil's Brigade, The Wild Bunch, The Christmas Tree, The Wild Rovers, The Revengers, Breezy, Open Season, The Towering Inferno, Network, Damien-Omen II, Fedora, When Time Ran Out, The Earthling.

HOLDSWORTH, GERARD (D.S.O., O.B.E.): b. Stourbridge (Worcester), Eng., Dec. 27, 1904; e. Tettenhall College (Staffordshire). Began career as rubber planter; ent. m.p. ind. 1930 with Publicity Films Ltd.; joined J. Walter Thompson Co. 1933; Royal Navy 1939–45; man. dir. Signal Films Ltd. 1946; dir. Wallace Productions Ltd. 1947; formed Gerard Holdsworth Prod. 1950 & Screen Audiences Ltd., 1951; man. dir., Rank Screen Services Ltd., 1954; res. 1959 to re-form Gerard Holdsworth, Ltd., and Gerard Holdsworth Prods. Ltd. 1971: Involvement with video-cassettes and programming for new outlets.

HOLLENDER, ALFRED L.: Advertising executive. b. Chicago, Ill.; e. U. of Illinois. Was associated with Radio Stations WIND-WJJD, Chicago as continuity ed., program dir. & asst. to pres.; entered military service in 1943; exec. v.p. & partner of Louis G. Cowan, Inc., exec. v.p. and dir. radio-TV dept., Grey Adv. Agency; pres., Grey Int'l.

HOLLIMAN, EARL: Actor. b. Tennassas Swamp, Delhi, La., Sept. 11. e. Louisiana State U. U.S.L.A.
PICTURES INCLUDE: Girls of Pleasure Island, Destination Gobi, East of Sumatra, Devil's Canyon, Tennessee Champ, Bridge at Toko-Ri, Broken Lance, Big Combo, I Died a Thousand Times, Forbidden Planet, Giant, Burning Hills, Gunfight at the OK Corral, The Rainmaker, Hot Spell, Visit to a Small Planet, The Power.

HOLLINGER, HY: Executive. b. New York, N.Y. e. CCNY, Columbia Sch. of Journalism; reporter, Upper Darby Review, The Morning Telegraph; Warner Bros.; reporter on Variety, Paramount Pictures Corp.; publ. mgr.; Dir., European prod. publicity, London; Paramount Pictures Corp. Dir. adv. & publicity; assoc. editor, Variety.

HOLLOWAY, STANLEY: Actor. b. London, Eng.; London stage debut 1919 in Kissing Time. Screen debut 1921 in The Rotters; from 1933 in many Brit. features. On Broadway & London in My Fair Lady, 1956–59. Toured Australia in The Pleasure of His Company, 1977.
PICTURES INCLUDE: One Night With You, Hamlet, Snowbound, Noose, The Winslow Boy, Another Shore, Passport to Pimlico, The Perfect Woman, Old Wild Oat, Lavender Hill Mob, The Magic Box, The Happy Family, Meet Me Tonight, Titfield Thunderbolt, Beggar's Opera, Meet Mr. Lucifer, A Day to Remember, Fast & Loose, An Alligator Named Daisy, Jumping for Joy, No Trees in the Street, Alive and Kicking, No Love for Johnnie, My Fair Lady, In Harms Way, Ten Little Indians, The Sandwich Man, Mrs. Brown You Have a Lovely Daughter, 1969; The Private Life of Sherlock Holmes, Run a Crooked Mile, Flight

of The Doves, Up the Front! (1972), Journey into Fear, Dangerous Journey.

TV: Sunday Night at London Palladium, The Mikado, Amer. TV, Lerner and Loewe of Broadway, Our Man Higgins series, The Fantastiks, Perry Como Show, Bell Telephone Hour, Dean Martin Show, Red Skelton Show, Bell Telephone Hour, Tribute to Alan Lerner, Danny Kaye Show, Dean Martin Show, Blanding Castle, What's In It For Harry, Dr. Jekyll and Mr. Hyde.

HOLLOWAY, STERLING: Actor. b. Cedartown, Ga.; e. Ga. Military Acad., Atlanta, Amer. Acad. of Dramatic Art.

THEATRE: N.Y. Plays include: Shepherd of the Hills, The Failures, Garrick Gaieties (4 editions), Donna Magana; vaude.; night clubs; radio; U.S. armed forces, 1943.

PICTURES INCLUDE: Walk in the Sun, Death Valley, Beautiful Blonde from Bashful Bend, Her Wonderful Lie, Alice in Wonderland, Live a Little, Love a Little, The Jungle Book (voice).

HOLM, CELESTE: Actress. b. New York City, Apr. 29. p. Theodor Holm and Jean Parke Holm. Ed. Univ. School for Girls, Chicago, Francis W. Parker, Chicago, Lyceé Victor Durui (Paris), Chicago U & UCLA.

THEATRE: On Bdwy incl. Time of Your Life, Return of the Vagabond, Papa Is All, Oklahoma, Bloomer Girl, Affairs of State, Anna Christie, The King and I, Third Best Sport, Invitation to a March, A Month in the Country; Theatre-in-Concert for the US State Department in 8 countries May–July 1966. Appeared on B'way 1975–76, Habeas Corpus.

PICTURES INCLUDE: The Little Girls in Blue, won Academy Award 1947, Gentlemen's Agreement, Come to the Stable, All About Eve, Snake Pit, Road House, Chicken Every Sunday, Everybody Does It, Champagne for Caesar, Tender Trap, High Society, Bachelor Flat, Doctor, You've Got To Be Kidding, Tom Sawyer, Bittersweet Love.

TV: A Clearing House in the Wood, Play of the Week, Cinderella.

RADIO: People at the U.N.

HOLT, DENIS: Associate Producer. 30 years in the industry working on major feature pictures. Currently a director of Winkast Programming Ltd., based at Pinewood Studios, England.

HOLT, PATRICK: Actor. b. Cheltenham, England, 1912; e. Christ's Hospital. From 1936–39 played in repertory. London stage debut, "Saloon Bar," 1939. Enlisted in Royal Artillery, 1940; served in 1st Punjab Reg., Indian Army, 1942–46. On screen first, 1938, "Return of the Frog."

PICTURES INCLUDE: Sword of Honor, Convoy, Hungry Hill, Frieda, October Man, When the Bough Breaks, Mark of Cain, My Sister and I, Fly Away Peter, Portrait from Life, Master of Bankdam, A Boy A Girl and A Bike, Marry Me, Boys in Brown, Guilt Is My Shadow, Golden Link, Men of Sherwood Forest, Miss Tulip Stays the Night, The Dark Avenger, Alias John Preston, Stolen Assignment, Gelignite Gang (The Dynamiters), Suspended Alibi, Count of Twelve, Fortune Is a Woman, Monty's Double, Further Up the Creek, Too Hot To Handle, The Challenge, Guns at Batasi., 13 East Street, Ivanhoe, Serena, Ghengis Khan, Thunderball, Murderers Row, Hammerhead, The Desperadoes, When Dinosaurs Ruled the Earth, Cromwell, No Blades of Grass, Young Winston, Psychomania, Legend of the Werewolfe, The Wild Geese, Sea Wolves.

TV: King Richard the Lionheart (series), African Patrol, Rendez-vous, Flying Doctor Series, The Avengers, The Liars, The Saint series, The Commander, Mr. Rose, No Hiding Place, Randall and Hopkirk, Man Charged, Whom God Hath Joined, War and Peace, Father Dear Father, Emmerdale Farm, Shabby Tiger, Howerd's History of England, Crown Court, Warship, Holding On, Mother Knows Best, Poldark, The Survivors, Rob Roy, Whodunnit, Philby, Burgess & Maclean, Eagle of the IXth, Lillie, Family Affair.

HOMEIER, SKIP: Actor. r.n. George Vincent Homeier. b. Chicago, Oct. 5, 1930. e. U.C.L.A. Started in radio, 1936–43; on B'way stage, Tomorrow the World, 1943–44.

PICTURES INCLUDE: Tomorrow the World, Boy's Ranch, Mickey, Arthur Takes Over, The Big Cat, The Gunfighter, Halls of Montezuma, The Black Widow, Cry Vengeance, Dakota Incident, The Captives, No Road Back, Decision at Durango, Showdown.

TV: Playhouse 90, Alcoa Hour, Kraft Theatre, Studio 1, Armstrong Circle Theatre, Alfred Hitchcock, etc.

HOMER, RAYMOND R.: Producer /director: Queen of Diamonds. Executive producer: Dream City, Double Identity, Left Hand of the Law, Swiss Conspiracy, The Inheritance. Producer: Shadow of a Killer, The Pawn, The Kids, Sharpies, For Love of Anna.

HONG, WILSON S.: Cinematographer. b. Butte, Mont., Dec. 18, 1934; ed. Montana State University, Brooks Institute of Photography; 1965 Free lance photographer for national magazine and world-wide newspaper syndication; 1966, Photographic Director of U.S. Forest Service Fire & Research Division; 1967, first cameraman on various documentaries, industrials, commercials, sports specials.

PICTURES INCLUDE: Bigfoot, Operation North Slope, John Wayne's 'No Substitute for Victory', The Hellcats, Dear Dead Delilah, Zodiac Killer, Velvet Vampire, Mrs. McGrudy, The Day The Adults Died, Sundown in Watts, Parallax View, 1776, Don't Go West, Drum, White Buffalo, MacArthur, An Enemy of the People, Sergeant Pepper's Lonely Hearts Club Band, Mulefeathers, Winterkills, Mission to Glory, The Unfinished, They Only Kill Their Masters, The Fearless Five.

TELEVISION: Snowmobile Grand Prix (ABC), Indianapolis International Drag Races (ABC), The Great Outdoors (23 episodes, ABC), Thank you America (spec.), The Unser Story (ABC), Gun Hawks (pilot), Keep it Up (pilot), Where are they Now? (pilot), Hunting and Fishing the North American Continent (spec.), The Blue Knight, A Dream for Christmas, The Toy Game, Moose (pilot), The Jerry Show, Apple's Way, The Moneychangers, Young Maverick, Rudi Gernreich/Future, Ours, Max Factor and Pepsi-Cola Commercials, The Groovy Seven (pilot).

HOPE, BOB: Actor. b. Eltham, England., May 29, 1903. Started in vaude.; plays include: Roberta, Ziegfeld Follies, Red, Hot & Blue; author, They Got Me Covered, I Never Left Home, So This Is Peace. Voted one of ten best Money-Making Stars in M.P. Herald-Fame Poll, 1941–47, 49–53. On radio and TV.

PICTURES INCLUDE: Big Broadcast of 1938, College Swing, Give Me a Sailor, Thanks for the Memory, Never Say Die, Some Like It Hot, Cat and Canary, Road to Singapore, Ghost Breakers, Road to Zanzibar, Caught in the Draft, Louisiana Purchase, My Favorite Blonde, Road to Morocco, Nothing But the Truth, They Got Me Covered, Star Spangled Rhythm, Let's Face It, Road to Utopia, Princess and Pirate, Monsieur Beaucaire, My Favorite Brunette, Where There's Life, Road to Rio, Paleface, Sorrowful Jones, Great Lover, Fancy Pants, Lemon Drop Kid, My Favorite Spy, Son of Paleface, Road to Bali, Off Limits, Here Come the Girls, Casanova's Big Night, Seven Little Foys, That Certain Feeling, Iron Petticoat, Beau James, Paris Holiday, Alias Jesse James, Facts of Life, Bachelor In Paradise, Road to Hong Kong, Call Me Bwana, A Global Affair, I'll Take Sweden, Boy Did I Get a Wrong Number, Eight on the Lam, The Private Navy of Sgt. O'Farrell, How to Commit Marriage, Cancel My Reservation.

HOPE, HARRY: Producer, director, writer. e. UCLA, Etudes Universitaires Internationales, Ph.D. Entered m.p. industry as special effect man, Republic Studios, 1944; assoc. prod., Star Productions, 1945; prod. for Exploitation Films, 1951; formed Blue Bird Film Co.; Taiwan; prod., dir., wrote 22 features for Flame Films, Hong Kong, including Like The Gull, 1967, which won creative classical film award at Asian Film Festival. In 1967, co-founder, gen. mgr. and prod., Western International Motion Pictures, Inc., which merged with Inter-Associates to form First Leisure Corp., of which Hope was prod. and v.p. chg. of foreign operations. In 1973 withdrew Inter-Associates from FLC and now operating it as indep. prod.-dist. co.

HOPKINS, ANTHONY: Actor. b. Port Talbot, 1941. Trained at Royal Academy of Dramatic Arts. Joined National Theatre, gaining fame on stage in England, then TV and films.

PICTURES INCLUDE: White Bus, Lion in Winter, Hamlet, The Looking Glass War, When Eight Bells Toll, Young Winston, The Girl from Petrovka, Audrey Rose, A Bridge Too Far, International Velvet, Magic, Change of Seasons, The Elephant Man.

TV: QB VII, All Creatures Great and Small, The Bunker, Peter and Paul.

HOPKINS, BO: Actor. B. Greenwood, S.C. Studied with Uta Hagen in N.Y. then went to Calif. with Desilu Playhouse training school in Hollywood. Parts in several prods. for that group won him an agent, an audition with director Sam Peckinpah and his first role in latter's The Wild Bunch.

PICTURES INCLUDE: Monte Walsh, The Culpepper Cattle Co., The Moonshine War, White Lightning, The Getaway, The Man Who Loved Cat Dancing, American Graffiti, The Nickel Ride, The Day of the Locust, Posse, The Killer Elite, A Small Town in Texas, More American Graffiti, The Fifth Floor.

TV: Doc Elliott (series).

HOPPER, DENNIS: Actor. b. Dodge City, Kans., May 17, 1936. e. San Diego, Calif., public schools.

TV: Medic, Loretta Young Show.

PICTURES INCLUDE: Jagged Edge, Rebel Without a Cause, Giant, Wrote, dir. starred in Easy Rider, The Last Movie, Hex, The American Friend, King of the Mountain.

HOPPER, JERRY: Director. b. Guthrie, Okla., July 29, 1907. Wrote radio scripts; asst. dir. & actor. Universal, MGM; casting office, Paramount; Combat/photog—U.S. Army, m.p. div.; asst. edit. dept. head, Paramount; dir., Paramount.

PICTURES INCLUDE: The Atomic City, Hurricane Smith, Pony Express, Alaska Seas, Secret of the Incas, Naked Alibi, Smoke Signal, Private War of Major Benson, One Desire, Square Jungle, Never Say Goodbye, Toy Tiger,

Shark Fighters, Missouri Traveler, Blueprint for Robbery, Maharlica, Madrone.

TV: pilots—Bachelor Father, Leave it to Beaver, Naked City, Wagon Train, Witchita Town. Many television productions.

HORDERN, MICHAEL: Actor. b. Berkhampstead, England, 1911. e. Brighton College. early career in business before stage appearance, 1937. M.P. debut 1939. TV debut 1946. 1939–45 Naval Service.

PICTURES INCLUDE: Passport to Pimlico, The Constant Husband, Alexander the Great, the Black Prince, Storm Over The Nile, Pacific Destiny, The Baby and the Battleship, The Spanish Gardener, No Time for Tears, Windom's Way, Monty's Double, Girls at Sea, Moment of Danger, Sink the Bismarck, Man in the Moon, El Cid, Cleopatra, V.I.P.s, Dr. Syn, The Yellow Rolls Royce, Ghengis Khan, The Spy Who Came in From the Cold, Khartoum, Cast a Giant Shadow, A Funny Thing Happened on the Way to the Forum, Taming of the Shrew, The Jokers, How I Won the War, I'll Never Forget What's 'Is Name, Prudence and the Pill, The Bed-sitting Room, Where Eagles Dare, Anne of the Thousand Days, Futtocks End, Some Will, Some Won't, Up Pompeii, The Possession of Joel Delaney (USA), Pied Piper, Blood Will Have Blood, England Made Me, Girl Stroke Boy, Alice's Adventures in Wonderland, Theatre of Blood, The Mackintosh Man, Quilp, Barry Lyndon (narrator), The Slipper and the Rose, Joseph Andrews, The Medusa Touch, Wildcats of St. Trinians.

TV: Doctor's Dilemma, The Great Adventure, The Witness, The Indifferent Shepherd, Dock Brief, Mr. Kettle & Mrs. Moon, Guinea Pig, The Gathering Dusk, Farewell My City, Flowering Cherry, I Have Been Here Before, Without the Grail, The Outstation, The Square, Any Other Business, The Stone Dance, The Quails, A Waltz on the Water, August for the People, Land of My Dreams, Condemned to Acquittal, Nelson, The Browning Version, Whistle and I'll Come to You, The Man Who Murdered in Public, A Crack in the Ice, Sir Jocelyn the Minister Would Like A Word, Six Dates With Barker, Don Juan in Hell, Tartoffe, Tall Stories, The Magistrate, Edward VII, King Lear, Cakes and Ale, Chester Mystery Cycle, Paddington Bear (story teller), The Saints Go Marching In, Mrs. Bixby and the Colonel's Coat, Romeo and Juliet, The Tempest.

HORNBECK, WILLIAM W.: Prod. executive. b. Los Angeles, Calif., Aug. 23, 1901. Lt. Col. in Signal Corps, U.S. Army, World War II (Legion of Merit). Entered m.p. ind. 1916 in film lab., Keystone Comedies; to cutting room; then editor supvr., Mack Sennett through 1933, 1934 to England with Alexander Korda and London Films; ed. The Scarlet Pimpernel; in 1935 supervising ed. for London Films: The Ghost Goes West, Things to Come, Drums, Sanders of the River, Four Feathers, among others. In 1946 apptd. asst. to vice-pres. in charge of studio operations, Republic Pictures. Later, supervising editor, Liberty Films: It's a Wonderful Life, State of the Union. Then Paramount, edited The Heiress, Shane. Academy Award for film ed., Place in the Sun, 1951. Edited Act of Love in France 1953, The Barefoot Contessa in Italy 1954. Then Warner Bros. for Giant in 1955 and The Quiet American for United Artists in Italy 1957. I Want to Live, 1958. A Hole in the Head, and to England for Suddenly Last Summer 1959. Appointed supervisor of editorial operations Universal Studio, 1960. Vice pres. Universal Pictures, 1966. Nominated for Academy Award, 4 times.

HORNE, DAVID: Actor. b. Balcome, Sussex, July 14, 1898; e. Eton & Sandhurst. Began screen career 1931.

PICTURES INCLUDE: Doomed Cargo, The Mill on the Floss, The Wrecker, Four Dark Hours, The First and the Last, Inspector Hornleigh Goes To It, Chamber of Horrors, Spitfire, Adventure in Blackmail, Rake's Progress, Seventh Veil, Men of Two Worlds, Gaiety George, The Magic Bow, Saraband for Dead Lovers, Easy Money, Martin Luther, Spaceways, Five Pound Note, Policewoman, Wedding Gift, The Intruder, 3 Cases of Murder, Beau Brummell.

HORNE, LENA: Vocalist, actress. b. Brooklyn, N.Y.

THEATRE: Blackbirds, Dance With Your Gods.

Radio with Noble Sissle, Charlie Barnet, other brands. Floor shows at Cotton Club, Cafe Society, Little Troc, etc. Started screen career 1942.

PICTURES INCLUDE: Panama Hattie, Cabin in the Sky, Stormy Weather, I Dood It, Thousands Cheer, Broadway Rhythm, Swing Fever, Two Girls and a Sailor, Ziegfeld Follies, Till the Clouds Roll By, Words and Music, Meet Me in Las Vegas, Death of a Gunfighter, The Wiz.

HORNER, HARRY: Director. b. Holic, Czechoslovakia, July 24, 1910; e. U. of Vienna, Dept. of Architecture, 1928–33; Acad. of the Theatre, Vienna, 1930–32, Max Reinhardt's Seminary. Joined Max Reinhardt Thea. Co., Vienna and Salzburg Festivals; to U.S. as asst. to Reinhardt on pageant, The Eternal Road. Stage designer, N.Y. theatre 10 yrs. (Lady In The Dark, Family Portrait, others). First m.p. as prod. designer, 1938, Our Town (co-credit, Wm. Cameron

Menzies). later Little Foxes, Stage Door Canteen. Army service, 1942–45; designed Winged Victory for Air Force. In 1949, won Acad. award black and white art dir., The Heiress. Other films designed: Born Yesterday, Separate Tables, They Shoot Horses; Acad. nomination, The Hustler; (Acad. award). Since 1959 prod., dir., TV series, The Royal Canadian Mounted Police; exec. prod., dir., Enterprise Films of Can., Anglo Ent. Films, London; co-prod., Fahrenheit 451, 1966, They Shoot Horses, Don't They? (Acad. nom.), Who Is Harry Kellerman?, Up the Sandbox (Streisand)

FURTHER PICTURES INCLUDE: Born Yesterday, He Ran All the Way, Androcles and the Lion, Outrage. Films Directed: Beware My Lovely, Red Planet Mars, Vicki, New Faces, Life in the Balance, Step Down to Terror, Lonesome Gun, Wild Party Man From Del Rio, Winner of 2 acad. awards, 6 acad. nominations for Art Dir. 1975: The Black Bird, Harry and Walter Go To New York, Audrey Rose, The Driver, Moment by Moment, The Jazz Singer.

TV: Omnibus, Cavalcade, Reader's Digest, Author's Playhouse, Four Star Theatre, Gunsmoke, Revue Productions, Dupont Theatre.

OPERA: designer & director at San Francisco Opera, Metrop. Opera N.Y. Vancouver Festivals Hollywood Bowl Operas designed & directed: David, Joan at the Seake, Magic Flute. Amer. Premiere of New Opera, Midsummers Night Dream. Designed Idiots Delight, Ahmanson Theatre, 1970, winner, L.A. Drama Critics Award, best stage design. Designed Time of the Cuckoo, Ahmanson Theatre 1974.

HORTON, ROBERT: Actor. b. Los Angeles, July 29, 1924. e. Miami Univ., U.C.L.A. U.S. Coast Guard; many legit. plays; many radio & TV appearances; co-star, Wagon Train; screen debut in The Tanks Are Coming.

PICTURES INCLUDE: Return of the Texan, Pony Soldier, Apache War Smoke, Bright Road, The Story of Three Loves, Code Two, Arena, Prisoner of War, Men of the Fighting Lady, The Green Slime.

HORWICH, FRANCES R.: b. Ottawa, Ohio. e. U. of Chicago, Ph.B., 1929; Columbia U., M.A., 1933; Northwestern U., Ph.D., 1942; hon. deg., D. Ped., Bowling Green (Ohio) State U., 1954; Grade-sch. teacher, Evanston, Ill., 1929–32; supvr., nursery schools, Chicago, 1932–35; dir., jr. kindergarten, Winnetka, Ill., 1935–38; dean of educ., Pestalozzi Froebel Teachers Coll., Chicago, 1938–40; counsellor of student teachers, Chicago Teachers Coll., 1940–42; dir., Hessian Hills Sch., N.Y., 1943–45; prof., U. of N.C., 1945–46; Roosevelt U., 1947–52; supvr. of children's programs, NBC, 1952–56; Miss Frances on TV show, Ding Dong School, NBC, 1955–56; WGN-TV, 1957–58; I.T.C. syndication, 1959; ed. dir., The Curtis Publishing Co., 1962–66; dir. of children's programs at WFLD-TV Chicago, 1966–68.

TV PROGRAMS: Time For Children with Miss Francis, Time for Parents with Miss Francis, 1966–67; Sunday in Chicago segment, WMAQ-TV, 1969.

HORWITZ, LEWIS M.: Exhibitor, Producer. b. Cleveland, Ohio, Sept. 14, 1931. e. Miami University, Ohio State University, Western Reserve University. 1943, popcorn boy, Haltnorth Theatre, Cleveland, Ohio; 1950, assistant manager, State Theatre, Cuyaghoga Falls, Ohio; 1953, booker, Washington Theatre Circuit, Cleveland; 1956, film buyer, Washington Theatre Circuit; 1959, Head Film Buyer, Washington Theatre Circuit; 1960, partner and chief executive officer, Washington Theatre Circuit; 1965, secretary-treasurer, Global Screen Associates, Inc., Los Angeles; 1966, indep. producer, A Man Called Dagger; 1967, formed independent production company—LMH Productions; 1967–70, independent producer, Metro-Goldwyn-Mayer Studios, Culver City; 1971, independent producer, Woodshed Films; 1972–73, exec., General Cinema Corporation, Boston; 1973–74, producer of The Prisoners, which was invited Berlin, Moscow and Belgrade International Film Festivals. 1974–75, head film buyer, Royal Cinemas, Inc.

HOUGH, JOHN: Director. Worked in British film prod. in various capacities; impressed execs. at EMI-MGM Studios, Elstree, London, so was given chance to direct The Avengers series for TV. Began theatrical films with Sudden Terror for prod. Irving Allen, 1971.

PICTURES INCLUDE: Twins of Evil, Treasure Island, The Legend of Hell House, Dirty Mary Crazy Larry, Escape to Witch Mountain, Return to Witch Mountain, Brass Target, Watcher in the Woods.

HOUSEMAN, JOHN: Producer, director, writer. r.n. J. Haussmann. b. Rumania, Sept. 22, 1902. e. Clifton Coll., Eng. Moved to Argentina 1923 to conduct wheat export business. To U.S., Canada, 1925; contrib. to magazines; adapt. plays from German, French. In 1932 prod. Four Saints in Three Acts; later dir. Valley Forge, Panic, for Theatre Guild. Assoc. with Orson Welles in founding Mercury Theat., 1937; apptd. assoc. prof. English at Vassar same yr. Prod. Julius Caesar, Native Son for stage. Co-author Woodrow Wilson (prod. on stage as In Time to Come), bought by 20th Century-Fox. Wrote radio scripts for Helen Hayes. Exec. Selznick Prod., 1941–42. Chief of overseas radio div. OWI, 1942–43. In 1943–44 (joint s.p.) Jane Eyre; New York stage; dir. Lute Song, 1948; King Lear, 1950; Coriolanis, 1953.

PICTURES INCLUDE: Miss Susie Slagle's, The Unseen, Blue Dahlia, Letter from an Unknown Woman, They live By Night, The Company She Keeps; prod. On Dangerous Ground, Holiday For Sinners, The Bad and The Beautiful, Julius Caesar, Executive Suite, Her Twelve Men, Moonfleet, The Cobweb, Lust For Life, All Fall Down, Two Weeks in Another Town, In The Cool of the Day. Actor: The Paper Chase, 1973, Rollerball, 1975, Three Days of the Condor, St. Ives, The Cheap Detective, The Fog, Wholly Moses.

TV: Paper Chase (series).

HOVEY, TIM: Actor. b. Los Angeles, Calif., June 19, 1945. Child model; on TV in Lassie.

PICTURES INCLUDE: Queen Bee, Private War of Major Benson, Toy Tiger, Everything But the Truth, Man Afraid, Slim Carter. Money Women and Guns.

TV: Playhouse 90, Lux Theatre, Kraft Theatre, Matinee Playhouse, Schiltz Playhouse, G.E. Theatre, Cimarron City.

HOWARD, CY: Producer, director. b. Milwaukee, Wis., Sept. 27, 1915. e. U. of Minnesota, U. of Wisconsin. Entered radio Station KTRH, Houston, Tex. as writer, prod.; served 1 yr. Army Air Corps; to WBBM, Chicago, as writer, prod., actor, 1942; to Jack Benny's radio writing staff; actor, Storm Operation (stage), 1943; to ABC as writer, comedian on What's New program; to NBC where orig. wrote Palmolive Party; radio writer for Milton Berle, Danny Thomas, Bert Lahr, Jerry Lewis; orig. My Friend Irma, Life with Luigi, radio and TV shows; to Hall B. Wallis Prod. as writer and assoc. prod. My Friend Irma; exec. prod., Desilu Studios, created and produced Harrigan & Son, Westward Ho, Fair Exchange, My Friend Irma Goes West (films), That's My Boy; writer, Marriage on the Rocks; co-writer: Won Tonton, The Dog Who Saved Hollywood; director, Lovers & Other Strangers and Every Little Crook and Nanny.

HOWARD, CYRIL: Managing Director of Rank's Pinewood Studios, England. Formerly Secretary and general manager of the studios. Joined Rank Organization 1942.

HOWARD, KEN: Actor. b. El Centro, CA, March 28. e. Yale Drama School. Left studies to do walk-on in Bdwy. musical, Promises, Promises. Starred at Thomas Jefferson in 1776 on Bdwy. (Theatre World Award).

PICTURES: Tell Me That You Love Me, Junie Moon (debut), Such Good Friends, 1776.

TELEVISION: Series: Manhunter, Bonanza, Medical Center, Adam's Rib, The White Shadow. Movie: The Trial of George Armstrong Custer.

STAGE: Child's Play, Seesaw, 1600 Pennsylvania Avenue, The Norman Conquests, Equus.

HOWARD, ROBERT T.: Executive. b. Red Bank, N.J. e. Univ. of Virginia, Columbia Univ. (N.Y.). Began prof. career as NBC page, joining guest relations staff in N.Y., 1947. Moved up to NBC TV research dept., where worked in program testing and audience measurement. Became head of research for NBC Radio Spot Sales in 1953; 1955, promoted to acct. exec. in same dept. Joined TV Spot Sales in 1959 and named natl. sales mgr. of WNBC-TV, New York in 1963 named gen. mgr. of KNBC, Los Angeles. Elected v.p. of NBC a month later. Returned to N.Y. and named pres. of NBC TV Network April 1, 1974. Elected to NBC bd. and named exec. v.p.; 1977, v.p. & gen. mgr. WNBC TV, New York; 1980, pres. & chm., Citicom Communications Co.

HOWARD, RON: Actor. b. Duncan, Okla., March 1, 1954. e. Univ. of South Calif. Acting debut at age of two with parents, Rance and Jean Howard, in The Seven Year Itch at Baltimore's Hilltop Theatre. Two years later travelled to Vienna for his first film, The Journey. Many TV appearances over years. Is brother of Clint Howard, also actor from childhood.

PICTURES INCLUDE: The Journey, Wild Country, The Music Man, Courtship of Eddie's Father, Happy Mother's Day . . . Love, George, American Graffiti, The Spikes Gang, The Shootist, More American Graffiti.

TELEVISION: Red Skelton Hour, Playhouse 90, Dennis, the Menace, Many Loves of Dobie Gillis, Five Fingers, Twilight Zone, Dinah Shore Show, Andy Griffith Show (regular), The Fugitive, Dr. Kildare, Big Valley, I Spy, Danny Kaye Show, Gomer Pyle, USMC, The Monroes, The FBI, Judd for the Defense, Daniel Boone, Lancer, Land of the Giants, Gentle Ben, Gunsmoke, Disney TV films (A Boy Called Nuthin', Smoke), Happy Days (regular).

HOWARD RONALD: Actor. b. Norwood, England; e. Tonbridge School and Jesus Coll.; p. the late Leslie Howard. m. Jean Millar. Reporter, Allied Newspapers. In British armed forces.

PICTURES INCLUDE: While the Sun Shines, 1946; Night Beat, My Brother Jonathan, Bond Street, Queen of Spades, Now Barabbas, Portrait of Eve, Double Confession, Assassin for Hire, The Browning Version, Tom Brown's School Days, Street Corner (Both Sides of the Law), Rustle of Silk, Drango; No Trees in the Street, Babette Goes to War, Come September (Italy), Monster of Highgate, The Naked Edge, Bomb in the High Street, The Curse of the Mummy's Tomb.

TV: Sherlock Holmes, Robin Hood, The Man Who Was Two, Mary Britten, M.D., Four Just Men.

HOWARD, SANDY: Producer. b. 1927. Ent. m.p. ind. 1946.

PICTURES INCLUDE: Perils of the Deep, One Step to Hell, Jack of Diamonds, Tarzan and the Trappers, A Man Called Horse, Man in the Wilderness, Together Brothers, Neptune Factor, The Devil's Rain, Sky Riders, The Last Castle, Embryo, Magna I—Beyond the Barrier Reef, The Battle, Island of Dr. Moreau, City on Fire, Death Ship (exec. prod.).

TV: Over 50 TV series.

HOWARD, TREVOR: Actor. b. Kent, England, Sept. 29, 1916; e. Clifton Coll., Bristol, Royal Acad. of Dramatic Art. Stage debut: Revolt in a Reformatory, 1933; played Petruchio in Old Vic production of The Taming of the Shrew and in James Bridie's The Anatomist. Screen debut: The Way Ahead, 1943. In H. M. Forces in World War II.

PICTURES INCLUDE: Brief Encounter, Way to the Stars, Green for Danger, So Well Remembered, Passionate Friends, Third Man, Golden Salamander, Odette, Outcast of the Islands, Lovers of Lisbon (French), The Clouded Yellow, The Gift Horse, Heart of the Matter, Stranger's Hand, Cockelshell Heroes, Run for the Sun, Around the World in 80 Days, Interpol, Manuela, The Key, Roots of Heaven, Moment of Danger, Sons and Lovers, Mutiny On the Bounty, Father Goose, The Great Spy Mission, Von Ryan's Express, The Sabateur Code Name-Morituri, The Lion, Man in the Middle, Pretty Polly, A Matter of Innocence, The Battle of Britain, Ryan's Daughter, Pope Joan, Ludwig, 11 Harrowhouse, Who?, Hennessy, Conduct Unbecoming, The Bawdy Adventures of Tom Jones, The Last Remake of Beau Geste, Superman, Hurricane, Meteor, The Sea Wolves.

TELEVISION: Hedda Gabler, Mr. Disraeli, Napoleon, Catholics, Night Flight.

HOWELLS, URSULA: Actress. b. Sept. 17, 1922. e. St. Paul's Sch., London. Stage debut, 1939, at Dundee Repertory with Bird in Hand followed by several plays inc. Springtime for Henry in N.Y., 1951; m.p. debut in Flesh and Blood, 1950; TV debut in Case of the Frightened Lady for BBC, 1948.

TV: Many appearances including The Small Back Room, A Woman Comes Home, For Services Rendered, Mine Own Executioner, The Cocktail Party.

PICTURES INCLUDE: The Oracle (Horse's Mouth), Track the Man Down, They Can't Hang Me, Keep It Clean, Long Arm (Third Key), Death and The Sky Above, Mumsy, Nanny, Sonny, and Girly.

HOWERD, FRANKIE: Performer. b. York, Eng., e. Shooters Hill, London, Sch. Stage debut, Sheffield Empire, 1946. Film: Runaway Bus; BBC radio & TV appearances include Tons of Money, Frankie Howerd Show, Howerd Crowd.

PICTURES INCLUDE: Jumping for Joy, An Alligator Names Daisy, The Lady Killers, A Touch of the Sun, Further Up the Creek, Cool Mikado, Fast Lady, The Great St. Trinian's Train Robbery, Carry On Doctor, Up Pompeii, Up the Chastity Belt, Up The Front, The House in Nightmare Park, Sgt. Pepper's Lonely Hearts Club Band.

TV: BBC series. Comedy Playhouse, Frankie Howerd Show, Up The Convicts—Series (4) (Australia 1975), The Frankie Howerd Show—Series (13) (Canada 1976), Up Pompei.

STAGE: Old Vic Midsummers Night's Dream, A Funny Thing Happened on the Way to the Forum, Way Out in Piccadilly, Wind in the Sassafras Trees.

HUBBARD, GORDON: Executive. b. Los Angeles, Calif., Aug. 11, 1921. e. Santa Monica City Coll. Air Force, 1940–45; sls. office, Maidenform Bra Co., 1945; ret., Air Force, 1950; special training program for sls. contracts and representation, Pacific Title, 1953; worked two yrs. in plant, in laboratory and optical depts., then represented the company in the field, acct. exec., Pacific Title; pres., Pacific Title.

HUDGINS, TORRENCE B.: Film Buyer. b. Merkel, Tex. e. SMU. Interstate Theatres, Inc. 1923–52; Trans-Texas Theatres, 1951–54, advertising; Cinema Art Theatres Inc., 1954–1974, film buyer and advertising. 1974–78 Torrence Hudgins Buying and Booking Service.

HUDIS, NORMAN: Writer. b. London, England. Now based in L.A.

PICTURES INCLUDE: 6 Carry On comedies, 2 Man From U.N.C.L.E. features.

TV: Many series include own series, Our House.

HUDSON, ROCK: Actor. r.n. Roy Fitzgerald. b. Winnetka, Ill., Nov. 17, 1925; e. New Trier H.S. Winnetka. U.S. Navy, 1944–46; m.p. debut in Fighter Squadron; No. 1 top moneymaking star M.P. Herald-Fame poll, 1957–65.

PICTURES INCLUDE: Undertow, I was a Shoplifter, One-Way Street, Peggy, Winchester 73, Tomahawk, Fat Man, Air Cadet, Iron Man, Bright Victory, Desert Hawk, Here Come the Nelsons, Bend of the River, Has Anybody Seen My Gal, Scarlet Angel, Horizons West, Lawless Breed,

Seminole, Sea Devils, Golden Blade, Back to God's Country, Gun Fury, Taza Son of Cochise, Magnificent Obsession, Bengal Brigade, Captain Lightfoot, One Desire, All that Heaven Allows, Never Say Goodbye, Giant, Written on the Wind, Battle Hymn, Something of Value, Pylon, Farewell to Arms, This Earth Is Mine, Pillow Talk, The Last Sunset, Come September, Lover, Come Back, The Spiral Road, A Gathering of Eagles, Mans Favorite Sport, Strange Bed Fellows, Send Me No Flowers, A Very Special Favor, Blindfold, Seconds, Tobruk, Ice Station Zebra, A Fine Pair, Darling Lilli, The Hornet's Nest, Pretty Maids All in a Row, Showdown, Embryo, Avalanche, The Mirror Crack'd.
TV: MacMillan and Wife series.

HUGGINS, ROY: Writer, director. b. Litelle, Wash., July 18, 1914; e. U. of Calif. 1935–39; U. of Calif. Grad. Sch., 1939–41; m. Adele Mara, actress. Spec. rep., U.S. Civil Service Comm., 1941–43; industrial eng., 1943–46; writer 3 novels and many stories for Sat. Eve. Post; pres., Public Arts, Inc., 1968. V.P., 20th Century-Fox TV, 1961.
PICTURES INCLUDE: I Love Trouble, Too Late for Tears, Lady Gambles; story, Fuller Brush Man, Good Humor Man; adap., Woman in Hiding; collab., s.p., Sealed Cargo; Sp., dir., Hangman's Knot; collab. s.p., Gun Fury, Three Hours to Kill; s.p., Pushover; Prod. motion picture A Fever in the Blood for Warner Bros.
TV: Prod. Warner Bors. Presents Cheyenne series, anthologies, 1955–56; Conflict (series); Produced Pilots of Colt .45, 77 Sunset Strip, Maverick, Prod. Maverick, 1957–58; won Emmy Award 1958. Created, The Fugitive, 1962; v.p., MCA Revue, 1963; exec.-prod. Run For Your Life, 1965; exec. prod., The Outsiders, The Bold Ones, Alias Smith and Jones, Toma, 1968–74. ABC Movie of Week, Pretty Boy Floyd. 1974: Co-creator of The Rockford Files pilot and series for NBC; 1975: Co-creator of City of Angels for NBC; 1976: executive producer of Captains and the Kings, a segment of Best Sellers for NBC. 1977: exec. prod. of Aspen, a segment of best sellers for NBC; 1978: exec. prod. of Wheels, a segment of The Big Event for NBC.

HUGHES, KATHLEEN: Actress. r.n. Betty von Gerkan; b. Hollywood, Calif., Nov. 14, 1928; e. L.A. City Coll., UCLA. m. Stanley Rubin, producer, mother of 4, Michael played Baby Matthew on Peyton Place. Studied drama; under contract, 20th-Fox, 1948–51; starred in 7 Year Itch 1954, La Jolla Playhouse; parts m.p.; signed by UI, 1952.
PICTURES INCLUDE: For Men Only, Sally and Saint Anne, Golden Blade, It Came From Outer Space, Thy Neighbor's Wife, Glass Web, Dawn at Socorro, Cult of the Cobra, Three Bad Sisters, Promise Her Anything, The President's Analyst, The Late Liz, The Take.
TV: Bob Cummings Show, Hitchcock, 77 Sunset Strip, G.E. Theatre, Bachelor Father, The Tall Man, Dante, Tightrope, Markham, I Dream of Jeannie, Peyton Place, Gomer Pyle, Kismet, Ghost and Mrs. Muir, Bracken's World, The Survivors, Julia, Here's Lucy, To Rome with Love, The Interns, The Man and the City, Mission Impossible, The Bold Ones, Lucas Tanner, Marcus Welby, Barnaby Jones, Medical Center, Babe (mov.).

HUGHES, KEN: Writer, dir. b. Liverpool, Eng. Ent. ind. as sound engineer, BBC, 1940; dir., doc. films. Novels: High Wray, The Long Echo.
TV: Script of serials Solo for Canary, An Enemy of the State; Sammy (Eddie in USA); The Haunting, Lenin in 1917 (Fall of Eagles); The Voice (Dial M For Murder).
PICTURES INCLUDE: Joe Macbeth, Confession, The Trials of Oscar Wilde, The Small World of Sammy Lee, Arrivederci Baby, Casino Royale, Chitty Chitty Bang, Bang, Cromwell, The Internecine Project, Sextette.
AWARDS INCLUDE: Golden Globe, Emmy, Script Writer of Year, W.G. Merit Award.

HUGO, LAURENCE: Actor. b. Berkeley, Calif. e. U. of Calif.
THEATRE: On Broadway in Skin of Our Teeth, Decision, Born Yesterday, Stalag 17.
TV: Studio One, Omnibus, Danger, The Web, Mama, over the CBS-TV network.

HUKE, BOB, B.S.C.: Cinematographer. Ent. m.p. ind. 1937, Asst. cameraman Pygmalion, French Without Tears, etc.; 1939–44 Royal Navy. 1945–9 camera operator Great Expectations, Uncle Silas, Seven Days To Noon and others. 1950–56 Brazil. Contract dir. of photo. for Cia Cinematographica Vera Cruz, 1957–59 dir. own company, Zenith. 1960. dir. photo, 3 Dinah Shore Shows, Spain, Paris, Copenhagen. NBC 1961. Dir. photo. Reach For Glory, The War Lover, The Very Edge, 1962; The Brain, 8 Dinah Thomas Shows in Europe. 1963 Sandres of the River. 1964, Ballad in Blue, License to Share. TV & Cinema Commericals, 1955. 1966, 2nd Unit You Only Live Twice; 1968, 2nd Unit, Battle of Britain, 1969; dir. photo, Virgin and Gypsy. 1971; Under Milk Wood.

HUNNICUT, GAYLE: Actress. b. Fort Worth, Texas, February 6, 1943. e. BA (with honors) University of California, Los Angeles, (UCLA) Theater Arts & English major. Early career, community theatres in Los Angeles. Ent. m.p. ind. 1967.

PICTURES INCLUDE: PJ (New Face in Hell), Eye of the Cat, Marlowe, Fragment of Fear, The Freelance, Voices, Running Scared, New Face in Hell, Scorpio, L'Homme Sans Visage, The Spiral Staircase, The Sell Out, Tony Siatta, Once in Paris, One Take Two, Fantomas.
TV: Man and Boy, The Golden Bowl, The Ripening Seed, Fall of Eagles, The Switch, Humboldts Gift, The Life and Death of Dylan Thomas, Return of the Saint, Martian Chronicles, A Man Called Intrepid.
THEATRE: The Ride Across Lake Constance, Twelfth Night, The Tempest, Dog Days, The Admirable Crichton, A Woman of No Importance.

HUNT, BILLY H.: Executive, attorney. b. Alton, Ill., Aug. 19, 1926. e. University of Southern California, University of California, Berkley, Juris Doctor, 1957. Attorney, Morrison, Forster, Holloway, Schuman & Clark, 1957–59; attorney for Mitchell, Silberberg & Knupp, working in legal dept. at Columbia Pictures, 1959–63; entertainment, corporate, labor law for entertainment companies at Mitchell, Silberberg & Knupp, was exec. v.p. of Association of Motion Picture and Television Producers, Inc., 1972–75; pres. of Central Casting Corporation, 1972–75; named exec. v.p. of Motion Picture Association of America, 1973–75.

HUNT, G. CARLETON: Executive. b. Bridgeport, Conn., Jan. 5, 1908. With Warner Bros. Theatres, 1929–35; with New England Theatres, 1935–38; with stage groups, 1938–41; with RKO Studios, 1941–51; secy., gen. mgr., Unicorn Theatres, 1952–53; pres., General Film Labs., 1953–62; Chairman of the Board; Pacific Industries, Inc. 1962–64, pres., Glen Glenn Sound Co., now bd. chm.; Pres. DeLuxe General Inc., 1964–1972. Retired 1973.
MEMBER: Acad. of M.P. Arts & Sciences, Acad. of TV Arts & Sciences; Assoc. mem. ASC; past pres. SMPTE, v.p. UNIATEC.

HUNT, MARSHA: Actress. b. Chicago, Ill., Oct. 17, 1917. Started screen 1935.
B'WAY PLAYS INCLUDE: Devils Disciple, Joy to the World, Legend of Sarah, Born in Texas, Tunnel of Love, The Paisley Convertible.
PICTURES INCLUDE: Virginia Judge, College Holiday, Easy to Take, Blossoms in the Dust, Panama Hattie, Joe Smith American, These Glamour Girls, Winter Carnival, Irene, Pride and Prejudice, Flight Command, Cheers for Miss Bishop, Trial of Mary Dugan, Thousands Cheer, None Shall Escape, Lost Angel, Cry Havoc, Bride by Mistake, Music for Millions, Valley of Decision, A Letter for Evie, Smash-Up, Carnegie Hall, Raw Deal, Take One False Step, Actors and Sin, Happy Time, No Place To Hide, Bombers B-52, Blue Denim, Johnny Got His Gun.
TV: Philco, Studio One, Ford Theatre, Show of Shows, G.E. Theatre, Climax, Hitchcock, Peck's Bad Girl Series, The Defenders, Twilight Zone, Cains Hundred, Gunsmoke, The Breaking Point, Outer Limits, Profiles in Courage, Ben Casey, Accidental Family, Run For Your Life, My Three Sons, The Outsiders, Name of the Game, Univ.'s 120, Ironside, Marcus Welby, M.D., Police Story, The Young Lawyers.

HUNT, PETER: Director—Editor. b. London, England. 1928. e. Romford England—Rome, Italy. London School of Music. Actor English Rep. Entered film as camera asst. Documentary, later asst editor documentary, then asst editor features. London Films then editor—credits incl. Hill in Korea, Admirable Crichton, Scripting films. Editor: Cry From the Streets, Greengage Summer (Loss of Innocence in USA), Ferry To Hong Kong, H.MS Defiant (Damn the Defiant in USA), Supervising editor/2nd Unit Director, Dr. No, Call Me Bwana, From Russia With Love, Goldfinger, Ibcress File, Thunderball, You Only Live Twice, . . . associate producer, Chitty Chitty Bang Bang. . . . Director, On Her Majesty's Secret Service, Gullivers Travels (Live & Animation) Gold, Shout At The Devil, at present filming for Golden Harvest Group (USA), Death Hunt.

HUNT, PETER H.: Director. b. Pasadena, Calif., Dec. 16, 1938. e. Hotchkiss, Yale, Yale Drama School. m. actress Barbette Tweed. Director for Williamston Theatre since 1957. Lighting designer on Bdwy. (1963–69).
PICTURES INCLUDE: 1776, Give 'Em Hell, Harry, Bully, A New Start.
TV: Adams Rib (pilot and series), Hello Mother Goodbye (pilot), Ivan the Terrible (pilot), Quark (pilot), Mixed Nuts (pilot), Flying High (pilot), Wilder and Wilder (pilot), Rendezvous Hotel (pilot).
STAGE: 1776 (London & Bdwy), Georgy (Bdwy.), Scratch (Bdwy.), Goodtime Charley (Bdwy.), Give 'Em Hell Harry (Tour), Magnificent Yankee (Kennedy Center), Bully (Tour).

HUNT, WILLIE: Executive. b. Van Nuys, Ca., Oct. 1, 1941. e. Utah State Univ. (BA, 1963). Married to actor Tim Considine. Started in industry as secretary at Warner Bros., 1965; named exec. secty. to Ted Ashley, WB, 1969; story analyst, WB, 1974; story editor, WB, 1975; named West Coast story editor for WB, 1978; joined MGM in 1979 as v.p., motion picture development.

HUNTER, KIM: Actress. r.n. Janet Cole; b. Detroit, Mich., Nov. 12, 1922. e. Miami Beach, Fla. schools; m. Robert Emmett,

Dec., 1951; daughter and son. Started career in summer stock, Gant Gaither Theatre, Fla.; Theatre of the 15, Coral Gables; Hendersonville, N.C.; Baltimore, Md.; Pasadena, Calif. Community Playhouse appeared in Arsenic and Old Lace; others. Screen debut; in leading role, The Seventh Victim, David O. Selznick; other films, Tender Comrade, When Strangers Marry, You Came Along; then, to England to co-star in Stairway To Heaven, A Canterbury Tale; then N.Y. stage in A Streetcar Named Desire (Pulitzer Prize play); signed by Elia Kazan to play orig. role in screen version for which Academy Award as best supporting actress, 1951. N.Y. stage; Darkness at Noon, The Chase, Children's Hour, Tender Trap, Write Me A Murder, bdway., 1961–62; films, Anything Can Happen; Deadline U.S.A., Storm Center, Bermuda Affair, Young Stranger, Money, Women & Guns, Lilith; 1961 American Shakespeare Festival, Stratford, Conn., As You Like It, Troilus and Cressida, Macbeth.

TV APPEARANCES: Climax, Lux Video, G.E. Theatre, U.S. Steel Hour, Omnibus, Playhouse 90, The Play of the Week, Hallmark Hall of Fame, Hitchcock, Arrest and Trial, TWTWTW, Jackie Gleason Show, Hawk, Mannix, Disney's Wonderful World of Color, Bonanza, CBS Playhouse, NET, 1970: Eternal Light, David Frost Show, Young Lawyers, Bracken's World. 1971: Bold Ones, In Search of America (Special), Medical Center, Gunsmoke, Cannon, Columbo. 1972: Night Gallery, Owen Marshall, Love, American Style, Young Dr. Kildare, The Evil Touch. 1973: Mission: Impossible, NBC Mystery Movie, Marcus Welby, M.D., Hec Ramsey, Griff, The Police Story, ''Unwed Father''—ABC Movie-of-the-Week, Ironside; This Is The Life, Insight, Lucas Tanner, Wide World of Mystery, and Movies of the Week: Born Innocent, Bad Ronald, Ellery Queen, This Side of Innocence, Once An Eagle, Gibbsville, Hunter, Baretta, Crazy Annie received Emmy nomination; Oregon Trail, and Backstairs at the White House; Stubby Pringle's Christmas, Project UFO, 1978; The Rockford Files, Specter on the Bridge (movie), 1979; Edge of Night (1978–80—Emmy nomination; FDR, The Last Year, 1980; Skokie, 1981.

BROADWAY: Weekend, 1968. The Penny Wars, 1969. The Women, 1973; Nat'l Tour: And Miss Reardon Drinks a Little, 1971–72; In Praise of Love (1975 summer tour), The Cherry Orchard (1976, off B'way), Elizabeth The Queen (Buffalo, N.Y.), Semmelweiss (1977, Buffalo, N.Y.), The Bell of Amherst (1978, New Jersey); The Little Foxes (1980, Berkshire Theatre Festival), To Grandmother's House We Go, 1981.

PICTURES INCLUDE: Planet of the Apes, The Swimmer, Beneath the Planet of the Apes, Escape from the Planet of the Apes, Dark August.

AUTHOR: Kim Hunter—Loose in the Kitchen (Domina Books).

HUNTER, ROSS: Producer. r.n. Martin Fuss. b. Cleveland, Ohio, May 6; e. Western Reserve U., M.A. School teacher, 1938–43; actor, Columbia Pictures, 1944–46; returned to school teaching; stage prod. & dir.; m.p. dialogue dir.; assoc. prod. U-I, 1950–51; prod., U-I, 1951. Moved production Co. from Universal to Columbia, April 1, 1971. Moved to Paramount, Oct. 1, 1974.

PICTURES INCLUDE: Louisiana Hayride, Ever Since Venus, Bandit of Sherwood Forest, Groom Wore Spurs, Take me to Town, All I Desire, Tumbleweed, Taza Son of Cochise, Magnificent Obsession, Naked Alibi, Yellow Mountain, Captain Lightfoot, One Desire, The Spoilers, All That Heaven Allows, There's Always Tomorrow, Battle Hymn, Tammy and the Bachelor, Interlude, My Man Godfrey, The Wonderful Years, Stranger in My Arms, Imitation of Life, Pillow Talk, Portrait in Black, Midnight Lace, Back Street, Flower Drum Song, Tammy and the Doctor, The Thrill of It All, The Chalk Garden, I'd Rather Be Rich, The Art of Love, Madame X, The Pad, Thoroughly Modern Millie, Rosie, Airport, Lost Horizon.

HUNTER, TAB: Actor. b. New York, N.Y., July 11, 1931. U.S. Coast Guard; odd jobs. discovered in 1948.

PICTURES INCLUDE: The Lawless, Island of Desire, Gun Belt, Steel Lady, Return to Treasure Island, Track of the Cat, Battle Cry, Sea Chase, Burning Hills, Girl He Left Behind, Lafayette Escadrille, Gunman's Walk, Damn Yankees, That Kind of Woman, Pleasure of His Company, The Golden Arrow, War Gods of the Deep, Ride the Wild Surf, Hostile Guns, Life and Times of Judge Roy Bean.

HUNTLEY, RAYMOND: Actor. b. Birmingham, England, Apr. 23, 1904. On stage from 1922 repertory, tour; London debut in ''Back to Methuselah'' 1924; N.Y. debut in ''Venetian Glass Nephew'' 1931; m.p. debut 1934; many TV appearances.

PICTURES INCLUDE: Rembrandt, Knight Without Armour, Night Train to Munich, They Came to a City, Pimpernel Smith, Freedom Radio, Way Ahead, I See a Dark Stranger, School for Secrets, Broken Journey, So Evil My Love, Mr. Perrin and Mr. Traill, It's Hard to Be Good, Passport to Pimlico, Trio, I'll Never Forget You, The Last Page, Laxdale Hall, Meet Mr. Lucifer, Mr. Denning Drives North, Hobson's Choice, Orders Are Orders, Constant Husband, Geordie, The Prisoner, Doctor at Sea, Dam Busters, Teck-

man Mystery, Green Man, Brothers in Law, Room at the Top, Carlton-Browne of the F.O., Suspect, A French Mistress, Pure Hell of St. Trinians, Only Two Can Play, Waltz of The Toreadors, Crooks Anonymous, On the Beat, Carry On Nurse, The Great St. Trinian's Train Robbery, Hostile Witness, The Gaunt Woman, Arthur! Arthur!, Young Winston, That's Your Funeral, Symptoms.

HURLOCK, ROGER W.: Pres. Hurlock Cine-World. b. Cambridge, Md., May 30, 1912. e. Baltimore City College; ent. m.p. ind. as publicist, Hippodrome Theatre, Balt.; asst. mgr., Lessor-operator Imperial and Majestic Theatres, Balt., 1931–35; real estate, bldg., farming, Md. and Alaska, 1936–58; elected bd. mem., Allied Artists, 1958; asst. to pres., 1961–63; chmn. budget comm., 1963; chmn. policy comm., 1964; c.p. exec. comm. member, 1964; v.p., chf. operating officer 1965; chmn. exec. comm., 1966; pres., 1967. pres., Hurlock Cine-World, 1969.

HURT, JOHN: Actor. b. Shirebrook, Derbyshire, Jan. 22, 1940. e. St. Martin's School for Art, London. Professional debut in 1962 in British film, The Wild and the Willing.

PICTURES: A Man for All Seasons, Before Winter Comes, Sinful Davey, In Search of Gregory, 10 Rillington Place, Forbush and the Penguins, East of Elephant Rock, Disappearance, Spectre, Pied Piper of Hamelin, The Ghoul, Little Malcolm, The Shout, Midnight Express, Alien, Heaven's Gate, The Elephant Man, Partners.

TELEVISION: Playboy of the Western World, A Tragedy of Two Ambitions, Green Julia, Nijinsky, Shades of Green, Ten from the Twenties, The Pedlar, The Naked Civil Servant, I, Claudius, Crime and Punishment.

STAGE: The Dwarfs, Little Malcolm and His Struggle Against the Eunuchs, Man and Superman, Belcher's Luck, Ride a Cock Horse, The Caretaker, Romeo and Juliet, Ruffian on the Streets, The Dumb Waiter, Travesties, The Arrest.

HURT, MARY BETH: Actress. e. NYU School of Arts. Stage debut in 1973 in N.Y. Shakespeare Festival prod., More Than You Deserve. Other stage work includes Trelawny of the Wells, Father's Day.

PICTURES: Interiors, Head Over Heels, Change of Seasons.

TELEVISION: Secret Service (NET Theatre), Kojak, etc.

HURT, R.N.: Circuit executive. b. Veedersburg, Ind., Jan. 30, 1902; e. Brown's Business Coll., Danville, Ill.; m. Entered m.p. ind. as operator at Veedersburg for H. C. Whisler, 1918–22; owned, oper. Lyric Edinburgh, Ind.; 1920; for six months, operator and later booker Lincoln Paris, Ill., for Mrs. L. Jarodsky. To Crown Point, Ind., Palace Theatre, manager four years; State, Princeton, in 1930 as mgr.; later owner. Sold out to E. E. Alger, 1932 and became mgr. Apollo, Princeton. Transferred to main office, Alger Circuit as booker in 1934, then gen. mgr. oper. in 10 towns controlling 14 theatres. Left 1945; Dixon Theatre Co., 1945–46; Isis Theatre, Toluca, Ill., 1946–48; returned to Alger Sept. 1948–58; booker, Kerasotes Theatres, hdq. Springfield, Ill., 1958–71. Mgr., Times, Danville, Ill., Oct. 1, 1971. Retired.

HURT, WILLIAM: Actor. b. Washington, D.C. 1951. e. Tufts, Julliard. Leading actor with New York's Civic Repertory Company since 1976, appearing in among other plays, The Fifth of July, My Life, Ulysses in Traction, The Runner Stumbles, Hamlet, Childe Byron.

FILMS: Altered States (debut), Eyewitness, Body Heat.

TELEVISION: Verna: USO Girl.

HUSSEIN, WARIS: Director. b. India, 1938. TV incl: Sleeping Dog, Death of a Teddy Bear, Toggle, Spoiled, Days In the Trees, A Passage to India, Girls in Uniform, St. Joan, A Casual Affair, Divorce His, Divorce Hers, Shoulder To Shoulder, Gorges Sand, Chips With Everything, The Glittering Prizes, Love Letters on Blue Paper, Sarah Bernhardt, Blind Love, Romance, Daphne Laureola, Waiting for Sheila, Armchair Thriller, Edward and Mrs. Simpson, Death Penalty, And Baby Makes Six.

PICTURES INCLUDE: A Touch of Love, Quackser Fortune, Melody, The Possession of Joel Delaney, Henry VIII and His Six Wives.

HUSTON, JOHN: Director, writer. b. Aug. 5, 1906, Nevada. Mo. p. Walter Huston. In 1938: collab. s.p., Amazing Dr. Clitterhouse, WB. In 1939: Juarez, In 1940: Dr. Ehrlich's Magic Bullet, WB. In 1941: High Sierra, Sergeant York, WB.; dir., s.p., The Maltese Falcon, WB, in 1942: dir. In This Our Life, Across the Pacific, WB. U.S. documentaries (dir.).

PICTURES INCLUDE: Three Strangers, Treasure of the Sierra Madre, Key Largo, WB. 1949 founded Horizon Films with S.P. Eagle, Were Strangers, The Asphalt Jungle, The Red Badge of Courage, The African Queen, Moulin Rouge, Beat the Devil, Moby Dick, The Misfits, Freud, List of Adrian Messenger, The Night of the Iguana, The Bible, Reflections in a Golden Eye, Candy, acted in De Sade, Walk with Life and Death, The Kremlin Letter, The Deserter, acted in Man in the Wilderness, Fat City, The Life and Times of Judge Roy Bean (dir. & acted), Battle for the Planet of the Apes (actor), The McIntosh Man, Chinatown (actor), The Wind and The Lion (actor), The Man Who Would Be King (dir.), Winter Kills (actor), Wise Blood (dir.), Victory (dir.).

TV: The Rheinmann Exchange.

HUSTON, VIRGINIA: Actress. b. Omaha, Neb., Apr. 24, 1925. Did radio and stage work while in school; acted at Omaha Community playhouse; started in m.p. with RKO 1945.

PICTURES INCLUDE: Nocturne, Out of the Past, Tarzan's Peril, The Highwayman, Racket, Flight to Mars, Night Stage to Galveston, Sudden Fear, Knock on Wood.

HUTNER, MEYER MICHAEL: Executive. b. Brooklyn, N.Y., July 11. e. St. John's U., Brooklyn; m. Roberta Bogart. Reporter, ed., N.Y. Post, Journal American; pub. dir., Billy Rose Enterprises, with 20th Century-Fox as newspaper contact, pub. dir., 1948–55; adv. pub. dir., Samuel Goldwyn Prod., 1956; nat. pub. mgr. Warner Bros., 1956–60; v.p., dir. & pub., Astor Pictures, 1961; apptd. pub. mgr., United Artists Corp., July 1962; pub. dir. 1965; exec. ass't in chg. publicity Paramount Pictures, 1966. v.p. chg. adv. publicity, Filmways, 1967. World-Wide pub., dir. United Artists, 1969. Eastern Co-ordinator, adv.-pub., Columbia Pictures, 1975; joined 20th Century Fox as natl. pub. director, Oct., 1976. Appt. Warner Bros., dir. special projects, 1980.

HUTTON, BETTY: Actress. b. Battle Creek, Mich., Feb. 26, 1921. Made screen debut 1942.

PICTURES INCLUDE: The Fleet's In, Star Spangled Rhythm, Happy Go Lucky, Miracle of Morgan's Creek, Incendiary Blonde, And the Angels Sing, Here Come the Waves, Duffy's Tavern, The Stork Club, Perils of Pauline, Annie Get Your Gun, Let's Dance, The Greatest Show on Earth, Somebody Loves Me, Spring Reunion.

TV: Goldie.

HUTTON, BRIAN, G.: Director. b. N.Y., N.Y.

PICTURES INCLUDE: The Wild Seed (Universal); The Pad (Universal); Sol Madrid (MGM); Where Eagles Dare (MGM); Kelly's Heroes (MGM); X, Y, and Zee, Night Watch, The First Deadly Sin.

HUTTON, LAUREN: Actress. b. Charleston, S.C. e. Univ. of So. Florida, Sophie Newcombe College. As model featured on more covers than any other American.

PICTURES: Paper Lion (debut, 1968), Little Fauss and Big Halsey, The Gambler, Gator, Welcome to L.A., A Wedding, American Gigolo, Zorro, the Gay Blade, Paternity.

HUTTON, ROBERT: Actor. r.n. R. Winne. b. Kingston, N.Y., June 11, 1920. e. Blair Acad., N.J. In summer stock prior to screen career, 1943.

PICTURES INCLUDE: Destination Tokyo, Janie, Roughly Speaking, Hollywood Canteen, Too Young to Know, Love and Learn, Always Together, Steel Helmet, New Mexico, Racket, Slaughter Trail, Casanova's Big Night, Cinderella; co-prod., star, The Slime People; asso. prod., Now It Can Be Told. The Vulture, You Only Live Twice, They Came From Beyond Space, Torture Garden, Tales From the Crypt.

HUTTON, TIMOTHY: Actor. b. Malibu, CA, 1961. Father, late actor Jim Hutton. In plays in high school; toured with father in Harvey during vacation. Theatrical film debut in Ordinary People (1980).

TELEVISION: Movies: Zuma Beach, Best Place To Be, Baby Makes Six, Sultan and the Rock Star, Young Love, First Love, Friendly Fire.

PICTURES: Ordinary People, Taps.

HUYCK, WILLARD: Writer-Director. e. USC. Went to work as reader for Larry Gordon, executive at American-International Pictures; named Gordon's asst., working on scene rewrites for AIP films. First screen credit on The Devil's Eight as co-writer with John Milius, also USC graduate. Left AIP to write original scripts, joining with Gloria Katz. Both signed by Francis Ford Coppola to write and direct films for his America Zoetrope but projects never materialized. Co-wrote American Graffiti with Katz (1973) and Lucky Lady (1975). Huyck made directorial debut in 1979 with French Postcards, co-written with Katz, who also produced.

HYAMS, JEROME: Executive. b. July 19, 1915, N.Y.C. e. New York Univ.; with Guaranteed Pictures Co., 1937; mgr., Commonwealth Pictures Corp., 1938; U.S.N., 1941–45; returned to Commonwealth 1945; sales mgr., Commonwealth Film & TV, Inc., 1948; apptd. v.p. chg. sales, Commonwealth; organ. Hygo TV Films, Inc., 1951; dir. of sync. dist. for Screen Gems, 1957; exec. v.p., gen. mgr., Screen Gems Inc. Pres. Screen Gems, 1968; senior exec. v.p. Columbia Pictures Industries, Inc., 1973, created Chief Operating Officer.

HYAMS, JOSEPH: Adv. & pub. exec. b. N.Y., Sep. 21, 1927. e. N.Y. Univ.; ent. industry, 1947. Various publicity posts, 20th Century-Fox, Columbia Pictures, 1947–55; eastern pub. mgr., Figaro Prods., 1955–56; West Coast pub. mgr., Hecht-Hill-Lancaster, 1955–58; pub. adv. dir., Batjac Prods. 1959–60 national adv. & pub. dir., Warner Bros., Seven Arts, 1960. v.p., Warner Bros., Inc., 1970.

HYAMS, PETER: Director-Writer. b. N.Y.C., July 26, 1943. e. Hunter College, Syracuse Univ. Joined CBS news staff N.Y. and made anchor man. Filmed documentary on Vietnam in 1966. Left CBS in 1970 and joined Paramount in Hollywood as writer. Hired by ABC to direct TV features.

PICTURES INCLUDE: Busting (s.p., dir.), Our Time (dir.), Peeper, Telefon (co-s.p.), Capricorn One (s.p., dir.), The Hunter (co. s.p.), Outland (dir., s.p.).

TV: The Rolling Man, Goodnight My Love (both s.p., dir.).

HYDE, JOHN W.: Executive. b. Jackson, MI. e. New York University, B.A. 1963. Joined ABC upon graduation from N.Y.U. 1963 hired by MCA-Universal as executive assitant to then-v.p. Ned Tanen. As Tanen's assistant, became assoc. prod. on several MCA features. Also wrote, produced and directed musical shorts for MCA Records. 1969 joined Filmways, Inc. as v.p. and exec. asst. to then-pres. Richard R. St. Johns. 1972 formed own company, Acmelab, Ltd., multifaceted special effects, commercial and post-production facility, which included Cinefex, Videoconversion and Acme Film Laboratories. 1976 Hyde sold Acmelab to produce The Ravagers for Columbia Pictures. During production of that film, Hyde rejoined Richard St. Johns as v.p. of the Guinness Film Group. 1977 Hyde became vice president in charge of production for all Guiness films.

TV INCLUDES: The Andy Williams Show, The Lloyd Thaxton Show.

PICTURES INCLUDE: Games, Midnight Patient, Skulduggery, The Ravagers, Death Hunt, Rituals, The Uncanny, Silent Flute (Circle of Iron), Matilda, The Wanders, Nightwing, The Mountain Men, The Final Countdown, A Change of Seasons, Dead & Buried, American Pop and Venom.

HYDE, TOMMY: Executive. r.n. Thomas L. b. Meridian, Miss., June 29, 1916. e. Lakeland H.S., grad., 1935. Worked, E.J. Sparks Theatres, 1932–41; Florida State Theatres, 1941–42. U.S. Navy, 1942–46. Florida State Theatres, 1946–47; city mgr. (Tallahassee); Talgar Theatres, 1947–58; v.p. and gen. mgr., Kent Theatres, 1958–81; vice-pres., Motion Picture Films, Inc.; pres., NATO of Florida, 1961–62; chmn. bd. 1963–70.

HYER, MARTHA: Actress. b. Fort Worth, Tex., Aug. 10, 1930; e. Northwestern U., Pasadena Playhouse.

PICTURES INCLUDE: Thunder Mountain, Indian Summer, Roughshod, Velvet Touch, The Lawless, Outcast of Black Mesa, Salt Lake Raiders, Frisco Tornado, Abbott and Costello Go to Mars, Scarlet Spear, So Big, Sabrina, Kiss of Fire, Paris Follies of 1956, Francis in the Navy, Red Sundown, Showdown at Abilene, Kelly and Me, Battle Hymn, Mister Cory, My Man Godfrey, Paris Holiday, Once Upon a Horse, Houseboat, Some Came Running, Big Fisherman, Best of Everything, Ice Palace, Desire In the Dust, The Right Approach, The Last Time I Saw Archie, Girl Named Tamiko, Man From the Diner's Club, Wives and Lovers, Pyro, The Carpetbaggers, First Man in the Moon, Blood On the Arrow, Bikini Beach, Sons of Katie Elder, The Chase, Night of the Grizzly, Picture Mommy Dead, The Happening, Some May Live, House of a Thousand Dolls, Once You Kiss A Stranger, Crossplot.

HYLAND, DICK IRVING: Writer-producer-management. b. N.Y.C., Aug. 22, 1906. e. Syracuse U. Reporter N.Y. Evening Journal, ed., trade pubs., adv., publicity dir. for Mills Artists, Inc., publicity dir. Warner Bros., Pres., Cinemasters, Inc., film prod. co. Made over 100 short subjects in conjunction with James Roosevelt-Mills Co., also commercial films. In Hollywood, 20 feature screen credits as writer-producer at Universal, R.K.O., Col. Became V.P. Frank Cooper Associates, Inc., artists management, 6 years. V.P. The Jaffe Agency, Inc. Currently Pres., Dick Irving Hyland Associates, literary agents, packagers. Guest lecturer U. So. Calif., Amer. Nat. Theater Academy. Pac. Coast Writers Conf. Recipient Wisdom Award of Honor for advancement of knowledge, learning and research in education.

I

IANNUCCI, SALVATORE J.: Executive. b. Brooklyn, N.Y., Sept. 24, 1927. e. NYU 1949 B.A., Harvard Law School 1952 L.L.D. 2 yrs. legal departments RCA and American Broadcasting Company, Inc.; 14 yrs. with CBS Television Network: asst. dir. of bus. affairs, dir. of bus. affairs, v.p. of bus. affairs; 2 yrs. v.p. admin. National General Corp.; 2' yrs. pres. of Capital Records; 4½ yrs. Corpor. Vice pres. and dir. of Entertainment Div. of Playboy Enterprises, Inc.; 4 yrs. partner with Jones, Day, Reavis & Pogue in Los Angeles office, handling entertainment legal work; Presently, pres. Filmways Entertainment, Inc. and sr. v.p., Filmways, Inc.

IMMERMAN, WILLIAM J.: Producer. b. 1937. Joined 20th Century-Fox in 1972 as v.p., business affairs. Promoted 1975 to senior vice pres., administration and worldwide business affairs of the Feature Film Division. Previously was with American International Pictures for 6 yrs. as v.p. business affairs & assoc. counsel. From 1963–65 was deputy dist. atty. for Los Angeles County. Presently bd. chm. of Cinema Group, Inc. Exec. prod., Highpoint.

INGALLS, DON: Producer, writer. b. Humboldt, Nebr. e. George Washington U. Columnist, Washington Post; producer-writer, ATV England and Australia; writer-producer, Have Gun Will Travel, CBS, also produced for TV: The Travels of Jamie McPheeters, The Virginian, Honey West, Serpico, Kingston: Confidential. Exec. story consultant The Sixth Sense, ABC.
   WRITER: Gunsmoke, Have Gun Will Travel, The Bold Ones, Marcus Welby M.D., Mod Squad, Star Trek, Honey West, Bonanza, The Sixth Sense, Then Came Bronson, Police Story, World Premier Movie, Shamus, Flood, Capt. America, The Initiation of Sarah, others. Currently prod.-writer for TV's Fantasy Island.
   FEATURE FILMS: Airport-1975, Story and Screenplay. Who's Got the Body?

INGELS, MARTY: Actor. b. Brooklyn, N.Y., Mar. 9, 1936. U.S. Infantry 1954–58. Ent. show business representing Army, Name That Tune. Stage: Sketchbook revue, Las Vegas.
   TV: Phil Silvers Show, Steve Allen, Jack Paar, Playboy Penthouse, Bell Telephone Hour, Manhunt, Ann Southern Show, Peter Loves Mary, The Detectives, Joey Bishop Show, Hennessey, Dick Van Dyke Show, I'm Dickens . . . He's Fenster, Burke's Law, Hollywood Palace.
   PICTURES INCLUDE: Ladies Man, Armored Command, Horizontal Lieutenant, Wild & Wonderful.

INGIS, ROBERT L.: Executive. b. Brooklyn, N.Y., Feb. 19, 1935. e. N.Y.U. Accounting staff, S. D. Leidesdorf & Co., 1956–61; officer of Kalvex, Inc., 1961 to present.

INGSTER, BORIS: Writer, director. In 1935; collaborated on adaptation, The Last Days of Pompeii, RKO. In 1936: Dancing Pirate, RKO. In 1937: collaborated on screen play Thin Ice, 20th-Fox. In 1938: Happy Landing.
   PICTURES INCLUDE: Judge Steps Out, Southside 1–1000; Something for the Birds, Abdullah's Harem, California-story, Cloak & Dagger, The Amazing Mrs. Holliday.
   TV: Wagon Train, The Alaskans, The Roaring 20's, Travel of Jaimie McFeathers, The Man From U.N.C.L.E.

IRELAND, JILL: Actress. b. London, England, 1936. Began career in music halls of England at age of 12; went on to sing, dance and entertain at London's Palladium, in cabarets and a tour of the continent in ballet. Began acting in West End repertory; then signed to major film studio contract at 16 by J. Arthur Rank. Screen debut as ballet dancer in Oh, Rosalinda, first of 14 feature films for Rank.
   PICTURES INCLUDE: Three Men in a Boat, Hell Drivers, Robbery Under Arms, Carry On, Nurse, Raising the Wind, Twice Round the Daffodils, Villa Rides, Rider on the Rain, Cold Sweat, The Family, Someone Behind the Door, The Mechanic, The Valdez Horses, The Valachi Papers, Breakout, Hard Times, Breakheart Pass, From Noon Till Three.
   TV: Shane (series), The Man from U.N.C.L.E., Ben Casey, Night Gallery, Daniel Boone, Mannix, Star Trek (series).

IRELAND, JOHN: Actor. b. Vancouver, B.C., Jan. 30, 1915; m. Stock 5 yrs. To Hollywood, 1945.
   THEATRE: On N.Y. stage: Macbeth, Moon Is Down, Native Son, Counter Attack, etc.
   PICTURES INCLUDE: A Walk in the Sun, Wake Up and Dream, Red River, The Gangsters, Roughshod, All The King's Men, Return of Jesse James, Vengeance Valley, Red Mountain, Basketball Fix, Bushwackers, Hurricane Smith, 49th Man, Combat Squad, Southwest Passage, Security Risk, Steel Cage, Outlaw Territory, Fast and Furious, Good Die Young, Queen Bee, Hell's Horizon, Faces in the Dark, I Saw What You Did, Fort Utah, Once Upon a Time in the West, The Adventurers, The Dirty Heroes, Escape to the Sun, Farewell, My Lovely.

IRETON, GLENN F.: Executive. b. Hammond, N.Y., July 11, 1906. e. Colgate Univ. Actor, stock in Balt., Md., Englewood, N.J.; vaude.; juvenile lead in Lew Cantor's, The Skull; musician, Frank Silver's orch., Loew's Theatres, NYC, publicity, Montclair, Commodore Hotels; 24-hour man. carnival, Endy Bros. Railroad shows; Public relations dir. Warner Bros., Canada, 1940–47. Free-lance publicist & promoter, 1947–50. Occupation film prod, Japan, 1951. Editor & publisher, and co-founder with wife (Kikuko M. Ireton) of Far East Film News in 1953, renamed Movie Marketing in 1961, Movie/TV Marketing in 1966.

IRETON, KIKUKO MONICA: Managing Editor. Movie/TV Marketing; Tokyo, Japan. b. May 22, 1929. e. Seijo Gaguen, Tokyo. Daughter of late Shoichiro Kobayashi, manager of Bank of Japan in New York (1937–41) and later director. Co-founder with husband (Glenn F. Ireton) of Far East Film News in 1953, renamed Movie Marketing in 1961, Movie/TV Marketing in 1966.

IRVING, GORDON: Film, stage, TV Journalist and Broadcaster. b. Annan, Scotland, Dec. 4, 1918. e. Dunfries Acad., Scotland, Edinburgh Univ., grad. M.A. Hons. Classics.

Writer on show business since 1939. Columnist for 18 years with Daily Record and Sunday Mail, Glasgow. Contributor to "The Performer," former weekly of variety Artistes' Federation and The Stage, London.
   AUTHOR: The Devil on Wheels, Annie Laurie Story, Great Scot! (Harry Lauder biography), The Good Auld Days (Story of Scotland's Music-Hall), Brush Up Your Scotland!, The Wit of the Scots, The Wit of Robert Burns, Take No Notice, etc. Contributor to trade and fan magazines and journals in Britain, America and South Africa. Free lance writer for worldwide publications. Official correspondent of Stage, London "Variety," New York "Daily Variety," Hollywood, Argus South African Newspapers in Johannesburg, Durban, Cape Town, etc.

IRWIN, CHRISTOPHER: Producer-Executive. b. England 1948. e. University of Sussex, Eng., from where he holds a B.A. degree in social studies. From 1967 to 1969 worked as freelance producer-presenter for BBC Radio Brighton. Was with the Federal Trust (the institute concerned with European affairs) 1969 to 1975, during which time worked for the Secretariat of the North Atlantic Assembly. Joined the BBC's External Services as talks producer in 1975, moving in 1977 to the BBC's central Secretariat. From 1977 to 1978 was seconded to the International Institute for Strategic Studies. In 1978 went to Scotland as Secretary, BBC Scotland, and was closely associated with early stages of Radio Scotland. Is a member of BBC's Future Policy Group, the "think tank" of the Corporation. Appointed Head of Radio Scotland May 1980.

ISAACS, PHIL: Executive. b. N.Y.C., May 20, 1922. e. City College of N.Y., 1938–42. In U.S. Navy, 1943–46. Joined Paramount Pictures in 1946 as bookers asst., N.Y. exch.; following year was booker. In 1951 branch mgr. in Washington. In 1955 named mgr. of Rocky Mountain Div. and in 1957 made asst. east sales mgr. In 1966 was Eastern-Southern sls. mgr. In 1967 joined Cinema Center Films as v.p. domestic dist. In 1972 named v.p., marketing, for Tomorrow Entertainment; Joined Avco-Embassy 1975 as v.p., gen. sls. mgr., named exec. v.p., 1977. 1978 joined General Cinema Corp. as v.p. Now v.p., gen. sls. mgr., Orion Pictures.

IVANO, PAUL: Director of Photography. r.n. Paul Ivanichevitch. b. Nice, France, May 13, 1900. e. Lycee de Nice. First director of photography to start air-shots from a helicopter (They Live by Night, Johnny Belinda, Criss Cross, My Four Sons, Japanese War Bride, etc.)
   PICTURES INCLUDE: Chubasco, Lizzie, Three and a Day, Champagne for Caesar, The Seagull, Shanghai Gesture, Blond Venus, The Suspect, The Impostor, Flesh and Fantasy, Queen Kelly, For Men Only, Hold Back Tomorrow, Johnny Belinda (exteriors & helicopter shots), The Gangster, Black Angel, Frozen Ghost, Dead Man's Eyes, Black Dawn.
   TV: The Jim Backus Show, The Lawless Years, Westinghouse Playhouse, Screen Director's Playhouse, The Texan, Telephone Time, Please Don't Eat the Daisies, Daktari, Man From Uncle, Family Affair.

IVERS, IRVING N.: Executive. Worked for 10 years in radio and TV in variety of executive capacities in station management before entering film business. Joined Columbia Pictures in 1973, serving as director of mktg. and dir. of adv. 1973–77; named Canadian sls. mgr. 1977–78; v.p. of adv./pub. 1978–80. Now with 20th Century-Fox as snr. v.p. of adv./pub./promo.

IVES, BURL: Ballad singer. b. Hunt Township, Ill., June 14, 1909. e. Teacher's College, Charleston, Ill. Professional football player, itinerant worker, radio singer, specializing ballads.
   STAGE: On B'way in Cat on a Hot Tin Roof.
   PICTURES INCLUDE: Smoky, Green Grass of Wyoming, Station West, So Dear to My Heart, Sierra, East of Eden, The Big Country, Cat on a Hot Tin Roof, Day of the Outlaw, Our Man in Havana, Robin and the Seven Hoods, Just You and Me, Kid.

J

JABLONOW, SCOTT: Exhibitor Executive. b. St. Louis, Mo., Feb. 27, 1950. e. Arizona State Univ. Joined Mid-America Theatres as film buyer in 1971, named president in February, 1979. Member of board of National Endowment for Arts; served on Short Film Showcase.

JACKS, ROBERT L.: Producer. b. Oxnard, Calif., June 14; e. Santa Monica City Coll.; U.S.C. U.S. Navy; expl. dept., 20th-Fox, 1949; then story dept.; admin. asst. to prod. Julian Blaustein & Samuel G. Engel; prod., 1952.
   PICTURES INCLUDE: Lure of the Wilderness, Man on a Tightrope, Desert Rats, Prince Valiant. Prod (with late Leonard Goldstein) as Panoramic Prod. for 20th-Fox: The Gorilla, Gambler from Natchez, Man in the Attic, Princess of the Nile; The Raid, Siege at Red River, Three Young

Texans, White Feather, A Life in the Balance, Robt. Jacks Prods.: Killer Is Loose, A Kiss Before Dying, Proud Ones, Bandido, Man from Del Rio, Roots of Heaven, Darryl Zanuck Prods.; prod. rep. 20th Century-Fox, 1963; Man in the Middle, The Third Secret, Guns at Batasi, Zorba the Greek; prod. exec. 20th Century-Fox TV, 1964. Prod.; Victor Borge Show (pilot), 1964; Three Coins in the Fountain (pilot), 1964; The Man Who Never Was, 1965; Custer (pilot), 1967; Honeymoon With a Stranger (ABC Movie of Week), 1969; Arnie (pilot), 1970; Bandolero (film), The Undefeated (film).

TELEVISION: Eight Is Enough (series), 1977–78; State Fair (1 hour pilot); Crunch (2 hour pilot); The Waltons (series), 1972–1976; Lovejoy (pilot); Pomroy's People (pilot/co-creator); The Girls of Huntington House (MOW); Binary (MOW); The Homecoming (CBS 2 hour special); Do Not Fold, Spindle or Mutilate (MOW); A Girl and a Boy (MOW); Wild, Wild West Revisited (special), Mr. Horn (miniseries); Young Pioneers (mini-series); Young Love, First Love (MOW); Murder Can Hurt You (MOW); More Wild Wild West (MOW); A Matter of Death & Life (MOW); The Day the Loving Stopped (MOW), A Few Days in Weasle Creek (MOW).

JACKSON, BRIAN: Actor. film/stage prod. b. Bolton, England, 1931. Early career in photography then numerous stage performances incl. Old Vic, Royal Shakespeare. Ent. film/TV industry 1958. Formed Quintus Plays, 1965; formed Brian Jackson Productions 1966; formed Hampden Gurney Studios Ltd. 1970. Co-produced The Others 1967; presented The Button, 1969; co-produced the documentary film Village in Mayfair, 1970; 1971: Formed Brian Jackson Films Ltd.; produced Yesterday, The Red Deer; 1972: produced The Story of Tutankhamen.

TV INCLUDES: Moon Fleet, Private Investigator, Life of Lord Lister, Z Cars, Vendetta, Sherlock Holmes, Mr. Rose, Hardy Heating International, Nearest and Dearest, The Persuaders, The Paradise Makers, The New Avengers, Smugglers Bay, The Tomorrow People, Secret Army, Last Visitor for Hugh Peters.

PICTURES INCLUDE: Incident in Karandi, Carry On Sergeant, Gorgo, Jack the Ripper, Taste of Fear, Heroes of Telemark, Only the Lonely, The Deadly Females, The Revenge of the Pink Panther.

STAGE INCLUDES: Mame, Drury Lane, Fallen Angels, South African Tour, Seasons with Old Vic and Royal Shakespeare Co., In Praise of Love.

JACKSON, FREDA: Actress. b. Nottingham, Eng., Dec. 29, 1909; e. U. Coll., Nottingham. Stage debut 1933, Northampton Repertory Theatre; London debut 1936, Old Vic; screen debut in Canterbury Tale, 1942.

PICTURES INCLUDE: Henry V, Beware of Pity, Great Expectations, No Room at the Inn, Flesh and Blood, Women of Twilight, The Good Die Young, The Crowded Day, The Enchanted Doll, Bhowani Junction, Last Man to Hang, The Flesh Is Weak, Brides of Dracula, Greyfriar's Bobbie, Shadow of the Cat, Attempt to Kill, West Eleven, Monster of Terror, The Third Secret, Gwangi, Tom Jones, Clash of the Titans.

TV: Macadam and Eve, Sorry Wrong Number, Trial of Marie Lafarge, Release, Colombe, Maigret in Montmartre, Sergeant Musgrave's Dance, Dr. Finlay's Casebook, Sunset, Knock On Any Door, The Spies, Adam Adamant, Midland Profile, Owen Md., The Kilvert Diaries, She Fell Among Thieves, Randall and Hopkirk, The Old Curiosity Shop.

JACKSON, GLENDA: Actress. b. Birkenhead, England, 1938. Ent. m.p. ind. 1955.

PICTURES INCLUDE: Marat-Sade, Negatives, Women In Love, The Music Lovers, Sunday, Bloody Sunday, Mary Queen of Scots, Triple Echo, The Nelson Affair, A Touch of Class, The Maids, The Tempter, The Romantic Englishwoman, Hedda, Sarah, Nasty Habits, House Calls, Stevie, The Class of Miss McMichael, Lost and Found.

TV: Queen Elizabeth.

JACKSON, GORDON: Actor. b. Glasgow, Scotland, Dec. 19, 1923; e. Glasgow. On radio since 1939; screen debut in "Foreman Went to France" 1940.

PICTURES INCLUDE: Nine Men, San Demetrio, Millions Like Us, Pink String & Sealing Wax, Captive Heart, Against the Wind, Eureka Stockade, Whiskey Galore, Floodtide, Stop Press Girl, Bitter Springs, Happy Go Lovely, The Lady with the Lamp, Meet Mr. Lucifer, Malta Story, Castle in the Air, Quartermass Experiment, Pacific Destiny, Baby and the Battleship, Sailor Beware, Seven Waves Away (Abandon Ship), As Long As You're Happy, Hell Drivers, Rockets Galore, Bridal Path, Yesterday's Enemy, Blind Date, Cone of Silence, Tunes of Glory, Greyfriar's Bobbie, Mutiny on the Bounty, The Great Escape, The Long Ships, Those Magnificent Men in Their Flying Machines, The Great Spy Mission, The Ipcress File, Cast A Giant Shadow, Fighting Prince of Donegal, Night of the Generals, Triple Cross, The Eliminator, Prime of Miss Jean Brodie, Run Wild, Run Free, Hamlet, Scrooge, Kidnapped, Madame Sin, Russian Roulette, Spectre, Golden Rendezvous, Medusa Touch, Raising Daisy Rothschild.

TV: Numerous TV appearances incl: Upstairs, Downstairs, The Professionals.

JACKSON, JAY: Performer. b. Stockdale, Ohio. e. Miami Univ. of Ohio, Ohio State Univ. Actor & announcer, many radio shows; U.S. Army; m.c., Twenty Questions TV show; Masquerade Party, Perry Como Show, Father Knows Best.

JACKSON, JOHN HENRY: Executive. b. New York, April 27, 1916. e. Holy Cross Academy, 1930; Professional Children's School, 1934; Georgia Tech, 1936. Performed as vaudeville artist touring Europe, 1928–29; Fair dates and indoor circus, 1929–35; Texas Centennial, 1936; George Abbott's Too Many Girls, 1938. Joined Radio City Music Hall, 1943 with Glee Club; stage manager, 1944–51; director of stage operations, 1958; v.p., 1970; prod., 1971; pres., Tri-Marquee Productions, Ltd., 1979.

JACKSON, KATE: Actress. b. Birmingham, Ala., Oct. 29. e. Univ. of Mississippi, Birmingham Southern Univ. Did summer stock before going to N.Y. to enter American Academy of Dramatic Arts, appearing in Night Must Fall, Constant Wife, Little Moon of Alban, etc. Worked as model and became tour guide at NBC. First role on TV in Dark Shadows (series).

PICTURES INCLUDE: Thunder and Lightning, Dirty Tricks, Making Love.

TV: The Jimmy Stewart Show (pilot). Movies: Killer Bees, The Shrine of Lorna Love, The Jenny Storm Homicide. Series: Charlie's Angels (regular).

JACKTER, NORMAN: Executive. b. New York City, May 18, 1922. e. N.Y. City Coll. Entered industry directly from school. Spent 35 years with Columbia Pictures, holding all jobs from booker thru division mgr. Was v.p. dist. from 1964–73. Also v.p., marketing, for Radnitz/Mattel Prods. Inc. Now indep. prod. and dist. consultant.

JACKTER, RUBE: Sales executive. b. New York City, Dec. 12, 1900. Entered m.p. ind. 1913 with Jesse L. Lasky Feature Play Co. in sales dept., joined Samuel Goldwyn upon org. Goldwyn Pictures Corp. as spcl. rep.; to Fox Film Corp. as Fox News staff cameraman, also a special rep. in charge of Fox News sales. Resigned to go with Universal and in 1924 left to join Columbia as first special field rep. and assisted in nationalizing Columbia Film Exchanges; then gen. sales mgr.; v.p., 1958.

JACOBS, BARRY: Executive. b. London, England, 1924. Ent. m.p. ind. 1938. Served in RAF 1943–46. Circuit rep. Warner Bros. 1938–59. Overseas sales rep. independent producers 1960–62. Formed Eagle Films Ltd. dist. organisation UK 1962. Entered prod. 1969. Exec. prod. The Wife Swappers, Groupie Girl, Bread, Naughty, The Love Box, Sex and The Other Woman, On the Game, Eskimo Nell.

JACOBY, FRANK DAVID: Director/Producer. b. New York, N.Y., July 15, 1925. Hunter College, Brooklyn College. m. Doris Storm, producer/director educational films, actress. 1949–52: NBC network TV director; 1952–56: B.B.D.O., Biow Co., TV producer/director; 1956–58 Metropolitan Educational TV Association, Director of Production; 1958–65: United Nation, film producer/director; 1965 to present: President, Jacoby/Storm Productions, Inc., Westport, Conn., documentary, industrial, educational films and filmstrips. Clients include Burlington Industries, United Federation of Teachers, USIA, Time/Life, Inc., Xerox Corp., Random House, Publ., Lippincott Co., Globe Publ., Harper & Row, IBM, Heublein, G.E., and Pitney Bowes. Winner, Sherwood Award, Peabody Award. Member, Director's Guild of America; winner, Int'l TV & Film Festival, National Educational Film Festival, American Film Festival.

JACOBY, JOSEPH: Producer-Director-Writer. b. Brooklyn, N.Y., 1942. e. N.Y. Univ. School of Arts and Sciences, majoring in m.p. As undergraduate worked part-time as prod. asst. on daytime network TV shows and as puppeteer for Bunin Puppets. In 1963 joined Bill Baird Marionettes as full-time puppeteer, working also on Baird film commercials. Made feature m.p. debut as prod.-dir of Shame, Shame, 1968.

PICTURES INCLUDE: Hurry Up, or I'll Be 30, The Great Georgia Bank Hoax (co.-prod., dir., s.p.).

JACON, BERNARD: Executive. b. Louisiana. Manager, promotion, Small & Strausberg Theatres, New York; buyer & gen. mgr., Mantell Theatres N.Y., gen. mgr. & assoc., Rockaway Beach Theatres, Universal Pictures, home office & field, br. operations & sales. Mgr., sales & dist. (Continental Films) Superfilms Distribution Corp., New York 1946–49; vice-pres. in chg. of sales & dist., Lux Film Distributing Corp., N.Y. 1949–52; v.p. sales, dist. IFE Releasing, 1952–55; org. nat'l distrib. co., Jacon Film Distributors, Inc., as pres., 1956; nat'l consultant to independent distributors, producers & exhibitors, member of the Pioneers & Variety; 1979, formed Bernie Jacon, Inc., nat'l. co-ordinator for producers and distributors.

JACQUES, ROBERT C.: Film editor. b. Cincinnati, Ohio, Feb. 24, 1919. e. U. of Mich., U.S.C. Asst. film ed., RKO Radio 1939–42; film ed., Pathe News, 1942–44; chief film ed., NBC Television, 1944–48; prod. chief, Ziv TV film dept. 1948–51; free lance m.p. film ed., 1951–52; supervising film ed., prod. mgr., American Film Prod., 1952–53; prod. supvr., ed., Telenews and Screen Gems 1953; film ed.,

RKO Radio, 1953–55; supervising film ed., George Blake Enterprises, 1955–57; v.p. Peter Elgar Productions 1957–60; supv. film editor, Transfilm-Caravel Inc. 1960–62; v.p. in chg. of completion, Filmex, Inc., 1962. V.P. in charge of completion, Filmex Inc. 1962–69. Free lance film editor, May–Nov. 1969. V.P. of own co., Double Image Inc., film and videotape editorial service, Nov. 1969 to date.

JAECKEL, RICHARD HANLEY: Actor. b. Long Beach, N.Y., Oct. 10, 1926; e. Hollywood High School, 1943. Performed odd jobs upon graduation, with plans toward entering Navy when of age; worked as delivery boy in mail room, 20th Century-Fox; signed for role of Baby Marine, in Guadalcanal Diary.
PICTURES INCLUDE: The Gunfighter, Sea Hornet, Hoodlum Empire, My Son John, Come Back Little Sheba, Big Leaguer, Sea of Lost Ships, Shanghai Story, Violent Men, Apache Ambush, Sands of Iwo Jima, Fragile Fox, The Dirty Dozen, Sometimes a Great Notion, Ulzanas Raid, Pat Garrett and Billy the Kid, The Outfit, Chosen Survivors, The Drowning Pool, Part II—Walking Tall, Twilights Last Gleaming.
TV: U.S. Steel Hour, Elgin Hour, Goodyear Playhouse, Kraft, Firehouse (movie).

JAEGER, ANDREW P.: Executive. b. New York City, Oct. 15, 1917. e. Fordham, Columbia U. American Tobacco Co., 1937–41 as asst. to sales & adv. division head; trainee through managing director, Puerto Rican office of 20th Century-Fox Int'l, 1946–49; network dir., film programming, Dumont TV Network, 1949–53; v.p. sales & program devel., Procker Syndications Int'l, 1953–57; network salesman, division mgr., Ziv Television Programs (later United Artists TV), 1957–63; Latin American supervisor, 1963–66; account exec., Telcom Inc., and program consultant to film buyers, 1966–69; sales mgr., then V.P. and currently president, Allied Artists Television, 1969 to present.

JAFFE, HERB: Executive-Producer. b. New York, N.Y. e. Brooklyn Coll., Columbia U. Press agent; then talent agent, MCA personal appearance div.; sales exec., MCA-TV, Ltd., syndic. film div.; eastern sales mgr., Motion Pictures for Television; joined Official Films as v.p., sales mgr.; Herb Jaffe Assoc. 1957; sold Herb Jaffe Assoc. to Ashley-Steiner-Famous Artists, Inc.; v.p. in prod., United Artists, 1965; v.p. of West Coast Operations, 1966. 1970, v.p. charge of World-Wide prod., 1973 entered field of independent motion picture production.
PICTURES: The Wind and the Lion, Demon Seed, Who'll Stop the Rain, Time After Time, Those Lips, Those Eyes, Motel Hell, Jinxed.

JAFFE, LEO: Executive. b. April 23, 1909. e. New York U. Columbia, 1930; v.p., Columbia Pictures, January, 1954; 1st v.p., treas., member of board, 1956; v.p. & treas., 1958; exec. v.p., Columbia Pictures, 1962; Pres. Columbia Pictures, 1968; pres., Columbia Pictures Industries, Inc, 1970, president & chief executive officer Columbia Pictures Industries, Inc., 1973; chm., August, 1973, Chairman of Board of directors since Aug., 1973.

JAFFE, SAM: Talent agent. b. New York City, May 21, 1901. In 1920 joined Mayer-Schulberg prod. org. as studio mgr.; later prod. mgr., prod. B.P. Schulberg Prod. 1922; 1923–29 prod. mgr. & exec. mgr. Paramount Studios; 1930–32 prod. mgr. & asst. to David O. Selznick, RKO Radio; 1933 asst. to Sam Briskin, Columbia. In 1934 became partner Schulberg-Feldman-Jaffe, talent agents, Hollywood; 1935 org. Sam Jaffe, Inc., Sam Jaffe, Ltd.; later dissolved; then headed Jaffe Agency; Ind. prod., head Sam Jaffe Prod., 1959; prod., The Sullivans, Damon & Pythias, co-prod., Born Free; executive producer, Theatre of Blood.

JAFFE, SAM: Actor. b. New York City, Mar 8, 1896. Went on stage 1915, member Washington Square Players, N.Y.; toured with Shakespearean Company; later in many N.Y. stage prods. (Samson and Delilah, The God of Vengeance, The Jazz Singer, Grand Hotel, A Doll's House, etc.). On screen 1933.
PICTURES INCLUDE: The Scarlet Empress, Lost Horizon, Gunga Din, 13 Rue Madeleine, Gentleman's Agreement, The Barbarian and the Geisha, Ben Hur, Les Espions, Rope of Sand, The Asphalt Jungle (Venice Int. Film Festival Award, Best Male Performance), Under the Gun, I Can Get It for You Wholesale, Day the Earth Stood Still, Guns for San Sebastian, The Great Bank Robbery, Dunwich Horror, Bedknobs and Broomsticks.
TV: Ben Casey series, Bonanza, Daniel Boone, Play of he Week, The Lovers (ABC movie of the week), Quarantine (World Premiere), Night Gallery, The Old Man Who Cried Wolf, Enemies (Hollywood Television Theatre), Ghost Story, Love, American Style, Owen Marshall, QB VII, Streets of San Francisco, S.W.A.T, Harry O, Medical Story.

JAFFE, STANLEY R.: Producer. b. New Rochelle, N.Y., July, 1940. Graduate of University of Pennsylvania's Wharton School of Finance. Joined Seven Arts Associates, 1962; named exec. ass't to president, 1964; later, head of East Coast TV programming. Produced Goodbye, Columbus,

in 1968 for Paramount; then joined that company as exec. v.p., 1969. Produced A New Leaf, 1970. Named pres. of Paramount in 1970; resigned June 10, 1971 to form own prod. unit. First film: Bad Company (1972); Man on the Swing, Bad News Bears. Joined Columbia as v.p. of global prod. in 1976, but resigned to be independent producer. 1979: Kramer vs. Kramer.

JAFFE, STEVEN-CHARLES: Prducer. b. 1954. e. Univ. of So. Calif. (cinema). Worked on production in Holland and Switzerland; served as prod. asst. on The Wind and the Lion in Spain. Assoc. prod. on Demon Seed (written by brother Robert); served as location mgr. on Who'll Stop the Rain; assoc. prod. on Time After Time. Full producer on Those Lips, Those Eyes.

JAFFE, WILLIAM B.: Attorney. b. New York City, Mar. 11, 1904; e. Union Coll. 1926, A.B.; Columzia U. Law School 1929, LL.B.; m. Evelyn Annenberg. Assoc. Nathan Burkan 1929–35; gen. counsel Allied Artists; 1933–69 spcl. counsel to interests financing independent prod.; to leading personalities m.p. ind.; dir. MPPDA rep. Columbia; gen. counsel & dir. Allied Artists Internat'l 1933–69; chmn. Manning Plan, State of N.Y.; counsel, War Manpower Commission, N.Y. Region Spec. counsel to Revlon, Inc., in TV field; s.p. counsel Triangle Pub.; chmn., Art Advisory Committee Dartmouth College; trustee, Union Coll., Schenectady, N.Y. Vice Chr. & Bd. of Gov. Jewish Museum, N.Y.C.; Benefactor Metropolitan Museum of Art; Patron, Museum of Modern Art, Group Chairm. United Hospital Fund 1964–69; Trustee, Phi Epsilon Pi Foundation. Recipient Phi Epsilon Pi Achievement Award, 1964; Doctor Humane Letters, Dartmouth College 1964; Trustee Mt. Sinai Hospital, N.Y., N.Y. Eye & Ear Infirmary. Partner, law firm, Shea, Gallop, Climenko & Gould.

JAFFEY, HERBERT: Executive. b. Somerville, N.J., Cap't. U.S. Army, pressbook writer, 20th Century-Fox; theatre management, Loew's; field exploitation, United Artists, Ad. pub. dir. 20th Century-Fox Int and Inter-Amer. Corp.; dir., adv. & publicity, Rugoff Theatres; Independent Film Prod.; Paramount Foreign Advertising & Publicity Manager, screenplay writer.

JAGGER, DEAN: Actor. b. Lima, Ohio, Nov. 7, 1903; e. Wabash Coll. (Crawfordsville, Ind.). On N.Y. stage, stock, vaudeville. Screen debut 1929 in Woman from Hell. Academy Award sup. role 1949 for 12 O'Clock High.
PICTURES INCLUDE: College Rhythm, Home on the Range, Car 99, Woman Trap, 13 Hours By Air, Woman in Distress, Escape by Night, Brigham Young, Western Union, Valley of the Sun, I Escaped from the Gestapo, North Star, Alaska, When Strangers Marry, Pursued, Driftwood, Dark City, Rawhide, Warpath, Denver and Rio Grande, My Son John, It grows on Trees, The Robe, Executive Suite, Private Hell 36, White Christmas, Bad Day at Black Rock, The Eternal Sea, On the Threshold of Space, It's a Dog's Life, Red Sundown, Great Man, Three Brave Men, The Nun's Story, Cash McCall, Elmer Gantry, Parrish, Jumbo, Stay way Joe, Firecreek, Smith, The Kremlin Letter, Vanishing Point, Tiger by the Tail.
TV: Glass House, Mr Novak (series), Brotherhood of the Bell, The Lie.

JAGLOM, HENRY: Director-Writer-Editor. b. New York. Studied acting, writing and directing at Univ. of Pennsylvania and with Actors Studio. Did off-Bdwy. shows; went to West Coast where appeared in TV series (Gidget, The Flying Nun, etc.). Started shooting documentary film in Israel during Six Day War; turned it into 3-hr. silent film. Hired to edit Easy Rider by producer Bert Schneider. Acted in Drive, He Said and Last Movie. Directed first feature, A Safe Place, in 1971.
PICTURES: Tracks (1977); Sitting Ducks (1980).

JAHNCKE, ERNEST LEE, JR.: Executive. b. New Orleans, La., Aug. 8, 1912. e. U.S. Naval Acad., 1933. Officer, U.S. Navy; traffic clerk, NBC, 1937–39; station rel. dept., 1939–41; active duty, U.S. Naval Reserve, 1941–46; joined station rel. dept., American Broadcasting Co., 1946; mgr., stat. rel., 1948–49; v.p., stat. rel., 1949–51; v.p. in charge of radio network, 1951–52; v.p., asst. to pres., ABC 1952–56; v.p., asst. to bd. chmn., Edward Petry & Co., Inc.; 1957–59; div., Standards & Practices, NBC, 1960–61; Vice pres., 1962–69; East. Dir., American Humane Ass'n, 1970.

JAMES, CLIFTON: Actor. b. N.Y.C., 1922. e. Oregon Univ. Studied at Actors Studio. Made numerous appearances on stage and TV, as well as theatrical films.
PICTURES INCLUDE: On The Waterfront, The New Centurions, Live and Let Die, The Last Detail, Bank Shot, Juggernaut, The Man with the Golden Gun, Rancho DeLuxe.

JAMES, DENNIS: Performer. b. Jersey City, N.J. Aug. 24, 1917. e. St. Peter's Coll., Jersey City. TV personality for over 30 years. Formerly M.C., actor, sports commentator in Radio; award winning sports commentator for wrestling, 25 TV first to credit; currently pres., Dennis James Prod.
TV: Chance of a Lifetime, High Finance, First Impressions, What's My Line, PDQ, Your All-American College Show; host new Price Is Right, Nightime; Host, "Name That Tune," Daytime.

JAMES, HARRY: Band leader. b. Albany, Ga. Mar. 15, 1916. With Mighty Haag Circus as child; contortionist until 1922; trumpet player until 1931; with Benny Goodman band; formed own orchestra 1939-till present. Dot records, 1966 Capitol, MGM, Columbia, London Records, Longines, RCA Readers Digest Albums & Sheffield Lab.
PICTURES INCLUDE: Syncopation, Private Buckaroo, Springtime in the Rockies, Best Foot Forward, Two Girls and a Sailor, Bathing Beauty, Do You Love Me, If I'm Lucky, Carnegie Hall, mus. dir., Young Man With a Horn, To Catch a Thief, Anything Goes.

JAMES, LAURA: Actress. b. Hazelton, Penn., 1933. e. The Theatre Wing, The American Academy of Dramatic Arts, 1948-50; worked Off-Broadway, Summer Stock, TV; starred in West Coast premieres of The Second Man, Champagne Complex.
PICTURES INCLUDE: Four Girls in Town, St. Francis of Assisi.
TV: Matinees Theatre, The Big Story, Day in Court, Divorce Court, Official Detective, Congressional Investigator, Sheriff of Cochise; now working overseas.

JAMES, POLLY: Writer. b. Ancon, Canal Zone; e. Smith Coll. Newspaper work, Panama; with trade mag., N.Y.; screen writer since 1942.
PICTURES INCLUDE: Mrs. Parkington, The Raiders, Redhead from Wyoming, Quantrill's Raiders.
TV: Several shows.

JANIS, HAROLD E.: Producer. b. July 8, 1906. e. Peddie, Columbia School of Journalism. AP Latin American reporter; INS feature writer; War ser. U.S.A. 1941-42, major; U.S. Dept. of State information ser., 1945-47; Radio Stat. WMCA 1934-40. Joined NBC 1950 as program exec., assigned to Show of Shows; exec. prod. Martha Raye Show, Caesar's Hour, Bob Hope Show, Max Liebman presents, others inc. Jackie Gleason, Martin & Lewis; joined Sid Caesar as prod. Sid Caesar Invites You; exec. prod. Shellrich Corp.

JANNI, JOSEPH: Producer. b. Milan, Italy, May 21, 1916. e. Milan University; Rome Film School. Entered m.p. industry 1941. Assistant producer. Founded Vic Films Ltd.
PICTURES INCLUDE: Own productions: The Glass Mountain, White Corridors, Something Money Can't Buy, Romeo and Juliet (co-prod.), A Town Like Alice (prod.); The Captain's Table, Savage Innocents, A Kind of Loving, Billy Liar, Darling, Modesty Blaise, Far From The Madding Crowd, Poor Cow, In Search of Gregory, Sunday, Bloody Sunday, Made, Yanks (co-prod.).

JARMAN, CLAUDE, JR.: Actor. b. Nashville, Tenn., Sept. 27, 1934; e. MGM School. Film debut in "Yearling," 1946.
PICTURES INCLUDE: High Barbaree, Sun Comes Up, Intruder in the Dust, Roughshod, Outriders, Inside Straight, Rio Grande, Hangman's Knot, Fair Wind to Java, Great Locomotive Chase.

JARRATT, ALFRED: Executive. b. London, England. Ent. m.p. ind. 1928 with W&F Film Services as sales rep. Joined Gaumont British Distributors as circuit rep. 1933-37; Grand National Pictures 1937-39; Army Career 1939-46; gen. sales man. Walt Disney Productions in London prior to going to Paramount Pictures, Australia, 1968. Appt. man. dir. Paramount Pictures (UK) Ltd., 1972. From 1973 man. dir., C.I.C. (UK).

JARRE, MAURICE: Composer. b. Lyon, France, 1924. Studied at Paris Cons. Was orchestra conductor for Jean Louis Barrault's theatre company four years. In 1951 joined Jean Vilar's nat'l theatre co., composing for plays by Shakespeare, Moliere, O'Neill, Eliot, and Victor Hugo. Started writing music for films in 1952.
PICTURES INCLUDE: Hotel des Invalides, La Tete contre les Murs, Eyes without a Face, Crack in the Mirror, Sundays and Cybele, The Longest Day, Lawrence of Arabia (AA, 1962), The Collector, Is Paris Burning?, Weekend at Dunkirk, Dr. Zhivago (AA 1965), Night of the Generals, The Professionals, Grand Prix, Five Card Stud, Isadora, The Damned, Ash Wednesday, The Life and Times of Judge Roy Bean, The Mackintosh Man, The Effect of Gamma Rays on Man-in-the-Moon Marigolds, Island at the Top of the World, Mandingo, Posse, Winter Kills, The Black Marble.

JARRICO, PAUL. Writer, Producer. b. Los Angeles, Jan. 12, 1915.
PICTURES INCLUDE: Salt of the Earth, Tom, Dick & Harry (Academy nomination), Thousands Cheer, The Search (Academy Award), The White Tower, Not Wanted, The Girl Most Likely.

JARROTT, CHARLES: Director. b. London, England June 16, 1927. Son of British businessman and former singer-dancer at Gaiety Theatre. Joined British Navy; wartime service in Far East. After military service turned to theatre as asst. stage mgr. with Arts Council touring co. In 1949 joined Nottingham Repertory Theatre as stage dir. and juvenile acting lead. In 1953 joined new company formed to tour Canada; was leading man and became resident leading actor for Ottawa Theatre. In 1955 moved to Toronto and made TV acting debut opposite Katharine Blake whom he later wed. In 1957 made directing debut in TV for Canadian Bdcstg. Co. Became CBC resident dir. Moved to London to direct for Armchair Theatre for ABC-TV. Then became free-lance dir., doing stage work, films, TV.
PICTURES INCLUDE: Anne of the Thousand Days, Mary, Queen of Scots, Lost Horizon, The Dove, The Littlest Horse Thieves, The Other Side of Midnight, The Last Flight of Noah's Ark.
TELEVISION: The Hot Potato Boys, Roll On, Bloomin' Death, Girl in a Birdcage, The Picture of Dorian Gray, Rain, The Rose Affair, Roman Gesture, Silent Song, The Male of the Species, The Young Elizabeth, A Case of Libel, Dr. Jekyll and Mr. Hyde.
STAGE: The Duel, Galileo, The Basement, Tea Party, The Dutchman, etc.

JASON, RICK: Actor. b. New York City, May 21, 1926. e. American Academy of Dramatic Arts.
THEATRE: Broadway debut: Now I Lay Me Down To Sleep (Theatre World award).
PICTURES INCLUDE: Sombrero, Saracen Blade, This Is My Love, Lieutenant Wore Skirts, Wayward Bus.
TV: The Case of the Dangerous Robin, Combat.

JAY, MORTY: Exec.-prod. r.n., Morton Saroff. b. Brooklyn, N.Y., Oct. 15, 1924. e. Brooklyn Coll. Pianist arranger, Sammy Kaye, 1953-54; mus. dir., Crew Cuts, 1955-61; v.p., Japsina Enterprises Inc., since 1961; v.p., Motivation Concepts of America, since 1962; v.p., International Concepts Inc., since 1963; indep. mus. arranger, since 1963; prod., commercials.
TV: Ed Sullivan Show, Masquerade Party, Stage Show.

JEFFEE, SAUL: Executive. b. Elizabeth, N.J., March 30, 1918. Established the Movielab, Inc., 1936, pres., bd. chmn., & chief exec. officer. Fellow, SMPTE, Treas.; Pres. & chm., Movielab Theatre Service; Pres. Assoc. of Cinema Labs, 1963; American Tech. Rep. & Deleg. in the U.S.-U.S.S.R. Cult. Exch. 1965; Ch. Enter. & Commu. Div., U.J.A., 1967-68; Life member, Motion Picture Pioneers, Friars, City Athletic Club; Author of Narcotics—An American Plan, chmn. Bd. of Trustees, Lorge School; Chm., Movielab-Hollywood, Inc., vice chrm., Film Society of Lincoln Center, Patron, Lincoln Center for The Performing Arts, Mem. Bd. of Gov. U.J.A., life member, chm., Life Patron Program, Variety Clubs International Patentee, Professional Motion Picture Equipment, Trustee, Federation of Jewish Philanthropies; Trustee, Will Rogers Hospital & Research Center; Mason (Shriner, 32 deg); Life Member, The Jewish Chautaqui Society. Member, Boy Scouts Advisory Committee on Scouting For The Handicapped; Fairview Country Club, Greenwich, Connecticut; Advisory Board, Cinema Lodge No. 1366 B'nai B'rith. Academy of Motion Picture Arts & Sciences; Mayor of N.Y.C. Advisory Council on Motion Pictures. Member, Natl. Academy of TV Arts & Sciences.

JEFFREYS, ANNE: Actress. b. Goldsboro, N.C.
PICTURES INCLUDE: I Married an Angel, Step Lively, Dillinger, Sing Your Way Home, Trail Street, Riffraff, Return of the Bad Men, Boys' Night Out.
THEATRE: On Bway. in Street Scene, Kiss Me Kate, Romance, Three Wishes for Jamie, Kismet.
TV: Topper, Love That Jill, many guest appearances, Delphi Bureau.
STOCK: Camelot, King & I, Kismet, Song of Norway, Bells Are Ringing, Marriage Go Round, No Sex Please, We're British, Take Me Along, Carousel, Anniversary Waltz, Do I Hear a Waltz, Ninotchka, Pal Joey, Name of the Game, Destry Rides Again, The Merry Widow, Bitter Sweet, Desert Song, High Button Shoes, Sound of Music.

JEFFRIES, LIONEL: Actor. b. Forest Hill, London, England. Ent. m.p. ind. 1952.
PICTURES INCLUDE: The Nun's Story, Two-Way Stretch, The Trials of Oscar Wilde, Fanny, The Notorious Landlady, The Wrong Arm of the Law, First Men in the Moon, Call Me Bwana, The Truth About Spring, You Must Be Joking, The Crimson Blade, Arrividerci Baby, Spy with the Cold Nose, Journey to the Moon, Camelot, Chitty Chitty Bang Bang, Eye Witness, The Prisoner of Zenda. Dir. s.p., Railway Children, 1970. Gingerbread House, Dir. Baxter, Dir. s.p., The Amazing Mr. Blunden, The Water Babies, Cream in My Coffee.

JENKINS, ALLEN: Actor. r.n. Al McConegal. b. New York, Apr. 9, 1900; e. Amer. Acad. Dramatic Arts, N.Y.
THEATRE: On stage: What Price Glory, Rain, The Last Mile, The Front Page, Five Star Final. In play & m.p. Blessed Event.
PICTURES INCLUDE: Three on a Match, I am a Fugitive from a Chain Gang, 42nd Street, Bureau of Missing Persons, Twenty Million Sweethearts, Big Shakedown, Whirlpool, Footsteps in the Dark, Ball of Fire, Tortilla Flat, Falcon Takes Over, Maisie Gets Her Man, They All Kissed the Bride, Wonder Man, Hat Box Mystery, Senator Was Indiscreet, Inside Story, Behave Yourself, Crazy Over Horses, Let's Go Navy, Oklahoma Annie, Wac from Walla Walla, Doctor, You've Got to Be Kidding.

JENKINS, CHARLES: Animation producer. b. Yorkshire, England, 1941. Ent. m.p. ind. 1957. Joined T.V.C. as gen. ass't 1958. Animated and prod. various prods. Joined Dick Williams, pioneered use of Oxberry Camera for animation, 1966. Esta. Trickfilm Ltd., prod. optical effects for Yellow Submarine, 1967.

JENKINS, DAN: Public Relations Executive. b. Montclair, N.J., Dec. 5, 1916. e. Univ. of Va., 1938. U.S. Army, 1940–45; major, infantry. P.R. officer, Hq. Eighth Army. Mng. ed., Motion Picture Magazine, 1946–48; editor, Tele-Views Magazine, 1949–50; TV editor, columnist, Hollywood Reporter, 1950–53; Hollywood bureau chief, TV Guide, 1953–63; v.p., exec. dir., TV dept., Rogers, Cowan & Brenner, Inc., 1963–71. Formed Dan Jenkins Public Relations, Inc., 1971. Joined Charles A. Pomerantz Public Relations, Ltd. as v.p., 1975, while retaining own firm. Mem. bd. trustees, Natl. Academy of TV Arts & Sciences; bd. gov., Hollywood chapter, Natl. Academy of TV Arts & Sciences, 1967–71. Rejoined Rogers & Cowan, 1979. Reactivated own firm, 1981.

JENKINS, GEORGE: Art dir. b. Baltimore, Md.; e. Univ. of Pennsylvania. Holly-N.Y. art dir. since 1946; TV pictures for Four Star Playhouse and revue productions; NBC-TV opera, Carmen; color dir., CBS-TV, 1954; NBC color spec. Annie Get Your Gun, 1957; TV music with Mary Martin, 1959.
STAGE: Mexican Hayride, I Remember Mama, Dark of the Moon, Lost in the Stars, Bell, Book & Candle, Bad Seed, Happiest Millionaire, Two for the Seesaw, Icecapades. Jones Beach spec., Song of Norway, Paradise Island, Around the World in 80 Days, Mardi Gras, Miracle Worker, Critics Choice, A Thousand Clowns, Jennie, Generation, Wait Until Dark, Only Game in Town, Night Watch, Sly Fox.
PICTURES INCLUDE: Best Years of Our Life, Secret Life of Walter Mitty, Miracle Worker, Mickey One, Up The Down Staircase, Wait Until Dark, Subject Was Roses Klute, 1776, Paper Chase, Parallax View, Night Moves, Funny Lady. Won Oscar 1977 for All the President's Men, Comes A Horseman, China Syndrome, Starting Over, The Postman Always Rings Twice, Rollover.

JENNINGS, TALBOT: Writer. b. Shoshone, Ida.; e. Harvard, M.A.; Yale Drama Sch.; playwright, N.Y. & London.
PICTURES INCLUDE: Mutiny on the Bounty, Good Earth, Romeo and Juliet; Rulers of the Sea, Spawn of the North, Northwest Passage, Edison the Man, So Ends Our Night, Landfall, Frenchman's Creek, Anna and the King of Siam, Black Rose, Across the Wide Missouri, Landfall, Knights of the Round Table, Escape to Burma, Pearl of the South Pacific, Untamed, The Naked Maja, Gunsight Ridge, The Sons of Katy Elder.

JEPHCOTT, SAMUEL C.: Executive. b. 1944, Southampton, England. e. Arts Educational School, London. Entered industry as child actor The Grove Family BBC TV, 1956. Eight years in advertising producing TV Commercials. Emigrated to Toronto, Canada in 1968. Exec. Secty., Directors Guild of Canada, 1969–72. Film production management, 1972–75. Joined Compass Film Sales Ltd., a division of Quadrant Films Ltd. 1975–77. Joined Nielsen-Ferns Intl. Ltd. in chg. of distribution. Is secretary of the Canadian Association of Motion Picture Producers. Now supvr. of prod., Nielsen-Ferns Intl. Ltd.
PICTURES INCLUDE: The Hard Part Begins 1973, Odyssey Films (prod. Manager); Sunday In The Country, 1973, Quadrant (2nd A.D.); Me, 1974, Muddy York Prods. (prod. Manager); Lions For Breakfast, 1974, Burg Prod. (prod. Manager); It Seemed Like A Good Idea At The Time, 1975, Quadrant (2nd A.D.); Love at First Sight, 1976 (prod. accountant) Quadrant; Find The Lady, 1976 (stills) Quadrant; The New Avengers, TV, 1977 (prod. manager) Neilson-Ferns Inc.

JERGENS, ADELE: Actress. b. Brooklyn, N.Y., Nov. 28, 1922. Began career in musical shows during summer vacation at 15; won contest, New York's World Fair, as model; appeared on New York stage; night clubs, U.S. and abroad.
PICTURES INCLUDE: Edge of Doom, Side Street, A&C Meet the Invisible Man, Sugarfoot, Try and Get Me, Show Boat, Somebody Loves Me, Aaron Slick From Punkin' Crick, Overland Pacific, Miami Story, Fireman Save My Child, Big Chase, Strange Lady in Town, The Cobweb.

JESSEL, IAN: Executive. b. London, England, 1939. e. Oxford. Joined Rank Organisation in 1962 as graduate trainee and became responsible for acquisition of indep. product. Formed Target International Pictures in 1968. In 1970 joined World Film Sales becoming man. dir. 1972. World Film Sales merged with ITC in 1974. Elected to board 1975. Appointed dir. Classic Cinemas and ITC Film Distributors (UK), 1979. Appt. man. dir. ITC Films Int., 1980.

JEWISON, NORMAN P.: Producer-director. b. Canada. e. Malvern Collegiate Institute, Toronto, 1940–44; Victoria College, Univ. of Toronto, 1946–50 (BA).
TV: Exec. prod. of 8 Judy Garland shows; prod.-dir., Judy Garland specials.
PICTURES INCLUDE: 40 Pounds of Trouble, The Thrill of It All, Send Me No Flowers, Art of Love, The Cincinnati Kid, The Russians Are Coming, The Russians Are Coming. Dir. In The Heat of the Night. Prod.-dir. Gaily, Gaily, Prod.: The Landlord, Fiddler on the Roof, Prod./dir.: Jesus Christ Superstar; Prod.: Billy Two Hats; Prod.-dir.: Rollerball. Prod.-dir.: F.I.S.T.; co-prod.-dir.: And Justice For All.

JOELS, MERRILL E.: Performer. b. Hartford, Conn.; began career, Hartford, 1930; organ. Mark Twain Masquers Thea.; radio, New York since 1945; TV since 1946; actor, announcer, narrator; over 500 TV shows; feature, Army, Navy and industrial films; narr., children's records, dir., AFTRA; member, The Players; Credits also Off-Broadway, Summer Stock, Daytime TV Drama. Announcer and Co-host WEVD Home Show 27 years. Announcer-engineer, WEVD.
AUTHOR: Acting is a Business, How to Get Into Show Business, Touring in Theatre of Peretz and Three by Chayefsky; Talking Books for Library of Congress.

JOFFE, CHARLES H.: Executive. b. Brooklyn, N.Y. e. Syracuse Univ. Joined with Jack Rollins to set up management-production org., clients including Woody Allen, Dick Cavett, Ted Bessell, Billy Crystal, Robert Klein, David Letterman, Martin Mull, Tom Poston, Robin Williams.
PICTURES INCLUDE: Produced: Don't Drink the Water, Take the Money and Run, Everything You Always Wanted to Know About Sex but Were Afraid To Ask, Love and Death, Annie Hall, House of God, Arthur. Exec. Prod.: Play It Again, Sam, Bananas, Sleeper, Arthur.
TV: Woody Allen specials.

JOFFE, EDWARD: producer, director, writer. b. Johannesburg, S. Africa. e. Marist Brothers College and Univ. of the Witwatersrand. Worked in m.p., theatre, commercial radio and as Journalist before ent. TV ind. in Britain 1957 as writer/prod with ATV. Has prod. & dir. some 3000 progs. 1959–61 staff prod. Granada TV. 1962 prod./dir. Grampian TV. 1966–7 dir. film The Price of a Record-r.u. Int. Emmy Award, Special Mention XXI Salerno Film Fest. Prod. dir. Columbia's Folk and So Many Partings, successive ITV entries Golden Harp TV Fest. 1968 prod. dir. Tony Hancock series in Australia; prod. dir. ind. film Will Ye No' Come Back Again for ITV; prod. dir. film Up At The Cross. 1969 ATV Network dir. This Is . . . 1970 prod. dir. The Golden Shot. 1971–2 Senior Production Lecturer Thomson TV College. 1972 dir. for London Television Service, and Thames Television, co-prod., dir. Sound Scene. 1972–73 dir. Opportunity Knocks! Today, The David Nixon Show, Magpie. Contract Prod/Dir. Thames TV. 1976–80. Productions include Problems (1st UK. Adult Sex Series), Finding Out, Writer's Workshop, About Books series.

JOHNS, GLYNIS: Actress. b. Durban, So. Africa, Oct. 5, 1923; daughter of Mervyn Johns, actor, and Alys Steele, pianist; e. In London stage from 1935 (Buckie's Bears, The Children's Hour, A Kiss for Cinderella, Quiet Week-End; Gertie, N.Y. stage, 1952; Major Barbara, N.Y., 1956–57.) On screen 1936: South Riding. Voted one of top ten British Money-making stars in Motion Picture Herald-Pathe poll, 1951–54.
STAGE: N.Y. 1964, Too Good to Be True, London, 1967: The King's Mare; 1970, Come As You Are. 1971–2 Tour of Britain, Canada and USA in The Marquise, A Little Night Music, NY 1973 (Emmy Award.)
PICTURES INCLUDE: Murder in Family, Prison Without Bars, Mr. Brigg's Family, 49th Parallel, Adventures of Tartu, Half-Way House, Perfect Strangers, This Man Is Mine, Frieda, An Ideal Husband, Miranda, Third Time, Lucky Mr. Proback, The Great Manhunt, Flesh and Blood, No Highway in the Sky, Appointment With Venus (Island Rescue), Encore, The Card (The Promoter), The Sword and the Rose, Rob Roy, Personal Affair, The Weak and the Wicked, The Seekers (Land of Fury) The Beachcomber, Mad About Men, Court Jester, Josephine and Men, Loser Takes All, Day They Gave Babies Away, Another Time Another Place, Shake Hands With the Devil, The Sundowners, The Spider's Web, The Chapman Report, Mary Poppins, Dear Brigitte, Don't Just Stand There, Lock Up Your Daughters, Vault of Horror.
TV: Own series (US): Glynis. Guest star TV includes: Dr. Kildare, Roaring Twenties, Naked City, The Defenders, Danny Kaye Show, Noel Coward's Star Quality, Mrs. Amworth, All You Need Is Love, Across A Crowded Room.

JOHNS, MERVYN: Actor. b. Pembroke, Wales, Feb. 18, 1899; married; p. non-prof.; e. Llandovery College. Abandoned study of dentistry for stage.
PICTURES INCLUDE: Lady in Danger, Guynor, Foreign Affairs, Pot Luck, Everything Is Thunder, Dishonour Bright, Storm in a Teacup, Jamaica Inn, Midas Touch, Girl in the News, Next of Kin; San Demetrio, London: Half-Way House, Twilight Hour, Dead of Night, Pink String and Sealing Wax, Captive Heart, Captain Boycott, Counterblast, Edward My Son, Quartet, Helter Skelter, Diamond City, Tony Draws a Horse, The Magic Box, A Christmas Carol, Tall Headlines, The Oracle, Master of Ballantrae, The Valley of Song, Romeo & Juliet, The Blue Peter, Moby Dick, Shield of Faith, 1984, Intimate Stranger, The Tunnel, Counterfeit Plan,

Doctor at Large, My Friend Charles, Dangerous Drugs, The Gypsy and the Gentleman, The Devil's Disciple, Once More With Feeling, Moment of Truth, No Love for Johnnie, Francis of Assisi, The Day of the Triffids, The Old Dark House, The Victors, 80,000 Suspects, Fifty-five Days at Peking, For He's a Jolly Bad Fellow, The Heroes of Telemark, The National Health, Q.B. VII, The Confessional.

TV: Many appearances, including Danger Man, The Avengers, The Sullivan Brothers, The Strauss Family, The Adventurer, Crown Court, Beryl's Lot, A Thinking Man As Hero, Kilvert's Diaries, The New Avengers, Shoestring.

JOHNSON, BEN: Actor. b. Pawhuska, Okla. Stunt rider & performer in rodeos, touring country; did stunt work in War Party; m.p. debut in Mighty Joe Young.

PICTURES INCLUDE: Three Godfathers, She Wore a Yellow Ribbon, Wagonmaster, Rio Grande, Wild Stallion, Fort Defiance, Shane, Rebel in Town, The Wild Bunch, The Undefeated, Chisum, The Last Picture Show (Academy Award, Best Supporting Actor, 1971), Junior Bonner, The Getaway, Dillinger, The Train Robbers, Kid Blue, The Sugarland Express, Bite The Bullet, Hustle, The Town That Dreaded Sundown, The Greatest, Grayeagle, The Swarm, The Hunter, Terror Train.

JOHNSON, CELIA: Actress. b. Richmond, Surrey, England, Dec. 18, 1908. e. Royal Acad. Dram. Art, London; m. Peter Fleming. On stage from 1928. London debut 1929 in A Hundred Years Old; N.Y. debut as Ophelia in Hamlet, 1931; screen debut 1942 in In Which We Serve.

THEATRE: Appearances include The Artist and the Shadow, The Circle, Death Takes a Holiday, The Wind and the Rain, Pride and Prejudice, Old Music, Sixth Floor Brit.

PICTURES INCLUDE: This Happy Breed, Brief Encounter, Dear Octopus. Received N.Y. Critics Award best perf. 1948 in Brief Encounter; 1947, This Happy Breed; pictures since include: Astonished Heart, I Believe In You, Holly & the Ivy, Captain's Paradise, Kid for Two Farthings, Good Companions, The Prime of Miss Jean Brodie.

JOHNSON, G. GRIFFITH: Executive. b. New York, Aug. 15, 1912; e. Harvard U., 1934, (AM), 1936, (Ph.D.), 1938; U.S. Treasury Dept., 1936–39; Dept. of Comm., 1939–40; O.P.A. & predecessor agencies, 1940–46; consulting economist, 1946–47; dir., Econ. Stab. Div., Nat'l. Security Resources Bd., 1948–49; chief econ., U.S. Bur. of Budget, 1949–50; econ. advisor to Econ. Stab. Admin. 1950–52; Exec. v.p. MPEAA, 1965, MPAA, 1971; Asst. Sec'y of State for Economic Affairs, 1962-65; v.p. MPAA, 1953–62; Author of several books & articles.

JOHNSON J. BOND: Producer, Exec. b. Fort Worth, Texas, June 18, 1926. e. Texas Wesleyan Coll., B.S., 1947; Texas Christian Univ. M. Ed., 1948; Southern Methodist Univ., B.D., 1952; Ph.D., Univ. of Southern Calif., 1967. Army Air Forces, WW II; public information officer, captain, U.S. Marine Corps. Korean War. Formerly member Marine Corps Reserve, Motion Picture Production Unit, Hollywood. Now Colonel, U.S. Army Reserve. Newspaper reporter, Fort Worth Star-Telegram, 1942–48; pres., West Coast News Service, 1960; pres.; exec. prod., Bonjo Prods., Inc., 1960, President, chief executive officer, Cine-Media International, 1975 managing partner, Capra-Johnson Productions, Ltd., 1978.

PICTURES INCLUDE: Sands of Iwo Jima, Retreat Hell, Flying Leathernecks; photographed aerial portions, Jamboree 53, Norfleet, Devil at My Heels, Kingdom of the Spiders, Ordeal at Donner Pass, Place of the Dawn, Lies I Told Myself, Backstretch, Airs Above The Ground, The Jerusalem Concert, The Berkshire Terror, The Seventh Gate.

TV: Creator, story consultant, tech. advisor, Whirlpool, 1962, one hour dramatic series for Screen Gems/CBS-TV, Executive Producer, Creator, On The Go. (½ hour TV News-Sports series), 1977, Coasties (1 hour TV series), 1978, Desert Rangers (1 hour series) 1979. Producer, Fandango (series), 1981.

JOHNSON, LAMONT: Director, producer, actor. b. Stockton, Calif.; e. UCLA.

TV: The Defenders, Profiles in Courage, Twilight Zone, That Certain Summer, My Sweet Charlie, The Execution of Pvt. Slovik, Fear On Trial.

PLAYS: The Egg, Yes is For a Very Young Man; dir., two operas, L.A. Philharmonic, 1964; founder, dir., UCLA Professional Theatre Group.

THEATRICAL PICTURES INCLUDE: McKenzie Break, A Gunfight, The Grundstar Conspiracy, You'll Like My Mother, The Last American Hero, Lipstick, One on One, Somebody Killed Her Husband, Cattle Annie and Little Britches.

JOHNSON, LAURIE: Composer, mus.; dir. b. 1927. Studied Royal College of Music.

STAGE: Lock Up Your Daughters, Pieces of Eight, The Four Musketeers.

TV: Themes for No Hiding Place, Echo Four-Two, Score, When the Kissing Had to Stop, The Avengers, Jason King, Shirley's World, The Avengers, Thriller, The New Avengers, The Professionals, The Botanic Man, The Adventure.

PICTURES INCLUDE: Good Companions, Moonraker, Girls at Sea, Operation Bullshine, Tiger Bay, I Aim at the Stars, Spare The Road, What a Whopper, Bitter Harvest, Seige of the Saxons, Dr. Strangelove, The First Men in The Moon, Beauty Jungle, East of Sudan, Hot Millions, And Soon the Darkness, Mister Jerico, Cause for Alarm, The Beltstone Fox, Hedda, It Lives Again, All Things Bright and Beautiful.

JOHNSON, RICHARD: Actor. b. Essex, England, 1927. Studied at RADA. First stage appearance Opera House, Manchester, then played in John Gielgud's repertory season, 1944. Served in Royal Navy 1945–48. Subsequent stage appearances incld. The Mad Woman of Chaillot, The Lark. Visited Moscow with Peter Brook's production of Hamlet. Royal Shakespeare Thea.: Stratford & London, 1957–62. Royal Shakespeare Company 1972–73. National Theatre, 1976–77.

PICTURES INCLUDE: The Haunting, 80,000 Suspects, Moll Flanders, Operation Crossbow, Khartoum, La Strega in Amore, Deadlier than the Male, The Rover, Danger Route, Twist of Sand, Oedipus The King, Trajan's Column, Lady Hamilton, Some Girls Do, Julius Caesar, The Deserters, The Beloved, Hennessy, Aces High, The Four Feathers.

JOHNSON, RUSSELL: Actor. b. Ashley, Pa. e. Girard College, Actors Laboratory, L.A.: W.W. II, Army Air Corps.

PICTURES INCLUDE: For Men Only, The Greatest Story Ever Told.

TV: Black Saddle, Climax, You Are There, Rawhide, Twilight Zone, Gilligan's Island.

JOHNSON, VAN: Actor. b. Newport, R.I., Aug. 28, 1916. Began in vaudeville; then on N.Y. stage New Faces of 1937, Eight Men of Manhattan, Too Many Girls, Pal Joey. On screen 1941 in Murder in Big House. Voted one of the top ten Money Making Stars in Motion Picture Herald-Fame Poll 1945–46.

PICTURES INCLUDE: War Against Mrs. Hadley, Dr. Gillespie's New Assistant, Pilot No. 5, Dr. Gillespie's Criminal Case, Guy Named Joe, Three Men in White, Two Girls and a Sailor, Thirty Seconds Over Tokyo, Ziegfeld Follies, Between Two Women, Thrill of Romance, Week-End at the Waldorf, Romance of Rosy Ridge, Bride Goes Wild, State of the Union, Command Decision, In the Good Old Summertime, Scene of the Crime, Battleground, Big Hangover, Three Guys Named Mike, Grounds for Marriage, Go For Broke, Too Young To Kiss, It's A Big Country, Invitation, When In Rome, Washington Story, Plymouth Adventure, Confidentially Connie, Remains to Be Seen, Easy to Love, Caine Mutiny, Siege at Red River, Men of the Fighting Lady, Brigadoon, Last Time I Saw Paris, End of the Affair, Bottom of the Bottle, Miracle in the Rain, 23 Paces to Baker Street, Slander, Kelly and Me, The Lost Blitzkreig, Beyond This Place, Subway in the Sky, Web of Evidence, Enemy General, Wives and Lovers, Where Angels Go . . . Trouble Follows, Eagles Over London.

JOHNSTON, MARGARET: Actress. e. Sydney Univ., Australia. London stage debut: Murder Without Crime. Screen debut: Rake's Progress, 1945.

TV: Always Juliet, Taming of the Shrew, Man With a Load of Mischief, Light of Heart, Autumn Crocus, Androcles and the Lion, Sulky Five, Windmill Near a Frontier, The Shrike, The Out of Towners, Looking for Garrow, The Typewriter, The Glass Menagerie, That's Where The Town's Going, The Vortex.

PICTURES INCLUDE: A Man About the House, Portrait of Clare, The Magic Box, Knave of Hearts, Touch and Go, Night of the Eagle, The Nose on My Face, Life at the Top, Schizo, Mr. Sebastian.

THEATRE: Ring of Truth, The Masterpiece, Lady Macbeth, Merchant of Venice, Measure for Measure, Othello.

JOHNSTONE, DAVID: b. Kilmarnock, Scotland, July 4, 1926. e. Ayr Academy. Journalist: Ayrshire Post; Glasgow Herald. Night News Editor Scottish Daily Mail; Scottish Correspondent News Chronicle. Joined Scottish Television May, 1958 as News Editor. Later producer, director. Originated daily magazine, Here and Now. Producer ITV World Cup (part) 1976. Head of News, Current Affairs, Documentaries and Sport. Assistant controller of programmes; controller (now director) of programmes 1977.

JOLLEY, STAN: Producer-Director-Production Designer-Art Director. b. New York City, May 17, 1926. e. Univ. of S. Calif., col. of architecture, son of actor I. Stanford Jolley. In Navy in World War II. Has acted in capacities listed for many feature films and TV series.

PICTURES INCLUDE: Producer and Production Designer: Knife For the Ladies. Assoc. Producer and Prod. Designer, The Good Guys & The Bad Guys, 2nd Unit director, Superman. Production Designer: Weeds, Caddyshack, Cattle Annie and Little Britches, Americathon (also second unit director), Swarm, Drum, Framed, Dion Brothers, Mixed Company, Walking Tall, Terror In The Wax Museum, Night of The Lepus (also second unit director), War Between Men & Women, Law Man, The Phynx. Art

Director: Young Billy Young, Ride Beyond Vengeance, Broken Saber, The Restless Ones, Mail Order Bride, Toby Tyler, Nine Lives of Elfego Baca. Assoc. producer & prod. designer & 2nd unit director, Happily Ever After.
TV FEATURES: 2nd Unit Director and Production Designer: Swiss Family Robinson, Voyage of The Queen, Woman Hunter, Production Designer: Like Normal People, Howard Hughes, Flood, Voyage of The Yes, The Stranger, Punch & Jody.
TV SERIES: Art Director: Walt Disney Presents, Pete & Gladys, Gunsmoke, Mr. Ed., Branded, Voyage to The Bottom of The Sea, Land of The Giants, O'Hara, etc.

JONES, BARRY: Actor. b. Guernsey (Channel Islands) March 6, 1893. Stage debut in 1921 acting extensively in London and United States. Film debut in Arms and the Man, 1931. During World War II, in Royal Navy.
PICTURES INCLUDE: Dancing with Crime, Frieda, Uneasy Terms, Seven Days to Noon, Clouded Yellow, White Corridors, Plymouth Adventure, Return to Paradise, Prince Valiant, Brigadoon, Demetrius and the Gladiators, Glass Slipper, Alexander the Great.
THEATRE: Starred B'way in Mis-Alliance.

JONES, CAROLYN: Actress. b. Amarillo, Texas, 1933.
STAGE: Summer and Smoke, Live Wire.
TV: Colgate Comedy Hour, Schlitz Playhouse of Stars, Dragnet, Burke's Law, The Addams Family, Roots.
PICTURES INCLUDE: Turning Point, Road to Bali, Military Policeman, Desiree, House of Wax, Invasion of the Body Snatchers, Seven Year Itch, Big Heat, Man Who Knew Too Much, Tender Trap, Opposite Sex, Bachelor Party, King Creole, Last Train from Gun Hill, Man in the Net, A Hole in the Head, Ice Palace, Sail a Crooked Ship, A Ticklish Affair, Heaven with a Gun.

JONES, CHUCK: Producer, Director, Writer. b. Spokane, Wash., Sept. 21, 1912. e. Chouinard Art Institute. Dir., Warner Bros. Animation until 1962 where he created and directed Roadrunner & Coyote, Pepe le Pew; directed and helped create Bugs Bunny, Porky Pig, Daffy Duck etc. Created Snafu character, U.S. Armed Services. Co-prod., wrote, dir., Bugs Bunny Show, ABC-TV. Headed MGM Animation Dept. dir. How the Grinch Stole Christmas, Horton Hears a Who, The Dot and the Line, Pogo, The Phantom Tollbooth. Lecturer and teacher at many universities. Currently independent, Chuck Jones Enterprises, Producer, Director, Writer (for ABC-TV) The Cricket in Times Square; A Very Merry Cricket; Yankee Doodle Cricket and (for CBS-TV) Rudyard Kipling's Rikki-Tikki-Tavi; The White Seal; Mowgli's Brothers, Saint-Saëns' The Carnival of the Animals, Ogden Nash lyrics, with Daffy Duck & Bugs Bunny; and most recently, A Connecticut Rabbit in King Arthur's Court, based on Mark Twain's original story, with Bugs Bunny, Daffy Duck, Porky Pig, Elmer Fudd, etc., two specials featuring Raggedy Ann and Andy in The Great Santa Claus Caper and The Pumpkin Who Couldn't Smile; plus a feature compilation of past work: Chuck Jones' Bugs Bunny Road Runner Movie. Most recently: Daffy Duck's Thanks-for-Giving Special and Bugs Bunny's Bustin' Out All Over. Recipient Academy Award for best animated cartoons for Scenti-Mental Reasons-1950, The Dot and The Line-1965; best documentary short subject for So Much for So Little, 1950. Honored with retrospectives at Deauville Film Fest (1978) British Film Institute (1979).

JONES, CHUCK: Public Relations Executive. b. Detroit, Mich., Dec. 6, 1942. e. Michigan State University (B.A. Advertising) U.S. Marine Corps 1964–66. Staff writer, Pacific Stars & Stripes, Tokyo, Japan and DaNang, Vietnam. Contributing editor, Leatherneck Magazine, Naval Aviation News, Navy Times. Entered motion picture industry 1969. Critic/writer Motion Picture Daily, 1969. Publicist, Harold Rand & Co., Public Relations, 1970–71. Publicist, American International Pictures, 1971. Radio/TV, newspaper, magazine & syndicate contact, United Artists Corp., 1972–73. Established Chuck Jones Public Relations in 1973 and has been pres. since then.

JONES, CLARK R.: Prod. dir. b. Clearfield, Pa., April 10, 1920. e. Northwestern U.
TV SHOWS INCLUDE: The Tony Awards, Peter Pan, Sleeping Beauty Ballet, Ford 50th Anniversary Show, Caesar's Hour, Your Hit Parade, Jack & the Beanstalk; Romeo & Juliet, Perry Como, Bell Telephone Hour, Carol Burnett series; Carol Channing and Pearl Bailey on Broadway, Tony Awards, 6 Rms Riv Vu, Twigs, CBS 50th Anniversary, Emmies, Miss USA, Miss Universe.

JONES, DAVID: CBE, publicity director, EMI Film and Theatre Corporation, Ltd. Director of the Corpn. and also of EMI Cinemas. b. London, Eng., 1913. Entered industry through the CEA Organ, "Cinematograph Times"; editorial assistant RKO-Radio, 1930–36; served in advertising and editorial sections, London "Hollywood Reporter"; rejoined RKO-Radio as exploiteer, appointed press representative, 1938; became director of publicity, 1942 until 1958, chairman, FIPC, 1951–52, 1956–62; president, FIPC, 1952–54, 1960–63; Press Guy, Variety Club of Gt. Britain, 1949–50,

1953–63, Chief Barker, Variety Club, 1964, International Press Guy Variety Club of Great Britain, 1965–66, 1968–71. European Press Guy, 1967–76. Int. Press Guy, 1977–80.

JONES, DEAN: Actor. b. Morgan County, Ala., Jan. 25, 1936; e. Asbury College, Wilmore, Ky.; prof. debut as blues singer, New Orleans; U.S. Navy, 1953.
TV: Ensign O'Toole, The Teddy Bears.
STAGE: There Was a Little Girl, Company.
PICTURES INCLUDE: Handle With Care, Never So Few, Under the Yum-Yum Tree, The New Interns, That Darn Cat, Two On A Guillotine, The Ugly Daschshund, Monkeys, Go Home, Blackbeard's Ghost, The Love Bug, The $1,000,000 Duck, Snowball Express, Mr. Super Invisible, The Shaggy D.A., Herbie Goes to Monte Carlo, Born Again.

JONES, GRIFFITH: Actor. b. London, England. e. University College, London; Royal Academy Dramatic Art (gold medal 1932). In H.M. Forces, World War II. Stage debut, London, 1930, in Carpet Slippers; N.Y. debut 1935 in Escape Me Never. Many stage successes. In many Brit. pictures from 1932.
PICTURES INCLUDE: Escape Me Never, Four Just Men, Atlantic Ferry, This Was Paris, The Day Will Dawn, Uncensored, Henry V. Rake's Progress, Wicked Lady, They Made Me a Fugitive, Good Time Girl, Miranda, Look Before You Love, Once Upon a Dream, Honeymoon Deferred, Star of My Night, Scarlet Web, The Sea Shall Not Have Them, Face in the Night, Wanted on Voyage, The High Wall, Hidden Homicide, Strangler's Web, Decline and Fall.
PLAYS: The Moonraker, Quadrille, Alice Thro' the Looking Glass, Love Machine, Dead on Nine, The Entertainer, Expresso, The Sound of Murder, Treasure Island, Two Accounts Rendered, The Cavern, The Doctor's Dilemma, Jockey Club Stakes. 1973, Nottingham P'House, 1974 Crucible, Sheffield. Member of Royal S'Peare Co. 1975–80.
TV: The Breaking Point, The Ware Case, When in Rome, A Moment in the Sun, Hell Hath no Fury, Margret, No Hiding Place, The Collection, By Invitation Only, A Woman of No Importance, Freedom in September, Blythe Spirit, Treasure Island, The Three Sisters, Emergency Ward, Vendetta, The Cabinet Papers, Man in a Suitcase, Boy Meets Girl, Troubleshooters, Strange Report, Avengers, Inside Man, A Matter of Principle, Doom Watch, Warm Feet, Warm Heart, Paul Temple, The Persuaders, The Lotus Eaters, The Black Arrow, Arrow, Spy Trap, Crown Court, Fallen Eagles, The Apple Cart, Comedy of Errors, Macbeth.

JONES, JENNIFER: Actress. r.n. Phyllis Isley. b. Tulsa, Okla., e. Northwestern U., Amer. Acad. Arts; daughter of Phil R., Flora Mae (Suber) Isley, exhib.; m. David O. Selznick prod. Toured with parents stock company as child; in summer stock in East; little theat. East & West. Began screen career (as Phyllis Isley) in several Republic Westerns, first major role 1943 as Marie Soubirous in The Song of Bernadette, Winning Academy Award 1943 (best performance by an actress).
PICTURES INCLUDE: Since You Went Away, Love Letters, Duel in the Sun, Cluny Brown, Portrait of Jennie, We Were Strangers, Madame Bovary, Carrie, Wild Heart, Ruby Gentry, Indiscretion of an American Wife, Beat the Devil, Love Is a Many-Splendored Thing, Good Morning Miss Dove, Man in the Gray Flannel Suit, Barretts of Wimpole Street, Farewell to Arms, Tender Is the Night, The Idol, Angel, Down We Go, The Towering Inferno.

JONES, QUINCY: Composer. b. 1935. Formerly in trumpet section of Lionel Hampton's band; has played with Dizzy Gillespie, Count Basie before scoring films.
PICTURES INCLUDE: In the Heat of the Night, In Cold Blood, (Acad. Award nom.), The Pawnbroker, Mirage, The Slender Thread, Made In Paris, Walk, Don't Run, Banning, The Deadly Affair, Enter Laughing, A Dandy in Aspic, The Counterfeit Killer, For Love of Ivy, The Split, Bob & Carol & Ted & Alice, The Lost Man, Cactus Flower, John and Mary, The Last of the Mobile Hotshots, The Out-of-Towners, They Call Me Mister Tibbs, Brother John, Dollars, The Anderson Tapes, The Hot Rock, The New Centurions, The Getaway.

JONES, SHIRLEY: Actress. b. Smithon, Pa., March 31.
THEATRE: Appeared with Pittsburgh Civic Light Opera in Lady in the Dark, Call Me Madam. Broadway: South Pacific, Me and Juliet, Maggie Flynn.
PICTURES INCLUDE: Oklahoma, Carousel, Bobbikins, Elmer Gantry, Pepe, A Ticklish Affair, The Secret of My Success, Fluffy, The Happy Ending, Beyond the Posiedon Adventure.
TV: Silent Night, Lonely Night, The Partridge Family (series).

JONES, TOMMY LEE: Actor. b. Texas. Worked in oil fields; studied acting at Harvard, where earned a degree in English. Broadway debut in A Patriot for Me; appeared in Four in a Garden, Ulysses in Nighttown, Fortune and Men's Eyes. Film debut in Love Story (1970).

PICTURES: Jackson County Jail, Rolling Thunder, The Betsy, Eyes of Laura Mars, Coal Miner's Daughter, Back Roads.
TELEVISION: The Amazing Howard Hughes.

JORDAN, HENRIETTA: Exec. b. New York, N.Y., Feb. 26. Ent. m.p. ind. as ass't to exec. v.p., UPA Pictures, 1950; v.p. in charge of sales, Format Prods, Inc. v.p. and assoc. prod., 1962–71. Assoc. prod. Levitow-Hanson Films, Inc., 1972–74; Producer, Image West, Ltd., 1975.

JORDAN, MARION F.: Executive. b. Hungary of Polish parents. e. grammar school in Yugoslavia, military academies in Austria and Poland, and Trade Academy of Warsaw. Entered m.p. ind. in 1928 as pub. in Paramount's Warsaw office; named mgr. of branch in Katowice. In 1930 named Para. mgr. in Yugoslavia; 1938, gen. mgr., Poland. After German invasion of Poland went with wife to India, where, from 1940 to 1946, he again served Para., the last four years as gen. mgr. of the territory. In 1946 transferred to H.O. (N.Y.); in 1947 was loaned to the Motion Picture Export Assn., which he represented until 1950 as gen. mgr., West Germany. For brief period turned exhib. in Providence, R.I.; re-entered dist. as Univ.-Intl.'s Latin-Amer. supvr. in 1959. Moved following year to Paris as Cont. sales mgr. In 1958 named U-I's Cont. mgr.; in 1960 joined Columbia Pictures as v.p. and Cont. mgr.; headquartered in Paris. In 1966 transferred to N.Y.; same year was promoted to exec. v.p. of Col. Intl. In 1974 named special repr. for product acquisition, headquartered in Europe.

JORY, VICTOR: Actor. b. Dawson City, Canada, Nov. 28, 1902. e. Calif. U. Won National Guard wrestling and boxing championship.
THEATRE: On stage: Berkeley Square, Tonight or Never, What Every Woman Knows, The Truth Game, etc. Wrote New York stage production, Five Who Were Mad.
PICTURES INCLUDE: (Screen debut, 1932) Sailor's Luck; Hoppy Serves a Writ, Leather Burners, Unknown Guest, Gallant Blade, Cariboo Trail, The Highwayman, Flaming Feather, Cave of Outlaws, Son of Ali Baba, Toughest Man in Arizona, Man from the Alamo, Valley of the Kings, Cat-Women of the Moon, Sabaka, Mandsu, Blackjack Ketchum Desperado, Cheyenne Autumn, The Miracle Worker, A Time for Dying, Papillon.

JOSEPH, KENNETH. Executive. b. New York City, July 15, 1922. e. Syracuse U. Entered industry as announcer and program director of various NY radio stations, including WNYC, 1946–53; exec. in various capacities of United Artists Television and predecessor companies, 1953–68; exec. v.p., syndication, Four Star Entertainment Corp., 1968–70; exec. v.p., world-wide syndication, Metromedia Producers Corp., 1970 to present.

JOURDAN, LOUIS: Actor. b. Marseille, France, June 19, 1921. Stage actor, prior to m.p.
PICTURES INCLUDE: Her First Affair, La Boheme L'Arlesienne, La Belle, Adventure, Felicie Nanteuil, The Paradine Case, Letter from an Unknown Woman, Madame Bovary, Bird of Paradise, Anne of the Indies, The Happy Time, Three Coins in the Fountain, No Minor Voices, Decameron Nights, The Swan, Julie, Gigi, Streets of Montmartre, Story of the Count of Monte Cristo, VIP's, Made in Paris, A Flea in Her Ear, To Commit a Murder, Silver Bears.

JUDD, EDWARD: Actor. b. Shanghai, 1934. e. Far East. Stage; The Long and the Short and the Tall, The Tinker. Numerous TV appearances.
PICTURES INCLUDE: The Day the Earth Caught Fire, Stolen Hours, The World Ten Times Over, Mystery Submarine, The Long Ships, First Men On The Moon, Strange Bedfellows, Invasion, Island of Terror, The Vengeance of Shee, Shakedown.

JUDELSON, DAVID N.: Executive. e. Graduated NYU Coll. of Engineering. Started business career in family's manufacturing business in N.J. Following military service with U.S.A. Engineers Corp. joined Gulf & Western and in 1959 was elected a director. In 1965 was appointed chairman of the exec. comm. and the following year became exec. v.p. of Gulf & Western; elected pres., 1967.

JUNKIN, RAYMOND: Executive. b. New York, N.Y., Nov. 4, 1918. e. Univ. of Alabama, Univ. of Penn. Air Force, World War II. Eastern sls. mgr., Robert H. Clark Co., southwestern sls. mgr., then ass't to president; v.p., director of sales, Official Films, Inc., 1951–58; self-employed as a film and program consultant, 1959–60; pres. Program Sales, Inc.; gen. sls. mgr., Programs For Television, Inc., since 1961; v.p. & gen. mgr., Screen Gems (Canada), Ltd.; v.p. Domestic Sales Mgr. Screen Gems Internat'l; 1967 gen. sls. mgr., Trans-Lux TV Corp., v.p. & gen. sls. mgr., 1968 to date. CTV Television Network Ltd.

JURADO, KATY: Actress. r.n. Maria Christina Jurado Garcia. b. Guadalajara, Mexico, 1927. Numerous Mexican films m.p. columnist for Mexican publications; American m.p. debut in Bullfighter and the Lady.

PICTURES INCLUDE: High Noon, San Antone, Arrowhead, Broken Lance, The Racers, Trial, Trapeze, Man from Del Rio, The Badlanders, One Eyed Jacks, Barabbas, A Convenant with Death, Pat Garrett and Billy the Kid.

JURGENS, CURT: Actor. b. Munich, Germany, Dec. 12, 1915. Leading man on German stage, turning to films in 1939.
PICTURES INCLUDE: Les Heros Sont Fatigues, An Eye for an Eye, Without You It Is Night (aiso dir.), And Woman Was Created, Me and the Colonel, The Enemy Below, The Devil's General, Inn of the Sixth Happiness, The Blue Angel, Ferry to Hong Kong, I Aim at the Stars, Tamango, Lord Jim, The Threepenny Opera, Das Liebeskarussel, The Assassination Bureau, The Battle of Neretva, Nicholas and Alexandra, Vault of Horror, The Spy Who Loved Me.

JUROW, MARTIN: Producer. b. New York, N.Y. e. William and Mary, Harvard Law School. Associated with MCA, William Morris, pres., Famous Artists; prod., G & E Productions; co-prod. with Richard Shepherd Jurow-Shepherd Productions.
PICTURES INCLUDE: The Hanging Tree, The Fugitive Kind, Love In a Goldfish Bowl, Breakfast At Tiffany's, The Great Race, Highroad Films.

JUSTIN, GEORGE: Executive. Major credits include producer on Middle of the Night and The Tiger Makes Out; assoc. prod. for Marathon Man and On the Waterfront; prod. exec. on The Goddess and Twelve Angry Men. V.p. & exec. prod. mgr. at Paramount Pictures; four years; left to join Columbia as prod. exec. where was assoc. prod. for The Deep and prod. exec. on The Eyes of Laura Mars. In April, 1979 joined Orion Pictures; named exec. prod. mgr. Promoted to v.p./exec. prod. mgr. in April, 1980.

JUSTIN, JOHN: Actor. b. London, Nov. 23, 1917; e. Bryanston (Dorset). Stage debut, repertory at Plymouth 1933; entered m.p. ind. in 1939. Many TV appearances.
PICTURES INCLUDE: Thief of Bagdad, Journey Together, The Sound Barrier, The Village, Melba, Crest of the Wave, King of the Khyber Rifles, The Man Who Loved Redheads, The Teckman Mystery, Untamed, Safari, Crime Passionelle, Guilty?, Island in the Sun, Spider's Web, Les Hommes Veulent, Vivre, The Savage Messiah, Barcelona Kill, Lisztomania, Valentino, The Big Sleep.

K

KAEL, PAULINE: Critic. b. June 19, 1919, Sonoma County, CA. e. Univer. of Calif. at Berkeley (1936–40), majoring in philosophy. Managed two art theaters in Calif. for which she wrote program notes. Broadcast weekly about films on Pacifica network. Made experimental shorts. Has written on films for many magazines. Since 1968 movie critic for The New Yorker
AUTHOR: I Lost it at the Movies, Kiss Kiss Bang Bang, Going Steady, The Citizen Kane Book, Deeper into Movies, Reeling, When the Lights Go Down.
AWARDS: Guggenheim Fellow, 1964; George Polk Memorial Award for Criticism, 1970; The National Book Award, 1974, for Deeper into Movies; Front Page Award for best magazine column in 1974 from Newswomen's Club of N.Y.

KAHN, MADELINE: Actress-Singer. Broadway bow in New Faces of '68. Featured in off-Broadway musical Promenade. Trained as opera singer and appeared in La Boheme, Showboat, Two by Two, Candide.
PICTURES INCLUDE: What's Up Doc? (debut), Paper Moon, From the Mixed-Up Files of Mrs. Basil E. Frankweiler, Blazing Saddles, At Long Last Love, Young Frankenstein, The Adventures of Sherlock Holmes' Smarter Brother, Won Ton Ton, High Anxiety, The Cheap Detective, Simon, Happy Birthday, Gemini, Wholly Moses, First Family, History of the World—Part I.
RECENT THEATRE: In the Boom Boom Room, On the Twentieth Century.

KAHN, MILTON: Publicist. b. Brooklyn, N.Y. May 3, 1934, e. Syracuse and Ohio University; BSJ 1957, formed Milton Kahn Associates, Inc. in 1958.

KAHN, RICHARD: Executive. b. New Rochelle. N.Y., Aug. 29, 1929; e. Wharton School, U. of Penn., B.S., 1951; U.S. Navy, 3 yrs.; joined Buchanan & Co., 1954; ent. m.p. ind., pressbook writer, Columbia Pictures, 1955; exploitation mgr., 1958; adv. and pub., 1963; natl. dir. of adv., pub. and exploitation, 1963; v.p., 1969; 1974 v.p. in chg. of special marketing projects; 1975; moved to MGM as v.p. in chg. of worldwide advertising, publicity and exploitation; 1978, named sr. v.p. in chg. worldwide mktg. & pres., MGM Intl. 1980, elected bd. of governors, m.p. Academy of Arts & Sciences.

KALB, MARVIN: TV news reporter. e. CCNY: Harvard, M.A., 1953; Russian Language School, Middlebury College. Worked for US State Dept., American Embassy, Moscow; CBS News, 1957; writer, reporter-researcher. Where We Stand: reporter-assignment editor; Moscow Bureau Chief, 1960–63; first dip. corres., Washington Bureau, 1963.

BOOKS: Eastern Exposure, Dragon in the Kremlin, A Day in the Life of Ivan Denisovich, Roots of Involvement, The U.S. in Asia, 1784–1971.

KALISCH, BERTRAM: Writer, supervising editor. TV Consultant, film documentaries. b. New York City, June 5, 1902; e. U.S. Naval Acad., '24, Began as reporter; Wash. corresp. 1924–29, man. ed. Army & Navy Journal 1926–29; asst. ed. RKO Pathe News, 1934–37; chief script writer, MGM News of the Day. Also author & supvr. many short subjects. Army from June, 1941; exec. prod., A.A.F. training films, TFPL, Wright Field. 1941–43; pub. rel. pictorial officer, 12th Army Group 1944; G.H.Q. Photo Officer, Pacific. 1945; Army Pictorial Center, 1948–1950, 1954–1956; Office Sec. of Defense 1950–64; Chief, Audio-Visual Div., Executive Producer Sec. Defense Film Reports. Member: Broadcast Pioneers, Academy TV Arts & Science, Overseas Press Club, Nat'l Headliner's Club.

KALISH, EDDIE: Executive. Joined Paramount Pictures in 1975 as dir. of intl. mktg.; later named v.p., worldwide pub. & promo. In 1980 appt. senior v.p., mktg. 1981, named United Artists v.p.—domestic mktg.

KALSER, KONSTANTIN: Executive. b. Munich, Germany, Sept. 4, 1920; e. Switzerland, and UCLA in United States. Color photographer, newsreel cameraman, founded Marathon International Prods., Inc., pres., executive producer; Crashing the Water Barrier, 1956 (Acad. Award); Give and Take (Venice Award), The Carmakers, Chris Award. Director, The One for the Road, 1973 Gold Award, Internatl. Film & TV Festival in N.Y. Director, We Did It! 1978 Gold Medal Intl. Film & TV Festival of N.Y.; Production Executive, The Unknown War 1978 Grand Award, Intl. Film & TV Festival of N.Y.

KAMBER, BERNARD M.: Executive. e. U. of Pa. New England exploitation rep. U.A. 1940; Army service 1941–43; dir. special events dept. U.A., 1943; asst. to Gradwell L. Sears, nat'l distrib. chmn. 6th War Loan Drive; dir. pub. 7th War Loan Drive, 1943–47; dir. pub. & prom. Eagle Lion Classics, 1951; org. Kamber Org., pub. rel. rep. for ind. prod. v.p. sales, adv. pub. Ivan Tors Prod. Greene-Rouse Prods.; June 1953; exec. asst. Hecht-Hill-Lancaster, chg. of N.Y. off., 1957; v.p. Hecht-Hill-Lancaster Companies, 1958; formed Cinex Distr. Corp., 1962; Pres. Cinex and Posfilm, Inc.; 1967 v.p. in chg. sls. Du Art Film Lab. Inc; 1975 joined Technicolor, Inc.

KAMEN, STANLEY A.: Executive. b. Jan. 13, 1928, New York City. e. Washington and Lee U. grad. 1948; Law School, grad. 1950; member, N.Y. Bar; atty., New York office, William Morris Agency; agency representative on West Coast, 1954. U.S. Navy, 1944–46.

KAMEY, PAUL: Executive. b. New York, N.Y., Aug. 25, 1912. Worked on newspapers including NY Journal American. Ent. m.p. industry 1938; worked for MGM and 20th Century Fox; during war, writer, Office of War information; joined Universal, 1949; eastern pub. mgr., Universal Pictures. 1968, Freelance publicist.

KAMINS, BERNIE: Publicist. b. Cambridge, Mass., Jan. 2, 1915; e. Harvard U., B.A. Harvard U. corresp. various newspapers and press services while in coll.; joined Russell Birdwell & Assoc., publicists unit man. Paramount studios. Author screen story Forty Thieves; co-author Sky Princess. Dir. adv. & publ. Harry Sherman Prod.; then Charles R. Rogers Prod.; apptd. same Principal Artists Prods., April, 1944; later same yr. joined Chas. R. Rogers Prods.; identical posts Cagney Prod. Inter-American Prod., Jesse L. Lasky Prod. Author, The Copy Rider; pub. relations, Hollywood Actors Council; 1953. instructor, propaganda, UCLA; 1953–54 pub. Peter Goelet Ent. Nat'l Bd. of Review of M.P., Inc.; 1954–57. p.r. and exec. v.p. national Audience Board, Inc.; p.d. Clarion Enterprises, 1956; p.d. Romson Productions, 1957; p.r. Guy Madison Prod., 1958; Julian Lesser Prod., Principal Securities, 1959. Pacific Title and Art Studio p.r., Counsel, 1960; elected pres. Opinion Builders, Inc., 1961. Exec. hd. of United Republican Finance Committee of Los Angeles County, 1962; Buddy Ebsen Enterprises (Turquoise Prods.), 1963; finance pub. rel. counsel. Herts-Lion International Corp., 1963–64; acting P.R. chmn., Republican State finance committee; P.R. chmn., Western US Amer. Jewish Comm., 1964; Publicists Assoc. Awards Comm. 1966–67. V.P. Commu. Rel. South. Calif. Industry-Educ. Council, 1966–68; Co-ord. Harvard Med. School Alumni Assoc. 1967; Exec. Sect. Insurance Research Foundation, 1968. Statewide education comm. of Calif. State Chamber of Commerce. National advisory comm. for UCLA Allied Health Projects Div.; staff, UCLA Alumni & Development; board member, Foundation for California Community Colleges; Advisory board, L.A. City Board-of-Education on Unified School District Proposal for Utilization of UHF-TV Channel 58; Exec. Secty., American Consumers Council, 1966–; Member, general advisory board, Santa Monica College; 1972–; Exec. Secty., Foundation of Oral and Maxillofacial Surgery Inc., 1976–, 1977 appointed to Los Angeles County Youth Commission; 1977—UCLA Chancellor's Associates member. 1978—lecturer on P.R. for Community Organizations, West Los

Angeles College. 1979—lecturer, same, Santa Monica College. 1979—Appointed to Board of Directors of International Students Center, UCLA, 1979—Coordinator and public relations consultant, Foundation for Effective Government Inc.

KANE, CAROL: Actress. b. Cleveland, Ohio, 1952. Began professional acting career at age 14, touring in The Prime of Miss Jean Brodie. Other stage credits include, Arturo UI, The Enchanted, The Tempest, Macbeth, Tales of the Vienna Woods, etc.
PICTURES: Wedding in White, The Last Detail, Carnal Knowledge, Hester Street, Dog Day Afternoon, Annie Hall, The World's Greatest Lover, The Muppet Movie, When a Stranger Calls.

KANE, STANLEY D.: Judge. b. Minneapolis, Minn., Dec. 21, 1907; e. U. of Minn., B.A. (magna cum laude, 1930), M.A., 1931; Minn. Coll. of Law, LL.B., 1940. Instructor, U. of Minn., 1930–33; exec. sec. Allied Theatre Owners of the Northwest, 1933–37; city attorney, Golden Valley, Minn., 1940–63; City Atty., Champlin, Minn., 1955–60; on faculty, Minn. Coll. of Law, 1940–44; trial attorney & trial examiner, NLRB, Minneapolis, New Orleans, N.Y., 1943–46; special, gen. counsel, Puerto Rico Labor Relations Bd., 1946; exec. vice-pres. & gen. counsel, North Central Allied Independent Theatre Owners, 1946–63; recording sec. Allied States Assn., 1947 to 1956; Dist. Court Judge, Hennepin County, 1963; elected to 6-yr. term, 1964; re-elected, 1970.

KANIN, FAY: Writer. b. New York, N.Y. e. Elmira Coll., U.S.C., m. Michael Kanin, writer. Contrib. fiction to mags.; mem. and officer of WGA., AMPAS. also bd. mem. of latter.
PICTURES INCLUDE: Blondie for Victory, Sunday Punch, My Pal Gus, Rhapsody, The Opposite Sex, Teacher's Pet, Swordsman of Siena, The Right Approach.
BROADWAY: Goodbye My Fancy, His and Hers, Rashomon, The Gay Life.
TELEVISION: Heat of Anger, CBS Friday Night Movie 1972; Tell Me Where It Hurts, CBS General Electric Theater, 1974.

KANIN, GARSON: Director, writer. b. Rochester, N.Y., Nov. 24, 1912; e. American Acad. Dram. Arts; m. Ruth Gordon, actress. Musician actor, appearing in Spring Song, Little Ol' Boy, and others. Prod. assist. George Abbott on Three Men on a Horse, Brother Rat, Room Service; dir. Hitch Your Wagon, Too Many Heroes, Broadway plays; In June, 1937, Samuel Goldwyn's prod. staff, 1938, joined RKO, prod.-dir. contract. In 1942: prod. for U.S. Office of Emergency Management. Joined armed forces, World War II; co-dir. True Glory.
PICTURES INCLUDE: A Double Life, Adam's Rib, Born Yesterday, Marrying Kind, Pat and Mike, It Should Happen to You, Next Time I Marry, Man to Remember, Great Man Votes, Bachelor Mother, My Favorite Wife, They Knew What They Wanted, Tom, Dick and Harry, From This Day Forward, The Girl Can't Help It, The Rat Race, High Time, The Right Approach, Where It's At, Some Kind of a Nut, Woman of the Year, The More the Merrier.
THEATRE: Born Yesterday, The Smile of the World, The Rat Race, The Live Wire, A Gift of Time, Do Re Mi, Come on Strong, The Amazing Adele, The Good Soup, Dreyfus in Rehearsal. (Writer &/or Dir.) Dir.: The Rugged Path; Years Ago; How I Wonder; The Leading Lady; The Diary of Anne Frank; Into Thin Air; Small War on Murray Hill; Hole in the Head; Sunday in New York; Funny Girl; I Was Dancing; A Very Rich Woman; We Have Always Lived in a Castle; Idiot's Delight; Ho! Ho! Ho!
BOOKS: Remembering Mr. Maugham, Cast of Characters, Tracy and Hepburn; Hollywood; Blow Up A Storm; The Rat Race; A Thousand Summers; One Hell of an Actor; It Takes a Long Time to Become Young; Moviola, Smash, Together Again!

KENIN, MICHAEL: Writer. b. Rochester, N.Y., Feb. 1, 1910; m. Fay Mitchell. Member SWG, officer; WGA, AMPAS. Commercial artist, musician, N.Y. prior to m.p. career; contrib. fiction mags.; s.p. Panama Lady, They Made Her a Spy, 1939.
PICTURES INCLUDE: Anne of Windy Poplars, Woman of the Year, Sunday Punch, The Cross of Lorraine, Centennial Summer Honeymoon, A Double Life, My Pal Gus, When I Grow Up, Rhapsody, The Opposite Sex, Teacher's Pet, The Right Approach, The Swordsman of Siena, The Outrage, How to Commit Marriage.
BROADWAY: Goodbye My Fancy, Seidman and Son, His and Hers, Rashomon, The Gay Life.

KANTER, HAL: Writer, director, producer. b. Savannah, Ga., Dec. 18, 1918. Writer, Danny Kaye Show, Amos 'n Andy, Bing Crosby Show, Ed Wynn TV Show, 1949; creator, writer, prod., stager, George Gobel Show; writer, Paramount, 1951–54; dir.: RKO Radio, 1956; Prod., dir., writer, Kraft Music Hall, 1958–59; exec. prod., TCF-TV; Valentine's Day; writer, prod. dir. Chrysler Theatre 1966–67. Creator W.D.P., Julia, NBC, 1968–71; creator W.D.P.; Jimmy Stewart (NBC), 1971. W.P. Many TV specials. 1975–76 exec. prod. All In The Family (CBS). Sup. Prod. Chico & The Man (NBC),

1976–77; exec. prod., WB-TV; 1978; prod./writer, Lucille Ball Prod., 1979–80; dir./writer, ABC TV Movies, 1980; Walt Disney Prods., 1981.

PICTURES INCLUDE: My Favorite Spy, Off Limits, Road to Bali, Casanova's Big Night, About Mrs. Leslie, Money from Home, Artists and Models, Mardi Gras, Rose Tattoo, Married a Woman, Loving You, Once Upon a Horse, Blue Hawaii, Pocketful of Miracles, Bachelor in Paradise, Move Over, Darling, Dear Brigitte.

KANTER, JAY: Executive. b. 1927. Entered industry with MCA, Inc., where was v.p. Left after more than 20 yrs. to become pres. of First Artists Production Co., Ltd. In 1975 joined 20th-Fox as v.p. prod.; 1976, named sr. v.p., worldwide prod. Named v.p., The Ladd Co., 1979.

KANTOR, IGO: Producer, Film Editor. b. Vienna Austria, Aug. 18, 1930. e. UCLA, AA. 1950. BS, 1952. MS, 1954. Foreign corres., Portugal magazine, FLAMA, 1949–57, music supvr., Screen Gems, Columbia 1954–63; post-prod. supvr., film ed., features, TV; assoc. prod., 1963–64; prod., exec., International Entertainment Corp., 1965. pres., Synchrofilm, Inc., post-production co. and Duque Films, Inc., production co. 1968–74. 1975—present, produced and edited films.

PICTURES INCLUDE: Bye Bye Birdie, Under the Yum Yum Tree, Gidget Goes to Rome, A House Is Not a Home, Pattern for Murder, Willy. Co.-prod., editor: Assault on Agathon (1975); assoc., prod., editor, Dixie Dynamite (1976); prod., editor, music supvr., Kingdom of the Spiders; assoc. prod., The Dark (1977); prod. supvr., Good Luck Miss Wyckoff, (1978); prod., Hardly Working,: (1980); Kill and Kill Again (1981).

KAPER, BRONISLAU: Composer. b. Warsaw, Poland Feb. 5, 1902; e. Warsaw Cons. of Music. Wrote concert music, songs and music for films in Warsaw, Berlin, Vienna, London and Paris.

PICTURES INCLUDE: Gaslight, Without Love, Mrs. Parkington, Green Dolphin Street, That Forsyte Woman, Naked Spur, Lili (Acad. Award, 1953), Saadia, Glass Slipper, Quentin Durward, Forever Darling, The Prodigal, The Swan, Brothers Karamazov, Don't Go Near the Water, Auntie Mame, Green Mansions, San Francisco, Butterfield 8, Night at the Opera, Red Badge of Courage, Day at The Races, Mutiny on The Bounty, Lord Jim.

KAPLAN, BORIS: Executive. b. New York City, Sept. 23, 1897; m.; e. Coll. of City of New York. General mgr. of Selwyn Theatrical Enterprises, 1925–32. Prod. Plays for legitimate stage, Broadway; joined Paramount Pictures Corp., 1933; head of eastern casting and talent dept., Paramount 1936–62; independent casting dir.; m.p. consultant

KAPLAN, GABRIEL: Actor/Comedian. b. Brooklyn, N.Y., March 31. After high school worked as bellboy at Lakewood, N.J. hotel, spending free time studying comedians doing routines. Put together a comedy act, landing engagements in small clubs and coffee houses all over U.S. Made several appearances on Tonight Show, Merv Griffin Show, Mike Douglas Show, etc. Has played Las Vegas clubs.

TV: Welcome Back, Kotter.

PICTURES INCLUDE: Fast Break, Tulips, Nobody's Perfect.

KAPLAN, MURRAY M., Executive. In motion picture distribution since 1936. Distributor for Warner Bros., Paramount, Monogram, Eagle-Lion, United Artists, Allied Artists, Cinemation Industries. Became independent distributor in 1950, independent producer in 1966. Co-founder of PRO-International Films, 1975; 1978, formed M & M Films, to produce and distribute worldwide. Member: Motion Picture Pioneers of America.

KARLIN, FRED: Composer. Won Academy Award for Best Song for For All We Know (from Lovers and Other Strangers) and Emmy for original music in The Autobiography of Jane Pittman on TV. Adapted Huddie Ledbetter melodies for film Leadbelly.

PICTURES INCLUDE: Up the Down Staircase, Yours, Mine and Ours, The Sterile Cuckoo, Westworld, Gravy Train, Mixed Company, Leadbelly, Loving Couples.

KARLIN, MYRON D.: Executive. b. Revere, Mass., Sept. 21, 1918. e. UCLA. Joined m.p. business in 1946 as gen. mgr. for MGM in Ecuador. Two yrs. later assigned same spot for MGM in Venezuela. In 1952–53 was gen. sales mgr. for MGM in Germany, after which held same post in Argentina, returning to Germany as mgr. dir. in 1956. Named mgn. dir. for United Artists in Italy. 1960–68 was pres. of Brunswick Int'l., while also serving as advisor to World Health Organization and UNESCO. In 1969 was European mgr. for MGM and mgn. dir. in Italy. Joined Warner Bros. Int'l. in May, 1970 as v.p. of European dist. In March, 1972 appt. v.p. in chg. of int'l. operations for WB; 1977, appt. pres., WB Intl. & exec. v.p., Warner Bros., Inc.

KARLSON, PHIL: Director. b. Chicago, Ill., 1908. r.n. Philip N. Karlstein.

PICTURES INCLUDE: The Phoenix City Story, Gunman's Walk, Hell to Eternity, Key Witness, The Secret Ways, The Young Doctors, Kid Gallahad, Rampage, The Si-

lencers, A Time for Killing, The Long Ride Home, The Wrecking Crew, Hornet's Nest, Ben, Walking Tall, Framed.

KASTNER, ELLIOTT: Executive. b. N.Y.C. Was agent before becoming indep. prod., financing and personally producing 23 feature films in 9 yrs. Based in London.

PICTURES INCLUDE: Harper, Kaleidoscope, Sweet November, Laughter in the Dark, Where Eagles Dare, When Eight Bells Toll, X, Y, & Zee, The Nightcomers, Fear Is The Key, The Long Goodbye, Cops and Robbers, Jeremy, 11 Harrowhouse, Rancho Deluxe, 92 in the Shade (exec. prod.,) The Missouri Breaks (co-prod.), Equus (co-prod.), The Big Sleep (co-prod.); ffolkes (prod.)

KATLEMAN, HARRIS L.: Executive. b. Omaha, Neb., Aug. 19, 1928. e. U.C.L.A. (B.A. in Admin., 1949). Joined MCA in 1949; in 1952 transferred to N.Y. as head of TV Packaging Dept. Left to join Goodson-Todman Prods. in 1955, where named v.p., 1956; exec. v.p., 1958; sr. exec. v.p., 1968. Was directly responsible for all film prod. in L.A., including such shows as The Rebel, Branded, The Richard Boone Show (Emmy nominations, Fame Award of Year), and Don Rickles Show, on which was exec. prod. Joined Metro-Goldwyn-Mayer in 1972 as v.p. of MGM-TV; promoted following year to pres., MGM-TV and sr. v.p. of MGM, Inc. Resigned as pres. of MGM-TV September, 1977. Formed Bennett/Katleman Productions under contract to Columbia Pictures. Exec. prod.: From Here to Eternity, Salvage 1; 1980, named bd. chm. 20th-Fox Television.

KATSELAS, MILTON: Director. b. Pittsburgh. e. drama dept. Carnegie Tech (now Carnegie Mellon Univ.). Has directed more than 30 stage prods., including in New York, The Rose Tattoo and Camino Real (both revivals), The Zoo Story, Butterflies Are Free, etc.

PICTURES INCLUDE: Butterflies Are Free (debut), 40 Carats, Report to the Commissioner, When You Comin' Back, Red-Ryder.

KATT, WILLIAM: Actor. Son of Barbara Hale and Bill Williams. e. Orange Coast College. Majored in music, playing piano and guitar. Acted with South Coast Repertory Theatre, later working in production at the Abmanson and Mark Taper Theatres in L.A. Made theatrical film debut in Carrie.

PICTURES INCLUDE: Carrie, First Love, Big Wednesday, Butch and Sundance: The Early Days.

KATZ, GLORIA: Producer-Writer. e. UCLA Film School. Joined Universal Pictures as editor, cutting educational films. Later joined forces with Willard Huyck, whom she had met at UCLA. Pair signed by Francis Ford Coppola to write and direct for his newly created company, American Zoetrope. Projects didn't materialize but Katz and Huyck teamed to write script for America Graffiti for director Paul Lucas. Wrote Lucky Lady (1975) together. Katz made debut as producer with French Postcards in 1979 which co-wrote with Huyck, who directed.

KATZ, MARTY: Producer-Writer. b. Landsburg, West Germany, Sept. 2, 1947. e. UCLA, Univ. of Maryland. Combat pictorial unit commander, US Army; 1st Lt. US Army Southeast Asia Pictorial Unit, Vietnam, 1969; awarded Bronze Star. Director, film production operations, ABC 1971–76; exec. v.p., prod., Quinn Martin Productions, 1976–77; prod., movies for TV, QM, 1977–78; producer for Paramount Pictures, 1979–80; formed Marty Katz Productions in 1980.

TELEVISION: Supervised production for Love Among the Ruins, Eleanor and Franklin, Eleanor and Franklin: The White House Years. Produced for Paramount: 11th Victim, Catalina C-Lab.

PICTURES: The Man, Nashville, Sounder II.

KATZ, NORMAN B.: Executive. b. Scranton, Penna., Aug. 23, 1919. e. Columbia Univ. In U.S. Army 1941–46 as intelligence officer, airborne forces. Entered m.p. industry in 1947 with Discina Films, Paris, France, as prod. asst. Named exec. asst. to head of prod. in 1948. In 1950 named v.p. Discina Int'l. Films and in 1952 exec. v.p. In 1954 joined Associated Artists Prods. as foreign mgr.; named dir. of foreign operations in 1958. In 1959 became dir. of foreign operations for United Artists Associated. 1961 joined Seven Arts Associated Corp. of v.p. in chg. of foreign operations; named exec. v.p., Seven Arts Prods. Int'l. in 1964. Named exec. v.p. Warner Bros.—Seven Arts Int'l. in 1967. In 1969 appt. exec. v.p. and chief exec. off. Warner Bros. International and bd. mem. of Warner Bros. Inc. In 1974 named snr. v.p. int'l. div. of American Film Theatre. Pres. of Cinema Arts Associated Corp. 1979, exec. v.p. and bd. member, American Communications Industries and pres., chief exec. off. of ACI subsidiary, American Cinema.

KAUFMAN, HAL: Creative director, TV writer-producer. b. New York, N.Y., Dec. 16, 1924; e. U. of Texas. 1943–44; U. of Michigan. 1944–47. Started career as petroleum geologist, Western Geophysical Co., 1947–48; TV writer-prod-dir., KDYL-TV, Salt Lake City, 1948–49; prog. dir., WLAV-TV, Grand Rapids, 1949–51; prod. mgr., WOOD-TV, Grand

Rapids, 1951–54; Radio-TV dir., Webber Advertising Agency, Grand Rapids, 1951–54; TV writer-prod., Leo Burnett Company, Chicago, 1954–56; TV writer-prod., Gordon Best Company, Chicago, 1956–59; senior writer, TV/Radio creative dept., Needham, Louis & Brorby, Inc., 1959; vice-pres., asst. copy dir., Needham, Louis & Brorby, Inc., 1962; dir., TV, Radio prod., Needham, Louis & Brorby, Inc., 1963; dir., broadcast design, production, Needham, Louis & Brorby, Inc., 1964; assoc. creat. dir., asst. Exec. v.p., Needham, Harper & Steers, Inc., 1965; Creat. dir. L.A., 1966; Sr. v.p. and Member Bd. of Dir., 1966. Aug. 1969, creative & marketing consultant in Beverly Hills. Aug., 1970, v.p., principle, Kaufman, Vinson, Lansky, Inc., Beverly Hills and San Diego; Aug. '72, Exec. V.P., principle, Kaufman, Lansky Advertising, Inc., Los Angeles and San Diego, Member, Directors Guild of America, SAG, AFTRA. 1979, program dir., Z Channel, Theata Cable TV. 1979 named snr. v.p./adv. & p.r. & asst. to pres. & bd. chmn., World Airways, Inc.

KAUFMAN, J. L. (Les): Publicist. b. Chicago, Ill., June 3: e. Morgan Park (Ill.) Military Acad. Police reporter, City News Bureau, Chicago. In 1926 adv. dept., Balaban & Katz Theats. In 1929 pub. Paramount Public Theats. To Columbia, 1933 asst. exploit, dir. In 1938 adv. & pub. dir., Fanchon & Marco Serv. Corp., St. Louis. Adv.-pub. dir., Republic Studios, 1944–46; Nat'l adv. pub. dir., International Pictures Corp. In 1947 named studio pub. dir., Universal-International; sales prom. counsel, Kaiser-Frazer Corp., 1950; v.p. in chge. West Coast, Ettinger Co., 1950; v.p. Grant Adv. Inc., Hollywood, Detroit, 1952–55; v.p., adv. dir., UPA Pictures, Inc., 1956; P.R. dir., Fedderson Productions & Lawrence Welk, 1957; My Three Sons, Hollywood Palladium, 1961, Family Affair, To Rome with Love. The Smith Family; pres., Hollywood Press Club, 1964–65, 1967–68. Bd. governors—NATVAS, Hollywood chapter.

KAUFMAN, LEONARD: Executive, attorney. b. New York, N.Y., April 30, 1913. e. C.C.N.Y., Fordham U. School of Law, 1933–36. LL.B. admitted New York Bar, 1937. U.S. Supreme Ct.; Law offices of Nathan Burkan, 1933–36; law offices of Schwartz & Frohlich. 1936–49, Member legal staff Paramount Pictures Corp. 1949–67, gen. counsel, 1964–67; Mem. law firm, Kaufman & Kaufman, 1969–75; Kommel, Rogers, Kaufman, Lorber & Shenkman 1975–78; Assoc. Bar City New York, American Bar Assoc., New York State Bar Assoc., President Cinema, Radio, TV Unit, B'nai B'rith, Motion Picture Pioneers, Variety Clubs Intl. Gen. Counsel, Variety Club, N.Y.

KAUFMAN, LEONARD B.: Producer, writer, director. b. Newark, N.J., Aug. 31. e. N.Y.U. In World War II served with Army Special Services writing and directing camp shows. Nat'l magazine writer, 1945–48; radio writer, including Errol Flynn Show, 1948–50; radio and TV writer, 1950–52. Headed own public relations firm: Kaufman, Schwartz, and Associates, 1952–64. Joined Ivan Tors Films as writer-prod., 1964. Films Corp., 1958.
PICTURES INCLUDE: Clarence, the Cross-eyed Lion, Birds Do It, Story.
TV: Daktari, Ivan Tors' Jambo, O'Hara, U.S. Treasury (CBS) pilot feature and series for Mark VII Prods.

KAUFMAN, PHILIP: Writer-Director. b. Chicago, Oct. 23, 1936. e. Univ. of Chicago, Harvard Law School. Was teacher in Europe before turning to film medium.
PICTURES INCLUDE: Goldstein, Fearless Frank, The Great Northfield, Minnesota Raid, The White Dawn, Invasion of the Body Snatchers, The Wanderers.

KAUFMAN, SIDNEY: Producer, Completion Guarantor. b. N.Y. Mar. 28, 1910. e. Cornell, N.Y.U., C.C.N.Y., L.I.U., Member faculty New School for Social Research, 1938–59. Newspaper editor; film critic, WQXR, N.Y., 1936–40. Production staff Walter Wanger, MGM. America associate—Pascal, Del Guidice, etc.; producer-writer-director numerous documentaries. Writer-prod. The Sorcerer's Village (1958—Continental); Behind the Great Wall (writer-adapter) 1959; man. dir. Grand Prize Films Ltd., London, 1960 release Macbeth (exec. prod.); since 1952, pres., Grand Prize Films, Inc., importer, dist. over 400 foreign features, since 1958, providing completion bonds, guarantor and prod. exec. numerous dom. and foreign features; Pres. Performance Guarantees, Inc.; Pres., Jermyn Venture Capitol Corp.

KAUFMANN, CHRISTINE: Actress. b. Lansdorf, Graz, Austria, Jan. 11, 1945. e. attended school in Munich, Germany. Film debut as a dancer. Salto Mortale at 7 yrs of age.
PICTURES INCLUDE: Rosenrosli (Little Rosie), Schweigende Engel (Silent Angel), Maedchen in Uniform, Winter Vacation, The Last Days of Pompeii, Red Lips, Town Without Pity, Taras Bulba (first American-made film), Murder in the Rue Morgue.

KAY, EDWARD: Musical director, composer. b. New York City, Nov. 27, 1898; e. U. of Pennsylvania; later musical study. Became musical director, vaudeville, New York stage productions; similar work in radio. Musical director, Gau-

mont-British, 1932–33. To Hollywood, 1933, as musical director, Paramount, Allied Artists.
PICTURES INCLUDE: Highway Dragnet, Thunder Pass, Treasure of Ruby Hills, Big Tip Off, Las Vegas Shakedown, Betrayed Women, Night Freight, Toughest Man Alive.

KAY, GILBERT LEE: Director-Writer. b. Chicago, Ill., June 28. e. Los Angeles City Coll. Was asst. dir. at various studios from 1942–53; started directing on own in 1954. Formed Pearly Gate Productions, London.
PICTURES INCLUDE: Three Bad Sisters, The Tower, Ocean's 11 (s.p.), Comeback, (s.p.), Take Five (s.p.), Fame! (s.p.), Anything for Money (s.p.), The Wrong Mrs. Wright, Now It Can Be Told (s.p.), It Happened in Lisbon (s.p.), The Secret Door, A Harvest of Evil (s.p., dir.), Sometimes I Love You (s.p.), White Comanche, Ragan, Devil May Care, Maybe September (s.p.), Recent screenplays: The Oedipus Vendetta, The Lotus Affair, Candle in the Wind, Royal Flush.
TV: Directed: Treasury Men in Action, Man Behind the Badge, Reader's Digest, Passport To Danger, Hollywood Profile, Highway Patrol, Arabian Nights, Telephone Time, Silent Service, The Grey Ghost, Man with a Camera, Adventures in Paradise, Shotgun Slade, Perry Mason, Follow the Sun, Frontier Circus. Wrote: The Uncivil Engineer, 8:46 to Southampton.
PLAYS: Directed: Two Faced Coin, Some Call It Love, French without Tears, Burlesque, London by Night, The Man from Madrid, Paris, With Love. Wrote and Directed: West End, Please Omit Flowers, The Girl From Nolo.

KAY, GORDON: Producer. b. Montreal, Canada, Sept. 6, 1916; e. Williams Coll. (Mass.); married. Asst. prod. Republic 1946, assoc. prod., 1947. apptd. secy.-treas.; exec. asst. to head of prod. at Republic, Feb., 1951; prod., Univ. 1955; pres. Gordon Kay & Assoc., 1958.
PICTURES INCLUDE: Wild Frontier, Bandits of Dark Canyon, Oklahoma Badlands, Bold Frontiersman, He Rides Tall, Fluffy, Taggart, Gunpoint, Beardless Warriors.

KAYAMA, YUZO: Actor. b. April 11, 1937. e. law school Keio Univ. Debut Toho Studio 1959 in Man Against Man.
PICTURES INCLUDE: Westward desperado, Man from the East, Blood in the Sea, Three Dolls series, Bull of Ginza, Tsubaki Sanjuro.

KAYE, DANNY: Actor. b. Brooklyn, N.Y., Jan. 18, 1913. On stage summer theatres; toured U.S. in act La Vie Paree; in night clubs; toured Orient, 1934; m.p. debut in Up in Arms, 1944; formed prod. co. Nov., 1952; Ambassador-at-Large UNICEF-U.N. Children's Fund. Recipient of Scopus Laureate for 1977; first award for International Distinguished Service from the United Nations Children's Fund; Honorary Degree from Colgate University, Doctor of Humane Letters.
TV: The Secret Life of Danny Kaye, numerous Danny Kaye Specials, Danny Kaye Show. Danny Kaye's "Look In" at Metropolitan Opera since 1973; televised, 1975. Won Emmy Award for Best Children's Special, 1975.
BROADWAY: Straw Hat Revue, Play's The Thing, Death Takes a Holiday, Lady in the Dark, Let's Face It, Two by Two, 1970–71.
PICTURES INCLUDE: Wonder Man, Kid from Brooklyn, Secret Life of Walter Mitty, Song Is Born, Inspector General, On the Riviera, Hans Christian Andersen, Knock on Wood, White Christmas, Court Jester, Merry Andrew, The Five Pennies, On the Double, Man for the Diners' Club, The Madwoman of Chaillot.

KAZAN, ELIA: Director. b. Constantinople, Turkey, Sept. 7, 1909; e. Williams Coll., Yale Dramatic School. With Group Theatre as apprentice & stage mgr.; on stage, 1934–41; plays include: Waiting for Lefty, Golden Boy, Gentle People, Five-Alarm Lilliom; m.p. acting debut in Blues in the Night, 1941; stage dir.; won Critics Award best direction of Skin of Our Teeth. All My Sons, Streetcar Named Desire, Death of a Salesman, Cat on a Hot Tin Roof; also dir.: One Touch of Venus, Harriet, Jacobowsky and the Colonel, Tea and Sympathy, Dark at the Top of the Stairs, J.B., Sweet Bird of Youth; co-dir., prod., Lincoln Center Repertory Theatre; dir., After The Fall, But For Whom Charlie; m.p. dir., 1944; Academy Award best direction, 1947, for Gentleman's Agreement; author novel, The Arrangement, 1967–68, novel, The Assassins; 1974 novel, The Understudy.
PICTURES INCLUDE: City of Conquest, Tree Grows in Brooklyn, Boomerang, Sea of Grass, Panic in the Streets, Pinky, Streetcar Named Desire, Viva Zapata, Man on a Tightrope, On the Waterfront (Acad. Award, best dir., 1954), East of Eden, Baby Doll, Face in the Crowd, Wild River, Splendor In the Grass, America, America, The Arrangement, The Visitors, The Last Tycoon.

KEACH, STACY: Actor. b. 1942. Began professional acting career as Marcellus, Player King in Joseph Papp's 1964 production of Hamlet in Central Park. Performances since have won three Obie Awards, Vernon Rice Drama Desk Award for Macbird, Drama Desk Award, Tony Nomination for Indians.
CREDITS: The Heart Is A Lonely Hunter, End of the

Road, The Traveling Executioner, Brewster McCloud, Doc, Judge Roy Bean, The New Centurions, Fat City, Long Day's Journey Into Night (Stage), Macbird (Stage), Indians (Stage), Hamlet (Stage), Luther, Gravy Train, Caribe (TV Series), The Killer Inside Me, Conduct Unbecoming, Street People, The Squeeze, Gray Lady Down, The Adventures of Pedro and Man, The Ninth Configuration, Longriders, Directed Six Characters In Search Of An Author and Incident At Vichy; Deathtrap (stage), Hughie (stage), The Long Riders (star & exec. prod.), Road Games (film), Butterfly (film), Barnum (stage).

KEACH, SR., STACY: Executive. b. Chicago, May 29, 1914. Father of actors, Stacy and James. e. Northwestern Univ. (MA). Was instructor in theatre arts at Northwestern and Armstrong College and dir. at Pasadena Playhouse before entering industry. For 4½ yrs. under contract at Universal Pictures; 3 yrs. at RKO; had own productions on NBC, CBS. In 1946 began producing and directing industrial stage presentations for Union Oil Co. and from then on became full-time prod. of m.p. and stage industrial shows. In 1946 formed Stacy Keach Productions, of which he is pres. In addition to directing, producing and writing he occasionally appears as actor in films.

KEATON, DIANE: Actress. b. So. Calif. e. Santa Ana College. Appeared in summer stock and studied at Neighborhood Playhouse in N.Y. Made prof. debut in Bdwy. prod. of Hair (1968); then co-starred with Woody Allen in Play It Again, Sam, repeating role for film version.
PICTURES INCLUDE: Lovers and Other Strangers, The Godfather, Play It Again, Sam, Sleeper, The Godfather, Part II, Love and Death, I Will . . . I Will . . . for Now, Harry and Walter Go to New York, Annie Hall, Looking for Mr. Goodbar, Interiors, Manhattan, Reds.

KEEL, HOWARD: Actor. r.n. Harold Keel. b. Gillespie, Ill., April 13, 1917. e. high school, Fallbrook, Calif.; m. Helen Anderson, dancer; d. Kaiya Liane. Stage and screen. Began career following George Walker scholarship award for singing, L.A.; appeared in plays, Pasadena Auditorium, concerts; won awards, Mississippi Valley and Chicago Musical Festivals. Stage debut: Carousel, 1945; principal role (Oklahoma). Screen debut, The Small Voice, London, 1948.
PICTURES INCLUDE: Annie Get Your Gun, Pagan Love Song, Three Guys Named Mike, Show Boat, Texas Carnival, Callaway Went Thataway, Lovely to Look At, Desperate Search, Ride Vaquero, Fast Company, Kiss Me Kate, Calamity Jane, Rose Marie, Seven Brides for Seven Brothers, Deep in My Heart, Jupiter's Darling, Kismet, Floods of Fear, Big Fisherman, Armored Command, Arizona Bushwackers.
PLAYS: Saratoga, No Strings.

KEESHAN, BOB: Performer. b. Lynbrook, N.Y., June 27, 1927. e. Fordham U. As network page boy became assistant to Howdy Doody's Bob Smith and originated role of Clarabelle the Clown; created children's programs Time for Fun (1953), Tinker's Workshop (1954), Captain Kangaroo (1955), Mister Mayor, 1965.

KEITEL, HARVEY: Actor. b. Brooklyn, N.Y. Served in U.S. Marine Corps. Over 10 yrs. experience in summer stock, repertory and little theatre after study at Actors Studio with Lee Strasberg and Frank Corsaro. Read for male lead in collegiate film prod. of Who's That Knocking at My Door?; Martin Scorsese, director, gave him the role. Has since become repertory member of Scorsese films.
PICTURES INCLUDE: Who's That Knocking at My Door?, Street Scenes, Mean Streets, Alice Doesn't Live Here Anymore, Taxi Driver, Mother, Jugs and Speed, Welcome to L.A., The Duellists, Fingers, Blue Collar, Bad Timing, The Border.

KEITH, BRIAN: Actor. b. Bayonne, N.J., Nov. 14, 1921; p. Robert Keith, actor. U.S. Marines, 1942–45; worked in stock co., radio shows, comm. films for TV; on B'way in Mr. Roberts, Darkness at Noon; dramatic TV shows including: Studio One, Suspense, Philco Playhouse, star of Crusader; m.p. debut in Arrowhead.
PICTURES INCLUDE: Jivaro, Alaska Seas, Bamboo Prison, Violent Men, Tight Spot, Five Against the House, Storm Center, Run of the Arrow, Nightfall, Sierra Baron, Those Calloways, The Raiders, The Young Philadelphians, Dino, A Tiger Walks, The Parent Trap, The Hallelujah Trail, Rare Breed, Nevada Smith, Reflections in a Golden Eye, Krakatoa, East of Java, Gaily, Gaily, Suppose They Gave a War and Nobody Came, McKenzie Break, Scandalous John, Something Big, The Yakuza, The Wind and the Lion, Nickelodeon, Hooper, Meteor, Charlie Chan and the Curse of the Dragon Queen.

KELLER, HARRY: Prod.-dir. b. Los Angeles, Calif., Feb. 22, 1913. Film ed., Nat'l Screen Service, Universal, Republic, 1936–50; dir., Republic 1950–53; TV dir., Loretta Young show, 1954–55; dir., Univ. Int., 1956–57; dir. Walt Disney, 1958–59; dir., Universal, 1960–62; for Univ. Prod-Dir. 1963–69; prod., WB, 1970–71.

PICTURES INCLUDE: The Unguarded Moment, Brass Bottle, Send Me No Flowers, That Funny Feeling, Voice in the Mirror, Tammy Tell Me True, Mirage, Texas Across the River, In Enemy Country, Skin Game.

KELLER, MARTHE: Actress. b. Switzerland. Started acting in France and attracted attention of U.S. directors after appearing in Claude Lelouch's And Now My Love.
PICTURES INCLUDE: The Devil by the Tail (debut), And Now my Love, Marathon Man, Black Sunday, Bobby Deerfield, Fedora, The Formula.

KELLERMAN, SALLY: Actress. b. Long Beach, Calif., June 2, 1936. e. Hollywood High. Studied acting in N.Y. at the Actors Studio and in Hollywood with Jeff Corey.
TV: Mannix, It Takes a Thief, Chrysler Theatre.
PICTURES INCLUDE: The Boston Strangler, The April Fools, M*A*S*H, Brester McCloud, Last of the Red Hot Lovers, Lost Horizon, Slither, Rafferty and the Gold Dust Twins, The Big Bus, Welcome to L.A., A Little Romance, Foxes, Loving Couples.

KELLERS, FREDERIC: Executive. b. Hackensack, N.J., Aug. 22, 1929. e. Wilmington College. Ohio. Wilmington Theatre. Ohio. 1947–49; Assoc. Film, Inc., N.Y., 1949–51; assistant box office treasurer, Radio City Music Hall, 1951–66; box office treasurer, 1966. Dir. Theas. Opera, 1967; v.p., operations, 1976; 1979, admissions mgr. Radio City Music Hall Productions; 1981, dir., house operations.

KELLEY, PATRICK: Executive. Joined MCA in 1950 as agent; with them for 20 years; named v.p. in chg. of talent for Universal's theatrical and TV project in 1964. Left MCA in 1970 to form First Artists with star partners Barbra Streisand, Sidney Poitier, Paul Newman (later joined by Steve McQueen and Dustin Hoffman). Resigned 1975 as F.A. bd. chmn. to head Pan Arts Corp., prod. co. of which George Roy Hill is bd. chmn.
PICTURES INCLUDE: A Little Romance (exec. prod.).

KELLOGG, PHILIP M.: executive. b. March 17, 1912, Provo, Wash. e. UCLA. Special feature writer for Hearst papers and magazines, 1933–34; MGM story dept., production dept., Irving Thalberg unit, 1934–35; Warner Bros. Film editor, 1935–41; Berg-Allenberg Agency, 1941–50; U.S. Naval Reserve officer, 1941–46; William Morris Agency, 1950-present, co-head of m.p. dept., dir. WMA, Ltd., London.

KELLY, DUKE: Actor-producer-director-writer. b. Dodge City, Kan., Aug. 26, 1936. e. Wichita State Univ., Fla. State Coll. (masters and doctorate); Masters in cinemagraphic arts. Phd, Archeology. Was in pro sports (football, baseball, boxing) and sgt. in U.S. Marines during Korean War. Also was deputy sheriff, high rigger, lumberjack and truck driver; professional parachutist for National Air Show, stock car driver, writer, lecturer and teacher. Began m.p. career as stunt man and horse wrangler; graduated to bit parts and eventually featured and supporting roles in both TV and m.p. Wrote scripts during first few years of career to supplement acting income. Did many legit theatre musicals, comedies and dramas. Worked radio and TV as personality; sang and danced in supper clubs, wrote music, etc Produced, wrote, directed and starred in seven features made by own co., Film Center Productions.
PICTURES INCLUDE: Producer-Director-Writer: Night of the Werewolf, Walk Home from Hell, Gunhawks, Gunner, Ride the Hot Wind, My Name is Legend, Conquest of Condor Valley. Director: Seven Men To Sundown, The Red Mask, Donovan. Actor: Ten Men from Now, Advise and Consent, The Alamo, Mustang, Walk Home from Hell, Gunhawks, Gunner, Ride the Hot Wind, Liberty Valance, Ride the High Country, My Name Is Legend, Conquest of Condor Valley, etc.
TV: Producer-Director-Writer: The Celebrity Gold Show, Movie Quiz, Box 777, The Costume Shop. Actor: 26 Men, Gunsmoke, F.B.I., Cannon, etc. Host of Celebrity Golf Show, Comedy Capers, Nightmare.

KELLY, GENE: Actor. b. Pittsburgh, Pa., Aug. 23, 1912. e. Penn State U., U. Pittsburgh. Bricklayer, concrete mixer, soda clerk, dance instructor before going on stage, in N.Y. prods. (Leave It to Me, One for the Money, The Time of Your Life, Pal Joey). On screen 1942 in For Me and My Gal; Summer Stock.
PICTURES INCLUDE: Pilot No. 5, Du Barry Was a Lady, Thousands Cheer, The Cross of Lorraine, Christmas Holiday, Anchors Aweigh, Cover Girl, Ziegfeld Follies, Pirate, Three Musketeers, Words and Music, Take Me Out to the Ball Game, Black Hand, On the Town, An American in Paris, Singin' in the Rain, It's A Big Country, Devil Makes Three, Brigadoon, Crest of the Wave, Deep in My Heart, Invitation to the Dance, It's Always Fair Weather, The Happy Road, Les Girls, Special Academy Award for advancing dance films, Gigot, A Guide for the Married Man, The Young Girls of Rochefort, Hello, Dolly!, The Cheyenne Social Club, 40 Carats, That's Entertainment, That's Entertainment, Part Two, Viva, Knievel!, Xanadu.

KELLY, GRACE: Actress. b. Philadelphia, Pa., Nov. 12; e. Amer. Acad. of Dramatic Arts, 1947–49. Amateur theatricals; several B'way plays; summer stock; TV plays; m.p. debut in 14 Hours.
PICTURES INCLUDE: High Noon, Mogambo, Dial M for Murder, Rear Window, Green Fire, Country Girl (Academy Award, best perf., 1954), Bridges at Toko-Ri, To Catch a Thief, The Swan, High Society.

KELLY, J. ARTHUR: Writer, producer, director. b. Brantford, Canada, 1922; served in Canadian Army Infantry (overseas), 1940–45; editor, publisher, Brantford Weekly Star, Brantford Merchants' Shopping Guide, 1947; sales mgr., C.K.P.C. Brantford, 1955; wrote, prod., This Most Gallant Affair, The Abbey On Monte Casino, The Samaritans, The Swimming Cases At Whistling, Ginsberg Isn't Guilty; wrote play, Wait For Me; own firm. Arthur J. Kelly Productions; dir., prod., Maytime Festival, Brantford, Ontario, Canada 1964. New play, He Hanged His Son. Dir. prod. Brantorama Historical Pageant Parade, 1967, Wrote, prod. dir. for Hotel Theatre, Onwonsyshon, 1968. 1970, wrote, prod., dir., Am I Really Joe Sholopka?; 1970, wrote, prod., dir., Standup and Shout About It; wrote, prod., dir., What In the Hell Ever Happened to Purgatory?; wrote, prod., dir., Is Mrs. Maloney' Our Only Hope?

KELLY, JIM: Actor. b. Paris, Ky. e. Univ. of Louisville. Studied karate at univ., winning trophies and int'l. middleweight championship. Opened school for karate in L.A. Did modelling and TV commercials. Was technical advisor for fight scenes on Melinda and played role in it.
PICTURES INCLUDE: Enter the Dragon (debut), Black Belt Jones, Three the Hard Way.

KELLY, NANCY: Actress. b. Lowell, Mass., March 25, 1921. e. Immaculate Conception Acad., N.Y.; St. Lawrence Acad., L.I.; Bentley Sch. for Girls. In number of pictures as child, and on stage in Susan and God (N.Y. prod. 1937). In 1938 on screen.
PICTURES INCLUDE: Torando, Women in Bondage, Gamblers Choice, Show Business, Double Exposure, Song of the Sarong, Woman Who Came Back, Murder in the Music Hall, Crowded Paradise, Bad Seed.
STAGE: Season in the Sun, 1950–51; Bad Seed, 1954–55.

KEMENY, JOHN: Producer. B. Budapest, Hungary. Producer for National Film Board of Canada, 1957–69. Formed International Cinemedia Center, Ltd. in 1969 in Montreal, as partner.
PICTURES INCLUDE: The Apprenticeship of Duddy Kravits, White Line Fever, Shadow of the Hawk, La Castles.

KEMP, JEREMY: Actor. b. Chesterfield, England, 1935. e. Abbottsholme School, Central School of Speech and Drama. Service with Gordon Highlanders. Early career on stage incl. Old Vic Theatre Company, 1959–61. Recent theatre: Celebration, Incident at Vichy, Spoiled, The Caretaker. National Theatre, 1979–80.
TV: Z Cars, The Lovers of Florence, The Last Reunion, Colditz, Brassneck, Rhinemann Exchange, Lisa, Goodbye, Henry VIII, St. Joan, The Winter's Tale.
PICTURES INCLUDE: Cast a Giant Shadow, Operation Crossbow, The Blue Max, Assignment K, Twist of Sand, Strange Affair, Darling Lilli, The Games, The Saltzburg Connection, The Blockhouse, The Bellstone Fox, 7% Solution, A Bridge Too Far, East of Elephant Rock, Caravans, The Prisoner of Zenda.

KEMP, MATTY: Producer, director, writer. b. Rockville Centre, N.Y. St. Paul's School, Hempstead, N.Y. Entered m.p. as actor-writer 1926 Universal Pictures; variously employed by Mack Sennett, Fox, Paramount, RKO, prod. Authors' Guild show for radio and musical shorts. Served in U.S. Army 1942–45 in signal corps pictorial, information education, and training film branch. Prod. dir. for series of musical shorts Universal 1945, formed Cameo Productions (Calif.) 1946; formed Masque Productions with Pene Raymond 1948.
PICTURES INCLUDE: (prod. dir.) Linda Be Good, Million Dollar Weekend; (Story) The French Line, (Writer, prod. dir.) Pan American Showtime, 13 half hour musical series, (prod. dir.) Meet the Family, series of 3 with Arthur Lake, (prod. dir.) Adventurous Hobby series 3 segments, (Story prod. dir.) The Birth of a Legend, documentary on Mary Pickford and Douglas Fairbanks, (Story, co-producer) America's Sweetheart feature documentary, Managing director production executive, Mary Pickford Co.

KEMP-WELCH, JOAN: Free lance, TV director-producer, actress. First appearance on stage 1927. Subsequently many stage parts and stage directorial assignments. First appeared in films 1938. Films included 60 Glorious Years, They Flew Alone, The Citadel, Busman's Honeymoon. West End theatre prods. include: Dead on Nine, Vicious Circle, Our Town, Desire Under the Elms. Since 1954 TV dir. Received TV Oscar for Light Entert., 1958. Desmond Davis Award for services to TV 1963. Silver Dove Monte Carlo

Award, 1961. The Lover, awarded Prix Italia 1963 (drama). Many other productions, incl. musicals, ballet, drama, series, outside broadcasts. Dear Octopus, The Birthday Party, The Collection, View from the Bridge, Electra, 3 Sisters, A Midsummer Nights Dream, Dangerous Corner. Upstairs, Downstairs; prod. Armchair Theatre, 1973–74. 1974–75. French Without Tears, Wait Till Dark, The Price, Cranford Musical. The Other Side of the Swamp, Romeo & Juliet, The Circle, Hay Fever, It Happened in Harrods.
TV: The Piano. 1977–78 In South Africa, The Deep Blue Sea, The King Fisher, The Monkey Walk, Cause Celebre, Your Place or Mine, Home, The Unvarnished Truth, I Am Who I Am, Happy Birthday.

KENNEDY, ARTHUR: Actor. b. Worcester, Mass., February 17, 1914; p. Dr. and Mrs. J. T. Kennedy; e. Carnegie Institute of Technology; m. Mary Cheffey, prof. Has worked for George M. Cohan; Guthrie McClintic, Marc Connelly and others well known to theatregoers. Film debut: City for Conquest.
PICTURES INCLUDE: Champion, They Died With Their Boots On, High Sierra, Strange Alibi, Knockout, Highway West, Air Force, Devotion, Boomerang, The Window, Chicago Deadline, The Glass Menagerie, Red Mountain, Bright Victory, Bend of the River, Rancho Notorious, Girl in White, Lusty Men, Man from Laramie, Trial, Naked Dawn, Desperate Hours, Crashout, Rawhide Years, Peyton Place, Some Came Running, Claudelle Inglish, Adventures of a Young Man, Barabbas, Laurence of Arabia, Italiano Brava Gentle, Stay Away Joe, A Minute to Pray, a Second to Die, Hail Hero, Shark, My Old Man's Place, The Sentinel.

KENNEDY, BURT: Director. b. Muskegon, Mich. Began as writer of TV and film scripts, and most recently was writer, producer and director of Combat series.
PICTURES INCLUDE: Mail Order Bride. The Rounders, The Money Trap, Return of the Seven, The War Wagon, Support Your Local Sheriff, Young Billy Young, The Devil's Backbone, Dirty Dingus Magee, Support Your Local Gunfighter, Hannie Caulder, The Train Robbers (also s.p.).

KENNEDY, DOUGLAS: Actor. b. Sept. 14, 1915. New York. e. Deerfield Academy, Mass., Amherst College. In armed services, World War II.
PICTURES INCLUDE: Opened By Mistake, Women Without Names, Those Were the Days, The Way of All Flesh, Northwest Mounted Police, The Round-Up, Nora Prentiss, Dark Passage, Possessed, The Unfaithful, Look for the Silver Lining, I Was An American Spy, Callaway Went Thataway, Fort Osage, Indiana Uprising, For Men Only, China Corsair, Last Train From Bombay, Ride the Man Down, Torpedo Alley, War Paint, Gun Belt, Sea of Lost Ships, Lone Gun, Massacre Canyon, Big Chase, Sitting Bull, Cry Vengeance, Wyoming Renegades, Eternal Sea, Strange Lady in Town, Wiretapper, Fastest Guitar Alive.
TV: Steve Donovan Western Marshal series.

KENNEDY, GEORGE: Actor. b. N.Y., N.Y., Feb. 18, 1927. f. orchestra leader at N.Y. Proctor Theatre, m. dancer with Le Ballet Classique in vaudeville. At 2 acted in touring co. of Bringing Up Father. At 7, disc jockey with his own radio show for children. Joined W.W. II Army at 17, earned two Bronze Stars and combat and service ribbons. In Army 16 years, became Capt. and Armed Forces Radio and TV officer. 1957, opened first Army Information Office, N.Y. Served as technical advisor to Phil Silver's Sergeant Bilko TV series. Began acting in 1959 when discharged from Army.
TV: Sugarfoot, Cheyenne.
PICTURES INCLUDE: Lonely Are the Brave, Strait Jacket, The Silent Witness, Island of the Blue Dolphins, The Man From the Diners Club, Little Shepherd of Kingdom Come, Mirage, See How They Run, McHale's Navy, Charade, In Harm's Way, The Sons of Katie Elder, Shenandoah, Hush . . . Hush Sweet Charlotte, The Dirty Dozen, Hurry Sundown, Cool Hand Luke (Acad. Award Best Supporting Actor), The Ballad of Josie, Jolly Pink Jungle, Bandolerol, The Boston Strangler, Guns of the Magnificent Seven, Gaily, Gaily, The Good Guys and the Bad Guys, Airport, . . . tick . . . tick . . . tick, Zigzag, Dirty Dingus Magee, Fool's Parade, Lost Horizon, Cahill, Thunderbolt and Lightfood, Airport 1975, Earthquake, The Human Factor, Airport '77, Death on the Nile, Brass Target, The Concorde—Airport '79, Death Ship.

KENNEDY, JOSEPH: Executive. b. New York City. Joined United Artists in 1968 as salesman out of Boston branch. Named Chicago sls. mgr. (1969–72); Jacksonville branch mgr. (1972–78); southern div. mgr. (1978–79). In 1980 named v.p. & asst. gen. sls. mgr. responsible for UA eastern sls. territories.

KENNEY, H. WESLEY: Producer-Director, stage, TV, film. b. Dayton, O., grad. Carnegie Tech. Four-time Emmy winner; 1974–75 dir., All in the Family; exec. prod. Days of Our Lives; 1979–81, dir., Ladies Man, Filthy Rich.

KENT, JEAN: Actress. b. London, Eng., June 29, 1921. e. Marist Coll., Peekham, London; p. prof. Fields & Norrie. First stage appearance at 3 and at 10 played in parents' act; chorus girl at Windmill Theatre, London, 1935; 2 yrs. repertory; Screen debut: It's That Man Again, 1941.
    PICTURES INCLUDE: Trottle True, Her Favorite Husband, The Reluctant Widow, The Woman in Question, The Browning Version, Big Frame, Before I Wake, Shadow of Fear, Prince and the Showgirl, Bon Jour Tristesse, Grip of the Strangler, Beyond This Place, Please Turn Over, Bluebeard's Ten Honeymoons, Shout At the Devil.
    TV: A Call on the Widow, The Lovebird, The Morning Star, November Voyage, Love Her to Death, The Lion and the Mouse, The Web, Sir Francis Drake series, Yvette, Emergency Ward 10, County Policy, Coach 7, Smile On the Face of the Tiger, No Hiding Place, Kipling, This Man Craig, The Killers, Vanity Fair, A Night with Mrs. Da Tanka, United serial. The Family of Fred, After Dark, Thicker than Water series, The Young Doctors, Brother and Sister, Up Pompei, Steptoe and Son, Doctor at Large, Family at War, K is for Killing, Night School, Tycoon series.

KENT, JOHN B.: Theatre executive and attorney. b. Jacksonville, Fla., Sept. 5, 1939. e. Yale Univ., Univ. of Fla., Law School, N.Y. Univ. grad. school of law (LLM in taxation, 1964). Partner in Kent, Watts, Durden, Kent & Mickler (1967 to present); Pres. & dir., Kent Investments, Inc. (1977 to present); dir. and off. Kent Theatres, Inc. and affiliated corps (1961 to present); v.p. and gen. counsel, (1970 to present). Was pres. 1967–70 when resigned to devote full time to law practice. NATO dir. (1972) and Presidents' Advisory Cabinet, 1979 to present) v.p. NATO of Fla., 1968–72, dir; 1973 to present. Member of Rotary Club of Jacksonville, Fla. Bar Ass'n., American Bar Ass'n., American Judicature Society.

KENYON, CURTIS: Writer.
    TV PLAYS: Cavalcade of America, Fireside Theatre, Schlitz Playhouse, U.S. Steel Hour, 20th Century-Fox Hour.
    PICTURES INCLUDE: Woman Who Dared, Lloyds of London, Wake Up and Live, Love and Hisses, She Knew All the Answers, Twin Beds, Seven Days' Leave, Thanks for Everything, Princess and the Pirate, Bathing Beauty, Fabulous Dorseys, Tulsa, Two Flags West.

KERASOTES, GEORGE G.: Exhibitor. b. Springfield, Ill., Mar. 27, 1911; e. U. of Ill. 1929–33, Lincoln Coll. of Law 1934–36. Entire career in m.p. ind.; chmn. bd., United Theatres Owners of Illinois; pres., Kerasotes Theatres, Mo., Ill.: pres. Theatre Owners of America, 1959–60; chmn. of board of TOA 1960–62; chmn. ACE Toll TV com.; bd. mem. Code Appeal Board; mem. exec. comm. NATO, bd. of dir. NATO. chairman NATO non-theatrical committee, dir. Sangamon Home Savings Assoc. Pres. Kerasotes Theatres; pres., St. Anthony's Church, Springfield, Ill.

KERKORIAN, KIRK: Executive. b. Fresno, CA, June 6, 1917. e. Los Angeles public schools. Served as capt., transport command, RAF, 1942–44. Commercial air line pilot from 1940; founder Los Angeles Air Service (later Trans Intl. Airlines Corp.), 1948; Intl. Leisure Corp., 1968; controlling stockholder, Western Airlines, 1970; chief exec. officer, MGM, Inc., 1973–74; chm. exec. com., vice-chm. bd., 1974—

KERR, DEBORAH: Actress. b. Helensburgh, Scotland, Sept. 30, 1921; e. Phyllis Smale Ballet Sch.; m. Anthony Bartley. On stage 1939 in repertory. Began Brit. screen career 1940 in Major Barbara; voted "Star of Tomorrow" Motion Picture Herald-Fame Poll, 1942. Voted one of top ten British money-making stars in Motion Picture Herald-Fame Poll, 1947. B'way debut in Tea & Sympathy, 1953.
    PICTURES INCLUDE: Major Barbara, Love on the Dole, Hatler's Castle, The Day Will Dawn, The Avengers, Perfect Strangers, Colonel Blimp, Black Narcissus, The Hucksters, If Winter Comes, Edward My Son, Please Believe Me, King Solomon's Mines, Quo Vadis, Thunder in the East, Prisoner of Zenda, Dream Wife, Julius Caesar, Young Bess, From Here to Eternity, End of the Affair, King and I, Proud and Profane, Tea and Sympathy, Heaven Knows Mr. Alison, Affair to Remember, Count Your Blessings, Beloved Infidel, Sundowners, The Grass Is Greener, The Innocents, The Naked Edge, The Chalk Garden, Night of the Iguana, Marriage On the Rocks, Casino Royale, Eye of the Devil, The Gypsy Moths, The Arrangement.

KERR, FRASER: Actor. b. Glasgow, Scotland, 1931. Early career in repertory. Tours of Canada and America. Ent. TV 1956. Series incl. Emergency Ward 10, Dixon of Deck Green, Murder Bag. Many Shakespeare plays. Radio: BBC Drama Rep. Co., 39 Steps, The Ringer, The Bible, What Every Woman Knows.
    STAGE & TV: Night Must Fall, Never a Cross Word, The Inside Man, On the Buses, Dr. Finlay's Casebook, Wicked Woman, Madelaine July, Doctor in the House, Counterstrike, Genevieve's Walk, Juno and the Paycock, Aquarius, Ev, Upstairs and Downstairs, Cover to Cover, Janine, Robert the Bruce, Caliph of Bagdad, Watch it, Sailor!, The Fosters, Weekend World, Doctor at Sea, Dads Army, Al-

gernon Blackwood, Waiting for Sheila, Weekend Show, Mind Your Language, Yes, Minister.
    PICTURES INCLUDE: What a Whopper, Carry on Regardless, Way of McEagle, Thomasina, Theatre of Death, Tom, Dick and Harriet, Granny Gets the Point, Nothing But The Night, The Lord of the Rings, Kidnapped, The Derelict.
    RECORD PRODUCER: Tales of Shakespeare Series, The Casket Letters of Mary Queen of Scots.

KERR, JOHN: Actor. b. New York, N.Y., Nov. 15, p. Geoffrey Kerr, actor, and June Walker, actress. e. Harvard U., B.A., Columbia U., M.A. Actor in summer stock, TV; on Broadway in Bernardine, Tea and Sympathy, All Summer Long.
    PICTURES INCLUDE: The Cobweb, Gaby, Tea and Sympathy, The Vintage, South Pacific, Girl of the Night, Pit and the Pendulum, Seven Women from Hell.
    TV: Peyton Place.

KERSHNER, IRVIN: Director. b. Phila., Pa., April 29, 1923. e. Tyler School Fine Arts of Temple Univ., 1946, Art Center School, Univ. of Southern Calif. Designer, photography, adv., documentary, architectural; doc. film maker, U.S.I.S., Middle East, 1950–52; dir., cameraman, TV doc., Confidential File, 1953–55; dir.-prod.-writer, Ophite Prod.
    PICTURES INCLUDE: Stakeout on Dope Street, Young Captives, Hoodlum Priest, The Luck of Ginger Coffey, A Fine Madness, The Flim Flam Man, Loving, Up the Sandbox, S*P*Y*s, Return of a Man Called Horse, Raid on Entebbe. (TV in U.S.): Eyes of Laura Mars, The Empire Strikes Back.
    TV: The Rebel, Naked City, numerous pilots and other nat'l shows.

KEYES, EVELYN: Actress. b. Port Arthur, Texas; e. high school; began career as a dancer in night clubs; m. Artie Shaw.
    PICTURES INCLUDE: The Buccaneer, Union Pacific, Gone with the Wind, A Thousand and One Nights, The Jolson Story, Mating of Millie, Johnny OX'Clock, Enchantment, Mr. Soft Touch, The Prowler, The Killer That Stalked New York, Smuggler's Island, The Iron Man, One Big Affair, Shoot First, 99 River Street, Hell's Half Acre, Top of the World, Seven-Year Itch, Around the World in 80 Days.

KIBBEE, ROLAND: Writer, producer, director. b. Monongahela, Pa., Feb. 15, 1914; e. L.A. City Coll., 1932–33. Radio writer: The Grouch Club, Fred Allen Show, Groucho Marx Show, Fanny Brice Show; Play: Easy Does It; Magazine Humor: Atlantic, Saturday Review, Script, Holiday.
    SCREENPLAYS: Night in Casablanca, Angel On My Shoulder, Ten Tall Men, The Crimson Pirate, Vera Cruz, The Devil's Disciple, Top Secret Affair, The Desert Song, Now You See It, Now You Don't, producer & writer; Valdez Is Coming, executive producer & writer; Brock's Last Case, producer; Moll Flanders, The Midnight Man, writer, producer, director.
    TV: The Ford Show, Ford Startime, The Bob Cummings Show, The Virginian, The Hitchcok Hour; Madigan, The Bob Newhart Show, It Takes A Thief, The Deputy, producer, creator, writer; prod., Madigan, Columbo; prod., creator, writer, McCoy. Exec. prod., The Family Holvak; prod., Barney Miller.

KIDDER, MARGOT: Actress. b. Yellowknife, Canada, Oct. 17, 1948.
    PICTURES: Gaily, Gaily, Quackser Fortune Has a Cousin in the Bronx, Sisters, The Great Waldo Pepper, Superman, Mr. Mike's Mondo Video, The Amityville Horror, Willy and Phil, Superman II.

KILEY, RICHARD: Actor. b. Chicago, Ill., Mar. 31, 1922; e. Loyola U. Started prof. career radio, Jack Armstrong, All American Boy.
    STAGE: Streetcar Named Desire, Misalliance, Kismet, Time Limit, No Strings, Man of LaMancha, Her First Roman.
    PICTURES INCLUDE: The Mob, The Sniper, Eight Iron Men, Pick-Up on South Street, Blackboard Jungle, Phoenix City Story, Spanish Affair, Pendulum, The Little Prince, Looking for Mr. Goodbar.

KILLIAM, PAUL: Producer-performer. b. Mass., Sept. 12, 1916. e. Harvard. News supervisor, WOR-Mutual; prod.-performer TV Hometown. Matinee in NY units for CBS-TV Morning Show, NBC-TV Home Show; ind. prod. cartoons, shorts, comedies: prod. film series, Paul Killiam Show, Movie Museum, Silents Please.

KIMBLEY, DENNIS: Sales Manager, Motion Picture Sales, Kodak Ltd., in U.K. Early career in Kodak Testing Dept. responsible for quality control motion picture films. Joined Marketing Division 1966. Chairman BKSTS Film 75 and film 79 Conference Committee. President BKSTS 1976–78.

KIMMINS, ANTHONY: Director, writer. b. Harrow Middlesex, England, Nov. 10, 1901; e. R.N. Coll., Dartmouth. Capt. in Royal Navy, World War II. Playwright (While Parents Sleep, Night Club Queen, Chase the Ace, Winter Sport, The Amorous Prawn.) Began screen career 1934 in How's

Chances?; since author variously orig., s.p., collab., dial., many Brit. features (Talk of the Devil, Come On George, Laburnum Grove, etc.); in 1936 dir. & s.p. All at Sea; pictures dir. since include I See Ice, It's in the Air, Trouble Brewing. In 1946 returned to m.p. to write, produce and direct.

PICTURES INCLUDE: Mine Own Executioner, Bonnie Prince Charlie, Flesh and Blood, Mr. Denning Drives North, Who Goes There (Passionate Sentry), Captain's Paradise, Smiley, Smiley Gets a Gun, The Amorous Prawn.

KING, ALAN: Actor-Producer. b. New York, N.Y. Author, Anybody Who Owns His Own Home Deserves It, Help I'm a Prisoner in a Chinese Bakery.

TV: The Tonight Show, Kraft Music Hall, Comedy is King. Prod-star NBC-TV specials. Hosts and guest star, Tonight Show. Stars semi-annually at Sands Hotel, Las Vegas, Seventh Avenue (mini-series).

STAGE: The Impossible Years, The Investigation, Dinner At Eight, A Lion in Winter, Something Different.

PICTURES INCLUDE: Bye Bye Braverman, Anderson Tapes, Just Tell Me What You Want. Producer: Happy Birthday, Gemini.

KING, ANDREA: Actress, r.n. Georgette Barry; b. Paris, France; e. Edgewood High School, Greenwich, Conn.; m. N.H. Willis, attorney. Started career on N.Y. stage, following high school; in Growing Pains & Fly Away Home, Boy Meets Girl, Angel Street (Boston); Life with Father (Chicago); signed by Warner, 1943. Screen debut: The Very Thought of You. TV actress, CBS.

PICTURES INCLUDE: My Wild Irish Rose, Ride the Pink Horse, Mr. Peabody and the Mermaid, Song of Surrender, Southside 1-1000l, Dial 1119, Lemon Drop Kid, Mark of the Renegade, World In his Arms, Red Planet Mars, Daddy's Gone A-Hunting.

KING, HENRY: Director "Champion of Champion Directors" in Fame ratings. b. Christiansburg, Va., Jan 24, 1896. Worked for Norfolk & Western R.R. in many depts.; toured in stock, circuses, vaudeville, burlesque; on N.Y. stage in "Top O' the Morning"; m.p. actor, Pathe studios; writer-dir.; producer; exec. head Inspiration Co.; with Fox Film Co., remaining after merger with 20th-Century Pictures Co.

PICTURES INCLUDE: 23½ Hours Leave, Tol'able David, Fury, White Sister, Stella Dallas, Romola, Winning of Barbara Worth, Woman Disputed, Over the Hill, Carolina, State Fair, Country Doctor, Ramona, Lloyds of London, In Old Chicago, Alexander's Ragtime Band, Jesse James, Little Old New York, Stanley and Lingstone, Maryland, Chad Hanna, Yank in the R.A.F., Black Swan, Song of Bernadette, Wilson, Bell for Adano, Margie, Captain from Castile, Deep Waters, Twelve O'Clock High, The Gunfighter, I'd Climb the Highest Mountain, David and Bathsheba, Wait Till the Sun Shines, Nelly, Snows of Kilimanjaro, O. Henry's Full House, King of the Khyber Rifles, Untamed, Love Is a Many Splendored Thing, Carousel, The Sun Also Rises, This Earth Is Mine, Tender Is the Night.

KING, HERMAN: Producer. b. Chicago, Ill. Was engaged in vending machine business; mfr. Hollywood Talkitone Soundie Projectors; org. prod. co., King Bros. Prod. (with bros. Maurice and Franklin), 1941.

PICTURES INCLUDE: When Strangers Marry, Dillinger, Suspense, The Gangster, The Dude Goes West, Badman of Tombstone, Gun Crazy, Southside 1-1000, Drums in the Deep South, Mutiny, The Ring, Carnival Story, The Brave One, Gorgo, Captain Sinbad, Maya, Return of The Gunfighter, Heaven with a Gun.

TV: Maya series, King International Corp.

KING, MURRAY J.: Prod.-Exec. b. Chelsea, Mass., Jan. 13, 1914. e. Columbia U., B.S., M.A., 1936; film cutter, 1936; film cutter, asst. ed., Monogram Pictures. Hollywood, 1937–41; Air Corps Captain, WW. II, 1942–46; own studio, Murray King Pictures, Inc., 1947–54; dubbing studio, Mexico, 1954–55; dubbing studio, Havana, Cuba, 1956–60; partner, Miller International Corp. 1961; pres., Miller International Corp., 1964. Pres. Vidata International Corp., 1968 to 1976; President of M-K Communications Corp. 1977 to date, produced feature pictures as follows: The Doll That Took the Town; Bad Girls Don't Cry; Television Series: The Adventures of Blinkey; Producer; Film Publishers Group, Inc.

KING, PEGGY: Singer. b. Greensburg, Pa., 1931. Worked as secretary, then singer with band; morning radio show, Cleveland; recording artist; featured singer, George Gobel Show.

KING, PERRY: Actor. b. Alliance, Ohio, e. Yale. Studied with John Houseman at Julliard.

PICTURES INCLUDE: The Possession of Joel Delaney (debut), Slaughterhouse-Five, Big Truck, Poor Clare, The Lords of Flatbush, Mandingo, The Wild Party, Lipstick, Andy Warhol's Bad, The Choirboys, A Different Story.

TV: Medical Center, Hawaii Five-O, Apple's Way, Cannon.

KING, PETER: Executive. b. London, Eng., 1928. e. Marlborough College, Oxford U.; bd., Shipman & King Cinemas Ltd., 1956; borough councillor, 1959–61; chmn., London & Home counties branch, CEA, 1962–63; pres., CEA, 1964; dir. film ind. Defense Organization dir., Grade Org. 1966–68; man. dir. Shipman & King Cinemas Ltd., 1959–68. Ch. man. dir. Paramount Pictures (U.K.) Ltd. Britain, 1968–70. Man., dir., EMI Cinemas and Leisure Ltd., 1970–74. Vice pres. National Youth Theatre, Governor, National Film School, Chairman: King Publications Ltd.

KINGMAN, DONG: Fine Artist. b. Oakland, Calif., Mar. 31, 1911. e. Hong Kong 1916–1920; 1928, mem. motion picture co., Hong Kong branch; 1935; began to exhibit as fine artist in San Francisco; promotional, advertising or main title artwork for following films: World of Suzie Wong, Flower Drum Song, 55 Days of Peking, Circus World, King Rat, The Desperados, The Sand Pebbles, Lost Horizon-1973. 1966–7, created 12 paintings for Universal Studio Tour for posters and promotion; 1968, cover painting for souvenir program for Ringling Bros.-Barnum and Bailey Circus; treasurer for Living Artist Production since 1954; 1968, became art director for Greater Amusements. Exec. V.P. 22nd-Century Films, Inc. since 1968, Prod. & dir. short, Hongkong Dong. Also short subject film Dong Kingman, filmed and directed by James Wong Howe.

KINGSLEY, DOROTHY: Writer. (Mrs. William W. Durney): b. New York City, Oct. 14. e. Detroit Arts and Crafts Acad. Radio writer for Bob Hope, 1938; Edgar Bergen, 1939–43.

PICTURES INCLUDE: Date With Judy, Neptune's Daughter, Two Weeks With Love, Angels in the Outfield, Texas Carnival, It's a Big Country, When In Rome, Small Town Girl, Dangerous When Wet, Kiss Me Kate, Seven Brides for Seven Brothers, Jupiter's Darling, Don't Go Near the Water, Pal Joey, Green Mansions, Can-Can, Pepe, Half a Sixpence, Valley of the Dolls.

TV: Created series, Bracken's World.

KINGSLEY, WALTER: Executive. b. New York, Oct. 20, 1923. e. Phillips Academy, Andover; Amherst Coll., B.A., 1947. Charter member Big Brothers of Los Angeles. WCOP, Boston, 1947–50; Ziv Television Programs, Inc., 1950–58; President, Independent Television Corp., 1958–61. Member bd. dir. Big Brothers of Amer.; pres. Kingsley Co., 1962–66; exec. v.p. Wolper Prods. Metromedia Prods. Corp., 1966–72; faculty, Inter-Racial Council of Business Opportunity, N.Y.C.; commercial real estate development, 1972-present.

KINOSHITA, KEISUKE: Director. b. Japan, 1912. Entered Shochiku studio as film processor and progressed to director.

PICTURES INCLUDE: Twenty-four Eyes, Sun and Rose, Wild Chrysanthemum, A Japanese Tragedy, Times of Joy and Sorrow, Snow Flurry, Candle in the Wind, Carmen's Pure Love.

KINOY, ERNEST: Writer. Started career in radio writing sci. fic. programs (X Minus One, Dimension X). Created and wrote religious radio show, The Eternal Light. Moved in to TV and wrote for nearly all dramatic shows, including Studio One, Philco Playhouse, Playhouse 90.

PICTURES INCLUDE: Brother John, Buck and the Preacher, Leadbelly.

TV: The Defenders, Naked City, Dr. Kildare, Jacob and Joseph (special), David, the King (special).

KIRK, PHYLLIS: Actress. b. Syracuse, N.Y., Sept. 18. Perfume repr. model, Conover Agcy.; B'way play debut in My Name Is Aquilon; actress, summer stock; screen debut in Our Very Own; B'way production of Point of No Return.

TV: The Thin Man.

PICTURES INCLUDE: A Life of Her Own, Two Weeks With Love, Mrs. O'Malley and Mr. Malone, Three Guys Named Mike, About Face, Iron Mistress, Thunder Over The Plains, House of Wax, Crime Wave, River Beat, Canyon Crossroads, City After Midnight.

KIRNER, MICHAEL: Actor. b. April 2, 1944. e. Drama schools Munich and Rome.

PICTURES INCLUDE: Dangerous Journey, The Hot Country, The Devil from Cape Town, Operation Yellow Viper, African Story, The Manipulator, Sfida Nella Citta del Oro, The Big Game, Snow From Hell.

KITT, EARTHA: Actress, singer. b. Columbia, S.C. Professional career started as dancer in Katherine Dunham group; toured U.S., Mexico & Europe with group, then opened night club in Paris; in Orson Welles stage prod. of Faust for European tour; N.Y. night clubs; stage in U.S., New Faces; at Macambo Hollywood, 1953; author, Thursday's Child; on screen, 1954, New Faces; 1958, The Mark of the Hawk, St. Louis Blues, Anna Lucasta.

KLEES, ROBERT E.: Executive. b. New York, N.Y., Feb. 21, 1927. e. Duke Univ. (1947–51); Univ. of Calif. Graduate School of Management (1973–75). U.S. Navy, 1944–46; Union Carbide Corp., 1951–57; director of communications, Beckman Instruments, Inc., 1957–69; co-founder and v.p., mktg., International Biophysics Corp., 1969–73; v.p., mktg., Deluxe General, Inc., 1975 to date. Member: Academy of m.p. Arts & Sciences. Academy of TV Arts & Sciences, American Film Institute, Hollywood Radio and TV Society, SMPTE. Associate Member: American Cinema Editors, American Society of Cinematographers.

KLEIN, ALLEN: Producer. b. Dec. 18, 1931. Pres. ABKCO industries, Inc.
PICTURES INCLUDE: Force of Impulse, Pity Me Not, Mrs. Brown, You've Got A Lovely Daughter, Stranger in Town, The Stranger Returns, Samuri on a Horse, The Silent Stranger, Pete, Pearl & The Pole, The Grand Bouffe, Come together, Let It Be, The Holy Mountain, El Topo, The Concert for Bangladesh, The Greek Tycoon.

KLEIN, EUGENE V.: Executive. b. New York, Jan. 29, 1921. e. New York University. U.S. Air Force 1941–46; Chmn. of bd. and chief executive officer. Nat'l Gen. Corp. various entertainment group subsidiaries, Nat'l Gen. Prods., Inc., Nat'l Gen. Pictures Corp., Nat'l Gen. TV Dist., Inc., Nat'l Gen. TV Prods., Inc., Edu. Film Prods., Inc., NGC Broadcasting Corp.

KLEIN, HAL: Producer. b. Chicago, Ill., Aug. 20, 1914. e. UCLA. Asst. Dir., 20th Fox; prod. mgr., Associate Producer features and TV, U.S., Europe, Africa. Presently, Aubrey Schenck Enterprises.
PICTURES INCLUDE: War Party, Forst Courageous, Convict Stage, Don't Worry, Ambush Bay, Kill a Dragon, Impasse, More Dead Than Alive, Barquero, Angel Unchained.

KLEIN, HAROLD J.: Executive. b. New York, N.Y., e. U. of West Virginia, N.Y. Law School; reviewer, sales staff. Showman's Trade Review; booker, Brandt Theatres; booker, later vice-pres., gen. mgr., J&J Theatres, 1941–59; account executive, Exec. vice-pres., dir. of world-wide sales, ABC Films, Inc., N.Y., Pres., Klein Film Assn.; Exec. Vice President, Plitt Theatres, Inc.

KLEIN, MALCOLM C.: Executive. b. L.A., Calif., Nov. 22, 1927. e. UCLA, grad., 1948, U. of Denver; Prod. dir. managment, KLAC-TV (KCOP), L.A., 1948–52; acct. exec., KABC-TV, 1952–56; asst. gen. sales mgr., KABC-TV, 1956–59; exec. vice-pres. gen. mgr., NTA Broadcasting, N.Y., 1959; v.p.; gen. mgr., RKO-General-KHJ-TV, 1960; joined National General Corp. 1968, vice-pres. Creative Services and Marketing. Pres. National General Television Productions, Inc.; Pres. NGC Broadcasting Corp.; 1971, pres. Filmways TV Presentations; 1972, pres. Malcolm C. Klein & Assoc. mgmt. & mktg. consultants; 1973 gen'l. exec. Sterling Recreation Organization & Gen'l Mgr. Broadcast Division; pres., American Song Festival. Now exec. v.p., Telease Inc. & American Subscription Television; and mgt. & mktng. consultant.

KLEIN, PAUL L.: Television Executive. e. Brooklyn Coll. Veteran of U.S. Army Air Corps. Research analyst with Biow Co., ad agency, 1953–54; research manager for Doyle Dane Bernbach ad agency, 1955–60. Started with NBC in 1961 as supervisor, ratings, and rose to position of v.p., audience measurement in October, 1965. In August, 1970, left NBC to found Computer Television Inc., first independent pay-per-view TV co. in world. Time, Inc. bought his interest in CTI. Returned to NBC in March, 1976, as v.p., network mktg. & planning; then named v.p., programs. Appointed exec. v.p., programs, NBC-TV, November, 1977.

KLEINER, HARRY: Writer, producer. b. Phila., Penna. e. Temple University (B.S.); Yale University (M.F.A.).
TV: Writer: The Virginian, Bus Stop, musical Robin Hood, Rosenberg Trial.
PICTURES INCLUDE: Screenplay: Carmen Jones, Street With No Name, Miss Sadie Thompson, Salome, Garment Jungle (also prod.), Fantastic Voyage, Bullitt (co-s.p.), Le Mans, Overlords.
TV: Robin Hoods, Rosenberg Trial.

KLINE, FRED W.: Publicist. b. Oakland, CA May 17, 1918. e. U. Calif. Berkeley; M.P. pub. rel. since 1934; pres. The Fred Kline Agency; pres. Kline Communications Corporation; Owner, Fred Kline Agency, Inc.; Kline Communications Corp.; Fred W. Kline Prod., Inc.; Capitol News Service, Sacramento; L.A. News Bureau; Capitol Radio News Service, Inc.; Commissioner, Motion Picture Council, State of California; Commissioner, Los Angeles Fire Services Commission.

KLINGER, HENRY: Eastern story editor, 20th Century-Fox Film Corp. b. New York, N.Y., Mar. 15, 1908. e. CCNY, BA; NYU, BBA. Assoc. ed., Chatterbox, nat'l mag., 1931–33; pres. Booklovers' Guild, 1930–33; freelance story dept. work, RKO, Cosmopolitan & Fox Films, 1931–33; story dept., pub. contract, Fox, 1934; asst. story ed., 20th-Fox, 1936; acting story ed., 1941; assoc. story ed., 1942; story ed., 1956; exec. story ed., 1964; exec. aide, 1971–73. Lecturer, Author.

KLINGER, MICHAEL: Producer. Managing Dir. Michael Klinger Ltd., Avton Film Productions.
PICTURES INCLUDE: Cul-de-Sac, Repulsion, Saturday Night Out, The Projected Man, Yellow Teddy Bears, Black Torment, Study in Terror, The Penthouse, Baby Love, Something to Hide, Get Carter, Pulp, Rachel's Man, Tomorrow Never Comes, Gold, Shout at the Devil. Exec. Prod. Confessions series, Blood Relatives.

KLUGMAN, JACK: Actor. b. Philadelphia, Pa., April 27. e. Carnegie Tech. m. Brett Somers. After several menial jobs appeared on Broadway in Saint John, Stevedore; later understudied in Mister Roberts, taking over the doctor role; recent stage work includes Gypsy.
PICTURES INCLUDE: Timetable, Twelve Angry Men, Cry Terror, The Scarface Mob, Days of Wine and Roses, I Could Go On Singing, The Yellow Canary, Act One, Hail Mafia, The Detective, The Split, Goodbye Columbus, Who Says I Can't Ride a Rainbow?, Two Minute Warning.
TV: The Defenders (Emmy Award for role in 'Blacklist' segment), The FBI, Ben Casey, 90 Bristol Court, etc.; The Odd Couple (Emmy, 1971 and 1973), Quincy.

KLYNN, HERBERT DAVID: Producer. b. Cleveland, O., Nov. 11, 1917; e. Ohio State U., 1937, Cleveland S. of Art Western Reserve U., 1939. Fine art painter, exhibitor, 1939; animation dir., U.S. Govt. m.p. unit, 1941–44; color dir., UPA, 1943–50; exec. prod. mgr., UPA, 1954–56; vice-pres., exec. prod., UPA, 1956–57; TV comm., industry films 1955–59; formed own co., Format Films, Oct. 1959; pres., Format Films, Inc., 1960–63; started Herb Klynn and Assoc., 1963; formed Format Productions Inc., 1964, pres., exec.

KNIGHT, ARTHUR: Critic, educator. b. Phila., Pa., Sept. 3, 1916. e. CCNY. BA 1940. Asst. curator Museum of Modern Art Film Library, 1939–49; film consultant CBS-color television, Omnibus, Odyssey, Seven Lively Arts, etc.; film courses at CCNY, New School for Social Research, Hunter College; contributor to Encyclopedia Britannica, Collier's Encyclopedia, etc.; author: "The Liveliest Art," The Hollywood Style; film critic, Westways; Director, Hollywood Reporter; formerly Saturday Review; prof. USC Cinema Division.

KNIGHT, DAVID: Actor. b. Niagara Falls, N.Y., Jan. 16, 1928. e. Whittier College, Calif.; 1944–52 teacher Putney School, Vermont; 1952–53 student Royal Academy of Dramatic Art.
LONDON STAGE: Trial of Mary Dugan, The Tenth Man, How to Succeed in Business Without Really Trying, Caine Mutiny Court Martial.
PICTURES INCLUDE: Young Lovers (Chance Meeting), Out of the Clouds, Lost, Eyewitness, Across the Bridge, V.I., The Story of David, Nightmare, Bedtime Story.
TV: Lincoln in Illinois, Berkeley Square, The Philadelphia Story, The Unquiet Spirit, A Question of Pride, Trial and Error.

KNIGHT, ESMOND: Actor, b. East Sheen, Surrey, Eng., May 4, 1906; m. Nora Swinburne, 1946. Stage debut 1925 in "Merchant of Venice," London; Birmingham Repertory; Paris, 1929 in "Maya"; N.Y. stage: The Emperor's Clothes.
LONDON STAGE: Age of Consent, Bell, Book and Candle, Caine Mutiny Court Martial, The Country Wife, The Russian, The Lady from the Sea, Becket, Two Star for Comfort, Last Old Vic Season, Getting Married, Martin Luther King, Spithead Mutiny, Mister, Three Sisters, Henry V, Agincourt—The Archer's Tale, Crime and Punishment, Family Reunion.
TV: Nicholas Nickleby, Our Mutual Friend, The Queen and the Welshman, The Silver Box, David and Broccoli, Barnaby Rudge, Knight Errant, Danger Man, The Age of Kings, A for Andromeda, Ghosts, Lysistrata, The Midnight Men, Murder in the Cathedral, To Bury Caesar, She's a Free Country, The Queen and the Rebel, Crime and Punishment, Jacobean Theatre, The Last Reunion, Gideon's Way, Dr. Finlay's Casebook, The Spies, Lord Ringo, The Rat Catchers, The Parachute, The Gamblers, More Best Sellers, The Troubleshooters, Z-Cars, The Casual Affair, Dr. Who, Faith, Queen Elizabeth I, Public Eye, Withered Arm, Shades of Green, Ballet Shoes, Quiller, I Claudius, Kilvert Diaries, Supernatural, Romeo & Juliet, Rebecca.
PICTURES INCLUDE: Dandy Dick, Waltzes from Vienna, Pagliacci, What Men Live By, Contraband, This England, Silver Fleet, Halfway House, Canterbury Tale, Henry V, Black Narcissus, Uncle Silas, Holiday Camp, Hamlet, Red Shoes, Wild Heart, The River, Helen of Troy, Richard III, Count of Monte Cristo, Prince and the Showgirl, Sailor of Fortune, O.S.S., Third Man on the Mountain, Sink the Bismarck, Peeping Tom, The Man Who Came In From The Cold, Anne of a Thousand Days, The Yellow Dog, Robin & Marian.

KNIGHT, SHIRLEY: Actress. b. Goessell, Kansas, 1937. e. University of Wichita, University of California. Joined the Pasadena Community Playhouse.
PICTURES INCLUDE: Five Gates to Hell (debut), Ice Palace, The Dark At the Top of the Stairs, (Acad. Award nom.) The Couch, Sweet Bird of Youth, House of Women, Flight from Ashiya, The Group, Dutchman, Petulia, The Counterfeit Killer, The Rain People, Juggernaut, Beyond the Poseidon Adventure, Endless Love.

KNIGHT, TED: Actor. b. Terryville, CT, Dec. 7, 1923. r.n., Tadeus Wladyslaw Konopka. e. Randall Sch. Dramatic Arts. U.S. Army, 1942–44. Started with various radio stations in New York City; emcee, newsman, host for late-night movies at TV stations. Hollywood film debut, 1957; Bdwy. stage debut, 1977. formed Kono Prods.
TELEVISION: Mary Tyler Moore Show, Ted Knight Show, Ted Knight Musical-Comedy Variety Special Special (CBS).

KNOECHEL, ROBERT F.: Executive. b. Cincinnati, Ohio. e. University of Cincinnati. ZIV Television—1953 budget, cost control-local auditor, 1958 controller of West Coast; Independent companies, 1962–64 location auditing; Ivan Tor Films—1965 controller, 1967 exec. and studio mgr. in Miami, Florida; Columbia Pictures—1969 assistant controller; ABC Pictures Corp.—1971 controller; Warner Bros.—1972 asst. studio controller; The Burbank Studios—1974 controller, 1979 treas. and member exec. comm. and EDP steering comm. Trustee SAG Pension & Welfare—Inception to 1964. Trustee & Chairman—Miami, Florida IA Pension Plan 1967–68.

KNOPF, EDWIN H.: Producer, writer. b. New York City, Nov. 11, 1899; e. MacKenzie School and Amherst. On the legitimate stage for eight years in New York and Germany. Entered picture business in 1928 with Paramount. Wrote Mr. Imperium, Free Love, etc.; collaborated on lyrics, Reckless; s.p. Picadilly Jim. Head of Scenario Department, MGM, 1936–39; prod. Samuel Goldwyn Pictures.
PICTURES INCLUDE: The Cross of Lorraine, Cry Havoc, Valley of Decision, Sailor Takes a Wife, Secret Heart, Cynthia, B.F.'s Daughter. Edward My Son, Malaya, Fearless Fagan, Scandal at Scourie, Lili, Great Diamond Robbery, Glass Slipper, King's Thief, Diane, Gaby, The Vintage, Tip on a Dead Jockey, Fast Company, Border Legion, Slightly Scarlet, Only Saps Work, Santa Fe Trail, Light of the Western Stars, Nice Women, Law and the Lady.

KNOTTS, DON: Actor. b. Morgantown, W.VA, July 21, 1924. e. West Virginia Univ., Univ. of Arizona. Drafted into US Army where became part of show called Stars and Grapes, teamed with comedian Mickey Shaughnessy. After schooling resumed, was offered teaching fellowship but went to New York to try acting instead. Appeared on radio and TV, leading to role in No Time for Sergeants on Bdwy.; appeared in film version.
PICTURES: It's a Mad, Mad, Mad, Mad World, The Incredible Mr. Limpet, The Shakiest Gun in the West, The Apple Dumpling Gang, Herbie Goes to Monte Carlo, The Apple Dumpling Gang Rides Again.
TELEVISION: Garry Moore Show, Steve Allen Show, Andy Griffith Show (played Barney Fife), The Don Knotts Show, Three's Company.

KNOWLES, PATRIC: Actor. r.n. Reginald Lawrence Knowles; b. Horsforth, Yorkshire, England, Nov. 11, 1911. Joined Abby Repertory Theatre, 1930; m.p. debut (Ireland) in Irish Hearts, 1934; on London stage in By Appointment; U.S. m.p. debut in Charge of the Light Brigade, 1936; served in Canadian RAF & as civilian instructor USAF, World War II.
PICTURES INCLUDE: Honours Easy, Mister Hobo, Two's Company, Give Me Your Heart, It's Love I'm After, Expensive Husbands, Adventures of Robin Hood, How Green Was My Valley, Forever and a Day, Of Human Bondage, Bride Wore Boots, Ivy, Kitty, Monsieur Beaucaire, Dream Girl, Big Steal, Quebec, Three Came Home, Mutiny, Tarzan's Savage Fury, Jamaica Run, Flame of Calcutta, World Ransom, Khyber Patrol, No Man's Woman, Band of Angels, Auntie Mame, The Way West, In Enemy Country, The Devil's Brigade, Chisum, The Man, Terror in the Wax Museum, Arnold.

KNOX, ALEXANDER: Actor. b. Strathroy, Ont., Jan. 16, 1907. e. Western Ontario U. Author, novels: Bride of Quietness, Night of the White Bear, The Enemy I Kill, Raider's Moon, The Kidnapped Surgeon; plays, Old Master, The Closing Door, Red On White. Many TV appearances.
STAGE: (NY) Romeo and Juliet, The Three Sisters, Jupiter Laughs, Jason, The Closing Door; (London) The Jealous God, Winter Journey, Henry VIII, Geneva, King of Nowhere, Return to Tyassi, Burnt Flower Bed, When Dead Awaken.
PICTURES INCLUDE: The Sea Wolf, This Above All, Commandos Strike at Dawn, None Shall Escape, Over 21, Wilson, Sign of the Ram, Judge Steps Out, Sister Kenny, I'd Climb the Highest Mountain, Saturday's Hero, Sleeping Tiger, Divided Heart, Crack in the Mirror, The Viking, The Night My Number Came Up, Reach for the Sky, High Tide at Noon, Davy, Operation Amsterdam, The Longest Day, Wreck of the Mary Deare, Man in the Middle, Woman of Straw, Mr. Moses, Accident, Villa Rides, Shalako, Skullduggery, Puppet on a Chain, Khartoum, Nicholas and Alexandra, Potsdam.

KNOX, GORDON: Executive. b. Greenville, Texas, May 10, 1909. e. Univ. of Missouri; married. In addition to making commercials for several years has been employed by Warner Bros., Caravel Films and Walter Wanger Prods. Joined Princeton Film Center in 1940; Pres. SKS Prod. Inc., Santa Fe, N.M. Pres., PAC Productions, Inc., Princeton, N.J.

KOBAYASHI, MASAKI: Director. b. Japan, Feb. 4, 1916. e. Waseda Univ. Joined Shochiku 1941 as asst. Director. Army. Rejoined Shochiku 1946.
PICTURES INCLUDE: No Greater Love, Road to Eternity, A Soldier's Prayer, Black River, Room with Thick Walls, Somewhere Beneath Wide Sky, Fountainhead, I'll Buy You, The Human Condition, The Inheritance.

KOCH, HOWARD: Writer. b. New York City, Dec. 12, 1902. e. St. Stephen's Coll., '22. B.A.; Columbia Law School, '25. LL.B. Hon. degree Doctor of Human Letters, Bard Coll., 1972. Playwright (Give Us This Day, In Time To Come, Straitjacket). Began screen career collab. s.p. The Sea Hawk. Radio: Invasion from Mars radio play for (Orson Welles broadcast); book: The Panic Broadcast (Little, Brown & Co.); Academy Award best s.p. (Casablanca). As Time Goes By, Memoirs of a Writer in Hollywood, New York and Europe under contract to Harcourt, Brace and Jovanovich for publication in the summer of 1979.
PICTURES INCLUDE: The Letter, Shining Victory, In This Our Life, Casablanca, Mission to Moscow, Letter From an Unknown Woman, The Thirteenth Letter, The War Lover, The Fox, Loss of Innocence, No Sad Songs for Me, Sergeant York, Three Strangers.

KOCH, HOWARD W.: Prod., dir. b. New York, N.Y., Apr. 11, 1916. Runner on Wall St., asst. cutter, 20th-Fox; asst. dir., 20th-Fox, Eagle Lion, MGM; 2nd unit dir.; freelance; prod. Aubrey Schenck Prod.; 1961–64, exec. prod. Frank Sinatra Enterprises; v.p., chg. prod., Paramount Pictures Corp., 1965. Elected pres. of the Academy of Motion Picture Arts and Sciences, June 2, 1977. On June 11, 1977, elected to the National Board of Directors Guild of America for two year term.
TV: Director, Miami Undercover, The Untouchables, Maverick, Cheyenne, Hawaiian Eye.
PICTURES INCLUDE: War Paint, Beachhead, Yellow Tomahawk, Shield for Murder, Big House USA, Crime Against Joe, Emergency Hospital, Ghost Town, Broken Star, Rebel in Town, Pharaoh's Curse, Three Bad Sisters, Fort Yuma, Desert Sands, Quincannon Frontier Scout, Black Sleep, Hot Cars, "X-1," Sergeants 3, The Manchurian Candidate, Come Blow Your Horn, Four For Texas, Robin and the Seven Hoods, None But the Brave, The Odd Couple, On A Clear Day You Can See Forever, Plaza Suite, Star Spangled Girl, (Prod.), Last of the Red Hot Lovers (Prod.), Badge 373 (Prod.-Dir.) 1973, (Prod.) Once Is Not Enough; MATI (prod.), 1977; Airplane! (prod.), 1980; Dragonslayer (exec. prod.), 1981; Some Kind of Hero (prod.), 1982.

KOHLER, FRED, JR.: Actor.
PICTURES INCLUDE: The Prisoner of Shark Island, Sins of Man, Pigskin Parade, Hold That Coed, Young Mr. Lincoln, Big Bonanza, Why Girls Leave Home, Feudin', Fussin' and A-Fightin', Spoilers of the Plains, Baron of Arizona, Hollywood Thrill-Makers, Racing Blood.

KOHN, HOWARD E., II: Executive. b. McKeesport, Pa. National dir. of adv., publicity, roadshow dept., United Artists; indep. prod., Hidden Fear, 1957; pres. Lioni-Warren-Kohn, Inc., 1958; national roadshow dir., Columbia Pictures, Porgy & Bess, 1959; World wide co-ordinator, national co-ordinator adv. & pub. for El Cid, June 1961; named world wide co-ordinator adv., pub. all Samuel Bronston Productions, April 1962; pres. Starpower Inc., 1968; exec. v.p., Avanti Films, 1970; v.p. Avariac Prods., 1971; pres., Blossom Films, 1973. Elected member of ASCAP, 1975. Pres., Avanti Associates, 1976.

KOHNER, FREDERICK: Writer. b. Teplitz-Schoenau, Czechoslovakia, Sept. 25, 1905; p. Julius and Helen Kohner; e. Ph.D., Sorbonne Univ., Paris, Univ. of Vienna, Austria; married. Was newspaper feature writer on Berliner Tageblatt and Prager-Czechoslovaki Tagblatt. wrote book, "Film is Art," history of film development.
NOVELS: Seven Rooms in Hollywood, Kiki of Montparnasse, The Skier, Gidget, Cher Papa, Gidget Goes Hawaiian, The Contintal Kick, Mister, Will You Marry Me, Affairs of Gidget, Gidget Goes to Rome, Gidget in Love, The Gremmie, Gidget Goes Parisienne, 1967, Gidget Goes New York. Biography: The Magician of Sunset Boulevard (story of Paul Kohner), Amanda, a love story.
TV: Revue, Four Star, Fireside, Schlitz Playhouse.
STAGE: (collab.) Bees and the Flowers, Stalin, Allee.
PICTURES INCLUDE: Burning Secret, La Crise Est Finie, Sins of Men, Mad About Music, It's a Date, Men in Her Life, Tahiti Honey, Patrick the Great, Lake Placid Serenade, Pan Americana, Three Daring Daughters, Bride for Sale, Nancy Goes to Rio, Hollywood Story, Never Wave at a Wac, Toy Tiger.

KOHNER, SUSAN: Actress. b. L.A., Calif., Nov. 11, 1936. e. Univ. of Calif., 1954–55.
TV: Alcoa Hour, Schlitz Playhouse, Four Star Theatre,

Matinee Theatre, Climax, Suspicion, Playhouse 90, Route 66, Dick Powell Theatre.
STAGE: Love Me Little, He Who Gets Slapped, A Quiet Place, Rose Tatoo, Bus Stop, St. Joan, Sunday in New York, Take Her She's Mine, Pullman Car, Hiawatha.
PICTURES INCLUDE: To Hell and Back, The Last Wagon, Dino, Imitation of Life, The Big Fisherman, The Gene Krupa Story, All the Fine Young Cannibals, By Love Possessed, Freud.

KONTOS, SPERO L.: Thea. Equip. Dealer. b. Chicago, Ill., Dec. 17, 1922. e. Illinois Inst. of Technology, B.S. BM., eng.; ECLA Ent. Ind. as Chicago exhib., 1937; thea. mgmt. until 1942. U.S. Army, 1942–46; sis. eng., Abbott Theatre Equip. Co., 1946–48; sis. mgr., 1948–51; gen. mgr. 1951–54; sis. mgr. John P. Filbert Co. Inc., 1954–59; hd. Century 70/35 mm. projector program, 1959–60; Filbert Co., v.p. chg. sis. & eng., 1960–64; pres., 1964; pres. Theatre Equipment Dealers Assoc., 1965–67; bd. chm., TEDA, 1967–69; chief barker, L.A. Variety, 1971–72; pres., Megaron Corp., 1973, Academy of Motion Picture Arts & Sciences, 1975.

KOPELMAN, JEAN R.: Producer. b. New York, N.Y., Apr. 5, 1927; e. Middlebury (Vt.) Coll. clerical work, CBS radio & TV, 1946–47; first girl prog. asst. in prod. dept., CBS-TV, 1948; prod. mgr., Goodson-Todman Prod.
TV: Winner Take All, It's News to Me, What's My Line, Name's the Same, I've Got a Secret, Two for the Money, Beat the Clock, Choose Up Sides, Number Please, The Match Game, (NBC-TV).

KORBAN, BERNARD: Executive. b. New York City, Nov. 28, 1923; e. RCA Inst. of Tech., NYU. U.S. Army 1942–46; 1951–58, Public Relations and Promotions for Davega Stores; 1959–62, exploitation fieldman for Universal Pictures; 1962–66, supvr. of fieldmen and exploitation activities; 1966–68, exec. in chrg. field activities; exec. assist. to v.p., adv. pub. and promotion; 1972 dir. of exploitation, National General Pictures; 1973, dir. of Marketing, promotion and worldwide distribution for Brut Prods; 1974, dir. of mkt., Avco Embassy Pictures, 1975, vice pres. of advertising/publicity/promotion, Cine Artists Pictures Corp.; advertising/publicity, United Artists Corp. West Coast ad. mgr.; now UA v.p., West Coast adv.

KORMAN, HARVEY: Actor-Director. b. Chicago, Feb. 15, 1927. e. Wright Junior College. Began dramatic studies at Chicago's Goodman School of Drama at the Arts Institute. Acted in small roles in Broadway plays and did TV commercials until break came as comedian for Danny Kaye Show on TV. Staged comedy sketches for Steve Allen variety series in 1967. Became Carol Burnett's leading man on her show in 1967 and continued as regular to present. Has directed two episodes of The New Dick Van Dyke Show.
PICTURES INCLUDE: Actor: Three Bites of an Apple, Lord Love a Duck, Last of the Secret Agents, The April Fools, Blazing Saddles, Huckleberry Finn, High Anxiety, Americathon, First Family, History of the World—Part I.
TV: The Danny Kaye Show, Carol Burnett Show.

KORTY, JOHN: Director, Producer, Writer, Cameraman, Animator. b. 1936; B.A. Antioch College 1959; President, Korty Films, Inc., Mill Valley, CA.
THEATRICAL FEATURES: Alex & the Gypsy (Fox 1976); Oliver's Story (Paramount 1978). TELEVISION FEATURES: The Autobiography of Miss Jane Pittman (CBS 1974), Emmy, DGA Award; Farewell to Manzanar (NBC 1976), Humanitas, Christopher Awards; Forever (CBS 1977); A Christmas Without Snow (CBS 1980). INDEPENDENT FEATURES: Crazy Quilt (1964); Funnyman (1967); Riverrun (1969.) DOCUMENTARIES: Who Are the DeBolts? (ABC 1978), Oscar, Emmy, DGA Award; Cant It Be Anyone Else? (ABC 1980); Stepping Out: the DeBolts Grow Up, (HBO 1980). SHORT FILMS: The Language of Faces (AFSC 1961); Imogen Cunningham, Photographer (AFI grant 1970); The Music School (PBS 1975). ANIMATION: Breaking the Habit (1964), Oscar Nominee; Various children's films; Segments for Sesame Street and The Electric Company.

KORVIN, CHARLES: Actor. r.n. Geza Korvin Karpathi: b. Czechoslovakia, Nov. 21; e. U. of Paris, Sorbonne, 1933–36. Cameraman, dir., documentary films in Europe; to U.S.A. in 1937; Barter Theatre, 1940–42; on B'way, Dark Eyes, 1943; m.p. debut in Enter Arsene Lupin, 1945.
PICTURES INCLUDE: This Love of Ours, Temptation, Berlin Express, Killer That Stalked N.Y., Lydia Bailey, Tarzan's Savage Fury, Sangaree, Ship of Fools, The Man Who Had Power Over Women.

KOSCINA, SYLVA: Actress. b. Yugoslavia, Aug. 22, 1933. Grew up in Italy; as model placed under contract for films by Carlo Ponti.
PICTURES INCLUDE: The Railroad Man (debut), Juliet of the Spirits, Deadlier Than the Male, The Hornet's Nest, Casanova & Co., Sunday Lovers.

KOSINER, HARRY: Executive. b. New York City, Jan. 29. e. City Coll. N.Y. Stenographer, Fox Films, 1923; asst. to pres., Deluxe Lab., N.Y. 1930–36; eastern rep. Walter

Wanger Prod., 1937–40; assistant to western div. mgr. United Artists, 1941–42; on staff m.p. bur., OWI, 1943; apptd. same yr. east. rep. Edward Small Prods., hdqts. N.Y.; home office staff, Columbia Pictures, 1951; v.p. National Screen Service, 1965.

KOSLECK, MARTIN: Actor. b. Barkotse. Pommern Mar. 24, 1907. Six years with Max Reinhardt's dramatic school and theatre in Berlin.
PICTURES INCLUDE: Espionage Agent, Calling Philo Vance, Nurse Edith Cavell, Bomber's Moon, North Star, Secrets of Scotland Yard, Hitler Gang, Gangs of the Waterfront, The Spider, The Wife of Monte Cristo, Pursuit to Algiers, The Frozen Ghost, The Mummy's Curse, Crime of the Century, Assigned to Danger, Smuggler's Cove, Something Wild, 36 Hours, Morituri, The Flesh Eaters.

KOSTER, HENRY: Director. b. Berlin, May 1, 1905. Comm. artist, cartoonist, newspaperman, critic; scenarist, Ufa, Terra, Aafa, Berlin; dir. Berlin, Vienna, Budapest, to Hollywood, 1936.
PICTURES INCLUDE: 100 Men and a Girl, Rage of Paris, It Started With Eve, Spring Parade, Music for Millions, Two Sisters from Boston, The Bishop's Wife, Come to the Stable, Inspector General, My Blue Heaven, Harvey, No Highway in the Sky, Mr. Belvedere Rings the Bell, Elopement, seq. O. Henry's Full House, Stars & Stripes Forever, My Cousin Rachel, The Robe, Desiree, A Man Called Peter, Good Morning Miss Dove, Power and the Prize, My Man Godfrey, Flower Drum Song, Mr. Hobbs Takes a Vacation, Take Her, She's Mine, Dear Brigitte, The Singing Nun.

KOTCHEFF, WILLIAM THEODORE: Director. b. Toronto, Canada, 1931. Ent. TV ind. 1952. After five years with Canadian Broadcasting Crop. joined ABC-TV in London, 1957.
PLAYS INCLUDE: Of Mice and Men, Desperate Hours, The Human Voice, Edna the Inebriate Woman, Signalman's Apprentice, Lights Out, Rx for the Defence.
STAGE: Progress The Park, Play With A Tiger, Luv, Maggie May, The Au Pair Man, Have You Any Dirty Washing, Mother Dear?
PICTURES INCLUDE: Life At The Top, Two Gentlemen Sharing, Outback, Billy Two Hats, The Apprenticeship of Duddy Kravitz, Fun with Dick and Jane, Who Is Killing The Great Chefs of Europe?, North Dallas Forty (also co-s.p.), Captured.

KOTTO, YAPHET: Actor. Has many stage credits, including starring roles on Broadway in The Great White Hope and The Zulu and the Zayda. Off-Bdwy.: Blood Knot, Black Monday, In White America, A Good Place To Raise a Boy.
PICTURES INCLUDE: The Limit (star, prod.), Nothing But a Man, The Liberation of L.B. Jones, Live and Let Die, Across 110th Street, Truck Turner, Bone, Report to the Commissioner, Sharks' Treasure, Hey Good Lookin', Friday Foster, Drum, Blue Collar, Brubaker.

KOVAKS, LASZLO: Cinematographer.
PICTURES INCLUDE: Hell's Angels On Wheels, The Savage Seven, Targets, Easy Rider, That Cold Day In the Park, Getting Straight, Alex In Wonderland, The Last Movie, Marriage of a Young Stockbroker, The King of Marvin Gardens, Pocket Money, What's Up, Doc?, Paper Moon, Huckleberry Finn, For Pete's Sake, Freebie and the Bean, Shampoo, Baby Blue Marie, Harry and Walter Go to New York, New York, New York, F.I.S.T., The Last Waltz, Paradise Alley, Butch and Sundance: The Early Days, The Runner Stumbles, Heart Beat.

KRAMER, JEROME: Executive-Producer-Director. b. Los Angeles, 1945. Graduated USC Law School 1971. Joined Braverman Productions, Inc. 1971; named exec. v.p. Co-producer with Charles Braverman of network specials (21 Years of A.I.P., Horror Hall of Fame), show titles (Rhoda, Cher) corporate and promotional films for Xerox, Petersen Publishing, etc. Producer and director of various television commercials (for Chevrolet, United Artists Records, Gulf Oil), educational films for United States Information Agency, special films and montages.

KRAMER, LARRY: Writer, producer. b. Bridgeport, Conn. U.S.A., 1935. e. Yale Univ. B.A. 1957. Ent. m.p. ind. 1958. Story edit. Columbia Pictures, N.Y. London 1960–65. Asst. to David Picker and Herb Jaffe, UA, 1965. Assoc. prod. and additional dialogue Here We Go Round The Mulberry Bush, 1968. Writ. prod. Women in Love, 1969. Writer: Lost Horizon, 1971; A Sea Change, 1972.

KRAMER, SIDNEY: Sales executive. b. New York City. e. LL.B., New York Law School and C.C.N.Y., married. Gen. sales mgr., RKO Pathe, June 1953; dir. and v.p. Cellofilm Corp. 1941–56; foreign sales mgr., RKO Radio, 1954–59; v.p. Cinemiracle Intl. 1960–61; v.p. T.P.E.A., 1960–61; foreign sls. mgr., Cinerama, Inc., 1962–65; Exec. Commonwealth Theatres, Puerto Rico, Inc., 1965–68; Exec. v.p. Cobian Jr. Enterprises Inc. 1968. M.P. consultant-exhibition, dist., foreign and Caribbean area, Oct., 1968 to 1970. Pres. Cequi Internat'l. Inc.; 1970–1980; vice. pres. of UAPR, Inc., Puerto Rico, U.A. Eastern Theatres, Inc.

KRAMER, STANLEY E.: Executive producer, director. b. New York City, Sept. 29, 1913; e. N.Y.U., B.Sc. 1933. Entered m.p. ind. via back lot jobs; with MGM research dept.; film cutter 3 yrs.; film ed.; m.p. & radio writer; served in U.S. Signal Corps, 1st Lt.
PICTURES INCLUDE: Champion, Home of the Brave, The Men, Cyrano de Bergerac, Death of a Salesman, High Noon, My Six Convicts, The Sniper, The Four Poster, The Happy Time, Eight Iron Men, 5,000 Fingers of Dr. T, Wild One, The Juggler, Caine Mutiny, Not As a Stranger, Pride and the Passion; prod. dir., s.p., The Defiant Ones, On the Beach, Inherit the Wind, Judgment at Nuremberg; prod., dir., It's a Mad, Mad, Mad, Mad World, Invitation To A Gunfighter, prod., Ship of Fools, Prod. Dir. Guess Who's Coming to Dinner, The Secret of Santa Vittoria, R.P.N.*, Bless the Beasts and Children, Oklahoma Crude, The Domino Principle, The Runner Stumbles.

KRAMS, ARTHUR: Set decorator. b. New York, N.Y., July 15, 1912. e. Parsons School of Design, New York and Paris, 1928–31. Interior designer, decorator, Chicago, 1931–34; New York, 1934–39; Los Angeles, 1939–45; set decorator, MGM, 1945–54; set decorator, Paramount, 1954.
PICTURES INCLUDE: Luxury Liner, Merry Widow, Lili, Story of Three Loves, Student Prince, To Catch A Thief, Rose Tattoo, Court Jester, Arists and Models, Man Who Knew Too Much, The Rainmaker, Wild Is the Wind, The Mating Game, Bye, Bye Birdie, The Carpetbaggers, Where Love Has Gone, Sylvia, Marriage On The Rocks, The Swinger, Good Times, Caper of The Golden Bulls, Barefoot in The Park, The President's Analyst, Hang 'Em High, How Sweet It Is.

KRANTZ, STEVE: Exec. b. New York, N.Y., May 20, 1923. e. Columbia U., B.A. Dir. progs., NBC, New York, 1953; dir. prog. dev., Screen Gems, N.Y., 1955; v.p.; gen. mgr. Screen Gems, Canada, 1958; dir. int sls., 1960; formed Krantz Films, Inc. 1964.
TV: Steve Allen Show, Kate Smith Show, Hazel, Dennis the Menace, Winston Churchill—The Valiant Years, Telefilms, Marvel Super Heroes, Rocket Robin Hood, Animated Films.
PICTURES INCLUDE: Fritz the Cat, Heavy Traffic (prod.).

KRASNA, NORMAN: Producer, writer. b. Corona, L.I. (N.Y.C.), Nov. 7, 1909; e. New York U., Columbia U., Brooklyn (N.Y.) Law School Asst. drama ed., N.Y. Morning World; drama ed., N.T. Graphic; on N.Y. staff Exhibitors Herald-World; asst. publicity dir., Warner Bros. Studios; from 1932 variously author & collab. orig. & s.p. many pictures.
STAGE PLAYS: Louder, Please, Small Miracle, Dear Ruth, John Loves Mary, Kind Sir, Who Was That Lady I Saw You With, Sunday in New York.
PICTURES INCLUDE: Fury, Richest Girl in the World, Hands Across the Table, Bachelor Mother, The Devil and Miss Jones, It Started With Eve, Academy Award, best orig. s.p. 1943 (Princess O'Rourke, Warner), Practically Yours, The Big Hangover, White Christmas, The Ambassador's Daughter, Indiscreet, Who Was That Lady?, My Geisha, Sunday in New York, I'd Rather Be Rich.
Screen Writers Guild Laurel Award, 1959, Joined U.S. Air Force; formed Wald-Krasna Prod., distrib. through RKO 1950; sold interest to Wald, May, 1952. Formed Monovale Prod. 1956.

KRAUSS, OSCAR: Executive. b. Brooklyn, N.Y. e. City College of N.Y., Architecture; Pratt Institute, Advertising Design, Artist, Paramount Pictures, 1936; 20th Century-Fox, 1936–40; Buchanan & Co., 1940; art dir., Lord & Thomas, 1941; U.S. Coast Guard, 1942–46; art dir., Republic Pictures, 1946–48; Monroe-Greenthal, Co., 1948–58; Oscar Krauss Advertising, Inc., pres., owner.

KREIMAN, ROBERT T.: Executive. b. Kenosha, Wis., Sept. 16, 1924. Served W. W. II Capt Army Corps of Engineers-ETO. e. Stanford, 1941; Univ. of Wis., 1942 — 1946–49. Dir., sales training, mgr., audio visual sales, Bell & Howell Co., 1949–58; V.P., Argus Cameras, Inc., 1958–61; V.P., gen. mgr., Commercial & Educ. Div., Technicolor 1961–69, v.p. gen. mgr., The Suburban Companies; 1969–71: pres. and chief exec. officer, Deluxe General, Inc. Pres. and Director of Movietonews, Inc. Bd. chm. Keith Cole Photograph, Inc. 1972–1978. bd. chm., pres. and chief exec. officer, Pace International Corp., 1969 to present. past pres. of UCLA Executive Program Ass'n. Fellow SMPTE, Member M.P. Academy; TV Academy; assoc. mem., American Society of Cinematographers.

KRESS, HAROLD F.: Director, film editor. b. Pittsburgh, Pa., June 26, 1913. e. U. of Calif., L.A. Film ed., Command Decision, Madame Curie, Mrs. Miniver, The Yearling; crime shorts; 5-reel Army documentary short, Ward Care for Psychotic Patients. Member: Acad. of M.P. Arts and Sciences, Screen Directors Guild, Film Editors Guild.
PICTURES INCLUDE: Painted Hills, No Questions Asked, Apache War Smoke, Ride Vaquero, Saadia, Rose Marie, Valley of the Kings, The Cobweb, The Prodigal, I'll Cry Tomorrow, Teahouse of the August Moon, Silk Stockings, Until They Sail, Merry Andrew, Imitation General, The World, The Flesh and The Devil, Count Your Blessings, Home from the Hills, The Greatest Story Ever Told, Walk Don't Run, Alvarez Kelly, Academy Award for Film Editing on How the West Was Won.
FILM EDITOR: Poseidon Adventure, The Iceman Cometh, 99-44/100ths % Dead, The Towering Inferno.

KREUGER, KURT: Actor. b. St. Moritz Switzerland, July 23, 1917; e. U. Lausanne, U. London. Came to U.S. 1937, partner in travel bureau: acted in Wharf Theat. group. Cape Cod, 1939; Broadway debut in Candle in the Wind with Helen Hayes, 1941.
PICTURES INCLUDE: Mademoiselle Fifi, Hotel Berlin, Paris Underground, Dark Corner, Unfaithfully Yours, Fear, The St. Valentine's Day Massacre, What Did You Do in the War Daddy?

KRIER, JOHN N.: Executive. b. Rock Island, Ill. e. Augustana Coll. Joined A. H. Blank Theatres, 1924: Grad. Publix Theatres Manager Training School, 1930: managed theatres in Illinois, Iowa, Nebraska; joined Intermountain Theatres, Salt Lake City, 1937: appointed Purchasing Head, 1946: buyer-booker, 1952: v.p., gen. mgr., 1955: appt. v.p. gen. mgr. ABC Theas., Arizona, 1968: appt. v.p. director Film Buying ABC Theatres of California & ABC Intermountain Theatres, Feb. 1972. Became consultant ABC Southern Theatres, 1974. Joined Exhibitors Relations Inc. as partner, 1978.

KRIM, ARTHUR B.: Attorney. b. New York City, 1910. e. Columbia U., B.A., '32, 1932 became member law firm Philips, Nizer, Benjamin & Krim, N.Y. elected pres. United Artists Feb. 20, 1951; chairman of bd., 1969 to January 1978; Ch. of Board, Orion Pictures Company, March, 1978.

KRISTOFFERSON, KRIS: Actor-singer. b. Brownsville, Texas, 1937. e. Pomona College, Oxford Univ. (Rhodes Scholar). Joined U.S. Army briefly and taught English Literature at West Point. Started writing songs (country music) and hits have included Me and Bobby McGee, Why Me, Lord, Sunday Mornin' Comin' Down, etc. Film debut in Cisco Pike, 1971. Continues to make records, do concert tours and appear in films.
PICTURES: Cisco Pike, Pat Garrett and Billy the Kid, Blume in Love, Bring Me the Head of Alfredo Garcia, Alice Doesn't Live Here Anymore, Vigilante Force, The Sailor Who Fell from Grace with the Sea, A Star Is Born, Semi-Tough, Convoy, Heaven's Gate, Roll-Over.

KRITZMAN, SERGE: production designer, architect. b. Yugoslavia, July 8, 1914. e. Royal U. of Zagreb, Royal Academy of Arts. Wrote, dir. and acted in featurette Dr. Faust, 1933; designed interior Royal Yugoslav Pavilion, N.Y. World's Fair, 1939. Public Relations officer, Yugoslav Embassy, 1940–42; tech. div. 20th Century Fox Studios, 1943; organized Century Theatres; art div., mgr. facilities KFJ-TV, 1953; member bd. of gov. Acad. TV Arts and Sciences, 1964–67; chairman P.R. committee Society of Motion Picture Art Directors; pres. Hollywood chapter TV Acad., 1967–68.
PICTURES INCLUDE: The Glass Wall, Ride the High Iron, Life of Christ, Crime in the Streets, Flight to Hong Kong, The Fuzzy Pink Nightgown, Time Limit, Porgy and Bess, The Cabinet of Dr. Caligari, Promise Her Anything, Miss Lonelyhearts, Gunfight at Dodge City, The Big Bounce.
TV: Schlitz Playhouse of Stars series, James Mason series, The Fugitive, Batman, Dick Tracy, City Beneath the Sea, Frank Sinatra, Roman and the Renegade.

KRONICK, WILLIAM: Writer-director. b. Amsterdam, N.Y. e. Columbia College, A.B.; U.S. Navy photography; wrote, dir. featurette, A Bowl of Cherries, 1961.
TV DOCS: Wrote, dir., prod. Mysteries of the Great Pyramid; George Plimpton Specials; National Geographic, et. al.
FEATURE FILMS: Horowitz in Dublin (dir., s.p.); King Kong (2nd unit dir.); The 500 Pound Jerk (dir., TV movie).

KRONSBERG, JEREMY: Writer/Actor/Associate Producer. b. Sept. 15, Denver. Former contract player with 20th Century Fox; former dialogue director for The Perry Mason Show.
SCREENPLAY: Every Which Way But Loose, Rule Golden.

KRUEGER, CARL: Producer, writer. b. Chicago, Ill., Oct. 8, 1908. U.S. Air Force, 1925–31; press agent for Olsen and Johnson, Max Reinhardt, others; exploit. dir., United Artists Corp.; in charge of spec. events. Paramount; writer. 20th Century-Fox, then freelance; served in U.S. Air Force, World War II.
PICTURES INCLUDE: Thunderbirds prod. Thunderbolt, Golden Gloves Story, Comanche, Sabre Jet.

KRUGER, HARDY: Actor. b. Berlin, Germany, April 12, 1928; ent. m.p. ind. 1943; on stage since 1945.
PICTURES INCLUDE: The One That Got Away, Bachelor of Hearts (Rank). German version of The Moon is Blue (U.A.). 1959: The Rest is Silence (German film of Hamlet), Blind Date (Britain). He has also starred in twenty-four

German films. 1960: Filming in France and Germany. 1961–62: Films include: Taxi Pour Tobrouk (France), Hatari (Paramount, Hollywood). 1962: Les Dimanches de Ville d'Avray (France), etc. 1963: Le Gros Coup (France). 1964: Les Pianos Mecaniques (France), Le Chant Du Monde (France). 1965: Flight of the Phoenix (Hollywood) 1966: The Defector (U.S.A.), La Grande Sauterelle (France). 1967: Le Franciscain de Bourge (France). 1968–9: The Battle of the Neretva, The Red Tent, The Nun of Monza, The Secret of Santa Vittoria (Israel). 1973–74: Le Solitaire (France), Barry Lyndon (England). 1974–75: Paper Tiger (England/Germany), Potato Fritz (Germany). 1976: A Bridge Too Far (England/U.S.A.), L'Autopsie d'un Monstre (France). 1977: The Wild Geese (England).

KRUGER, JEFFREY S.: Concert impresario., Prod. Film Dist., Music Publ. and gramophone records exec. b. London, Eng., Apr. 19, 1931. Produced feature films Rock You Sinners; Sweet Beat; The Amorous Sex. Distributor of over 34 feature films including I Want To Be A Woman, Dial Rat For Terror, Equinox, The Shooting, Smashing The Crime Syndicate, A Whale of A Tale, The Good Time Outlaws. Exec. Prod. and worldwide dist. musical specials (Prod. in assoc. BBC). TV productions include one-hour musical specials of Anne Murray, Glen Campbell, Jacksons, Marvin Gaye, David Soul, Jerry Lee Lewis and series The Other Broadway. Concert presentations incl. ownership Flamingo Club and The Temple Club and via the Kruger Organisation, Sarah Vaughan, Billy Eckstine, Chet Baker, Garland Wilson, Thelma Carpenter, Billie Holiday, Glen Campbell, Diana Trask, Charlie Rich, Susan Maughan, Desmond Dekker, Roy Clark, Anne Murray, Jack Benny, Charley Pride, P.J. Proby, Connie Smith, Faron Young, Gladys Knight and the Pips, Helen Reddy, Wayne Newton, Dionne Warwick, Frank Gorshin, Trini Lopez, Buddy Greco, Stylistics, Supremes, George Burns, Marty Allen, Tony Bennett, Lena Horne, Barry White, Love Unlimited, Marvin Gaye, Chi-Lites, Bill Anderson, Sonny Terry, Brownie McGhee, Ray Stevens, Loretta Lynn, Jack Jones, Elaine Starr, David Soul, Jacksons, War, Blood, Sweat and Tears, Frankie Valli and the Four Seasons. Music publ. through Songs For Today. Own record production and distribution via Bulldog Records and Visual and Audio Leisure Co. Ltd. Director The Kruger Organisation (Concerts) Ltd. Songs For Today Ltd. Ember Enterprises Inc. Visual and Audio Leisure Co. Ltd. Hillbrow Productions Ltd.

KUBRICK, STANLEY: Producer, director, writer. b. New York, N.Y., July 26, 1928; e. Taft H.S. Staff photog., Look magazine; writer, prod., dir., documentaries including Day of the Fight, Flying Padre; prod., dir., s.p., Fear and Desire, Killer's Kiss; dir., s.p., The Killing; writer-dir., Paths of Glory; dir. Spartacus; prod. dir., Lolita; prod. dir., writer, Dr. Strangelove; prod. dir., writer, 2001; A Space Odyssey; A Clockwork Orange; Barry Lyndon; The Shining.

KUERTZ, SR., CHARLES H.: Executive. b. Cincinnati, O., Nov. 1, 1923. e. Roger Bacon Catholic High School. Started as usher in theatre industry in 1939 with M. Marcus Enterprises. Ran theatres in Ft. Wayne and Cincinnati. From 1950 to 1957 co-owned and operated three drive-in theatres in Nashville. Built other theatres around that area for various cos. From 1957 to 1961 was with Holiday Amusement Co., Cincinnati, as gen. mgr. Holiday sold to Martin Theatres which he joined in 1961 starting as dist. mgr. in Nashville, running 44 theatres. Became exec. v.p. for Martin in July, 1972; elected pres., 1979.

KUHN, THOMAS G.: Executive. b. Chicago, Ill., Nov. 10, 1935. e. Northwestern Univ., 1957; Univ. of So. Calif. (MBA), 1966. Singer on Roulette Records, 1958–59. KNBC-TV sales 1960–62; NBC business affairs, 1962–64; NBC mgr. live night time progs., 1965–67; dir. live night time progs., 1968–69. Warner Bros. TV, v.p. program dev. 1970; v.p. TV prod., 1971; exec. prod., Alice (WB-CBS), 1976; exec. prod., The Awakening Land (WB-NBC), 1977; exec. v.p. for Alan Landsburg Prods., 1977; exec. prod., Torn Between Two Lovers, 1978; exec. prod., The Jayne Mansfield Story, 1980. Staff, v.p., west coast, for RCA Selectavision Video Discs, 1980.

KULIK, SEYMOUR (BUZZ): Producer-dir. b. N.Y.C., TV: Lux Video, Kraft; joined CBS-TV as prod.-dir., 1956; dir., You Are There, Climax, Playhouse 90, Defenders, Dr. Kildare, Twilight Zone, Dick Powell Playhouse; exec. prod., Kentucky Jones. 1964: v.p. chg. West Coast Prods., Bob Banner Associates Inc., 1965; 1967 Prod-Dir. with Paramount Studios, Brian's Song (TV); Shamus.
PICTURES INCLUDE: Warning Shot, The Riot, Villa Rides, The Hunter, Pursuit.

KUNO, MOTOJI: Sr. Managing Director. Tokyo Shibaure Electric Co., (Toshiba), Tokyo, Japan. Graduated Law Dept., Tokyo Imperial Univ. Mar., 1923. Became Toshiba auditor June, 1941; dir. June, 1942; sr. managing dir. Nov., 1948, perm. auditor Apr. 1949; dir. Fem., 1950; exec. dir. May, 1952; sr. managing dir. May, 1958.

KUPPER, W. J.: Executive. b. New York, N.Y., Oct. 17, 1896. World Film Corp. 2 yrs.; h.o. 20th-Fox, Aug., 1919; asst. mgr. Dallas, 1920; br. mgr., Washington, Oct. 1921; later, br. mgr., Albany, Charlotte, Pittsburgh, Chicago; asst. gen. sales mgr., h.o., Jan., 1924; spcl. rep., 1928; west div. mgr., Aug., 1932; gen. sales mgr., U.S., Canada, 1942; mag. dir., 20th-Fox Films of Gt. Brit., 1947–54; v.p., gen. sales mgr. Chromart Colour Org., England; 1954. Member: M.P. Pioneers; Variety Club of Gt. Brit.

KURALT, CHARLES: TV News Correspondent. b. Wilmington, NC. e. Univ. of North Carolina. Reporter-columnist for Charlotte News until joining CBS News as writer in 1956. Promoted to news assignment desk in 1958. Became first host of CBS News series, Eyewitness, in 1960. Named CBS News chief Latin American correspondent (based in Rio de Janeiro) in 1961 Appt. CBS News chief west coast correspondent in 1963; transferred to New York, 1964. Has worked on CBS Reports, CBS News Specials, and On the Road series for CBS Evening News with Walter Cronkite (latter 11 years). Now anchor man for CBS News Sunday Morning.

KURI, EMILE: Set decorator. b. Mexico City, Mex., June 11, 1907; e. Chaminade Coll., 1924–27. Interior decorator Be Hennesey Art Studio, 1929–32; then set decorator property dept. dir.
PICTURES INCLUDE: I'll Be Seeing You, Silver Queen, Spellbound, Duel in the Sun, Paradine Case, The Heiress (Academy Award, 1949), A Place in the Sun, Carrie, Shane, The Actress, Executive Suite, 20,000 Leagues Under the Sea (Academy Award, 1954); in charge of interior exterior decorations Disneyland. Several Golden Chair Awards (L.A. Furniture Mart). Mem.: Nat'l Acad. of TV Arts and Sciences, American Institute of Interior Designers, Bd. of Gov. Acad. of M.P. Arts and Sciences (1959–69). Honorary Sir Knights of Royal Rosarians, State of Oregon (1970), Decorating Consultant, Disney World, Fla.

KURODA, TOYOJI: Executive. b. Tokyo. April 29, 1920. e. Waseda Univ. Joined Motion Picture Producers Association 1945; appointed inspectorate Board of Trade in export film division 1948. On occasion of founding of Association for Diffusion Japanese Films Abroad (UniJapan Film) became manager.

KUROSAWA, AKIRA: Director. b. Japan. March 23, 1910. Entered PCL Studio 1936 and made director 1943.
PICTURES INCLUDE: Sanshiro Sugata, The Most Beautiful, Those Who Tread on The Tiger's Tail, No Regrets For Our Youth, The Quiet Duel, Scandal, Stray Dog, Rashomon, The Seven Samurai, The Drunken Angel, The Lower Depths, The Idiot, Ikiru, I Live in Fear, The Hidden Fortress, Throne of Blood, Yojimbo, High and Low, Red Beard, The Bad Sleep Well, Sanjourno, Kagemusha.

KURTZ, GARY: Producer-Director. b. Los Angeles, 1941. e. Univ. of So. Calif., Cinema School. Began prof. career during college. Has worked as cameraman, soundman, editor for Roger Corman, other prods. Also worked on documentaries. Was asst. dir. for two Monte Hellman westerns, Ride in the Whirlwind, The Shooting. Was prod. supvr. for The Hostage before being drafted into Marines. Spent 2 yrs. in Photo Field as cameraman, editor and still photo.
PICTURES INCLUDE: Two-Lane Blacktop (asst. prod.), Chandler (asst. prod.), American Graffiti (co.-prod.); Star Wars (prod.), The Empire Strikes Back (prod.).

KUTNER, MARTIN: Executive. Joined Paramount Pictures in 1971 as eastern div. mgr.; has held various positions in sls. dept. Named v.p., gen. sls. mgr.; in 1980 appt. senior v.p., domestic distribution.

KWIT, NATHANIEL TROY, JR.: Executive. b. N.Y.C., 1941. B.A. Cornell Univ.; M.B.A. New York Univ. 1964–68, American Broadcasting Co., Inc., exec. asst. to pres. of ABC Films. 1968–71, National Screen Service Corp., New York branch mgr., asst. genl. sls. mgr. 1971, founder , CEO Audience Marketing, Inc., later acquired by Viacom International as operating subsidiary. 1974 named v.p. marketing services, Warner Bros., Inc. 1979, named v.p. in charge video and special markets division, United Artists Corp.; 1981, named sr. v.p. in chg. VA television, video, special market div.

KYO, MACHIKO: Actress. b. Osaka, Japan. e. Osaka, Japan. Dancer in Osaka and Tokyo music halls; entered films 1948 with Daiei Studio; has appeared in numerous Japanese films.
PICTURES INCLUDE: Rashomon, Gate of Hell, Golden Demon, Story of Shunkin, Tales of Genji, Street of Shame, Teahouse of the August Moon, Ugetsu.

L

LADD, JR., ALAN: Executive. b. Los Angeles, Oct. 22, 1937. Motion picture agent, Creative Management Associates, 1963–69. M.p. producer, 1969–73; produced 9 films in 4 yrs. Joined 20th Century-Fox in 1973 in chg. of creative affairs in feature div. Promoted to v.p., production, 1974. In 1975 named sr. v.p. for worldwide prod.; 1976, promoted to pres. of 20th Century-Fox Pictures. Resigned & formed The Ladd Co., 1979.

LADD, CHERYL: Actress. b. Huron, S.D., July 2, 1951. r.n. Cheryl Stoppelmoore. M. film actor David Ladd. Joined professional Music Shop Band while in elementary school; left with it on tour, ending up in Los Angeles. Cast as voice of Melody character in animated Josie and the Pussycats. Studied acting with Milton Katselas. Did TV commercials, small parts in TV, made film Jamaica Reef (unreleased).
TELEVISION: Series: Charlie's Angels. Guest star on Ben Vereen. . . . His Roots, General Electric's All-Star Anniversary, John Denver and the Ladies, Police Woman, Happy Days, Switch, etc. Had own special, Cheryl Ladd. TV movie: A New Start.

LAKE, ARTHUR: Actor. r.n. Arthur Silverlake; b. Corbin, Ky. Stage debut at 3 yrs. of age; m.p. debut in silent Western 1924; sound m.p. debut Air Circus 1928; in vaudeville; on radio in "Blondie and Dagwood" series; owner of plastics household products co.; org. Arthur Lake Productions.
PICTURES INCLUDE: Sweet Sixteen comedies, Cradle Snatchers, Dance Hall, Annapolis Salute, Everybody's Doing It, There Goes My Heart, Blondie series, Sixteen Fathoms Deep.

LAMARR, HEDY: Actress. b. Vienna. At 15 starred in Ecstasy (awarded top Italian film-prize).
PICTURES INCLUDE: Algiers, I Take This Woman, Lady of the Tropics, Boom Town, Comrade X, Come Live With Me, Ziegfeld Girl; H. M. Pulham, Esq.; Tortilla Flat, Crossroads, White Cargo, Heavenly Body, Conspirators, Strange Woman, Samson and Delilah, A Lady Without a Passport, Dishonored Lady, Experiment Perilous, Let's Live a Little, Copper Canyon, My Favorite Spy, Story of Mankind, The Female Animal.

LAMAS, FERNANDO. Actor-Director. b. Buenos Aires, Jan. 9, 1925. e. Argentina, Spain, Italy. Trained at Teatro Experimental. After over 24 European and Latin-American films came to Hollywood under contract to MGM in 1951. Starred in more than 20 Hollywood films.
PICTURES INCLUDE: Rich, Young and Pretty, Lady and The Law, The Merry Widow, Sangaree, The Girl Who Had Everything, Dangerous When Wet, Diamond Queen, Jivaro, Rose Marie, The Girl Rush, 100 Rifles, The Cheap Detective. Dir.: Magic Fountain, The Violent Ones.
Several Box Office Awards and The New York Drama Critics Award for his Broadway play, Happy Hunting, international award for Place In Glory (wrote s.p.) 1967; debut as director: several TV segments of Run for Your Life. Has directed segments of The Bold Ones, Mannix, Alias Smith & Jones, The Rookies, S.W.A.T., Carl Reiner Show, and Starsky and Hutch.

LAMB, GIL: Actor. b. Minneapolis, Minn., June 14, 1906; e. U. Minn. On stage before screen debut 1939 in The Fleet's In, Lambs Clubs (N.Y.) On screen 1943.
PICTURES INCLUDE: Riding High, Rainbow Island, Practically Yours, Hit Parade of 1947, Make Mine Laughs, Humphrey Takes a Chance, Bye Bye Birdie, The Gnome-Mobile, Blackbeard's Ghost, The Love Bug.

LAMOUR, DOROTHY: Actress. b. Dec. 10, 1914, New Orleans, La.; e. Spence's Business Sch. Miss New Orleans 1931; sang on radio programs; screen debut in Jungle Princess 1938.
PICTURES INCLUDE: Spawn of the North, St. Louis Blues, Man About Town, Disputed Passage, Johnny Apollo, Typhoon, Road to Singapore, Caught in the Draft, Star Spangled Rhythm, Road to Utopia, Practically Yours, Medal for Benny, Duffy's Tavern, My Favorite Brunette, Road to Rio, Wild Harvest, Miracle Can Happen, Lulu Belle, Girl from Manhattan, Lucky Stiff, Slightly French, Manhandled, The Greatest Show on Earth, Road to Bali, Road to Hong Kong, Donovan's Reef, The Phynx.

LANCASTER, BURT: Actor. b. New York City, Nov. 2, 1913; e. N.Y.U. Was circus acrobat, in vaudeville; served in U.S. Army Special Service in Italy & N. Africa, World War II; screen debut in The Killers, 1946. Formed Hecht-Lancaster Orgn. in partnership with Harold Hecht.
PICTURES INCLUDE: Desert Fury, I Walk Alone, Brute Force, Sorry Wrong Number, Kiss the Blood Off My Hands, Criss Cross, All My Sons, Rope of Sand, Mister 880, Flame and the Arrow, Vengeance Valley, Ten Tall Men, Jim

Thorpe—All American, Crimson Pirate, Come Back Little Sheba, South Sea Woman, From Here to Eternity, His Majesty O'Keefe, Apache, Vera Cruz, The Kentuckian, Rose Tattoo, Trapeze, The Rainmaker, Gunfight at the OK Corral, Sweet Smell of Success, Separate Tables, The Devil's Disciple, Elmer Gantry, The Young Savages, Birdman of Alcatraz, The Leopard, Seven Days in May, Hallelujah Trail, The Swimmer, The Gypsy Moths, Castlekeep, Airport, Valdez Is Coming, Lawman, Ulzana's Raid, Scorpio, Executive Action, The Midnight Man (prod., dir. & star), Conversation Piece, Buffalo Bill and the Indians, The Cassandra Crossing, Twilight's Last Gleaming, The Island of Dr. Moreau, 1900, Go Tell the Spartans, Cattle Annie and Little Britches, Atlantic City.

LANCHESTER, ELSA: Actress and authoress. b. London, England; m. Charles Laughton. Acted in London, New York. At 16, started the Children's Theatre in London. Acted in London and New York with her husband. First British film was The Constant Nymph, silent version; The Private Life of Henry VIII, 1933, London Films. In 1935: David Copperfield, Naughty Marietta, MGM, and The Bride of Frankenstein, U. In 1936: The Ghost Goes West, Rembrandt, UA-London Films. In 1938: the Beachcomber, Mayflower-Par. In 1938: authoress of Charles Laughton and I. In 1939–40: Hollywood and on stage. In 1941: on screen, Ladies in Retirement, Col. In 1942: Son of Fury, Tales of Manhattan, 20th-Fox. In 1943: Forever and a Day, Lassie Come Home, Passport to Adventure, Witness for the Prosecution, Bell, Book and Candle.
PICTURES INCLUDE: The Spiral Staircase, The Razor's Edge, Northwest Outpost, Bishop's Wife, Come to the Stable, Secret Garden, Inspector General, Buccaneer's Girl, Mystery Street, Frenchie, Petty Girl, Androcles and the Lion, Dreamboat, Les Miserables, The Girls of Pleasure Island, Hell's Half Acre, Three Ring Circus, Glass Slipper, Mary Poppins, That Darn Cat, Blackbeard's Ghost, Easy Come Easy Go, Rascal, Me, Natalie, My Dog, The Thief, Willard, Arnold, Murder by Death.
TV: Studio One, Omnibus, Schlitz Playhouse, John Forsythe Show, Dick Cavett, Johnny Carson, Merv Griffin, David Frost Shows. Guest appearances on Mannix, Bill Cosby, To Catch a Thief, Then Came Bronson, Lucy Show.

LANDAU, ELY A.: Executive. b. New York, N.Y., Jan. 20, 1920; formed National Telefilm Associates, Inc., 1954; org. NTA Film Network, 1956; pres., chmn. of bd., National Telefilm Associates, Inc., 1957; resigned, 1961; formed Ely Landau Company, Inc., 1963; dist. The Servant, King and Country, Umbrellas of Cherbourg; prod. Long Day's Journey Into Night, The Fool Killer, The Pawnbroker, A Face of War, The Madwoman of Chaillot. Prod. King—A Filmed Record—Montgomery to Memphis, 1968; organized, directed one-night simultaneous charity showing 633 theatres U.S., 1970; 1972 Formed American Film Theatre, and the Ely Landau Organization, Inc. 1973–74 produced Iceman Cometh, Rhinoceros, The Homecoming, A Delicate Balance, Luther, Lost In The Stars, Burley Galileo, In Celebration, The Man in the Glass Booth, 1978: The Greek Tycoon. 1980: Hopscotch.

LANDAU, MARTIN: Actor. b. N.Y.C., 1934. Cartoon and staff artist on N.Y. Daily News; studied 3 yrs. at Actors Studio.
PICTURES INCLUDE: Pork Chop Hill, North by Northwest, Gazebo, Stagecoach to Dancer's Rock, Cleopatra, The Hallelujah Trail, The Greatest Story Ever Told, Nevada Smith, A Town Called Hell, Black Gunn, Strange Shadows in an Empty Room.
TV: Mission Impossible (1966–68), etc.
STAGE: Middle of the Night, Uncle Vanya, Stalag 17, Wedding Breakfast, First Love, The Goat Song.

LANDAU, RICHARD H.: Writer. b. New York City, Feb. 21, 1914; e. U. Arizona, Yale U. With Samuel-Landau agency handling writers and stories; shorts dept. writer MGM 1939; writer for RKO Radio since 1942; wrote documentaries and raining films for U.S. Army.
PICTURES INCLUDE: Gun in His Hand, Strange Confession, Challenge in the Night, Back to Bataan, Little Iodine, Christmas Eve, Crooked Way, Johnny One Eye, Roadblock, Lost Continent, F.B.I. Girl, Stolen Face, Bad Blonde, Spaceways, Sins of Jezebel, Blackout, Deadly Game, A Race for Life, Pearl of the South Pacific, Creeping Unknown.

LANDERS, ALBERT R: Executive. b. Goshen, Ind., May 22, 1920. e. Duke U., U. of Cincinnati Grad School. Crosley Broadcasting, dir. of TV film opers., 1946–52; dir. of TV film opers., ABC-TV, Hollywood; 1953–55; ass't. to pres., General Film Laboratories, 1955–64; v.p. West Coast opers., DeLuxe General, Inc., 1964 to 1969; asst. gen. mgr., MGM Laboratories, 1970–77.

LANDON, MICHAEL: Actor-Writer-Director. b. Forest Hills, N.Y., Oct. 31. e. U.S.C. Was athlete before signed by Warner Bros. to attend acting school. Roles in films and TV followed; big break came with Bonanza.
TV: Actor: Restless Gun, Bonanza, Little House on the Prairie. Guest appearances on Variety Shows. Writer-

Director: Love Came Laughing (Love Story series). Director: Roy Campanella Story. Producer: Little House on the Prairie.

LANDRES, PAUL: Director. b. New York, N.Y., Aug. 21, 1912. e. U.C.L.A. Started as asst. Film Editor at Universal 1931. Editor 1937 to 1949 of many feature films. Director of feature films and TV since 1949. Under Directorial contract to Warner Bros. 1961–62. Twenty-two feature films for theatrical release. Last film "Son of a Gunfighter" made in Spain for MGM release.
PICTURES INCLUDE: Miracle of the Hills, Johnny Rocco, Vampire, Flame Barrier, Oregon Passage, Last of the Badmen.
TV: 91 hour episodes of various series including among many others: The Outcasts, Bonanza, Daktari, The Rifleman, 77 Sunset Strip, Maverick, Hawaiian Eye, etc.

LANDSBURG, ALAN: Executive, producer. b. New York City, May 10, 1933. e. New York University. Producer for NBC News Dept., 1951–59; producer-writer, CBS, 1959–60; exec. prod., Wolper Productions/Metromedia Producers Corp., 1961–70; pres., Alan Landsburg Productions, 1970–present.

LANG, CHARLES: Cinematographer. b. Bluff, Utah, March 27, 1902. e. Lincoln H.S., Los Angeles, U.S.C. Entered m.p. ind. with Paramount Film Laboratory, then asst. cameraman; dir. of photography, Paramount, 1929–52; then freelance.
PICTURES INCLUDE: A Farewell to Arms (Academy Award for best photography, 1933); Ghost and Mrs. Muir, A Foreign Affair, September Affair, Ace in the Hole, Sudden Fear, Sabrina, Queen Bee, Man from Laramie, The Rainmaker, Some Like It Hot, The Magnificent Seven, Facts of Life, One-Eyed Jacks, Summer and Smoke, Charade, Father Goose, Wait Until Dark, Inside Daisy Clover, Hotel, Flim Flam Man, The Stalking Moon, Cactus Flower, Bob & Carol & Ted & Alice, The Love Machine, Doctors' Wives, Butterflies Are Free.

LANG, DAVID: Writer. b. New York City, Nov. 30, 1913. Was in Merchant Marine three years. Joined Charles Mintz Studio (Columbia) as cartoonist. Moved to MGM cartoon dept. 1938–40. Radio writer, Calling All Cars, KNX, Los Angeles, 1941. Contract writer at MGM, 1941–43. Yank on the Burma Road, Gambler's Choice, Hired Gun, North West Mounted Police. For Par. Midnight Manhunt, People Are Funny, Caged Fury, One Exciting Night. For Warner Bros. Flaxy Martin, Smart Money. For Columbia, Chain of Circumstance, Ambush at Tomahawk, The Nebraskan, Black Horse Canyon for U.I. Also Screaming Eagles, Hellcats of the Navy, Buckskin Lady. For PRC, Queen of Burlesque.
TELEVISION: Cheyenne, 87th Precinct, Ford Theatre, Gallant Men, Westinghouse Theatre, Adventures in Paradise, Bonanza, Trackdown, Wanted Dead or Alive, Rifleman, Rawhide, Have Gun Will Travel. At least two hundred credits in above series. Novelist. Oedipus Burning. Publisher, Stein and Day.

LANG, JENNINGS: Executive. b. New York City, May 28, 1915. e. St. John's Univ. & Law School. m. actress-singer Monica Lewis. Went into law practice in 1937 with Seligsburg and Lewis, m.p. law specialists. In 1938 went to Hollywood and became 2nd asst. dir. at Grand National Studios. Opened own office as actor's agent; first client, comedian Hugh Herbert. In 1940 joined Jaffe Agency; made partner and v.p. in 1942. Was pres. from 1948 to May, 1950, when resigned to join MCA. Worked in all phases of MCA operations; in 1952 made v.p. of MCA TV Ltd., and bd. mem. Involved with prod. and sales of TV prods. from inception of Revue (now Universal City Studios) in 1950. Organized Revue's New Projects Dept., creator and exec. in chg. of prog. dev. Involved with creation and sales of such series as Wagon Train, The Robert Cummings Show, Bachelor Father, Wells Fargo, Mike Hammer, etc. Most recently has been supvr. of Universal's World Premiere films, airing on Tuesday Night at the Movies and Saturday Night at the Movies (NBC).
Made Executive Producer at MCA (Universal) for motion pictures. Executive Producer on following films: Winning, They Might Be Giants, Puzzle of a Downfall Child, Coogan's Bluff, The Beguiled, Act of the Heart, Tell Them Willie Boy is Here, Play Misty for Me, Pete 'N Tillie, High Plains Drifter, Slaughterhouse Five, Charley Varrick, Breezy, The Great Waldo Pepper, Airport '75, Earthquake, Joe Kidd, The Great Northfield Minnesota Raid, The Eiger Sanction, Airport 1977, The Front Page, The Hindenburg. Producer: Swashbuckler, Roller Coaster, House Calls, Nunzio, Airport '79—The Concorde, Little Miss Marker, The Nude Bomb.

LANG, OTTO: Producer-Director, Four Academy Award nominations for Cinemascope Specials, Twentieth Century-Fox Film Corp. Saga of Western Man; ABC-TV Specials—The Legend of Cortez; Beethoven: Ordeal and Triumph.
TV: Man from U.N.C.L.E.; Daktari; Iron Horse; Cheyenne; Dick Powell Show; Zane Gray Theatre; Ann Sothern Show; Rifleman; Bat Masterson; Seahunt; The Deputy;

Surfside 6; Hawaiian Eye. Prod. Twentieth Century Fox Hour. Dir. Man and the Challenge; Aquanauts; World of Giants. Dir. feature for Cinerama: Search for Paradise, Lancer, Felony Squad.
PICTURES: Prod., Call Northside 777; Five Fingers; White Witch Doctor. Specialist for foreign locations. Many segments for This World of Ours; Wide, Wide World. 1969. Assoc. prod: Tora! Tora! Tora!, 20th Century-Fox.

LANGAN, GLENN: Actor. b. Denver, Colo., July 8, 1917; e. Wheatridge H.S. Started career as asst. mgr. Elitch Gardens, Denver; traveled to N.Y., worked at odd jobs, until walk-on part in play, Swing Your Lady; signed by Hollywood after appearance in A Kiss for Cinderella, oppos. Luise Rainer.
PICTURES INCLUDE: Riding High, Four Jills in a Jeep, Something For The Boys, Margie, Homestretch, Forever Amber, Iroquois Trail, Treasure of Monte Cristo, Rapture, Hangman's Knot, One Girl's Confession, 99 River Street, Big Chase, Mutiny in Outer Space.

LANGE, HOPE: Actress. r.n. Hope Elise Ross Lange; b. Redding Ridge, Conn., Nov. 28; e. Reed Coll., Portland, Ore. & Barmore Jr. Coll., N.Y. Parents: John Lange, musician (Arr. music for stage shows, including Show Boat); Minnette Buddecke Lange, actress. Prof. stage debut at age 12 in The Patriots on Broadway; then in The Hot Corner; seen on TV by 20th-Fox prod. Buddy Adler and signed for Bus Stop, her screen debut.
PICTURES INCLUDE: Jesse James, Peyton Place, The Young Lions, In Love and War, The Best of Everything, A Pocketful of Miracles, How the West Was Won, Love is a Ball, Jigsaw, Death Wish.
TV: The Ghost and Mrs. Muir, The New Dick Van Dyke Show, That Certain Summer, I Love You—Goodbye.

LANGELLA, FRANK: Actor. Studied acting at Syracuse Univ.; later in regional repertory, summer stock, and on and off Bdwy. Film debut in The Twelve Chairs (1970).
PICTURES: Diary of a Mad Housewife, Dracula, Those Lips, Those Eyes, Sphinx.

LANGFORD, FRANCES: Singer-actress. b. Lakeland, Fla.; e. Southern Coll. Stage experience in vaudeville, nightclubs, national radio programs. In 1935: collab. on lyrics and appeared in Every Night at Eight, Collegiate Broadway Melody of 1936, Palm Springs, Born to Dance, The Hit Parade, Hollywood Hotel, Dreaming Out Loud, Too Many Girls, The Hit Parade of 1941, All-American Coed, Swing It Soldier, Mississippi Gambler, Yankee Doodle Dandy, This Is the Army, Career Girl, The Girl Rush, Dixie Jamboree, Radio Stars on Parade, People Are Funny, Deputy Marshall, Purple Heart Diary, Glenn Miller Story; TV appearances with Don Ameche.

LANGNER, PHILIP: Producer, b. New York, N.Y., Aug. 24, 1926. e. Yale U. President of The Theatre Guild and Theatre Guild Films, Inc. Producer the Westport Country Playhouse 1947–53. Joined The Theatre Guild 1954. Produced 28 plays on Broadway for the Theatre Guild including the Matchmaker, Bells Are Ringing, The Tunnel of Love, Sunrise At Campobello, A Majority of One, The Unsinkable Molly Brown, A Passage To India, Seidman and Son, The Royal Hunt of the Sun, The Homecoming, Absurd Person Singular and Golda.
FILMS: Producer of The Pawnbroker, Slaves and Born To Win. Associate Prod., Judgment At Nuremberg, and A Child Is Waiting.

LANSBURY, ANGELA: Actress. b. London, England, Oct. 16, 1925. e. South Hampstead School for Girls, England; Academy of Music, London; Feagin Dramatic School, N.Y.; p. Moyna Macgill, actress; also rel. to Robert B. Mantell, actor, & Rt. Hon. George Lansbury, gov't. official. Screen debut in "Gaslight," 1943, which won Hollywood Foreign Correspondents' Assoc. award.
PICTURES INCLUDE: National Velvet, Picture of Dorian Gray, Harvey Girls, Hoodlum Saint, Till the Clouds Roll By, Tenth Avenue Angel, If Winter Comes, State of the Union, Three Musketeers, Red Danube, Samson and Delilah, Kind Lady, Mutiny, Remains to be Seen, Purple Mask, A Lawless Street, A Life at Stake, Court Jester, Please Murder Me, A Breath of Scandal, All Fall Down, In the Cool of the Day, The Manchurian Candidate, Mr. Buddwing, Dear Heart, Something for Everyone, Bedknobs & Broomsticks, Death on the Nile, The Mirror Crack'd.
BROADWAY: Mame, Dear World, Gypsy.

LANSBURY, BRUCE: Executive. b. London, England, Jan. 12, 1930. e. UCLA. m. actress Moyna Macgill. writer, prod. KABC-TV, Los Angeles, 1957–59; joined CBS-TV, 1959, was ass't dir., program dev., Hollywood, director for daytime and nighttime programs, producer of Great Adventure series; and v.p., programs, New York; 1964–66, indep. prod., Broadway stage; 1966–69 producer, Wild Wild West, CBS series; 1969–72, prod. Mission: Impossible, Paramount Movies of Week; now v.p., creative affairs, Paramount TV.

LANSING, SHERRY: Executive. b. Chicago, July 31, 1944. e. Northwestern Univ. Taught math, English and drama in L.A. city high schools, 1966–69. Acted in films (Loving, Rio Lobo) and numerous TV shows. Story editor for Wagner Intl. Prod. Co., 1972–74. Talent Associates, in chg. West Coast development (all projects), 1974–75. Appt. MGM story editor, 1975. In 1977 named MGM v.p. of creative affairs, Nov., 1977, appointed vice pres., production, at Columbia Pictures. Sept., 1978, named sen. v.p., production, for Columbia Pictures. January, 1980, appointed pres., Twentieth Century-Fox Productions.

LANTZ, WALTER: Animated cartoon producer. b. New Rochelle N.Y., April 27, 1900. Producer and creator of Woody Woodpecker, Andy Panda, Chilly Willy. Started with Gregory La Cava, 1916 with Katzenjammer Kids, Happy Hooligan and Krazy Kat. Joined J. R. Bray in 1922, producing Col. Heeza Liar, Dinky Doodle. Started with Universal Pictures in 1928. Produced first Technicolor cartoon for Paul Whiteman's King of Jazz. Produced Oswald Rabbit. Created Woody Woodpecker in 1941. Produced the first Woody Woodpecker TV show in 1957. Toured the Pacific War Zone on a handshake tour for the USO, with wife Gracie, the voice of Woody Woodpecker. Has been awarded the Golden Globe Award, the ASIFA Award, and in 1979 the OSCAR for achievement in the field of animation. Now producing the Woody Woodpecker TV show.

LARDNER, RING W., JR.: Writer. b. Chicago, Aug. 19, 1915; married; p. Ring W. and Ellis A.; e. Phillips Acad. and Princeton U. Was reporter on New York Daily Mirror. Publ. writer, Selznick International. Shared Academy Award with Michael Kanin. Orig. Screenplay, Woman of the Year, 1942. PICTURES INCLUDE: The Cross of Lorraine, Tomorrow the World, Forever Amber, Forbidden Street, Four Days Leave, Cloak and Dagger, The Cincinnati Kid, M*A*S*H, The Greatest.

LARKIN, JAMES J.: Executive. B. Brooklyn, N.Y., Nov. 2, 1925; e. Columbia U., 1947–52. U.S. Air Force, 1943–46; BOAC rep. to entertainment ind., 1948–60; pres. Transportation Counselors Inc., 1960–62; pres., Larkin Associates, Inc., 1962–65; exec. Radio N.Y. Worldwide, 1965–68, V.P. Grolier Educational Corp., 1968–69; V.P. Visual Informational Systems, 1969–73. Pres., Business Television Services, Inc., 1973; exec. prod., Madhouse Brigade, 1977–79; prod.-writer, All Those Beautiful Girls, 1979–80.

LARSEN, KEITH: Actor. e. Univ. of Utah. Little theatre work. TV: Series: The Hunter, Brave Eagle. PICTURES INCLUDE: Green Glove, Son of Belle Star, Chief Crazy Horse, Desert Sands, Night Freight, Arrow in the Dust, Dial Red O, Security Risk, Wichita, Women of the Prehistoric Planet.

LARSON, G. BENNETT: Executive. Joined KDYL, Salt Lake City as announcer, prog. mgr., 1926. Prod., dir., NBC, New York, 1929–34. Shows included Ed Wynn Texaco Show, Fleischmann House and Chase & Sanborn Hour. Radio exec. with Joseph Katz Co., Ruthrauff & Ryan, and Young & Rubicam, 1934–42. Gen. mgr. and part owner of WWDC, Washington, 1942–45. Mgr. of WPEN, Phila., 1945–47. v.p. of TV, WCAU-TV 1947–1950, App'd v.p. and gen. mgr., WPIX, New York, 1950; pres., Intermountain Broadcasting Corporation, KDYL AM-FM & TV, Salt Lake City, Utah, Exec. v.p. and gen. mgr. of Flower City Television Corporation, WOKR-TV, Rochester, New York, 1979–80, pres. Larson/Walker & Co., media brokers, Los Angeles; pres., G. Bennett Larson & Associates (broadcast consultants), 1981.

LASKY, JESSE JR.: Writer. b. New York City, Sept. 19, 1910; p. Jessie and Bessie Gains Lasky; e. Blair Academy, Hun School of Princeton, Grand Central School of Art, U. Of Dijon; entered m.p. industry, foreign dept., Paramount, Spain, 1930. Was censorship editor for Paramount on story board. Assistant to Sol Wurtzel Fox.
NOVELS INCLUDE: Curtain of Life, No Angels in Heaven, Spendthrift, Naked in a Cactus Garden, The Offer (with Pat Silver), autobiography, Whatever Happened to Hollywood?
OTHER MATERIAL: Three books of verse. Short stories published in Cosmopolitan Magazine; The Gehenna of the Bone; (plays) Hope and Pray and Private Beach (in collab.); Ghost Town: (collab. s.p. or story) Secret Agent; The Red Head (s.p.); Back in the Saddle; The Singing Hill (collab. s.p.); Steel Against the Sky (film script); Union Pacific; Northwest Mounted Police; Reap the Wild Wind; (collab. narr.) Land of Liberty, dir. orig. story, s.p. Omaha Trail; U.S. Army, 1942–46; (collab. s.p.) Unconquered. Samson and Delilah; (orig. s.p.) Sickle or Cross Thief of Venice (Italy); (s.p.) Women Without Names, City of Violence (Italy); (s.p.) Lorna Doone, Mask of the Avenger, Never Trust a Gambler, The Brigand, The Silver Whip, (collab. s.p.) Mission Over Korea, (story) Salome, (collab. s.p.) Hell and High Water, Iron Glove, (s.p.) Pearl of the South Pacific, Hot Blood, (collab. s.p.) Ten Commandments, (collab. s.p.) The Buccaneer, John Paul Jones, (collab. with Pat Silver) Wizard of Bagdad, Pirates of Tortuga, River Gambler, 7 Women From Hell, The Land Grabbers (orig. story), One of Those Things (English version).
TV: Naked City, Rescue 8, Shannon, 7 of the New Breed (in collab. with Pat Silver), Avengers, Danger Man, The Saint, The World of Lowell Thomas, The Baron, The Protectors, and four musical specials for BBC; Ten Who Dared (serial with Pat Silver).

LASSER, LOUISE: Actress. b. New York City. e. Brandeis Univ., New Sch. for Social Research. Appeared on stage before theatrical film debut in 1965 with What's New, Pussycat?
PICTURES: What's Up, Tiger Lily?, Take the Money and Run, Bananas, Everything You Always Wanted to Know About Sex, Such Good Friends, Slither.
TELEVISION: Masquerade, Mary Hartman, Mary Hartman (series); The Lie, Isn't It Shocking? (movies).

LASTFOGEL, ABE: Talent agent, William Morris Agency, Inc., hdqts., Beverly Hills, Calif., bd. chmn., 1969.

LATIMER, JONATHAN: Writer.
PICTURES INCLUDE: Lady in the Morgue, Last Warning, Phantom Raiders, Topper Returns, Night Has a Thousand Eyes, Beyond Glory, Redhead and Cowboy, Plunger of the Sun, Botany Bay, Night in New Orleans, Glass Key, Nocturne, They Won't Believe Me, Big Clock, Sealed Victory, Alias Nick Beal, Copper Canyon.

LA TOREE, CHARLES: Actor. b. New York City, Apr. 15, 1900. e. Columbia U. Long career on stage in character parts. Screen debut in Louisiana Purchase.
PICTURES INCLUDE: My Sister Eileen, Life Begins at 8:30, Casablanca, Mission to Moscow, Song of Bernadette, Enger Arsene Lupin, Hairy Ape, Uncertain Glory, Panhandle, 711 Ocean Drive.

LATSIS, PETER C.: Publicist. b. Chicago, Ill., Mar. 9, 1919. e. Wright Junior College, Chicago, Newspaper reporter, Chicago Herald-American, 1942–45; Army, 1943; joined Fox West Coast Theatres, Los Angeles, in theatre operations 1945; adv.-pub. dept. 1946; asst. dir. adv.-pub. 1955; press rep. National Theatres, 1958; press relations dir., National General Corp., 1963; home office special field pub. repr., American International Pictures, 1973; Filmways Pictures, 1980.

LATTUADA, ALBERTO: Director. b. Milan, Italy, 1914. Son of Felice Lattuada, musician, opera composer, and writer of scores of many of son's films. Studied architecture; founded the periodical Cominare. Later founded Italian Film Library, of which he is still pres. Also, pres., Cinema D'Essay. First screen work as scriptwriter and asst. dir. of two films, 1940.
PICTURES INCLUDE: Mill on the Po, Anna, The Overcoat, La Lupa, Love in the City, White Sister, Flesh Will Surrender, Without Pity, The She Wolf, Tempest, The Unexpected, Mafioso, The Mandrake, Matchless, The Betrayal, The Steppe, Oh, Serafina, Stay As You Are.

LAUGHLIN, TOM: Actor-Producer-Director-Writer. b. Minneapolis e. Univ. of Indiana, Univ. of Minn. where had athletic scholarships. m. actress Delores Taylor. Travelled around world, studying in Italy with Dr. Maria Montessori. Established, ran a Montessori school in Santa Monica for several yrs. Worked his way to Hollywood, where acted in bit parts until stardom came in Born Losers in 1967. Produced and starred in Billy Jack and The Trial of Billy Jack, also writing s.p. with wife under pseudonym Frank Christina. Heads own prod. co., Billy Jack Enterprises.
PICTURES INCLUDE: South Pacific, Tea and Sympathy, Gidget, Born Losers, Billy Jack, The Trial of Billy Jack, The Master Gunfighter, Billy Jack Goes to Washington.

LAUNDER, FRANK: Writer, director, producer. b. Hitchen, Eng., 1907, e. Brighton, Brit. civil svce.; dramatist; entered m.p. ind. as writer, 1930; Scenario ed., Gainsborough; org. Individual Pictures, Ltd., 1944 now called Launder-Gilliat and Company.
PICTURES INCLUDE: Lady Vanished, Night Train, Young Mr. Pitt, Millions Like Us, 2,000 Women, Notorious Gentleman, Green For Danger, Dulcimer Street, Great Manhunt, The Story of Gilbert and Sullivan, The Constant Husband, the Adventurers, Captain Boycott, Blue Lagoon, Happiest Days of Your Life, Lady Godiva Rides Again, The Belles of St. Trinians, Only Two Can Play, Joey Boy, The Great St. Trinian's Train Robbery.

LAURENCE, DOUGLAS: Producer. b. Totowa, N.J., Dec. 16, 1922. U.S. Air Force. 1947–50; wrote, prod., dir., shows for NBC Radio. Exec. prod. talent buyer for Teleways Radio, TV Prod. 1958–59; ent. dir., Flamingo Hotel. Advisor to Brazilian govt. on building film industry.
PICTURES INCLUDE: Quick Before It Melts, Mister Buddwing, Doctor You've Got to Be Kidding, Speedway, Stay Away Joe, Live a Little Love a Little, The Outside Man, Rio Man.
STAGE: General Motors Motorama, L.A. Home Show, Calif., Wisc., Texas State Fairs, Ford Motor Auto Shows, Stay Eastern Univ. Dance Troupe, Jazz America.

TV: Strange Wills, John Charles Thomas Show, Sons of he Pioneers, All Star Hit Parade, John Gunther's High Road.

LAURENTS, ARTHUR: Writer-Director. b. New York City, e. Cornell, B.A. 1937. First professional writing as radio script writer in 1939. In Army 1941-45.
STAGE PLAYS: Author: Home of the Brave, The Bird Cage, The Time of the Cuckoo, West Side Story, Gypsy, Hallelujah, Baby! Director: Invitation to a March, I Can Get It For You Wholesale. Author-Director: Anyone Can Whistle, Do I Hear a Waltz?
SCREENPLAYS: Rope, Caught, Anastasia, The Way We Were (from his own novel), The Turning Point.

LAURIE, JOHN: Actor. b. Dumfries, Scotland, Mar. 25, 1897. Architect; on stage.
PICTURES INCLUDE: Juno and the Paycock, Red Ensign, Thirty-Nine Steps, Convoy, Sailors Three, Dangerous Moonlight, Fanny, By Gaslight, Henry V., Way Ahead, Medal for the General, Caesar and Cleopatra, Agitator, I Know Where I'm Going, School for Secrets, Brothers, Jassy, Uncle Silas, Hamlet, Bonnie Prince Charlie, Mine Own Executioner, Flood Tide, Treasure Island, Trio, No Trace, Pandora & Flying Dutchman, Happy Go Lovely, Laughter in Paradise, Encore, Saturday Island, The Black Knight, Devil Girl from Mars, Richard III, Rockets Galore, Campbell's Kingdom, Kidnapped, Ladies Who Do, The Siege of the Saxons, The Reptile, Mr. 10½, Dad's Army, Doctor Phibes, One of Our Dinosaurs Is Missing.
TV INCLUDES: Dad's Army, Red Gauntlet, Tales of Mystery, Late Night Line Up, Call My Bluff, Quiz Ball, The Gnomes of Dulwich, Justice Is A Woman, Eyeless in Gaza, A Midsummer Night's Dream, Jackanory, Nation Wide.

LAURIE, PIPER: Actress. r.n. Rosetta Jacobs. b. Detroit, Mich. Jan. 22, 1932. e. Los Angeles H.S. Acted in school plays, signed by U.I. in 1949; m.p. debut in Louisa; Broadway, The Glass Menagerie (revival).
PICTURES INCLUDE: The Milkman, Francis Goes to the Races, Prince Who Was A Thief, Son of Ali Baba, Has Anybody Seen My Gal, No Room for the Groom, Mississippi Gambler, Golden Blade, Dangerous Mission, Johnny Dark, Dawn at Socorro, Smoke Signal, Ain't Misbehavin', Until They Sail, The Hustler, Carrie, Ruby.

LAVEN, ARNOLD: Director-Producer. b. Chicago, Ill., Feb. 23, 1922; with W.B. 1940-42; U.S. Army 1942-45; dialogue dir., 1946-50.
PICTURES INCLUDE: Without Warning, Vice Squad, Down Three Dark Streets, The Rack, Slaughter on 10th Ave., Anna Lucasta, The Glory Guys, Rough Night in Jericho, Sam Whiskey.
TELEVISION: Part creator and director TV pilots: The Rifleman, Robert Taylor's Detectives, The Plainsmen. Many TV films.

LAVERY, EMMET G., JR.: Producer. Poughkeepsie, N.Y., Aug. 10, 1927. e. UCLA: AB, 1950; LL.B., 1953. Private practice, law, dealing w. entertainment matters, 1953-64; resident counsel subscription TV, 1964-65; dir. of business affairs, 20th Century-Fox TV, 1965-67; v.p. in chg. business affairs, Paramount Television, 1967-71, exec. v.p., Paramount Television, 1972-1974, prod. Paramount Television and Paramount Pictures 1974-1975; prod. Serpico (series) for Paramount TV-NBC-TV, 1976, Prod.: The Ghost of Flight 401 (NBC) The Victim: An Anatomy of a Mugging (CBS).

LAVIN, LINDA: Actress. b. Portland, Me. Oct. 15. e. College of William & Mary. First professional job in chorus of Camden County (N.J.) Music Circus. Worked in plays both off and on Broadway before turning to TV, where guest-starred on such series as Family, Rhoda, Phyllis and Harry O; had recurring role in Barney Miller—all before advent of her own series, Alice.

LAW, JOHN PHILIP: Actor. b. Hollywood, 1937. e. University of Hawaii. Trained at Repertory Theatre of Lincoln Center under Elia Kazan. Did numerous Italian films before discovery in U.S.
PICTURES INCLUDE: The Russians Are Coming, The Hawaiians, Barbarella, Von Richtofen and Brown, The Last Movie, The Love Machine, The Golden Voyage of Sinbad, The Cassandra Crossing, Tarzan, the Ape Man.

LAWFORD, PETER: Actor. b. London, England, Sept. 7, 1923; e. priv. On screen at 7 in Brit. prod. "Old Bill"; U.S. m.p. debut in "Lord Jeff" 1938; parking lot attendant; usher Westwood Village Theatre, Hollywood.
PICTURES INCLUDE: Thunderbirds, Mrs. Miniver, Yank at Eton, Eagle Squadron, Someone to Remember, Man from Down Under, White Cliffs of Dover, Paris After Dark, Canterville Ghost, Picture of Dorian Gray, Two Sisters from Boston, Cluny Brown, My Brother Talks to Horses, It Happened in Brooklyn, My Brother Talks to Horses, It Happened in Brooklyn, On an Island With You, Easter Parade, Julia Misbehaves, Little Women, Red Danube, Please Believe Me, Royal Wedding, Kangaroo, Just This Once, Hour of Thirteen, You For Me, Rogue's March, It Should Happen to You, Never So Few, Exodus, Ocean's 11, Sergeants 3, Advise & Consent, Dead Ringer, Sylvia,

Harlow, The Oscar, Salt and Pepper, Skidoo, Hook, Line and Sinker, Buona Sera, Mrs. Campbell, April Fools, One More Time, They Only Kill Their Masters, That's Entertainment, Rosebud.
TV: Dear Phoebe, The Thin Man; pres., Chrislaw Prods., Inc., A Step Out of Line, Ellery Queen, The Doris Day Show.

LAWRENCE, BARBARA: Actress. b. Carnegie, Okla., Feb. 24, 1930; e. UCLA: mother Berenice Lawrence. Child model; successful screen try-out, 1944; screen debut in Billy Rose Diamond Horse Shoe.
PICTURES INCLUDE: Margie, Captain from Castile, You Were Meant for Me, Give My Regards to Broadway, Street With No Name, Unfaithfully Yours, Letter to Three Wives, Mother is a Freshman, Thieves Highway, Two Tickets to Broadway, Here Come the Nelsons, The Star, Arena, Paris Model, Her 12 Men, Oklahoma, Man With a Gun, Pay The Devil, Joe Dakota.

LAWRENCE, JODY: Actress. r.n. Josephine Lawrence Goddard. b. Fort Worth, Tex., Oct. 19, 1930; e. Beverly Hills H.S.; Hollywood Professional Sch. Signed by Columbia; m.p. debut in Mask of Avenger.
PICTURES INCLUDE: Family Secret, Son of Dr. Jekyll, Ten Tall Men, The Brigand, All Ashore, Capt. John Smith & Pocahontas, Scarlet Hour, Leather Saint.

LAWRENCE, MARC: Actor. b. New York City; e. City Coll. N.Y. On stage in Sour Mountain, Waiting for Lefty.
PICTURES INCLUDE: White Woman, Little Big Shot, Dr. Socrates, Road Gang, San Quentin, I Am the Law, While New York Sleeps, Dillinger, Flame of Barbary Coast, Club Havana, Don't Fence Me In, The Virginian, Life with Blondie, Yankee Fakir, Captain from Castile, I Walk Alone, Calamity Jane and Sam Bass, The Asphalt Jungle, Hurricane Island, My Favorite Spy, Girls Marked Danger, Helen of Troy, Custer of the West, Nightmare in the Sun.

LAWRENCE, STEVE: Actor. b. New York City, July 8, 1935. Singer in nightclubs and on TV.
PICTURES INCLUDE: Stand Up and Be Counted, The Blues Brothers.
TELEVISION: Steve and Eydie Celebrate Irving Berlin.

LAWSON, JOHN HOWARD: Writer. b. 1894, New York City; e. Williams Coll., 1914; ed. American Red Cross Bulletin in Rome, 1918. Wrote Broadway plays Loud Speaker, Processional, and others. With MGM, then freelance with Wanger, Goldwyn, 20th-Fox.
PICTURES INCLUDE: Sahara, Counter-Attack, Smash-Up.

LAWSON, SARAH: Actress. b. London, Eng., Aug. 6, 1928. e. Heron's Ghyll School (Sussex). stage debut in Everyman (Edinburgh Festival) 1947; screen debut in The Browning Version, 1949.
PICTURES INCLUDE: Street Corner, You Know What Sailors Are, Blue Peter, It's Never Too Late, Links of Justice, Three Crooked Men, Man with a Dog, Night Without Pity, The World Ten Times Over.
TV: Face to Face, River Line, Whole Truth, Lady From the Sea, Mrs. Moonlight, Silver Card, An Ideal Husband, Love and Money, Rendezvous, Invisible Man, Saber Buccaneers, White Hunter, Flying Doctor, On the Night of the Murder, Haven in Sunset, The Odd Man, Zero 1 series.

LAWYER, M.H. (A.C.R.A.): Distributor. b. Dec. 3, 1909. Bank official, 1927-49; with United Film Services, Jal Hind Pictures & Indo-Pak Film Corp., Karachi, before 1947; former secy., chmn., pres., M.P. Society of Sind & Baluchistan; secy. & treas., Sind & Baluchistan Film distrib. Synd.; pres. Famous Films, Pakistan.

LAY, BEIRNE, JR.: Writer, producer. b. Berkeley Springs, W. Va., Sept. 1, 1909; e. Yale U., B.A. Graduate as 2nd Lt. Army Air Corps Res. (pilot) 1933; col., AFRes, 10 yrs. active duty, Commander 487 Bomb Gp., 8th Air Force; Contributor to Post, Harpers, Fortune, Reader's Digest.
BOOKS: I Wanted Wings, I've Had It, 12 O'Clock High, Someone Has To Make It Happen, Earthbound Astronauts, I'm an Endangered Species.
PICTURES INCLUDE: I Wanted Wings, 12 O'Clock High, Above and Beyond, Strategic Air Command, Toward the Unkown, The Gallant Hours.

LAYE, EVELYN: Actress, singer. b. London, England, July 10, 1900. London stage debut 1918 The Beauty Spot. Subseq. in numerous musicals, dramas, London, including The Merry Widow, Madame Pompadour, Lilac Time, Blue Eyes, The New Moon, Paganini, Wedding in Paris, The Amorous Prawn, Strike a Light!, Let's All Go Down the Strand, Phil the Fluter, No Sex Please, We're British (1971-72). B'way stage debut, 1929, Bitter Sweet; m.p. debut 1927 silent production The Luck of the Navy.
PICTURES INCLUDE: One Heavenly Night, Waltz Time, Princess Charming, Evensong, The Night is Young, Make Mine a Million, Theatre of Death, Within and Without, Say Hello to Yesterday.
TV: Stars and Garters, Not Just An Act; 1969: Late Night

Line Up, The Golden Shot, The Simon Dee Show, The David Niven Show, This Is Your Life, Ommnibus.
PUBLICATION: Boo To My Friends (Autobiography).

LAZARUS, ERNA: Assoc. Producer Screen Writer. e. Columbia University, M.P. Industry major studio credits include: Hollywood or Bust, Martin & Lewis, sole story sole s.p.; Flareup, starring Raquel Welch, assoc. producer; Dancing in Manhattan, sole story-sole screenplay; Little Miss Big, sole screenplay-story; Michael O'Halloran, sole screenplay; Blonde From Brooklyn, sole story-sole s.p. Nobody's Sweetheart Now, story-screenplay, Meet Me After the Show, Betty Grable, original story; and others.
TV: Petticoat Junction, Donna Reed Show, Bewitched; Hawaiian Eye; Surfside Six; Mr. & Mrs. North; Ford Theatre, Irene Dunne, Sister Veronica; associate producer-head writer, Thomas Mitchell series, Mayor of the Town; Robert Taylor Detectives, and others.
RADIO: New York and Hollywood top comedy and dramatic shows.

LAZARUS, PAUL N.: Executive. b. Brooklyn, N.Y., March 31, 1913. e. Cornell U., B.A., '33. In U.S. Army, World War II. Entered m.p. ind. 1933 as gen. asst., press book dept., Warner Bros.; pres., AMPA, 1939–40. Joined Buchanan & Co., 1942 as m.p. account exec. To United Artists 1943 as dir. adv. & pub. Named asst. to pres., July 1948; joined Columbia exec. staff, New York, Aug. 1950; elected v.p. Columbia, Jan., 1954–62; exec. vice-pres. Samuel Bronston Prods., 1962–64; v.p., chg. Motion Pictures, Subscription Television Inc., 1964; exec. officer and partner, Landau Releasing Organization, 1964–65, exec. v.p., member bd. of dir., Nat'l Screen Serv. Corp., 1965–75. Lecturer and consultant, Film Studies Dept., Univ. of California at Santa Barbara. 1975 to present.

LAZARUS III, PAUL N.: Motion Picture Executive. Third generation film exec. Began career with Palomar Pictures Int'l. as exec. v.p.; joined ABC Pictures Corp. as v.p. in chg. of creative affairs. Mng. dir., CRM Productions, maker of educational films; v.p. for motion pictures. Marble Arch Productions.
PICTURES INCLUDE: Extreme Close-Up, Westworld, Futureworld, Capricorn One, Hanover Street.

LAZARUS, THEODORE R.: Executive. b. Brooklyn, N.Y., Aug. 5, 1919. e. Yale U. B.A., 1940. Adv. mgr., Eagle Lion Classics, 1951; adv., sales prom. mgr., WMGM, New York, 1951; then with Donahue and Coe adv. agency; secy., treas., George Blake Enterprises, TV film prod. firm, 1955; v.p. Gommi-TV, 1956; Charles Schlaifer and Co., Inc., 1957; adv. mgr., Paramount Pictures Corp., 1964; pres., Cinema Lodge, B'nai B'rith, 1968–71.

LAZARUS, THOMAS L.: Executive. b. New York, N.Y., Oct. 5, 1942. e. Boston U., 1960–62; New School for Social Research, 1962; acct. exec. Donahue and Coe, Inc., 1962–63; asst. to adv. mgr., Twentieth Century-Fox, 1963–64; adv. mgr., Seven Arts Pictures, 1964–66; acct. exec. Chas. Schaiffer & Co., 1966; exec. coordinator adv., MCA, 1966–70; dir. creative services, 1970; writer, prod., dir. for CRM Productions, 1971–4.
PICTURES: Just You and Me Kid (story credit)
TELEVISION: Screenplay: Revenge or Justice, Charlie's Angels (The Jade Trap), The President's Mistress, Columbo, The Survival of Melissa, The Boys Next Door, etc.

LEACHMAN, CLORIS: Actress. b. Des Moines, Iowa, June 30, 1930. e. Northwestern Univ. Broadway stage, television, motion pictures.
TV: Lassie, A Brand New Life, The Migrants, Phyllis (series).
PICTURES INCLUDE: Butch Cassidy and the Sundance Kid, The Steagle, The Last Picture Show, (Acad. award best supporting actress, 1971), Dillinger, Daisy Miller, Young Frankenstein, Crazy Mama, High Anxiety, The North Avenue Irregulars, Scavenger Hunt, History of the World—Part I.

LEADER, ANTON MORRIS: Director-producer. b. Boston, Mass., e. Hebrew Coll., New Eng. Conservatory of Music. Dir., announcer, actor, Boston radio stations; prod. mgr., WMCA, N.Y.; Army Air Corp.; prod. dir., NBC; winner, Variety Showmanship Award, Peabody Award for Words at War; winner Brotherhood Award, Peabody Award for Eternal Light; Western Heritage Award, dir. TV Film, The Horsefighter (The Virginian); inst., Fordham U., prod., dir., Suspense, CBS; prod., dir., writer Columbia Pictures; prod., U-1;
PICTURES INCLUDE: It Happens Every Thursday, Sally and St. Anne, Go Man Go!, Children of the Damned, Cock-eyed Cowboys of Calico County.
TV: The Virginian, Rawhide, Tarzan, Daniel Boone, Playhouse 90, Father of the Bride, It Takes a Thief, Ironside, Star Trek, Lost in Space, I Spy, Get Smart, Hawaii Five-O, Firehouse, Movin' On, This Is The Life.

LEAN, DAVID: Director. b. Croydon, England, Mar. 25, 1908; e. Leighton Park. Entered m.p. ind. 1928 as camera asst. Graumont Pictures; asst. dir. & ed.; co-dir. 1942; dir.

PICTURES INCLUDE: Escape Me Never, Pygmalion, Invaders, In Which We Serve, This Happy Breed, Blithe Spirit, Brief Encounter, Great Expectations, Oliver Twist, Madeleine, One Woman's Story. The Sound Barrier, Hobson's Choice, Summertime, The Bridge on the River Kwai (Academy Award 1957, best direction), Lawrence of Arabia, Dr. Zhivago, Ryan's Daughter.

LEAR, NORMAN: Producer-Director-Writer. Began in TV as co-writer of weekly one-hour variety show, The Ford Star Revue in 1950. Followed as writer for Dean Martin and Jerry Lewis on the Colgate Comedy Hour and for the Martha Raye and George Gobel TV shows. With partner, Bud Yorkin, created and produced such specials as Another Evening with Fred Astaire, Henry Fonda and the Family, An Evening with Carol Channing, and The Many Sides of Don Rickles. In 1965 their company also produced the original Andy Williams Show. Moved into motion pictures in 1963, writing and producing Come Blow Your Horn.
PICTURES: Never Too Late (prod.), Divorce-American Style (s.p.), The Night They Raided Minsky's (co. prod., co-s.p.), Start the Revolution without Me (co.-prod.), Cold Turkey, (s.p., prod., dir.).
RECENT TELEVISION: Exec. prod. of All in the Family, Maude, Good Times, The Jeffersons, Mary Hartman, Mary Hartman, One Day at a Time, The Baxters, Palmerstown.

LEARNED, MICHAEL: Actress. b. Washington, D.C. Studied ballet and dramatics in school. Many stage credits include Under Milkwood, The Three Sisters, A God Slept Here, etc.; resident performances with Shakespeare festivals in Canada, Stratford, CT, and San Diego, CA. Gained fame on hit TV series, The Waltons, as the mother, Olivia. Theatrical film debut in 1980, Touched by Love.
TELEVISION: Gunsmoke, Police Story, Widow, Little Mo, etc.

LE BORG, REGINALD: Director. b. Vienna, Austria Dec. 11; e. U. Vienna, B.A.; Sorbonne, Paris; Columbia U. Banker, playwright & stage dir., Europe; then staged musical and operatic sequences, Columbia, Paramount. To MGM as dir. short subjects. In 1941 joined Universal. Entered U.S. armed services, 1942; returned to Universal, 1944; Rec'd citation from OWL; free lance since 1946. Wrote Academy Award winning short Heavenly Music, 1945. directed two films in England, one in Mexico.
PICTURES INCLUDE: She's for Me, The Mummy's Ghost, Calling Dr. Death, Weird Woman, Dead Man's Eyes, Jungle Woman, Destiny, Honeymoon Ahead; San Diego, I Love You; (prod.), Philo Vance's Secret Mission; (dir.) Fighting Fools, Hold That Baby, The Squared Circle, Young Daniel Boone, Wyoming Mail, Triple Cross, G.I. Jane; Models, Inc., Bad Blonde, Great Jesse James Raid, Sins of Jezebel, Joe Palooka, Champ, Port Said, Fall Guy, Formed Cosmos Prod., prod., White Orchid (dir.), Black Sleep, Voodoo Island, War Drums, The Dalton Girls.
TV: for Sovereign, 4 Star, Schlitz Playhouse, Wire Service, Navy Log, Maverick, Desilu Revue; Court of Last Resort, Warner Bros., Screen Gems, MGM, Ziv; recent features: The Flight That Disappeared, Deadly Duo, The Diary of A Madman, The Eyes of Annie Jones, So Evil, My Sister.

LEDER, HERBERT JAY: Writer-director, producer. b. New York City, Aug. 15, 1922. e. B.A., PHD. Play Doctor on Broadway; Director TV dept., Benton and Bowles Adv. chg. all T.V. & Film production, 13 yrs.; Features: writer, Fiend Without a Face; writer-director co-prod., Pretty Boy Floyd; writer-director, co-producer, Nine Miles to Noon; writer, Love Keeps No Score of Wrongs; writer, prod-dir., The Frozen Dead, It; Mia, writer-dir., Candyman, writer-director; writer, The Winners, The Way It Is, The Cool Crazies. Sponsored Films: Child Molester, Bank Robber, Shoplifter, Untouchables.

LEDERER, RICHARD: Executive. b. New York, N.Y. Sept. 22, 1916; e. Univ. of Virginia. B.S., 1938; Free lance writer, 1939–41; U.S. Army. Cryptanalyst, Signal Intell. Serv 1941–45; Adv. copywriter, Columbia Pictures, 1946–50; Adv. copywriter, Warner Bros., 1950–53; copy chief, Warner Bros., 1950–53; copy chief, Warner Bros., 1953–57; Asst. Nat'l Adv. mgr., Warner Bros. studios, 1957–1959; Prod., theatrical, TV. Warner Bros. studios, 1959–60; Dir. of adv., publicity, Warner Bros. Pictures, 1960; v.p. Warner Bros. Pictures, 1963. V.P. production, Warner Bros. Studio, 1969–70; indep. prod. to May, 1971, when returned to WB as adv.-pub., v.p. Now independent producer. 1980: Hollywood Knights.

LEE, ANNA: Actress. b. England; seen in First a Girl, The Camels Are Coming, You're in the Army Now, King Solomon's Mines.
PICTURES INCLUDE: Flesh and Fantasy, Summer Storm, Abroad with Two Yanks, High Conquest, Ghost and Mrs. Muir, Best Man Wins, Fort Apache, Prison Warden, This Earth is Mine.
Many TV shows.

LEE, CHRISTOPHER: Actor. b. London, England, May 27, 1922. e. Wellington College. Served RAF 1940–46. Ent. m.p. ind. 1947. Over 40 TV films. Recent TV: How The West Was Won.

PICTURES INCLUDE: Corridor of Mirrors, Hamlet, Moulin Rouge, Moby Dick, River Plate, Truth About Women, Tale of Two Cities, Curse of Frankenstein, Dracula, Man Who Could Cheat Death, The Mummy, Too Hot to Handle, Beat Girl, City of the Dead, Two Faces of Dr. Jekyll, The Terror of the Tongs, The Hands of Orlac, Taste of Fear, The Devil's Daffodil, Pirates of Blood River, Devil's Agent, Red Orchid, Valley of Fear, Katharsis, Faust '63, The Virgin of Nuremberg, The Whip and the Body, Carmilla, The Devil Ship Pirates, The Gorgon, The Sign of Satan, The House of Blood, The Dunwich Horror, Dr. Terror's House of Horrors, She, The Skull, The Mask of Fu Manchu, Dracula, Prince of Darkness, Rasputin, Theatre of Death, Circus of Fear, The Brides of Fu Manchu, Five Golden Dragons, Diabolica, Vengeance of Fu Manchu, Night of the Big Heat, The Pendulum, The Face of Eve, The Devil Rides Out, The Blood of Fu Manchu, The Crimson Altar, Dracula Has Risen from the Grave, The Oblong Box, De Sade 70, Scream and Scream Again, The Magic Christian, Julius Caesar, One More Time, Count Dracula, Bloody Judge, Taste the Blood of Dracula, Private Lives of Sherlock Holmes, El Umbragolo, Scars of Dracula, House That Dripped Blood, I Monster, Hannie Caulder, Dracula 72, Horror Express, Creeping Flesh, Death Line, Nothing but the Night, The Wicker Man, Poor Devil, Dark Places, Dracula Is Dead?, Eulalie Quitte les champs, The Three Musketeers, Earthbound, Man With The Golden Gun, The Four Musketeers, Killer Force, Diagnosis-Murder, Whispering Death, The Keeper, To The Devil a Daughter, Pere Et Fils, Airport 77, Alien Encounter, The End of the World, Return from Witch Mountain, Caravans, The Silent Flute, The Passage, The Pirates, Jaguar Lives, Arabian Adventure.

LEE, JOHN: Actor. b. Launceston, Tasmania, March 31, 1928. Early career on Australian stage and radio. Ent. m.p. ind. in England 1957.

PICTURES INCLUDE: Dunkirk, Cat Girl, Silent Enemy, Flying Scot, Gypsy and The Gentleman, Under Ten Flags, The Liar, Seven Keys, The Secret Partner, Dr. Crippen, Stitch in Time, Go Kart Go, Space Flight.

TV: Adventures of the Sea Hawk, International Detective, Rendezvous, Flying Doctor, Danger Man, Shadow Squad, Man and Superman, A Man Involved, Aren't We All, Probation Officer, Ladies of the Corridor, Golden Girl, After the Crash, The Net, Emergency Ward 10, Zero One, Sapper Series, Dr. Fancy, The Shifting Heart, Sergeant Cork, Dr. Who, The Materialists, The July Plot.

LEE, PEGGY: Singer, actress. r.n. Norma Egstrom; b. Jamestown, N.D., May 26, 1920. Began career as night club vocalist in Fargo & radio singer, WDAY, then with Sev Olsen, bandleader, Minneapolis, Will Osborne; Benny Goodman; collab. (with Dave Barbour) popular songs, Manana, It's a Good Day, What More Can a Woman Do? Leading feminine vocalist. TV & records; screen debut in Mr. Music (Bing Crosby); singer on Bing Crosby program, CBS, TV appearances.

PICTURES INCLUDE: Jazz Singer, Pete Kelly's Blues, act., collab. songs, Lady and the Tramp.

LEE, PINKY: Performer, r.n. Pincus Leff. b. St. Paul, Minn. Started in musical comedy stock, vaudeville; with Gus Edwards troupe; then toured vaudeville circuits as solo act; appeared in burlesque, Broadway musicals; star, Earl Carrolls Theatre Restaurant, Hollywood, 1942–46; star of Pinky Lee Show, NBC network.

PICTURES INCLUDE: Lady of Burlesque, That's My Gal, In Old Amarillo, South of Caliente.

LEEDS, MARTIN N.: Film-TV Executive. b. New York City, Apr. 6, 1916. e. NYU, BS, 1936; J.D., 1938. Admitted N.Y. Bar, 1938, Calif. Bar, 1948; dir. indsl. relations Wabash Appliance Corp., 1943–44; indsl. bus. relations cons. Davis & Gilbert. 1944–45; dir. indsl. relations Flying Tiger Lines, 1947; dir. bus. affairs CBS. TV div., 1947–53; exec. v.p. Desilu Productions, Inc., 1953–60; v.p. Motion Picture Center Studios, Inc.: mem. Industry comm. War Manpower Comm., 1943; chmn. Com. to form Television Code of Ethics; U.S. Army 1941. Mem. Los Angeles Bar Assn.; exec. v.p. in chg. of West Coast oper. & member of bd. of dir. Talent Associates—Paramount Ltd., Hollywood, 1962; TV production consultant; exec. v.p., Electronovision Prods. Inc., 1964; TV prod. & MP prod. consultant, 1965. Pres., chief exec. officer member of bd., Beverly Hills Studios, Inc., 1969, senior v.p., American Film Theatre, 1973; 1975, motion picture and TV attorney & consultant.

LEENHOUTS, LEWIS GRANT: Executive. b. Los Angeles, California; m. Edith Hargrave. From 1934–1938 variously stunt man, unit manager, cutter & asst. dir., Collab. orig. story No More Women, wrote orig. Heroes at Leisure. In 1939 wrote training films, U.S. Officer of Education; 1940–41 assoc. prod., writer, dir., Caravel Films Inc.; 1942–45 head of planning and production U.S. Navy Training Film &

Motion Picture branch, Navy Dept.; 1946–47 gen. mgr. in charge of prod., National Educational Films, Inc. Later coordinator-producer, Industry Film Project, Motion Picture Assoc.; prod. California's Golden Beginning, Paramount assoc. chief and head of prod., International M.P. Div., U.S. Dept. of State, 1950–51; exec. v.p., Cinerama, Inc., 1952–53; planning and prod. head, Ford Foundation Fund for Adult Education, 1954, v.p., prod. head Cinerama, Inc., 1955–60. Ind. producer; prod. consultant Macbeth, Compass Prods. and Grand Prize Films, London; pres., Leehouts Prods., Inc., 1961; prod., 20th Century Fox, Movietone Digest, Children's Digest, 1963; Prod. Consultant, Cascade Pics. of Calif., 1964–65; 1967, dir. prod., Breakfast At the Capitol; prod., New Sounds in Africa; prod. head, Eddie Albert, Inc., 1971.

LEE-THOMPSON, J.: Writer, Director, Producer. On Brit. stage; writer of stage plays including: Murder Without Crime, Cousin Simon, Curious Dr. Robson (collab.) Thousands of Summers, Human Touch. Writer and m.p. director.

PICTURES INCLUDE: The Yellow Balloon, Weak and the Wicked, Yield To The Night, Woman In The Dressing Gown, Ice Cold in Alex, No Trees in the Street, Tiger Bay, I Aim at the Stars, The Guns of Navarone, Taras Bulba, Cape Fear, Kings of the Sun, What A Way to Go, John Goldfarb, Please Come Home, Return From the Ashes, MacKenna's Gold, Battle for the Planet of the Apes, Before Winter Comes, Country Dance, Conquest of the Planet of the Apes, Huckleberry Finn, The Reincarnation of Peter Proud, St. Ives, The White Buffalo, The Greek Tycoon, The Passage, Cabo blanco, Happy Birthday To Me.

LEEWOOD, JACK: Producer. b. New York City, N.Y., e. Upsala Coll., Newark U. and New York U. From 1926–31 with Gottesman-Stern circuit as usher, asst. and relief mgr.; 1931–43 Stanley-Warner mgr. of Ritz, Capitol and Hollywood theatres 1943–47. Joined Warner Bros. field forces in Denver-Salt Lake; Seattle-Portland, 1947–52. Dir. pub. & adv. Screen Guild Prod.; Lippert Productions; prod. exec. in chge. story dept.; 1953–56 Allied Artists; 1957–62 Prod. 20th Cent. Fox; 1965–68 prod., Universal; 1976–78. Affiliated Theatre Serrio; 1978–79. Aubrey/Hammer Prod.

PICTURES INCLUDE: Holiday Rhythm, Gunfire, Hi-Jacked; Roaring City, Danger Zone, Lost Continent, F.B.I. Girl, Pier 23, Train to Tombstone, I Shot Billy the Kid, Bandit Queen, Motor Patrol, Savage Drums, Three Desperate Men, Border Rangers, Western Pacific Agent, Thundering Jets, Lone Texan, Little Savage, Alligator, People, 13 Fighting Men, Young Jesse James, Swingin' Along, We'll Bury You, 20,000 Eyes, Thunder Island, the Plainsman, Longest 100 Miles, Escape to Mindanao, Dallas Cowboys Cheerleaders, When Hell Was in Session.

LEFFERTS, GEORGE: Producer, writer, director. b. Paterson, N.J., dir., numerous award-winning TV series, films, exec. prod.-Time-Life films 1977–78; prod./writer, Movie of the Week (NBC) 1977–78. Biog: Who's Who in America, Who's Who in the World. 1975 Emmy Award Benjamin Franklin Specials (CBS).

TV: 1969 Emmy Award, prod. Hallmark Hall of Fame "Teacher Teacher," 1963 Emmy Award, wrote, prod., directed Purex Specials for Women. 1965 Producer's Guild Award, exec. prod. "Breaking Point" series. Other shows: The Bill Cosby Show, Studio One, Kraft Theatre, Chrysler Theatre, Sinatra Show, Lights Out, Alcoa, The Harness (Movie of the Week), The Bold Ones, Exec. prod., Bing Crosby Productions, prod., NBC 10 yrs, Independent.

PICTURES INCLUDE: The Stake, Mean Dog Blues, 1977–78, The Living End, The Boat, The Teenager.

BROADWAY: The Boat, 1968, Hey, Everybody, 1970.

LEFKO, MORRIS E.: b. March 30, 1907. Entered m.p. ind. as poster clerk; booker, salesman, br. mgr., Indianapolis, RKO, June 1941; br. mgr., Pittsburgh, July 1944; East Central dist. mgr., July, 1948; appt. sales exec. of Ten Commandments Unit. Para. Film Dist. Corp., N.Y.C. 1956; v.p. in chg. sls., Michael Todd Co., 1958. Joined MGM, Inc., July 1960 sls. mgr., of road shows, Ben-Hur, King of Kings, Mutiny on the Bounty; vice pres., gen. sales mgr., MGM, 1963. Exec. consultant to Pres., Cinema 5 Ltd., Jan. 1970. v.p., Network Cinema Corp., 1972; American Film Theatre, Ely Lando Co., Nov., 1972; v.p., sls. mgr. Brut Prods., 1976.

LEFKOWITZ, NAT: Chairman Emeritus, William Morris Agency, Inc. b. July 24, 1905, Brooklyn. e. CCNY School of Business Adm., grad. 1926, CPA: Brooklyn Law School, grad. 1938-LLM: admitted to NYS bar, Nov., 1938. Community activities: United Jewish Appeal; Federation of Jewish Philanthropies; M.P. Pioneers; Variety Clubs International Cinema Lodge B'nai B'rith; member, National Academy of TV Arts & Sciences, board of trustees of Will Rogers Hospital and O'Donnell Memorial Research Laboratories; Boy Scouts of America; USO bd.; N.Y. City Athletic Club; Dellwood Country Club, Friars Club, Variety Club, Trustee, Natl. Conf. of Christians & Jews, 1980.

LE GALLIENNE, EVA: Actress—Producer. b. London, England, 1899. Stage career began in 1914. Founded Civic Repertory Theatre in 1926, starring in and directing such classics as Hedda Gabler, Romeo and Juliet, Alice in Wonderland, Camille, The Cherry Orchard. Also co-founder of American Repertory Theatre; toured with National Repertory Theatr.

TELEVISION: Alice in Wonderland, The Corn Is Green, The Bridge of San Luis Rey, Mary Stuart, The Royal Family (Emmy award, 1977).

PICTURES: Prince of Players, The Devil's Disciple, Resurrection.

LEGG, STUART: Producer. b. London, England, August 31, 1910. m. e. Marlborough Coll., 1923–28; St. John's Coll., Cambridge, 1928–31. Began as dir. and ed., prod. of documentary and public information shorts. From 1931–32, with British Instructional Films; 1932–34, Empire Marketing Board film unit; 1934–37, G.P.O. Film Unit; 1937–38. Film Centre, London; 1938–39, Strand Films, London; 1939–42. National Film Board, Ottawa. In 1945, head N.Y. br., John Grierson's co.; editor, World in Action, shorts enterprises.

LEGRAND, MICHEL JEAN: Composer-Conductor. b. France, 1931. Son of well-known arranger, composer and pianist, Raymond Legrand. At 11 Michel, a child prodigy, entered Paris Cons. and graduated nine years later with top honors in composition and as solo pianist. In late Fifties turned to composing for films and has composed, orchestrated and conducted scores of more than 50 films.

PICTURES INCLUDE: Lola, Eva, Vivre Sa Vie, La Baie des Anges, The Umbrellas of Cherbourg, Banda a Part, Un Femme Mariee, Les Demoiselles de Rochefort, Ice Station Zebra, The Thomas Crown Affair, Pieces of Dreams, The Happy Ending, Wuthering Heights, The Go-Between, Summer of '42, Picasso Summer, The Nelson Affair, Breezy, The Three Musketeers, Sheila Levine, Gable and Lombard, The Hunter.

TV: Brian's Song.

LEHMAN, ERNEST: Writer-Producer, Director. b. New York City. e. City College of New York. Began career as financial editor and free-lance short story and novelette writer. Recently published first novel, The French Atlantic Affair. First screenplays were Executive Suite, Sabrina, Sweet Smell of Success, based on own novelette.

PICTURES INCLUDE: The King and I, Somebody Up There Likes Me, North by Northwest, From the Terrace, West Side Story, The Prize, The Sound of Music. Became a prod.-wr. for first time with Who's Afraid of Virginia Woolf? Prod.-wr. Hello Dolly; prod.-wr.-dir., Portnoy's Complaint; Family Plot (s.p.), Black Sunday (co.-s.p.).

LEHMAN, GLADYS: Writer, Scenarios identified with such Reginald Denny pictures as Out All Night, Clear the Deck, On Your Toes and Companionate Trouble; joined Columbia in 1929.

SCRIPTS INCLUDE: The Little Accident, A Lady Surrenders, The Cat Creeps, Many a Slip, Seed, Strictly Dishonorable, Back Street, Embarrassing Moments, Nice Women, Good Girls Go to Paris, Blondie, Two Girls and a Sailor, Thrill of a Romance, Her Highness and the Bellboy, This Time for Keeps, collab. s.p. Luxury Liner, Golden Girl.

LEHR, MILTON H.: Director, producer, writer. b. Sept. 10, 1918. m. Harriet Smerling, 1942. e. Ohio U., A.B., 1938; Ohio State U., B.S., 1939; Virginia Polytech., M.S., 1940; Tex. A.&M. cand., PhD., 1941. Pres., Int'l Prods., Puerto Rico, 1949–60; pres., Int'l Video Prods., Miami, London, Madrid, 1960–70.

PICTURES & TV: Legend of Juggler, 1970; The Ray Anthony Show, 26 one-hr. Films, 1969; Prof. Irwin Corey Special, 1969; Swinging Scene of Ray Anthony (RKO-General), 1968; 240 musical shorts for Scopitone, Color Sonics and Automatic Canteen, 1966–67; Robert Taylor Presents Cugat in Madrid, 1965; Command Performance with Edmundo Ros, 26 ½-hr. Progs. for BBC, 1964; The Latin Touch, 26 ½-hr. progs. for Rheingold and RKO-General, 1960–61; Showtime, 212 1-hr. progs. (General Motors in Spanish) 1957–60; Telemundo, Puerto Rico, 1953–57; Televisa, Caracas, 1952; CMQ, Havana, 1949–51.

LEIBMAN, RON: Actor. e. Ohio Wesleyan Univ. Joined Actor's Studio in N.Y.; first professional appearance in summer theatre production of A View from the Bridge.

STAGE: The Premise, We Bombed in New Haven, Cop Out, Room Service, I Oughta Be in Pictures.

PICTURES INCLUDE: Where's Poppa (debut), The Hot Rock, Slaughterhouse Five, Your Three Minutes Are Up, Super Cops, Won Ton Ton, Up the Academy, Zorro, the Gay Blade.

TV: A Question of Guilt (ff), Kaz (series).

LEIBOWITZ, SAM: Executive. b. New York City, Feb. 12, 1913. Service mgr., Reel Photos, 1931–4; svg. mgr., Consolidated Film Ind., 1935; Apco Photo Co., Inc., treas., 1936–62; Apco-Apeda Photo Co., Inc., 1962–present, pres. & chief operating officer.

LEIDER, GERALD J.: Producer. b. Camden, New Jersey, May 28, 1931. e. Syracuse Univ. 1953; Bristol Univ., Eng. 1954 Fulbright Fellowship in Drama. m. Susan Trustman, son

Matthew Trustman, born April 14, 1972, son Kenneth Harold, born June 18, 1975. 1955 MCA, Inc., N.Y.; 1956–59 theatre producer in N.Y., London; Shinbone Alley, Garden District, and Sir John Gielgud's Ages of Man. 1960–61; director of special programs, CBS/TV; 1961–62, dir. of program sales, CBS-TV; 1962–69, vice pres., television operation, Ashley Famous Agency, Inc. Sept. 1969–Dec. 1974, pres. Warner Bros. Television, Burbank. Jan. 1975–Dec. 1976, exec. vice pres. foreign production Warner Bros. Pictures, Rome. Jan. 1977–present, independent producer under Jerry Leider Productions.

PICTURES: Wild Horse Hank, The Jazz Singer (1980).

TELEVISION: And I Alone Survived, Willa, The Hostage Tower.

LEIGH, JANET: Actress, r.n. Jeanette Helen Morrison; b. Merced, Calif., July 6, 1927. e. College of Pacific (music). Screen debut in Romance of Rosy Ridge, 1947.

PICTURES INCLUDE: If Winter Comes, Hills of Home, Words and Music, Act of Violence, Little Women, That Forsyte Woman, Red Danube, Doctor and the Girl, Holiday Affair, It's a Big Country, Two Tickets to Broadway, Strictly Dishonorable, Angels in the Outfield, Just This Once, Naked Spur, Confidentially Connie, Houdini, Walking My Baby Back Home, Prince Valiant, Living It Up, Black Shield of Falworth, Rogue Cop, My Sister Eileen, Pete Kelly's Blues, Safari, The Vikings, The Perfect Furlough, Psycho, The Manchurian Candidate, Bye, Bye, Birdie, Wives and Lovers, Kid Rodello, Grand Slam, Hello Down There, One Is A Lonely Number, Night of the Lepus, Boardwalk, The Fog.

LEIGH, SUZANNA: Actress. b. England, 1945. Studies at the Arts Educational School and Webber Douglas School. Film debut 1961 in Oscar Wilde, followed by Bomb in the High Street. 1964: TV series made in France, Three Stars. 1965–6: Under contract to Hal Wallis and Paramount, Boeing Boeing, Paradise Hawaiian Style, 1966: The Deadly Bees, Deadlier Than The Male. 1967: The Lost Continent. 1968: Subterfuge. TV film series in West Indies, One On An Island. 1969: TV play, The Plastic People. 1970.

PICTURES INCLUDE: To Love a Vampire, Beware My Brethren, Son of Dracula.

TV: The Persuaders.

LEISER, HENRI: Producer. b. Anbergue, France. Jan. 30, 1903; e. U. Strasburg, Berlin. Paris LL.D. Co-prod., prod. & pres. 1922–39 of Alpha Films, Inc., Monaco; Artem, Paris; Les Films, Paris; ARTIP, Cuba; assoc. Wm. Morris, Jr., personal repr. Villa Lobos; vice-pres. Villa Lobos Music Corp. & Teleconcert Corp.; independent prod. with Henry Souvaine, Inc.

PICTURES INCLUDE: Brothers Karamazoff, Living Corpse, One Night in London, Burning Heart, Incomplete Marriage, Variety, Three Valises.

TV: Tele Bingo, Sandy's Kiddy Club.

LELOUCH, CLAUDE: Director-Cinematographer. b. Paris, France, Oct. 30, 1937. Began m.p. career with short subjects, 1956; French military service, motion picture department, 1957–60; formed Films 13, 1960; publicity Films and Scopitones, 1961–62.

PICTURES INCLUDE: Le Propre de L'homme (Man's Own), L'amour avec des Si (Love With Ifs), Une fille et des Fusils (Guns and a Girl), To be A Crook, Un Homme et une Femme (A Man and A Woman), Vivre pour Vivre (Live for Life), Life, Love, and Death, Love Is a Funny Thing (dir., photog., s.p.); The Crook (dir., photog., s.p.) Adventure Is Adventure (prod., dir., s.p.). Smic, Smac, Smoc, La Bonne Anne, Another Man, Another Chance.

LEMLEIN, NEAL C.: Executive. e. Tulane Univ.; New York Univ. Began career at Young & Rubicam in N.Y.; later joined Doyle Dane Bernbach, Inc., where named snr. acct. exec. assigned to 20th-Fox feature films account and CBS-TV Entertainment Division. In March, 1980, joined Universal Pictures as dir. of mktg.

LEMMON, JACK: Actor. b. Boston, Mass. Feb. 8; e. Harvard U. Stage debut as a child; radio actor on soap operas; stock companies; U.S. Navy, WWII; many TV shows; B'way debut in Room Service 1953; other Broadway shows include: Face of a Hero (1960) and Tribute (1978). Other legitimate theatre appearances include: Idiot's Delight (1970, Los Angeles), Juno and the Paycock (1975, Los Angeles), Tribute (1979, Denver and Los Angeles). m.p. debut in It Should Happen to You.

PICTURES INCLUDE: Three for the Show, Phfft, My Sister Eileen, Mr. Roberts (Academy Award, best supporting actor, 1955), You Can't Run Away From It, Fire Down Below, Operation Mad Ball, Bell Book and Candle, It Happened to Jane, Some Like It Hot, The Apartment, The Wackiest Ship in the Army, Notorious Landlady, Days of Wine and Roses, Irma La Douce, Under the Yum Yum Tree, Good Neighbor Sam, How To Murder Your Wife, The Great Race, The Fortune Cookie, Luv, The Odd Couple, The April Fools, The Out of Towners. Debut as director: Kotch, 1971, The War Between Men and Women, 's Wonderful, 's Marvelous, 's Gershwin (TV Emmy Award 1972),

Save the Tiger (Academy Award, Best Actor), Avanti, The Prisoner of Second Avenue, The Front Page, The Entertainer (TV in U.S.), Alex & The Gypsy, Airport '77, The China Syndrome (Cannes festival award for best actor, 1979), Tribute.

LEMONT, JOHN: Producer, director, screenwriter. e. Canada, U.S.A. and England. Ent. m.p. ind. as actor and writer/technician. Early career working on features and documentaries. Service with Army Kinematograph Service as writ./dir. A.B.P. Director of Trans-Oceanic Telefilm Productions, Zodiac Productions Ltd., Venture Productions Ltd. V. Chmn. Writers Guild of Gt. Britain. Awards: WGGB Laurel, Edgar Allen Poe, NY/USA Festival Gold Award.
PICTURES INCLUDE: Vacation Rhythm, The Patrol, The Green Buddha, Cross Channel, Missing Person, Harvest of the Seas, People's Playground, Port of London, Mirror and Markheim, And Women Shall Weep, The Shakedown, Konga, The Frightened City, Deep Waters, Horse Called Jester, Woman On the Stair.
TV: Fabian of the Yard, British Heritage, Frances Drake, Strange Study, Errol Flynn Theatre, Ivanhoe; prod., Sixpenny Corner, Dir. The Glorification of Al Toolum; dir. Witness in The Dark; TV Playhouse series.

LEON, SOL: Executive. b. July 2, 1913, New York City. e. N.Y.U., CCNY, Brooklyn Law School, BBL, master of law. V.p., TV Dept., William Morris Agency, N.Y.C.

LEONARD, HERBERT B.: Producer. b. New York, Oct. 8, 1922. e. New York University. Columbia Pictures, 1940. Naval Aviator, 1941–46. Prod. mgr., Sam Katzman Prod., 1946–48; formed Herbert B. Leonard Prod., 1954. TV debut as prod., Rin Tin Tin Series. Formed Norber Prod., Inc., with Norman Blacburn, 1955, prod. Circus Boy, TV series. Formed Lancer Prod., prod. Tales of the Bengal Lancers, TV series, 1956. Formed Wilbert Prod., Inc. with Cinefilm, Inc., prod. Rescue 8 TV series, 1958. Formed Shelle Prod., Inc., prod. Naked City, TV series, 1958 and Route 66, TV series. Formed Leonard Films, Inc., prod. motion picture Popi for United Artists, 1968–69; joined Allied Artists Int'l., TV Prods.

LEONARD, SHELDON: Actor. r.n. Sheldon Leonard Bershad. b. New York, N.Y., Feb. 22, 1907; e. Syracuse U., B.A. Theatre mgr., Publix; N.Y. stage, 10 yrs.; sec., Directors Guild of America. 3 Emmy awards, Sylvania award, 4 TV Director of the Year nominations by D.G.A.
PICTURES INCLUDE: Another Thin Man, Tall, Dark and Handsome, Tortilla Flat, Rise and Shine, Lucky Jordan, Somewhere in the Night, Her Kind of Man, Its a Wonderful Life, The Gansters, If You Knew Susie, Sinbad the Sailor, My Dream Is Yours, Take One False Step, Iroquois Trail, Here Come the Nelsons, Young Man with Ideas, Stop You're Killing Me, Diamond Queen, Money from Home, Guys and Dolls; dir. Real McCoys, Pocketful of Miracles.
TV: 1953–56: dir. Make Room for Daddy, Damon Runyon, G.E. Theatre, Electric Theatre, Jewelers' Showcase, Jimmy Durante Show; prod.-dir. Danny Thomas Show; package & exec. prod., Andy Griffith Show, Dick Van Dyke Show; exec. prod., Gomer Pyle, U.S.M.C., I Spy, My World and Welcome To It. In 1975 starred in Big Eddie (CBS), 1977, exec. prod. and co-star in Top Secret.

LEONE, ALFRED: Producer, b. Nov. 30, 1926. In entertainment industry since 1958. Assistant producer for Braken Productions and Hallmark Productions. In 1968 formed Europa-America in Rome, Italy. 1974, formed Leone Intl. SPA in Rome. In 1978 opened offices in Beverly Hills. Produced and distributed over 35 films, among them: Vengeance, Four Times That Night, Baron Blood, Lisa And The Devil, House of Exorcism, Love by Appointment, Gold of the Amazon Women, The Snake.

L'EPINE-SMITH, ERIC: Producer, director, writer. b. Thornton Heath Eng. m. Brenda Cameron. Stage as actor, prod. playwright, formed own co. Adivah Films; joined Wieland's Agency; apptd. dir. of co.; casting dir. Warner Bros. 1st Natl.; assoc. prod. Edward Dryhurst Productions, then prod. Now artists' mgr., L'Epine-Smith, Ltd.
PICTURES INCLUDE: Down on the Farm, Pitchfork and Powder-Puff, Making a Man of Him, House of Silence, Five Pound Man, Coming of Age, While I Live, Noose, Romantic Age, Come Die My Love.

LERNER, ALAN JAY: Playwright, lyricist.
N.Y. STAGE PLAYS: What's Up, The Day Before Spring, Brigadoon (N.Y. Drama Critics Award 1947), Love Life With Weill, 1948, Paint Your Wagon, My Fair Lady, NY Drama Critic Award, Tony Award, Donaldson Award (1956), Camelot, with Frederick Loewe; Grammy Award, On A Clear Day You Can See Forever with Burton Lane; Coco with Andre Previn; Gigi, with Frederick Loewe (Tony Award best score 1973–74); 1600 Pennsylvania Avenue with Leonard Bernstein (1976); Carmelia (1979).
SCREEN PLAYS: Royal Wedding, An American In Paris (Academy Award, best s.p., best song, 1958), My Fair Lady,

Camelot, Paint Your Wagon, On A Clear Day You Can See Forever, The Little Prince.

LERNER, JOSEPH: Producer, director, writer. m. Geraldine Lerner, film ed. radio stage mgr. & actor on Broadway; with RKO, Columbia and Republic as dir.; dial. dir., writer, 2nd unit dir., test dir., dir.-writer & head of special productions U.S. Army Signal Corps Photographic Center; writer of commercial and educational films 1946–47; vice-pres. in chg. of prod. Visual Arts Productions 1947; vice-pres. in chg. of prod. Laurel Films 1949; prod.-dir., TV Gang-busters series, Grand Tour series; Girl on the Run, com. ind. films, Three Musketeers series TV, dir.-prod., 1961; Director, producer, writer, MPO Videotronics, Inc. 1967–1973. President, The Place for Film Making, Inc.; pres., Astracor Associates Ltd. in production: The Ditch Digger's Daughter, The Little Hat, The Mapmakers. Also lecturer and instructor at New York University, Wm. Patterson College.
CREDITS INCLUDE: (writer-dir.) Fight Never Ends; (prod.-writer) Kings of the Olympics, Olympics Cavalcade; (prod.-dir.-writer) United Nations Case Book (for CBS-TV), C-Man; (prod.-dir.) Guilty Bystander, Mr. Universe, writer, director co-producer, The Dark of Day.

LEROY, MERVYN: Producer, director, b. San Francisco, Calif., Oct. 15, 1900. In vaudeville before entering m.p. ind. as contrib. comedy & other situations. From 1927 dir. many pictures, & from 1927 variously dir. & prod. In 1942 apptd. dir. supvr. Hollywood prod. for coordinator Inter-Amer. Affairs. In 1955 orig. own prod. co., Mervyn LeRoy Prods.; A "Champion Directors" in Fame ratings Special Acad. Award 1945 for dir. The House I Live In. In 1976 won the Irving Thalberg Award.
PICTURES INCLUDE: Wizard of Oz, King and the Chorus Girl, High Pressure, Thirty Seconds Over Tokyo, I Am a Fugitive from a Chain Gang, Hard to Handle, Gold Diggers of 1933, Five Star Final, Oil for the Lamps of China, Little Caesar, Tugboat Annie, Anthony Adverse, Three Men on a Horse, Escape, Johnny Eager, Random Harvest, Madame Curie, Without Reservations, Homecoming, Little Women, Any Number Can Play, East Side West Side, Quo Vadis, Lovely to Look At, Million Dollar Mermaid, Latin Lovers, Rose Marie, Mister Roberts, Strange Lady in Town, Bad Seed, Toward the Unknown, No Time for Sergeants, Home Before Dark, The FBI Story, Wake Me When It's Over, Majority of One, The Devil at 4 O'Clock.

LESLIE, ALEEN: Writer. b. Pittsburgh, Pa., Feb. 5, 1908; e. Ohio State U. Contributor to magazines; columnist Pittsburgh Press; orig. & wrote radio series A Date with Judy 1941–50. Bway play Slightly Married, 1943; wrote, prod. Date with Judy, TV series; author, The Scent of the Roses, The Windfall.
PICTURES INCLUDE: Doctor Takes a Wife, Affectionately Yours, Henry Aldrich Plays Cupid, Stork Pays Off, Henry Aldrich Gets Glamour, It Comes Up Love, Rosie the Riveter, Father Was a Fullback, Father Is a Bachelor.

LESLIE, JOAN: Actress. Star of Tomorrow, 1946. r.n. Joan Brodell; b. Detroit, Mich., January 26, 1925; p. Agnes and John Brodell; e. St. Benedicts, Detroit; Our Lady of Lourdes, Toronto; St. Mary's Montreal; Immaculate Heart. H.S., Los Angeles. Modeled for color photography advertising or Eastman Kodak Co. Bd. of dir. Damon Runyon Foundation. Now on bd. of dir., St. Anne's Hospital.
PICTURES INCLUDE: The Sky's the Limit, This Is the Army, Yankee Doodle Dandy, Thank Your Lucky Stars, Rhapsody in Blue, Cinderella Jones, Hollywood Canteen, Where Do We Go From Here?, Too Young to Know, Repeat Performance, Northwest Stampede, Born To Be Bad, Skipper Surprised His Wife, Man in the Saddle, Toughest Man in Arizona, Hellgate, Woman They Almost Lynched, Flight Nurse, Jubilee Trail, Hell's Outpost, Revolt of Mamie Stover, Police Story.
TV: Ford Theatre, G.E. Theatre, Queen for a Day, The Keegans (MOW), Various commercials.

LESSER, SEYMOUR H. Executive. b. New York City, Nov. 9, 1929. e. Pace U., C.C.N.Y. Public accounting, 1953–60; asst. corporate controller & mgr. of accounting, Metro-Goldwyn-Mayer, 1960–68; gen'l mgr., financial v.p., Robbins Music Corp., 1968–70; financial consultant for entertainment industry, 1970–73; treasurer, Allied Artists Pictures Corp.

LESTER, MARK: Actor. b. Oxford, England, 1958. Ent. m.p. ind. 1963.
PICTURES INCLUDE: Allez France, Our Mother's House, 1967; Oliver, 1968; Run Wild, Run Free, 1969; The Boy Who Stole the Elephant, Eye Witness, SWALK (Melody), Black Beauty, Whoever Slew Auntie Roo?, Redneck, Crossed Swords.
TV: Special for Disney in Hollywood. 1970: American series for Krofft Television Productions, Scalawag, 1972; Graduation Trip, 1972; Danza Alla Porto Gli Olmi (Italian Entry Berlin '75), Seen Dimly Before Dawn '75.
STAGE: The Murder Game '76; The Prince & The Pauper '76.

LESTER, RICHARD: Director, composer. b. Philadelphia, Pa., 1932. Early career: dir. and mus. dir. TV, CBS, Phila., CBC-TV, Toronto. Ent. m.p. ind. 1957. TV: dir. TV Goon Shows. Composed (with Reg. Owen) Sea War Series. Films: Composed and dir., Running, Jumping and Standing Still Film.
PICTURES INCLUDE: It's Trad, Dad, Mouse On the Moon, Hard Day's Night, The Knack, Help! A Funny Thing Happened on the Way to the Forum, How I Won The War, Petulia, The Bedsitting Room, The Three Musketeers, Juggernaut, The Four Musketeers, Royal Flash, Robin & Marian, The Ritz, Butch and Sundance: The Early Days, Cuba, Superman II.

LETTER, LOUIS N.: Executive. b. New York, N.Y., August, 1937. e. Brooklyn College Business Administration, v.p. and dir. of operations, Century Theatres, New Hyde Park, N.Y.

LEVEE, MICHAEL: Producer. e. Stanford Univ. Four years as U.S. Navy officer in World War II. After service went to work for father's company, M.C. Levee Agency. In 1947 formed Levee-Stark Agency with Ray Stark. Joined MCA in 1950; 1952, appt. v.p. in chg of TV division. When MCA phased out of agency business became exec. v.p. at CMA. Later joined Robert Radnitz as exec. v.p. of Radnitz/Mattel division of Mattel Toys, formed to finance family-oriented films. In 1975 rejoined Starr as exec. v.p. of Rastar Group. Left to produce independently.
PICTURES: The Black Bird (exec. prod.), Casey's Shadow (exec. prod.), Slow Dancing in the Big City (co.-prod.).

LEVEN, BORIS: Art director, production designer. b. Moscow, Russia. e. Certificate of Beaux Arts Inst. of Design, N.Y., U.S.C.—Bachelor of Architecture degree. Painter of water colors, many awards in architectural competitions; sketch artist, set designer, Paramount Studios, 1933–35; asst. art dir., Major Pictures Corp., 1936; art dir., 20th Century-Fox, 1937–38, 41–42, 45–46, Universal, 1947–48, freelance from 1948. Nominated for Acad. Award 8 times. Academy award in art direction for West Side Story. Member: Academy of M.P. Arts & Sciences, Soc. of M.P. & TV Art Dirs. Delta Phi Delta, Tau Sigma Delta, Skull & Dagger. U.S. Army Air Force 1942–45.
PICTURES INCLUDE: Alexander's Ragtime Band, Tales of Manhattan, Shanghai Gesture, Hello Frisco Hello, I Wonder Who's Kissing Her Now, Criss-Cross, Mr. Peabody and The Mermaid, The Senator Was Indiscreet, Sudden Fear, The Star, Silver Chalice, Giant, Anatomy of Murder, West Side Story, Two For the Seesaw, The Sound of Music, The Sand Pebbles, Star! A Dream of Kings, The Andromeda Strain, The New Centurions, Jonathan Livingston Seagull, Mandingo, New York, New York, The Last Waltz.

LEVEY, ARTHUR: Pres., Skiatron Electronics & Television Corp.; Skiatron Broadcasting Co. b. New York City, 1903. Film industrialist operating in London and New York. Developed unique inventions, including Skiatron dark-trace tube used in Berlin Airlift and atomic tests, etc. Ultrasonic system of large-screen TV. Also Subscriber-Vision system of subscription television, etc. Member: Masons (Anima Lodge, London).

LE VIEN, JACK: Producer/Director. b. N.Y., N.Y., 1918; film ed., reporter, Pathe News; military service, 1941–46; news ed., gen. mgr., v.p., Pathe News; chmn, American Newsreel Assoc., 1956–59; dir. of prod., Hearst Metrotone News; prod. in assoc., ABC-TV, The Valiant Years; exec. prod., Black Fox; prod. The Finest Hours, A King's Story; chmn., exec. prod., Le Vien Films Ltd.; prod.; Other World of Winston Churchill (NBC, BBC), The Gathering Storm, Walk With Destiny, The Amazing Voyage of Daffodil & Daisy, The Queens Drum Horse, Where The Lotus Fell, Churchill and the Generals.

LEVIN, IRVING H.: Executive. b. Chicago, Ill., Sept. 8, 1921. e. grad., U. of Ill. U.S. Air Force, 1943–45; entered m.p. ind. as partner of Kranz-Levin Pictures and Realart Pictures of Calif. Inc.; indep. exch. in 1948; formed Mutual Prod, 1952; pres., Filmakers Releasing Org., 1953; secy., Filmakers Prod., Inc., 1952; pres. AB-PT Pictures Corp., 1956; pres., exec. prod., Oakhurst Television Prod., Inc., Sindee Prod., Inc.; pres., exec. prod. Atlas Enterprises, Inc.; pres., prod. Atlantic Pictures, 1959; exec. vice-pres., mem. of bd. of dir., National General Corp. (formerly NT&T) 1961 and Pres. National General Prod. Inc. 1966 and Pictures Corp. 1967. Pres. and chief operating officer, NGC. In 1975 formed Levin-Schulman Prods.

LEVIN, IRVING M.: Executive. b. San Francisco, Oct. 1916. ent. Theatre work, managing showhouses 1932; div. dir., San Francisco Theatres, circuit, 1945–79; bd. of dir., S.F. Theatres, Inc., 1945–68; pres., bd. of dir. pres. Blind Babies Foundation, 1958–79; Chief Barker, Variety Club of Northern Calif., Tent 32, 1957–58; bd. of dir., S.F. Chamber of Commerce, 1961–63; Star of Solidarity Award—Italian Gov., 1960; founded S.F. Film Festival, 1957; exec., dir., of Festival, 1957–64. President, NATO of Northern California, 1971–72; Chairman, Northern California Theatre Assn.; Chm., Theatre Assn. California.

LEVIN, JACK H.: Executive. b. New York City, Aug. 19. e. Technical Inst. New York. Mutual Film Co. 1916; F.I.L.M. Club to 1923; Film Board Trade to 1927; founded Copyright Protection Bureau, 1927–45; orig. audit bureau for m.p. ind. 1941; founded Confidential Reports, Inc. 1944; founded Certified Reports 1951, founded Certified Investigations, 1952. Representing theatre owners-theatre inspections and ticket integrity tests. Also market research and industrial investigations.
AUTHOR: 1932: Bootlegging. 1934: Arguments in favor of Federal Registration. 1939: Marriage, Morals and Mothballs. 1943: Marriage, Morals and War, for U.S. Army.
Pres. Assoc. of Licensed Detectives of N.Y. State (1962–63); Chief Barker, Int. Variety Club Tent 35 (1964–66). Currently Nat'l. Comm. Vocational Service, B'nai B'rith.

LEVINE, HOWARD A.: Executive. Served in legal depts. of advertising agencies, BBDO and Ogilvy & Mather, before joined legal dept. of Paramount Pictures as counsel to mktg. div. in 1976. In 1979 appt. exec. dir.—prod. mktg. for Paramount's motion picture div.

LEVINE, JOSEPH E.: Executive. b. Boston, Massachusetts, Sept. 9, 1905. Entered motion picture industry as owner of theatre in New Haven, Connecticut. Entered national distribution in 1943. Named "Pioneer of the Year", Variety Club of N.Y.; "Showman of the Year", 1960. Named "Producer of the Year" by Allied States Assoc. of M.P. Exhibitions, 1962. Named "Master Showman of the World" by TOA, 1963; winner of Cecil B. DeMille Award for "Showman of the Year" from Hollywood Foreign Press, 1964; winner First Annual Award, Conference of Personal Mgrs., East, for outstanding contributions to World of Entertainment, 1965. President Avco Embassy Pictures. Resigned 1974 to form own co. Joseph E. Levine Presents.
PICTURES INCLUDE: Hercules, 1959; Two Women, 1962; Boccaccio '70, The Sky Above, The Mud Below, Long Day's Journey Into Night, Federico Fellini's 8½, The Easy Life, Yesterday, Today and Tomorrow, Marriage Italian Style, Divorce Italian Style, The Carpetbaggers, Zulu, Casanova '70, Darling, Woman Times Seven, The Graduate, The Producers, The Lion in Winter, Carnal Knowledge, Day of the Dolphin, A Bridge Too Far, Magic.

LEVINE, MARTIN: Executive. b. Brooklyn, N.Y., June 29, 1909. e. Syracuse U., Brooklyn Law. Prod. of The Roosevelt Story, doc.; pioneer in fgn. film dist. in U.S., pres. of Cinema Lodge, B'nai B'rith; former vice pres. & bd. member, Motion Picture Pioneers; Mem. MPP; former first asst. chief barker, Variety clubs of America, Tent No. 35. Active with J.D.A., A.D.L.; v.p. nat. fund cabinet of B'nai B'rith. Exec. v.p., William Brandt Theatres, 1957. Former chmn., A.D.L. m.p. industry, 1962. Mem. bd. dirs. I.T.O.A. Chmn. M.P. Boy Scout Drive, 1958–59; National Jewish Home, 1960–61. Chmn. N.Y. Regional Board A.D.L., 1962–63, Chmn., M.P. Federation of Jewish Philanthropies, 1962–63. Awards: 6 by foreign govts. for promotion of foreign films in U.S.; I.F.I.D.A., special citation; Torch of Liberty Award, A.D.L., 1968. Elected to bd. of dir., Motion Picture Pioneers, elected to Crew, Variety Tent 35; 1972, President, Brandt Theatres.

LEVINSON, BARRY: Producer. b. New York, 1932. Ent. m.p. ind. 1956. Chairman of Board of the Cinema Fund.
PICTURES INCLUDE: The Only Way, First Love, The Night Visitor, The Amazing Mr. Blunden, Catholics, Who, The Internecine Project (also wrote).

LEVINSON, NORM: Executive. b. New Haven, Conn., March 17, 1925. Started theatre business as usher for Loew's Theatres, 1940. U.S. Army, 1943–46. Returned Loew's Theatres managerial positions New Haven and Hartford, Connecticut. MGM press representative, Minneapolis, Jacksonville, Atlanta, Dallas. General Manager, Trans-Texas Theatres, Dallas. President, Academy Theatres, Inc., Dallas. Promoted Championship Boxing, Dallas and Johannesburg, South Africa. Executive Vice President, Cobb Theatres, Birmingham, Alabama. Member of the President's Advisory Committee of NATO. Chairman of the Alabama Advertising Committee for NATO.

LEVINSON, RUTH POLOGE: Executive. b. N.Y., N.Y., Oct. 5. e. CCNY, NYU; public relations, Arthur P. Jacobs, 1957; adv. publ. dept. J. Arthur Rank to 1959; assistant national dir. of advertising, publ., and exploitation, American International Pictures to 1979 when established Ruth Pologe Levinson Group Public Relations & Marketing & Personal Management.

LEVITT, RUBY REBECCA: Set decorator. b. Corinth, N.Y., Sept. 10, 1907; e. Pratt Inst., Brooklyn. Buyer, interior decorator, department stores; store mgr.; set decorator, Universal, since 1944.
PICTURES INCLUDE: Letter From an Unknown Woman, Magnificent Obsession, The Shrike, Six Bridges to Cross, Private War of Major Benson, This Earth Is Mine, Pillow Talk, 40 Pounds of Trouble, For the Love of Money, Sound of Music, Willie Boy, The Scavengers, Colossus, Change of Habit, Andromeda Strain, Vanished, Happy Birthday,

Wanda June, The Other, Freebie and The Bean, The Manchn Eagle, Chinatown, Once Is Not Enough, Let's Do It Again, Harry and Walter Go To New York, A Star Is Born, New York-New York, Looking for Mr. Goodbar, The One The Only, Matilda, Promises in the Dark, The Jazz Singer.

TV: Mr. Ed, Addams Family, Double Life of Henry Phyffe, Movies of the Week, ABC, Banyon TV Series, Genesis II, Name of the Game, Love Story, Having Babies, Return Engagement.

Staff Decorator for television commercials, Filmways of California, Inc. Staff of Filmways of Calif., 1966. Universal Studios, 1968.

LEVY, BERNARD: Executive. b. Jacksonville, Florida. e. Brooklyn Law School, L.L.B. Legal staff of Superintendent of Insurance of the State of New York in the rehabilitation and liquidation of guaranteed title and mortgage companies, 1934–36; private practice of law, 1936–46; legal staff, Paramount Pictures, Inc., 1946–50; legal staff, United Paramount Theatres, 1950–51; exec. asst. to Edward L. Hyman, vice-pres., American Broadcasting Companies, Inc., in chg. of theatre administration, north, 1951–62; apptd. exec. liaison officer for southern motion picture theatres, ABC, Inc., 1962–64; exec. liaison officer, m.p. theas., ABC, Inc., 1965–72; vice pres., ABC Theatre Division, 1973. Retired, 1976.

LEVY, BUD: Executive. b. Jackson Heights, N.Y. April 3, 1928. e. New York Univ. Exec. v.p. Trans-Lux Corp., N.Y. Member: Variety Clubs Int'l., M.P. Pioneers, bd. of Indep. Theatres Owners Ass'n.; dir., Trans-Lux Corp.; New York area chm., Will Rogers Memorial Fund; Member, President's Advisory Board-NATO; director: NATO, TOP, CATO. Elected pres., Trans-Lux Corp., 1980.

LEVY, DAVID: Executive. b. Philadelphia, Pa., January 2, 1913; e. Wharton, U. of Pa.; exec. v.p., Four Star International, Inc. As v.p. & assoc. dir., Young & Rubicam. Inc., 1938–59, acquisitions for clients include: Father Knows Best, Goodyear Playhouse, Life of Riley, Gunsmoke. Was v.p. in charge of network TV programs & talent, NBC, 1959–61.

TV: Bonanza, Dr. Kildare, Dick Powell Show, Saturday Night at the Movies, Bat Masterson, Klondike, Americans, Outlaws, The Addams Family, Double Life of Henry Phyffe, The Chameleons, The Gods of Foxcroft Carbor House, as well as numerous TV plays.

LEVY, HERMAN M.: Attorney, New Haven, Conn. b. New Haven, Conn., Sept. 27, 1904; e. Yale, B.A, '27, Yale Law School, LL.B., '29; Phi Beta Kappa, was in legal dept. RCA Photophone; newspaper reporter; admitted to Connecticut bar, 1929. In 1939 elected exec. secy. of MPTO of Connecticut. In 1943: Elected general counsel MPTOA. Elected gen. counsel, Theatre Owners of America, 1947–63. Pres., New Haven County Bar Assn., 1964; legislative agent, Conn. Assn. of Theatre Owners.

AUTHOR: More Sinned Against . . . Natl. Bd. of Review Magazine, 1941. Proving the Death of a Non-Resident Alien, Conn. Bar Journal, 1950; Need for a System of Arbitration M.P. Ind., Arbitration Journal, 1950; reprint of Industry Case Digest, 20th Century-Fox vs. Boehm in the Journal (Screen Producers Guild); Book Review of Antitrust in the Motion Picture Industry, by Michael Conant (Univ. of Calif. Law Review).

LEVY, JULES V.: Producer. b. Los Angeles, Calif., Feb. 12, 1923; e. U.S.C. Property dept., W.B., 1941; Army Air Force, 1942–45.

PICTURES INCLUDE: The Vampire, Return of Dracula, Vice Squad, Without Warning, Down Three Dark Streets, Geronimo, Glory Guys, Clambake, Scalphunters, Sam Whiskey, Underground, McKenzie Break, The Hunting Party, The Honkers', McQ, Brannigan, White Lightning, Gator, Kansas City Bomber, Rally.

TV: Rifleman, Robert Taylor's Detectives, Law of the Plainsman, The Big Valley.

LEVY, NORMAN: Executive. b. Bronx, New York, Jan. 3, 1935. e. City College. In 1957 joined Universal Pictures, holding various sales positions; 1967, went to National General Pictures, ultimately being named v.p. and exec. asst. to pres.; 1974, Columbia Pictures, v.p., gen. sls. mgr. In 1975 named Columbia exec. v.p. in chg. of domestic sls.; 1977, exec. v.p., mktg; 1978. pres., Columbia Pictures Domestic Distribution. In 1980 joined 20th-Fox as pres. of Entertainment Group.

LEVY, ROBERT S.: Producer. b. New York, N.Y. Dec. 15, 1932; e. Columbia U., 1951–55, BA; mgt. consultant, Ernest L. Loen & Assoc., 1955–63; bd. of dir. American Marketing Assoc., 1960–61; v.p., 1963; prod. Lullaby, 1963; pres. Pebble Productions, prod., A Comedy Tale of Fanny Hill; assoc. prod., The Todd Killings, 1971; assoc. prod., Some Call It Loving, 1975.

LEWINE, ROBERT F.: Executive. b. New York, N.Y., Apr. 16, 1913; e. Swarthmore Coll. Worked for restaurant chain, in real estate; U.S. Navy, 1942; creative staff, Cine-Television Studios, Inc.; v.p. in charge of oper., 1946; formed own co., 1947, for prod. of TV comm., industrial m.p.; also eastern rep., Dudley Films; radio-TV dir., Hirshon-Garfield, Inc., 1953; eastern prog. dir., ABC, 1953; dir., ABC-TV network prog. dept., 1954; v.p. in charge of programming and talent ABC-TV network, 1956; v.p., NBC, prog. dept. chg. nighttime programming, 1957; v.p. network programs, 1958; v.p. Figaro, Inc., 1958; v.p. programs, CBS Films, 1959; v.p. programs, Hollywood CBS Television Network, Apr., 1962; officer Acad. TV Arts & Sciences from 1954, Exec. comm., dir., Acad. TV Arts & Sciences. Pres., N.Y. Chapter 1959; nat'l. pres., 1961; nat'l. trustee, 1961–63; National pres., Academy TV Arts & Sciences, 1961–63; first vice pres., dir., Academy TV Arts & Sciences Foundation; pres., 1964; exec. v.p., Creative Management Associates Ltd.; v.p., Warner Bros., TV Pres. Nat'l Acad. of Television Arts and Sciences; trustee, Columbia College, L.A., Calif.; trustee, American Women in Radio and Television Foundation. 1977-NBC Television Network, exec. prod. dir.; chairman, PAW Society (Preservation of Animal Wildlife); Member International Advisory Council, Population Institute; Chairman of the Board, Riverside Broadcasting Company.

LEWIS, ARTHUR: Producer—Director—Writer. b. New York City. e. Univ. of So. Calif. and Yale. Began career as writer and assoc. prod. on the Jones Family TV series. Five years in U.S. Army; returned to screenwriting before producing Three Wishes for Jamie on Broadway and producing and directing Guys and Dolls in London's West End. In mid-60s produced plays with Bernard Delfont at Shaftesbury Theatre in London.

PICTURES: Producer: Loot, Baxter, The Killer Elite, Brass Target.

TELEVISION: Brenner, The Asphalt Jungle (prod.writer).

LEWIS, BERNARD: Executive. b. Brooklyn, N.Y., May 18, 1912. e. Bklyn Coll., N.Y.U. Reporter, feature writer, Bklyn. Daily Eagle, 1935-37; A.P., 1937-40; pub. dept., Paramount, 1940-44; spec. events dir., then asst. to dir. of adv., 20th-Fox, 1944-46; first pub. mgr. then exploit., prom. mgr., I.F.E., 1952-55; adv. pub. dir., Kingsley International Pictures, 1956-60; own pub. rel. org., The Bernard Lewis Company, 1960 to present. Lecturer at N.Y.U. on motion pictures.

LEWIS, CLAUDE P. JR.: Executive. b. Hutchinson, Kans., e. Howard U.; NYU, B.A., 1949. adv. dept., 20th Century-Fox, 1950; staff copywriter, 1951; copy chief, 1962; asst. adv. mgr., 1966; adv. mgr.; div. of adv., East Coast, 1979.

LEWIS, DAVID: Executive. b. Mass. e. N.Y.U.; ent. m.p. ind., 1925; with MGM in Paris, Madrid, Lisbon; mgr., Central America MGM. 1930; mgr., Cuba: mgr. Japan; Argentina, 1937; Brazil, 1939; since 1945 in Europe, headquarters Paris; vice pres., MGM. International and Regional dir. for Europe. 1968, pres. Two World Enterprises.

LEWIS, EDWARD: Producer. Began entertainment career as script writer, then co-produced The Admiral Was a Lady and teamed with Marion Parsonnet to bring the Faye Emerson Show to TV. Subsequently prod. first Schlitz Playhouse and China Smith series. Was v.p. of Kirk Douglas' indep. prod. co., where was assoc. prod. and writer-prod. Collaborated with John Frankenheimer on 8 films.

PICTURES INCLUDE: Lizzie (assoc. prod.), The Careless Years (prod., s.p.), Spartacus, The Last Sunset, Lonely Are the Brave, The List of Adrian Messenger, Seconds, Grand Prix, The Fixer (exec. prod.), The Gypsy Moths (exec.), I Walk the Line (exec.), The Horsemen, The Iceman Cometh (exec.).

LEWIS, HAROLD G.: Executive. b. New York City, Sept. 18, 1938. e. Union College; graduated 1960, electrical engineer. Joined ATA Trading Corp. in 1960 and has been pres. since 1977. Producer of feature animation. Importer and exporter for theatrical and TV features, documentaries, series, classics, etc.

LEWIS, JERRY: Actor. b. Newark, N.J., Mar. 16, 1926. e. Irvington H.S. m. Patti Palmer, vocalist, Jimmy Dorsey & Ted Florita bands; has six sons. Began his career in school theatricals, at 14, earned plaque by American Red Cross for amateur show, Mosque Theatre. Formed comedy-team with Dean Martin (singer, straight man) at 500 Club, Atlantic City, N.J., 1946; appeared Latin Casino, Phila., then other nightclubs, on NBC television; played many m.p. theatres; signed by Hal Wallis; team m.p. debut in My Friend Irma (see biog. Dean Martin). Voted Most Promising Male Star in Television in m.p. Daily's 2nd annual TV poll, 1950. Voted (as team) one of top ten money making stars in m.p. Herald-Fame poll, 1951, 1953–54–57. Number 1, 1952; best comedy team in m.p. Daily's 16th annual radio poll, 1951, 1952, 1953; 1956 formed Jerry Lewis Prods. Inc., functions as prod., dir., writer & star.

PICTURES INCLUDE: My Friend Irma Goes West, At War With the Army, That's My Boy, The Stooge, Sailor Beware, Jumping Jacks, The Caddy, Scared Stiff, Money From Home, Living It Up, Three Ring Circus, You're Never Too Young, Artists and Models, Pardners, Hollywood or Bust,

Delicate Delinquent, Sad Sack, Rock-A-Bye Baby, Geisha Boy, Don't Give Up the Ship, Visit to A Small Planet, Cinderfella, Bellboy, The Ladies Man, The Errand Boy, It's Only Money, The Nutty Professor, Who's Minding the Store?, The Patsy, The Disorderly Orderly, Boeing-Boeing, The Family Jewels, Three on a Couch, Way . . . Way Out, The Big Mouth, Don't Lower the Bridge Raise the River, Hook Line and Sinker, Which Way to the Front?, One More Time, Hardly Working (star, dir., co-s.p.).

LEWIS, JOSEPH H.: Director. b. New York, N.Y., Apr. 6. e. DeWitt Clinton H.S. Camera boy, MGM; then asst. film ed. in chge. film ed., Republic; dir. in chge. 2nd units; dir. Universal; U.S. Signal Corps., WW II; dir. RKO, Columbia, W.B.
PICTURES INCLUDE: My Name is Julia Ross, So Dark the Night, Jolson Story, The Swordsman, Return of October, Undercover Man, Gun Crazy, Lady Without Passport, Retreat Hell!, Desperate Search, Cry of the Hunted, Big Combo, A Lawless Street.
TV: Rifleman series, Barbara Stanwyck Show: The Big Valley.

LEWIS, JUDY: Actress. b. Los Angeles, Nov. 6, 1936. e. New York School of Interior Design, Duchesne Residence School, N.Y., Marymount School, L.A.; mother Loretta Young.
TV: The Outlaws, The Secret Storm, Policewoman, Apple's Way, Streets of San Francisco, FBI.
BROADWAY: Mary, Mary.

LEWIS, LESTER: talent rep. b. New York, N.Y. Sept. 12, 1912. e. H.S. of Commerce, N.Y. Pres. Lester Lewis Associates, Inc., talent agency.

LEWIS, MICHAEL J.: Composer. b. Wales, 1939. First film score 1968, The Mad Woman of Chaillot, won Ivor Novello Award for best film score. 1973: first Broadway musical, Cyrano, Grammy Nomination '74, Caesar & Cleopatra (T.V. '76).
PICTURES INCLUDE: The Man Who Haunted Himself, Julius Caesar. 1970: Upon This Rock,1971: Unman, Wittering and Zigo, Running Scared, Baxter, Theatre of Blood, 11 Harrowhouse, 92 In The Shade, Russian Roulette, The Stick-Up, The Medusa Touch, The Legacy, The Passage, The Unseen, Sphinx.

LEWIS, MONICA: Singer, actress. b. Chicago, Il., May 5. e. Hunter Coll., N.Y. p. Leon Lewis, concert pianist, former medical dr. CBS; Jessica Lewis, child star with Nazimova; member Ben Greet's Shakespearean players, sang leading roles. Chicago Opera Co.; now vocal teacher. Started career as radio singer, own show, WMCA, N.Y.; on Beat the Band, 1946; co-star Chesterfield program; sang leading role, Girl Crazy, Ford Sunday Evening Hour, Own program, Monica Makes Music; co-star Revere Camera show. Among first ten feminine singers in country on recording polls. Vocalist: Stork Club, Astor Roof, Copacabana, Persian Room.
PICTURES INCLUDE: Inside Straight, Excuse My Dust, The Strip, Everything I Have is Yours, Affair With a Stranger.

LEWIS, ROGER H.: Executive. b. New York, N.Y., Mar. 14, 1918. e. Lafayette Coll., Easton, Pa. 1939; postgrad. U.C.L.A., Columbia. Apprentice in adv. pub. dept. Warner, 1939; U.S. Army, WW II; spec. asst. to dir. of adv., pub. & exploit., 20th-Fox; v.p. creative dir. Monroe Greenthal Co.; adv. mgr. United Artists, 1952–55; nat'l dir. of adv. pub. and exploit, 1956; v.p. adv. pub. expl. 1959. Resigned June 1961 to enter independent film production. Exec. v.p. Garrick Films; prod. The Pawnbroker; TV script, The Defenders. Exec. Horizon Pictures; prod. The Swimmer; prod. exec. National General; script consultant, Universal-TV; prod. exec. W.B.; exec. producer, Shaft, 1971; Co-Producer, Shaft's Big Score, 1972; producer, Shaft in Africa, 1973. Now exec. v.p., Max Youngstein Enterprises.

LEWIS, TOM: Producer, b. Troy, N.Y. e. Union College, Schenectady, N.Y. m. Loretta Young, Prod. dir., Schenectady WTAM; prod. head Cleveland, 1934; prog. mgr. NBC Cleveland Div. 1935; radio prod.; Young and Rubicam, 1937; then radio supervisor, mgr. of radio dept. v.p. radio prod., Hollywood offices. Now v.p. stockholder, member of plan. bd., v.p. Audience Research, Inc., 1941; U.S. Army World War II; created and became commandant Armed Forces Radio Service; awarded Legion of Merit. Excellent Order of British Empire, degree of Honorary Office of His Majesty the King of England; Knight of Malta; introduced Aldrich Family on Kate Smith Hour, developed program's subsequent format; also assoc. with Screen Guild Theatre, Fred Allen Show, Jack Benny Show; prod. writer, Cause for Alarm, MGM. Pres. Lewislor Prod., prod. rewriter Loretta Young Show, 1953–55; v.p. and head of TV-Radio dept., C.J. LaRoche and Co., Inc., New York; dir. Nat. Soc. of TV prod.; dir. of Academy of TV Arts and Sciences, bd. of dir. Beverly Hills Hotel.

LEWIS, WYNDHAM O.B.E. (L.R.A.M., A.T.C.L.): Exhibitor. b. Briton Ferry, S. Wales, 1910. e. Neath Grammar School. Studied music at Royal Academy of Music; entered m.p. industry at Regal Marble Arch. 1929. Joined Odeon The-

atres 1937. Served as Flying Officer RAF, 1940–45; returned to take over as man. dir. West of England Cinemas and assoc. companies; now booking director of circuit of 9 cinemas. Justice of the Peace for the City of Cardiff. President Cinematograph Exhibitors Assoc., 1966–69.

LIBERACE: Performer, pianist, r.n. Wladziu Valentino Liberace. b. Milwaukee, Wis., May 16, 1920. e. Wisconsin College of Music. Guest soloist with Chicago Symphony at 16, then hotel, night club entertainer, concert and recording artist. Own TV shows since 1952; m.p. debut in Sincerely Yours.

LIBERMAN, FRANK P.: Publicist, b. N.Y., N.Y., May 29, 1917. e. Cheshire Acad., Conn. 1934; Lafayette College, Easton, Pa., B.A. 1938. m. Patricia Harris, casting dir. Worked as copy boy, NY Daily News, 1938–39. Began career as publicist at Warner Bros., home office as messenger, 1939, promoted to pressbooks dept., transferred to Warner's Chicago office as field exploitation man. U.S. Signal Corps, 1941, public relations officer, Army Pictorial Service, on temporary duty with War Dept., Bureau of Public Relations in Pentagon. Discharged as Capt., 1946. Rejoined Warner Bros. on coast 2 years, 1947, est. own public relations office. Owner, Frank Liberman and Associates, Inc.

LICCARDI, VINCENT G.: Executive. b. Brooklyn, N.Y., Started as messenger at Universal Pictures, adv. dept. handling co-operative adv. Universal, asst. adv. mgr. on Around the World in 80 Days, Michael Todd Co., asst. to exec. co-ord. of States & Adv. on Spartacus; National Exploit. Dir., Continental; National Dir. of Adv. & Publi., Continental; Nat. Dir. Adv. & Publi., Braintree Prod., adv. pub. mgr. Allied Artists, ad. mgr. Paramount, National Dir. Adv.-Pub., UMC Pictures, Screenwriter, Playboy to Priest, The Rivals, The Rivals-Part II, The Greatest Disaster of All Time, The Lady on the 9:40.

LIDER, EDWARD W. Executive. b. New Bedford, Mass., March 13, 1922. e. Dartmouth, Harvard Law. Served as attorney-at-law, 1948–50. President & treasurer, Fall River Theatres Corp. & Nathan Yamins Enterprises, 1950 to present; member of bd., Theatre Owners of New England; past pres., Theatre Owners of New England; past member of bd. & past treas., Allied States Assoc. of M.P. Exhibitors; general manager of Sonny & Eddy's Theatres in Boston: Exeter St., Academy, Harvard Square, Central Square, Allston C1nema-C2nema and Galeria Theatres.

LIEBER, PERRY W.: Publicist. b. Pleasant Prairie, Wis., June 1, 1905; e. U. of Illinois. Was in adv. dept. of J. P. Seaburg Co., Chicago, Ill. Pub. dept. RKO Radio Studio 1930; publ. dir. 1939; nat'l dir. pub., exploit. supv. N.Y. office, 1953–55. 20th Century-Fox pub. dept. 1956; in chg. studio adv. pub. dept., 20th Century Fox Studio, Aug. 1962. 1966 pub. dept. 20th Century-Fox. Mgr./P.R. Summa Corp. since 1970, Consultant, P.R., Summa Corp. since July, 1977.

LIEBERFARB, WARREN: Executive. e. Wharton School of Commerce and Finance, Univ. of Penna (BS, Economics); Univ. of Michigan (Master of Business Admin.). Started career in industry at Paramount Pictures as dir. of mktg. and exec. asst. to Stanley Jaffe, then pres. Later joined 20th-Fox as v.p.—special market dist. (cable, pay-TV, non-theatrical), also representing 20th in all MPAA matters on cable and pay/TV. Joined Warner Bros. as v.p., exec. asst. to Ted Ashley, bd. chm.; later named v.p., intl. adv-pub. In 1979 joined Lorimar as v.p., of Lorimar Productions, Inc., the parent company, based in New York. Promoted to snr. v.p.

LIEBERSON, SANDY: Executive. b. 1936. 1979, named pres. of 20th-Fox Productions, which company he joined in 1977 as v.p.—European production. Previously an independent producer (Performance, Bugsy Malone, Jabberwocky, etc.). Prior to that exec. in chg. of European operations of Creative Management Associates. In 1980 named int'l. v.p. for Ladd Co., based in London.

LIEBLING, HOWARD: Executive. Began career in publicity with 20th-Fox in N.Y. as magazine contact, following which was N.Y. press repr. for Stanley Kramer, pub. mgr. for United Artists, and natl. pub. mgr. for MGM on West Coast. Rejoined Fox in July, 1975 as prod. pub. mgr.

LIEBMAN, MAX: Producer-director. m. Sonya; writer. Career in theatre; producer Tars and Spars for U.S. Coast Guard; discovered Danny Kaye, Sid Caesar, Betty Garrett, Jules Munshin, Imogene Coca, Mati and Hari, Jerome Robbins, etc.; prod.-dir. Your Show of Shows since 1949; prod. Bob Hope's TV debut and NBC series color spectaculars; also Max Liebman Presents. Look award for best prod., 1950–52; Emmy Awards 1951–52; U.S. Steel Specials 1960–61.

LIGHTMAN, M.A., JR.: Exhibitor. b. Nashville, Tenn., Apr. 21, 1915; e. Southwestern U., Vanderbilt U., 1936, B.A. bd. chmn. Malco Theatres, Inc., Memphis, Tenn.

LINDBLOM, GUNNEL: Actress-Director. b. Gothenburg, Sweden, 1931. Discovered by Ingmar Bergman while studying at drama school of Gothenburg Municipal Theatre (1950–

53); she moved to Malmo, where he was director of the local Municipal Theatre. Under Bergman's direction she played in Easter, Peer Gynt, Faust, etc. between 1954–59. Later appeared in many Bergman films. Since 1968 has been on staff of Stockholm's Royal Dramatic Theatre, assisting Bergman and then beginning to direct on her own. Made film debut as director with Summer Paradise in 1977.
PICTURES INCLUDE: Actress: The Seventh Seal, Wild Strawberries, The Virgin Spring, Winter Light, The Silence, Rapture, Loving Couples. Director: Summer Paradise.

LINDEN, HAL: Actor. b. Bronx, N.Y., March 20. e. City College New York. Began career as saxophone player and singer, playing with bands of Sammy Kaye, Bobby Sherwood, etc. Drafted and performed in revues for Special Services. After discharge enrolled at N.Y.'s American Theatre Wing; appeared on Bdwy. in Bells Are Ringing, replacing Sydney Chaplin. On many TV talk and variety shows.
THEATRE: On a Clear Day, Wildcat, Something More, Subways Are for Sleeping, Ilya Darling, Apple Tree, Three Men on a Horse, Pajama Game, The Rothschilds.
TELEVISION: Host on ABC series, Animals Animals Animals; Barney Miller.
PICTURE: When You Comin' Back Red Ryder?

LINDFORS, VIVECA: Actress. b. Uppsala, Sweden, Dec., 1920; e. Royal Dramatic School, Stockholm. Stage debut in Ann-Scofi Hedvig school prod. Screen debut in The Crazy Family, 1941; reached stardom in If I Should Marry the Minister. U.S. screen debut in Night Unto Night.
PICTURES INCLUDE: Adventures of Don Juan, Dark City, Flying Missile, Gypsy Fury, No Sad Songs For Me, Journey Into Light, Four In a Jeep, The Raiders, No Time for Flowers, Run for Cover, Captain Dreyfus, Coming Apart, Puzzle of a Downfall Child, The Way We Were, Welcome to L.A., Girl Friends, A Wedding, Voices, The Hand.

LINDNER, TERRELL M.: Executive. b. Dromana, Australia. Aug. 10, 1915. Entered m.p. ind. in pub. dep. Columbia Pictures, Melbourne, Australia, 1942. Columbia mgr. Western Australia, Dec. 1946. gen. mgr. Columbia, New Zealand, 1948. United Artists home office rep. for India, Burma, Pakistan, Ceylon, 1952. apptd. United Artists dist. supvr. for Southeast Asia. hdqts. Bombay. Dec. 1953. Rank overseas. 1957. Opened West Indies offices. man. dir. Rank Filmes do Brasil, 1958. man. dir. Filmcenter Internacional Ltda., Brazil, (successors Rank) 1970.

LINKLETTER, ART: Emcee, prod. b. Moose Jaw, Saskatchewan, Canada, July 17, 1912. e. San Diego State Coll. Radio prg. mgr., San Diego Exposition, 1935; radio pgm. mgr. S.F. World's Fair, 1937–39; freelance radio ann. and m.c. 1939–42; m.c. People are Funny since 1942. Starred Inside Beverly Hills, NBC-TV, 1955; exec. prod. host, NBC-TV spec. Salute to Baseball, 1956; host, Art Linkletter's Secret World of Kids, NBC-TV's Ford Startime, 1959; 1969 House Party series became the Linkletter Show.
Author of: The Secret World of Kids, 1959, Kids Say the Darndest Things, 1957, Linkletter Down Under, 1969, Yes, You Can, 1979.

LINSON, ART: Producer-Director. b. Chicago. e. UCLA. Was rock music manager before turning to film production. Debuted as director also with Where the Buffalo Roam.
PICTURES INCLUDE: Rafferty and the Gold Dust Twins, (co.-prod.), Wash, American Hot Wax (also co-s.p.), Melvin and Howard.

LIPPERT, ROBERT J., JR.: Producer. director, film editor. b. Alameda, Calif. Feb. 28, 1928. e. St Mary's College 1946; all conference Football 1947. Film Editor of 65 motion pictures. Produced and directed nine pictures for Lippert Pictures and 20th Century Fox. Present position is president, for Lippert Theatres headquartered in San Francisco.

LIPSTONE, HOWARD H.: Executive. producer. b. Chicago, Ill., Apr. 28. e. UCLA, Univ. of So. Calif. Ass't to gen. mgr. at KLTA, 1950–55; program dir. at KABC-TV, 1955–65; exec. ass't to pres. at Selmur Prods., ABC subsidiary, 1965–69. Ivan Tors Films & Studios as exec. v.p., 1969–70; pres., Alan Landsburg Prods., 1970 to present.

LIPTON, DAVID A.: Executive. b. Chicago, Nov. 6, 1906. U.S. Army, WW II. Entered m.p. ind. 1921 as office boy, Balaban & Katz, Chicago; in 1922 joined pub. dept.; in 1929 transf. Detroit; in 1930 joined Famous Players Canadian Corp., org. pub. dept.; ret'd to Chicago office 1931; res. 1933 to become publ. dir. for Sally Rand. In 1937 joined CBS, N.Y. as press relations counsel. Named publ. dir. Universal N.Y., 1938; later to West Coast as studio publ. dir. In 1941 to N.Y. as dir. adv. publ. & exploit.; Columbia; returned to Universal as exec. coordinator of adv. & promotion, 1946; nat'l dir. adv. pub., Jan. 1949; elected v.p. in chge. adv. pub.; 1974, MCA Discovision, Inc., public relations director.

LISTER, MOIRA: Actress. b. Capetown, So. Africa. e. Holy Family Convent, Johannesburg. Stage debut at 6 yrs. of age in Vikings of Heligoland; screen debut in Shipbuilders, 1943. Numerous TV appearances.
PICTURES INCLUDE: Love Story, Wanted for Murder, Don Chicago, Uneasy Terms, So Evil My Love, Another Shore, Once a Jolly Swagman, Run for Your Money, Pool of London, White Corridors, Something Money Can't Buy, Cruel Sea, Grand National Night, Limping Man, Trouble in Store, John and Julie, Deep Blue Sea, Seven Waves Away, The Yellow Rolls Royce, Joey Boy, Double Man, Stranger in the House.

LITTO, GEORGE: Executive. b. Philadelphia, Dec. 9, 1930. e. Temple Univ. Joined William Morris Agency in New York and then became indep. literary agent. Opened own office in Hollywood, 1962. Packaged film and TV productions, including six films for Robert Altman. 1981, named chmn. bd. & CEO, Filmways.
PICTURES INCLUDE: That Cold Day in the Park, M*A*S*H, McCabe and Mrs. Miller, Images, Brewster McCloud, Thieves Like Us (debut as exec. prod.), Drive-In (exec. prod.), Dressed To Kill (prod.). Blow Out (prod.). TV: Hawaii Five-O.

LITVINOFF, SI: Producer. b. New York City, April 5, 1929. e. Adelphi College (A.B.); NYU School of Law (LLB). Theatrical lawyer, personal and business manager in New York until 1967 when left firm of Barovick, Konecky & Litvinoff to produce plays and films.
PICTURES: The Queen, All the Right Noises, Walkabout, A Clockwork Orange (exec. prod.), Glastonbury Fayre (exec. in chg. prod.); The Man Who Fell to Earth (exec. prod.).
STAGE: Leonard Bernstein's Theatre Songs, Cry of the Raindrop, Girl of the Golden West, Little Malcolm and His Struggle Against the Eunuchs, I and Albert (London).

LIVINGSTON, BLANCHE: Advertising and publicity. b. New York City. e. Columbia University. m. Albert Levi. Began with trade paper, handled publicity for Fox Theatres in Manhattan and Brooklyn. Joined RKO Theatres publicity dept.; became nat'l. dir. adv.-pub., RKO Stanley-Warner theatres. Past secretary and v.p. AMPA. Retired July, 1977.

LIVINGSTON, JAY: Comp. & Lyric. b. McDonald, Pa., March 28, 1915; e. U. Pa., 1937, UCLA, 1964–65, Army, World War II. Accompanist and arranger for various NBC singers and singing groups 1940–42, N.Y.; author music and special material for Olsen & Johnson, including various editions of Hellzapoppin, and Sons O'Fun; began composing picture songs, 1944. Under contract to Paramount, 1945–55; then free lance. Composed songs for over 100 films.
SONG HITS INCLUDE: G'bye Now, Stuff Like That There, To Each His Own, Golden Earrings, Silver Bells, Buttons and Bows (Acad. Award, 1949), Mona Lisa (Acad. Award, 1951), Que Sera Sera (Acad. Award, 1957), Tammy (Acad. nom.), Almost In Your Arms (Acad. nom.), Bonanza (TV Theme), Mister Ed (TV Theme), Dear Heart, (Acad. nom.), Wish Me a Rainbow, In the Arms of Love, Never Let Me Go, As I Love You, All the Time, Maybe September, Collab. music and lyrics for B'way show Oh Captain! 1958; Let It Ride, 1961. Two songs for Sugar Babies, 1980.
PICTURES INCLUDE: The Paleface, Fancy Pants, The Lemon-Drop Kid, Houseboat, Tammy and the Bachelor, The Man Who Knew Too Much, Dear Heart, The Night of the Grizzly, This Property is Condemned, The Oscar, Never Too Late, Harlow, What Did You Do In The War Daddy?, Wait Until Dark, Red Garters, Sorrowful Jones.

LIVINGSTON, JEFFERSON: Advertising executive. With MGM as pub., 1937–42; U.S. Army Air Force, 1943–45. Joined J. Arthur Rank Org., 1946 and loaned to U.A. for roadshow release of Henry V. Joined Universal, 1947, charge road show and promotion, Hamlet, etc. In charge adv. & pub. J. Arthur Rank prod., released through U-1, 1950; apptd. Eastern adv. mgr. Universal, 1951; U-1. exec. coord. sales, adv. 1959; v.p., & dir. of adv. & publicity, Mirisch Company, 1962; exec. v.p., Harold Robbins International, 1972.

LIVINGSTONE, PERCY: Executive. b. Leeds, England, 1913. e. City of Leeds School, School of Accountancy. Entered m.p. industry Aug. 1931 in clerical capacity with old Fox Company. Joined sales force 3 years later; appointed Dublin Branch Manager, 1939; attached to Head Office, 1945 southern district mgr.; 1948; assistant sales mgr., 1951; sales mgr., 1956; dir. of sales, 1957; bd. member; gen. sales mgr. Warner-Pathe Dist., 1959; man. dir. 20th Century-Fox, 1961; 20th Cent.-Fox Inter'l, N.Y., 1967; sr., v.p., 20th-Fox Intl. Corp., 1975; Chrm. 20th-Fox Film Co. Ltd. 1977; Chrm., 20th-Fox Productions Ltd.

LLOYD, EUAN: Producer. b. Rugby (Warwick), Dec. 6, 1923. e. Rugby. Entered m.p. ind. in 1939 as theatre manager, then pub. dir.; dir. of Publ. Rank, 1946; joined Associated British-Pathe, Ltd. in same capacity; 1952 asst. to prod., Warwick Film Prod. Ltd. v.p. Highroad Productions, 1962–64. Rep. Europe Goldwyn's Porgy & Bess 1959.
PICTURES INCLUDE: April in Portugal, Heart of Variety, Invitation to Monte Carlo, The Secret Ways, Genghis Khan, Poppy Is Also A Flower, Murderer's Row, Shalako, Catlow,

The Man Called Noon, Paper Tiger, The Wild Geese, The Sea Wolves.

LLOYD, NORMAN: Producer. b. Jersey City, N.J., Nov. 8, 1914. e. N.Y.U., 1932. Acted on B'wy in: Noah, Liberty Jones, Everywhere I Roam, 1935–44; in various stock companies.
PICTURES INCLUDE: (actor) Spellbound, The Southerner, Green Years, Limelight. Prod. asst. on Arch of Triumph and The Red Pony, 1946. Assoc. prod. on The Alfred Hitchcock Show, 1957 (TV) and exec. prod. 1963. Also prod. of Up Above the World, Universal feature film; prod. of TV package deal, 2 hr. film.
STAGE: The Cocktail Party, The Lady's Not for Burning, Madame Will You Walk, The Golden Apple.

LO BIANCO, TONY: Actor. Has performed on N.Y. stage as well as in films and TV. Won Obie Award for performance in Yanks 3, Detroit 0, Top of the Seventh. Also acted on stage in The Office, The Rose Tattoo, The Royal Hunt of the Sun, etc.
PICTURES INCLUDE: The French Connection, The Honeymoon Killers, F.I.S.T., Bloodbrothers.

LOCKE, SONDRA: Actress. Debut in The Heart Is a Lonely Hunter (1968).
PICTURES: The Second Coming of Suzanne, Willard, A Reflection of Fear, The Outlaw—Josey Wales, The Gauntlet, Every Which Way But Loose, Bronco Billy, Any Which Way You Can.

LOCKHART, JUNE: Actress. p. Gene and Kathleen Lockhart. On TV in Lassie series.
PICTURES INCLUDE: All This and Heaven Too (1940, Warner Bros.), Sergeant York, Miss Annie Rooney (1942, United Artists), Meet Me in St. Louis, Son of Lassie, White Cliffs of Dover, Keep Your Powder Dry, Bury Me Dead, T-Men, It's a Joke, Son, Time Limit.

LOCKWOOD, GARY: Actor. b. Van Nuys, Calif., 1937. Began in Hollywood as stuntman.
PICTURES INCLUDE: Tall Story, Splendor in the Grass, Wild in the Country, The Magic Sword, It Happened at the World's Fair, Firecreek, 2001: A Space Odyssey, They Came to Rob Las Vegas, Model Shop, The Body, R.P.M., Stand Up and be Counted.

LOCKWOOD, JULIA: Actress. b. Bournemouth, Enl., Aug. 23, 1941, daughter of Margaret Lockwood. M.P. debut in Hungry Hill, 1946. Stage and TV debut, 1953.
PICTURES INCLUDE: I Have a Teenage Daughter, Please Turn Over, No Kidding.
STAGE: Alice in Wonderland, Goldilocks, Peter Pan, Servant of Two Masters, Birds on the Wing, Jockey Club Stakes, The Mating Game, Out On A Limb, Sextet.
TV: Royalty and Life With Father series, Your Obedient Servant, The Exam, Six Proud Walkers, Compact, The Flying Swan, Birds on the Wing.

LOCKWOOD, MARGARET: Actress. b. Karachi, Pakistan, Sept. 15, 1916. e. R.A.D.A. Stage experience; pictures, from 1935. Voted one of the top ten British money-making stars in Motion Picture Herald-Fame Poll, in 7 successive years, 1944–50; top actress, 1946; won National Film Award, 1946, 1947, 1949. London stage, 1954.
PICTURES INCLUDE: Wild Justice, Lorna Doone, Midshipman Easy, Amateur Gentleman, Beloved Vagabond, Street Singer, Bank Holiday, Lady Vanishes, Rulers of the Sea, Stars Look Down, Night Train, Two on a Weekend, Quiet Wedding, Girl in the News, Alibi, Man in Grey, Love Story, Place of One's Own, I'll Be Your Sweetheart, Wicked Lady, Bedelia, Hungry Hill, Jassy, The Bad Sister, Madness tf the Heart, Highly Dangerous, Trent's Last Case, Laughing Anne, Trouble in the Glen, Cast a Dark Shadow, Spiders Web, The Slipper & The Rose.
LONDON STAGE: Subway In the Sky, Suddenly It's Spring, Signpost to Murder, An Ideal Husband, The Others, On a Foggy Day, Lady Frederick, Relative Valves (1973), Double Edge.
TV: Last of Mrs. Cheyney, Murder Mistaken, Call It a Day, The Great Adventure, The Royalty, Your Obedient Servant, That Lady, Yorky, Palace of Strangers, The Human Jungle (series), The Flying Swan, Justice Is a Woman, Five Finger Exercise (1971), Justice series (1972–74).

LOCKWOOD, ROGER: Executive. b. Middletown, Conn., June 7, 1936. e. Ohio Wesleyan Univ. Sports writer for Akron Beacon Journal, 1960–62. On executive staff of Lockwood & Gordon Theatres; exec. v.p. SBC Theatres, 1969–73. In 1974 asst. to exec. v.p., General Cinema Corp. In 1975 formed Lockwood/Friedman Film Corp., buying-booking and distribution organization. Pres., Theatre Owners of New England, 1971–72; pres., Young NATO 1965–67; bd. of dir. NATO, 1962-present; pres., Jimmy Fund; present; 1979–80, Variety Club of New England, pres.

LOEFFLER, LOUIS: Film editor, with 20th-Fox many years.
PICTURES INCLUDE: 4 Men & a Prayer, Rose of Washington Square, Swanee River, Forever Amber, Iron Curtain, Call Me Mister, We're Not Married, My Cousin Rachel,

Titanic, How to Marry a Millionaire, Women's World, Man with the Golden Arm, Tall Men.

LOEWE, FREDERICK: Composer. b. Vienna June 10, 1904. Studied piano at Stern Conservatory; at 13 was youngest solo pianist to appear with Berlin Symphony Orchestra. Came to U.S. in 1924; played organ at Keith Albee's, Brooklyn. Became partner with Alan Jan Lerner for series of stage musicals, many of them filmed.
PICTURES INCLUDE: Brigadoon, Paint Your Wagon, My Fair Lady, Gigi, Camelot, The Little Prince.

LOGAN, JIMMY: Com., exhib. b. Glasgow, Scotland, 1928. p. Jack Short, May Dalziel, vaudeville act. Started as asst. theatre manager. On stage in vaudeville with the Logan Family. Began in radio in It's All Yours, weekly series on Scottish BBC. Joined Howard & Wyndham Ltd. as principal comedian in pantomime and summer revue. Televised in network shows from London and Glasgow. Appeared in Royal Variety Performance at Palladium, London, Nov. 1957; Scottish Royal Variety Performance, 1958. Starred in film, Floodtide; promoted stage comedy, Wedding Fever, 1962, 1964; chmn. Logan Theatres Ltd., 1964.
TV: Own series BBC-TV; Jimmy Logan Entertains, The Jimmy Logan Show series.

LOGAN, JOSHUA: Director, writer, producer. b. Texarkana, Tex., Oct. 5, 1908; e. Princeton U., Moscow Art Theatre.
STAGE: Camille, On Borrowed Time, I Married an Angel, Knickerbocker Holiday, Star in Your Eyes, Morning's at Seven, Charley's Aunt, By Jupiter, Happy Birthday, John Loves Mary, South Pacific, Mister Roberts, Wish You Were Here, Picnic, Fanny.
PICTURES INCLUDE: Garden of Allah, History is Made at Night, I Met My Love Again, Mister Roberts (collab.), Picnic, Fanny, Camelot, Paint Your Wagon.

LOLLOBRIGIDA, GINA: Actress. b. Subiaco, Italy, 1928. e. Acad. of Fine Arts, Rome, m.p. debut (Italy) in Love of a Clown.
PICTURES INCLUDE: The City Defends Itself, The White Line, Fanfan the Tulip, Times Gone By, Beat the Devil, Crossed Swords, The Great Game, Beauties of the Night, Wayward Wife, Bread Love and Dreams, Bread Love and Jealousy, Young Caruso, World's Most Beautiful Woman, Trapeze, Hunchback of Notre Dame, Solomon and Sheba, Never So Few, Go Naked in the World, Come September, Imperial Venus, Woman of Straw, That Splendid November, Hotel Paradisio, Buona Sera, Mrs. Campbell, Bambole, Plucked.

LOM, HERBERT: Actor. b. Prague. e. Prague U. Stage training London Embassy, Old Vic—Sadlers Wells and Westminster Schools. First British Picture 1941 (Mein Kampf—My Crimes); on TV, The Human Jungle Series.
PICTURES INCLUDE: Tomorrow We Live, Secret Mission, Young Mr. Pitt, Dark Tower, Cage of Gold, Whispering Smith vs. Scotland Yard, Two on the Tiles, Mr. Denning Drives North, Hell is Sold Out, Gaunt Stranger, Rough Shoot, The Net, The Love Lottery, Star of India, Beautiful Stranger, The Ladykillers, War and Peace Action, Fire Down Below, Hell's Drives, Chase a Crooked Shadow, Passport to Shame, Roots of Heaven, The Big Fisherman, North-West Frontier, I Aim at the Stars, Spartacus, Mysterious Island, Mr. Topaz, The Frightened City, El Cid, Tiara Tahiti, The Phantom of the Opera, Horse Without a Head, A Shot in the Dark, Uncle Tom's Cabin, Return From the Ashes, Gambit, The Assignment, Three Faces of Eve, Villa Rides, Doppelganger, Mr. Jericho, Dorian, Mark of the Devil, Count Dracula, Murders in the Rue Morgue, Dark Places, Death in Persepolis, Return of the Pink Panther, The Pink Panther Strikes Again, Charleston, Revenge of the Pink Panther, The Man with Bogarts' Face, Hopscotch, The Acts of Peter and Paul.

LOMBARDO, GOFFREDO: Executive. b. Naples, Italy, May 13, 1920. President Titanus Films.
PICTURES INCLUDE: Rocco and His Brothers, Sodom and Gomorrah, The Leopard, Four Days of Naples.

LOMITA, SOLOMON: Executive. b. New York City, April 23, 1937. Entire industry career with United Artists Corp. as follows: adm., intl. dept., 1962; asst., intl. sales, same year. 1963, asst. intl. print mgr.; 1965, intl., print mgr. In 1973 appt. dir. of film services. 1981, v.p., film services.

LONDON, JULIE: Singer-Actress. b. Santa Rosa, Calif., Sept. 26, 1926. r.n. Julie Peck. Launched as actress by agent Sue Carol (wife of Alan Ladd) who arranged screen test, followed by contract for 6 films. As singer has appeared in nightclubs and recorded.
PICTURES INCLUDE: The Red House, The Fat Man, The Great Man, Saddle the Wind, Man of the West, The Third Voice.
TELEVISION: Perry Como Show, Steve Allen Show, Ed Sullivan Show, Emergency (series).

LONDON, MILTON H.: Exhibitor. b. Detroit, Mich., Jan. 12, 1916. e. U. of Mich. BA, 1937. Wayne U. Law School, 1938. Theatre owner since 1937. U.S. Army 1943–46. Invented Ticograph system of positive admissions control for theatres, 1950; pres. Theatre Control Corp., 1950–62; secy-treas. Co-op. Theas. of Michigan Inc., 1956–63; exec. comm., Council of M.P. Organizations, 1957–66; dir. M.P. Investors, 1960–67; exec. dir. Allied States Assoc. of M.P. Exhib., 1961–1966; exec. dir. National Assoc. of Theatre Owners, 1966–1969 pres., NATO of Michigan, 1954–74; pres. Metropolitan Exhibitors, Inc., adv. & pub. rel. Mich. State Fire Safety Bd., Chief Barker, Variety Club of Detroit, Tent No. 5. 1975–76; Life Patron, Variety Clubs International; Mich. Chairman, Motion Picture Pioneers.

LONERGAN, ARTHUR: Art director. b. New York City, Jan. 23, 1906. e. Columbia U. Instructor in history of architecture, NYU; architect with N.Y. School of Decoration and Design; joined MGM as illustrator in art dept., 1938; free-lance art dir., 1945; pres. Soc. of M.P. Art Dir., 1952–54; Acad. Award nomination, art. dir., The Oscar. 1975-The Georges Melies Award for outstanding cinematic achievement for art direction in Science Fiction category.
TV: Loretta Young show, The Falcon, Mr. and Mrs. North, Topper, Life of Riley, Adventures of Hiram Holiday, Hitchcock Presents, GE Theatre, M. Squad, Restless Gun. etc.
PICTURES INCLUDE: Song in My Heart, Intrigue, Tender Years, Maneaters of Kumaon, Pitfall, Outpost in Morocco, Ride Vaquero, The Actress, It's Always Fair Weather, Tender Trap, Ransom, Forbidden Planet, On the Double, My Geisha, Who's Got the Action, Papa's Delicate Condition, A New Kind of Love, Who's Sleeping in My Bed, Robinson Caruso On Mars, Tickle Me, Red Line 7000, The Caper of the Golden Bull, Yours Mine and Ours, How Sweet It Is, Che, M*A*S*H*, Plaza Suite.

LONGSTREET, STEPHEN: Writer. b. New York City, April 18, 1907; e. Rutgers U.; Parsons Coll.; Rand Sch., London, B.A. Humorist, cartoonist (New Yorker, Collier's, etc.) 1930–37; ed. Free World Theat., radio plays; ed. film critic, Saturday Review of Literature, 1940, U.S. at War, Time 1942–43; writer for screen from 1942. On staff U.C.L.A. Elected pres. Los Angeles Art Assoc. 1970. 1974: appointed Prof. English Dep. Univ. of So. Calif. Modern Writing Course.
WRITINGS: Decade, The Golden Touch, The Gay Sisters, Last Man Around the World, Chico Goes to the Wars, Pedlocks, Lion at Mornino, Promoters, Boy in the Model T, Sometimes I Wonder, Wind at My Back, The Young Men of Paris, The Wilder Shore, War Cries on Horseback, Yoshiwara, Geishas and Courtesans, Canvas Falcons, Men and Planes of World War I, We All Went to Paris. New publications in 1973: Chicago 1860–1919, (show business & society), Divorcing (a novel); The General (novel, 1974), All Star Cast, 1977; The Queen Bees (1979).
STAGE: High Button Shoes.
PICTURES INCLUDE: The Gay Sisters, Golden Touch, Stallion Road, Jolson Story, Silver River, Helen Morgan Story, First Traveling Saleslady, Untamed Youth, Duel in the Sun, Greatest Show on Earth, Streets of Montmarte, The Crime, Uncle Harry, Rider on a Dead Horse.
TV: Cassey Jones Clipper Ship, Agent of Scotland Yard, m.c. author of The Sea, NBC; m.c. Press & Clergy, 1960–63; Viewpoint, CBS, 1963–65; series Boy in the Model T, Young Man From Boston, 1967, Blue and the Grey, Donald O'Connor Show, John J. Anthony talk shows, L.A. Guest; Art Linkletter Show, CBS Boutique, Writers Guild, Comm. of Public Relations. Film and Book critic for Readers' Syndicate since 1970. Professor performing arts dept. Univ. So. Calif. since 1973, where he is in 1979, presenting 12 great silent films, The Art & Entertainment of Silent Films in the cinema section of the college.

LONSDALE, PAMELA: Producer/director. Born Pinner, England. Entered TV 1960. m. Reginald Collin. Series include Tempo, Lion, Witch And Wardrobe, Smith, Ace of Wands. Rainbow, Shadows. 1975 Won British Academy Award—best childrens programme. 1979: exec. prod. Children's Drama Thames TV.

LOORAM, MARY HARDEN: Executive of National Catholic Office for Motion Pictures; (now U.S. Catholic Conference Division of Film Broadcasting) Chairman, International Federation of Catholic Alumnae M.P. Dept. (official reviewing group NCOMP). b. Brooklyn, N.Y. Chmn., M.P. Bureau 1926–52, asst. nat'l chmn. 4 yrs.; chmn. since 1932. Hon. deg. Fordham U. 1948. Member: Attorney General's Juvenile Delinquency Panel, Washington; White House Conference, 1950; Nat'l Catholic Theatre Conference; Honor: Pro Ecclesia et Pontifice, 1942. Member bd. dir. St. Joseph's College, Emmitsburg; Lady of the Holy Sepulchre, 1957; Sienna Medal (outstanding Catholic woman of the year), 1958; Lady Grand Cross, Holy Sepulchre, 1961; Woman of Achievement—Women's International Exposition, 1961. Nat'l Laymen's Award, 1968. Retired Aug. 1970 after 35 yrs. as an exec. mem. of Legion, NCOMP.

LOOS, ANITA: Writer. b. Sissons, Calif. Author novels & plays.
PICTURES INCLUDE: Gentlemen Prefer Blondes, New York Hat, Ex-Bad Boy, The Struggle, Midnight Mary; Hold Your Man, Lady of the Night, Red Headed Woman, Blondes of the Follies, Biography of Bachelor Girl, Girl from Missouri, Social Register, Riff Raff, San Francisco, Mama Steps

Out, Saratoga, The Women, Susan and God, They Met in Bombay, I Married an Angel.

LOOS, MARY: Writer. b. San Diego, Calif. May 6, 1914. e. Stanford U., 1933. Actress m.p.; in public relations field N.Y. 1938; jewelry designer for Paul Flato; author of novel Return in the Vineyard, 1945. secy. Voyager Films, Inc., literary exec. M. J. Frankovich Prod. Novel: The Beggars Are Coming, Bantam Books, 1974, Belinda, 1976; The Barstow Legend, 1978.
PICTURES INCLUDE: Rose Marie, Maytime, Crusades, Cleopatra, Mr. Belvedere Goes to College, Mother Was a Freshman, Ticket to Tomahawk, When Willie Comes Marching Home, Father Was a Fullback, I'll Get By, Meet Me After the Show, Let's Do It Again, The French Line, Gentlemen Marry Brunettes, Over-Exposed, Woman's World.

LORD, JACK: Actor-writer-artist-director. b. N.Y.C., Dec. 30, 1930. e. N.Y.U. (Chancellor Chase scholarship), B.S. Artist, represented in various museums including Metropolitan Museum of Art, Museum of Modern Art, Brooklyn Museum, in New York. Bibliotheque National, Paris; British Museum; Fogg Museum, Harvard University. St. Gandens Plaque for Fine Arts; creator of Tramp Ship, McAdoo, Yankee Trader, The Hunter TV series. On Bway in Traveling Lady (Theatre World Award), Cat on a Hot Tin Roof. Fame Award, new male star, 1963, mem. of Directors Guild of America.
PICTURES INCLUDE: Court Martial of Billy Mitchell, Williamsburg Story, Tip On a Dead Jockey, God's Little Acre, Man of the West, The Hangman, True Story of Lynn Stuart, Walk Like a Dragon, Doctor No, Doomsday Flight, Ride to Hangman's Tree, Counterfeit Killer.
TV: Leads on all networks, including Omnibus Constitution series, Playhouse 90, Goodyear Playhouse, Studio One, U.S. Steel, etc. (Film shows incl.) Have Gun Will Travel, Untouchables, Naked City, Rawhide, Bonanza, The Americans, Route 66, Gunsmoke, Stagecoach West, Dr. Kildare, Greatest Show on Earth, Combat, Chrysler Theatre, 12 O'Clock High, The Loner, Laredo, The FBI, The Invaders, The Fugitive, The Virginian, Man from UNCLE, High Chaparral, Ironside, Star of Stoney Burke and Hawaii Five-O series, also director of Death with Father, How to Steal a Masterpiece; Honor Is An Unmarked Grave, The Bells Toll At Noon, Top of the World, Why Won't Linda Die? Dir.: Who Says Cops Don't Cry? episodes of Hawaii Five-O. Creator, director, and exec. Producer of M Station: Hawaii (2-hr film for TV), 1979.

LORD, ROSEMARY: Actress—Writer. b. Born May 16; Taunton, Somerset England. Entered industry in 1965. After various theatre work did several television appearances: Softly, Softly; Spyder's Web; 30 Minute Theatre; Rivals of Sherlock Holmes; etc. Also TV & film work in France, Germany and Holland. Now living in Hollywood, writing for major publications in UK & USA, and developing television scripts. Member: British Equity, U.S. Equity, SAG, Publicists Guild.
PICTURES INCLUDE: Actress: The Whisperers, Dr. Jekyll & Sister Hyde, The Watchers, Touch of Class, Duchess and the Dirtwater Fox, Return from Witch Mountain.

LOREN, SOPHIA: Actress. b. Rome, Italy, Sept. 20, 1934. e. Naples. m.p. debut, 1952.
PICTURES INCLUDE: Africa Beneath the Seas, Village of the Bells, Good People's Sunday, Neapolitan Carousel, Day in the District Court, Pilgrim of Love, Aida, Two Nights with Cleopatra, Our Times, Attila, Scourge of God, Too Bad She's Bad, Pride and the Passion, Gold of Naples, Boy on a Dolphin, Scandal in Lorrinto, Miller's Beautiful Wife, Desire Under the Elms, Houseboat, The Black Ordeal, That Kind of Woman, Heller With a Gun, Anatomy of Love, Breath of Scandal, Heller in Pink Tights, Bay of Naples, Two Women, El Cid, Boccaccio 70, Il Coltello nello Piaga, French, The Fall of the Roman Empire, The Great Spy Mission, Lady L, Marriage Italian Style, Judith, Arabesque, The Countess from Hong Kong, Happily Ever After, More than a Miracle, Ghosts—Italian Style, Sunflower, The Priest's Wife, Lady Liberty, White Sister, Man of La Mancha, The Voyage, The Verdict, The Cassandra Crossing, A Special Day, Angela, Brass Target, Firepower.

LOSEY, JOSEPH: Director, writer, producer, teacher. Chevalier de l'Orde des Arts erdes Lettres (1957) Litterarum Humaniorum Doctorem (Darthmouth College 1973). b. La Crosse, Wis., Jan. 14, 1909. e. Dartmouth C., 1929, B.A.; Harvard Grad. Sch. of Arts & Sciences 1930. Play & book reviewer, N.Y. Times, N.Y. Herald-Tribune, theatre mags., Saturday Review of Literature, 1930–31. Stage mgr.; actor, expmt. N.Y. stage plays; for Theatre Guild, others, 1931–32; stage mgr. at opening of Radio City Music Hall, 1932; dir. & co-prod., Little Ol' Boy, Jayhawker, Galileo on Bdwy, among many others, also, Living Newspapers for Federal Theatre, N.Y.; became m.p. dir. in 1937. Documentary & comml. films (40) incl. A Child Went Forth (distrib. by State Dept.); Youth Gets a Break (Nat'l Youth Adminis.); Petroleum and His Cousins (New York World's

Fair, 1939); educational films (60) as dir. Rockefeller Foundation, Human Relations Commission Film Project; Gun in His Hand (Crime Doesn't Pay short subj.), The Boy With Green Hair, The Lawless, The Prowler, M, the Big Night, Encounter. To Britain in 1953; on London stage in: The Wooden Dish, A Night at the Ball.

PICTURES INCLUDE: Time Without Pity, Blind Date (Chance Meeting), The Criminal, The Damned, Eva, The Servant, King and Country, Modesty Blaise, Accident, Boom, Secret Ceremony, Figures in a Landscape, The Go-Between, (Palme d' Or Award, Cannes 1971), The Assassination of Trotsky, A Doll's House, Galileo, The Romantic Englishwoman. Mr. Klein, Les Routes du Lud, Mozart's Don Giovanni.

LOUIS, JEAN: Designer. b. Paris, France, Oct. 5, 1907. Head designer, Hattie Carnegie, 7 yrs., before accepting post as Chief Designer Columbia Pictures. Later Universal Studios. Free lance in m.p. & TV. Pres. Jean-Louis, Inc.

LOUISE, TINA: Actress. b. New York, N.Y. e. Miami U., N.Y. Neighborhood Playhouse, Actors Studio, B'way.

STAGE: Two's Company, The Fifth Season, Almanac, Li'l Abner.

PICTURES INCLUDE: God's Little Acre, For Those Who Think Young, The Wrecking Crew, How to Commit Marriage, The Happy Ending, The Stepford Wives.

TV: Gilligan's Island, Mannix, Ironside, Kung Fu, Police Story, Kojak.

LOVE, BESSIE: Actress. b. Midland, Texas, Sept. 10, 1898. Began screen career with Triangle, Vitagraph, Callahan films. Early pictures. On stage, repertory, London (Love in Idleness). On staff Ealing Studio as technician, 1943. Co-mgr. and entertainer, Red Cross Hospital Unit, Great Britain, 1944.

PICTURES INCLUDE: Penny of Top Hill, Lovey Mary, Human Wreckage, The Eternal Three, Gentle Julia, Torment, Those Who Dance, The Lost World, The Purple Dawn, Dress Parade, The King of Main Street, The Song and Dance Man, Has Anybody Here Seen Kelly, Sally of the Scandals, Broadway Melody, Hollywood Revue of 1929, The Idle Rich, The Road Show, Chasing Rainbows, Conspiracy, The Swellhead, Morals for Women, Live Again, Atlantic Ferry.

STAGE: Gone With the Wind (London, 1972).

LOVE, JAMES A.: Producer. b. May 1, 1918; began film career, Warner Bros., 1938–41; mil. serv., Motion Picture Div., U.S. Coast Guard, WW II. chief film ed., Princeton Film Center; prod-dir. Cineffects Productions; pres., Lalley & Love Inc., 1952; changed firm name to James Love Productions, 1955; founded Monitor Film Distributors, 1964.

TV: Professor Yes 'n' No, Mary Margaret McBride, commercials for Democratic and Republican Conventions (1956); prod.-dir., industrial films; assoc. prod., Ballad of Gavilan; assoc. prod., By Jupiter.

LOVY, ALEX: Producer, director. b. Passaic, N.J. dir. Univ. Studios; assoc. prod. dir. Flintstones, Yogi Bear, Huckleberry Hound; dir., What a Wonderful Feeling. pres., Alex Lovy Productions, Inc.

LOWE, PHILIP L.: Executive. b. Brookline, Mass. Apr. 17, 1917. e. Harvard. Army, 1943–46. Checker, Loew's 1937–39; treasurer, Theatre Candy Co., 1941–58; Pres., ITT Sheraton Corp., 1969–70; pres., Philip L. Lowe and Assoc.; dir., First Artists, Teleprompter.

LOWE, PHILIP M.: Executive. b. 1944. e. Deerfield Academy, Harvard College (cum laude in psychology, 1966); Columbia Business School (1968). Work experience includes major marketing positions at General Foods, Gillette, Gray Advertising, and Estee Lauder Cosmetics before co-founding Cinema Centers Corp. and Theatre Management Services in Boston. Is professor marketing at Bentley College; consultant to major multi-national corporations. In 1978 named new head of Natl. Assoc. of Concessionaires, previously serving NAC as treas., v.p.

LOY, MYRNA: Actress. r.n. Myrna Williams. b. Helena Mont., Aug. 2, 1905; e. Westlake Sch. for Girls. Appeared in stage presentations, Grauman's Chinese theatre, then Hollywood. On screen in What Price Beauty, 1925; thereafter in many pictures, variously starred, co-starred & featured. Voted one of the ten best Money Making Stars in Motion Picture Herald-Fame Poll, 1937, 38.

STAGE: Marriage-Go-Round, There Must Be A Pony, Good Housekeeping, Barefoot in the Park, Dear Love, The Women, Don Juan in Hell, Relatively Speaking.

PICTURES INCLUDE: Last of the Duanes, Transatlantic, Arrowsmith, Vanity Fair, Animal Kingdom, The Prizefighter and the Lady, The Thin Man, Evelyn Prentice, Wife Versus Secretary, After the Thin Man, Test Pilot, The Rains Came, Another Thin Man, Third Finger, Left Hand; Shadow of the Thin Man, The Thin Man Goes Home, Best Years of Our Lives, Mr. Blanding Builds His Dream House, Red Pony, If This Be Sin, Cheaper by the Dozen, Belles on Their Toes, Ambassador's Daughter, Lonely hearts, From

the Terrace, Midnight Lace, The April Fools, Airport 1975, The End, Just Tell Me What You Want.

TV: Meet Me in St. Louis, Minerva, George Gobel, Perry Como, Happy Birthday—June Allyson Show, Family Affair, The Virginians, Do Not Spindle or Mutilate, Death Takes a Holiday, The Couple Takes a Wife, Ironside, The Elevator, It Happened at Lakewood Manor, Summer Solstice.

LUBCKE, HARRY R.: Cons. TV engineer, registered patent agent. b. Alameda, Calif., Aug. 25, 1905. Married to Jean MacRae. e. U. of Calif. 1929. B.S. Holds numerous U.S. and foreign patents on television. In 1931: station W6XAO went on air on what is now television Channel No. 2 to become first station of kind in nation. New Mt. Lee studios built at cost of $250,000 in 1941, housing then largest TV stage 100x60x30 ft. Pioneered present television standard of 525 line (Aug., 1940). In 1942, television programs to promote war bonds sale. 1942–46 dir. war research for which certificates of commendation were received from Army & Navy.

MEMBER: RTPB, Panel 6, on television standards and various sub-committees since inception, and of Nat'l Television Systems Committee, which preceded it. Pres., Acad. TV Arts & Sciences, 1949. Dir. TV Don Lee Broadcasting System to Dec. 31, 1950; Consulting eng., CBS, thereafter consulting practice restricted to TV eng. electronics, program prod., 1951; cons. TV engineer, 1951; registered patent agent, 1952. Life Fellow, 1951, IEEE, AAAS, SMPTE, 1967. Board of Governors, Patent Law Association of Los Angeles, 1974. Life Member National Academy of Television Arts & Sciences, member engineering Emmy Awards Committee. Member Blue Ribbon panel Emmy Awards Committee; member ANTA 1977, Life Member, Actor's Fund of America, 1978; Diamond Circle, of Pacific Pioneer Broadcasters, 1980.

LUBER, BERNARD: b. Philadelphia, PA., May 18, 1908. Dickinson College and Law School, Carlisle, PA., 1928. Law work in New York City until 1930. Admitted to New York Bar. National publicity and theater operations for Paramount Publix Theaters until 1937. Joined Paramount Hollywood Studios 1937 as studio attorney. 1942–45 assoc. head of Paramount talent and casting dept. Head of talent and casting dept. of Republic Studios until 1947. General Manager of Jack Benny's Amusement Enterprises to 1950. Organized and part-owner of Pine-Thomas Productions, producers of 75 feature films. Organized, part owner and co-producer (with R. Polk) World Artists, producers of series of concert films, featuring Heifetz, Rubenstein, Piatigorsky and Marian Anderson, etc., for NBC Network. Laurel Award for Of Men and Music, feature film featuring concert artists. 1951, produced 26 half-hour films of Superman featuring George Reeves. From 1952 to 1964 produced feature films and tv series (for ABC Exclusive) in Hollywood, New York, London, Paris, Rome, Munich and Athens, etc. From 1965 and continuing to present, pres. of Celebrity Concert Corporation, importing cultural music films and recordings, and USA representative of Melodiya and Mezhkniga, Soviet Recording Industry, exporting Soviet recordings from USSR and importing American Recordings to USSR.

LUBIN, ARTHUR: Director. b. Los Angeles, Calif. Since 1935 has directed numerous pictures.

PICTURES INCLUDE: Buck Privates in the Navy, Hold That Ghost, Keep 'Em Flying, Ride 'Em Cowboy, Eagle Squadron, Phantom of the Opera, White Savage, Ali Baba and the Forty Thieves, Delightfully Dangerous, Francis, Queen for a Day, Francis Goes to the Races, Rhubarb, Francis Covers the Big Town, Francis Goes to West Point, It Grows on Trees, South Sea Woman, Star of India, Lady Godiva, Francis in the Navy, Footsteps in the Fog, First Traveling Saleslady, Escapade in Japan, The Thief of Baghdad, The Incredible Mr. Limpett, Rain for a Dusty Summer, Night in Paradise, The Spider Woman Strikes Back, New Orleans, Impact, Queen for a Day, Star of India, Hold On!

TV: Maverick (Henry Fonda episodes), 77 Sunset Strip, Bonanza, the entire Mister Ed series (prod.-dir.).

LUCAS, GEORGE: Producer-Director-Writer. b. 1945. e. USC (cinema). Made short film called THX and won National Student Film Festival Grand Prize, 1967. Signed contract with WB. Ass't. to Francis Ford Coppola on The Rain People, during which Lucas made 2-hr. documentary on filming of that feature. Debut as director with THX 1138 for WB.

PICTURES INCLUDE: THX 1138 (dir., co-s.p.), American Graffiti (dir., co-s.p.), Star Wars (dir., s.p.); More American Graffiti (exec. prod.); The Empire Strikes Back (exec. prod.); Raiders of the Lost Ark (exec. prod.).

LUDWIG, IRVING H.: Executive. b. Nov. 3, 1910. e. Savage School, Rivoli Theatre, N.Y., mgr., theatre oper., Rugoff and Becker, 1938–39; opened first modern art type theatre, Greenwich Village, 1940. With Walt Disney Prod. in charge of theatre oper. on Fantasia in various cities, 1940–

41; buyer-booker, Rugoff and Becker, 1942–45; film sales admin., Walt Disney Prod. home office, 1945–53; v.p. and domestic sales mgr., Buena Vista Dist. Co., 1953; pres. gen. sales mgr., 1959–80. Now exec. consultant

LUFKIN, DAN W.: Executive. Chairman of Exec. Comm., Columbia Pictures Industries (appt. July, 1978). Co-founder of Donaldson, Lufkin & Jenrette Securities Corp., investment banking and brokerage firm. Served as first commissioner of Dept. of Environmental Protection for State of Connecticut. Joined Columbia board in November, 1977.

LUFT, HERBERT G.: Writer. b. Essen, Germany, Aug. 21. Started career as journalist; came to U.S. 1940, to Hollywood, 1943. Magazine writer, film ed., researcher, translator, prod. asst., 1944. Adapt. M: prod. mgr., collab. s.p. This Is Freedom, Secret of Giving, Springtime in Copenhagen, Hong Kong Affair, Why Must I Die, Night Raiders, Syndicated Hollywood Columnist, writer, prod. exec., chmn. Int'l Film Comm.; pres. Hollywood Foreign Press, 1966–1968. Production Exec. Getty Picture Corp. (1969) (treas.); Flare-Up, Zeppelin, 1970. Shellia, 1970; Rage, 1971/72, Associate producer, The Mutation, (England) 1972/73. Assoc. producer The Devil's Men (1975), Shoot (1976); vice pres. in charge of production, Getty Picture Corp. (1976).

LUKE, KEYE: Actor, artist. b. Canton, China, 1904. e. Franklin High Sch., Seattle; Formerly artist for Fox West Coast Theats. & RKO Studios; also technical advisor on Chinese films. Screen debut as actor in Painted Veil, 1935.
STAGE: Flower Drum Song (3 yr).
PICTURES INCLUDE: Charlie Chan series, Oil for the Lamps of China, King of Burlesque, The Good Earth, International Settlement, Sued for Libel, Disputed Passage, Dragon Seed, Three Men in White, Between Two Women, First Yank in Tokyo, Tokyo Rose, Sleep My Love, Hell's Half Acre, World for Ransom, Bamboo Prison, Love is a Many Splendored Thing, 80 Days Around the World, Their Greatest Glory, Battle Hell, Fair Winds to Java, Nobody's Perfect, Project X, The Chairman, The Hawaiians, Noon Sunday, Won Ton Ton, Amsterdam Kill, Just You and Me, Kid.
TV: Gunsmoke, Danger, December Bride, Crusader, Wireservice, Crossroads, Soldiers of Fortune, My Little Margie, Annie Oakley, Ray Milland Show, Medic, Citizen Chang, Climax, Jerry Jewis, Trackdown, Perry Mason Show, The Littlest Hobo, This Is the Life, Smothers Bros., I Spy, FBI, Wackiest Ship in Army, Mickey Rooney Show, Johnny Quest, Kentucky Jones, Never Too Young, Bob Hope Chrysler Show, Family Affair, Big Valley, Dragnet, It Takes a Thief, Star-Trek, Adventures of Huck Finn, The Outsider, Scooby Doo, Paris 7000, Johnny Carson Show, Marcus Welby, M.D., Adam 12, Hawaii 5-0, Dinah Shore Show, The Lucy Show, Anna and the King of Siam, Kung Fu, Amazing Chan and Chan Clan, Follow The Sun, Target, The Corruptors, Fair Exchange, Cannon, Cat Creature, Love American Style, Judgement—trial of Yamashita, Judge Dee, Khan, Harry O, MASH, Quincy, How the West Was Won, Meeting of Minds, Vegas, Battle of the Planets, The Yee Family, Might Man and Yukk, Rickety Racket, Tang Face, Charlie's Angels, Reach for the Sun, Fly Away Home, Brothers, Adventures of Goldie Gold, etc.

LUKE, PETER: Playwright director. Author of plays for TV: Small Fish Are Sweet, 1958; Pigs Ear with Flowers, 1960; Roll on Bloomin' Death, 1961; A Man on Her Back (with William Sansom), 1965; Devil a Monk Won't Be, 1966. Wrote and directed films for BBC-TV: Anach 'Cuan (about the late Sean O Riada) 1967; Black Sound—Deep Song (About Federico Garcia Lorca) 1968; Author of Stage play, Hadrian VII, first produced at Birmingham rep in 1967 and at time of going to press has been playing in one part of the world or another ever since. Stage Play, Bloomsbury. Author of autobiography, Sisyphus & Reilly, publ., 1972, Prod. Phoenix Theatre 1974.

LUMET, SIDNEY: Director. b. Philadelphia, Pa., June 15, 1924. e. Professional Children's Sch.; Columbia U. Child actor in plays: Dead End, George Washington Slept Here, My Heart's in the Highlands. U.S. Armed Forces, WW II, 1942–46; dir. summer stock, 1947–49; taught acting, H.S. of Prof. Arts. Assoc. dir. CBS, 1950, dir. 1951.
TV: Mama, Danger, You Are There, Omnibus, Best of Broadway, Alcoa, Goodyear Playhouse.
PICTURES INCLUDE: 12 Angry Men, Stage Struck, That Kind of Woman, Fugitive Kind, A View From the Bridge, Long Day's Journey into Night, Fail Safe, The Pawnbroker, The Hill, The Group, The Deadly Affair, Bye Bye Braverman, The Sea Gull, The Appointment, Last of the Mobile Hot-Shots, The Anderson Tapes, Child's Play, The Offence, Lovin' Molly, Serpico, Murder on the Orient Express, Dog Day Afternoon, Network, Equus, The Wiz, Just Tell Me What You Want, Prince of the City, Deathtrap.

LUPINO, IDA: Actress-director. b. London, England, Feb. 4, 1918. e. Royal Academy of Dramatic Art, London. Daughter of Stanley Lupino, English stage and screen comedian. Brit. m.p. debut in "Her First Affair," 1932; in U.S.

m.p. 1934; ent. independent prod., variously dir., prod. collab. s.p. and acting.
PICTURES INCLUDE: Money for Speed, High Finance, High Sierra, Ladies in Retirement, Moontide, Hard Way, Devotion, Man I Love, Escape Me Never, Deep Valley, Road House, Lust for Gold, Not Wanted, Never Fear, Outrage, Hard Fast & Beautiful, On Dangerous Ground, Beware My Lovely, The Hitch-Hiker, Jennifer, The Bigamist, Private Hell 36, Women's Prison, Big Knife, While the City Sleeps, Trouble With Angels, Junior Bonner, The Devil's Rain, The Food of the Gods.
TV: Mr. Adams and Eve. No. 5 Checked Out, The Trial of Mary Surrat, Honey West, Virginian, I Love a Mystery, Sam Benedict, Untouchables, G. E. Theater, Have Gun Will Travel, Thriller, Mr. Novac, Hong Kong, The Rogues, Chrysler Theatre, Kraft Theatre, Gilligan's Island, The Ghost and Mrs. Muir, The Bill Cosby Show, To Catch a Thief, Mod Squad, Family Affair.

LURASCHI, LUIGI G.: Exec. b. London, Jan 7, 1906. e. U. of Zurich. Long Island Studio, Paramount, 1929; home officer mgr. For. dept. hd, For. & dom. Censorship; Hollywood to 1960. Asst. Prod., Dino De Laurentiis Prod. 1960–65; asst. to pres. for prod. activities, Paramount, 1965. 1967 continental prod. exec. Paramount-Rome. Now v.p., intl.

LYDON, JAMES: Actor. b. Harrington Park, N.J., May 30, 1923; e. St. Johns Mil. Sch. On NY stage in Prologue to Glory, Sing Out the News. On screen 1939, Back Door to Heaven.
PICTURES INCLUDE: Thoroughbreds, Naval Academy, Henry Aldrich series, Twice Blessed, Life With Father, Out of the Storm, Joan of Arc, Miss Mink of 1949, Tucson, Gasoline Alley, Island in the Sky, The Desperado, Battle Stations, My Blood Runs Cold (assoc. prod.), Brainstorm, An American Dream, A Covenant With Death, First to Fight, The Cool Ones, Chubasco, Countdown, Assignment to Kill, The Learning Tree, Scandalous John.
TV: Frontier Circus (assoc. prod.), Wagon Train, Alfred Hitchcock hour, McHale's Navy, 77 Sunset Strip, Mr. Roberts

LYLES, A. C.: Producer. b. Jacksonville, Florida. May 17. e. Andrew Jackson High School; Paramount Publix's Florida Theatre, 1928; interviewed Hollywood celebrities, Jacksonville Journal, 1932; mail boy, Paramount Studios, Hollywood, 1937; publicity dept., 1938; hd. of adv., publ. dept., Pine-Thomas unit at Paramount, 1940; assoc. prod., The Mountain; prod., Short Cut to Hell; assoc. prod., Rawhide. President, A. C. Lyles Productions, Inc. (Paramount Pictures).
PICTURES INCLUDE: Raymie, The Young and the Brave, Law of the Lawless, Stage to Thunder Rock, Young Fury, Black Spurs, Hostile Guns, Arizona Bushwackers, Town Tamer, Apache Uprising, Johnny Reno, Waco, Red Tomahawk, Fort Utah, Buckskin, Rogue's Gallery, Night of the Lepus, The Last Day.

LYNCH, DAVID: Director-Writer. b. Montana, 1947. e. Pa. Academy of Fine Arts, where received an independent filmmaker grant from America Film Institute. Made 16mm film, The Grandmother. Accepted by Center for Advanced Film Studies in Los Angeles, 1970. Wrote and directed Eraserhead (with partial AFI financing) which became cult movie. Co-wrote and directed The Elephant Man (1980).

LYNCH, RICHARD: Actor. Made Bdwy. debut in The Devils, latter both on and off Bdwy in The Balcony, Lion in Winter, etc. Film debut in Scarecrow (1973).
PICTURES: The Premonition, Steel, The Formula.
TELEVISION: Vampire.

LYNCH, T. MURRAY: Executive. b. St. Thomas, Ontario, July 22, 1920. Capitol Theatre, St. Thomas, Ont.; R.C.A.F., Capitol Theatre, London, Ont.; Capitol Theatre, Halifax, N.S.; Paramount Theatre, Moncton, N.B.; Avalon Mall Theatre, St. John's Newfoundland: City supervisor, St. John's; Maritime and Newfoundland district mgr., Famous Players Canadian Corp., Sept. 1, 1968; office in Capitol Theatre, Halifax, N.S.

LYNDE, PAUL: Actor. b. Mt. Vernon, Ohio, June 13. e. Northwestern U. After club circuit appeared on Broadway in New Faces of 1952, then Bye Bye Birdie; films include The Glass Bottom Boat, Bye Bye Birdie, Under the Yum-Yum Tree, Send Me No Flowers, The Villain.
TV: Bewitched, The Paul Lynde Show, Hollywood Squares.

LYNDON, VICTOR: Producer. b. London. Ent. m.p. ind. as asst. dir., Gainsborough Pictures, 1946–56; prod. mgr., 26 feature pictures; since 1957 prod., assoc. prod., pictures for Columbia, United Artists, M-G-M, Paramount, British Lion.
PICTURES INCLUDE: as prod. mgr. The African Queen, Albert R.N., The Admirable Crichton, As assoc. prod., Dr. Strangelove, Darling, 2001 A Space Odyssey. As prod., Spare The Rod, Station Six—Sahara, The Optimists.

LYNN, ANN: Actress. b. London, England. Ent. films and TV, 1958.

PICTURES INCLUDE: Naked Fury, Piccadilly Third Stop, The Wind of Change, TV film series: The Cheaters, The Other Side of the Underneath.
TV: After The Show, All Summer Long, Trump Card, Man at the Top, The Expert, Hine, The Intruders, Too Far, King Lear, The Zoo Gang. Recent films incl: The Uncle, Morning Tide, Shot In The Dark, Black Torment, Four In The Morning, Baby Love, Hitler—The Last Ten Days, Estuary, Who Pays The Ferryman, The Professionals, Zeticula, Westway. The Perfect House, Minder, To the Sound of Guns, Crown Court.

LYNN, JEFFREY: Actor. b. Auburn, Mass., 1909: e. Bates Coll. m.p. debut in 1938.
PICTURES INCLUDE: Four Daughters, Yes My Darling Daughter, Daughters Courageous, Espionage Agent, Roaring Twenties, Four Wives, Child Is Born, Fighting 69th, It all Came True, All This and Heaven, Too; My Love Came Back, Four Mothers, Million Dollar Baby, Law of the Tropics, Body Disappears, For the Love of Mary, Black Bart, Letter to Three Wives, Strange Bargain, Home Town Story, Up Front, Captain China, Lost Lagoon, Tony Rome.
BROADWAY: (Revival) Dinner at Eight

LYNN, ROBERT: Director, producer. 100 TV films. Assoc. prod. for Mid-Atlantic Films. 1970 prod. The Railway Children.
TV: Space 1999.
PICTURES INCLUDE: Dr. Crippen, Postman's Knock, Victim 5, Mozambique, Coast of Skeletons, Carnival of Killers, 2nd unit dir., Superman.

LYON, EARLE: Producer, Executive. b. Waterloo, Ia., April 9, 1923. e. UCLA. Entered m.p. industry 1947. Independent prod. 1954–55 and 1958–59; 20th Century-Fox prod., 1956–57; at Columbia, 1959–60; Universal, 1960–63; developed new TV projects with Bob Banner Assoc., 1963; v.p. and gen. mgr. United Pictures Corp.
PICTURES INCLUDE: Silent Raiders, The Lonesome Trail, The Silver Star, Stagecoach Fury, The Quiet Gun, The Rawhide Trail, The Rebel Set, The Destructors, Cyborg 2087, Dimension 5, Destination Inner Space, Haunting at Castle Montego, The Ten Billion Dollar Caper, Panic in the City.
TV: Tales of Wells Fargo.

LYON, FRANCIS D. "PETE": Director. b. Bowbells, N.D., July 29. e. Hollywood H.S., Univ. of Calif. at L.A.; writer, prod., dir., OWI, W.W. II; assoc. with training, exploitation and information films. Maj. U.S. Army Signal Corps.
PICTURES INCLUDE: Shape of Things to Come, Knight Without Armour, Rembrandt, Intermezzo, Adam Had Four Sons, The Great Profile, Four Sons, Daytime Wife, Body and Soul, He Ran All the Way, Crazylegs, The Bob Mathias Story, Walt Disney's The Great Locomotive Chase, The Oklahoman, Gunsight Ridge, Bailout at 43,000, Escort West, Cinerama South Seas Adventure, The Young and The Brave, Destination Inner Space, The Destructors, The Money Jungle, The Girl Who Knew Too Much, Tiger By the Tail.
TV: Laramie, Perry Mason, Zane Grey Theatre, Bus Stop, M. Squad, Wells Fargo, Draft Suspense Theatre, etc.

LYON, SUE: Actress. b. Davenport, Iowa, July 10, 1946. e. Hollywood Prof. School.
PICTURES INCLUDE: Lolita, Seven Women, Night of he Iguana, The Flim Flam Man, Evel Knievel.

LYONS, RICHARD E.: Producer. b. Boston, Mass., 1921; e. Titlon Jr. Coll. & Dartmouth College. Eastern sls. dept., MGM Pictures, 1533–41: Field Photographic Br., U.S. Navy, 1941–46; eastern artist, repertoire exec., MGM Records, 1946–55; story ed., Edward Small Prod., 1955–56; assoc. story ed., Univ., 1956–57; staff prod., MGM Studios, 1960.
PICTURES INCLUDE: Frontier Gun, The Sad Horse, The Miracle of the Hills, Ride The High Country, Mail Order Bride, The Rounders, The Plainsman, Winchester 73, Stranger on the Run, Something for a Lonely Man, Coogan's Bluff, Death of a Gunfighter, Dirty Dingus Magee.
TV: The Daughters of Joshua Cabe, The Jerico Mile (ABC-TV), Shootout in A One Dog Town (ABC-TV movie of the week, 1973). The Daughters of Joshua Cabe Return (ABC-TV M.O.W.); Welcome to Xanadu. (ABC-TV M.O.W.), Kate Bliss and the Ticker Tape Kid (ABC-TV M.O.W.), Roughnecks (4 hr. mini series), I Married Wyatt Earp (NBC-TV M.O.W.).

LYONS, STUART: Producer. b. Manchester, England, 1928. e. Manchester University. Ent. m.p. ind. 1955. Asst. dir. TV series 1955–56. Casting dir. Associated British, 1956/60. Freelance cast. dir., 1960/63. Joined 20th Century-Fox Productions as cast. dir., 1963. Appt. director 20th Century-Fox Productions Ltd., 1967, man. dir. 1968. 1971: left Fox on closure Europe prod. Joined Hemdale Group as head of production, May, 1972. Left Hemdale Aug. 1973 to resume indep. prod.
PICTURES INCLUDE: As casting director: Those Magnificent Men in Their Flying Machines, High Wind in Jamaica, Rapture, The Blue Max, Cleopatra, The Prime of

Miss Jean Brodie, The Chairman. As indep. producer: The Slipper & The Rose, Meetings with Remarkable Men.

M

MAC ARTHUR, JAMES: Actor. b. Los Angeles, Calif., Dec. 8, 1937; e. Harvard. p. Helen Hayes, Charles MacArthur. Stage debut, summer stock; The Corn Is Green, 1945; Life With Father, 1953.
PICTURES INCLUDE: The Young Stranger, The Light in the Forest, The Third Man on the Mountain, Kidnapped, Swiss Family Robinson, The Interns, Spencer's Mountain, The Love-Ins, Cry of Battle, Angry Breed.
TV: Strike a Blow, Hawaii Five-O.

MACAULAY, FRED: Producer-Executive. b. Sollas, North Uist, in Western Isles of Scotland, 1925. e. Dunskellar and Paible public schools, Inverness Royal Academy, and University of Edinburgh. Was engaged 1950 to 1954 on the Linguistic Survey of Scotland for Edinburgh University. Actively supported over many years the School of Scottish Studies at Edinburgh, and is recognised for encouraging the use of the Gaelic language in Scotland. Associated with BBC Gaelic-language broadcasting since joining the BBC in 1954. Was head of the BBC's Gaelic dept. at Glasgow for 15 years. Manager of Radio Highland, BBC community station at Inverness, since January 1980.

MAC DONALD, PHILIP: Writer. b. Scotland; e. St. Paul's School, London. Novelist, playwright. Began screen career 1933.
PICTURES INCLUDE: Sahara, Action in Arabia, The Body Snatcher, Strangers in the Night, Dangerous Intruder, Man Who Cheated Himself, Circle of Danger, Mask of the Avenger, Ring of Fear, Tobor the Great.

MAC GRAW, ALI: Actress. b. 1938. Was top fashion model.
PICTURES INCLUDE: Goodbye Columbus, Love Story, The Getaway, Convoy Players, Just Tell Me What You Want.

MACK, IRVING: Executive. b. Centerville, Iowa, Aug. 26, 1895. Started in show business as asst. pub. man. to Ralph Thomas Kettering, White City Amusement Park, Chicago; 3 yrs. ass't pub. man., Jones, Linich & Schafer; in 1917 pub. exploit. mgr., Universal, Chicago. In 1919 started Filmack Trailer Co.; at one time published local Chicago trade paper and was Chicago rep. for Film Daily. Chief barker Variety Club, 1951; member of Covenant Club, Chicago, Prudence Masonic Lodge, Cinema Lodge, B'nai B'rith. Now chm. bd. Filmack Corp. One of original founders of Variety Club of Ill. (Tent 26).

MACKERRAS, SIR CHARLES, CBE 1974. Knighted 1979: TV music conductor. b. Schenectady, N.Y., Nov. 17, 1925; e. Sydney Grammar School, (Australia); Sydney Conservatorium of Music, Prague Academy of Music. Principal oboist Sydney Symphony Orchestra, 1943–46; conductor, Sadlers Wells Opera, 1948–54; permanent conductor BBC Concert Orchestra, 1954–56; Ballet arrangements Pineapple Poll, Lady & The Fool. Now conducts regularly all principal British orchestras recordings, concerts, TV. etc.; also European Festivals & concert tours S. Africa, Australia, Russia, Scandinavia and USA. 1st Cond. Hamburg State Opera, 1966–70. Musical dir. English Nat. Opera Co. 1970–77. Chief guest conductor BBC Symphony Orch. 1977. Conductor many TV operas notably Otello, Billy Budd, La Boheme, Macbeth.

MAC LAINE, SHIRLEY: Actress. b. Richmond, Va., April 24, 1934; e. Washington and Lee H.S., Arlington, Va. Dancer, singer; signed by Hal Wallis; m.p. debut in Trouble with Harry. Producer of film documentary on China, The Other Half of the Sky, Author of 2 best-selling books: Don't Fall off the Mountain and You Can Get There from Here.
PICTURES INCLUDE: Artists and Models, Around the World in 80 Days, The Matchmaker, Some Came Running, Ask Any Girl, Career, Can-Can, The Apartment, All in a Night's Work, Two Loves, My Geisha, The Children's Hour, Two for the Seesaw, Irma La Duce, What A Way To Go, John Goldfarb Please Come Home, The Yellow Rolls Royce, Gambit, Woman Times Seven, Sweet Charity, Two Mules for Sister Sara, Desperate Characters, The Possession of Joel Delaney, The Turning Point, Being There, Loving Couples, Change of Seasons.
TV: Shirley's World, Specials.

MAC LEAN, IAN: Actor. b. London, England, 1894. On Brit. stage from 1918. Recent plays: Fifty-Fifty, The Sleeping Clergyman. Screen debut in Brit. picture Brewsters Millions, 1930.
PICTURES INCLUDE: Marigold, Arsenal Stadium Mystery, A Week in Paris, Murder Will Out, Confidential Lady, Atlantic Ferry, Young Mr. Pitt, The Reporter, Shipbuilders, Dreamin', Twilight Hour, Carabana, Headline, Appoint-

ment With Crime, Calling Paul Temple, Story of Shirley Yorke, Floodtide.

MAC MAHON, ALINE: Actress. b. McKeesport, Pa., May 3, 1899; e. Erasmus Hall, Barnard College Stage experience; Once in a Lifetime, Candida, others. Screen debut 1931 in Five Star Final.
PICTURES INCLUDE: The Mouthpiece, One Way Passage, Gold Diggers of 1933, World Changes, Babbitt, Side Streets, Mighty McGurk, Search, Roseanna McCoy, Flame and the Arrow, Eddie Cantor Story, Man From Laramie, All the Way Home.

MAC MURRAY, FRED: Actor. b. Kankakee, Ill., Aug. 30, 1908; e. Carroll College, Wis. Sang and played in orchestra to earn tuition. To Hollywood with band; extra roles on screen; to N.Y. with comedy stage band, then joined "Three's a Crowd" revue; vaudeville circuits, night clubs. Began screen career 1935.
PICTURES INCLUDE: Grand Old Girl, Beyond Suspicion, Murder He Says, Double Indemnity, Oregon Trail, The Absent Minded Professor, The Happiest Millionaire, Follow Me Boys, Charlie and the Angel, Car 99, Gilded Lily, Hands Across the Table, Bride Comes Home, Alice Adams, Trail of the Lonesome Pine, Maid of Salem, Exclusive, True Confession, Men with Wings, Coconut Grove, Sing You Sinners, Cafe Society, Invitation to Happiness, Honeymoon in Bali, Smoky, Pardon My Past, Suddenly It's Spring, Egg and I, Singapore, A Miracle Can Happen, Miracle of the Bells, Don't Trust Your Husband, Family Honeymoon, Never a Dull Moment, Callaway Went Thataway, Millionaire for Christy, Fair Wind to Java, The Moonlighter, Caine Mutiny, Pushover, Woman's World, Far Horizons, There's Always Tomorrow, At Gunpoint, Rains of Rachipur, Gun For a Coward, Quantez, Good Day for a Hanging, The Shaggy Dog, Face of a Fugitive, The Oregon Trail, Bon Voyage, Son of Flubber, Kisses For My President, The Swarm.
TV: My Three Sons (12 years).

MACNAUGHTON, ROBERT: Actor. b. New York City, Dec. 19, 1966. Entered entertainment industry in 1979.
TELEVISION: Angel City.
STAGE: Critic's Choice, Thousand Clowns, Camelot.

MACQUITTY, WILLIAM: Prod. Author. b. Ireland.
PICTURES INCLUDE: Feature Prod., The Way We Live, Blue Scar, The Happy Family, Street Corner, The Beachcomber, Above Us The Waves, Black Tent, A Night to Remember, The Informers.
AUTHOR: Abu Simbel, Great Botanical Gardens of The World, Buddha, Persia the Immortal Kingdom, Tutankhamen the Last Journey, Princes of Jade, The World in Focus, Island of Isis, The Wisdom of the Ancient Egyptians, Rameses The Great, Master of the World, Our World in Colour, Inside China.

MAC RAE, GORDON: Singer, actor. b. East Orange, N.J., Mar. 12, 1921, p. Wee Willie Mac Rae, early radio star. Child actor on radio, in stock, on stage in Three to Make Ready, juvenile soloist in Ray Bolger revue, with Millpond Playhouse, Roslyn, L.I., radio, TV singer.
PICTURES INCLUDE: Big Punch, Look for the Silver Lining, Backfire, Return of the Frontiersman, Tea for Two, West Point Story, On Moonlight Bay, Standing, About Face, By the Light of the Silvery Moon, Desert Song, 3 Sailors and a Girl, Oklahoma, Carousel, Best Things in Life Are Free.

MAC RAE, JEAN: Actress. b. Montreal, Quebec, Mar. 24, 1930. M. Harry Lubcke. Worked for National Film Bd. of Canada, Canadian Bdcst. Corp., and repertory theatre in Canada; U.S. studios, including MGM, 20th-Fox, Columbia, and Paramount; as TV studios at Desilu and 20th-Fox.

MADDEN, BILL: Executive. b. New York City, March 1, 1915; e. Boston U. Joined Metro-Goldwyn-Mayer as office boy, 1930; student salesman, 1938; asst. Eastern div. mgr., 1939; U.S. Navy, 1942–46; Boston salesman, M.G.M., 1947–53; Philadelphia branch mgr., 1954–59; Midwest div. sales mgr., 1960–68; roadshow sales mgr., 1969; v.p., general sales mgr., M.G.M.; corp., v.p. & gen. sls. mgr., MGM, 1973; retired from MGM, 1975; 1976-present, exec. consultant to motion picture industry; lecturer at UCLA.

MADISON, GUY: Actor. r.n., Robert Moseley. b. Bakersfield, Calif., Jan. 19, 1922; e. Bakersfield Jr. Coll.; m. Sheila Connolly, U.S. Navy; m.p. debut in Since You Went Away, 1944; Wild Bill Hickok radio and TV shows, Star of Tomorrow, 1954.
PICTURES INCLUDE: Till the End of Time, Honeymoon, Texas, Brooklyn and Heaven, Massacre River, Drums in the Deep South, Red Snow, Charge at Feather River, The Command, Five Against the House, Beast of Hollow Mountain, Last Frontier, On the Threshold of Space, Hilda Crane, Bullwhip, Gunmen of The Rio Grande, Sandokan Fights Back, Sandokan Against the Leopard of Sarawak, Mystery of Thug Island, Shatterhand, Payment in Blood.

MAESTRI, CHARLES J.: Exhibitor. b. San Francisco, Calif., m.; e. Univ. of San Francisco, 1930. Paramount booker. San Francisco, 1930–33. In 1933 West Coast Theatres booker; pres., Oregon-California Theatres, Inc.

MAGEE, PATRICK: Actor. b. 1924, County Armagh, N. Ireland. Stage work before entering films.
PICTURES INCLUDE: The Birthday Party, Hard Contract, Barry Lyndon, Telefon, The Bronte Sisters, Rough Cut, Sir Henry at Rawlinson's End.

MAGILL, MORT: Sales executive. b. Philadelphia, Pa., Oct. 10, 1907; e. U. of Pennsylvania, B.S. 1927. Silk salesman in southern U.S. 9 yrs.; salesman United Artists, Harrisburg 1936; city salesman Philadelphia 1938; br. mgr. Pittsburgh 1941; br. mgr. Philadelphia; part-owner Principal Films 1949; district mgr. for M.P. Sales Corp., Philadelphia & Pittsburgh 1949; br. mgr., U.A. Philadelphia; dist. mgr. Buena Vista, (Phila., Pittsburgh, Washington) 1954; dist. mgr. Nat'l Gen. Pictures, 1971, independent distribution in partnership with John Turner-Firm called Turner-Magill, Inc., covering New York, Washington, Philadelphia and Pittsburgh. Firm now called Magill Films, Inc.

MAHIN, JOHN LEE: Writer. b. Evanston, Ill. From 1930 author, collaborator many screenplays MGM pictures. Received 3 Oscar nominations, 3 WGA nominations, Photoplay Gold Medal, Laurl Award (WGA).
PICTURES INCLUDE: Scarface, Beast of the City, The Wet Parade, Captains Courageous, Chained, Love on the Run, The Prizefighter and The Lady, Naughty Marietta, Small Town Girl, Wife vs Secretary, The Devil is a Sissy, The Last Gangster, Too Hot to Handle, Sabotage Agent, The Spiral Road, The Horse Soldiers, North To Alaska, Hell Below, Johnny Eager, Dr. Jekyll and Mr. Hyde, Tortilla Flat, Down to Sea in Ships, Love That Brute, Show Boat, Quo Vadis, My Son John, Mogambo, Elephant Walk, Lucy Gallant, Bad Seed, Eskimo, Treasure Island, Red Dust, Boom Town, No Time for Sergeants, Heaven Knows Mr. Allison, Moment to Moment.

MAHONEY, JOCK: Actor. r.n. Jacques O'Mahoney. b. Chicago, Ill., Feb. 7, 1919. e. U. of Iowa. Fighter pilot instructor, U.S.M.C.; enter m.p. ind. as stuntman; then started in westerns; TV show, Range Rider, many appearances on Loretta Young Show.
PICTURES INCLUDE: Away All Boats, Day of Fury, Showdown at Abilene, Battle Hymn, I've Lived Before, Land Unknown, Joe Dakota, Money, Women & Guns, Moro Witch Doctor, Walls of Hell, Tarzan Goes to India, Tarzan's Three Challenges.

MAIBAUM, RICHARD: Writer, Producer. b. New York City, May 26. educ. NYU, Univ. of Iowa, B.A., M.A., Ph. Beta Kappa. Plays on Broadway: The Tree, Birthright, Sweet Mystery of Life, See My Lawyer (1939), Member, Shakespearean Repertory Theatre in New York as player, 1933, From 1935 to 1942 worked on screenplays in Hollywood: MGM (They Gave Him a Gun, Stablemates, etc.); Columbia (Amazing Mr. Williams); Paramount (I Wanted Wings); 20th-Fox (Ten Gentlemen from West Point). Army, 1942–46, dir. Combat Film Div., final rank Lt. Col. To Para. prod.-writer, 1946, wrote-produced O.S.S., Song of Surrender; collab. & prod. The Great Gatsby. Prod. Sainted Sisters, The Big Clock, Bride of Vengeance, Dear Wife, No Man of Her Own, Capt. Carey, U.S.A.; free lance, 1953; collab. s.p., Paratrooper; adapt., Hell Below Zero; writer of Teleplays; exec. prod. MGM-TV, 1958–60.
PICTURES INCLUDE: Ransom, Cockleshell Heroes, Bigger Than Life, Zarak, Tank Force, Killers of Kilimanjaro, The Day They Robbed the Bank of England, Battle at Bloody Beach, Dr. No, From Russia With Love, Goldfinger, Thunderball, Chitty, Chitty, Bang Bang, On Her Majesty's Secret Service, Diamonds Are Forever, The Man With The Golden Gun, The Spy Who Loved Me, For Your Eyes Only.

MAIDMENT, GEORGE JOSEPH: Executive. Apptd. chief continental auditor, Fox Film Co., Ltd., 1924; was later comptroller of that co. and of Fox Britsh Movietonews, Ltd.; dir., Fox British Pictures, Ltd. 1933, treas. & secy., Columbia Pictures Corp., Ltd., Columbia Pictures Export Ltd., and Columbia British Productions, Ltd. In War Service as regional officer. Ministry Home Security, then on production planning for engineering and aircraft, finally on reorganization work. Ministry of Agriculture. 1944; gen. mgr., London Films Export, Ltd. 1947 gen. mgr., Omnia Films Ltd., Producers Representations Ltd., 1951 gen. mgr. Pendennis Pictures Corp. Ltd., Tower Films Ltd., Pax Films Ltd., Vicar Prod. Ltd., Orb. Prod. Ltd., Orb. Intl. Ltd. Fellow, Inst. of Chartered Accountants, Fellow Chartered Institute of Secretaries; Fellow, Institute of Linguists.

MAIN, DAVID: Writer, Producer. b. Essex, England, 1929. Extensive television experience in Britain producing and directing for A.T.V., Granada, A.B.C. and B.B.C. Emigrated to Canada in 1960. Directed Moment of Truth for N.B.C., and Quentin Durgens M.P. for C.B.C., Famous Jury Trials for 20th Century Fox. In 1977–78 directed King of

Kensington, Le Club, A Gift to Last for CBC. President of Velvet Screen Plays Ltd. a subsidiary of Quadrant Films Ltd.

PICTURES INCLUDE: Sunday In The Country, 1973 (story & co-writer), and It Seemed Like A Good Idea At The Time, 1975 (co-writer); Find The Lady, 1976 (story, co-writer, co-producer); Double Negative, 1978 (co-prod.); Nothing Personal, 1979 (co-prod.).

MAJORS, LEE: Actor. b. Wyandotte, Mich., April 23, 1940. m. actress-model Farrah Fawcett-Majors. Star athlete in high school; turned down offer from St. Louis Cardinals in final year at Eastern Kentucky State College to pursue acting career. In L.A. got job as playground supervisor for park dept while studying acting at MGM Studio.

PICTURES INCLUDE: Will Penny (debut), The Liberation of L. B. Jones.

TV: The Big Valley, The Man From Shiloh, The Six Million Dollar Man. Movies: The Ballad of Andy Crocker, Weekend of Terror, The Gary Francis Powers Story.

MALDEN, KARL: Actor. r.n. Malden Sekulovich. b. Gary, Ind., Mar. 22, 1914.

B'WAY PLAYS: Golden Boy, Key Largo, Flight to West, Missouri Legend, Uncle Harry, Counterattack, Truckline Cafe, All My Sons, Streetcar Named Desire, Desperate Hours, Desire Under the Elms.

PICTURES INCLUDE: Boomerang, The Gunfighter, Where the Sidewalk Ends, Hall of Montezuma, Streetcar Named Desire, (Acad. Award best supporting actor, 1951), The Sellout, Diplomatic Courier, Operation Secret, Ruby Gentry, I Confess, Take the High Ground, Phantom of the Rue Morgue, On the Waterfront, Bombers B-52, Desperate Hours, Fear Strikes Out, Egghead, The Hanging Tree, One Eyed Jacks, Parrish; dir., Time Limit, Billion Dollar Brain, Hot Millions, Blue Hotel, Patton, Cat O'Nine Tails, Wild Rovers, Summertime Killer, Beyond the Poseidon Adventure, Meteor.

TV: Streets of San Francisco, Captains Courageous.

MALICK, TERENCE: Producer-Writer-Director. b. Texas, 1945. e. Harvard. Attended Oxford on Rhodes scholarship. Worked for Newsweek, Life and The New Yorker; lectured for year in philosophy at M.I.T. Studied at American Film Institute in Bev. Hills and made short funded by AFI.

PICTURES INCLUDE: Badlands (prod., dir., s.p.), Days of Heaven (s.p., dir.).

MALLE, LOUIS: Director. b. Thumeries, France, 1932. Started in film industry as assistant to Robert Bresson. Began career somewhat ahead of most young French directors referred to as the Nouvelle Vague (New Wave). Became internationally known with Les Amants (The Lovers) in 1958. Has also acted in films.

PICTURES INCLUDE: The World of Silence (co-dir. with J. Y. Cousteau); A Man Escaped (asst. to Bresson); Elevator to the Gallows, The Lovers, Zazie in the Metro, Private Life, Vive Le Tour, The Fire Within, Bon Baisers de Bangkok, Viva Maria, The Thief, William Wilson, Phantom India, Murmur of the Heart, Humain, Trop Humain, Lacombe, Lucien, Black Moon, Pretty Baby, Atlantic City.

MALLERS, ANTHONY: Theatre Owner. b. Portland, Ind., Oct. 4, 1933. e. Indiana Univ. (B.S., business admin.). Entered industry in 1957. Now pres. of Mallers Theatres, headquartered in Muncie, Ind.

MALMUTH, BRUCE: b. Brooklyn. e. City Coll., Brooklyn Coll. Acted in college productions. Moved to California and obtained job as page at TV center. In Army assigned to special services as director; reassigned to New York. Upon release began 10-year production stint in TV commercials. Debut as director of feature with Nighthawks, 1981.

MALONE, DOROTHY: Actress. b. Chicago, Ill., Jan. 30, 1930, e. So. Methodist U. Screen debut in The Big Sleep, 1946.

PICTURES INCLUDE: Young at Heart, Battle Cry, Pillars of the Sky, Written on the Wind (Acad. Award, best supporting actress, 1956), Man of a Thousand Faces, The Last Voyage, The Last Sunset, Beach Party, Abduction, Golden Rendezvous, Winter Kills.

TV: Dick Powell Theatre, Dr. Kildare, Bob Hope Show, Jack Benny Show, The Untouchables, The Greatest Show On Earth, Peyton Place.

MALTZ, ALBERT: Writer. b. Brooklyn, N.Y., Oct. 28, 1908; e. Columbia U., B.A., 1930; Yale Sch. Drama. From 1932 author, playwright, novelist ("The Cross and the Arrow" 1944). From 1933–37, exec. bd., Theat. Union. Instructor in playwriting. Sch. Adult Educ., N.Y.U., 1937–41; also ed. Equality, 1937–38. Began screen writing 1941. Paramount. Acad. Award in documentaries (Moscow Strikes Back). 1943.

MEMBER: Author's League (council 1935–41); Amer. Arbitration Soc. (arbitor, from 1938).

PICTURES INCLUDE: This Gun for Hire, Destination Tokyo, Pride of the Marines, Cloak and Dagger, Naked City, Two Mules for Sister Sara.

MAMOULIAN, ROUBEN: Director. b. Tiflis, Caucasus (Russia), Oct. 8, 1897; e. Lycee Montaigne, Paris, Moscow U., (law).

Stage dir. since 1918; first English prod., Beating on the Door, London, 1922; came to U.S., 1923; prod. dir., Eastman Theatre, Rochester, N.Y., 1923–26; dir. operas, operetta, musicals; organizer, 1925, dir., 1925–26, Eastman Theatre School; dir. Oklahoma for Berlin Art Festival, 1951; dir. Oklahoma! for Paris, France (Salut a La France), 1955; Oklahoma! for Rome, Milan, Naples and Venice, Italy; author of short stories, verse, articles; pub. books: Abigayil, 1964; "Shakespeare's Hamlet, A New Version," 1966; 1966. prod. Hamlet; 1967. Tribute to R.M.'s 40th Anniv. on stage & screen at Mod. Art in N.Y.; 1968, Festival of R.M. Films at National Film Thea. in London, Washington, D.C., and Montreal. Tribute to Rouben Mamoulian: Retrospectives of all his films and personal appearances for discussion at: San Francisco International Film Festival, Science Center in Toronto, Canada, Museum of Science in Buffalo, New York, University of California at Los Angeles, University of South Florida, Yale University, New York (all in 1971). Seminar for USA Educators by Rouben Mamoulian at the American Film Institute, 1970. Guest of Honor of U.S.S.R. at the International Film Festival in Moscow, 1971. The Art of Survival—symposium at University of Southern California, 1972. Musical Mamoulian—Retrospective of R.M.'s musical films at the Academy of Motion Pictures Arts & Sciences, Hollywood, 1972. Publication: Foreword to the book Chevalier, 1973. Retrospective showing of Rouben Mamoulian's films at UCLA, 1973. Special showing of Blood and Sand and discussion at Filmex, Hollywood, 1973. President of the international jury at the International Film Festival of San Sebastian, Spain, 1973. Festival of Mamoulian's films in San Sebastian, 1973. Festival of Rouben Mamoulians films at the Cinematheque Francaise, Paris, France, 1973. Symposium on the Coming of Sound to the American Film 1925–1940—George Eastman House, Rochester, New York, 1973. Showing of Dr. Jekyll & Mr. Hyde and stage appearance Filmex 1974—Hollywood, 1974. Festival of Mamoulian's films in Sydney and Melbourne, Australia, 1974. Establishment of the "Rouben Mamoulian Award for the Best Australian Short Film" in perpetuity, June, 1974. Shtwing of Mamoulian musicals and appearance at the American Film Institute's "History of American Musicals" at Kennedy Center of Performing Arts, Washington, D.C., Sept., 1974. Guest of honor and member of international jury at International Film Festival, Tehran, Iran, 1974. Guest of Honor at festivities in Ispahan, Shiraz and Persipolis, December, 1974. Lecture on "The State of films and the state of the World" at Washington Club, Washington, D.C., December, 1974. Lectures, seminar and showing of Mamoulian films at University of California at Santa Barbara, February, 1975.

BROADWAY PLAYS: Porgy, Marco's Millions, Wings over Europe, Congai, A Month in the Country, Solid South, Farewell to Arms, Porgy and Bess, Oklahoma, Sadie Thompson, Carousel, St. Louis Woman, Lost in the Stars, Arms and the Girl.

PICTURES INCLUDE: Applause, City Streets, Dr. Jekyll and Mr. Hyde, Love Me Tonight, Song of Songs, Queen Christine, We Live Again, Becky Sharp, Gay Desperado, High, Wide and Handsome, Golden Boy, Mark of Zorro, Blood and Sand, Rings On Her Fingers, Summer Holiday, Silk Stockings, Never Steal Anything Small (co-author) 1959.

MANASSE, GEORGE: Producer. b. Florence, Italy, Jan. 1, 1938; e. U. of N.C. Producer, GSF Productions, Inc.; for Cannon was assoc. prod., Joe, Jump; prod. Who Killed Mary What's Her Name; for GSF was exec. prod., Journey Through Rosebud, Change in the Wind.

MANBY, C. R.: Executive. b. Battle Creek, Mich., Feb. 24, 1920; e. Hillsdale Coll., Mich., A.B., 1942; Harvard Grad. School of Bus. Admin., 1953; v.p. RKO General Inc., 1955–58; pres. Show Corp. of Amer., 1958–75. Now sr. v.p., RKO General, Inc. & pres., RKO Pictures, Inc.

MANCINI, HENRY: Composer. b. 1922. Arranged music for the Glen Miller Story, The Benny Goodman Story, then began composing scores.

PICTURES INCLUDE: Touch of Evil, High Time, Breakfast at Tiffany's (AA, 1961), Bachelor in Paradise, Hatari, The Pink Panther, Charade, A Shot in the Dark, Dear Heart, What Did You Do in the War, Daddy?, Two for the Road, Visions of Eight, Oklahoma Crude, 99 44/100s½ Dead, The White Dawn, The Girl from Petrovka, The Great Waldo Pepper, W. C. Fields and Me, The Pink Panther Strikes Again, Silver Streak, Revenge of the Pink Panther, Who Is Killing the Great Chefs of Europe?, Prisoner of Zenda, Nightwing, "10," Little Miss Marker, Change of Seasons, Back Roads, "S.O.B.".

MANCUSO, FRANK G.: Executive. b. Buffalo, N.Y., July 25, 1933. e. State Univ. of New York. Film buyer and operations supvr. for Basil Enterprises, theatre circuit, from 1958 to 1962. Joined Paramount as booker in Buffalo branch, 1962. Named sls. repr. for branch in 1964 and branch mgr. in 1967. In 1970 appt. v.p./gen. sls. mgr., Paramount Pictures Canada, Ltd., becoming pres. in 1972. In 1976 relocated with Paramount in U.S. as western div. mgr. in L.A. In Jan., 1977, appt. gen. sls. mgr. of N.Y. office; two months later promoted to v.p.—domestic distribution; 1979, named exec. v.p., distribution & mktg.

MANDEL, HARRY: Theatre executive. b. New York City, dir., adv. & publicity, RKO Theatres, 1938; added duties asst. to v.p. theatre operations, 1952; v.p. theatre operations, 1957; pres., 1961–66.

MANDELL, ABE: Executive. e. U. of Cincinnati. Entered broadcasting as actor on Cincinnati radio station prior to WW II. Served U.S. Army in Southwest Pacific, 1942–45. Formed independent motion picture distribution company in the Far East. Company, which became the largest independent motion picture distributor in the Far East, also operated and owned motion picture theaters throughout the Phillipine Islands and Indonesia, 1946–56; network-regional sales exec., Ziv Television, 1956–58; dir. foreign operations, Independent Television Corporation, 1958; v.p.-foreign oper., 1960; v.p.-sales and adm., 1961; exec. v.p., 1962; pres. 1965. In 1976 ITC changed its corporate name from Independent Television Corp. to ITC Entertainment, Inc. President to date of ITC Entertainment.

MANGANO, SILVANA: Actress. b. Rome, Italy. e. Dance Academy of Jia Ruskaja. Model to 1949; m.p. debut in L'Elisir D'Amore.
PICTURES INCLUDE: Bitter Rice, Lure of Sila, Musolino, the Brigand; Anna, Ulysses, Mambo, Gold of Naples, This Angry Age, Tempest, Five Branded Women, Barabbas, Teorama, Death in Venice, Decameron, Ludwig, Conversation Piece.

MANHEIM, MANNIE: Producer, writer. b. Syracuse, N.Y., Nov. 13; e. Syracuse U. Newspaper ed.; m.p. & mag. writer; radio & TV writer & prod.

MANKIEWICZ, DON M.: Writer. b. Berlin, Germany, Jan. 20, 1922. p. Herman J. Mankiewicz e. Columbia, B.A., 1942; Columbia Law School. Served in U.S. Army, 1942–46; reporter, New Yorker magazine, 1946–48; author of novels, See How They Run, Trial, It Only Hurts a Minute; magazine articles, short stories.
TV: Studio One, On Trial, One Step Beyond, Playhouse 90, Profiles in Courage.
PICTURES INCLUDE: Trial, I Want to Live.
TV PILOTS: Ironside, Marcus Welby, M.D., Sarge; Lanigan's Rabbi (collaboration); Rosetti and Ryan (collab.)

MANKIEWICZ, JOSEPH L.: Writer, director. b. Wilkes-Barre, Pa., Feb. 11, 1909; e. Columbia U. Asst. corr. in Berlin, Chicago Tribune; Ufa studio, translating subtitles into Eng. for release in Eng. & U.S.; returned to U.S. 1929 to join brother, Herman, on Paramount writing staff; MGM, 1933; Fox, 1943–51; dir., La Boheme, Metropolitan Opera House, 1953.
PICTURES INCLUDE: Skippy, Million Dollar Legs, If I Had a Million, Alice in Wonderland, Fury, Gorgeous Hussy, Mannequin, Three Comrades, Shopworn Angel, Philadelphia Story, Woman of the Year, Keys of the Kingdom, Dragonwyck, Somewhere in the Night, No Way Out, Late George Apley, Ghost and Mrs. Muir, House of Strangers, Letter to Three Wives, All About Eve, 1950, People Will Talk, 5 Fingers, Julius Caesar, Barefoot Contessa, Guys and Dolls, Quiet American, Suddenly Last Summer, The Honey Pot, There was a Crooked Man, Sleuth.

MANKIEWITZ, TOM: Writer. Specializes in adventure/suspense films.
PICTURES INCLUDE: The Sweet Ride (debut), Diamonds Are Forever, Live and Let Die, The Man with the Golden Gun, Mother, Jugs and Speed, The Cassandra Crossing, The Eagle Has Landed.

MANKOWITZ, WOLF: Author, playwright, producer & impresario. B. London, 1924. Journalist. Ent. m.p. in 1952. Musical play based his story Expresso Bongo, 1958. Musical play, Make Me An Offer, 1959; Belle, 1961; Pickwick, 1963; Passion Flower Hotel.
PICTURES INCLUDE: Make Me An Offer, Kid For Two Farthings, The Bespoke Overcoat, Trapeze, Expresso Bongo, The Millionairess, The Long and Short and Tall, The Day The Earth Caught Fire, Where the Spies Are, Assassination Bureau 1969; Bloomfield, 1970: Black Beauty, Treasure Island. 1973: The Hireling.
TV: Make Me An Offer, The Baby, The Girl, It Should Happen To A Dog, Conflict, The Killing Stones, A Cure for Tin Ear, The Model Marriage, ABC of Show Business, The Battersea Miracle, Dickens of London, 1976–77.

MANN, ABBY: Writer. b. Philadelphia. e. N.Y.U. First gained fame on TV; adapted own teleplay Judgment at Nuremberg into theatrical film.
PICTURES INCLUDE: Judgment at Nuremberg, A Child Is Waiting, Ship of Fools, The Detective, Report to the Commissioner.

MANN, DANIEL: Director. b. New York, N.Y., Aug. 8, 1912. e. Erasmus Hall, Brooklyn; Professional Children's School. Started as musician in resort hotels; then in Canada, on road; U.S. Army, World War II; then received scholarship to Neighborhood Playhouse, N.Y.; dir. teaching, TV dir.
BROADWAY: Come Back Little Sheba, Rose Tattoo, Streetcar Named Desire (City Center prod.), Paint Your Wagon.
PICTURES INCLUDE: Come Back Little Sheba, About Mrs. Leslie, Rose Tattoo, I'll Cry Tomorrow, Teahouse of the August Moon, Hot Spell, Last Angry Man, Mountain Road, Butterfield 8, Ada, Judith; A Dream of Kings, Who's Got the Action?, Who's Been Sleeping in my Bed?, For Love of Ivy, Willard, The Revengers, Maurie, Interval, Lost in the Stars, Matilda.

MANN, DELBERT: Director, Producer. b. Lawrence, Kans., Jan. 30, 1920; e. Vanderbilt Univ., Yale Univ., U.S. Air Force, 1942–45; stage mgr., summer stock, dir. Columbia, S.C. Town Theatre, 1947–49; asst. dir., NBC-TV, 1949; dir., NBC-TV, 1949–55. Past pres. Directors Guild of America.
PROGRAMS: Philco-Goodyear TV Playhouse, Producer's Showcase, Omnibus, Playwrights '56, Playhouse 90, Ford Star Jubilee, Lights Out, Mary Kay and Johnny, The Little Show, Masterpiece Theatre, Ford Startime.
STAGE: A Quiet Place, Speaking of Murder, Zelda, opera: Wuthering Heights; New York City Center.
PICTURES INCLUDE: Marty (Academy Award, best director, 1955), Bachelor Party, Desire Under the Elms, Separate Tables, Middle of the Night, The Dark at the Top of the Stairs, The Outsider, Lover Come Back, That Touch of Mink, A Gathering of Eagles, Dear Heart, Quick Before It Melts, Mister Buddwing, Fitzwilly, The Pink Jungle, Kidnapped, Birch Interval, Night Crossing.
TV: Heidi, David Copperfield, Jane Eyre. The Man Without A Country, A Girl Named Sooner, Breaking Up, Tell Me My Name, Home To Stay, All Quiet on the Western Front, To Find My Sons.

MANN, MICHAEL: Producer-Director-Writer. b. Chicago. e. Univ. of Wisc., London Film School. From 1965–72 directed commercials and documentaries in England, including Insurrection for NBC in Paris during the 1968 riots. Directed short film, Jaunpuri, winner of Juris Prize at Cannes Film Festival. Returned to U.S. in 1972 to direct documentary, 18 Days Down the Line. Wrote for prime-time TV (episodes of Starsky and Hutch, Police Story, Vegas).
PICTURE: Thief (exec. prod., s.p., dir.).
TELEVISION: The Jericho Mile (s.p., dir.). (DGA, 1980 best director award).

MANN, TED: Chairman of the Board, Mann Theatres Corp. of California. b. Wishek, N.D. Acquired first theatre in St. Paul, MN; then acquired and built 25 theatres and drive-ins in Minnesota; acquired National General Theatres circuit of 266 theatres in 1973. Produced Buster and Billie, Lifeguard and Brubaker. Now in production with Dragons of Krull.

MANNE, S. ANTHONY: Executive. b. New York, N.Y., July 19, 1940. e. Wharton School Univ. of Pa. (B.S., economics). Joined Columbia Pictures 1963; international dept. 1964; asst. mgr., Brazil, 1968; mgr., Brazil, 1972–76. Joined JAD Films, 1976; appointed v.p. 1978, exec. v.p., 1979.

MANSON, ARTHUR: Executive. b. Brooklyn, N.Y., Feb. 21, 1928; e. CCNY, grad. (Inst. Film Technique) '45; editor, American Traveler, U.S. Army, 1946; Advance agent, co. mgr., Henry V, U.S., 1948–50; producer's publ. rep., Stanley Kramer Distributing Corp., Samuel Goldwyn Productions, Lopert Films, dir. of adv. and publ., MGM Pictures of Canada, Ltd., 1952–53; publ. and adv. rep., Cinerama Corp., 1953–58; worldwide ad-pub Cinerama (wide screen process) 1958–60; adv. mgr., Columbia Pictures, 1961–62; nat'l dir. of adv., publ., Dino De Laurentiis, 1962–64; exec. asst. to v.p. chg. adv. & pub., 20th Century-Fox, 1964–67; v.p. chg, adv. & pub. Cinerama. Inc., and Cinerama Releasing Corp.; 1967–74; exec. v.p., sales & marketing, BCP, service of Cox Broadcasting Corp., 1974–75; v.p. chg. worldwide adv.-pub. Warner Bros., 1976. In 1977 formed own company, Cinemax Mkt. & Dist. Corp. and is pres.

MANULIS, MARTIN: Prod.-dir. b. N.Y.C. May 30, 1915; e. Columbia Univ., B.A. 1935. Head of prod. John C. Wilson, 1941–49; mgr. dir., Westport Country Playhouse, 1945–50; dir. B'way plays; staff prod. & dir. CBS-TV, 1951–58; head prod. 20th-Fox Television. Now pres. Martin Manulis Prods. Ltd.
BROADWAY: Private Lives, Made in Heaven, The Philadelphia Story, Pride's Crossing, Laura, The Men We Marry, The Hasty Heart, The Show Off.
TV: Suspense, Studio One, Climax, Best of Broadway, Playhouse 90.
PICTURES INCLUDE: Days of Wine and Roses, The Out-Of-Towners, Luv, Duffy.

MANVELL, ROGER (PhD., Litt. D.): Author, Co. Director, broadcaster, screen, TV writer. b. Oct. 10, 1909; e. Kings School Peterborough, London Univ. During World War II with films div. of Min. of Information, mem. Screen Dir. Guild (U.S.); chmn. British Radio & Television Writer's Ass'n. 1953–56; dir. British Film Academy, 1947–59; Consultant Soc. Film and Television Arts (formerly British Film Academy), 1959–75. Visiting fellow Univ. of Sussex; gov. and hd. of Dept. Film Hist., London Film School, 1967–75. Author numerous books on film and T.V. New Cinema in U.S.A., 1968; New Cinema in Britain (1969). The German Cinema, Shakespeare and Film (1971); Films & The 2nd World War (1974), Charles Chaplin (1974). Editor, International Encyclopedia of Film (1972). Theater and film (1979). Ingmar Bergman (1980) Art & Animation (1980). Apptd. Bingham Prof. of Humanities, University of Louisville, 1973. Visiting Prof. Film, Boston Univ., Mass., U.S.A. 1975–81.

MARA, ADELLE: Actress. r.n. Adelaida Delgado; b. Dearborn, Michigan, April 28. m. Roy Huggins. Singer, dancer with Xavier Cugat orchestra; Col. contract.
PICTURES INCLUDE: Shut My Big Mouth, Blondie Goes to College, Alias Boston Blackie, You Were Never Lovelier, Riders of the Northwest Mounted, Magnificent Rogue, Passkey to Danger, Traffic in Crime, Exposed, The Trespasser, Blackmail, Campus Honeymoon, Sands of Iwo Jima, Sea Hornet, Count The Hours, Wake of the Red Witch, Back from Eternity.

MARAIS, JEAN: Actor. b. Cherbourg, France, Dec. 11, 1913; e. Coll. St. Germain, Lycee Janson de Sailly & Lycee Condorcet Painter; photog; stage actor; French Air Army; m.p. debut in Pavillon Brule.
PICTURES INCLUDE: Carmen, Eternal Return, Beauty and the Beast, Ruy Blas, Les Parents Terribles, Secret of Mayerling, Souvenir, Orpheus, Eagle with Two Heads, Inside a Girl's Dormitory, Royal Affairs in Versailles, Paris Does Strange Things, Le Capitan, Le Bossu La Princesse de Cleves, Le Capitaine Fracasse, Honorable Stanilleu, Agent Secret, Patute, Fantomas, Le Gentleman de Cocody.

MARANS, MARDI: Executive. b. 1949. ed. Univ. of Calif. (1971 graduate). Worked in L.A. office of Doyle Dane Bernbach ad agency. Joined Warner Bros. in March, 1975, as asst. to media director. In 1979 appt. v.p. and director of media for WB, responsible for planning and executing placement of all advertising in U.S. and Canada for films distributed by so. Also serves as consultant to intl. div. on use of media in other countries.

MARCH, ALEX: Producer. b. Brooklyn, N.Y. 1920. Actor in stock cos.; later turned to dir.; U.S. Air Force World War II; on Broadway in Look Ma I'm Dancing; then script ed., casting dir., Philco Playhouse; assoc. prod., Nash Airflyte Theatre; joined CBS-TV as script ed., You Are There; prod., Pentagon UCA, Studio One Summer Theatre.

MARCH, DONALD: Production Executive. Held senior programming positions with ABC-TV network and Robert Stigwood Organization before joining CBS in 1977 as director, special projects, motion pictures for TV and mini-series. Later promoted to v.p., motion pictures for TV. Left CBS to serve as pres. of Filmways' theatrical division in early 1979; later that year rejoined CBS as v.p., theatrical films, with responsibility for selection, development and production of pictures for theatrical release.

MARCUS, BEN D.: Chairman of the Board & Chief Executive Officer, The Marcus Corporation, parent company of Marcus Theatres Corporation, Milwaukee, Wis. b. Poland, Aug. 10, 1911. e. U. of Minn., 1934. Promotion, adv. dept., Minn. Journal, 1933–35; entered exhib. in Wis.; now owns & operates 83 theatres 13 drive-ins; pres., nat'l dir., Wis. Allied Theatre Owners, 1950–51–56–57; dir. Wis. Allied Theatre Owners, 1950–51; nat'l dir., 1952; state chmn., Movietime U.S.A., 1951; nat'l pres., Allied States Assn., 1954; chmn., Audience Poll award. State of Wis., 1955; mem., Prod. Code Review Board, 1962–65; chief barker Variety Club, Milwaukee, 1954; COMPO triumvirate rep. Allied States Assn., 1958–65; chmn. exec. comm., Allied States Assn., 1963–65. Treas. Nato; chmn. of bd. NATO of Wisc., treas, nat'l NATO, Code and Rating Appeals Bd., 1968–79; v.p.; Variety International, 1977–79. Received NATO-Walt Disney Humanitarian Award, 1977.

MARCUS, LOUIS: Producer, Director, Writer. b. Cork, Ireland, 1936. e. Natl. Univ. of Ireland (B.A., 1959). Based in Dublin since 1959, where has made nearly 30 theatrical documentary films. Produces and directs for Louis Marcus Documentary Film Production of Dublin and Louis Marcus Films Ltd. of London. In 1964 appt. by Irish govt. as bd. mem. of Dublin's Abbey Theatre. In 1972 appt. by govt. as mem. of Cultural Relations Comm. of Dept. of Foreign Affairs. Elected mem. of Academy of M.P. Arts & Sciences (short subject branch) 1974.
PICTURES INCLUDE: Fleadh Cheoil, Horse Laughs, Woes of Golf, Children at Work, Conquest of Light.
AUTHOR: The Irish Film Industry (1968).

MARDEN, MICHAEL: Executive. e. Princeton Univ. Joined CBS in N.Y. in 1957. Later was TV prog. exec. for Benton & Bowles, Inc. Returned to CBS in April, 1966 as gen. prog. exec. for the network in N.Y. Named director, feature films, and was responsible for the CBS Late Movie (premiere:

1972). In June, 1976 named director, motion pictures for TV and mini-series, Hollywood.

MARENSTEIN, HAROLD: exec. b. New York, N.Y., e. C.C.N.Y., 1937. Shipping, picture checking service, Warner Bros., 1935–45; Booking, Loew's Inc., 1945–48; Booking, contracts, Selznick Rel. Org., 1948–51; contracts, Paramount, 1951–52; asst. sls. gr., International Rel. Org., 1952; asst. sls. mgr., Janus Films, 1961–64; sls. exec., Rizzoli Films, 1965; 1967, nat'l. sales dir., Continental Dist.; gen. sales mgr., Cinemation Industries, 1968. v.p-sales, dir., Cinemation Industries, 1971; 1976, gen. sls. mgr., General National Films; 1980, gen. sls. mgr., Lima Productions.

MARGO: Actress. r.n. Maria Marguerita Guadalupe Boldao y Castilla. b. Mexico City, May 10, 1918. Starred as dancer by Xavier Cugat at Waldorf Astoria, elsewhere; on N.Y. stage (Winterset, Masque of Kings, The Outward Room).
PICTURES INCLUDE: Winterset, Lost Horizon, Crime Without Passion, The Leopard Man, Viva Zapata!, I'll Cry Tomorrow.

MARGOLIN, JANET: Actress. b. New York City, 1943. e. N.Y. High School of Performing Arts. Discovered by Frank Perry while playing in Bdwy. show, Daughter of Silence, and hired by him for lead in David and Lisa.
PICTURES: The Greatest Story Ever Told, Bus Riley's Back in Town, Morituri, Nevada Smith, Enter Laughing, Buena Sera, Mrs. Campbell, Take the Money and Run, Annie Hall, Last Embrace.

MARGRAF, GUSTAV B.: Executive. b. Cape Giradeau, Mo., May 14, 1915; e. Southeast Missouri State Coll. and Duke Univ. Law Sch.; attorney with Cahill, Gordon, Zachry & Reindel 1939–48; v.p., gen. atty., NBC, 1948–53; v.p. for talent NBC, 1953–55; gen. counsel, dir. and v.p. Reynolds Metal Co.; mgng. dir., British Aluminum Co., Ltd.; pres., chmn. bd., Canadian British Aluminum Co., Ltd.; v. chmn., Manicouagan Power Co., chmn., Aluminum Wire & Cable Co. Ltd.; chr. dir., Reynolds Jamaica Mines, Metal Development Corp., Caribbean Steamship Co., Haitian Mines Inc.; chmn. Aluminum Foils Ltd.; pres. Aluminum Fed. of Gt. Britain.

MARGULIES, IRWIN: Attorney, executive. b. Austria. June 24, 1907; e. N.Y.U., BA, 1929; N.Y.U. Law Sch., LL.B., 1931. Assoc. with father in m.p. theatres, 1918; treas., counsel or Jayem Management Corp.; MGM legal dept., N.Y., 1930–42; asst. to v.p.; gen. counsel J. Robert Rubin, 1943–47; asst. secy, counsel, MGM Intern'l Films. Inc., 1945–47; in private practive since 1947. Member Calif. bar since 1948; counsel for many m.p. prod. & dist., cos., literary gencies, radio & TV prod., dist., & personalities; 1954–67 v.p. Horizon Pict. Inc.; 1967, v.p. in charge of bus. affairs, Warner-7 Arts; 1969, with Harry Saltzman; exec. prod., "Digby—The Biggest Dog in The World."

MARGULIES, LYNNE (BARKETT): Actress-Film Maker. b. Feb. 28, 1957 Sylmar, CA. Began film career in 1977 working both in front of and behind the camera. Second ranking executive in Nautilus Films.
PICTURES: Teenage Cruisers, Highriders, The Aftermath.

MARGULIES, STAN: Producer. b. New York, N.Y. Dec. 14, 1920. e. De Witt Clinton High School, New York Univ., B.S., June, 1940; Army Air Force, May, 1942; pub. rels. Air Force and the Infantry, wrote service magazines, newspapers including Yank; spec. feature writer & asst. Sunday editor, Salt Lake City Tribune; publicist, RKO Studios, Hollywood, March, 1947; continued publicity with CBS-Radio, 20th Century-Fox, Walt Disney Productions. Bryna Films, 1955; became vice-pres., 1958; also served exec. prod., TV series, Tales of the Vikings; prod. aide. Spartacus.
PICTURES INCLUDE: 40 Pounds of Trouble, Those Magnificent Men In Their Flying Machines, Don't Just Stand There, The Pink Jungle, If It's Tuesday, This Must Be Belgium, I Love My Wife, Willy Wonka and the Chocolate Factory, One Is A Lonely Number, Visions of Eight.
TV: The Morning After, I Will Fight No More Forever, Collision Course, Roots, Roots: The Next Generation, Moviola, Murder Is Easy.

MARIN, RICHARD: Actor-Writer. b. Los Angeles, July 13, 1946. Teamed with Tommy Chong in improvisational group. Has made comedy recordings with him.
PICTURES: Cheech and Chong's Up in Smoke, Cheech and Chong's Next Movie, Cheech and Chong's Nice Dreams.

MARKHAM, MONTE: Actor. b. Monatee, Fla., June 21. e. Univ. of Ga. Military service in Coast Guard after which joined resident theatre co. at Stephens College, Missouri, where also taught acting. Joined ACT Theatre, San Francisco, for three years. Made TV debut in Mission: Impossible episode then starred in two series.
PICTURES INCLUDE: One Is a Lonely Number, Hour of the Gun, Guns of the Magnificent Seven, Midway, Airport '77.

TELEVISION: The Second Hundred Years (series), Mr. Deeds Goes to Town (series), The New Perry Mason (series), Visions (movie), The Astronaut (movie), Death Takes a Holiday (movie).
BROADWAY: Irene.

MARKLE, FLETCHER: Writer, director, producer. b. Canada, March 27, 1921. Writer, dir., prod. Canadian Broadcasting Co. & BBC, London, 1942–46; prod., dir. Studio One series, CBS, 1947–48; Ford Theatre, CBS, 1948–49; writer, ed. & narrator The Robot Bomb, prize-winning doc. short, 1941; first m.p. dir. Jigsaw, 1949; thereafter Night Into Morning, The Man With a Cloak; prod. Studio One series, CBS, 1952–53; prod., dir., Life with Father, CBS-TV, 1953–55; Front Row Center, 1955. Contributing dir. and/or prod. to various TV film series: Mystery Theatre, Panic, No Warning, Colgate Theatre, Lux Playhouse, M Squad, Buckskin, Rendezvous, Tales of the Vikings, Thriller, Hong Kong, 1956–61. Dir. Father of the Bride, 1961; dir. m.p., The Incredible Journey, 1962; Telescope series, CBC-TV, 1963–72. Head of TV Drama, Canadian Broadcasting Corp. 1970–73, Exec. prod., CBC-TV features and writer in residence. University of Toronto, 1974–75.

MARKOE, JERRY: Composer-Arranger-Conductor. b. New York, N.Y. March 22, 1941. e. Manhattan School of Music (BM, MM in composition, 1968); Julliard School of Music. Winner of ASCAP music for theatre awards.
MUSICALS: Macbird, Fair Play for Eve, Another Time.
MUSIC FOR FILM, THEATER and TV: Faust, The Chinese Wall, He Who Gets Slapped, Ethan Frome, The Lion in Winter, Indulgences in the Louisville Harem, The Cycle, The Ancient Art of Tai Chi.
CHILDREN'S MUSICALS FOR STAGE & TV: Alice in Wonderland, Punch & Judy, Alladin, Cinderella, The Black Princess, Forgotten Treasure, Androcles and the Lion.

MARKOWITZ, ROBERT: Director. Mostly on TV before theatrical debut in Voices, 1979.
TELEVISION: The Deadliest Season, Song of Myself, With All Deliberate Speed, The 34th Star, The Storyteller.

MARKS, ALFRED: Actor-Comedian. b. London, TV, own series, Alfred Marks Time with wife, comedienne Paddie O'Neil.
PICTURES INCLUDE: Desert Mice, There Was A Crooked Man, Weekend With Lulu, The Frightened City, She'll Have To Go.
TV: Blanding's Castle, Hobson's Choice, Paris 1900, The Memorandum.

MARKS, ARTHUR: Producer, Director, Writer, Film Executive. b. Los Angeles, Calif., Aug. 2, 1927. M. Has 4 children. At 19 began work at MGM Studios as Production Messenger. Became Asst. Dir. in 1951, youngest tf. member of Directors Guild of Amer., 1957. Prod. of Perry Mason TV Show from 1961–66. Dir. of over 100 Perry Mason episodes. Prod.-dir.-writer of feature film togetherness. Writer-director tf Class of '74, writer-director of Bonnie's Kids, writer-director of The Roommates, producer-director of Detroit 9000, producer-director of The Centerfold Girls, director of A Woman For All Men, executive producer of Wonder Woman, executive producer, The Candy Snatchers. President and board member of Arthur Prod., Inc. & Arm Service Co. Exec. head of prod., Henry Plitt Prods.
RECENT CREDITS: Bucktown (dir.), Friday Foster (prod., dir.) J.D.'s Revenge (prod.-dir.), Monkey Hustle (prod., dir.).

MARKSON, BEN: Writer. b. Creston, Ia., Aug. 6. Army Capt., W.W. II. Reporter, magazine writer columnist, playwright (Is My Face Red?). Joined Warners, 1932 as writer; since author orig. s.p. dial., adapt., collab., many pictures. Writes many TV plays.
PICTURES INCLUDE: Here Comes the Navy, Woman-Wise, Danger, Love at Work, Is My Face Red?, Brides Are Like That, Half-Naked Truth, Lady Killer, That I May Live, White Cockatoo, Goodbye Again, Great Mr. Nobody, The Beautiful Cheat, A Close Call for Boston Blackie, Prison Ship, The Falcon in San Francisco, Mr. District Attorney, It Happened on Fifth Ave., Edge of Eternity, With My Face to The Enemy.

MARLEY, J. PEVERELL: Cameraman. b. San Jose, Calif., Aug. 14, 1901; Chief cameraman for C. B. DeMille for The Ten Commandments, The Volga Boatman, King of Kings.
PICTURES INCLUDE: Night and Day, Of Human Bondage, Two Mrs. Carrolls, Life with Father, Off Limits, House of Wax, Serenade.

MARLOW, LUCY: Actress. r.n. Lucy Ann McAleer; b. Los Angeles, Calif., Nov. 20, 1932; e. U. of Ariz.
PICTURES INCLUDE: A Star Is Born, Lucky Me, Tight Spot, My Sister Eileen, Queen Bee, Bring Your Smile Along.

MARLOWE, HUGH: Actor. r.n. Hugh Hipple. b. Philadelphia, Pa. Formerly radio announcer. Little Theatre actor; won recognition on London stage. In N.Y. plays. Began screen career 1936. TV series Ellery Queen.
N.Y. PLAYS: Kiss the Boys Goodbye, Margin for Error, Land Is Bright, Lady in the Dark.

PICTURES INCLUDE: Marriage Is a Private Affair, Meet Me in St. Louis, Mrs. Parkington, Come to the Stable, 12 O'Clock High, All About Eve, Rawhide, Mr. Belvedere Rings the Bell, Day the Earth Stood Still, Wait Till the Sun Shines Nellie, Bugles in the Afternoon, Way of a Gaucho, Monkey Business, Stand at Apache River, Casanova's Big Night, Garden of Evil, Illegal, Earth vs. the Flying Saucers, Castle of Evil, The Last Shot You Hear.

MARLOWE, LOUIS J.: Producer, director. r.n. L. J. Goetten. b. St. Cloud, Minn., Jan. 4, e. Hollywood H.S., USC. Prop man, asst. dir., unit mgr., dr. special effects, shorts, second units Warner Bros., freelance dir. comedy series; Director features both theatrical and TV programs.

MARLY, FLORENCE: Actress. b. Czechoslovakia, June 2; e. Sorbonne, Paris. Appeared in 9 films in France inc. L'Alibi, Cafe de Paris, Les Maudits; also films in Argentina, Czechoslovakia.
PICTURES INCLUDE: Sealed Verdict, Tokyo Joe, Tokyo File 212, Gobs and Gals, Queen of Blood, Games.

MARRIOTT, PETER: Executive. b. Isle of Wright, England, 1921. Ent. ind. 1949. Assoc. prod. TV series Douglas Fairbanks Presents. Assoc. prod. Chase A Crooked Shadow, Moment of Danger, etc. Man. dir. Desilu Sales Inc. Dir. U.K. and Continental TV Sales 20th Century-Fox. Now man. dir. and dir. European operations NBC International (G.B.) Ltd.

MARSHALL, E. G.: Actor. b. Minnesota. Acting debut with Oxford Players, 1933. Numerous TV appearances on all networks; m.p. debut in House on 92nd St.
BROADWAY: Jason, Jacobowsky and the Colonel, Skin of Our Teeth, Iceman Cometh, Woman Bites Dog, The Survivors, The Gambler, The Crucible, The Little Foxes.
PICTURES INCLUDE: 13 Rue Madeleine, Call Northside 77, Caine Mutiny, Pushover, Bamboo Prison, Broken Lance, Silver Chalice, Left Hand of God, Scarlet Hour, 12 Angry Men, Bachelor Party, Town Without Pity, The Chase, Tora, Tora, Tora, The Bridge at Remagen, The Pursuit of Happiness, Interiors, Superman II.
TV: The Defenders, The Bold Ones.

MARSHALL, LARRY: Comedian, actor, writer, songwriter. b. Clarkston, Scotland. Trained Rutherglen repertory theatre. Own daily lunchtime television show for eight years. Appeared in many major television drama series; own evening shows; Comedy and panel games.

MARSHALL, PENNY: Actress. b. New York City, Oct. 15. m. actor Bob Reiner. Dropped out of Univ. of New Mexico to teach dancing. Acted in summer stock before going to Hollywood to make TV debut in The Danny Thomas Hour.
TV: The Bob Newhart Show, The Mary Tyler Moore Show, Chico and the Man, The Odd Couple (regular), Laverne & Shirley (regular). Movie: Let's Switch.

MARSHALL, PETER: Actor-TV Show Host. b. Huntington, W. Va., March 30. r.n. Pierre La Cock. Began career as NBC page in N.Y.C. Did plays both on and off Bdwy., starring with Julie Harris in Skyscraper. Teamed with the late Tommy Noonan in comedy act for nightclubs, guesting on Ed Sullivan Show and other variety shows. In 1974 made Las Vegas stage debut and since has been headliner there and in Reno and Lake Tahoe.
PICTURES INCLUDE: Ensign Pulver, The Cavern, Americathon.
TV: Two of the Most (local N.Y. show), The Hollywood Squares (host).

MARSHALL, TRUDY: Actress. b. Brooklyn, N.Y. Commercial photographers' model before entering pictures, 1942.
PICTURES INCLUDE: Secret Agent of Japan, Girl Trouble, Sentimental Journey, Dragonwyck, Talk About a Lady, Boston Blackie and the Law, Alias Mr. Twilight, Too Many Winners, Joe Palooka in the Knockout, Key Witness, Fuller Brush Man, Disaster, Shamrock Hill, Mark of Gorilla, The President's Lady.

MARSHALL, WILLIAM: Actor. b. Chicago, Ill., Oct. 12, 1917. In 1936, vocalist with Fred Waring's Orchestra; from 1937 orch. leader; on stage 1943, Army Air show Winged Victory. Screen debut 1940 in Sante Fe Trail.
PICTURES INCLUDE: Flowing Gold, City for Conquest, Flying with Music, Murder in the Music Hall, Earl Carroll's Sketchbook, That Brennan Girl, Calendar Girl, Blackmail, Adventures of Captain Fabian, Seven Different Ways.

MARSHALL, ZENA: Actress. b. Kenya (East Africa). e. France and finishing school in Ascot (England). Made her stage debut in repertory. Many TV appearance U.S. and England including Bob Hope show, Harpers W.I., Ghost Squad.
PICTURES INCLUDE: Marry Me, Dark Interval, Blind Man's Bluff, Love's a Luxury, Deadly Nightshade, My Wife's Family, Bermuda Affair, Let's Be Happy, Dr. No, The Guilty Party, Those Magnificent Men In Their Flying Machines, The Terrornauts.
TV: International Detective, Invisible Man, Dial 999,

Danger Man, Sir Francis Drake, Man of The World, Human Jungle, Sentimental Agent, Court Martial.

MARTA, JACK: Cameraman, Republic Studios. b. Butte, Montana, 1905; e. Los Angeles public schools. Began as laboratory worker for Fox. Then to Columbia. Later with Republic.
PICTURES INCLUDE: In Old Sacramento, Bells of San Angelo, Bill and Cool, Fair Wind to Java, Jubilee Trail, Timberjack, Last Command, Come Next Spring, Maverick Queen.

MARTEL, GENE: Producer, director. b. New York, N.Y., June 19, 1916. e. C.C.N.Y., University of Alabama, Sorbonne, Paris; newspaperman, New York and Birmingham, Ala.; dancer, actor, choreographer, director Broadway; prod. dir., many documentaries; films for State Department, others; dir. for Paramount Pictures. Joined Princess Pictures 1952 to make films in Europe; formed own company, Martel Productions Inc., 1954.
PICTURES INCLUDE: Check-mate, Double-barrelled Miracle, The Lie, Double Profile, Sergeant and the Spy, Black Forest, Eight Witnesses, Fire One, Phantom Caravan, Doorway to Suspicion, Diplomatic Passport, Immediate Disaster.

MARTIN, AL: Writer since 1932, including: (s.p.) The Last Alarm; (orig., s.p.) Flying Wild; (collab. orig., s.p.) Mississippi Gambler; (s.p.) Stagecoach Buckaroo, The Devil with Hitler; (joint orig. s.p.) Gang Busters, serial: s.p., Amazon Quest; orig. story, Standing Room Only, Adventures of Rusty; s.p., Nine Girls, Strange Mrs. Crane; collab. s.p. Racing Luck; s.p., Army Bound, In the Money.
TV: Trouble with Father, Mystery Theatre, Ramar of the Jungle, Joe Palooka, Hank McCune Show, Wild Bill Hickok, Craig Kennedy Series, Mayor of the Town, Ford Theatre, Frontier Doctor, Lone Ranger, Damon Runyon Theatre, Roy Rogers, Screen Gems, Dupont Theatre, Gray Ghost, Restless Gun, Whirlybird, Trouble Shooters, Huckleberry Finn (serial), Spark Tarzan, 77 Sunset Strip, Man Trap, Laramie, My Favorite Martian; co-creat., My Living Doll.

MARTIN, CHARLES E.: Writer, director, producer. e. NYU, N.J. Law Sch.; under contract to MGM, Universal and Twentieth Century Fox; pres., Forward Films, Inc.
PICTURES INCLUDE: My Dear Secretary, No Leave No Love, Death of a Scoundrel, If He Hollers Let Him Go, Remember Vivian Valentine, Seduction American Style, How to Seduce a Woman, Hotshot, The Cop Who Played God, One Man Jury, Dead on Arrival, Muffet Ann Marvel, And Now It Can Be Told.
TELEVISION: Tallulah Bankhead Show, Gertrude Lawrence Show, Philip Morris Playhouse. Wrote 500 scripts.

MARTIN, DEAN: Actor. b. Steubenville, Ohio, June 17, 1917. e. Steubenville High School. Was amateur prizefighter; worked at odd jobs, mill hand, gasoline attendant, prior to acting career. Joined Jerry Lewis, comedian at 500 Club, Atlantic City, N.J., as straight man-singer, 1946; played many theatres, night clubs (see biography: Jerry Lewis). Team m.p. debut: My Friend Irma. Voted (with Jerry Lewis) one of the top ten Money-Making Stars in Motion Picture Herald-Fame poll, 1951, 1953–55; Number One, 1952.
PICTURES INCLUDE: My Friend Irma Goes West, At War With the Army, That's My Boy, The Stooge, Sailor Beware, Jumping Jacks, The Caddy, Scared Stiff, Money from Home, Living It Up, Three Ring Circus, You're Never Too Young, Artists and Models, Pardners, Hollywood Or Bust, 10,000 Bedrooms, The Young Lions, Some Came Running, Rio Bravo, Career, Who Was That Lady?, Bells Are Ringing, Ocean's 11, Ada, Sergeants 3, Who's Got the Action?, Toys In the Attic, Who's That Sleeping in My Bed, Robin and the Seven Hoods, Kiss Me Stupid, Sons of Katie Elder, Rough Night in Jericho, How To Save a Marriage, Airport, The Ambushers, The Wrecking Crew, Something Big, Showdown, Mr. Ricco, The Cannonball Run.
TV: Club Oasis, Dean Martin Show. Golden Globe Award.

MARTIN, DEWEY: Actor. b. Katemcy, Texas, Dec. 8: e. U. of Ga., Louisiana State Teachers Coll. U.S. Navy, W.W. II; actor, little theatres & stock; m.p. debut in Knock on Any Door.
PICTURES INCLUDE: The Thing, Big Sky, Tennessee Champ, Prisoner of War, Men of the Fighting Lady, Land of the Pharaohs, Desperate Hours, Proud and Profane, 10,000 Bedrooms.

MARTIN, DON: Writer. b. Phila., Pa., April 3, 1911; e. Girard Coll., U. Delaware, B.A.; George Washington U. Law School; husband of Tamara, actress, Journalist, Washington Post, Star, 1932–33; gen. mgr., Diamond State Theat. Co., 1933–34; newspaper, magazine, radio writer, 1934–42. Successively with Columbia, United Artists, MGM, RKO-Radio publicity depts. Joined 20th-Fox writing dept., 1943.
PICTURES INCLUDE: Devil's Cargo, Appointment with Murder, Shakedown, Shed No Tears, The Creeper, Lost Tribe, Arrow in the Dust, Lone Gun, Shield for Murder, Stranger on Horseback, Double Jeopardy, No Man's Woman, Deadliest Sin, Quincannon Frontier Scout, Emer-

gency Hospital, Hot Cars, Brass Legend, Storm Rider. The Pretender, Lighthouse, Hat Box Mystery, Triple Threat, Search for Danger, Destination Murder, The Man Is Armed, Violent Road, Operation Tobruk, The Four Deuces.
TV: Playhouse of Stars, Racket Squad, Fireside Theatre, Mr. District Attorney, Trouble With Father, Rebound, Celebrity Theatre, Cheyenne, Sheriff of Chochise, Whirly-birds, The Violent Road.

MARTIN, EDWIN DENNIS: Executive. b. Columbus, Ga., Jan. 30, 1920, e. grad., Univ. of Georgia, B.S., 1940; Anti Air Craft Artillery, past pres. TOA, International.

MARTIN, HENRY H.: Executive. b. Holcomb, Miss., March 22, 1912. Joined Universal poster clerk, Oklahoma City, 1935; then booker, then salesman. Military service 1943–46. Rejoined Universal as salesman, Oklahoma City, then branch manager; to Dallas as branch manager, 1948, to district manager, 1951, to New York as southern division manager 1956; general sales manager, 1957. Elected v.p. Universal Pictures Co., Inc., Nov. 2, 1959. Namedv.p. of MCA, Inc., Dec., 1972 and president of Universal, Jan. 1, 1973.

MARTIN, MARIAN: Actress. b. Philadelphia, June 7, 1916. e. Bayonne School, Switzerland. On stage in Follies of 1933, George White's Scandals, and others.
PICTURES INCLUDE: Sinners in Paradise, Deadline for Murder, Suspense, Cinderella Jones, Queen of Burlesque, Angel on My Shoulder, That's My Girl, That Brennan Girl, Lighthouse, Thunder in the Pines, Come to the Stable, Key to the City, Dakota Lil.

MARTIN, MARY: Actress. b. Wetherford, Texas, Dec. 1, 1914; e. Ward-Belmont Sch., Nashville, Tenn.; m.p. debut in 1939.
STAGE: Lute Song, Leave It to Me, One Touch of Venus, South Pacific, Annie Get Your Gun, Kind Sir, Peter Pan, Jennie, I Do I Do.
PICTURES INCLUDE: Great Victor Herbert, Rhythm on the River, Love Thy Neighbor, Kiss the Boys Goodbye, New York Town, Birth of the Blues, Happy Go Lucky, Night and Day.
TV: Ford anniversary show, Rodgers & Hammerstein Cavalcade show. Peter Pan, Together with Music (with Noel Coward).

MARTIN, MILLICENT: Actress, singer. Toured U.S. The Boy Friend, 1954–57.
STAGE: Expresso Bongo, The Crooked Mile, Our Man Crichton, Tonight at 8, The Beggars Opera, Puss 'n Boots, The Card, Absurd Person Singular, Aladdin, Side By Side By Sondheim, Move Over Mrs. Markham, Meet Mr. Stewart.
TV: International Detective Series, Millie, That Was the Week That Was, Harry Moorings; own series, Mainly Millicent, Kiss Me Kate; 1966 own series, Millicent TV; 1967: London Palladium Color Show, USA, Danny Kaye, Piccadilly London; From a Bird's Eye View (own series); Tom Jones show, Englebert Humperdinck show.
PICTURES INCLUDE: The Horsemaster, The Girl on the Boat, Nothing But the Best, Alfie, Stop the World I Want To Get Off.

MARTIN, R. E.: Exhibitor. b. Columbus, Ga., March 25, 1917. e. grad., Univ. of Georgia, B.S.C., 1939. Co-owner, Martin Theatre Circuit; co-owner, TV stations, WTVM, Columbus, Ga., WTVC, Chattanooga, Tenn.; partner, The Marbro Co.; dir., Columbus Transportation Co.; exec. comm., TOA; pres., Junior Achievement; past pres., Columbus Chamber of Commerce; dir., Y.M.C.A.; member, Rotary Club.

MARTIN, RICHARD: Producer-Director. b. New York City, Feb. 2, 1938. e. Harvard. Stage and TV actor in N.Y. from 1959 to 1969; writer from 1969–73.
PICTURES INCLUDE: The Bengal Tiger, The Chase Expedition, Jaws of Death (also s.p.).

MARTIN, ROY E., Jr.: Executive. b. Columbus, Ga., March 25, 1917; e. U. of Ga., (BSC); Troy State (MSC, 1979); Retired.

MARTIN, STEVE: Actor. b. Waco, TX, 1946. e. Long Beach Coll., UCLA. Writer for various TV comedy shows (Smothers Brothers, Sonny & Cher, etc.). Acted on TV in Steve Martin—A Wild and Crazy Guy, Steve Allen Comedy Hours, Comedy Is Not Pretty, etc.
PICTURES: The Kids Are Alright, The Muppet Movie, The Jerk.

MARTIN, TONY: Singer, musician, actor. b. Oakland, Calif., Dec. 25, 1913; e. Oakland H.S.; St. Mary's Coll.; m. Cyd Charisse, actress-dancer. Sang, played saxophone & clarinet in high school band, engaged by nearby theatres for vaudeville; with Five Red Peppers, jazz group at 14 yrs.; two yrs. later with band, Palace Hotel, San Francisco; radio debut Walter Winchell program, 1932; joined Tom Gerund's band, World's Fair Chicago, 1933; played night clubs. First starring radio show, Tune Up Time (singer & emcee); on Burns and Allen program; own show for Texaco, Carnation Contented Hour.
RECORDINGS INCLUDE: Begin the Beguine, Intermezzo, The Last Time I Saw Paris, I'll See You in My Dreams, Domino, September Song.

PICTURES INCLUDE: Sing Baby Sing, Follow The Fleet, You Can't Have Everything; Ali Baba Goes to Town, Music in My Heart, Ziegfield Girl, Till The Clouds Roll By, Cabash, Two Tickets to Broadway, Here Come the Girls, Easy to Love, Deep in My Heart, Hit the Deck, Quincannon Frontier Scout, Let's Be Happy, The Big Store.

MARTINI, ALLEN V.: Executive. b. San Francisco, Dec. 14, 1919. e. Stanford U. Since resigning from Air Force ent. m.p. ind., 1945. Executive capacity RKO Studios; partner Filmakers Prod.; 1950; United Artists Television, 1953; associated with National General Corporation since 1963; man. dir., Carthay Center Productions Ltd., National General's subsidiary, London, 1966; vice-pres., National General Productions Inc.; formerly vice-president, National General Television Corporation.

MARTINS, ORLANDO: Actor, singer, b. Lagos, Nigeria; e. Eko High School, Lagos, Stage debut, Stevedore, 1937; creen debut; Men Of Two Worlds, 1946.
PICTURES INCLUDE: The Hasty Heart, Where No Vultures Fly, West Of Zanzibar, Simba, Safari, Seven Waves Away, Naked Earth, The Nun's Story, Sapphire, Frankie & Johnnie, Cry the Beloved Country, In Judea, This Book Is News, Killers of Kilimanjaro, Sammy Going South, Call Me Bwana, Mister Moses.

MARTON, ANDREW: Director. b. Budapest, Hungary, Jan. 26, 1904. Vita Film, Vienna, 1922; to Hollywood with Ernst Lubitsch, 1923; started directing in Berlin, then in London, Wolf's Clothing, Secret of Stamboul, School for Husbands; in Hollywood, Little Bit of Heaven, Gentle Annie, Gallant Bess.
PICTURES INCLUDE: King Solomon's Mines, Wild North, Storm Over Tibet, Devil Makes Three, Gypsy Colt, Prisoner of War, Men of the Fighting Lady, Green Fire, Underwater Warrior, Cinerama Seven Wonders of the World, It Happened In Athens, The Longest Day, The Thin Red Line, Crack in the World, Clarence the Crosseyed Lion, Around the World Under The Sea, Birds Do It, Africa-Texas Style.
TV: Man and The Challenge, Daktari, Cowboy in Africa, The Sea Hunt.

MARVIN, LEE: Actor. b. New York, N.Y., Feb. 19, 1924. Played in summer stock cos.; Bway. debut in Billy Budd; m.p. debut in You're in the Navy Now.
PICTURES INCLUDE: Diplomatic Courier, We're Not Married, Down Among the Sheltering Palms, Eight Iron Men, Stranger Wore a Gun, Big Heat, Gun Fury, Wild One, Caine Mutiny, Gorilla at Large, The Raid, Bad Day at Black Rock, Life in the Balance, Violent Saturday, Not As a Stranger, Pete Kelly's Blues, I Died a Thousand Times, The Rack, Shack Out on 101, Attack!, The Killers, Ship of Fools, Cat Ballou, The Professionals, The Dirty Dozen, Point Blank, Sergeant Ryker, Paint Your Wagon, Monte Walsh, Pocket Money, Prime Cut, Emperor of the North, The Spikes Gang, The Iceman Cometh, The Klansman, Great Scout and Cathouse Thursday, Shout at the Devil, Death Hunt.

MARX, SAMUEL: Writer-producer.
PICTURES INCLUDE: Lassie Come Home, This Man's Navy, My Brother Talks to Horses, The Beginning or End, A Lady Without Passport, Grounds for Marriage, Kiss of Fire, Ain't Misbehavin', Waterloo, Rome, The Ravine.

MASEFIELD, JOSEPH R.: Executive, Producer, Director, Writer. b. N.Y., N.Y., June 20, 1933, 1950 American Academy of Dramatic Arts. Writer-performer, club work (as Steve Parker). Later, actor in stock; formed EEF Film Productions, 1956; prod. A Story Like Two (short), A City Eats (doc.). In m.p. as unit mgr., asst. dir. and prod. mgr. Later writer and film editor: Montage (Time-Life); Ages of Man (IBM); Festival of Two Worlds (Bell Telephone Hour) and special, The New Face of Israel. Asst. dir., prod. mgr., Mitgebracht Aus New York (German TV), The Devils Doubloon, (feature); Writer-director, Citizen Smith, feature documentary. Co-director and assoc. prod. Hear My Song, (Cavalier Films), 1969 producer The Spy. 1969, vice pres. in charge of prod. PCI, Inc. Public Relations director, The Max Steiner Music Society; pres., Joseph R. Masefield & Associates. In 1974, formed Majer Prods. with Steve Jerro.
PICTURES INCLUDE: A New Life, The Vanquished, Trio, Living Planet, The Burning Man.

MASLANSKY, PAUL: Producer.—Director—Writer. Studied filmmaking at Cinemateque Francais where made a documentary (Letter from Paris) which won Cannes Festival award. Asst. dir. on Counterfeit Traitor; followed by prod. mgr. on several films in Europe, including The Running Man and Jason and the Argonauts. Wrote and produced Gothic horror films, including Castle of the Living Dead. Covered Israeli war in 1967 with CBS film group; spent year in Russia on The Red Tent, followed by The Blue Bird. Filmed Big Truck and Poor Claire in Israel; Miracles Still Happen in Brazil.
PICTURES: Damnation Alley (co-prod.), When You Comin' Back, Red Ryder (co-prod.).

MASON, JAMES: Actor. b. Huddersfield, Yorkshire, England, May 15, 1909; e. Marlborough Coll.; Peterhouse Coll., Cambridge; m. Pamela Kellino, actress & writer. On stage from 1931, tour. repertory; London debut 1933 in "Gallows Glorious"; other appearances include "Bonnett Over the Windmill," "Road to Rome," "Divorce for Christabel," "Jupiter Laughs." Screen debut 1935 in "Late Extra"; since in numerous Brit. feature pictures. Voted one of top ten Brit. money-making stars in Motion Picture Herald-Fame Poll: 1944, 45, 46, 47, 48.
PICTURES INCLUDE: The Mill on the Floss, Fire Over England, The Return of the Scarlet Pimpernel, I Met a Murderer, This Man Is Dangerous, Hotel Reserve, They Were Sisters, Seventh Veil, Wicked Lady, Odd Man Out, Upturned Glass, Patient Vanishes, Man of Evil, Hatter's Castle, Place of One's Own, Caught, Pandora and The Flying Dutchman, Lady's Possessed, Desert Fox, 5 Fingers, Botany Bay, Story of Three Loves, Prisoner of Zenda, Face to Face (Secret Share), Julius Caesar, Desert Rats, Man Between, Prince Valiant, A Star Is Born, 20,000 Leagues Under the Sea, Forever Darling, Bigger than Life, Island in the Sun, North by Northwest, Journey to The Center of The Earth, A Touch of Larceny, The Decks Ran Red, Marriage-Go-Round, Lolita, The Pumpkin Eater, Lord Jim, Georgy Girl, The Deadly Affair, The Seagull, Mayerling, Age of Consent, Child's Play, The Last of Sheila, The Mackintosh Man, 11 Harrowhouse, Mandingo, Voyage of the Damned, Cross of Iron, Heaven Can Wait, The Boys from Brazil, Murder by Decree, The Passage, ffolkes.

MASON, KENNETH: Executive. b. Rochester, N.Y. Sept. 21, 1917. e. Washington and Jefferson College; Univ. of Rochester (graduate work). Began career with Eastman Kodak Co. in Kodak Park cine processing dept. in 1935; transferred following year to film developing dept. at Kodak Research Laboratories. Returned to college in 1938 to complete studies and returned to Kodak year later to same dept. Later joined film planning dept., remaining there until entering military service in 1943. Returned to Kodak in 1946 as staff engineer in Kodak Office motion picture film dept. In 1950 appt. mgr. of Midwest Division of m.p. film dept.; became gen. mgr., Midwest Division, m.p. products sales dept. in 1963; named sls. mgr. of New York City region in 1965; appt. regional sls. mgr. of Pacific Southern Region, Hollywood, in 1970. On Jan. 1, 1974 appt. mgr., product programs and research, Motion Picture and Audiovisual Markets Division, Kodak Office. On March 18, 1974 named gen. mgr. of that division. Elected asst. v.p. of co. on March 28, 1974, v.p., Dec. 11, 1978.
MEMBER: Board of Trustees of Washington and Jefferson College; past pres. of Society of Motion Picture & Television Engineers, honorary fellow of British Kinematograph Sound & Television Society; mbr. of University Film Assn., Academy of TV Arts and Sciences, Motion Picture Academy, American Society of Cinematographers, Variety Club.

MASON, MARSHA: Actress. b. St. Louis. m. Neil Simon. Came to N.Y. to continue dramatic studies and embark on theatre career. Appeared off-Broadway (Happy Birthday, Wanda June, Deerpark) and on Broadway (Cactus Flower). Now member of American Conservatory Theatre, San Francisco.
PICTURES INCLUDE: Blume in Love (debut), Cinderella Liberty, Audrey Rose, The Goodbye Girl, The Cheap Detective, Promises in the Dark, Chapter Two, Only When I Laugh.
TV: Love of Life (series), Brewsie and Willie, Cyrano de Bergerac.

MASON, PAMELA: Actress, writer. b. Westgate. England. Mar. 10, 1918; Stage debut 1936, The Luck of the Devil, London; also playwright (in collab. James Mason, Flying Blind, Made in Heaven), Author novels This Little Hand, A Lady Possessed, The Blinds Are Down, Ignoramus, Began Brit. screen career 1938, I Met a Murderer (orig. story & s.p.; cast); also in They Were Sisters, 1944. In 1946 (s.p. & Cast) The Upturned Glass; (acted) Pandora and the Flying Dutchman; acted, collab. s.p. Lady Possessed, syndicated TV, Pamela Mason Show, author Marriage Is the First Step Toward Divorce. Syndicated TV The Weaker Sex?; author, The Female Pleasure Hunt; lectures at women's clubs countrywide.

MASSEN, OSA: Actress. b. Denmark, Copenhagen. Jan. 13, 1916.
PICTURES INCLUDE: Honeymoon in Bali, Honeymoon for Three, A Woman's Face, Accent on Love, You'll Never Get Rich, The Devil Pays Off, Ireland, Strange Journey, Night Unto Night, Deadline at Dawn, Gentleman Misbehaves, Rocketship XM.

MASSEY, DANIEL: Actor. b. London, Eng., Oct. 10, 1933. e. Eaton and King's Colleges f. Raymond Massey. Active on stage and TV.
PICTURES INCLUDE: Girls at Sea, Upstairs and Downstairs, The Queen's Guard, Go to Blazes, Moll Flanders,

The Jokers, Star!, Fragment of Fear, Mary, Queen of Scots, Victory.

MASSEY, RAYMOND: Actor. b. Toronto, Canada, Aug. 30, 1896; s. Chester D. and Anna Vincent Massey, e. Appleby School, Oakville, Ont.; Belliol Coll., Oxford; Litt. D. (hon) Lafayette U.; Hobart Coll., Smith Coll., LL.D. (hon.) Queens U., Kingston, Ont. m. Dorothy Ludengton. Canadian Field artillery officer, World War I; wounded in Belgium; then with Siberian Expeditionary Force; on stage in England, 1922; since then in many plays in England and U.S.
THEATRE: Ethan Frome, Abe Lincoln in Illinois, Pygmalion, John Brown's Body; dir. numerous stage plays.
PICTURES INCLUDE: Has appeared in more than 60 motion pictures. The Scarlet Pimpernel, Things to Come, The Prisoner of Zenda, Abe Lincoln in Illinois, Hurricane, Possessed, Mourning Becomes Electra, Fountainhead, Arsenic and Old Lace, Santa Fe Trail, Sugarfoot, Dallas, David and Bathsheba, Come Fill the Cup, Prince of Players, Battle Cry, East of Eden, Seven Angry Men, The Naked and the Dead, McKenna's Gold.
TV: Dr. Kildare.

MASSIE, PAUL: Actor. b. Ontario, Canada. July 7, 1932. Early career on Canadian stage. Attended Central School, London, 1952, later jnd. Scottish National Children's Theatre. Entered m.p. ind. 1954 in Orders to Kill.
PICTURES INCLUDE: High Tide at Noon, Sapphire, Libel, The Two Faces of Dr. Jekyll, The Rebel, The Pot Carriers, Raising the Wind.
STAGE: Cat On a Hot Tin Roof.
TV: The Mark of the Warrior, The Last of the Brave, Ring Around the Moon, Secret Mission and Her Romeo.

MASTORAKIS, NICO: Writer-Director. b. Athens, Greece, 1941. Writer of novels and screenplays. Books include Fire Below Zero and The Ephesus Scrolls (co-author).
PICTURES: The Next One (s.p., dir.).

MASTROIANNI, MARCELLO: Actor. b. Fontane Liri, Italy, Sept. 28, 1924. e. U. of Rome theatrical company. Draftsman in Rome, 1940–43. Theatrical debut in Rome in Angelica, 1948.
PLAYS INCLUDE: Death of a Salesman, Streetcar Named Desire, Ciao Rudy.
PICTURES INCLUDE: Three Girls from Rome, The Miller's Beautiful Wife, Fever to Live, The Ladykillers of Rome, Love a La Carte, Days of Love, La Dolce Vita, White Nights, Divorce Italian Style, La Notte, A Very Private Affair, Bell Antonio, Where the Hot Wind Blows, The Organizer, 8½, Yesterday, Today and Tomorrow, Marriage Italian Style, Casanova '70, The 10th Victim, The Poppy Is Also a Flower, Shoot Loud, Louder . . . I Don't Understand, The Stranger, A Place for Lovers, Leo the Last, Diamonds for Breakfast, Sunflower, Jealousy Italian Style, The Priest's Wife. Formed indep. prod. co., Master Films, 1966; What?, The Grande Bouffe, Massacre in Rome, Down the Ancient Stairs, The Sunday Woman, A Special Day, Stay As You Are, Blood Feud, City of Women.

MATHEWS, CAROLE: Actress. b. Montgomery, Ill., Sept. 13. e. Aurora, Ill. H.S. Started as night club, radio entertainer; to Hollywood, 1944.
PICTURES INCLUDE: Massacre River, Great Gatsby, Special Agent, Meet Me at the Fair, Swamp Woman, Port of Heil, Shark River, Treasure of Ruby Hills, Requirement for a Redhead, Look In Any Window, Thirteen Men, Female Fiend, Tender Is The Night, End of the Road.
TV: Steel Hour, Kraft Theatre, Lux Video, Hitchcock Presents, Studio One, Californians, Texan, 77 Sunset Strip, Perry Mason, Four Star Theatre, M-Squad, Death Valley Days, Guestward Ho, Two Faces West, Johnny Midnight, Pete & Gladys, 87th Precinct, Ben Casey.

MATLACK, JACK D.: Theatre executive, publicist. b. Manton, Calif., Feb. 22, 1914; e. Chico, Calif. State Teachers Coll. Entered m.p. ind. as doorman Criterion, Medford, Ore.; then mgr. dir.; joined J.J. Parker Theatres, Portland, Ore., 1943; as exec. asst. to pres. and adv. dir. eight theatres; now pres. Jack Matlack Promotions. Portland, Ore. N.W.P.R. for studios; well known showman, winner 20 exploit. awards including Grand (Silver) Quigley Award, 1943; Quigley Star Showmanship Award, 1942–44; numerous Quigley Pub. citations; cited by U.S. Govt. for outstanding contrib. to World War II effort; active as civic worker; on bd. Portland, Ore. C. of C. Kiwanis, Portland City Planning Comm., Oregon Advertising Club; named First Citizen of Portland, 1944.

MATOFSKY, HARVEY: Executive. b. Bklyn., N.Y., Jan. 12, 1933. e. Washington Square Coll., N.Y.U., 1950–52; Brooklyn Coll., B.A., 1954; Sorbonne, 1956; New York Film Institute, 1959. New York Times newspaper. 1952–54; U.S. Army Intelligence, Austria. Italy. 1954–56. Ent. m.p. industry, reporter. Independent Film Journal; assoc. editor. 1957; publicity dept., United Artists, 1959; international publicity dir., Embassy Pictures, 1960; apptd., dir., adv. & pub., Morningside Worldwide Pictures, 1961; appt. European publicity coordinator Embassy Pictures. Rome, 1963;

publicity coordinator: The Wonders of Aladdin, Jason and the Golden Fleece, The Old Dark House, Ballad of the Running Man, Gidget Goes to Rome, "8½", Ghost at Noon, prod. dir. motion picture shorts N.Y. Film Institute. Executive vice pres. Marstan Productions (1969), and coproducer of the Alberto Moravia film "Crime at the Tennis Club" and TV special Upon this Rock. Author, s.p. The Stranger (based on Lillian Ross novel). Formed and is pres. RHM Music and Records, Ltd. London. Pres. of RHM Productions. 1973: produced Zandy's Bride.

MATSOUKAS, NICHOLAS JOHN: Executive. b. Pylos-Navarino, Greece, June 13, 1903. e. U. of Chicago, Ph.D. 1929. Editorial staff of Chicago Daily News; ran own public relations office; adv., prom. dir., Cinema Art Theatre Chicago, 1932; pub. relations dir. and campaign mgr., Greek War Relief Assn. 1940–41; dir. adv. pub. and community Service dept., Skouras Theatres Corp. since 1941; nat'l. dir., adv., pub. & exploitation, Magna Theatres Corp.; nat'l. campaign dir., Will Rogers Memorial Hospital, Saranac Lake, N.Y., American Korean Foundation; producer, show, It's Up to You, National Food Admin., U.S. Dept. of Agriculture; adv., pub. dir., United Artists Theatre Circuit, Inc., Rivoli Theatre; pres., Movie Bonus Corp.

MATTHAU, WALTER: Actor. b. New York, Oct. 1, 1923. Served in Air Force WW II. Studied journalism at Columbia, then acted in summer stock. First Broadway role, 1948, in Anne of a Thousand Days.
THEATRE: Will Success Spoil Rock Hunter? and The Odd Couple.
PICTURES INCLUDE: A Face in the Crowd, The Kentuckian, Slaughter on Tenth Avenue, Indian Fighter, No Power on Earth, Middle of the Street, Onion Head, Voice in the Mirror, King Creole, Lonely Are the Brave, Strangers When We Meet, Who's Got the Action, The Gangster Story, Charade, Goodbye Charlie, Mirage, The Fortune Cookie, A Guide for the Married Man, The Odd Couple, Candy, Cactus Flower, Hello Dolly, A New Leaf, Plaza Suite, Pete 'n' Tillie, Charley Varrick, The Laughing Policeman, The Taking of Pelham 1,2,3, The Front Page, The Sunshine Boys, The Bad News Bears, Casey's Shadow, House Calls, California Suite, Little Miss Marker, Hopscotch, First Monday in October.

MATTHEWS, JESSIE: (O.B.E.) Actress, Singer. b. London, England, March 11, 1907. London stage debut 1919 in Bluebell in Fairyland. Subseq. in numerous musicals, dramas, London. Starred on U.S. stage in Andre Charlot's Revue of 1924, Wake Up and Dream (1929–30), The Lady Comes Across (1941), Jessie Matthews in Concert (1979).
STAGE (London): One Damn Thing After Another, This Year of Grace, Wake Up and Dream, Ever Green, Hold My Hand, Sally Who?, Come Out to Play, Wild Rose, Maid to Measure, Sweethearts and Wives, Sauce Tartare, Five Finger Exercise, A Share in the Sun, The Water Babies (1973), The Jessie Matthews Show (1976), Lady Windermere's Fan (1978–79).
PICTURES INCLUDE: The Beloved Vagabond, Straws in the Wind, This England, Out of the Blue, There Goes the Bride, The Man From Toronto, The Midshipmaid, The Good Companions, Friday the Thirteenth, Waltzes from Vienna, Evergreen, First A Girl, It's Love Again, Head Over Heels, Gangway, Sailing Along, Climbing High, Forever and a Day (in Hollywood), Candles At Nine, Victory Wedding (as director), Life is Nothing without Music, Making the Grade, Tom Thumb, The Hound of the Baskervilles (1978).
TELEVISION: This is Your Life, The Apple Cart, Stars and Garters, Dolly, The Nicest Man in the World, Angels, Another Opening Another Show, Nanny's Boy (in the BBC series, Jubilee), Parkinson, Edward and Mrs. Simpson (1978), The Winter Ladies (1979), Tales of the Unexpected (1980).

MATURE, VICTOR: Actor. b. Louisville, Ky., Jan. 29, 1916. TV retail store; trainee, Pasadena Theatre, Playbox Theatre; on B'way in Lady in the Dark; U.S. Coast Guard, WW II.
PICTURES INCLUDE: Housekeeper's Daughter, One Million B.C., Captain Caution, No No Nanette, I Wake Up Screaming, Shanghai Gesture, Song of the Islands, My Gal Sal, Footlight Serenade, Seven Days Leave, My Darling Clementine, Moss Rose, Kiss of Death, Cry of the City, Red Hot and Blue, Fury at Furnace Creek, Easy Living, Samson and Delilah, Wabash Avenue, Stella, Gambling House, Las Vegas Story, Androcles and the Lion, Million Dollar Mermaid, Something for the Birds, Glory Brigade, Affair with a Stranger, The Robe, Veils of Bagdad, Dangerous Mission, Betrayed, Demetrius & The Gladiators, The Egyptian, Chief Crazy Horse, Violent Saturday, Last Frontier, Safari, Zarak Pickup Alley, Tank Roce, The Bandit of Zhobe, Escort Wst., Big Circus, Timbuktu, Hannibal, The Tartars, After the Fox, Every Little Crook and Nanny, Won Ton Ton, the Dog That Saved Hollywood, Firepower.

MAURER, MAURICE (Ziggy): Executive. b. New York City, Aug. 25, 1914; e. Alfred U. Started in m.p. theatre field as usher, Palace Theatre, N.Y.; mgr. Fox theatres there; owned &

oper. Stanley Theatre; dir. Lopert Films, Inc.; v.p. in charge of oper., Astor, Victoria, Bijou theatres, N.Y.; owner, oper., Central Theatre; dir. Mayand the Brave, House of The Seven Hawks, High Time.

MAUREY, NICOLE: Actress. b. France. Studied dancing; French films include Blondine, Pamela, Le Cavalier Noir; stage appearances in France; U.S. debut in Little Boy Lost.
PICTURES INCLUDE: Secret of the Incas, Bold and the Brave, House of The Seven Hawks.

MAY, ELAINE: Actress, Screenwriter. b. Philadelphia, Pa., April 21, 1932. Repertory theatre in Chicago, 1954; comedy team with Mike Nichols, 1955.
PICTURES INCLUDE: Luv, Enter Laughing. 1970: writer, dir., star, A New Leaf; dir., The Heartbreak Kid; dir., s.p., Mikey and Nicky. 1978: co-s.p. Heaven Can Wait; actress, California Suite.

MAYEHOFF, EDDIE: Comedian. b. Baltimore, Md., July 7; e. Yale Sch. of Music. Adv. salesman, 1932; dance band leader, 6 yrs.; on radio with Norman Corwin; own show, Eddie Mayehoff on the Town; night clubs; B'way shows.
THEATRE: Let Freedom Sing, Early to Bed, Rhapsody, Billy Rose's Concert Varieties, Season in the Sun, Visit to a Small Planet.
TV: Adventures of Fenimore J. Mayehoff.
PICTURES INCLUDE: That's My Boy, The Stooge, Off Limits, Artists and Models, How to Murder Your Wife, Luv.

MAYER, BEN: Executive. b. Nov. 22, 1925. e. Manchester All Saints School of Art (England); Royal College of Art. President, Ben Mayer Design, Inc.

MAYER, GERALD: Producer, director. b. Montreal, Canada; p. both deceased: Jerry G., mgr. MGM studio, and Rheba G. Mayer (later Mrs. Hal Elias); e. Stanford (Journalism); corr. for San Francisco Examiner; pres. Sigma Delta Chi, prof. journalism soc. Navy lieut. amphibious forces, World War II. Entered m.p. ind. in prod. dept. MGM studios; first dir. job Dial 1119.
PICTURES INCLUDE: Dial 1119, Inside Straight, Sellout, Holiday for Sinners, Bright Road (Christopher Award for direction), The Marauders, African Drumbeat, and The Man Inside (Canadian).
TV: Canadian Broadcasting Corp. (prod./dir., TV Drama), prod. The Swiss Family Robinson (British-Canadian TV series). Director for U.S. TV: One Last Ride (mini-series), Lou Grant, Eight Is Enough, Quincy, Logan's Run, Mannix, Mission Impossible, Police Surgeon, Cimarron Strip, Peyton Place, Judd for the Defense, Bonanza, The Fugitive, Chrysler Thea., Ben Casey, Slattery's People, Profiles in Courage, The Defenders, Gunsmoke, etc.

MAYER, MICHAEL F.: Attorney-Executive. b. White Plains, N.Y., Sept. 8, 1917; Harvard College B.S., 1939; Yale Law School L.L.B., 1942. Armed Forces 1942–46, Air Medal (1945); vice-pres. Kingsley International Pictures Corp., 1954–62. Executive Director and General Counsel, Independent Film Importers and Distributors of America Inc. (IFIDA), 1959–67. Special Counsel, French Society of Authors, Composers and Publishers, 1961-to date; British Performing Rights Society, 1962–67. Author: Foreign Films on American Screens (1966); Divorce and Annulment (1967); What You Should Know About Libel and Slander (1968); Rights of Privacy (1972); The Film Industries (1973)—revised edition published in 1978). Lecturer on motion picture problems at N.Y.U., Stanford, Univ. of Pennsylvania, Dartmouth and New York State University (Albany). Teacher of courses on Business Problems in Film, New School (1971 to present). Is secty. of Film Society of Lincoln Center, Inc.

MAYER, ROGER LAURANCE: Executive. b. New York City, Apr. 21, 1926. e. Yale Univ. (1948 graduate); Yale Law School (1951 graduate). In 1952 was practicing attorney; joined Columbia Pictures that year as atty. and named corp. exec., 1957. Left in 1961 to join MGM Studio as asst. gen. mgr. Since with MGM as follows: v.p., operations, 1964; v.p., administration, 1975 to present. Also exec. v.p., MGM Laboratories, 1974 to present.
MEMBER: Los Angeles County Bar Assn., Los Angeles Copyright Society, Academy of Motion Picture Arts & Sciences. Chm. & trustee for both Directors Guild Pension Plan and Producers Guild Pension Plan.

MAYER, SEYMOUR R.: Executive. b. New York, N.Y., July 30, 1912; e. N.Y.C. schools. Mgr. Loew's Theatres; div. mgr. Loew's in-town theatres, 1933; Armed Forces, WW II, as Major in charge of overseas m.p. service; with Loew's International: 1959, 1st v.p.; MGM Int'l.: Jan., 1963: May, 1969, pres., MGM Int'l.; Worldwide sales Sagittarius Prods., N.Y., May, 1970; pres., MSD Int'l. worldwide sales.

MAYES, WENDELL: Writer. b. Hayti, Missouri e. Johns Hopkins, Columbia. Military service in Pacific, World War II. Began career as actor legit theatre, turned to writing for television. Gained television recognition before moving to Hollywood as motion picture writer.
PICTURES INCLUDE: Spirit of St. Louis, The Way to the

Gold, Enemy Below, The Hunters, From Hell to Texas, The Hanging Tree, Anatomy of A Murder, Advise And Consent, In Harm's Way, Von Ryan's Express, Hotel, The Stalking Moon, The Poseidon Adventure, The Revengers, Bank Shot, Death Wish, Love & Bullets, Charlie, Go Tell The Spartans.

MAYO, VIRGINIA: Actress. r.n., Virginia Jones. b. St. Louis, Mo.; e. St. Louis dramatic school. With Billy Rose's Diamond Horseshoe; then N.Y. stage (Banjo Eyes).
PICTURES INCLUDE: Kid from Brooklyn, Best Years of Our Lives, Secret Life of Walter Mitty, Out of the Blue, Smart Girls Don't Talk, The Girl From Jones Beach, Flaxy Martin, Colorado Territory, Always Leave Them Laughing, Flame and the Arrow, West Point Story, Along the Great Divide, Captain Horatio Hornblower, Painting the Clouds with Sunshine, Starlift, She's Working Her Way Through College, Iron Mistress, She's Back on Broadway, South Sea Woman, Devil's Canyon, King Richard & the Crusaders, Silver Chalice, Pearl of the South Pacific, Great Day in the Morning, Proud Ones, Congo Crossing, Big Land, Young Fury, Fort Utah, Castle of Evil.

MAZURKI, MIKE: Actor. b. Ukrainian descent; Tarnopal, Austria, Dec. 25, 1909; e. Manhattan Coll., New York, B.A., 1930; married. Toured United States and Canada as heavyweight wrestler. Screen debut 1941 in Shanghai Gesture.
PICTURES INCLUDE: Killer Dill, I Walk Alone, Unconquered, Nightmare Alley, Relentless, Neptune's Daughter, Come to the Stable, Rope of Sand, Samson & Delilah, Light Touch, Criminal Lawyer, Ten Tall Men, My Favorite Spy, The Egyptian, New Orleans Uncensored, New York Confidential, Blood Alley, Kismet, Davy Crockett, King of the Wild Frontier, Comanche, Around the World in 80 Days, Mad, Mad, Mad, Mad World, Four for Texas, Cheyenne Autumn, 7 Women, Bullwhip Griffin, Challenge to be Free, The Magic of Lassie, The Man with Bogart's Face.

MAZURSKY, PAUL: Producer-Director-Writer-Actor. b. Brooklyn, N.Y. April 25, 1930. Started acting in 1951 in the theatre, TV and films. Was nightclub comic 1954–1960 and directed plays. Began association with Larry Tucker by producing, directing, writing and performing in Second City, semi-improvisational revue. For four years they wrote the Danny Kaye TV show and created and wrote the Monkees series. First theatrical film I Love You, Alice B. Toklas (1969) which he wrote with Tucker and both men acted as exec. prod.
PICTURES INCLUDE: Bob and Carol and Ted and Alice, (dir., co-s.p.), Alex in Wonderland (dir., co-s.p., actor), Blume in Love (dir., s.p., prod., actor), Harry and Tonto (prod., dir., co-s.p.); Next Stop, Greenwich Village (prod., dir., s.p.); "Unmarried Woman (prod., dir., s.p.); A Man, A Woman and A Bank (actor): Willie and Phil (prod., dir., s.p.).

McCALL, JOAN: Actress-Writer. b. Grahn, Kentucky. e. Berea College, Starred on Broadway in Barefoot In The Park, The Star Spangled Girl, A Race of Hairy Men, and road companies of Barefoot In The Park, Star Spangled Girl, and Don't Drink The Water, Los Angeles Company of Jimmy Shine.
PICTURES INCLUDE: Grizzly, Act of Vengeance, The Devil Times Five. Screenwriter: The Predator, The Concision, Fly Away Home. 1980: Staff writer for The Days of Our Lives, Currently staff writer for Another World (both daytime soaps) under the pen name Joan Pommer.

McCALLUM, DAVID: Actor. b. Scotland, Sept. 19, 1933. Early career in rep. theatres and dir. plays for Army. Ent. m.p. Ind. 1953.
PICTURES INCLUDE: The Secret Place, Hell Drivers, Robbery Under Arms, Violent Playground, A Night to Remember, The Long and the Short and the Tall, Billy Budd, Freud, The Great Escape, The Greatest Story Ever Told, To Trap A Spy, Three Bits of the Apple, Sol Madrid, Mosquito Squadron, Watcher in the Woods.
TV: The Man From Uncle, The Invisible Man.

McCALLUM, JOHN: Actor, Producer, Director. b. Brisbane, Australia, CBE. Mar. 14, 1918; e. Royal Academy Dramatic Arts; served in Australian Imperial Forces. World War II. Appeared in repertory with Old Vic & Stratford-on-Avon seasons. On stage, 1937 in Judgment Day, Australian tour, 1955–56; on screen first 1944, Australia is Like This. Asst. man. dir. J. C. Williamson Theatres, Ltd., Australia, 1958; man. dir., 1960–66. Resigned chmn. Williamson-Powell Int. Films, 1965; chmn. Fauna Prod.; dir. Relatively Speaking on stage in Australia, 1968. Dir.; Plaza Suite, My Fair Lady, for Australian stage, 1969–70. Prod. TV Series, Skippy, Barrier Reef, Boney, Shannons Mob; London Stage 1973–74 Constant Wife. 1974 Comedy Theatre, Melbourne. 1976 Chichester Fest. 1976–77 The Circle. Exec. prod. Bailey's Bird, TV series.
PICTURES INCLUDE: A Son Is Born, Joe Goes Back, Root of All Evil, The Loves of Joanna Godden, It Always Rains on Sunday, Miranda, The Calendar, A Boy, a Girl and a Bike, Traveler's Joy, The Woman in Question, Valley of the Eagles, Lady Godiva Rides Again, Derby Day (Four Against Fate), Trent's Last Case, The Long Memory, Melba,

Devil on Horseback, Trouble in the Glen, Smiley (in Australia), Safe Harbour, Nickel Queen (dir.); The Z Men (prod.).

McCAMBRIDGE, MERCEDES: Actress. b. Joliet, Ill., March 17; e. Mundelein College Chicago, Ill., B.A. Did some radio work while in college; opposite Orson Welles two seasons, on Ford Theatre, other air shows; New York stage in: Hope for the Best, 1945; others: Place of Our Own, Twilight Bar, Woman Bites Dog, The Young and Fair; left latter play for Hollywood. Screen debut: All the King's Men (Academy Award for best supporting actress, 1950); own radio show, 1952.
PICTURES INCLUDE: Lightning Strikes Twice, Inside Straight, The Scarf, Johnny Guitar, Giant, A Farewell to Arms, Suddenly Last Summer, Cimarron, Angel Baby, Last Generation, Jigsaw, 99 Women, Thieves, The Concord-Airport '79.
AUTHOR: The Two of Us.
TV: Numerous appearances.

McCARTHY, FRANK: Producer. b. Richmond, Va., June 8, 1912. e. Virginia Military Institute and U. of Virginia, serving at VMI as instructor and tactical officer, and as police reporter for Richmond News-Leader, 1933–37. Press agent for producer George Abbott, 1937–39. During WW II was Asst. Secy. and later Secy. of War Dept. General Staff and military secy. to General George C. Marshall. Decorated with U.S. Distinguished Service, U.S. Legion of Merit, Order of the British Empire. Brigadier General in Army Reserve, Retired. In 1945, named Asst. Secy. of State for Administration; joined MPAA 1946 as asst. to v.p., later European mgr. Signed by 20th Century-Fox two years later as exec. and prod. Co-prod. Decision Before Dawn; prod., Sailor of the King, A Guide for the Married Man, Patton, Fireball Forward; at Universal, MacArthur.

McCARTHY, KEVIN: Actor. b. Seattle, Wash., Feb. 15; e. Minnesota U. Acted in sch. plays, stock; B'way debut in Abe Lincoln in Illinois. In U.S. Army; m.p. debut: Death of A Salesman.
PLAYS INCLUDE: Flight to West, Winged Victory, Truckline Cafe, Joan of Lorraine, Biography, Death of a Salesman, Anna Christie.
PICTURES INCLUDE: Drive a Crooked Road, Gambler from Natchez, Stranger on Horseback, Annapolis Story, Nightmare, Invasion of the Body Snatchers, A Big Hand for the Little Lady, Hotel, Kansas City Bomber, Buffalo Bill and the Indians, Hero at Large, Those Lips, Those Eyes.

McCLORY, SEAN: Actor. b. Dublin, Ireland, March 8, 1924; e. Jesuit Coll., U. of Galway. With Gaelic Theatre, Galway; Abbey Theatre. Dublin. Brought to U.S., in 1946 under contract to RKO Pictures. Produced and directed numerous plays, member of the Directors Guild of America and is the author of the produced drama, Moment of Truth.
PLAYS INCLUDE: Shining Hour, Juno and the Paycock, Anna Christie, Escape to Autumn, King of Friday's Men, Lady's Not for Burning, Billy Budd, Dial M for Murder, The Winslow Boy, Shadow of A Gunman, Saint Joan.
PICTURES INCLUDE: Film debut: Dick Tracy vs. The Claw, Rough-Shod, Beyond Glory, Daughter of Rosie O'Grady, Storm Warning, Lorna Doone, What Price Glory, The Quiet Man, Diane, Island in the Sky, Ring of Fear, Them, Long Grey Line, Cheyenne Autumn, Plunder of the Sun, Anne of the Indies, I Cover the Underworld, Botany Bay, Man in the Attic, Guns of Fort Petticoat, Kings Thief, Moonfleet, Bandolero, Day of the Wolves, Valley of the Dragons, Follow Me Boys, Rogues March, The Gnomobile, Well of the Saints, In Search of the Historical Jesus, Roller Boogie.
TV: Matinee Theatre, Climax, Lost in Space, My Three Sons, Suspense, The Untouchables, Hitchcock, Thriller, Bonanza, Gunsmoke, Mannix, Little House On The Prairie, S.W.A.T., The New Daughters of Joshua Cabe, The Captains And The Kings, Once An Eagle, Fish, Columbo, How the West Was Won. Co-starred in two series: The Californians, also directing several episodes, and Kate McShane and General Hospital.

McCLURE, WENDY: Actress, Dancer. b. Glasgow, Scotland, March 9, 1934. m. David Knight. e. Lowther College, North Wales. On London stage from 1955 in The Punch Revue, Alice Through the Looking Glass, Zuleika. M.P. debut in 1956 in Helen of Troy.
PICTURES INCLUDE: Helen of Troy, It's A Wonderful World, The Girl on the Boat, The Comedy Man, A King in New York.
TV: Knock on Any Door, Dr. Finlay's Casebook, The Newcomers, Over to Una, Z-Cars, The Borderers, Young Man in Trouble.

McCLURE, WILLIAM K.: Producer-Director. b. Knoxville, Tenn., Sept. 8, 1922; e. U. Tennessee & Catholic U., Washington, D.C. Contact man Washington staff, Pathe Newsreel, 1942; Los Angeles staff, 1943; asst. dir., "This Is America" series, 1943. Combat photographer, U.S. Army, 1944–46; Pub. mgr., RKO Pathe, Inc., 1947; Cameraman, corr., Warner Pathe Newsreel, 1948–51; Cameraman-corr., in Europe,

Middle East for See It Now, CBS-TV, 1951–52, London, 1953; dir., cameraman, See It Now, 1952–54, Report on Africa. 1955–56, Burma, Buddhism. Neutralism, 1957, Watch on the Ruhr, 1958; dir. oper. Europe Small World. 1958–59. Prod., CBS Reports, co-prod.: CBS Reports, Iran Brittle Ally 1959, Berlin: End of the line 1960. Prod., CBS Reports: Britain, Blood Sweat and Tears, plus 20 1961 prod., Mr. Europe and the Common Market; prod., Germany Since Hitler; Adenauer Sums-up; prod., DeGaulle: The Challenge, DeGaulle: Roots of Power, East Europe, Satellites Out of Orbit; prod., CBS News, Henry Moore: Man of Form; Eur. prod., Town Meeting of the World, 1965–66. Prod. 1967 If you're appalled at my Texas I'm bewildered with your England. Prod. 1968 Don't Count the Candles.

McCRARY, TEX: Performer. r.n. John Reagan. b. Calvert, Tex., 1910. e. Exeter Acad., Yale. m. Jinx Falkenburg. Began journalistic career on N.Y. World Telegram and Literary Digest; Asst. to Arthur Brisbane on N.Y. Mirror, ed. chief 1933–41; writer and dir. of newsreels for Pathe Films; U.S. Air Force, WW II; author of First of Many.

McCREA, JOEL: Actor. b. Los Angeles, Calif., Nov. 5, 1905; e. Pomona College; husband of Frances Dee, actress. Stage experience: amateur dramatics and community plays taking male lead in "The Patsy," "Laff That Off" and "The Little Journey." In many pictures since 1932.
PICTURES INCLUDE: In 1940 He Married His Wife, Primrose Path, Foreign Correspondent. In 1941 Reaching for the Sun, Sullivan's Travels. In 1942 The Great Man's Lady, The Palm Beach Story. In 1943 The More the Merrier, Virginian, Ramrod, Four Faces West, South of St. Louis, Outriders, Colorado, Territory, Stars in My Crown, Saddle Tramp, Cattle Drive, San Francisco Story, Lone Hand, Shoot First, Border River, Black Horse Canyon, Stranger on Horseback, Wichita, First Texan, The Oklahoman, Trooper Hook, Fort Massacre, The Gunfight at Dodge City, Ride the High Country, Mustang Country.

McCULLOUGH, JIMMIE B.: Producer-Director. b. Mansfield, La., May 12, 1929. e. UCLA (1955). U.S. Marine Corps Reserve 1948–50; Ziv Studio, Hollywood, 1949–56: Acted on TV: Highway Patrol, CBS Playhouse 90, The Shadow, Teenage Monster, Crime File. Officer-director, American Metal Window Co., 1959–63. Owned and operated Macco Prod. Co., Inc., 1966–72. Now heads Jim McCullough Prods., Inc., Ry-Mac Intl. Film Dist., Inc., and Macco Prods., Inc.
PICTURES: Shepherd of the Hills (prod.-dir.), Where the Red Fern Grows (co-prod.), Creature from Black Lake (prod.-dir.), Charge of the Model Ts (prod.-dir.).

McDOWALL, BETTY: Actress. b. Syndey, Australia; e. Mt. Bernard Convent, N. Sydney. Early career radio, stage in Australia; ent. BBC TV, 1952; since in West End plays, many TV and radio plays and films.
STAGE: Age of Consent, Ghost Train, The Kidders, The Dark Halo, Period of Adjustment, Rule of Three, Signpost to Murder, Hippolytus, The Winslow Boy, Woman in a Dressing Gown, As Long As It's Warm, Caprice—In A Pink Palazzo, Sweet Bird of Youth, There was an Old Woman, What the Butler Saw, Two Dozen Red Roses, A Boston Story, The Man Most Likely To . . . ., Sleeping Partner.
TV: Mid-Level and Glorification of Al Toolum, The Black Judge, Phone Call for Matthew Quade, Thunder on the Snowy, Shadow of Guilt, Traveling Lady, Torment, Biography, Notes for a Love Song, Esther's Altar, The Corridor People, The Braden Beat, The Douglas Fairbanks, Ivanhoe, The Foreign Legion, Fabian of the Yard, Four Just Men, Flying Doctor, No Hiding Place, 'Z' Cars, Days of Vengeance, Flower of Evil, Outbreak of Murder, Call Me Sam, The Prisoner, Public Eye, The Forgotten Door, All Out for Kangaroo Valley, Barry Humphries Scandals, Castle Haven, Albert and Victoria, Follyfoot, The Man Who Came to Dinner, Anne of Avoniea, Little Lord Fauntleroy, The Bass Player and the Blond (4 plays), The Gingerbread Lady.
PICTURES INCLUDE: First lead in England, Timelock, She Didn't Say No, Jack the Ripper, The Shiralee, Jackpot, Dead Lucky, Spare the Rod, Golliwog, Echo of Diana, First Men in the Moon, Ballad in Blue, The Liquidators, Willy Wagtails by Moonlight.

McDOWALL, MALCOLM: Actor. b. Leeds, England, June 1943. Was spear-holder for the Royal Shakespeare Co. in season of 1965–66 when turned to TV and then to films. Made debut in small role in Poor Cow, 1967.
PICTURES INCLUDE: If. . . . , Figures in a Landscape, The Raging Moon, A Clockwork Orange, O Lucky Man!, Royal Flash, Aces High, Voyage of the Damned, Caligula, The Passage, Time after Time.

McDOWALL, RODDY: Actor (Star of Tomorrow, 1944.) b. London, England, Sept. 17, 1928; e. St. Joseph's London. First appeared in Murder in the Family at age of 8. Later, You Will Remember, The Outsider, Just William, Hey, Hey, U.S.A., This England, all made in England. In 1940 signed by 20th Century-Fox.

PICTURES INCLUDE: Man Hunt, How Green Was My Valley, Confirm or Deny, Son of Fury, On the Sunny Side, The Pied Piper, My Friend Flicka, Lassie Come Home, White Cliffs of Dover, Macbeth, Act, assoc. prod., Rocky, Kidnapped, Big Timber, Tuna Clipper, Black Midnight, Killer Shark, Steel Fist, The Subterraneans, Midnight Lace, Cleopatra, The Longest Day, The Greatest Story Ever Told, Shock Treatment, That Darn Cat, The Loved Ones, The Third Day, Daisy Clover, Bullwhip Griffin, Lord Love A Duck, The Defector, It, The Cool Ones, Planet of the Apes, Hello, Down There, Midas Run, Escape from the Planet of the Apes, Conquest of the Planet of the Apes. Directorial Debut: The Devil's Widow, 1971. Actor: The Legend of Hellhouse, The Poseidon Adventure, Arnold, Funny Lady, The Cat from Outer Space, Scavenger Hunt, Charlie Chan and the Curse of the Dragon Queen.
THEATRE: On B'way in Misalliance, Escapade, Doctor's Dilemma, No Time for Sergeants, Good as Gold, Compulsion, Handful of Fire, Look After Lulu, The Fighting Cock, 1959–60, Camelot, 1960–61, The Astrakhan Coat, 1966.
RADIO & TV: Stratford Shakespearean festival, 1955.

McEVEETY, BERNARD: Director. Comes from film family; father was pioneer as unit mgr. at New York's Edison Studios; brothers Vincent, also a dir., and Joseph, writer are at Disney Studios. Bernard's career began in 1953 at Paramount where was asst. dir. for 6 yrs. Earned full dir. responsibility on The Rebel, TV series.
PICTURES INCLUDE: Napoleon and Samatha, One Little Indian, The Bears and I.
TV: Episodes on Bonanza, Gunsmoke, Combat and Cimarron Strip (also prod.)

McEVEETY, VINCENT: Director. Joined Hal Roach Studios in 1954 as second asst. dir. Then to Republic for The Last Command. First Disney assignments: Davy Crockett shows and Mickey Mouse Club. Moved to Desilu as first asst. dir. on The Untouchables; made assoc. prod. with option to direct. Did segments of many series, including 34 Gunsmoke episodes. First theatrical film: Firecreek, 1968.
PICTURES INCLUDE: $1,000,000 Duck, The Biscuit Eater, Charley and the Angel, Superdad, The Strongest Man in the World, Gus, Treasure of Matecumbe. Herbie Goes to Monte Carlo.
TELEVISION: High Flying Spy.

McFADDEN, FRANK: Publicist. b. San Diego, Calif., June 3, 1914. e. Southwestern Bus. Coll. Pub. dept., Warner Bros. Studio, 1933–35; asst. pub. dir., Universal Studio, 1936–53; adv., pub. dir., Leonard Goldstein Prod., 1954; president pub. rel. agency, McFadden and Eddy, Inc., 1955; partner, McFadden, Strauss & Irwin, 1963. TV, 1956. Became partner in ICPR in 1975.

McGANNON, DONALD H.: Executive. b. Sept. 9, 1920. New York, N.Y.; e. Fordham U., Fordham Sch. of Law. Network exec., gen. mgr., owned, operated stations, DuMont Television Network, 1952–55; pres. chmn. of bd., Westinghouse Broadcasting Co., Inc., Ind., Md., Del., 1955; pres. chmn. of bd. Television Advertising Representatives, Inc.; chmn. of bd., AM Radio Sales Co.; chmn., WBC Productions, Inc.; Chmn., WBC Program Sales, Inc.; Chmn. The Advertising Council; Pres., National Urban League; Chmn., Connecticut Commission for Higher Education; chmn., Permanent research Comm., 1964 dis. serv. award, National Association of Broadcasters; dir., The Advertising Council, Inc.; dir. Radio Advertising Bureau; dir., Academy of Television Arts and Sciences Foundation; dir., Radio Free Europe; Communications Subcommittee, Community Relation Service; advsr. Pontifical Commission for Communications Media. Adv. North American Vatican Radio.

McGAVIN, DARREN: Actor. b. San Joaquin Valley, Calif., May 7, 1922. e. C. of the Pacific.
PLAYS INCLUDE: Death of a Salesman, My Three Angels, The Rainmaker, The Lovers, Dinner at Eight (revived).
PICTURES INCLUDE: Summertime, The Man with the Golden Arm, Court Martial of Billy Mitchell, Beau James, Delicate Delinquent, The Great Sioux Massacre, Bulley For a Badman, Mission Mars. Directorial Debut: Happy Mother's Day . . . Love, George (1973). Actor: Airport '77.
TV: Mike Hammer, The Outsider, The Night Stalker.

McGOOHAN, PATRICK: Actor. b. New York. Early career in repertory in Britain. London stage 1954 in Serious Charge; 1955 Orson Wells' Moby Dick. Ent. films 1955.
PICTURES INCLUDE: Passage Home, High Tide at Noon, Hell Drivers, The Gypsy and the Gentleman, Nor the Moon by Night, Two Living, One Dead, All Night Long, The Quare Fellow, Thomasina, Dr. Syn, Ice Station Zebra, The Moonshine War, Brass Target, Scanners.
TV: Plays and star of ATV's Danger Man series; also directed some of these; Secret Agent, The Prisoner.

McGOWAN, BROTHERS: Dorrell & Stuart. Writers, Directors, Producers. (Dorrell) b. Winnetka, Ill., (Stuart) b. Wilmette,

III. In m.p. ind. since 1930. Producers. Independent production since 1950. TV series: Death Valley Days, Sky King, The Littlest Hobo. Features: Tokyo File, Japan—Bashful Elephant, Austria; Hellfire, Showdown, The Littlest Hobo, Snowfire, Billion Dollar Hobo, U.S. Feature, Mister Too Little now in release.

McGOWAN, ROBERT A.: Writer. b. Denver, Colo., May 22, 1901. Cartoonist; from 1923–29, writer of Hal Roach "Our Gang" comedies for his uncle, Robert Francis McGowan. Directed under the name of Anthony Mack, s.p., Babes in Toyland, collab. s.p., Too Many Parents, Boy Friend shorts for Warner-Vitagraph, N.Y. Prod. manager, four technicolor shorts. Wrote new series "Our Gang" comedies for MGM.

McGRATH, THOMAS J.: Producer. b. New York City. e. Washington Square Col. of N.Y.U. (B.A. 1956), N.Y.U. School of Law (LLB 1960). Has practiced law in N.Y.C. from 1960 to date. Became indep. prod. with Deadly Hero in 1976; Author, Carryover Basis Under The 1976 Tax Reform Act, published in 1977.

McGREAL, E. B. "MIKE": Executive. b. Bellingham, Wash., Aug. 13, 1905. e. U. of So. Calif. Camera dept., MGM, 1929–34; exec. dir. of photog., Warner Bros., 1934–54; v.p., Houston Fearless Corp., pres., Houston Color Film Lab. of Calif., 1954–56; Exec. dir., spec. photographic effects, 20th Century Fox, 1957–59; pres. Producers Service Corp., 1960–70. Currently president and owner of B.M.C. Corporation, McGreal and Hunt. Member—Academy of Motion Picture Arts & Sciences, Society of Motion Picture & Television Engineers, British Kinematograph Sound & Television Society.

McGREGOR, CHARLES: Executive. b. Jersey City, N.J., April 1, 1927. e. N.Y.U. 1958–1969, Co-founder, pres. and chief exec. officer, Banner Films, Inc. (World Wide TV Distribution), 1955–1958, salesman and div. mgr., Flamingo Films (domestic TV Dist.). 1953–55; Professional mgr. ABC Music Publishing. 1951–53: Prod. and partner Telco Prods. and G&M Productions (prods. of network and local shows). 1969–77: exec. v.p. in chg. of w-w dist., WB-TV; 1977: pres. WB-TV Distribution.

McGUIRE, DON: Writer, director. b. Chicago, Ill., Feb. 28, 1919. U.S. Army, 4 yrs.; press agent, Chicago and Hollywood; newsman, Hearst papers, Chicago; then actor, writer.
PICTURES INCLUDE: Double Deal, Dial 1119, Meet Danny Wilson, Willie and Joe in Back at the Front, Walking My Baby Back Home, Three Ring Circus, Bad Day at Black Rock, Artists and Models, Johnny Concho, Delicate Delinquent, Suppose They Gave a War and Nobody Came.
TV: Writer, dir. & co-prod., Hennessey series, creator, series Not for Hire; creator, writer, prod. series, Don't Call Me Charlie.
AUTHOR: Novels, The Day Television Died, 16000 Floogle Street.

McGUIRE, DOROTHY: Actress. b. Omaha, Neb., June 14, 1919; e. Ladywood convent, Indianapolis; Pine Manor, Wellesley, Mass.
STAGE: Bachelor Born, Our Town, My Dear Children, Swinging the Dream, Claudia, Legend of Lovers, Night of the Iguana (1976).
PICTURES INCLUDE: Claudia, Tree Grows in Brooklyn, Enchanted Cottage, Spiral Staircase, Claudia and David, Gentleman's Agreement, Mister 880, Callaway Went Thataway, I Want You, Make Haste to Live, Invitation, 3 Coins in the Fountain, Trial, Friendly Persuasion, Old Yeller, This Earth Is Mine, Remarkable Mr. Pennypacker, Dark at The Top of the Stairs, Summer Place, Susan Slade, Flight of the Doves.
TELEVISION: Rich Man, Poor Man.

McHUGH, FRANK: Actor. b. Homestead, Pa., May 23, 1899. Child actor in For His Children's Sake; on stage N.Y. and London.
PLAYS INCLUDE: Fall Guy, Tenth Avenue, Excess Baggage, Conflict, Show Girl.
PICTURES INCLUDE: If Men Played Cards as Women Do 1928; Top Speed Bright Lights, Easy Come, Easy Go, Kiss Me Again, Dawn Patrol, Toast of the Legion, Back Street, Her Cardboard Lover, Going My Way, Gold Diggers of 1935, Footlight Parade, Marine Raiders, Bowery to Broadway, Medal for Benny, State Fair, Mighty Joe Young, Pace That Thrills, My Son John, It Happens Every Thursday, Lion is in the Streets, There's No Business Like Show Business.

McHUGH, JAMES: Agent/Manager. b. Boston, Mass., Oct. 21, 1915; e. Holy Cross Coll. Joined MCA 1939. U.S. Army 1944–46. MCA-British and European, 1945–50. Formed James McHugh, Talent Agency 1953. Pres., Artists Mgr. Corp., pres., Turquoise Prod., Inc., v.p. investment consultant, Miguel Prod. and Ebsen Ent., Inc. Present clients: B. Ebsen, Brian Keith, Leo Penn, Alan Fudge.

McINTIRE, JOHN: Actor. b. Spokane, Wash., June 27, 1907; e. Local schools; m. Jeanette Nolan, actress; Radio announcer, actor teamed with wife.
PICTURES INCLUDE: Asphalt Jungle, Francis, Saddle Tramp, Winchester '73, Ambush, Scene of the Crime, You're in the Navy Now, Under the Gun, Raging Tide, Westward the Women, World in His Arms, Glory Alley, Sally & St. Anne, Horizons West, Lawless Breed, Mississippi Gambler, The President's Lady, Lion Is In the Street, War Arrow, Apache, Four Guns to the Border, Yellow Mountain, Far Country, Stranger on Horseback, Scarlet Coat, Phoenix City Story, Backlash, The Spoilers, The Kentuckian, World in My Corner, Away All Boats, The Tin Star, Who Was That Lady, Flaming Star, Two Rode Together, Summer & Smoke, Herbie Rides Again.
TV: Wagon Train, Naked City, The Virginian.

McINTOSH, STANLEY: Educator, executive b. Stewardson, Ill., Mar. 7, 1908. e. East Ill. University, B.Ed.; Northwestern U., M.A. Tchr., prin. Evanston, Ill. pub. schls.; Asst. Supt. Cook Co., Ill. pub. schools; Instr. Northwestern U.; visitng lecturer, U. of Iowa; prof. lectr. American U.; Regional dir., war training films, U.S. Office of Educ.; assoc. research & prod., Encyclopaedia Britannica Films, Inc.; appt. to MPAA, 1947 as asst. dir. educational service; in 1958 made dir. educational & community service; since 1955 ex. dir. Teaching Film Custodians; org. pres., CINE, 1957–58; appt. Consultant Indiana U. on merger of TFC-Indiana U., May 1973. Retired 1976.

McKELLAR, KENNETH: Singer. b. Paisley, Scotland. singer, stage prods., radio & TV; appeared, concerts, Edinburgh International Festival; toured, Scots Concert groups; created role, Jamie in A Wish For Jamie, A Love for Jamie. Many BBC-TV and ITV appearances in V.K. Records regularly.

McKENNA, SIOBHAN: Actress. b. Belfast, Ireland, May 24, 1923; e. St. Louis Convent, Monaghan; National Univ. of Ireland, B.A. Stage debut at Abbey Theatre, 1943; then London stage in The White Steed, 1947. Screen debut: Hungry Hill, 1946. London film and stage parts, also stage in Dublin; interested in development of Gaelic Theatre in Galway for which she has translated several plays including G. B. Shaw's Saint Joan.
PICTURES INCLUDE: Daughter of Darkness, The Lost People, The Adventurers, King of Kings, Of Human Bondage, Dr. Zhivago.
STAGE: (London) Saint Joan; (N.Y.) Chalk Garden.
TV: appearances in U.S

McKINNEY, BILL: Actor. b. Tennessee, Sept. 12.
PICTURES INCLUDE: Hollywood Secret File; She Freak; The Road Hustlers; Smack; Breakheart Pass; Josey Wales; Deliverance; Junior Bonner; Judge Roy Bean; Kansas City Bomber; The Outfit; Thunderbolt & Lightfoot; Parallax View; Every Which Way But Loose; The Gauntlet; For Pete's Sake.
THEATRE: No Time For Sergeants; A Cook For Mr. General; Time Limit; Bus Stop; Of Mice And Men; The Garbage Hustler; Roadside; As You Like It; Hassan Of Bagdad; No Place To Run; Career; Hat Full Of Rain; The Gamblers; The Devil's Disciple; All My Sons; Deadwood Dick; Chanticleer; Hoot And Holler; War And Peace; Grapes Of Wrath; El Camino Real; The Little Prince.
TV: Showcase for Success; The Monkeys; Holvak; Baretta; Bronk; Sarah; Bold Ones; Smith & Jones; McCloud; Columbo; Ironside; Pvt. Slovak; The Healers.

McLAGLEN, ANDREW V.: Dir. b. London, Eng., July 28, 1920. e. U. of Virginia, 1939–40. prod. dept., Lockheed Aircraft Corp., 1944–44; asst. m.p. dir., 1944–54; dir., 1955–65; dir., CBS-TV. 1956–63.
PICTURES INCLUDE: Man in the Vault, Gun the Man Down, The Abductors, Freckles, The Little Shepherd of Kingdom Come, McLintock!, Shenandoah, The Rare Bree, Seven Men From Now, The Way West, The Ballad of Josie, Monkeys, Go Home, Devil's Brigade, Bandolero, The Undefeated, Fool's Parade, Something Big, One More Train To Rob, Cahill, U.S. Marshall, Mitchell, The Last Hard Men, The Wild Geese, ffolkes, The Sea Wolves.
TV: Gunsmoke, Have Gun—Will Travel, Perry Mason, Rawhide, The Lineup, The Lieutenant, etc.

McLERIE, ALLYN: Actress. b. Grand Mere, Quebec, Canada, Dec. 1, 1926; e. High School, N.Y. Dancer since 15 in many B'way shows.
SHOWS INCLUDE: One Touch of Venus, On the Town, Finian's Rainbow, Where's Charley, Miss Liberty, Time Limit.
PICTURES INCLUDE: Where's Charley, Desert Song, Calamity Jane, Phantom of the Rue Morgue, Battle Cry, They Shoot Horses, Don't They?, The Cowboys, Jeremiah Johnson, The Magnificent Seven Ride, Cinderella Liberty.

McMAHON, ED: Performer. b. Detroit, Mich., March 6, 1923. e. Boston Coll.; Catholic U. of America, B.A., 1949. U.S. Marines, 1942–53.
TV: Tonight Show, Monitor, Fortune Phone, Who Do You Trust, The Missing Links, commercials.
THEATRE: Stock Bdwy., Impossible Years.
PICTURES INCLUDE: The Incident, Fun with Dick and Jane.

McMAHON, JOHN J.: Executive. b. Chicago, Ill., 1932. e. Northwestern U. Served with U.S. Army in Korea, beginning career on WGN-TV, Chicago; associated with ZIV-United Artists TV Productions during 1950's; joined American Broadcasting Company in 1958; v.p. & gen. mgr., WXYTZ-TV, Detroit, then KABC-TV, Los Angeles, 1968; v.p., ABC, 1968–72; joined National Broadcasting Company in 1972 as v.p., programs, west coast, NBC-TV; president, Hollywood Radio & Television Society; board member, Permanent Charities Committee. June, 1980, named pres. of Carson Prods. (Johnny Carson's prod. co.).

McNALLY, STEPHEN: Actor r.n. Horace McNally; b. New York City, July 29; e. Fordham U., LL.B. In school dramatics; practiced law 2 yrs.; N.Y.; stage, films, 1942.
PICTURES INCLUDE: Winchester 73, Wyoming Mail, No Way out, Air Cadet, Apache Drums, Raging Tide, Lady Pays Off, Devil's Canyon, Make Haste to Live, A Bullet Is Waiting, Man From Bitter Ridge, Tribute to a Bad Man, Once You Kiss a Stranger, Black Gunn.

McNAMARA, THOMAS J.: Executive. b. New York, N.Y. e. N.Y. schools, Pace University, C.P.A. Price Waterhouse, 1943–1947; chief accountant, Motion Picture Association of America, Inc., 1948; asst. treas., 1955; treas. AMPECA, 1961, and AFRAM Films, 1973; treas. MPAA and MPEA, 1977.

McNEIL, ROBERT A.: Exhibitor. b. San Francisco, Cal., Jan. 14, 1889; e. public schools of San Francisco; m. Started show career when 17. Sang on stage, also operated projection machine and played in three shows a week in San Francisco. Worked on Pantages circuit for two years. Expanded theatre enterprises after San Francisco fire, owning five houses. Joined E. H. Emmick in forming Golden State Circuit in 1927. Associated with Mike Naify of T. and D. Jr. Enterprises to form United California Theatres, Inc., sold interest to Naify, retired; maintains interest in small San Francisco chain.

McNELLIS, MAGGI: Performer; b. Chic. Ill.; e. Rosemont Coll., Mundelein Coll.; m. Clyde Newhouse; began as singer in Chic. and New York clubs; radio shows; Maggi's Private Wire, Maggi's Magazine; on various TV shows.
TV: Maggi's Private Wire, ABC, Leave It to the Girls, ABC, NBC, Say It with Acting, ABC, Crystal Room, NBC, Maggi McNellis Show, WABC, WABD, N. Y.

McNICHOL, KRISTY: Actress. Made debut at age of 7 performing in commercials. Given regular role in Apple's Way; began appearing on such series as Love, American Style and The Bionic Woman. Attracted attention of Spelling-Goldberg Productions, who cast her as Buddy Lawrence in Family series.
PICTURES: The End, Little Darlings, The Night the Lights Went Out in Georgia, Only When I Laugh.
TELEVISION: Movies: Like Mom, Like Me, Summer of My German Soldier, My Old Man.

McQUEENEY, ROBERT: Actor. b. Bridgeport, Conn., March 5. e. Taft School, Watertown, Bard College; lieutenant, U.S. Army; prof. debut, summer theatre group, Jennerstown, Pa.
SHOWS INCLUDE: Billy Budd, Dial M for Murder, Affairs of State, Fragile Fox, Macbeth, Rain, The Second Man, The Tender Trap, Brainstorm, The Glory Guys.
TV: Robert Montgomery Presents, Philco, Kraft Theatre, Studio One, Omnibus Playwrights '56, Love of Life, The Guiding Light, The Gallant Men.

McWILLIAMS, HARRY KENNETH: Publicity executive. b. Middlesboro, Ky., July 20, 1907; e. Colorado U.; Denver Sch. of Tech. 1930–32 sales mgr., Acme Film Co., Bowles; Ted Bates Adv., Inc. Entered m.p. ind. 1927 as theat. & pub. mgr., Harry E. Huffman Theats., Denver, Col.; in 1928 partner, Filmcraft Labs., Denver (trailers, commercial and scenic short subjects). In 1928 joined Publix Theats. Corp.; 1941 joined Columbia Picture exploit. dept.; in Jan. 1944 named exploit. mgr. dir. adv. pub. rel. Screen Gems, Inc., TV sub. Col.; Pict., Jan. 1953-May, 1954; pres., gen. sales mgr. Air Programs, Inc., May 1954; asst. dir. adv., pub., exploit. Magna Theatres Corp., 1955–56; ass't gen. man. Original Amateur Hour Program 1959–60; prod. Academy Award Exhibitor Kit, 1961–62, ass't to Oscar Doob "Ben-Hur" dept., MGM, 1959; prom. Samuel Bronston 1959; Columbia, 1960; pub. rel. U. of Cincinnati, 1961; co-ordinator of Community Relations; co-ordinator, New York City, Movie News, MPA, ad-pub. committee, co-ordinator, Academy Award News, TOA, 1963; p.r. council. Currently p.r. consultant NATO. Publisher of theatre ad book, 1975.

MEAD, THOMAS: Newsreel editor, producer. b. Tecumseh, Mich., Dec. 7, 1904; e. Wabash Coll. Was reporter, Chicago Daily News, prior to entering m.p. ind.; prod. Universal-Internat'l Newsreel & Variety View short subjects since 1938.

PICTURES INCLUDE: Snow Capers, Cheating in Gambling, Four Years Before the Mast, Tiny Terrors Make Trouble, Thundering Rails, Fun at the Zoo (1950), Landscape of Silence & Perils of the Forest, Hottest 500, Blond Empire, Venice of the East; man. dir., Universal-International Newsreel, New York.

MEADES, KENNETH RICHARDSON: Communications Consultant. b. Montreal, Can., March 2, 1943; e. Cote des Neiges Comm. Coll., Geo. Williams U., Sta. Ana Coll., Western Tech. Inst. Obtained first class Radiotelephone lic. with FCC; eng. dept., CFCF Radio & TV, 1960–63; technician with Broadcast Engineering Services, Garden Grove, Calif.; presently priv. consultant.

MEANEY, DONALD V.: Executive. b. Newark, N.J. e. Rutgers Univ. School of Journ. Worked as reporter for Plainfield (N.J.) Courier-News, Newark Evening News. Became news director of radio station WCTC in New Brunswick N.J. and later for WNJR, Newark. Joined NBC in 1952 as news writer; two years later became nat'l. TV news editor. Promoted to mgr., national news, 1960 and mrg., special news programs, 1961. Appt. dir. of news programs 1962 and gen. mgr., NBC News, 1965; v.p., news programming, NBC, 1967; v.p. news, Washington, 1974; mrg. dir., affiliate & intl. liaison, 1979.

MEDAK, PETER: Director. b. Budapest, Hungary. Entered industry in 1956 in London with AB-Pathe as trainee. Worked sound, editing and camera depts. Later was asst. dir., second unit dir. on various action pictures. In 1963 under contract to Universal Pictures, where started directing TV films. In 1967 under contract to Paramount Pictures.

PICTURES INCLUDE: Kaleidoscope (assoc. prod., 2nd unit dir.), Funeral in Berlin (2nd unit dir.), Fathom (assoc. prod.; 2nd unit dir.) Negatives (dir.), Day in the Death of Joe Egg (dir.), Ruling Class (dir.), Ghosts in the Noonday Sun (dir.).

TV: Third Girl from the Left, The Babysitters, The Dark Secret of Black Bayou.

MEDAVOY, MIKE: Executive. b. Shanghai, China, Jan 21, 1941. Lived in China until 1947 when family moved to Chile. Came to U.S. in 1957. e. UCLA, graduating in 1963 with honors in history dept. Started working in mail room at Universal Studios and became a casting director, from which he went to work for Bill Robinson as an agent trainee. Two years later joined GAC and CMA where he was a v.p. in the motion picture department. In 1971 joined IFA as vice-president in charge of motion picture dept. Represented American and foreign creative talents, among whom were Jane Fonda, Donald Sutherland, Michelangelo Antonioni, Jean-Louis Trintignant, Karel Reisz, Steven Spielberg, Robert Aldrich, George Cukor, John Milius, Terry Malick, Raquel Welch, Gene Wilder and Jeanne Moreau. While at IFA was involved in packaging The Sting, Young Frankenstein, Jaws and others, before joining United Artists Corp. in May, 1974, as senior v.p. in chg. of West Coast prod. In 1978 named exec. v.p., Orion Pictures Co. Is also pres. of Filmex, Inc. Member: UCLA Chancellors and Associates, The American Film Institute, the Board of Crossroads School; Board of Governors, Academy of Motion Picture Arts & Science and member of the visiting committee to the Dept. of Public Relations of Boston Museum of Fine Arts.

MEDFORD, DON: Director. b. Detroit, Mich.; e. Purdue U., U. of N.C., B.A., Yale U., M.F.A., actor, stage mgr., summer theatres; producer, B'way stage, Christopher Award.

TV: Kraft Theatre, General Electric Theatre, Alfred Hitchcock Presents, Climax, Twilight Zone, U.S. Steel Hour, Dick Powell, Eleventh Hour, Dr. Kildare, Fugitive, 12 O'clock High, The FBI, Man From UNCLE, Cimarron Strip, Baretta, Police Story, Kaz, Streets of San Francisco, Dynasty, Odd Job, The Changeling, Zorro, The Gay Blade.

FILMS: The Hunting Party, The Organization, The November Plan, Incident in San Francisco, The Coach.

MEDINA, PATRICIA: Actress. b. London, Eng. In many British films.

PICTURES INCLUDE: Secret Journey, Hotel Reserve, Don't Take It to Heart, Waltz Time. U.S. screen debut: Secret Heart, 1946; others: Moss Rose, Foxes of Harrow, Sangaree, Drums of Tahiti, Phantom of the Rue Morgue, Black Knight, Pirates of Tripoli, Duel on the Mississippi, Uranium Boom, Stranger At My Door, The Killing of Sister George.

MEDLEY, WM. THOMAS: Actor-singer. b. Hollywood, Calif., Sept. 19, 1940. Mem., Righteous Bros. rec. team.

TV: Shindig, The Danny Kaye Show, Ed Sullivan Show.

PICTURES INCLUDE: Beach Ball, Swingin' Summer.

MEDMAN, EDWARD A: Executive. b. Philadelphia, Pa. Nov. 11, 1937. e. University of Pennsylvania (Wharton School) 1955–58; University Pennsylvania Law School 1958–61, JDS; Joined General Counsel's Staff National Labor Relations Board, Washington, D.C., 1962–66; Trial Attorney

NLRB, New York 1966–69; Joined Law firm of Poletti, Freidin, Prashker, Feldman & Gartner, 1969; Senior Labor Attorney, National Broadcasting Company 1970–72; Joined The Burbank Studios, Dec. 1972, v.p., legal/business affairs and chm. of exec. committee.

MEDWIN, MICHAEL: Actor, writer, producer. b. Eng., 1925; e. Institut Fischer. Switzerland. Stage debut 1940; m.p. acting debut in Root of All Evil, 1946.

PICTURES INCLUDE: My Sister and I, Mrs. Christopher, Gay One, Children of Chance, Operation Diamond, Black Memory, Just William's Luck, Ideal Husband, Picadilly Incident, Night Beat, Courtney's of Curzon Street, Call of the Blood, Anna Karenina, William Comes to Town, Woman Hater, Look Before You Love, Forbidden, For Them That Trespass, Queen of Spades, Trottie True, Boys in Brown, Trio, Long Dark Hall, Curtain Up, Street Corner (Both Sides of the Law). I Only Asked, Carry on Nurse, Wind Cannot Read, Heart of a Man, Crooks Anonymous, It's All Happening, Night Must Fall, I've Gotta Horse, 24 Hours To Kill, Charlie Bubbles, If . . . , Spring and Port Wine, O Lucky Man! Prod., Gumshoe, Law and Disorder.

TV: Granada's Army Game, The Love of Mike, Three Live Wires, Memorial Films Ltd.

THEATRE: Spring and Port Wine, Joe Egg, Forget-me-not Lane, Chez Nous, Alpha Beta.

MEEKER, RALPH: Actor: b. Minneapolis, Minn., Nov. 21, 1920; e. Northwestern U. In school plays; served in U.S. Navy.

THEATRE: On B'way in Doughgirls, Strange Fruit, Cyrano de Bergerac, Mr. Roberts, Streetcar Named Desire (also road co.), Picnic, Mrs. Dally; off-B'way: House of Blue Leaves.

PICTURES INCLUDE: Teresa, Four in a Deep Shadow, Sky, Somebody Loves Me, Glory Alley, The Naked Spur, Jeopardy, Code Two, Big House U.S.A., Kiss Me Deadly, Desert Sands, Ada, Dirty Dozen, Gentle Giant, The DEVIL'S Eight, I Walk the Line, Anderson Tapes, The Happiness Cage, Food of the Gods, Winter Kills.

TV: Lost Flight (Special).

MELAMED, DAVID J.: Executive. b. N.Y., Dec. 11, 1911; e. NYU; accountant, Columbia Pictures Corp., 1933–35; acct., RKO Radio Pictures, 1935–40; comptroller, Pathe Labs., Inc., 1941–43; U.S. Army, 1943–46; treas., Eagle Lion Films, 1947–51; exec. v.p., dir., 1952–58; dir. of adm., asst. to chmn. of bd., Nat'l General Corp., 1959–61; v.p., finance, American International Pictures, 1961.

MELCHIOR, IB: Director, writer. b. Copenhagen, Denmark, Sept. 17, 1917. p. Lauritz Melchior; e. Coll., Stenhus, Denmark, 1936. Actor, stage mgr., English Players, 1937–38; co-dir., 1938; actor in 21 stage prod. in Europe and U.S. on radio; set designer; stage man. dept., Radio City Music Hall, 1941–42; U.S. Military Intelligence, 1942–45; writer, dir., m.p. shorts for TV, 1947–48; TV actor, 1949–50; assoc. dir., CBS-TV, July, 1950; assoc. prod., G-L Enterprises, 1952–53; dir., Perry Como Show, 1951–54; dir. March of Medicine, 1955–56; writer, dir. of M.P. & TV films. 1957. Documentary writ. & dir. awarded Top Award by Nat'l. Comm. for Films for Safety, 1960. Golden Scroll Award, Academy of Science Fiction, Best Writing, 1976.

PICTURES INCLUDE: When Hell Broke Loose, Live Fast Die Young, The Angry Red Planet, Reptilicus, Journey to the Seventh Planet, The Case of Patty Smith, Robinson Crusoe on Mars, The Time Travellers, Ambush Bay, Planet of the Vampires, Death Race 2000.

AUTHOR: Novel, Order of Battle, 1972, Sleeper Agent, 1975, The Haigerloch Project, 1977, The Watchdogs of Abaddon, 1979, The Marcus Device, 1980.

MELFORD, AUSTIN: Actor, author, director. b. Alverstoke. England, Aug. 24, 1884; Actor & prod., Theatre Royal, Drury Lane, London, Gaiety Theatre, London, and others.

STAGE PLAYS: (Author) It's a Boy, Battling Butler, Night of the Garter, Nippy, Bob's Your Uncle, Blue for a Boy.

PICTURES INCLUDE: Oh, Daddy, Car of Dreams, Getting Married, We'll Smile Again, Heaven Round the Corner, Champagne Charlie, Sailors Three.

MELNICK, DANIEL: Executive. b. N.Y.C., April 21, 1934. e. N.Y. Univ. In 1954 was staff prod. for CBS-TV; then exec. prod., East Side West Side and N.Y.P.D. Joined ABC-TV as v.p. in chg. of programming. Partner in Talent Associates. Joined MGM as v.p. in chg. of prod.; in 1974 named sr. v.p. & worldwide head of prod.; 1977 in charge of worldwide production, Columbia Pictures; named pres., 1978. Resigned to be indep. prod. (now at 20th-Fox).

PICTURES INCLUDE: Straw Dogs, That's Entertainment! (exec. prod.); That's Entertainment, Two! (co-prod.); All That Jazz (exec. prod.); Altered States (exec. prod.); First Family (prod.).

MELNIKER, BENJAMIN: Motion Picture Producer—Attorney; b. Bayonne, N.J., e. Brooklyn College; LL.B., Fordham Law School, Loew's Theatres usher, private law practice, employed Legal Department Metro-Goldwyn-Mayer, vice president and general counsel, 1954–1969, executive vice president, 1968–1970, resigned from MGM December 1971;

also member MGM bd. dir. and mem. MGM exec. com.; Adjunct associate professor, New York Law School; former motion picture chmn. Anti-Defamation League, B'nai B'rith; Mem. Am., N.Y. State bar assns., Bar Assn. City N.Y., Acad. Motion Picture Arts and Scis.

MELSON, JOHN: Writer-Lyricist. b. Anderson, Ind., Dec. 17, 1930. e. Univ. of Paris (La Sorbonne, 1952 B.A.) and Univ. of Madrid (P.G. studies, 1953–4). m. Maria Perschy, actress. Reporter, Detroit Labor News, 1951; taught French and Italian in various commercial schools in Paris, 1954–5; orchestra musician 1946–50. Script writer for films since 1962. Member: WGAW, BMI.
PICTURES INCLUDE: Battle of the Bulge (co-story, co-s.p.); Savage Pampas (co-s.p.); Cauldron of Blood (co-story, co-s.p.); Simon Bolivar (co-story, co-s.p.); Special Delivery (co-story, co-s.p.); Where Time Began (co-story, co-s.p.); Love and Bullets, Charlie (co-s.p.); The Animal (co-s.p.).
TV: Hawaii Five-O.
SONG LYRICS: Like a Dream (from the Summertime Killer); Cotton Candy Kingdom and The Familiar Stranger (both from Where Time Began).

MENGERS, SUE: Talent Agent. b. Bronx, N.Y. Started as receptionist, secretary with Music Corp. of America in New York. In 1963 became agent in small partnership. Two years later joined Creative Management Associates and sent to Hollywood. Now with Intl. Creative Mgt. (co. formed by merger of CMA and Marvin Josephson Associates). Clients include Barbra Streisand, Gene Hackman, Ryan O'Neal, Tatum O'Neal, Ali MacGraw, Cybill Shepherd, Peter Bogdanovich, Sidney Lumet, Arthur Penn, Nick Nolte, Robin Williams, Roman Polanski, Michael Caine.

MERCHANT, LAWRENCE H., JR.: Producer. b. Cambridge, Mass. e. Boston Latin School, Hebron Academy, Maine, Columbia University, New York University. Pres., Educational Book Div., Prentice-Hall; pres., Pillsbury Productions; prod. exec., TV-Today, Home, Tonight, Milton Berle, Show of Shows, Hallmark Hall of Fame, Eye Witness, R. Montgomery Presents, Wide, Wide World, Walter Winchell; TV advisor, Gen. Dwight D. Eisenhower; prod. CBS films; pres., Kachina Productions.
PICTURES INCLUDE: Hands of Dr. Maniacal, Back Track, Present Tense of Love.

MERCOURI, MELINA: Actress, b. Athens; schooling and training in Athens, fluent in French, German and English; Stage debut on Athens stage in avant-garde work; early stage career in Paris. Also made vocal recordings.
PLAYS INCLUDE: Morning Becomes Electra, La Nuit de Samaracande, Les Compagnons de la Marjolaine, Il Etait une Gare, Le Moulin de la Galette; to Greece 1954, in Stella. Also: A Streetcar Named Desire, Helen or the Joy of Living, The Queen of Clubs, The Seven Year Itch, Sweet Bird of Youth, Ilya Darling.
PICTURES INCLUDE: Stella, The Gypsy and the Gentleman, The Law, Never on Sunday, Phaedra, The Victors, Topkapi, He Who Must Die, 10:30 P.M. Summer, A Man Could Get Killed, Gaily, Gaily, Promise at Dawn, Earthquake, Once is Not Enough, Nasty Habits, A Dream of Passion.

MEREDITH, BURGESS: Actor. b. Cleveland, Ohio, Nov. 16, 1909; e. Amherst Coll., M.A. (hon.). m. Kaja Sundsten. Capt. U.S. Army Air Corps, World War II. On stage 1929 Civic Repertory Co., N.Y.
STAGE PLAYS: Little Ol' Boy, She Loves Me Not, The Star Wagon, Winterset, High Tor, Remarkable Mr. Pennypacker, etc.
PICTURES INCLUDE: Began screen career 1936 in Winterset. Idiot's Delight, Of Mice and Men, Second Chorus, That Uncertain Feeling, Tom, Dick and Harry, Street of Chance, Miracles Can Happen, Story of G.I. Joe, Diary of a Chambermaid, Magnificent Doll, Mine Own Executioner, Man on the Eiffel Tower, Gay Adventure, Joe Butterfly, Advise and Consent, Hurry Sundown, Fortune Garden, Stay Away Joe, McKenna's Gold, Hard Contract, There Was a Crooked Man, The Clay Pigeon, Such Good Friends, Golden Needles, The Day of the Locust, 92 in the Shade, The Hindenburg, Burnt Offerings, Rocky, The Sentinel, The Manitou, Foul Play, Magic, The Great Georgia Bank Hoax, Golden Rendezvous, Rocky II, When Time Ran Out, Clash of the Titans, True Confessions, Rocky III.

MERKE, UNA: Actress. b. Covington, Ky., Dec. 10, 1903.
PLAYS INCLUDE: Two by Two, Poor Nut, Pigs, Gossipy Sex, Coquette, Salt Water, Ponder Heart, Take Me Along.
PICTURES INCLUDE: Eyes of the World, Abraham Lincoln, Command Performance, Daddy Long Legs, Private Lives, Reunion in Vienna, Bombshell, Day of Reckoning, Merry Widow, Born to Dance, Saratoga, Road to Zanzibar, Twin Beds, This Is the Army, It's a Joke Son, Bride Goes Wild, Emergency Wedding, My Blue Heaven, Rich, Young and Pretty, Golden Girl, Millionaire for Christy, With A Song in My Heart, I Love Melvin, The Kentuckian, Bundle

of Joy, The Mating Game, Summer and Smoke, Summer Magic, A Tiger Walks.
TV: Studio 1, Kraft Theatre, Playhouse 90, Climax; I Spy.

MERMAN, ETHEL: Actress. r.n. Ethel Zimmerman; b. Jan. 16, 1909, Astoria, N.Y.; e. William Cullen Bryant H.S. Astoria. Started as secretary, then nightclubs, vaudeville.
THEATRE: Girl Crazy, George White's Scandals, Take a Chance, Red Hot and Blue, Stars in Your Eyes, Du Barry Was a Lady, Panama Hattie, Something for the Boys, Annie Get Your Gun, Call Me Madam, Happy Hunting, Hello Dolly!
PICTURES INCLUDE: We're Not Dressing, Big Broadcast of 1936, Anything Goes, Alexander's Ragtime Band, Call Me Madam, There's No Business Like Show Business, It's a Mad, Mad, Mad, Mad World.

MERRALL, MARY: Actress. b. Liverpool, England; e. convents in Belgium and London; m. Franklyn Dyall. First stage appearance in 1907. Managed Abbey Theatre, Dublin, in 1918 with Franklyn Dyall and produced several plays. Has toured Canada, U.S. and South Africa; many plays since. On screen in 1939–40; Dr. O'Dowd & since in many British films.
PICTURES INCLUDE: Squadron Leader X, Dead of Night, Pink String and Sealing Wax, This Man Is Mine, Nicholas Nickleby, They Made Me a Fugitive, Three Weird Sisters, Badgers Green, For Them That Trespass, Trio, The Late Edwina Black, Out of True, Tale of Five Cities, Encore, Meet Me Tonight, Pickwick Papers, Weak and the Wicked, Duel in the Jungle, Belles of St. Trinians, Pay-Roll Robbery, Green Buddha, Its Great To Be Young, Campbell's Kingdom, Family Doctor, Camp on Blood Island, Spare the Rod, Everything I Have, Moll Flanders, Futtocks End.
TV: The Guardians, Idle at Work, Cider with Rosie, I can See It All, His Lordship Entertains, Kate, Justice, Hunter's Walk, Willy.

MERRICK, DAVID: Producer. b. Hong Kong, 1911. Famed Broadway stage impresario with long record of hits, including Fanny, The Matchmaker, Hello, Dolly!, Look Back in Anger, The Entertainer, Jamaica, World of Suzie Wong, Gypsy, Take Me Along, Becket, Sunday in New York, Oliver!, I Do! I Do!, Private Lives, etc. Recent: 42nd Street.
PICTURES: Child's Play (debut), The Great Gatsby, Semi-Tough, Rough Cut.

MERRILL, DINA: Actress. r.n. Nedinia Hutton; b. N.Y.C. Dec. 9, 1925. e. George Washington Univ., 1940–41; American Academy of Dramatic Arts, 1942–44. Fashion model, 1941–42. Acting debut: Here Today, Mrs. January and Mr. X, Newport 1942.
PLAYS INCLUDE: My Sister Eileen, Major Barbara, Misalliance.
PICTURES INCLUDE: Debut, Desk Set, Catch Me If You Can, Operation Petticoat, Butterfield 8, Young Savages, I'll Take Sweden, The Greatest, A Wedding, Just Tell Me What You Want.
TV: debut, Kate Smith Show 1956; Four Star Theatre, Playwrights '56, Climax!, Playhouse 90, Westinghouse Presents, The Investigators, Checkmate, The Rogues, Bob Hope Presents, To Tell the Truth.

MERRILL, GARY: Actor. b. Hartford, Conn.; e. Loomis Prep. School, Bowdoin Coll., Trinity Coll. Stage career started in 1937, minor role, stage play, The Eternal Road; toured, Brother Rat co.; then, Morning Star, See My Lawyer; on air in Young Dr. Malone, Helen Hayes Theatre, Theatre Guild, Gangbusters, Superman; army service 1941–45; upon disch. to stage in Born Yesterday, At War With the Army. Screen debut: Slattery's Hurricane, supporting role, then Twelve O'Clock High.
PICTURES INCLUDE: Where the Sidewalk Ends, All About Eve, The Frogmen, Decision Before Dawn, Another Man's Poison, Phone Call From a Stranger, Girl in White, Night Without Sleep, Blueprint for Murder, Black Dakotas, Human Jungle, Pleasure of His Company, The Woman Who Wouldn't Die, Clambake, The Incident, The Last Challenge, The Power, Huckleberry Finn, Thieves.
TV: The Mask, Justice, Dr. Kildare.

MERSON, MARC: Producer. b. New York City, Sept. 9, 1931. e. Swarthmore. Entered Navy in 1953; assigned as publicist to Admiral's Staff of Sixth Fleet Command in the Mediterranean. Upon discharge joined trade paper Show Business as feature editor. Joined CBS-TV as asst. to casting editor. Left after 3 yrs. to work for Ely Landau as casting dir., packager and sometime producer of The Play of the Week on TV. Returned to CBS for 3-yr. stint doing specials and live programs. Left to organize Brownstone Productions as indep. prod. Now partner with Alan Alda in Helix Productions to package and produce TV shows.
PICTURES INCLUDE: The Heart Is a Lonely Hunter, People Soup (short), Leadbelly.
TV: Stage 67, Androcles and the Lion, Dummler & Son (pilot), The David Frost Revue (synd. series), We'll Get By.

MESMER, MARIE: Drama, film reviewer. b. Newark, N.J. Feb. 14, 1920; e. Syracuse Univ., Brooklyn (N.Y.) Inst. of Arts & Sciences; Radio adv. Crowell Pub. Co., 2 yrs.; danced with Ted Lewis and orchestra on tour; exhibiting artist in art galleries throughout U.S. for number years; currently drama reviewer Los Angeles (Calif.) Daily News, specializing in covering jazz music & personalities. Member: Los Angeles Press Club.

MESSENGER, GARY L.: Executive. b. Fresno, Calif., Jan. 14, 1941. e. University of Southern California-Cinema. 1967, joined MCA, Inc., asst. to exec. v.p.; 1970, independent motion picture & television producer; 1976, v.p. director production services, The Burbank Studios. Member of USC Cinema Circulus, Producers Guild of America.

METZLER, ROBERT: Writer. b. Buffalo, N.Y., Dec. 26, 1914; e. U. of S. California. Joined MGM writing staff 1939. In 1941: collaborated on screenplay Riders of the Purple Sage, 20th-Fox. In 1942: Sundown Jim, Dr. Renault's Secret; (s.p.) Circumstantial Evidence; (adapt.) The Undercover Woman.

MEYER, RICHARD C.: Producer, exec. film editor, screen writer, b. Frankfurt, Ger., 1920. e. Herne Bay Coll., Eng.; UCLA; cameraman, George Stevens' Special Motion Picture Coverage Unit; film ed., re-recording spvr., Louis de Rochemont; film dir., Prockter Prods.; co-org., Robert Lawrence Prods., free lance film ed., TV & m.p.; v.p., International Operation, Ass. Prod. Dino de Laurentiis.
PICTURES INCLUDE: Lost Boundaries, Seven Angry Men, King Oedipus, Crime in the Streets, The Wild Party, Hot Rod Rumble, Pyro, The Castilian, Young Jesse James, Return of the Fly, Jazz Party, Forbidden Dreams, The Babysitter, Alaska Passage, Men In War, God's Little Acre, Anna Lucasta, Spartacus, Happy Anniversary, Three in the Attic, Winning, Waterloo, Capone, Butch Cassidy and the Sundance Kid.
TV: Jack Benny Show, The Big Story, Grand Old Opry, Dear Phoebe, Farmer's Daughter, Wackiest Ship in the Army, Danny Thomas Anthology, The Iron Horse, The Outcasts, The Bold Ones, Police Story, King.

MEYER, RUSS: Producer, director. b. Oakland, Calif.; in 1942 joined Army Signal Corps, learned m.p. photography and shot combat newsreels.
PICTURES INCLUDE: The Immoral Mr. Teas, Eve and the Handyman, Finders Keepers, Lovers Weepers, Goodmorning and Goodbye, Vixen, Beyond the Valley of The Dolls, The Seven Minutes, and Sweet Suzy.

MEYERS, ROBERT: Executive. b. Mount Vernon, N.Y., Oct. 3, 1934. e. N.Y.U. Entered m.p. industry as exec. trainee in domestic div. of Columbia Pictures, 1956. Sales and adv., 1956–60; transferred to sales dep't. Columbia Pictures International, N.Y., posts there included supervisor of international roadshows and exec. ass't. to continental mgr. Joined National General Pictures as v.p.-foreign sales, 1969. Created JAD Films International Inc. in Feb. 1974 for independent selling and packaging of Motion Pictures around the world. September, 1977, joined Lorimar Productions Inc. as senior vice pres. of Lorimar Distribution International. Became pres. in April, 1978. Joined Filmways Pictures in 1980, named pres. & co-o. Is pres. of American Film Mktg. Assn.

MICHAELI, JOHN EDWARD: Executive. b. Los Angeles, Calif., Nov. 20, 1938; e. Mt. Carmel H.S., Sta. Monica City Coll., S. California State University, B.A., 1965; M.A. 1977. Merch. buyer & dir. of Adv., Maymart div. of May Co.; police beat reporter, KGIL; pub. ed. Bunker-Ramo Corp.; Off. boy then publicist, MGM, 1965; v.p. communications, Hanna-Barbera Prods.

MICHAUD, HENRI: Executive. b. Ismailia, Egypt, Sept. 24, 1912. e. H.E.C. (Commercial Acdmy.), Paris, 1932. Warner Bros., Paris, 1934, 1944. Paramount Internat'l Films, 1944–68; pres. Para. Intern'l; co-chmn., Cinema Int'l Corp., July, 1970. Co-chairman A.M. Film Consultants Ltd. 1977.

MICHAUD, HENRY A.: Executive. b. Gastonia, N.C., Mar. 19, 1914. e. Loyola Coll., Tech. School (Science) 1932–37. Amateur photographer. Cameraman on animation and title stand, Associated Screen News, 1939; cameraman, Naval and Air Force training films, industrial and tourist films, 1940–47. Partner, founded, Phoenix Studios, 1947 which later was reorganized as Omega Prods., 1951; in chg. technical services, multiple camera shooting methods, rear-projection techniques, etc., using 16mm negative for TV shows, 1952; dir. on numerous industrial and government films. Pres., Assoc. of Motion Picture Producers and Labs. of Canada, 1961. v.p. Omega Prod. of Montreal.

MICHEL, WERNER: Producer. b. Detmold, Germany March 5, 1910. e. U. of Berlin, U. of Paris, Ph.D. Radio writer, dir., co-author two Broadway revues, 1938, 1940; dir. French feature films; dir. Broadcast Div., Voice of America, 1942–46; prod., dir., CBS, 1946–48; asst. prog. dir., CBS, 1948–50; dir. of Kenyon and Eckhart TV dept., 1950–52; prod.,

DuMont TV network, 1952–55; dir., Electronicam TV-Film Prod., 1955–56; prod., Benton and Bowles; Procter and Gamble, 1956–57; v.p. & dir. TV-radio dept., Reach, McClinton Advertising, Inc., 1957–62; consultant, TV Programming & Comm'l-Prod., N. W. Ayer & Son, Inc.; v.p., dir., TV dept. SSC&B Advertising, 1963, pgm. exec., ABC-TV, Hollywood, 1975; director, dramatic programs, 1976; sr. v.p., creative affairs, MGM-TV, 1977; exec. v.p., Wrather Entertainment Intl., 1979; sr. v.p., programs, MGM-TV, 1980.

MICHELET, MICHEL: Composer. b. Kieff, Russia. Prof., Kieff & Vienna Conserv.; composed concert compositions, ballets, stage music; ent. m.p. industry, composed scores 105 films, France; to U.S. 1941; author many concert compositions.
PICTURES INCLUDE: Voice in the Wind (AA nom.), Hairy Ape (AA nom.), Music for Millions, The Chase, Lured, Siren of Atlantis, Man on the Eiffel Tower, Once a Thief, Tarzan's Peril, Fort Algiers, Un Missionaire, Le Secret de Soeur Angele, Petersburger, Nachte, Challenge (Tribute to Modern Art). Also did scores for many U.S. Information Service documentaries; arr. of Russian music Anastasia; Afrodife (score); The January (orig. songs & arr. of Russian music). Member: French Soc. of Composers (SACEM).

MICHELL, KEITH: Actor. b. Adelaide, Australia. Early career as art teacher, radio actor; toured Australia with Stratford Shakespearean Co. 1952–53; Stratford Memorial Theatre 1954–55, Old Vic Theatre 1956–7. Irma la Douce, Chichester, Art of Seduction, The First 400 Years, Robert & Elizabeth, Kain, The King's Mare, 1969: Don Quijote in Man of La Mancha, London, N.Y. 1970: Abelard & Heloise, London; 1971, NY and LA, 1972, Hamlet, London, in October 1973 apptd. Artistic Director, Chichester Festival Theatre.
TV: Pygmalion, Act of Violence, Mayerling Affair, Tiger At The Gates, Traveller Without Luggage, Guardian Angel, Wuthering Heights, The Bergonzi Hands, Ring Round The Moon, Spread of the Eagle, The Shifting Heart, Loyalties, Soldier in Love, Hallmark Hall of Fame, series; Kain, The Ideal Husband, The Six Wives of Henry VIII (series). Keith Michell at various London theatres, Dear Love.
PICTURES INCLUDE: True As A Turtle, Dangerous Exile, Gypsy and the Gentleman, The Hellfire Club, All Night Long, Seven Seas to Calais, Prudence and the Pill, House of Cards, Henry VIII and his Six Wives, Moments.

MIDDLETON, RAY: Actor. b. Chicago, Ill.; e. Illinois (music); Julliard School of Music, N.Y.C. With Detroit Civic Opera House; started in play, Roberta; in Chicago Opera Co. 1936: to Hollywood.
PICTURES INCLUDE: Knickerbocker Holiday, George White's Scandal's, American Jubilee, Lady for a Night, Girl from Alaska, I Dream of Jeannie, Sweethearts on Parade, Jubilee Trail, I Cover the Underworld, Road to Denver, 1776.
STAGE: Annie Get Your Gun, South Pacific, Man of La Mancha.

MIDLER, BETTE: Actress-Singer. b. Honolulu, 1945. e. Univ. of Hawaii. Appeared on Bdwy. in Fiddler on the Roof; Salvation, 1970; Tommy, Seattle Opera Co., 1971. Gained fame as singer-comic in nightclubs and cabarets. Has toured extensively with own stage shows: Divine Miss M, Clams on the Half-Shell, etc.
PICTURES: The Rose, Divine Madness, Jinxed.

MIFUNE, TOSHIRO: Actor. b. Tsingtao, China, April 1, 1920. e. Japanese schools. Served five years Japanese army. Joined Toho Studio 1946.
PICTURES INCLUDE: Snow Trail, Drunken Angel, Eagle of Pacific, Seven Samurai, I Live in Fear, Legend of Musashi, Throne of Blood, Rikisha Man, Three Treasures, Last Gunfight, I Bombed Pearl Harbor, Rose in Mud, Rashomon, Yojimbo, Animus Trujano (Mexican), Kiska, Red Beard, High and Low, Judo Saga, The Lost World of Sinbad, Hell in the Pacific, Paper Tiger, Midway, Winter Kills, 1941, Shogun.

MIDGEN, CHESTER L.: Executive. b. New York, N.Y., May 21, 1921; e. CCNY, B.A., 1941, Columbia U. LLB 1947; Member New York Bar. Attorney for National Labor Relations Board 1947–51. Currently National Executive Secretary, Screen Actors Guild; v.p., California Labor Federation, AFL-CIO. Vice Pres., Associated Actors and Artists of America, AFL-CIO. Vice pres., Hollywood Film Council. Executive committee Motion Picture and Television Fund. Trustee, John L. Dales Scholarship Fund. Trustee, Producers-Screen Actors Guild Pension and Welfare Funds. Board Member, Partnership for the Arts. Vice-chairman, State of California Motion Picture Development Council.

MIKELL, GEORGE: Actor. b. Lithuania. In Australia 1950–6 acting with Old Vic Co. Ent. films 1955. TV 1957. To England 1957; since appeared in numerous film and TV prod.
TV: Counsel at Law, Six Eyes on a Stranger, The Mask of a Clown, Green Grows the Grass, Opportunity Taken, OSS Series, Espionage, The Danger Man, Strange Report,

The Survivors, The Adventurer, Colditz, The Hanged Man, Quiller, Martin Hartwell, Flambards, Sweeney, The Secret Army, Sherlock Holmes.

PICTURES INCLUDE: The Guns of Navarone, The Password Is Courage, The Great Escape, Deadline for Diamonds, Where The Spies Are, The Spy Who Came in From the Cold, I Predoni Del Sahara, Sabina, The Double Man, Attack on the Iron Coast, Zeppelin, Young Winston, Scorpio, The Tamarind Seed, Sweeney Two, The Sea Wolves, Escape to Victory.

STAGE: Five Finger Exercise, Altona, The Millionairess, Love from a Stranger, Portrait of A Queen.

MILES, LORD: C.B.E. Actor, dir., writer. b. Hillingdon, Middlesex, Sept. 27, 1907; e. Pembroke Coll., Oxford. Brit. stage debut 1930 in Richard III, London. Brit. screen debut in Channel Crossing. Awarded C.B.E., 1953; founded Mermaid Theatre, 1959.

PICTURES INCLUDE: Pastor Hall, The Big Blockade, This Was Paris; (collab. s.p.) Thunder Rock; The Day Will Dawn, One of Our Aircraft Is Missing, In Which We Serve; (author, co-dir., actor) Tawney Pipit; Carnival, Great Expectations, Fame is the Spur, Nicholas Nickleby, Guinea Pig, Never Let Me Go, Moby Dick, Man Who Knew Too Much, Zarak, Tiger In the Smoke, Fortune Is a Woman, Smallest Show on Earth, St. Joan, Tom Thumb, Sapphire, Heavens Above, Run Wild, Run Free, The Specialist.

TV: Treasure Island, etc.

MILES, SARAH: Actress. b. 1941; e. R.A.D.A.; film debut, Term of Trial.

PICTURES INCLUDE: The Servant, The Ceremony, Six-Sided Triangle, Those Magnificent Men In Their Flying Machines, Blowup, Ryan's Daughter, Lady Caroline Lamb, The Man Who Loved Cat Dancing, The Sailor Who Fell from Grace with the Sea, The Big Sleep.

THEATRE: Vivat! Vivat Regina!

MILES, VERA: Actress. b. Boise City, Okla., Aug. 23, 1930. e. public schools, Pratt and Wichita, Kans.

TV: Climax, Pepsi Cola Playhouse, Schlitz Playhouse, Ford Theatre.

PICTURES INCLUDE: For Men Only, Rose Bowl Story, Charge at Feather River, Pride of the Blue Grass, Wichita, The Searchers, 23 Paces to Baker Street, Autumn Leaves, Wrong Man, Beau James, Web of Evidence, FBI Story, Touch of Larceny, Five Branded Women, Psycho, The Spirit Is Willing, Gentle Giant, Sergeant Ryker, Kona Coast, It Takes All Kinds, Hellfighters, The Wild Country, One Little Indian.

MILFORD, JOHN: Actor.

TV: Delvecchio; Code R; Little House On The Prairie; ABC Circle Short Story Theatre; Hip; $6 Million Man; Bionic Woman; Police Story; Streets Of San Francisco; Gemini Man; The Hunter; Faith for Today; Barnaby Jones; Blue Knight; Policewoman; Cannon; Joe Forrester; Medical Story; Men In Green; The Name Of The Game; Gold Ones; Mannix; The Magician; Twelve O'Clock High; The Invaders; Firehouse; The Sound Of Anger; The Sixth Sense; The Plainsman; Tombstone Territory; The Lieutenants; Columbo; The FBI; Petrocelli; Longstreet; Mod Squad; Dan August; King Of Diamonds; Men In Space; High Chaparral; Family Affair; Toma; Ironside; Rifleman; Jesse James; Wyatt Earp; Gunsmoke; The Virginian; Big Valley; Bonanza; Hawkins; Guns Of Will Sonnett; Robert Taylor Detectives.

PICTURES INCLUDE: Brannigan's Rebels; The Ten Commandments; For Pete's Sake; Heart Of The Rebel; Marty; Gunfight At Commanche Creek.

THEATRE: What Every Woman Knows; Pygmalion; The Prime Of Miss Jean Brodie; Happy Birthday, Wanda June; Silent Night, Lonely Night; Child's Play; Diary Of A Scoundrel; Miss Julie; Apollo Of Bellac; Do You Know The Milky Way; The Vigil; Portrait Of A Madonna; State Of The Union; Night Must Fall; The Long Voyage Home; Murder In The Cathedral; The Male Animal; The Admirable Crichton; Aria De Capo; Nothing But The Truth; The Happy Prince; The Purging of Simon Madden; Peterson House; Where Is Thy Victory; Harry; Noon And Night; Room Service; The American Nightmare.

MILGRAM, HENRY: Theatre Executive. b. Philadelphia, April 20, 1926. e. Univ. of Pa., Wharton School. In industry 35 years; now exec. v.p. Milgram Theatres. Variety Club Board Member for past 15 years, past president and chairman of the Board of Variety Club of Phila.; presently Variety Club Intl. Ambassador. Board member: Moss Rehabilitation Hospital, Likoff Cardiovascular Institute, Hahnemann Medical College & Hospital of Phila.

MILIUS, JOHN: Writer-Director. b. 1945. e. L.A. City College, USC (cinema course). While at latter won National Student Film Festival Award. Started career as ass't. to Lawrence Gordon at AIP. Began writing screenplays, then became director with Dillinger.

PICTURES INCLUDE: Devil's 8, Evil Knievel, The Life and Times of Judge Roy Bean, Jeremiah Johnson (co-s.p.), Dillinger (s.p.-dir.), Magnum Force (o.-s.p.), The Wind

and the Lion (s.pm., dir.), Big Wednesday (dir. co-s.p.); Apocalypse Now (s.p.); 1941 (exec. prod.-co. s.p.)..

MILLAND, RAY: Actor. r.n. Reginald Truscott-Jones; b. Neath, Wales, Jan. 3, 1908; e. King's Coll.

PICTURES INCLUDE: Ambassador Bill, Payment Deferred, Bolero, One Hour Late, Glass Key, Big Broadcast of 1937, Three Smart Girls, Easy Living, Ebb Tide, Wise Girl, Beau Geste, French Without Tears, Irene, Doctor Takes a Wife, Lady Has Plans, Reap the Wild Wind, Are Husbands Necessary, Major and the Minor, Crystal Ball, Forever and a Day, Lady in the Dark, Kitty, Acad. Award best perf. ("Lost Weekend") 1945; Well-Groomed Lady, California, Imperfect Lady, Trouble With Women, Golden Earrings, Big Clock, Wings Over Honolulu, So Evil My Love, Sealed Verdict, Alias Nick Beal, It Happens Every Spring, Life of Her Own, Copper Canyon, Woman of Distinction, Circle of Danger, Night Into Morning, Rhubarb, Close to My Heart, Something to Live For, Bugles in the Afternoon, The Thief, Jamaica Run, Let's Do It Again, Dial M for Murder, Girl on the Red Velvet Swing; act. A Man Alone, Lisbon: act., Three Brave Men, River's Edge, Premature Burial, Panic in Year Zero, Man with the X-Ray Eyes, Love Story, Frogs, The House in Nightmare Park, Gold, Escape to Witch Mountain, The Last Tycoon, Battlestar Galactica, Oliver's Story.

TV: Rich Man, Poor Man, Seventh Avenue, Testimony of Two Men.

MILLAR, STUART: Producer-Director. b. New York, N.Y., 1929. e. Stanford; Sorbonne, Paris. Ent. industry working for Motion Picture Branch, State Dept., Germany. documentaries, Army Signal Corps, Long Island, Germany; journalist, International News Service, San Francisco; assoc. prod.-dir., The Desperate Hours; assoc. prod.-dir., Friendly Persuasion.

PICTURES INCLUDE: The Young Stranger; Stage Struck; Birdman of Alcatraz. I Could Go On Singing, The Young Doctors, Stolen Hours, The Best Man, Paper Lion, Little Big Man, When The Legends Die, Rooster Cogburn.

MILLER, ANN: Actress. r.n. Lucille Ann Collier; b. Houston, Tex., Apr. 12, 1923; e. Albert Sidney Johnson H.S., Houston; Lawler Prof., School, Hollywood. Studied dance as child; played West Coast vaudeville theatres, Screen debut: New Faces of 1937.

STAGE: George White's Scandals, 1940, Mame, 1969.

PICTURES INCLUDE: Life of the Party, Stage Door, New Faces of 1937, Radio City Revels, Having a Wonderful Time, Room Service, You Can't Take It With You, Too Many Girls, Time Out for Rhythm, Priorities on Parade, Reveille With Beverly, Jam Session, Eve Knew Her Apples, Thrill of Brazil, Easter Parade, The Kissing Bandit, On the Town, Watch the Birdie, Texas Carnival, Two Tickets to Broadway, Lovely To Look At, Small Town Girl, Kiss Me Kate, Deep in My Heart, Hit the Deck, Opposite Sex, Great American Pastime.

MILLER, BEVERLY: Distributor. b. Huntsdale, Mo., April 8, 1906. Entered m.p. ind. in Mo. as exhib., 1925; salesman, National Screen Service, in midwest 1926–36; opened own bus., 1936 Producers Releasing Co., 1941; sold to Pathe Industries, 1945; branch mgr., Producers Releasing Co.; dist. mgr., Eagle Lion to 1948. Operated drive-ins 1949 to 1968, sold out to Mid-America Theatres, St. Louis, Missouri. exec. pres. United M.P. Assoc.; Pres. Mercury Film Co., Inc. Also v.p. Four Associates Ltd. Cinema Project Number One, producing movies in the Philippines.

MILLER, CHERYL: Actress. b. Sherman Oaks, Calif., Feb. 4, 1943. e. ULCA, Los Angeles Conservatory of Music.

PICTURES INCLUDE: First film, Casanova Brown, age 19 days. Appeared in over 100 films as child, more recently in The Monkey's Uncle, Clarence the Cross-Eyed Lion, The Initiation, The Man From Clover Grove, Doctor Death.

TV: Perry Mason, Bachelor Father, Flipper and as co-star in Daktari, Donna Reed, Leave it to Beaver, Farmers Daughter, Wonderful World of Color, Dobie Gillis, Bright Promise, Love American Style, Emergency, Cades County.

MILLER, DAVID: Director. b. Paterson, N.J., Nov. 28, 1909. U.S. Army, World War II. Film ed. 1930, Columbia; Walter Futter prods. In 1933 short subjects ed. MGM; then dir. short subjects. Dir. features 1941.

PICTURES INCLUDE: Billy the Kid, Sunday Punch, Flying Tigers, Love Happy, Top O The Morning, Our Very Own, Saturday's Hero, Sudden Fear, Twist of Fate, Diane, Opposite Sex, The Story of Esther Costello, Midnight Lace, Backstreet, Lonely are the Brave, Captain Newman, MD, Hammerhead, Hail Hero, Executive Action, Bittersweet Love, Best Place To Be, Goldie and The Boxer, Love for Rent.

MILLER, DICK (RICHARD): Actor/Writer. b. N.Y.C., Dec. 25, 1928. e. CCNY, Columbia Univ. School of Dramatic Arts. Commercial artist, Psychologist; Bellevue Mental Hygiene Clinic, Queens General Hospital Psychiatric dept. U.S. Navy, WWII. Boxing champ, U.S. Navy.

Semi-pro football. Broadway stage, radio; Disc jockey, The Dick Miller Show, WMCA, WOR-TV Over 500 live shows. Did first live night talk show, Midnight Set, CBS Wrote, produced and directed many early radio and TV shows. Wrote Screenplays; T.N.T. Jackson, Which Way To The Front, Four Robe Out and others.

PICTURES INCLUDE: Has appeared in over 65 features, including: Not of This Earth, Thunder Over Hawaii, Rock All Night, Sorority Girl, The Terror, Bucket Of Blood, Little Shop Of Horrors, Targets, War Of The Satelittes, The Long Ride Home, St. Valentine Day Massacre, Capone, Executive Action, White Line Fever, Cannonball, Mr. Billion, N.Y., N.Y.

MILLER, JASON: Writer-Actor. Entered regional playwriting contest during high school in Scranton, Penna. and since has moved back and forth between acting and writing. Wrote That Championship Season, winner of N.Y. Drama Critics Best Play award, 1972, Tony Award, 1973, and Pulitzer Prize for Drama.

PICTURES INCLUDE: The Exorcist (actor), That Championship Season (s.p.), The Nickel Ride (actor), A Home of our Own (actor), Fitzgerald in Hollywood (actor), A Love Story (s.p.).

MILLER, J.P.: Writer. b. San Antonio, Tex., Dec. 18, 1919. e. Rice Univ., 1937–41, Yale Drama School, 1946–47. U.S. Navy, Lieut., 1941–46; pub. poetry, short stories.

ORIGINAL DRAMAS INCLUDE: Philco TV Playhouse: Hide and Seek, Old Tasslefoot, The Rabbit Trap, The Pardon-me Boy; Playhouse 90, Days of Wine and Roses, CBS Playhouse, The People Next Door, The Unwanted, The Lindbergh Kidnaping Case, Gauguin The Savage.

PICTURES INCLUDE: The Rabbit Trap, (story, s.p.) Days of Wine and Roses, (story, s.p.) The Young Savages, (coauthor, s.p.) Behold A Pale Horse, (s.p.) The People Next Door (story, s.p.), Helter Skelter (s.p.)

NOVELS: The Race for Home, Liv.

MILLER, JAMES P.: Executive. Began m.p./industry career in 1971 in legal dept. of United Artists (N.Y.). Left to go with Paramount Pictures in legal dept.; then moved to Columbia in 1977 as snr. counsel; later assoc. gen. counsel. In 1979 named Warner Bros. v.p.—studio business affairs.

MILLER, MARVIN: Actor, narrator, writer. b. St. Louis, Mo., July 18, 1913. e. Washington U., A.B., 1930–34. Radio stations KWK, WIL, KMOX, St. Louis 1931–39; since free lance; announcer & actor on numerous major network radio shows, Chicago & Los Angeles. Member: Mason, Scottish Rite; Legion of Honor Order of DeMolay; Shrine; poetry groups; Motion Picture, TV and Recording Academies, Pacific Pioneer Broadcasters.

PICTURES INCLUDE: Johnny Angel, Intrigue, Off Limits, Forbidden, Shanghai Story, Peking Express, The Naked Ape, Where Does it Hurt?, I Wonder Who's Killing Her Now, Prime Time, Kiss Daddy Goodbye.

Narrated many award-winning industrial, educational, military films. UPA cartoons, Disney, DePatie-Freleng Filmation, Hanna-Barbera. Actor or anncr. filmed and live TV.

TV: Star, Millionaire, CBS-TV; Narrator, FBI; Star, Aquaman, Fantastic Voyage; Narr., Electrawoman, Burrud Nature Specials, Bigfoot & Wildboy.

Recorded entire Talking Bible, other talking books, Audio Book; Two Grammy awards for Dr. Seuss Children's Records, RCA Victor. Synd. radio, Marvin Miller, Storyteller; Almanac.

MILLER, MAX B.: Executive. Father, Max Otto Miller, producer silent features and shorts. e. Los Angeles Valley Coll., UCLA, Sherwood Oaks Coll. Writer of articles on cinema for American Cinematographer and other publications. Owns and manages Fotos Intl., entertainment photo agency with offices in 46 countries. Recipient of Golden Globe Award in 1976 for Youthquake, documentary feature. Chm. of bd. of Hollywood Foreign Press Ass'n. since 1976.

MILLER, NAT: Executive. b. London, 1909. Joined Granada Theatres 1924; appointed chief booker. Own organization, ORB Productions Ltd., 1954; man. dir. Animated Motion Pics., Ltd.

PICTURES INCLUDE: Secret Tent and Grove Family Film series, Nudist Paradise, Death Over My Shoulder, That Kind of Girl, Yellow Teddybears.

TV: TV film series. UK Film Distribution.

MILLER, ROBERT ELLIS: Director. Worked on Broadway and TV before feature film debut with Any Wednesday (1966).

PICTURES INCLUDE: Sweet November, The Heart Is a Lonely Hunter, The Buttercup Chain, Big Truck and Poor Claire, The Girl from Petrovka, The Baltimore Bullet.

TV: The Voice of Charlie Pont, And James Was a Very Small Snail.

MILLER, RONALD W.: Producer. b. April 17, 1933, Los Angeles, e. U. of Southern Calif. Football player with Los Angeles Rams. Two years U.S. Army. 1957 joined Walt Disney Productions as 2nd asst. dir. Old Yeller. Assoc. prod. TV series Walt Disney Presents; assoc. or co-prod.

additional 37 episodes Disney TV. Exec. prod. Walt Disney's Wonderful World of Color. 1980, named pres., Disney Productions.

PICTURES INCLUDE: Bon Voyage, Summer Magic, Son of Flubber, Moon Pilot, The Misadventures of Merlin Jones, A Tiger Walks, The Monkey's Uncle, That Darn Cat, Robin Crusoe, U.S.N., Monkey's Go Home, Prod. of: Never A Dull Moment, The Boatniks, The Wild Country, No Deposit, No Return, Treasure of Matecumbe, Freaky Friday, The Littlest Horse Thieves, Herbie Goes to Monte Carlo, Pete's Dragon, Candleshoe, Return from Witch Mountain, Cat from Outer Space, The North Avenue Irregulars, The Black Hole, Midnight Madness, Watcher in the Woods, The Last Flight of Noah's Ark.

Assisted Walt Disney, Pageant Direct 1960 U.S. Olympics. By 1968, v.p., exec. prod. mem. bd. of dir. Walt Disney Productions.

MILLER, WINSTON: Writer. b. St. Louis, Mo., June 22, 1910; e. Princeton U. In 1935 entered m.p. ind.

PICTURES INCLUDE: Good Morning, Judge, Song of Texas, Home in Indiana, One Body Too Many, They Made Me a Killer, Double Exposure, My Darling Clementine, Relentless, Station West, Last Outpost, Rocky Mountain, Hong Kong, Blazing Forest, Carson City, The Vanquished, Boy from Oklahoma, Jivaro, Bounty Hunter, Run for Cover, Far Horizons, Lucy Gallant, Tension at Table Rock, April Love, A Private's Affair, Hound Dog Man, Escapade In Japan, Mardi Gras.

MILLS, HAYLEY: Actress. b. London, Eng., April 18, 1946. e. Elmhurst Boarding School, Surrey. m.p. debut Tiger Bay. 1959; Pollyanna, 1960; signed Disney contract 1960.

PICTURES INCLUDE: The Parent Trap, Whistle Down the Wind, The Castaways, Summer Magic, The Chalk Garden, The Moonspinners, The Truth About Spring, Sky West and Crooked, Trouble With Angels, The Family Way, Pretty Polly, A Matter of Innocence, Twisted Nerve, Take a Girl Like You, Sillouettes, What Changed Charley Farthing, The Diamond Hunters.

MILLS, SIR JOHN: Actor, Producer. b. Suffolk, England, February 22, 1908. m. Mary Hayley Bell. Previously clerk. Film actor since 1933. In 1942: "The Young Mr. Pitt." "In Which We Serve," One of top ten money-making Brit. stars in Motion Picture Herald-Fame Poll, 1945, 1947, 1949–50, 1954, 1956–58, Oscar for Ryans Daughter.

PICTURES INCLUDE: We Dive at Dawn, This Happy Breed, Blue for Waterloo, Cottage To Let, Way to the Stars, Waterloo Road, Great Expectations, So Well Remembered, October Man, Scott of the Antarctic, Operation Disaster, Mr. Denning Drives North, Gentle Gunman, Long Memory, Hobson's Choice, End of the Affair, Colditz Story, Above Us the Waves, Escapade, It's Great to be Young, Around the World in 80 Days, War and Peace, Baby and the Battleship, Town on Trial, Monty's Double, Dunkirk, Summer of the 17th Doll, Tiger Bay, Swiss Family Robinson, Tunes of Glory, The Singer Not The Song, Flame In the Streets, Tiara Tahiti, The Valiant, The Chalk Garden, The Truth About Spring, The Great Spy Mission, King Rat, The Wrong Box, 1965; dir., Sky West and Crooked; acted, The Family Way, Cowboy in Africa, Chukka, A Black Veil For Lisa, Oh! What a Lovely War, Run Wild, Run Free, Ryan's Daughter, Adam's Woman, Dulcima, Oklahoma Crude, Young Winston, Lady Caroline, The Human Factor, Trial By Combat, Lamb, The Big Sleep.

STAGE: Good Companions, 1975; Great Expectations, 1976; Separate Tables, 1977.

MILNER, JACK: Exec. Prod. b. Jersey City, N.J., Nov. 2, 1910. e. Roosevelt H.S., L.A., Calif. M.P. industry 1927. Worked many phases from laboratory-camera-editorial dept. to financing and co-producing feature pictures; formed Milner Bros. Productions with brother Dan Milner, 1955; prod. Phantom from 10,000 Leagues, From Hell It Came, Jail Break, etc.

TV: prod. My Dog Sheppy, From Here to Now, Come As You Are.

MILNER, MARTIN: Actor. b. Detroit, Mich., Dec. 28. e. USC. m.p. debut in Life with Father, 1947; U.S. Army 1952–54, directed 20 training films.

PICTURES INCLUDE: Sands of Iwo Jima, The Halls of Montezuma, Operation Pacific, The Captive City, Battle Zone, Mr. Roberts, Pete Kelly's Blues, On the Threshold of Space, Gunfight at the O.K. Corral, Sweet Smell o' Success, Marjorie Morningstar, Too Much, Too Soon, Compulsion, 13 Ghosts, Valley of the Dolls.

TV: Route 66 (4 yrs.), Adam-12 (6 yrs), Swiss Family Robinson.

MILO, GEORGE: Set Decorator. r.n. George Milo Vescia. b. New York, N.Y., Dec. 19, 1909. e. High School, Art Schools; landscape, seascape, still life painter, portrait sculptor; set decorator since 1937.

TV: Republic Studios, Revue Studios; Dangerous Assignment, Stories of the Century, Thriller, Alfred Hitchcock, Checkmate, General Electric.

PICTURES INCLUDE: Wake of the Red Witch, Fair Wind

to Java, Borderline, Jubilee Trail, Make Haste to Live, Eternal Sea, Last Command, Come Next Spring, Psycho, Judgement at Nuremberg, The Last Cowboy, That Touch of Mink, The Birds.

MIMIEUX, YVETTE: Actress. b. Los Angeles, Calif., Jan. 8. e. Vine Street School, Le Conte Junior High, Los Angeles, Los Ninos Heroes de Chapultepec, Mexico City, Hollywood High School, Calif. Appeared with a theatrical group, Theatre Events; Sympn. Concert: Persphone, Oakland Orchestra, 1965, N.Y. Philharmonic, Linc. Ctr., L.A. Philharmonic, Hollywood Bowl.
PICTURES INCLUDE: debut, Time Machine, Where the Boys Are, The Four Horsemen of the Apocalypse, Light in the Piazza, The Wonderful World of the Brothers Grimm, Diamond Head, Toys In the Attic, Joy In The Morning, Reward, Monkeys Go Home, Dark of the Sun, Caper of the Golden Bulls, Picasso Summer, Three in the Attic, Skyjacked, The Neptune Factor, Jackson County Jail, The Black Hole.
TV: Tyger Tyger, 1964. 1970: series, Most Deadly Game, Death Takes A Holiday, Black Noon.
STAGE: I Am A Camera, 1963; Owl and the Pussycat, 1966.
CONCERTS: Persephane—Houston Symphony, London Royal Philharmonic.

MINDLIN, MICHAEL, JR.: Executive. b. New York, N.Y. e. Columbia U., 1940–41; Duke U., 1941–43. U.S. Air Force; short subject pub., W.B., 1946–47; assoc., George & Dorothy Ross pub., 1947; pub., adv. dir., Ballet Russe de Monte Carlo, 1947–49; asst. to prod. Joseph Kaufman, 1950; with We the People, radio & TV show, 1950–51; Alfred Katz pub. & mgt., 1951–53; adv. & pub. dir., Lopert Films, 1953, pub., Hecht-Lancaster, 1955; adv., pub. dir., Figaro, Inc., 1956–58; assoc. prod. David Merrick Prod., 1958–59; formed prod. co. with Raoul Levy, 1959; v.p. chg. adv., publ., Filmways, Inc., 1963, v.p. prod., Filmways, Inc., 1968. Formed own prod. co. 1969, v.p., prod., Warren Bros., 1972–74; Paramount Pictures, Producer, 1974–75; Frank Yablans Enterprises, 1975.

MINER, WORTHINGTON C.: Theatrical producer. e. Buffalo, N.Y.; e. Kent School; Yale Univ.; Cambridge Univ., England. m. Frances Fuller, actress. Started theatrical career 1925; author and dir. RKO Radio Pictures, 1933–34; mem. of exec. bd. of Theatre Guild, 1937; entered TV, 1939; developed and produced TV shows.
TV: Studio One, Toast of the Town, the Goldbergs, Medic, Play of the Week; Ely Landau Associates. exec. prod., The Pawnbroker, The Fool Killer.
1964–68, pres. American Acad. of Dram. Arts.

MINNELLI, LIZA: Actress-singer. b. 1946; p. Judy Garland & Vincente Minnelli; After repertory work & off-broadway roles starred on Broadway in Flora, The Red Menace (Tony award).
PICTURES INCLUDE: Charlie Bubbles, The Sterile Cuckoo, Tell Me That You Love Me Junie Moon, Cabaret, That's Entertainment!, Lucky Lady, Silent Movie, A Matter of Time, New York, New York, Arthur.

MINNELLI, VINCENTE: Director. b. Chicago, Ill. Feb. 28. Toured with Minnelli Brothers Dramatic Tent Show as child; joined Balaban & Katz to assist in staging presentations; then to N.Y. Paramount in same work; stage Du Barry (N.Y.); art dir., Radio City Music Hall 3 yrs.; prod. At Home Abroad, Ziegfeld Follies, Very Warm for May (N.Y.). Screen debut, 1943.
PICTURES INCLUDE: Cabin in the Sky, I Dood It, Meet Me in St. Louis, The Clock, Ziegfeld Follies, Yolanda and the Thief; Undercurrent, The Pirate, Madame Bovary, Father of the Bride, Father's Little Dividend, An American in Paris, Bad & the Beautiful, Three Loves, The Bandwagon, Long Long Trailer, Brigadoon, The Cobweb, Kismet, Lust for Life, Tea and Sympathy, Designing Woman, Gigi, The Reluctant Debutante, Some Came Running, Home from the Hill, Bells Are Ringing, Four Horsemen of the Apocalypse, Two Weeks in Another Town, Courtship of Eddie's Father, Goodbye Charlie, The Sandpiper, On a Clear Day You Can See Forever, A Matter of Time.

MINSKY, HOWARD G.: Writer-Producer-Sales and Distribution Exec. Paramount-Twentieth Century-Fox. Agency Exec. Wm. Morris. Pres. Cinema Consultants. Produced Love Story. 1970.

MIRANDA, ISA: Actress. r.n. Ines Sampietro. b. Milan, Italy, July 5, 1917. m. Alfredo Guarini, producer. Typist; stage actress; made debut in 1934.
PICTURES INCLUDE: Darkness, Everybody's Lady, Red Passport, White Lady of Maharadscha, You Are My Happiness (German), Hotel Imperial & Adventure in Diamonds (U.S.), Malombra, Zaza, Mistake to Be Alive, Pact with the Devil, Walls of Malapaga, La Ronde, Seven Deadly Sins, Secret Conclave, Before the Deluge, Secret of Helen, Rasputin, We Women, Summertime, The Yellow Rolls Royce, The Great Train Robbery, The Shoes of the Fisherman.

MIRISCH, DAVID: Executive. b. Gettysburg, Pa., July 24, 1935. e. Ripon College. United Artists Corp., 1960–63; former exec. with Braverman-Mirisch adv. public rel. firm.

MIRISCH, MARVIN E.: Executive. b. New York, N.Y., March 19, 1918. e. College of the City of New York, B.A., 1940. Print dept., contract dept., asst. booker, N.Y. exch.; head booker, Grand National Pictures, Inc., 1936–40; officer, gen. mgr., vending concession operation 800 theatres, Midwest, Theatres Candy Co., Inc., Milwaukee, Wisc., 1941–52; exec., corporate officer in chg., indep. producer negotiations, other management functions, Allied Artists Pictures, Inc., 1953–57; Chmn. of Bd., Chief Exec. Officer in chg. of all business affairs, admin. & financing, distr. liaison, The Mirisch Company, Inc., 1957 to present. Member of Board of Governors and currently vice-president of Academy of Motion Picture Arts & Sciences. Member Motion Picture Pioneers. Currently president of Academy of MPAA Foundation; vice chm., AMPTP.

MIRISCH, WALTER: Producer. b. New York City, Nov. 8, 1921; e. U. Wisconsin, 1942; Harvard Grad. Sch. Business Admin., 1943. In m.p. indust. with Skouras Theatres Corp., 1938–40; Oriental Theatre Corp., 1940–42. 1945 with Monogram, A.A.; apptd. exec. prod. Allied Artists, July, 1951; pres. and exec. head of prod. The Mirisch Corporation 1969; pres. Screen Prod. Guild; 1962, mem. bd. dir., MPAA; bd. Gvnrs., Academy of Motion Pictures Arts and Sciences, 1964; 1967, pres., Center Thea. Group of L.A.; bd. dir., Wisconsin Alum. Assn.; bd. of dir. Cedars-Sinai Medical Center, Bd. of Advisors, California State University—Northridge, Board of Governors, Academy of Motion Picture Arts & Sciences—1972. President, Permanent Motion Picture Charities Committee 1962–63; President, Academy of Motion Picture Arts & Sciences—1973–77.
PICTURES INCLUDE: By Love Possessed, Two for the Seesaw, Toys in the Attic, Hawaii, Fitzwilly, In the Heat of the Night, They Call Me Mister Tibbs, The Organization, Mr. Majestyk, Midway, Gray Lady Down, Same Time, Next Year, Prisoner of Zenda, Dracula.

MITCHELL, ANDREW: Producer. b. Giffnock, Scotland, 1925. e. Fettes College, Edinburgh; early career, banking; Associated British Picture Corporation, Elstree Studios; gen. mgr., Elstree Distributors, 1961; dir., Kenwood Films Ltd., 1963; assoc. prod., Hand in Hand, The Young Ones, Summer Holiday, French Dressing, Wonderful Life. 1965; Pro., Up Jumped a Swagman. Asst. to mgr. dir., Assoc. British Prods., Ltd. Prod. con. Associated British Productions Ltd. 1969–70: Film Finances, Mng. dir., Leslie Grade Film Ltd. 1973. Mng. Dir. E.M.I. Elstree Studios. 1977 Prod. Are You Being Served?

MITCHELL, CAMERON: Actor. b. Dallastown, Pa., Nov. 4, 1918. e. Theatre School (New York City); New York Theatre Guild, 1938–40; on stage with Lunt & Fontanne, "Taming of the Shrew." Radio announcer, sportscaster before joining U.S. Army Air Forces 1942–44. Star of Tomorrow, 1954.
PICTURES INCLUDE: Mighty McGurk, High Barbaree, Cass Timberlane, Leather Gloves, The Sellout, Death of a Salesman, Japanese War Bride, Flight to Mars, Man in the Saddle, Outcasts of Poker Flat, Okinawa, Les Miserables, Pony Soldier, Powder River, Man on a Tightrope, How To Marry a Millionaire, Hell & High Water, Gorilla At Large, Garden of Evil, Desiree, Strange Lady in Town, Love Me Or Leave Me, House of Bamboo, Tall Men, View from Pompey's Head, Carousel, Monkey on My Back, Face of Fire, Inside The Mafia, The Unstoppable Man, The Last of the Vikings, Three Came to Kill, Blood and Black Lace, Ride in the Whirlwind, Hombre, Island of the Doomed, Nightmare in Wax, Buck and the Preacher, Slaughter, The Midnight Man, The Klansman, Viva, Knievel!, The Swarm.
TV: High Chapparel, Andersonville Trial, Swiss Family Robinson.

MITCHELL, GUY: Singer. actor. b. Detroit, Mich., Feb. 22, 1927 e. High Sch., San Francisco. Studied singing; U.S. Navy, 1945–46; singer, radio stations; vocalist with Carmen Cavallaro orch.; sings with Columbia records; m.p. debut in Those Redheads from Seattle; since in: Red Garters.
TV: Guy Mitchell TV Show, Whispering Smith Series NBC.

MITCHELL, JACK: Executive. b. Paris, Kentucky, Nov. 3, 1918. District mgr. for Schine Theatres; joined Wometco in 1963; now vice-pres. & General Manager for Wometco's Florida theatres and Director of Advertising & Promotion, Wometco Entertainment Division, Wometco Enterprises, Inc. Five-time winner, Box Office Showman of the Year Award. Member—Advertising Committee, NATO National; Board of Directors, NATO of Florida; Member—A.D.S.; Serve on Action Committee—Greater Miami Chamber of Commerce; Member—Ad Club of Greater Miami; Chairman—NATO of Florida Advertising. National winner . . . 1st place . . . Film Day contest. Winner, Show-o-Rama Showman Award 1977. Elected pres. NATO of Fla., 1979; NATO nat'l. bd. of directors, 1980.

MITCHELL, JOHN H.: Executive. b. Rochester, N.Y., Apr. 27, 1918; e. University of Michigan. radio dept., Erwin Wasey & Co., 1939; mgr. sales service dept., Mutual Broadcasting System, 1939; U.S. Navy; WVET and Honel Corp., 1946; dir. of television, United Artists, 1948; v.p. & gen. mgr. UA television dept., to 1952; Screen Gems, Inc., 1952; on bd. dirs., 1961, and first v.p. Columbia Pictures Ind., Inc. 1969 Pres. Screen Gems Div. of Columbia Pictures Industries; 1973, pres. Columbia Pictures Television, Division of Columbia Pictures Industries, and executive vice president of Columbia Pictures Industries Inc. 1975, elected to board of directors of Columbia Pictures Industries; 1975, elected pres. of Hollywood Radio and Television Society. Resigned all offices-Columbia Pictures Industries 1977. Formed John H. Mitchell Co., Inc. 1977. Located in Los Angeles, television program and distribution consultants. First v.p.-Academy of Television Arts & Sciences, 1978–79; chmn., Academy of TV Arts & Sciences, forum luncheons, 1979–80; pres., Academy of TV Arts & Sciences, 1980–82.

MITCHELL, STEVE: Actor. b. New York, Dec. 15; e. Univ. of Wisconsin; grad. Feagin School of Drama, New York. U.S. Navy World War II and Korean War. Summer stock, Hilltop Md. Bway appearances Diamond Lil. Toured with Strike a Match. Screen debut in Walk East on Beacon St. 1952. M.P. and TV rep. State of Ark. (consultant).
PICTURES INCLUDE: Above and Beyond, Tender Hearts, Battle Circus, Fearless Feagin, Gypsy Colt, Gunsight Ridge, Big Combo, The Killing, Deep Six, Terror in a Texas Town, Seven Men From Now, China Doll, Submarine Sea Hawk, Girl in the Red Bikini, Most Dangerous Man Alive, Cause of Death, Once A Thief, Nevada Smith, Young Runaways.

MITCHUM, JIM: Actor. b. Los Angeles, May 8, 1941. m. actress Wendy Wagner. Son of Robert Mitchum. e. Univ. High School in L.A. Went directly from school to Hollywood Professional School. On-job prof. training at Barter Theatre in Virginia.
PICTURES INCLUDE: Thunder Road (debut), The Last Time I Saw Archie, The Victors, Ambush Bay, Tramplers, In Harm's Way, Invisible Six, Moonrunners, Beat Generation, Ride the Wild Surf, Trackdown.

MITCHUM, ROBERT: Actor. b. Bridgeport, Conn., Aug. 6, 1917. Odd jobs; to California; joined Long Beach Players Guild; appeared in Hopalong Cassidy series with William Boyd; in Westerns 8 yrs. RKO.
PICTURES INCLUDE: Story of G.I. Joe, Undercurrent, Pursued Locket, Til' the End of Time, Desire Me, Crossfire, Out of the Past, Rachel and the Stranger, Blood on the Moon, Red Pony, Big Steal, His Kind of Woman, Where Danger Lives, Her Forbidden Past, Macao, Racket, One Minute to Zero, Lost Men, Angel Face, White Witch Doctor, Second Chance, She Couldn't Say No, River of No Return, Track of the Cat, Night of the Hunter, Not as a Stranger, Man with the Gun, Foreign Intrigue, Bandido, Heaven Knows Mr. Allison, Fire Down Below, Wonderful Country, Home from the Hill, Sundowners, The Last Time I Saw Archie, Cape Fear, The Longest Day, List of Adrian Messenger, Two for the Seesaw, Rampage, Mr. Moses, El Dorado, Anzio, Villa Rides, Five Card Stud, Secret Ceremony, Young Billy Young, Good Guys and the Bad Guys, Ryan's Daughter, Going Home, Wrath of God, Friends of Eddie Coyle, The Yakuza, Farewell My Lovely, Midway, The Last Tycoon, Amsterdam Kill, The Big Sleep, Matilda.

MITOSKY, ALAN P.: Executive. b. Philadelphia, March 13, 1934. e. Univ. of Penna., School of Fine Arts (BFA, 1957). Was curator of museums in Phila. (1957–65) and later assoc. dir. of Philadelphia Civic Center, handling performing arts and film programs, promotion of trade shows, conventions, etc. In 1970–2 v.p., production, Madison Square Garden. In 1972 named pres. Leisure Presentations of America, packaging and producing film properties and rock and pop concerts. In 1974 named gen. mgr. Dragon Aire Ltd. and No Moss Films, handling distribution of theatrical properties. In 1975 pres. of Coliseum Films and Athena Films Ltd., natl. theatrical film dist., prod., foreign sales and prod. repr. in 1977—project administrator, National Endowment for the Arts Short Film Showcase—dist. of special films.

MIZIKER, RONALD D.: Producer. b. Cleveland, OH, Oct. 14, 1941. e. Univ. of New Mexico, Univ. of So. Calif. Began career as cameraman in 1961 at educational TV station in Albuquerque; soon after produced, wrote and directed variety of TV programs; two series nationally televised weekly on NET network. Following graduate work at Univ. of So. Calif. in 1965 became producer for 50-50 Club, syndicated daily talk show for AVCO Broadcasting Corp. Joined entertainment div. of Walt Disney Prods. in 1969; was dir. of show development, creating entertainment and parades for Disneyland, Walt Disney World, etc. Left in 1978 to be independent TV producer and director and to produce live events and spectaculars. Formed own company, R.D. Miziker & Associates. Recent credits: Perry

Como's Christmas in New Mexico, 25 Years of Mouseketeers, Wonderful World of Disney segments.

MOBERLY, LUKE: Producer, director, writer. b. Richmond, Ky., Nov. 1, 1925. e. Univ. of Cincinnati, 1947, Univ. of Miami, 1951. Designed and built studio buildings; designer and set builder.
PICTURES INCLUDE: Country A-Go-Go, The Misfits, Gavilan, Devil's Sisters, Go-Go-A-Go-Go, etc. Wrote screenplay: Psychedelic, Rhinemans Seven, Ride Roxie Ride, In the Skin with Me, Easy Little Laura, Old Time Religion. Dir. and prod.: Moonlight Maniac, Assoc., prod.: That Nice Boy, writer, producer, director.: Sweet Talker, Skunk Ape, Moberly/Gordon Studios Inc. Production Company for feature films, 1975.

MOCIUK, YAR W.: Executive. b. Ukraine, Jan. 26, 1927. e. CCNY, World Univ., Peoples Univ. of Americas (Puerto Rico). Expert in field of m.p. care and repair; holds U.S. patent for method and apparatus for treating m.p. film. Has also been film producer and director. Founder and pres. of C&M Films Service, Inc. until 1973. Now chm. of bd. and pres. of Filmtreat International Corp. Member: M.P. & TV Engineers; Univ. Film Assn. Pres., Ukrainian Cinema Assn. of America.

MOGER, ART: Publicity executive-Author. b. Boston, Mass., April 4. e. Boston U. Coll. of Journalism (BS) Cartoonist & caricaturist, stage & screen attractions; feature writer. nat. mag.; script writer, guest appearances with Fred Allen, and many radio, TV shows (Mike Douglas Show, Merv Griffin); creator cartoon strip Seymour Shoze, dealing with m.p. and comic strip, Groucho, based on Groucho Marx: orig., About Faces, puzzle series; in 1937 syndicated cartoon series; pressbook cartoonist; handled personal appearances of celebrities. Pub. exec., Warner Bros. & other m.p. cos. Holds record for "My Favorite Jokes" in Parade Magazine. (8 consecutive times) First honorary trustee of Nat'l. Broadcasters Hall of Fame; member Sigma Delta Chi, professional journalism society.
AUTHOR: You'll Dial Laughing, Pros and Cons, Some of My Best Friends Are People, The Complete Pun Book, Everybody Loves an Underdog; pres., Advertising Enterprises, Boston; exec., Amuse-A-Menu Corp.; dorArt Enterprises; pres. and originator Tub Thumpers of Amer.

MOGER, STANLEY H.: Executive. Pres., SFM Entertainment, Exec. Vice Pres., SFM Media Corp. b. Boston, Nov. 13, 1936. e. Colby Coll., Waterville, ME (BA, 1958). m. Marcia Fleishman, May 29, 1960, children—Robin 19, Wendy 16; announcer/TV personality/WVDA and WORL (Boston) 1953–54; WGHM (Skowhegan) 1955–56; WTWO-TV (Bangor) 1955; WMHB (Waterville) 1956–57; WTVL (Waterville); US Army reserve, 1958–64, with calls to active duty in 1958–59 and 1961–62; account exec., NBC Films/California National Productions, Chicago; 1959–60, asst. sales manager, Midwest, Hollingbery Co., Chicago, 1960–63, and New York 1963–66; account executive, Storer Television Sales, 1966–69; co-founded SFM, Sept. 29, 1969. In 1978, named pres., SFM Entertainment which is responsible for the revival of Walt Disney's "Mickey Mouse Club," "The Adventures of Rin-Tin-Tin"; Mobil Showcase Network; SFM Holiday Network. Executive producer-"Television-Annual 1978–79," ABC-TV Network; Executive producer-"Your New Day" with Vidal Sassoon.
PROPERTIES INCLUDE: SFM Holiday Network, SFM Documentary Network, Car Care Central, Your New Day with Vidal Sassoon, March of Time series, Nightside, Sparrow, Co-Packager Superstars-ABC-TV and Battle of the Network Stars ABC-TV; Network Sales: Adventures of the Wilderness Family-ABC-TV; Across the Great Divide-CBS-TV; Mysteries from Beyond Earth-NBC-TV; To the Ends of the Earth-PBS.

MOLINARO, EDOUARD: Director. b. Bordeaux. Made amateur films at university and launched professional career via award-winning technical shorts. First feature film, Le Dos au Mur (1957).
PICTURES INCLUDE: Girls for the Summer, A Ravishing Idiot, Gentle Art of Seduction, La Cage Aux Folles (also Part II), Sunday Lovers.

MOLL, ELICK: Writer. b. New York City, Mar. 20, 1907; e. U. Illinois; U. Chicago. Short story writer, novelist, playwright; Seidman and Son, Memoir of Spring, Night Without Sleep, Image of Tallie; with Samuel Goldwyn, MGM, Fox; stories appear in magazines, texts on short story; won 2nd prize O'Henry Memorial Award Prize Stories 1937.
PICTURES INCLUDE: You Were Meant for Me, Wake Up and Dream, House on Telegraph Hill, Night Without Sleep, Storm Center, Spring Reunion.
TV: Playhouse 90, Chrysler Theatre, others.

MONACO, EITEL: Executive. b. Montazzoli, Chieti, Italy, May 16, 1903; e. LLD. Gen. mgr., film div. in State Dept. for Popular Culture to Italian armistice; vice-pres., ENIC; gen. secy., ANICA (Italian Association of Producers & Distributors); pres., 1950; pres., Unitalia, promoting Italian m.p. throughout the world.

MONASH, PAUL: Producer-Writer. b. New York City. e. Univ. of Wisconsin, Columbia Univ. Was in U.S. Army Signal Corps and Merchant Marine; newspaper reporter; high school teacher; and civilian employee of U.S. gov't. in Europe. Wrote two novels: How Brave We Live, The Ambassadors. Entered industry writing TV scripts on such shows as Playhouse 90, Studio One, Theatre Guild of the Air, Climax, etc. Authored two-part teleplay which launched The Untouchables. In 1958 won Emmy award for The Lonely Wizard, dramatization of life of German-born electrical inventor Charles Steinmetz. Made m.p. debut as exec. prod. of Butch Cassidy and the Sundance Kid, 1969.
  PICTURES INCLUDE: Slaughterhouse-Five (prod.), The Friends of Eddie Coyle (prod., s.p.), The Front Page (prod.), Carrie (prod.).

MONICELLI, MARIO: Director. b. Rome, Italy, May 15, 1915. Ent. m.p. industry in production; later co-authored, collab., comedies. Dir.: Big Deal on Madonna Street, The Great War, Tears of Joy, Boccaccio '70, The Organizer.

MONKHOUSE, BOB: TV-radio-cabaret comedian & comedy writer. b. Beckenham, Kent, June 1, 1928; e. Dulwich College. Debut 1948 while serving in RAF, own radio comedy series 1949–75 (winters), own TV series, BBC 1952–56, ITV 1956–78. Several West End revues, Boys from Syracuse (Theatre Royal, Drury Lane, 2 yrs.); Come Blow Your Horn, (Prince of Wales); The Gulls; others. Films include: Carry On, Sergeant; Weekend with Lulu; Dentist in the Chair; She'll Have to Go; Bliss of Mrs. Blossom; others. Major cabaret attraction U.K., Australia, Hong Kong. British star of numerous TV series including: What's My Line?; Who Do You Trust?; Mad Movies; Quick On The Draw; Bob Monkhouse Comedy Hour; The Golden Shot (8 years); Celebrity Squares (3 years, ongoing); I'm Bob, he's Dickie! (1978 series). Regular dramatic guest spots ITV & BBC-TV.

MONKS, JOHN, JR.: Writer, actor, prod., dir. b. Brooklyn, N.Y. e. Virginia Military Institute, A.B.; actor, stock, b'way, radio, m.p. U.S. Marines, 1942; commissioned Major, 1945. Playwright Co-author Brother Rat.
  PICTURES INCLUDE: Brother Rat, Co-author Brother Rat And A Baby, Strike Up the Band, The House on 92nd Street, 13 Rue Madeleine, Wild Harvest, Dial 1119., The West Point Story, People Against O'Hara. Where's Charley. So This Is Love, Knock On Any Door, No Man Is An Island.
  TV: Climax, 20th Century-Fox Hour, Gen. Electric Theatre; CBS Special High Tor; Creator serial Paradise Bay.

MONTAGNE, EDWARD J.: Producer-director. b. Brooklyn; e. Loyola University, of Notre Dame. RKO Pathe, 1942; U.S. Army, 1942–46; prod. many co. after army.
  PICTURES INCLUDE: Tattooed Stranger, The Man With My Face, McHale's Navy, McHale's Navy Joins The Air Force, P.J.
  TV: Man Against Crime, Cavalier Theatre, The Vaughn Monroe Show, The Hunter, I Spy, McHale's Navy; exec. prod. of film-CBS-N.Y., Phil Silvers Show. Prod. & head of programming, Wm. Esty Adv. Co., 1950; Program consultant, William Esty Co.; v.p. Universal TV prod. & dir.: 5 Don Knotts features; prod.: Andy Griffith, Angel in My Pocket, Ellery Queen, A Very Missing Person, Short Walk to Daylight, Hurricane, Terror on the 40th Floor, Francis Gary Powers, Million Dollar Ripoff.

MONTALBAN, RICARDO: Actor. b. Mexico City, Mex., Nov. 25, 1920. Appeared in Mexican pictures 1941–45; to U.S.
  PICTURES INCLUDE: Fiesta, On an Island With You, Kissing Bandit, Neptune's Daughter, Battleground, Mystery Street, Right Cross, Two Weeks with Love, Across the Wide Missouri, Mark of Renegade, My Man and I, Sombrero, Border Incident, Latin Lovers, Saracen Blade, Life in The Balance, Sayonara, Hemingway's Adventures of a Young Man, The Reluctant Saint, Love Is a Ball, Sol Madrid, Blue, Sweet Charity, Conquest of the Planet of the Apes, The Train Robbers.
  TELEVISION: Series: Fantasy Island.

MONTAND, YVES: Actor, singer. r.n. Yvo Livi. b Monsumano, Italy. Worked as a truck loader, waiter in dock-side bar, and barber. Performed in Marseilles as singer in clubs and music halls. m. Simone Signoret, actress, 1951.
  PICTURES INCLUDE: Etoile Sans Lumiere, Les Portes de La Nuit, L'Idole, Souvenir Perdus, Le Salaire de la Peur (Wages of Fear), Nostri Tempi, Mar, Napoleon, Les Heros Sont Fatiques, Marguerite de la Nuit, Uomini e Lupi, Les Sorcieres de Salem (The Crucible), La Lunga Strada, Un Denomme Squarcio, Le Pere et L'enfant, La Loi (Where the Hotwind Blows), Let's Make Love, Sanctuary, My Geisha, Goodbye Again, The Sleeping Car Murders, La Guerre est Finie, Is Paris Burning?, Grand Prix, Live for Life, Z, On A Clear Day You Can See Forever, The Vow, State of Siege.

MONTGOMERY, DOREEN: Writer. e. Edinburgh University (M.A.).
  PICTURES INCLUDE: Lassie from Lancashire, Room 13, Meet Mr. Penny, Dead Men Tell No Tales, Poison Pen, Just William, Bulldog Sees It Through, At Villa-Rose, House of the Arrow, Flying Squad, Man in Grey, Fanny by Gaslight, Dream of Olwen, Second Mrs. Elliott, Shadow of the Eagle, Scarlet Web, One Jump Ahead, Narrowing Circle, Dance Little Lady, You Can't Escape, Murder Reported, Island of Dreams.
  TV: Fairbanks series, Aggie series: Fabian of the Yard. Last of the Mohicans, Charlie Chan, William Tell, Invisible Man, Danger Man, Zero One, Dr. Finlay's Casebook, Taxi, The Avengers, No Hiding Place, Borderers, Who-dun-it.
  BOOK: Voices in the Dark, Play, The Summer House.

MONTGOMERY, GEORGE: Actor. r.n. George Montgomery Letz; b. Brady, Mont., Aug. 29, 1916; e. U. of Montana. Armed Services, World War II.
  PICTURES INCLUDE: Cisco Kid and the Lady (1939), Star Dust, Young People, Charter Pilot, Jennie, Cowboy and the Blonde, Accent on Love, Riders of the Purple Sage, Last of the Duanes, Cadet Girl, Roxie Hart, Ten Gentlemen from West Point, Orchestra Wives, China Girl, Brasher Doubloon, Three Little Girls in Blue, Lulu Belle, Belle Starr's Daughter, Girl From Manhattan, Sword of Monte Cristo, Texas Rangers, Indian Uprising, Cripple Creek, Pathfinder, Jack McCall Desperado, Fort Ti, Gun Belt, Battle of Rogue River, Lone Gun, Masterson of Kansas, Seminole Uprising, Robbers' Roost, Too Many Crooks, Stallion Trail, The Steel Claw, Watusi, Samar, Hallucination Generation, Hostile Guns.

MONTGOMERY, ROBERT: Actor, director, producer. r.n. Henry Montgomery, Jr.; b. Beacon N.Y., May 21, 1904. Captain, U.S. Naval Reserve, World War II. Entered m.p. for MGM 1929. Captain, U.S. Naval Reserve, World War II Exec. prod. Cagney-Montgomery Prod. Consultant to President of U.S. on all radio and TV, 1952–60.
  PLAYS: Dawn Mack, Arlene O'Dare, One of the Family.
  PICTURES INCLUDE: College Days, So This is College, Untamed, Their Own Desire, On the Set, Single Standard, Free and Easy, Sins of the Children, Big House, Private Lives, Letty Lynton, When Ladies Meet, Another Language, Night Flight, Riptide, Vanessa—Her Love Story, Petticoat Fever, Last of Mrs. Cheyney, Yellowjack, Cat and the Canary, Haunted Honeymoon, Rage in Heaven, Here Comes Mr. Jordan, They Were Expendable, Saxon Charm, Secret Land, June Bride, (dir. acted in) Lady in the Lake, Eye Witness, Ride the Pink Horse, Once More My Darling, The Gallant Hours.

MOONJEAN, HANK: Producer-Director. Began as asst. dir. at MGM. Later turned to producing.
  PICTURES INCLUDE: Assoc. Prod.; The Great Gatsby, WUSA. Exec. Prod.: The Fortune, The End. Producer: Hooper, Smokey and the Bandit II, The Incredible Shrinking Woman, Paternity.

MOORE, CONSTANCE: Actress. b. Sioux City, Iowa, Jan. 18, 1922. Sang on radio; Lockheed prog., 2 yrs; Jurgen's Show, 2 yrs. Screen debut 1938. TV shows, nightclubs. N.Y. Stage: The Boys From Syracuse, My Daughter.
  PICTURES INCLUDE: Prison Break, A Letter of Introduction, I Wanted Wings, Take A Letter Darling, Show Business, Delightfully Dangerous, Earl Carroll Sketchbook, In Old Sacramento, Hit Parade of 1947.

MOORE, DICKIE: Actor. b. Los Angeles, Cal., Sept. 12, 1925. Began picture career when only 11 months old, appearing with John Barrymore in The Beloved Rogue.
  PICTURES INCLUDE: Oliver Twist, Peter Ibbetson, Dangerous Years, Out of the Past, Eight Iron Men, Member of the Wedding.

MOORE, DUDLEY: Actor-Writer-Musician. b. England. e. Oxford, graduating in 1958. Toured British Isles with jazz group before joining with three other Englishmen to put on revue, Beyond the Fringe, which was a hit in U.K. and N.Y. Appeared later with Peter Cook in N.Y. in Good Evening.
  PICTURES: Monte Carlo or Bust, The Bed Sitting Room, Bedazzled, Foul Play, "10", Wholly Moses, Arthur.

MOORE, ELLIS: Executive. b. New York, N.Y., May 12, 1924. e. Washington and Lee U., 1941–43. Newspaperman in Arkansas, Tenn., 1946–52; Joined NBC 1952; mgr. of bus. pub., 1953; dir., press dept., 1954; dir., press & publicity, Dec. 22, 1959; vice-pres., 1961; pub. rel. dept., Standard Oil Co. (N.J.), 1963–66; v.p. press relations, ABC-TV Network, 1966–68; v.p. public relations ABC-TV Network, 1968–70; v.p. public relations, ABC, 1970, v.p. public relations, ABC, Inc., 1972; v.p. corporate relations, ABC, Inc., 1979.

MOORE, GARRY: Performer. r.n. Thomas Garrison Morfit; b. Baltimore, Md., Jan. 31, 1915. Continuity writer, WBAL; announcer, sports commentator, KWK, St. Louis; comedian, writer, Club Matinee show, Chicago; Everything Goes, N.Y.; teamed with Jimmy Durante on radio to 1947; m.c., Take It or Leave It, Breakfast in Hollywood.
  TV: Star of Garry Moore Show, I've Got A Secret. Best TV daytime show: Fame Poll, 1958; To Tell The Truth.

MOORE, KIERON: Actor. b. Skibereen, Co. Cork, Eire, 1925; e. St. Mary's Coll. (Dublin). Stage debut, 1945 in Desert Rats; appeared in Red Roses For Me. Film debut 1947 in A Man About The House.
PICTURES INCLUDE: Anna Karenina, Mine Own Executioner, Ten Tall Men, David and Bathsheba, Saints and Sinners, Naked Heart, Honeymoon Deferred, Man Trap (Man in Hiding), Conflict of Wings (Fuss Over Feathers), Green Scarf, Blue Peter, Satellite in the Sky, Three Sundays to Live, The Key, The Angry Hills, The Day They Robbed the Bank of England, League of Gentlemen, The Seige of Sidney Street, Faces of Evil, Lion of Sparta, Steel Bayonet, I Thank a Fool, Double Twist, The Day of the Triffids, The Thin Red Line, The Main Attraction, Crack in the World, Son of a Gunfighter, Never Love a Savage, Run Like a Thief, Custer of the West, Ryan International, The Dolmetsch Story, Zoo Gang, The Progress of Peoples, The Parched Land.

MOORE, KINGMAN T.: Director. b. Macon, Ga., Sept. 13, 1919; e. Wharton Sch. of Finance, U. of Pa., BS; Member: Lambs Club, Phi Delta Theta, Actor, 1939–41; U.S. Army, 1941–46; asst. cutter, RKO Radio Pictures, 1946–47; production asst., 1947–48; CBS-TV, N.Y., 1948–49; NBC-TV, N.Y., Hollywood, 1949–52; dir. CBS shows include: Places Please, Backstage with Barry Wood, Kobbs Korner, Adventures in Jazz.
TV: Candid Camera, Lights Out, Your Show of Shows, Colgate Comedy Hour.

MOORE, MARY TYLER: Actress. b. Brooklyn. N.Y., Dec. 29, 1936; Began as professional dancer.
TV: Steve Canyon, Richard Diamond, 77 Sunset Strip, Hawaiian Eye, Bachelor Father; feature role on The Dick Van Dyke Show (2 emmy awards); star, The Mary Tyler Moore Show, Mary.
PICTURES INCLUDE: X-15, Thoroughly Modern Millie, Don't Just Stand There, What's So Bad About Feeling Good, Change of Habit, Ordinary People.

MOORE, ROBERT: Director. b. Washington, D.C. Studied and taught drama at Catholic University. Acted on Broadway as a teen-ager in Jenny Kissed Me, later appeared in Cactus Flower and Everything in the Garden. His staging of The Boys in the Band attracted the attention of Neil Simon, and he directed Simon's Promises, Promises, Last of the Red Hot Lovers and The Gingerbread Lady.
TV: Rhoda, Thursday's Game (movie).
PICTURES INCLUDE: Tell Me That You Love Me, Junie Moon (actor), Murder by Death (theatrical debut as director), The Cheap Detective (dir.); Chapter Two (dir.).

MOORE, ROGER: Actor. Dir. b. London, England, Oct. 14 e. Art School, London; Royal Acad. of Dramatic Art.
PLAYS: Mr. Roberts, I Capture the Castle, Little Hut, others.
BROADWAY: A Pin to See the Peepshow.
TV: Maverick, The Alaskans, Ivanhoe, The Saint, The Persuaders.
PICTURES INCLUDE: Last Time I Saw Paris, Interrupted Melody, King's Thief, Diane, The Miracle, Gold of the Seven Saints, Rachel Cade, Rape of the Sabines, No Mans Land, Crossplot, The Man Who Haunted Himself, Live and Let Die, Gold, The Man with the Golden Gun, That Lucky Touch, Street People, Shout at the Devil, Sherlock Holmes in New York, The Spy Who Loved Me, The Wild Geese, Escape To Athena, Moonraker, ffolkes, The Sea Wolves, Sunday Lovers, For Your Eyes Only, The Cannonball Run.

MOORE, TERRY: Actress. r.n. Helen Koford; b. Los Angeles, Cal., Jan. 1, 1932; mother Luella Bickmore, actress. Photographer's model as a child; on radio; with Pasadena Playhouse 1940; in m.p. 1933.
PICTURES INCLUDE: Gaslight, Son of Lassie, Sweet and Low Down, Shadowed, Devil on Wheels, Return of October, Mighty Joe Young, He's a Cockeyed Wonder, Gambling House, Two of a Kind, Sunny Side of the Street, Star of Tomorrow: 1958, Man on a Tightrope, Beneath the 12-mile Reef, King of the Khyber Rifles, Daddy Long Legs, Shack Out on 101, Postmark for Danger, Come Back Little Sheba, Bernardine, Why Must I Die?, Platinum High School, A Private's Affair, Cast a Long Shadow, City of Fear, Black Spurs, Town Tamer, Waco, A Man Called Dagger.

MOORE, THOMAS W.: Executive. e. U of Mo.; Naval aviator, USNR, 1940–45. Adv. dept., Star, Meridian, Miss.; v.p., adv. mgr., Forest Lawn Memorial Park; account exec., CBS-TV Film Sales, Los Angeles; gen. sales mgr., CBS-TV Film Sales, 1956; v.p. in chg. programming & talent, 1958; pres., ABC-TV Network, 1962; chmn. bd., Ticketron, 1968; pres., Tomorrow Entertainment, Inc. 1971.

MORAN, DOLORES: Actress. b. Stockton, Cal., 1926. Screen debut, 1941.
PICTURES INCLUDE: Yankee Doodle Dandy, The Hard Way, Old Acquaintances, Man I Love, Christmas Eve, Johnny One Eye, Count The Hours, Silver Lode.

MORE, KENNETH: Actor. b. Gerrards Cross (Buckinghamshire), England, Sept. 20, 1914; e. Victoria College, Jersey (Channel Islands). Stage debut at Windmill Vaudeville Theatre, 1937; screen debut in Scott of the Antarctic, 1948. Voted one of Top Ten British Moneymaking Stars in M.P. Herald-Fame poll, British and International poll, 1955–56. Many TV appearances, incl. On Approval.
STAGE: Our Man Crichton, The Forsythe Saga, The Secretary Bird, The Winslow Boy, Getting On, Signs of the Times.
v   PICTURES INCLUDE: Now Barabbas, The Clouded Yellow, No Highway, Appointment with Venus, Franchise Affair, Brandy for the Parson, Yellow Balloon, Never Let Me Go, Genevieve, Our Girl Friday (Adventures of Sadie), Doctor in the House, Raising a Riot, Deep Blue Sea, Reach for the Sky, Admirable Crichton, Sheriff of Fractured Jaw, Next to No Time, A Night To Remember, The 39 Steps, Northwest Frontier, Sink the Bismarck, The Man in the Moon, The Greengage Summer, Some People, We Joined the Navy, The Comedy Man, The Mercenaries, Fraulein Doktor, Oh! What a Lovely War, Battle of Britain, Scrooge, Slipper and the Rose, Leopold in the Snow.

MOREAU, JEANNE: Actress. b. Paris, France, 1928. e. Nat'l Conservatory of Dramatic Art. Stage debut in Comedie Francaise, acting there until 1952 when she joined the Theatre Nationale Populaire, Director: Lumiere (film), 1976.
PLAYS: A Month in the Country, La Machine Infernale, Pygmalion, Cat on a Hot Tin Roof.
PICTURES INCLUDE: The She-wolves, Elevator to the Scaffold, The Lovers, Le Dialogue Des Carmelites, Les Liaisons Dangereuses, Moderato Cantabile, La Notte, Jules and Jim, A Woman is a Woman, Eva, The Trial, Bay of Angels, The Victors, Le Feu Follet, Diary of a Chambermaid, The Yellow Rolls-Royce, The Train, Mata Hari, Viva Maria, Mademoiselle, Chimes at Midnight, Sailor From Gibraltar, The Bride Wore Black, The Immortal Story, Great Catherine, Monte Walsh, Alex in Wonderland, The Little Theatre of Jean Renoir, The Last Tycoon, Mr. Klein.

MORENO, RITA: Actress. b. Humacao, Puerto Rico, Dec. 11, 1931. Spanish dancer since childhood; night club entertainer; m.p. debut in 1950.
PICTURES INCLUDE: Pagan Love Song, Toast of New Orleans, Singin' in the Rain, The Ring, Cattle Town, Latin Lovers, Jivaro, Yellow Tomahawk, Garden of Evil, Untamed, Seven Cities of Gold, Lieutenant Wore Skirts, King and I, This Rebel Breed, Summer and Smoke, West Side Story, The Night of the Following Day, Marlowe, Popi, Carnal Knowledge, The Ritz, Happy Birthday, Gemini, The Four Seasons.

MORGAN, ANDRE: Producer. b. Morocco, 1953. e. Univ. of Kansas, majoring in Oriental languages-literature. Met Raymond Chow and joined his film production co. in Hong Kong. Produced Enter the Dragon, Bruce Lee kung-fu picture. Now acts as prod. on Golden Harvest's Chinese language films as well as new division established to produce English-language films.
PICTURES INCLUDE: Enter the Dragon, The Amsterdam Kill, The Boys in Company C.

MORGAN, DENNIS: Actor. r.n. Stanley Morner; b. Prentice, Wisc., Dec. 10, 1920; e. Carroll Coll. Started with State Lake Theat., Chicago. Toured midwest in Faust, sang in Empire Room of Palmer House, Chicago, appeared on NBC programs and sang lead in Xerxes. Screen debut, 1936.
PICTURES INCLUDE: Susy, The Fighting 69th, Three Cheers for the Irish, My Wild Irish Rose, Two Guys from Milwaukee, Two Guys from Texas, Cheyenne, Perfect Strangers, To the Victor, One Sunday Afternoon, Raton Pass, Pretty Baby, Painting the Clouds with Sunshine, Star of Tomorrow (1941), This Woman is Dangerous, Cattle Town, Gun That Won the West, Pearl of the South Pacific, Uranium Boom.

MORGAN, HARRY: Actor. r.n. Harry Bratsburg; b. Detroit, Mich., Apr. 10, 1915; e. U. Chicago. Screen debut 1942.
TV: December Bride, Pete and Gladys, MASH, Dragnet, etc.
PLAYS: Gentle People, My Heart's in the Highlands, Thunder Rock, Night Music, Night Before Christmas.
PICTURES INCLUDE: To the Shores of Tripoli, Loves of Edgar Allen Poe, Orchestra Wives, Dragonwyck, Appointment with Danger, The Highwayman, When I Grow Up, The Well, Blue Veil, Bend of the River, Scandal Sheet, My Six Convicts, Boots Malone, High Noon, What Price Glory, Stop You're Killing Me, Arena, Torch Song, Glenn Miller Story, About Mrs. Leslie, Forty-Niners, Far Country, Not As a Stranger, Backlash, Strategic Air Command, Support Your Local Sheriff, Charlie and the Angels, Snowball Express, The Apple Dumpling Gang, The Greatest, Cat from Outer Space.

MORGAN, MICHELE: Actress. r.n. Simone Roussel; b. Paris, France, Feb. 29, 1920; e. Dieppe, dramatic school, Paris. Decided on acting career at 15 yrs., won role at 17 opposite Charles Boyer in Gribouille (later filmed as The Lady in Question, Hollywood). Made several pictures abroad; to U.S. 1940. First Amer. film Joan of Paris, 1942.

PICTURES INCLUDE: The Chase, Symphonie Pastorale, Fallen Idol, Fabiola, 7 Deadly Sins, Moment of Truth, Daughters of Destiny, Naked Heart, Proud and the Beautiful, Grand Maneuver, Oasis, Lost Command, Benjamin.

MORGAN, TERENCE: Actor. b. London, Eng., Dec. 8, 1921; e. Ewell Castle, Surrey & R.A.D.A. Stage debut: There Shall Be No Night, London 1943; m.p. debut: Hamlet, 1948.
PICTURES INCLUDE: Capt. Horatio Hornblower, Encore, Mandy, It Started in Paradise, Steel Key, Street Corner, Turn the Key Softly, Always a Bride, Forbidden Cargo, Dance Little Lady, Femina, Svengali, They Can't Hang Me, March Hare, It's a Wonderful World, The Scamp, Tread Softly Stranger, The Shakedown, Picadilly Third Stop, The Curse of the Mummy's Tomb, The Penthouse, Hide and Seek, The Lifetaker.
TV: Sir Francis Drake, The Persuaders, etc.

MORIARTY, MICHAEL: Actor. b. Detroit, 1942. e. Dartmouth. Studied at London Academy of Music and Dramatic Arts. Appeared with New York Shakespeare Festival, Charles Street Playhouse (Boston), Alley Theatre (Houston) and Tyrone Guthrie Theatre (Minneapolis). Broadway debut in The Trial of the Catonsville Nine.
PICTURES: Glory Boy (debut), Hickey & Boggs, Shoot It, Bang the Drum Slowly, The Last Detail, Report to the Commissioner, Who'll Stop the Rain.
TV: The Glass Menagerie, Girls of Summer, The Deadliest Season, Holocaust.
STAGE: Find Your Way Home, Richard III

MORIN, ROBERT B.: Executive. b. New York, N.Y. Nov. 24. e. Harvard Coll., Merch, Mgr., ad agency. AAP sis., 1955; AAP mgr. program sls., 1956; eastern sls. mgr., MGM-TV, 1957; sls. mgr., Lopert-UA, 1959; v.p., Allied Artists TV; formed Scandia Films, pres., 1965; joined RKO, 1966, in chg. foreign operations; 1968, pres. Lin Medallion Pict. Corp.; 1970–73, Talent Associates; 1973–76, exec. v.p.; Heritage Eng.; 1976–78, v.p., MGM TV; 1978 to present, pres. Lorimar Syndication; 1980, exec. v.p., 20th Century Fox.

MORITZ, MILTON I: Executive. b. Pittsburgh, Pa., Apr. 27, 1933; e. Woodbury College, grad. 1955. Owned, operated theatres in L.A., 1953–55; U.S. Navy 1955–57; American International Pictures asst. gen. sls. mgr., 1957; nat'l. dir. of adv. and publ., 1958; v.p. and bd. mem. of American International Pictures, 1967; 1975, named Senior v.p.; in 1980 formed own co., The Milton I. Moritz Co., Inc., Inc., mktg. & dist consultant. Pres. of Variety Club of Southern California Tent 25, 1975–76.

MORLEY, KAREN: Actress. r.n. Mabel Linton; b. Ottumwa, Iowa; e. Calif. U. Campus Baby Star, 1931; bit part in Scarface, 1932.
PICTURES INCLUDE: Arsene Lupin, Fast Life, Gabriel Over the White House, Dinner at Eight, Crime Doctor, Thunder in the Night, Devil's Squadron, Beloved Enemy, Outcast. Pride and Prejudice, Jealously, Unknown, 13th Hour, Framed, Six Gun Serenade, Code of the Saddle, M..

MORLEY, ROBERT: Actor, writer. b. Wiltshire, England, May 26, 1908; e. Royal Acad. Dram. Arts, London. U.S. Air Force, 1943; prod., assoc. prod., Captain Gallant, Arsen, Chicot, Forbidden Cargo; TV Series: Captain Gallant; Scene of the Crime; TV Advisor, Telepictures of Morroco, Telerama, Ltd., Eng., 1954–59; helped org., Alliance of TV Film Producers; prod., Telarama, Inc., Georgetown Films, Inc., 1960; prod., dir., TV film series closeup, Telefilm, Inc. Presently president, Creative Assoc., Inc. and co-prod. with Helen Ainsworth; exec. prod. with Leon Fromkess, The Long Corridor.
PLAYS: Brit. stage debut London 1929 in Treasure Island, also tour and repertory; N.Y. debut 1938 in Oscar Wilde; other appearances include Great Romancer, Pygmalion; 1948, Edward My Son, co-author, lead London and B'way stage; author several plays (Short Story, Goodness, How Sad, Staff Dance).
PICTURES INCLUDE: Marie Antoinette, You Will Remember, Major Barbara, Big Blockade, This Was Paris, Foreman Went to France, Young Mr. Pitt, I Live in Grosvenor Square, Outcast of the Islands, African Queen, Edward My Son, Curtain Up, The Final Test, Melba, Gilbert & Sullivan, Beat the Devil, Beau Brummell, Rainbow Jacket, Good Die Young, Quentin Durward, Loser Takes All, Six Months Grace, Full Treatment, Hippo Dancing, Around the World in 80 Days, Sheriff of Fractured Jaw, The Journey, The Doctor's Dilemma, Battle of the Sexes, Libel, Oscar Wilde, Go To Blazes, The Young Ones, Nine Hours to Rama, Murder at the Gallop, Topkapi, Amanda, Take Her She's Mine, Genghis Khan, Hot Enough for June, The Alphabet Murders, Sinful Davey, Hot Millions, Some Girls Do, The Trygon Factor, Song of Norway, The Blue Bird, Who Is Killing the Great Chefs of Europe?, Scavenger Hunt, The Human Factor, The Great Muppet Caper.
TV: Call My Bluff (series), Charge!

MORRICONE, ENNIO: Composer-Arranger. b. Rome. Studied with Goffredo Petrassi at the Academy of Santa Cecilia in Rome.
PICTURES INCLUDE: A Fistful of Dollars, El Greco, Fists in the Pocket, Matcheless, Theorem, Once Upon a Time in the West, Investigation of a Citizen, The Bird with the Crystal Plumage, Cat O'Nine Tails, The Red Tent, Four Flies in Grey Velvet, The Decameron, The Black Belly of the Tarantula, Battle of Algiers, Burn, Partner, Orca, The Heretic, Exorcist II, 1900, Days of Heaven, The Island.

MORRIS, HOWARD: Actor. b. New York, N.Y., Sept. 4, 1919; e. N.Y.U. U.S. Army, 4 yrs.; dir., Who's Minding the Mint, Don't Drink the Water.
BROADWAY: Hamlet, Call Me Mister, John Loves Mary, Gentlemen Prefer Blondes.
TV: Your Show of Shows, Caesar's Hour.

MORRIS, NELSON: Producer. b. Warsaw, Poland, July 25, 1920; e. Columbia Univ., 1939. Began in m.p. ind. in 1930 as child actor, Paramount Studio, Astoria, L.I.; photographer, Life Mag., 1939–43; WWII, training film div. Army Pictorial Service. After war continued career in advertising, industrial and mag. photography. Org., American Society of Magazine Photographers. Formed, Nelson Morris Prods., 1953; engaged in prod. of industrial and doc. film; prod. films for TV, theatrical feature films; producer, stage prod., Bicycle Ride to Nevada. Now pres., Astoria Pictures Corp.

MORRIS, OSWALD: Cinematographer. b. London. Left school at 16 to work for two years as camera dept. helper at studios. Was lensman for cameraman Ronald Neame who gave Morris first job as cameraman; in 1949 when Reame directed The Golden Salamander he made Morris dir. of photography.
PICTURES INCLUDE: The Golden Salamander, The Card, The Man Who Never Was, Mister Moses, Moulin Rouge, Beat the Devil, Moby Dick, Heaven Knows, Mr. Allison, The Roots of Heaven, Reflections in a Golden Eye, The Mackintosh Man, Oliver!, Scrooge, The Pumpkin Eater, The Hill, The Spy Who Came in from the Cold, A Farewell to Arms, The Key, The Guns of Navarone, Lolita, Term of Trial, Fiddler on the Roof, Sleuth, The Odessa File, The Man Who Would Be King, Seven Per Cent Solution, Just Tell Me What You Want, The Great Muppet Caper.

MORRIS, R.A.: Executive. b. London, England, 1925; e. Imperial Services College, Windsor. Served Royal Navy 1942–46. Ent. m.p. ind. Animation Dept. Polytechnic Studios 1947; AB-Pathe, 16MM salesman, 1948; assist. to overseas sales mgr.; 1949; overseas sales mgr.; 1952; joined ABC-TV develop world-wide dist. TV films, 1958; res. to form Programme Exchange Ltd., 1960; formed Anthony Morris (London) Ltd., 1968.

MORRIS, RICHARD: Director, writer. b. San Francisco, Cal., May 14, 1924; e. Burlingame High School, 1939–42, Chouinard Art Institute, 1946–47; Neighborhood Playhouse, 1947–48; U.S. Army special services, writing shows, Victory Bond; Universal-Int., talent dept., writing, directing skits, writing music for acting class and Korean War entertainment troups; s.p. Take Me to Town, Finders Keepers.
AUTHOR, STAGE: The Unsinkable Molly Brown, Golden Gate, Tomato Pie.
PICTURES INCLUDE: If a Man Answers, I Married a Psychiatrist, It Seems There Were These Two Irishmen, Thoroughly Modern Millie, The Man Who Was Magic, Change of Habit.
TV: Wrote & dir. teleplays, Loretta Young Show, wrote & dir. The Pearl (Loretta Young Show), wrote teleplays, Private Secretary, Ford Theatre, Kraft Television Theatre, dir., The Wild Swans (Shirley Temple Show-Christopher Award).

MORRIS, SEYMOUR: Executive. b. Aug. 26, 1906. Started in show business with B.S. Moss, juvenile theatricals; entered m.p. ind. with C.B.C. Pictures on adv. accessories; exp. dept., U.A., Columbia. Ran own theatres, N.Y. State; mgr., upstate N.Y. theatres, Skouras Bros., until 1933; then mgr., dist. mgr., Schine; dir. of adv., pub., pub. rel., Schine Ent. Inc., including theatres, hotels, radio station etc. In 1961 opened own adv. & p.r. agency, Seymour Morris Associates Inc.; also pres. of Northeast Film Enterp. (1967); pres. PMK Prod. Inc.

MORRIS, WILLIAM, JR.: Consultant, retired president, William Morris Agency, Inc. b. New York, Oct. 22, 1899.

MORRISSEY, PAUL: Writer-Director. b. New York City. e. Fordham Univ. Service in Army; worked for insurance co. and Dept. of Public Welfare before becoming film-maker. Was involved in indep. film prod. for four years prior to joining Andy Warhol with whom he worked on such films as Chelsea Girls, Four Stars, Bike Boy, Nude Restaurant, Lonesome Cowboys, Blue Movie, L'Amour, Women in Revolt.
PICTURES INCLUDE: Flesh, Trash, Heat, Andy Warhol's Frankenstein, Dracula.

MORRISON, BURT: Executive. Joined 20th Century-Fox in 1963; named snr. financial officer for 20th Century-Fox Pictures. In 1980 named v.p., finance & administration, for The Ladd Company.

MORROW, DON: Announcer, actor, narrator. b. Stamford, Conn., Jan. 29; e. Syracuse U., Southern Methodist U., Wesconn. Currently spokesman for Ford, and IBM.

MORROW, JEFF: Actor. b. New York, N.Y., Jan. 13; e. Pratt Institute. Worked as commercial illustrator. Many radio and TV appearances including TV, Iron Horse.
01   BROADWAY: Romeo and Juliet, St. Joan, January Thaw, Billy Budd, Three Wishes for Jamie, Lace on Her Petticoat, The Suspects.
    PICTURES INCLUDE: The Robe, Flight to Tangier, Siege at Red River, Tanganyika, Sign of the Pagan, Captain Lightfoot, This Island Earth, World in My Corner, Creature Walks Among Us, Giant Claw, Story of Ruth, Harbor Lights.

MORROW, VIC: Actor, writer, director. b. Bronx, N.Y., Feb. 14, 1932; e. Florida Southern College, Paul Mann's N.Y. Actors' Workshop. Dir., off-Broadway, Deathwatch, The Maids; The Firstborn, Desilu Prof. Theatre Workshop, pres., The Firstborn; appeared in A Streetcar Named Desire, summer stock; dir., A Man Called Sledge, Columbia Pictures.
    PICTURES INCLUDE: Blackboard Jungle, Survival, Tribute to a Badman, Men in War, God's Little Acre, Cimarron, Portrait of a Mobster, Last Year at Malibu, Sledge, Deathwatch, Step out of Line, Police Story, The Bad News Bears, Treasure of Matecumbe, Message from Space.
    TV: Bonanza, The New Breed, The Untouchables, The Rifleman, G.E. Theatre, The Outlaws, Combat, world premiere, The Glass House (CBS Movie of the Week), Roots, Captain and the Kings.

MORSE, ROBERT: Actor. b. Newton, Mass., May 18. Served U.S. Navy. Studied with American Theatre Wing, New York, where he had small role in film The Proud and the Profane, 1956. Following radio work, appeared on Broadway stage in The Matchmaker, 1956.
    BROADWAY: Say, Darling, Take Me Along, How to Succeed in Business Without Really Trying, Sugar.
    PICTURES INCLUDE: The Matchmaker, Honeymoon Hotel, Quick Before it Melts, The Loved One, Oh Dad Poor Dad, How to Succeed in Business Without Really Trying, Guide for the Married Man, The Boatniks.
    TV: That's Life series.

MORSE, TERRY: Director. b. St. Louis, Mo., Jan. 30, 1906. Started in cutting room dept., First National, 1922; film ed., dir., Warner Bros.
    PICTURES INCLUDE: Lady in Ermine, Heart of New York, Misbehaving Ladies, Dragon Murder Case, Personality Kid, Massacre, I Love for Love, Front Page Woman, Case of the Curious Bride, Woman in Red, Stolen Holiday, Patient in Room 18, Crime School, Waterfront, On Trial, Smashing the Money Ring, Heart of the North, British Intelligence, No Place to Go, Dick Tracy, Fog Island, Tulsa, Rogue River, Journey Into Light, Ruby Gentry, Unknown World, The Moonlighter, Top Banana, Gang Busters, Godzilla King of the Monsters, Taffey & the Jungle Hunter, Young Dillinger.

MORTON, ARTHUR: Composer, arranger. b. Duluth, Minn., Aug. 8, 1908; e. U. of Minn., 1929. Composer for various film cos. including Universal, RKO, United Artists; with Columbia since 1948.
    PICTURES INCLUDE: Night Life of the Gods, Princess O'Hara, Riding On Air, Fit for a King, Turnabout, Walking Hills, The Nevadan, Rogues of Sherwood Forest, Father is a Bachelor, Never Trust a Gambler, Harlem Globetrotters, Big Heat, Pushover, He Laughed Last.
    ORCH. ARRANGEMENTS: Laura, Smokey, From Here to Eternity, Jolson Story, Salome, Phfft, No Sad Songs For Me, Born Yesterday, Long Gray Line, Man from Laramine, My Sister Eileen, Queen Bee, Picnic, Jubal, Autumn Leaves, Johnny Concho, Harder They Fall, 3:10 to Yuma, Full of Life, Garment Jungle, They Came to Cordura, Strangers When We Meet, Touch of Mink, Critics Choice, Diamond Head, Toys in the Attic, Man from the Diners' Club, Von Ryan's Express, The Saboteur, Code Name—Morituri, In Harm's Way, What a Way to Go, The New Interns, Rio Conchos, Dear Briggitte, Our Man Flint, Planet of the Apes, Flim Flam Man, Justine, Patton, Tora Tora Tora, Mephisto Waltz, Ballad of Cable Hogue, Traveling Executioner, Escape from the Planet of the Apes, Cold Turkey, Wild Rovers, The Other, Ace Eli, One Little Indian, The Don is Dead, Papillon, Chinatown, Breakout, The Wind and the Lion, Logan's Run, The Omen, Islands in the Stream, Passover Plot, Twilight's Last Gleaming, Damnation Alley, MacArthur, Capricorn One, Coma, The Swarm, Omen II (Damien), Boys from Brazil, Magic, Superman, Alien, Players, Meteor, Star Trek, Inchon, Masoda, The Final Conflict, Outland, Raggedy Man, Night Crossing.
    TV: Black Saddle, Laramie, Bus Stop, Follow the Sun, My Three Sons, Peyton Place, Medical Center, Daniel Boone, Lancers, National Geographic, Say Goodbye, How

to Stay Alive, Hooray For Hollywood, The Waltons, Apple's Way, Medical Story.

MOSES, CHARLES ALEXANDER: Executive, producer, publicist. b. Chicago, Ill., March 1, 1923; e. Northwestern U. School of Journ., Aernoautical U. (B.S.), Englewood Eve. Jr. Coll. Prod. radio-TV shows, pub. rel. dir., Goldblatt Bros., Chicago, 1944–50; Prod. Radio Free Europe, Munich, 1951–52; spec. rep., RKO Radio Pictures, 1952; European adv.-pub. dir., United Artists, Paris, 1953–56; dir., adv., pub. and exploit., Bel-Air Prod., 1956–58; pub. exec., Screen Gems, Warners, Mirisch; own p.r. firm, Hollywood, 1959; adv., pub. and p.r. dir., Sinatra Enterprises, 1962; dir., adv., pub. and exploit., Associates and Aldrich Co., 1964; exec.-in-charge, Universal Picts. N.Y. domestic and foreign dept., Universal Studios adv., pub., and exploit. rep., Europe, Universal Picts. associate studio pub. dir., 1966–68. Orig. Story, Frankenstein, 1970. Pres., Pub. Guild of America, 1962–67. Pres., Charles A. Moses Co., 1968.

MOSES, GILBERT: Director. New York Stage director; m.p. debut Willie Dynamite, 1973; The Fish That Saved Pittsburgh, 1979.
    STAGE: Ain't Supposed to Die a Natural Death, Slave Ship.
    TV: Roots.

MOSS, ARNOLD: Actor-dir. b. New York, Jan. 28; e. CCNY, BA; Columbia U., MA; New York U., Ph.D.; Teacher, B'klyn Coll. 1932–39; visiting prof., U. of Conn. 1973; Pace U., 1975; College of William and Mary, 1976; Purdue U., 1977. Neighborhood Playhouse School of the Theatre, 1974–76. Theatre, film & TV actor-director.
    PICTURES INCLUDE: Temptation, Loves of Carmen, Reign of Terror, Border Incident, Kim, Mask of the Avenger, My Favorite Spy, Viva Zapata, Salome, Casanova's Big Night, Bengal Brigade, Hell's Island, Jump Into Hell, The 27th Day, The Fool Killer, Caper of the GOLDEN Bulls, Gambit.

MOSS, CHARLES B., JR.: Theatre Executive and Producer. b. New York City, Aug. 29, 1944. e. Univ. of Penn. (B.A., 1966), Boston Univ. School of Law (LIB, 1969). Was asst. prof. of law at Boston Univ. 1969–70. Entered ind. as v.p. of B.S. Moss Enterprises, 1970; now pres. Has produced three films: Let's Scare Jessica to Death, Stigma, Diary of the Dead.

MOSS, FRANK L.: Writer-producer. b. New York, N.Y.; e. Duke & Columbia U: Reporter, drama & film critic, N.Y.; U.S. Army Air Force, 1942–46.
    PLAYS: author: Glamour Girl, Call To Arms, (colab), So Goes The Nation, (colab), Some People's Children, American Pastoral, City On A Hill.
    PICTURES INCLUDE: The Unvanquished, Whiphand, Carribean, Sangaree, Papago Wells, The Half Breed, Sweetheart of Sigma Chi. MILITARY: 22 Air Force Training Films; 17 documentaries.
    TV PILOTS: Outer Limits, Grand Jury, The Texan.
    TV SCRIPTS: Telephone Hour, Four Star Playhouse, Winston Churchill's Valiant Years, Route 66, Wagon Train, Laramie, Wild, Wild West, The Texan, G.E. Theater, Wire Service, U.S. Marshall, M-Squad, Stoney Burke, Tales of The Texas Rangers, T.V. Reader's Digest, Sheriff of Cochise, Whirlybirds, Line-Up, Wyatt Earp, Rin Tin Tin, Walter Winchell File, Daniel Boone, Man Who Never Was, Felony Squad, Richard Diamond, Lassie, Like The Rich People, Hired Mother, Shenandoah, Counterspy, White Hunter.

PROD-STORY Ed: Screen Televideo, Sovereign Prod., Wire Service, T.V. Reader's Digest, Wyatt Earp.

MOUND, FRED: Executive. b. St. Louis, Mo., April 10, 1932. e. St. Louis Univ., Quincy Coll. 1946–52, assoc. with father, Charles Mound, at Park Theatre in Valley Park, Mo.; 1952–53, Universal Pictures (St. Louis); 1953, booker, UA, St. Louis; 1955 promoted to salesman in Kansas City; 1957, salesman, St. Louis; 1962, Indianapolis branch mgr. In 1967 named UA regional mgr., Dallas and in 1970 became S.W. Div. mgr; 1977–78, asst. gen. sls. mgr. for Southern, N.W. and S.W. division, operating out of Dallas. In June, 1978 appt. v.p., asst. gen. sls. mgr. of UA.

MOYLAN, WILLIAM J: (M.B.K.S.) Producer-director, script editor and researcher, journalist. Entered m.p. ind. 1927; credits include 59 features and over 200 shorts; in charge prod. in various studios 1933–42; prod. and ed. Indian News Parade for Indian Govt. and war corr. with India and South East Asia Commands, 1943–46; prod. information films of India 1947; Indep. prod. documentaries in Ireland 1948; dir. eastern language versions De Lane Lea Process Ltd., 1949–51; films advisor to Pakistan Govt. apptd. by Commonwealth Relations Office under Tech. Co-op. Scheme of the Colombo Plan, 1952–58; overseas adv. De Lane Lea Process, 1959–60. Founded Munster House Prods. in Ireland, 1961.

MUGGERIDGE, MALCOLM: Journalist, TV interviewer. b. Sanderstead Surrey, Mar. 24, 1903; e. Selhurst Grammar School & Selwyn Coll., Cambridge. Lecturer at Egyptian

Univ., Cairo, 1927–30; served on several newspapers including Manchester Guardian, Calcutta Statesman, Evening Standard; with Army (Legion of Honor, Croix de Guerre with Palm Medaille de la Reconnaissance Francaise), 1939–45; Daily Telegraph Washington Correspondent, 1946–47; deputy editor, Daily Telegraph, 1950–52; editor, Punch, 1953; ent. TV 1951 as interviewer on Panorama program.

MUHL, EDWARD E.; Executive and Producer. b. Richmond, Ind. Feb. 17, 1907; gen. mgr., Universal 1948–53; v.p., chg. production 1953–68.

MUIR, GRAEME: TV producer, actor. b. London, Feb., 1916; e. Oundle and St. John's, Oxford. Awarded Silver Medal Royal Academy of Dramatic Art 1938; first broadcast in Alcestis, 1940; many TV plays since; now freelance producer.
TV: Its Magic, The Dancing Years, Showtime, Perchance to Dream, Gilbert and Sullivan, Brothers In Law, Mr. Justice Duncannon, Christmas Night with the Stars, The Marriage Lines, Charley's Aunt, Comedy Playhouse, The Whitehall Worrier, Harry Worth, Not in Front of the Children, The Very Merry Widow, Bachelor Father, Birds on the Wing, My Wife Next Door, Oh Father!, Second Time Around, It Ain't Half Hot Mum, Oneupmanship, You're Only Young Twice, Life Begins at Forty, Hows' Your Mother?

MUIR, E. ROGER: Producer. b. Canada, Dec. 16, 1918. e. U. of Minn. Partner Minn Advertising Services Co., Photographer, Great Northern Railway; motion picture producer Army Signal corps; NBC TV producer, Howdy Doody, exec. producer, Concentration. Now pres. Nicholson-Muir Prods, TV program packager, U.S. Spin-Off, Pay Cards, Canada Pay Cards, Headline Hunters, Definition, Celebrity Dominoes; co-creator Newlywed Game, exec. prod. I Am Joe's Heart, I Am Joe's Lung, I Am Joe's Spine, I Am Joe's Stomach, The New Howdy Doody Show, Supermates, Second Honeymoon, Groaner, Generation Jury.

MULDAUR, DIANA: Actress. Began on New York stage then turned to films and TV, appearing on numerous major network shows.
PICTURES INCLUDE: The Swimmer, Number One, The Lawyer, One More Train To Rob, The Other, Chosen Survivors.

MULHOLLAND, ROBERT E.: Executive. e. Northwestern Univ. Joined NBC News as newswriter in Chicago in 1962. In 1964 made midwestern field producer for Huntley-Brinkley Report. In 1964 moved to London as European producer for NBC News; 1967, named Washington producer of Huntley-Brinkley Report. Transferred to L.A. in 1967 to be director of news, west coast. Named exec. prod. of NBC Nightly News. In 1973 appt. v.p., NBC news.; 1974 exec. v.p. of NBC News. In 1977 appt. pres. of NBC Television Network; also elected to board of directors.

MULLIGAN, ROBERT: Director. b. Bronx, N.Y.; e. Fordham U., A.B. With CBS-TV, asst. supvr. in radio oper.; prod. asst. on Suspense, TV; then asst. dir. & dir.: TV Playhouse, NBC, Alcoa-Goodyear, Studio One, Playhouse 90, Hallmark Hall of Fame.
PICTURES INCLUDE: Fear Strikes Out (1957), The Rat Race, The Great Imposter, Come September, To Kill a Mockingbird, The Spiral Road, Love with the Proper Stranger, Baby the Rain Must Fall, Inside Daisy Clover, Up the Down Staircase, Pursuit of Happiness, Summer of '42, The Other, The Nickel Ride, Bloodbrothers, Same Time Next Year.

MURPHY, BEN: Actor. b. Jonesboro, Ark., March 6. e. Univ. of Ill. (B.S., political science).
TV: Alias Smith and Jones, The Name of the Game, Grif, Gemini Man (all series).

MURPHY, GEORGE: U.S. Senator. b. New Haven, Conn., July 4, 1902; e. Yale U. Toolmaker for Ford Co., miner, real estate agent, nightclub dancer, actor. On stage from 1927 (Good News, Of Thee I Sing, Roberta, etc.). Screen debut 1934 in Kid Millions. Member: Screen Actors Guild (pres.); Nat'l. Com. WAC. Spcl. Academy Award "for interpreting m.p. ind. correctly to country at large," 1940; chmn., Hollywood Coordinating Com.; bd. mem., USO Inc.; v.p., Acad. of M.P. Arts & Sciences; div. of pub. rel., MGM, 1954–58; bd. mem. & past pres., Screen Actors Guild; bd. mem., M.P. Relief Fund. Joined Desilu Productions as v.p. in chg. public affairs, 1959; v.p., bd. of dir., Technicolor Corp. Elected U.S. Senator, California.
PICTURES INCLUDE: I'll Love You Always, You're a Sweetheart, London by Night, Broadway Melody of 1938, Risky Business, Two Girls on Broadway, A Girl, a Guy and a Gob, Tom, Dick and Harry, Ringside Maisie, Mayor of 44th Street, For Me and My Gal, Powers Girl, This Is the Army, Up Goes Maisie, Arnelo Affair, Cynthia, Tenth Avenue Angel, Big City, Battleground, Border Incident, No Questions Asked, Talk About a Stranger, It's a Big Country, Walk East on Beacon, Jamboree (Boy Scout film), This is the Army, Broadway Melody.

MURPHY, JOHN F.: Theatre executive. b. Brooklyn, N.Y., Mar. 25, 1905; e. CCNY. Entire career with Loew's Theatres; started over 45 yrs. ago as asst. mgr. Hillside & Valencia Theatres, Jamaica, N.Y.; apptd. gen. mgr. in chg. of out-of-town Theatres, 1942–54; v.p., Loew's Theatres, Aug., 1954; dir., Loew's Theatres, Oct., 1956; exec. v.p., Loew's Theatre, 1959; ret. July 1963; continues on bd. as advisor and director.

MURPHY, MARY: Actress. b. Washington, D.C., Jan. 26; e. University High Sch., Santa Monica, 1949; m.p. debut in Lemon Drop Kid.
PICTURES INCLUDE: Carrie, When Worlds Collide, Atomic City, Turning Point, Come Back Little Sheba, Off Limits, Houdini, Main Street to Broadway, Wild One, Beachhead, Mad Magician, Make Haste to Live, Sitting Bull, Hell's Island, Desperate Hour, A Man Alone, Maverick Queen, Zex, Harlow, Junior Bonner.

MURPHY, RICHARD: Writer, director. b. Boston, Mass.; e. Williams Coll. Entered m.p. ind. 1937. Capt. U.S. Army Sig. Corps, SWPA, 1942–45. Contract writer, 20th Century-Fox, 1945–54. Writer-prod., 20th-Fox, 1964–72; pres. Cinecom World Ent. Ltd., 1974.
PICTURES INCLUDE: Boomerang, Deep Waters, Cry of the City, Panic in the Streets, You're in the Navy Now, Les Miserables, Desert Rats, Broken Lance, Three Strips in the Sun, Wackiest Ship in the Army, Compulsion, Last Angry Man.
TV: Our Man Higgins, Screen Gems, creator, TV series, The Felony Squad.

MURRAY, BARBARA: Actress. b. London, England, Sept. 27, 1929. Stage debut in Variety, 1946; screen debut in Badger's Green, 1948. Various TV appearances.
PICTURES INCLUDE: Passport to Pimlico, Don't Ever Leave Me, Boys in Brown, Poets Pub, Tony Draws a Horse, Dark Man, Frightened Man, Mystery Junction, Another Man's Poison, Hot Ice, Street Corner (Both Sides of the Law), Meet Mr. Lucifer, Doctor At Large, Campbell's Kingdom, A Cry from the Streets, Girls in Arms.

MURRAY, BILL: Actor. b. Chicago. Was pre-med student; left to join brother, Brian, in Second City, the Chicago improvisational troupe. Appeared with brother on radio, National Lampoon Show, and in off-Bdwy. revue, of same name. Hired by ABC for Saturday Night Live; then by NBC.
PICTURES: Meatballs (debut), Where the Buffalo Roam, Caddyshack, Stripes.

MURRAY, DON: Actor-director. writer. b. Hollywood, Calif., July 31, 1929.
PLAYS: Insect Comedy, Rose Tattoo, The Skin of Our Teeth, The Hot Corner, Smith (a musical), The Norman Conquests.
PICTURES INCLUDE: Bus Stop, Bachelor Party, Hatful of Rain, The Hoodlum Priest, Advise & Consent, Baby the Rain Must Fall, Sweet Love, Bitter, The Cross and the Switchblade, Conquest of the Planet of the Apes, One Man's Way, The Plainsman, Escape From East Berlin, Shake Hands with the Devil, From Hell to Texas, Confessions of Tom Harris, Call Me by My Rightful Name, The Borgia Stick, Deadly Hero, Damien, Endless Love.

MURRAY, JAN: Performer. b. New York, N.Y., Performed in nightclubs, vaudeville, B'way, radio, TV, films. Was m.c., Songs for Sale, and Sing It Again, CBS-TV; TV guest star many programs; on Dollar a Second, ABC; Jan Murray Time, NBC; Treasure Hunt, ABC.
PLAYS: A Funny Thing Happened on the Way to the Forum.
PICTURES INCLUDE: Who Killed Teddy Bear?

MURRAY, KEN: Actor. r.n. Don't Court. b. New York, N.Y. On N.Y. stage as master of ceremonies; also Hollywood stage in Blackouts of 1942–49. Screen debut 1929 in Half Marriage. Since in numerous features and short subjects.
PICTURES INCLUDE: Leathernecking, For a Sweetheart, Swing Sister Swing, A Night at Earl Carroll's, Swing It Soldier, Juke Box Jenny, Special Academy award 1947 (Bill and Coo)., Follow Me Boys, The Power, The Man Who Shot Liberty Valance, Sound of Flubber.
TV: Ken Murray Show TV; p. d., act.: Marshall's Daughter; prod.: Where Were You, El Coyote, Hollywood, My Home Town, Hollywood Without Makeup.
BROADWAY: Ken Murray's Hollywood.
LITERARY: The Golden Days of San Simeon—Doubleday, 1971, Now in 8th Edition.

MUSANTE, TONY: Actor. b. Bridgeport, Conn., June 30, 1936. e. Oberlin College. Taught High School, directed local theatre, then appeared off-Broadway and on Dupont Show of the Month (Ride With Terror).
PICTURES INCLUDE: Once A Thief, The Incident, The Detective, A Professional Gun, The Love Circle, The Bird With The Crystal Plumage, The Last Run, Anonymous Venetian.
TV: Toma (series).

MUSCHAMP, THOMAS: Writer. b. London, Eng., May 27, 1917; e. Wm. Ellis School, Hampstead. Prof. prod. plays include: One Man's Meat, Bella Vista, Out of Season, Bridge of Sighs, Monday to Saturday, I Dreamt I Dwelt in Marble Halls, Stranger in Manhattan, Tie the Noose Tighter. TV scripts include: A Girl for George, Bridge of Sighs; in German, Gwendoline.

MUSTO, MICHAEL J.: Producer-writer B. N.Y.C. Jan. 16, 1917; e. S. Niagara U. Apprentice for J. J. Shubert. Comedy Workshop, N.Y.C. W-Co.P Hellzapoppin, Wrote, Prod. Dir. Burlesque shows and stage revues. Prod. Industrial Films, Commercials, Operas, Fund Raising Shows. Prod. Films: The Glass House, Phenomena 7-7, Down Tin Pan Alley, Single Room Furnished, Educated Heart, Agnes, Spring Fancy, The Atheist, Man Who Cried Wolf, Several Robert Montgomery Presents, Hallmark Hall of Fame, TV Specials, The Bold Ones, Strange Is The Wind. Wrote: Due-Bill Marriage, Spring Fancy, Granada, Seppi and His Brothers, Amato and The Yenta, The Cliffdwellers, Other. Owner. Empire Films and Cinema City Studios. Manager, Ruth Burch.

MUTSU, IAN YONOSUKE: Producer-Distributor. b. London, England, Jan. 14, 1907. e. Univ. of Birmingham, England. Journalist 1931–48. Daily Express, UPI, etc.; Japan repr. MGM-Hearst Metrotone News, U.S. Newsreel Pool, later Telenews, UPI-Movietone News, ITN London; 1952 pres. International Motion Picture Co. for news coverage, documentaries, custom films for worldwide clients; 1966 agent BBC TV sales, Modern Talking Picture Service NYC; 1973 founded Mutsu Inc. (Canada). Productions include numerous documentaries on Japan, Japanese background flms for overseas clients.

MYERS, JULIAN F.: Public relations. b. Detroit, Mich., Feb. 22, 1918; e. Wayne Univ., 1935–37, Univ. Southern Calif., 1937–39. Distribution, Loew's Detroit, 1941–42; asst. story editor, idea man, Columbia, 1942–46; publicist, 20th Century-Fox, 1948–62; public relations, Julian F. Myers, Inc., 1962; pres., Myers Studios, Inc., 1966; pres., New Horizons Broadcasting Corp., 1968–69; snr. publicist American Intl. Pictures, 1970–80. Executive Board Hollywood Press Club; member Variety Clubs; Academy of Motion Pictures Arts & Sciences; Board of Governors Film Industry Workshops, Inc. 1977, western vice-pres., The Publicists Guild; Recipient of Publicists Guild's Robert Yeager Award; 1979, re-elected western v.p., Publicists Guild. First male member Hollywood Women's Press Club. Co-founder HANDS (Hollywood Answering Needs of Disaster Survivors). Member, m.p. Pioneers. Winner, 1980 Publicists Guild Les Mason Award. Instructor in publicity, UCLA, 1979. Filmways Pictures, pub. dept., 1980–81.

MYERS, PETER S.: Executive. b. Toronto, Ont., Canada, May 13, 1920; e. U. of Toronto, R.C.A.F. 1941–46. Salesman, Warner, 1946; Toronto br. mgr., Eagle Lion, 1947; Toronto br. mgr., 20th Century-Fox, 1948; Canadian div. mgr., 1951; Canadian gen. mgr., 1955; man. dir. Canada, 1959; gen. sales mgr. in chg. of dom. distribution, 1968; v.p., 1969; named snr. v.p., domestic dist., 1979; snr. v.p., 20th-Fox Entertainment, 1980.

MYERSON, BERNARD: Executive. b. New York, N.Y., March 25, 1918. Entered m.p. ind. with Fabian Theatres, 1938–63, last position as exec. v.p.; joined Loew's Theatres as v.p., 1963; exec. v.p. and board member, Loew's Corp.; pres. Loew's Theatres, 1971. Mem. of Executive Committee Greater N.Y. Chapter, National Foundation of March of Dimes; Board of Directors and President of Will Rogers Memorial Fund; Mem. National Assn. Theatre Owners (dir., exec. com.); Motion Pictures Assn. Am. (dir.); Motion Picture Pioneers (pres.) Clubs: Variety (dir.).

MYERSON, BESS: Executive, entertainer. b. New York, N.Y.; e. Hunter Coll., 1945; hon. degree, Doctor of Humane Letters, L.I. Univ., Doctor of Public Service, Seton Hall, 1972. Miss America 1945; guest soloist with N.Y. Philharmonic, 1946; starred in several network TV programs; co-star, The Big Payoff; panelist, I've Got a Secret, Tournament of Roses, Miss America Pageant, Candid Camera. Commissioner, N.Y. City Dept. of Consumer Affairs, 1969–73. Consumer consultant, Citibank and Bristol-Myers. Syndicated columnist, contributing ed. Red Book Magazine, TV & Radio consumer documentaries.

N

NADEL, ARTHUR: Producer, director, writer. b. New York, N.Y. Film editor for Paramount, 20th Century-Fox, Walt Disney, U.S. Air Force m.p. div., United Artists; superv. editor, McCann-Erickson; prod., dir., writer, Universal; v.p., Levy-Gardner-Laven.
PICTURES INCLUDE: Clambake, Lola, Underground, No Trumpets, No Drum.

TV: The Rifleman, The Plainsman, Great Adventure, Arrest and Trial, Kraft Theatre, The Virginian, Day Valley, Daniel Boone, Cowboy in Africa, Bonanza, Delphi Bureau, Banyon, Streets of San Francisco: NBC Specials, Welcome Home (Emmy Winner): This Year in Jerusalem, Vortex in Oatmeal, Universal Studios, The Chase: NBC Special, Crime Without Punishment: executive consultant Filmation Studios, Shazam, The Secrets of Isis.

NADER, GEORGE: Actor. b. Pasadena, Calif.; e. Occidental College, B.A., Pasadena Playhouse. Served in U.S. Navy. Many TV appearances, m.p. debut in Monsoon. First novel, Chrome, recently published by Putnam's.
PICTURES INCLUDE: Carnival Story, Miss Robin Crusoe, Sins of Jezebel, Fours Guns to the Border, Six Bridges to Cross, Lady Godiva, Second Greatest Sex, Away All Boats, Congo Crossing, Unguarded Moment, Four Girls in Town, Man Afraid, Joe Butterfly, Nowhere to Go, The Secret Mark of D'artagnan, The Great Space Adventure, Zigzag, Walk by the Sea, The Human Duplicators, Sumuru, House of a Thousand Dolls, Alarm on 83rd Street, Murder at Midnight, Count-Down for Manhattan, Dynamite in Green Silk, The Check and Icy Smile, The Murder Club From Bklyn, Death in a Red Jaguar, End Station of the Damned, Bullets on Broadway, Beyond Atlantis.
TV: Letter to Loretta, Fireside Theatre, Chevron Theatre, Ellery Queen, Man and the Challenge, Shannon.

NAIFY, MARSHALL: Executive. b. Sacramento, Calif., March 23, 1920; e. U. So. Calif. U.S.A.F. Ch. exec. comm., United Artists Theatre Circuit Inc.; pres., Magna Pictures Corp.

NAIFY, ROBERT: Pres., United Artists Theatre Circuit Inc.; exec. v.p., Magna Pictures Corp.

NAKAMURA, MOTOHIKO: Executive. b. Tokyo, Japan, Aug. 10, 1929. e. U. of California at Berkeley, U. of Pennsylvania, Tokyo University. Joined Fuji Film Co., Ltd. in Tokyo, 1953; assigned to Japan Camera Center, New York City, 1956–67; North American rep. for Fuji Photo Film Co., Ltd., 1957–63; assistant export sales mgr., Fuji Photo Co., Ltd. in charge of international marketing of all products, 1964–71; exec. v.p., resident mgr., Fuji Photo Film U.S.A., Inc.

NALLE, BILLY: Theatre concert organist, popular field, ASCAP composer. b. Fort Myers, Fla.; graduate, The Julliard School. Over 5000 major TV shows from New York; now artist-in-residence, Wichita Theatre Organ, Inc. Reader's Digest, Telarc & WTO Records Artist. Public Relations: Billy Nalle Music, Wichita.

NAPIER, ALAN: Actor. b. In 1930, Caste, Nettleford; In a Monastery Garden, Hagen; Loyalties, ATP, 1933; Wings Over Africa, Premier Stafford, 1936; For Valour, Capitol, 1937; Wife of General Ling, Four Just Men, 1938.
PICTURES INCLUDE: The Uninvited, The Song of Bernadette, Action in Arabia, Ministry of Fear, The Hairy Ape, Mlle. Fifi, Dark Waters, Hanover Square, Isle of the Dead, Three Strangers, High Conquest, Driftwood, Forever Amber, Macbeth, Joan of Arc, Hills of Home, Tripoli, Highwayman, Strange Door, Blue Veil, Across the Wide Missouri, Big Jim McLain, Young Bess, Julius Caesar, Desiree, Moonfleet, Court Jester, Miami Expose, Mole People, Until They Sail, Journey to the Center of the Earth, Batman.
TV: Many TV dramatic shows and Batman series.

NARIZZANO, SILVIO: Producer-Director. b. Montreal, Canada, 1927. e. Univ. of Bishop's, Lennoxville, Quebec. (B.A.). Was active as actor-director in Canadian theatre before going to England for TV and theatrical film work.
PICTURES INCLUDE: Director: Under Ten Flags (co-dir.), Die! Die! My Darling!, Georgy Girl, Blue, The Man Who Had Power Over Women, Loot, Redneck, The Sky Is Falling. Producer: Negatives, Fadeout, Redneck.

NASH, N. RICHARD: Writer.
BROADWAY: author: Second Best Bed, The Young and Fair, See the Jaguar, The Rainmaker, Girls of Summer, Handful of Fire, Wildcat, 110 in the Shade, The Happy Time, Echoes.
PICTURES INCLUDE: Nora Prentiss, Vicious Years, The Rainmaker, Porgy and Bess, Sainted Sisters, Dear Wife, Welcome Stranger, Dragonfly.
TV: Many TV plays for Television Playhouse, U.S. Steel, General Electric.
NOVEL: Cry Macho, East Wind, Rain, The Last Magic, Aphrodite's Cave.
PHILOSOPHY: The Athenian Spirit, The Wounds of Sparta.

NATHAN, WYNN: Executive. e. U. of So. Calif. Casting dept., Universal, 1941; then U.S. Air Force 4 yrs.; asst. oper. mgr., Universal, 1946; talent agent, Wm. Morris Agency; talent agent, Century Artists; then United TV Programs; v.p., MCA, 1954; v.p. chg. syndication & bd. of dir., MCA; pres., TV Marketeers, 1961; v.p. & gen. mgr. Metromedia Program Sales, 1966; vice president, Worldwide Syndication Time-Life Television 1970-May, 1981. Now pres. & chief exec. officer, Lionheart TV Intl.

NATHANSON, MORTON: Publicist. b. Fayetteville, Tenn., July 27, 1918; e. N.Y.U. Legitimate stage press agent for Katharine Cornell, Group Theatre, Theatre Guild, Michael Todd, Playwrights' Co., others. Entered m.p. ind. as publicity staff writer, United Artists; then Eastern adv., pub. dir., Samuel Goldwyn Prod. and Liberty Films; pub. mgr., Paramount, Horizon; pub. dir., U.A., 1952–60; dir., internat'l adv., pub., U.A., 1960–62; headed own public relations co., 1962–67, then v.p., Ruder & Finn, Inc., 1967–71; public relations dir., Nat'l. Multiple Sclerosis Society, 1972–73.

NATHANSON, NAT: Executive. b. Detroit, Mich. Entered m.p. ind. 1935 with United Artists as salesman, Denver exch.; to Chicago, 1937; mgr., Milwaukee office, 1941–44; br. mgr., Chicago 1944; br. mgr., San Francisco 1945; br. mgr., Chicago 1947; apptd. Eastern & Canadian gen. sales mgr., Feb. 1950; sales exec., Allied Artists, 1952; midwest dist. mgr., Chicago, Sept. 1954; asst. gen. sales mgr., 1963; gen. sls. mgr., 1965. Member: Variety (chief Barker, Tent 26, Chic.; Charter mem. Tent 32, San Francisco), Variety Internat'l Property Master, 1954–55. Pres., Producers Releasing Organization, 1966; cent. div. mgr, 20th Century-Fox, 1967; Eastern & Canadian sales mgr., Four Star Excelsior, 1970; Central Divison mgr., Allied Artists Pictures Corporation headquartering in Chicago, 1970; International Ambassador Variety Club International, 1973–79.

NATWICK, MILDRED: Actress. b. Baltimore, Md., June 19, 1908; e. Bryn Mawr Sch., Baltimore, Bennett Sch., Millbrook. Prof. stage debut in Carry Nation, 1932; London debut in Day I Forget.
    PLAYS: Wind and the Rain, Distaff Side, End of Summer, Love From a Stranger, Candida, Missouri Legend, Stars in Your Eyes, Grass Harp, Blithe Spirit (Barter Theatre award), Waltz of the Toreadors (nominated for Tony), The Firstborn, The Good Soup, Critic's Choice, Barefoot in the Park, Our Town, Landscape, 70, Girls 70 (nominated for Tony), Bedroom Farce.
    PICTURES INCLUDE: Long Voyage Home, Enchanted Cottage, Yolanda and the Thief, Late George Apley, Woman's Vengeance, Three Godfathers, Kissing Bandit, She Wore a Yellow Ribbon, Cheaper by the Dozen, Quiet Man, Against All Flags, Trouble with Harry, Court Jester, Teenage Rebel, Tammy and the Bachelor, Barefoot in the Park (nominated for Oscar), If It's Tuesday This Must be Belgium, Trilogy, The Maltese Bippy, Daisy Miller, At Long Last Love.
    TELEVISION: Blithe Spirit (nominated for Emmy), House Without an Xmas Tree, Thanksgiving Treasure, Money to Burn, The Snoop Sisters (Emmy award), The Easter Promise, Little Women, McMillan & Wife, Hawaii Five-O, Love Boat, You Can't Take It With You.

NAZARRO, CLIFF: Actor. b. New Haven, Conn., January 31, 1904. Stock, vaudeville, master of ceremonies in all leading theatres. Appeared with "Two Marjories" in Vitaphone No. 2116. In 1936: "Romance Rides the Range," Spectrum.
    PICTURES INCLUDE: Outside of Paradise, a Desperate Adventure, King of the Turf, St. Louis Blues, Arise, My Love, In Old Colorado, Mr. Dynamite, Artists and Models Abroad, Dive Bomber, Night of January 16, World Premiere, Rookies on Parade, Sailors on Leave, Blondie Goes to College, Melody for Three, You'll Never Get Rich, Pardon My Stripes, Call of the Canyon, Hillbilly Blitzkrieg, Shanty-town, I'm from Arkansas, Swing Hostess, Gentleman Joe Palooka.

NEAGLE, ANNA (DAME): (D.B.E.) Actress, producer. r.n. Marjorie Robertson. b. Forest Gate, England, Oct. 20, 1904; m. Herbert Wilcox C.B.E. Teacher of dancing, world championship finalist. On London stage, m.p. debut 1929 in Mary Was Love (as Marjorie Robertson), then changed her name to Anna Neagle and appeared in Should a Doctor Tell? and The Chinese Bungalow. Then put under contract by Herbert Wilcox. Voted top British moneymaking actress Motion Picture Herald-Fame poll six years, 1947–52. Voted top box office star in the world 1949. International Gold Medal five times as Best Actress of the Year. National Film Award for Spring in Park Lane, 1948; Odette in 1951. Created C.B.E. in 1952. D. B. G. 1969.
    PLAYS: London stage: In Andre Charlot and C. B. Cochran revues, including This Year of Grace and Wake Up and Dream (London and Broadway); starred in Stand Up and Sing; others: As You Like It, Twelfth Night, Peter Pan, Emma, The Glorious Days, The More The Merrier, 1965–71. Charlie Girl. 1973; No, No Nanette.
    PICTURES INCLUDE: Goodnight Vienna, The Flag Lieutenant, The Little Damozel, Bitter Sweet, The Queen's Affaire, Nell Gwyn, Peg of Old Drury, Limelight, The Three Maxims, London Melody, Victoria the Great, Sixty Glorious Years, (to Hollywood 1939–42 for:) Nurse Edith Cavell, Irene, No No Nanette, Sunny, and Forever and a Day. (Back to England to star in:) They Flew Alone (in U.S. Wings and the Woman), Queen Victoria, The Yellow Canary, I Live in Grosvenor Square (in U.S. A Yank in London), Piccadilly Incident, The Courtneys of Curzon Street,

Spring in Park Lane, Elizabeth of Ladymead, Maytime in Mayfair, Odette, The Lady With a Lamp, Derby Day, Lilacs in the Spring (in U.S. Let's Make Up), King's Rhapsody, My Teenage Daughter, No Time for Tears, The Man Who Wouldn't Talk, The Lady Is a Square. Produced: These Dangerous Years, Wonderful Things, The Heart of a Man.
    TV: The Spice of Life (BBC-TV), What's My Line (BBC-TV), Juke Box Jury (BBC TV), Day by Day (Southern Television), Sunday Night at the London Palladium (AtV), The Elstree Story (ABC), The Magic Box (ABC), The Golden Shot (ATV) and numerous interviews. Her two television drama appearances in A Letter From the General (Anglia), and Shadow on the Sun (Anglia) both had record viewing audiences of over 20 million.

NEAL, PATRICIA: Actress. b. Packard, Ky., Jan. 20, 1926; e. Northwestern U. Doctor's asst., cashier, hostess, model, jewelry store clerk. In summer stock; Broadway debut in "Another Part of the Forest" 1947, winning the Donaldson & Drama Critic Awards, also in Children's Hour. M.p. debut in John Loves Mary, 1948. Academy Award—Best Actress, 1963.
    TV: The Bastard.
    PICTURES INCLUDE: Fountainhead, Hasty Heart, Bright Leaf, Three Secrets, Breaking Point, Raton Pass, Operation Pacific, Day the Earth Stood Still, Weekend With Father, Diplomatic Courier, Washington Story, Something for the Birds, Face in the Crowd, Hud (Academy Award), Psych 59, In Harms Way, The Subject Was Roses, The Night Digger, Baxter!, Happy Mother's Day . . . Love, George, The Passage (1978), Ghost Story.

NEAME, RONALD: Cinematographer, producer, director. b. 1911; e. U. Coll. Sch., London; son, Elwin Neame, London photog. & Ivy Close, m.p. actress. Entered m.p. ind. 1928; asst. cameraman on first full-length Brit. sound "blackmail," dir. by Alfred Hitchcock, 1929; became chief cameraman & lighting expert, 1934; in 1945 joint assoc. prod., Noel Coward Prods.
    PICTURES INCLUDE: Elizabeth of England, Invitation to the Waltz, Brief Ecstasy, It's in the Air, Gaunt Stranger, Four Just Men, Major Barbara, A Yank in the R.A.F. (Brit. flying sequence), One of Our Aircraft is Missing, In Which We Serve, This Happy Breed, Blithe Spirit, Brief Encounter, Great Expectations, Oliver Twist, Passionate Friends, Take My Life, Magic Box, Golden Salamander, The Card (The Promoter), Million Pound Note (Man With a Million), Man Who Never Was, Seventh Sin, Windom's Way, The Horse's Mouth, Tunes of Glory, Escape From Zahrain, I Could Go on Singing, The Chalk Garden, Mister Moses, Gambit, The Prime of Miss Jean Brodie, Scrooge, The Poseidon Adventure, The Odessa File, Meteor, Hopscotch, First Monday in October.

NEBENZAL, SEYMOUR: Producer. b. New York City. July 22, 1899. Began prod. 1925 in Berlin (M. Ariane, West Front 1918, Beggar's Opera): then prod. Mayerling, Betrayal in Paris. Prod. in U.S. from 1940; in 1945 pres. & exec. prod., Nero Films, Inc., Hollywood.
    PICTURES INCLUDE: We Who Are Young, Summer Storm, Whistle Stop, The Chase, Heaven Only Knows, M.

NEEDHAM, HAL: Director. In industry over 25 years. Was popular stuntman and second unit action director before full directorial debut with Smokey and the Bandit.
    PICTURES: Hooper, The Villain, Smokey and the Bandit II, The Cannonball Run.
    TELEVISION: Hal Needham's Wild World of Stunts (syndicated series he wrote, directed and starred in): Directed Death Car on the Freeway (movie); Stunts Unlimited.

NEFF, HILDEGARDE: Actress, author. r.n. Hildegard Knef. b. Ulm, Germany, Dec. 28, 1925; e. Art Acad., Berlin. Film cartoonist for UFA, Berlin; on Berlin stage after war; appeared in German films: Murderers Are Among Us, Between Yesterday and Tomorrow, Film Without Title, The Sinner. On B'way in: Silk Stockings. U.S. m.p. debut in Decision Before Dawn. Author of best-selling autobiography, 1971.
    PICTURES INCLUDE: Diplomatic Courier, Night Without Sleep, Snows of Kilimanjaro, Holiday for Henrietta, Man Between, Svengali, Subway in the Sky, Mozambique.

NEGULESCO, JEAN: Director. b. Rumania (Craiova), Feb. 29, 1900; e. Liceul Carol Univ., Rumania. Stage dir., artist, painter, Came to U.S. in 1927.
    PICTURES INCLUDE: The Mask of Dimitrios, The Conspirators, Nobody Lives Forever, Three Strangers, Humoresque, Deep Valley, Johnny Belinda, Road House, Forbidden Street, Three Came Home, Under My Skin, Mudlark, Take Care of My Little Girl, The Full House, Phone Call From a Stranger, Lydia Bailey, Lure of the Wilderness, Titanic, Scandal at Scourie, How to Marry a Millionaire, The Rains of Ranchipur, Woman's World, Three Coins in The Fountain, Daddy Long Legs, Boy on a Dolphin, The Gift of Love, A Certain Smile, Count Your Blessings, The Best of Everything, Jessica, The Pleasure Seekers, Hello, Goodbye.

NELSON, BARRY: Actor. r.n. Robert Neilson. b. Oakland, Calif.; e. U. of Calif. London stage: No Time for Sergeants, 1957.
PICTURES INCLUDE: A Guy Named Joe, Winged Victory, Man with My Face, First Traveling Saleslady, Mary, Mary, The Borgia Stick, Airport, Pete 'n Tillie, The Shining.
BROADWAY: Light Up the Sky, Rat Race, Moon is Blue, Mary, Mary, Cactus Flower, Everything in the Garden, Seascape, The Norman Conquests, The Act.
TV: series: The Hunter, My Favorite Husband, Washington: Behind Closed Doors.

NELSON, DAVID: Actor. b. New York, N.Y., Oct. 24, 1936; e. Hollywood H.S., U. of Southern Calif.
PICTURES INCLUDE: Here Comes the Nelsons, Peyton Place, The Remarkable Mr. Pennypacker, Day of the Outlaw, The Big Circus, "30," The Big Show, No Drums, No Bugles, The Wheel, The Sinners.
TV: Adventures of Ozzie and Harriet; dir.: Easy To Be Free (special), OK Crackerby series.

NELSON, EDWARD, J.: Executive. b. July 15, 1911, St. Louis, Mo. e. Iowa State. Started as commercial m.p. & aerial photographer. With National Theatre Supply, 1934–42. AAFMPS, mgr., engineering E.To., 1942–52. Joined Ballantyne of Omaha in 1952; made pres. 1973, which post now holds. Member: T.E.A. pres., May 1974–76. and bd. mbr., 1970–74. SMPTE. Variety Club. Nominated for Academy Award 1973 for designing VIP, automated projection system.

NELSON, GENE: Dancer, actor. r.n. Gene Berb. b. Seattle, Wash., March 24, 1920; e. Santa Monica, Calif. H.S. Began dancing and ice skating in school; joined Sonja Henie ice show; played in This is the Army, World War II; after discharge, featured in It Happens on Ice, Center Theatre, New York. To Hollywood for I Wonder Who's Kissing Her Now; joined Hollywood group prod. stage musical, Lend an Ear; to Warner for Daughter of Rosie O'Grady.
PICTURES INCLUDE: Tea for Two, West Point Story, Lullaby of Broadway, Painting the Clouds With Sunshine, Starlift, She's Working Her Way Through College, She's Back on Broadway, Three Sailors and a Girl, Crime Wave, Oklahoma, Way Out, Atomic Man, So This Is Paris. Directed, The Hand of Death, Hootenany Hoot, The Cool Ones, Your Cheatin' Heart, Kissin' Cousins, Wake Me When the War is Over, The Letters, Harum Scarum.
TV: Directed Mod Squad, I Dream of Jeannie, Hawaii Five-O, Farmer's Daughter, Donna Reed Show, Burke's Law, Felony Squad, Laredo, The Rifleman, The Wackiest Ship, Iron Horse, FBI, The Rookies.
Broadway: Follies, 1970; Music, Music, 1974.

NELSON, HARRIET: r.n. Harriet Hilliard. b. Des Moines, Iowa, July 18; e. High Sch., Kansas City, m. Ozzie Nelson. Appeared in dramatic & musical roles in shows; singer with Ozzie Nelson band; on radio shows: Believe It or Not, Seeing Stars, Red Skelton, Adventures of Ozzie & Harriet. Appeared in m.p.: Here Come the Nelsons.
TV: Adventures of Ozzie & Harriet, ABC-TV.
STAGE: Marriage-Go-Round; rec.: Ozzie & Harriet.
PLAYS: Impossible Years, State Fair.

NELSON, LORI: Actress. r.n. Dixie Kay Nelson; b. Santa Fe, N.M., Aug. 15, 1933; e. High Sch., L.A. Child actress; photographer's model; m.p. debut in Ma and Pa Kettle at the Fair.
PICTURES INCLUDE: Bend of the River, Francis Goes to West Point, All I Desire, All-American, Walking my Baby Back Home, Tumbleweed, Underwater, Destry, Revenge of the Creature, I Died a Thousand Times, Sincerely Yours, Mohawk, Day the World Ended, Pardners, Hot Rod Girl.
TV: How to Marry a Millionaire, Wagon Train, Laramie, Bachelor Father.

NELSON, RALPH: Producer, director, playwright, actor. b. New York City. Stage actor 1933–41; Wrote play, Angels Weep, for Cleveland Playhouse, 1943; also two Bdwy. plays: Mail Call (1944) and The Wind Is Ninety (1945). Directed plays: Here's Mama (1952); The Trouble-Makers (1953) and The Man in the Dog Suit (1957). From 1948 to 1960 directed over 1,000 dramatic shows on all TV networks. Has made film appearances in many pictures he produced and/or directed, now president Rainbow Productions. Honorary Doctor of Humane Letters, Columbia College, 1975.
PICTURES INCLUDE: Director: Requiem for a Heavyweight, Lilies of the Field, (also prod.) Soldier in the Rain, Fate Is the Hunter, Father Goose, Duel at Diablo, (also prod.) Charly, (also prod.) Counterpoint, Tic-Tic-Tic, Soldier Blue, Flight of the Doves, (also prod.) The Wrath of God, (also prod.) The Wilby Conspiracy, Embryo, A Hero Ain't Nothin' But a Sandwich, Because He's My Friend, You Can't Go Home Again. Screenplays: The Man in the Funny Suit, Flight of the Doves, The Wrath of God.
TV: Director: Playhouse 90, Studio One, Philco Playhouse, G.E. Theatre, Ford Startime, Omnibus, ABC Theatre, Elgin Hour, Dick Powell Theatre, Dupont Show of the Month, Front Row Center, Climax, Desilu Playhouse, and specials: Cinderella, Aladdin, This Happy Breed, Nut-

cracker Suite. Producer: Climax Series, Studio One, The Old Vic Hamlet, The Man in the Funny Suit, Doyle Against the House, Three Soldiers, John J. Digges, Farmer's Daughter (pilot). Christmas, Lilies of the Field.

NELSON, RAYMOND E.: Executive. b. Cleveland, O., Feb. 12, 1907; e. Baldwin-Wallace Univ. Eastern prod. mgr., NBC: supervisor of TV, Mutual; prod.-conductor, light operas; stock co. dir.; prod.-dir. TV shows on all networks: Television Follies, Fashions on Parade, Western Theatre, Boys from Boise, etc.; prod.-dir.-writer, Rod and Gun Club of the Air on Mutual, radio and TV; prod., dir., Story Time, ABC-TV. Pres., Keystone Ad Agency, Nelson Prod., Inc.; dir. of spot sales, TV Bureau of Adv.; v.p., gen. mgr., NTA Film Network.

NELSON, RICK: Actor, singer. r.n. Eric Hilliard Nelson. b. Teaneck, N.J., May 8, 1940; e. Hollywood H.S. Recording artist, Decca Records.
PICTURES INCLUDE: Here Comes the Nelsons, The Wackiest Ship in the Army, Rio Bravo, A Story of Three Loves, Love and Kisses.
TV: Adventures of Ozzie and Harriet.

NEPOMUCENO, LUIS: Producer, director. b. Manila, Philippines, July 24, 1930; e. De La Salle College, Manila, Phil., New York Inst. of Photography, N.Y. Tech. Ass't. to pres., Nepomuceno Productions, 1946–54; gen. mgr., Mepro, Inc., 1954–59; pres., Film Advertising Media Exhibitions, Inc., 1959 to date; pres., Luis Nepomuceno & Sons, Inc., 1961 to date; pres., Filipino Theas. Ass'n., 1969. Awards include: Filipino Academy of Motion Pictures Arts & Sciences 3 Awards 1968, 8 Awards 1969. Grand Prix, 2nd & 3rd Manila Film Festivals; 6 Awards, 4th Manila Film Festival. Asian Film Festivals: 2 Awards 14th Festival, 4 Awards 15th Festival.
PICTURES INCLUDE: Tears in the Dark, Manila, Open City, Because of a Flower, Heaven on Earth, Mountain Maiden, The Beggar, A Time for Dying, The Hunted.

NETTER, DOUGLAS: Motion Picture and Television Producer. V.P., gen. mgr., Todd A.O., 1955–1957. Sam Goldwyn Prods., N.Y. gen. mgr., 1958–1960. Formed own company rep. producers, 1961–1967. V.P Jalem Prod., 1968–1969. Exec. v.p. MGM, 1969–1974. Produced Mr. Ricco in 1975. American Co-Producer, The Wild Geese, 1977. Producer—Louis L'Amour's The Sacketts, 4 hour mini-series for NBC 1978. Exec. Producer—The Buffalo Soldiers, NBC pilot 1979. Produced Brian Garfield's Wild Times, a 4 hour mini-series, Metromedia, 1980. Produced Roughnecks, 4 hour mini-series, Metromedia, 1980. L'Amour's Cherokee Trail for Walt Disney Productions and CBS, 1981.

NETTLETON, LOIS: Actress. e. Studied at Goodman Theatre, Chicago. Replaced Kim Hunter in Darkness At Noon on Broadway.
PLAYS INCLUDE: Cat on a Hot Tin Roof, Silent Night, Lonely Night, God & Kato Murphy, The Wayward Stork, The Rainmaker, A Streetcar Named Desire.
PICTURES INCLUDE: Period of Adjustment, Come Fly With Me, Mail Order Bride, Valley of Mystery, Bamboo Saucer, The Good Guys and the Bad Guys, Dirty Dingus Magee, The Sidelong Glances of a Pigeon Kicker, The Honkers, Echoes of a Summer.

NEUMAN, ALAN: Producer, director. b. New York City. July 25, 1924; e. N.Y. Univ., B.A. American Theatre Wing. Dir., NBC-TV, 1947; prod., dir. of over 4000 TV shows; winner of 48 Nat'l Awards for excellence in TV. Now pres., Alan Neuman Prods.
TV: Exploring the Unknown (NBC Big Event), Person to Person, America Pause-Coke Special, Wide Wide World, General Motors Special Show, Inner Sanctum film series, Colgate Comedy Hour, Lights Out, Blind Date, Chevrolet Teletheatre, We the People, Kate Smith Show, Believe It or Not, Little Show, Dagmar's Canteen, Meet the Press, Ellery Queen; exec. prod.: College of the Air, Beat the Odds, Let. T, Laugh-In, This Is Your Life, You Asked For It.

NEWBERY, CHARLES BRUCE: Executive. b. Melbourne, Australia; e. All Saints Grammar School, Melbourne and Melbourne U. Entered m.p. ind. with Hoyt's Theatres, Ltd., Melbourne, 1929; publ. mgr., Fox Studios, Eng., 1934; controller, Fox Newsreel Theatres, 1935; managing dir., Fox Films, India, 1937; Supvr., India, China, Malaya, Fox Films, 1940; Film advisor, Government of India, 1941; estab. film studios & Newsreel for Government of India. suprv. Far East & Australia, Republic, 1945; supvr. Middle, Near and Far East. Republic, 1947; supvr. Eng. & Europe, Republic, 1948; estab. Republic Productions Great Britain, 1952; v.p. bd. mem. dir. of sales, Republic, U.S.A., 1953; pres., Charles Newbery Assoc., Newbery-Warden Associates, London, 1960; mgr. dir., Santor Film Prods., Amerion Prods., Inc., 1964; sen. v.p., bd. mem., administration, In-Flight Motion Pictures Inc., v.p., Intransit Motion Pictures, Inc., 1965. Senior v.p. Sales and Marketing 1967, President and Chief Operating Office, May 1973; vice chm. bd., Inflight, June 1979; dir. of mktg., Life Services Co.,

of America June, 1979; vice chm. bd., Inflight and sls.—Europe, East and Africa, 1980.
PICTURES INCLUDE: Deadlier Than the Male, Catch Me if You Can, Kiss Her Goodbye.

NEWBROOK, PETER: Producer and director of photography. Entered m.p. ind. 1934, Warner Bros. Studios, Teddington. Chmn. Titan Film Distributors Ltd.
PICTURES INCLUDE: After working on such pictures as The Sound Barrier, The Captain's Paradise, Hobson's Choice, Summer Madness, The Deep Blue Sea, Anastasia, The Bridge on the River Kwai; became dir. photog.: Lawrence of Arabia (2nd unit), 1961; In The Cool of the Day, That Kind of Girl, 1962; The Yellow Teddybears, Saturday Night Out, 1963; The Black Torment, 1964. Prod. and photog; Gonks Go Beat, 1965; prod. and photog; The Sandwich Man, 1966; Press For Time, Corruption, The Smashing Bird I Used to Know; Bloodsuckers, She'll Follow You Anywhere, Crucible of Terror, The Asphyx, The Wonderful World of Greece.

NEWCOM, JAMES E.: Associate producer. b. Indianapolis, Ind., Aug. 29, 1907; e. U. California. Reader, MGM, 1926, then in stocks and bonds with E. F. Hutton; then actor and film editing dept., MGM, 1930; film ed. 1933; asst. prod., 1952.
PICTURES INCLUDE: Gone With the Wind, Trial, Since You Went Away, Annie Get Your Gun, Trial, Somebody Up There Likes Me, Wings of Eagles, Until They Sail, Farewell to Arms, The Inn of the Sixth Happiness; Revue Television; Paramount Studios. Nine Hours to Rama, The Impossible Years, editor: Tora Tora Tora.

NEWGARD, ROBERT M.: Executive. b. Des Moines, Iowa, Jan. 14, 1925; e. U. of Notre Dame, 1948; Mirisch Bros., Theatres Candy Co., built and operated theas. in midwest, 1948–50; operated record dist. business 1949–53, Columbia and MGM records; prod. shows at KTTV Hollywood, 1952; Interstate Television Subsidiary Allied Artists, dist. and prod'n of TV films, 1953–56; midwestern and western sales mgr., Screen Gems, 1956–66; v.p. world syndication, Paramount Television, 1967–73; now v.p., intl. mkt., Film Services Corp.

NEWHART, BOB: Actor-Comedian. b. Chicago, Sept. 5, 1929. e. Loyola Univ. In Army 2 yrs.; then law school; left to become copywriter and accountant. Acted with theatrical stock co. in Oak Park; hired for TV man-in-street show in Chicago. Recorded comedy album for Warner Bros. Record Co., The Button Down Mind of Bob Newhart, which was big hit. Followed by two more successful albums. Did series of nightclub engagements and then acquired own TV variety series in 1961. Frequently appears in Las Vegas and headlines college concerts. Has guested on most major TV variety and comedy series.
PICTURES INCLUDE: Cool Millions, Catch 22, Cold Turkey, First Family.
TV: The Bob Newhart Show, Thursday's Game (movie).

NEWLAND, JOHN: Director, actor. b. Cincinnati, Ohio. Musicals, many TV appearances. Actor, dir., Robert Montgomery Show, My Lover, My Son.

NEWLEY, ANTHONY: Actor, writer, composer, singer. b. Sept. 24, 1931.
PICTURES INCLUDE: Cockleshell Heroes, Battle of the River Plate, Port Afrique, Fire Down Below, Good Companions, X the Unknown, High Flight, No Time to Die, The Man Inside, The Bandit, The Lady is a Square, Idle on Parade, Killers of Kilimanjaro, Let's Get Married, Jazz Boat, In The Nick, The Small World of Sammy Lee, Dr. Dolittle, 1966; Can Hieronymus Merkin Ever Forget Mercy Humpee and Find True Happiness?, Sweet November, Quilp (star, music) Willie Wonka and the Chocolate Factory (score); Summer Tree (dir.).
TV: Sammy, Sunday Night Palladium, The Strange World of Gurney Slade (series), Saturday Spectaculars, The Johnny Darling Show, Hollywood Squares, Merv Griffin Show, The Tonight Show, Anthony Newley Special (London).
PLAYS: West End stage; Stop The World—I Want to Get Off. N.Y. stage: Roar of the Greasepaint (wrote, composed with Leslie Bricusse), Good Old Bad Old Days.

NEWMAN, ALFRED S.: Executive. b. Brooklyn, N.Y., Nov. 16, 1940. e. New York University. Public relations work for Equitable Life Insurance, Trans World Airlines prior to joining Columbia Pictures in 1968 as writer in publicity dept.; named New York publicity mgr., 1970; national publicity mgr., 1972; joined MGM as East adv't-pub. dir., 1972; named director of adv't, pub. and promotion, 1974; named v.p., worldwide adv., pub., promo., 1978.

NEWMAN, DAVID: Writer. b. N.Y.C., Feb. 4, 1937. e. Univ. of Mich. (M.S., 1959). Was writer-editor at Esquire Magazine where he met Robert Benton, an art director, and formed writing partnership. All credits co-written with Benton.
PICTURES INCLUDE: Bonnie and Clyde, There Was a Crooked Man, Floreana, What's Up, Doc?, Money's Tight, Bad Company, Superman (co-s.p.), Superman II (co-s.p.).

STAGE: It's a Bird . . . It's a Plane . . . It's Superman (libretto), Oh! Calcutta (one sketch).

NEWMAN, EDWIN: News Correspondent. Joined NBC News in 1952, based in N.Y. since 1961. Reports news on NBC-TV and often assigned to anchor instant specials. Has been substitute host on Today, appeared on Meet the Press and has reported NBC News documentaries. Hosts interview series, Speaking Freely, on WNBC-TV, N.Y.C. station of NBC.

NEWMAN, JOSEPH M.: Producer, Director, writer. b. Logan, Utah. Aug. 7, 1909. Started as office boy MGM, 1925; jobs in production dept. to 1931; asst. to George Hill, Ernst Lubitsch, etc., 1931–37; asstd. in organization of MGM British studios 1937; dir. short subjects 1938; dir. "Crime Does Not Pay" series 1938–42; Major in U.S. Army Signal Corps 1942–46; dir. 32 Army Pictorial Service Pictures. Member: AMPAS, SDG Masons.
PICTURES INCLUDE: Northwest Rangers, Abandoned, Jungle Patrol, Great Dan Pitch, 711 Ocean Drive, Lucky Nick Cain, Guy Who Came Back, Love Nest, Red Skies of Montana, Outcasts of Poker Flat, Pony Soldier, Dangerous Crossing, Human Jungle, Kiss of Fire, This Island Earth, Flight to Hong Kong, Fort Massacre, Big Circus, Tarzan The Ape Man, King of the Roaring Twenties, Twenty Plus Two, The George Raft Story, Thunder of Drums.

NEWMAN, MARTIN H.: Executive. b. Brooklyn, N.Y. m. Nov. 16, 1913; e. N.Y.U., 1934, Certified Public Accountant (N.Y.); Century Theatres, 1936–1974, exec. v.p. 1966–1974; National Association of Theatre Owners, 1975–1977; exec. dir., Will Rogers Memorial Fund, 1977.

NEWMAN, NANETTE: Actress-writer. b. Northampton, England; m. to Brian Forbes. Ent. films in 1946 and TV in 1951.
TV: The Glorious Days, The Wedding Veil, Broken Honeymoon, At Home, Trial by Candlelight, Diary of Samuel Pepys, Faces in the Dark.
FILMS INCLUDE: The Personal Affair, The League of Gentlemen, The Rebel, Twice Around the Daffodils, The L-Shaped Room, Wrong Arm of the Law, Of Human Bondage, Seance on a Wet Afternoon, The Wrong Box, The Whisperers, Deadfall, The Madwoman of Chaillot, The Raging Moon, (U.S. title: Long Ago Tomorrow), The Stepford Wives, It's A 2'2" Above the Ground World (The Love Ban), Man at the Top, International Velvet.
RECENT TV: Balzac (BBC), Fun Food Factory, TV series, Stay with Me Till Morning.

NEWMAN, PAUL: Actor. Director. b. Cleveland, Ohio, Jan. 26, 1925. e. Kenyon Coll., Yale School of Drama. Summer stock; on Broadway in Picnic, The Desperate Hours, Sweet Bird of Youth, Baby Want A Kiss.
TV: Philco, U.S. Steel, Playhouse 90.
PICTURES INCLUDE: The Silver Chalice, The Rack, Somebody Up There Likes Me, The Long, Hot Summer, Cat on a Hot Tin Roof, Rally Around the Flag Boys, The Young Philadelphians, Exodus, The Hustler, Sweet Bird of Youth, Adventures of a Young Man, Hud, A New Kind of Love, The Prize, The Outrage, What a Way to Go, Lady L., Harper, Hombre, Cool Hand Luke, The Secret War of Harry Frigg, Winning, Butch Cassidy and the Sundance Kid. Dir. Rachel, Rachel. Formed First Artists Prod. Co. Ltd. 1969 with Sidney Poitier, Steve McQueen and Barbra Streisand, 1971; actor, director, Sometimes A Great Notion; Pocket Money (actor), 1971; Life & Times of Judge Roy Bean, 1972, The Effect of Gamma Rays (dir., 1972), The Mackintosh Man, The Sting, The Towering Inferno, The Drowning Pool, Buffalo Bill and the Indians, Slap Shot, Quintet, When Time Ran Out, Fort Apache, The Bronx, Absence of Malice.

NEWMAN, ROBERT V.: Executive. b. New Haven, Conn., Publicity director and mgr. for George Broadhurst, George M. Cohan, George White, etc.; dir. publicity "Abie's Irish Rose." Broadway stage prod., first 14 mos.; then prod. N.Y. plays ("Off Key," "The Sap from Syracuse," "The Poor Nut," "Twelve Miles Out," "Bad Girl," "Old Man Murphy," "Storm Song," "Trick for Trick," etc.). 1942–43 exec. asst., handling scripts & stories for Wm. Goetz, exec. prod., 20th-Fox; v.p. Republic Prod., Inc.; also asst. secy.-treas., Republic Pictures Corp. 1944–51; v.p. Samuel Goldwyn Prod., 1951–58; Pres. Batjac Prod. 1958 to 1963; founded San Remo Prods, 1963; Paramount Pictures 1964–67; exec. prod. & dir. of studio operations, 1967–70; in chg. of Quaker Oats m.p. div., 1970–72; exec. and gen. mgr. Hughes Productions, 1972–77; Executive Paramount Pictures, 1978.

NEWMAN, SAMUEL: Producer, writer, attorney. b. Jersey City, New Jersey, Dec. 14, 1919; e. N.Y.U. USFV College of Law, B.A., Juris Doctor; Captain, Armed Forces, WW II; writ. prod. Armed Forces Radio Service; freelance, contract writ. 30 m.p.; asst. exec. prod., Columbia Pictures; Pres., Samuel Newman Prods., Inc.; Head writer, story consultant, Perry Mason Show, CBS-TV 1960–64; head writer, story consultant, associate producer, Tarzan Series, NBC-TV, 1966–67; practicing licensed member, California and Federal Bar.

NEWMAN, SYDNEY.: (F.R.S.A.) Chief Creative Consultant for Canadian Film Development Corp. b. Toronto, Canada. Studied painting, drawing, commercial art at Central Techn. Schl. To Hollywood in 1938. Joined National Film Board of Canada under John Grierson. Prod. over 300 shorts. Later became exec. prod. all Canadian government cinema films, 1947–52; Canadian Broadcasting Corp., 1952, as dir. outside broadcasts, features and documentaries. Later became drama sup. and prod. Canadian Television Theatre. Joined ABC-TV in England, 1958. as sup. of drama and producer of Armchair Theatre; Head of Drama Group, TV, BBC, 1963. Commissioned and prod. first TV plays by Arthur Hailey, Harold Pinter, Alun Owen, Angus Wilson, Peter Lake. Fellow Society of Film & TV Arts, 1968; Prod. Associated British Pictures. SFTA award 1968; Zeta award, Writers Guild, Gt. Btn., 1970. 1970: Special advisor, ch. dir., Broadcast Programmes branch, Canadian Radio & TV Commission, Ottawa. Aug., 1970: Appt. Canadian Govt. Film Commissioner and chm., National Film Board of Canada; Trustee, National Arts Centre, Ottawa; board member, Canadian Broadcasting Corporation, Canadian Film Development Corp., Canadian Picture Pioneers Special Award. Special Advisor on Film to the Secretary of State for Canada, 1975–77; pres., Sydney Newman Enterprises.

NEWMAN, WALTER BROWN: Writer.
PICTURES INCLUDE: Ace in the Hole (co-s.p.), Underwater, The Man with the Golden Arm (co-s.p.), The True Story of Jesse James, Crime and Punishment, USA, The Interns (co-s.p.), Cat Ballou (co-s.p.).

NEWTON-JOHN, OLIVIA: Actress-Singer. b. Cambridge, England. Brought up in Melbourne, Australia, where won first talent contest at 15, with prize trip to England. Stayed there 2 yrs. performing as part of duo with Australian girl singer, Pat Carroll, in cabarets and on TV. Started recording; several hit records. Became a regular guest on TV series, It's Cliff Richard. Gained world-wide prominence as singer, winning several Grammys and other music awards.
PICTURES: Grease, Xanadu.

NEY, RICHARD: Actor, writer, prod., financier. b. N.Y. e. Columbia Univ., B.A. Acted in RCA TV demonstration, New York World's Fair; on stage in "Life with Father." On screen 1942 in Mrs. Miniver, War Against Mrs. Hadley, In armed services, World War II. Many TV shows. Financial advisor consultant, Richard Ney and Associates; financial advisor, lecturer; author, The Wall Street Jungle.
PICTURES INCLUDE: Late George Apley, Ivy, Joan of Arc, The Fan, Secret of St. Ives, Lovable Cheat, Babes in Bagdad, Miss Italia, Sergeant and The Spy.

NIBLEY, SLOAN: Writer. b. Ore.; e. U. of Utah, U.C.L.A., m. Linda Stirling, actress, Three yrs. U.S. Navy; employed as writer at major studios; contributor to mags.; wrote many western pictures incl.: Carson City, Springfield Rifle; prod., and writer many TV shows on film and live TV for Ralph Edwards.

NICHOLS, MIKE: Actor-Director. b. Berlin, Ger., Nov. 6, 1931. e. Chicago U. Compass Players, teamed with Elaine May; night clubs.
TV: Broadway, An Evening with Mike Nichols and Elaine May.
STAGE: Barefoot in the Park, The Knack, Luv, The Odd Couple, The Apple Tree, The Little Foxes, Plaza Suite, Uncle Vanya, The Prisoner of 2nd Avenue, Streamers, Comedians, The Gin Game. Produced Annie, 1976.
PICTURES INCLUDE: Who's Afraid of Virginia Woolf, The Graduate, Catch 22, Carnal Knowledge, The Day of the Dolphin, The Fortune.

NICHOLSON, ELWOOD J.: Cinematographer, research engineer, physicist. b. Dewitt Co., Clinton, Ill., Mar. 8, 1908; e. Chicago Eng. Coll., D.E.E. 1925; Amer. Eng. Coll., N.Y.C., Ph.D., 1929, 1927 cameraman & technician U.S. Army Air Corps, Panama; 1928 photog. & tech. Chas. A. Lindbergh; 1929 aerial photog. skywriting, Curtiss Field, L.I.; 1930 pilot & photog., newsreels & Curtiss Flying Service; 1931 newsreel cameraman, prod. & ed., Bermuda; 1932, Natl. Theat. Supply; 1934 designed equip. for Billy Rose's Jumbo, N.Y.C.; 1935 newsreels; 1936 designed equip. sound & lighting Max Reinhardt's Eternal Road, N.Y.C.; 1937–40 eng., George Teegue Process, Hollywood; 1940–44 research eng., U.S. Army Wright Field, Dayton, Ohio; 1944–45 photo research developing color tem. meter; color photog. & design eng., Wolff Studios, Hollywood. In 1947 designed & built new type 16mm sound on film recorder; invented "Cinematic" sound; mag. tape; electro devices.
PICTURES INCLUDE: Pansy the Horse, Clyde Beatty series, Operation Airstrip, Drink Up series.
MEMBER: SMPTE, IATSE. Sec'y, treas., Magna-Sound, Inc., 1954.

NICHOLSON, EMRICH: Art director. b. Shelburn, Ind., Sept. 4, 1913. e. Yale U., B.F.A.; Chouinard Art School. Pres., Nicholson-Maier Co. (architects); wrote Contemporary Shops in the U.S. 1943; joined art dept. Paramount 1941; apptd. art dir. 1946.
PICTURES INCLUDE: Black Bart, Highwayman, One Touch of Venus, Sleeping City, Walking My Baby Back Home, Magnificent Obsession, Sign of The Pagan. Retired, 1969.

NICHOLSON, JACK: Producer, director, actor, writer. b. Neptune, N.J.; April 22, 1936. Began career in cartoon department of MGM. Made acting debut in Hollywood stage production of Tea and Sympathy.
PICTURES INCLUDE: (Acting credits) The Shooting, Psych Out, Hell's Angels on Wheels, Little Shop of Horrors, The Raven, Ride the Whirlwind, Flight to Fury, Ensign Pulver, Too Young To Live, Studs Lonigan, Cry Baby Killer, Easy Rider, Five Easy Pieces, Carnal Knowledge, A Safe Place, (Writing credits) The Trip, Head, Flight to Fury, Ride the Whirlwind, Drive, He Said. (Producing credits) Ride the Whirlwind, The Shooting, Head, Drive, He Said. Directing debut with Drive, He Said, 1971. Acting: The Last Detail, 1973, Chinatown, Tommy, The Passenger, The Fortune, One Flew Over the Cuckoo's Nest, The Missouri Breaks, The Last Tycoon, Goin' South (also dir.), The Shining, The Postman Always Rings Twice, The Border, Reds.

NICHOLSON, ROBERT (NICK): Producer, actor, composer, arranger. b. Buffalo, N.Y. Musical dir., WBEN, WGR Buffalo, N.Y.; Musical dir., Howdy Doody, Ruff & Reddy, Top Dollar, Look To Win, How Do You Rate. Prod., Do, Re, Mi. VP., Nicholson-Muir Prod. Package Prod. creator Newlyweds Game, Matches 'n Mates, Big Spender, Pay Cards, Video Encyclopedia, Reader's Digest "Joe" series, The Joy of Sewing, Headline Hunters, Family Challenge, Ladies 'n Gentlemen.

NICKELL, PAUL: Director. e. Morehead, Ky., State Teachers College, U. of No. Carolina English instructor, North Carolina State College; then cameraman, asst. dir., dir. WPTZ, Philadelphia; dir. CBS-TV 1948.
TV: Studio One, Best of Broadway, Climax, Playhouse 90.

NICOL, ALEX: Actor, Director. b. Ossining, N.Y., Jan. 20, 1919; e. Fagin Sch. of Dramatic Arts, Actor's Studio; U.S. Cavalry.
THEATRE: Forward the Heart, Sundown Beach, Hamlet, Richard II, South Pacific, Mr. Roberts, Cat on a Hot Tin Roof.
PICTURES INCLUDE: Sleeping City, Target Unknown, Air Cadet, Raging Tide, Meet Danny Wilson, Red Ball Express, Because of You, Tomahawk, Redhead From Wyoming, Lone Hand, Law and Order, Champ for a Day, Black Glove, Heat Wave, About Mrs. Leslie, Dawn at Socorro, Strategic Air Command, Man from Laramie, Great Day in the Morning, Sincerely Yours, Five Branded Women, Via Margutta, Under 10 Flags, Gunfighters at Casa Grande. Dir., Sleeping Skull, Then There Were Three. Acted in: The Brutal Land, Bloody Mama, Homer, The Gilded Cage. Director: Point of Terror. Actor: Hells Black Night: Director: Screaming Skull, Then There Were Three.

NIELSEN, LESLIE: Actor. b. Regina, Sask., Canada, Feb. 11. e. Victoria H.S., Edmonton. Disc jockey, announcer for Canadian radio station; studied at Neighborhood Playhouse; N.Y. radio actor summer stock.
TV APPEARANCES: Studio One, Kraft, Philco Playhouse, Robert Montgomery Presents, Pulitzer Prize Playhouse, Suspense, Danger, Justice, Man Behind the Badge, Death of a Salesman, The New Breed, Swamp Fox, Peyton Place, Ben Casey, Wild Wild West, The Virginian, The Loner.
PICTURES INCLUDE: Vagabond King, Forbidden Planet, Ransom!, Opposite Sex, Hot Summer Night, Tammy and the Bachelor, Night Train To Paris, Harlow, Dark Intruder, Beau Geste, Gunfight in Abilene, The Reluctant Astronaut, Counterpoint, Rosie, Dayton's Devils, How to Commit Marriage, Change of Mind, The Resurrection of Zachary Wheeler, The Poseidon Adventure, Viva, Knievel!, City on Fire, Airplane!

NIEMEYER, HARRY: Publicist. b. New York, N.Y., May 31, 1909. Drama ed. St. Louis Times; pub. depts., Warner Bros., RKO, Paramount and Columbia. In January, 1946 appointed asst. pub. dir., Benedict Bogeaus Prods. Hollywood correspondent St. Louis Post-Dispatch. Apptd. pub. dir. Samuel Bischoff Prod., 1948; Universal-International studio pub. dept., 1949; asst. pub. dir., 1958; Free lance pub., major studios, 1965–71.

NIGH, JANE: Actress. r.n. Bonnie Lenora Nigh. b. Hollywood, Calif., Feb. 25, 1926; e. Polytechnic H.S., Long Beach, Calif. Defense plant worker.
PICTURES INCLUDE: Something for the Boys; State Fair, Dragonwyck, Unconquered, Give My Regards to Broadway, Red, Hot and Blue, Blue Grass of Kentucky, County

Fair, Captain Carey, U.S.A., Blue Blood, Disc Jockey, Fort Osage, Rodeo.

NILES, FRED A.: Executive. b. Milwaukee, Wisc., Sept. 12, 1918. e. Univ. of Wisc. Was radio news commentator and capt. of office of educ. and information of U.S. Army in World War II. Now heads own film studio, Fred A. Niles Communications Centers, Inc., Chicago.

NIMOY, LEONARD: Actor. b. Boston, Mass., 1931. Along with active career in films, TV and stage, has been writer and photographer. Author of three books of own photography and poetry, as well as autobiography, I Am Not Spock. Has also been speaker on college lecture circuit.
PICTURES: Queen for a Day, Rhubarb, The Balcony, Catlow, Invasion of the Body Snatchers, Star Trek—The Film.
TELEVISION: Star Trek, Mission: Impossible, etc.
STAGE: Equus, Sherlock Holmes, Vincent (one-man show).

NIMS, ERNEST: Executive. b. Des Moines, Iowa, Nov. 15, 1908; e. U. of Iowa; started in film cutting dept., Fox Films, 1930; film editor, with Walter Wanger, Republic and International Pictures, 1931–46; supervising film ed., head of ed. dept., Universal-International, 1947–52; ed. exec., U-I, 1952–62; assoc. prod., CBS, Rawhide, 1959–61; post-production exec. Universal Pictures, 1962–73, named v.p., 1966.

NIVEN, DAVID, JR.: Executive. b. London, Dec. 15, 1942. Joined William Morris Agency in Beverly Hills in 1963. Transferred same yr. to New York; in next five yrs. worked for agency's European offices in Rome, Madrid and London. In 1968 joined Columbia Pictures' U.K. office as a prod. exec.; 1972, named mg. dir. of Paramount Pictures in U.K. In 1976 became indep. prod., forming partnership with Jack Wiener.
PICTURES INCLUDE: The Eagle Has Landed, Escape to Athena.

NIVEN, DAVID: Actor. b. Kirriemuir, Scotland, Mar. 1; e. Sandhurst Coll. Served in Highland Light Infantry in Malta; advanced military training Eng.; in lumber camp Canada; newspaper writer briefly; laundry messenger; repr. of London wire firm in U.S., gunnery instructor to revolutionists in Cuba; serviced with Brit. Army 1939–45, rising from 2nd Lt. to Col.; m.p. debut 1935.
PICTURES INCLUDE: Without Regret, Rose Marie, Dodsworth, Beloved Enemy, Charge of the Light Brigade, Dinner at the Ritz, Four Men and a Prayer, Three Blind Mice, Dawn Patrol, Bluebeard's Eighth Wife, Wuthering Heights, Raffles, Eternally Yours, Kiss in the Dark, Enchantment, Kiss for Corliss, Happy Go Lovely, Toast of New Orleans, Soldiers Three, Lady Says No, Island Rescue, The Moon is Blue, Love Lottery, O'Leary Night (Tonight's the Night), King's Thief, Birds and the Bees, Around the World in 80 Days, My Man Godfrey, Separate Tables, Ask Any Girl, Happy Anniversary, Please Don't Eat the Daisies, Guns of Navarone, Guns of Darkness, Best of Enemies, Captive City, 55 Days At Peking, The Pink Panther, King of the Mountain, Conquered City, Island of the Blue Dolphins, Lady L, The Eye of The Devil, Casino Royale, The Extraordinary Seaman, Eye of the Devil, Before Winter Comes, The Brain, The Statue, Vampira, Paper Tiger, No Deposit, No Return, Murder by Death, Candleshoe, Death on the Nile, Escape to Athena, Rough Cut, The Sea Wolves.
AUTHOR: Round the Rugged Rocks, The Moon is a Balloon, 1972.

NIX, WILLIAM PATTERSON: Attorney. b. Philadelphia, April 10, 1948. e. Georgetown Univ. (A.B., 1970), Antioch Graduate School (M.A., 1971), Hofstra Univ. School of Law (J.D., 1976). New York University School of Law (LL.M., 1979). In 1976 joined the legal staff of the Motion Picture Association of America. Handles copyright and literary property matters, in addition to censorship legislation, piracy matters, and First Amendment litigation on behalf of producers, distributors and exhibitors. Serves as counsel to the MPAA Title Registration Bureau and counsel to the MPAA Classification and Rating Administration Code for Advertising.

NIZER, LOUIS: Attorney. b. London, Eng., Feb. 6, 1902; e. Columbia Coll., B.A., 1922; Columbia Univ. Law School, LL.B., 1924. At college won Curtis Oratorical Prize (highest award for oratory at Columbia) twice; won recognition from U.S. Govt. for oratory, various Liberty Loan drives. Since 1920 member firm Phillips, Nizer, Benjamin, Krim & Ballon; attorney, exec. secy., New York Film Board of Trade 1928 and thereafter; attorney many important personalities in films, stage, opera; counsel to m.p. cos., theatrical prod., also film, stage, radio exec.; trial counsel many litigations involving contract, copyright disputes.
AUTHOR: Writer, legal and other subj.; author (books) My Life in Court, Between You and Me, What to Do With Germany, Thinking on Your Feet, New Courts of Industry. Books: The Jury Returns, Analysis and Commentary on the Official Warren Commission Report on the Assassination of President John F. Kennedy. Legal Essays; author (articles); My Most Unforgettable Character, How Nazi Courts Operate, Analysis of Standard Exhibition Contract, Analysis of Motion Picture Code, Freeing the Judge, New Concepts in the Law of Radio, An Analysis of the Wagner Act, Recent Developments in Law of Plagiarism, The Implosion Conspiracy, Reflections Without Mirrors.
MEMBER: American Bar Assn., Bar Assn. of New York; hon. member, AMPA; identified Red Cross drives, March of Dimes drives; was chmn., theatrical div. La Guardia & Dewey campaigns; gen. counsel to MPAA, 1966.

NOBLE, PETER: Writer, producer, actor, TV personality. b. London, Eng., June 18; e. Hugh Myddelton Sch.; Latymer Sch. Author several books on m.p. ind.; writer & conducts movie radio prog. for B.B.C. & Luxembourg (Film Time, Movie-Go-Round, Peter Noble's Picture Parade). Formed Peter Noble Productions, 1953; Acted in many pictures; Ed. Screen International 1975.
PICTURES INCLUDE: Production assoc., Runaway Bus; asst. prod., to Dorothy a Son; co-prod., s.p. Fun at St. Fanny's; s.p., Three Girls in Paris; assoc. prod., Lost; s.p., Captain Banner; prod., Strange Inheritance; London Columnist; Hollywood Reporter etc. 1967–75.
AUTHOR: Editor, British Film Year Book; author of biographies of Bette Davis, Erich Von Stroheim, Ivor Novello, Orson Welles. Author book, I Know That Face. Wrote screenplays, the King of Soho, Love in the Limelight, The Story of Ivor Novello, etc.
TV: Find the Link, Other Screen, Film Fanfare, Movie Memories, Yakity Yak, Startime, Thank Your Lucky Stars, Juke Box Jury, Simon Dee Show, Star Parade, Who's Whose, Movie Magazine, The Big Noise, The Name Game, Line Up, Tea Break, Today. Prod. consult. On The Braden Beat, The Frost Program, Dee Time. 1969–70 Prod. Cons. Simon Dee Show. Appeared on Anything You Can Do Looks Familiar, Password, Etc. 1971–1975. Wrote scripts and prod. consultant Movie Quiz (series). Appears frequently on Today TV series. 1976, Two's Company, Looks Familiar. Prod. con. Musical Time Machine BBC2 series, Talking about films on radio, including BBC Star Sound, Radio Luxembourg, Film Faces, etc.

NOIRET, PHILIPPE: Actor. b. France, 1931. Has played character roles in numerous international films.
PICTURES INCLUDE: Zazie dans le Metro, Les Copains, The Night of the Generals, Topaz, Murphy's War, A Time for Loving, The Serpent, Let Joy Reign Supreme.

NOLAN, LLOYD: Actor. b. San Francisco, Calif.; e. Santa Clara Prep. School; Stanford U. In 1927 joined Pasadena Community Theat.; later in road co. of play The Front Page; in such stage prods. as Cape Cod Follies, High Hat, Reunion in Vienna, Americans, One Sunday Afternoon, Caine Mutiny Court Martial. Screen debut in Stolen Harmony, 1934.
PICTURES INCLUDE: Guadalcanal Diary, Bataan, Circumstantial Evidence, Captain Eddie, The House on 92nd Street, Lady in the Lake, Somewhere in the Night, Wild Harvest, Two Smart People, Green Grass of Wyoming, Street With No Name, Sun Comes Up, Easy Living, Bad Boy, The Lemon Drop Kid, Island in the Sky, Crazylegs, Last Hunt, Santiago, Abandon Ship, Hatful of Rain, Peyton Place, Susan Slade, Circus World, Sergeant Ryker, Airport, Earthquake.
TV: Julia.

NOLTE, C. ELMER, JR.: Executive v.p., b. Baltimore, Md., Oct. 19, 1905. Managing dir., FOH. Durkee Enterprises, Baltimore. Pres., NATO of Md., 1955–56; treas., 1957–59; pres., 1952–66, 67–69.

NOLTE, NICK: Actor. b. Omaha, Nebr., 1942. Attended 5 colleges in 4 yrs. on football scholarships, including Pasadena City College and Phoenix City College. Joined Actors Inner Circle at Phoenix and appeared in several plays. Did stock in Colorado. In 1968 joined Old Log Theatre in Minneapolis and after 3 yrs. left for New York, appearing at Cafe La Mama. Went to L.A. and did several TV series before big break in mini-series Rich Man, Poor Man as Tom Jordache.
PICTURES INCLUDE: Return to Macon County Line, The Deep, Who'll Stop the Rain, North Dallas Forty, Heart Beat, Cannery Row.
TV: Guested on Medical Center, Gunsmoke, etc. Starred in Rich Man, Poor Man, Book I. Movies: Feather Farm.

NORDEN, CHRISTINE: Actress, singer. r.n. Mary Lydia Thornton. b. Sunderland, England, Dec. 28, 1924. m. Jack Clayton, director (q.v.). On British stage in Tell the World, 1942; Take It Easy, 1944; Cinderella, 1951–52; The Marriage-Go-Round, 1979–80. On Broadway in Tenderloin, 1960–61; The Butler and Egg Man, 1966; Marat de Sade, 1967; Scuba Duba, 1968 etc. Signed by Sir Alexander Korda 1945 to seven year contract with London Films and Metro Goldwyn Mayer.
PICTURES INCLUDE: Night Beat, Mine Own Executioner, An Ideal Husband, Idol of Paris, A Yank Comes Back (in U.S.: A G.I. Returns), Saints and Sinners, The

Interrupted Journey, Black Widow, A Case for PC 49, Reluctant Heroes.

TELEVISION: Angel's Ransom, The Virginia Graham Show, Playhouse 90, Give My Regards to Broadway, Time to Spare, Love and Marriage.

NORMAN, STANLEY: Producer-Director. b. Dec. 22, 1921. e. Filmacademy Berlin.

PICTURES INCLUDE: The Hot Country, Dangerous Journey, Land without Grace, The Devil from Cape Town, Nobodies Land, Operation Yellow Viper, The Man Who Came To Kill, El Cisco, Tests to Kill, The Spy Pit, Taste of Savage, The Manipulator, The Big Game, In a Colts Shadow.

NORRIS, CHARLES GLENN: Executive. b. Taylorsville, N.C., Nov. 24, 1906; e. Nat'l U. Law Sch., Wash., D.C. Asst. poster clerk, Fox Film Co.; 1928; booker, Wash., D.C., 1934; ad-sales mgr., Aug., 1935; salesman, Phila.; Wash., July, 1937; Baltimore, July, 1944; br. mgr., Wash., Jan. 1946; dist. mgr., July, 1946; br. mgr., Wash., Apr., 1948; Atlantic div. mgr., Wash., Jan., 1952; eastern sales mgr., April, 1954; central Canadian sales mgr., April, 1956; asst. gen. sales mgr., April, 1959; gen. sls. mgr., 1960–69; exec. capacity in distribution, 20th Century-Fox, The Glenoris Corp.

MEMBER: Variety Club, English Speaking Union, M.P. Pioneers.

NORRIS, EDWARD: Actor. b. Philadelphia, Pa.; e. Culver Mil. Acad. Ran away to sea; later reporter on Philadelphia Ledger, Philadelphia Bulletin & Morning Record. Joined Philadelphia Professionals, then to Theatre Union Group, N.Y. On stage (Doomsday Circus). Screen debut Queen Christina, 1934.

PICTURES INCLUDE: Boys' Town, Dr. Ehrlich's Magic Bullet, Mystery of Marie Roget, Great Impersonation, Decoy, Heartaches, Trapped by Boston Blackie, Forgotten Women, Breakthrough, Killer Shark, Highway 301, Murder Without Tears, The Kentuckian.

NORRIS, KATHI: Performer. b. Newark, Ohio. e. Univ. of Chicago; banker; acct. exec., Grant Advertising, Inc., 1940–45; columnist and writer, 1944–46; star, TV, Kathi Norris Show, WABD, WNBC, 1949–54; Today Show, NBC, 1954; spokeswoman, General Electric television shows, NBC, CBS, ABC, 1954–57; hostess-narrator, True Story, NBC TV, 1957–61; panelist, Leave It to the Girls, 1962–63; radio-TV spokeswoman, Ralston Purina, 1962–64; syndication and commercials, 1964–66.

NORRIS, ROBERT: Executive. b. Santa Rosa, California, 1924. Ent. ind. 1955 as op. man, TV-Aud. Measurement, then in 1956 advt. controller and appt. to board ABC TV 1963 with responsibility company's TV film development. Then exec. director ABC Television Films Ltd., and appoint. man. director Associated British-Pathe Ltd., 1967; appt., man. dir., Anglo-EMI Film Dist., 1970; now man. dir., Film & TV Marketing Service Ltd. and dir. Walport Telmar Ltd., dir. Trantel Ltd.

NORTH, ALEX: Composer. b. Chester, Pa., Dec. 4, 1910; e. Curtis Inst., 1928–29; Juilliard Sch. of Music, 1932–34. Composer for ballet, radio, TV, theatre; U.S. Army, 1942–46; Guggenheim Fellowship, 1947–48; comp., 40 documentary films, 1937–50; comp. Revue for Clarinet & Orch. for Benny Goodman, 1947. Member ASCAP; Dramatists Guild.

PICTURES INCLUDE: Streetcar Named Desire, Death of a Salesman, Viva Zapata, Les Miserables, Pony Soldier, Member of the Wedding, Go Man Go, Desiree, Unchained, The Racers, Man with the Gun, Rose Tatoo, I'll Cry Tomorrow, Cleopatra (Composers and Lyricists Award, best film score, 1964), Shoes of the Fisherman Golden Globe Award; best film score 1968), The Children's Hour, The Misfits, Spartacus, The Rainmaker, The Agony and the Ecstacy, Who's Afraid of Virginia Woolf?, A Dream of Kings, Willard, Pocketmoney, Rebel Jesus, Once Upon a Scoundrel, Lost in the Stars, (musical director) Journey Into Fear, Shanks, Bite the Bullet, Somebody Killed Her Husband, Wise Blood, Carny, Dragonslayer. 14 Acad. Awards nominations.

NORTH, EDMUND H.: Writer. b. New York City, e. Stanford Univ., U.S. Army Signal Corps, five yrs., World War II, sep. as major.

PICTURES INCLUDE: One Night of Love, I Dream Too Much, Dishonored Lady, Flamingo Road, Young Man with a Horn, In a Lonely Place. collab. Only the Valiant; s.p. Day the Earth Stood Still, Outcasts of Poker Flat; collab. s.p., Destry, Far Horizons, Proud Ones; s.p. Cowboy; screen story and s.p., Sink the Bismarck!; collab. s.p., H.M.S. Defiant; collab. story and s.p. Patton; story and collab. s.p. Meteor.

NORTH, SHEREE: Actress. r.n. Dawn Bethel. b. Los Angeles, Calif., Jan. 17. e. Hollywood H.S. Amateur dancer with USO at 11; prof. debut at 13; many TV appearances; on Broadway in Hazel Flagg.

PICTURES INCLUDE: Excuse My Dust, Living It Up, How To Be Very Very Popular, Lieutenant Wore Skirts, Best

Things in Life Are Free, Way to the Gold, Destination Inner Space, The Gypsy Moths, Charley Varick, The Outfit, Breakout, The Shootist, Telefon.

TV: Eddie.

NOSSECK, MAX (Alexander M. Norris): Director. b. Nakel, Poland, Sept. 19, 1902. e. U. of Berlin; studied art in Vienna; stage actor four years Poland and Germany. In 1919: Actor, assist. dir., film ed., dir. (DLS Berlin, Biograph, U.F.A.). In 1931: dir. The Unhappy Man, DLS Berlin. In 1938: first picture in Portuguese; also dir. in Spain, France, Holland; dir. Gado Bravo, Overture to Glory, Girls Under 21. In U.S., 1939–40.

PICTURES INCLUDE: The Brighton Strangler, Dillinger, Black Beauty, Return of Rin-Tin-Tin, Kill or Be Killed, the Hoodlum.

NOVAK, KIM: Actress. r.n. Marilyn Novak. b. Feb. 13, 1933. e. Wright Junior Coll., Los Angeles City Coll. Started as model, named World's Favorite Actress, Brussels World Fair; m.p. debut in Pushover.

PICTURES INCLUDE: Phfft, Five Against the House, Picnic, Man with the Golden Arm, Eddy Duchin Story, Jeanne Eagels, Pal Joey, Middle of the Night, Bell, Book and Candle, Vertigo, Pepe, Strangers When We Meet, The Notorious Landlady, Boys' Night Out, Of Human Bondage, Kiss Me, Stupid, The Amorous Adventures of Moll Flanders, The Legend of Lylah Clare, The Great Bank Robbery, Tales That Witness Madness, The White Buffalo, The Mirror Crack'd.

NYKVIST, SVEN: Cinematographer. b. 1922, Sweden. Became internationally known through photographing most of Ingmar Bergman's pictures.

PICTURES INCLUDE: Sawdust and Tinsel, Karin Mansdotter, The Silence, Loving Couples, Persona, Hour of the Wolf, Cries and Whispers (AA), The Dove, Black Moon, Scenes from a Marriage, The Magic Flute, Face to Face, The Tenant, The Serpents' Egg, Pretty Baby, Autumn Sonata, King of the Gypsies, Hurricane, Starting Over, Willie and Phil, The Postman Always Rings Twice.

NYREN, DAVID O.: Prod. b. Des Moines, Iowa, Nov. 9, 1924. e. Columbia U., 1945–47. U.S. Marine Corps, 1943–45; radio & TV prod. supervision, W. Wallace Orr Adv. Agency, 1947–49; radio & TV dir., Ruthrauff & Ryan, Baltimore, 1949; TV supervisor & commercial prod. TV shows, Ruthrauff & Ryan, N.Y., 1950; also dir. of new program development & talent, 1951–52; radio-TV acct. exec., Dancer-Fitzgerald-Sample, 1952–55; vice-pres. in chge. of TV programming, 1955. Sr. V.P. in chg. TV Programs, 1966; David Nyren Prods., 1971.

O

OAKLAND, SIMON: Actor. b. N.Y.C., 1922. Was prof. violinist. Spent 3½ yrs. in military service, World War II. Studied Amer. Thea. Wing. First appeared on Bdwy. in Skipper Next to God. Has done summer stock and TV.

PICTURES INCLUDE: The Brothers Karamazov, I Want To Live, Who Was That Lady?, The Rise and Fall of Legs Diamond, Psycho, Murder, Inc., West Side Story, Follow That Dream, Third of a Man, Wall of Noise, The Raiders, The Satan Bug, The Plainsman, The Sand Pebbles, Tony Rome, Chubasco, Scandalous John, Chato's Land, Emperor of the North, Happy Mother's Day.

OATES, WARREN: Actor. b. Depoy, Kentucky.

PICTURES INCLUDE: The Rise and Fall of Legs Diamond, Private Property, Ride the High Country, The Land We Love, Mail Order Bride, The Rounders, Major Dundee, Return of the Seven, In the Heat of the Night, The Split, The Wild Bunch, The Shooting, There Was a Crooked Man, Two-Lane Blacktop, The Hired Hand, Tom Sawyer, Dillinger, The Thief Who Came to Dinner, Kid Blue, Badlands, The White Dawn, Bring Me The Head of Alfredo Garcia, Cockfight, Race with the Devil, 92 in the Shade, Drum, Brinks' Job, 1941, Stripes, The Border.

OBER, PHILIP: Actor. b. Fort Payne, Ala., March 23, 1902. e. Princeton Univ., 1919–21; Adv. bus., Brooklyn Edison Co., Liberty Magazine, Collier's and the Spur, 1922–32.

STAGE: The Animal Kingdom, She Loves Me Not, Personal Appearance, Kiss the Boys Goodbye, Mr. and Mrs. North, Junior Miss, Craig's Wife, Dear Ruth, Light Up the Sky.

PICTURES INCLUDE: The Secret Fury, Never A Dull Moment, The Magnificent Yankee, The Dull Knife, The Washington Story, Come Back, Little Sheba, My Mother and Mr. McChesney, From Here to Eternity, About Mrs. Leslie, Broken Lance, Tammy, Escapade in Japan, The High Cost of Loving, 10 North Frederick, Torpedo Run, North by Northwest, The Mating Game, Beloved Infidel, Let No Man Write My Epitaph, Elmer Gantry, The Facts of Life, Go Naked In The World, The Ugly American, The

Brass Bottle, The Ghost and Mr. Chicken, The Assignment.

TV: Lux Video Thea., Climax, Screen Gems, etc. 1952–67.

MEMBER: Council, Actor's Equity Assoc., 1947; Bd. of Governors Screen Actors Guild, 1954.

OBOLER, ARCH: Writer. b. Chicago, Ill.; e. U. Chicago. Began writing for radio 1936 as author Lights Out, "Arch Oboler's Plays," Plays for Americans; 5 vols. radio scripts published; collab. s.p. Escape.

PICTURES INCLUDE: Bewitched, Arnelo Affair, Five, The Twonky. Org. Arch Oboler Prod., August, 1952. Prod. Bwana Devil, 1952, first 3-D feature, winner Peabody Award. Writer, dir., exec. prod., 1 & 1, 1961. Prod., writer, dir. The Bubble, (in space-vision).

O'BRIAN, HUGH: Actor. b. Rochester, N.Y., Apr. 19, 1930; r.n. Hugh J. Krampe; Univ. of Cincinnati; U.S. Marine Corps; actor, stock cos.; actor with many m.p. cos.

PICTURES INCLUDE: Young Lovers, Never Fear, Vengeance Valley, Little Big Horn, On the Loose, The Cimarron Kid, Red Ball Express, Sally and Saint Anne, The Raiders, The Lawless Breed, Meet Me at the Fair, Seminole, Man from the Alamo, Back to God's Country, Saskatchewan, Fireman Save My Child, Drums Across the River, Broken Lance, There's No Business Like Show Business, White Feather, The Fiend Who Won the West, Twinkle in God's Eye, Brass Legend, Rope Law, Come Fly With Me, Love Has Many Faces, In Harm's Way, Ten Little Indians, Ambush Bay, Cowboy in Africa, Harpy, Killer Force, The Shootist, Game of Death.

TV: Wyatt Earp, ABC; Special Dial M for Murder; Hallmark Hall of Fame, A Punt, A Pass and A Prayer; It's a Man's World. TV movie: Wild Women, ABC, Probe, NBC series, Tomorrow is Now, Space In the Age of Aquarius, Search (NBC series) Murder on Flight 502 (ABC Movie), Fantasy Island (ABC series), Cruise Into Terror (ABC movie).

THEATRE: B'way Plays: Destry Rides Again, First Love, Guys and Dolls. National co. of Cactus Flower.

Pres. H.O.B. Inc. Bev. Hills, 1956. Pres., Flounder: Hugh O'Brian Youth Foundation; Nat'l Chmn., Cystic Fibrosis Research Foundation 1969–74, Pres. Thalians 1956–57; Founder Hugh O'Brian Annual Acting Awards at UCLA.

O'BRIAN, JACK: Journalist. b. Buffalo, N.Y., Aug. 16, 1914. Worked on various N.Y. and Buffalo papers in many capacities since 1932; N.Y. Herald Tribune, N.Y. World-Telegram drama critic & N.Y. columnist, AP 1943–49; Radio-TV Ed., N.Y. Journal American 1949–65 Voice of B'way columnist syndicated to more than 150 newspapers by King Features; author, Great Godfrey and many magazine articles. Since 1965, daily radio show via WOR, N.Y.C.

O'BRIAN, PETER: Producer. b. Toronto, 1947. e. University of Toronto, Emerson College, Boston. Assistant dir. in feature films, television series, and commercials. Prod. for Quadrant Films Ltd., 1975. Also pres. of Muddy York Motion Pictures Ltd.

PICTURES INCLUDE: Me (prod.) 1974; The Mourning Suit (Line Producer) 1974; Clown Murders (principal) 1975; Love At First Sight (prod.) 1975; Blood and Guts, 1977; Fast Company, 1978.

O'BRIEN, EDMOND: Actor. b. New York, Sept. 10, 1915; e. Fordham U. one year, won scholarship at Neighborhood Playhouse School of the Theatre; m. Olga San Juan, prof. On stage: Daughters of Atrios, Hamlet, Parnell Family Portrait, Henry IV. On Orson Welles Radio program. Signed by RKO.

PICTURES INCLUDE: The Hunchback of Notre Dame, A Girl, A Guy and A Gob, Parachute Battalion, Obliging Young Lady, Powder Town, Victory, The Killers, The Web, Double Life, Another Part of the Forest, Fighter Squadron, Act of Murder, For Love of Mary, White Heat, Redhead and the Cowboy, Admiral Was a Lady, DOA, 711 Ocean Drive, Between Midnight and Dawn, Two of a Kind, Silver City, Warpath, Denver and the Rio Grande, Turning Point, Hitch-Hiker, Julius Caesar, Man in the Dark, China Venture, The Bigamist; act., co-dir., Shield for Murder; act. Shanghai Story, Barefoot Contessa (Acad. Award, best supporting actor, 1954); Pete Kelly's Blues, D-Day the Sixth of June, The Rack, 1984, Girl Can't Help It, The Third Voice, The Last Voyage, The Great Impostor, The Man Who Shot Liberty Valance, Moon Pilot, Birdman of Alcatraz, Fantastic Voyage, The Viscount, The Love God, The Wild Bunch, To Commit a Murder, They Only Kill Their Masters, 99 and 44/100ths ½ Dead.

TV: Johnny Midnight, 1960; 333 Montgomery Street, MGM-TV, NBC, 1962. Flesh and Blood, Sam Benedict (series).

O'BRIEN, GEORGE: Actor. b. San Francisco, Calif., Apr. 19, 1900; e. Santa Clara Coll.; medical student, then U.S. Navy. In amateur theatricals. Entered m.p. ind. as asst. cameraman, stunt man, double, finally actor.

PICTURES INCLUDE: The Iron Horse, The Man Who Came Back, The Roughneck, The Johnstown Flood, Is Zat So?, Sharpshooters, Honor Bound, Blindfold, Noah's Ark,

My Wild Irish Rose; since 1939 in many Westerns (RKO); Fort Apache, She Wore a Yellow Ribbon, Gold Raiders, Cheyenne Autumn.

O'BRIEN, LIAM: Writer. b. New York, N.Y., March, 1913; e. Fordham U., Manhattan Coll., A.B., 1935. Author B'way play Remarkable Mr. Pennypacker, 1953.

PICTURES INCLUDE: Chain Lightning, Redhead and the Cowboy, Of Men and Music, Diplomatic Courier, Here Comes the Groom, The Stars Are Singing, Young at Heart.

O'BRIEN, MARGARET: Actress. b. Los Angeles, Calif., Jan. 15, 1937. Screen debut at 4 in Babes in Arms, Acad. Award best child actress, 1944. Voted one of ten best money-making stars in Motion Picture Herald-Fame Poll 1945–46.

PICTURES INCLUDE: Journey for Margaret, Dr. Gillespie's Criminal Case, Lost Angel, Thousands Cheer, Jane Eyre, The Canterville Ghost, Meet Me in St. Louis, Music for Millions, Our Vines Have Tender Grapes, Three Wise Fools, Unfinished Dance, Tenth Avenue Angel, Secret Garden, Big City, Little Women, Her First Romance, Anabelle Lee, Diabolic Wedding.

O'BRIEN, PAT: Actor. b. Milwaukee, Wis., Nov. 11, 1899; e. Marquette U.; Great Lakes Naval Training Station; Sargent School, N.Y. In stock; on Broadway in Man's Man, Up and Up; on the road in Coquette, Front Page; m.p. debut in "Front Page" 1932; org. with Phil Ryan, 1944, Terneen Productions.

PICTURES INCLUDE: Flying High, Final Edition, Virtue, Strange Case of Clara Deane, Air Mail, Destination Unknown, Bureau of Missing Persons, Flirtation Walk, Oil for the Lamps of China, Angels With Dirty Faces, Knute Rockne, Flowing Gold, Bombardier, The Iron Major, His Butler's Sister, Marine Raiders, Having Wonderful Crime, Secret Command, Man Alive, Perilous Holiday, Crack-Up, Riffraff, Fighting 69th, Fighting Father Dunne, The Boy With Green Hair, The Fireball, Johnny One Eye, Criminal Lawyer, People Against O'Hara, Okinawa, Jubilee Trail, Ring of Fear, Inside Detroit, The Last Hurrah, Town Tamer, The End, Ragtime.

O'BRIEN, VIRGINIA: Actress. b. Los Angeles, Calif. On stage in "Meet the people." Screen debut 1940 in Hullabaloo; now retired.

PICTURES INCLUDE: The Big Store, Lady Be Good, Ringside Maisie, Ship Ahoy, Panama Hattie, DuBarry Was a Lady, Thousands Cheer, Meet the People, Two Girls and a Sailor, The Harvey Girls, Ziegfeld Follies, Till Clouds Roll By, The Showoff, Merton of the Movies.

O'CONNELL, JACK: Producer-Director-Writer-Lyricist. b. Boston. After Germany in WWII got BA Princeton MBA Harvard. After being copy group head at D'Arcy and McCann advertising and doing 500 TV commercials entered feature films working with Fellini on La Dolce Vita, then asst. director to Antonioni on L'Avventura, then writer-producer-director Greenwich Village Story, Revolution, Christa (a.k.a. Swedish Fly Girls), City Women. Features have been invited by critics to represent U.S. at Cannes, Locarno, Berlin and Venice Festivals.

O'CONNOR, CARROLL: Actor. b. New York City, Aug. 2, 1925. e. University College, Dublin & U. of Montana. Three years with Dublin's Gate Theatre, then N.Y. where stage credits include Ullyses in Nighttown, Playboy of the Western World, The Big Knife; m.p. debut in Fever in the Blood, 1960.

PICTURES INCLUDE: By Love Possessed, Lonely Are The Brave, Cleopatra, In Harm's Way, What Did You Do In The War Daddy?, Hawaii, Not With My Wife You Don't, Waterhole No. 3, The Devil's Brigade, For Love Of Ivy, Kelly's Heroes, Doctors' Wives, Law and Disorder.

TV: US Steel Hour, Armstrong Circle Theatre, Kraft Theatre, All In The Family (Emmy, Golden Globe awards), Of Thee I Sing.

AUTHOR: Ladies of Hanover Tower (play); Little Anjie Always, The Great Robinson (screenplays).

O'CONNOR, DONALD: Actor. Star of Tomorrow, 1943. b. Chicago, Ill., Aug. 28, 1925. In vaudeville with family and "Sons o' Fun" (Syracuse, N.Y.) before screen debut 1938 in Sing You Sinners; in number other pictures 1938–39 (Sons of the Legion; Tom Sawyer, Detective, Beau Geste, On Your Toes, etc.); in vaudeville 1940–41, then resumed screen career with What's Cookin'?, 1942. Entered armed services, 1943.

PICTURES INCLUDE: Private Buckaroo, Give Out, Sisters, When Johnny Comes Marching Home, It Comes Up Love, Mr. Big, Top Man, Patrick the Great, Follow the Boys, The Merry Monahans, Bowery to Broadway, This Is the Life, Something in the Wind, Are You With It? Feudin', Fussin' and a-Fightin'. Yes Sir, That's My Baby, Francis series, Curtain Call at Cactus Creek, The Milkman, Double Crossbones, Singin' In the Rain, I Love Melvin, Call Me Madam, Walking My Baby Back Home, There's No Business Like Show Business, Anything Goes, Buster Keaton Story, Cry for Happy, That Funny Feeling, That's Entertainment, Ragtime.

TV: Colgate Comedy Hour, 1953–54. Voted best TV performer, M.P. Daily poll, 1953, The Donald O'Connor Show.

O'DONNELL, WILLIAM: Exhibitor. b. Chicago, Ill. Grad., 18 years on B'way; 19 yrs. Interstate Circuit, Dallas; Pres., Cinema Art Theatres, Inc., Dallas, 1956.

OFFENHAUSER, WILLIAM H., JR.: Executive, engineer; b. Brooklyn, N.Y., May 8, 1904; e. Columbia U., RCA, 1929–32; inventor MGM squeezetrack, 1929; contractor, Army Sig. Corps, 1933–34; sales eng., J. A. Maurer, Inc., 1936–39; mgr., Precisions Films Labs., N.Y., & v.p., mem. of bd., J. A. Maurer, 1939–43; project eng., Johns Hopkins U., 1942–43; consultant, Sig. Corps Photo Center, 1944–45; consultant, film in color TV, CBS, 1946–47, 1949–51; research project, Cornell U. Med. Coll., 1947–49; consultant, Telenews Prod., 1951–52; v.p., Andre Debrie of America, Inc., 1953; ind. consultant, films & TV, 1954. 1960–61, (Photo Staff) M.I.T. Lincoln Laboratory, Lexington, Mass. Author, 16mm Sound Motion Pictures—A Manual; co-author, Microrecording-Industrial and Library Microfilming; ind. consultant, Films, TV, biological Acoustics and Biophysics; 1968, pres. Radio Club of America; 1969–73 Bd. Dir. Radio Club of America.

O'HANLON, GEORGE: Actor. b. B'klyn., N.Y., Nov. 23, 1917; e. La Salle Acad., Providence, R.I. p. Sam Rice and Luly Beeson, prof., served in U.S. Air Corps, 1942–45. Appeared in stock, vaudeville and Broadway musicals. On screen first, 1941, New Wine.
PICTURES INCLUDE: The Hucksters, Headin' for Heaven, Triple Cross, Spirit of West Point, Are You With It? star in Joe McDoakes series: Park Row, Cattle Town, Tanks Are Coming, Lion & the Horse, Battle Stations, Million Dollar Duck.
TV: Real George, Life of Riley, Bop Girl, Desilu Playhouse, Pantomime Quiz.

O'HARA, GERRY: Director. b. Boston-Lincs., England 1924. e. St. Mary's Catholic School, Boston. Junior Reporter Boston Guardian. Entered industry in 1942 with documentaries and propaganda subjects. Dir. debut 1963 That Kind of Girl.
PICTURES INCLUDE: Game for Three Lovers; Pleasure Girls (wrote & dir.); Maroc 7; Love in Amsterdam; All the Right Noises (orig. screenplay & dir.).
TV: The Avengers; Man in a Suitcase, Journey into the Unknown.

O'HARA, MAUREEN: Actress. r.n., Maureen FitzSimons. b. Dublin. Abbey School of Acting. Won numerous prizes for elocution. Under contract to Erich Pommer-Charles Laughton. Co-starred, Abbey & Repertory Theatre: Jamaica Inn, Mayflower Pictures, 1939; Hunchback of Notre Dame, RKO. In 1940: A Bill of Divorcement, Dance, Girls, Dance, RKO. In 1941: They Met in Argentina, RKO; How Green Was My Valley, 20th-Fox. In 1942: To the Shores of Tripoli, Ten Gentlemen from West Point, The Black Swan.
PICTURES INCLUDE: The Fallen Sparrow, Buffalo Bill, The Spanish Main, Do You Love Me?, Miracle on 34th Street, Foxes of Harrow, The Homestretch, Sitting Pretty, Woman's Secret, Forbidden Street, Sentimental Journey, Sinbad the Sailor, Father Was a Fullback, Comanche Territory, Tripoli, Bagdad, Rio Grande, At Sword's Point, Kangaroo, Flame of Araby, Quiet Man, Against All Flags, Redhead from Wyoming, War Arrow, Fire Over Africa, Magnificent Matador, Lady Godiva, Long Gray Line, Everything But the Truth, Wings of Eagles, The Deadly Companions, Our Man in Havana, Mr. Hobbs Takes a Vacation, McLintock, Spencer's Mountain, The Parent Trap, The Rare Breed, The Battle of Villa Fiorita, How Do I Love Thee:, Big Jake, The Red Pony.

O'HERLIHY, DAN: Actor. b. Wexford Ireland; e. National U. of Ireland. Actor with Abbey Theatre, Dublin Gate, Langford Prod.; announcer on Radio; Eireann; on Broadway in The Ivy Green.
PICTURES INCLUDE: Odd Man Out, Macbeth, At Swords Point, Actors and Sin, Adventures of Robinson Crusoe, Black Shield of Falworth, Bengal Brigade, Purple Mask, Virgin Queen, That Woman Opposite, City After Midnight, 100 Rifles, The Tamarind Seed, MacArthur.

OHMART, CAROL: Actress. b. Salt Lake City, Utah, June 3. e. Lewis and Clark H.S., Spokane. Newspaper writer, model, radio actress.
TV: Versatile Varieties, Studio One, Philco Playhouse, Colgate Comedy Hour.
THEATRE: On Broadway in Kismet.
PICTURES INCLUDE: Scarlet Hour; Wild Party; House On Haunted Hill, Scavengers.

O'HORGAN, TOM: Director. e. DePaul Univ. At age 12 wrote opera, Doom on the Earth. Is also musician, singer, actor. Responsible for developing many revolutionary off-off Bdwy. artistic innovations in such productions as The Maids, Tom Paine, Futz.
PICTURES INCLUDE: Futz, Rhinoceros.

STAGE: Broadway: Hair, Lenny, Jesus Christ, Superstar, Inner City, Dude.

OHTANI, HIROSHI: Executive. b. Tokyo, Nov. 2, 1910. e. Kobe Commercial C. 1935; entered Shochiku Co., Ltd., 1936; exec. dir. 1937; man. dir. 1944; dir. Taisho-kan Theatre Co., Ltd. 1948; dir. Chuei Co., Ltd. 1953; man. dir. 1953; aud. Schochiku Co., 1954; pres. 1960–62; pres., Chugai motion picture chain, 1962.

O'KEEFE, ALLAN J.: Exhibitor. b. Minneapolis, Minn. e. St. Thomas Coll., St. Paul, Minn.; Univ. of Minnesota, Minneapolis; m. railroading with Soo Line; salesman, Belden-Evans Shirt Co., Minneapolis; Western Theatre Equipment Co., 1919–21; W. W. Hodkinson Corp., 1921; Robertson-Cole, 1922; Goldwyn Cosmopolitan and Metro Goldwyn 1923–24; Producers Distributing Corp. 1925; then br. mgr. Producers Distr. Corp; Pathe Exchange, Inc., Salt Lake City, Utah 1926–30; br. mgr. Pathe and RKO Pathe Dist. Corp., Los Angeles, 1930–31; br. mgr., Universal, Portland, Ore. 1932–33; Los Angeles 1933–May, 1938; west. dist. mgr. 1938; west div. sales mgr. 1943; asst. gen. sales mgr. 1946–50; west coast exhib., 1951–53; v.p. in chge. of sales, Polalite Co., July, 1953. In exhibition since 1953.

OKON, TED: Producer-director. b. New Kensington, Pa., Oct. 27, 1929. e. U. of Pittsburgh, BA 1949. Started career as radio announcer, disk jockey; John Harris Enterprises, theatres and Ice Capades, 1 year; prod. dir., WDTV-TV, Pittsburgh, formed Togo Productions prod. live and film TV shows: Reach, Yates and Matoon. TV-radio dir. 1956; TV-radio pro. dir. Reach McClinton & Co., 1957. sr. v.p. pro. TV comm. Benton and Bowles Adv. 1958–63; Exec. TV prog. dir. art., Ogilvy, Benson & Mather Adv. 1963–65; v.p. prog. dir. Van Praag Prod.; Exec. prod. Girl Game, TV show, 1966; Pres. Rough & Ready, 1966–69; Pres. prod-dir. Tape 16, Teletronics 1969–70; Pres. 1970's Productions; Exec. prod. Women's Clubhouse, TV show, Pres., exec. prod., Pennysaver Productions, Inc., TV programming syndication. Exec. prod. The Pennysaver Place, Dance Party '76, $50,000 Crossword, Sho-Biz-Quizz, Polka Party, Salsa Time, Northstage Theatre Restaurant.

OLEMERT, THEODORA: Producer/writer. Doctor of Law Criminology of Paris University. Entered films through documentaries on child delinquency. Worked during the war as assistant to Prof. Rene Cassin on Franco/British cultural relations including films. Afterwards joined Jean Benoit-Lévy, chief of the United Nations Film Section. Formed Triangle Films Ltd. for international coproductions; associated with l'Editon Française Cinematographique (Paris).
PRODUCED: Leonardo da Vinci, G. B. Shaw, Chopin, Teiva, The Sixth Day of Creation, Salvador Dali, Is Venice Sinking?, Edith Piaf and Corsica. Co-produced: Midnight Episode, Van Gogh, Molière, Mont St. Michel and Chinese Theatre. Preparing further films for international releases.

OLIN, MILTON E.: Executive. b. Chicago, Ill., Jan. 25, 1913. e. U. of Chicago, Ph.B., 1934; American Theatre Wing, N.Y., 1946–47. Freelance nightclub MC. radio & TV writer, radio actor; charter member AFRA, 1932; writer, World Broadcasting System, 1946; radio transcription sales, Ray Block Enterprises & Richard H. Ullman, Inc., 1947–51; div. sales mgr., United Artists TV Corp., 1951–54; TV sales rep., WABC-TV, N.Y., 1954; nat'l sales mgr., Telefilm Enterprises, TV exec., Walt Disney Prod., 1956–60.

OLIVER, ANTHONY: Actor, author. b. July 4, 1923. e. Monmouth, R.A.F., 1940–46; stage debut, 1946; numerous plays; pictures; TV debut, 1946; many TV plays for BBC & ITV. Writes & tells own stories for TV. Authority on antiques. Author of The Victorian Staffordshire Figure and a novel, The Pew Group.

OLIVIER, LORD. (Sir Laurence Olivier): Actor. b. Dorking, England, May 22, 1907. On stage, London, N.Y. since 1925. Recent plays include, Caesar & Cleopatra, Anthony & Cleopatra, London, 1951, N.Y. 1952; Venus Observed, London 1950; Sleeping Prince, London, 1953; Shakespeare Season, Stratford-upon-Avon, 1955; The Entertainer, London, N.Y., 1957–58; Titus Andronicus European Tour 1957; Coriolanus Stratford-upon-Avon, 1959. Rhinoceros, London, 1960; Becket, N.Y., 1960 & Tour 1961. dir., Chichester festival Theatre; 1962, dir., The Chances, The Broken Heart; Uncle Vanya, dir., acted, 1965; Othello, 1964. dir., National Theatre, 1962; Hamlet, Uncle Vanya. Recruiting Officer 1963–64. Othello Master Builder 1963–65; dir., The Crucible, 1965; Moscow, Berlin, Othello And Love For Love 1965; dir. Juno and the Paycock, 1965–66. Tour of Canada with National Thea. Co. in Love for Love, Dance of Death, Flea in Her Ear, 1967, Home and Beauty, 1969, Shylock in The Merchant of Venice, 1970; Long Day's Journey Into Night, 1972–74; Dir. Amphitryon 38, 1971; Saturday, Sunday, Monday, 1973; The Party, 1973; Eden End, 1974.
PICTURES INCLUDE: As You Like It, Fire Over England, Divorce of Lady X, Wuthering Heights, Rebecca, Pride and Prejudice, That Hamilton Woman, Demi Paradise,

Henry V (dir. & cast), Hamlet (prod., dir. & cast), Acad. Award, Best Actor, 1948, Carrie, Beggar's Opera, Richard III (prod., dir. & cast), Prince & the Showgirl, Devil's Disciple, Spartacus, The Entertainer, Term of Trial, Bunny Lake Is Missing, Othello, Khartoum, Shoes of the Fisherman, Oh! What a Lovely War, Battle of Britain, Dance of Death, David Copperfield. THREE SISTERS, Sleuth, Nicholas & Alexandra, Lady Caroline Lamb, 7½ Solution, Marathon Man, A Bridge Too Far, The Betsy, The Boys from Brazil, A Little Romance, Dracula, Clash of the Titans, Inchon, The Jazz Singer.

TV: John Gabriel Borkman, London. The Moon and Sixpence, N.Y.; The Power & The Glory, N.Y., Uncle Vanya, Long Day's Journey Into Night, 1973, Merchant of Venice, 1973, World at War, 1973, Love Among the Ruins, 1975, Jesus of Nazareth 1976. Prod. and acted in The Collection, Cat on a Hot Tin Roof. Prod. and dir. Hindle Wakes. Pres. and acted in Come Back Little Sheba, Daphne Laureola. Prod. and acted in Saturday Sunday Monday, Brideshead Revisited.

O'LOUGHLIN, GERALD STUART: Actor. b. N.Y.C., Dec. 23, 1921. e. Blair Academy, Lafayette Coll., U. of Rochester, Neighborhood Playhouse; U.S. Marine, WW II.
THEATRE: Broadway: Streetcar, Shadow of a Gunman, Dark at the Top of the Stairs, A Touch of the Poet, Cook For Mr. General, One Flew Over The Cuckoo's Nest, Calculated Risk. Off Broadway: Who'll Save the Plowboy, Harry, Noon & Night.
PICTURES INCLUDE: Lovers and Lollypops, Cop Hater, Hatful of Rain, Ensign Pulver, A Fine Madness. In Cold Blood, The Valachi Papers, Desperate Characters, The Organization, Twilight's Last Gleaming.
TV: The Defenders, Ben Casey, Dr. Dildare, 12 O'clock High, For the People, Going My Way, Naked City, Alcoa Premiere.

OLSON, CARL: Executive. Joined United Artists in 1954 as branch mgr. for Des Moines. Named Minneapolis branch mgr., 1958; promoted to asst. gen. sls. mgr. in 1961. Named western div. mgr. in 1964. In 1960 appt. v.p. & asst. gen. sls. mgr. responsible for UA western regions.

OLSON, NANCY: Actress. b. Milwaukee, Wis.; e. U. of Wisconsin, Univ. of California, Los Angeles; m. Alan Jay Lerner composer, writer. No prof. experience prior to films.
PICTURES INCLUDE: Union Station, Canadian Pacific, Sunset Boulevard, Mr. Music, Submarine Command, Force of Arms, So Big, Boy From Oklahoma, Battle Cry, Pollyanna, The Absent-Minded Professor, Smith!, Airport 1975.

O'NEAL, FREDERICK: Actor-Director-Lecturer. b. Brooksville, Miss., Aug. 27, 1905. e. public schools of Brooksville and St. Louis, Mo., New Theatre School, American Theatre Wing. Acted primarily on stage. Is now pres. of Associated Actors and Artists of America.
PICTURES INCLUDE: Pinky, No Way Out, Something of Value, Anna Lucasta, Take a Giant Step.
TV: Car 54, Where Are You (series, 1961–62).

O'NEAL, PATRICK: Actor. b. Ocala, Fla., 1927. e. Univ. of Fla. Neighborhood Playhouse. In stock cos. before N.Y. TV, 1951.
PICTURES INCLUDE: The Mad Magician, The Black Shield of Falworth, From the Terrace, A Matter of Morals, The Cardinal, In Harm's Way, King Rat, Chamber of Horrors, A Fine Madness, Alvarez Kelly, Matchless, The Assignment, Where Were You When the Lights Went Out?, The Secret Life of an American Wife, Castle Keep, Stiletto, Corky, The Way We Were, The Stepford Wives.

O'NEAT, RON: Actor. b. Utica, N.Y. e. Ohio State Univ. Spent 8 yrs. at Karamu House in Cleveland (inter-racial theatre) from 1957 to 1966, taking part in 40 plays. 1967–68 spent in N.Y. teaching acting in Harlem. Appeared in all-black revue 1968, The Best of Broadway, then in summer stock. Acted off-Broadway in American Pastorale and The Mummer's Play. 1970 joined Joseph Papp's Public Theatre. Big break came with No Place To Be Somebody, which won him top acting honors: the Obie, the Clarence Derwent, the Drama Desk and the Theatre World Awards.
PICTURES INCLUDE: None, The Organization, Super Fly, Super Fly TNT, The Master Gunfighter, When a Stranger Calls, The Final Countdown.
TV: The Interns (guest).
STAGE: Tiny Alive, The Dream of Monkey Mountain.

O'NEAL, RYAN: Actor, r.n. Patrick Ryan O'Neal. b. Los Angeles, Calif., April 20, 1941. Began as stand-in, then stuntman, then actor in "Tales of the Vikings," series, in Germany, 1959; freelanced in Hollywood; Screen Gems Pilots, Donny Dru, Our Man Higgins, and co-starred in series made from Empire; co-star, Peyton Place, ABC-TV.
PICTURES INCLUDE: The Big Bounce, The Games, Love Story, Wild Rovers, What's Up Doc, Paper Moon, The Thief Who Came To Dinner, Barry Lyndon, Nickelodeon, A Bridge Too Far, The Driver, Oliver's Story, Green Ice, Partners, So Fine.

O'NEAL, TATUM: Actress. b. Los Angeles, 1964. Daughter of Ryan O'Neal and Joanna Moore. Won A.A. for debut performance in Paper Moon.
PICTURES INCLUDE: Paper Moon, The Bad News Bears, Nickelodeon, International Velvet, Little Darlings.

O'NEIL, THOMAS F.: Executive. b. Kansas City, Mo., Apr. 18, 1915. e. Holy Cross Coll., 1933–37. Employed by General Tire and Rubber Co., 1937–41; U.S. Coast Guard, 1941–46; v.p., dir., Yankee Network, Boston, 1948–51; pres. chmn. of bd. RKO General, Inc., since 1952. Arranged purchase RKO Radio by General Teleradio, Inc. from Howard Hughes, July, 1955; chairman of the Board, RKO General, Inc.; chmn. & dir. General Tire & Rubber Co.

ONTKEAN, MICHAEL: Actor. b. Canada, 1950. e. Univ. of New Hampshire. son of Leonard and Muriel Cooper Ontkean, actors.
PICTURES INCLUDE: Slap Shot, Voices, Willie and Phil, Making Love.
TELEVISION: The Rookies (series).

OPATOSHU, DAVID: Actor. b. N.Y.C., Jan. 30; e. Morris High School. U.S. Army, 1942–46; played character roles, The Group Theatre at 19; appeared on Broadway.
THEATRE: Me and Molly, Once More With Feeling, Silk Stockings, The Reclining Figure, The Wall, Bravo Giovanni.
PICTURES INCLUDE: Cimmarron, Naked City, The Brothers Karamazov, Exodus, Act of Mercy, Best of Enemies, Enter Laughing, Romance of a Horse Thief.

OPOTOWSKY, STAN: Executive. e. Tulane Univ. Served in U.S. Marine Corps as combat corr. and later joined United Press, working in New Orleans, Denver, and New York. Published own weekly newspaper in Mississippi before returning to N.Y. to join New York Post as mgr. editor and traveling natl. corr. Is also cinematographer and film editor. Joined ABC News as TV assignment editor; named asst. assignment mgr. In 1974 named dir. of operations for ABC News TV Documentaries. In 1975 named dir. of TV News Coverage, ABC News.
AUTHOR: TV: The Big Picture, The Longs of Louisiana, The Kennedy Government, Men Behind Bars.

OPPENHEIMER, GEORGE: Writer. b. New York, N.Y., Feb. 7, 1900. e. Williams Coll., 1916–20; Harvard, 1921. Alfred A. Knopf, publishers, 1921–25; co-founder, Viking Press, 1925–33; WWII, 1942–45; playwright; short stories; radio.
PICTURES INCLUDE: Rendezvous, We Went to College, Libeled Lady, Day at the Races, Married Before Breakfast, Adventures of Don Juan; Anything Can Happen, Tonight We sing, Decameron Nights.
TV: 30 Topper plays.

OPPENHEIMER, JESS: Producer, director, writer. b. San Francisco, Calif., Nov. 11, 1913. e. Stanford U.; radio, Packard Hour, Fred Astaire, 1937–39; head writer, Screen Guild Program, 1939–40; Writer: Rudy Vallee, John Barrymore Show, 1939–41; head writer, prod., dir., Baby Snooks, 1943–48; writer, prod., dir., Lucille Ball, My Favorite Husband, 1948–51.
TELEVISION: Creator, head writer, prod., I Love Lucy, The Glynis Johns Show. Prod., Get Smart, Gen. Motors 50th Anniversary Program, Danny Kaye Special, Emmy Show. Creator, prod., The Debbie Reynolds Show. Prod., writer: Ford Startime Special, Bob Hope Chrysler Hours (also dir.); creator, prod.-dir., Angel series. Writer, All in the Family.

OPPENHEIMER, PEER J.: Executive. e. Georgetown University, UCLA. Founder and pres. of O&O Productions, 1960–64, founder and pres. of HeiRaMatt Productions, 1964. Exec. prod. at CCC Films, Berlin, 1965–66. Pres. of Elite Syncopation, Ltd. London, 1973. Producer of over 22 films including Operation CIA, Lady Hamilton, Kashmir Run, Nashville Girl, Emma Mae, Cassanova and Company. Cofounder and vice-pres. of PRO-International Films, 1975- . West coast editor of Family Weekly since 1954. Member, Writers' Guild of America. Guest lecturer, UCLA.

ORIOLO, JOSEPH: Executive. b. Union City, N.J., Feb. 21, 1913. e. Union Hill High, Cooper Union, Hudson Coll. of Art Animator, Max Fleisher Studios, 1932–42. Est. own studios, specializing in animated commercials, educationals, industrials and film strips, 1943–58. Vice-pres., exec. prod., Felix the Cat Prod., also Felix the Cat syndicated newspaper strip, 1958–61; prod., dir., Mighty Hercules series; exec. vice pres., Adventure Cartoons, Television, Inc.

ORKIN, AD: Executive. b. Jackson, Miss., Dec. 7, 1922. e. Univ. of Miss. With Trans World Airlines as flt. eng. 1945–50. Now co-owner of Orkin Amusements in Jackson.

ORLEBECK, LESTER: Director, film editor. b. Sheboygan, Wis., June 26, 1907. e. Carroll Coll., Waukesha, Wis. Entered m.p. ind. as lab. tech. with Bennett Laboratories 1925; with Mascot as film ed. 1930. Edited many outdoor & feature pictures including first Gene Autry, Roy Rogers & Don Barry series (Republic). Worked on many Westerns.

In 1942 dir. 60 MM Motor, Horsemanship Mounted for U.S. Army. Western films since.

O'ROURKE, JOHN J.: Executive. b. N.Y., N.Y., July 3, 1922. e. City College of New York, 1950. Entered the industry 1939 Music Hall/New York. 20th Century Fox Film Corp. 1941–59, asst. to dir. of exploitation, MGM, 1960–62; asst. exploitation mgr. Astor Pictures 1962–63; exploitation mgr. 1963–67; National dir. of exploitation Avco Embassy Pictures, 1967; national co-ordinator roadshows, United Artists, 1968; asst. roadshow mgr. Universal Pictures. 1969 joined Cinemation Industries as dir. advertising, publicity and exploitation. 1974, v.p., Harry K. McWilliams Assoc. Advertising, 1977, vice pres., Benjamin Philip Associates, Inc., Advertising.

ORR, WILLIAM T.: Executive. b. New York City, Sept. 27, 1917. e. Coburn School, Rumsey Hall, Philips Exeter Academy. Impersonator, Meet the People, revue. Contract, Warner Bros. Joined U.S. Air Force, 1942. Assigned, production duties. Air Force's first motion picture unit, 1945. Joined Warner Bros. staff, 1946. Entertained, various night clubs and acting on Broadway stage, New York. Returned to Warner Bros., 1947 as exec. talent dept. and shortly named asst. to Steve Trilling, exec. asst. to Mr. Warner. Chg., studio's TV opers., 1955 as exec. prod. vice-pres., Warner Bros. Pictures, Inc., Nov. 29, 1957–62; vice-pres. in chg. of prod. both features and television, March 1961 to March 1962; vice-pres. in chg. of television production, 1962–63; prod., Sex and the Single Girl; asst. to pres., exec. prod., TV div., J. L. Warner, 1963–65; formed Wm. T. Orr Co., 1966, for prods. of M.P.s and TV films.
   PICTURES INCLUDE: My Love Came Back, Thieves Fall Out, Navy Blues and Three Sons O'Guns, The Mortal Storm, The Big Street, Unholy Parners, Wicked, Wicked (exec. prod.).

ORSATTI, VICTOR M.: Executive. b. Los Angeles, Cal., Nov. 25, 1905. e. U. Southern Calif., B.A., 1928. Played baseball with St. Louis Cardinals; test pilot at Lockheed during World War II; artists' rep., Hollywood, since 1933; pres., Sabre prod.; pres., Calhoun-Orsatti Enterprises.

ORTH, MARION: Writer. b. Chicago; e. Knickerbocker Hall, Indianapolis, Ind., and St. Helen's Hall, Portland, Ore. Sold her first story in 1918 to Lois Weber for a picture which took her to Los Angeles; began writing for the screen; has been connected with Universal, First National, Famous Players and DeMille; went to Fox to descript for Come to My House; later did scripts for Sharp Shooters, Street Angel, Hangman's House, and many others for major companies.

OSBORN, ANDREW: Actor-Prod., BBC-TV. b. London, Eng., April 9, 1912. e. Christ's Hospital. Stage debut with Channing Pollock's The Enemy, 1931; played leading parts many stage plays 1935–38; ran own theatre. TV debut as actor, 1936.
   TV: Adventure Story, Ghosts, Justice, Mourning Becomes Electra, Richard of Bordeaux, Hamlet, Wandering Jew, High Fidelity. Starred in serials, incl. Stand By to Shoot, The Six Proud Walkers, The Naked Lady, Solo for Canary; as prod. and dir. over 70 stage prod. TV; prod. and dir., Gentle Maiden, People of the Night, Goldfish in the Sun, One Morning Near Troodos, The Devil Came from Dublin, Flight of the Dove, etc. Serials: Crime of the Century, Common Room, The Man Who Sold Death. TV series: Maigret, Dr. Finlay's Casebook. Head of series dept. BBC-TV, for ten years. Drama series incl: Troubleshooters, Colditz, Lotus Eaters, Softy Softly, Trial, Detective, Menace, Champion House, The Mask of Janus, Adam Adament, Doomwatch, Fall of Eagles, Onedin Line, The Borderers, Pike, The Expert, Sherlock Holmes, Vendetta, Cluff, The Spies, Shadow of the Tower, The regiment. 1974 returned to production. Prod. Walk With Destiny, When The Boat Comes In, series, The Aphrodite Inheritance, serial.

OSBORNE, JOHN: Dramatist. b. London, England, 1929.
   AUTHOR: Plays, includ. 1956: Look Back in Anger. 1957: Epitaph for George Dillon. 1958: The Entertainer. 1959: The World of Paul Slickey. 1961: Luther. 1963: Plays for England. 1964: Inadmissible Evidence. Films of his plays include Look Back in Anger, The Entertainer. Film scripts: Tom Jones (Oscar, 1964). Plays: A Patriot for Me, A Bond Honoured, Time Present, The Hotel in Amsterdam, West of Suez, Hedda Gabler (adaptn.).
   TV: The Right Prospectus, Very Like A Whale, A Subject of Scandal and Concern.

OSCO, WILLIAM: Producer. b. Akron, OH, Aug. 17, 1948. Pres., General National Enterprises (dist.), since 1967; pres., Bill Osco Productions (films) since 1969; pres., Cybelle Productions (films) since 1979.
   PICTURES: Flesh Gordon, Alice in Wonderland, Easter Sunday.

OSGOOD, STANTON M.: Executive. b. Berlin, N.H., e. Dartmouth Coll., B.A. Mgr. Fox Metropolitan Playhouse, Paramount, and worked on short subjects with Fred Waller,

1936–37; market analyst, Young & Rubicam, 1939–41; U.S. Navy, 1942–46; supvr., shorts, RKO Pathe, 1946–48; dir. of TV prod., CBS-TV, 1948–50; NBC, 1950–56, asst. dir., TV oper.; mgr., film prod. & theatre TV; gen. mgr., Paramount Sunset Corp., 1956–58; Ted Bates & Co., adv. agency, 1958–62; bus. mgr., Will Rogers Memorial Hospital, Saranac Lake, N.Y., 1962; special asst. to the president, Pratt Institute, 1969; bond sales prom. rep., U.S. Treasury, Savings Bond Div., 1971.

OSMOND, DONNY: Singer/TV Host. b. Ogden, Utah, Dec. 9, 1958. Seventh of 9 children, he was fifth member of family to become professional singer. (Four brothers, Alan, Wayne, Merrill and Jay, are original and present members of Osmond Bros., who originally sang barbershop quartet.) Donny made debut at 4 on Andy Williams Show. Donny has had 12 gold albums. Is now co-host of Donny & Marie on TV with sister.

OSMOND, MARIE: Singer/TV Host. b. Ogden, Utah, Oct. 13, 1959. Began career at age of 7 while touring with her brothers. Her first album, Paper Roses, became a gold one. Appears as co-host with brother Donny on TV's Donny & Marie.

O'SULLIVAN, KEVIN P.: Executive. b. N.Y.C., April 13, 1928. e. Queens College, Flushing, N.Y. Associated with television 33 yrs., initially as a talent; later as businessman. Entered entertainment world after winning first prize in Arthur Godfrey Talent Scouts competition in 1948. 1950–55—professional singer, actor on TV, in theatre, night clubs. 1955–57—on radio-TV promotion staff, Ronson Corp. 1958–61 salesman, Television programs of America. 1961–67—director of program services, Harrington, Righter and Parsons. In 1967 joined ABC Films, domestic sales div. as v.p. & gen. sales mgr. In Jan., 1969 named v.p., gen. mgr., ABC Films, Inc.; in April same yr. named pres. In July 1970 made pres., ABC Int'l. TV, while retaining position as pres., ABC Films. In April, 1973 become pres., chief operating officer, Worldvision Enterprises, Inc., co. formed to succeed ABC Films when FCC stopped networks from TV program dist.

O'SULLIVAN, MAUREEN: Actress. b. Boyle, Eire, May 17; e. convents in Dublin, London; finishing sch., Paris. On screen numerous pictures, various Hollywood cos. from 191. On many TV shows.
   PICTURES INCLUDE: The Big Shot, MGM Tarzan series, Tugboat Annie, The Barretts of Wimpole Street, The Thin Man, David Copperfield, Anna Karenina, Cardinal Richelieu, The Voice of Bugle Ann, A Day at the Races, Big Clock, Bonzo Goes to College, All I Desire, Mission Over Korea, Duffy of San Quentin, Steel Cage, Never Too Late.
   STAGE: The Front Page (1971), No Sex Please, We're British (1973).

OSWALD, GERD: Director. b. Berlin, Germany. Father Richard Oswald, Austrian prod. dir., founder of UFA. Child actor, Vienna 1938; asst. dir., Monogram, Republic, Goldwyn, Paramount; 1949–53, 20th-Fox, prod. mgr., 2nd unit dir., test dir. 1954, 20th-Fox, assoc., prod., Man on a Tightrope, Nightpeople. Prod. Oasis, 1955–58, dir., U.A., A Kiss Before Dying, San Sebastian Film Festival nominee; Brass Legend; Crime of Passion; Fury at Showdown; Valerie; Paris Holiday. 1959–67, dir., Columbia, Screaming Mimi. Prod.-dir., screenplay Germ., prod. The Day the Rains Came; J. Arthur Rank-Allied Artists: Brainwashed, Bombay, & Venice Film Festival nominee; dir., 20th-Fox, The Longest Day (St. Mere-Eglise Seq.). Prod. Dir. Italo-French, Co-prod., The Scarlet Eye; dir., Universal, Agent from H.A.R.M. 1970. Story prod.-dir. Warner Bros. 80 Steps to Jonah, outstanding merit award by motion picture council; 1971 prod.-dir., A.I.P., Bunny O'Hare; 1976, dir. European co-prod.; To The Bitter End.
   TV: Ford Theatre, G.E. Hour, Playhouse 90, Perry Mason, Rawhide, Black Saddle, The Virginian, Outer Limits (Soldier episode won HUGO award at world Sci-Fi convention), Fugitive, Blue Light, Felony Squad, Michner's Adventure in Paradise, Star Trek, Shane, Daniel Boone, Gentle Ben, Bonanza, It Takes A Thief, James Garner's Nichols.

OSWALD, RICHARD: Producer, director. b. Vienna, Austria. e. Vienna Dramatic School. Actor, dir., Vienna stage; entered m.p. industry as prod. dir., 1914; formed own co. in 1916. Prod., dir. more than 100 films in Europe, came to Hollywood, 1933.
   PICTURES INCLUDE: Lady Hamilton, Lilac Time, White Horse Inn, Lucrezia Borgia, Hound of the Baskervilles, Cagliostro, Dreyfus, My Song Goes Round the World, Storm of Asia, Captain of Kopenick, Isle of the Missing Men, Lovable Cheat, Devil on Broadway, Don Carlos, Countless Maritza, Mayerling (TV).

O'TOOLE, PETER: Actor. b. Ireland, Aug. 2, 1932. Studied at R.A.D.A. Early career with Bristol Old Vic. London Stage in The Long, the Short and the Tall. 1960, with the Strat-

ford-on-Avon Company. Ent. films 1959 in Kidnapped. Partner with Jules Buck, Keep Films, Ltd.
PICTURES INCLUDE: The Savage Innocents, The Day They Robbed the Bank of England, Lawrence of Arabia, Becket, Lord Jim, What's New Pussycat, How to Steal a Million, The Night of the Generals, The Bible, Great Catherine, The Lion in Winter, Goodbye Mr. Chips, Brotherly Love, Murphy's War, Under Milk Wood, The Ruling Class, Man of La Mancha, Rosebud, Man Friday, Foxtrot, Caligula, The Stunt Man.
TELEVISION: Masada (mini-series).

O'TOOLE, STANLEY: Producer. Earliest experience with production costs; worked on Cleopatra, Singer, Not the Song, No Love for Johnny, Victim, etc. In 1966 named chief cost acct. for Paramount in U.K.; 1967, promoted to prod. exec. Worked on Downhill Racer, Running Scared, etc. Produced The Last of Sheila in 1972 for W.B.; 1974–75 was in Prague working on Operation Daybreak. Produced The Seven-Per-Cent Solution for Universal. Formed own Martinat Co. and produced for WB The Squeeze. Recent credits: The Boys from Brazil, Nijinsky.

OTWELL, RONNIE RAY: Theatre Executive. b. Carrollton, Ga., Aug. 13, 1929. e. Ga. Inst. Tech. Entered industry as mgr., Bremen Theatre (Ga.), 1950; dir. pub., adv., Martin Theatres, Columbus (Ga.), 1950–63; v.p., dir. Martin Theatres of Ga., Inc., 1963, Martin Theatres of Ala., Inc., 1963; dir. Martin Theatres of Columbus, 1963; sr. v.p., Martin Theatres Companies, 1971. Member: NATO, Ga., NATO, Columbus C of C; Columbus Mus. Arts & Crafts; Assn. U.S. Army.

OWEN, ALUN: Writer. b. Liverpool, Eng., 1925.
STAGE: A Little Winter Love, Maggie May, Progress to the Park, The Rough and Ready Lot, There'll Be Some Changes Made, Norma (Mixed Doubles), Shelter, Fashion of Your Time.
TV: The Ruffian, Not Trams to Lime Street, After the Funeral, Lena O My Lena (for ITV's Armchair Theatre); The Rose Affair (two awards, 1961), Ways of Love, You Can't Win 'Em All, A Hard Knock, Dare to be a Daniel, The Stag, The Strain, A Local Boy, Ruth, Funny, Pal, Giants and Ogres, The Piano Player, The Web Flight, Buttons, Lucky, Left. Ronnie Barker and Forget-me-not series.
PICTURES INCLUDE: The Criminal, A Hard Day's Night, Minding the Shop, Park People, You'll Be the Death of Me, McNeil, Cornelius, Emlyn.

OWEN, BILL: Actor. b. Acton, Eng., Mar. 14, 1915. Screen debut in Way to the Stars. Numerous TV appearances.
PICTURES INCLUDE: School for Secrets, Daybreak, Dancing With Crime, Easy Money, When the Bough Breaks, My Brother's Keeper, Martha, Parlor Trick, The Roundabout, Trottie True, Once a Jolly Swagman, A Day to Remember, You See What I Mean, Square Ring, Rainbow Jacket, Ship That Died of Shame, Not so Dusty, Davy, Carve her Name with Pride, Carry on Sergeant, Carry on Nurse, Night Apart, Shakedown, Hell Fire Club, Carry on Regardless, Carry on Cabby!, Secret of Blood Island, Georgy Girl, Headline Hunters, O Lucky Man!, Kadoyng, In Celebration, When The Screaming Stopped, Comeback.

OWENS, GARY: Performer, broadcaster. b. Mitchell, S.D., May 10, 1936; e. Wesleyan U. Disc Jockey, KMPC, Hollywood; winner of Gavin Poll, 1966–69; named TV Radio Mirror top D.J. of year, 1970; named top D.J. in U.S. by Billboard, 1971–72; among top three TV announcers in U.S. in 'FAME' poll for three years; regular performer, "Rowan & Martin's Laugh-In" since inception in 1968.

OXBERRY, JOHN: b. New Rochelle, N.Y., March 17, 1918. Executive. Asst. photog. to Margaret Bourke-White, 1931–32; assoc. A.P. Lane Film Studio, 1932–38; assoc., R. J. Irwin, prod. photog., 1938–41; U.S. Army Signal Corps., 1941–45; cameraman, Tech Film Studio, N.Y., 1945–46; head, camera dept. Mini Toons Inc., 1946–47; pres. Animation Equipment Co., 1947–61; pres., Oxberry Corp., 1962–69; pres. Ox Products, 1971.

P

PAAR, JACK: Actor. b. Canton, O., May 1, 1918; radio announcer in Cleveland & Buffalo; served in U.S. Armd Forces World War II; entertained in Pacific zone with 28th Special Service Div. On radio with own show; m.p. debut in Variety Time, 1948. CBS-TV; Jack Paar Show, NBC-TV.
PICTURES INCLUDE: Walk Softly Stranger, Footlight Varieties, Love Nest, Down Among the Sheltering Palms.

PACINO, AL: Actor gained attention as stage actor.
STAGE: The Indian Wants the Bronx, (Obie award), Does a Tiger Wear A Necktie? (Tony Award), The Connection,

Hello Out There, Tiger at the Gates, The Basic Training of Pablo Hummel (Tony Award).
PICTURES INCLUDE: Panic in Needle Park (debut), The Godfather, Scarecrow, Serpico, The Godfather II, Dog Day Afternoon, Bobby Deerfield, And Justice for All, Cruising.

PACKARD, FRED M.: Producer. b. Los Angeles, Calif., March 14, 1919; e. Los Angeles City Coll.; m. Shelagh Mary Rank, d. of J. Arthur Rank, c. Susan & Fred Arthur Rank. Radio commentator, sports and news; personal mgr. Joe Reichman and orch.; adv. pub. rep. Bing Crosby; officer in chge. film ed. dept. & prod. Army films, U.S. Army Pictorial Service in England, France, 1935–41; actor (bit, feat. roles) including East Side of Heaven; film ed. dept. RKO studio; Universal in various dept.; pres. Fred M. Packard Prod., thereafter and since, to Columbia as prod.

PAGANO, JO: Writer. b. Denver, Col., Feb. 5, 1906. From 1930, novelist, short story writer, screen writer and comm., illustrator, 1936 with Goldwyn. Over 100 filmed teleplays.
PICTURES INCLUDE: (collab. orig. s.p. co-prod.) That's the Spirit, (novel basis, s.p.) Try and Get Me (adapted from own novel) The Condemned, (collab. s.p.) Hotel Berlin, Adventures in Silverado, Jungle Goddess, Murder Without Tears, Security Risk.

PAGE, GALE: Actress. r.n. Sally Rutter. b. Spokane, Wash., 1918.
PICTURES INCLUDE: Crime School, The Amazing Dr. Clitterhouse, Four Daughters, Heart of the North, You Can't Get Away With Murder, Daughters Courageous, Naughty But Nice, Indianapolis Speedway, Four Wives, A Child is Born, They Drive by Night, Knute Rockne—All American, Four Mothers, Time of Your Life, Anna Lucasta, About Mrs. Leslie.

PAGE, GERALDINE: Actress. b. Missouri. m. Rip Torn. After summer stock & off-broadway roles, to Broadway and m.p. Theatre awards include Drama Critics' Circle (2).
STAGE: Mid-Summer, The Immoralist, Summer and Smoke (revival), The Rainmaker, Separate Tables, Sweet Bird of Youth, Strange Interlude, The Three Sisters, Angela, Black Comedy, Sarah Siddons, Theatre World, Donaldson.
PICTURES INCLUDE: Hondo, Summer and Smoke, Sweet Bird of Youth (academy nominations), Toys in the Attic, Dear Heart, The Happiest Millionaire, You're a Big Boy Now, Trilogy, Whatever Happened to Aunt Alice, Beguiled, J.W. Coop, The Day of the Locust, Nasty Habits, Interiors, Honky Tonk Freeway.
TV: A Christmas Memory, The Thanksgiving Visitor (Emmy awards), Barefoot in Athens, The Name of the Game.

PAGE, PATTI: Performer. r.n. Clara Ann Fowler. b. Claremore, Pkla. 1927. e. Univ. of Tulsa. Staff performer, radio stat. KTUL, Tulsa; m. Charles O'Curran. Appeared on CBS radio show; star Patti Page Show, TV film series, The Big Record; author, Once Upon a Dream.
PICTURES INCLUDE: Elmer Gantry, Dondi, Boys Night Out.

PAGET, DEBRA: Actress. r.n. Debralee Griffin. b. Denver, Colo., Aug. 19, 1933. e. drama & dancing privately. Stage debut in Marry Wives of Windsor, 1946; in Jeanne D'Arc little theatre prod.; m.p. debut in Cry of the City, 1948.
PICTURES INCLUDE: House of Strangers, Broken Arrow, Fourteen Hours, Bird of Paradise, Anne of the Indies, Belles on Their Toes, Les Miserables, Stars & Stripes Forever, Prince Valiant, Demetrius & the Gladiators, Princess of the Nile, Gambler from Natchez, White Feather, Seven Angry Men, Last Hunt, Ten Commandments, Tales of Terror, The Haunted Palace.

PAIGE, BOB: Performer. r.n. John Arthur Page. b. Indianapolis, Ind., Dec. 2; e. UCLA. Singer, amateur theatricals, usher Fox West Coast theatres; singer, KGER, Long Beach, Cal., announcer; program dir., KMTR, Hollywood; played films Columbia, Paramount, Universal; 30 films.
TV: Fireside Theatre, Pepsi-Cola Playhouse, Lux Theatre, Studio One, Kraft; 1957, host on Bride and Groom; 1958 co-star Bess Myerson, Big Payoff.

PAIGE, JANIS: Actress (Star of Tomorrow, 1947). r.n. Donna Mae Jaden. b. Tacoma, Wash., Sept. 16, 1923. Sang with Tacoma Opera Co. m.p. debut, 1944, Hollywood Canteen, N.Y. stage in 1951, and TV in 1956.
STAGE: Two Gals and a Guy, Fugitive Lady, Pajama Game, It's Always Jan.
PICTURES INCLUDE: Of Human Bondage, The Time the Place and the Girl, Two Guys from Milwaukee, Her Kind of Man, Cheyenne, Love and Learn, Wallflower, Winter Meeting, One Sunday Afternoon, Romance on High Seas, House Across the Street, Younger Brothers, Mr. Universe, Remains to be Seen, Please Don't Eat the Daisies, The Caretakers, Welcome to Hard Times.

PAINE, CHARLES F.: Executive. b. Cushing, Texas, Dec. 23, 1920. e. Stephen F. Austin University, pres. Tercar Theatre Company; pres., NATO of Texas, 1972–73. NATO board member, 1973 to present; Motion Picture Pioneers member; Variety Club of Texas member.

PAKULA, ALAN J.: Producer-director. b. New York, N.Y., April 7, 1928. e. Yale U. Prod. apprentice, MGM, 1950; prod. asst., Para. 1951; prod. Para., 1955. Own prod. co., Pakula-Mulligan Prod. Stage prod. and m.p. dir. prod.
STAGE: Comes a Day, Laurette, There Must Be a Pony.
PICTURES INCLUDE: Fear Strikes Out, To Kill a Mockingbird, Love with the Proper Stranger, Baby the Rain Must Fall, Inside Daisy Clover, Up the Down Staircase, The Stalking Moon, The Sterile Cuckoo, Klute, Love and Pain and the Whole Damned Thing, The Parallax View, All the President's Men, Comes a Horseman, Starting Over (co.-prod., dir.). Roll-over.

PALANCE, JACK: Actor. b. Lattimer, Pa., Feb. 18, 1920. e. U. of N. Car. Professional fighter; U.S. Air Corps. Broadway stage and m.p.
STAGE: The Big Two, Temporary Island, The Vigil, Streetcar Named Desire, Darkness at Head.
PICTURES INCLUDE: Star of Tomorrow, Flight to Tangier, Man in the Attic, Sign of the Pagan, Silver Chalice, Kiss of Fire, Big Knife, I Died a Thousand Times, Attack!, Lonely Man, House of Numbers, Ten Seconds to Hell, Warriors Five, Barabbas, Contempt, Torture Garden, Kill a Dragon, They Came to Rob Las Vegas, The Desperadoes, Che, The Mercenary, Justine, Legion of the Damned, A Bullet for Rommel, The McMasters, Monte Walsh, Companeros, The Horsemen, The Professionals, Oklahoma Crude, Craze, The Four Deuces, The Diamond Mercenaries.
TV: Dr. Jekyll and Mr. Hyde, Dracula, Bronk (series).

PALEY, WILLIAM S.: Corp. Officer. b. Chicago, Sept. 28, 1901. e. U. of Penn. Took over operation Columbia Broadcasting System (now CBS, Inc.) as pres. 1928; chairman of the board since January, 1946; built network to leading position and est. innovations in broadcasting. During war on leave to supervise OWI radio in Mediterranean area. Chief of radio of Psychological Warfare Division, SHAEF, 1944-45; Dep. Chief info. Control Div. of U.S.G.C.C. 1945; Colonel, A.U.S. Deputy Chief Psychological Warfare Division, SHAEF, 1945; pres. & dir., William S. Paley Foundation, Inc.; pres. & dir. Greenpark Foundation, Inc. Founder and Chairman of The Board of Trustees of The Museum of Broadcasting; trustee, Emeritus Columbia University; trustee and chairman, Museum of Modern Art. Trustee North Shore University Hospital 1949-73, Co-Chairman emeritus of the Board. Decorations include the Legion of Merit, Medal of Merit. Legion of Honor, Croix de Guerre with Palm. Chairman of President's Materials Policy Comm., 1951-52, which issued report, "Resources for Freedom."

PALLOS, STEVEN: Producer. b. Budapest, Hungary, Journalist before entering m.p. ind. Began prod. & dist. in France & Continental Europe. Entered partnership with Sir Alexander Korda in 1929; later formed with him London Film Prod. From 1943-46 Brit. Army, head Psychological Warfare Br., Film Div., Italy; dir. Pendennis Pictures Corp., Ltd., Gibraltar Prods., Ltd., Britannia Film Distributors, Ltd.
RECENT PICTURES INCLUDE: Where the Spies Are, Captain Nemo & The Underwater City, Catch Me a Spy, The Glorious Musketeers.

PALMER, BETSY: Actress. b. East Chicago, Ind., Nov. 1, 1929. e. De Paul U. Actress in stock; on Broadway in Grand Prize, Affair of Honor, Roar Like a Dove.
TV: Studio One, Philco Playhouse, Danger, U.S. Steel Hour, Martin Kane, Climax, Kraft Theatre, Today, The Garry Moore Show, I've Got a Secret.
PICTURES INCLUDE: Mister Roberts, Long Gray Line, Queen Bee, The Tin Star, The Last Angry Man.

PALMER, GREGG: Actor. r.n. Palmer Lee. b. San Francisco, Calif., Jan. 25, 1927; e. U. of Utah. U.S. Air Force, 1945-46; radio announcer, disc jockey; then to Hollywood; many TV appearances.
PICTURES INCLUDE: Cimarron Kid, Battle at Apache Pass, Son of Ali Baba, Red Ball Express, Francis Goes to West Point, Sally and St. Anne, The Raiders, Back at the Front, Redhead From Wyoming, Column South, Veils of Bagdad, Golden Blade, The All American, Taza Son of Cochise, Magnificent Obsession, Playgirl, To Hell and Back, Creature Walks Among Us, Hilda Crane, Zombies of Mora Tau, Revolt of Fort Laramie, Rebel Set, Thundering Jets, Forty Pounds of Trouble, Night Hunt, The Undefeated, Chisum, Rio Lobo, Big Jake, Providencia (Italy), Ci Risiamo Vero Providencia (Italy & Spain). The Shootist, The Man with Bogart's Face.
TV: Movie of the week: Go West Young Girl, Hostage Heart, True Grit.

PALMER, LILLI: Actress. b. Austria. m. Carlos Thompson, act. N.Y. stage in 1952, Bell Book & Candle; London stage (same play) in 1955. On TV in Lilli Palmer Presents.
STAGE: (London) Suite in 3 Keys. (N.Y.) Venus Observed, Love of 4 Colonels.

PICTURES INCLUDE: Secret Agent, Silent Barrier, Sunset in Vienna, Command Performance, Man With 10 Faces, Girl Must Live, Chamber of Horrors, Thunder Rock, Gentle Sex, English Without Tears, Cloak and Dagger, Notorious Gentleman, Body and Soul, Beware of Pity, My Girl Tisa, No Minor Vices, Her Man Gilbey, Wicked City, Long Dark Hall, The Four Poster, Main Street to Broadway, Is Anna Anderson Anastasia?, But Not For Me, Conspiracy of Hearts, Counterfeit Traitor, The Pleasure of His Company, Adorable Julia, The Flight of the White Stallions, The Great Spy Mission, Operation Crossbow, Le Tonnerre De Dieu, Le Voyage DuPere, Nobody Runs Forever, Hard Contract, Marquis De Sade, La Residencia, Oedipus the King, What the Peeper Saw, Murders in the Rue Morgue, The House That Screamed, The Boys from Brazil.

PALMER, MARIA: Actress. b. Vienna, Austria, Sept. 5, 1924. e. College de Bouffement, summa cum laude; studied interpretive dance, ballet and drama. Vienna Academy of Music & the Interpretive Arts. Award at International Dance Congress, 1936; youngest member, Reinhardt's Theatre in der Josefstadt, Vienna, 1938-39; m.p. debut in Mission to Moscow.
STAGE: The Moon is Down, The Vigil, The Girl on the Via Flaminia, The Heiress, A Streetcar Named Desire, Dial M for Murder, The Diary of Anne Frank, The Happy Time.
PICTURES INCLUDE: Mission to Moscow, Days of Glory, Lady on a Train, The Other Love, The Web, Surrender, Strictly Dishonorable, By the Light of the Silvery Moon, Nostradamus and the Queen, Three for Jamie Dawn, Flight Nurse, City of Women.
TV: The Diamond Necklace, Schlitz Playhouse, Lux Video, Montgomery Presents, Matinee, Playhouse 90, Desilu Playhouse, One Step Beyond, Rawhide, Sincerely Maria Palmer (wrote and starred).

PAM, JERRY: Publicist. b. London, England, Oct. 17, 1926. e. Cambridge, London Univ. Reporter, Paris & London; free lance writing, Australia; 1950-53. To U.S. in 1953, on Hollywood Reporter, drama ed. Beverly Hills Citizen, 1953-54; publicist, Moulin Rouge, MGM studios; drama ed., Valley Times 1959-61; partner, Pam and Joseph pub. rel. counsellors; est. Jerry Pam & Associates, pub. rel., April 1965; formed Guttman & Pam, Ltd., 1971. Exec. prod., Highpoint, 1979.

PAMPANINI, SILVANA: Actress. b. Rome, Italy, Sept. 25, 1925. e. Academy of St. Cecilia. Studied singing, several concert appearances. Elected Miss Italia of 1946-47; m.p. debut in Secret of Don Giovanni.
PICTURES INCLUDE: Second Ark, Twin Trouble, O.K. Nero, City Stands Trial, A Husband for Anna, Songs of Half a Century, Songs Songs Songs, Matrimony, Enchanting Enemy, A Day in District Court, Loves of Half a Century, Slave of Sin, Orient Express, Merry Squadron, Princess of the Canary Islands, Mademoiselle Gobette, Don Juan's Night of Love, Roman Tales.

PAN, HERMES: Dance director. In 1935, handled Roberta, RKO stage ensembles. In 1938 won Academy honors for dance direction Damsel in Distress.
PICTURES INCLUDE: Top Hat, Old Man Rhythm, In Person, I Dream Too Much, Follow the Fleet, Swing Time, Shall We Dance, Radio City Revels, Let's Dance, Three Little Words, Excuse My Dust, Texas Carnival, Lovely to Look At, Sombrero, Kiss Me Kate, Student Prince, Hit the Deck, Jupiter's Darling, Meet Me in Las Vegas, Porgy and Bess, Can-Can, Flower Drum Song, Cleopatra, My Fair Lady, Finian's Rainbow, Darling Lilli, The Lost Horizon.
TV: An Evening with Fred Astaire (Emmy Award, choreography), Astaire Time, Sounds of America, Star-times Academy Awards of Songs, Remember How Great, Frances Langford Show.

PANAMA, CHARLES A. (CHUCK): Publicist. b. Chicago, Ill., Feb. 2, 1925. e. Northwestern U., Beloit College, UCLA. Publicist, Los Angeles Jr. Chamber of Commerce; staff So. Calif. sports ed., Los Angeles bureau, INS; pub. 20th Century-Fox Studios; adv. pub. dir., Arcola Pics.; opened L.A. office, John Springer Associates. Assoc. with Jerry Pam & Assoc. Account exec. Rogers, Cowan & Brenner, Inc.; dir. m.p. div., Jim Mahoney & Assoc. v.p. Guttman & Pam, Ltd.; ast. pub. dir., 20th-Fox TV.

PANAMA, NORMAN: Writer, prod., dir. b. Chicago, Ill., April 21, 1918. e. U. Chicago, PhB., 1936. Writer, radio (Bob Hope, Phil Baker, Rudy Vallee); sketches N.Y. stage (Schubert revue Keep off the Grass, 1939). Began screen career as writer 1941; wrote, co-prod. & dir., with Melvin Frank, Li'l Abner, Facts of Life, The Road to Hong Kong, Mr. Blandings Builds His Dream House.
PICTURES INCLUDE: My Favorite Blonde, Happy Go Lucky, Star-Spangled Rhythm, Thank Your Lucky Stars, And the Angels Sing, Road to Utopia, Duffy's Tavern, Our Hearts Were Growing Up, Monsieur Beaucaire, It Had to Be You, Return of October, The Reformer and the Redhead, Strictly Dishonorable, Callaway Went Thataway, Above and Beyond, Knock on Wood, White Christmas, Court Jester, Not With My Wife You Don't, How to Commit

Marriage, Coffee, Tea, or Me. 1975 wrote and directed: I Will, I Will . . . For Now. 1977: directed, Barnaby and Me; 1978 wrote Fade In—Fade Out, The Stewardesses, Li'l Abner, for NBC-TV, 1979. Recent works: Co-authored The Glass Bed (novel), and two plays: A Talent for Murder & The Bats of Portobello.

PANTAGES, CLAYTON G.: Executive. b. Hartford, March 6, 1927. e. Trinity Coll. Served various executive posts for 11 years with 20th Century-Fox; gen. sales mgr. Magna Pictures; Pres., International Coproductions, Inc.

PAPAS, IRENE: Actress. b. near Corinth, Greece. Entered dramatic school at 12. At 16 sang and danced in variety shows. Film debut in 1951 Greek film, Lost Angels; 1958 Greek Popular theatre in Athens.
STAGE: The Idiot, Journey's End, The Merchant of Venice, Inherit the Wind, That Summer, That Fall, Iphigenia in Aulis.
PICTURES INCLUDE: Dead City, The Unfaithful, Atilla the Hun, Theodora, Whirlpool, Tribute to a Bad Man, The Guns of Navarone, Antigone (Best Actress Award, Salonika Film Festival), Electra (Best Actress Award, Salonika Film Festival), Zorba the Greek, The Brotherhood, Anne of a Thousand Days, Z, A Dream of Kings, A Ciascuno il Suo, The Odyssey, The Trojan Women, Moses, Mohammed, Messenger of God, Lion of the Desert.

PAPAZIAN, STEVEN J.: Executive. b. San Diego, CA., July 10, 1944. e. California State University at Northridge. 1968 joined Warner Bros. production cost and auditing dept. 1972, the Burbank Studios—exec. asst. to the president; 1975 director-management services; 1978 director-production services; 1979 v.p.-production services. Member of exec. comm.

PARK, ROBERT H.: Executive. b. Atlanta, Georgia, May 11, 1916. e. University of Texas; Attorney for Jefferson Amusement Co.; now bd. chm., Tercar Theatre Company.

PARKER, BENJAMIN R.: Producer-director. b. New Haven, Conn., Sept. 16, 1909. e. U.C.L.A., Los Angeles and Yale Drama Sch. In m.p. indust. 1939, indep. prod. George Washington Carver. During WW II, dir. 23 training films for Army Air Corps; transferred Signal Corps, Photographic Center, Astoria, L.I., made 39 one-reel musical subjects; many shorts as prod., dir., for General Film prod. Co.

PARKER, ELEANOR: Actress. B. Cedarville, Ohio, June 26, 1922. In Cleveland play group; in summer stock Martha's Vineyard; at Pasadena Community Playhouse.
PICTURES INCLUDE: They Died With Their Boots On, Buses Roar, Mission to Moscow, Between Two Worlds, Very Thought of You, Crime By Night, Last Ride, Never Say Goodbye, Pride of the Marines, Of Human Bondage, Escape Me Never, Woman in White, Voice of the Turtle, Chain Lightning, Caged, Three Secrets, Valentino, Millionaire for Christy, Detective Story, Scaramouche, Above and Beyond, Escape from Fort Bravo, Naked Jungle, Valley of the Kings, Many Rivers to Cross, Interrupted Melody, Man with the Golden Arm, King and Four Queens, Lizzie, Seventh Sin, Home from the Hill, Return to Peyton Place, Madison Avenue, The Oscar, An American Dream, Warning Shot, The Eye of the Cat, The Sound of Music, Sunburn.
TV: Bracken's World, Vanished.

PARKER, FESS: Actor. b. Fort Worth, Tex., Aug. 16, e. U. of Tex., U. of So. Calif. US Navy, 1943–46; national co., Mr. Roberts, 1951; m.p. debut, Untamed Frontier, 1952.
PICTURES INCLUDE: No Room for the Groom, Springfield Rifle, Thunder Over the Plains, Island in the Sky, Kid from Left Field, Take Me to Town, Them, Battle Cry, Davy Crockett, King of the Wild Frontier, Davy Crockett and the River Pirates, Great Locomotive Chase, Westward Ho the Wagons, Old Yeller, The Light in the Forest, The Hangman, The Jayhawkers, Hell Is For Heroes, Smoky.
TV: Mr. Smith Goes to Washington series, Daniel Boone series, Jonathan Winters, Walt Disney Presents, Ed Sullivan, Phyllis Diller, Joey Bishop, Dean Martin, Red Skelton, Glen Campbell.

PARKER, JAMESON: Actor. b. Baltimore, Md. e. Beloit College. Professional stage debut in Washington Theatre Club production, Caligula. Acted with Arena Stage in D.C.; worked in dinner theatres and summer stock. Moved to N.Y., working in TV commercials and touring in play, Equus. Feature film debut in The Bell Jar (1979).
PICTURES: A Small Circle of Friends.
TELEVISION: Series: Somerset, One Life to Live. Movies: Women at West Point, Anatomy of a Seduction.

PARKER, SUZY: Actress. r.n. Cecelia Parker. b. San Antonio, Tex. Oct. 28; e. Schools in N.Y. & Florida. Began career at 17 as fashion model; became known as highest paid fashion model and cover girl in U.S.; to Paris under contract to fashion magazine; m.p. debut as model in Funny Face; signed by 20th-Fox prod. chief Buddy Adler for part opposite Cary Grant in Kiss Them For Me.

PICTURES INCLUDE: Ten North Frederick, The Best of Everything, Circle of Deception, The Interns.

PARKER, WILLARD: Actor. r.n. Worster Van Eps. b. New York City, Feb. 5, 1912. Meter reader; tennis pro; on stage in Johnny Belinda; screen debut in Slight Case of Murder, 1938; in Westerns.
PICTURES INCLUDE: What a Woman, Fighting Guardsman, One Way to Love, Relentless, Wreck of the Hesperus, You Gotta Stay Happy, Calamity Jane and Sam Bass, Bandit Queen, Emergency Wedding, Hunt the Man Down, Caribbean, The Vanquished, Sangaree, Kiss Me Kate, Great Jesse James Raid, The Earth Dies Screaming, Waco, The Great Waltz.

PARKHURST, PEARCE: Owner, novelty adv., ent. b. Gloucester, Mass., Apr. 12, 1919; e. Gloucester H.S., 1936; entered m.p. ind. at Union Hill Theatre, Gloucester, 1931; mgr., New Star, Dover-Foxcroft, Me., 1937; mgr., 1st drive-in, Methuen, Mass. for E.M. Loew, 1946; 1st Lt. Air Force; mgr. theatres in Karachi, India; New England, Va., Indiana, Ohio, N.C. Mich., Fla., Md., Penn., Ky.; present post, 1964, 1st prize winner, nat'l pub. m.p. contest, 1949 scroll winner, 2nd quarter, 1st place winer, 3rd, 4th qtrs. Quigley Awards for Showmanship, 1950. Member: Variety Club, 1950; Allied Theatres of Mich.; apptd. 2nd v.p. 1954; first v.p. 1955; Michigan Allied Chairman State Allied Convention 1953. Mgr. Round Table, M.P. Herald; Lansing C. of C.: Amer. Legion; Veterans of Fgn. Wars; Nat'l Geo. Soc.; Nat'l Travelers Club. Adv. Specialty Guild, Premium Adv. Assn. of America, Inc.; operator own spec. adv. business, Pearce Parkhurst Enterprises, 1968, catering to theatre trade; with COMPO regional committee, 1954–55; Idea Advertising Budco Quality Theatres, 1967; Chakeres Theatres, 1964; Florida State Theatres, 1968; adv. spec. distrib. to theatre trade, 1969–82. Also mail order business with complete line Elvis Presley souvenirs for trade and public, 1977–82.

PARKINSON, ALLEN: Executive. b. Rexburg, Idaho, Jan. 26, 1910. e. Utah Agricultural College, Logan, Utah; pres. Sleepeze Drug Co.; dir of sls., Mercury Record Company, pres. Movieland Wax Museum.

PARKS, BERT: Announcer, m.c. b. Atlanta, Ga. Announcer, then chief announcer in Atlanta radio station; announcer, network, N.Y., for Eddie Cantor; m.c. for Xavier Cugat's show; U.S. Army, WWII; radio shows include Break the Bank, Stop the Music, Double or Nothing.
TV: Break the Bank, Stop the Music.

PARKS, GORDON: Director, writer, photographer, composer. Photo-journalist.
AUTHOR: The Learning Tree; A Choice of Weapons; A Poet and His Camera; Whispers of Intimate Things; In Love; Born Black, Moments Without Proper Names, Flavio, To Smile in Autumn, Shannon.
PICTURES INCLUDE: The Learning Tree, Shaft, Shaft's Big Score, Super Cops, Leadbelly.

PARKS, MICHAEL: Actor. b. 1938. Made m.p. debut in Wild Seed, 1964.
PICTURES INCLUDE: Bus Riley's Back in Town, The Bible, The Idol, The Happening, The Last Hard Men, Sidewinder One. ffolkes, Hard Country.
TV: Along Came Bronson (series, numerous TV movies. 1973: Can Ellen Be Saved? 1976: Savage Bees.

PARKS, RICHARD: Executive. e. Duke University; University of North Carolina (M.A. in theatre arts). Taught theatre arts at Duke. Associated with Curtis Brown, Ltd., literary agency, for 8 years, specializing in m.p. rights for literary materials and representing authors. Joined United Artists in December, 1978, as exec. asst. to Steven Bach, then snr. v.p. for east coast production. In 1980 promoted to v.p.—production.

PARRISH, ROBERT R.: Director, producer. b. Columbus, Georgia, Jan. 4; actor before joining RKO in 1933, first as assistant director, then film editor. With various companies since, including 20th Century-Fox, Universal, Columbia, United Artists, J. Arthur Rank, etc. Won Academy Award, best film editing, Body and Soul, 1947. U.S. Navy 1941–45; won documentary Academy Award, 1942 and 1943 for Battle of Midway and December 7th. Formed own independent production company, Trimark Productions, Inc., 1955.
PICTURES INCLUDE: City Lights, All Quiet on the Western Front, The Divine Lady, A Double Life, Caught, No Minor Vices, All the King's Men, Cry Danger (dir.) The Mob, San Francisco Story, Assignment—Paris, My Pal Gus, Shoot First, The Purple Plain, Lucy Gallant, Fire Down Below, Saddle the Wind, The Wonderful Country, In the French Style, Up From the Beach, Casino Royale, The Bobo, Duffy, A Town Called Bastard, Flashman.

PARRY, GORDON: Director, producer. b. Aintree, Liverpool, Eng., July 24, 1908; p. Studied electrical eng. before entering m.p. ind. as actor in 1929. Joined Gaumont-British in 1931 as assist. dir. and remained for four years, then prod. mgr. Rock Studios. Returned to GB as assist. to Walter Forde on King of the Damned. Left GB to become prod. mgr. for Soskin Prod. Ltd. and Amalgamated Studios; prod. television in conjunction with E.M.I. Author radio plays and short stories. Unit mgr. Ealing Studios propaganda shorts department. In 1942 under contract to Two Cities Films, 2nd unit.

PICTURES INCLUDE: In Which We Serve, The Demi-Paradise, English Without Tears, The Way to the Stars, Beau Brummell, Bond Street, Third Time Lucky, Now Barabbas, Three Men and a Girl, Midnight Episode, Tom Brown's Schooldays, Night Was Our Friend, Women of Twilight, Innocents of Paris, Front Page Story, Fast and Loose, Yank in Ermine, Sailor Beware, Touch of the Sun, Surgeon's Knife, Tread Softly Stranger, Friends and Neighbors, The Navy Lark.

TV: Robin Hood.

PARSONS, ESTELLE: Actress. b. Marblehead, Mass. e. Connecticut College for Women, Bachelor's Degree in Political Science. Attended Boston U. Law School. Helped harvest crops in England with the Women's Land Army. Was active in politics; worked for the Committee for the Nation's Health in Wash. and the Republican Finance Committee in Marblehead, Mass. Joined NBC-TV's Today Show as prod. asst.; then writer, feature producer and commentator. Appeared in two Julius Monk revues, Jerry Herman's Nightcap and the Three-Penny Opera. Dramatic stage debut, Mrs. Dally Has A Lover (won Theatre World Award). Has appeared with the Lincoln Center Repertory Theatre, Mahagonny. Acad. Award, Best Supporting Actress for Bonnie and Clyde.

STAGE: Next Time I'll Sing to You (Obie Award), In the Summer House (Obie Award), Ready When You Are, C.B. Malcolm, The Seven Descents of Myrtle, and Miss Reardon Drinks a Little, The Norman Conquests, Ladies of the Alamo, Miss Margarida's Way, Pirates of Penzance.

PICTURES INCLUDE: Rachel, Rachel, Don't Drink the Water, Strangers, Watermelon Man, I Never Sang For My Father, I Walk the Line, Two People, For Pete's Sake.

PARSONS, HARRIET: Producer, writer. b. Burlington, Ia. e. Wellesley Coll.; daughter of the late Louella O. Parsons, Hearst syn. m.p. columnist. Joined MGM scenario staff 1928, assoc. ed. Photoplay Magazine, 1929–30; mag. contrib. 1930–33; columnist, Universal Service, International News Service, 1931–44; on m.p. staff Los Angeles Examiner, 1935–44; Hollywood commentator, NBC, 1938; author, prod., dir. Screen Snapshots, Columbia, 1933–40; in 1940 joined Republic as writer, prod., dir., commentator of Meet the Stars series; assoc. prod. Republic, 1941–43. prod., writer, RKO 1943–55; 1956 TCF-TV. Member: Wellesley Alumnae Assn., Zeta Alpha, Hollywood Women's Press Club, Producers Guild of America, Acad. of M.P. Arts & Sciences.

PICTURES INCLUDE: The Enchanted Cottage, Night Song, I Remember Mama, Never a Dull Moment, Clash by Night, Susan Slept Here.

PARSONS, LINDSLEY: Pres., Completion Service Co., Hollywood. Mng. dir., Linpar Cinema Completion Corp., Toronto. b. Tacoma, Wash., Sept. 12. e. U. Calif. (L.A.) On ed. staff City News Service, L.A.: Alhambra Post-Advocate; Calexico Chronicle; Santa Rosa Press Democrat; Humboldt Times; San Marino News (ed. & pub.). Joined Monogram 1931 as pub. dir. In 1933 author s.p. Sagebrush Trails; then wrote orig. s.p. Westerns for Monogram, Republic, Grand Nat'l. In 1939 assoc. prod. Tough Kid; from 1940 prod. numerous westerns; prod. Wayne Morris & James Oliver Curwood series for Allied Artists; prod. Motion Pictures Int'l, 1956–72.

PICTURES INCLUDE: Rocky Rhythm Inn, Casa Manana, Big Timber, Call of the Klondike, Sierra Passage, Yukon, Manhunt, Yellow Fin, Northwest Territory, Desert Pursuit, Torpedo Alley, Jack Slade, Loophole, Cry Vengeance, Finger Man, Return of Jack Slade, Come On, The Intruder, Cruel Tower, Dragon Wells Massacre, Portland Expose, Oregon Passage, Wolf Larsen, Crash Boat, The Purple Gang, Mara of the Wilderness, Good Times, The Big Cube, Bravo Hennessey, Coasts of War.

TV: Gray Ghost TV series.

PARTON, DOLLY: Singer-Composer-Actress. b. Sevierville, TN, Jan. 19, 1946. Gained fame as country music singer, composer and radio and TV personality. Many awards for recordings.

PICTURES: Nine to Five, The Best Little Whorehouse in Texas.

TELEVISION: Porter Wagoner Show, Cass Walker program, Bill Anderson Show, Wilbur Bros. Show.

PARTRIDGE, DEREK: Actor. Born London, England. 1935. Educated Charterhouse. Entered business in 1958 as documentary scriptwriter/assistant director with Film Producer's Guild. Films (as actor): Incident At Midnight, The Verdict, The Murder Game, The High Bright Sun, King and Country, Thunderball, Where The Spies Are. 1966–67: In

Rome, films: 7 Donne Per I MacGregor, Madigan's Millions, Cjmango, Don Giovannino. 1968–70: In Hollywood, TV: Star Trek, Robin Hood, My Friend Tony. Films: The Killing of Sister George, Fiuggi (Rome). 1971–72: Acting in Britain (after 5 years abroad). Many TV plays and series. TV commercials, voice-overs, commentaries. 1971: Directed and filmed clay-pigeon shooting film in Europe for ICI.

PASSER, IVAN: Director-Writer. b. Czechoslovakia. Began career as writer.

PICTURES INCLUDE: Writer: Loves of Blonde, Fireman's Ball. Director: Intimate Lighting, Born To Win, Law and Disorder, Crime and Passion, The Silver Bears, Cutter and Bone.

PASSMORE, HENRY: Producer. b. London, Eng., Nov. 28, 1905. e. Univ. College School (London). Enter m.p. ind. in 1929; gen. mgr. A.C.T. Films, Ltd.; joined Grendon Films, 1954; org. Croydon Passmore Prod., Ltd.; prod., Delavine Affair, Children Galore; prod. supvr., Charter Film Prod., Ltd., Guild Holdings & Augusta Prod. Man. dir. Reporters International, 1969; consult. prod. to De Beers Ind. Diamond Div.

PICTURES INCLUDE: Brothers in Law, Lucky Jim.

PASTER, GARY M.: Executive. b. St. Louis, Missouri, July 4, 1943. e. University of Missouri—B.A., U.C.L.A., U.S.C.—Graduate School of Business. 1970 joined Columbia Pictures, assistant to v.p. of facilities and operations division; 1972 joined The Burbank Studios as assist. to the president and as treasurer. 1976 v.p.—administration and chairman of the exec. committee. September, 1977 president. Board of Directors/Trustees: Contract Services Administration Trust Fund, St. Joseph Medical Center Institute, Permanent Charities Committee of Entertainment Industry. Member: Academy of Motion Picture Arts and Sciences, Academy of Television Arts and Sciences, Los Angeles Film Development Council, Advisory Commission—California Motion Picture Council, Hollywood Radio and T.V. Society. Board member of the Permanent Charities Committee of the Entertainment Industry, Board of Trustees of the St. Joseph Medical Center Foundation Board of Trustees Oakwood School, and alternate Trustee of the Contract Services Administration Trust Fund.

PASTERNAK, JOE: Producer. b. Szilagysomlyo, Hungary, Sept. 19, 1901. 2nd asst. dir. Paramount 1923; asst. dir. Universal (Hollywood), 1926, then prod. mgr. Berlin; made pictures in Vienna and Budapest, returned to Hollywood 1937; assoc. prod. then prod. A "Champion of Champion producers" in Fame Ratings.

PICTURES INCLUDE: Zwei Menschen, Unter Falscher Flagge, Grosse Scehnsucht, Unsichtbare Front, Fraulein Paprika, Gruss Und Gruss, Veronika, Scandal in Budapest, Csibi, Spring Parade, Katherine, Three Smart Girls, 100 Men and a Girl, Mad About Music, That Certain Age, Three Smart Girls Grow up, Destry Rides Again, It's a Date, Nice Girl, It Started With Eve, Presenting Lily Mars, Thousands Cheer, Two Girls and a Sailor, Music for Millions, Thrill of a Romance, Anchors Aweigh, Her Highness and the Bellboy, Two Sisters from Boston, Holiday in Mexico, No Leave No Love, This Time for Keeps, Three Daring Daughters, On an Island With You, Date With Judy, In the Good Old Summertime, Big City, Unfinished Dance, Nancy Goes to Rio, Summer Stock, That Midnight Kiss, Toast of New Orleans, The Great Caruso, Rich, Young and Pretty, The Strip, Merry Widow, Skirts Ahoy!, Because You're Mine, Small Town Girl, Latin Lovers, Easy to Love, Flame and the Flesh, Student Prince, Athena, Hit the Deck, Love Me or Leave Me, Meet Me in Las Vegas, Opposite Sex, 10,000 Bedrooms, This Could be the Night, Where the Boys Are, Jumbo, A Ticklish Affair, Girl Happy, Penelope.

PATERSON, NEIL: Novelist, screenwriter. b. Scotland, 1916. e. Edinburgh Univ. War Service Lt. R.N.V.R. Early career as novelist. Awarded Atlantic Award in Literature, 1946. Dir. Grampian TV Chmn. of Production; films of Scotland. Vice-chmn. Scottish Arts Council; Gov. Pitlochry Thea.; Gov. National Film School. Former Gov. British Film Institute. Member Arts Council Gt. Britain.

NOVELS: The China Run, Behold Thy Daughter and Delilah, Man on the Tight Rope.

PICTURES INCLUDE: Man on a Tight Rope, The Little Kidnappers, Woman for Joe, High Tide at Noon, The Shiralee, Innocent Sinners, Room at the Top (s.p. Acad. Award, 1960), The Spiral Road, The Golden Fool, The Forty Days of Musa Dagh, Keeper of My Heart.

PATRICK, C. L.: Theatre Executive. b. Honaker, Va., Dec. 6, 1918. Pres. of Fuqua Industries, which owns Martin Theatres and Gulf States Theatres. Prior to this was pres. and chm. of Martin Theatres. Member NATO exec. Comm.; International Ambassador of Variety; Motion Picture Pioneer of the Year in 1976.

PATRICK, GEORGE: Art director, b. Salida, Colo. May 21, 1905. e. U. of So. Calif., 1923–27. Entered m.p. ind. as junior draftsman, First National Pictures, 1928; asst. art dir., art dir. for many prod.; designed, supervised construction of Frontierland section of Disneyland, 1955.

PICTURES INCLUDE: Deadline U.S.A., Beneath the 12-Mile Reef, The Racers.

PATRICK, NIGEL: Actor, director. b. London, Eng., May 2, 1913; e. private. Stage debut in The Life Machine, 1932. Screen debut, Mrs. Pim of Scotland Yard 1939; served with H.M. Forces, 1939–46. Top ten British money making star, 1952, 1953.

PICTURES INCLUDE: Uneasy Terms, Spring in Park Lane, Noose, Silent Dust, Jack of Diamonds, The Perfect Woman, Operation Disaster, Trio, Pandora & the Flying Dutchman, The Browning Version, Young Wives Tale, Encore, The Sound Barrier, Who Goes There, Meet Me Tonight, Pickwick Papers, Grand National Night (Wicked Wife), Forbidden Cargo, Sea Shall Not Have Them, Prize of Gold, All for Mary, Raintree County, How to Murder a Rich Uncle, Count Five and Die, The Man Inside, Sapphire, League of Gentlemen, The Trials of Oscar Wilde, Johnny Nobody, The Informers, The Battle of Britain, The Virgin Soldiers, The Executioner, Tales from the Crypt, The Great Waltz, The Mackintosh Man, The Silver Bears.

TV: Zero One series.

PATTERSON, RICHARD L.: Executive. b. St. Louis, Mo., November 1924. B.A. U.C.L.A., 1950; graduate work and teaching Theatre Arts Dept., U.C.L.A. until 1952; film dept. and dir. TV until 1955; H.N. Swanson Literary Agency handling TV dept.; head literary dept., Wm. Morris Agency to 1959; chmn., man. dir. Paramount British Pictures, Ltd., 1959; chmn. Seven Arts Prods. (U.K.) Ltd.: dir. Bryanston Seven Arts, 1961; assoc. Of Human Bondage; prod. The Wild Affair. Joined Christopher Mann Ltd., 1964; int. man. dir., P.L. Representation, 1967; prod. exec. MGM, 1972.

PAUL, M. B.: Cameraman, director. r.n. Morrison Bloomfield Paul. b. Montreal, Canada. Sept. 30. e. De Paul U.; newsreel, publicity picture service; partner, Seymour Studios, 1930–33; film test biz. own studio. Hollywood, 1933–35; prod. adv. films, asst. in N.Y. E.W. Hammons, 1945–47; Acad. Award, one-piece color translucent background system, 1950. Dir. of photography, optical effects, Daystar, United Artists, Outer Limits, 1963; designed, patented, Scenoramic process, 1965. Camera, Paradise Road. Features, Film project supervision A/V consult. Sceno 360 surround system development. Mem. AMPAS, Friars, SMPTE.

PAUL, RALPH: Announcer, m.c. b. Denver, Oct. 11, 1920. e. U. of Denver, 1945. Prod., dir. news ed. announcer, m.c. & narrator for radio stations KVOD, Denver; KTSM, El Paso; WITH, Baltimore; WOR, N.Y.; now free-lance, radio & TV, N.Y.

TV: Strike It Rich, Sound Stage, Television Playhouse.

PAULEY, JANE: Program Hostess-Reporter. b. Indianapolis, Ind., Oct. 31, 1950. e. Indiana Univ. Involved in Indiana state politics before joining WISH-TV, Indianapolis, as reporter. Co-anchored midday news reports and anchored weekend news reports. Co-anchor of nightly news at WMAQ-TV, NBC station in Chicago. Joined Today show in October, 1976, as featured regular, prior to which had made guest appearances on that program.

PAVAN, MARISA: Actress, r.n. Marisa Pierangeli. b. Cagliari, Sardinia, June 19, 1932; e. Torquado Tasso coll.; s. Pier Angeli, actress. Came to U.S. 1950; m.p. debut in What Price Glory.

PICTURES INCLUDE: Down Three Dark Streets, Drum Beat, Rose Tattoo, Diane, Man in the Gray Flannel Suit, John Paul Jones, Solomon and Sheba, Midnight Story.

PAVLIK, JOHN M.: Executive. b. Melrose, Iowa, Dec. 3, 1939. e. Univ. of Minnesota, B.A. 1963. Reporter, Racine (Wis.) Journal-Times, San Bernardino (Calif.) Sun-Telegram, 1963–66; Writer, News Bureau, Pacific Telephone, Los Angeles, 1966–68; assistant director of public relations, Association of Motion Picture and Television Producers, 1968–72; director of public relations, 1972–78; vice-president, 1978–79; executive administrator, Academy of Motion Picture Arts and Sciences, 1979–present. Member, board of trustees and Executive Committee, and chairman, Awards and Honors Committee, Motion Picture and Television Fund; member, board of directors, Permanent Charities Committee of the Entertainment Industries; member, board of directors, Hollywood Chamber of Commerce; vice-president, Los Angeles Film Development Committee, 1977–78, member, executive council, 1974–; special consultant, California Motion Picture Council, 1974–79.

PAVLOW, MURIEL: Actress. b. June 27, 1924. e. England, France & Switzerland. Stage debut in Dear Octupus, 1938; screen debut in Quiet Wedding.

PICTURES INCLUDE: Night Boat to Dublin, Shop at Sly Corner, It Started in Paradise, The Net (Project M7), Malta Story, Conflict of Wings (Fuss Over Feathers), Doctor in the House, Simon and Laura, Reach for the Sky, Eye Witness, Tiger in the Smoke, Doctor at Large, Rooney, Whirlpool, Meet Miss Marple.

PAXTON, JOHN: Writer. b. Kansas City, Mo., Mar. 21, 1911. e. U. Missouri, B.J. 1934. Publicist, 1935–36; assoc. ed., Stage mag. 1937–39; free lance 1939–41; pub. New York Theatre Guild, 1941. To Hollywood as writer 1942.

PICTURES INCLUDE: Murder My Sweet, Cornered, So Well Remembered, Cross Fire, My Pal Wolf, Crack-Up, Rope of Sand, Of Men and Music, Fourteen Hours, Wild One, The Cobweb, Prize of Gold, Pick-up Alley, How to Murder a Rich Uncle, On the Beach, Kotch.

PAY, WILLIAM: Executive. b. London, England; joined London office Quigley Publications. Served in RAF, 1941–46; rejoined Quigley; dir. Burnup Service Ltd., 1951; London news ed., Quigley Pub., 1955. Dir., Quigley Pub. Ltd., 1961; appt. mgr. dir., 1963; mgr. dir., Burnup Company. Appt. Sec. British Kinematograph Sound & TV Society. Conference Co-ordinator biennial Intern. Technology Conferences in London, 1975–81.

PAYNE, JOHN: Actor. b. Roanoke, Va.; e. Mercersburg Acad., Pa., Roanoke Coll. of Virginia and Columbia. On radio programs. Stage debut, 1973, Good News.

PICTURES INCLUDE: Dodsworth, Wings of the Navy, Indianapolis Speedway, Kid Nightingale, Star dust, Maryland, Great Profile, Tin Pan Alley, King of the Lumberjacks, Tear Gas Squad, Great American Broadcast, Sun Valley Serenade, Week-End in Havana, Remember the Day, To the Shores of Tripoli, Hello Frisco Hello, The Dolly Sisters, Sentimental Journey, Razor's Edge, Wake Up and Dream, Miracle on 34th Street, Larceny, Saxon Charm, El Paso, Crooked Way, Captain China, Eagle and Hawk, Passage West, Crosswinds, Blazing Forest, Caribbean, The Vanquished, Kansas City, Confidential, Raiders of the 7 Seas, 99 River Street, Rails into Laramie, Silver Lode, Hell's Island, Santa Fe Passage, Road to Denver, Tennessee's Partner, Slightly Scarlet, Rebel in Town, Bail Out at 43,000, Hidden Fear.

PAYNE, NORMAN: Artists' and writers' manager. b. London, England. Ent. entertainment ind., 1939. Early career music, then formed talent agency, J.P. Productions, 1945. Later bought by MCA, 1951. Became dir. MCA and head of light ent. for theatres and TV throughout Europe. On MCA terminating reformed agency, Albemarle Scripts (London) Ltd. and Albemarle Films Int., including Norman Payne Agency, TV offices also in Germany & Australia.

PEACH, MARY: Actress. b. Durban, South Africa, 1934. Ent. films 1957. TV appearances include Ghosts, The Rat Wife, The Master Builder, Love Story, Hadley, Somerset Maugham, Can You Keep a Secret?, Cat on a Hot Tin Roof, Blind Love, Disraeli, Children at the Gods, Fox.

PICTURES INCLUDE: Room at the Top, Follow That Horse, No Love for Johnnie, A Gathering of Eagles, Ballad in Blue, Scrooge.

RECENT THEATRE: Birthday Run, The Marriage, When the Music Stops, Hilda, Don't Gas the Blacks, Old Times, The Chairman, The Autumn Garden.

PEAKER, E. J.: Actress, singer, dancer. Edra Jeanne Peaker, b. Tulsa, Okla., Feb. 22. e. Univ. of New Mexico, Univ. of Vienna, Austria. Stage debut Bye, Bye Birdie; m.p. debut Hello, Dolly. Films include All American Boy.

TV: That's Life series, The Flying Nun, That Girl, Movie of Week, Love American Style, Odd Couple, Police Woman, Rockford Files, Get Christy Love.

PECK, GREGORY: Actor, producer. b. La Jolla, Calif. April 5, 1916; U. Calif.; Neighborhood Playhouse Sch. of Dramatics. On dramatic stage (The Doctor's Dilemma, The Male Animal, Once in a Lifetime, The Play's the Thing, You Can't Take It With You, Sons and Soldiers, etc.); on screen 1944 in Days of Glory. Voted one of ten best Money-Making Stars Motion Picture Herald-Fame Poll, 1947, 1952. Co-prod. and starred in Big Country, for his company, Anthony Productions; prod. the Trial of the Catonsville Nine, The Dove (St. George Productions).

PICTURES INCLUDE: Keys of the Kingdom, Valley of Decision, Spellbound, Yearling, Duel in the Sun, Macomber Affair, Gentleman's Agreement, Paradine Case, Yellow Sky, 12 O'Clock High, Great Sinner, The Gunfighter, Only the Valiant, David and Bathsheba, Captain Horatio Hornblower, World in His Arms, Snows of Kilimanjaro, Roman Holiday, Night People, Man With a Million, Purple Plains, Man in the Gray Flannel Suit, Moby Dick, Designing Woman, The Bravados, Pork Chop Hill, On the Beach, Beloved Infidel, Guns of Navarone, Cape Fear, To Kill a Mocking Bird, Captain Newman, M.D., Behold a Pale Horse, Mirage, Arabesque, MacKenna's Gold, Stalking Moon, The Chairman, Marooned, I Walk the Line, Shootout, Billy Two Hats, The Omen, MacArthur, The Boys from Brazil, The Sea Wolves.

PECKINPAH, SAM: Writer-director. b. Fresno, Calif., Feb. 21, 1925. e. B.A., Fresno State College; M.A. University of Southern Calif. TV writer, Gunsmoke, awarded Writers Guild nom. for Best Writing Achievement in TV for specific segment. 20th Century Fox Hour, nom. from Writers Guild Best Achievement in TV. Created the Rifleman (dir. first five shows). Wrote script for Dick Powell's Zane Grey Theatre which became the pilot for the Westerner, which he wrote, prod. and dir. The Westerner received Producers Guild Nom. as Best Filmed Series. Also wrote-dir., Klondike and Stage 1967 production of Noon Wine (Screen Directors Guild Award.) Member: Directors Guild of America, Writers Guild of America, Acad. of M.P. Arts & Sciences.

PICTURES INCLUDE: Deadly Companions, Ride the High Country (won Belgian Film Festival Grand Prize, Mexican Film Festival Award, Best Film); Major Dundee, The Glory, Guys (writer), Villa Rides (writer), The Wild Bunch, The Ballad of Cable Hogue, Straw Dogs, Junior Bonner, The Getaway, Pat Garrett and Billy the Kid, Bring Me the Head of Alfredo Garcia, The Killer Elite, The Cross of Iron, Convoy.

PEERCE, LARRY: Director. b. Bronx, N.Y.
PICTURES INCLUDE: One Potato, Two Potato, The Incident, Goodbye Columbus, The Sporting Club, The Big TNT Show, A Separate Peace, Ash Wednesday, The Other Side of the Mountain, Two Minute Warning, The Other Side of the Mountain-Part II, The Bell Jar, Why Would I Lie?

PELLATT, JOHN: Production Executive. Abandoned school for theatre at age of 14. Became stage manager before serving in H.M. Forces. Then became assistant director for Warner Bros., MGM, London Films, etc. Since 1955 worked as prod. manager/assoc. producer with British Lion, Columbia, Paramount, United Artists, Ivan Tors, American International. Also while assistant gen. prod. mgr. 20th Century Fox, associated with Inn of Sixth Happiness, Roots of Heaven, The Blue Angel, Sons and Lovers, Sink the Bismark.
TV: Series for Incorporated Television Espionage. Worked in Europe, Middle and Far East, India, East and North Africa, Congo, Bahamas, Australia, Hollywood, Southern Africa.
PICTURES INCLUDE: Noose, The Wooden Horse, Silent Dust, Lavender Hill Mob, Man in the White Suit, Ivanhoe, Innocents in Paris, Mogambo, Knights of the Round Table, A Kid for Two Farthings, Oh Rosalinda, The Twelve Days of Christmas, The Captain's Paradise, Zarak Khan, The Green Man, St. Trinians, Only Two Can Play, They're a Weird Mob, Age of Consent, Count Five and Die, Help, The Revolutionary, Wuthering Heights, Elephant Country, Who Slew Auntie Roo, Tower of Evil, The Zoo Gang TV series, Born Free TV series (Kenya), The Diamond Mercenaries (Killer Force in Us), One Away. (South & S.W. Africa).

PENN, ARTHUR: Director. b. Philadelphia. e. Black Mountain College, Asheville, N.C., and Universities of Perugia and Florence in Italy. Began as TV dir. in 1953, twice winner of Sylvania Award. Dir. stage plays Two for the Seesaw, Miracle Worker, Toys in the Attic, All the Way Home, Golden Boy. Entered m.p. as dir. of Left-Handed Gun in 1958.
PICTURES INCLUDE: Miracle Worker, Micky One, The Chase, Bonnie and Clyde, Alice's Restaurant, Little Big Man, Visions of Eight, Night Moves, The Missouri Breaks, Four Friends.

PEPPARD, GEORGE: Actor. b. Detroit, Mich., Oct. 1, e. Dearborn H.S., Carnegie Tech., BA, Fine Arts. U.S. Marine Corps. Legit. stage debut, Pittsburgh Playhouse, 1949. Worked as mason, construction laborer, fencing instructor, Braddock, Pa. Signed by Sam Spiegel to appear in The Strange One.
STAGE: Girls of Summer, The Pleasure of His Company.
PICTURES INCLUDE: Pork Chop Hill, Home from the Hill, The Subterraneans, Breakfast At Tiffany's, How the West Was Won, The Victors, The Carpetbaggers, The Third Day, Operation Crossbow, The Blue Max, Tobruk, Rough Night in Jericho, P.J., House of Cards, What's So Bad About Feeling Good, Pendulum, Cannon for Cordoba, The Executioner, One More Train to Rob, The Groundstar Conspiracy, Newman's Law, Damnation Alley, Five Days From Home, Your Ticket Is No Longer Valid, Battle Beyond the Stars, Race to the Yankee Zephyr.
TV: Little Moon of Alban, Suspicion, U.S. Steel Hour, Alfred Hitchcock Presents, Matinee Theatre, Alcoa-Goodyear Playhouse, Studio One, Hallmark Hall of Fame, Banacek, The Bravos, Doctors Hospital, Story of Dr. Sam Sheppard, Crisis in Mid-Air, Torn Between Two Lovers.

PEPPER, L. J.: Exhibitor. Entered industry with Wilby-Kincey org., Selma, Alabama, 1923, while still in Selma H.S. With Wilby-Kincey 23 years. Opened own Center Theatre, Kingsport, Tenn., 1949. Went to Birmingham to open Eastwood Mall Theatre, 1964. General mgr., Cobb Theatres, two years. General mgr. Jefferson Amusement Co. with theatres in Birmingham and Selma, Ala.

PEPPERCORN, CARL: Executive. b. New York. e. NYU. Ent. film ind. FBO (forerunner of RKO), held var. sls. positions,

home office and branches. Lt. Comm. US Navy, WW II; pres. Military Bank of Naples, sales mgr. NY branch RKO; asst. to Eastern sales mgr., RKO; gen'l sales mgr., RKO Canada; pres. Dairy-maid Chocolate Co., Toronto; v.p. Fairweather Dept. Stores, Canada; chmn. bd. Andako Mining Co., Canada; v.p. & gen'l sales mgr. Continental Dist. Inc.; v.p. & gen'l sales mgr. Embassy Pictures, Inc.; exec. v.p. and gen'l sales mgr. Cinema V Inc, pres. & sls. mgr., U.M. Film Distributors and Peppercorn-Wormser Film Distributors; Diversified Film Representatives, Inc., Peppercorn Film Enterprises.

PERAKOS, SPERIE P.: Executive. b. N. Britain, Conn., Nov. 12, 1915. e. Cheshire Acad., Yale, Harvard Law School, Student mgr., Stanley-Warner thtrs., 1939-40; Perakos thtrs., 1940-41; Fellow, Pierson Coll., Yale, 1946-present; Yale Alumni Bd., 1949 to present; Yale Alumni Film Bd. 1952 to present; member Alumni Council for Yale Drama School; past pres. Yale Club of N. Britain, Conn.; dir. of Films & Filmings Seminars, Pierson Coll., Yale; prod. Antigone, 1962; pres. Norma Film Prod., Inc., 1962 to present. Past pres. and now chm. Yale's Peabody Museum Associates and member of the University Council of the Peabody Museum. Pres., Perakos Theatres.

PERCIVAL, LANCE: Actor, singer. b. Sevenoaks, Kent, England, 1933.
PICTURES INCLUDE: V.I.P.'s, Yellow Rolls Royce, Mrs. Brown You've Got A Lovely Daughter, Darling Lili.
TV: That Was The Week That Was, Lance Percival Show.

PEREIRA, HAL: A.I.A. Art Director. Unit art dir., Paramount, 1942-46, special assignments. Paramount Home Office exec. staff for domestic and international companies 1947-50; appointed super. art dir., all films Paramount Studios, 1950; art dir., Rose Tatoo (Academy Award, best black & white art dir., 1955). 29 Academy nominations; 1968 design consul. William L. Pereira & Assoc., consultant motion pictures, theatres, television, leisure parks. Staff: Loyola Marymount University. School of Communications & Fine Arts 1976-78.

PERGAMENT, HARVEY: Producer, distributor; b. Detroit, Mich. June 18. e. Ohio State U.; NYU. With Air Transport Command, Army Air Forces, World War II. From 1928-37 gen. mgr. & sec. Film Exchange, Inc., N.Y. in 1937 org. and was pres., Pictorial Film Library, Inc.; gen. foreign sales mgr., Natl. Pictures, Inc., N.Y. Resigned 1940 to form Cavalcade Pictures; also Crystal Pictures, Inc.; ed. foreign language versions After Mein Kampf, Adventure in Music; disposed of interest in Crystal Pictures on entering armed forces, 1944. In 1945 formed Cavalcade Pictures, Hollywood; pres. thereafter; Cavalcade Television Programs, Inc. & Cavalcade Pictures Int'l Corp., 1951; foreign sales rep.; Eve Prods. Inc.; Essence Prods.; Phaeton Int'l Pics.; Savoy Road Show Pics.; Bernard Glasser Prod., Balut Prod., Belish Prod. Inc., Unusual Films, Inc., Interfilm Nassau Ltd., Timely Prods., Inc., Fountain Films, Woo Woo Prods., Sudan Prods., Inc., Lyman Dayton Prods., Inc., IPC Prod. Corp., VIP, Ltd., Doc-Art Prods., Premier Investment Corp., Zenith Int'l Films, Iota Prod., Lau Film Co., (Hong Kong), Ausable Co., Inc., Samwa Co. (Korea), Cosa Nueva Prod., R.M. Film Intern'l, Ad-Art Agency, Bill Copeland Prod.

PERINAL, GEORGES: Cinematographer. b. Paris, France, 1897. Ent. m.p. ind. 1913 as cameraman, French pictures; silent pictures until 1929; Jean de la Lune, David Golder, etc.; from 1929 several pictures for Rene Clair, Souls les Toits de Paris, Le Million, A Nous La Liberte, 14 Juillet; in 1933 to England; since cameraman many feature pictures for various Brit. cos. (London Films, B&D, United Artists, 20th-Fox, MGM-Korda, etc.); Acad. Award, color photog., 1940, Thief of Bagdad.
PICTURES INCLUDE: The Private Life of Henry VIII, Catherine the Great, Escape Me Never, Rembrandt, I Claudius, Under the Red Robe, Drums, The Four Feathers, Dangerous Moonlight, First of the Few, Colonel Blimp, Perfect Strangers, Man About the House, Ideal Husband, Fallen Idol, Forbidden Street, The Mudlark, No Highway in the Sky, House on the Square, Three Cases of Murder, Man Who Loved Redheads, Woman for Joe, Satellite in the Sky, Loser Take All, Lady Chatterley's Lover, King in New York, St. Joan, Bonjour Tristesse, Tom Thumb, Honeymoon, Serious Charge, Once More With Feeling, The Day They Robbed the Bank of England, Oscar Wilde.

PERKINS, ANTHONY: Actor. b. New York City, Apr. 14, 1932. Columbia U., Rollins College. Broadway stage in Tea and Sympathy. Dr. Steambath, 1970. Wrote s.p. Last of Sheila, 1973.
TV: Kraft Theatre, Studio One, U.S. Steel Hour, Armstrong Theatre.
PICTURES INCLUDE: The Actress, Friendly Persuasion, The Lonely Man, Fear Strikes Out, The Tin Star, This Bitter Earth, Desire Under the Elms, The Matchmaker, Green Mansions, On the Beach, Tall Story, Psycho, Goodbye Again, Phaedra, The Trial, The Fool Killer, The Champagne Murders, Pretty Poison, Catch 22, Someone Be-

hind the Door, Ten Days' Wonder, WUSA, Play It As It Lays, Lovin' Molly, Murder on the Orient Express, Mahogany, Remember My Name, Winter Kills, The Black Hole, ffolkes.
STAGE: Greenwillow, Look Homeward Angel, Steambath, Equus.

PERKINS, JOHN HENRY ROWLAND II: Executive. b. July 10, 1934, Los Angeles. e. Univ. So. Calif., UCLA. Joined William Morris Agency, 1959; exec. in TV dept. In January, 1975, co-founded Creative Artists Agency, of which is senior partner and first pres. Member Hollywood Radio & TV Society since 1964, and Academy of TV Arts & Sciences since 1962.

PERLMUTTER, DAVID M.: Producer. b. Toronto, Canada, 1934. e. University of Toronto. Pres., Quadrant Films Ltd.
PICTURES INCLUDE: The Neptune Factor, 1972; Sunday In The Country, 1973; It Seemed Like A Good Idea At The Time, 1974; Love at First Sight, Find the Lady, 1975; Blood and Guts, The Third Walker, Two Solitudes, 1977; Fast Company, 1978; Double Negative, Nothing Personal, 1979; Misdeal, Love, 1980.

PERREAU, GIGI: Actress. r.n. Ghislaine Perreau; b. Los Angeles, Calif. Feb. 6; sister of Janine Perreau & Richard Miles, prof. m.p. debut in Madam Curie 1943; many stage and TV guest appearances.
PICTURES INCLUDE: Dark Waters, Abigail, Dear Heart, Family Honeymoon, Roseanna McCoy, High Barbaree, Song of Love, Green Dolphin Street, Two Girls and a Sailor, Shadow on the Wall, My Foolish Heart, For Heaven's Sake, Never a Dull Moment, Reunion in Reno, Lady Pays Off, Weekend With Father, Has Anybody Seen My Gal, Bonzo Goes to College, There's Always Tomorrow, Man in the Gray Flannel Suit, Dance With Me Henry, Tammy Tell Me True, Journey to the Center of Time, Hell on Wheels.

PERRIN, NAT: Writer. With Arthur Sheekman wrote series of radio broadcasts for the Marx Brothers. With Sheekman in 1933 wrote additional dialogue on Duck Soup. Par. Collab. s.p. Roman Scandals, many others. CBS-TV West Coast, exec. prod., color programs.
PICTURES INCLUDE: Kid Millions, Rose of the Rancho, Dimples, Pigskin Parade, Stowaway, Don't Tell the Wife, New Faces of 1937, On Again—Off Again, Swing Fever, Whistling in Brooklyn, Abbott and Costello in Hollywood, Song of the Thin Man, Petty Girl, Tell It To The Judge, Miss Grant Takes Richmond, Emergency Wedding.

PERRINE, VALERIE: Actress. b. Phoenix, 1944. e. Univ. of Arizona. Was showgirl in Las Vegas before discovered by agent Robert Walker who got her contract with Universal Pictures. Film debut in Slaughterhouse Five.
PICTURES INCLUDE: The Last American Hero, Lenny (N.Y. Film Critics Award, best supporting actress), W. C. Fields and Me, Mr. Billion, Superman, The Electric Horseman, Can't Stop the Music, Superman II, The Border.

PERRY, ANTHONY: Producer. b. London, England, 1929. Ent. m.p. ind. 1948 with Two Cities story dept. asst. story ed., Rank Prods. Wrote orig. story and prod. asst. Simba. Prod., The Secret Place in 1957. Created and prod. TV series, Interpol Calling, 1959; founded Eyeline Films, prod. many Brit. prize-winning commercials. Sold Eyeline Films, 1963; wrote, dir. Emma, 1964–65, res. prod. Keep Films/Embassy Prods., London, 1966–67; prod. Dare I Weep, Dare I Mourn, for ABC-TV, and Fernandel TV series. Admin. Yellow Submarine, joined Trickfilm as man. dir. Chmn. Film & TV Copyrights, Ltd.
PICTURES INCLUDE: The Impersonator, Girl on Approval, The Party's Over.

PERRY, EARL: Circuit Executive. b. Aug. 11, 1921. e. Tulane Univ. Spent 4 yrs. as Air Force officer in World War II. Worked for Twentieth Century Fox for four years; then entered exhibition in 1951 as vice pres. and gen. mgr. of Pittman Theatres; in 1965, formed Ogden-Perry Theatres, and as pres., operates theatres in Louisiana, Mississippi, Tennessee, and Florida. Past President of NATO of Louisiana; director-at-large for National Association of Theatre Owners; Past Chief Barker of Variety Club Tent 45.

PERRY, FRANK: Director, producer, writer. served as apprentice, Westport, Conn. Country Playhouse; spent nine years in stock as stage mgr.; prod. mgr., and managing director. U.S. Army, 1952–54; director-observer, Actors Studio, 1955; Theatre Guild, 1956–60; s.p. (with Eleanor Perry) Somersault, David and Lisa, and others.
PICTURES INCLUDE: The Swimmer, Ladybug, Ladybug, David and Lisa, Last Summer, Trilogy, Diary of a Mad Housewife, Doc, Play It As It Lays, The Man on the Swing, Rancho Deluxe, Mommie Dearest.

PERSCHY, MARIA: Actress. b. Eisenstadt, Austria, Sept. 23, 1940. e. Max Rheinhardt Seminar (Vienna). m. John Melson, writer. Started in 1958 with German film (Nasser Asphalt) and has appeared in over 50 European and U.S. features. Has also appeared on European TV. Recipient of Laurel Award in 1963.

PICTURES INCLUDE: Man's Favorite Sport, Squadron 633, Ride the High Wind, Murders in the Rue Morgue, Last Day of the War, The Desperate Ones, The Tall Woman, Witch Without a Broom, etc.
TV: General Hospital, Hawaii Five-O.

PERSKY, LESTER: Executive. b. New York City, July 6, 1927. e. Brooklyn College. Officer in U.S. Merchant Marine, 1945–48. Founder and pres. of own adv. agency, 1951–1964. Theatrical stage producer, 1966–69. Produced Fortune and Men's Eyes for MGM in 1971. In 1973 creative director and co-owner Persky Bright Org. (owner-financier of numerous motion pictures for private investment group). Films include Last Detail, Golden Voyage of Sinbad, For Pete's Sake, California Split, The Man Who Would be King, The Front, Shampoo. Also financing/production services for Hard Times, Taxi Driver, Missouri Breaks, Bound for Glory, Sinbad and the Eye of the Tiger. Now pres. and chief exec. officer, Lester Persky Productions, Inc.
PICTURES: Produced Equus, Hair, Yanks, Lone Star.

PERSOFF, NEHEMIAH: Actor. b. Jerusalem, Israel, Aug. 14, 1920. e. Hebrew Technical Inst., 1934–37; Actors Studio electrician, 1937–39; signal maint., N.Y.C. Subway, 1939–41.
STAGE: Only in America, Galileo, Richard III, King Lear, Peter Pan, Peer Gynt, Tiger At the Gates, Colombe, Mont Serrat.
PICTURES INCLUDE: Fate is the Hunter, Al Capone, Some Like It Hot, The Harder They Fall, The Badlanders, Men In War, This Angry Age, The Big Show, The Greatest Story Ever Told, The Wild Party, The Power, Mrs. Pollifax—Spy, Red Sky at Morning, Psychic Killer, Voyage of the Damned.
TV: Philco-Goodyear Show, Kraft, Producers Showcase, Danger, You Are There, Untouchables, Route 66, Naked City, Wagon Train, Rawhide, Gunsmoke, Thriller, Hitchcock Thriller, Bus Stop, Five Fingers, Mr. Lucky.

PERTWEE, JON: TV performer. b. London, July 7, 1919. e. Sherborne, Royal Academy Dramatic Art. Early career, Arts League Traveling Theatre, 5 yrs. repertory; regularly on radio, TV, music hall, cabaret and circus.
PICTURES INCLUDE: Murder At the Windmill, Miss Pilgrim's Progress, Will Any Gentleman?, Gay Dog, It's A Wonderful Life, Mr. Drake's Duck, A Yank in Ermine, Ugly Duckling, Just Joe, Not a Hope in Hell, Nearly A Nasty Accident, Ladies Who Do, Carry on Cleo, I've Gotta Horse, Carry On Cowboy, Carry On Screaming, A Funny wthing Happened On the Way To The Forum, Up in the Air, The Hod, March of the Desert, One of our Dinosaurs is Missing, The House That Dripped blood, The Island of Young Tigers.
TV: Own series, Sunday Night, London Palladium Compere Variety Show, Doctor Who series, Who Dunnit, Worzel Gummidge.
RADIO: Navy Lark.
STAGE: See You Inside, A Funny Thing Happened On The Way To The Forum, There's A Girl In My Soup, Oh Clarence, My Dear Gilbert, The Bedwinner, Don't Just Lie There, Say Something, Irene, Touch It Light.

PERTWEE, MICHAEL: Writer. b. April 14, 1916. e. Sherborne School and France. Early career, journalist; ent. m.p. ind. 1937. Co-author, co-presentation many BBC plays and serials; many appearances panel games.
PICTURES INCLUDE: Laughter in Paradise, On Monday Next, Top Secret, Happy Ever After, Now and Forever, Against the Wind, Interrupted Journey, The Naked Truth, Too Many Crooks, Bottoms Up, Make Mine Mink, It Started in Naples, In the Doghouse, Mouse on the Moon, Ladies Who Do, Finders Keepers, Strange Bedfellows, A Funny Thing Happened on the Way to the Forum, Salt and Pepper, One More Time, Don't Just Lie There Say Something, Digby the Biggest Dog in the World.
TV: Rainy Day, Strictly Personal, Grove Family, Man in a Moon, The Frightened Man, Yakity Yak (ATV 1956), The Old Campaigner, Terry Thomas series, B and B series, Never a Cross Word, Six of Rix, Men of Affairs.
STAGE: The Four Musketeers, Drury Lane, Done It Again, Don't Just Lie There Say Something, Birds of Paradise, A Bit Between the Teeth, Six Of One, Ace In A Hole, Find the Lady.

PESCOW, DONNA: Actress. b. Brooklyn, NY, March 24. e. American Academy of Dramatic Arts. Started career on summer tour in Ah Wilderness in 1975. Did bit in ABC daytime series, One Life to Live. Film debut in Saturday Night Fever (1977). Regular on ABC-TV series, Angie.

PETERS, BERNADETTE: Actress. b. New York City, Feb. 28, 1944. Professional debut at age 5 on TV's Horn & Hardart Children's Hours. Stage debut with NY City Center production of The Most Happy Fella. Screen debut, Ace Eli and Rodger of the Skies.
PICTURES INCLUDE: W.C. Fields & Me, Vigilante Force, Silent Movie, The Jerk, Tulips, Pennies from Heaven, Heartbeeps.

PETERS, BROCK: Actor. b. Harlem, N.Y.C. e. Univ. of Chicago. Had numerous featured roles on and off Bdwy. in road and stock cos., nightclubs, TV. Toured with DePaur Infantry Chorus 3 seasons. Made m.p. debut, Carmen Jones, 1955.
PICTURES INCLUDE: Carmen Jones, Porgy and Bess, To Kill a Mockingbird, The L-Shaped Room, The Pawnbroker, Black Girl, Soylent Green, Lost in the Stars.
STAGE: King of the Dark Chamber, Othello, The Great White Hope, Lost in the Stars, Framed.

PETERS, JON: Producer. b. Van Nuys, CA, 1947. Started hairstyling business; built it into multi-million-dollar firm before turning film producer. Formed Jon Peters Organization. 1980, joined with Peter Guber and Neil Bogart to form The Boardwalk Co.
PICTURES INCLUDE: A Star Is Born, The Eyes of Laura Mars, The Main Event, Die Laughing, Caddyshack.

PETERS, ROBERT C.: Executive. With Paramount Pictures since 1967 holding variety of financial posts: controller, TV div.; v.p., finance-west coast; pres., non-theatrical & educational dist. div. in 1980 appt. snr. v.p. for Paramount, assuming responsibility for all west coast administration, studio operations, post-production, personnel, industrial relations and Paramount Sound Systems, Inc. Continues responsibility for Paramount merchandising and has taken over talent relations.

PETERSEN, CLIFF: TV producer-director. b. Oct. 20, 1906. Ashland, Wis. on radio, Duluth; mem. vocal groups; joined Don McNeill's Breakfast Club cast 1936 with vocal group; later joined ABC mid-west prod. staff; assigned to Breakfast Club, 1945; superviser, Don McNeill's TV Club.

PETERSON, S. DEAN: Executive. b. Toronto, Canada, December 18, 1923. e. Victoria College, University of Toronto. WWII service RCNVR; 1946 TV newsreel cameraman NBC; founded own production company in 1947; incorporated Dordean Realty Limited to acquire new studios 1959; formed Peterson Production Limited in 1957 to make TV commercials and sponsored theatrical shorts; has international awards as producer, director, director of photography; formed Studio City Limited in 1965 to produce television series and features acquiring an additional studio complex and backlot in Kleinberg, Ontario; 1972 formed SDP Communications Ltd. to package M.P. and TV; 1970 incorporated Intermedia Financial Services Limited to provide specialized financing and consultation to companies in M.P. and TV industries.
Past-President Canadian Film and Television Association, mbr. Variety Club, Tent 28; Canadian Society of Cinematographers; Directors Guild of America, Directors Guild of Canada, SMPTE.

PETERSON, EDGAR: Television producer. b. Mobile, Ala., Jan. 12, 1913. e. Harvard. Theat. & radio prod.; N.Y., 1935–36; asst. to dir. div. info., Resettlement Admin., Wash.; specialist in Public Info.; writer, dir. documentary films, 1938–41; civ. assoc. to Col. Frank Capra. Prod. Why We Fight series, 1942–45; prod. asst. to Dore Schary, Vanguard Films; assoc. prod. Spiral Staircase; exec. asst. RKO 1947; spec. research & writing for Div. of Int'l M.P., U.S. State Dept.; prod. TV shows; secty./ treas., Cornwall Prods., prod. of Janet Dean Series; mgr. script & story dept. CBS-TV; assoc. prod., then prod., Climax, CBS-TV; CBS consultant, London; exec. prod. CBS-TV. Created format and prod. techniques for Winston Churchill series, the Valiant Years, N.Y., London prod. operations and supv. writers, Hollywood, N.Y., London, 1961; writer-dir., Jack Douglas Organizations, prod. in France for series, Keyhole. U.A. TV writer; NTA-GOETZ Series, The Giants, prod., creator, The Nobel Prize, 1962; wrote orig. story and s.p. The Black Veil; created, wrote TV series, A Letter for Me, Americans Abroad; script and book, musical version Tom Sawyer, orig. treatment, s.p., Islandia, 1963. Consult. to Subscription TV in 1964; 1965–67 s.p. Assault in Eden. TV Emmy for The Pharmacist's Mate, starring Gene Raymond and Brian Donlevy. Won first Emmy for hour length film made especially for TV for program, Pulitzer Prize Playhouse; writer-editor for U.S. History Society biographical encyclopedia, The People Book, Hollywood, 1973; writer/editor, Research Associates, 1973-present. Currently, TV/MP writer.
PICTURES INCLUDE: Spiral Staircase, Till the End of Time, The Farmer's Daughter, Bachelor & Bobby Soxer (all asst. prod.), Assault in Eden, Northward the Coast.
TV: Pulitzer Prize Playhouse, Amazing Mr. Malone, Wonderful Town. Prod., Climax (CBS), Front Row Center (CBS), exec. prod. Westinghouse Summer Theatre, (CBS).

PETERSON, PAUL: Actor. b. Glendale, Calif., Sept. 23, 1945. e. Valley Coll. Mouseketeer (TV).
PICTURES INCLUDE: Houseboat, This Could Be the Night.
TV: The Donna Reed Show, Playhouse 90, Lux Video Theatre, GE Theatre, The Virginian, Ford Theatre, Valentine's Day, Shindig.

PETERSON, RICHARD W.: Executive. b. Denver, Colo., June 15, 1949. e. Col. School of Broadcasting; Harper Coll. Joined Kennedy Theatres, Chicago, 1966. In 1968 went with Great States Theatres (now Plitt Theatres), Chicago. Was city mgr. of Crocker and Grove Theatres, Elgin, Ill. In 1973 joined American Automated Theatres, Oklahoma City, as dir. of adv., pub. Promoted to dir. of U.S. theatre operations.

PETRIE, DANIEL: Director.
PICTURES INCLUDE: Lifeguard, Buster and Billie; Spy With A Cold Nose; The Idol; Stolen Hours; Raisin in the Sun; The Bramble Bush, The Betsy, Resurrection, Fort Apache, The Bronx.
THEATRE: Shadow of My Enemy; Who'll Save The Plowboy?; Mornin' Sun; Monopoly, The Cherry Orchard, Volpone.
TV FILMS: Sybil, Eleanor and Franklin, Eleanor and Franklin: The White House Years, Silent Night, Lonely Night, Harry Truman, Plain Speaking.

PETROU, DAVID MICHAEL: Writer-Producer. b. Washington, D.C., Nov. 3, 1949. e. Univ. of MD (BA); Georgetown Univ. (MA). Publicity assoc., Psychiatric Institutes of America, Washington, D.C., 1971; assoc. dir. of publicity & film liaison, Random House, 1974; guest lecturer, screen writing & film production, The American University Consortium, Washington, D.C., spring, 1980; Woodrow Wilson Fellowship, 1971. Entered industry in 1975. Joined Salkind Organization in chg. of literary projects. Worked in numerous production capacities on Crossed Swords, Superman, Superman II. 1977, exec. in chg. of literary development, Salkind. Wrote Crossed Swords (1978) and The Making of Superman. Co-authored screenplay, Shoot to Kill. 1978–79, promotional development on Time after Time for Warner Bros.; working on novel, The Hostess; dir., special projects Joseph Kennedy Foundation. Organized U.S. premiere of Superman II.

PEVERALL, JOHN: Producer. b. Islington, England. Started in entertainment industry in 1945 in mail room of J. Arthur Rank Prods. Promoted to asst. dir. Time out for military service in Royal Air Force Air-Sea Rescue Unit. Resumed career as asst. dir. and unit prod. mgr. on several films produced in Britain and throughout Europe. In 1969 became associated with newly-formed Cinema Center Films as prod. exec. in London. When firm suspended activities became freelance as asst. dir.
PICTURES INCLUDE: Conduct Unbecoming and The Man Who Fell to Earth (both assoc. prod.), The Deer Hunter (prod.).

PEVNEY, JOSEPH: Director, actor. b. New York City; e. N.Y.U., 1933; m. Mitzi Green, former child star; actress, nightclub entertainer. Began career in vaudeville at 13 as jr. mem. song & dance team; later stage in Home of the Brave. US Army ETO WW II.
STAGE: Counsellor at Law, Key Largo, Native Son; (dir.) Swan Song, Let Freedom Sing.
PICTURES INCLUDE (acting) Nocturne, Outside The Wall, Body & Soul; (dir.) Counsellor at Law, Key Largo, Native Son, Stage Door, Lady from Texas, Meet Danny Wilson, Iron Man, Flesh and Fury, Just Across the Street, Because of You, Desert Legion, It Happens Every Thursday, Back to God's Country, Yankee Pasha, Playgirl, Three Ring Circus, Six Bridges to Cross, Foxfire, Female on the Beach, Away All Boats, Congo Crossing, Tammy and the Bachelor, Man of a Thousand Faces, Cash McCall, Crowded Sky, Night of the Grizzly.

PEYSER, JOHN: Producer, director. b. New York, N.Y., Aug. 10, 1916; e. Colgate U., 1938. In TV ind. since 1939, with Psychological Warfare Div., ETO., WW II; pres. Peypacproductions, Madrid.
TV: Director: Hawaii Five-0, Mannix, Movin On, Swiss Family Robinson, Bronk, Combat Untouchables, Rat Patrol, etc.
FEATURE FILMS: Spain, The Open Door: Kashmiri Run; Honeymoon with a Stranger; Four Rode Out; Massacre Harbor.

PHILBIN, JACK: Producer. b. Lynn, Mass., e. Boston U., U.C.L.A. Started in Hotel management. Personal mgr., Glenn Miller 1939; Johnny Long 1942; Perry Como, 1944; Jackie Gleason 1948; v.p. General Artists Corp. 3 years; exec. prod., Jackie Gleason Show, Stage Show, The Honeymooners, America's Greatest Bands, CBS prod., The Vic Damone Show, The Big Record, exec. prod. Jackie Gleason American Scene Magazine TV Show, CBS-TV, 1962–63, Jackie Gleason Show 1965–74; Jackie Gleason Specials 1975–1980.

PHILLIPS, BILL: Actor. b. Washington, D.C. e. George Washington U. On N.Y. stage, Alice in Wonderland, Lightnin', etc. On screen 1940 in City for Conquest.
PICTURES INCLUDE: Larceny, Inc., Sergeant York, Action in the North Atlantic, Johnny Come Lately, See Here, Private Hargrove, Thirty Seconds Over Tokyo, Harvey Girls, Holiday in Mexico, Till Clouds Roll By, Sea of Grass, Liv-

ing in Big Way, Easy Living, Big Jack, Johnny Allegro, Customs Agent, Chain Gang, Bugles in the Afternoon, New York Confidential.

PHILLIPS D. JOHN: Motion Picture Theatre Consultant. b. New York City. Advertising and publicity mgr. Borden Co. Produce Sales Div., 1933–36; adv. & pub. mgr., Paul R. Dillon Co., Inc., 1936–41. Became field exploitation rep., United Artists Corp., 1941–42; Short Subjects & Paramount News adv. & pub. mgr. Paramount Pictures, 1942–47; exec. dir. Metropolitan Motion Pictures Theatres Assn., 1947–79, New York.

PHILLIPS, JULIA: Producer. b. Brooklyn, N.Y. e. Mt. Holyoke College. Production asst. at McCall's Magazine; later became textbook copywriter for Macmillan. In 1970 she and her husband, Michael, formed a company with actor Tony Bill (Bill/ Phillips Productions) to develop film projects.
PICTURES INCLUDE: Steelyard Blues, The Sting, Taxi Driver, The Big Bus, Close Encounters of the Third Kind.

PHILLIPS, LESLIE: Actor, producer. b. London, April 20, 1924. Early career as child actor. Ent. m.p. ind. 1935.
PICTURES INCLUDE: High Flight, Les Girls, Smallest Show on Earth, Carry On Nurse, King Ferdinand of Naples, This Other Eden, The Navy Lark, Doctor in Love, Please Turn Over, Watch Your Stern, No Kidding, Week-End With Lulu, VIP, Carry on Constable, Raising the Wind, In the Doghouse, Crooks Anonymous, Fast Lady, Father Came Too, Doctor in Clover, You Must Be Joking, Maroc 7, Some Will Some Won't, Doctor in Trouble, The Magnificent 7 & Deadly Sins, Not Now Darling, Don't Just Lie There, Spanish Fly, Not Now Comrade.
TV: Our Man At St. Marks Impasse, The Gong Game, Time and Motion Man, Reluctant Debutante, A Very Fine Line, The Suit, The Culture Vultures (series), Edward Woodward Show, Casanova 74 (series).

PHILLIPS, MICHAEL: Producer b. Brooklyn, N.Y., Nov. 10, 1916. Mgr. & prof. pugilist (featherweight), 1930–36. Ent. m.p. ind. as secy to Ray Milland, 1937; apptd asst. dir., U.S. Army Special Service Div., 1942–45; script ed. & prod. activities, Eddie Bracken Radio Prod. until 1949 (orig. & s.p.) Double Cross; formed own prod. co. Demyrtha Prod., Inc. 1950. In 1970 formed prod. co. with wife, Julia, and Tony Bill.
PICTURES INCLUDE: Steelyard Blues, The Sting, Taxi Driver, The Big Bus, Close Encounters of the Third Kind, Heartbeeps, Cannery Row.

PICERNI, PAUL: Actor. b. New York, N.Y. Dec. 1, 1922. e. Lovola U., Los Angeles. U.S. Air Force 1943–46; head of drama dept. Mt. St. Mary's College, 1949–50; TV credits include Untouchables (co-star).
TV: Philco Playhouse, Climax, Lux, Loretta Young Show, Desilu, Kojak, Mannix, Police Story, Lucy Special.
PICTURES INCLUDE: Breakthrough, I Was a Communist for the FBI, Mara Maru, Desert Song, She's Back on Broadway, House of Wax, Shanghai Story, To Hell and Back, Miracle in the Rain, Bobby Ware is Missing, Omar Khayyam, Brothers Rico, Young Philadelphian, The Young Marrieds, The Scalphunters, Airport, Kotch.

PICKENS, SLIM: r.n. Louis Bert Lindley, Jr.; b. Kingsberg, Calif., June 29, 1919; e. High School, Hanford, Calif. With rodeos since age of 12; m.p. debut in Rocky Mountain; since in many Rex Allen Westerns.
PICTURES INCLUDE: Sun Shines Bright, Boy from Oklahoma, The Outcast, Santa Fe Passage, Last Command, When Gangland Strikes, Stranger At My Door, Great Locomotive Chase, One-Eyed Jacks, Dr. Strangelove, The Honkers, Pat Garrett and Billy the Kid, Blazing Saddles, Rancho Deluxe, White Line Fever, Mr. Billion, The Swarm, Beyond the Poseidon Adventure, 1941, Tom Horn, Honeysuckle Rose.

PICKER, ARNOLD M.: Executive. b. New York, Sept. 19, 1913; m.; p. Celia and David V. Picker; e. Coll. of City of New York, U. of London; joined Columbia's foreign dept. in June, 1935. Asst. to foreign mgr.; then vice-pres. 1945, Columbia International Corp.; v.p. charge foreign dist., Oct., 1951; exec. v.p. UA, and in charge all distribution, June 1961; chmn. exec. com., 1967. Retired.

PICKER, DAVID V.: Executive. b. New York City, May 14, 1931; e. Dartmouth Coll., B.A., 1953. Father Eugene Picker, exec. Loew's Theatres. Ent. industry in 1956 as adv. pub. & exploitation liaison with sls. dept, United Artists Corp.; exec. v.p. U.A. Records; asst. to Max Youngstein, v.p.; v.p. U.A.; first v.p. UA; pres. 1969. Resigned 1973 to form own production co. In 1976 joined Paramount Pictures as pres. of m.p. div. Now exec. v.p., Lorimar Productions.
PICTURES INCLUDE: Juggernaut, Lenny, Smile, Royal Flash, Won Ton Ton, The One and Only, Oliver's Story, The Jerk.

PICKER, EUGENE D.: Executive b. New York City, Nov. 17, 1903; married; p. David V. and Celia C. Picker; e. N.Y.U. and School of Business. Started with father in Bronx theatres; joined Loew's Inc., 1920; in charge circuit opera-

tions, New York City area, 1945; v.p. Loew's Theatres, Sept. 1954; member bd. of dir., 1956, exec. v.p. Sept. 1958; pres. Loew's Theatres, March 1959. Res. 1961 as pres. Loew's Theatres; joined U.A. as v.p., July 1961. Joined Trans-Lux Corp. as exec. v.p., Jan. 1967; pres. & chief oper. Officer of Entertainment Division of Trans-Lux Corp.; Exec. consultant motion picture industry Jan. 1, 1974 and Pres. E.D.P. Films Inc. as of June 1974; pres. NATO, 1969–71, ch. bd., 1971–72, Bd. dir., Will Rogers Hospital, bd. ch. At present member board of directors, Trans Lux Corp. and Foundation of Motion Picture Pioneers and Broadway Association.

PICKMAN, JEROME: Executive. b. New York, N.Y., Aug. 24, 1916; e. St. John's U.; B'klyn Law Sch. of St. Lawrence U., LL.B. Reporter N.Y. newspapers, 1930–40; U.S. Army, WW II, adv. dept. 20th-Fox, 1944–46; Eagle-Lion Films, 1947; Paramount, April 1949; v.p., dir., adv. & pub., Paramount Film Dist Corp., 1951–60; v.p. domestic gen. sls. mgr., Paramount Film Dist. Co., N.Y. till 1962; sls. exec. Columbia Pictures 1963–67; pres. Continental Div. of Walter Reade Org., 1967–70; pres., Levitt-Pickman Film Corp., 1971; snr. v.p., domestic distribution, Lorimar Productions, 1979.

PICKMAN, MILTON EUGENE: Executive. b. N.Y.C. e. Columbia U., LL.B; St. Lawrence U. Reporter, Brooklyn Daily Eagle, 1925–29; asst. Florenz Ziegfeld Publicity, 1929–31; mgr. & agent, name bands, 1932–40; exec. M.C.A., 1933–36; U.S. Army, 1942–45; eastern studio rep. & asst. to Harry Cohn, Columbia, 1945; own agency, 1948–51; v.p. & gen. mgr., Wald-Krasna Prod., RKO, 1952; exec. asst. to Jerry Wald, v.p. in charge of prod., Columbia, 1952–54; v.p. of TV prog., Screen Gems Prod.; gen. mgr. Samuel Goldwyn Prod., 1958; prod. exec. and asst. to Buddy Adler, v.p., chg. of prod., 20th Century Fox Studios; exec. v.p., American Entertainment Enterprises.

PICKUS, ALBERT M.: Exhibitor. b. New Haven, Conn., Mar. 20, 1903; e. Washington and Lee U., 1920–24, B.S. Accountant, auditor, New Haven; ent. m.p. ind., 1926; owner, Stratford Theatre, Stratford, Conn.; dir., MPTO of Conn., 1953–59; v.p., TOA, 1953–57; asst. pres. TOA rep. to COMPO, 1957–58; chmn. exec. com. TOA, 1959; exec. com., ACE, 1959; pres. TOA, 1959–61; chmn. of bd., 1962.

PIDGEON, WALTER: Actor. b. East St. John, New Brunswick, Canada, Sept. 23, 1898. Prof. career began with Elsie Janis in At Home, in which they toured U.S. & England. Made Victor phonograph records; then vaudeville with Elsie Janis. Pres., Screen Actors Guild, 1953.
STAGE: No More Ladies, Something Gay, The Night of January 16, There's Wisdom in Women, Happiest Millionaire.
PICTURES INCLUDE: Her Private Life, Bride of the Regiment, Mlle. Modiste, Going Wild, The Gorilla, Journal of a Crime, Big Brown Eyes, Fatal Lady, Happiest Millionaire, Youngest Profession, Madame Curie, Mrs. Parkington, Week-End at the Waldorf, Holiday in Mexico, Secret Heart, If Winter Comes, Julia Misbehaves, Command Decision, Red Danube, That Forsythe Woman, The Miniver Story, Soldiers Three, Calling Bulldog Drummond, Unknown Man, The Sellout, Million Dollar Mermaid, The Bad and the Beautiful, Scandal At Scourie, Dream Wife, Executive Suite, Men of the Fighting Lady, Last Time I Saw Paris, Deep in the Heart, Hit the Deck, Forbidden Planet, The Rack, Voyage to the Bottom of the Sea, Advise & Consent, Warning Shot, Funny Girl, Skyjacked, The Neptune Factor, Harry in Your Pocket, Two Minute Warning.

PIERCE, FREDERICK S.: Executive. e. Bernard Baruch School of B.A., City College N.Y. Served with U.S. Combat Engineers in Korean War. Associated with Benj. Harrow & Son, CAP, before joining ABC in 1956. Served as analyst in TV research dep.; prom. to supvr. of audience measurements, 1957, named mgr. next year. In 1961 made dir. of research; 1962 dir. of research, sales devel. Named dir. of sales planning, sales devel. April, 1962; elec. v.p., Feb. 1964 and made nat. dir. of sales for TV. In 1968 named v.p., planning; March. 1970 named asst. to pres. In July 1972, named v.p. in chg. ABC TV planning and devel. and asst. to pres. ABC TV, March, 1973. Named sr. v.p., ABC TV, Jan., 1974. Elected pres., ABC Television Division, October, 1974.

PIERSON, FRANK: Producer-Director-Writer. b. 1925. Was correspondent for Time Magazine before entering show business as story editor of TV series, Have Gun, Will Travel. Later served as both producer and director for show. Developed a number of properties for Screen Gems before writing theatrical screenplays.
PICTURES INCLUDE: Cat Ballou (co-s.), Cool Hand Luke, (s.p.), The Anderson Tapes, (s.p.), The Looking Glass War, (s.p., dir.) Dog Day Afternoon, (s.p.), A Star Is Born (dir., s.p.), King of the Gypsies (dir., s.p.).

PILCHER, TONY: Executive. b. Boston, England, 1936. e. Shrewsbury School. Ent. m.p. industry 1960 with Anglo-Scottish Pictures. Became prod. exec. 1961, German rep.

and exec. 1968. Joined AB-Pathe as German rep., TV and Advertising Films division 1964. TV prod. Heumann Ogilvy & Mather, Frankfurt, 1966; prod. Chambers and Partners; Guild TV Services and freelance, 1967–69. Prod. Wace Film Prods., 1970; Signal Films, 1971; Rayant TV, 1972; Filmshop, 1979.

PILE, SUSAN: Executive. Now director of West Coast adv. & pub. for m.p. division of Paramount Pictures. Had six-year stint with Diener, Hauser, Bates Advertising Agency (L.A.); worked at Lion Gates Films; headed own mktg. firm in association with Marykay Powell (clients including Cinema 5, 20th-Fox, Filmex 1976, etc.). Unit publicity on films for Warner Bros., Universal; also publicist at latter co.

PINCUS, IRVING: Producer. b. New York, N.Y. e. N.Y. Univ. Indep. TV prod., 1949–63; creator-prod.; The Real McCoys, Ellery Queen, Mr. Imagination. Theatre prod. The Good, co-author; The More The Merrier, Higher and Higher, ind. prod. Prod. feature, To Find a Man, Col., 1971.

PINE, HOWARD: Producer. b. New York, N.Y., April 4, 1917. e. Stanford U. Asst. dir., Pine-Thomas Prod., then prod. mgr.; prod. Universal.
PICTURES INCLUDE: Cult of the Cobra, Man from Bitter Ridge, Private War of Major Benson, Running Wild, Nightmare.

PINK, SIDNEY: Producer, director, writer. b. Pitts., Pa., Mar. 6, 1916. e. Univ. of Pitts., B.S., 1934–37; U.S.C., Law, 1940–41. Projectionist, mgr., booker, Warner Bros., Pa., Fox West Coast, United Artists Theatres, Calif. Prod. budget mgr., Something to Sing About and Lost Horizon.
PICTURES INCLUDE: Bwana Devil, Angry Red Planet, Green-Eyed Elephant, Reptilicus, Journey to The Seventh Planet, Operation Camel, Valley of the Swords, Madigan's Millions.

PINKHAM, RICHARD R.: Executive. b. New York, N.Y. April 11, 1914. e. Yale U., 1932–36. Time, Inc., 3 yrs.; Lord and Thomas, 1 yr.; Herald Tribune, 5 yrs.; mgr. of TV planning, NBC, 1951–52; exec. prod., Today, 1952–54; exec. prod. Home, Tonight, 1954; dir. of participating prog., 1954; v.p. participating prog., 1954–55; v.p. in charge of TV programs, 1955–56; v.p. of adv. 1957; senior v.p. in chg. media, programs, bd. Ted Bates & Company, Inc. senior v.p. in chg. media, programs, bd. dir. Vic Chairman of the Board, 1976, Ted Bates & Company, Inc. from which retired 1979. Now pres., Alden Rey Enterprises.

PINSKER, ALLEN: Executive. b. New York City, Jan. 23, 1930. e. N.Y. Univ. Mgr., Hempstead Theatre, 1950. In 1954 joined Island Theatre Circuit as booker-buyer; named head buyer 1958. In 1969 joined United Artists Eastern Theatres as film buyer; head buyer, 1969, v.p., 1970. Named v.p. United Artists Theatre Circuit, 1972. In 1973 named UAET exec. v.p., member bd., 1974.

PIPER, FREDERICK: Actor. b. London, England, Sept. 23, 1902. On British stage from 1922. m.p. debut 1932 in Brit. picture The Good Companions.
PICTURES INCLUDE: Four Just Men, Jamaica Inn, Spare a Copper, 49th Parallel, The Big Blockade, Pink String and Sealing Wax, Hue and Cry, Loves of Joanna Godden, The October Man, Master of Bankdam. It Always Rains on Sunday, Escape, My Brother's Keeper, Don't Ever Leave Me, Fly Away Peter, Passport to Pimlico, Look Before You Love, Blue Lamp, Brandy for the Parson, Hunted (Stranger in Between), Home at Seven (Murder on Monday), Escape Route, Conflict of Wings (Fuss Over Feathers), Rainbow Jacket, Lease of Life, Doctor at Sea, Man in the Road, Passionate Stranger, Suspended Alibi, Doctor at Large, Se sation, Second Fiddle, Birthday Present, Barnacle Bill, Dunkirk. A Touch of Larceny, The Day They Robbed the Bank of England, Dead Luckey, The Frightened City, VIP, What A Carve-Up, Only Two Can Play, Postman's Knock, Reach for Glory, Ricochet, Becket, One Way Pendulum, Catacombo, He Who Rides A Tiger, Burke and Hare.
TV: Gert, Maude, Hindle Wakes, Mornings at Seven, The Green Bay Tree, Time Out of Mind, The Breaking Point, The Citadel, Emergency Ward 10, Zero One, Harpers West One, The Human Jungle, The Teachers, Guilty Party, Sergeant, Corky, Rupert of Hentzav, The Bender, The Hidden Truth, Danger Man, The Brothers Karamazov, Tea Party, The Long House, 199 Park Lane, Dixon of Dock Green, the Idiot, Weavers Green, The Prisoner, The Happy Sacking, Great Expectations, The Man Behind You, Approach to Living.

PIROSH, ROBERT: Writer, director, producer. S.p. credits include Battleground (solo orig. s.p. Academy Award winner), Hell Is For Heroes, What's So Bad About Feeling Good, S.P.-dir. credits include Go For Broke, Washington Story, Valley of the Kings.
TV: (Wrote, prod. pilots) Laramie, Combat. (Writer) Hawaii Five-0, Ellery Queen, Mannix, Bonanza, Ironside, The Waltons, Barnaby Jones, The Bold Ones, etc.

PISIER, MARIE-FRANCE: Actress. b. Indochina. First discovered by Francois Truffaut who cast her in L'Amour a Vingt

Ans. When film completed returned to school for degree in political science. Continued to work in films.
PICTURES: Trans-Europe Express, Stolen Kisses, Celine et Julie Vont en Bateau, Cousin Cousine, Souvenirs d'en France, Barocco, The Other Side of Midnight, French Postcards.

PLANCK, ROBERT: Cinematographer.
PICTURES INCLUDE: It's Great to be Alive, Life in the Raw, Jane Eyre, Last of the Mohicans, By Secret Command, Canterville Ghost, Secrets in the Dark, Cass Timberlane, It Happened in Brooklyn, Three Musketeers, Luxury Liner, Little Women, Madame Bovary, Summer Stock, Royal Wedding, Texas Carnival, Scandal at Scourie, Torch Song, Rhapsody.
TV: My Three Sons.

PLATT, MILT: Executive. b. New York City. e. CCNY, RCA Institute, Ohio State U.; US Army 1942–46; div. mgr., RKO Radio Pictures until 1957; gen. sls. mgr. Continental Dist., 1957–65; vice-pres. & gen. sls. mgr. Sherpix, 1965; v.p. & gen. sls. mgr., Comet Film Distributors, Inc., 1965; v.p. & sls. mgr., Times Film Corp., 1968. Pres. Eagle Amusement Co., 1970. Appointed member of the Appeals Board of the MPA rating system, 1971; pres. of Pisces Group, Ltd., 1972; v.p. & gen. sls. mgr., International Co-productions, Inc., 1974. pres., Milton Platt Co., 1975. Member governing committee, IFIDA.

PLEASENCE, DONALD: Actor. b. Worksop, England, Oct. 5, 1919. Repertory, first London appearance in Twelfth Night. RAF, WW II. Since London stage, NY stage, ent. m.p. ind. 1953.
STAGE: Vicious Circle, Saint's Day, Hobson's Choice, The Rules of the Game, The Lark, Ebb Tide, The Caretaker, Poor Bitos, The Man in the Glass Booth, Wise Child (N.Y.); voted actor of the year, 1958.
PICTURES INCLUDE: Manuela, The Man in the Sky, Heart of a Child, Tale of Two Cities, Battle of the Sexes, The Shakedown, The Horsemasters, Spare the Rod, No Love for Johnnie, The Caretaker, The Great Escape, The Greatest Story Ever Told, Hallelujah Trail, Fantastic Voyage, Cul-de-Sac, You Only Live Twice, Matchless, 13, Will Penny, Arthur! Arthur, THX 1138, Soldier Blue, Outback, Jerusalem File, Pied Piper, Innocent Bystanders, Death Line, Wedding in White, The Rainbow Boys, The Black Windmill, Journey Into Fear, Escape to Witch Mountain, Hearts of the West, The Devil Within Her, The Last Tycoon, Passover Plot, Trial by Combat, The Eagle Has Landed, Goldenrod, Oh God!, Fear, the Uncanny, Telefon, Escape from New York.
TV: Fate and Mr. Browne, Small Fish are Sweet, The Silk Purse, A House of His Own, The Traitor, The Millionairess, The Cupboard Machinal, The Hatchet Man, The Bandstand, Ambrose, Thou Good and Faithful servant, Call Me Daddy, Taste, The Fox Trot, Omnibus, Julius Caesar, Occupations, The Joke, The Cafeteria, Hindle Lakes, Sgt. Peppers Lonely Heart's Club Band, Halloween.

PLESHETTE, EUGENE: Executive. b. Jan. 7, Brooklyn, N.Y. e. CCNY & LaSalle U., Para. Tech. Acting School; stage actor; assoc. prod. and dir. three off-Broadway plays; treas. and house mgr. N.Y. Paramount; v.p. Reid-Singer Music; exec. mgr. Brooklyn Paramount thea., 1945; mgn. dir. 1953; v.p. in chg. of ABC Merchandising Inc., AB-PT, Inc. and American Broadcasting Co., 1962; exec. v.p., MSG-ABC Prods., Inc. 1965; exec. v.p. Don Reid TV Prod.; 1975, President, Pleshette Associates.

PLESHETTE, SUZANNE: Actress. b. New York, N.Y. Jan. 31. e. Performing Arts H.S., Finch College, Syracuse U. Broadway debut, Compulsion; m.p. debut Geisha Boy; major TV shows including The Bob Newhart Show, 1972.
PICTURES INCLUDE: Rome Adventure, The Birds, 40 Pounds of Trouble, Wall of Noise, A Rage to Live, Youngblood Hawke, A Distant Trumpet, The Ugly Dachshund, Bullwhip Griffin, Fate is the Hunter, Mr. Buddwing, Nevada Smith, Blackbeard's Ghost, The Power, If It's Tuesday This Must Be Belgium, Suppose They Gave a War and Nobody Came, Support Your Local Gunfighter, The Shaggy D.A., Oh, God! Book II.
STAGE: The Cold Wind and the Warm, The Golden Fleecing, The Miracle Worker, Compulsion, Two for the Seesaw.

PLESKOW, ERIC: Executive. b., Vienna, Austria. Served as film officer, U.S. War dept., 1946–48; entered industry in 1948 as asst. gen. mgr., Motion Picture Export Association, Germany; 1950–51, continental rep. for Sol Lesser Prods.; joined United Artists in 1951 as Far East Sales Mgr.; named mgr., S. Africa, 1952; mgr., Germany, 1953–58; exec. asst. to continental mgr., 1958–59; asst. continental mgr., 1959–60; continental mgr., 1960–62; v.p. in charge of foreign distribution, 1962; exec. v.p. & chief operating off., Jan. 1, 1973; pres. & chief exec. off., Oct. 1, 1973. Resigned in 1978 to becomes pres. and chief exec officer of Orion Pictures.

PLITT, HENRY G.: Executive. b. New York, Nov. 26, 1918. e. Syracuse U. St. Lawrence U. Law School. War service, 6 yrs.; Paramount Pictures International Corp.; United Detroit Theatres; asst. gen. mgr., North Ohio Theatres Corp.; div. mgr., then v.p., Paramount Gulf Theatres, New Orleans; pres. gen. mgr. Paramount Gulf Theatres; pres., ABC Films, 1959–65; Pres. ABC Great States Inc., Great States Theas. 1966; v.p. Prairie Farmer publications, 1971, v.p., ABC Theatre Holdings, Inc.; 1974, purchased Northern Theatre Circuit from American Broadcasting Company, consisting of 127 theatres, naming these theatres Plitt Theatres, Inc., of which he is pres. 1978, purchased rest of ABC theatres from American Broadcasting Company consisting of 272 screens, and will rename them Plitt Theatres.

PLUMMER, CHRISTOPHER: Actor. b. Toronto, Canada. Stage career started with English repertory group visiting Canada; toured U.S. in Nina, 1953; Bway debut in The Constant Wife, 1954; on road and in N.Y. with The Dark is Light Enough; American Shakespeare Festival at Stratford, Conn., in Julius Caesar and The Tempest; Shakespeare Festival at Stratford, Ontario, in Henry V, Twelfth Night, and Hamlet; on Bway in The Lark and Cyrano.
   TV: Oedipus Rex, Omnibus, After the Fall, The Shadow Box.
   PICTURES INCLUDE: Stage Struck, Inside Daisy Clover, The Sound of Music, Triple Cross, The Battle of Britain, The Royal Hunt of the Sun, Lock Up Your Daughters, The Phyx, The Return of the Pink Panther, Conduct Unbecoming, The Man Who Would Be King, International Velvet, The Silent Partner, Murder by Decree, Hanover Street, Somewhere in Time, Eyewitness.

PLUNKETT, PATRICIA: Actress. b. Streatham, Eng., Dec. 17, 1928; e. Royal Acad. Dram. Art. Stage debut in Pick Up Girl, 1946; m.p. debut in It Always Rains on Sundays.
   STAGE: Girl Who Couldn't Quite, French Without Tears, The Brothers, Family Upstairs.
   PICTURES INCLUDE: Bond Street, For Them That Trespass, Landfall, Murder Without Crime, Mandy (Crash of Silence), Crowded Day, Dunkirk, Three Survived.
   TV: African Patrol, Jungle Boy series, The Big Thirst, Emergency Ward 10.

PLUNKETT, WALTER: Costume designer. b. Oakland, Calif., June 5, 1902. e. U. of Calif. Began career as actor, vaudeville & stock lo., San Francisco; designed first stage costumes for vaudeville chorus on tour, costume designer. N.Y. stage and Metropolitan Opera House.
   PICTURES INCLUDE: Gone With the Wind, Lust for Life, Raintree County, Pollyanna, Bells are Ringing, How the West was Won.

PODELL, ALBERT N.: Executive. b. New York City, Feb. 25, 1937. e. Cornell U., U. of Chicago. Articles editor, Playboy Magazine, 1959–61; dir. of photog., Argosy Magazine, 1961–64; account exec. on 20th Century-Fox at Diener, Hauser, Greenthal, 1966–68; national advertising dir., Cinema Center Films, 1969; account supervisor on Columbia Pictures at Charles Schlaifer; creator & dir. of Annual Motion Picture Advertising Awards sponsored by Cinema Lodge, B'nai B'rith.

PODESTA, ROSSANA: Actress. b. Tripoli, 1934. Discovered in Italy by French director, Leonide Moguy, who starred her in Tomorrow Is Another Day. For 15 years appeared only in films by her husband, Marco Cicario; now divorced.
   PICTURES INCLUDE: Cops and Robbers, La Red, Ulysses, Helen of Troy, Santiago, The Golden Arrow, Il Prete Sposato, Seven Golden Men, Pano, Burro e Marmelate, The Quiet Countrywoman, Sunday Lovers, Stasi.

PODHORZER, MUNIO: Executive. b. Berlin, Germany, Sept. 18. e. Jahn-Realgymnasium. U. of Berlin Medical School. U.S. Army, 1943–47; pres. United Film Enterprises, Inc.; formerly secy.-treas. 86th St. Casino Theatre, N.Y.; former v.p. Atlantic Pictures Corp.; former pres. Casino Films, Inc.; former pres. Film Development Corp.; former rep. Export-Union of the German Film Ind.; former U.S. rep. Franco-London Film, Paris; former pres., Venus Productions Corp.; former U.S. rep. Atlas Int'l Film GmbH, Munich; former U.S. rep. Bavaria Atelier Gesellschaft U.S. past rep. Israfilm Ltd., Tel-Aviv; past rep. Tigon British Film Prod., London; past rep. Equiluz Films, Madrid, past rep. Airport Cine, Hawaii. Member: Variety Club, Cinema Lodge, B'nai B'rith, Past Board of Governors IFIDA; past pres. CID Agents Assoc. Former gen. foreign sales mgr., theatrical division of National Telefilm Associates. Presently representing Atlas Film—AV, Germany; Barcino Films, S.A., Spain; Filme Scorpio, Mexico; Eagle Films Ltd., United Kingdom; Les Films Du Capricorne, S.R.L., Italy; Les Films Jacques Leitienne, France; Nero Films Classics U.S.A.; Schongerfilm, Germany; Europgroup Film Distributors of France; Profilmes, S.A., Spain; KFM Films, Inc. U.S.A.; Signo Producciones, Spain; Les Films D'Alma, France; Intra Films, Italy; Elektra Films, Greece.

PODHORZER, NATHAN: Executive. b. Brody, Poland, Nov. 27, 1919. e. City Coll. of N.Y., Rutgers Univ., U. of So. Calif. U.S. Army, 1942–46; documentary film prod., Israel, 1946–57; vice pres., secy., United Film Enterprises, Inc.

POITIER, SIDNEY: Actor. b. Feb. 24, 1924; e. Nassau. Formed First Artists Prod. Co. Ltd., 1969, with Paul Newman and Barbra Streisand.
   STAGE: Lysistrata, Anna Lucasta, Freight.
   PICTURES INCLUDE: No Way Out, Cry the Beloved Country, Red Ball Express, Go Man Go, Blackboard Jungle, Good-Bye My Lady, Edge of the City, Something of Value, Porgy and Bess, All the Young Men, Devil at Four O'Clock, A Raisin in the Sun, The Long Ships, Lilies of the Field, Slender Thread, A Patch of Blue, Duel at Diablo, To Sir With Love, In the Heat of the Night, Guess Who's Coming to Dinner, The Lost Man, They Call Me Mister Tibbs, Brother John, For Love of Ivy, Buck and the Preacher, A Sweet December (dir., star), Uptown Saturday Night (dir., star), The Wilby Conspiracy, Let's Do It Again (dir., star), A Piece of the Action (dir.-star), Stir Crazy (dir.).

POLANSKI, ROMAN: Director/Writer. b. Paris, France, 1933. Lived in Poland from age of three. Early career, Art School in Cracow; five years State Film College at Lodz. Wrote and dir. Two Men In a Wardrobe, Le Gros et Le Maigre, Mammals. From 1961 wrote and dir. Knife in the Water (Poland), Repulsion, Cul-De-Sac, The Vampire Killers, Rosemary's Baby, Macbeth, What?, Chinatown. Co-scripted & Dir. The Tenant (Paris).

POLIER, DAN A.: Executive. b. Atlanta, Ga. e. Ga. Mil. Acad. and U. of Ill. m. Leila Michalove. Sports columnist, Charlotte (N.C.) News; sports editor, army wkly, Yank; entered m.p. industry adv. dept. 20th Century-Fox; head of booking dept. Fox West Coast Theatres; v.p. and director of film buying NT&T Amusement Corp.; v.p. and co-director theatre operations, National General Corp. (formerly NT&T); named v.p. in chg. of production, National General Productions, Inc., 1967. Joined Radnitz/Mattel Productions in 1972 as v.p. in chg. of distribution for Sounder; v.p. Mann Theatres Corp. of Calif., 1973. Rejoined Radnitz/Mattel Productions, 1975, as vice pres. in charge of marketing. Now gen. sls. mgr. New World Pictures.
   PICTURES INCLUDE: Cheyenne Social Club, Stalking Moon, Dream of Kings, Daddy's Gone Hunting, Grasshopper, El Condor, How Sweet It Is, Baby Maker.

POLL, MARTIN H.: Producer. b. New York. e. Wharton School, U. of Pa.; pres. Gold Medal Studios, 1956; prod. Love Is a Ball, Sylvia, The Lion in Winter, The Appointment, The Magic Garden of Stanley Sweetheart, The Man Who Loved Cat Dancing, Night Watch, Love and Death (exec. prod.); The Sailor who Fell From Grace with the Sea, Somebody Killed Her Husband, The Dain Curse, Nighthawks.

POLLACK, SYDNEY: Director, actor. b. South Bend, Ind., July 1. m. Claire Griswold. e. Neighborhood Playhouse, Assistant to Sanford Meisner at Neighborhood Playhouse. Appeared as actor on B'way in A Stone for Danny Fisher, The Dark is Light Enough. As TV actor: Playhouse 90 segments, Shotgun Slade, 15 Ben Caseys, A Cardinal Act of Mercy (won 5 Emmy nominations), The Game on Bob Hope-Chrysler Theatre (won Emmy for direction), Two is the Number. Dir. debut in 1960. Dir. play at UCLA, P.S. 193. Prepared the American version of The Leopard.
   PICTURES INCLUDE: The Slender Thread (dir.), This Property is Condemned, The Scalphunters, Castle Keep, They Shoot Horses, Don't They?, Jeremiah Johnson, The Way We Were, The Yakuza, Three Days of the Condor, Bobby Deerfield, The Electric Horseman, Absence of Malice.

POLLEXFEN, JACK: Producer, director, writer. b. San Diego, Calif., June 10, 1918. e. Los Angeles City Coll. Newspaperman, magazine writer, playwright: prod. for RKO, United Artists, Columbia, Allied Artists.
   PICTURES INCLUDE: Son of Sinbad, At Swords Point, Secret of Convict Lake, Desert Hawk, Lady in the Iron Mask, Dragon's Gold, Problem Girls, Captive Women, Captain Kidd and the Slave Girl, Neanderthal Man, Captain John Smith and Pocahontas, Return to Treasure Island, Sword of Venus, 1000 Years from Now, Daughter of Dr. Jekyll, Monstrosity.

POLONSKY, ABRAHAM: Director, writer. b. N.Y.; e. CCNY, BA., Columbia Law School. Taught at City College 1932 until war. Wrote s.p. Golden Earrings, I Can Get it For You Wholesale. Wrote novels: The Discoverers, The World Above, The Season of Fear. Wrote orig. story and s.p. Body and Soul; collab. s.p. and directed Force of Evil. Blacklisted from 1951–66. Coll. s.p. Madigan 1968; dir. and s.p. Tell Them Willie Boy is Here, 1970; dir. Romance of a Horse Thief, 1971.

PONTI, CARLO: Producer. b. Milan, Italy, Dec. 11, 1913. Univ. of Milan 1934. Prod. first picture in Milan, Little Old World; prod. Lux Film Rome; prod. first of a series of famous Toto pictures, Toto Househunting.
   PICTURES INCLUDE: A Dog's Life, The Knight Has Ar-

rived. Musolino, The Outlaw, Romanticism, Sensuality, The White Slave, Europe 1951, Toto in Color, The Three Corsairs, Ulysses, The Woman of the River, An American of Rome, Attila, War and Peace, The Last Lover, The Black Orchid, That Kind of Woman, Marriage Italian Style, The Great Spy Mission, Happily Ever After, The Girl and the General, Sunflower, Best House in London, Lady Liberty, White Sister, What?, Andy Warhol's Frankenstein, The Passenger, The Cassandra Crossing, A Special Day.

POOLE, FRANK S.: Executive. b. London, England, 1913. e. Dulwich Coll, 1925–31. Ent. m.p. ind. 1931. Early career with Pathe Pictures, Twickenham Film Distributors, until joining 20th Century Fox as London Branch Office Supervisor 1939. War service 1940–46. Rejoined Fox 1946–53; appt. Leed Branch mgr. 1954–59; supv. 1959–61; asst. sls. mgr., 1961 until joined Frank Film Distrib. as asst. sls. mgr. 1962. Appt. sls. mgr. July 1965, and to board as dir. of sls. Aug. 1965. Appt. gen. mgr. 1968; int. man. dir. 1969; appt. man. dir. July 1970; appt. dir. Rank Overseas Film Dist. Ltd., 1972; apptd. co-chmn Fox-Rank Distributors Ltd., Dec. 1972; appt. vice-chairman Rank Film Distributors Ltd. 1977. 1975, elected to Committee of Cinema & TV Veterans. Oct., 1978, retired from Rank Organisation. Appt. chmn., Appeal Tribunal for the Film Industry. Appt. chm., Grebelands Mgt. Committee & to exec. council of CTBF, 1979, assoc. Geoff Reeve & Associates. 1980, chm. & mng. dir., Omandry Intl. Ltd.

POPE, EDWARD J.: Producer, writer. b. Rye, N.Y., Aug. 3, 1919. e. Western Reserve Academy, 1938; Yale University, 1942. m. H.I.H. Princess Niloufer. World record, all-American swimmer, 1940–42; Commander, USNR, 1942–45; author, History of U.S. Navy, WW II; author, with Marechal Juin, La Defense Nationale, 1946; awarded Exceptional Civil Service Medal; Cross of Malta; Commandante, Grand Order of Merit Italian Republic; Commander, Order of Medjidiye; junior writer, MGM, 1946; prod., writer documentaries, 2 Academy Award nominations, 1947–48; prod. Seaboard Studios, ABC-TV studios, 1949; prod. film seq. Robert Montgomery Presents and 10 Million Bros. (Germany). Producer, Dumont TV, 1950; Auerbach Film Enterprises, 1950–51; ass. prod. 70 US TV films, Europe, 1951–53; v.p., exec. prod. Alpha Omega Films (France), 1954–55; chief int'l and pub. rel. U.S. Defense Dept. Europe, 1956–64; exec. prod., Compagnie Francaise De Coproduction Internationales (France) 1965–69; v.p. General Productions S.A., 1968–69; and Giroux Films, S.A. 1969; associate prod., Sweet Hunter; prod. 12 + 1; pres., H.I. Management SA (Holiday Inns) Europe.

POPKIN, HARRY M.: Exhibitor, producer. b. N.Y.C., e. Jarvis Collegiate Sch., Toronto, Canada; U. of Cal. Started career as cashier, ticket-seller, asst. to mgr., Gore Bros. Theatre Circuit, Los Angeles; became mgr. & 3 yrs. later theatre owner, L.A.; acq. other theatres, formed Eastland Circuit; purchases Gore Bros. interests; ent. sports world, oper. major auditorium, L.A., San Francisco, Oakland; first m.p. prod. all-Negro film, then, feature picture And Then There Were None; financed other ind. prod. Since 1949 org. ind. prod. unit, Hollywood; world-wide offices.
PICTURES INCLUDE: Impact, Champagne for Caesar, Second Woman, The Well, The Thief, Top Banana.

PORTER, DON: Actor. b. Miami, Okla. e. Oregon Inst. of Tech. Wide theatre work; then m.p. roles. U.S. Army, 3 yrs.
TV: Co-star, Private Secretary, Ann Sothern Show, Gidget, Bionic Woman, Hawaii Five-0, Switch, Love Boat, Three's Company, The President's Mistress, The Murder That Wouldn't Die, The Last Song, Dallas.
STAGE: The Best Man, Any Wednesday, Generation, Plaza Suite, The Price, How To Succeed in Business Without Really Trying, Harvey.
PICTURES INCLUDE: The Racket, The Savage, 711 Ocean Drive, Because You're Mine, Our Miss Brooks, Bachelor in Paradise, Youngblood Hawke, The Candidate, 40 Carats, Mame, White Line Fever, The Last Resort.

PORTER, RAND: Actor/writer/producer. b. Los Angeles, Nov. 9, 1933. e. Tulane Univ. Child actor on stage 1946–50; radio, 1950–51. 1955–64, radio, TV personality. Made films in France and U.S. 1949–56. Producer from 1964–present.

POST, TED: Producer, director. b. Brooklyn, N.Y., dir. many stage plays; dir. CBS-TV Repertoire Thea.; Producer-dir., NBC-TV Coney Island of the Mind.
TV: Studio One, Ford Theatre, Playhouse of Stars, Fred Astaire Show, Gunsmoke, Rawhide, Twilight Zone, Wagon Train, Combat, Peyton Place, Alcoa, Defenders, Route 66, Baretta, and Columbo. Movies: Dr. Cook's Garden, Girls in One Office, Cagney & Lacey, Night Stars, Five Desperate Women. etc.
MINI-SERIES: Rich Man, Poor Man.
PICTURES INCLUDE: Go Tell The Spartans, Magnum Force, Hang 'em High, Beneath The Planet Of The Apes, The Harrad Experiment, Good Guys Wear Black, Whiffs.

POTTER, BRIDGET: Executive. Married, author Robert Wool. Served as assoc. prod. of Dick Cavett Show; in chg. TV

development for Palomar Pictures Intl. Joined ABC-TV, being named v.p. of prime time program development—east coast. In 1980 appointed v.p., Lorimar Productions, in chg. of m.p. and TV development for east coast.

POWELL, CHARLES, M.: Executive. b. New York, Feb. 17, 1934. B.S. NYU/Journalism. Columbia Pictures National Publicity Manager, National Exploitation Manager, 1959–69. Paramount Pictures, National Publicity Coordinator, 1963–64. WNBC-Radio/TV, Advertising/Promotion Manager 1965. Director adv., pub. for M. J. Frankovich 1969–71. Joined MGM as dir. adv. pub.-expl. in 1972; named div. v.p. & corp. v.p., 1974; Columbia Pictures, v.p. advertising/publicity/exploitation 1975. Universal Pictures, sr. v.p., 1976–80. Currently bd. chm., Powell & Young, m.p. consultants. Board of Governors, Acad. of Motion Picture Arts & Sciences, since 1973. Founder & President, Synagogue for the Performing Arts, L.A.

POWELL, DILYS C.B.E.: Journalist. b. Bridgenorth, England. e. Bournemouth H.S. & Somerville College, Oxford. Film critic, London Sunday Times 1939–1976; now critic films on TV; Film critic, Punch, frequent broadcaster, author of several books; member of Independent Television Authority, 1954–57. Mem., Cinematograph Films Council, 1965–69.

POWELL, JANE: Actress. r.n. Suzanne Burce. b. Portland, Ore., Apr. 1. Had own radio program over KOIN, Portland; singer on natl. networks; m.p. debut in Song of the Open Road, 1944, Star of Tomorrow, 1948.
PICTURES INCLUDE: Holiday in Mexico, Three Daring Daughters, Luxury Liner, Date With Judy, Nancy Goes to Rio, Two Weeks With Love, Royal Wedding, Rich Young and Pretty, Small Town Girl, Three Sailors and a Girl, Seven Brides for Seven Brothers, Athena, Deep in My Heart, Hit the Deck, Girl Most Likely, The Enchanted Island.
STAGE: Irene (Broadway, 1974).

POWELL, WILLIAM: Actor. b. Pittsburgh, Pa., July 29, 1892; e. American Acad. Dram. Arts, New York. First appearance in The Ne'er Do Well, N.Y., 1912; then in stock & touring in Within the Law, The King, and others; on N.Y. stage 1920 in Spanish Love. m.p. debut, 1920, Sherlock Holmes; numerous pictures since. Voted one of the best Money-Making Stars in M.P. Herald-Fame Poll 1937.
PICTURES INCLUDE: Four Feathers, One Way Passage, Evelyn Prentice, The Thin Man, Rendezvous, After the Thin Man, The Last of Mrs. Cheney, Shadow of the Thin Man, Crossroads, Youngest Profession, Heavenly Body, Thin Man Goes Home, The Senator Was Indiscreet, Life with Father, Mr. Peabody and the Mermaid, Take One False Step, Dancing in the Dark, It's a Big Country, Treasure of Lost Canyon, The Girl Who Had Everything, How to Marry a Millionaire, Mister Roberts.

POWER, MALA: Actress. r.n. Mary Ellen Powers. b. San Francisco, Calif., Dec. 29, 1921; p. George and Dell Powers, latter, dramatic coach. e. Max Reinhardt Dramatic School, Hollywood, Calif.; U. of Calif., Los Angeles. Pasadena Playhouse in For Keeps, 1946; Distant Isle; Actor's Lab, Hollywood; did considerable radio work.
PICTURES INCLUDE: Outrage, Edge of Doom, Cyrano de Bergerac, Rose of Cimarron, City Beneath the Sea, City That Never Sleeps, Geraldine, Yellow Mountain, Rage at Dawn, Bengazi, Tammy and the Bachelor, Storm Rider, Flight of the Lost Balloon, Daddy's Gone-A-Hunting.

POWERS, C. F. (MIKE) JR.: Executive. b. San Francisco, March 6, 1923. e. at Park College, Mo., Columbia University, N.Y., graduated University of Oregon. Entered film business with P.R.C. in Portland, Oregon, 1947. Became Eagle Lion branch mgr. in Portland, 1950, and then United Artists. Moved to Seattle, Wash. as branch mgr. of 20th Century Fox, 1960. Was then western division mgr. for 20th Century Fox until 1967, then western division mgr. for Cinerama till 1973. Became exec. v.p., head film buyer for Robert L. Lippert Theatres, Transcontinental Theatres and Affiliated Theatres until 1978. Present position, western division mgr. for Filmways Pictures. President of Catholic Entertainment Guild of Northern Calif.; past Chief Barker of Variety Club Tent 32, San Francisco.

POWERS, STEFANIE: Actress. b. Hollywood, CA, Nov. 2, 1942. Theatrical m.p. debut in Among the Thorns. TV debut in The Girl from U.N.C.L.E. series.
PICTURES: Experiment in Terror, McClintock, Warning Shot, Escape to Athena.
TELEVISION: Feather and Father series, Washington: Behind Closed Doors (mini-series), Hart to Hart (series).

PRAGER, ALICE HEINECKE: Music executive. b. N.Y.C., Aug. 2, 1930; d. Paul and Ruth (Colin) Heinecke; grad. Russell Sage Coll., 1951; grad. study N.Y.U. With SESAC, Inc., N.Y.C., 1946– , now exec. v.p., mng. dir.; pres. The Personal Touch, Inc. Named hon. citizen, Tenn., Fla.; Zonta, International Radio and TV Execs. Soc., Int'l & Am. (mem. adv. bd) women in radio and TV, A.I.M., Broadcast Pioneers, Advertising Women of N.Y. (Editor, Ad Libber).

PRATLEY, GERALD: Commentator. b. and e. London, Eng. Joined Canadian Broadcasting Corp., 1946; writer, narrator and producer of The Movie Scene and Music from the Films; asst. member British Film Academy, dir. Canadian Film Institute 1953; chairman Toronto and District Film Council 1956; co-dir. & founder A.G.E. Film Society, Toronto; contributor to US and European film journals; film consult., Canadian Centennial Comm. Chmn., Canadian Film Awards; director, Stratford Film Festival; director, Ontario Film Institute, Toronto. Prof. of film, York Univ., Univ. of Toronto. Seneca College, McMaster Univ.

PRATT, CHARLES A.: Executive. b. Chicago, Oct. 17, 1923. e. Culver Military Academy, 1942; Amherst College, 1949. Worked for General Foods and Alberto-Culver before joining NBC. Now pres. Bing Crosby Productions.

PRELOCK, EDWARD P.: Executive. b. Cleveland, Ohio, Sep. 1, 1934. e. University of Kansas, B.A., 1958, J.D., 1963. Defensive end, Cleveland Brown and Saskatchewan Roughriders, 1958; personnel director, Transport Company of Texas, Honolulu, Hawaii, 1959–61; Justice of the Peace, Lawrence Township, Kansas, 1962–63; director of labor relations, Walt Disney Productions, 1964–75; was executive vice-president of Association of Motion Picture and Television Producers, (AMPTP), 1975–77; first vice. pres., AMPTP, 1977– ; President, Central Casting Corporation, 1976. Chairman of the Board, Contract Services Administration Trust Fund, 1976–; president, Animated Film Producers Association, 1971–; member, board of directors, Permanent Charities Committee of the Entertainment Industries, 1976–; member, board of directors, AMPTP, 1973–.

PREMINGER, OTTO: Director, producer, actor. b. Vienna, Austria, Dec. 5, 1906. e. U. Vienna. At 17 became actor with Max Reinhardt troupe at Theatre-in-the-Josefstadt, Vienna; later dir. that theat.; 1935–40, stage prod. & dir. in U.S. and on faculty Drama Sch. Yale U.; NY stage dir. Autobiography, Preminger, published 1977 by Doubleday.
STAGE: Margin for Error, The Moon is Blue, Critics Choice, Full Circle.
PICTURES INCLUDE: Royal Scandal, Forever Amber, Laura, Centennial Summer, Daisy Kenyon, In the Meantime Darling, Fallen Angel, Whirlpool, Where the Sidewalk Ends, The 13th Letter, Angel Face, The Moon is Blue, River of No Return, Carmen Jones, Court Martial of Billy Mitchell, Man With the Golden Arm, St. Joan, Bonjour Tristesse, Porgy and Bess, Anatomy of a Murder, Exodus, Advise & Consent, The Cardinal, In Harm's Way, Bunny Lake is Missing, Hurry Sundown, Skidoo, Tell Me That You Love Me Junie Moon, Such Good Friends, Rosebud, The Human Factor.

PRENTISS, PAULA: Actress. r.n. Paula Ragusa. B. San Antonio, Texas, March 4; e. Northwestern U.; Bachelor degree in drama, 1959; on TV in He & She; on stage in As You Like It, Arf!
PICTURES INCLUDE: Where the Boys Are, The Honeymoon Machine, Bachelor in Paradise, Man's Favorite Sport, Catch 22, Move, The World of Henry Orient, In Harms Way, What's New Pussycat?, Scraping Bottom, Last of the Red Hot Lovers, The Parallax View, The Stepford Wives, The Black Marble.

PRESLE, MICHELINE: Actress. r.n. Micheline Chassagne. b. Paris, France, Aug. 22, 1922; e. Raymond Rouleau Dram. Sch. m.p. debut in Je Chante; on stage in Colinette. Am. Stram Gram, Spectacle des Allies; to U.S., 1945.
PICTURES INCLUDE: Jeunes Filles en Detresse, L'Histoire de Rire, La Nuit Fantastique, Felicie Nanteuil, Seul Amour, Faibalas, Boule de Suif, Jeux Sont Faix, Diable au Corps, Under My Skin, American Guerilla in the Philippines, Adventures of Captain Fabian, Sins of Pompeii, House of Ricordi.

PRESNELL, ROBERT R., JR.: Writer. b. Chicago, Ill., July 21, 1914. e. Weymouth Coll., England; U. of Geneva; Harvard U., Stanford U., B.A. m. Marsha Hunt. Police reporter, Milwaukee Journal, 1937–38; copywriter, Young and Rubicam, 1938–40; then freelance writer; author of novel, Edgell's Island.
TV: Dr. Kildare, McCloud, Twilight Zone, Alcoa Premiere, 11th Hour, The Virginians, World Premiere, Bracken's World, Universal 120, Ritual of Evil, Banacek, Columbo, Love Story, Secret Night Caller (NBC movie of week), Smashup on Interstate 5 (ABC 2-hr. film).
PICTURES INCLUDE: Man in the Attic, Legend of the Lost, Conspiracy of Hearts, Let No Man Write My Epitaph, The Third Day.

PRESSMAN, EDWARD R.: Producer. b. N.Y.C., ed. Fieldston School. grad., Stanford Univ.; studied at London School of Economics. Began career with film short, Girl, in collaboration with director Paul Williams in London. They formed Pressman-Williams Enterprises.
PICTURES INCLUDE: Out of It, The Revolutionary, Dealing: or the Berkeley to Boston Forty Brick, Lost Bag Blues, Sisters, Badlands (exec. prod.), Phantom of the Paradise; Paradise Alley (exec. prod.): Old Boyfriends (prod.); The Hand (prod.).

PRESSMAN, MICHAEL: Producer-Director. b. New York City, July 1, 1950. e. CA Inst. of Arts. Comes from show business family; was actor in college.
PICTURES INCLUDE: The Great Texas Dynamite Chase, The Bad News Bears Breaking Training, Boulevard Nights, Those Lips Those Eyes.
TELEVISION: Like Mom, Like Me.

PRESTON, ROBERT: Actor. b. Newton Highlands, Mass.; e. Pasadena Playhouse, m.p. debut in 1938 in King of Alcatraz.
PICTURES INCLUDE: Illegal Traffic, Disbarred, Union Pacific, Beau Geste, Typhoon, Moon Over Burma, Northwest Mounted Police, New York Town, Macomber Affair, Wild Harvest, Tulsa, Big City, Lady Gambles, Whispering Smith, Blood on the Moon, Sundowners, Best of the Bad Men, My Outlaw Brother, When I Grow Up, Cloudburst, Face to Face (Bride Comes to Yellow Sky), Last Frontier, Dark at the Top of the Stairs, The Music Man, Junior Bonner, Child's Play, Mame, Semi-Tough, "S.O.B," Victor/Victoria.
STAGE: The Music Man (Tony Award), A Lion in Winter, I Do, I Do (Tony Award), Mack and Mabel, Sly Fox.

PREVIN, ANDRE: Composer, Conductor. b. Berlin, Germany, Apr. 6, 1929; composed and conducted over 50 m.p. scores; currently music director, Pittsburgh Symphony Orchestra, & conductor emeritus of London Symphony Orchestra. Guest conductor of most major symphony orchestras in U.S. and Europe.
PICTURES INCLUDE: Three Little Words, Cause for Alarm, It's Always Fair Weather, Bad Day at Black Rock, Invitation to the Dance, Catered Affair, Designing Woman, Silk Stockings, Gigi (Academy Award), Porgy and Bess (Academy Award), Subterraneans, Bells are Ringing, Pepe, Elmer Gantry, Four Horsemen of the Apocalypse, One Two Three, Two for the Seesaw, Long Day's Journey Into Night, Irma LaDouce (Academy Award), My Fair Lady (Academy Award), Goodbye Charlie, Inside Daisy Clover, Fortune Cookie, Thoroughly Modern Millie, Valley of the Dolls, Paint Your Wagon, The Music Lover.

PREVIN, STEVE: Producer, executive. b. New York, 1925. Film editor Universal studios 1941; to Europe 1951 as dir. Foreign Intrigue, TV series. Also dir. TV Sherlock Holmes, Captain Gallant, The Vikings; 1960 joined Disney, dir. Almost Angels, Waltz King, Escapade in Florence; 1965 Eon Productions; London, as TV exec.; joined Paramount in London as European prod. exec.; 1967, Paramount, London, prod. exec.; 1969, Commonwealth United, London, Eur., prod. exec.; prod. exec. Don't Look Now; '74 1975 v.p. in charge of European production Filmways Pictures.

PRICE, FRANK: Executive. b. 1930. e. Michigan State Univ., following naval service. Joined CBS in N.Y. in 1951 as story editor and writer. Moved to Hollywood in 1954, serving as story editor first at Screen Gems and then NBC (Matinee Theatre). In 1959 joined Universal as an assoc. prod. and writer. In 1961 named exec. prod. of The Virginian TV series. Appt. exec. prod. of Ironside; later did It Takes a Thief and several World Premiere movies. In 1964 named v.p. of Universal TV; 1971, sr. v.p.; 1974, pres. Also v.p., MCA, Inc. In 1978 left to join Columbia as pres. of new company unit, Columbia Pictures Productions.

PRICE, ROGER: Performer. b. Charleston, W. Va., Mar. 6, 1920; e. U. of Michigan, American Acad. of Art, Max Reinhardt Dramatic Workshop. Appeared at many night clubs, many TV guest appearances; writing credits include the Don Knotts Show, Governor & J.J., Bob Hope, The Partners, The Bluffers. V.P. of Price, Stern, Sloan Publishers.
TV: Toast of the Town, Arthur Godfrey's Friends, Gary Moore Show, This Is Show Business, Jack Parr, Get Smart, Johnny Carson. creator of: The Kallikaks (NBC); The Waltons, McMillan and Wife, Mike Douglas.
PICTURES: Mame, Day of the Locust, The Strongest Man in the World, Mixed Company, At Long Last Love, Pete's Dragon, The Devil and Max Devlin, Love on the Run.

PRICE, VINCENT: Actor. b. St. Louis, Mo., May 27, 1911; e. Yale U., U. of London, Nuremberg U.
PICTURES INCLUDE: The Song of Bernadette, Buffalo Bill, The Eve of St. Mark, Wilson, The Keys of the Kingdom, Laura, A Royal Scandal, Leave Her to Heaven, Dragonwyck, Shock, Long Night, Moss Rose, Three Musketeers, Rogues Regiment, The Web, The Bribe, Baron of Arizona, Champagne for Caesar, Bagdad, His Kind of Woman, Adventures of Captain Fabian, Las Vegas Story, House of Wax, Dangerous Mission, Mad Magician, Son of Sinbad, Serenade, While the City Sleeps, Mysterious House of Usher, Return of the Fly, The Bat, The Tingler, House on Haunted Hill, House of Usher, Pit and Pendulum, Tales of Terror, The Mask of the Red Death, War Gods of the Deep, Dr. Gold Foot and the Sex Machine, The House of 1,000 Dolls, More Dead Than Alive, The Oblong Box,

Scream and Scream Again, Dr. Phibes, Dr. Phibes Rise Again!, Theatre of Blood, Madman, Scavenger Hunt.

PRIES, RALPH W.: Executive. b. Atlanta, Ga. August 31, 1919. Graduated Georgia Tech. Former President, Ogden Food Service Corporation. Board Member: First Federal Savings & Loan of Philadelphia; National Foundation—March of Dimes; Moss Rehabilitation Hospital; St. Christopher's Hospital for Children; William Likoff Cardiovascular Institute of Hahnemann Medical College and Hospital; Police Athletic League; Motion Picture Pioneers; Board Member and Past International President: Variety Clubs International; Board Member: Will Rogers Hospital, Hahnemann Medical College & Hospital.

PRIESTLEY, J.B.: Writer. b. Bradford, Yorkshire, England, Sept. 13, 1894. Many of his novels and plays made into films; also authored several orig. s.p., add. dial., acted in advisory capacity on scripts both Hollywood and England. Pres. Screenwriters Assoc., London, 1944–45. Devised, appeared in Lost City on TV, and You Know What People Are, TV series 1955.
  PICTURES INCLUDE: The Foreman Went to France, Britain at Bay, Priestley's Postcripts, Battle for Music, They Came to a City, Last Holiday, An Inspector Calls.

PRINCE, HAROLD: Director-Producer. b. New York, N.Y. Jan. 30, 1928. e. Pennsylvania U. Working as stage mgr. for George Abbott on three shows, later co-produced, produced and/or directed the following: The Pajama Game, Damn Yankees, New Girl In Town, West Side Story, Fiorello!, Tenderloin, Take Her, She's Mine, A Call on Kuprin, A Funny Thing Happened on the Way to the Forum, She Loves Me, The Matchmaker (revival), Fiddler On The Roof, Poor Bitos, Baker Street, Flora, The Red Menace, Superman, Cabaret, Zorba, Company, Follies, The Great God Brown, The Visit, Love for Love (the last three all revivals), A Little Night Music, Candide and Pacific Overtures, Side by Side by Sondheim, Some of My Best Friends, On The Twentieth Century and Evita (London, 1978, Broadway 1979, Los Angeles, Australia & Chicago, 1980; Vienna & Mexico City, 1981), Sweeney Todd (Broadway, 1978; London, 1980) and also directed the operas Ashmadei and Silverlake for N.Y. City Opera, Girl of Golden West for Chicago Lyric Opera Co. and San Francisco Opera and Willie Stark for Houston Grand Opera.
  MOVIES DIRECTED: Something for Everyone and A Little Night Music. Authored: Contradictions, Notes on Twenty-Six Years in the Theatre (Dodd, Mead & Co., New York, 1974).

PRINCE, WILLIAM: Actor. b. Nichols, N.Y., Jan. 26, 1913; with Maurice Evans, actor, 2 yrs., radio announcer. On N.Y. stage, Ah Wilderness; m.p. debut in 1943.
  STAGE: Guest in the House, Across the Board on Tomorrow Morning, The Eve of St. Mark, John Loves Mary, As You Like It, I Am a Camera, Forward the Heart, Affair of Honor, Third Best Sport, The Highest Tree, Venus at Large, Strange Interlude, The Ballad of the Sad Cafe, Mercy Street.
  PICTURES INCLUDE: Destination Tokyo, Cinderella Jones, The Very Thought of You, Roughly Speaking, Objective Burma, Pillow to Post, Lust for Gold, Cyrano de Bergerac, Secret of Treasure Mountain, Macabre, Sacco and Vanzetti, The Heartbreak Kid, The Stepford Wives, Rollercoaster, The Cat from Outer Space, The Promise.

PRINZ, LE ROY: Producer, director. b. St. Joseph, Mo., July 14, 1895. Ran away from home at 15; shipped on freighter; joined French Foreign Legion, in French aviation corps & 94th Aerial Squad, World War I; remained after war; dir. dances Folies Bergere, Paris, then Spain & Switzerland; ret. to U.S., 1920; trained student aviators in Mexico; to US 1925 after So. America; back to dance direction; to Hollywood 1931, on choreography for C. B. DeMille, including Sign of the Cross, The Crusaders; many films for Paramount including several road series with Crosby and Hope; to Warner where conceived & dir. musical sequences in all Warner musicals 1940–53; dir. Boy and His Dog, Academy Award short subject, 1948; choreography, Ten Commandments; industrial films, 1959; New York Life—American Tel. & Tel. 1960–61; Prinz Prod., Inc., Japan, Hong-Kong films; exec. prod. Valley Music Hall Theatre Round, Salt Lake City; pres. 1966 prod. dir. for Arameta Enterprises; Films U.S. Navy, pres. Jai-Alai Arameta Enterprises; Films U.S. Navy, pres. Jai-Alai Corp. of Calif. 1969. Exposition 70, Tokyo, Japan, 1971, commercial films, Warner Bros., Seven Arts, Texaco; pres., Mini Fronton of Calif.
  PICTURES INCLUDE: Yankee Doodle Dandy, Desert Song, This Is The Army, Night and Day, Helen Morgan Story, Sayonara, South Pacific.

PRIZEK, MARIO: TV Producer-director. b. Edmonton, Alberta, Canada, 1922. e. U. of Alberta, U. of British Columbia.
  TV: Bamboula, Parade, Socrates, A Month in the Country, The Diary of a Scoundrel, Peer Gynt, Queen After Death, The Unburied Dead, Gianni Schicci (opera), Colombe, Ring

Around the Moon, Three Sisters, The Zoo Story, The Dumb Waiter, Gallileo.

PROVINE, DOROTHY: Actress. b. Deadwood, S.D., Jan. 20, 1937; e. U. of Washington.
  TV: The Alaskans, The Roaring 20's.
  PICTURES INCLUDE: The Bonnie Parker Story, It's A Mad, Mad, Mad World, Good Neighbor Sam, The Great Race, That Darn Cat, Who's Minding the Mint?

PRYOR, RICHARD: Actor. At age 7 played drum with professionals. Appearances on TV (Johnny Carson, Merv Griffin, Ed Sullivan) established him as standup comic. Wrote TV scripts for Lily Tomlin and Flip Wilson; co-author of film, Blazing Saddles. Several albums are best-selling hits.
  PICTURES INCLUDE: Actor: Lady Sings the Blues, Bingo Long and the Travelin' All Stars, Silver Streak, Greased Lightning, Which Way Is Up? Blue Collar, The Wiz, California Suite, Wholly Moses, In God We Trust, Stir Crazy, Bustin' Loose (star, co-prod.).

PRYOR, THOMAS M.: Journalist. b. New York, NY, May 22, 1912. Joined NY Times, 1929; m.p. dept. 1931 as reporter, editor, asst. film critic; Hollywood bureau chief, corres., NY Times, 1951–59; editor, Daily Variety, 1959.

PUCKHABER, RALPH L.: Executive. b. Flat Rock, N.C., June 28, 1921. e. Rollins Coll. Theatre. mgr., Orlando, West Palm Beach, Miami 1938–54; adv. m.p. dir., Palm Beach, 1943–54; spec. prom & group sls rep for FST—Magna, Todd, MGM, Col., Fox, UA., 1954–63; dir. adv. pub., ABC Florida State Theatres, Inc., 1963. In 1974 named adv. p.r., publ dir. for ABC Southeastern Theatres (Fla.-Ga.-Ala.).

PULLING, M. J. L. (C.B.E.), M.A., C. ENG. FIEE. Engineer. b. Sandown, Isle of Wight, May 30, 1906; e. Marlborough Coll., King's Coll., Cambridge. With telephone and radio companies in various technical capacities 1929–34; joined BBC in eng. information dept., 1934; asst. to asst. chief eng. 1937; in charge of sound recording dept. 1941; senior supt. eng. TV service, 1950; con. TV service eng., 1956; asst. dir. eng., 1962, Deputy dir., eng. 1963; Chmn. Electronics and Comm. Sec. I.E.E. 1959–60; mem. council, 1963–66; retired from BBC, 1967; Consultant Telecommunications Engineering.

PURCELL, NOEL: Actor. b. Dublin, Eire. Dec. 23, 1900; e. Irish Christian Brothers, Dublin. Made stage debut as child actor; later played leading roles in most of Sean O'Casey & other Abbey Theatre plays at Gaietey, Dublin; also starred as comedian in vaudeville prod. including Something in the Air, Royal Flesh, others at Theatre Royal, Dublin. Screen debut, Odd Man Out, 1946.
  PICTURES INCLUDE: Captain Boycott, The Blue Lagoon, Talk of a Million, No Resting Place, Encore, Appointment with Venus (Island Rescue), Crimson Pirate, Decameron Nights, Father's Doing Fine, Pickwick Papers, Grand National Night (Wicked Wife), The Seekers (Land of Fury), Doctor in the House, Svengali, Moby Dick, Doctor at Sea, Lust for Life, Jacqueline, Watch Your Stern, The Millionairess, Mutiny on the Bounty, Lord Jim, Drop Dead Darling, I Spy, Sinful Davy, Violent Enemy, Where's Jack?

PURDOM, EDMUND: Actor. b. Welwyn Garden City, England, Dec. 19. e. St. Ignatius Coll., London. Played leads, character roles for Northampton Rep. Co., Kettering Rep., two seasons at Stratford-On-Avon; London stage in Way Things Go, Malade Imaginaire, Romeo and Juliet, played in Caesar and Cleopatra, Anthony and Cleopatra, London and N.Y.; TV and radio appearances N.Y. & London.
  PICTURES INCLUDE: Titanic, Julius Caesar, Student Prince, The Egyptian, Athena, The Prodigal, King's Thief, Moment of Danger, Rasputin, The Comedy Man, The Beauty Jungle.

PURDY, RAI: Producer. b. London, Eng., Nov. 10, 1910; e. Canada. Owned & operated Rai Purdy Prod., Toronto for 12 yrs. Canada's largest ind. radio prod. co.: dir. narr., Out of the Night; C.O. of Canadian Army Shows. Overseas, with rank of Lt. Col., 1950–56 prod. dir. CBS N.Y.: dir. prog. Scottish TV Ltd, Glasgow, 1957–60 TV prod. Toronto, Canada, 1960.

PYKE, REX: Film-Television Producer/Director. Recent productions include Akenfield, Landscape, Eric Clapton's Rolling Hotel, Van Morrison in Ireland and Woodstock in Europe 1979.

Q

QUAID, DENNIS: Actor. b. Houston, TX Apr. 9, 1954. e. Houston Univ. Appeared in Houston stage productions before leaving for Hollywood. Movie debut: September 30, 1955 (1978).
  PICTURES INCLUDE: Crazy Mama, Our Winning Sea-

son, Seniors, Breaking Away, Gorp, The Long Riders, All Night Long, Caveman, The Night the Lights Went Out in Georgia.

QUAID, RANDY: Actor. Discovered by Peter Bogdanovich while still jr. at Drama Dept. at Univ. of Houston and cast in his The Last Picture Show (1971).
PICTURES INCLUDE: What's Up, Doc?, Paper Moon, Lolly-Madonna XXX, The Last Detail, The Apprenticeship of Duddy Kravitz, Breakout, The Missouri Breaks, Bound for Glory, The Choirboys, Midnight Express, The Long Riders.

QUALEN, JOHN: Actor. b. Vancouver, B.C.; m. Pearle Larson, 1924. Daughters: Meredith Kilpatrick, Kathleen Roberts, Elizabeth Bacon. e. studied declamation under Eliss Day; bachelor of oratory, also degree in dietetics. Played piano, flute & saxo U.S. phone in concert tours, Canada & On stage in Street Scene, Counsellor at Law, (later in film versions); m.p. debut in Arrowsmith.
TV: Mr. Ed, Andy Griffith Show, Hazel, Danny Thomas Show, Partridge Family.
PICTURES INCLUDE: Casablanca, Adventure, The Fugitive, Grapes of Wrath, My Girl Tisa, Big Steal, Jackpot, Woman on Run, Flying Missile, Belle Le Grand, Hans Christian Andersen, Ambush at Tomahawk Gap, I the Jury, Student Prince, High & the Mighty, Passion, Unchained, Sea Chase, At Gunpoint, The Searchers, Johnny Concho, Country Doctor, Two Rode Together, The Man Who Shot Liberty Valance, The Prize, The Seven Faces of Dr. Lao, Cheyenne Autumn, Sons of Katie Elder, Patch of Blue, Big Hand for the Little Lady, Firecreek, Criss Cross.

QUAYLE, ANTHONY: Actor, stage producer. b. Lancashire, England, 1913. Early career acting Old Vic Co., Elsinore and on tour Continent, North Africa. Army service, 1939–45; joined Stratford Memorial Theatre as director & actor 1948; many plays and acted Shakespearean roles; m.p. debut 1955, Oh Rosalinda; many TV credits in U.S. & England; Moses, David & Saul, Q.B. VII (Emmy). Recent TV: Ice Age, Henry IV.
PICTURES INCLUDE: Battle of the River Plate, The Wrong Man, No Time for Tears, Woman in a Dressing Gown, The Man Who Would Not Talk, Ice Cold in Alex, Serious Charge, Tarzan's Greatest Adventure, Guns of Navarone, H.M.S. Defiant, Lawrence of Arabia, The Fall of the Roman Empire, East of Sudan, Operation Crossbow, MacKenna's Gold, Before Winter Comes, Anne of A Thousand Days, Everything You Always Wanted to Know About Sex*, Bequest to the Nation, Tamarind Seed, The Eagle Has Landed, Murder by Decree.

QUEEN, ROBERT I.: Writer, author, publicist. b. Aug. 12, 1919; e. CCNY, 1942; reporter, Bronx Home News, 1936–41; information & editorial specialist, U.S. Civil Service (pub. rel.) 1942–55; admin. asst. to pres., Cinema Diorama Adv. Agency in chg., Radio-TV-Press Rel., 1955–56; night copy, headline ed., Journal of Commerce, 1956; dir., Radio-TV 1956–58, Greater New York Fund, writer of GNYF documentaries, GNYF variety shows and panel interview shows. Writer Nick Kenny WABD-TV shows; Operation Maverick, WPIX-TV Army Recruiting Service series; Suspense and The Web shows as free lance writer, CBS Radio Network Press Inf. Dept., copy ed. 1958, 1959 Press Consult. Cong. Alfred E. Santangello, 1960–63; Author: Emigres in Wartime, 1940; Creative PR in Planning Spec. Events Planning Special Events, 1958; co-author with wife, Elephant Comes to Play; own pub. rel. firm, 1955–73; p.r. counsel to NYC Transit Police PBA (1967–69); p.r. counsel-legislative aide, Hon. Thomas J. Manton (D. Queens) 1971; p.r. council, 1971–72, Councilman Morton Povman, 1971; p.r. counsel to State Sen. John R. Dunne (1969–70); teaching consult., Sch. of Contin. Prof. Studies, Pratt Institute; N.Y., N.J. Corres. Press Wire Services, Pub. rel. consultant, 1972, Thomas J. Manton Campaign for Congress; (1973–75) Public Affairs Officer, The Methodist Hospital in Brooklyn and concurrently, Community Relations-Public Relations Aide to State Assemblyman Leonard P. Stavisky, Chairman, Committee on Education; (1973–77) Public Relations Counsel to N.Y. State Senator Jeremiah B. Bloom; 1977 to 1979. Public relations counsel, Jeremiah B. Bloom for Governor Campaign, (1978). P.R. Counsel to N.Y. State Assemblyman Saul Weprin (1979 to date).

QUICK, ROBERT E.: Executive. b. Milwaukee, Wis., Aug. 8, 1917. Joined Loew's Inc., while attending Marquette U.; 1936–42, Loew's Inc., ad sales mgr. booker, apprentice salesman; 1943, adm. asst. Seattle and St. Louis Regional Offices, AAFMPS (formerly Army M.P. Service); 1945, mgr., New Orleans branch. AAFMPS; 1946, gen. man., MIDPAC M.P.S., Hawaii; 1948, ex. asst., HQ AAFMPS, Washington, D.C.; 1949, chief, European M.P.S., Nurenburg, Germany; 1952, dep. chief, AAFMPS Worldwide, Washington, D.C.; 1958, chief, AAFMPS Worldwide.

QUIGLEY, MARTIN, JR.: Editor, writer. b. Chicago, Ill., Nov. 24, 1917. e. A. B. Georgetown Un; M.A., Ed. D, Columbia U., M.P. Herald, Oct. 1939; spcl. ed. rep., M.P. Herald & M.P. Daily, May, 1941; wartime film work in U.S., England,

Eire & Italy, Dec. 1941–Oct. 1945; assoc. ed., Quigley Pub., Oct. 1945; ed. M.P. Herald July, 1949; also edit. dir. of all Quigley Pub., 1956; pres. Quigley Pub. Co., 1964; author, Great Gaels, 1944, Roman Notes, 1946, Magic Shadows—the Story of the Origin of Motion Pictures, 1948. Editor, New Screen Techniques, 1953; m.p. tech. section, Encyclopaedia Brit., 1956; co-author, Catholic Action in Practice, 1963. Co-author: Films in America, 1929–69, 1970. Pres., QWS, Inc., educational consultants, 1975. Village of Larchmont, N.Y., trustee, 1977–79; mayor, 1980–81.

QUIGLEY, WILLIAM J.: Executive. b. New York City, July 6, 1951. e. Wesleyan Univ. (BA). From 1973 to 1974 was advt. circulation mgr. for Quigley Publishing Co. Taught school in Kenya in 1974; returned to U.S. to join Grey Advt. as media planner. In 1975 joined Walter Reade Organization as asst. film buyer; promoted to head film buyer in 1977.

QUILLAN, EDDIE: Actor. b. Philadelphia, Pa., March 31, 1907; p. Sarah Owen and Joseph Quillan, professionals; stage training playing in the Quillan act with his family. On the screen in Up and At 'Em.
PICTURES INCLUDE: Night Work, Big Money, A Little Bit of Everything, The Big Shot, Dark Mountain, This Is the Life, Moonlight and Cactus, Song of the Sarong, A Guy Could Change, Sensation Hunters, Sideshow, Brigadoon, Did You Hear the One About the Traveling Saleslady?, Angel in My Pocket, How to Frame a Figg.

QUINE, RICHARD: Actor. b. Detroit, Mich., Nov. 12, 1920. In U.S. Coast Guard during WW II; in vaudeville 6 yrs.; also on radio in 1938. NY stage debut in Very Warm for May, then in My Sister Eileen. First appearance on screen in The World Changes, 1932; variously acted, prod. & dir. many films.
PICTURES INCLUDE: Babes on Broadway, Tish, My Sister Eileen, For Me and My Gal, Dr. Gillespie's New Assistant, Stand By for Action, We've Never Been Licked, Rookie Fireman, Sunny Side of the Street, Purple Heart Diary, Rainbow Round My Shoulder, Sound Off, All Ashore, Cruisin' Down the River, Pushover, So This is Paris, Solid Gold Cadillac, Full of Life, Mad Ball, Drive a Crooked Road, Bell Book and Candle, It Happened to Jane, Strangers When We Meet, The World of Suzie Wong, Notorious Landlady, Paris When It Sizzles, Sex and the Single Girl, How to Murder Your Wife, Synanon, Oh Dad Poor Dad Mama's Hung You In The Closet and I'm Feeling So Sad, Hotel (dir.), A Talent for Loving (dir.), "W" (dir.), Prisoner of Zenda (dir.).
TV: The Jean Arthur Show (exec. prod.).

QUINLAN, KATHLEEN: Actress. b. Pasadena, CA. Played small role in film, One Is a Lonely Number, while in high school. Also did bit in American Graffiti. Major role debut in Lifeguard (1976).
PICTURES: Airport '77, I Never Promised You a Rose Garden, The Promise, The Runner Stumbles, Sunday Lovers.

QUINN, ANTHONY: Actor. b. Mexico, Apr. 21, 1915. Began on screen, 1936 Acad. Award, best supp. actor, Viva Zapata, 1952, Lust for Life, 1956.
PICTURES INCLUDE: Guadalcanal Diary, Buffalo Bill, Irish Eyes Are Smiling, China Sky, Back to Bataan, Where Do We Go From Here?, Black Gold, Tycoon, The Brave Bulls, Mask of the Avenger, The Brigand, World in His Arms, Against All Flags, Ride Vaquero, City Beneath the ea, Seminole, Blowing Wild, East of Sumatra, Long Wait, Magnificent Matador, Ulysses, Naked Street, Seven Cities of Gold, La Strada, Attila the Hun, Lust for Life, Wild Party, Man from Del Rio, Ride Back, Hunchback of Notre Dame, The River's Edge, Hot Spell, Black Orchid, Last Train From Gun Hill, Warlock, Heller With a Gun, Heller in Pink Tights, Savage Innocents, The Guns of Navarone, Barabbas, Requiem for a Heavy-weight, Behold a Pale Horse, Zorba the Greek, High Wind in Jamaica, The Visit, Guns for San Sebastian, The Secret of Santa Vittoria, A Dream of Kings, Flap, A Walk in the Spring Rain, R.P.M.*, Across 110th Street, Deaf Smith and Johnny Ears, The Don Is Dead, Mohammad, Messenger of God, The Greek Tycoon, Caravans, The Passage, Lion of the Desert.

QUINN, STANLEY J., JR.: Producer, director. b. Brooklyn, N.Y., Mar. 18, 1915; e. Princeton U., 1932–36. Radio writer for Edgar Bergen show; mgr., J. Walter Thompson radio dept. in Australia, 1941–43; war corresp., 1943–45; radio prod. J. Walter Thompson, 1946; prod., dir., Kraft TV Theatre, NBC, 1947–53; ABC, Oct. 1953; vice pres., J. Walter Thompson, June 1954; exec. prod. Lux Video Theatre, 1954; pres. Quinn, McKenney Prod.; v.p. head radio, TV dept., D.C.S.&S.; prod., Grey Adv. for Revlon commercials. Dir. of Admin. MGM-TV Studios 1963–64; dir. Radio-TV Center U. of Conn. 1965–76. Commercial dir. Kraft Foods, 1964–72; Director, Radio/TV Div., CIMT, Univ. Conn., 1976–80. Freelance TV dir., 1980.

R

RABINOVITZ, JASON: Executive. b. Boston, MA., Aug. 17, 1921. e. Harvard College where elected to Phi Beta Kappa. Following World War II service as military intelligence captain with paratroops, took MBA degree at Harvard Business School in 1948. Started in industry in 1949 as asst. to secty.-treas., United Paramount Theatres. Asst. controller, ABC, 1953; adm. v.p., ABC-TV, 1956; joined MGM as asst. treas., 1957; named MGM-TV gen. mgr., director of business & financial affairs, 1958; treas. & chief financial officer, MGM, Inc., 1963; advanced to financial v.p. & chief financial officer, 1967. In 1971 named exec. v.p., Encyclopedia Brittanica Education Corp.; sr. v.p., American Film Theatre, 1974–75. Rejoined MGM as v.p./financial asst. to the pres., 1976. Elected v.p. finance, 1979.

RACHMIL, LEWIS J.: New York City, July 3, 1908. e. NYU, Yale University School of Fine Arts, Art Director, producer at Paramount, RKO, Columbia, United Artists, director and studio exec. v.p. Ziv-United Artists; v.p. Mirisch-U.A.; v.p. ABC Pictures Corp.; presently v.p. and executive production manager, MGM.

RACKMIL, MILTON R.: Executive. b. New York City. e. NYU. Certified Public Accountant prior to assoc. with Brunswick Record Co. 1929; co-founder Decca Records, 1934; pres. Decca Records, 1949; pres. and member of board of dir. Universal Pictures, 1952, after Decca bought controlling stock interest in Universal; pres. emeritus, Universal, 1973.

RADIN, PAUL: Producer. b. N.Y.C. ed. N.Y.U. m. Writer Decla Dunning. After college went in adv. Became v.p. in chg of m.p. div. of Buchanan & Co. During the war posted in Middle East as film chief for Office of War Information for that area. On return to U.S. assigned by Buchanan to ad campaign for Howard Hughes' The Outlaw. Turned to talent mgr., joining the Sam Jaffe Agency. Then joined Ashley-Famous Agency. Became exec. prod. for Yul Brynner's indep. prod. co. based in Switzerland, with whom made such films as The Journey, Once More with Feeling, Surprise Package.
PICTURES INCLUDE: Born Free, Living Free, Phase IV, The Blue Bird.

RADNER, GILDA: Actress. Writer. Began career as part of Toronto's Second City improvisational group. Moved to New York when John Belushi invited her to work with him on National Lampoon Radio Hour for which she wrote and performed. Soon after joined TV's Saturday Night Live. Appeared in Bdwy. in one-woman show, Gilda Radner—Live from New York, which was filmed for theatrical movie.
PICTURES: First Family, Gilda Live.

RADNITZ, ROBERT B.: Producer. b. Great Neck, N.Y.; e. U. of Virginia. Taught 2 years at U. of Virginia, then became reader for Harold Clurman; wrote several RKO "This is America" scripts, then to Broadway where co-prod., The Frogs of Spring; prod. The Young and the Beautiful; to Hollywood working at United Artists, then as story consultant for 20th Century-Fox; prod. A Dog of Flanders (first feature) in 1960. Board of Directors, Producer Guild of America, last 3 years first producer with retrospective at Museum of Modern Art. First producer honored by joint resolution of both houses of Congress, 1973. Sounder received four Academy Award nominations: best picture, best actor, best actress, best screenplay. Pres. Radnitz Productions, Ltd.
PICTURES INCLUDE: Misty, Island of the Blue Dolphins, And Now Miguel, My Side of the Mountain, The Little Ark, Sounder, Where The Lilies Bloom, Birch, Interval, Sounder II, A Hero Ain't Nothin' But a Sandwich, Mary White (TV-Emmy for best screenplay, 1978).

RAFELSON, BOB: Producer-Director-Writer. b. N.Y.C., 1935. After Army Service did program promotion for a radio station; then hired by David Susskind to read scripts. Became script supervisor of Play of the Week for Susskind and Ely Landau; wrote 34 adaptations for the series. Joined Screen Gems in California, developing program idea for Jackie Cooper, then head of TV prod. arm of Columbia. Later formed BBS Productions with Burt Schneider and Steve Blauner; their first film, Head.
PICTURES INCLUDE: Head (co-s.p.); Five Easy Pieces (co-prod., dir.), The King of Marvin Gardens (prod.-dir.), Stay Hungry (co-prod., co-s.p., dir.), The Postman Always Rings Twice (co. prod.-dir.).

RAFFERTY, FRANCES: Actress. b. Sioux City, Iowa, June 26, 1922; e. U. of California, premedical student UCLA. TV show, December Bride, CBS.
PICTURES INCLUDE: Seven Sweethearts, Private Miss

Jones, Girl Crazy, War Against Mrs. Hadley, Thousands Cheer, Dragon Seed, Honest Thief, Mrs. Parkington, Barbary Coast Gent, Hidden Eye, Abbott and Costello in Hollywood, Adventures of Don Coyote, Money Madness, Lady at Midnight, Old Fashioned Girl, Rodeo, Shanghai Story.

RAFFIN, DEBORAH: Actress. b. Los Angeles, Calif., March 13, 1953. e. Valley College. Was active fashion model before turning to acting when discovered by Ted Witzer. Made m.p. debut in 40 Carats (1973).
PICTURES INCLUDE: The Dove, Once Is Not Enough, The Sentinel, Touched by Love.
TELEVISION: Haywire.

RAGSDALE, CARL V.: Director, producer. b. Illmo, Missouri, May 16, 1925. e. Washington U., St. Louis and Denison U., Ohio. U.S. Navy M.P. Officer, WW II and Korea; CPT, US Naval Reserve. v.p. industrial m.p. prod., Depicto Films, 1954–61; started Carl Ragsdale Associates, 1962; pres. and exec. prod. Sun Dial Films, Inc. 1963–69. Winner of Academy Award for Best Documentary Short of 1966. Nominated for Academy Award for Best Documentary Short of 1967.

RAINES, ELLA: Actress. r.n. Ella Wallace Raines Olds. b. Snoquainde Falls, Wash., Aug. 6, 1921. e. U. Wash. Winner dramatic scholarships; actress little theatre groups; on screen 1943 in Corvette K-225.
PICTURES INCLUDE: Phantom Lady, Enter Arsene Lupin, Hail the Conquering Hero, The Suspect, Strange Affair of Uncle Harry, Time Out of Mind, The Web, Brute Force, Senator was Indiscreet, Impact, Dangerous Profession, Walking Hills, Fighting Coast Guard, Ride the Man Down.

RAINS, ROBERT H.: Executive. b. N.Y., N.Y., Aug. 12, 1921. e. USC, NYU: Air Force 3 yrs.; publicist, Int'l Pictures 1946; dir. of radio activities, Universal-Int'l Pictures, 1946; asst. casting dir., 1952; dir. Radio-TV activities, 1955; exec. in chg. of TV press dept., Universal City Studios, 1961; Universal v.p. 1966. Retired April 21, 1978.

RAKOFF, ALVIN: Producer, director. b. Toronto, Canada. e. Toronto U. Early career as journalist. Dir. in French & U.S. T.V. England, Canada Emmy Award Winner, 1968 for Call Me Daddy.
STAGE: Hamlet.
PICTURES INCLUDE: On Friday at 11, The Comedy Man, Crossplot, Hoffman, Say Hello to Yesterday, City of Fire, Death Ship, Dirty Tricks.
TV: The Caine Mutiny, Court Martial, Requiem for a Heavyweight, Our Town, The Velvet Alley, A Town Was Turned to Dust, Jokers Justice, Call Me Back, Day Before Atlanta, Heart to Heart, The Seekers, Sweet War Man, The Move after Checkmate, The Stars in My Eyes, Call Me Daddy, Summer & Smoke, Don Quixote, Shadow of a Gunman, The Impeachment of Andrew Johnson, Cheap in August, In Praise of Love, Nicest Man in the World, Dame of Sark, The Kitchen, Romeo and Juliet.

RAKSIN, DAVID: Composer. b. Philadelphia, Pa., Aug. 4, 1912. e. U. of Pennsylvania, studied music with Isadore Freed and Arnold Schoenberg. Composer of music for films, ballet, dramatic and musical comedy, stage, radio and TV, symphony orchestra and chamber ensembles. Arranger of music of Chaplin film, Modern Times; pres. Composers and Lyricists Guild of America, 1962–70; film cartoons include Madeline and The Unicorn in the Garden (UPA), professor of Music and Urban Semester, U.S.C., and Faculty, UCLA School of Music.
PICTURES INCLUDE: Laura, Secret Life of Walter Mitty, Smoky, Force of Evil, Across the Wide Missouri, Carrie, Bad and the Beautiful, Apache, Suddenly, Big Combo, Jubal, Hilda Crane, Separate Tables, Al Capone, Night Tide, Too-Late Blues, Best of the Bolshoi (music for visual interludes), Two Weeks in Another Town, The Redeemer, Invitation to a Gunfighter, Sylvia, A Big Hand for the Little Lady, Will Penny, Glass Houses, What's the Matter with Helen?
TV: Wagon Train, Five Fingers, Journey, Life With Father, Tender is the Night, Father of the Bride, Ben Casey, Breaking Point, Prayer of the Ages, Report from America, Medical Center, The Olympics (CBC).

RALSTON, GIL: Producer, writer. b. Los Angeles, 1912. e. American Acad. N.Y. stage, mgr. Broadway shows, then writer dir., NBC radio; radio dir., exec. prod. Proctor and Gamble, radio shows include Ransom Sherman Show, Junior Miss, Truth or Consequences, Lowell Thomas, Red Skelton Show independent TV prod, packaging firm exec. prod. 1948; exec. prod. CBS-TV dramatic shows, N.Y.; dir. network programs, N.Y. CBS-TV 1956. Exec. prod. High Adventure, 1957; writer, Naked City, Route 66, Ben Casey.
TV: Cavalcade of America, General Electric Theatre, Suspense.

RALSTON, RUDY Producer. b. Prague, Czechoslovakia, Jan. 30, 1918. e. grad. eng. Realka U. Came to U.S. & joined Consolidated Lab.; exec. Republic Prod.; prod. Republic, 1950.

Ram-Rap

PICTURES INCLUDE: No Man's Woman, Double Jeopardy, Terror at Midnight, Hell's Crossroads, The Lawless Eighties, Last Stagecoach West, Man Who Died Twice.

RAMPLING, CHARLOTTE: Actress. b. Sturmer, England, 1946. e. Jeanne D'Arc Academie pour Jeune Filles, Versailles; St. Hilda's, Bushey, England. Ent. m.p. ind. 1966. TV credits include: Six More for BBC, The Superlative Seven-Avenger series, Mystery of Cader Iscom, The Fantasists, What's in it for Henry, Zinotchka, Sherlock Holmes.
PICTURES INCLUDE: The Knack, Rotten to the Core, Georgy Girl, The Long Duel, Sequestro di Persona, The Damned, Three, Ski Bum, Corky, Tis Pity She's a Whore, The Six Wives of Henry VIII, Asylum, The Night Porter, Giordano Bruno, Zardoz, Caravan to Vaccares, Yuppi Dui La Chair De L'orchidee, Farewell My Lovely, Foxtrot, Orca, The Mauve Taxi, Stardust Memories.

RAMSAY, PATRICK: b. Bristol, Eng., 1926. e. Marlborough College and Jesus College, Cambridge (M.A. History), Eng. Served with Royal Naval Volunteer Reserve (Fleet Air Arm) 1944–46. Joined British Broadcasting Corporation 1949 as a report writer in monitoring service. Became assistant, appointments dept., 1953 and three years later re-joined BBC External Services as senior administrative assistant. In charge of news administration, radio and television 1958 to 1963, helping develop the U.K. regional television news network for BBC. 1963, appointed planning manager (projected arrangements), television. 1966 assistant controller, programme services, television, then assistant controller, program planning, television, from December 1969. Controller, programme services, television, April 1972. Appointed controller, BBC-Scotland, May 1979.

RAND, HAROLD: Executive. b. N.Y., Aug. 25, 1928. e. L.I.U., B.S. 1948–50; City Coll. of N.Y., 1945–46; U.S. Army 1946–48; ent. m.p. ind. 1950, pub. dept. 20th-Fox; variety of posts incl. writer, trade press, newspaper contacts; joined Walt Disney's Buena Vista pub. mgr., 1957; pub. mgr. Paramount Pictures, 1959; formed own pub. rel. firm, 1961; dir. of pub. Embassy Picture Corp. 1962; dir. of world pub. 20th Century Fox 1962; resigned 1963; dir. of adv. & pub., Landau Co, 1963; dir. world pub., Embassy Pictures, 1964; est. Harold Rand & Co., Inc., 1966, pres; Co-formed Talent Four Artists, Ltd. in 1975 to produce motion pictures. Harold Rand & Co. acting as feature film packager and producer's representative. Now pres. of Satellite Consultants, Ltd. (SACON), production & mktg. co. for TV and home video mkts.

RANDALL, TONY: Actor. b. Tulsa, Okla. e. Northwestern U. Prof. N.Y. debut as actor in Circle of Chalk; then in Candida and others; U.S. Army 1942–46; radio actor on many shows.
STAGE: Corn is Green, Anthony & Cleopatra, Caesar & Cleopatra, Inherit the Wind, Oh Men Oh Women, Oh Captain, The Sea Gull, The Master Builder.
PICTURES INCLUDE: Oh Men Oh Women, Will Success Spoil Rock Hunter, No Down Payment, The Mating Game, Pillow Talk, Adventures of Huckleberry Finn, Let's Make Love, Lover Come Back, Boys' Night Out, 7 Faces of Dr. Lao, Send Me No Flowers, Fluffy, The Alphabet Murders, Bang! You're Dead, Hello Down There, Everything You Always Wanted to Know About Sex*, Foolin' Around, Scavenger Hunt.
TV: One Man's Family, TV Playhouse, Mr. Peepers, Max Liebman Spectaculars, Sid Caesar, Dinah Shore, Playhouse 90, Odd Couple, The Tony Randall Show.

RANDOLPH, ELSIE: Actress, singer. b. London, England, Dec. 9, 1904. London stage debut 1919 in The Girl for the Boy. M.p. debut 1932 in Alfred Hitchcock's Rich and Strange.
STAGE (London): Battling Butler, Toni, Madame Pompadour, Boodle, Sunny, Peggy-Ann, That's A Good Girl, Follow Through, Wonder Bar, Stand Up and Sing, Mr. Whittington, This'll Make You Whistle, Room for Two, Top Hat and Tails, The Maid of the Mountains, It's Time to Dance, Great Day, Is Your Honeymoon Really Necessary?, No Other Verdict, The Lost Generation, What A Racket!, Lord Arthur Savile's Crime, The Cure for Love (1978).
PICTURES INCLUDE: Brother Alfred, Life Goes On, Rise and Shine, Night of the Garter, Yes, Mr. Brown, That's A Good Girl, This'll Make You Whistle, Smash and Grab, Cheer the Brave, Sky Riders, Frenzy (1972), Charleston (1977).
TV: Harper's West One, Stars and Garters, The Jimmy Logan Show, Fraud Squad, Tales of Piccadilly, Father Brown, Z-Cars, The Coffee Lace, Thriller, Within These Walls (1977), Edward and Mrs. Simpson (1978).

RANSOHOFF, MARTIN: Executive. b. New Orleans, La., 1927. e. grad., Colgate Univ. Adv., Young & Rubicam, 1948–49; slsmn, writer, dir., Gravel Films, 1951; formed own co., Filmways, 1952; industrial films, commercials; formed Filmways TV Prods., Filmways, Inc., Filmways of Calif. chmn. bd. Filmways, Inc., resigned from Filmways in 1972 and formed own independent motion picture and television production company.

TV: Mister Ed, The Beverly Hillbillies, Petticoat Junction, The Addams Family.
PICTURES INCLUDE: The Amereicanization of Emily, The Sandpiper, Boys Night Out, The Loved One, The Cincinnati Kid, See No Evil, Ten Rillington Place, King Lear, Topkapi, Fuzz, Castle Keep, Ice Station Zebra, Catch 22, Save The Tiger, The White Dawn, Silver Streak (exec. prod.), The Wanderers, Change of Seasons, American Pop.

RAPF, MATTHEW: Producer, writer. b. New York City, Oct. 22, 1920; e. Dartmouth Coll., B.A. 1942; p. Harry Rapf, producer. U.S. Navy, World War II as Lt. (j.g.).
PICTURES INCLUDE: Adventures of Gallant Bess s.p., co-prod., assoc. prod., story, The Sellout; prod., Desperate Search, Big Leaguer, Half a Hero.
TV: Loretta Young Show, Frontier, Great Gildersleeve, The Web, Jefferson Drum, Man From Blackhawk, Two Faces West, Ben Casey, Slattery's People, Iron Horse, Young Lawyers, Hardcase, Terror In the Sky, Shadow On the Land, Marcus-Nelson Murders, Kojak, Switch, Roctor's Hospital, Eischied, Oklahoma City Rolls, Gangster Chronicles.

RAPHAEL, FREDERIC: Writer. b. Chicago, 1931. e. Charterhouse, St. John's College, Cambridge. First novel pub., 1956, subsequently, The Earlsdon Way, The Limits of Love, A Wild Surmise, The Graduate Wife, The Trouble With England, Lindmann, Orchestra and Beginners. 1970: Like Men Betrayed. 1971: Who Were You With Last Night. 1972: April, June and November. 1973: Richard's Things. 1975: California Time. 1976: The Glittering Prizes. 1979: Sleeps Six & Other Stories. Ent. m.p. ind., 1956. Several plays for ATV, 1960–62. First feature film credits 1964. Nothing But The Best; 1965, Darling; Ac. Awd. for original screenplay. 1967: Two For The Road, Far From The Madding Crowd. 1971: A Severed Head. 1974: Daisy Miller. 1976: The Glittering Prices, Rogue Male. 1978: Roses, Roses . . . ; School Play, Something's Wrong, The Oresteia of Aeschylus. 1979: From the Greek and An Early Life (plays); Best of Friends (TV).

RAPHAELSON, SAMSON: Writer. b. New York City, March 30, 1896. e. U. Illinois. English instructor at U. Illinois; police reporter on N.Y. Times; has written short stories, plays, essays, screen plays.
WRITINGS INCLUDE: (plays) Jazz Singer, Young Love, Wooden Slipper (director), Accent on Youth, White Man, Skylark, dir., Jason, dir., Perfect Marriage, Hilda Crane; book: The Human Nature of Playwriting; (s.p.) Shop Around the Corner, Heaven Can Wait, Green Dolphin Street, That Lady in Ermine, Suspicion, Trouble in Paradise, The Merry Widow, Smiling Lieutenant, One Hour With You, Broken Lullaby (The Man I Killed) Angel, A Prince in Disguise. Visiting prof. of playwriting, Univ. Illinois, 1948. Adjunct Professor, Film Division, and Drama Department, Columbia University, since 1976. Received Laurel Award for lifetime screenwriting achievement from Writers Guild of America, 1977. Honorary degree, Doctor of Humane Letters, Col. Univ., 1981. Stories and articles in Esquire, New Yorker, Sat. Evening Post, etc.

RAPHEL, DAVID: Executive. b. Boulogne-s/Seine, France, Jan. 9, 1925; e. University in France. Entered m.p. ind. as asst. to sales mgr. in France, 20th-Fox, 1950–51; asst. mgr. in Italy, 1951–54; mgr. in Holland, 1954–57; asst. to European mgr. in Paris, 1957–59; European mgr. for TV activities in Paris, 1959–61; Continental mgr. in Paris, 1961–64, transferred to N.Y. as vice-pres. in chge. of international sales, 1964; named pres., 20th Century-Fox International, 1973. In Feb., 1975, also appointed senior vice-pres., worldwide marketing, feature film division, for 20th-Fox, headquartered in Los Angeles. In November, 1976, joined ICM, appointed director general of ICM (Europe) headquartered in Paris. In 1979 elected pres. ICM with headquarters in Los Angeles.

RAPPER, IRVING: Director. b. London, Eng.; e. New York U., B.A. Assoc. Gilbert Miller in Stage prod. dir. Animal Kingdom, Firebird, Five Star Final, etc.
PICTURES INCLUDE: Shining Victory, One Foot in Heaven, The Gay Sisters, The Adventures of Mark Twain, Rhapsody in Blue, The Corn is Green, Deception; Now, Voyager; Voice of the Turtle, Anna Lucasta, The Glass Menagerie, Another Man's Poison, Forever Female, Bad For Each Other, The Brave One, Marjorie Morningstar, The Miracle, Joseph and His Brethren, Pontius Pilate, The Christine Jorgensen Story, Born Again, Justus.

RAPPOPORT, GERALD J.: Executive-Film Producer. b. New York, N.Y., 1925. e. New York University. U.S. Marine Corps. 1955–1958—pres., Major Artists Representatives Corp.; 1958–1960—director of Coast Sound Services, Hollywood; 1957 to present, pres., Sewan Music Publishers. 1961 to present, repre., major Eastern European film producers. 1970 to present, dir., International Film Exchange Ltd., New York and Paris, and pres. of Family Entertainment Corp.

215

RATHER, DAN: News Correspondent. Joined CBS News in 1962 as chief of southwest bureau in Dallas. White House Correspondent, 1964 to 1974. Covered top news events, from Democratic and Republican national conventions to President Nixon's trip to Europe (1970) and to Peking and Moscow (1972). Anchored CBS Reports, 1974–75. Presently co-editor of 60 minutes (since 1975) and anchors Dan Rather Reporting on CBS Radio Network (since 1977). Winner of numerous awards, including 5 Emmys.

RAVETCH, IRVING: Director, scenarist, producer. m. Harriet Frank.
PICTURES INCLUDE: The Long Hot Summer, The Sound and the Fury, Home from the Hill, The Dark at the Top of the Stairs, Hud, Hombre, The Reivers (also prod.), Conrack (co. s.p.), Norma Rae (co.-s.p.).

RAWLINSON, A. R.: Writer. b. London, August 9: e. Rugby School, Pembroke College. Cambridge. In Queen's Royal Regiment, World War I: ship repairer & coal exporter (Liverpool & London) 1919–26; professional writer since 1929; in m.p. since 1930; assoc. prod. 1936; scenario ed. Brit. Natl. Films, Ltd. 1938; Lt. Col. British Army, World War II; scenario ed. & assoc. prod. Nettlefold Films, Ltd. 1948.
WRITINGS INCLUDE: (plays) Five Farthings, Magnolia Street, This Desirable Residence, Chain Male, Private Life of Helen of Troy, Birth-mark, Scarlet Thread, Troubadour, (s.p. & orig. play) Leap Year.
PICTURES INCLUDE: Jew Suss, Man of the Moment, Man Who Knew Too Much, Strange Boarders, Spies of the Air, Gaslight, Chinese Bungalow, Face at the Window, This England, White Unicorn, My Sister & I, Calling Paul Temple, Story of Shirley Yorke, Dark Secret, Paul Temple's Triumph; assoc. prod. Wall of Death. Prod. There Was a Young Lady, Broken Horseshoe; prod., s.p. Black Riders, Stock Car, Cloak Without Dagger, Man, dir., Balblair Prod. Ltd. 1954; 1961 s.p. Gaolbreak.
TV: Scripts for Douglas Fairbanks Prod., CBS Assoc. Rediffusion: Granada TV; TV serials B.B.C.; Diary of Samuel Pepys, Lorna Doone, Infamous John Friend, The Moonstone, Amelia, Kipling Series (BBC). Lord Glenaldy, serial BBC (sound). A Bottle of Rum, Captain Barnstead, Kipling Puck of Pook's Hill, Rewards and Fairies, Tales of The Supernatural, series. BBC: Light That Failed, Hursham Rew, Pilgrim's Way, The Gwaine Inheritance, Windows on the Beach, Three Kipling Love Stories, Traitor's Gate, M'sieur from Armenteers, A Theatre in the Family, Jacobs Ladder, Too Much Music, The Shoplifter, Four From The Days Work, A Quest for Witches.

RAY, ALDO: Actor. r.n. Aldo DaRe. b. Pen Argyl, Pa., Sept. 25, 1926: e. U. of Calif. U.S. Navy, June, 1944–May, 1946: constable. Crockett, Calif., Nov. 1950–Sept. 1951: m.p. debut in Saturday's Hero.
PICTURES INCLUDE: Star of Tomorrow. 1954: since in Marrying Kind, Pat and Mike, Let's Do It Again, Miss Sadie Thompson, Battle Cry, We're No Angels, Three Stripes in the Sun, Nightfall, Men in War, God's Little Acre, Four Desperate Men, Day They Robbed the Bank of England, Sylvia, What Did You Do in the War Daddy?, To Kill A Dragon, Dead Heat on a Merry-Go-Round, Welcome To Hard Times, The Power, Green Berets, The Violent Ones, Angel Unchained, And Hope To Die, Psychic Killer, Seven Alone.

RAY, MICHEL: Actor. b. Gerrard Cross. Buckinghamshire, England, 1945, e. Lycee Francais, London.
PICTURES INCLUDE: Divided Heart, Brave One.

RAYBURN, GENE: Performer. b. Christopher, Ill., Dec. 22. e. Knox Coll., Galesburg, Ill. NBC guide; with many radio stations as announcer in Baltimore, Philadelphia, N.Y.; U.S. Army Air Force, 1942–45, Rayburn and Finch, show, WNEW, N.Y., 1945–52; Gene Rayburn Show, NBC radio; TV shows: Many appearances as host-humorist on game shows, variety shows, drama shows. Summer stock: leads in comedies.
BROADWAY: Bye Bye Birdie, Come Blow Your Horn.
TV: Helluva Town, Amateur's Guide to Love, The Match Game.

RAYE, MARTHA: Actress. b. Butte, Mont.: p. Reed and Hooper, professionals. On stage: sang and did comedy with Paul Ash's orchestra; was in Earl Carroll's Sketch Book; Lew Brown's Calling All Stars. Appeared in night clubs.
PICTURES INCLUDE: Rhythm on the Range, The Big Broadcast of 1937, Hideway Girl, College Holiday, Par, Waikiki Wedding, Mountain Music, Artists and Models, Double or Nothing, Par. Pin Up Girl, Four Jills and a Jeep, Monsieur Verdoux, Pufnstuf, The Concorde—Airport '79.
TV: All Star Revue, Martha Raye Show, NBC.

RAYMOND, GENE: Actor. r.n. Raymond Guion, b. N.Y.C., Aug. 13, 1908. Air Force Reserve, WW II; formed ind. prod. co., Masque Prod., 1949; broadway starred Shadow of My Enemy, 1957, National Co., The Best Man 1960.
STAGE: Why Not?, The Potters, Cradle Snatchers, Take My Advice, Say When, Mirrors, Jones, Young Sinners.
PICTURES INCLUDE: Personal Maid, Ladies of the Big House, The Night of June 13th, Forgotten Commandments, If I Had A Million, Red Dust, Sadie McKee, Brief Moment, I am Suzanne, Flying Down to Rio, The House on 56th Street, Seven Keys to Baldpate, Hooray for Love, Zoo in Budapest, Behold My Wife, Mr. and Mrs. Smith, Walking On Air, Coming Out Party, Life of the Party, She's Got Everything, The Woman in Red, Ann Carver's Profession, Transient Lady, The Best Man.
TV: Star-host, TV Fireside Theatre and TV Reader's Digest; Lux Video Theatre, Robert Montgomery Presents, Climax, Playhouse 90, Kraft Theatre, Red Skelton, U.S. Steel Hour, Uncle, Girl from Uncle, Laredo, Ironsides, Julia, Judd, etc.

RAYMOND, PAULA: Actress. r.n. Paula Ramona Wright, b. San Francisco, Calif.: e. San Francisco Jr. Coll. 1942. Started career in little theatre groups, San Francisco; leading roles, Ah! Wilderness, Peter Pan, other plays; model, Meade-Maddick Agency; TV appearance 1949.
PICTURES INCLUDE: Devil's Doorway, Inside Straight, Duchess of Idaho, Crisis, Grounds For Marriage, Tall Target, Texas Carnival, The Sellout, Bandits of Corsica, City That Never Sleeps, Beast from 20,000 Fathoms, King Richard & the Crusaders, Human Jungle, Gun That Won the West, The Flight That Disappeared, 5 Bloody Graves, Blood of Dracula's Castle.

RAYNOR, LYNN S.: Prod. Executive. b. 1940. Child Actor 1944–54. Continued acting through 1963. Managed Civic Theatre, L.A. prod. The Balcony, The Crawling Arnold Review. Joined Television Enterprises, 1965; Commonwealth United Entertainment, 1968 as prod. supvr.; later headed business affair Europe. In 1973 opened London office for Vidtronics Co. 1974, formed Parazone Entertainment. In 1976–77 producer, Public Bdg. Network; 1976–78, producer, James Flocker Enterprises.
TELEVISION: Waiting for Godot (co.-prod., 1977); Camp Wilderness (series, 1978–79); Marilyn (ABC movie); Ghosts That Still Walk, Alien Encounters (both docu-dramas).

READER, RALPH (C.B.E.): Performer, producer. b. Crewekerne Somerset, May 25, 1903; e. Crewekerne School and St. John's, Cardiff. Early career graduating from New York chorus boy to dance dir., prod.; has produced 34 shows in London theatres; with R.A.F. throughout War as intelligence officer and show-producer; creator. Gang Shows; responsible for 151 productions at Royal Albert Hall, several films; author of three books; BBC disc jockey in Housewives Choice program.
TV: It's A Great Life series, BBC, Chance of A Lifetime, Radio Luxembourg, Ralph Reader Parade, Saturday spectacular, Window of the West, Flying High, U.S.A. TV Series, A.B.C. Calling At Random, Mid-day Special, Starlight Hour, Interview Time, Golden Shot, Festival of Remembrance, A Star Remembers, Scenes Familiar, Right with the Stars, This is your Life, Showman Ralph Reader, Pebble Mill at One.
RADIO: Startime, Radio Look Who's Here, Aut, & Comp. Summer Holiday, You Can't Go Wrong If You're Right, Happy Family, All For The Boys, David Coleman Series, Golden Shot, Be My Guest radio series, Pete Murray Show, Russ Conway Show, Portrait, Keith Fordyce program. Author of Plays: The Hill, Next Door, Great Oaks. 1972: variety show tour, Ralph Reader and the Stars of Tomorrow; 40th year, The Gang Show, Portrait (2nd edition), Nationwide. Series BBC W. "Showman."

READICK, ROBERT: Actor. b. 1926. New York; e. Prof. Children's Sch.
BROADWAY: George Washington Slept Here, All in Favor, Biggest Thief in Town.
PICTURES INCLUDE: Harrigan's Kid, Canterville Ghost.
TV: That Wonderful Guy, Plainclothesman, Two Girls Named Smith, Big Story.

REAGAN, CHARLES M.: b. Lawrenceburg, Ind., June 30, 1896; e. U. Notre Dame, B.S., '17. In Hotel business before entering m.p. ind. 1920 as salesman Cincinnati branch; apptd. mgr. Indianapolis exch., 1922; dist. mgr. Cincinnati, Indianapolis, Louisville, 1925; mgr. Chicago dist., 1932; west iv. mgr., 1934; asst. gen. sales mgr., 1941; vice-pres. & dir., Paramount Pictures, Inc., Paramount Film Distributing Corp.; pres. & dir., Paramount Films Service Ltd. (Canada). Domestic & Canadian distrib. & vice-pres., April, 1944. Resigned, Feb., 1949; joined MGM, sales executive; v.p. chge. dom. sales, 1952–57; vice pres. Denham Theatre Inc.; 540–15th St. Inc.; Empire Theatres, Inc.

REAGAN, RONALD: Actor. b. Tampico, Illinois, Feb. 6, 1911. e. high school and Eureka College; m. Nancy Davis; lifeguard. Wrote weekly sports column for a Des Moines, Iowa newspaper; broadcast sporting events. Signed as actor by Warner Bros. in 1937. In World War II. 1942–45, capt., USAAF. Actor until 1966 on TV as well. Program supvr., General Electric Theatre, Death Valley Days. Gov., California, 1967–74. Businessman and rancher. Elected Pres. of U.S., 1980.
PICTURES INCLUDE: Love Is On the Air, Submarine D-1, Sergeant Murphy, Swing Your Lady, Accidents Will

Happen, Cowboy from Brooklyn, Boy Meets Girl, Girls on Probation, Going Places, Dark Victory, Naughty but Nice, Hell's Kitchen, Kings Row, Juke Girl, Desperate Journey, This is the Army, The Killers, That Hagen Girl, Night Unto Night, Voice of the Turtle, John Loves Mary, Girl from Jones Beach, Hasty Heart, Louisa, Last Outpost, Bedtime for Bonzo, Storm Warning, Hong Kong, She's Working Her Way Through College, Winning Team, Tropic Zone, Law & Order, Prisoner of War, Cattle Queen of Montana, Tennessee's Partner, Hellcats of the Navy, The Killers (1964).

REARDON, BARRY: Executive. Began industry career with Paramount Pictures; named v.p.; left to join General Cinema Theatres Corp. as snr. v.p. Now with Warner Bros. as exec. v.p. & gen. sls. mgr. of domestic distribution co.

REASON, REX: Actor. b. Berlin, Germany, Nov. 30, 1928. e. Hoover H.S., Glendale, Calif. Worked at various jobs; studied dramatics at Pasadena Playhouse.
PICTURES INCLUDE: Storm Over Tibet, Salome, Mission Over Korea, Taza Son of Cochise, This Island Earth, Smoke Signal, Lady Godiva, Kiss of Fire, Creature Walks Among Us, Raw Edge, Miracle of The Hills, The Rawhide Trail.

REASONER, HARRY: News correspondent. b. Dakota, Iowa. Apr. 17, 1923; e. Stanford Univ., Univ. of Minnesota. Beg. journalism career, reporter, Minneapolis Times 1941–43; U.S. Army, WW II. Ret. to Times, drama critic 1946–48. Author, book, Tell Me About Women, 1946; newswriter, radio station WCCO. CBS affiliate. Minn., 1950–51; writer U.S. Information Agency Manila, 1951–54; news-dir., KEYD-TV (now KMSP-TV). Minn., 1954; Joined CBS News, N.Y., 1956; ABC News 1970–78. Rejoined CBS 1978.

REDDY, HELEN: Singer. b. Australia, Oct. 25, 1942. Parents were producer-writer-actor Max Reddy and actress Stella Lamond. e. in Britain. Began career at age four as singer and had appeared in hundreds of stage and radio roles with parents by age of 15. Came to New York City in 1966, subsequently played nightclubs, appeared on TV. First single hit record: I Don't Know How To Love Him (Capitol). Grammy Award, 1973, as best female singer of year for I Am Woman. Other Gold singles: Delta Dawn, Leave Me Alone, Angle Baby. Gold Albums: Love Song for Jeffrey, Free & Easy, No Way to Treat a Lady, I Don't Know How To Love Him, Music, Music. Platinum albums: I Am Woman, Long Hard Climb, Helen Reddy's Greatest Hits. Most Played Artist by the music operators of America; American Music Award 1974; Los Angeles Times Woman of the Year (1975); No. 1 Female Vocalist in 1975 and 1976; Record World, Cash Box and Billboard; one of the Most Exciting Women in the World because of her strong convictions, beauty and intelligence—International Bachelor's Society (1976).
PICTURES: Airport 1975 (debut), Pete's Dragon.
TV: David Frost Show, Flip Wilson Show, Mike Douglas Show, etc. The Helen Reddy Show (Summer, 1973, NBC), Permanent host of Midnight Special. Appearances on Tonight Show, Mac Davis Show. Hosted Merv Griffin Show, Sesame St.—Children's Workshop Prod., Tonight Show, Muppet Show.

REDELINGS, LOWELL E.: Columnist & Editor. b. Park Ridge, Ill.; e. U.S.C., B.S. Sports writer Hollywood Citizen-News 1935; sports ed. 1939; film ed. 1943–62; motion picture editor, Evening Outlook, Santa Monica, Feb. 1962–64; Film Columnist, Evening Outlook, to 1965; film drama critic, Los Angeles Herald-Examiner, 1965–66; Holly. Correspondent, Quigley Pub. Co., 1967; Land Developer, 1968; 1970–75, amusements ed., Hicks-Deal Publications to May, 1975. Now retired.

REDFORD, ROBERT: Actor. b. Santa Monica, Calif., Aug. 18, 1937. University of Colorado, left to travel in Europe, 1957. Attended Pratt Institute and American Academy of Dramatic Arts. m. Lola Van Wangemen.
BROADWAY: Walk-on in Tall Story, also in The Highest Tree, Sunday in New York, Barefoot in the Park.
PICTURES INCLUDE: Warhunt, 1961; Situation Hopeless, But Not Serious, Inside Daisy Clover; The Chase, This Property Is Condemned, Barefoot in the Park, Tell Them Willie Boy is Here, Butch Cassidy and the Sundance Kid, Downhill Racer, The Crow Killer, The Hot Rock, The Candidate, Jeremiah Johnson, The Way We Were, The Sting, The Great Gatsby, The Great Waldo Pepper, Three Days of the Condor, All The President's Men, A Bridge Too Far, The Electric Horseman, Brubaker. Director: Ordinary People (AA).
TV: The Iceman Cometh, In the Presence of Mine Enemies, (Playhouse 90).

REDGRAVE, LYNN: Actress. b. London, England, 1943. Ent. m.p. and TV, 1962.
PICTURES INCLUDE: Tom Jones, Girl With Green Eyes, Georgy Girl, The Deadly Affair, Smashing Time, The Virgin Soldiers, The Last of the Mobile Hot-Shots, Viva la Muerta Tua, Every Little Crook and Nanny, Everything You Always

Wanted to Know About Sex*, The National Health, The Happy Hooker, The Big Bus, Sunday Lovers.
TV: Pretty Polly, Ain't Afraid to Dance, The End of the Tunnel, I Am Osango, What's Wrong with Humpty Dumpty, Egg On the Face of the Tiger, Blank Pages, A Midsummer Night's Dream, Pygmalion, Turn of the Screw, William, Vienna 1900, Daft as a Brush, Not For Women Only, Co-host U.S. talkshow (NBC).

REDGRAVE, SIR MICHAEL: Actor, author. b. Bristol, Eng., March 20, 1908; m. Rachel Kempson; p. Roy Redgrave & Margaret Scudamore, prof.; e. Clifton Coll., Magdalene Coll., Cambridge. Author of two plays, publications, 1959. The Mountebank's Tale (novel). The Aspern Papers (play). Public schoolmaster three years. Started stage career in 1934, Liverpool Repertory.
STAGE: In 1936; Old Vic Season. 1937; Thunder Rock, Beggars Opera, Tiger and the Horse 1960, Out of Bounds 1962, Uncle Vanya (Chichester Festival 1962–63); mem., Nat. Theatre Cox., 1963–64. In 1938 signed long-term contract with Gainsborough, G.B.
PICTURES INCLUDE: Browning Version, Importance of Being Earnest, Green Scarf, Sea Shall Not Have Them, Confidential Report, Dam Busters, Night My Number Came Up, Oh Rosalinda!, 1984, Town Without Pity, The Quiet American, Law and Disorder, Shake Hands with the Devil, The Wreck of The Mary Deare, No! My Darling Daughter, The Innocents, The Loneliness of the Long-Distance Runner, Young Cassidy, The Hill, The Heroes of Telemark, Oh What a Lovely War, Goodbye Mr. Chips, The Lady Vanishes, Stolen Life, Stars Look Down, Way to the Stars, Dead of Night, Kipps Jeannie (Girl in Distress), Thunder Rock, The Go-Between.
Entered Royal Navy 1941. Voted among first ten Money Making Stars in British productions in Motion Picture Herald-Fame Poll, 1942, 1946, 1955.
STAGE: Tiger at the Gates, The Sleeping Prince, 1956; New York, 1961–62; The Complaisant Lover, Voyage Round My Father, 1972.

REDGRAVE, VANESSA: Actress. b. 1937. Early career with Royal Shakespeare Company. Ent. m.p. 1958 in Behind the Mask.
TV: A Farewell To Arms, Katherine Mansfield.
STAGE: Daniel Deronda, Cato Street, The Threepenny Opera, Twelfth Night, As You Like It, Taming of the Shrew, Cymbeline, The Sea Gull, The Prime of Miss Jean Brodie, Anthony & Cleopatra, Design for Living, Macbeth, Lady from the Sea.
PICTURES INCLUDE: Morgan, A Suitable Case for Treatment, A Man for All Seasons, Blow-up, Red and Blue, 1967 to Hollywood for Camelot, Charge of the Light Brigade, Isadora, Oh! What a Lovely War, The Seagull, A Quiet Place in the Country, Drop Out, Trojan Women, The Devils, La Vacanza, Mary Queen of Scots, Murder on the Orient-Express, Out of Season, Seven-per-cent Solution, Julia, Agatha, Yanks, Bear Island.

REDSTONE, EDWARD S.: Exhib. b. Boston, Mass., May 8, 1928. e. Colgate U., B.A., 1949; Harvard Grad. School of Bus. Admin., M.B.A., 1952; v.p., treas., Northeast Drive-In Theatre Corp.; v.p.; Theatre Owners of New England, 1962; chmn., advis. comm., mem. bd. dirs., TOA; gen. conven. chmn., joint convention TOA & NAC, 1962; pres. National Assn. of Concessionaires, 1963; chief barker. Variety Club of New England, 1963; pres., Theatre Owners of New England; gen. chmn., 35th annual reg. convention.

REDSTONE, MICHAEL: Exhibitor. b. Boston, Mass., Apr. 11, 1902. Built first drive-in in N.Y., 1938. Chief Barker of Variety Club of New England, 1957–58; treas. of Jimmy Fund; member of exec. comm. of the Children's Cancer Research Foundation. Chmn of the board and treas., Northeast Theatre Corp., Boston.

REDSTONE, SUMNER M.: Exhib. b. Boston, Mass., May 27, 1923. e. Harvard Coll., 1944; Harvard Law School, 1947. Law sec., U.S. Court of Appeals, 9th Circuit, 1947–48; instr., U. of San Francisco Law School, Labor Man. School, 1947; spec. asst. to U.S. Attorney Gen., 1948–51; partner, Ford, Bergson, Admans, Borkland and Redstone; President attny., Northeast Theatre Corp.; mem., asst. pres., TOA, 1960–63; pres., 1964–65. Chairman of The Board 1965–66.

REED, DONNA: Actress. r.n. Donna Mullenger. b. Denison, Ia., Jan. 27, 1921; e. Los Angeles City Coll. In school plays, then on screen.
PICTURES INCLUDE: The Getaway; Shadow of the Thin Man, Bugle Sounds, Courtship of Andy Hardy, The Human Comedy, The Man from Down Under, See Here, Private Hargrove, The Picture of Dorian Gray, Gentle Annie, They Were Expendable, Faithful in My Fashion, It's a Wonderful Life, Green Dolphin Street, Beyond Glory, Chicago Deadline, Saturday's Hero, Scandal Sheet, Hangman's Knot, Raiders of the 7 Seas, The Caddy, From Here to Eternity, (Best Supporting Actress Academy Award 1953), Gun Fury, They Rode West, Three Hours to Kill, The Last Time I Saw

Paris, Far Horizons, Benny Goodman Story, Ransom!, Backlash, Beyond Mombasa.
TV: Donna Reed Show.

REED, MAXWELL: Actor. b. Larn, Ireland, 1920. Has been sailor, Merchant Navy; during World War II served as pilot officer, R.A.F. Spent 18 months in repertory. TV appearances.
PICTURES INCLUDE: Screen debut in 1946 in The Years Between, Daybreak, The Brothers, Dear Murderer, Holiday Camp, Dark Man, Sea Devils, Square Ring, Brain Machine, Roadhouse Girl, Before I Wake (Shadow of Fear), Helen of Troy, A Time for Killing, Love is a Funny Thing, The Line Up.

REED, OLIVER: Actor. b. Wimbledon, England, Feb. 13, 1938.
PICTURES INCLUDE: The Rebel, His and Hers, Beat Girl, The Angry Silence, League of Gentlemen, Two Faces of Dr. Jekyll, Sword of Sherwood Forest, Bulldog Breed, Paranoic, No Love for Johnnie, Curse of the Werewolf, Pirates of Blood River, Curse of Captain Clegg, The Damned, The Party's Over, Scarlet Blade, Assassination Bureau, Shuttered Room, The System, Brigand of Kandahar, The Trap, I'll Never Forget What's His Name, Hannibal Brooks, The Jokers, Oliver, The Girl Getters, Women in Love, Take a Girl Like You, The Lady in the Car, Hunting Party, The Devils, Zero Population Growth, Sitting Target, Triple Echo, Fury Rides the Wind, Dirty Weekend, Revolver, Blue Blood, Three Musketeers, Death in Persepolis, Tommy, The Four Musketeers, Ten Little Indians, Royal Flash, Sell Out, Burnt Offerings, The Great Scout and Cathouse Thursday, The Prince and the Pauper, Assault on Paradise, Tomorrow Never Comes, The Big Sleep, The Class of Miss MacMichael, The Broad, Lion in the Desert.

REED, PETER: Executive. Ent. m.p. ind. 1937. Early career with Union Cinemas, General Film Distributors, Warner Bros. RAF Bomber Command 1939–45. UA Salesman, 1945–50. Paramount, 1950–70. Appt. sales man. Paramount 1963 and to brd. dir. 1966. Formed Carthay Center Distributors Ltd., now NGC Distrs. Ltd., subsidiary of National General Corporation, in May 1970. With NBC withdrawal from UK distribution in 1972, formed Eton Films as ind. venture. 1973: joined Anglo-EMI in exec. capacity. Man. Dir. Cathay Films (Uk) Ltd. 1974. UK Rep. Theatrical Dist. N.T.A.

REED, PHILIP: Actor. b. New York City; e. Cornell U. Left coll. in freshman yr. to join Hoboken, N.J. stock co.; later in vaudeville & on N.Y. stage (Grand Street Follies, Grand Hotel, Ziegfeld Follies of 1931, Serena Blandish, Melody, My Dear Children).
PICTURES INCLUDE: Female, The House on 56th Street, Lost Lady, Dr. Monica, Old Acquaintance, People Are Funny, Big Town After Dark, Song of Sheherizade, Pirates of Monterey, Bandit Queen, Tripoli, Davy Crockett, Indian Scout, Target, Take Me to Town, Girl in the Red Velvet Swing, Harem Scarem.

REEVE, CHRISTOPHER: Actor. b. New York City, Sept. 25, 1952. e. Cornell (BA); graduate work at Julliard. National tour with Irregular Verb to Love, co-starring with Celeste Holm. Went to England, visiting repertory theatres; hired for backstage work by Old Vic. Returned to U.S.; played role on daytime TV series, Love of Life. On Bdwy. with Katharine Hepburn in A Matter of Gravity.
PICTURES: Superman, Somewhere in Time, Superman II, Deathtrap.

REEVES, HAZARD, E.: Executive b. Baltimore, Md., July 6, 1906. e. Georgia Inst. of Technology, B.S. 1928; In research eng. dept., Columbia Phonograph Co., 1928; asst. chief eng., Stanley Recording Co., 1929; chief eng., 1930–31; consultant Harvard Film Foundation, 1930–32; chief eng., Standard Sound Co., 1932–33; founder, Reeves Sound Studios, Inc., 1933 (now Cinetel, Inc.); Audio Devices, Inc., 1937; Reeves Industries, Inc., 1946; co-founder, Reeves-Ely Laboratories, Inc., 1942 (now a division of Dynamics Corporation of America); co-founder, 1947, and first pres., Cinerama, Inc.; chmn. bd., Reeves Telecom Corp., Realtron Corp.

REEVES, STEVE: Actor. b. Glasgow, Mont., Jan. 21, 1926. Delivered newspapers. Mr. Pacific, Mr. America, Mr. World, Mr. Universe; ent. theatrical field, Kismet. Appeared The Vamp, Wish You Were Here.
PICTURES INCLUDE: Athena, Goliath and the Barbarians, Sword of Siracusa, Judos, David and Goliath, Hercules, Giant of Marathon, Last Days of Pompeii, Hercules Unchained, White Warrior, Morgan the Pirate, The Thief of Baghdad, The Trojan Horse, The Private Prince, A Long Ride From Hell.

REGAN, PHIL: Singer and actor. b. Brooklyn, N.Y., May 28, 1906. While a boy was a boatman at Charleston, S.C., navy yard. Was a clerk in an oil company; clerked in different parts of the country, then became a court clerk in New York, finally a detective. After voice was trained, sang for Columbia Broadcasting System. Was signed by WB.
PICTURES INCLUDE: The Key, Housewife, Dames in

1934, Sweet Rosie O'Grady, Swing Parade of 1946, Sunbonnet Sue, Three Little Words.
TV: Many appearances and several radio shows.

REHME, ROBERT G.: Executive. b. Cincinnati, Ohio, May 5, 1935. e. Univ. of Cincinnati. 1953, mgr., RKO Theatres, Inc., Cincinnati; 1961, adv. mgr., Cincinnati Theatre Co.; 1966, dir. of field adv., United Artists Pictures; 1969, named dir. of pub. and ass't gen. sls. mgr., United Artists Pictures; 1972, pres., B&R Theatres and v.p., April Fools Films; 1976, v.p. & gen. sls. mgr., New World Pictures; Feb. 1978, joined Avco Embassy Pictures as snr. v.p. & chief operating officer; Dec. 1978, named exec. v.p.; 1979, named pres., Avco Embassy Pictures, Inc. 1981, joined Universal Pictures as pres. of distribution & marketing.

REILLY, CHARLES E., JR.: Communications Executive. e. St. Joseph's College, Network Liaison, TV Guide Magazine; asst. to the v.p. & dir., corporate relations, Young & Rubicam, 1964–66; executive dir., National Catholic Office for Radio, 1966–71; Secretary, Catholic Communications Foundation (CCF) 1968–77; exec. v.p., Patrick Carr Associates 1971–73; corp. exec. Communispond Inc. of J. Walter Thompson Co., 1973–76; v.p., Speech Dynamics subsidiary, Ogilvy & Mather International, 1976–77; pres., In-Person Communications Inc. 1977–present.

REILLY, CHARLES NELSON: Actor-Director. b. New York City, Jan. 13, 1931. e. Univ. of Conn. On Broadway mostly in comedy roles before turning to TV and films. Recently directed stage plays.
PICTURES INCLUDE: A Face in the Crowd, Two Tickets to Paris, The Tiger Makes Out.
TELEVISION: Broadway of Lerner and Lowe, Ghost and Mrs. Muir, Dean Martin Show.

REINAUER, RICHARD: Executive. b. Chicago, Ill., April 28, 1926. e. Univ. of Ill.; grad. 1952; prod., dir., free lance, 1952–59; bus. mgr., asst. prod., Showcase Theatre Evanston, 1952; prod., dir., NBC, Chicago, 1953–55; film dir., Kling Studios, 1956; asst. dir., Foote Cone & Belding, 1956–59; dir., radio, TV & m.p., American Medical Assoc., 1959–63; Communications Counselors, 1963–64; exec. dir., TV Arts & Sciences Foundation, 1964; pres., Acad. of TV Arts & Sciences, Chicago Chapter, 1970–72. assoc. prod. & asst. dir. Wild Kingdom & asst. to pres., Don Meier Prods., 1965-present. Member-Illinois Nature Preserve Commission.

REINER, CARL: Performer; b. New York, N.Y., March 20, 1923. Comedian on B'way, Call Me Mr., Inside U.S.A., Alive and Kicking; m.p. The Russians are Coming; on TV in Your Show of Shows, first Bob Hope Show, Caesar's Hour; Sid Caesar Invites You, 1958; prod.-writer, The Dick Van Dyke Show, CBS (Emmy Award-writing Comedy) 1961–62. Prod., The New Dick Van Dyke Show 1973; Heaven Help Us, 1975–76.
PICTURES INCLUDE: The Gazebo, writ. orig. s.p. The Thrill of It All, dir. co-author & co-prod. The Comic; Generation. A Performer: It's a Mad, Mad, Mad, Mad World; Happy Anniversary, Gidget Goes Hawaiian, The End. Co-author & dir: Enter Laughing; Dir: Where's Poppa, Oh, God!, The One and Only, The Jerk.
RECORDINGS: Carl Reiner and Mel Brooks, The 2000 Year Old Man, The 2001 Year Old Man, 2013 Year Old Man.
AUTHOR: Enter Laughing, Something Different, B'way.

REINHARDT, GOTTFRIED: Producer. writer. b. Berlin, Germany, p. Max Reinhardt, noted theatrical prod.; Else Reinhardt, actress; brother, Wolfgang Reinhardt, prod.; e. Berlin. Began career at 19 as asst. to prod. Ernst Lubitsch, father's friend, with m.p. Design For Living; asst. to Walter Wanger; later to Bernard H. Hyman (Saratoga; San Francisco). Wrote orig. story, I Live My Life, The Great Waltz; collab. Bridal Suite; book for NY musicals, Rosalinda, Helen of Troy. U.S. Army service, Signal Corps. 1942–46.
PICTURES INCLUDE: Comrade X, Rage in Heaven, Two-Faced Woman, (co-prod.) Homecoming, Command Decision, The Great Sinner, The Red Badge of Courage, Invitation, Young Man With Ideas, (dir. 2 seq.) Story of Three Loves, Betrayed, Town Without Pity, Hitler: The Last Ten Days (prod., co. s.p.).

REINHART, ALICE: Actress. b. San Francisco, Calif., May 6. Legit. theatre work, 1928–49; appeared in stock, numerous Broadway plays; radio work since 1930; shows include Woman in My House, The Whistler, Life Can Be Beautiful, many other shows on all networks; on stage, American Dream in Hollywood.
TV: Stage 13, Man Behind the Badge, Big Town, O. Henry Series, Dragnet, Crusader, The Donna Reed Show.
PICTURES INCLUDE: Lieutenant Wore Skirts, The Iron Sheriff, Bachelor Flat.

REISENBACH, SANFORD E.: Executive. e. N.Y. University. Associated with Grey Advertising for 20 years; exec. v.p. and pres. of Grey's leisure/entertainment division in N.Y. In August, 1979, joined Warner Bros. as exec. v.p. in chg. of worldwide adv. & pub.

REISNER, ALLEN: Director. b. N.Y.C.
FEATURES: The Day They Gave Babies Away; St. Louis Blues.
FEATURES FOR TV: The Captain And the Kings; Mary Jane Harper Cried Last Night, Your Money Or Your Wife; To Die In Paris; The Cliff; Skag.
TV: Film; Kojak, Hawaii Five-0, Cannon, Mannix Etc. Live: Playhouse 90, Studio One, Climax, Etc.

REISS, JEFFREY C.: Executive. b. Brooklyn, N.Y., April 14, 1942. e. Washington Univ., St. Louis (B.A., 1963). Consultant at N.Y. Univ. and Manhattanville College and instructor at Brooklyn College before entering industry. Agt. in literary dept. for General Artists Corp., 1966. Supervised development in N.Y. of Tandem Prods. for Norman Lear, 1968. Produced off-Bdwy. plays 1968–70. Dir. of progm. devel. for Cartridge TV, Inc. (mfg. of video-players-recorders) 1970–73. Joined ABC Entertainment as director of network feature films, 1973–75. Joined Viacom International Inc. as vice pres. of Premium Television services in 1976, promoted to pres. of Showtime Entertainment, Inc., the pay television subsidiary, in 1977. Appt. exec. v.p., Viacom Entertainment Group, 1980.

REISS, STUART A.: Set decorator. b. Chicago, Ill., July 15, 1921. e. L.A. High Sch., 1939. Property man, 20th-Fox, 1939–42; U.S. Army Air Corps, 1942–45; set decorator, 20th-Fox since 1945; 6 Acad. nom.; 2 Acad. Awards, Diary of Anne Frank & Fantastic Voyage.
PICTURES INCLUDE: Titanic, How to Marry a Millionaire, Hell and High Water, There's No Business Like Show Business, Soldier of Fortune, Seven Year Itch, Man in the Grey Flannel Suit, Teen Age Rebel, What a Way to Go, Doctor Doolittle, Fantastic Voyage, Oh God! Swarm, Beyond the Poseidon Adventure, Carbon Copy, All the Marbles.

REISZ, KAREL: Director. b. Czechoslovakia, 1926. e. Britain. Wrt. Technique of Film Editing for British Film Academy. Worked with British Film Institute and National Film Library, 1954; co. dir. (with Tony Richardson) Momma Don't Allow, 1957; prod. Every Day Except Christmas, 1958; dir. We Are the Lambeth Boys, 1959–60; dir. Saturday Night & Sunday Morning, 1962; prod. This Sporting Life, 1963; dir. Night Must Fall, 1966; dir. Morgan, 1968; dir. Isadora; The Gambler. Dir. On the Road. (BBC-TV). Dir. Who'll Stop the Rain (1978), The French Lieutenant's Woman, 1981 (also co-prod.).

RELPH, MICHAEL: Producer, director, writer, designer. 1942 art dir. Ealing Studios then assoc. prod. to Michael Balcon on The Captive Heart, Frieda, Kind Hearts and Coronets, Saraband (also designed: nominated Oscar). 1948 appt. producer and formed prod/dir. partnership Basil Dearden (until 1972). 1971–76 Governor Brit. Film Institute. Chairman B.F.I. Prod. Board. Chairman Film Prod. Assoc. of G.B., member Films Council.
PICTURES INCLUDE: (For Ealing) The Blue Lamp (Brit. Film Academy: Best Brit. Film 1950), I Believe in You, The Gentle Gunman, The Square Ring, The Rainbow Jacket, Out of the Clouds, The Ship That Died of Shame, Davy (for Rank). Lion!, The Smallest Show on Earth. (For Rank) Violent Playground, Rockets Galore (Island Fling U.S.) Sapphire (Brit. Film Academy: Best Brit. Film 1959) 1960 Founder Dir. Allied Film Makers: Prod. The League of Gentlemen, Man in The Moon (Co-author S.P.) Victim, Life For Ruth (Walk in the Shadow U.S.) Also produced: Secret Partner (For M.G.M.), All Night Long (For Rank), The Mind Benders (For Anglo). A Place To Go (Author S.P.) For United Artist Produced: Woman of Straw (Co-author S.P.) Masquerade (Co-author S.P.) For Paramount produced, wrote and designed The Assassination Bureau. For E.M.I. produced The Man Who Haunted Himself (Co-author S.P.). 1978 Exec. prod., Scum, co-prod., An Unsuitable Job for a Woman. Exec. in chg. U.K. prod., Kendon Films Ltd.

RELYEA, ROBERT E.: Executive. b. Santa Monica, Calif., May 3, 1930. e. UCLA (B.S.), 1952). In Army 1953–55. Started production of films in 1968 with Bullitt. Now exec. v.p. in chg. of worldwide prod. for Melvin Simon Productions.
PICTURES INCLUDE: Bullitt, The Reivers, Day of the Dolphin.

REMBUSCH, TRUEMAN T.: Exhibitor. b. Shelbyville, Ind., July 27, 1909; f. Frank J. Rembusch, pioneer exhibitor; e. Notre Dame U. Sch. of Commerce, 1928; m. Mary Agnes Finneran. Ent. m.p. ind., 1928, servicing sound equip., father's circuit; became mgr., 1932; elect. bd. of dir., Allied Theatre Owners of Ind., 1936–45, pres. 1945–51, 1952–53; dir. chmn. Allied TV Committee, 1945–50; pres. Allied States Assn., 1950–51; 1952, named by Allied as one of triumvirate heading COMPO; elected chmn. Joint Com. on Toll TV, 1949; Nov. 1953 named by Gov. of Indiana as dir. State Fair Board. Currently pres. Syndicate Thea., Inc., Franklin, Ind. member, In Notre Dame Club of Indianapolis (Man of Yr., 1950); BPOE, Antelope Club, 4th Degree K of C, Meridian Hills Country Club, Marco Island Country Club and Hillview Country Club of Franklin. American Radio Relay League (amateur & commerce, licenses); OX5 Aviation Pioneers; awarded patent, recording & counting device, 1951; dir. Theatre Owners of Indiana; dir. to NATO; dir. NATO member ad hoc comm; 1972 chair., NATO Statistical Committee; presently chm., trade practice comm.; 1976-NITE Award service to Independent Exhibition.

REMICK, LEE: Actress. b. Boston, Dec. 14, 1937. e. Miss Hewitt's Sch., Barnard Coll. Started in summer stock; on tour in Jenny Kisses Me, The Seven Year Itch, Paint Your Wagon; first N.Y. stage appearance, Be Your Age; major TV shows incl. Studio 1, Playhouse 90, Armstrong Circle Theatre; m.p. debut in A Face In the Crowd.
PICTURES INCLUDE: The Long Hot Summer, Anatomy of a Murder, Wild River, Sanctuary, Experiment in Terror, The Days of Wine and Roses, The Wheeler Dealers, Travelin' Lady, Baby the Rain Must Fall, Hallelujah Trail, Hard Contract, A Severed Head, Sometimes A Great Notion, A Delicate Balance, Hennessy, The Omen, Telefon, The Medusa Touch, The Europeans, The Competition, Tribute.

REPP, ED EARL: Writer; TV, White Savage, Incident at Yuma, many others.
PICTURES INCLUDE: West of Cheyenne, Rawhide Ranger, Silver City Raiders, Six Gun Gospel, Trigger Trail, Texas Panhandle, Fighting Frontiersman, Guns of Hate, many Westerns, currently featured in western history magazines.

RESNAIS, ALAIN: Director. b. Cannes, France, 1922. Began career as asst. dir. to Nicole Vedres on compilation of film for Paris 1900. During '50s worked as asst. editor and editor; experimented with making his own 16mm films. Did series of shorts on various painters, culminating with documentary on Van Gogh (1948), which he co-directed with Robert Hessens, with whom he later filmed Guernica. Co-directed The Statues Also Die with Chris Marker.
PICTURES INCLUDE: Night and Fog, Hiroshima, Mon Armour, Last Year at Marienbad, Muriel, La Guerre Est Finie, Je t'Aime, Je t'Aime, Stavisky; Providence, Mon Oncle d'Amerique.

RETCHIN, NORMAN: Writer, producer. b. Chicago. May 6, 1919. e. U. of Pa., 1940. U.S. Air Force, 1943–45; J. Walter Thompson adv. agency, 1946–51; story ed. & assoc. prod. Screen Televideo Co., 1951–55; story ed. Clover Prod. 1955; stage, orig. bk. and lyrics, The Genius Farm; TV, orig. prod., The Untouchables.
PICTURES INCLUDE: Uranium Boom, (collab.) Leather Saint, Ride Out for Revenge, Mission Mars, Into Thin Air, (orig. story).

RETTIG, TOMMY: Actor. b. Jackson Heights, N.Y., Dec. 10, 1941; on stage in Annie Get Your Gun; TV series, Lassie.
PICTURES INCLUDE: Gobs and Gals, Paula, Lady Wants Mink, 5000 Fingers of Dr. T., So Big, River of No Return, The Raid, The Egyptian, The Cobweb, At Gunpoint.

REVERE, ANNE: Actress. b. New York City, June 25, 1907; e. Wellesley Coll., B.A., m. Samuel Rosen, director. On stage, Stuart Walker Stock Co., 1928–29, Double Door, 1933–34. Children's Hour, 1934–37, org. & dir. Surry Theat., Maine, N.Y., 1936–39; Acad. Award best supporting role (National Velvet), 1945.
PICTURES INCLUDE: Double Door, Howards of Virginia, Men of Boys Town, Remember the Day, Star Spangled Rhythm, Song of Bernadette, National Velvet, Keys of the Kingdom, Sunday Dinner for a Soldier, Dragonwyck, Forever Amber, Body and Soul, Gentleman's Agreement, Place in the Sun, Great Missouri Raid, Tell Me That You Love Me Junie Moon, Birch Interval.

REVILL, CLIVE: Actor. b. Wellington, New Zealand, Ent. m.p. ind. 1965.
STAGE: Irma La Douce, The Mikado, Oliver, Marat/Sade, Jew of Malta, Sherry, Chichester Season, The Incomparable Max (N.Y.), Sherlock Holmes (NY).
PICTURES INCLUDE: Bunny Lake is Missing, Once Upon a Tractor, Modesty Blaise, A Fine Madness, Kaleidoscope, The Double Man, Fathom, Italian Secret Service, Nobody Runs Forever, Shoes of the Fisherman, Assassination Bureau, The Private Life of Sherlock Holmes, The Buttercup Chain, A Severed Head, Boulevard de Rhum, Avanti!, Flight to the Sun, The Legend of Hell House, The Little Prince, The Black Windmill, Ghost in the Noonday Sun, One of Our Dinosaurs Is Missing, Galileo, Matilda.
TV: Chicken Soup with Barley, Volpone, Bam, Pow, Zapp. Candida, Platonov, A Bit of Vision, Mill Hill, The Piano Player, Hopcroft in Europe, A Sprig of Broome, Ben Franklin in Paris, Pinocchio, The Great Houdini, Show Business Hall of Fame, Feather and Father, Winner Take All, The New Avenger, Licking Hitler, Columbo, Centennial, A Man Called Sloane, Nobody's Perfect, Marya, Moviola, Diary of Anne Frank.

REYNOLDS, BURT: Actor/Director. b. Waycross, Ga., Feb. 11, 1936. Former Fla State U football star, won fame as actor on TV in series: Riverboat, Gunsmoke, Hawk and Dan August.
PICTURES INCLUDE: Armored Command, Angel Baby,

Operation CIA, Navajo Joe, Impasse, Shark, Sam Whiskey, 100 Rifles, Fade-In, Skullduggery, Everything You Wanted To Know About Sex, Fuzz, Deliverance, Shamus, White Lightning, The Man Who Loved Cat Dancing, The Longest Yard, W.W. & The Dixie Dancekings, At Long Last Love, Hustle, Lucky Lady, Gator (dir.-star), Silent Movie, Nickelodeon, Smokey & The Bandit, Semi-Tough, The End (dir-star), Hooper, Starting Over, Rough Cut, Smokey & The Bandit II, Cannonball Run, Paternity, Sharky's Machine (dir.-star).

REYNOLDS, CLARKE: Writer, producer. b. Bklyn, N.Y. e. U. of Missouri; pub. rel. NYC, pub. with WAAM-TV, Baltimore.
PICTURES INCLUDE: Disc-Jockey, Shotgun, Chisera, Gunmen of Laredo, Imperial Venus, Gunfighters of Casa Grande, Gringo, Genghis Khan, Son of A Gunfighter, The Viking Queen, The Viscount, Warhead, Shalako, The Marauders, The Red Sun, Private Navy, Operation Thunderbolt, Cruise Missile, Night Games.
TV: Celebrity Playhouse, Damon Runyon Theatre, Cheyenne, 20th Century-Fox Hour, Lux Video Hour, West Point, Whiplash, Playhouse 90, Walter Winchell File, Wells Fargo, Tombstone Territory, The Texan, Peter Gunn, Wagon Train, U.S. Marshall, Zane Grey Theatre, Broken Arrow (pilot), The Beachcomber, The Deputy, The Investigators, Cain's Hundred, Created Man Without a Gun.

REYNOLDS, DEBBIE: Actress. r.n. Mary Frances Reynolds. b. El Paso, Tex., April 1, 1932. e. Burbank & John Burroughs H.S., Burbank, Calif. With Burbank Youth Symphony during h.s.; beauty contest winner (Miss Burbank) 1948, signed by Warner Bros.; on stage in Personal Appearances, Blis-Hayden Theater, Star of Tomorrow, 1952.
PICTURES INCLUDE: The Daughter of Rosie O'Grady, Three Little Words, Two Weeks With Love, Mr. Imperium, Singing in the Rain, Skirts Ahoy, I Love Melvin, Give a Girl a Break, Affair of Dobie Gillis, Susan Slept Here, Athena, Hit the Deck, Tender Trap, Catered Affair, Bundle of Joy, Tammy and the Bachelor, The Mating Game, Say One for Me, It Started With A Kiss, The Gazebo, The Rat Race, Pleasure of His Company, Second Time Around, How the West Was Won, Goodbye Charlie, The Unsinkable Mollie Brown, The Singing Nun, Divorce, American Style, What's The Matter With Helen?, That's Entertainment!
TV: The Debbie Reynolds Show.
STAGE: Irene.

REYNOLDS, JOYCE: Actress. b. San Antonio, Texas, Oct. 7, 1924; e. UCLA. School plays including role of Alice in Alice in Wonderland at UCLA, contracted by Warner Bros. in 1942, appearing in Yankee Doodle Dandy, George Washington Slept Here, Mark Twain, Constant Nymph, Janie, Always Together, Wallflower, Girl School, Dangerous Inheritance.

REYNOLDS, MARJORIE: Actress. b. Buhl, Idaho, Aug. 12, 1921. On screen as child 1923 & later (Scaramouche, Svengali, Revelation, etc.).
PICTURES INCLUDE: Murder in Greenwich Village (1937), College Humor, Holiday Inn, Star-Spangled Rhythm, Dixie, Ministry of Fear, Up in Mabel's Room, Three Is a Family, Duffy's Tavern, Bring on the Girls, Meet Me on Broadway, Heaven Only Knows, Bad Men of Tombstone, Great Jewel Robber, Rookie Fireman, Home Town Story, No Holds Barred, Models, Inc., Silent Witness.
TV: The Life of Riley (series).

REYNOLDS, SHELDON: Writer, producer, director. b. Philadelphia, Pa., 1923. e. NYU. Radio-TV writer; programs include My Silent Partner, Robert Q. Lewis Show, We the People, Danger; writer, prod., dir. Foreign Intrigue film; prod. dir. s.p. collab. story, Foreign Intrigue.

REYNOLDS, STUART: Producer. b. Chicago, Ill., March 22, 1907. e. Chicago law schools. Adv. exec., Lord and Thomas, BBD & O. General Mills; sales exec. Don Lee-Mutual; formed Stuart Reynolds Prod., TV films.
TV: General Electric Theatre, Cavalcade of America, Your Jeweler's Showcase, Wild Bill Hickok, educational/training films; Eye of the Beholder.

RHEINER, SAMUEL: Executive. b. NYC. e. NYU, BCS; Fordham U. Joined Paramount as asst. to James R. Cowan; asst. org. Publix Stage Show dept.; then gen. mgr. Artists Booking Office (Paramount sub.); in chg. cost control Paramount theat., N.Y. & Bklyn, Rivoli, Rialto, Criterion theats., N.Y.; gen. mgr. scenic & costume depts., Publix Theats. In 1937 tr. to Paramount Studios, reorg. music dept. Resigned 1939 to enter independent prod. becoming v.p. Boris Morros Prods. (Flying Deuces); org. Nat'l Pictures Corp. of Calif. (Second Chorus, Tales of Manhattan). In 1945 assoc. prod. David L. Loew Prod. Artists, Inc.; The Southerner prod. Inner Sanctum; treas. Horizon Pictures, Inc.
PICTURES INCLUDE: The Southerner, The Stranger, Carnegie Hall, Inner Sanctum, The Prowler, When I Grow Up, African Queen, Melba, On the Waterfront, Bridge on the River Kwai, The Strange One, The Chase, Suddenly Last Summer, Lawrence of Arabia, Night of the Generals,

The Swimmer, Nicholas and Alexandra, The Happening, The Last Tycoon.

RHODES, E. A.: Exhibitor. b. Cape Town, S.A. 1900. Father, one of first cinema exhibitors in Transvaal. Joined m.p. ind. 1916 with Schlesinger Org., later in Britain with P.D.C. & U.A., 1941 mgr. with The Classic Cinemas. Took control Booking Dept. 1945; apptd. chmn. and managing dir. 1962; retired from Classic 1973. Chmn. London CEA 1956–57, 1967–68, 1969–73. Pres., National Assoc., Bingo Clubs, 1967. Chmn, 1968. Pres. Cinema Theatre Assoc. 1972–77. Pres. Cinema Veterans Soc., 1975–76 Prop. Curzon Cinemas, Eastbourne.

RICH, IRENE: Actress. b. Buffalo, N.Y. Oct. 13, 1897. e. St. Margaret's Episcopal School; painting. Real estate saleswoman; stock farmer; on radio, in night clubs, vaudeville.
PICTURES INCLUDE: Exalted Flapper, Lady Windemere's Fan, Lost Lady, Craig's Wife, They Had to See Paris, So This is London, Down to Earth, That Certain Age, Mortal Storm, Lady in Question, Queen of the Yukon, Keeping Company, This Time for Keeps, Angel and the Badman, Calendar Girl, New Orleans, Fort Apache, Joan of Arc.

RICH, JOHN: Producer-Director. b. Rockaway Beach, N.Y., July 6, 1925. e. U. of Michigan, B.A., Phi Beta Kappa, 1948; M.A. 1949 Sesquicentennial Award, 1967; bd. of dir., Screen Dir. Guild of America, 1954–1960; v.p. 1958–1960 Founder-Trustee, Producers-Directors Pension Plan, chmn. of bd. 1965, 1968, 1970; treasurer, Directors Guild of America, 1966–67; v.p. 1967–72.
TV: Academy Awards, The Dick Van Dyke Show, 1963; All in the Family, 1972 (director); All in the Family, 1973 (producer); Directors Guild Award, Most Outstanding Directorial Achievement, 1971.
PICTURES INCLUDE: Boeing-Boeing; The New Interns; Wives and Lovers; Roustabout; Easy Come, Easy Go.

RICHARD, CLIFF: Singer and actor. b. 1940. Ent. show business 1958 in TV series Oh Boy. Other TV includes Sunday Night at the London Palladium, several Cliff Richard Shows; film debut in Serious Charge, 1959; star, play Aladdin, London Palladium Theatre, 1964–65. Top British Singer, 1960–66.
PICTURES INCLUDE: Expresso Bongo, The Young Ones, Summer Holiday, Wonderful Life, Voted top box-office Star of Grt. Britain, 1962–63, 1963–64. Finder's Keepers, Two a Penny, Take Me High.

RICHARDS, JEFF: Actor. r.n. Richard Mansfield Taylor. b. Portland, Ore. Nov. 1. e. Tacoma, Wash. H.S., U.S.C. served in U.S. Navy, 1943–46; professional baseball.
PICTURES INCLUDE: Kill the Umpire, Tall Target, The Strip, Angels in the Outfield, The Sellout, Above and Beyond, Desperate Search, Code Two, Big Leaguer, Crest of the Wave, Seven Brides for Seven Brothers, Many Rivers to Cross, The Marauders, It's A Dog's Life, Waco, Johnny Belinda.

RICHARDS, THOMAS LLOYD: Producer-Writer. b. Cardiff, Wales. Entered industry in London at Stoll Studios in 1926, working in production and as 3rd asst. director. Named 1st asst. dir. for producer Herbert W. Wilcox, going to Hollywood to work on Wilcox films starring Anna Neagle: No, No, Nanette, Nurse Edith Cavell, Sunny, and Irene. Worked for RKO Studios as 1st asst. dir., acting in that capacity for Without Reservations, etc. Joined Four Star Productions (TV producers) as v.p. in chg. prod. Produced 24 in Untouchables series at Desilu. Prod. assoc. of many TV special and features for TV; also special consultant to producers of TV series and mini-series.

RICHARDSON, SIR RALPH: Actor. b. Cheltenham Gloucestershire, England, Dec. 19, 1902; m. Merial Forbes; made first appearance on stage in 1921 as Lorenzo in The Merchant of Venice; joined Birmingham Repertory Theatre 1926 and has appeared in many plays, particularly Shakespearean prod.; hobbies: Drawing, modeling, literature, aviation, squash, racquets. In 1934 appeared in Friday the 13th, GB; Return of Bulldog Drummond, BIPUA. In 1942, The Day Will Dawn, Soskin-Gen. Film, The Avengers, Par. In 1943, The Silver Fleet, The Volunteer, Released from Fleet Air Arm; then repertory, Old Vic, London. Knighted in New Year's Honor's List, 1947, British money-making star, 1953.
PICTURES INCLUDE: School for Secrets, Anna Karenina, The Fallen Idol, Heiress, Outcast of the Islands, Home at Seven (Murder on Monday), Holly & the Ivy, The Sound Barrier, Richard III, Smiley, Passionate Stranger, Our Man in Havana, Exodus, Lion of Sparta, Long Day's Journey Into Night, Woman of Straw, Dr. Zhivago, Khartoum, The Wrong Box, 1968, Battle of Britain, Oh! What A Lovely War, The Bed Sitting Room, Looking Glass War, David Copperfield, 1972: Oh Lucky Man; Alice in Wonderland, A Doll's House, Rollerball, Dragonslayer.

RICHARDSON, TONY: Director. b. Shipley, Yorks; England, 1928. e. Wadham Coll., Oxford, where he dir. number prod. for O.U.D.S. Began career with BBC TV and directed such plays as Othello and The Gambler. In 1955 joined English

Stage Co. as Assoc. Artistic Dir. Started with Look Back in Anger, Member of the Wedding, 1958 at Shakespeare Memorial Theatre. 1960, N.Y. co-dir., A Taste of Honey. Recent stage work, dir., Seagull and St. Joan of the Stockyards, Threepenny Opera, I Claudius. Ent. m.p. ind. 1958 to dir. prod. Look Back in Anger, The Entertainer, 1959–60; prod. Saturday Night and Sunday Morning.
PICTURES INCLUDE: A Taste of Honey, Loneliness of the Long Distance Runner, Tom Jones, The Loved One, Mademoiselle, The Sailor from Gibralter, Red and Blue, Charge of the Light Brigade, Laughter in the Dark, Hamlet, Ned Kelly, A Delicate Balance, Dead Cert, Joseph Andrews.

RICHMAN, MARK: Actor. b. Philadelphia, Pa. Stage credits incl. End as a Man, Masquerade, The Zoo Story, Detective Story, Rose Tattoo.
PICTURES INCLUDE: Friendly Persuasion, Dark Intruder, Agent for H.A.R.M., For Singles Only.
TV: Cain's Hundred.

RICHMOND, TED: Producer. b. Norfolk, Va., June 10, 1912; e. Mass. Inst. Tech. Ent. m.p. ind. as publicity dir., RKO Theats.; later mgr. Albany dist. Pub. dir. Fabian circuit, N.Y.: Paramount upper N.Y. state theats.; Grand Nat'l Pictures. Author Grand Nat'l series Trigger Pal, Six Gun Rhythm. Formed T. H. Richmond Prods., Inc., 1941.
PICTURES INCLUDE: Hit the Hay, The Milkman, Kansas Raiders, Shakedown, Smuggler's Island, Strange Door, Cimarron Kid, Bronco Buster, Has Anybody Seen My Gal, No Room for the Groom, Weekend with Father, The Mississippi Gambler, Desert Legion, Column South, Bonzo Goes to College, Forbidden, Walking My Baby Back Home, Francis Joins the Wacs, Bengal Brigade, (Formed Copa Prod. with Tyrone Power, 1954) Count Three and Pray, Nightfall, Abandon Ship, Solomon and Sheba, Charlemagne. Formed Ted Richmond Prod. Inc. for MGM release, 1959. Reactivated Copa Prod. Ltd., England, 1960. Produced for MGM: Bachelor in Paradise, Advance to the Rear; for Paramount, Pancho Villa; for Mirisch-U.S., Return of the 7; Independent, Red Sun; Producer, Papillon-Allied Artists, various distributors.

RICHTER, W. D.: Writer. b. Connecticut. e. USC Film School.
PICTURES: Slither, Peeper, Nickelodeon, Invasion of the Body Snatchers, Dracula, Brubaker, All Night Long.

RICKETSON, FRANK H., JR.: Executive. b. Leavenworth, Kan. e. U. Ky., LL.B. U. Denver. On ed. staff Kansas City Star, The Denver Post. Member exploitation Dept., Famous Players-Lasky Corp., 1921–24. Pres. Consolidated Theatres 1924 to 1929, Pres. Fox Inter-Mountain Theatres, 1934 to 1957, v.p. & gen. mgr. of Theatre Operations, National Theatres, Inc., 1956–58. Author of The Management of Motion Picture Theatres, Europe after the Marshall Plan, Opportunity Needs a Selling, Gems from a Thousand Sources. Retired director, Public Service Co. of Colorado, Continental Airlines, United Banks of Colorado, Cheyenne Newspapers Inc., Frontier Broadcasting Co., honorary bd. Central City Opera House Assn., Denver Museum of Natural History, first individual elected to Rocky Mountain Motion Picture Association Hall of Fame; member of the Colorado Motion Picture and Television Advisory Commission.

REISNER, DEAN: Writer. Began career as director: Bill and Coo, 1947. Has collaborated on following screenplays, among others: Coogan's Bluff, Dirty Harry, Play Misty for Me.

RIFKIN, JULIAN: Exhibitor. b. Boston, May 26, 1915. e. MIT. Member bd. of dir. Allied States Assoc. of M.P. Exhibitors, and Theatre Owners of America. Pres. Theatre Owners of New England 1961–63. Chairman bd. Theatre Owners of New England 1964–65. Past pres. Allied Artists Corp. of New England. Pres., 1968–69, chmn. of bd. Nat'l Assoc. of Theatre Owners, 1970. Pres. Rifkin Theatres. Pres. Cinema Centers Corp. Chm. NATO Code and Rating Comm., 1968–79.

RIGG, DIANA: Actress. Formerly with the Royal Shakespeare Co. at Aldwych Theatre, 1962–64. Ent. TV in The Avengers series, 1965. Ent. films 1967.
PICTURES INCLUDE: The Assassination Bureau, On Her Majesty's Secret Service, The Great Muppet Caper. 1970–71, on London and NY stage.

RISI, DINO: Director. b. Italy, 1916. Studied medicine but left for film job as assistant in Mario Soldati's Giacomo L'Idealista. Interned in Switzerland in World War II. Returned home to make documentaries and short films before directing Vacanze col Gangster in 1952.
PICTURES INCLUDE: Sign of Venus, Poveri ma Bellis, Ill Sorpasso, Scent of a Woman, Sunday Lovers.

RISSIEN, EDWARD L.: Executive. b. Des Moines, IA. e. Grinnell Coll., Stanford Univ. (B.A., 1949). Army Air Force, World War II. Bdwy. stage, mgr., 1950–53; v.p., Mark Stevens Prods., 1954–56; prod. v.p., Four Star, 1958–60; prog. exec., ABC-TV, 1960–62; v.p., Bing Crosby Prods., 1963–66; v.p.,

Filmways TV Prods.; assoc. producer, Columbia, 1968–69; indep. producer, 1970; prod., WB, 1971; exec. v.p., Playboy Prods., 1972–80; consultant & indep. prod., 1981–82.
PICTURES INCLUDE: Snow Job (prod., WB); Castle Keep (exec. prod.); Julius Vrooder (prod., Fox); Saint Jack (exec. prod.).
TELEVISION: Minstrel Man (exec. prod., CBS); A Whale for the Killing (exec. prod., ABC); Ocean View Park (exec. prod., ABC); Big Bob Johnson (exec. prod., NBC).

RITCHIE, MICHAEL: Director. b. Waukesha, Wisc., 1938. e. Harvard Univ. where he directed first production of Arthur Kopit's play, Oh Dad, Poor Dad, Mama's Hung You in the Closet and I'm Feeling So Sad. Professional career began as ass't. to Robert Saudek on Ford Foundation's Omnibus TV series. Later became assoc. prod. and then dir. on Saudek's Profiles in Courage series. Then had dir. assignments on top series (Man from U.N.C.L.E., Dr. Kildare, The Big Valley, Felony Squad).
PICTURES INCLUDE: Downhill Racer, Prime Cut, The Candidate, Smile (also prod.), The Bad News Bears, Semi-Tough, An Almost Perfect Affair, The Island, Bette Midler's Divine Madness.
TELEVISION: Man from U.N.C.L.E., Dr. Kildare, The Big Valley, Felony Squad, Run for Your Life, The Outsider (pilot).

RITT, MARTIN: Dir. b. N.Y., N.Y. Mar. 2. e. Elon Coll., Burlington, Ky, Started as actor in Golden Boy. N.Y. stage: studied acting under Elia Kazan; dir. stage; Mr. Peebles and Mr. Hooker, The Man, Set My People Free, A View From the Bridge, N.Y.; acted in 150 and dir. 100 TV dramas.
TV: Danger.
PICTURES INCLUDE: Edge of the City (first screen dir.), No Down Payment, The Long Hot Summer, The Black Orchid, The Sound and the Fury, Adventures of a Young Man, Hud (also co-producer), The Outrage, Spy Who Came In From the Cold, Hombre, The Brotherhood, The Molly Maguires, The Great White Hope, Sounder, Pete 'n' Tillie, Conrack, The Front, Casey's Shadow, Norma Rae, Back Roads. Acted: End of the Game.

RITTER, JOHN: Actor. b. Hollywood. Father was late Tex Ritter, country-western star. Married, actress Nancy Morgan. Attended Hollywood High School. Interest in acting began at Univ. of So. Calif. in 1968. Appeared with college cast at Edinburgh Festival; later with Eva Marie Saint in Desire under the Elms. Gained fame as star of TV series, Three's Company.
PICTURES: Americathon, Hero at Large, Wholly Moses, They All Laughed.
TELEVISION: Leave Yesterday Behind.

RIVE, KENNETH: Executive. b. London, England, July 26, 1919. Early career as actor, radio compere, theatrical agent. Served in Intell. Corps. during WWII. After demob. theatre sup. and gen. man. cinema co. promoted dir. 1947. Started in continental exhibition forming Gala Film Distrib. Ltd., 1950. Now man. dir. Gala Film Dist., Carlton & Majestic Cinemas & Dance Hall Ltd., Cosmopolitan Film Dist. Ltd., Gala-Jacey Enterprises Ltd., Berkeley & Continentale (Holdings) Ltd., Gala TV Prod. Ltd., Galaworldfilm Prod. Ltd., Gala Maintenance Ltd.; 1966, mgr. dir. Grade-Rive Ltd., Gala Co-Productions, Ltd., Gala Int'l Film & TV Enterprises, Ltd. Film Industry Defence Org., Malta United Film Corp. Ltd., Children's Film Foundation Ltd., International Films Theatre Ltd.
PICTURES INCLUDE: During One Night, The Boys, Devil Doll, Curse of Simba.

RIVERA, GERALDO: TV Reporter. b. N.Y.C., July 4, 1943. e. Univ. of Arizona, Columbia School of Journalism. Started legal career then switched to journalism, making several TV documentaries on such subjects as institutions for retarded, drug addiction, migrant workers, etc. Joined WABC-TV, New York, in 1970.
TV: Geraldo Rivera: Good Night America; Good Morning America (contributor). 20/20.

RIVKIN, ALLEN: Writer, producer. b. Hayward, Wis., Nov. 20, 1903. Newspaperman, novelist, playwright. Authored 85 s.p. including Farmer's Daughter, Battle Circus, Prisoner of War, Joe Smith American, Eternal Sea, Big Operator.
TV: Prod. Troubleshooters series, 1960 Democratic Nat'l Convention; author (with Laura Kerr) Hello, Hollywood; past pres. scr. br. and currently dir. pub. rel., WGAW, liaison rep., Legal Advisory Committee on m.p. & TV of the American Bar Assn. Recipient of Morgan Cox and Valentine Davies awards.

RIVKIN, JOE: Production executive. b. Hartford, Conn. Exploit. dir., Pathe, also artist mgr. then to Hal Roach. In armed services Pres. Carthay Prod., v.p. gen. mgr. Wald & Krasna Prod., 1951; talent exec. Allied Artists Pictures. Now with Wm. Morris Agency.

RIX, BRIAN: C.B.E. Actor, manager. b. Yorkshire, England, 1924. e. Bootham Sch., York. Ent. m.p. ind. 1951.

TV: Farces, 1956–72, over 80. Men of Affairs (series); A Roof over My Head (series).
PICTURES INCLUDE: Reluctant Heroes, What Every Woman Wants, Up to His Neck, Dry Rot, Wanted on Voyage, And the Same to You, The Night We Dropped a Clanger, The Night We Got the Bird, Nothing Barred, Don't Just Lie There Say Something!

ROACH, HAL, JR.: President, owner Hal Roach Studios. Unit mgr. 20th Century-Fox, 1944–45; gen. mgr., Rainbow Prod., 1945–46. Member of Acad. of M.P. Arts & Sciences, M.P. Producers Assoc., Pres. Alliance of TV Film Producers; treas. & bd. member and former pres. of Acad. of TV Arts & Sciences; pres. Rabco Corp., Hal Roach Prod., chmn. exec. officer, dir., F. I. Jacobs, Detroit; past chmn. bd., Mutual Broadcasting System, bd. member, Vitapix Corp.; gen, exec., TV Prod., Seven Arts Associated.
PICTURES INCLUDE: Block Heads, A Chump at Oxford, One Million B.C., Road Show, All American Co-ed, Calaboose, Prairie Chickens, Army Training films, Physical Education & Military Training, Military Justice of Court Martials, Fighting Man series.
TV: Stu Erwin Show, Racket Squad, Public Defender, My Little Margie, Passport to Danger, Screen Directors Playhouse, Stories of John Nesbitt, Code 3, Charlie Farrell Show, Gale Storm Show, Blondie, Forest Ranger.

ROBARDS, JASON, JR.: Actor. b. Chicago, July 26, 1922. Served in Navy during WW II. Studied acting at Acad. of Dramatic Arts. Began with Children's World Theatre, radio parts, asst. stage mgr. on Stalag 17. First major break 1953 in play American Gothic, followed by The Iceman Cometh, Long Day's Journey into Night, Toys in the Attic. After the Fall, others; to Hollywood, 1958.
PICTURES INCLUDE: The Journey, By Love Possessed, Long Day's Journey Into Night, Tender is the Night, Act One, A Thousand Clowns, Any Wednesday, The St. Valentine's Day Massacre, The Night They Raided Minsky's, Hour of the Gun, The Loves of Isadora, Once Upon a Time in the West, Ballad of Cable Hogue, Fools, Johnny Got His Gun, Murders in the Rue Morgue, Pat Garrett and Billy the Kid, All the President's Men, Julia, Comes a Horseman, Hurricane, Raise the Titanic! Caboblanco.
TV: Washington: Behind Closed Doors.

ROBBIE, SEYMOUR MITCHELL: Producer, director.
TV: Studio One, Omnibus, Play of the Week, Jackie Gleason Show, The Man From U.N.C.L.E., Eleventh Hour, Dupont Show of the Week, F Troop, Mr. Roberts, Amos Burke, Honey West, Disney Wonderful World of Color, Felony Squad, Lost in Space, Name of the Game, Hawaii Five-0, It Takes a Thief, High Chapparal, Mannix, Mission: Impossible, Cannon (TV film), F.B.I., Mod Squad, Streets of San Francisco, Kojak, Moving On.
PICTURES INCLUDE: C.C. & Company, 1970, Marco.

ROBBINS, BURTON: Executive. Chm. & chief exec. officer, National Screen Service Corp. b. New York City, Feb. 2. e. New Rochelle, N.Y. public schools; Clark Prep, Hanover, N.H.; Vanderbilt University, Nashville, Tenn. Entered motion picture industry 1941 as trainee at National Screen Service Philadelphia branch. Subsequently served as salesman and asst. branch manager at NSS Albany, N.Y. and Detroit branches, respectively. Entered U.S. Army Air Corps in January, 1942, Anti-Aircraft Artillery O.C.S. Wilmington N.C. October 1943, U.S. Army Air Corps European theatre June 1944 to September 1945. Separated from Army of U.S. as First Lieutenant, December 1945. Rejoined NSS January 1946, subsequently appointed head of advertising accessories division. 1953, appointed asst. to the pres., and elected vice-pres. in charge of sales in September 1955. Elected president and chief executive officer, August 1963, and chairman of the board and chief executive officer February, 1979. Past Motion Picture Industry chairman Federation of Jewish Philanthropies; past trustee of Central Synagogue in New York City; past vicepres. & current director, Will Rogers Memorial Fund; past treas. and current vice-pres. & director, Foundation of Motion Picture Pioneers; past pres., Cinema Unit B'nai B'rith in New York City; and currently int. chm., Variety Clubs International.

ROBBINS, MATTHEW: Writer-Director. e. Univ. of S. Calif. School of Cinema. Writes scripts in collaboration with Hal Barwood, Robbins branching out into directing also with Corvette Summer in 1978.
PICTURES INCLUDE: Scripts, all with Barwood: The wsugarland Express, The Bingo Long Traveling All-Stars and Motor Kings, Corvette Summer (also dir.); Dragonslayer (also dir.).

ROBERT, PATRICIA HARRISON. Executive. b. Atlanta, Ga., March 31, 1939. e. Manhattanville College of the Sacred Heart, Ecole Francaise (Paris), U. of Virginia Graduate School. Dir. of pub. & pub. relations, Gerald Rafshoon Advertising, 1965–69; drama critic, Atlanta Magazine, 1965–68; drama critic, feature writer, The Atlanta Constitution, 1968–69; asst. to publicity director, The Walter Reade Organization, 1969–70; director of publicity—public re-

lations, Radio City Music Hall, 1970. Became Director of Advertising—Public Relations July, 1973.

ROBERTS, BEN: Writer. r.n. Ben Eisenberg. b. New York, N.Y. Mar. 23, 1916. e. N.Y.U., 1932–35. Free lance pub. rel. counsel, 1938; collab. on Broadway shows, Merry Widow, Jackpot, Dream with Music, Portrait in Black.
PICTURES INCLUDE: (collab. s.p.) White Heat, Goodbye My Fancy, Captain Horatio Hornblower, Come Fill the Cup, White Witch Doctor, O. Henry's Full House, King of the Khyber Rifles, Green Fire, Serenade.

ROBERTS, CURTIS: Producer. b. Dover, England. e. Cambridge U. Child actor. England, Germany; numerous pictures for Rank Org.; prod. England, on Broadway in Gertie, Island Visit; co-prod. on Broadway, Horses in Midstream, Golden Apple, Tonight or Never; tour and N.Y. 1965, The Journey, B'way, 1965.
TV: Rendezvous, Deadly Species, Top Secret, The Ilona Massey Show, When In Rome, Ethan Frome, Black Chiffon, Monaco.
PICTURES INCLUDE: An Actress in Love, La Die, Hypocrite, Jet Over the Atlantic, The Vixen, Farewell Party, Polly's Return, Rain Before Seven, Halloween, Malaga, My Dear Children, Bus Stop, Eve Arden Show, Rose-Marie Show.
BOOKS: History of Summer Theatre, The History of Vaudeville, Other Side of the Coin, 1969, History of Music (Popular) 1900–70. 1970, History of English Music Halls (1972), Latta (1972). Then There Were Some (1979).
TOURS: Blithe Spirit, Showboat, Kiss Me Kate, Generation, The Camel Bell, Farewell Party, Twentieth Century, Great Sebastians, Goodbye Charlie, Time of the Cuckoo, Under Papa's Picture, Everybody's Gal, Divorce Me Darling, Gingerbread Lady, September Son, 1975, Same Time Next Year.

ROBERTS, LYNNE: Actress (also known as Mary Hart); b. El Paso, Tex., Nov. 22, 1922. e. Lawler Prof. Sch. On stage prior to screen debut in Dangerous Holiday, 1937.
PICTURES INCLUDE: My Buddy, Big Bonanza, Girls of the Big House, The Chicago Kid, Winter Wonderland, Eyes of Texas, Sons of Adventure, Timber Trail, Trouble Preferred, Madonna of the Desert, Secret Service Investigator, Call of Klondike, Blazing Sun, Great Plane Robbery, The Blazing Forest, Because of You, Port Sinister.

ROBERTS, MARGUERITE: Writer. b. Clarks, Neb. m. John Sanford, novelist.
PICTURES INCLUDE: Honky Tonk, Dragon Seed, Ziegfeld Girl, Sea of Grass, If Winter Comes, Ambush, Escape, Soldiers Three, Diamond Head, Love Has Many Faces, Five Card Stud, Norwood, Shootout, Red Sky At Morning, True Grit.

ROBERTS, STANLEY: Writer. b. New York, N.Y. May 17, 1916. e. C.C.N.Y.
PICTURES INCLUDE: Sing While You're Able, Thanks for Listening, Anything for a Thrill, Under Western Skies, Penthouse Rhythm, Song of the Thin Man, Louisa, Curtain Call at Cactus Creek, Up Front, Death of a Salesman, Story of Will Rogers, Caine Mutiny.

ROBERTS, WILLIAM: Writer-Producer. b. Los Angeles. e. USC.
PICTURES INCLUDE: You For Me, Fast Company, Easy To Love, Her 12 Men, Private War of Major Benson, The Sheepman, The Mating Game, The Magnificent Seven, Wonderful World of the Brothers Grimm, Come Fly With Me, The Devil's Brigade, The Bridge At Remagen, One More Train to Rob, Red Sun, The Last American Hero, Posse.
TV: head writer, Life With Father; created Donna Reed Show.

ROBERTSON, CLIFF: Actor. b. La Jolla, Calif., 1925.
STAGE: Mr. Roberts, Late Love, The Lady and the Tiger, The Wisteria Tree, Orpheus Descending.
TV: Philco-Goodyear, Studio One, Robert Montgomery presents; Man Without a Country (movie); Washington: Behind Closed Doors.
PICTURES INCLUDE: Picnic, Autumn Leaves, Battle of the Coral Sea, As the Sea Ranges, Underworld, USA, The Big Show, Gidget, All in a Night's Work, The Interns, PT 109, The Best Man, 633 Squadron, Masquerade, The Honey Pot, The Devil's Brigade, Charly, (Academy Award, Best Actor, 1969), Too Late the Hero, The Great Northfield, Minnesota Raid, J. W. Coop (director, actor); Man On a Swing, Three Days of the Condor, Midway, Shoot.

ROBERTSON, DALE: Executive, actor, producer (Star of Tomorrow, 1951), r.n. Dayle; b. Oklahoma City, Okla., July 14, 1923; e. Oklahoma Military Coll. Prof. prizefighter; U.S. Army Sept. 1942–June 1945; m.p. debut in Fighting Man of the Plains.
PICTURES INCLUDE: Caribou Trail, Two Flags West, Call Me Mister, Take Care of My Little Girl, Golden Girl, Lydia Bailey, Return of the Texan, Outcasts of Poker Flat, O. Henry's Full House, Farmer Takes a Wife, Gambler from Natchez, Sitting Bull, Son of Sinbad, Day of Fury, Law of the Lawless, Blood on the Arrow, The Walking Major, The

Coast of Skeleton, The One-Eyed Soldier, The Last Ride of the Daltons, Dakota Incident, View from the Terrace, Fast and Sexy, Hell's Canyon.
TELEVISION: (series) Wells Fargo, The Iron Horse, Death Valley Days, Hollywood Palace. (films) Melvin Purvis, Kansas City Massacre.

ROBERTSON, F. J.: Producer. b. London, England, 1916. Early career as pianist, musical comedy, writer (composer) stage revues, pantomime. Theatre manager. Ent. TV 1954 as writer; created Goldhawk Studios of which man. dir. 1964, prod. The Little Ones, Columbia release.

ROBIN, DANY: Actress. b. Paris, France. Dancer since child. Played at the opera; acted on stage in Paris, then m.p.
PICTURES INCLUDE: Thirst of Men, Naughty Martine (L'Eventail); American Language debut in Act of Love, 1954. Holiday for Henrietta, Topaz.

ROBIN, LEO: Lyricist. b. Pittsburgh, Pa., April 6, 1900. e. U. of Pittsburgh. Became actor in New York after some time in Carnegie Tech. drama dept., then newspaperman publicist.
STAGE: Girl in Pink Tights, Hit the Deck, Greenwich Village Follies, Judy, Bubbling Over; to Hollywood 1929, formed musical partnerships with Richard Whitting, Ralph Rainger.
SONGS: Hallelujah, June in January, Louise, Prisoner of Love, Beyond the Blue Horizon, My Ideal, No Love No Nothin'.
PICTURES INCLUDE: Innocents of Paris, Monte Carlo, Little Miss Marker, Big Broadcast of 1935, Big Broadcast of 1937, Big Broadcast of 1938 (Award 1938 for best song, Thanks for the Memory), Waikiki Wedding, Paris Honeymoon, Gulliver's Travels, Coney Island, Gang's All Here, My Gal Sal, The Time The Place and the Girl, Just for You, Meet Me After the Show, Small Town Girl, Latin Lovers, Hit the Deck, My Sister Eileen.

ROBSON, FLORA: Actress. b. South Shields, England, March 28, 1902. e. Palmers Green High School, R.A.D.A. Before film career was factory welfare worker and on leg. stage.
PICTURES INCLUDE: Dance Pretty Lady, One Precious Year, Catherine the Great, Fire Over England, Farewell Again, Wuthering Heights, The Lion Has Wings, Poison Pen, We Are Not Alone, Invisible Stripes, The Sea Hawk, Bahama Passage, Saratoga Trunk, Great Day, Years Between, Black Narcissus, Frieda, Holiday Camp, Caesar and Cleopatra, Saraband for Dead Lovers, Good Time Girl, Tall Headlines, Malta Story, Romeo and Juliet, High Tide at Noon, No Time for Tears, The Gypsy and the Gentleman, Innocent Sinners, Murder at the Gallop, Guns at Ratasi, Young Cassidy, Those Magnificent Men in Their Flying Machines, Seven Women, The Kings Story, The Eye of the Devil, The Shuttered Room, Cry on the Wind, Fragment of Fear, Cry in the Wind, The Cellar, The Beloved, Dominque, Les Miserables, Clash of the Titans.
STAGE: Black Chiffon (1959), The Importance of Being Ernest, Ring Around the Moon.
TV: Corn is Green, Message for Margaret, The Return, Humanity, The Untouchable, Mother Courage, The Gentle Shade, The Human Jungle, The Misunderstanding, David Copperfield, The Old Ladies, Brighton Belle, Something for the Children, Heidi, Mr. Lollipop, The Shrimp and The Anemone, The Oresteia of Aeschylus, The Man Called Intrepid, Rebecca.

"ROCHESTER": See Eddie Anderson.

ROCKERT, JOHN F.: Executive. b. Kansas City, Mo., Oct. 29, 1924, e. Univ. So. Calif. In U.S. Navy, 1942–45. Joined Universal Pictures in 1951; left in 1957 to start independent productions. From 1960 to 1968 handled indep. roadshow distribution (4-walling). In 1969 formed CineWorld Corporation, natl. dist. co., of which he is pres. In 1975–76 did tax shelter financing for 13 films. Currently involved in distribution, production packaging and intl. co-production.

RODGERS, GABY: Actress. b. Frankfort, Germany, Mar. 29, 1928; e. Mt. Holyoke Coll., 1944–48. Barter Theatre Award, 1950; summer stock, many TV shows.
TV: Suspense, Philco Playhouse, Danger, Robert Montgomery, Pulitzer Prize Playhouse, Kraft TV Theatre, Omnibus.
PICTURES INCLUDE: Kiss Me Deadly.

ROEG, NICHOLAS: Director-Cameraman. b. London Aug. 15, 1928. Entered film industry through cutting rooms of MGM's British Studios, dubbing French films into English. Moved into prod. as clapper boy and part of photographer Freddie Young's crew. Next became camera operator (Trials of Oscar Wilde, The Sundowners). Had first experience as cameraman on TV series (Police Dog and Ghost Squad). Feature film debut as cameraman on Doctor Crippen. Debut as director on Performance; co-directed with Donald Cammell. First solo dir. film, Walkabout.
PICTURES INCLUDE: Cameraman: The System, Every Day's a Holiday, The Caretaker, Nothing But the Best, A

Funny Thing Happened on the Way to the Forum, Fahrenheit 451, Far from the Madding Crowd, Petulia. Director-Cameraman: Performance (co.-dir.), Walkabout, Don't Look Now, The Man Who Fell To Earth, Bad Timing.

ROGELL, ALBERT S.: Producer and director. b. Oklahoma City, Okla., Aug. 21, 1901; e. public school and h.s., Spokane, Wash., Washington State Coll.; m. Irma Warner; camera man; cutter, titler, author, dir. Has been assoc. with First Nat'l, Universal, FBO and Tiffany. Ent. m.p. ind. 1916 with Washington M.P. Co., Spokane. Went to Hollywood, 1917, as assist. to George Loane Tucker, prod. of The Miracle Man; joined Andrew J. Callahan Prod. In 1921 made Hollywood's first coop. film, costing $1,200 which C.B.C. bought; prod. Hallroom Boys series for Columbia. Then joined Western Pictures Exploitation Co. In 1925 joined Universal for two years, dir. 8 pic. a year; to First Nat'l & dir. Shepherd of the Hills, Aloha, Mamba, Tiffany Tip Off.
PICTURES INCLUDE: Magnificent Rogue, Earl Carroll, Sketchbook, Heaven Only Knows, Song of India, Northwest Stampede, Admiral Was a Lady, Shadow of Fear.
TV: Ford Theatre, 20th Century Hour, Broken Arrow, etc.

ROGERS, CHARLES (BUDDY): Actor. b. Olathe, Kan., Aug. 13, 1904; m. Mary Pickford; p. Maude & Bert Henry Rogers; e. U. of Kansas, and was trained for screen in Paramount Picture School. Appeared in Fascinating Youth and others. In armed services WW II. In 1945 named v.p. & treas. Comet Prods., Inc. Assoc. prod. Sleep My Love, 1950, pres. PRB, Inc., prod. radio, video shows.
PICTURES INCLUDE: Wings, My Best Girl, Get Your Man, Abie's Irish Rose, The Lawyer's Secret, Road to Reno, Working Girls, This Reckless Age, Best of Enemies. Fox: Take a Chance, Dance Band, Old Man Rhythm, One In a Million, Let's Make a Night of It, This Way Please, Golden Hoofs, Mexican Spitfire's Baby, Sing for Your Supper, Mexican Spitfire at Sea, Mexican Spitfire Sees a Ghost, Don't Trust Your Husband.

ROGERS, FRED: Entertainer & producer. b. Latrobe, PA, 1928. e. Rollins College (BA, music composition). In 1951 served as asst. prod. of NBC-TV's The Voice of Firestone and NBC-TV Opera Theatre. Later promoted to network floor dir., supervising Your Lucky Strike Hit Parade, Kate Smith Hour, etc. In Nov., 1953, joined WQED-TV in Pittsburgh, educational TV station, to handle programming. In 1954 started Children's Corner series, writing, producing and performing; it ran 7 years. In 1963 was ordained minister of United Presbyterian Church, dedicated to working with children and families through TV. Same year introduced character of Mister Rogers on Canadian Bdctg. Corp. of 15-min. daily program. Ran for one year—was similar in content to Neighborhood of Make-Believe segments on present half-hour program, Mister Rogers' Neighborhood. In 1964 programs were incorporated into larger, half-hour format on ABC affiliate in Pittsburgh. In 1966, 100 programs acquired by Easter Educational Network, broadcast in Pittsburgh, and seen for first time in other cities. Program now carried over 250 PBS stations.
AWARDS: George Foster Peabody, NET Special, Saturday Review TV, General Federation of Women's Club, Ralph Lowell, Gabriel, ten honorary doctoral degrees from universities. Emmy—(1980) Outstanding Individual Achievement in Children's Programming; Abe Lincoln Distinguished Communications Recognition Award.

ROGERS, GINGER: Actress. r.n. Virginia Katherine McMath; b. Independence, Mo., July 16, 1911. On stage in vaudeville, m.p. theat. presentations & musical comedy (Girl Crazy;). On screen from 1930. Academy Award, best performance by an actress. 1940 (Kitty Foyle, RKO Radio); voted among ten best Money-Making Stars in M.P. Herald-Fame Poll 1935, '37. In numerous pictures including Young Man of Manhattan, Gold Diggers of 1933, and others.
PICTURES INCLUDE: 42nd Street, Flying Down to Rio, The Gay Divorcee, Top Hat, Swing Time, The Story of Irene & Vernon Castle, Having Wonderful Time, Bachelor Mother, Tom Dick & Harry, Vivacious Lady, Stage Door, Primrose Path, Kitty Foyle, Roxie Hart, The Major & the Minor, Once Upon a Honeymoon, Lady in the Dark, Tender Comrade, I'll be Seeing You, Week-End at the Waldorf, Heartbeat, Magnificent Doll, It Had to Be You, Barkeleys of Broadway, Perfect Strangers, Groom Wore Spurs, Storm Warning, We're Not Married, Dream Boat, Monkey Business, Forever Female, Black Widow, Twist of Fate, Tight Spot, First Traveling Saleslady, Oh! Men, Oh! Women, Teenage Rebel, Harlow, The Confession.
TV: Como Show, Pontiac, Pat Boone, Dinah Shore, Bob Hope, Ed Sullivan, Hollywood Palace, Chrysler, Steve Allen, Jack Benny, Cinderella.

ROGERS, HENRY C.: Publicist. b. Irvington, N.J., April 19, 1914; e. U. of Pa., 1934, bd. chm., Rogers & Cowan, Inc.

ROGERS, JOHN W.: Producer. b. Buffalo, N.Y. 1916; p. Charles R. Rogers, prod.; e. U.S.C., 2nd asst. dir., 20th-Fox, then asst. dir., 5 yrs.; assoc. prod., Pine-Thomas prod.; U.S. Army, 4 yrs.; indep. Prod.; assoc. prod., U-I, 1951; prod., 1952.

PICTURES INCLUDE: Powers Girl, Fabulous Dorseys, Buccaneer's Girl, Iron Man, Raging Tide, Here Come the Nelson's, Red Ball Express; prod., Spirit of West Point, Law and Order, War Arrow, Ride Clear of Diablo, Black Horse Canyon.

ROGERS, LAWRENCE H., II: Executive. b. Trenton, N.J. Sept. 6, 1921; e. Princeton U. 1942, U.S. Army, 1942–1946; WSAZ, Huntington, W. Va. Radio & TV, V.P. & Gen. Mgr., 1949–55; WSAZ, Inc., President, 1955–59; Taft Broadcasting Co., v.p., 1959–63; Taft Broadcasting Co., President, 1963–1976. Vice Chairman, Hanna-Barbera Productions, L.A., Calif. and Cinemobile Systems, Hollywood. Director: Cine Artists International, Hollywood; Cincinnati Financial Corp.; Inter-Ocean Insurance Co., Cinti.; Cardinal Fund, Ohio; Federal Reserve Bank of Cleveland, Cincinnati Branch; Theater Development Fund, New York; Greater Cincinnati Foundation; Rockford College, Rockford, Ill.

ROGERS, PETER: Executive. b. Rochester, Eng., Feb. 20, 1916; e. Kings School, Rochester, Journalist in theatre and BBC; joined G. W. H. Productions 1941 as script writer; with Gainsborough Studios; asst. scenario ed. to Muriel Box; assoc. prod.; personal asst. to Sydney Box 1949.

PICTURES INCLUDE: Dear Murderer, Holiday Camp, When the Bough Breaks, Here Come the Huggetts, Huggetts Abroad, Vote for Huggett, It's Not Cricket, Marry Me, Don't Ever Leave Me, Appointment with Venus (Island Rescue), The Clouded Yellow, The Dog and the Diamonds (Children's Film Found.), Up to His Neck, You Know What Sailors Are, Cash on Delivery, To Dorothy A Son, Gay Dog, Circus Friends, Passionate Stranger, After the Ball, Time Lock, My Friend Charles, Chain of Events, Carry on Sergeant, Flying Scott, Cat Girl, Solitary Child, Carry On Teacher, Carry On Nurse, Carry On Constable, Please Turn Over, Watch Your Stern, The Tommy Steele Story, The Duke Wore Jeans, No Kidding, Carry On Regardless, Raising the Wind, Twice Around the Daffodils, Carry on Cruising, The Iron Maiden, Nurse on Wheels, Carry on Cabby, This is My Street, Carry On Jack, Carry On Spying, Carry On Cleo, The Big Job, Carry on Cowboy, Carry on Screaming, Don't Lose Your Head, Follow that Camel, Carry on Doctor, Carry on Up the Khyber, Carry on Camping, Carry on Assault, Carry on Henry, Quest, Revenge, Carry on At Your Convenience, All Coppers Are . . . Carry on Matron, Carry on Abroad, Bless This House, Carry on Girls, Carry on Dick, Carry on Behind, Carry on England, The Best of Carry On, Carry on Emmannuelle.

TV: Ivanhoe series, Carry on Laughing.

ROGERS, RICHARD H.: Executive. b. New York, Jan. 26, 1926. e. Colby Coll., Waterville, Me. Served in U.S. Army during WW II with Engineers. Joined Ziv TV in research and asst. to film ed. on Yesterday's Newsreel, 1948; sales dept., 1949; Flamingo Films, handling midwest sales, 1950; R. Monroe Prod., sales mgr. of TV properties, 1952; southeastern sales mgr. Sterling TV, 1954; PR dept., Shell Oil, 1955; acct. exec. Modern Talking Picture Service, 1957; elected v.p. and eastern sales mgr., 1962; v.p. for theatre division, 1965. Pres. of RHR Filmedia, Inc.

ROGERS, RODDY: Producer. b. Philadelphia; e. St. George's School. R.I.; U. of Pa. asst. acct. exec., Gray & Rogers Adv. Agency, Phila., 1946–48; stage mgr. and lighting coordinator at WFIL-TV, 1948; operations correlator, 1949; prod., dir., 1950; exec. prod. for WFIL-TV, 1951, prod. dir. Paul Whiteman TV Teen Club for ABC and Youth on the March, both on ABC-TV; dir. TV prod., WFIL-TV, 1953, mgr. radio, TV prod., Ward Wheelock Co., New York, 1954; prog. prod., radio-TV account supervisor N. W. Ayer & Son, 1955, N.Y.; chge. network sup. Ayer, N.Y. 1958; v.p., mgr. home office Ayer, 1959, pres. Agency Services Co.; pres. E. H. Rogers & Co., 1969.

ROGERS, ROY: Actor. Family name originally Leonard Slye. b. Cincinnati, O. Nov. 5, 1911. Radio singer; many m.p. from 1937. Voted No. 1 Money-Making Western Star in M.P. Herald-Fame, 1943–54 inclusive; also voted one of ten best money-making stars in 1945, '46. Acting & prod. TV films, 1952 with wife, Dale Evans; one-hour spectaculars, Chevy Show, 1959–60; contracted for several TV specials and for nationwide appearances with Roy Rogers touring show in Canada & U.S., 1962; State Fairs, Rodeo's since 1962; TV series.

PICTURES INCLUDE: Under Western Stars, The Old Barn Dance, Rep. in 1938; Billy the Kid Returns, Come On Rangers, Rough Riders, Round-Up, Frontier, Pony Express, Southward Ho!, In Old Caliente, Wall Street Cowboy, Heart of the Golden West, Sunset Serenade, Son of Paleface.

ROGERS, TED: Producer. b. Cleveland, O., Oct. 21, 1920. e. Cornell U.; dir. prog.; prod. I.T.C.

ROGERS, WILL, JR.: Actor. b. New York, N.Y. Oct. 20, 1912; p. late Will Rogers, actor; e. Stanford U., 1935. Publisher,

ed., Beverly Hills Citizen; for. corresp.; elected congressman from Calif.; U.S. Army, WW II; m.p. debut in Story of Will Rogers, since in Eddie Cantor Story, Boy From Oklahoma.

ROHM, MARIA: Actress. b. Vienna, Austria, 1949. Early career with Burgtheater in Vienna. Ent. TV 1963, Films 1966. Films incl: Million Eyes of Sumuru, Five Golden Dragons, House of a Thousand Dolls, 99 Women, Blood of Fu Manchu, Justine, Venus in Furs, Eugenie, Black Beauty, Treasure Island, Call of the Wild, The Assassin Is Not Alone, Ten Little Indians, End of Innocence. Flight to Hell, TV Series, Quatermain.

ROLAND, GILBERT: Actor. r.n. Luis Alonso. b. Juarez, Mexico, Dec. 11, 1905; p. Mr. & Mrs. Francisco Alonso, father a bull-fighter in Spain. e. private schools in Mexico.

PICTURES INCLUDE: Captain Kidd, Pirates of Monterey, Dude Goes West, Malaya, We Were Strangers, Crisis, The Furies, The Torch, Bullfighter and Lady, Mark of Renegade, Ten Tall Men, My Six Convicts, Glory Alley, Miracle of Fatima, Apache War Smoke, Bad & the Beautiful, Thunder Bay, Diamond Queen, Beneath the 12-Mile Reef, French Line, Underwater, The Racers, That Lady, The Wild Innocents, Eyes of Father Thomasino, The Big Circus, Samar, Cheyenne Autumn, The Reward, High Chaparral, Christian Licorice Store, Islands in the Stream, Caboblanco, Barbarosa.

TV: Bonanza, Alfred Hitchcock Presents, The FBI, Gunsmoke, The Fugitive, etc.

ROLEY, SUTTON: Director. b. Belle Vernon, Pa. Made dir. debut in live TV on Lights Out. Directed many live NBC-TV shows in "golden days" including Macbeth, with Judtih Anderson and Maurice Evans. Moved to L.A.: joined Ziv-UA and wrote, produced and directed Target. Was asst. prod. on Men of Annapolis.

PICTURES INCLUDE: Chosen Survivors.

TELEVISION: The Fugitive, Name of the Game, Gunsmoke, Rawhide, Mannix, Mission Impossible, Lost in Space, Bonanza, The Invaders, and many TV feature films.

ROLLE, ESTHER: Actress. b. Pompano Beach, Fla., Nov. 8. e. New School for Social Research. One of original members of Negro Ensemble Co. in N.Y. Has appeared both off and on Bdwy and in several TV series.

TELEVISION: Guest roles in N.Y.P.D., Like It Is, The Winners. Regular on series: Maude, Good Times. Film: I Know Why the Caged Bird Sings.

ROLLINS, JACK: Executive. Joined in partnership with Charles H. Joffe (see bio) to set up management-production org. Involved in production of many Woody Allen films with Joffe.

TV: Dick Cavett Show (exec. prod.).

ROMAN, LAWRENCE: Writer. b. Jersey City, N.J., May 30, 1921. e. UCLA, 1943.

PICTURES INCLUDE: (collab.) Drums Across the River, Vice Squad, (collab.) Naked Alibi, (collab.) One Desire, Man From Bitter Ridge, (s.p.) Kiss Before Dying, The Sharkfighters, (s.p.) Slaughter on Tenth Avenue, The Swinger, Author B'way play s.p. Under the Yum Yum Tree, Author B'way play P.S. I Love You. s.p. Paper Lion, collab. Red Sun, orig. s.p. A Warm December; wrote play, Buying Out, prod. in Buffalo, N.Y.; wrote play Crystal Chandelier, prod. in Stockbridge, Mass. McQ, (orig. s.p.) The Mayflower Number; (orig. s.p.) Abracadabra (org. s.p), Skeletons (orig. s.p.); Lovers Three (orig. s.p.). Broadway play: If! If! If!, Omar Bradley (TV special movie).

ROMAN, RUTH: Actress. b. Boston, Mass., Dec. 23; p. professionals; e. Girls H.S., Boston; Bishop Lee Dramatic Sch. Started career with little theatre groups: New Eng. Repertory Co., Elizabeth Peabody Players. Screen debut in Universal serial, Queen of the Jungle, then minor roles; author stories, The Whip Son, The House of Seven Gables.

PICTURES INCLUDE: Good Sam, Belle Starr's Daughter, Whip Son, House of Seven Gables, The Window, Champion, Barricade, Beyond the Forest, Always Leave Them Laughing, Colt .45, Three Secrets, Dallas, Strangers on a Train, Tomorrow is Another Day, Invitation, Starlift, Mara Maru, Young Man With Ideas, Blowing Wild, Far Country, Shanghai Story, Tanganyika, Down Three Dark Streets, Joe Macbeth, Bottom of the Bottle, Great Day in the Morning, Rebel in Town, Bitter Victory, Look in Any Window, Miracle of the Cowards (Spanish prod.), Love Has Many Faces.

TV: Naked City, Route 66, The Defenders, Breaking Point, Eleventh Hour, Producers Showcase, Dr. Kildare, The Long Hot Summer, Go Ask Alice (movie).

ROMERO, CESAR: Actor. b. New York City, Feb. 15, 1907; e. Collegiate Sch., Riverdale Country Sch. In U.S. Coast Guard, WW II. In 1927 on N.Y. stage.

PICTURES INCLUDE: Wintertime, Coney Island, Captain from Castile, Show Them No Mercy, Beautiful Blonde from Bashful Bend, Deep Waters, That Lady in Ermine, Once a Thief, The Jungle, Lost Continent, FBI Girl, Happy Go Lovely, Scotland Yard Inspector, Prisoners of the Casbah, Shadow Man, The Americano, Vera Cruz, The Racers, Leather Saint, Ocean's 11, The Computer Wore Tennis Shoes, Madigan's Millions, Now You See Him, Now You Don't, The Spectre of Edgar Allan Poe, The Strongest Man in the World, Carioca Tiger, and The Story of Father Kino.

ROONEY, MICKEY: Actor. r.n. Joe Yule, Jr.; b. Brooklyn, N.Y., Sept. 23, 1922; son of Joe Yule & Nell Carter, vaudeville performers. U.S. Army, WW II; in vaudeville during early infancy with parents and others before m.p. debut and after; from age of 5 to 12 created screen version of Fontaine Fox newspaper comic character Mickey McGuire in series of short subjects of that title, also appeared in number of features (Not to be Trusted, Orchids and Ermine, The King, etc.). Adopting name of Mickey Rooney, ret. to vaudeville; resumed screen career 1934. Special Academy Award 1940; for Andy Hardy characterization; voted among first ten Money-Making Stars in M.P. Herald-Fame Poll. 1938–43.

PICTURES INCLUDE: The Strip, Sound Off, Off Limits, All Ashore, Slight Case of Larceny, Drive a Crooked Road, Bridges at Toki-Ri, Atomic Kid, Twinkle in God's Eye, Bold and the Brave, Magnificent Roughnecks, The Last Mile, Big Operation, Private Lives of Adam and Eve, Platinum High School, King of the Roaring 20's, Breakfast at Tiffany's, It's a Mad, Mad, Mad, Mad World, Everything's Ducky. The Secret Invasion, The Extraordinary Seaman, The Comic, The Cockeyed Cowboys of Calico County, Skidoo, Pulp, Richard, B.J. Presents, That's Entertainment!, The Domino Principle, Pete's Dragon, The Black Stallion, Arabian Adventure.

TV: Playhouse 90, Pinocchio, Eddie, Somebody's Waiting, The Dick Powell Theater, Mickey.

ROONEY, PAT: Performer stage, nightclubs, pictures. Producer. e. Denver Univ.; Santa Monica College; Univ. Cal. Los Angeles; Marquette Univ. Entertainer vaudeville, theatres, stage, TV and pictures. Captain U.S. Army Air Corps, during Korean War. Entertained troops Far East Commands. Producer, 1960, C.B.S. Films Inc., producing TV pilots and series. 1962, formed Pat Rooney Prods. with Del E. Webb, hotel and construction exec. 1963–68, producer for Jerry Buss Prods. c/o Paramount Pictures, Hollywood, making feature films.

MAJOR PICTURES INCLUDE: Dime With A Halo, Danger Pass, Caged, Law of the Lawless, Requiem for a Gunfighter, Bounty Killer, Young Once, Hells Angels, Fools, Christmas Couple, Black Eye, Jan and Dean.

ROOT, WELLS: Writer. b. Buffalo, N.Y. e. Yale, Drama ed., NY World; dramatic and film critic, Time mag.; fiction, articles, various magazines; many TV dramas, various programs.

PICTURES INCLUDE: I Cover the Waterfront, Tiger Shark, Bird of Paradise, Prisoner of Zenda, Magnificent Obsession, Texas Across the River.

ROSE, ALEX: Producer. r.n. Alexandra Rose. Started in m.p. distribution with Medford Films, marketing low-budget pictures. Later became asst. sls. mgr. for New World Pictures, working in all phases of distribution. In 1972 met Tamara Asseyev and joined her in co-producing, starting with Drive-In, released by Universal.

PICTURES INCLUDE: With Tamara Asseyev: Drive-In, I Wanna Hold Your Hand, Big Wednesday, Norma Rae.

ROSE, DAVID: Composer, conductor. b. London, England, June 15, 1910. To U.S. 1914; studied music, Chicago Coll. of Music; pianist with Chicago orchestras; staff arranger for several radio stations; mus. dir., West Coast network; while in U.S. Army, comp. dir. of Winged Victory; songs include Holiday for Strings, Our Waltz.

PICTURES INCLUDE: Texas Carnival, Rich Young & Pretty, The Clown, Bright Road, Jupiter's Darling, Port Afrique.

TV: Musical dir., Red Skelton Show; composer-conductor, Bonanza. Emmy, Fred Astaire special.

ROSE, DAVID E.: Producer. B. Kansas City, Mo. 1895. Ent. industry in 1930 in assoc. Douglas Fairbanks; v.p. gen. mgr. United Artists Studios; same posts with Goldwyn. Prod. and dir. UA Corp. until 1938 when he went to England to become chmn., man. dir. of all Paramount companies in Great Britain; currently prod. as David E. Rose Productions, Inc.

PICTURES INCLUDE: Island of Desire, Sea Devils, End of the Affair, Port Afrique, The Safecracker, The House of the Seven Hawks.

ROSE, JACK: Writer. b. Warsaw, Poland, Nov. 4, 1911; e. Ohio U. 1934, B.A. m. Audrey Mary Rose, writer, prod. Paramount Pictures, L.A.

PICTURES INCLUDE: Ladies Man, Sorrowful Jones, The Great Lover, It's A Great Feeling, Pale Face, My Favorite Brunette, Road to Rio, Daughter of Rosie O'Grady, Always Leave Them Laughing, On Moonlight Bay, Riding High, I'll See You in My Dreams, Room for One More, April in Paris, Trouble Along the Way, Living it Up, Seven Little Foys, Houseboat, Five Pennies, Beau James, It Started in Naples, Double Trouble, Papa's Delicate Condition, Who's Got the Action?, Who's Been Sleeping in My Bed?, A Touch of Class, the Duchess and the Dirtwater Fox.

ROSE, JACK: Exhibitor. b. Chicago, May 23, 1897. e. U. of Chicago, Ph.D. Clerk, stenographer, private secretary, in Navy during WW I, and accountant. Was assist. br. mgr. for Selznick Pictures, Film Classics of Illinois, Warner, then slsmn. for Warners and assoc. with James Coston as film buyer for Coston booking circuit; formed own booking and buying exchange; secretary and treas. Indiana-Illinois Theatres, Inc.; also film buyer, Chief Barker, Variety Club of Illinois, 1946–47; Nat'l Canvassman, 1947–48; Intern'l Rep. 1950–53. Member: Covenant Club of Ill., Exec. Club of Chicago, Masons, American Legion; trustee, Chicago Sinai Congreg., M.P. Pioneers.

ROSE, JOHN C.: Writer, producer. b. Chicago, Ill., Nov. 7, 1905. e. Dartmouth College. Free lance commercial art, sls, prom. & adv. N.Y. 1929–33; jr. acct. exec. Young & Rubicam, Inc., N.Y. 1933; bus. mgr., radio dept. Compton Adv., Inc. N.Y. 1934–36; story ed. & story research dir., Walt Disney, 1936–42; headed Disney survey, South America, State Dept.; W.W. II worked on Frank Capra's "Why We Fight" films, orig. "G.I. Movies," officer-in-chg. motion pictures & graphics, U.S. Army Education Program, 1942–44; v.p. chg. prod., Pathescope Co. of America, 1945; Indie Prods., Hollywood, 1945–51; Chief of Health Education Films, Korean War, U.S. Navy, 1951–53; consultant, Indie TV Prod., 1954–61; formed & pres. Nugget Prods., Inc. 1962; Organized Film Industry Development Co. of Iran, 1975. Ret., 1976.

PICTURES INCLUDE: The Incredible Mr. Limpet.

ROSE, REGINALD: Writer, b. New York, 1921. e. C.C.N.Y. Worked as clerk, publicist, Warner Bros.; adv. acct. exec., copy chief; US Air Force, WW II; first TV play, Bus to Nowhere, 1951; since then numerous TV plays, Studio One, other programs.

PICTURES INCLUDE: Crime in the Streets, 12 Angry Men, The Man in the Net, Somebody Killed Her Husband, The Wild Geese, The Sea Wolves.

TELEVISION: Studs Lonigan.

ROSE, STEPHEN: Executive. Entered m.p. industry in 1964 with Columbia Pictures; named adv. dir. In 1970 joined Cinema V Distributing, Inc. as dir. of adv.; left in 1971 to take post at Cinemation Industries, where was named v.p. and bd. member. In 1975 joined Paramount Pictures as dir. of adv.; promoted to v.p./adv. In 1979 formed Barrick Prods. with Gordon Weaver, of which co. he is pres.

ROSE, SYDNEY: Producer. b. 1939. Ent. ind. 1956 as freelance writer/photographer, 1959–61: publicity director Films de France Ltd. 1961–3: independent film publicist. 1963–8: Artistes' management company in association with Frankie Vaughan. 1968: Formed independent artistes' agency. 1970–4: Executive agent M.A.M. Agency Ltd. 1975: Independent film producer. 1977: Exec. prod., The Kids are Alright. 1979: Co-prod., Five Star Five.

ROSE, WILLIAM: Screen writer. b. Jefferson City, U.S.A. Ent. m.p. ind. in Britain, 1947.

PICTURES INCLUDE: Gift Horse (Glory at Sea), Genevieve, The Maggie (High and Dry), Touch and Go, The Ladykillers, Man in the Sky, Davy, The Smallest Show on Earth, It's A Mad, Mad, Mad, World, The Russians are Coming, The Russians are Coming, The Flim Flam Man, Guess Who's Coming to Dinner, The Secret of Santa Vittoria.

ROSENBERG, FRANK P.: Producer. b. New York City, Nov. 22, 1913. e. Columbia U., N.Y.U. Joined Columbia 1929; writer m.p. & radio; exploit. mgr.; 1941; apptd. national dir. adv., publicity, exploitation, Columbia Pictures Feb. 1944. Pub. dir. M.P. Victory Loan, 1945; dir. pub. Columbia Pictures Studios, Hollywood, Jan. 1946. Resigned 1947 to enter production. Co-prod. Man Eater of Kumaon. Collab. adapt., assoc. prod. Where the Sidwalk Ends.

PICTURES INCLUDE: Secret of Convict Lake, Return of the Texan, The Farmer Takes a Wife, King of the Khyber Rifles, Illegal, Miracle in the Rain, Girl He Left Behind, One-Eyed Jacks, Critic's Choice, Madigan, exec. prod., The Steagle, prod. The Reincarnation of Peter Proud; sole adaptation, Gray Lady Down.

TV: Exec. prod. and prod. for Schlitz Playhouse programs during 1957–58; exec. prod., Arrest and Trial, 1963–64; exec. prod. Kraft Suspense Theatre, 1964–65; v.p. MCA Universal 1964.

ROSENBERG, MARK: Executive. Started career in magazine publishing field in New York. Adv. exec. with Seiniger & Associates; agent in m.p. dept. of IFA (later became ICM). With literary agency of Adams, Ray, Rosenberg. In 1978 joined Warner Bros., as v.p., prod.; in 1980 promoted to snr. v.p. of prod.

ROSENBERG, RICK: Producer. b. Los Angeles. e. L.A. City College, UCLA. Started career in mail room of Columbia Pictures, then asst. to prod. Jerry Bresler on Major Dundee and Love Has Many Faces. Asst. to Col. v.p., Arthur Kramer. Was assoc. prod. on The Reivers and in 1970 produced first feature, Adam at Six A.M., with Bob Christiansen, with whom co-produced all credits listed below.
PICTURES INCLUDE: Adam at Six A.M., Hide in Plain Sight.
TV: Features: Suddenly Single, The Glass House, A Brand New Life, The Man Who Could Talk to Kids, The Autobiography of Miss Jane Pittman, I love You . . . Goodbye, Queen of the Stardust Ballroom, Born Innocent, A Death in Canaan, Strangers.

ROSENBERG, STUART: Director-Producer. b. New York City, 1927. e. New York University.
PICTURES INCLUDE: Murder, Inc., Cool Hand Luke, The April Fools, WUSA, Pocket Money, The Laughing Policeman, The Drowning Pool, Voyage Of The Damned, The Amityville Horror, Brubaker. Has made over 300 TV shows for such series as The Untouchables, Naked City, The Defenders, Espionage. Chrysler Theatre, Emmy Award, 1962

ROSENCRANS, LEO S.: Writer. b. Linesville, Pa. e. Findlay Coll., B.A., O.B., LHD. NBC, 1931–34; radio ed. U.S. Office of Education, 1935–36; commercial m.p. since 1937; v.p., Creative Dept., Jerry Fairbanks Prods. of Calif., since 1951; more than 500 m.p., radio and TV credits.

ROSENFELT, FRANK E.; Executive. b. Peabody, Mass., Nov. 15, 1921. e. Cornell Univ. (B.S.) & Cornell Law School (L.L.B.). Served as atty. for RKO Radio Pictures, before joining MGM in 1955 as member of legal dept. Appt. secty. in 1966. Named v.p., gen. counsel in 1969 and pres. in 1973. In 1974 also named chief exec. officer. As of May, 1980, is bd. chm. & ch ef exec. officer. Member: Bd. of Governers, Academy of M.P. Arts & Sciences, bd. of trustees, American Film Institute.

ROSENFIELD, JONAS, JR.: Publicity executive. b. Dallas, Texas. e. U. of Miami, A.B. In U.S. Navy, World War II. Warner Bros. pressbook copy department, adv. mgr. Walt Disney, Adv. copywriter Donahue & Coe. Advertising copy chief 20th Century-Fox. Pres. N.Y. Screen Publicists Guild. In July 1942, ex-officio member industry's War Activities Committee. In 1945 apptd. asst. adv. mgr., 20th Cent.-Fox; adv. mgr., 1949–51; dir. of pub. rel. for Italian Films Export 1952; v.p. chg. adv. prom., pub. IFE Releasing Corp., 1953–55; exec. asst. to Paul Lazarus; v.p. of Columbia Pictures, 1955; exec. in chg., avd., pub. expl., Columbia, 1958; v.p. in chg. adv. pub. expl. Columbia, 1960; elected v.p., Columbia Int'l Pictures Corp., 1962; elected gen. exec. officer, Columbia Pictures, 1962; vice president, worldwide advertising, publicity and promotion, Twentieth Century-Fox, 1963–77; film mktg. consultant, 1977–78; lecturer in mktg., University of So. Calif., 1978–79; v.p. in chg. of worldwide mktg., Melvin Simon Productions, 1979. In 1980 named snr. v.p.; 1981, joined Filmways Pictures as exec. v.p., worldwide adv./pub., promo.

ROSENSTEIN, GERTRUDE: Director. b. New York, N.Y. e. Barnard Coll., B.A. Neighborhood Playhouse. exec. asst. to George Balanchine & Lincoln Kirstein, NYC Ballet. Assoc. with Gian Carlo Menotti, Festival of Two Worlds, Spoleto, Italy.
TV: Assoc. dir., NBC Opera, Emmy Awards, election coverages, Kennedy inauguration, Huntley-Brinkley Report, Kennedy Memorial Mass; dir.; Concentration; TV staff dir., NBC. Now free-lance director.

ROSENTHAL, BUD: Executive. b. Brooklyn, N.Y., Mar. 21, 1934. e. Brooklyn College, B.A. 1954, New York U.; U.S. Army, 1954–56; college correspondent, N.Y. Times; ent. m.p. ind. as associate editor, Independent Film Journal, 1957. Joined Columbia Pictures publicity dept. as trade paper contact and news writer, 1959; newspaper and syndicate contact 1960; appointed national publicity mgr., Columbia Pictures Corp., 1962–67; asst. prod. Something For Everyone; pub. dir., Anderson Tapes, Such Good Friends; story ed. and casting dir., Sigma Prods., 1972–75; associate producer, Broadway play, Full Circle, 1973, assoc. prod., Rosebud, 1974; dir. intl. press relations; The Bluebird, 1975; Warner Bros. project coordinator, Superman, 1977–79.

ROSENTHAL, ROBERT M.: Producer. b. N.Y.C., Dec. 28, 1936. e. Lawrence Academy, Mass., 1952–56. U. of Penn., The Wharton School, 1956–60. Pictorial Officer, Prod.-dir. for U.S. Army Signal Corp., 1960–62; Chief, U.S. Army Production Facilities, France, 1961–62. Production mgr., Gurney Productions Inc., 1963; comptroller, Jalor Productions Inc., 1964; pres. Rosenthal Productions Inc., 1964; prod. Lieut. Wolf, I Wonder Why, Been Down So Long It Looks Like Up To Me.

ROSI, FRANCESCO: Director. b. Naples, Italy, 1922. Apprenticed as asst. to Visconti and Antonioni; directed first feature La Sfida (The Challenge) in 1958.
PICTURES INCLUDE: Salvatore Giuiliano, Hands Over the City, More Than a Miracle, Just Another War, Lucky Luciano, The Mattei Affair, Eboli.

ROSIAN, PETER F.: Executive. b. Persia, Sept. 11, 1902; e. NYU. Commonwealth Pictures, N.Y., 1923; later office mgr.; booker, MGM, 1925, then salesman, spcl. sales rep, br. mgr., Grand Nat'l, Cleveland, 1937; N.Y. 1938, spcl. sales rep., Universal, 1939; br. mgr., Cincinnati, 1940; dist. mgr. hdqts., Cincinnati, 1941; dist. mgr. 1951, Cleveland; regional sales mgr. 1958, Cleveland. Retired from MCA, 1970. Organized Personal Film Research Co.

ROSMARIN, CHARLES: Manager. b. London, England, Jan. 27, 1911. Insurance agent; district mgr. Columbia Pictures 1931; mgr. Venezuela office 1944; mgr. Monogram Pictures, Argentina 1946; mgr. RKO Radio Pictures, Argentina, 1949; gen. sales mgr. Europe—Near East, hdqtrs. Paris 1953; gen. mgr. Europe, Near East, 1958; gen. mgr. Metro-Goldwyn-Mayer, Italy, 1961; European rep., RKO General Films, 1968.

ROSS, DIANA: Singer-Actress. B. Detroit, Mich. Formed musical group at age 14 with two friends, Mary Wilson and Florence Ballard. In 1960 they auditioned for Berry Gordy, head of Motown Record Corp. and were hired to sing backgrounds on records for Motown acts. After completing high school, the trio was named the Supremes and went on tour with Motor Town Revue. Over period of 10 yrs. Supremes had 15 consecutive hit records and once had five consecutive records in no. one spot on charts. In 1969 Diana Ross went on her own, appearing on TV and in nightclubs. Made film debut in Lady Sings the Blues, 1973.
PICTURES INCLUDE: Lady Sings the Blues, Mahogany, The Wiz.
TV: Diana! (spec.).

ROSS, FRANK: Producer-writer. b. Boston, Mass., Aug. 12, 1904; e. Exeter and Princeton. President, Frank Ross Inc. In 1939, asst. prod. Of Mice and Men, UA, Roach. In 1941, producer, The Devil and Miss Jones, RKO. Co-author of story and s.p. The More the Merrier. Spec. Acad. Award (1945) for prod. The House I Live In, short subject on tolerance.
PICTURES INCLUDE: The Lady Takes a Chance, Flame and the Arrow, The Lady Says No, The Robe, Demetrius and the Gladiators, Rain of Ranchipur, Kings Go Forth, Mr. Moses, Maurie (prod.).

ROSS, HERBERT: Director. b. New York City, May 13. Resident Choreographer A.B.T., Choreographer on Broadway for I Can Get It For You Wholesale, Tovarich, Anyone Can Whistle, Do I Hear a Waltz, On a Clear Day You Can See Forever, The Apple Tree. Broadway Director: Chapter Two. I Ought To Be in Pictures. Ent. m.p. ind. as choreographer/musical sequences dir.
PICTURES INCLUDE: As Director/Choreographer: Funny Girl. As director: Goodbye Mr. Chips, The Owl and the Pussycat, Play It Again, Sam, The Last Of Sheila (produced and directed), Funny Lady, The Sunshine Boys, The Seven-Per-Cent Solution (produced and directed), The Turning Point (produced and directed), The Goodbye Girl, California Suite, Nijinsky, Pennies from Heaven (prod.-dir.).
TV: Bell Telephone Hour, Fred Astaire Special.

ROSS, KATHARINE: Actress. b. Los Angeles, Calif., Jan. 29, 1943. e. Santa Rosa College. Joined the San Francisco Workshop, appeared in The Devil's Disciple, The Balcony, 1962, poetry festival. TV debut, 1962 in Sam Benedict segment.
TV: Doctors at Work, World Premiere, The Longest Hundred Miles, Ben Casey, The Bob Hope-Chrysler Theatre, The Virginian, Wagon Train, Kraft Mystery Theatre, the Lieutenant, The Road West. Acted in the UCLA theatre Arts prod. of King Lear.
PICTURES INCLUDE: Shenandoah, Mister Buddwing, The Singing Nun, Games, The Graduate (nom. for Acad. Award, Best Actress; voted Most Promising Female Newcomer, Golden Globe Award), Hellfighters, Butch Cassidy and the Sundance Kid, Tell Them Willie Boy is Here, They Only Kill Their Masters, The Stepford Wives, Voyage of the Damned, The Betsy, The Swarm, The Legacy, The Final Countdown.

ROSS, KENNETH: Writer. b. London, Sept. 16, 1941.
TV: The Roundelay, ATV Network, 1963. The Messenger, CBC Network, 1966.
THEATRE: The Raft, Hampstead Theatre, London, 1964. Under The Skin, Citizens' Theatre, Glasgow, 1968. Mr. Kilt & The Great I Am, Hampstead Theatre, London, 1970.
PICTURES INCLUDE: Entered industry 1970. Brother Sun, Sister Moon, 1970. Slag, 1970. Original story and screenplay, The Reckless Years, 1971. Abelard & Heloise, 1971. The Day of the Jackal (nominated for Writers' Guild, SFTA, and Golden Globe Awards), 1971–72. The Devil's Lieutenant, 1972. The Odessa File (nominated for Writers' Guild Award), 1973–74. Original story and screenplay,

Quest, 1974–75. Original story and screenplay, Lorenzo The Magnificent, 1975.

ROSS, LANNY: Singer, M.C., Actor. b. Seattle, Washington, Jan. 19, 1906; e. Yale 1928. Columbia Law, Juilliard, 1933. AAU title 1927–28; qualified 1928 Olympics, Star of Showboat NBC 1932–37; retired from track to sing. Town Hall debut, 1936; Showboat, 1932–36. Radio; Packard Mardi Gras, Hit Parade Franco American, Camel Caravan; U.S. Army, Major 1943–46; Ivory Show. First musical show on TV Swift Show 1947–49. Concert Tour of U.S. 1949–54. WCBS Radio, The Lanny Ross Show 1954–61, Telephone Hour, 1963; Today Show, 1964; Les Crane Show, 1965; Joe Franklin, 1973; Salvation Army Banquet, Palm Beach, 1973–75. Records include Jolly Doctor Dolliwell, Silver Dollar Country Album.
PICTURES INCLUDE: Melody in Spring, College Rhythm, The Lady Objects, Stage Door Canteen.

ROSSO, LEWIS, T.: Executive. b. Hoboken, N.J., Feb. 3, 1911. Ent. m.p. ind. 1930; prod. & mgt. for Consolidated Film Ind., 1930–44; Republic Prod., 1944–50; prod. mgr. Republic, 1950–55; asst. sec'y and asst. treas. Republic Pictures Corp., 1959; exec. asst. to exec. prod. mgr., 20th Century-Fox Films, 1960; plant mgr., Samuel Goldwyn Studios, 1961–71; exec. admin. asst. to gen'l mgr., The Burbank Studios, 1972–81.

ROTH, CY: Writer, producer, director. b. Chicago, Ill., Mar. 16, 1912; e. U. of Calif. at L.A. Formed and headed Cy Roth Productions, later formed and was pres. Saturn Films, Inc.
PICTURES INCLUDE: Flight to Outer Space, Caballero Jones, Spanish Territory, Top Secret, Solar Rescue, Crawling Hand, Stone Dragon, Battle at Silver Pass, Passport to Freedom, Danger at Ghost Town; dir. Combat Squad; prod. dir. s.p. Air Strike, Fire Maidens of Outer Space.
TV: Prod., dir., writer. Adventures of Rainbow Riley; writer, Central Allied Intelligence, Tokyo Police, Attack Squadron, The Twisted Black Cross; dir., Rheingold Theatre, Outlaw Queen; prod., dir., s.p., Attack Squadron, Nuremberg, Growing Wild; prod., dir. Horrors of the Black Forest. Heads C.R. Ent.

ROTH, PAUL A.: Executive, born Asheville, N.C., March 28, 1930. U. of N.C., A.B. Political Science 1948–51. George Washington Univ. Law School 1951–52. U.S. Army 1952–55. Dist. Mgr. Valley Enterprises, Inc. 1955–56. Vice Pres. Roth Enterprises, Inc. 1956–65. Pres. Roth Enterprises, Inc. 1965-present. President NATO of Virginia 1971–73. Chairman of Board NATO of Virginia, 1973–1975. Member National NATO Board, 1971-present. Executive Committee NATO of Metro-D.C. 1970-present. Variety Club Tent 11 Board Member 1959–65. President National NATO, 1973–75; chairman National NATO board of directors 1975-77. Co-Chairman Motion Picture Energy Conservation Council, 1973-present. Member Foundation Motion Picture Pioneers, 1973-present. Director & advisory committee, Will Rogers Hospital, 1973-present. Trustee American Film Institute, 1973–75.

ROTH, RICHARD A.: Producer. b. Bev. Hills, 1943. e. Stanford U. Law School. Worked for L.A. law firm before beginning film career as lawyer and literary agent for Ziegler-Ross Agency. In 1970 left to develop s.p. Summer of '42 with Herman Raucher.
PICTURES INCLUDE: Summer of '42, Our Time, The Adventures of Sherlock Holmes Smarter Brother, Julia, Outland.

ROTHA, PAUL: Producer and director. b. London, 1907. e. London U., Slade School of Art. Ent. film ind. in art dept. of British Int'l in 1928. Visited America 1937–38 and advised General Education Board (Rockefellor Foundation) and Museum of Modern Art Film Library, N.Y., regarding documentary film technique. Managing dir. Paul Rotha Productions, Ltd., London; ex-chmn., 1953 vice-chmn. fellow, British Film Academy.
AUTHOR: (film books) The Film Till Now, Celluloid Documentary Film, Movie Parade, Television in the Making, Rotha on the Film, The Innocent Eye, The Biography of Robert J. Flaherty, Head of documentary BBC-TV, 1953–55.
PICTURES INCLUDE: Contact, Shipyard, Face of Britain, Today We Live, Future's in Air, World of Plenty, Night Shift, Children of the City, Land of Promise, A City Speaks, The World is Rich, World Without End (with Basil Wright), No Resting Place, Cat and Mouse, Cradle of Genius, The Life of Adolf Hitler, The Silent Raid.

ROTHKIRCH, Dr. EDWARD V.: Producer. b. July 30, 1919; e. Friedrich Wilhelm U., Berlin; Rockhurst Coll., Midwestern College. Prod. asst., research, Pan American Prod., 1941; research, Pacific Films, 1942; U.S. Air Force, 1942–44; asst. prod., Pan American Productions, 1945; analyst, Cambridge Prod., 1947; assoc. prod., Pentagon Films, 1949; assoc. prod., Reelestic Pictures, 1950; assoc. prod. Cambridge-Meran Prod. Co., 1951; assoc. exec. prod., Cambridge Prod., 1954; also v.-p. Continental Prod. Services;

assoc. exec. prod. Trinity Hill Productions, produced Pan-American Highway 1954, The Keepers TV series, 1953–58, Famous Women of the Bible, 1955–58; To the Stars TV series, 1954–58; also sec.-treas. Crusader Records and v.p. Orbit Records. Member of many professional societies, director International Association of Independent Producers, presently Executive Producer—Galaxie Productions, and Encore Records also Executive Editor, Intercontinental Media Service, Ltd.

ROTHMAN, MO: Executive. b. Montreal, Canada, Jan. 14, 1919. Royal Canadian A.F., WW II. Student trainee, Universal, India; mgr., Malaysia; mgr. prod. Worldwide Rep. for Edward Small, 1950; intern'l sales dept. U.A., 1952; sales mgr. for Continent, Near East, 1955; Cont'l mgr., 1957; v.p. int'l oper., 1960; exec. v.p., Columbia Pict. Int'l, 1960; v.p. world distrib. 1966; exclusive distributor all media, Chaplin Pictures, 1971.

ROUNDTREE, RICHARD: Actor. b. New Rochelle, N.Y. e. Southern Illinois University. Former model, Ebony Magazine Fashion Fair; joined workshop of Negro Ensemble Company, appeared in Kongi's Harvest, Man, Better Man, Mau Mau Room; played lead role in Philadelphia road company of The Great White Hope before film debut.
PICTURES INCLUDE: Shaft, Shaft's Big Score, Shaft in Africa, Charley One-Eye, Earthquake, Man Friday, Diamonds, Escape to Athena.
TV: Shaft (series, 1973), Firehouse (movie), Roots.

ROUSE, RUSSELL: Prod., dir., writer. b. New York City. ed. U.C.L.A. Formed Greene-Rouse Prods. with Clarence Greene. Acad. Oscar co-orig. story Pillow Talk. Acad. award nom. co-orig. s.p. The Well. 2 Writers Guild nominations. Writers Guild award outstanding teleplay: One Day In The Life of Ivan Denisovitch.
PICTURES INCLUDE: Prod., collab. s.p. The Town Went Wild. Orig. story Yokel Boy. Collab. orig. s.p. The Home Front, D.O.A. Co-author Pillow Talk. Dir. and collab. s.p. The Well, The Thief, Wicked Woman, New York Confidential, Fastest Gun Alive, House of Numbers, Thunder in the Sun, A House Is Not A Home, The Oscar, Dir. Caper of the Golden Bulls. Dir. and collab. Prod.-writer T.V. series: Tightrope.

ROWE, ROY: Owner-operator, Rowe Amusement Co., Burgaw, N.C. b. Burgaw, May 29, 1905; e. U. of No. Car. Eng. instructor, private bus. coll., 1926–29; Publix Sch. for Mgrs., N.Y., 1930–31; mgr. theatres, Spartanburg, S.C.; Greensboro & Raleigh, N.C.; mgr., Warner Theatre, Pittsburgh, Pa., 1931–34; city mgr. for Warner Theatres, Washington, Pa., 1934–35; opened own theatres in N.C. 1935; member N.C. Senate, 1937, 1941, 1945, 1949, 1957, 1965; House of Rep., 1943; Major, Civil Air Patrol, WWII; pres. Carolina Aero Club, 1943–44; chmn. N.C. Aeronautics Comm., 1941–49; dir. Theatre Owners N. & So. Car. 1943–45; pres., Theatre Owners of S.C. & N.C. 1944–45; pres. Assn. of Governing Boards of State Universities, 1964. Owned and operated motel, Carolina Beach, N.C., 1965–67., Rowe Insurance Agency, 1967–69. Mem. Exec. Bd., U. of N.C. Trustees, 1969. Principal Clerk N.C. Senate 1969–75. Retired. Now water color artist and world traveller.

ROWLAND, ROY: Director. b. New York City, Dec. 31; e. U. of So. California (law). Script clerk; asst. dir.; asst. to late W. S. Van Dyke on Tarzan pictures; dir. of shorts, "How to" Benchley series; Crime Does Not Pay series. Pete Smith Specialties.
PICTURES INCLUDE: Think First, Stranger in Town, Lost Angel, Our Vines Have Tender Grapes, Tenth Avenue Angel, Night patrol, Ski Soldier, Boys' Ranch, Romance of Rosy Ridge, Killer McCoy, Scene of the Crime, Outriders, Excuse My Dust, Two Weeks With Love, Bugles in Afternoon, 5000 Fingers of Dr. T. Affair with a Stranger, The Moonlighter, Witness to Murder, Rogue Cop, Many Rivers to Cross, Hit the Deck, Meet Me in Las Vegas, Slander, Somewhere I'll Find Him, Gun Glory, The Seven Hills of Rome, The Girl Hunters, Gunfighters of Casa Grande, They Called Him Gringo, Tiger of the Seven Seas, Thunder Over the Indian Ocean.

ROWLAND, WILLIAM: Producer, director. b. Philadelphia, Pa., Sept. 12, 1900; e. U. of Pa. Actor: vaude., prod.; play prod.; author; prod. shorts, Universal, 1931–32; prod. features Moonlight and Pretzels, Take a Chance, Sweet Surrender, I Loved an Actress; prod., dir. in chge. Spanish prod., RKO, 1937; Spanish Acad. Award for best prod., dir., Perfidis, 1939; won highest Spanish awards for prod. dir., author, Harvest of Hate, 1940; prod. dir., Int'l Forum series, Follies Girl.
PICTURES INCLUDE: Song for Miss Julie, Flight to Nowhere, Women in the Night.

ROWLANDS, GENA: Actress. b. Cambria, Wisc. June 19, 1936. e. Univ. of Wisc. Came to New York to attend American Academy of Dramatic Arts, where met and married John Cassavetes. Made Bdwy. debut as understudy and then succeeded to role of the Girl in The Seven Year Itch. Launched as star with part in The Middle of the Night, which she played 18 mos. Then brought to Hollywood to make film debut in The High Cost of Living (1958).

PICTURES INCLUDE: Lonely Are the Brave, The Spiral Road, A Child Is Waiting, Tony Rome, Faces, Minnie and Moskowitz, A Woman Under the Influence, Two Minute Warning, The Brinks' Job, Gloria.

TV: The Philco TV Playhouse, Studio One, Alfred Hitchcock Presents, Dr. Kildare, Bonanza, The Kraft Mystery Theatre, Columbo.

ROWLEY, JOHN H.: Executive. b. San Angelo, Tex., Oct. 6, 1917. e. U. of Tex., 1935–39. v.p. United Artists Theat. Cir. Inc., Rowley United Div.: past president, NATO of Texas; part Int'l Chief barker, Variety Clubs Int'l; past pres., TOA; pres., Variety Foundation of Texas.

ROYLE, SELENA: Actress. b. New York City, Nov. 6, 1904; d. Edwin Milton Royle & Selena Fetter, pro. Made debut on N.Y. stage, 1921 in Launcelot & Elaine. Has appeared in numerous N.Y. prod.; on radio starred in Woman of Courage, Kate Hopkins, and many others. On screen 1941 in Stage Door Canteen.

PICTURES INCLUDE: The Sullivans, Mrs. Parkington, This Man's Navy, Main Street After Dark, Courage of Lassie, Green Years, Gallant Journey, No Leave, No Love, Night and Day, Summer Holiday, Wild Harvest, Cass Timberlane, Smart Woman, You Were Meant for Me, Joan of Arc, You're My Everything, My Dream Is Yours, Bad Boy, Big Hangover, Branded, Dammed Don't Cry, The Heiress, He Ran All the Way, Come Fill the Cup, Robot Monster, Murder Is My Beat.

ROZSA, MIKLOS: Composer. b. April 18, 1907, Budapest, Hungary. e. Leipzig Conservatory. Wrote great number of symphonic and chamber music works. Composed music for many m.p. In 1936, Knight Without Armor, Acad. Award best music scoring for drama or comedy (Spellbound) 1945; best music scoring for drama or comedy (Double Life) 1947; Ben-Hur, 1959. Pres., Screen Composers Assn. 1956. Cesar of French Academy for Providence, 1978.

PICTURES INCLUDE: Jungle Book, Song to Remember, Double Idemnity, The Killers, Madame Bovary, The Lost Weekend, Spellbound, Asphalt Jungle, Quo Vadis, Ivanhoe, Julius Caesar, Story of Three Loves, Plymouth Adventure, Young Bess, Knights of the Round Table, A Time to Love and a Time to Die, The World the Flesh and the Devil, Ben Hur, Lust for Life, Something of Value, King of Kings, El Cid, Sodom and Gomorra, The VIP's, The Power, The Green Berets, The Private Life of Sherlock Holmes, Sinbad's Golden Voyage, Providence, Secret Files of J. Edgar Hoover, Fedora, Last Embrace, Time After Time, Eye of the Needle.

RUBIN, STANLEY: Producer, writer. b. New York, N.Y. Oct. 8, 1917; ed. UCLA, 1933–37. Phi Beta Kappa. Writer—radio, magazines, pictures, 1937–41; U.S. Army Air Force, 1942–45; writer, prod., owner, Your Show Time, Story Theatre TV series; producer, RKO, 20th-Fox, U.I.

PICTURES INCLUDE: The Narrow Margin, My Pal Gus, Destination Gobi, River of No Return, Destry, Francis in the Navy, Behind the High Wall, Rawhide Years, Promise Her Anything, The President's Analyst, The Take.

TV: Ghost and Mrs. Muir, Bracken's World, The Man and the City.

RUDDY, ALBERT S.: Producer. b. Montreal, Canada, March 28, 1934. e. U. of So. Calif., B.S. in Design, School of Architecture, 1956.

PICTURES INCLUDE: The Wild Seed (Pennebaker); prod.; Little Fauss & Big Halsey (Alfran Prods.), Paramount Studios Prod.; Making It (Alfran Prods.—for 20th Century Fox); prod. The Godfather (Albert S. Ruddy Production, Inc. for Paramount). 1974: The Longest Yard, Coonskin, both for Para. 1978: Matilda. 1981: The Cannonball Run.

RUDIE, EVELYN: Actress, Singer, Songwriter. r.n. Evelyn Rudie Bernauer. b. Hollywood, Calif. March 28. e. Hollywood H.S., U.C.L.A. At 19, after childstar career in TV and films, stage debut at Gallery Theatre in Hollywood as songwriter, musical director, choreographer and star performer: Ostrogoths and King of the Schnorrers. Currently Producer, Artistic Director at Santa Monica Playhouse; founder of own repertoire Company; among major productions: Backstreet, Dreamplay, and musicals Anatol-Anatol, Attorney at Love, Author-Author, The Alchemist, etc. Screen debut as child performer Daddy Longlegs. Received Emmy Nomination for first TV leading role, Eloise, Playhouse 90, 1956.

PICTURES INCLUDE: The Wings of Eagles, Gift of Love. Filmdom's Famous Fives critics award, 1958.

TV: Hostess with the Mostess, Playhouse 90, Dinah Shore, Red Skelton Show, George Gobel Show, Omnibus, Matinee Theatre, Hitchcock presents, Gale Storm Show, Jack Paar, Wagon Train, G.E. Theatre, 77 Sunset Strip, etc.

RUGOFF, DONALD S.: Executive. b. Brooklyn, N.Y., Feb. 7, 1927. e. Woodmere Academy, Harvard; U.S. Navy, 1944–

46; dir. Motion Picture Theatres Assoc.; pres. Cinema 5 Ltd.

RUGOLO, PETE: Composer, arranger. b. Sicily, Italy, Dec. 25, 1915. To U.S., 1919; e. San Francisco State Coll., Mills Coll., Oakland. Armed Forces, 1942–46; pianist, arr. for many orch. including Stan Kenton; m.p. and TV.

PICTURES INCLUDE: The Strip, Skirts Ahoy, Glory Alley, Latin Lovers, Easy to Love, Jack the Ripper.

TV: Richard Diamond, The Thin Man, Thriller.

RULE, ELTON H.: Executive. b. Stockton, CA, 1917. e. Sacramento Coll. With Amer. Bdg. Cos., Inc., since 1952; gen. sls. mgr., KABC-TV, 1953–60; gen. mgr., 1961–8; pres., ABC TV Network 1968–70; group v.p. Am. Bdg. Cos. Inc., 1969–72; pres., ABC div. 1970–72; pres., chief operating officer, mem. exec. comm., Amer. Bdg. Cos. since 1972.

RULE, JANICE: Actress. b. Cincinnati, O., Aug. 15, 1931; e. Wheaton & Glenhart H.S., Glen Ellyn, Ill. Dancer 4 yrs. in Chicago & New York nightclubs; stage experience in It's Great To Be Alive, as understudy of Bambi Lynn; in chorus of Miss Liberty; Picnic, 1953. Screen debut, Goodbye My Fancy.

PICTURES INCLUDE: Starlift, Holiday for Sinners, Rogue's March, Woman's Devotion, Gun for a Coward, Subterraneans, Invitation to a Gunfighter, The Chase, Welcome to Hard Times, The Ambushers, Kid Blue, 3 Women.

RUNCIMAN, ALEX: Director-producer. b. Santa Cruz, Calif., May 30, 1924. e. U. of So. Calif., B.A., 1949; M.A., 1951; Ph.D., 1959. Served in U.S. Army, 1943–46; radio work, 1946–49; in prod. department, CBS, 1953; staff dir., 1954; has dir. panel, news, educational, variety programs, Television Journal, 1959–60; prod. Eye on St. Louis, 1960–61; prod. award-winning public service programs; Host of Metroplex Series, 1963.

RUSH, BARBARA: Actress. b. Denver, Colo. Jan. 4. e. U. of Calif. First stage appearance at age of ten, Loberto Theatre, Santa Barbara, Calif., in fantasy, Golden Ball; won acting award in coll. for characterization of Birdie, (The Little Foxes); scholarship, Pasadena Playhouse Theatre Arts Coll.

PICTURES INCLUDE: The First Legion, Quebec, Molly, When Worlds Collide, Flaming Feather, Prince of Pirates, It Came From Outer Space, Taza Son of Cochise, Magnificent Obsession, Black Shield of Falworth, Captain Lightfoot, Kiss of Fire, World in My Corner, Bigger Than Life, Oh Men! Oh Women!, Harry Black and the Tiger, The Young Philadelphians, Bramble Bush, Strangers When We Meet, Come Blow Your Horn, Robin and the Seven Hoods, Hombre, Airport, The Man, Superdad, Can't Stop the Music.

RUSH, RICHARD: Director, producer, writer; wrote, dir. prod., Too Soon To Love (U.I.), 1960; Of Love and Desire (Fox), 1963; dir. A Man Called Dagger (MGM) 1965; dir. Fickle Finger of Fate, 1966; dir. Thunder Alley, 1966; dir. Hell's Angels on Wheels, 1967; dir. wrote Psych-Out, 1967; dir. Savage Seven, 1968; dir., prod. Getting Straight (Columbia), 1970, dir. prod. Freebie and the Bean (Warner Bros.) 1974; dir., prod. wrote, The Stunt Man (Fox), 1980.

RUSSELL, CHARLES W.: Producer, b. N.Y.C., Mar. 31, 1918. Actor, m.p. & radio.

PICTURES INCLUDE: The Purple Heart, The Late George Apley.

TV: CBS-TV prod., You Are There, Danger.

RUSSELL, EDWARD: Executive. b. Chicago, June 12, 1945. e. Columbia Coll. Started with industry in Chicago as asst. adv. mgr. for Plitt Theatres, 1968–70; asst. adv. mgr., midwest div., MGM, 1970–72; midwest adv. mgr., United Artists, 1972–74; midwest adv. mgr., Filmways (AIP), 1974–77; in 1977 made natl. dir. of cooperative adv. & field promo. for Filmways; promoted in 1980 to exec. asst. to the v.p. of worldwide adv., promo., pub. Member: Academy of M.P. Arts & Sciences.

RUSSELL, JACK: Performer. b. Saratoga Spr., N.Y., Sept. 22, 1919. e. Rollins College, 1945–47. U.S. Air Force, 1940–45; appeared in B'way shows including: Sleepy Hollow, Heaven on Earth, As the Girls Go, Alive & Kicking; many nightclubs as singer; on NBC-TV opera, Pagliacci, 1951; guest star N.Y.C. Opera, 1953; featured aqua show, A Night in Venice, 1952–53; singer, Your Show of Shows, NBC-TV, 1950–53.

RUSSELL, JANE: Actress. b. Bemidji, Minn., June 21, 1921; e. Max Reinhardt's Theatrical Workshop & Mme. Ouspenskaya. Photographer's model; m.p. debut in Outlaw, 1943.

PICTURES INCLUDE: Young Widow, Paleface, Montana Belle, His Kind of Woman, Double Dynamite, Macao, Son of Paleface, Las Vegas Story, Gentlemen Prefer Blondes, French Line, Underwater, Gentlemen Marry Brunettes, Foxfire, Tall Men, Hot Blood, Revolt of Mamie Stover, Fuzzy Pink Nightgown, Darker Than Amber, Born Losers, Fate Is The Hunter, Waco.

RUSSELL, JOHN: Actor. b. Los Angeles, Calif., Jan. 3, 1921; e. U. of Calif. Served in U.S. Marine Corps. 1942–44, as 2nd Lt. m.p. debut in Frame-Up.
PICTURES INCLUDE: Story of Molly X, Gal Who Took the West, Slattery's Hurricane, Yellow Sky, Sitting Pretty, Forever Amber, Somewhere in the Night, Within These Walls, Don Juan Quilligan, Bell for Adano, Barefoot Mailman, Man in the Saddle, Hoodlum Empire, Oklahoma Annie, Fair Wind to Java, Sun Shines Bright, Jubilee Trail, Hell's Outpost, Last Command, Rio Bravo, Yellowstone Kelly, Fort Utah.

RUSSELL, KEN: Director. b. Southampton, England, 1927. e. Walthamstow Art School. Early career as dancer, actor, stills photographer, TV documentary film-maker. Ent. TV ind. 1959. Made 33 documentaries for BBC-TV.
PICTURES INCLUDE: Prokofiev, Elgar, Bartok, The Debussy films, Isadora Duncan, Song of Summer—Delius, Dance of the Seven Veils, French Dressing, Billion Dollar Brain, Women in Love, The Music Lovers, The Devils, The Boy Friend, Savage Messiah, Mahler, Tommy, Lisztomania, Valentino, Altered States.

RUSSELL, ROBERT: Performer. b. Passaic, N.J., Baritone, Philadelphia Grand Opera Co.; then radio work as quizmaster, m.c., singer, gagwriter, composer, writer spec. material; m.c., writer, composer, dir. eleven Miss America pageants; staged, wrote, dir. five Miss Universe pageants.
TV: Birthday Party, Bonny Maid Show, It's in the Bag, Toast of the Town, Live Like a Millionaire; now m.c. Stand Up and Be Counted, CBS-TV; pres. Pageant Productions, Inc.

RUSSELL, THERESA: Actress. b. San Diego, CA, 1957. e. Burbank High School. Studied at Actors' Studio in Hollywood. Professional film debut in The Last Tycoon (1977).
PICTURES: Straight Time, Bad Timing/A Sensual Obsession.
TELEVISION: Blind Ambition (mini-series).

RUTHERFORD, ANN: Actress. b. Toronto, Canada, 1924. Trained by mother (cousin of Richard Mansfield); with parents in stock as child; later on Los Angeles radio programs. Screen debut, 1935.
PICTURES INCLUDE: Laramie Trail, Happy Land, Bermuda Mystery, Two O'Clock Courage, Bedside Manner, The Madonna's Secret, Murder in the Music Hall, Secret Life of Walter Mitty, Operation Haylift, Adventures of Don Juan, They Only Kill Their Masters.

RYAN, ARTHUR N.: Executive. Joined Paramount in N.Y. in 1967 as asst. treas; later made dir. of admin. and business affairs, exec. asst. to Robert Evans and asst. scty. In 1970 appt. v.p.–prod. adm. In 1975 named senior v.p. handling all prod. operations for Paramount's m.p. and t.v. divisions, including supvr. of physical prod., business affairs, studio operations and coordination with co.'s creative personnel and filmmakers. Named asst. to the Chairman and Chief Executive Officer 1976; Chairman and President Magicam, Inc.; Chairman Fortune General Corp.; Chairman Paramount Communications; co-chm. of scholarship comm. of Academy of Motion Picture Arts and Sciences; trustee of Univ. Film Study Center in Boston. Joined Technicolor in August 1976 as pres., chief operating officer and director. Chairman Technicolor Audio-Visual Systems International, Inc.; director Technicolor S.P.A.; director Technicolor Film International; and chairman of executive committee, Technicolor Graphic Services, Inc.; director, Technicolor, Inc.; chairman, Technicolor Fotografica, S.A.; Chairman Technicolor Film International Service Company, Inc.; director and Deputy Chairman Technicolor Limited; director, The Vidtronics Company, Inc.; Permanent charities committee of the Entertainment Industry; Hollywood Canteen Foundations. Dir., Calif. Institute of Arts.

RYAN, MITCHELL: Actor. b. Louisville, Ky. was New York stage actor working off-Bdwy. for Ted Mann and Joseph Papp; on Bdwy. in Wait Until Dark. Member of Arena Stage group in Washington.
PICTURES INCLUDE: Monte Walsh, The Hunting Party, My Old Man's Place, High Plains Drifter, The Friends of Eddie Coyle, Magnum Force.

RYAN, PEGGY: Actress, r.n. Margart Irene Ryan. b. Long Beach, Calif., August 28, 1924. Before entering pictures appeared in vaudeville; on TV in Hawaii Five-0.
PICTURES INCLUDE: Top of the Town, The Women Men Marry, The Flying Irishman, She Married a Cop, Girls Town, Miss Annie Rooney, Private Buckaroo, Give Out, Sisters, Top Man, Mr. Big, Patrick the Great, The Merry Monahans, Follow the Boys, Babes on Swing Street, Bowery to Broadway, Merrily We Sing, That's the Spirit, This Is the Life, Here Come the Co-eds.
STAGE: Everybody, Men in Her Diary, Shamrock Hill, There's a Girl in My Heart, All Ashore.

RYAN, SHEILA: Actres. r.n. Katherine Elizabeth McLaughlin; b. Topeka, Kansas, June 8, 1921; e. Le Conte Jr. H.S., Hollywood H.S.
PICTURES INCLUDE: Something for the Boys, The Caribbean Mystery, Lone Wolf in London, Cobra Strikes, Caged Fury, Western Pacific Agent, Mask of the Dragon, Jungle Manhunt, On Top of Old Smoky, Pack Train.

RYDELL, MARK: Producer-Director-Actor. b. 1934. Studied acting with Sanford Meisner of N.Y. Neighborhood Playhouse. Became member of Actors Studio. Was leading actor for six years on daytime CBS serial, As The World Turns. Made Broadway debut in Seagulls over Sorrento and film bow in Crime in the Streets. Went to Hollywood as TV director (Ben Casy, I Spy, Gunsmoke, etc.). Theatrical feature debut: The Fox. Partner with Sidney Pollack in Sanford Prods., film, TV prod. co.
PICTURES INCLUDE: Director: The Fox, The Receivers, The Cowboys, Cinderella Liberty (also prod.), Harry and Walter Go To New York. Actor: The Long Goodbye.

RYDER, LOREN L.: Technical executive. b. Pasadena, Calif., Mar. 9, 1900; e. U. Calif., B.A. research engineer, telephone, telegraph 1924–25; radio importer 1926; asst. mgr. ShermanClay radio-phono. depts. 1927–28; head of sound dept. Paramount Pictures Corp., 1936–57; pres. Ryder Sound Services Inc., Ryder Magnetic Sales Corp., v.p. Nagra Magnetic Recorders. War Research consultant, National Defense Research Committee and Office of Scientific Research & Development, Washington; past pres. Soc. of M.P. & Television Engineers; recipient War-Navy Research Award; member, Academy of M.P. Arts & Sciences; recipient of Academy Awards for sound quality, sound effects in Spawn of the North, first use of fine-grain film, introduction of magnetic recording, development of Vista-Vision; past national sec'y., Academy of Television Arts & Sciences.

RYLANDER, ALEXANDER S.: Executive. b. N.Y.C., Jan. 9. Columbia, 1941; organ, spec. events dept., 1946; expl. mgr., Jan. 1953; exploit. dir., NBC, 1955; dir. prom. services, 1959; vice pres., promotion, 1961; staff v.p. spec. projects, RCA, 1966. v.p. news & information, 1967.

RYSKIND, MOORIE: Writer. e. Columbia U. Co-auth. Many plays including Of Thee I Sing, Animal Crackers, Louisiana Purchase, Currently columnist, syndicated by Human Events.
PICTURES INCLUDE: Palmy Days, Animal Crackers, Night at the Opera, Anything Goes, Ceiling Zero, Rhythm on the Range, My Man Godfrey, Luckiest Girl in the World, Room Service, Man About Town, Penny Serenade, Claudia, Where Do We Go From Here?, Heartbeat.

S

SACKS, SAMUEL: Attorney, agent. b. New York, N.Y., March 29, 1908. C.C.N.Y., St John's Law School, LL.B, 1930. Admitted Calif. Bar, 1943; priv. prac., law, N.Y. 1931–42; attorney, William Morris Agency, Inc., Sept. 1942; head of west coast TV business affairs, 1948–75. bd. of dir., Alliance of Television Film Producers, 1956–60. L.A. Copyright Society Treasurer, Beverly Hills Bar Assn., Los Angeles Bar Assn., American Bar Assn.; Academy of TV Arts & Sciences; Hollywood Radio & TV Society. Pres. Adat Shalom Synagogue, 1967–69, chmn. of bd., 1969–71; pres., American Field Service West L.A. Chapter 1970–72, United Synagogue of America (west region), v.p.; counsel, entertainment field, Simon & Sheridan, 1975–

SAFER, MORLEY: News Correspondent. b. Toronto. e. Univ. of Western Ontario. Started as corresp. and prod. with Canadian Broadcasting Corp. Joined CBS News as head of Saigon Bureau, 1965. Chief of CBS London bureau 1967–70. Joined 60 minutes as co-editor in Dec., 1970.

SAFFLE, M.W. "BUD": Executive. b. Spokane, Wash., June 29, 1923. e. Univ. of Wash. In service 1943–46. Started in m.p. buiness as booker, 1948. Entire career with Saffle Theatre Service as buyer-booker; named pres. in 1970. Also pres. of Grays Harbor Theatres, Inc., operating theatres in Aberdeen, Wash. Also operates d.i. in Centralia, Wash. On bd. of NATO of Wash. for 15 yrs; pres. of same for 2 terms and secty.-treas. 6 yrs. Elected to National NATO bd. in 1972. Founder of Variety Tent 46, serving as chief barker three times.

SAFIR, SIDNEY: Executive. b. Vienna, Aust., Feb. 2, 1923. e. London U. Ent. m.p. ind. 1940, Shipman & King Cinemas; RKO Radio Picture, 1941; salesman, British Lion, 1943; European sls. mgr., Lion Int'l, 1958; gen. sls. mgr. Lion Int'l, 1960; president, Lion Int'l Inc., 1965; man. dir. Lion Int'l Ltd. 1969; dir., British Lione Film Ltd., 1972.

SAINT, EVA MARIE: Actress. b. Newark, N.J., July 4, 1924. e. Bowling Green State U., Ohio. Radio, TV actress; on Broadway in Trip to Bountiful; m.p. debut in On the Waterfront (Acad. Award, best supporting actress, 1954).
PICTURES INCLUDE: That Certain Feeling, Raintree County, Hatful of Rain, North by Northwest, Exodus, All

Fall Down, Grand Prix, The Stalking Moon, Loving, Cancel My Reservation.
TV: How the West Was Won.

ST. JACQUES, RAYMOND: Actor-Director. Began career as actor, asst. dir. and fencing dir. for American Shakespeare Festival, Stratford, Conn. Made prof. acting debut in off-Bdwy. play, High Name Today. Made m.p. debut, Black Like Me, 1964.
PICTURES INCLUDE: The Pawnbroker, The Comedians, Mr. Moses, Madigan, Mister Buddwing, The Green Berets, Uptight, If He Hollers Let Him Go, Change of Mind, Cotton Comes to Harlem, Cool Breeze, Come Back Charleston Blue, Book of Numbers (also dir. debut), Lost in the Stars.
STAGE: The Blacks, Night Life, The Cool World, Seventh Heaven.

ST. JAMES, SUSAN: Actress. b. Los Angeles, Aug. 14, 1946. e. Conn. College for Women. Was model for six years; then signed to contract by Universal Pictures.
TELEVISION: The Name of the Game (series), McMillan & Wife (series), numerous shows.
PICTURES INCLUDE: What's So Bad About Feeling Good?, Jigsaw, P.J., Where Angels Go . . . Trouble Follows, Magic Carpet, Outlaw Blues, Love at First Bite, How to Beat the High Cost of Living, Carbon Copy.

ST. JOHN, BETTA: Actress. b. Hawthorne, Calif., Nov. 26. B'way debut in Carousel; then in South Pacific in N.Y. & London; m.p. debut in Dream Wife; since many more m.p., TV films.
PICTURES INCLUDE: All the Brothers were Valiant, The Robe, Dangerous Mission, Saracen Blade, Student Prince, Law vs. Billy the Kid, Alias John Preston, Naked Dawn, Tarzan and the Lost Safari, High Tide at Noon, City of the Dead.

ST. JOHNS, RICHARD R.: Executive Producer. b. Los Angeles, CA. e. Stanford University, B.A. 1953; Doctorate of Jurisprudence, Stanford Law School 1954. Joined law firm O'Melveny & Meyers 1954, specializing in entertainment law. 1963 became partner in law firm. 1968 became senior v.p., Filmways, Inc., becoming president and chief operating office in 1969. 1972, formed Richard R. St. Johns and Associates, independent management and packaging firm. Formed Guinness Film Group in 1975, branching out into full-scale motion picture production.
PICTURES: (exec. prod.): The Uncanny, Death Hunt, Matilda, The Silent Flute (Circle of Iron), Nightwing, The Wanderers, The Mountain Men, The Final Countdown, A Change of Seasons, Dead & Buried, American Pop and Venom.

SAKS, GENE: Director—Actor. b. N.Y.C., Nov. 8, 1921. e. Cornell Univ. m. actress Bea Arthur. Attended Dramatic Workshop of the New School for Social Research. Active in off-Broadway in 1948–49, forming cooperative theatre group at Cherry Lane Theatre. Joined Actor's Studio, followed by touring and stock. Also appeared in live TV dramas (Philco Playhouse, Producer's Showcase). Directed many Broadway plays before turning to film direction with Barefoot in the Park (1967).
PICTURES INCLUDE: Director: Barefoot in the Park, The Odd Couple, Last of the Red Hot Lovers, Mame, Cactus Flower. Actor: A Thousand Clowns, Prisoner of Second Avenue, The One and Only.
BROADWAY: Director: Enter laughing, Nobody Loves an Albatross, Generation, Half a Sixpence, Mame. Actor: Middle of the Night, Howie, The Tenth Man, A Shot in the Dark, A Thousand Clowns, Same Time, Next Year.

SALANT, RICHARD S.: Executive. b. New York, N.Y., Apr. 14, 1914; e. Harvard Coll. A.B., 1931–35; Harvard Law Sch., 1935–38; Atty. Gen.'s com on Admin. Procedure, 1939–41; Office of Solicitor Gen., U.S. Dept. of Justice, 1941–43; U.S. Naval Res., 1943–46; assoc., Roseman, Goldmark, Colin & Kave, 1946–48; then partner, 1948–51; pres. CBS news div., 1961–64; v.p. special asst. to pres. CBS, Inc., 1964; pres., CBS news div., 1966; mem. bd. of dir., CBS, Inc. 1964–69; vice chm., NBC bd., 1979–.

SALE, RICHARD: Writer, director. b. New York, N.Y., Dec. 17, 1911; e. Washington & Lee, A.B., 1934; m. Irma Foster, designer. Author novels, over 400 published stories; honor roll Best Short Stories, 1935; ent. m.p. ind. with Paramount, 1944; member: WGAW, DGA: Acad. of M.P. Arts & Sciences, Authors League of Amer., BMI: pres. Voyager Films, Inc.; v.p. Libra Productions, Inc.
PICTURES INCLUDE: Strange Cargo, Rendezvous with Annie, Spoilers of the North, Campus Honeymoon, Lady at Midnight, Calendar Girl, Inside Story, Dude Goes West, Mother is a Freshman, Father Was a Fullback, When Willie Comes Marching Home, Mr. Belvedere Goes to College, Ticket to Tomahawk, I'll Get By, Driftwoods Meet Me After the Show, Half Angel, Let's Make It Legal, Girl Next Door, My Wife's Best Friend, Let's Do It Again, Torpedo Run, French Line, Suddenly, Women's World, Gentlemen Marry Brunettes, Abandon Ship, The Oscar, The White Buffalo.

SALETRI, FRANK R.: Producer-Director-Writer. b. Chicago, Jan. 20, 1928. Is criminal trial lawyer, member of State of Calif. bar. Heads FRSCO Prods., Ltd., m.p. prod.
PICTURES INCLUDE: Black Frankenstein—Blackenstein (s.p., prod.); Black the Ripper (s.p., dir.); The Return of the Ghost of the Son of the Bride of the House of Frankenstein, 1984 (s.p., dir.), The Skid Row Slasher, s.p., dir; The Secret of the Maltese Falcon, s.p., dir; Annually prod., s.p. & dir. for The Academy of Science Fiction, Horror and Fantasy Films. Annually proe., s.p. & dir. for The Annual Count Dracula Society 'Ann Radcliffe' Awards. (Both are documentaries).

SALKIND, ALEXANDER: Producer. b. Danzig/Gdansk, of Russian extraction. Grew up in Berlin where father, Miguel, produced films. Went to Cuba with father to assist him in film production. First solo venture a Buster Keaton comedy, 1945. Returned to Europe where made many pictures in Spain, Italy, France and Hungary.
PICTURES INCLUDE: The Three Musketeers, The Four Musketeers, Superman.

SALKIND, ILYA: Producer. b. Mexico City. e. Univ. of London. Grew up in many countries as father, Alexander, produced films. First film job as production runner on The Life of Cervantes for father. Was assoc. prod. on Light at the Edge of the World.
PICTURES: The Three Musketeers, The Four Musketeers, Superman, Superman II (exec. prod.).

SALKOW, SIDNEY: Director, writer. b. New York City, June 16, 1911; e. City Coll. N.Y., B.A. Harvard Law Sch. Stage dir. & prod. asst. number N.Y. dram. prods. (Dir. Bloodstream, Black Tower, etc.) and mgr. summer theat. From 1933 variously dialogue dir., assoc. dir., writer & dir. numerous pictures Paramount, Universal, Republic, Columbia, etc.; dir. number of pictures in Lone Wolf series (for Columbia), Tillie the Toiler, Flight Lieutenant, etc. In armed service, WW II.
PICTURES INCLUDE: Millie's Daughter, Bulldog Drummond at Bay, Admiral Was a Lady, Fugitive Lady, Golden Hawk, Scarlet Angel, Pathfinder, Prince of Pirates, Jack McCall Desperado, Raiders of the 7 Seas, Sitting Bull, Robbers' Roost, Shadow of the Eagle, Las Vegas Shakedown, Toughest Man Alive, Chicago Confidential, Iron Sheriff, Great Sioux Massacre, Martin Eden.
TV: Created, prod. dir., This is Alice series for Desilu, Lassie, Fury, Wells Fargo series. Headed prod. for F&F Prod. in Rome, 1967–71.

SALMI, ALBERT: Actor. b. Coney Island, N.Y. After serving in World War II, studied—1948–54—with Dramatic Workshop, American Theatre Wing, Actors Studio. Appeared in many off-Bdwy. plays and live TV prods. Big hit on Bdwy. in Bus Stop. Other plays include The Rainmaker and The Brothers Karamazov. Has appeared in over 20 feature films and over 200 TV shows.
PICTURES INCLUDE: The Lawman, Something Big, The Deserter, The Crazy World of Jules Vrooder, Empire of the Ants, Dragonslayer.
TV: Gunsmoke, Barnaby Jones, etc.

SALT, WALDO: Writer. b. Chicago, Ill., Oct. 18, 1914. e. Stamford U., 1934, A.B. Taught dramatics & music, Menlo Jr. Coll., 1935; served as civilian consultant writer, Army films, OWI Overseas Film Burea, 1945.
PICTURES INCLUDE: Shopworn Angel, Tonight We Raid Calais, Rachel & the Stranger, M, Wild Man of Borneo, Mr. Winkle Goes to War, The Flame & the Arrow, Midnight Cowboy, Gang That Couldn't Shoot Straight, Serpico, The Day of the Locust, Coming Home.

SALTER, HANS J: Composer, conductor. e. U. Acad. of Music, Vienna-Austria, Mus. dir.: Volksopera, Vienna; State Oper. Berlin; Metropole Theatre, Berlin; comp., cond., UFA, Berlin, 1929–33; European br., Universal, 1934–36; to U.S., Univ. 1938–47, 1950–52, wrote over 150 scores.
PICTURES INCLUDE: It Started With Eve, His Butler's Sister, Scarlet Street, Magnificent Doll, The Spoilers, Frenchie, Flesh and Fury, Golden Horde, The Sign of the Ram, Frightened City, Ghost of Frankenstein, Black Friday, House of Frankenstein, The Wolfman, Hold That Ghost, The Invisible Man Returns, the Mummy's Hand, Man-Eater of Kumaon, This Island Earth, Tomahawk, The Battle of Apache Pass, Please Believe Me, Apache Drums, Untamed Frontier, Lover Come Back, Thunder on the Hill, Bend of the River, Against All Flags, Black Shield of Falworth, Sign of the Pagan, Far Horizons, Man Without a Star, Wichita, Autumn Leaves, Red Sundown, Hold Back the Night, Rawhide Years, The Oklahoman, Three Brave Men, Pay the Devil, Law of the Trigger, Female Animal, Raw Wind in Eden, The Wild and the Innocent, Bat Masterson Story, Man in the Net, Come September, Follow That Dream, If a Man Answers, Bedtime Story, The Warlord, Beau Geste, Return of the Gunfighter.
TV: Wichita Town, Laramie, The Law and Mr. Jones, The Virginian, Wagon Train, Lost in Space, Maya.

SALTZMAN, HARRY: Producer. b. October, 1915. St. John, N.B., Canada. Ent. film ind. 1945.

PICTURES INCLUDE: The Iron Petticoat, Look Back in Anger, The Entertainer, Saturday Night, Sunday Morning; formed Lowndes Prods. Ltd., 1964 and prod.: Dr. No, Call me Bwana, From Russia With Love, Goldfinger, The Ipcress File, Thunderball, Funeral in Berlin, You Only Live Twice, Billion Dollar Brain, Play Dirty, Battle of Britain, On Her Majesty's Secret Service, Tomorrow, The Man With the Golden Gun, Nijinsky.

TV: Prod. Robert Montgomery Show, Capt. Gallant of the Foreign Legion.

SALZBURG, JOSEPH S.: Producer, editor. b. New York, N.Y., July 27, 1917. Film librarian, then rose to v.p. in chge. of prod., Pictorial Films, 1935–42; civilian chief film ed. U.S. Army Signal Corps Photo Center, 1942–44; U.S. Army Air Forces, 1944–46; prod. mgr., Pictorial Films, 1946–50; prod. mgr. Associated Artists Prod., then M.P. for TV, 1950–51; org. m.p. prod. & edit. service for theatrical, non-theatrical & TV films; prod. mgr., dir. of films oper., official Films. Oct. 1956; prod. sup. tech. dir. Lynn Romero Prod. features and TV; assoc. prod. Lynn Romero Prod. TV series, Counterthrust; v.p., sec'y, B.L. Coleman Assoc., Inc. & Newspix, Inc. 1961; pres. National Production Assoc., Inc. 1962, chief of production, UPI Newsfilm, 1963. Prod. a/c Fred A. Niles Comm. Center, 1966. Appt. v.p., F.A. Niles Communications Centers, N.Y., 1969. In 1979 appointed in addition exec. producer & gen. mgr., F.A. Niles Communication Centers Inc., N.Y. studio.

SALZBURG, MILTON J.: Producer. b. New York, N.Y., Dec. 17, 1912. Book publishing field, N.Y.; film librarian; ed. instructional film, Dealers in Death; founder & pres. Pictorial Films, Inc., prod. instructional & topical shorts; pres. Academic Film Co. & Academic Prod. of Hollywood; sold Pictorial to Pathe Industries, remaining as pres., 1945; pres. 1946; sales mgr., Post Pictures, 1946; re-purchased Pictorial Films & pres. Nov. 1961; pres. Cornell Films; prod., Pattern for Survival, documentary film & Target: U.S.A., industrial film; pres. Novel Films, Dec. 1952; pres. Award TV Corp. (prod. Jimmy Demaret Golf series, Golden Era of Boxing), pres. Birad Corp., prod. dist. educat. films, 1960 pres. Productions Unlimited, Inc., producers of 16 mm educational films. Prod. 1963 Life Cycle of WASP, Cine Golden Eagle, Pre-Historic Animals, 1965 Story of Rice. Prod. Instincts of an Insect which has won Blue Ribbon, American Film Festival; Chris Award, Columbus Film Festival; Golden Eagle at Cine; Silver Hugo at Chicago Film Festival. 1967, v.p. & gen. sales mgr., Fleetwood Films, 1970, pres. Non-Theatrical Div., United Productions of America, DEI Industres, Inc. Left UPA in 1971 to reactivate Productions Unlimited, Inc., producing shorts and supplying films to govt. agencies.

SAMETH, JACK: Executive Producer, Producer, Director. Syracuse U., US Army. ABC TV 1950–63. NET 1963–67. ABC TV 1967–69 NET 1969–77. Executive Director, ABC TV News. Now exec. prod., special programs, WNET.

SAMPSON, LEONARD E.: Exhibitor. b. New York, N.Y. Oct., 1918. e. CCNY (B.B.A. '39). Entered m.p. industry as stagehand helper and usher, Skouras Park Plaza, Bronx 1932–36; asst. mgr. Gramercy Park, 1937–38; mgr., 5th Avenue Playhouse, 1939–41; mgr., Ascot Bronx, 1941–42. In Army 1942–46. On return entered into partnership with cousin Robert C. Spodick in Lincoln, a New Haven art house. Organized Nutmeg Theatres, operating 6 art and conventional theatres in Conn., associated with Norman Bialek in Westport and Norfolk. Sold Nutmeg in 1968 to Robert Smerling. Retains partnership with Spodick in New Haven's York Sq., Lincoln, and Crown. Built Groton, Conn., Cinemas I and II in 1970 and Norwich, Conn., Cinema I & II, 1976 and acquired Village Cinemas I & II, Mystic, in association with Spodick and William Rosen.

SAMUELS, ABRAM: Executive. b. Allentown, Pa., Sept. 15, 1920. e. Lehigh U. U.S. Army 1942–46; pres. Automatic Devices Co. 1946–76; named bd. chm. in 1976.

SAMUELSON, DAVID W.: F.B.K.S., A.R.P.S., B.S.C.: Executive. b. London, England, 1924. Son of early producer G.B. Samuelson. Joined ind. 1941 with British Movietone News. Later film cameraman, 1947. Left Movietone 1960 to join family company, Samuelson Film Service Ltd. Past president British Kinematograph Sound & TV Soc., Chmn. Inc. Ass. Kine. Mans. V.P. UNIATEC. Author of Motion Picture Camera and Lighting Equipment, Motion Picture Camera Techniques, Motion Picture Camera Data.

SAMUELSON, PETER GEORGE WYLIE: Producer. b. London, England, October 16, 1951. Masters Degree: English Literature, Cambridge University. Early career as interpreter and production assistant. Production Manager: 1973, Speed Merchants. 1974, High Velocity. 1975, One by One. 1976, Return of the Pink Panther. 1977, Santa Fe 1836. 1978, produced: A Very Big Withdrawal. 1979, partner: Kinesis Productions, is motion picture development and production company. Executive president and chief officer.

SAMUELSON, SYDNEY: C.B.E. Hon. F.B.K.S. B.S.C. Executive. b. London, England 1925. Early career as cinema projectionist 1939–42. Gaumont British News 1942–43. Royal Air Force 1943–47. Asst. cameraman, cameraman, director/cameraman. Founded Samuelson Film Service, 1955. Man. dir. Panavision Corp. of Calif. Ltd. 1965. Chrnn. and Chief Executive dir. Samuelson Film Service Ltd., Trustee British Academy of Film and Television Arts (chm. of Council, 1973–76). Governor British Society of Cinematographers. Executive member of Council, Cinema and Television Benevolent Fund. Pres., Television Veterans, 1980–81.

SANDERS, DENIS: Writer-producer-director, executive SRS Productions. b. New York City, Jan. 21, 1929. e. UCLA (M.A. 1954). Awards include 2 Academy Awards, A Time Out of War 1954; Czechoslovakia, 1968 in 1970. Made over 70 documentaries including Trial: City and County of Denver v.s. Lauren R. Watson; Arbitration: The Truth of the Matter.

FEATURES INCLUDE: Elvis, That's The Way It Is, MGM: Soul To Soul, Cinerama; One Man's Way, UA: War Hunt, UA: Crime and Punishment, USA.

SANDERS, HONEY: Actress, Singer. b. N.Y.C. TV; Edge of Night, CBS/TV; film, radio commercials.

STAGE: Gentlemen Prefer Blondes, Plain and Fancy, High Button Shoes, Carousel, Pajama Game, Damn Yankees, Diary of Anne Frank, Matchmaker, View From the Bridge.

SANDERS, NAT: Executive. b. New York City, Mar 4, 1892; e. C.C.N.Y., 1912. Publicity dir. & pub. rel. counsel; independent business mgr. for m.p. stars and directors; with sales dept. Commonwealth Pictures, Inc.; gen. mgr. Sanders Films; gen. mgr. Film Alliance of U.S. Inc.; pres. The Baker's Wife, Inc.; pres. Leo Films, Inc.; vp. English Films, Inc.; pres. Film Renters, Inc.; gen. mgr., United Motion Pictures Org., gen. mgr., Times Film Corp.; southern dist. rep.: Lopert Films, Inc., Janus Films, Inc., Audubon Films, Continental Distribution Corp., Mishkin Motion Pictures, Inc.; member: M.P. Pioneers, Variety Clubs International Sect'y, National Assoc. M.P. Ind., Motion Picture Pioneers of Florida.

SANDERS, TERRY BARRETT: Producer, director, writer. b. New York, Dec. 20, 1931. e. UCLA, 1951; Co-prod., photographed, A Time Out of War, 1954. Academy award best two-reel subject, and won first prize Venice Film Festival, etc.; co-wrote The Day Lincoln Was Shot, CBS-TV; s.p. The Naked and the Dead; prod. Crime and Punishment— USA., prod. War Hunt; prod. and dir. Portrait of Zubin Mehta for U.S.I.A. Assoc. dean, Film School, Calif. Instit. of the Arts.

TV: Prod. dir., Hollywood and the Stars, The Legend of Marilyn Monroe, National Geographic Society specials; exec. v.p., American Film Foundation.

SANDS, ERNEST: Executive. b. Newark, N.J., May 5, 1924. e. NYU, B.S., 1947. Sales exec., Warner Bros., 1947–59; film buyer, Fabian Theatres, 1960–61; gen. sales mgr., Astor Pic., 1962; gen. sales mgr., Allied Artists, 1963–64; asst. gen. sales mgr., Paramount, 1965; v.p. asst. gen. sales mgr., Paramount, Resigned 1969. Ivan Tors Films Inc., sales exec., 1970; v.p. gen. sales mgr., Cannon Releasing Corp., 1970–1973; Sands Film Co. Inc. president, March, 1973, Distributor and Producer's Representative.

SANDS, JOHNNY: Actor. r.n. John Harp; b. Lorenzo, Tex., Apr. 29, 1927. Started in school plays; screen debut in Stranger, 1946.

PICTURES INCLUDE: Till the End of Time, Affairs of Geraldine, Born to Speed, Blaze of Noon, Bachelor and the Bobby-Soxer, Fabulous Texan, Admiral Was a Lady, Lawless, Two Flags West, Aladdin and His Lamp, Basketball Fix.

SANDS, TOMMY: Singer. b. Chicago, Aug. 27, 1937; e. Schools there and Greenwood, La. Father, Benny Sands, pianist with stage bands. Started career as guitar player, singer when 10, at KWKH station, Shreveport, followed by other radio app.; TV with Ernie Ford, then Kraft TV show The Singin' Idol; recording contract won him million record sales of "Teen Age Crush."

PICTURES INCLUDE: Sing Boy Sing, Mardi Gras, Love in a Goldfish bowl, Babes in Toyland, The Longest Day.

SANFORD, CHARLES: Musical Director. b. June 17, 1905, N.Y.C. Has been conducting since age of 15; asst. Cond. NY Hippodrome; district musical supervisor, RKO; conducted various shows, assoc. cond. to Alexander Smallens, Porgy and Bess.

TV: Musical dir., Admiral Broadway Review, 1948; Your Show of Shows, 1950–54; Bob Hope, 1950–51; Elgin American Show, 1950; Beatrice Lillie Show, 1950–51; Max Liebman Presents, 1954–56; Producer's Showcase, 1957–58; Jerry Lewis, Patrice Munsel Shows; 1959–60 Max Liebman Specials, Phil Silvers, Sid Caesar Specials.

SANGER, GERALD: (C.B.E., J.P.): Director, British Movietone News, Ltd. b. Su-biton, Eng., May 23, 1898; married. e. Shrewsbury School and Kebie Coll., Oxford. Lieut., Royal Marines, 1917–19. Secretary of Hon. Esmond Harmsworth, M.P. (Lord Rothermere), 1921–29. Ed. Brit. Movietone News, 1929–53; dir., Assoc. Newspapers Ltd., 1944–63; F. Hewitt & Son (1927) Ltd. 1954: News Holdings Ltd., 1954; Associated-Rediffusion Ltd., 1954–56; Daily Mail & Gen. Trust Ltd., 1963.

SANGSTER, JIMMY: Producer, director, screenwriter. Ent. m.p. ind. 1943. Prod. man. for Break in the Circle, Men of Sherwood Forest, X the Unknown.
PICTURES INCLUDE: Man on the Beach, The Curse of Frankenstein, The Trollenberg Terror, The Georkel, The Blood of the Vampire, Dracula, Intent to Kill, The Revenge of Frankenstein, Jack the Ripper, The Mummy, The Brides of Dracula, The Man Who Could Cheat Death, The Siege of Sydney Street, The Criminal, The Hell Fire Club, See No Exit, 1960 prod. and scripted Taste of Fear for Hammer Films 1961. Prod. The Savage Guns; 1962; prod. s.p. Maniac, Nightmare, Devil Ship Pirates; prod. Hysteria, s.p., The Giants, Paranoiac, 1963; s.p. Brainstorm, 1964; prod., s.p. The Nanny, s.p. Deadlier Than the Male, The Bridge of Newgate Jail, 1965; 1966 s.p. Java Weed, s.p. The Anniversary. 1967 prod. 1968 s.p. Doubled in Diamonds, Hide and Seek, Foreign Exchange, Private I (prod.) 1969; s.p. The Killing Game, The Claw, Touchfeather. 1970 wrote, prod. dir. The Horror of Frankenstein; dir. Lust for a Vampire, 1971; co-wrote s.p. Gingerbread House, Murder by Month Club, A Taste of Evil, The Goldfish Bowl, s.p. prod., dir. Fear in the Night, 1971. 1973: Screenplay: The Fairytale Man. 1974: s.p. The Monstrous Defect. 1977: s.p. The Legacy. 1980: s.p., Phobia.
TV: Writing credits include: Motive for Murder, The Assassins, I Can Destroy the Sun, 1972, exec. story consultant Screen Gems-NBC short story series, McCloud, Banacek, Cannon, Ironside, etc. 1977–78; prod. CBS series, Young Dan'l Boone; wrote & produced pilot for CBS: Ebony Ivory and Jade; wrote pilot for ABC: Adventure (Columbia TV); wrote pilot for NBC: Murder in Music City; The Concrete Cowboys (CBS-movie); Holiday (CBS pilot); Once Upon a Spy.

SANSOM, LESTER A.: Producer. b. Salt Lake City, Utah. e. University of Utah. Radio singer under name of Jack Allen, 1930; ent. m.p. ind. in editorial dept., Fox Film Corp., Dec. 1931; served in U.S. Navy as head of film library, Washington, D.C., 1942–45; head of edit. dept. & post-prod., Allied Artists, since 1953; assoc. prod. Skabenga; prod., co-writer, Battle Flame; assoc. prod. Hell to Eternity, exec. prod. The Thin Red Line, prod. Crack in the World; prod. Bikini Paradise, Battle of the Bulge, Cluster of the West, Co-prod., Krakatoa—East of Java; exec. prod. 12 + 1.

SAPERSTEIN, HENRY G.: Executive. b. Chicago, Ill., June 2, 1918. e. U. of Chicago. Theatre owner, Chicago, 1943–45; pres. Television Personalities, Inc., 1955–67 Mister Magoo, Dick Tracy, TV shows, 1960–62; 1960–67 Glen Films, Inc.; prod., All-Star Golf, 1958–62; prod. Championship Bowling, 1958–60; prod. Ding Dong School, 1959–60; pres. owner, UPA Pictures, Inc., prod. Gay Purr-ee, animated features. Mr. Magoo, Dick Tracy cartoon series, Mr. Magoo's Christmas Carol. Prod. War of the Gargantuas, Invasion of the Astros, What's Up, Tiger Lily?, T-A-M-I, T.N.T. Show, Turnon, Tune In Drop Out, 1968; Hell in the Pacific. Pres. Screen Entertainment Co., Benedict Pictures Corp., United Prod. of America; pres. H.G. Saperstein & Associates. Producer: The Vaudeville Thing; Tchaikovsky Competition, Gerald McBoing Boing Show.

SARAFIAN, RICHARD C.: Director. b. New York City. Studied medicine and law before entering film industry with director Robert Altman doing industrial documentaries. Made documentaries before starting TV career.
TV: Gunsmoke, Bonanza, Guns of Will Sonnet, I Spy etc.
PICTURES: Andy (debut, 1965), Run Wild, Run Free, Ballad of a Badman, Fragment of Fear, Man in the Wilderness, Vanishing Point, Lolly Madonna (XXX), The Man Who Loved Cat Dancing, The Next Man (also co-prod.), Sunburn.

SARANDON, SUSAN: Actress. b. New York. e. Catholic University. Came to New York to pursue acting, first signing with Ford Model Agency. Made film debut in Joe. Also appeared on TV in A World Apart series. Co-produced film, The Last of the Cowboys.
PICTURES INCLUDE: The Great Waldo Pepper, The Rocky Horror Show, Lovin' Molly, The Front, assoc. cond. to Alexander Smallens, Porgy Page, Dragonfly, Walk Away Madden, The Other Side of Midnight, Pretty Baby, King of the Gypsies, Loving Couples, Atlantic City.

SARGENT, ALVIN: Writer. Began career as writer for TV, then turned to theatrical films.
PICTURES INCLUDE: The Stalking Moon, Gambit, The Sterile Cuckoo, The Effect of Gamma Rays on Man in the Moon Marigolds, Love and Pain (and the whole damn thing), Julia, Bobby Deerfield, Straight Time, Ordinary People.

SARGENT, DICK: Actor. b. Carmel, CA, 1933. Veteran of over 140 TV shows, 17 feature films and four TV series.
PICTURES: Captain Newman, M.D., Operation Petticoat, Mardi Gras, Bernadine, Hardcore, etc.
TELEVISION: Bewitched.

SARGENT, JOSEPH: Director.
PICTURES INCLUDE: The Taking of Pelham One, Two, Three, MacArthur, Goldengirl.
TV: The Marcus-Nelson Murders (Emmy award for tv movie that was pilot for Kojak series), The Night That Panicked America, Sunshine, Tribes, Hustling.

SARGENT, THORNTON: Executive. b. Wichita, Kans., June 22, 1902. e. U. of Mich., A.B. 1922, M.A., 1923. Instructor U. of Mo.; drama ed. St. Louis Times; adv.-pub. dir. Skouras Thea., 1932; Fox studio pub. 1933; pub. dir. Fox West Coast Thea., 1934; dist. mgr. L.A. first-runs 1935–43; training films div. Bur. Aeronautics and asst. officer in chg., Naval Photo Center, Hollywood; dir. adv. and pub. rel. Fox West Coast Thea., 1946; Lou Smith Associates, 1958; sales mgr. UPA Pictures, 1960; Sargent-Bourne Publicity, 1961–68. Public Relations consultant, 1968–81.

SARGOY, EDWARD A.: Attorney. b. New York City. e. C.C.N.Y., B.S., 1921, Columbia U. Law Sch., LL.B., 1924. Admitted to N.Y. bar. Specialist in copyright & m.p. law. Member Law firm of Sargoy & Stein, New York City, later known as Sargoy, Stein & Hanft, spec. counsel nationally for 11 major m.p. distrib. cos. in copyright infringement and distribution, from Jan. 1946 until his retirement, December, 1970. Now counsel. Compiler and annual reviser of U.S. Copyright Law Digest for Martindale—Hubbell Law Directory, 1948–76. Technical consultant to U.S. Delegation, for Inter-American Copyright Convention signed in Washington, D.C., June 1946, and Universal Copyright Conv., signed in Geneva, Sept. 1952. Chairman, Committee Copyrights Assn. Bar City of N.Y., 1957–60, formerly chairman of: Copyright Subsection of Amer. Bar Assn. and of its Committees on Copyright on Int'l Copyright, and on Program for Copyright Law Revision. Author of "U.C.C. Protection in the U.S.A." In June 1958 issue of N.Y. Univ. Law Review, and contributions to other legal periodicals. Lecturer on copyright and m.p. law in courses at Practicing Law Institute and in various law schools. Panelist in various bar association copyright symposia; pres. Copyright Society of the U.S.A., 1963–67.

SARLUI, ED: Executive. b. Amsterdam, Holland, Nov. 10, 1925. Owner, Peruvian Films, S.A.; pres., Radio Films of Peru, S.A.; pres. Bryant Films Educatoriana, S.A.; partner, United Producers of Colombia Ltd.; pres. Royal Film N.V.; pres., United Producers de Centroamerica, S.A.; pres. United Producers de Mexico, S.A.; pres. United Producers Int'l, Inc.

SARNOFF, ROBERT W.: Executive. b. New York, N.Y., July 2, 1918; Harvard U., B.A., 1939; Columbia Law Sch. 1940. In office of Coordinator of Info., Wash., D.C., Aug. 1941; the U.S. Navy, Mar. 1942; asst. to publisher, Gardner Cowles, Jr., 1945; mem. of staff Look Mag., 1946, with NBC, 1948–65; pres., Dec. 1955–58; chmn. bd., 1958; bd. of dir. RCA, 1957; chmn bd. chief exec. officer, NBC, 1958–65; pres. RCA, 1966; Chief Exec. Officer, 1968; bd. chmn., 1970–75. Mem., TV Pioneers, 1957; pres., 1952–53; International Radio & TV Society, Broadcasters Committee for Radio Free Europe. Am Home Products, Inc., dir., of Business Committee for the Arts.

SARNOFF, THOMAS: Executive. b. New York, N.Y., Feb. 23, 1927. e. Phillips Academy, Andover, Mass., 1939–43, Princeton U., 1943–45, Stanford U. grad. 1948, B.S. in E.E., Grad School of Bus. Admin. 1948–49. Sgt., U.S. Army Signal Corps, 1945–46; prod. & sales, ABC-TV, Hollywood, 1949–50; prod. dept. MGM, 1951–52; asst. to dir. of finance and oper., NBC, 1952–54; dir. of prod. and bus. affairs, 1954–57; vice pres., prod. and bus. affairs, 1957–60; v.p. adm. west coast, 1960–62; v.p. west coast, 1962; exec. v.p. 1965–77; bd. of dir., NBC prods 1961–77; bd of dir. Hope Enterprises 1960–75; dir. NABCAT, Inc. 1967–75; dir. Valley County Cable TV, Inc. 1969–75; Pres. NBC Entertainment Corp. 1972–77; Pres. Sarnoff International Enterprises, Inc. 1977– . Past pres. Research Foundation at St. Joseph Hospital of Burbank; past pres. Permanent Charities of the Entertainment Ind.; past ch. bd. of trustees, National Acad. of TV Arts and Sciences.

SARRAZIN, MICHAEL: Actor. r.n. Jacques Michel Andre Sarrazin. b. Quebec, Canada, May 22, 1940. Began acting at 17 on CBC TV; signed by Universal, 1965, appearing on several TV shows.
PICTURES INCLUDE: Gunfight in Abilene (debut), The Film-Flam Man, The Sweet Ride, Journey to Shiloh, A Man Called Gannon, Eye of the Cat, In Search of Gregory, They Shoot Horses, Don't They?, The Pursuit of Happiness, Sometimes a Great Notion, Believe in Me, Harry in Your

Pocket, For Pete's Sake, The Reincarnation of Peter Proud, Scaramouche, The Gumball Rally, Caravans.
TOWER: Chrysler Theatre, The Virginian, World Premiere.

SASSOWER, HARVEY L.: Advertising director. b. N.Y., July 28, 1945. e. CCNY (B.A. in adv.); 1968 asst. to adv. mg., United Artists. 1969, asst. to adv. dir., 20th Century-Fox, 1969, appointed adv. mgr. of ABC Pictures Corp., dir. of adv., ABC Pictures, 1970; pres., Universal Spectrum, Inc. (design & adv. studio). Art director; author.

SATENSTEIN, FRANK: Producer-director. b. N.Y.C., Oct. 7, 1924; e. Cornell Univ., Columbia Univ. U.S. Air Force; bd. chm. & dir., American Book—Stratford Press Inc.; dir., Standard Security Life Insurance Co. of New York; dir. Trans-Lux Corp.
THEATRE: Are You With It, Deep Are The Roots, The Greatest of These, Eagle-Lion.
PICTURES INCLUDE: Open Secret, Closeup.
TV: Ken Murray Show, Frank Sinatra Show, The Show Goes On, Strike It Rich, I've Got a Secret, Robert Q. Lewis, Godfrey's Talent Scouts, Jackie Gleason Show, What's My Line, Timex Show, Red Buttons.

SAUL, OSCAR: Writer. b. Brooklyn, N.Y., e. B'klyn Coll. Coauthor play, Medicine Show; m.p. ed., U.S. Public Health Svce; numerous radio and tv plays.
PICTURES INCLUDE: collab. s.p., Once Upon a Time, Strange Affair; collab. story, Road House, Lady Gambles; s.p., Woman in Hiding, Secret of Convict Lake; adapt., Streetcar Named Desire; collab. sp. p., Thunder on the Hill, Affair in Trinidad; prod., Let's Do It Again; collab. s.p. Helen Morgan Story; s.p. Joker Is Wild; collab. story Naked Maja; collab. s.p. Second Time Around, Major Dundee; s.p. The Silencers; collab. s.p. Man and Boy. Novel: The Dark Side of Love (NBC movie).

SAVAGE, DAVID: Executive Producer & Advertising Executive. b. New York, N.Y., March 17, 1924. e. Columbia U., 1945. In research development & testing div., Eastman Kodak Co., 2 yrs.; adv. mgr. asst. nat'l sales mgr., Official Films; org., film dept. mgr. WCBS-TV; dir. of film procurement, CBS; mgr. of film procurement, NBC 1953; exec. v.p., Bernard L. Schulbert; pres., Theatrical Enterprises div.; prod., indiv. shows.; v.p. in chg. radio, TV, acct. sup., Lynn Baker Inc., 1959; v.p. in chg. m.p. prod., TV prog. Gerald Prods., 1962; pres., Gerald's Clef-10 Prods. Inc.; mgr. planning, merchandising, Recorded Tape Dept., RCA Records, 1966; Promo. Mgr. Special Products Marketing RCA Records Div; pres., Response Industries, Inc., (adv. agency), 1970 which became affiliate of McCann Erickson, and was v.p. of McCann Erickson in addition to continuing as pres. of R.I.

SAVAGE, JOHN: Actor. Studied at American Academy of Dramatic Arts. In Manhattan organized Children's Theatre Group which performed in Public Housing. Has appeared in many plays both on and off Bdwy. Won Drama Circle Award for performance in One Flew Over the Cuckoo's Nest in Chicago and Los Angeles.
PICTURES: Bad Company, Steelyard Blues, All the Kind Strangers, The Deer Hunter, Hair, The Onion Field, Cattle Annie and Little Britches, Inside Moves.
STAGE: Fiddler on the Roof, Ari, Siamese Connections, The Hostage, American Buffalo.
TELEVISION: Eric, Gibbsville (series).

SAVALAS, TELLY: Actor. b. Garden City, N.Y., Jan. 21, 1924. r.n. Aristotle Savalas, e. Col. Univ. (B.S.). Joined Information Services of State Dep't.; made exec. dir. Then named sr. dir. of news, special events for ABC, where created Your Voice of America series. Acting career began with debut in Bring Home a Baby on Armstrong Circle Theatre TV.
PICTURES INCLUDE: Birdman of Alcatraz, Young Savages, Cape Fear, Man from the Diner's Club, Battle of the Bulge, Greatest Story Ever Told, Beau Geste, Dirty Dozen, Buona Sera, Mrs. Campbell, Crooks and Coronets, Kelly's Heroes, On Her Majesty's Secret Service, Killer Force, Lisa and the Devil, Capricorn One, Escape to Athena, Beyond the Poseidon Adventure.
TELEVISION: Mongo's Back in Town (movie), Visions (movie), The Marcus-Nelson Murders (movie), Kojak (series).

SAWELSON, MEL: Executive b. Los Angeles, Calif., Sept. 5, 1929. e. USC 1947–48, UCLA 1948–49. Entered M.P. industry in 1947; mgr., Acme Film Laboratories, Inc., 1952; pres., Sports-TV, 1957–59; produced, Olympic Films, International Olympic Organization, 1956; produced, Big 10 Hilites, PCC Hilites, All American Game of the Week, 1957–59; 1st m.p. lab. exec. to install videotape, 1959; created Acme-chroma process of transferring color videotape to film; pres., Acme Film & Videotape Labs., 1967–71; v.p. Consolidated Film Industries, 1971, exec. v.p. 1972; pres., Glen Glenn Sound Co., 1972.

SAXON, JOHN: Actor. b. Brooklyn, N.Y., Aug. 5, 1935. Model; m.p. debut: Running Wild.
PICTURES INCLUDE: The Unguarded Moment, Rock

Pretty Baby, Summer Love, The Restless Years, The Reluctant Debutante, Cry Tough, Portrait in Black, The Unforgiven, The Plunderers, Posse from Hell, War Hunt, Nightmare, Evil Eye, For Singles Only, Joe Kidd, Enter The Dragon, Black Christmas, Strange Shadows in an Empty Room, The Electric Horseman.

SCHACKER, MARSHALL: Producers representative. b. Los Angeles, Calif., Jan. 10, 1922. e. Univ. of Southern Calif., 1939–42. U.S. Army Signal Corps., 1942–45. Bus. rep., Indep. M.P. Prods. in Hollywood, 1945–48; talent, prog. dept. exec., National Broadcasting Co., 1948–52. Producers representative specializing in representation of European m.p. companies, 1952 to present.
CURRENTLY REPRESENTING: Italy: Titanus, Documento Films, Malenotti, Cirac, CCM; France: Terra Film, Les Films Agiman, Cormoran Film, Fides Film, Rialto Film, Arpa; England: Regal Films International, Ltd. Pres., Premiere Films, Inc., Premiere Video, Inc.

SCHAEFER, CARL: Publicist, b. Cleveland, Ohio, Sept. 2. e. U.C.L.A., contr. to mag., including Vanity Fair, Hollywood Citizen-News, 1931–35; Warner Bros., 1935.; Huesped de Honor, Mexico, 1943; OSS WWII, 1944–45; Int'l Comt. AMPS, chmn. 1966–67; Italian Order of Merit, 1957; Chevalier de l'ordre de la Couronne, Belgium, 1963. Pres., Foreign Trade Assn. of Southern Calif., 1954; chmn. of bd., 1955; British-American C. of C., 1962; Chevalier French Legion d'Honneur, 1955; Comm. Hollywood Museum; dir., International Relations, Warner Bros. Seven Arts Int'l Corp., 1960; formed own firm, Carl Schaefer Enterprises, 1971. Dir. pub. rel., British-American Chamber of Commerce, 1971; dir. pub. rel. Iota International Pictures, 1971; dir. pub. rel. Lyric Films International, 1971; bureau chief (Hollywood) Movie/TV Marketing, 1971; managing dir., International Festival Advisory Council, 1971; dir. pub. rel. & adv. Francis Lederer Enterprises (Inc. American National Academy of Performing Arts, and Canoga Mission Gallery) 1974; West Coast rep. Angelika Films of N.Y. 1974, Hwd. rep Krowitz/Geiger Products. 1975– ; Hwd. corresp. Movie News, S'pore, & Femina, Hong Kong, 1974– ; member Westn. Publications Assn. 1975– ; field rep. Birch Records 1975; Hollywood rep. Antena Magazine, Buenos Aires; dir pub rel Style Magazine. Coordinator Hollywood Reporter Annual Key Art Awards; coordinator Hollywood Reporter Annual Marketing Concept Awards; executive committee & historian ShoWesT.

SCHAEFER, GEORGE: Producer, director. b. Wallingford, Conn., Dec. 16, 1920. e. Lafayette Coll., Yale Drama School. Dir. for Broadway stage; assoc. prod., Teahouse of the August Moon; prod., N.Y. City Center Theatre Co., 1949–52; dir., Dallas, Tex., State Fair musicals, 1952–58; prod., dir., B'way Play: Write Me a Murder, The Last of Mrs. Lincoln; dir. for TV.
TV: Including Macbeth, Little Moon of Alban; Victoria Reginia; The Magnificient Yankee, A War of Children; In This House of Brede, F. Scott Fitzgerald & The Last of the Belles, Truman At Potsdam, Sandburg's Lincoln, Amelia Earhart; Our Town; Blind Ambition; Here There Be Dragons, Voyage of the Mayflower, Barry Manilow: One Voice, The Bunker, People vs. Jean Harris; prod.-dir., Hallmark Hall of Fame. Pres. Compass Prod., Inc. Pres., Directors Guild of America.
PICTURES: Dir., Generation, Pendulum, Doctor's Wives, Once Upon a Scoundrel, An Enemy of the People.

SCHAEFER, JACK: Writer. b. Cleveland, O., Nov. 19, 1907. e. Oberlin Coll., Columbia U. edit. & pub., Theatre News, 1935–40, The Movies, 1939–41.
AUTHOR: Short stories for TV anthologies; Shane, First Blood, Jeremy Rodock, Company of Cowards, Monte Walsh, The Great Endurance Horse Race.

SCHAFER, NATALIE: Actress. b. New York, N.Y. e. Merrill School and Hamilton Institute.
B'WAY: Lady in the Dark, Susan and God, The Doughgirls.
PICTURES INCLUDE: Marriage is a Private Affair, The Snake Pit, Molly and Me, Dishonored Lady, Susan Slade, 40 Carats, The Day of the Locust.
TV: I Love Lucy, Route 66, 77 Sunset Strip, Thriller, The Beverly Hillbillies, Gilligan's Island.

SCHAFFNER, FRANKLIN: Director. b. Tokyo, Japan, May 30, 1920; e. Franklin & Marshall Coll. U.S. Navy, W.W. II; Dir. Person to Person, Studio One. Kaiser-Aluminum Hour, Playhouse 90; Emmy Best dir. 1945–55.
PICTURES INCLUDE: The Stripper, 1962, The Double Man, The Best Man, Planet of the Apes, Patton, Nicholas and Alexandra, Papillon, Islands in the Stream, The Boys from Brazil, The Sphinx.

SCHARY, DORE: Writer-producer-director. b. Newark, N.J., Aug. 31, 1905. Little theatre dir., actor in stock; playwright, Too Many Heroes, Sunrise at Campobello, The Highest Tree, The Devil's Advocate, Banderol; newspaper, mag. columnist author orig. & s.p. alone and in collab., numerous pictures from 1932.

Pres. & chief exec. off., Theatre Vision Inc., 1972; pres. & chief exec. officer, Schary Productions, Inc., 1973.

PICTURES INCLUDE: Boys Town, Young Tom Edison, Edison the Man; Acad. award, best orig., Boys Town, 1938; in 1942 appt. exec. prod. MGM; prod., Journey for Margaret, The War Against Mrs. Hadley, Lassie Come Home, Joe Smith, American, Lost Angel, Bataan, I'll Be Seeing You, Till the End of Time, The Spiral Staircase, The Farmer's Daughter, The Bachelor and the Bobby-soxer, Mr. Blanding Builds His Dream House, The Window, The Set-up, Crossfire, Bad Day at Black Rock, Go For Broke, The Swan, Designing Woman, Lonely Hearts, Sunrise at Campobello, writer, prod., dir., Act One.

Joined Vanguard Films, 1943, as prod. exec.; v.p. in chg. prod., RKO Radio Pictures, 1947; July 1948 to Dec. 1956, v.p. in chg. prod. MGM. A Champion of Champion Producer Fame ratings. Formed indep. co., 1958.

STAGE: Author, co-prod. with Theatre Guild, Sunrise at Campobello; author, co-prod. with Theatre Guild and dir., The Highest Tree; co-prod. with Theatre Guild and dir., The Unsinkable Molly Brown; dramatized, prod., dir., The Devil's Advocate; co-prod. with Theatre Guild and dir., Something About A Soldier; co-prod., dir., The Zulu & the Zayda. Dramatized and produced Herzl.

SCHATZBERG, JERRY: Director. b. N.Y.C. Early career in photography as asst. to Bill Helburn.

PICTURES INCLUDE: Puzzle of a Downfall Child, Panic in Needle Park, Scarecrow, Sweet Revenge (prod.-dir.), The Seduction of Joe Tynan, Huckleberry Rose.

SCHEIDER, ROY: Actor. b., Orange, N.J. e. Franklin and Marshall College where he won the Theresa Helburn Acting Award twice. First professional acting in N.Y. Shakespeare Festival 1961 prod. of Romeo and Juliet. Became member of Lincoln Center Repertory Co. and acted with Boston Arts Festival, American Shakespeare Festival, Arena Stage (Wash., D.C.) and American Repertory Co.

PICTURES INCLUDE: Loving, Paper Lion, Stiletto, Star!, Puzzle of a Downfall Child, Klute, The French Connection, The Outside Man, The Seven Ups, The Inheritor, Sheila Levine, Jaws, Marathon Man, Sorcerer, Jaws II, Last Embrace, All That Jazz.

TV: Hallmark Hall of Fame, Studio One, N.Y.P.D.

STAGE: Richard III, Stephen D, Sergeant Musgrave's Dance, The Alchemist.

SCHELL, MARIA: Actress. b. Vienna, 1926. Sister of Maximilian Schell. Made debut at 12 in Swiss film, The Gravel Pit. Subsequently appeared in many British and American films.

PICTURES INCLUDE: Angel with a Trumpet, The Heart of the Matter, So Little Time, The Magic Box, The Brothers Karamazov, The Hanging Tree, Cimarron, The Odessa File, Voyage of the Damned, The Twist, Superman.

SCHELL, MAXIMILIAN: Actor. b. Vienna, Dec. 8, 1930.

TV: Shows include: Playhouse 90, Judgment at Nuremberg, The Fifth Column, Turn The Key Deftly.

PICTURES INCLUDE: Children, Mother and the General, The Young Lions, Judgment at Nuremberg, Five Finger Exercise, The Condemned of Altona, Return from the Ashes, The Deadly Affair, Counterpoint, The Desperate Ones, The Castle, Krakatoa East of Java, The Odessa File. Dir., starred First Love; The Man in the Glass Booth (actor), End of the Game (dir., co-prod.), St. Ives, A Bridge Too Far, Cross of Iron, Julia, Players, The Black Hole.

SCHENCK, AUBREY: Producer. b. Brooklyn, N.Y., Aug. 26, 1908; e. Cornell U.; N.Y.U. With law firm of O'Brien, Driscoll & Raftery; buyer & attorney for Natl. Theaters, 1936; prod. for 20th Century-Fox 1945; exec. prod. Eagle Lion 1946; contract prod. Universal Internatl. 1948; Aubrey Schenck Productions, Inc.

PICTURES INCLUDE: Shock, Johnny Comes Flying Home, Strange Triangle, Repeat Performance, T-Men, Mickey, It's a Joke Son, Trapped, Port of New York, Wyoming Man, Undercover Girl, Fat Man, Target Unknown; formed own co. to prod. War Paint, Beachhead. Also: Yellow Tomahawk, Shield for Murder, Big House, U.S.A., Crime Against Joe, Emergency Hospital, Ghost Town, Broken Star, Rebels in Town, Pharaoh's Curse, Three Bad Sisters, Fort Yuma, Desert Sands, Quincannon, Frontier Scout, Black Sleep, Hot Cars, War Drums, Voodoo Island, Revolt at Fort Laramie, Tomahawk Trail, Untamed Youth, Girl in Black Stockings, Bop Girl Goes Calypso, Up Periscope, Violent Road, Reckless, Frankenstein 1970, Wild Harvest, Robinson Crusoe On Mars, Don't Worry, Ambush Bay, Kill a Dragon, Impasse, More Dead Than Alive, Barquero, Daughters of Satan.

TV: Miami Undercover, series.

SCHERICK, EDGAR J: Executive Producer. e. Harvard Univ.; elected to Phi Beta Kappa. Introduced Wide World of Sports on TV thru his co., Sports Programs, Inc. Was v.p. in chg. of network programming at ABC-TV. Now pres. of Palomar Pictures Int'l.

PICTURES INCLUDE: For Love of Ivy, The Birthday Party, Take the Money and Run, They Shoot Horses, Don't They?, The Killing of Sister George, Sleuth, The Heartbreak Kid, Law and Disorder, The Stepford Wives, I Never Promised You a Rose Garden.

SCHERMER, JULES: Associate producer. In 1942: True to the Army, Henry Aldrich, Editor, Par. In 1943: Henry Aldrich Gets Glamour, Par.; collab. s.p. The Sullivans.

PICTURES INCLUDE: Framed, Man From Colorado, Criss-Cross, Illegal Entry, Union Station, Pride of St. Louis, Lydia Bailey, Pickup on South Street, Pushover, Carthay Center Prods. Inc., 1965. Prod., A Dream of Kings.

SCHIAVONE, JAMES: Executive. b. Niagara Falls, N.Y., Nov. 14, 1917. e. U. of Michigan. Started career as newspaperman; general manager WWJ-AM-FM-TV, Detroit, 1952–68; v.p.-gen. mgr., KSAT-TV, San Antonio, Tex., 1969-present.

SCHICK, ELLIOT: Executive. b. Brooklyn, N.Y., Dec. 24, 1924. e. Brooklyn Coll. (B.A.), New School for Social Research (drama workshop, directing 1945–46). Author of book for Ballet Theatre, Manfred; book, The Administration of the Economic and Social Council. 1942–48, prod. & dir. radio shows for WNYC, N.Y.C., composed and arranged music for radio and stage production; 1946–48 dialogue director, Republic Studios; 1948–50, prod. & dir. TV shows and commercials, Nova Productions; 1950–51, editor, United Nations Film Div.; 1951–53, editor, Candid Camera; 1953–55, asst. studio mgr., American Natl. Studios; 1955–56, prod. mgr., Gross-Krasne; 1956–60, prod. & dir. industrials, commercials, documentaries, Fred Niles, Chicago; 1960–63, dir., commercials, Hollywood Film Commercials; 1964–65; prod. & dir. live and video tape shows for KCET; 1965–69, asst., dir. for TV series: 12 O'Clock High, Time Tunnel, Star Trek and features: Hombre, Hard Contract, Bloody Mama, Billy Jack, Tora, Tora, Tora; 1969–72, prod. mgr. for features: 3 in the Attic, Up in the Cellar, Bunny O'Hare, Honkers, Hickey and Boggs, Kansas City Bomber, White Lightning; 1973–77 spvr. prod. for AIP on Sugar Hill, Return to Macon County, Cooley High, Futureworld, Island of Dr. Moreau in 1977 joined EMI Films, Inc. as v.p. prod.; 1978, exec.-in-chg.-prod., Deer Hunter; 1980, produced The Earthling; 1981, prod., Private Benjamin (TV series), supvr. prod., Pippin (TV).

SCHIFRIN, LALO: Composer, b. Buenos Aires. Father was conductor of Teatro Colon in B.A. for 30 years. Schifrin studied with Juan Carlos Paz in Arg. and later Paris Cons. Returned to homeland and wrote for stage, modern dance, TV. Became interested in jazz and joined Dizzie Gillespie's band in 1962 as pianist and composer. Settled in L.A.

PICTURES INCLUDE: The Cincinnati Kid, The Liquidator, Cool Hand Luke, The President's Analyst, The Fox, Kelly's Heroes, Magnum Force, Man on a Swing, The Four Musketeers, Voyage of the Damned, The Eagle Has Landed, Rollercoaster, The Manitou, Boulevard Nights, Escape to Athena, The Amityville Horror, The Nude Bomb, The Competition, Caveman.

SCHILLER, FRED: Playwright, screen & TV writer, radio producer. Awarded: Literary Prize, for McCall magazine story Ten Men and a Prayer. National Member of Smithsonian Institution, Member of Societè Des Auteurs et Compositeurs Dramatiques. Was chief corres. European Newspaper Feature Services, exploitation director. RKO Radio Studios. Honored by the Univ. of Wyoming for literary achievements with a special Fred Schiller Collection for their library.

PICTURES FOR: MGM, Columbia, RKO, Republic and Henri Sokal Films, Paris.

TV: TV writer; NBC All Star Special adapt., George Bernard Shaw's play, Inca of Persualem. All in all 53 TV plays, Four Star Playhouse, The Millionaire, Loretta Young Show, Charlie Chan, Desilu, Colonel Flack, The Veil, Manhunt, The Islanders, The Beachcomber, Follow the Sun, The Third Man, The Americans You Don't Know; Two 90 min. TV specials, Finder Bitte Melden, Vienna, and Demandez Vickey!, Paris. TV Pilot, Comedy Series Diet Fever, ABC.

STAGE: Come On Up (U.S.), Anything Can Happen (London), Demandez Vicky (Paris), Finder Please Return (Athens, Madrid), Finder Bitte Melden (Berlin, Hamburg, Vienna).

SCHILLER, LAWRENCE J.: Producer-Director. b. New York City, Dec. 28, 1936. Photo-journalist with Life Magazine & Saturday Evening Post, 1958–70; collaborated on numerous books including three by Norman Mailer: The Executioner's Song, Marilyn, and The Faith of Graffiti; Muhammad Ali with Wilfrid Sheed; Minamata with Eugene Smith.

PICTURES: The Man Who Skied Down Everest (editorial concept & direction); Lady Sings the Blues, Butch Cassidy & the Sundance Kid (conceived and executed special still montages & titles); The American Dreamer (prod./dir.).

TELEVISION: Hey, I'm Alive (prod./dir.); The Trial of Lee Harvey Oswald (prod.); The Winds of Kitty Hawk (prod.).

SCHIMEL, ADOLPH: Lawyer. b. Vienna, Austria. U.S., 1904 naturalized. 1910 e. A.B. Coll, City of N.Y., 1920; LL.B., Harvard 1923; Admitted to N.Y. bar, 1924, since practiced in N.Y.; Sec'y., Universal Pictures since 1945; v.p., gen. counsel, Universal & subsids., 1950 to 1972. Mem: law com. (chmn.), 1955 to 1972 MPA, Bar Assn. of the City of New York, American Bar Assn; consultant to Universal since 1972.

SCHIMMEL, HERBERT D.: Executive. b. New York, N.Y., October 15, 1927. e. University of Pennsylvania, Wharton School. C.P.A., partner with M. Schimmel and Co. prior to entering m.p. industry in 1966 as treasurer, Europix Consolidated Corp.; pres., 1968; pres., Europix International Ltd., 1971.

SCHINE, G. DAVID: Executive. Film exhibitor until 1966 in New York, Ohio, Kentucky, Maryland, Delaware, and West Virginia. Exec. prod. of French Connection, 1971. Writer, prod., dir. of That's Action!, 1977. Chief Exec. officer of Schine Productions (production) and Epic Productions, Inc. (distribution), and Studio Television Services, Inc.

SCHLAIFER, CHARLES: Executive. President, Charles Schlaifer and Company, Inc., advertising agency with offices in New York and Los Angeles. b. Omaha, Nebr. Reporter Daily News, World-Herald, (Omaha). In 1928 apptd. adv. mgr. Paramount theatres, Omaha; then of Publix theats., Omaha; then of Tri-State circuit, Neb., Iowa; 1936–42 managing dir. United Artists Theats., San Francisco; advisor, nat'l adv., United Artists prod. In 1942 apptd. adv. mgr. 20th Cent.-Fox; named asst. dir. adv., publicity & exploitation, 1944; appt'd. dir. of advertising, publicity, exploitation and radio, 1945. Resigned 20th-Fox post, Feb. 1, 1949, to establish own adv. agency. Pres., Charles Schlaifer & Co., Inc. Chmn. advertising advisory council, MPAA; instructor at New School of Social Research, N.Y., on m.p.; revised m.p. adv. code; permanent chmn. first MPAA pub rel. com. Member; Nat'l Advisory Mental Health Council to U.S. Surgeon General; vice-chmn. bd. of gov., Nat'l Assn. of Mental Health. Lecturer, writer on adv. & mental health bd. of gov., Menninger Foundation; founder, co-chmn., Nat'l Mental Health Comm., secy., treas., Joint Comm. on Mental Illness & Health; expert witness Congress, govt. hearings. Elected Hon. Fellow of the Amer. Psychiatric Assn., 1959; V. chmn., trustee in chg., Mental Health and Mental Retardation Facilities, N.Y. State; 1964; secy., treas., Joint Commission Mental Health for Children; vice chmn. bd. Foundation for Child Mental Welfare, 1963. Member bd. trustees Research Foundation 1966. Member White House Conference on the Handicapped, 1952–65; elected honorary fellow, Post Graduate Psychiatric Institute, 1968. Hon. Doctor of Letters, John F. Kennedy College, Wahoo, Neb., 1969; Chmn. N.Y. State Health and Mental Hygiene Facilities Improvement Corp., 1970; Hon. Fellow—American Ortho Psychiatric Assoc., 1970; Hon. Fellow British Royal Society of Health. Wisdom Award Hon. Wisdom Mag., 1969; social conscience award Karen Horney Clinic, 1972. Chairman, New York State Facilities Development Corp., 1973– ; Advisory Council to the National Institute of Mental Health & to the Surgeon General of the U.S. 1976–

SCHLANG, JOSEPH: Executive. b. N.Y.C. Feb. 24, 1911, e. N.Y.U. Owner and leader in N.Y.C. real estate, partner of N.Y. Stock Exchange firm and exec. dir. of many enterprises. Pres. of International Opera Co. & Opera Presentations, Inc. Has produced two weekly radio programs: Opera Stars of Tomorrow and 100 & More Ways to Improve N.Y.C. since April, 1973. Opera Presentations, Inc., a non-profit corp. distributes and exhibits opera, ballet and art films throughout America and the school system. Over 100 cultural films owned by Schlang are supplied to Opera Presentations free to use.

SCHLESINGER, JOHN: Director. b. London, England. 1960: Wrote and dir. Terminus for British Transport Films (Golden Lion, best doc., Venice); The Class. Some episodes The Valiant Years series.
PICTURES INCLUDE: 1961: A Kind of Loving (Golden Bear, Berlin); 1962–63; Billy Liar; 1964–65: Darling (New York Film Critics Award); 1966–67: Far From the Madding Crowd. 1968: Midnight Cowboy (Best dir. and film, S.F.T.A. and 'Oscars'), 1970: Sunday, Bloody Sunday (Best dir. and film, S.F.T.A.), Visions of Eight (sequence), The Day of the Locust, Marathon Man, Yanks, Honky Tonk Freeway.

SCHLONDORFF, VOLKER: Director. b. Wiesbaden, Germany, Mar. 31, 1939. Studied in France, acquiring degree in political science in Paris. Studied at French Intl. Film School, before becoming asst. to Jean-Pierre Melville, Alain Resnais, and Louis Malle Debut film, Der Junge Torless (Young Torless), 1965.
PICTURES: A Degree of Murder, 1966; Michael Kohlhass, 1968; The Sudden Fortune of the Poor People of Kombach, 1970; Die Moral der Rugh Halbfass, 1971; A Free Woman, 1972; The Lost Honor of Katharine Blum,

1975; Le Coup de Grace, 1976; Valeska Gert, 1977; The Tin Drum, 1979.

SCHLOSSBERG, JULIAN: Producer-Distributor-Radio Host. b. N.Y.C. Jan. 26, 1942. e. N.Y.U. Joined ABC-TV network 1964 as asst. acct. rep.; named acct. rep. 1965; 1966, joined Walter Reade Organization as asst. v.p. chg. of TV; 1969, moved to WRO Theatre Div.; 1970, joined faculty of School of Visual Arts; 1971, named v.p. of WRO Theatres; 1972, Jan., 1976, joined Paramount Pictures as v.p. in charge of feature film acquisition. Since 1978 pres. & owner of Castle Hill Productions; 1974, prod. & moderated An Evening with Joseph E. Levine at Town Hall, N.Y.C.; 1974 to 1980, host of radio show Movie Talk on WMCA (N.Y.C.), WMEX (Boston), and WICE (Providence).
PICTURES INCLUDE: Ten from Your Show of Shows, No Nukes.
THEATRE: It Had To Be You.

SCHLOSSER, HERBERT S.: Executive. b. Atlantic City, N.J. e. Princeton U., Yale Law. Joined law firm of Phillips, Nizer, Benjamin, Krim & Ballon, 1954; attorney, California National Productions (subsidiary of National Broadcasting Company) 1957; v.p. & gen. mgr., 1960; director, talent & program administration, NBC television network, 1961; v.p., talent & program admin., 1962; v.p. programs, west coast, 1966–72; exec. v.p., NBC-TV, 1972; president, NBC Television Network, 1973, pres. & chief operating officer, NBC, April 1, 1974–76; Pres. & chief executive officer, 1977–78; exec. V.P. RCA 1978.

SCHLUSSELBERG, MARTIN: Film Executive. b. Sept. 1936. e. Yeshiva Univ. Booking clerk. UA. 1956; head booker, Citation Films, 1958; head booker, Desilu Dist., Co., 1961; head booker, and asst. to gen. sls. mgr., Medallion Pictures Corp., 1963; World Ent. Corp., 1966, Sales Mgr.; Crystal Pictures, 1978, sls. mgr., v.p.

SCHMIDT, WOLF: Producer-Distributor. b. Freiburg/Br., Germany, June 30, 1937. Came to U.S. 1962 as free-lance journalist. Started producing in 1969, distributing independently since 1972.
PICTURES INCLUDE: Ski Fever (prod.), Stamping Ground (co-prod.), Young Hannah (exec. prod.), Things Fall Apart (prod.), The Passover Plot (prod.), Run For the Roses (co-prod.).

SCHNEER, CHARLES H.: Producer, b. Norfolk, Va., May 5, e. Columbia College; pres., Morningside Prods. Inc. & Pictures Corp.; 1956. Founded Andor Films 1974.
PICTURES INCLUDE: Prod. The 3 Worlds of Gulliver, The 7th Voyage of Sinbad, I Aim at the Stars, Face of a Fugitive, Good Day for a Hanging, Battle of the Coral Sea, Tarawa Beachhead, Mysterious Island, Jason and the Argonauts, First Men In The Moon, Half A Sixpence, Land Raiders, Valley of Gwangi, The Executioner, The Golden Voyage of Sinbad, Sinbad & The Eye of the Tiger, Clash of the Titans.

SCHNEIDER, DICK: Prod.-dir. b. Cazadero, Calif., Mar. 7; e. Coll. of the Pacific; U.S. Navy, WWII.
TV: Dough Re Mi, NBC-TV, Wide Wide World, NBC-TV, Colgate Comedy Hours, Beatrice Lilly & Jackie Gleason Comedy Hours, Henry Morgan Show, Kate Smith Show, Big Story, Treasury Men in Action, Doorway to Danger, Today Show, Home, Tonight Show, General Mills Circus; dir. coverage of political conventions; dir. NBC-TV coverage, Princess Margaret's Wedding and Paris Summit conference; dir. Eleanor Roosevelt Specials, 1959–60; Something Special 61, At This Very Moment, Inauguration, Gemini, Emmys, 1962, 1963, 1964; Papal Mass for all networks at Yankee Stadium, 1965–66; 1966–67 Tonight Show, Orange Bowl, Macy's Parade; Jr. Miss Pageant; 1967–70 College Queen, Emmy Award. Prod.; Macy's Parade, 1968–69 Orange Bowl Parade, 1968–69; Prod.-dir., NBC Expt in TV, New Communication; prod., Big Sur; prod.-dir., Jr. Miss Pageant, 1968–69; dir. Dream House, ABC; dir. Who, What or Where, NBC; produced in 1970: Macy's Parade, Junior Miss, Orange Bowl Parade. 1971–79 Macy's Parade, Stars and Stripes; in 1972: Post Parade, Stars and Stripes 1973–75; Rose Parade 1974–80; Salute to Sir Lew; Jeopardy; NBC Star Salute, 1980; Emmy winner, 1980; Rose Parade, 1981; Star Salute, 1981.

SCHNEIDER, JOHN A.: Exec. b. Chicago, Ill., Dec. 4, 1926. e. Notre Dame, B.S. U.S.N.R., 1943–47, Exec. assignments with CBS-TV, in Chicago and New York City 1950–58; VP, gen. mgr. WCAU-TV, Philadelphia 1958–64; WCBS-TV, New York City 1964–65; pres. CBS-TV Network 1965–66; pres. CBS/Broadcast Group 1966–69, 1971–77; exec. VP CBS Inc. 1969–71, TV and MP consultant 1977–79; consultant WCI, 1979; pres., CEO Warner Amex Satellite Entertainment Corp., 1980.

SCHNEIDER, ROMY: Actress. b. Vienna, Austria, Sept. 23, 1938. Parents Magda Schneider and Wolf Albach-Retty, of the stage. Debut on screen when 15. Appeared in 10 films produced on the Continent in four years. Introduced in U.S., 1958, as star of The Story of Vickie.
PICTURES INCLUDE: Forever, My Love; Boccaccio '70;

Good Neighbor Sam, Triple Cross, Otley, My Lover, My Son, The Hero, Ludwig, The Infernal Trio.

SCHNEIER, FREDERICK: Executive. b. New York, N.Y., May 31, 1927; e. N.Y. Univ., 1951, bus. admin., N.Y.U. Grad. Sch., MBA, 1953. Dir. Sls. planning, Mutual Broadcasting System, 1947–53; media research dir., RKO Teleradio, 1953–55; RKO Teleradio Advisory Comm., 1955–56; exec. staff RKO Teleradio & dir., marketing services, 1956–58; exec. vice-pres., Showcorporation, 1958–71; v.p. TV programming, RKO General, 1972–1973; v.p.; Hemdale Leisure Corporation, 1973–79. Joined Viacom Enterprises as v.p., feature films, 1979. Appt. sr. v.p., program acquisitions & motion pictures, 1980.

SCHNUR, JEROME: Producer-director. b. N.Y.C., July 30, 1923; e. Carnegie Tech. Film prod. & dir. many indep. cos., 1939–43; prod., dir., training films, U.S. Air Force 1943–46; indep. film prod., Hollywood, 1946–50: on bd. of dir., Alson Prod., Inc. & Burwood Pictures Corp.; prod., dir., CBS-TV, N.Y., 1950–51; prod., dir., Goodson-Todson Prod., 1951–56; pres., Holiday Prod., indep. TV prod., 1956; Metropole Prod., indep. film prod., 1956; exec. prod. chg. creative prog. Frank Cooper Assoc., 1958; pres., Jerome Schnur Prods., Inc. Packager and Producer TV and Film.
TV: It's News to Me, Two for the Money, The Name's the Same, What's My Line, Beat the Clock, Robert Q. Lewis Show, Judge for Yourself, Holiday film series, Fred Allen Show, Dotto, Make the Connection, Scene of the Crime, Who Pays, Shari Lewis Show, Bell Telephone Hour, U.S. Steel Spec., Private Eye—Private Eye, exec. prod., United Fund Simulcast This Is My Town; writer, dir., Mark of Cain, CBS-TV, Chronicle, Science Special, Tomorrow Was Yesterday; dir., L'Enfance du Christ, CBS-TV; exec. prod., Supermarket Sweep, ABC-TV; dir., Michelangelo's Pauline Chapel. CBS News spec.; dir., Jeptha's Daughter. St. Joan. TV ballet specials. Exec. Prod. Everybody's Talking; dir. Missions of San Antonio; Light in the Wilderness, and David Wept (all CBS). Exec. Prod. Politithon 1970—PBS. Exec. Prod. & Dir. "Threatened Paradise" (PBS) "A Time To Live" (PBS) 1972; Director "Questions of Abraham" Special Contata (CBS) "American Ballet Theatre Special" (PBS) "Luther" (CBS) 1973. Exec. prod., Musical Chairs, Strategy, others, 1974; Director, Joffrey ballet, PBS special; dir. Jerusalem Symphony, CBS spec.; 1977; dir. Song of Songs, CBS spec., 1978, Director, All Star-Jazz Show, CBS Special 1976. Recipient 1970–71 Peabody Award, 1970–71 Saturday Review Award, 1972 Emmy Citation; 1975 Ohio State Award.

SCHOENFELD, JOE: Executive. b. June 2, 1907. New York City. e. New York City Schools. Reporter, Hearst newspapers, 1924–32; reporter & editor, Variety, 1932–43; William Morris Agency, 1944–50; editor, Daily Variety, 1950–59; M.P. agency exec., William Morris, 1959–1974; film prod. present.

SCHOENFELD, LESTER: Executive. b. Brooklyn, N.Y., Dec. 6, 1916; e. C.C.N.Y., 1934–38, Asst. mgr., Randforce Amusement, 1936–38; mgr., Rugoff & Becker circuit, 1938–47; mgr., Golden & Ambassador Theatres, 1948; print & sales dept., Film Classics, 1948–50; chg. of Theatrical, non-theatrical & TV dist., Brit. Info. Serv.; est. Lester A. Schoenfeld Films, 1958.

SCHONFELD, NORMAN J.: Theater Executive. b. Newark, N.J., June 25, 1934, e. University of PA, BA 1955, Navigator, U.S.A.F., 1957, sls. rep. Bache & Co. 1963, v.p. Tiger Films, Inc., 1966 founder and president, Wood Theater Group.

SCHORR, JOSE: Advertising and Publicity Specialist; e. Cornell Univ. Contributor to McCall's, The New Yorker, Redbook, Fortune, This Week, Saturday Evening Post. Joined Columbia as adv. and pub. writer. Ed., Columbia Mirror. National mag. and syndicate pub. contact. Co-author Sensible Dieting (Knopf). Army, 1942–45; Sec'y. Soc. of Mag. Writers; adv. writer, 20th Century-Fox, Donahue & Coe. Universal, Solters & Sabinson.

SCHRADER, PAUL: Writer. b. Grand Rapids, Mich., 1946. e. Columbia Univ., U.C.L.A. (Master's in Cinema). Served as film critic for L.A. Free Press and Cinema 1970, 1971, 1972. First screenplay was The Pipeliner (unproduced).
PICTURES INCLUDE: The Yakuza, Taxi Driver, Close Encounters of the Third Kind, Rolling Thunder, Blue Collar (co-s.p., dir.), Hardcore (s.p., dir.), Old Boyfriends (co-s.p.), American Gigolo (s.p., dir.), Raging Bull (co-s.p.).

SCHREIBER, EDWARD: Producer. b. Jersey City, N.J., Mar. 30, 1913. e. John Marshall Coll., Jersey City. Joined Warner Bros., 1936, press contact, then pub. dir., WB Vitaphone Studio, pub. and adv. dir., War Activities Comm., 1942. Joined Century Theatres, dir. adv., pub., 1946. Left ind., 1949 became builder 10 yrs. Ret., m.p. industry as independent prod., screenplay writer, Mad Dog Coll. Kathie's Lot (19 min.); Useless Mouths (20 min.); Cassals Conducts (28 min.); Acad. Award winner. Prod. off B'way: Unfair to Goliath.

SCHULBERG, BUDD WILSON: Writer. b. New York City, Mar. 27, 1914; son of B. P. Schulberg, prod.; e. Dartmouth Coll. Publicist, Paramount Pictures, 1931; writer for screen from 1932; addit. dial., A Star Is Born; collab. s.p., Little Orphan Annie; orig. & collab. s.p., Winter Carnival. Weekend for Three; collab. orig., City Without Men; adap. Government Girl. Armed services World War II. Author, 3 best-selling novels including The Disenchanted. Harder They Fall; story, s.p., On the Waterfront (Acad. Award & Writers Guild Award, 1954), Face in a Crowd, Wind Across the Everglades. Recent books: Everything That Moves (novel), Motion Pictures: Memories of a Hollywood Prince.

SCHULMAN, WILLIAM B.: Advertising executive. b. Dayton, O., July 2, 1916; e. Ohio State U., B.A., 1940; Columbia U. Lieut. Comm. U.S. Navy. WWII. In 1945 with Universal home office exploitation dept.; New England pub. and exploitation mgr., Universal. 1946. Became dir. adv. publ. & exploit., member bd. dir. Realart Pictures; gen. mgr. Screen Ad Adv. Agency, Inc.; adv. mgr. Sharmark Ent. Inc.

SCHUMAN, EDWARD L.: Executive vice president & partner, Quartet Films. b. Lisbon, Conn., Sept. 3, 1916. e. Wayne Univ., 1932–34, Univ. of Michigan, 1934–37. Mathematician, 1937–51, assistant actuary, Detroit City Employees Pension Fund. Pres., Studio Theatre Corp., Detroit, 1951 to 1975; pres. Studio 8 Theatre Corp., Detroit, 1953 to 1975; secy.-treas., Studio New Center Theatre Corp. of Detroit, 1975; v.p. and gen. mgr. Art Theatre Guild, 1954–60; v.p. Rugoff Theatres, N.Y., 1960–1963. V.p. and bd. member, Walter Reade Organization 1975: Associate producer Broadway play, Same Time Next Year, The Comedians, and Anna Christie. Assoc. prod. of First Monday in October.

SCHUSTER, HAROLD: Director. b. Cherokee, Ia., Aug. 1.
PICTURES INCLUDE: Marine Raiders, My Friend Flicka, So Dear to My Heart, Girl Trouble, Wings of the Morning, Zanzibar, The Tender Years, Postman Didn't Ring, A Very Young Lady, Exposed, Bombers Moon, Spring Tonic, Breakfast in Hollywood, Dinner at the Ritz, Strange Cargo, Framed, On the Sunnyside, Small Town Deb, Kid Monk Baroni, Ma He's Making Eyes at Me, Swing That Cheer, Jack Slade, Loophole, Security Risk, Port of Hell, Tarzan's Hidden Jungle, Finger Man, Return of Jack Slade, Black Beauty, Portland Expose, Dragon Wells, Massacre.
TV PLAYS: Playhouse of Stars, Ellery Queen, The Line-Up, Wire Service, Meet McGraw, The Gray Ghost, U.S. Marshall, Death Valley Days, Wichita Town, Man With a Camera, The Californians, The Outlaws, Laramie.
TV: Deacon St., Overland Trail, Death Valley Days, Tombstone Territory, Zane Grey Theatre, Twilight Zone, Surfside Six.

SCHUTE, MARTIN: Producer. Began as asst. dir. to Lewis Milestone; then graduated to prod. supervisor on Gentlemen Marry Brunettes for United Artists in 1955. Spent 3 years with Columbia Pictures in London. Became gen. mgr. of Otto Preminger's production co. during making of Exodus.
PICTURES INCLUDE: The Cardinal (assoc. prod.), Bunny Lake Is Missing (assoc. prod.), Maroc 7 (exec. prod.), The Lion in Winter (prod. exec.), Macho Callahan (co-prod.), Miss Julie (co-prod.), Not Now Darling (co-prod.), The Tempter (co-prod.), Not Now Comrade (prod.), Silver Bears (exec. prod.).

SCHWAB, LAURENCE, JR.: Producer, director, writer. b. Mar. 31, 1922, N.Y.C. Prod., dir., documentary films, TV films & shows.
PICTURES INCLUDE: American Inventory, Soldiers of Fortune, Stakeout.
TV: The Clock, Lights Out, Kate Smith Hour, Amazing Mr. Malone, NBC Matinee Theatre.

SCHWARTZ, ARTHUR: Producer, composer. b. Brooklyn, N.Y. e. New York U., J.D., A.B.; Columbia U., M.A.; Phi Beta Kappa. Member ASCAP, Authors League Amer., Dramatists Guild. Teacher N.Y. public schools; practiced law; then turned to music; composer songs & scores many N.Y. musicals.
MUSICALS INCLUDE: The Band Wagon, Flying Colors, Revenge With Music, Between the Devil, Stars in Your Eyes, Inside U.S.A., A Tree Grows in Brooklyn, By the Beautiful Sea.
PICTURES INCLUDE: Composing for screen includes scores for Girl From Paris, Under Your Spell, Navy Blues. score, collab. story Thank Your Lucky Stars; prod., Cover Girl; music, The Time, the Place and the Girl, Excuse My Dust, Dangerous When Wet, The Bandwagon, You're Never Too Young.

SCHWARTZ, ARTHUR H.: Lawyer. b. New York, N.Y., Nov. 18, 1903; e. Columbia Coll. & Law Sch. Asst. U.S. atty. for so. dist. of N.Y.; 1926–33; chief, Prohibition Div., 1931–33; assoc. with Nathan Burkan, 1933; member Schwartz & Frohlich since 1936 (became Schwartz, Burns, Lesser & Jacoby, 1970); now Special Counsel, Burns, Jackson, Miller, Summit & Jacoby; trial counsel in litigation affecting m.p.

ind. including copyright problems, contract, labor, work; counsel to N.Y. State Jt. Legislative Com. on Legislative Practices, Procedures & Expenditures, 1943–46; N.Y. State Republican campaign mgr., 1944; counsel to N.Y. State Temporary Comm. on Need for State U.; N.Y. State Comm. on Co-Ord., of State Affairs, 1947–60; counsel N.Y.S. Republican Com.; member of N.Y.S. Law Revision Comm. 1960–1974 of N.Y.S. Comm. on Judicial & Legislation Salaries 1972-to-date Justice of N.Y. State Supreme Court 1952, former pres. N.Y. County Lawyers Assn. Chairman. NY 5 Board of Electors, 1974–75; Board of Editors, N.Y. Law Journal 1976–

SCHWARTZ, BERMUDA: Publicist. b. Deal, N.J., July 30, e. Seton Hall University; grad. Transylvania University, Newspaper editor, radio personality, Ice Capades; Mutual Radio Network; Broadway publicity; head, Schwartz, O'Heney, Thompson Inc., N.Y. pub./rel. firm. Motion picture publicity, Studio City, North Miami, Fla., Ivan Tors, Miami, Fla.

SCHWARTZ, BERNARD: Producer. Brought to Hollywood by the late Howard Hughes to watch his film interests; Schwartz teamed with atty. Greg Bautzer to package movie deals for clients. Re-cut number of Buster Keaton's silent movies into documentary anthologies (The Golden Age of Comedy, When Comedy Was King, etc.). Subsequently made TV series, One Step Beyond, followed by The Wackiest Ship in the Army, Miss Teen International specials, etc. Named pres., Joseph M. Schenck Enterprises, for which made Journey to the Center of the Earth, Eye of the Cat, A Cold Wind in August, I Passed for White, The Shattered Room, Trackdown. Presently partnered with Alan Silverman of Essaness Theatres. 1979, produced Coal Miner's Daughter.

SCHWARTZ, LESLIE R.: Exhibitor. b. New York City, June 7, 1915; e. Lehigh U., 1937. Entered m.p. ind. with Century Theatres Construction Co., 1937–39; film buyer, Century Theatres, 1940–42; personnel exec. 1942–43; U.S. Army service, 1943–45; with Andrews, Inc., Century Theat. concessions, 1945–48; apptd. gen. theatre mgr. 1948; pres., 1955. Member: Pi Lambda Phi; North Shore Country Club; pres., Metropolitan Motion Picture Assn., 1960–62; pres., 1955–present.

SCHWARTZ, SOL A.: Executive. b. New York City; e. New York University; m. Marion Phillips; s. Leonard. Started career with RKO circuit as assistant manager Alhambra Theatre, New York, 1922; mgr. Cameo, Momart, Orpheum & Prospect, Fordham, Albee theatre; western zone mgr. 1942; gen. mgr. RKO out-of-town theatres, 1944, then v.p. RKO theatres; pres., gen. mgr., RKO Theatres, Inc., Jan. 1, 1951; v.p. Columbia Pictures Corp., Mar. 3, 1961; v.p., theatres, 20th-Fox, 1968.

SCOFIELD, PAUL: Actor. b. Hurstpierpoint, England, Jan. 21, 1922. Gained greatest fame on London stage during much Shakespeare and modern plays, including Staircase and Desire Under the Elms.
PICTURES INCLUDE: That Lady, Carve Her Name with Pride, The Train, A Man for All Seasons (Oscar, 1966), King Lear, Scorpio, A Delicate Balance.

SCOGNAMILLO, GABRIEL A.: Art director. b. New York, N.Y., Oct. 27, 1906; e. Royal Acad. of Fine Arts, Italy, 1922–25; N.Y. Sch. of Fine & Applied Arts, France, 1925. Architectural designer; stage scenery; Paramount, Long Island, 1928; Braunberger-Richebe Studios, Paris, 1930–33; MGM, 1934; in armed forces, 1942–46; returned to MGM, 1946.
PICTURES INCLUDE: Man Proof, Babes on Broadway, Thousands Cheer, Great Caruso, Lovely to Look At, Story of Three Loves, Latin Lovers, Strange Lady in Town, World of Tomorrow (Disneyland).
TV: Ozzie & Harriet, Westinghouse Playhouse, MGM-TV.

SCORSESE, MARTIN: Writer-Director-Editor. Began career while film arts student at N.Y. Univ., doing short, It's Not Just You, Murray.
PICTURES INCLUDE: Editor: Woodstock, Medicine Ball Caravan, Elvis. Director: Who's That Knocking at My Door? Boxcar Bertha, Mean Streets (also co-s.p.), Alice Doesn't Live Here Anymore, Taxi Driver, New York, New York, The Last Waltz (also actor), Raging Bull.

SCOTT, ADRIAN: Producer. b. Arlington, N.J., Feb. 6, 1912; e. Amherst Coll. Assoc. ed. stage mag. before entering m.p. prod. In 1940 collab. s.p. Keeping Company; later Parson of Panamint, We Go Fast, Mr. Lucky. In 1943 joined RKO-Radio as prod. (Farewell, My Lovely). In 1944 prod. My Pal, Wolf.
PICTURES INCLUDE: (collab. adapt.) Miss Susie Slagle's (prod.) Cornered, So Well Remembered, Crossfire.

SCOTT, ALLAN: Writer. In 1933 wrote play, Goodbye Again, Warner. In 1934: collaborated on screen play of Let's Try Again, By Your Leave, RKO-Radio.
PICTURES INCLUDE: s.p. So Proudly We Hail; orig. s.p. I Love a Soldier; collab. orig. s.p. Here Come the Waves;

s.p. Let's Dance; collab. adapt., s.p. Wait Till the Sun Shines Nellie; assoc. prod., s.p. Four Poster; collab. s.p., 5000 Fingers of Dr. T.

SCOTT, BARBARA: Sr. Vice President & General Attorney, MPAA. e. Wellesley College, Yale U. School of Law. Began career as law clerk to Judge Charles Wyzanski of U.S. District Ct. in Mass. 1949, joined law firm of Poletti, Diamond, Roosevelt, Freiden, Mackay; 1950, associated w. Dwight, Royall, Harris, Koegel, Caskey. In 1959 joined staff Motion Picture Assoc. of America as Associate counsel specializing in censorship matters. Member bd. of dir. Wiltwyck, Federation of Protestant Welfare Agencies, New York Philharmonic. Member N.Y.C. Board of Ethics, N.Y. Convention Center Corp., N.Y. Community Trust, N.Y.C. Bar Assoc., Citizens Comm. for Children and American Civil Liberties Union. Successor Trustee Yale Corporation.

SCOTT, GEORGE C.: Actor, Director. b. Wise, Va., Oct. 18, 1927. Served 4 years Marine Corps. e. University of Missouri, appeared in varsity productions, summer stock, Shakespeare.
THEATRE: Off-Broadway in Richard III, As You Like It, Children of Darkness, Merchant of Venice, Desire Under the Elms, Antony and Cleopatra; Broadway in Comes a Day, The Andersonville Trial, The Wall, The Little Foxes, Plaza Suite, Uncle Vanya, director All God's Chillun Got Wings, director-actor Death of a Salesman, Sly Fox.
PICTURES INCLUDE: Film debut in Hanging Tree, 1959. Anatomy of a Murder, The Hustler, List of Adrian Messenger, Dr. Strangelove, The Bible, Film-Flam Man, Patton, They Might Be Giants, The Last Run, Hospital, The New Centurions, Oklahoma Crude, The Day of the Dolphin, The Hindenburg, Islands in the Stream, Crossed Swords, Movie Movie, Hardcore, The Changeling, The Formula, Taps.
Director-Actor, Rage; Director-Producer-AQCTOR, The Savage is Loose.
TV: Major TV playhouses including Dupont Show of the Month, Playhouse 90, Hallmark Hall of Fame, Kraft Theatre, Omnibus, Armstrong Theatre, Play of the Week, NBC Sunday Showcase, Dow Hour of Great Mysteries, Esso Theatre; East Side, West Side series; The Crucible, Jane Eyre, The Price, Fear on Trial, Beauty and the Beast; directed The Andersonville Trial.

SCOTT, GORDON: Actor. r.n. Gordon M. Werschkul. b. Portland, Ore., Aug. 3, 1927. e. Oregon U. U.S. Army, 1944–47; then worked as fireman, cowboy, life guard; signed by Sol Lesser Prod. for role of Tarzan; debut in Tarzan's Hidden Jungle; since in: Tarzan and the Lost Safari, Tarzan's Greatest Adventure, The Tramplers.

SCOTT, GORDON L. T.: Producer. b. Edinburgh, Scotland, January 3, 1920. e. George Watson's Boys College. Served H.M. Forces 1939–46. Ent. m.p. ind. 1946 as 3rd asst. dir. with Ealing Studios. 1948: 1st asst. dir. on Passport to Pimlico, Train of Events; joined Associated British 1949 and worked on The Dancing Years, The Franchise Affair, Laughter in Paradise, Angels One Five, Isn't Life Wonderful, Will Any Gentleman, Rob Roy; 1953 prod. man. The Weak and the Wicked, It's Great to be Young, The Dam Busters; 1956 appt. production exec. asst.; prod. Look Back in Anger, Sands of the Desert, Petticoat Pirates, The Pot Carriers, The Punch & Judy Man, Crooks in Cloisters, Forbush and the Penguins, Voices, The Maids, Snow Children, Out of Season, Hedda, The Abbess. Left Associated British 1969. Currently freelance. Recent Prods: Spectre Hanover Street.
TV: (Prod): International Detective Series, The Avengers, Pathfinders, The Maids, Snow Children, A Man Called Intrepid.

SCOTT, IAN: Mng. dir. Thames TV, Ltd. Early career as chartered accountant. Ent. m.p. ind. 1958.

SCOTT, JANETTE: Actress. b. Morecambe (Lancs), Eng., Dec. 14, 1938; e. Lycee Francaise De Londres. Stage debut in Third Person 1951; since in Peter Pan; screen debut in Went the Day Well at age of 2½.
PICTURES INCLUDE: No Place for Jennifer, The Galloping Major, No Highway, Background, Helen of Troy, As Long As They're Happy, Now and Forever, Good Companions, Happy Is the Bride, Lady Is a Square, Devil's Disciple, School for Scoundrels, His and Hers, Double Bunk, The Old Dark House, Paraoniac, The Beauty Jungle, Crack in the World, The White Savage.
TV: Many appearances including Dashing White Sergeant, A Man's Woman, Cinderella, Six Wonderful Girls, Amos Burke.

SCOTT, LIZABETH: Actress. b. Scranton, Pa. e. Marywood College, Pennsylvania, and Alviene Sch. of Drama, New York. Toured with Hellzapoppin show; fashion model, understudied Tallulah Bankhead in N.Y. prod., Skin of Our Teeth. Screen debut in You Came Along, 1946.
PICTURES INCLUDE: Strange Love of Martha Ivers, Dead Reckoning, Desert Fury, I Walk Alone, Pitfall, Company

She Keeps, Red Mountain, Two of a Kind, Racket, Stolen Face, Scared Stiff, Bad for Each Other, Silver Lode, The Weapon, Loving You, Pulp.

Many TV shows.

SCOTT, MARGARETTA: Actress. b. London, England, Feb. 13, 1912; e. Conv. of Holy Child, London; Royal Acad. Dram. Art. In provincial rep. prior to London debut 1929 in, Her Shop; thereafter in numerous London productions. Screen debut 1934.

TV & PICTURES INCLUDE: Fanny by Gaslight, Man from Morocco, The First Gentleman, Mrs. Fitzherbert, Calling Paul Temple, Case of Shirley Yorke, Where's Charley, Landfall, Last Man to Hang, Town on Trial, Devil's General, Mayerling Story, You Never Can Tell, Long Sunset, The Heiress, Henry IV of Pimandello, Adventure Story, Second Mrs. Tanquery, Queen in Hamlet, Maigret, The Weather in the Streets, Member of the Family, Nicked at the Bottle, End of Term, File on Harry Jordan, The Importance of Being Earnest, Mr. Aitch, Upstairs and Downstairs, Elizabeth R., The Poisoning of Charles Bravo, The Duchess of Duke Street, What Every Woman Knows, All Creatures Great and Small, Tales of the Unexpected, Murder Trap, Racing Game, Together.

SCOTT, MARTHA: Actress. b. Jamesport, September 22, 1916; e. U. Michigan. In little theatres over U.S.; summer stock N.Y.; on radio with Orson Welles; film debut in "Our Town" 1940.

PICTURES INCLUDE: Cheers for Miss Bishop, They Dare Not Love, One Foot in Heaven, In Old Oklahoma; Hi Diddle Diddle; So Well Remembered, When I Grow Up, Desperate Hours, Ten Commandments, Airport 1975, Turning Point.

PLAYS INCLUDE: Soldier's Wife, Voice of the Turtle, The Number, Male Animal, Remarkable Mr. Pennypacker.

SCOTT, MORTON W.: Executive. b. San Francisco, Calif., Jan. 17; e. Stanford U. Pres., Studio City Television Productions, Inc.

SCOTT, RANDOLPH: Actor. b. Orange Co., Va., Jan. 23, 1903; e. U. of No. Car. On stage west coast; m.p. debut in Sky Bridge, 1931.

PICTURES INCLUDE: Roberto, Follow the Fleet, My Favorite Wife, Trail Street, The Gunfighters, Christmas Eve, Albuquerque, Return of the Bad Men, Coroner Creek, Canadian Pacific, Fighting Man of the Plains, Doolins of Oklahoma, Walking Hills, Cariboo Trail, The Nevadan, Colt .45, Sugarfoot, Sante Fe, Fort Worth, Man in the Saddle, Starlift, Carson City, Man Behind the Gun, Hangman's Knot, Thunder Over the Plains, Stranger Wore a Gun, Riding Shotgun, Bounty Hunter, Ten Wanted Men, Rage at Dawn, Tall Man Riding; act., assoc. prod., Lawless Street, Westbound, The Name's Buchanan. Ride Lonesome, Comanche Station, Ride the High Country.

One of Top Ten Money-Making Stars, M.P. Herald-Fame Poll, 1950-53. Retired.

SCOTT, WALTER M.: Set decorator. b. Cleveland, Ohio, Nov. 7. 1906. e. U.S.C., 1929; Chouinard School of Art. Interior decorator, Fred B. Martin Co., 1929-30, asst. mgr., United Studios, 1930-31; joined Fox Film Corp., 1931; asst. set decorator, 1932; set decorator, 1933; set decorator, 20th Century-Fox, 1935; supervising set decorator, 1952-72. Now consultant decorator for Fox.

PICTURES INCLUDE: Twenty-one Academy Nominations—6 oscars for Robe, King and I, Diary of Ann Frank, Cleopatra, Fantastic Voyage, Hello, Dolly, On Board of Governors of the Academy of Motion Picture Arts and Sciences 1968-76, 1980-81.

SCULLY, JOE: Talent Executive-Casting Director-Producer. b. Kearney, N.J., March 1, 1926. e. Goodman Memorial Theatre of the Art Institute of Chicago, 1946. m. Penelope Gillette. Acted until 1951. CBS-TV, N.Y. Casting Dir., Danger You Are There, Omnibus, The Web, 1951-56. 1956-60, CBS-TV, Associate Prod., Studio One, Dupont Show of the Month, Playhouse 90. 1962-64, CBS Stations Div. KNXT, Producer, Repertoire Workshop. 1965-70 Casting Dir. 20th Century-Fox Films. 1970-74 Independent Casting Director. 1974-75 Universal TV, Casting Dir. 1975, NBC-TV, Manager, Casting & Talent. 1978, Re-established Joe Scully-Casting independent Service to the industry.

PICTURES INCLUDE: Hello Dolly, In Like Flint, Valley of the Dolls, Planet of the Apes, The Flim-Flam Man, Sounder, Lady Sings the Blues, Play It As It Lays, The Stone Killer, Parallax View, Lifeguard, Man in the Glass Booth, Middle Age Crazy, Death Wish II.

TV: Peyton Place, Room 222; Pilots: Julia, The Ghost & Mrs. Muir. 1970, Joe Scully Casting, Indep., The Bill Cosby Show. 1971: TV Feature, Thief, Missiles of October, Earth II; Series: Search, Bonanza, Nichols, Snoop Sisters, Columbo, Switch, McMillan & Wife, Tales of the Unexpected.

SCULLY, PETER R.: Producer. b. Arlington, Mass., June 14, 1920; e. Mass. Inst. of Tech., 1939. With Ross Federal Research Corp. N.Y. (consumer studies) 1939-40; studied, Feagin School Dramatic Art. N.Y., to Universal as con-

tract actor, then film ed., 1940-41; U.S. Marine Corps until 1945; film ed. Univ-Internat'l 1945-48; became m.p. prod. indep. cos., releasing through Monogram Prod., Inc. (Mayfair Pictures, Inc. & Motion Pictures, Inc.)

PICTURES INCLUDE: Father's Wild Game, Father Takes The Air, Son of Belle Star.

SCUSE, DENNIS GEORGE (M.B.E.): Executive. b. Ilford, England, May 19, 1921. e. Park School; Mercers' School, London. British Army, Royal Artillery, 1939; command entertainment officer, Ceylon Army, 1941-42; joined British Army Broadcasting Service, Italy, 1944-46; overseas div., BBC, 1947; loaned to Forces Broadcasting Service, Middle East, 1948-50; dir., British Forces network, Germany, 1950-57; ret., BBC-TV, senior planning asst., Jan. 1958; chief asst., light entertainment dept., BBC-TV,1960; apptd., chief asst. (TV) BBC N.Y. office, Sept. 1960; apptd., BBC rep. in U.S., July, 1962; gen. mgr., Television Enterprises, 1963; gen. mgr., Radio Enterprises 1968.

SEARS, HEATHER: Actress. b. London, 1935. Early career in repertory; m.p. debut, 1956.

PICTURES INCLUDE: Dry Rot, Story of Esther Costello (Golden Virgin), Room at the Top, The Siege of Pinchgut, Sons and Lovers, The Phantom of the Opera, Saturday Night Out, The Black Torment, Great Expectations.

TV: Death of the Heart, Our Town, Ring Around the Moon, The Paraguana Harp, Cymbals at Your Door, An Inspector Calls, A Reason for Staying, Trial Run, Giaconda Smile, First Love, The Informer, Footprints in the Jungle, Somerset Maugham series.

STAGE: Look Back in Anger, The Apollo de Bellac, The Seashell, South, The Door, The Caucasian Chalk Circle, Chichester Festival Theatre, How the Other Half Lives, Cause Celebre, Blithe Spirit, Antigone, War and Peace, Macbeth, etc.

SECOMBE, HARRY: Singer, comedian, actor. b. Swansea, Wales, Sept. 8, 1921; e. m.p. debut, Penny Points to Paradise, 1951; awarded, C.B.E., 1963. 1963-64: London stage starring in Pickwick. 1965: same role New York stage. 1967-68 The Four Musketeers, 1975 The Plumber's Progress.

PICTURES INCLUDE: Forces Sweetheart, Down Among the Z Men, Trilby, Davy, Jet Storm, Oliver, The Bed Sitting Room, Song of Norway, Rhubarb, Doctor in Trouble, The Magnificent Seven Deadly Sins, Sunstruck.

TV: Numerous appearances, incl. own series: Secombe and Friends, The Harry Secombe Show, etc. Also special version, Pickwick. Author of Twice Brightly, Goon for Lunch.

SEGAL, GEORGE: Actor. b. N.Y., N.Y., Feb. 13, 1934. m. Marion Sobol. e. Columbia U. 1955. B.A. Worked as janitor, ticket-taker, soft-drink salesman, usher and under-study at N.Y.'s Circle in the Square theatre. Acting debut: Downtown Theatre's revival of Don Juan.

THEATRICAL CREDITS INCLUDE: 1956 revival: The Iceman Cometh, N.Y. Shakespeare Festival's Antony and Cleopatra, Leave It To Jane, The Premise (satiric improvisational revue), Rattle of a Simple Man, The Knack.

Formed a nightclub singing act with Patricia Scott. Record album of ragtime songs and banjo music: The Yama, Yama Man. Dir. debut: Bucks County Playhouse prod. Scuba Duba.

TV: Death of A Salesman, Of Mice and Men, The Desperate Hours.

PICTURES INCLUDE: The Young Doctors (1961), The Longest Day, Act One, The New Interns, Invitation to A Gunfighter, Ship of Fools, King Rat, The Lost Command, Who's Afraid of Virginia Woolf? (Acad. Award nom.), The Quiller Memorandum, The St. Valentine's Day Massacre, Bye Bye Braverman, No Way to Treat a Lady, The Southern Star, The Bridge at Remagen, The Girl Who Couldn't Say No, Loving, The Owl and the Pussycat, Where's Poppa?, Born to Win, Hot Rock, A Touch of Class, Blume in Love, The Terminal Man, California Split, The Black Bird, Russian Roulette, The Duchess and the Dirtwater Fox, Fun with Dick and Jane, Rollercoaster, Who Is Killing The Great Chefs of Europe?, Lost and Found, The Last Married Couple in America, Carbon Copy.

SEGAL, MAURICE: Publicist. b. New York, N.Y., July 22, 1921; e. C.C.N.Y., 1937-41. Entered m.p. ind., adv. dept., 20th Fox, 1941-42; U.S. Army 1942-46; feature writer, pub. dept., 20th Fox, April, 1946; asst. to dir., adv., pub., Century Circuit, 1947; press book dept., Paramount, 1949; trade press rep. 1950; trade press rep. RKO Radio, Nov. 1952; res. to join Richard Condon-Kay Norton, publicists, May, 1953; adv., pub. dept., U-I. Sept. 1954; asst. pub. mgr., United Artists Apr. 1957. Hollywood pub.-exploit., coordinator, 1958; exec. in chg. of M.P. press dept., Universal City Studios, 1966; West Coast adv.-pub. dir., National Gen. Pictures, 1971; Pres., Maurice E. Segal Co., 1974; div., West Coast operations, Charles Schlaifer & Co., 1976; v.p., Max Youngstein Enterprises, 1979; exec. v.p., Taft Intl. Pictures, 1980.

SEIDMAN, LLOYD: Adv. exec. b. Brooklyn, N.Y., 1913. e. Columbia U., B.A., 1932; NYU School Business Administration. adv. dept., Montgomery Ward; M.P. dept., Lord & Thomas Adv. Agency, 1935; Donohue & Coe, 1936; v.p., 1942–61; pres., Educ. Science Div., U.S. Industries Inc., 1961; v.p., West, Weir & Bartel, 1963–65; exec. staff, v.p., Charles Schlaifer & Co., 1965; acct. superv. adv., Loew's Theatres; Jack Tinker & Partners, 1968; acct. superv. CBS Films (Cinema Center Films); vice-president, 1969, Blaine-Thompson Company.

SEIGENFELD, EDWARD P.: Executive. b. New York City, January 2, 1937. e. Fieldston School, Johns Hopkins, NYU School of Law. At National Broadcasting Company was asst. adv. mgr., 1961; mgr., W. Coast adv., 1962–65; national adv. mgr., 1965–67; adv. mgr., Paramount Pictures Corp., 1967–68; account supervisor, Charles Schlaifer & Co., 1968–71; At Allied Artists Pictures Corp.: dir. of adv. & pub., 1971; vice president, adv. & pub., 1971 to 1978 when joined United Artists as v.p. of adv./pub.

SELBY, DAVID: Actor. b. Morganstown, W. Va. e. W. Va. Univ. Acted in outdoor dramas in home state and did regional theatre elsewhere. Was ass't. instructor in lit. at So. Ill. Univ.
PICTURES INCLUDE: Up the Sandbox, Super Cops, Lady in Blue, Night of Dark Shadows, Rich Kids, Rich and Famous.
TV: Dark Shadows (series), Washington: Behind Closed Doors, Telethon, Family, etc.

SELF, WILLIAM: Producer. b. Dayton, Ohio, June 21, 1921. e. Univ. of Chicago, 1943; prod.-dir., Schlitz Playhouse of Stars, 1952–56; prod., The Frank Sinatra Show, 1957; exec. prod., CBS-TV, The Twilight Zone, Hotel De Paree. 1960–61 exec. prod., 20th Century-Fox TV. Hong Kong, Adventures in Paradise, Bus Stop, Follow The Sun, Margie; v.p. in chg. of prod., 20th Century-Fox TV, 1962; exec. v.p., 1964. Pres., FOX TV 1969; v.p. 20th Century Fox Film Corp., 1969; pres. of William Self Productions, Inc., partner, Frankovich/Self Productions; 1975; vice-pres., programs, Hollywood CBS Television Network, 1976; 1977, v.p. motion pictures for television and miniseries, CBS Television Network.

SELIG, ROBERT WILLIAM: Exhibitor. b. Cripple Creek, Colo., e. U. of Denver, 1932, B.A.; Doctorate, 1959. Vice pres., Pacific Theatres. Lifetime Trustee, U. of Denver. Member Kappa Sigma, Omicron Delta Kappa, Beta Gamma Sigma; Nat'l Methodist Church Foundation; Chairman, Theatre Association of California; board of directors and, Advisory Committee, Los Angeles Chamber of Commerce.

SELLARS, ELIZABETH: Actress. b. Glasgow, Scotland, May 6, 1923; e. Queenswood, Hatfield. Memb. Lincolns Inn. Stage debut with Wilson Barrett Co. in Laburnum Grove, Glasgow.
PLAYS INCLUDE: Remarkable Mr. Pennypacker, South Sea Bubble, Tea & Sympathy, The Sound of Murder; 1960–61: Stratford upon Avon.
PICTURES INCLUDE: m.p. debut in Floodtide. Also: Madeleine, Prime of Miss Jean Brodie, Guilt Is My Shadow, Cloudburst, Hunted (Stranger in Between), Night Was Our Friend, Gentle Gunman, Long Memory, Barefoot Contessa, Desiree, Prince of Players, Three Cases of Murder, Last Man to Hang, Man in the Sky, The Shiralee, Jetstorm, The Day They Robbed the Bank of England, The Moment of Truth, Middle of Nowhere, 55 Days at Peking, The Chalk Garden, The Hireling.
TV: Many appearances include: Still Life, Too Late for the Mashed Potato, Harbour Island, The Happy Ones, The Sound of Murder, R 3 (series), Family Christmas, Person to Person, Person Unknown, Shades of Greene, Beasts.

SELLER,, THOMAS: Writer. b. San Francisco, Calif. e. Stanford U., Yale Drama School. Armed Forces, World War II; contract writer. MGM, 8 years.
PICTURES INCLUDE: Andy Hardy Meets Debutante, Tish, The Man From Down Under, The Black Arrow.
TV WRITER FOR: Rawhide, Laramie, Combat, Private Secretary, The Ann Sothern Show, Playhouse of Stars, Riverboat, The Tall Man, Death Valley Days, Cimarron City, Cavalcade of America, The Lone Ranger, The Stu Erwin Show, Walt Disney's Wonderful World of Color, The FBI, Bonanza, The Virginian, Kentucky Jones.

SELLERS, ARLENE: Producer. In partnership as attorneys in L.A. for 20 years with Alex Winitsky before they turned to financing and later production of films.
PICTURES INCLUDE: (co-prod. with Winitsky) End of the Game, The Seven-Per-Cent Solution, Cross of Iron, Night Calls, Silver Bears, Cuba.

SELTZER, JULES: Executive. b. New York City, Sept. 4, 1908; e. U. of Penn. Adv. and pub. depart., Fox Theatres Corp., Roxy Theatre, N.Y. District pub. Publix Theatres, Florida. Publ. depart., Warner Brothers Theatres, Philadelphia, for seven years. In 1937; Quigley Silver Showmanship Awards winner. Adv. and pub. dir., Warner Brothers theatres, Philadelphia, for two years, then pub. representative for Hal

Roach. In 1940; joined Western Advertising. Resigned March, 1943, to join U.S. Navy. Returned to Hal Roach Studios dir. pub., 1945: 20th-Fox Studios, 1949. Retired 1973.

SELTZER, WALTER: Executive. b. Philadelphia, Pa., Nov. 7, 1914; e. U. of Penn.; married. Publicity man for Warner Bros. Theatres, Philadelphia; Fox West Coast Theatres; to Hollywood with MGM 1936–39; Columbia, 1940–41. Enlisted U.S. Marine Corps, 1941–44. Pub. dir., Hal Wallis, 1945–54; v.p. in chg. adv & pub., Hecht-Lancaster Orgn., Feb., 1954–55; assoc. prod., The Boss; partner, Glass-Seltzer, pub. rel. firm; v.p. & exec. prod, Pennebaker Production. Vice pres., M.P. & TV Fund.
PICTURES INCLUDE: One-Eyed Jacks, Shake Hands With the Devil, Paris Blues, The Naked Edge, Man in the Middle, Wild Seed, War Lord, Beau Geste, Will Penny, Number One, Darker Than Amber, The Omega Man, Skyjacked, Soylent Green, The Cay, The Last Hard Men.

SEMEL, TERRY: Executive. b. New York City, Feb. 24, 1943. e. C.C.N.Y. (MBA, 1967). Was with C.P.A. accounting firm 1965–66. Entered ind. with Warner Bros. in 1966 as br. mgr., New York, Cleveland, Los Angeles. From 1971 to 1973 was domestic sls. mgr. for CBS—Cinema Center Films. In 1973 joined Buena Vista as v.p., gen. sls. mgr. In 1975 went to Warner Bros. as v.p., gen. sls. mgr. In 1978 named exec. v.p. and chief operating officer.

SEN, BACHOO: Producer/director/distributor. Born 1934, Calcutta, India. Entered industry 1950 in India and 1958 in U.K. Director of English Film Co. Ltd., English Film Co. (Exports) Ltd. and English Film Co. (Productions) Ltd. 1968: Produced: Her Private Hell, Loving Feeling. 1969: Produced: Love Is A Splendid Illusion. 1972: Sex Is Beautiful, Love-Hungry Girls. 1973: Tenderness. 1975: Erotic Inferno, The Intruders. 1970: Formed The English Film Co. 1974: Consultant, Superground, Ltd. and Active Video Ltd.

SENDREY, ALBERT: Music composer, arranger, conductor. b. Chicago, Ill., 1921; e. Trinity Coll. Music, London, U.S.C., Paris & Leipzig Conservatories. Winner, Chi. Symphony Orch. prize for First Symphony, 1941; 1948, Reichhold Award Detroit Symph. Orch. for 2nd Symphony. Ohio Sesquicentenn. Award for Overture, Johnny Appleseed, 1953; One Act Opera: The Telltale Stones, 1964; arr., Mary Martin at Radio City Music Hall, 1965. Compose, arr., orch. for many plays, films and TV.
MEMBER: M.P. Academy, ASCAP, CLGA, ASMA, TV Academy.
BROADWAY: orch., arr.: Peter Pan, Ziegfeld Follies, New Faces, At the Grand, Pink Jungle, The Great Waltz, Turn to the Right.
PICTURES INCLUDE: The Yearling, Three Musketeers, Father's Little Dividend, Duchess of Idaho, Royal Wedding, Easy to Love, Great Caruso, American in Paris, Brigadoon, Athena, Finian's Rainbow, Guys and Dolls, Meet Me in Las Vegas, Opposite Sex, High Society, Raintree County, Let's Be Happy, Ride the High Country, Hallelujah Trail, The Hook, The Comancheros, Nevada Smith, The Oscar, Thoroughly Modern Millie, Hello Down There, Private Navy of Sgt. O'Farrell, Hard Times, Soul of Nigger Charley.
TV: comp. music: Laramie, Wagon Train, Ben Casey, Wolper Documentaries, Americans Abroad, J. F. Kennedy Anthology; Young Man from Boston, collab. with Harry Sukman, High Chaparral, Bonanza (with D. Rose), The Monroes, Ken Murray's Hollywood, SWAT collab. B. de Vorzon, Hard Times, collab.

SERNAS, JACQUES: Actor-Producer. b. Lithuania, July 30, 1925. Became naturalized French citizen, studying medicine in Paris. Was amateur boxer when heard Jean Gabin needed an acting boxer for The Mirror, in which he made professional debut as actor. Has appeared in over 80 films, made in recent years primarily in Italy, now his home.
PICTURES INCLUDE: Lost Youth, The Golden Salamander, Helen of Troy, Jump into Hell, The First Night, La Dolce Vita, 55 Days in Peking, F.B.I.: Operation Baalbeck (also prod.), Operation Gold in the Balearic Islands (also prod.), Super Fly TNT.
TV: The School of the Painters of Paris (prod. only), The 18th Century Seen Through Its Famous Painters (prod. only), The Red Triangle (Ital. series).

SERPE, RALPH B.: Producer. b. Portland, Me., Dec. 23, 1914; e. Columbia U. Ind. thea. agent, 1936. U.S. Army, Spec. Services, 1942. v.p., Scalera Films, 1946; v.p., Italian Films Export, 1948; U.S. rep., assoc. prod., exec. asst., Dino De Laurentiis, 1952.
PICTURES INCLUDE: War and Peace, Ulysses, The Tempest, Under Ten Flags, Yovanka, Barabbas, The Bible, Drum, The Brinks' Job.

SETTON, MAXWELL: Producer. b. Cairo, Egypt, Oct. 24, 1909; e. Clifton Coll., London U., Sorbonne, Paris U. Called to bar, 1931; practiced before H.B.M. Supreme Court & International Mixed Courts of Egypt, 1931–35; to Mayflower Pictures Corp. as legal adviser, 1937; mem. bd. & joint man. dir., 1939. Served with H. M. Forces, 1939–46. With Rank Org., 1949; with Aubrey Baring in Mayflower Pictures; formed Marksman Films Ltd. & prod. Twist of Fate. Man. dir. Bryanston Films Ltd. and Bryanston Seven Arts Ltd., Pax Films until June 1962; exec. in chg. prod., Columbia Pictures, Rome & Paris, 1962; mgr. dir., Columbia (British) Pictures Ltd., 1964; v.p. Columbia Pictures Intern'l., 1965–69; chmn, & man. dir., Paramount British Pictures Ltd. to 1972; now independent.

PICTURES INCLUDE: Prod: Spider and the Fly, Cairo Road, So Little Time, Golden Mask, Appointment in London, They Who Dare; (Marksman Films Ltd.) prod: Twist of Fate; co-prod: Footsteps in the Fog; prod: Wicked As They Come, Town on Trial, I Was Monty's Double, Beyond This Place.

SEVAREID, ERIC: News commentator. b. Velva, N.D., Nov. 26, 1912; e. U. of Minn., Paris. Started career as reporter: Minneapolis Journal, Paris Herald Tribune, United Press; joined CBS radio news staff in Paris at outbreak of World War II; with CBS radio, TV since; nat. corres; retired (1977).
BOOKS: author: Not So Wild a Dream, In One Ear, Small Sounds in the Night, This is Eric Sevareid.

SEWALL, BARBARA JEAN: Publicist. b. Holly, Colo., Jan. 6; e. UCLA; pub. dir. & adv. mgr., Saks Fifth Ave., Beverly Hills; Hollywood Athletic Club; U.S. rep., Chile films, Santiago; RKO, Goldwyn, MGM; Edward Small Prod., Warner Bros., 20th Century-Fox, Cinerama, owner public relations office Hollywood since 1971.

SEYMOUR, DAN: Actor. b. Chicago, Ill., Feb. 22, 1915. Performer burlesque, nightclubs. Stage, screen and TV actor.
PLAYS: Rain, Amphitryon 38, Room Service, and others.
PICTURES INCLUDE: Casablanca, To Have and Have Not, Confidential Agent, Intrigue, Key Largo, Johnny Belinda, Rancho Notorious, Maru Maru, Glory Alley, Face to Face, The System, Second Chance, Big Heat, Human Desire, Moonfleet, Buster Keaton Story, Sad Sack, Watusi, Return of the Fly, Leader of the Pack, The Mummy, The Way Things Were, Soft Touch, Escape from Witch Mountain, Rainbow Island.
TV: Casablanca, Restless Gun, Perry Mason, Untouchables, Holiday Inn, This Gun for Hire, 77 Sunset Strip, Hawaiian Eye, Get Smart, My Mother The Car, Batman, U.N.C.L.E., Beverly Hillbillies, Voyage to the Bottom of the Sea, My Favorite Martian, Don't Eat the Daisies, The Bob Hope Show, Kojak, The Chase, Barbary Coast, Fantasy Island.

SHADOWS, THE. Instrumental vocal group. Ent. films and TV, 1958 as accompanying group to Cliff Richard. Now stars in own right. Voted 3rd Most Popular International Artists in American Billboard 1963–64. Film debut in Serious Charge. Many TV shows in England and Ed Sullivan Show in America. EMI recording stars. Stars, score writers, play: Aladdin. London Palladium Theatre; 1966 Finders Keepers. 1967 Cinderella.
PICTURES INCLUDE: Expresso Bongo, The Young Ones, Summer Holiday, Wonderful Life; 1964, Christopher Miles dir. them as leads in Rhythms and Greens.

SHAFTEL, JOSEF: Producer, director, writer. b. Cleveland, Ohio, 1919. Early career violinist, musician, newspaper correspondent, photographer, screen writer, director. Ent. m.p. ind. 1949.
PICTURES INCLUDE: prod: Man Who Watched the Trains Go By, Naked Dawn, No Place to Hide, Naked Hills, The Biggest Bundle of Them All, The Bliss of Mrs. Blossom, The Last Grenade, Goodbye Gemini, Say Hello to Yesterday, The Statue, The Trojan Women, Soul to Soul, Assassination of Trotsky, Where Does it Hurt?, Redneck, Alice's Adventures in Wonderland.
TV: 1962–63 prod: The Untouchables.

SHAGAN, STEVE: Writer. b. New York City. Apprenticed in night school little theatres, film lab chores, stagehand jobs. Wrote, produced and directed film short, One Every Second; moved to Hollywood in 1959. Was IATSE man, working as grip, stagehand, electrician to support film writing. Was freelance advertising man and publicist; produced "Tarzan" TV show. In 1968 began writing and producing two-hour films for TV.
PICTURES INCLUDE: Save the Tiger (prod., s.p.), Hustler (s.p.), Voyage of the Damned (co.-s.p.), The Formula (s.p., prod.).
TV: Writer-producer: River of Mystery, Spanish Portrait, Sole Survivor, A Step Out of Line, etc.

SHALIT, GENE: b. N.Y.C., 1932. e. Univ. of Illinois. Started as free-lance writer; joined NBC Radio Network, working on Monitor. Has been book and film critic, sports and general columnist. In January, 1973 replaced Joe Garagiola as featured regular on Today Show.

SHAMROY, LEON: Cameraman. b. New York, N.Y., July 16, 1901; e. Cooper Union, N.Y., CCNY, Columbia U. (mech. eng.); m. Mary Anderson, actress. Asst. to Nicholas J. Shamrov, developer Lawrence motor. Turned to cinema-

tography & since cameraman various Hollywood prods. Academy Awards: color cinemaphotography, Black Swan, 1943; Wilson, 1945; Leave Her to Heaven, 1946; Cleopatra, 1964. Look Awards: Wilson, 1945; 10 O'Clock High, 1949. Holds 20th-Fox contract.
PICTURES INCLUDE: Call Me Madam, The Robe, King of the Khyber Rifles, The Egyptian, There's No Business Like Show Business, Daddy Long Legs, Love Is a Many-Splendored Thing, King and I, South Pacific, Porgy and Bess, Cleopatra, The Cardinal, What a Way to Go!, John Goldfarb Please Come Home, The Agony and The Ecstasy, Planet of the Apes, Justine.

SHANE, MAXWELL: Writer, director, producer. b. Paterson, N.J.; e. U.C.L.A., Univ. of South. Calif. Law School. Hollywood film trade journal ed. and in exec. posts publicity & adv. depts., number of film cos. & theat. circuits, Los Angeles, Portland, Ore., N.Y.; later writer, Fanchon & Marco Revues; then pres., Hillman-Shane Adv. Agency Inc., Hollywood. Sole author or collab. orig s.p., dir., many feature films and TV shows.
PICTURES INCLUDE: Tornado, Gambler's Choice, The Navy Way, Minesweeper, Timber Queen, One Body Too Many, Cowboy in Manhattan, Dark Mountain, High Powered, Double Exposure, Scared Stiff, Tokyo Rose, People Are Funny, Seven Were Saved, Fear in the Night, Adventure Island, City Across the River, Wait Till The Sun Shines Nellie, The Glass Wall, Human Desire, Three Hours to Kill, Hell's Island, Naked Street, Nightmare.
TV: M Squad, Checkmate, Thriller, Virginian; wrote numerous other TV dramatic shows.

SHAPIRO, BYRON M.: Executive b. Hill City, Minn., Aug. 15, 1918. e. Univ. of Minn. (graduated 1940). Served in U.S. Army Air Corp., 1941–44. Entered m.p. industry as booker with Columbia in Minneapolis, 1944, later becoming branch mgr. in Des Moines (1951), St. Louis (1957), Minneapolis, (1958). Named western div. mgr. for Columbia in 1966. In 1974 appt. MGM v.p. domestic dist.

SHAPIRO, IRVIN: Executive. Formerly newspaperman; m.p. reviewer; director of national publicity campaigns. Publicity, RKO; active in ind. dist. & in export & import. Now pres., Films Around the World, Inc.; Filmworld Export Corp. which represents leading film producers and distributors throughout the world.

SHAPIRO, JACOB: Executive. b. Harbin, China, Aug. 26, 1928; e. Gakushuin Univ. (Peers' School), Tokyo, Japan, B.A. Pol. Sci. Joined Columbia Pictures Intl., N.Y., 1961; Japan sales manager, 1961–65; Puerto Rico gen. mgr., 1965–68; appointed Japan and South Korea gen. mgr., Columbia, 1968; from 1970 Columbia supv. for Philippines concurrently with Japan & South Korea gen. mgr.

SHAPIRO, KEN: Producer-Director-Writer-Actor. b. New Jersey, 1943. e. Bard College. Was child actor on tv and teacher in Brooklyn before opening "world's first video theatre" in East Village of Manhattan: Channel One, 90 mins. of TV lampoons and original material shown on TV monitors to live audience. Took 16 mm material on college dates with success, culminating in feature film: The Groove Tube (1974).

SHAPIRO, ROBERT K.: Executive. b. New York, N.Y., Feb. 12; e. CCNY, St. John's Coll. Usher, Rialto Theatre, N.Y., 1928; chief of service, 1929; Paramount Theatre, N.Y., 1930; treas. asst. mgr., Rivoli, Criterion, B'klyn Paramount Theatres, 1930–33; treas., Paramount Theatre, 1933; asst. mgr., 1936; house mgr., 1941; mgr., 1945; exec mgr., 1953; managing dir., 1954; coord., TV network progs., Western Div., American Broadcasting, 1964. Member: Variety Club of N.Y.; past pres., Cinema Lodge, B'nai B'rith, Trustee Agva Youth Fund; pres., Metropolitan Motion Picture Theatres Assn., 1962–64, Head of Int. Motion Pic. Div. 1974.

SHAPIRO, ROBERT W.: Executive. b. Brooklyn, N.Y., 1938. Joined William Morris Agency, Inc., 1958. dir. and head of motion picture dept., William Morris Agency (UK) Ltd., 1969; man. dir., 1970. 1974 vice president William Morris, Inc. In March, 1977 joined Warner Bros. as exec. v.p. in chg. of worldwide production. 1981, named WB pres., theatrical production div.

SHARIF, OMAR: Actor. b. Alexandria, Egypt, April 10, 1932. r.n. Michel Shahoub; e. Victoria College, Cairo. pres. of College Dramatic Society; m. Faten Hamama. Starred in 21 Egyptian and two French films prior to Lawrence of Arabia.
PICTURES INCLUDE: The Blazing Sun, 1955 (debut), Goha, 1959, Lawrence of Arabia, Ghengis Khan, The Fall of the Roman Empire, The Yellow Rolls-Royce, Behold a Pale Horse, Doctor Zhivago, Night of the Generals, More Than a Miracle, McKenna's Gold, Che!, Funny Girl, The Appointment, Mayerling, The Horsemen, The Burglars, The Tamarind Seed, The Mysterious Island of Captain Nemo, Juggernaut, Funny Lady, Crime and Passion, The Baltimore Bullet, Green Ice.

SHARP, ALAN: Writer. b. Glasgow, Scotland. Writes western screenplays.
PICTURES INCLUDE: The Hired Hand, Ulzana's Raid, Billy Two Hats, Night Moves.

SHARP, DON: Writer, director. b. Hobart, Tasmania, Australia, 1922. Early career as actor in Australia. Ent. m.p. ind. in England with Group Three as screenwriter, 1951. Began directing 1955 with doc. children's films, 2nd unit work and filmed TV series.
PICTURES INCLUDE: Kiss of the Vampire, It's All Happening, Devil Ship Pirates, Witchcraft, Those Magnificent Men in Their Flying Machines (2nd unit), Curse of the Fly, The Face of Fu Manchu, Rasputin—The Mad Monk, Our Man in Marrakesh, The Brides of Fu Manchu, Rocket to the Moon, Taste of Excitement, The Violent Enemy, Puppet on a Chain, Psychomania, Dark Places, Callan, Hennessy, The Four Feathers, The 39 Steps, Bear Island.

SHARPS, WALLACE S.: (B.Sc.): Executive. b. London, England, 1927. Manager, photographic subsidiary A.E.I. Group, visual aids consultant, exec. prod., T.V. Commercials, Ltd.; head of TV dept., Smee's Advertising Ltd.; founded Sharps Television Services Ltd., 1957. Consultant to TV Audience Measurement Ltd.; Univ. lect. on Int'l. Communications; Author of "Sharp's Colour Chart and Grey Scale," "Advertising and Production Techniques for Commercial Television," Dictionary of Cin. and Sound Recording, Tape Recorder Manual; gen. ed., Fountain Press Movie-books series, Cons. Ed. Broadcasting.
Member: NAEB of USA.

SHAVELSON, MELVILLE: Writer, director. b. B'klyn, N.Y., April 1, 1917; e. Cornell U. 1937, A.B. Radio writer: We The People, Bicycle Party, 1937, Bob Hope Show, 1938–43. Screen writer; apptd. prod., Warner Bros, 1951. Conceived for TV: Make Room for Daddy, My World and Welcome To It. Author: book, How To Make a Jewish Movie. Lualda, The Great Houdinis, The Eleventh Commandment, Ike. Pres., Writers Guild of America, West, 1969–71, 1979–81. Pres., Writers Guild Foundation, 1978–81.
PICTURES INCLUDE: Princess & The Pirate, Wonder Man, Kid From Brooklyn, Sorrowful Jones, It's a Great Feeling, Daughter of Rosie O'Grady, Always Leave Them Laughing, Where There's Life, On Moonlight Bay, I'll See You in My Dreams, Room For One More, April in Paris, Trouble Along the Way, Living It Up, Seven Little Foys, Beau James, Houseboat, It Started in Naples, The Five Pennies, On the Double, The Pigeon That Took Rome, A New Kind of Love, Cast a Giant Shadow, Yours Mine and Ours, The War Between Men and Women, Mixed Company.
TV FEATURES: The Legend of Valentino, The Great Houdinis, Ike.

SHAW, EDWARD S.: Producer-Actor-Executive. b. Buffalo, N.Y., July 13, 1939. e. El Camino College. Began as child actor on radio, joined CBS-TV in 1957, then owner/president of p.r./adv. firm under his own banner.
PICTURES INCLUDE: Actor; Sergeant Rutledge, Claudell English, Palm Springs Weekend, Rise & Fall of Legs Diamond, PT-109, Critics Choice. Production: Assoc. prod. Harlow, Give 'em Hell Harry; Exec. prod. Half A House, Aftermath; Co-prod., Hollywood Knight, Lady Taxi Driver; Prod., The Josephine Baker Story.

SHAW, SEBASTIAN: Actor. b. Holt, England, May 29, 1905; e. Gresham School, Slade School of Art before screen career; m. Margaret Delamere; p. Dr. Geoffrey Shaw (musician) and Mary Shaw. British m.p. debut 1930 in Caste. In R.A.F. World War II.
PICTURES INCLUDE: Get Your Man, Brewster's Millions, Ace of Spades, Jury's Evidence, Tomorrow We Live, Men Are Not Gods, Farewell Again, The Squeaker, Spy in Black, Too Dangerous to Live, The Flying Squad, Allas the Bulldog, East of Piccadilly, Glass Mountain, Landfall, Feature Story, Laxdale Hall, It Happened Here, 1968, Midsummer Night's Dream.

SHAWLEE, JOAN: Actress. b. Forest Hills, N.Y., March 5, 1929; e. Calif. & N.Y. high schools. Powers model, night club entertainer.
PLAYS: By Jupiter, Connecticut Yankee in King Arthur's Court.
TV: Abbott and Costello TV show, series: Aggie.
PICTURES INCLUDE: Marrying Kind, Something for the Birds, Conquest of Space, A Star is Born, Francis Joins the Wacs, Some Like it Hot, The Apartment, Critic's Choice, Irma LaDouce, All the Fallen Angels, Tony Rome, Live a Little, Love a Little, Willard, One More Train To Rob.

SHAWN, DICK: Actor. r.n. Richard Schulefand. b. Buffalo, N.Y., December 1; e. U. of Miami. Actor, play: For Heaven's Sake, Mother, A Funny Thing Happened on the Way to the Forum. Worked night club circuit, 5 yrs.
PICTURES INCLUDE: Wake Me When it's Over, It's a Mad Mad Mad Mad World, The Producers, The Happy Ending.
TV: Max Liebman TV Spectaculars, Mary (series).

SHAYNE, ROBERT: Actor. b. Yonkers, N.Y. On N.Y. stage, on screen 1943 in Shine on Harvest Moon.
PLAYS: Claudia, Night of January 16th, Both Your Houses, Yellow Jack, Whiteoaks, Without Love, etc.
PICTURES INCLUDE: Mr. Skeffington, Christmas in Connecticut, Welcome Stranger, Neanderthal Man, North by Northwest, The Arrangement, Tora Tora Tora, Barefoot Executive, Million Dollar Duck.
TV: Marcus Welby, M.D., Doris Day Show, S.W.A.T., Emergency, Superman series, etc.

SHEAFF, DONALD J.: Executive. b. Oct. 23, 1925; e. U.C.L.A., 1948, Pierce College, 1957. Served 4 yrs. during WW II in Navy Air Corps in South Pacific. 1946, joined Technicolor Motion Picture Div. in supervisory capacity; 1957, lab. supervisor, Lookout Mountain Air Force Station, handling Top Secret film for Air Force and Atomic Energy Commission. Est. and org. the installation of Vandenberg Air Force Base Lab. facilities, which Technicolor designed. 1961 joined Panacolor Corp., 1963 joined Pacific Title and Art Studio in charge of color control for special effects and titles. Returned to Technicolor Corp. 1966, appt'l. Plant Mgr. of Television Div., Oct. 1966, V.P. & Gen. Mgr. of the Television Div., July, 1973 appt v.p. & gen. mgr., Motion Picture Division; 1976, mgr., special visual effects, Universal City Studios. Member: SMPTE, Nat'l Academy of Television Arts & Sciences. Has conducted scientific seminars for SMPTE.

SHEDLO, RONALD: Producer. b. Los Angeles, 1940. Secretary to Errol Flynn, 1956. Asst. prod. Strangers in the City, 1961. Prod. The Whisperers, 1966. Prod. The Reckoning, Day of Locust, Letters from Frank, Back Roads.

SHEELER, MARK: Actor. r.n. Morris Sheeler. b. New York, N.Y., April 24, 1923; e. UCLA. Disc jockey 1942–48. Air Corp. Photog. during war. Voices, animated cartoons, commercials. M.p. debut in Born Yesterday.
PLAYS: Hillbarn Thea., Calif.: Harvey, The Happy Time, Time of Your Life, Amphitryon 38, etc.
PICTURES INCLUDE: The High and the Mighty, Blood Alley, It Came From Beneath the Sea, Apache Warrior, Tank Battalion, P.O.W., Book of Israel, Why Must I Die?, Irma La Douce, The Raven, Elmer Gentry, How the West Was Won, Mary Poppins, Unsinkable Molly Brown, Sound of Music, After the Fox, Elmer Gantry, See the Man Run, Capricorn I, Damien, Omen II, The Hand.
TV: Hitchcock Presents, Kraft Thea., Day in Court, Defenders, East Side, West Side, Dr. Kildare, The Fugitive, Mr. Ed, Jack Benny Show, Life of Riley, Man from Uncle, Doctors & the Nurses, The Invaders, Batman, Here's Lucy, Dennis the Menace, Andy Griffith, Marcus Welby, Banacek, Moses the Lawgiver, All My Children, Kojak, Charlie's Angels, Police Woman, The Tonight Show, Mash, Fantasy Island, Photo Clinic (PBS), The C.C. Connection, Nero Wolfe, House Calls.

SHEEN, MARTIN: Actor. r.n. Ramon Estevez. b. Dayton, O., Aug. 3, 1940.
PICTURES INCLUDE: The Subject Was Roses, The Incident, Catch 22, No Drums, No Bugles, Rage, Pickup on 101, Badlands, The Cassandra Crossing, The Little Girl Who Lives Down the Lane, Apocalypse Now, The Final Countdown.
TV: That Certain Summer, Letters for Three Lovers, The Execution of Private Slovik, The California Kid, The Missiles of October, Sweet Hostage, etc.

SHEFFIELD, JOHN: Actor. b. Pasadena, Calif., April 11, 1931; e. UCLA. Stage debut at 7 in On Borrowed Time. Created screen role of Tarzan's son; in Tarzan pictures since.
PICTURES INCLUDE: Babes in Arms, Little Orvie, Bomba series, creating name part in Million Dollar Baby, Knute Rockne, Roughly Speaking, Cisco Kid.
TV: series: Bantu the Zebra Boy.

SHEFTER, BERT: Composer, conductor. b. Russia, May 15, 1904; e. Carnegie Inst. of Tech., Curtis Inst., Damrosch Inst. Member of piano team, Gould & Shefter, on radio & in theatres; org. own band; concert pianist; comp., cond. for many films and TV.
PICTURES INCLUDE: compose, conduct: Tall Texan, No Escape, Great Jesse James Raid, Sins of Jezebel, The Big Circus, The Fly, Lost World, Jack the Giant Killer, Monkey on My Back, Cattle King, Curse of the Fly, Last Man on Earth, Voyage to the Bottom of the Sea, The Bubble, Dog of Flanders.
TV: Written shows for Sunset Strip, Surfside, Hawaiian Eye, Maverick, Sugarfoot, Lawman, Bourbon St., Roaring 20's.

SHEINBERG, SIDNEY JAY: Executive. b. Corpus Christi, TX, Jan. 14, 1935. e. Columbia Coll. (Ab, 1955); LLB, 1958). Admitted to Calif. bar, 1958; assoc. in law U. Cal. Sch. Law, Los Angeles, 1958–59; Joined MCA, Inc, 1959. Pres., TV div., 1971–74; exec. v.p., parent co., 1969–73. Named MCA pres., 1973.

SHELDON, DAVID: Director-Writer-Producer. b. New York City. e. Yale Univ., School of Drama (M.F.A.), Principia College

241

(B.A.). Directed N.Y. & L.A. companies of The Star Spangled Girl, Alley Oop, Jimmy Shine, etc. Co-founded The Gateway Playhouse in N.Y. where produced & directed over 50 plays and musicals. From 1972–74 was exec. in chg. of development at American Intl. Pictures supervising various production & post-production aspects of such as Dillinger, The Frogs, Macon County Line, Slaughter, Dr. Phibes, Boxcar Bertha, Heavy Traffic, etc.

PICTURES INCLUDE: Producer-Writer, Sheba, Baby, Grizzly, The Evil, Project: Kill. Producer: Just Before Dawn. Director: Satellite, The Predator, Lovely But Deadly.

SHELDON, JAMES: Director. b. New York, N.Y.; e. U. of N.C. Page boy, NBC; announcer-writer-dir., NBC Internat'l Div.; staff dir., ABC radio; staff prod. dir., Young & Rubicam; free lance prod. dir. of many programs live and film, N.Y. and Hollywood.

TV: prod., dir.: Mr. Peepers, Armstrong Circle Theatre, Robert Montgomery Presents, Schlitz Playhouse, West Point, Zane Grey Theatre, The Millionaire, Desilu Playhouse, Perry Mason, Twilight Zone, Route 66, Naked City, The Virginian, Alfred Hitchcock Presents, Fugitive, Espionage, Defenders, Nurses, Bing Crosby Show, Family Affair, Wonderful World of Disney, Man From UNCLE, Felony Squad, That Girl, Ironside, My World and Welcome To It, To Rome With Love, Owen Marshall, Room 222, Gidget Grows Up (ABC Movie), Apple's Way, Love American Style, McMillan and Wife, Sanford and Son, Ellery Queen, Rich Man, Poor Man II, Family, MASH, Switch, Loveboat, With This Ring (ABC Movie), Sheriff Lobo, Gossip Columnist (movie), Knott's Landing, The Waltons, 240-Robert, Nurse.

SHELDON, SIDNEY: Writer-Producer-Novelist. b. Chicago, Feb. 11, 1917. e. Northwestern Univ. Novels made into films include Other Side of Midnight and Bloodline.

PICTURES INCLUDE: Bachelor and the Bobbysoxer, Easter Parade, Annie Get Your Gun, Dream Wife, Jumbo, Pardners, You're Never Too Young, Birds and the Bees, Three Guys Named Mike, Remains To Be Seen, Gambling Daughters, Dangerous Lady.

TELEVISION: Created Patty Duke Show; Created and produced I Dream of Jeannie and Nancy.

SHENSON, WALTER: Producer. b. San Francisco, Calif.; e. Stanford U., Calif.; Ent. m.p. ind. 1941; studio exec., writing, prod., prom. shorts, trailers, Columbia; sup. publ., expl., London, Columbia European production, 1955.

PICTURES INCLUDE: prod.: The Mouse That Roared, A Matter of WHO, The Mouse on the Moon, A Hard Day's Night, Help!, 30 is a Dangerous Age, Cynthia, Don't Raise the Bridge Lower the River, A Talent for Loving, Welcome to the Club (prod.-dir.), The Chicken Chronicles (co-prod.).

SHEPARD, SAM: Writer-Actor. b. Fort Sheridan, Ill. Grew up in California, Montana and South Dakota. Lives near San Francisco, where, in addition to writing, runs a drama workshop at the Univ. of California at Davis. Recipient of Brandeis Univ. Creative Arts Citation (1976) and American Academy of Arts and Letters Award (1975).

PLAYS INCLUDE: Cowboys and Rock Garden (double bill), Chicago, Icarus' Mother, and Red Cross (triple bill—1966 Obie Award), La Turista (1967 Obie), Forensic and the Navigators, Melodrama Play, Tooth of Crime (1973 Obie), Back Dog Beast Bait, Operation Sidewinder, 4-H Club, The Unseen Hand, Mad Dog Blues, Shaved Splits, Rock Garden, Curse of the Starving Class (1978 Obie), Buried Child, etc.

ACTOR: Days of Heaven, Resurrection.

SHEPHERD, CYBILL: Actress-singer. b. Memphis, Tenn., February 18. e. Hunter Col., NYU, USC. Was fashion model before acting debut in 1971. Debut record album, Cybill Does It . . . To Cole Porter (Paramount), 1974.

PICTURES INCLUDE: The Last Picture Show (debut), The Heartbreak Kid, Daisy Miller, At Long Last Love, Taxi Driver, Special Delivery, Silver Bears.

SHEPHERD, RICHARD: Producer. b. Kansas City, Mo., June 4, 1927. e. Stanford Univ. In U.S. Naval Reserve, 1944–45. Entered ent. field as exec. with MCA, 1948, functioning in radio, TV, and m.p. fields until 1956, with time out for U.S. Army, 1950–52. In 1956 became head of talent for Columbia Pictures. In 1962 joined CMA talent agency on its founding, becoming exec. v.p. in chg. of m.p. div. Left to join Warner Bros. in Aug., 1972, as exec. v.p. for prod. Resigned Oct. 1, 1974 to become indep. prod. In 1976 named MGM sr. vp. & worldwide head of theatrical prod.

PICTURES INCLUDE: Twelve Angry Men, The Hanging Tree, The Fugitive Kind, Breakfast at Tiffany's (prod.), Alex and the Gypsy, Robin and Marian.

SHER, ABBOTT J.: Executive. b. Duluth, Minn., Oct. 21, 1918; e. U. of Minnesota. Sls. mgr., Sher Packing Co., 1938–39; U.S. Army, 1942–45. Mgr., Jayhawk Thea., Kansas City, Kan., 1947–48; office mgr., Exhibitors Film Delivery & Service Co., 1949–54; sec., Exhibitors Film Delivery, 1955; theatre operator; vice-pres., sec., Exhibitors Film Delivery & Service Co., Inc., 1960; pres., M.P. Ass'n of Greater Kansas City, 1960; bd. of dir., United Theatre Owners Heart

of America, 1960–61; bd. of dir., Northtown Theatre Corp., Kansas City, Mo., 1961–62; secy. United Theatre Owners Heart of America, 1963; treas., 1964; v.p., 1965; pres. United Motion Pict. Assoc., 1967–68; Dough Guy, Variety Clubs International, Kansas City Tent No. 8, 1974; asst. chief barker, 1975–76; chief barker, Variety Clubs Int. Kansas City Tent 8, 1978–79.

SHER, JACK: Writer, producer, director. b. Minneapolis, Minn. e. U. of Minnesota. Syndicated newspaper columnist; contrib. mag. articles (fiction & non-fiction). U.S. Army, WW II.

BROADWAY: The Perfect Setup, 1963.

BOOKS: author: The Cold Companion, 12 Sports Immortals, 12 More Sports Immortals.

PICTURES INCLUDE: collab. s.p.: My Favorite Spy, Off Limits; s.p.: Kid from Left Field; addit. dial.: Shane; s.p., collab. story: World in My Corner; collab. s.p.: Walk the Proud Land, Joe Butterfly; s.p., dir.: Four Girls in Town; s.p., dir.: Kathy O, The Wild and the Innocent; collab. s.p., dir.: 3 Worlds of Gulliver; collab. s.p.: Paris Blues; s.p., dir.: Love in a Goldfish Bowl; s.p.: Critic's Choice; collab. s.p.: Move Over Darling, produced and wrote "Goodby Raggedy Ann," produced "Slither."

SHER, LOUIS K.: Executive. b. Columbus, Ohio, Feb. 25, 1914; e. Ohio State Univ., 1933. Exec., Stone's Grills Co., 1934–37; owned & operated, Sher Vending Co., 1937–43. U.S. Army, 1943–46. V.p., Sons Bars & Grills, 1947–54; org. & pres., Art Theatre Guild, 1954; opened art theatres for first time in many cities, org. opera film series, film classic series and similar motion picture activities in many cities. Org., Film Festival at Antioch Coll., 1960; pioneer in fighting obscenity laws in Ohio; operates 43 theatres in midwest and western states. Co-producer of the musical broadway production Shenandoah and American Dance Machine.

SHERDEMAN, TED: Writer, producer, director. b. Lincoln, Neb.; e. U. of Nebraska, Creighton U.

PICTURES INCLUDE: Lust For Gold, Scandal Sheet, Breakthrough, Retreat Hell, Winning Team, Eddie Cantor Story, Riding Shotgun, Them, McConnell Story, Toy Tiger, Away All Boats, Maracaibo, St. Louis Blues, Hell to Eternity, A Dog of Flanders, The Big Show, Misty, Island of the Blue Dolphins, And Now Miguel, My Side of the Mountain, Latitude Zero.

TV: Wagon Train, Zane Grey, Californians, Astronaut, Hazel, Men Into Space, My Favorite Martian, Bewitched, Family Affair, The Monroes, Flying Nun.

SHERMAN, AL: Producers Representative, Film and public relations consultant. b. New York. N.Y., April 27; e. Columbia U., CCNY. Film & pub. consultant, Royal Norwegian Information Service, Wash., D.C.; Wash.; pres., Sherman Films, Inc.; American rep., Films of Scotland, Edinburgh, Scotland; Patria Film Prods. Ltd., London; British Films Ltd., London. Member: Silurians; Educational Film Library Association; American Federation of Film Societies; M.P. Pioneers, American Film Institute.

SHERMAN, EDWARD: Talent agent. b. Russia, Jan. 12, 1903. Entered vaudeville agency field Philadelphia and New York 1920; estab. Edward Sherman Agency, New York; in 1941 estab. branch Hollywood, Calif.; org. & pres., MPM Corp. to distribute films for television, 1947; also org. & pres., Glove TV Corp., 1952; formed Edward Sherman (personal mgt.), 1956.

SHERMAN, GEORGE: Director. b. New York, N.Y.

PICTURES INCLUDE: The Bandit of Sherwood Forest, Red Canyon, Yes Sir That's My Baby, Sword in the Desert, Comanche Territory, Sleeping City, Spy Hunt, Tomahawk, Target Unknown, Golden Horde, Steel Town, Raging Tide, Against All Flags, Battle at Apache Pass, The Lone Hand, Veils of Bagdad, War Arrow, Border River, Johnny Dark, Dawn at Socorro, Chief Crazy Horse, Count Three and Pray, Treasure of Pancho Villa, Comanche, Reprisal, Flying Fontaines, Enemy General. Formed Shergari Corp. with F.H. Ricketson, Jr., and Ted R. Gamble made For the Love of Mike; dir.: Panic Button, Wounds of Hunger, Jaquin Murieta, Smokey, Big Jake. In 1976 wrote, produced, and directed Artie-Charley and Friend, indep. feature.

TV: Prod. and/or dir. for 20th Century-Fox, and NBC, CBS. 1978, prod., Little Mo (TV movie NBC), Man O'War and Trudy (TV movie ABC).

SHERMAN, RICHARD M.: Composer, lyricist. b. New York, N.Y., June 12, 1928; e. Bard Coll. B.A. 1949. Info. & Educ. Br., U.S. Army, 1953–55. Songwriter, composer, Walt Disney Prods.

SONGS: Things I Might Have Been, Tall Paul, Christmas in New Orleans, Mad Passionate Love, Midnight Oil, You're Sixteen, Pineapple Princess, Lets Get Together, Maggie's Theme, Chim Chim Cheree, Comedy Album: Smash Flops.

PICTURES INCLUDE: Nightmare, The Cruel Tower, Absent Minded Professor, The Parent Trap, Big Red, The Castaways, Moon Pilot, Bon Voyage, Legend of Lobo, Summer Magic, Miracle of the White Stallions, The Sword

in the Stone, Merlin Jones, Mary Poppins, Those Calloways, The Monkey's Uncle, That Darn Cat, Symposium of Popular Songs, Winnie the Pooh, Bedknobs & Broomsticks, Tom Sawyer (s.p. and score.), Huckleberry Finn.
TV: Wonderful World of Color, Bell Telephone Hour.

SHERMAN, ROBERT B.: Composer, lyricist. b. New York, N.Y., Dec. 19, 1925; e. Bard Coll., B.A., 1949. U.S. Army, WWII, 1943–45. Songwriter, 1952–60; pres., Music World Corp., 1958; songwriter, composer, Walt Disney, 1960–65.
SONGS: Things I Might Have Been, Tall Paul, Young & In Love, Midnight Oil, Pineapple Princess. You're 16, Let's Get Together, Maggie's Theme, Chim Chim Cheree.
PICTURES INCLUDE: Absent Minded Professor, The Parent Trap, Big Red, The Castaways, Moon Pilot, Bon Voyage, Legend of Lobo, Miracle of the White Stallions, Summer Magic, The Sword in the Stone, Merlin Jones, Mary Poppins, Those Calloways, The Monkey's Uncle, That Darn Cat, Winnie the Pooh, Symposium of Popular Songs, Bedknobs & Broomsticks, Tom Sawyer (s.p. and score.), Huckleberry Finn.
TV: Wonderful World of Color, Bell Telephone

SHERMAN, ROBERT M.: Executive. Entered ind. as agent for MCA; later joined Arthur P. Jacobs pub. rel. firm. Became acc't. exec. when Jacobs merged with Rogers & Cowan. In 1964 joined CMA; 1967 made v.p. in m.p. div., serving both in London and Hollywood. In 1972 formed own prod. co., Layton Prods., with first film, Scarecrow for WB. In 1973 prod. Night Moves, also for WB. In 1974 named v.p., prod., for 20th-Fox. Returned to independent prod.: The Missouri Breaks, Convoy.

SHERMAN, SAMUEL M.: Producer, director, writer. b. New York, N.Y.; e. CCNY, BA. Entered m.p. ind. as writer, cameraman, film ed., neg. & sound cutter; nat'l mag. ed., Westerns Magazine, 1959; pres., Signature Films; prod., dir., TV pilot, The Three Mesquiteers, 1960; prod., Pulse Pounding Perils, 1961; helped create, ed.,dir., Screen Thrills Illustrated; exec. prod., Screen Thrills; v.p., Golden Age Films, 1962; prod., Joe Franklin's Silent Screen, 1963; N.Y. rep., Victor Adamson Productions; owns world rights; The Scarlet Letter; 1965; N.Y. rep., Tal Prods., Hlywd.; adv. & pub., Hemisphere Pictures; ed., autobiog., Joe Bonomo; prod., writer, Chaplin's Art of Comedy, The Strongman; prod., Hollywood's Greatest Stuntman; story adapt., Fiend With the Electronic Brain. 1967, prod. Spanish version Chaplin Su Arte Y Su Comedia; tech. consul., Hal Roach Studios, NBC, Music from the Land; 1968, N.Y. rep. East West Pict. of Hollywood. 1968, N.Y. rep., Al Adamson Prods. of Hollywood; post-prod'n consultant: The Fakers, Creatures of the Prehistoric Planet; sales U.K. of U.S. product; promo. consultant, Love is a Woman, Blood Fiend, Brides of Blood, The Ghastly Ones. 1969, post prod'n and promo. consultant, Blood Demon, Mad Doctor of Blood Island. Ed.-in-chief, bk., The Strongman. Prod'n consultant, Satan's Sadists, The Blood Seekers. Pres., Independent-International Pictures Corp, assoc. prod. Horror of the Blood Monsters, Blood of Ghastly Horror; Producer-Writer Brain of Blood; prod. supervisor Dracula vs. Frankenstein; Exec. prod. Angels, Wild Women; pres., Producers Commercial Productions Inc.; producer-writer, The Naughty Stewardesses; producer, Girls For Rent; producer TV special, Wild, Wild World of Comedy; executive producer, The Dynamite Brothers; producer-writer, Blazing Stewardesses; production consultant, In Search of Dracula; executive producer, Cinderella 2000; producer & orig. story, Team-Mates; Chairman of Creditors' Committee, Allied Artists Television Corp.; president, Independent-International Entertainment, TV div. Independent-International Pictures Corp.

SHERMAN, VINCENT: Director. b. Vienna. Ga., July 16, 1906; e. Oglethorpe U. B.A. Writer, actor, dialogue dir., then prod. dir.
PICTURES INCLUDE: Dir.: Underground, Saturday's Children, Flight from Destiny, Old Acquaintances, In Our Time, Mr. Skeffington, Pillow to Post, Nora Prentiss, The Unfaithful, Adventures of Don Juan, Somewhere in the City, Hasty Heart, Damned Don't Cry, Harriet Craig, Goodbye, My Fancy, Lone Star, Assignment—Paris; prod. dir.: Affair in Trinidad, The Young Philadelphians, The Naked Earth, Second Time Around.
TV: 25 episodes of Medical Center; 3 Westside Medical; 6 Baretta; 4 Waltons; 2 Doctors Hospital; The Last Hurrah (movie); Women at West Point (movie); The Yeagers (pilot), Bogey, The Dream Merchants.

SHERRIN, NED: Producer, director, writer. Early career writing plays and musical plays. Prod., dir., ATV Birmingham, 1955–57; prod., Midlands Affairs, Paper Talk, etc. Joined BBC-TV 1957 and produced many TV talk programmes. Novels: (with Caryl Brahms) Cindy-Ella or I Gotta Shoe (also prod. as stage play), Rappell 1910, Benbow Was His Name.
TV: England: prod.: Ask Me Another, Henry Hall Show, Laugh Line, Parasol. Assoc. prod.: Tonight series. Little Beggars, 1962; prod., creator: That Was The Week That

Was, 1962–63; prod., dir.: Benbow Was His Name (co-author), 1964; Take a Sapphire (co-author), The Long Garden Party, The Long Cocktail Party. ABC of Britain revue. Prod., dir.: thrice-weekly series Not So Much a Programme, More a Way of Life, 1964–65. Appearances inc. Your Witness, Quiz of The Week, Terra Firma, Who Said That, The Rather Reassuring Programme, Song by Song.
PICTURES INCLUDE: prod.: The Virgin Soldiers (with Leslie Gilliat), Every Home Should Have One, Up Pompeii, Girl Stroke Boy (co-author with Caryl Brahms), Up the Chastity Belt, Rentadick, The Garnet Saga, Up the Front, The National Health, The Cobblers of Umbridge (dir. with Ian Wilson).

SHIELDS, BROOKE: Actress. b. New York City, May 31, 1965. Discovered at age 11 months by photographer Francesco Scavullo to pose in Ivory Snow ads. Later became Breck girl in commericals; appeared in Richard Avenon's Colgate ads for 3 yrs.
PICTURES INCLUDE: Alice Sweet Alice (Communion), Pretty Baby, Tilt, King of the Gypsies, Wanda Nevada, Just You and Me, Kid, The Blue Lagoon, Endless Love.
TV: The Prince of Central Park, After the Fall.

SHIELDS, WILLIAM A.: Executive. b. New York City, 1946. e. El Camino College and California State College. Entered the motion picture industry in 1966 when he went to work for Pacific Theatres. Other industry affiliations included: MGM sales department, Los Angeles and Denver, 1970; New World Pictures, Western Division manager, 1972; branch manager, 20th Century-Fox, Washington, 1973; New York district manager, 20th Century-Fox, 1973–75. Joined Mann Theatres Corporation of California as head booker in 1975. Gen. sls. mgr.'Far West Films, 1977–79; joined Avco Embassy as Western div. mgr., promoted to asst. gen. sls. mgr., 1980; promoted to v.p.-gen. sls. mgr., January, 1981.

SHIMA, KOJI: Director. b. Japan. Entered m.p. ind. as actor, 1930; then asst. dir., director. Dir., Daiei M. P. Co. (now defunct). Presently indep. director.
PICTURES INCLUDE: Golden Demon, Phantom Horse.

SHINBACH, BRUCE D.: Executive. b. South Bend, Ind., June, 1939. e. Univ. of Colorado, (B.A. 1963), N.Y. Institute of Finance, Northwestern Univ. (M.A., 1965). Stockbroker for Harris, Upham & Co., 1964, shopping center developer, Dixie Associates, 1966 to present. Pres., Monarch Theatres.

SHIPMAN, BARRY: Writer. b. S. Pasadena, Cal., Feb. 24, 1912. Parents professional. M.p. writer since 1936. U.S.M.C.R. photog. officer 1942–46. 43 sole s.p. credits including Montana Territory for Col., 1946–52.

SHIPMAN, KENNETH: Producer. b. London, England, 1930. Electro-mechanical engineer, entered m.p. ind. as assistant dir., Riverside Studios, 1949; mgr., Southhall Studios; dept. chmn., Bryanston Films; formed Kenneth Shipman Productions, 1964; prod., The System, exec. prod., Burke and Hare, Au Pair Girls.

SHIRE, DAVID: Composer.
PICTURES INCLUDE: Farewell My Lovely, The Conversation, All the President's Men, Saturday Night Fever, Old Boyfriends, Norma Rae, The Night the Lights Went Out in Georgia.

SHIRE, TALIA: Actress. Raised on road by her father, arranger-conductor Carmine Coppola, who toured with Broadway musicals. After 2 yrs. at Yale School of Drama she moved to L.A. where appeared in many theatrical productions. Is sister of Francis Ford Coppola.
PICTURES INCLUDE: The Dunwich Horror, Gas-s-s, The Christian Licorice Store, The Outside Man, The Godfather, The Godfather, Part II, Rocky, Old Boyfriends, Rocky II, Windows.
TV: Rich Man, Poor Man, Kill Me If You Can.

SHIVAS, MARK: Producer/Director. TV credits incl: Margins Of The Mind. Presenter of Cinema. The Six Wives of Henry VIII, Casanova, The Edwardians, The Evacuees, The Glittering Prizes, Abide With Me, Rogue Male, 84 Charing Cross Road, The Three Hostages, She Fell Among Thieves, Professional Foul, Telford's Change, On a Giant's Shoulders. Film: Exec. prod. Henry VIII and His Six Wives, Richards' Things.

SHONFELD, PHIL: Executive. Began career in sls. dist. at Universal Pictures. Later asst. to western sls. mgr. for National General and western dist. mgr. for Buena Vista. Joined Warners in November, 1976 as asst. to v.p. & gen. sls. mgr. In 1979 promoted to v.p.—sls. admin., continuing to head playdate and contract depts. while becoming involved in all aspects of sls. dept.

SHORE, DINAH: Singer. r.n. Frances Rose Shore. b. Winchester, Tenn., Mar. 1, 1920; e. Vanderbilt U., B.A. 1939; m. George Montgomery. Became singer WNEW, N.Y., 1938; joined NBC as sustaining singer, 1938; started contract RCA-Victor, 1940; star Chamber Music Soc. of Lower Basin

St. program, 1940; joined Eddie Cantor radio pgm., 1941; star own radio program, General Foods, 1943; entertained troops European Theatre of operations, 1944; radio program, Procter & Gamble. Star TV show, Chevrolet, 1951–61; Dinah Shore Specials, 1964–65. 1969: Dinah Shore Special, Like Hep. 1970–71: Dinah's Place, Dinah!

AWARDS: Awarded New Star of Radio Motion Picture Daily Poll and World Telegram-Scripps-Howard Poll, 1940; Best Popular Female Vocalist M.P. Daily Fame's Annual Poll Radio and TV 1941–61; Michael Award Best Female Vocalist, Radio and TV, 1950, 51, 52; Billboard Award; Favorite Female Vocalist in radio, 1949; Billboard Award Favorite Female Vocalist in records, 1947; Gallup Poll One of Most Admired Women in the World, 1958–61; 6 Emmy Awards 1954 to 59. Recording of songs by Decca; Los Angeles Times Woman of the Year Award, 1957; TV-Radio Mirror mag. award, best female singer, radio, 1952, 53, 56, 57, 58; TV-Radio Mirror mag. award, TV's Best Musical Variety Show, 1956, 58, 59; Peabody TV Award, 1957; Fame's Critics' Poll, Best Female Vocalist, 1958, 63; Hollywood Foreign Press Assn's Golden Globe Award, 1959; Radio-TV Daily, Female Vocalist of the Year, 1949, 56.

SHORE, SIG: Producer. b. New York City. Served as navigator in Air Force, World War II. First job in films in pub. dept. at Warner Bros. Formed own ad agency on West Coast; then turned to TV production with The Errol Flynn Theatre. Engaged by David O. Selznick Films to dist. its films to TV outlets. Entered theatrical distribution, importing Hiroshima, Mon Amour, The 400 Blows, etc. In mid-50s became involved in cultural exchange program of US State Dept., importing and distributing Soviet films. Returned to TV production, turning out over 250 shows, including The Outdoor World for Shell Oil. Headed co. for Ivan Tors which made Flipper, Daktari, Gentle Ben series. In 1970 formed Plaza Pictures for theatrical dist.
PICTURES INCLUDE: Super Fly, Super Fly TNT, That's The Way of the World.

SHOWALTER, MAX: Actor, composer. s.n. Casey Adams. b. Caldwell, Kans., June 2, 1917; e. Caldwell H.S.; Pasadena Playhouse. Composed background music for films: Vicki, Return of Jack Slade. Arrangements for records.
BROADWAY: Knights of Song, Very Warm for May, My Sister Eileen, Showboat, John Loves Mary, Make Mine Manhattan, Lend an Ear.
PICTURES INCLUDE: Always Leave Them Laughing, With a Song in My Heart, What Price Glory, My Wife's Best Friend, Niagara, Destination Gobi, Dangerous Crossing, Vicki, Night People, Naked Alibi, Never Say Goodbye, Bus Stop, Down Three Dark Streets, Designing Woman, Female Animal, Voice In the Mirror, The Naked and the Dead, It Happened in June, Elmer Gantry, Return to Peyton Place, Summer and Smoke, Music Man, Smog, Bon Voyage, My Six Loves, Lord Love a Duck, The Anderson Tapes.

SHULMAN, MAX: Writer. b. St. Paul, Minn., March 14, 1919; e. U. of Minn., B.A., 1942.
NOVELS: Barefoot Boy with Cheek, Feather Merchants, Zebra Derby, Sleep Till Noon, Rally Round the Flag Boys.
BROADWAY: Barefoot Boy with Cheek, Tender Trap.
PICTURES INCLUDE: collab. story: Always Leave Them Laughing; Collab. story, s.p.: Confidentially Connie; story, s.p.: Affairs of Dobie Gillis, Half a Hero.
TV: Creator: The Many Loves of Dobie Gillis.

SHUMATE, HAROLD: Writer. b. Austin, Texas; e. Texas and Missouri. Wrote short stories, worked on newspaper; sold first story to motion pictures 1916; came to Los Angeles 1923; written over 100 motion pictures for major studios, several books, innumerable television stories and scripts.

SHUPERT, GEORGE T.: b. Alpena, Mich., July 24, 1904; e. U. Mich., 1926. Investment banking, Detroit, Mich., 1926–38; found George T. Shupert & Co., 1936; dir. of sales, commercial film div., Paramount Pictures, 1940–42; TV dept. 1942–51; v.p., dir., commercial TV oper., Paramount TV Prod., Inc.; v.p. Peerless TV Prod., Inc.; v.p., gen. mgr., United Artists Television Corp.; v.p., ABC Film Syndication, Aug., 1953; pres., March, 1954; v.p. chg., TV, MGM, 1959–61; named director, TV sales, v.p., 20th Century-Fox TV, 1961–64; pres., Sunrise Broadcasting Co., 1965–77. Director, American Video Corp., (Cable TV) Pompano Beach, Fla.

SHURPIN, SOL: Executive. b. New York, N.Y., Feb. 22, 1914; e. Pace Institute, 1936. Law stenog., 1932–33; Joe Hornstein, Inc., 1933–41; National Theatre Supply, 1941–48; purchased interest in Raytone Screen Corp., became v.p., 1948; pres., Raytone, 1952; pres., Technikote Corp., which succeeded Raytone Screen, 1956-present; sole owner, Technikote Corp., 1962.

SHYLEN, BEN: Editor emeritus of Boxoffice.

SIDARIS, ANDY: Producer, director. b. Chicago, Ill., Feb. 20, 1932. e. Southern Methodist University, B.A. in Radio-TV. Began television career in 1950 in Dallas, Texas as a director at station WFAA-TV; now pres., The Sidaris Company.

PICTURES INCLUDE: Dir., Stacey, The Racing Scene, M*A*S*H football sequences, Seven (prod.-dir.).
TV: Dir., The Racers/Mario Andretti/Joe Leonard/Al Unser, ABC's Championship Auto Racing, ABC's NCAA Game of the Week, 1972 Summer Olympics, 1968 Summer Olympics (won Emmy Award), Wide World of Sports, The Racers/Craig and Lee Breedlove, dir.: The Burt Reynolds Late Show, dir., Kojak episode, Nancy Drew, Dukes of Hazzard.

SIDNEY, GEORGE: Director, producer. b. New York, N.Y. 1916; son of L. K. Sidney, veteran showman and v.p. MGM and Hazel Mooney, actress. From 1932 at MGM as test, second unit and short subjects dir. Several Academy Awards for shorts, Our Gang Comedies, Pete Smith, etc. In 1941 made feature dir., MGM. Pres., Directors' Guild of America, 16 yrs; spec. presidential assignment to Atomic Energy Commission and U.S. Air Force; 1961–66, Pres., Hanna-Barbera Productions; Doctorate of Science Hanneman Medical University and Hospital. Mem. ASCAP
PICTURES INCLUDE: dir., prod.: Free and Easy, Pacific Rendezvous, Pilot No. 5, Thousands Cheer, Bathing Beauty, Anchors Aweigh, Harvey Girls, Cass Timberlane, Three Musketeers, Red Danube, Key to the City, Annie Get Your Gun, Holiday in Mexico, Show Boat, Scaramouche, Young Bess, Kiss Me Kate, Jupiter's Darling, Eddie Duchin Story, Jeanne Eagels, Pal Joey, Who Was That Lady, Pepe, Bye Bye Birdie, A Ticklish Affair, Viva Las Vegas, Who Has Seen the Wind?, U.N. special; The Swinger, Half A Sixpence.

SIDNEY, SYLVIA: Actress. b. New York, N.Y., Aug. 8, 1910; e. Theatre Guild School. On stage, then screen debut in Through Different Eyes.
PLAYS: Nice Women, Crossroads, Bad Girl, The Gentle People, etc.
PICTURES INCLUDE: City Streets, Five Minutes from the Station, Ladies of the Big House, Confessions of a Co-Ed, An American Tragedy, The Miracle Man, Merrily We Go to Hell, Madame Butterfly, Blood on the Sun, Mr. Ace, Searching Wind, Love from a Stranger, Les Miserables, Violent Saturday, Behind the High Wall, Summer Wishes, Winter Dreams, I Never Promised You a Rose Garden, Damien-Omen II.
TV: Raid on Entebbe.

SIEGEL, DON: Director. b. Chicago, Ill., Oct. 26, 1912; e. Jesus Coll., Cambridge U. (England). Has appeared with the Royal Academy of Dramatic Arts, London, and Contemporary Theatre Group, Hollywood. Joined Warner Bros. as asst. film librarian, 1934; became asst. cutter and head of insert dept. Organized montage dept.; wrote and dir. all montages.
PICTURES INCLUDE: dir.: Star in the Night and Hitler Lives (two Academy Awards for distinctive achievement for shorts, 1945). dir.: The Verdict, Night Unto Night, Big Steal, Duel at Silver Creek, No Time For Flowers, Count the Hours, China Venture, Riot in Cell Block 11, Private Hell 36, Annapolis Story, Invasion of the Body Snatchers, Madigan, Coogan's Bluff, Two Mules for Sister Sara, The Beguiled, Dirty Harry; appeared in Play Misty for Me, Charley Varrick, Black Windmill, The Shootist, Telefon, Escape from Alcatraz, Rough Cut.

SIEGEL, SIMON B.: Financial vice-president, treas., American Broadcasting Paramount Theatres & mem. bd. of dir. Started career in ind. 1929, comptroller's staff Paramount Pictures, Inc.; asst. to comptroller of the company's theatre div., 1941; comptroller, 1949; joined United Paramount Theatres, 1950; in 1953 named treasurer when ABC & UPT were merged; named financial v.p. and treas., 1957; exec. vice-pres., ABC-Paramount Theatres.

SIEGEL, SOL C.: Producer. b. New York City, Mar. 30, 1903; e. Columbia U. Joined Republic Pictures 1934 as exec. prod. To Paramount 1940 as exec. prod. of unit. In 1944 entered indep. prod. with Kiss and Tell. Returned to Paramount 1945. Prod. Blue Skies, Welcome Stranger, Perils of Pauline; prod. 20th Century-Fox, 1946; indep. prod. releasing through MGM, 1955; became vice-president in charge of production MGM Studios, April, 1958. A Champion of Champion Producers, in Fame ratings. Independent Prod. Unit 1964 Columbia Pict.; and Paramount Pict. 1966.
PICTURES INCLUDE: Letter to Three Wives, House of Strangers, I Was a Male War Bride, Panic in the Streets, Prince of Foxes, Stella, My Blue Heaven, Fourteen Hours, Deadline U.S.A., What Price Glory, Dream Boat, Monkey Business, Call Me Madam, The President's Lady, Gentlemen Prefer Blondes, Three Coins in the Fountain, Broken Lance, There's No Business Like Show Business, High Society, Man on Fire, Les Girls, Merry Andrew, Some Came Running, The World, The Flesh and the Devil, Home from the Hill, Alvarez Kelly, Walk Don't Run, No Way to Treat a Lady.

SIGNORET, SIMONE: Actress. r.n. Simone Kaminker. b. Wiesbaden, 1921. Appeared in roles as extra. First break in Les

Visiteurs Du Soir. Attended classes at Solange Sicard's school.
PICTURES INCLUDE: Le Couple Ideal, 1945, Les Demons de L'Aube, 1945, Macadam, 1946, Fantomas, 1947, Dedee D'Anvers, 1948, Guerriers Dans L'Ombre, 1948, L'Impasse des Deux Anges, 1948, Maneges, 1949, Swiss Tour B, XV, 1949, La Ronde, 1950. Ombre & Lumiere, 1950, Casque D'or (Golden Marie—Acad. Award, London, 1953), Therese Raquin, 1953, Les Diaboliques, 1954, The Crucible, Room at the Top, 1958, The Day and The Hour, Ship of Fools, The Sleeping Car Murders, The Deadly Affair, Games, The Seagull, The Confession, Le Chat, Madame Rosa.
STAGE: Les Sorcieres de Salem.

SILBER, ARTHUR: Executive. b. Phila., Pa., Feb. 13, 1919. e. Univ. of Penna. Engineer, U.S. Navy. Owner, Silabert Corp. operator of Lawrence Park theatre, also Able-Silber Theatres & Concessions, Phila., Pa.; pres., Silber-Stoltz Corp.; 1966, Westcoast film buyer and western division manager for General Cinema; 1972-v.p., Avco Triplex Cinema (General Cinema of California); June, 1972, purchased Exhibitor Service Inx.; January, 1975, exec. v.p., Mann Theatres; June, 1975, pres. of Four Stars Cinema Corp. & Four Stars of Ohio; v.p., film, Pacific Theatres, 1977.

SILBERKLEIT, WILLIAM B.: Executive. e. New York University, Full Colonel, USAF. Pres., Tommy J Productions, independent producer: Bonnie's Kids, Roommates, Centerfold Girls, Linda Lovelace for President, Alice Cooper's Welcome to My Nightmare, A Woman for All Men. In 1975 became chm. and co-founder of Pro-International Films. Executive producer for PRO-International: Young Lady Chatterly, Once Upon a Girl, Detroit 9000, Emma Mae.

SILLIPHANT, STIRLING: Executive-Writer. b. Detroit, Mich., Jan. 16, 1918. e. U. Southern California, B.A., 1938; married. On pub. staff, Walt Disney Productions, Burbank, 1938–41; 1941–42, exploit. & pub., Hal Horne Org. for 20th Century-Fox in New York & other key cities, 1942–43, asst. to Spyros P. Skouras. U.S. Navy, World War II. Since 1946, 20th-Fox; in chge. special events and promotions, June 1949; apptd. Eastern pub. mgr. Aug, 13, 1951; prod., Joe Louis Story; co-prod., collab. s.p., 5 Against the House; screenwriter, producer, Naked City, Route 66, The Slender Thread, In the Heat of the Night; s.p., Marlowe; collab., s.p., The Liberation of L. B. Jones; s.p., A Walk in the Spring Rain; p., Shaft, Shaft in Africa, (s.p.). The New Centurions (s.p.), The Poseidon Adventure, (s.p.), The Towering Inferno (s.p.), The Killer Elite (co.-s.p.), The Enforcer (co.-s.p.), Telefon (co-s.p.), The Swarm, When Time Ran Out.

SILVER, JOAN MICKLIN: Writer-Director. b. Omaha, Nebr., 1935. e. Sarah Lawrence College. Began career as writer for educational films. Original s.p., Limbo, purchased by Universal Pictures. In 1972 Learning Corp. of Am. commissioned her to write and direct a 30-min. documentary, The Immigrant Experience. Also wrote and directed two children's films for same co. First feature was Hester Street, which she wrote and directed.
PICTURES INCLUDE: Hester Street (s.p., dir.); Bernice Bobs Her Hair (short, s.p.-dir., later shown on TV), Between the Lines (dir.); Head Over Heels (s.p., dir.).

SILVER, LEON J.: Executive. b. Boston, Mass., March 25, 1918. e. U. of So. Calif., 1935–38. Independent prod. of short subjects, 1939; story analyst, Paramount, 1940, film writer, U.S. Army Pictorial Service, 1941–45; free lance writer, 1946; film writer. prod., U.S. Public Health Service, 1946–51, asst. chief, foreign film prod., U.S. Dept. of State, 1951–54; acting chief, domestic film prod., U.S. Information Agency, 1955. Division Chief, Worldwide Documentary Film & Television Product, U.S. Information Agency, Apr. 6, 1968, 1978 to present, sr. advisor iv, film production. Resigned, 1980. Now TV network writer-producer-novelist.

SILVER, MILTON: Advertising executive. b. New York City. U.S. Army World War I. Co-ed. Who's Who on Screen and Little Movie Mirror books; co-author Broadway stage production, The Mystery Ship; dir. adv., exploit., Universal Pictures, trailer ed, adv. manager, National Screen Service; exec. asst. to dir. adv. pub. Republic Pictures; to Souvaine Selective Pictures as adv., pub. dir., 1951; adv. pub. dept. United Artists 1953. Free lance writer since 1960.

SILVER, PAT: Writer. co-s.p., Wizard of Baghdad, Pirates of Tortuga, orig. story, s.p., 7 Woman From Hell, The Golden Touch, Dare To Be Free; prod., Ghost Town.
TV: Mables Fables Series, Rescue 8, New Breed, Shannon, Paladin.

SILVER, RAPHAEL D.: Producer. b. Cleveland, Ohio, 1930. e. Harvard College and Harvard Graduate School of Business Adm. Is pres. of Midwestern Land Devel. Corp. and Hodgson Houses, Inc. In 1973 formed Midwest Film Productions to produce Hester Street, written and directed by his wife, Joan Micklin Silver. Also distributed film in-

dependently. Also produced Between the Lines, directed by wife. Directed On the Yard.

SILVERMAN, FRED: b. N.Y.C. Sept., 1937. e. Syracuse Univ., Ohio State (Master's in TV and theatre arts). Joined WGN-TV, indep. sta. in Chicago. Came to N.Y. for exec. post at WPIX-TV, where stayed only six weeks when CBS-TV hired him as dir. of daytime programs. Named v.p.—programs June, 1970. In May, 1975 left CBS to become pres., ABC Entertainment. In June, 1978, named pres. and chief exec. officer of NBC.

SILVERMAN, RON: Producer-writer. b. Los Angeles, Calif., June 13, 1933. e. UCLA, 1951–53, U. of Arizona, 1953–55; reporter reviewer, Daily Variety, 1957–61; asst. to prod.-dir. Mark Robson, Red Lion Films, 20th Century-Fox, 1961–62; assoc. prod., Daystar Productions, 1961; v.p., 1964; assoc. prod. Crackerby TV series, 1965. Prod. exec., Warner Bros. TV, 1966; prod. & exec. Ted Mann Prods., 1967.
PICTURES INCLUDE: Buster and Billie (prod.), 1974, Lifeguard, Brubaker.
TV: Wild Wild West (writer), 1967.

SILVERMAN, SYD: Executive. b. N.Y., Jan. 23, 1932. e. The Manlius School, 1946–50; Princeton Univ., 1950–54. Lt., U.S. Army, 1954–56. Publisher, Variety and Daily Variety, executive editor, Weekly Variety.

SILVERS, PHIL: Actor. b. Brooklyn, N.Y., May 11, 1912; in vaudeville as boy tenor, later comedian in burlesque, then on dramatic stage, See My Lawyer, Yokel Boy; Tom, Dick and Harry. On screen 1940 in The Hit Parade.
PICTURES INCLUDE: You're in the Army Now, Roxie Hart, My Gal Sal, Footlight Serenade, Just Off Broadway, Coney Island, Cover Girl, Four Jills in a Jeep, A Lady Takes a Chance, Something for the Boys, Take It or Leave It, Diamond Horseshoe, Don Juan Quilligan, A Thousand and One Nights, If I'm Lucky, Summer Stock, Top Banana, Lucky Me, You'll Never Get Rich, 1955; 40 Pounds of Trouble, Mad, Mad, Mad World. A Guide for the Married Man, Buona Sera, Mrs. Campbell, The Boatniks, The Strongest Man in the World, Won Ton Ton, The Chicken Chronicles, The Cheap Detective.
TV: Noted Best Comedian and Best Television Performer in M.P. Daily's 2nd annual television poll, 1950.
THEATRE: Broadway Shows: High Button Shoes, Top Banana (Tony Award, best male star, 1951), Do Re Mi, A Funny Thing Happened On the Way to the Forum (Tony Award, best male actor-musical, 1972).

SILVERS, SID: Actor, writer, song writer. b. Brooklyn, N.Y., Jan. 1, 1908. On stage with Phil Baker for 7 yrs., as stooge & collab., many songs; began screen writing, 1930; Oh, Sailor, Behave; Follow The Leader, Par.
PICTURES INCLUDE: (collab. story, s.p. & appeared) Bottoms Up, Born To Dance; (collab. s.p. & appeared) Broadway Melody of 1936, (collab. story) Broadway Melody of 1938; (collab. music) Walking On Air; (add. dial. & appeared) 52nd Street; (collab. s.p.) Kentucky Kernels, The Gorilla, The Fleet's In, For Me and My Gal. Collab. s.p., Two Tickets to Broadway; collab. story, The Stooge.

SILVERSTEIN, MAURICE: Executive. b. Syracuse, N.Y., March 1, 1912; booker, salesman, MGM domestic dep't; International Dep't, MGM; supervisor Southeast Asia Hdqts. Singapore, MGM, 1938–42; OWI chief, film distribution for Europe, hdqts. London, during World War II; asst. sales supervisor, Far East, MGM; regional director, Latin America, 1947; liaison exec. to handle independent productions MGM, 1956; vice-pres., MGM International, 1957; first vice-pres., 1958; pres., MGM International, 1963; vice-pres., parent company, Metro-Goldwyn-Mayer Inc. 1970; Silverstein Int'l Corp., pres.

SILVESTER, VICTOR: (O.B.E.) Musical director. b. Wembley, England. e. St John's Leatherhead, John Lyons, Harrow. Exclusive BBC contract; with his orchestra, Records exclusively for Pye Records.

SIMMONS, JEAN: Actress. b. London, Jan. 31, 1929. e. Aida Foster Sch., London. m. Richard Brooks, director, writer. Screen debut 1944, in Give Us the Moon. Voted one of top ten British money-making stars in M.P. Herald-Fame Poll, 1950–51.
PICTURES INCLUDE: Mr. Emmanuel, Ki s the Boys Goodbye, Sports Day, Caesar and Cleopatra, Way to the Stars, Great Expectations, Hungry Hill, Black Narcissus, The Women In the Hall, Blue Lagoon, Hamlet, Adam and Evelyn, Trio, So Long as the Fair, Cage of Gold, The Clouded Yellow, Androcles and the Lion (U.S. film debut), Angel Face, Young Bess, Affair with a Stranger, The Actress, The Robe, She Couldn't Say No, A Bullet Is Waiting, The Egyptian, Desiree, Footsteps in the Fog, Guys and Dolls, Hilda Crane, This Could be the Night, Until They Sail, Home Before Dark, Spartacus, The Grass Is Greener, All the Way Home, Elmer Gantry, Divorce American Style, Rough Night in Jericho, The Happy Ending (Acad. Award nom.).

SIMMONS, JOHN: Producer, director, writer, creative consultant. e. St. Clement Danes, the Univ. of London, the Temple. Assoc. with many adv. doc. feature & TV films. Numerous International Festival awards, incl. Oscar nomin.; creative dir., Cinevista Ltd.; wrote, The Blue Bird, Loganberry Fair (lyrics, etc.), devised adv. campaigns, The Guns of Navarone, Summer Holiday; creative dir., John Simmons Creative Consultants Ltd. Join The Tea Set, Shell, Ovaltine, Waddington, Tide, Terylene, Marks & Spencer, Schweppes, Crown, Cleveland, Gold Camera Award (1st Place) for The Bosch Equation, U.S. Int. Ind. Film Festival, 1974. 1st Prize San Francisco Fest. 1975. Dev. & Dir. Cinema Ad. Awards, 1976. Corr. to Fin. Times, Variety, Campaign etc. Gold Camera Award 1977 for Stop Her, Silver Award, New York Fest. Consultant, Rank Advertising Awards (cinema) and commercial radio. Best radio commercial Award 1977. Award, Cannes 1978, 'A Clear Edge.'

SIMMONS, STANLEY: Producer, director. b. New York City, May 8, 1915. e. McBurney Preparatory School. Entered m.p. ind. 1930; pres. own distributing co.; advance man on roadshow m.p. 5 yrs.; ed. Hollywood shorts & features; apptd. managing dir. Amer. Museum of Natural History's exhibit at N.Y. World's Fair; film ed.; prod.-dir. Carnival in Brazil, 1941; served in U.S. Army 1942–45, as prod.-dir.-ed. over 100 documentaries & head of special trailer dept. ETO; supvr. color Western feature series; prod. head of Realart Productions, Inc.; lab. & exchange rep. for Soundies Distributing Corp.; prod. mgr. North Amer. Video Productions, Inc.
PICTURES INCLUDE: (prod.-dir. for video) It's a Woman's World series, Album of Songs (musical series), spots for Life Cigarettes and others. 9 Acapello musicals.

SIMMS, FRANK: Announcer. b. Tulsa, Okla., June 8, 1921. e. U. of Tulsa, 1946. Radio announcer, U.S. Air Force, WWII; announcer, KVOO, Tulsa, to N.Y., 1953.
TV: I Love Lucy, My Little Margie, Public Defender, Garry Moore Show.

SIMON, MELVIN: Executive. b. N.Y.C., Oct. 21, 1926. e. City College, New York (BBA, 1949); graduate work at Indiana Univ. Law School. Owns and operates, in partnership with two brothers, over 90 shopping centers in U.S. In 1978 formed Melvin Simon Productions, privately owned corp., to finance films.
MEMBER: Friars Club; N.Y. div.; 1978, v.p.; In-tl. Council of Shopping Centers; 1978, commerce and industry chm. of muscular dystrophy; mem. bd., Indiana Repertory Theatre 1978, corporate sponsor: Indianapolis 500 Festival, Indianapolis Museum of Arts, Indianapolis Children's Museum; Indianapolis Zoological Society.

SIMON, NEIL: Playwright. b. Bronx, N.Y. Wrote comedy for radio with brother, Danny, also TV scripts for Sid Caesar, Red Buttons, Jackie Gleason.
PLAYS INCLUDE: Barefoot in the Park, The Odd Couple, Sweet Charity, The Star Spangled Girl, Plaza Suite, Promises, Promises, The Last of the Red Hot Lovers, The Gingerbread Lady. Adapted several of own plays to screen and wrote original s.p., The Out-of-Towners.
PICTURES: Sunshine Boys, Murder by Death, The Goodbye Girl, The Cheap Detective, California Suite, Seems Like Old Times, Only When I Laugh.

SIMONE, SIMONE: Actress. b. April 23, 1914, Marseilles, France. Played in many films in Europe, among them Les Beaux Jours and Lac aux Dames. On stage in Toi C'est Moi, and others.
PICTURES INCLUDE: Girl's Dormitory, Ladies in Love, Seventh Heaven, Love and Kisses, Josette, Johnny Doesn't Live Here Any More, Silent Bell, Temptation, Harbor, Lost Women, La Ronde, Pit of Loneliness, Le Plaisir.

SIMPSON, GARRY: Producer, director, writer. e. Stanford U. Major shows with NBC-TV: Jimmy Durante Show, Armstrong Circle Theatre, Ed Wynn Show, Philco TV Playhouse, Ballet Theatre. Awards: Academy of TV Arts & Sc., Sylvania. Documentary film writer-producer awards: International Film & TV Festival, Chicago Film Festival, Broadcast Media Awards. Currently, pgm mgr., Vermont Ed. TV Network.

SIMPSON, DONALD C.: Executive. b. Alaska, 1946. e. Univ. of Oregon (Phi Beta Kappa). Began m.p. career as Warner Bros.' acct. exec. with Jack Woodell Agency in San Francisco in 1969. In 1971 joined WB as member of adv./mktg. group, handling special projects. In 1975 joined Paramount Pictures as prod. exec. for Motion Picture Division. Promoted in 1977 to v.p. in chg. of prod. for division. 1980, appt. snr. v.p., in chg. of world-wide prod.

SIMS, JOAN: Actress. b. London, England, 1930.
PICTURES INCLUDE: Dry Rot, Off the Record, No Time for Tears, Just My Luck, The Naked Truth, The Captain's Table, Passport to Shame, Emergency Ward 10, Most of the 'Carry On' films, Doctor in Love, Watch Your Stern, Twice Round The Daffodils, The Iron Maiden, Nurse on Wheels, Doctor in Clover, Doctor in Trouble, The Garnett Saga, Not Now Darling, Don't Just Lie There Say Something, Love Among the Ruins, One of Our Dinosaurs Is Missing.
TELEVISION: Born and Bred, Worzel Gummidge.

SINATRA, FRANK: Actor, singer. b. Hoboken, N.J., 1915. Sportswriter; then singer on radio various N.Y. stations; joined Harry James orchestra, later Tommy Dorsey. On screen 1943 in Reveille with Beverly. Spec. Academy Award 1945 for acting in The House I Live In, short subject on tolerance; Academy Award 1953.
PICTURES INCLUDE: Higher and Higher, Step Lively, Anchors Aweigh, It Happened in Brooklyn, Till the Clouds Roll By, Miracle of the Bells, Kissing Bandit, Take Me Out to the Ball Game, On the Town, Double Dynamite, Meet Danny Wilson, From Here to Eternity (Acad. Award. best supporting actor, 1953), Suddenly, Young at Heart, Not as a Stranger, Guys and Dolls, Tender Trap, Man With the Golden Arm, Johnny Concho, High Society, Around The World in 80 Days, Pride and the Passion, The Joker is Wild, Pal Joey, Kings Go Forth, Some Came Running, A Hole in the Head, Never So Few, Ocean's 11, Devil at Four O'Clock, Sergeants 3, The Manchurian Candidate, Come Blow Your Horn, The List of Adrian Messenger, 4 for Texas, Robin and the Seven Hoods, None But the Brave (dir.), Von Ryan's Express, Marriage on the Rocks, Cast a Giant Shadow, Assault on a Queen, The Naked Runner, Tony Rome, The Detective, Lady in Cement, Dirty Dingus Magee, That's Entertainment!, The First Deadly Sin.
TV: The Frank Sinatra Show, numerous specials, etc. Won both an Emmy and a Peabody Award. Hersholt Humanitarian Award, 1971. 1977: Contract on Cherry Street (movie).

SINCLAIR, ANDREW: Director, writer. Early career as novelist and historian, playwright. Published 18 books in U.K., U.S.A. Entered m.p. ind. 1968.
PICTURES INCLUDE: s.p.: Before Winter Comes, Adventures in the Skin Trade, The Voyage of the Beagle, You?; dir., writer: The Breaking of Bumbo, 1970; dir., writer: Under Milk Wood, 1971; prod. Malachi's Cove, 1973. Writ. The Representative, 1976; The Scarlet Letter; Martin Eden.

SINCLAIR, MARY: Actress. r.n. Mary Cook. b. San Diego, Nov. 15. Model; summer stock; TV debut, CBS, 1949. Screen debut in Arrowhead, 1953.
TV: Fireside Theatre, Studio One, Suspense, Pulitzer Prize Playhouse. Under contract CBS TV, 1951.

SINDELL, BERNARD I.: Talent agent b. Nob. 27, 1912. e. Western Reserve Univ.; vice-pres., Jaffe Agency, 1944–57; talent agent, the Sindell Agency, 1957.

SINDEN, DONALD: Actor. b. Plymouth, England, Oct. 9, 1923. Stage debut 1941 in fit-up shows; TV debut 1948; screen debut in 1953, Cruel Sea.
PICTURES INCLUDE: The Cruel Sea, Mogambo, A Day to Remember, You Know What Sailors Are, Doctor in the House, The Beachcomber, Mad About Men, Simba, Above Us the Waves, Josephine and Men, An Alligator Named Daisy, Black Tent, Eyewitness, Tiger in the Smoke, Doctor at Large, Rockets Galore, The Captain's Table, Operation Bullshine, Your Money or Your Wife, The Siege of Sydney Street, Twice Around the Daffodils, Mix Me a Person, Decline and Fall, Villain, Rentadick, The National Health, The Day of the Jackal, The Island at the Top of the World.
TV: Bullet in the Ballet, Road to Rome, Dinner With the Family, Odd Man In, Love from Italy, The Frog, The Glove, The Mystery of Edwin Drood, The Happy Ones, The Comedy of Errors, The Wars of the Roses, The Red House, Blackmail, A Bachelor Gray, Our Man at St. Marks (3 series), The Wind in the Tall Paper Chimney, A Woman Above Reproach, Call My Bluff, Relatively Speaking, Father Dear Father, The 19th Hole, Seven Days in the Life of Andrew Pelham (serial), The Assyrian Rejuvenator, The Organization (serial), The Confederacy of Wives, Tell It to The Chancellor, Two's Company (4 series), All's Well That Ends Well.

SINGER, A: Managing Director BBC Radio 1978. b. Bradford, York, England, Jan. 21, 1927; e. Giggleswick High School, Bradford Grammer Sch. Entered m.p. ind. 1943; dir. 8 films; worked as unit mgr. in Austria; TV as BBC prod., 1949; prod. 80 programs of events and features. Joined Scottish Region 2-year attachment. N.Y. office, BBC as TV officer working with American TV networks and local stations, Oct., 1953; ret. to London, 1956; prod. BBC-TV, Eye on Research and Science Intl. series; Asst. Head Outside Broadcasts 1959; exec. producer for E.B.U.; on first programme exchange between Europe and America 1962; Head of Outside Broadcasts Feature and Scientific Programmes, 1963. Head of features group, BBC Television, 1967. Controller BBC 2, 1974.

SINGLETON, PENNY: Actress. r.n. Dorothy McNulty. b. Philadelphia, Pa., September 15; e. Columbia U. First Broadway success came as top comedienne in Good News., exec. pres. AGVA.
BROADWAY: Follow Through, Hey Nonny Nonny.

PICTURES INCLUDE: Innumerable films in Blondie series; Young Widow.

SINN, ROBERT S.: Executive. b. Philadelphia, Pa., March 9, 1930; e. U. of Pa., A.B., M.S. Pres., Ultronic Systems Corp., 1960–70; chmn., The Wall Street Venture Capital Corp.; chmn., Microwave Semiconductor Corp.; chmn., Medical Electroscience & Pharmaceuticals Inc.; backer, Joe. Founder GSF Productions, Inc.

SIODMAK, CURT: Director. e. U. of Zurich. Engineer, newspaper reporter, writer in Berlin; novelist, including "F.P.1 Does Not Answer," adapt. 1932 for Ufa. Originals and screenplays in France and England including France (Le Bal), Transatlantic Tunnel, GB.
PICTURES INCLUDE: In U.S. originals and screenplays, many pictures including Her Jungle Love, Aloma of the South Sea, Par.; Invisible Woman; basis: Son of Dracula; s.p.: The Mantrap; (orig.) House of Frankenstein; collab. orig. s.p.: Shady Lady; s.p.: Beast with Five Fingers; collab. s.p., story: Berlin Express; collab. s.p.: Tarzan's Magic Fountain, Four Days Leave; dir.: Bridge of the Gorilla; collab. s.p., dir.: The Magnetic Monster; s.p.: Riders to the Stars; story, s.p.: Creature with the Atom Brain; story: Earth vs. the Flying Saucers.

SIRK, DOUGLAS: Director, writer. b. Denmark, April 26, 1900; e. U. Hamberg, Munich. Prod. for UFA, stage actor & producer, newspaperman. From 1944, dir., Hollywood.
PICTURES INCLUDE: Sleep My Love, Lured, Slightly French, Shockproof, Mystery Submarine; prod. dir.: The First Legion; dir.: Thunder on the Hill, Lady Pays Off, Weekend With Father, Has Anybody Seen My Gal?, No Room for the Groom, Meet Me at the Fair, Take Me to Town, All I Desire, Taza Son of Cochise, Magnificent Obsession, Sign of the Pagan, Captain Lightfoot, There's Always Tomorrow, All That Heaven Allows, Battle Hymn, Written on the Wind, A Time to Love and a Time to Die, Imitation of Life.

SKELTON, RED: Actor, comedian. r.n. Richard Skelton. b. Vincennes, Ind. Joined medicine show at 10; later in showboat stock, minstrel shows, vaudeville, burlesque, circus. Screen debut 1939 in Having Wonderful Time. On radio from 1936. Red Skelton Show, TV, since 1950. Composer of music, writer of short stories and painter.
PICTURES INCLUDE: Flight Command, Lady Be Good, The People vs. Dr. Kildare, Whistling in the Dark, Whistling in Dixie, Ship Ahoy, Maisie Gets Her Man, Panama Hattie, Du Barry Was a Lady, Thousands Cheer, I Dood It, Whistling in Brooklyn, Bathing Beauty, Ziegfeld Follies, Fuller Brush Man, Southern Yankee, Neptune's Daughter, Yellow Cab Man, Three Little Words, Watch the Birdie, Excuse My Dust, Texas Carnival, Lovely to Look At, The Clown, Half a Hero, Great Diamond Robbery, Public Pigeon No. 1, Those Magnificent Men and Their Flying Machines.

SKILES, MARLIN: Composer. b. Harrisburg, Pa., Dec. 17, 1906; e. Froehlich Sch. of Music, Harrisburg. Pianist for several dance orch.; mus. dir., pianist, arr. for Paul Whiteman, Irving Aaronson, others; to Hollywood, 1932; comp., arr. for radio & many m.p.
PICTURES INCLUDE: com., arr.: Over 21, Jolson Story, Gilda, Tonight and Every Night, Dead Reckoning, Callaway Went Thataway, Rose Bowl Story, Battle Zone, The Maze, Fighter Attack, Pride of the Blue Grass, Arrow in the Dust, Dial Red O, Annapolis Story, many Bowery Boys features, Sudden Danger.

SKIRBALL, JACK H.: Producer. b. Homestead, Pa., June 23, 1896. (LLD. & D.H.L.) Was with Alco Films, Cincinnati, and Metro. Later on advisory bd., div. mgr., Educational; assoc. with Wm. N. Skirball in Skirball Brothers Ohio Theatres; sales mgr. Educational, 1932. In 1932–38: in chg. prod. & distrib. for Educational. Resigned July, 1939, to take up indep. prod. In 1944–45 formed Skirball-Manning Prod. with B. Manning. Pres., Films for Television, Inc. Produced stage play, N.Y.: Jacobowsky and the Colonel, 1944. General Intl. Film Co., Inc. Recipient M.P. Pioneers Award 1925.
PICTURES INCLUDE: producer, independently: Half a Sinner (U.); Miracle on Main Street (Col.); El Milagro de la Calle Major (20th-Fox). Franchise holder with William N. Skirball for Ohio on WB, Columbia, Educational. In 1940, assoc. prod., Frank Lloyd's The Howards of Virginia (Col.); In 1941: The Lady From Cheyenne, This Woman is Mine (U.). In 1942 formed Jack H. Skirball Prod., Inc.; prod.: Saboteur (U.) In 1943, Shadow of a Doubt, It's in the Bag, then; Guest Wife, So Goes My Love, The Secret Fury, Payment on Demand, A Matter of Time.

SKIRBALL, WILLIAM N.: Exhibitor. b. Homestead, Pa. Began career with Metro in Des Moines & Chicago; states rights distrib., Cleveland; assoc. with brother, Jack H. Skirball (of Skirball-Manning prod. team), educational films br. mgr.; also brother of Joseph Skirball, first nat'l franchise owner, Pittsburgh. Currently partner Skirball Bros. circuit (10 theatres, Ohio), hdqts., Cleveland, Ohio.

SKLAR, MICHAEL: Producer. b. Philadelphia, e. Temple U. Beg. career in broadcasting field, free lancing, script writer, radio: Grand Central, First Nighter, Superman, 1939; producer, ed., writer, WMCA, N.Y., Five Star Final; joined CBS-TV, 1948 You Are There; New World A'Coming, 1947 radio prod.; wrote-prod., The Greatest Drama, series of film biog. of famous people, Fox Movietone; Eye on the World, Talkaround, The Good Morning Show, CBS-TV; prod., New Frontiers, 1956; prod., Conquest, 1957 presented in cooperation with the American Assoc. for the Advancement of Science, 1960; prod., writer, Intertel, U.S.A. 1961–62; Britain Postscript to Empire, Mexico—The Unfinished Revolution; prod., writer, Exploring The Universe, 1962; prod., Mayer-Sklar Prods., 1962–63; prod., writer, Intertel, U.S.A., 1964; This Question of Color; prod. exec., Confidential—For Women, 1966, prod., How it Happened.

SKOLSKY, SIDNEY: Columnist, Producer. b. New York, N.Y., May 2, 1905; e. N.Y. Univ.; p. Louis and Mildred Skolsky. Press agent on Broadway for Sam H. Harris, George White, Earl Carroll and others; weekly feature Tintypes for the N.Y. Sun and then to New York Daily News as columnist. In 1935, collab. on story, The Daring Young Man, 20th-Fox. In 1937 resigned as Hollywood columnist for Daily News; to New York Daily Mirror, then New York Post. Column syndicated by United Features.
PICTURES INCLUDE: prod.: The Jolson Story, 1946; Eddie Cantor Story, 1953.
TV: special: prod.: Hollywood, the Golden Era, 1961.

SLATER, DAPHNE: Actress. b. Bayswater, London, England, March 3, 1928; e. Haberdashers' Askes Sch.; Royal Acad. Dramatic Arts. Stage debut: The Rising Generation, 1945; several plays including King Lear; m.p. debut in Courtneys of Curzon Street, 1947; TV debut for BBC in I Want To Be An Actor, 1946.
TV: Emma, Shout Aloud Salvation, All the Year Round, They Fly by Twilight, Pride and Prejudice, The Affair at Assino, Beau Brummell, Jane Eyre, Precious Bane, The Dark Is Light Enough, Mary Rose, Julius Caesar, Berkeley Square, Less Than Kind, The Burning Glass, Persuasion, The Winslow Boy, She Stoops to Conquer, Nothing to Pay, The Father, The Bald Prima Donna, The Big Breaker, The Cocktail Party, Photo Finish, The Seagull, Love Story, Emergency Ward 10, Jackanory, The First Freedom, Man of Our Times, The Jazz Age, Callan, The Piano Tuner, Happy Ever After, The Pretenders, Virtue, Elizabeth R, The Staff Room, Footprints in the Sand.

SLATZER, ROBERT FRANKLIN: Writer, Director, Producer, Author; b. Marion, Ohio; April 4, 1927; e. Ohio State Univ., UCLA, 1947; Radio news commentator sportscaster, wrote radio serials; adv. dir., Brush-Moore Newspapers; feature writer, Scripps-Howard Newspapers; adv. exec., The Columbus Dispatch; syndicated columnist, New York Journal-American; write several guest columns for Walter Winchell and Dorothy Kilgallen; author of several western short stories and novels; wrote, directed, produced many industrial films, documentaries, sports specials and commercials; 1949–51, writer for Harry "Pop" Sherman Productions, Monogram Pictures, Republic Studios, Eagle-Lion Films; 1951, publicist, Hope Enterprises; Pub. Dir., Paramount Pictures; 1952, personal manager to Marilyn Monroe, Ken Maynard, James Craig, Gail Russell and other stars; 1953, story editor and assoc. prod., Joe Palooka Productions; 1953–57, staff writer Universal Studios, RKO Radio Pictures, MGM, Columbia and Paramount Studios; 1958, formed Robert F. Slatzer Productions; 1960, exec. in chg. of prod., Jaguar Pictures Corp.; 1963–65, president, Slatzer Oil & Gas Company; 1966–67, board director, United Mining & Milling Corp.; 1967–70, wrote and directed several feature films; 1970–74, exec., Columbia Pictures Corp.; 1974, resumed producing and financing features and television films; 1976, honored as "Fellow", Mark Twain Institute.
PICTURES INCLUDE: White Gold, The Obsessed, Mike and the Heiress, Under Texas Skies, They Came To Kill, Trail of the Mounties, Jungle Goddess, Montana Desperado, Pride of the Blue, Green Grass of Wyoming, The Naked Jungle, Warpaint, Broken Lance, Elephant Walk, South of Death Valley, The Big Gusher, Arctic Flight, The Hellcats, Bigfoot, John Wayne's 'No Substitute for Victory', Joniko—Eskimo Boy, Operation North Slope, Don't Go West, Mulefeathers, The Unfinished, Single Room Furnished, Viva Zapata.
TELEVISION: The Great Outdoors, Adventures of White Arrow, Let's Go Boating, The Joe Palooka Story, Amos & Andy, I am the Law, Files of Jeffrey Jones, Fireside Theatre, the Unser Story, Year of Opportunity (Award winning spec.), The Big Ones, Ken Maynard's West, Where are They Now?, The Groovy Seven, The Untouchables, The Detectives, Wild Wild West, Wagon Train, Playhouse 90, Highway Patrol, David Frost Special, Today Show.
AUTHOR: (novels) Desert Empire, Rose of the Range, Rio, Rawhide Range, The Cowboy and the Heiress, Daphne, Campaign Girl, Scarlet, The Dance Studio Hucksters, Born to be Wild, Single Room Furnished, The West is Still Wild,

Gusher, The Young Wildcats; (Biographies) The Life and Curious Death of Marilyn Monroe, The Life and Legend of Ken Maynard, Who Killed Thelma Todd?, The Duke of Thieves, Bing Crosby—The Hollow Man.

SLAVIN, GEORGE: Writer. b. Newark, N.J., 1916; e. Bucknell U., Drama Dept., Yale U.
PICTURES INCLUDE: story, collab. s.p., Intrigue; collab. story, Woman on Pier 18; collab. s.p., The Nevadan, Mystery Submarine; collab. story & s.p. Peggy, Red Mountain, City of Bad Men; collab. story, Weekend with Father, Thunder Bay, Rocket Man; collab. story, collab s.p., Smoke Signal, Uranium Boom; collab. s.p., Desert Sands.

SLEZAK, WALTER: Actor. b. Vienna, Austria, May 3, 1902; son of Leo Slezak, opera singer. In banking business before becoming actor Ufa; also on Berlin stage. In 1930 to U.S. for N.Y. stage production Meet My Sister; other roles N.Y. stage followed. First U.S. screen role in Once Upon a Honeymoon, RKO; on B'way, in My 3 Angels, Fanny.
PICTURES INCLUDE: Fallen Sparrow, Lifeboat, And Now Tomorrow, The Spanish Main, Cornered, Sinbad the Sailor, Born to Kill, Riffraff, Pirate, Inspector General, Yellow Cab Man, Bedtime for Bonzo, People Will Talk, Confidentially Connie, Call Me Madam, White Witch Doctor, Steel Cage, The Gazebo, Come September, Swinger's Paradise, Emil and the Detectives, 24 Hours To Kill, Dr. Coppelius, Black Beauty.

SLOAN, JOHN R.: Producer. e. Merchiston Castle, Edinburgh, 1932–39; asst. dir. and prod. man. Warners, London, Hollywood; 1939–46, Army Service.
PICTURES INCLUDE: Sea Devils, The End of the Affair, Port Afrique, Abandon Ship, The Safecracker, Beyond this Place, The Killers of Kilimanjaro, Johnny Nobody, The Reluctant Saint, The Running Man, The Last Command, To Sir With Love, Fragment of Fear, Dad's Army, Lord Jim, No Sex Please We're British, The Odessa File, Force From Navarone.

SLOCOMBE, DOUGLAS: Cinematographer. b. England, 1913. Former journalist.
PICTURES: Dead of Night, The Captive Heart, Hue and Cry, The Loves of Joanna Godden, It Always Rains on Sunday, Saraband for Dead Lovers, Kind Hearts and Coronets, Cage of Gold, The Lavender Hill Mob, The Man in the White Suit, The Titfield Thunderbolt, Man in the Sky, The Smallest Show on Earth, Tread Softly, Stranger, Circus of Horrors, The Young Ones, The L-Shaped Room, Freud, The Servant, Guns at Batashi, A High Wind in Jamaica, The Blue Max, Promise Her Anything, The Vampire Killers, Fathom, Robbery, Boom, The Lion in Winter, The Italian Job, The Music Lovers, Murphy's War, Jesus Christ Superstar, The Great Gatsby, Rollerball, Hedda, Nasty Habits, Julia, Lost and Found, Nijinsky, Raiders of the Lost Ark.
TELEVISION: Love Among the Ruins, The Corn Is Green, etc.

SMAKWITZ, CHARLES A.: e. Syracuse University, named by Warner Bros. as dist. mgr. Albany, Troy and Utica, and named as zone mgr. Warner Bros., New York State Theatres. Made zone mgr. of Stanley Warner Theatres for the State of New Jersey and New York State Theatres added to N.J. Zone and made headquarters in Newark, N.J. in 1955, transferred to New York City home office as national director of public relations, publicity, advertising for Stanley Warner Corp. nation-wide. In the various areas was Mayor's Rehabilitation and Urban Development Com. of Albany, State Albany Chairman War Activities Committee, National Public Dir. Red Cross Fund Organized Albany V.C. Tent #9 and served as Chief Barker 3 years, 1949–1952, elected National Representative V.C. of America. Member N.Y. State Program and Planning Committee, Pres. Heart Assn. of Albany County, N.J. State Chairman Nat. Conf. of Christian and Jews 1955–62. Organized and Pres. of Syr. Un. of Greater, N.Y. Served as Office of V.C. of N.Y. Assistant to Spyros R. Skoveas 1969–71, served as International-Ambassador at large of V.C. International Consultant exhibition, production, promotion, real estate and public relations.

SMART, RALPH: Writer, producer, director. b. London, Eng., 1908. Dir. documentaries and wrote s.p. for features 1927–40; prod. films for Royal Australian A.F. 1940–44; assoc. prod. The Overlanders, prod. dir. and s.p. Bush Christmas in Australia; ret. to England to dir. Boy, Girl and a Bike, Bitter Springs, Never Take No for An Answer, Always a Bride; dir. TV series Robin Hood, 1955–56; exec. prod. Incorporated Television programme Co., 1957; series William Tell, The Invisible Man, prod. author, 2 series, Danger Man; now freelancing.

SMART, ROY L.: Exhibitor. b. Clayton, Ala. e. U. of Ala., drama critic, city ed. Birmingham Age-Herald; U.S. Naval Air Corps, mgr. theatres, Ala., Fla., Carolinas; dist. mgr. Wilby-Kincey theatres, N.C. & S.C. assistant gen. mgr., hdqts., Charlotte, N.C.; during WW II Naval Aviation Cadet Selection Bd., Naval Officer Procurement Comm., co-ordinator

War Activities Comm. for N.C. & S.C. Variety Club, past chief barker; American Legion, past vice commander; Kiwanis, past pres.; City School Commissioner, Charlotte, N.C.; past pres. Charlotte City Club; v.p. Charlotte Country Club; m.p. pioneer; bd. member, Charlotte Symphony Orch.

SMIGHT, JACK: Director. b. Minneapolis, Minn., 1926
PICTURES INCLUDE: I'd Rather Be Rich, The Third Day, Harper, Kaleidoscope, The Secret War of Harry Frigg, No Way to Treat a Lady, Strategy of Terror, The Illustrated Man, The Travelling Executioner, Rabbit Run, Dr. Frankenstein, Frankenstein: The True Story, Airport 1975, Midway, Damnation Alley, Fast Break, Loving Couples.
TV: Banacek, Columbo, etc.

SMITH, ALEXIS: Actress. b. Penticton, Can., June 8, 1921; e. Los Angeles City Coll. In summer stock British Columbia; star in coll. prod., Night of January 16th; in m.p. for Warner Bros.
PICTURES INCLUDE: Smiling Ghost, Dive Bomber, Steel Against the Sky, Gentleman Jim, Thank Your Lucky Stars, Constant Nymph, Conflict, Adventures of Mark Twain, Rhapsody in Blue, Horn Blows at Midnight (Star of Tomorrow, 1943), One More Tomorrow, Night and Day, Of Human Bondage, Stallion Road, Two Mrs. Carrolls, Woman in White, Decision of Christopher Blake, Whiplash, South of St. Louis, Any Number Can Play, One Last Fling, Undercover Girl, Wyomying Hall, Montana, Here Comes the Groom, Cave of the Outlaws, Turning Point, Split Second, Sleeping Tiger, Eternal Sea, The Young Philadelphians, Once Is Not Enough, The Little Girl Who Lives Down the Lane, Casey's Shadow.
BROADWAY: Follies, 1971, Platinum, 1978.

SMITH, A. BERKELEY: TV commentator, producer. b. Bournemouth, Eng., Dec. 8, 1918. e. Blundell's Sch., St. Andrews U. Royal Artillery, 1939–46; lecture tour, U.S., 1945; prod.-comment., BBC North American service, 1946; to U.N. Assembly, New York, for BBC home service, 1949; TV as BBC outside broadcasts prod., 1949; devised, prod. sports & farming series with other documentaries; Comm. State Occasions. Theatre Shows, etc., 1951; prod. Show Places series; prod. exchange program from R.T.F. Paris; commentator Coronation & all State visits, 1953; prod. Arenascope, programs radio show, 1954; asst. head TV outside broadcasts. Feb. 1955; head outside broadcasts Southern Television Ltd., 1958; asst. Con. Programs, 1961; Con. Programs (Southern TV Ltd), 1964; dir. Southern TV, 1965, Left Dec. 75, Dir. ITV Prog. Planning, 1976.

SMITH, CHARLIE MARTIN: Actor. b. 1955. e. Calif. State Univ. f. is animation artist Frank Smith.
PICTURES INCLUDE: The Culpepper Cattle Company, Fuzz, The Spikes Gang, American Graffiti, More American Graffiti.
TELEVISION: The Brady Bunch, Monte Nash.

SMITH, CONSTANCE: Actress. r.n. Constance Smyth. b. Limerick, Ire.; e. St. Louis Convent. Began career as model for Noel Mayne; winner of beauty contest Screen Magazine. Free-lance actress, studios in Eng., prior to Hollywood m.p. debut in The Mudlark.
PICTURES INCLUDE: Brighton Rock, Now Barrabas, Trottie True, Murder at the Window, Blackmail, The Perfect Woman, Room to Let, The 13th Letter, I'll Never Forget You, Red Skies of Montana, Treasure of the Golden Condor, Lure of the Wilderness, Taxi, Man in the Attic, Big Tipoff.

SMITH, HOWARD K.: News commentator. b. Ferriday, La., May 12, 1914. e. Tulane Univ., 1936. Heidelberg U., Germany; Oxford U., Rhodes Scholarship. United Press, London, 1939; United Press Bureau, Copenhagen; United Press, Berlin, 1940; joined CBS News, Berlin corr., 1941. Reported on occupied Europe from Switzerland to 1944; covered Nuremberg trials, 1946; ret. to U.S., moderator, commentator or reporter, CBS Reports, Face the Nation, Eyewitness to History, The Great Challenge, numerous news specials. Sunday night news analysis. CBS News Washington corr., 1957; chief corr. & mgr., Washington Bureau, 1961; joined, ABC News, Jan. 1962. News and Comment, ABC news. Anchorman and Commentator, ABC Evening News. Author: Last Train from Berlin, 1942, The State of Europe, 1949. Washington, D.C.—The Story of Our Nation's Capital, 1967.

SMITH, HY: Executive. b. New York City, June 3, 1934. e. Baruch School, CCNY, BBA. Joined Paramount Pictures 1967, foreign ad.-pub coordinator; 1969-joined United Artists as foreign ad-pub mgr., named int'l. ad-pub dir., 1970; named v.p.; intl. adv-pub. 1976; Appointed vice pres. worldwide Advertising, publicity and promotion, July 1978; 1981, named first v.p., adv./pub./promo.

SMITH, JACLYN: Actress. b. Houston, Texas, Oct. 26. Started acting while in high school and studied drama and psychology at Trinity Univ. in San Antonio. Appeared in many commercials as model.
PICTURES INCLUDE: Bootleggers, The Adventures.

TV: McCloud, Get Christy Love, The Rookies, World of Disney, Switch, Charlie's Angels (regular).

SMITH, JACQUELINE: Executive. b. Phila., Pa., May 24, 1933. e. Antioch College, 1954. m. William Dale Smith, novelist (pseudonym David Anthony). Actress, Bermudiana Theatre in Bermuda, The Antioch Theatre in Ohio and several little theatres in Washington, D.C.; with the Stanford U. Players. Did research and writing for RCA, worked as a nursery school teacher and directed Little Theatre groups in the West Coast area. 1957: wrote and produced over 100 weekly children's programs at KPIX, San Francisco. Promotion director at WPIX-TV, N.Y. Worked with CBS TV Network for over 5 yrs. as general prog. exec. and exec. prod. of CBS West Coast Daytime Programs. Currently director of special projects at Warner Bros. Television Dept. and executive producer of Warner Bros. Animation Division.

SMITH, JOSEPH P.: Executive. b. Bklyn, N.Y. e. Columbia Univ. Started career Wall Street; joined RKO Radio Pictures, served in sales and managerial posts; exec. vice-pres., Lippert Productions, Hollywood; formed, president, Telepictures, Inc; pres., Pathe Pictures, Inc., Pathe News, Inc.

SMITH, KATE: Performer. r.n. Kathryn Elizabeth S. b. Greenville, Va., May 1, 1909; on Broadway in musicals, Honeymoon Lane, Hit the Deck, Flying High; joined Ted Collins for radio prog., 1931; various variety programs followed; started daytime prog. as commentator, 1938, now has daytime Kate Smith Hour and weekly Kate Smith Evening Hour on NBC-TV in N.Y.

SMITH, KENT: Actor. On screen from 1943 in Forever and a Day, Hitler's Children, This Land is Mine; N.Y. stage, The Autumn Garden and The Wild Duck.
PICTURES INCLUDE: Youth Runs Wild, The Cat People, Three Russian Girls, The Spiral Staircase, Nora Prentiss, Magic Town, Voice of the Turtle, Fountainhead, Damned Don't Cry, My Foolish Heart, Paula, Commanche, The Balcony, Covenant with Death, Games, Kona Coast, Assignment to Kill, Pete an' Tillie, Cops and Robbers.
TV: Richard II, Profiles in Courage, The Outer Limits, Peyton Place.

SMITH, MAGGIE: Actress. b. Ilford, England, 1934. Early career Oxford Playhouse. Numerous TV appearances Britain, America.
PICTURES INCLUDE: Nowhere to Go, The V.I.P.s, Young Cassidy, Othello, The Honey Pot, Hot Millions, The Prime of Miss Jean Brodie (Acad. Award, Best Actress), Oh What a Lovely War, Love and Pain, Travels with my Aunt, Murder by Death, Death on the Nile, California Suite (AA), Clash of the Titans.

SMITH, MAURICE: Producer, director, writer. b. London, England, May 12, 1939. e. St. Ignatius College. Prior to entering m.p. industry, worked in bank in England, on newspaper in Canada, pool hustler, general contractor in Los Angeles, Calif.
PICTURES INCLUDE: The Glory Stompers, Scream Free, Cycle Savages, Hard Trail, Diamond Stud, Love Swedish Style, November Children, How Come Nobody's On Our Side, Joys of Jezebel.

SMITH, RAY E.: Executive. v.p., asst. sect. & asst. treas., buyer & booker, union negotiator, Jamestown Amusement Co., Inc. & Shea Enterprises, New York, N.Y., b. Oct. 10, 1908. e. Northhampton Commercial College, 1930.

SMITH, ROGER: Actor. b. South Gate, Calif., Dec. 18, 1932. e. U. of Arizona, started career at age 7, one of the Meglin Kiddies, appearing at the Mayan Theater, Wilshire, Ebell.
PICTURES INCLUDE: No Time to be Young, Crash Landing, Operation Madball, Man of a Thousand Faces, Never Steal Anything Small, Aunti Mame, Rogues Gallery.
TV: The Horace Heidt Show, Ted Mack Original Amateur Hour, 77 Sunset Strip, writer, ABC-TV, sings, composes, American folk songs.

SMITH, WILLIAM: Actor.
PICTURES: Twilight's Last Gleaming, The Frisco Kid, Any Which Way You Can.
TELEVISION: Rich Man, Poor Man, Hawaii 5-0

SMOLEN, DONALD E.: Executive. b. New York City, Aug. 10, 1923; e. NYU 1943, Pratt Institute 1947, Ecole Des Beaux Arts 1949. Art dept. Fox, 1940–41; art dept. Kayton Spiero Advtg., 1942; illustrator designer, Gilbert Miller Studios 1946–49; free lance illustrator, designer, 1951–65 servicing such accounts as UA, Fox, Warner Bros., TWA, Ford Motors; dir. of adv., UA. Resigned 1974 to form own co., Donald E. Smolen and Associates, consultant for m.p. adv.; 1975 merged to form Smolen, Smith and Connolly, advertising and marketing consultants to m.p. industry. Created ad campaigns for All the Presidents' Men, Fiddler on the Roof, Rocky, Superman, Star Wars.

SNAPER, WILBUR: Exhibitor. b. Perth Amboy, N.J., Oct. 30, 1911. e. Yale U. 1933, N.J. Law, 1935. Pres. Snaper Theatres, New York, nat'l pres. Allied States Assn.; partner 1957. Member: Yale Club, Variety Club, N.Y. Bridge Club; pres. Triangle Theatres; pres., AIT Theatres, N.J.; pres. Triangle Theatres.

SNELL, PETER R.E.: Producer. b. 1941. Prod.: 1967: Winters Tale, Some May Live, A Month in the Country, Carnaby 68. 1968: Subterfuge. 1969–70: Juliet Ceasar, Goodbye Gemini. 1971: Anthony and Cleopatra. 1972: The Wicker Man. Appt. head of prod. and man. dir. British Lion 1973. Joined Robert Stigwood group 1975. Hennessy. 1976: Returned to indep. prod. 1978: Bear Island. 1980: Goodbye California.

SNODGRESS, CARRIE: Actress. b. Chicago, IXLL., Oct 27; e. Northern II The nois U. Acted with Goodman Theatre where plays include All Way Home, Oh What a Lovely War, Caesar and Cleopatra and Tartuffe (Sarah Siddons Award, 1966).
PICTURES INCLUDE: Rabbitt, Run, Diary of a Mad Housewife, The Fury.
TV: World Premier (Silent Night, Lonely Night, The Whole World is Watching), The Outsider, The Virginian, Judd for the Defense, Medical Center, Marcus Welby, M.D.

SNOWDEN, ALEC CRAWFORD: Independent producer b. Leeds. Ent. m.p. ind. as asst. dir. with Stoll Film Co. Later with Fuller Hayward Theatre Corp., New Zealand; subsequently with British Films Ltd., G-B Screen Services, Spectator Films; Merton Park Studios Ltd. Instigated and prod. Edgar Lustgarten Scotland Yard series.
PICTURES INCLUDE: Brain Machine, Case of the Red Monkey, Confession (Deadliest Sin), Timeslip, Dial 999 (Way Out), Intimate Stranger (The Guilty Secret), The Hypnotist, Counterfeit Plan, Man in the Shadow, The Key Man, Escapement, The Strange Awakening, Broth of a Boy, This Other Eden, Over the Odds.

SNOWDON, LEIGH: Actress. b. Memphis, Tenn., June 28, 1932. e. Lambeth College, Jackson, Tenn. Model, TV appearances.
PICTURES INCLUDE: Kiss Me Deadly, All That Heaven Allows, Francis in the Navy, Rawhide Years, Square Jungle, Creature Walks Among Us, Outside the Law.

SNYDER, TOM: Newscaster, show host. b. Milwaukee, May 12, 1936. e. Marquette Univ. First job in news dept. of WRIT, Milwaukee. Subsequently with WSAV-TV, Savannah; WAII-TV, Atlanta; KTLA-TV, Los Angeles; and KYW-TV, Philadelphia, before moving to KNBC in Los Angeles in 1970 as anchorman for weeknight newscast. Named host of NBC-TV's Tomorrow program in Oct., 1973, and moved to N.Y.C. in Dec., 1974, at which time began as anchorman of one-hour segment of NewsCenter 4. In Aug., 1975, inaugurated the Monday-thru-Friday editions of NBC News Update, one-minute prime time news spot. Now host for Tommorow talk show.

SNYDER, WILLIAM L.: Producer, executive. b. Baltimore, Md., Feb. 14, 1920; e. B.A. The John Hopkins U., 1940. Lt. Comnder., U.S. Navy WWII, 1941–45. Established Rembrandt Films, N.Y.C., 1948 as importer and dist. of foreign films. Co-prod. White Mane (UA, dom.), winner Cannes Fest. Grand Prize, seven other int'l awards, 1945. Prod. 13 Tom & Jerry Cartoons (MGM) and more than 100 Miss Nightingale, She, Little Lord Fauntleroy, The Secret Army (2 series). Popeye and Krazy Kat cartoons for U.S. TV plus number cartoons (Para.)., 1956. Won Academy Award for cartoon Munro (Para.), 1961. Rec'd Academy nominations for Self Defense for Cowards (1962), The Game (1963), How to Avoid Friendship (1964) and Nudnik (1965). Prod. cartoon feature Alice in Paris (Childhood Prodns.), 1966. Prod. I a Woman II, 1968:(Chevron Picts.), and The Daughter (Chevron Picts.), 1970.

SOAMES, RICHARD: Executive. b. London, England, 1936. Joined Film Finances Ltd. 1972; Appt. director Film Finances Ltd., 1977: Appt. man. dir. 1979. Appt. pres. Film Finances Canada Ltd.

SOBLE, RON: Actor. b. Chicago, March 28, 1932. e. Univ. of Michigan. Served U.S. Army, 11th Airborne, in Japan. Studied acting in New York and was member of Jose Quintero's Circle in the Square Players. Acted in such plays as Romeo and Juliet, Murder in the Cathedral, The Petrified Forest; prod. assoc. on TV series Suspense and Danger, and appeared in 56 series. Co-star in The Monroes TV show.
PICTURES INCLUDE: Navajo Run, Al Capone, The Cincinnati Kid, Joe Kidd.

SOBOL, LOUIS: New York columnist, N.Y. World-Journal-Tribune and other papers. b. New Haven, Conn., Aug. 10, 1896. Universal short series, Down Memory Lane, 1933. Contributor of articles and short stories to nat'l mags. Broadcast Lucky Strike Cigarettes for 10 weeks; Ludwig Baumann 39 weeks, Borden's 26 weeks; ABC network 45 weeks; first novel published, Six Lost Women, also Some Days Were Happy & Along the B'way Beat, 1951. Appeared several times at Loew's State Theatre, New York, with own unit; also one week at Palace Theatre. Broadway columnist, N.Y. Evening Graphic, 1929–31; joined Journal-American and Hearst newspapers 1931. Author s.p., Bill's Gay Nineties, collab. s.p., Need for Each Other; Broadway Beat & The Longest Street; ABC network.

SOCHIN, IRVING: Executive. b. Boston, Mass., Mar. 15, 1910; e. English H.S., 1927. In vaude., night clubs with own band & act; salesman, U.A., May, 1938; city salesman, U.A., Cincinnati, 1940; 20th Fox, Cincinnati, 1941; 20th Fox sales mgr., Cincinnati, 1942–46; acting br. mgr., Indianapolis, 1946. Headed booking, buying co., Theatre Owners Corp., to Aug. 1947; then Cincinnati br. mgr., Universal to Jan. 1, 1950; sales mgr., U.I. spcl. films div. asst. to gen. sales mgr. 1952–53. Short subjects sales mgr., gen. sales man. for Rank Film Dist. of America, Inc., 1957–58. Member: Masonic Lodge; Variety Club (past chief barker), Cincinnati Tent 3, 1947–48; spec. rep., Continental Pictures, 1960; v.p., gen. sls. mgr.; Times Film Corp., 1961–64; v.p., gen. sls. mgr., Rizzoli Film Distribs. Inc. 1964; West div. mgr. 20th-Fox, 1969; Fox western div. mgr., 1969–75; Fox special films head, 1975; West div. mgr. Ganma III, 1976–77; 1978, vice pres. and gen'l sales mgr. of Vadib International Films, San Francisco based distribution co. Now retired.

SOFAER, ABRAHAM: Actor. b. Rangoon, Burma, Oct. 1, 1896. Stage debut 1921 in Chas. Doran Shakespeare Co.'s first London appearance, Glorianna, 1925; starred in several London productions & subsequently Old Vic & Stratford-on-Avon; broadcaster & TV star; played in many British films; Broadway stage and films in Hollywood.
PICTURES INCLUDE: His Majesty O'Keefe, Elephant Walk, The Naked Jungle, Out of the Clouds, Bhowani Junction, Sinbad, King of Kings, Head.

SOLDATI, MARIO: Director. b. Turin, Italy, 1906. e. Superior Institute of the History of Art, Rome. Lecturer, Columbia U.; author of America First Love, other books; m.p. dir. since 1939.
PICTURES INCLUDE: O.K. Nero, Wayward Wife, Stranger's Hand, Don Juan's Night of Love.

SOLO, ROBERT H.: Executive. Early career as agent with Ashley-Famous; later production as exec. asst. to Jack Warner and Walter MacEwen at Warner Bros. In London prod. Scrooge for Cinema Center Films, 1970; co-prod. The Devils, 1971; 1971, named WB v.p., foreign production 1974, named exec. v.p., prod. at Burbank Studio. Now indep. prod. Invasion of the Body Snatchers, 1978, for United Artists; The Awakening (EMI-Orion), 1980; I, The Jury (American Cinema), 1981.

SOLOMON, FLORENCE: Executive. b. New York City. e. Hunter College. Research mgr. & Ligon Johnson's copyright title search firm, 1937–65; dir. for research, Entertainment Copyright Research Co., Inc., 1965–1968; ASCAP (Music Index-Library) 1968-present. Pres. Cinema History Correspondent Society assoc. ed. TV Movies, research associate, The Great Movie Series, The Slapstick Queens, The Paramount Pretties, The MGM Stock Co.; The RKO Gals, The Glamour Girls, The Great Spy Pictures, Actors' Television Credits, 1950–1972; Good Dames, Hollywood's Great Love Teams, Liza! Elvis!, The Debonairs, The Swashbucklers, Hollywood Players: The Forties, The Great Gangster Pictures, Hollywood Players: The Thirties, The Great Western Pictures, the All-Americans, Leading Ladies, The Great Science Fiction Pictures, Hollywood Character Actors, Film Actors Guide: Western Europe, Hollywood on Hollywood, Hollywood Beauties, The Funsters, The Forties Gals, Actors TV Credits: Supplement I, The Hollywood Regulars, Best of MGM: The Golden Years.

SOLOMON, MICHAEL JAY: TV Executive. b. Jan. 20, 1938. e. Emerson in Boston; N.Y.U. Evening School of Commercial while working at first job with United Artists in 1956. Became student booker. Hired by Seymour Florin as booker for one year; returned to UA in intl. dept. January, 1960 went to Panama as asst. to mgr. of Central America. Transferred to Bogota after one yr.; made mgr. of UA in Peru and Bolivia. In 1964 joined MCA Latin American div., reorganizing office in Mexico and later opening office in Brazil. Made v.p., 1968, of MCA-TV. Supervised Latin American and Caribbean div.; 1973 made head of feature film sales to tv stations internationally while still supervising MCA business in Latin America. Resigned 1977 to form Michael Jay Solomon Films International, Inc. & Solomon International TV Newsletter. In 1978 formed Telepictures Corporation to distribute films worldwide and enter production.

SOLOMON, THEODORE GEORGE: Executive. b. Jan. 5, 1920, e. LSU, 1941. Advisor/Consultant to Gulf States Theatres, New Orleans, LA, operating theatres in Alabama, Louisiana, Mississippi, and Texarkana; Past chm. of the National Association of Theatre Owners, past president of the National Association of Theatre Owners.

SOLOW, SIDNEY PAUL: Executive. b. Jersey City, N.J., Sept., 15, 1910. e. New York Univ., 1926–30; chief chemist, Consolidated Film Industries, 1932–36; plant supt., 1937–42;

gen. mgr., 1942; Lecturer, University of Southern California (USC), Department of Cinema, 1947–66; Pacific Coast Section, SMPTE, 1948–49; assoc. member, American Society of Cinematographers, 1948-present; chmn. docum. comm., Acad. of M.P. Arts & Sciences, 1951–56; bd. of dir., Acad. of TV Arts & Sciences, 1953; pres., Consolidated Film Industries, 1954 to 1977 when named chrn. exec. comm.; v.p. Republic Pictures Corp., 1954; chmn. scientific & technical awards comm., Acad. of M.P. Arts & Sciences; treas., SMPTE, 1959–60; Permanent Charities Comm., 1958; campaign chmn, Permanent Charities, 1961; mot. pic. section chmn, United Jewish Welfare Fund, 1966; professor, USC, 1966 to present; Honarary Life Member, American Cinema Editors, 1965; Honorary Member, Delta Kappa Alpha, Nat'l Cinema Fraternity, 1972; Winner of Progress Medal, SMPTE, 1974. Elected fellow British Kinematograph & TV Society, 1978.

SOLT, ANDREW: Writer. b. Budapest, Hungary, June 7, 1916; e. St. Stephen's Coll.
PICTURES INCLUDE: They All Kissed the Bride, Without Reservations, Joan of Arc, Little Women, Jolson Story, In a Lonely Place, Thunder on the Hill, Lovely to Look At; orig. s.p. For the First Time.
TV: Hitchcock Presents, Ford Theatre, Douglas Fairbanks Presents, Wire Service, General Electric Theatre, BBC and Stuttgart TV.
STAGE: 1973, Geld In Der Tasche, produced by Theatre am Kurfurstendamm, West Berlin.

SOLTZ, CHARLENE E.: Executive. b. New London, Conn. e. Mitchell College and University of Bridgeport. Entered motion picture industry in 1970 as assistant to director of press information for Motion Picture Association of America, Inc. In 1970 named director of press information.

SOMERS, SUZANNE: Actress. b. San Bruno, CA, Oct. 16, 1946. e. Lone Mountain, San Francisco College for Women. Pursued modeling career; worked as regular on Mantrap, syndicated talk show. Did summer stock and theatrical films. Wrote books: Touch Me Again, Some People Live More Than Others. Biggest TV success in Three's Company series.
PICTURES: Bullitt, Daddy's Gone A-Hunting, Fools, Magnum Force, American Graffiti, Yesterday's Hero, Nothing Personal.
TELEVISION: One Day at a Time, Lotsa Luck, The Rockford Files, Starsky & Hutch, The Rich Little Show, Battle of the Network Stars, Us Against the World, Love Boat, etc. TV movies: Happily Ever After, The Princess and the Lumberjack, Zuma Beach, Ants.

SOMMER, ELKE: Actress. b. Germany, 1941. To Britain 1956 English. Ent. films in Germany, 1958, and since made films in Germany and Italy incl. Friend of the Jaguar, Traveling Luxury, Heaven and Cupid, Ship of the Dead. 1960: made debut in British films.
PICTURES INCLUDE: Don't Bother to Knock, The Victors, The Money Trap, Love the Italian Way, A Shot in the Dark, The Venetian Affair, Deadlier than the Male, Frontier Hellcat. Under contract to ABPC; The Corrupt Ones, The Wicked Dreams of Paula Schultz, They Came to Rob Las Vegas, The Wrecking Crew, Baron Blood, Percy, Zeppelin, Ten Little Indians, Lisa and the Devil, The Prisoner of Zenda.

SONDERGAARD, GALE: Actress. b. Litchfield, Minn.; m. Herbert Biberman dir.; e. Univ. of Minnesota, A.B. On stage in Strange Interlude, Red Rust, and others. In 1936: Anthony Adverse, W.B. In 1937: Maid of Salem, Par.; Seventh Heaven, 20th-Fox. Ranked first in Academy 1936 awards as outstanding actress in supporting role for Anthony Adverse, The Life of Emile Zola, W.B.
PICTURES INCLUDE: Isle of Forgotten Sins, The Strange Death of Adolph Hitler, The Climax, The Invisible Man's Revenge, Gypsy Wildcat, Christmas Holiday, Enter Arsene Lupin, Anna and the King of Siam, Road to Rio, Pirates of Monterey, East Side, West Side, Return of a Man Called Horse.

SONENFELD, OTTO: Producer, distributor. Former br. mgr., RKO, Czechoslovakia, ind. prod. German & Czech films, latter including Erotikon (silent), Ecstasy, first with Hedy Lamarr, Revolution of Blood and Mud, first Czech feature-length doc.; first Israeli prod. Adama (Tomorrow is a Wonderful Day); oper. as Forum Films, hdqts., Tel-Aviv. Also rep. Korda-London Film, London & Lux Films, Rome and Israel; member Int'l Fed. of Film Prod., Paris.

SORIANO, DALE: Publicist, b. Brooklyn, N.Y. Ent. m.p. Ind. as a reelboy in projection room, later usher, sign painter, manager, film booker stagehand (NBC-CBS-ABC). Orchestra leader, director of info. for various N.Y.C. depts., licenses, real estate, law, public events and firearms control board. Publicist for Americana festivals, various veteran organizations. V.F.W., A.L., D.A.V., C.W.V. and Army & Navy Union and many philanthropic organizations. World War II served with 1st Marine Div. U.S.M.C. in S.W. Pacific thea. of oper. 1960–68 v.p. Publicists Association, I.A.T.S.E.

conducted many TV and vet columns for the Brooklyn Eagle and independent newspapers. Show*Biz Column 1st for the Brooklyn Daily Bulletin. Also stage, records, movies, radio and TV Editor. Pres. of Lighthouse Productions and pres. of Flatlands Chamber of Commerce; pres. National Council of Civic Assn. Member of Motion Picture Pioneers, National Publicists Association, and American Newspaper Guild.

SORRELL, HELENA: Dramatic coach. b. Edinburgh, Scotland, Dec. 30. e. Royal Academy of Dramatic Arts, London, Eng., and Edinburgh, Scotland. Toured England, Ireland, Scotland and Wales as dramatic actress and director. With Jessie Bonstelle, Detroit, six seasons as actress and director in Bonstelle Prod.; dir of Bonstelle Dramatic School, Detroit. Studied singing, piano, music and dancing abroad and in America. Played and toured all over America and Canada in such stage plays as The Fool, Autumn Crocus, Dinner at Eight, Death Takes a Holiday, Peter Ibbesten, Design for Living, Cynara, Philip Goes Forth. Picture career; dramatic coach, RKO Radio Studios, Selznick, 20th-Fox.

SORVINO, PAUL: Actor. b. New York City. Acted on Bdwy.; broke into films with Where's Poppa in 1970.
PICTURES: Day of the Dolphin, Made for Each Other, The Gambler, A Touch of Class, Oh, God, Bloodbrothers, Slow Dancing in the Big City, The Brink's Job, Lost and Found, Cruising.
TELEVISION: Seventh Avenue, Tell Me Where It Hurts, etc.

SOTHERN, ANN: Actress. b. Valley City, N.D., Jan. 23, 1923; e. Washington U.; p. Annette Yde-Lake, opera singer. On stage, in m.p. since 1934.
PICTURES INCLUDE: Let's Fall in Love, Melody in Spring, Three Hearts for Julia, Swing Shift Maisie, Cry Havoc, Thousands Cheer, Maisie series, April Showers, Letter to Three Wives, Judge Steps Out, Words and Music, Nancy Goes to Rio, Blue Gardenia, Lady in a Cage, Sylvia, Chubasco, The Killing Kind, Golden Needles, Crazy Mama, The Manitou.
TV: Private Secretary, Ann Sothern Show, Captain and the Kings.

SOUL, DAVID: Actor. b. Chicago, Aug. 28. Attended several colleges but gave up studies to pursue a career in music. Made 25 singing appearances on The Merv Griffin Show where was spotted and given screen test. Signed contract with Screen Gems and given starring role in ABC-TV series, Here Come the Brides.
PICTURES INCLUDE: Johnny Got His Gun, Magnum Force, Dog Pound Shuffle.
TV: Guest Star: The Streets of San Francisco, Cannon, Medical Center, The Rookies, Ironside, Star Trek, McMillan and Wife, Dan August, Circle of Fear, Owen Marshall, Counselor at Law. Movies: The Disappearance of Flight 412, Intertect, Movin' On, Little Ladies of the Night. Series: Starsky and Hutch.

SPACEK, SISSY: Actress. b. Quitman, Texas. Christened Mary Elizabeth. Cousin of actor Rip Torn. Was photographic model; attended acting classes in New York under Lee Strasberg.
PICTURES INCLUDE: Prime Cut (debut), Ginger in the Morning, Badlands, Carrie, Welcome to L.A., 3 Women, Heart Beat, Coal Miners' Daughter, Raggedy Man.
TV: The Girls of Huntington House, The Migrants, Katherine (all TV movies), two episodes of The Waltons.

SPALLA, JOSEPH SALVATORE "RICK": Executive, producer. b. Sandusky, Ohio, May 22, 1923. e. Ohio State U. 1943 and 1946; U. of So. Calif., B.A., 1953. m. Shirley Egland. Studied voice while teenager, soloist with Sandusky High a cappella choir, Ohio State U. Chorus and Men's Glee Club & OSU Symphonic Choir. To Hollywood, 1946, as City Messenger. Member, Screen Extras Guild, Screen Actors Guild. Co-owner of cab co. 1953–54, cameraman with Hollywood Prod. Co., travel series: The Open Road and document series, Before Your Eyes. 1954–56, one of the founders, prod. head and v.p., Bill Burrud Prod., Inc. Started half-hour weekly series, Wanderlust (later syndicated as Vagabond). Prod. supervisor and co-creator of Assignment America, 1956–57, v.p. and gen. mgr. of Jet TV and Film Prods., Inc. Exec. prod. of TV: The Open Road. Creator and exec. prod. of High Road to Danger, 1957–62, formed RSVP, Rick Spalla Video Productions. Prod. Those Faraway Places, Enchanted Lands. Created series, Guest Shot, 1962–67, formed Hollywood Newsreel Syndicate, Inc., sub. of RSVP; created, prod. Hollywood Backstage TV series, prod., dir. Hollywood's Fantastic Artists and Models Ball (TV special); producer-director of TV series, Portrait of a Star, (12 hour-long specials) also TV series Holiday on Wheels. Owns millions of feet of film on stars, newsreel, travelogue footage etc. Producer of TV commercials and industrial films.

SPARKS, ROBERT: Producer. b. West Union, Ohio; e. U. of Cincinnati Law School; assoc. prod. Para., 1932; story

ed., RKO, 1935; prod. Columbia, 1938; U.S.M.C., 1942; Univ., 1946; exec. prod. RKO, 1947; exec. prod. CBS TV network, 1955–59; dir. syndication, Screen Gems, Hollywood, 1959–62; exec. prod., CBS, 1962; exec. prod., MGM TV, 1963.

SPECKTOR, FREDERICK: Executive. b. April 24, 1933, Los Angeles. e. Univ. of So. Calif., UCLA. M.P. agent, Ashley Famous Agency, 1962–64; Artists Agency Corp., 1964–68; exec. M.P. dept., William Morris Agency, 1968-78; exec. Creative Artists Agency, 1978–present.

SPELLING, AARON: Executive. Was actor/writer before becoming producer at Four Star in 1957. In 1967, formed Thomas/Spelling Productions to produce several series and movies, including Mod Squad. In 1969, formed his own company, Aaron Spelling Productions, and then in 1972, partnered with Leonard Goldberg to produce The Rookies, Charlie's Angels, Fantasy Island, Starsky and Hutch, Hart to Hart, and under his own company banner, Love Boat, Vegas, Dynasty, and a total of 92 movies for television.

SPENCER, LESLIE B.: Exhibitor. b. Boston, Nov. 17, 1938. Father was late exhibitor Leslie Beudsler. Pres., Community Playhouse, Inc., Wellesley Hills, MA.

SPENGLER, PIERRE: Producer. b. Paris, 1947. Went on stage at 15; returned to language studies at Alliance Francaise. Entered film industry as production runner and office boy. Teamed for first time with friend Ilya Salkind on The Light at the Edge of the World, produced by Alexander Salkind.
PICTURES INCLUDE: Bluebeard, The Three Musketeers, The Four Musketeers, Crossed Swords, Superman, Superman II.

SPENSER, JEREMY: Actor. b. Ceylon, 1937; e. Downshill School, Farnham, England. Ent. films 1947 in Anna Karenina.
PICTURES INCLUDE: It's Great To Be Young, The Prince and the Showgirl, Wonderful Things, Ferry to Hong Kong, Roman Spring of Mrs. Stone, Vengeance, King and Country, He Who Rides a Tiger.

SPERLING, MILTON: Producer. b. New York City. e. C.C.N.Y., Shipping clerk Paramount Newsreel; messenger boy, Paramount, Astoria studio; script clerk, United Artists studio, Hollywood, secy. to Darryl Zanuck, Warner Bros.; secy. to Hal B. Wallis, assoc. prod.; Edward Small Prod.; asst. to Winfield Sheehan, Fox Films; screen writer 20th-Fox, Four Sons, Sing, Baby, Sing, Thin Ice, Cisco Kid; apptd. prod.; served in U.S. Marines as Capt. 3½ yrs; prod. Sun Valley Serenade, Hello, Frisco, Hello, Crash Dive, Rings on Her Fingers; To the Shores of Tripoli; Iwo Jima; documentary m.p.; org. & pres. of U.S. Pictures, 1945.
PICTURES INCLUDE: Cloak and Dagger, Pursued, Three Secrets, The Enforcer, Distant Drums, Retreat Hell, Blowing Wild, prod. collab. story & s.p. Court Martial of Billy Mitchell; supv. prod. Top Secret Affair, Marjorie Morningstar; prod. collab. s.p. The Bramble Bush; prod. collab. s.p., Merrill's Marauders; collab. prod. s.p. Battle of the Bulge; prod., collab. Captain Apache.
TV: Black Market Baby (MOW, ABC), Brave New World (exec. prod., NBC. mini-series); The Dream Merchants (exec. prod., OPT series).

SPEWACK, BELLA: Writer. b. Hungary, 1899. e. Washington Irving H.S., 1917. m. Samuel Spewack, 1922; writer. Reporter N.Y. Call, N.Y. Mail, N.Y. World, N.Y. Evening World; feature writer, N.Y. Herald Tribune, N.Y. Times; nat'l pub. dir. Camp Fire Girls, then Girl Scouts; asst. to husband for corr. for N.Y. World, Russia, 1922–26; author plays with husband include: Solitaire Man, Poppa, War Song, Clear All Wires, Spring Song, Boy Meets Girl, Leave It to Me, Kiss Me Kate, My Three Angels, Festival. Member: Dramatists Guild; SWG; pres., N.Y. Girls Scholarship Fund.
PICTURES INCLUDE: Clear All Wires, Boy Meets Girl, Cat and the Fiddle, Rendezvous, The Nuisance, Three Loves of Nancy, My Favorite Wife, When Ladies Meet, Weekend at the Waldorf, Move Over Darling, We're No Angels (based on play My Three Angels).
TV: Mr. Broadway, Kiss Me Kate, My Three Angels, The Enchanted Nutcracker, Kiss Me Kate, BBC.

SPIEGEL, LARRY: Producer-Writer-Director. b. Brooklyn, New York. e. Ohio Univ. With CBS-TV 1960–66; Benton & Bowles, 1966–67; Wells, Rich, Green, 1967–71; BBD&O, 1972–73. Now co-heads Spiegel-Bergman Productions.
PICTURES INCLUDE: Hail (s.p.); Book of Numbers (s.p.); Death Game (prod.); Stunts (prod.); Spree (direc./s.p.); Phobia (prod.); Pure Escape (prod.).
TV: Alexander (s.p., prod.); Incredible Indelible Magical Physical Mystery Trip (s.p.); Bear That Slept Through Christmas (s.p.); Never Fool With A Gypsy Ikon (s.p.); Mystery Trip Through Little Red's Head (s.p.); Planet of Apes (animated) (s.p.).

SPIEGEL, SAM: Producer. b. Jaroslau, Poland, Nov. 11, 1903. e. University of Vienna; with Universal 1930–33, producing German and French films in Berlin for European distribution. Independent producer 1933–37 in Europe. In 1941, co-producer with Boris Morns of Tales of Manhattan.

PICTURES INCLUDE: The Stranger, 1945; We Were Strangers with John Huston (Horizon Prod.), The Prowler, When I Grow Up, African Queen, Melba, On the Waterfront (Acad. Award, best picture, 1954); The Strange One, Bridge on the River Kwai (Acad. Award, best picture, 1957); Suddenly Last Summer, 1959; Lawrence of Arabia, Dangerous Silence, The Chase, The Night of the Generals, The Happening, The Swimmer, Nicholas and Alexandra, The Last Tycoon.

SPIEGEL, TED: Publicist. b. New York City. e. N.Y.U., B.S. 1948. Joined Columbia Pictures 1948 in adv. copy, exploitation, pub. depts.; foreign public rel., Columbia International 1956. Spec. adv., pub. rep., Kingsley Int'l Pictures, 1960; spec. asst. to pres. Kingsley Int'l Pictures, 1962; mgr. dir., theatre operations, The Landau Co., 1963; pub. exec., Embassy Pics. Corp., 1964; dir. pub., Avco Embassy Pictures, 1968. In 1976 joined A. Stirling Gold as dir. adv./pub. relations. In 1978 named acct. exec. for Solters & Roskin.

SPIELBERG, STEVEN: b. Cincinnati, 1947. e. Calif. State Coll. Made home movies as child; completed first film with story and actors at 12 yrs. old in Phoenix. At 13 won film contest for 40-min. war movie, Escape to Nowhere. At 16 made 140-min. film, Firelight. At CSC made five films. First professional work, Amblin', 20 min. short which led to signing contract with Universal Pictures.
TV: Duel, Something Evil.
PICTURES INCLUDE: The Sugarland Express, Jaws, Close Encounters of the Third Kind, I Wanna Hold Your Hand (exec. prod.), 1941, Used Cars (exec. prod.), Raiders of the Lost Ark; Poltergeist (prod.-s.p.), E.T. and Me (dir.).

SPIER, WILLIAM: Producer, director, novelist, radio-TV writer; m. June Havoc. Network exec., producer; prod. radio shows including March of Time, Columbia Work Shop, Adventures of Sam Spade, Philip Morris Playhouse, Suspense; co-dir. film, Lady Possessed.
TV: The Clock, 1951; Fred Waring, Omnibus, 1952–53; Medallion Theatre, Willy, 1954–55; Perry Mason, 1956; scripts for Omnibus, The Clock, 20th Century-Fox Hour, The Lineup, Reader's Digest, Passing Parade, Alfred Hitchcock, Steve Canyon, Peter Gunn, Desilu, Playhouse 90, The Untouchables, 77 Sunset Strip, Bourbon Street, Dragnet, Richard Diamond, CIC, The Islanders, Thin Man, etc. Winner of Peabody Award, Look Magazine, Mystery Writers of America, Writers' Guild Award, best hour script of 1961.

SPIGELGASS, LEONARD: Writer. Early pictures include: collb. s.p. Letter of Introduction, Service DeLuxe, Unexpected Father, Boys from Syracuse; collab. story, s.p. All Through the Night, Tight Shoes; s.p. Butch Minds the Baby, Big Street, Youngest Profession; U.S. armed forces, WW II.
PICTURES INCLUDE: Perfect Marriage, So Evil My Love, I Was a Male War Bride, Mystery Street, Night Into Morning, Law and the Lady, Because You're Mine, Scandal at Scourie, Athena, Deep in My Heart, Ten Thousand Bedrooms, Silk Stockings, A Majority of One, Gypsy.
TV: Climax, Playhouse 90.
STAGE: A Majority of One, Dear Me, The Sky is Falling, The Wrong Way Light Bulb, Look to the Lillies.

SPIKINGS, BARRY: Executive. b. 1939. Ent. m.p. ind. 1963. Jnt. Mang. Dir. British Lion Films Ltd., 1975. Co-prod. Conduct Unbecoming, Man Who Fell To Earth, 1976. Appt. jnt. man. dir. EMI Films Ltd., 1977. Prod. The Deer Hunter, Convoy. 1979, appt. chm. & chief exec., EMT Film & Theatre Corp.; chm. & chief exec, EMI Films, Ltd., chm. EMI Cinemas, Ltd.; chm., Elstree Studios, Ltd. Named dir. of Associated Film Dist. (USA). Chm. EMI-TV Programs, Inc., 1980, appt. chm. chief exec., EMI Films Group.

SPIRES, JOHN B.: Executive. b. New York, N.Y. e. N.Y.U. Assistant manager Tribune Theatre, N.Y., 1934–36; Paramount Pictures lab., 1936–42; Capt. U.S. Army, 1942–46; Major U.S. Reserves, 1946–48; foreign rep., RKO, Europe, 1946; asst. foreign mgr., United World Films, 1947–48; in charge 16mm foreign oper., Universal 1949; asst. to European gen. mgr., Universal International, 1950; European gen. mgr., Continental Europe, Near East, Universal International, 1955; gen. mgr., foreign film sales, MCA-TV, 1958; dir., TV sis., UK, Europe, MGM-TV, 1961; dir., Int'l TV sis., MGM-TV, 1964; named v.p. OF MGM-TV, 1973; snr. v.p., MGM-TV, 1978. Founded Phoenix Intl. TV Associates, 1980; pres., Phoenix Intl.

SPITZ, HENRY: Producer. b. Paterson, N.J., Mar. 4, 1905. e. N.Y.M.A. Gen. mgr., Quackenbush Dept. Stores; on bd. Preakness Hill Country Club & Barnet Memorial Hosp.; v.p. Marshall-Matherson dept. store, 1930–34; ent. m.p. ind. as prod. & bus. mgr., Cameo, 1935; assoc. prod., Cameo-Imperial Pictures, 1936; asst. prod. mgr. & asst. dir. Conn Prod.; asst., prod. mgr. Universal.
PICTURES INCLUDE: I Demand Payment, High Hat,

Here's Flash Casey, Headleys at Home, Hawaiian Nights, Private Affairs; assoc. prod. Two Dollar Bettor, Sabre Jet, Commanche.

SPITZER, MARIAN: Writer. b. New York City. e. NYU. m. Harlan Thompson, writer. Was reporter on Brooklyn Times, then N.Y. Globe, in dramatic dept. Did publicity for B.F. Keith Circuit, Shubert & Edgar Selwyn. First short story pub. in 1924 by Smart Set. Novels include Who Would Be Freed? and A Hungry Young Lady. Was in editorial dept. Fox, then contract writer. Became asst. to chmn. of ed. board. Paramount.
PICTURES INCLUDE: Dolly Sisters, Look for the Silver Lining.

SPIVAK, LAWRENCE E.: TV-radio producer. b. N.Y. e. Harvard U. LL.D. (hon.) Wilberforce U.; Litt.D. (hon.) Suffolk U. L.H.D. (hon.) Tampa U. Began as bus. mgr., Antiques Mag., 1921–30; asst. to the pub., Hunting and Fishing, Nat. Sportsman mags., 1930–33; bus. mgr., American Mercury, 1934–39; pub., 1939–44; editor, pub., 1944–50; founder, pub. until 1954, Ellery Queen's Mystery Mag., The Mag. of Fantasy and Science Fiction, Mercury Mystery Books, Bookseller Mysteries, Jonathan Press Books; producer, panel member, TV program, Meet the Press. Recipient two Peabody Awards. Winner of Emmy Award for outstanding achievement in Coverage of Special Events and Honor Award from University of Missouri for Distinguished Service in Journalism.

SPODICK, ROBERT C.: Exhibitor. b. New York City, Dec. 3, 1919; e. CCNY, 1940; ent. m.p. ind. as errand boy Skouras Park Plaza, Bronx 1932–33; reel boy, asst. mgr., Loew's Theatres; mgr., Little Carnegie and other art theatres; exploitation man, United Artists. Acquired Lincoln, New Haven art house in 1945 in partnership with cousin Leonard E. Sampson; developed Nutmeg Theatre circuit, which was sold in 1968 to Robert Smerling. Now operates in Groton, Ct., Cinemas I and II; Norwich Cinemas I and II and Village Cinemas I & II in Mystic in Partnership with Sampson and William Rosen; also Whalley Lincoln, Crown, York Sq., Theatres in New Haven. Pres., Allied of Conn., 1962–64; Pres. NATO of Conn. 1968–73. Past chm. exec. comm., Conn. Ass'n of Theatre Owners.

SPRINGSTEEN, R. G.: Director. b. Tacoma, Wash., Sept. 8, 1904; e. U. Washington. With Universal Studios 1930; asst. dir. Fox; asst. dir. & dir. Republic.
PICTURES INCLUDE: Out of the Storm, Hellfire, Red Menace, Singing Guns, Honeychile, Toughest Man in Arizona, Gobs & Gals, Perilous Journey, Geraldine, I Cover the Underworld, Cross Channel, When Gangland Strikes, Come Next Spring, Track the Man Down, Secret Venture, Double Jeopardy, Johnny Reno, Red Tomahawk.

STACK, ROBERT: Actor. b. Los Angeles, Calif., Jan. 13, 1919; e. U. So. Calif.; dramatic school. In U.S. Armed Forces, WW II.
PICTURES INCLUDE: First Love, When the Daltons Rode, Mortal Storm, Little Bit of Heaven, Nice Girls, Badlands of Dakota, To Be or Not To Be, Eagle Squadron, Men of Texas, Fighter Squadron, Date With Judy, Miss Tatlock's Millions, Mr. Music, Bullfighter and the Lady, My Outlaw Brother, Bwana Devil, War Paint, Conquest of Cochise, Sabre Jet, Iron Glove, High & the Mighty, House of Bamboo, Good Morning Miss Dove, Great Day in the Morning, Written on the Wind, John Paul Jones, Last Voyage, Killers of Killimanjaro, The Caretakers, The Corrupt Ones, Story of a Woman, 1941, Airplane!.
TV: The Untouchables, Name of the Game.

STAFFORD, BRENDAN J. (B.S.C.): Director lighting cameraman. Has served as photographer various documentary companies, including Student Nurse, Sports Day, Journey for Jeremy, Riders of the Forest, etc. Directed Mediaeval Monastery, A Nation Once Again, Proud Canvas, A Car is Born, etc., 1947–48. Photography, Fortune Lane, Via London, Cape Cargoes, etc. Directed, Our Country: 1948–49, directed Stranger at My Door; directed and photographed approx. 40 TV films; 1949–50. Photographed Paul Temple Triumphs, E.C.A. film on Britain; dir. Marshall Plan for Ireland; dir. and photo. 8 TV films, 1950–51; formed Irish Film Prods. Made Portrait of Dublin; photographed The Promise, 1951–55; formed Meridan Films, Ltd.; dir. The Armchair Detective, Men Against the Sun, etc.; photo. The Wallet, Circumstantial Evidence, The Night Won't Talk, etc.; dir. of photo. to Douglas Fairbanks series and Fabian of the Yard series; photo. Eight O'Clock Walk, Bang You're Dead, Checkmate, Profile, One Jump Ahead, Find the Lady, Hide-Up, Murder Reported, There's Always a Thursday, The Hostage, Curse of Nostradamus, The Shakedown, Woman Shall Weep, Witness in the Dark, Your Money or Your Wife. 1969: Crossplot, The Promise, Dangerous Hands.
TV: Gay Cavalier, Files of the O.S.S., Errol Flynn, White Hunter, William Tell, Invisible Man, Danger Man series, 1960–61. The Pursuers, One Step Beyond, Sir Francis Drake series; 1962, part Third Man series, Man of the World series; Sentimental Agent series; 1963, Danger Man; 1964,

Danger Man (Secret Agent), 1965–66, The Man Who Never Was, The Prisoner, 1966–67; 1968, The Saint, 1969 UFO Series; 1970 2nd UFO series; 1971, The Protectors series; 1972, The Pathfinders series and 2nd The Protectors series; 1975 The Protectors, Space 1999; 1976/7 Commercials and Documentaries.

STAGGS, JACK E.: Executive Director, Motion Picture and Television Fund. b. Los Angeles, August 10, 1920. A registered pharmacist, he is a Fellow of the American College of Apothecaries and Member of American College of Hospital Administrators. Educated Idaho Southern and Columbia Universities. Served in World War II as Chief Pharmacist Mate in the Navy. Former chief administrator of So. Nevada Memorial Hospital of Las Vegas. Joined Motion Picture and Television Fund Sept. 1, 1968.

STAHL, AL: Executive. Syndicated newspaper cartoonist; asst. animator, Max Fleischer, gag ed. Terrytoons; U.S. Signal Corps; opened own studios, 1946; prod. first animated TV cartoon show; pres., Animated Prod., prod. live and animated commercials; member of bd. NTFC.

STALLONE, SYLVESTER: Actor-Writer. b. New York City, July 6, 1946. After high school taught an American College of Switzerland instructing children of career diplomats, young royalty, etc. Returned to U.S. in 1967 and graduated from Univ. of Miami in 1969. Came to New York to seek acting career, taking part-time jobs, including usher for Walter Reade Theatres. Then turned to writing, selling several TV scripts. Back to acting with lead role in The Lords of Flatbush.
PICTURES INCLUDE: Capone, Death Race 2000, Rocky (also s.p.), F.I.S.T. (actor, co. s.p.), Paradise Alley (actor, s.p., dir.), Rocky II (actor, s.p., dir.), Nighthawks, Victory, Rocky III.

STAMP, TERENCE: Actor. b. London, England, 1938. After stage experience. Alfie On Broadway. Recent stage: Dracula, The Lady from the Sea.
PICTURES INCLUDE: Billy Budd, Term of Trial, The Collector, Modesty Blaise, Far from the Madding Crowd, Poor Cow, Blue, Tales of Mystery, Theorem, The Mind of Mr. Soames, A Season in Hell, Hu-Man, The Divine Creature, Strip-Tease, Superman, Meetings With Remarkable Men, The Thief of Baghdad, Together, Superman II.

STANDER, LIONEL: Actor. b. New York City. e. coll.; N.Y. stage, 1952.
PICTURES INCLUDE: Scoundrel, Page Miss Glory, Gay Deception, Music Goes 'Round, Mr. Deeds Goes to Town, Meet Nero Wolfe, Guadalcanal Diary, Big Show-Off, Specter of the Rose, In Old Sacramento, Kid From Brooklyn, Gentleman Joe Palooka, Pal Joey, Mad Wednesday, Call Northside 777, Unfaithfully Yours, Trouble Makers, Two Gals and a Guy, St. Benny the Dip, Cul de Sac, A Dandy in Aspic, The Gang That Couldn't Shoot Straight, Pulp, The Black Bird, The Cassandra Crossing, New York, New York, Matilda, 1941.

STANFILL, DENNIS C.: Executive. b. Centerville, Tenn., April 1, 1927; e. Lawrenceburg H.S., Annapolis, Oxford U., M.A. After active duty in the Navy served in foreign affairs section, office of Chief of Naval Operations; resigned commission & joined Lehman Brothers, as corporate finance specialist, 1959–65; v.p., finance, Times Mirror Company, 1965–69; ent. m.p. ind. as exec. v.p., finance, 20th Century-Fox & member of Fox board & exec. committee, 1969; named pres. 20th Century-Fox, March, 1971; named chmn., chief exec. officer, Sept. 1971. Resigned, 1981.

STANG, ARNOLD: Performer, b. Chelsea, Mass., Sept. 28, 1927. Radio, 1935–50; on B'way, in five plays and in m.p. and short subjects; guest appearances on TV shows.
TV: Milton Berle, Danny Thomas, Perry Como, Ed Sullivan, Red Skelton, Frank Sinatra, Wagon Train, Top Cat, Batman, Bonanza, Bob Hope, Danny Kaye, Broadside, Jackie Gleason, Emergency, Feeling Good, Chico & The Man, Super Jaws & Catfish.
PICTURES INCLUDE: Man with the Golden Arm, The Wonderful World of the Brothers Grimm, It's a Mad, Mad, Mad, Mad World, Pinocchio in Outer Space, Dondi, Alakazam the Great, Hello Down There, Skidoo, Walt Disney's Aristocats, Raggedy Ann & Andy, Gang That Couldn't Shoot Straight, We Go Polo, That's Life.

STANLEY, PHYLLIS: Actress. b. London, England, Oct. 30. e. Beauclair Sch., London. On London stage in 1932–35.
STAGE: The Miracle, Words & Music, The Town Talks, Oh! You Letty, Happy Returns, Lights Up.
PICTURES INCLUDE: Side Street Angel (m.p. debut), St. Martin's Lane, Jeannie, One Exciting Night, Next of Kin, The Case of Lady Brooke, Lovely to Look At, Take Me To Town, Her 12 Men, Strange Lady in Town, Black Sleep, Seventh Veil.
TV: Fireside Theatre, Ford Theatre, Four Star Playhouse (Schlitz Playhouse, Lux Video Theatre, Matinee Theatre).

STANWYCK, BARBARA: Actress. r.n. Ruby Stevens; b. Brooklyn, N.Y., July 16, film debut, Locked Door, 1929.

PICTURES INCLUDE: Ladies of Leisure, Night Nurse, So Big, Bitter Tea of General Yen, Brief Moment, Woman in Red, Annie Oakley, Plough and the Stars, Stella Dallas, Mad Miss Manton, Union Pacific, Golden Boy, Meet John Doe, Two Mrs. Carrolls, B.F.'s Daughter, Sorry, Wrong Number, Lady Gambles, East Side, West Side, Thelma Jordan, The Furies, No Man of Her Own, To Please a Lady, Man With a Cloak, Clash by Night, Jeopardy, All I Desire, Titanic, Blowing Wild, The Moonlighter, Executive Suite, Witness to Murder, Violent Men, Double Indemnity, Ball of Fire, Cattle Queen of Montana, Escape to Burma, There's Always Tomorrow, Maverick Queen, These Wilder Years, Crime of Passion, Trooper Hook, Forty Guns, Walk on the Wild Side, Roustabout, The Night Walker.
TV: Guest, Jack Benny, Ford, Zane Grey, Alcoa-Goodyear; 4 yrs., 1965–69, The Big Valley.

STAPLETON, JEAN: Actress. b. New York City, Jan. 19, 1923. e. Wadleigh High School. Summer stock in New Hampshire, Maine, Mass., and Penna. First Broadway appearance in In the Summer House.
STAGE: Damn Yankees, Bells Are Ringing, Something Wild, Up the Down Staircase, Cold Turkey, Klute.
TV: All in the Family.

STAPLETON, MAUREEN: Actress. b. Troy, N.Y., June 21, 1925. Studied acting with Herbert Berghof in N.Y. in 1944 and became member of Actors Studio. Broadway debut, 1946, in The Playboy of the Western World. Other early roles in: Antony and Cleopatra, Detective Story, The Bird Cage. Became a star in 1951 in The Rose Tattoo and later acted in 27 Wagons Full of Cotton, Orpheus Descending, The Glass Menagerie. m.p. debut 1949 in Lonelyhearts. Recent play: Gingerbread Play (Tony Award), 1970–71.
PICTURES INCLUDE: Fugitive Kind, View from the Bridge, Bye Bye Birdie, Airport, Plaza Suite, Interiors, The Runner Stumbles, On the Right Track, Reds.
TV: Tell Me Where It Hurts (movie), Queen of the Stardust Ballroom, Cat on a Hot Tin Roof.

STARGER, MARTIN: Executive. e. N.Y. City Coll. Serviced in U.S. Army Signal Corp., where prod. training films. Joined BBDO, starting in TV prod. dept.; later made v.p. & assoc. dir. of TV. Joined ABC in April 1966, as v.p. of programs, ABC-TV, East Coast. In March, 1968, prom. to v.p. and natl prog. dir; in 1969 named v.p. in chg. progr. Named pres., ABC Entertainment, July 17, 1972. In June, 1975 formed Marstar Productions Inc., M.P. & TV production company of which he is pres. In March 1978 formed Marble Arch Productions, of which he is pres.

STARK, RAY: Producer. e. Rutgers U. Began career after WWII as agent handling radio scripts, and later literary works for such writers as Costain, Marquand and Hecht. Joined Famous Artists Agency, where he represented such personalities as Marilyn Monroe, Kirk Douglas and Richard Burton; in 1957, resigned exec. position to form Seven Arts Prods. with Eliot Hyman, serving as exec. v.p. and head of production until July, 1966, when he left to take on personal production projects, including Reflections in a Golden Eye and Funny Girl.
PICTURES INCLUDE: The Sunshine Boys, Robin and Marian, Murder by Death, Casey's Shadow, The Cheap Detective, California Suite, The Electric Horseman, Chapter Two, Seems Like Old Times.

STARR, EVE: Columnist. b. Chicago, Ill., May 1. e. Columbia Univ., Miami Univ., Julliard Sch. of Music. Radio-TV playwright, feature writer, actress. Hollywood foreign correspondent; m.p. writer, newspapers, mags.; m.p. columnist, Hollywood Citizen-News; Daily syndicated TV column, Inside TV—General Features Synd.; feature column, Tell It To Eve, International Newspapers; Traveling With Eve, Nat'l Syndicated Travel Column.

STEEL, ANTHONY: Actor. b. London, Eng., May 21, 1920; e. private schools, South Ireland & Cambridge. Film debut in Saraband for Dead Lovers.
PICTURES INCLUDE: Portrait from Life, Christopher Columbus, Helter Skelter, Poet's Pub, The Blue Lamp, The Wooden Horse, Laughter in Paradise, The Mudlark, Where No Vultures Fly (Ivory Hunter), Another Man's Poison, Emergency Call, Something Money Can't Buy, The Planter's Wife (Outpost in Malaya), Malta Story, Master of Ballantrae, Albert, R.N. (Break to Freedom), West of Zanzibar, Sea Shall Not Have Them, Passage Home, Storm Over the Nile, Black Tent, Checkpoint, Valerie, A Question of Adultery, Harry Black, Honeymoon, The Switch.

STEELE, TOMMY: Performer. b. London, 1936. Early career Merchant Navy. First TV and film appearances, 1956. Composed and sang title song for The Shiralee.
PICTURES INCLUDE: Kill Me Tomorrow, The Tommy Steele Story, The Duke Wore Jeans, Tommy the Toreador, Light Up the Sky, It's All Happening, The Happiest Millionaire, Half A Sixpence, Finian's Rainbow, Where's Jack?
TV: Tommy Steele Spectaculars, Richard Whittington Esquire (Rediffusion), Ed Sullivan Show, Gene Kelly Show, Perry Como Show, Twelfth Night, The Tommy Steele Hour,

Tommy Steele in Search of Charlie Chaplin, Tommy Steele And A Show, Quincy's Quest.

STEIGER, ROD: Actor. b. Westhampton, N.Y., Apr. 14, 1925; e. Westside H.S., Newark, N.J. Served in U.S. Navy, then employed in Civil Service; studied acting at N.Y. Theatre Wing Dramatic Workshop Actors' Studio; numerous TV plays; on Broadway in ANTA prod. of Night Music; m.p. debut in On the Waterfront.
PICTURES INCLUDE: Big Knife, Oklahoma! Court Martial of Billy Mitchell, Jubal, Harder They Fall, Back from Eternity, Run of the Arrow, Unholy Wife, Al Capone, Seven Thieves, The Mark, Reprieve, 13 West Street, Hands Upon the City, The Time of Indifference, The Pawnbroker, In the Heat of the Night, The Girl and the General, No Way to Treat a Lady, And There Came a Man, The Illustrated Man, Three Into Two Won't Go, Duck, You Sucker, Happy Birthday, Wanda June, Waterloo, The Lolly-Madonna War, Lucky Luciano, Hennessy, W. C. Fields and Me, F.I.S.T., The Amityville Horror, Lion of the Desert, Cattle Annie and Little Britches.

STEIN, JOSEPH L.: Attorney. b. Portland, Me.; e. NYU, NYU Law Sch., LL.B. Admitted to N.Y. Bar. Specialist in copyright and m.p. law. Member of Sargoy & Stein, New York until Dec. 1970 when he retired, becoming counsel to firm. Compilers and annual revisers of U.S. Copyright Law Digest for Martindale-Hubbell Law Directory. Special counsel nationally for ten major m.p. dist. cos. in copyright & dist. matters. Former member: American Bar Assn. and of its Copyright Subsection's Committees on Anti-Trust Matters, 1951–54, on Copyright Office Affairs. 1953–55, 1959–63, 1966–67, on Copyright Law Revision, 1955–56, 1963–65, on Int. Copyrights, 1956–57, 1966–67, on Cooperation with Other Sections, 1956–57, on authors, 1959–61, and on Related Rights, 1957–59; American Patent Law Assn.: American Judicature Society; National Panel of Arbitrators of American Arbitration Assn.; American Society of International Law; American Foreign Law Soc.; Assn. of the Bar of City of New York; N.Y. County Lawyers' Assn.; N.Y. State Bar Assn.; Fed. Bar Assn. of N.Y., N.J. & Conn.; dir., N.Y. Tuberculosis & Health Assn., Inc.

STEIN, RONALD: Composer, conductor, pianist, teacher, filmmaker. b. St. Louis, Mo., April 12, 1930. e. Washington Univ., St. Louis, 1947–51, Yale Univ., New Haven, 1951–52, U.S.C., Los Angeles, 1960–63 U.S. Army, 1952–54. Music director's asst. Municipal Opera, St. Louis, 1950–51, 1954; asst. music dir., Greek Theatre, 1955; asst. prof. of music, Calif. State Univ. at Northridge, 1960–61; assoc. mus. dir., Phoenix Star Theatre, 1964. 78 m.p. scores since 1955; Documentary film director, writer, editor, photographer. U.S. Educational Films (Administrator). Professor of Music, Univ. Colorado, 1980.
PICTURES INCLUDE: The Littlest Hobo, Raymie, Legend of Tom Dooley, Premature Burial, Of Love and Desire, Dime With A Halo, Psych-Out, Dementia 13, The Rain People, Getting Straight, The Prisoners, Dateline Yesterday TV series, (Editorial Supervisor). National Parks—A Road For The Future (Photographer, Editor), The Eye of The Mind (Writer, Director).

STEINBERG, HERB: b. New York, N.Y. July 3, 1921; e. CCNY, 1937–41. Capt. U.S. Army, 1942–46; pub. PRC, 1946, Eagle Lion, 1946–49, Paramount 1949; pub. mgr. 1951; expl. mgr., 1954; studio adv. & pub. dir., 1958; exec. chg. of spec. proj., press dept., Universal City Studio, 1963; dir., adv. & mkt. Universal Studio Tours, 1971; 1974 v.p., MCA Recreation Services advertising & marketing; 1978, v.p., Universal Pictures.

STELLINGS, ERNEST G.: Exhibitor. b. Petersburg, Ind.; e. Washington, Ind., H.S. Ent. m.p. ind. 1912; theatre mgr., Washington, Ind., 1918; mgr. Wilmington, N.C., 1920; mgr., Wilmington Theatres, 1923–1939; joined information of Everett Enterprises, Charlotte, N.C., 1939; with Everett Enterprises. Stewart and Everett Theatres, 1939–62; leased two Charlotte theatres, 1951; v.p. Stellings-Gossett Theatres. Dir. Theatre Owners of N.C. and S.C.; pres. TOA, 1956–58; lifetime mem., TOA exec. comm.

STELLOFF, SKIP: Producer. b. N.Y.C., Aug. 10, 1925, e. U.S. Naval Academy; U.S. Navy, 1943–51; WWDC Radio, Wash., D.C., 1951–52; Ziv Television, 1952–56; sls. mgr.; C&C Television, 1956–58; pres., Heritage Productions, 1958–60.

STEMBLER, JOHN H.: Executive. b. Miami, Fla., Feb. 18, 1913; e. U. of Florida Law School, 1937. Asst. U.S. att., South. dist. of Fla., 1941; U.S. Air Force, 1941–45; pres. Georgia Theatre Co., 1957; NATO finance chm. member exec. comm. and past pres.; Major Gen. USAF (Ret) bd. chm., National Bank of Georgia.

STEPHEN, SUSAN: Actress. b. London, Eng., July 16, 1931; e. Eastbourne and Royal Acad. of Dramatic Art. Screen debut in His Excellency, 1951.
PICTURES INCLUDE: Stolen Face, Treasurer Hunt, Father's Doing Fine, Luxury Girls, The Red Beret (Paratrooper), House Across the Lake, Private Man, Golden Ivory,

For Better For Worse, As Long As They're Happy, Value for Money, His Excellency, Pacific Destiny, Barretts of Wimpole Street, Carry on Nurse.
TV: Little Women, Birdcage Room, No Hero, Pillars of Midnight.

STERLING, JAN: Actress. r.n. Jane Sterling Adriance. b. April 3, 1923. e. Private tutors; Fay Compton Sch. of Dramatic Art, London. N.Y. stage debut: Bachelor Born.
STAGE: Panama Hattie, Present Laughter, John Loves Mary, Two Blind Mice, Front Page, Over 21, Born Yesterday.
PICTURES INCLUDE: Johnny Belinda (debut), Appointment with Danger, Mating Season, Union Station, Skipper Surprised His Wife, Big Carnival, Caged, Rhubarb, Flesh and Fury, Sky Full of Moon, Pony Express, The Vanquished, Split Second, Alaska Seas, High & the Mighty, Return From the Sea, Human Jungle, Women's Prison, Female on the Beach, Man with the Gun, 1984, The Harder They Fall, Love in a Goldfish Bowl, The Incident, The Minx.

STERLING, ROBERT: Actor. r.n. William Sterling Hart; b. Newcastle, Pa., Nov. 13, 1917; e. U. of Pittsburgh; m. Anne Jeffreys, actress. Fountain pen salesman, day laborer, clerk, industrial branch credit mgr., clothing salesman on West Coast; served as pilot-instructor U.S. Army Corps. 3 yrs.
PICTURES INCLUDE: Blondie Meets the Boss, Only Angels Have Wings, Manhattan Heartbeat, Yesterday's Heroes, Gay Caballero, Penalty, I'll Wait for You, Get-Away, Ringside Maisie, Two-Faced Woman, Dr. Kildare's Victory, Johnny Eager, This Time for Keeps, Somewhere I'll Find You, Secret Heart, Roughshod, Bunco Squad, Sundowners, Show Boat, Column South.
TV: Topper.

STERN, ALFRED E. F.: Public relations executive. b. Boston, Mass., Aug. 4. e. Boston U. Reporter, editor, Lowell Sun, Quincy Patriot-Ledger, Dartmouth News; publicist, RKO Radio Pictures, 1946–54; publicity dir., 1955; West Coast publicity dir., NTA, 1958; own public relations org., Alfred E. F. Stern Co., 1960.

STERN, EDDIE: Film buyer. b. New York City, Jan. 13, 1917. e. Columbia Sch. of Journalism; head film buyer and booker, specializing in art theatres, for Rugoff and Becker, N.Y.; Captain, USAF; joined Wometco Ent. in 1952 as asst. to film buyer; now v.p. motion picture theatre film buying and booking, Wometco Enterprises, Inc.

STERN, EZRA E.: Attorney. b. New York, N.Y., Mar. 22, 1908. e. Southwestern U. 1930, LL.B.; pres., Wilshire Bar Assn. Former legal counsel for So. Calif. Theatre Owners Association. Member: Calif. State Bar; member, Int'l Variety Clubs; former chief barker, Variety Club So. Calif. Tent 25; pres., Variety Int'l Boys' Club; board of dir., Los Angeles Metropolitan Recreation & Youth Services Council; bd. of trustees, Welfare Planning Council, Los Angeles Region; former mem. Los Angeles Area Council, Boys' Club of America; pres., Variety International Boys' Club 1976–77 and 1979–80. Member bd., Will Rogers Institute, M.P. Pioneers.

STERN, STANLEY L.: Executive. b. Philadelphia, Dec. 31, 1917. Major, USAF, World War II & Korea. Entire working career with Wometco Enterprises, starting as usher in 1933. Served as theatre mgr., m.p. booker, in chg. of real estate and insurance, before taking over Wometco Theatre Division in 1973. Elected v.p., 1959, sr. v.p., in 1967, dir. in 1972. Placed in chg. Wometco Entertainment Division, 1976.
MEMBER: VCI, Tent 33, Motion Picture Pioneers. Past v.p. and dir., American Society of Insurance Management; v.p. and dir. NATO of Florida; mem. bd., NATO.

STERN, STEWART: Writer. b. New York, N.Y., Mar. 22, 1922. e. Ethical Culture Schools, 1927–40; U. of Iowa, 1940–43; Rifle Squad Leader, S/Sgt. 106th Inf. Div., 1943–45; actor, asst. stage mgr., The French Touch, B'way, 1945–46; dialogue dir. Eagle-Lion Studios, 1946–48. 1948 to date: screenwriter.
TV: (Plays) Crip, And Crown Thy Good, Thunder of Silence, Heart of Darkness, Sybil.
PICTURES INCLUDE: Teresa, Benjy (orig. s.p.) Rebel Without a Cause, The Rack, The James Dean Story, The Outsider, The Ugly American, Rachel, Rachel, The Last Movie, Summer Wishes—Winter Dreams (orig. s.p.).

STERNAD, RUDOLPH: Producer, designer, art director. b. N.Y., Oct. 6, 1905. e. Cooper Union Inst., 1922–23; Beaux Arts, 1924; Chouinand, 1925; arch. designer, Society M.P. Art Directors; designer, MGM, Fox, United Artists, Univ. Studios, 1926–34; art dir., 20th-Fox, Old Chicago, Suez, etc. 1934–40; art dir. Columbia Studios, More the Merrier, Talk of the Town, Craig's Wife, 1001 Nights, You Were Never Lovelier, etc.; prod. designer, Stanley Kramer Prod., 1948–62.
PICTURES INCLUDE: Champion, Home of the Brave, The Men, Cyrano de Bergerac, High Noon, Death of a Salesman, Four Poster, Caine Murder, Not as a Stranger, The Defiant Ones, On the Beach, Judgment at Nurem-

berg, Pressure Point, A Child Is Waiting, It's a Mad, Mad, Mad, Mad World.

STEVENS, ANDREW: Actor. b. Memphis, Tenn., 1956. Son of actress Stella Stevens. e. Memphis Messick H.S. Studied acting with Strasberg, David Craig, Vincent Chase, and Robert Easton. Began on TV, later playing in feature films.
PICTURES INCLUDE: Shampoo, Day of the Animals, Vigilante Force, The Boys in Company C, The Fury, Death Hunt.
TV: Adam-12, Apple's Way, The Quest, Police Story, Shazan, Once an Eagle (mini-series), Oregon Trail, Pumper One. Movies: S Secrets, The Last Survivors, The Werewolf of Woodstock, The Bastard (mini-series), The Rebels (mini-series), Beggarman Thief, Topper.

STEVENS, CONNIE: Actress. r.n. Concerta Ann Ingolie. b. Brooklyn, N.Y., August 8, 1938. e. Sacred Heart Academy, Hollywood Professional School; began career as winner of several talent contests in Hollywood; prof. debut, Hollywood Repertory Theatre's prod. Finian's Rainbow; recordings include: Kookie, Kookie, Lend Me Your Comb, 16 Reasons, What Did You Make Me Cry For, From Me to You, They're Jealous of Me, A Girl Never Knows.
TV: Hawaiian Eye, Wendy and Me, Sex Symbol (movie).
PICTURES INCLUDE: Eighteen and Anxious, Young and Dangerous, Drag Strip Riot, Rock-a-Bye Baby, Parish, Susan Slade, Palm Springs Weekend, Cruise A-Go-Go, The Grissom Gang, Last Generation.

STEVENS, CRAIG: Actor. b. Liberty, Mo.; e. U. Kansas. Played in coll. dramatics. On screen 1941 in Affectionately Yours.
PICTURES INCLUDE: Since You Went Away, The Doughgirls, Roughly Speaking, Too Young to Know, Humoresque, The Man I Love, That Way With Women, Night Unto Night, Love and Learn, Lady Takes a Sailor, Phone Call from a Stranger, French Line, Where the Sidewalk Ends, Duel on the Mississippi, The Name's Buchanan, Gunn, Limbo Line, The Snoop Sisters, "S.O.B.".
TV: Lux Video Theatre, Four Star Playhouse, Loretta Young Show, Schlitz Playhouse, Peter Gunn, Dinah Shore, Ernie Ford Shows, Chevvy Show, Summer on Ice, Person to Person, Man of the World series (ATV England); Mr. Broadway, The Millionaire, Name of the Game, The Bold Ones.
STAGE: Here's Love, King of Hearts, Plain and Fancy, Critics Choice, Mary Mary; Nat. Co. Cactus Flower.

STEVENS, GEORGE, JR.: Director, producer. b. Los Angeles, Calif., Apr. 3, 1932. e. Occidental College, 1949–53, B.A., 1st Lieut. U.S. Air Force; TV dir., Alfred Hitchcock Presents, Peter Gunn, 1957–61; prod. asst. Giant Productions, 1953–54; prod. asst. Mark VII, Ltd., 1956–57; assoc. prod., dir., The Diary of Anne Frank, 1957–59; assoc. prod., dir., The Greatest Story Ever Told, 1959–62; dir. M.P. Service, U.S. Information Agency 1962–67; chmn., U.S. deleg. to Film Festivals at Cannes (1962, 1964), Venice (1962, 1963), Moscow (1963); prod. John F. Kennedy; Years of Lightning, Day of Drums; co-chm., American Film Institute. Producer, America at the Movies (1976). Executive producer of The American Film Institute's Salute to James Cagney for which he was awarded an Emmy by National Academy of Television Arts and Sciences on May 19, 1975; producer/writer, American Film Institute's Salutes, 1973–81; executive producer, The Stars Salute America's Greatest Movies, 1977; producer/writer, The Kennedy Center Honors, 1978–80; producer/writer, America Entertains Vice Premier Deng, 1978.

STEVENS, K. T.: Actress. r.n. Gloria Wood. b. Hollywood, Calif.; e. U. So. Calif.; d. late Sam Wood, director.
STAGE: You Can't Take It With You, The Man Who Came to Dinner, My Sister Eileen, Nine Girls, St. Joan.
PICTURES INCLUDE: (debut) Peck's Bad Boy, The Great Man's Lady, 1942; Nine Girls, Address Unknown, Kitty Foyle, Harriet Craig, Vice Squad, Tumbleweed, Missile to the Moon.

STEVENS, LEE: Executive Administrator. b. March 10, 1930, New York City. e. NYU School of Commerce, grad. 1951 BS; NYU Law School, grad. 1957, Jurist Doctor, member of NY bar. With William Morris Agency 28 years. Now exec. v.p. & chief operating officer.

STEVENS, LESLIE: Executive, writer, producer, director. b. Wash., D.C., Feb. 3, 1924. e. Westminster School, London, Yale Drama School, American Theatre Wing, N.Y.C. Sold first play, The Mechanical Rat at 15; wrote six plays for summer stock groups, 1941–42; U.S. Air Force, 1943; pres., exec. prod. Daystar Prods.; writer, producer, director, film TV and features.
STAGE: Bullfight (off B'way) 1953–54; wrote, Broadway: Champagne Complex, 1954; The Lovers, 1956; The Marriage-Go-Round, 1958; The Pink Jungle, 1959.
TV: For Playhouse 90: Invitation to a Gunfighter, Charley's Aunt, Rumors of Evening, The Violent Heart, Portrait of a Murderer, The Second Man; Kraft TV Theatre, Duel; Four Star Playhouse, Award, Producers Showcase, Bloomer Girl; created, prod., dir. Stoney Burke, ABC series, 1962, created, prod., dir. Outer Limits, pilot It Takes a Thief; exec. prod. series, ABC; prod.-writer pilot McCloud, NBC; exec. prod. series; exec. prod. Men From Shiloh series; exec. prod., writer-dir., Name of the Game, Warner Bros. (Leslie Stevens Productions), 1971, prod.-writer, pilot of Search, exec. prod. of NBC: series creator, CATV series Movie of Today, Paperback Playhouse, Earthside Missile Base. Exec. prod., Universal Studios, Invisible Man, 1975. Supervising prod. Gemini Man, 1976 pilot and series.
PICTURES INCLUDE: author, The Left-Handed Gun 1958; co-prod.-wrote-dir. Private Property 1959; wrote, The Marriage-Go-Round 1960; wrote-prod.-dir. Hero's Island 1961.

STEVENS, MARK: Actor. r.n. Richard Stevens. b. Cleveland, Ohio, Dec. 13; e. privately; Beaux Arts and Sir George Williams Sch. of Fine Arts, Montreal. Had varied career before appearing on stage and radio in Canada; later joined station WAKB in Akron; then prod. mgr., WJW, Akron. Screen debut in Objective Burma.
PICTURES INCLUDE: God Is My Co-Pilot, Pride of the Marines, From This Day Forward, The Dark Corner, I Wonder Who's Kissing Her Now, Between Midnight and Dawn, Katie Did It, Little Egypt, Reunion in Reno, Mutiny, Big Frame, Torpedo Alley, Jack Slade, Cry Vengeance, Timetable, September Storm, Fate Is the Hunter, Frozen Alive, Sunscorched.
TV: Martin Kane, NBC; Big Town, NBC; prod., starred, script. Formed Mark Stevens Prod., Mark Stevens Television Prod., 1955.

STEVENS, STELLA: Actress. b. Hot Coffee, Mississippi, Oct. 1, 1938. e. Attended Memphis State University. Modeled in Memphis when she was discovered by talent scouts. Was briefly a term contract actress at 20th Century-Fox, later under exclusive contract to Paramount, then Columbia.
PICTURES INCLUDE: Say One For Me, The Blue Angel, Li'l Abner, Too Late Blues, Man Trap, The Courtship of Eddie's Father, The Nutty Professor, Advance to the Rear, Synanon, The Secret of My Success, The Silencers, The Ballad of Cable Hogue, Stand Up & Be Counted, Slaughter, The Poseidon Adventure, Arnold, Las Vegas Lady, Cleo Jones and the Casino of Gold, Nickelodeon, The Manitou.
TV: Five episodes of Ben Casey.

STEVENSON, PARKER: Actor. b. Philadelphia, June 4. e. Princeton Univ. Began professional acting career by starring in film, A Separate Peace, while high school senior, having attracted attention through work on TV commercials.
PICTURES INCLUDE: A Separate Peace (debut), Our Time, Lifeguard.
TV: The Streets of San Francisco, Gunsmoke, Hardy Boys Mysteries. Guest and host on several talk shows and specials.

STEVENSON, ROBERT: Director, writer. b. London, 1905. Educated Shrewsbury, Cambridge U. Under contract British companies 1929–39; Selznick, 1939–43. American citizenship 1940. U.S. Army, War Department, Italian campaign, 1943–46. Novel, Darkness in the Land; scripted Tudor Rose. Selznick, 1946–49; RKO 1949–52. TV scripting 15 shows; directed over 100 TV shows.
TV: Cavalcade of America, Ford Theatre, Playhouse of Stars, G.E. Theatre, Hitchcock Presents, 20th Century Fox Hour, Gunsmoke, 1952–56. Walt Disney, 1956 to present.
PICTURES INCLUDE: Nine Days a Queen, To the Victor, Back Street, Jane Eyre, To the Ends of the Earth, Walk Softly Stranger, My Forbidden Past, Dishonored Lady, Las Vegas Story, Johnny Tremaine, Old Yeller, In Search of the Castaways, The Mis-Adventures of Merlin Jones, The Absent-Minded Professor, Son of Flubber, That Darn Cat, Kidnapped, Darby O'Gill and the Little People, Blackbeard's Ghost, The Gnome-Mobile, The Monkey's Uncle, Mary Poppins, The Love Bug, Bedknobs and Broomsticks, Herbie Rides Again, Island at the Top of the World, One of Our Dinosaurs is Missing, The Shaggy D.A.

STEWART, ELAINE: Actress. b. Montclair, N.J., May 31, 1929. Usherette & cashier, m.p. theatre, Montclair; model, Conover Agcy., 1948; many TV shows; screen debut in Sailor Beware; Star of Tomorrow, 1954.
PICTURES INCLUDE: Sky Full of Moon, The Bad and the Beautiful, Desperate Search, Code Two, Slight Case of Larceny, Young Bess, Take the High Ground, Brigadoon, Adventures of Hajji Baba, Tattered Dress, Rise and Fall of Legs Diamond, Most Dangerous Man Alive.

STEWART, HUGH: Producer. b. Falmouth, Cornwall, Dec. 14, 1910. e. Clayesmore School, St. John's College, Cambridge; ent m.p. ind. 1932; editor, Gaumont British, 1932.
PICTURES INCLUDE: Man Who Knew Too Much, London Films: Dark Journey, Storm in a Teacup, Action for Slander, South Riding, Q Planes, Spy in Black. Army Service, 1939–45. Co-producer with Frank Capra of Anglo-US War Film, Tunisian Victory; True Glory. An Ideal Husband, Trottie True, Night Without Stars, Long Memory,

255

Up To His Neck, Man of the Moment, Up in the World, Just My Luck, Innocent Sinners, The Square Peg, Follow a Star, Make Mine Mink, The Bulldog Breed, In the Doghouse, On the Beat, A Stitch In Time, The Intelligence Men, The Early Bird, That Riviera Touch, The Magnificent Two, All at Sea, Mr. Horatio Knibbles, Anoop and The Elephant, The Flying Sorcerer, The Chiffy Kids (two series), High Rise Donkey.

STEWART, JAMES: Actor b. Indiana, Pa., May 20, e. Mercersburg Acad.; Princeton U. With Falmouth Stock Co., Cape Cod; on N.Y. stage in Goodbye Again; stage mgr. for Camille with Jane Cowl (Boston). Won Acad. Award for best performance 1940; joined U.S. Air Forces 1942, commissioned Col. 1944. Voted one of top ten money-making stars; M.P. Herald-Fame poll, 1950, 52, 54, 57; No. 1 Money-Making Star, 1955. 1968, Screen Actors Guild Award. Mem.: Bd. of Trustees, Princeton U. Trustee, Claremont College; exec. bd. of Los Angeles Council of Boy Scouts of America, bd. of dirs., Project Hope.
STAGE: Spring in Autumn, All Good Americans, Yellow Jack, Journey at Night, Harvey.
PICTURES INCLUDE: Murder Man, Rose Marie, Wife vs. Secretary, Next Time We Love, Speed, Gorgeous Hussy, Born to Dance, Seventh Heaven, You Can't Take It With You, Vivacious Lady, Mr. Smith Goes to Washington, Philadelphia Story, It's A Wonderful World, Destry Rides Again, Shop Around the Corner, Mortal Storm, It's a Wonderful Life, Magic Town, Call Northside 777, Rope, You Gotta Stay Happy, Stratton Story, Malaya, Winchester '73, Broken Arrow, Harvey, Jackpot, No Highway in the Sky, Greatest Show on Earth, Carbine Williams, Bend of the River, Naked Spur, Thunder Bay, Glenn Miller Story, Far Country, Rear Window, Strategic Air Command, Man From Laramie, Man Who Knew Too Much, Spirit of St. Louis, Night Passage, Vertigo, Bell Book and Candle, FBI Story, The Mountain Road, Two Rode Together, Man Who Shot Liberty Valance, Mr. Hobbs Takes a Vacation, How the West Was Won, Take Her, She's Mine, Cheyenne Autumn, Dear Brigitte, Shenandoah, The Rare Breed, Flight of the Phoenix, Firecreek, Bandolero, Cheyenne Social Club, Fool's Parade, That's Entertainment, The Shootist, Airport '77, The Big Sleep.
TV: Hawkins, 1973.

STEWART, JAY: Broadcast Announcer. b. Sept. 6, Summitville, Indiana. Was Monty Hall's sidekick on "Let's Make A Deal" for 14 years, currently is doing The Joker's Wild and Tic Tac Dough.

STEWART, MARILYN: Public Relations Executive. b. New York City. e. Hunter College. Singer, composer, artists mgr.—latter two hobbies; first was profession that began prior to entry into industry. Entered Ind. as scty. in 1960 to Si Seadler, MGM dir. of adv. Promoted in 1963 to asst. to Seadler, who was then dir. adv.-pub.-prom. for special projects at MGM. Left in 1964 to become prom.-pub. dir. for Verve/Folkways Records; duties also included a&r and talent-scouting. In 1966 joined 20th-Fox as radio/tv pub. coordinator. In 1969 went to Para. Pictures as mag. pub. coordinator. In Aug. '70 named worldwide director of pub. for Para., including creation of overall mkt. concepts, becoming 1st woman to be appointed to that position at major co. Campaigns included Love Story and The Godfather. In 1972 opened own p.r. firm, The Mediary, specializing in m.p. pub. Headquarters in N.Y.; repr. in L.A. Has represented American Film Theatre, The Lords of Flatbush, Bang the Drum Slowly, A Very Big Withdrawal, The Kids Are Alright, Autumn Sonata, The Tin Drum, L.A. Film Exposition, Michael Moriarty, etc.

STEWART, MARTHA: Actress. r.n. Martha Haworth, b. Bardwell, Ky., Oct. 7, 1922; m. Joe E. Lewis, prof. vocalist, Glenn Miller and Claude Thornhill bands; appeared in Copacabana, N.Y.; star Lucky Strike Hit Parade, 1943. On screen first, 1945 Doll Face.
PICTURES INCLUDE: Johnny Comes Flying Home, I Wonder Who's Kissing Her Now, Daisy Kenyon, Are You With It?, Convicted, In a Lonely Place, Aaron Slick from Punkin Crick.

STEWART, PEGGY: Actress. b. West Palm Beach, Fla., June 5, 1923; in 1933 was champion swimmer, Georgia; acq. honors in horseback riding. Taught riding in Calif. at age of 14. On San Francisco stage: Great American Family, Goodnight Ladies.
PICTURES INCLUDE: Wells Fargo, That Certain Age, Back Street, All This and Heaven Too, Pride of Maryland, The Longhorn, Vengeance Trail, Kansas Territory, Montana Incident, The Way West, The Animals, Pickup on 101.

STIGWOOD, ROBERT: Executive. b. Adelaide, Australia, 1934. e. Sacred Heart College. Began career as copywriter for Aust. ad agency; at 21 left home for England. Series of first jobs led to his opening a London theatrical agency. Began casting commercials for TV; produced records for clients. Became first independent record producer in Great Britain. In mid '60s joined forces with Brian Epstein, manager of Beatles, to become co-mgr. of NEMS Enterprises.

At Epstein's death formed own company, launching careers of such artists as Bee Gees, Cream, etc. Moved into theatre production in London: Hair, Jesus Christ Superstar, Pippin, Oh! Calcutta! Evita. Entered film production with Jesus Christ Superstar. Formed RSO Records in 1973.
PICTURES INCLUDE: Jesus Christ Superstar, Tommy, Saturday Night Fever, Grease, Sgt. Pepper's Lonely Hearts Club Band, Moment by Moment, Times Square (co.-prod.), The Fan.

STOCKWELL, DEAN: Actor. b. Hollywood, Calif., Mar. 5; p. Harry and Betty Veronica Stockwell; e. L.I. public schools and Martin Milmore, Boston. On stage in Theatre Guild prod. Innocent Voyage. Has appeared on radio in Death Valley Days and Dr. Christian.
PICTURES INCLUDE: (debut) Anchors Aweigh, The Valley of Decision, Abbott and Costello in Hollywood, The Green Years; named in 1949 M.P. Herald-Fame Stars of Tomorrow poll; Home Sweet Homicide, The Mighty McGurk, The Arnelo Affair, The Romance of Rosy Ridge, Song of the Thin Man, Gentleman's Agreement, Deep Waters, Down to Sea in Ships, Boy With Green Hair, Secret Garden, Happy Years, Kim, Stars in My Crown, Cattle Drive, Compulsion, Sons and Lovers, Long Day's Journey Into Night, Psych-out, The Dunwich Horror, The Last Movie, The Loners.

STODDARD, BRANDON: Executive. e. Yale Univ., Columbia Law School. Was program ass't. at Batton, Barton, Durstine and Osborn before joining Grey Advertising, where was successively, program operations supvr., dir. daytime programming, v.p. in chg. of TV, radio programming. Joined ABC in 1970; named v.p. daytime programs for ABC Entertainment, 1972; v.p. children's programs, 1973. Named v.p., motion pictures for TV, 1974. In 1976 named v.p. dramatic prog rams and motion pictures for television. In June, 1979, named pres., ABC Motion Pictures.

STOLBER, DEAN: Executive. b. Philadelphia, Penna., Sept. 2, 1944. e. Harvard (A.B., 1966); NYU School of Law (J.D., 1969). Acted on Broadway and in TV before starting career in law and business affairs in films. 1979, sr. v.p., business affairs, for United Artists Corp.; 1981 named exec. v.p.

STOLL, GEORGE: Musical director, MGM. b. Minneapolis, Minn., May 7, 1905. Was musical director Bing Crosby Woodbury program, CBS for two years; Camel Cigarette program, CBS for two years; Shell Oil program, NBC, 2 years. Violin soloist for a number of years touring U.S. and Canada. In 1936 appeared in MGM short product; musical dir. numerous films for MGM. Acad. Award best scoring musical picture (Anchors Aweigh) 1945.
PICTURES INCLUDE: Neptune's Daughter, Two Weeks with Love, I Love Melvin, Dangerous When Wet, Rose Marie, Flame & the Flesh, Student Prince, Athena, Hit the Deck, Love Me or Leave Me, Meet Me in Las Vegas.

STOLLER, MORRIS: Executive. b. New York, N.Y., Nov. 22, 1915. e. C.C.N.Y., BBA 1933; N.Y.U., CPA 1935, Brooklyn Law School, LLB, 1937; joined William Morris agency in 1936; president, Permanent Charities Comm., 1962; director and officer, Artist's Mgr. Guild, 1950–67; dir. St. Jude Hospital, 1955–67; presently bd. chm., chief operating officer, William Morris Agency.

STOLNITZ, ART: Executive. b. Rochester, N.Y. March 13, 1928. e. University of Tennessee. U.S. Navy Air Force. Legal dept., William Morris Agency, 1953, dir. business affairs, ZIV, 1959; dir. new program development, ZIV-United Artists, 1960; literary agent, MCA, 1961; dir. business affairs, Selmur Productions, Selmur Pictures, 1963; v.p. ABC Pictures, 1969; v.p. Metromedia Producers Corporation, 1974, executive v.p. Metromedia Producers Corporation; 1975 exec. v.p. and prod. Charles Fries Prods. 1976, prod. Edgar J. Scherick Productions; 1976–77 prod., Grizzly Adams (TV); 1977, v.p. business affairs, Warner Bros.-TV; 1980, snr. v.p., business affairs.

STOLOFF, VICTOR: Producer, writer, director, editor; e. French Law U. Ac. Fines Arts. Prod. dir. writer of award winning documentaries (Warner Bros. release); Prod. dir. writer first U.S. film made in Italy, When in Rome; First U.S. film made in Egypt; Collaborator William Dieterle films; Contract; writer, dir. to Sidney Buchman, Columbia, S.p. Volcano, The Sinner, Shark Reef.
TV: Ford Theater, Lloyd Bridges series, NBC, National Velvet, CBS High Adventure, with Lowell Thomas, Journey Around the World, Prod. Writ. Of Love and Desire; producer-director, Intimacy, Prod. on location 22, Hawaii Five-0, The 300 Year Weekend, Why? Director (orig. s.p.). Created Woman of Iran, first of TV series. 1977: producer-director: The Washington Affair.

STOLTZ, ARNOLD T.: Publicity executive. b. New York; e. Washington, U., St. Louis. Worked as reporter, publicity adv. man, 1933–37. Was pub. dir. and mgr., Warner and Loew theatres. Was radio commentator under name of Solly Wood. Pen name, Franc Arnold. Winner Quigley Silver Grand Award for exploitation, 1941. In 1942 named exploitation mgr., United Artists. In July, 1945 named natl. dir. and pub. PRC Pictures; then sales rep. Resigned 1947 to enter prod.; exec. prod. Movie Star, American Style. Joined Famous Players Corp.; adv., pub. dir., 1965; v.p. & gen. sales mgr., 1966. pres. Movie-Rama Color Corp., 1967; exec. prod. Tell Me in the Sunlight, The Golden Poodle.

STONE, ANDREW L.: Producer, director. b. Calif., July 16, 1902; e. U. Calif. Ent. ind. 1918 at Universal San Francisco exch.; later author, prod., dir. series of pictures for Paramount; prod., dir. for Sono-Art; 1932–36. org. and oper. Race Night company; prod., dir., The Girl Said No, 1936; Stolen Heaven, Say It in French, The Great Victor Herbert, Magician Music, 1940. Dir. Stormy Weather; formed Andrew Stone Prods., 1943.
PICTURES INCLUDE: Hi Diddle Diddle, Sensations of 1945, Bedside Manner, Bachelor's Daughter, Fun on a Weekend, Highway 301, Confidence Girl, Steel Trap, Blueprint for Murder, Night Holds Terror, Julie, Cry Terror, The Decks Ran Red, The Last Voyage, Ring of Fire, Password is Courage, Never Put It in Writing, Secret of My Success, Song of Norway, The Great Waltz.

STONE, BURTON S.: Executive. b. Feb. 16, 1928; e. Florida So. Coll; Pres., Deluxe General, Inc. and Deluxe Laboratories. Was film ed., Hollywood Film Co. 1951–53; serv. mgr., sales mgr. and gen. mgr., Consolidated Film Inds., 1953–61; nat'l sales mgr., Movielab, 1961–63; pres., All Service Film Laboratories, 1963–68; v.p. Technicolor, Inc., 1968–70. Pres., Precision Film Labs., 1970–78.
MEMBER: Board of directors, Will Rogers Hospital; member, Academy of M.P. Arts & Sciences; assoc. member, American Society of Cinematographers; member, SMPTE; trustee, Motion Picture Laboratory Technicians, Local 702 IATSE, Pension and Welfare Fund; member, Cinema Lodge, B'nai B'rith, Variety Club 1035, N.Y., Motion Picture Pioneers. University Film Producers, Association of Cinema Laboratories.

STONE, EZRA C.: Actor, director, producer. b. New Bedford, Mass., Dec. 2, 1917; e. American Acad. of Dramatic Arts, N.Y., 1934–35; actor: National Junior Theatre, 1931; WCAU, Phila., 1930–34; vaudeville, Steel Pier, Atlantic City, N.J., 1931–32; WMHA & Plays & Players Productions, Phila., 1928–30; Broadway: Parade, Ah Wilderness, Oh Evening Star, Three Men on a Horse, Room Service, Brother Rat; created Henry Aldrich, What a Life, The Alchemist, She Stoops to Conquer; prod. asst. to George Abbott, 1935–40; created Henry Aldrich on radio's Aldrich Family, 1938; starred, Those Were the Days, Paramount, 1939, This is the Army, Warners 1943, USAAF, 1941–45; directed on Broadway: See My Lawyer, 1939, Reunion in New York, 1940.
STAGE: This is the Army, 1942, January Thaw, 1946, At War With the Army, 1949, To Tell You the Truth, 1947, Me and Molly, 1948, Wake Up Darling, 1956, Make a Million, 1958, The Man That Corrupted Hadleyburg, 1951, The Pink Elephant, 1953, Dear Ruth, 1961, Come Blow Your Horn, 1962, God Bless Our Bank, Fallen Angels, 1963; Finishing Touches (1978); Dracula—The Vampire King (1978).
PICTURES INCLUDE: (docum.) I.B.M., American Heart Assn. Chapman Coll., University of Judaism, Jewish Theological Seminary; dir. live action sequences for The Daydreamer; The Forty Million (producer, director, co-narrator).
TV: Aldrich Family, Danny Thomas, Ed Wynn, Ezio Pinza, Martha Raye, Fred Allen, Herb Shriner, Life With Father, Sid Caesar, Joan Davis, dir. Joe and Mabel, prod., dir. Bachelor Father, Angel, The Hathaways, spec. Affairs of Antol, Shari Lewis, Bob Hope, My Living Doll, Munsters, Karen, Tammy, O.K. Crackerby, Please Don't Eat the Daisies; dir., writer Woody Allen pilot, Loredo, Pistols & Petticoats, Petticoat Junction, Phyllis Diller Show, Lost in Space, Tammy Grimes show, Julia, Flying Nun, Debbie Reynolds, The Jimmy Stewart Show, Lassie, Sandy Duncan Show, Tribute to the Lunts, Love American Style, Bob Newhart, Space Academy, ABC Circle Playhouse Project UFO, Actor, (PBS Paul Muni, biography film). Did 200 documentary films for IBM. Has over 25 intl. film awards; Grand Prize, Barcelona Int'l Film Festival.
AUTHOR: Coming Major, 1945, co-author; Deems Taylor; Puccini Opera, 1951; contributor to: Variety, Magazine Digest, N.Y. Post; Equity Magazine, etc. Teacher: American Acad. Dramatic Arts, assoc. dir., American Theatre Wing; American College Theatre Festival, Princeton, Yale, U.C.L.A.; dir., David Library of Amer. Revolution.

STONE, MARIANNE: Actress. b. London, England. Studied Royal Acad. of Dramatic Art, making her first appearance West End stage in The Kingmaker, 1946. Since then has appeared in numerous films.
TV: Maigret, Bootsie and Snudge, Jimmy Edwards Show, Wayne and Schuster Show, Roy Hudd Show, Harry Worth Show, Steptoe and Son, Informer, Love Story, Father Dear Father, Bless This House, The Man Outside, Crown Court, Public Eye, Miss Nightingale, She, Little Lord Fauntleroy, The Secret Army (2 series).
PICTURES INCLUDE: Brighton Rock, Seven Days to

Noon, The Clouded Yellow, Wrong Arm of the Law, Heavens Above, Stolen Hours, Nothing But the Best, Curse of the Mummy's Tomb, Hysteria, The Beauty Jungle, A Hard Day's Night, Battle of a Simple Man, Echo of Diana, Act of Murder, Catch Us If You Can, You Must Be Joking, The Countess from Hong Kong, The Wrong Box, To Sir With Love, 1967–68; The Bliss of Mrs. Blossom, Here We Go Round the Mulberry Bush, Carry on Doctor, The Twisted Nerve, The Best House in London, Oh! What a Lovely War, 1970; The Raging Moon, There's a Girl in My Soup, All the Right Noises, Assault, Carry On at Your Convenience, All Coppers are . . . , Carry on Girls, Penny Gold, The Vault of Horror, Percy's Progress, Confessions of a Window Cleaner, Carry on Dick, That Lucky Touch, Sarah, Carry on Behind, Confessions From a Holiday Camp, The Chiffy Kids, What's Up Superdoc?; The Class of Miss McMichael, The Human Factor, Dangerous Davies.

STONE, PETER: Writer. Won Oscar in 1964 for Father Goose; Emmy for segment of The Defenders.
PICTURES INCLUDE: Charade, Arabesque, Mirage, Sweet Charity, The Taking of Pelham One Two Three, 1776 (adapted own stage musical book to screen), Silver Bears, Who Is Killing the Great Chefs of Europe?, Why Would I Lie?

STONEMAN, JAMES M.: Executive. b. Jan. 16, 1927. Pres., Interstate Theatres Corp., Boston.

STOREY, FREDERICK: Executive. b. Columbus, Georgia, Nov. 12, 1909. e. Georgia Tech. Adv. staff Atlanta Journal, 1933–38; adv. staff C. P. Clark Adv. Agcy., 1938; partner 1940; U.S. Navy, 1941–46; staff Georgia Theatre Co., 1946; v.p. 1947–52. Founded Storey Theatres Inc., Atlanta, Ga.; 1952, now chm. exec. comm./(formerly pres.) of Georgia State Theatres; dir. numerous theatre cos.; officer, dir. radio, TV firms; v.p. treas., dir., Motion Picture Theatre Owners of Georgia, member, NATO, member, pres., advisory council.

STORKE, WILLIAM F.: Executive. b. Rochester, N.Y. e. Univ. of Calif. In Navy in World War II. First position with NBC Hollywood guest relations staff, 1948. Moved to continuity acceptance dept. as comm. editor. Prom. to asst. mgr, comm. supvr. before joining NBC West Coast sales dept., 1953. Transferred to N.Y. as progr. acct. exec., 1955; named administrator, participating prog. sales, Nov., 1957. Named dir., participating program sales, 1959. Named dir., program adm., NBC-TV, Jan., 1964; in Feb. elected v.p., program adm. In 1967 named v.p., programs, East Coast; Nov. 1, 1968, appt. v.p., special programs, NBC TV Network; 1979, pres., Claridge Group, Ltd.

STORM, GALE: Actress. r.n. Josephine Cottle. b. Bloomington, Texas, April 5, 1922. In high school became interested in dramatics. To films, 1940.
PICTURES INCLUDE: Between Midnight and Dawn, Underworld Story, Curtain Call at Cactus Creek, Al Jennings of Oklahoma, Texas Rangers, Woman of the North Country.
TV: My Little Margie, Oh Susanna, radio show.

STRAIGHT, BEATRICE: Actress. b. Old Westbury, N.Y. 1918. Trained in classics; won Tony award early in career for best actress in Arthur Miller's The Crucible. Many films and TV programs.
PICTURES: Patterns, The Nun's Story, Phone Call from a Stranger, Network (AA), The Promise, The Formula, Endless Love.
STAGE: A Streetcar Named Desire, Phedre, The Heiress, Ghosts, The Lion in Winter, etc.
TELEVISION: Beacon Hill, many specials.

STRAMER, HUGO: Executive. b. Budapest, Hungary. Up to 1957 man. dir. of RKO in various Latin American territories. Joined Paramount Pictures 1957 as man. dir. for Argentine, Uruguay and Paraguay. 1960: man. dir. Paramount Pictures Germany. 1963–69 Continental man. for Paramount in Paris. Then man. dir. Cinema Int'l Corp. (UK). 1972, joined MPEAA in London. 1973, apptd CIC man. dir. for Argentina, Uruguay and Paraguay.

STRASBERG, LEE: Acting Instructor-Director-Actor. b. Nov. 17, 1901, Bodanov (then Austria-Hungary, now in U.S.S.R.). At 8 moved to New York with family. Began acting in teens at settlement house; soon began directing. Studied at American Laboratory Theatre under Richard Boleslavski and Maria Ouspenskaya, who had studied with Stanislavski, founder of Moscow Art Theatre. Founded Group Theatre in early '30s; since 1949 artistic director of Actors Studio, known for acting technique called The Method.
STAGE CREDITS: Supervised productions of Marathon '33, Baby Wants a Kiss, Blues for Mr. Charlie, revivals of Strange Interlude, The Three Sisters, etc.
PICTURES: Actor: The Godfather, Part II (AA nominee), And Justice for All, Going in Style, Boardwalk.

STRASBERG, SUSAN: Actress. b. New York, N.Y.; e. there. Parents: Lee Strasberg, stage dir. & dir. of Actors Studio, and Paula Miller, actress. Made stage debut in off-Bway.

production of Maya; on TV in series, The Marriage, The Duchess and the Smugs, Catch a Falling Star; starred on Bway. in The Diary of Anne Frank.

PICTURES INCLUDE: Picnic, Stage Struck, Scream of Fear, Adventures of a Young Man, The Trip, Psych-Out, The Name of the Game is Kill, Rollercoaster, The Manitou, In Praise of Older Women.

STRASSBERG, STEPHEN: Publicist. B. New York, N.Y.; e. C.C.N.Y., B.S.S., joined Loew's Inc., 1940; served in U.S. Army, WW II; publicist with Republic Pictures, 1946–49; asst. nat'l adv. dir., Film Classics, 1949–50; pub. dir., Eagle Lion Classics, 1950; publicist Lopert Films, Inc., 1951; dir. of adv., pub., Imperial Films, 1953; pub. dir., WABC, WABC-TV, N.Y., 1955; asst. dir., Press Information; ABC, 1957; dir. press info. ABC-TV Network, 1958; dir., News Information, ABC-TV Network, 1975.

STRATTON, JOHN: Actor. b. Clitheroe, England, 1925; e. Royal Grammar School, Clitheroe. Early career in repertory; m.p. and TV debut 1948.

TV: The First Mrs. Fraser, The Confidential Clerk, Adams Apple, You Know What People Are (series). Death of a Salesman, Quatermass in The Pit, The Wind and the Rain, The Secret Kingdom, Kipps, The Dobson Fund, The Problem of Mary Winshaw, A Perfect Woman, Climate of Fear, Thank You and Goodnight, What's In It for Walter, A Free Weekend, Workshop Limits, 24 Hour Call, 2 Cars, The Odd Man, It's Dark Outside, For the West, Man in Room 17, Julie's Gone, The Trouble Shooters, Turn out the Lights, Mr. Rose, The Black Doctor, Sir Arthur Conan Doyle, The Newcomers, Tickle Time, Letters from the Dead, Z Car, Wanted Single Gentleman, Swiftly Softly, Fall of the Goat, City '68, Artists in Crime, The First Lady, Print and Be Damned, The Expert, Resurrection (serial), Sherlock Holmes, Measure of Malice, The Elusive Pimpernel (serial), The Pallisers, Fall of the Eagles, Clayhanger, Trinity Tales, Witch of Pendle, When We Are Married, Just William, Backs to the Land.

PICTURES INCLUDE: Small Back Room, Seven Days to Noon, Appointment With Venus (Island Rescue), Happy Family, Cruel Sea, Long Arm, Man In the Sky, Seven Waves Away (Abandon Ship), The Challenge, Strangler's Web.

STRAUSBERG, SOLOMON M.: Exhibitor, attorney. b. N.Y.C. Feb. 16, 1907. e. U. of P., 1927, B.S. in Econ.; Columbia U. Law Sch., 1930, J.D.; St. John's U. Law Sch. 1931, L.L.M. U.S. Navy, Lt. Comdr. Supply Corps, 1942–45; chmn. of bd. & pres. Interboro Circuit Inc., New York City. Member: Variety Club, Cinema Lodge, M.P. Pioneers; pres. Metropolitan M.P. Theatres Assn., Inc., 1956; chmn. of bd., Metro. M.P. Theatres Assn., 1958–61.

STRAUSS, JOHN: Publicist. b. N.Y. Apr. 2, 1913; e. Yale U., B.A., 1935. Securities trader & analyst, Mabon & Co., N.Y. 1935–41; New Eng. factory rep., Star Rubber Co., 1941; city sales rep., W.B., Buffalo, 1941–45; unit pub., W.B., Burbank, 1945; asst. pub. dir., PRC., 1946; unit pub., Enterprise Prod., 1946–47; pub., Columbia Studios, 1947–48; Pres., McFadden, Strauss & Irwin, Inc., pub. rel. counsellors for personalities, m.p. TV & indust. accts., Los Angeles, New York, Palm Springs, London, Paris.

STRAUSS, PETER: Actor. b. Croton-on-Hudson, N.Y., 1947. e. Northwestern Univ. Spotted at N.U. by talent agent and sent to Hollywood. Debut in Hail Hero (1969). Has acted at Mark Taper Theatre in Dance Next Door, The Dirty Man.

PICTURES: Hail, Hero!, Soldier Blue, The Trail of the Catonsville Nine, The Last Tycoon.

TELEVISION: Man Without a Country, Attack on Terror, Rich Man, Poor Man, The Forgotten Kennedy, Masada.

STRAUSS, PETER E. Executive. b. Oct. 7, 1940. e. Oberlin College, London School of Economics, Columbia University School of Law (L.L.B.), 1965). Vice pres., University Dormitory Development Co., 1965–68; v.p., Allart Cinema 16, 1968–69; v.p. Production, Allied Artists, 1969–70; v.p. operations and member of board, Allied Artists Pictures Corp., 1970; June 14, 1974 elected exec. v.p. Joined Rastor Films; left to become independent.

STRAUSS, RICHARD: b. Chicago, Ill.; e. Northwest U., Fordham U., Univ. of Illinois (also graduate work U. of Ill., U.S.C.). President of Bevelite-Adler Co. Past pres. TESMA; bd. secty. TEA, Calif. Sign Ass'n., Exhibit rules of Nat'l. Electric Sign Ass'n.; Variety Club, life member; bd. of dir., National Electric Sign Assn.

STREEP, MERYL: Actress. b. Bernardsville, N.J. April 22, 1949. Gained fame on N.Y. stage in such plays as Trelawny of the Wells, The Taming of the Shrew, The Cherry Orchard, Happy End, etc.

PICTURES: Julia, Manhattan, The Deer Hunter, The Seduction of Joe Tynan, Kramer vs. Kramer (AA, best supporting actress, 1979), The French Lieutenant's Woman, Stab.

TELEVISION: Holocaust.

STREISAND, BARBRA: Singer, actress. b. New York, April 24, 1942. e. Erasmus H.S., Brooklyn. Appeared in New York

night clubs. On Broadway in I Can Get It For You Wholesale, debut 1962; Funny Girl.

PICTURES INCLUDE: (debut) Funny Girl, Hello Dolly, On A Clear Day You Can See Forever, The Owl and the Pussycat, What's Up Doc?, Up the Sandbox, The Way We Were, For Pete's Sake, Funny Lady, A Star is Born, (star, prod.), The Main Event (star, co-prod.), All Night Long.

TV: My Name is Barbra, Color Me Barbra, Bell of 14th Street, A Happening in Central Park.

STRICKLYN, RAY: Actor. b. Houston, Texas, October 8; e. University of Houston.

PLAYS INCLUDE: Broadway debut in Moss Hart's The Climate of Eden. Tour: Stalag 17. Off-B'way: The Grass Harp. Alley Theatre, Houston: Mourning Becomes Electra, Long Day's Journey Into Night, etc. Los Angeles: Starred in Compulsion and The Caretaker.

FILMS INCLUDE: The Proud and the Profane, Crime In the Streets, Somebody Up There Likes Me, Catered Affair, The Last Wagon, Return of Dracula, 10 North Frederick, The Remarkable Mr. Pennypacker, The Big Fisherman, The Plunderers, The Lost World, Young Jesse James, Track of Thunder, Arizona Raiders, Shuffle.

AWARDS: Broadway Theatre World Award; two Hollywood Foreign Press Golden Globe nominations (10 North Frederick and The Plunderers).

STROCK, HERBERT L.: Prod.-writer, dir., film editor. b. Boston, Mass., Jan. 13, 1918. e. Univ. of So. Calif., A.B., M.A. in cinema; prof., of Cinema, Univ. of So. Calif., 1941. Started career, publicity leg man, Jimmy Fidler, Hollywood columnist; editorial dept., MGM, 1941–47; pres., IMPPRO, Inc., 1955–59; assoc. prod.-supv. film ed., U.A.; dir., AIP; dir., Phoenix Films. Pres., Herbert L. Strock Prods.

PICTURES INCLUDE: Storm Over Tibet, Magnetic Monster, Riders to the Stars, The Glass Wall, Gog, Battle Taxi, Donovan's Brain, Rider on a Dead Horse, Devil's Messenger, Brother on the Run, One Hour of Hell, Witches Brew, Blood of Dracula, I Was a Teenage Frankenstein, The Crawling Hand. Director; Brother On the Row, Monster. Writer-film editor, Hurray for Betty Boop (cartoon).

TV: Highway Patrol, Harbor Command, Men of Annapolis, I Led Three Lives, The Veil, Dragnet, 77 Sunset Strip, Maverick, Cheyenne, Bronco, Sugarfoot, Colt 45, Science Fiction Thea., Seahunt, Corliss Archer, Bonanza, Hallmark Hall of Fame, The Small Miracle, Hans Brinker, The Inventing of America (specials) for World Vision Intl.; What Will We Say to a Hungry World (5 hr. Telethon), They Search for Survival (special). NBC specials, Flipper (series). Documentaries: Atlantis, Legends, UFO Journals.

STROSS, RAYMOND: Producer, exhibitor. b. Leeds, England, May 22, 1916. b. Abington, Oxford. Ent. m.p. ind. 1933, worked at Sound City, other studios as exec. until 1938; then prod., exhibitor; formed Raymond Stross Theatres; re-entered production, 1950.

PICTURES INCLUDE: Hell is Sold Out, Tall Headlines, Man Who Watched the Trains Go By, Rough Shoot (Shoot First), Star of India, Jumping for Joy, As Long as They're Happy, An Alligator Named Daisy, A Touch of the Sun, The Flesh is Weak, A Question of Adultery, The Angry Hills, A Terrible Beauty, The Mark, Very Edge, The Leather Boys, Ninety Degrees in the Shade, The Fox, I Want What I Want, The Woman Who Rode Away.

STRUDWICK, SHEPPERD: Actor. b. Hillsboro, N.C., Sept. 22, 1907; e. U. of N.C. 1928, B.A. Stage experience since 1933; member Phi Beta Kappa Naval officer 1942–45.

STAGE: Both Your Houses, Let Freedom Ring, End of Summer, As You Like It, Christopher Blake, Affairs of State, Ladies of the Corridor.

PICTURES INCLUDE: (debut) Congo Maizie, 1940; Flight Command, Remember the Day, Edgar Allen Poe, Joan of Arc, Enchantment, The Red Pony, All the King's Men, A Place in the Sun, Eddie Duchin Story, Autumn Leaves, That Night, Sad Sack, Psychomania, The Daring Game, Cops and Robbers.

STRUTHERS, SALLY: Actress. b. Portland, OR, 1948.

PICTURES: The Phynx, Charlotte, Five Easy Pieces, The Getaway.

TELEVISION: Summer Bros. Smothers Show, Tim Conway Comedy Hour, All in the Family (series). Films: The Great Houdinis, Aloha Means Goodbye, Hey, I'm Alive.

STULBERG, GORDON: Executive. b. Toronto, Canada, Dec. 17, 1923; e. U. of Toronto, B.A., Cornell Law, LLB. Was assoc. & member, Pacht, Ross, Warne & Bernhard; ent. m.p. ind. as exec. asst. to v.p., Columbia Pictures Corp., 1956–60; v.p. & chief studio admin. off., 1960–67; pres. of Cinema Center Films (div. of CBS) 1967–71; pres. 20th Century-Fox, Sept. 1971–75; 1980, named pres. & chief operating officer, PolyGram Pictures. Member of N.Y. & Calif. bars.

STURDIVANT, B. VICTOR: Circuit executive. b. Gurdon, Ark., April 5, 1901; e. Crossett, Ark., Baylor U., Waco, Tex. Specialized journalism followed by newspaper work as reporter several Texas papers, news ed., Memphis (Tenn.)

News-Scimitar, city ee., Jacksonville, Fla. Journal, staff corresp. and then mgr. southern bureau (Atlanta, Ga.) International News Service. Three yrs. adv. & pub. counsel automobile ind. Became affiliated with Skouras-Publix Theat. in 1930. Joined Fox West Coast theatres August 1932, oper. various districts throughout So. Calif. until June, 1942, when apptd. div. mgr. No. Calif. with headquarters in San Francisco. Originator-organizer Los Angeles Theatre Defense Bureau Dec. 7, 1941; national campaign dir., M.P. Ind. Fourth War Loan; v.p. Calif. War Chest; pres., California Theatres Assn., Inc. Latin Amer. mgr., Nat'l Theats. Amusement Co.; org. Espectaculos Victor Sturdivant, Rio de Janerio, Brazil, dist. m.p. & TV films, manage talent Latin America. Owner-mgr. Silver Crest Ent.; pres. Sturdivant, Inc., Yuma, Ariz.; pres. Yuma City Cham. Comm.; Yuma City Man of the Year, 1967; chmn. exec. comm., Citizens' Conference of Arizona Courts; mem. Gov. of Arizona Advis. Bd.; pres. NATO of Arizona.

STURGES, JOHN ELIOT: Director. b. Jan. 3, Oak Park, Ill. e. Marin Jr. Coll. asst. in blueprint dept., RKO-Radio Pictures, 1932; art dept; asst. film ed.; prod. asst., David O. Selznick; film ed.; Captain, Air Corps, WW II; directed, edited, 45 documentaries, training films.
PICTURES INCLUDE: The Man Who Dared, Shadowed, Alias Mr. Twilight, For the Love of Rusty, Keeper of the Bees, Best Man Wins, Sign of the Ram, The Walking Hills, The Capture, Mystery Street, Right Cross, The Magnificent Yankee, Kind Lady, The People vs. O'Hara, The Girl in White, Jeopardy, Fast Company, Escape from Fort Bravo, Bad Day at Black Rock, Gunfight at the O.K. Corral, The Old Man and the Sea, Last Train from Gun Hill, Never So Few, The Magnificent Seven, By Love Possessed, Sergeants Three, A Girl Named Tamiko, The Great Escape, The Satan Bug, Hallelujah Trail, Hour of the Gun, Ice Station Zebra, Marooned, Joe Kidd, McQ, The Eagle Has Landed.

STURGIS, NORMAN: Director, actor, writer. b. Dallas, Tex. 1922; prod., Your Navy Sings, Evanston; TV dir. Space X, Theaterama, Plays Anthology, The Viewers, TV commercials, educational films and newsfilms.
TV: The Web, Gunsmoke, Twilight Zone, Alcoa Goodyear Theatre, Bat Masterson, The Untouchables.
PICTURES INCLUDE: Solid Gold Cadillac, Bernardine, Mardi Gras, Compulsion.

STYNE, JULE: Composer, producer, r.n. Jules Stein. b. London, Eng. To U.S. as a child; guest piano soloist with Chicago Symph. Orch. at 8; played with many dance bands; gen. mus. dir. Granada & Marbro Theat., Chicago; vocal coach, arranger, conductor & comp. for several m.p. studios; entertainment consult.
SONGS: I've Heard That Song Before, It's Magic, I'll Walk Alone, It's Been a Long, Long Time; Let It Snow, 3 Coins in the Fountain (Acad. Award in collab. Sammy Cahn, 1954), People.
STAGE: High Button Shoes, Gentlemen Prefer Blondes, Two on the Aisle, Hazel Flagg, Gypsy, Sugar, Peter Pan, Bells Are Ringing, Funny Girl.
PICTURES INCLUDE: Kid from Brooklyn, It Happened in Brooklyn, Romance on the High Seas, It's a Great Feeling, West Point Story, Meet Me After the Show, Living It Up, My Sister Eileen.

SUBOTSKY, MILTON: Writer, producer. b. New York, 1921. Early career studying engineering. Wrote, dir. and edited doc. & educational films. Ent. m.p. ind. 1938. Wrote and prod. live TV programmes 1941. Wrote & prod. TV film series Junior Science 1954. Wrote & co-prod. Rock, Rock, Rock; Jamboree, The Last Mile, Timegate, in USA. In England: City of the Dead, It's Trad Dad, Just for Fun, Dr. Terror's House of Horrors, Dr. Who and The Daleks, Daleks' Invasion Earth 2150 A.D., The Skull, The Psychopath, The Deadly Bees, The Terrornauts, They Came From Beyond Space, Torture Garden, Danger Route, The Birthday Party, Thank You All Very Much (Brit. title: A Touch of Love), Scream and Scream Again, The Mind of Mr. Soames, The House That Dripped Blood, I Monster, What Became of Jack and Jill, Tales From the Crypt, Asylum, Vault of Horror, And Now the Screaming Starts, Madhouse, From Beyond the Grave, The Beast Must Die, The Land That Time Forgot, At The Earth's Core, The Uncanny, Dominique, The Martian Chronicles, The Monster Club.

SUCHER, HENRY: Writer. b. New York City, Sept. 3, 1900; e. N.Y.U. With A.E.F., WW I. M. Pearl Krex, Reporter, N.Y. Globe, then mag. ed. (Nugents, Garment Weekly, The Brooklynite); publicity adv. copywriter; contrib. light satirical verses and humorous bits to the Sat. Eve. Post, Colliers, The New Yorker and other nat'l mags. Began screen career 1941 with collab. orig. s.p. The Miracle Kid. In 1942 wrote Soundies for Roosevelt-Coslow-Mills Corp. Wrote serials, Jack Holt, G. Man, and others for Larry Darmoor at Columbia Studios. Contract writer, Eagle-Lion Studios.
PICTURES INCLUDE: Captive Wild Woman, The Mummy's Tomb, Mug Town, The Mummy's Ghost (adapt.

& collab. orig.), The Frozen Ghost, Jungle Woman, Your Fate Is In Your Hands, Lines of Destiny; short subjects released by RKO; now v.p. Edward Finney Prod., v.p. Boots and Saddles Pictures, Inc.

SUGAR, JOSEPH M.: Executive. b. New York City. e. N.Y.U. Ent. m.p. ind. 1938 in contract dept., Republic Pictures; ent. U.S. Army Air Forces, 1942; asst. contract mgr. PRC, then mgr.; when PRC merged with Eagle Lion continued as mgr. contract dept.; then exec. asst. to dist. v.p.; to U.A.N.Y. exchange, Jan. 1, 1953; v.p. sales, Magna Theatre Corp., 1959; member: Cinema Lodge, B'nai B'rith; road show mgr., 20th Century-Fox, 1962; v.p. chg. dom. distrib., 1963; exec. v.p. Warner-Seven Arts, 1967; pres. Cinerama Rel. Corp., 1968; pres., Gamma III Dist. Co., 1975; May, 1976: Joe Sugar, Inc., pres.; 1978, joined AIP as exec. v.p., worldwide sls. and pres. of AIP Distributing Co. which is now Filmways Pictures

SUGARMAN, HAROLD: Executive. b. New York City, Oct. 17, 1905; m.; e. New York Univ. Joined Paramount foreign sales dept., 1927. In charge foreign versions and adapt. at Paramount Astoria studio, Long Island City, 1928–31. Dist. mgr., UA Latin American distribution 1932–36. Prod. ind. pictures in Hollywood, 1936–40. Org. and head Universal Studio foreig.i dept., 1941–46. Transf. to Universal New York office, 1946 to org. and head 16 mm. overseas oper. Apptd. v.p. in chge. of export, United World Films, Inc., 1947; apptd. superv. So. Europe, Universal-International, hdqts., Rome, Italy, 1950; prod. & sales exec. Archer Television Prod., 1952. dist. & prod. exec. dir., of Chancellor Films.

SUHOSKY, BOB: Publicist. b. Philadelphia, Pa., Nov. 23, 1928. Marine Corps 1946–57; 20th Century Fox Television, publicist, 1959, publicity director, 1964–70; pres. Bob Suhosky Assoc., public relations, 1971–77. Chairman, Suhosky & Hardiman Public Relations, 1977 to date. Wrote s.p. for Lone Star Girls (theatrical film) and Code R (TV).

SULLIVAN, BARRY: Actor. r.n. Patrick Barry. b. New York, N.Y., Aug. 29, 1912; e. N.Y.U., Temple U. Usher in theat.; buyer for dept. stores; N.Y. stage: The Man Who Came to Dinner, Brother Rat, Idiot's Delight, The Land is Bright, Caine Mutiny Court Martial, etc.
PICTURES INCLUDE: Woman of the Town, Lady in the Dark, Rainbow Island, Two Years Before the Mast, And Now Tomorrow, Duffy's Tavern, Three Guys Named Mike, Cause for Alarm, Grounds for Marriage, Life of Her Own, Nancy Goes to Rio, Inside Straight, Payment on Demand, Mr. Imperium, No Questions Asked, Unknown Man, Skirts Ahoy, Bad & the Beautiful, Jeopardy, Cry of the Hunted, China Venture, Loophole, Her 12 Men, Miami Story, Playgirl, Queen Bee, Texas Lady, Maverick Queen, Strategic Air Command, Purple Gang, Seven Ways from Sundown, Light in the Piazza, War Lords of Outer Space, Stage to Thunder Rock, Buckskin, Tell Them Willie Boy Is Here, Earthquake, The Human Factor, Oh, God!, Caravans.

SULLIVAN, J. CHRISTOPHER: Actor. b. Greenville, TX, Sept. 15, 1932. e. Prairie View A & M Univ. Stage debut in The Sign in Sidney Brustein's Window. Also appeared in Hatful of Rain, Anna Lucasta, Ceremonies in Dark Old Men. First black to teach at any predominantly white university in the south; is instructor of speech and communications at Univ. of Texas (Austin) since 1964.
PICTURES INCLUDE: Night Call Nurses, The Venetian Affair, The Lost Man, Body Heat.
TELEVISION: The White Shadow, Jeffersons, Good Times, One Day at a Time, General Hospital, Serpico, etc.

SULLIVAN, REV. PATRICK J., S.J., S.T.D.: Director, Office for Film & Broadcasting, U.S. Catholic Conference. b. New York, N.Y., March 25, 1920; e. Regis H.S.: Georgetown U., A.B., 1943; Woodstock Coll. M.A., 1944; Fordham U., 1945–47; S.T.L. Weston Coll., 1947–51; S.T.D. Gregorian U. (Rome), 1952–54; Prof. of Theology, Woodstock Coll., 1954–57; editor-in-chief, Film & Broadcasting Review; prod. TV and radio network religious programming. Consultor, Pontifical Commission for Social Communications; member executive committee, International Catholic Film Organization (O.C.I.C.); member, Board of Management, International Catholic Radio and Television Association (UNDA).

SULTAN, ROGER H.: Executive. b. Algiers, C.P.A.; e. U. of Algiers, LL.B. pub. adv. slsmn., 1934–35; thea. exploit., Algiers, 1936–39; French Army, 1939–40, 1943–45; bkr., slsmn., film distrib. co., N. Africa, 1941–42, 1945–46; auditor, office mgr., asst. supvsr., Atlantic Div., Warner Bros., Brazil, 1947–51; br. mgr., spvsr., No. Div., Allied Artists, Brazil, 1953–57; mgr., Allied Artists Chile, 1957–62; asst. gen. sls. mgr. (for.), Allied Artists Int., New York, 1962–64; v.p., gen. sls. mgr., 1965; pres., gen. sls. mgr., 1968–70; producer's rep.

SUMMERFIELD, ELEANOR: Actress. b. London, Eng., Mar. 7, 1921. Stage debut in Cornelius, 1939; screen debut in London Belongs to Me (in U.S.A., Dulcimer Street), 1947.
PICTURES INCLUDE: Take My Life, All Over the Town,

No Way Back, The Third Visitor, Scrooge, Laughter in Paradise, Mandy, Top Secret, Isn't Life Wonderful, Street Corner (Both Sides of the Law), Face the Music, Murder by Proxy, Lost, It's Great to be Young, Odongo, No Road Back, A Cry from the Streets, The Millionairess, Spare the Rod, Don't Bother to Knock, Petticoat Pirates, On the Fiddle, Act of Mercy, On the Beat, The Running Man, The Yellow Hat, Private Eye, Foreign Exchange, Some Will, Some Won't, Watcher in the Woods.

TV: (BBC, indep.) My Wife's Sister, The Two Charles (series), The Invasion, Dickie Henderson Shows, Night Train to Surbiton, Many A Slip, World of Wooster, David Copperfield, The Suede Jacket, Haunted, You're Lovely in Black, Misleading Cases, East of Eden, Tennis, Elbow, Foot Game, Murder at the Panto, Now Take My Wife, Madly in Love, Kate, Simon Fenton's Story, Kept on a String, Password, Husband of the Year, The Overnight Bag, The Rather Reassuring Show, Murder at the Wedding, Pig in the Middle.

SUNDBERG, CLINTON: Actor, b. Appleton, Minn., Dec. 7; e. Hamline U. Teacher of English literature; in New England stock cos.; on London and N.Y. stage.

STAGE: Silent Witness, She Loves Me Not, Boy Meets Girl, Room Service, Arsenic and Old Lace, Over 21, Diary of Anne Frank, Mary, Mary.

PICTURES INCLUDE: Undercurrent, Undercover Maisie, Living in a Big Way, Song of Love, Hucksters, Kissing Bandit, Easter Parade, Good Sam, Date With Judy, Words and Music, Command Decision, In the Good Old Summertime, Key to City, Annie Get Your Gun, Toast of New Orleans, Fat Man, As Young As You Feel, Belle of New York, Girl Next Door, Main Street to Broadway, The Caddy, Birds and the Bees, Wonderful World of Brothers Grimm, How the West Was Won.

SUNSHINE, MORTON: International Executive Director, Variety Clubs International, 1975 to present. b. Brooklyn, N.Y., Sept. 20, 1915. B.S. in S.S. (1935), LL.B. (1938), J.S.D. (1939); admitted to N.Y. Bar 1939. Federal Bar 1941. Practicing attorney, 1941–44; Federal investigator with U.S.C.S.C. 1944–45; business mgr., Independent Theatre Owners Assn. 1945–46; exec. dir. since 1946; member COMPO tax & legis. com., 1950; sp. rep. Org. of M.P. Ind. of City of N.Y., 1952–55; exec. coord. Tony Awards dinner Amer. Theatre Wing, 1958–60, Sophie Tucker Golden Jubilee; ind. trib. to Jimmy Durante; Will Rogers; A. Montague; Herman Robbins; S. H. Fabian; Rodgers-Hammerstein; Eric Johnston; Diamond Jubilee, Stagehands, 1962. Danny Thomas; indus. pub. rel. consultant; exec. coord. IFIDA Int'l Film Awards Dinners; pres. cabinet, Nat'l Assn. of Theatre Owners, Exec. dir., Variety Club of N.Y., 1970; Consultant to American Film Institute, 1973–75; executive director, Motion Picture Pioneers, 1970–75; Editor-Publisher, Independent Film Journal, 1947–75.

SURTEES, BRUCE: Cinematographer. Son of Robert L. Surtees.

PICTURES INCLUDE: Play Misty for Me, Dirty Harry, The Great Northfield Minnesota Raid, The Beguiled, High Plains Drifter, Blume in Love, Joe Kidd, Lennie (A.A. nomination), Leadbelly, Sparkle, Big Wednesday, Escape from Alcatraz.

SURTEES, ROBERT L.: Cinematographer. b. Covington, Ky., Aug. 9, 1906; e. Withrow H.S., Cincinnati, Ohio, 1925. Ent. m.p. ind. as asst. cameraman, Universal Pictures Corp., 1927–29; Universal, Berlin, 1929–30; ret'd to U.S.; since with First Nat'l, Warner Bros., Pathe, MGM; won Look Mag. Award for Film Achievement, 1950; member: ASC. 13 A.A. nominations; winner 3 times.

PICTURES INCLUDE: Our Vines Have Tender Grapes, Thirty Seconds Over Tokyo, Intruder in the Dust. Acad. Award, best color photog., King Solomon's Mines, 1950; best photog. The Bad and the Beautiful, 1952; Merry Widow, Mogambo, Trial, Oklahoma, The Swan, Raintree County, Merry Andrew, Ben Hur (AA), Mutiny on the Bounty, The Hallelujah Trail, The Collector, The Satan Bug, Lost Command, Doctor Dolittle, Sweet Charity, Summer of '42, The Cowboys, The Other, The Sting, The Great Waldo Pepper, The Hindenburg, A Star is Born, The Turning Point, Same Time Next Year, Bloodbrothers.

SUSSAN, HERBERT: Producer. b. New York, N.Y., Feb. 24, 1921. e. N.Y.U. U. of So. Calif. Radio writer, prod. 1937–42; series included American Rhapsody, Theme and Variations; m.p. prod., Army Air Forces, 1942; supervised prod., dir. films in Far East on effects of atomic bombs in Japan, life and culture, 1945–46; dir. film coverage, Louis de Rochemont, 1947; author of 3 photo books on Japan; assoc. dir., CBS TV 1948, worked on Suspense, Mama, Studio One, others. prod. dir., 1949: dir. 54th St. Revue, Ken Murray Show, Eddie Fisher Show, Christmas with the Stars; prod., dir. Guy Lombardo Show; sen. prod. Wide Wide World, 1955–58; natl. dir. sp. prog. NBC-TV, 1958–60; pres. Herbert Sussman Ent.

SUSSKIND, DAVID: Producer—TV Talk Show Host. b. New York City, 1920. Producer of TV shows, founder of production co., Talent Associates; host of own syndicated interview program (The David Susskind Show; formerly called Open End.) Notable for producing TV adaptations of famous plays: Glass Menagerie, The Crucible, Death of a Salesman, etc. In 1970 Norton Simon, Inc. acquired his co., renaming it Talent Associates—Norton Simon for theatrical as well as TV film production. Sold in 1977 to Time-Life Films.

SUTHERLAND, DONALD: Actor b. St. John, New Brunswick, Canada, July 17. m. Shirley Douglas, actress. e. U. of Toronto. At 14 became a radio announcer and disc jockey. Worked in a mine in Finland. Theatre includes: The Male Animal (debut), The Tempest (Hart House Theatre, U. of Toronto), Two years at London Acad. of Music and Dramatic Art. Spent a year and a half with the Perth Repertory Theatre in Scotland, the repertory at Nottingham, Chesterfield, Bromley and Sheffield. London stage debut: August for the People.

STAGE: On a Clear Day You Can See Canterbury, The Shewing Up of Blanco Posnet, The Spoon River Anthology.

PICTURES INCLUDE: The Castle of the Living Dead, Dr. Terror's House of Horrors, The Dirty Dozen, Oedipus the King, Interlude, Joanna. The Split, Start the Revolution Without Me, The Act of the Heart, M⅛A⅛S⅛H⅛, Kelly's Heroes, Little Murders, Alex in Wonderland, Klute, F.T.A., Steelyard Blues, Lady Ice, Don't Look Now, S⅛P⅛Y⅛S⅛, The Day of the Locust, Casanova, The Eagle Has Landed, 1900, National Lampoon's Animal House, Invasion of the Body Snatchers, Murder by Decree, Nothing Personal, Ordinary People, Gas, Eye of the Needle.

TV: (British) Gore Vidal's Marching to the Sea, Albee's The Death of Bessie Smith, Hamlet at Eisinore, The Saint, The Avengers, Gideon's Way, The Champions.

SUTTON, JAMES T.: Executive. b. Calif., Sept. 13 e. Columbia U.; film inspector, U.S. Government; overseas m.p. service, WW II; co-owner, gen. mgr., Hal Davis Studios; hd. TV commercial div., Allan Sandler Films; Academy Art Pictures; pres., chmn. of bd., exec. prod., Royal Russian Studios, Inc., western hemisphere div.; pres. exec. prod. Gold Lion Prods., Inc.; pres. exec. prod. James T. Sutton-John L. Carpenter Prods.; pres., exec. dir., Airax Corp.; pres. of Skyax (div. of Airax).

SUTTON, JOHN: Actor. b. Rawalpindi, India, Oct. 22, 1908; e. Wellington, Coll.; Sandhurst (England). Spent 8 yrs. hunting in Africa; became veldt rancher; managed tea plantation; lived in China, Malaya, Philippines; studied voice in Los Angeles; became tech. adv. on films with British background; then actor. On screen 1937.

PICTURES INCLUDE: Jane Eyre, The Hour Before the Dawn, Claudia and David, Captain from Castile, Three Musketeers, Bagdad, Second Woman, Second Face, Payment on Demand, David and Bathsheba, Thief of Damascus, Captain Pirate, Golden Hawk, My Cousin Rachel, Sangaree, East of Sumatra, The Bat.

SUTTON, REGINALD: Sound technician. b. London, Oct. 24, 1916. e. Acton County School, Kent College, Canterbury, Regent Street Polytechnic. Early career with BBC engineering div.; ent. m.p. ind. with British Movietonews; following news-reel work recorded whole Royal Tour of Australasia 1953–54 for Flight of the White Heron in CinemaScope; other CinemaScope recordings include Supersonic Age, Birthday Parade, Pastimes and Pleasures; TV features, commercials. Chief of sound, Samuelson Film Service Ltd., 1960. Location facilities and Westrex Magnetic Transfer suite, Formed own company, Soundways Ltd., recording sound for m.p., 1960.

SWALLOW, NORMAN: Producer. b. Manchester, Eng., Feb. 17, 1921. e. Manchester Grammar Sch., Keble Coll. (Oxford U.). British Army 1941–46; BBC as writer-prod. of docum., 1946; wrote 3 docum. films, 1948; TV as docum. prod., 1950; prods. include American Looks at Britain, with Howard K. Smith for CBS, Wilfred Pickles at Home series; orig. Speaking Personally series with appearance of people like Bertrand Russell; co-prod. TV coverage of Britain's general election, 1951; ed. prod. BBC monthly prog. Special Inquiry, 1952–56; World is Ours, 1954–56; study tour Middle East, India, Pakistan, Ceylon, 1956–57; writer, prod. Line of Defense, I Was a Stranger; asst. head films for BBC, 1957; writer-prod., On Target, 1959; apptd. chief asst. (doc. & gen.), BBC-TV, 1960; asst. editor, Panorama, BBC-TV, 1961. Joined Denis Mitchell films, May 1963; writer, prod., Pomp and Pageantry, The Right to Health, A Wedding on Saturday, 1964; The End of a Street, 1964; exec. prod., Report from Britain, 1964; writer, prod., Youth, British, Football; co-prod. This England. prod. A Railwayman for Me, 1966; co-prod. Ten Days That Shook the World, 1967. Co-prod. The Long Bridge, 1968. prod., dir., The Three Happiest Years; exec. prod. Omnibus series, 1968–70. Writer, prod., dir. To Leningrad With Love; exec. prod. Omnibus Series, 1968–72. Writer, co-prod. Eisenstein, 1970. BBC-TV Head of Arts Features 1972–4.

Prod-dir. series A Lasting Joy 1972. Exec. Prod. Granada TV since 1974 of The Christians, This England, Clouds of Glory. Winner Desmond Davis Award (UK) 1977.

SWANN, FRANCIS: Writer. b. Annapolis, Md., July 17, 1913; e. Princeton U.; Johns Hopkins U. 1935. Stage experience, 8 yrs., actor, musician, dir., wrote plays: Out of the Frying Pan, Family Man, Bad Angel, Follies of 1910, Paradise Island, Dear God, Send Us a Producer, Country Bumpkins; fiction writer. Novels pub.: The Brass Key, Greenwood, Royal Street, You'll Hang, My Love, Hermit's Island, Hellgate Plantation, Hacienda Triste, House of Terror; nat'l pub.; U.S. Navy, 1942–46. Member: Dramatists Guild, Writers Guild of America, Authors League of America.
PICTURES INCLUDE: Shine on Harvest Moon, The Gay Intruders, Time Place & the Girl, Love & Learn, Jungle Patrol, Tarzan's Peril, 711 Ocean Drive, Barefoot Mailman, One Big Affair, Force of Impulse, Instant Love, Candy Man, A Very Rich Man, Cover Up, Make Your Own Bed.

SWANSON, GLORIA: Actress. b. Chicago, Ill., Mar. 27, 1899; e. schools in Key West, Puerto Rico, Chicago Art Inst. Screen debut at old Essanay Studios (Elvira Farina, The Meal Ticket); then to Keystone (The Nick of Time Baby, Teddy at the Throttle, Haystacks and Steeples, etc.); next with Sennett Comedies (Pullman Bride) 1917; Triangle (Her Decision, You Can't Believe Everything, Wife or Country, Secret Code, etc.).
PICTURES INCLUDE: (under Cecil B. DeMille) Don't Change Your Husband, For Better For Worse, Male and Female, Why Change Your Wife, The Affairs of Anatol; later in Paramount films The Great Moment, The Gilded Cage, My American Wife, Prodigal Daughter, Bluebeard's Eighth Wife, others; among Alan Dawn prods. The Humming Bird, Society Scandal, Manhandled, Wages of Virtue, Madame Sans Gene, Stage Struck. In 1926 formed own corp. to prod. pictures for release through United Artists; first film The Lovers of Sonya; later Sadie Thompson, The Trespasser, What a Widow, Indiscreet, Tonight or Never. In 1935 Music in the Air (Fox); in 1941 Father Takes a Wife (RKO), 1949, Sunset Boulevard; Three for Bedroom C, When Comedy Was King, Airport-1975.
THEATRE: New York stage: Twentieth Century, 1951; Nina, 1952; Butterflies Are Free, 1970–73.
TV: Killer Bees (movie of the week), 1974.

SWANSON, ROBERT E.: Musician. b. New York, Dec. 1, 1920. e. N.Y.U. Arranging, performing in bands 10 yrs.; singing commercial for Piel's Beer, 1948; since creating, prod. musical com. radio, TV. pres. Robert Swanson Prod. Inc.

SWAYZE, JOHN CAMERON: Reporter, commercial spokesman. b. Wichita, Kansas, Apr. 4, 1906; e. Univ. of Kansas; Anderson-Milton Dramatic Sch. Reporter and ed., Kansas City, Mo. Journal-Post; news dept. KMBC, Kansas City; head of news, NBC western network, Hollywood; NBC radio news reports, N.Y.C.; covered political conv. TV 1948–52; began News Caravan on NBC in 1949–56; panel mem. Who Said That, 1949–51; Watch the World on NBC-TV, 1948–50; Sightseeing With The Swayzes (with family) NBC-TV, 1953; news program, ABC, 1957. Host: Circle Theatre, NBC, and panel member, To Tell the Truth, CBS. Voted best news commentator, M.P. Daily TV Poll, 1951–55.
MEMBER: Lambs and Players clubs; National Press Club, Greenwich, Conn., CC.

SWEDROE, JEROME D.: Executive. b. N.Y.C., September 7, 1925. e. NYU, B.S. Entered industry 1949 bookkeeping dept. Skouras Theatres Corp. Advanced through dept. to Comptroller in March 1962 and v.p. June 1964. Appointed exec. v.p. in charge operations of the chain, name had been changed to United Artists Eastern Theatre Circuit, Inc., in April, 1967; promoted v.p. parent company, UATC, January 1968. Resigned to join Cinecom March 3, 1969. Elected director Aug. 1969; joined Redstone Management Co., June, 1971; named v.p., operations, U.S. Cinema Corp., December, 1971, consultant October, 1973.

SWENSON, S.A.G.: Producer, distributor. b. Stockholm, Sweden. e. Stockholm, London, & N.Y. Entered m.p. industry in N.Y., 1921; Swedish mgr. Warner, 1923–35, pres. Wirefilm, Swedish prod. & distrib. Co., since 1935; prod. 50 feature films; Swedish rp. Korda London Films 1947–60; Disney 1954–56. Member: Various trade ass'ns Sweden, France, U.S.A. Now operates TV & theatrical import & export in Sweden & New York: Scandinavia—Wire—Films.

SWERLING, JO: Writer. b. Russia, Apr. 8, 1897. Newspaper & mag. writer; author vaude. sketches; co-author plays, The Kibitzer, Guys and Dolls.
PICTURES INCLUDE: s.p., The Kibitzer, Guys and Dolls; s.p., Platinum Blonde, Washington Merry-Go-Round, Dirigible, Man's Castle; collab. s.p., Whole Town's Talking; s.p., No Greater Glory, Pennies from Heaven, Double Wedding, Made for Each Other; collab. s.p., The Westerner; s.p., Confirm or Deny, Blood and Sand; collab. s.p., Pride of the Yankees; story, Lady Takes a Chance; s.p.,

Crash Dive, Lifeboat, Leave Her to Heaven, Thunder in the East.
TV: collab. The Lord Don't Play Favorites, NBC.

SWIFT, ALLEN: Performer. b. New York City, Jan. 16, 1924; Actor vaudeville, legitimate stage, radio and TV shows, including Bob Hope, Eddie Cantor, Jackie Gleason shows; voices for Mighty Mouse and UPA features and commercials; now announcer-master of ceremonies.

SWIFT, DAVID: Producer, director, writer. b. Minneapolis, 1919. Served with 8th Air Force in England, WW II. Entered m.p. ind. in Walt Disney animation dept. After service, comedy writer for radio. Later, starting in 1949, TV drama writer for Philco Playhouse, Studio One, Kraft Theatre, Omnibus. Created Mr. Peepers, Jamie. Writer-dir. Playhouse 90, Rifleman, Wagon Train, Climax, others. First feature film Pollyana (writer-dir.).
PICTURES INCLUDE: The Parent Trap, The Interns, Love Is a Ball, Under the Yum Yum Tree; pr.-dir.-writer, Good Neighbor Sam, How to Succeed in Business Without Really Trying.

SWIFT, LELA: Director.
TV: Studio One, Suspense, The Web, Justice, Dupont Show of the Week, Purex Specials For Women, (Emmy Award) Dark Shadows, Norman Corwin Presents, ABC Late Night 90 min. Specials, ABC Daytime 90 min. Play Break. Won three Emmy awards for best director of day-time serial: Ryan's Hope (1977, 1979, 1980).

SWIMMER, SAUL: Producer-director. b. Uniontown, Pa. e. Carnegie Tech Drama Dept. Producer-director of Melephant. Winner, Gold Leaf Venice Award, 1959. Director: Force of Impulse. Exec. prod. The Wounds of Hunger; prod. dir. Around the World of Mike Todd (Embassy Pictures TV Special, 1967), 1965–67; TV series development for Screen Gems. Advisor: CBS-TV Children's Film Festival (1967). In Charge of Production: Mrs. Brown, You've Got a Lovely Daughter, Only Lovers Left Alive; Stranger in the Night.
PICTURES INCLUDE: Cometogether (co-prod., dir.), The Concert for Bangladesh (dir.), Blindman (prod.).

SWINK, ROBERT E.: Film editor, Director. b. Rocky Ford, Colo., June 3, 1918; married. Joined editorial dept., RKO Radio, 1936; apptd. film ed., 1941. In U.S. Army Signal Corps, 1944–45; supv. editor, Fox studio. Edited numerous productions.
PICTURES INCLUDE: Detective Story, Carrie, Roman Holiday, Desperate House, Friendly Persuasion, The Big Country, The Diary of Anne Frank, The Young Doctors, The Children's Hour, The Best Man, The Collector, How To Steal A Million, Flim Flam Man, Funny Girl, The Liberation of L. B. Jones, The Cowboys, Skyjacked, Lady Ice, Papillion, Three the Hard Way, Rooster Cogburn, Midway, Islands in the Stream, Gray Lady Down, The Boys From Brazil, The In-Laws, Going in Style, The Sphinx.

SWIT, LORETTA: Actress. b. Passaic, NJ, Nov. 4, 1937. Stage debut in Any Wednesday. Toured in Mame for year. Arrived in Hollywood in 1969 and began TV career. Theatrical film debut in Stand Up and Be Counted, 1972.
PICTURES: Freebie and the Bean, Race with the Devil, "S.O.B."
TELEVISION: MASH, Gunsmoke, Mannix, Hawaii Five-0, Mission: Impossible, The Doctors, Cade's County. Films: Shirts/Skin, Coffeeville, Valentine, Mirrors, Mirror, The Walls Came Tumbling Down.

SWOPE, HERBERT BAYARD, JR.: Director, producer, ctm-mentator. b. N.Y. e. Horace Mann Sch., Princeton Univ. U.S. Navy, 1941–46; rejoined CBS-TV as remote unit dir., 1946 directing many "firsts" in sportscasting; winner, Variety Show Management Award for sports coverage & citation by Amer. TV Society, 1948; joined NBC as dir., 1949; prod. dir., 1951; Lights Out, The Clock, The Black Robe, dir., Robt. Montgomery Presents; winner, Sylvania, 1952. TV Award Outstanding Achievement in Directorial Technique; became executive producer, NBC-TV in charge of Wide, Wide World; directed Arsenic & Old Lace on Best of Broadway, CBS-TV, 1955; dir. Climax, CBS-TV, Film prod., 20th Century-Fox, Hilda Crane, Three Brave Men, True Story of Jesse James, The Bravados, The Fiend who Walked the West; 1960–62; exec. prod. 20th-Fox TV: many Loves of Dobie Gillis, Five Fingers; dir. co-prod. on Broadway, Step On A Crack, Fragile Fox, Fair Game for Lovers. 1970–72 exec. at NYC Off-Track Betting Corp. 1973–74; vice-president, Walter Reade Organization, Inc.; 1975–76 producer-host, This Was TV, Growth of a Giant; 1976–77 commentator, Swope's Scope (radio); Critic (TV); column Swope's Scope, Palm Beach (FLA) pictorial.

SYKES, ERIC: Scriptwriter, comedian. b. Oldham, England, 1924. Early career actor; ent. TV industry, 1948; wrote first three series, BBC's Educating Archie and radio, TV comedy series for Frankie Howard, Max Bygraves, Harry Secombe. BBC panel show member. Longterm contract ATV, 1956; own BBC series, 1958–65, Sykes Versus TV, The Frankie Howard Show; Sykes and a Big, Big Show, 1971,

1978 19th Year BBC-TV series. Toured extensively in Big Bad House. 1977 Summer Show Sykes. 1978 Tour of Sykes to Rhodesia, Australia, Canada, The Plank, Rhubarb.

PICTURES INCLUDE: Watch Your Stern, Invasion Quartet, Village of Daughters, Kill or Cure, Heavens Above, The Bargee, One Way Pendulum, Those Magnificent Men in Their Flying Machines, Rotten to the Core, The Liquidator, Spy With The Cold Nose. 1967, Dir. s.p. The Plank, Shalako, The Monte Carlo Rally, Theatre of Blood.

SYLBERT, ANTHEA: Executive. b. New York. e. Barnard (B.A.); Parsons School of Design (M.A.). Early career in costume design with range of Bdwy., off-Bdwy. and m.p. credits (Rosemary's Baby, F.I.S.T., Shampoo, The Fortune, A New Leaf, The Heartbreak Kid. Two A.A. nominations for creative costume designs for Julia and Chinatown. Joined Warner Bros. in October, 1977, as v.p., special projects, acting as liaison between creative executives, production dept., and creative talent producing films for company. In October, 1978, named v.p., production (projects included One Trick Pony, Personal Best, etc.). In March, 1980 appointed v.p.—production, for United Artists, working on Stab, Jinx, Swing Shift.

SYMS, SYLVIA: Actress. b. London, 1934. e. Convent and Grammar Schools. Film debut, 1955, My Teenage Daughter.

PICTURES INCLUDE: No Time For Tears, Birthday Present, Woman In A Dressing Gown, Ice Cold in Alex, The Devil's Disciple, Moonraker, Bachelor of Hearts, No Trees in the Street, Ferry to Hong Kong, Expresso Bongo, Conspiracy of Hearts, The World of Suzie Wong, Flame in the Streets, Victim, Quare Fellow, Punch & Judy Man, The World Ten Times Over, East of Sudan, The Eliminator, Operation Crossbow, The Big Job, Hostile Witness, The Marauders, The White Cold, Danger Route, Run Wild, Run Free, The Desperados, The Tamarind Seed, Give Us This Day, There Goes the Bride.

TV: The Human Jungle (series), Something to Declare, The Saint (series), The Baron (series), Bat Out of Hell, Department in Terror, Friends and Romans, Strange Report, Half-hour Story, The Root of All Evil, The Bridesmaid, Clutterbuck, Movie Quiz, My Good Woman, Looks Familiar, Love and Marriage, The Truth About Verity, I'm Bob, He's Dickie, Blankety Blank.

T

TAFFNER, DONALD L.: Executive. b. New York City. e. St. Johns University. William Morris Agency, 1950–59; Paramount Pictures. 1959–63; D. L. Taffner Ltd., 1963-present.

TALBOT, JOSEPH T. (Brud): Producer-Director-Actor. b. NYC, Sept. 16, 1938. e. Deerfield Academy, University of Virginia, Welsh Drama Workshop. Co-producer, actor: Force of Impulse, 1961; Without Each Other, 1962; Wounds of Hunger, 1963; co-star, Finger on the Trigger, 1964; Production supervisor TV special "Around the World of Mike Todd." 1965. Producer, Soundblast '66, musical spectacular Yankee Stadium, 1966. Producer-director TV commercials & documentaries, Filmex, Inc., 1966–69. Producer-director TV Documentary, The Singlehanders. President Dana Films Ltd., 1969–72; prod. Run Before the Wind, (Official m.p. rep. to Bicentennial Council of the Thirteen Original States), 1972–73 Executive in charge of Production Cinemation Industries; 1976–78 pres., Truesdale Pictures Ltd.

OTHER PICTURES: The Case of the Smiling Stiff (prod., dir.); The Black Pearl (co.-prod.); Willie Sutton, Bank Robber (Prod.)

TALBOT, LYLE: Actor. r.n. Lysle Hollywood. b. Pittsburgh, Pa., Feb. 8, 1904. In Army Air Corps, World War II. First screen appearance in Vitaphone short; then in Love Is a Racket, 1932.

PICTURES INCLUDE: Up in Arms, Sensations of 1945, One Body Too Many, Dixie Jamboree, Gambler's Choice, Strange Impersonation, Vicious Circle, Mutineers, Sky Dragon, The Jackpot, Sea Tiger, Down Among the Sheltering Palms, Star of Texas, Capt. Kidd & the Slave Girl, Tobor the Great, Steel Cage, There's No Business Like Show Business, Jail Busters, Sudden Danger.

MEMBER: Masonic Lodge (Shriner), Lambs, Masquers, American Legion.

TAMBLYN, RUSS: Actor. b. Los Angeles, Calif., Dec. 30. e. No. Hollywood H.S. West Coast radio shows; on stage with little theatre group; song-and-dance act in Los Angeles clubs, veterans hospitals.

PICTURES INCLUDE: Boy with Green Hair, Reign of Terror, Samson and Delilah, Deadly Is the Female, Kid from Cleveland, Captain Carey, U.S.A., Father of the Bride, As Young As You Feel, Father's Little Dividend, Winning Team, Retreat Hell, Take the High Ground, Seven Brides for Seven Brothers, Many Rivers to Cross, Hit the Deck,

Last Hunt, Fastest Gun Alive, Young Guns, Don't Go Near the Water, Peyton Place, High School Confidential, Tom Thumb, Cimarron, West Side Story, Wonderful World of the Brothers Grimm, The Haunting, Long Ships, Son of Gunfighter, The Last Movie.

TANDY, JESSICA: Actress. b. London, Eng., June 7, 1909; wife of Hume Cronyn. On London, N.Y. stage, 1928–42.

THEATRE: N.Y. stage. Streetcar Named Desire, Hilda Crane, The Four Poster, Coward In Two Keys; The Way of the World, Eve and A Midsummer Night's Dream at Stratford Festival 1976, Canada; limited tours of Many Faces of Love 1974, 75, 76 and for CBC, Canada 1977; performed in The Gin Game Long Wharf Thea., New Haven, Conn. June 1977; Long Day's Journey Into Night, Theatre London, London, Canada 1977. Appeared in The Gin Game, Pulitzer Prize Winning Play at The Golden Thea. N.Y.C. 1977–78, and toured with it in U.S., Toronto, London and U.S.S.R., 1979.

PICTURES INCLUDE: The Green Years, Forever Amber, A Woman's Vengeance, September Affair, The Desert Fox, Adventures of a Young Man, Butley, A Light In The Forest, The Birds, Honky Tonk Freeway, Stab, Garp.

TANEN, NED: Executive. b. Los Angeles. e. UCLA (law degree). Joined MCA, Inc. 1954; Appd. v.p. in 1968. Brought Uni Records, since absorbed by MCA Records, to bestseller status with such artists as Neil Diamond, Elton John, Olivia Newton-John. First became active in theatrical film prod. in 1972. In 1975 began overseeing feature prod. for Universal. In 1976 named pres. of Universal Theatrical Motion Pictures, established as div. of Universal City Studios to encompass all theatrical film prod. activities.

TANKERSLEY, ROBERT K.: Executive. b. Decatur, Ill., July 31, 1927. In U.S. Navy, 1945–46; Marine Corps, 1949–55. With Natl. Theatre Supply as salesman in Denver 13 yrs. 1959 to present, pres. Western Service & Supply, Denver, theatre equip. form. Also is v.p. theatre chain, Theatre Operators, Inc., Bozeman, Mont. Member: Theatre Equipment Assn. (past pres.), National NATO (presently dir.), Rocky Mt. Motion Picture Assn. (past pres.), SMPTE, Motion Picture Pioneers.

TANNER, WINSTON R.: Exhibitor. b. Appomattox, Va., Feb. 10, 1905. e. U. of Richmond. Entered m.p. ind., 1939 as asst. to owner, mgr. Free State Victoria Theatres, Kenbridge, Va.; dir. partner Kendig-Tanner Theatres, 1942; bought partner's interest in 1957; operator Tanner Theatres 7 houses, in Va.; operates Winston R. Tanner booking-buying service.

TANTO, GYULA PAL: Director, journalist, publicist. b. Budapest, Hungary, 1927. Ent. m.p. ind. 1947 as press officer MGM, Budapest; film critic, Nepsport (Hungarian daily newspaper), 1949–56; worked for Cinevision Film Makers Inc. London as pub. dir. several films, 1960; sports tech. adviser Olympic films, Rome, 1960; Tokyo, 1964; Mexico City, 1968; editor of Balkan Press, film section since 1969.

DIRECTOR: Football World Cup, Olympia Games (1972) Munich (1976) Montreal Miss World, 1971–74 1975–76 (TV), World Swimming Championship, Belgrade; 1st Gymnastic World Cup, Sport in Scotland.

TAPS, JONIE: Producer. Executive. Columbia Studio.

PICTURES INCLUDE: Jolson Story, Down to Earth, Thrill of Brazil. Produced: When You're Smiling, Sunny Side of Street, Sound Off, Rainbow Round My Shoulder, All Ashore, Cruisin' Down the River, Drive a Crooked Road, Three for the Show, Bring Your Smile Along, He Laughed Last, Shadow on the Window.

MEMBER: Friars Club, Hillcrest Country Club.

TARADASH, DANIEL: Writer. Director. b. Louisville, Ky., Jan. 29, 1913. e. Harvard Coll., BA, 1933; Harvard Law Sch., LL.B., 1936. Passed N.Y. Bar, 1937; won nationwide playwriting contest, 1938; U.S. Army W.W. II.

PICTURES INCLUDE: collab. s.p. Golden Boy, A Little Bit of Heaven, Knock on Any Door; s.p., Rancho Notorious, Don't Bother to Knock, From Here to Eternity (Acad. Award 1953); Desiree; collab. story, s.p. and dir., Storm Center; s.p., Picnic, Bell Book and Candle; The Saboteur Code Name—Morituri; col. s.p. Hawaii; collab. s.p. Castle Keep, s.p. Doctors' Wives; Collab. s.p. The Other Side of Midnight. Pres. Screen Writers Branch, WGA, 1955–56; v.p., Writers Guild of America, West 1956–59; mem. Writers Guild Council, 1954–65; mem., bd. of govnrs. M.P. Acad. of Arts & Sciences, 1964–74, and v.p. 1968–70; chmn., trustee, Producers-Writers Guild Pension plan 1960–73. Mem. Bd. of Trustees of American Film Institute 1967–73. WGA's Valentine Davies Award, 1971. Pres., Academy M.P. Arts & Sciences, 1970–73, member of Board of Trustees, Entertainment Hall of Fame Foundation. Member, Public Media General Programs panel for the National Foundation for the Arts, Pres. Writers Guild of America, West, 1977–1979. Nat'l. chm., Writers Guild of America, 1979–81.

TARNOFF, JOHN B.: Executive. b. New York City, Mar. 3, 1952. e. UCLA (motion pictures & TV, 1973–74); Amherst College (BA, 1969–73). Named field exec. with Taylor-Laughlin Distribution (company arm of Billy Jack Enterprises) 1974; left in 1975 to be literary agent with Bart/Levy, Inc.; later with Michael Levy & Associates, Paul Kohner/Michael Levy Agency; Headed TV dept., Kohner/Levy, 1979. Now v.p., motion picture development, for MGM.

TASCO, RAI: Actor, announcer. r.n. Ridgeway Tasco. b. Boston, Mass., Aug. 12, 1917. e. Boston English High. 1935. U.S. Army, 1935–45. Grad., Cambridge School of Radio & TV, New York, 1950. Appeared in most TV and radio dramatic shows, New York and Hollywood; Broadway & films; dramatic instructor.

TATUM, DONN B.: Executive. b. Los Angeles, January 9, 1913. e. Stanford, Oxford. Chairman of Board, Walt Disney Prods. 1943, lawyer, RCA and ABC. 1949, v.p., counsel, Dir. of Don Lee Companies. Gen. Mgr., KABC, dir. of Television, Western Division ABC. 1956, prod. business mgr. for Walt Disney Productions; exec. v.p. Disneyland, v.p. TV sales; v.p. and adm. asst. to pres. and exec. comm.; exec. v.p.; president; now Chrmn. of Bd. Member of Bd. of Dir. of Bank of America, NT&SA; a director of Greyhound Corp, Union Oil Co. of Calif.; director of Kings County Development; director and pres. John Tracy Clinic; director of Community Television of So. Calif. (Ch. 28); dir. & v.p. Community Building Funds of So. Calif.; trustee of Calif. Institute of the Arts, the Salk Institute & the Disney Foundation.

TAVERNIER, BERTRAND: Director-Writer. b. Lyon, April 25, 1941. After 2 yrs. of law study, quit to become film critic. Partner for 6 yrs. with Pierre Rissient in film promotion company, during which time he studied all aspects of filmmaking. Debut picture: The Watchmaker of St. Paul in 1974.
PICTURES INCLUDE: Let Joy Reign Supreme (dir., cowriter), The Judge and the Assassin.

TAYLOR, ANTHONY: Producer. b. Los Angeles, Calif., Feb. 5, 1931. e. U. of So. Cal.; USAF 1954–56; mem. Chicago Board of Trade, 1962–65; columnist, L.A. Herald Examiner, 1964–65; also mem. N.Y Mercantile Exchange, Chicago Mercantile Exchange; partner commodity Futures Co., Westwood, Calif.; 1966, produced feature Incubus; 1966, award for motion picture excellence, San Francisco Int'l Film Festival; 1967, award Incubus, Cork Int'l Film Festival, Ireland; 1968: prod. feature, Possession.

TAYLOR, DELORES: Actress-Writer. b. Winner, So. Dak. e. Univ. of So. Dak., studying commercial art. m. Tom Laughlin. First TV experience was heading art dept. at RCA wholesale center in Milwaukee. Made feature film debut as actress in Billy Jack in 1971. Wrote s.p. with husband for that and the sequel, The Trial of Billy Jack, under pseudonym Teresa Christina.
PICTURES INCLUDE: Billy Jack, The Trial of Billy Jack.

TAYLOR, DON: Actor-Director. b. Freeport, Pa., Dec. 13. e. Pennsylvania State Univ. Appeared in Army Air Corps' Winged Victory; on stage & screen; author short stories, radio dramas, one-act plays, TV shows, both ½ hour and hour.
PICTURES INCLUDE: Actor: Girl Crazy, Naked City, For the Love of Mary, Battleground, Father of the Bride, Father's Little Dividend, Submarine Command, Flying Leathernecks, Blue Veil, Japanese War Bride, Stalag 17, The Girls of Pleasure Island, Destination Gobi, Johnny Dark, I'll Cry Tomorrow, Bold and the Brave. Director: Jack of Diamonds, Five Man Army, Escape from The Planet of the Apes, Tom Sawyer, Echoes Of A Summer, The Great Scout and Cathouse Thursday, The Island of Dr. Moreau, Damien-Omen II, The Final Countdown.

TAYLOR, ELIZABETH: Actress. b. London, Eng., Feb. 27, 1932; e. Bryon House, London, When 3 years old danced before Princess Elizabeth, Margaret Rose. Came to U.S. on outbreak World War II. In 1943–44 screen debut Lassie Comes Home.
PICTURES INCLUDE: National Velvet, Life with Father, Cynthia, Courage of Lassie, Little Women, White Cliffs of Dover, Jane Eyre, Date With Judy, Conspirator, Big Hangover, Father of the Bride, Father's Little Dividend, Love Is Better Than Ever, Place in the Sun, Ivanhoe, The Girl Who Had Everything, Rhapsody, Elephant Walk, Beau Brummell, Last Time I Saw Paris, Giant, Raintree Country, Suddenly, Last Summer, Butterfield 8, Cleopatra, The V.I.P.'s, The Night of the Iguana, Who's Afraid of Virginia Woolf, The Taming of the Shrew, The Sandpiper, Doctor Faustus, The Comedians, Reflections In A Golden Eye, Boom!, Secret Ceremony, The Only Game in Town, X, Y, and Zee, Hammersmith Is Out, Night Watch, Ash Wednesday, That's Entertainment!, The Driver's Seat, The Blue Bird, A Little Night Music, The Mirror Crack'd.

TAYLOR, KENT: Actor. r.n. Louis Weiss. b. Nashua, Iowa, May 11, 1907. In many feature productions from 1931.
PICTURES INCLUDE: Merrily We Go to Hell, Blonde Venus, Death Takes a Holiday, Mrs. Wiggs of the Cabbage Patch, Alaska, Bomber's Moon, Roger Touhy—Gangster,

Notorious Gentleman, Dangerous Millions, Deadline for Murder, Second Chance, Crimson Key, Half Past Midnight, Western Pacific Agent, Payment on Demand, Playgirl, Slightly Scarlet, Track the Man Down, Secret Venture, Ghost Town, Iron Sheriff.
TV: Boston Blackie.

TAYLOR, LAWRENCE: Writer. b. Atlanta, Ga.; e. Northwestern U., '33. Reporter, dramatic critic, foreign correspondent 1934–40; writer radio, m.p., 1940–42; U.S.A.F., 1942–45; writer, m.p. story consultant. TV since 1945, U.S. and England.
PICTURES INCLUDE: Dixie Jamboree, Philo Vance's Secret Mission, Devil Ship, Bulldog Drummond Strikes Back; (story basis) Lady Without a Passport; (collab. s.p.) Jackie Robinson Story, Candelario (coll. with son, Heath).

TAYLOR, MICHAEL: Executive. b. New York City. e. Univ. of Miami (English, Drama). Worked at producing for stage before joining United Artists in 1973 as trainee. Named asst. to v.p. in chg. of production. Appointed exec. in chg. of production in London, where worked in acquisition and production of properties, working on such pictures as The Spy Who Loved Me, Valentino, The Pink Panther Strikes Again, etc. Left U.A. to form Taylor/Wigutow Productions with former U.A. executive Dan Wigutow. First film of new company: Last Embrace (1979).

TAYLOR, ROD: Actor. b. Sydney, Australia, Jan. 11, 1929. e. Fine Arts College. Started out as artist then turned to acting on stage. After co-starring in film Long John Silver, to Hollywood in 1954. First film The Virgin Queen, followed by Giant, Separate Tables and Step Down to Terror. Also made a number of TV appearances. Formed own company, Rodler, Inc., for TV-film production.
PICTURES INCLUDE: Ask Any Girl, The V.I.P.s, The Birds, Sunday in New York, Young Cassidy, The Time Machine, Seven Seas to Calais, A Gathering of Eagles, 36 Hours, Do Not Disturb, The Glass Bottom Boat, Hotel, Chuka, Dark of the Sun, The Hell with Heroes, Zabriskie Point, The Train Robbers, Trader Horn, The Deadly Trackers.

TEITELBAUM, PEDRO: Executive. b. Porto Alegre, Rio Grande Do Sul, Brasil, Nov. 21, 1922. e. Colegio Uniao, Brasil, 1942 (CPA); Univ. of Porto Alegre, Brasil, 1945 (economics & business admin.) 1939; Columbia Pictures; 1943, Warner Brothers; 1958, Latin-American supervisor for Republic Pictures; 1957, producer, distributor, exhibitor in Brasil; 1968, area supervisor for United Artists; 1973, v.p. intl. sales; 1975, v.p. international sales & distribution; 1976, senior v.p. and foreign manager. In Jan., 1977, joined CIC as senior exec. v.p. Named pres., July, 1977.

TELLER, IRA: Executive. b. New York, N.Y., July 3, 1940. e. CCNY 1957–61; NYU Graduate Sch. of Arts, 1961–62; publicist, Pressbook Dept., 20th Century Fox., 1961–62; asst. to adv. mgr., Embassy Pictures Corp., 1962–63; asst. adv. mgr., Columbia Pictures Corp.; 1963; adv. mgr., Columbia Pictures Corp., 1964, 1964–65; asst. to chmn. of bd., Diener, Hauser, Greenthal Agy., 1966; adv. mgr., 20th Century-Fox, 1966–67; 1967, adv. dir. 20th Cent.-Fox; Dir. of Adv., Nat'l General Pictures Corp., 1969; eastern dir., adv.-pub., 1972; National Director, Adv-Pub., 1973; Bryanston Distributors, Inc. v.p. adv.-pub., 1974; Cine Artists Pictures Corp. v.p. adv-pub., 1975; Lorimar Productions, v.p., adv.-marketing, 1976–77. 1977-present, pres. Ira Teller and Company, Inc.

TEMPLE, SHIRLEY JANE: Actress. b. Santa Monica, Calif., April 23, 1929. In 1932 screen debut, Red Haired Alibi. In 1933 To the Last Man; then leading figure in Baby Burlesque series Educational shorts until Stand Up and Cheer (1934), which resulted in career as child star.
PICTURES INCLUDE: Baby Takes a Bow, Bright Eyes, Now I'll Tell, Change of Heart, Little Miss Marker, Now and Forever, The Little Colonel, Our Little Girl, Curly Top, The Littlest Rebel, Captain January, Poor Little Rich Girl, Dimples, Stowaway, Wee Willie Winkle, Heidi, Rebecca of Sunnybrook Farm, Little Miss Broadway, Just Around the Corner, Little Princess, Susannah of the Mounties, The Blue Bird, Young People. In 1941 Kathleen. In 1942 Miss Annie Rooney. Voted one of ten best Money-Making Stars in Motion Picture Herald-Fame Poll, 1934–39. Since You Went Away, I'll Be Seeing You, Kiss and Tell, That Hagen Girl, Honeymoon, Fort Apache, Bachelor and the Bobby-Soxer, Mr. Belvedere Goes to College, Adventure in Baltimore, Story of Seabiscuit, Kiss for Corliss.
TV: Hostess, fairy tale series.

TENNANT, WILLIAM: Executive. Partner in literary agency of Ziegler, Ross, and Tennant. Turned to m.p. production with Cleopatra Jones for Warner Bros., following with writing and producing of sequel, Cleopatra and the Casino of Gold. In 1975 joined Columbia Pictures as v.p.-prod., headquartering at Burbank Studios. Named pres., Casablanca Filmworks; now pres., PolyGram Pictures m.p. division.

TERRY, SIR JOHN: Film Finance Consultant. b. London, England, 1913; e. Mill Hill School. Early career as solicitor.

Entered m.p. ind. Film Producers Guild 1946–47; then legal dept. Rank Organization until 1949; joined National Film Finance Corporation; its chief solicitor 1949–57; sec., 1956–57; appt. man. dir., 1958–78.

TERRY-THOMAS: Actor, comedian. r.n. Thomas Terry Hoar Stevens. b. London, England, July 14, 1911; e. Ardingly College, Sussex.
PICTURES INCLUDE: Private's Progress, The Green Man, Lucky Jim, Tom Thumb, I'm All Right, Jack, Too Many Crooks, Make Mine Mink, School for Scoundrels, A Matter of WHO, Bachelor Flat, Operation Snatch, Kill or Cure, The Mouse on the Moon, It's a Mad, Mad, Mad, Mad World, Wild Affair, Strange Bedfellows, How to Murder Your Wife, Those Magnificent Men in Their Flying Machines, Rocket to the Moon, Guide for the Married Man, Kiss The Girls and Make Them Die, The Perils of Pauline, Blast Off, 2000 Years Later, Where Were You When the Lights Went Out?, Don't Raise the Bridge, Lower the River, How Sweet It Is!, Arabella, Dr. Phibes, and many films made in Europe, Side By Side, Spanish Fly, The Amorous Adventures of Tom Jones, The Last Remake of Beau Geste, Hound of the Baskervilles.
TV: (U.S.) Danny Kaye Show, Garry Moore Show, Andy Williams Show, Jack Paar Show, Judy Garland Show, Burke's Law (series) Red Skelton Show.

TESICH, STEVE: Writer. b. Yugoslavia. e. Indiana Univ., Columbia. Came to U.S. at age 14. While doing graduate work in Russian literature at Columbia left to begin writing. Taken up by American Place Theatre which did his play, The Carpenters, in 1970 and then six others. Wrote screenplays; first produced was Breaking Away, 1979.

TETZLAFF, TED: Director. b. Los Angeles, Calif., June 3, 1903. Joined camera dept. Fox Studios, became first cameraman; dir., 1940; served in U.S. Air Corps as a Major, World War II.
PICTURES INCLUDE: cameraman: Enchanted Cottage, Notorious; dir.: World Premiere, Riffraff, Fighting Father Dunne, Window, Johnny Allegro, Dangerous Profession, Gambling House, White Tower, Under the Gun, Treasure of Lost Canyon, Terror on a Train, Son of Sinbad.

TEWKESBURY, JOAN: Writer. e. Univ. of So. Calif. Directed and choreographed Little Theatre prods. in L.A. area; taught in theatre arts depts. of three universities: Univ. of So. Calif., Immaculate Heart and Mount St. Mary's. Became script supvr. for Robert Altman on McCabe & Mrs. Miller.
PICTURES INCLUDE: Thieves Like Us (co. s.p.), Nashville.

THALHIMER, JR., MORTON G.: Theatre Executive. b. Richmond, Va., June 27, 1924. e. Dartmouth Coll. (1948, B.A.). Univ. of Va. (1959). In Navy in World War II. Joined Century Theatres as trainee 1948; Jamestown Amusement, 1949–50. Now pres. Neighborhood Theatre, Inc. Charter member of Theatre Owners of America; continuing member of NATO, served on finance comm. and Trade Practice comm. bd. member and past president of NATO of Va. (1973–75.) Mem. Variety Club Int'l., Tent 11; patron life member, Variety Club of Israel, Tent 51.

THATCHER, HEATHER: Actress. b. London, England. London stage debut in Girl From Ciro's, 1916. Entered m.p. ind. as extra in 1916.
PLAYS: Naughty Princess, Sally, Constant Wife, School for Husbands, Lucky Break, Full House.
PICTURES INCLUDE: (Hollywood pictures since 1936): Hour of Thirteen, Duel in the Jungle.

THACHER, RUSSELL: Producer-Writer. b. Hackensack, N.J. e. Bucknell Univ., N.Y.U. Author of novels: The Captain, The Tender Age, A Break in the Clouds. Editor Omnibook Magazine, 1946–58; Book of the Month Club, 1958–63. Exec. story editor, MGM, 1963–69. Exec. prod., MGM, 1969–72.
PICTURES INCLUDE: Travels with My Aunt (assoc. prod.), Soylent Green, The Cay, Last Hard Men.

THAXTER, PHYLLIS: Actress. b. Portland, Me., Nov. 20, 1921; e. St. Genevieve School, Montreal. Screen debut in Thirty Seconds Over Tokyo.
PLAYS: What A Life, There Shall Be No Night, Claudia. Take Her She's Mine.
PICTURES INCLUDE: Week-End at the Waldorf, Bewitched, Tenth Avenue Angel, Sign of the Ram, Blood on the Moon, The Breaking Point, Fort Worth, Jim Thorpe—All American, Come Fill the Cup, She's Working Her Way Through College, Operation Secret, Springfield Rifle, Women's Prison, World of Henry Orient, Superman.
TV: Wagon Train, Alfred Hitchcock, Twilight Zone, Purex Specials For Women, Playhouse 90, The Fugitive, Defenders, etc.

THOMAS, BILL: Fashion designer. b. Chicago, Ill., Oct. 13, 1921; e. U. of S.C., A.B. 1941. Art Center, Los Angeles, 1941. Started career as designer on assignment to USO shows; Theatre Royle, Brisbane, Australia; from duty with

U.S. A.F., 1941–46. Asst. to Irene, Irene Inc., 1948; asst. costume designer MGM Studios 1947–48; U-I Studios 1949–59; currently free lance.
PICTURES INCLUDE: High Time, Beloved Infidel, By Love Possessed, Babes in Toyland.

THOMAS, DANNY: Actor. r.n. Amos Jacobs. b. Deerfield, Mich., Jan. 6. Night club entertainer; on radio and TV, films.
TV: Own TV show, The Danny Thomas Show, CBS-TV, 1953–64; NBC-TV specials 1964–66, Danny Thomas Show, 1967–68; CBS-TV Specials 1967 & 1970. Make Room for Grandaddy series 1970–71, ABC-TV; The Practice, 1976–77; NBC-TV.
PICTURES INCLUDE: Unfinished Dance, Big City, Call Me Mister, I'll See You in My Dreams, Jazz Singer.

THOMAS, GERALD: Producer, director. b. Hull, England, 1920. Entered m.p. industry 1946.
PICTURES INCLUDE: Tony Draws a Horse, Appointment With Venus, Venetian Bird, Sword and the Rose, A Day to Remember, Mad About Men, Doctor in the House, Above Us the Waves, A Novel Affair, After the Ball, Timelock, Vicious Circle, Chain of Events, Solitary Child, The Duke Wore Jeans, Carry On Sergeant, Carry on Nurse, Carry on Teacher, Please Turn Over, Carry on Constable, Watch Your Stern, No Kidding, Carry On Regardless, Raising The Wind, Twice Around the Daffodils, Carry on Cruising, The Iron Maiden, Nurse On Wheels, Call Me a Cab, Carry on Jack, Carry on Spying, Carry On Cleo, The Big Job, Carry On Cowboy, Carry on Screaming, Don't Lose Your Head, Follow That Camel, Carry on Doctor, Carry On Up The Khyber, Carry on Up the Jungle, Carry on Loving, Carry on Camping, Carry On Again, Doctor, Carry On, Henry, Carry On At Your Convenience, Carry On Matron, Carry on Abroad, Bless This House, Carry On Girls, Carry On Dick, Carry On Behind, Carry On England, That's Carry On, Carry On Emmannuelle.
TV: Prod. and dir. Rob Roy, serial. Prod. Carry on Christmas for Thames TV. Dir. Carry On Dick, Prod., Carry On Laughing. Dir. Best of Carry On. Prod. Odd Man Out, series.

THOMAS HARRY E.: Exhibitor. b. Monroe, La., May 22, 1920; e. L.S.U. 1938–41. Psychological Branch of Army Air Force, 1942–46. Past pres., secy., and treas. of NATO of Mississippi. Dir. of Design & Const. & Sec. Gulf State Theatres Inc. Retired 1978.

THOMAS, HOWARD: Executive. b. CWM. Monmouthshire. Entered m.p. ind. in 1944. Newspaper columnist & feature writer; adv. copywriter; writer of revue sketches, books, radio plays; mgr. sponsored radio dept., London Press Exchange, Ltd.; BBC prod. & orig. The Brains Trust. Prod.-in-chief, Associated British-Pathe, Ltd.; managing dir., ABC Television Ltd., 1956. Appt. dir., Associated British Picture Corp., 1964; div. dir., EMI, Ltd., 1970; man. dir., Thames TV, 1968–74; Thames TV Int. Ltd., pres., Cinema TV Veterans, 1979–80. Dir., Argus Press Ltd.

THOMAS, JAMES: Critic, producer. b. Huddersfield, York, England, June 9, 1922; e. Huddersfield Coll. Reporter, Huddersfield Daily Examiner, 1946–47; Yorkshire Evening Post, 1947–48; London, News-Chronicle, 1948–50; radio & TV corres. and spec. writer on entertainment, News Chronicle, 1950; TV editor, Daily Express, 1957. Assoc. ed., The Time, The Place and The Camera, ATV series, 1961–62. Ed., The Braden Beat, 1963. Prod., On the Braden Beat, 1964–65. 1965–67 TV columnist, Daily Express.

THOMAS, LOWELL: Commentator. b. Woodington, Darke County, Ohio, Apr. 6, 1892; e. Northern Indiana Univ., Denver Univ., Princeton Univ., Kent College of Law. Instructor, Eng. Lit., Princeton, 1914; lecturer, biographer, historian and film producer until 1930 when broadcaster for CBS; commentator on first TV news program for NBC, 1939; & on first daily TV prog., 1940; foreign commentator during WWII; now, commentator on own daily prog. for CBS. Chmn. bd., then vice chmn., Cinerama Prod. Corp., 1952; pres., 1953–54; exec. prod., High Adventure, TV series; TV series in conjunct'n with BBC, The World of Lowell Thomas; co-founder, Capital Cities Broadcasting Corp.

THOMAS, MARLO: Actress. b. Detroit, Nov. 21, 1938. f. is Danny Thomas. e. U. of Southern Calif. Started career with small TV roles, summer stock. Appeared in London stage prod. of Barefoot in the Park. Debut in own TV series, That Girl, 1966. Most Promising Newcomer Awards from both "Fame" and "Photoplay."
PICTURES INCLUDE: Jenny, Thieves.

THOMAS, RALPH: Director. b. Hull, Yorkshire, England, Aug. 10, 1915; e. Tellisford College, Clifton and University College, London. Journalist in early career, entered m.p. ind. 1932 as film ed.; service with 9th Lancers, 1939–45; then film director.
PICTURES INCLUDE: prod.: The Clouded Yellow, Appointment with Venus (Island Rescue), Day to Remember, Travellers' Joy, Venetian Bird, Once Upon a Dream, Doctor in the House, Mad about Men, Above Us the Waves, Doctor At Sea, Iron Petticoat, Checkpoint, Doctor at Large,

Campbell's Kingdom, A Tale of Two Cities, The Wind Cannot Read, The 39 Steps, Upstairs and Downstairs, Conspiracy of Hearts, Doctors in Love, No Love for Johnnie, No, My Darling Daughter, A Pair of Briefs, The Wild & The Willing, Doctor in Distress, Hot Enough for June, The High Bright Sun, Agent 008¾, Doctor in Clover, Deadlier Than the Male, Nobody Runs Forever, Some Girls Do, Doctor in Trouble, Percy, Quest, The Love Ban, Percy's Progress, A Nightingale Sang in Berkeley Square.

THOMAS, RICHARD: Actor. b. N.Y.C., June 13, 1951. e. Col. Univ. Made TV Debut at age 7 and featured in several series.
PICTURES INCLUDE: Last Summer, Red Sky at Morning, The Todd Killings, Cactus in the Snow, You'll Like My Mother, September 30th, 1955.
TELEVISION: Medical Center, Marcus Welby, M.D., The F.B.I., The Waltons (regular).

THOMAS, ROBERT G. ("BOB"): Producer-Director. b. Glen Ridge, N.J., July 21, 1943. e. Univ. of Bridgeport, Fairleigh Dickinson Univ. Produced educational radio programs, 1962, WPKN-FM. Asst. stage manager at Meadowbrook Dinner Theatre, 1963. In March, 1964 began career as TV cameraman for New York stations. Worked both full-time and free-lance for major TV and video tape studios. In January, 1968, started Bob Thomas Productions and began producing business/sales films and TV commercials. Has 8 awards from natl. film festivals; nominated for 5 Emmys for TV series called The Jersey Side he produced for WOR-TV.
PICTURES: Shorts: Valley Forge with Bob Hope, New Jersey—200 Years. Road-Eo '77.
TV: The Jersey Side (talk/entertainment), Jersey People (weekly talk/entertainment program); $10,000 Touchdown (game show); Sir Reginald and the 3rd Dimension (Children's Show) 3-D Television—for local TV station promotion "The First Annual Comedy Awards" (TV Special).

THOMAS, ROBERT J. ("BOB"): Columnist, Associated Press, Hollywood. b. San Diego, Cal., Jan. 26, 1922; p. George H. Thomas, publicist; e. U. of Calif., L.A. Joined Associated Press staff, Los Angeles, 1937; corr. Fresno, 1944; Hollywood since 1944. Writer mag. articles; appearances, radio; orig. story Big Mike.
BOOKS: author: The Art of Animation, King Cohn, Thalberg, Selznick, Winchell, Secret Boss of California, The Heart of Hollywood, Howard, The Amazing Mr. Hughes, Weekend '33, Marlon, Portrait of the Rebel as an Artist, Walt Disney, An American Original; Bud and Lou, The Abbott and Costello Story; The Road to Hollywood (with Bob Hope), The One and Only Bing, Joan Crawford.

THOMAS, WILLIAM C.: Producer, writer, director. b. Los Angeles, Calif., Aug. 11, 1903; e. U. of So. Calif. From 1925–30 publicity Pantages Theats.; Fox West Coast Theats.; pub. dept., Columbia; writer, Paramount, RKO; prod. from 1936; partner, Pine Thomas Prod.
PICTURES INCLUDE: Scared Stiff, co-prod.: Dangerous Passage, Double Exposure, High Powered; co-prod. & dir.: Midnight Manhunt; dir. & co-prod.: They Made Me a Killer; co-prod. & dir.: Big Town, Tokyo Rose, Hot Cargo, Swamp Fire, People Are Funny, I Cover Big Town, Fear in the Night, Seven Were Saved, Danger Street, Jungle Flight, Albuquerque, El Paso, Capt. China, Eagle and the Hawk, The Lawless, Tripoli, Last Outpost, Crosswinds, Passage West, Hong Kong, Caribbean, Blazing Forest, Tropic Zone, The Vanquished, Jamaica Run, Sangaree, Those Redheads from Seattle, Jivaro, Hell's Island, Run for Cover, Far Horizons, Lucy Gallant, Nightmare, The Big Caper, Bailout at 43,000, High Seas Hijack (co-producer with Toho Films Ltd.); Crusin' High (prod. writer).

THOMOPOULOS, ANTHONY D.: Executive. b. 1938. e. Georgetown Univ. Began career in broadcasting at NBC, 1959, starting as mailroom clerk and moving to radio division in prod. & admin. Shortly named to post in International Division Sales, involved with programming for stations and in developing TV systems for other nations. Joined Four Star Entertainment Corp. as dir. of foreign sales, 1964; named v.p., 1965; exec. v.p., 1969. In 1970 joined RCA SelectaVision Div. as dir. of programming. In 1971 joined Tomorrow Entertainment as v.p. In 1973 joined ABC as v.p., prime-time programs in N.Y.; 1974, named v.p., prime-time TV creative operations, ABC Entertainment. In 1975 named v.p. of special programs, ABC Entertainment; 1976 made v.p., ABC-TV, assisting pres. Frederick S. Pierce in supervising all activities of the division. In Feb., 1978 named pres. of ABC Entertainment.

THOMPSON, CARLOS: Actor. b. Buenos Aires, Argentina, June 7; e. National U., Buenos Aires. Stage & screen actor in Argentina; Hollywood m.p. debut in Fort Algiers, 1953.
PICTURES INCLUDE: Flame and the Flesh, Valley of the Kings, Magic Fire.

THOMPSON, JACK: Actor. b. Sydney, Australia, Aug. 31, 1940. e. Queensland Univ. Joined drama workshop at school; first part was in TV soap opera as continuing character.

PICTURES INCLUDE: A Sunday Too Far, The Chant of Jimmy Blacksmith, Breaker Morant (Australian award), The Earthling.

THOMPSON, MARSHALL: Actor. r.n. James Marshall Thompson; b. Peoria, Ill., Nov. 27; e. Occidental Coll., L.A. In school dramatics; studied for clergy; wrote play Faith, prod. by Westwood Players; in Westwood Players as actor; m.p. debut in Reckless Age, 1944.
PICTURES INCLUDE: They Were Expendable, Gallant Bess, Valley of Decision, Homecoming, B.F.'s Daughter, Words and Music, Command Decision, Roseanna McCoy, Battleground, Dial 1119, Devil's Doorway, Mystery Street, Tall Target, Basketball Fix, My Six Convicts, Rose Bowl Story, The Caddy, Battle Taxi, Port of Hell, Cult of the Cobra, Crashout, To Hell and Back, Clarence, The Cross-eyed Lion, Around the World Under the Sea.

THOMPSON, SADA: Actress. b. Des Moines, Sept. 27, 1929. e. Carnegie Inst. of Technology, Pittsburgh. First N.Y. stage appearance in Under Milkwood with Dylan Thomas. Bdwy. career has produced many awards topped by The Effects of Gamma Rays, for which she won Obie, Drama Desk, Variety Poll.
TV: Sandburg's Lincoln, The Entertainer, Our Town. Series: Family (regular).

THOMSON, ALAN: Studio Publicity manager, EMI Elstree Studios Ltd. e. in Scotland. Early career in Glasgow with his father, well-known cinema manager. Ent. journalism on staff film magazine, other Scottish publications. Ent. m.p. with Associated British Productions 1953. Appt. studio pub. mgr. 1956.

THOR, JEROME: Performer. b. Brooklyn, N.Y., Jan. 5, 1920; e. Neighborhood Playhouse. On B'way in He Who Gets Slapped, My Sister Eileen, Doughgirls, Golden Boy, etc.; on TV in Studio One, Suspense, Danger, Foreign Intrigue, Rogue for Hire, Riot in Juvenile Prison.

THORPE, RICHARD: Director. b. Hutchinson, Kan., Feb. 24, 1896; m. Belva Kay, prof. In vaudeville, stock & musical comedy, 1915–18. Now retired.
PICTURES INCLUDE: cast, Torchy Comedies, Three O'Clock in the Morning, Burn 'Em Up Barnes, Flame of Desire; dir. since 1933. dir., Night Must Fall, Ivanhoe, Double Wedding, Crowd Roars, Earl of Chicago, Huckleberry Finn, White Cargo, Two Girls and a Sailor, Sun Comes Up, Big Jack, Challenge to Lassie, Malaya, Black Hand, Three Little Words, Vengeance Valley, The Great Caruso, Unknown Man, It's a Big Country, Carbine Williams, Prisoner of Zenda, The Girl Who Had Everything, All the Brothers Were Valiant, Knights of the Round Table, Student Prince, Athena, Quentin Durward, The Prodigal, The Tartars, Honeymoon Machine, Horizontal Lieutenant, Follow The Boys, The Truth About Spring, That Funny Feeling, Scorpio Letters, Last Challenge, Retired.

THULIN, INGRID: Actress, director. b. Solleftea, Sweden, Jan. 27, 1929. m. Harry Schein, founder and head of Sweden's Film Institute. Made acting debut at 15 at the Municipal Theatre in Norrkoping. Studied at Stockholm's Royal Dramatic Theatre. Worked with Malmo repertory. Appeared on Swedish stage in Gigi, Peer Gynt, Two for the Seesaw, Twelfth Night, Miss Julie. Has directed plays in Stockholm. N.Y. stage debut: 1967: Of Love Remembered.
PICTURES INCLUDE: For Ingmar Bergman: Wild Strawberries, Brink of Life (Best Actress Award, Cannes Film Festival), The Magician, Winter Light, The Silence, The Hour of the Wolf, The Ritual, Night Games, The Bathers, Adelaide, La Guerre Est Finie, The Four Horsemen of the Apocalypse, Return From Ashes, The Damned, Cries and Whispers, Moses, The Cassandra Crossing. Dir. short film: Devotion.

THUNDER, CLOUD, CHIEF: Actor. r.n. Victor Daniels. b. Muskogen, Okla., April 12, 1899. Worked on cattle ranches, in mining, as boxer; became rodeo performer, stunt man. Entered pictures 1929. In many films since.
PICTURES INCLUDE: Fighting Seabees, Buffalo Bill, Sonora, Stagecoach, Romance of the West, Senator Was Indiscreet, Ambush, Ticket to Tomahawk, Colt 45.

THURSTON, CAROL: Actress. b. Forsyth, Mont.; e. Montana U.; Bliss-Hayden School of Acting. With father in amateur theatricals prior to screen debut.
PICTURES INCLUDE: Swamp Fire, Jewels of Brandenburg, Last Round-Up, Rogue's Regiment, Arctic Manhunt, Apache Chief, Flaming Feather, Arctic Flight, Conquest of Cochise, Killer Ape, Yukon Vengeance.

TIDYMAN, ERNEST: Writer. b. Cleveland. Began crime reporting at 14. After long experience as newspaperman started writing fiction at 42. Wrote the novels on which the Shaft films were based.
PICTURES INCLUDE: The French Connection (AA), Shaft, Shaft's Big Score, High Plains Drifter, Report to the Commissioner (Co-s.p.), Street People (Co-s.p.).

TIERNEY, GENE: Actress. b. Brooklyn, N.Y., Nov. 20, 1920; e. St. Margaret's School, Brilmont, Switzerland; Miss Farmer's School, Farmington, Conn.
PICTURES INCLUDE: Return of Frank James, Hudson's Bay, Tobacco Road, Belle Starr, Sundown, Shanghai Gesture, Son of Fury, Heaven Can Wait, Laura, Bell for Adano, Leave Her to Heaven, Dragonwyck, Razor's Edge, Ghost and Mrs. Muir, Iron Curtain, That Wonderful Urge, Whirlpool, Where the Sidewalk Ends, Night and the City, Mating Season, On the Riviera, Secret of Convict Lake, Way of a Gaucho, Close To My Heart, Plymouth Adventure, Never Let Me Go, Personal Affair, The Egyptian, Black Widow, Left Hand of God, Advise & Consent.

TIERNEY, LAWRENCE: Actor. b. Brooklyn, N.Y., Mar. 15, 1919; e. Manhattan Coll. Track athlete (natl. championship Cross Country Team, N.Y. Athletic Club). On stage as actor. Screen debut 1943 in The Ghost Ship.
PICTURES INCLUDE: Youth Runs Wild, Dillinger, Mama Loves Papa, Badman's Territory, Step By Step, San Quentin, Devil Thumbs a Ride, Born to Kill, Bodyguard, Kill or Be Killed, Best of the Bad Men, Shakedown, Greatest Show on Earth, Hoodlum, Bushwackers, Steel Cage, Custer of the West, Such Good Friends.

TIFFIN, PAMELA: Actress. b. Oklahoma City, Okla., Oct. 13. e. Hunter College. Started modeling as a teenager. Film debut in Summer and Smoke.
PICTURES INCLUDE: One Two Three, State Fair, Come Fly With Me, For Those Who Think Young, The Pleasure Seekers, The Hallelujah Trail, Harper, Paranoia, Kiss The Other Sheik, Viva Max.
PLAY: Dinner at Eight.

TILLSTROM, BURR: Performer. b. Chicago, Oct. 13, 1917. e. Univ. of Chicago. With WPA-Chicago Park Dist. Theatre, 1936; traveled with puppet, marionette, stock shows; mgr. puppet exhibits and marionette Theatre, Marshall Field & Co., Chicago (performed on experimental television for RCA), 1939; sent to Bermuda by RCA to do ship to shore television broadcasts 1940; creator and impresario puppet troupe headed by Kukla and Ollie on show "Kukla, Fran and Ollie" with Fran Allison since 1947 (pioneered in television when he presented puppets on Balaban and Katz 1st telecast. Stat. WBKB. Chicago, 1941). Winner two Peabody awards and three national Academy of TV Arts & Science Emmy awards; hon. Doctorate of Letters, Hope College, Holland, Mich., 1972.

TINKER, GRANT A.: Executive. b. Stamford, Conn., Jan. 11, 1926. e. Dartmouth College, 1947. m. Mary Tyler Moore. Joined NBC radio prog. dept. 1949. In 1954 with McCann-Erickson ad agency, TV dept. In 1958, Benton & Bowles Ad Agency, TV dept. From 1961–66 with NBC, v.p., programs, West Coast; v.p. in chg. of programming, N.Y., 1966–67. Joined Universal Televison as v.p., 1968–69; 20th-Fox, v.p., 1969–70. Became pres. MTM Enterprises, Inc. 1970. Named NBC pres., 1981.

TINLING, JAMES: Director. b. Seattle, Wash., May 8, 1889; e. U. Washington. Started in m.p. as prop boy for Century Studios; wrote comedies 2 yrs.; stunt man; dir.
PICTURES INCLUDE: Silk Legs, Don't Marry, Very Confidential, Exalted Flapper, True Heaven, Words and Music, Fox, Flood, Mr. Moto's Gamble, Boy Friend, Riders of the Purple Sage, Crime Buster, Rendezvous, Deadline for Murder, Strange Journey, Dangerous Millions, Roses Are Red, Second Chance, Night Wind, Trouble Preferred, Tales of Robin Hood.
TV films.

TISCH, LAURENCE A.: Executive. b. Bklyn, N.Y., March 5, 1923. e. N.Y. Univ., 1941; Univ. of Pa. Wharton School, 1942; Harvard Law School, 1946. Pres. Tisch Hotels, Inc., 1950–59; Pres. Americana Hotel, Inc., Miami Beach, 1956–59; Chmn. of bd. and chief executive officer of Loews Corp since 1960. Also chmn. of bd. of CNA Financial Corp since 1974.

TISCH, PRESTON ROBERT: Executive. b. Bklyn., N.Y., April 29, 1926. e. Bucknell U. Lewisberg, Pa., 1943–44; B.A., U. Mich., 1948. Pres. Loew's Corporation.

TODD, ANN: Actress. e. Central School of Speech Training & Dramatic Art.
BRITISH STAGE PLAYS INCLUDE: Service, When Ladies Meet, Man in Half-Moon Street, Peter Pan, Brit., Lottie Dundass.
PICTURES INCLUDE: Squeaker, Seventh Veil, Perfect Strangers, Gaiety George, Hollywood debut in Paradine Case. Ret. to theatre Feb., 1951 in stage version, Seventh Veil, So Evil My Love; Old Vic. Theatre, 1954–55: Doctor's Dilemma, Four Winds, Duel of Angels, One Woman's Story, Daybreak, Madeleine, The Sound Barrier, Green Scarf, Time Without Pity, Taste of Fear, Son of Captain Blood, Ninety Degrees in The Shade, The Human Factor.
TV: Many appearances and TV films, New York, Hollywood. London incl.: Camille, The Vortex, The Door, Snows of Kilimanjaro, TV film, Hollywood. 1964: Prod., travelogue in Nepal, Love Story, Reading for Glory. Makes own Diary Documentaries and appears in them. Films for cinema and TV incl. Thunder in Heaven, Thunder of Gods, Thunder of Kings. Persian Fairy Tale. Force in the Sun, Thunder of Silence. Recent TV appearance, The Last Target.

TODD, RICHARD: Actor. b. Dublin, Eire, June 11, 1919. e. Shrewsbury. In repertory, 1937; founder-member, Dundee Repertory Theatre, 1939; distinguished war service, 1939–46; Dundee Repertory, 1946–48; screen debut, 1948; For Them That Trespass, 1948. 1970 Founder-Director Triumph Theatre Productions.
PICTURES INCLUDE: The Hasty Heart, Lightning Strikes Twice (USA), Robin Hood, The Venetian Bird, Sword and the Rose, Rob Roy, A Man Called Peter (USA), Virgin Queen (USA), The Bed, Dam Busters, D-Day the Sixth of June (USA), Marie Antoinette, Yangtse Incident, Chase a Crooked Shadow, The Naked Earth, Danger Within, The Long the Short and the Tall, The Hellions, Never Let Go, The Longest Day, The Boys, The Very Edge, exec. prod., star own prod. Don't Bother to Knock, Operation Crossbow, Coast of Skeletons, Asylum, The Big Sleep.
STAGE: 1966–67, An Ideal Husband; 1967–68, Dear Octopus. Co-founder, Triumph Theatre Prods., Ltd. Plays since 1970: Roar Like a Dove, Grass Is Greener, The Marquise, 1972. (USA). Sleuth, 1972–73 (Australia). Thunder by Numbers 1973, The Hollow Crown 1974–75, Equus. 1975, Sleuth, 1976, On Approval, Quadrille, 1977; This Happy Breed, 1980.

TODDY, TED: President, Toddy Picture Co., Toddy Prod., Inc., Dixie National Pictures, Inc., Consolidated National Film Exchanges; v.p., Acceptance Film Corp. b. New York City, June 15, 1912. Worked three years at Universal. For 12 years Columbia, Atlanta. Then formed Dixie Film Exchange in Atlanta. In 1940 purchased Million Dollar Pictures of Supreme Pictures and formed Consolidated National Film Exchanges. In 1941: consolidated as Toddy Pictures Co., prod. under Dixie National Pictures banner, Mr. Washington Goes to Town, Lucky Ghost, Up Jumped the Devil, Professor Creeps. Under Sepia Art Co., prod. One Round Jones, etc.; own ex. in Atlanta, Dallas, Chicago, New York and Los Angeles. Member: War Prod. Bd.

TODMAN, HOWARD: Executive. b. N.Y.C., Nov. 24, 1920; e. Hamilton College 1941; dir. business affairs, Goodson-Todman Productions; treas., Goodson-Todman Associates, Inc.; v.p. & treas., Goodson-Todman Enterprises, Ltd.; Treasurer, Peak Prods., Inc.; Treas. Goodson-Todman Bcstg. Inc.; v.p. Price Productions, Inc.; v.p. Celebrity Productions, Inc.; chm., N.Y. Cancer Crusade, radio & TV.

TOGNAZZI, UGO: Actor. b. Cremona, Italy, March 23, 1922. Graduate of law. Started entertainment career in 1945 as comic in music hall revues. Film career began in 1950 with Les Cadets de Gascogne. Has produced four films and a detective series for TV. Also acted on stage.
PICTURES INCLUDE: His Women, The Fascist, Queen Bee, The Magnificent Cuckold, Question of Honor, Barbarella, Property Is No Longer a Theft, La Cage Aux Folles, La Cage II, Sunday Lovers.

TOM, C.Y.: Cinematographer and distributor. b. Toy Shan, Kwangtung, China, Nov. 6, 1907; graduated N.Y. Institute of Photography 1926; photographed newsreels for The Great Wall Film Co. of Shanghai; in New York, 1926–29; in charge of production, Shanghai, 1929–32. Studied production techniques in Hollywood. Toured Europe, managing Chinese vaudeville, 1934–35. Studio mgr. and dir. photography for Chi Ming Motion Picture Co., 1935–41. President, Chinamerica Film Exchange and Chinamerica Film Studio, Hong Kong and Shanghai. Distributor, Monogram, Film Classics and Telenews, Hong Kong, Macao and China; asst. man. dir., Capitol Theatre, Hong Kong, 1948–59.

TOMBES, ANDREW: Actor. b. Ashtabula, Ohio; p. nonprofessionals; e. public schools and Phillips Exeter Academy; married. Appeared in vaudeville and in musical comedies including The O'Brien Girl, Ziegfeld Follies of 1922, and other stage musicals. In 1933 appeared in Moulin Rouge, UA-20th-Cent. From 1934 in many productions, principal Hollywood companies.
PICTURES INCLUDE: Can't Help Singing, Singing Sheriff, Night Club Girl, Goin' to Town, Don't Fence Me In, Frontier Gal, G.I. Honeymoon, Lake Placid Serenade, Oh You Beautiful Doll, Oklahoma Annie, I Dream of Jeanie, How To Be Very Very Popular.

TOMBRAGEL, MAURICE: Writer.
PICTURES INCLUDE: Legion of Lost Flyers, Horror Island, Mutiny in the Arctic, Two Senoritas from Chicago, Lone Wolf in Mexico, Return of the Whistler, Prince of Thieves, The Creeper, Highway 13, Thunder in the Pines, Sky Liner, Arson Inc., Motor Patrol, Fort Bowie, Moon Pilot, s.p. Monkeys Go Home; v.p. Running Wild, Golden Circle Prods., 1973.
TV: Wild Bill Hickcok, Stories of the Century, Annie Oakley, Soldiers of Fortune, Western Marshal, Wyatt Earp,

Frontier Doctor, Texas Rangers, Sergeant Preston, Adventures of Jim Bowie, Bat Masterson, Walt Disney's Elfego Baca, John Slaughter TV series, Life of Johann Strauss, Escapade in Florence, Bristle Face. Gallegher series, The Tenderfoot series. For Disney, The Treasure of San Marco (2 parts), The Gentle Ben Series.

TOMLIN, LILY: Actress. b. Detroit. e. Wayne State Coll. Started inventing characters for comedy sketches in college, used them in cafe and night club dates. In December, 1969, first appeared on Laugh-In, TV series, gaining national attention.
TV: Laugh-In, The Lily Tomlin Show, Lily.
PICTURES INCLUDE: Nashville, The Late Show, Moment by Moment, Nine to Five, The Incredible Shrinking Woman.
RECORDS: This Is a Recording, And That's The Truth.

TOMLINSON, DAVID: Actor. b. May 17, 1917; e. Tonbridge Sch. On stage first, 1934 in "Outward Bound." Screen debut, 1938, "Name, Rank and Number."
PICTURES INCLUDE: Way to the Stars, School for Secrets, Quiet Wedding, Miranda, Easy Money, Sleeping Car to Trieste, Chiltern Hundreds, So Long at the Fair, Wooden Horse, Broken Journey, Hotel Sahara, Castle in the Air, Made in Heaven, Landfall, Three Men in a Boat, Carry on Admiral, Up the Creek, Further Up the Creek, Follow That Horse, Tom Jones, Mary Poppins, The Truth About Spring, City In the Sea, The Liquidator, The Love Bug, Bed Knobs & Broomsticks, From Hong Kong with Love, Wambling Free, Dominique, Fiendish Plot of Dr. Fu Manchu.

TOOMEY, REGIS: Actor. b. Pittsburgh, Pa., Aug. 13, 1902; e. U. Pittsburgh; Carnegie Inst. of Technology (drama); on N.Y. & London stage 5 yrs.; film debut in Alibi, 1929.
PICTURES INCLUDE: Spellbound, Big Sleep, Her Sister's Secret, Guilty, High Tide, Magic Town, Bishop's Wife, Boy With Green Hair, Mighty Joe Young, Come to the Stable, Cry Danger, Tall Target, People Against O'Hara, Show Boat, My Six Convicts, Battle at Apache Pass, Just For You, My Pal Gus, Never Wave at a Wac, It Happens Every Thursday, High and the Mighty, Top Gun, Guys and Dolls, Great Day in the Morning, 3 for Jamie Down, Dakota Incident, Warlock, Guns of the Timberland, The Day of the Gun, The Last Sundown, Journey to the Bottom of the Sea, Man's Favorite Sport, Peter Gunn, Change of Habit, Run Shadow Run, The Carey Treatment.
TV: Four Star Theatre, December Bride, Hey Mulligan, Dodsworth, Richard Diamond (series), Shannon (series), Burke's Law (series), Petticoat Junction (series).

TORME, MEL: Singer, actor. b. Chicago, Ill., Sept. 13. Singing debut at age of 4; won radio audition 1933; on radio; composed song "Lament to Love"; with Chico Marx's orchestra as drummer, arranger & vocalist 1942; served in U.S. Army, World War II; m.p. debut in "Higher and Higher" 1943; org. vocal group "Meltones"; many recordings; in night clubs.
PICTURES INCLUDE: Pardon my Rhythm, Good News, Let's Go Steady, Janie Gets Married, Night and Day, Good News, Words and Music, Duchess of Idaho, Girls Town, Walk Like A Dragon.

TORN, RIP: Actor. b. Temple, Tex., Feb. 6, 1931. e. Texas A&M, Univ. of Texas. Served in army. Signed as understudy for lead in Cat on a Hot Tin Roof on Broadway.
PICTURES INCLUDE: Baby Doll, A Face in the Crowd, King of Kings, The Cincinnati Kid, You're a Big Boy Now, Beach Red, Sol Madrid, Beyond the Law, Coming Apart, Maidstone, Tropic of Cancer, Payday, Crazy Joe, Birch Interval, The Man Who Fell to Earth, Nasty Habits, Coma, The Seduction of Joe Tynam, One Trick Pony, First Family.

TORS, IVAN: Writer, producer, director. b. Budapest, Hungary, June 12, 1916; e. U. of Budapest and Fordham U., N.Y. While in Europe wrote numerous plays, incl. Mimi, Keep Your Distance, Wind Without Rain, During World War II with Army Air Forces and O.S.S. Wrote orig. story, Below the Deadline; (collab. s.p.) Song of Love; w)s.p.) That Forsyte Woman; (s.p.) In Good Old Summertime; (collab. s.p.) Watch the Birdie; story, 49 Men; co-prod. collab. s.p. Storm Over Tibet; prod. collab. s.p. The Glass Wall, The Magnetic Monster; prod., Riders to the Stars; prod., story G.O.G.; co-prod., Battle Taxi; prod. Underwater Warriors. For Ziv-TV, prod. Science Fiction Theatre, Ripcord, Aquanauts, Man and the Challenge, Sea Hunt. Member of Faculty, Department of Psychiatry and Behavioral Sciences, University of California, Irvine.
PICTURES INCLUDE: Flipper, Rhino, Flipper's New Adventure, Zebra in the Kitchen, Clarence the Cross-eyed Lion, Around the World Under the Sea, Birds Do It, Namu the Killer Whale; Africa, Texas Style, Gentle Giant, Daring Game, Hello Down There, Island of the Lost, The Aquarians. directed, produced March of the Desert; Where the Lions Rule.
RECENT PICTURES: Escape from Angola (exec. prod.), Galyon File (exec. prod., dir.).
TV: Flipper, Daktari, Cowboy in Africa, Gentle Ben,

Jambo, Primus, Elephant Country, NBC special. 26 segments Encyclopedia of Wildlife; 3 one-hour Specials, Orientation and Navigation; Labyrinth of Odor; Pain in Nature, Danny and The Mermaid, CBS.

TOTTER, AUDREY: Actress. b. Joliet, Ill., Dec. 20. In many stage plays. On radio 1939–44; film debut in "Main Street" 1944.
PLAYS INCLUDE: Copperhead, Stage Door, Late Christopher Bean, My Sister Eileen.
PICTURES INCLUDE: Her Highness and the Bellboy, Dangerous Partners, Sailor Takes a Wife, Cockeyed Miracle, Lady in the Lake, High Wall, Beginning or the End, Unsuspected, Alias Nick Beal, Saxon Charm, Any Number Can Play, Tension, Set-Up, Under the Gun, Blue Veil, Sellout, F.B.I. Girl, Assignment-Paris, My Pal Gus, Woman They Almost Lynched, Cruisin' Down the River, Man in the Dark, Mission Over Korea, Champ for a Day, Massacre Canyon, Women's Prison, A Bullet for Joey, Vanishing American, Chubasco.
TV: Medical Center.

TOWERS, HARRY ALAN: Executive and producer. b. London, England, 1920. Prod. and wrote: 1963: Sanders of the River; 1964: Code Seven Victim Five.
PICTURES INCLUDE: City of Fear, Mozambique, Coast of Skeletons, Sandy the Seal, 24 Hours to Kill, The Face of Fu Manchu, Ten Little Indians, Marrakesh, Circus of Fear, The Brides of Fu Manchu, Sumuru, Five Golden Dragons, The Vengeance of Fu Manchu, Jules Verne's Rocket to the Moon, House of a Thousand Dollas, The Face of Eve, Blood of Fu Manchu, 99 Women, Girl From Rio, Marquis de Sade's Justine, Castle of Fu Manchu, Venus in Furs. 1969: Philosophy in the Boudoir, Eugenie, Dorian Gray, Count Dracula, The Bloody Judge. Black Beauty, Night Hair Child, The Call of the Wild, Treasure Island, White Fang, Death in Persepolis, Ten Little Indians, End of Innocence, Black Cobra, Black Velvet-White Silk, Night of The High Tide, King Solomon's Treasure.

TOWNE, ROBERT: Writer. Was member of Warren Beatty's production staff on Bonnie and Clyde and made contributions to that screenplay.
PICTURES INCLUDE: Villa Rides, The Tomb of Ligeia, The Last Detail, Chinatown, Shampoo (co-s.p.), The Yazuka (co-s.p.).

TOWNSEND, CLAIRE: b. 1953. e. Princeton. Joined 20th Century-Fox in 1976; named west coast story editor & v.p., creative affairs. Left in 1978 to go to United Artists, where named v.p. of production, responsible for managing the acquisition, development and production of feature films.

TOWNSEND, LEO: Writer. b. Faribault, Minn., May 11, 1908; e. Minnesota U. Formerly radio and feature story magazine writer. In 1942 collab. s.p., It Started With Eve, collab. orig. s.p. Seven Sweethearts.
PICTURES INCLUDE: The Amazing Mrs. Halliday, Can't Help Singing, Chip Off the Old Block, Night and Day, Southside E-1000, One Big Affair, Dangerous Crossing, Siege at Red River, A Life in the Balance, White Feather, Running Wild, Fraulein, The Black Hand, Shadow On the Window, Flight to Hong Kong, That Way With Women, Seven Sweethearts, I'd Rather Be Rich, Bikini Beach, Beach Blanket Bingo, How to Stuff a Wild Bikini, Fireball 500.
TV: Jane Wyman Theatre, Wagon Train, Maverick, 77 Sunset Strip, Hawaiian Eye, Dinah Shore Chevy Show, Shirley Temple Show, Perry Mason, Bourbon Street Beat, Beulah, Bachelor Father, Surfside Six, Destry, Patty Duke Show, Gidget, Man From U.N.C.L.E., My Three Sons, The Munsters, Batman, Andy Griffith Show, Bewitched.

TOWNSEND, PAULINE SWANSON: Writer. b. Athen, Ohio, e. Ohio University. Former Hollywood head of Tom Fizdale and Robert S. Taplinger p.r. agencies. Fiction and non-fiction writer for most national magazines.
TV: Death Valley Days, Patty Duke Show, Gidget, The Munsters, Batman, Andy Griffith Show, Bewitched.

TOYE, WENDY: Director. e. privately. Early career, ballet actress, dir., plays and musicals; entered m.p. industry 1952; dir., Stranger Left No Card (Award winning Short Cannes Festival 1953).
PICTURES INCLUDE: Three Cases Of Murder, Teckman Mystery, Raising A Riot, On The 12th Day (Nom. Best Short America 1955), All For Mary, True as a Turtle, We Joined The Navy, The Kings Breakfast.
STAGE: As You Like It, Majority Of One, Fledermaus, Orpheus in the Underworld, La Vie Parisienne, Virtue in Danger, Midsummer Night's Dream, Robert & Elizabeth, On the Level. Dir., Tribute to Noel Coward, Phoenix Th., Great Waltz, Soldiers Tale, Show Boat, Cowardly Custard, Stand and Deliver, She Stoops to Conquer, R Loves J, The Confederacy, Italian Girl in Algiers, Made in Heaven, Follow the Star, Make Me a World, Oh Mr. Porter, Once More With Music, Colette.
TV: Esme Divided, Chelsea at Nine, Orpheus in the Underworld, The Soldiers Tale, Cliff in Scotland, Girls Wanted,

Istanbul, A Goodley Manor for a Song, Girls, Girls, Girls, All Star Golden Gala ATV, Follow the Star.

OPERAS: Seraglio, Don Pasquale, The Impresario, Italian Girl in Algiers, The Merry Widow.

TRAMBUKIS, WILLIAM J.: Executive. b. July 26, 1926. Began career as usher with Loews in Providence, R.I. 1941. Served 1943–46 with Navy Seabees. Recipient of Quigley Awards. Managed/supervised Loews Theatres in several New England cities, Harrisburg, Pa., Syracuse, Rochester, Buffalo, N.Y., Washington, D.C., Richmond, Norfolk, Va., Toronto, Canada, Atlanta, Ga. Appt. Loews NorthEastern Division mgr. 1964, Loews gen. mgr. 1975: v.p. in 1976.

TRAVERS, BILL: Actor, Producer, Director. b. Newcastle-on-Tyne, England. Actor in repertory co.; London stage in Cage Me a Peacock, Damask Cheek, Square Ring, I Captured the Castle, 1961; A Cook for Mr. General (Broadway); Royal Shakespeare Theatre Co., 1962. Abraham Cochrane, 1964. Peter Pan, 1970.
PICTURES INCLUDE: Square Ring, Romeo and Juliet, Geordie, Footsteps in the Fog, Bhowani Junction, Barretts of Wimpole Street, Smallest Show on Earth, Seventh Sin, Passionate Summer, Bridal Path, Gorgo, The Green Helmet, Two Living—One Dead, Born Free, Duel at Diablo, A Midsummer Night's Dream, Ring of Bright Water, Boulevard du Rhum, The Belstone Fox, River of Sand, Bloody Ivy.
TV: A Cook for the General (Kraft), Episode, A Giant Is Born (U.S.A.), Espionage, Rawhide, CBS Voice of America (Rome), Lorna Doone, The Admirable Crichton, The Lion at World's End, Christian the Lion. Prod. dir. The Wild Doges of Africa, Baboons of Gombe, A Prospect of Whales, The Hyena Story, Death Trap, The Lions of the Serengeti, The Queen's Garden.

TRAVIS, RICHARD: Actor. r.n. William Justice. b. Carlsbad, N.M., Apr. 17, 1913. Started career in radio as announcer, sportscaster; writer and publisher of Cinemag. (theatrical tabloid); 3 yrs. U.S. Army.
PICTURES INCLUDE: The Man Who Came To Dinner, Postman Didn't Ring, Big Shot, Escape from Crime, Busses Roar, Truck Busters, Mission to Moscow, Last Ride, Jewels of Brandenburg, Alaska Patrol, Sky Liner, Operation Haylift, Passage West, Roaring City, Mask of Dragon, Lost Women, Girl in the Red Velvet Swing, Speed to Spare, Pier 21, Fingerprints Don't Lie, Annapolis Story, City of Shadows.
TV: Lucky Strike Theatre, Racket Squad, Lone Ranger, Schlitz Playhouse, Loretta Young Show, Treasury Men in Action, Pepsi Cola Playhouse, Ray Milland Show, Pride of the Family, The Falcon, Fury, Crossroads; host-narrator, Code 3, Missile to the Moon.

TRAVOLTA, JOHN: Actor. b. Englewood, N.J., Feb. 18, 1955. Quit school at 16 to pursue theatre career; first stage role in Who Will Save the Plowboy? Did off-Bdwy prod. of Rain; next to Broadway in Grease. Toured with latter for 10 months. Also in Over Here on Bdwy. with Andrew Sisters for 10 months.
PICTURES INCLUDE: Carrie, Saturday Night Fever, Grease, Moment by Moment, Urban Cowboy, Blow Out.
TV: Emergency, Owen Marshall, The Rookies, Medical Center, Welcome Back, Kotter (regular). Movie: The Boy in the Plastic Bubble.

TREE, DOROTHY: Actress. b. Brooklyn, N.Y. May 21, 1909; e. Cornell U.; m. Michael Uris, m.p. writer. On stage in: Street Scene, Clear All Wires, Torch Song, m.p. debut in "Life Begins" 1932; retired from screen 1943; wrote for m.p. in collab. with Michael Uris.
PICTURES INCLUDE: (cast) East of Fifth Avenue, Woman in Red, Night at the Ritz, Great Garrick, Having Wonderful Time, Confessions of a Nazi Spy, City in Darkness, Abe Lincoln in Illinois, Hitler Dead or Alive, Edge of Darness, Men, Asphalt Jungle, No Sad Songs for Me.
Under contract to Stanley Kramer Productions 1950.

TREEN, MARY LOU: Actress. b. St. Louis, Mo.; p. Helene Sullivan Treen, prof.; e. Ramona Convent; Denishawn School; Marion Morgan Dancers. With Fachon & Marco revues; on circuits; in early Bryan Foy short subjects; on stage in Little Boy Blew In; screen debut in Hot Tires.
PICTURES INCLUDE: Happiness Ahead, Strange Impersonation, From This Day Forward, She Wouldn't Say Yes, One Exciting Week, Let's Live a Little, The Stooge, Sailor Beware, Let's Do It Again, The Caddy, When Gangland Strikes, Birds and the Bees, Rockabye Baby, Paradise Hawaiian Style.

TREMAYNE, LES: Actor. b. London, England, Apr. 16, 1913; Northwestern U., Chicago Art Institute; Columbia, UCLA. First professional appearance in British m.p., 1916, with mother; stock, little theatres, vaudeville, 1925–40; entered radio field, 1931; numerous shows on all networks.
SHOWS INCLUDE: Woman in My House (with wife, Alice Reinheart), Errand of Mercy, You Are There, One Man's Family, Heartbeat Theatre, The First Nighter (lead 7 yrs.); on Broadway in Heads or Tails, Detective Story.

TV: Lux Video Theatre, 20th Century-Fox Hour, Navy Log, One Man's Family, Meet Millie, The Millionaire, The Whistler, Truth or Consequences, NBC Matinee, The Girl, O'Henry series, Rin Tin Tin, Bachelor Father, The Texan, Adventures of Ellery Queen, Court of Last Resort, Rifleman, State Trooper, Rescue 8, June Allyson-Dupont Show, Wagon Train, M Squad, Hitchcock Presents, Mr. Ed., Perry Mason.
PICTURES INCLUDE: The Racket, Blue Veil, Francis Goes to West Point, It Grows on Trees, I Love Melvin, Under the Red Sea, Dream Wife, War of the Worlds, Susan Slept Here, Lieutenant Wore Skirts, Unguarded Moment, Everything But the Truth, Monolith Monsters, Perfect Furlough, North by Northwest, Say One for Me, The Gallant Hours, The Angry Red Planet, The Story of Ruth.
Blue ribbon award for best perf. of the month for A Man Called Peter; dir. Hollywood Repertory Theatre, 1957; pres. Hollywood Actors' Council, 1951–58; various stage appearances, narrator of Air Force film, 1958; chmn. Actors Div. workshop com. Acad. TV Arts & Sciences; Member of The Workshop Comm. of the Hollywood M.P. & TV Museum Commission.

TRENT, JOHN: Director, Producer, Writer. b. London, England, 1935. e. London. Emigrated to Toronto, Canada in 1961. Pres. of Five Continents Prods. Ltd. Extensive television production including: Moment of Truth for NBC, Wojeck, Quentin Durgens M.P., and Whiteoaks of Jalna for CBC.
PICTURES INCLUDE: The Bushbaby, 1968, for MGM (prod.-dir.); Homer, 1969 for Palomar/Cinema Centre (dir.); The Man Who Wanted To Live Forever, 1970 for ABC/National General (dir.), Dead Of Night, 1972 for Quadrant (exec. prod.), Sunday In The Country, 1973 for Quadrant (dir.-writer), It Seemed Like A Good Idea At The Time, 1975 for Quadrant (dir.-co-writer), Middle Age Crazy, Misdeal.
TV: The Fighting Men and Riel for CBC.

TREVOR, CLAIRE: Actress. b. New York City; e. Amer. Acad. of Dram. Arts; Columbia U.; m. Milton H. Bren. On Broadway in Party's Over, Whistling in the Dark, Big Two.
PICTURES INCLUDE: Life in the Raw, Last Trail, Mad Game, Jimmy and Sally, Stagecoach, Allegheny Uprising, Dark Command, Murder, My Sweet, Johnny Angel, Crack-Up, Bachelor's Daughters, Born to Kill, Raw Deal, Valley of the Giants, Babe Ruth, Velvet Touch, Key Largo (Acad. Award), Lucky Stiff, Best of the Bad Men, Border Line, Hoodlum, Empire, Hard, Fast and Beautiful, My Man and I, Stop, You're Killing Me, Stranger Wore a Gun, High and the Mighty, Man Without a Star, Lucy Gallant, The Mountain, Majorie Morningstar, Two Weeks in Another Town, The Stripper, How to Murder Your Wife, Capetown Affair.
TV: Dodsworth (Academy Emmy).

TREXLER, CHARLES B.: Exhibitor. b. Wadesboro, N.C., Feb. 8, 1916. From 1937 to Nov. 1948 was practicing CPA except for 2 yrs. in U.S. Army in World War II. Joined Stewart & Everett Theatres in 1948 as controller. In March, 1953 named gen. mgr.; Jan. 1, 1954, exec. v.p.; treas.; May, 1962 named pres. Retains title as treas. bd. mbr., NATO of North and South Carolina; v.p. & bd. mbr., National NATO.

TRIKONIS, GUY: Director. b. New York City. Started career in chorus of West Side Story on Bdwy. Turned to direction, making low-budget "weekenders" (films shot in 12 days only on weekends).
PICTURES: Moonshine County Express, The Evil, Touched by Love.
TELEVISION: Dark Side of Terror, Dressed To Kill, The Last Convertible (final three hours).

TRINDER, TOMMY: TV performer. b. London, March 24, 1909. Early career, music halls. Starred London Palladium 1939, Top Of The World 1940, Best Bib and Tucker 1942, Happy And Glorious 1944, Here, There And Everywhere 1947, Fancy Free 1951, Variety and several Command Performance shows. Entered m.p. industry 1936.
PICTURES INCLUDE: Almost A Honeymoon, Laugh It Off, Sailors Three, The Foreman Went To France, Champagne Charlie, Fiddlers Three, Bitter Springs, You Lucky People.
TV: Master of Ceremonies, Sunday Night At The London Palladium (ATV), My Wildest Dream, BBC, The Trinder Box.

TRINTIGNANT, JEAN-LOUIS: Actor. b. Aix-en-Provence, France, Dec. 11, 1930. m. Nadine Marquand. Theatre debut: 1951, To Each According to His Hunger. Then Mary Stuart, Macbeth (at the Comedie de Saint-Etienne). 1955 screen debut.
PICTURES INCLUDE: Si Tous Les Gars Du Monde, La Loi Des Rues, And God Created Woman, Club De Femmes, Les Liaisons Dangereuses, L'Ete Violent, Austerlitz, La Millieme Fenetre, Plein Feux Sur L'Assasin, Coeur Battant, L'Atlantide, The Game of Truth, Horace 62, Les Sept Peches Capitaux (7 Capital Sins), Le Combat Dans L'Ile, The Easy Life, Il Successo, Nutty, Naughty Chateau, Les

Pas Perdus, La Bonne Occase, Mata-Hari, Meurtre A L'Italienne, La Longue Marche, Le 17eme Ciel, Un Jour A Paris, Is Paris Burning?, The Sleeping Car Murder, A Man and a Woman, Enigma, Safari Diamants, Trans-Europ-Express, Mon Amour, Mon Amour, Un Homme A Abattre, La Morte Ha Fatto L'Uovo, Les Biches, Grand Silence, Z, Ma Nuit Chez Maud (My Night at Maud's), The Conformist, The Crook, Without Apparent Motive, The Outside Man, The French Conspiracy, Les Violons du Bal, The Sunday Woman.

TROELL, JAN: Writer-Director-Cinematographer. b. Sweden, 1931. Was teacher before entering industry. In early 60s photographed Bo Widerberg's first film, The Pram. Became apprentice in TV; made m.p. debut as director in 1965 with Stay in the Marshland.
PICTURES INCLUDE: Here Is Your Life, Eeny, Meeny, Miny, Mo., The Emigrants, The New Land, Zandy's Bride.

TROSPER, GUY: Writer. b. Lander, Wyo. Started as reader, Samuel Goldwyn; then story ed.; screen writer since 1941.
PICTURES INCLUDE: collab. s.p., Stratton Story; s.p., Devil's Doorway, Inside Straight; story; Pride of St. Louis; collab. s.p., Many Rivers to Cross; s.p., The Americano, Girl He Left Behind.

TRUFFAUT, FRANCOIS: Director, writer, critic. b. Paris, France, Feb. 6, 1932. Started working at 14 as office boy, messenger, and welder in a factory. Org. and ran small cineclubs in Paris. Journalist in the m.p. section of "Work and Culture." Served in French Army 1951–53. Joined the m.p. section of the Ministry of Agriculture. Critic with Les Cahiers Du Cinema. 1955, 16mm short: Une Viste. 1956: became asst. to Roberto Rossellini, prepared three films (never produced). 1966: wrote The Cinema of Alfred Hitchcock. Acted in Close Encounters of the Third Kind.
FILMS DIRECTED INCLUDE: 1958, Les Mistons (won Dir. Award, Brussels film festival; Prix des Jeunes Spectactuers (Belgium); Germany's Gold Medal; U.S.A. Blue Ribbon Award); 1959 Histoire D'eau (short); 1959: The Four Hundred Blows (Grand Prix Cannes; Grand Prix Fr. Catholic Office Cannes, N.Y. Critics Award for Best Foreign Film; David O. Selznick Award, Oscar for best story written directly for screen); Shoot the Piano Player (Prize for photography in Germany; New Critics Prize France); Jules and Jim (Prix del la Mise en Scene, Mar del Plata and Acapulco Festivals; Danish Oscar Bodil for best European film of the year); 1962, Love at Twenty; 1963, Soft Skin; The Bride Wore Black; Stolen Kisses; Mississippi Mermaid; The Wild Child; Bed and Board; Two English Girls, Such a Gorgeous Kid Like Me, La Nuit Americain, The Story of Adele H, The Man Who Loved Women.

TRYON, TOM: Actor. b. Hartford, Conn., Jan. 14. 1926. e. Yale U. Served in U.S. Navy, World War II, studied at Art Students League; with Cape Playhouse, Dennis, Mass., as set painter, asst. stage mgr., actor; prod. asst., CBS; then TV actor.
PLAYS INCLUDE: Wish You Were Here, Cyrano de Bergerac, Richard III.
PICTURES INCLUDE: m.p. debut in Scarlet Hour; since in Screaming Eagles, Three Violent People, Moon Pilot, Marines Let's Go, The Cardinal, The Glory Guys.
AUTHOR: The Other, Crowned Heads.

TSUKASA, YOKO: Actress. b. Tottori, Japan, Aug. 20, 1934. e. Kyoritsu College; joined Toho Studio 1954 after period as magazine cover girl.
PICTURES INCLUDE: Don't Die My Darling, Blue Beast, Eternity of Love, End of Summer, Three Treasures, Yojimbo (The Bodyguard), Women of Design.

TUCHOCK, WANDA: Writer, producer. b. Pueblo, Colo., Mar. 20; e. U. of Calif., B.A. Wrote many pictures, directed Finishing School.
PICTURES INCLUDE: Hallelujah!, The Champ, Sporting Blood, Susan Lennox, Nob Hill, Sunday Dinner for a Soldier, The Homestretch, Foxes of Harrow.
Member: SWG; Acad. of M.P. Arts & Sciences, NSTP.

TUCKER, FORREST: Actor. b. Plainfield, Ind., Feb. 12, 1919; e. George Wash. U., Wash., D.C. Screen debut, 1940, in The Western, foll. by 42 feature roles, 1940–51, first starring role, Rock Island Trail, Rep., 1950. Star of Tomorrow, 1952. Member: Masquers Club of Hollywood, Lakeside Golf.
PICTURES INCLUDE: The Yearling, The Howards of Virginia, Never Say Goodbye, Warpath, Sands of Iwo Jima, Oh! Susanna; Crosswinds, Fighting Coast Guard, Wild Blue Yonder, Flaming Feather, Bugles in the Afternoon, Hoodlum Empire, Montana Belle, Hurricane Smith, Ride the Man Down, San Antone, Flight Nurse, Pony Express, Jubilee Trail, Laughing Anne, Trouble in the Glen, Rage at Dawn, Vanishing American, Finger Man, Night Freight, Paris Follies of 1956, Break in the Circle, Counterplot, The Night They Raided Minsky's, Auntie Mame, Barquero, Chisum, The Wild McCullochs.
TV: Crunch and Des, F Troop; Rad. Show: WCFL, Chicago.

Chicago Co., Plaza Suite, Oct. 1968 to June, 1969. Now assoc. prod. Drury Lane Theatre, Ill. Mem., Lambs Club, Friars Club, N.Y. Opened Nat'l Co., Music Man, L.A., on tour.

TUCKER, MELVILLE: Executive. b. New York City, Mar. 4, 1916; e. Princeton U. Asst. purchasing agent Consolidated Laboratories, N.Y., 1934–36; sound effects & picture ed., Republic Productions, Inc. 1936–8; then asst. production mgr. & first asst. dir., 1938–42; served in U.S. Army 1942–46; asst. prod. Republic 1946; assoc. producer, 1947–52; prod., Universal 1952–54; prod. exec. v.p., Universal, 1955–70; prod.-Verdon Prods., 1971–present.
PICTURES INCLUDE: The Missourians, Thunder in God's Country, Rodeo King and the Senorita, Utah Wagon Train. U-I prod., 1953: Drums Across the River, Black Shield of Falworth; production exec. U-I, 1954–71. prod., Verdon Prod., prod. A Warm December, 1972; prod., Uptown Saturday Night, Producer, Let's Do It Again, 1975; prod., A Piece of the Action, 1977; exec. prod., Stir Crazy, 1980.

TULIPAN, IRA H.: Publicist. b. New York City. e. N.Y.U. 1934, B.S. Entered m.p. ind. as theatre mgr., Boston, 1934; pub. dept. Warner Bros. home office, 1935–40; joined 20th Century-Fox 1942; U.S. Army service 1943–46; returned to Fox upon disch., feature writer, press book ed.; trade paper contact; newspaper contact; pub. mgr. 1955; ass't dir. adv. pub. expl. Columbia Pictures. 1960; exec. adm. asst. to adv., publ., v.p., Columbia, 1963; dir. overseas prod. pub., 1966. Returned to U.S. in 1978 as eastern pub.-coordinator.

TULLY, MONTGOMERY: Director-writer. b. Ireland. e. Kings College, U. London, B. Sc. Before entering m.p. indus. in 1929 as writer, was in advertising bus.; wrote short stories. Apptd. dir.-writer, 1937; documentaries, 1929–44.
PICTURES INCLUDE: (dir. & s.p.) Murder in Reverse, Spring Song, Mrs. Fitzherbert; (s.p.) Waltz Time, For You Alone, and Lisbon Story, Punchdrunk (s.p.); Boys in Brown (dir. s.p.); Tale of Two Cities, Five Women (dir.); orig. s.p. Berlin Story; dir. Girdle of Gold, Small Town Story, 36 Hours, The Diamond, Five Days, Devil's Point, The Hypnotist, Counterfeit Plan; dir., s.p., Dial 999 (Way Out), No Road Back, One Man's Secret; dir. Scotland Yard and Man From Interpol series. Dir.: Jackpot, Dead Lucky, The House on Marsh Road, The Man Who Was Nobody, 1959–61; Third Alibi, She Knows Y'Know, Out of the Fog, Checkmate, 1961–62; Clash By Night, Boy With A Flute, 1964–65. Dir. Who Killed The Cat? The Terrornauts, Battle Beneath the Earth, 1966. s.p. The Hawks; s.p. The Ballbreakers, 1967–68. The Fighting Contessa, 1969.

TULLY, TOM: Actor. b. Durango, Colo., Aug. 21. Appeared in many New York plays.
PLAYS INCLUDE: Time of Your Life, White Steed, Jason and Ah, Wilderness.
PICTURES INCLUDE: Came to Hollywood 1943. Since: Till the End of Time, Kiss and Tell, I'll Be Seeing You, The Unseen, Destination Tokyo, Intrigue, Scudda Hoo Scudda Hay, Killer McCoy, Illegal Entry, Branded, Tomahawk, Caine Mutiny, Love Me Or Leave Me, Soldier of Fortune, Behind the High Wall, 10 North Frederick, The Wackiest Ship in the Army, Blood on the Moon, Coogan's Bluff.
TV: The Lineup (network series), Philco Playhouse, Ford Theatre, Celebrity Playhouse, Front Row Center, San Francisco Beat, Alfred Hitchcock. 1959–61: dir., s.p., Strange Awakening, I Only Asked, Price of Silence, Man From Interpol (series) Jackpot, Dead Lucky, The House In March Road, The Man Who Was Nobody. 1962: Third Alibi, She Knows Y'Know, Out of the Fog. 1963–64: Checkmate, Clash By Night, Boy With A Flute.

TUNBERG, KARL: Writer. b. Spokane, Wash. From 1937 collab. many Hollywood s.p.
PICTURES INCLUDE: You Can't Have Everything, My Lucky Star, Hold That Co-Ed, Down Argentine Way, Yank in the RAF. In 1942 (collab. s.p.) My Gal Sal, Orchestra Wives, Lucky Jordan, (collab. s.p.) Dixie, Standing Room Only, Bring on the Girls; (prod. & collab. s.p.) Kitty; (prod.) You Gotta Stay Happy; (collab. s.p.) Love That Brute, Night Into Morning, Law and the Lady, Because You're Mine, Scandal at Scourie, Valley of the Kings; s.p. Beau Brummell, Scarlet Coat, Seventh Sin, Ben Hur, s.p. Count Your Blessings; s.p. Libel, Taras Bulba; s.p., I Thank A Fool; s.p. The Seventh Dawn, Harlow (story); col. s.p., Where Were You When the Lights Went Out?

TUNICK, EUGENE: Executive. b. Cincinnati, Ohio, Oct. 21, 1920. e. Hughes High School, 1934–38; Univ. of Cincinnati, 1938–39. 1941, shipping clerk, RKO, Cincinnati. 1942, Armed Forces. 1944–45, Third Booker, Second Booker, Office Manager-RKO Cincinnati, 1946, Salesman, West Virginia and Ohio for RKO, Cincinnati. 1948, Sales-manager, RKO. 1949, Salesmanager, Eagle Lion, N.Y.C. Oct. 1949–51, Branch Manager Eagle Lion, Indianapolis. 1951–52, Lippert Branch Mgr. Indianapolis. 1952–53, Lippert franchise holder, Cincinnati. Dec. 1954, United Artists Branch Mgr. Philadelphia. 1957, District Mgr. U.A., Phila. Sept. 1961, Eastern and Canadian Div. Mgr. U.A., N.Y. June 1968, Assistant General Sales Mgr., National General Pictures. June 1969, V.P. and General Sales Mgr. National General Pictures. Jan. 1, 1970, Executive V.P. General Sales Mgr. NGP; exec. v.p., Mid States Theatres, 1971; exec. v.p., National Amusements (Redstone), 1975; 1977, v.p. General Cinema Theatres (Western Div.); 1978, v.p. in charge of Special Projects, Amer. Int'l Pictures; later in year named v.p. & gen. sls. mgr.; 1979, v.p. & gen. sls. mgr., Filmways; promoted to exec. v.p. & gen. sls. mgr.; 1981.

TUNICK, IRVE: Writer. b. New York, N.Y.; e. N.Y.U. and Georgetown U. Commenced writing career with radio scripts; later senior writer (TV) for Cavalcade of America and You Are There, stories produced by Studio One and Armstrong Circle Theatre; five radio and TV scripts won Peabody Awards; script editor for Princess Pictures 1953–55; orig. s.p. for Lady of Vengeance; s.p. for High Hell.

TURELL, SAUL J.: Writer, Producer, Executive. b. N.Y.C., Jan. 20, 1921. e. City Coll., U. of Chicago. B.A.—Univ. of The State of N.Y. Started Sterling Films, 1946; merged Walter Reade-Sterling, 1961; pres., 1961–65. Presently: pres., Janus Films Inc. Adjunct Assoc. Prof. N.Y.U.
PICTURES INCLUDE: The Great Chase, The Love Goddesses, My Home Is Copacabana, The Art of Film Series, Robeson: A Film Tribute. (Oscar, 1980).
TV: King's Crossroads, Adventure Theatre, Killiam Show, Movie Museum, Silents Please, The Big Moment, Hollywood The Golden Years, The Legend of Valentino.
PRIZE WINNING SHORT SUBJECTS INCLUDE: Sandy Steps Out, Hot Ice, The Princess and the Dragon, Death in the Arena, The Fun Factory.

TURFKRUYER, MARC: Journalist. Pres. Antwerp Sec. of the Belgian Film Press Assn.; editor of Weekblad Cinema, the oldest Belgian trade paper; contributor to the daily paper Volksgazet (Antwerp) and to the weeklies ABC and Het Toneel, Motion Picture Herald (New York); Pres., International Film Press Assn.

TURMAN, LAWRENCE: Producer. b. Los Angeles, 1926. e. UCLA. In textile business 5 years, then joined Kurt Frings Agency; left in 1960 to form Millar-Turman Prods.
PICTURES INCLUDE: (prod.) The Young Doctors, I Could Go on Singing, The Best Man. Formed own prod. co., Lawrence Turman, Inc., to make The Flim-Flam Man, The Graduate, Pretty Poison, The Drowning Pool, First Love, Heroes, Walk Proud, Caveman (co-prod.).

TURNER, CLIFFORD: Producer. b. Leeds, England, 1913. ent. m.p. industry as cutting room asst. Gaumont British. Edited number early British pictures, before going to Hollywood in 1935. Subsequently edited for Warners, Columbia, Universal, Fox. Returned to England 1948 to edit The Small Back Room. Dir. and assoc. producer since 1950 in Hollywood and New York. Formed Boulevard Film Productions Ltd., Screen Biographies International Inc., Television Enterprises Inc. Four Against the Bank of England. 1972: Utrillo. 1975, Rose of Cimarron, 1976 Mystery of the General Grant; La Cicatrice, The Valadon Story.

TURNER, LANA: Actress. b. Wallace, Idaho, Feb. 8, 1921; p. Virgil Turner, prof.
PICTURES INCLUDE: They Won't Forget, Great Garrick, Adventures of Marco Polo, Love Finds Andy Hardy; Rich Man, Poor Girl; Dramatic School, Calling Dr. Kildare, These Glamour Girls, Dancing Coed. Two Girls on Broadway, We Who Are Young, Ziegfeld Girl, Dr. Jekyll and Mr. Hyde, Johnny Eager, Slightly Dangerous, Youngest Profession, Marriage Is a Private Affair, Keep Your Powder Dry, Week-End at the Waldorf, Postman Always Rings Twice, Green Dolphin Street, Cass Timberlane, Homecoming, Three Musketeers, Life of Her Own, Mr. Imperium, The Merry Widow, Bad & the Beautiful, Latin Lovers, Flame & the Flesh, Betrayed, The Prodigal, Sea Chase, Rains of Ranchipur, Diane, Lady and the Flyer, Imitation of Life, Portrait in Black, By Love Possessed, Bachelor in Paradise, Who's Got the Action?, Love Has Many Faces, Madame X, The Big Cube, Persecution, Bittersweet Love.
TV: The Survivors.

TUSHINGHAM, RITA: Actress. b. Liverpool, England, 1942. Student at Liverpool Playhouse, Motion pic. debut 1961 in A Taste of Honey.
PICTURES INCLUDE: The Leather Boys, A Place to Go, Girl With Green Eyes, The Knack, Dr. Zhivago, The Trap, Smashing Time, Diamonds for Breakfast, The Guru, The Bedsitting Room, Straight on 'til Morning, Situation, Instant Coffee, The Human Factor, Rachel's Man, The Slum Boy, Green Eyes, The Black Journal, Bread, Butter and Jam, Mysteries.

TUTIN, DOROTHY: Actress. b. London, Eng., Apr. 8, 1930; e. St. Catherine's School Bramley, Guildford (Surrey). Stage debut in The Thistle & the Rose, 1949.
PLAYS INCLUDE: Much Ado About Nothing, The Living Room, I Am a Camera, The Lark, Wild Duck, Juliet, Ophelia, Viola, Portia, Cressida, Rosalind, The Devils, Once More With Feeling, The Cherry Orchard, Victoria Regina-Portrait of a Queen, Old Times, Peter Pan, What Every Woman

Knows, Month in the Country, Macbeth, Antony and Cleopatra, Undiscovered Country, Reflections.
PICTURES INCLUDE: Screen debut in The Importance of Being Earnest. Also: The Beggar's Opera, A Tale of Two Cities, Cromwell, Savage Messiah.
TV: Living Room, Victoria Regina, Invitation to a Voyage, Antigone, Colombe, Carrington V.C., The Hollow Crown, Scent of Fear, From Chekhov With Love, Anne Boleyn in The Six Wives of Henry VIII, Flotsam and Jetsam, Mother & Son, South Riding, Willow Cabins, Ghosts, Sister Dora.

TWIGGY: Recording Artiste. b. London, Sept. 19, 1949. r.n. Leslie Hornby. m. actor Michael Witney. At 17 regarded as world's leading high fashion model. Made m.p. debut in The Boy Friend (1971).
TV: Hosted and starred in major American & British music shows including Twiggy (UK), Twiggy and Friends (UK), and Juke Box (US).
PICTURES INCLUDE: W, There Goes the Bride, The Blues Brothers.

TWYMAN, ALAN P.: Executive. b. Dayton, Ohio, May 30, 1934. e. Univ. of Cincinnati. Twyman Films, Inc. sales 1958, vice pres.-pres., 1975. NAVA board of directors, 1964–1969; pres 1970, chm. of bd., 1972.

TYLER, BEVERLY: Actress. r.n. Beverly Jean Saul. b. Scranton, Pa., July 5, 1928; e. Scranton H.S. Church choir singer; on radio, TV.
PICTURES INCLUDE: Green Years, My Brother Talks to Horses, Beginning or End, The Palomino, The Fireball, Cimarron Kid, Battle at Apache Pass.

TYRRELL, SUSAN: Actress. b. San Francisco, 1946. Made first prof. appearance with Art Carney in summer theatre tour prod. of Time Out for Ginger. Worked in off-Bdwy. prods. and as waitress in coffee house before attracting attention in Lincoln Center Repertory Co. prods. of A Cry of Players, The Time of Your Life, Camino Real.
PICTURES INCLUDE: The Steagle, Shoot Out, Fat City, Catch My Soul, Islands in the Stream, Andy Warhol's Bad, I Never Promised You A Rose Garden, Another Man, Another Chance, September 30, 1955.

TYSON, CICELY: Actress. b. New York City, Dec. 19, 1933.
PICTURES INCLUDE: A Man Called Adam, The Comedians, The Heart Is a Lonely Hunter, Sounder, A Hero Ain't Nothin, But a Sandwich, The Concorde—Airport '79.
TELEVISION: The Autobiography of Miss Jane Pittman, Roots, East Side, West Side, A Woman Called Moses, King.

U

UGGAMS, LESLIE: Singer. b. New York, May 25, 1943. e. Professional Children's Sch., grad., 1960. Juilliard. Beg. singing career age 5. TV debut: age 7, Johnny Olsen's TV kids. Records for Columbia Records.
STAGE: Hallelujah Baby.
RADIO: Peter Lind Hayes-Mary Healy Show, Milton Berle, Arthur Godfrey, Star Time.
TV: Milton Berle Show, Name That Tune, Jack Paar Show, Garry Moore, Sing Along With Mitch.

ULLMAN, ELWOOD: Writer. b. Memphis, Tenn.; e. Washington U., St. Louis, BA. Newspaper reporter, St. Louis Post-Dispatch; m.p., TV & mag. writer.
PICTURES INCLUDE: Martin and Lewis, Abbott and Costello, Bowery Boys films, Kettle films, Battle Flame, Three Stooges, Tickle Me, Dr. Goldfoot and The Bikini Machine.
FICTION: Country Gentleman, Sat. Eve. Post, Esquire, etc.

ULLMANN, LIV: Actress. b. Japan of Norwegian parents. Accompanied parents to Canada when World War II began and later returned to Norway. Was catapulted to fame in a succession of Swedish films directed by Ingmar Bergman.
PICTURES INCLUDE: Swedish: Persona (debut), Hour of the Wolf, Shame, The Passion of Anna, The Emigrants, Cries and Whispers; American: The Devil's Imposter (formerly Pope Joan), Lost Horizon, 40 Carats, Zandy's Bride, The Abdication, Face to Face, A Bridge Too Far, The Serpent's Egg, Autumn Sonata.

UNGER, ANTHONY B.: Executive Producer. b. New York, Oct. 19, 1940. e. Duke Univ. and Univ. of Southern Calif. Prod. ass't Third Man, TV series, 1961. v.p. Unger Productions, Inc., 1964; v.p. Landau-Unger Co., Inc., 1965; v.p. Commonwealth United Entertainment in London, 1968.
PICTURES INCLUDE: 1966: assoc. prod., The Desperate Ones. 1968: assoc. prod., The Madwoman of Chaillot. 1969: exec. prod., The Battle of Neretva, The Magic Christian, Julius Caesar. 1970: exec. prod., The Devil's Widow. 1973: exec. prod., Don't Look Now.

UNGER, KURT: Producer. b. Berlin, Jan. 10, 1922. Entered ind. in 1939 in chg. m.p. entertainment British troops in Middle East. Subsequently distributor for United Artists Corp. in Israel and Italy.
PICTURES INCLUDE: Judith, Best House in London, Puppet on a Chain, Pope Joan (The Devil's Imposter).

UNGER, STEVEN A.: Executive. Started as independent prod. and dist. of theatrical and TV films. In June, 1978, joined Universal Pictures Intl. Sales as foreign sls. mgr. Named v.p. Universal Theatrical Motion Pictures in 1979, responsible for licensing theatrical or TV features not handled by C.I.C. in territories outside U.S. & Canada. In 1981 joined CBS Theatrical Films as int'l. v.p., sls.

URICH, ROBERT: Actor. b. Toronto, Ohio, Dec. 19. e. Florida State Univ. (BA in radio and TV communications). Appeared in university plays. Was sales account executive at WGN Radio, Chicago, before turning to stage acting.
TELEVISION: The FBI, Gunsmoke, Kung Fu, Marcus Welby, MD, S.W.A.T., Boy & Carol & Ted & Alice, Soap, Tabitha, The Love Boat, Vega$.
PICTURE: Magnum Force.

URQUHART, ROBERT: Actor, writer. b. Scotland, October 16, 1922. e. George Heriots, Edinburg. Served in Merchant Navy 1938–45; stage debut, Park Theatre, Glasgow; screen debut: You're Only Young Twice, 1951.
PICTURES INCLUDE: Isn't Life Wonderful, The House Of The Arrow, Knights Of The Round Table, Happy Ever After (Tonight's The Night), Golden Ivory, The Dark Avenger, You Can't Escape, Yangtse Incident, Curse of Frankenstein, Dunkirk, The Trouble with Eve, Danger Tomorrow, Foxhole in Cairo, Murder in Mind, The Bulldog Greed, 55 Days At Peking, The Break, Murder at the Gallup, The Syndicate, The Limbo Line, The Looking Glass War, Brotherly Love (Country Dance).
TV: Tamer Tamed, Infinite Shoeblack, Morning Departure, The Human Touch, The Iron Harp, Sleeping Clergyman, The Naked Lady, For Services Rendered, The Bright One, Jango, Murder Swamp, She Died Young, Plane Makers series, Reporter, Inheritors series; 1976 series: Mr. Goodall, The Nearly Man, The Button Man, Happy Returns.
AUTHOR: (Wrote TV) House of Lies, End of the Tether, Landfall, The Touch of a Dead Hand.

USTINOV, PETER: Actor, writer, dir. b. London, Eng., 1921; e. Westminster Sch. In Brit. Army, World War II. On Brit. stage from 1937. Screen debut 1941 in Brit. picture Mein Kampf, My Crimes.
PICTURES INCLUDE: The Goose Steps Out, One of Our Aircraft Is Missing, Let the People Sing, The Way Ahead, The True Glory, (collab. s.p.) The Way Ahead; (wrote, dir. & co-prod.) School for Secrets, Vice Versa; (adapt., dir., co-prod.) Private Angelo, Odette, Quo Vadis, Hotel Sahara, The Egyptian, Beau Brummell, We're No Angels, Lola Montez, The Spies, An Angel Flew Over Brooklyn, The Sundowners, Spartacus; prod., scripted, acted, Romanoff and Juliet; dir., prod./scpt., acted, Billy Budd, Topkapi, John Goldfarb Please Come Home; prod. dir., Lady L., Blackbeard's Ghost, The Comedians, Hot Millions, Viva Max. Dir. and acted, Hammersmith Is Out, acted Big Truck, Poor Clare, Logan's Run, Treasure of Matecumbe, One of Our Dinosaurs Is Missing, Le Taxi Mauve, The Last Remake of Beau Geste, Doppio Delitto, Death on the Nile, Charlie Chan and the Curse of the Dragon Queen, The Great Muppet Caper.
STAGE: Romanoff and Juliet, N.Y., London; and 17 other plays. Dir., acted, Photo Finish; wrote, Life In My Hands, The Unknown Soldier and His Wife, Half Way Up The Tree.

V

VACCARO, BRENDA: Actress. b. Brooklyn, N.Y., Nov. 18, 1939. e. Thomas Jefferson High School, Dallas; studied two yrs. at Neighborhood Playhouse in N.Y. Was waitress and model before landing first Bdwy. role in Everybody Loves Opal. Toured in Tunnel of Love and returned to N.Y. for role in The Affair. Won Tony for best supporting actress in Cactus Flower.
PICTURES INCLUDE: Midnight Cowboy (debut), I Love My Wife, Summertree, Going Home, Once Is Not Enough, Airport '77, House by the Lake, Capricorn One, The First Deadly Sin, Zorro, the Gay Blade.
TV: The F.B.I., The Name of the Game, The Helen Reddy Show, The Shape of Things (special), Sunshine (tv movie), etc.

VALE, EUGENE: Writer. b. April 11, 1916. e. Zurich, Switzerland. m. Evelyn Wahl. Story and s.p., The Second Face, The Shattered Dream, 1954 SWG award nom., best written telefilm; The Dark Wave. 1957, m.p. academy award nominations.

TV: Four Star Playhouse, Fireside Theatre, 20th Century Fox Hour, Schlitz Playhouse, Hollywood Opening Night, NBC, Crusader, Lux Video Theatre, Danger, CBS, Chevron Theatre, Douglas Fairbanks, Pepsicola Playhouse, Waterfront, Christophers, Cavalcade of America, Hallmark Hall of Fame.
AUTHOR: Technique of Screenplay Writing.

VALENTE, CATERINA: Singer. b. Paris, France.
RECORDINGS INCLUDE: Malaguena, in German; I Happen to Like New York.
TV: The Bing Crosby Show, The Ed Sullivan Show, The Entertainers.

VALENTI, JACK J.: Executive. b. Sept. 5, 1921. e. Univ. of Houston, B.A., 1946; Harvard, MBA, bus. admin., 1948. Air force pilot in European theatre, WWII; adv. and pub. rel. exec. in Houston; special asst. and advisor to Pres. Lyndon B. Johnson, 1963–66; pres., MPAA; elected pres., MPAA, MPEA and AMPTP, June, 1966.

VALENTINO, THOMAS J.: Chairman, Thomas J. Valentino, Inc. b. New York, N.Y., Apr. 27, 1907; e. high sch. Cartoonist; piano & organ tuner, R. Wurlitzer Co., then Starr Piano Co., 1924–29; Gennett Recording Co., N.Y.; synchronized sound shorts, feature films; sound consultant, Major Records, N.Y.; owns large library of mood music & sound effects. Elected v.p., Recording Ass'n of America, 1969–71.

VALLEE, RUDY: Actor, r.n. Hubert Prior Vallee; b. Island Pond, Vt., July 28, 1901; e. U. of Maine, Yale U. After college began career in entertainment as singer with dance orchestra; org. own band, Connecticut Yankees, popular dance orchestra, later also feature various New York musicals and on radio. First screen dramatic work in The Vagabond Lover, RKO; later various shorts and feature appearances with orchestra. In 1942 role in The Palm Beach Story, Par. In 1943, Happy Go Lucky, Par. In World War II chief petty officer (bandmaster) U.S. Coast Guard. In 1945 formed (with Leslie Charteris) Saint Enterprises, Inc.
PICTURES INCLUDE: Man Alive, People Are Funny, It's in the Bag, The Fabulous Suzanne, Bachelor and Bobby Soxer, Beautiful Blonde from Bashful Bend, Father Was a Fullback, Mother Is a Freshman, Admiral Was a Lady, Mad Wednesday, Ricochet Romance, Gentlemen Marry Brunettes, How to Succeed in Business Without Really Trying, Live a Little, Love a Little.

VALLI, ALIDA: Actress. b. Pola, Italy, May 31, 1921. e. M.P Academy, Rome (dramatics); m. Oscar de Mejo, pianist-composer. In Italian m.p.; won Venice Film Festival Award in "Piccolo Monde Antico" (Little Old World).
PICTURES INCLUDE: Vita Ricomincia, Giovanna; to U.S. 1947; U.S. m.p. debut in Paradine Case, 1947; later pictures: Miracle of the Bells, The Third Man, Walk Softly Stranger, White Tower, Lovers of Toledo, Stranger's Hand, The Castilian, Ophelia, Spider's Stratagem, The Cassandra Crossing, Susperia, 1900.

VALLIN, RICK: Actor. b. Russia; son of Nedja Yatsenko, ballerina. In stage stock, radio; joined Pasadena Playhouse, 1942. Screen debut 1942.
PICTURES INCLUDE: King of the Stallions, Nearly Eighteen, Corregidor, Lady from Chungking, A Night for Crime, Panther's Claw, Northwest Outpost, Two Blondes and a Redhead, Jungle Jim, Shamrock Hill, Comanche Territory, Aladdin and His Lamp, Magic Carpet, Woman in the Dark, Jungle Manhunt, Strange Fascination, Voodoo Tiger, Star of Texas, many Westerns, Bowery to Bagdad, Treasure of Ruby Hills, Dial Red O.

VALLONE, RAF: Actor. b. Turin, Italy; e. U. of Turin. Newspaper writer; m.p. debut in Bitter Rice.
PICTURES INCLUDE: Under the Olive Tree, Anna, Path of Hope, White Line, Rome 11 O'Clock, Strange Deception, Anita Garibaldi, Daughters of Destiny, Teresa Raquin, Riviera, The Secret Invasion. 1961: Two Women, El Cid, A View From the Bridge, Phaedra, Kiss The Girls and Make Them Die, The Desperate Ones, The Cardinal, The Italian Job, The Kremlin Letter, Summertime Killer, Rosebud, The Human Factor, The Other Side of Midnight, The Greek Tycoon, Lion of the Desert.

VAN CLEEF, LEE: Actor. b. Somerville, N.J., Jan. 9, 1925. e. Somerville H.S., 1942. Joined U.S. Navy, 1942; asst. mgr. in summer camp, public accountant; then joined little theatre group.
PICTURES INCLUDE: High Noon, Beast from 20,000 Fathoms, Vice Squad, The Nebraskan, Gypsy Colt, Arrow in the Dust, Yellow Tomahawk, Dawn at Socorro, Princess of the Nile, Ten Wanted Men, The Conqueror, Big Combo, Treasure of Ruby Hills, I Cover the Underworld, Road To Denver, Posse from Hell, The Man Who Shot Liberty Valance, A Man Alone, Vanishing American, Tribute to a Bad Map, For a Few Dollars More, The Good, The Bad and The Ugly, The Big Gundown, Death Rides a Horse, Day of Anger, Barquero, El Condor, The Magnificent Seven Ride, Return of Sabata, Escape from New York.

VAN DOREN, MAMIE: Actress. r.n. Joan Lucille Olander. b. Rowena, S.D., Feb. 6, 1933. e. Los Angeles High Sch. Secy. law firm, L.A.; prof. debut as singer with Ted Fio Rita orch.
THEATRE: Appeared in many stock plays incl.: Once in a Lifetime, Boy Meets Girl, Come Back Little Sheba.
PICTURES INCLUDE: (m.p. debut) Forbidden; All American, Yankee Pasha, Francis Joins the Wacs, Ain't Misbehavin, Second Greatest Sex, Running Wild, Star in the Dust, Untamed Youth, Girl in Black Stockings, Teachers Pet, The Navy Vs. The Night Monsters.

VAN DYKE, DICK: Actor. b. West Plains, Mo., Dec. 18, 1925. U.S.A.F., WWII. partner, ad. agency, nightclub acts: Merry Mutes, Eric and Van.
THEATRE: The Girls Against the Boys, Bye Bye Birdie.
PICTURES INCLUDE: Bye Bye Birdie, Mary Poppins, What a Way to Go. The Art of Love, Lieutenant Robinson Crusoe, Divorce American Style, What's New Fitzwilly?, Chitty Chitty Bang Bang, Some Kind of Nut, The Comic, Cold Turkey, The Runner Stumbles.
TV: The Merry Mute Show, The Music Shop, The Dick Van Dyke Show (variety prog.), Cartoon Theater, The New Dick Van Dyke Show, The Carol Burnett Show.

VAN FLEET, JO: Actress. b. Oakland, Calif. e. College of the Pacific. Neighborhood Playhouse.
THEATRE: On Broadway in Winter's Tale, Whole World Over, Closing Door, King Lear, Flight into Egypt, Camino Real, Trip to Bountiful (Tony Award); Look Homeward Angel (Critics Award); The Glass Menagerie; Off Broadway: The Alligators, Oh Dad, Poor Dad, Mama's Hung You In The Closet and I'm Feeling So Sad.
PICTURES INCLUDE: East of Eden (Academy Award, best supporting actress, 1955); I'll Cry Tomorrow (Look Award), Rose Tattoo, This Angry Age, King and Four Queens, Gunfight at the OK Corral; Wild River, Cool Hand Luke, I Love You, Alice B. Toklas, Gang Who Couldn't Shoot Straight, The Tenant.
TELEVISION: Cinderella, Bonanza, Mod Squad, Power, etc.

VAN HEUSEN, JIMMY: Composer. b. Syracuse, N.Y., Jan. 26, 1919. e. Syracuse U. Pianist with publishing houses; songs for many m.p. including Sunday, Monday or Always, Swinging on a Star (Acad. Award 1944), Sunshine Cake, etc.
PICTURES INCLUDE: Road to Rio, Emperor Waltz, Connecticut Yankee, Mr. Music, Riding High, Road to Bali, Little Boy Lost, All the Way (Academy Award), Call Me Irresponsible (Academy Award), won Emmy for Love and Marriage; Songwriters Hall of Fame.

VAN PALLANDT, NINA: Actress. b. Copenhagen, Denmark. e. Univ. of So. Calif. Returned to Denmark where married Baron Frederik Van Pallandt with whom she had appeared as folk singer throughout Europe. Made 3 films with him; went on world tour together. Now divorced. Has appeared in New York as singer.
PICTURES: The Long Goodbye, A Wedding, Quintet, American Gigolo, Cloud Dancer, Cutter and Bone.
TELEVISION: The Sam Shepherd Murder Case.

VAN PATTEN, DICK: b. N.Y.C., Dec. 9. Began career as child actor with Bdwy. debut at 7 yrs., playing son of Melvyn Douglas in Tapestry in Gray. Has worked since in stage, radio, TV, films.
PICTURES INCLUDE: Making It, Joe Kidd, Soylent Green, Dirty Little Billy, Westworld, Gus, Treasure of Matecumbe, High Anxiety.
TV: Series: Mama, The Partners, The New Dick Van Dyke Show, Eight Is Enough. Guest Roles: Arnie, The Rookies, Cannon, Banyon, The Little People, The Streets of San Francisco, When Things Were Rotten.
STAGE: The Lady Who Came to Stay, O Mistress Mine, On Borrowed Time, Ah, Wilderess, Watch on the Rhine, The Skin of Our Teeth, Kiss and Tell, Mister Roberts, I Was Dancing.

VAN PEEBLES, MELVIN: Director, writer, composer. Was navigator-bombardier in Air Force, drove cable car in San Francisco.
AUTHOR: A Bear for the F.B.I., Don't Play Me Cheap (play) won 1st prize, Belgian Festival; and photo-essay book on cable cars. Albums of his own music: Brer Soul, Ain't Supposed to Die a Natural Death. Composed music for Watermelon Man.
PICTURES INCLUDE: The Story of a Three-Day Pass, Watermelon Man, Sweet Sweetback.
MEMBER: French Director's Guild; one of first Black directors to be member of Directors Guild of America.
STAGE: Ain't Supposed to Die a Natural Death, Don't Play Us Cheap.

VAN PRAAG, WILLIAM: Executive, Producer, Director, Writer, Editor. Advertising Consultant. b. N.Y.C., Sept. 13, 1924. e. CREI, Columbia Univ.; U.S. Army, 1942. Paramount, 1945; Brandt Bros. Prods., 1946; NBC, 1947; v.p. Television Features, 1948. Devlpd. vidicon system in m.p. prod., 1949. Started, pres., Van Praag Prod. Inc. 1951. Formed Ernst-

Van Praag, Inc. 1971, a communications and marketing counseling firm (N.Y., Brussels, Tokyo). Pres., International Film, TV and A-V Producers Ass'n, 1969, Creator of Van-O-Vision. Winner of commercial, short subject and feature theatrical awards. Author of Color Your Picture, Primer of Creative Editing, and Van Praag's Magic Eye. Past pres., Film Producer's Ass'n, mem. DGA, SAG, 71 IATSE, National Academy of TV Arts and Sciences, International Radio and TV Executive Society and Soc. of MP and TV Engineers.

VAN RIKFOORD, HAROLD C.: Producer. b. New York, Jan. 1, 1935. e. Bryant H.S., grad., 1952; N.Y. Univ. Errand bty, stage mgr., N.Y., 1954–57. Co-prod. two Broadway plays. Prod., The Long Ride Home, Rome, 1957; prod., short subject films; prod., Moment of Crisis, 1959; prod., television pilot films; exec. prod., Jonathan Shields Prod.

VAN TAALINGEN, J.TH.: b. Amsterdam, Holland, Oct. 16, 1921. Joined Nederlandse Bioscoopbond 1946. Apptd. general director Nederlandse Bioscoopbond 1970.

VAN THAL, DENNIS: Executive. b. London, June 4, 1909. e. University College. Early career musical dir.; war service, Royal Navy; entered m.p. industry 1946; casting dir. Pinewood Studios; dir., Myron Selznick Ltd.; joined dir. Alexander Korda as prod. assoc.; 1953; apptd. dir., Big Ben Films, 1955; joined Ealing Films, 1956; prod. assoc. Anastasia; assoc. prod. The Admirable Crichton, Barnacle Bill, The Scapegoat; mgr. London Management, Ltd.

VAN VOLKENBURG, J. L.: Executive. b. Sioux City, Ia., Dec. 6, 1903. e. U. of Minn. Batten, Barton, Durstine, Osborne adv. agency, 1928; CBS, Inc., since 1932; v.p. CBS and pres. CBS-TV Div.; ret. Jan., 1957; pres. McCann, Erickson Prod., Inc., 1960.

VANCE, DENNIS: TV Producer, director. b. Birkenhead, England, 1924. Service in Merchant Navy & Fleet Air Arm. Early career with BBC and Rank Organization making film debut in Hungry Hill. Others: Hamlet, Saraband for Dead Lovers, Christoper Columbus, Landfall, Shadow of the Eagle; 1952, prod. for BBC Inc. Public Prosecutor, Mr. Betts Runs Away; 1956 drama supv., and later prod. supv. ABC-TV, 1959–60 dir., U.S. Steel Hour and play of The Week, N.Y.; 1961: dir. Henry IV Part 1, Old Vic. 1961–64 ATV prod. dir. 1964: Gen. man. Caribbean Broadcasting Corp. set up TV in West Indies. 1966: Returned to ATV and Thames TV. Contract prod. dir.
TV: The Misfit, Man at the Top, Spyders Web.

VANCE, LEIGH: Scriptwriter and producer. b. Harrogate, England 1922. Early career; reporter, critic. Ent. TV 1951, then films, many TV scripts; 1961, won Edgar Allan Poe Award, 1969, brought to Hollywood by Paramount. In 1973 exec. story consultant and producer, Cannon; 1974, exec. story consultant, Caribe; 1975, prod., Bronk. 1976: Exec. prod., Baretta & Switch, 1977/8: Prod., Switch.
PICTURES INCLUDE: The Flesh Is Weak, Heart of a Child, Picadilly Third Stop, Women Shall Weep, The Shakedown, Eyes of Youth, The Frightened City, It's All Happening Dr. Crippen, Outcast, Walk Like A Man, Cross Plot, Tall Cool Girl, The Black Windmill.
TV: Mannix, Mission Impossible, many pilots, The Avengers, The Saint, Cannon, Caribe, Bronk, Baretta, Switch.

VARDA, AGNES: Photographer-Director-Writer. b. France, 1928. Started as still photographer for The Theatre National Populaire de Jean Vilar. Became a photo-journalist. In 1954 wrote and directed first film, La Pointe Courte. Afterwards made both documentaries and features.
PICTURES INCLUDE: Cleo from 5 to 7, Le Bonheur, Les Creatures, Lion's Love, One Sings, The Other Doesn't.

VAUGHN, ROBERT: Actor. b. New York City, 1932. Played Napoleon Solo in The Man From U.N.C.L.E. TV series.
CREDITS: Hell's Crossroads, No Time to Be Young, Unwed Mother, Good Day for a Hanging, The Young Philadelphians, The City Jungle (Acad. Award nom.), The Magnificent Seven, The Big Show, The Caretakers, To Trap a Spy, The Spy With My Face, One Spy too Many, The Venetian Affair, How to Steal the World, Bullitt, The Bridge at Remagen, The Mind of Mr. Soames, If It's Tuesday, This Must Be Belgium, Julius Caesar, The Statue, The Clay Pigeon, One of Our Spies Is Missing (TV, Great Britain), The Spy In the Green Hat (TV, Great Britain), The Towering Inferno, Starship Invasions, "S.O.B.".
AUTHOR: Only Victims, 1972.
TV: Washington: Behind Closed Doors.

VEITCH, JOHN: Executive. b. New York City, June 22, 1920. Started production career as asst. director and moved through ranks as prod. mgr., assoc. prod., prod., second unit dir., and exec. prod. mgr. Appointed Columbia Pictures exec. asst. prod. mgr., 1961; became exec. prod. mgr., 1963. Named v.p. & exec. prod. mgr., 1966; promoted in 1977 to exec. v.p. & exec. prod. mgr. of worldwide physical productions. In 1979 named pres. of Columbia Pictures Productions.

VELAISE, ROBERT: Executive. e. Zurich U.; ent. production 1957; formed Vauban Productions of Paris, Robert Velaise Productions, Ltd., of London, 1961; prod., Les Oeufs de l'Autruche, Nina, Geliebte Hochstaplerin, Give Me Ten Desperate Men, The Wrong Arm of the Law, The Go-Between.

VELAZCO, ROBERT E.: r.n. Emil Velazco, Jr. b. Dallas, Texas, Jan 1, 1924. e. Columbia Univ., Business Administration 1942–43. Started in film business with father, Emil Velazco, 1942. Following yrs. worked for Emil Velazco, Inc., NTA, Ross Gaffney, Inc. During this time worked on over 8,500 productions from 5 sec. to feature films. In charge of Velazco, Inc., Kansas City, Mo., 1947–49. Owner and pres., Musifex Co., Inc., 1958. Opened Musifex Inc. Arlington, Va., 1972. Two films scored by Velazco nominated for Academy Award, 1978 and 1980.

VELDE, DONALD L.: Executive. b. Tremont, Ill., Sept. 10, 1902. e. Bradley Prep, Swarthmore Coll. Paramount Pictures, 1922–40; National Screen Service, 1940–48; chairman, Donald L. Velde, Inc.

VELDE, JAMES R.: Executive. b. Bloomington, Ill., e. Illinois Wesleyan Univ. Entered m.p. ind. as night shipper Paramount ex. Detroit, 1934; then city salesman, office mgr. until joining Army, 1943, rejoining same ex. upon dischge., 1946; to Paramount, Washington as Baltimore city salesman, same yr.; br. mgr. Selznick Rel. Org. Pittsburgh, 1948; salesman Eagle-Lion Classics, Pittsburgh, 1949; br. mgr. ELC, Des Moines, 1949; br. mgr., ELC, Detroit, 1950; west coast dist. mgr., United Artists, April, 1951; Western div. mgr. UA, 1952; gen. sales mgr., 1956; v.p., 1958; dir., UA, 1968; sr. v.p., 1972. Retired, 1977.

VENTURA, LINO: Actor. b. Italy, 1918. French resident since age of 8. Was professional wrestler until injury ended career in ring. First acting appearance in Touchez pas au Grisbi (1953) opposite Jean Gabin. Veteran of over 50 films.
PICTURES: Marie Octobre, Crooks in Clover, Les Aventuriers, The Valachi Papers, Wild Horses, Sunday Lovers, etc.

VERNON, ANNE: Actress. r.n. Edith Antoinette Alexandrine Vignaud. b. Paris, Jan. 24. e. Ecole des Beaux Arts, Paris. Worked for French designer; screen debut in French films; toured with French theatre group; first starring role, Le Manneuin Assassine 1948.
PICTURES INCLUDE: Ainsi Finit La Nuit, A Warning to Wantons, Patto Col Diavolo, A Tale of Five Cities, Shakedown, Song of Paris, Edward and Caroline, Terror on a Train.

VERONA, STEPHEN: Director. e. School of Visual Arts. Directed some 300 commercials before turning to feature films in 1972, which he wrote as well.
PICTURES: Pipe Dreams, Boardwalk.

VERSOIS, ODILE: Actress. b. Paris, June 15, 1930. e. Paris. Early career in ballet at Paris Opera; worked on stage in France, Belgium, Switzerland and North Africa; screen debut in 1947 with films in France and Italy.
PICTURES INCLUDE: (In England) Into the Blue, A Day to Remember, Young Lovers (Chance Meeting), To Paris With Love, Checkpoint, Ruler Without Crown, Passport to Shame, Docks, Nude in a White Car.

VETTER, RICHARD: Exec. b. San Diego, Calif., Feb. 24, 1928. e. Pepperdine Coll., B.A., 1950; San Diego State Coll., M.A., 1953, U.C.L.A., Ph.D., 1959. U.S. Navy: aerial phot., 1946–48, reserve instr., San Diego County Schools, 1951–54; asst. prof., audio-vis. commun., U.C.L.A., 1960–63. Inventor, co-dev., Dimension 150 Widescreen Process. 1957–63: formed D-150 Inc., 1963; exec. v.p. mem.: SMPTE, Technical & Scientific Awards Committee, AMPAS.

VICTOR, HARVEY L.: Executive. b. New York. e. Carnegie Inst. of Technology, N.Y. University. Acct. exec., Television Programs of America; acct. supv., Official Films Inc.; acct. exec., various ad. agencies; N.Y. mgr., Special Devices, Inc.; vice-pres., gen. sls. mgr., Jayark Films Corporation 1958; pres., Harvey Victor Films, Ltd., 1964.

VIDOR, KING WALLIS: Director. b. Galveston, Tex., Feb. 8, 1895. e. Peacock Military Academy, San Antonio, Tex.; Tome College, Port Deposit, Md.
PICTURES INCLUDE: Turn in the Road, La Boheme, The Crowd, Big Parade, Hallelujah, Billy the Kid, Street Scene, The Champ, Cynara, Bird of Paradise, Stranger's Return, Our Daily Bread. In 1936 produced, directed and collaborated on screen story Texas Rangers. Stella Dallas, The Citadel, Northwest Passage, Comrade X, H.M. Pulham, Esq.; (prod. dir.) An American Romance. In Jan., 1949, signed term contract with Warners TV show; Lights Diamond Jubilee, 1954. Duel in the Sun, Fountainhead, Ruby Gentry, Man Without a Star, War and Peace, Solomon and Sheba.

VIETHEER, GEORGE C.: Executive. b. New York, N.Y., Feb. 27, 1910. e. Norwich U., B.S., 1932; Syracuse U, M.S., 1933. U.S. Army officer, 1933–37; chief service bureau, later Wash. rep. Panama Canal & R.R. Co., 1937–41; deputy dir., personnel, Office of Emergency Mgt., 1941–43; U.S. Army, 1943–46; mem., Nat'l Comm. on Manpower Shortages, 1946; deputy dir., personnel, U.S. Dept. of Commerce, 1946–50; U.S. rep. to U.N. Public Admin. Conf., 1950; deputy asst. admin. Econ. Stab. Agency, 1951; mgr., Washington office, MPAA, 1952; subsequently v.p., MPEAA and also v.p. American Motion Picture Export Co. (Africa) and v.p., Afram Films, Inc. Author: various pubs., articles on bus. mgt. Retired since 1977.

VILAS, WILLIAM H.: Executive. e. Harvard U.; U. Minnesota, B.A. Dunwoody Institute. In adv. & sales management; wrote, prod. or supervised over 100 productions for TV, industrial or theatre release; organized & supervised film training projects for U.S. Armed Forces, World War II: v.p., Wilding Pictures Prod.; special consultant for OSS; prod. of theatrical, TV & non-theatrical m.p. For pub. rel.; recent TV: Terry and the Pirates, series on film, dir., motion picture & television dept. & account exec., J. M. Mathes, Inc., N.Y.; chmn. bd. gov. Yankee Highway Assn.; dir. Citizens Assn. of Conn.; pub. Brotherhood Press. Clubs; Pequet Yacht, Southport, Conn., Harvard, New Canaan, Conn.

VILLECHAIZE, HERVE: Actor. b. Paris, France, April 23, 1943. Sought career as artist, studying in Paris and then coming to New York to the Art Students League. Studied acting with Julie Bovasso. First film, The Guitar, shot in Spain. On Broadway in Elizabeth the First and Gloria and Esperenze. Also performed mime in N.Y. City Opera productions.
PICTURES: Hollywood Blvd. No. 2, Hot Tomorrow, The Man with the Golden Gun, Crazy Joe, The Gang That Couldn't Shoot Straight, Seizure, The One and Only.
TELEVISION: Fantasy Island (regular).

VINCENT, JAN-MICHAEL: Actor. b. Denver, Colo., July 15. e. Ventura City (Calif.) College as art major. Joined National Guard. Discovered by agent Dick Clayton. Hired by Robert Conrad to appear in his film, Los Bandidos, made in Mexico. Signed to 6-mo. contract by Universal, for which made Journey to Shiloh. Then did pilot TV movie for 20th-Fox based on Hardy Boys series of book. Originally called self Michael Vincent; changed after The Undefeated.
PICTURES INCLUDE: Los Bandidos, Journey to Shiloh, The Undefeated, Going Home, The Mechanic, The World's Greatest Athlete, Buster and Billie, Bite the Bullet, White Line Fever, Baby Blue Marine, Vigilante Force, Shadow of the Hawk, Damnation Alley, Big Wednesday, Hooper, Defiance, Hard Country.
TV: Lassie, Bonanza, The Banana Splits Adventure Hour, The Survivors (series), Tribes (movie released theatrically abroad), The Catcher (movie), Sandcastle (movie).

VINCENT, JR., FRANCIS T: Executive. President & chief exec. officer of Columbia Pictures Industries (appt. July, 1978). e. William College, Yale Law School. 1968–78, partner in law firm of Caplin & Drysdale, specializing in corporate banking and securities matters. Since March 1, 1978, assoc. dir. of, Division of Corporation Finance of Securities & Exchange Commission. Trustee of William College & Hotchkiss School.

VINCENT, JUNE: Actress. r.n. Dorothy June Smith. b. Harrods, Ohio. Concert pianist; photographer's model. On dramatic stage, The Family. Screen debut Second Honeymoon, 1937.
PICTURES INCLUDE: The Climax, Ladies Courageous, Can't Help Singing, Shed No Tears, Creeper, Counterspy Meets Scotland Yard, Secrets of Monte Carlo, Colorado Sundown, Night Without Sleep, Wac From Walla Walla, Clipped Wings, City of Shadows.

VINCENT, KATHARINE: Actress. r.n. Ella Vincenti. b. St. Louis, Missouri, May 28, 1919. e. Two years of high school, left in 1937 to go on the stage. m. Pandeno Descanto, producer.
THEATRE: Broadway shows include: Love or Bust, 1938; Could She Tell?, 1939; Banners of 1939; Czarina Smith, 1940. Numerous road show tours.
PICTURES INCLUDE: Peptipa's Waltz, 1942 (debut), Error in Her Ways, 1943, Skin Deep, 1944, The Hungry, Voodoo Village, Welcome to Genoa, 1950, Unknown Betrayal, 1956, The Hooker, 1962 (Descanto films).
TV: The Untouchables, Moses, The Lawgiver.

VINER, MICHAEL: Producer-Writer. b. 1945. e. Harvard, Georgetown. Served as aide to Robert Kennedy; was legman for political columnist Jack Anderson. Settled in Hollywood, where worked for prod. Aaron Rosenberg, first as prod. asst. on three Frank Sinatra films; then asst. prod. on Joaquin Murietta. In music industry was record producer, manager, executive, eventually heading own division, at MGM. Debut as writer-producer in 1976 with TV special, Special of the Stars. Theatrical film debut as prod.-co-writer of Touched by Love, 1980.

VITALE, JOSEPH A.: Actor. b. New York City, Sept. 6, 1901. In 1924, on dramatic stage (Hold on to Your Hats, Page Miss

Glory, All Editions, I'd Rather Be Right, Common Ground). Screen debut, 1943.

PICTURES INCLUDE: None But the Lonely Heart, Lady Luck, Road to Rio, Where There's Life, Connecticut Yankee, Illegal Entry, Red Hot and Blue, Paleface, Fancy Pants, My Friend Irma Goes West, Stop You're Killing Me, Stranger Wore a Gun, Square Jungle, Rumble On the Docks, Apache Rifles.

TV: Climax, Lineup, Bengal Lancers, Wagon Train, Schlitz Playhouse, Cimmaron City, Telephone Time, Wyatt Earp, Rawhide, Red Skelton, The Thin Man, M Squad, Dawson, Ben Casey, Empire, Hazel, Mr. Ed, To Rome With Love, Fisherman's Wharf (pilot).

VITALE, MILLY: Actress. b. Rome, Italy. July 16, 1938. e. Lycee Chateaubriand, Rome. Has appeared in numerous Italian films.

PICTURES INCLUDE: The Juggler, Seven Little Foys, Breath of Scandal.

VLECK, JOSEPH V.: Executive. b. Fort Morgan, Colorado. e. U. of Denver, School of Theatre and Graduate School Business Adm. Fox-Intermountain Theatres Denver, Ogden, Pocatello, La Junta; foreign film program director. Promotion manager, 1962 National General Theatres home office advertising department, appointed director adv. and publicity, 1965; now with Mann Theatres as dir. of adv.

VOGEL, JESSE: Writer, Composer. b. New York, N.Y., Oct. 24, 1925. e. CCNY, B.S.Sc., 1947; Paris Conservatory of Music, 1949; dir., Vogel Films, Paris, post-production services, English and Foreign versions. Screenplays: Carmen, Baby; Therese and Isabelle. Produced: Who's Harriet? My Pleasure Is My Business.

VOHS, JOAN: Actress. r.n. Elinor Joan Vohs. b. St. Albans, L.I., N.Y., July 30, 1931; e. Andrew Jackson H.S., Professional Children's School. Radio City Music Hall Rockette at 16; Bdwy play; Parlor Story; many TV shows.

TV: Readers Digest, Stage Seven, Dear Phoebe, Ray Bolger Show, Robert Cummings Show, Stage 7, Frontier, Schlitz Playhouse, Lux Video Theatre.

PICTURES INCLUDE: My Dream Is Yours, Girl from Jones Beach, Inspector General, Yes Sir That's My Baby, Vice Squad, Fort Ti, Crazylegs, Sabrina, Cry Vengeance, Fort Yuma, Terror at Midnight.

VOIGHT, JON: Actor. b. Yonkers, N.Y. Dec. 29, 1938. e. Archbishop Stepinac High School, White Plains, N.Y.: Catholic University, Bachelor of Fine Arts Degree, 1960; studied acting at the Neighborhood Playhouse and in private classes with Sanford Meisner, four yrs. Off-Broadway in: A View From the Bridge (revival), 1964. Won the Theatre World Award for Broadway prod. That Summer, That Fall. Played Romeo, San Diego Shakespeare Festival.

TV: Public Broadcast Lab.'s The Dwarf, also Gunsmoke, Cimarron Strip.

PICTURES INCLUDE: Fearless Frank, Hour of the Gun, Midnight Cowboy (Acad. Award nom., Best Actor), Out of It, Catch 22, The Revolutionary, All American Boy, Deliverance, Conrack, The Odessa File, End of the Game, Coming Home, The Champ, Lookin' To Get Out (also co-s.p.).

VOLONTE, GIAN MARIA: Actor. b. Milan, April 9, 1933. e. Rome's National Academy of Dramatic Art (1957 graduate). Entered on professional theatrical career, playing Shakespeare and Racine, along with modern works, Sacco and Vanzetti and The Deputy. On TV in Chekov's Uncle Vanya and Dostoyevsky's The Idiot. First major film roles in Un Uomo da Bruciare (1961) and Il Terrorista (1963). Called self John Welles in credits for "spaghetti westerns."

PICTURES INCLUDE: For a Fistful of Dollars, For a Few Dollars More, Investigation of a Citizen Above Suspicion, The Working Class Goes to Heaven, Wind from the East, Sacco and Vanzetti, L'Attenat, Slap the Monster on Page One, Just Another War, The Mattei Affair, Lucky Luciano, Eboli.

VON SYDOW, MAX: Actor. b. Lund, Sweden, April 10. m. Keratin Olin, actress, 1951. Theatrical debut in a Cathedral School of Lund prod. of The Nobel Prize. Served in the Swedish Quartermaster Corps two yrs. Studied at Royal Dramatic Theatre School in Stockholm. Tour in municipal theatres. Has appeared on stage in Stockholm, London, Paris and Helsinki in Faust, The Legend and The Misanthrope. 1954 won Sweden's Royal Foundation Cultural Award.

PICTURES INCLUDE: Wild Strawberries, Brink of Life, The Magician, The Seventh Seal, The Virgin Spring, Through a Glass Darkly, Winter Light, Hawaii, The Greatest Story Ever Told, The Reward, Hour of the Wolf, Shame, The Kremlin Letter, The Passion of Anna, The Immigrants, Night Visitor, The Emigrants, The New Land, Three Days of The Condor, Voyage of the Damned, Exorcist II: The Heretic, March or Die, Flash Gordon, Victory.

VONDERHAAR, RAYMOND T.: Executive. b. Rugby, No. Dak., Nov. 1, 1919. e. St. Cloud State. Spent entire career in exhibition. Pres., Allied Theatre Assn., 1963–64; pre., NATO North Central States, 1965–76; National NATO bd., 1965–80; also memb. exec. comm. 1965–80; NATO No. Central, chm., 1976–80.

VORHAUS, BERNARD: Director. In 1933, wrote and directed Money for Speed (UA-British).

PICTURES INCLUDE: 1934, directed The Ghost Camera (Radio-British), Crime on the Hill (BIP) and Night Club Queen (Universal-British); 1935: Broken Melody (APD), Blind Justice (Universal-British), Ten Minutes Alibi (BL), Street Song (Radio-British). In 1936; directed Last Journey, Twickenham; Dark World, Fox British. Associate producer Broken Blossoms; director, Dusty Ermine, Twickenham; Cotton Queen, Rock Studios, Bury Me Dead, Winter Wonderland, The Spiritualist, So Young, So Bad, Pardon My French.

VYE, MURVYN: Actor, singer. b. Quincy, Mass., July 15, 1913. e. Yale U., 1937.

THEATRE: Hamlet, The Live Wire, The Number, All In Fun, Something for the Boys, Oklahoma, Carousel.

PICTURES INCLUDE: Golden Earrings, Connecticut Yankee, Road to Bali, Destination Gobi, Pickup on South Street, Green Fire, Escape to Burma, Pearl of the South Pacific, Best Things in Life are Free, Al Capone, Pay or Die.

TV: Studio One, U.S. Steel, Ford Theater, Lux Video, Celebrity Playhouse, Schlitz Playhouse, etc.

W

WADLEIGH, MICHAEL: Director. b. Akron, Ohio, Sept. 24, 1941. e. Ohio State U., B.S., B.A., M.A., Columbia Medical School. Directed Woodstock.

WAGENHEIM, CHARLES: Actor. From 1941 in Meet Boston Blackie, Fingers at the Window, Halfway to Shanghai, Sin Town, I Escaped from the Gestapo.

PICTURES INCLUDE: Colonel Effingham's Raid, The House on 92nd Street, Summer Storm, Dark Corner, Pirates of Monterey, Scudda-Hoe! Scudda-Hay, Cry of City, Lady Without Passport, House on Telegraph Hill, Vicki, Beneath the 12-Mile Reef, Canyon Crossroads, Blackjack Ketchum, Desperado.

WAGGONER, LYLE: Actor. b. Kansas City, Kan., April 13, 1935. e. Washington Univ., St. Louis. Was salesman before becoming actor with road co. prod. of Li'l Abner. Formed own sales-promo co. to finance trip to Calif. for acting career in 1965. Did commercials, then signed by 20th-Fox for new-talent school.

TELEVISION: The Carol Burnett Show, It's Your Bet (host), The New Adventures of Wonder Woman.

WAGNER, LINDSAY: Actress. b. Los Angeles, June 22. Appeared in school plays in Portland, Oregon; studied singing and worked professionally with rock group. In 1968 went to L.A. and decided to make acting her career. Signed to Universal contract in 1971.

PICTURES INCLUDE: Two People, Paper Chase, Second Wind, Nighthawks.

TV: The F.B.I., Owen Marshall, Counselor at Law, Night Gallery, The Bold Ones, Marcus Welby, M.D., The Rockford Files, The Six Million Dollar Man, The Bionic Woman.

WAGNER, RAYMOND JAMES: Executive. b. College Point, L.I., N.Y., Nov. 3, 1925. e. Middlebury College & Williams College. Joined Young & Rubicam, Inc., as radio-TV commercial head in Hollywood, 1959–50. Head of pilot development, Universal Studios, 1960–65. Produced Petulia for Warner Bros. (1967) and was exec. prod. of Loving for Columbia (1969). Presently v.p. of production (features) or MGM.

WAGNER, ROBERT: Actor. b. Detroit, Feb. 10, 1930; e. Saint Monica's H.S. Film debut in, Halls of Montezuma.

PICTURES INCLUDE: The Frogmen, Let's Make It Legal, With A Song in My Heart, What Price Glory, Stars and Stripes Forever, The Silver Whip, Titanic, (Star of Tomorrow, 1953). Beneath the 12-Mile Reef, Prince Valiant, Broken Lance, White Feather, Kiss Before Dying, The Mountain, True Story of Jesse James, Stopover Tokyo, The Hunters, In Love and War, Say One for Me, Between Heaven and Hell, All the Fine Young Cannibals, Sail a Crooked Ship, The Longest Day, The War Lover, The Condemned of Altona, Harper, Banning, The Biggest Bundle of Them All, Don't Just Sit There, Winning, The Towering Inferno, Midway, The Concord—Airport '79.

TV: It Takes A Thief series; Madame Sin; Switch (series), Cat on a Hot Tin Roof, Pearl, Hart to Hart.

WAKELY, JIMMY: Actor, singer, songwriter. b. Mineola, Ark., Feb. 16, 1914. Began as farmer, then singer, radio, Oklahoma City, Decca recordings. Author lyrics & music numerous hillbilly songs (Too Late, I'll Never Let You Go). Screen debut 1939 in Saga of Death Valley; collab. on music Six Lessons from Madame La Zonga, 1941. From 1939 in many Westerns various cos. (Paramount, Universal, Republic, etc.); producing Westerns independently; act., Marshal's Daughter, Arrow in the Dust.

WALD, MALVIN: Writer, producer. b. New York City, N.Y., Aug. 8. e. Brooklyn College, B.A., J.D. Woodland University College of Law, graduate work Columbia U., New York University U.S.C. Newspaper reporter and editor, publicist, social worker, radio actor. Screenplays and original stories for Columbia, 20th-Fox, UA, MGM, WB; U.S. Air Force; tech. sgt., wrote 30 documentary films for film unit.
PICTURES INCLUDE: The Naked City (Acad. Award nomination, best story); Behind Locked Doors, The Dark Past, Ten Gentlemen from West Point, The Powers Girl, Two in a Taxi, Undercover Man, Outrage, On the Loose; (assoc. producer and sec.-treas., Filmakers Pictures, Inc.); Battle Taxi, Man on Fire, Al Capone, Venus in Furs. In Search of Historic Jesus. Legend of Sleepy Hollow. Shorts: Employees Only (Academy Award nomin., best sht. doc.), Boy Who Owned a Melephant (Venice Children's Film Festival gold medal), Unarmed in Africa, The Policeman, James Weldon Johnson, Me An Alcoholic?
TV: Many credits including Playhouse 90, Hollywood: The Golden Years, The Rafer Johnson Story, D-Day, Project: Man in Space, Biography of A Rookie, Alcoa-Goodyear Hour, Climax, Shirley Temple Storybook, Peter Gunn, Perry Mason, Dobie Gillis, Combat, Daktari, (Associate Prod.) Primus, California Tomorrow, prod. Mod Squad, Untamed World, Around the World of Mike Todd, The Billie Jean King Show, Life and Times of Grizzly Adams, Mark Twain's America, Greatest Heroes of the Bible, Littlest Hobo. Exec. prod., 20th Century Fox TV Documentary Unit, 1963–64 writer-prod. U.S.I.A. 1964–65; writer-prod., Ivan Tors Films, 1965–69; prof., U.S.C., Division of Cinema; Writer's Guild of America, Acad. of Motion Picture Arts and Sciences, co-author of book, Three Major Screenplays. Contributor to book, Close-Ups. Published s.p., Naked City.

WALD, RICHARD C.: Executive. b. New York City. e. Columbia College, Clare College (Cambridge). Joined the New York Herald Tribune in 1951 as Columbia College correspondent; religion editor, political reporter; foreign correspondent (London, Bonn), 1959–63; associate editor, 1963–65; managing editor from 1965 until paper ceased publication in 1966; Sunday editor, World Journal Tribune, 1966; managing editor, Washington Post, 1967; vice president, Whitney Communications Corp., 1967–68; joined National Broadcasting Company as vice president, NBC News, 1968; exec. v.p., 1972; president, NBC News, 1973.

WALDMAN, WALTER: Publicist. b. New York City. e. CCNY, Columbia U. Newspaper reporter; magazine writer; radio-television-film critic; radio news writer, Current Events, Triangle Publications; The Bronx Home News; Grolier Society; Netherlands Information Bureau, station WLIB; free-lance New York Times and New York Herald Tribune; writer, press book dept., 20th Century-Fox; copy writer, advertising dept., Republic Pictures; writer, Variety, Box-office Magazine; publicity writer, copy chief, publicity dept., Paramount Pictures; publicity copy chief, contact, United Artists.

WALKEN, CHRISTOPHER: Actor. b. Astoria, N.Y., Mar. 31, 1943. Began career in off-Bdwy. musical revue, Best Foot Forward, starring Liza Minnelli. Continued in musicals until cast in original Bdwy. production of The Lion in Winter, winning Clarence Derwent Award for performance as King Philip. Switched to dramatic roles, winning Obie Award for title role in Kid Champion and Theater World Award for performance in N.Y. City Center revival of Rose Tattoo.
PICTURES INCLUDE: The Anderson Tapes (debut), Next Stop, Greenwich Village, Roseland, Santa Fe—1936, The Sentinel, Annie Hall, The Deer Hunter, Heaven's Gate, The Dogs of War, Pennies from Heaven.

WALKER, CARDON E.: Executive. b. Rexburg, Idaho, Jan. 9, 1916. e. UCLA, Los Angeles; B.A. 1938. Four years Officer, U.S. Navy. Started with Walt Disney Productions 1938; camera, story, unit director short subjects, budget control. Headed, 1950, adv. & pub. 1956, v.p. in chg. of adv. & sales. 1960 member bd. of dir. & exec. comm. 1965 v.p., mkt. 1967 exec. v.p. operations. 1968, exec. v.p. and chief operating officer; pres., 1971; Nov. 1976 pres. and chief executive officer; June, 1980, named bd. chm. & chief exec. officer.

WALKER, CLINT: Actor. b. Hartford, Ill., May 30, 1927. e. schools there. Joined Merchant Marine 1944, worked as sheet metal worker, carpenter, other jobs in Alton, Ill.; set out with wife and infant daughter for oil fields in Texas; decided to try acting. Got screen test at Paramount Studios for Cecil B. De Mille; later landed contract to star in Cheyenne TV films at Warner.
PICTURES INCLUDE: Fort Dobbs, Yellowstone Kelly, None But the Brave, Pancho Viva, Maya, Night of the Grizzly, Gold of the Seven Saints, Send Me No Flowers,

The Dirty Dozen, The Great Bank Robbery, Sam Whisky, More Dead Than Alive, etc.

WALKER, DAVID PAT: b. Glasgow, Scotland, 1928. Joined British Broadcasting Corporation as studio manager in Glasgow, became radio producer, then a production assistant in television. Joined BBC in Northern Ireland as that station's only television producer in 1960. Became assistant head of programmes, BBC, Northern Ireland, then rejoined BBC Scotland in similar post 1970. Head of programmes, Scotland, 1973, and Head of network productions at Scotland 1978. Comes from theatrical family, sister Amanda Walker being an actress and his mother, Madeleine Christie, actress in TV, films, theatre and radio. Assistant controller, BBC Scotland, June 1979.

WALKER, JOSEPH: Cameraman. From 1928 cinematographer many Columbia productions. Member Amer. Soc. Cinematographers (second vice-pres. 1944–45). Inventor of Electra-Zoom Lens used in TV stations; chief eng., Radio Optical Research Co., Hollywood, retired.
PICTURES INCLUDE: It Happened One Night, Mr. Deeds Goes to Town, Lost Horizon, Here Comes Mr. Jordan, Jolson Story, Affair in Trinidad, Born Yesterday.

WALKER, MARTIN: Singer, actor. b. Dundee, Scotland, Jan. 6, 1938. e. N.J., Yonkers, N.Y. high schools. B'way stage play 3 Wishes for Jane; winner Godfrey Talent Scouts, CBS-TV, Paul Whiteman Show, ABC-TV; guest on Morey Amsterdam Show, Johnny Olsen Show, Johnny Andrew Show etc.; recording artist, Pinky Records.

WALKER, NANCY: Actress-Director. b. Philadelphia, May 10, 1922. As child toured Europe with her parents, The Barto and Mann vaudeville team. Pursued career as serious vocalist until George Abbott steered her toward comedy when she auditioned for Broadway prod., Best Foot Forward. Directed film, Can't Stop the Music (1980).
STAGE: On the Town, Barefoot in the Park, Phoenix '55, Fallen Angels, Copper and Brass, Pal Joey, Wonderful Town, Girls Against the Boys, Look Ma, I'm Dancing, Along Fifth Avenue, Lucky Me.
PICTURES INCLUDE: Best Foot Forward, Girl Crazy, Broadway Rhythm, Meet the People, Stand Up and Be Counted, Forty Carats, Won Ton Ton, Murder by Death.
TV: Nearly every major TV show, plus series: McMillan & Wife, Rhoda, The Nancy Walker Show, Blansky's Beauties.

WALLACE, CHARLES: Producer, writer, director. b. Temple, Texas, May 5, 1930. e. New Mexico Military Institute; Arizona State Univ. Ent. industry, announcer engineer, KTYL, Phoenix, 1948; prod. dir., KVAR, Phoenix, 1950; prod. dir., Wide Wide World, NBC-TV, 1955–58; prod. dir., writer, NBC News overseas, U.S. Air Force Power for Peace, 1956; assoc. prod. writer, Twenty-Six Men, ABC-TV, 1958; prod. dir., writer, American Pauses spectaculars, CBS-TV Zane Grey Theatre, Johnny Ringo, Wyatt Earp, Robert Taylor Show, 1959; prod. writer, Four Star pilots, Hardcase-Yuma, 1959; writer, Wells Fargo, NBC-TV, Ichabod and Me, 1960; writer, Death Valley Days, U.S. Air Force Classified Documentaries; writer, Screen Gems, Whirlpool pilot, 1961; prod., Lum 'n Abner, Four Star TV, 1962.

WALLACE, IRVING: Writer. b. Chicago, Ill., March 19, 1916. e. Williams Inst., Berkeley, Calif., 1935–36. For. correspondent in Japan & China, Liberty Mag., 1940; U.S. Army doing m.p. & photog.; covered France, Germany, Spain for Sat. Evening Post, Collier's, Reader's Digest, 1946, 1947, 1949, 1953.
AUTHOR: The Fabulous Originals, 1955; The Square Pegs, 1957; The Sins of Philip Fleming, 1959; The Fabulous Showman, 1959; The Chapman Report, 1960; The Twenty-Seventh Wife, 1961; The Prize, 1962; The Three Sirens, 1963; The Man, 1964; The Sunday Gentleman, 1965; The Plot, 1967. The Writing of One Novel, 1968; The Seven Minutes, 1969; The Nympho and Other Maniacs, 1971; The Word, 1972, The Fan Club, 1974; The People's Almanac, 1975; The R Document, 1976.
PICTURES INCLUDE: story, collab. s.p., West Point Story; s.p., Meet Me at the Fair; collab. s.p., Desert Legion, Gun Fury; collab. story and s.p., Split Second; s.p., The Burning Hills, Bombers B-52; novel (basis for film), The Chapman Report, The Prize, The 7 Minutes, The Man.

WALLACE, JEAN: Actress. b. Chicago, Oct. 12, 1930. As teenager signed by Paramount as contract player and studied at Actors Laboratory (Method School) in Hollywood. Later, switched to 20th Century-Fox. In 1951 went to Argentina to star in first film, Native Son. Board of Directors Permanent Charities Committee and (Womens Auxiliary), Antans (The Womens Auxiliary of the American National Theater and Academy); hospitality chm., Beverly Hills P.T.A.
PICTURES INCLUDE: Storm Fear, The Big Combo, The Man on the Eiffel Tower, The Devil's Hairpin, Maracaibo, The Sword of Lancelot, Beach Red, No Blade of Grass. bd. of dir. of Screen Smart Set.

WALLACE, MIKE: TV commentator, interviewer. b. Brookline, Mass., May 9, 1918. e. Univ. of Michigan; 1939. Night Beat,

WABD, N.Y., 1956; The Mike Wallace Interview, ABC, 1956–58; Newspaper col., Mike Wallace Asks, N.Y. Post, 1957–58; News Beat, WNTA-TV, 1959–61; The Mike Wallace Interview, WNTA-TV, 1959–61; Biography, 1962; correspondent, CBS News, 1963, CBS Radio: Personal Closeup, Mike Wallace at Large; Co-editor, 60 Minutes, CBS News.

WALLACH, ELI: Actor. b. Brooklyn, N.Y., Dec. 7, 1915. e. U. of Texas. Capt. in Medical Admin. Corps during WW II. After college acting, appeared in Summer stock. Made Broadway debut in Skydrift, 1945, followed by Antony & Cleopatra, The Rose Tattoo, Major Barbara, Rhinoceros, Luv. Charter member, Actors Studio in 1947.
PICTURES INCLUDE: first film Baby Doll. Also: The Magnificent Seven, Seven Thieves, The Misfits, The Victors, Hemingway's Adventures of A Young Man, How the West Was Won, Act One, Genghis Khan, The Moonspinners, Lord Jim, How to Steal a Million, The Good, the Bad and the Ugly, The Tiger Makes Out, Band of Gold, How to Save a Marriage and Ruin Your Life, A Lovely Way to Die, Ace High, The Brain, Zigzag, The People Next Door, Romance of a Horse Thief, Cinderella Liberty, Crazy Joe, Movie Movie, The Hunter.
TV: Studio 1, Philco Playhouse, Playhouse 90; Won Emmy for A Poppy Is Also a Flower.

WALLACH, GEORGE: Producer, writer, dir. b. New York, N.Y., Sept. 25, 1918; e. N.Y.U. Actor in theatre & radio 1938–45; U.S. Navy 1942–45; supvr. radio-TV Div. of Amer. Thea. Wing 1946–48; prod.-dir. WNEW, 1947–48; program mgr. WNYC 1948–50; prod.-writer-dir. for WNBC-WNBT, 1950; Dir., news, spec. events WNBT-WNBC, 1951–52; prod. mgr., NBC Film Div. since 1953; CBS-TV; formed George Wallach Prod., 1956; prod. dir. It Happened in Havana, appt. TV officer, U.S.I.A., 1957. Film-TV-film officer American Embassy, Bonn, Germany, 1961. Film-TV officer American Embassy; Tehran, Iran, 1965–66; m.p. Prod. Officer, JUSPAO, American Embassy, Saigon, 1966; prod.-dir.-wr., Greece Today, 1967–68. Exec. prod.-dir., George Wallach Productions, spec. doc., travel, and industrial films, chairman, Film-TV Dept., N.Y. Institute of Photography, 1968–75; Prof. film-TV-radio, Brooklyn Coll., 1975–80; presently special projects officer, DGA, N.Y.
PICTURES INCLUDE: NBC-producer. Inner Sanctum, The Falcon, His Honor Homer Bell, Watch the World; assoc. prod., prod. mgr., Bwana Devil; dir., Wanted, CBS-TV series.

WALLIS, HAL B.: Producer. b. Chicago, Ill.; m. Martha Hyer, actress. Entered m.p. ind. 1922, learning exhib. & distrib. as mgr. Los Angeles theat. Later in pub. dept., Warner Bros. Then variously with Principal Pictures Corp.; First Nat'l (studio mgr., prod. mgr.); Warner Bros. in chge. prod. From 1933 prod. many features; established Hal Wallis Prods., 1944. Academy-Irving Thalberg Award, 1938, 1943. Partner with Joseph Hazen in Wallis-Hazen Prod. rel. via Paramount. Wallis-Hazen dissolved June 1953.
PICTURES INCLUDE: Little Caesar, Five Star Final, Dawn Patrol, Midsummer Night's Dream, The Story of Louis Pasteur, Anthony Adverse, Zola, Jezebel, King's Row, Sergeant York, The Male Animal, In This Our Life, Yankee Doodle Dandy, Desperate Journey, Now Voyager, Casablanca, Saratoga Trunk, Love Letters, The Affairs of Susan, You Came Along, Strange Love of Martha Ivers, Searching Wind, Sorry Wrong Number, The Accused, Bitter Victory, The Furies, Desert Fury, I Walk Alone, Rope of Sand, My Friend Irma, My Friend Irma Goes West, Dark City, September Affair, Red Mountain, That's My Boy, The Stooge, Peking Express, Sailor Beware, Jumping Jacks, Come Back Little Sheba, Scared Stiff, Cease Fire, Money from Home, About Mrs. Leslie, Three Ring Circus, Rose Tattoo, Artists and Models, Hollywood or Bust, The Rainmaker, Gunfight at the OK Corral, Loving You, Wild Is the Wind, Sad Sack, Last Train from Gun Hill, Don't Give Up the Ship, Hot Spell, King Creole, Career, Visit to A Small Planet, All In A Night's Work, G.I. Blues, Summer and Smoke, Blue Hawaii, A Girl Named Tamiko, Girls! Girls! Girls!, Wives & Lovers, Fun in Acapulco, Becket, Roustabout, The Sons of Katie Elder, Boeing-Boeing, Easy Come, Easy Go, Barefoot in the Park, 5 Card Stud, True Grit, Norwood, Anne of the Thousand Days, Red Sky at Morning, Shoot Out, Mary, Queen of Scots, The Partner with Joseph Hazen in Wallis-Hazen Prod. rel. via Public Eye, The Nelson Affair, The Don Is Dead, Rooster Cogburn.

WALSH, DERMOT: Actor, playwright. b. Dublin, Eire, Sept. 10, 1924; e. St. Mary's Coll., University Coll., Four Courts (Dublin), Abbey School of Acting. With Longford Productions. Dublin Gate Theatre, screen debut in Hungry Hill 1947.
PICTURES INCLUDE: Jassy, Mark of Cain, To the Public Danger, My Sister and I, Third Time Lucky, Torment, Frightened Many, Ghost Ship, Counterspy, Floating Dutchman, Straw Man, Blue Parrot, On the Night of the Full Moon, Bond of Fear, The Hide-Out, On the Stroke of Nine, Sea Fury, Sea of Sand, The Bandit, The Flesh and the Fiends, Shoot to Kill, The Challenge, The Clock Struck

Three, Tarnished Heroes, Tell Tale Heart, The Breaking Point, The Trunk, Bedelia, Woman of Mystery, Chain of Events, The Crowning Touch, Make Mine a Million, Crash Dive, The Witness, Emergency, The Cool Mikado, The Switch, Echo of Diana, Infamous Conduct.
TV: Richard The Lionheart (series), Too Late for the Mashed Potato, Court Martial, Love Me Like A Brother, Softly Softly.

WALSH, KAY: Actress. b. London, Eng., 1915. Dancer in Andre Charlot revues; screen debut in How's Chances, 1934.
PICTURES INCLUDE: In Which We Serve, This Happy Breed, The October Man, Vice Versa, Oliver Twist, Stage Fright, Last Holiday, The Magnet, Encore, Meet Me Tonight (Tonight at 8:30), Young Bess, Stranger in Between, Lease Of Life, Rainbow Jacket, Cast a Dark Shadow, Now and Forever, The Horse's Mouth, Tunes of Glory, Reach for Glory, 80,000 Suspects, A Study in Terror, Beauty Jungle, Gideon's Way, The Baron, The Witches, He Who Rides A Tiger, The Ruling Class.

WALSH, RICHARD F.: President Emeritus International Alliance Theatrical Stage Employees and M.P. Machine Operators. b. Brooklyn, N.Y., 1900. In 1917 became apprentice stage electrician; 1920 full member Local 4, Brooklyn stagehand union IATSE & MPMO. Stage electrician various theatres. In 1924 elected pres. Local 4. 1926 business agent: 1934 int'l vice-pres. IATSE & MPMO; Nov., 1941 named pres. by exec. board; elected pres. by convention June, 1942; re-elected International pres. by convention thereafter; v.p., AFL-CIO, 1956. ch. of bd., Will Rogers Hospital, pres., Union Label Dept, retired as IATSE president in 1974.

WALSTON, RAY: Actor-Director. b. New Orleans, Louisiana, Nov. 22, 1918. Dir. of Bdwy-musical, Damn Yankees, 1974.
TV: You Are There, Producers Showcase, There Shall Be No Night, Studio One, Playhouse 90, My Favorite Martian.
PICTURES INCLUDE: South Pacific, Damn Yankees, Kiss Them For Me, Say One for Me, The Tall Story, The Apartment, Portrait In Black, Convicts Four, Wives and Lovers, Who's Minding the Store, Kiss Me Stupid, Caprice, Paint Your Wagon, The Sting, Popeye.

WALTER, JESSICA: Actress. b. Brooklyn, N.Y., Jan. 31. e. High School of Performing Arts. Studied at Bucks County Playhouse and Neighborhood Playhouse. Many TV performances plus lead in series, For the People. Broadway debut in Advise and Consent, 1961. Also, Photo Finish (Clarence Derwent Award), Night Life, A Severed Head.
PICTURES INCLUDE: Lilith, The Group, Grand Prix, Bye Bye Braverman, Number One, Play Misty For Me, Going Ape.
TV: Love of Life, Ironside, Amy Prentiss.

WALTERS, BARBARA: TV Personality. b. Boston, 1931. e. Sarah Lawrence Coll. Began working in TV right after graduation. Joined Today in 1961 as writer, making occasional on-camera appearances. In 1963 became full-time on camera. In April, 1974, named permanent co-host. Also hosts own synd. prog., Not for Women Only. In 1976 joined ABC-TV.

WALTERS, CHARLES: Director. b. Pasadena, Calif., Nov. 17; e. Univ. Southern California. On stage in Fanchon & Marco shows, 1934; in dance team Versailles Club, 1935.
STAGE: (cast) Musical Parade, Jubilee, Transatlantic Rhythm, Show Is On, Between the Devil, I Married An Angel, DuBarry Was a Lady; stage dir.: Let's Face It, Banjo Eyes.
PICTURES INCLUDE: (dir. dance sequences in m.p.) Seven Days' Leave, Presenting Lily Mars, Girl Crazy, Best Foot Forward, Meet Me in St. Louis, Abbott & Costello in Hollywood, Ziegfeld Folies, Summer Holiday; dir. Good News, Easter Parade, Barkleys of Broadway, Summer stock, Three Guys Named Mike, Texas Carnival, Belle of New York, Lili, Dangerous When Wet, Torch Song, Easy to Love, Glass Slipper, Tender Trap, High Society, Don't Go Near the Water, Ask Any Girl, Please Don't Eat the Daisies, Two Loves, Jumbo, The Unsinkable Molly Brown, Walk, Don't Run.
TV: Here's Lucy and The Governor and J.J.; 2 Lucille Ball Specials.

WANAMAKER, SAM: Actor, stage producer, film director. b. Chicago, 1919. e. Drake University. On Broadway stage as actor, producer, presenter. Hollywood films incl.: My Girl Tisa. British films incl: Give Us This Day, Mr. Denning Drives North. London West End stage: Winter Journey, The Big Knife, The Threepenny Opera, The Rainmaker. 1955: starred in film The Secret. 1956–58: Acting, producing London and Liverpool stage. 1959–60: Acting at Stratford-on-Avon. Numerous TV plays incl.: The Big Wheel, The White Death and dir. A Young Lady of Property, 1960: Film, The Criminal. 1961–62: Acting on New York stage in The Far Country. TV productions: The Defenders, Oedipus Rex, etc. Film: Taras Bulba. 1963: prod. dir. Children From Their Games, N.Y. stage.

TV: CBS special, Russian Self Impressions. Man of World, TV series. 1962: Stage, Washington D.C., Rhinoceros, Arms and The Man. Opera productions, King Priam, Forza Del Destino, etc. 1963: Dir., A Case of Libel (N.Y.). TV: Espionage, Outer Limits. Film: Man in the Middle (London). 1964–65: Acted in Macbeth (Chicago) and films, Those Magnificent Men In Their Flying Machines, The Spy Who Came In From The Cold, The Warning Shot, The Day The Fish Came Out, Voyage of the Damned. Dir. The Executioner. Dir. several The Defenders TV series (N.Y.), 1968; The Eliminator, The Chinese Visitor. 1971; Catlow. 1972; Sinbad and the Eye of the Tiger, 1977; Founder and exec. dir. Globe Playhouse Trust; starred BBC film Arturo Ul. 1973. Dir. Sydney Opera House Opening. War & Peace. 1974. Acted in The Law. Prod. Bankside Festival. U.S. Tour Shakespeare's globe. 1980: Private Benjamin, The Competition.

WARBURTON, JOHN: Actor. b. Liverpool, Eng., e. Oxford U. With British Army, World War I; then on stage Liverpool Repertory Theatre. To U.S. 1920.
STAGE: Journey's End, Bird In the Hand, Dishonorable Lady.
PICTURES INCLUDE: on screen 1933 in Cavalcade. Also: Chi Ci, Becky Sharp, Sisters, Saratoga Trunk, The White Cliffs, Marriage Is a Private Affair, Confidential Agent, Living in a Big Way, City Beneath the Sea, East of Sumatra, Royal African Rifles.

WARD, BILL: O.B.E., f.r.s.a. b. Plymouth, Devon, Jan. 19, 1916. e. Hoe Grammar School. Early career eng. asst., BBC; entered TV industry 1936; technical asst., 1936–37; War service; studio manager BBC 1941; presentation asst. 1946; prod. 1947; senior prod. light ent., 1950–55; joined Associated Television Ltd., 1955; prod. controller 1956. Judge at Golden Rose Festival, Montreux, Covered Mexico Olympics, ITV 1966, Exec. prod. ITV World Cup, delegate Prix Italia Festival. 1967, Judge Cannes O.B. Festival. 1968 Apptd. exec. dir. & dir. of programs, ATV Network. 1971 chmn. ITV Sports committee, Dep. Man. Dir. & Dir. Progs. ATV Network.
TV: Sunday Night at the Palladium, Golden Hour, Royal Variety Show, 1964.

WARD, BURT: Actor/Executive. b. July 6, California. Is pres. of Entertainment Management Corp. and Entertainment Licensing Corp., fan club and merchandising companies, respectively.
TV: Batman.

WARD, SARAH E.: Executive. b. Warrenton, Va., April 5, 1920. 1949–1962, office clerical positions with RKO, 20th Century-Fox, Todd AO Corp; v.p. sales mgr. for Europix Consolidated Corp., 1968; v.p.—sec'y for Europix International Ltd., 1971.

WARD, SIMON: Actor. b. London, England, 1941. Ent. ind. 1964.
TV: Spoiled, Chips With Everything, 1969. Films incl. Frankenstein Must Be Destroyed, I Start Counting, Young Winston, Hitler—The Last Ten Days, The Three Musketeers, The Four Musketeers, Children of Race, Deadly Strangers, All Creatures Great & Small, Aces High, The Battle Flag, Holocaust 2000.

WARDEN, JACK: Actor. b. Newark, N.J., 1925. With Margo Jones theatre in Dallas.
TV: Philco Goodyear Producer's Showcase, Kraft, Raid on Entebbe.
THEATRE: View from the Bridge, Very Special Baby.
PICTURES INCLUDE: From Here to Eternity, 12 Angry Men, Edge of the City, Bachelor Party, Escape from Zahrain, The Thin Red Line, Summertree, Who Is Harry Kellerman?, The Sporting Club, Welcome to the Club, Billy Two Hats, The Apprenticeship of Duddy Kravitz, Shampoo, All the President's Men, Heaven Can Wait, Death on the Nile, And Justice for All, Being There, The Great Muppet Caper, Carbon Copy.

WARING, FRED: Musician. b. Tyrone, Pa., June 9, 1900; e. Penn State. Choral & orchestral conductor, star & producer many seasons concert, radio, stage & television; winner many national awards; strongly identified with music education through Waring Music Workshop & Shawnee Press at Delaware Gap in Pennsylvania. Member Lambs, N.Y.

WARNER, DAVID: Actor. b. Manchester, England, 1941. Made London stage debut in Tony Richardson's version of A Midsummer Night's Dream. Four seasons with Royal Shakespeare Co.
PICTURES INCLUDE: Tom Jones, Morgan, Work Is a Four Letter Word, The Bofors Gun, The Fixer, The Seagull, Michael Kohlhaas, The Ballard of Cable Hogue, Perfect Friday, Straw Dogs, A Doll's House, Tales from the Crypt, Providence, Cross of Iron, Silver Bears. The Concorde—Airport '79, Time After Time, The Island.

WARNER, JACK JR.: Producer. b. San Francisco, Calif., Mar. 27, 1916; p. Jack L. Warner, and Mrs. Albert S. Rogell; e.

Beverly Hills High Sch., B.A., U. of Southern Calif. Entered Warner New York office studying distrib. and exhib. for 1½ years. Transferred to prod. dept. at West Coast studios, then to short subject dept. as assoc. prod. As Reserve Officer called to active duty in 1942 and served as combat photo unit officer in 164th Signal Photo Co. for one year. Transf. to Signal Corps Photographic Center, Astoria, N.Y., where participated in prod. Army Signal Corps Training Films. Was asst. to chief of training films prod. In 1944 assigned to Hq. First U.S. Army Group to assist in planning combat photography for invasion of Europe. Until cessation of hostilities was asst. chief Photo Branch Office of Chief Signal Officer in 12th Army Group and on fall of Germany was on staff of General Eisenhower in Frankfurt as asst. and acting photo officer, Office of the Chief Signal Officer, Theatre Service Forces European Theatre (TSFET). Released from active duty April 20, 1945. Commissioned Lt. Col. Signal Corps Reserve. In 1947 with Warner Bros. Pictures Distrib. Corp., making survey of exhib. and distrib. as related to prod.; liaison between Warner and Assoc. Brit. Pictures on The Hasty Heart, 1948–49; org. Jack M. Warner Prod., Inc., 1949; first film, The Man Who Cheated Himself, distrib. by 20th Cent.-Fox; prod. dept., Warner Bros., 1951; prod. exec. Warners 1953. In charge of TV film prod. for Warners 1955; exec. in charge of television comm. and ind. film dept., Warner Bros. 1956; v.p., Warner Bros. Pictures, Inc., Jan. 1958; Warner association terminated Jan. 1959. Reactivated independent motion picture company Jack M. Warner Prod. Future activities motion picture production of feature television and industrial films; pres., Jack Warner Prods., Inc., prod. theatrical films, 1961; prod., dir., Brushfire; Commissioned Colonel, Signal Corps. U.S. Army Reserve, 1962; 1977–78: Producer, TV series & films for theatrical and TV, Jack Warner Pdns; writer, 1979–81.

WARREN, CHARLES MARQUIS: Director, producer, writer b. Baltimore, Md.; e. Baltimore City College. Commander U.S. Navy, World War II; then to Hollywood. Writer for screen, magazines; author of books.
BOOKS INCLUDE: Only the Valiant, Valley of the Shadow, Wilderness, Deadhead.
PICTURES INCLUDE: Only the Valiant, Beyond Glory, Redhead and the Cowboy, Streets of Laredo, Springfield Rifle, Day of the Evil Gun, Little Big Horn, Hellgate, Pony Express, Arrowhead, Flight to Tangier, 7 Angry Men, Trooper Hook, Tension at Table Rock, Cattle Empire, Charro!, Down to the Sea, Time of the Furies.
TV: Creator of Gunsmoke, Rawhide, Gunslinger, and the Virginian, series as well as prod.-dir.-writer. Exec. prod. on Iron Horse series.

WARREN, GENE: Executive. Pres. of Excelsior Prods., production co. specializing in special effects and animation. Has headed 2 other cos. of similar nature over past 20 years, functioning at various times as prod., dir., studio prod. head and writer. Producer-Director of following shorts: The Tool Box, Suzy Snowflake, Santa and the Three Dwarfs, Land of the Midnight Sun and these documentaries/training films: Mariner I, Mariner III, Apollo, U.S. Navy titles.
Special effects on theatrical features including, Black Sunday, McNamara's Band, Satan's School for Girls, My Name Is John, The Power, 7 Faces of Dr. Lao, Wonderful World of the Brothers Grimm, The Time Machine, Tom Thumb, etc. TV series include The Man from Atlantis, Land of the Lost, Star Trek, Outer Limits, Twilight Zone, Mission Impossible, etc.

WARREN, HARRY: Song writer, director. b. Brooklyn, N.Y., Dec. 24, 1893. Asst. dir. Vitagraph Studio, Brooklyn; song writer various N.Y. shows: Sweet and Low, Crazy Quilt; writer songs in many pictures since sound, including several WB Gold Diggers series, Wonder Bar, Down Argentine Way, Tin Pan Alley, also dramatic pictures. Academy Award for best motion picture song, Lullaby of Broadway, from Gold Diggers, 1935; (with Mack Gordon) for best motion picture song, 1943 (You'll Never Know from Hello Frisco Hello); 1946 (On the Atchison Topeka & Santa Fe (from Harvey Girls).
SONGS INCLUDE: (m.p.) Serenade in Blue, At Last, That's Amore, Chattanooga Choo-Choo.
PICTURES INCLUDE: Texas Carnival, Just for You, Skirts Ahoy, The Caddy, Artists and Models, Birds and the Bees.

WARRICK, RUTH: Actress. b. St. Louis, June 29. In 1941: "Citizen Kane," "Obliging Young Lady," RKO; "The Corsican Brothers," UA-Small. In 1942: "Journey Into Fear," RKO. In 1943: "Forever and a Day," RKO. On TV in Peyton Place.
PICTURES INCLUDE: The Iron Major, Secret Command, Mr. Winkle Goes to War, Guest in the House, China Sky, Driftwood, Daisy Kenyon, Arch of Triumph, The Great Dan Patch, Make Believe, Ballroom, Three Husbands, Let's Dance, One Too Many, Roogie's Bump.

WASHBURN, DERIC: Writer. b. Buffalo, N.Y. e. Harvard Univ. (English lit.). Has written number of plays, including The Love Nest and Ginger Anne.
PICTURES: Silent Running (co-s.p.), The Deer Hunter, The Border.

WASILEWSKI, VINCENT, T.: Executive. b. Athens, Ill. e. Univ. of Ill., Coll. of Engineering, 1940; U.S. Air Force, Sept. 1942–Oct. 1945; ret. to Univ. of Ill., bachelor degree in political science, 1948, degree of Doctor of Jurisprudence, 1949; admitted to the Illinois Bar, 1950; joined staff of the National Association of Broadcasters, Oct. 12, 1949; chief attorney, Feb. 1953; mgr., government relations, Aug. 1955; v.p., governmental affairs, NAB, June 1960; exec. v.p., NAB, Aug. 1961; pres., Jan. 1965.

WASSERMAN, DALE: Writer, producer. b. Rhinelander, Wis., Nov. 2, 1917. Stage: lighting designer, dir., prod.; dir. for attractions, S. Hurok; began writing, 1954. Founding member & Trustee of O'Neill Theatre Centre; Artistic Director Midwest Playwrights Laboratory; member Motion Picture Academy; awards include Emmy, Tony, Critics Circle (Broadway), Outer Circle; Writers Guild, etc.
TV: The Fog, The Citadel, The Power and the Glory, Engineer of Death, The Lincoln Murder Case, I Don Quixote, Elisha and the Long Knives, and others.
PLAYS: Livin' the Life, 998, One Flew Over the Cuckoo's Nest, The Pencil of God, Man of La Mancha, Play With Fire.
PICTURES INCLUDE: Cleopatra, The Vikings, The Sea and the Shadow, Quick, Before It Melts, Mister Buddwing, A Walk With Love and Death, Man of La Mancha.

WASSERMAN, LEW: Chairman of the bd., Chief Executive Officer, MCA, Inc., Universal City Studios, Universal City, Calif.

WATERBURY, RUTH: Executive. b. Rensselaer, N.Y.; e. private and public schools, Albany, N.Y.; m. late Harold Cary. Feature writer, New York World, New York Daily News ed. Photoplay Mag. In 1938 superv. ed. for films, all Macfadden publications; Louella Parsons Hollywood staff, 1945–64; Books: Elizabeth Taylor, 1964, Richard Burton, 1965.

WATERHOUSE, KEITH: writer. b. Leeds, England, 1929. Early career as journalist, novelist. Author of There is a Happy Land, Billy Liar, Jubb, The Bucket Shop. Ent. m.p. ind. 1960, s.p. (with Willis Hall).
PICTURES INCLUDE: Whistle Down The Wind, A Kind of Loving, Billy Liar, Man in the Middle, Pretty Polly, Lock Up Your Daughters, The Valiant, West Eleven.
TV: (series): Inside George Webley, Queenie's Castle, Budgie, Billy Liar, There is a Happy Land.

WATERS, GEORGE, W.: Writer, producer, executive. b. Washington, D.C., Dec. 24, 1900; e. Catholic Univ. of America, 1923. Reporter, Times-Herald, Wash., D.C., 1923–25; Reporter, state ed., Washington Evening Star, 1925–30; City ed., Wash. Times-Herald, 1936–43; city ed., Miami Daily News, 1943–47; dir. of publicity Int'l Polo, Miami Seahawks pro football team, night clubs, etc., 1950; senatorial accts., press relations, Wash., D.C., 1950–55; co-author, assoc. prod., Tank Battalion, 1958; co-author, pictures: Speed Crazy, Why Must I Die?
TV: Scene of the Crime; Segments; Violence Comes Easy, Collector's Item. Georgetown Films.

WATERSTON, SAM: Actor. b. Cambridge, Mass., Nov. 15, 1940. e. Yale Univ. Began acting on stage in New York (Indians, Halfway Up a Tree, The Trial of the Catonsville Nine) and in Los Angeles (Meeting by the River, Volpone, etc.). Won Drama Desk Award as best actor for role in Joseph Papp production of Much Ado About Nothing (1972–73 Broadway season).
PICTURES INCLUDE: Three, Savages, The Great Gatsby, Rancho de Luxe, Journey into Fear, Capricorn One, Interiors, Heaven's Gate.
TV: Much Ado About Nothing, The Glass Menagerie.

WATKINS, GARTH: Actor. b. London, Aug. 8, 1922. e. University College School. Served in Royal Air Force 1944–45. Entered films in 1945 with role in The Captive Heart.
PICTURES INCLUDE: Bedelia, Gaiety George, A Matter of Life and Death, The Hanging Judge, Goodbye Mr. Chips, Cromwell, The Rise and Fall of Michael Rimmer, Virgin Witch, Fright, Naughty, Twins of Evil, Mary, Queen of Scots, Steptoe and Son, Henry VIII, Cinderella, The Omen.
TV: People in Conflict (Canada).

WATLING, JACK: Actor. b. Chingford, London, Eng., Jan. 13, 1923. e. Italia Conti Stage Sch. Stage debut in Where the Rainbow Ends, 1936; m.p. debut in 60 Glorious Years, 1937.
PICTURES INCLUDE: Goodbye, Mr. Chips, We Dive at Dawn, Day Will Dawn, Demi Paradise, Way Ahead, Journey Together, Easy Money, Winslow Bay, Quartet, Courtneys of Curzon Street, Once a Sinner, Naked Heart, White Corridors, Under Capricorn, Private Information, Father's Doing Fine, Meet Mr. Lucifer, Trouble in The Glen, Sea Shall Not Have Them, Confidential Report, Admirable

Crichton, A Night to Remember, Sink the Bismarck, The Night We Sprang A Leek, Nearly A Nasty Accident, Mary Had A Little, Three On A Spree, Edgar Wallace, The Nanny, 11 Harrow House.
TV: Crime on My Hands, No Medals, Disturbance, Manor at Northstead, Devil Makes Three, Aren't We All, World of Tim Fraser, No Hiding Place, Zero I, Hancock Half Hour, Anna Karenina, Both Ends Meet, Loyalties, Ghost Squad, Tales of Mystery, Dixon of Dock Green, The Planemakers, Love Story, Six of the Best, The Power Game, Dixon of Dock Green, Mickey Dunne, Emergency Ward 10, Dr. Who, Softly Softly, No That's Me Over Here, The Power Game, The Pathfinders, Spike Milligan, The Mackinnons, Many Wives of Patrick, The Cedar Tree, The Doctors' Daughters.

WATT, HARRY: Director. b. Edinburgh, Scotland, Oct. 18, 1906. e. Edinburgh Acad.; Edinburgh U. Joined Empire Marketing Board Film Unit, 1931; asst. Robert Flaherty on Man of Aran. Wrote and dir. number of documentaries including Six-thirty Collection, Night Mail, North Sea. Since outbreak of war worked with Crown Film Unit on propaganda films, including Squadron 992, Britain at Bay, Dover Front Line, Target for Tonight, London Can Take It, and Christmas Under Fire. In 1942;: associated Ealing Studios (s.p., dir.) Nine Men; (dir.) Fiddlers Three, 1946; wrote and dir. The Overlanders in Australia, 1947; Eureka Stockade, Australia, 1949; Where No Vultures Fly (Ivory Hunter), West of Zanzibar; in Africa, 1950–54; exec. prod., Granada TV, 1955; rejoined Ealing Films; wrote, dir., People Like Maria; s.p. dir., Siege of Pinchgut; The Lion.

WAX, MO.: Publisher and editor of Film Bulletin. b. Philadelphia. e. Villanova U. Also pres., Audienscope, Inc., Entertainment research organization.

WAYLAND, LEN: Actor. b. California, Dec. 28. e. Junior College, Modesto, California. Wrote, prod. weekly radio series 1939–41, KPAS, KTRB, Calif. Service, radar navigator, 1941–45; en. theatre, Tobacco Road, 1946; 1973, formed Len Wayland Prods. for production of theatrical pictures and TV series. In 1976–77: produced/directed, Don't Let It Bother You. 1978, pro./dir., You're not there yet, for own company.
THEATRE: Played summer and winter stock 1947–49. B'way; Streetcar Named Desire, 1949; war; toured as lead, Heaven Can Wait, 1951; My Name Is Legion, 1952–53; toured, Love of Four Colonels, 1953, Stalag 17, 1954. Lead, NBC-TV serial, A Time to Live, 1954. NBC-TV, First Love, 1955; Armstrong Circle Theatre, Justice, Sgt. Bilko, Kraft Theatre, etc., 1956–58; NBC-TV, Dr. Weaver, From These Roots, 1958–61. Off Broadway prod., USA, 1960; on Broadway; A Man For All Seasons, 1962.
TV: Profiles In Courage, Dr. Kildare, Gunsmoke, Slattery's People, Ben Casey, A Noise in The World, 1967, Love Is A Many Splendored Thing, 1969; Dragnet, Outsider, 1970; Ironside, Name of the Game, The Bold Ones, Daniel Boone, The Virginian, Project U.F.O., Sam.

WAYNE, DAVID: Actor, r.n. Wayne McKeekan; b. Travers City, Mich., Jan. 30, 1916; e. Western Michigan land, 1936; in marionette shows, 1937.
THEATRE: Finian's Rainbow, Mister Roberts, Teahouse of the August Moon.
PICTURES INCLUDE: Portrait of Jennie, Adam's Rib, Reformer and the Redhead, My Blue Heaven, Stella, M, Up Front, As Young As You Feel, With a Song in My Heart, Wait 'Til the Sun Shines, Nellie; Down Among the Sheltering Palms, The I Don't Care Girl, We're Not Married, O. Henry's Full House, Tonight We Sing, How to Marry a Millionaire, Hell and High Water, Tender Trap, Last Angry Man, The Big Gamble, The Andromeda Strain, The African Elephant (narrator), Huckleberry Finn, The Front Page, The Apple Dumpling Gang.

WAYNE, JOEL: Executive. Had career as art director before joining Grey Advertising in 1962, where headed staff of 250 and was responsible for all TV, radio and print campaigns in behalf of General Foods, Procter and Gamble, B.F. Goodrich, Revlon, etc., as exec. v.p & creative director. Left in 1980 to become Warner Bros., v.p. in chg. of creative advertising, headquartered in Burbank.

WAYNE, MICHAEL A.: Executive. r.n. Michael A. Morrison. b. Los Angeles, Calif., Nov. 23, 1934. f. John Wayne. e. Loyola H.S., Loyola Univ., B.B.A. Asst. dir., various companies, 1955–56; asst. dir., Revue Prods., 1956–57; pres. Batjac Prods. and Romina Prods., 1961; asst. to producer: China Doll, 1957; Escort West, 1958; The Alamo, 1959; prod., McClintock, 1962; co-prod., Cast Giant Shadow, 1965; prod. The Green Berets, 1967; exec. prod. Chisum, 1968; prod. Big Jake, 1970; prod. The Train Robbers, 1972; prod. Cahill, U.S. Marshall, 1972; exec. prod. McQ, 1973, Brannigan, 1974.

WAYNE, PATRICK: Actor. b. 1939. Son of John Wayne. Made film debut at age 11 in Rio Grande.
PICTURES INCLUDE: The Searchers, The Alamo, The Comancheros, McClintock, The Bears and I, Mustang Country, Sinbad and the Eye of the Tiger.

WEAVER, DENNIS: Actor, director. b. Joplin, Mo., June 4, 1925. e. Univ. of Oklahoma, B.A. fine arts, 1948.
TV: Chester, in Gunsmoke, 1955–64; title role, Kentucky Jones, NBC series, 1964–65; Gentle Ben, 1967–69; Mc-Cloud, 1970–76, The Forgotten Man, Duel, The Rolling Man, The Great Man's Whiskers, McCloud, (1970–77); Terror on the Beach, Intimate Strangers (ABC) 1977, Pearl (1978), Centennial (1978); Stone (series, 1979–80). Movies: Amber Waves, Dr. Mudd (1980).
PICTURES INCLUDE: Duel at Diablo, Way Way Out, Gentle Giant, A Man Called Sledge, What's the Matter with Helen?, The Gallant Hours, Batangas.

WEAVER, MARJORIE: Actress. b. Grossville, Tenn., Mar. 2, 1913; e. U. of Kentucky, Indiana U. Played with McCauley Stock Co.; Billy Rose's Shrine Minstrels. In 1936 appeared in China Clipper, WB; from 1937 in many 20th Century-Fox pictures.
PICTURES INCLUDE: Let's Face It, Pardon My Rhythm, You Can't Ration Love, The Great Alaskan Mystery, Shadows of Suspicion, Fashion Model, Leave It to Blondie, We're Not Married.

WEAVER, SYLVESTER L., JR.: Executive. b. Los Angeles, Calif., Dec. 21, 1908; e. Dartmouth Coll. CBS, Don Lee Network, 1932–35; Young & Rubicam adv. agency, 1935–38; adv. mgr.,"American Tobacco Co., 1938–47; v.p. Young & Rubicam, 1947–49; joined NBC as v.p., chg. TV, 1949; appt'd v.p.chg. NBC Radio & TV networks, 1952; vice-chmn. bd., NBC, Jan., 1953; pres., NBC, Dec., 1953; bd. chmn., Dec. 1955; own firm, 430 Park Avenue., N.Y.C., 1956; chmn. of bd. McCann-Erickson Corp. (Intl.), 1959; pres., Subscription TV, Inc. Comm. Consultant in Los Angeles, Cal. and President, Weaver Productions, Inc.

WEBB, JACK: Actor, Producer, Director. b. Santa Monica, California, Apr. 2, 1920; e. Belmont H.S., Los Angeles. Began radio career, San Francisco, 1945, announcer, writer, actor. Army Air Forces WWII. 1942–45; freelance radio actor, title role, Pat Novak, 1946 in San Francisco; Johnny Modero, Pier 23, 1947, Los Angeles; created "Dragnet" 1949; created "Pete Kelly's Blues" 1950; "Dragnet" winner Best Mystery Show and Most Popular Star of Tomorrow categories, M.P Daily's 15th annual radio poll 1950–51; Best Mystery Show, TV & radio, 1953–54; winner Best Mystery Show, Academy of Television Arts and Sciences 1952–54; winner Look magazine award, Best Director, 1954. Director, star, "Dragnet" TV film series; prod. TV series, Pete Kelly's Blues, D.A.:'s Man, True, Dragnet, 1967–70; Adam-12, 1968–74; The D.A., 1970–71; O'Hara, U.S. Treasury, 1970–71; Emergency, 1971–75; Chase, 1973, The Rangers, 1974–75 and Mobile Two, 1975; Project UFO (1978).
PICTURES INCLUDE: Sunset Boulevard, Appointment With Danger, The Men, Halls of Montezuma, You're in the Navy Now; prod. act., dir., Dragnet, Pete Kelly's Blues, The D.I.-30-; The Last Time I Saw Archie.

WEBB, JERRY: Editor. b. Indianapolis, Ind. Feature editor, supervision, Fox Studio, 1929–33; 20th Century-Fox, 1934–57. supv. film editor, Bonjour Tristese, London, 1957; film editor, Yovanka, Under Ten Flags, Roma, 1959–60; Esther and The King, Roma, 1960; Lion of Sparta, Athens, London, 1961; supv. editor, Damon & Pythias, Roma, 1962. 1964 entered commercial field. 1968: invented new anamorphic method of photography and printing of film: Vertiscope.

WEBB, ROBERT A.: Film editor, writer. b. Springfield, Ill., May 27, 1911. Film editor, Goldwyn, 20th-Fox; served 3½ years with John Ford's Naval Photog. Unit & headed film editorial unit at Nurnberg Internat'l Military Trials; ed. many short film sketches, Omnibus (TV), 1953; ed., Patti Page Shows. Member: M.P. Film Editors, Soc. of M.P. Film Editors, Acad. of TV Arts & Sciences.

WEBB, ROBERT D.: Director.
PICTURES INCLUDE: assoc. prod., Lure of the Wilderness; dir., Glory Brigade, Proud Ones. Prod., dir.: Threshold of Space, Seven Cities of Gold, Beneath the 12 Mile Reef, White Feather, The Jackals, Capetown Affair, Love Me Tender.

WEBBER, ROBERT: Actor. b. Santa Ana, Calif., Oct. 14. e. Belmont High, Van Nuys High, Compton Jr. Coll. USMC, 1943–45. Summer stock. Co-starred, Wonderful Town, American Pavilion, Brussels World Fair, 1958.
THEATRE: Two Blind Mice, Goodbye My Fancy, Royal Family, No Time for Sergeants, Orpheus Descending, Fair Game, A Loss of Roses, Period of Adjustment.
PICTURES INCLUDE: Highway 301, Twelve Angry Men, The Stripper, The Sandpiper, The Third Day, Harper, The Silencers, The Hired Killer, Dead Heat on a Merry-Go-Round, Don't Make Waves, The Dirty Dozen, The Big Bounce, The Great White Hope, The French Mistress, $(Dollars), Every Man Is My Enemy, Bring Me the Head of Alfredo Garcia, Midway, Casey's Shadow, The Choirboys; The Revenge of the Pink Panther, Ten, Private Benjamin, S.O.B., Sunday Lovers, Wrong Is Right.
TV: Over 400 shows from 1947 through 1979.

WEBSTER, DAVID: Dir. Public Affairs, BBC. b. Taunton, England, 1931. Joined BBC News in 1953. Moved to BBC Television Current Affairs 1959 and worked on Face to Face and Lifeline before going to Panorama in 1959. Panorama producer until start of BBC-2 in 1964, when he left to run Enquiry, Encounter on BBC-2. Returned to Panorama as Deputy Editor, becoming Editor in 1967. Appt. Assistant Head of Current Affairs Group, Television 1970. For five years (1971–76) BBC rep. in the USA. Chairman of the International Council of the National Academy of Television Arts and Sciences 1974–75. In 1976 returned to England to become the BBC's Controller of Information Services. Appt. Director, Public Affairs 1977.

WEBSTER, M. COATES: Writer. b. East Orange, N.J. December 15, 1906. e. U. Pa., Wesleyan U. On stage 8 yrs. Wrote 3 novels (published) Showboy, Derelict Alley, Strange Fraternity.
PICTURES INCLUDE: Klondike Kate; collab., story, s.p., Adventures of a Rookie; (s.p.) Blonde Ransom; (collab. s.p.) Jungle Captive; (s.p.) Strange Confession, I'll Remember April, Song of Arizona, Frisco Tornado, Rough Riders of Durango, Desert of Lost Men, Captive of Billy the Kid, Leadville Gunslinger, Montana Belle.

WECHSLER, LAZAR: Producer. b. Poland, 1896; e. Polytechnical Inst. of Zurich. Set up first film co. in Switzerland making documentary & pub. shorts.
PICTURES INCLUDE: Wings Over Ethiopia, This Is China, Marie Louise (Acad. Award, best s.p.), The Last Chance, The Search, Four in a Jeep, The Village, Heidi, Heidi and Peter, It Happened in Broad Daylight, The Marriage of Mr. Mississippi, Shadows Growing Longer, The Right to Be Born (The Doctor Speaks Out).

WEILER, GERALD E.: Producer. b. Mannheim, Germany, May 8, 1928. e. Harvard, 1946–48; Columbia, B.S., 1949–51; NYU Grad. Sch., 1951–53; writer, WHN, N.Y. writer, sports ed., news ed., Telenews Prod., Inc., 1948–52; asst. to prod., Richard de Rochemont, Vavin, Inc., 1952; U.S. Army, 1953–55; v.p., 1955–73; President, Weiler Communications Inc. 1973.

WEINBERG, HERMAN G.: Writer, film editor. b. New York City, Aug. 6, 1908. e. Inst. Musical Art (N.Y.). Entered m.p. ind. 1927 as musical consultant in scoring of silent foreign films for various little theats., N.Y. Then U.S. correspondent various European film publications; Close-Up (Switzerland), 1928–33; Film Art (London) 1929–30; Cinema Quarterly (Edinburgh) 1930–31; Cinea Pour Tous (Paris) 1931; Intercine (official publication of film div., League of Nations, Rome) 1932; Sight & Sound, British Film Institute, London; ed. and titled many foreign prod., dir., Autumn Fire, 1930. In 1950, U.S. correspondent Filmkunst, Vienna; Bianco e Nero, Rome; Cinema, Rome; also ed. series Indexes on Directors for British Film Institute; U.S. corr. Cahiers du Cinema; Filmkunst, Vienna; Film, Venice; Film, Munich; former film ed. Liberty Mag.; prod. supvr. The Knife Thrower; ed., U.S. edition, 50 Years of Italian Cinema, 50 Years of Opera and Ballet in Italy; syndicated column, Coffee, Brandy and Cigars; contrib. to newspapers, mags.; author: Sin & Cinema; cont. to anthologies, 20 Years of Cinema in Venice. Introd. to Art of the Movies, The Cinema Between Two World Wars; film critic; Film Culture, Film Quarterly, Playboy Magazine, 1960–76, Instructor, film history. The City College, N.Y.: Juror at San Francisco film festival, 1960; Vancouver film festival, 1961; prep. exhibit, Homage to Erich Von Stroheim, Montreal Film Festival, 1964. Work in progress: an autobiography.
AUTHOR: Josef Von Sternberg. Editions Seghers, Paris, 1966 and American edition by E. P. Dutton, 1967, The Lubitsch Touch, E. P. Dutton, 1968, Saint Cinema, D.B.S. Publications, 1970. The Complete Greed, Arno Press, 1972. Revised edition, E. P. Dutton, 1973. Revised edition "Saint Cinema" (Dover) 1973, Stroheim: A Pictorial Record (Dover 1974), The Complete 'Wedding March' (Little, Brown) 1975. Revised edition, "The Lubitsch Touch" (Dover) 1977.

WEINBLATT, MIKE: Television Executive. e. Syracuse Univ. Served in Army as counter-intelligence agent, mostly in Japan (1952–53). Joined NBC in 1957; has headed two major TV network functions—talent/program admin. & sls. Joined network business affairs dept. in 1958 as mgr., business affairs, facilities operations; rose to post of director, pricing & financial services before moving to sales in November, 1962, as mgr., participating program sales. Named v.p., eastern sales, NBC-TV, 1968. Named v.p., talent & program admin., October, 1968; promoted to v.p. sales, February, 1973. January, 1975 named snr. v.p., sales; later became exec. v.p. Appointed exec. v.p. & gen. mgr. of NBC TV network in August, 1977.

WEINSTEIN, HENRY T.: Executive prod. b. New York, N.Y. July 12, 1924. e. C.C.N.Y., Carnegie Institute of Technology. Entered theatre as dir., 1950. Stage mgr. for Herman Shumlin. Dir. of: the Bratte Theatre, Cambridge, Mass., Margo Jones Theatres, Dallas, Theatre, Theatre in the Round, Houston, Texas. Prod. for Theatre Guild, N.Y. 1957–59. 1960–65 producer 20th Century-Fox, M.G.M. 1970–75 executive in charge of production, American Film Theatre. Presently executive in charge of production for L.C. Entertainment.

PICTURES INCLUDE: Tender is the Night, Joy in the Morning, Cervantes, Madwoman of Chaillot, The Battle of Neretva, Magic Christian, A Delicate Balance, The Homecoming, The Iceman Cometh, Lost In the Stars, Butley, Luther, Rhinoceros, Galileo, The Man In the Glass Booth, In Celebration.

TV: Play of the Week series, prod. 1959–60.

WEINSTEIN, PAULA: Executive. Started as theatrical agent with William Morris and International Creative Management. With Warner Bros. 1976–78 as production v.p.; left to go to 20th-Fox in same capacity. Named Fox snr. v.p., worldwide production. In 1980 appointed v.p.-production of The Ladd Company, headquartering at Burbank Studios offices of firm.

WEINTRAUB, FRED: Executive, producer. b. April 27, 1928, Bronx, N.Y. e. U. of Pennsylvania Wharton School of Business, Owner of The Bitter End Coffeehouse to 1971. Personal management, Campus Coffee House Entertainment Circuit; TV Production Hootenanny, Popendipity; syndicated TV show host: From The Bitter End; motion picture production; v.p., creative services, Warner Bros. 1969, executive in charge of Woodstock; producer motion pictures, Weintraub-Heller Productions, 1974, Enter The Dragon, Rage, Black Belt Jones, Truck Turner, Golden Needles, Animal Stars, Hot Potato, The Ultimate Warrior, Dirty Knights Work, Those Cuckoo Crazy Animals, Crash, Outlaw Blues, The Pack, The Promise, Tom Horn, Battle Creek Brawl, Force: Five.

WEINTRAUB, SY: Executive. b. New York City, 1923. e. Univ. of Missouri (B.A., Bach, of Journalism, 1947); graduate of American Theater Wing. Started career in 1949 forming with associates a TV syndication co., Flamingo Films, Inc., which merged with Associated Artists to form Motion Pictures for Television, Inc., largest syndicator at that time. He originated Superman and Grand Ol'Opry series for TV. In 1958 bought Sol Lesser Prods., owners of film rights for Tarzan, and began producing and distributing Tarzan films through Banner Productions, Inc. Also formerly chmn. of bd. of Panavision, Inc.; bd. mem. and pres. of National General Television Corp., and pres. of KMGM-TV in Minneapolis. In 1978 named chm. of Columbia Pictures Industries' new Film Entertainment Group, also joining Office of the Chief Executive of CPI.

WEIS, DON: Writer, director, producer. b. Milwaukee, Wis., May 13, 1922; e. U. of Southern Calif. No prior bus. experience.

PICTURES INCLUDE: (dial. dir.) Body & Soul, Red Pony, Champion, Home of the Brave, The Men; (dir.) Letter From a Soldier, sequence in It's a Big Country, Bannerline, Just This Once, You for Me, I Love Melvin, Remains To Be Seen, A Slight Case of Larceny, Half a Hero, Affairs of Dobie Gillis, Adventures of Haiji Baba, Ride the High Iron, Catch Me If You Can, Gene Krupa Story, Critic's Choice, Looking for Love, The King's Pirate, Repo.

TV: Dear Phoebe, Best TV director, 1956, 1958. Screen Dir. Guild, The Longest Hundred Miles, It Takes a Thief, Ironside, M.A.S.H., Happy Days, Planet of the Apes, Bronk, Petrocelli, The Magician, Mannix, Night Stalker, Barbary Coast, Courtship of Eddie's Father, Starsky & Hutch, Hawaii Five-O, Chips, Charlie's Angels, Love Boat, Fantasy Island

WEIS JACK: Producer-Director-Writer-Cinematographer-Film Editor. b. Tampa, Fla., October 1, 1932. e. Notre Dame (BS); Master Univ. of Chicago. Was in U.S. Air Force six yrs. Founded Associated Productions/Associated Advertising Productions, Inc. in New Orleans in Aug., 1967, and has been involved in over 120 films and approx. 1,500 commercials. Produced, directed and wrote original s.p.s for several HEW youth rehabilitation pictures. Member: Cinematography Local 666, Chicago IATSE; Film Editor Local 780, IATSE, Chicago; Directors Guild of America; Writers Guild of America.

PICTURES INCLUDE: Quadroon (dir.), Storyville (prod., dir., s.p.), Damballa (prod., dir., s.p.); creature from Hony Island Swamp (prod.-dir., s.p.); Lehia (prod., dir., camera), You Never Gave Me Roses, (s.p., prod., dir.); The Perfect Circle (TV-s.p., prod., dir.); Crypt of Dark Secrets (prod., dir., s.p.); Mardi Gras Massacre, prod., dir., s.p., editor.

WEISBERG, BRENDA: Writer. b. Rowne, Poland. Magazine writer, social service, public health, drama instructor. Married to the late Morris Meckler.

PICTURES INCLUDE: s.p., China Sky; s.p., When a Girl's Beautiful, Burning Cross, Port Said, Rusty series, Girl's School; collab. s.p., Isle of Samoa; collab. orig., Reunion in Reno, Alias Mr. Twilight, King of the Wild Horses, Little Tough Guy, s.p. Shadowed. Collaborator, Scarlet Claw, Ding Dong Williams, Babes On Swing Street, Weird Woman, The Mummy's Ghost, The Mad Ghoul, Keep 'Em Slugging, Mug Town, Tough As They Come, Mob Town,

There's One Born Every Minute, Hit the Road, Sing Another Chorus, You're Not So Tough.

TV: Fireside Theatre, Philco Theatre, Matinee Theatre.

AUTHOR: U(short stores) Woman's Home Companion, Collier's. American Mercury (Mencken's) Plain Talk, Forum

WEISBORD, SAM: Executive. b. New York, N.Y., Sept. 21, 1911. William Morris Agency, Inc., 1929; Bd. of Directors, Cedars-Sinai, Medical Center bd. of dirs. Menninger Foundation; Board of Directors Motion Picture and Television Fund. Exec. member Board of Directors, President & Chief Exec. Officer, William Morris Agency.

WEISER, MARTIN: Publicist. b. New York City, Oct. 27, 1916. e. U. of Rochester, 1936. Pub. dept. Warner Bros., N.Y., 1936–40; exploitation dir., western states, 1940–45; studio exploitation head, 1945–50; adv. pub. head, Lippert Pictures, 1950. Partner, Weiser and Thomas, Inc., 1954; pres., Marty Weiser Co., prom. Columbia Studio, 1959; Pub. dept., Warner Bros. Studios, 1961; Paramount Studios, 1962; asst. ad. pub. dir., Allied Artists Pictures, 1963; studio exploitation director Warner Bros. 1964; west coast advertising and exploitation co-ordinator for Warner Bros. Inc., 1973.

WEISS, FRITZ: Producer, director. Dir. of first anti-Hitler film, Vagabond, 1930. Dir. I am a Gypsy, 1934 film was confiscated in Vienna with its negative by Goebbels. Emigrated to England in 30's. Worked during WWII as prod. in the English theatre and as director-editor for the British Ministry of Information on anti Nazi propaganda and documentary films. Prod. mgr. of The Journey, Our Man in Vienna, and Mayerling. Director of Austrian TV Screen play for The Sex Commandment and Naked Odyssey.

WEISSMAN, MURRAY: Executive. b. New York City, Dec. 23, 1925. e. U. of Southern California. As an editor and news reporter for Fairchild Publications worked on Women's Wear Daily, Footwear News, Supermarket News, 1949–52; promotion mgr., TV Guide, 1952; asst. publicity director, KABC-TV, 1953–60; asst. dir. of press info., CBS, 1960–66; mgr., TV press dept., Universal Studio, 1966–68; executive in charge of m.p. press dept., Universal Studios & asst. secty., Universal Pictures, 1968–76; marketing exec., Columbia Pictures, 1976–77; vice pres. of advertising & publicity, Lorimar Productions, 1977; vice pres., ICPR Public Relations Company, 1978.

WEISSMAN, SEYMOUR J.: Executive, producer, director. Weissman Franz Productions. b. Brooklyn, N.Y., May 28, 1931. e. Kenyon Coll., Eng. Lit., A.B., 1953; Univ. of Southern Calif., Cinema, 1955. Unity Films, 1954; Henry Strauss & Co., 1954; Dir. of motion pictures, White Sands Proving Grounds, N.M., 1954–55; M.P.O., 1955; Coleman Prod., 1956; prod. dir., Dynamic Films, Inc., 1958–59; prod., dir., Viston Assoc., 1959–64; dir., VPI Prods., 1966.

WEISSMULLER, JOHNNY: Actor. b. Chicago, Ill., June 2, 1904. e. Chicago U. Champion swimmer. Screen debut 1932 in Tarzan, the Ape Man.

PICTURES INCLUDE: Tarzan's Desert Mystery, Swampfire, Tarzan and the Amazons, Tarzan and the Mermaids, Jungle Jim, The Lost Tribe, Fury of the Congo, Jungle Manhunt, Forbidden Land, Others in Jungle Jim film & TV series.

WEITMAN, ROBERT M.: Executive. b. New York City, August 18, 1905. e. Cornell University. Attended Paramount Managers' Training School. Assigned to Rialto Theatre, assistant manager, in 1926. Promoted to manager, Brooklyn Paramount. City manager of New York Paramount Public Theatres. Appointed managing director of New York Paramount Theatre in 1935. Managing dir. of N.Y. and Brooklyn Paramount Theatres. Vice-pres. United Paramount Theatres, supervising southern and Philadelphia houses; v.p. American Broadcasting-Paramount Theatres, Inc. in chge. of programming and talent; v.p. in charge of program development, CBS-TV, 1956; v.p. chge. prod. MGM-TV, 1960; v.p. in chg. prod., MGM, Inc., 1962; member MGM bd. directors; resigned MGM, July, 1967; v.p. in charge of studio production, Columbia, July, 1967. Dec., 1969 formed own prod. company.

WEITZNER, DAVID: Executive. b. New York, Nov. 13, 1938. e. Michigan State U. Entered industry in 1960 as mem. Columbia Pictures adv. dep't; later with Donahue and Coe as ass't exec. and Loew's Theatres adv. dep't; later with Embassy Pictures, adv. mgr.; dir. of adv. and exploitation for Palomar Pictures Corp.; v.p. in charge of adv., pub., and exploitation for ABC Pictures Corp.; v.p., entertainment/leisure div., Grey Advertising; v.p., worldwide adv., 20th Century Fox; now exec. v.p. adv./pub./promo., Universal Pictures.

WELCH, PETER: Actor. b. London, England, 1922. Early career as draughtsman. Formed own rep. company, later 5 years in various reps. Ent. m.p. ind. 1955.

TV: Three Tough Guys, Robin Hood, Doctor Morelle, The Chigwell Chicken, A Candle to the Madonna, Twelfth Night, Othello, Shadow Squad, William Tell, The Queen's

Corporal, No Hiding Place, Life of Falstaff, The Enemy, The Odd Man, The Lark, Dixon on Dock Green, Z Cars, The Plane Makers, Hancock, Cause of Death, The Discharge of Trooper Lusby, North and South, The Expert, The Trouble-Shooters, Spytrap, Smith, The Strange Report. The Carnforth Practice, Softly, Softly, The Healing, Dickens of London, Snacker Emmerdale Farm, Law and Order, series. Limbo Connection, serial; Fox series.

THEATRE: Rights of Man, Broken Sword, All in a Good Time, Cromwell at Drogheda, A Man and his Wife, Candida, Little Foxes, Whose Life Is It Anyway?

PICTURES INCLUDE: Doctor Syn, The Secret of Blood Island, The Legend of Young Dick Turpin, Astronaut at the Court of King Arthur.

WELCH, RAQUEL: Actress. r.n. Raquel Tejada. b. Chicago, Ill. e. La Jolla H.S. Fashion and photographic modeling. Co-hostess. Hollywood Palace.

PICTURES INCLUDE: Roustabout, A House is Not a Home, Swinging Summer, Fantastic Voyage, Shoot Louder . . . I Don't Understand, One Million Years B.C., Fathom, Bedazzled, The Biggest Bundle of Them All, The Queens, Bandolero, Lady in Cement, 100 Rifles, Flare Up, The Magic Christian, Myra Breckinridge, Hannie Caulder, Kansas City Bomber, Fuzz, The Last of Sheila, The Three Musketeers, The Four Musketeers, The Wild Party, Mother, Jugs and Speed, Crossed Swords.

WELCH, ROBERT L.: Producer, writer. b. Chicago, Ill., Nov. 23, 1910. e. Northwestern U., U. of Illinois. In stock as actor-prod. Hedgerow Theatre, Phila.; with Pasadena Community Playhouse & Padua Hills Theatre; on radio wrote & prod. Kate Smith, Fred Allen & Jack Benny shows, originated Henry Aldrich shows with Young & Rubicam, N.Y.; prod. all U.S. Armed Forces radio shows, World War II; writer-prod. Paramount Pictures Corp.

PICTURES INCLUDE: (collab. s.p.) Variety Girl; (prod.) Paleface, Sorrowful Jones, Top O' the Morning, Fancy Pants, Mr. Music, The Lemon Drop Kid, Son of Paleface. Writer, prod., NBC-TV, 1953.

MEMBER: Lambs, AMPAS, Screen Writers Guild, Producers Guild, American Legion.

WELD, TUESDAY: Actress. b. New York, Aug. 27, 1943. e. Hollywood Professional School. Began modeling at 4 yrs. Film debut, Rock, Rock, Rock.

PICTURES INCLUDE: Rally Round The Flag, Boys! The Five Pennies, The Private Lives of Adam and Eve, Return to Peyton Place, Wild in the Country, Bachelor Flat, Lord Love a Duck, Pretty Poison, I Walk the Line, A Safe Place, Play It As It Lays, Looking for Mr. Goodbar, Who'll Stop the Rain, Thief.

TV: The Many Loves of Dobie Gillis.

WELDEN, BEN: Actor. b. Toledo, Ohio, 1901. First appeared on the stage in 1926 at the Central Park Theatre, New York; then on London stage. Has appeared in many British and Hollywood film productions.

PICTURES INCLUDE: It's in the Bag, Appointment With Murder, Search for Danger, Fighting Fools, Sorrowful Jones, Tales of Robin Hood, All Ashore, Killers from Space, Steel Cage, Ma and Pa Kettle at Waikiki, Hidden Guns.

WELDON, JOAN: Actress. b. San Francisco, Calif., Aug. 5, 1933. e. San Francisco Conservatory of Music, U. of Calif. at Berkeley, City Coll. in San Francisco. Sang in chorus of San Francisco Grand Opera Co.; then L.A. Civic Light Opera Co.; m.p. debut in The System, 1953.

PICTURES INCLUDE: So This Is Love, Stranger Wore a Gun, The Command, Riding Shotgun, Them, Deep in My Heart.

WELK, LAWRENCE: Orchestra leader. b. Strasburg, N.D., March 11. Played accordion community dances, church socials, etc. Started own group. Biggest Little Band in America. Played hotels, ballrooms, music became known as Champagne Music. Signed Aragon Ballroom, Pacific Ocean Park, Calif., 1951, with weekly television show. Champagne Music Makers, ABC-TV, July 2, 1955; The Lawrence Welk Show, ABC; signed lifetime contract, Hollywood Palladium, July 1961. Recording: Calcutta, 1961; syndicated network show started 1971.

WELLES, ORSON: Producer, writer, actor. b. Kenosha, Wis.; p. Richard Head Welles, inventor, Beatrice Ives Welles, concert pianist; e. Todd School at Woodstock, Ill.

RADIO: March of Time, The Shadow, Campbell Playhouse. co-producer of Julius Caesar, Doctor Faustus, Horse Eats Hat, Macbeth, Shoemaker's Holiday, Heartbreak House.

PICTURES INCLUDE: in 1941: producer, director, writer and star of Citizen Kane, RKO. In 1942: produced, wrote and directed, The Magnificent Ambersons, RKO. Produced and wrote Journey into Fear, RKO, in 1943: Jane Eyre, 20th-Fox. In 1945 author column Orson Welles Almanac in N.Y. Post. Tomorrow Is Forever, Lady from Shanghai, (s.p., dir., prod., acted in) Macbeth; Prince of Foxes, Black Magic, Third Man, Black Rose, Trent's Last Case, Trouble in the Glen, Three Cases of Murder; act,

prod., dir., Othello; act. Moby Dick, Compulsion, The Tartars; dir. star, Mr. Arkadin; prod., dir., wrt., The Trial; prod., dir., Chimes at Midnight (Falstaff); dir., starred, The Immortal Story. Acted in: Casino Royale, The Sailor From Gibraltar, I'll Never Forget What's 'is Name, Oedipus the King, The Southern Star, House of Cards, The Kremlin Letter, Start the Revolution Without Me, Catch 22, A Safe Place, Necromancy, F for Fake, Voyage of the Damned.

TV: The Man Who Came to Dinner.

WELLS, FRANK G.: Executive. b. March 4, 1932, Calif. e. Pomona College, 1949–53; Oxford U., 1953–55; Rhodes Scholarship Jurisprudence; U.S. Army, Infantry first lieutenant, 1955–57; Stanford Law School, 1957–59; joined Gang, Tyre & Brown (entertainment industry law firm) 1959; partner, 1962–69; mem., State Bar of Calif., American Bar Assoc., Los Angeles County Bar Assoc., pres., Warner Bros. Inc.

WELSH, CHARLES L.: b. New York, N.Y., June 7, 1906. e. Morris H.S., 1923. Press dept., N.Y. Hippodrome, 1919; B.F. Keith's Theats., 1921–29; United Trailer Svce., 1930; Meyer-Rigger Lab., 1931; partner Welgot Trailer Svce., 1932; mgr. special film div. Nat'l Screen Service, 1959. Pres., Summit Screen Service, 1967.

WELTMAN, PHILIP: Executive. b. Brooklyn, N.Y., July 16, 1908. e. Brooklyn College, 1923–27, N.Y.U., 1928–30, N.Y. Stock Exch. Inst., 1934–36. New York stock exchange firm, Chas. E. Quincey & Co., 1930–38; joined William Morris Agency, N.Y. office, 1938; trans. to coast, 1947; U.S. Armed Forces, 1943–45, battlefield commission, rec'd Croix de Guerre; transferred to Coast, 1947; Sr. exec., TV div.

WELTNER, GEORGE: Executive. b. Chicago, Ill., Aug. 16, 1901; e. B.S., Columbia, 1922. Entered foreign dept. of Paramount, 1922; asst. to head, Paramount Internat'l, 1934; asst. mgr., v.p., 1944; pres., Paramount Internat'l Films 1945; dir. of domestic and foreign sales, distrib., Paramount Pictures; pres., Paramount Film Dist. Corp., 1955; v.p. Paramount Pictures Corp., exec. vice-pres., Paramount Pictures Corp., 1962; pres., 1964; resigned, 1967, rank of cmmdr. in Order of Merit, Italian Republic, 1966. La Medaille de Vermeil, Conseil Municipal de Paris, 1966; Medal of Honor Veterans of Foreign Wars, 1966.

WENDERS, WIM: Director. b. Dusseldorf, Germany, 1945. Studied from 1967 to 1970 at Filmhochschule in Munich. Worked as film critic. In 1967 made first short films (Schauplatze) and three others before first feature, Summer in the City, in 1970.

PICTURES INCLUDE: Die Angst DesTormanns Beim Elfmeter, The Scarlet Letter, Aus Der Familie Der Panzerechsen, Falsche Bewegung, Alice in the Cities, The Goalie's Anxiety at the Penalty Kick, Kings of the Road, The American Friend.

WERLE: Costume designer. Real name Dan Werle. b. Chicago, Ill. e. Chicago Art Institute. Started as designer for New York wholesale house; later, Hattie Carnegie; Chez Paree in Chicago; opened own business, California, 1945. Designer for seven seasons Loretta Young hostess-gowns on The Loretta Young Show, NBC-TV. Also Rosemary Clooney Show; Playhouse 90; free lance, consul. designer; pres., man. designer, Werle Originals Inc. mem., Costume Designers Guild; has designed for television appearances Merle Oberon, Claudette Colbert, Ava Gardner, etc. Contracted to design for Barbara Stanwyck Theatre, Rosemary Clooney Show, Playhouse 90; now making clothes for special shows, also selling to top specialty stores throughout U.S. and Canada. Opened new salon feat. Coutoure and Custom Gowns, Dresses, Suits, boutique div., 1971. Designed for That Girl (ABC); Lana Turner's Town Hall & TV appearances, 1975.

WERNER, OSKAR: Actor, director, producer. b. Vienna, Austria, Nov. 13, 1922. Actor with repertory gp., Burg Theatre, Vienna.

PICTURES INCLUDE: Angel With a Trumpet, Eroica, Wonder of Our Days, Wonder Boy, Decision Before Dawn, Last Ten Days, Jules Et Jim, Ship of Fools, Interlude, The Shoes of the Fisherman, Voyage of the Damned.

TV: prod., dir., cast: A Certain Judas.

WERTMULLER, LINA: Writer-Director. b. Rome. After graduating high school enrolled in drama school. Began working in theatre in 1951; spent decade doing everything from puppetry to stage managing to writing and directing for radio and TV. Began film career as asst. to Fellini on 8½ in 1962. Following year wrote and directed first film, The Lizards. Had big TV success with series called Gian Burasca and then returned to theatre for a time.

PICTURES: This Time, Let's Talk About Men, The Seduction of Mimi, Love and Anarchy, All Screwed Up, Swept Away, Seven Beauties, A Night Full of Rain.

WESTCOTT, HELEN: Actress. r.n. Myrthas Helen Hickman. b. Hollywood, Calif; e. L. A. Jr. Coll., 1946. In play The Drunkard, at 7, for 9 yrs.; many radio shows.

PICTURES INCLUDE: Midsummer Night's Dream (as

child), Adventures of Don Juan, Girl from Jones Beach, Mr. Belvedere Goes to College, Whirlpool, Dancing in the Dark, The Gunfighter, Three Came Home, Secret of Convict Lake, Phone Call from a Stranger, Return of Texan, With a Song in My Heart, Loan Shark, A&C Meet Dr. J. & Mr. H., Charge at Feather River, Hot Blood, The Last Hurrah.

WESTON, JACK: Actor. b. 1915. Began career in 1934 in children's division of Cleveland Playhouse. In Army in World War II. Success came in Broadway hit, Season in the Sun. Was frequent performer in top TV shows during 1950s. Film debut in Stage Struck in 1958.
PICTURES INCLUDE: Stage Struck, Please Don't Eat the Daisies, All in a Night's work, The Honeymoon Machine, It's Only Money, Palm Springs Weekend, The Incredible Mr. Limpet, Mirage, The Cincinnati Kid, Wait Until Dark, The Thomas Crown Affair, The April Fools, Cactus Flower, A New Leaf, Fuzz, Marco, Gator, The Ritz, Cuba, The Four Seasons.
TELEVISION: Studio One, Philco Theatre, Kraft Playhouse, Rod Browning of the Rocket Rangers.

WESTON, JAY: Producer. b. New York City, March 9, 1929. e. NYU. Operated own pub. agency before moving into film prod. In 1965 launched Weston Production; sold orig. s.p., The War Horses, to Embassy Pictures; acquired and marketed other properties. Became prod. story exec. for Palomar-ABC Pictures in 1967.
PICTURES INCLUDE: For Love of Ivy (co.-prod.), Lady Sings the Blues (co.-prod.), W. C. Fields and Me, Chu Chu and the Philly Flash.
STAGE: Does a Tiger Wear a Necktie (co.-prod.).

WESTON, ROBERT R.: Executive. b. N.Y., e. Peekskill Military Acad., Fordham Univ., Publicity dir., WFUV-FM, 3 yrs.; copy writer, Columbia Pictures, asst. accnt. exec.; Donahue & Coe, asst. adv. mgr., United Artists adv. dir., Embassy Pictures, v.p., asst. to exec. v.p.; v.p. asst. to pres., resigned to become independent film producer, 1971. Presently pres., Harold Robbins Int'l., film prod. co. Prod.: The Betsy.

WEVER, WARREN: Talent agent. b. Dennison, Texas, Feb. 20; e. Col. Univ., 1938–39; UCLA, 1939–41, B.A. casting dir., Warner Bros., 1942–53; talent agent, Wynn Rocamora Agency, 1953–60; the Mitchell J. Hamilburg Agency, 1960. Formed own agency, Warren Wever Artists' Mgt., 1970.

WEXLER, HASKELL: Cinematographer, director. b. 1926. Photographed educational and industrial films before features.
PICTURES INCLUDE: The Savage Eye, The Bus, The Hoodlum Priest, Angel Baby, A Face In the Rain, America, America, The Best Man, The Loved One, Who's Afraid of Virginia Woolf, In the Heat of the Night, The Thomas Crown Affair. Co-produced, directed, wrote, Medium Cool. 1972: Trial of Catonsville Nine, Interview Allende, American Graffiti, One Flew Over the Cuckoo's Nest, Introduction to the Enemy, Bound for Glory, Days of Heaven.

WHEELER, LYLE: Art director. b. Woburn, Mass., Feb. 12, 1905; e. U. So. Calif. Mag. illustrator, industrial designer before entering m.p. ind. as art dir. of Garden Of Allah. In 1944 apptd. supervising art dir. 20th Century-Fox. Academy Award, in collab. art-direction black & white for Anna and the King of Siam; Gone With The Wind, color art dir., collab., The Robe, 1953. Love Is a Many-Splendored Thing, Daddy Longlegs, The Diary of Anne Frank (AA, 1959), Journey to the Center of the Earth, The Cardinal.

WHELDON, SIR HUW. P. (O.B.E., M.C.): Producer, executive, author. Consultant, NBC, personnel and electronics, etc. b. Prestatyn (Wales), May 7, 1916; e. Friars Bangor; Soester Gymnasium (Germany); London Univ. With Airborne Division during War; dir for Wales Arts Council, 1946; entered TV 1952, produced TV programmes. Head of Documentary and Music Programmes, BBC TV, 1964; controller of programs BBC TV, 1965–68; managing director of television, BBC, 1969. 1975. Chrm. Court of Governors, LSE., pres., Royal TV Society (Wales); Governor Royal Coll. of Art, National Film School, London Festival Ballet. Trustee: National Portrait Gallery, Knighted 1976. Hon. D. Litt (Ulster), Hon. Fellow (LSE).
TV: Television Talks, 1954; also: Press Conference, Is This Your Problem, Orson Welles Sketchbook, All Your Own, Men in Battle, Men of Action, Monitor, Portraits of Power, Royal Heritage, Library of Congress.

WHITE, JESSE: Actor. b. Buffalo, N.Y., Jan. 13, 1919; e. Akron, O., H.S. Did odd jobs, then salesman; radio, vaudeville, burlesque, nightclubs and little theatre work; Broadway stage debut in Moon is Down, 1942; other shows include Harvey, Born Yesterday, etc. Has appeared on numerous radio and TV shows, regular on Danny Thomas, Ann Southern Shows.
PICTURES INCLUDE: Harvey, Death of a Salesman, Callaway Went Thataway, Million Dollar Mermaid, Witness to Murder, Forever Female, Not As a Stranger, Bad Seed, Back from Eternity, Designing Woman, Marjorie Mor-

ningstar, Legs Diamond, Fever in the Blood, Sail a Crooked Ship, It's Only Money, The Yellow Canary, It's a Mad, Mad, Mad, Mad World, Looking For Love, A House Is Not a Home, Bless the Beasts and Children, The Cat from Outer Space.

WHITE, JULES J.: Producer, director. Started as juvenile actor, film editor, assist. cameraman, gag writer, dir., shorts and features; exec. prod., short subjects, Columbia, 1933–58; prod. and/or dir., over six hundred shorts, including the Three Stooges several features; co-prod., CBS-TV; prod., free lance.

WHITE, LAWRENCE R.: Executive. b. 1926. e. Syracuse U. Began career as producer-director for the Dumont Television Network in 1948. Dir. of programming, Benton & Bowles, Inc., 1951; joined CBS TV network as v.p., daytime programming, 1959; dir. of program development, CBS, 1963; joined NBC television network in 1965 as v.p., daytime programs; v.p. programs, east coast, 1969; v.p. programs, NBC-TV, 1972; ind. prod. affiliated with CPT, 1975.

WHITE, LEONARD: Producer, director, actor. b. Sussex, Eng. TV dir., prod., CBS-TV (Canada), T.W.W. Ltd. T.T. TV & ABC-TV; Jupiter Thea., Inc.; Crest Theatre; Royal Alexandra Thea.; Toronto Thea., 1953–57. England, Playhouse, Oxford, Perth Repertory Thea., Hornchurch, Guilford Repertory Thea. Belgrade Thea., Coventry. Actor: U.S.A. debut in A Sleep of Prisoners, 1951–52; London West End. In the White Devil, He Who Gets Slapped, Macbeth, Still She Wished for Company, Point of Departure.
PICTURES INCLUDE: The Dark Man, The Large Rope, River Beat, Hunted, Martin Luther, Passage Home, Breakout, Circumstantial Evidence, At the Stroke of Nine, etc.
TV: All networks, G. Britain and CBC (Canada). Prod., ABC-TV, 1960–68. Inside Story series, Armchair Mystery Thea., series. Police Surgeon series, The Avengers, series, Out of This World, series, Armchair Theatre series. Prod., 1968–69; prod., Thames Television, 1969–70. Drama consultant CBC-TV Toronto.

WHITE, PAUL: Executive, producer, director. b. New York, N.Y.; e. Columbia U. Worked for N.Y. Times, N.Y. & Wash., D.C., managing ed., Nation-Wide News Service; publisher of first consumer weekly radio magazine "Radio Review"; ed.-publisher of "Key Magazine"; home office exec. Paramount Pictures. Author, alone & in collab., books including I Find Treason. Served in U.S. Marine Corps as officer-in-chg. combat photography in the Pacific WWII, prod. & dir. wire recording of first sound ever made of actual war conditions under battle fire in the Marshalls. Joined Selznick Releasing Org. as gen. mgr. of European operations 1946; formed own co., Paul White Productions, Inc. 1948; v.p. & dir., Procter Prod., Inc.; pres., PSI-TV 1953. v.p. Subscription TV in chg. pgmg; pioneer cablevision and Pay-TV; pres. MCI; created 11 audio-visual inventions; exec. consultant posts; RCA; Impresario S. Hurok and his org; chm. exec. comm, The Education Guild; 1979–80, bd. chm. Palolite 4D Systems.
PICTURES INCLUDE: Battle of the Marshalls, Saipan, Tinian, To the Shores of two Jima, Song of Siam, Pearl of the Orient, Land of Fair Dinkum, Unusual Sports, Flying Doctor.
TV: film series started & supervised incl.: Playhouse of Stars, China Smith, Play of The Week, Orient Express, prod. & dir. "The Keys to Peace" (Pope Paul's U.S. Visit); exec. prod. two 90-min TV Specials, "The Bolshoi Ballet" Bicentennial project; OP Sail 1976, The Tall Ships; Int'l. Productions (features & TV).

WHITE, ROY B.: Executive, exhibitor. b. Cincinnati, Ohio. e. University of Cincinnati. Flight engineer, U.S. Air Force during World War II; worked in sales department of 20th Century-Fox, 1949–52; began in exhibition, 1952; pres., Mid-States Theatres; past president, National Association of Theatre Owners, Chairman of the Board, National Association of Theatre Owners: Board of Trustees—American Film Institute, NATO of Ohio, v.p., Motion Picture Pioneers, Will Rogers Hospital, Nat'l. Endowment for Arts.

WHITE, WILFRID HYDE: Actor. b. Gloucestershire, Eng.; e. Marlborough Coll. Stage debut, 1925; screen debut in Rembrandt, 1936. TV appearances.
PICTURES INCLUDE: The Winslow Boy, Britannia Mews, Adam and Evelyn, The Third Man, Golden Salamander, Trio, Mr. Drake's Duck, The Browning Version, Outcast of the Islands, Mr. Denning Drives North, Gilbert & Sullivan, Million Pound Note (Man With a Million), Betrayed, Duel in the Jungle, Rainbow Jacket, To Dorothy, A Son, Quentin Durward, March Hare, The Silken Affair, Libel, North West Frontier, Two-Way Stretch, Let's Make Love, On the Double, Ada, The Castaways, Crooks Anonymous, My Fair Lady (Hollywood), 1964; You Must Be Joking, Ten Little Indians, The Sandwich Man, Marrakesh.

WHITELAW, BILLIE: Actress. b. Coventry, England. Acted on radio and television since childhood. Winner of the TV Actress of the Year; Variety Club Actress of the Year 1960.

British Academy Award 1969. U.S. National Society of Film Critics Award for Best Supporting Actress, Variety Club, 1977. Evening New, Best Film Actress, 1977.

STAGE: 3 years with National Theatre of Great Britain. Revue: England, My England. Stage plays include: Progress to the Park, A Touch of the Poet, Othello, Tretawney of the Wells, After Haggerty, Not I, Alphabetical Order, Footfalls, Molly, The Greeks, Happy Days.

PICTURES INCLUDE: No Love for Johnnie, Mr. Topaze, Hell Is a City, Payroll, Charlie Bubbles, The Adding Machine, Twisted Nerve, Start the Revolution Without Me, Leo the Last, Eagle in a Cage, Gumshoe, Frenzy, Nightwatch, The Omen, Leopard in the Snow, The Water Babies.

TV: Over 100 leading roles incl. No Trains to Lime Street, Lady of the Camelias, Resurrection, The Pity of it All, You and Me, A World of Time, Dr. Jekyll and Mr. Hyde, Poet Game, Sextet (8 plays for BBC), Wessex Tales, The Fifty Pound Note, Supernatural (2 plays), Three plays by Samuel Beckett, Eustace and Hilda, The Oresteia of Aeschylus, The Haunted Man, The Bad Soldier Schultz.

WHITFIELD, RICHARD ALLEN: Producer-Executive. b. Goldsboro, N.C., 1946. e. Univ. of North Carolina. Adv. writer-producer for American Brands, Pepsicola, 1970–73; TV-film producer, industrial-educational, 1973–77; v.p., adv., Independents International Films, Inc., distributor, 1978; v.p.-producer, Rick Friedberg & Associates, 1979; pres. Golden Image Motion Picture Corp., feature production, 1980.

PICTURES INCLUDE: K-GOD (exec. prod.), Used Cars (video segments prod.), Bones of Peking (prod.).

WHITMAN, STUART: Actor. b. San Francisco, Calif., Feb. 1; e. Los Angeles City Coll. Army Engineers June 1945 to Sept. 1948, Engineers at Fort Lewis, Wash.; while in army, became light heavyweight boxer. Studied drama, L.A. City Coll., 2 yrs.; attended Ben Bard's training sch. for actors, became member of Chekhov group, and Arthur Kennedy famed local Stage Society. Joined tent show, Here Comes Mr. Jordan, then TV and pictures.

PICTURES INCLUDE: When Worlds Collide, The Day The Earth Stood Still, China Doll, Darby's Rangers, Johnny Trouble, Hell Bound, Seven Men from Now, No Sleep Till Dawn, Ten North Frederick, These Thousand Hills, The Deck Ran Red, The Sound and The Fury, Hound Dog Man, The Story of Ruth, Murder, Inc., Francis of Assisi, The Fiercest Heart, The Mark, The Comancheros, Reprieve, The Day and the Hour, Signpost to Murder, Rio Conchos, Sands of Kalahari, An American Dream, Last Escape, Last Generation, Night of the Lepus, Crazy Mama, Call Him Shatter, Las Vegas Lady, Strange Shadows in an Empty Room.

TV: The Crowd Pleaser (Alcoa-Goodyear), Highway Patrol, Dr. Christian, Hangman's Noose (Zane Grey).

WHITMORE, JAMES: Actor. r.n. James Allen Whitmore, Jr. b. White Plains, N.Y., Oct. 1; e. Yale U. In Yale Drama School players; co-founder Yale radio station, 1942; U.S. Marine Corps, World War II; in USO, in American Wing Theatre school, in stock. Broadway debut in Command Decision, 1947; m.p. debut in Undercover Man. Star of Tomorrow.

PICTURES INCLUDE: Battleground, Asphalt Jungle, Next Voice You Hear, Mrs. O'Malley and Mr. Malone, Outriders, Please Believe Me, Across the Wide Missouri, It's a Big Country, Because You're Mine, Above and Beyond, Girl Who Had Everything, All the Brothers Were Valiant, Kiss Me Kate, The Command, Them, Battle Cry, McConell Story, Last Frontier, Oklahoma, Face of Fire, Eddie Duchin Story, Who Was That Lady?, Black Like Me, Chuka, Water Hole No. 3, Nobody's Perfect, Planet of the Apes, Madigan, The Split, Guns of the Magnificent Seven, Chato's Land, Where the Red Fern Grows, Give 'em Hell, Harry, The Serpent's Egg, The First Deadly Sin.

TV: The Law and Mr. Jones.

WHITTAKER, WILLIAM: Producer. Entered m.p. ind. as asst. dir. prod. man. with Gaumont British 1932. War service 1939–45. Joined Associated British Picture Corporation as prod. man 1946 Producer 1954. From 1960 Con. of AB Productions. 1970: independent producer.

PICTURES INCLUDE: (from 1946) prod.: Dam Buster, No Time for Tears, Ice Cold in Alex, The Rebel, The Cracksman, The Bargee, Mister Ten Per Cent, Judith, Universal Soldier.

WHITTINGHAM, JACK: Writer, producer, b. London, England, 1910; e. Charterhouse and Lincoln College, Oxford. Formerly journalist Daily Express, Morning Post.

PLAYS: Return Ticket, Ill Wind.

PICTURES INCLUDE: Q. Planes (Clouds Over Europe); orig. s.p.: Escape to Danger, Welcome Mr. Washington, Twilight Hour, Waltz Time, Green Fingers, Hunted; orig. story and s.p.: Kiss the Bride Goodbye, The Lisbon Story, Counterblast, The Dancing Years, Cage of Gold, Pool of London, I Believe in You, The Divided Heart, The Prince and the Pauper, While the Storm Lasts; prod., story, s.p.:

The Birthday Present; orig. story, coliab. s.p.: Mandy, West of Zanzibar; collab. story, orig. s.p.: Thunderball.

WICKES, MARY: Actress. e. Washington U., Doctor of Arts (hon.), 1969.

THEATRE: (B'way) The Man Who Came to Dinner, Town House, Stage Door, Danton's Death. Dramatic & musical comedy stock includes: St. Louis Municipal Opera, Starlight Theatre, Houston Music Theatre.

PICTURES INCLUDE: The Man Who Came to Dinner, Now, Voyager, White Christmas, The Music Man, The Trouble With Angels, Where Angels Go Trouble Follows, Napoleon and Samantha, Snowball Express.

TV: The Halls of Ivy, The Danny Thomas Show, Dennis the Menace, Bonino, Hitchcock Presents, Studio One, Playhouse 90.

WIDEM, ALLEN M.: Author, editor. b. Hartford, Conn., Feb. 14, 1925; e. Univ. of Connecticut, B.S. In U.S. Army, 1943–46, as Army corr., European Theatre of Oper. Author, m.p. scripts, radio and TV properties and stage plays. Amusements-TV editor and columnist, Hartford, Connecticut, Times.

WIDMARK, RICHARD: Actor. b. Sunrise, Minn., Dec. 26; e. Lake Forest U. Instructor, 1938. On radio, then stage, films.

PICTURES INCLUDE: Kiss of Death, Cry of the City, Road House, Street With No Name, Yellow Sky, Down to the Sea in Ships, Slattery's Hurricane, Night and the City, Panic in the Streets, No Way Out, Halls of Montezuma, The Frogmen, Red Skies of Montana, Don't Bother to Knock, O. Henry's Full House, My Pal Gus, Destination Gobi, Pickup on South Street, Take the High Ground, Hell & High Water, Broken Lance, Prize of Gold, The Cobweb, Backlash, Last Wagon, Saint Joan, Warlock, Kingdom of Man, The Long Ships, Run for the Sun, The Alamo, Judgment at Nuremberg, How the West Was Won, The Way West, Madigan, Death of a Gunfighter, When The Legends Die, Murder on the Orient Express, Twilight's Last Gleaming, The Domino Principle, Rollercoaster, Coma, The Swarm.

WIENER, JACK: Executive. b. Paris, France, June 8, 1926. Pub. rep., MGM, New Orleans, Jacksonville, Fla., 1952–56; joined Columbia Pictures Int. Corp., 1956, continental publicity mgr., Columbia, Paris; v.p., Columbia Pics. Int'l., 1966; continental prod. exec., 1968; v.p. Columbia Pictures Corp., 1970. In 1972 became indep. prod., making Vampira and The Eagle Has Landed.

WIESEN, BERNARD: Producer, Director, Executive. b. New York City, Oct. 6. e. College of the City of New York (B.B.A.) Pasadena Playhouse College of Theatre (Master of Theatre Arts), Dramatic Workshop of New School. Is pres. of M.A.N. International Productions.

PICTURES INCLUDE: Producer-Director: Fear No More. Asst. Director on films, including The King and I, The Left Hand of God, The Rains of Ranchipur, To Catch a Thief, The Trouble with Harry.

TV: Director: How to Marry A Millionaire, Valentine's Day. Assoc. Producer: Valentine's Day, Three on an Island, Cap'n Ahab, Sally and Sam. Assoc. Prod: Daniel Boone. Producer/Director: Julia, Co-Producer-Director: The Jimmy Stewart Show. Prod. Exec.: Executive Suite (pilot). Exec. Paramount TV, director of current programming.

STAGE: First Monday in October (Bdwy.)

WIESENTHAL, SAM: Executive. b. New York, N.Y., Jan. 26, 1909; e. N.Y.U., 1929. In story dept., Universal Pictures 1929–31; asst. to pres., 1931–39; v.p., gen mgr. & dir. of General Service Studios & producing companies since 1942, exec. v.p., assoc. producer many films. pres., Olympic Prod., 1964.

PICTURES INCLUDE: Bridge at San Luis Rey, Dark Waters, The Macomber Affair, Cry Danger, with W. R. Frank; Second Chance (RKO) The Americano, Bengazi, Tension at Table Rock, The Day They Gave Babies Away, The Jack Dempsey Story.

WILCOX, CLAIRE: Actress. b. Toronto, Canada, 1955. Photographer's model, 3 yrs. of age; appeared on numerous national magazine covers; TV commercials; signed contract, Curtis Enterprises.

PICTURES INCLUDE: 40 Pounds of Trouble, Wives and Lovers.

TV: Harris Versus the World.

WILCOXON, HENRY: Actor. b. British West Indies, Sept. 8, 1905. r.n. Harry Wilcoxon. On London stage from 1925; made his first sound film appearance in 1931 in The Perfect Lady (BL). Named assoc. prod. by Cecil B. DeMille on Greatest Show on Earth. Produced The Buccaneer (1959), in which also acted.

PICTURES INCLUDE: The Flying Squad, 1931, The Lovelorn Lady, 1931, (BIP); A Taxi to Paradise, and many others. Since 1942: The Man Who Wouldn't Die, (20th-Fox), Mrs. Miniver, Johnny Doughboy, Unconquered, Crusades, Samson and Delilah, Miniver Story, Scaramouche, The War Lord, The Private Navy of Sgt. O'Farrell, Man in the Wilderness.

WILD, JACK: Actor. b. Lancashire, England, 1952. m.p. debut in Oliver, 1968. To Hollywood 1969 to star in H. R. Pufnstuf TV series for Krofft Television Productions. Under contract to Hemdale Group.
PICTURES INCLUDE: Pufnstuf, Oliver!, Swalk, Flight of the Doves, Pied Piper, The 14.
TV: Our Mutual Friend, The Government Inspector.

WILDE, ARTHUR L.: Executive. b. San Francisco, Calif., May 27, 1918. S.F. Daily News; Matson Lines; pub. dept., Warner Bros., 1936; dir. exploitation, CBS; pub. dir., Hal Wallis Prod.; pub. dept., Paramount; pub., Hecht-Hill-Lancaster; v.p., Arthur Jacobs, public rel.; Blowitz-Maskell Publicity Agency; pub. dir., C. V. Whitney Pictures; gen. v.p., 1958; owner, pub.-ad. agency, The Arthur L. Wilde Co., 1961–65; freelance publicist, 1965–66; pub. rel. consultant, Marineland of Florida, 1965; unit publicity dir., United Artists, National General, Paramount, 1966–69; free lance publicity, 1971; unit publicist, MGM, Paramount, United Artists, 1972–74; staff position; Features Publicity at Paramount Pictures, 1973. Free lance unit publicist again in 1976 at Universal, Paramount and Lorimar Productions. 1978–79, Columbia Pictures & Universal Studios; 1980, Marble Arch. Prods. & Northstar Intl. Pictures; 1981, studio pub. mgr., 20th Century-Fox.

WILDE, CORNEL: Actor, producer, director, author. b. New York, Oct. 13, 1918; e. Columbia & City Coll., N.Y. Art Sch., Budapest; Columbia Med. School; studied drama with Strasberg, Bulgakov, Chekov. First screen role, 1941, High Sierra.
STAGE: Moon Over Mulberry Street, Love is Not So Simple, Daughters of Altreus, Having a Wonderfuyl Time, Romeo & Juliet.
PICTURES INCLUDE: Wintertime, A Song to Remember, The Perfect Snob, A Thousand and One Nights, Leave Her to Heaven, Bandit of Sherwood Forest, Centennial Summer, Forever Amber, The Homestretch, It Had to be You, Walls of Jericho, Roadhouse, Four Days Leave, Two Flags West, Greatest Show on Earth, At Sword's Point, Saadia, Passion, Woman's World, Big Combo, Scarlet Coat, Hot Blood, Star of India, Beyond Mombasa, Omar Khayyam, Edge of Eternity, Constantine the Great; act., prod., dir.: Storm Fear, Maracaibo; act., prod., dir., cowriter: The Devil's Hairpin, The Sword of Lancelot; act., prod., dir.: The Naked Prey; act., prod., dir., co-author s.p.: Beach Red; prod., dir., co-author s.p.: No Blade of Grass; prod., dir., act., screenplay: Sharks' Treasure; actor: The Fifth Musketeer.

WILDER, BILLY: Producer, director, writer. b. Austria, June 22, 1906. Newspaperman active Vienna, Berlin; then author screen story People on Sunday, s.p.: Emil and the Detectives (in Museum of Modern Art), UFA. Wrote, dir., Mauvaise Graine, Paris. To Hollywood 1934, (collab. s.p) Bluebeard's Eighth Wife, Ninotchka, What a Life, Midnight, Arise My Love, Ball of Fire, Hold Back the Dawn. Head Film Section, Psych. Warfare Div., U.S. Army, 1945, Am. Zone, Germany.
PICTURES INCLUDE: collab. s.p., dir.) The Major and the Minor, Five Graves to Cairo, Double Indemnity, The Emperor Waltz, A Foreign Affair. Academy Award for dir., best s.p. (collab.) for Lost Weekend, 1945. Academy Award for best story & s.p. (collab.) for Sunset Boulevard, 1950; (collab. s.p., dir., prod) The Big Carnival, Stalag 17, Sabrina, Love in the Afternoon, Some Like it Hot, The Apartment (Academy Award for best direction, best story, and s.p., best picture, 1960); One, Two, Three, Irma La Douce; (collab. s.p., dir. co-prod.) Seven Year Itch; (collab. s.p. & dir.) Spirit of St. Louis; (collab. s.p. & dir.) Witness for the Prosecution; (prod., dir., collab.) Kiss Me, Stupid, The Fortune Cookie, The Private Life of Sherlock Holmes, Avanti, The Front Page, Fedora.

WILDER, GENE: Actor. b. Milwaukee, Wis., 1935. e. University of Iowa. Joined Bristol Old Vic company in England, became champion fencer; in New York, worked as chauffer, fencing instructor, etc. Before N.Y. off-Broadway debut in Roots.
BROADWAY: The Complaisant Lover, Mother Courage, Luv.
PICTURES INCLUDE: Bonnie and Clyde, The Producers, Start the Revolution Without Me, Quacker Fortune Has an Uncle in the Bronx, Willie Wonka and the Chocolate Factory, Everything You Always Wanted to Know About Sex*, Blazing Saddles, Rhinoceros, Young Frankenstein, The Little Prince, Adventures of Sherlock Holmes Smarter Brother (s.p., dir., star), Silver Streak, The World's Greatest Lover (s.p., dir., star), The Frisco Kid, Stir Crazy, Sunday Lovers, (dir., s.p., act.).

WILDER, W. LEE: Producer, director. b. Austria; e. U. Vienna. Awards: First prize 1950 Venice Film Festival musical documentary category.
PICTURES INCLUDE: The Vicious Circle, Shadows of Fire, The Pretender, Once a Thief, Three Steps North, Phantom from Space, Killers from Space, Snow Creature,

Big Bluff, Manfish, Man Without a Body, Fright, Spy in the Sky, Bluebeard's Ten Honeymoons.

WILK, TED: Theatrical agent. b. Minneapolis, Minn., Jan. 5, 1908. e. U. of Mich., 1926–30. Publix Theatres, Duluth, Minn., 1930; Warner Bros., Minneapolis, 1932–33; Film Daily, Hollywood, 1934–40; U.S. Army, 1941–46; Lou Irwin agency 1946–61; Ted Wilk Agency, since 1961.

WILKINSON, ROBERT: Executive. Came to Universal in 1941 as student booker in Memphis branch. Spent 4 years in Marines; then returned to Memphis as salesman, branch mgr.; later mgr. of Dallas branch, then district and regional mgr. Named Universal asst. gen. sls mgr. in 1964. Appt. exec. v.p. in chg of domestic dist. in 1978.

WILLIAMS, BERT: Executive, actor. b. Newark, N.J., April 12, 1922. e. USC Navy, 1942–45. Summer Stock, 1940–41; world's prof. diving champion, 1945–48; star diver, Larry Crosby, Buster Crabb, Johnny Weismuller, Dutch Smith Shows, 1945–48; writer, asst. prod., Martin Mooney Prods., PRC, Goldwyn Studios; pres., Bert Prods., Bert Williams Motion Picture Producers and Distributors, Inc. Member, M.P. Academy of Fine Arts & TV Academy of Arts & Science.
THEATRE: roadshow plays include: Cat on a Hot Tin Roof, Hamlet, Run From The Hunter, Sugar and Spice.
PICTURES INCLUDE: Actor, Angel Baby; prod., dir., actor, The Nest of the Cuckoo Birds; actor, Around the World Under the Sea; s.p. auth. Deathwatch 28; actor, Twenty Eight Watched, prod. dir. Adventure To Treasure Reef. s.p. Knife Fighters. orig. story & s.p.; Black Freedom; A Crime of Sex; The Masters (actor). Crazy Joe, Serpico, Lady Ice, The Klansman, Report to the Commissioner, Tracks, All the President's Men, From Noon Till Three. (all actor); While Buffalo (actor), Helter Skelter (actor), Shark Bait (writer), The Big Bus (actor). Actor: Wanda Nevada, Horn, Sunnyside, Cuba, The Last Resort, The All Night Treasure Hunt. Recent acting: Tom Horn, Kill Castro, Midnight Madness.
TV: Flipper, Sea Hunt, prod., Speargun, Gentle Ben, The Law (pilot) and Police Story (actor). Recent actor: Get Christy Love, General Hospital, Columbo, Brenner for the People (actor), Mayday 40,000 Feet (actor) Jigsaw John (Blue Knight episode). Actor: Police Woman, Chips, Mobil One, Street Killing, East of Eden, etc. Produced, directed & wrote pilot, Fifth St. Gym. Appeared on Mike Douglas Show & Johnny Carson Show.

WILLIAMS, BILL: Actor. r.n. William Katt. b. Brooklyn, N.Y. e. Pratt Inst., Brooklyn. In U.S. Army, World War II. Began as professional swimmer; later with Municipal Opera House, St. Louis; then on vaudeville tour, U.S. & England. Screen debut 1944 in "Murder in the Blue Room."
PICTURES INCLUDE: Thirty Seconds Over Tokyo, Those Endearing Young Charms, Blue Blood, Great Missouri Raid, Operation Haylift, Cariboo Trail, Havana Rose, Rose of Cimarron, Son of Paleface, Bronco Buster, Pace That Thrills, Torpedo Alley, Racing Blood, Outlaw's Daughter, Apache Ambush, Hell's Horizon, Wiretapper, Broken Star, Dogs Best Friend, Buckskin, Tickle Me, Scandalous John.

WILLIAMS, BILLY DEE: Actor. b. New York City, April 6, 1937. Studied acting with Paul Mann and Sidney Poitier at actor's workshop in Harlem. Was child actor; Broadway adult debut in The Cool World in 1961.
STAGE: A Taste of Honey, Hallelujah, Baby.
PICTURES INCLUDE: The Last Angry Man (debut), The Out-of-Towners, The Final Comedown, Lady Sings the Blues, Hit!, Mahogany, The Bingo Long Travelling All-Stars, The Empire Strikes Back, Nighthawks.
TV: Brian's Song, The Glass House and appearances on series: The F.B.I., The Interns, Mission Impossible, Mod Squad.

WILLIAMS, BOB: Writer. b. Sioux Falls, S.D., Oct. 19, 1913.
PICTURES INCLUDE: collab. s.p., Treat 'Em Rough, Overland Mail Robbery, Pride of the Plains, Youth on Trial, Sergeant Mike; s.p., Lone Texas Ranger, Trail to Vengeance, many Westerns; colab. s.p., Stage to Tucson.

WILLIAMS, CARA: Comedienne. r.n. Bernice Kamiat. b. Brooklyn, N.Y. e. Holywood Professional Sch.; ent. ind., 20th Century Fox, child actress.
PICTURES INCLUDE: Boomerang, Something For the Boys, Meet Me In Las Vegas, Never Steal Anything Small, The Defiant Ones, The Man From the Diners' Club, Doctors' Wives.
TV: Pete and Gladys, Alfred Hitchcock Presents, Desilu Playhouse, The Jackie Gleason Show, Henry Fonda Special, The Cara Williams Show.

WILLIAMS, CARL W.: Executive. b. Decatur, Ill., March 9, 1927. e. Illinois State Normal U., B.S., 1949; UCLA, M.A., 1950. dir. adv. photo., Clark Equipment Co., 1951–54; film dir., WKAR-TV, E. Lansing, Mich., 1954–56; Prod., dir., Capital Films, E. Lansing, Mich., 1957; dir., A-V Laboratory, UCLA, 1957–63; co-dev. Dimension 150 Widescreen process, 1957; formed D-150 Inc., 1963; Filbert Co., 1970, v.p., 1977.
MAMPAS, SMPTE, AFI, Variety Club, Tent 25.

WILLIAMS, CHARLES: Actor, writer. b. Albany, N.Y., Sept. 27, 1898. Appeared on stage in "Rio Rita," dialogue for vaudeville and stage. To Fox Studios, Hollywood, 1931. In 1933 appeared in Gambling Ship. In 1935 collab. music and lyrics, Gigolette; collab. orig. s.p. Arm of the Law, Midnight Limited.
PICTURES INCLUDE: The Girl from Monterey, Where Are Your Children? (collab. orig. & s.p.) Hollywood and Vine; (cast) End of the Road, Identity Unknown, Doll Face, Heldorado, Due Goes West, Grand Canyon.

WILLIAMS, CINDY: Actress. b. Van Nuys, Calif. Aug. 22. e. L.A. City Coll. Appeared in high school and college plays; first prof. role in Roger Corman's film Gas. Made TV debut in Room 222 and had continuing role.
PICTURES INCLUDE: Beware the Blob, Drive, He Said, The Christian Licorice Store, Travels with My Aunt, American Graffiti, The Conversation, Mr. Ricco, The First Nudie Musical, More American Graffiti.
TV: Episodes of The Funny Side, The Neighbors, Barefoot in the Park, My World and Welcome to It, Love, American Style, Nanny and the Professor, The Bobby Sherman Show—Getting Together; The Migrants (movie), Laverne and Shirley.

WILLIAMS, DERICK: Cinematographer. b. Nottingham, Eng., 1906. e. Brighton Coll.; Nottingham U. Cinematog., 1929; first cameraman & experimental work on Evans color process, 1930; head camera dept., Gainsborough Pictures, 1932; org. camera dept., Nat'l Studios, Sydney, Australia, 1935.
PICTURES INCLUDE: In Which We Serve, Way Ahead, Way to the Stars, Beware of Pity, For Them That Trespass, Lady Possessed; mgr. dir., Derick Williams Prod., Ltd.; Voice of London, Ltd.

WILLIAMS, DIAHN: Actress. b. Gainesville, Fla., June 30. e. Univ. of Miami (BA, psychology, speech), also attended Univ. of Florida, UCLA. m. Thomas J. McGrath, prod. & atty. Started as fashion model in New York, France, Germany. Top woman exec. as assoc. dir. of pub. rel. at Chesebrough-Ponds, 1971–72.
PICTURES INCLUDE: Chair de Poule, Another Nice Mess, Deadly Hero.
TV: Harry's Girls (series, 1963–64), Somerset (series, 1973–74) and guest-starred in many TV shows, including I Spy, Get Smart, Tarzan, Here Comes the Brides, Andy Griffith Show, G.E. Theatre, etc.

WILLIAMS, ELMO: Film editor. b. Oklahoma City, Okla., Apr. 30, 1913. Film editor 1933–39, with British & Dominion Studio, England. Since then with RKO-Radio as film editor for numerous major productions; Academy Award, best film ed. (collab.) High Noon, 1952; dir. film ed., Tall Texan; prod. dir., ed., The Cowboy; ed., 20,000 Leagues Under the Sea; dir. Apache Kid; second unit dir., film ed. The Vikings; dir. 2nd Unit DFZ prod., The Big Gamble; assoc. prod., The Longest Day; mgr., dir., 20th Century Fox Prod. Ltd. Producer: Tora! Tora! Tora! v.p., worldwide production, 20th Century-Fox Film, 1971. President Ibex Films. Exec. v.p., Gaylord Prods., 1979.
TV: co-prod. dir., Tales of the Vikings.

WILLIAMS, ESTHER: Actress. b. Los Angeles, Calif., Aug. 8, 1923. e. U. of So. Calif. Swimmer San Francisco World's Fair Aquacade; professional model. On screen 1942 in Andy Hardy Steps Out.
PICTURES INCLUDE: A Guy Named Joe, Bathing Beauty, Thrill of a Romance, This Time for Keeps, Ziegfeld Follies, Hoodlum Saint, Easy to Wed, Fiesta, On an Island With You, Take Me Out to the Ball Game, Neptune's Daughter, Pagan Love Song, Duchess of Idaho, Texas Carnival, Skirts Ahoy!, Million Dollars Mermaid, Dangerous When Wet, Easy to Love, Jupiter's Darling, Unguarded Moment, The Big Show. Voted one of Top Ten Money-Making Stars in M.P. Herald-Fame poll, 1950.

WILLIAMS, GEORGE EMLYN (C.B.E.) Writer, actor, producer. b. Mostyn, Flintshire, Wales, Nov. 26, 1905. e. Christ Church, Oxford, M.A., LL.D. (Hon.). On London stage from 1927 (And So to Bed, The Case of the Frightened Lady, Wild Decembers, Night Must Fall, The Corn is Green, etc.); also author many plays (Glamour, The Late Christopher Bean, Night Must Fall, He Was Born Gay, The Corn is Green, The Light of Heart, etc.). Began Brit. screen career 1932 as actor in The Case of the Frightened Lady; author variously adapt. or dial. Friday the Thirteenth. Evergreen, This England, In 1945 on Brit. stage; author & cast the Wind of Heaven, Trespass, Accolade, Charles Dickens Mixed Bill & Bleak House, Someone Waiting.
PICTURES INCLUDE: Broken Blossoms, The Citadel, Jamaica Inn, The Stars Look Down, The Girl in the News, Major Barbara, You Will Remember, Hatter's Castle, Last Days of Dolwyn, Three Husbands, Scarf, Another Man's Poison, Ivanhoe, Deep Blue Sea, I Accuse, Beyond This Place, The Wreck of the Mary Deare, The L-Shaped Room, The Eye of the Devil.
TV: The Winslow Boy, The Defenders, Yob and Nabob.

BOOKS: George, Beyond Belief, Emlyn, Doctor Crippen's Diary, Headlong.

WILLIAMS, GRANT: Actor. b. New York, N.Y., Aug. 18, 1930. e. Queens Coll., U. of Ill., N.Y.C.; U.S. Air Force, 1943–52. Pub. work. MCA acted with Barter Theatre, Abingdon, Va., summer stock, road cos.; many TV dramatic shows; m.p. debut in Red Sundown.
PICTURES INCLUDE: Showdown at Abilene, Written on the Wind, Outside the Law, Four Girls in Town, Incredible Shrinking Man, Monolith Monsters, The Leech.

WILLIAMS, JOHN: Composer. b. New York City, Feb. 8, 1932. e. UCLA, Juilliard School. Worked as session musician in '50s; began career as film composer in late '50s. Considerable experience as musical director and conductor as well as composer.
PICTURES INCLUDE: I Passed for White, Because They're Young, The Secret Ways, Bachelor Flat, Diamond Head, Gidget Goes to Rome, The Killers, None But the Brave, John Goldfarb Please Come Home, The Rare Breed, How To Steal A Million, The Plainsman, Not with My Wife You Don't, Penelope, A Guide for the Married Man, Fitzwilly, Valley of the Dolls, Daddy's Gone A-Hunting, Goodbye Mr. Chips (mus. supvr. & dir.), The Reivers, Jane Eyre, Fiddler on the Roof (musc. dir.), The Cowboys, Images, Pete 'n' Tillie, The Poseidon Adventure, Tom Sawyer (musc. supvr.), The Long Goodbye, The Man Who Loved Cat Dancing, The Paper Chase, Cinderella Liberty, Conrack, The Sugarland Express, Earthquake, The Towering Inferno, The Eiger Sanction, Jaws, Family Plot, The Missouri Breaks, Midway, Black Sunday, Star Wars, Encounters of the Third Kind, The Fury, Jaws II, Meteor, Quintet, Dracula, Raiders of the Lost Ark.
TV: Once Upon a Savage Night, Sergeant Ryker, Heidi.

WILLIAMS, MURIEL: Actress. e. Leland Powers Dramatic School, Boston. Played in stock. Cape Playhouse, Dennis, Mass.; with nat'l co. Autumn Garden, Heaven Can Wait; with late husband formed model, prod. agency, Hart Model Agency; commentator for fashion shows.
TV: frequent appearances; series: Brighter Day, CBS-TV.

WILLIAMS, OSCAR: Writer-Producer-Director. e. San Francisco State Univ., getting degree in film, TV. Was director's intern on The Great White Hope (directed by Martin Ritt) through the American Film Institute.
PICTURES INCLUDE: The Final Comedown (s.p., prod. dir.); Black Belt Jones (s.p., assoc. prod.) Five on the Black Hand Side (dir.), Truck Turner (s.p.), Hot Potato (s.p., dir.).

WILLIAMS, PAUL: Composer. b. Omaha. Began career at studios as set painter and stunt parachutist. Bit and character parts in commercials followed. Seen briefly in The Chase and The Loved One. Became song writer, collaborating briefly with Biff Rose and later with Roger Nichols, with whom wrote several best-sellers, including We've Only Just Begun, Rainy Days and Mondays, Just an Old-Fashioned Love Song, etc.
PICTURES INCLUDE: Cinderella Liberty (score), Phantom of the Paradise (actor, score), Bugsy Malone (score), A Star Is Born (songs).

WILLIAMS, PAUL: Director. First gained attention as director of film short, Girl, which won Golden Eagle award. Made in collaboration with producer Edward R. Pressman, with whom he formed Pressman-Williams Enterprises.
PICTURES INCLUDE: Out of It, The Revolutionary, Dealing: or the Berkeley to Boston Forty Brick, Lost Bag Blues, Nunzio.

WILLIAMS, RICHARD: Producer-painter-film animator. b. March, 1933, Toronto, Canada. Entered industry in 1955. Founded Richard Williams Animation Ltd. in 1962, having entered films by producing The Little Island (1st Prize, Venice Film Festival) in 1955. His company produces TV commercials, entertainment shorts and animated films. Also designed animated feature titles for such films as What's New Pussycat?, A Funny Thing Happened On The Way To The Forum, Casino Royale, etc. (20 feature titles in 6 years). 1969: Animated sequences: Charge of the Light Brigade (Woodfall). 1971: A Christmas Carol, animated TV special for ABC-TV. His company makes TV commercials for England, America, France and Germany. His films have won awards at Festivals at Venice, Edinburgh, Mannheim, Montreal, Trieste, Melbourne, West Germany, New York, Locarno, Vancouver, Philadelphia, Zagreb, Hollywood, Cork, Los Angeles. 1973: Won Hollywood Oscar, Best Cartoon.

WILLIAMS, ROBERT: Actor. b. Glencoe, Ill.; Dartmouth U., B.A. Member: Psi Upsilon, Dartmouth Club, University Club (Chicago).
THEATRE: Burlesque, Strictly Dishonorable, Let Freedom Ring, Sailor Beware, Room Service, Eve of St. Mark.
PICTURES INCLUDE: The Girl in the Case, Secret Command, That Wonderful Urge, Apartment for Peggy, Dark Past, It Happens Every Spring, Oh, You Beautiful Doll, The Lawless, Mister 880, Groom Wore Spurs.

WILLIAMS, ROBERT X., JR.: Exhibitor, attorney. b. Taylor, Miss., Nov. 16, 1900. e. U. of Miss. Law Sch.; m. owner & mgr. Lyric Theatre, Oxford, Miss. since 1917; active in oper. to prevent adverse legislation (theatres); del., Nat'l Democratic Conventions, Phila. & Chicago; chmn. campaign funds for Democratic Party, 2nd Congressional Dist., Miss.; chmn. Roosevelt Electors of Oxford; treas. Pat Harrison campaign, Lafayette Co.; pres. De Soto Memorial Highway Assn. of Miss.; secy.-treas. Jackson to Jackson Highway Ass'n.

MEMBER: MPTO of Ark., Miss. & Tenn. (pres.); MPTO of Miss. (pres.); mayor, City of Oxford; Rotary (dir. Oxford); Shriner; Soldiers of Soil Div. of Lafayette Co. (sgt.); U. of Miss. Alumni Assn., 2nd Congressional Dist. (chmn.).

WILLIAMS, ROBIN: Actor—Comedian. b. Edinburgh, Scotland. Family moved to U.S. when he was one year old. e. Claremont Men's College (Calif.), College of Marin (Calif.), studying acting at latter. Continued studies at Julliard in New York. As San Francisco club performer appeared at Holy City Zoo, Intersection, the Great American Music Hall and The Boardinghouse. In Los Angeles performed as stand-up comedian at Comedy Store, Improvisation, and The Ice House. First TV appearance on Laugh In, followed by The Great American Laugh Off.

TELEVISION: Mork and Mindy, America Tonight, Ninety Minutes Live, The Alan Hamel Show.

PICTURES: The Last Laugh, Popeye, The World According to Garth.

WILLIAMS, ROGER: Pianist, concert-film-TV personality. b. Omaha, Oct. 1. e. Drake U., Idaho State Coll. Hon. Ph.D. Midland and Wagner Colls. Served U.S. Navy WWII. Appeared as guest artist in number of films. Public debut on TV's Arthur Godfrey Talent Scouts and Chance of a Lifetime. Other TV appearances include Ed Sullivan, Hollywood Palace, Kraft Summer Series, Celanese Special. Tours in addition to U.S. and Australia. Concert Halls—Japan, Mexico, Union of South Africa. Recorded 50 Albums, Kapp (now MCA) Records, with sales over 15 million albums.

WILLIAMS, TENNESSEE: Playwright. r.n. Thomas Lanter Williams. b. Columbus, Miss., Mar. 26, 1914. e. U. of Mo., 1931–33; Washington U., St. Louis, 1936–37; U. of Iowa, A.B., 1938.

AUTHOR: (plays) Battle of Angels, Glass Menagerie, You Touched Me; Pulitzer Prize for Streetcar Named Desire, 1947 and Cat On a Hot Tin Roof, Camino Real 1954; Summer and Smoke, Rose Tattoo, Orpheus Descending; Sweet Bird of Youth, Period of Adjustment, Slapstick Tragedy, The 7 Descents of Myrtle, In a Bar of a Tokyo Hotel, Small Craft Warnings, Novel: The Roman Spring of Mrs. Stone.

PICTURES INCLUDE: collab s.p., Glass Menagerie; s.p. Streetcar Named Desire, Rose Tattoo, Night of the Iguana.

WILLIAMS, TREAT: Actor. b. Rowayton, Conn. e. Franklin and Marshall College. Landed role on Bdwy. in musical, Over There! also played leading role in Grease on Bdwy. Film debut in The Ritz.

PICTURES: Deadly Hero, The Eagle Has Landed, Hair, 1941, Why Would I Lie?, Pursuit, Prince of the City.

WILLIAMSON, FRED: Actor. b. Gary, Ind., March 5. e. Northwestern Univ. Spent 10 yrs. playing pro football before turning to acting.

PICTURES INCLUDE: M*A*S*H*, Tell Me That You Love Me, Junie Moon, The Legend of Nigger Charley, Hammer, Black Caesar, The Soul of Nigger Charley, Hell Up in Harlem, That Man Bolt, Crazy Joe, Three Tough Guys, BLACK Eye, Three the Hard Way, Bucktown.

TV: Julia (series), Police Story, Monday Night Football.

WILLIAMSON, NICOL: Actor. b. England, 1939. Has played many classical roles with Royal Shakespeare Co., including Macbeth, Molvolio, and Coriolanus. Starred on Broadway in Inadmissible Evidence; musical debut in Rex.

PICTURES INCLUDE: Six Sided Triangle, Inadmissible Evidence, The Bofors Gun, Laughter in the Dark, The Reckoning, Hamlet, The Jerusalem File, The Seven-Per-Cent Solution, The Goodbye Girl (cameo), The Cheap Detective, The Human Factor, Excalibur.

WILLIAMSON, PATRICK: President-Columbia Pictures International Corp., New York Apptd. June 1978. b. England, Oct. 1929. Joined Columbia Pictures London office 1944-career spanned advertising & publicity responsibilities until 1967 when apptd. managing director Columbia Great Britain in 1971. Also man. dir. on formation of Columbia-Warner. Promoted to executive position in Columbia's home office, New York, April, 1973 and headed international operations since Feb. 1974.

WILLIS, GORDON: Cinematographer. Acted two summers in stock at Gloucester, MA, where also did stage settings and scenery. Photographer in Air Force; then cameraman, making documentaries. In TV did commercials and documentaries.

PICTURES INCLUDE: End of the Road, Loving, The Landlord, Little Murders, Bad Company, Klute, Up the

Sandbox, The Paper Chase, The Godfather, The Parallax View, The Godfather, Part II, All the President's Men, September 30, 1955, Annie Hall, Comes a Horseman, Interiors. Director: Windows (1980; debut).

WILLIS, TED: Screenwriter and dramatist.

PICTURES INCLUDE: The Blue Lamp (orig. treatment), Good-Time, Trouble in Store, One Good Turn, Top of the Form, Up to His Neck, Woman in a Dressing Gown, The Young and the Guilty, Great to Be Young, No Trees in the Street, The Horsemasters, Flame in the Streets, Bitter Harvest.

TV: Dixon of Dock Green, Big City, Look in Any Window, Strictly for the Sparrows, Scent of Fear, Inside Story, Hot Summer Night, Sergeant Cork, The Four Seasons of Rosie Carr, The Sullivan Brothers, Knock On Any Door, Virgin of the Secret Service, Crime of Passion, Black Beauty, Hunter's Walk.

WILLOUGHBY, GEORGE W.: (GFPE). Producer. b. Bergen, Norway. e. Oslo University. First, writer and journalist; ent. m.p. industry as assistant dir. and film editor; dir. pictures in Sweden, Norway; formed distribution cos. in Oslo and Stockholm. Prod. in England since 1950. Consultant for Guaranty of Completion Company, City Share Trust Ltd.

PICTURES INCLUDE: prod. Bar Barson, I Killed; dir. Panique, assoc. prod. Valley of Eagles, Hell Below Zero, Action of the Tiger; prod. Passionate Summer, Beat Girl; assoc. prod., Nothing but the Best; prod., Masque of The Red Death, The City Under the Sea, Love in Amsterdam, Who'd Want to Kill a Nice Girl Like You?, Squeeze a Flower, The Man Outside, Outback, Wake in Fright, Summer Rain, Age of Innocence, Boardwalk.

WILLS, SIR, JOHN SPENCER: Executive. b. London, Aug. 10, 1904. e. Merchant Tailors' School. Became connected with automobile industry 1922 and appointed dir. (later man. dir. and deputy chmn.), chmn. of British Electric Traction Co., Ltd., 1939; formerly chairman, Rediffusion, Ltd. chmn., Rediffusion Television Ltd.; apptd. program contractor to Independent Television Authority; chmn., dir. many other public companies; governor, Royal Shakespeare Theatre, 1946–74. Chartered Inst. Transport (pres., 1950–51); mem. council, Soc. of the Royal Opera House, 1962–74; v. patron, Theatre Royal Windsor Trust, 1965.

WILSON, FLIP: Performer. b. Newark, N.J. r.n. Clerow Wilson. Left school at 16 to join Air Force; played clubs in Fla. & Bahamas until 1965 when guest appearance on NBC began; The Flip Wilson Show debuted 1970–71 season, NBC.

PICTURE: The Fish That Saved Pittsburgh.

WILSON, NORMAN: (OBE). Editor. b. Edinburgh, Scotland. ed. The Living Cinema, formerly ed. Cinema Quarterly; assoc. ed. World Film News; author scripts for British documentaries and book Presenting Scotland: A Film Survey; attached to British Ministry of Information, World War II; ed. Film Forum, Documentary. Chmn. Edinburgh Film Guild, Edinburgh International Film Festival, 1947–60; Films of Scotland Com.; Governor, Brit. Film Inst.

WILSON, RICHARD: Producer, director. b. McKeesport, Pa., Dec. 25, 1915. e. Denver U. actor, announcer, Denver radio stations; radio actor, N.Y.; actor, asst. stage mgr., stage mgr., prod. asst. with Mercury Theatre, 1937–38; mgr., prod., summer theatres, 1939–40; assoc. with all Orson Welles films & radio shows to 1951; U.S. Air Force, 1942–45; assoc., prod., then prod., U-I.

PICTURES INCLUDE: assoc. prod., Lady from Shanghai, Macbeth, Ma and Pa Kettle on Vacation, Ma and Pa Kettle Go to Waikiki, Redhead from Wyoming; prod., Ma and Pa Kettle at Home, Golden Blade, Man with a Gun, Kettles in the Ozarks; dir. The Big Boodle; co-writer, dir. Man with a Gun; co-writer, dir., Raw Wind in Eden; dir., Al Capone; collab. s.p., dir. Invitation to a Gunfighter, Three in the Attic (prod.-dir.).

WILSON, SCOTT: Actor. b. Atlanta, Ga., 1942. Was college athlete on basketball scholarship when injured and had to leave school. Moved to L.A. and enrolled in local acting class. Made film debut, In Cold Blood, 1968.

PICTURES INCLUDE: The Grissom Gang, The Gypsy Moths, Castle Keep, In the Heat of the Night, The New Centurions, Lolly-Madonna XXX, The Great Gatsby.

WILSON, WARREN: Writer, producer. b. Boston, Mass., May 11, 1909. On stage under name Warren Burke. Began writing for screen 1941; screenplay Blondie Goes to College, Col. in 1942; Tanks a Million, UA; Sing Your Worries Away, RKO; Helzapoppin, Strictly in the Groove.

PICTURES INCLUDE: (collab., s.p.) She Gets Her Man; (story, prod.) Her Lucky Night; (collab. s.p.) If You Knew Susie; (org. s.p.) Square Dance Katy; (s.p.) Big Timber.

WINCHELL, PAUL: Performer. b. New York, N.Y., 1924. e. School of Industrial Arts. At 13 won first prize Major Bowes Radio Amateur Hour; signed by Ted Weems; created Jerry Mahoney when 17; ventriloquist & star own Paul Winchell-Jerry Mahoney show, NBC-TV.

WINDSOR, MARIE: Actress. b. Maryvale, Utah, Dec. 11, 1924. r.n. Emily Marie Bertelson. Winner of beauty contests, including Miss Utah. Worked as telephone girl, dancing teacher. Trained for acting by Maria Ouspenskaya.
PICTURES INCLUDE: Song of the Thin Man, Force of Evil, Dakota Lil, Little Big Horn, The Narrow Margin, The Eddie Cantor Story, The Bounty Hunter, Swamp Woman, The Killing, The Story of Mankind, Critics Choice, Mail Order Bride, Chamber of Horrors, Support Your Local Gunfighter, One More Train To Rob, Cahill, U.S. Marshall, The Outfit, Freaky Friday.

WINELAND, LLOYD G.: Theatre Executive. b. Washington, D.C., 1917. e. George Washington Univ. (A.B.), 1937. Pres., Wineland Theatres. Bd. mbr., TOA, 1962066; on bd. of NATO of Metropolitan D.C., 1939–81. Circuit owns and operates four Maryland drive-ins and triple indoor cinema.

WINITSKY, ALEX: Producer. In partnership as attorneys in L.A. for 20 years with Arlene Sellers before they turned to financing and later production of films.
PICTURES INCLUDE: (co-prod. with Winitsky) End of the Game, The Seven-Per-Cent Solution, Cross of Iron, Night Calls, Silver Bears, Cuba.

WINKLER, HENRY: Actor. b. New York City, Oct. 30, 1946. e. Emerson College, Yale School of Drama. Appeared with Yale Reportory Co.; returned to N.Y. to work in radio. Did 30 TV commercials before starring in The Great American Dream Machine and Masquerade on TV.
PICTURES INCLUDE: The Lords of Flatbush (debut), Crazy Joe, Heroes, The One and Only.
TV: The Mary Tyler Moore Show, The Bob Newhart Show, The Paul Sand Show, Rhoda, Happy Days (regular), Laverne & Shirley. Movie: Katherine.

WINKLER, IRWIN: Producer. b. N.Y.C. e. N.Y. Univ. With I. Robert Chartoff formed production co., Chartoff-Winkler Prods. All films co-produced with Chartoff.
PICTURES INCLUDE: Double Trouble, Point Blank, The Split, They Shoot Horses, Don't They?, The Strawberry Statement, Leo The Last, Believe in Me, The Gang That Couldn't Shoot Straight, The New Centurions, Up the Sandbox, The Mechanic, Busting, SPY's, The Gambler, Breakout, Rocky, Nickelodeon, New York, New York, Valentino, Comes a Horseman, Uncle Joe Shannon, Raging Bull.

WINNER, MICHAEL: Producer, director, writer. b. London, Eng. 1935. e. Cambridge U.; ent. m.p. ind. as columnist, dir., Drummer Films.
TV: White Hunter series, Dick and the Duchess series.
PICTURES INCLUDE: orig. s.p., Man With A Gun; prod. dir., writ., Shoot to Kill, Swiss Holiday, Climb Up the Wall, Out of the Shadow, Some Like it Cool, Girls, Girls, Girls, It's Magic, Behave Yourself; formed, Scimitar Films; prod. dir., Haunted England, Play It Cool, The Mikado; dir., West 11; co-prod., dir., The System; co-author, dir. You Must Be Joking; co-prod. author. dir. The Jokers; prod. dir. I'll Never Forget What's 'Is Name; prod. dir., Hannibal Brooks, co-prod. dir., The Games prod, dir. Lawman, prod. dir., The Nightcomers, Chato's Land; dir. The Mechanic, Scorpio, The Stone Killer 1973, Death Wish, (prod. dir.), 1974 Won Ton Ton, The Dog That Saved Hollywood (prod., dir.), 1975. Prod. dir. The Sentinel, 1976, The Big Sleep, 1977; Firepower, 1978.

WINSTEN, ARCHER: Motion picture critic, New York Post. b. Seattle, Wash., September 18, 1904; p Harry J. Winsten and Nell Archer. e. Princeton University, 1926. Varied newspaper experience before joining New York Post as columnist 1933; present post, 1936; ski ed., N.Y. Post since 1942.

WINTERS, DEBORAH: Actress. b. Los Angeles. e. Professional Children's School, New York City, began studying acting with Stella Adler at age 13. Acting debut at age six in TV Commercials.
CREDITS: Me, Natalie, Hail Hero!, The People Next Door, Kotch, The People Next Door (TV production) Class of '44.

WINTERS, DAVID: Choreographer, actor, director. b. London, April 5. Acted in both Broadway and m.p. version of West Side Story. Directed and acted in number of TV shows. Choreography credits include films Viva Las Vegas, Billie, Send Me No Flowers, Tickle Me, Pajama Party, Girl Happy, The Swinger, Made in Paris, Easy Come, Easy Go, Was choreographer for TV series Hullabaloo and Steve Allen Show, and several TV specials.

WINTERS, JERRY: Producer, director. b. Waterbury, Conn., Aug. 18, 1917. e. Antioch College, B.A., 1940. Photog., 1940–42; U.S. Air Force, 1942–46; photog., Hollywood, 1946–47; prod. assoc. Tonight on Broadway, CBS-TV, 1949; assoc. prod., College Bowl, ABC-TV, 1950–51; in charge N.Y. film prod., Television Varieties, Inc., 1951–54; Production head Eldorado Int'l Pictures Corp., 1964–67; vice president, Edutornics Corp., 1968; pres. Giralda Pros., 1971.

PICTURES INCLUDE: prod., Renoir; prod.-dir., Herman Melville's Moby Dick, Speak to Me Child; prod; English version, The Loves of Liszt.

WINTERS, JONATHAN: Performer. b. Dayton, Ohio, Nov. 11, 1925. e. Kenyon College. Disc jockey, Dayton and Columbus stations; night club comedian.
TV: And Here's the Show, Columbus—TV, NBC Comedy Hour, Jonathan Winters Show, NBC-TV.
PICTURES INCLUDE: It's A Mad, Mad, Mad, Mad World, The Loved One, Viva Max, The Fish That Saved Pittsburgh.

WINTERS, RICHARD J.: Executive. b. New York City, Oct. 3, 1928. e. Columbia Univ. Started in film industry in 1952 in pub. dep't., RKO Pictures; joined 20th-Fox in 1954 in pub. dept, first as nat'l. mag. contact then dir. of special events; went to MGM 1957 as nat'l. mag. contact, named N.Y. mag. mgr., 1959; nat'l. pub. dir., 1961.; in 1969 named nat'l. pub. dir. for Columbia Pictures. Worked on production pub. assignments for MGM and Paramount in 1972. Named nat'l. dir. adv.-pub.-prom., Paramount TV, 1973; promoted to exec. dir. adv./pub./promo., 1977.

WINTERS, ROLAND: Actor. b. Boston, Mass., Nov. 22, 1905. Appeared on stage and in stock, 1923–33; numerous radio programs, 1933–47. On screen in 13 Rue Madaleine, Return of October. Starred as Charlie Chan in pictures for Monogram.
PICTURES INCLUDE: West Point Story, Follow the Sun, Inside Straight, She's Working Her Way Through College, Jet Pilot, So Big.

WINTERS, SHELLEY: Actress. r.n. Shirley Schrift. b. St. Louis, Mo., Aug. 18, 1922. e. Wayne U. Clerked in 5 & 10 cent store; in vaudeville; on dramatic stage (Conquest, Night Before Christmas, Meet the People, Rosalinda, etc.). On screen 1944 in Nine Girls, Sailor's Holiday. N.Y. stage; A Hatful of Rain, Girls of Sumer, Minnie's Boys.
PICTURES INCLUDE: Double Life, Cry of the City, Larceny, Take one False Step, Johnny Stool Pigeon, Great Gatsby, South Sea Sinner, Winchester '73, Place in the Sun, Untamed Frontier, My Man and I, Tennessee Champ, Executive Suite, Saskatchewan, Playgirl, Mambo, Night of the Hunter, I Am a Camera, Big Knife, Treasure of Pancho Villa, I Died a Thousand Times, Cash on Delivery, Diary of Anne Frank, Young Savages, Lolita, Chapman Report, A House is Not a Home, A Patch of Blue, Alfie, Enter Laughing, The Scalphunters, Wild in the Streets, Buena Sera Mrs. Campbell, The Mad Room, Bloody Mama, What's the Matter with Helen?, The Poseidon Adventure, Cleopatra Jones, Something To Hide, Blume in Love, Diamonds, Next Stop Greenwich Village, The Tenant, Pete's Dragon, City on Fire, "S.O.B."

WINTMAN, MELVIN R.: Theatre Executive. b. Chelsea, Mass., June 28, 1918. e. Univ. of Mass., Northeastern Univ. (degree of juris doctor). Major, infantry, AUS, World War II. Attorney. Now exec. v.p. & dir. General Cinema Corp., Boston, pres. & dir. GCC Theatres, Inc., Boston, dir. Will Rogers Memorial Fund. Former pres. Theatre Owners of New England (1969–70); past dir. NATO (1969–70); treas., Nat'l Assoc. of Concessionaires (1960).

WISBERG, AUBREY: Writer, producer, director. b. London, Eng., Oct. 20; e. Columbia U. Newspaper writer, radio, TV dramatist U.S. Eng., Australia, radio diffusionist, Paris, France. Author novels Bushman at Large, Patrol Boat 999, This Is the Life; plays Virtue, Inc., Whiphand.
PICTURES INCLUDE: s.p., prod. The Man From Planet X, Captive Women, Sword of Venus, The Neanderthal Man, Capt. John Smith & Pocahontas, Problem Girls, Dragon's Gold, Capt. Kidd & the Slave Girl, Return to Treasure Island, Murder is My Beat, The Women of Pitcairn Island, Port Sinister, Submarine Raider, Counter Espionage, Escape in the Fog, U-Boat Prisoner, Power of the Whistler, Adventures of Rusty, After Midnight, The Wreck of the Hesperus, The Big Fix, Betrayal from the East. The Falcon's Adventure, Son of Sinbad, At Swords Point, Hit Parade, They Came to Blow Up America, Bombers Moon, Rendezvous 24, The Lady in the Iron Mask, The Steel Lady, Treasure of Monte Cristo, Road to the Big House, The Burning Cross, St. Montana Mike, Casanova's Big Night, So Dark the Night, The Desert Hawk, s.p. Just Before Dawn, Out of the Depths, Target Minus Forty, Mission Mars, Ride the Wild Wind, Hercules in N.Y., Evil in the Blood.

WISDOM, NORMAN: Actor, singer, comedian. Musical and legit. b. London, Eng. Many London West End Stage shows including Royal Command Performances. New York Broadway shows include Walking Happy and Not Now Darling. Two Broadway awards. Films include Trouble in Store (Academy Award) and 19 others mostly for the Rank Organization and United Artists. Latest American film, The Night They Raided Minsky's.

WISE, ROBERT: Producer, director. b. Winchester, Ind., Sept. 10, 1914; e. Franklin Coll., Franklin, Ind. No prior bus. experience. Ent. m.p. ind. in cutting dept. RKO, 1933; sound cutter, asst. ed.,; film ed., 1939; dir., 1943; to 20th-Century-

Fox, 1949; ass'n. Mirisch Co. independent prod. 1959; assn. MGM independent prod., 1962; assn. 20th Century Fox Independent Prod. 1963. Partner, Filmakers Group, The Tripar Group.

PICTURES INCLUDE: The Body Snatchers, Blood on the Moon, The Set Up, Day the Earth Stood Still, Captive City, So Big, Executive Suite, Helen of Troy, Tribute to a Bad Man, Somebody Up There Likes Me, Until They Sail, Run Silent Run Deep, I Want to Live, Odds Against Tomorrow, West Side Story, Two For the Seesaw, The Haunting, The Sound of Music, The Sand Pebbles, Star!, The Andromeda Strain, Two People, The Hindenburg, Audrey Rose, Star Trek.

WISEMAN, JOSEPH: Actor. b. Montreal, Canada. Began acting in the thirties, including Bdwy. stage, radio, m.p. and later TV.

PICTURES INCLUDE: Viva Zapata, Les Miserables, The Silver Chalice, The Garment Jungle, Dr. No, Bye Bye Braverman, The Night They Raided Minsky's The Valachi Papers, The Apprenticeship of Duddy Kravitz, The Betsy.

STAGE: King Lear, Golden Boy, The Diary of Anne Frank, Uncle Vanya, The Last Analysis, Enemies, etc.

WITHERS, GOOGIE: Actress. b. Karachi, India, Mar. 12, 1917. Trained as a dancer under Italia Conti, Helena Lehmiski & Buddy Bradley; stage debut Victoria Palace in Windmill Man, 1929. Best Actress Award, Deep Blue Sea, 1954. Began screen career at 18. TV also. Theatrical tours Australia, Sun Award, Best Actress, 1974.

PICTURES INCLUDE: Traveler's Joy, Night and the City, White Corridors, Derby Day, Devil on Horseback, Safe Harbor, Nickel Queen.

STAGE: (Britain) Winter Journey, Deep Blue Sea, Hamlet, Much Ado About Nothing. (Australian) Plaza Suite, Relatively Speaking, Beckman Place, Woman in a Dressing Gown, The Constant Wife, First Four Hundred Years, Roar Like a Dove, The Cherry Orchard, An Ideal Husband. (London) Getting Married, Exit the King. (New York) The Complaisant Lover. Chichester Festival Theatre and Haymarket, London, in The Circle, The Kingfisher, Importance of Being Earnest.

TV: Series, Within These Walls.

WITHERS, JANE: Actress. b. Atlanta, Ga. By 1934 attracted attention as child player on screen, after radio appearance in Los Angeles and experimental pictures parts, in 1934 in Fox production Bright Eyes, Ginger; thereafter to 1942 featured or starred in numerous 20th-Fox prod. Voted Money-Making Star M.P. Herald-Fame Poll 1937, 1938.

PICTURES INCLUDE: North Star, Johnny Doughboy, My Best Gal, Faces in the Fog, Dangerous Partners, Affairs of Geraldine, Danger Street, Giant, The Right Approach, Captain Newman.

WIZAN, JOE: Producer. Started in industry as agent for William Morris Agency. Left to form London Intl. Artists, Ltd. in association with Richard Gregson, Alan Ladd, Jr. and Mike Gruskoff. When firm dissolved joined Creative Management Associates as v.p. in chg. of creative services. In 1969 formed own indep. prod. co. 1981, named pres., CBS Theatrical Film Div.

PICTURES: Jeremiah Johnson, Junion Bonner, Prime Cut, The Last American Hero, Audrey Rose, Voices, And Justice for All.

WIZEMAN, JR. DONALD G.: Executive. b. Fort Smith, Ark., Nov. 17, 1944. e. Old Dominion Univ. Formed Wizeman & Associates, Ltd. Advertising Agency and Artus Specialty Company in 1967; is pres. of both. In 1971 formed Filmakers, Ltd. which also heads.

PICTURES INCLUDE: Moonchild (exec. prod.), Come Out of the Bathroom Hannibal Fry (exec. prod.).

WOLCOTT, JAMES L.: Executive. b. Wilmington, Del. e. Williams Coll., Harvard Bus. Sch.; Wilmington Trust Co., banking dept.; Fox Film Corp. New York legal dept.; Fox Movietonews cutter, asst. ed. short subjects dept.; Fox Film Corp. publicity dept.; deLuxe Lab.; 10th Century-Fox Studios asst. dir., head of test dept.; March of Time prod. mgr., ed. board; Audience Research, Inc. v.p. and gen. mgr.; Pathe Laboratories, Inc. sales v.p., exec. v.p. and director; Pathecolor, Inc. pres. and director; Transamerica Releasing Corp. pres. and director; Dorado Int'l Corp. pres. and director; James Wolcott Productions, Inc. pres. and director.

WOLF, EMANUEL, L.: Executive. b. Brooklyn, N.Y., Mar. 27, 1927. e. Syracuse U.B.A., 1950; Maxwell School, Syracuse U. M.A. 1952; Maxwell Scholar in Public Admin.- Economics; Chi Eta Sigma (Econ. Hon.). 1952–55. Management consultant, exec. office of Secretary of Navy & Dept. of Interior, Wash., D.C. 1956. National dir. of Program & Admin. of a Veterans Org. 1957–61. Pres. E. L. Wolf Associates, Washington, D.C. 1961–Jan. 1965. Treasurer, Kalvex, Inc. Dec. 1962. Director Kalvex, Inc. March 1963. Dir. Allied Artists Pictures Corp. Jan. 1965. Pres. Kalvex, Inc. April 1966–present, pres. & chmn. of the Bd. Kalvex, Inc.; Chmn. of the Bd. Vitabath, Inc.; Chmn. of the

Bd. Lexington Instruments; pres. & chairman of the Bd. Pharmaceutical Savings Plan, Inc. Syracuse U. Corporate Advisory Board, American Committee for the Weizmann Institute of Science (Bd. of Directors). Pres. and Chmn. of Bd., Allied Artists Pictures Corp: January, 1976: pres., bd. chm. & chief executive officer of Allied Artists Industries Inc., created by Merger of Allied Artists Pictures Corp., Kalvex Inc. and PSP, Inc.

WOLF, HERBERT: Producer. b. New York, N.Y., July 11, 1917. e. N.Y.U., 1937. Radio & TV prod. Wolf Presentations, Inc. TV: (N.Y.) Masquerade Party, Break the Bank, Hold That Note, Keep Talking, Window Shopping.

WOLF, THOMAS HOWARD: TV news exec. b. New York, N.Y., April 22, 1916; e. Princeton, B.A., magna cum laude, 1937. Time & Life Mag. 1937–39; 1937–39 NEA (Scripps-Howard) 1940–46; European mgr., NEA, 1942–46. War correspondent, ETO, MTO) NBC radio correspondent, Paris, 1944–45; co-owner, pres., Information Prod., Inc. founded 1951; co-owner, chairman. Butterfield & Wolf, Inc. founded 1959; prod. CBS series. Tomorrow, 1960; exec. prod., CBS daily live Calendar Show, 1961–62; senior prod., ABC News Report, 1963; exec. prod., ABC Scope, 1964–66. v.p. dir. of TV Documentaries, 1966; v.p., dir. of TV Public Affairs, 1974; dir. TV Cultural Affairs, 1976.

WOLFF, LOTHAR: Producer, director, president: Lothar Wolff Productions Inc. b. Bromberg, Ger. Asst. prod., March of Time. WWII; Officer in Charge, U.S. Coast Guard M.P. section; head, Marshall Plan film section, Paris, 1949–50; M.P. advisor to Indonesian Govt. 1953–55; v.p. & prod., Louis de Rochemont Assoc.; prod. & co-author, Martin Luther, produced: Question Seven, 3 half hour Planet Earth Films (Natl Academy of Sciences), Fortress of Peace (Swiss Govt. Cinerama); assoc. prod. Lost Boundaries, Walk East on Beacon, Windjammer, Roman Spring of Mrs. Stone. Series executive producer for Time-Life Films (The World We Live In; Other people, Other Places; Wild, Wild World of Animals). 1976–77: Consultant Eductl. Film Division, Natl. Geographic; Editorial Director, I Sought my Brother, Harvard U./WQED; Producer, The Joy of Bach, Luthern Film Associates, a 90-minute special.

WOLFSON, MITCHELL: Executive. b. Key West, Fla., Sept. 13, 1900. Ent. m.p. ind. as exhibitor, Miami, 1924; later co-owner Wometco Circuit; bd. chm. & pres. Wometco Ent. Inc.; TV stations. WTVJ Miami: WLOS-TV, Asheville, N.C.; WLOS-FM, Asheville, KVOS-TV, Bellingham, Wash.; KVOS-TV (BC) Ltc., Vancouver, B.C.; Seaquarium, Miami; bottling: Coca Cola and WZZM-TV, Grand Rapids, Mich., WWHT, Newark, N.J.; STV and CATV. Automatic vending firms. Founder, Audubon House, Key West, 1939 elected City Councilman, Miami Beach; 1943 Mayor; bd. chm.; chm. City of Miami Off-Street Parking Board; in 1949 chmn. TOA TV comm. Clubs; Rotary, Elks, Shriners, Lt. Col. U.S. Army, WW II; trustee Mt. Sinai Hospital; LL.D., U. of Miami; bd. chm., Financial Federal Savings & Loan Assn.; director and member, executive board, National Association of Theatre Owners; mem. Variety Club.

WOLFSON, RICHARD: Executive. b. New York City, Jan. 7, 1923. e. Harvard Coll. Yale Law School, 1945–47, law sect'y to Justice Wiley Rutledge, U.S. Supreme Court; law instructor at NYU Law School; later received Guggenheim Fellowship; 1952, joined Wometco Ent. as counsel and asst. to pres.; named v.p. and dir. in 1959 and senior v.p. in 1962; named exec. v.p. and general counsel in 1973; named chmn., exec. comm., 1976; co-author of Jurisdiction of the Supreme Court of the United States and author of articles in various legal publications.

WOLPER, DAVID L.: Executive. b. New York, N.Y., Jan. 11, 1928. e. Drake U., U. of So. Calif., Treas., Flamingo Films, 1948; merged with Associated Artist to form M.P. for TV, Inc., acting as v.p. in chge of West Coast oper., 1950; v.p. reactivated Flamingo Films, 1954; also pres. Harris-Wolper Pictures, Inc.; pres. Wolper Prod. 1958; pres. Dawn Prod.; v.p. Bd. Dir. Metromedia, 1965; pres. Wolper Pictures Ltd. 1967; ch. of bd. Wolper Prod., Inc., 1967; pres. Wolper Pictures, 1968; pres. Wolper Productions, 1970; pres. & ch. of bd. of dir. The Wolper Organization, Inc., 1971; married Gloria Diane Hill, July 11, 1974.

TV & M.P.: The Race For Space, 1958; Story of . . . series, 1962–63; Biography series, 1962–63; Hollywood and the Stars series, 1963–64; The Making of the President, 1960, 1964, 1968; Men in Crisis series, 1964; Four Days in November feature, 1965; National Geographic Society Specials, 1965–68, 1971–75; The March of Time series, 1965–66; The Rise and Fall of the Third Reich, 1967–68; The Undersea World of Jacques Cousteau, 1967–68; If It's Tuesday, This Must Be Belgium feature, 1968; Plimpton specials, 1970–72; Say Goodbye, 1971; Willy Wonka and the Chocolate Factory feature, 1971; Appointment With Destiny series, 1971–73; Visions of Eight feature, 1973; American Heritage specials, 1973–74; Primal Man specials, 1973–75; Get Christie Love! series, 1974; Judgment specials, 1974; Birds Do It, Bees Do It feature, 1974; Chico and the Man series, 1974–; Smithsonian Specials, 1974–;

Sandburg's Lincoln, 1974–76; Welcome Back, Kotter series, 1975–.

WOOD, NATALIE: Actress. b. San Francisco, Calif., 1938. p. father, noted designer, set decorator, Hollywood studios; mother, ballet dancer. Screen debut: Tomorrow is Forever.
PICTURES INCLUDE: Ghost and Mrs. Muir, Miracle on 34th Street, Driftwood, Bride Wore Boots, Green Promise, One Desire, Scudda-Hoo ScuddaHay; Chicken Every Sunday, Father Was a Fullback, No Sad Songs for Me, Jackpot, Never a Dull Moment, Our Very Own, Blue Veil, Just for Your, The Star, Rebel Without a Cause, Cry in the Night, The Searchers, Burning Hills, Girl He Left Behind, Bombers B-52, Marjorie Morningstar, Kings Go Forth, Cash McCall, Splendor in the Grass, West Side Story, Gypsy, Love with a Proper Stranger, Sex and the Single Girl, Inside Daisy Clover, This Property is Condemned, Penelope, Bob and Carol and Ted and Alice, Peeper, Meteor, The Last Married Couple in America.
TV: Cat on a Hot Tin Roof.

WOODHAM-SMITH, GEORGE IVON: Solicitor. b. London, England, Dec. 20, 1895. 1st Lt., Machine Gun Corps., Brit. Army, World War I, studied law; also journalist. Since 1928 partner in Richards Butler & Co., London law firm. In charge of legal work for the Rank Org.

WOODLAND, NORMAN: Actor. b. Dusseldorf, Germany, March 16, 1910; e. Edward VI School. Stratford-on-Avon. Spent several years in repertory cos.; joined BBC 1939 and spent 6 yrs. as commentator; stage career largely assoc. with Shakespearean and classical plays; TV appearances; screen debut in Hamlet.
PICTURES INCLUDE: Escape, I Know You, All Over the Town, Background, Romeo and Juliet, Master Plan, Richard III, Teenage Daughter, Guilty, No Road Back, The Bandit, Rough and the Smooth.

WOODS, DONALD: Actor.
PICTURES INCLUDE: Watch on the Rhine, Roughly Speaking, 13 Ghosts, Kissin' Cousins, Moment to Moment, A Time to Sing.
STAGE: Two for the Seesaw, L.A., 1961; Rosmersholm, NYC, 1962; One by One, NYC, 1964; Soldier, You Can't Take It With You, Chicago, 1969; Twelfth Night, Assasination 1865, Chicago, 1969–71.
TV: G.E. Theatre, Wagon Train, Thrillers, Sunset Strip, Ben Casey, Laramie, The Rebel, The Law and Mr. Jones, The Roaring 20's, Wild Wild West, Bonanza.

WOODWARD, EDWARD: O.B.E. Actor, Singer. b. Croydon, England. LPs. 1 Gold Disc.
TV: Sword of Honour, Callan series. Over 300 TV plays latest: Bassplayer and Blonde, Saturday, Sunday, Monday, and 1990 series. Television Actor of the Year, 1969–70; also Sun Award Best Actor 1970, 71, 72.
PICTURES INCLUDE: Becket, File on the Golden Goose, Murders in the Rue Morgue, Julius Caesar, The Listener, Young Winston, Sitting Target, Hunted, Wicker Man, Callan, Stand Up Virgin Soldiers, Breaker Morant.
THEATRE: 16 West End Plays and Musicals. Latest: On Approval.

WOODWARD, JOANNE: Actress. b. Thomasville, Ga., Feb. 27; e. La. State U. Studied at Neighborhood Playhouse Dramatic Sch. m. Paul Newman, N.Y.; appeared in many TV dramatic shows; on B'way in Picnic; m.p. debut in Count Three and Pray.
PICTURES INCLUDE: Kiss Before Dying, Three Faces of Eve (Academy Award 1957, best actress); Long Hot Summer, No Down Payment, Rally Round the Flag Boys, The Sound and the Fury, From the Terrace, Fugitive Kind, Paris Blues, The Stripper, A New Kind of Love, Signpost to Murder, A Big Hand for the Little Lady, Rachel, Rachel (Acad. Award nom.); Winning, USA, The Effect of Gamma Rays on Man-in-the-Moon Marigolds, Summer Wishes, Winter Dreams, The Drowning Pool, The End.
TV: Sybil, See How She Runs.

WOODY, CHESTER F.: Actor. b. Zoar Valley, Colo., Aug. 13, 1934; e. U. of Colo. Writer, stories, songs, lyrics used on radio, TV.
PICTURES INCLUDE: The Glenn Miller Story, The Mob, Monsters of the Deep, Hit the Deck, The Rangers, The Big Circus, Gangland, Adventure Is our Destiny, Freed, Distant Field Are Greener, And Now My Love, Murder at Midnight, The Queen's Guard, Look Back and Cry.

WOOLF, JOHN: Chairman Romulus Films, Ltd. Man. dir. British and American Film Holdings. Exec. dir., Anglia Television Ltd. Mem. Cinematograph Films Council. Bd. of man. Services Kinema Corp.
PICTURES INCLUDE: Pandora and the Flying Dutchman, African Queen, Moulin Rouge, Beat the Devil, Carrington V.C., I am a Camera, Sailor Beware, Three Men in a Boat, The Story of Esther Costello, Room at the Top, The L-Shaped Room, Life At The Top, Oliver! (Oscar for best film 1969), The Day of the Jackal, The Odessa File.

WOOLNER, LAWRENCE H.: Executive. b. St. Louis, Mo. e. Fairfax High School, L.A. After discharged from U.S. Army at end of World War II started drive-in theatre in New Orleans. Formed Woolner Bros. Pictures there in 1955. Later moved to Hollywood, entering distribution and production as Woolner Bros. Pictures. In 1970 started New World Pictures as pres. in chg. sales, dist. In 1971 started own company, Dimension Pictures.

WORKER, ADRIAN: Producer. b. Kempston, England, 1916. e. public school. Bedford. Early career as accountant; joined Rank Organization, then prod. sup. Highbury Studios; studio man., Islington studios; freelance prod. man. 1949.
PICTURES INCLUDE: Another Man's Poison, Mr. Drake's Duck. Joined Warwick on formation 1952. Prod. sup. Red Beret (Paratrooper), Hell Below Zero, The Black Knight, Prize of Gold; prod., Safari, Beyond Mombasa. Formed Zonic Prod. 1956; prod. Naked Earth, Intent to Kill; assoc. prod. Danger Within, I'm All Right Jack; man. dir. Shepperton Studios, 1959; 1976, prod. Fern, the Red Deer for Children's Film Foundation; 1978, Kidnapped (TV series).

WORMSER, IRVING: Executive. b. Feb. 1, 1900. Booking, sales, Pathe Films, 1916–24; state right operation, 1924–30; Columbia Pict. sales, 1930–44; eastern sales mgr., Film Classics. 1944–46; exec. sales, gen. sales mgr., Columbia, 1946–54; co-owner, St. Cloud circuit, 1949–55; v.p. gen. sales mgr., Dist. Corp. of Amer., 1954–58; pres. Continetal Dist. Inc., 1958–66; prod. rep. for Palomar Pictures; now v.p.-tres. of both U.M. Film Distributors and Peppercorn-Wormser.

WORMSER, RICHARD: Writer. b. New York, N.Y., Jan. 30, 1908. e. Princeton U. Publicist. 1927–32; fiction writer, Street & Smith, 1932–34; freelance fiction writer, 1934–41; forest officer. U.S. Forest Service. 1941–45; then free lance m.p.; magazine writer; novels include Pass through Manhattan, Lonesome Quarter, Road to Carmichael's.
PICTURES INCLUDE: s.p., In Self Defense; collab. orig., The Showdown; orig. s.p. Fort Dodge Stampede.

WORTH, IRENE: Actress. b. 1916. Bdwy. debut in The Two Mrs. Carrolls, after which went to London where made her home. Appeared with Old Vic and Royal Shakespeare Co.; returned to U.S. to appear on Bdwy. in the Cocktail Party, Toys in the Attic, Sweet Bird of Youth, Cherry Orchard; etc.
PICTURES: Orders to Kill (British AA as best actress), King Lear, Nicholas and Alexander, Rich Kids, Eyewitness.
TELEVISION: The Lady from the Sea, The Duchess of Malfi, The Way of the World, Prince Orestes, etc.

WOWCHUK, HARRY N.: Actor, Writer, Photographer, Producer, Executive. b. Phila. Pa. Oct. 16, 1948. e. Santa Monica City College, U.C.L.A. Theater Arts, 1970. Started film career as actor, stunt-driver-photographer. T.V. and commercial credits include: Warner Bros.; Columbia Records; R.C.A.; Playboy Magazine; T.V. Guide; Seal Test; Camel Cigarettes; Miller High Life; American Motors; Camera V; A&W Rootbeer; Harold Robbins Productions. Former exec. v.p. International Cinema, in charge of prod. and distribution; V.P. J. Newport Film Productions; pres., United West Productions.
PICTURES INCLUDE: The Lost Dutchman, Las Vegas Lady, This Is A Hijack, Tidal Wave, Tunnel Vision, Incredible 2-Headed Transplant, Jud, Bad Charleston Charlie, Some Call It Loving, Summer School Teachers, Five Minutes of Freedom, Pushing Up Daisies, Money-Marbles-Chalk, The Models, Love Swedish Style, Up-Down-Up, Sunday's Child, Soul Brothers, Freedom Riders, Perilous Journey, Claws of Death, Georgia Peaches.

WOWCHUK, NICHOLAS: Executive, Producer, Writer, Editor, Financier. b. Philadelphia, Pa. e. St. Basil's College, U.C.L.A. Founder-publisher: All-American Athlete Magazine; Sports and Health Digest; The Spectator. Former sports writer: Phila. Evening Public Ledger; Phila. Daily Record; Phila. Inquirer. Founder & board chairman: Mutual Realty Investment Co.; Mutual Mortgage Co., Beverly Hills, Calif. President: Mutual General Films, Bev. Hills, Calif.; Abbey Theatrical Films, N.Y.C.; Mutual Film Distribution Co.; Mutual Recording & Broadcasting Enterprises.
PICTURES INCLUDE: Exec. Prod.: Perilous Journey; Incredible 2-Headed Transplant, Pushing Up Daisies; Money-Marbles-Chalk; Five Minutes Of Freedom; The Campaign; Claws of Death. Prod.: Scorpion's Web; Pursuit; Brave Men; Sea of Despair; The Hetman; Cossack's In Battle; The Straight White Line; Tilt, Rooster, To Live . . . You Gotta Win.

WRATHER, JACK: Producer. b. Amarillo, Texas, May 24, 1918; e. U. of Texas; m. Bonita Granville, actress. Oil producer since 1938. During WW II, U.S. Marine Corps. Producer Jack Wrather Productions, Inc. & Freedom Prod.
PICTURES INCLUDE: The Guilty, High Tide, Perilous Waters, Strike It Rich, Guilty of Treason, Lone Ranger, The Magic of Lassie, The Legend of the Lone Ranger. co-owner: KFMB-TV, San Diego; KERO-TV, Bakersfield, Calif.;

Muzak Corp.; pres. Lone Ranger, Television, Inc., Lassie Television, Inc., Sergeant Preston of the Yukon; owner Disneyland Hotel. pres., Wrather Corp. Director, Tele-PromTer. Chm. of board, Wrather Entertainment Intl. Director, Continental Airlines.

WRAY, FAY: Actress. b. Alberta, Canada, Sept. 10, 1907. m. Robert Riskin, writer. On stage in Pilgrimage Play, Hollywood, 1923; m.p. debut in Gasoline Love; thereafter in many m.p. for Paramount to 1930; then in films for various Hollywood and Brit. prod.
PICTURES INCLUDE: Small Town Girl, Treasure of the Golden Condor, Rock Pretty Baby, Tammy, Out of Time.
TV: Pride of the Family, ABC-TV.

WRIGHT, BASIL: Producer and direcor. b. London, June 12, 1907. Educated at Sherborne school, Corpus Christi College, Cambridge. Assistant, 1929, to John Grierson and was associated with him in creation of "documentary" film in England.
PICTURES INCLUDE: The Country Comes to Town, O'er Hill and Dale, Windmill in Barbadoes, Cargo from Jamaica, and Liner Cruising South for Empire Marketing Bd. in 1931–33. In 1934 made The Song of Ceylon and awarded First Prize and Prix de Gouvernement at Brussels Film Festival in 1935. With Henry Watt directed Night Mall for GPO Film Unit, under prod. of John Grierson. In 1937 founded Realist Film Unit. Exec. prod., Film Centre, Ltd., 1939–44. In 1945, prod. in chge, Crown Film Unit. In 1946 adv. to Dir. Gen. of M.O.I.; prod. dir. Waters & Time for Festival of Britain, 1950–51; made World Without End for Unesco. 1953: with Gladys Wright prod. The Immortal Land and Greek Sculpture; prod. dir. A Place for Gold, 1960, 1962–68 Lecturer at U. of C., Los Angeles, 1975 Guest of Honour Melbourne Film Festival; 1975–76 Lecture Tour USA, Canada. 1977–78 Visiting Lecturer Temple Univ., Philadelphia.

WRIGHT, TERESA: Actress. b. New York City, Oct. 27, 1918. m. Divorced from Niven Busch and Robert Anderson. Ent. m.p. 1941, The Little Foxes, Goldwyn-RKO. In 1942: Pride of the Yankees, Goldwyn-RKO, Mrs. Miniver, MGM Acad. Award 1942 supporting role (Mrs. Miniver).
PICTURES INCLUDE: Shadow of a Doubt, Casanova Brown, Best Years of Our Lives, Trouble with Women, Pursued, Imperfect Lady, Enchantment, The Capture, The Men, Something to Live For, California Conquest, Steel Trap, Count the Hours, The Actress, Track of the Cat, Hail Hero, The Happy Ending, Roseland, Somewhere in Time.
STAGE: Tours: Mary, Mary, Tchin-Tchin, The Effect of Gamma Rays on Man-in-the-Moon Marigolds, Noel Coward in Two Keys, The Master Builder. Regional Theatre: Long Days, Journey into Night, You Can't Take It With You, All The Way Home. New York: Life with Father, Dark at the Top of the Stairs, I Never Sang for My Father, Death of a Salesman, Ah, Wilderness!, Morning's at Seven

WRIGHT, TONY: Actor. b. London, Dec. 10, 1925. Stage debut in repertory, South Africa; screen debut; Flanagan Boy, 1951.
PICTURES INCLUDE: A Toi De Jouer Callaghan, Plus De Whiskey, Pour Callaghan (France), Jumping for Joy, Jacqueline, Tiger in the Smoke, Seven Thunders, Broth of a Boy, Faces in the Dark, In the Wake of a Stranger, Journey to Nowhere, The Liquidator.
TV: Compact, Marriage Lines, No Hiding Place, The Saint, Mystery Theatre, Curtains for Sheila, Crossroads, Make Me A Widow, Wednesday's Train, Onedin Line, 6 Saints, Persuaders, The Jensen Code, Follow Me, Kidnapped.

WRIGHT, WILLIAM H.: Producer. b. Lawrenceburg, Ind., Apr. 29, 1902; e. Indiana U. Reporter, Cincinnati Post, Indianapolis Star; exploit. dept., Paramount, Columbus, Ohio, 1925; Long Island studio pub. dept, 1926; Hollywood studio, 1927; asst. to Selznick, Schulberg, others, 1931; asst. to Selznick, MGM, 1935; to Harry Cohn, Columbia, 1936; prod. asst. to Selznick, 1937; free lance writer, 1940; staff writer, MGM, 1941; prod., 1944–53; prod. Columbia, 1955; Warner Bros., 1963–64; Paramount, 1964. Trustee, M.P. & TV Fund.
PICTURES INCLUDE: Letter for Evie, Three Wise Fools, Bride Goes Wild, Act of Violence, Skipper Surprised His Wife, Black Hand, Stars in My Crown, Mrs. O'Malley and Mr. Malone, People Against O'Hara, Shadow in the Sky, Love Is Better Than Ever; co-prod. Young Man with Ideas; prod. The Clown, The Naked Spur, Dead Ringer, A Distant Trumpet; documentary, Williamsburg, The Story of a Patriot; collab. s.p., The Sons of Katie Elder.
TV: prod. Adventures of Jim Bowie, Barbara Stanwyck Theatre; co-creator, Kentucky Jones, NCB.

WUNSCH, ROBERT J.: Executive. e. Yale. Literary agent—first with Adams, Ray & Rosenberg; later with Intl. Famous Agency. Entered indep. motion picture production; co-producer of Slap Shot, and exec. producer of Defiance. Named dir. of motion pictures for TV at CBS. Left to join United Artists as v.p., production, West Coast, in June, 1979.

WYATT, JANE: Actress. b. Aug. 10, 1913, New York: e. Miss Chapin's School, Barnard College; m. Edgar B. Ward. Joined Apprentice School, Berkshire Playhouse, Stockbridge, Mass. Understudied in Tradewinds and The Vinegar Tree. Appeared in Give Me Yesterday and the Tadpole. In 1933 succeeded Margaret Sullivan in Dinner at Eight. m.p.: New York stage, The Autumn Garden, 1951; other plays, The Bishop Misbehaves, Conquest, Eveninsong, The Mad Hopes.
PICTURES INCLUDE: Great Expectations, The Navy Comes Through, The Kansan, None But the Lonely Heart, Boomerang, Gentlemen's Agreement, No Minor Vices, Bad Boy, Canadian Pacific, Pitfall, Task Force, Our Very Own, My Blue Heaven, Man Who Cheated Himself, Criminal Lawyer, Lost Horizon, Never Too Late, Treasure of Matecumbe.
TV: Father Knows Best, winner 3 Emmy Awards (6 yrs.), Bob Hope Chrysler Theater, The Virginian, Wagon Train, U.S. Steel Hour, Bell Telephone Hour, Hostess moderator, Confidential For Women, My Father My Mother. Guest star—Star Trek, Barefoot in the Park Pilot CBS-TV, The Ghost and Mrs. Muir, Here Come the Brides, Love American Style, ABC Movie of Week, Guest star, the Men of Shiloh, Alias Smith and Jones, Kraft Music Hall; co-star, Hollywood TV Theater, Katherine (guest star), Tom Sawyer; Father Knows Best Reunion, A Love Affair, Amelia Earhart, Superdome, Fantasy Island, Love Boat, The Nativity, The Millionaire.

WYMAN, JANE: Actress. r.n. Sarah Jane Fulks. b. St. Joseph, Mo., Jan. 4, 1914. In 1936: My Man Godfrey, U; Cain and Mabel, Smart Blonde, Warner. From 1937 in many Hollywood pictures. In 1942: Larceny, Inc., My Favorite Spy, Footlight Serenade. Voted one of top ten money-making stars in M.P. Herald-Fame poll 1954. TV show: Fireside Theatre.
PICTURES INCLUDE: Princess O'Rourke, Doughgirls, Make Your Own Bed, Crime by Night, Lost Weekend, One More Tomorrow, Night and Day, The Yearling, Cheyenne, Magic Town; academy award, best actress, Johnny Belinda, 1948, Three Guys Named Mike, Here Comes the Groom, Blue Veil, Just for You, Story of Will Rogers, Let's Do It Again, So Big, Magnificent Obsession, Lucy Gallant, All That Heaven Allows, Miracle in the Rain, Pollyanna, Holiday for Lovers, Bon Voyage, How to Commit Marriage.

WYMORE, PATRICE: Actress. b. Miltonvale, Kans., Dec. 17; p. James A. Wymore, oper. exhib. film delivery service throughout Kans.; ret. Began career as child performer, tent shows, county fairs, vaudeville; later, toured night clubs in middle west, own song & dance act; modelled, Chicago understudy Betty Bruce, U Up in Central Park, played role Hollywood Bowl; then, NY stage, Hold It! All For Love; radio & TV roles.
PICTURES INCLUDE: Screen debut: Tea for Two, 1950, then Rocky Mountain, I'll See You In My Dreams, Star-Lift, Big Trees, Man Behind the Gun, She's Working Her Way Through College, She's Back on Broadway, Chamber of Horrors.

WYNN, KEENAN: Actor. b. New York City, July 27, 1916. s. of Ed Wynn (died June 19, 1966). e. St. John's Military Acad. New York stage, radio stock in Skowhegan, Me.
PICTURES INCLUDE: See Here, Private Hargove, Since You Went Away, Marriage Is a Private Affair, Between Two Women, The Clock, Without Love, Week-End at the Waldorf, What Next Corporal Hargrove?, The Hucksters, B.F.'s Daughter, Three Musketeers, Neptune's Daughter, Annie Get Your Gun, Three Little Words, Royal Wedding, Kind Lady, Angela in the Outfield, Texas Carnival, Phone Call from a Stranger, Fearless Fagan, Sky Full of Moon, Desperate Search, Battle Circus, Code Two, All the Brothers Were Valiant, Kiss Me Kate, Long Long Trailer, Tennessee Champ, Men of the Fighting Lady, Glass Slipper, The Marauders, Running Wild, Man in the Gray Flannel Suit, Shack Out on 101, Johnny Concho, Great Man, Some Came Running, A Hole in the Head, King of the Roaring Twenties, Absent-Minded Professor, Warning Shot, Welcome to Hard Times, The War Wagon, Point Blank, Finian's Rainbow, McKenna's Gold, Smith, Once Upon A Time in the West, 80 Steps to Jonah, Cancel My Reservation, Pretty Maids All in a Row, The Animals, B.J. Presents, The Mechanic, Snowball Express, Wild in the Sky, Herbie Rides Again, Nashville, The Devil's Rain, The Shaggy D.A., Orca, Just Tell Me What You Want.

WYNN, MAY: Actress. r.n. Donna Lee Hickey. b. New York, Jan. 8, 1930; e. Newtown H.S., Elmhurst, L.I. Model; chorus girl, then singer, dancer; played bits in Hollywood; then The Caine Mutiny, They Rode West, Violent Men.

WYNN, TRACY KEENAN: Writer. Fourth generation of show business; son of actor Keenan Wynn; grandson of Ed Wynn; great-grandson of Frank Keenan Wynn, Irish Shakespearean actor who made Bdwy. debut in 1880.
PICTURES INCLUDE: The Longest Yard, The Deep (co. s.p.).

TV: The Glass House, Tribes, The Autobiography of Miss Jane Pittman.

WYNNE, DONALD. Production executive and writer. b. Surrey, England 1918. Early career: actor, camera prod. assistant. Ent. m.p. industry 1935; served in Army 1938–46; since prod. man., assoc. prod. Concanen, Nettlefold, Pan Productions.
PICTURES INCLUDE: Fabian of the Yard series, On Such a Night, prod. sup. Rank Screen Services. Wrote, dir. prod. for African Film Prod. in S. and E. Africa; Donald Wynne Prods. Ltd.

WYNTER, DANA: Actress. b. London, England. June 8. e. Rhodes U. On stage in London; TV appearances include Robert Montgomery Show, Suspense, Studio One, U.S. Steel Hour.
PICTURES INCLUDE: Invasion of the Body Snatchers, View from Pompey's Head, D-Day, The Sixth of June, Something of Value, Fraulein, Shake Hands with the Devil, In Love and War, Sink the Bismarck, The List of Adrian Messenger, Airport.
TV: Playhouse 90, Dick Powell Show, Wagon Train, Virginian, Burkes Law, Bob Hope Presents, Alfred Hitchcock, Twelve O'clock High, The Rogues, Ben Casey, FBI Story, My Three Sons, Wild Wild West, The Man Who Never Was.

Y

YABLANS, FRANK: Executive. B. Brooklyn, N.Y. Aug. 27, 1935. Ent. m.p. ind. as Warner Bros. booker, 1957. Warner Bros. salesman in N.Y., Boston, Milwaukee, Chicago, 1957–59. Milwaukee br. mgr. Buena Vista, 1959–66. Midwest sales mgr., Sigma III, 1966. Eastern sales mgr., 1967, sales v.p. 1968. V.P. general sales mgr., Paramount Pic. Corp., 1969; v.p.-dist., April 1970; sr. v.p.-mkt., Oct., 1970; exec. v.p., April 1971; named pres. May, 1971. In Jan., 1975, became an independent producer, his company called, Frank Yablans Presentations Inc.
PICTURES: Silver Streak (exec. prod.), The Other Side of Midnight (prod.), The Fury (prod.), North Dallas Forty (prod. & co-s.p.s.).

YABLANS, IRWIN: Executive. b. Brooklyn, N.Y. Began career in industry at WB in 1956 after two-yr. stint in Germany with U.S. Army. Held m.p. sales posts in Washington, D.C., Albany, Detroit, Milwaukee and Portland. In 1962 joined Paramount as L.A. mgr.; in 1964 made western sales mgr. In 1972 entered production as assoc. prod. on Howard W. Koch's Badge 373. First prod. on own: The Education of Sonny Carson (1974). Now pres. of Compass Int'l. Pictures.
PICTURES: Halloween, Roller Boogie (both exec. prod.), Roller Boogie (exec. prod., story), Fade To Black (story).

YATES, PETER: Producer, director. b. 1929. Ent. m.p. ind. as studio man and dubbing asst. with De Lane Lea. Asst. dir. The Entertainer, The Guns of Navarone, A Taste of Honey. Stage: dir. The American Dream, The Death of Bessie Smith.
TV: Danger Man, The Saint (series).
PICTURES INCLUDE: Summer Holiday, One Way Pendulum, Robbery, Bullitt, John and Mary, Murphy's War, The Hot Rock, The Friends of Eddie Coyle, For Pete's Sake, Mother, Jugs and Speed, The Deep, Breaking Away, Eyewitness.

YAWITZ, PAUL A.: Writer. b. St. Louis, Mo. Feb. 5, 1905; e. U. Missouri; U. Washington. Member: Zeta Beta Tau. Publicist, Ned Wayburn Enterprises, Fox Film Corp.; Broadway columnist, N.Y. Mirror; writer, prod., RKO. Started screen career 1937.
PICTURES INCLUDE: (orig. s.p.) She Has What It Takes, They Knew What They Wanted (orig. s.p.); Affairs of Annabelle (orig. s.p.); Go Chase Yourself (orig. s.p.); The Chance of a Lifetime; (collab. s.p.) The Racket Man, Beauty for Sale; Breakfast for Two; (s.p.) I Love a Bandleader, Boston Blackie Booked on Suspicion; (orig.) A Close Call for Boston Blackie; (collab. story) Walk Softly, Stranger; collab. s.p. Models, Inc. (orig. s.p.); The Black Scorpion. Editor Beverly Hills Courier.

YORDAN, PHILIP: Writer. b. Chicago, Ill. e. University of Ill., B.A., Kent Coll. Law, LL.D. Author, producer, playwright (Anna Lucasta). Began screen writing 1942 with collab. s.p. Syncopation.
PICTURES INCLUDE: Unknown Guest, Johnny Doesn't Live Here, When Strangers Marry, Dillinger, Whistle Stop, The Chase, Suspense; play & s.p. Anna Lucasta, House of strangers; s.p. Edge of Doom; collab. s.p. Detective Story, (Acad. Award nomination) Mary Maru, s.p.; Houdini, Blowing Wild; collab. s.p., Man Crazy, Naked Jungle; s.p., Johnny Guitar; story, Broken Lance (Acad Award 1954); adapt. Conquest of Space; collab. s.p. Man from

Laramie, Last Frontier; prod. s.p. Harder They Fall, Men In War, No Down Payment, God's Little Acre; s.p. Bravados, Time Machine, The Day of the Outlaw, Studs Lonigan, King of Kings; collab., El Cid, 55 Days at Peking, Fall of the Roman Empire; prod., Crack in the World, Battle of the Bulge, Royal Hunt of the Sun, Brigham, Cataclysm.

YORK, DICK: Actor. r.n. Richard Allen York. b. Fort Wayne, Ind., Sept. 4, 1928. e. De Paul U. Drama School. Appeared on radio shows; commercial m.p. actor; on Broadway in Tea and Sympathy, Bus Stop; TV appearances.
TV: Omnibus, Robert Montgomery Show, Mr. D.A., The Web, Wagon Train, Alfred Hitchcock, Twilight Zone, Route 66, Going My Way, Bewitched.
PICTURES INCLUDE: Inherit the Wind, Cowboy, They Came to Cordura, My Sister Eileen, Three Stripes in the Sun.

YORK, MICHAEL: Actor. b. Fulmer, England, 1942. Early career with Oxford University Dramatic Society and National Youth Theatre; later Dundee Repertory, National Theatre.
TV: The Forsyte Saga, Rebel in the Grave, Great Expectations, Jesus of Nazareth, True Patriot, Much Ado About Nothing, A Man Called Intrepid.
STAGE: Any Just Cause, Hamlet, Outcry (Broadway), Ring Round The Moon (Los Angeles).
PICTURES INCLUDE: The Taming of the Shrew, Accident, Red and Blue, Smashing Time, Romeo and Juliet, The Strange Affair, The Guru, Alfred The Great, Justine, Something for Everyone, Zeppelin, La Poudre D'Escampette, Cabaret, England Made Me, Lost Horizon, The Three Musketeers, Murder on the Orient Express, The Four Musketeers, Conduct Unbecoming, Logan's Run, Seven Nights in Japan, The Last Remake of Beau Geste, The Island of Dr. Moreau, Fedora, The Riddle of the Sands.

YORK, SUSANNAH: Actress. b. London, 1942. Ent. TV 1959. Appearances include: The Crucible The Rebel and the Soldier, The First Gentleman, The Richest Man in the World. Ent. films in 1960.
PICTURES INCLUDE: Tunes of Glory, There Was a Crooked Man, Greengage Summer, Freud, Tom Jones, While the Tiger Sleeps, The Seventh Dawn, Scene Nun—Take One, Sands of Kalahari, Scruggs, Kaleidoscope, A Man for All Seasons, Sebastian, The Killing of Sister George, Oh What a Lovely War, The Battle of Britain, Lock Up Your Daughters, They Shoot Horses Don't They? (Acad. Award nom.), Brotherly Love, Zee & Co., Happy Birthday Wanda June, Images, The Maids, Gold, Conduct Unbecoming, Heaven Save Us From Our Friends, Sky Riders, The Silent Partner, Superman, The Shout, Superman II, Falling in Love Again, Alice Loophole, The Awakening.
TV: Slaughter of St. Teresa's Day, Kiss On A Grass Green Pillow, Fallen Angles, Prince Regent, Second Chance.
STAGE: A Cheap Bunch of Flowers, Wings of the Dove, A Singular Man, Man and Superman, Mrs. Warren's Profession, Peter Pan, Appearances.

YORKIN, BUD: Producer-director. r.n. Alan "Bud" Yorkin. b. Washington, Pa., Feb. 22, 1926. e. Carnegie Tech., Columbia U. U.S. Navy, 1942–45; prod., dir., NBC-TV.
TELEVISION: Song at Twilight, Martin & Lewis Show, Abbott and Costello Show, Ritz Bros. Show, Spike Jones Show; writer, prod. dir., Tony Martin Show, 1954–55; dir., George Gobel Show, 1954–55; prod. dir., The Ernie Ford Show 1956–57; owner. co-prod. All In The Family; Sanford and Son; Maude; Good Times; What's Happening!!; Carter Country.
PICTURES: Dir. Never Too Late; Divorce American Style; Inspector Clouseau; prod.-dir. Start the Revolution Without Me; Thief Who Came to Dinner; co-prod.-dir. Come Blow Your Horn; exec.-prod. The Night They Raided Minsky's; Cold Turkey.

YOSHISAKA, KIYOJI: Executive. b. Shanghai, China 1908. e. Thomas Hambury College, Shanghai. Ent. ind. 1930 RCA Victor of China, 1932 Victor Talking Machine, 1938 Manchuria Talking Machine, 1940 Victor of Japan. Left Photophone Div. of Victor in 1950 for Tokyo Theatre Supply 1950–58; 1959–63 Rhythm Friend Corp.; exec. dir.s Nichior 1964–66; became consultant Nihon Eiga Shizai 1966 and after name changed to Toshiba Photo Phone became mgr. trade. div. 1969 then dir. and gen. mgr. of trade div. in 1970. Retired.

YOUNG, ALAN: Actor. r.n. Angus Young; b. North Shield, Northumberland, England, Nov. 19, 1919. Sign painter; cartoonist, acted first as monologuist at 13 years in Canada; radio comedian 10 yrs. in Canada and U.S.; served in Canadian Navy as sub-lt. 1939–42; wrote, dir. and acted in comedy broadcasts; TV: Alan Young Show, Mister Ed; m.p. debut in Margie 1946.
PICTURES INCLUDE: Chicken Every Sunday, Mr.Belvedere Goes to College, Aaron Slick from Punkin Crick, Androcles and the Lion, Gentlemen Marry Brunettes, Tom Thumb, Time Machine.

YOUNG, BUDDY: Executive. b. New York City, June 15, 1935; e. CCNY, UA publicity dept. 1952; asst. pub. mgr., UA 1963;

pub. dir. Fox, Oct. 1965; west coast coordinator of adv. and publicity UA. In 1975 joined Columbia Pictures as worldwide dir. of adv.-pub.-exp. In 1976 named MGM adv.-pub. co-ordinator. Joined Universal Pictures in 1976 as dir. of pub. & promo. promoted to v.p. of advertising, publicity and promotion; 1980, partner in m.p. consulting firm, Powell & Young.

YOUNG, BURT: Actor-Writer. Worked at variety of jobs (boxer, trucker, etc.) before turning to acting and joining Actor's Studio. Appeared in off-Bdwy. plays which led to Hollywood career.
    PICTURES INCLUDE: Cinderella Liberty, The Gambler, The Killer Elite, Chinatown, Rocky, The Choirboys, Convoy, Uncle Joe Shannon (actor, s.p.), All the Marbles.
    TV: MASH, Baretta, etc.

YOUNG, CARROLL: Writer. b. Cincinnati, Ohio, Oct. 9, 1908; e. St. Xavier Coll. Publicist for Pathe Studios, Fox West Coast Theatres, RKO Studios, MGM, 1930–35; story ed. Sol Lesser Prod., Ernst Lubitsch Prod., 1936–40; asst. to exec. prod., RKO, 1941; U.S. Army Air Force, 1942–44.
    PICTURES INCLUDE: story, collab. s.p. Tarzan Triumphs; story, Tarzan's Desert Mystery; story, s.p. Tarzan and Leopard Woman, Tarzan and Mermaids; s.p. many in Jungle Jim series, Hidden City, The Jungle; story, Lost Continent; collab. s.p. Tarzan and the She-Devil; story s.p. Cannibal Attack; collab. story & s.p. Apache Warrior; collab. s.p. She-Devil, The Deerslayer; collab. s.p. Machete. Asst. to prod. Lewis Milestone Prods.

YOUNG, FREDDIE: Cinematographer. b. 1902. Ent. m.p. ind. 1917. Early career as cameraman and directing for Gaumont Film Co., British and Dominion Film Corp., MGM British, Army Training Films, now freelance.
    PICTURES INCLUDE: Victoria The Great, Sixty Glorious Years, Nell Gwyn, Goodbye Mr. Chips, Edward My Son, Ivanhoe (Oscar Nom.), Bhowani Junction, Greengage Summer, Lawrence of Arabia (Oscar award), Macbeth, Doctor Zhivago (Oscar award), The Deadly Affair, You Only Live Twice, Battle of Britain, Ryan's Daughter (Oscar), Nicholas and Alexandra (Oscar Nom.), Luther, The Tamarind Seed, Great Expectations, The Blue Bird, Permission to Kill, The Man In the Iron Mask, Rough Cut.

YOUNG, HAROLD: President, Harold Young Prod., Inc. e. Columbia U. Film ed., Warner Bros., MGM, First Natl. Studios; co-writer, Brit. & Dominions; superv. ed., Paramount Studios, Paris; also Alexander Korda's Brit. and French prod. units. Dir. The Scarlet Pimpernel, for Korda; then to Hollywood.
    PICTURES INCLUDE: Time Bomb, Hi Ya Chum, Mexican Fiesta, The Frozen Ghost, The Three Caballeros (live action parts), I'll Remember April, Jungle Captive, Song of the Sarong, Citizen Saint, Roogie's Bump, Carib Gold.

YOUNG, IRWIN: Executive. b. N.Y.C. e. Perkiomen School, Lehigh Univ., B.S., 1950. Pres., Du Art Film Laboratories, Inc.

YOUNG, LORETTA: Actress. r.n. Gretchen Young; b. Salt Lake City, Utah, Jan. 6, 1913. e. Ramona Convent, Alhambra, Calif. Immaculate Heart College, Hollywood. After small part in Naughty But Nice, lead in Laugh Clown, Laugh. Played in almost 100 films. Won Academy Award best perf. (Farmer's Daughter) 1947; NBC-TV Loretta Young Show, 1953–61; CBS-TV New Loretta Young Show 1962; won TV Acad. Awards, 1954–56–59. Has won innumerable other awards.

YOUNG, MORRIS: Executive. b. South Shields, England, 1919. Ent. m.p. industry 1935. Managing dir. United Artists until 1977. Appt. man. dir. Rank Film Distributors Ltd.

YOUNG ROBERT: Actor. b. Chicago, Ill., Feb. 22, 1907. Star numerous pictures before and after sound; from 1932 in many productions, various Hollywood producers; star. weekly TV show, Father Knows Best.
    PICTURES INCLUDE: Claudia, Sweet Rosie O'Grady, The Canterville Ghost, Secrets in the Dark, The Enchanted Cottage, Those Endearing Young Charms, Claudia and David, Lady Luck, They Won't Believe Me, Crossfire, Sitting Pretty, Adventures in Baltimore, And Baby Makes Three, Bride for Sale, Second Woman, That Forsyte Woman, Goodbye My Fancy, Half-Breed, Secret of the Incas.
    TV: Marcus Welby, M.D.

YOUNG, TERENCE: Director, writer. b. Shanghai, China, June 20, 1915; e. Cambridge U. Served with Guards Armoured Div. WWII; ent. m.p. ind. 1936 at BIP Studios.
    PICTURES INCLUDE: On the Night of the Fire, On Approval, Dangerous Moonlight; Theirs is the Glory, dir., Corridor of Mirrors, One Night With You, Woman Hater, They Were Not Divided, The Valley of the Eagles, Red Beret (Paratrooper), That Lady, Safari, Storm Over the Nile, Action of the Tiger, Serious Charge, Black Tights, Dr. No, From Russia With Love, Moll Flanders, Thunderball, Triple Cross, The Rover, Wait Until Dark, Mayerling, The Christmas Tree, The Red Sun, Grand Slam, The Va-

lachi Papers, War Goddess, The Klansman, Jackpot, Bloodline.

YOUNGSTEIN, MAX E.: Executive, b. New York City, March 21, 1913; e. Fordham U., LL.B.; Brooklyn Law School, LL.M.; Business mgr., Hal Horne Org., 1941–42; asst. dir. adv., pub. & exploit. 20th Fox, 1941–3; asst. dir. studio special services dept. 20th Fox, 1943. Pub. dir., Motion Picture & Special events section. War Finance Div., U.S. Treas., 1944–5. Dir., ad. pub. and exploitat., 1945–46, exec. v.p., Stanley Kramer Story Prods.; Eagle Lion Films, 1946. Named v.p. in charge adv., pub. and exploitat., 1949. Res. May, 1949 to become dir. adv., pub. exp. & member exec. com. Paramount Pictures; v.p. & dir. Paramount Film Dist. Corp., June, 1950; v.p. & nat'l dir. adv. pub. & partner United Artists, Feb. 26, 1951; appointed gen. v.p., member of board, 1955. Pres. United Artists Records & United Artists Music, 1957–62; exec. vice pres. Cinerama, Inc., pres. Cinemiracle, Jan. 1962, indep. producer, 1972; President, Max E. Youngstein Enterprises Inc.; exec. prod., Best of Cinerama, Man In The Middle; prod. Fail Safe, The Money Trap, Co-Prep. The Dangerous Days of Kiowa Jones, Welcome to Hard Times, Prod. Young Billy Young. 1972, v.p. Todd-AO Corp.; 1973, pres., Taylor-Laughlin Dist. Co.; senior v.p., Billy Jack Prods. National Student Film Corp.; v.p. Billy Jack Records & Publishing. 1975, Distrib., prod., merchandising, and marketing consultant to Filmation, Optimus Productions, Moonrunners Ltd., AFC Dist. Co., Grey Advertising., and Geo. Litto Productions. Consultant to New World Pictures on Tidal Wave; to High Key Limited Partnership on Big Mo; to Sequoia Pictures on Stunts; to Shirley MacLaine Enterprises. 1976, appointed general film consultant to Reader's Digest. Consultant to the Barry Film Company on Suzanne. Consultant to George Litto Productions on Obsession and Drive-In. 1977 consultant to Bart-Palevsky productions on Fun with Dick and Jane and Island in the Stream. Advisor on The Amsterdam Kill. Consultant to Rico-Lion for Olly, Olly Oxen Free with Katherine Hepburn. Consultant to Golden Harvest International Ltd., Hong Kong (Paragon Films, Golden Films). Co-executive producer of the Diahann Carroll Television Specials. 1978, consultant George Peppard's Five Days From Home; Robert Mitchum's Amsterdam Kill and Power Play with Peter O'Toole. 1979, consultant Roy Disney's Shamrock Productions Pacific High, Rank Film Distributors, Taft Broadcasting (Hanna-Barbera), Encore Productions' Celebration, Ralph Waite's On The Nickel, Bobrun Productions' Running and Selkirk Films' "Bear Island." 1980–81, bd. chm. & chief exec. officer, Taft International Pictures, Inc. Member of the Board of Governors of the Producers Guild. Lecturer on motion pictures at the University of Southern California, Stanford University and Dartmouth University. Member of the Motion Picture Pioneers Foundation, and one of the founders of the Children's Asthmatic and Research Home in Denver, Colorado. Member of the Board of Governors of Albert Einstein College of Medicine in New York City.

Z

ZAMPA, LUIGI: Director. b. Rome, Italy, 1905. Playwright studied at Experimental Film Center, Rome, 1935–38; script writer, director.
    PICTURES INCLUDE: American on Vacation, To Live in Peace, Difficult Years, Angelina, The White Line, City on Trial, Two Gentlemen in a Carriage, His Last 12 Hours, We Women, Woman of Rome, Art of Getting Along.

ZAMPI, GIULIO: Associate producer. b. London, Eng., Sept. 29, 1923; p. Mario Zampi; e. Rome U. Ed. to Marcel Varnel, then to Mario Zampi; dir. of Anglofilm Ltd. & Transocean Films Ltd.
    PICTURES INCLUDE: Phantom Shot, Fatal Night, Shadow of the Past, Come Dance with Me, Third Time Lucky, Laughter in Paradise, Top Secret, I Have Chosen Love, Happy Ever After (Tonight's the Night), Now and Forever, The Naked Truth, Too Many Crooks, Bottoms Up, Five Golden Hours.

ZANUCK, RICHARD DARRYL: Executive. b. L.A., Calif., Dec. 13, 1934; e. Stanford U. 1952–56; f. Darryl Zanuck. Story dept., 20th Century Fox, 1954; N.Y pub. dept., 1955; asst. to prod., Island in the Sun, 1957; The Sun Also Rises, 1956; v.p., Darryl F. Zanuck Prod. 1958; prod., Compulsion, 1959, DFZ Prod.; 20th Century Fox; prod., Sanctuary, 1961; prod., The Chapman Report, 1962; asst. to prod., The Longest Day, 1962; president's prod. rep., 20th Century Fox Studio 1963; v.p. charge prod., 20th Fox; pres., 20th Fox TV exec. v.p. chge. prod., 20th Fox, 1967. 1968: Chmn. of Bd., Television div., 20th Century Fox, 1969: Pres., 20th Century Fox Film Corp. Joined Warner Bros., March 1971, as sr. exec. v.p.; Resigned July, 1972 to form Zanuck-Brown Production Company, Universal Pictures.

Films under Z/B Company released: "Sssssssss," 1973; "The Sugarland Express," 1974; "Willie Dynamite," 1973; "The Sting," 1973; "The Black Windmill," 1974, The Girl from Petrovka, 1974; Jaws, 1975; Jaws 2, 1978; The Island, 1980; Neighbors, 1981.

ZEFFIRELLI, FRANCO: Director. b. Italy, 1922. Was stage director before entering film industry.
PICTURES INCLUDE: The Taming of the Shrew, Romeo and Juliet, Brother Sun, Sister Moon, The Champ, Endless Love.

ZEMECKIS, ROBERT: Director-Writer. b. Chicago 1952. e. USC's School of Cinema. At USC wrote, produced and directed a 14-minute film, A Field of Honor, which won special jury award at Second Annual Student Film Awards sponsored by M.P. Academy of Arts & Sciences, plus 15 international honors. Has film editing background, having worked as cutter on TV commercials in Illinois. Also cut films at NBC News, Chicago, as summer job. After schooling went to Universal to observe on set of TV series, McCloud. Wrote script for that series in collaboration with Bob Gale. Turned to feature films, directing I Wanna Hold Your Hand and co-writing s.p. with Gale and co-writing 1941 with him.

ZENS, WILL: Producer-director. b. Milwaukee, Wis., June 26, 1920. e. Marquette Univ. and Univ. of Southern Calif. BA, MA. Wrote, produced and directed many TV shows. Formed Riviera Productions in 1960 to produce theatrical motion pictures.
TV: Punch & Trudy, Your Police, Aqua Lung Adventures.
PICTURES INCLUDE: Capture That Capsule, The Starfighters, To the Shores of Hell, Road to Nashville, Hell on Wheels, From Nashville with Music, Yankee Station, Help Me . . . I'm Possessed!

ZETTERLING, MAI: Actress, director. b. Sweden, May 24, 1925. e. Ordtuery Sch. & Theater Sch. First m.p.: Sweden, Frenzy. Has made numerous stage and screen appearances since in Sweden. British screen debut, Frieda. Since 1969 directing plays & films in Sweden. Won Golden Lion at Venice in 1964 for The War Game.
PICTURES INCLUDE: Bad Lord Byron, Quartet, Portrait from Life, Romantic Age, Blackmailed, Hell is Sold Out, Desperate Moment, Knock on Wood, Dance Little Lady, Prize of Gold, Seven Waves Away (Abandon Ship), The Truth About Women, Jetstorm, Faces in the Dark, Piccadilly Third Stop, Offbeat, Only Two Can Play, The Main Attraction. 1965-66 wrote, dir. Loving Couples, Night Games. 1968: Dr. Glas, The Girls, The Rain Hat, We Have Many Names.
TV: Idiot's Delight, Mayerling, Doll's House, Dance of Death, etc. dir. doc. for BBC and in Sweden.

ZIEFF, HOWARD: Director. Started as artist and photographer, working as newsreel photographer for L.A. TV station. Went to N.Y. to do still photography; became top photo artist in advertising. Turned to film direction with Slither in 1972.
PICTURES INCLUDE: Slither, Hearts of the West, House Calls, The Main Event.

ZIFFER, FELIX C.: Lawyer. b. Staniscawow, Poland. Aug. 8, 1930. e. Yale U., 1947-51; Columbia U. Law School, 1952-55; law practice, since 1955; rep. many firms in music & record fields inc. United Artists (spec. counsel), J. Arthur Rank Organization (gen. counsel); pres., International Entertainment Corp.

ZIFKIN, WALTER: Executive. b. July 16, 1936. New York City. e. UCLA A.B. 1958; USC LL.B. 1961. CBS legal dept., 1961-63; William Morris Agency 1963-present; exec. vice-pres. WMA 1974.

ZIGMOND, JERRY: Exhibitor. b. Denver, Colo.; e. U. of Denver, and Chicago; m. Joined Paramount 1926; managed theatres in Los Angeles and Denver; later with J. H. Cooper Circuit, Lincoln, Neb.; managing dir., Newman Theatre, Kansas City; then exec. theatre dept., Paramount Theatres, home office; in charge of Paramount San Francisco Theatres; div. mgr. West Coast, United Paramount, L.A. ABC-TV dir. of Promotional Activities for M.P. Acad. Awards Telecast (1961-64) and ABC-TV dir. of exploitation, Western div.

ZIMBALIST, EFREM, JR.: Actor. b. New York, Nov. 30, 1923. Fay School, Southboro, Mass.; St. Paul's, Concord, N.H., Yale. Studied drama, Neighborhood Playhouse, N.Y. Stage debut, The Rugged Path. Shows with American Repertory Theatre; Henry VIII, Androcles and the Lion, What Every Woman Knows, Yellow Jack, Appeared, Hedda Gabler. Co-prod., The Medium, The Telephone, The Consul, (Critics Award, Pulitzer Prize) Barrymore Theatre. m.p. debut, House of Strangers. Gave up acting after death of his wife and served as asst. to father, Curtis Institute of Music for 4 yrs. Returned to acting, stock co., Hammonton, N.J., 1954. Appeared in TV series.
TV: Philco, Goodyear Playhouse, U.S. Steel Hour, Maverick, 77 Sunset Strip, The FBI.
PICTURES INCLUDE: Bomber B-52, Band of Angels, The Deep Six, Violent Road, Girl on the Run, Too Much Too Soon, Home Before Dark, The Crowded Sky, A Fever in the Blood, By Love Possessed, Chapman Report, The Reward, Harlow (electronovision), Airport 1975.

ZINNEMAN, FRED: Director. b. Vienna, Australia, Apr. 29, 1907; e. Vienna U. (law). Studied violin as a boy; after law, studied photographic technique, lighting & mechanics (Paris); asst. cameraman 1 yr. Paris; came to U.S. 1929; extra in m.p. All Quiet on the Western Front, 1930; asst. to Berthold Viertel, script clerk & asst. to Robert Flaherty, 1931; dir. Mexican documentary The Wave; short subjects dir., MGM, winning Academy Award for That Mothers Might Live, 1938; feature dir. 1941; winner of first Screen Directors' Award 1948 with The Search. 4 N.Y. Film Critics Awards; 2 Director's Guild Annual Awards; 3 Acad. Awards.
PICTURES INCLUDE: The Seventh Cross, The Search, The Men, Teresa, High Noon (N.Y. Film Critics Award), Benjy, short for L.A. Orthopedic Hosp. for which Academy Award, best doc. short, 1951; Member of the Wedding, From Here to Eternity (Acad. Award, best dir., 1953, N.Y. Film Critics Award, Directors Guild Award), Oklahoma, Hatful of Rain, Nun's Story (N.Y Film Critics Award), Sundowners, Behold a Pale Horse, A Man for All Seasons, Day of the Jackal, Julia.

ZINNEMANN, TIM: Producer. Began career in industry as film editor; then asst. dir. on several films. Production mgr. for several projects; assoc. prod. on The Cowboys and Smile. Produced Straight Time for Warners with Stanley Beck.
PICTURES: A Small Circle of Friends, The Long Riders.
TELEVISON: The Jericho Mile (ABC).

ZOUARY, MAURICE H.: Executive. b. Brooklyn, N.Y., July 17, 1921; e. Sch. of Industrial Design & Art, 1937; Trans-Lux Theatres, 1941; U.S. Armed Forces, 1943; production, acct. exec. ad agencies; Bud Gamble Prod., 1948; TV dept., Edward S. Kellogg Agency, L.A.; formed Zouary TV-Film Prod., 1950; prod. supvr. Films for Industry, 1950-52; TV prod., Grey Adv. Agency, 1952-54; prod. new commercials div., Guild Films, 1955-56; prod. Dore Prod., 1956-57; reactivated Zouary TV Film Prod., 1957; formed Filmvideo Releasing Corp. film stock shot library, 1957. Prod.: Freedom (feature film); Prod. Kiddie Camera (TV series); Prod.: The Vaudevillains (TV special); Prod.: Dr. DeForest. In 1975 formed TV National Releasing Corp., supplier of TV programming.

ZSIGMOND, VILMOS: Cinematographer. b. Hungary. e. National Film School. Began career photographing Hungarian Revolution of 1956. Later escaped from Hungary with friend Laszlo Kovacs, also a cinematographer.
PICTURES: McCabe and Mrs. Miller, Images, Deliverance, Scarecrow, The Long Goodbye, Cinderella Liberty, Sugarland Express, Obsession, Close Encounters of the Third Kind, The Deer Hunter, Heaven's Gate.

ZUGSMITH, ALBERT: Producer, director, writer. b. Atlantic City, N.J., Apr. 24, 1910. e. U. of Va. Pres. Intercontinental Broadcasting Corp.; ed. publ. Atlantic City Daily World; v.p. Smith Davis Corp.; Chmn. of bd., Continental Telecasting Corp., Television Corp. of America; assoc. ed. American Press; pres. World Printing Co.; exec. CBS; pres., American Pictures Corp.
PICTURES INCLUDE: Written on the Wind, Man in the Shadow, Red Sundown, Star in the Dust, Tarnished Angels, The Incredible Shrinking Man, The Girl in the Kremlin, The Square Jungle, Female on the Beach, Touch of Evil, Captive Women, Sword of Venus, Port Sinister; Invasion U.S.A., Top Banana, Paris Model, Slaughter on Tenth Avenue, The Female Animal, High School Confidential, Night of the Quarter Moon, Beat Generation, The Big Operator, Girls Town, Platinum High School, Private Lives of Adam and Eve, Dondi, College Confidential, Confessions of an Opium Eater, The Great Space Adventure, On Her Bed of Roses, Fanny Hill, The Rapist! author, Private Lives of Adam and Eve, The Beat Generation, How to Break Into the Movies, The Chinese Room, Street Girl, The President's Girl Friend, The Phantom Gunslinger, Sappho, Darling, Menage A Trois, Two Roses and a Goldenrod, The Friend Neighbors, Why Me, God?, Tom Jones Rides Again, etc.

Pictures

*CREDITS FOR FEATURE FILMS,
SEPTEMBER, 1980–AUGUST, 1981

*FEATURE RELEASES, 1955–1980

CREDITS FOR FEATURE FILMS

September, 1980–August, 1981

Major credits for feature films screened for the trade press in New York and reviewed in Quigley Publications' newsletter, Motion Picture Product Digest.

All Night Long .... Universal

Producers: Leonard Goldberg and Jerry Weintraub. Director: Jean-Claude Tramont. Screenplay: W.D. Richter. In color. Running time: 99 minutes. MPAA Rating: R. Release date: March 6, 1981.
Players: Gene Hackman, Barbra Streisand, Diane Ladd, Dennis Quaid, Kevin Dobson, William Daniels, Ann Doran, Jim Nolan.

Altered States ....Warner Bros.

Executive Producer: Daniel Melnick. Producer: Howard Gottfried. Director: Ken Russell. Screenplay: Sidney Aaron, from the novel of the same name by Paddy Chayefsky. In color. Running time: 105 minutes. MPAA Rating: R. Release date: December, 1980.
Players: William Hurt, Blair Brown, Bob Balaban, Charles Haid, Thaao Penghlis, Miguel Godreau, Dori Brenner, Peter Brandon, Charles White Eagle.

An American Werewolf in London .... Universal

A Lycanthrope Films Limited production for PolyGram Pictures. Producer: George Folsey, Jr. Executive Producers: Peter Guber and Jon Peters. Director-Writer: John Landis. Music: Elmer Bernstein. Cinematography: Robert Paynter. Editor: Malcolm Campbell. In color. Running time: 97 minutes. MPAA Rating: R. Release date: August 21, 1981.
Players: David Naughton, Jenny Agutter, Griffin Dunne, John Woodvine, Brian Glover, David Schofield, Lila Kane, Paul Kember, Don McKillop, Frank Oz.

Any Which Way You Can ....

Executive Producer: Robert Daley. Producer: Fritz Manes. Director: Buddy Van Horn. Screenplay: Stanford Sherman, based on characters created by Jeremy Joe Kronsberg. In color. Running time: 115 minutes. MPAA Rating: PG. Release date: December 17, 1980.
Players: Clint Eastwood, Sondra Locke, Geoffrey Lewis, William Smith, Harry Guardino, Ruth Gordon, Michael Cavanaugh, Barry Cobin, Roy Jenson, Bill McKinney, William O'Connell, John Quade, Al Ruscio.

American Pop .... Columbia

Bakshi Productions/Aspen Productions. Producers: Martin Ransohoff and Ralph Bakshi. Director: Mr. Bakshi. Screenplay: Ronnie Kern. In color. Running time: 98 minutes. MPAA Rating: R. Release date: February, 1981.
Players: Featuring the Voices of Ron Thompson, Marya Small, Jerry Holland, Lisa Jane Persky, Jeffrey Lippa, Roz Kelly.

Arthur ....Warner Bros.

An Orion Pictures release. Producer: Robert Greenhut. Executive Producer: Charles H. Joffe. Writer-Director: Steve Gordon. Music: Burt Bacharach. Cinematography: Fred Schuler. Editor: Susan E. Morse. In color. Running time: 96 minutes. MPAA Rating: PG. Release date: July 17, 1981.
Players: Dudley Moore, Liza Minnelli, John Gielgud, Geraldine Fitzgerald, Jill Eikenberry, Stephen Elliott, Red Ross, Barney Martin, Thomas Barbour, Anne de Salvo, Marjorie Barnes.

Atlantic City ....Paramount

International Cinema Corp. A John Kemeny—Denis Heroux production. Executive Producers: Joseph Beaubien and Gabriel Boustant. Producer: Mr. Heroux. Director: Louis Malle. Screenplay: John Guare. In color. Running time: 105 minutes. MPAA Rating: Release date: April, 1981.
Players: Burt Lancaster, Susan Sarandon, Kate Reid, Michel Piccoli, Hollis McLaren, Robert Joy, Al Waxman, Robert Goulet, Moses Znaimer, Harvey Atkin, Eleanor Beecroft, Norma Dell'Agnese, Louis Del Grande.

The Awakening ....Warner Bros.

Orion Pictures Company. Producer: Robert Solo. Director: Mike Newell. Screenplay: Allan Scott, Chris Bryant and Clive Exton, based on the novel, "The Jewel of the Seven Stars," by Bram Stoker. In color. Running time: 100 minutes. MPAA Rating: R. Release date: October, 1980.
Players: Charlton Heston, Susannah York, Jill Townsend, Patrick Drury, Bruce Myers, Nadim Sawalha, Miriam Maygolyes, Ian.

Back Roads ....Warner Bros.

A CBS Theatrical Films presentation. Meta-Films Associates, Inc. Produced in association with Marion Rosenberg. Producer: Ronald Shedlo. Director: Martin Ritt. Screenplay: Gary DeVore. In Panavision and color. Running time: 94 minutes. MPAA Rating: R. Release date: March, 1981.
Players: Sally Field, Tommy Lee Jones, David Keith, Miriam Colon, Michael Gazzo, Dan Shor, M. Emmet Walsh, Barbara Babcock, Nell Carter, Alex Colon, Lee de Broux, Ralph Seymour, Royce Applegate.

Bad Timing/A Sensual Obsession .... World Northal

A Rank Organization Production. A Sondra Gilman/Louise Westergaard presentation. Producer: Jeremy Thomas. Director: Nicolas Roeg. Screenplay: Yale Udoff. In color. Running time: 122 minutes. MPAA Rating: X. Release date: October, 1980.
Players: Art Garfunkel, Theresa Russell, Harvey Keitel, Denholm Elliott, Daniel Massey, Dana Gillespie.

Beyond the Reef .... Universal

A Dino DeLaurentiis Co. production. Producer: Raffaella DeLaurentiis. Director: Frank C. Clark. Screenplay: Louis LaRusso II and Jim Carabatsos, from the novel by Clement Richer. In color. Running time: 91 minutes. MPAA Rating: PG. Release date: May, 1981.
Players: Dayton Ka'ne, Maren Jensen, Kathleeen Swan, Keahi Farden, Oliverio Maciel Diaz, Joseph Ka'ne.

Blow Out .... Filmways

Producer: George Litto. Writer-Director: Brian De Palma. Music: Pino Donaggio. Cinematography: Vilmos Zsigmond. Editor: Paul Hirsch. In color. Running time: 108 minutes. MPAA Rating: R. Release date: July 24, 1981.
Players: John Travolta, Nancy Allen, John Lithgow, Dennis Franz, Peter Boyden, Curt May, Ernest McClure, Dave Roberts, Maurice Copenald, Claire Carter, John Aquino, John Hoffmeister, Patrick McNamara, Terrence Currier, Tom McCarthy, Dean Bennett.

Body Heat .... Warner Bros.

A Ladd Company release. Producer: Fred T. Gallo. Director-Writer: Lawrence Kasdan. Music: John Barry. Cinematography: Richard H. Kline. Editor: Carol Littleton. In color. Running time: 113 minutes. MPAA Rating: R. Release date: August 28, 1981.

Players: William Hurt, Kathleen Turner, Richard Crenna, Ted Danson, J.A. Preston, Mickey Routke, Kim Zimmer, Jane Hallaren, Lanna Saunders, Carola McGuinness, Michael Ryan, Larry Marko.

Borderline .... Associated Film Dist.

A Lord Grade presentation. Producer: James Nelson. Director: Jerrold Freedman. Screenplay: Steve Kline and Mr. Freedman. In Panavision and color. Running time: 106 minutes. MPAA Rating: PG. Release date: October, 1980.

Players: Charles Bronson, Bruno Kirby, Bert Remsen, Michael Lerner, Kenneth McMillan, Ed Harris, Karmin Murcelo, Enrique Castillo, A. Wilford Brimley, Norman Alden, James Victor, Panchito Gomez, John Ashton, Lawrence Casey.

Breaker Morant
.... New World Pictures/Quartet Films

A South Australian Film Corp. presentation. Producer: Matt Carroll. Director: Bruce Beresford. Screenplay: Mr. Beresford, Jonathan Hardy, and David Stevens, from a play by Kenneth Ross. In color. Running time: 108 minutes. MPAA Rating: PG. Release date: February, 1981.

Players: Edward Woodward, Jack Thompson, John Waters, Bryan Brown, Charles Tingwell, Frank Wilson, Terence Donovan, Vincent Ball, Lewis Fitzgerald, Rod Mullinar.

Bustin' Loose .... Universal

A Richard Pryor Production. Producers: Richard Pryor and Michael S. Glick. Director: Oz Scott. Screenplay: Roger L. Simon. Adaptation: Lonne Elder, III. Story: Richard Pryor. In color. Running time: 94 minutes. MPAA Rating: R. Release date: May, 1981.

Players: Richard Pryor, Cicely Tyson, Robert Christian, George Coe, Bill Quinn, Roy Jenson, Fred Carney, Peggy McCay, Alphonso Alexander, Kia Cooper, Edwin DeLeon, Jimmy Hughes, Edwin Kinter, Tami Luchow, Angel Ramirez, Janet Wong.

Caddie .... Atlantic Releasing Corp.

Australian Film Commission. Producer: Anthony Buckley. Director: Donald Crombie. Screenplay: Joan Long, based on the book, "Caddie, A Sydney Barmaid—an autobiography written by herself." In color. Running time: 107 minutes. No MPAA Rating. Release date: February, 1981.

Players: Helen Morse, Takis Emmanuel, Jack Thompson, Jacki Weaver, Melissa Jaffer, Ron Blanchard, Drew Forsythe, Kirrili Nolan, Lynette Currin.

The Cannonball Run ...... 20th Century-Fox

A Golden Harvest presentation. Producer: Albert S. Ruddy. Executive Producer: Raymond Chow. Director: Hal Needham. Screenplay: Brock Yates. Music: Al Capps. Cinematography: Michael Butler. Editors: Dom Cambern and William D. Gordean. In color. Running time: 95 minutes. MPAA Rating: PG. Release date: June, 1981.

Players: Burt Reynolds, Roger Moore, Farrah Fawcett, Dom DeLuise, Dean Martin, Sammy Davis, Jr., Jack Elam, Adrienne Barbeau, Terry Bradshaw.

Cattle Annie and Little Britches .. Universal

A King-Hitzig Production. Producers: Rupert Hitzig and Alan King. Executive Producers: John Daly and Derek X. Dawson. Director: Lamont Johnson. Screenplay: David Eyre and Robert Ward, based on a screen story by Ward from his novel. In color. Running time: 97 minutes. MPAA Rating: PG. Release date: May, 1981.

Players: Burt Lancaster, John Savage, Rod Steiger, Diane Lane, Amanda Plummer, Scott Glenn, Redmond Gleeson, William Russ, Ken Call, Buck Taylor, John Quade.

Caveman .... United Artists

A Turman-Foster Company production. Producers: Lawrence Turman and David Foster. Director: Carl Gottlieb. Screenplay: Rudy De Luca and Mr. Gottlieb. In color. Running time: 91 minutes. MPAA Rating: PG. Release date: April, 1981.

Players: Ringo Starr, Barbara Bach, Dennis Quaid, Shelley Long, John Matuszak, Avery Schreiaber, Jack Gilford.

A Change of Seasons ..... 20th Century-Fox

A Film Finance Group presentation. Executive Producer: Richard R. St. Johns. Producer: Martin Ransohoff. Director: Richard Lang. Screenplay: Erich Segal, Ronni Kern, and Fred Segal, based on a story by Erich Segal. In color. Running time: 102 minutes. MPAA Rating: R. Release date: December, 1980.

Players: Shirley MacLaine, Anthony Hopkins, Bo Derek, Michael Brandon, Mary Beth Hurt, Ed Winter, Paul Regina.

Cheech and Chong's
Nice Dreams
.... Columbia

A C. & C. Brown Production. Producer: Howard Brown. Director: Thomas Chong. Screenplay: Mr. Chong and Richard "Cheech" Marin. Music: Harry Betts. Cinematography: Charles Correll. Editors: Tom Avildsen and Tony Lombardo. In color. Running time: 97 minutes. MPAA Rating: R. Release date: June 5, 1981. Players: Thomas Chong, Richard "Cheech" Marin, Stacy Keach, George Craig Brown, Jimmy Fame, Evelyn Guerrero, Peter Jason, Suzanne Kent, Michael Masters, Paul Reubens, Tim Rossovich, Dr. Tomothy Leary, James Faracci, Jeff Pomerantz.

Chu Chu and the Philly Flash
.... 20th Century-Fox

A Jay Weston production from Melvin Simon Productions. Producer: Mr. Weston. Director: David Lowell Rich. Screenplay: Barbara Dana from a story by Henry Barrow. Muic: Pete Rugolo. Cinematography: Victor J. Kemper. Editor: Argyle Nelson. In color. Running time: 100 minutes. MPAA Rating: PG. Release date: August, 1981.

Players: Alan Arkin, Carol Burnett, Jack Warden, Danny Aiello, Adam Arkin, Danny Glover, Sid Haig, Vincent Schiavelli, Ruth Buzzi, Vito Scotti, Lou Jacobi.

City of Women .... New Yorker Films

Gaumont/Opera production. Director: Federico Fellini. Screenplay: Fellini, Bernardino Zappoini and Brunello Rondi. In color. Running time: 138 minutes. No MPAA Rating. Release date: April, 1981.

Players: Marcello Mastroianni, Ettore Manni, Anna Brucnal, Bernice Stegers, Donatella Maniani, Sara Tafuri, Jole Silvani, Carla Terizzi, Katren Gabelein.

Clash of the Titans .... United Artists

A Metro-Goldwyn-Mayer presentation. Producers: Charles H. Schneer and Ray Harryhausen. Director: Desmond Davis. Screenplay: Beverley Cross. Music: Laurence Rosenthal. Cinematography: Ted Moore. Editor: Timothy Gee. In color. Running time: 118 minutes. MPAA Rating: PG. Release date: June, 1981.

Players: Harry Hamlin, Judi Bowker, Burgess Meredith, Maggie Smith, Ursula Andress, Claire Bloom, Sian Phillips, Flora Robson, and Laurence Olivier as Zeus.

Coast to Coast .... Paramount

A Steve Tisch—Jon Avnet production. Director: Joseph Sargent. Screenplay: Stanley Weiser. In color. Running time: 95 minutes. MPAA Rating: PG. Release date: October 3, 1980.

Players: Dyan Cannon, Robert Blake, Quinn Redeker, Michael Lerner, Maxine Stuart, Bill Lucking, Ellen Gerstein, Patricia Conklin, David Moody.

The Competition .... Columbia

A Rastar/William Sackheim production. Producer: Mr. Sackheim. Director: Joel Oliansky. Screenplay: Mr. Oliansky, from a story by himself and Mr. Sackheim. In color. Running time: 129 minutes. MPAA Rating: PG. Release date: December, 1980.

Players: Richard Dreyfuss, Amy Irving, Lee Remick, Sam Wanamaker, Joseph Cali, Ty Henderson, Vickie Kriegler, Adam Stern, Bea Silvern, Philip Sterling, Gloria Stroock, Delia Salvi.

Condorman ....Buena Vista

Walt Disney Productions. Executive Producer: Ron Miller. Producer: Jan Williams. Director: Charles Jarrott. Screenplay: Marc Stirdivant, suggested by "The Game of X" by Robert Sheckley. Music: Henry Mancini. Cinematography: Charles F. Wheeler. Editor: Gordon D. Brenner. In Panavision and color. Running time: 90 minutes. MPAA Rating: PG. Release date: August, 1981.

Players: Michael Crawford, Oliver Reed, Barbara Carrera, James Hampton, Jean-Pierre Kalfon, Dana Elcar, Vernon Dobtcheff, Robert Arden.

Cutter and Bone .... United Artists

A Gurian Entertainment Production. Producer: Paul R. Gurian. Director: Ivan Passer. Screenplay: Jeffrey Alan Fiskin, based on the novel by Newton Thornburg. In color. Running time: 109 minutes. MPAA Rating: R. Release date: March, 1981.

Players: Jeff Bridges, John Heard, Lisa Eichhorn, Ann Dusenberry, Stephen Elliott, Arthur Rosenberg, Nina Van Pallandt, Patricia Donahue, Geraldine Baron.

Deadly Blessing .... United Artists

An InterPlanetary Production from PolyGram Pictures. Producers: Micheline and Max Keller and Pat Herskovic. Director: Wes Craven. Screenplay: Glenn M. Benest, Matthew Barr and Mr. Craven, based on a story by Benest and Barr. Music: James Horner. Cinematography: Robert Jessup. Editor: Richard Bracken. In color. Running time: 102 minutes. MPAA Rating: R. Release date: August 14, 1981.

Players: Maren Jensen, Susan Buckner, Sharon Stone, Jeff East, Lisa Hartman, Lois Nettleton, Ernest Borgnine, Coleen Riley.

Death Hunt .... 20th Century-Fox

An Albert S. Ruddy Production. Producer: Murray Shostak. Director: Peter Hunt. Screenplay: Michael Grais and Mark Victor. In color. Running time: 96 minutes. MPAA Rating: R. Release date: May, 1981.

Players: Charles Bronson, Lee Marvin, Andrew Stevens, Carl Weathers, Ed Lauter, Scott Hylands, Angie Dickinson, Henry Beckman, William Sanderson, John Cedar, James O'Connell, Len Lesser, Dick Davalos.

The Devil and Max Devlin ......Buena Vista

A Walt Disney production. Producer: Jerome Courtland. Director: Steven Hilliard Stern. Screenplay: Mary Rodgers. In color. Running time: 96 minutes. MPAA Rating: PG. Release date: February, 1981.

Players: Elliott Gould, Bill Cosby, Susan Anspach, Adam Rich, Julie Budd, David Knell.

Dirty Tricks .... Avco Embassy

A Filmplan International production. Executive Producers: Victor Solnicki, Pierre David, and Arnold Kopelson. Producer: Claude Heroux. Director: Alvin Rakoff. Screenplay: William Norton, Sr., Eleanor Elias Norton, Thomas Gifford and Camille Gifford, from a novel by Thomas Gifford. In color. Running time: 91 minutes. MPAA Rating: PG. Release date: May, 1981.

Players: Elliott Gould, Kate Jackson, Arthur Hill, Rich Little, Nick Campbell, Angus McInnes, Michael Kirby, Michael McNamara, Martin McNamara.

Divine Madness ....Warner Bros.

A Ladd Company release. Producer-Director: Michael Ritchie. Executive Producer: Howard Jeffrey. Writers: Jerry Blatt, Bette Midler, and Bruce Vilanch. In Panavision and color. Running time: 94 minutes. MPAA Rating: R. Release date: September, 1980.

Players: Bette Midler and the Harlettes: Jocelyn Brown, Ula Jedwig, Diva Gray.

The Dogs of War .... United Artists

A Norman Jewison/Patrick Palmer production. Producer: Larry DeWaay. Director: John Irvin. Screenplay: Gary DeVore and George Malko, based on a novel by Frederick Forsyth. In Panavision and color. Running time: 101 minutes. MPAA Rating: R. Release date: February, 1981.

Players: Christopher Walken, Tom Berenger, Colin Blakely, Hugh Millais, Paul Freeman, Jean-Francois Stevenin, Jobeth Williams, Robert Urquhart, Winston Ntshona.

Dragonslayer .... Paramount

A Barwood/Robbins Production. Producer: Hal Barwood. Director: Matthew Robbins. Screenplay: Mr. Barwood and Mr. Robbins. Music: Alex North. Cinematography: Derek Vanlint. Editor: Tony Lawson. In Panavision and color. Running time: 110 minutes. MPAA Rating: PG. Release date: June 26, 1981.

Players: Peter MacNicol, Caitlin Clarke, Ralph Richardson, John Hallam, Peter Eyre, Albert Salmi, Sydney Bromley, Chiloe Salaman, Emrys James, Roger Kemp, Ian McDiarmid, Ken Shorter, Jason White.

The Earthling .... Filmways

A Samuel Z. Arkoff presentation. Executive Producer: Stephen W. Sharmat. Producers: Elliot Schick and John Strong. Director: Peter Collinson. Screenplay: Lanny Cotler. In color. Running time: 98 minutes. MPAA Rating: PG. Release date: February, 1981.

Players: William Holden, Ricky Schroder, Jack Thompson, Olivia Hammett, Jane Harders, Alwyn Kurts, Pat Evison, Redmond Phillips, Willie Fennell, Allan Penney, Walter Pym, Harry Neilson, Tony Barry.

The Elephant Man .... Paramount

A Brooksfilms production. Executive Producer: Stuart Cornfeld. Producer: Jonathan Sanger. Director: David Lynch. Screenplay: Christopher DeVore, Eric Bergren, and Mr. Lynch, based on "The Elephant Man and Other Reminiscences" by Sir Frederick Treves and in part on "The Elephant Man: A Study in Human Dignity," by Ashley Montagu. In Panavision and black-and-white. Running time: 125 minutes. MPAA Rating: PG. Release date: October, 1980.

Players: Anthony Hopkins, John Hurt, Anne Bancroft, John Gielgud, Wendy Hiller, Freddie Jones, Michael Elphick, Hannah Gordon, Helen Ryan, John Standing, Dexter Fletcher, Lesley Dunlop, Phoebe Nicholls, Pat Gorman, Claire Davenport.

Endless Love .... Universal

A Polygram Pictures presentation. Producer: Dyson Levell. Executive Producer: Keith Barish. Director: Franco Zeffirelli. Screenplay: Judith Rascoe, based on the book by Scott Spencer. Music: Jonathan Tunick. Cinematography: David Watkin. Editor: Michael J. Sheridan. In color. Running time: 110 minutes. MPAA Rating: R. Release date: July 17, 1981.

Players: Brooke Shields, Martin Hewitt, Shirley Knight, Don Murray, Richard Kiley, Beatrice Straight, Jimmy Spader, Ian Ziering, Robert Moore, Penelope Milford, Jan Miner.

Escape from New York ...... Avco Embassy

A Debra Hill Production. Producers: Larry Franco and Ms. Hill. Director: John Carpenter. Screenplay: Mr. Carpenter and Nick Castle. Music: Mr. Carpenter in association with Alan Howarth. Cinematography: Dean Cundey. Editor: Todd Ramsay. In color. Running time: 102 minutes. MPAA Rating: R. Release date: July, 1981.

Players: Kurt Russell, Lee Van Cleef, Ernest Borgnine, Donald Pleasence, Isaac Hayes, Season Hubley, Harry Dean Stanton, Adrienne Barbeau.

Excalibur ....Warner Bros.

An Orion Pictures presentation. Producer-Director: John Boorman. Screenplay: Rospo Pallenberg and Mr. Boorman, adapted from Malory's "Le Morte D'Arthur" by Mr. Pallenberg. In color. Running time: 140 minutes. MPAA Rating: R. Release date: April 10, 1981.

Players: Nigel Terry, Helen Mirren, Nicholas Clay, Cherie Lunghi, Paul Geoffrey, Nicol Williamson, Robert Addie, Gabriel Byrne, Keith Buckley, Katrine Boorman, Liam Neeson, Corin Redgrave, Niall O'Brien, Patrick Stewart, Clive Swift, Ciarin Hinds, Liam O'Callaghan, Michael Muldoon, Charley Boorman.

Eye of the Needle .... United Artists

A Kings Road production. Producer: Stephen Friedman. Director: Richard Marquand. Screenplay: Stanley Mann, based on the novel by Ken Follett. Music: Miklos Rozsa. Cinematography: Alan Hume. Editor: Sean Barton. In color. Running time: 111 minutes. MPAA Rating: R. Release date: July 24, 1981.

Players: Donald Sutherland, Kate Nelligan, Ian Bannen, Christopher Cazenove, Faith Brook, Barbara Ewing, David Hayman, Alex McCrindle, Philip Martin Brown, Rupert Frazer, Jonathan Nicholas Haley.

Eyes of a Stranger ....Warner Bros.

A Georgetown Production. Producer: Ronald Zerra. Director: Ken Wiederhorn. Screenplay: Mark Jackson and Eric L. Bloom. In Panavision and color. Running time: 85 minutes. MPAA Rating: R. Release date: March 27, 1981.

Players: Lauren Tewes, Jennifer Jason Leight, John DiSanti, Peter DuPre, Gwen Lewis, Kitty Lunn, Timothy Hawkings, Ted Richert.

Eyewitness ....20th Century-Fox

Producer-Director: Peter Yates. Screenplay: Steve Tesich. In color. Running time: 102 minutes. MPAA Rating: R. Release date: March, 1981.

Players: William Hurt, Sigourney Weaver, Christopher Plummer, James Woods, Irene Worth, Kenneth McMillan, Pamela Reed, Albert Paulsen, Steven Hill, Morgan Freeman. Alice Drummond, Sharon Goldman, Chao-Li Chi.

Fade to Black .... American Cinema

A Leisure Investment Company & Movie Ventures Ltd. production. Executive producers: Irwin Yablans and Sylvio Tabet. Producers: George G. Braunstein and Ron Hamady. Writer-Director: Vernon Zimmerman. In color. Running time: 100 minutes. MPAA Rating: R. Release date: October, 1980.

Players: Dennis Christopher, Tim Thomerson, Gwynne Gilford, Linda Kerridge, Morgan Paull, James Luisi, Eve BrentAshe, John Steadman, Marcie Barkin, Mickey Rourke, Peter Horton, Hennen Chambers, Melinda Fee, Norman Burton.

The Fan ....Paramount

RSO Films, Ltd. Producer: Robert Stigwood. Executive Producer: Kevin McCormick. Director: Edward Bianchi. Screenplay: Priscilla Chapman and John Hartwell, based on the novel by Bob Randall. In color. Running time: 95 minutes. MPAA Rating: R. Release date: May 15, 1981.

Players: Lauren Bacall, James Garner, Maureen Stapleton, Hector Elizondo, Michael Biehn, Anna Maria Horsford, Kurt Johnson, Feiga Martinez, Reed Jones, kaiulani Lee, Charles Blackwell.

Fear No Evil .... Avco Embassy

A LaLoggia Productions picture. Producers: Frank LaLoggia and Charles M. LaLoggia. Director-Writer: Frank LaLoggia. In color. Running time: 99 minutes. MPAA Rating: R. Release date: January, 1981.

Players: Stefan Arngrim, Elizabeth Hoffman, Kathleen Rowe McAllen, Frank Birney, Daniel Eden, Jack Holland, Barry Cooper, Alice Sachs, Paul Haber, Roslyn Gugino.

The Final Conflict ....20th Century-Fox

A Harvey Bernhard production in association with Mace Neufeld. Producer: Mr. Bernhard. Director: Graham Baker. Screenplay: Andrew Birkin, based on characters created by David Seltzer. In Panavision and color. Running time: 109 minutes. MPAA Rating: R. Release date: March 20, 1981.

Players: Sam Neill, Rossano Brazzi, Don Gordon, Lisa Harrow, Barnaby Holm, Mason Adams, Robert Arden, Tommy Dugan, Leueen Willoughby, Louis Mahoney, Marc Boyle, Richard Oldfield, Milos Kirek, Tony Vogel.

The First Deadly Sin .....Filmways Pictures

An Elliott Kastner presentation of an Artanis-Cinema VII production. Executive Producers: Frank Sinatra and Mr. Kastner. Producers: George Pappas and Mark Shaker. Director: Brian Hutton. Screenplay: Mann Rubin, based on the novel by Lawrence Sanders. In color. Running time: 112 minutes. MPAA Rating: R. Release date: October, 1980.

Players: Frank Sinatra, Faye Dunaway, David Dukes, George Coe, Brenda Vaccaro, James Whitmore, Martin Gabel, Joe Spinell, Jeffrey de Munn, Anthony Zerbe, Fred Fuster.

First Family ....Warner Bros.

An Indie-Prod production. Producer: Daniel Melnick. Director-Writer: Buck Henry. In color. Running time: 97 minutes. MPAA Rating: R. Release date: December 25, 1980.

Players: Gilda Radner, Bob Newhart, Madeline Kahn, Richard Benjamin, Bob Dishy, Harvey Korman, Austin Pendleton, Rip Torn, Fred Willard, Julius Harris, John Hancock, Maurice Sherbanee, Buck Henry, Shatsmi Sarume Dance Troupe.

First Monday in October ....Paramount

A Paul Heller production. Producers: Paul Heller and Martha Scott. Director: Ronald Neame. Screenplay: Jerome Lawrence and Robert E. Lee, based on their play. Music: Ian Fraser. Cinematography: Fred J. Koenekamp. Editor: Peter E. Berger. In color. Running time: 95 minutes. MPAA Rating: R. Release date: August 21, 1981.

Players: Walter Matthau, Jill Clayburgh, Barnard Hughes, Jan Sterling, James Stephens, Joshua Bryant, Wiley Harker, F.J. O'Neill, Charles Lampkin, Lew Palter, Richard McMurray, Herb Vigran.

Flash Gordon .... Universal

A Dino De Laurentiis presentation. Director: Mike Hodges. Screenplay: Lorenze Semple, Jr., from an adaptation by Michael Allin, based on characters created by the late Alex Raymond. In color. Running time: 113 minutes. MPAA Rating: PG. Release date: December 5, 1980.

Players: Sam Jones, Melody Anderson, Topol, Max Von Sydow, Ornelia Muti, Timothy Dalton, Brian Blessed, Peter Wyngrade, Mariangela Melato, Richard O'Brien.

For Your Eyes Only .... United Artists

Eon Productions, Ltd. Executive Producer: Michael G. Wilson. Producer: Albert R. Broccoli. Director: John Glen. Screenplay: Richard Maibaum and Mr. Wilson. Music: Bill Conti. Cinematography: Alan Hume. Editor: John Grover. In Panavision and color. Running time: 128 minutes. MPAA Rating: PG. Release date: June 26, 1981.

Players: Roger Moore, Carole Bouquet, Topol, Lynn-Holly Johnson, Julian Glover, Cassandra Harris, Jill Bennett, Michael Gothard, John Wyman, Jack Hedley, Louis Maxwell, Desmond Llewelyn, Geoffrey Keen, Walter Gotell, and John Wells and Janet Brown.

The Formula .... United Artists

An MGM presentation. Producer-Writer: Steve Shagan, script based on his own book. Director: John Avildsen. In color. Running time: 117 minutes. MPAA Rating: R. Release date: December, 1980.

Players: George C. Scott, Marlon Brando, Marthe Keller, John Gielgud, G.D. Spradlin, Beatrice Straight, Richard Lynch, John Van Dreelen, Robin Clarke, Ike Eisenmann.

Fort Apache, The Bronx ... 20th Century-Fox

Time-Life Films. Produced in association with the Producer Circle Co. Executive Producer: David Susskind. Producers: Martin Richards and Gill Champion. Director: Daniel Petrie. Screenplay: Heywood Gould. In color. Running time: 120 minutes. MPAA Rating: R. Release date: February, 1981.

Players: Paul Newman, Edward Asner, Ken Wahl, Danny Aiello, Rachel Ticotin, Pam Grier, Kathleen Beller, Tito Goya, Miguel Pinero, Jaime Tirelli, Lance William Guecia, Ronnie Clanton, Clifford David.

The Four Seasons .... Universal

Producer: Martin Bregman. Director-Writer: Alan Alda. In color. Running time: 108 minutes. MPAA Rating: PG. Release date: May 22, 1981.

Players: Alan Alda, Carol Burnett, Len Cariou, Sandy Dennis, Rita Moreno, Jack Weston, Bess Armstrong, Elizabeth Alda, Beatrice Alda, Robert Hitt, Kristi McCarthy, David Stackpole.

The Fox and the Hound ....Buena Vista

A Walt Disney production. Producer: Wolfgant Reitherman. Executive Producer: Ron Miller. Directors: Art Stevens, Ted Berman, and Richard Rich. Story: Larry Clemmons, Ted Berman, Peter Young, Steve Hulett, David Michener, Burny Mattinson, Earl Kress, and Vance Gerry, from the book by Daniel P. Mannix. In color. Running time: 83 minutes. MPAA Rating: G. Release date: July, 1981.

Players: Voices of Mickey Rooney, Kurt Russell, Pearl Bailey, Jack Albertson, Sandy Duncan, Jeannette Nolan, Pat Buttram, John Fiedler, John McIntire, Dick Bakalyan, Paul Winchell, Keith Mitchell, Corey Feldman.

Friday the 13th Part II ....Paramount

Producers: Steve Miner and Dennis Murphy. Director: Mr. Miner. Screenplay: Ron Kurz, based on characters created by Victor Miller. In color. Running time: 87 minutes. MPAA Rating: R. Release date: May, 1981.

Players: Amy Steel, John Furey, Adrienne King, Kirsten Baker, Stu Charnc, Warrington Gillette, Walt Gorney, Marta Kober, Tom McBride, Bill Randolph, Lauren-Marie Taylor, Russell Todd.

Gallipoli ....Paramount

A Robert Stigwood and Rupert Murdoch presentation for Associated R&R Films Pty. Ltd. Producers: Mr. Stigwood and Patricia Lovell. Director: Peter Weir. Screenplay: David Williamson, based on a story by Mr. Weir. Music: Brian May. Cinematography: Russell Boyd. Editor: William Anderson. In Panavision and color. Running time: 110 minutes. MPAA Rating: PG. Release date: August 28, 1981.

Players: Mark Lee, Bill Kerr, Ron Graham, Harold Hopkins, Charles Yunupingu, Heath Harris, Gerda Nicolson, Brian Anderson, Mel Gibson, Robert Grubb, Tim McKenzie.

Gas ....Paramount

Producer: Claude Heroux. Executive Producers: Victor Solnicki and Pierre David. Director: Les Rose. Screenplay: Richard Wolf. In color. Running time: 94 minutes. MPAA Rating: R. Release date: July, 1981.

Players: Donald Sutherland, Susan Anspach, Howie Mandel, Sterling Hayden, Sandee Currie, Peter Aykroyd, Keith Knight, Helen Shaver, Alf Humphries.

Gloria ....Columbia

Producer: Sam Shaw. Director-Writer: John Cassavetes. In color. Running time: 121 minutes. MPAA Rating: PG. Release date: October, 1980.

Players: Gena Rowlands, Buck Henry, Julie Carmen, John Adames, Tony Knesich, Gregory Cleghorne, Lupe Garnica, Jessica Castillo, Tom Noonan, Ronald Maccone, John Finnegan, Basilio Franchina.

Going Ape ....Paramount

A Hemdale Production. Producer: Robert L. Rosen. Director-Writer: Jeremy Joe Kronsberg. In color. Running time: 89 minutes. MPAA Rating: PG. Release date: April 10, 1981.

Players: Tony Danza, Jessica Walter, Stacey Nelkin, Danny De Vito, Art Metrano, Frank Sivero, Rick Hurst, Howard Mann.

The Great Muppet Caper .... Universal

A Lord Grade presentation. An Associated Film Distribution Corp. release. Executive Producer: Martin Starger. Producers: David Lazer and Frank Oz. Director: Jim Henson. Screenplay: Tom Patchett, Jay Tarses, Jerry Juhl, and Jack Rose. Music and Lyrics: Joe Raposo. Cinematography: Oswald Morris. Editor: Ralph Kemplen. In color. Running time: 95 minutes. MPAA Rating: G. Release date: June 26, 1981.

Players: Charles Grodin, Diana Rigg, John Cleese, Robert Morley, Peter Ustinov, Jack Warden, and the Muppet Performers by Jim Henson, Frank Oz, Dave Goelz, Jerry Nelson and Richard Hunt.

The Hand ....Warner Bros.

An Orion Pictures release. A Jon Peters presentation of an Edward R. Pressman production. Producer: Mr. Pressman. Director-Writer: Oliver Stone based upon the novel, "The Lizard's Tale," by Marc Brandel. In color. Running time: 108 minutes. MPAA Rating: R. Release date: April, 1981.

Players: Michael Caine, Andrea Marcovicci, Annie McEnroe, Viveca Lindfors, Nicholas Hormann, Rosemary Murphy, Dave Maddow, Bruce McGill.

Happy Birthday To Me .... Columbia

A John Dunning—Andre Link Production. Director: J. Lee Thompson. Screenplay: John Saxton, Peter Jobin and Timothy Bond, from a story by Mr. Saxton. In color. Running time: 108 minutes. MPAA Rating: R. Release date: May, 1981.

Players: Melissa Sue Anderson, Glenn Ford, Lawrence Dan, Sharon Acker, Frances Hyland, Tracy Bregman, Lisa Langlois.

Hard Country .... Universal

An Associated Film Distribution release. Producers: David Greene and Mack Bing. Director: Mr. Greene. Screenplay: Michael Kane. In color. Running time: 104 minutes. MPAA Rating: PG. Release date: March, 1981.

Players: Jan-Michael Vincent, Kim Basinger, Michael Parks, Gailard Sartain, Tanya Tucker, Sierra Pecheur, John Chappell, Daryl Hannah.

Hardly Working ....20th Century-Fox

Producers: James M. McNamara and Igo Kantor. Director: Jerry Lewis. Screenplay: Michael Janover and Mr. Lewis, from a story by the former. In color. Running time: 91 minutes. MPAA Rating: PG. Release date: April 3, 1981.

Players: Jerry Lewis, Susan Oliver, Roger C. Carmel, Deanna Lund, Harold J. Stone, Steve Franken, Buddy Lester, Leonard Stone, Jerry Lester, Billy Barty.

Heaven's Gate .... United Artists

Joann Carelli, producer. Michael Cimino, writer-director. In 70mm Panavision and color. Running time: 205 minutes, plus intermission. MPAA Rating: R. Release date: November, 1980, (limited); February, 1981, (general).

Players: Kris Kristofferson, Christopher Walken, John Hurt, Sam Waterston, Brad Dourif, Isabelle Huppert, Joseph Cotten, Jeff Bridges, Roseanne Vela, Ronnie Hawkins, Geoffrey Lewis, Nicholas Woodeson, Stefan Shcherby, Waldemar Kalinowski, Terry Quinn, John Conley, Margaret Benczak, James Knoveloch, Erika Petersen, Paul Koslo, Robin Barlett, Tom Noona.

He Knows You're Alone ...... United Artists

A Metro-Goldwyn-Mayer presentation. A Lansbury/Beruh production. Executive Producers: Edgar Lansbury and Joseph Beruh. Producer: George Manasse. Director: Armand Mastrianni.

Screenplay: Scott Parker. In color. Running time: 94 minutes. MPAA Rating: R. Release date: September, 1980.

Players: Don Scardino, Caitlin O'Hearney, Elizabeth Kemp, Tom Rolfing, Lewis Arlt, Patsy Pease, James Rebhorn, Tom Hanks, Dana Barron, Joseph Leon.

History of the World—Part I
.... 20th Century Fox

Brooksfilms Limited. Written, Produced and directed by Mel Brooks. In Panavision and color. Running time: 86 minutes. MPAA Rating: R. Release date: June 12, 1981.

Players: Mel Brooks, Dom DeLuise, Madeline Kahn, Harvey Korman, Cloris Leachman, Ron Carey, Sid Caesar, Gregory Hines, Pamela Stephenson, Shecky Greene, Mary-Margaret Humes.

Honky Tonk Freeway .... Universal

An Associated Film Distribution Corp. release. An EMI Films production. Producers: Don Boyd and Howard W. Koch, Jr. Director: John Schlesinger. Screenplay: Ed Clinbon. In color. Running time: 107 minutes. MPAA Rating: PG. Release date: August 21, 1981.

Players: Beau Bridges, Beverly D'Angelo, William Devane, Teri Garr, Paul Jabra, Hume Cronyn, Jessica Tandy, Geraldine Page, Daniel Stern, Howard Hesseman, Deborah Rush, Joe Grifasi, George Dzunda, Ron Frazier, David Rasche.

The Howling .... Avco Embassy

International Film Investors and Wescom Productions. Executive Producers: Daniel H. Blatt and Steven A. Lane. Producers: Michael Finnell and Jack Conrad. Director: Joe Dante. Screenplay: John Sayles and Terence H. Winkless, based on the novel by Gary Brandner. In color. Running time: 91 minutes. MPAA Rating: R. Release date: March, 1981.

Players: Dee Wallace, Patrick Macnee, Dennis Dugan, Christopher Stone, Belinda Balaski, Kevin McCarthy, John Carradine, Slim Pickens, Elizabeth Brooks, Robert Picardo, Margie Impert.

The Idolmaker .... United Artists

A Koch/Kirkwood Production. Producers: Gene Kirkwood and Howard W. Koch, Jr. Director: Taylor Hackford. Screenplay: Edward Di Lorenzo. In color. Running time: 119 munutes. MPAA Rating: PG. Release date: November, 1980.

Players: Ray Sharkey, Tovah Feldshuh, Paul Land, Peter Gallagher, Joe Pantoliano, Maureen McCormick, John Aprea, Richard Bright, Olympia Dukakis, Steven Apostlee Peck.

The Incredible .... Shrinking Woman
Universal

A Lija Production. Executive Producer—Writer: Jane Wagner. Producer: Hank Moonjean. Director: Joe Schumacher. In color. Running time: 88 minutes. MPAA Rating: PG. Release date: January 30, 1981.
Players: Lily Tomlin, Charles Grodin, Ned Beatty, Henry Gibson, Elizabeth Wilson, Mark Blankfield, Maria Smith, Pamela Bellwood, John Glover, Nicholas Hormann, James McMullan, Shelby Balik, Justin Dana, Richard A. Baker and Mike Douglas as himself.

In God We Trust .... Universal

A Howard West/George Shapiro production. Director: Marty Feldman. Screenplay: Mr. Feldman and Chris Allen. In color. Running time: 97 minutes. MPAA Rating: PG. Release date: September 26, 1980.

Players: Marty Feldman, Peter Boyle, Louis Lasser, Wilfred Hyde-White, Richard Pryor, Andy Kaufman, Severn Darden, Eddie Parkes, Stephanie Ross, Richard A. Roth.

Inside Moves .... Associated Film Dist.

A Goodmark Production. Producers: Mark M. Tanz and R. W. Goodwin. Director: Richard Donner. Screenplay: Valerie Curtin and Barry Levinson, based on the novel by Todd Walton. In color. Running time: 113 minutes. MPAA Rating: PG. Release date: December, 1980.

Players: John Savage, David Morse, Diana Scarwid, Amy Wright, Tony Burton, Bill Henderson, Steve Kahan, Jack O'Leary, Bert Remsen, Harold Russell, Pepe Serna, Harold Sylvester, Arnold Williams.

It's My Turn .... Columbia

A Rastar—Martin Elfand production. Producer: Mr. Elfnad. Director: Claudia Weill. Screenplay: Eleanor Bergstein. In color. Running time: 91 minutes. MPAA Rating: R. Release date: October, 1980.

Players: Jill Clayburgh, Michael Douglas, Charles Grodin, Beverly Garland, Steven Hill, Teresa Baxter, Joan Copeland, John Gabriel, Charles Kimbrough, Roger Robinson, Jennifer Salt, Daniel Stern, Diane Wiest.

The Jazz Singer ......Associated Film Dist.

EMI Films. Producer: Jerry Leider. Director: Richard Fleischer. Screenplay: Herbert Baker, as adapted by Stephen H. Foreman from the play by Samson Raphaelson. In color. Running time: 115 minutes. MPAA Rating: PG. Release date: December 19, 1980.

Players: Neil Diamond, Laurence Olivier, Lucie Arnaz, Catlin Adams, Franklyn Ajaye, Paul Nicholas, Sully Boyar, Mike Kellin, James Booth, Luther Waters, Oren Waters, Rod Gist, Walter Janowitz, Janet Brandt.

Kagemusha .... 20th Century-Fox

Toho Co., Ltd. and Kurosawa Productions. Executive producers: Akira Kurosawa and Tomoyuki Tanaka. Executive Producers, international version: Francis Ford Coppola and George Lucas. Director: Mr. Kurosawa. Screenplay: Mr. Kurosawa and Masato Ide. Running time: 161 minutes. MPAA Rating: PG. Release date: October, 1980. In Japanese with English titles.

Players: Tatsuya Nakadai, Tsutomu Yamazaki, Kenichi Hagiwara, Jinpachi Nezu, Shuji Otaki.

King of the Mountain .... Universal

A PolyGram Pictures production. Producer: Jack Frost Sanders. Director: Noel Nosseck. Screenplay: H.R. Christian. In color. Running time: 90 minutes. MPAA Rating: PG. Release date: April, 1981.

Players: Harry Hamlin, Joseph Bottoms, Deborah Van Valkenburgh, Richard Cox, Dennis Hopper, Dan Hagerty, Seymour Cassel, Jon Sloan.

Knightriders ....United Film Dist. Co.

A Laurel Production. Producer: Richard P. Rubinstein. Director-Writer: George A. Romero. In color. Running time: 145 minutes. MPAA Rating: R. Release date: April 10, 1981.

Players: Ed Harris, Gary Lahti, Tom Savini, Amy Ingersoll, Patricia Tallman, Christine Forrest, Warner Shook, Brother Blue, Cynthia Adler, John Amplas, Ken Hixon, John Hostetter, Albert Amerson.

La Cage Aux Folles II
.... United Artists

A French—Italian co-production. Les Productions Artistes Associes (Paris); DM. Produzione s.r.l. (Rome). Executive Producer: Marcello Danon. Director: Edouard Molinaro. Screenplay: Francis Veber, based on a story by himself, Jean Poiret, and M. Danon. In color. Running time: 100 minutes. MPAA Rating: R. Release date: February, 1981. In French with English subtitles.

Players: Ugo Tognazzi, Michel Serrault, Marcel Bozzuffi, Paola Borboni, Giovanni Vettorazzo, Glauco Onorato, Roberto Bisacco, Benny Luke, Michael Galabru.

The Legend of The Lone Ranger
.... Universal

A Lord Garde/Jack Wrather Presentation. A Martin Starger Production. Producer: Walter Coblenz. Director: William A. Fraker. Screenplay: Ivan Goff & Ben Roberts and Michael Kane and Wil-

liams Roberts. Adaptation: Jerry Derloshon. In color. Running time: 98 minutes. MPAA Rating: PG. Release date: May, 1981.
Players: Klinton Spilsbury, Michael Horse, Christopher Lloyd, Matt Clark, Juanin Clay, Jason Robards, John Bennett Perry, David Hayward, John Hart, Richard Fransworth, Lincoln Tate, Ted Flicker.

Lion of the Desert .....United Film Dist. Co.

A Falcon International production. Producer-Director: Moustapha Akkad. Screenplay: H.A.L. Craig. In Panavision and color. Running time: 162 minutes. MPAA Rating: PG. Release date: April, 1981.
Players: Anthony Quinn, Oliver Reed, Rod Steiger, John Gielgud, Irene Papas, Raf Vallone, Gastone Moschin, Takis Emmanuel, Stefano Patrizi, Sky Dumont, Robert Brown, Eleonora Stathopoulous, Andrew Keir, Rodolfo Bigotti.

Loving Couples ....20th Century-Fox

A Time—Life Films presentation. Executive Producer: David Susskind. Producer: Renee Valent. Director: Jack Smight. Screenplay: Martin Donovan. In color. Running time: 96 minutes. MPAA Rating: PG. Release date: October, 1980.
Players: Shirley MacLaine, James Coburn, Susan Sarandon, Stephen Collins, Sally Kellerman, Nan Martin, Shelly Batt, Bernard Behrens, Anne Bloom, Fred Carney, Helena.

Melvin and Howard .... Universal

A Linson—Phillips—Demme production. Producers: Art Linson and Don Phillips. Director: Jonathan Demme. Screenplay: Bo Goldman. In color. Running time: 93 minutes. MPAA Rating: R. Release date: November, 1980.
Players: Paul Le Mat, Jason Robards, Mary Steenburgen, Michael J. Pollard, Jack Kehoe, Pamela Reed, Dabney Coleman, John Glover, Charles Napier, Charlete Holt, Gloria Grahame.

Middle Age Crazy ....20th Century-Fox

A Sid and Marty Krofft presentation. Producers: Robert Cooper and Ronald Cohen. Produced with participation of the Canadian Film Development Corp. Director: John Trent. Screenplay: Carl Kleinschmitt. In color. Running time: 95 minutes. MPAA Rating: R. Release date: August, 1980.
Players: Bruce Dern, Ann-Margret, Graham Jarvis, Eric Christmas, Helen Hughes, Geoffrey Bowes, Michael Kane, Diane Dewey, Vivian Reis, Patricia Hamilton, Anni Lantuch, Deborah Wakeham, Gina Dick.

The Mirror Crack'd ....Associated Film Dist.

EMI Films. Producers: John Brabourne and Richard Goodwin. Director: Guy Hamilton. Screenplay: Jonathan Hales and Barry Sandler, based on the book by Agatha Cristie. In color. Running time: 105 minutes. MPAA Rating: PG. Release date: December 19, 1980.
Players: Angela Lansbury, Geraldine Chaplin, Tony Curtis, Edward Fox, Rock Hudson, Kim Novak, Elizabeth Taylor, Marella Oppenheim, Wendy Morgan, Margaret Courtenay, Charles Gray, Maureen Bennett.

Modern Romance ....

Producers: Andrew Scheinman and Martin Shafer. Director: Albert Brooks. Screenplay: Mr. Brooks and Monica Johnson. In color. Running time: 93 minutes. MPAA Rating: R. Release date: March, 1981.
Players: Albert Brooks, Kathryn Harrold, Tyann Means, Bruno Kirby, Jane Hallaren, Karen Chandler, Dennis Kort, Bob Einstein, Virginia Feingold, Thelma Leeds, Candy Castillo.

Mon Oncle d'Amerique
.... New World Pictures

Producer: Philippe Dussart in co-production with Andrea Films and T.F.I. Director: Alain Resnais. Screenplay: Jean Gruault, based on the works of Henri Laborit. In color. Running time: 123 minutes. No MPAA Rating. Release date: December, 1980.

Players: Gerard Depardieu, Nicole Garcia, Roger-Pierre, Marie Dubois, Nelly Borgeaud, Pierre Arditi, Gerard Darrieu, Philippe Laudenbach, Professor Henri Laborit.

My Bloody Valentine ....Paramount

Produced with participation of the Canadian Film Development Corp. and Famous Players Ltd. Producers: John Dunning, Andre Link and Stephen Miller. Director: George Mihalka. Screenplay: John Beaird. In color. Running time: 91 minutes. MPAA Rating: R. Release date: February, 1981.
Players: Paul Kelman, Lori Hallier, Neil Affleck, Keith Knight, Alf Humphreys, Cynthia Dale, Helene Udy, Rob Stein, Tom Kovacks, Terry Waterland, Carl Marotte, Jim Murchison, Gina Dick, Peter Cowper, Don Francks, Patricia Hamilton, Larry Reynolds, Jack Van Evera.

Nighthawks .... Universal

A Martin Poll/Production Company production. Producer: Mr. Poll. Director: Bruce Malmuth. Screenplay: David Shaber, from a story by himself and Paul Sylbert. In color. Running time: 98 minutes. MPAA Rating: R. Release date: April 10, 1981.
Players: Sylvester Stallone, Billy Dee Williams, Lindsay Wagner, Persis Khambatta, Nigel Davenport, Rutger Hauer, Hilarie Thompson, Joe Spinell, Walter Mathews, E. Brian Dean, Caesar Cordova, Charles Duval, Tony Munafo.

The Night the Lights Went Out in Georgia ....Avco Embassy

G.L. Productions, Ltd. Producers: Elliot Geisinger, Howard Kuperman, Ronald Saland and Howard Smith. Executive Producers: William and Carole Blake. Director: Ronald F. Maxwell. Screenplay: Bob Bonney. Music: David Shire. Cinematography: Bill Butler. Editor: Anne Goursaud. In color. Running time: 120 minutes. MPAA Rating: PG. Release date: June, 1981.
Players: Kristy McNichol, Dennis Quaid, Mark Hamill, Sunny Johnson, Don Stroud, Arlen Dean Snyder, Barry Corbin, Lulu McNichol, Royce Clark.

Nine to Five ....20th Century-Fox

An IPC Films production. Producer: Bruce Gilbert. Director: Colin Higgins. Screenplay: Mr. Higgins and Patricia Resnick, from a story by the latter. In color. Running time: 110 minutes. MPAA Rating: PG. Release date: December 19, 1980.
Players: Jane Fonda, Lily Tomlin, Dolly Parton, Dabney Coleman, Sterling Hayden, Elizabeth Wilson, Henry Jones, Lawrence Pressman, Marian Mercer.

Nobody's Perfect .... Columbia

Producer: Mort Engelberg. Executive Producer: Ted Swanson. Director: Peter Bonerz. Screenplay: Tony Kenrick, based on his novel. In color. Running time: 96 minutes. MPAA Rating: PG. Release date: July, 1981.
Players: Gabe Kaplan, Alex Karras, Robert Klein, Susan Clark, Paul Stewart, Alex Rocco, Arthur Rosenberg, James Cromwell, Bobby Ramsen, John Di Santi, Ric Applewhite, Will Knickerbocker, Peter Bonerz.

Oh God! Book II ....Warner Bros.

Producer-Director: Gilbert Cates. Screenplay: Josh Greenfeld, Hal Goldman, Fred S. Fox, Seaman Jacobs, and Melissa Miller, based on a story by Mr. Greenfeld. In color. Running time: 94 minutes. MPAA Rating: PG. Release date: October, 1980.
Players: George Burns, Suzanne Pleshette, David Birney, Louanne, John Louie, Conrad Janis, Anthony Holland, Hugh Downs.

One-Trick Pony ....Warner Bros.

Producers: Michael Tannen and Michael Hausman. Director: Robert M. Young. Screenplay: Paul Simon. In color. Running time: 98 minutes. MPAA Rating: R. Release date: October 3, 1980.
Players: Paul Simon, Blair Brown, Rip Torn, Joan Hackett, Allen Goorwitz, Mare Winningham, Michael Pearlman, Lou Reed, Steve Gadd, Eric Gale, Tony Levin, Richard Tee, Harry Shearer, The B-52s, Sam and Dave, The Lovin' Spoonful, and Tiny Tim.

Ordinary People .... Paramount

A Wildwood Enterprises Production. Producer: Ronald L. Schwary. Director: Robert Redford. Screenplay: Alvin Sargent, based on the novel by Judith Guest. In color. Running time: 124 minutes. MPAA Rating: R. Release date: September, 1980.

Players: Donald Sutherland, Mary Tyler Moore, Judd Hirsch, Timothy Hutton, M. Emmet Walsh, Elizabeth McGovern, Dinah Manoff, Fredric Lehne, James B. Sikking, Basil Hoffman, Quinn Redeker, Mariclare Costello, Meg Mundy, Elizabeth Hubbard, Adam Baldwin, Scott Doebler.

Outland .... Warner Bros.

A Ladd Company Release. Producer: Richard A. Roth. Writer-Director: Peter Hyams. In Panavision and color. Recorded in Dolby Stereo. Running time: 109 minutes. MPAA Rating: R. Release date: May, 1981.

Players: Sean Connery, Peter Boyle, Frances Sternhagen, James B. Sikking, Kika Markham, Clarke Peters, Steven Berkoff.

Popeye .... Paramount

A presentation of Paramount Pictures and Walt Disney Productions. Executive producer: C.O. Erickson. Producer: Robert Evans. Director: Robert Altman. Screenplay: Jules Feiffer. In Technovision and color. Running time: 114 minutes. MPAA Rating: PG. Release date: December 12, 1980.

Players: Robin Williams, Shelley Duvall, Ray Walston, Paul Dooley, Paul L. Smith, Richard Libertini, Donald Moffat, MacIntyre Dixon, Roberta Maxwell, Donovan Scott, Allan Nicholls, Wesley Ivan Hurt.

The Postman Always Rings Twice
.... Paramount

Lorimar Productions, Inc. A Northstar International picture made in association with CIP-Europaische Treuhand AG, Germany. Producers: Charles Mulvehill and Bob Rafelson. Director: Mr. Rafelson. Screenplay: David Mamet, based on the novel by James M. Cain. In color. Running time: 125 minutes. MPAA Rating: R. Release date: March (special); April, 1981 general.

Players: Jack Nicholson, Jessica Lange, John Colicos, Michael Lerner, John P. Ryan, Anjelica Huston, William Traylor, Tom Hill, Jon Van Ness, Brian Farrell, Raleigh Bond, William Newman, Albert Henderson.

Prince of the City .... Warner Bros.

An Orion Pictures Company release. Producer: Burtt Harris. Executive Producer: Jay Presson Allen. Director: Sidney Lumet. Screenplay: Ms. Allen and Mr. Lumet, based on the book by Robert Daley. Music: Paul Chihara. Cinematography: Andrzej Bartkowiak. Editor: John J. Fitzstephens. In color. Running time: 167 minutes. MPAA Rating: R. Release date: August, 1981 (limited); October, (general).

Players: Treat Williams, Jerry Orbach, Richard Foronjy, Don Billett, Kenny Marino, Carmine Caridi, Tony Page, Norman Parker, Paul Roebling, Bob Balaban, James Tolkan, Steve Inwood, Lindsay Crouse, Matthew Laurance, Tony Turco, Ron Maccone, Ron Karabatsos, Tony DiBenedetto, Tony Munafo, Robert Christian.

Private Benjamin .... Warner Bros.

A Goldie Hawn/Nancy Meyers Production. Producers-Writers: Ms. Meyers, Charles Shyer, and Harvey Miller. Director: Howard Zieff. In color. Running time: 110 minutes. MPAA Rating: R. Release date: October 10, 1980.

Players: Goldie Hawn, Eileen Brennan, Armand Assante, Robert Webber, Sam Wanamaker, Barbara Barrie, Albert Brooks, Mary Kay Place, Harry Dean Stanton.

Raging Bull .... United Artists

A Robert Chartoff—Irwin Winkler Production. Produced in association with Peter Savage. Director: Martin Scorsese. Screenplay: Paul Schrader and Mardik Martin, based on the book of the same name by Jake La Motta, with Joseph Carter and Peter Savage. In black-and-white with sequences in color. Running time: 128 minutes. MPAA Rating: R. Release date: November, (limited); December, 1981 (general).

Cast: Robert De Niro, Cathy Moriarty, Joe Pesci, Frank Vincent, Nicholas Colasanto, Theresa Saldana, Frank Adonis, Mario Gallo, Frank Topham, Lori Anne Flax, Joseph Bono, James V. Christy, Bernie Allen, Bill Mazer, Bill Hanrahan, Rita Benett, Mike Miles.

Raiders of the Lost Ark .... Paramount

Lucasfilm Ltd. Producer: Frank Marshall. Director: Steven Spielberg. Screenplay: Lawrence Kasdan, from a story by George Lucas and Philip Kaufman. Music: John Williams. Cinematography: Douglas Slocombe. Editor: Michael Kahn. In Panavision and color. Running time; 115 minutes. MPAA Rating: PG. Release date: June 12, 1981.

Players: Harrison Ford, Karen Allen, Paul Freeman, Ronald Lacey, John Rhys-Davies, Denholm Elliott, Wolf Kahler, Anthony Higgins, Alfred Molina, Vic Tablian, Don Fellows.

Resurrection .... Universal

Producers: Renee Missel and Howard Rosenman. Director: Daniel Petrie. Screenplay: Lewis John Carlino. In color. Running time: 103 minutes. MPAA Rating: PG. Release date: October, 1980.

Players: Ellen Burstyn, Sam Shepard, Richard Farnsworth, Roberts Blossom, Clifford David, Pamela Payton-Wright, Jeffrey DeMunn, Eva Le Gallienne, Lois Smith, Madeleine Thornton-Sherwood, Richard Hamilton, Carlin Glynn, Lane Smith, Penelope Allen.

Sam Marlow, Private Eye . 20th Century-Fox

Melvin Simon Productions. Producer-Writer: Andrew J. Fenady, based on his novel. Director: Robert Day. In color. Running time: 111 minutes. MPAA Rating: PG. Release date: October, 1980.

Players: Robert Sacchi, Franco Nero, Michelle Phillips, Olivia Hussey, Misty Rowe, Victor Buono, Herbert Lom, Sybil Danning, Dick Bakalyan, Gregg Palmer, Jay Robinson, George Raft, Yvonne de Carlo.

Savage Harvest .... 20th Century-Fox

Producers: Ralph Helfer and Sandy Howard. Director: Robert Collins. Screenplay: Robert Blees and Robert Collins, based on a story by Ralph Helfer and Ken Noyle. In color. Running time: 86 minutes. MPAA Rating: PG. Release date: May, 1981.

Players: Tom Skerritt, Michelle Phillips, Shawn Stevens, Ann-Marie Martin, Derek Partridge, Arthur Malet, Tana Helfer.

Scanners .... Avco Embassy

A Filmplan International Production. Executive Producers: Victor Solnicki and Michael Ironside. Producer: Claude Heroux. Director-Writer: David Cronenberg. In color. Running time: 103 minutes. MPAA Rating: R. Release date: January, 1981.

Players: Jennifer O'Neill, Stephen Lack, Patrick McGoohan, Lawrence Dane, Charles Shamata, Adam Ludwig, Michael Ironside, Victor Desy, Robert Silverman.

The Sea Wolves .... Paramount

A Lorimar presentation. Made by Richmond Light Horse Productions Ltd. for Varius A. G. An Anglo-American-Swiss Enterprise. Producer: Euan Lloyd. Director: Andrew V. McLaglen. Screenplay: Reginald Rose, based on "Boarding Party" by James Leasor. In color. Running time: 120 minutes. MPAA Rating: PG. Release date: June, 1981.

Players: Gregory Peck, Roger Moore, David Niven, Trevor Howard, Barbara Kellerman, Patrick Macnee, Kenneth Griffith, Patrick Allen, Wolf Kahler, Robert Hoffmann, Dan Van Husen.

Second Hand Hearts .... Paramount

A Lorimar Pictures production. Producer: James William Guerclo. Director: Hal Ashby. Screenplay: Charles Eastman. In color. Running time: 102 minutes. MPAA Rating: PG. Release date: May, 1981.

Players: Robert Blake, Barbara Harris, Collin Boone, Ambert Rose Gold, Jessica Standbury, Bert Remsen, Sondra Blake, Shirley Stoler, Woodrow Chambliss.

Seems Like Old Times .... Columbia

A Rastar Production. Producer: Ray Stark. Director: Jay Sandrich. Screenplay: Neil Simon. In color. Running time: 102 minutes. MPAA Rating: PG. Release date: December 19, 1980.

Players: Goldie Hawn, Chevy Chase, Charles Grodin, Robert Guillaume, Harold Gould, George Grizzard, Yvonne Wilder, T.K. Carter, Judd Omen, Marc Alaimo.

Somewhere in Time .... Universal

A Rastar/Stephen Deutsch production. Producer: Stephen Deutsch. Director: Jeannot Szwarc. Screenplay: Richard Matheson, based on his novel, "Bid Time Return." In color. Running time: 103 minutes. MPAA Rating: PG. Release date: October 3, 1980.

Players: Christopher Reeve, Jane Seymour, Christopher Plummer, Teresa Wright, Bill Erwin, George Foskovec, Susan French, John Alvin, Eddra Gale.

"S.O.B." .... Paramount

A Lorimar Pictures presentation. Producers: Blake Edwards and Tony Adams. Writer-Director: Blake Edwards. Music: Henry Mancini. Cinematography: Harry Stradling. Editor: Ralph E. Winters. In color. Running time: 121 minutes. MPAA Rating: R. Release date: July 1, 1981.

Players: Julie Andrews, William Holden, Marisa Berenson, Larry Hagman, Robert Loggia, Stuart Margolin, Richard Mulligan, Robert Preston, Craig Stevens, Loretta Swit, Robert Vaughn, Robert Webber, Shelly Winters.

Sphinx .... Warner Bros.

An Orion Pictures production. Executive Producer: Franklin J. Schaffner. Producer: Stanley O'Toole. Director: Mr. Schaffner. Screenplay: John Byrun, adapting the novel by Robin Cook. In Panavision and color. Running time: 119 minutes. MPAA Rating: PG. Release date: February 11, 1981.

Players: Lesley-Anne Down, Frank Langella, Maurice Ronet, Sir John Gielgud, Vic Tablian, Martin Benson, John Rhys-Davies, Nadim Sawalha, Tutte Lemkow, Safed Jaffrey, Eileen Way, William Hootkins, Mark Kingston.

Stardust Memories .... United Artists

A Jack Rollins-Charles H. Joffe production. Producer: Robert Greenhut. Director-Writer: Woody Allen. In black-and-white. Running time: 88 minutes. MPAA Rating: PG. Release date: October, 1980.

Players: Woody Allen, Charlotte Rampling, Jessica Harper, Marie-Christine Barrault, Tony Roberts, Daniel Stern, Amy Wright, Helen Hanft, John Rothman, Anne DeSalvo, Joan Neuman, Ken Chapin, Leonardo Cimino.

Stir Crazy .... Columbia

Producer: Hannah Weinstein. Director: Sidney Poitier. Screenplay: Bruce Jay Friedman. In color. Running time: 114 minutes. MPAA Rating: R. Release date: December 12, 1980.

Players: Gene Wilder, Richard Pryor, Georg Stanford Brown, Jobeth Williams, Miguelangel Suarez, Craig T. Nelson, Barry Corbin, Charles Weldon, Nicholas Coster, Joel Brooks, Jonathan Banks, Erland Van Lidth De Jeude.

Stripes .... Columbia

An Ivan Reitman Film. Producers: Mr. Reitman and Dan Goldberg. Director: Mr. Reitman. Screenplay: Len Blum, Mr. Goldberg, and Harold Ramis. Music: Elmer Bernstein. Cinematography: Bill Butler. Editors: Eva Ruggiero, Michael Luciano, and Harry Keller. In color. Running time: 105 minutes. MPA Rating: R. Release date: June 26, 1981.

Players: Bill Murray, Harold Ramis, Warren Oates, P.J. Soles, Sean Young, John Candy, John Larroquette, John Voldstad, John Diehl, Lance LeGault, Roberta Leighton.

Student Bodies .... Paramount

A Universal Cinema Inc. production. Producer: Allen Smithee. Executive Producers: Jerry Belson and Harvey Miller. Director-

Writer: Mickey Rose. Music: Gene Hobson. Cinematography: Robert Ebinger. Editor: Kathryn Ruth Hope. In color. Running time: 86 minutes. MPAA Rating: R. Release date: August, 1981.

Players: Kristen Riter, Matthew Goldsby, Richard Brando, Joe Flood, Joe Talarowski, Mimi Weddell, Carl Jacobs, Peggy Cooper, Janice E. O'Malley.

The Stunt Man .... 20th Century-Fox

A Melvin Simon production. Producer-Director: Richard Rush. Screenplay: Lawrence B. Marcus, from an adaptation by Mr. Rush of the novel by Paul Brodeur. In color. Running time: 129 minutes. MPAA Rating: R. Release date: August, 1981.

Players: Peter O'Toole, Steve Railsback, Barbara Hershey, Allen Goorwitz, Alex Rocco, Sharon Farrell, Adam Roarke, Phillip Bruns, Chuck Bail.

Sunday Lovers .... United Artists

A Metro-Goldwyn-Mayer presentation. Viaduc Productions, S.A. Producer: Leo Fuchs. Directors: Edouard Molinaro, Bryan Forbes, Dino Risi and Gene Wilder. Screenplay: Francis Veber, Leslie Bricusse, Age & Scarpelli, and Mr. Wilder. In color. Running time: 125 minutes. MPAA Rating: R. Release date: February, 1981.

Players: England: Roger Moore, Denholm Elliott, Lynn Redgrave, Priscilla Barnes. America: Gene Wilder, Kathleen Quinlan, Dianne Crittenden. France: Lino Ventura, Robert Webber, Catherine Salviat. Italy: Ugo Tognazzi, Rossana Podesta, Sylva Koscina, Beba Loncar.

Superman II .... Warner Bros.

An International Film Production Inc. picture. An Alexander Salkind presentation. An Alexander and Ilya Salkind production. Producer: Pierre Spengler. Director: Richard Lester. Screenplay: Mario Puzo, David Newman, and Leslie Newman, from a story by Mr. Puzo. In Panavision and color. Running time: 127 minutes. MPAA Rating: PG. Release date: June 19, 1981.

Players: Gene Hackman, Christopher Reeve, Ned Beatty, Jackie Cooper, Sarah Douglas, Margot Kidder, Jack O'Halloran, Valerie Perrine, Susannah York, Clifton James, E.G. Marshall, Marc McClure, Terence Stamp.

Take This Job and Shove It
.... Avco Embassy

A Cinema Group presentation. Producer: Greg Blackwell. Executive Producers: William J. Immerman and J. David Marks. Director: Gus Trikonis. Screenplay: Barry Schneider, from a story by Jeffrey Bernini and Mr. Schneider. Music: Billy Sherrill. Cinematography: James Devis. Editor: Richard Belding. In color. Running time: 100 minutes. MPAA Rating: PG. Release date: May, 1981.

Players: Robert Hays, Art Carney, Barbara Hershey, David Keith, Tim Thomerson, Martin Mull, Eddie Mull, Eddie Albert, Penelope Milford.

Tarzan, The Ape Man .... United Artists

A Metro-Goldwyn-Mayer presentation. A Svengali Production. Producer: Bo Derek. Director: John Derek. Screenplay: Tom Rowe and Gary Goodard, based on characters created by Edgar Rice Burroughs. Music: Perry Botkin. Cinematography: John Derek. Editor: James B. Ling. In color. Running time: 112 minutes. MPAA Rating: R. Release date: July 24, 1981.

Players: Bo Derek, Richard Harris, John Phillip Law, Miles O'Keefe, Akushula Selayah, Steven Strong, Maxime Philoe, Leonard Bailey, Wilfrid Hyde-White, Laurie Mains, Harold Ayer.

The Tempest .... World Northal

A Boyd's Co. production. Producers: Sarah Radclyffe, Guy Ford and Mordecai Schreiber. Executive Producer: Don Boyd. Director-Adapter: Derek Jarman. In color. Running time: 95 minutes. Release date: October, 1980.

Players: Heathcote Williams, Karl Johnson, Toyah Willcox, Peter Bull, Richard Warwick, Elisabeth Welch, Jack Birkett, Ken Campbell, David Meyer, Christopher Biggins, Neil Cunningham, Peter Turner.

Terror Train .... 20th Century-Fox

An Astral Bellevue-Pathe production. Producer: Harold Greenberg. Director: Roger Spottiswoode. Screenplay: T. Y. Drake. In color. Running time: 97 minutes. MPAA Rating: R. Release date: October, 1980.

Players: Ben Johnson, Jamie Lee Curtis, Hart Bochner, David Cooperfield, Derek MacKinnon, Sandee Currie, Timothy Webber, Anthony Sherwood, Howard Busgang, Steve Michaels, Greg Swanson, D. D. Winters, Joy Boushel, Victor Knight.

Tess .... Columbia

A Franco-British co-production: Renn Productions (France) and Burrill Productions (England) with the participation of the Societe Francaise De Production (S.F.P.). Producers: Claude Berri and Timothy Burrill. Executive Producer: Pierre Grunstein. Director: Roman Polanski. Screenplay: Gerard Brach, Mr. Polanski and John Brownjohn, based on the novel, "Tess of the D'Ubervilles" by Thomas Hardy. In color. Running time: 170 minutes. MPAA Rating: PG. Release date: February, 1981.

Players: Nastassia Kinski, Peter Firth, Albert Simono, Brigid Erin Bates, Jeanne Biras, John Bett, Leigh Lawson.

Thief .... United Artists

Michael Mann/Cann Productions. Producers: Jerry Bruckheimer and Ronnie Caan. Director: Michael Mann. Screenplay and Screen Story: Mr. Mann, based on "The Home Invaders" by Frank Hohimer. In color. Running time: 118 minutes. MPAA Rating: R. Release date: March, 1981.

Players: James Caan, Tuesday Weld, Willie Nelson, James Belushi, Robert Prosky, Tom Signorelli, Dennis Farina, Nick Nickeas, W. R. (Bill) Brown, Norm Tobin, John Santucci, Gavin MacFadyen.

This Is Elvis .... Warner Bros.

A David L. Wolper production. Produced, directed, and written by Malcom Leo and Andrew Solt. In color and black-and-white. Running time: 109 minutes. MPAA Rating: PG. Release date: May, 1981.

Players: Elvis Presley, David Scott, Paul Boensch 3rd, Johnny Harra, Lawrence Kobler, Rhonda Lyn, Debbie Edge, Larry Raspberry. Narration: Ral Donner, Joe Esposito, Linda Thompson, Lisha Sweetnam, Virginia Kiser, Michael Tomack.

Times Square .... Associated Film Dist.

An EMI Films release. Producers: Robert Stigwood and Jacob Brackman. Director: Alan Moyle. Screenplay: Mr. Brackman, from a story by Mr. Moyle and Leanne Unger. In Panavision and color. Running time: 111 minutes. MPAA Rating: R. Release date: October 17, 1980.

Players: Tim Curry, Trini Alvarado, Robin Johnson, Peter Coffield, Herbert Berghof, David Marguilies, Anna Maria Horsford, Michael Margotta, J. C. Quinn, Miguel Pinero.

Tribute .... 20th century-Fox

A Turman-Foster Company production. Producers: Joel B. Michaels and Garth H. Drabinsky. Director: Bob Clark. Screenplay: Bernard Slade, based on his play. In color. Running time: 125 minutes. MPAA Rating: PG. Release date: December, 1980 (limited); February, 1981 (general).

Players: Jack Lemmon, Robby Benson, Lee Remick, Colleen Dewhurst, John Marley, Kim Cattrall, Gale Garnett, Teri Keane.

Under the Rainbow .... Warner Bros.

An Orion Pictures Company release. An Innovisions/ECA presentation. Producer: Fred Bauer. Director: Steve Rash. Screenplay: Pat McCormick, Harry Hurwitz, Martin Smith, Pat Bradley and Fred Bauer, based on a story by Bauer and Bradley. Music: Joe Renzetti. Cinematography: Frank Stanley. Editor: David Blewitt. In color. Running time: 98 minutes. MPAA Rating: PG. Release date: July 31, 1981.

Players: Chevy Chase, Carrie Fisher, Eve Arden, Joseph Maher, Robert Donner, Billy Barty, Mako, Cork Hubbert, Pat McCormick, Adam Arkin, Richard Stahl, Freeman King.

Victory .... Paramount

A Lorimar Pictures presentation. Producer: Freddie Fields. Director: John Huston. Screenplay: Evan Jones and Yabo Yablonsky, from a story by Mr. Yablonsky, Djordje Millcevic, and Jeff Maguire. Music: Bill Conti. Cinematography: Gerry Fisher. Editor: Roberto Silvie. In color. Running time: 117 minutes. MPAA Rating: PG. Release date: July, 1981.

Players: Sylvester Stallone, Michael Caine, Pele, Max Von Sydow, Daniel Massey, Carole Laure.

Wolfen .... Warner Bros.

An Orion Pictures release. Producer: Rupert Hitzig. Executive Producer: Alan King. Director: Michael Wadleigh. Screenplay and Story: David Eyre and Mr. Wadleigh, based on the novel by Whitley Strieber. Music: James Horner. Cinematography: Gerry Fisher. Editors: Chris Lebenzon, Dennis Dolan, Martin Bram, and Marshall M. Borden. In Panavision and color. Running time: 115 minutes. MPAA Rating: R. Release date: July 24, 1981.

Players: Albert Finney, Diane Venora, Edward James Olmos, Gregory Hines, Tom Noonan, Dick O'Neill, Dehl Beri, Peter Michael Goetz, Sam Gray, Ralph Bell, Max M. Brown, Annie Marie Photamo, Sarah Felder.

Zorro, The Gay Blade ..... 20th Century-Fox

A Melvin Simon Production. Producers: George Hamilton and C. O. Erickson. Executive Producer: Mr. Simon. Director: Peter Medak. Screenplay: Hal Dresner, based on a story by himself, Greg Alt, Don Moriarty, and Bob Randall. Music: Ian Fraser. Cinematography: John A. Alonzo. Editor: Hillary Jane Kranze. In color. Running time: 93 minutes. MPAA Rating: PG. Release date: July 17, 1981.

Players: George Hamilton, Lauren Hutton, Brenda Vaccaro, Ron Leibman, Donovan Scott, James Booth, Helen Burns, Clive Revill, Eduardo Noriega.

FEATURE PICTURES
January 1, 1955—August 1, 1980

[In the following listings (R) indicates release dates; (CS) indicates CinemaScope; (VV) indicates VistaVision; (SS) indicates Super-Scope; (T) indicates Technirama; (P) Panavision; (D-150) Dimension-150; (D) Dyalscope; (F) Franscope; (U) Ultrascope; (VS) VistaScope; (M) Megascope; (R) Regalscope; (H) Hammerscope; (TE) Techniscope. All films released starting in 1974 in color unless otherwise indicated.]

	Length In Mins.

a.k.a. CASSIUS CLAY 85
UNITED ARTISTS. (R) November, 1970. Documentary on Mohammad Ali.

AARON LOVES ANGELA 98
COLUMBIA. (R) December, 1975. Kevin Hooks, Irene Cara.

ABANDON SHIP 100
COLUMBIA. (R) May, 1957. Tyrone Power, Mai Zetterling.

ABBOTT AND COSTELLO MEET THE MUMMY 79
UNIVERSAL. (R) June, 1955. Abbott and Costello.

ABBY 91
AMERICAN INTERNATIONAL. (R) December, 1974. William Marshall, Carole Speed.

ABDICATION, THE 103
WARNER BROS. (R) October, 1974. Peter Finch, Liv Ullmann.

ABDUCTORS, THE 80
TWENTIETH CENTURY-FOX. (R) July, 1957. Victor McLaglen, George Macready.

ABDULLAH'S HAREM 88
TWENTIETH CENTURY-FOX. (R) June, 1956. Gregory Ratoff, Kay Kendall. Color.

ABOMINABLE DR. PHIBES, THE 93
AMERICAN INTERNATIONAL. (R) May, 1971. Vincent Price, Joseph Cotten. Color.

ABOMINABLE SNOWMAN, THE 85
TWENTIETH CENTURY-FOX. (R) October, 1957. Forrest Tucker, Peter Cushing.

ABOVE US THE WAVES 92
REPUBLIC. (R) October 26, 1956. John Mills, John Gregson.

ABSENT MINDED PROFESSOR, THE 97
BUENA VISTA. (R) April, 1961. Fred MacMurray, Nancy Olson.

ABYSSES, LES (Fr., Eng. titles) 90
KANAWHAX. (R) November, 1964. Francine Berge, Colette Berge.

ACCIDENT 105
CINEMA V. (R) April, 1967. Dirk Bogarde, Stanley Baker. Color.

ACCURSED, THE 78
ALLIED ARTISTS. (R) July, 1958. Robert Bray, Donald Wolfit.

ACCUSED OF MURDER 74
REPUBLIC. (R) December, 1956. David Brian, Vera Ralston. Color.

ACE ELI AND RODGER OF THE SKIES 92
TWENTIETH CENTURY-FOX. (R) April, 1973. Cliff Robertson, Pamela Franklin. Color.

ACE HIGH 123
PARAMOUNT. (R) October, 1969. Eli Wallach, Terrence Hill, Bud Spencer. Color.

ACROSS 110TH STREET 102
UNITED ARTISTS. (R) December, 1972. Anthony Quinn, Anthony Franciosa. Color.

ACROSS THE BADLANDS 55
COLUMBIA. (R) September 14, 1950. Charles Starrett, Smiley Burnette.

ACROSS THE BRIDGE (Brit.) 103
RANK. (R) January, 1958. Rod Steiger, Maria Landi.

ACROSS THE RIVER 85
DEBEMA. (R) April, 1965. Lou Gilber, Kay Doubleday.

ACT OF THE HEART 103
UNIVERSAL. (R) October 1970. Genevieve Bujold, Donald Sutherland. Color.

ACT ONE 110
WARNER BROS. (R) December, 1963. George Hamilton, Jason Robards, Jr.

ACTION OF THE TIGER (Cs) 93
METRO-GOLDWYN-MAYER. (R) August, 1957. Van Johnson, Martine Carol.

ACTIVIST, THE 86
REGIONAL. (R) December, 1969. Michael Smith, Leslie Gilbrum. Color.

	Length In Mins.

ADA (Cs) 108
METRO-GOLDWYN-MAYER. (R) August, 1961. Susan Hayward, Dean Martin. Color.

ADALEN 31 (Swed., Eng. titles) 115
PARAMOUNT. (R) October, 1969. Peter Schildt, Kerstin Tidelius. Color.

ADAM AT 6 A.M. 100
NATIONAL GENERAL. (R) September, 1970. Michael Douglas, Lee Purcell. Color.

ADDING MACHINE, THE 100
REGIONAL. (R) September, 1969. Phyllis Diller, Milo O'Shea, Billie Whitelaw. Color.

ADELAIDE (Fr., Eng. titles) 86
SIGMA III. (R) February, 1969. Ingrid Thulin, Jean Sorel, Sylvia Fennec. Color.

ADORABLE CREATURES 106
CONTINENTAL. (R) January, 1956. Martine Carol, Danielle Darrieux.

ADORABLE JULIA 94
SEE-ART. (R) April, 1964. Lilli Palmer, Charles Boyer.

ADRIFT 102
MPO. (R) July, 1971. Rade Markovic, Paula Pritchett. Color.

ADVANCE TO THE REAR (P) 97
METRO-GOLDWYN-MAYER. (R) April, 1964. Glenn Ford, Stella Stevens.

ADVENTURE OF SHERLOCK HOLMES' SMARTER BROTHER 91
TWENTIETH CENTURY-FOX. (R) December, 1975. Gene Wilder, Madeline Kahn.

ADVENTURERS, THE 171
PARAMOUNT. (R) March, 1970. Bekim Fehmiu, Ernest Borgnine, Candice Bergen. Color.

ADVENTURES OF A YOUNG MAN (Cs) 145
TWENTIETH CENTURY-FOX. (R) June, 1962. Richard Beymer, Diane Baker. Color.

ADVENTURES OF BULLWHIP GRIFFIN, THE 110
BUENA VISTA. (R) March, 1967. Roddy McDowall, Suzanne Pleshette. Color.

ADVENTURES OF HUCKLEBERRY FINN, THE (Cs) 107
METRO-GOLDWYN-MAYER. (R) May, 1960. Tony Randall, Patty McCormack. Color.

ADVENTURES OF SADIE (Brit.) 88
TWENTIETH CENTURY-FOX. (R) May, 1955. Joan Collins, Kenneth More. Color.

ADVISE AND CONSENT (P) 139
COLUMBIA. (R) June, 1962. Henry Fonda, Charles Laughton.

AFFAIR IN HAVANA 70
ALLIED ARTISTS. (R) October, 1957. John Cassavetes, Raymond Burr.

AFFAIR IN RENO (N) 75
REPUBLIC. (R) February 15, 1957. John Lund, Doris Singleton.

AFFAIR OF THE SKIN, AN 102
ZENITH. (R) January, 1964. Kevin McCarthy, Herbert Berghof.

AFFAIR TO REMEMBER, AN (Cs) 114
TWENTIETH CENTURY-FOX. 1957. Cary Grant, Deborah Kerr. Color

AFRICA ADDIO (TS) 125
RIZZOLI. (R) January, 1967. Documentary. Color.

AFRICA-TEXAS STYLE! 106
PARAMOUNT. (R) May, 1967. Hugh O'Brian, John Mills. Color

AFRICAN ELEPHANT, THE 92
NATIONAL GENERAL. (R) October, 1971. Documentary.

AFRICAN LION, THE 75
BUENA VISTA. (R). October 10, 1955. Documentary. Color.

AFRICAN MANHUNT 65
REPUBLIC. (R) January 5, 1955. Myron Healey, Karin Booth.

AFRICAN SAFARI 98

	Length In Mins.

CROWN INTERNATIONAL. (R) February, 1969. Documentary. Color.

AFTER THE FOX (P) **103**
UNITED ARTISTS. (R) December, 1966. Peter Sellers, Victor Mature. Color.

AFTER YOU COMRADE **84**
CONTINENTAL. (R) April, 1967. Jamie Uys, Bob Courtney. Color.

AGATHA **98**
WARNER BROS. (R) February, 1979. Dustin Hoffman, Vanessa Redgrave.

AGE OF CONSENT **98**
COLUMBIA. (R) January, 1970. James Mason, Helen Mirren. Color.

AGENT FOR H.A.R.M. **84**
UNIVERSAL. (R) February, 1966. Mark Richman, Wendell Corey. Color.

AGENT 8¾ **98**
CONTINENTAL. (R) June, 1965. Dirk Bogarde, Sylvia Koscina. Color.

AGONY AND THE ECSTASY, THE (Todd-AO) **140**
TWENTIETH CENTURY-FOX. (R) October, 1965. Charlton Heston, Rex Harrison. Color.

AIN'T MISBEHAVIN' **82**
UNIVERSAL. (R) July, 1955. Rory Calhoun, Piper Laurie, Jack Carson, Mamie Van Doren. Color.

AIR PATROL **70**
TWENTIETH CENTURY-FOX. (R) July, 1962. Willard Parker, Merry Anders.

AIR STRIKE **67**
LIPPERT. (R) May 6, 1955. Richard Denning, Gloria Hean.

AIRPLANE **88**
PARAMOUNT. (R) July, 1980. Robert Hayes, Julie Hagerty.

AIRPORT (Todd-AO) **137**
UNIVERSAL. (R) March, 1970. Burt Lancaster, Dean Martin, Jean Seberg.

AIRPORT 1975 .... **106**
UNIVERSAL. (R) October, 1974. Charlton Heston, Karen Black.

AIRPORT '77 (P) **113**
UNIVERSAL. (R) May, 1977. . Jack Lemmon, Lee Grant.

AL CAPONE **105**
ALLIED ARTISTS. (R) March 26, 1959. Rod Steiger, Fay Spain.

ALAKAZAM THE GREAT **85**
AMERICAN INTERNATIONAL. (R) July, 1961. Animated Cartoon. Color.

ALAMO, THE **199**
UNITED ARTISTS. (R) October, 1960. John Wayne, Richard Widmark. Color.

ALASKA PASSAGE (RS) **71**
TWENTIETH CENTURY-FOX. (R) February, 1959. Bill Williams, Lyn Thomas.

ALBERT SCHWEITZER **80**
DE ROCHEMONT. (R) January, 1957. Documentary. Color.

ALEX IN WONDERLAND **109**
MGM. (R) December, 1970. Donald Sutherland, Jeanne Moreau. Color.

ALEXANDER THE GREAT (CS) **141**
UNITED ARTISTS. (R) April, 1956. Richard Burton, Frederic March, Claire Bloom. Color.

ALF AND FAMILY **100**
SHERPIX. (R) August, 1972. Warren Mitchell, Randy Nichols. Color.

ALFIE (TS) **114**
PARAMOUNT. (R) October, 1966. Michael Caine, Shelley Winters. Color.

ALFRED THE GREAT (P) **125**
MGM. (R) October, 1969. David Hemmings, Michael York. Color.

ALREDO ALFREDO **100**
PARAMOUNT. (R) December, 1973. Dustin Hoffman, Stefania Sandrelli.

ALI BABA AND THE SEVEN MIRACLES OF THE WORLD (Cs) **79**
AMERICAN INTERNATIONAL. (R) November, 1961. Cartoon Feature. Color.

ALIAS JESSE JAMES **92**
UNITED ARTISTS. (R) March, 1959. Bob Hope, Rhonda Fleming. Color.

ALIAS JOHN PRESON (Brit.) **71**
ASSOCIATED. (R) November, 1955. Alexander Knox, Betta St. John.

ALICE DOESN'T LIVE HERE ANYMORE **113**
WARNER BROS. (R) January, 1975. Ellyn Burstyn, Kris Kristofferson.

ALICE IN WONDERLAND IN PARIS AND WHITE MANE **90**
CHILDHOOD PRODUCTIONS. (R) February, 1966. Animated.

ALICE'S ADVENTURES IN WONDERLAND **100**

	Length In Mins.

AMERICAN NATIONAL ENTERPRISES. (R) November, 1972. Ralph Richardson, Fiona Fullerton, Peter Sellers. Color.

ALICE'S RESTAURANT **111**
UNITED ARTISTS. (R) August, 1969. Arlo Guthrie, Pat Quinn, James Broderick. Color.

ALIEN **124**
TWENTIETH CENTURY-FOX. (R) May, 1979. Tom Skeritt, Sigourney Weaver.

ALL-AMERICAN BOY, THE (P) **118**
WARNER BROS. (R) November, 1973. Jon Voight, Carol Androsky.

ALL AT SEA (Brit.) **87**
METRO-GOLDWYN-MAYER. (R) January, 1958. Alec Guiness, Irene Brownee.

ALL FALL DOWN **111**
METRO-GOLDWYN-MAYER. (R) April, 1962. Eva Marie Saint, Warren Beatty.

ALL HANDS ON DECK (Cs) **98**
TWENTIETH CENTURY-FOX. (R) April, 1961. Pat Boone, Buddy Hackett. Color.

ALL IN A NIGHT'S WORK (VV) **94**
PARAMOUNT. (R) March, 1961. Dean Martin, Shirley MacLaine. Color.

ALL MINE TO GIVE **87**
UNIVERSAL. (R) January, 1958. Glynis Johns, Cameron Mitchell. Color.

ALL NEAT IN BLACK STOCKINGS **96**
NATIONAL GENERAL. (R) October, 1969. Victor Henry, Susan George. Color.

ALL SCREWED UP (Ital., English titles) **105**
NEW LINE CINEMA. (R) January, 1976. Luigi Diberti, Lina Polito.

ALL THAT HEAVEN ALLOWS **89**
UNIVERSAL. (R) January, 1956. Jane Wyman, Rock Hudson. Color.

ALL THAT JAZZ **123**
TWENTIETH CENTURY-FOX. (R) December, 1979. Roy Scheider, Jessica Lange.

ALL THE FINE YOUNG CANNIBALS (Cs) **122**
METRO-GOLDWYN-MAYER. (R) September, 1960. Natalie Wood, Robert Wagner. Color.

ALL THE LOVING COUPLES **85**
U-M. (R) October, 1969. Norman Aldren, Gloria Manon, Scott Graham. Color.

ALL THE PRESIDENT'S MEN **135**
WARNER BROS. (R) April, 1976. Robert Redford, Dustin Hoffman.

ALL THE WAY HOME **103**
PARAMOUNT. (R) October, 1963. Jean Simmons, Robert Preston.

ALL THE YOUNG MEN **86**
COLUMBIA. (R) August, 1960. Alan Ladd, Sidney Poitier.

ALL THESE WOMEN **80**
JANUS. (CR) October, 1964. Jark Kulle, Georg Funkquist. Color.

ALLIGATOR NAMED DAISY, AN (VV) **84**
RANK. (R) October, 1957. Donald Sinden, Diana Dors. Color

ALLIGATOR PEOPLE, THE (Cs) **74**
ALLIED ARTISTS. (R) July, 1959. Beverly Garland, George Macready.

ALMOST ANGELS **93**
BUENA VISTA. (R) October, 1962. Peter Weck, Sean Scully. Color.

ALMOST PERFECT AFFAIR, AN **93**
PARAMOUNT. (R) April, 1979. Keith Carradine, Monica Vitti.

ALOHA, BOBBY AND ROSE **89**
COLUMBIA. (R) April, 1975. Paul Le Mat, Dainne Hull.

ALONE AGAINST ROME (Totalscope) **100**
MEDALLION. (R) 1960. Jeffrey Lang, Rosanna Podesta. Color.

ALPHABET MURDERS, THE **90**
METRO-GOLDWYN-MAYER. (R) May, 1966. Tony Randall, Anita Ekberg.

ALPHAVILLE (Fr., Eng. titles) **100**
PATHE CONTEMPORARY. (R) October, 1965. Eddie Constantine, Anna Karina.

ALVEREZ KELLY (P) **116**
COLUMBIA. (R) October, 1966. William Holden, Richard Widmark, Color.

ALVIN PURPLE **92**
SANDS FILM CO. (R) October, 1975. Graeme Blundell, George Whaley.

AMAZING COLOSSAL MAN, THE **81**
AMER. INT. PICS. (R) September, 1957. Glenn Langan, Cathy Downs.

AMAZING GRACE **99**
UNITED ARTISTS. (R) August, 1974. Moms Mabley, Slappy White.

AMAZING TRANSPARENT MAN, THE **60**

307

Length In Mins.

AMERICAN INTERNATIONAL. (R) July, 1960. Marguerite Chapman, Douglas Kennedy.

AMAZON TRADER, THE 41
WARNER BROTHERS. (R) September 8, 1956. John Sutton, Maria Fernandez. Color.

AMBASSADOR's DAUGHTER, THE (Cs) 102
UNITED ARTISTS. (R) September, 1956. Olivia de Havilland, John Forsythe, Myrna Loy. Color.

AMBUSH AT CIMARRON PASS (Rs) 87
TWENTIETH CENTURY-FOX. (R) March, 1958. Scott Brady, Margia Dean.

AMBUSH BAY 109
UNITED ARTISTS. (R) September, 1966. Hugh O'Brian, Mickey Rooney. Color.

AMBUSHERS, THE 102
COLUMBIA. (R) December, 1967. Dean Martin, Senta Berger. Color.

AMERICA, AMERICA 174
WARNER BROS. (R) February, 1964. Stathis Giallelis, Frank Wolff.

AMERICAN DREAM, AN 107
WARNER BROS. (R) October, 1966. Stuart Whitman, Janet Leigh. Color.

AMERICAN FRIEND, THE 127
NEW YORKER FILMS. (R) October, 1977. Bruno Ganz, Dennis Hopper.

AMERICAN GIGOLO 115
PARAMOUNT. (R) February, 1980. Richard Gere, Lauren Hutton.

AMERICANIZATION OF EMILY, THE 117
METRO-GOLDWYN-MAYER. (R) December, 1964. James Garner, Julie Andrews.

AMERICANO, THE 85
RKO RADIO. (R) January 29, 1955. Glenn Ford, Ursula Theiss. Color.

AMERICATHON 85
UNITED ARTISTS. (R) August, 1979. Peter Riegert, Harvey Korman.

AMITYVILLE HORROR, THE 117
AMERICAN INTERNATIONAL. (R) July, 1979. James Brolin, Margot Kidder.

AMOROUS ADVENTURES OF MOLL FLANDERS, THE (P) 126
PARAMOUNT. (R) May, 1965. Kim Novak, Richard Johnson. Color.

AMSTERDAM KILL, THE (P) 92
COLUMBIA. (R) March, 1978. Robert Mitchum, Bradford Dillman.

ANASTASIA (Cs) 105
TWENTIETH CENTURY-FOX. (R) December, 1956. Ingrid Bergman, Yul Brynner, Helen Hayes. Color.

ANATOMY OF A MARRIAGE (Fr., Eng. titles) .... 96 & 97
JANUS. (R) October, 1964. Marie-Jose Nat, Jacques Charrier. (Two-Parts).

ANATOMY OF A MURDER 160
COLUMBIA. (R) July, 1959. James Stewart, Lee Remick.

AND HOPE TO DIE. 99
TWENTIETH CENTURY-FOX. (R) November, 1972. Robert Ryan, Jean-Louis Trintingant, Lea Massari. Color.

AND JUSTICE FOR ALL 120
COLUMBIA. (R) October, 1979. Al Pacino, Jack Warden.

AND NOW FOR SOMETHING COMPLETELY DIFFERENT 88
COLUMBIA. (R) August, 1972. Graham Chapman, John Cleese. Color.

AND NOW MIGUEL 95
UNIVERSAL. (R) June, 1966. Pat Cardi, Michael Ansara.

AND NOW MY LOVE (Fr., Eng. titles) 121
AVCO-EMBASSY. (R) March, 1975. Marthe Keller, Andre Dussolier.

AND NOW THE SCREAMING STARTS 87
CINERAMA. (R) April, 1973. Peter Cushing. Color.

AND SO TO BED (Germ., Eng. titles) 112
MEDALLION. (R) May, 1965. Hildegard Knef, Lilli Palmer.

AND SOON THE DARKNESS 98
LEVITT-PICKMAN. (R) April, 1971. Pamela Franklin, Michele Dotrice. Color.

AND SUDDENLY IT'S MURDER (Cs) 90
ROYAL. (R) January, 1964. Alberto Sordi, Dorian Gray.

AND THERE CAME A MAN 90
BRANDON. (R) April, 1968. Rod Steiger, Adolfo Celi. Color.

ANDERSON TAPES, THE 98
COLUMBIA. (R) June, 1971. Sean Connery, Dyan Cannon. Color.

ANDROMEDA STRAIN, THE (P) 130
UNIVERSAL. (R) March, 1971. Arthur Hill, David Wayne.

ANDY 86
UNIV. (R) February, 1965. Norman Alden, Tamara Day Karhanova.

Length In Mins.

ANDY HARDY COMES HOME 80
METRO-GOLDWYN-MAYER. (R) August, 1958. Mickey Rooney, Patricia Breslin.

ANDY WARHOL'S BAD 105
NEW WORLD. (R) May, 1977. Carroll Baker, Perry King.

ANDY WARHOL'S DRACULA 106
BRYANSTON. (R) January, 1975. Joe Dallesandro, Udo Kier.

ANDY WARHOL'S FRANKENSTEIN 95
BRYANSTON. (R) May, 1974. Joe Dallesandro, Monique Van Vooren.

ANGEL BABY 97
ALLIED ARTISTS. (R) May, 1961. George Hamilton, Mercedes McCambridge.

ANGEL IN MY POCKET 105
UNIVERSAL. (R) April, 1969. Andy Griffith, Jerry Van Dyke, Kay Medford. Color.

ANGEL LEVINE, THE 104
UNITED ARTISTS. (R) August, 1970. Harry Belafonte, Zero Mostel, Ida Kaminska. Color.

ANGEL WHO PAWNED HER HARP, THE (Brit.) 73
ASSOCIATED ARTISTS. (R) February, 1956. Felix Aylmer, Diane Cilento.

ANGEL WORE RED, THE 99
METRO-GOLDWYN-MAYER. (R) September, 1960. Ava Gardner, Dirk Bogarde.

ANGELA 81
TWENTIETH CENTURY-FOX. (R) April, 1955. Dennis O'Keefe, Mara Lane.

ANGELS FROM HELL 86
AMERICAN INTERNATIONAL. (R) June, 1968. Tom Stern, Arlene Martel. Color.

ANGELS OF DARKNESS (Ital., Eng. dial.) 84
EXCELSIOR. (R) February, 1957. Linda Darnell, Anthony Quinn.

ANGRY HILLS, THE (Cs) 105
METRO-GOLDWYN-MAYER. (R) June, 1959. Robert Mitchum, Stanley Baker.

ANGRY RED PLANET, THE 83
AMER. INT'L. PICS. (R) 1960. Gerald Mohr, Les Treymayne. Color.

ANIMAL FARM (Brit.) 75
DISTRIBUTORS CORP. OF AMERICA. (R) January, 1955. Cartoon. Color.

ANIMAL WORLD, THE 82
WARNER BROTHERS. (R) June 23, 1956. Documentary. Color.

ANIMALS ARE BEAUTIFUL PEOPLE 92
WARNER BROS. (R) March, 1975. Documentary.

ANNA LUCASTA 97
UNITED ARTISTS. (R) March, 1959. Eartha Kitt, Sammy Davis, Jr.

ANNAPOLIS STORY 81
ALLIED ARTISTS. (R) April 10, 1955. John Derek, Diana Lynn. Color.

ANNE AND EVE 89
CHEVRON. (R) July, 1970. Gio Petre, Marie Liljedhal. Color.

ANNE OF THE THOUSAND DAYS (P) 145
(R) January, 1970. Richard Burton, Genevieve Bujold. Color.

ANNIE HALL 94
UNITED ARTISTS. (R) April, 1977. Woody Allen, Diane Keaton.

ANNIVERSARY, THE 95
TWENTIETH CENTURY-FOX. (R) Feb., 1968. Bette Davis, Christian Roberts. Color.

ANOTHER MAN, ANOTHER CHANCE 136
UNITED ARTISTS. (R) November, 1977. James Caan, Genevieve Bujold

ANOTHER TIME, ANOTHER PLACE (VV) 98
PARAMOUNT. (R) June, 1958. Lana Turner, Barry Sullivan.

ANY GUN CAN PLAY 105
GOLDEN EAGLE. (R) September, 1969. Edd Byrnes, Gilbert Roland. Color.

ANY NUMBER CAN WIN (D) 112
METRO-GOLDWYN-MAYER. (R) October, 1963. Jean Gabin, Alain Delon.

ANY WEDNESDAY 109
WARNER BROS. (R) December, 1966. Jane Fonda, Jason Robards. Color.

ANYONE CAN PLAY 88
PARAMOUNT. (R) September, 1968. Ursula Andress, Virna Lisi, Claudine Auger. Color.

ANYTHING GOES (VV) 106
PARAMOUNT. (R) April, 1956. Bing Crosby, Donald O'Connor, Jeanmarie, Mitzi Gaynor. Color.

ANZIO 117
COLUMBIA. (R) June, 1968. Robert Mitchum, Peter Falk, Earl Holliman. Color.

APACHE AMBUSH 68

Length In Mins.

COLUMBIA. (R) August, 1956. Joan Crawford, Cliff Robertson.

AUTUMN SONATA 97
NEW WORLD PICTURES. (R) October, 1979. Ingrid Bergman, Liv Ullmann.

AVANTI 144
UNITED ARTISTS. (R) December, 1972. Jack Lemmon, Juliet Mills. Color.

AVENGER, THE 108
MEDALLION. (R) January, 1965. Steve Reeves, Cupia Marlier. Color.

AWAY ALL BOATS (VV) 114
UNIVERSAL. (R) August, 1956. Jeff Chandler, Julie Adams, George Nader, Lex Barker. Color.

B

B.S., I LOVE YOU 99
20TH CENTURY-FOX. (R) March, 1971. Peter Kastner, Joanna Barnes. Color.

BABES IN TOYLAND 105
BUENA VISTA. (R) December, 1961. Ray Bolger, Rommy Sands. Color.

BABETTE GOES TO WAR (Cs) 103
COLUMBIA. (R) March, 1960. Brigette Bardot, Jacques Charrier. Color.

BABY BLUE MARINE 90
COLUMBIA. (R) April, 1976. Jan Michael-Vincent, Glynnis O'Connor.

BABY DOLL 114
WARNER BROTHERS. (R) December 29, 1956. Karl Malden, Carroll Baker, Eli Wallach.

BABY FACE NELSON 85
UNITED ARTISTS. (R) November, 1957. Mickey Rooney, Carolyn Jones.

BABY LOVE 102
AVCO-EMBASSY. (R) March, 1969. Ann Lynn, Keith Barron, Linda Hayden. Color.

BABY MAKER, THE 109
NATIONAL GENERAL. (R) October, 1970. Barbara Hershey, Collin Wilcox-Horne. Color.

BABY THE RAIN MUST FALL 100
COLUMBIA. (R) January, 1965. Lee Remick, Steve McQueen.

BABYSITTER, THE 90
CROWN INTERNATIONAL. (R) October, 1969. Patricia Wymer, George E. Carey.

BACHELOR FLAT (Cs) 92
TWENTIETH CENTURY-FOX. (R) January, 1961. Tuesday Weld, Richard Beymer. Color.

BACHELOR IN PARADISE (Cs) 109
METRO-GOLDWYN-MAYER. (R) November, 1961. Bob Hope, Lana Turner. Color.

BACHELOR PARTY, THE 93
UNITED ARTISTS. (R) April, 1957. Don Murray, E.G. Marshall.

BACK DOOR TO HELL 68
TWENTIETH CENTURY-FOX. (R) January, 1965. Jimmie Rodgers, Conrad Maga.

BACK FROM ETERNITY 97
UNIVERSAL. (R) September, 1956. Robert Ryan, Anita Ekberg, Rod Steiger.

BACK FROM THE DEAD (Cs) 75
TWENTIETH CENTURY-FOX. (R) September, 1957. Arthur Franz, Peggie Castle.

BACK STREET 107
UNIVERSAL. (R) November, 1961. Susan Hayward, John Gavin.

BACKFIRE (Fr., Eng. titles) 97
ROYAL. (R) April, 1965. Jean-Paul Belmondo, Jean Seberg.

BACKLASH 84
UNIVERSAL. (R) April, 1956. Richard Widmark, Donna Reed. Color.

BAD COMPANY 91
PARAMOUNT. (R) October, 1972. Jeff Bridges, Barry Brown. Color.

BAD DAY AT BLACK ROCK (Cs) 81
METRO-GOLDWYN-MAYER. (R) January 7, 1955. Spencer Tracy, Anne Francis. Color.

BAD MAN'S COUNTRY 68
WARNER BROS. (R) August, 1958. George Montgomery, Buster Crabbe.

BAD NEWS BEARS, THE 105
PARAMOUNT. (R) April, 1976. Walter Matthau, Tatum O'Neal.

BAD NEWS BEARS IN BREAKING TRAINING, THE 97
PARAMOUNT. (R) August, 1977. William Devane, Clifton James.

BAD SEED, THE 129

Length In Mins.

WARNER BROTHERS. (R) September 29, 1956. Nancy Kelly, Patty McCormick.

BADGE #73 115
PARAMOUNT. (R) August, 1973. Robert Duvall, Verna Bloom.

BADGE OF MARSHAL BRENNAN, THE 78
ALLIED ARTISTS. (R) May 26, 1957. Jim Davis, Carl Smith.

BADLANDERS, THE (Cs) 83
METRO-GOLDWYN-MAYER. (R) August, 1958. Alan Ladd, Ernest Borgnine. Color.

BADLANDS 95
WARNER BROS. (R) May, 1974. Martin Sheen, Sissy Spacek.

BADLANDS OF MONTANA 75
TWENTIETH CENTURY-FOX. (R) May, 1957. Rex Reason, Margia Dean.

BAIL OUT AT 43,000 78
UNITED ARTISTS. (R) May, 1957. John Payne, Karen Steel.

BALCONY, THE 84
CONTINENTAL. (R) March, 1963. Shelley Winters, Peter Falk.

BALLAD OF A SOLDIER (Russian: Eng. titles) 89
ARTKINO. (R) December, 1960. b&w.

BALLAD OF CABLE HOGUE, THE 120
WARNER BROS. (R) March, 1970. Jason Robards, Stella Stevens. Color.

BALLAD OF JOSIE, THE (T) 102
UNIVERSAL. (R) February, 1968. Doris Day, Peter Graves. Color.

BALLAD OF LOVE, A (Russian, Eng. Titles) 45
ARTKINO. (R) February 19, 1966. Victoria Fyodorova, Valentin Smirnitsky.

BALTIMORE BULLET, THE 103
AVCO EMBASSY. (R) April, 1980. James Coburn, Omar Sharif.

BAMBOLE (Ital., with English Titles) 111
ROYAL FILMS INT'L. (R) June, 1965. Virna Lisi, Nino Manfredi.

BAMBOO PRISON, THE 80
COLUMBIA. (R) January, 1955. Robert Francis, Dianne Foster.

BANANA PEEL 97
PATHE-CONT. (R) January, 1965. Jeanne Morreau, Jean-Paul Belmondo.

BANANAS 82
UNITED ARTISTS. (R) May, 1971. Woody Allen, Louise Lasser. Color.

BAND OF ANGELS 127
WARNER BROS. (R) August, 1957. Clark Gable, Yvonne DeCarlo. Color.

BAND OF OUTSIDERS (Fr., Eng. Titles) 95
ROYAL FILMS INTERNATIONAL. (R) March, 1966. Anna Karina, Sami Frey.

BANDIDO (Cs) 92
UNITED ARTISTS. (R) September, 1956. Robert Mitchum, Ursula Thiess. Color.

BANDIT OF ZHOBE, THE (Cs) 80
COLUMBIA. (R) April, 1959. Victor Mature, Anthony Newly. Color.

BANDITS OF ORGOSOLO 98
PATHE-CONT. (R) May, 1964. Michele Lossu, Peppaddu Cuccu.

BANDOLERO 106
TWENTIETH CENTURY-FOX. (R) July, 1968. James Stewart, Dean Martin, Raquel Welch, George Kennedy. Color.

BANG, BANG, YOU'RE DEAD 92
AMERICAN INTERNATIONAL. (R) August, 1966. Tony Randall, Senta Berger. Color.

BANG THE DRUM SLOWLY 97
PARAMOUNT. (R) August, 1973. Michael Moriarty, Robert de Niro.

BANK SHOT 85
UNITED ARTISTS. (R) July, 1974. George C. Scott, Joanna Cassidy.

BANNING (TS) 102
UNIVERSAL. (R) August, 1967. Robert Wagner, Anjanette Comer. Color.

BARABAS (T-70) 134
COLUMBIA. (R) December, 1962. Anthony Quinn, Silvana Mangano. Color.

BARBARELLA 98
PARAMOUNT. (R) October, 1968. Jane Fonda, John Phillip Law, Anita Pallenberg. Color.

BARBARIAN AND THE GEISHA, THE (Cs) 104
TWENTIETH CENTURY-FOX. (R) October, 1958. John Wayne, Elko Ando. Color.

BARBARIANS, THE 80
ALLIED ARTISTS. (R) December, 1957. Pierre Cresoy, Helene Remy.

BAREFOOT BATTALION (Germ., Eng., titles) 63

Length In Mins.

TWENTIETH CENTURY-FOX. (R) July, 1956. Maria Costi, Nicos Fermas.

BAREFOOT EXECUTIVE, THE 95
BUENA VISTA. (R) April, 1971. Kurt Russel, Joe Flynn. Color.

BAREFOOT IN THE PARK. 106
PARAMOUNT. (R) June, 1967. Robert Redford, Jane Fonda. Color.

BARON BLOOD 90
AMERICAN INTERNATIONAL. (R) October, 1972. Elke Sommer, Joseph Cotten. Color.

BARQUERO 115
UNITED ARTISTS. (R) May, 1970. Lee Van Cleef, Warren Oates. Color.

BARRETTS OF WIMPOLE STREET, THE (Cs) 105
METRO-GOLDWYN-MAYER. (R) February 1, 1957. Jennifer Jones, Bill Travers. Color.

BARRY LYNDON 185
WARNER BROS. (R) December, 1975. Ryan O'Neal, Marisa Berenson.

BARTLEBY 78
MARON. (R) February, 1972. Paul Scofield, John McEnery. Color.

BASHFUL ELEPHANT, THE 82
ALLIED ARTISTS. (R) February, 1962. Molly Mack, Helmut Schmid.

BAT, THE 80
ALLIED ARTISTS. (R) August, 1959. Vincent Price, Agnes Moorehead.

BATMAN 105
20TH CENTURY-FOX. (R) August, 1966. Adam West, Burt Ward. Color.

BATTLE AT BLOODY BEACH 60
TWENTIETH CENTURY-FOX. (R) June, 1961. Audie Murphy, Sal Mineo. Color.

BATTLE BENEATH THE SEA 92
MGM. (R) May, 1968. Kerwin Mathews, Vivian Ventura. Color.

BATTLE BEYOND THE SUN 75
AMERICAN INTERNATIONAL. (R) April, 1963. Ed Perry, Arla Powell.

BATTLE CRY (Cs) 148
WARNER BROTHERS. (R) March 12, 1955. Van Heflin, Aldo Ray. Color.

BATTLE FLAME 75
ALLIED ARTISTS. (R) April, 1959. Ronny Pennell, Ronnie Knox.

BATTLE FOR THE PLANET OF THE APES, THE 90
TWENTIETH CENTURY-FOX. (R) June, 1973. Roddy McDowall, Claude Akins. Color.

BATTLE HELL 112
DCA DIST. (R) 1956. Richard Todd, Akim Tamiroff. b&w.

BATTLE HYMN (Cs) 108
UNIVERSAL. (R) March, 1957. Rock Hudson, Martha Hyer. Color.

BATTLE IN OUTER SPACE 90
COLUMBIA. (R) June, 1960. Ryo Ikebe, Kyoko Angai. Color.

BATTLE OF ALGIERS (Algerian, Eng. titles) 123
ALLIED ARTISTS. (R) 1967. Jean Martin, Yacef Saadi. b&w.

BATTLE OF BLOOD ISLAND 64
THE FILM GROUP. (R) May, 1960. Richard Devon, Ron Kennedy.

BATTLE OF BRITAIN, THE (P) 133
UNITED ARTISTS. (R) October. Laurence Olivier, Ralph Richardson, Michael Caine. Color.

BATTLE OF NERETVA, THE (P) 102
AMERICAN INTERNATIONAL (R) February, 1971. Yul Brynner, Orson Welles. Color.

BATTLE OF THE BULGE (Ultra Panavision) 163
WARNER BROTHERS. (R) January, 1966. Henry Fonda, Robert Shaw. Color.

BATTLE OF THE CORAL SEA, THE 80
COLUMBIA. (R) November, 1959. Cliff Robertson, Gia Scala.

BATTLE OF THE VILLA FIORITA, THE (P) 111
WARNER BROS. (R) June, 1965. Maureen O'Hara, Rossano Brazzi. Color.

BATTLESTAR GALACTICA 120
UNIVERSAL. (R) May, 1979. Lorne Green, Richard L. Hatch.

BATTLE STATIONS 81
COLUMBIA. (R) February, 1956. John Lund, William Bendix, Keefe Brasselle.

BATTLE TAXI 82
UNITED ARTISTS. (R) January, 1955. Sterling Hayden. Arthur Franz.

BAWDY ADVENTURES OF TOM JONES, THE 94
UNIVERSAL. (R) 1976. Nicky Henson, Trevor Howard.

BAXTER! 100

Length In Mins.

NATIONAL GENERAL. (R) February, 1973. Scott Jacoby, Patricia Neal, Britt Eckland. Color.

BAY OF THE ANGELS (Fr., Eng. titles) (Cs) 85
PATHE-CONT. (R) November, 1964. Jeanne Moreau, Claude Mann.

BAYOU 84
UNITED ARTISTS. (R) June, 1957. Peter Graves, Lita Milan.

BEACH BALL 83
PARAMOUNT. (R) October, 1965. Edd Byrnes, Chris Noel.

BEACH BLANKET BINGO (P) 98
AMERICAN INTERNATIONAL. (R) April, 1965. Frankie Avalon, Annette Funicello. Color.

BEACH PARTY (P) 100
AMERICAN INTERNATIONAL. (R) August, 1963. Bob Cummings, Dorothy Malone. Color.

BEACH RED 105
UNITED ARTISTS. (R) September, 1967. Cornel Wilde, Rip Torn. Color.

BEACHCOMBER, THE (Brit.) 82
UNITED ARTISTS. (R) January, 1955. Glynis Johns, Robert Newton. Color.

BEAR AND THE DOLL, THE 90
PARAMOUNT. (R) October, 1971. Brigitte Bardot, Jean-Pierre Cassel. Color.

BEARS AND I, THE 89
BUENA VISTA. (R) October, 1974. Patrick Wayne, Chief Dan George.

BEAST FROM A HAUNTED CAVE 75
THE FILM GROUP. (R) October, 1959. Michael Forest, Sheila Carol.

BEAST IN THE CELLAR 104
CANNON. (R) April, 1971. Beryl Reid, Flora Robson. Color.

BEAST OF BUDAPEST 72
ALLIED ARTISTS. (R) February, 1958. Gerald Milton, John Hoyt.

BEAST OF HOLLOW MOUNTAIN, THE (Cs) 79
UNITED ARTISTS. (R) August, 1956. Guy Madison, Patricia Medina. Color.

BEAST WITH 1,000,000 EYES 71
AMERICAN RELEASING CORP. (R) January, 1956. Paul Birch, Lorna Thayer.

BEASTS OF MARSEILLES, THE 70
LOPERT. (R) July, 1959. Stephen Boyd, James Robertson Justice.

BEAT GENERATION, THE (Cs) 95
METRO-GOLDWYN-MAYER. (R) July, 1959. Steve Cochran, Mamie Van Doren.

BEATSVILLE 72
ALLIED ARTISTS. (R) June, 1959. Gregg Palmer, Kathleen Crowley.

BEAU GESTE (T) 105
UNIVERSAL. (R) July 20, 1966. Guy Stockwell, Doug McClure. Color.

BEAU JAMES (VV) 105
PARAMOUNT. (R) July, 1957. Bob Hope, Vera Miles. Color.

BEAUTIFUL BUT DANGEROUS 103
TWENTIETH CENTURY-FOX. (R) February, 1958. Gina Lollobrigida, Victorio Gassman. Color.

BEBO'S GIRL 106
READE-STERLING. (R) November, 1964. Claudia Cardinale, George Chakiris.

BECAUSE THEY'RE YOUNG 102
COLUMBIA. (R) March, 1960. Dick Clark, Michael Callan.

BECKET (P-70) 148
PARAMOUNT. (R) Special March, 1964. Richard Burton, Peter O'Toole. Color.

BED AND BOARD (Fr., with English Titles) 95
COLUMBIA. (R) January, 1971. Jean-Pierre Leaud, Claude Jade. Color.

BED SITTING ROOM, THE 90
UNITED ARTISTS. (R) October, 1969. Rita Tushingham, Ralph Richardson, Peter Cook. Color.

BEDAZZLED (P) 107
TWENTIETH CENTURY-FOX. (R) December, 1967. Peter Cook, Raquel Welch. Color.

BEDEVILLED (Cs) 85
METRO-GOLDWYN-MAYER. (R) April 22, 1955. Anne Baxter, Steve Forrest. Color.

BEDFORD INCIDENT, THE 102
COLUMBIA. (R) October, 1965. Richard Widmark, Sidney Poitier. Color.

BEDKNOBS AND BROOMSTICKS 117
BUENA VISTA. (R) November, 1971. Angela Lansbury, David Tomlinson. Color.

BEDTIME STORY 99
UNIVERSAL. (R) July, 1964. Marlon Brando, David Niven. Color.

BEEN DOWN SO LONG IT LOOKS LIKE UP TO ME 90

	Length In Mins.

PARAMOUNT. (R) October, 1971. Barry Primus, Linda De Coff. Color.

BEFORE THE REVOLUTION (Ital., Eng. titles) 112
NEW YORKER. (R) July, 1965. Adriana Asti, Francesco Barilli.

BEFORE WINTER COMES 102
COLUMBIA. (R) March, 1969. David Niven, Topol, Anna Karina, John Hurt. Color.

BEGINNING OF THE END 73
REPUBLIC. (R) June 1957. Peter Graves, Peggi Castle.

BEGUILED, THE 105
UNIVERSAL. (R) April, 1971. Clint Eastwood, Geraldine Page. Color.

BEHIND THE GREAT WALL (Totalscope) 96
CONTINENTAL. (R) 1959. Documentary. Narrated by Chet Huntley. Color.

BEHIND THE HIGH WALL 85
UNIVERSAL. (R) July, 1956. Tom Tully, Sylvia Sidney.

BEHOLD A PALE HORSE 113
COLUMBIA. (R) August, 1964. Gregory Peck, Anthony Quinn.

BEING THERE 125
UNITED ARTISTS. (R) December, 1979. Peter Sellers, Shirley MacLaine.

BELIEVE IN ME 88
METRO-GOLDWYN-MAYER. (R) September, 1971. Michael Sarrazin, Jacqueline Bisset. Color.

BELL, BOOK AND CANDLE 103
COLUMBIA. (R) January, 1959. James Stewart, Kim Novak. Color.

BELLBOY, THE 72
PARAMOUNT. (R) July, 1960. Jerry Lewis, Alex Gerry.

BELLE DE-JOUR (Fr.) 100
ALLIED ARTISTS. (R) April, 1968. Catherine Deneuve, Genevieve Page. Color.

BELLE SOMMERS 63
COLUMBIA. (R) 1962. Polly Bergen, David Janssen.

BELLES OF ST. TRINIAN'S, THE (Brit.) 90
ASSOCIATED ARTISTS. (R) January, 1955. Alastair Sim, Joyce Grenfell.

BELL JAR, THE 112
AVCO EMBASSY. (R) March, 1979. Marilyn Hassett, Julie Harris.

BELLS ARE RINGING (Cs) 127
METRO-GOLDWYN-MAYER. (R) July, 1960. Judy Holliday, Dean Martin. Color.

BELOVED INFIDEL (Cs) 123
TWENTIETH CENTURY-FOX. (R) November, 1959. Gregory Peck, Deborah Kerr. Color.

BEN 95
CINERAMA. (R) June, 1972. Lee Harcourt Montgomery, Joseph Campanella. Color.

BEN-HUR (MGM Camera 65) 212
METRO-GOLDWYN-MAYER. (R) Special. November, 1959. Charlton Heston, Jack Hawkins. Color.

BENEATH THE PLANET OF THE APES (P) 95
20TH CENTURY-FOX. (R) July, 1970. James Franciscus, Kim Hunter. Color.

BENGAZI (SS) 79
RKO RADIO. (R) September 14, 1955. Richard Conte, Richard Carlson, Mala Powers.

BENJAMIN (Fr.) 100
PARAMOUNT. (R) March, 1968. Pierre Clementi, Michele Morgan. Color.

BENNY GOODMAN STORY, THE 110
UNIVERSAL. (R) February, 1956. Steve Allen, Donna Reed. Color.

BERNADINE (Cs) 95
TWENTIETH CENTURY-FOX. (R) July, 1957. Pat Boone, Terry Moore. Color.

BERSERK! 96
COLUMBIA. (R) Jan., 1968. Joan Crawford, Ty Hardin. Color.

BEST HOUSE IN LONDON, THE 94
MGM. (R) September, 1969. David Hemmings, Joanna Pettet, George Sanders. Color.

BEST MAN, THE 102
UNITED ARTISTS. (R) May, 1964. Henry Fonda, Cliff Robertson.

BEST OF ENEMIES, THE (T) 104
COLUMBIA. (R) September, 1962. David Niven, Alberto Sordi. Color.

BEST OF EVERYTHING, THE (Cs) 121
TWENTIETH CENTURY-FOX. (R) October, 1959. Hope Lange, Stephen Boyd. Color.

BEST OF WALT DISNEY'S TRUE-LIFE ADVENTURES .. 89
BUENA VISTA. (R) October, 1975. Documentary.

BEST THINGS IN LIFE ARE FREE, THE (Cs) 104
TWENTIETH CENTURY-FOX. (R) September, 1956. Gordon McRae, Ernest Borgnine, Dan Dailey, Sheree North. Color.

BETRAYED WOMEN 70

ALLIED ARTISTS. (R) July 17, 1955. Carole Mathews, Tom Drake.

BETSY, THE 120
ALLIED ARTISTS. (R) February, 1978. Laurence Olivier, Robert Duvall.

BETTER A WIDOW 105
UNIVERSAL. (R) March, 1969. Virna Lisi, Peter McErnery, Gabrielle Ferzetti. Color.

BETWEEN HEAVEN AND HELL (Cs) 94
TWENTIETH CENTURY-FOX. (R) October, 1956. Robert Wagner, Terry Moore. Color.

BETWEEN THE LINES 101
MIDWEST FILM PRODS. (R) April, 1977. John Heard, Lindsay Crouse

BETWEEN TIME AND ETERNITY 96
UNIVERSAL. (R) September, 1950. Lilli Palmer, Willy Birgel. Color.

BEWARE OF CHILDREN 80
AMERICAN INTERNATIONAL. (R) April, 1961. Leslie Phillips, Geraldine McEwan.

BEYOND A REASONABLE DOUBT 80
UNIVERSAL. (R) September, 1956. Dana Andrews, Joan Fontaine.

BEYOND ALL LIMITS 115
OMAT. (R) May, 1961. Jack Palance, Maria Felix. Color.

BEYOND CONTROL 89
MISHKIN. (R) June, 1971. Anthony Baker.

BEYOND MOMBASA 90
COLUMBIA. (R) June, 1957. Donna Reed, Cornel Wilde. Color.

BEYOND THE DOOR 100
FILM VENTURES INTERNATIONAL. (R) May, 1975. Juliet Mills, Richard Johnson.

BEYOND THE GREAT WALL (Mandarin) 100
FRANK LEE. (R) August, 1967. Lin Dai, Chao Lei. Color.

BEYOND THE LAW 96
GROVE. (R) October, 1968. Rip Torn, George Plimpton, Norman Mailer, Micky Knox. b&w.

BEYOND THE POSEIDON ADVENTURE 122
WARNER BROS. (R) May, 1979. Michael Caine, Sally Field

BEYOND THE TIME BARRIER 80
AMERICAN INTERNATIONAL. (R) July, 1960. Robert Clarke, Darlene Tompkins.

BEYOND THE VALLEY OF THE DOLLS (P) 109
20TH CENTURY-FOX. (R) June, 1970. Dolly Read, Cynthia Myers. Color.

BHOWANI JUNCTION (Cs) 110
METRO-GOLDWYN-MAYER. (R) June 8, 1956. Ava Gardner, Stewart Granger. Color.

BIBLE . . . IN THE BEGINNING, THE (D-150) 175
20th CENTURY-FOX. (R) September, 1966. George C. Scott, Ava Gardner. Color.

BIG BANKROLL, THE 106
ALLIED ARTISTS. (R) September, 1961. Stephen Boyd, Juliette Greco.

BIG BEAT, THE 82
UNIVERSAL. (R) March, 1958. William Reynolds, Andra Martin. Color.

BIG BLUFF 70
UNITED ARTISTS. (R) June, 1955. John Bromfield, Martha Vickers.

BIG BOODLE, THE 83
UNITED ARTISTS. (R) January, 1957. Errol Flynn, Rosanna Rory.

BIG BOUNCE, THE 102
WARNER BROS.-7 ARTS. (R) March, 1969. Ryan O'Neal, Leigh Taylor Young, James Daly. Color.

BIG BUS, THE 88
PARAMOUNT. (R) July, 1976. Joseph Bologna, Stockard Channing.

BIG BUST OUT, THE 80
NEW WORLD PICTURES. (R) March, 1973. Vonetta McGee, Gordon Mitchell. Color.

BIG CAPER, THE 84
UNITED ARTISTS. (R) April, 1957. Rory Calhoun, Mary Costa.

BIG CIRCUS, THE (Cs) 108/12
ALLIED ARTISTS. (R) July, 1959. Victor Mature, Red Buttons. Color.

BIG COMBO, THE 89
ALLIED ARTISTS. (R) February 13, 1955. Cornel Wilde, Richard Conte.

BIG COUNTRY, THE (T) 168
UNITED ARTISTS. (R) August, 1958. Gregory Peck, Jean Simmons. Color.

BIG CUBE, THE 91
WARNER BROS.-7 ARTS. (R) March, 1969. Lana Turner, George Chakiris, Richard Egan. Color.

BIG FISHERMAN, THE 180
BUENA VISTA. (R) August, 1959. Howard Keel, Susan Kohner.

Length In Mins.

BIG FIX, THE 108
UNIVERSAL. (R) October, 1979. Richard Dreyfuss, Susan Anspach.

BIG GUNDOWN, THE 90
COLUMBIA. (R) August, 1968. Lee Van Cleef, Thomas Milan, Luisa Rivelli. Color.

BIG HAND FOR THE LITTLE LADY, A 95
WARNER BROTHERS. (R) June 1, 1966. Henry Fonda, Joanne Woodward. Color.

BIG HOUSE, U.S.A. 82
UNITED ARTISTS. (R) March, 1955. Broderick Crawford, Ralph Meeker.

BIG JAKE (P) 110
NATIONAL GENERAL. (R) June, 1971. John Wayne, Richard Boone. Color.

BIG KNIFE, THE 111
UNITED ARTISTS. (R) November, 1955. Jack Palance, Ida Lupino, Wendell Cory, Shelley Winters.

BIG LAND, THE 93
WARNER BROTHERS. (R) February 23, 1957. Alan Ladd, Virginia Mayo, Edmond O'Brien. Color.

BIG MOUTH, THE 107
COLUMBIA. (R) July, 1967. Jerry Lewis, Harold J. Stone. Color.

BIG NIGHT, THE 74
PARAMOUNT. (R) February, 1960. Randy Sparks, Venetia Stevenson.

BIG OPERATOR, THE (Cs) 91
METRO-GOLDWYN-MAYER. (R) September, 1959. Mickey Rooney, Steve Cochran. b&w.

BIG RED 93
BUENA VISTA. (R) June, 1962. Walter Pidgeon, Gilles Payant. Color.

BIG RED ONE, THE 113
UNITED ARTISTS. (R) July, 1980. Lee Marvin, Mark Hamill.

BIG SHOW, THE (Cs) 118
TWENTIETH CENTURY FOX. (R) May, 1961. Esther Williams, Cliff Robertson. Color.

BIG SLEEP, THE (P) 100
UNITED ARTISTS. (R) March, 1978. Robert Mitchum, Sarah Miles.

BIG T.N.T. SHOW, THE 98
AMERICAN INTERNATIONAL. (R) January, 1966. Folk n' Rock Musical.

BIG TIP OFF 78
ALLIED ARTISTS. (R) March 20, 1955. Richard Conte, Constance Smith.

BIG WEDNESDAY (P) 125
WARNER BROS. (R) Summer, 1978. Jan-Michael Vincent, William Katt.

BIGGER THAN LIFE (Cs) 95
TWENTIETH CENTURY-FOX. (R) August, 1956. James Mason, Barbara Rush. Color.

BIGGEST BUNDLE OF THEM ALL, THE (P) 100
MGM. (R) Jan., 1968. Edward G. Robinson, Vittorio De Sica. Color.

BIKINI BEACH (P) 100
AMERICAN INTERNATIONAL. (R) July, 1964. Frankie Avalon, Annette Funicello.

BILLIE 87
UNITED ARTISTS. (R) September, 1965. Patty Duke, Jim Bakus. Color.

BILLION DOLLAR BRAIN (P) 108
UNITED ARTISTS. (R) December, 1967. Michael Caine, Francoise Dorleac. Color.

BILLY BUDD (Cs) 112
ALLIED ARTISTS. (R) June, 1962. Peter Ustinov, Robert Ryan.

BILLY JACK 112
WARNER BROS. (R) May, 1971. Tom Laughlin, Delores Taylor. Color.

BILLY LIAR 96
CONTINENTAL. (R) November, 1963. Tom Courtenay, Julie Christie.

BILLY ROSE'S JUMBO (P) 125
METRO-GOLDWYN-MAYER. (R) December, 1962. Doris Day, Stephen Boyd. Color.

BILLY TWO HATS 99
UNITED ARTISTS. (R) March, 1974. Gregory Peck, Desi Arnaz, Jr.

BIMBO THE GREAT 96
WARNER BROS. (R) June, 1961. Charles Holm, Eleanor Marlowe. Color.

BINGO LONG TRAVELING ALL-STARS AND MOTOR KINGS, THE 111
UNIVERSAL. (R) July, 1976. Billy Dee Williams, James Earl Jones.

BIRCH INTERVAL 105
GAMMA III. (R) May, 1976. Eddie Albert, Rip Torn.

BIRD WITH THE CRYSTAL PLUMMAGE, THE (Te) 98
UMC PICTURES. (R) September, 1970. Tony Musante, Suzy Kendall. Color.

Length In Mins.

BIRDMAN OF ALCATRAZ 143
UNITED ARTISTS. (R) August, 1962. Burt Lancaster, Karl Malden.

BIRDS, THE 120
UNIVERSAL. (R) April, 1963. Rod Taylor, Jessica Tandy. Color.

BIRDS AND THE BEES, THE (VV) 94
PARAMOUNT. (R) May, 1956. George Gobel, Mitzi Gaynor, David Niven. Color.

BIRDS DO IT 95
COLUMBIA. (R) Aug. 1966. Soupy Sales, Tab Hunter. Color.

BIRDS IN PERU 95
REGIONAL. (R) November, 1968. Jean Seberg, Maurice Ronet, Piette Brasseur, Danielle Darrieux. Color.

BIRDS, THE BEES, AND THE ITALIANS, THE (Ital., Eng. Titles) 115
SEVEN ARTS. (R) April, 1967. Virna Lisi, Gastone Moschin.

BIRTHDAY PARTY, THE 127
CONTINENTAL. (R) December, 1968. Robert Shaw, Patrick McGee, Dandy Nichols. Color.

BITE THE BULLET (P) 131
COLUMBIA. (R) June, 1975. Gene Hackman, Candice Bergen.

BITTER VICTORY (Cs) 83
COLUMBIA. (R) March, 1958. Richard Burton, Curt Jurgens.

BITTERSWEET LOVE 92
AVCO-EMBASSY. (R) October, 1976. Lana Turner, Robert Lansing.

BLACK AND WHITE IN COLOR (Fr., Eng. titles) 90
ALLIED ARTISTS. (R) April, 1977. Jean Carmet, Jacques Dufilho.

BLACK BEAUTY 106
PARAMOUNT. (R) November, 1971. Mark Lester, Walter Slezak. Color.

BLACK BELT JONES 87
WARNER BROS. (R) January, 1974. Jim Kelly, Gloria Henry.

BLACK BIRD, THE 98
COLUMBIA. (R) December, 1975. George Segal, Stephane Audran.

BLACK CAESAR 93
AMERICAN INTERNATIONAL. (R) February, 1973. Fred Williamson, D'Urville Martin. Color.

BLACK DUKE, THE 90
PRODUCTION RELEASING. (R) July, 1964. Cameron Mitchell, Gloria Milland. Color.

BLACK EYE 98
WARNER BROS. (R) May, 1974. Fred Williamson, Rosemary Forsyth.

BLACK GIRL 97
CINERAMA. (R) January, 1973. Brock Peters, Leslie Uggams, Claudia McNeil. Color.

BLACK GOLD 98
WARNER BROS. (R) June, 1963. Philip Carey, Diane McBain.

BLACK GUNN 94
COLUMBIA. (R) December, 1972. Jim Brown, Martin Landau. Color.

BLACK HOLE, THE 97
BUENA VISTA. (R) December, 1979. Maxmillian Schell, Anthony Perkins.

BLACK KLANSMAN, THE 88
U.S. FILMS. (R) June 26, 1966. Richard Glidden, Rima Kutner.

BLACK LIKE ME 107
READE-STERLING. (R) May, 1974. James Whitmore, Dan Priest.

BLACK MAMA, WHITE MAMA 87
AMERICAN INTERNATIONAL. (R) January, 1973. Margaret Markov, Pam Grier. Color.

BLACK MARBLE, THE 113
AVCO EMBASSY. (R) March, 1980. Robert Foxworth, Paula Prentiss.

BLACK MOON 100
TWENTIETH CENTURY-FOX. (R) November, 1975. Cathryn Harrison, Therese Giehse.

BLACK ON WHITE 80
AUDUBON. (R) October, 1969. Anita Sanders, Nino Segurino, Terry Carter. Color.

BLACK ORCHID, THE (VV) 93
PARAMOUNT. (R) March, 1959. Sophia Loren, Anthony Quinn.

BLACK ORPHEUS (Brazilian, Eng. titles) 98
LOPERT. (R) 1960. Bruno Mello, Marpessa Dawn. Color.

BLACK SABBATH 99
AMERICAN INTERNATIONAL. (R) May, 1964. Boris Karloff, Mark Damon. Color.

BLACK SCORPION, THE 83

Length In Mins.

Length In Mins.

WARNER BROS. (R) October, 1957. Richard Denning, Mara Corday.

BLACK SLEEP, THE 83
UNITED ARTISTS. (R) June, 1956. Basil Rathbone, Akim Tamiroff.

BLACK SPURS 81
PARAMOUNT. (R) May, 1965. Rory Calhoun, Terry Moore. Color.

BLACK STALLION, THE 125
UNITED ARTISTS. (R) October, 1979. Kelly Reno, Mickey Rooney.

BLACK SUNDAY (P) 145
PARAMOUNT. (R) April, 1977. Robert Shaw, Bruce Dern.

BLACK SUNDAY 84
AMERICAN INTERNATIONAL. (R) February, 1961. Barbara Steele, John Richardson.

BLACK TENT, THE (VV) 85
RANK. (R) July, 1957. Anthony Steel, Donald Sinden.

BLACK THURSDAY (Fr., Eng. titles) 92
LEVITT-PICKMAN. (R) December, 1974. Christine Pascal, Christian Rist.

BLACK TUESDAY 80
UNITED ARTISTS. (R) January, 1955. Edward G. Robinson, Peter Graves.

BLACK VEIL FOR LISA 88
COMMONWEALTH UNITED. (R) October, 1969. John Mills, Luciana Paluzzi. Color.

BLACK WHIP, THE 77
TWENTIETH CENTURY-FOX. (R) December, 1956. Hugh Marlowe, Colleen Gray.

BLACK WINDMILL, THE (P) 106
UNIVERSAL. (R) June, 1974. Michael Caine, Donald Pleasence.

BLACK ZOO, THE 88
ALLIED ARTISTS. (R) May, 1963. Michael Gough, Jeanne Cooper. Color.

BLACKBEARD'S GHOST 107
BUENA VISTA. (R) February, 1968. Peter Ustinov, Suzanne Pleshette. Color.

BLACKBOARD JUNGLE, THE 101
METRO-GOLDWYN-MAYER. (R) March 25, 1955. Glenn Ford, Anne Francis.

BLACKJACK KETCHUM, DESPERADO 76
COLUMBIA. (R) April, 1956. Howard Duff, Maggie Mahoney. Color.

BLACULA 92
AMERICAN INTERNATIONAL. (R) July, 1972. William Marshall, Denis Nichols. Color.

BLADE 90
JOSEPH GREEN PICTURES. (R) December, 1973. John Marley, Jon Cypher.

BLAST OF SILENCE 77
UNIVERSAL. (R) July, 1961. Allen Baron, Molly McCarthy.

BLAZING SADDLES (P) 94
WARNER BROS. (R) February, 1974. Cleavon Little, Gene Wilder.

BLESS THE BEASTS AND CHILDREN 109
COLUMBIA. (R) July, 1971. Bill Mumy, Barry Robins. Color.

BLINDFOLD (P) 102
UNIVERSAL. (R) June, 1966. Rock Hudson, Claudia Cardinale. Color.

BLINDMAN 105
20TH CENTURY-FOX. (R) March, 1972. Tony Anthony, Ringo Starr. Color.

BLISS OF MRS. BLOSSOM, THE 93
PARAMOUNT. (R) October, 1968. Shirley MacLaine, Richard Attenborough, James Booth. Color.

BLOB!, THE 82
PARAMOUNT. (R) October, 1958. Steve McQueen, Aneta Corseaut. Color.

BLONDE BAIT 71
ASSOCIATED FILM. (R) April 2, 1956. Beverly Michaels, Jim Davis.

BLONDE BLACKMAILER 58
ALLIED ARTISTS. (R) January, 1958. Richard Arlen, Susan Shaw.

BLONDE SINNER, THE (Brit.) 73
ALLIED ARTISTS. (R) Nov. 18, 1956. Diana Dors, Michael Craig.

BLOOD ALLEY (Cs) 118
WARNER BROTHERS. (R) October 1, 1955. John Wayne, Lauren Bacall. Color.

BLOOD AND BLACK LACE 90
ALLIED ARTISTS. (R) 1965. Cameron Mitchell, Eva Bartok. Color.

BLOOD AND LACE 87
AMERICAN INTERNATIONAL. (R) March, 1971. Gloria Grahame, Milton Selzer. Color.

BLOOD AND ROSES (T) 74

PARAMOUNT. (R) September, 1961. Mel Ferrar, Elsa Martinelli. Color.

BLOOD AND STEEL 63
TWENTIETH CENTURY-FOX. (R) November, 1959. John Lupton, James Edwards.

BLOOD BATH 69
AMERICAN INTERNATIONAL. (R) March, 1966. William Campbell, Marissa Mathes.

BLOOD BROTHERS 116
WARNER BROS. (R) October, 1979. Paul Sorvino, Tony Lo Bianco, Richard Gere.

BLOOD FIEND 70
HEMISPHERE. (R) January, 1969. Christopher Lee, Julian Glover.

BLOOD OF DRACULA 68
AMERICAN INTERNATIONAL. (R) November, 1957. Sandra Harrison, Louise Lewis.

BLOOD OF DRACULA'S CASTLE 84
CROWN INTERNATIONAL. (R) December, 1969. John Carradine, Paula Raymond.

BLOOD OF THE VAMPIRE 87
UNIVERSAL. (R) November, 1958. Donald Wolfit, Barbara Shelly. Color.

BLOOD ON SATAN'S CLAW 100
CANNON. (R) April, 1971. Patrick Wymark, Michele Dotrice. Color.

BLOOD ON THE ARROW 91
ALLIED ARTISTS. (R) November, 1964. Dale Robertson, Martha Hyer. Color.

BLOOD ON THE BALCONY (Ital., Eng. titles) 92
JILLO. (R) August, 1964. Documentary.

BLOODTHIRSTY BUTCHERS 79
MISHKIN. (R) January, 1970. John Miranda, Anabella Wood. Color.

BLOODY BROOD 111
ALLIED ARTISTS. (R) October, 1960. Barbara Lord, Jack Bett.

BLOODY MAMA 92
AMERICAN INTERNATIONAL PICTURES. (R) March, 1970. Shelley Winters, Don Stroud, Pat Hingle. Color.

BLOODY PIT OF HORROR 74
PACEMAKER PICTURES. (R) March, 1969. Mickey Hagitay.

BLOW-UP 110
METRO-GOLDWYN-MAYER. (R) April, 1967. Vanessa Redgrave, David Hemmings. Color.

BLUE 103
PARAMOUNT. (R) April, 1968. Terence Stamp, Joanna Pettit. Color.

BLUE ANGEL, THE (Cs) 107
TWENTIETH CENTURY-FOX. (R) September, 1959. Curt Jurgens, May Britt. Color.

BLUE BIRD, THE 95
TWENTIETH CENTURY-FOX. (R) May, 1976. Elizabeth Taylor, Jane Fonda.

BLUE COLLAR 110
UNIVERSAL (R) February, 1978. Richard Pryor, Harvey Keitel.

BLUE DENIM (Cs) 89
TWENTIETH CENTURY-FOX. (R) August, 1959. Carol Lynley, Brandon de Wilde.

BLUE HAWAII (P) 101
PARAMOUNT. (R) November, 1961. Elvis Presley, Joan Blackman. Color.

BLUE LAGOON, THE 104
COLUMBIA. (R) June, 1980. Brooke Shields, Christopher Atkins.

BLUE MAX, THE (Cs) 156
20TH-CENTURY FOX. (R) June, 1966. George Peppard, James Mason. Color.

BLUE PETER, THE (Alt. title: NAVY HEROES) 93
DCA DIST. (R) 1957. Greta Gynt, Kieron Moore. Color.

BLUE WATER, WHITE DEATH 100
NATIONAL GENERAL. (R) June, 1971. Documentary.

BLUEBEARD 125
CINERAMA. (R) August, 1972. Richard Burton, Raquel Welch, Joey Heatherton. Color.

BLUEBEARD (Alt. title: LANDRU) 118
Michele Morgan, Hildegarde Neff. Color.

BLUEBEARD'S TEN HONEYMOONS 92
ALLIED ARTISTS. (R) May, 1960. George Sanders, Corinne Calvert.

BLUEPRINT FOR ROBBERY 87
PARAMOUNT. (R) January, 1961. Jay Barney, J. Pat O'Malley.

BLUES BROTHERS, THE 133
UNIVERSAL. (R) June, 1980. John Belushi, Dan Aykroyd.

BLUES FOR LOVERS 89
20TH CENTURY-FOX. (R) September, 1966. Ray Charles, Tom Bell.

BLUME IN LOVE 117

	Length in Mins.

WARNER BROS. (R) July, 1973. George Segal, Susan Anspach. Color.

BOARDWALK 98
ATLANTIC RELEASING. (R) November, 1979. Ruth Gordon, Lee Strasberg.

BOATNIKS, THE 100
BUENA VISTA. (R) July, 1970. Robert Morse, Stephanie Powers. Color.

BOB & CAROL & TED & ALICE 104
COLUMBIA. (R) November, 1969. Robert Culp, Natalie Wood, Elliott Gould, Dyan Cannon. Color.

BOBBIE JO AND THE OUTLAW 89
AMERICAN INTERNATIONAL. (R) April, 1976. Marjoe Gortner, Lynda Carter.

BOBBIKINS (Cs) 89
TWENTIETH CENTURY-FOX. (R) June, 1960. Max Bygraves, Shirley Jones.

BOBBY DEERFIELD (P) 123
COLUMBIA, (R) October, 1977. Al Pacino, Marthe Keller.

BOBBY WARE IS MISSING 66
ALLIED ARTISTS. (R) October 23, 1955. Neveille Brand, Arthur Franz.

BOBO, THE 105
WARNER BROS.-SEVEN ARTS. (R) September, 1967. Peter Sellers, Britt Ekland. Color.

BOCCACCIO 70 145
AVCO EMBASSY, (R) 1962. Sophia Loren, Anita Ekberg. Color.

BODY, THE 111
MGM. (R) February, 1971. Documentary.

BOEING, BOEING 102
PARAMOUNT. (R) Christmas, 1965. Tony Curtis, Jerry Lewis. Color.

BOFORS GUN, THE 106
UNIVERSAL. (R) September, 1968. Nicol Williamson, Jan Holm, David Warner, Richard O'Callaghan. Color.

BOLD AND THE BRAVE, THE (SS) 90
RKO RADIO. (R) April 18, 1956. Wendell Corey, Mickey Rooney, Don Taylor, Nicole Maurey.

BOLSHOI BALLET, THE 99
RANK FILM DISTRIBUTORS OF AMERICA. (R) January, 1958. Galina Ulanova. Color.

BOLSHOI BALLET 67 76
PARAMOUNT. (R) September, 1966. Ballet documentary. Color.

BOMB FOR A DICTATOR, A. 73
MEDALLION. (R) 1960. Pierre Fresnay, Michel Auclair. b&w.

BOMBAY TALKIE 110
MERCHANT/IVORY. (R) November, 1970. Shashi Kapoor.

BOMBERS B-52 (Cs) 106
WARNER BROS. (R) November, 1957. Natalie Wood, Karl Malden. Colo.

BON VOYAGE 130
BUENA VISTA. (R) June, 1962. Fred MacMurray, Jane Wyman. Color.

BONJOUR TRISTESSE (Cs) 94
UNITED ARTISTS (R) February, 1958. Deborah Kerr, David Niven. Color.

BONNE SOUPE, LA (Cs) 97
INTERNATIONAL CLASSICS. (R) March, 1964. Annie Girardot, Marie Bell.

BONNIE AND CLYDE 111
WARNER BROS.-SEVEN ARTS. (R) September, 1967. Warren Beatty, Faye Dunaway. Color.

BONNIE PARKER STORY, THE (Superama) 79
AMER. INT. PICS. (R) May, 1958. Dorothy Provine, Jack Hogan.

LE BONHEUR 87
CLOVER FILMS. (R) May, 1966 Jean-Claude Drouot, Claire Drouot. Color.

BOOK OF NUMBERS 80
AVCO-EMBASSY. (R) April, 1973. Raymond St. Jacques, Freda Payne. Color.

BOOM 113
UNIVERSAL. (R) July, 1968. Elizabeth Taylor, Richard Burton, Noel Coward. Color.

BOP GIRL 79
UNITED ARTISTS. (R) July, 1957. Mary Kaye Trio, Mudy Tyler.

BORA BORA 90
AMER. INT. PICS. (R) February, 1970. Haydee Politoff, Corrado Pani, Color.

BORN AGAIN 110
AVCO EMBASSY. (R) October, 1978. Dean Jones, Anne Francis.

BORN FREE (P) 95
COLUMBIA. (R) April, 1966. Virginia McKenna, Bill Travers. Color.

BORN LOSERS 112

	Length In Mins.

AMERICAN INTERNATIONAL. (R) September, 1967. Jeremy Slate, Tom Laughlin. Color.

BORN RECKLESS 79
WARNER BROS. (R) May, 1959. Mamie Van Doren, Jeff Richards.

BORN TO WIN 90
UNITED ARTISTS. (R) October, 1971. George Segal, Paula Prentiss, Karen Black. Color.

BORSALINO (Fr. titles) 123
PARAMOUNT. (R) October, 1970. Jean-Paul Belmondo, Alain Delon. Color.

BOSS, THE 89
UNITED ARTISTS. (R) October, 1956. John Payne, Doe Avedon.

BOSTON STRANGLER, THE 116
TWENTIETH CENTURY-FOX. (R) October, 1968. Tony Curtis, Henry Fonda, George Kennedy. Color.

BOTTOM OF THE BOTTLE, THE (Cs) 88
TWENTIETH CENTURY-FOX. (R) January, 1956. Van Johnson, Joseph Cotten, Ruth Roman, Jack Carson. Color.

BOUCHER, LE 90
CINERAMA. (R) December, 1971. Jean Yanne, Stephane Audran. Color.

BOULEVARD NIGHTS 102
WARNER BROS. (R) March, 1979. Richard Yniguez, Danny De La Paz.

BOUND FOR GLORY 147
UNITED ARTISTS. (R) February, 1977. David Carradine, Ronny Cox.

BOUNTY KILLER, THE (TE) 92
EMBASSY. (R) July, 1965. Dan Duryea, Rod Cameron. Color.

BOWERY TO BAGDAD 84
ALLIED ARTISTS. (R) January 2, 1955. Bowery Boys.

BOY. . . A GIRL, A 85
CINEMA J. (R) April, 1969. Dino Martin Jr., Karen Steele.

BOY AND THE PIRATES, THE 82
UNITED ARTISTS. (R) April, 1960. Charles Herbert, Susan Gordon. Color.

BOY CRIED MURDER, THE 86
UNIVERSAL. (R) March, 1966. Veronica Hurst, Phil Brown. Color.

BOY, DID I GET A WRONG NUMBER 99
UNITED ARTISTS. (R) June, 1966. Bob Hope, Elke Sommer, Phyllis Diller. Color.

BOY FRIEND, THE 110
METRO-GOLDWYN-MAYER. (R) December, 1971. Twiggy, Christopher Gable. Color.

BOY NAMED CHARLIE BROWN, A. 85
NATIONAL GENERAL CORP. (R) March, 1970. Cartoon. Color.

BOY ON A DOLPHIN (Cs) 111
TWENTIETH CENTURY-FOX. (R) April, 1957. Sophia Loren, Alan Ladd. Color.

BOY TEN FEET TALL, A (Cs) 88
PARAMOUNT. (R) January, 1965. Edward G. Robinson, Fergus McClelland. Color.

BOY WHO CAUGHT A CROOK 72
UNITED ARTISTS. (R) October, 1961. Wanda Hendrix, Don Beddoe.

BOY WHO CRIED WEREWOLF, THE 93
UNIVERSAL. (R) August, 1973. Kerwin Mathews, Elaine Devry.

BOY WHO STOLE A MILLION 84
PARAMOUNT. (R) September, 1960. Virgillo Texera, Maurice Reyna.

BOYS FROM BRAZIL, THE 124
TWENTIETH CENTURY-FOX. (R) October, 1979. Gregory Peck, Laurence Olivier.

BOYS IN COMPANY C, THE (R) 125
COLUMBIA. (R) February, 1978. Stan Shaw, Andrew Stevens.

BOYS IN THE BAND, THE 120
NATIONAL GEN. CORP. (R) April, 1970. Kenneth Nelson, Leonard Frey, Cliff Gorman, Laurence Luckinbill. Color.

BOYS' NIGHT OUT (Cs) 115
METRO-GOLDWYN-MAYER. (R) June, 1962. Kim Novak, James Garner. Color.

BOYS OF PAUL STREET, THE 108
TWENTIETH CENTURY-FOX. (R) March, 1969. Anthony Kemp, William Burleigh, John Moulder-Brown. Color.

BRAIN, THE 100
PARAMOUNT. (R) October, 1969. David Niven, Jean-Paul Belmondo, Bourvil. Color.

BRAIN EATERS, THE 60
AMERICAN INTERNATIONAL. (R) October, 1958. Edwin Nelson, Alan Frost.

BRAIN MACHINE, THE (Brit.) 72

Length In Mins.

WARNER BROS. (R) October, 1972. Bob Hope, Eva Marie Saint. Color.

CANDIDATE, THE 110
WARNER BROS. (R) July, 1972. Robert Redford, Don Porter. Color.

CANDLESHOE 101
BUENA VISTA. (R) February, 1978. David Niven, Helen Hayes.

CANDY 126
CINERAMA. (R) December, 1968. Ewa Aulin, Charles Aznavour, Marlon Brando, Richard Burton, James Coburn. Color.

CANNIBAL GIRLS 80
AMERICAN INTERNATIONAL. (R) October, 1972. Eugene Levy, Andrea Martin. Color.

CANNON FOR CORDOBA 104
UNITED ARTISTS. (R) October, 1970. George Peppard, Giovanna Ralli. Color.

CAN'T STOP THE MUSIC 118
ASSOCIATED FILM DIST. (R) June, 1980. Village People, Valerie Perrine. Color.

CANYON CROSSROADS 83
UNITED ARTISTS. (R) February, 1955. Richard Basehart, Phyllis Kirk.

CANYON RIVER (Cs) 80
ALLIED ARTISTS. (R) August 5, 1965. George Montgomery, Marcia Henderson. Color.

CAPE FEAR 105
UNIVERSAL. (R) May, 1962. Gregory Peck, Robert Mitchum.

CAPER OF THE GOLDEN BULLS, THE 104
EMBASSY. (R) May, 1967. Stephen Boyd, Yvette Mimieux. Color.

CAPONE 101
20TH CENTURY-FOX. (R) April, 1975. Ben Gazzara, Susan Blakely.

CAPRICE (CS) 98
TWENTIETH CENTURY-FOX. (R) June, 1967. Doris Day, Richard Harris. Color.

CAPRICORN ONE 127
WARNER BROS. (R) June, 1978. Elliott Gould, James Brolin.

CAPTAIN FROM KOEPENICK, THE 93
DCA DIST. (R) 1956. Heinz Ruhmann. Color.

CAPTAIN KRONOS: VAMPIRE HUNTER 91
PARAMOUNT. (R) June, 1974. Horst Janson, John Carson.

CAPTAIN LIGHTFOOT (Cs) 91
UNIVERSAL. (R) March, 1955. Rock Hudson, Barbara Rush. Color.

CAPTAIN NEMO AND THE UNDERWATER CITY (P) 105
MGM. (R) March, 1970. Robert Ryan, Chuck Conners, Nanette Newman. Color.

CAPTAIN NEWMAN, M.D. 126
UNIVERSAL. (R) April, 1964. Gregory Peck, Tony Curtis. Color.

CAPTAIN SINBAD 85
METRO-GOLDWYN-MAYER. (R) June, 1963. Guy Williams, Heidi Bruhl. Color.

CAPTAIN'S TABLE, THE 90
TWENTIETH CENTURY-FOX. (R) September, 1960. John Gregson, Peggy Cummins. Color.

CAR, THE (R) 95
UNIVERSAL. (R) May, 1977. James Brolin, Kathleen Lloyd.

CAR WASH 97
UNIVERSAL. (R) September, 1976. Franklyn Ajaye, Sully Boyar.

CARAVANS 127
UNIVERSAL. (R) November, 1978. Anthony Quinn, Michael Sarrazin.

CARAVAN TO VACCARES 84
BRYANSTON. (R) February, 1976. Charlotte Rampling, David Birney.

CARDINAL, THE (P-70) 175
COLUMBIA. (R) Special in December, 1963. Tom Tryon, Carol Lynley. Color.

CAREER 105
PARAMOUNT. (R) November, 1959. Dean Martin, Anthony Franciosa.

CAREER GIRL 61
ASTOR-WOODBURN FILMS. (R) May, 1960. June Wilkinson, Charles Robert Keane. Color.

CAREER GIRL 69
PBC PICTURES. (R) January 11, 1944. Frances Langford, Craig Wood.

CARELESS YEARS, THE 70
UNITED ARTISTS. (R) September, 1957. Dean Stockwell, Natalie Trundy.

CARESSED 81
JOSEPH BRENNER ASSOCIATES. (R) October, 1965. Robert Howay, Angela Gann.

CARETAKER, THE (formerly THE GUEST) 105

JANUS. (R) January, 1964. Alan Bates, Donald Pleasence, Robert Shaw.

CARETAKERS, THE 97
UNITED ARTISTS. (R) August, 1963. Robert Stack, Polly Bergen.

CAREY TREATMENT, THE 100
METRO-GOLDWYN-MAYER. (R) March, 1972. James Coburn, Jennifer O'Neil. Color.

CARMEN JONES (Cs) 107
TWENTIETH CENTURY-FOX. (R) January, 1955. Dorothy Dandridge, Harry Belafonte. Color.

CARNAL KNOWLEDGE 100
AVCO EMBASSY. (R) July, 1971. Jack Nicholson, Art Garfunkle. Color.

CARNIVAL OF CRIME 83
CROWN. (R) June, 1964. Jean-Pierre Aumont.

CARNY 108
UNITED ARTISTS. (R) May, 1980. Gary Busey, Jodie Foster.

CAROLINA CANNONBALL 74
REPUBLIC. (R) January 28, 1955. Judy Canova.

CAROUSEL (Cs) 128
TWENTIETH CENTURY-FOX. (R) February, 1956. Gordon MacRae, Shirley Jones, Cameron Mitchell. Color.

CARPETBAGGERS, THE 150
PARAMOUNT. (R) April, 1964. Carroll Baker, George Peppard. Color.

CARRIE 98
UNITED ARTISTS. (R) November, 1976. Sissy Spacek, Piper Laurie.

CARRY IT ON 80
MARON. (R) September, 1970. Documentary. Joan Baez, David Harris.

CARRY ON CLEO 92
GOVERNOR FILMS. (R) October, 1965. Sidney James, Amanda Barrie. Color.

CARRY ON CONSTABLE 86
GOVERNOR. (R) November, 1961. Sidney James, Eric Ranker.

CARRY ON DOCTOR 95
AMERICAN INTERNATIONAL. (R) November, 1972. Francis Bigger, Kenneth Williams. Color.

CARRY ON NURSE 87
GOVERNOR. (R) June, 1960. Terence Longdon, Kenneth Connor.

CARRY ON SPYING 87
GOVERNOR. (R) February, 1965. Barbara Windsor, Kenneth Williams.

CARRY ON TEACHER 86
GOVERNOR. (R) October, 1962. Kenneth Connor, Charles Hawtry.

CARTHAGE IN FLAMES 95
COLUMBIA. (R) March, 1961. June Suarez, Anne Heywood. Color.

CARTOUCHE 73
RKO. (R) August, 1957. Richard Basehart, Patricia Roc.

CARTOUCHE (D) 124
EMBASSY. (R) July, 1964. Jean-Paul Belmondo, Claudia Cardinale. Color.

CASANOVA 70 113
EMBASSY. (R) July, 1965. Marcello Mastroianni, Virna Lisi. Color.

CASE AGAINST BROOKLYN, THE 82
COLUMBIA. (R) June, 1958. Darren McGavin, Maggie Hayes.

CASE OF THE NAVES BROTHERS, THE 93
EUROPIX INTERNATIONAL. (R) September, 1972. Raoul Cortez, Juca De Olivere. Color.

CASE OF THE RED MONKEY (Brit.) 73
ALLIED ARTISTS. (R) June 26, 1955. Richard Conte, Rona Anderson.

CASEY'S SHADOW (P) 117
COLUMBIA (R) March, 1978. Walter Matthau, Alexis Smith.

CASH McCALL 102
WARNER BROS. (R) January, 1960. James Garner, Natalie Wood. Color.

CASH ON DELIVERY 82
RKO RADIO. (R) January 15, 1956. Shelley Winters, Peggy Cummins.

CASH ON DEMAND 84
COLUMBIA. (R) February, 1962. Peter Cushing, Andre Morrell.

CASINO ROYALE (P) 130
COLUMBIA. (R) April, 1967. Peter Sellers, Ursula Andress and all-star cast. Color.

CASSANDRA CROSSING, THE (P) 125
AVCO-EMBASSY. (R) February, 1977. Sophia Loren, Richard Harris.

CAST A DARK SHADOW (Brit.) 84
DIST. CORP. OF AMER. (R) November, 1957. Dirk Bogarde, Margaret Lockwood.

Length In Mins.

CAST A GIANT SHADOW (P) 142
UNITED ARTISTS. (R) April, 1966. Kirk Douglas, Senta Berger. Color.

CAST A LONG SHADOW 82
UNITED ARTISTS. (R) July, 1959. Audie Murphy, Terry Moore. Color.

CASTILIAN, THE 129
WARNER BROS. (R) October, 1963. Spartaco Santony, Teresa Velasquez.

CASTLE, THE 90
CONTINENTAL. (R) March, 1969. Maximillian Schell, Cordula Tranto W, Trudik Daniel. Color.

CASTLE KEEP (P) 105
COLUMBIA. (R) July, 1969. Burt Lancaster, Patrick O'Neal, Jean-Pierre Aumont. Color.

CASTLE OF EVIL 80
UNITED PICTURES. (R) October, 1969. Scott Brady, Virginia Mayo.

CAT, THE 87
EMBASSY. (R) Summer, 1966. Roger Perry, Peggy Ann Gardner. Color.

CAT AND MOUSE (German; Eng. titles) 92
GROVE. (R) February, 1970. Lars Brandt, Peter Brandt, Wolfgang Neuss. b&w.

CAT BALLOU 97
COLUMBIA. (R) August, 1965. Jane Fonda, Lee Marvin. Color.

CAT GIRL, THE 67
AMER. INT. PICS. (R) September, 1957. Barbara Shelley, Robert Ayers.

CAT ON A HOT TIN ROOF 108
METRO-GOLDWYN-MAYER. (R) September, 1958. Elizabeth Taylor, Paul Newman. Color.

CAT O'NINE TAILS, THE 112
NATIONAL GENERAL. (R) May, 1971. Karl Malden, James Franciscus. Color.

CATCH MY SOUL 95
CINERAMA. (R) March, 1974. Richie Havens, Lance Le Gault.

CATCH 22 (P) 121
PARAMOUNT. (R) June, 1970. Alan Arkin, Richard Benjamin, Jon Voight, Orsen Welles. Color.

CATERED AFFAIR, THE 93
METRO-GOLDWYN-MAYER. (R) June 22, 1956. Bette Davis, Ernest Borgnine, Debbie Reynolds, Barry Fitzgerald.

CATHERINE & CO. (French; English titles) 99
WARNER BROS. (R) March, 1976. Jane Birkin, Patrick Dewaere.

CATLOW 101
UNITED ARTISTS. (R) October, 1971. Yul Brynner, Richard Crenna. Color.

CATS, THE (Swedish; Eng. titles) 93
NSF. (R) February, 1969. Eva Dahlbeck, Isa Quensel, Gio Petre. b&w.

CATTLE EMPIRE (Cs) 82
TWENTIETH CENTURY-FOX. (R) February, 1958. Joel MacCrea, Gloria Talbott. Color.

CATTLE KING 88
METRO-GOLDWYN-MAYER. (R) June, 1963. Robert Taylor, Joan Caufield.

CAVERN, THE 83
TWENTIETH CENTURY-FOX. (R) November, 1965. Rosanna Schiaffino, Joan Saxon.

CELEBRATION AT BIG SUR 82
20TH CENTURY-FOX. (R) April, 1971. Musical documentary. Joan Baez, John Sebastian. Color.

CELL 2455, DEATH ROW 77
COLUMBIA. (R) May, 1955. William Campbell, Robert Campbell.

CEREMONY, THE 105
UNITED ARTISTS. (R) December, 1963. Laurence Harvey, Sarah Miles.

CERTAIN SMILE (Cs) 106
TWENTIETH CENTURY-FOX. (R) August, 1958. Rossano Brazzi, Joan Fontaine. Color.

CESAR AND ROSALIE 110
CINEMA V. (R) December, 1972. Yves Montand, Romy Schneider. Color.

CHA-CHA-CHA-BOOM! 72
COLUMBIA. (R) October, 1956. Stephen Dunne, Alix Talton.

CHAIN OF EVIDENCE 64
ALLIED ARTISTS. (R) January 6, 1957. Bill Elliott, James Lydon.

CHAIRMAN, THE (P) 102
20th CENTURY-FOX. (R) July, 1969. Gregory Peck, Anne Heywood, Arthur Hill. Color.

CHALK GARDEN, THE 105
UNIVERSAL. (R) June, 1964. Deborah Kerr, Hayley Mills. Color.

CHALLENGE FOR ROBIN-HOOD, A 85

Length In Mins.

TWENTIETH CENTURY-FOX. (R) August, 1969. Barrie Ingham, James Hayter, Leon Greene, Peter Blythe. Color.

CHAMBER OF HORRORS 99
WARNER BROS. (R) September, 1966. Patrick O'Neal, Cesare Danova. Color.

CHAMP, THE 121
UNITED ARTISTS. (R) April, 1979. Jon Voight, Faye Dunaway.

CHAMPAGNE MURDERS, THE 98
UNIVERSAL. (R) March, 1968. Anthony Perkins, Maurice Ronet. Color.

CHANCE MEETING 96
PARAMOUNT. (R) March, 1960. Hardy Kruger, Micheline Presle.

CHANDLER 88
METRO-GOLDWYN-MAYER. (R) December, 1971. Warren Oates, Leslie Caron. Color.

CHANGE IN THE WIND, A 87
CINERAMA. (R) November, 1972. William Devane, Anne Meara. Color.

CHANGE OF HABIT 93
UNIVERSAL. (R) November, 1969. Elvis Presley, Mary Tyler Moore, Barbara McNair. Color.

CHANGE OF MIND 96
CINERAMA. (R) October, 1969. Raymond St. Jacques, Susan Oliver, Leslie Nielson. Color.

CHANGES 93
CINERAMA. (R) February, 1969. Kent Lane, Michele Carey, Manuela Thiess.

CHAPMAN REPORT, THE 125
WARNER BROS. (R) October, 1962. Efram Zimbalist, Jr., Shelley Winters. Color.

CHAPPAQUA 82
REGIONAL. (R) November, 1967. Jean-Louis Barrault, Conrad Rooks.

CHAPTER TWO 124
COLUMBIA. (R) December, 1979. James Caan, Marsha Mason.

CHARADE 114
UNIVERSAL. (R) January, 1964. Cary Grant, Audrey Hepburn. Color.

CHARGE OF THE LIGHT BRIGADE, THE 128
UNITED ARTISTS. (R) October, 1968. Trevor Howard, Vanessa Redgrave, John Gielgud. Color.

CHARLEY AND THE ANGEL 93
BUENA VISTA. (R) March, 1972. Fred MacMurray, Cloris Leachman. Color.

CHARLEY ONE-EYE 107
PARAMOUNT. (R) May, 1973. Richard Roundtree, Roy Thinnes. Color.

CHARLEY VARRICK (P) 111
UNIVERSAL. (R) October, 1973. Walter Matthau, Joe Don Baker.

CHARLIE BUBBLES 91
REGIONAL. (R) February, 1968. Albert Finney, Liza Minnelli. Color.

CHARLIE THE LONESOME COUGAR 75
BUENA VISTA. (R) October, 1967. Ron Brown, Brian Russell. Color.

CHARLOTTE (French; Eng. titles) 100
GAMMA III. (R) June, 1975. Sirpa Lane, Roger Vadim.

CHARLOTTE'S WEB 94
PARAMOUNT. (R) March, 1973. Cartoon. Color.

CHARLY 106
CINERAMA. (R) October, 1968. Cliff Robertson, Claire Bloom, Leon Janney. Color.

CHARRO! 98
NGC. (R) April, 1969. Elvis Presley, Ina Balin, Lynn Kellogg. Color.

CHARTROOSE CABOOSE 75
UNIVERSAL. (R) August, 1969. Molly Bee, Ben Cooper. Color.

CHASE, THE (P) 135
COLUMBIA. (R) February, 1966. Marlon Brando, Jane Fonda. Color.

CHASE A CROOKED SHADOW 87
WARNER BROS. (R) March, 1958. Richard Todd, Anne Baxter.

CHASTITY 85
AMER. INT. PICS. (R) June, 1969. Cher, Barbara London. Color.

CHATOS'S LAND 100
UNITED ARTISTS. (R) May, 1972. Charles Bronson, Jack Palance. Color.

CHE! (P) 96
20th CENTURY-FOX. (R) June, 1969. Omar Sharif, Jack Palance. Color.

CHEAP DETECTIVE, THE 92
COLUMBIA. (R) June, 1978. Peter Falk, Ann-Margaret.

CHECKPOINT 84
RANK. (R) June, 1957. Anthony Steel, Odile Versois. Color.

	Length In Mins.

CHEECH AND CHONG'S NEXT MOVIE 99
UNIVERSAL. (R) July, 1980. Richard Marin, Thomas Chong.

CHERRY, HARRY & RAQUEL 71
EVE PRODUCTIONS. (R) December, 1969. Linda Ashton, Charles Napier. Color.

CHEYENNE AUTUMN (Super P-70) 160
WARNER BROS. (R) December, 1964. Richard Widmark, Caroll Baker. Color.

CHEYENNE SOCIAL CLUB 103
NATIONAL GENERAL. (R) June, 1970. James Stewart, Henry Fonda, Shirley Jones. Color.

CHICAGO CONFIDENTIAL 74
UNITED ARTISTS. (R) September, 1957. Brian Keith, Beverly Garland.

CHICKEN CHRONICLES, THE 94
AVCO EMBASSY. (R) October, 1977. Phil Silvers, Ed Lauter.

CHICAGO SYNDICATE 84
COLUMBIA. (R) July, 1955. Dennis O'Keefe, Abe Lane.

CHIEF CRAZY HORSE (Cs) 86
UNIVERSAL. (R) April, 1955. Victor Mature, Suzan Ball. Color.

CHILD IS WAITING, A 102
UNITED ARTISTS. (R) January, 1963. Burt Lancaster, Judy Garland.

CHILDISH THINGS 85
FILMWORLD. (R) June, 1969. Don Murray, Linda Evans.

CHILDREN OF THE DAMNED 90
METRO-GOLDWYN-MAYER. (R) January, 1964. Ian Henry, Alan Badel.

CHILDREN'S HOUR, THE 109
UNITED ARTISTS. (R) March, 1962. Audrey Hepburn, Shirley MacLaine.

CHILD'S PLAY 100
PARAMOUNT. (R) October, 1972. Robert Preston, Beau Bridges, James Mason. Color.

CHINA! 65
JANUS. (R) May, 1965. Documentary. Color.

CHINA DOLL 85
UNITED ARTISTS. (R) August, 1958. Victor Mature, Lili Hus.

CHINA GATE (Cs) 97
TWENTIETH CENTURY-FOX. (R) May, 1957. Nat King Cole, Gene Barry.

CHINA IS NEAR (Ital.) 108
ROYAL. (R) January, 1968. Glauco Mauri, Elda Tattoli.

CHINA SYNDROME, THE 122
COLUMBIA. (R) March, 1979. Jane Fonda, Jack Lemmon, Michael Douglas. Color.

CHINATOWN (P) 130
PARAMOUNT. (R) July, 1974. Jack Nicholson, Faye Dunaway.

CHINESE CONNECTION, THE 105
NATIONAL GENERAL. (R) April, 1973. Bruce Lee, James Tien. Color.

CHISUM 111
WARNER BROS. (R) July, 1970. John Wayne, Christopher George, Ben Johnson. Color.

CHITTY CHITTY BANG BANG 142
UNITED ARTISTS. (R) December, 1968. Dick Van Dyke, Sally Ann Howes, Lionel Jeffries. Color.

CHLOE IN THE AFTERNOON 97
COLUMBIA. (R) September, 1972. Bernard Verly, Zouzou. Color.

CHOIRBOYS, THE 119
UNIVERSAL. (R) December, 1977. Charles Durning, Lewis Gossett, Jr.

C.H.O.M.P.S. 89
AMERICAN INTERNATIONAL. (R) December, 1979. Wesley Eure, Valerie Bertinelli.

CHOSEN SURVIVORS 99
COLUMBIA. (R) May, 1974. Jackie Cooper, Alex Cord.

CHRISTIAN LICORIC STORE, THE 90
NATIONAL GENERAL. (R) November, 1971. Beau Bridges, Maud Adams. Color.

CHRISTINE JORGENSON STORY, THE 98
UNITED ARTISTS. (R) June, 1970. John Hansen, Joan Tompkins. Color.

CHRISTMAS THAT ALMOST WASN'T, THE 95
CHILDHOOD. (R) November, 1966. Rossano Brazzi, Paul Tripp. Color.

CHRISTMAS TREE, THE 110
CONTINENTAL. (R) October, 1969. William Holden, Virna Lisi. Color.

CHROME AND HOT LEATHER 91
AMERICAN INTERNATIONAL. (R) August, 1971. William Smith, Tony Young. Color.

CHRONICLE OF A SUMMER (Fr., Eng. titles) 88
PATHE-cont. (R) May, 1965. Documentary.

CHUBASCO (P) 100
WARNER BROS.-7 ARTS. (R) June, 1968. Richard Egan, Susan Strasberg. Color.

	Length In Mins.

CHUKA 105
PARAMOUNT. (R) May, 1967. Rod Taylor, Ernest Borgnine. Color.

CID, EL (T-70) 160
ALLIED ARTISTS. (R) December, 1961. Charlton Heston, Sophia Loren. Color.

CIMARRON (Cs) 147
METRO-GOLDWYN-MAYER. (R) March, 1961. Glenn Ford, Maria Schell. Color.

CINCINNATI KID, THE 113
METRO-GOLDWYN-MAYER. (R) November, 1965. Steve McQueen, Edward G. Robinson. Color.

CINDERELLA LIBERTY (P) 117
TWENTIETH CENTURY-FOX. (R) February, 1974. James Caan, Marsha Mason.

CINDERFELLA 88
PARAMOUNT. (R) December, 1960. Jerry Lewis, Ed Wynn. Color.

CIRCLE OF DECEPTION (Cs) 100
TWENTIETH CENTURY-FOX. (R) February, 1961. Bradford Dillman, Suzy Parker.

CIRCLE OF LOVE (Fr., Eng. titles) 105
READE-STERLING. (R) March, 1965. Jane Fonda, Maurice Ronet. Color.

CIRCUS GIRL 88
REPUBLIC. (R) April 20, 1956. European Cast. Color.

CIRCUS OF HORRORS 88½
AMERICAN INTERNATIONAL. (R) May, 1960. Anton Diffring, Erika Remberg. Color.

CIRCUS WORLD. (Cinerams, Super T-FO) 135
PARAMOUNT. (R) June, 1964. John Wayne, Claudia Cardinale. Color.

CISCO PIKE 100
COLUMBIA. (R) October, 1971. Karen Black, Gene Hackman. Color.

CITY AFTER MIDNIGHT 84
STATER RIGHTS-RKO. (R) September, 1959. Phyllis Kirk, Dan O'Herlihy.

CITY OF FEAR 81
COLUMBIA. (R) February, 1959. Vince Edwards, Lyle Talbot.

CITY OF FEAR 90
ALLIED ARTISTS. (R) May, 1965. Terry Moore.

CITY OF SHADOWS 70
REPUBLIC. (R) June 1, 1955. Victor McLaglen, John Baer.

CITY ON FIRE 101
AVCO EMBASSY. (R) September, 1979. Barry Newman, Susan Clark.

CLAIRE'S KNEE 110
COLUMBIA. (R) February, 1971. Jean-Claude Brialy, Aurora Cornu, Beatrice Romand. Color.

CLAMBAKE (P) 99
UNITED ARTISTS. (R) November, 1967. Elvis Presley, Shelley Fabares. Color.

CLARENCE THE CROSS-EYED LION 98
METRO-GOLDWYN-MAYER. (R) April, 1965. Marshall Thompson, Betsy Drake. Color.

CLASS OF '44 (P) 105
WARNER BROS. (R) April, 1973. Gary Grimes, Gerald Houser. Color.

CLAUDELLE INGLISH 99
WARNER BROS. (R) September, 1961. Diane McBain, Arthur Kennedy.

CLAUDINE 92
TWENTIETH CENTURY-FOX. (R) April, 1974. Diahann Carroll, James Earl Jones.

CLAY PIGEON 97
METRO-GOLDWYN-MAYER. (R) August, 1971. Telly Savales, Robert Vaughn. Color.

CLEOPATRA (TODD-AO) 243
TWENTIETH CENTURY-FOX. (R) Special. June, 1963. Elizabeth Taylor, Richard Burton. Color.

CLEOPATRA JONES (P) 89
WARNER BROS. (R) July, 1973. Tamara Dobson, Bernie Casey. Color.

CLEOPATRA JONES AND THE CASINO OF GOLD (P) .. 96
WARNER BROS. (R) July, 1975. Tamara Dobson, Stella Stevens.

CLEOPATRA'S DAUGHTER (U) 93
McDALLION (R) February, 1963. Debra Paget, Robert Alda. Color.

CLIMAX, THE (Ital.) 97
LOPERT. (R) September, 1967. Ugo Tognazzi, Stefania Sandrelli.

CLOCKWORK ORANGE 137
WARNER BROS. (R) December, 1971. Malcolm McDowell, Patrick Magee. Color.

CLOPORTES (Fr., Eng. titles) (Cs) 102
INTERNATIONAL CLASSICS. (R) April, 1966. Lino Ventura, Charles Aznavour. Color.

CLOSE ENCOUNTERS OF THE THIRD KIND (P) 135

	Length In Mins.

COLUMBIA. (R) November, 1977. Richard Dreyfuss, Francois Trauffaut.

CLOSELY WATCHED TRAINS (Czech.) 89
SIGMA III. (R) October, 1967. Vaclav Neckar, Jitka Nendova.

CLOUDS OVER ISRAEL 102
HAROLD CORNSWEET-ISRAEL. (R) May, 1966. Co-Prod. Yiftach Spector, Ehud Banal.

CLOWNS, THE 91
LEVITT-PICKMAN. (R) June, 1971. Documentary. Color.

C'MON, LET'S LIVE A LITTLE (TS) 85
PARAMOUNT. (R) April, 1967. Bobby Lee, Jackie DeShannon. Color.

COALMINER'S DAUGHTER 125
UNIVERSAL. (R) March, 1980. Sissy Spacek, Tommy Lee Jones.

COAST OF SKELETONS (T) 90
SEVEN ARTS. (R) November, 1965. Richard Todd, Derek Nimmo. Color.

COBRA, THE (TS) 93
AMERICAN INTERNATIONAL. (R) January, 1968. Anita Ekberg, Dana Andrews. Color.

COBWEB, THE (Cs) 124
METRO-GOLDWYN-MAYER. (R) July 15, 1955. Richard Widmark, Lauren Bacall, Charles Boyer, Gloria Grahame. Color.

COCKEYED COWBOYS OF CALICO COUNTY, THE 99
UNIVERSAL. (R) April, 1970. Dan Blocker, Nanette Fabray, Jim Backus. Color.

COCKLESHELL HEROES, THE (Cs) 97
COLUMBIA. (R) May, 1956. Jose Ferrer, Trevor Howard. Color.

CODE 7, VICTIM 5! (TS) 83
COLUMBIA. (R) February, 1965. Lex Barker, Ann Smyrner. Color.

COFFY 90
AMERICAN INTERNATIONAL. (R) May, 1973. Pam Grier. Color.

COLD TURKEY 106
UNITED ARTISTS. (R) February, 1971. Dick Van Dyke, Bob Newhart. Color.

COLE YOUNGER GUNFIGHTER (Cs) 79
ALLIED ARTISTS. (R) February, 1958. Frank Lovejoy, Abby Dalton. Color.

COLLECTOR, THE 119
COLUMBIA. (R) June, 1965. Terence Stamp, Samantha Eggar. Color.

COLLEGE CONFIDENTIAL 90
UNIVERSAL. (R) August 1960. Steve Allen, Jayne Meadows.

COLOR ME DEAD 97
COMMONWEALTH UNITED. (R) October, 1969. Tom Tryon, Carolyn Jones. Color.

COLOSSUS OF NEW YORK, THE (VV) 70
PARAMOUNT. (R) June, 1958. Ross Martin, Mala Powers.

COLOSSUS OF RHODES, THE (Supertotalscope) (Ital.: dubbed) 127
MGM. (R) 1960. Rory Calhoun, Lea Massi.

COLOSSUS: THE FORBIN PROJECT 100
UNIVERSAL. (R) May, 1970. Eric Braeden, Susan Clark. Color.

COMA (P) 112
UNITED ARTISTS. (R) February, 1978. Genevieve Bujold, Michael Douglas.

COMANCHE (Cs) 87
UNITED ARTISTS. (R) March, 1956. Dana Andrews, Linda Cristal. Color.

COMANCHE STATION (Cs) 74
COLUMBIA. (R) March, 1960.

COMANCHEROS, THE (Cs) 107
TWENTIETH CENTURY-FOX. (R) November, 1961. John Wayne, Stewart Whitman. Color.

COME BACK CHARLESTON BLUE 100
WARNER BROS. (R) June, 1972. Godfrey Cambridge, Raymond St. Jacques. Color.

COME BLOW YOUR HORN (P) 112
PARAMOUNT. (R) June, 1963. Frank Sinatra, Lee J. Cobb. Color.

COME FLY WITH ME (P) 109
METRO-GOLDWYN-MAYER. (R) April, 1963. Dolores Hart, Hugh O'Brian. Color.

COME NEXT SPRING 92
REPUBLIC. (R) March 9, 1956. Ann Sheridan, Steve Cochran. Color.

COME ON, THE (SS) 83
ALLIED ARTISTS. (R) April 15, 1955. Ann Baxter, Sterling Hayden.

COME SEPTEMBER (Cs) 112
UNIVERSAL. (R) June, 1961. Rock Hudson, Gina Lollobrigida. Color.

COME SPY WITH ME 85

	Length In Mins.

20th CENTURY-FOX. (R) January, 1967. Troy Donahue, Andrea Dromm. Color.

COMEDIANS, THE (P) 160
MGM. (R) December, 1967. Richard Burton, Elizabeth Taylor. Color.

COMEDY OF TERRORS, THE (P) 88
AMERICAN INTERNATIONAL. (R) December, 1963. Vincent Price, Peter Lorre. Color.

COMES A HORSEMAN 119
UNITED ARTISTS. (R) October, 1978. James Caan, Jane Fonda.

COMIC 95
COLUMBIA. (R) November, 1969. Dick Van Dyke, Michelle Lee, Mickey Rooney. Color.

COMING APART 110
(R) Ooctober, 1969. Rip Torn, Viveca Linfors, Sally Kirkland. b&w.

COMING HOME 127
UNITED ARTISTS. (R) February, 1978. Jane Fonda, Jon Voight.

COMMITTEE, THE 90
COMMONWEALTH UNITED ENTERTAINMENT. (R) March, 1969. Don Sturdy, Carl Gottlieb, Christopher Ross. Color.

COMPANEROS 107
CINERAMA. (R) April, 1972. Franco Nero, Jack Palance. Color.

COMPANY OF KILLERS 83
UNIVERSAL. (R) August, 1970. Van Johnson, Ray Milland. Color.

COMPULSION (Cs) 103
TWENTIETH CENTURY-FOX. (R) April, 1959. Orson Welles, Diana Varsi.

COMPUTER WORE TENNIS SHOES, THE 90
BUENA VISTA. (R) February, 1970. Kurt Russell, Caesar Romero. Color.

CONCERT FOR BANGLADESH, THE 100
20th CENTURY-FOX. (R) April, 1972. Rock Concert. Documentary. Color.

CONCORDE—AIRPORT '79, THE 109
UNIVERSAL. (R) August, 1979. Alain Delon, Susan Blakely.

CONDEMNED OF ALTONA, THE (Cs) 114
TWENTIETH CENTURY-FOX. (R) October, 1963. Sophia Loren, Maximillian Schell.

CONDUCT UNBECOMING 107
ALLIED ARTISTS. (R) October, 1975. Michael York, Richard Attenborough.

CONFESSION, THE (French; Eng. titles) 138
PARAMOUNT. (R) December, 1970. Yves Montand, Simone Signoret. Color.

CONFESSIONS OF A WINDOW CLEANER 90
COLUMBIA. (R) November, 1975. Robin Askwith, Anthony Booth.

CONFESSIONS OF AN OPIUM EATER 85
ALLIED ARTISTS. (R) May, 1962. Vincent Price, Linda Ho.

CONFORMIST, THE (Ital.; Eng. titles) 110
PARAMOUNT. (R) December, 1970. Jean-Louis Trintignant, Stefania Sandrelli. Color.

CONGO CROSSING 83
UNIVERSAL. (R) July, 1956. Virginia Mayo, George Nader. Color.

CONGRESS DANCES (Ger.) (Cs) 90
REPUBLIC. (R) January, 1957. Hannelore Ballman. Color.

CONJUGAL BED, THE 90
AVCO EMBASSY. (R) 1963. Ugo Tognazzi, Marina Vlady. b&w.

CONQUERED CITY 91
AMERICAN INTERNATIONAL. (R) January, 1965. David Niven, Ben Gazzara.

CONQUEROR, THE (Cs) 111
RKO RADIO. (R) March 28, 1956. John Wayne, Susan Hayward, Pedro Armendariz. Color.

CONQUEROR WORM, THE 87
AMERICAN INTERNATIONAL. (R) May, 1968. Vincent Price, Ian Ogilvy. Color.

CONQUEST OF SPACE 81
PARAMOUNT. (R) March, 1955. Walter Brooks, Eric Fleming. Color.

CONQUEST OF THE PLANET OF THE APES 88
20th CENTURY-FOX. (R) June, 1972. Roddy McDowall, Don Murray. Color.

CONRACK (P) 106
TWENTIETH CENTURY-FOX. (R) March, 1974. Jon Voight, Paul Winfield.

CONSTABLE AND THE CROSS (Totalscope) 114
AVCO EMBASSY. (R) 1962. Cornel Wilde, Belinda Lee. Color.

CONTEMPT (Cs) 103
EMBASSY. (R) October, 1964. Brigitte Bardot, Jack Palance. Color.

Length In Mins.

CONTEST GIRL (Cs) 102
CONTINENTAL. (R) May, 1966. Ian Hendry, Janette Scott. Color.

CONVERSATION, THE 112
PARAMOUNT. (R) April, 1974. Gene Hackman, John Cazale.

CONVICT STAGE 71
TWENTIETH-CENTURY-FOX. (R) June, 1965. Harry Lauter, Donald Berry.

CONVOY (P) 111
UNITED ARTISTS. (R) June, 1978. Kris Kristofferson, Ali MacGraw.

COOGAN'S BLUFF 94
UNIVERSAL. (R) November, 1968. Clint Eastwood, Lee J. Cobb, Susan Clark. Color.

COOL AND THE CRAZY, THE 78
AMERICAN INTERNATIONAL PICTURES. (R) March, 1958. Gigi Pereau.

COOL BREEZE 101
METRO-GOLDWYN-MAYER. (R) April, 1972. Thalmus Rasulala, Judy Pace. Color.

COOL HAND LUKE 129
WARNER BROS.-SEVEN ARTS. (R) October, 1967. Paul Newman, George Kennedy. Color.

COOL ONES, THE (P) 95
WARNER BROS. (R) April, 1967. Roddy McDowall, Debbie Watson. Color.

COOL WORLD, THE 105
CINEMA V. (R) April, 1964. Hampton Clanton, Carl Lee.

COOLEY HIGH 107
AMERICAN INTERNATIONAL. (R) June, 1975. Glynn Turman, Lawrence-Hilton Jacobs.

COONSKIN 83
BRYANSTON. (R) August, 1975. Barry White, Charles Gordone.

COP, THE 100
AUDUBON. (R) May, 1971. Michel Bouquet, John Garko. Color.

COP HATER 75
UNITED ARTISTS. (R) September, 1958. Robert Loggia, Gerald O'Laughlin.

COP OUT 95
CINERAMA. (R) January, 1968. James Mason, Geraldine Chaplin. Color.

COPPER SKY (Cs) 77
TWENTIETH CENTURY-FOX. (R) September, 1957. Jeff Morrow, Coleen Gray.

COPS AND ROBBERS 89
UNITED ARTISTS. (R) August, 1973. Cliff Gorman, Joe Bologna.

CORNBREAD EARL AND ME 95
AMERICAN INTERNATIONAL. (R) June, 1975. Moses Gunn, Keith Wilkes.

CORRIDORS OF BLOOD 89
METRO-GOLDWYN-MAYER. (R) April, 1963. Boris Karloff, Betta St. John.

CORRUPT ONES, THE (TE) 92
WARNER BROS. (R) February, 1967. Robert Stack, Elke Sommer. Color.

CORRUPTION 91
COLUMBIA. (R) December, 1968. Peter Cushing, Sue Lloyd, Noel Trevarthon. Color.

CORVETTE SUMMER (P) 110
UNITED ARTISTS. (R) June, 1978. Mark Hamill, Annie Potts.

COSMIC MAN, THE 72
ALLIED ARTISTS. (R) January, 1959. Bruce Bennett, John Carradine.

COSSACKS, THE (Totalscope) 113
UNIVERSAL. (R) May, 1960. Edmund Purdom, John Drew Barrymore. Color.

COTTON COMES TO HARLEM 97
UNITED ARTISTS. (R) June, 1970. Godfrey Cambridge, Raymond St. Jacques, Calvin Lockhart. Color.

COUCH, THE 100
WARNER BROS. (R) March, 1962. Grant Williams, Shirley Knight.

COUNT FIVE AND DIE 92
TWENTIETH CENTURY-FOX. (R) March, 1958. Jeffrey Hunter, Anne Marie Duringer.

COUNT THREE AND PRAY (Cs) 102
COLUMBIA. (R) October, 1955. Van Heflin, Joanne Woodward. Color.

COUNT YORGA, VAMPIRE 91
AMERICAN INTERNATIONAL. (R) June, 1970. Robert Quarry, Roger Perry. Color.

COUNT YOUR BLESSINGS (Cs) 102
METRO-GOLDWYN-MAYER. (R) April, 1959. Deborah Kerr, Rossano Brazzi. Color.

COUNTDOWN (P) 101
WARNER BROS.-SEVEN ARTS. (R) February, 1968. James Caan, Joanna Moore. Color.

Length In Mins.

COUNTDOWN AT KUSINI 101
COLUMBIA. (R) April, 1976. Ruby Dee, Greg Morris.

COUNTERFEIT CONSTABLE, THE 86
SEVEN ARTS. (R) November, 1966. Robert Dhery. Color.

COUNTERFEIT KILLER, THE 95
UNIVERSAL. (R) January, 1970. Jack Lord, Shirley Knight.

COUNTERFEIT PLAN, THE 86
WARNER BROTHERS. (R) May 11, 1957. Zachary Scott, Peggie Castle.

COUNTERFEIT TRAITOR, THE 140
PARAMOUNT. (R) July, 1962. William Holden, Lilli Palmer. Color.

COUNTERFEITERS OF PARIS, THE 90
METRO-GOLDWYN-MAYER. (R) July, 1962. Jean Gabin, Bernard Blier.

COUNTERPLOT 76
UNITED ARTISTS. (R) October, 1959. Forrest Tucker, Allison Hayes.

COUNTESS DRACULA 94
TWENTIETH CENTURY-FOX. (R) October, 1972. Ingrid Pitt, Nigel Green. Color.

COUNTESS FROM HONG KONG, A 108
UNIVERSAL. (R) April, 1967. Marlon Brando, Sophia Loren. Color.

COUNTRY GIRL, THE 104
PARAMOUNT. (R) March, 1955. Bing Crosby, Grace Kelly, William Holden.

COUNTRY MUSIC 93
UNIVERSAL. (R) November, 1972. Marty Robbins, Sammy Jackson. Color.

COUNTRY MUSIC HOLIDAY 81
PARAMOUNT. (R) May, 1958. Ferlin Husky, Zsa Zsa Gabor.

COUPLE, THE (Russ.) 103
ARTKINO. (R) August, 1967. Ivan Marin, Vera Kuznetsoya.

COURT JESTER, THE (VV) 101
PARAMOUNT. (R) March, 1958. Danny Kaye, Glynis Johns. Color.

COURT MARTIAL (Brit.) 105
KINGSLEY. (R) August, 1955. David Niven, Margaret Leighton.

COURT MARTIAL OF BILLY MITCHELL, THE (Cs) 100
WARNER BROTHERS. (R) December 31, 1955. Gary Cooper, Charles Bickford, Ralph Bellamy, Rod Steiger. Color.

COURTSHIP OF EDDIE'S FATHER, THE (P) 117
METRO-GOLDWYN-MAYER. (R) March, 1963. Glenn Ford, Shirley Jones. Color.

COUSIN, COUSINE (French with English titles) 95
LIBRA FILMS. (R) September, 1976. Marie-Christine Barrault, Victor Lamoux.

COUSINS, THE (French; Eng. titles) 112
CONTINENTAL. (R) 1959. Claude Brialy, Gerard Blain.

COVENANT WITH DEATH, A 97
WARNER BROS. (R) February, 1967. George Maharis, Laura DeVon. Color.

COVER GIRL KILLER! 61
FANFARE. (R) May, 1960. Harry H. Corbett, Felicity Young.

COVER ME, BABE (P) 89
20th CENTURY-FOX. (R) November, 1970. Robert Forster, Sondra Locke. Color.

COWBOY 92
COLUMBIA. (R) March, 1958. Glenn Ford, Jack Lemmon. Color.

COWBOYS, THE 128
WARNER BROS. (R) February, 1972. John Wayne. Color.

CRACK IN THE MIRROR (CS) 97
TWENTIETH CENTURY-FOX. (R) May, 1960. Orson Welles, Juliette Greco.

CRACK IN THE WORLD 96
PARAMOUNT. (P) February, 1965. Dana Andrews, Janette Scott. Color.

CRASH LANDING 76
COLUMBIA. (R) 1958. Gary Merrill, Nancy Davis.

CRASHING LAS VEGAS 62
ALLIED ARTISTS. (R) April 22, 1956. Leo Gorcey, Hunts Hall.

CRASHOUT 82
FILMAKERS. (R) April, 1955. William Bendix, Arthur Kennedy.

CRAZE 96
WARNER BROS. (R) July, 1974. Jack Palance, Diana Dors.

CRAZY JOE 100
COLUMBIA. (R) February, 1974. Peter Boyle, Paula Prentiss.

CRAZY MAMA 82

	Length In Mins.

AMERICAN INTERNATIONAL. (R) March, 1959. Dick
Contino, Sandra Giles.

DADDY'S GONE A-HUNTING 108
NATIONAL GENERAL. (R) July, 1969. Carol White,
Paul Burke. Color.

DAGMAR'S HOT PANTS, INC. 94
AMERICAN INTERNATIONAL. (R) November, 1971.
Diana Kjaer, Anne Grete. Color.

DAISY MILLER 91
PARAMOUNT. (R) May, 1974. Cybill Shepherd, Barry
Brown.

DAKOTA INCIDENT 88
REPUBLIC. (R) July 23, 1956. Linda Darnell, Dale Robertson. Color.

DALTON GIRLS, THE 71
UNITED ARTISTS. (R) December, 1957. Merry Anders,
Lisa Davis.

DAMIEN—OMEN II (P) 110
20th CENTURY-FOX. (R) June, 1978. William Holden,
Lee Grant.

DAM BUSTERS, THE (Brit.) 102
WARNER BROTHERS. (R) July 16, 1955. Richard Todd,
Ursula Jeans, Michael Redgrave.

DAMN CITIZEN 88
UNIVERSAL. (R) March, 1958. Keith Anders, Lisa
Davis.

DAMN THE DEFIANT (Cs) 101
COLUMBIA. (R) September, 1962. Alec Guinness, Dirk
Bogarde. Color.

DAMN YANKEES 110
WARNER BROS. (R) September, 1958. Tab Hunter,
Gwen Verdon. Color.

DAMNATION ALLEY (P) 92
20th CENTURY-FOX. (R) October, 1977. Jan-Michael
Vincent, George Peppard.

DAMNED, THE 160
WARNER BROS. (R) January, 1970. Dirk Bogarde, Ingrid Thulin, Helmet Berger. Color.

DAMON AND PYTHIAS 99
METRO-GOLDWYN-MAYER. (R) September, 1962.
Guy Williams, Don Burnett. Color.

DANCE LITTLE LADY (Brit.) 87
TRANS-LUX. (R) January, 1956. Mai Zetterling, Terence
Morgan. Color.

DANCE WITH ME HENRY 80
UNITED ARTISTS. (R) December, 1956. Abbott and
Costello.

DANDY IN ASPIC. A (P) 107
COLUMBIA. (R) April, 1968. Laurence Harvey, Tom
Courtenay. Color.

DANGER: DIABOLIK 102
PARAMOUNT. (R) May, 1968. John Phillip Law, Marisa
Mell. Color.

DANGER ROUTE 90
UNITED ARTISTS. (R) February, 1968. Richard Johnson, Diana Dors. Color.

DANGEROUS EXILE (VV) 90
RANK FILM DISTRIBUTORS OF AMERICA. (R) October, 1958. Louis Jourdan, Belinda Lee. Color.

DANGEROUS YOUTH 98
WARNER BROTHERS (R) June, 1958. George Baker,
Frankie Vaughn.

DANIEL BOONE, TRAIL BLAZER 76
REPUBLIC. (R) September 14, 1956. Bruce Bennett,
Lon Chaney. Color.

DARBY O'GILL AND THE LITTLE PEOPLE 93
BUENA VISTA. (R) July, 1959. Janet Munro, Albert
Sharpe. Color.

DARBY'S RANGERS 121
WARNER BROS. (R) January, 1958. James Garner,
Etchika Choureau.

DARING GAME 100
PARAMOUNT. (R) April, 1968. Lloyd Bridges, Nico
Minardos. Color.

DARK AT THE TOP OF THE STAIRS, THE 124
WARNER BROS. (R) October, 1960. Robert Preston,
Dorothy McGuire. Color.

DARK INTRUDER 59
UNIVERSAL. (R) October, 1965. Leslie Nielsen, Gilbert
Green.

DARK OF THE SUN 105
MGM. (R) July, 1968. Rod Taylor, Yvette Mimieux, Jim
Brown. Color.

DARK PURPOSE 90
UNIVERSAL. (R) February, 1964. Shirley Jones, Rossano Brazzi. Color.

DARK RIVER (ARG.) 90
TIMES. (R) February, 1956. Adriana Bennett.

DARKER THAN AMBER 97
NATIONAL GENERAL. (R) August, 1970. Rod Taylor,
Suzy Kendall. Color.

DARLING (Brit.) 122

	Length In Mins.

EMBASSY. (R) August, 1965. Laurence Harvey, Dirk
Bogarde.

DARLING LILI (P) 136
PARAMOUNT. (R) January, 1970. Julie Andrews, Rock
Hudson. Color.

DARWIN ADVENTURE, THE 91
TWENTIETH CENTURY-FOX. (R) October, 1972. Nicholas Clay, Ian Richardson. Color.

DAUGHTER OF DR. JEKYLL 71
ALLIED ARTISTS. (R) July, 1957. John Agar, Gloria
Talbott.

DAUGHTERS OF DARKNESS 87
MARON. (R) July, 1971. Delphine Seyrig, John Karlen.
Color.

DAUGHTERS OF SATAN 92
UNITED ARTISTS. (R) October, 1972. Tom Selleck,
Barra Grant. Color.

DAVID AND GOLIATH (Cs) 95
ALLIED ARTISTS. (R) April, 1961. Orson Welles, Ivo
Payer. Color.

DAVID AND LISA 94
CONTINENTAL. (R) February, 1963. Keir Dullea, Janet
Margolin.

DAVY CROCKETT AND THE RIVER PIRATES 85
BUENA VISTA. (R) July 17, 1956. Fess Parker, Buddy
Ebsen. Color.

DAVY CROCKETT, KING OF THE WILD FRONTIER 95
BUENA VISTA. (R) June, 1955. Fess Parker, Buddy Ebsen. Color.

DAWN OF THE DEAD 125
UNITED FILM DIST. (R) April, 1979. David Enge, Ken
Foree.

DAY AND THE HOUR, THE (Franscope) 104
METRO-GOLDWYN-MAYER. (R) February, 1964. Si-
mone Signoret, Stuart Whitman.

DAY FOR NIGHT 116
WARNER BROS. (R) October, 1973. Jacqueline Bisset,
Valentina Cortese.

DAY IN THE DEATH OF JOE EGG, A 106
COLUMBIA. (R) June, 1972. Alan Bates, Janet Suzman.
Color.

DAY MARS INVADED EARTH, THE (Cs) 70
TWENTIETH CENTURY-FOX. (R) February, 1963.
Kent Taylor, Marie Windsor.

DAY OF ANGER (P) 109
NATIONAL GENERAL. (R) November, 1969. Lee Van
Cleef. Color.

DAY OF FURY, A 78
UNIVERSAL. (R) May, 1956. Dale Robertson, Mara
Corday. Color.

DAY OF THE BAD MAN, THE (Cs) 81
UNIVERSAL INTERNATIONAL (R) April, 1953. Fred
MacMurray, Joan Waldon. Color.

DAY OF THE DOLPHIN, THE 104
AVCO-EMBASSY. (R) December, 1973. George C.
Scott, Trish Van Devere.

DAY OF THE EVIL GUN 95
MGM. (R) March, 1968. Glenn Ford, Arthur Kennedy.
Color.

DAY OF THE JACKAL, THE 142
UNIVERSAL. (R) May, 1973. Edward Fox, Delphine
Seyrig. Color.

DAY OF THE LOCUST, THE 140
PARAMOUNT. (R) May, 1975. Donald Sutherland,
Karen Black.

DAY OF THE OUTLAW 90
UNITED ARTISTS. (R) July, 1959. Robert Ryan, Burl
Ives.

DAY OF THE TRIFFIDS, THE (Cs) 119
ALLIED ARTISTS. (R) July, 1962. Howard Keel, Nicole
Maurey. Color.

DAY THE EARTH CAUGHT FIRE, THE 90
UNIVERSAL. (R) May, 1962. Edward Judd, Janet
Munro, Leo McKern.

DAY THE FISH CAME OUT, THE 109
INTERNATIONAL CLASSICS. (R) October, 1967. Tom
Courtenay, Candice Bergen. Color.

DAY THE HOT LINE GOT HOT, THE 100
COMMONWEALTH UNITED. (R) December, 1969.
George Chakiris, Robert Taylor, Color.

DAY THE WORLD ENDED, THE 90
AMERICAN RELEASING CORP. (R) January, 1956.
Richard Denning, Lori Nelson.

DAY THEY ROBBED THE BANK OF ENGLAND, THE 85
METRO-GOLDWYN-MAYER. (R) August, 1960. Aldo
Ray, Elizabeth Sellars.

DAY TO REMEMBER, A (Brit.) 72
REPUBLIC. (R) March 29, 1955. Stanley Holloway, Joan
Rice.

DAYDREAMER, THE 101
EMBASSY. (R) Summer, 1966. Animagic-Live
action/animation. Color.

DAYS OF HEAVEN 95

	Length In Mins.

PARAMOUNT. (R) December, 1961. Jerry Lewis, Brian Donlevy.

ESCAPADE IN JAPAN 92
UNIVERSAL. (R) November, 1957. Teresa Wright, Cameron Mitchell.

ESCAPE BY NIGHT 75
ALLIED ARTISTS. (R) September, 1964. Terence Longdon, Jennifer Jayne.

ESCAPE FROM ALCATRAZ 112
PARAMOUNT. (R) June, 1979. Clint Eastwood.

ESCAPE FROM EAST BERLIN 94
METRO-GOLDWYN-MAYER. (R) November, 1962. Don Murray, Christine Kaufmann.

ESCAPE FROM HELL 80
CROWN. (R) June, 1964. Mark Stevens.

ESCAPE FROM REDROCK (RS) 75
TWENTIETH CENTURY-FOX. (R) January, 1958. Brian Donlevy, Eilene Janssen.

ESCAPE FROM SAN QUENTIN 81
COLUMBIA. (R) November, 1957. Johnny Desmond, Merry Anders.

ESCAPE FROM TERROR 70
COOGAN-ROGERS. (R) March, 1960. Jackie Coogan, Mona Knox. Color.

ESCAPE FROM THE PLANET OF THE APES 98
TWENTIETH CENTURY-FOX. (R) June, 1971. Roddy McDowell, Kim Hunter. Color.

ESCAPE FROM ZAHRAIN 93
PARAMOUNT. (R) June, 1962. Yul Brynner, Sal Mineo. Color.

ESCAPE TO ATHENA (P) 100
ASSOCIATED FILM DIST. (R) June, 1979. Roger Moore, Telly Savalas.

ESCAPE TO BURMA (SS) 87
RKO RADIO. (R) April 9, 1955. Barbara Stanwyck, Robert Ryan. Color.

ESCAPE TO NOWHERE (French; Eng. titles) 118
PEPPERCORN-WORMSER. (R) August, 1974. Lina Ventura, Lea Massari.

ESCAPE TO THE SUN 105
CINEVISION. (R) October, 1972. Laurence Harvey, Josephine Chaplin. Color.

ESCAPE TO WITCH MOUNTAIN 98
BUENA VISTA. (R) March, 1975. Eddie Albert, Ray Milland.

ESCORT WEST (Cs) 75
UNITED ARTISTS. (R) January, 1959. Victor Mature, Elaine Stewart.

ESTHER AND THE KING (Cs) 109
TWENTIETH CENTURY-FOX. (R) December, 1960. Joan Collins, Richard Egan. Color.

ETERNAL SEA, THE 103
REPUBLIC. (R) May 5, 1955. Sterling Hayden, Alexis Smith.

EVA 115
TIMES FILM (R) June, 1965. Jeanne Moreau, Stanley Baker.

EVE 97
COMMONWEALTH UNITED. (R) April, 1969. Celeste Yarnall, Robert Walker, Herbert Lom.

EVE AND THE DRAGON (Cs) 80
AMERICAN INTERNATIONAL. (R) February, 1960. Color.

EVEL KNIEVEL 90
FANFARE. (R) July, 1971. George Hamilton, Sue Lyon. Color.

EVENING WITH THE ROYAL BALLET, AN 90
SIGMA III. (R) September, 1965. Rudolph Nureyev, Margot Fonteyn. Color.

EVERY BASTARD A KING 93
CONTINENTAL. (R) April, 1970. Pier Angeli, William Berger. Color.

EVERY DAY IS A HOLIDAY 76
COLUMBIA. (R) July, 1966. Marisol, Angel Peralta. Color.

EVERY LITTLE CROOK AND NANNY 92
METRO-GOLDWYN-MAYER. (R) June, 1972. Victor Mature, Lynn Redgrave. Color.

EVERYTHING BUT THE TRUTH 83
UNIVERSAL. (R) December, 1956. Maureen O'Hara, John Forsythe, Tim Hovey. Color.

EVERYTHING YOU ALWAYS WANTED TO KNOW ABOUT SEX AND WERE AFRAID TO ASK 87
UNITED ARTISTS. (R) August, 1972. Woody Allen, Gene Wilder, Lynn Redgrave. Color.

EVERYTHING'S DUCKY 81
COLUMBIA. (R) November, 1961. Mickey Rooney, Buddy Hackett.

EVERY WHICH WAY BUT LOOSE 114
WARNER BROS. (R) December, 1978. Clint Eastwood, Sondra Locke.

EVIL OF FRANKENSTEIN 86

	Length In Mins.

UNIVERSAL. June, 1964. Peter Culshing, Kiwi Kingston. Color.

EXECUTIONER, THE 107
COLUMBIA. (R) June, 1970. George Peppard, Joan Collins. Color.

EXECUTIVE ACTION 91
NATIONAL GENERAL. (R) November, 1973. Burt Lancaster, Robert Ryan.

EXODUS (P) 212
UNITED ARTISTS. (R) December, 1960. Paul Newman, Eva Marie Saint. Color.

EXORCIST, THE 121
WARNER BROS. (R) December, 1973. Ellen Burstyn, Max von Sydow.

EXORCIST II: THE HERETIC (P) 110
WARNER BROS. (R) June, 1977. Linda Blair, Richard Burton.

EXPERIMENT IN TERROR 123
COLUMBIA. (R) April, 1973. Glenn Ford, Lee Remick.

EXPLOSION 96
AMER. INT. PICS. (R) March, 1970, Don Stroud, Gordon Thomson. Color.

EXPLOSIVE GENERATION, THE 89
UNITED ARTISTS. (R) October, 1961. William Shatner, Patty McCormack.

EXPRESSO BONGO 108
CONTINENTAL. (R) April, 1960. Laurence Harvey, Sylvia Syms.

EXTERMINATING ANGEL, THE (Span.) 91
ALTURA. (R) August, 1967. Silvia Pinal, Jose Baviera.

EXTRAORDINARY SEAMAN, THE 80
METRO-GOLDWYN-MAYER. (R) January, 1969. David Niven, Faye Dunaway, Alan Alda, Mickey Rooney. Color.

EXTREME CLOSE-UP 90
NATIONAL GENERAL. (R) May, 1973. James McMullan, Kate Woodville, Color.

EYE FOR AN EYE, AN 92
EMBASSY. (R) June, 1966. Robert Lansing, Pat Wayne, Slim Pickens. Color.

EYE OF THE CAT 102
UNIVERSAL. (R) June, 1969. Michael Sarrazin, Gayle Hunnicutt, Eleanor Parker. Color.

EYE OF THE DEVIL 92
MGM. (R) September, 1967. David Niven, Deborah Kerr.

EYE OF THE NEEDLE, THE (Italian with English titles) .. 97
ELDORADO. (R) July, 1965. Vittorio Gassman, Annette Stroyberg.

EYES OF ANNIE JONES, THE 85
20th CENTURY-FOX. (R) 1964. Richard Conte, Francesca Annis.

EYES OF LAURA MARS (P) 104
COLUMBIA. (R) August, 1978. Faye Dunaway, Tommy Lee Jones

F

F.B.I. CODE 98 94
WARNER BROS. (R) June, 1964. Robert P. Cannon, Fred Vitale.

F.B.I. STORY, THE 149
WARNER BROS. (R) October, 1959. James Stewart, Vera Miles. Color.

F.I.S.T 143
UNITED ARTISTS. (R) April, 1978. Sylvester Stallone, Rod Steiger.

FM 110
UNIVERSAL. (R) April, 1978. Michael Brandon, Eileen Brennan

F.T.A. 94
AMERICAN INTERNATIONAL. (R) July, 1972. Jane Fonda, Donald Sutherland, Peter Boyle. Color.

FABULOUS WORLD OF JULES VERNE 95
WARNER BROS. (R) June, 1961. Lou Tuck, Ernie Navara.

FACE IN THE CROWD, A 126
WARNER BROS. (R) June, 1957. Andy Griffith, Patricia Neal.

FACE OF A FUGITIVE 81
COLUMBIA. (R) May, 1959. Fred MacMurray. Color.

FACE OF FIRE 80
ALLIED ARTISTS. (R) August, 1959. Cameron Mitchell, James Whitmore.

FACE OF FU MANCHU, THE (TE) 96
SEVEN ARTS. (R) October, 1965. Christopher Lee, Nigel Green. Color.

FACE OF WAR, A 77
FEATURE FILM. (R) March, 1968. Documentary.

FACE TO FACE (Swedish; English sub-titles.) 136

	Length In Mins.			Length In Mins.

PARAMOUNT. (R) April, 1976. Liv Ullmann, Erland Josephson.

FACES 127
CONTINENTAL. (R) November, 1968. John Marley, Gena Rowlands, Fred Draper, Lynn Carter. b&w.

FACES IN THE DARK 84
STATES RIGHTS. (R) September, 1964. John Gregson, Mai Zetterling.

FACTS OF LIFE, THE 103
UNITED ARTISTS. (R) December, 1960. Bob Hope, Lucille Ball.

FAHRENHEIT 451 111
UNIVERSAL. (R) January, 1967. Oskar Werner, Julie Christie. Color.

FAIL SAFE 111
COLUMBIA. (R) October, 1964. Dan O'Herlihy, Walter Matthau.

FAIR IS THE KEY 105
PARAMOUNT. (R) March, 1973. Suzy Kendall, Barry Newman. Color.

FALL GIRL 83
MEDALLION. (R) 1961. John Agar, Greta Chi. b&w.

FALL OF THE HOUSE OF USHER, THE (Cs) 85
AMERICAN INTERNATIONAL. (R) July, 1960. Vincent Price, Mark Damon. Color.

FALL OF THE ROMAN EMPIRE, THE (P) 180
PARAMOUNT. (R) Special in March, 1964. Sophia Loren, Stephen Boyd. Color.

FALSTAFF 115
PEPPERCORN-WORMSER-SALTZMAN. (R) February, 1967. Orson Welles, Jeanne Moreau, Keith Baxter, John Gielgud.

FAME 127
UNITED ARTISTS. (R) May, 1980. Eddie Barth, Irene Cara.

FAMILY HONOR 104
CINERAMA. (R) February, 1973. Anthony Page. Color.

FAMILY JEWELS, THE 100
PARAMOUNT. (R) June, 1965. Jerry Lewis, Donna Butterworth. Color.

FAMILY PLOT 120
UNIVERSAL. (R) April, 1976. Karen Black, Bruce Dern.

FAMILY WAY, THE 115
WARNER BROS-SEVEN ARTS. (R) June, 1967. Hayley Mills, John Mills. Color.

FANDO & LIS (Spanish; Eng. titles) 82
CANNON. (R) February, 1970. Sergio Klainer, Diana Mariscal.

FANNY 133
WARNER BROS. (R) July, 1961. Maurice Chevalier, Leslie Caron. Color.

FANNY HILL 91
CINEMATION. (R) Diana Kjaer, Hans Ernbank.

FANTASTIC PLASTIC MACHINE, THE 93
CROWN. (R) May, 1969. Nat Young, Bob McTavish, George Greenough. Color.

FANTASTIC VOYAGE (Cs) 105
20th CENTURY-FOX. (R) October, 1966. Stephen Boyd, Raquel Welch. Color.

FANTOMAS (Cs) 105
LOPERT PICTURES. (R) April, 1966. Marais, Lonis De Funes. Color.

FANTOME DE LA LIBERTE, LE (French; Eng. titles) 104
20th CENTURY-FOX. (R) November, 1974. Adrianna Asti, Julien Bertheau.

FAR COUNTRY, THE 97
UNIVERSAL. (R) February, 1955. James Stewart, Ruth Roman. Color.

FAR FROM THE MADDING CROWD (70mmP) 175
MGM. (R) Special. September, 1967. Julie Christie, Terence Stamp. Color.

FAR HORIZONS, THE (VV) 106
PARAMOUNT. (R) June, 1955. Charlton Heston, Fred MacMurray. Color.

FAREWELL, MY LOVELY 97
AVCO-EMBASSY. (R) August, 1975. Robert Mitchum, Charlotte Rampling.

FAREWELL TO ARMS, A (Cs) 150
TWENTIETH CENTURY-FOX. (R) December, 1957. Rock Hudson, Jennifer Jones. Color.

FARMER, THE (P) 98
COLUMBIA. (R) March, 1977. Gary Conway, Angel Tompkins.

FASCIST, THE (Ital. with English Titles) 102
EMBASSY. (R) June, 1965. Ugo Tognazzi, Georges Wilson.

FAST AND SEXY (T) 96
COLUMBIA. (R) September, 1960. Gina Lollobrigida, Dale Robertson. Color.

FAST BREAK 107
COLUMBIA. (R) March, 1979. Gabriel Kaplan, Harold Sylvester.

FASTEST GUITAR ALIVE, THE 85

METRO-GOLDWYN-MAYER. (R) May, 1967. Roy Orbison, Sammy Jackson. Color.

FASTEST GUN ALIVE, THE 89
METRO-GOLDWYN-MAYER. (R) July 6, 1956. Glenn Ford, Jeanne Crain

FAT CITY 96
COLUMBIA. (R) August, 1972. Stacy Keach, Jeff Bridges, Susan Tyrell. Color.

FATE IS THE HUNTER (CS) 106
TWENTIETH CENTURY-FOX. (R) October, 1964. Glenn Ford, Nancy Kwan.

FATHER GOOSE 115
UNIVERSAL. (R) January, 1965. Cary Grant, Leslie Caron. Color.

FATHER OF A SOLDIER (Russian; Eng. titles) 83
ARTKINO. (R) February 19, 1966. Georgi Makharashvilli, Sergo Zakhariadze.

FATHOM (CS) 99
TWENTIETH CENTURY-FOX. (R) August, 1967. Raquel Welch, Tony Franciosa. Color.

FATSO 94
TWENTIETH CENTURY-FOX. (R) February, 1980. Dom DeLuise, Anne Bancroft.

FEAR, The (Greek) 102
TRANS-LUX. (R) October, 1967. Alexis Damianos, Mary Chronopoulou.

FEAR STRIKES OUT (VV) 100
PARAMOUNT. (R) March, 1957. Anthony Perkins, Karl Malden.

FEARLESS FRANK 79
AMERICAN INTERNATIONAL. (R) December, 1969. Jon Voight, Monique Van Vooren. Color.

FEARLESS VAMPIRE KILLERS, OR PARDON ME, BUT YOUR TEETH ARE IN MY NECK (P) 94
MGM. (R) November, 1967. Sharon Tate, Jack MacGowran. Color.

FEARMAKERS, THE 83
UNITED ARTISTS. (R) October, 1958. Dana Andrews, Dick Foran.

FEDORA 116
UNITED ARTISTS. (R) April, 1979. William Holden, Marthe Keller.

FELLINI SATYRICON (P) 127
UNITED ARTISTS. (R) March, 1970. Martin Potter, Hiram Keller. Color.

FELLINI'S AMARCORD (Italian; Eng. titles) 127
NEW WORLD. (R) October, 1974. Magali Noel, Bruno Zanin.

FELLINI'S CASANOVA 158
UNIVERSAL. (R) February, 1977. Donald Sutherland, Tina Aumont.

FELLINI'S ROMA 120
UNITED ARTISTS. (R) October, 1972. Federico Fellini, Stefano Majore. Color.

FEMALE ANIMAL, THE (CS) 84
UNIVERSAL INTERNATIONAL. (R) April, 1958. Hedy Lamarr, Jane Powell.

FEMALE FIENDS 71
CINEMA ASSOCIATES. (R) April, 1960. Lex Barker, Carole Mathews.

FEMALE JUNGLE 71
AMERICAN INTERNATIONAL. (R) June 15, 1966. Jayne Mansfield, Lawrence Tierney.

FEMALE ON THE BEACH 97
UNIVERSAL. (R) September, 1955. Joan Crawford, Jeff Chandler.

FERNANDELL THE DRESSMAKER (FR.) 84
UNION. (R) August, 1957. Fernandel, Suzy Delair.

FERRY CROSS THE MERSEY 86
UNITED ARTISTS. (R) February, 1965. Gerry and the Pacemakers.

FERRY TO HONG KONG (CS) 118
TWENTIETH CENTURY-FOX. (R) April, 1961. Curt Jergens, Orson Welles. Color.

FESTIVAL 90
PEPPERCORN-WORMSER. (R) November, 1967. Documentary.

FEVER HEAT 100
PARAMOUNT. (R) May, 1968. Nick Adams. Color.

FEVER IN THE BLOOD, A 117
WARNER BROS. (R) January, 1961. Efrem Zimbalist, Jr., Angie Dickinson.

FFOLKES 99
UNIVERSAL. (R) April, 1980. Roger Moore, James Mason.

FIDDLER ON THE ROOF 181
UNITED ARTISTS. (R) November, 1971. Topol, Norma Crane, Leonard Frey, Molly Picon. Color.

FIEND WHO WALKED THE WEST, THE (CS) 101
TWENTIETH CENTURY-FOX. (R) August, 1958. Hugh O'Brian, Robert Evans.

FIEND WITHOUT A FACE 94

Length In Mins.

METRO-GOLDWYN-MAYER. (R) June, 1958. Marshall Thompson, Terrence Kilburn.

FIENDISH PLOT OF DR. FU MANCHU, THE 108
WARNER BROS. (R) August, 1980. Peter Sellers, Helen Mirren.

FIERCEST HEART, THE (CS) 91
TWENTIETH CENTURY-FOX. (R) April, 1961. Stuart Whitman, Juliet Prowse. Color.

FIFTH HORSEMAN IS FEAR, THE (Czech) 100
GIGMA III. (R) May, 1968. Miraslav Machacek, Olga Schenplugova.

55 DAYS AT PEKING (T-70) 150
ALLIED ARTISTS. (R) Special. May, 1963. Charlton Heston, Ava Gardner. Color.

FIGHTING CHANCE, THE 70
REPUBLIC. (R) December 15, 1955. Rod Cameron, Julie London, Ben Cooper.

FIGHTING PRINCE OF DONEGAL, THE 89
BUENA VISTA. (R) October, 1966. Peter McEnery, Susan Hampshire. Color.

FIGHTING TROUBLE 61
ALLIED ARTISTS. (R) September 16, 1956. Huntz Hall, Stanley Clements.

FIGURES IN A LANDSCAPE (P) 109
NATIONAL GENERAL. (R) July, 1971. Robert Shaw, Malcolm McDowell. Color.

FILE OF THE GOLDEN GOOSE 105
UNITED ARTISTS. (R) November, 1969. Yul Brynner, Charles Gray. Color.

FILLMORE 105
20th CENTURY-FOX. (R) June, 1972. Rock Concert Documentary. Color.

FINAL COUNTDOWN, THE 103
UNITED ARTISTS. (R) July, 1980. Kirk Douglas, Martin Sheen.

FINDERS KEEPERS 89
UNITED ARTISTS. (R) April, 1967. Cliff Richard. Color.

FINE MADNESS, A 112
WARNER BROTHERS. (R) June 25, 1966. Sean Connery, Joanne Woodward, Patrick O'Neill. Color.

FINE PAIR, A 89
NATIONAL GENERAL. (R) May, 1969. Rock Hudson, Claudia Cardinale, Thomas Milan. Color.

FINEST HOURS, THE 114
COLUMBIA. (R) October, 1964. Documentary on Sir Winston Churchill. Color.

FINGER MAN 82
ALLIED ARTISTS. (R) June 19, 1955. Frank Lovejoy, Peggie Castle.

FINGER OF GUILT (Brit.) 71
RKO. (R) November, 1956. Richard Basehart, Mary Murphy.

FINGER ON THE TRIGGER (T) 87
ALLIED ARTISTS. (R) November, 1965. Rory Calhoun, James Philbrook. Color.

FINIAN'S RAINBOW 145
WARNER BROS.-7 ARTS. (R) October, 1968. Fred Astaire, Petula Clark, Don Francks. Color.

FIRE DOWN BELOW (CS) 116
COLUMBIA. (R) July, 1957. Rita Hayworth, Robert Mitchum. Color.

FIREPOWER 104
ASSOCIATED FILM DIST. (R) April, 1979. Sophia Loren, James Coburn.

FIRE WITHIN, THE 110
NEW YORKER FILMS. (R) May, 1968. Maurice Ronet, Lena Skerla, Jeanne Moreau.

FIREBALL 500 (P) 92
AIP. (R) June 29, 1966. Frankie Avalon, Chill Wills, Annett Funicello. Color.

FIRECREEK (P) 104
WARNER BROS.-SEVEN ARTS. (R) February, 1968. James Stewart, Henry Fonda. Color.

FIREMAN'S BALL, THE 73
CINEMA V. (R) October, 1968. Jan Vostroil, Josef Sebanek.

FIREMAN'S BALL, THE (Czech; Eng. titles) 73
CINEMA V. (R) October, 1968. Vaclay Stockel, Josef Svet, John Vostrcil. Color.

FIRST CIRCLE, THE 98
PARAMOUNT. (R) January, 1973. Gunther Malzacher, Elzbieta Czyzewska. Color.

FIRST LOVE 88
PARAMOUNT. (R) November, 1977. William Katt, Susan Dey.

FIRST LOVE 90
UMC PICTURES. (R) October, 1970. Maxmilian Schell, Dominique Sanda. Color.

FIRST MAN INTO SPACE 76
METRO-GOLDWYN-MAYER. (R) February, 1959. Marshall Thompson, Maria Landi.

FIRST MEN IN THE MOON (P) 107

Length In Mins.

COLUMBIA. (R) October, 1964. Edward Judd, Lionel Jeffries. Color.

FIRST NUDIE MUSICAL, THE 100
PARAMOUNT. (R) March, 1976. Stephen Nathan, Cindy Williams.

FIRST TEXAN, THE (CS) 82
ALLIED ARTISTS. (R) June 29, 1956. Joel McCrea, Felicia Farr. Color.

FIRST TIME, THE 90
UNITED ARTISTS. (R) April, 1969. Jacqueline Bisset, Wes Stern, Rick Kelman, Wink Roberts. Color.

FIRST TO FIGHT (P) 97
WARNER BROS. February, 1967. Chad Everett, Marilyn Dein. Color.

FIRST TRAVELING SALESLADY, THE 92
UNIVERSAL. (R) August, 1956. Ginger Rogers, Barry Nelson. Color.

FISH THAT SAVED PITTSBURGH, THE 104
UNITED ARTISTS. (R) November, 1979. Julius Erving, Jonathan Winters.

FISTFUL OF DOLLARS, A (T) 98
UNITED ARTISTS. (R) January, 1967. Clint Eastwood, Marianne Koch. Color.

FISTS IN THE POCKET (Italian) 105
PEPPERCORN-WORMSER. (R) December, 1967. Lou Castel, Paola Pitagora.

FISTS OF FURY 103
NATIONAL GENERAL. (R) May, 1973. Bruce Lee, Tien Foong. Color.

FITZWILLY (P) 102
UNITED ARTISTS. (R) December, 1967. Dick Van Dyke, Barbara Feldon. Color.

FIVE AGAINST THE HOUSE 84
COLUMBIA. (R) June, 1955. Guy Madison, Kim Novak.

FIVE BOLD WOMEN 82
CITATION FILMS. Jeff Morrow, Merry Anders.

FIVE BRANDED WOMEN 108
PARAMOUNT. (R) May, 1960.

FIVE CARD STUD 103
PARAMOUNT. (R) July, 1968. Dean Martin, Robert Mitchum, Inger Stevens. Color.

FIVE EASY PIECES 96
COLUMBIA. (R) September, 1970. Jack Nicholson, Karen Black. Color.

FIVE FINGER EXERCISE 108
COLUMBIA. (R) June, 1962. Rosalind Russell, Jack Hawkins.

FIVE FINGERS OF DEATH 104
WARNER BROS. (R) March, 1973. Lo Lieh, Wang Ping. Color.

FIVE GATES TO HELL (CS) 107
TWENTIETH CENTURY-FOX. (R) October, 1959. Neville Brand, Benson Fong.

FIVE GOLDEN HOURS 90
COLUMBIA. (R) June, 1961. Cyd Charisse, Ernie Kovaks.

FIVE GUNS TO TOMBSTONE 71
UNITED ARTISTS. (R) February, 1961. James Brown, John Wilder.

FIVE GUNS WEST 78
AMERICAN RELEASING CORP. (R) April, 1955. John Lund, Dorothy Malone. Color.

FIVE MAN ARMY, THE 107
MGM. (R) February, 1970. Peter Graves, James Daly. Color.

FIVE MILES TO MIDNIGHT. 110
UNITED ARTISTS. (R) March, 1963. Sophia Loren, Anthony Perkins.

FIVE MILLION YEARS TO EARTH 98
TWENTIETH CENTURY-FOX. (R) February, 1968. James Donald, Barbara Shelley. Color.

FIVE ON THE BLACK HAND SIDE 96
UNITED ARTISTS. (R) October, 1973. Clarice Taylor, Leonard Jackson.

FIVE PENNIES, THE (VV) 157
PARAMOUNT. (R) August, 1959. Barbara Bel Geddes, Danny Kaye. Color.

FIVE STEPS TO DANGER 80
UNITED ARTISTS. (R) January, 1957. Sterling Hayden, Ruth Roman.

FIVE WEEKS IN A BALLOON (CS) 101
TWENTIETH CENTURY-FOX. (R) August, 1962. Red Buttons, Fabian. Color.

FIXER, THE 132
METRO-GOLDWYN-MAYER. (R) December, 1968. Alan Bates, Dirk Bogarde, Georgia Brown. Color.

FLAME AND THE FIRE 80
CONTINENTAL. (R) March, 1966. Documentary. Color.

FLAME OF THE ISLANDS 90
REPUBLIC. (R) January 6, 1958. Yvonne De Carlo, Zachary Scott, Howard Duff. Color.

FLAME OVER INDIA (CS) 130

	Length In Mins.

ASSOCIATED ARTISTS. (R) June, 1955. Anna Neagle, Michael Wilding.

FOUR BAGS FULL (Fr.) 84
TRANS-LUX. (R) September, 1957. Jean Gabin, Bourvil.

FOUR BOYS AND A GUN 78
UNITED ARTISTS. (R) January, 1957. Frank Sutton, Tarry Treen.

FOUR CLOWNS 97
20th CENTURY-FOX. (R) September, 1970. b&w.

"4-D MAN" 85
UNIVERSAL. (R) October, 1959. Robert Lansing, Lee Meriwether. Color.

FOUR DAYS IN NOVEMBER 120
UNITED ARTISTS. (R) November, 1964. Documentary.

FOUR DAYS OF NAPLES 124
METRO-GOLDWYN-MAYER. (R) March, 1963. Regina Blanchi, Aldo Giuffre.

FOUR DESPERATE MEN 96
CONTINENTAL. (R) 1960. Aldo Ray, Heather Sears. b&w.

FOUR FAST GUNS 72
UNIVERSAL. (R) February, 1960. James Craig, Martha Vickers.

FOUR FLIES ON GREY VELVET (TE) 110
PARAMOUNT. (R) August, 1972. Michael Brandon, Mimsy Farmer. Color.

4 FOR TEXAS 124
WARNER BROS. (R) December, 1963. Frank Sinatra, Dean Martin. Color.

FOUR GIRLS IN TOWN (CS) 85
UNIVERSAL. (R) January, 1957. George Nader, Julie Adams. Color.

FOUR HORSEMEN OF THE APOCALYPSE (CS) 158
METRO-GOLDWYN-MAYER. (R) February, 1962. Glenn Ford, Ingrid Thulin. Color.

FOUR MUSKETEERS, THE (P) 103
20th CENTURY-FOX. (R) March, 1975. Oliver Reed, Raquel Welch, Richard Chamberlain.

FOUR SKULLS OF JONATHAN DRAKE, THE 70
UNITED ARTISTS. (R) June, 1959. Eduard Franz, Grant Richards.

FOUR WAYS OUT (Ital.-Eng. dubbed) 77
CARROLL. (R) September, 1956. Gina Lollobrigida.

FOX, THE 110
CLARIDGE. (R) January, 1968. Anne Heywood, Sandy Dennis, Keir Dulles. Color.

FOXES 106
UNITED ARTISTS. (R) March, 1980. Jodie Foster, Scott Baio.

FOXFIRE 91
UNIVERSAL. (R) July, 1955. Jeff Chandler, Jane Russell. Color.

FOXHOLE IN CAIRO 79
PARAMOUNT. (R) January, 1961. James Robertson Justice, Albert Lieven.

FOXIEST GIRL IN PARIS, THE (Fr.) 100
TIMES. (R) 1957. Martine Carol, Miscla Auer. b&w.

FRAGMENT OF FEAR 96
COLUMBIA. (R) September, 1971. David Hemmings, Gayle Hunnicutt. Color.

FRAMED 106
PARAMOUNT. (R) August, 1975. Joe Don Baker, Conny Van Dyke.

FRANCIS IN THE HAUNTED HOUSE 80
UNIVERSAL. (R) August, 1956. Mickey Rooney, Virginia Welles.

FRANCIS IN THE NAVY 80
UNIVERSAL. (R) August, 1955. Donald O'Connor, Martha Hyer.

FRANCIS OF ASSISI (CS) 111
TWENTIETH CENTURY-FOX. (R) August, 1961. Bradford Dillman, Dolores Hart. Color.

FRANKENSTEIN-1970 (CS) 83
ALLIED ARTISTS. (R) July 6, 1958. Boris Karloff, Jana Lund.

FRANKENSTEIN AND THE MONSTER FROM HELL 93
PARAMOUNT. (R) June, 1974. Peter Cushing, Shane Briant.

FRANKENSTEIN CONQUERS THE WORLD (Tohoscope) Japan 87
AMER. INT'L. PICS. (R) Nick Adams.

FRANKENSTEIN CREATED WOMAN 92
20th CENTURY-FOX. (R) March, 1967. Peter Cushing, Susan Denberg. Color.

FRANKENSTEIN MEETS THE SPACE MONSTER 78
ALLIED ARTISTS. (R) 1965. James Karen, Nancy Marshall. b&w.

FRANKENSTEIN MUST BE DESTROYED 101
WARNER BROS. (R) February, 1970. Peter Cushing, Simon Ward. Color.

FRANKIE AND JOHNNY 87
UNITED ARTISTS. (R) April, 1966. Elvis Presley, Donna Douglas. Color.

FRANTIC (French) 90
TIMES. (R) June, 1961. Jeanne Moreau, Maurice Ronet.

FRATERNITY ROW 101
PARAMOUNT. (R) April, 1977. Peter Fox, Gregory Harrison.

FRAULEIN (CS) 90
TWENTIETH CENTURY-FOX. (R) May, 1958. Mel Ferrer, Dana Wynter. Color.

FRAULEIN DOKTOR 102
PARAMOUNT. (R) May, 1969. Suzy Kendall, Kenneth More, Capucine, James Booth. Color.

FREAKY FRIDAY 95
BUENA VISTA. (R) February, 1977. Barbara Harris, Jodie Foster.

FRECKLES (CS) 84
TWENTIETH CENTURY-FOX. (R) September, 1960. Martin West, Carol Christensen. Color.

FREEBIE AND THE BEAN (P) 113
WARNER BROS. (R) December, 1974. Alan Arkin, James Caan.

FRENCH CANCAN (Fr.) 98
UMPO. (R) April, 1956. Jean Gabia, Francis Armoul. Color.

FRENCH CONNECTION, THE 104
20th CENTURY-FOX. (R) October, 1971. Gene Hackman, Fernando Rey, Roy Scheider. Color.

FRENCH CONNECTION II 118
20th CENTURY-FOX. (R) June, 1975. Gene Hackman, Fernando Rey.

FRENCH CONSPIRACY, THE 125
CINE GLOBE. (R) November, 1973. Jean Louis Trintignant, Michel Piccoli.

FRENCH POSTCARDS 95
PARAMOUNT. (R) October, 1979. Miles Chapin, Blanche Baker.

FRENZY 116
UNIVERSAL. (R) June, 1972. Jon Finch, Barry Foster, Alec McCowen. Color.

FREUD 139
UNIVERSAL. (R) December, 1962. Montgomery Clift, Susannah York.

FRIDAY FOSTER 89
AMERICAN INTERNATIONAL. (R) December, 1975. Pam Grier, Yaphet Kotto.

FRIEND OF THE FAMILY (Fr., English titles) 95
INTERNATIONAL CLASSICS. (R) November, 1965. Jean Marais, Danielle Darrieux.

FRIENDLY PERSUASION 137
ALLIED ARTISTS. (R) November 25, 1956. Gary Cooper, Dorothy McGuire. Color.

FRIENDS 102
PARAMOUNT. (R) April, 1971. Sean Bury, Anicee Alvina. Color.

FRIENDS OF EDDIE COYLE, THE (P) 103
PARAMOUNT. (R) July, 1973. Robert Mitchum, Peter Boyle. Color.

FRIGHTENED CITY, THE 97
ALLIED ARTISTS. (R) October, 1962. Herbert Lom, John Gregson.

FRISCO KID, THE 122
WARNER BROS. (R) July, 1979. Gene Wilder, Harrison Ford.

FRISKY (Ital.) 96
DISTRIBUTORS CORP. OF AMERICA. (R) November, 1955. Gina Lollobrigida, Vittorio De Sica.

FRITZ THE CAT 78
CINEMATION. (R) April, 1972. Animated Adult Feature. Color.

FROGS 91
AMERICAN INTERNATIONAL. (R) March, 1972. Ray Milland, Adam Roarke. Color.

FROM EAR TO EAR (WS) 81
CINEMATION. (R) January, 1971. Nicole De Bonne, Daniele Argence. Color.

FROM HELL IT CAME 71
ALLIED ARTISTS. (R) August, 1957. Tod Andrews, Tina Carver.

FROM HELL TO TEXAS (CS) 100
TWENTIETH CENTURY-FOX. (R) June, 1958. Don Murray, Diane Varsi. Color.

FROM HERE TO ETERNITY 118
COLUMBIA. (R) September, 1953. Burt Lancaster, Montgomery Clift, Deborah Kerr, Frank Sinatra, Donna Reed.

FROM NOON TILL THREE 100
UNITED ARTISTS. (R) August, 1976. Charles Bronson, Jill Ireland.

FROM RUSSIA WITH LOVE 118
UNITED ARTISTS. (R) April, 1964. Sean Connery, Daniela Bianchi. Color.

FROM THE MIXED-UP FILES OF MRS. BASIL E. FRANKWEILER 105

Length In Mins.

GENE KRUPA STORY, THE 101
COLUMBIA. (R) December, 1959. Sal Mineo, Suzan Kohner.
GENERALE DELLA ROUVERE 129
CONTINENTAL. (R) 1960. Vittorio DeSica, Hannes Messmer. b&w.
GENERATION 104
AVCO EMBASSY. (R) December, 1969. David Janssen, Kim Darby, Carl Reiner. Color.
GENTLE GIANT 93
PARAMOUNT. (R) October, 1967. Dennis Weaver, Vera Miles. Color.
GENTLE RAIN, THE 110
COMET. (R) May, 1966. Christopher George, Lynda Day, Fay Spain.
GENTLE TOUCH, THE 86
RANK. (R) August, 1957. George Baker, Belinda Lee.
GENTLEMEN MARRY BRUNETTES (Cs) 97
UNITED ARTISTS. (R) October, 1955. Jane Russell, Jeanne Crain. Color.
GEORGE RAFT STORY 106
ALLIED ARTISTS. (R) December, 1961. Ray Danton, Jayne Mansfield.
GEORGIA, GEORGIA 91
CINERAMA. (R) March, 1972. Diana Sands, Dirk Benedict. Color.
GEORGY GIRL 100
COLUMBIA. (R) October, 1966. James Mason, Lynn Redgrave.
GERONIMO! 101
UNITED ARTISTS. (R) April, 1962. Chuck Connors, Kamala Devi. Color.
GERVAISE (Fr.) 89
CONTINENTAL. (R) November, 1957. Maria Schell, Francoise Perier.
GET CARTER 110
MGM. (R) February, 1971. Michael Caine, John Osborne. Color.
GET ON WITH IT (Brit.) 88
GOVERNOR. (R) August, 1965. Bob Monkhouse, Kenneth Connor.
GET TO KNOW YOUR RABBIT 93
WARNER BROS. (R) June, 1972. Tom Smothers, Orson Welles. Color.
GET YOURSELF A COLLEGE GIRL 86
METRO-GOLDWYN-MAYER. (R) November, 1964. Mary Ann Mobley, Joan O'Brien. Color.
GETAWAY, THE (TAO) 122
NATIONAL GENERAL. (R) December, 1972. Steve McQueen, Ali MacGraw. Color.
GETTING STRAIGHT 124
COLUMBIA. (R) June, 1970. Elliott Gould, Candice Bergen. Color.
GHOST AND MR. CHICKEN, THE (T) 90
UNIVERSAL. (R) May, 1966. Don Knotts, Joan Staley. Color.
GHOST DIVER 76
TWENTIETH CENTURY-FOX. (R) October, 1957. James Craig, Audrey Totter.
GHOST IN THE INVISIBLE BIKINI, THE (P) 82
AMERICAN INTERNATIONAL. (R) April, 1966. Tommy Kirk, Deborah Walley. Color.
GHOST OF DRAGSTRIP HOLLOW 65
AMERICAN INTERNATIONAL. (R) July, 1959. Jody Fair, Martin Braddock.
GHOST OF THE CHINA SEA 79
COLUMBIA. (R) September, 1958. David Brian, Lynn Bernay.
GHOST TOWN 75
UNITED ARTISTS. (R) March, 1956. Kent Taylor, Marian Carr.
GHOSTS, ITALIAN STYLE 92
METRO-GOLDWYN-MAYER. (R) January, 1969. Sophia Loren, Vittorio Gassman, Marlo Adorf. Color.
GIANT 201
WARNER BROTHERS. (R) November 24, 1956. Rock Hudson, Elizabeth Taylor, James Dean. Color.
GIANT BEHEMOTH, THE 83
ALLIED ARTISTS. (R) March, 1959. Gene Evans, Andre Morell.
GIANT CLAW, THE 76
COLUMBIA. (R) June, 1957. Jeff Morrow, Mara Corday.
GIANT FROM THE UNKNOWN 77
ASTOR. (R) 1958. Buddy Baer, Bob Steel. b&w.
GIANT GILA MONSTER, THE 73
McLENDON. (R) November, 1959. Don Sullivan. Lisa Simone.
GIANT OF MARATHON, THE (D) 92
METRO-GOLDWYN-MAYER. (R) May, 1960. Steve Reeves, Mylene Demongeot. Color.
GIDEON OF SCOTLAND YARD 91
COLUMBIA. (R) February, 1959. Jack Hawkins, Anna Massey. Color.

Length In Mins.

GIDGET (Cs) 95
COLUMBIA. (R) April, 1959. James Darren, Sandra Dee. Color.
GIDGET GOES HAWAIIAN 102
COLUMBIA. (R) June, 1961. James Darren, Michael Callan. Color.
GIDGET GOES TO ROME 101
COLUMBIA. (R) August, 1963. Cindy Carol, James Darren. Color.
GIDRAH, THE THREE-HEADED MONSTER (TO) 85
CONTINENTAL. (R) October, 1965. Yosuke Natsuki, Yuriko Hoshi. Color.
GIFT OF LOVE, THE (Cs) 105
TWENTIETH CENTURY-FOX. (R) February, 1958. Lauren Bacall, Robert Stack. Color.
GIGANTIS 78
WARNER BROS. (R) June, 1959. Hiroshi Koizumi, Sotsuko Wakayama.
GIGI (Cs) 116
MGM. (R) December, 1958. Maurice Chevalier, Leslie Caron. Color.
GIGOT 104
TWENTIETH CENTURY-FOX. (R) November, 1962. Jackie Gleason, Katherine Kath. Color.
GILDA LIVE 91
WARNER BROS. (R) March 28, 1980. Gilda Radner, Father Guido Sarducci.
GIMME SHELTER 91
CINEMA V. (R) December, 1970. Documentary. The Rolling Stones. Color.
GIRL, AND THE GENERAL, THE 105
MGM. (R) October, 1967. Rod Steiger, Virna Lisi. Color.
GIRL CAN'T HELP IT, THE (Cs) 97
TWENTIETH CENTURY-FOX. (R) December, 1956. Tom Ewell, Jayne Mansfield, Edmond O'Brien. Color.
GIRL FRIENDS 86
WARNER BROS. (R) August, 1978. Melanie Mayron, Eli Wallach
GIRL FROM PETROVKA, THE (P) 104
UNIVERSAL. (R) August, 1974. Goldie Hawn, Hal Holbrook.
GIRL GETTERS, THE 93
AIP. (R) June, 1966. Oliver Reed, Jane Merrow.
GIRL HAPPY (P) 96
METRO-GOLDWYN-MAYER. (R) April, 1965. Elvis Presley, Shelley Fabares. Color.
GIRL HE LEFT BEHIND, THE 103
WARNER BROTHERS. November 10, 1956. Tab Hunter, Natalie Wood.
GIRL HUNTERS, THE (P) 103
COLORAMA. (R) June, 1963. Mickey Spillane, Shirley Eaton.
GIRL IN BLACK STOCKINGS, THE 73
UNITED ARTISTS. (R) October, 1957. Lex Barker, Anne Bancroft.
GIRL IN THE KREMLIN, THE 81
UNIVERSAL. (R) May, 1957. Lex Barker, Zsa Zsa Gabor.
GIRL IN THE RED VELVET SWING, THE (Cs) 109
TWENTIETH CENTURY-FOX. (R) October, 1955. Ray Milland, Joan Collins, Farley Granger. Color.
GIRL MOST LIKELY, THE 98
UNIVERSAL. (R) February, 1958. Jane Powell, Cliff Robertson. Color
GIRL NAMED TAMIKO, A (P) 110
PARAMOUNT. (R) February, 1963. Laurence Harvey, France Nuyen. Color.
GIRL OF THE NIGHT 93
WARNER BROS. (R) October, 1960. Anne Francis, Lloyd Nolan.
GIRL ON A MOTORCYCLE, THE 91
CLARIDGE. (R) November, 1968. Alain Delon, Marianne Faithfull, Roger Mutton. Color.
GIRL RUSH, THE (VV) 65
PARAMOUNT. (R) September, 1955. Rosalind Russell, Fernando Lamas. Color.
GIRL WHO COULDN'T SAY NO, THE 83
20th CENTURY-FOX. (R) November, 1969. Virna Lisi, George Segal, Lila Kedrova. Color.
GIRL WHO KNEW TOO MUCH, THE 96
COMMONWEALTH UNITED. (R) September, 1969. Adam West, Nancy Kwan. Color.
GIRL WITH GREEN EYES 91
LOPERT. (R) August, 1964. Rita Tushingham, Peter Finch.
GIRLS! GIRLS! GIRLS! 106
PARAMOUNT. (R) November, 1962. Elvis Presley, Stella Stevens. Color.
GIRLS IN PRISON 87
AMERICAN INTERNATIONAL. (R) July 15, 1956. Richard Denning, Joan Taylor.
GIRLS ON THE BEACH 80
PARAMOUNT. (R) May, 1965. Martin West, Noreen Corcoran. Color.

	Length In Mins.

GIRLS TOWN 92
METRO-GOLDWYN-MAYER. (R) October, 1959. Mel Torme, Mamie Van Doren.

GIT! 92
AVCO EMBASSY. (R) June, 1965. Jack Chaplain, Heather North, Leslie Bradley.

GIVE 'EM HELL, HARRY! 102
THEATRE TELEVISION. (R) 1976. James Whitmore.

GLADIATORS SEVEN (T) 92
METRO-GOLDWYN-MAYER. (R) May, 1964. Richard Harrison, Lordana Nusciak. Color.

GLASS BOTTOM BOAT (P) 110
METRO-GOLDWYN-MAYER. (R) July, 1966. Doris Day, Rod Taylor. Color.

GLASS HOUSES 90
COLUMBIA. (R) January, 1972. Bernard Barrow, Jennifer O'Neill. Color.

GLASS SLIPPER, THE 94
METRO-GOLDWYN-MAYER. (R) April 8, 1955. Leslie Caron, Michael Wilding. Color.

GLASS TOMB, THE 59
LIPPERT. (R) April 15, 1955. John Ireland.

GLEN AND RANDA 94
UMC. (R) August, 1971. Steven Curry, Shelley Plimpton. Color.

GLOBAL AFFAIR, A 84
METRO-GOLDWYN-MAYER. (R) February, 1964. Bob Hope, Lilo Pulver.

GLORY (SS) 100
RKO RADIO. (R) January 11, 1956. Margaret O'Brien, Walter Brennan, Charlotte Greenwood. Color.

GLORY GUYS, THE (P) 112
UNITED ARTISTS. (R) July, 1965. Tom Tryon, Harve Presnell. Color.

GLORY STOMPERS, THE (Colorscope) 85
AMERICAN INTERNATIONAL. (R) November, 1967. Dennis Hopper, Chris Noel. Color.

GNOME-MOBILE, THE 90
BUENA VISTA. (R) July, 1967. Walter Brennan, Karen Dotrice. Color.

GO-BETWEEN, THE 116
COLUMBIA. (R) Fall, 1971. Julie Christie, Alan Bates, Margaret Leighton, Michael Redgrave. Color.

GO GO MANIA (T) 70
AMERICAN INTERNATIONAL. (R) May, 1965. The Beatles, The Animals. Color.

GO NAKED IN THE WORLD (Cs) 103
METRO-GOLDWYN-MAYER. (R) February, 1961. Gina Lollobrigida, Anthony Franciosa. Color.

GO TELL THE SPARTANS 114
AVCO EMBASSY. (R) June, 1978. Burt Lancaster, Marc Singer.

GOAL! (TS) 106
COLUMBIA. (R) February, 1967. Soccer Documentary. Color.

GOD IS MY PARTNER (R) 82
TWENTIETH CENTURY-FOX. (R) July, 1957. Walter Brennan, John Hoyt.

GODDESS, THE 105
COLUMBIA. (R) May, 1958. Kim Stanley, Lloyd Bridges.

GODDESS OF LOVE, THE (Cs) 65
TWENTIETH CENTURY-FOX. (R) December, 1960. Belinda Lee, Jack Sernas. Color.

GODFATHER, THE 78
PARAMOUNT. (R) March, 1972. Marlon Brando, Al Pacino, James Caan. Color.

GODFATHER, PART II, THE 200
PARAMOUNT. (R) December, 1974. Al Pacino, Robert Duvall.

GOD'S LITTLE ACRE 110
UNITED ARTISTS. (R) May, 1958. Aldo Ray, Robert Ryan.

GODSPELL 103
COLUMBIA. (R) April, 1973. Victor Garber, David Haskell. Color.

GODZILLA, KING OF THE MONSTERS (Jap.; Eng. dubbed) 80
EMBASSY. (R) April, 1956. Raymond Burr.

GODZILLA vs. THE THING (Tohoscope) 90
AMERICAN INTERNATIONAL. (R) October, 1964. Akira Takarada, Yuriko Hoshi. Color.

GOIN' DOWN THE ROAD 90
CHEVRON. (R) October, 1970. Doug McGrath, Paul Bradley. Color.

GOIN' SOUTH 105
PARAMOUNT. (R) October, 1978. Jack Nicolson, Mary Steenburgen.

GOING HOME 100
METRO-GOLDWYN-MAYER. (R) November, 1971. Robert Mitchum, Brenda Vaccaro. Color.

GOING IN STYLE 97

	Length In Mins.

WARNER BROS. (R) December 25, 1979. George Burns, Art Carney, Lee Strasberg.

GOING STEADY 79
COLUMBIA. (R) February, 1958. Molly Bee, Alan Reed, Jr.

GOLD (P) 120
ALLIED ARTISTS. (R) October, 1974. Roger Moore, Susannah York.

GOLD FOR THE CAESARS (CinemaScope) 86
METRO-GOLDWYN-MAYER. (R) June, 1964. Jeffrey Hunter, Mylene Domongeot. Color.

GOLD OF NAPLES, THE (Ital.) 107
DISTRIBUTORS CORPORATION OF AMERICA. (R) February, 1957. Silvana Mangano, Vittorio DeSica, Sophia Loren, Toto.

GOLD OF THE SEVEN SAINTS (Warnerscope) 83
WARNER BROS. (R) April, 1961. Clint Walker, Roger Moore.

GOLDEN AGE OF COMEDY, THE 78
DCA DIST. (R) 1958. Laurel & Hardy, Charlie Chaplin. b&w.

GOLDEN ARROW, THE (T) 91
METRO-GOLDWYN-MAYER. (R) April, 1964. Tab Hunter, Rossana Podesta. Color.

GOLDENGIRL 104
AVCO EMBASSY. (R) June, 1979. Susan Anton, James Coburn.

GOLDEN DEMON, THE (Jap.) 95
HARRISON. (R) January, 1956. Jun Negami. Color.

GOLDEN NEEDLES (P) 93
AMERICAN INTERNATIONAL. (R) July, 1974. Joe Don Baker, Elizabeth Ashley.

GOLDEN VOYAGE OF SINBAD, THE 105
COLUMBIA. (R) March, 1974. John Philip Law, Caroline Munro.

GOLDFINGER 108
UNITED ARTISTS. (R) December, 1964. Sean Connery, Gert Ferbe. Color.

GOLDSTEIN 82
ALTURA. (R) May, 1965. Lou Gilbert, Ellen Madison.

GOLIATH AND THE BARBARIANS (Totalscope) 90
AMERICAN INTERNATIONAL. (R) December, 1959. Steve Reeves, Chelo Alosso. Color.

GOLIATH AND THE DRAGON (Colorscope) 90
AMERICAN INTERNATIONAL. (R) November, 1960. Mark Forrest, Broderick Crawford. Color.

GOLIATH AND THE VAMPIRES (Totalscope) 91
AMERICAN INTERNATIONAL. (R) May, 1964. Gordon Scott, Gianna Maria Canale. Color.

GONE ARE THE DAYS! 97
HAMMER. (R) September, 1963. Ruby Dee, Ossie Davis.

GONE WITH THE WIND (70mm) 220
MGM. (R) October, 1967. Clark Gable, Vivian Leigh. Color.

GONG SHOW MOVIE, THE 89
UNIVERSAL. (R) May, 1980. Chuck Barris, Robin Altman.

GOOD DAY FOR A HANGING 85
COLUMBIA. (R) January, 1959. Fred MacMurray, Maggie Hayes. Color.

GOOD DIE YOUNG, THE 100
UNITED ARTISTS. (R) February, 1955. Richard Basehart, Gloria Grahame.

GOOD GUYS AND THE BAD GUYS, THE (P) 91
WARNER BROS. (R) November, 1969. Robert Mitchum, George Kennedy, Tina Louise. Color.

GOOD MORNING, MISS DOVE (Cs) 107
TWENTIETH CENTURY-FOX. (R) November, 1955. Jennifer Jones, Robert Stack. Color.

GOOD NEIGHBOR SAM 130
COLUMBIA. (R) June, 1964. Jack Lemmon, Romy Schneider. Color.

GOOD, THE BAD, AND THE UGLY, THE (T) 161
UNITED ARTISTS. (R) December, 1967. Clint Eastwood, Eli Wallach, Lee Van Cleef. Color.

GOOD TIMES 91
COLUMBIA. (R) May, 1967. Sonny and Cher. Color.

GOOD TIMES, WONDERFUL TIMES 70
ROGOSIN. (R) August, 1966. Documentary.

GOODBYE AGAIN 120
UNITED ARTISTS. (R) August, 1961. Ingrid Bergman, Yves Montand.

GOODBYE CHARLIE (Cs) 117
TWENTIETH CENTURY-FOX. (R) December, 1964. Tony Curtis, Debbie Reynolds. Color.

GOODBYE, COLUMBUS 105
PARAMOUNT. (R) June, 1969. Richard Benjamin, Ali MacGraw, Jack Klugman. Color.

GOODBYE GEMINI 90
CINERAMA. (R) September, 1970. Judy Geeson, Martin Potter. Color.

GOODBYE GIRL, THE 110

Length In Mins.

WARNER BROS. (R) December, 1977. Richard Drey-fuss, Marsha Mason.

GOODBYE MR. CHIPS (P) 151
MGM. (R) November, 1969. Peter O'Toole, Petula Clark, Sian Phillips, Michael Redgrave. Color.

GOODBYE MY LADY 95
WARNER BROS. (R) May 12, 1956. Brandon de Wilde, Walter Brennan.

GORDON'S WAR (P) 90
TWENTIETH CENTURY-FOX. (R) August, 1973. Paul Winfield, Carl Lee.

GORGO 76
METRO-GOLDWYN-MAYER. (R) February, 1961. Bill Travers, Will Sylvester. Color.

GORGON, THE 83
COLUMBIA. (R) February, 1965. Peter Cushing, Christopher Lee. Color.

GOSPEL ACCORDING TO ST. MATTHEW, THE (Ital., Eng. titles) 135
CONTINENTAL DISTRIBUTING. (R) February 17, 1966. Enrique Irazoque, Margherita Caruso.

GOSPEL ROAD, THE 83
TWENTIETH CENTURY-FOX. (R) March, 1973. Johnny Cash, Robert Elfstrom. Color.

GRADUATE, THE (P) 105
EMBASSY. (R) December, 1967. Anne Bancroft, Dustin Hoffman. Color.

GRAND BOUFFE, THE 122
ABKCO FILMS. (R) October, 1973. Marcello Mastroianni, Michel Piccoli.

GRAND MANEUVER, THE (Fr.) 107
UMPO. (R) October, 1956. Michele Morgan. Gerard Philipe. Color.

GRAND OLYMPICS 120
TIMES FILM. (R) April, 1964. 1960 Rome Olympics. Color.

GRAND PRIX (Super Panavision) 175
METRO-GOLDWYN-MAYER. (R) December, 1966. James Garner, Eva Marie Saint. Color.

GRAND SLAM (TE) 121
PARAMOUNT. (R) January, 1968. Edward G. Robinson, Janet Leigh. Color.

GRAND SUBSTITUTION, THE (Shawscope) (Chinese; Eng. titles) 116
FRANK LEE INTERNATIONAL. (R) November, 1965. Li Li-Hus, Ivy Ling Po. Color.

GRASS IS GREENER, THE (T) 102
UNIVERSAL. (R) January, 1961. Cary Grant, Jean Simmons. Color.

GRASSHOPPER, THE 95
NATIONAL GENERAL. (R) May, 1970. Jacqueline Bisset, Jim Brown, Joseph Cotten. Color.

GRAVY TRAIN, THE 95
COLUMBIA. (R) July, 1974. Stacy Keach, Frederic Forest.

GRAYEAGLER 104
AMERICAN INTERNATIONAL. (R) December, 1977. Ben Johnson, Iron Eyes Cody.

GRAY LADY DOWN (P) 110
UNIVERSAL. (R) March, 1978. Charlton Heston, David Carradine.

GRAZIE, ZIA 93
AVCO-EMBASSY. (R) January, 1969. Lisa Gastoril, Lou Castel, Gabriel Ferzetti. b&w.

GREASE (P) 110
PARAMOUNT. (R) June, 1978. John Travolta, Olivia Newton-John.

GREASED LIGHTNING 96
WARNER BROS. (R) July, 1977. Richard Pryor, Beau Bridges.

GREAT ADVENTURE, THE (Swed.) 75
DE ROCHEMONT. (R) September, 1955. Non-Professional Cast.

GREAT AMERICAN PASTIME, THE 89
METRO-GOLDWYN-MAYER. (R) December, 1956. Tom Ewell, Anne Francis.

GREAT ESCAPE, THE (P) 168
UNITED ARTISTS. (R) July, 1963. Steve McQueen, James Garner. Color.

GREAT GATSBY, THE 148
PARAMOUNT. (R) April, 1974. Robert Redford, Mia Farrow.

GREAT GEORGIA BANK HOAX, THE 88
WARNER BROS. (R) November, 1978. Richard Basehart, Ned Beatty.

GREAT IMPOSTOR, THE 112
UNIVERSAL. (R) February, 1961. Tony Curtis, Edmond O'Brien.

GREAT LOCOMOTIVE CHASE, THE (Cs) 85
BUENA VISTA. (R) June 20, 1956. Fess Parker, Jeffrey Hunter. Color.

GREAT MAN, THE 92
UNIVERSAL. (R) February, 1957. Jose Ferrer, Dean Jagger, Keenan Wynn.

Length In Mins.

GREAT NORTHFIELD MINNESOTA RAID, THE 91
UNIVERSAL. (R) April, 1972. Cliff Robertson, Robert Duvall. Color.

GREAT RACE, THE (P) 170
WARNER BROS. (R) Special. June, 1966. Jack Lemmon, Tony Curtis. Color.

GREAT SANTINI, THE 118
WARNER BROS. (R) October, 1979. Robert Duvall, Blythe Danner, Michael O'Keefe.

GREAT SCOUT AND CATHOUSE THURSDAY, THE 102
AMERICAN INTERNATIONAL. (R) June, 1976. Lee Marvin, Oliver Reed.

GREAT SIOUX MASSACRE, THE (Cs) 91
COLUMBIA. (R) September, 1965. Joseph Cotten, Darren McGavin. Color.

GREAT SIOUX UPRISING, THE 80
U-I. (R) July, 1958. Jeff Chandler, Faith Domergue. Color.

GREAT SPY CHASE, THE 87
AMERICAN INTERNATIONAL. (R) May, 1966. Lino Ventura, Bernard Blair.

GREAT ST. LOUIS BANK ROBBERY, THE 86
UNITED STATES. (R) February, 1959. Steve McQueen, David Clarke.

GREAT TRAIN ROBBERY, THE 111
UNITED ARTISTS. (R) February, 1979. Sean Connery, Donald Sutherland.

GREAT WALDO PEPPER, THE (T-AO 35) 106
UNIVERSAL. (R) March, 1975. Robert Redford, Bo Svenson.

GREAT WALTZ, THE 135
METRO-GOLDWYN-MAYER. (R) October, 1972. Mary Costa, Horst Buchholz, Rossano Brazzi. Color.

GREAT WAR, THE (Cs) 118
UNITED ARTISTS. (R) October, 1961. b&w.

GREAT WHITE HOPE, THE 103
TWENTIETH CENTURY-FOX. (R) December, 1970. James Earl Jones, Jane Alexander. Color.

GREATEST, THE 100
COLUMBIA. (R) May, 1977. Muhammad Ali, Ernest Borgnine.

GREATEST STORY EVER TOLD, THE (Cinerama, P-70) 195
UNITED ARTISTS. (R) Specialty. Max Von Sydow, Charlton Heston. Color.

GREED IN THE SUN (Cs) 122
METRO-GOLDWYN-MAYER. (R) September, 1965. b&w.

GREEK TYCOON, THE 106
UNIVERSAL. (R) May, 1978. Anthony Quinn, Jacqueline Bisset.

GREEN BERETS, THE 141
WARNER BROS.-7 ARTS. (R) July, 1968. John Wayne, David Janssen, Jim Hutton. Color.

GREEN BUDDHA, THE (Brit.) 61
REPUBLIC. (R) July 9, 1955. Wayne Morris, Mary Germaine.

GREEN FIRE (Cs) 100
METRO-GOLDWYN-MAYER. (R) January 21, 1955. Grace Kelly, Stewart Granger. Color.

GREEN HELMET, THE 88
METRO-GOLDWYN-MAYER. (R) April, 1961. Bill Travers, Nancy Walters.

GREEN MAGIC (Ital.-Eng. narration) 83
I.F.E. (R) May, 1955. Documentary. Color.

GREEN MANSIONS 104
METRO-GOLDWYN-MAYER. (R) April, 1959. Audrey Hepburn, Anthony Perkins.

GREEN SCARF, THE (Brit.) 96
ASSOCIATED ARTISTS. (R) January, 1955. Michael Redgrave, Ann Todd, Leo Glenn.

GREEN SLIME, THE 85
METRO-GOLDWYN-MAYER. (R) May, 1969. Robert Horton, Luciana Paluzzi. Color.

GREEN-EYED BLONDE, THE 73
WARNER BROS. (R) December, 1957. Susan Oliver, Linda Plowman.

GREENGAGE SUMMER 93
COLUMBIA. (R) April, 1961. Kenneth Moore, Danielle Darrieux. Color.

GREENWICH VILLAGE STORY 95
SHAW INT. (R) July, 1963. Robert Hogan, Melinda Plank.

GREETINGS 88
SIGMA III. (R) December, 1968. Robert De Niro, Jonathan Warden.

GREYFRIARS BOBBY 90
BUENA VISTA. (R) October, 1961. Donald Crisp, Laurence Nals.

GRIMM'S FAIRY TALES FOR ADULTS ONLY ... 76
CINEMATION. (R) February, 1971. Marie Liljedhal, Ingrid Von Bergen. Color.

GRISSOM GANG, THE 125

	Length In Mins.

HAVE ROCKET WILL TRAVEL 76
COLUMBIA. (R) August, 1959. Moe Howard, Larry Fine.

HAVING A WILD WEEKEND 91
WARNER BROTHERS. (R) June, 1965. Dave Clark Five.

HAWAII (P) 189
UNITED ARTISTS. (R) October, 1966. Julie Andrews, Max Von Sydow. Color.

HAWAIIANS, THE 134
UNITED ARTISTS. (R) June, 1970. Charlton Heston, Geraldine Chaplin, John Phillip Law. Color.

HAWKS AND THE SPARROW, THE (Ital.) 91
BRANDON. (R) July, 1967. Toto, Ninetto Davoli.

HE LAUGHED LAST 77
COLUMBIA. (R) August, 1956. Frankie Laine, Lucy Marlowe. Color.

HE RIDES TALL 84
UNIVERSAL. (R) April, 1964. Tony Young, Dan Duryea.

HE WHO MUST DIE 129
LOPERT. (R) May, 1965. Melina Mercouri.

HEAD 86
COLUMBIA. (R) November, 1968. Peter Tork, David Jones, Michael Nesmith, Mickey Dolenz. Color.

HEAD OF A TYRANT (Totalscope) 94
UNIVERSAL. (R) June, 1960. Massimo Girotti, Isabelle Corey. Color.

HEADLESS GHOST, THE (D) 63
AMERICAN INTERNATIONAL. (R) April, 1959. Richard Lyon, Lilian Sottane.

HEADLINE HUNTERS 90
REPUBLIC. (R) September 15, 1955. Rod Cameron, Julie Bishop.

HEAD OVER HEELS 99
UNITED ARTISTS. (R) October, 1979. John Heard, Mary Beth Hurt.

HEAR ME GOOD (VV) 80
PARAMOUNT. (R) October, 1957. Hal March, Joe E. Ross. Color.

HEART BEAT 109
WARNER BROS. (R) January, 1980. Nick Nolte, Sissy Spacek.

HEART IS A LONELY HUNTER, THE 125
WARNER BROS.-7 ARTS. (R) October, 1968. Alan Arkin, Leurinda Barrett, Stacy Keach, Jr. Color.

HEART OF SHOW BUSINESS, THE 40
COLUMBIA. (R) June, 1957. All Star Cast.

HEART OF THE MATTER, THE (Brit.) 100
ASSOCIATED ARTISTS. (R) November, 1954. Trevor Howard, Maria Schell.

HEARTBREAK KID, THE 104
TWENTIETH CENTURY-FOX. (R) December, 1972. Cybill Shepherd, Charles Grodin, Eddie Albert. Color.

HEARTS AND MINDS 112
WARNER BROS. (R) March, 1975. Documentary.

HEARTS OF THE WEST 102
UNITED ARTISTS. (R) October, 1975. Jeff Bridges, Andy Griffith.

HEAT 100
WARHOL. (R) October, 1972. Joe Dallesandro, Sylvia Miles. Color.

HEAVEN CAN WAIT 100
PARAMOUNT. (R) June, 1978. Warren Beatty, Julie Christie.

HEAVEN KNOWS, MR. ALLISON (Cs) 107
TWENTIETH CENTURY-FOX. (R) March, 1957. Deborah Kerr, Robert Mitchum. Color.

HEAVEN ON EARTH 84
JB FILMS. (R) January, 1961. Barbara Florian, Charles Fawcett. Color.

HEAVEN WITH A GUN 101
METRO-GOLDWYN-MAYER. (R) May, 1969. Glenn Ford, Carolyn Jones, Barbara Hershey. Color.

HEAVY TRAFFIC 82
AMERICAN INTERNATIONAL. (R) August, 1973. Joseph Kaufman, Beverly Hope Atkinson.

HEDDA 100
BRUT PRODS. (R) February, 1976. Glenda Jackson, Timothy West.

HEIDI 95
WARNER BROS.-7 ARTS. (R) March, 1968. Eva Maria Singhammer, Gertraud Mittermayr. Color.

HEIDI AND PETER (Swiss-Eng. dubbed) 89
UNITED ARTISTS. (R) December, 1955. Elisbeth Sigmund, Heinrich Getler. Color.

HELEN MORGAN STORY, THE (Cs) 118
WARNER BROS. (R) September, 1957. b&w.

HELEN OF TROY (Cs) 118
WARNER BROTHERS. (R) February 11, 1956. Rossana Podesta, Jack Sernas. Color.

HELGA 87

AMERICAN INTERNATIONAL. (R) August, 1968. Ruth Gassman. Color.

HELL BENT FOR LEATHER (Cs) 82
UNIVERSAL. (R) February, 1960. Audie Murphy, Felicia Farr. Color.

HELL BOUND 79
UNITED ARTISTS. (R) October, 1957. John Russell, June Blair.

HELL CANYON OUTLAWS 72
REPUBLIC. (R) October, 1957. Dale Robertson, Brian Keith.

HELL DRIVERS (VV) 91
RANK FILM DISTRIBUTORS OF AMERICA. (R) May, 1958. Stanley Baker, Herbert Lom.

HELL, HEAVEN OR HOBOKEN 100
NTA. (R) September, 1959. M.E. Clifton Jones, Joan Mills.

HELL IN KOREA 82
HAL ROACH. (R) July, 1959. George Baker, Harry Andrews.

HELL IN THE PACIFIC 103
CINERAMA. (R) January, 1969. Lee Marvin, Toshiro Mifune. Color.

HELL IS A CITY 96
COLUMBIA. (R) November, 1960. Stanley Baker, Maxine Audley.

HELL IS FOR HEROES 90
PARAMOUNT. (R) June, 1962. Steve McQueen, Bobby Darin.

HELL ON DEVIL'S ISLAND (Cs) 74
TWENTIETH CENTURY-FOX. (R) September, 1957. Helmut Dantine, William Talman.

HELL ON FRISCO BAY (Cs) 98
WARNER BROTHERS. (R) January 28, 1956. Alan Ladd, Edward G. Robinson, Joanne Dru. Color.

HELL SHIP MUTINY 66
REPUBLIC. (R) December, 1957. Jon Hall, John Carradine.

HELL SQUAD 64
AMERICAN INTERNATIONAL. (R) July, 1958. Wally Campo, Frederic Gavlin.

HELL TO ETERNITY 132
ALLIED ARTISTS. (R) August, 1960. Jeffrey Hunter, David Janssen.

HELL WITH HEROES, THE 102
UNIVERSAL. (R) September, 1968. Rod Taylor, Claudia Cardinale. Keven McCarthy. Color.

HELLCATS OF THE NAVY 82
COLUMBIA. (R) May, 1957. Ronald Reagan, Nancy Davis.

HELLFIGHTERS, THE 121
UNIVERSAL. (R) January, 1969. John Wayne, Katherine Ross, Jim Hutton. Color.

HELLO, DOLLY! (Todd-AO) 148
20th CENTURY-FOX. (R) December, 1969. Barbara Streisand, Walter Matthau, Michael Crawford. Color.

HELLO DOWN THERE 98
PARAMOUNT. (R) March, 1969. Jim Backus, Tony Randall, Janet Leigh. Color.

HELLO-GOODBYE 107
20th CENTURY-FOX. (R) July, 1970. Michael Crawford, Curt Jurgens, Genevieve Gilles. Color.

HELL'S ANGELS 69
Tom Stern, Jeremy Slate, Conny Van Dyke.

HELL'S BELLES 95
AMERICAN INTERNATIONAL. (R) April, 1969. Jeremy Slate, Adam Roarke, Jocelyn Lane. Color.

HELL'S CROSSROADS (N) 73
REPUBLIC. (R) March 8, 1957. Stephen MacNally, Peggie Castle.

HELL'S FIVE HOURS 76
ALLIED ARTISTS. (R) February, 1958. Steven McNally, Coleen Gray.

HELL'S HORIZON 90
COLUMBIA. (R) December, 1955. John Ireland, Maria English.

HELL'S ISLAND (VV) 84
PARAMOUNT. (R) May, 1955. John Payne, Mary Murphy.

HELLSTROM CHRONICLE, THE 90
CINEMA 5. (R) July, 1971. Insect documentary. Color.

HELP! 90
UNITED ARTISTS. (R) August, 1965. The Beatles. Color.

HEMINGWAY'S ADVENTURES OF A YOUNG MAN (Cs) 145
TWENTIETH CENTURY-FOX. (R) June, 1962. Richard Beymer, Diane Baker. Color.

HENNESSY 103
AMERICAN INTERNATIONAL. (R) August, 1975. Rod Steiger, Lee Remick.

HENRY VIII AND HIS SIX WIVES 125
LEVITT-PICKMAN. (R) September, 1973. Keith Michell, Donald Pleasence.

	Length In Mins.

HERBIE GOES TO MONTE CARLO 105
BUENA VISTA. (R) July, 1977. Dean Jones, Don Knotts.
HERBIE RIDES AGAIN 89
BUENA VISTA. (R) Summer, 1974. Helen Hayes, Ken Berry.
HERCULES 103
WARNER BROS. (R) July, 1959. Steve Reeves.
HERCULES IN THE HAUNTED WORLD (Totalscope 100)
 91
WOOLNER. (R) October, 1964. Reg Park, Christopher Lee. Color.
HERCULES, SAMSON AND ULYSSES (Ital. dubbed) ... 85
MGM. (R) 1965. Kirk Morris, Richard Lloyd. Color.
HERCULES UNCHAINED (Cs) 97
EMBASSY-WARNER BROS. (R) July, 1960. Steve Reeves, Sylva Koscina. Color.
HERE COMES THE JETS (R) 71
TWENTIETH CENTURY-FOX. (R) June, 1959. Steve Brodie, John Doucette. b&w.
HERE WE GO ROUND THE MULBERRY BUSH 96
LOPERT. (R) March, 1968. Barry Evans, Judy Geeson. Color.
HERO, THE 97
AVCO-EMBASSY. (R) August, 1972. Richard Harris, Romy Schneider. Color.
HERO AT LARGE 99
UNITED ARTISTS. (R) February, 1980. John Ritter, Anne Archer
HEROD THE GREAT (Totalscope) 89
ALLIED ARTISTS. (R) December, 1960. Edmund Purdom, Sylvia Lopez. Color.
HEROES 113
UNIVERSAL. (R) November, 1977. Henry Winkler, Sally Field.
HEROES DIE YOUNG 76
ALLIED ARTISTS. (R) November, 1960. Erika Peters, Scott Borland.
HEROES OF TELEMARK, THE (P) 131
COLUMBIA. (R) January, 1966. Kirk Douglas, Richard Harris. Color.
HERO'S ISLAND (P) 91
UNITED ARTISTS. (R) September, 1962. James Mason, Neville Brand. Color.
HESTER STREET 90
MIDWEST FILMS. (R) September, 1975. Steven Keats, Carol Kane.
HEY BOY! HEY GIRL! 81
COLUMBIA. (R) May, 1959. Louis Prima, Keely Smith.
HEY, LET'S TWIST 80
PARAMOUNT. (R) December, 1961. Joey Dee, Teddy Randazzo.
HEY THERE, IT'S YOGI BEAR 90
COLUMBIA. (R) June, 1964. Animated Feature. Color.
HI, MOM! 87
SIGMA 3. (R) April, 1970. Robert DeNira, Jennifer Salt. Color.
HICKEY AND BOGGS 111
UNITED ARTISTS. (R) September, 1972. Bill Cosby, Robert Culp. Color.
HIDDEN FEAR 83
UNITED ARTISTS. (R) July, 1957. John Payne, Conrad Nagel.
HIDDEN GUNS 66
REPUBLIC. (R) January 29, 1956. Bruce Bennett, Richard Arlen.
HIDDEN HOMICIDE 70
REPUBLIC. (R) February, 1959. Griffith Jones, Patricia Lafran.
HIDE AND SEEK 90
UNIVERSAL. (R) February, 1964. Ian Carmichael, Janet Munro.
HIDE IN PLAIN SIGHT (P) 93
UNITED ARTISTS. (R) March, 1980. James Caan, Jill Eikenberry.
HIDING PLACE, THE 145
WORLD WIDE PICTURES. (R) Fall, 1975. Julie Harris, Eileen Heckart.
HIGH 82
BRENNER. (R) April, 1969. Astri Thorvik, Lanny Beckman. b&w.
HIGH ANXIETY 91
20th CENTURY-FOX. (R) February, 1978. Mel Brooks, Madeline Kahn.
HIGH BALLIN' 100
AMERICAN INTERNATIONAL. (R) May, 1978. Peter Fonda, Jerry Reed.
HIGH COMMISSIONER 93
CINERAMA. (R) September, 1968. Rod Taylor, Christopher Plummer, Lili Palmer. Color.
HIGH COST OF LIVING, THE (Cs) 87
METRO-GOLDWYN-MAYER. (R) March, 1958. Jose Ferrer, Anthony Newley.
HIGH FLIGHT (Cs) 85

COLUMBIA. (R) April, 1958. Ray Milland, Anthony Newley.
HIGH HELL 87
PARAMOUNT. (R) January, 1958. John Derek, Elaine Stewart.
HIGH INFIDELITY (Ital. with English Titles) 120
MAGNA. (R) June, 1965. Nino Manfredi, Fulvia Franco.
HIGH PLAINS DRIFTER 105
UNIVERSAL. (R) April, 1973. Clint Eastwood, Verna Bloom. Color.
HIGH POWERED RIFLE, THE 60
TWENTIETH CENTURY-FOX. (R) September, 1960. Willard Parker, Allison Hayes.
HIGH SCHOOL BIG SHOT 70
THE FILM GROUP. (R) July, 1959. Tom Pittman, Virginia Aldridge.
HIGH SCHOOL CONFIDENTIAL! (Cs) 85
MGM. (R) June, 1958. Russ Tamblyn, Jan Sterling.
HIGH SCHOOL HELL CATS 68
AMERICAN INTERNATIONAL. (R) July, 1959. Yvonne Line, Brett Halsey.
HIGH SOCIETY (VV) 107
METRO-GOLDWYN-MAYER. (R) Special, 1957. Bing Crosby, Grace Kelly, Frank Sinatra. Color.
HIGH SOCIETY 61
ALLIED ARTISTS. (R) April 17, 1955. Leo Gorcey, Huntz Hall.
HIGH TERRACE, THE (Brit.) 70
ALLIED ARTISTS. (R) December 9, 1956. Dale Robertson, Lois Maxwell.
HIGH TIME (Cs) 103
TWENTIETH CENTURY-FOX. (R) September, 1960. Bing Crosby, Fabian. Color.
HIGH, WILD AND FREE 105
AMERICAN INTERNATIONAL. (R) April, 1968. Documentary. Color.
HIGH WIND IN JAMAICA, A (Cs) 135
TWENTIETH CENTURY-FOX. (R) June, 1965. Anthony Quinn, James Coburn. Color.
HILDA CRANE (Cs) 87
TWENTIETH CENTURY-FOX. (R) April, 1956. Jean Simmons, Guy Madison, Jean Pierre Aumont. Color.
HILL, THE 123
METRO-GOLDWYN-MAYER. (R) October, 1965. Sean Connery, Harry Andrews.
HILL 24 DOESN'T ANSWER (Israel-Eng. dial.) 102
CONTINENTAL. (R) November, 1955. Michael Wager, Haya Hararit.
HILLS RUN RED, THE (T) 89
UNITED ARTISTS. (R) September, 1967. Thomas Hunter, Henry Silva. Color.
HINDENBURG, THE 125
UNIVERSAL. (R) December, 1975. George C. Scott, Anne Bancroft.
HIPPODROME 90
Gerhard Reidmann, Willy Birgel. Color.
HIRED GUN, THE (Cs) 85
METRO-GOLDWYN-MAYER. (R) September, 1957. Rory Calhoun, Anne Francis.
HIRED HAND, THE 93
UNIVERSAL. (R) August, 1971. Peter Fonda, Warren Oates. Color.
HIRED KILLER, THE (TS) 94
PARAMOUNT. (R) March, 1967. Robert Webber, Franco Nero. Color.
HIRELING, THE 108
COLUMBIA. (R) June, 1973. Sarah Miles, Robert Shaw. Color.
HIS EXCELLENCY (Brit.) 84
JOSEPH BRENNER. (R) February, 1956. Eric Portman, Cecil Parker.
HIT! (P) 134
PARAMOUNT. (R) October, 1973. Billy Dee Williams, Richard Pryor.
HIT AND RUN 84
UNITED ARTISTS. (R) March, 1957. Cleo Moore, Hugo Hass.
HIT THE DECK (Cs) 112
METRO-GOLDWYN-MAYER. (R) March 4, 1955. Jane Powell, Tony Martin, Debbie Reynolds. Color.
HITLER 78
ALLIED ARTISTS. (R) July, 1961. Richard Basehart.
HITLER: THE LAST TEN DAYS 106
PARAMOUNT. (R) May, 1972. Alec Guiness, Simon Ward. Color.
HOA BINH 93
TRANSVUE. (R) September, 1971. Phi Lan, Huynh Cazenas. Color.
HOLD BACK THE NIGHT 75
ALLIED ARTISTS. (R) July 29, 1956. John Payne, Mona Freeman.
HOLD BACK TOMORROW 75

	Length In Mins.

UNIVERSAL. (R) November, 1955. Cleo Moore, John Agar.

HOLD ON (P) 85
METRO-GOLDWYN-MAYER. (R) April, 1966. Peter Blaire Noone, Karl Green. Color.

HOLD THAT HYPNOTIST 61
ALLIED ARTISTS (R) February 24, 1957. Huntz Hall, Stanley Clements.

HOLE IN THE HEAD, A (Cs) 120
UNITED ARTISTS. (R) July, 1959. Frank Sinatra. Edward G. Robinson. Color.

HOLIDAY FOR HENRIETTA (Fr.) 103
ARDEE. (R) January, 1955. Dany Robin, Hildegarde Neff.

HOLIDAY FOR LOVERS (Cs) 102
TWENTIETH CENTURY-FOX. (R) July, 1959. Clifton Webb, Jane Wyman. Color.

HOLLYWOOD KNIGHTS, THE 91
COLUMBIA. (R) May, 1980. Robert Wuhl, Fran Drescher.

HOLLYWOOD OR BUST (VV) 95
PARAMOUNT. (R) December, 1956. Dean Martin, Jerry Lewis, Anita Ekberg. Color.

HOMBRE (P) 111
20th CENTURY-FOX. (R) April, 1967. Paul Newman, Frederic March. Color.

HOME BEFORE DARK 137
WARNER BROS. (R) November, 1958. Jean Simmons, Dan O'Herlihy.

HOME FROM THE HILL (Cs) 150
METRO-GOLDWYN-MAYER. (R) March, 1960. Robert Mitchum, Eleanor Parker. Color.

HOME IS THE HERO 83
SCOA. (R) February, 1961. Arthur Kennedy, Walter Macken.

HOME OF YOUR OWN, A (Brit.) 43
CINEMA V. (R) July, 1965. Comedy.

HOMEBODIES 96
AVCO-EMBASSY. (R) September, 1974. Peter Brocco, Frances Fuller.

HOMECOMING, THE 116
AFT DISTRIBUTING. (R) Special, 1973. Cyril Cusack, Ian Holm.

HOMER 95
NATIONAL GENERAL. (R) September, 1970. Don Scardino, Alex Nicol, Tisa Farrow. Color.

HOMICIDAL 87
COLUMBIA. (R) June, 1961. Glenn Corbett, Patricia Breslin.

HONEY POT, THE 131
UNITED ARTISTS. (R) May, 1967. Rex Harrison, Susan Hayward. Color.

HONEYMOON HOTEL (P) 89
METRO-GOLDWYN-MAYER. (R) August, 1964. Robert Goulet, Nancy Kwan. Color.

HONEYMOON KILLERS, THE 108
CINERAMA. (R) February, 1970. Shirley Stoler, Tony LoBianco, Mary Jane Higby. b&w.

HONEYMOON MACHINE, THE (Cs) 100
METRO-GOLDWYN-MAYER. (R) August, 1961. Steve McQueen, Brigid Bazlen. Color.

HONEYSUCKLE ROSE (P) 119
WARNER BROS. (R) July, 1980. Willie Nelson, Dyan Cannon.

HONG KONG AFFAIR 79
ALLIED ARTISTS. (R) May 11, 1958. Jack Kelly, May Wynn.

HONG KONG CONFIDENTIAL 64
UNITED ARTISTS. (R) November, 1958. Gene Barry, Beverly Tyler.

HONKERS, THE 110
UNITED ARTISTS. (R) February, 1972. James Coburn, Louis Nettleton, Slim Pickens. Color.

HOODLUM PRIEST, THE 101
UNITED ARTISTS. (R) April, 1961. Don Murray, Larry Gates.

HOOK, THE (P) 98
METRO-GOLDWYN-MAYER. (R) February, 1963. Kirk Douglas, Robert Walker.

HOOK LINE AND SINKER 92
COLUMBIA. (R) April, 1969. Jerry Lewis, Peter Lawford, Anne Francis. Color.

HOOKED GENERATION, THE 92
ALLIED ARTISTS. (R) April, 1969. Jeremy Slate, Steve Alaimo, John Davis Chandler. Color.

HOOPER 97
WARNER BROS. (R) July, 1978. Burt Reynolds, Jan-Michael Vincent.

HOOTENANNY HOOT 91
METRO-GOLDWYN-MAYER. (R) August, 1963. Peter Breck, Ruta Lee.

HORIZONTAL LIEUTENANT, THE (Cs) 90
METRO-GOLDWYN-MAYER. (R) March, 1962. Jim Hutton, Paula Prentiss. Color.

HORNET'S NEST 100
UNITED ARTISTS. (R) September, 1970. Rock Hudson, Sylva Koscina. Color.

HORROR HOUSE 79
AMER. INT. PICS. (R) May, 1970. Frankie Avalon, Jill Haworth, Dennis Price. Color.

HORROR OF DRACULA 82
UNIVERSAL INTERNATIONAL. (R) June, 1958. Peter Cushing, Melisa Stribling. Color.

HORROR OF PARTY BEACH, THE 78
20th CENTURY. (R) 1964. John Scott, Alice Lyon.

HORROR OF THE BLACK MUSEUM (Cs) 95
AMERICAN INTERNATIONAL. (R) April, 1959. Michael Gough, Graham Gurnow. Color.

HORSE IN THE GREY FLANNEL SUIT 113
BUENA VISTA. (R) November, 1968. Dean Jones, Diane Baker, Lloyd Bochner. Color.

HORSE SOLDIERS, THE 119
UNITED ARTISTS. (R) July, 1959. John Wayne, William Holden. Color.

HORSEMEN, THE (P) 109
COLUMBIA. (R) June, 1971. Omar Sharif, Leigh Taylor-Young. Color.

HORSE'S MOUTH, THE 93
UNITED ARTISTS. (R) March, 1959. Alec Guinness. Kay Walsh. Color.

HOSPITAL, THE 104
UNITED ARTISTS. (R) December, 1971. George C. Scott, Diana Rigg. Color.

HOSTILE GUNS (TE) 91
PARAMOUNT. (R) July, 1967. George Montgomery, Yvonne deCarlo. Color.

HOT ANGEL, THE 73
PARAMOUNT. (R) December, 1958. Jackie Loughery, Edward Kemmer.

HOT BLOOD (Cs) 85
COLUMBIA. (R) March, 1956. Jane Russell, Cornel Wilde. Color.

HOT CAR GIRL 71
ALLIED ARTISTS. (R) August, 1958. Richard Bakalyan, June Kenney.

HOT CARS 60
UNITED ARTISTS. (R) August, 1956. John Bromfield, Joi Lansing.

HOT MILLIONS 120
METRO-GOLDWYN-MAYER. (R) October, 1968. Peter Ustinov, Maggie Smith, Karl Malden. Color.

HOT ROCK, THE 101
20th CENTURY-FOX. (R) January, 1972. Robert Redford, George Segal, Zero Mostel. Color.

HOT ROD GANG 72
AMER. INT. PICS. (R) June, 1958. John Ashley, Jody Fair.

HOT ROD GIRL 75
AMERICAN INTERNATIONAL. (R) July 15, 1956. Lori Nelson, John Smith.

HOT ROD RUMBLE 79
ALLIED ARTISTS. (R) May 12, 1957. Leigh Snowden, Richard Hartunian.

HOT RODS TO HELL 92
METRO-GOLDWYN-MAYER. (R) March, 1967. Dana Andrews, Jeanne Crain. Color.

HOT SHOTS 61
ALLIED ARTISTS. (R) December 23, 1956. Huntz Hall, Stanley Clements.

HOT SPELL (VV) 86
PARAMOUNT. (R) June, 1958. Shirley Booth, Anthony Quinn.

HOT SUMMER NIGHT 86
METRO-GOLDWYN-MAYER. (R) February 15, 1957. Leslie Nielsen, Colleen Miller.

HOTEL 124
WARNER BROS. (R) March, 1967. Rod Taylor, Catherine Spaak. Color.

HOTEL PARADISO (P) 100
METRO-GOLDWYN-MAYER. (R) November, 1966. Alec Guinness, Gina Lollobrigida. Color.

HOUND DOG MAN (Cs) 87
TWENTIETH CENTURY-FOX. (R) November, 1959. Fabian, Carol Lynley. Color.

HOUND OF THE BASKERVILLES 84
UNITED ARTISTS. (R) June, 1959. Peter Cushing.

HOUR OF DECISION (Brit.) 74
ASTOR. (R) January, 1957. Jeff Morrow, Hazel Court.

HOUR OF THE GUN (R) 100
UNITED ARTISTS. (R) October, 1967. James Garner, Jason Robards. Color.

HOUR OF THE WOLF (Swed.) 88
LOPERT. (R) April, 1968. Liv Ullmann, Max von Sydow.

HOURS OF LOVE, THE (Ital. English Titles) 89

343

	Length In Mins.

20TH CENTURY-FOX. (R) March, 1967. James Coburn, Lee J. Cobb. Color.

IN PRAISE OF OLDER WOMEN **108**
AVCO EMBASSY. (R) February, 1979. Tom Berenger, Karen Black.

IN SEARCH OF GREGORY **90**
UNIVERSAL. (R) Julie Christie, Michael Sarrazin, John Hunt. Color.

IN SEARCH OF THE CASTAWAYS **100**
BUENA VISTA. (R) December, 1962. Hayley Mills, Maurice Chevalier. Color.

IN THE COOL OF THE DAY (P) **89**
METRO-GOLDWYN-MAYER. (R) June, 1963. Jane Fonda, Peter Finch. Color.

IN THE FRENCH STYLE **105**
COLUMBIA. (R) September, 1963. Jean Seberg, Stanley Baker.

IN THE HEAT OF THE NIGHT **109**
ALLIED ARTISTS. (R) August, 1967. Rod Steiger, Sidney Poitier. Color.

IN THE MONEY **81**
ALLIED ARTISTS. (R) February, 1957. Huntz Hall, Stanley Clements.

IN THE YEAR OF THE PIG **101**
PATHE. (R) November, 1969. Documentary. b&w.

INADMISSIBLE EVIDENCE **96**
PARAMOUNT. (R) June, 1968. Nicol Williamson, Eleanor Fazan, Jill Bennet. b&w.

INCIDENT AT PHANTON HILL **88**
UNIVERSAL. (R) July, 1966. Robert Fuller, Dan Duryea. Color.

INCIDENT IN AN ALLEY **84**
UNITED ARTISTS. (R) 1961. Charles Warfield, Erin O'Donnell.

INCREDIBLE JOURNEY, THE **80**
BUENA VISTA. (R) October, 1963. Emile Genest, John Drainie. Color.

INCREDIBLE MELTING MAN, THE **86**
AMERICAN INTERNATIONAL. (R) February, 1978. Alex Rebar, Burr DeBenning.

INCREDIBLE MR. LIMPET, THE **99**
WARNER BROS. (R) March, 1964. Donn Knotts, Carole Cook. Color.

INCREDIBLE PETRIFIED WORLD, THE **70**
GOVERNOR FILMS. (R) April, 1960. John Carradine, Robert Clarke.

INCREDIBLE SHRINKING MAN, THE **81**
UNIVERSAL. (R) April, 1957. Grant Williams, Randy Stuart.

INCREDIBLE 2-HEADED TRANSPLANT, THE **87**
AMERICAN INTERNATIONAL. (R) April, 1971. Bruce Dern, Pat Priest. Color.

INCREDIBLY STRANGE CREATURES, THE **82**
FAIRWAY. (R) 1964. Cash Flagg, Carolyn Brandt. Color.

INDESTRUCTIBLE MAN, THE **78**
ALLIED ARTISTS. (R) March 18, 1956. Lon Chaney, Casey Adams.

INDIAN FIGHTER (Cs) **83**
UNITED ARTISTS. (R) December, 1955, Kirk Douglas, Elsa Martinelli. Color.

INDIAN PAINT **91**
EAGLE-INTERNATIONAL. (R) February, 1966. Johnny Crawford, Jay Silverheels. Color.

INDISCREET **100**
WARNER BROS. (R) July, 1958. Cary Grant, Ingrid Bergman.

INFORMATION RECEIVED **77**
UNIVERSAL. (R) July, 1962. Sabina Sesselman, Wiliam Sylvester.

INHERIT THE WIND **127**
UNITED ARTISTS. (R) November, 1960. Spencer Tracy, Fredric March.

INHERITOR, THE **111**
HERA FILMS. (R) October, 1973. Jean-Paul Belmondo, Carla Gravina.

INN OF THE SIXTH HAPPINESS, THE (Cs) **156**
TWENTIETH CENTURY-FOX. (R) December, 1958. Ingrid Bergman, Curt Jurgens. Color.

INNOCENT BYSTANDERS **111**
PARAMOUNT. (R) January, 1973. Stanley Baker, Geraldine Chaplin. Color.

INNOCENT, THE (Italian, Eng. titles) **112**
ANALYSIS FILM RELEASING. (R) February, 1979. Giancarlo Giannini, Laura Antonelli.

INNOCENTS, THE (Cs) **100**
TWENTIETH CENTURY-FOX. (R) January, 1962. Deborah Kerr, Michael Redgrave.

INNOCENTS IN PARIS (Brit.) **90**
TUDOR. (R) March, 1955. Alastair Sim, Claire Bloom, Margaret Rutherford.

INSECT WOMAN, THE (Jap., Eng. titles) **123**
NIKKATSU. (R) June, 1964. Sachiko Hidari, Jitsuko Yoshimura.

INSERTS **117**
UNITED ARTISTS. (R) February, 1976. Richard Dreyfuss, Jessica Harper.

INSIDE DAISY CLOVER (P) **128**
WARNER BROTHERS. (R) February, 1966. Natalie Wood, Christopher Plummer. Color.

INSIDE DETROIT **82**
COLUMBIA. (R) January, 1956. Dennis O'Keefe, Pat O'Brien.

INSIDE OUT **97**
WARNER BROS. (R) November, 1975. Telly Savalas, Robert Culp, James Mason.

INSPECTOR CLOUSEAU **94**
UNITED ARTISTS. (R) June, 1968. Alan Arkin, Delia Boccardo, Frank Finlay. Color.

INTENT TO KILL (CS) **89**
TWENTIETH CENTURY-FOX. (R) February, 1959. Richard Todd, Betsy Drake.

INTERLUDE **113**
COLUMBIA. (R) July, 1968. Oscar Werner, Barbara Ferris, Virginia Meskell. Color.

INTERLUDE (Cs) **90**
UNIVERSAL. (R) September, 1957. June Allyson, Rossano Brazzi. Color.

INTERNATIONAL VELVET **126**
UNITED ARTISTS. (R) July, 1978. Tatum O'Neal, Christopher Plummer

INTERNS, THE **121**
COLUMBIA. (R) August, 1962. Michael Callan, Cliff Robertson.

INTERRUPTED MELODY (Cs) **106**
METRO-GOLDWYN-MAYER. (R) July 1, 1955. Glenn Ford, Eleanor Parker. Color.

INTERVAL **84**
AVCO-EMBASSY. (R) June, 1973. Merle Oberon, Robert Wolders. Color.

INTIMACY **87**
GOLDSTONE FILM ENTERPRISES, INC. (R) May, 1966. Jack Ging, Nancy Malone.

INTRUDER, THE (Brit.) **84**
ASSOCIATED ARTISTS. (R) January, 1955. Jack Hawkins, George Cole.

INVASION OF THE BODY SNATCHERS **114**
UNITED ARTISTS. (R) December, 1978. Donald Sutherland, Brooke Adams.

INVASION OF THE BODY SNATCHERS (SS) **80**
ALLIED ARTISTS. (R) February 5, 1956. Kevin McCarthy, Dana Wynter.

INVASION OF THE SAUCERMEN **75**
AMERICAN INTERNATIONAL. (R) June, 1957. Steve Terrell, Gloria Castillo.

INVASION OF THE STAR CREATURES **70**
AMER. INT'L. PICS. (R) 1963. Bob Ball, Frankie Ray. b&w.

INVASION 1700 .... **112**
MEDALLION. (R) January, 1965. Jeanne Crain, John Drew Barrymore. Color.

INVASION QUARTET **87**
METRO-GOLDWYN-MAYER. (R) October, 1961. Bill Travers, Spike Milligan.

INVESTIGATION OF A CITIZEN ABOVE SUSPICION (Italian, Eng. titles) **115**
COLUMBIA. (R) December, 1970. Gian Maria Volonte, Florinda Bolkan. Color.

INVINCIBLE GLADIATOR, THE (TS) **96**
7 ARTS. (R) 1963. Richard Harrison, Isabel Corey. b&w.

INVINCIBLE SIX, THE **96**
CONTINENTAL. (R) July, 1970. Stewart Whitman, Elke Sommer. Color.

INVISIBLE AVENGER **90**
REPUBLIC. (R) December, 1958. Richard Derr, Helen Westcott.

INVISIBLE BOY, THE **85**
METRO-GOLDWYN-MAYER. (R) October, 1957. Richard Ever, Phillip Abbot.

INVISIBLE INFORMER, THE **87**
REPUBLIC. (R) August, 1956. Linda Stirling, William Henry.

INVISIBLE INVADERS **67**
UNITED ARTISTS. (R) June, 1959. John Agar, Jean Byran.

INVITATION TO A GUNFIGHTER **91**
UNITED ARTISTS. (R) November, 1964. Yul Bryner, Janice Rule. Color.

INVITATION TO THE DANCE **92**
METRO-GOLDWYN-MAYER. (R) March 1, 1957. Gene Kelly, Nora Kaye. Color.

IPCRESS FILE, THE (TE) **106**
UNIVERSAL. (R) October, 1965. Michael Caine, Nigel Green. Color.

IRMA LA DOUCE (P) **149**
UNITED ARTISTS. (R) July, 1963. Jack Lemmon, Shirley MacLaine. Color.

COLUMBIA. (R) August, 1957. Kim Novak, Jeff Chandler.

JENNIFER ON MY MIND 90
UNITED ARTISTS. (R) November, 1971. Michael Brandon, Tippy Walker. Color.

JENNY 88
CINERAMA. (R) January, 1970. Marlo Thomas, Alan Alda. Color.

JEREMIAH JOHNSON (P) 107
WARNER BROS. (R) December, 1972. Robert Redford. Color.

JERK, THE 93
UNIVERSAL. (R) December, 1979. Steve Martin, Bernadette Peters.

JERUSALEM FILE, THE 94
METRO-GOLDWYN-MAYER. (R) March, 1972. Bruce Davison, Nicol Williamson. Color.

JESSE JAMES MEETS FRANKENSTEIN'S DAUGHTER 88
EMBASSY. (R) 1966. John Lupton, Estelita.

JESSICA. 112
UNITED ARTISTS. (R) April, 1962. Angie Dickinson, Maurice Chevalier. Color.

JESSIE'S GIRLS 86
MANSON DISTRIBUTING. (R) April, 1975. Ben Frank, Sandra Currie.

JESUS 117
WARNER BROS. (R) October, 1979. Brian Deacon.

JESUS CHRIST SUPERSTAR (TAO) 106
UNIVERSAL. (R) July, 1973. Ted Neeley, Carl Anderson. Color.

JET ATTACK 68
AMERICAN INT. PICS. (R) February, 1958. John Agar, Audrey Totter.

JET PILOT 112
UNIVERSAL. (R) October, 1957. John Wayne, Janet Leigh. Color.

JIGSAW 97
BEVERLY PICTURES. (R) June, 1965. Jack Warner, Ronald Lewis.

JIM—THE WORLD'S GREATEST 90
UNIVERSAL. (R) February, 1976. Gregory Harrison, Robbie Wolcott.

JIMI HENDRIX 102
WARNER BROS. (R) October, 1973. Documentary.

JOANNA 107
TWENTIETH CENTURY-FOX. (R) November, 1968. Genevieve Waite, Calvin Lockhart, Christian Doermer. Color.

JOCK PETERSEN 97
AVCO-EMBASSY. (R) November, 1975. Jack Thompson, Jacki Weaver.

JOE 107
CANNON. (R) July, 1970. Peter Boyle, K. Callan, Dennis Patrick. Color.

JOE BUTTERFLY (Cs) 90
UNIVERSAL. (R) July, 1957. Audie Murphy, George Nader. Color.

JOE DAKOTA 79
UNIVERSAL. (R) September, 1957. Jock Mahoney, Luana Patten. Color.

JOE HILL 114
PARAMOUNT. (R) October, 1971. Thommy Berggren, Anja Schmidt. Color.

JOE KIDD 88
UNIVERSAL. (R) July, 1972. Clint Eastwood, Robert Duvall, John Saxon. Color.

JOE MACBETH 90
COLUMBIA. (R) February, 1956. Paul Douglas, Ruth Roman.

JOHN AND MARY (P) 92
20th CENTURY-FOX. (R) December, 1969. Dustin Hoffman, Mia Farrow, Michael Tolan. Color.

JOHN F. KENNEDY: YEARS OF LIGHTNING, DAY OF DRUMS 87
EMBASSY. (R) April, 1966. Documentary.

JOHN GOLDFARB, PLEASE COME HOME (Cs) 96
TWENTIETH CENTURY-FOX. (R) April, 1965. Shirley MacLaine, Peter Ustinov. Color.

JOHN PAUL JONES (T) 126
WARNER BROS. (R) July, 1959. Robert Stack, Macdonald Carey. Color.

JOHNNY CASH—THE MAN, HIS WORLD, HIS MUSIC .. 94
CONTINENTAL. (R) September, 1969. Documentary. Color.

JOHNNY CONCHO 84
UNITED ARTISTS. (R) July, 1956. Frank Sinatra, Phyllis Kirk.

JOHNNY COOL 101
UNITED ARTISTS. (R) October, 1963. Henry Silva, Elizabeth Montgomery.

JOHNNY GOT HIS GUN 112
MARKETING & DISTRIBUTION CO. (R) August, 1971. Timothy Bottoms, Donald Sutherland. Color.

JOHNNY NOBODY 88
MEDALLION. (R) November, 1965. Nigel Patrick, Yvonne Mitchell.

JOHNNY RENO (TE) 83
PARAMOUNT. (R) March, 1966. Dana Andrews, Jane Russell. Color.

JOHNNY ROCCO 84
ALLIED ARTISTS. (R) December, 1958. Stephen McNally, Richard Eyer.

JOHNNY TIGER 102
UNIVERSAL. (R) April, 1966. Robert Taylor, Geraldine Brookes. Color.

JOHNNY TREMAIN 80
BUENA VISTA. (R) July, 1957. Hal Stalmaster, Luana Patten. Color.

JOHNNY TROUBLE 80
WARNER BROS. (R) September, 1957. Ethel Barrymore, Cecil Kellaway.

JOKER, THE 86
UNITED ARTISTS. (R) October, 1961. Francois Maistre, Anne Tonietti.

JOKER IS WILD, THE (VV) 123
PARAMOUNT. (R) October, 1957. Frank Sinatra, Mitzi Gaynor.

JOKERS, THE (Brit.) 94
UNIVERSAL. (R) June, 1967. Michael Crawford, Oliver Reed. Color.

JONATHAN LIVINGSTON SEAGULL (P) 115
PARAMOUNT. (R) December, 1973. Documentary.

JORY 95
AVCO-EMBASSY. (R) November, 1972. John Marley, Robby Benson. Color.

JOURNEY 125
METRO-GOLDWYN-MAYER. (R) February, 1959. Yul Brynner, Deborah Kerr. Color.

JOURNEY THROUGH ROSEBUD 93
CINERAMA. (R) March, 1972. Robert Forster, Kristoffer Tabori. Color.

JOURNEY TO FREEDOM 60
REPUBLIC. (R) June, 1957. Jacques Scott, Genevieve Aumont.

JOURNEY TO JERUSALEM, A 95
SIGMA III. Leonard Bernstein, Isaac Stern.

JOURNEY TO SHILOH 101
UNIVERSAL. (R) June, 1968. James Caan, Michael Sarrazin, Brenda Scott. Color.

JOURNEY TO THE CENTER OF THE EARTH (Cs) 132
TWENTIETH CENTURY-FOX. (R) December, 1959. Pat Boone, James Mason. Color.

JOURNEY TO THE FAR SIDE OF THE SUN 99
UNIVERSAL. (R) September, 1969. Roy Thinnes, Ian Hendry, Patrick Wymark. Color.

JOURNEY TO THE LOST CITY 95
AMERICAN INTERNATIONAL. (R) October, 1960. Debra Paget, Paul Christian. Color.

JOURNEY TO THE SEVENTH PLANET 80
AMER. INT'L. PICS. (R) 1962. John Agar, Greta Thyssen. Color.

JOY HOUSE (Franscope) 98
METRO-GOLDWYN-MAYER. (R) November, 1964. Alain Delon, Jane Fonda.

JOY IN THE MORNING (P) 133
METRO-GOLDWYN-MAYER. (R) June, 1965. Richard Chamberlain, Yvette Mimieux. Color.

JOY RIDE 85
ALLIED ARTISTS. (R) October, 1958. Rad Fulton, Ann Doran.

JOYRIDE 92
AMERICAN INTERNATIONAL. (R) June, 1977. Desi Arnaz, Robert Carradine.

JUBAL (Cs) 101
COLUMBIA. (R) May, 1956. Glenn Ford, Ernest Borgnine, Rod Steiger. Color.

JUDEX 91
CONTINENTAL. (R) April, 1966. Michel Vitold, Channing Pollock.

JUDGE AND THE SINNER, THE 94
CASINO. (R) June, 1964. Heinz Ruehmann, Karin Baal.

JUDGEMENT AT NUREMBERG 176
UNITED ARTISTS. (R) Special. October, 1961. Spencer Tracy, Burt Lancaster.

JUDITH (P) 109
PARAMOUNT. (R) February, 1966. Sophia Loren, Peter Finch. Color.

JUGGERNAUT 109
UNITED ARTISTS. (R) September, 1974. Richard Harris, Omar Sharif.

JUKE BOX RACKET 62
BRENNER. (R) May, 1960. Steve Karmen, Arlene Corwin.

JUKE BOX RHYTHM 81
COLUMBIA. (R) April, 1959. Jack Jones, Jo Morrow.

JULIA 117

	Length In Mins.

LAST REMAKE OF BEAU GESTE, THE 83
UNIVERSAL. (R) July, 1977. Ann-Margret, Marty Feldman, Michael York.

LAST RUN, THE (P) 92
MGM. (R) July, 1971. George C. Scott, Tony Musante. Color.

LAST SAFARI, THE 115
PARAMOUNT. (R) November, 1967. Kaz Garas, Stewart Granger. Color.

LAST SHOT YOU HEAR, THE 87
LIPPERT. (R) 1969. Hugh Marlowe, Zena Walker.

LAST STAGECOACH WEST 67
REPUBLIC. (R) July, 1957. Jim Davis, Mary Castle.

LAST SUMMER 97
ALLIED ARTISTS. (R) 1969. Barbara Hershey, Richard Thomas, Bruce Davison, Cathy Burns. Color.

LAST SUNSET, THE 115
UNIVERSAL. (R) July, 1961. Rock Hudson, Kirk Douglas. Color.

LAST TANGO IN PARIS 132
UNITED ARTISTS. (R) February, 1972. Marlon Brando, Maria Schneider. Color.

LAST TEN DAYS, THE 113
COLUMBIA. (R) April, 1956. Documentary.

LAST TIME I SAW ARCHIE, THE 98
UNITED ARTISTS. (R) June, 1961. Robert Mitchum, Jack Webb.

LAST TRAIN FROM GUN HILL (VV) 94
PARAMOUNT. July, 1959. Kirk Douglas, Anthony Quinn. Color.

LAST TYCOON, THE 122
PARAMOUNT. (R) February, 1977. Robert DeNiro, Tony Curtis. Color.

LAST VALLEY, THE (Todd-AO) 126
CINERAMA. (R) February, 1971. Michael Caine, Omar Sharif. Color.

LAST VOYAGE, THE 91
METRO-GOLDWYN-MAYER. (R) February, 1960. Robert Stack, Dorothy Malone. Color.

LAST WAGON, THE (Cs) 99
TWENTIETH CENTURY-FOX. (R) September, 1956. Richard Widmark, Felicia Farr. Color.

LAST WALTZ, THE 115
UNITED ARTISTS. (R) April, 1978. Bob Dylan, Joni Mitchell.

LAST WAVE, THE 106
WORLD NORTHAL. (R) Feburary, 1979. Richard Chamberlain.

LAST WOMAN OF SHANG 107
SHAW. (R) December, 1964. Lin Dai, Nam Koong-Woon. Color.

LAST WORLD, THE (Cs) 90
TWENTIETH CENTURY-FOX. (R) July, 1960. Michael Rennie, Jill St. John. Color.

LATE SHOW, THE 94
WARNER BROS. (R) February, 1977. Art Carney, Lily Tomlin.

LATITUDE ZERO 99
NATIONAL GENERAL. (R) May, 1970. Joseph Cotten, Cesar Romero. Color.

LAUGHING POLICEMAN, THE 112
TWENTIETH CENTURY-FOX. (R) December, 1973. Walter Matthau, Bruce Dern.

LAUGHTER IN THE DARK 101
LOPERT. (R) May, 1969. Nicol Williamson, Anna Karina, Jean-Claude Durot. Color.

LAUREL AND HARDY'S LAUGHING 20'S 91
METRO-GOLDWYN-MAYER. (R) September, 1965. Stan Laurel, Oliver Hardy.

LAW AND DISORDER (P) 103
COLUMBIA. (R) October, 1974. Carroll O'Connor, Ernest Borgnine.

LAW AND JAKE WADE, THE (Cs) 86
MGM. (R) June, 1958. Robert Taylor, Richard Widmark. Color.

LAW OF THE LAWLESS (T) 87
PARAMOUNT. (R) March, 1964. Dale Robertson, Yvonne de Carlo. Color.

LAWLESS EIGHTIES 70
REPUBLIC. (R) May, 1958. Buster Crabbe, John Smith.

LAWLESS STREET, A 78
COLUMBIA. (R) December, 1955. Randolph Scott, Angela Lansbury. Color.

LAWMAN 99
UNITED ARTISTS. (R) August, 1971. Burt Lancaster, Robert Ryan, Lee J. Cobb. Color.

LAWRENCE OF ARABIA (P) 221
COLUMBIA. (R) Special. December, 1962. Peter O'Toole, Sir Alex Guinness. Color.

LAWYER, THE 120
PARAMOUNT. (R) January, 1970. Barry Newman, Harry Gould, Diana Muldaur. Color.

LAY THAT RIFLE DOWN 71

	Length In Mins.

REPUBLIC. (R) July 7, 1955. Judy Canova, Robert Lowery.

LE MANS (P) 106
NATIONAL GENERAL. (R) July, 1970. Steve McQueen. Color.

LE VIOL 81
FREENA. (R) September, 1968. Bibi Anderson, Bruno Cremer, Frederic de Pasquale. Color.

LEADBELLY 126
PARAMOUNT. (R) March, 1976. Roger E. Mosley, Paul Benjamin.

LEARNING TREE, THE (P) 107
WARNER BROS. (R) September, 1969. Kyle Johnson, Alex Clarke, Estelle Evans. Color.

LEASE OF LIFE (Brit.) 93
I.F.E. (R) March, 1956. Robert Donat, Kay Walsh. Color.

LEATHER BOYS, THE (Br. T.) 105
RLP PICTURES. (R) November, 1965. Rita Tushingham, Colin Campbell.

LEATHER SAINT, THE (VV) 86
PARAMOUNT. (R) June, 1956. John Derek, Paul Douglas, Jody Lawrence, Cesar Romero. Color.

LEECH WOMAN, THE 77
UNIVERSAL. (R) June, 1960. Coleen Gray, Grant Williams.

LEFT HAND OF GOD, THE (Cs) 87
TWENTIETH CENTURY-FOX. (R) September, 1955. Humphrey Bogart, Gene Tierney. Color.

LEFT HANDED GUN, THE 102
WARNER BROTHERS. (R) May, 1958. Paul Newman, Lita Milan.

LEGACY, THE 102
UNIVERSAL. (R) September, 1979. Katharine Ross, Sam Elliott.

LEGEND OF HELL HOUSE, THE 90
TWENTIETH CENTURY-FOX. (R) June, 1973. Roddy McDowall, Pamela Franklin. Color.

LEGEND OF LOBO, THE 67
BUENA VISTA. (R) November, 1962. Documentary. Color.

LEGEND OF LYLAH CLARE, THE 130
METRO-GOLDWYN-MAYER. (R) November, 1968. Kim Novak, Peter Finch, Ernest Borgnine. Color.

LEGEND OF NIGGER CHARLEY, THE 99
PARAMOUNT. (R) May, 1972. Fred Williamson, Durville Martin. Color.

LEGEND OF THE LOST (T) 109
UNITED ARTISTS. (R) December, 1957. John Wayne, Sophia Loren.

LEGEND OF TOM DOOLEY, THE 79
COLUMBIA. (R) June, 1959. Michael Landon, Jack Hogan.

LEGION OF THE DOOMED 75
ALLIED ARTISTS. (R) September 21, 1958. Bill Williams, Dawn Richard.

LEGIONS OF THE NILE (Cs) 91
TWENTIETH CENTURY-FOX. (R) December, 1960. Linda Cristal, Georges Marchal. Color.

LEMONADE JOE (Czech.) 84
ALLIED ARTISTS. (R) November, 1967. Karel Fiala, Olga Schoberova.

LENNY 112
UNITED ARTISTS. (R) November, 1974. Dustin Hoffman, Valerie Perrine. b&w.

LEO THE LAST 103
UNITED ARTISTS. (R) May, 1970. Marcello Mastroianni, Billie Whitelaw, Calvin Lockhart. Color.

LEOPARD, THE (Cs) 165
TWENTIETH CENTURY-FOX. (R) October, 1963. Burt Lancaster, Alain Delon. Color.

LEPKE (P) 110
WARNER BROS. (R) June, 1975. Tony Curtis, Anjanette Comer.

LES BICHES (Fr.) 99
VIP. (R) 1968. Stephane Audran, Jacqueline Sassard, Jean Louis Trintignant. Color.

LES CREATURES 93
NEW YORKER FILMS. (R) April, 1969. Catherine Deneuve, Michael Piccoli, Eva Dahlbeck. Color.

LES GAULOISES BLEUES (French, Eng. titles) 93
LOPERT. (R) May, 1969. Annie Giardot, Jean Pierre Kalfon, Nella Bielski. Color.

LES GIRLS (Cs) 114
METRO-GOLDWYN-MAYER. (R) November, 1957. Gene Kelly, Mitzi Gaynor. Color.

LES LIASONS DANGEREUSES 105
ASTOR. (R) December, 1961. Gerard Philipe, Jeanne Moreau.

LET IT BE 80
UNITED ARTISTS. (R) May, 1970. The Beatles. Color.

LET JOY REIGN SUPREME (Fr., Eng. titles) 120

	Length In Mins.

LOST IN THE STARS 114
AFT DISTRIBUTING. (R) Special, 1974. Brock Peters, Melba Moore.

LOST LAGOON 79
UNITED ARTISTS. (R) February, 1958. Jeffrey Lynn, Peter Donat.

LOST MAN, THE 122
UNIVERSAL. (R) July, 1969. Sidney Poitier, Joanna Shimkus, Al Freeman. Color.

LOST MISSILE, THE 70
UNITED ARTISTS. (R) December, 1958. Robert Loggia, Ellen Parker.

LOST WORLD, THE (Cs) 98
TWENTIETH CENTURY-FOX. (R) July, 1960. Michael Rennie, Jill St. John. Color.

LOST WORLD OF SINBAD, THE 95
AMERICAN INTERNATIONAL. (R) March, 1965. Toshiro Mifume, Makoto Satoh. Color.

LOVE A LA CARTE (Ital., Eng. titles) 98
PROMENADE. (R) January, 1965. Simone Signoret, Marcello Mastroianni.

LOVE AFFAIR (Yugoslav.) 90
BRANDON. (R) Feb., 1968. Eva Ras, Ruzica Sokic.

LOVE AND DEATH 82
UNITED ARTISTS. (R) June, 1975. Woody Allen, Diane Keaton.

LOVE AND KISSES 87
UNIVERSAL. (R) November, 1965. Rick Nelson, Jack Kelly. Color.

LOVE AND MARRIAGE (Ital.; Eng. titles) 106
EMBASSY. (R) September, 1966. Lando Buzzanca, Sylva Koscina.

LOVE AND PAIN (AND THE WHOLE DAMN THING) .. 110
COLUMBIA. (R) May, 1973. Maggie Smith, Timothy Bottoms. Color.

LOVE AT FIRST BITE 96
AMERICAN INTERNATIONAL. (R) April, 1979. George Hamilton, Susan Saint James.

LOVE BUG, THE 107
BUENA VISTA. (R) April, 1969. Dean Jones, Michele Lee, David Tomlinson. Color.

LOVE GOD, THE 101
UNIVERSAL. (R) August, 1969. Don Knotts, Anne Francis, Edmund O'Brien. Color.

LOVE GODDESSES, THE 87
CONTINENTAL. (R) March, 1965. Marlene Dietrich, Lillian Gish.

LOVE HAS MANY FACES 105
COLUMBIA. (R) February, 1965. Lana Turner, Cliff Robertson. Color.

LOVE IN A GOLDFISH BOWL 88
PARAMOUNT. (R) June, 1961. Tommy Sands, Fabian. Color.

LOVE IN 4 DIMENSIONS (Ital.; Eng. titles) 108
ELDORADO PICTURES INTERNATIONAL. (R) September, 1965. Michele Mercier, Sylva Koscina.

LOVE IN THE AFTERNOON 125
ALLIED ARTISTS. (R) July, 1957. Gary Cooper, Audrey Hepburn.

LOVE-INS, THE 91
COLUMBIA. (R) July, 1967. James McArthur, Susan Oliver. Color.

LOVE IS A BALL (P) 111
UNITED ARTISTS. (R) March, 1963. Glenn Ford, Hope Lange. Color.

LOVE IS A FUNNY THING (Fr.: Eng. titles) 110
UNITED ARTISTS. (R) March, 1970. Jean-Paul Belmondo, Annie Girardot. Color.

LOVE IS A MANY SPENDORED THING (Cs) 102
TWENTIETH CENTURY-FOX. (R) August, 1955. William Holden, Jennifer Jones. Color.

LOVE ISLAND 68
ASTOR PICTURES. (R) May, 1960. Paul Valentine, Eva Gabor. Color.

LOVE MACHINE, THE 108
COLUMBIA. (R) August, 1971. John Phillip Law, Dyan Cannon, Robert Ryan. Color.

LOVE ME OR LEAVE ME (Cs) 108
METRO-GOLDWYN-MAYER. (R) June 10, 1955. Doris Day, James Cagney. Color.

LOVE ME TENDER (Cs) 89
TWENTIETH CENTURY-FOX. (R) November, 1956. Elvis Presley, Richard Egan, Debra Paget.

LOVE ON A PILLOW (Cs) 102
ROYAL FILMS. (R) December, 1963. Brigitte Bardot, Robert Hossen. Color.

LOVE SLAVES OF THE AMAZONS 81
UNIVERSAL. (R) December, 1957. Don Taylor, Grianna Segale. Color.

LOVE STORY 90
PARAMOUNT. (R) December, 1970. Ali MacGraw, Ryan O'Neil, John Marley, Ray Milland. Color.

LOVE WITH THE PROPER STRANGER 100

	Length In Mins.

PARAMOUNT. (R) February, 1964. Natalie Wood, Steve McQueen.

LOVED ONE, THE 116
METRO-GOLDWYN-MAYER. (R) October, 1965. Robert Morse, Jonathan Winters.

LOVELY WAY TO DIE, A 104
UNIVERSAL. (R) October, 1968. Kirk Douglas, Sylva Koscina, Eli Wallach. Color.

LOVEMAKER, THE (Spain) 99
TRANS-LUX. (R) March, 1958. Betsy Blair, Jose Suarez.

LOVER BOY (Brit.) 85
TWENTIETH CENTURY-FOX. (R) October, 1955. Gerard Philipe, Valerie Hobson, Joan Greenwood.

LOVER COME BACK 107
UNIVERSAL. (R) March, 1962. Doris Day, Rock Hudson. Color.

LOVERS AND LOLLIPOPS 80
TRANS-LUX. (R) April, 1956. Lori March, Gerald O'Loughlin.

LOVERS AND OTHER STRANGERS 106
CINERAMA. (R) August, 1970. Gig Young, Anne Jackson. Color.

LOVES AND TIMES OF SCARAMOUCHE, THE 91
AVCO-EMBASSY. (R) March, 1976. Michael Sarrazin, Ursula Andress.

LOVES OF A BLONDE, THE (Czech; Eng. titles) 88
PROMINENT. (R) December, 1966. Hana Brejchova, Vladimir Pucholt.

LOVES OF ISADORA, THE 131
UNIVERSAL. (R) June, 1969. Vanessa Redgrave, James Fox, Ivan Tchenko, Jason Robards. Color.

LOVES OF ONDINE, THE 106
FACTORY FILMS. (R) December, 1969. Ondine, Viva, Joe Dallesandro.

LOVES OF SALAMMBO (Cs) 72
TWENTIETH CENTURY-FOX. (R) October, 1962. Jeanne Valerie, Jacques Sernas. Color.

LOVIN' MOLLY 98
COLUMBIA. (R) March, 1974. Anthony Perkins, Beau Bridges, Blythe Danner.

LOVING 90
COLUMBIA. (R) March, 1970. George Segal, Eva Marie Saint. Color.

LOVING COUPLES (Swedish; Eng. titles) 113
PROMINENT. (R) September, 1966. Harriet Anderson, Gunnel Lindblom.

LOVING YOU (VV) 101
PARAMOUNT. (R) July, 1957. Elvis Presley, Lizabeth Scott. Color.

LUCK OF GINGER COFFEY, THE 100
READE-STERLING. (R) September, 1964. Robert Shaw, Mary Ure.

LUCKY LADY 117
TWENTIETH CENTURY-FOX. (R) December, 1975. Liza Minnelli, Gene Hackman, Burt Reynolds.

LUCKY LUCIANO 110
AVCO-EMBASSY. (R) 1975. Gian-Maria Volonte, Rod Steiger.

LUCY GALLANT (VV) 104
PARAMOUNT. (R) December, 1955. Jane Wyman, Charlton Heston, Claire Trevor, Thelma Ritter. Color.

LUDWIG 173
METRO-GOLDWYN-MAYER. (R) March, 1973. Helmut Berger, Trevor Howard, Romy Schneider. Color.

LUNA 141
TWENTIETH CENTURY-FOX. (R) October, 1979. Jill Clayburgh, Matthew Barry.

LURE OF THE SWAMP (Cs) 75
TWENTIETH CENTURY-FOX. (R) June, 1957. Marshall Thompson, Joan Vohs.

LUST FOR LIFE (Cs) 122
METRO-GOLDWYN-MAYER. (R) September 15, 1956. Kirk Douglas, Anthony Quinn. Color.

LUTHER 112
AFT DISTRIBUTING. (R) Special, 1974. Stacy Keach, Patrick Magee.

LUV (P) 95
COLUMBIA. (R) August, 1967. Peter Falk, Jack Lemmon, Elaine May. Color.

M

M*A*S*H (P) 116
20TH CENTURY-FOX. April, 1970. Elliott Gould, Donald Sutherland, Sally Kellerman. Color.

MA AND PA KETTLE AT WAIKIKI 79
UNIVERSAL. (R) April, 1955. Marjorie Main, Percy Kilbride.

MA BARKER'S KILLER BROOD 89
FILM SERVICE. (R) June, 1960. Lurene Tuttle, Tris Coffin.

	Length In Mins.

MACABRE 73
ALLIED ARTISTS. (R) March, 1958. William Prince, Jacqueline Scott.

MACABRO 87
TRANS AMERICAN. (R) July, 1966. Documentary. Color.

MACARTHUR 130
UNIVERSAL. (R) July, 1977. Gregory Peck.

MACBETH 139
COLUMBIA. (R) December, 1971. John Finch, Francesca Annis. Color.

MACHETE 75
UNITED ARTISTS. (R) December, 1958. Mari Blanchard, Albert Dekker.

MACHINE GUN KELLY 84
AMERICAN INTERNATIONAL. (R) May, 1958. Charles Bronson, Susan Cabot.

MACHINE GUN McCANN 94
COLUMBIA. (R) September, 1970. John Cassavetes, Peter Falk. Color.

MACHO CALLAHAN (P) 99
AVCO-EMBASSY. (R) August, 1970. David Janssen, Jean Seberg. Color.

MACK, THE 100
CINERAMA. (R) March, 1973. Max Julien, Carol Speed. Color.

MACKENNA'S GOLD 128
COLUMBIA. (R) May, 1969. Gregory Peck, Omar Sharif, Telly Savalas. Color.

MACKINTOSH MAN, THE 105
WARNER BROS. (R) August, 1973. Paul Newman, James Mason.

MACON COUNTY LINE 89
AMERICAN INTERNATIONAL. (R) June, 1974. Alan Vint, Cheryl Waters.

MACUMBA LOVE 86
UNITED ARTISTS. (R) June, 1960. Ziva Rodann, William Wellman, Jr.

MAD ADVENTURES OF "RABBI" JACOBS, THE 96
TWENTIETH CENTURY-FOX. (R) September, 1973. Louis de Funes, Suzy Delair.

MAD AT THE WORLD 71
FILMAKERS. (R) May, 1955. Frank Lovejoy, Keefe Brasselle.

MAD DOG COLL 86
COLUMBIA. (R) May, 1961. John Chandler, Neil Nephew.

MAD-DOGS AND ENGLISHMEN (Todd-AO) 114
MGM. (R) April, 1971. Rock Music. Documentary. Joe Cocker. Color.

MAD LITTLE ISLAND 94
RANK FILM DISTRIBUTORS OF AMERICA. (R) February, 1959. Jeannie Carson, Donald Sinden. Color.

MAD ROOM, THE 92
COLUMBIA. (R) March, 1969. Stella Stevens, Shelley Winters, Skip Ward. Color.

MADAM WHITE SNAKE (Shawscope) (Chinese, Eng. titles) 105
FRANK LEE. (R) October, 1965. Lin Dai, Chao Lei. Color.

MADAM X 100
UNIVERSAL. (R) March, 1966. Lana Turner, John Forsythe. Color.

MADAME BUTTERFLY (Ital.) 114
I.F.E. (R) May, 1956. Kaoru Yachigusa, Michiko Tanaka. Color.

MADAME ROSA (Fr., Eng. titles) 105
ATLANTIC RELEASING. (R) March, 1978. Simone Signoret, Claude Dauphin.

MADDALENA (Ital.-Eng. dubbed) 90
I.F.E. (R) December, 1955. Marta Toren, Gino Cervi. Color.

MADDALENA 105
INT'L CO-RODS. (R) November, 1971. Lisa Gastoni, Eric Wolfe. Color.

MADE FOR EACH OTHER 107
20TH CENTURY-FOX. (R) December, 1971. Rene Taylor, Joseph Bologna. Color.

MADE IN ITALY (Ital.; Eng. titles) (TE) 101
ROYAL INTERNATIONAL. (R) May, 1967. Anna Magnani, Virna Lisi. Color.

MADE IN PARIS (P) 103
METRO-GOLDWYN-MAYER. (R) February, 1966. Ann-Margret, Louis Jourdan. Color.

MADEMOISELLE (P) 103
LOPERT. (R) August, 1966. Jeanne Moreau, Ettore Manni.

MADIGAN (T) 101
UNIVERSAL. (R) May, 1968. Richard Widmark, Inger Stevens. Color.

MADIGAN'S MILLIONS 79
AMERICAN INTERNATIONAL. (R) December, 1969. Dustin Hoffman, Elsa Martinelli. Color.

	Length In Mins.

MADISON AVENUE (Cs) 94
TWENTIETH CENTURY-FOX. (R) January, 1962. Dana Andrews, Barbara Eden.

MADWOMAN OF CHAILLOT, THE 145
WARNER BROS. (R) October, 1969. Katharine Hepburn, Charles Boyer, Edith Evans. Color.

MAEDCHEN IN UNIFORM (German with English titles) 91
SEVEN ARTS. (R) June, 1965. Lilli Palmer, Romy Schneider.

MAFISO 100
ZENITH. (R) July, 1964. Alberto Sordi, Norma Bengell.

MAGIC 106
TWENTIETH CENTURY-FOX. (R) November, 1978. Anthony Hopkins, Ann-Margret.

MAGIC BOY 83
METRO-GOLDWYN-MAYER. (R) April, 1962. Cartoon. Color.

MAGIC CHRISTIAN, THE 93
COMMONWEALTH UNITED. (R) February, 1970. Peter Sellers, Ringo Starr, Raquel Welch. Color

MAGIC FIRE 85
REPUBLIC. (R) March 29, 1956. Yvonne DeCarlo, Carlos Thompson, Rita Gam. Color.

MAGIC FLUTE, THE (Swedish; Eng. titles) 136
SURROGATE RELEASING. (R) October, 1975. Ulrik Cold, Josef Kostlinger.

MAGIC GARDEN OF STANLEY SWEETHEART, THE 113
MGM. (R) June, 1970. Don Johnson, Diane Hull, Holly Near. Color.

MAGIC SWORD, THE 80
UNITED ARTISTS. (R) April, 1962. Basil Rathbone, Estelle Winwood. Color.

MAGIC WEAVER, THE 87
ALLIED ARTISTS. (R) 1965. Color.

MAGIC WORLD OF TOPO GIGIO, THE 75
COLUMBIA. (R) December, 1965. Fantasy. Color.

MAGNIFICENT CONCUBINE, THE (Chinese, Eng. titles) 97
FRANK LEE. (R) June, 1966. Li Li-Hus, Yen Chuan. Color.

MAGNIFICENT CUCKOLD, THE (Ital., Eng. titles) 113
CONTINENTAL. (R) April, 1965. Claudia Cardinale, Ugo Tognazzi.

MAGNIFICENT MATADOR, THE (CS) 94
TWENTIETH CENTURY-FOX. (R) June, 1955. Maureen O'Hara, Anthony Quinn. Color.

MAGNIFICENT ROUGHNECKS 73
ALLIED ARTISTS. (R) July 22, 1956. Jack Carson, Mickey Rooney.

MAGNIFICENT SEVEN, THE (P) 126
UNITED ARTISTS. (R) November, 1960. Yul Brynner, Eli Wallach. Color.

MAGNIFICENT SEVEN RIDE, THE 100
UNITED ARTISTS. (R) August, 1972. Lee Van Cleef, Michael Callan. Color.

MAGNUM FORCE (P) 124
WARNER BROS. (R) December, 1973. Clint Eastwood, Hal Holbrook.

MAGUS, THE 116
TWENTIETH CENTURY-FOX. (R) Jan., 1969. Anthony Quinn, Michael Caine, Candice Bergen. Color.

MAHLER 115
MAYFAIR FILM GROUP. (R) February, 1975. Robert Powell, Georgina Hale.

MAIDEN FOR A PRINCE, A (Ital.) 92
ROYAL INTERNATIONAL. (R) September, 1967. Vittorio Gassman, Virna Lisi. Color.

MAIDS, THE 95
AFT. (R) 1975. Glenda Jackson, Susannah York.

MAIL ORDER BRIDE (P) 83
METRO-GOLDWYN-MAYER. (R) February, 1964. Buddy Ebsen, Keir Dullea. Color.

MAIN ATTRACTION, THE 96
METRO-GOLDWYN-MAYER. (R) November, 1962. Pat Boone, Nancy Kwan.

MAIN CHANCE, THE 60
EMBASSY. (R) July, 1966. Gregoire Aslan, Tracy Reed.

MAIN EVENT, THE 112
WARNER BROS. (R) June, 1979. Barbara Streisand, Ryan O'Neal.

MAJOR DUNDEE (P) 124
COLUMBIA. (R) April, 1965. Charlton Heston, Richard Harris. Color.

MAJORITY OF ONE, A 153
WARNER BROS. (R) February, 1962. Rosalind Russell, Alec Guinness. Color.

MAKE ME AN OFFER (Brit.) 88
ASSOCIATED ARTISTS. (R) February, 1956. Peter Finch, Adrienne Corri. Color.

MAKE MINE MINK 101
CONTINENTAL. (R) December, 1960. Terry-Thomas, Athene Seyler.

MAKING IT 97

	Length In Mins.

TWENTIETH CENTURY-FOX. (R) April, 1971. Kristoffer Tabori, Marlyn Mason. Color.

MALAGA (Brit.) 97
WARNER BROS. (R) 1962. Trevor Howard. Dorothy Dandridge.

MALAMONDO 79
MAGNA. (R) November, 1964. Documentary. Color.

MALCOLM X 92
WARNER BROS. (R) May, 1972. Documentary Biography. Color.

MALE COMPANION (Fr., Eng. titles) 92
INTERNATIONAL CLASSICS. (R) January, 1966. Jean-Pierre Cassel, Catherine Deneuve. Color.

MALIZIA 98
PARAMOUNT. (R) February, 1974. Laura Antonelli, Turi Ferra.

MALTESE BIPPY, THE (P) 92
MGM. (R) June, 1969. Dan Rowan, Dick Martin, Carol Lynley. Color.

MAMBO 94
PARAMOUNT. (R) April, 1955. Silvana Mangano, Shelley Winters, Vittorio Gassman.

MAME (P) 132
WARNER BROS. (R) April, 1974. Lucille Ball, Beatrice Arthur.

MAN, A WOMAN, AND A BANK, A 100
AVCO EMBASSY. (R) October, 1979. Donald Sutherland, Brooke Adams.

MAN, THE 94
PARAMOUNT. (R) August, 1972. James Earl Jones, Martin Balsam. Color.

MAN AFRAID (CS) 64
UNIVERSAL. (R) June, 1957. George Nader, Phyllis Thaxter.

MAN ALONE, A 96
REPUBLIC. (R) October 17, 1955. Ray Milland, Mary Murphy. Color.

MAN AND A WOMAN, A 102
ALLIED ARTISTS. (R) July, 1966. Anouk Aimee, Jean-Louis Trintignant. Color.

MAN AND BOY 98
LEVITT-PICKMAN. (R) March, 1972. Bill Cosby, Leif Erickson. Color.

MAN CALLED ADAM, A 102
EMBASSY. (R) July, 1966. Sammy Davis, Louis Armstrong.

MAN CALLED DAGGER, A 82
MGM. (R) January, 1968. Terry Moore, Jan Murray. Color.

MAN CALLED FLINTSTONE, THE 87
COLUMBIA. (R) August, 1966. Animation. Color.

MAN CALLED GANNON, A 105
UNIVERSAL. (R) May, 1969. Tony Franciosa, Michael Sarrazin, Judi West. Color.

MAN CALLED HORSE, A (P) 114
NATIONAL GENERAL. (R) April, 1970. Richard Harris, Judith Anderson. Color.

MAN CALLED NOON, THE 97
NATIONAL GENERAL. (R) September, 1973. Richard Crenna, Stephen Boyd.

MAN CALLED PETER, A (CS) 119
TWENTIETH CENTURY-FOX. (R) April, 1955. Richard Todd, Jean Peters. Color.

MAN CALLED SLEDGE, A 90
COLUMBIA. (R) March, 1971. James Garner, Dennis Weaver. Color.

MAN COULD GET KILLED, A (P) 99
UNIVERSAL. (R) April, 1966. James Garner, Melina Mercouri. Color.

MAN ESCAPED, A (Fr.) 94
CONTINENTAL. (R) November, 1957. Robert Bresson.

MAN FOR ALL SEASONS, A 120
COLUMBIA. (R) December, 1966. Paul Scofield, Wendy Hiller. Color.

MAN FROM BITTER RIDGE, THE 80
UNIVERSAL. (R) June, 1955. Lex Barker, Mara Corday. Color.

MAN FROM BUTTON WILLOW, THE 84
UNITED SCREEN ARTS. (R) January, 1965. Animated Western. Color.

MAN FROM DEL RIO 93
UNITED ARTISTS. (R) October, 1956. Anthony Quinn, Katy Jurado.

MAN FROM GALVESTON, THE 57
WARNER BROS. (R) January, 1964. Jeff Hunter, Preston Foster.

MAN FROM GOD'S COUNTRY (CS) 70
ALLIED ARTISTS. (R) January, 1958. George Montgomery, Randy Stuart. Color.

MAN FROM LARAMIE, THE (CS) 104
COLUMBIA. (R) August, 1955. James Stewart, Arthur Kennedy. Color.

MAN FROM O.R.G.Y., THE 92

CINEMATION. (R) April, 1970. Robert Walker, Steve Rossi. Color.

MAN FROM THE DINERS' CLUB, THE 96
COLUMBIA. (R) April, 1963. Danny Kaye, Cara Williams.

MAN IN A COCKED HAT 88
LION INTERNATIONAL. (R) May, 1960. Terry-Thomas, Peter Sellers.

MAN IN THE DARK 80
UNIVERSAL. (R) March, 1965. William Sylvester, Barbara Shelley.

MAN IN THE GRAY FLANNEL SUIT, THE (CS) 152
TWENTIETH CENTURY-FOX. (R) March, 1956. Gregory Peck, Jennifer Jones, Fredric March. Color.

MAN IN THE MIDDLE (CS) 94
TWENTIETH CENTURY-FOX. (R) January, 1964. Robert Mitchum, France Nuyen.

MAN IN THE NET, THE 97
UNITED ARTISTS. (R) April, 1959. Alan Ladd, Carolyn Jones.

MAN IN THE ROAD 83
REPUBLIC. (R) April 12, 1957. Derek Farr, Ella Raines.

MAN IN THE SHADOW (CS) 80
UNIVERSAL. (R) January, 1958. Jeff Chandler, Orson Welles.

MAN IN THE STORM 112
TOHO CO. (R) August, 1969. Toshiro Mifune.

MAN IN THE VAULT 73
UNIVERSAL. (R) December, 1956. Anita Ekberg, William Campbell.

MAN IN THE WILDERNESS 105
WARNER BROS. (R) November, 1971. Richard Harris, John Bindon. Color.

MAN INSIDE, THE (CS) 89
COLUMBIA. (R) December, 1958. Jack Palance, Anita Ekberg.

MAN IS ARMED, THE 76
REPUBLIC. (R) October 19, 1956. Dane Clark, William Talman, May Wynn.

MAN OF A THOUSAND FACES (CS) 122
UNIVERSAL. (R) October, 1957. James Cagney, Dorothy Malone.

MAN OF LA MANCHA 130
UNITED ARTISTS. (R) December, 1972. Sophia Loren, Peter O'Toole. Color.

MAN OF THE WEST (CS) 100
UNITED ARTISTS. (R) October, 1958. Gary Cooper, Julie London. Color.

MAN ON A STRING 92
COLUMBIA. (R) May, 1960. Ernest Borgnine, Kerwin Mathews.

MAN ON A SWING (P) 110
PARAMOUNT. (R) March, 1974. Cliff Robertson, Joel Grey.

MAN ON FIRE 96
METRO-GOLDWYN-MAYER. (R) July, 1957. Bing Crosby, Inger Stevens.

MAN ON THE PROWL 86
UNITED ARTISTS. (R) December, 1957. Mala Powers, James Best.

MAN ON THE ROOF (Swedish with English titles) 110
CINEMA 5. (R) April, 1977. Carl-Gustaf Lindstedt, Hakan Serner.

MAN OR GUN (N) 79
REPUBLIC. (R) May, 1958. Macdonald Carey, Audrey Totter.

MAN OUTSIDE, THE 97
ALLIED ARTISTS. (R) March, 1969. Van Heflin, Heidelinde Weis, Pinkas Braun. Color.

MAN-TRAP (P) 90
PARAMOUNT. (R) September, 1961. Jeffrey Hunter, David Janssen.

MAN UPSTAIRS, THE 89
LION INT. (R) August, 1959. Richard Attenborough, Bernard Lee.

MAN WHO COULD CHEAT DEATH, THE 83
PARAMOUNT. (R) September, 1959. Anton Diffring, Hazel Court. Color.

MAN WHO COULDN'T WALK 63
FALCON. (R) March, 1964. Eric Pohlman, Peter Reynolds.

MAN WHO DIED TWICE, THE (N) 70
REPUBLIC. (R) June, 1958. Rod Cameron, Vera Ralston.

MAN WHO HAD POWER OVER WOMEN, THE 89
AVCO EMBASSY. (R) November, 1970. Rod Taylor, Carol White. Color.

MAN WHO KNEW TOO MUCH, THE (VV) 120
PARAMOUNT. (R) June, 1956. James Stewart, Doris Day. Color.

MAN WHO LOVED CAT DANCING, THE (P) 114
METRO-GOLDWYN-MAYER. (R) July, 1973. Burt Reynolds, Sarah Miles. Color.

MAN WHO LOVED REDHEADS, THE (Brit.) 89

**Length
In Mins.**

TAYLOR-LAUGHLIN. (R) October, 1975. Tom Laughlin, Ron O'Neal.

MASTER OF THE WORLD 104
AMERICAN INTERNATIONAL. (R) June, 1961. Vincent Price, Charles Bronson. Color.

MASTER PLAN, THE (Brit.) 77
ASTOR. (R) February, 1955. Wayne Morris.

MASTER SPY, THE 71
ALLIED ARTISTS. (R) July, 1964. Stephen Murray, June Thornburn.

MASTER TOUCH, THE 101
WARNER BROS. (R) May, 1974. Kirk Douglas, Florinda Bolkan.

MASTERS OF THE CONGO JUNGLE (CS) 80
TWENTIETH CENTURY-FOX. (R) December, 1959. Documentary. Color.

MASTERSON OF KANSAS 73
COLUMBIA. (R) January, 1955. George Montgomery, Nancy Gates. Color.

MATCHLESS 104
UNITED ARTISTS. (R) October, 1967. Ira Furstenberg, Patrick O'Neal. Color.

MATCHMAKER, THE (VV) 101
PARAMOUNT. (R) August, 1958. Shirley Booth, Anthony Perkins.

MATILDA 105
AMERICAN INTERNATIONAL. (R) July, 1978. Elliott Gould, Robert Mitchum.

MATING GAME, THE (CS) 96
METRO-GOLDWYN-MAYER. (R) March, 1959. Debbie Reynolds, Tony Randall. Color.

MATTEI AFFAIR, THE 118
PARAMOUNT. (R) May, 1973. Gian Maria Volonte, Luigi Squarzina. Color.

MATTER OF INNOCENCE, A (TS) 102
UNIVERSAL. (R) February, 1968. Hayley Mills, Trevor Howard. Color.

MAURIE 113
NATIONAL GENERAL. (R) August, 1973. Bernie Casey, Bo Swenson.

MAURIETA 108
WARNER BROTHERS. (R) September, 1965. Jeffrey Hunter, Arthur Kennedy. Color.

MAVERICK QUEEN, THE (Naturama) 90
REPUBLIC. (R) May 3, 1956. Barbara Stanwyck, Barry Sullivan, Scott Brady, Mary Murphy. Color.

MAYA (P) 91
METRO-GOLDWYN-MAYER. (R) June, 1966. Clint Walker, Jay North. Color.

MAYERLING 140
METRO-GOLDWYN-MAYER. (R) February, 1969. Omar Sharif, Catherine Deneuve, James Mason. Color.

McCABE AND MRS. MILLER 120
WARNER BROS. (R) July, 1971. Warren Beatty, Julie Christie. Color.

McCLINTOCK (P) 127
UNITED ARTISTS. (R) November, 1963. John Wayne, Maureen O'Hara. Color.

McCONNELL STORY, THE (CS) 107
WARNER BROTHERS. (R) September 3, 1955. Alan Ladd, June Allyson. Color.

McGUIRE, GO HOME! 101
CONTINENTAL. (R) April, 1966. Dirk Bogarde, George Chakiris. Color.

McHALE'S NAVY 90
UNIVERSAL. (R) September, 1964. Ernest Borgnine, Joe Flynn. Color.

McHALE'S NAVY JOINS THE AIR FORCE 92
UNIVERSAL. (R) July, 1965. Joe Flynn, Tim Conway. Color.

McKENZIE BREAK, THE 103
UNITED ARTISTS. (R) October, 1970. Brian Keith, Helmut Griem. Color.

McMASTERS 89
CHEVRON. (R) June, 1970. Burl Ives, Brock Peters, David Carradine. Color.

McQ (P) 116
WARNER BROS. (R) February, 1974. John Wayne, Eddie Albert.

ME AND THE COLONEL 109
COLUMBIA. (R) October, 1958. Danny Kaye, Curt Jurgens.

ME, NATALIE 111
NATIONAL GENERAL. (R) August, 1969. Patty Duke, James Farentino, Salome Jens. Color.

MEAN STREETS 110
WARNER BROS. (R) October, 1973. Robert de Niro, Harvey Keitel.

MEATBALLS 92
PARAMOUNT. (R) July, 1979. Bill Murray, Harvey Atkin.

MECHANIC, THE 95

UNITED ARTISTS. (R) October, 1972. Charles Bronson, Jan-Michael Vincent. Color.

MEDICINE BALL CARAVAN 90
WARNER BROS. (R) August, 1971. Rock Concert Tour Documentary. Color.

MEDITERRANEAN HOLIDAY (Wonderama) 130
CONTINENTAL. (R) March, 1964. Travelogue. Color.

MEDIUM COOL 110
PARAMOUNT. (R) September, 1969. Robert Forster, Vera Bloom, Peter Bonerz. Color.

MEDUSA TOUCH, THE 110
WARNER BROS. (R) April, 1978. Richard Burton, Lee Remick.

MEET ME IN LAS VEGAS (CS) 112
METRO-GOLDWYN-MAYER. (R) March 9, 1956. Dan Dailey, Cyd Charisse. Color.

MEIN KAMPF 110
COLUMBIA. (R) May, 1961. Documentary.

MELINDA 109
METRO-GOLDWYN-MAYER. (R) August, 1972. Calvin Lockhart, Rosalind Cash. Color.

MELODY 103
LEVITT-PICKMAN. (R) April, 1971. Jack Wild, Mark Lester. Color.

MEN IN WAR 104
UNITED ARTISTS. (R) February, 1957. Robert Ryan, Aldo Ray.

MEN OF SHERWOOD FOREST (Brit.) 77
ASTOR. (R) September, 1956. Don Taylor, Eileen Moore. Color.

MENACE IN THE NIGHT 78
UNITED ARTISTS. (R) October, 1958. Griffith Jones, Lisa Gastoni.

MEPHISTO WALTZ, THE 115
TWENTIETH CENTURY-FOX. (R) March, 1971. Alan Alda, Jacqueline Bisset. Color.

MERCENARY, THE 105
UNITED ARTISTS. (R) March, 1970. Franco Nero, Tony Musante, Jack Palance. Color.

MERRILL'S MARUADERS 98
WARNER BROS. (R) June, 1962. Jeff Chandler, Ty Hardin. Color.

MERRY ANDREW (CS) 103
MGM. (R) April, 1958. Danny Kaye, Pier Angeli. Color.

MERRY-GO-ROUND (Hungary) 90
TRANS-LUX. (R) April, 1958. Bela Harsi, Manyi Kiss.

MERRY WIVES OF WINDSOR, THE 97
SIGMA III. (R) March, 1966. Norman Foster, Colette Boxy. Color.

MESSAGE FROM SPACE 105
UNITED ARTISTS. (R) November, 1978. Vic Morrow, Sonny Chiba.

METEOR (P) 103
AMERICAN INTERNATIONAL. (R) October, 1979. Sean Connery, Natalie Wood.

MGM'S BIG PARADE OF COMEDY 109
METRO-GOLDWYN-MAYER. (R) September, 1964. Stars of Past and Present.

MIAMI EXPOSE 73
COLUMBIA. (R) September, 1956. Lee J. Cobb, Patricia Medina.

MICHAEL AND HELGA 87
AMERICAN INTERNATIONAL. (R) April, 1969. Ruth Gassmann, Felix Franchy. Color.

MICKEY ONE 93
COLUMBIA. (R) October, 1965. Warren Beatty, Hurd Hatfield, Alexandra Stewart.

MIDAS RUN 103
CINERAMA. (R) May, 1969. Richard Crenna, Anne Heywood, Fred Astaire. Color.

MIDDLE OF THE NIGHT 118
COLUMBIA. (R) July, 1959. Kim Novak, Fredric March.

MIDNIGHT COWBOY 119
UNITED ARTISTS. (R) May, 1969. Dustin Hoffman, Jon Voight, Sylvia Miles. Color.

MIDNIGHT EXPRESS 120
COLUMBIA. (R) October, 1978. Brad Davis, Bo Hopkins.

MIDNIGHT LACE 108
UNIVERSAL. (R) November, 1960. Doris Day, Rex Harrison. Color.

MIDNIGHT MADNESS 110
BUENA VISTA. (R) February, 1980. David Naughton, Debra Clinter.

MIDNIGHT MAN, THE 117
UNIVERSAL. (R) May, 1974. Burt Lancaster, Susan Clark.

MIDNIGHT STORY, THE (CS) 89
UNIVERSAL. (R) August, 1957. Tony Curtis, Marisa Pavan.

MIDSUMMER NIGHT'S DREAM, A (P) 93
COLUMBIA. (R) Special. January, 1962. Suzanne Farrell, Edward Villella. Color.

	Length In Mins.

	Length In Mins.			Length In Mins.

MONKEY IN WINTER 104
METRO-GOLDWYN-MAYER. (R) February, 1963. Jean Gabin, Jean-Paul Belmondo.

MONKEYS, GO HOME! 101
BUENA VISTA. (R) February, 1967. Maurice Chevalier, Dean Jones. Color.

MONKEY ON MY BACK 93
UNITED ARTISTS. (R) May, 1957. Cameron Mitchell, Dianne Foster.

MONKEY'S UNCLE, THE 87
BUENA VISTA. (R) July, 1965. Tommy Kirk, Annette. Color.

MONOLITH MONSTERS, THE 77
UNIVERSAL. (R) December, 1957. Grant Williams, Lola Albright.

MONSTER ON THE CAMPUS 76
UNIVERSAL. (R) November, 1958. Arthur Franz, Joanna Moore.

MONSTER THAT CHALLENGED THE WORLD, THE 83
UNITED ARTISTS. (R) June, 1957. Tina Holt, Audrey Dalton.

MONTE CARLO STORY, THE (Technirama) 99
UNITED ARTISTS. (R) August, 1957. Marlene Dietrich, Vittorio de Sica. Color.

MONTE WALSH (P) 106
NATIONAL GENERAL. (R) October, 1970. Lee Marvin, Jeanne Moreau. Color.

MONTEREY POP 80
LEACOCK PENNEBAKER. (R) Otis Redding, Scott Mackenzie, Jimi Hendrix. Color.

MONTY PYTHON AND THE HOLY GRAIL 90
CINEMA V. (R) May, 1975. Graham Chapman, John Cleese.

MOON PILOT 98
BUENA VISTA. (R) April, 1962. Tom Tryon, Brian Keith. Color.

MOON-SPINNERS, THE 118
BUENA VISTA. (R) July, 1964. Hayley Mills, Peter McEnery. Color.

MOON WOLF 85
ALLIED ARTISTS. (R) 1966. Carl Moehner, Ann Savo. b&w.

MOON ZERO TWO 100
WARNER BROS. (R) March, 1970. James Olson, Catherina Von Schell. Color.

MOONFLEET (CS) 89
METRO-GOLDWYN-MAYER. (R) June 24, 1955. Stewart Granger, Viveca Lindfors. Color.

MOONRAKER (P) 126
UNITED ARTISTS. (R) June, 1979. Roger Moore, Lois Chiles.

MOONRUNNERS 102
UNITED ARTISTS. (R) July, 1975. Jim Mitchum, Kiel Martin.

MOONSHINE WAR, THE (P) 100
MGM. (R) August, 1970. Patrick McGoohan, Richard Widmark. Color.

MORALS SQUAD 57
BRENNER. (R) May, 1960. Bob O'Connell, Beverly Bennett.

MORE 120
CINEMA V. (R) December, 1969. Mimsy Farmer, Heinz Engelmann, Klaus Grunberg. Color.

MORE AMERICAN GRAFFITI (P) 111
UNIVERSAL. (R) August, 1979. Candy Clark, Bo Hopkins, Ron Howard.

MORE DEAD THAN ALIVE 104
UNITED ARTISTS. (R) May, 1969. Clint Walker, Vincent Price, Anne Francis. Color.

MORE THAN A MIRACLE (Franscope) 105
MGM. (R) November, 1967. Sophia Loren, Omar Sharif. Color.

MORGAN 97
CINEMA V. (R) April, 1966. Vanessa Redgrave, David Warner.

MORGAN THE PIRATE (CS) 95
METRO-GOLDWYN-MAYER. (R) July, 1961. Steve Reeves, Valerie Larange. Color.

MORITURI (CS) 123
TWENTIETH CENTURY-FOX. (R) August, 1965. Marlon Brando, Yul Brynner.

MOSQUITO SQUADRON 90
UNITED ARTISTS. (R) November, 1970. David McCallum, Suzanne Neve. Color.

MOST DANGEROUS MAN ALIVE 82
COLUMBIA. (R) June, 1961. Ron Randell, Debra Paget.

MOTHER KUSTERS GOES TO HEAVEN (German with English titles) 108
NEW YORKER FILMS. (R) March, 1977. Brigette Mira, Ingrid Caven.

MOTHRA 100
COLUMBIA. (R) May, 1962. Franky Sakari, Hiroshi Koizymix. Color.

MOTORCYCLE GANG 78
AMERICAN INTERNATIONAL. (R) October, 1957. Steve Terrell, Ann Neyland.

MOUNTAIN, THE (VV) 105
PARAMOUNT. (R) November, 1956. Spencer Tracy, Robert Wagner, Claire Trevor. Color.

MOUNTAIN MEN, THE 102
COLUMBIA. (R) July, 1980. Charlton Heston, Brian Keith.

MOUNTAIN ROAD, THE 102
COLUMBIA. (R) June, 1960. James Stewart, Lisa Lu.

MOUSE THAT ROARED, THE 83
COLUMBIA. (R) November, 1959. Peter Sellers, Jean Seberg. Color.

MOVE (P) 90
20TH CENTURY-FOX. (R) August, 1970. Elliott Gould, Genevieve Waite, Paula Prentiss. Color.

MOVE OVER DARLING (CS) 103
TWENTIETH CENTURY-FOX. (R) December, 1963. Doris Day, James Garner. Color.

MOVIE MOVIE 105
WARNER BROS. (R) January, 1979. George C. Scott, Trish Van Devere.

MOZAMBIQUE (TE) 98
SEVEN ARTS. (R) February and March, 1966. Steve Cochran, Hildegarde Neff. Color.

MRS. BROWN YOU'VE GOT A LOVELY DAUGHTER 95
METRO-GOLDWYN-MAYER. (R) June, 1968. Peter Noone, Barry Whitwam, Keith Hopwood. Color.

MRS. POLLIFAX, SPY 110
UNITED ARTISTS. (R) March, 1971. Rosalind Russell, Darren McGavin. Color.

MUGGER, THE 74
UNITED ARTISTS. (R) November, 1958. Kent Smith, Nan Martin.

MUMMY'S SHROUD, THE 90
20TH-FOX-SEVEN ARTS. (R) March, 1967. Andre Morell, John Phillips. Color.

MUMSY, NANNY, SONNY, GIRLY 101
CINERAMA. (R) May, 1970. Michael Bryant, Ursula Howells, Vanessa Howard. Color.

MUNSTER GO HOME! 96
UNIVERSAL. (R) July, 1966. Fred Gwynne, Yvonne DeCarlo. Color.

MUPPET MOVIE, THE 94
ASSOCIATED FILM DIST. (R) June, 1979. Guest Stars.

MURDER AHOY! 93
METRO-GOLDWYN-MAYER. (R) September, 1964. Margaret Rutherford, Lionel Jeffries.

MURDER AT 45 R.P.M. (Fr.) 105
MGM. (R) 1960. Danielle Darrieux, Michael Auclair.

MURDER AT THE GALLOP (P) 81
METRO-GOLDWYN-MAYER. (R) July, 1963. Margaret Rutherford, Robert Morley.

MURDER BY CONTRACT 81
COLUMBIA. (R) December, 1958. Vince Edwards, Michael Granges.

MURDER BY DECREE 120
AVCO EMBASSY. (R) February, 1979. Christopher Plummer, James Mason.

MURDER CZECH STYLE (Czech.; Eng. titles) 90
ROYAL. (R) August, 1968. Rudolf Hrusinsky, Kveta Fialova, Vaclav Voska. b&w.

MURDER GAME, THE 75
20TH CENTURY-FOX. (R) April, 1966. Ken Scott, Maralandi.

MURDER, INC. 103
TWENTIETH CENTURY-FOX. (R) June, 1960. Stuart Whitman, May Britt.

MURDER IS MY BEAT 77
ALLIED ARTISTS. (R) February 27, 1955. Barbara Payton, Paul Langton.

MURDER MUST FOUL (P) 90
METRO-GOLDWYN-MAYER. (R) September, 1964. Margaret Rutherford, Stringer Davis.

MURDER ON APPROVAL (Brit.) 70
RKO RADIO. (R) May 30, 1956. Tom Conway.

MURDER ON THE CAMPUS 61
COLORAMA. (R) September, 1963. Terence Longdon, Donald Gray.

MURDER ON THE ORIENT EXPRESS (P) 127
PARAMOUNT. (R) December, 1974. Albert Finney, Lauren Bacall, Ingrid Bergman.

MURDER SHE SAID 87
METRO-GOLDWYN-MAYER. (R) January, 1962. Margaret Rutherford, Arthur Kennedy.

MURDERERS' ROW 108
COLUMBIA. (R) December, 1966. Dean Martin, Ann-Margaret. Color.

MURDERS IN THE RUE MORGUE 86
AMERICAN INTERNATIONAL. (R) July, 1971. Jason Robards, Christine Kaufman, Herbert Lom. Color.

MURIEL 115

Length In Mins.

GOLDEN EAGLE. (R) April, 1969. Akio Takahashi, Kuniko Ishii, Koji Mitsui. b&w.

NANNY, THE 93
TWENTIETH CENTURY-FOX. (R) November, 1965. Bette Davis, Wendy Craig.

NAPOLEON AND SAMANTHA 91
BUENA VISTA. (R) July, 1972. Johnny Whitaker, Jodie Foster, Michael Douglas. Color.

NASHVILLE (P) 159
PARAMOUNT. (R) June, 1975. Ronee Blakley, Keith Carradine, Lily Tomlin.

NASTY HABITS 91
BRUT PRODS. (R) March, 1977. Glenda Jackson, Melina Mercouri, Geraldine Page.

NASTY RABBIT, THE (T) 85
FAIRWAY INT. (R) December, 1964. Mischa Terr, Arch Hall, Jr. Color.

NATIONAL LAMPOON'S ANIMAL HOUSE 109
UNIVERSAL. (R) July, 1978. John Belushi, Tim Matheson.

NATURAL ENEMIES 100
CINEMA 5. (R) November, 1979. Hal Holbrook, Louise Fletcher.

NAVAJO RUN 79
AMERICAN INTERNATIONAL. (R) December, 1964. Johnny Seven, Virginia Vincent.

NAVY VS. THE NIGHT MONSTER, THE 90
FEAT. FILM CORP. OF AMER. (R) 1965. Anthony Eisley, Mamie Van Doren. Color.

NAVY WIFE 83
ALLIED ARTISTS. (R) May 20, 1956. Joan Bennett, Gary Merrill, Shirley Yamaguchi.

NAZARIN (Spanish; Eng. titles) 92
ALTURA. (R) June, 1968. Francisco Rabal, Rita Macedo, Marga Lopez. b&w.

NEA (French; Eng. titles) 101
LIBRA FILMS. (R) August, 1978. Samy Frey, Ann Zacharias.

NEARLY A NASTY ACCIDENT 86
UNIVERSAL. (R) April, 1962. Jimmy Edwards, Kenneth Connor.

NECROMANCY 82
CINERAMA. (R) November, 1972. Orson Welles, Pamela Franklin. Color.

NED KELLY 100
UNITED ARTISTS. (R) June, 1970. Mick Jagger, Allen Bickford, Geoff Gilmour. Color.

NEGATIVES 90
CONT. (R) November, 1968. Peter McEnery, Diane Cilento, Glenda Jackson. Color.

NELSON AFFAIR, THE 118
UNIVERSAL. (R) May, 1972. Glenda Jackson, Peter Finch. Color.

NEPTUNE FACTOR, THE (P) 97
TWENTIETH CENTURY-FOX. (R) May, 1973. Ben Gazzara, Yvette Mimieux. Color.

NETWORK 121
UNITED ARTISTS. (R) February, 1977. Faye Dunaway, William Holden.

NEVADA SMITH (P) 130
PARAMOUNT. (R) July, 1966. Steve McQueen, Karl Malden. Color.

NEVER A DULL MOMENT 100
BUENA VISTA. (R) June, 1968. Dick Van Dyke, Edward G. Robinson, Dorothy Provine. Color.

NEVER LET GO 90
CONTINENTAL. (R) June, 1963. Richard Todd, Peter Sellers.

NEVER LOVE A STRANGER 91
ALLIED ARTISTS. (R) May 4, 1958. John Drew Barrymore, Lita Milan.

NEVER ON SUNDAY 97
LOPERT PICTURES. (R) October, 1960.

NEVER PUT IT IN WRITING 93
ALLIED ARTISTS. (R) April, 1964. Pat Boone, Milo O'Shea.

NEVER SAY GOODBYE 97
UNIVERSAL. (R) March, 1956. Rock Hudson, Cornel Borchers, George Sanders. Color.

NEVER SO FEW (Cs) 124
METRO-GOLDWYN-MAYER. (R) December, 1959. Frank Sinatra, Gina Lollobrigida. Color.

NEVER STEAL ANYTHING SMALL (Cs) 92
UNIVERSAL. (R) March, 1959. James Cagney, Shirley Jones. Color.

NEVER TOO LATE (P) 105
WARNER BROTHERS. (R) December, 1965. Paul Ford, Maureen O'Sullivan. Color.

NEW ANGELES, THE (Ital., Eng. titles) 94
PROMENADE. (R) May, 1965. Episodes on Italian Life.

NEW CENTURIONS, THE 103
COLUMBIA. (R) August, 1972. George C. Scott, Stacy Keach, Jane Alexander. Color.

Length In Mins.

NEW INTERNS, THE 123
COLUMBIA. (R) June, 1964. Michael Callan, Barbara Eden.

NEW KIND OF LOVE, A 110
PARAMOUNT. (R) October, 1963. Paul Newman, Joanne Woodward. Color.

NEW LAND, THE 161
WARNER BROS. (R) October, 1973. Max von Sydow, Liv Ullmann.

NEW LEAF, A 102
PARAMOUNT. (R) April, 1971. Walter Matthau, Elaine May. Color.

NEW ORLEANS UNCENSORED 70
COLUMBIA. (R) March, 1955. Arthur Franz, Beverly Garland.

NEW YORK CONFIDENTIAL 87
WARNER BROTHERS. (R) March 12, 1955. Broderick Crawford, Marilyn Maxwell.

NEW YORK, NEW YORK 155
UNITED ARTISTS. (R) June, 1977. Liza Minnelli, Robert De Niro.

NEWMAN'S LAW 98
UNIVERSAL. (R) May, 1974. George Peppard, Roger Robinson.

NEXT MAN, THE 108
ALLIED ARTISTS. (R) November, 1976. Sean Connery, Cornelia Sharpe.

NICE GIRL LIKE ME, A 90
AVCO EMBASSY. (R) December, 1969. Barbara Ferris, Harry Andrews, Gladys Cooper. Color.

NICE LITTLE BANK THAT SHOULD BE ROBBED, A (Cs) 87
TWENTIETH CENTURY-FOX. (R) December, 1958. Tom Ewell, Mickey Rooney.

NICHOLAS AND ALEXANDRA 187
COLUMBIA. (R) December, 1971. Michael Jayston, Janet Suzman. Color.

NICKEL RIDE, THE 99
20TH CENTURY-FOX. (R) January, 1975. Jason Miller.

NICKELODEON (P) 122
COLUHBIA. (R) December, 1976. Ryan O'Neal, Burt Reynolds.

NIGHT AMBUSH (VV) 93
RANK FILM DISTRIBUTORS OF AMERICA. (R) July, 1958. Dick Bogarde, Marius Goring.

NIGHT CREATURES 81
UNIVERSAL. (R) June, 1962. Peter Cushing, Yvonne Romain. Color.

NIGHT DIGGER, THE 110
MGM. (R) May, 1971. Patricia Neal, Pamela Brown. Color.

NIGHT FIGHTERS, THE 74
ALLIED ARTISTS. September, 1960. Robert Mitchum, Dan O'Herlihy.

NIGHT FREIGHT 79
ALLIED ARTISTS. (R) August 28, 1955. Forrest Tucker, Barbara Britton.

NIGHT GAMES (Swed.; Eng. titles) 104
MONDIAL. (R) December, 1966. Ingrid Thulin, Keve Hjelm.

NIGHT HOLDS TERROR, THE 86
COLUMBIA. (R) September, 1955. Jack Kelly, Hildy Parks.

NIGHT MOVES (P) 100
WARNER BROS. (R) June, 1975. Gene Hackman.

NIGHT MUST FALL 105
METRO-GOLDWYN-MAYER. (R) March, 1964. Albert Finney, Susan Hampshire.

NIGHT OF DARK SHADOWS 97
METRO-GOLDWYN-MAYER. (R) September, 1971. David Shelby, Grayson Hall. Color.

NIGHT OF THE BLOOD FEAST 65
AMERICAN INTERNATIONAL. (R) August, 1958. Michael Emmet, Angela Greeney.

NIGHT OF THE FOLLOWING DAY, THE 93
UNIVERSAL. (R) March, 1969. Marlon Brando, Rita Moreno, Richard Boone. Color.

NIGHT OF THE GENERALS, THE (P) 148
COLUMBIA. (R) February, 1967. Peter O'Toole, Omar Sharif. Color.

NIGHT OF THE GRIZZLY (TE) 102
PARAMOUNT. (R) May, 1966. Clint Walker, Martha Hyer. Color.

NIGHT OF THE HUNTER, THE 93
UNITED ARTISTS. (R) September, 1955. Robert Mitchum, Shelley Winters.

NIGHT OF THE IGUANA, THE 125
METRO-GOLDWYN-MAYER. (R) August, 1964. Richard Burton, Ava Gardner.

NIGHT OF THE LEPUS 88
METRO-GOLDWYN-MAYER. (R) October, 1973. Stuart Whitman, Janet Leigh. Color.

NIGHT OF THE LIVING DEAD, THE 90

	Length In Mins.

CONT. (R) October, 1968. Judith O'Dea, Russell Streiner. b&w.

NIGHT OF THE QUARTER MOON (Cs) 96
METRO-GOLDWYN-MAYER. (R) February, 1959. Julie London, John Drew Barrymore.

NIGHT PASSAGE (T) 90
UNIVERSAL. (R) August, 1957. James Stewart, Audie Murphy. Color.

NIGHT PORTER, THE 117
AVCO-EMBASSY. (R) October, 1975. Dirk Bogarde, Charlotte Rampling.

NIGHT RUNNER, THE 79
UNIVERSAL. (R) February, 1957. Ray Danton, Colleen Miller.

NIGHT THE WORLD EXPLODED, THE 64
COLUMBIA. (R) June, 1957. Kathryn Grant, William Leslie.

NIGHT THEY KILLED RASPUTIN, THE 87
BRIGADIER FILMS. (R) 1962. Edmund Purdom. John Drew Barrymore.

NIGHT THEY RAIDED MINSKY'S, THE 100
UNITED ARTISTS. (R) December, 1968. Jason Robards, Britt Eklund. Color.

NIGHT TIDE 84
AMERICAN INTERNATIONAL. (R) April, 1963. Dennis Hopper, Linda Lawson.

NIGHT TO REMEMBER, A 123
RANK FILM DISTRIBUTION OF AMERICA. (R) March, 1959. Kenneth More, Ronald Allen.

NIGHT TRAIN TO PARIS 65
TWENTIETH CENTURY-FOX. (R) November, 1964. Leslie Nelson, Alizia Gur.

NIGHT VISITOR, THE 102
UMC PICTURES. (R) February, 1971. Max von Sydow, Trevor Howard. Color.

NIGHT WALKER, THE 86
UNIVERSAL. (R) January, 1965. Robert Taylor, Barbara Stanwyck.

NIGHT WATCH, THE (Fr. Eng. titles) 118
CONSORT/ORION. (R) April, 1964. Michael Constantin, Jean Keraudy.

NIGHT WATCH 99
AVCO-EMBASSY. (R) August, 1973. Elizabeth Taylor, Laurence Harvey.

NIGHTCOMERS, THE 95
AVCO EMBASSY. (R) February, 1972. Marlon Brando, Stephanie Beacham. Color.

NIGHTFALL 78
COLUMBIA. (R) February, 1957. Aldo Ray, Brian Keith.

NIGHTMARE (H) 83
UNIVERSAL. (R) June, 1964. David Knight, Moira Redmond.

NIGHTMARE 89
UNITED ARTISTS. (R) June, 1956. Edward G. Robinson, Kevin McCarthy.

NIGHTMARE CASTLE 93
ALLIED ARTISTS. (R) July, 1966. Barbara Steele, Paul Miller.

NIGHTMARE IN THE SUN 81
ZODIAC. (R) January, 1965. Ursula Andress, John Derek. Color.

NIGHTMARE IN WAX 87
CROWN INTL. (R) December, 1969. Scott Brady, Cameron Mitchell.

NIGHTWING 105
COLUMBIA. (R) June, 1979. Nick Mancuso, David Warner.

NIGHTS OF CABIRIA (Ital.) 110
LOPERT. (R) November, 1957. Guiletta Massina, Francois Ferrier.

NIGHTS OF LUCRETIA BORGIA, THE (Totalscope) 106
COLUMBIA. (R) August, 1960. Belinda Lee, Jacques Sernas. Color.

NIJINSKY 125
PARAMOUNT. (R) March, 1980. Alan Bates, George De La Pena.

NIKKI, WILD DOG OF THE NORTH 74
BUENA VISTA. (R) July, 1961. Jean Coutu, Emile Genest. Color.

NINE DAYS OF ONE YEAR 102
ARTKINO. (R) December, 1964. Alexi Batalov, Innokenty Smoktunovsky.

NINE HOURS TO RAMA (Cs) 125
TWENTIETH CENTURY-FOX. (R) April, 1963. Horst Buchholz, Jose Ferrer. Color.

NINE LIVES OF FRITZ THE CAT, THE 76
AMERICAN INTERNATIONAL. (R) July, 1974. Cartoon.

1900 245
PARAMOUNT. (R) December, 1977. Robert De Niro, Gerard Depardieu.

1984 91

COLUMBIA. (R) September, 1956. Edmond O'Brien, Jan Sterling.

1941 (P) 118
UNIVERSAL. (R) December, 1979. Dan Aykroyd, Ned Beatty.

90 DEGREES IN THE SHADE 90
LANDAU/UNGER. (R) October, 1966. Anne Heywood, James Booth.

99 AND 44/100% DEAD (P) 97
TWENTIETH CENTURY-FOX. (R) July, 1974. Richard Harris, Edmond O'Brien.

99 WOMEN 90
COMMONWEALTH UNITED. (R) April, 1969. Maria Schell, Mercedes McCambridge. Color.

92 IN THE SHADE 91
UNITED ARTISTS. (R) August, 1975. Peter Fonda, Warren Oates.

NO BLADE OF GRASS 97
MGM. (R) October, 1970. Nigel Davenport, Jean Wallace. Color.

NO DOWN PAYMENT (Cs) 105
TWENTIETH CENTURY-FOX. (R) October, 1957. Joanne Woodward, Sherry North.

NO DRUMS, NO BUGLES 85
CINERAMA. (R) August, 1971. Martin Sheen. Color.

NO MAN IS AN ISLAND 114
UNIVERSAL. (R) October, 1962. Jeffrey Hunter, Marshall Thompson. Color.

NO MAN'S WOMAN 70
REPUBLIC. (R) October 27, 1955. Marie Windsor, Patrick Knowles.

NO MORE EXCUSES 82
IMPACT FILMS. (R) January, 1968. Robert Downey, Allen Noel.

NO, MY DARLING DAUGHTER! 96
ZENITH. (R) February, 1964. Michael Redgrave, Michael Craig.

NO NAME ON THE BULLET (Cs) 77
UNIVERSAL. (R) February, 1959. Audie Murphy, Charles Drake. Color.

NO NUKES 103
WARNER BROS. (R) July, 1980. Jackson Browne, David Crosby.

NO PLACE TO HIDE 72
ALLIED ARTISTS. (R) August 26, 1956. David Brian, Keenan Wynn. Color.

NO PLACE TO LAND (N) 78
REPUBLIC. (R) October, 1958. John Ireland, Mari Blanchard.

NO TIME FOR BREAKFAST (French; Eng. titles) 100
BOURIA FILM ENTERPRISES. (R) September, 1978. Annie Girardot, Jean-Pierre Cassel.

NO TIME FOR SERGEANTS 111
WARNER BROS. (R) July, 1958. Andy Griffith, Myron McCormick.

NO TIME TO BE YOUNG 82
COLUMBIA. (R) August, 1957. Robert Vaughn, Roger Smith.

NO TREE IN THE STREET 96
SEVEN ARTS. (R) January, 1964. Sylvia Syms, Herbert Lom.

NO WAY TO TREAT A LADY 108
PARAMOUNT. (R) March, 1968. Rod Steiger, Lee Remick. Color.

NOBODY WAVED GOODBYE 80
CINEMA V. (R) April, 1965. Peter Kastner, Julie Biggs.

NOBODY'S PERFECT (TE) 103
UNIVERSAL. (R) January, 1968. James Whitmore, Doug McClure. Color.

NONE BUT THE BRAVE (P) 110
WARNER BROS. (R) February, 1965. Frank Sinatra, Clint Walker. Color.

NOOSE FOR A GUNMAN 69
UNITED ARTISTS. (R) May, 1960. Jim Davis, Lyn Thomas.

NORMA RAE 110
TWENTIETH CENTURY-FOX. (R) March, 1979. Sally Field, Beau Bridges, Ron Leibman.

NORMAN . . . IS THAT YOU? 91
UNITED ARTISTS. (R) September, 1976. Redd Foxx, Pearl Bailey.

NORTH AVENUE IRREGULARS, THE 100
BUENA VISTA. (R) February, 1979. Edward Herrmann, Barbara Harris.

NORTH BY NORTHWEST (VV) 136
METRO-GOLDWYN-MAYER. (R) July, 1959. Cary Grant, Eva Marie Saint. Color.

NORTH DALLAS FORTY 120
PARAMOUNT. (R) August, 1979. Nick Nolte, Mac Davis.

NORTH TO ALASKA (Cs) 122
TWENTIETH CENTURY-FOX. (R) November, 1960. John Wayne, Stewart Granger. Color.

Length In Mins.

UNITED ARTISTS. (R) December, 1969. George Lazenby, Diana Rigg, Telly Savalas. Color.

ON MY WAY TO THE CRUSADES I MET A GIRL WHO ... 93
WARNER BROS. (R) September, 1969. Tony Curtis, Monica Vitti. Color.

ON THE BEACH 133
UNITED ARTISTS. (R) December, 1959. Gregory Peck, Ava Gardner.

ON THE DOUBLE 92
PARAMOUNT. (R) July, 1961. Danny Kaye, Dana Wynter, Color.

ON THE THRESHOLD OF SPACE (Cs) 96
TWENTIETH CENTURY-FOX. (R) March, 1956. Guy Madison, Virginia Leith. Color.

ON THE YARD 102
MIDWEST FILMS. (R) January, 1979. John Heard, Thomas Waites.

ONCE A THIEF 107
METRO-GOLDWYN-MAYER. (R) September, 1965. Alain Delon, Ann-Margret.

ONCE IN PARIS 100
LEIGH & McLAUGHLIN. (R) November, 1978. Wayne Rogers, Gayle Hunnicutt.

ONCE IS NOT ENOUGH (P) 120
PARAMOUNT. (R) June, 1975. Kirk Douglas, Alexis Smith.

ONCE MORE WITH FEELING (Technirama) 92
COLUMBIA. (R) February, 1960. Yul Brynner, Kay Kendall. Color.

ONCE UPON A HORSE (Cs) 85
UNIVERSAL. (R) September, 1958. Dan Rowan, Dick Martin.

ONCE UPON A TIME IN THE WEST (P) 165
PARAMOUNT. (R) July, 1969. Henry Fonda, Jason Robards, Charles Bronson. Color.

ONCE YOU KISS A STRANGER 106
WARNER BROS. (R) December, 1969. Paul wburke, Carol Lynley, Martha Hyer. Color.

ONE AND ONLY, THE 95
PARAMOUNT. (R) February, 1978. Henry Winkler, Kim Darby.

ONE AND ONLY, GENUINE, ORIGINAL FAMILY BAND, THE 110
BUENA VISTA. (R) April, 1968. Walter Brennan, Buddy Ebsen. Color.

ONE DAY IN THE LIFE OF IVAN DENISOVICH 100
CINERAMA. (R) June, 1971. Tom Courtenay, Alfred Burke. Color.

ONE DESIRE 94
UNIVERSAL. (R) August, 1955. Anne Baxter, Rock Hudson. Color.

ONE-EYED JACKS (VV) 141
PARAMOUNT. (R) Special. March, 1961. Marlon Brando, Karl Malden. Color.

ONE FLEW OVER THE CUCKOO'S NEST 129
UNITED ARTISTS. (R) November, 1975. Jack Nicholson, Louise Fletcher.

ONE FOOT IN HELL (Cs) 90
TWENTIETH CENTURY-FOX. (R) July, 1960. Alan Ladd, Don Murray. Color.

101 DALMATIANS 80
BUENA VISTA. (R) March, 1961. Feature Cartoon. Color.

100 RIFLES 110
TWENTIETH CENTURY-FOX. (R) April, 1969. Jim Brown, Raquel Welch, Burt Reynolds. Color.

ONE LITTLE INDIAN 90
BUENA VISTA. (R) June, 1973. James Garner. Color.

ONE MAN'S WAY 100
UNITED ARTISTS. (R) February, 1964. Don Murray, Diana Hyland.

ONE MILLION YEARS B.C. 91
20TH CENTURY-FOX. (R) April, 1967. Raquel Welch, John Richardson. Color.

ONE MORE TIME 93
UNITED ARTISTS. (R) May, 1970. Sammy Davis, Jr., Peter Lawford, Ester Anderson. Color.

ONE MORE TRAIN TO ROB 108
UNIVERSAL. (R) May, 1971. George Peppard, Diana Muldaur.

ONE OF OUR DINOSAURS IS MISSING 97
BUENA VISTA. (R) July, 1975. Helen Hayes, Peter Ustinov.

ONE ON ONE 98
WARNER BROS. (R) August, 1977. Robby Benson, Annette O'Toole.

ONE POTATO, TWO POTATO 92
CINEMA V. July, 1964. Barbara Barrie, Bernie Hamilton.

ONE SINGS, THE OTHER DOESN'T (Fr., Eng. titles) 105
CINEMA 5. (R) October, 1977. Valerie Mairesse, Therese Liotard.

ONE SPY TOO MANY 102

Length In Mins.

METRO-GOLDWYN-MAYER. (R) September, 1966. Robert Vaughn, David McCallum. Color.

ONE THAT GOT AWAY, THE (Brit.) 106
RANK. (R) March, 1958. Hardy Kruger, Colin Gordon.

1,001 ARABIAN NIGHTS 70
COLUMBIA. (R) December, 1959. Mister Magoo. Color.

1000 CONVICTS AND A WOMAN 92
AMERICAN INTERNATIONAL. (R) October, 1971. Alexandra Hay, Sandor Eles. Color.

ONE, TWO, THREE (P) 108
UNITED ARTISTS. (R) December, 1961. James Cagney, Arlene Francis.

ONE WAY OUT 60
RANK. (R) December, 1957. Jill Adams, Lyndon Brook.

ONE WAY PENDULUM 85
LOPERT. (R) January, 1965. Eric Sykes, George Cole.

ONIBABA (TOHOSCOPE) 99
TOHO. (R) February, 1965. Nobuko Otowa, Jitsuko Yoshimura.

ONION FIELD, THE 126
AVCO-EMBASSY. (R) September, 1979. John Savage, James Woods.

ONIONHEAD 110
WARNER BROS. (R) October, 1958. Andy Griffith, Felicia Farr.

ONLY GAME IN TOWN, THE (P) 113
20TH CENTURY-FOX. (R) February, 1970. Elizabeth Taylor, Warren Beatty. Color.

ONLY ONE NEW YORK 75
EMBASSY. (R) October, 1964. Documentary.

ONLY TWO CAN PLAY 106
KINGSLEY INT. (R) March, 1962.

ONLY WHEN I LARF 104
PARAMOUNT. (R) February, 1969. Richard Attenborough, David Hemmings, Alexandra Stewart. Color.

OPERATION AMSTERDAM 105
TWENTIETH CENTURY-FOX. (R) June, 1960. Peter Finch, Eva Bartok.

OPERATION BIKINI 83
AMERICAN INTERNATIONAL. (R) April, 1963. Tab Hunter, Frankie Avalon.

OPERATION BOTTLENECK 78
UNITED ARTISTS. (R) February, 1961. Ron Foster, Milko Takax.

OPERATION CAMEL 70
AMERICAN INTERNATIONAL. (R) August, 1961. Nora Hayden, Louis Reynard. Color.

OPERATION C.I.A. 90
ALLIED ARTISTS. (R) 1965. Burt Reynolds, John Hoyt. b&w.

OPERATION CONSPIRACY 69
REPUBLIC. (R) September, 1957. Phillip Friend, Mary Mackenzie.

OPERATION CROSSBOW (P) 116
METRO-GOLDWYN-MAYER. (R) July, 1965. Color.

OPERATION DAMES 74
AMERICAN INTERNATIONAL. (R) March, 1959. Eve Meyer, Check Henderson.

OPERATION EICHMANN 92
ALLIED ARTISTS. (R) March, 1961. Werner Klemperer, Ruta Lee.

OPERATION KID BROTHER (TS) 104
UNITED ARTISTS. (R) October, 1967. Neil Connery, Daniela Bianchi. Color.

OPERATION MAD BALL 105
COLUMBIA. (R) November, 1957. Jack Lemmon, Ernie Kovacs.

OPERATION MALAYA (Brit.) 80
AMERICAN RELEASING CORP. (R) October, 1955. Documentary.

OPERATION PETTICOAT 124
UNIVERSAL. (R) December, 1959. Cary Grant, Tony Curtis. Color.

OPERATION SNAFU 89
AMERICAN INTERNATIONAL. (R) February, 1965. Sean Connery, Stanley Holloway.

OPERATION SNATCH 83
CONTINENTAL. (R) September, 1962. Terry-Thomas, George Sanders.

OPPOSITE SEX, THE (Cs) 117
METRO-GOLDWYN-MAYER. (R) October 26, 1956. June Allyson, Ann Sheridan, Joan Collins, Dolores Gray. Color.

OPTIMISTS, THE 110
PARAMOUNT. (R) October, 1973. Peter Sellers, Donna Mullane.

ORCA (P) 92
PARAMOUNT. (R) July, 1977. Richard Harris, Charlotte Rampling.

OREGON PASSAGE (Cs) 81
ALLIED ARTISTS. (R) January, 1958. John Erickson, Lola Albright. Color.

OREGON TRAIL, THE (Cs) 88

Length In Mins.

UNITED ARTISTS. (R) October, 1968. Alan Alda, Lauren Hutton, Sugar Ray Robinson. Color.

PAPER MOON 102
PARAMOUNT. (R) May, 1973. Ryan O'Neal, Tatum O'Neal.

PAPILLON (P) 150
ALLIED ARTISTS. (R) December, 1973. Steve McQueen, Dustin Hoffman.

PARADISE ALLEY 108
UNIVERSAL. (R) November, 1978. Sylvester Stallone.

PARADISE, HAWAIIAN STYLE 91
PARAMOUNT. (R) Summer, 1966. Elvis Presley, Suzanna Leigh.

PARADISE LAGOON (The Admirable Crichton) 94
COLUMBIA. (R) April, 1958. Kenneth Moore, Diane Cilento. Color.

PARALLAX VIEW, THE (P) 100
PARAMOUNT. (R) June, 1974. Warren Beatty, Paula Prentiss.

PARANOIA (Cromoscope) 91
COMMONWEALTH UNITED. (R) October, 1969. Carroll Baker, Lou Castel. Color.

PARANOIAC 80
UNIVERSAL. (R) May, 1963. Janette Scott, Oliver Reed.

PARATROOP COMMAND 83
AMERICAN INTERNATIONAL. (R) February, 1959. Richard Bakalyan, Jack Hogan.

PARDNERS (VV) 85
PARAMOUNT. (R) August, 1956. Dean Martin, Jerry Lewis. Color.

PARENT TRAP, THE 124
BUENA VISTA. (R) June, 1961. Hayley Mills, Maureen O'Hara. Color.

PARIS BLUES 98
UNITED ARTISTS. (R) October, 1961. Paul Newman, Joanne Woodward.

PARIS DOES STRANGE THINGS 86
WARNER BROTHERS. (R) March 2, 1957. Ingrid Bergman, Mel Ferrer. Color.

PARIS FOLLIES OF 1958 78
ALLIED ARTISTS. (R) November 27, 1955. Forrest Tucker, Margaret Whiting. Color.

PARIS HOLIDAY (T) 100
UNITED ARTISTS. (R) March, 1958. Bob Hope, Fernadel.

PARIS IN THE MONTH OF AUGUST 94
TRANS-LUX. (R) March, 1968. Charles Aznavour, Susan Hampshire.

PARIS SECRET 84
CINEMA V. (R) September, 1965. Documentary. Color.

PARIS WHEN IT SIZZLES 110
PARAMOUNT. (R) April, 1964. William Holden, Audrey Hepburn. Color.

PARISIENNE, LA 85
UNITED ARTISTS. (R) August, 1958. Brigitte Bardot, Charles Boyer. Color.

PARRISH 137
WARNER BROS. (R) July, 1961. Troy Donahue, Claudette Colbert. Color.

PARSON AND THE OUTLAW, THE 71
COLUMBIA. (R) September, 1957. Anthony Dexter, Sonny Tufts.

PART 2 WALKING TALL 109
AMERICAN INTERNATIONAL. (R) July, 1975. Bo Svenson, Luke Askew.

PARTY, THE (P) 99
UNITED ARTISTS. (R) April, 1968. Peter Sellers, Claudine Longet. Color.

PARTY CRASHERS, THE 76
PARAMOUNT. (R) September, 1958. Connie Stevens, Robert Driscoll.

PARTY GIRL (Cs) 99
METRO-GOLDWYN-MAYER. (R) September, 1958. Robert Taylor, Cyd Charisse. Color.

PARTY'S OVER, THE (Brit.) 94
ALLIED ARTISTS. (R) 1966. Oliver Reed, Catherine Woodville.

PASSAGE, THE (T) 99
UNITED ARTISTS. (R) March, 1979. Anthony Quinn, James Mason, Malcolm McDowell.

PASSAGES FROM FINNEGAN'S WAKE 94
GROVE PRESS. (R) November, 1967. Martin J. Kelly, Jane Reilly.

PASSENGER, THE 122
UNITED ARTISTS-MGM. (R) April, 1975. Jack Nicholson, Maria Schneider.

PASSION OF ANNA, THE (Swedish; Eng. titles) 99
UNITED ARTISTS. (R) May, 1970. Liv Ullman, Bibi Anderson, Max Von Sydow. Color.

PASSPORT TO CHINA 75
COLUMBIA. (R) March, 1961. Richard Basehart, Lisa Gastoni.

Length In Mins.

PASSPORT TO TREASON (Brit.) 70
ASTOR. (R) June, 1956. Rod Cameron, Lois Maxwell.

PASSWORD IS COURAGE, THE 116
METRO-GOLDWYN-MAYER. (R) January, 1963. Dirk Bogarde, Maria Perschy.

PAT GARRETT AND BILLY THE KID (P) 106
METRO-GOLDWYN-MAYER. (R) May, 1973. James Coburn, Kris Kristofferson. Color.

PATCH OF BLUE, A (P) 105
METRO-GOLDWYN-MAYER. (R) March, 1966. Sidney Poitier, Shelley Winters.

PATHS OF GLORY 88
UNITED ARTISTS. (R) January, 1958. Kirk Douglas, Ralph Meeker.

PATSY, THE 103
PARAMOUNT. (R) July, 1964. Jerry Lewis, Ina Balin. Color.

PATTERNS 83
UNITED ARTISTS. (R) March, 1956. Van Heflin, Ed Begley, Everett Sloane.

PATTON (D-150) 170
20th CENTURY-FOX. (R) February, 1970. George C. Scott, Karl Malden. Color.

PAUL AND MICHELLE (P) 103
PARAMOUNT. (R) May, 1974. Anicee Alvina, Sean Bury, Keir Dullea.

PAWNBROKER, THE 110
ALLIED ARTISTS-LANDAU. (R) April, 1965. Rod Stieger, Geraldine Fitzgerald.

PAWNEE 80
REPUBLIC. (R) September, 1957. George Montgomery, Bill Williams. Color.

PAY OR DIE 111
ALLIED ARTISTS. (R) July, 1960. Ernest Borgnine, Zohra Lampert.

PAYDAY 103
CINERAMA. (R) February, 1973. Rip Torn, Anna Capri. Color.

PAYMENT IN BLOOD 90
COLUMBIA. (R) December, 1968. Guy Madison, Edd Byrnes, Louise Barrett. Color.

PAYROLL 94
ALLIED ARTISTS. (R) July, 1962. Michael Craig, Francoise Prevost.

PEACEMAKER, THE 82
UNITED ARTISTS. (R) November, 1956. James Mitchell, Risemari Bowe.

PEACH THIEF 84
BRANDON. (R) September, 1969. Nevena Kokanova, Mikhail Mikhailov. b&w.

PEARL OF THE SOUTH PACIFIC (SS) 85
RKO RADIO. (R) July 4, 1955. Virginia Mayo, Dennis Morgan, David Farrar. Color.

PEEPER 87
TWENTIETH CENTURY-FOX. (R) September, 1975. Michael Caine, Natalie Wood.

PENDULUM 106
COLUMBIA. (R) January, 1969. George Peppard, Jean Seberg, Richard Riley. Color.

PENELOPE (P) 97
METRO-GOLDWYN-MAYER. (R) December, 1966. Natalie Wood, Ian Bannen. Color.

PENTHOUSE, THE 100
PARAMOUNT. (R) October, 1967. Suzy Kendall, Terence Morgan. Color.

PEOPLE NEXT DOOR, THE 93
AVCO EMBASSY. (R) September, 1970. Julie Harris, Eli Wallach, Deborah Winters. Color.

PEOPLE THAT TIME FORGOT, THE 90
AMERICAN INTERNATIONAL. (R) July, 1977. Patrick Wayne, Doug McClure.

PEPE (Cs) 195
COLUMBIA. (R) Special. December, 1960. Cantinflas, Dan Dailey. Color.

PERCY 103
MGM. (R) April, 1971. Hywel Bennett, Elke Sommer. Color.

PERFECT COUPLE, A 110
TWENTIETH CENTURY-FOX. (R) April, 1979. Paul Dooley, Marta Heflin.

PERFECT FRIDAY 94
CHEVRON. (R) October, 1970. Stanley Baker, Ursula Andress. Color.

PERFECT FURLOUGH, THE (Cs) 93
UNIVERSAL. (R) January, 1959. Tony Curtis, Janet Leigh. Color.

PERFORMANCE 106
WARNER BROS. (R) August, 1970. James Fox, Mick Jagger. Color.

PERILS OF PAULINE 90
UNIVERSAL. (R) July, 1967. Pat Boone, Pamela Austin. Color.

PERIOD OF ADJUSTMENT 112

Length In Mins.

PARAMOUNT. (R) June, 1979. Ali MacGraw, Dean-Paul Martin.

PLAYGIRL AND THE WAR MINISTER, THE 90
UNION. (R) November, 1963. Joan Greenwood, Cecil Parker.

PLAZA SUITE 115
PARAMOUNT. (R) June, 1971. Walter Matthau, Maureen Stapleton. Color.

PLEASE DON'T EAT THE DAISIES (Cs) 111
METRO-GOLDWYN-MAYER. (R) April, 1960. Doris Day, David Niven. Color.

PLEASE! MR. BALZAC (Fr.) 99
DIST. CORP. OF AMER. (R) October, 1957. Daniel Gelin, Brigitte Bardot.

PLEASE MURDER ME 78
DISTRIBUTORS CORP. OF AMERICA. (R) March, 1956. Angela Lansbury, Raymond Burr.

PLEASE TURN OVER 86
COLUMBIA. (R) December, 1960. Ted Ray, Jean Kent.

PLEASURE OF HIS COMPANY, THE 114
PARAMOUNT. (R) August, 1961. Fred Astaire, Debbie Reynolds. Color.

PLEASURE SEEKERS, THE (Cs) 107
TWENTIETH CENTURY-FOX. (R) January, 1965. Ann-Margaret, Carol Lynley. Color.

PLUNDER ROAD (R) 72
TWENTIETH CENTURY-FOX. (R) December, 1957. Gene Raymond, Carolyn Craig.

PLUNDERERS, THE 94
ALLIED ARTISTS. (R) November, 1960. Jeff Chandler, John Saxon.

PLUNDERERS OF PAINTED FLATS (N) 72
REPUBLIC. (R) January, 1959. Corine Calvet, John Carroll.

POACHER'S DAUGHTER, THE 74
SHOW CORP. OF AMERICA. (R) June, 1960. Julie Harris, Harry Brogan.

POCKET MONEY 102
NATIONAL GENERAL. (R) February. 1972. Paul Newman, Lee Marvin. Color.

POCKETFUL OF MIRACLES (P) 136
UNITED ARTISTS. (R) December, 1961. Glenn Ford, Bette Davis. Color.

POE'S TALES OF TERROR 90
AMERICAN INTERNATIONAL. (R) August, 1962. Vincent Price, Peter Lorre. Color.

POINT BLANK (P) 92
MGM. (R) October, 1967. Lee Marvin, Angie Dickinson. Color.

POINT OF ORDER 97
POINT FILMS. (R) January, 1964. McCarthy hearings.

POLICE DOG STORY, THE 62
UNITED ARTISTS. (R) February, 1961. Jim Brown, Merry Anders.

POLICE NURSE 64
TWENTIETH CENTURY-FOX. (R) May, 1963. Ken Scott, Merry Anders.

POLLYANA 134
BUENA VISTA. (R) July, 1960. Hayley Mills, Jane Wyman. Color.

POOR COW 104
NATIONAL GENERAL CORPORATION. (R) February, 1968. Terence Stamp, Carol White. Color.

POP CORN 85
SHERPIX. (R) December, 1970. Mick Jagger & The Rolling Stones, Jim Hendrix. Color.

POP! 115
UNITED ARTISTS. (R) June, 1969. Alan Arkin, Rito Moreno, Miguel Alehandro. Color.

POPPY IS ALSO A FLOWER, THE 100
COMET. (R) October, 1966. Senta Berger, Stephen Boyd. Color.

PORGY AND BESS (Todd-AO) 146
COLUMBIA. (R) Special. June, 1959. Sidney Poitier, Dorothy Dandridge. Color.

PORK CHOP HILL 97
UNITED ARTISTS. (R) May, 1959. Gregory Peck.

PORT AFRIQUE 92
COLUMBIA. (R) October, 1956. Phil Carey, Pier Angeli. Color.

PORTLAND EXPOSE 72
ALLIED ARTISTS. (R) August, 1957. Edward Binns, Carolyn Craig.

PORTNOY'S COMPLAINT 101
WARNER BROS. (R) July, 1972. Richard Benjamin, Karen Black, Lee Grant. Color.

PORTRAIT IN BLACK 112
UNIVERSAL. (R) July, 1960. Lana Turner, Anthony Quinn. Color.

PORTRAIT OF A MOBSTER 108
WARNER BROS. (R) April, 1961. Vic Morrow, Leslie Parrish.

PORTRAIT OF A SINNER 96

Length In Mins.

AMERICAN INTERNATIONAL. (R) February, 1961. Nadja Tiller, Tony Britton.

PORTRAIT OF AN UNKNOWN WOMAN 86
UNIVERSAL. (R) May, 1958. Ruth Leuwerik, O.W. Fisher.

POSEIDON ADVENTURE, THE (P) 117
TWENTIETH CENTURY-FOX. (R) December, 1972. Gene Hackman, Shelley Winters, Ernest Borgnine. Color.

POSSE FROM HELL 89
UNIVERSAL. (R) May, 1969. Audie Murphy, John Saxon. Color.

POSSESSION OF JOEL DELANEY, THE 105
PARAMOUNT. (R) May, 1972. Shirley MacLaine, Perry King. Color.

POSTMARK FOR DANGER 84
RKO RADIO. (R) January 1956. Terry Moore. Robert Beatty.

POUND 92
UNITED ARTISTS. (R) August, 1970. Joe Madden, James Green. Color.

POWER (P) 109
MGM. (R) February, 1968. George Hamilton, Suzanne Pleshette. Color.

POWER AND THE PRIZE, THE (Cs) 89
METRO-GOLDWYN-MAYER. (R) October, 1956. Robert Taylor, Elizabeth Mueller.

PREMATURE BURIAL 8
AMERICAN INTERNATIONAL. (R) March, 1962. Ray Milland, Hazel Court. Color.

PREMONITION, THE 95
AVCO-EMBASSY. (R) February, 1976. Sharon Farrell, Richard Lynch.

PRESIDENT'S ANALYST, THE (P) 104
PARAMOUNT. (R) December, 1967. James Coburn, Godfrey Cambridge. Color.

PRESSURE POINT 91
UNITED ARTISTS. (R) September, 1962. Sidney Poitier, Bobby Darin.

PRETTY BABY 109
PARAMOUNT. (R) April, 1978. Brooke Shields, Keith Carradine.

PRETTY MAIDS ALL IN A ROW 92
MGM. (R) May, 1971. Rock Hudson, Angie Dickinson. Color.

PRETTY POISON 89
TWENTIETH CENTURY-FOX. (R) September, 1968. Anthony Perkins, Tuesday Weld, Beverly Garland. Color.

PRICE OF FEAR, THE 79
UNIVERSAL. (R) May, 1956. Merle Oberon, Lex Barker.

PRIDE AND THE PASSION, THE (VV) 182
UNITED ARTISTS. (R) July, 1957. Cary Grant, Frank Sinatra. Color.

PRIEST'S WIFE, THE 106
WARNER BROS. (R) February, 1971. Marcello Mastroianni, Sophia Loren. Color.

PRIME CUT 91
NATIONAL GENERAL. (R) June, 1972. Gene Hackman, Lee Marvin. Color.

PRIME OF MISS JEAN BRODIE, THE 116
TWENTIETH CENTURY-FOX. (R) March, 1969. Maggie Smith, Robert Stephens, Pamela Franklin. Color.

PRIME TIME, THE 70
ESSANJAY. (R) May, 1960. JoAnn Le Compte, Frank Roche.

PRINCE AND THE SHOWGIRL, THE 117
WARNER BROS. (R) July, 1957. Marilyn Monroe, Laurence Olivier. Color.

PRISONER, THE (Brit.) 91
COLUMBIA. (R) March, 1956. Alec Guinness, Jack Hawkins.

PRISONER OF SECOND AVENUE, THE (P) 99
WARNER BROS. (R) March, 1975. Jack Lemmon, Anne Bancroft.

PRISONER OF THE IRON MARK 80
AMER. INT'L PICS. (R) 1969. Michael Lemoine, Wandisa Guida. Color.

PRISONER OF THE VOLGA (Totalscope) 102
PARAMOUNT. (R) May, 1960. John Derek, Elsa Martinelli. Color.

PRISONER OF ZENDA, THE 108
UNIVERSAL. (R) May, 1979. Peter Sellers, Lionel Jeffries.

PRIVATE LIFE OF SHERLOCK HOLMES, THE (P) 125
UNITED ARTISTS. (R) November, 1970. Robert Stephens, Colin Blakely. Color.

PRIVATE LIVES OF ADAM AND EVE, THE 87
UNIVERSAL. (R) December, 1960. Mickey Rooney, Mamie Van Doren.

PRIVATE NAVY OF SGT. O'FARRELL, THE 92

	Length In Mins.

UNITED ARTISTS. (R) June, 1968. Bob Hope, Phyllis Diller. Color.

PRIVATE PROPERTY. 79
CITATION FILMS. (R) April, 1960. Kate Manx, Corey Allen.

PRIVATE WAR OF MAJOR BENSON, THE 105
UNIVERSAL. (R) August, 1955. Charlton Heston, Julie Adams. Color.

PRIVATE'S AFFAIRS, A (Cs) 105
TWENTIETH CENTURY-FOX. (R) August, 1959. Sal Mineo, Christine Carere. Color.

PRIVATE'S PROGRESS (Brit.) 96
DISTRIBUTORS CORPORATION OF AMERICA. (R) September, 1956. Richard Attenborough, Dennis Price, Ian Carmichael. Color.

PRIVILEGE 103
UNIVERSAL. (R) September, 1967. Paul Jones, Jean Shrimpton. Color.

PRIZE, THE 136
METRO-GOLDWYN-MAYER. (R) December, 1963. Paul Newman, Edward G. Robinson. Color.

PRIZE OF GOLD, A 98
COLUMBIA. (R) June, 1955. Richard Widmark, Mai Zetterling. Color.

PRODIGAL, THE (Cs) 110
METRO-GOLDWYN-MAYER. (R) May 6, 1955. Lana Turner, Edmund Purdom. Color.

PRODUCERS, THE 88
EMBASSY. (R) June, 1968. Zero Mostel, Gene Wilder. Color.

PROFESSIONALS, THE (P) 117
COLUMBIA. (R) November, 1966. Burt Lancaster, Lee Marvin. Color.

PROFESSIONALS, THE 68
AMERICAN INTERNATIONAL (R) July, 1961.

PROJECT X 97
PARAMOUNT. (R) June, 1968. Christopher George, Greta Baldwin, Monte Markham. Color.

PROJECTED MAN, THE (TE) 77
UNIVERSAL. (R) February, 1967. Bryant Haliday, Mary Peach. Color.

PROJECTIONIST, THE 85
TED MARON. (R) January, 1971. Chuck McCann, Ina Balin. Color.

PROMISE, THE (P) 97
UNIVERSAL. (R) March, 1979. Kathleen Quinlan, Stephen Collins.

PROMISE AT DAWN 103
AVCO EMBASSY. (R) January, 1971. Melina Mercouri, Assaf Dagan. Color.

PROMISE HER ANYTHING 98
PARAMOUNT. (R) March, 1966. Warren Beatty, Leslie Caron. Color.

PROMISES IN THE DARK 115
WARNER BROS. (R) November, 1979. Marsha Mason, Ned Beatty.

PROUD AND THE BEAUTIFUL, THE (Fr.) 94
KINGSLYE. (R) June, 1956. Michele Morgan, Gerard Philipe.

PROUD AND THE PROFANE, THE (VV) 111
PARAMOUNT. (R) August, 1956. William Holden, Deborah Kerr.

PROUD ONES, THE (Cs) 94
TWENTIETH CENTURY-FOX. (R) May, 1956. Robert Ryan, Virginia Mayo, Jeffrey Hunter. Color.

PROUD REBEL, THE 105
BUENA VISTA (DISNEY.) (R) June, 1958. Alan Ladd, Olivia De Haviland. Color.

PROVIDENCE 104
CINEMA 5. (R) February, 1977. Ellen Burstyn, Dirk Bogarde, John Gielgud. Color.

PRUDENCE AND THE PILL 92
TWENTIETH CENTURY-FOX. (R) July, 1968. Deborah Kerr, David Niven, Robert Coote. Color.

PSYCHE 59 94
ROYAL. (R) April, 1964. Curt Jergens, Patricia Neal.

PSYCHE OUT 98
AMERICAN INTERNATIONAL. (R) April, 1968. Susan Strasberg, Jack Nicholson. Color.

PSYCHIC KILLER 90
AVCO EMBASSY. (R) December, 1975. Jim Hutton, Julie Adams.

PSYCHO 109
PARAMOUNT. (R) August, 1960. Anthony Perkins, Vera Miles.

PSYCHO CIRCUS 65
AMERICAN INTERNATIONAL. (R) May, 1967. Christopher Lee, Leo Genn.

PSYCHOUT FOR MURDER (WS) 88
TIMES FILM (R) January, 1971. Rosanno Brazzi, Adrienne La Russa. Color.

PSYCOPATH, THE (TE) 83

	Length In Mins.

PARAMOUNT. (R) May 1966. Patrick Wymark, Margaret Johnson. Color.

PT 109 (P) 140
WARNER BROS. (R) July, 1963. Cliff Robertson, Ty Hardin. Color.

PUBLIC EYE, THE 90
UNIVERSAL. (R) August, 1972. Mia Farrow, Topol, Michael Jayston. Color.

PUBLIC PIGEON NO. ONE 79
UNIVERSAL. (R) June, 1957. Red Skelton, Vivian Blaine. Color.

PUFNSTUF 94
UNIVERSAL. (R) June, 1970. Jack Wild, Billie Hayes, Martha Raye. Color.

PULP 95
UNITED ARTISTS. (R) October, 1972. Michael Caine, Mickey Rooney. Color.

PUMPKIN EATER, THE 110
ROYAL INT. (R) November, 1964. Ann Bancroft, Peter Finch.

PUPPET ON A CHAIN 97
CINERAMA. (R) April, 1972. Sven-Bertil Taube, Barbara Parkins. Color.

PURPLE GANG, THE 83
ALLIED ARTISTS. (R) January, 1960. Barry Sullivan, Robert Blake.

PURPLE HILLS, THE (CS) 60
TWENTIETH CENTURY-FOX. (R) October, 1961. Gene Nelson, Joanna Barnes. Color.

PURPLE MASK, THE (Cs) 82
UNIVERSAL. (R) July, 1955. Tony Curtis, Colleen Miller. Color.

PURPLE PLAIN, THE (Brit.) 100
UNITED ARTISTS. (R) April, 1955. Gregory Peck, Win Min Than. Color.

PURSUIT OF HAPPINESS, THE 98
COLUMBIA. (R) February, 1971. Michael Sarrazin, Barbara Hershey. Color.

PURSUIT OF THE GRAF SPEE (VV) 106
RANK. (R) November, 1957. John Gregson, Anthony Quayle. Color.

PUSHER, THE 81
UNITED ARTISTS. (R) January, 1960. Kathy Carlyle, Felice Orlandi.

PUSSYCAT, PUSSYCAT, I LOVE YOU 99
UNITED ARTISTS. (R) March, 1970. Ian McShane, John Gavin, Severn Darden. Color.

PUTNEY SWOPE 84
CINEMA 5. (R) July, 1969. Stanley Gottlieb, Allen Garfield. b&w.

PUZZLE OF A DOWNFALL CHILD 104
UNIVERSAL. (R) November, 1970. Faye Dunaway, Barry Primus. Color.

PYRO 99
AMERICAN INTERNATIONAL. (R) April, 1964. Barry Sullivan, Martha Hyer.

PYX, THE (P) 111
CINERAMA. (R) October, 1973. Karen Black, Christopher Plummer.

Q

QUACKSER FORTUNE HAS A COUSIN IN THE BRONX 90
UMC. (R) July, 1970. Gene Wilder, Margot Kidder. Color.

QUANTEZ (Cs) 80
UNIVERSAL. (R) October, 1957. Fred MacMurray, Dorothy Malone. Color.

QUANTRILL'S RAIDERS (Cs) 75
ALLIED ARTISTS. (R) April 27, 1958. Steve Cochran, Gale Robbins. Color.

QUARE FELLOW, THE 85
AJAY PICTURES. (R) October, 1966. Patrick McGoohan, Sylvia Syms.

QUE SEAS FELIZ (Span.) 102
COLUMBIA. (R) March, 1960. Miguel Acoves Mevia, Rosita Quintana.

QUEEN, THE 68
GROVE PRESS. (R) June, 1968. Documentary. Color.

QUEEN BEE 95
COLUMBIA. (R) November, 1955. Joan Crawford, Barry Sullivan.

QUEEN OF BABYLON (Ital.-Eng. dial.) 109
TWENTIETH CENTURY-FOX. (R) July, 1956. Rhonda Fleming, Ricardo Montalban. Color.

QUEEN OF BLOOD 81
AMERICAN INTERNATIONAL. (R) March, 1966. John Saxon, Basil Rathbone. Color.

QUEEN OF OUTER SPACE (Cs) 80

Length In Mins.

ALLIED ARTISTS. (R) September, 1958. Zsa Zsa Gabor, Eric Fleming. Color.

QUEEN OF THE PIRATES 80
COLUMBIA. (R) August, 1961. Gianna Maria Canale, Massimo Serato.

QUEENS, THE 110
ROYAL. (R) March, 1968. Raquel Welch, Claudia Cardinale. Color.

QUENTIN DURWARD (Cs) 101
METRO-GOLDWYN-MAYER. (R) October 21, 1955. Robert Taylor, Kay Kendall, Robert Morley. Color.

QUEST FOR A LOST CITY 60
RKO RADIO. (R) May 4, 1955. Dana and Ginger Lamb. Color.

QUICK BEFORE IT MELTS (CP) 98
METRO-GOLDWYN-MAYER. (R) February, 1965. George Maharis, Robert Morse. Color.

QUICK GUN, THE (T) 88
COLUMBIA. (R) May, 1964. Audie Murphy, Merry Anders. Color.

QUIET AMERICAN, THE 120
UNITED ARTISTS. (R) January, 1958. Audie Murphy, Michael Redgrave. Color.

QUIET GUN, THE 77
TWENTIETH CENTURY-FOX. (R) January, 1957. Forrest Tucker, Cleo Moore.

QUIET PLACE IN THE COUNTRY, A 106
LOPERT. (R) August, 1970. Franco Nero, Vanessa Redgrave. Color.

QUILLER MEMORANDUM (P) 105
TWENTIETH CENTURY-FOX. (R) January, 1967. George Segal, Alec Guinness. Color.

QUINCANNON, FRONTIER SCOUT 83
UNITED ARTISTS. (R) May, 1956. Tony Martin, Peggie Castle. Color.

QUINTET 122
TWENTIETH CENTURY-FOX. (R) February, 1979. Paul Newman, Vittorio Gassman.

R

R.P.M.* 92
COLUMBIA. (R) September, 1970. Anthony Quinn, Ann-Margret. Color.

RA EXPEDITIONS, THE 93
UNIVERSAL. (R) August, 1974. Documentary.

RABBIT, RUN 94
WARNER BROS. (R) October, 1970. James Caan, Anjanette Comer. Color.

RABBIT TRAP, THE 75
UNITED ARTISTS. (R) June, 1959. Ernest Borgnine, David Brian.

RACE FEVER 90
ALLIED ARTISTS. (R) March, 1965. Joe Morrison, David Blanchard. Color.

RACE WITH THE DEVIL 88
TWENTIETH CENTURY-FOX. (R) June, 1975. Peter Fonda, Warren Oates.

RACERS, THE (Cs) 112
TWENTIETH CENTURY-FOX. (R) February, 1955. Kirk Douglas, Bella Darvi, Gilbert Roland. Color.

RACHEL, RACHEL 101
WARNER BROS.-7 ARTS. September, 1968. Joanne Woodward, James Olsen, Kate Harrington. Color.

RACK, THE 100
METRO-GOLDWYN-MAYER. (R) November 2, 1956. Paul Newman, Walter Pidgeon, Wendell Corey, Edmond O'Brien, Anne Francis.

RAFFERTY AND THE GOLD DUST TWINS (P) 92
WARNER BROS. (R) February, 1975. Alan Arkin, Sally Kellerman.

RAGE (P) 100
WARNER BROS. (R) November, 1972. George C. Scott, Richard Basehart. Color.

RAGE 103
COLUMBIA. (R) December, 1966. Glenn Ford, Stella Stevens. Color.

RAGE AT DAWN 87
RKO RADIO. (R) March 26, 1955. Randolph Scott, Mala Powers. Color.

RAGE TO LIVE, A (P) 101
UNITED ARTISTS. (R) May, 1965. Suzanne Pleshette, Ben Gazzara. b&w.

RAGGEDY ANN & ANDY (P) 84
TWENTIETH CENTURY-FOX. (R) April, 1977. Animated cartoon.

RAID ON ROMMEL 99
UNIVERSAL. (R) February, 1971. Richard Burton, Wolfgang Preiss.

RAIDERS, THE 80

Length In Mins.

UNIVERSAL. (R) November 1952. Richard Conte, Viveca Lindfors. Color.

RAIDERS, THE 75
UNIVERSAL. (R) May, 1964. Robert Culp, Brian Keith. Color.

RAIDERS FROM BENEATH THE SEA, THE 78
TWENTIETH CENTURY-FOX. (R) January, 1965. Ken Scott, Merry Anders.

RAIDERS OF LEYTE GULF, THE 80
HEMISPHERE. (R) July, 1963. Jennings Sturgeon, Efren Reves.

RAIDERS OF OLD CALIFORNIA 72
REPUBLIC. (R) November, 1957. Jim Davis, Arleen Whelan.

RAILROAD MAN, THE (Ital., Eng. Titles) 105
CONTINENTAL. (R) October, 1965. Pietro Germi, Luisa Della Noce.

RAILWAY CHILDREN, THE 108
UNIVERSAL. (R) October, 1971. Dinah Sheridan, Bernard Cribbens, Jenny Agutter. Color.

RAIN PEOPLE, THE 101
(R) September, 1969. James Caan, Shirley Knight, Robert Duvall. Color.

RAINMAKER, THE (VV) 121
PARAMOUNT. (R) February, 1957. Katharine Hepburn, Burt Lancaster. Color.

RAINS OF RANCHIPUR, THE (Cs) 104
TWENTIETH CENTURY-FOX. (R) December, 1955. Lana Turner, Richard Burton, Fred MacMurray, Joan Caulfield, Michael Rennie. Color.

RAINTREE COUNTY (Camera 65) 185
METRO-GOLDWYN-MAYER. (R) Special. October, 1957. Elizabeth Taylor, Montgomery Clift. Color.

RAISE THE TITANIC (T) 122
ASSOCIATED FILM DIST. (R) August, 1980. Jason Robards, Richard Jordan.

RAISIN IN THE SUN, A 128
COLUMBIA. (R) April, 1961. Sidney Poitier, Claudia McNeil.

RAISING A RIOT (Brit.) 90
CONTINENTAL. (R) May, 1957. Kenneth More, Ronald Squire. Color.

RALLY 'ROUND THE FLAG BOYS! (Cs) 106
TWENTIETH CENTURY-FOX. (R) February, 1959. Paul Newman, Joanne Woodward. Color.

RAMPAGE 98
WARNER BROS. (R) October, 1963. Robert Mitchum, Elsa Martinelli. Color.

RAMPARTS OF CLAY 85
CINEMA 5. (R) February, 1971. Leila Schenna. Color.

RANCHO DELUXE 93
UNITED ARTISTS. (R) March, 1975. Jeff Bridges, Sam Waterston.

RANSOM! 104
METRO-GOLDWYN-MAYER. (R) January 20, 1956. Glenn Ford, Donna Reed.

RAPE OF MALAYA, THE (Brit.) 107
LOPERT. (R) 1956. Virginia McKenna, Peter Finch.

RAPTURE (Cs) 105
INTERNATIONAL CLASSICS. (R) September, 1965. Melvyn Douglas, Dean Stockwell.

RARE BREED, THE (P) 97
UNIVERSAL. (R) February, 1966. James Stewart, Maureen O'Hara. Color.

RASCAL 85
BUENA VISTA. June, 1969. Steve Forrest, Bill Mumy, Elsa Lanchester. Color.

RASPUTIN—THE MAD MONK (Cs) 92
TWENTIETH CENTURY-FOX. (R) April, 1966. Christopher Lee, Barbara Shelley. Color.

RAT FINK 90
CINEMA DISTRIBUTORS OF AMERICA. (R) February, 1966. Schuyler Hayden.

RAT RACE, THE 105
PARAMOUNT. (R) July, 1960. Tony Curtis, Debbie Reynolds. Color.

RATTLE OF A SIMPLE MAN 96
READE-STERLING. (R) December, 1964. Harry H. Corbett, Diane Cilento.

RAVAGERS, THE 79
HEMISPHERE. (R) December, 1965. John Saxon, Fernando Poe, Jr.

RAVEN'S END (Danish; Eng. Titles) 100
NEW YORKER. (R) August, 1970. Thommy Berggren, Keve Hjelm.

RAW EDGE 76
UNIVERSAL. (R) September, 1956. Rory Calhoun, Yvonne de Carlo. Color.

RAW WIND IN EDEN (Cs) 89
UNIVERSAL. (R) October, 1958. Esther Williams, Jeff Chandler. Color.

RAWHIDE BREED 68

Length In Mins.

NATIONAL GENERAL. (R) June, 1972. William Holden, Ernest Borgnine. Color.

REVOLT AT FORT LARAMIE 78
UNITED ARTISTS. (R) March, 1957. John Dhener, Gregg Palmer. Color.

REVOLT IN THE BIG HOUSE 79
ALLIED ARTISTS. (R) November, 1958. Gene Evans, Robert Blake.

REVOLT OF MAMIE STOVER, THE (Cs) 98
TWENTIETH CENTURY-FOX. (R) April, 1956. Jane Russell, Richard Egan. Color.

REVOLT OF THE SLAVES, THE 99
UNITED ARTISTS. (R) May, 1961. Rhonda Fleming, Lang Jeffries. Color.

REVOLUTION 86
LOPERT. (R) August, 1968. Documentary. Color.

REVOLUTIONARY, THE 100
UNITED ARTISTS. (R) July, 1970. Jon Voight, Jennifer Salt, Seymour Cassel. Color.

REWARD, THE (Cs) 92
TWENTIETH CENTURY-FOX. (R) October, 1965. Max Von Sydow, Yvette Mimieux. Color.

RHINO! 91
METRO-GOLDWYN-MAYER. (R) May, 1964. Harry Guardino, Robert Culp. Color.

RHINOCEROS 101
AFT DISTRIBUTING. (R) Special, 1974. Zero Mostel, Gene Wilder, Karen Black.

RICH KIDS 96
UNITED ARTISTS. (R) August, 1979. Trini Alvarado, Jeremy Levy.

RICHARD III (Brit.) (VV) 155
LOPERT. (R) March, 1956. Laurence Olivier, Claire Bloom, Ralph Richardson, John Gielgud. Color.

RIDE A CROOKED TRAIL (Cs) 87
UNIVERSAL. (R) September, 1958. Audie Murphy, Gia Scala. Color.

RIDE A VIOLENT MILE 80
TWENTIETH CENTURY-FOX. (R) December, 1957. John Agar, Penny Edwards.

RIDE A WILD PONY 91
BUENA VISTA. (R) April, 1976. Michael Craig, John Meillon.

RIDE BACK, THE 79
UNITED ARTISTS. (R) May, 1957. Anthony Quinn, William Conrad.

RIDE BEYOND VENGEANCE 108
COLUMBIA. (R) April, 1966. Chuck Connors, Michael Rennie. Color.

RIDE LONESOME (Cs) 73
COLUMBIA. (R) February, 1959. Randolph Scott, Karen Steele. Color.

RIDE OUT FOR REVENGE 79
UNITED ARTISTS. (R) November, 1957. Rory Calhoun, Gloria Grahame.

RIDE THE HIGH COUNTRY (Cs) 94
METRO-GOLDWYN-MAYER. (R) May, 1962. Randolph Scott, Joel McCrea. Color.

RIDE THE HIGH IRON 74
COLUMBIA. (R) January, 1957. Don Taylor, Sally Forrest.

RIDE THE WILD SURF 101
COLUMBIA. (R) July, 1964. Fabian, Tab Hunter. Color.

RIDE TO HANGMAN'S TREE, THE 90
UNIVERSAL. (R) July, 1967. Jack Lord, James Farentino. Color.

RIDE, VAQUERO 90
MGM. (R) July 17, 1958. Robert Taylor, Ava Gardner, Howard Keel. Color.

RIDER ON A DEAD HORSE 72
ALLIED ARTISTS. (R) May, 1962. John Vivyan. Lisalu.

RIDER ON THE RAIN (French; Eng. Titles) 115
AVCO EMBASSY. (R) May, 1970. Marlene Jobert, Charles Bronson, Annie Cordy. Color.

RIFIFI (Fr.) 118
UMPO. (R) June, 1956. Jean Servais, Carl Mohner.

RIFIFI IN TOKYO 89
METRO-GOLDWYN-MAYER. (R) April, 1963. Karl Boehm, Michael Vitold.

RIGHT APPROACH, THE (Cs) 92
TWENTIETH CENTURY-FOX. (R) May, 1961. Frankie Vaughn, Juliet Prowse.

RING-A-DING RHYTHM! 78
COLUMBIA. (R) September, 1962. Helen Shapiro, Craig Douglas.

RING OF BRIGHT WATER 107
CINERAMA. (R) June, 1969. Bill Travers, Virginia McKenna. Color.

RING OF FIRE 91
METRO-GOLDWYN-MAYER. (R) May, 1961. David Janssen, Joyce Taylor. Color.

RING OF TREASON 89

PARAMOUNT. (R) June, 1964. Bernard Lee, Margaret Tyzack.

RINGS AROUND THE WORLD 98
COLUMBIA. (R) September, 1966. Circus Documentary narrated by Don Ameche. Color.

RIO BRAVO (C) 141
WARNER BROS. (R) April, 1959. John Wayne, Dean Martin.

RIO CONCHOS (Cs) 107
TWENTIETH CENTURY-FOX. (R) October, 1964. Richard Boone, Stuart Whitman. Color.

RIO LOBO (P) 114
NATIONAL GENERAL. (R) December, 1970. John Wayne, Jorge Rivero. Color.

RIOT 97
PARAMOUNT. (R) January, 1969. Jim Brown, Gene Hackman, Ben Carruthers. Color.

RIOT IN JUVENILE PRISON 71
UNITED ARTISTS. (R) April, 1959. John Hoyt, Marcia Henderson.

RIOT ON SUNSET STRIP 85
AMERICAN INTERNATIONAL. (R) March, 1967. Aldo Ray, Mimsy Farmer. Color.

RIP OFF 90
J. CINEMAX. (R) September, 1972. Don Scardino, Ralph Endersby. Color.

RISE AND FALL OF LEGS DIAMOND, THE 101
WARNER BROS. (R) February, 1960. Ray Danton, Karen Stecie.

RISING OF THE MOON, THE 81
WARNER BROS. (R) August, 1957. Frank Lawton, Dennis O'Day.

RITUAL, THE (Swedish; Eng. Titles) 75
JANUS. (R) September, 1969. Ingrid Thulin, Anders Ek.

RITZ, THE 91
WARNER BROS. (R) September, 1976. Jack Weston, Rita Moreno.

RIVALS 101
AVCO-EMBASSY. (R) August, 1972. Joan Hackett, Scott Jacoby. Color.

RIVER CHANGES, THE 91
WARNER BROTHERS (R) March 24, 1956. Rossana Rory, Harold Maresch.

RIVERRUN 87
COLUMBIA. (R) April, 1970. John McLiam, Louise Ober, Mark Jenkins. Color.

RIVERS EDGE, THE (Cs) 87
TWENTIETH CENTURY-FOX. April, 1957. Ray Milland, Debra Paget, Anthony Quinn. Color.

RIVIERA (Ital.-Eng. dubbed) 68
I.F.E. (R) September. 1956. Martine Carol. Color.

ROAD HOUSE GIRL (Brit.) 68
ASTOR. (R) June, 1955. Sandra Dorn, Marwell Reed.

ROAD TO DENVER 90
REPUBLIC. (R) June, 16, 1955. John Payne, Mona Freeman. Color.

ROAD TO HONG KONG, THE 91
UNITED ARTISTS. (R) June, 1962. Bing Crosby, Bob Hope.

ROAD TO SALINA (P) 96
AVCO-EMBASSY. (R) February, 1971. Rita Hayworth, Robert Walker. Color.

ROADIE (P) 105
UNITED ARTISTS. (R) June, 1980. Meat Loaf, Kaki Hunter.

ROADRACERS, THE 78
AMERICAN INTERNATIONAL. (R) March, 1959. Joel Lawrence, Marian Collier.

ROBBER'S ROOST 82
UNITED ARTISTS. (R) May, 1955. Robert Montgomery, Richard Boone.

ROBBERY 113
EMBASSY. (R) October, 1967. Stanley Baker, Joanna Pettet. Color.

ROBBERY UNDER ARMS 83
RANK FILM DISTRIBUTORS OF AMERICA. (R) May, 1958. Peter Finch, Ronald Lewis. Color.

ROBIN AND MARIAN 107
COLUMBIA. (R) April, 1976. Sean Connery, Audrey Hepburn.

ROBIN AND THE SEVEN HOODS (P) 123
WARNER BROS. (R) June, 1964. Frank Sinatra, Dean Martin. Color.

ROBIN HOOD 83
BUENA VISTA. (R) December, 1973. Cartoon.

ROBINSON CRUSOE ON MARS (Ts) 110
PARAMOUNT. (R) June, 1964. Paul Mantee, Vic Lundin. Color.

ROCK-A-BYE (VV) 108
PARAMOUNT. (R) July, 1958. Jerry Lewis, Marilyn Maxwell. Color.

ROCK ALL NIGHT 65

Length In Mins.

UNITED ARTISTS. (R) May, 1966. Carl Reiner, Eva Marie Saint, Alan Arkin.

RX MURDER (Cs) 65
TWENTIETH CENTURY-FOX. (R) August, 1958. Rick Jason, Marius Goring.

S

S.O.S. PACIFIC 92
UNIVERSAL. (R) July, 1960. Eddie Constantine, Pier Angeli.

S*P*Y*S 87
TWENTIETH CENTURY-FOX. (R) June, 1974. Elliott Gould, Donald Sutherland.

SABAKA 81
UNITED ARTISTS. (R) February, 1955. Boris Karloff, Reginald Denny. Color.

SABATA (TE) 107
UNITED ARTISTS. (R) October, 1970. Lee Van Cleef, William Berger. Color.

SABU AND THE MAGIC RING 61
ALLIED ARTISTS. (R) March, 1958. Sabu, William Marshall.

SACCO AND VANZETTI 120
UMC. (R) November, 1971. Gian Maria Volonte, Riccardo Cucciolla. Color.

SAD HORSE, THE (Cs) 81
TWENTIETH CENTURY-FOX. (R) March, 1959. David Ladd, Chill Wills. Color.

SAD SACK, THE (VV) 98
PARAMOUNT. (R) December, 1957. Jerry Lewis, David Wayne.

SADDLE THE WIND (Cs) 84
METRO-GOLDWYN-MAYER. (R) March, 1958. Robert Taylor, Julie London. Color.

SAFARI (Cs) 91
COLUMBIA. (R) June, 1956. Victor Mature, Janet Leigh. Color.

SAFE AT HOME 83
COLUMBIA. (R) April, 1962. Mickey Mantle, Roger Maris.

SAFE CRACKER, THE 96
METRO-GOLDWYN-MAYER. (R) January, 1958. Ray Milland, Barry Jones.

SAFE PLACE, A 94
COLUMBIA. (R) October, 1971. Tuesday Weld, Orson Welles. Color.

SAGA OF HEMP BROWN, THE (Cs) 79
UNIVERSAL. (R) October, 1958. Rory Calhoun, Beverly Garland. Color.

SAIL A CROOKED SHIP 88
COLUMBIA. (R) January, 1962. Robert Wagner, Dolores Hart.

SAILOR FROM GIBRALTAR, THE 89
LOPERT. (R) April, 1967. Jeanne Moreau, Ian Bannen.

SAILOR WHO FELL FROM GRACE WITH THE SEA, THE 105
AVCO-EMBASSY. (R) April, 1976. Sarah Miles, Kris Kristofferson.

ST. IVES 93
WARNER BROS. (R) August, 1976. Charles Bronson, Jacqueline Bisset.

SAINT JOAN 110
UNITED ARTISTS. (R) June, 1957. Richard Widmark, Richard Todd.

SAINTLY SINNERS 78
UNITED ARTISTS. (R) February, 1962. Don Beddoe, Ellen Corby.

SALESMAN 90
MAYSLES. (R) April, 1969. Paul Brennan, Charles McDevitt, James Baker. b&w.

SALT AND PEPPER 101
UNITED ARTISTS. (R) July, 1968. Sammy Davis, Jr., Peter Lawford, Michael Bates. Color.

SALO, 120 DAYS OF SODOM (It., Eng. titles) 117
ZEBRA RELEASING. (R) October, 1977. Paolo Bonacelli, Giorgio Cataldi.

SALT OF THE EARTH 104
INDEPENDENT PRODUCTIONS. (R) October, 1965. Rosvara Revueltas, Juan Chacon.

SALTO (Polish; Eng. titles) 104
KANAWHA. (R) August, 1966. Zbigniew Cybulski, Gustaw Holoubek.

SALUT L'ARTISTE (French; English sub-titles) 96
ARCHER KING. (R) February, 1976. Marcello Mastrioianni, Francoise Fabian.

SAM WHISKEY 96

Length In Mins.

UNITED ARTISTS. (R) March, 1969. Burt Reynolds, Clint Walker, Ossie Davis. Color.

SAMAR 89
WARNER BROS. (R) May, 1962. George Montgomery, Gilbert Roland. Color.

SAME TIME, NEXT YEAR 119
UNIVERSAL. (R) March, 1979. Ellen Burstyn, Alan Alda.

SAMSON AND THE SEVEN MIRACLES OF THE WORLD (Colorscope) 78
AMER. INT'L. PICS. (R) 1963. Gordon Scott, Yoko Tani. Color.

SAMSON AND THE SLAVE QUEEN (Colorscope) 86
AMER. INT'L. PICS. (R) 1964. Alan Steel, Pierre Brice. Color.

SAMURAI (Jap.) 92
FINE ARTS. (R) November, 1955. Toshiro Mifune. Color.

SAMURAI ASSASSIN 122
TOHO-MIFUNE. (R) March, 1965. Toshiro Mifune, Keiju Kobayashi.

SANCTUARY (Cs) 90
TWENTIETH CENTURY-FOX. (R) March, 1961. Lee Remick, Yves Montand.

SAND PEBBLES, THE (P) 195
20TH CENTURY-FOX. (R) December, 1966. Steve McQueen, Richard Attenborough. Color.

SANDOKAN THE GREAT (TS) (Ital., dubbed) 105
MGM. (R) 1965. Steve Reeves, Genevieve Grad.

SANDPIPER, THE (P) 116
METRO-GOLDWYN-MAYER. (R) June, 1965. Elizabeth Taylor, Richard Burton. Color.

SANDRA (Ital., Eng. titles) 100
ROYAL FILM INTERNATIONAL. (R) January, 1966. Claudia Cardinale, Michael Craig.

SANDS OF BEERSHEBA 90
LANDAUUNGER. (R) May, 1966. Diane Baker, David Opatoshu.

SANDS OF KALAHARI (P) 119
PARAMOUNT. (R) November, 1965. Stuart Whitman, Stanley Baker. Color.

SANTA CLAUS CONQUERS THE MARTIANS 80
EMBASSY. (R) November, 1964. John Call, Leonard Hicks. Color.

SANTA FE PASSAGE 90
REPUBLIC. (R) May 12, 1955. John Payne, Faith Domergue. Color.

SANTIAGO 93
WARNER BROTHERS. (R) July, 1956. Alan Ladd, Rossana Podesta. Color.

SAPPHIRE 92
UNIVERSAL. (R) November, 1959. Nigel Patrick, Yvonne Mitchell. Color.

SASQUATCH 96
NORTH AMERICAN PRODUCTIONS. (R) January, 1976. George Lauris.

SATAN BUG, THE (P) 114
UNITED ARTISTS. (R) March, 1965. George Maharis, Richard Basehart. Color.

SATAN NEVER SLEEPS (Cs) 126
TWENTIETH CENTURY-FOX. (R) March, 1962. William Holden, Clifton Webb. Color.

SATAN'S SATELLITES 70
REPUBLIC. (R) May, 1958. Judd Holdren, Aline Towne.

SATCHMO THE GREAT 63
UNITED ARTISTS. (R) September, 1957. Louis Armstrong, Leonard Bernstein.

SATELLITE IN THE SKY (Brit.) (Cs) 85
WARNER BROTHERS. (R) July 21, 1956. Kieron Moore, Louis Maxwell. Color.

SATURDAY MORNING 82
COLUMBIA. (R) May, 1971. Group Therapy Documentary. Color.

SATURDAY NIGHT FEVER 120
PARAMOUNT. (R) December, 1977. John Travolta, Karen Lynn Gorney.

SATURDAY NIGHT AND SUNDAY MORNING 90
CONTINENTAL. (R) March, 1961. Albert Finney, Shirley Anne Field.

SAVAGE! 81
NEW WORLD PICTURES. (R) February, 1973. James Inglehart, Carol Speed. Color.

SAVAGE GUNS, THE (Metroscope) 90
MGM. (R) 1962. Richard Basehart, Don Taylor. Color.

SAVAGE INNOCENTS (T-170) 110
PARAMOUNT. (R) February, 1961. Anthony Quinn, Yoko Tani. Color.

SAVAGE IS LOOSE, THE 114
CAMPBELL DEVON. (R) November, 1974. George C. Scott, Trish van Devere.

SAVAGE MESSIAH 100
METRO-GOLDWYN-MAYER. (R) October, 1972. Dorothy Tutin, Scott Anthony. Color.

	Length In Mins.

METRO-GOLDWYN-MAYER. (R) May, 1966. Tony Russell, Helga Line. Color.

SECRET VENTURE (Brit.) 68
REPUBLIC. (R) November 10, 1955. Kent Taylor, Jane Hylton.

SECRET WAR OF HARRY FRIGG, THE (TE) 119
UNIVERSAL. (R) April, 1968. Paul Newman, Sylvia Koscina. Color.

SECRET WAYS, THE 112
UNIVERSAL. (R) April, 1961. Richard Widmark, Sonja Ziemann.

SECRET WORLD 94
20th CENTURY-FOX. (R) July, 1969. Jacqueline Bisset, Giselle Pascal, Pierre Zimmer. Color.

SECRETS OF MONTE CRISTO, THE (Dyaliscope) 70
MGM. (R) 1961. Rory Calhoun. Color.

SECRETS OF THE REEF 72
CONTINENTAL. (R) July, 1956. Life Underwater. Color.

SEDUCED AND ABANDONED (Ital., Eng. Titles) 125
CONTINENTAL. (R) July, 1964. Stefania Sandrelli, Saro Urzi.

SEDUCTION OF JOE TYNAN, THE 107
UNIVERSAL. (R) August, 1979. Alan Alda, Barbara Harris.

SEE NO EVIL 89
COLUMBIA. (R) September, 1971. Mia SQARROW, Dorothy Alison. Color.

SEMI-TOUGH 108
UNITED ARTISTS. (R) November, 1977. Burt Reynolds, Kris Kristofferson.

SEMINOLE UPRISING 74
COLUMBIA. (R) May, 1955. George Montgomery, Karin Booth. Color.

SEND ME NO FLOWERS 100
UNIVERSAL. (R) November, 1964. Rock Hudson, Doris Day. Color.

SENIOR PROM 82
COLUMBIA. (R) January, 1959. Jill Corey, Paul Hampton.

SENSE OF LOSS, A 135
CINEMA V. (R) October, 1972. Documentary. Color.

SENTINEL, THE 89
UNIVERSAL. (R) February, 1977. Chris Sarandon, Cristina Raines.

SEPARATE PEACE, A 105
PARAMOUNT. (R) October, 1972. John Heyl, Parker Stevenson. Color.

SEPARATE TABLES 98
UNITED ARTISTS. (R) February, 1959. Deborah Kerr, Rita Hayworth.

SEPTEMBER STORM (Cs) 99
TWENTIETH CENTURY-FOX. (R) October, 1960. Joanne Dru, Mark Stevens. Color.

SEPTEMBER 30, 1955 101
UNIVERSAL. (R) January, 1978. Richard Thomas, Susan Tyrell.

SERAFINO (Ital., Eng. Titles) 96
ROYAL. (R) May, 1970. Adriano Celentano, Francesca Romana Coluzzi. Color.

SEREGENTI SHALL NOT DIE 84
ALLIED ARTISTS. (R) October, 1961. Documentary. Color.

SERENADE 121
WARNER BROTHERS. (R) April 21, 1956. Mario Lanza, Joan Fontaine, Sarita Montiel. Color.

SERGEANT, THE 107
WARNER BROS.-7 ARTS. (R) January, 1969. Rod Steiger, John Phillip Law, Ludmila Mikael. Color.

SERGEANT DEADHEAD (P) 89
AMERICAN INTERNATIONAL. (R) August, 1965. Frankie Avalon, Deborah Walley. Color.

SERGEANT RUTLEDGE 111
WARNER BROS. (R) May, 1960.

SERGEANT RYKER 86
UNIVERSAL. February, 1968. Lee Marvin, Vera Miles. Color.

SERGEANT WAS A LADY, THE 72
UNIVERSAL. (R) November, 1961. Martin West, Venetia Stevenson.

SGT. PEPPER'S LONELY HEARTS CLUB BAND. (P) 111
UNIVERSAL. (R) July, 1978. Peter Frampton, Barry Gibb.

SERGEANT'S 3 (P) 112
UNITED ARTISTS. (R) February, 1962. Frank Sinatra, Dean Martin.

SERIAL 91
PARAMOUNT. (R) March, 1980. Martin Mull, Tuesday Weld.

SERPENT'S EGG, THE 120
PARAMOUNT. (R) February, 1978. Liv Ullmann, David Carradine.

SERPICO 130

	Length In Mins.

PARAMOUNT. (R) February, 1974. Al Pacino, John Randolph.

SERVANT, THE 115
LANDAU. (R) 1964. Dirk Bogarde, James Fox.

SEVEN ANGRY MEN 90
ALLIED ARTISTS. (R) March 27, 1955. Raymond Massey, Debra Paget.

SEVEN BEAUTIES (Italian; English sub-titles) 115
CINEMA 5. (R) January, 1976. Giancarlo Giannini, Fernando Rey.

SEVEN CITIES OF GOLD (Cs) 103
TWENTIETH CENTURY-FOX. (R) September, 1955. Richard Egan, Michael Rennie, Jeffrey Hunter, Anthony Quinn, Rita Moreno. Color.

SEVEN DAYS FROM SUNDOWN 86
UNIVERSAL. (R) September, 1960. Audie Murphy, Barry Sullivan. Color.

SEVEN DAYS IN MAY 120
PARAMOUNT. (R) February, 1964. Burt Lancaster, Kirk Douglas.

SEVEN DWARFS TO THE RESCUE, THE 84
CHILDHOOD. (R) January, 1965. Rosanna Podesta, Roberto Risso.

SEVEN FACES OF DR. LAO 100
METRO-GOLDWYN-MAYER. (R) March, 1964. Tony Randall, Arthur O'Connell. Color.

SEVEN GOLDEN MEN 87
WARNER BROS.-7 ARTS. (R) May, 1969. Rosanna Podesta, Philippe Leroy, Gastone Moschin. Color.

SEVEN GUNS TO MESA 69
ALLIED ARTISTS. (R) March, 1958. Charles Quinlivan, Lola Albright.

SEVEN HILLS OF ROME (T) 107
METRO-GOLDWYN-MAYER. (R) January, 1958. Mario Lanza, Renato Rascel. Color.

SEVEN LITTLE FOYS, THE (VV) 95
PARAMOUNT. (R) July, 1955. Bob Hope, Milly Vitale. Color.

SEVEN MEN FROM NOW 78
WARNER BROTHERS. (R) August 4, 1956. Randolph Scott, Gail Russell. Color.

SEVEN MINUTES, THE 115
20TH CENTURY-FOX. (R) July, 1971. Wayne Maunder, Marianne McAndrew. Color.

SEVEN-PER-CENT SOLUTION, THE 113
UNIVERSAL. (R) October, 1976. Alan Arkin, Vanessa Redgrave, Robert Duvall.

SEVEN SEAS TO CALAIS (Cs) 99
METRO-GOLDWYN-MAYER. (R) March, 1963. Rod Taylor, Keith Michell.

SEVEN SURPRISES 77
QUARTET INT. (R) September, 1964. Claude Jutra, Wallace Jensen. Color.

SEVEN THIEVES (Cs) 102
TWENTIETH CENTURY-FOX. (R) January, 1960. Edward G. Robinson, Rod Steiger.

SEVEN-UPS, THE 103
TWENTIETH CENTURY-FOX. (R) December, 1973. Roy Scheider, Tony Lo Bianco.

SEVEN WOMEN (P) 93
METRO-GOLDWYN-MAYER. (R) January, 1966. Anne Bancroft, Sue Lyon. Color.

SEVEN WOMEN FROM HELL (Cs) 88
TWENTIETH CENTURY-FOX. (R) October, 1961. Patricia Owens, Denise Darcel.

SEVEN YEAR ITCH, THE (Cs) 105
TWENTIETH CENTURY-FOX. (R) June, 1955. Marilyn Monroe, Tom Ewell. Color.

1776 (P) 148
COLUMBIA. (R) November, 1972. William Daniels, Howard DaSilva, Ken Howard. Color.

7TH CAVALRY 75
COLUMBIA. (R) December, 1956. Randolph Scott, Barbara Hale. Color.

7TH DAWN, THE 128
UNITED ARTISTS. (R) July, 1964. William Holden, Susannah York. Color.

SEVENTH JUROR, THE (Fr., Eng. titles) 90
TRANS-LUX. (R) January, 1964. Daniele DeLorme, Bernard Blier.

SEVENTH SIN, THE (Cs) 94
METRO-GOLDWYN-MAYER. (R) June, 1957. Eleanor Parker, Bill Travers. Color.

7TH VOYAGE OF SINBAD, THE (Dynamation) 89
COLUMBIA. (R) December, 1958. Kerwin Mathews, Kathryn Grant. Color.

SEVERED HEAD A 96
COLUMBIA. (R) April, 1971. Lee Remick, Richard Attenborough. Color.

SEX AND THE SINGLE GIRL 114
WARNER BROS. (R) January, 1965. Tony Curtis, Natalie Wood. Color.

SEX KITTENS GO TO COLLEGE 94

	Length In Mins.

ALLIED ARTISTS. (R) October, 1960. Mamie Van Doren, Tuesday Weld.

SEX OF ANGELS, THE (TE) 104
LOPERT. (R) December, 1969. Rosemarie Dexter, Laura Troschel. Color.

SHACK OUT ON 101 80
ALLIED ARTISTS. (R) December 4, 1955. Terry Moore, Frank Lovejoy, Keenan Wynn.

SHADOW MAN 77
LIPPERT. (R) October 16, 1963. Cesar Romero.

SHADOW OF FEAR (Brit.) 76
UNITED ARTISTS. (R) June, 1956. Mona Freeman, Jean Kent.

SHADOW OF THE CAT, THE 79
UNIVERSAL. (R) June, 1961. Andre Morell, Barbara Shelley.

SHADOW OF THE EAGLE (Brit.) 93
UNITED ARTISTS. (R) July, 1955. Richard Greene, Valentina Cortesa.

SHADOW ON THE WINDOW, THE 73
COLUMBIA. (R) March, 1957. Phil Carey, Betty Garrett. Color.

SHAFT 100
MGM. (R) July, 1971. Richard Roundtree, Gwen Mitchell. Color.

SHAFT IN AFRICA (P) 113
METRO-GOLDWYN-MAYER. (R) June, 1973. Richard Roundtree, Frank Finlay. Color.

SHAFT'S BIG SCORE 105
METRO-GOLDWYN-MAYER. (R) June, 1972. Richard Roundtree, Moses Gunn. Color.

SHAGGY D.A., THE 92
BUENA VISTA. (R) December, 1976. Dean Jones, Tim Conway, Suzanne Pleshette.

SHAGGY DOG, THE 104
BUENA VISTA. (R) April, 1959. Fred MacMurray, Jean Hagen. Color.

SHAKE HANDS WITH THE DEVIL 110
UNITED ARTISTS. (R) June, 1959. James Cagney, Don Murray.

SHAKE, RATTLE AND ROCK 77
AMERICAN INTERNATIONAL. (R) October 31, 1956. Fats Domino, Lisa Gaye.

SHAKEDOWN, THE 91
UNIVERSAL. (R) February, 1961. Terence Morgan, Hazel Court.

SHAKESPEARE WALLAH 115
MERCHANT IVORY PRODUCTIONS. (R) March 22, 1966. Shashi Kapoor, Felicity Kendal.

SHAKIEST GUN IN THE WEST, THE (T) 101
UNIVERSAL. (R) May, 1968. Don Knotts, Barbara Rhoades. Color.

SHALAKO 113
CINERAMA. (R) November, 1968. Sean Connery, Brigitte Bardot, Stephen Boyd. Color.

SHAME (Swedish, Eng. titles) 100
LOPERT. (R) January, 1969. Liv Ullman, Max Von Sydow, Gunnar Bjornstrand. Color.

SHAMELESS OLD LADY, THE (Fr., Eng. titles) 95
CONTINENTAL. (R) September, 1966. Sylvie, Malka Ribovska.

SHAMPOO 112
COLUMBIA. (R) February, 1975. Warren Beatty, Julie Christie, Goldie Hawn.

SHAMUS 98
COLUMBIA. (R) January, 1973. Burt Reynolds, Dyan Cannon. Color.

SHANKS 93
PARAMOUNT. (R) October, 1975. Marcel Marceau.

SHARK FIGHTERS, THE (Cs) 73
UNITED ARTISTS. (R) November, 1956. Victor Mature, Karen Steele. Color.

SHARK'S TREASURE 95
UNITED ARTISTS. (R) May, 1975. Cornel Wilde, Yaphet Kotto.

SHE (Cs) 105
METRO-GOLDWYN-MAYER. (R) June, 1965.

$ta04SHE-CREATURE 77
AMERICAN INTERNATIONAL. (R) July 25, 1956. Maria English, Chester Morris.

SHE DEVIL, THE 77
TWENTIETH CENTURY-FOX. (R) April, 1957. Mari Blanchard, Albert Dekker.

SHE GODS OF SHARK REEF 65
AMERICAN INTERNATIONAL. (R) August, 1958. Don Durant, Lisa Montell.

SHE PLAYED WITH FIRE 95
COLUMBIA. (R) September, 1958. Jack Hawkins, Arlene Dahl.

SHEBA, BABY 90
AMERICAN INTERNATIONAL. (R) March, 1975. Pam Grier, Austin Stoker.

SHEEP HAS FIVE LEGS, THE (Fr.) 93
UMPO. (R) August, 1955. Fernandel.

SHEEPMAN, THE (Cs) 85
MGM. (R) May, 1958. Glenn Ford, Shirley MacLaine. Color.

SHEILA LEVINE IS DEAD AND LIVING IN NEW YORK (P) 112
PARAMOUNT. (R) February, 1975. Jeannie Berlin, Roy Scheider.

SHELL SHOCK 75
PARADE. (R) February, 1964. Beach Dickerson, Carl Crow.

SHENANDOAH 105
UNIVERSAL. (R) April, 1965. James Stewart, Doug McClure. Color.

SHEPHERD GIRL, THE (Shawscope) (Chinese, Eng. titles) 105
FRANK LEE. (R) September, 1965. Julie Yeh Feng, Kwan Shan. Color.

SHERIFF OF FRACTURED JAW, THE (Cs) 103
TWENTIETH CENTURY-FOX. (R) January, 1959. Kenneth More, Jayne Mansfield. Color.

SHINBONE ALLEY 84
ALLIED ARTISTS. (R) April, 1971. Animated Feature. Voices of Eddie Bracken, Carol Channing. Color.

SHINING, THE 146
WARNER BROS. (R) May, 1980. Jack Nicholson, Shelley Duvall.

SHIP OF FOOLS 150
COLUMBIA (R) September, 1965. Oskar Werner, Simone Signoret.

SHIP THAT DIED OF SHAME, THE (Brit.) 79
CONTINENTAL. (R) August, 1956. Richard Attenborough, George Baker.

SHIP WAS LOADED, THE (Brit.) 81
GEORGE K. ARTHUR. (R) September, 1959. David Tomlinson, Peggy Cummins.

SHOCK CORRIDOR 101
ALLIED ARTISTS. (R) August, 1963. Peter Breck, Constance Towers.

SHOCK TREATMENT (Cs) 94
TWENTIETH CENTURY-FOX. (R) February, 1964. Stuart Whitman, Lauren Bacall.

SHOCK TROOPS (Fr., Eng. titles) 106
UNITED ARTISTS. (R) September, 1968. Jean Claude Brialy, Bruno Cremer, Jacques Perrin. Color.

SHOES OF THE FISHERMAN 157
METRO-GOLDWYN-MAYER. (R) Special. Anthony Quinn, David Janssen, Oskar Werner. Color.

SHOOT 94
AVCO-EMBASSY. (R) June, 1976. Cliff Robertson, Ernest Borgnine.

SHOOTIST, THE 99
PARAMOUNT. (R) July, 1976. John Wayne, Lauren Bacall.

SHOOTOUT 94
UNIVERSAL. (R) June, 1971. Gregory Peck, Robert F. Lyons. Color.

SHOOT-OUT AT MEDICINE BEND 87
WARNER BROS. (R) May, 1957. Randolph Scott, James Craig.

SHOP ON MAIN STREET, THE (Czech., Eng. titles) 128
PROMINENT. (R) January, 1966. Josef Kroner, Ida Kaminska.

SHORT CUT TO HELL (VV) 89
PARAMOUNT. (R) September, 1957. Robert Ivers, Georgann Johnson.

SHOT GUN 80
ALLIED ARTISTS. (R) April 24, 1955. Sterling Hayden, Yvonne de Carlo. Color.

SHOT IN THE DARK, A (P) 101
UNITED ARTISTS. (R) July, 1964. Peter Sellers, Elke Sommer. Color.

SHOUT AT THE DEVIL (P) 128
AMERICAN INTERNATIONAL. (R) November, 1976. Lee Marvin, Roger Moore, Barbara Parkins.

SHOWDOWN 99
UNIVERSAL. (R) June, 1973. Dean Martin, Rock Hudson. Color.

SHOWDOWN 79
UNIVERSAL. (R) May, 1963. Audie Murphy, Kathleen Crowley.

SHOWDOWN AT ABILENE 80
UNIVERSAL. (R) October, 1956. Jock Mahoney, Martha Hyer. Color.

SHOWDOWN AT BOOT HILL (Rs) 71
TWENTIETH CENTURY-FOX. (R) June, 1958. Charles Bronson, Robert Hutton.

SHRIKE, THE 88
UNIVERSAL. (R) September, 1955. Jose Ferrer, June Allyson.

SHUTTERED ROOM, THE 100

Length In Mins.

WARNER BROS.-SEVEN ARTS. (R) January, 1968. Gig Young, Carol Lynley. Color.

SICILIAN CLAN, THE (P) (Fr., Eng. titles) 12
20TH CENTURY-FOX. (R) June, 1970. Jean Gabin, Alain Delon. Color.

SIDDHARTHA 86
COLUMBIA. (R) July, 1973. Shashi Kapoor, Simi Garewal. Color.

SIDECAR RACERS 100
UNIVERSAL. (R) August, 1975. Ben Murphy, Wendy Hughes.

SIDEWINDER ONE 97
AVCO-EMBASSY. (R) August, 1977. Marjoe Gortner, Michael Parks.

SIDNEY SHELDON'S BLOODLINE 116
PARAMOUNT. (R) June, 1979. Audrey Hepburn, Ben Gazzara.

SIEGE OF SYRACUSE (D) 97
PARAMOUNT. (R) February, 1962. Rossano Brazzi, Tina Louise. Color.

SIEGE OF THE SAXONS 85
COLUMBIA. (R) August, 1963. Janette Scott, Ronald Lewis. Color.

SIERRA BARON (Cs) 80
TWENTIETH CENTURY-FOX. (R) July, 1958. Brian Keith, Rick Jason. Color.

SIERRA STRANGER 74
COLUMBIA. (R) May, 1957. Howard Duff, Gloria McGhee.

SIGN OF THE GLADIATOR (Colorscope) 92
AMERICAN INTERNATIONAL. (R) October, 1959. Anita Ekberg, George Marshall. Color.

SIGN OF ZORRO, THE 91
BUENA VISTA. (R) June, 1960. Guy Williams.

SIGNPOST TO MURDER (P) 74
METRO-GOLDWYN-MAYER. (R) February, 1965. Joanne Woodward, Stuart Whitman.

SILENCE, THE (Sw., Eng. titles) 95
JANUS. (R) February, 1964. Ingrid Thulin, Gunnel Lindblom.

SILENCERS, THE 105
COLUMBIA. (R) March, 1966. Dean Martin, Stella Stevens. Color.

SILENT ENEMY, THE 91
UNIVERSAL. (R) November, 1958. Laurence Harvey, Dawn Addams.

SILENT MOVIE 86
TWENTIETH CENTURY-FOX. (R) July, 1976. Mel Brooks, Marty Feldman.

SILENT NIGHT, EVIL NIGHT 100
WARNER BROS. (R) May, 1975. Olivia Hussey, Keir Dullea.

SILENT RUNNING 90
UNIVERSAL. (R) March, 1972. Bruce Dern, Cliff Potts. Color.

SILENT WORLD, THE 86
COLUMBIA. (R) January, 1957. Deep Sea Documentary. Color.

SILK STOCKINGS (Cs) 117
METRO-GOLDWYN-MAYER. (R) July, 1957. Fred Astaire, Cyd Charisse. Color.

SILKEN AFFAIR, THE (Brit.) 96
DIST. CORP. OF AMER. (R) November, 1957. David Niven, Genevieve Page.

SILVER BEARS 113
COLUMBIA. (R) April, 1978. Michael Caine, Cybill Shepherd.

SILVER CHALICE, THE (Cs) 137
WARNER BROTHERS. (R) February 5, 1955. Virginia Mayo, Jack Palance. Color.

SILVER STAR, THE 73
LIPPERT. (R) March 25, 1955. Edgar Buchanan, Marie Windsor.

SILVER STREAK 110
TWENTIETH CENTURY-FOX. (R) December, 1976. Gene Wilder, Jill Clayburgh.

SIMBA (Brit.) 99
LIPPET. (R) September 9, 1955. Dirk Bogarde. Color.

SIMON 97
WARNER BROS. (R) March, 1980. Alan Arkin, Madeline Kahn.

SIMON AND LAURA (Brit.) 91
UNITED ARTISTS. (R) July, 1956. Peter Finch, Kay Kendall. Color.

SIMON KING OF THE WITCHES 89
FANFARE. (R) May, 1971. Andrew Pine, Brenda Scott. Color.

SIMON OF THE DESERT (Mex. dubbed) 45
ALTURA FILMS. (R) August, 1968. Silvia Pinal, Claudio Brook. b&w.

SINBAD AND THE EYE OF THE TIGER (Dynarama) 114
COLUMBIA. (R) May, 1977. Patrick Wayne, Taryn Power.

Length In Mins.

SINCERELY YOURS 115
WARNER BROTHERS. (R) November 26, 1955. Liberace, Joanne Dru, Dorothy Malone. Color.

SINFUL DAVEY 95
UNITED ARTISTS. (R) March, 1969. John Hurt, Pamela Franklin, Nigel Davenport. Color.

SING AND SWING 75
UNIVERSAL. (R) December, 1964. David Hemmings, John Pike.

SING BOY SING (Cs) 91
TWENTIETH CENTURY-FOX. (R) January, 1958. Tommy Sands, Lili Gentle.

SINGER, NOT THE SONG, THE (Cs) 129
PARAMOUNT. (R) January, 1962. John Mills, Dirk Bogarde. Color.

SINGING NUN, THE(P) 98
METRO-GOLDWYN-MAYER. (R) April, 1966. Debbie Reynolds, Ricardo Montalban. Color.

SINK THE BISMARCK! (Cs) 97
TWENTIETH CENTURY-FOX. (R) February, 1960. Kenneth More, Dana Wynter.

SINS OF POMPEII (Ital., Eng. dubbed) 73
VISUAL DRAMA. (R) December, 1955. Micheline Prelle, George Marchal.

SINS OF RACHEL CADE, THE 123
WARNER BROS. (R) April, 1961. Angie Dickinson, Peter Finch. Color.

SISTERS 94
AMERICAN INTERNATIONAL. (R) March, 1973. Margot Kidder, Jennifer Salt. Color.

SISTERS, THE (Greek, Eng. titles) 95
BRENNER. March, 1969. Petros Fissoun, Elli Fotiou, Nicos Rizos. b&w.

SITTING DUCKS 90
UNITED FILM DIST. (R) April, 1980. Michael Emil, Zack Norman.

SITTING TARGET 93
METRO-GOLDWYN-MAYER. (R) February, 1972. Oliver Reed, Jill St. John. Color.

SITUATION HOPELESS-BUT NOT SERIOUS 97
PARAMOUNT. (R) October, 1965. Alec Guinness, Michael Connors.

SIX BLACK HORSES 80
UNIVERSAL. (R) June, 1962. Audie Murphy, Dan Duryea. Color.

SIX BRIDGES TO CROSS 96
UNIVERSAL. (R) February, 1955. Tony Curtis, Julie Adams.

SIX DAYS TO ETERNITY 88
P.W. Documentary. (R) October, 1968. Color.

633 SQUADRON (P) 101
UNITED ARTISTS. (R) June, 1964. Cliff Robertson, George Chakiris. Color.

SIX PACK ANNIE 88
AMERICAN INTERNATIONAL. (R) December, 1975. Lindsay Bloom, Jana Bellan.

SKABENGA 61
ALLIED ARTISTS. (R) May 29, 1955. Documentary.

SKI BUM, THE 94
AVCO EMBASSY. (R) January, 1971. Zalman King, Charlotte Rampling. Color.

SKI FEVER 98
ALLIED ARTISTS. (R) March, 1969. Martin Miller, Claudia Martin, Frankie Avalon. Color.

SKI ON THE WILD SIDE 104
SIGMA III. (R) August, 1967. Documentary. Color.

SKI PARTY (P) 90
AMERICAN INTERNATIONAL. (R) June, 1965. Frankie Avalon, Dwayne Hickman, Color.

SKI TROOP ATTACK 61
THE FILM GROUP. (R) May, 1960. Frank Wolff, Michael Forrest.

SKIDOO 98
PARAMOUNT. (R) December, 1968. Jackie Gleason, Carol Channing, Frankie Avalon. Color.

SKIN GAME 102
WARNER BROS. (R) October, 1971. James Garner, Lou Gossett. Color.

SKULL, THE (TE) 83
PARAMOUNT. (R) September, 1965. Peter Cushing, Patrick Wymark. Color.

SKULLDUGGERY (P) 105
UNIVERSAL. (R) March, 1970. Burt Reynolds, Susan Clark. Color.

SKY ABOVE, THE MUD BELOW, THE 90
AVCO EMBASSY. (R) 1962. Narrated by William Peacock. Color.

SKY RIDERS 91
TWENTIETH CENTURY-FOX. (R) March, 1976 James Coburn, Susannah York.

SKYJACKED 100
METRO-GOLDWYN-MAYER. (R) May, 1972. Charlton Heston, Yvette Mimieux, Walter Pidgeon. Color.

	Length In Mins.

SLAMS, THE 91
METRO-GOLDWYN-MAYER. (R) August, 1973. Jim Brown, Judy Pace.
SLANDER 81
METRO-GOLDWYN-MAYER. (R) January 18, 1957. Van Johnson, Ann Blyth.
SLAP, THE (French; English sub-titles) 98
SILVER SCREEN. (R) January, 1976. Lina Ventura, Annie Giradot.
SLAP SHOT 122
UNIVERSAL. (R) March, 1977. Paul Newman, Strother Martin.
SLAUGHTER 92
AMERICAN INTERNATIONAL. (R) August, 1972. Jim Brown, Stella Stevens. Rip Torn. Color.
SLAUGHTER ON TENTH AVENUE 82
UNIVERSAL. (R) November, 1957. Richard Egan, Jan Sterling.
SLAUGHTERHOUSE FIVE 104
UNIVERSAL. (R) April, 1972. Michael Sacks, Ron Leibman. Color.
SLAUGHTER'S BIG RIP OFF 92
AMERICAN INTERNATIONAL. (R) July, 1973. Jim Brown, Brock Peters. Color.
SLAVE, THE (Cs) 110
METRO-GOLDWYN-MAYER. (R) May, 1963. Steve Reeves, Jacques Sernas. Color.
SLAVE TRADE IN THE WORLD TODAY 86
READE-STERLING. (R) November, 1964. Documentary. Color.
SLAVES 110
CONTINENTAL. (R) September, 1969. Stephen Boyd, Dionne Warwick, Ossie Davis. Color.
SLEEPER 88
UNITED ARTISTS. (R) December, 1973. Woody Allen, Diane Keaton.
SLEEPING BEAUTY (Ger., Eng. dubbed) 70
CHILDHOOD PRODUCTIONS. (R) October, 1965. Fantasy. Color.
SLEEPING BEAUTY (Ballet) 90
ROYAL FILMS INTL. (R) April, 1966. Alla Sizova, Yuri Soloview. Color.
SLEEPING BEAUTY (T) 75
BUENA VISTA. (R) March, 1959. Animated. Color.
SLEEPING CAR MURDER, THE (Fr., Eng. titles) 90
SEVEN ARTS. (R) February, 1966. Simone Signoret, Yves Montand.
SLENDER THREAD, THE 98
PARAMOUNT. (R) January, 1966. Sidney Poitier, Anne Bancroft.
SLEUTH 138
TWENTIETH CENTURY-FOX. (R) December, 1972. Laurence Olivier, Michael Caine. Color.
SLIGHTLY SCARLET (SS) 90
RKO RADIO. (R) February 8, 1956. John Payne, Arlene Dahl, Rhonda Fleming. Color.
SLIM CARTER 82
UNIVERSAL. (R) November, 1957. Jock Mahoney, Julie Adams.
SLIPPER AND THE ROSE, THE (P) 128
UNIVERSAL. (R) February, 1977. Richard Chamberlain, Gemma Craven. Color.
SLITHER 97
METRO-GOLDWYN-MAYER. (R) March, 1973. James Caan, Peter Boyle, Sally Kellerman. Color.
SLOGAN (Fr., Eng. titles) 94
ROYAL. (R) April, 1970. Serge Gainsbourg, Jane Birkin. Color.
SLOW DANCING IN THE BIG CITY 101
UNITED ARTISTS. (R) November, 1978. Paul Sorvino, Anne Ditchburn.
SMALL CHANGE (French with English titles) 104
NEW WORLD. (R) October, 1976. Geory Desmoudeaux, Philippe Goldman.
SMALL CIRCLE OF FRIENDS, A 112
UNITED ARTISTS. (R) March, 1980. Brad Davis, Karen Allen.
SMALL TOWN IN TEXAS, A 95
AMERICAN INTERNATIONAL. (R) June, 1976. Timothy Bottoms, Susan George.
SMALL WORLD OF SAMMY LEE, THE 105
SEVEN ARTS (R) August, 1963. Anthony Newley, Julia Foster.
SMALLEST SHOW ON EARTH, THE (Brit.) 80
TIMES. (R) November, 1957. Bill Travers, Virginia McKenna.
SMIC, SMAC, SMOC 90
CINERAMA. (R) January, 1972. Catherine Allegret, Amidou. Color.
SMILE 113
UNITED ARTISTS. (R) July, 1975. Bruce Dern, Barbara Feldon.

SMILES OF A SUMMER NIGHT (Swed.) 108
RANK. (R) February, 1958. Vlla Jacobson, Eva Dahlbeck.
SMILEY (Aust.) (Cs) 91
TWENTIETH CENTURY-FOX. (R) January, 1957. Ralph Richardson, Colin Peterson. Color.
SMILEY GETS A GUN (Cs) 89
TWENTIETH CENTURY-FOX. (R) January, 1959. Keith Calvert, Dame Sybil Thorndike. Color.
SMITH! 112
BUENA VISTA. (R) April, 1969. Glenn Ford, Nancy Olson, Dean Jagger. Color.
SMOKE SIGNAL 88
UNIVERSAL. (R) March, 1955. Dana Andrews, Piper Laurie. Color.
SMOKEY AND THE BANDIT 97
UNIVERSAL. (R) May, 1977. Burt Reynolds, Sally Field.
SMOKEY AND THE BANDIT II 102
UNIVERSAL. (R) August, 1980. Burt Reynolds, Sally Fields.
SMOKY 103
20TH CENTURY-FOX. (R) September, 1966. Fess Parker, Diana Hyland. Color.
SNAKE WOMAN, THE 68
UNITED ARTISTS. (R) 1961. John McCarthy, Susan Travers.
SNIPER'S RIDGE (Cs) 61
TWENTIETH CENTURY-FOX. (R) March, 1961. Jack Ging, Stanley Clements.
SNOOPY COME HOME 90
NATIONAL GENERAL. (R) July, 1972. Animated Feature. Color.
SNORKEL, THE 74
COLUMBIA. (R) July, 1958. Peter Van Eyck, Betta St. John.
SNOW JOB 90
WARNER BROS. (R) February, 1972. Jean-Claude Killy, Daniele Gaubert. Color.
SNOW QUEEN, THE 70
UNIVERSAL. (R) May, 1960. Cartoon Feature. Color.
SNOW TREASURE 85
ALLIED ARTISTS. (R) October, 1968. James Franciscus, Bente Nielsen, Paul Austad. Color.
SNOW WAS BLACK, THE (Fr.) 104
CONTINENTAL. (R) November, 1956. Daniel Gelin.
SNOW WHITE (Ger., Eng. dubbed) 74
CHILDHOOD PRODUCTIONS. (R) October, 1965. Fantasy. Color.
SNOW WHITE AND THE THREE STOOGES (Cs) 107
TWENTIETH CENTURY-FOX. (R) June, 1961. Carol Heiss, The Three Stooges. Color.
SNOWBALL EXPRESS 99
BUENA VISTA. (R) December, 1972. Dean Jones, Nancy Olson. Color.
SNOWFIRE 73
ALLIED ARTISTS. (R) May 18, 1958. Molly McGowan, Don McGownan. Color.
SO THIS IS PARIS 96
UNIVERSAL. (R) January, 1955. Tony Curtis, Gloria de Haven. Color.
SODOM AND GOMORRAH (Cs) 154
TWENTIETH CENTURY-FOX. (R) January, 1963. Stewart Granger, Pier Angeli. Color.
SOFT SKIN, THE (Fr. Eng. titles) 120
CINEMA V. (R) October, 1964. Jean Desailly, Francoise Dorleac.
SOL MADRID (P) 90
MGM. (R) February, 1968. David McCallum, Stella Stevens. Color.
SOLDIER BLUE (P) 112
AVCO EMBASSY. (R) August, 1970. Candice Bergen, Peter Strauss. Color.
SOLDIER IN THE RAIN 88
ALLIED ARTISTS. (R) November, 1963. Jackie Gleason, Steve McQueen.
SOLDIER OF FORTUNE (Cs) 96
TWENTIETH CENTURY-FOX. (R) June, 1955. Clark Gable, Susan Hayward. Color.
SOLID GOLD CADILLAC, THE 99
COLUMBIA. (R) October, 1956. Judy Holliday, Paul Douglas.
SOLOMON AND SHEBA (T) 139
UNITED ARTISTS. (R) December, 1959. Yul Brynner, Gina Lollobrigida. Color.
SOME CALL IT LOVING 103
CINE GLOBE. (R) November, 1973. Zalman King, Carol White.
SOME CAME RUNNING (Cs) 127
METRO-GOLDWYN-MAYER. (R) January, 1959. Frank Sinatra, Shirley MacLaine. Color.
SOME KIND OF NUT 89
UNITED ARTISTS. (R) November, 1969. Dick Van Dyke, Angie Dickinson, Rosemary Forsyth. Color.
SOME LIKE IT HOT 120

Length In Mins.

UNITED ARTISTS. (R) March, 1959. Marilyn Monroe, Tony Curtis.

SOMEBODY KILLED HER HUSBAND (P) 97
COLUMBIA. (R) September, 1978. Farrah Fawcett, Jeff Bridges.

SOMEBODY UP THERE LIKES ME 113
METRO-GOLDWYN-MAYER. (R) Special. 1957. Paul Newman, Pier Angeli.

SOMEONE BEHIND THE DOOR 97
CINERAMA. (R) December, 1971. Charles Bronson, Anthony Perkins. Color.

SOMETHING BIG 108
NATIONAL GENERAL. (R) November, 1971. Dean Martin, Brian Keith. Color.

SOMETHING FOR EVERYONE 112
NATIONAL GENERAL. (R) September, 1970. Angela Lansbury, Michael York. Color.

SOMETHING OF VALUE 113
METRO-GOLDWYN-MAYER. (R) June, 1957. Rock Hudson, Dana Wynter.

SOMETHING WILD 112
UNITED ARTISTS. (R) May, 1961. Carroll Baker, Ralph Meeker.

SOMETIMES A GREAT NOTION 114
UNIVERSAL. (R) November, 1971. Paul Newman, Henry Fonda, Lee Remick. Color.

SON OF A GUNFIGHTER (Cs) 92
METRO-GOLDWYN-MAYER. (R) May, 1966. Russ Tamblyn, Kieron Moore. Color.

SON OF CAPTAIN BLOOD, THE 88
PARAMOUNT. (R) April, 1964. Sean Flynn, Allessandra Panaro. Color.

SON OF FLUBBER 100
BUENA VISTA. (R) February, 1963. Fred MacMurray, Nancy Olson.

SON OF ROBIN HOOD, THE (Cs) 81
TWENTIETH CENTURY-FOX. (R) July, 1959. Al Hedison, June Laverick. Color.

SON OF SAMSON (Total Scope) 89
MEDALLION. (R) 1961. Mark Forest, Chelo Alonso. Color.

SON OF SINBAD (SS) 88
RKO RADKO. (R) June 1, 1955. Dale Robertson, Sally Forrest. Color.

SON OF SPARTACUS, THE (Ital. dubbed) 102
MGM. (R) 1962. Steve Reeves, Jacques Sernas.

SONG AND THE SILENCE, THE 80
CLOVERHOUSE. (R) February, 1969. Annita Koutsouveli, Harry Rubin, Jim Murphy. b&w.

SONG OF NORWAY (Super Panavision) 138
CINERAMA. (R) November, 1970. Florence Henderson, Toraly Maurstad. Color.

SONG OVER MOSCOW 94
ARTKINO. (R) November, 1964. Herbert Rappaport, Olga Zabotinka. Color.

SONG REMAINS THE SAME, THE 136
WARNER BROS. (R) October, 1976. Led Zeppelin.

SONG WITHOUT END (Cs) 130
COLUMBIA. (R) August, 1960. Dirk Bogarde, Capucine. Color.

SONNY & JED 87
K-TEL MOTION PICTURES. (R) Special, 1973. Thomas Milian, Telly Savalas.

SONS AND LOVERS (Cs) 103
TWENTIETH CENTURY-FOX. (R) August, 1960. Trevor Howard, Dean Stockwell.

SONS OF KATIE ELDER, THE (P) 122
PARAMOUNT. (R) June, 1965. John Wayne, Dean Martin. Color.

SORCERER 121
PARAMOUNT and UNIVERSAL. (R) June, 1977. Roy Scheider.

SORCERERS, THE 87
ALLIED ARTISTS. (R) January, 1968. Boris Karloff, Catherine Lacey. Color.

SORORITY GIRL 60
AMER. INT. PICS. (R) October, 1957. Susan Cabot, Dick Miller.

SORROW AND THE PITY, THE 260
CINEMA V. (R) March, 1972. Documentary.

SOUL OF NIGGER CHARLIE, THE 98
PARAMOUNT. (R) June, 1973. Fred Williamson. Color.

SOUL TO SOUL 96
CINERAMA. (R) August, 1971. Black Concert Documentary. Color.

SOUND AND THE FURY, THE (Cs) 115
TWENTIETH-CENTURY-FOX. (R) March, 1959. Yul Brynner, Joanne Woodward. Color.

SOUND OF LAUGHTER, THE 75
UNION. (R) December, 1963. Ed Wynn, Bing Crosby and All Star Cast.

SOUND OF MUSIC, THE (Todd-AO) 171

Length In Mins.

TWENTIETH CENTURY-FOX. (R) Special. March, 1965. Julie Andrews, Christopher Plummer. Color.

SOUNDER 105
TWENTIETH CENTURY-FOX. (R) October, 1972. Cicely Tyson, Paul Winfield. Color.

SOUTH PACIFIC (Todd-AO) 171
TWENTIETH CENTURY-FOX. (R) March, 1958. Special. Rossano Brazzi, Mitzi Gaynor. Color.

SOUTHERN STAR, THE 104
COLUMBIA. (R) July, 1969. George Segal, Ursula Andress, Orson Wells. Color.

SOYLENT GREEN 97
METRO-GOLDWYN-MAYER. (R) April, 1973. Charlton Heston, Edward G. Robinson. Color.

SPACE CHILDREN, THE 69
PARAMOUNT. (R) June, 1958. Adam Williams, Michel Ray.

SPACE FLIGHT I-CI (Brit.) 65
20TH CENTURY-FOX. (R) 1965. Bill Williams, Norma West.

SPACE MASTER X-7 (Rs) 71
TWENTIETH CENTURY-FOX. (R) June, 1958. Bill Williams, Lyn Thomas.

SPACEWAYS 76
LIPPERT. (R) August 7, 1953. Howard Duff, Eva Bartok.

SPANISH AFFAIR, THE (VV) 95
PARAMOUNT. (R) October, 1957. Richard Kiley, Carmen Savilla. Color.

SPANISH GARDENER, THE (VV) 95
RANK. (R) October, 1957. Dirk Bogarde, Jon Witeley.

SPARKLE 99
WARNER BROS. (R) April, 1976. Philip M. Thomas, Irene Cara.

SPARROWS CAN'T SING 93
JANUS. (R) May, 1963. James Booth, Barbara Windsor.

SPARTACUS (T-70) 198
UNIVERSAL. (R) Special. October, 1960. Kirk Douglas, Laurence Olivier. Color.

SPECIAL DAY, A (It., Eng. titles) 110
CINEMA 5. (R) October, 1977. Sophia Loren, Marcello Mastroianni.

SPECIAL DELIVERY 99
AMERICAN INTERNATIONAL. (R) July, 1976. Bo Svenson, Cybill Shepherd.

SPECIAL DELIVERY 86
COLUMBIA. (R) September, 1955. Joseph Cotten, Eva Bartok.

SPECIAL SECTION (French; English sub-titles) 110
UNIVERSAL. (R) December, 1975. Louis Seigner, Michel Lonsdale.

SPECTRE OF EDGAR ALLAN POE, THE 85
CINERAMA. (R) April, 1974. Robert Walker, Jr., Cesar Romero.

SPEED CRAZY 75
ALLIED ARTISTS. (R) May, 1959. Brett Halsey, Yvonne Lime.

SPEEDWAY 100
MGM. (R) June, 1968. Elvis Presley, Nancy Sinatra. Color.

SPIDER, THE 72
AMERICAN INTERNATIONAL. (R) October, 1958. Ed Kemmer, June Kenny.

SPIKES GANG, THE 96
UNITED ARTISTS. (R) April, 1974. Lee Marvin, Gary Grimes.

SPINOUT (P) 95
METRO-GOLDWYN-MAYER. (R) November, 1966. Elvis Presley, Shelley Fabres. Color.

SPIRAL ROAD, THE 145
UNIVERSAL. (R) August, 1962. Rock Hudson, Burl Ives. Color.

SPIRIT IS WILLING, THE 100
PARAMOUNT. (R) July, 1967. Sid Caesar, Vera Miles. Color.

SPIRIT OF ST. LOUIS, THE (Cs) 135
WARNERS. (R) April 20, 1957. James Stewart. Color.

SPIRITS OF THE DEAD 117
AMER. INT. PICS. (R) July, 1969. Brigitte Bardot, Alain Delon, Jane Fonda. Color.

SPLENDOR IN THE GRASS 124
WARNER BROS. (R) October, 1961. Natalie Wood, Pat Hingle. Color.

SPLIT, THE 91
METRO-GOLDWYN-MAYER. (R) October, 1968. Jim Brown, Diahnn Carroll, Julie Harris. Color.

SPOILERS, THE 84
UNIVERSAL. (R) January, 1956. Jeff Chandler, Anne Baxter, Rory Calhoun. Color.

SPOILERS OF THE FOREST 68
REPUBLIC. (R) April 5, 1957. Rod Cameron, Vera Ralston. Color.

SPOOK CHASERS 62

	Length In Mins.

ALLIED ARTISTS. (R) June, 1957. Huntz Hall, Stanley Clements.

SPOOK WHO SAT BY THE DOOR 102
UNITED ARTISTS. (R) September, 1973. Lawrence Cook, Paula Kelly.

SPORTING CLUB, THE 105
AVCO-EMBASSY. (R) February, 1971. Robert Fields, Maggie Blye. Color.

SPRING REUNION 79
UNITED ARTISTS. (R) March, 1957. Betty Hutton, Dana Andrews.

SPY CHASERS 61
ALLIED ARTISTS. (R) July 31, 1955. Leo Gorcey, Huntz Hall.

SPY IN THE SKY 74
ALLIED ARTISTS. (R) July, 1958. Steve Brodie, Sandra Francis.

SPY IN YOUR EYE 88
AMERICAN INTERNATIONAL. (R) December, 1965. Brett Halsey, Pier Angeli. Color.

SPY WHO CAME IN FROM THE COLD, THE 112
PARAMOUNT. (R) February, 1966. Richard Burton, Claire Bloom.

SPY WHO LOVED ME, THE (P) 125
UNITED ARTISTS. (R) July, 1977. Roger Moore.

SPY WITH A COLD NOSE, THE 93
EMBASSY. (R) December, 1966. Laurence Harvey, Lionel Jeffries. Color.

SPY WITH MY FACE, THE 88
METRO-GOLDWYN-MAYER. (R) February, 1966. Robert Vaughn, Senta Berger. Color.

SQUAD CAR 62
TWENTIETH CENTURY-FOX. (R) September, 1960. Paul Bryar, Vici Raaf.

SQUARE JUNGLE, THE 86
UNIVERSAL. (R) January, 1956. Tony Curtis, Ernest Borgnine, Pat Crowley.

SQUARE RING, THE 73
REPUBLIC. (R) January 28, 1955. Jack Warner, Robert Beatty.

SQUIRM 92
AMERICAN INTERNATIONAL. (R) August, 1976. John Scardino, Patricia Pearcy.

ST. VALENTINE'S DAY MASSACRE, THE (P) 100
TWENTIETH CENTURY-FOX. (R) August, 1967. Jason Robards, George Segal. Color.

Sssssss 90
UNIVERSAL. (R) July, 1973. Strother Martin, Dirk Benedict. Color.

STAGE STRUCK 95
BUENA VISTA. (R) March, 1958. Henry Fonda, Susan Fonda, Susan Strasberg. Color.

STAGE TO THUNDER ROCK (TS) 82
PARAMOUNT. (R) June, 1964. Barry Sullivan, Marilyn Maxwell. Color.

STAGECOACH (Cs) 114
TWENTIETH CENTURY-FOX. (R) May-June, 1966. Ann-Margret, Red Buttons, Bing Crosby.

STAGECOACH TO DANCER'S ROCK 72
UNIVERSAL. (R) October, 1962. Warren Stevens, Martin Landau.

STAGECOACH TO FURY 76
TWENTIETH CENTURY-FOX. (R) October, 1956. Forrest Tucker, Mari Blanchard.

STAIRCASE (P) 96
20TH CENTURY-FOX. (R) August, 1969. Richard Burton, Rex Harrison. Color.

STAKEOUT ON DOPE STREET 83
WARNER BROTHERS. (R) April, 1958. Yale Wexler, Jonathan Haze.

STALKING MOON 109
NATIONAL GENERAL. (R) January, 1969. Eva Marie Saint, Gregory Peck, Robert Forster. Color.

STAND UP AND BE COUNTED 99
COLUMBIA. (R) May, 1972. Jacqueline Bisset, Stella Stevens. Color.

STAR! 175
TWENTIETH CENTURY-FOX. (R) October, 1968. Julie Andrews, Richard Crenna, Michael Craig. Color.

STAR IN THE DUST 80
UNIVERSAL. (R) June, 1956. John Agar, Mamie Van Doren. Color.

STAR IS BORN (Cs) 154
WARNER BROTHERS. (R) January 22, 1955. Judy Garland, James Mason. Color.

STAR IS BORN, A (P) 140
WARNER BROS. (R) December, 1976. Barbra Streisand, Kris Kristofferson.

STAR OF INDIA 84
UNITED ARTISTS. (R) June, 1956. Cornel Wilde, Jean Wallace. Color.

STAR TREK—THE MOTION PICTURE 132

	Length In Mins.

PARAMOUNT. (R) December, 1979. William Shatner, Leonard Nimoy.

STAR WARS (P) 123
TWENTIETH CENTURY-FOX. (R) June, 1977. Mark Hamill, Harrison Ford, Carrie Fisher.

STARDUST 107
COLUMBIA. (R) March, 1975. David Essex, Adam Faith.

STARSHIP INVASIONS 89
WARNER BROS. (R) January, 1978. Robert Vaughn, Christopher Lee.

START THE REVOLUTION WITHOUT ME 98
WARNER BROS. (R) February, 1970. Gene Wilder, Donald Sutherland. Color.

STARTING OVER 101
PARAMOUNT. (R) October, 1979. Burt Reynolds, Jill Clayburgh.

STATE FAIR (Cs) 118
TWENTIETH CENTURY-FOX. (R) April, 1962. Pat Boone, Bobby Darin. Color.

STATE OF SIEGE 115
CINEMA V. (R) April, 1973. Yves Montand, Renato Salvatori. Color.

STATION SIX SAHARA 99
ALLIED ARTISTS. (R) August, 1964. Carroll Baker, Ian Bannen.

STATUE, THE 72
CINERAMA. (R) February, 1971. David Niven, Vierna Lisi. Color.

STAY AS YOU ARE (Ital., Eng. titles) 95
NEW LINE CINEMA. (R) December, 1979. Marcello Mastroianni, Nastassia Kinski.

STAY AWAY JOE 102
MGM (R) April, 1968. Elvis Presley, Burgess Meredith. Color.

STAY HUNGRY 103
UNITED ARTISTS. (R) May, 1976. Jeff Bridges, Sally Field.

STEAGLE, THE 91
AVCO EMBASSY. (R) September, 1971. Richard Benjamin, Chill Wills, Cloris Leachman. Color.

STEEL BAYONET, THE (H) 84
UNITED ARTISTS. (R) March, 1958. Leo Genn. Kieron Moore.

STEEL CLAW, THE 96
WARNER BROS. (R) May, 1961. George Montgomery, Charlto Luna. Color.

STEEL JUNGLE, THE 86
WARNER BROTHERS. (R) March 31, 1956. Perry Lopez, Beverly Garland.

STEELYARD BLUES 92
WARNER BROS. (R) February, 1973. Jane Fonda, Peter Boyle. Color.

STEP DOWN TO TERROR 75
UNIVERSAL. (R) March, 1959. Colleen Miller, Charles Drake.

STEPFORD WIVES, THE (P) 115
COLUMBIA. (R) February, 1975. Katharine Ross, Paula Prentiss.

STERILE CUCKOO, THE 107
PARAMOUNT. (R) October, 1969. Liza Minelli, Wendell Burton. Color.

STEWARDESSES, THE (3-D) 93
SHERPIX. (R) November, 1970. Christina Hart, Michael Garrett. Color.

STIGMA 93
CINERAMA. (R) August, 1972. Philip M. Thomas, Harlan Poe. Color.

STILETTO 99
AVCO EMBASSY. (R) August, 1969. Alex Cord, Britt Eckland, Patrick O'Neal. Color.

STING, THE 129
UNIVERSAL. (R) December, 1973. Paul Newman, Robert Redford.

STOLEN HOURS 100
UNITED ARTISTS. (R) October, 1963. Susan Hayward, Michael Craig. Color.

STOLEN KISSES (French; Eng. titles) 90
LOPERT. (R) February, 1969. Jean Pierre Leaud, Delphine Seyrig, Michael Lonsdale. Color.

STONE KILLER, THE 95
COLUMBIA. (R) August, 1973. Charles Bronson, Martin Balsam.

STOOGE, THE 100
PARAMOUNT. (R) February, 1953. Dean Martin, Jerry Lewis.

STOP! LOOK! AND LAUGH! 78
COLUMBIA. (R) July, 1960. The Three Stooges.

STOP ME BEFORE I KILL! (M) 105
COLUMBIA. (R) June, 1961. Claude Dauphin, Diane Cilento.

STOP THE WORLD—I WANT TO GET OFF 98

**Length
In Mins.**

WARNER BROTHERS. (R) May, 1966. Tony Tanner, Millicent Martin. Color.

STOP TRAIN 349 95
ALLIED ARTISTS. (R) July, 1964. Jose Ferrer, Sean Flynn.

STOPOVER TOKYO (Cs) 100
TWENTIETH CENTURY-FOX. (R) October, 1957. Robert Wagner, Joan Collins. Color.

STORM CENTER 87
COLUMBIA. (R) September, 1956. Bette Davis, Kim Hunter.

STORM FEAR 87
UNITED ARTISTS. (R) January, 1956. Cornel Wilde, Jean Wallace, Dan Duryea.

STORM OVER THE NILE (Cs) 107
COLUMBIA. (R) June, 1956. Anthony Steel, Laurence Harvey. Color.

STORM RIDER, THE 70
TWENTIETH CENTURY-FOX. (R) March, 1957. Scott Brady, Mala Powers.

STORY OF A WOMAN 90
UNIVERSAL. (R) February, 1970. Bibi Andersson, Robert Stack, James Farentino. Color.

STORY OF ADELE H., THE (French; English sub-titles) 95
NEW WORLD PICTURES. (R) December, 1975. Isabelle Adjani, Bruce Robinson.

STORY OF ESTHER COSTELLO, THE 127
COLUMBIA. (R) October, 1957. Joan Crawford, Rossano Brazzi.

STORY OF MANKIND, THE 100
WARNER BROS. (R) November, 1957. Ronald Colman, Hedy Lamarr. Color.

STORY OF O, THE (French; Eng. titles) 97
ALLIED ARTISTS. (R) November, 1975. Corinne Clery, Udo Keir.

STORY OF RUTH, THE (Cs) 132
TWENTIETH CENTURY-FOX. (R) June, 1960. Stuart Whitman, Tom Tryon. Color.

STORY OF THE COUNT OF MONTE CRISCO, THE (D) .. 132
WARNER BROS. (R) June, 1962. Louis Jourdan, Yvonne Furneau.

STORY OF VICKIE (Ger.) 109
BUENA VISTA. (R) February, 1958. Romy Schneider, Adrian Haven. Color.

STORY ON PAGE ONE, THE (Cs) 123
TWENTIETH CENTURY-FOX. (R) January, 1960. Rita Hayworth, Anthony Franciosa.

STOWAWAY GIRL 87
PARAMOUNT. (R) September, 1957. Trevor Howard, Pedro Armendariz.

STOWAWAY IN THE SKY 82
UNITED ARTISTS. (R) June, 1962. Jack Lemmon, Andre Gille. Color.

STRAIGHT TIME 114
WARNER BROS. (R) March, 1978. Dustin Hoffman, Gary Busey.

STRAIT-JACKET 93
COLUMBIA. (R) January, 1964. Joan Crawford, Diane Baker.

STRANGE ADVENTURE, A 70
REPUBLIC. (R) August 24, 1956. Joan Evans, Ben Cooper.

STRANGE AFFAIR, THE 106
PARAMOUNT. (R) September, 1968. Michael York, Jeremy Kamp, Susan George. Color.

STRANGE AFFECTION 87
BRENNER. (R) November, 1959. Richard Attenborough, Dorothy Leigh.

STRANGE BEDFELLOWS 99
UNIVERSAL. (R) February, 1965. Rock Hudson, Gina Lollobrigida. Color.

STRANGE CASE OF DR. MANNING, THE 75
STATES-RIGHTS-REPUBLIC. (R) September, 1959. Ron Randall, Greta Gynt.

STRANGE INTRUDER 82
ALLIED ARTISTS. (R) September 2, 1956. Ida Lupino, Edmund Purdom.

STRANGE LADY IN TOWN (Cs) 112
WARNER BROTHERS. (R) April 30, 1955. Greer Garson, Dana Andrews. Color.

STRANGE ONE, THE 97
COLUMBIA. (R) May, 1957. Ben Gazzara, Julie Wilson.

STRANGE SHADOWS IN AN EMPTY ROOM (P) 99
AMERICAN INTERNATIONAL. (R) February, 1977. Stuart Whitman, John Saxon.

STRANGER, THE 105
PARAMOUNT. (R) January, 1968. Marcello Mastroianni, Anna Karina. Color.

STRANGER AT MY DOOR 85
REPUBLIC. (R) April 6, 1956. Macdonald Carey, Patricia Medina.

STRANGER IN MY ARMS, A (Cs) 83

**Length
In Mins.**

UNIVERSAL. (R) February, 1959. June Allyson, Jeff Chandler.

STRANGER IN TOWN (Brit.) 74
ASTOR. (R) May, 1957. Alex Nicol, Colin Tapley.

STRANGER IN TOWN, A 90
MGM. (R) April, 1968. Tony Anthony, Frank Wolf. Color.

STRANGER KNOCKS, A (Dan., Eng. titles) 81
TRANS LUX. (R) March, 1965. Preben Lerdorff Rye, Brigitte Federspiel.

STRANGER ON HORSEBACK 66
UNITED ARTISTS. (R) March, 1955. Joel McCrea, Miroslava. Color.

STRANGER RETURNS, THE 90
METRO-GOLDWYN-MAYER. (R) August, 1968. Tony Anthony, Dean Vadis, Daniele Vargas. Color.

STRANGER'S HANDS, THE (Brit.) 88
DISTRIBUTORS CORP. OF AMERICA. (R) March, 1955. Trevor Howard, Alida Valli.

STRANGERS WHEN WE MEET (Cs) 117
COLUMBIA. (R) July, 1960. Kirk Douglas, Kim Novak. Color.

STRANGLER, THE 89
ALLIED ARTISTS. (R) April, 1964. Victor Buono, David McLean.

STRATEGIC AIR COMMAND (VV) 114
PARAMOUNT. (R) July, 1955. James Stewart, June Allyson. Color.

STRAW DOGS 113
CINERAMA. (R) December, 1971. Dustin Hoffman, Susan George, David Warner. Color.

STRAWBERRY STATEMENT, THE 103
MGM. (R) June, 1970. Bruce Davison. Kim Darby. Color.

STRAY DOG (Jap., Eng. titles) 122
TOHO. (R) March, 1964. Toshiro Mifune, Takashi Shimura.

STREET FIGHTER 71
SAVAGE-BRENNER. (R) October, 1959. Vic Savage, Ann Atmar.

STREET OF DARKNESS. 60
REPUBLIC. (R) June, 1958. Robert Keys, John Close.

STREET OF SINNERS 76
UNITED ARTISTS. (R) September, 1957. George Montgomery, Geraldine Brooks.

STREET PEOPLE 92
AMERICAN INTERNATIONAL. (R) October, 1976. Roger Moore, Stacy Keach.

STREETCAR NAMED DESIRE 122
WARNER BROS. (R) March 22, 1952. Vivien Leigh, Marlon Brando.

STRIPPER, THE (Cs) 95
TWENTIETH CENTURY-FOX. (R) June, 1963. Joanne Woodward, Richard Beymer.

STRONGEST MAN IN THE WORLD, THE 92
BUENA VISTA. (R) February, 1975. Kurt Russell, Joe Flynn.

STUDS LONIGAN 95
UNITED ARTISTS. (R) September, 1960. Christopher Knight, Venetia Stevenson.

STUDY IN TERROR, A 94
COLUMBIA. (R) April, 1966. John Neville, Donald Houston. Color.

SUBJECT WAS ROSES, THE 107
METRO-GOLDWYN-MAYER. (R) November, 1968. Patricia Neal, Jack Albertson, Martin Sheen. Color.

SUBMARINE X-I 89
UNITED ARTISTS. (R) July, 1969. James Caan, David Sumner. Color.

SUBMARINE SEAHAWK 87
AMERICAN INTERNATIONAL. (R) February, 1959. John Bentley, Jan Brooks.

SUBTERRANEANS, THE (Cs) 86
METRO-GOLDWYN-MAYER. (R) August, 1960. Leslie Caron, George Peppard. Color.

SUBWAY IN THE SKY 85
UNITED ARTISTS. (R) September, 1959. Van Johnson, Hildegarde Neff.

SUCCESS, THE (Ital., Eng. titles) 103
AVCO EMBASSY. (R) 1965. Vittorio Gassmann, Anouk Aimee. b&w.

SUCCUBUS (Ger., Eng. titles) 93
AMERICAN. (R) April, 1969. Janine Reynaud, Jack Taylor, Howard Vernon. Color.

SUCH A GORGEOUS KID LIKE ME 95
COLUMBIA. (R) March, 1973. Bernadette Lafont, Claude Brasseur. Color.

SUCH GOOD FRIENDS 101
PARAMOUNT. (R) December, 1971. Dyan Cannon, James Coco, Lawrence Luckenbill. Color.

SUCKER, THE 101
ROYAL FILMS INTERNATIONAL. (R) June, 1966. Bourvil, Louis De Funes. Color.

	Length In Mins.

SUDDEN DANGER 65
ALLIED ARTISTS. (R) December 18, 1955. Bill Elliott, Tom Drake.

SUDDEN TERROR 95
NATIONAL GENERAL. (R) March, 1971. Mark Lester, Lionel Jeffries. Color.

SUDDENLY, LAST SUMMER 114
COLUMBIA. (R) January, 1960. Elizabeth Taylor, Katharine Hepburn.

SUGARLAND EXPRESS, THE (P) 108
UNIVERSAL. (R) April, 1974. Goldie Hawn, Ben Johnson.

SUICIDE BATTALION 75
AMER. INT. PICS. (R) February, 1958. Michael Connors, Jewell Lain.

SUICIDE MISSION 70
COLUMBIA. (R) November, 1956. Leif Larsen, Michael Aldridge.

SULLIVAN'S EMPIRE 85
UNIVERSAL. (R) August, 1967. Martin Milner, Linden Chiles. Color.

SUMMER AND SMOKE 116
PARAMOUNT. (R) February, 1962. Geraldine Page, Laurence Harvey. Color.

SUMMER LOVE 85
UNIVERSAL INTERNATIONAL. (R) April, 1958. John Saxon, Molly Bee.

SUMMER MAGIC 109
BUENA VISTA. July, 1963. Hayley Mills, Burl Ives. Color.

SUMMER OF '42 102
WARNER BROS. (R) April, 1971. Jennifer O'Neill, Gary Grimes. Color.

SUMMER PARADISE (Swed., Eng. titles) 113
CINEMA 5. (R) March, 1978. Birgktta, Valberg, Sif Ruud.

SUMMER PLACE, A 130
WARNER BROS. (R) November, 1959. Richard Egan, Dorothy McGuire. Color.

SUMMER WISHES, WINTER DREAMS 90
COLUMBIA. (R) October, 1973. Joanne Woodward, Martin Balsam.

SUMMERTIME 99
UNITED ARTISTS. (R) June, 1955. Katharine Hepburn, Rossano Brazzi. Color.

SUMMERTIME KILLER 100
AVCO-EMBASSY. (R) September, 1973. Christopher Mitchum, Karl Malden.

SUMMERTREE 88
COLUMBIA. (R) June, 1971. Michael Douglas, Jack Warden, Brenda Vaccaro. Color.

SUN ALSO RISES, THE (Cs) 129
TWENTIETH CENTURY-FOX. (R) September, 1957. Tyrone Power, Ava Gardner. Color.

SUNBURN 101
PARAMOUNT. (R) August, 1979. Farrah Fawcett, Charles Grodin.

SUNDAY BLOODY SUNDAY 106
UNITED ARTISTS. (R) October, 1971. Peter Finch, Glenda Jackson, Murray Head. Color.

SUNDAY IN NEW YORK. 105
METRO-GOLDWYN-MAYER. (R) February, 1964. Cliff Robertson, Jane Fonda. Color.

SUNDAY WOMAN, THE 110
TWENTIETH CENTURY-FOX. (R) September, 1976. Marcello Mastroianni, Jacqueline Bisset.

SUNDOWNERS, THE 133
WARNER BROS. (R) December, 1960. Deborah Kerr, Robert Mitchum. Color.

SUNFLOWER 101
AVCO-EMBASSY. (R) September, 1970. Sophia Loren, Marcello Mastroianni. Color.

SUNRISE AT CAMPOBELLO 143
WARNER BROS. (R) November, 1960. Ralph Bellamy, Greer Garson. Color.

SUNSHINE BOYS, THE 111
UNITED ARTISTS. (R) December, 1975. Walter Matthau, George Burns.

SUPER COPS, THE 94
UNITED ARTISTS. (R) March, 1974. Ron Liebman, David Selby.

SUPER FLY 98
WARNER BROS. (R) August, 1972. Ron O'Neal, Carl Lee. Color.

SUPER FLY T.N.T. 87
PARAMOUNT. (R) June, 1973. Ron O'Neal, Roscoe Lee Brown. Color.

SUPERBEAST 91
UNITED ARTISTS. (R) October, 1972. Craig Littler, Antoinette Bower. Color.

SUPERCHICK 92
CROWN INTERNATIONAL. (R) May, 1973. Joyce Jelson, Louis Quinn. Color.

	Length In Mins.

SUPERDAD 95
BUENA VISTA. (R) February, 1974. Bob Crane, Barbara Rush.

SUPERMAN (P) 143
WARNER BROS. (R) December, 1978. Marlon Brando, Gene Hackman, Christopher Reeve.

SUPPORT YOUR LOCAL GUNFIGHTER 92
UNITED ARTISTS. (R) May, 1971. James Garner, Suzanne Pleshette. Color.

SUPPORT YOUR LOCAL SHERIFF 92
UNITED ARTISTS. (R) April, 1969. James Garner, Joan Hackett, Walter Brennan. Color.

SUPPOSE THEY GAVE A WAR AND NOBODY CAME ... 113
CINERAMA. (R) June, 1970. Tony Curtis, Brian Keith, Ernest Borgnine. Color.

SURF PARTY 68
TWENTIETH CENTURY-FOX. (R) February, 1964. Bobby Vinton, Patricia Morrow.

SURPRISE PACKAGE 100
COLUMBIA. (R) November, 1960. Yul Brynner, Mitzi Gaynor.

SURRENDER HELL! 85
ALLIED ARTISTS. (R) August, 1959. Keith Andes, Susan Cabot.

SURVIVE 85
PARAMOUNT. (R) July, 1976. Hugo Stiglitz, Norma Lazareno.

SUSAN SLADE 110
WARNER BROS. (R) November, 1961. Troy Donahue, Connie Stevens. Color.

SUSPIRA 92
TWENTIETH CENTURY-FOX. (R) August, 1977. Jessica Harper, Joan Bennett.

SVENGALI (Brit.) 82
METRO/GOLDWYN-MAYER. (R) September 9, 1955. Hildegarde Neff, Derek Bond. Color.

SWAMP WOMAN 72
WOOLNER BROS. (R) April, 1956. Beverly Garland, Marie Windsor, Carole Mathews. Color.

SWAN, THE (Cs) 112
METRO-GOLDWYN-MAYER. (R) April 27, 1956. Grace Kelly, Alec Guinness, Louis Jourdan. Color.

SWAN LAKE 81
COLUMBIA. (R) January, 1960. M. Plisetskaya, N. Fadeychev. Color.

SWARM, THE 116
WARNER BROS. (R) July, 1978. Michael Caine, Katharine Ross.

SWASHBUCKLER 100
UNIVERSAL. (R) July, 1976. Robert Shaw, James Earl Jones.

SWEDEN—HEAVEN AND HELL 90
AVCO EMBASSY. (R) August, 1969. Semi-documentary. Color.

SWEDISH WEDDING NIGHT (Swed., Eng. titles) 96
ROYAL FILMS INTERNATIONAL. (R) November, 1965. Jarl Kulle, Lena Hansson.

SWEET AND SOUR (Fr., Eng. titles) 93
PATHE-CONTEMPORARY. (R) December, 1964.

SWEET BIRD OF YOUTH (Cs) 120
METRO-GOLDWYN-MAYER. (R) March, 1962. Paul Newman, Geraldine Page. Color.

SWEET BODY OF DEBORAH, THE 105
WARNER BROS.-7 ARTS. (R) March, 1969. Carroll Baker, Jean Sorel, Evelyn Stewart. Color.

SWEET CHARITY 151
UNIVERSAL. (R) February, 1969. Shirley MacLaine, Sammy Davis, Jr., Ricardo Montalban. Color.

SWEET CREEK COUNTY WAR, THE 99
IMAGERY FILMS. (R) March, 1979. Richard Egan, Albert Salmi.

SWEET JESUS, PREACHER MAN 106
METRO-GOLDWYN-MAYER. (R) May, 1973. Roger E. Morley, William Smith. Color.

SWEET LIGHT IN A DARK ROOM (Czech., Eng. titles) .. 93
PROMENADE. (R) June 1966. Dana Smutna, Ivan Mistrik.

SWEET LOVE, BITTER 92
FILM 2 ASSOCIATES. (R) January, 1967. Dick Gregory, Don Murray.

SWEET NOVEMBER 114
WARNER BROS-SEVEN ARTS. (R) April, 1968. Sandy Dennis, Anthony Newley. Color.

SWEET REVENGE (P) 85
UNITED ARTISTS. (R) May, 1977. Stockard Channing, Sam Waterston.

SWEET RIDE, THE 110
TWENTIETH CENTURY-FOX. (R) June, 1968. Tony Franciosa, Michael Sarrazin, Jacqueline Bisset. Color.

SWEET SMELL OF SUCCESS 96
UNITED ARTISTS. (R) June, 1957. Burt Lancaster, Tony Curtis.

SWEET SWEETBACK'S BAADASSSSS SONG 97

Length In Mins.

CINEMATION. (R) April, 1971. Melvin Van Peebles. Color.

SWEETHEARTS ON PARADE 90
REPUBLIC. (R) July 15, 1953. Ray Middleton, Eileen Christy. Color.

SWEPT AWAY . . . BY AN UNUSUAL DESTINY IN THE BLUE SEA OF AUGUST 116
CINEMA V. (R) September, 1975. Giancarlo Giannini, Mariangela Melato.

SWIMMER, THE 94
COLUMBIA. (R) May, 1968. Burt Lancaster, Janice Rule. Color.

SWIMMING POOL, THE 87
AVCO-EMBASSY. (R) August, 1970. Alain Delon, Romy Schneider. Color.

SWINGER, THE 81
PARAMOUNT. (R) November, 1966. Ann-Margret, Tony Franciosa. Color.

SWINGERS PARADISE (T) 82
AMERICAN INTERNATIONAL. (R) May, 1965. Cliff Richard, Walter Slezak. Color.

SWINGIN' MAIDEN, THE 81
COLUMBIA. (R) January, 1964. Michael Craig, Anne Helm. Color.

SWINGIN' SUMMER (TS) 80
UNITED SCREEN ARTS. (R) April, 1965. James Stacey, William A. Wellman, Jr. Color.

SWINGING ALONG (Cs) 74
LIPPERT. (R) 1962. Tommy Noonan, Pete Marshall, Barbara Eden. Color.

SWISS FAMILY ROBINSON (P) 128
BUENA VISTA. (R) December, 1960. John Mills, Dorothy McGuire. Color.

SWORD IN THE STONE, THE (T) 75
BUENA VISTA. (R) November, 1963. Animation. Color.

SWORD OF ALI BABA, THE 81
UNIVERSAL. (R) May, 1965. Peter Mann, Jocelyn Lane. Color.

SWORD OF DOOM (T) (Jap.) 122
TOHO. (R) May, 1967.

SWORD OF EL CID 85
PRODUCTION RELEASING. (R) July, 1964. Roland Carey, Chantel Deberg. Color.

SWORD OF SHERWOOD FOREST (M) 80
COLUMBIA. (R) January, 1961. Richard Greene, Peter Cushing. Color.

SWORD OF THE CONQUEROR (Cs) 95
UNITED ARTISTS. (R) September, 1962. Jack Palance, Eleanora Rossi Drago. Color.

SWORDSMAN OF SIENNA (Cs) 92
METRO-GOLDWYN-MAYER. (R) November, 1962. Stewart Granger, Sylva Koscina. Color.

SYLVIA 115
PARAMOUNT. (R) February, 1965. Carroll Baker, George Maharis.

SYMPHONY FOR A MASSACRE (Fr., Eng. Titles) 110
SEVEN ARTS. (R) May, 1965. Michel Auclair, Claude Dauphin.

SYNANON 107
COLUMBIA. (R) May, 1965. Edmond O'Brien, Chuck Connors.

T

T-BIRD GANG 75
THE FILM GROUP. (R) July, 1959. Ed Nelson, John Brinkley.

THX 1138 88
WARNER BROS. (R) March, 1971. Robert Duvall, Donald Pleasance. Color.

TABOOS OF THE WORLD 97
AMERICAN INTERNATIONAL. (R) May, 1965. Documentary. Color.

TAFFY AND THE JUNGLE HUNTER 90
ALLIED ARTISTS. (R) February, 1965. Jacques Bergerac, Manuel Padilla. Color.

TAGGART 85
UNIVERSAL. (R) February, 1965. Tony Young, Dan Duryea. Color.

TAKE, THE 93
COLUMBIA. (R) May, 1974. Billy Dee Williams, Eddie Albert.

TAKE A GIANT STEP 100
UNITED ARTISTS. (R) February, 1960. Johnny Nash, Estelle Hemsley.

TAKE A GIRL LIKE YOU 96
COLUMBIA. (R) October, 1970. Hayley Mills, Oliver Reed. Color.

TAKE A HARD RIDE 103
TWENTIETH CENTURY-FOX. (R) July, 1975. Jim Brown, Lee Van Cleef.

Length In Mins.

TAKE DOWN 107
BUENA VISTA. (R) March, 1979. Edward Herrmann, Lorenzo Lamas.

TAKE HER SHE'S MINE 98
TWENTIETH CENTURY-FOX. (R) November, 1963. James Stewart, Sandra Dee. Color.

TAKE IT ALL 90
LOPERT PICTURE. (R) April, 1966. Johanne, Claude Jutra.

TAKE THE MONEY AND RUN 85
CINERAMA. (R) August, 1969. Woody Allen, Janet Margolin, Marcel Hillaire. Color.

TAKING OF PELHAM ONE TWO THREE, THE (P) 102
UNITED ARTISTS. (R) October, 1974. Walter Matthau, Robert Shaw.

TAKING OFF 102
UNIVERSAL. (R) April, 1971. Buck Henry, Lynn Carlin. Color.

TALE OF TWO CITIES, A 117
RANK FILM DISTRIBUTORS OF AMERICA. (R) November, 1958. Dirk Bogarde, Dorothy Tutin.

TALES FROM THE CRYPT 92
CINERAMA. (R) March, 1972. Ralph Richardson, Joan Collins, Peter Cushing. Color.

TALES THAT WITNESS MADNESS 90
PARAMOUNT. (R) October, 1973. Kim Novak, Georgia Brown.

TALL BLOND MAN WITH ONE BLACK SHOE, THE 90
CINEMA V. (R) September, 1973. Pierre Richard, Bernard Blier.

TALL MAN RIDING 68
WARNER BROTHERS. (R) June 18, 1955. Randolph Scott, Dorothy Malone. Color.

TALL MEN, THE 121
TWENTIETH CENTURY-FOX. (R) October, 1955. Clark Gable, Jane Russell, Robert Ryan. Color.

TALL STORY 91
WARNER BROS. (R) April, 1960. Anthony Perkins, Jane Fonda.

TALL STRANGER, THE 83
ALLIED ARTISTS. (R) November, 1957. Joel McCrea, Virginia Mayo. Color.

TALL T, THE 78
COLUMBIA. (R) April, 1957.

TALL WOMEN, THE 92
ALLIED ARTISTS. (R) March, 1967. Anne Baxter, Maria Perschy. Color.

TAMAHINE (Cs) 85
METRO-GOLDWYN-MAYER. (R) March, 1964. Nancy Kwan, John Fraser. Color.

TAMANGO (Cs) 98
HAL ROACH. (R) August, 1959. Curt Jurgens, Dorothy Dandridge. Color.

TAMARIND SEED, THE (P) 123
AVCO-EMBASSY. (R) July, 1974. Julie Andrews, Omar Sharif.

TAMING OF THE SHREW, THE (P) 126
COLUMBIA/ROYAL FILMS. (R) March, 1967. Elizabeth Taylor, Richard Burton. Color.

TAMING SUTTON'S GAL (Naturma) 71
REPUBLIC. (R) September, 1957. John Lupton, Gloria Talbott.

TAMMY AND THE BACHELOR (Cs) 89
UNIVERSAL. (R) August, 1957. Debbie Reynolds, Leslie Neilsen. Color.

TAMMY AND THE DOCTOR 88
UNIVERSAL. (R) June, 1963. Sandra Dee, Peter Fonda. Color.

TAMMY AND THE MILLIONAIRE 80
UNIVERSAL. (R) July, 1967. Debbie Watson, Frank McGrath. Color.

TAMMY TELL ME TRUE 97
UNIVERSAL. (R) July, 1961. Sandra Dee, John Gavin. Color.

TANK BATTALION 89
AMERICAN INTERNATIONAL. (R) July, 1958. Don Kelly, Marjorie Hellen.

TANK COMMANDOS 79
AMERICAN INTERNATIONAL. (R) March, 1959. Robert Barron, Maggie Lawrence.

TANK FORCE (Cs) 81
COLUMBIA. (R) August, 1958. Victor Mature, Leo Genn. Color.

TARANTULA 80
UNIVERSAL. (R) December, 1955. John Agar, Mara Corday.

TARAS BULBA (P) 122
UNITED ARTISTS. (R) December, 1962. Tony Curtis, Yul Brynner. Color.

TARAWA BEACHHEAD 77
COLUMBIA. (R) November, 1958. Kerwin Mathews, Julie Adams.

TARGET ZERO 92

	Length In Mins.

WARNER BROTHERS. (R) December 10, 1955. Richard Conte, Peggie Castle.

TARGETS 92
PARAMOUNT. (R) August, 1968. Boris Karloff, Tim O'Kelley, Nancy Houeh. Color.

TARNISHED ANGELS, THE (Cs) 91
UNIVERSAL. (R) January, 1958. Rock Hudson, Robert Stack.

TARTARS, THE 83
METRO-GOLDWYN-MAYER. (R) June, 1962. Victor Mature, Orson Welles. Color.

TARZAN AND THE GREAT RIVER (P) 88
PARAMOUNT. (R) September, 1967. Mike Henry, Jan Murray. Color.

TARZAN AND THE JUNGLE BOY 90
PARAMOUNT. (R) May, 1968. Mike Henry, Rafer Johnson. Color.

TARZAN AND THE LOST SAFARI 80
METRO-GOLDWYN-MAYER. (R) May 3, 1957. Gordon Scott, Yolande Donland. Color.

TARZAN GOES TO INDIA (Cs) 86
METRO-GOLDWYN-MAYER. (R) July, 1962. Jock Mahoney, Mark Dana. Color.

TARZAN, THE APE MAN 82
METRO-GOLDWYN-MAYER. (R) October, 1959. Denny Miller, Joanna Barnes. Color.

TARZAN THE MAGNIFICENT 88
PARAMOUNT. (R) July, 1960. Gordon Scott, Betta St. John.

TARZAN'S DEADLY SILENCE 82
NATIONAL GENERAL. (R) April, 1970. Ron Ely, Jock Mahoney. Color.

TARZAN'S FIGHT FOR LIFE (Cs) 86
METRO-GOLDWYN-MAYER. (R) July, 1958. Gordon Scott, Eve Brent. Color.

TARZAN'S GREATEST ADVENTURE 90
PARAMOUNT. (R) July, 1959. Gordon Scott, Anthony Quayle. Color.

TARZAN'S HIDDEN JUNGLE 73
RKO RADIO. (R) February 16, 1955. Gordon Scott, Vera Miles.

TARZAN'S JUNGLE REBELLION 92
NATIONAL GENERAL. (R) May, 1970. Ron Ely, Manuel Padilla, Jr. Color.

TARZAN'S THREE CHALLENGES (D) 92
METRO-GOLDWYN-MAYER. (R) June, 1963. Jock Mahoney, Woody Strode. Color.

TASTE OF HONEY, A 100
CONTINENTAL. (R) May, 1962. Dora Bryan, Rita Tushingham.

TASTE THE BLOOD OF DRACULA 95
WARNER BROS. (R) September, 1970. Christopher Lee, Linda Hayden. Color.

TATTERED DRESS, THE (Cs) 93
UNIVERSAL. (R) April, 1957. Jeff Chandler, Jeanne Crain.

TATTOOED POLICE HORSE, THE 48
BUENA VISTA. (R) December, 1964. Sandy Sanders, Charles Seel. Color.

TAXI DRIVER 112
COLUMBIA. (R) February, 1976. Robert De Niro, Jodie Foster.

TAXI FOR TOBRUK (D) 90
SEVEN ARTS. (R) March, 1965. Charles Aznavour, Lino Ventura.

TCHAIKOVSKY 105
TIOMKIN. (R) December, 1971. Innokenti Smoktunovsky, Antonina Shuranova. Color.

TEA AND SYMPATHY (Cs) 122
METRO-GOLDWYN-MAYER. (R) Sept. 28, 1956. Deborah Kerr, John Kerr. Color.

TEACHER'S PET (VV) 120
PARAMOUNT. (R) April, 1958. Clark Gable, Doris Day.

TEAHOUSE OF THE AUGUST MOON, THE (Cs) 123
METRO-GOLDWYN-MAYER. (R) Dec., 1956. Marlon Brando, Glenn Ford. Color.

TEARS FROM SIMON (Brit.) 91
REPUBLIC. (R) January, 1957. David Farrar, David Knight. Color.

TECKMAN MYSTERY, THE 90
ASSOCIATED ARTISTS. (R) August, 1955. Margaret Leighton, John Justin.

TEENAGE BAD GIRL (Brit.) 100
DIST. CORP. OF AMER. (R) December, 1957. Anna Neagle, Sylvia Sims.

TEENAGE CAVE MAN 65
AMERICAN INTERNATIONAL. (R) July, 1958. Robert Vaughn, Leslie Bradley.

TEENAGE CRIME WAVE 77
COLUMBIA. (R) November, 1955. Tommy Cook, Mollie McCart.

TEENAGE DOLL 71

ALLIED ARTISTS. (R) September, 1957. June Kenney, Fay Spain.

TEENAGE MILLIONAIRE 84
UNITED ARTISTS. (R) August, 1961. Jimmy Clayton, Rocky Graziano.

TEENAGE REBEL (Cs) 94
TWENTIETH CENTURY-FOX. (R) November, 1956. Ginger Rogers, Michael Rennie.

TEENAGE REBELLION 81
TRANS AMERICAN. (R) May, 1967. Documentary.

TEENAGE WOLF PACK (Ger.) 89
DIST. CORP. OF AMER. (R) December, 1958. Henry Bookholt, Karen Beal.

TEENAGE ZOMBIES 73
GOVERNOR FILMS. (R) April, 1960. Don Sullivan, Katherine Victor.

TEENAGERS FROM OUTER SPACE 85
WARNER BROS. (R) June, 1959. David Love, Dawn Anderson.

TELEFON (P) 103
UNITED ARTISTS. (R) December, 1977. Charles Bronson, Lee Remick.

TELL ME IN THE SUNLIGHT 86
MOVIE-RAMA. (R) May, 1967. Steve Cochran, Shary Marshall.

TELL ME THAT YOU LOVE ME JUNIE MOON 113
PARAMOUNT. (R) June, 1970. Liza Minelli, Robert Moore, Ken Howard. Color.

TELL THEM WILLIE BOY IS HERE (P) 96
UNIVERSAL. (R) February, 1970. Robert Redford, Robert Blake, Katharine Ross. Color.

"10" 122
WARNER BROS. (R) October, 1979. Dudley Moore, Julie Andrews.

TEN COMMANDMENTS, THE (VV) 219
PARAMOUNT. (R) Special, 1957. Charlton Heston, Yul Brynner. Color.

TEN DAYS TO TULARE 77
UNITED ARTISTS. (R) November, 1958. Sterling Hayden, Grace Raynor.

TEN DAYS WONDER 100
LEVITT-PICKMAN. (R) April, 1972. Orson Welles, Anthony Perkins. Color.

TEN FROM YOUR SHOW OF SHOWS 92
WALTER READE. (R) February, 1972. Sid Caesar, Imogene Coca.

TEN LITTLE INDIANS 92
SEVEN ARTS. (R) January, 1966. Hugh O'Brian, Shirley Eaton.

TEN LITTLE INDIANS 98
AVCO-EMBASSY. (R) March, 1975. Oliver Reed, Elke Sommer.

TEN NORTH FREDERICK (Cs) 102
TWENTIETH CENTURY-FOX. (R) May, 1958. Gary Cooper, Diane Varsi.

10 RILLINGTON PLACE 109
COLUMBIA. (R) May, 1971. Richard Attenborough, Judy Geeson. Color.

TEN SECONDS TO HELL 93
UNITED ARTISTS. (R) July, 1959. Jeff Chandler, Jack Palance.

10:30 P.M. SUMMER 85
LOPERT. (R) November, 1966. Melina Mercouri, Romy Schneider. Color.

TEN THOUSAND BEDROOMS (Cs) 114
METRO-GOLDWYN-MAYER. (R) March 29, 1957. Dean Martin, Anna Maria Alberghetti. Color.

TEN WANTED MEN 80
COLUMBIA. (R) February, 1955. Randolph Scott, Jocelyn Brando. Color.

TEN WHO DARED 92
BUENA VISTA. (R) November, 1960. Brian Keith, John Beal. Color.

TENANT, THE 125
PARAMOUNT. (R) June, 1976. Roman Polanski, Isabelle Adjani.

TENDER IS THE NIGHT (Cs) 146
TWENTIETH CENTURY-FOX. (R) February, 1962. Jennifer Jones, Jason Robards, Jr. Color.

TENDER SCOUNDREL (Fr.) 99
EMBASSY. (R) August, 1967. Jean-Paul Belmondo, Nadja Tiller. Color.

TENDER TRAP, THE (Cs) 111
METRO-GOLDWYN-MAYER. (R) November 4, 1955. Frank Sinatra, Debbie Reynolds, David Wayne, Celeste Holm. Color.

TENNESSEE'S PARTNER (SS) 87
RKO RADIO. (R) September, 1955. John Payne, Ronald Reagan, Rhonda Fleming. Color.

TENSION AT TABLE ROCK 93
UNIVERSAL. (R) October, 1956. Richard Egan, Dorothy Malone. Color.

TENTH VICTIM, THE 92

Length In Mins.

EMBASSY. (R) December, 1965. Marcello Mastroianni, Ursula Andress. Color.

TEOREMA (Ital. dubbed) 98
CONTINENTAL. (R) May, 1969. Terence Stamp, Silvana Mangano. Color.

TERM OF TRIAL 113
WARNER BROS. (R) February, 1963. Laurence Olivier, Simone Signoret.

TERMINAL MAN, THE 100
WARNER BROS. (R) June, 1974. George Segal, Joan Hackett.

TERRACE, THE (Span., Eng. titles) 90
ROYAL. (R) November, 1964. Graciela Borges, Leonardo Favio.

TERROR, THE (VS) 81
AMERICAN INTERNATIONAL. (R) September, 1963. Boris Karloff, Jack Nicholson. Color.

TERROR AT MIDNIGHT 70
REPUBLIC. (R) April 27, 1956. Scott Brady, Joan Vohs.

TERROR FROM THE YEAR 5,000 68
AMERICAN INTERNATIONAL. (R) August, 1958. Joyce Holden, Ward Costello.

TERROR IN A TEXAS TOWN 80
UNITED ARTISTS. (R) September, 1958. Sterling Hayden, Sebastian Cabot.

TERROR IN THE JUNGLE 82
CROWN INTERNATIONAL. (R) March, 1969. Robert Burns, Fawn Silver.

TERROR IN THE WAX MUSEUM 95
CINERAMA. (R) May, 1973. Ray Milland, Maurice Evans. Color.

TERROR IS A MAN 89
VALIANT. (R) December, 1959. Francis Lederer, Greta Thyssen.

TERROR OF THE TONGS 80
COLUMBIA. (R) May, 1961. Christopher Lee, Geoffrey Toone. Color.

TERROR STREET 83
LIPPERT. (R) December 4, 1958. Dan Duryea, Alsy Albin.

TERRORNAUTS, THE 75
AVCO EMBASSY. (R) June, 1969. Simon Oates, Zena Marshall. Color.

TERRY WHITMORE, FOR EXAMPLE 98
GROVE. (R) November, 1969. Documentary. b&w.

TESS OF THE STORM COUNTRY (Cs) 85
TWENTIETH CENTURY FOX. (R) December, 1960. Diane Baker, Lee Philips. Color.

TEXAS ACROSS THE RIVER (T) 101
UNIVERSAL. (R) November, 1966. Dean Martin, Alain Delon. Color.

TEXAS CHAIN SAW MASSACRE, THE 87
BRYANSTON. (R) November, 1974. Marilyn Burns, Allen Danziger.

TEXAS LADY (SS) 80
RKO RADIO. (R) November 30, 1955. Claudette Colbert, Barry Sullivan. Color.

TEXICAN, THE (TS) 86
COLUMBIA. (R) 1966. Audie Murphy, Broderick Crawford. Color.

THANK GOD IT'S FRIDAY 90
COLUMBIA. (R) May, 1978. Hilary Beane, John Friedrich.

THANK HEAVEN FOR SMALL FAVORS (Fr., Eng. titles) 84
INT. CLASSICS. (R) January, 1965. Bourvil, Francis Blancho.

THANK YOU VERY MUCH 106
COLUMBIA. (R) August, 1969. Sandy Dennis, Ian McKellen, Michael Coles. Color.

THAT CERTAIN FEELING (VV) 103
PARAMOUNT. (R) July, 1956. Bob Hope, Eva Marie Saint. Color.

THAT COLD DAY IN THE PARK 113
COMMONWEALTH UNITED. (R) June, 1969. Sandy Dennis, Michael Burns, John Garfield, Jr.

THAT DARN CAT 116
BUENA VISTA. (R) December, 1965. Hayley Mills, Dean Jones. Color.

THAT FUNNY FEELING 93
UNIVERSAL. (R) September, 1965. Sandra Dee, Bobby Darin. Color.

THAT KIND OF WOMAN 92
PARAMOUNT. (R) September, 1959. Sophia Loren, Tab Hunter.

THAT LADY (Cs) 100
TWENTIETH CENTURY-FOX. (R) May, 1955. Olivia de Havilland, Gilbert Roland. Color.

THAT MAN BOLD 105
UNIVERSAL. (R) December, 1973. Fred Williamson, Byron Webster.

THAT MAN FROM RIO 114
LOPERT. (R) June, 1964. Jean-Paul Belmondo, Francoise Dorleac. Color.

THAT MAN GEORGE 92
ALLIED ARTISTS. (R) October, 1967. George Hamilton, Claudine Auger. Color.

THAT MAN IN ISTANBUL (T) 117
COLUMBIA. (R) February, 1966. Horst Bucholz, Sylvia Koscina. Color.

THAT NIGHT 88
UNIVERSAL. (R) September, 1957. John Beal, Augusta Dabney.

THAT SPLENDID NOVEMBER 93
UNITED ARTISTS. (R) June, 1971. Gina Lollobrigida, Paolo Turco. Color.

THAT TENNESSEE BEAT 84
20TH CENTURY-FOX. (R) October, 1966. Sharon DeBord, Minnie Pearl. Color.

THAT TOUCH OF MINK (P) 99
UNIVERSAL. (R) July, 1962. Cary Grant, Doris Day. Color.

THAT'S ENTERTAINMENT! 132
UNITED ARTISTS. (R) June, 1974. Fred Astaire, Bing Crosby, Gene Kelly.

THAT'S ENTERTAINMENT, PART 2 133
UNITED ARTISTS. (R) May, 1976. Fred Astaire, Gene Kelly.

THEATRE OF BLOOD 104
UNITED ARTISTS. (R) April, 1973. Vincent Price, Diana Rigg. Color.

THERE WAS A CROOKED MAN 125
WARNER BROS. (R) December, 1970. Kirk Douglas, Henry Fonda. Color.

THERE'S A GIRL IN MY SOUP 95
COLUMBIA. (R) December, 1970. Peter Sellers, Goldie Hawn. Color.

THERE'S ALWAYS TOMORROW 84
UNIVERSAL. (R) February, 1956. Barbara Stanwyck, Fred MacMurray, Joan Bennett.

THERE'S ALWAYS VANILLA 91
CAMBIST. (R) February, 1972. Roy Laine, Judith Streiner. Color.

THERESE (Fr., Eng. titles) 107
PATHE-CONTEMPORARY. (R) November, 1963. Jean-Paul Belmondo, Francoise Dorleac.

THERESE AND ISABELLE (Fr.) 118
AUDUBON. (R) May, 1968. Essy Persson, Anna Gael.

THESE ARE THE DAMNED 77
COLUMBIA. (R) July, 1965. MacDonald Carey, Shirley Anne Field.

THESE THOUSAND HILLS (Cs) 96
TWENTIETH CENTURY-FOX. (R) February, 1959. Don Murray, Richard Egan. Color.

THESE WILDER YEARS 91
METRO-GOLDWYN-MAYER. (R) Aug. 3, 1956. James Cagney, Barbara Stanwyck, Walter Pidgeon.

THEY ALL DIED LAUGHING 90
CONTINENTAL. (R) March, 1964. Leo McKern, Janet Murro.

THEY CALL ME MISTER TIBBS! 108
UNITED ARTISTS. (R) August, 1970. Sidney Poitier, Martin Landau, Barbara McNair. Color.

THEY CAME TO CORDURA (Cs) 123
COLUMBIA. (R) October, 1959. Gary Cooper, Rita Hayworth. Color.

THEY CAME TO ROB LAS VEGAS 130
WARNER BROS.-7 ARTS. (R) February, 1969. Gary Lockwood, Elke Sommer, Lee J. Cobb, Jack Palance.

THEY MIGHT BE GIANTS 88
UNIVERSAL. (R) March, 1971. George C. Scott, Joanne Woodward. Color.

THEY ONLY KILL THEIR MASTERS 97
METRO-GOLDWYN-MAYER. (R) November, 1972. James Garner, Katharine Ross. Color.

THEY SHOOT HORSES, DON'T THEY? 129
CINERAMA. (R) December, 1969. Jane Fonda, Michael Sarrazin, Susannah York, Gig Young. Color.

THEY WERE SO YOUNG 80
LIPPERT. (R) January 7, 1955. Scott Brady, Raymond Burr.

THEY WHO DARE (Brit.) 101
ASSOCIATED ARTISTS. (R) November, 1955. Dirk Bogarde, Akim Tamiroff. Color.

THIEF OF BAGHDAD, THE (Cs) 90
METRO-GOLDWYN-MAYER. (R) August, 1961. Steve Reeves, Georgia Moll. Color.

THIEF OF PARIS (Fr.) 119
LOPERT. (R) August, 1967. Jean-Paul Belmondo, Genevieve Bujold. Color.

THIEF WHO CAME TO DINNER, THE 105
WARNER BROS. (R) March, 1972. Ryan O'Neal, Jacqueline Bisset. Color.

THIEVES 103
PARAMOUNT. (R) February, 1977. Marlo Thomas, Charles Grodin.

THIEVES LIKE US 122

	Length In Mins.

UNITED ARTISTS. (R) February, 1974. Keith Carradine, Shelley Duvall.
THIN RED LINE, THE (Cs) 99
ALLIED ARTISTS. (R) June, 1964. Keir Dullea, Jack Warden.
THING THAT COULDN'T DIE, THE (Cs) 99
UNIVERSAL INTERNATIONAL. (R) June, 1958. William Reynolds, Andra Martin. Color.
THING WITH TWO HEADS, THE 93
AMERICAN INTERNATIONAL. (R) July, 1972. Ray Milland, Rosy Grier. Color.
THINGS OF LIFE, THE (French; Eng. titles) 88
COLUMBIA. (R) August, 1970. Romy Schneider, Michel Piccoli. Color.
THIRD DAY, THE (P) 119
WARNER BROTHERS. (R) August, 1965. George Peppard, Elizabeth Ashley. Color.
THIRD KEY, THE 84
RANK. (R) July, 1957. Jack Hawkins, John Stratton.
THIRD MAN ON THE MOUNTAIN, THE 105
BUENA VISTA. (R) November, 1959. Michael Rennie, James MacArthur. Color.
THIRD OF A MAN 81
UNITED ARTISTS. (R) October, 1962. James Drury, Jan Shepard.
THIRD SECRET, THE (Cs) 103
TWENTIETH CENTURY-FOX. (R) April, 1964. Stephen Boyd, Jack Hawkins.
THIRD VOICE, THE (Cs) 80
TWENTIETH CENTURY-FOX. (R) January, 1960. Edmund O'Brien, Julie London.
THIRTEEN FIGHTING MEN (Cs) 71
TWENTIETH CENTURY-FOX. (R) April, 1960. Grant Williams, Brad Dexter.
13 FRIGHTENED GIRLS 89
COLUMBIA. (R) July, 1963. Kathy Dunn, Murray Hamilton. Color.
13 GHOSTS 88
COLUMBIA. (R) July, 1960. Charles Herbert, Jo Morrow. Color.
13 WEST STREET 80
COLUMBIA. (R) May, 1962. Alan Ladd, Rod Steiger.
—30— 96
WARNER BROS. (R) November, 1959. Jack Webb, William Conrad.
30 FOOT BRIDE OF CANDY ROCK, THE 73
COLUMBIA. (R) August, 1959. Lou Costello, Dorothy Provine.
30 IS A DANGEROUS AGE, CYNTHIA 85
COLUMBIA. (R) March, 1968. Dudley Moore, Suzy Kendall. Color.
30 YEARS OF FUN 85
TWENTIETH CENTURY-FOX. (R) February, 1963. Film Clips.
39 STEPS, THE (Cs) 95
TWENTIETH CENTURY-FOX. (R) July, 1960. Kenneth More, Taina Elg. Color.
36 HOURS (P) 115
METRO-GOLDWYN-MAYER. (R) January, 1965. James Garner, Eva Marie Saint.
THIS ANGRY AGE (R) 100
COLUMBIA. (R) May, 1958. Anthony Perkins, Silvano Mangano. Color.
THIS BEAST MUST DIE! 93
CINERAMA. (R) April, 1974. Calvin Lockhart, Peter Cushing.
THIS COULD BE THE NIGHT (Cs) 105
METRO-GOLDWYN-MAYER. (R) May 17, 1957. Jean Simmons, Paul Douglas, Anthony Franciosa.
THIS EARTH IS MINE (Cs) 125
UNIVERSAL. (R) July, 1959. Rock Hudson, Jean Simmons. Color.
THIS HAPPY FEELING (Cs) 92
UNIVERSAL. (R) June, 1958. Debbie Reynolds, Curt Jurgens. Color.
THIS IS RUSSIA 67
UNIVERSAL. (R) January, 1958. Documentary. Color.
THIS ISLAND EARTH 87
UNIVERSAL. (R) June, 1955. Bart Roberts, Faith Domergue. Color.
THIS MAN MUST DIE (French; Eng. titles) 115
ALLIED ARTISTS. (R) August, 1970. Michel Duchaussoy, Caroline Cellier. Color.
THIS PROPERTY IS CONDEMNED 110
PARAMOUNT. (R) Summer, 1966. Natalie Wood, Robert Redford. Color.
THIS REBEL BREED 90
WARNER BROS. (R) March, 1960. Rita Moreno, Mark Damon.
THIS SPECIAL FRIENDSHIP (Fr.) 99
PATHE CONTEMPORARY. (R) November, 1967. Lacombrade, Didier Haudepin.
THIS SPORTING LIFE 129

	Length In Mins.

CONTINENTAL. (R) July, 1963. Richard Harris, Rachel Roberts.
THIS STRANGE PASSION (Mex.) 80
OMNIFILMS. (R) December, 1955. Arturo de Cordova.
THOMAS CROWN AFFAIR, THE 102
UNITED ARTISTS. (R) August, 1968. Steve McQueen, Faye Dunaway, Paul Burke. Color.
THOMASINE AND BUSHROD 95
COLUMBIA. (R) April, 1974. Max Julien, Venetta McGee.
THOROUGHLY MODERN MILLIE 138
UNIVERSAL. (R) April, 1967. Julie Andrews, Mary Tyler Moore. Color.
THOSE CALLOWAYS 131
BUENA VISTA. (R) November, 1964. Brian Keith, Vera Miles. Color.
THOSE DARING YOUNG MEN IN THEIR JAUNTY JALOPIES (P) 125
PARAMOUNT. (R) August, 1969. Peter Cook, Tony Curtis, Bourvil. Color.
THOSE FANTASTIC FLYING FOOLS (P) 92
AMERICAN INTERNATIONAL. (R) June, 1967. Burl Ives, Troy Donahue. Color.
THOSE LIPS, THOSE EYES (P) 106
UNITED ARTISTS. (R) August, 1980. Frank Langella.
THOSE MAGNIFICENT MEN IN THEIR FLYING MACHINES (Todd-AO) 152
TWENTIETH CENTURY-FOX. (R) June, 1956. Special. Stuart Whitman, Sarah Miles. Color.
THOUSAND CLOWNS, A 118
UNITED ARTISTS. (R) April, 1966. Jason Robards, Barbara Harris.
1,000 PLANE RAID, THE 94
UNITED ARTISTS. October, 1969. Christopher George, J.D. Cannon. Color.
THREAT, THE 66
WARNER BROS. (R) March, 1960. Robert Knapp, Linda Lawson.
THREE 104
UNITED ARTISTS. (R) December, 1969. Charlotte Rampling, Robie Porter, Sam Waterston. Color.
THREE BAD SISTERS 75
UNITED ARTISTS. (R) January, 1956. Maria English, Kathleen Hughes, Sara Shane, John Bromfield.
THREE BITES OF THE APPLE (P) 105
METRO-GOLDWYN-MAYER. (R) February, 1967. David McCallum, Sylva Koscina. Color.
THREE BRAVE MEN (Cs) 88
TWENTIETH CENTURY-FOX. (R) January, 1957. Ernest Borgnine, Ray Milland.
THREE CAME TO KILL 70
UNITED ARTISTS. (R) April, 1960. Cameron Mitchell, John Lupton.
THREE CASES OF MURDER (Brit.) 90
ASSOCIATE ARTISTS. (R) March, 1955. Orson Welles, Alan Badel.
THREE DAY PASS 103
SIGMA III. (R) May, 1968. Harry Barid, Nicole Berger.
THREE DAYS OF THE CONDOR 118
PARAMOUNT. (R) September, 1975. Robert Redford, Faye Dunaway.
THREE FACES OF EVE, THE (Cs) 91
TWENTIETH CENTURY-FOX. (R) October, 1957. Joanne Woodward, David Wayne.
THREE FOR JAMIE DAWN 81
ALLIED ARTISTS. (R) July 8, 1956. Laraine Day, Ricardo Montalban.
THREE FOR THE SHOW (Cs) 93
COLUMBIA. (R) April, 1955. Betty Grable, Marge and Gower Champion. Color.
THREE GIRLS DOWN 87
NEW WORLD PICTURES. (R) April, 1973. Robert Collins, Isabel Jewel. Color.
THREE GUNS FOR TEXAS 99
UNIVERSAL. (R) June, 1968. Neville Brand, Peter Brown. Color.
300 SPARTANS, THE (Cs) 114
TWENTIETH CENTURY-FOX. (R) September, 1962. Richard Egan, Sir Ralph Richardson. Color.
THREE INTO TWO WON'T GO 93
UNIVERSAL. (R) July, 1969. Claire Bloom, Rod Steiger, Judy Geeson. Color.
THREE LIVES OF THOMASINA, THE 97
BUENA VISTA. (R) December, 1963. Patrick McGoohan, Susan Hampshire. Color.
THREE MURDERESSES 90
TWENTIETH CENTURY-FOX. (R) February, 1960. Alain Delon, Mylene Demongeot.
THREE MUSKETEERS, THE (P) 105
TWENTIETH CENTURY-FOX. (R) June, 1974. Oliver Reed, Raquel Welch, Richard Chamberlain.
THREE ON A COUCH 109

	Length In Mins.

COMET. (R) February, 1967. Jean-Pierre Kalfon, Amidou, Janine Magnan.

TO BED . . . OR NOT TO BED (Ital., Eng. titles) 100
READE-STERLING. (R) December, 1963. Alberta Sordi, Barbara Wastenson.

TO CATCH A THIEF (VV) 97
PARAMOUNT. (R) September, 1955. Cary Grant, Grace Kelly. Color.

TO COMMIT A MURDER 91
CINERAMA. (R) January, 1970. Louis Jourdan, Senta Berger, Edmund O'Brien. Color.

TO DIE IN MADRID 85
ALTURA FILMS INTERNATIONAL. (R) September, 1965. Documentary.

TO DIE OF LOVE 110
METRO-GOLDWYN-MAYER. (R) February, 1972. Annie Girardot, Bruno Pradal. Color.

TO FIND A MAN 90
COLUMBIA. (R) January, 1972. Pamela Sue Martin, Darren O'Connor. Color.

TO HELL AND BACK (Cs) 100
UNIVERSAL. (R) October, 1955. Audie Murphy, Marshall Thompson. Color.

TO KILL A CLOWN 72
TWENTIETH CENTURY-FOX. (R) August, 1972. Alan Alda, Blythe Danner. Color.

TO KILL A MOCKINGBIRD 129
UNIVERSAL. (R) March, 1963. Gregory Peck, Mary Badham.

TO LOVE (Swed., Eng. titles) 88
PROMINENT. (R) November, 1964. Harriet Anderson, Zbigniew Cybulski.

TO PARIS WITH LOVE (Brit.) 78
CONTINENTAL. (R) April, 1955. Alec Guinness, Odile Versolfs. Color.

TO SIR WITH LOVE 105
COLUMBIA. (R) June, 1967. Sidney Poitier, Judy Geeson. Color.

TO TRAP A SPY 92
METRO-GOLDWYN-MAYER. (R) February, 1966. Robert Vaughn, David McCallum. Color.

TOBRUK (T) 110
UNIVERSAL. (R) February, 1967. Rock Hudson, George Peppard. Color.

TOBY TYLER 96
BUENA VISTA. (R) February, 1960. Kevin Corcoran, Henry Calvin. Color.

TODD KILLINGS, THE 93
NATIONAL GENERAL. (R) August, 1971. Robert F. Lyons, Richard Thomas. Color.

TOKYO AFTER DARK 80
PARAMOUNT. (R) January, 1959. Richard Long, Michi Kobi.

TOKYO OLYMPIAD (Cs) 93
JACK DOUGLAS ASSOCIATES. (R) January, 1966. Documentary. Color.

TOM HORN (P) 98
WARNER BROS. (R) March, 1980. Steve McQueen, Linda Evans.

TOM JONES 131
LOPERT. (R) October, 1963. Albert Finney, Susannah York. Color.

TOM SAWYER 100
UNITED ARTISTS. (R) June, 1973. Johnny Whitaker, Celeste Holm. Color.

TOM THUMB 98
METRO-GOLDWYN-MAYER. (R) December, 1958. Russ Tamblyn, Alan Young. Color.

TOMAHAWK TRAIL 60
UNITED ARTISTS. (R) February, 1957. Chuck Connors, Susan Cummings.

TOMB OF LIGEIA, THE 81
AMERICAN INTERNATIONAL. (R) January, 1965. Vincent Price, Elizabeth Shepherd. Color.

TOMBOY AND THE CHAMP 92
UNIVERSAL. (R) Apr., 1961. Candy Moore, Ben Johnson. Color.

TOMMY 111
COLUMBIA. (R) March, 1975. Ann-Margret, Oliver Reed.

TOMORROW AT TEN 80
GOVERNOR. (R) April, 1964. John Gregson, Robert Shaw.

TONKA 97
BUENA VISTA. (R) December, 1958. Sal Mineo, Jerome Courtland. Color.

TONY ROME (P) 109
TWENTIETH CENTURY-FOX. (R) November, 1967. Frank Sinatra, Jill St. John. Color.

TOO BAD SHE'S BAD (Ital.) 95
KINGSLEY. (R) December, 1955. Sophia Loren, Vittorio De Sica.

TOO LATE BLUES 100

	Length In Mins.

PARAMOUNT. (R) January, 1962. Bobby Darin, Stella Stevens.

TOO LATE THE HERO (P) 133
CINERAMA. (R) July, 1970. Michael Caine, Cliff Robertson. Color.

TOO MUCH TOO SOON 121
WARNER BROTHERS. (R) May, 1958. Dorothy Malone, Errol Flynn.

TOO SOON TO LOVE 85
UNIVERSAL. (R) March, 1960. Jennifer West, Richard Evans.

TOO YOUNG FOR LOVE (Ital.-Eng. dubbed) 88
I.F.E. (R) April, 1955. Marina Vlady, Pierre Michel Beck.

TOP GUN 73
UNITED ARTISTS. (R) December, 1955. Sterling Hayden, William Bishop.

TOP OF THE WORLD 90
UNITED ARTISTS. (R) May, 1955. Dale Robertson, Frank Lovejoy.

TOP SECRET AFFAIR 100
WARNER BROTHERS. (R) February 9, 1957. Kirk Douglas, Susan Hayward.

TOPAZ 125
UNIVERSAL. (R) December, 1969. John Forsythe, Michel Piccoli, Frederick Stafford. Color.

TOPKAPI 120
UNITED ARTISTS. (R) October, 1964. Melina Mercouri, Maximillian Schell. Color.

TORA! TORA! TORA! (P) 143
20TH CENTURY-FOX. (R) October, 1970. Jason Robards, Martin Balsam, E.G. Marshall. Color.

TORERO! 75
COLUMBIA. (R) November, 1957. Louis Precuna.

TORMENTED 75
ALLIED ARTISTS. (R) November, 1960. Richard Carlson, Susan Gordon.

TORN CURTAIN 128
UNIVERSAL. (R) August, 1966. Paul Newman, Julie Andrews. Color.

TORPEDO RUN (Cs) 98
METRO-GOLDWYN-MAYER. (R) October, 1958. Glenn Ford, Ernest Borgnine.

TORTURE GARDEN 93
COLUMBIA. (R) March, 1968. Jack Palance, Burgess Meredith. Color.

TOUCH, THE 113
CINERAMA. (R) July, 1971. Elliott Gould, Bibi Anderson, Max von Sydow. Color.

TOUCH AND GO (Brit.) 85
UNIVERSAL. (R) April, 1956. Jack Hawkins, Margaret Johnston. Color.

TOUCH AND GO (French; Eng. titles) 110
LIBRA FILMS. (R) July, 1975. Marlene Jobert, Michael York.

TOUCH OF CLASS, A (P) 105
AVCO-EMBASSY. (R) June, 1973. Glenda Jackson, George Segal. Color.

TOUCH OF EVIL 95
UNIVERSAL. (R) February, 1960. Orson Welles, Charlton Heston. b&w.

TOUCH OF HELL, A 87
GOVERNOR, (R) February, 1964. Anthony Quayle, Sarah Churchill.

TOUCH OF LARCENY, A 93
PARAMOUNT. (R) January, 1960. James Mason, George Sanders.

TOUCHABLES, THE 97
TWENTIETH CENTURY-FOX. (R) November, 1968. Judy Huxtable, Esther Anderson. Color.

TOUCHED BY LOVE 95
COLUMBIA. (R) April, 1980. Deborah Raffin, Diane Lane.

TOUGHEST GUN IN TOMSTONE 72
UNITED ARTISTS. (R) May, 1958. George Montgomery, Beverly Tyler.

TOUGHEST MAN ALIVE 72
ALLIED ARTISTS. (R) November 6, 1955. Dane Clark, Lita Milan.

TOWARD THE UNKNOWN 115
WARNER BROTHERS. (R) October 20, 1956. William Holden, Lloyd Nolan. Color.

TOWER OF LONDON 79
UNITED ARTISTS. (R) 1962. Vincent Price, Joan Freeman.

TOWERING INFERNO, THE (P) 165
20TH CENTURY-FOX. (R) December, 1974. Paul Newman, Steve McQueen.

TOWN OF TRIAL 96
COLUMBIA. (R) August, 1957. Charles Coburn, Barbara Bates.

TOWN TAMER (T) 89

391

	Length In Mins.

NEW LINE CINEMA. (R) July, 1974. Robert Joel, Curt Gareth.

VERY PRIVATE AFFAIR, A 94
METRO-GOLDWYN-MAYER. (R) September, 1962. Brigitte Bardot, Marcello Mastroianni. Color.

VERY SPECIAL FAVOR, A 104
UNIVERSAL. (R) August, 1965. Rock Hudson, Leslie Caron.

VICE AND VIRTUE (F) 108
METRO-GOLDWYN-MAYER. (R) March, 1965. Annie Girardot, Catherine Deneuve. b&w.

VICE RAID 71
UNITED ARTISTS. Feb., 1960. Edward G. Robinson.

VICTORS, THE (P) 175
COLUMBIA. (R) December, 1963. Vincent Edwards, George Hamilton.

VIEW FROM POMPEY'S HEAD, THE (Cs) 97
TWENTIETH CENTURY-FOX. (R) November, 1955. Richard Egan, Dana Wynter, Cameron Mitchell. Color.

VIGILANTE FORCE 89
UNITED ARTISTS. (R) April, 1976. Kris Kristofferson, Jan-Michael Vincent.

VIKING QUEEN, THE 91
TWENTIETH CENTURY-FOX. (R) September, 1967. Don Murray, Carita.

VIKING WOMEN, THE 70
AMER. INT. PICS. (R) December, 1957. Abby Dalton, Susan Cabot.

VIKINGS, THE (T) 114
UNITED ARTISTS. (R) July, 1958. Kirk Douglas, Tony Curtis. Color.

VILLA! (Cs) 72
TWENTIETH CENTURY-FOX. (R) October, 1958. Brian Keith, Cesar Romero. Color.

VILLA RIDES (P) 125
PARAMOUNT. (R) June, 1968. Yul Brynner, Robert Mitchum, Grazia Buccella. Color.

VILLAGE OF THE DAMNED, THE 78
METRO-GOLDWYN-MAYER. (R) January, 1961. George Sanders, Barbara Shelley.

VILLAGE OF THE GIANTS 81
EMBASSY. (R) October, 1965. Tommy Kirk, Johnny Crawford. Color.

VILLAIN (P) 90
MGM. (R) May, 1971. Richard Burton, Nigel Davenport. Color.

VILLAIN, THE 93
COLUMBIA. (R) July, 1979. Kirk Douglas, Ann-Margret.

VINTAGE, THE (Cs) 92
METRO-GOLDWYN-MAYER. (R) April 19, 1957. Mel Ferrer, Pier Angeli, John Kerr. Color.

VIOLATORS, THE 76
UNIVERSAL. (R) December, 1957. Arthur O'Connell.

VIOLENT FOUR, THE (Italian; Eng. titles) 98
PARAMOUNT. (R) September, 1968. Gian Marie Volonte, Thomas Milan, Margaret Lee. Color.

VIOLENT MEN, THE (Cs) 96
COLUMBIA. (R) January, 1955. Glenn Ford, Barbara Stanwyck. Color.

VIOLENT ROAD 86
WARNER BROTHERS. (R) May, 1958. Brian Keith, Dick Foran.

VIOLENT SATURDAY (Cs) 90
TWENTIETH CENTURY-FOX. (R) April, 1955. Victor Mature, Sylvia Sidney. Color.

VIOLONS DU BAL, LES (French; Eng. titles) 110
LEVITT-PICKMAN. (R) December, 1974. Marie-Josee Nat, Jean-Louis Trintignant.

VIRGIN AND THE GYPSY, THE 92
CHEVRON. (R) June, 1970. Joanna Shimkus, Franco Nero, Honor Blackman. Color.

VIRGIN QUEEN, THE (Cs) 92
TWENTIETH CENTURY-FOX. (R) August, 1955. Bette Davis, Richard Todd, Joan Collins. Color.

VIRGIN SOLDIERS, THE 96
COLUMBIA. (R) January, 1970. Lynn Redgrave, Hywel Bennett, Nigel Davenport. Color.

VISCOUNT, THE (Ts) 98
WARNER BROS. (R) May, 1967. Kerwin Matthews, Edmund O'Brien. Color.

VISIONS OF EIGHT 105
CINEMA V. (R) August, 1973. Documentary.

VISIT, THE (Cs) 90
TWENTIETH CENTURY-FOX. September, 1964. Ingrid Bergman, Anthony Quinn.

VISIT TO A SMALL PLANET 85
PARAMOUNT. (R) April, 1960. Jerry Lewis, Joan Blackman.

VISITORS, THE 87
UNITED ARTISTS. (R) February, 1972. Patrick McVey, Patricia Joyce.

	Length In Mins.

VITELLONI (THE YOUNG AND THE PASSIONATE) (Ital.) ... 103
JANUS. (R) October, 1956. Franco Fabrizi, Alberto Sordi.

VIVA KNIEVEL! 106
WARNER BROS. (R) June, 1977. Evel Knievel, Gene Kelly.

VIVA LAS VEGAS (P) 86
METRO-GOLDWYN-MAYER. (R) June, 1964. Elvis Presley, Ann-Margaret. Color.

VIVA MARIA (P) 119
UNITED ARTISTS. (R) Spring, 1966. Brigitte Bardot, Jeanne Moreau. Color.

VIVA MAX! 92
COMMONWEALTH UNITED. (R) December, 1969. Peter Ustinov, Pamela Tiffen, Jonathan Winters. Color.

VOICE IN THE MIRROR (Cs) 102
UNIVERSAL. (R) August, 1958. Richard Egan, Julie London.

VOICE OF THE HURRICANE 80
SELECTED PICTURES. (R) April, 1964. Muriel Smith, David Cole. Color.

VOICES 106
UNITED ARTISTS. (R) March, 1979. Michael Ontkean, Amy Irving.

VOLCANO 100
CINEMA 5. (R) October, 1977. Documentary.

VON RICHTOFEN AND BROWN 97
UNITED ARTISTS. (R) June, 1971. John Phillip Law, Don Stroud. Color.

VON RYAN'S EXPRESS (Cs) 117
TWENTIETH CENTURY-FOX. June, 1965. Color.

VOODOO ISLAND 76
UNITED ARTISTS. (R) February, 1957. Boris Karloff, Beverly Tyler.

VOODOO WOMAN 75
AMERICAN INTERNATIONAL. (R) March, 1957. Marla English, Tom Conway.

VOYAGE OF SILENCE 88
LOPERT. (R) September, 1968. Marco Pico, Ludmila Mikael. b&w.

VOYAGE OF THE DAMNED (P) 158
AVCO-EMBASSY. (R) February, 1977. Faye Dunaway, Max Von Sydow.

VOYAGE TO THE BOTTOM OF THE SEA (Cs) 105
June, 1961. Walter Pidgeon, Joan Fontaine. Color.

VOYAGE TO THE END OF THE UNIVERSE 75
AMERICAN INTERNATIONAL. (R) September, 1964. Dennis Stephans, Francis Smolen.

VULTURE, THE 91
PARAMOUNT. (R) May, 1967. Robert Hutton, Akim Tamiroff.

W

W.C. FIELDS AND ME 111
UNIVERSAL. (R) April, 1976. Rod Steiger, Valerie Perrine.

WUSA (P) 115
PARAMOUNT. (R) October, 1970. Paul Newman, Joanne Woodward. Color.

W.W. AND THE DIXIE DANCEKINGS 91
TWENTIETH CENTURY-FOX. (R) March, 1975. Burt Reynolds.

WACKIEST SHIP IN THE ARMY, THE (Cs) 99
COLUMBIA. (R) December, 1960. Jack Lemmon, Ricky Nelson. Color.

WACO (TS) 85
PARAMOUNT (R) September, 1966. Howard Keel, Jane Russell. Color.

WAGES OF FEAR, THE (Fr.) 100
DISTRIBUTORS CORP. OF AMERICA. (R) January, 1956. Yves Montand, Vera Clouzot.

WAIT UNTIL DARK 107
WARNER BROS.-SEVEN ARTS. (R) December, 1967. Audrey Hepburn, Alan Arkin. Color.

WAITING FOR CAROLINE 83
LOPERT. (R) July, 1969. Alexandria Stewart, Francoise Tasse. Color.

WAKAMBA 65
RKO RADIO. (R) June 29, 1955. African adventure. Color.

WAKE ME WHEN IT'S OVER (Cs) 126
TWENTIETH CENTURY-FOX. (R) April, 1960. Ernie Kovacs, Margo Moore. Color.

WALK A TIGHTROPE 69
PARAMOUNT. (R) June, 1964. Dan Duryea, Patricia Owens.

WALK, DON'T RUN (P) 117
COLUMBIA. (R) July, 1966. Cary Grant, Samantha Eggar. Color.

	Length In Mins.

WALK IN THE SHADOW (Brit.) 93
CONTINENTAL. (R) February, 1966. Michael Craig, Patrick McGoohan.

WALK IN THE SPRING RAIN, A (P) 100
COLUMBIA. (R) May, 1970. Ingrid Bergman, Anthony Quinn. Color.

WALK LIKE A DRAGON 95
PARAMOUNT. (R) June, 1960. Jack Lord, Nobu McCarthy.

WALK ON THE WILD SIDE 113
COLUMBIA. (R) February, 1962. Laurence Harvey, Capucine.

WALK PROUD 102
UNIVERSAL. (R) May, 1979. Robby Benson, Sarah Holcomb.

WALK TALL (Cs) 60
TWENTIETH CENTURY-FOX. (R) September, 1960. Willard Parker, Joyce Meadows. Color.

WALK THE DARK STREET 74
ASSOCIATED ARTISTS. (R) April, 1956. Chuck Connors, Don Ross.

WALK THE PROUD LAND (Cs) 88
UNIVERSAL. (R) September, 1956. Audie Murphy, Pat Crowley. Color.

WALK WITH LOVE AND DEATH, A 90
20TH CENTURY-FOX. (R) October, 1969. Anjelica Huston, Assaf Dayan. Color.

WALKABOUT 95
20TH CENTURY-FOX. (R) June, 1971. Jenny Agutter, David Gumpili. Color.

WALKING STICK, THE (P) 101
MGM. (R) April, 1970. David Hemmings, Samantha Eggar, Emlyn Williams. Color.

WALKING TALL 125
CINERAMA. (R) February, 1973. Joe Don Baker, Elizabeth Hartman. Color.

WALKING TARGET 74
UNITED ARTISTS. (R) August, 1960. Joan Evans, Ronald Foster.

WALL OF NOISE 112
WARNER BROS. (R) September, 1963. Suzanne Pleshette, Ty Hardin.

WALLS OF HELL, THE 88
HEMISPHERE. (R) October, 1964. Jock Mahony, Fernando Poe, Jr.

WALTZ OF THE TOREADORS 105
CONTINENTAL. (R) August, 1962. Peter Sellers, Dany Robin. Color.

WANDA 105
BARDENE INTERNATIONAL. (R) March, 1971. Barbara Loden, Michael Higgins.

WANDA NEVADA 102
UNITED ARTISTS. (R) May, 1979. Peter Fonda, Brooke Shields.

WANDERER, THE (French, Eng. titles) 103
(R) February, 1969. Brigitte Epssey, Jean Blaise, Alain Libolt. Color.

WANDERERS, THE 113
ORION PICTURES. (R) July, 1979. Ken Wahl, John Friedrich.

WAR AND PEACE (VV) 208
PARAMOUNT. (R) November, 1956. Audrey Hepburn, Henry Fonda, Mel Ferrer. Color.

WAR AND PEACE 132
CONTINENTAL. (R) Special. April, 1968. Ludmila Savelyeva, Sergei Bondarchuk. Color.

WAR BETWEEN MEN AND WOMEN, THE 108
NATIONAL GENERAL. (R) May, 1972. Jack Lemmon, Barbara Harris. Color.

WAR DRUMS 75
UNITED ARTISTS. (R) April, 1957. Lex Barker, Joan Taylor. Color.

WAR GAME, THE 47
PATHE CONTEMPORARY. (R) March, 1967. BBC Documentary by Peter Watkins.

WAR-GODS OF THE DEEP (Colorscope) 85
AMERICAN INTERNATIONAL. (R) May, 1965. Vincent Price, Tab Hunter. Color.

WAR HUNT 81
UNITED ARTISTS. (R) May, 1962. John Saxon, Robert Redford.

WAR IS HELL! 81
ALLIED ARTISTS. (R) February, 1964. Tony Russell, Baynes Barron.

WAR—ITALIAN STYLE (TS) 84
AMERICAN INTERNATIONAL. (R) January, 1967. Buster Keaton, Franco and Ciccio. Color.

WAR LORD, THE (P) 123
UNIVERSAL. (R) November, 1965. Charlton Heston, Richard Boone. Color.

WAR LOVER, THE 105
COLUMBIA. (R) November, 1962. Steve McQueen, Robert Wagner.

WAR OF THE COLOSSAL BEAST 68
AMERICAN INTERNATIONAL. (R) July, 1958. Dean Parkin, Sally Fraser.

WAR OF THE SATELLITES 72
ALLIED ARTISTS. (R) April 6, 1958. Susan Cabot, Dick Miller.

WAR OF THE ZOMBIES 85
AMERICAN INTERNATIONAL. (R) March, 1965. John Barrymore, Jr. Color.

WARKILL 100
UNIVERSAL. (R) May, 1968. George Montgomery, Tom Drake. Color.

WAR PARTY 91
TWENTIETH CENTURY-FOX. (R) March, 1965. Michael T. Miker, Davey Davidson

WAR WAGON, THE (P) 101
UNIVERSAL. (R) June, 1967. John Wayne, Kirk Douglas. Color.

WARLOCK (Cs) 121
TWENTIETH CENTURY-FOX. (R) April, 1959. Richard Widmark, Henry Fonda. Color.

WARM DECEMBER, A 100
NATIONAL GENERAL. (R) May, 1973. Sidney Poitier. Color.

WARNING SHOT 100
PARAMOUNT. (R) January, 1967. David Janssen, Ed Begley. Color.

WARRENDALE 100
GROVE PRESS. (R) September, 1968. b&w.

WARRIOR AND THE SLAVE GIRL, THE (Supercinescope) 89
COLUMBIA. (R) November, 1959. Gianna Maria Canale, Georges Marchal. Color.

WARRIOR EMPRESS, THE (Cs) 97
COLUMBIA. (R) May, 1961. Kerwin Mathews, Tina Louise. Color.

WARRIORS, THE 92
PARAMOUNT. (R) February, 1979. Michael Beck, James Remar.

WARRIORS, THE (Cs) 85
ALLIED ARTISTS. (R) September 11, 1955. Errol Flynn, Joanne Dru. Color.

WASP WOMAN, THE 73
THE FILMGROUP. (R) October, 1959. Susan Cabot, Fred Eisley.

WATERHOLE #3 (TS) 100
PARAMOUNT. (R) October, 1967. James Coburn, Margaret Blye. Color.

WATERLOO (P) 123
PARAMOUNT. (R) April, 1971. Rod Steiger, Christopher Plummer. Color.

WATERMELON MAN 97
COLUMBIA. (R) August, 1970. Godfrey Cambridge, Estelle Parsons. Color.

WATERSHIP DOWN 92
AVCO EMBASSY. (R) November, 1978. Cartoon.

WATTSTAX 102
COLUMBIA. (R) February, 1973. Isaac Hayes, Carla Thomas. Color.

WATUSI (Cs) 85
METRO-GOLDWYN-MAYER. (R) May, 1959. George Montgomery, Taina Elg. Color.

WAY OUT, THE 78
RKO RADIO. (R) April 11, 1956. Gene Nelsen, Mona Freeman.

WAY TO THE GOLD, THE (Cs) 94
TWENTIETH CENTURY-FOX. (R) May, 1957. Sheree North, Jeffrey Hunter. Color.

WAY . . . WAY OUT (Cs) 106
20TH CENTURY-FOX. (R) October, 1966. Jerry Lewis, Connie Stevens. Color.

WAY WE LIVE NOW, THE 110
UNITED ARTISTS. (R) May, 1970. Nicholas Pryor, Linda Simon, Joanne Miles. Color.

WAY WE WERE, THE (P) 118
COLUMBIA. (R) October, 1973. Barbara Streisand, Robert Redford.

WAY WEST, THE (P) 122
UNITED ARTISTS. (R) June, 1967. Kirk Douglas, Lola Albright. Color.

WAYWARD BUS, THE (Cs) 90
TWENTIETH CENTURY-FOX. (R) June, 1957. Jayne Mansfield, Dan Dailey.

WAYWARD GIRL, THE 71
REPUBLIC. (R) September, 1957. Marchia Henderson, Peter Walker.

WAYWARD WIFE, THE (Ital.—Eng. dubbed) 95
I.F.E. (R) January, 1955. Gina Lollobrigida, Alda Mangini.

WE ARE ALL MURDERERS (Fr.) 113
KINGSLEY. (R) January, 1957. Marcel Mouloudji, Raymond Pellegrin.

WE STILL KILL THE OLD WAY (Ital.) 90

	Length In Mins.

METRO-GOLDWYN-MAYER. (R) June, 1967. Tony Russell, Connie Gastoni. Color.

WILD, WILD WINTER (Te) 80
UNIVERSAL. (R) January, 1966. Gary Clarke, Chris Noel. Color.

WILL ANY GENTLEMAN? (Brit.) 84
STRATFORD. (R) January 3, 1955. George Cole, Veronica Hunt.

WILL PENNY 109
PARAMOUNT. (R) March, 1968. Charlton Heston, Joan Hackett. Color.

WILL SUCCESS SPOIL ROCK HUNTER? (Cs) 94
TWENTIETH CENTURY-FOX. (R) August, 1957. Jayne Mansfield, Tony Randall. Color.

WILLARD 95
CINERAMA. (R) June, 1971. Bruce Davison, Ernest Borgnine. Color.

WILLIE AND PHIL 116
TWENTIETH CENTURY-FOX. (R) August, 1980. Michael Ontkean, Ray Sharkey.

WILLIE DYNAMITE 102
UNIVERSAL. (R) January, 1974. Roscoe Orman, Diana Sands.

WILLY McBEAN AND HIS MAGIC MACHINE 94
MAGNA. (R) August, 1965. Puppet Fantasy.

WILLY WONKA AND THE CHOCOLATE FACTORY 110
PARAMOUNT. (R) June, 1971. Gene Wilder, Jack Albertson, Peter Ostrum. Color.

WIND ACROSS THE EVERGLADES 98
WARNER BROS. (R) September, 1958. Burl Ives, Christopher Plummer.

WIND AND THE LION, THE (P) 119
UNITED ARTISTS—MGM. (R) June, 1975. Sean Connery, Candice Bergen.

WIND CANNOT READ, THE 107
TWENTIETH CENTURY-FOX. (R) February, 1960. Dick Bogarde, Yoko Tani.

WINDJAMMER, (Cinemiracle & Cinerama) 127
LOUIS DE ROCHEMONT. (R) April, 1958. Travellogue Color.

WINDOM'S WAY 108
RANK FILM DISTRIBUTORS OF AMERICA. (R) November, 1958. Peter Finch, Mary Ure. Color.

WINDOWS 94
UNITED ARTISTS. (R) January, 1980. Talia Shire, Joseph Cortese.

WINGS OF CHANCE 76
UNIVERSAL. (R) April, 1961. Jim Brown, Frances Rafferty. Color.

WINGS OF EAGLES, THE 110
METRO-GOLDWYN-MAYER. (R) Feb. 22, 1957. John Wayne, Maureen O'Hara. Color.

WINK OF AN EYE 72
UNITED ARTISTS. (R) June, 1958. Doris Dowling, Jonathan Kidd.

WINNER, THE 82
NOELLE GILMORE AND ROBERT KINGSLEY. (R) June, 1965. Abdoulaye Faye, Marcel Bruchard.

WINNING 123
UNIVERSAL. (R) wjune, 1969. Paul Newman, Joanne Woodward, Robert Wagner. Color.

WINTER A GO-GO 88
COLUMBIA. (R) October, 1965. James Stacy, William Wellman, Jr. Color.

WINTER KILLS 97
AVCO EMBASSY. (R) May, 1979. Jeff Bridges, John Huston.

WINTERHAWK 98
HOWCO INTERNATIONAL. (R) 1975. Leif Ericson, Woody Strode.

WIRETAPPER 80
EMBASSY. (R) February, 1956. Bill Williams.

WISE GUYS, THE 100
UNIVERSAL. (R) June, 1969. Bourvil, Lino Ventura. Color.

WITCH WITHOUT A BROOM, A 86
PRODUCERS RELEASING ORG. (R) May, 1967. Jeff Hunter, Maria Perschy. Color.

WITCHCRAFT 79
20th CENTURY-FOX. (R) 1964. Lon Chaney, Jack w qedley. Color.

WITCHMAKER, THE 86
EXCELSIOR. (R) May, 1969. Anthony Eisley, Thordis Bandi.

WITH SIX YOU GET EGGROLL 95
NATIONAL GENERAL. (R) July, 1968. Doris Day, Brian Keith, Pat Caroll, Barbara Hershey. Color.

WITHOUT A STITCH (Danish; Eng. titles) 96
VIP. (R) January, 1970. Anne Grete, Ib Mossin. Color.

WITHOUT APPARENT MOTIVE 102
20th CENTURY-FOX. (R) May, 1972. Jean-Louis Trintignant, Dominique Sanda. Color.

WITNESS FOR THE PROSECUTION 114

	Length In Mins.

UNITED ARTISTS. (R) February, 1958. Tyrone Power, Marlene Dietrich.

WITNESSES, THE 82
ALTURE FILMS INTERNATIONAL. (R) August, 1967. Documentary.

WIVES AND LOVERS 103
PARAMOUNT. (R) October, 1963. Janet Leigh, Van Johnson.

WIZ, THE 133
UNIVERSAL. (R) October, 1978. Diana Ross, Michael Jackson.

WIZARD OF BAGHDAD, THE (Cs) 92
TWENTIETH CENTURY-FOX. (R) December, 1960. Dick Shawn, Diane Baker. Color.

WIZARDS 81
TWENTIETH CENTURY-FOX. (R) March, 1977. Animated cartoon.

WOLF DOG 69
TWENTIETH CENTURY-FOX. (R) July, 1958. Jim Davis, Allison Hayes.

WOLF LARSEN 83
ALLIED ARTISTS. (R) October, 1958. Barry Sullivan, Gita Hall.

WOMAN IN A DRESSING GOWN 93
WARNER BROS. (R) November, 1957. Yvonne Mitchell, Sylvia Syms.

WOMAN IN THE DUNES (Jap., Eng. titles) 128
PATHECONT. (R) October, 1964. Eiji Okada, Kyoko Kistlida.

WOMAN IS A WOMAN, A (Fr., Eng. titles) 80
PATHE-CONT. (R) November, 1964. Jean-Claude, Brialy, Ann Karina. Color.

WOMAN OBSESSED (Cs) 102
TWENTIETH CENTURY-FOX. (R) May, 1959. Susan Hayward, Stephen Boyd.

WOMAN OF STRAW 117
UNITED ARTISTS. (R) September, 1964. Gina Lollobrigida, Sean Connery. Color.

WOMAN OF THE RIVER 92
COLUMBIA. (R) September, 1957. Sophia Loren, Gerald Oury. Color.

WOMAN TIMES SEVEN 99
EMBASSY. (R) June, 1967. Shirley MacLaine, Alan Arkin. Color.

WOMAN WHO WOULDN'T DIE, THE 84
WARNER BROS. (R) May, 1965. Raymond Garth, Alice Taylor.

WOMAN'S DEVOTION, A 88
REPUBLIC. (R) November 9, 1956. Ralph Meeker, Janice Rule. Color.

WOMEN IN CAGES 78
NEW WORLD PICTURES. (R) January, 1973. Jennifer Gan, Judy Brown. Color.

WOMEN IN CELL BLOCK 7 100
AQUARIUS RELEASING. (R) August, 1974. Anita Strinberg, Eva Czemeys.

WOMEN IN LOVE 129
UNITED ARTISTS. (R) March, 1970. Alan Bates, Jennie Linden, Oliver Reed, Glenda Jackson. Color.

WOMEN OF PITCAIRN ISLAND 72
TWENTIETH CENTURY-FOX. (R) December, 1956. James Craig, Lynn Bari.

WOMEN OF THE PREHISTORIC PLANET 91
FEATURE FILM CORP. OF AMER. (R) 1965. Wendell Corey, Keith Larsen. Color.

WOMEN OF THE WORLD 107
EMBASSY. (R) July, 1963. Documentary. Color.

WOMEN'S PRISON 80
COLUMBIA. (R) February, 1955. Ida Lupino, Howard Duff.

WON TON TON, THE DOG WHO SAVED HOLLYWOOD . 92
PARAMOUNT. (R) May, 1976. Madeline Kahn, Bruce Dern.

WONDERFUL COUNTRY, THE 96
UNITED ARTISTS. (R) October, 1959. Robert Mitchum, Julie London.

WONDERFUL TO BE YOUNG (Cs) 92
PARAMOUNT. (R) October, 1962. Cliff Richard, Robert Morley. Color.

WONDERFUL WORLD OF THE BROTHERS GRIMM, THE (Cinerama) 129
METRO-GOLDWYN-MAYER. (R) Special. July, 1962. Laurence Harvey, Claire Bloom. Color.

WONDERS OF ALADDIN, THE (Cs) 93
METRO-GOLDWYN-MAYER. (R) December, 1961. Donald O'Connor, Noelle Adam. Color.

WOODSTOCK (P) 184
WARNER BROS. (R) March, 1970. Color.

WORLD BY NIGHT 103
WARNER BROS. (R) September, 1961. International Acts. Color.

WORLD BY NIGHT NO. 2 (T) 116
WARNER BROS. (R) July, 1962. Documentary. Color.

MOTION PICTURE HERALD

ON MICROFILM

MOTION PICTURE HERALD, the trade journal published by Quigley Publishing Company for 57 years, has been recorded on microfilm by Brookhaven Press for the period from 1915 through 1950.

Issues of the **HERALD** contain an invaluable record for the years when the industry went from infancy to maturity. Regular features include everything from reports on theatre architectural design to promotional stunts to descriptions of newsreels and shorts. Of special interest are the regularly published release charts which give the title, audience classificaiton, stars, release date and running time for all films.

Cost of the complete 61 reels of microfilm for 1915-50 is $2,500. Individual reels are available.

QUIGLEY PUBLISHING COMPANY, INC.
159 West 53rd Street, New York, N.Y. 10019

Services

Film Distributors
in Key Cities

ALBANY

Riverside Film Distributing, P.O. Box 255, Yorktown Hts., NY (914) 245-2910; Craig Clark.
United Artists Corp., 991 Broadway, 72204. (518) 462-5385; Franklin R. Meadow, br. mgr.
Wesco Film Service, Inc., 24 North 3 St., 12204. (518) 434-1289.

ATLANTA

Alliance International, 161 Spring St., NY 30303. (404) 524-7579.
American National, 3070 Presidential Drive, 30340; (404) 451-7861. Harvey Edwards.
Avco Embassy Pictures, 2812 New Spring Road. 30339. (404) 434-1391. Robert Benefield, div. mgr.
Benton Film Forwarding Co., 168 Baker St., N.W., (404) 577-2821. W. B. Langston, mgr.
Bradley Films, 1876 De Foor Ave., N.W., 30318. (404) 352-3316. Gordon Bradley.
Buena Vista Distribution Co., 3445 Peachtree Rd., N.E., 30326; (404) 266-8454.
Chappell Releasing Co., 2814 New Spring Rd., 30339; (404) 432-3361. Wayne Chappell, pres.
Clark Film, Inc., 2200 Northlake Pkwy., Tucker, GA 30084. (404) 491-7766. Lewis Owens.
Columbia Pictures, 2600 Century Parkway, N.E., 30345. (404) 325-9525. Henry Harrell, mgr.
Craddock Films, Inc., Atlanta Film Bldg., 161 Spring St., N.W.; Suite 417. (404) 523-5653.
Films Inc., 277 Pharr Rd., N.E.; Tel: (404) 237-0341.
General Film Distributing, 3950 Peachtree Rd., N.E. 30319; (404) 261-5363. C. L. Autry.
Harnell Independent Productions, 6065 Roswell Rd., 30328; (404) 256-3464. Walter Powell, gen. sls. mgr.
Independent Film Dist., Inc., 161 Spring St. N.E., Phone: 524-7579. Sam Davis, pres., Steve Davis, mgr./booker.
JACO Productions Inc., 207 Luckie St., N.W.; 524-4218.
Kay Exchange, 201 Luckie Street; 524-0261. Ike Katz, pres. Harry Katz, booker.
K-Tel Motion Pictures, 1645 Tully Circle, N.E., 30329; (404) 321-5973. Jim Bello.
Major Film Distributors Inc., 161 Spring St., N.W.; Tel: (404) 688-1339.
Modern TV, 4705 F. Bakers Ferry Rd.; (404) 696-2026. Bob Cole, TV manager.
New World Pictures, 1587 Northeast Expressway, 30313. (404) 321-2910, Jack Rigg.
Paramount Pictures Corp., 17 Executive Park Dr., N.E., 30329; (404) 325-7674. M. V. McAfee.
Toddy Pictures Co., Box 150, 30301; (404) 355-9654. Ted Toddy, pres.
Transvue Pictures Corp., 161 Spring St., N.W.; Tel: (404) 523-6566.
20th Century-Fox, 2200 Century Parkway, 30345. Jerry Smith, mgr.
United Artists, 401 W. Peachtree NE, Suite 1760, 30308; (404) 552-6386. Larry Terrell, mgr.
Universal Film Exchange, 205 Walton St., N.W., 30303; (404) 523-5081. Weber Howell, mgr.
Warner Bros. 2600 Century Pkwy., 30345. (404) 325-0301. Roy Donaldson.
Clem Williams Films Inc., 1277 Spring St., N.W., (404) 872-5353.

BOSTON

Association Films, 410 Great Road, Littleton, MA 01460. (617) 486-3518.
Atlantic Releasing Corp., 585 Boylston St., 02116; (617) 266-5400.
Avco Embassy Pictures, 509 Statler Office Bldg., 02116; (617) 482-3325. Marc Halpern.
Buena Vista Distribution Co., 31 St. James Ave., 02116. (617) 426-9360.
Columbia Pictures Corp., 20 Providence St., 02116. (617) 426-8980. Gasper Urban, mgr.
Filmways Pictures, 31 St. James Ave., 02116. (617) 542-0677.
Ellis Gordon Films, 46 Church St., 02116. Ellis Gordon, mgr.

Lockwood & Friedman Film Corp., 430 Park Sq. Bldg., 02116; (617) 482-9717.
National Film Service Operating Corp., 621 E. 1st St., 02127. (617) 268-6510. Jimmie Choukas, mgr.
New England Film Distributing, 31 St. James Ave., 02116; (617) 482-9025.
Paramount Film Distributing Corp., 31 St. James Avenue, 02116. (617) 426-1070. Joe Rathgeb.
Jud Parker Films, 46 Church St. 02116; (617) 542-0744.
Topar Films, Inc., 771 Truman Parkway, Hyde Park, MA 02136, (617) 361-1640.
20th Century-Fox, 31 St. James Ave., 02116; (617) 426-2180. Cary Brokaw.
United Artists Corp., Park Square Bldg., 31 St. James Ave., 02116. (617) 426-6540. Joseph Griffin, br. mgr.
Universal Film Exchanges, Inc., 44 Winchester St., 02116. (617) 426-8760. Joan Corrado, mgr.
Warner Bros. Pictures Dist. Corp., 31 St. James Ave., 02116; (617) 482-3290. Jeff Goldstein, mgr.

BUFFALO

Frontier Amusements Corp., 505 Pearl St., 14202. (716) 854-6752. Mannie Brown, pres.
Paramount Pictures, Inc., 300 Delaware Ave., 14202. (716) 856-3758. Anthony J. Mercurio, mgr.
United Artists Corp., 300 Delaware Ave., 14202. (716) 854-1500. William Abrams, br. mgr.
Wesco Film Service, 108 Gruner Rd., 14225. (716) 897-0467.

CHARLOTTE

Avco-Ambassy Pictures, 230 S. Tryon St., 28202; (704) 375-9827. Donald Osley.
Buena Vista Dist. Co. Inc., 230 S. Tryon St., 28202. (704) 373-0724.
Carolina Booking Service, 291 So. Church St., 28202; (704) 375-7787. Frank Lowry.
Carolina Film Service Inc., 5012 Hovis Rd.; (704) 394-3129. E. J. Poole (ship); Marg. Miller (off.)
Charlotte Booking & Film Dist. Services, 221 So. Church St., 28201; (704) 376-5569. J. R. McClure.
Christian Film Service Corp., 2308 E. 7 St.; 333-5249.
Cinema Film Distributing, 222 S. Church, 28201; (704) 332-8539. Ron Witherspoon.
Clark Film Inc., 230 S. Tryon St., 28202; (704) 376-5569. Bob McClure, branch mgr.
Columbia Pictures Corp., 230 S. Tryon St., 28202. (704) 332-2502. Ed McLaughlin.
Dominant Pictures Co., 230 S. Tryon, 28202; (704) 334-1391. Harry Kerr, mgr.
Galaxy Films, 222 S. Church St.; (704) 372-6747. W. R. James, mgr.
Howco Exchange, 301 So. McDowell, 28204; (704) 834-8510. J. Francis White.
International Amusement Corp., 222 So. Church St., 28202; (704) 332-4163.
JACO Productions, 222 So. Church St., 28202; (704) 375-2519. K. Rogers, Charlie Mincey, branch mgrs.
Paramount Film Dist. Corp., 230 S. Tryon St., 28202. (704) 374-0193. Joe L. Cutrell, mgr.
Premier Pictures, 221 So. Church St., 28202; (704) 332-5101. Jerry Helms.
Pyramid Films, 221 So. Church St., 28202. (704) 333-2894.
Queens City Advertising & Amusement, Inc., 221 So. Church St., 28202; (704) 375-4419. Hugh M. Sykes, Jr.
20th Century-Fox Film Corp., 230 So. Tryon St., 28202. Larry Jameson, mgr.
United Artists Corp. 230 So. Tryon St., 28202. (704) 332-5070. Philip Cutrell, mgr.
Universal Film Exchanges, Inc., 705 E. Morehead St.; (704) 333-5564. Bill McClure, mgr.
Variety Films Inc., 1170 Northwestern Bank Bldg, 28202. (704) 374-1611. Bob McClure, mgr.
Warner Bros. Pictures, 330 S. Tryon St., 28202. (704) 376-5611. Harold Duckett, br. mgr.

CHICAGO

Apache Films, 32 W. Randolph, 60601; (312) 782-5620. Harry Goodman.
Avco-Embassy Pictures Corp. 190 N. State St., 60601. (312) 346-6122. Haywood Mitchusson, br. mgr.
Azteca Films, Inc., 1233 S. Wabash Ave., 60605; WAbash 2-6186. Edward G. Edwards, br. mgr.
Buena Vista Distribution Co. Inc., 8550 W. Bryn Mawr Ave., 60631. (312) 693-8580.

Don Buhrmester & Assoc., Inc., 203 N. Wabash Ave., 60601; (312) 782-0988. Don Buhrmester.

Clark Service, Inc., 2265 W. St. Paul Ave. (312) 342-3140. Jack Bailey.

Columbia Pictures Corp., 8550 W. Bryn Mawr Ave., 60631. (312) 693-3500. Evan Williams.

Dudelson Film Distributing, 1325 So. Wabash Ave., 60605; (312) 922-3546. Moe Dudelson.

Gilbreth Film Co., 32 West Randolph St., 60601; (312) 726-6220. Jack Gilbreth.

J.M.G. Film Co., 32 West Randolph St., 60601; (312) 346-6916. Virgil Jones.

Kaplan-Continental Pictures, 203 No. Wabash Ave., 60601. (312) 782-8413. Sam Kaplan.

William Lange & Associates, 32 West Randolph St., 60601; (312) 332-1734. Bill Lange.

Modern Talking Picture Service, 2020 Prudential Plaza; (312) 337-3252. Edwin Swanson, vice pres.

Modern TV, 1587 Elmhurst Rd., Elk Grove Village, IL 60007; (312) 593-3256.

Paramount Pictures Corp., 111 E. Wacker Dr., 60601; (312) 565-1990. Jeff Blake, br. mgr.

Select Film Co., 32 West Randolph St., 60601; (312) 236-1233. Sam Seplowin.

Teitel Film Corp., 600 S. Michigan, 60605; 427-4551. Chas. Teitel, bd. chmn.

Topar Films, Inc., 345 Fullerton Parkway, 60614; (312) 348-0210. John McLaurin.

Twentieth Century-Fox Film Corp., 35 E. Wacker Dr., 60601. Ray Russo.

United Artists Corp., 203 N. Wabash Ave., 60601; (312) 236-7390. Lou Aurelio, br. mgr.

Universal Film Exchanges, 425 N. Michigan Ave., 60611. (312) 822-0513. W. Gehring, mgr.

Warner Bros. Dist. Corp., 550 W. Jackson Blvd., 60606; (312) 726-1658. Seymour Hite, div. mgr.

CINCINNATI

Avco Embassy Pictures, 35 E. Seventh St. 45202. (513) 381-8480. Robert Rosen, mgr.

Buena Vista Distribution Co., Inc., 636 Northland Rd., 45240. (513) 742-0900. Bob Bruce, mgr.

J.M.G. Film Co., 636 Northland Blvd., 45240. (513) 851-9933. Jay Goldberg, mgr.

MYCO Films, 617 Vine St., 45202; (513) 579-8090. Jo Harrison.

Paramount Pictures Corp., 414 Walnut St., 45202. Mike Share.

Regency Film Distributing, 617 Vine St., 45202; (513) 621-2955. William Blum.

C.J. Ruff Film Distributing Co., 1620 Harrison Ave., 45214; (513) 921-8200.

Edward Salzberg, Inc., 35 East Seventh St., 45202; (513) 241-3671.

States Film Service, 421 Bauer St. (513) 621-4240. Harry Jansen.

20th Century-Fox Film Corp., 617 Vine Street; 241-6460. Tony Knollman, br. mgr.

United Artists Corp., 35 E. 7th St., 45202. (513) 241-1546. Tom Morris, br. mgr.

Universal Film Exchanges, Inc., 1628 Central Parkway, 45210. (513) 421-3820. D. Coons, mgr.

Warner Bros. Pictures Dist. Corp., 414 Walnut St., 45202. (513) 241-6824. Bill Waynberg.

Zipp Film Distributors, 617 Vine. (513) 241-5548.

CLEVELAND

Academy Film Service, Inc., 2108 Payne Ave.; 696-0661. Blair Mooney, pres. M. M. Blaettner, mgr.

Avco Embassy Pictures, Three Common Park Sq., 44122; (216) 292-3973. Gordon Bugie, br. mgr.

Buena Vista Distribution Co., Inc., 29001 Cedar Rd., 44124. (216) 442-3270. Jerry Pokorski, mgr.

Cine-Pix, 2108 Payne Ave., 44114; (216) 781-0622. Jack Kaufman.

Columbia Pictures Corp., 23200 Chagrin Blvd., 44122. (216) 292-3610. Richard Sands, mgr.

Imperial Pictures, 2108 Payne Ave., 44114. (216) 621-9376.

SelecPictures Corp., 29001 Cedar Rd., Lyndhurst, OH 44124; (216) 461-9770. Jay Schultz, pres.

States Film Service, Inc., Warner Bldg., 2336 Payne Ave.; (216) 771-3723. Harry Lyman, mgr.

20th Century-Fox Film Corp., 29001 Cedar Rd., Lyndhurst, OH 44124. William Anderholt.

United Artists, Corp., 29001 Cedar Rd., Lyndhurst, OH 44124. (216) 461-1266. D. Buckley, mgr.

Universal Film Exchanges Inc., 1721 Superior Ave., 44114; (216) 771-0413. J. Ryan, br. mgr.

Warner Bros. Pictures Distrib. Corp., 29001 Cedar Road, Lyndhurst, 44124. (216) 473-0560. Andrew Silverman.

DALLAS

American National Enterprises, 11422 Harry Hines Blvd., 75229; (214) 243-5171. A. H. Watts.

Avco Embassy Pictures, 10300 N. Central Expressway, 75231; (214) 739-0327. Gene Haufler, br. mgr.

Buena Vista Distribution, 6060 N. Central Expressway, 75206; (214) 363-9494. Sebe Miller, dist. mgr.

Central Shipping & Inspection, 2500 S. Harwood St. (214) 421-5411. Wallace Jack, mgr.

Columbia Pictures, 10830 N. Central Expressway, 75231. (214) 750-0100. Jack Foley.

Crump Distributors, Inc., 1712 Commerce St., 75201. (214) 741-3370. Jim Crump.

Dal Art Film Exchange, 2017 Young St., 75201; (214) 748-8342. Fred Beiersdorf, pres.

Dimension General Eric Distributing, 10830 N. Central Expressway, 72531; (214) 692-7744. Eric Deneve, Don Scrugs.

Film Booking Service, 500 So. Ervay, Suite 603, 75201; (214) 744-3165. Bennie Lunch.

Films Incorporated, 1414 Dragon St., Dallas 75207; RI 1-4071. Estelle Redd, br. mgr.

G&M Film Distributors, 500 So. Ervay St., 75201; (214) 748-7093. Frank Meyers, Jake Guiles.

Jaco Productions, 500 So. Ervay St., 75201; (214) 748-6145. Bill Hill.

K-Tel Motion Pictures, 1010 W. Mockingbird, 75247; (214) 634-1726. Jerry Malone.

Major Film Distributors, 1907 Elm St., 75201; (214) 744-4069. Jack Durrell.

Orbit Films, 4411 N. Central Exp. 75205; (214) 522-7780. Al Weiner.

Paramount Pictures, 8350 N. Central Expressway, 75206. (214) 369-4600. Terry Kierzek.

Sack Amusement Enterprises, 1710 Jackson St., 75201. (214) RI 2-9445.

Southern Enterprises, 2344 Farrington St., 75207; (214) 634-2690. Carl Sims, gen. mgr.

Starline Pictures, 3220 Lemmon West, 75204; (214) 522-8300. James Prichard.

Topar Films, Inc., 1 No. Park East, 75201. (214) 691-7660. M. Parker, J. Kauffman.

Twentieth Century-Fox, 11351 Forest Central Dr., Richard King, br. mgr.

United Artists Corp., Suite 438, 6060 N. Central Expressway, 75206. (214) 692-0777. Enoch Stevens, mgr.

Universal Film Exchanges, Inc., 11551 Forest Central Dr., 75243. Bob Harris, br. mgr.

Variety Film Distributors, 4308 N. Central Expressway, 75206; (214) 827-7800. Vern Fletcher.

Warner Bros. Distributing Corp., 7424 Greenville Ave., 75231. (214) 691-6101. Jackie Stanley.

DENVER

Buena Vista Dist. Co., Inc., 88 Steele St., 80206. (303) 321-1200. Al Hemingway, mgr.

Columbia Pictures Industries, 1860 Lincoln, Suite 250. (303) 534-6341. William Kreigenhofer, mgr.

Crest Films, 1860 Lincoln St., 80203; (303) MA 3-1221. Jack Felix, branch mgr.

Denver Shipping & Inspection, 2118 Stout St. (303) 222-5616. Frank Norris, mgr.

Favorite Film of California, Inc., 1860 Lincoln, Suite 416; 623-1221. Dick Notti, br. mgr.

L. E. "Bill" Hobson, 130 Pearl St., 80203; (303) 722-9443. Bill Hobson.

Roy Hunt, 921 21st St., 80205. (303) 893-3998.

J&B Independent Films, 1860 Lincoln, 80203. (303) 255-0495.

McGee Film Distributing, 655 S. Alton Way. (303) 343-3413.

Mountain State Film Dist., 2140 Champa St., 80205; (303) 623-1377, Bates Farley.

Paramount Pictures Corp., 158 Fillmore St., 80206; Robert Fox.

20th Century-Fox Film Corp., 55 Steele St., Gary Erickson, br. mgr.

United Artists Corp., 88 Steele St., 80206. (303) 320-4907. Edna Gallagher, br. mgr.

Universal Film Exchanges, Inc., 801 21st St.; (303) 623-3281. Jack Box, br. mgr.

Warner Bros. Dist. Corp., 88 Steele St., 80206. (303) 355-4431. Jay Pekos.

DES MOINES

Columbia Pictures Corp., 1501 Ingersoll Ave., 50309. (515) 243-0105. Glenn Abrams, br. mgr.

D&D Enterprises, Inc., 311 Eleventh St., 50309. (515) 288-6006.

D&H Distributors, P.O. Box 4907, 50306. (515) 276-4263. Dick Haes.

Iowa Film Depot, 3123 Delaware Ave. (515) 265-1469. Art Trombley, mgr.

McCulloch Film Distributing, 500-A Produce Bank Bldg., 55403; (612) 333-2281. Stan McCulloch, owner.

National Screen Service Corp., 1005 High St.; 244-3911. Carl Sokolof, representative.

Paramount Film Distributing Corp., 1535 Linden St., 50309. (515) 288-3638. Charles A. Caliguiri, br. mgr.

Producers Distributing Co., 1219 Paramount Bldg., 50309; (515) 282-5157. Ken Weldon, Mike Weldon.

20th Century-Fox Film Corp., 3737 Woodland Ave., Mary Ann Shaughnessy.

United Artists Corp., 1213 Grand Ave., 50309. (515) 283-0481. George Bloxham.

DETROIT

American National Enterprises, 19400 W. 10 Mile Rd., Southfield, MI 48075; (313) 352-4282. Larry Bishop.

Avco Embassy Pictures, 23300 Greenfield Rd., Oak Park, 48237; (313) 968-3350. Pat Woolcott, bk. mgr.

Columbia Pictures Corp., 24100 Southfield Rd., Southfield 48075; (313) 557-2150.

D&R Distributors, 13131 Fenkell Ave., 48277; (313) 491-2180. Al Dezel, George Rossman.

Gail Film Distributors, 16300 W. 9 Mile Road, Southfield, MI 48075; (313) 557-5024. Arthur Weisberg, pres.

J.M.G. Films, 2330 Greenfield Road, Oak Park, 48237. (313) 968-0500.

Levin Film Distributors, 29501 Greenfield Rd., Southfield, MI, 48072; (313) 559-1101. Nate Levin.

National Film Service, 6111 Concord, 48211; (313) 923-2150. Ed McCauley, mgr.

Paramount Pictures, 23300 Greenfield Rd., Oak Park, 48237; (313) 968-8137. James Goldschlager.

R. Distributors, 13131 Fenkell, 48227. (313) 491-2180.

Regency Film Distributing, 24655 Southfield Road, Southfield, 48075; (313) 354-3245. Herb Gillis.

C.J. Ruff Films, 23300 Greenfield Road, Oak Park, 48237; (313) 968-7770. Dennis Glenn.

United Artists Corp., 24100 Southfield Rd., Southfield, MI 48075; (313) 557-5770. Robert Kapolintz, mgr.

Universal Film Exchanges, Inc., 55 Park St., Troy, MI 48099. (313) 583-1720. D. Gonda.

Warner Bros. Dist. Corp., 20820 Greenfield Road, Oak Park, MI 48237; (313) 564-5826. Don E. Martin, br. mgr.

HONOLULU, HI

Hawaii Nichibel Film Co. Inc., 728 9th Ave., 96816; (808) 737-3455.

Pacific Motion Picture Co. Ltd., 1190 Nuuanu Ave., 96817; (808) 538-1035.

Shochiku Films, 1387 N. Beretania St.; 964-444; 733-8181.

HOUSTON, TX

Conner, Charles M. Productions, 4713 Braeburn Drive, Bellaire, TX (713) 668-9900.

INDIANAPOLIS

Howco Films, 6385 N. Park Ave., 46220; (317) 251-5070. R. V. Jones.

Paramount Pictures, Inc., 428 Illinois Bldg.; 634-7563. John Kane, mgr.

States Film Service, 429 No. Senate Ave. (317) 638-3531. Robert Ahart, mgr.

United Artists Corp., 7002 No. Graham Rd., 46220. (317) 849-2714. Tom Morris.

Zipp Film Distributors, 718 N. Senate Ave. (317) 632-6873.

JACKSONVILLE, FL

Avco-Embassy Pictures, 101 Century 21 Dr., 32216. (904) 721-8365. James Dixon, br. mgr.

Buena Vista Distribution Co., Inc., Seaboard Coastline Bldg., 32202. (904) 358-1221. Bob Pollard, mgr.

Clark Film Inc., 905 North St., 32211; (904) 721-2122. Harry Clark, pres. Belton Clark, gen. mgr.

Columbia Pictures Corp., 9550 Regency Sq. Blvd., 32211. (904) 725-8891. Terry H. Tharpe.

Robert Farber Films, Guaranty Life Bldg.; 356-4232. Robert Farber, mgr.

General Film Productions, 128 E. Forsyth St.; 358-3641. Walter Powell, mgr.

Independent Film Exchange, 128 East Forsyth St.; 356-1475. Mrs. O. Glenn Gryder, mgr.; 1011 Houston St. (shipping station.)

Jacksonville Film Service, 2208 West 21 St., (904) 355-5447. B. D. Benton, Bert Benton, Jr.

Paramount Film Dist. Corp., 9550 Regency Square Blvd., 32211. (904) 725-6470. Al Stout, mgr.

South Eastern Entertainment, 10348 Atlantic Circle, 32216. (904) 356-7216. Robert Capps.

20th Century-Fox Film Corp., One Regency Place, 32211. Woodrow Townsend, mgr.

United Artists, Inc., 9550 Regency Square Blvd., Suite 203, 32211. (904) 724-4290. Joseph Kennedy, mgr.

Universal Film Exchanges, Inc., 331 E. Bay St., 32202; (904) 721-1250. G. F. Byro, br. mgr.

Warner Bros. Pictures Dist. Corp., 9550 Regency Square Blvd., 32211. (904) 721-0480. R. E. Heffner.

KANSAS CITY, MO

Avco-Embassy Pictures, 4638 J. C. Nichols Pkwy., 64112. (816) 931-4526. Jerry Brethour, mgr.

Buena Vista Distribution Co., 4210 Johnson Dr., 66205. (913) 362-9500. Jim Witcher, mgr.

Central Shipping & Inspection, 101 West 10th Ave.; (816) 471-0884. Earl E. Jameson, Jr.

Columbia Pictures Corp., 3130 Broadway; 64111. (816) 561-3021. James Domlon, mgr.

Marcus Film Distributing, 3773 W. 95th St., Overland Park, KS, 66206; (913) 381-6222. Ben Marcus, pres.

Mercury Film Co., 3865 W. 95th St., KS, Overland Park, 66206. (913) 383-3880. Bev. Miller.

Midwest Films, 3879 W. 95th St., Shawnee Mission, KS 66206; (913) 381-2058. Gene Irwin.

Motion Picture Booking Agency, 9427 Bluejacket; 888-6590.

Paramount Pictures Corp., 4200 Johnson Dr., Shawnee Mission, KS, 66205. (913) 831-9212. Mike Klein, br. mgr.

Sun International Productions, 25 East 12th St. (816) 471-0415.

Thomas/Shipp Film Distributing, 110 W. 18th St., 64108; (816) 421-1692. Howard Thomas, John Shipp.

20th Century-Fox Film Corp., 106 W. 34th St. Neill Blatt, br. mgr.

United Artists Corp., 1703 Wyandotte, 64108. (816) 471-1123. Morton Truog, br. mgr.

United National Distributors, 1703 Wyandotte, 64108. (816) 474-5330. Gene Irwin.

Universal Film Exchanges, Inc., 1700 Wyandotte St., 64108. (816) 421-5624. S. Miller, br. mgr.

Warner Bros. Distributing Corp., 2440 Pershing Rd., 64108 (816) 474-9909. Frank Rhodes, br. mgr.

LOS ANGELES

American National Enterprises, 6115 Selma Ave., (213) 467-8624.

Amerikana Film Co., 6255 West Sunset Blvd., L.A., 90046. (213) 464-3131.

Avco-Embassy Pictures, 956 Seward St., 90038. (213) 460-7200. Ross Merrin, br. mgr.

Azteca Films, Inc., 555 N. La Brea Ave., 90036; (213) 938-2413.

BFA Educational Media, 2211 Michigan Ave., Santa Monica, 90212. (213) 829-2901.

Seymour Borde Associates, 292 S. LaCienega, Beverly Hills, 90035; (213) 652-6785.

Beuna Vista Dist. Co. Inc., 350 S. Buena Vista St., Burbank, 91521. (213) 841-1000.

Carlyle Films Ltd., 6430 Sunset Blvd., 90028; (213) 466-0864.

Cavalcade Pictures, Inc., 959 N. Fairfax Ave., 90046; (213) 654-4144.

Columbia Pictures Corp., 8671 Wilshire Blvd., 90211. (213) 657-6410. Robert Humak, br. mgr.

Counselor Films, 8816 Sunset Blvd., L.A.; 90069; (213) 659-5720.

Crest Film Distributors, 116 No. Robertson Blvd., 90052; (213) 652-8844. J. Persell.

Crown International Pictures, 292 S. La Cienega Blvd., B.H. 90211; (213) 657-6700.

Dart Enterprises, 5421 Santa Monica Blvd., L.A.; (213) 464-9283.

Far West Films, 116 No. Robertson Blvd., 90048; (213) 659-5161.

Favorite Films of California, Inc., 292 La Cienega Blvd., B.H.; (213) 657-6700.

Film Investment Corp., 333 S. Beverly Drive, B.H.; 90211; (213) 553-5806.

Hollywood International Film Corp. of America, 1044 S. Hill St., L.A. 90015; (213) 749-2067.

Manson International, 9145 Sunset Blvd., 90069; (213) 273-8640. Michael F. Goldman, pres.

Modern Talking Picture Service, 1145 N. McCadden Place, 90038; (213) 462-2202. Jack Whalen, manager.

National Screen Service Corp., 2001 S. Cienega Blvd., L.A. 90034; (213) 871-0598.
Paramount Film Dist. Corp., 9440 Santa Monica Blvd., Beverly Hills, 90210. (213) 550-8600. Walter Lange.
Services Marketing & Distribution Co, P.O. Box 85, Ross, CA 94957.
Summit Film Distributors, 116 No. Robertson Blvd., 90048. (213) 652-7702.
Toho Co., Ltd., 834 S. La Brea Ave., 90036; (213) 933-5877.
Topar Films, Inc., 116 N. Robertson Blvd., 90048. (213) 657-5901. Rick Parker.
Tower Film Co., 8400 W. Sunset Blvd., L.A. 90069; (213) 654-4414.
Twentieth Century-Fox Film Corp., 9440 Santa Monica Blvd., 90210 (213) 550-1044. Donna Littman.
United Artists, 116 No. Robertson Blvd., 90048. (213) 657-7000. Robert Wood, mgr.
United Film Distributing Co., 291 S. La Cienega Blvd., B.H., 90211; (213) 657-6210. J. Crotly.
Universal Film Exchanges, Inc., 8901 Beverly Blvd., 90048. (213) 550-7461. J. Finn, mgr.
Warner Bros. Pictures Distributing Corp., 8484 Wilshire Blvd., 90211. (213) 653-9600. Shirley Becker.

MEMPHIS

Blue Ribbon Pictures, 942 Normandy Ave., 38137. (901) 683-3949.
Clark/Pabst Films, Inc., 1188 Perkins Rd. S. 38117; (901) 683-8182.
Dal-Art Films, Exchange, 4942 Normandy St., 39317. (901) 683-3949.
Dimension General, 138 Huling St., 38102; (901) 278-4442. Jeff Williams.
Don Kay Enterprises, 138 Huling St., 38102; (901) 527-4023. Fordyce Kaiser, branch mgr.
Film Transit, Inc., 291 Hernando St.; 525-6894.
Howco Exchange, 399 South 2nd St.; 526-8328. Charles Arendall, br. mgr.
Memphis Film Service Inc., Homewood Rd., (901) 365-7550. A. S. Crews, G. L. Brandon.
Paramount Pictures, 100 N. Main St., 38103. (901) 527-9575. Tom Donahue.
Starline Pictures, 100 N. Main Bldg., 38103; (901) 527-9424. Bailey Prichard, owner.
Tab Films, 1364 No. Watkins, 38108; (901) 274-6491. Charles Arendall.
United Artists, 1437 Central Ave., 38104. K. Keifer.

MILWAUKEE

Buena Vista Dist. Co., 212 W. Wisconsin Ave., 53203. (414) 273-5111. Carole Sutter, br. mgr.
Independent Film Distributor, 6421 Milwaukee Ave.; 771-9470. Fern Anderson, mgr.
Mescop Distributing, 9235 W. Capitol Dr., 53222; (414) 466-1700. Fred Florence, pres.
Milwaukee Film Center, Inc., 333 No. 25th St.; (414) 344-0300. Oliver Trampe, John Prostinak.
Theatres Service Co., 9235 W. Capitol Dr.; 462-7970. Don Perlewitz, mgr.
United Artists Corp., 212 W. Wisconsin Ave., 53203. (414) 271-6529. John McKenna, br. mgr.

MINNEAPOLIS

Action Films Inc., 7400 Metro Blvd., 941-7769.
Avco Embassy Pictures, 15 S. 9th St. (612) 339-2719. Dean Lutz, mgr.
Buena Vista Distribution Co., Inc., 6950 Wayzata Blvd., 55426. (612) 546-8533. Irving Marks, br. mgr.
Columbia Pictures Corp., 711 Hennepin Ave., 55403. (612) 333-6227. Jack Ignatowicz.
Independent Film Distributors, 2249 Pennsylvania Ave., So.; 545-7015. Abbott Swartz, owner.
Independent Film Service, 245 Second Ave. No.; (612) 335-2203. Jack Bradley, mgr.
William H. Lange & Associates, 2901 Pleasant Ave. So., 55408. (612) 827-5371. Leroy Smith.
McCulloch Film Distributing, 500-A Produce Bank Bldg., 55403; (612) 333-2281. Stan McCulloch, owner.
Mid West Entertainment, 704 Hennepin Ave., 55043; (612) 332-4523. James Payne.
Northwest Cinema, 1602 Midwest Plaza Bldg., 55402; (612) 332-3456. Irving Braverman.
Paramount Pictures Corp., 6950 Wayzata Blvd., 55426. (612) 544-0112. F. C. Myers, br. mgr.
Leroy Smith, 2901 Pleasant Ave., S., 55408. (612) 827-5371.
20th Century-Fox, 600 So. County Rd. ‡18. Aaron Rosen, mgr.

United Artists Corp., 711 Hennepin Ave., 55403. (612) 333-7276. Walter Badger, mgr.
Universal Film Exchanges, Inc., 6800 Shingle Creek Parkway, 55430. (612) 566-9620. Frank Zanotti, br. mgr.
Viking Films, 1228 Wagon Wheel Rd., Hopkins, Minn., 55343; (612) 338-3841. Jack Kelvie.

NEW HAVEN

New Haven Film Service, Inc., 90 Woodmont Rd., Milford, CT, 06460; (203) 878-1465. William Rosen, mgr.

NEW ORLEANS

Avco-Embassy Pictures, 1030 W. Central Expressway, 70130; (504) 739-0327. John Trickett, mgr.
Blue Ribbon Pictures, Inc., International Trade Mart, Suite 1400, 2 Canal St., 70130; 522-8788-89. George Pabst, owner.
Buena Vista Dist. Co., Inc., International Trade Mart, Suite 1438. 2 Canal St., 70130; (504) 525-2258. Larry Fine, mgr.
Clark/Pabst Film, Inc., P.O. Box 7865, Metairie, LA, 70010; (504) 733-3555.
Columbia Pictures Corp., 1001 Howard Ave., 70113 (504) 529-2461. Gene Gibbons.
Delta Visual Service, Inc., 715 Girod St.; 525-9061. F. J. Didier, pres.
Film Inspection Service, Inc., 2411 Edenborn Ave., Metairie, LA; (504) 883-5552. Weldon C. Wade, mgr. Dan M. Brandon, pres. & gen. mgr.
Goodrow, F. F. Distributor, 214 S. Liberty, 523-1474. F. F. Goodrow, owner.
I.F.I. Films, P.O. Box 8507, Metairie, LA 70011; (504) 837-6107. Charles Varnado.
Independent Films, Box 8007, Metairie, LA 70011. (504) 837-6106.
Jaco Productions, 822 Peroido, 70112; (504) 524-4218. Ken Rodgers.
Don Kay Enterprises, Inc., 1034 Carondelet, 524-2796.
Masterpiece Pictures, Inc., 215 S. Liberty St.; 522-8703. Mrs. Mamie Dureau, pres.
Paramount Pictures Corp., 3525 N. Causeway Blvd., Metairie, 70002. (504) 837-7751. David Garfinkle.
Southern Film Distributing, 143 N. Rampart St., 70112. (504) 581-6700.
Twentieth Century-Fox Distrib. Corp., 3829 Veterans Memorial Blvd., 70003. Jeff Lee, br. mgr.
United Artists Corp., 4900 Veterans Memorial Blvd., Metairie, LA 70002; (504) 885-7333. Greg Perash.
Universal Film Exchanges, Inc., 734A Martin Behrman Ave., Metairie, LA 70005. (504) 837-2631. N. Gazaway, mgr.
Warner Bros. Dist. Corp., 4539 Inlo Road, Metairie, LA 70002; (504) 456-1751. David Chinich, mgr.

NEW YORK

Audio-Brandon Films, 34 MacQuesten P'way S., Mt. Vernon, NY 10550; (914) 644-5051.
Avco Embassy Pictures Corp., 300 E. 42nd St., 10017; (212) 949-8900. Jerome Horowitz, br. mgr.
Bonded Film Distributors, (Division of Novo Communications, Inc.) 55 Main Street, Fort Lee, NJ 07024; (212) 557-6738. Joseph Marcy, mgr.
Bonded Services, (Division of Novo Communications, Inc.) 733 Third Avenue, New York, NY 10017; (212) 557-6700. Emanuel Kandel, exec. v.p.
Buena Vista Distribution Co., 477 Madison Ave., 10022. (212) 593-8900.
Cinema 5 Ltd., 595 Madison Ave., 421-5555.
Columbia Pictures, 711 Fifth Ave. (212) 751-4400. Joseph Curtin.
ITM Releasing Corp., 321 W. 44 St., 10036; (212) 582-6946.
Marvin Films, 1501 Broadway, 10036; (212) 354-5700. Marvin Friedlander, pres.
Modern Talking Picture Service, 45 Rockefeller Plaza, 10111; (212) 765-3100.
Modern TV, 2323 New Hyde Park Road, New Hyde Park, 11040; (516) 437-6300. Peter Glick, manager.
Paramount Film Distributing Corp., 1 Gulf & Western Plaza; 333-4600. Nat Stern.
Times Film Corp., 144 West 57 St., 10019; PL 7-6980.
Trans-Lux Distributing Corp., 625 Madison Ave., 10022; PLaza 1-3110.
20th Century-Fox Film Corp.; 40 W. 57th St., 10019 (212) 977-5500. Leo Fisch, mgr.
United Artists Corporation, 729 Seventh Ave., 10019. (212) 575-4897. Robert Shein, mgr.
United Film Dist. Co., 11 Middleneck Rd., Great Neck, NY 11021; (212) 895-7100. R. Hassanein.
Universal Film Exchanges, Inc., 445 Park Ave., 10022. (212) 759-7500. A. Quaedvlieg, mgr.

Warner Bros. Distributing Corporation, 75 Rockefeller Plaza, 10019. (212) 484-8960. Herb Gaines, NY sales mgr.

OKLAHOMA CITY

Conner, Charles M., Productions, 4713 Braeburn Dr., Bellaire, TX; (713) 668-9945.
O&A Film Lines, 708 W. Sheridan, 232-9900.
Okla. City Shipping & Inspection Bureau, 809 S.W. 7th; (405) 235-2553. Alfred Baird, mgr.
Screen Guild Productions of Oklahoma, Inc., 708 W. Sheridan; 232-4623. Harry McKenna, mgr.
United Artists Corp., 2000 Classen Blvd., 73106. (405) 528-2888. T. Dyksterhuis.

OMAHA

Buena Vista Film Dist. Co., Inc., 203 572; 393-2321.
Modern Sound Pictures Inc., 1402 Howard St., 68102; (402) 341-8476
Omaha Film Depot, Inc., office 1441 No. 11th St.; (402) 342-6576.

PHILADELPHIA

Alan Pictures, 900 Kings Highway North, Cherry Hill, NJ 08034; (215) 561-0800. Alan Strulson, pres.
Avco Embassy Pictures Corp., 425 15th St., 19102. (215) 563-8345. Tom Mihok, br. mgr.
Buena Vista Distribution, One Cherry Hill, Cherry Hill, NJ 08002. (609) 779-8804.
Capital Film Exchange, 309 N. 13th St. 19107. (215) 567-2698.
Columbia Pictures Corp. 1612 Market St., 19103. (215) 568-3889. Abe Dortheiner.
Filmways Pictures, 1530 Chestnut St., 19102; (215) 568-6684.
Magill Films, 1612 Market St., 19103; (215) 563-7428. Mort Magill.
M.Y. Film Co., Fox Theatre Bldg., 1612 Market St., 19103; (215) 665-9052. Emanuel Youngerman, pres.
Paramount, Fox Bldg., 1612 Market St., 19103. (215) 567-3672. Ralph Garman, br. mgr.
20th Century-Fox Film Corp., 1429 Walnut St., Louis Korte, br. mgr.
United Artists Corp., 117 S. 17th St., 19103. (215) 563-9500. Lew O'Neil.
Universal Film Exchanges, 1165 Marlkress Rd., Cherry Hill, NJ 08003. (609) 424-5045. P. Ciccotta, mgr.
Warner Bros. Pictures Dist. Corp., 400 Market St., 99106. (215) 928-9000. Frank Carroll.

PITTSBURGH

Cinema Consultants, Box 191, Grove City, PA 16127. (412) 458-8503.
New World Pictures of Pittsburgh, 107 6th St., (412) 391-0370. Morris Zyd, div. mgr.
John O'Glaus Agency, Box 18072, 15236. (412) 653-5493.
Paramount Pictures, Inc., Fulton Bldg., 107 6th St.; 281-9270; Don Hicks, mgr.
S. Perilman Films, Fulton Bldg., 107 6th St.; (412) 471-5535.
Pittsburgh Film Service, Inc., Bldg. 16, Nichol Ave., McKees Rocks, PA; (412) 771-2665. Peter Dana, Harold Tinker.
Screenguild Pictures, 415 Van Braam, 15219; (412) 281-1630. William Jenkins.
United Artists Corp., Fulton Bldg., 107 Sixth St.; 471-8960. David Litto, mgr.
Wheeler Films, 625 Fulton Bldg., 107 Sixth St., 15222. (412) 471-8960. David Litto.
Wheeler Film Co., 107 Sixth St., 15222; (412) 471-8225. Ross Wheeler, Jr.

PORTLAND, OR

Portland National Film Service, 2369 N.W. Quimby St. (503) 244-6205. Herb Kirsch, mgr.

ST. LOUIS

Avco-Embassy Pictures, 1750 S. Brentwood Blvd., 63144; (314) 962-7373. Jeannine Wieczorek, broker.
Kahan Film Distributors, 3974 Page Blvd.; (314) 371-6572. Meyer Kahan, mgr.
Kemp Film Distributors Corp., 539 No. Grand Blvd., 63103; (314) 535-1159. Stan Smith.
National Screen Service, 1001 Hanley Industrial Ct., 968-1730.
Paramount Pictures Corp., 539 N. Grand, 63103. (314) 533-4231. Barry Florin.
Thomas/Shipp Films, 539 N. Grand. (314) 535-1117.

United Artists Corp., 1750 So. Brentwood Blvd., 63144. (314) 533-0346. Edward Stevens.

SALT LAKE CITY

American Cinema, 555 East Fourth South. (801) 521-8161. Phillip G. Catherall, gen. sls. mgr.
American National Enterprises, 550 E. 200 South, 84102; (801) 521-9400. Ron Rodgers.
Avco Embassy Pictures, 2095 Douglas St. 84015. (801) 487-4700. Lyle Livsey, br. mgr.
Ed Brinn, Box 1714, 84410. (801) 355-4611.
JD Theatre Service, 1223 S. 20th St., East, 84108; (801) 466-1554. John Dahl.
20th Century-Fox Film Corp., 515 S. 700 East, 84102. Gordon Larsen.
United Artists, P.O. Box 11525, 84147; (801) 532-1224. Robert Loftis.

SAN FRANCISCO

Avco Embassy Pictures, 988 Market St., 94102. (415) 928-7400. Margaret Rykowski, br. mgr.
Buena Vista Dist. Co., Inc., 680 Beach St., 94109. (415) 441-7114. L. Pilmaier, mgr.
Cardinal Films, 1255 Post St., 94102; (415) 776-2626. R. Stafford.
Columbia Pictures, 595 Market St., 94105. (415) 546-7211. Robert Capps, Jr., mgr.
Favorite Films of Calif. Inc., 230 Hyde St.; (415) 776-4408. N. P. Jacobs, pres. Andy Anderson, br. mgr.
Modern TV, 149 New Montgomery St.; (415) 543-1666. Henry Henn, TV manager.
Pacific Film Enterprises, 1 Hallidie Plaza, 94102; (415) 479-8223. Paul Williams.
Paramount Pictures, Inc., 1700 Montgomery St., 94111; (415) 433-8660. R. Litvin.
Ted Reisch Enterprises, 1325 Laurel St., San Carlos, 94070. (415) 593-7060.
Thomas Brothers, 30 Berry St., 94107. (415) 664-1901.
20th Century-Fox Film Corp., 605 Market St., J. Edward Shugrue, br. mgr.
United Artists Corp., 681 Market St., 94105. (415) 441-5500. Mike Musarra.
United Film Dist. Co., 127 Golden Gate Ave., 94102; (415) 928-3200. James Peirson.
Universal Film Exchange, 693 Sutter St., 94102. (415) 776-3660. James B. Mooney, mgr.
Warner Bros. Pictures Distributing Corp., 544 Golden Gate Ave., 94102. (415) 474-5938. Mike Timko.

SEATTLE

Buena Vista Dist. Co. Inc., 2419 Second Ave., 98121. (206) 624-0186. Homer Schmitt, br. mgr.
Favorite Films, 2318 Second Ave., 98121; (206) 624-6234. Pete Tolins, br. mgr.
Northwest Diversified Entertainment, 2318 2nd Ave., MA 3-5380.
Paramount Pictures Corp., 975 John St., 98109; (206) 747-1176. Joe vogel.
Parnell Film Distributors Inc., 2318 Second Ave., 98121; (206) 624-2882.
Saffle's Theatre and TV Service, 975 John St., 98109; (206) 623-5177. M. W. "Bud" Saffle, pres.
Seattle National Film Services, 900 Maynard Ave., So; (206) 682-6685. Norman Jones, mgr.
20th Century-Fox Film Corp., 100 W. Harrison St., 98119. William Robinson.
United Artists Corp., 225-108th Ave., N.E. Bellevue, WA 98004. S. Amato, mgr.
U.S. Navy Dist. Booking Office, 13th Naval Dist.; LA 7-3863. L. D. Palermini, dr. spec. services.
Universal Film Exchange, Lake Villa Apts., 25010 106th St., Apt 8-201E, Kent, WA. (206) 859-1429.

WASHINGTON, DC

Associated Pictures Co., 8601 Liberty Rd., Randallstown, MD; (301) 922-6000, Philip Glazer, mgr.
Avco Embassy Picture Corp., 9470 Annapolis Rd., Lanham, MD (301) 577-2700. Fritz Goldschmidt, br. mgr.
Association-Sterling Films, 1701 N. Fort Meyer Drive, Arlington, VA; 525-4475. C. Edgar Bryant, sales mgr.
Buena Vista Dist. Co., 5205 Leesbury Pike, Baileys Crossroads, VA 22041; (703) 931-6876.
Clark Service, Inc., 3194 Bladensburg Rd. N.E.; (202) 526-0733. Dan McClafferty, mgr.

Columbia Pictures Corp., 2011 I St., N.W., 20006; (202) 466-6570. Martin Zeidman, br. mgr.

DOS Films, Box 87, Nokesville, VA 22123; (703) 368-4429. Doris Steffey.

Key Theatre Ent., 1325½ Wisconsin Ave., N.W., 20007; (202) 965-4401, David Levy.

Modern Talking Picture Service, Inc., 2000 "L" St. N.W. 20036; (202) 293-1222. Robert Kelley, pub. aff. dir.

Paramount Film Dist. Co., 5249 Duke St., Suite 306, Alexandria, VA 22304; (703) 751-1733. George Kelly.

Peerless Dist. Co., 4620 Wisconsin Ave., N.W.; EM 2-8712. Teddy Shull, owner.

20th Century-Fox Film Corp., 1156 15th Street, Suite 701, N.W.; 223-6320. Francis X. Gornley, br. mgr.

United Artists Corp., 7315 Wisconsin Ave., N.W., 20014. (301) 652-6658. Doug Potash, br. mgr.

Universal Film Exchanges, Inc. 6801 Kenilworth Ave. Riverdale, MD 20840. (301) 699-3200. Steve Turner, br. mgr.

Warner Bros. Dist. Corp., 7315 Wisconsin Ave., 20814; (301) 657-9221. Charles Jordan.

Wheeler Film Co., 4701 42nd St. N.W., 20016. (202) 244-1500. Ross Wheeler, Sr.

CANADA

CALGARY, ALTA.

Astral Films, Ltd., 3904—1st St. NE, T2R2E3. (403) 230-3345.

Bellevue Film Distributors, Ltd., 522—11th Ave., SW, T2R068 (403) 264-4660.

Columbia Pictures of Canada, Ltd., 3904—1st St. NE (403) 230-3345

Empire Films Ltd., 3811 Edmonton Trail. Maws Kitigawa, mgr.

Paramount Film Service Ltd., 1410 11th Ave., S.W. (403) 245-4306. Donald Popou, mgr.

United Artists Corp. Ltd., 1003 11th Ave., S.W. T2R0N4. (403) 264-0384. Barry Newstead, mgr.

Universal Films Ltd., 3811 Edmonton Trail; (403) 276-4466. Al Genaske, mgr.

Warner Bros. Pictures Dist. Co. Ltd., 1147 17th Ave., S.W., T2X-0B7. (403) 245-3933. Blain Covert, mgr.

MONTREAL, QUE.

Astral Films, Ltd., 175 Montpellier Blvd., (514) 748-6541.

Bellevue Film Distributors, Ltd., 708 Walnut St.

Cine Pix, Inc., 8275 Maynard St., H4P 2C8. (514) 342-2340.

Columbia Pictures of Canada, Ltd., 175 Montpellier Blvd.; (514) 748-6976.

France Film Company, 1405 Maisonneuve St. J. A. DeSeve pres. and gen. mgr.

International Film Distributors Ltd., 5801 Monkland Ave.; (514) 486-7355.

Paramount Film Service Ltd., 5887 Monkland, (514) 488-9186.

United Artists Corp. Ltd., 3290 Cavendish Blvd., H4B 2M7. (514) 489-8256. Alvin Himelfarb.

Universal Films, Ltd., 8444 St. Laurent Blvd.; (514) 382-8475. J. Hurtubise, br. mgr.

Warner Bros. Distributing Co. Ltd., 5890 Monkland Ave., Rm. 107. (514) 481-2763. Archie Cohen, mgr.

SAINT JOHN, N.B.

Astral Films, Ltd., 55 Bentley St.; (506) 693-3877. Darly Madill, mgr.

Bellevue Film Distributors, Ltd., 77 Germain St.; (506) 693-8601. Vince Winchester, mgr.

Columbia Pictures of Canada, Ltd., 55 Bentley St., L. Simon, mgr.

Paramount Film Service Ltd., 77 Germaine St. (506) 657-5660.

United Artists Corp., Ltd., 77 Germain St., E2L-4S4. Isadore Davis, br. mgr.

Universal Films Ltd., 77 Germain St.; (506) 652-1600. Don McKelvie, mgr.

TORONTO, ONT.

Ambassador Film Distributors, Ltd., 175 Bloor St. E, M4W1C8. (416) 960-3180. Leonard Herberman.

Astral Films Ltd., 720 King St., West, M5V 2T3. (416) 364-3894.

Bellevue Film Distributors, Ltd., 40 Lesmill Rd., Don Mills, Ont. M3B2T5; (416) 449-9322. Herbert S. Mathers, pres.

Columbia Pictures of Canada, Ltd., 720 King St. West. M5V 2T3. Sandra Genesove.

Frontier Amusements, Ltd., 3636 Victoria Park Ave; (416) 499-1106. Morey Hamat.

International Film Distributors, Ltd., 41A Avenue Rd.; (416) 968-2180.

Marden Film Distributors, 4750 Yonge St.; (416) 225-1113.

Modern Talking Picture Service, 143 Sparks Ave., Ontario M2H 255; (416) 498-7290.

Paramount Film Service Ltd., 146 Bloor St.; (416) 922-3600. Robert Lightstone, gen. sales mgr.

Saguenay Films, Ltd., 44 Eglinton Ave., W.; (416) 487-2421.

Twentieth Century-Fox Corp. Ltd., 720 King St., West. Cullen Hulse.

United Artists Corp. Ltd., 2180 Yonge St., M4S2B9. (416) 487-5371.

Universal Films, 2450 Victoria Park Ave.; (416) 491-3000.

Warner Bros. Distributing Co. Ltd., 70 Carlton St.; (416) 922-5145.

VANCOUVER, B.C.

Astral Films Ltd., 1644 W. 75 St., Larry Strick.

Bellevue Film Distributors, 788 Beatly St.; (604) 669-4738.

Columbia Pictures of Canada Ltd., 1644 W. 75 Ave.

Paramount Film Service, Ltd., 1646 West 75 Ave. (604) 263-2574. Chris Sullivan, mgr.

Prima Film, Inc., 1734 West Broadway, Suite 7; (604) 732-7421. Miss V. Hosford.

Sovereign Film Distributors, Ltd., 2416 Granville St.; MArine 3843. Fred Stone, mgr.

United Artists Corp., Ltd., 1682 West 7th Ave., V6K155. Thomas Lightburn, mgr.

Universal Films Ltd., 1200 W. 73 St.; (604) 263-1908. Bryan-Rudston Brown, mgr.

Warner Bros. Pictures Dist. Co. Ltd., 8041 Granville St. Roland Rickard, mgr.

WINNIPEG, MAN.

Astral Films, 20 Stevenson Rd.; (204) 632-1270.

Bellevue Film Distributors, 583 Ellice Ave.; (204) 774-4451.

Columbia Pictures of Canada Ltd., 20 Stevenson Rd.; (204) 632-1270

Paramount Film Service Ltd., 315 Donald St. (204) 943-1435.

United Artists Corp., Ltd., 365 Hargrave St., R3B2K3. Meyer Nackimson.

Universal Films Ltd., 583 Ellice Ave.; (204) 786-3397.

Warner Bros. Pictures Distributing Co., Ltd., 583 Ellice Ave. (204) 786-5513. Florent Boulet, mgr.

Distributors of Trailers

ATLANTA

NATIONAL SCREEN SERVICE, 1325 Logan Circle, N.W.; 351-1416. Robert Sedlak, br. mgr.

CINEMA CONCEPTS THEATRE SERVICE, INC., P.O. Box 720576, Atlanta 30328. (404) 396-1055.

BALTIMORE

ALPHA FILM LABORATORIES, Falls Rd.; CL 2-4150. Ernest Wood.

COLORAMA PRODT., 2805 Greenmount Ave.; 889-6777.

FOLKEMER PHOTO SERVICE, 9041 Chevrolet Drive, Ellicott City, MD; 465-7788.

HALLMARK FILMS, 1511 E. North Ave.; Ve 7-3516.

IDEAL PICTURES, 102 W. 25th St.; TU 9-9962. Nelson White.

KUNZ INC., 207 E. Patapsco Ave.; 355-7220.

LEWY FILM & SOUND STUDIOS, 853 N. Eutaw St.; 728-7000.

MONUMENTAL FILMS INC., Rockrose and Maiden Road; 462-1550.

QUALITY FILM LABS., 3010 Greenmount Ave.; 467-1744.

STANSBURY PHOTO FILMS, 2031 Merritt Ave.; 284-4625.

STARK FILMS, Patterson Village Shopping Center; 358-5044.

BOSTON

MASTER MOTION PICTURE COMPANY, 50 Piedmont St.;
HAncock 6-3592. Abner Racoo, mgr.
NATIONAL SCREEN SERVICE, 95-97 Broadway, 02116. (617)
542-4476. Joe Rossi, sls. mgr.

BUFFALO

CLARK SERVICE, INC., 108 Gruner Road, 14225; (716) 897-0467.
Robert Neffke, mgr.

CHARLOTTE

NATIONAL SCREEN SERVICE, 624 Anderson St., 28205; (704)
333-6628. Milton Lindner, mgr.

CHICAGO

FILMACK CORP., 1327 S. Wabash Ave., 60605; (312) 427-3395.
Joseph R. Mack, pres.
NATIONAL SCREEN SERVICE CORP., 1322 Wabash Ave., 60605;
(312) 427-8211. Paul Ayotte, sls. mgr.
UNIVERSAL IMAGES, LTD., 9504 E. 63rd Street, Kansas City,
MO 64133; (816) 358-6166. Garrett Tuck, president, resident
manager—R. M. Upham, P. O. Box 289, Clarendon Hills, IL
60514; (312) 323-6896.

CINCINNATI

NATIONAL SCREEN SERVICE, 1403 Central Parkway; (513) 621-
8900. David Fletcher, sls. mgr.

DALLAS

JAMIESON FILM CO., 3825 Bryan St.; TA 3-8158. Bruce Jamieson, pres.; Hugh V. Jamieson, Jr., exec. vice-pres.
NATIONAL SCREEN SERVICE, 7138 Envoy Court. (214) 634-
0101. Seymour Kaplan, sls. mgr.

DES MOINES

PARROT FILM SERVICE, 2125 Forest Ave.; 282-4211. Haydon
Peterson, mgr.

DETROIT

NATIONAL SCREEN SERVICE, 2943 Cass Ave., 48201; (313)
831-0790. Ivan Clavet, mgr.

KANSAS CITY, MO

NATIONAL SCREEN SERVICE CORP., 1800 Baltimore Ave.,
64108; 842-5893. William Lustig, sls. mgr.
UNIVERSAL IMAGES, LTD., 9504 E. 63rd Street, Kansas City,
MO 64133; (816) 358-6166. Garrett Tuck, president.

LOS ANGELES

MOONDIAL MANUFACTURING CORP. (dba) Barnett Film Ser-
vice, 8969 Sunset Blvd., Hollywood, CA 90069. (213) 271-4448.
Gabriel Barnett, pres.; Matilda Barnett, v.p.; Morton Breg-
man, sec.-treas. (Sponsored intermission music trailers).
NATIONAL SCREEN SERVICE, 2001 S. La Cienega Blvd., 90034;
836-1505. Richard Barnes, sls. mgr.
UTA, INC., 1658 Cordova St., 9007; (213) 734-0510. Joan Atamian
Bodin, pres.

MEMPHIS

TRI-STATE THEATRE SERVICE, 151 Vance Ave.; 525-8249. Bob
Blank, owner.

MINNEAPOLIS

UNIVERSAL IMAGES, LTD., 9504 E. 63rd Street, Kansas City,
MO 64133; (816) 358-6166. Garrett Tuck, president, resident
manager—J. H. McDonald, 913 Horn Drive, Minnetonka, MN
55343; (612) 545-8617.
SLY-FOX FILMS, INC., 1025 Currie Ave.: 336-6777; Earle C. Sly,
vice-pres.

NEW ORLEANS

NATIONAL SCREEN SERVICE, 5624 Jefferson Highway, Harahan, LA 70123; (504) 837-3570. Joseph Moll, sls. mgr.

NEW YORK CITY

MOTION PICTURE ADVERTISING CORP., 641 Lexington Ave.;
935-3434.
NATIONAL SCREEN SERVICE, 1600 Broadway, 10019; (212) 246-
5700

PITTSBURGH

NATIONAL SCREEN SERVICE, 107 Sixth St., (depot only). 281-
1808.

ST. LOUIS

CINE-GRAPHIC FILMS LABS INC., 101 N. 17th St.; GA 1-5827.
E. H. GOLDBERGER, 1210 Tamm; MI 7-7112.
HARDCASTLE FILM ASSOC., 7319 Wise; MI 7-4200.
PREMIER FILM AND RECORDING CORP., 3033 Locust; JE 1-
3555.
SHELBY STORCK AND CO. INC., 4746 McPherson Ave.; FO 1-
4200.
TECHNISONIC STUDIOS INC., 1201 S. Brentwood Blvd.; PA 7-
1055.

SAN FRANCISCO

MOTION PICTURE SERVICE CO., 125 Hyde St.; ORdway 3-
9162; Gerald L. Karski, pres.
NATIONAL FILM SERVICE, 35 Guy Place; 362-2182.

SEATTLE

NATIONAL SCREEN SERVICE CORP., 2413 Second Ave.; MAin
4-2882; Scott Dingler, br. mgr.

Film Carriers

ALBANY

CLARK SERVICE, INC., 24 North Third St., 12204; Tel.: (518)
434-1289; John Pemberton, mgr.
FIRLIK EXPRESS SERVICE INC., 141 South Hawk St.; Tel.:
(518) 463-3712; John Firlik, pres.
WESCO FILM SERVICE, INC., 24 N. Third St., 12204. (518) 434-
1289. John Pemberton.

ATLANTA

BENTON BROTHERS, 168 Baker St. N.W., 30313; (404) 577-
2821.
THEATRES SERVICE CO., 830 Willoughby Way, N.E., (404)
577-2821. W. B. Langston.

BOSTON

NFS OPERATING CORP., 621 East 1st St., 02127. (617) AN 8-
6510. Jimmie Choukas.

BUFFALO

OLIN FILM DELIVERY, 141 Nassau Ave., Kenmore; 875-4398.
SMITH & HOWELL FILM SERVICE, INC., 108 Gruner Road,
Cheektowaga.
SOUTHWESTERN FILM DELIVERY, 141 Nassau Ave., Ken-
more; Tel.: 875-4398.
WESCO FILM SERVICE, INC., 108 Gruner Rd., 14225. (716)
897-0467. Robert Neffke.

CHARLOTTE

CAROLINA FILM SERVICE, INC., 5012 Hovis Rd., 28203. (704)
394-3129. John H. Vickers.
CAROLINA DELIVERY SERVICE CO., INC., 1336 S. Graham
St.; 333-5196.
M&M SHIPPING SERVICE, 1336 So. Graham St., 28201.
OBSERVER TRANSPORTATION CO., 1600 W. Independence
Blvd.; Tel.: 377-5431.

CHICAGO

ALLIN EXPRESS SERVICE, 2101 S. Peoria, 60608; Tel.: 666-5407; J. B. Allin, owner.
CLARK FILM SERVICE, 222 No. Laflin St., 60607. (312) 829-3700. William Saley.
CONSOLIDATED FILM DELIVERY, 2270 S. Archer Ave.; 326-4120. Ralph McLaughlin, pres.
EMERY AIRFREIGHT, 686-7300; Chicago O'Hare Airport; Zip 60666, O'Hare Field; George Brown, mgr.
LAVIN BROS. FILM DELIVERY SERVICE, 6328 N. Richmond Ave.: BR 4-6450; William Lavin and Lewis Lavin, owners.
NOVO AIR FREIGHT, 2707 Coyle Ave., 593-7300; Donald C. Galloy, v.p. central region; Sid Weintraub, city mgr.
STANDARD TRUCKING CO., 2270 Archer Ave.; 225-1458; Richard McLaughlin, pres.

CINCINNATI

CLARK FILM SERVICE, 421 Bauer St., 45214. (513) 621-4240. Harry Jansen.
FILM SERVICE CO., 1717 Logan St.; 241-5986; Joseph Larkin, mgr.: 471-5848.
LAHMANN FILM SERVICE CO., 214 W. Elder St.; 421-2823; Lawrence Lahmann, mgr.
STATES FILM SERVICE, INC., 421 Bauer St., Tel.: 621-4240; Harry Jansen, mgr.

CLEVELAND

CLEVELAND FILM SERVICE, INC., 2336 Payne Ave., 44114. (216) 771-3723. Harry Lyman.
FILM TRANSIT CO., 2514 Bridge; 771-7636; P. L. Tanner, 3327 Montecello Blvd., Cleveland Heights, Yellowstone 2-4595; Art Marchland, 6545 Aylesworth Dr., TUxedo 5-0635.
STATES FILM SERVICE, INC., 2336 Payne Ave.; Tel.: 771-3723; Harry Lyman, mgr.; K. Wessel, owner.

COLUMBUS, OH

COLUMBUS-CINCINNATI TRUCKING CO., 939 N. 20th St.; 258-2913.

DALLAS

CENTRAL SHIPPING & INSPECTION, 2500 S. Harwood, 75215. (214) 421-5411; Wallace Jack, mgr.
FILM TRANSFER, 1066 W. Mockingbird La.; 637-6690.

DENVER

DENVER SHIPPING AND INSPECTION, 2118 Stout St., 80205. (303) 222-5616; Frank Norris, mgr.
SOUTHWESTERN FILM SERVICE, 2118 Stout St.; 244-2287; Sidney Johnson, mgr.

DES MOINES

D&H DISTRIBUTING, 421 Bower St., 45202.
IOWA FILM DEPOT, 3123 Delaware Ave., 50313. (515) 265-1469; Arthur Trombley, mgr.
NEWS FILM AGENCY, 2500 S. Harwood; HA 8-5181; Bill Durrett, mgr.
IOWA FILM DEPOT, 3123 Delaware, 50313. (515) 265-1469.
KING, H. W. DELIVERY SERVICE, 1320 Grand Ave.; 243-5269; Floyd L. King, mgr.

DETROIT

JAY G. TRUCKING SERVICE, 9237 Warwick; VE 8-5462; Jack Stahley, mgr.
NFS OPERATING CORPORATION, 6111 Concord Ave. 48211. (313) 923-2150. Ed McCauley.
PEP LINES TRUCKING CO., 15120 Third, Highland Park, TUlsa 3-3200.
ROE FILM SERVICE, Bad Axe, MI COngress 9-7927.
SULLIVAN'S FILM SERVICE, 2598 Chalmers, Detroit 48215; VA 1-4713; Ed Sullivan.

GRAND ISLAND, NB

RAPID FILM SERVICE, E. Lincoln Highway; Tel.: 382-4058.

HOBOKEN, NJ

HIGHWAY EXPRESS LINES, INC., Telephone in New York City, WHitehall 3-9188.

HOUSTON, TX

BLUE BONNET EXPRESS AGENCY, INC., 5009 Rusk; S. C. Kirby, mgr. WA 3-9101.
FILM EXPRESS AGENCY, 1402 Palmer; CA 5-4170; A. M. Westbrook, mgr.

INDIANAPOLIS

BRADFORD FILM TRANSIT CO., 718 N Senate Ave., 46202. (317) 636-2800. Don A. Pierce.
CLARK TRANSFER, INC., 429 N. Senate Ave., 46204. (317) 638-3531.
INDIANA TRANSIT SERVICE, 4300 W. Morris St., 46241. (317) 241-9321; Wm. R. Smith, mgr.

JACKSONVILLE

JACKSONVILLE FILM SERVICE, 2208 West 21st St. 32209; (904) 355-5447. B. D. Benton, mgr.

KANSAS CITY, MO

CENTRAL SHIPPING & INSPECTION, 101 West Tenth Ave. No., 64116. (816) 471-0884; Earl Jameson, Jr.
INDEPENDENT FILM SHIPPERS, 1800 Central, 64108. (816) 471-3348.

LINCOLN, NB

MILLS FILM TRANSFER, 1234 S. 9th St.; Tel.; 432-1197.

LOS ANGELES

AIR SEA FORWARDERS, 9009 La Cienega Blvd., L.A. 90045; (213) 776-1611.
B&W FILM DELIVERY, 1972 W. Washington Blvd., Los Angeles, CA; 735-8383.
BARNETT INTERNATIONAL FORWARDERS, INC. OF CALIF., 8635 Aviation Blvd., Inglewood, 90301; (213) 776-1178.
BARNETT/NOVO INTERNATIONAL CORP., P.O. Box 91100, Worldway Postal Center, Los Angeles, CA 90009.
BEEKAY FILM DELIVERY, 1972 W. Washington Blvd.; 733-0233.
BLISS FILM DELIVERY, 1120 S. Second St., Alhambra, CA; 282-9532.
FILM TRANSPORT COMPANY OF CALIFORNIA, 1525 West 23rd Street; 734-4141.
GARDNER'S DELIVERY SERVICE, INC., 11229 S. Prairie, Inglewood, CA; 978-9018.
GILBOY, INC., 8536 National Blvd., 90230; (213) 559-2722. James Hunter, mgr.
RAY HACKIE FILM SERVICE, 1613½ W. 20th, 90007.
NOVO INTERNATIONAL CORP., 8635 Aviation Blvd., Inglewood, 90301; (213) 776-1178.
SANTA BARBARA SPECIAL DELIVERY, 1972 W. Washington Blvd., Los Angeles; REpublic 4-5590.

MEMPHIS

FILM TRANSIT, INC., 291 Hernando St.; Tel.: 525-6894; Guilbert Brandon, president.
MEMPHIS FILM SERVICE, INC., 3931 Homewood Rd., 38118. (901) 365-7550. A. S. Crews.

MILWAUKEE

FILM CENTER, INC. 333 N. 25th St.; 342-3717; Oliver Trampe, mgr.
MILWAUKEE FILM CENTER, INC., 333 No. 25th St., 53233. (414) 344-0300. Oliver Trampe.
NOVO INT'L AIR FREIGHT CORP., 4930 S. 2, 482-3200.

MINNEAPOLIS

CENTURY MOTOR FREIGHT, INC., 3245-4th St. S.E. 55414; 645-9484; Steve Bonello, pres.
HYMAN FREIGHTWAYS, INC., 2690 Prior Ave. N., St. Paul; 633-7310; Eugene Pikovsky, pres.
INDEPENDENT FILM SERVICE, INC., 245 Second Ave. No., 55401. (612) 335-2203. Jim Perrin.

MIDDLEWEST MOTOR EXPRESS, Willmar. Minn.; Barney Johnson, owner.
MIDWEST MOTOR EXPRESS, 2778 Cleveland Ave. No., St. Paul; 633-5653; W. J. Greenstein, vice-president.
MIX TRANSFER, 701 N. 4th St.; 339-9646; Roy W. Mix, owner.
NOVO AIR FREIGHT, INC., 701 N. 4th St.; 336-5341.
PITTS FILM SERVICE, INC., 149 Jackson Ave. N., Hopkins, Minn.; 938-7290; Lawrence Johnson, pres.
RINGSBY UNITED SYSTEM, 2508 Kennedy St., N.E.; Tel.: 331-4330; Jerry Flanagan, terminal mgr.
TWIN CITIES NEWSPAPER SERVICE, INC., 1161 Selby Ave., St. Paul, 644-8810; Leo Loomis, Ed Riley, owners.
TWIN CITY FREIGHT, 2280 Ellis, St. Paul; 645-3661; W. E. Elshotz, Sr., pres.

NEW HAVEN

NEW HAVEN FILM SERVICE, 90 Woodmont Rd., 06460, Milford. (203) 878-1465. William Rosen.
ROSEN FILM DELIVERY SYSTEM, 1890 Dixwell Ave., Hamden: ATwater 8-9161.

NEW ORLEANS

FILM INSPECTION SERVICE, INC., 2411 Edenborn Ave., Metairie, LA 70001. (504) 833-5552. Ian Brandon.
NOVO AIR FREIGHT, 2411 Edenboro Ave., Metairie, LA; 837-0922.
SCHAFFER FILM SERVICE, INC., P.O. Box 9344, Metairie, LA; Tel.: 833-9670; Buddy Schaffer, owner/mgr.
TRANSWAY, INC., (A subsidiary of Novo).

NEW YORK CITY

BONDED SERVICES DIVISION, 733 Third Ave., 10017; (212) 557-6700.
HIGHWAY EXPRESS LINES, INC., 360-16 St., Hoboken, NJ; NY 267-5990.
HUDSON FILM DELIVERY CORP., 560 Main, Fort Lee, NJ; 201-947-5200.
STATE FILM DELIVERY, 560 Main. Fort Lee, NJ; 201-947-5200.
PRUDENTIAL FILM DISTRIBUTORS CORP., 630 Ninth Avenue; COlumbus 5-6884.
RAPID FILM DISTRIBUTORS, INC., 37-02 27th St., Long Island City, 11101; (212) 786-4600.
TRANS-WORLD INTERNATIONAL INC., 767 Fifth Ave., 755-9415.

OKLAHOMA CITY

MAGIC EMPIRE EXPRESS, 920 S.W. 2 Street; Tel.: CE 5-8543; Nolan Nuckols.
MISTLETOE EXPRESS SERVICE, INC., 111 N. Harrison; CE 6-1482; Jack LaMonte, mgr.
O&A FILM LINES, 706 W. Sheridan; CE 2-9900; Roy Avery, mgr.
OKLAHOMA CITY SHIPPING & INSPECTION, 8009 So. West 7th St., 73125. (405) 235-2553. Charles Baird.

OMAHA

OMAHA FILM DEPOT, 1441 N. 11th St., 68102. (404) 342-6576. Charles Janousek.

PHILADELPHIA

CLARK SERVICE INC., 829 No. 29th Street; (215) 232-3500.
HIGHWAY EXPRESS LINES, INC., 3200 S. 20th St., DE 6-6060.
STATES FILM SERVICE, INC., 130 Ferry Ave., Camden, NJ 08104. (215) LO 30303. Meyer Adelman.

PIERCE, NB

PIERCE FILM SERVICE, 512 S. Brown St., Tel.: 329-6365; Dale Hitz.

PITTSBURGH

EXHIBITORS SERVICE CO., 85 Helen St. McKees Rocks; 771-5010; George Callahan, Jr., pres.
KALLY EXPRESS EXHIBITORS SERVICE, 239 Calmar Dr., Verona, PA 15147; 731-9018; Ed M. Duva, owner.
PITTSBURGH FILM SERVICE, Building 16, Nichol Ave., McKees Rocks, 15136. (412) 771-2665; Pete Dana, mgr.

PORTLAND, OR

ADAMSON THEATRES, 909 N.W. 19th; CA 227-5684; Art Adamson, owner; Mark McDougal, mgr.
BELL, HOWARD FILM SERVICE, 907 N.W. 19th St.; 227-2932.
LOVETT INTERSTATE THEATRE SERVICE, 935 N.W. 19th Ave.; CA 4-6108; J. G. (Jack) Lovett, mgr.
PORTLAND NATIONAL FILM SERVICE, 2369 N.W. Quimby St., 97210. (503) 224-6205. Herb Krisch.

PORTSMOUTH, OH

HUNTINGTON/CINCINNATI TRUCKING LINES, LTD., 1006 Gay Street; Tel.: EL 3-7359.

ST. LOUIS

KAHAN FILM DISTRIBUTORS, 3974 Page Blvd., 63113. (314) 371-6572; Meyer Kahan, mgr.
LEWTON FILM SERVICE INC., 12721 San Clemente, 739-0717.

SALT LAKE CITY

NFS OPERATING CORP., 350 West Sixth St., 84110. (801) 364-7729. Rulon Hammer.
WYCOFF CO., INC., 560 S2W; 322-1361; Robert Andrus, mgr.

SAN ANTONIO, TEX.

TEXAS FILM SERVICE, 518 S. Main Ave.; Tel.: CA 7-9295.
VALLEY FILM SERVICE, 518 S. Main Ave.; Phone CA 7-9295.

SAN FRANCISCO

FILM MESSENGER SERVICE, 215 Golden Gate Ave.; 431-4074; Stan Draper, owner.
NFS OPERATING CORP., 35 Guy Place, 94105. (415) 362-2182. H. Przyborowski.

SEATTLE

INLAND NORTHWEST FILM SERVICE, INC., 2201 6th Ave., S.; Tel.: MU 2-4766; R. C. Kercheval, pres.
LOCAL FILM DELIVERY, INC., 900 Maynard South; MU 2-6663; Chas. D. Lawson, pres.
NATIONAL SCREEN SERVICE CORP., 2413 Second Ave.; MAin 4-2882; Arch McGlunchey, br. mgr.
NORTHWEST FILM SERVICE, INC., 79 S. Dearborn St.; MA 2-0241; Paul R. Grunewald, pres.
SEATTLE NATIONAL FILM SERVICE, 900 Maynard Ave., So., 98134. (206)

SYRACUSE, NY

SMITH & HOWELL FILM SERVICE, INC., 505 Burnet Ave.; 2-6836.

TOLEDO, OH

THEATRE TRANSPORT CO., 205 First St.; Tel.: OX 1-0711.

WASHINGTON, DC

MOLITCH FILM SERVICE, 3194 Bladensburg Rd., N.E. 20018. (202) 526-0733. Dan McClafferty.

Canada

CALGARY, ALTA.

FREDDIE'S TRANSPORT, Strathmore, Alta.; 382-3033; J. F. Teare, mgr.

MONTREAL, QUE.

MONTREAL MESSENGER SERVICE REG'D, 444 Notre Dame St. East; 288-1286; Harry A. Cohen, pres.

SAINT JOHN, N.B.

FITZPATRICK TRANSFER, 178 King St. E.; 693-5649; J. P. Fitzpatrick, mgr.

TORONTO, ONT.

MAVETY FILM DELIVERY LTD., 277 Victoria St.; EMpire 3-2413; William Pfaff.

Screening Rooms

ATLANTA

ATLANTA PREVIEW THEATRE, 161 Spring St., N.W.; (404) 523-0663.
20TH-CENTURY FOX EXCHANGE, 2200 Century Parkway, 30345.

BOSTON

E.M. LOEW THEATRES, 164 Tremont St., Boston, 02111. (617) 482-9200.
UNIVERSAL, 44 Winchester St., 02116. (617) 426-8760.

CHICAGO

H. & E. BALABAN THEATRES, 190 North State St., Chicago 60601; (312) 372-2262.
CHICAGO INTERNATIONAL FILM FESTIVAL, 235 Eugenie, Chicago 60614; (312) 644-3400.
DOUGLAS FILM INDUSTRIES, 10 W. Kinzie, 60610. (312) 664-7455.
ESSANESS THEATRES CORPORATION, 54 West Randolph, Chicago 60601. (312) 332-7465.
UNIVERSAL FILM EXCHANGES, INC., 425 North Michigan Avenue, Chicago 60601; (312) 822-0513.

CINCINNATI

20TH CENTURY-FOX FILM CORP., 617 Vine St.; (513) 241-6460.

DENVER

CENTURY SCREENING ROOM, 2100 Stout St.; (303) 534-7611.
THE FLICK THEATRE, Larimer Sq., 80202; (303) 244-9155.
WESTERN CINE SERVICE INC., 312 S. Pearl St., 80209; (303) 744-1017.

KANSAS CITY

COMMONWEALTH THEATRES, 215 W. 18th St., 64108. (816) 471-2390.
DICKINSON OPERATING CO., 5913 Woodson Rd., Mission, KS 66202. (316) 432-2334.

LOS ANGELES

ACADEMY AWARD THEATRE, 8949 Wilshire Blvd.; 278-8990.
AIDIKOFF, CHAS., SCREENING ROOM, 9255 W. Sunset Blvd., L.A.; 274-0866.
BEVERLY HILLS HOTEL, 9641 Sunset Blvd., Beverly Hills, CA 90210; 276-2251.
CENTRE FILMS INC., 1103 N. El Centro Ave., Hollywood 90038; (213) 466-5123.
CONSOLIDATED FILM INDUSTRIES, 959 Seward St., L.A. 90038; 462-3161.
DE LUXE GENERAL, 1546 N. Argyle Ave., L.A. 90028; 462-6171.
DIRECTORS GUILD OF AMERICA, 7950 W. Sunset Blvd., Los Angeles 90046; Tel.: 656-1220.
SAM GOLDWYN STUDIOS, 1041 N. Formosa Ave., L.A. 90046; 851-1234.
HOLLYWOOD SCREENING ROOM, 1800 N. Highland Ave., Suite 511, Hollywood 90028; (213) 466-1888.
DONALD H. NOSSECK THEATRE, 9229 Sunset Blvd., L.A. 90069; 274-4888.
MARTIN NOSSECK PROJECTION THEATRE, 9118½ Sunset Blvd., Hollywood, 90069. (213) 275-3037.

PREVIEW HOUSE, 7655 Sunset Blvd., L.A. 90046; (213) 876-6600.
JOE SHORE'S SCREENING ROOM, 9229 W. Sunet Blvd., L.A. 90046; (213) 274-4888.

MILWAUKEE

CENTRE THEATRE BLDG., 212 W. Wisconsin Ave., 53203, (608) 272-6020.
RKO-STANLEY WARNER THEATRES, INC., 5341 W. Fond du Lac Avenue (Capitol Court Theater); (608) 871-2213.

NEW YORK

(All major producers-distributors have screening rooms at their home offices in New York for their own use. Most also have screening room facilities at their New York exchanges).

CINE-METRIC THEATRE INC., 25 W. 45th St., 869-8670.
CINEMA 405 INC., 600 Madison Ave.; 759-5700.
FELDMAN, ARTHUR, 1585 Broadway, NY; 245-9738.
FIFTH AVENUE SCREENING ROOM, 4 West 56th St.; 541-5454.
MOVIELAB THEATRE SERVICE, INC., 619 W. 54th St.; 586-0360.
MUSEUM OF MODERN ART FILM LIBRARY, 11 W. 53rd St.; 956-7236.
PARK AVENUE SCREENING, INC., 445 Park Ave.; 688-3277.
PRECISION FILM LABS' SCREENING THEATRE, 630 Ninth Avenue. 489-8800.
PREVIEW THEATRE, 1600 Broadway; 246-0865.
RIZZOLI SCREENING ROOM, 712 5th Ave.; 397-3738.
ROSS-GAFFNEY INC., 21 W. 46 St.; 582-3744.
WESTSIDE SCREENINGS, INC., 311 West 43rd St.; 246-3838.

SAN FRANCISCO

MOTION PICTURE SERVICE CO., 125 Hyde St., (415) 673-9162.
THOMAS BROTHERS, 30 Berry St., 94107; (415) 664-1901.

TAMPA

POST PRODUCTION SERVICES, INC., 3808 San Nicholas St.; (813) 253-0400.

WASHINGTON

BYRON, INC., 65 K St., N.E.; (202) 783-2700.
CAPITAL FILM LABORATORIES, INC., 470 "E" St., S.W.; (202) 347-1717.
KOSTER FILM FACILITIES, INC., 1017 "E" St., S.W.; 544-4410.
NATIONAL CINE LABORATORIES, 4319 Rhode Island Ave., Brentwood, MD; 779-6800.

Canada

MONTREAL

ASSOCIATED SCREEN INDUSTRIES LTD., 2000 Northcliffe Ave.; (514) 484-1186.
CONSOLIDATED THEATRES LTD., 5887 Monkland Ave.; (514) 489-8461.
EMPIRE FILMS LTD., 8440 St. Lawrence; (514) 381-5961.
FRANCE FILM COMPANY, 1405 Maisonneuve St.; (514) 526-5971.
UNITED AMUSEMENT CORP. LTD., United Bldg., 5887 Monkland Ave.; (514) 489-8461.

TORONTO

FAMOUS PLAYERS CANADIAN CORP. LTD., 130 Bloor St., W.; (416) 964-5800.
FILM HOUSE, 22 Front St. W.; (416) 363-4321.
ODEON THEATRES (Canada) LTD., 225 Consumers Rd., Willowdale, Ont. (416) 491-1660.
PARAMOUNT FILM SERVICE, 111 Bond St.; (416) 366-8811.
TWENTIETH-CENTURY FOX CORP. LTD., 277 Victoria St.; (416) 364-3471.

Film Processing, Raw Stock, Preservation, Storage

Film Labs, Processing

ATLANTA
CINEMA PROCESSORS, INC., 2156 Faulkner Rd.; 30324. (404) 633-1448.
COLOR-GRAPHIC, 3184 Roswl Rd., N.W.; 30305. (404) 233-2174.
SOUTHERN FILM LAB INC., 2381 John Glenn Dr., Chambler, GA 30341. (404) 458-0026.
WOMETCO & CO. FILM LABS, INC., 3630 Peachtree Rd., N.W., 30305. (404)233-5387.

BOSTON
CINE SERVICE LABORATORIES, INC., 51 Kondazian St.; Watertown 02172; (617) 926-0210.
D-4 FILM STUDIOS, INC., 109 Highland Ave., Needham Hts., MA 02194. (617) 444-0226.
FILM SERVICE LAB, 62 Berkeley St.; 02116. (617) 542-1238.
MASTER MOTION PICTURE CO., 50 Piedmont St., 02116; (617) 426-3592.
SPORTS FILM LAB, 361 W. Broadway, 02127. (617) 268-8388.

CHICAGO
ASTRO COLOR LAB, 61 W. Erie, 60610. (312) 280-5500.
CINEMA VIDEO PROCESSORS, 211 East Grand Ave.; 60611. (312) 527-4050.
COLBURN LABORATORY, GEORGE W., INC., 164 North Wacker Drive, 60606. (312) 332-6286.
DOUGLAS FILM INDUSTRIES, INC., 10 W. Kinzie, 60630. (312) 664-7455.
EAGLE FILM LABORATORY, INC., 4971 N. Elston, 60630. (312) 282-7161.
EDITEL, INC., 301 E. Erie (312) 440-2360.
ESKAY FILM SERVICE, INC., 540 N. Lakeshore, 60611; (312) 467-6250.
SUPERIOR BULK FILM CO., 442 N. Wells; SUperior 7-4448.
TITLE-CRAFT, 2722 W. Lawrence, 60625. (312) 271-5731.

CINCINNATI
CINCINNATI FM LABS, 3705 Lonsdale St., 45227; (513) 271-5540.
FILM ART, INC., 2436 Vine St., 45220: (513) 621-4930.
MARATHON MOVIE LABORATORY, 2436 Vine St., 45219; (513) 621-5313.

CLEVELAND
FILM LAB SERVICE, 4117 Prospect Ave., 44103; (216) 881-4510.

COLUMBIA, SC
SOUTHEASTERN FILM COMPANY, 3604 Main St.; 29203; (803) 252-3753.

COLUMBUS, OH
JOHN R. BENNETT, 1617 Aberdeen Ave., 43211. (614) 263-7007.

DALLAS
PSI FILM LAB., 3011 Diamond Park Dr., 75247. (214) 631-5670.
SOUTHWEST FILM LABORATORY, INC., 3024 Fort Worth Ave., 75211. (214) 331-8347.

DAYTON
FILM ASSOCIATES, INC., 4600 S. Dixie Ave., 45439; (513) 293-2164.

DETROIT
DYNAMIC FILM SERVICE, 3028 E. Grand Blvd.; (313) 873-4720.
FILM CRAFT LAB., INC., 66 Sibley, 48201; (313) 962-2611.
THE JAM HANDY ORGANIZATION, 2792 E. Grand Boulevard 48211; (313) 845-2450.
PRODUCERS COLOR SERVICE, 2921 E. Grand Blvd.; (313) 874-1112.

HOLLYWOOD-LOS ANGELES
AMERICAN FILM IND., 1138 N. La Brea Ave., Hollywood 90038; (213) 467-1118.

AUDIO VISUAL HEADQUARTERS CORP., 515 S. Olive St., L.A. 90013; (213) 629-3661.
CINEMA RESEARCH CORP., 6860 Lexington Ave., L.A. 90038; (213) 461-3235.
CINE-CRAFT FILM LAB., 8764 W. Beverly, Hwd., 90048; 213-652-7357.
CINESERVICE, INC., 1459 N. Seward St., 90028. (213) 463-3178.
COLOR REPRODUCTION COMPANY, 7936 Santa Monica Blvd., Los Angeles 90046; 654-8010.
CONSOLIDATED FILM INDUSTRIES, 959 No. Seward St., Los Angeles 90038; (213) 462-3161.
CREST FILM LABORATTRIES, 1141 N. Seward St., L.A. (90038); (213) 462-6696.
DELUXE GENERAL INC., 1546 N. Argyle Ave., Hollywood, CA 90028; 462-6171; 1377 N. Serrano Ave., Hollywood, CA 90027; 462-6171
EASTMAN KODAK LABORATORY, 1017 N. Las Palmas Ave., Los Angeles 90038; (213) 465-7151.
FILMSERVICE LABORATORIES, INC., 6327 Santa Monica Blvd., Hollywood 90038; (213) 464-5141.
FLORA COLOR, 1715 N. Mariposa St., Hollywood 90027; (213) 663-2291.
FOTO-KEM INDUSTRIES, INC., 2800 W. Olive Ave., Burbank, 91505. (213) 846-3101.
HOLLYWOOD FILM ENTERPRISES, INC., 6060 Sunset Blvd., Los Angeles 90038; (213) 464-2181.
MANN, HAL, 7070 Santa Monica Blvd., Hollywood, CA 90038; (213) 466-3231.
METRO-GOLDWYN-MAYER LABS., 10202 W. Washington Bl. C.C. 90230; (213) 836-3000.
METRO-KALVAR, INC., 8927 W. Exposition Bl. L.A. 90034; (213) 870-1602.
MOVIELAB, 6823 Santa Monica Blvd., Los Angeles 90038; (213) 469-5981.
NEWSFILM LABORATORY, INC., 516 N. Larchmont Bl., LA 90004; (213) 462-8292.
PACIFIC TITLE AND ART STUDIO, 6350 Sánta Monica Blvd., Los Angeles 90038; (213) 464-0121.
PEERLESS FILM PROCESSING CORP., 730 Salem, Glendale; (213) 242-2181.
REVERSALS UNLIMITED, 6903 Melrose Ave., L.A. 90038; (213) 938-3641.
TECHNICOLOR INC. (Cinema Systems Division), 4050 Lankershim Bl., North Hollywood, 91608; (213) 769-8500.
UNITED COLOR LAB, INC., 835 N. Seward, 90038. (213) 461-9921.
YALE LABS, 1509 N. Gordon St., L.A. 90028; (213) 464-6181.

HOUSTON
A-V CORP., 2518 No. Blvd., 77006. (713) 523-6701.
THE PHOTOGRAPHIC LABORATORIES, 1926 W. Gray, 77019; (713) 529-5846.

INDIANAPOLIS, IND.
FILMCRAFT LABORATORIES, 5323 W. 86th St., 46268. (317) 299-7070.

MEMPHIS, TENN.
MOTION PICTURE LABORATORIES, INC., 781 S. Main St.; 38106. (901) 774-4944.

MIAMI, FLA.
CAPITAL FILM LABORATORIES, INC., 1998 N.E. 150 St., 33161. (305) 949-4252.
WOMETCO FILM LABS, INC., 65 N.W. Third St., 33128. (305) 377-2611.

MILWAUKEE, WISC.
CENTRAL FILM LABORATORY & PHOTO SUPPLY, 1003 North Third St.; 53203. (414) 272-0606.

NEW ORLEANS
PAN AMERICAN FILMS, 822 N. Rampart St., 70116; (504) 522-5364.

NEW YORK CITY

ACCURATE FILM LABS, 45 W. 45th St., 10036. (212) 730-0555.
BEBELL INC., 416 W. 45th St., New York 10036. (212) 245-8900.
BERKEY FILM PROCESSING, 77 E. 13 St., 10003. (212) 475-8700.
CINEFFECTS VISUALS INC., 115 West 45th St., 10036. (212) 575-5151.
CINELAB CORP., 475 Tenth Ave., 10019. (212) 244-7400.
CONTROL FILM SERVICE, 421 W. 54th St. 10019. (212) 245-1574.
DELUXE GENERAL INC., 630 Ninth Ave., 10036. (212) 489-8800.
DU-ART FILM LABORATORIES, 245 W. 55th St., 10019. (212) 757-4580.
FILMTRONICS LABS, 231 West 54th Street, 10019. (212) 586-3150.
GUFFANTI FILM LABORATORIES, INC., 630 Ninth Ave., 10036; (212) 265-5530.
HUEMARK FILMS INC., 277 East 44th Street, 10017. (212) 986-5066.
J & D LABS INC., 421 West 54th Street, 10019. (212) 581-4725.
KIN-O-LUX, INC., 17 West 45th Street, 10036. (212) 586-1880.
MEDIA FILM SERVICES, INC., 351 West 52nd Street, 10019. (212) 581-4995.
MOVIELAB, INC., 619 W. 54th St., 10019. (212) 586-0360.
PRECISION FILM LABORATORIES, 630 Ninth Ave., 10036. (212) 489-8800.
QUALITY FILM LABORATORIES CO., 619 W. 54 St., 10019. (212) 586-4912.
RAPID FILM TECHNIQUE, INC., 37-02 27th Street, L.I.City, 11101. (212) 786-4600.
TVC LABORATORIES, INC., NEW YORK, 311 W. 43rd St., New York, 10036. (212) 397-8600.
TECHNICOLOR INC., 321 W. 44th St., 10036. (212) 582-7310.
U.S. PHOTO EQUIPMENT, 40-13 104th St., Corona, 11368. (212) 672-3140.
WOMETCO FILM LABS, INC., 310 Cedar Lane, Teaneck, NJ 07666. (201) 836-6706.

NIAGARA FALLS, N.Y.

NIAGARA PHOTO CENTER, 726 Division Ave. 14305; (716) 285-2914.

OMAHA

CORNHUSKER FILM PROCESSING LAB., 1817 Vinton St., 341-4290.

PHILADELPHIA

NEWS REEL LABORATORY, 1733 Sansom St., Philadelphia 3; RIttenhouse 6-3892; Louis W. Kellman, pres.

PITTSBURGH

WRS MOTION PICTURE LAB., 210 Semple St., Pittsburgh 15213; (412) 683-6300.

PORTLAND, ORE.

FORDE MOTION PICTURE LABS., 2153 NE Sandy Blvd., 97232; (503) 234-0553.
KING FILM LAB., 1501 SW Jefferson St., 97201; (503) 224-8620.

SALT LAKE CITY, UTAH

STOCKDALE & CO., INC.—PHOTO-TECH. LAB., 200 E. 1st South St.; 521-3505.

SAN FRANCISCO

DINER, LEO FILMS INC., 332-350 Golden Gate Ave. 94102; (415) 775-3664.
HIGHLAND LABS., 90 Tehama St., 94105; (415) 986-5480.
D.D. MONACO FILM LABORATORY, 234 Ninth St., 94103. (415) 864-5350.
MULTICHROME LABORATORIES, 760 Gough St., 94102. (415) 431-6567.
PALMER, W.A., FILMS, INC., 611 Howard St., 94105. (415) 986-5961.

SEATTLE, WASH.

FORDE MOTION PICTURE LABORATORY, 306 Fairview Ave. N., 98109. (206) 682-2510.

SHREVEPORT, LA.

DELTA FILMS, 327 Market Street, 71101; (318) 423-2679.

SPRINGFIELD, MASS.

BAY STATE FILM PRODUCTIONS, INC., 35 Springfield St., Agawarm 01101. (413) 734-3164.

TAMPA, FLA.

BEACON FILM LABORATORY, 3705 N. Nebraska Ave., Tel.: (813) 248-4935.

WASHINGTON, D.C.

BYRON, INC., 65 K Street, N.E., 20002. (202) 783-2700.
CAPITAL FILM LABORATORIES, INC., 470 E St., S.W., 20024. (202) 347-1717.
WASHINGTON FILM LABORATORIES, INC., 1042 Wisconsin Ave., N.W., 20007. (202) 333-1162.

CANADA

MONTREAL, QUE.

ASSOCIATED SCREEN INDUSTRIES, LTD., 2000 Northcliffe Avenue. Montreal. Subsidiary of Du-Art Film Labs, Inc.
BELLEVUE-PATHE LTD., 2000 Northcliffe Ave., (514) 484-1186.
BIER, DAVID STUDIOS & FILM LABS., 265 Vitre St., West, Montreal.
QUEBEC FILM LABS, 1085 Rue St. Alexandre. (514) 861-5483.

OTTAWA, ONT.

GRAPHIC FILMS LTD., 19 Fairmont Ave.; (613) 728-3513.

TORONTO, ONT.

BELLEVUE-PATHE LTD., 9 Brockhouse Rd., (416) 259-7811.
BEST FILM LAB., 344 Jarvis St.; (416) 921-2137.
NORTHERN MOTION PICTURE LABORATORIES, LTD., 65 Granby St.; (416) 362-7631.

Film Preservation

THE CINECURE COMPANY, 1112 Lancaster Ave., Rosemont Pennsylvania, PA 19010 (215) 527-1855 Walter E. Shank, pres.
THE DURAFILM CO., 137 No. La Brea Ave., Hollywood, CA 90036. (213) 936-1156. Madelon Cohen, pres.
FILMLIFE INCORPORATED, Filmlife Bldg., 141 Moonachie Road, Moonachie, NJ 07074. (201) 440-8500. Marvin A. Bernard, bd. chm. & pres.
FILMTREAT INTERNATIONAL CORP., 250 W. 64 St., New York, NY 10023. (212) 799-2500. Y. W. Mociuk, pres. (See isplay ad on page 413.)
PEERLESS FILM PROCESSING CORPORATION, 250 W. 64th St., New York, NY 10023. (212) 242-2181. Y. M. Mociuk, pres.
RESEARCH TECHNOLOGY, INC., 4700 Chase Ave., Lincolnwood, IL 60646. 677-3000.

Photo Reproduction Labs

APCO-APEDA PHOTO CO., INC., 250 West 54th St., NY 10019, NY, (212) 586-5755.
BEBELL INC., 416 West 45th St., New York 10036; (212) 245-8900. 16mm. 35mm. reversal processing, black & white and color release prints. Slides and slide films, camera masters, dupes. Giant size color prints, plus transparencies.
FRANKLIN PHOTOS, INC., 353 West 48th St., N.Y., NY 10036. (212) CI 6-4255.

Film Storage Vaults

ATLANTA

ATLANTA FILM SERVICE, 161 Spring St., N.W.; Tel.: 524-5380. Geoffrey Tyers, pres. R. D. (Curly) Burns, mgr.
BENTON FILM FORWARDING CO., 168 Baker St., N.W.; 577-2821. William B. Langston, mgr.

HOLLYWOOD-LOS ANGELES

(Hollywood studios have own storage vaults)

BEKINS VAN AND STORAGE COMPANY, 1025 North Highland Avenue, (213) 466-9271.

BONDED SERVICES, INC., 8290 Santa Monica Blvd., 90046; (213) 654-7575.

CONSOLIDATED FILM INDUSTRIES, 959 No. Seward Street, Hollywood, CA 90038. (213) 462-3161. (Stores only film which Consolidated Laboratory is handling.)

EVCO REFRIGERATED FILM VAULTS, 838 N. Seward, Hollywood, 90038. (213) 464-9252.

HOLLYWOOD FILM CO., 956 N. Seward St. 90038; (213) 462-3284.

PRODUCERS FILM CENTER, 948 N. Sycamore Ave., 90038; (213) 851-1122.

NEW YORK CITY

BEKINS ARCHIVAL SERVICES, INC., 609 W. 51 St., 10019. (212) 489-7890.

BONDED SERVICES, 733 Third Avenue, New York, NY 10017; (212) 557-6700.

BONDED FILM STORAGE, 550 Main Street, NJ 07024; (212) 557-6732.

RAPID FILM TECHNIQUE, INC., 37-02 27 St., L.I. City 11101. (212) 786-4600.

TORONTO

BONDED FILMTREAT, 205 Richmond St. W.; (416) 363-6414.

CENTRAL FILM SHIPPING & STORAGE COMPANY, 277 Victoria St., Toronto; EM. 3-2909.

PEACOCK FILM STORAGE CO., Sheppard Ave., Agincourt, Ont.; HIckory 4-6135.

SPONSOR FILM SERVICES CORP. LTD., 443 Jarvis St., Toronto; WA 2-3159.

SYNDICATED FILM SERVICES LTD., 103 Church St., Toronto; EM. 4-1475.

Raw Stock Manufacturers

AGFA-GEVAERT, INC., (manufacturer, distributor 35mm 16mm color, black, white raw stock. Executive offices: 275 North St., Teterboro, NJ; 212 LO 5-7850 or 201 288-4100. Branches: 1025 Grand Central Ave., Glendale, CA, 91201, 213 246-8141; 6901 N. Hamlin Ave., Chicago, IL, 60645, 312 675-6000; 1019 Collier Rd., N.W., Atlanta, GA, 30318, 404-355-7450; 460 Tottem Pond Rd., Waltham, MA, 02154, 617-890-5430; 1355 Conant St., Dallas, TX, 75207, 214-ME1-7290; 31 East 28th St., New York City, 10016. (212) 685-6641; 1 West Hill Drive, Crocker Industrial Park, Brisbane, CA 94005. (415) 467-2330.

EASTMAN KODAK CO., 343 State St., Rochester, NY Tel.: (716) 325-2000. 1901 W. 22nd St., Oakbrook, IL 60521. Tel.: (312) 654-5300. 6706 Santa Monica Blvd., Hollywood, CA. Tel.: (213) 464-6131. 1133 Ave. of Americas, New York City 10036. Tel.: (212) 262-6000.

FUJI PHOTO FILM U.S.A., INC., (distributor of Fuji Professional Motion Picture Film) 350 Fifth Ave., N.Y., NY, 736-3335.

GAF CORP., Binghamton, NY 13902; (607) 729-6555.

GEVAERT COMPANY OF AMERICA, INC., (see Agfa-Gevaert).

ILFORD, INC., 70 W. Century Rd., Paramus, NJ 07562; (201) 265-6000.

3M COMPANY (MINNESOTA MINING & MANUFACTURING CO.), Photographic Products Division, manufacturer and distributor of Ferrania 3M motion picture films; 2501 Hudson Rd., St. Paul, Minn. 55101, (612) 733-0020; 845 Third Ave., New York, NY, (212) LT-1-1416; 6023 So. Garfield Ave., Los Angeles, CA 90022, (213) 685-9600.

RESEARCH TECHNOLOGY, INC., 4700 Chase Ave., Lincolnwood, IL 60646. (312) 677-3000.

Stock-Shot Film Libraries

HOLLYWOOD-LOS ANGELES

BUDGET FILMS, 4590 Santa Monica Blvd., L.A. 90029; 660-0187.

COLOR STOCK LIBRARY, INC., 910 N. Citrus Ave., (213) 466-1344.

EVCO LIBRARY, 838 N. Seward, Hollywood 90038; (213) 464-9252.

SHERMAN GRINBERG FILM LIBRARIES, INC., 1040 N. McCadden Pl., Hollywood, CA 90038; (213) 464-7491.

METRO-GOLDWYN-MAYER, 10202 W. Washington Blvd., Culver City, CA 90230; (213) 836-3000.

PRODUCERS LIBRARY SERVICE, 7325 Santa Monica Blvd., Hollywood 90046 (213) 851-2201.

ALLAN SANDLER FILM LIBRARIES, INC., 1001 No. Poinsetta Place, Hollywood; (213) 876-2021.

TRANS AMERICA FILM CORP., 1680 N. Vine St., L.A. 90028; 466-7575.

UNITED AIRLINES, (stock footage), 626 Wilshire Blvd., L.A. 90017; (213) 482-2000.

UNIVERSAL CITY STUDIOS, 100 Universal City, 91608; (213) 985-4321.

NEW YORK CITY

FOTOSONIC INC., 15 West 46th St., 10036. (212) JU 6-0355.

HEARST METROTONE NEWS, 235 E. 45 St. 10017. (212) 682-7690.

MOVIETONEWS, INC. FILM LIBRARY, (Subsidiary of 20th Century Fox), 1345 Ave. of Americas, 10019 (212) 397-8548.

MUSEUM OF MODERN ART FILM LIBRARY, 11 West 53rd Street, 10019. (212) CIrcle 5-8900.

SHERMAN-GRINBERG FILM LIBRARIES, INC., 630 Ninth Avenue, NY 10036; (212) 765-5170.

STOCK SHOTS TO ORDER, 521 Fifth Ave., New York, NY 10017. (212) 682-5844.

STRATFORD INTERNATIONAL FILM SEARCHERS, INC., 250 West 57th St., New York, JU 6-3828.

TELENEWS FILM CORP., 235 E. 45 St. 10019. (212) 682-5600.

Services for Producers

Advertising, In-Theatre

MOONDIAL MANUFACTURING CORP. (dba) Barnett Film Service, 8969 Sunset Blv., Hollywood, CA 90069. (213) 271-4448. Gabriel Barnett, pres.; Matilda Barnett, v.p.; Morton Bregman, sec.-treas. (Sponsored theatre clocks especially designed and perfected for advertising use in motion picture theatres.)

MOVIE MEDIA NETWORK, INC., 2600 Douglas Road, Coral Gables, FL 33134. (305) 448-0008. David I. Weiss, pres. (National program of in-theatre poster advertising; company installs posters of products and services for the general consumer public on the walls of theatre lobbies)

Animals and Trainers

EAST COAST

ANIMAL ACTORS INTERNATIONAL, INC., R.D.3 Box 221, Washington, NJ 07882 (201) 689-7539. Professionally trained animals for all media, natural filming locations.

ANIMAL TALENT SCOUTS, INC., 331 W. 18th St., New York, NY 10011. (212) 243-2700.

DAWN ANIMAL AGENCY, 160 W. 46th St., New York, NY 10036. (212) 757-9396.

WEST COAST

ANIMAL ACTORS OF HOLLYWOOD, 864 W. Carlisle Rd., Thousand Oaks, CA 91361 (805) 495-2122.

ANIMAL TRAINERS UNLIMITED, 12617 Foothill Blvd., Sylmar, CA 91342 (213) 896-0068.

LION ANIMAL RENTAL, Box 259, Ventura, CA 93001 (805) 648-6550.

PUMA PAW RANCH, P.O. Box 606, Rifle, CO 81650 (303) 625-2786.

WORKING WILDLIFE, Box 65, Acton, CA 93510 (805) 947-4041.

Animation

CALIFORNIA

BOSUSTOW, STEPHEN, PRODUCTIONS, 1649 Eleventh St., Santa Monica, CA 90404. (213) 394-0218.

HANNA BARBERA, 3400 West Cahuenga Blvd., Hollywood, CA 90028. (213) 466-1371.

IMAGINATION INC., 443 Jackson St., San Francisco, CA (415) 433-5480.

MONTROY SUPPLY CO., 4165 Beverly Blvd., Hollywood, CA (213) 662-2111.

QUARTET FILMS, INC., 5631 Hollywood Blvd., Los Angeles CA 90046. (213) 464-9225. Arthur Babbitt.

RUBY-SPEARS PRODUCTIONS, 3400 Cahuenga Blvd., W. Los Angeles, CA 90068. (213) 764-7700.

THOMAS BROTHERS, 30 Berry St., San Francisco, CA 94107. (415) 664-1901.

NEW YORK

ANIMATED CAMERA WORKSHOP, 51 East 42 St., N.Y., NY 10017 (212) 687-5009.

ANIMATED PRODUCTIONS, INC., 1600 Broadway, N.Y., NY 10019 (212) 265-2942.

BEBELL & BEBELL COLOR LABORATORIES, INC., 416 West 45th St., N.Y., NY 10036 (212) 245-8900.

ELINOR BUNIN PRODUCTIONS, INC., 30 East 60 St., N.Y., NY 10022 (212) 688-0759.

CLARK, IAN, 229 E. 96 St., New York, NY 10028 (212) 289-0998.

CREATIVISION, INC., 295 West 4th St., N.Y., NY 10012 (212) 924-3935.

GRANATO ANIMATION PHOTOGRAPHY INC., 15 West 46th St., N.Y., NY 10036 (212) 869-3231

HARVEY FAMOUS CARTOONS, 15 Columbus Circle, N.Y., NY 10024 (212) 582-2244.

HUBLEY STUDIO, 815 Park Ave., N.Y., NY 10021 (212) 744-8050.

LEO ANIMATION CAMERA SERVICE, 15 West 46th Street, N.Y., NY 10036 (212) 582-2515.

NATIONAL SCREEN SERVICE CORP., TV & INDUSTRIAL FILMS DIVISION, 1600 Broadway, N.Y., NY 10019 (212) CI 6-5700.

THE OPTICAL HOUSE, 25 West 45th St., N.Y., NY 10036 (212) 757-7840.

OVATION FILMS, 33 W. 46 St., N.Y., NY 10036 (212) 581-4406.

RAINBOW FILM EFFECTS, INC., 45 West 45th Street, N.Y., NY 10036 (212) 247-1676.

STAHL, AL, PRODUCTIONS, 1600 Broadway, New York, NY 10019 (212) CO 5-2942.

TELEMATED M.P., 51 East 42, N.Y., NY 10017 (212) 682-3434.

ZEPLIN PRODUCTIONS, 850 Seventh Ave., N.Y., NY 10019. (212) 582-6633.

Camera Sales, Rental, Repairs

NEW YORK

ARRIFLEX CO. OF AMERICA, P.O. Box 1050, Woodside, NY 11377 (212) 932-3403.

CAMERA MART, INC., 465 West 55th St., 10019 (212) 757-6977.

CAMERA SERVICE CENTER, 625 W. 54th St., 10019 (212) 757-0906.

CINE 60 INC., 630 Ninth Ave.; 10019 (212) JU 6-8782.

F&B/CECO/SOS, 315 W. 43rd St., New York 10036 (212) 586-1420.

FILM EQUIPMENT RENTAL CO., 419 W. 54 St., 10019 (212) 581-5474.

GENERAL CAMERA, 471 11th Ave.; 10018 (212) 594-8700.

NATIONAL CINE EQUIPMENT, INC., 4140 Austin Blvd., Island Park; (212) 799-4602.

OLDEN CAMERA & LENS CO., INC., 1265 Broadway; (212) 725-1234.

WILLOUGHBY CAMERA STORES, 110 W. 32 St., 10001 (212) LO 4-1600.

HOLLYWOOD

AKKAD INTERNATIONAL PRODS. INC., 8730 Sunset Blvd., CA 90069; (213) 657-7670.

AREMAC CAMERA CO., 5609 Sunset Blvd., L.A. 90028; (213) 469-2988.

ARMISTEAD, MARK INC., 1041 N. Formosa, L.A. 90046; (213) 467-6181.

BACH AURICON, INC., 6950 Romaine St., Hollywood 90038 (213) 462-0931.

BELL & HOWELL, 623 Rodier Drive, Glendale, CA; (213) 245-6631.

BIRNS & SAWYER, 1026 N. Highland Ave., Hollywood 90038; (213) 466-8211.

F&B/CECO/SOS, 7051 Santa Monica Blvd., L.A. 90038; (213) 466-9361.

GALLI, HERMAN, CAMERA SERVICE, 6804 Melrose Ave., L.A. 90038; (213) 931-4111.

GORDON ENTERPRISES, 5362 N. Cahuenga Blvd., N. Hollywood 91601; (213) 985-5500.

HOLLYWOOD CAMERA, 1255 No. La Brea Ave., 91603; (213) 783-1134.

HOLLYWOOD FILM CO., 956 Seward St., Hollywood, 90038; (213) 462-3824.

KENWORTHY SNORKEL CAMERA SYSTEMS, INC., P.O. Box 49851, L.A. 90049; (213) 476-4100.

MOLE-RICHARDSON CO., 937 N. Sycamore Ave., Hollywood, 90038; (213) 851-0111.

PILL, JACK & ASSOCIATES INC., 6370 Santa Monica Blvd., Hollywood, CA 90038; (213) 466-5391.

TECH-CAMERA RENTALS, INC., 6370 S. Monica Blvd., 90038; (213) 466-3238.

UPS STUDIO RENTALS, 6561 Santa Monica Blvd., Hollywood, CA 90038; (213) 461-1442.

Checking Theatre Attendance

CERTIFIED MARKETING SERVICES, INC., 120 N. Main St., New City, NY 10956; (914) 638-1021. National field interviews; in-theatre and telephone. William P. Smith, pres.

CERTIFIED REPORTS, INC., (CRI) Kinderhook, NY 12106; (518) 758-6403. Theatre checking; industry research. Harold Roth, pres.

VERIFIED REPORTS, INC., Hatfield Road, R. D. 1, Mahopac, NY 10541; (914) 628-6412. Blind (covert) theatre checking; national coverage. Diane Rosenblith, pres.

Commercial Jingles

AEOLUS PRODUCTIONS, INC., 119 West 57th St., N.Y., NY 10019 (212) 541-9388.

FAILLACE PRODUCTIONS, 207 East 45th Street, New York, NY; 687-9080. Tony Faillace.

MAMORSKY, ZIMMERMANN & HAMM, INC., 56 West 45th St., N.Y., NY 10036 (212) 986-1084.

MUSIC MAKERS, INC., 200 Central Park So., N.Y., NY 10019 (212) 245-3737.

Consultants

AMERICAN FILM PRODUCTIONS INC., 1540 Broadway, N.Y., NY 10019 (212) 582-1900.

BROADCAST INFORMATION BUREAU, 30 East 42 St., N.Y., NY 10017 (212) 687-1668.

FILM COUNSELORS, INC., 500 Fifth Ave., N.Y., NY 10022 (212) 736-7220.

FILM PLANNING ASSOCIATES, INC., 305 East 46th St., N.Y., NY 10017 (212) 725-9316.

NATIONAL SCREEN SERVICE CORP., TV & INDUSTRIAL FILMS DIVISION, 1600 Broadway, N.Y., NY 10019 (212) CI 6-5700.

RADIO FEATURES INC., 527 Madison Ave., N.Y., NY 10022 (212) EL 5-4616.

ROSS-GAFFNEY, 21 West 46th St., N.Y., NY 10036 (212) JU2-3744.

Costumes & Uniforms

NEW YORK

ANIMAL COSTUME CO., 236 West 55th Street, 10019 (212) 245-5199.

BROOKS-VAN HORN COSTUME CO. INC., 117 West 17th St., 10011 (212) 989-8000.

CHENKO STUDIO, 108 W. 45th st., 10036. (212) 582-1646.

EAVES COSTUME COMPANY, INC., 151 W. 46th Street, 10019 (212) 757-3730.

KARINSKA, MME., 6 West 61 St., 10023 (212) 247-3341.

WEST COAST

A-CINEMA HOLLYWOOD COSTUMERS, 5514 Hollywood Blvd., 90028; (213) 464-9894.

ACUNA, FRANK, 8212 Sunset Blvd., L.A. 90046; (213) 656-1413.

ADELE'S OF HOLLYWOOD, 5059 Hollywood Blvd., L.A. 90038; (213) 662-2231.

IC COSTUME RENTALS, 6121 Santa Monica Blvd., L.A. 90038; (213) 496-2056.

TUXEDO CENTER, 7360 Sunset Blvd., L.A., 90046 (213) 874-4200.

WESTERN COSTUME CO., 5335 Melrose Ave., Hollywood, CA 90038 (213) 469-1451.

Cutting Rooms

LOS ANGELES

F&B/CECO EDITING CENTER, 7051 Santa Monica, L.A., CA 90038 (213) 466-9361.

HORIZONTAL EDITING STUDIOS, 6253 Hollywood Blvd., Hollywood, CA 90028; (213) 461-4643.

NEW YORK

ANIMATED PRODS., INC., 1600 Broadway, New York, NY 10019. (212) 265-2942.

CAMERA MART, THE., 456 W. 55 St., New York, NY 10019 (212) 757-6977.

CRITERION FILM LABORATORIES, INC., 415 West 55th St., 10019 (212) 265-2180.

DE LUXE GENERAL INC., 630 Ninth Ave., New York, NY 10036 (212) 489-8800; 1546 N. Argyle Ave., L.A. 90038; (213) 462-6171.

MOVIELAB THEATRE SERVICE, 619 West 54th Street, New York, NY 10019 (212) 586-0360; 6823 Santa Monica Blvd., L.A.; (213) 469-5981.

PREVIEW HOUSE, 7655 W. Sunset Blvd., L.A. 90046; (213) 876-6600.

PREVIEW THEATRE, 1600 Broadway, New York, NY 10019 (212) 246-0865.

ROSS-GAFFNEY, INC., 21 West 46th St., New York, NY 10036 (212) 582-3744.

Editing Equipment

CIRO EQUIPMENT CORPORATION, 6820 Romaine St., Hollywood, CA (213) 467-1296. (8, 16, 35 & 70mm self-perforating film splicers and splicing tape) Barry Green, pres.

KLM ASSOCIATES, INC., 11810 Charen Lane, Potomac, MD. (301) 299-7259 (sells and rents film editing equipment; horizontal editing tables and related hardware) Mar McElroy, pres.

TWENTY-FOURTH FRAME, 303 Depot., N.W., P.O. Box 2167, Christiansburg, VA 24073. (703) 382-4135 (manufactures 35mm, 16mm, two-picture 3-sound, 8-plate flatbed editing machines) Ike Jeanes, owner.

Lighting Equipment

BARDWELL & McALLISTER, 7269 Santa Monica Blvd., Hollywood, CA 90038; (213) 876-4133.

BATES LIGHTING CO., 1215 Bates Ave., L.A. 90029; (213) 661-1262.

BIRNS & SAWYER, 1026 N. Highland Ave., L.A. 90038; (213) 466-8211.

BERKEY-COLORTRAN, INC., (A division of Berkey Photo, Inc.), 1015 Chestnut St., Burbank, CA 91502; (213) 843-1200; 842 Broadway, N.Y., 475-8700. (Berkey Photo).

BLAKE FILMS, 104 West Concord, St., Boston, MA 02118. (617) 267-7713.

BOKEN, INC., 349 West 48th St., N.Y., NY 10036 (212) LT 1-5626.

THE CAMERA MART, 456 West 55th St., N.Y., NY 10019; (212) 757-6977.

F&B/CECO/SOS, 315 W. 43rd St., N.Y. 10036; (212) 586-1420; 7051 Santa Monica Blvd.; 90038 (213) 466-9361.

ALAN GORDON ENTS., CO., 5342 Cahuenga, No. Hollywood, CA (213) 985-5500.

LEONETTI CINE RENTALS, 5609 Sunset Blvd., L.A., CA 90028; (213) 469-2987.

LIGHTING & PRODUCTION EQUIPMENT, INC., 1081 Memorial Drive, S.E. (rear) Atlanta, GA 30316. (404) 681-0130. W. Bruce Harlan, pres.

LOS ANGELES STAGE LIGHTING CO. LTD., 1451 Venice Blvd., L.A., CA 90006; (213) 384-1241.

MOLE-RICHARDSON CO., 937 N. Sycamore Ave., L.A. 90038; (213) 851-0111.

CHARLES ROSS, INC., 333 W. 52nd St., N.Y., NY 10019 (212) CI 6-5470.

TIMES SQUARE THEATRICAL & STUDIO SUPPLY CORP., 318 West 47th St., New York, NY 10019 (212) 245-4155.

Market Research

MARKET RESEARCH CORP. OF AMERICA, 122 E. 42nd St., New York, NY 10017. (212) 953-7240; 624 South Michigan Ave., 60605 (312) 939-1500.

NIELSEN, A.C., CO., Nielsen Plaza, Northbrook, IL 60062. (312) 498-6300; 1290 Ave. of Americas, N.Y., NY 10019. (212) 956-2500.

OPINION RESEARCH CORP., Research Park, Princeton, NJ 08540. (212) 489-1955.

POLITZ, ALFRED, RESEARCH, INC., 300 Park Ave. So., N.Y., NY 10010. (212) 982-7600.

THE PULSE, INC., 730 5th Ave., N.Y., NY 10019. (212) 586-3316.

ROPER ORGANIZATION, THE, 1 Park Ave., N.Y., NY 10017. (212) 679-3523.

SAN FRANCISCO RESEARCH GROUP, 2200 Sacramento St., Suite 1206, San Francisco, CA 94115.

SINDLINGER & CO., INC., Harvard & Yale Aves., Swarthmore, PA 19081. (215) 544-9000.

STARCH INRA HOOPER, INC., East Boston Post Rd., Mamaroneck, NY 10543 (914) 698-0800.

TRENDEX, INC., 477 Madison Ave., New York, NY 10017 (212) 752-7160.

VIDEODEX, INC., 342 Madison Ave., New York, NY 10017 (212) 687-8837.

Merchandisers

DISNEY, WALT, PRODUCTIONS, (Character Merchandising Division), 477 Madison Ave., N.Y., NY 10022 (212) 593-8900.

HARVEY FAMOUS CARTOONS, 15 Columbus Circle, N.Y., NY 10024 (212) 582-2244.

HODGE CO., MARGARET, 488 Madison Ave., N.Y., NY 10022; (212) 758-9230.

Music, Music Libraries and Music Cutting

ARIES SOUND INTERNATIONAL, 245 E. 63rd St., N.Y., NY 10021 (212) 838-4940.

EMIL ASCHER, INC., 666 Fifth Ave., N.Y., NY 10019 (212) 581-4504.

AUDIO DIRECTORS, INC., 325 West 19th St., N.Y., NY 10011 (212) 924-5850.

CHAPELL MUSIC LIBRARY, 810 Seventh Ave., New York, NY 10019 (212) 977-7213.

CORELLI-JACOBS FILM MUSIC INC., 25 West 45th St., N.Y., NY 10036 (212) 586-6673.

DE WOLFE MUSIC LIBRARY, 25 W. 45th St., N.Y., NY 10036 (212) 586-6673.

EDWARDS, CLEVE (composer-producer), 311 Pall Mall St., Columbia, SC 29201. (803) 252-3504.

FILM SCORES BY JERRY MARKOE, 11 Fort George Hill 13c, New York, NY 10040. (212) 567-6223. Jerry Markoe, composer-conductor.

FILMSOUNDS, INC., 128 East 41st Street, N.Y., NY 10017 (212) 867-0330.

MacGREGOR, C.P., CO., 729 South Western Ave., Los Angeles 90005, (213) 384-4191.

MUSIC FOR FILMS INC., 49 West 45th St., N.Y., NY 10036 (212) 247-3577.

MUSIC HOUSE INC., 16 East 48th St., N.Y., NY 10017 (212) 758-7773.

M.S.T.S. MUSIC, 1600 Broadway, N.Y., NY 10019 (212) 246-4687.

PIC COLOR CORP., 25 W. 45th St., New York, NY 10036 (212) 575-5600.

PICTURE SCORES, INC., 115 West 45th St., N.Y., NY 10036 (212) JU 6-1845.

ROSS-GAFFNEY, INC., 21 W. 46th St., N.Y. 10036 (212) 582-3744.

SCORE PRODUCTIONS, INC., 249 East 49th St., N.Y., NY 10021 (212) 751-2510.

THOMAS BROTHERS, 30 Berry St., Los Angeles, CA 94107 (415) 664-1901.

VALENTINO, THOMAS J., INC, 150 W. 46th St., N.Y., NY 10036 (212) 246-46675.

Properties and Scenery

BASCH, JOS. GALLERIES CO., 5755 Santa Monica Blvd., Hollywood 90038 (213) 463-5116.

CINEMA MERCANTILE CO., 5857 Santa Monica Blvd., L.A. 90038; (213) 467-1151.

CINEMA PROPS CO., 6161 Santa Monica Blvd., Hollywood, 90038 (213) 464-3191.

FANTASY FAIR, 4310 San Fernando Rd., Glendale, CA (213) 245-7367.

GROSH, R. L. (Scenic Studios), 4114 Sunset Blvd.; L.A., CA, 90028 (213) 662-1134.

HOUSE OF PROPS., 1117 Gower St., Hollywood, CA; 463-3166.

METRO-GOLDWYN-MAYER, INC., 10202 West Washington Blvd., Culver City, CA 90230. (213) 836-3000.

OMEGA STUDIO RENTALS, 5757 Santa Monica, Blvd., L.A., 90038 (213) 466-8201.

ROSCHU, 6514 Santa Monica Blvd., L.A., 90038 (213) 469-2749.

SILVESTRI STUDIOS, 1733 Cordova, Hollywood; (213) 735-1481.

WOOLF BILLY HOUSE OF MOTION PICTURE ACCESSORIES, INC., 1112 N. Beachwood Dr., Hollywood; (213) 469-5335.

Rental Studios and Production Facilities

ATLANTA
LIGHTING & PRODUCTION EQUIPMENT, INC., 1081 Memorial Drive, S.E. (rear), 30316. (404) 681-0130.

LOS ANGELES
R.L. BEVINGTON, INC., 650 N. Bronson, Hollywood, CA 90004; (213) 466-7778.

BURBANK STUDIOS, 4000 Warner Blvd., Burbank, CA 91522; 213-843-6000.

CARTHAY STUDIOS, INC., 5903-07 W. Pico Blvd., L.A. 90035. (213) 938-2106.

CBS STUDIO CENTER, 4024 N. Radford Ave., N. Hollywood, CA 91604; (213) 763-8411.

CINEMOBILE SYSTEMS, INC., 11166 Gault St., No. Hollywood (213) 764-9900.

COLUMBIA PICTURES CORP., Colgems Sq., Burbank, 91505; 213-843-6000.

CULVER CITY STUDIOS, INC., 9336 W. Washington 90230; (213) 871-0360.

FALCON STUDIOS, 5526 Hollywood Blvd., L.A. 90028; (213) 462-9356.

F&B/CECO OF CALIFORNIA, INC., 7051 Santa Monica Blvd., Hollywood 90038; (213) 466-9361.

GOLDWYN, SAMUEL STUDIOS, 1041 N. Formosa Ave., L.A. 90046. (213) 851-1234.

HOLLYWOOD GENERAL STUDIOS, 1040 N. Las Palmas Ave., L.A., 90038. (213) 469-9011.

METRO-GOLDWYN-MAYER INC., 10202 W. Washington Blvd., Culver City, CA 90230; (213) 836-3000.

MOLE-RICHARDSON CO., 937 N. Sycamore Ave., L.A. 90038; (213) 654-3060.

PARAMOUNT PICTURES CORP., 5451 Marathon St., 90038. (213) 463-0100.

PRODUCERS STUDIO, INC., 650 North Bronson Ave., Los Angeles 90004; (213) 466-8111.

U.P.A. PICTURES, INC., 4440 Lakeside Drive, Burbank, CA, 91505. (213) 849-6666.

UNIVERSAL CITY STUDIOS, 100 Universal City Plaza, Universal City Plaza, Universal City, 91608. (213) 985-4321.

MIAMI
LUKE MOBERLY STUDIOS AND PRODUCTIONS, 4810 S.W. 54, Ft. Lauderdale, FL; Tel.: 581-7508.

NEW YORK
ASTORIA MOTION PICTURE AND TELEVISION PRODUCTION CENTER, 35-11 35th Ave., Astoria. (516) 936-6827.

BOKEN, INC., 349 West 48th St., NY 10036; (212) 581-5507.

CINEMOBILE SYSTEMS, INC., 601 West 29th St., (212) 695-7585.

FILMWAYS, INC., 246 E. 127 (212) 876-7788.

NATIONAL SCREEN SERVICE CORPORATION, TV AND INDUSTRIAL FILMS DIVISION, 1600 Broadway, New York, NY 10017; (212) 246-5700.

PRODUCTION CENTER, 221 West 26th St., 10001; (212) 675-2211.

TITRA SOUND CORPORATION, 1600 Broadway, NY 10019; (212) PL 7-6681.

UNITED FILM ENTERPRISES, INC., 1546 Broadway, New York, NY 10036; (212) 586-1442.

TAMPA, FLORIDA
POST PRODUCTION SERVICES, 3808 San Nicholas St. (813) 253-0402.

Slides-Telops

BEBELL INC., 416 W. 45th St., N.Y., NY 10036 (212) 245-8900.
TWO BY TWO SLIDES, INC., 2 West 45 St., 10036. (212) 972-0744.

Sound and Recording Services

HOLLYWOOD
ALTEC SERVICE CORP., 1515 S. Manchester Ave., Anaheim (714) 774-2900.
ARTISAN SOUND RECORDERS, 1600 Wilcox Ave. Hollywood 90028. (213) 461-2751.
AUDIO EFFECTS COMPANY, 1600 N. Western Ave., Hollywood 90027 (213) 469-3692. (Complete recording services).
BURBANK STUDIOS, THE, 4000 Warner Blvd., Burbank, CA 91522; (213) 843-6000.
CINESOUND, 915 North Highland Ave., Hollywood, CA 90038; (213) 464-1155.
COLUMBIA PICTURES TELEVISION, 300 S. Colgens Square, Burbank, 91522; (213) 954-6000.
CONSOLIDATED FILM INDUSTRIES, 959 N. Seward St., L.A. 90038; (213) 462-3161.
DOLBY LABORATORIES, 5248 Buffalo Ave., Van Nuys, 91401. (213) 981-4123.
GLEN GLENN SOUND CO., 6624 Romaine St., Hollywood 90038. (213) 469-7221.
INDEPENDENT PRODUCERS SERVICE, 7370 Melrose Ave., Hollywood 90046; (213) 655-3599.
METRO-GOLDWYN-MAYER, 10202 W. Washington Blvd., Culver City 90230; (213) 836-3000.
NEWJACK SOUND RECORDERS, 1717 N. Highland Ave., L.A. 90038; (213) 466-6141.
PARAMOUNT STUDIOS, 5451 Marathon St., Hollywood 90038; (213) 468-5000.
PRODUCERS SOUND SERVICE, INC., 1223 N. Highland; (213) 462-6535.
QUALITY SOUND, 5625 Melrose Ave. 90038; (213) 467-7154.
RYDER SOUND SERVICES, INC., 1161 Vine St., Hollywood (213) 469-3511.
SCOTTSOUND, INC., 6110 Santa Monica Blvd. 90038; (213) 462-6981.
TODD-AO SOUND RECORDING SCORING, 1021 N. Seward St., Hollywood, 90038. (213) 463-1136.
TV RECORDERS, 6054 Sunset Blvd., Hollywood; (213) 469-8201.
UNIVERSAL CITY STUDIOS, 100 Universal City, Plaza, UC 91608; (213) 985-4321.
WARNER HOLLYWOOD, 1041 N. Formosa, Los Angeles, 90046; (213) 650-2500.
ZOETROPE STUDIOS, 1040 N. La Palmas, Hollywood 90038; (213) 469-9011.

NEW YORK
ADD SOUND, INC., 16 W. 46 St., 10036 (212) 575-0719.
AQUARIUS TRANSFER, 12 E. 46 St., 10017 (212) 581-0123.
AURA RECORDING, INC., 136 W. 52nd St., 10019 (212) 582-8105.
HIT FACTORY, THE, INC., 353 W. 48 St., 10036 (212) 581-9590.
IMAGE SOUND STUDIO, INC., 1619 Broadway, 10036 (212) 581-6717.
MAGNO SOUND, INC., 212 W. 48; 10036 (212) 757-8855.
MUSIC SOUND TRACK SERVICE, 1600 Broadway, 10019 (212) CIrcle 6-4687-8.
NATIONAL RECORDING STUDIOS, 730 Fifth Ave. 10019 (212) 757-6440.
RKO SOUND STUDIOS, 1440 Broadway, 10018 (212) 564-8000.
ROSS-GAFFNEY, INC., 21 W. 46th St., 10018 (212) 582-3745.
SOUND SHOP, THE, 304 E. 44 St., 10017 (212) 757-9800.
TITRA SOUND CORP., 1600 Broadway, 10019 (212) 757-6681.
THOMAS J. VALENTINO, 151 West 46th St., 10036 (212) 246-4675.

SAN FRANCISCO
DOLBY LABORATORIES, 731 Sansome St., 94111. (415) 392-0300.
THOMAS BROTHERS, 30 Berry St., 94107. (415) 664-1901.

WASHINGTON, DC
BYRON MOTION PICTURES INC., 65 K St., N.E.; 20002 (202) 783-2700.
CAPITAL FILM LABORATORIES, INC., 470 E. St., S.W.; 20024 (202) 347-1717.

Special Effects

NEW YORK
ACTION PRODUCTIONS, INC., 16 West 46 St., New York, NY 10036 (212) 391-2747.
ANIMATED CAMERA WORKSHOP, 51 East 42 St., N.Y., NY 10017. (212) 687-5009.
ANIMATED PRODUCTIONS, INC., 1600 Broadway, New York NY 10019 (212) 265-2942.
EUE/SCREEN GEM PRINTS, 222 East 44 St., New York, NY 10017 (212) 867-43030.
EXCEPTIONAL OPTICALS, INC., 17 East 45 St., New York, NY 10017 (212) 972-1760.
FILM OPTICALS, INC., 144 East 44 St., New York, NY 10017 (212) 697-4744.
I.F. STUDIOS, INC., 328 East 44 St., New York, NY 10017 (212) 683-4747.
MINI-EFFECTS, INC., 15 West 44 St., New York, NY 10036 (212) 869-0370.
NATIONAL SCREEN SERVICE CORP., TV & INDUSTRIAL FILMS DIVISION, 1600 Broadway, New York, NY 10019 (212) 246-5700.
OPTICAL HOUSE, INC., 25 West 45 St., New York, NY 10036 (212) 757-7840.
PROFESSIONAL OPTICALS, INC., 20 East 46 St., New York, NY 10017 (212) 682-1757.
RAINBOW FILMS EFFECTS, INC., 45 West 45 St., New York, NY 10036 (212) 247-1676.
TRI-PIX FILM SERVICE, INC., 49 West 45 St., New York, NY 10036 (212) JU 2-0650.
WORLD EFFECTS, INC., 20 East 46 St., New York, NY 10017 (212) 687-7070.

HOLLYWOOD
ANDERSON, HOWARD A., CO., Main Office: Paramount Studios, 5451 Marathon St., Hollywood, CA 90038 (213) 463-2336.
BRAVERMAN PRODS., INC., 8961 Sunset Blvd., L.A. 90069; (213) 278-5444.
CINEMA SERVICE, INC., 5725 Santa Monica Blvd., (213) 462-1376.
COAST SPECIAL EFFECTS, 4907 N. Lankershim Blvd., N. Hollywood, 91602. (213) 876-2021.
CONSOLIDATED FILM INDUSTRIES, 959 N. Seward St., 90038. (213) 462-3161.
FILM EFFECTS OF HOLLYWOOD, 1140 N. Citrus, Hollywood; (213) 469-5808.
MERCER RAY & CO., 4241 Normal Ave., (213) 663-9331.
MODERN FILM EFFECTS, 6824 Melrose Ave., 90030; (213) 938-2155.
OPTICAL PRINT SERVICES, INC., 1132 N. Vine St., Los Angeles 90038 (213) 462-7446.
PACIFIC TITLE & ART STUDIO, 6350 Santa Monica Blvd., Los Angeles 90038 (213) 464-0121.
VIDEOTAPE ENTERPRISES, 8610 Sunset Blvd., Los Angeles, 90069 (213) 659-4801.

Stop Watches

DUCOMMUN, M., CO., 48 Main St., Warwick, NY 10990.(914) 986-5757.
MARCEL WATCH CORP., 1180 Sixth Ave., N.Y., NY 10036. (212) 245-3355.
RACINE, JULES & CO., 85 Executive Rd., Elmsford, NY 10523. (914) 592-4760.

Sub-titles

WHITE ROSE CAPTION, INC., Sundvall Bldg., 83-90 Broadway, Elmhurst, Queens, NY 11373. (212) 271-3388. Negative subtitle cards—super-imposed negative and translations in most languages for motion pictures and TV. Ms. Rose Robles, pres.

Talent and Literary Agencies

Hollywood

ABRAMS-RUBALOFF & ASSOC., INC.,
9012 Beverly Blvd. (48), 273-5711
AGENCY FOR PERFORMING ARTS,
9000 Sunset Blvd. #.315 (69), 273-0744
AIMEE ENTERTAINMENT ASSOCIATES,
13749 Victory Blvd., Van Nuys, CA 91401; 994-9354.
ALVARADO, CARLOS.
8820 Sunset Blvd. (69), 652-0272
AMARAL AGENCY,
1000 Riverside Dr., Toluca Lake, 980-1013
ASSOCIATED BOOKING CORP.,
292 S. La Cienga Blvd., BH; 855-8051
AUER, MILES BOHM,
8344 Melrose Ave., Suite 29 (69), 462-6416
BARSKIN AGENCY,
11240 Magnolia Blvd., No. Hollywood; 985-2992.
BLAKE AGENCY, LTD.,
409 N. Camden Dr., BH, 278-6885
BLANCHARD, NINA,
1717 N. Highland (28), 462-7274
BLUMENTHAL ARTISTS AGENCY,
8833 Sunset Blvd., (69) 855-1403.
BREWIS AGENCY, ALEX,
8721 Sunset Blvd. (69), 274-9874
CALDER AGENCY,
4063 Radford, 91604; 508-7200.
CAREY-PHELPS-COLVIN,
1407 N. La Brea Ave. (28) 874-7780.
CENTURY ARTISTS, LTD.
9744 Wilshire Blvd. BH (90212) 273-4366
CHARTER MGMT.,
9000 Sunset Blvd. (69), 278-1690
CHARTWELL ARTISTS, LTD.,
1901 Ave. of Stars (67) 553-3600.
CHASIN-PARK-CITRON,
9255 Sunset Blvd., (69), 273-7190
COLTON & ASSOC., KINGSLEY,
321 S. Beverly Drive, BH, 277-5491
COMMERCIAL TALENT AGENCY,
8500 Wilshire, BH 90211; 855-0422
COMMERCIALS UNLTD.,
7461 Beverly Blvd. (36), 937-2220
CONNOR-CORFINO ASSOC., INC.,
14241 Ventura Blvd., Sherman Oaks, 981-1133
CONTEMPORARY-KORMAN,
132 Lasky Dr., BH, 274-7888
COUGLIN AGENCY, KERWIN,
10850 Riverside Dr., N. Hwd. 980-6100
CRONIN AGENCY, BERNYCE,
439 S. La Cienega Blvd. (48), 273-8144
CUMBER, LIL,
6515 Sunset Blvd. (28), 469-1919
CUNNINGHAM & ASSOC.,
261 S. Robertson, BH 90211; 855-1700
DIAMOND ARTISTS, LTD.,
8400 Sunset Blvd. (69), OL 4-5960
EISENBACH-GREENE-DUCHOW, INC.
760 N. LaCienega Blvd. L.A. (69), 659-3420
ENTERTAINMENT ENT.,
1680 Vine St. (28), 462-6001
F.C.A. AGENCY, INC.
1800 Century Park East (67) 277-8422
FELBER, WM.,
2126 Cahuenga Blvd. (68) 466-7629
FIELDS ASSOC., JACK,
9255 Sunset Blvd. (69), 278-1333
FLAIRE AGENCY,
8693 Wilshire, BH, 90211; 659-6721
FRINGS, KURT,
9440 Santa Monica Blvd., BH, 274-8881
GARRICK, DALE,
8831 Sunset Blvd. (69), 65 7-2661
GERSH AGENCY, PHIL.
222 N. Canon Dr., BH 274-6611
GIBSON, J. CARTER,
9000 Sunset Blvd. (69), 274-8813
GORDEAN-FRIEDMAN AGENCY, INC.,
9570 Wilshire, BH 90212; 273-4195

GRANITE AGENCY,
1920 S. La Cienega Blvd. (34), 934-8383
GREENVINE AGENCY,
9021 Melrose Av., (69), 278-5800
GREEN AGENCY, IVAN,
1888 Century Park East (67), 277-1541
GROSSMAN-STALMASTER AGENCY,
8730 Sunset Blvd. (69), 65 7-3040
HAMILBURG, MITCHELL,
292 S. La Cienga, BH, 657-1501
HECHT, BEVERLY,
8949 Sunset Blvd. (69), 278-3544
HUNT, GEORGE B.,
8350 Santa Monica Blvd. (46), 65 4-6600
HUSSONG AGENCY,
8271 Melrose Ave. (46), 655-2534
INGERSOLL, GEORGE,
6513 Hollywood Blvd. (28), 874-6434
INT'L CREATIVE MANAGEMENT,
8899 Beverly Blvd., (48), 550-4000
JUNIOR ARTIST UNLTD.,
4914 Lankershim Blvd., No. Hollywood. 762-9000
KELMAN, TONI AGENCY,
7813 Sunset Blvd. (46) 851-8822
KING AGENCY, HOWARD,
118 S. Beverly Dr., BH, 271-7294
KOHNER, PAUL,
9169 Sunset Blvd. (69), 271-5165
LAZAR, IRVING PAUL,
211 S. Beverly Dr., BH, 27 5-6153
LEONETTI, CAROLINE,
6526 Sunset Blvd. (28), 462-2345
LONGNECKER, ROBERT,
11704 Wilshire (25), 477-0039
LOO, BESSIE,
8730 Sunset Blvd. (69), 657-5888
LYONS, GRACE,
8730 Sunset Blvd. (69), 652-5290
McHUGH AGENCY, JAMES
8150 Beverly Blvd. (48), 651-2770
McMILLAN, HAZEL,
9426 Santa Monica Bl., BH, 276-9823
MEIKLEJOHN, WM.,
9250 Wilshire Blvd., Suite 412, BH, 273-2566
MESSENGER, FRED,
8235 Sunset Blvd. (46), 654-3800
MISHKIN AGENCY,
9255 Sunset Blvd. (69), 274-5261
MOORE, LOLA D.,
13848 Vanowen St., Van Nuys 91405; 276-6097
MORRIS, WILLIAM,
151 El Camino Dr., BH, 274-7451
M.T.A. ARTISTS' MGR.
4615 Melrose Ave. (29), 661-9888
MURPHY, MARY,
10701 Riverside Dr., NH, 985-4241
OLIVER & ASSOCS., MARINE,
8746 Sunset Blvd. (69), 657-1250
OTIS AGENCY, DOROTHY DAY,
6430 Sunset Blvd. (28), 461-4911
PEARSON, BEN,
606 Wilshire Blvd. SM (90401) 451-8414
PREMIERE ARTISTS & PROD.,
6399 Wilshire Blvd. (48), 651-3381
PRESCOTT, GUY,
8920 Wonderland Ave., (46), 656-1963
RAPER ENTERPRISES AGENCY
9441 Wilshire Blvd., (12) 273-7704
ROBINSON & ASSOC.,
132 S. Rodeo Dr. BH, 275-6114
ROBINSON-WEINTRAUB & ASSOCIATES,
554 S. San Vicente (48), 653-5802
ROSE, HAROLD,
8530 Wilshire Blvd., BH, 652-3961
RUSH, ART,
10221 Riverside Dr., No. Hwd., 985-3033
SACKHEIM AGENCY,
9301 Wilshire Blvd BH (90210) 276-3151
SANDERS, NORAH,
9255 Sunset Blvd. (69) 550-0797

SCHWARTZ & ASSOC., DON,
8721 Sunset Blvd. (69), 657-8910
SHAW, GLENN,
330 Barkam Blvd. (68), 851-6262
SHERRELL AGENCY LEW,
7060 Hollywood Blvd. (28), 461-9955
SHIPLEY-ISHIMOTO,
9163 Sunset Blvd. (69), CR 6-6251
SHREVE, DOROTHY,
1525 Superior Ave., Newport Beach, 92663; 642-3050
TANNEN & ASSOC. HERB,
6640 Sunset Blvd. (28), 461-3055
TOBIAS & ASSOCIATES,
1901 Ave. of Stars (67), 277-6211
TWENTIETH CENTURY ARTISTS,
13273 Ventura Bl., Studio City (91604) 990-8580
WEINER, JACK,
8721 Sunset Blvd. (69), 652-1140
WEVER, WARREN,
1104 S. Robertson Blvd. (35), 276-7065
WILK, TED,
9172 Sunset Blvd. (69), 273-0801
WOSK AGENCY, SYLVIA,
439 S. La Cienega (48), 274-8063
WRIGHT ASSOC., ANN,
8422 Melrose Pl., (69), 655-5040

New York

AGENCY FOR PERFORMING ARTS,
888 Seventh Ave., (10106) 582-1500.
ALEXANDER INC., WILLARD,
660 Madison Ave., (21), 751-7070
AMERICAN-INT'L TALENT,
166 W. 125th St., (27), 663-4626
ANDERSON, BEVERLY,
1472 Broadway, Ste. 806, (36), 279-5553
ASSOCIATED BOOKING CORP.,
1995 Broadway (23), 874-2400
ASTOR, RICHARD,
119 W. 57th St., (19), 581-1970
BISHOP, LOLA M.,
160 W. 46 (36) 997-1848
CASE, BERTHA,
345 W. 58 (19) 541-9451
COLEMAN-ROSENBERG AGCY.,
667 Madison Ave., (21), 838-0734
COOPER ASSOC., BILL,
16 E. 52nd St., (22), 758-6491
DEACY, JANE,
300 E. 75 (21) 652-4865
DIAMOND ARTISTS, LTD.,
119 W. 57th St., (19), 247-3025
DRAPER, STEPHEN AGENCY,
27 W. 57th St., (19), 421-5780
FORD—TALENT GROUP
344 E. 59th St., (22), 688-8628
GAGE GROUP, THE,
1650 Broadway, (19), 541-5250
HARTIG, MICHAEL,
527 Madison (22), 759-9163
HENDERSON/HOGAN AGENCY,
200 W. 57, (19), 765-5190
HUNT, DIANA,
44 W. 44th St., (36), 391-4971
HUNTER, JEFF,
119 W. 57th St., (19), 757-4995
INT'L CREATIVE MANAGEMENT,
40 W. 57th St., (19), 556-5600
JACOBSON/WILDER, INC.,
400 Madison Ave., (17), 759-0860
JAN J. AGENCY,
224 E. 46th St., (17), 490-1875
JORDAN, JOE TALENT AGCY.,
400 Madison Ave., (17), 838-4910
KAHN INC.,
853-7th Ave., (19), 582-1280
KENNEDY ARTISTS REP.,
881 7th Ave., (19), 675-3944
KING, ARCHER,
777 Seventh Ave. (19), 581-8513
KROLL, LUCY,
390 West End Ave., (24), 877-0556
LARNER, LIONEL LTD.,
850 7th Ave., (19), 246-3105
LEIGH, SANFORD,
527 Madison Ave., (22), 752-4450

LEWIS ASSOC., LESTER,
156 E. 52nd St., (22), 753-5082
McDERMOTT, MARGE,
214 E 39 (16) 889-1583
MARTINELLI ATTRACTIONS,
888 8th Ave., (36), 586-0963
M.E.W. COMPANY,
370 Lexington Ave., (17), 889-7272
MORRIS AGENCY, WM.,
1350 Ave. of Americas, (19), 586-5100
OPPENHEIM-CHRISTIE ASSOC.,
565 5th Ave., (17), 661-4330
OSCARD/FIFI AGENCY,
19 W. 44th St., (36), 764-1100
OSTERTAG, BARNA,
501 Fifth Ave., (17), 697-6339
PITT AGENCY, JOEL,
144 W. 57th St., (19), 765-6373
PREMIER TALENT ASSOC.,
3 E. 54 (22) 758-4900
RUBENSTEIN, BERNARD,
342 Madison Ave., (17), 986-1317
RYAN, CHARLES VERNON,
200 W. 57 (19) 245-2225
SCHULLER AGENCY, WM.,
667 Madison Ave., (22), 758-1919
SILVER, MONTY,
200 W. 57 (19) 765-4040
STEWART ARTISTS CORP.,
140 E. 63 (21) 752-0944
STROUD MGMT.,
18 E. 48th St. (17), 688-0226
TALENT REPS., INC.,
20 E. 53rd St., (22), 752-1835
THOMAS, JEAN,
342 Madison (17), 490-3954
THOMAS, MICHAEL,
22 E. 60th St., (22), 755-2616
TROY, GLORIA TALENT AGENCY,
1790 Broadway, (19), 582-0260
WATERS AGENCY, BOB,
510 Madison Ave., (22), 593-0543
WINANT III, WILLIAM A.,
30 Sutton Place; (22), 68 8-0768
WOLTERS, HANNS,
342 Madison Ave., (17), 867-9177
WRIGHT REPS., ANN,
137 E. 57th St., (22), 832-0110

Advertising & Publicity Representatives

Hollywood-Los Angeles-Beverly Hills

ABRAMS, BOB, AND ASSOCIATES, 2030 Prosser Ave., Los Angeles, 90025 475-7739
BARLOR ASSOCIATES, 428 North Palm Dr., Beverly Hills; 278-1998.
BLOWITZ & CANTON, INC., 9350 Wilshire Blvd., Beverly Hills, 90210; 275-9443.
BRAVERMAN-MIRISCH, INC., 9255 Sunset Blvd., Los Angeles 90069; 272-8608.
TOM BROCATO & ASSOCIATES, INC., 6380 Wilshire Blvd., Suite 1411, Los Angeles 90048 (213) 653-9570.
DICK BROOKS UNLIMITED, 9465 Wilshire Blvd., Beverly Hills, CA 90212; (213) 273-8477.
BYOIR, CARL, AND ASSOCIATES, INC., 900 Wilshire Blvd., Los Angeles 90019; 627-6421.
DRUXMAN, MICHAEL B. & ASSOCIATES, 8831 Sunset Blvd., Los Angeles, 90069; 652-5592.
EDELMAN, DANIEL, INC., 1901 Ave. of the Stars, Los Angeles 90067; 555-1560.
FRANKEN PUBLIC RELATIONS, 1101 S. Robertson; 272-7577.
GARRETT, MICKEY, ASSOCIATES, 3349 Cahuenga Boulevard West; Los Angeles 90068; 851-5075.
GELFOND, FORDON AND ASSOCIATES, 9808 Wilshire Blvd., Beverly Hills 90212; 273-1440.
GOODMAN/NEMOY, 6464 Sunset Blvd., Los Angeles, 90028, 464-1135.
HANSON & SCHWAM, 9229 Sunset Blvd., Los Angeles 90069; 278-1255.

HARSHE-ROTMAN & DRUCK, INC., 3345 Wilshire Blvd., Los Angeles; 90036; 385-5271.

JENNEY, NOREEN PUBLIC RELATIONS, 1901 Ave. of Stars, Los Angeles 90067. (213) 553-1983.

LEE & ASSOCIATES, 8727 West 3rd, Los Angeles 90048; 278-5300.

LEWIS & ASSOCIATES, 3440 Wilshire Blvd., Los Angeles; 381-7641.

LEWIS HERM & ASSOCIATES, 316 W. Rossmore, Los Angeles; 464-8189.

LIBERMAN, FRANK, AND ASSOCIATES, 9021 Melrose Ave., Los Angeles 90069; 278-1993.

MAHONEY, JIM & ASSOCIATES, 120 El Camino, Beverly Hills; 272-7861.

McKENZIE, KING & GORDON, 1800 N. Argyle, Hollywood 90028 (213) 466-3421.

RUDER & FINN OF CALIFORNIA, INC., 9300 Wilshire Blvd., Beverly Hills; 274-8303.

SAMUELSON, CHIEF, & ASSOCIATES, 7260 Hillside Ave., Los Angeles 90046; 966-6106.

SOLTERS, ROSKIN, AND FRIEDMAN, INC. 9255 W. Sunset Blvd., Los Angeles 90069; 275-5303.

SUHOSKY, BOB ASSOCIATES, 9110 W. Sunset Blvd., Los Angeles 90069; 272-2612.

TAMKIN ASSOCIATES, INC., 1122 Robertson Blvd., 90035. (213) 275-6122.

THOMPSON, J. WALTER CO., 10100 Santa Monica Blvd., Los Angeles, 90067; 553-8383.

New York

BECK, MYER P., 729 7th Ave., NY 10019; 24 5-5552.

BILLINGS, MARION, 200 West 57th St., NY; 581-4493.

BYOIR, CARL & ASSOCIATES, INC., 380 Madison Ave., 986-6100.

CANAAN, LEE ASSOCIATES LTD., 205 East 42nd St., 10017. 682-4155.

DAVIS, AL, PUBLICITY, 711 Third Ave., 557-1045

EISEN, MAX, 234 West 44th St., 391-1072.

GIFFORD/WALLACE, INC., 1211 Park Ave. 427-7600.

EDWARD GLASS/BARRY SCHOOR, 1600 Broadway, Suite 1003M, New York, NY 10019; (212) 246-6650; (212) 586-1846. Creators and producers of advertising campaigns for motion pictures.

GOODMAN, FRANK, 1776 Broadway; 246-4180.

GREY ADVERTISING AGENCY, 777 Third Ave., 751-3500.

HARSHE-ROTMAN & DRUCK, INC., 300 East 44th St., 661-3400.

MARCH FIVE, INC., 30 East 42nd St., 68 7-3484.

MASLANSKY-KOENIGSBERG, INC., 250 West 57th St., NY 10019 489-7390.

POST, MYRNA ASSOCIATES, 9 E. 53 St., 935-7122.

ROFFMAN, RICHARD H., ASSOCIATES, 697 West End Ave., NY; 74 9-3647.

ROGERS & COWAN, INC., 3 East 54; 486-7100.

RUDER & FINN, INC., 110 East 59th St.; 593-6400.

SOLTERS, ROSKIN, AND FREIDMAN, INC., 62 West 45th St., NY 10036; 840-3500.

WAX, MORTON D. PUBLIC RELATIONS, 1650 Broadway; NY; 247-2159.

WOLHANDER, JOE, ASSOCIATES, INC., 211 East 51st St., NY 10022; 759-2050.

YOUNG & RUBICAN INTERNATIONAL, 285 Madison; 59 53-2000.

Equipment and Supplies

* **MANUFACTURERS & SERVICES**

* **STUDIO EQUIPMENT**

* **REFRESHMENT PRODUCTS, EQUIP-MENT**

* **MANUFACTURERS & SERVICES**
  (By Product Classification)

* **SUPPLY DEALERS IN U.S. AND CANADA**

Manufacturers & Services

A-Wagner Zip Change, Inc.
(formerly WAGNER Sign Service)
3100 Hirsch Street, Melrose Park, IL 60160. Tel.: (312) 681-4100.
WAGNER brand slotted dimensional marquee letters in 4", 6", 8", 10" and 17" letters in red, green, blue or black plastic. Wagner brand marquee background with stainless steel frames and unbreakable Enduronamel Panel Assembly, low cost metal marquee for 8" or larger letters, ready to install. Zip-Change plastic or metal flat marquee letters in 6", 8", 10", 12", 15", 17", and 24". Letter changing Mechanical Hands. Letter storage cabinets. Rating Units (PG, R, G). Alumabar letter track. Sell thru theatre suppliers only.

Altec Lansing
1515 S. Manchester Avenue, Anaheim, CA 92803. Tel.: (714) 774-2900.
Manufacturers of amplifiers, loudspeakers, electronic devices, microphones and transformers "Voice of the theatre" speaker systems.

American Desk Manufacturing Co.
P.O. Box 429, Temple, TX; Tel.: (817) 773-1776.
Manufacturers of theatre seating.

American Playground Device Co.
Main Offices: 1801-1831 So. Jackson, P.O. Drawer 2599, Anderson, IN 46011. Tel.: (317) 642-0288.

Branch Offices: Nahma Blvd., Nahma, MI 49864. Tel.: (317) 642-0288.
Manufacturers of playground equipment, park benches, picnic tables, charcoal grills, flood lights and swimming pool equipment for drive-in theatres, and bicycle racks for theatres. Complete line of American approved extra-heavy-duty Park, Picnic, Playground, Swimming Pool, Beach and Dressing Room Equipment.

American Seating Company
Grand Rapids, MI 49504. Tel.: (616) 456-0433.

(District offices in principal cities)
Manufacturers of auditorium and theatre chairs and portable stacking chairs.

BRANCH OFFICES
CALIFORNIA: Manhattan Beach, 90266, 802 First St., P.O. Box 221; (213) 374-5330; E. D. Thompson. Mountain View, 94043, 2440 Charleston Rd.; (415) 964-6600; J. D. Laird.
GEORGIA: Marietta, 30067, 473 Indian Hills Trail; (404) 973-0385; J. DeFrancesco.
MASSACHUSETTS: Hingham, 02043, 12 Richard St.; (617) 749-7197; J. T. Corrigan.
MICHIGAN: Grand Rapids, 49504, 901 Broadway Ave., NW, (Main Office); (616) 456-0433, J. E. Sherry, (616) 456-0522, Q. R. Van Dore, (616) 456-0432; G. L. Courtney.
MISSOURI: Parkville, 64152, 10307 Mirror Lake Dr.; (816) 741-8195; J. W. Lamkin.
NEW JERSEY: Leonia, 07605, 135 Fort Lee Rd.; (201) 947-9506; R. K. Kenaga, D. A. Spadola.
TEXAS: Richardson, 75080; 312 N. Central Expressway, Suites 215-217; (214) 231-1419; J. K. Godwin.

ASC Technical Services Corp.
(formerly Altec Service Corporation)
Executive offices: P.O. Box 706, Plano, TX 75074 (214) 422-2160.
Nationwide sound service and full booth maintenance.

DIVISION OFFICES
Nick Markanich, regional supervisor, 7 Van Riper Ave., Pompton Plains, NJ 07444 (201) 483-5305.
Indianapolis, IN 46226: LaMar Michael, regional supervisor, 5857 N. Winthrop; (317) 257-1807.
Houston, TX 77092: B. R. Emerson, regional supervisor, 7119 Pine Grove Drive, (713) 523-9077.

Atlantic Audio Visual Corp.
630 Ninth Avenue, New York, NY 10036.
Projection system for mini or maxi theatres. Exlcusive U.S. Distributors for Zeiss Ikon Projection Equipment.

Automatic Devices Co.
2121 South 12th St., Allentown, Pa. 18103. Tel.: (215) 797-6000.
Manufacturers of stage, television, drapery and cubicle hardware.

Ballantyne of Omaha, Inc.
(A Subsidiary of Canrad-Hanovia, Inc.)
1712 Jackson Street, Omaha, NB 68102. Tel.: (402) 342-4444.
Complete sound and projection systems, from engineering and planning to construction and financing. Projectors, sound-heads, pedestals, rewind and automation. Transistorized or tube amplification. The complete package for mini, maxi, and multi-screened theatres, including platters. Sold only through selected theatre supply dealers.

Bauer Division, AIC Photo, Inc.
168 Glen Cove Road, Carle Place, NY 11514.
Super 8 movie cameras and projectors, 16 mm projectors.

Bausch & Lomb Incorporated
Scientific Optical Products Division
1400 North Goodman Street, Rochester, NY 14692. Tel.: (716) 338-6000.

Branch offices in principal cities.
Manufacturers of optical instruments of all types. BAL-cold glass reflectors.

Bevelite-Adler
14824 South Main Street, Gardena, CA 90248. Tel.: (800) 421-1256, (213) 321-5641.
Changeable marquee sign letters with Snap-Lok plastic 4", 6", 8", 10", 12", 15", 17", 24", red, green, blue, black; Stainless Steel frames with Plexiglas, Adlerite or glass; stainless steel, plastic, or aluminum track for mounting on any backgrounds, all of the above; for drive-ins, theatre marquees, and pylons. Also Pronto changeable letters and numbers from 3" to 42" plus Regency Injection Molded Changeable and permanent letters and numbers.

Brandt, Inc.
705 12th St., Watertown, WI 53094. Tel.: (414) 261-1780.
Manufacturers of coin sorting and counting machines, coin counting and packaging machines, automatic coin wrappers, currency and document counters.

Canrad-Hanovia, Inc.
100 Chestnut Street, Newark, NJ 07105.
Manufacturers of projection bulbs, Ballantyne projectors and Strong lamps.

CEMCORP (Consolidated Engineering & Manufacturing Corp.)
1515 Melrose Lane, Forest Hill, MD Tel.: 383-0036 and 879-3022.
Manufacturers and designers of ticket issuing equipment: "Automaticket" line, including Ticketaker control boxes, drive-in equipment, and ticket control systems.

Century Projector Corporation

1690 Oak, Lakewood NJ (201) 367-4434.

Manufacturers and distributors of motion picture equipment, sound reproducing equipment, automatic controls, and accessories.

Christie Electric Corp.

-8 3410 W. 67th St., Los Angeles, CA 90043. Tel.: (213) 750-1151.

Manufacturers of Xenolite consoles (lamphouse, rectifier power supply and projector based housed in one unit), dual sound system, and automatic system.

Cinematograph International, Inc.

341 W. 44th St., New York, NY 10036. Tel.: (212) 246-6285.

Distributors of automated theatre equipment and supplies; Cinemeccanica Victoria 70/35mm projectors in U.S.; complete Drive-In theatre equipment; projection-sound equipment and supplies; speaker systems; projection arclamps-rectifiers-generators; Xenon light systems; stage lighting, spotlighting, stage draperies; auditorium seats, carpets; display frames, marquee letters, boxoffice equipment; equipment for Studios, Schools, Auditoriums.

Dolby Laboratories Inc.

731 Sansome St., San Francisco, CA 94111. Tel.: (415) 392-0300.

Manufacturer of noise reduction and equalization equipment for theatres and studios.

Econo-Pleat—Phil Sperling

(A division of Eastwest Carpet Mills)

2664 So. La Cienga Blvd., Los Angeles, CA 90034. Tel: (213) 871-1690.

Manufacturers of acoustical fabric wall coverings.

Electronics Div. of Drive-In Theatre Mfg. Co.

709 North 6th St., Kansas City, KS 66101. Tel.: (913) 321-3978.

Manufacturers of drive-in speakers, junction boxes, directional lighting, box office electronic security systems, custom electronic design. Platter systems—automation.

EPRAD, Inc.

P.O. Box 4712, 123 W. Woodruff, Toledo, OH 43620. Tel.: (419) 243-8106.

Manufacturers of stereo-optical (SVA) sound processors, digital dimmers, drive-in speakers, car counters, electronic ordering equipment, all transistor optical sound amplifier systems, transistorized head amplifiers, burglar alarms, speaker baskets, boxoffice cash controls, in car heaters, junction boxes, car-check boxoffice cash control systems, all transistor drive-in theatre power amplifiers, programatic automation systems, sword-large reel film handling devices, sound heads, xenon lamphouses.

Forest Bay Construction Corp.

2 Lawson Ave., East Rockaway, NY 11518. Tel.: (516) 599-0070.

Experts in theatre design.

Goldberg Brothers, Inc.

P.O. Box 5345, Denver, CO 80217.

Manufacturers of automatic rewind equipment, including reels, tables, film cabinets and splicers. Also box office and lobby accessories.

Griggs International Inc.

Box 630, Belton, TX 76513. Tel.: (817) 939-3761.

Manufacturers of conventional and Push-Back theatre chairs, lobby and office furniture.

Gulistan Carpet, Division of J. P. Stevens & Co., Inc.

1185 Avenue of the Americas, New York, NY 10036. Tel.: (212) 575-2282.

Manufacturers of Gulistan carpets.

Hertner Divison, General Battery Corp.

12690 Elmwood Avenue, Cleveland, OH 44111. Tel.: (216) 252-4242.

Manufacturers of Hertner TransVerteRs, ballast rheostats, and control panels.

Heywood-Wakefield Company

National Sales Office, Public Seating Division: 3010 Tenth St., Menominee, MI 49858.

Manufacturers of theatre seating and lounge furniture.

Hurley Screen Company, Inc.

26 Sarah Drive, Farmingdale, NY 11735. Tel.: (516) 293-7140.

Manufacturers of Super-Optica, Super-Glo, Lenticlite 20, Silver-Glo, and MW-16 projection screens and screen frames.

Ideal Seating Corporation

North Berwick, ME (207) 676-2271.

Manufacturers of Mark IV & System 4 theatre seating.

The Imperial Electric Company

64 Ira Avenue, Akron, OH 44309. Tel.: (216) 253-9126.

Indiana Cash Drawer Company

.P.O. Box 236, Shelbyville, IN 46176. Tel.: (317) 398-6643.

Manufacturers of cash drawers.

Irwin Seating Company

3251 Fruitridge Road, P.O. Box 2429, Grand Rapids, MI 49501. Tel.: (616) 784-2621.

Manufacturers of theatre seating.

Kalart Victor Corporation

Hultenius Street, Plainville, CT 06062. Tel.: (203) 747-1663.

Manufacturers of audio-visual equipment and educational television systems including: 16mm sound and silent motion picture projectors: Tele-Beam large screen TV projectors; 16mm TV projectors; 16mm TV uniplex film chain; Multiplexer; Craig film editing and viewing equipment for super 8mm and 16mm film.

K-Hill® Signal Company, Inc.

326 West Third St., Uhrichsville, OH 44683. Tel.: (614) 922-0421.

Manufacturers of drive-in traffic counters. "One way" for boxoffice and flashing light for "exit" sneak-in protection.

Kinotone, Inc.

257 Tenth Avenue, Paterson, NJ 07524. Tel.: (201) 279-9700.

Distributors of projection and sound equipment.

Kneisley Electric Company

2501-9 Lagrange Street, P.O. Box 4692, Toledo, OH 43620. Tel.: (419) 241-1219.

Manufacturers of silicon rectifiers for carbon arcs; also power supplies and lamphouses for Xenon lamps. Silicon replacement stacks for selenium rectifiers, "sil-tubes" (silicon tubes) to replace gas-filled tubes in rectifiers and in exciter lamp supplies. Silicon exciter lamp suppliers, Xenon conversions for 16mm projectors, slide projectors, and for strong trouper. Xenon conversions for carbon arc lamphouses. Xenon "super-spot" lamp and Xenon conversion for strong follow spots.

Kollmorgen Corporation

347 King St., Northampton, MA 01060. Tel.: (413) 586-2330.
Manufacturers of special optics, and optical instruments.

Koneta Matting Division

700 Lunar Drive, Wapakoneta, OH 45895. Tel.: (419) 738-2155.
Manufacturers of rubber and vinyl entrance mats and matting, nylon top-vinyl back wipe off mats.

LaVezzi Machine Works, Inc.

900 North Larch Avenue, Elmhurst, IL 60126. Tel.: (312) 832-8990.
Manufacturers of parts for projector mechanisms and soundheads, including complete intermittent movement assemblies. Also special high precision machine parts for all types of motion picture equipment.

Manko Fabrics Company, Inc.

50 West 36th Street, New York, NY 10018. Tel.: (212) OX 5-7470.
Specialists in manufacturing seat covers, backs, etc. Large inventory nylons, vinyls, mohair fabrics.

The Marble Company, Inc.

P.O. Box 8218, Nashville, TN 37207 (615) 227-7772.
National manufacturer of Marble "Double Eagle" carbons, X-Cel Xenon bulbs and products, projections lens, projection reflectors, and Polecat (in-car radio sound).

Massey Seating Company, Inc.

100 Taylor Street, Nashville, TN 37208. (615) 242-2561.
Manufacturers of theatre seating, polyurethene foam cushions, tailored upholstery units and general seating supplies. Products distributed by leading theatre equipment dealers.

Miracle Equipment Co.

Box 275, Grinnell, IA 50112. Tel.: (515) 236-7536.
Manufacturers of drive-in playground equipment, outdoor fiberglass picnic tables and benches. Also coin-operated carousels, trackless trains, and liter-liminaters (trash receptacles).

National Theatre Supply Company

(Division of National Screen Service Corp.)

1600 Broadway, New York, NY 10019. Tel.: (212) 246-5700.
Vice Pres., Managing Director, Dan Miller.
Products: Theatre equipment and supplies.

National Ticket Company

1650 Broadway, New York, NY 10019 (212) 757-1426.
Ticket printers to theatres; roll-machine-reserved.

Neumade Products Corporation

720 White Plains Rd., Scarsdale, NY 10583. Tel.: (914) 725-4900. PLANT: 2485 Walden Ave., Buffalo, NY 14225. Tel.: (716) 684-0051.
Manufacturers of motion picture, audio visual, and television equipment and accessories, 8mm, 70mm, 35mm, and 16mm fields.

Nick Mulone & Son

Pittsburgh St., Cheswick, PA 15024. Tel.: (412) 274-6646 or 274-5994.
Manufacturers of wide screen frames, all types.

Novelty Scenic Studios

40 Sea Cliff Ave., Glen Cove, NY 11542. Tel.: (212) 895-8668, (516) 671-5940.
Stage curtains and drapes, wall coverings, tracks and stage equipment.

Optical Radiation Corporation

1300 Optical Drive, Azusa, CA 91702. Tel.: (213) 969-3344.
Manufacturer of ORCON lamphouses, Xenon bulbs, automation sound systems, and platters.

Osram Sales Corporation

P.O. Box 7062, R.D. No. 3, Jeanne Drive, Newburgh NY 12550. Tel.: (914) 564-6300.
U.S. distributor of OSRAM Xenon bulbs.

Panavision, Inc.

18618 Oxnard St., Tarzana, CA 91356.
Manufacturers and lessors of motion picture processes—Ultra Panavision 70, Super Panavision 70, Panavision 70 and Panavision 35.

Perey Turnstiles

535 Fifth Avenue, New York, NY 10017. (212) 599-0077.
Manufacturers of theatre turnstiles. Application engineering available

Poblocki and Sons

620 South First St., Milwaukee, Wis. 53204. Tel.: (414) 273-3333.
Manufacturers of marquees and canopies, signs, poster cases, etc.

Prestoseal Manufacturing Corp.

545 Meacham Ave., Elmont, NY 11003. Tel.: (516) 488-1155.
Manufacturers of motion picture and microfilm splicers.

Projected Sound, Inc.

469 Avon Ave., P.O. Box 112, Plainfield, Ind. 46168. Tel.: (317) 839-4111.
Manufacturers and suppliers of In-Car Speakers, Junction Boxes, cone units and component parts.

RCA

30 Rockefeller Plaza, New York, NY 10020. Tel.: (212) 689-7200.

RCA Service Company, Cherry Hill Offices, Camden, NJ 08101. Tel.: (609) 963-8000.

Theatre Service Field Offices

JERSEY CITY, 43 Edward J. Hart Road, Liberty Industrial Park; W. P. Browski, mgr.
CLEVELAND, OH, 20338 Progress Drive, Strongsville, OH, M. J. Duffield, mgr.
ATLANTA, 4508 Bibb Blvd., Tucker, GA, L. N. Howard, mgr.
SKOKIE, IL, 7620 Gross Pointe Rd.; R. H. Bunting, mgr.
HOLLYWOOD, 1501 Beach St., Montebello, CA, M. B. Solomon Jr., mgr.

Rangertone Research Inc.

509 Madison Ave., New York, NY 10022.
Manufacturers and distributors of 16 mm and 35 mm motion picture sound recorders, projectors, interlock systems, telecine and film chain projectors.

The Rank Organisation (Rank Film Equipment)

P.O. Box 70, Great West Rd., Brentford, Middlesex, England. Tel.: 01-568-92222; Telex: 24408; Cables: RANKAUDIO BRENTFORD.

(See under companies, in Great Britain Section.)

Schneider/ISCO

185 Willis Avenue, Mineola, NY 11501 (516) 747-5100.

Manufacturers of the CINELUX line of 70mm, 35mm, 16mm theatre projection lenses. Optical accessories include: outdoor lenses, Zoom lenses (16mm only), Magna-Com 65, ½x reverse and 2X anamorphics, 2″ and 1″ spacers, and thread changers. Special applications and designs also available upon request.

Selby Industries, Inc.

P.O. Box 277, Richfield, OH 44286. Tel.: (216) 659-6631.

Manufacturers and erectors of drive-in screen towers and prefabricated box offices; drive-in design consultants; speaker posts; canopies; and fencing.

Alexander Smith Carpets, Inc.

Sales Division: 919 Third Avenue, New York, NY 10016. Tel.: (212) MU 9-1300.

Manufacturers of carpeting.

Soundfold, Inc., A. Sickels

Box 2125, Dayton, OH 45429. Tel.: (513) 228-3773.

Manufacturers of low cost, acoustical and insulative fabric wall coverings.

Special Optics Heyer Shultz Div./Metal Optics

101 East Main St., Little Falls, NJ 07424.

Manufacturers of metal projection arc reflectors.

Stewart Filmscreen Corp.

1161 W. Sepulveda Blvd., Torrance, CA 90502. Tel.: (213) 326-1422.

Manufacturers of seamless, professional projection screens for motion pictures and TV.

Strand Century, Inc.

20 Bushes Lane, Elmwood Park, NJ 07407; Tel.: (201) 791-7000.

5432 W. 102nd St., Los Angeles, CA 90045; Tel.: (213) 776-4600.

Manufacturers of studio, stage and auditorium lighting fixtures and all types of dimmer control equipment.

Strong Electric Corporation

(A subsidiary of Canrad-Hanovia, Inc.)

P.O. Box 1003, 87 City Park Avenue, Toledo, OH 43697. Tel.: (419) 248-3741.

Manufacturers of carbon and xenon arc motion picture projection lamphouse for 16 and 35mm film, 2 × 2 and 3¼ × 4 xenon slide projectors. Associate DC power supplies. Tufcold and silver reflectors. Carbon and xenon arc, quartz halogen and incandescent follow spotlights.

Technikote Corporation

63 Seabring Street, Brooklyn, NY 11231. Tel.: (212) MAin 4-6429/6430.

Manufacturers of seamless projection Screens—Anti-static XR-171 Pearlescent Dust-resistant screen, Jetwhite screen, Lenticolar Screens, Hilux metallic screen, Matte white screen; drive-in screen paints, wood & metal screen frames; rope and pulley screens.

Theatrical Electronics

Box 706, Matthews, NC 28105.

Reel brackets, rewinds plastic reels, sankor lens, rebuilt used equipment. Everything for the booth.

Union Carbide Corp.—Carbon Products Division

270 Park Avenue, New York, NY 10017. Tel.: (212) 551-2345.

Sales Office: 120 So. Riverside Plaza, Chicago, IL 60606. Tel.: (312) 454-2000.

In Europe: Union Carbide Europe S.A., Rue Pedro-Meylan 5, CH-1211, Geneva 17, Switzerland. Tel.: (022) 47.44.11.

Manufacturers of carbons for motion picture projectors, spotlights and effect lights; brushes, carbon, graphite and metal-graphite for electric motors, generators and converters.

Williams Screen Company

1674 Summit Lake Blvd., Akron, OH 44314. Tel.: 745-0521.

Manufacturers of projection screens.

Edw. H. Wolk, Inc.

1241 S. Wabash Ave., Chicago, IL 60605. Tel.: (312) WE 9-2720-21-22(-)45.

Manufacturers of replacement parts for all American made projectors, arc lamps and sound reproducers, 26½″ Reel Arms for regular and automated projection. Deluxe & "Moto-Matic" Hand Rewinders. "Solfonic" Solar Cells & Power Pacs. Distributor of Naren Spot Lights, Ex-Cell Sand/Water Urns, G.E. & Westinghouse Projection and Exciter Lamps, Cetron Photo-Electric Cells, Bausch & Lomb Glass Silvered Reflectors & "Wolk" Rectifier Bulbs; Sav-A-Reel kits.

Studio Equipment

Ampex Corporation

401 Broadway, Redwood City, CA 94063 Tel.: 367-2011 TWX: 415-364-9034.

Glendale, CA: 500 Rodier Dr. 91201 213-245-9373.

Dallas, TX: 1615 Prudential Dr. 75235 214-637-5200.

Elk Grove Village, IL: 2201 Estes Ave. 60007 312-593-6000.

Hackensack, NJ: 75 Commerce Way 07601 201-489-7400.

Atlanta, GA: 1680 Tully Circle, N.E. 30329 404-633-4131.

Audio/Video recording equipment for industry/studios/radio & TV stations.

Amusement Supply Co.

208 West Montcalm, Detroit 48207. Tel.: WO 1-3440.

R. Ruben, owner.

Automatic Devices Co.

2121 South 12th St., Allentown, PA 18103. Tel.: (215) 797-6000.
Manufacturers of stage and drapery hardware.

Bach Auricon, Inc.

6950 Romaine St., Hollywood, CA 90038. Tel.: Hollywood 2-0931.
Manufacturers of "Filmagnetic" sound-on-film recording equipment and "Auricon" motion picture cameras.

Bell & Howell Company (Professional Equipment Division

7100 McCormick Road, Chicago, IL 60645. (312) 262-1600.
Professional film printers, duplicators and related accessories for motion picture film and video laboratories.

The Camera Mart, Inc.

456 W. 55th St., New York, NY 10019. Tel.: (212) PLaza 7-6977.
Sale & Rental of motion picture and TV equipment, both film & videotape.

F&B/CECO, Inc.

315 West 43rd St., New York, NY 10036. Tel.: (212) 974-4600. Cable: 'CINEQUIP'
Rental, sale and service of photographic equipment for motion picture and TV studios. Manufacturer of professional tripods, tripod heads, editing viewers, camera motors, editing tables and other professional motion picture production equipment. Distributor for Hajnal Snorkel lens systems.

Fiberbilt Photo Products Division of Ikelheimer-Ernst, Inc.

601 West 26th St., New York, NY 10001. Tel.: (212) OR 5-5820.
Manufacturers of cases and trunks for all types of motion picture equipment; also film cases.

Jack A. Frost

234 Piquette Avenue, Detroit, MI 48202. Tel.: 873-8030.
Studio and motion picture lighting equipment.

Galaxy Productions

5233 N.E. 15th St., Des Moines, IA 50313. Tel.: (515) 265-4208/09.
Lease mobile sleeping, and eating facilities, a power plant and heavy duty rigs for location work.

Grosh Scenic Studios

4114-4122 Sunset Blvd., Hollywood, CA 90029. Tel.: (213) 662-1134.
Design, manufacture and installation of theatrical stage draperies; custom and standard theatrical hardware.

Kliegl Bros. Universal Electric Stage Lighting Company, Inc.

32-32 48th Ave., Long Island City, NY 11101. Tel.: (212) 786-7474.
Manufacturers of Klieglights and lighting control equipment for TV studios, stage, auditorium and architural lighting specialties.

Magnasync-Moviola Corp., Subsidiary of Craig Corp.

5539 Riverton Avenue, North Hollywood, CA 91601. Tel.: (213) 763-8441.
Manufacturers of sound equipment, magnetic film recorders, reproducers and accessories, film to videotape transfer system, communication tape recorders, and film editing equipment and accessories.

Oxberry Berkey Technical

25-15 50th St., Woodside, L.I., NY Tel.: (212) 721-5555.

Branch Offices: 1015 Chestnut St., Burbank, CA; Burrell Way, Thetford, Norfolk, England.
Manufacturers of animation stands, optical printers, cameras, registration devices.

RCA

30 Rockefeller Plaza, New York, NY 10020. Tel.: (212) 598-5900.

Commercial Communications Systems Division, Broadcast Systems, Front and Cooper St., Camden, NJ 08102. Tel.: (609) 963-8000.

Commercial Communications Systems Division, Photophone Systems, 2700 West Olive Ave., Burbank, CA 91505. Tel.: (213) 849-6741.

Complete theatre service.

Ringold Theatre Equipment Co.

952 Ottawa N.W., Grand Rapids, Mich. 49503. Tel.: (616) 454-8852; Nights: (616) 949-0124. Paul Voudouris, president.

Branch Offices: 29525 Ford Rd., Garden City, MI 48135. Tel.: (313) 522-4650; Nights: (313) 722-8247. 7976 Broadview Rd., Broadview Heights, OH 44147. Tel.: (216) 526-2783.

429

Ritter Co. Studio Equipment

3325 Cahuenga Blvd., Hollywood, CA 90068. Tel.: (213) 851-3325.

Gas and Electric Wind Machines.

Roctronics Entertainment Lighting and Special Effects, Inc.

100-MPA Roctronics Park, Pembroke, MA 02359. (617) 826-8888.

Designers, manufacturers and sellers of entertainment lighting electronics (dimmers and color synthesizers) and special effects (foggers, bubblers, stroboscopes, laser beam scanners, animated displays).

Ross, Inc.

333 West 52nd St., New York, NY 10019. Tel.: (212) 246-5470.

Rental, sale and service of motion picture and TV lighting, grip equipment and generators. Sole distributor of Mole-Richardson Co. products in the State of New York.

S.O.S. Photo-Cine-Optics, Inc.

Main Office: 315 West 43 St., New York, NY 10036. (212) 974-4600.

Distributors, manufacturers and exporters of television production equipment. Includes 16 and 35mm studio and newsreel cameras; lenses and viewfinders; motion picture and TV accessories; animation equipment; lighting equipment for studio and video; sound recording equipment and accessories; theatre, preview and TV background projection equipment; editing and cutting room supplies; film handling equipment; printing and processing and laboratory testing equipment. All types of stage scenic materials.

Stewart Filmscreen Corp.

1161 W. Sepulveda Blvd., Torrance, CA 90502. Tel.: (213) 326-1422.

Manufacturers of complete line of Stewart Seamless, professional projection screens for rear projected backgrounds of all sizes in motion picture and TV studios, including screen frames and accessories; also seamless front projection screens for theatres and viewing rooms of all types.

Tru-Roll Corporation

622 Sonora Ave., Glendale, CA 91201. Tel.: (213) 243-9567 and 245-5741.

Designers and manufacturers of custom and standard theatrical hardware. Curved and straight drapery tracks, contour drapery rigging, motion picture screen frames, top and side screen masking rigging, motors and controls, motorized revolving stages, motorized bandwagons, orchestra enclosures, sliding panels, disappearing motion picture screens.

Westrex-Litton Industries, Inc.

2629 W. Olive Ave., Burbank, CA 91505. (213) 846-3394.

Westrex Recorders, re-recorders, mixers.

Branch Offices

Westrex Company Limited, Unit 1, Fairway Drive,, Bilton Fairway Industrial Estate, Greenford, Middlesex, UB6 8PW, England.
Westrex Company, Asia, 1302 Luk Hoi T-ng Bldg., 31, Queen's Road Central, Hong Kong.
Westrex Company, Asia, International House, Sec. 3, Hsin Yee Road, Taipei, Taiwan.
Westrex Company Italy, 65 via Constantine Maes, 00162 Rome, Italy, Cable: Westrex Rome, Tel.: 83 92 990.
Westrex Company Orient, C.P.O. Box 760, Tokyo, Japan, cable: Westrex Tokyo, Telex: J22612, Tel.: 211-6791.

XeTRON Corp.

10 Saddle Road, Cedar Knolls, NJ 07927 Tel.: (201) 267-8200.

Lorraine Carbon Division: Carbon electrodes for all motion picture applications. XeTRON Products Division: Professional 16, 35, and 70 mm projection equipment and accessories. Cinemaccanica 35mm and 70mm projectors, film, transports, sound systems, XeTRON xenon lamphouses, bulbs, platter transport, continuous loop transport, dimmer systems, projection lenses. Hortson and Fumeo 16mm projection systems.

Refreshment Products and Equipment

American Can Company—Dixie and Marathon Products

24th and Dixie Avenue, Easton, PA 18042. Tel.: 250-1400, and American Lane, Greenwich, CT 96830.

Manufacturers of paper products: plates, cups, bowls, towels, tissues, etc.

Paul F. Beich Co.

Bloomington, IL 61701. Tel.: (309)828-1311.

Manufacturers of 10¢ Bike Whiz. Complete line of other 10¢ bars and 15¢ Milk Chocolate caramel filled shells.

Blevins Popcorn Co.

Popcorn Village, Memphis, TN 38117. 813 Ridge Lake Blvd., P.O. Box 171233. Tel.: (901) 761-2062.

Processing Plants in Ridgway, IL and North Bend, NE

Concession supply branches in Atlanta, GA 30325, P.O. Box 20176 Sta. N., 2023 Hills Ave., N.W.: Cincinnati, OH 45246, 11705 Chesterdale Rd.: Dallas, TX 75226, P.O. Box 26264, 1901 S. Good-Latimer: Houston, TX 77206, P.O. Box 10243, 202 W. 38th St.: Jacksonville, FL 32203, P.O. Box 2752, 633 N. Myrtle Ave.: Louisville, KY 40214, 6224 Strawberry Lane: Memphis, TN 38116, P.O. Box 16834, 3143 Fleetbrook Dr.: Miami, FL 33152, P.O. Box 552901, 7851 N.W. 32nd Street: Nashville, TN 37209, P.O. Box 90766, 3098 Charlotte Ave.: New Orleans, LA 70181, P.O. Box 10585, 1017 Jefferson Hwy.: Omaha, NE 68101, P.O. Box 1282, 1608 Cuming St.: Tampa, FL 33601, P.O. Box 5461, 1212 N. 39th St.: West Terre Haute, IN 47885, Highway 40 West

Warehouses in Little Rock, AR, Knoxville, TN & North Loup, NE

Processors of raw popcorn and distributors of all high profit concession supplies and equipment.

Butler Fixture & Mfg. Co.

3939 So. Williams St., Denver, CO 80205. Tel.: (303) 572-3939.

Builders of theatre concession stands.

Canada Dry Corp. (Syrup Division)

100 Park Ave., New York, NY 10017. Tel.: (212) LE 2-4300.

Manufacturers of beverage syrups: Ginger Ale, Cola, Tahitian Treat, Hi-Spot, Orange, Cactus Cooler, Root Beer and others.

Castleberry's Food Co.
Box 1010, August, GA 30903.
Fast foods, sauces, packed foods.

Coca-Cola USA
P.O. Drawer 1734, Atlanta, GA 30301. Tel.: (404) 897-2121.
Manufacturers of soft drink syrups, Coca-Cola, Tab, Sprite, Fanta flavors, Fresca.

Continental Can Co. Bondware Division
633 Third Ave., New York, NY 10017. Tel.: 551-7000.
Paper cups for hot and cold drinks.

Crush International, Inc.
2201 Main St., Evanston, IL Tel.: (312) DAvis 8-8850 and MAin 5-0400.
Manufacturers of Hires Root Beer, Crush fruit syrups and Old Colony syrups.

Dr Pepper Company
5523 East Mockingbird Lane, P.O. Box 225086, Dallas, TX 75222. Tel.: (214) 824-0331.
Manufacturers of Dr Pepper and Sugar-Free Dr Pepper concentrates and fountain syrups.

Goetze's Candy Co., Inc.
3900 E. Monument St., Baltimore, MD 21205.
Candy designed exclusively for theatres; 3½ oz. 12 pack.

Greer Enterprises, Inc.
281 N. Grant Ave., Columbus, OH 43215. Tel.: CA 1-3245. Factory and Sales: 31 Chicago St., Quincy, MI 49082. Tel.: (517) 639-9825.
Manufacturers of combination frankfurter barbecue unit and bun warmer, Glenray manufacturers of Moist Heat Portable Steam Table (steamette).

Henry Heide, Inc.
P.O. Box 271, New Brunswick, NJ 08903. Tel.: (201) 846-2400.
Manufacturers of candy—Jujyfruits, Jujubes, Chocolate Flavor Babies, Candy Corn, Red Hot Dollars and drops.

Hershey Foods Corp. Hershey Chocolate and Confectionery Division
19 East Chocolate Avenue, Hershey, PA 17033. Tel.: (717) 534-4200
Manufacturers of chocolate and cocoa.

M.J. Holloway & Company
308 West Ontario, Chicago, IL 60610. Tel.: (312) 642-2700.
Manufacturers of candy—Milk Duds, Slo-Poke and Black Crow Suckers, Hi-noon bars, Zooper Dooper bars.

Hollywood Brands, Inc.
A subsidiary of Consolidated Foods Corp.

836 South Chestnut Street, Centralia, IL 62801. Tel.: (618) 532-4767.
Manufacturers of Pay Day, Butternut, Milk Shake, and Zero.

Jet Spray Corp.
195 Bear Hill Road, Waltham, MA 02154. Tel.: (617) 890-7700.
Manufacturers of visual display, electrically refrigerated carbonated and non-carbonated beverage dispensers, hot chocolate dispensers, freeze-dried coffee dispensers, coin operated coffee and chocolate dispensers, instant mashed potato dispensers, hot and cold tea dispenser.

Manley, Inc.
1920 Wyandotte, Kansas City 8, MO (Mail: P.O. Box 1006, Kansas City, MO 64141). Tel.: (816) 421-6155.
Manufacturers of popcorn machines, popcorn, popcorn seasoning and beverage dispensers. Theatre and Drive-In theatre concession stands.

M & M/Mars
High Street, Hackettstown, NJ 07840.
Manufacturers of M & M's Plain Chocolate Candies, Milky Way Milk Chocolate Bar, M & M's Peanut Chocolate Candies, 3 Musketeers bar, Snickers, Mars Almond, Mars Double Crunch, Sprint Chocolate Wafer, Snickers Peanut Munch, Milky Way Dark Chocolate Bar.

National Rejectors, Inc.
P.O. Box 1550, Hot Springs, AR 71901.
Coin and currency handling equipment. Branches in major cities.

Ogden Food Service
254 Franklin St., Buffalo, NY. Tel.: 852-3339.

Ogden Foods, Inc.
3660 S. Lawrence St. Philadelphia, PA 19148
Operators of Theatre Food Concessions—both Indoor Houses and Drive-Ins.

Pepsi-Cola Company
Purchase, NY
Manufacturers of Pepsi-Cola syrup and bottlers of Pepsi-Cola, Diet-Pepsi, Teem.

Peter Paul Codbury, Inc.
New Haven Road, Naugatuck, CT 06770.
Manufacturers of candy; Mounds, Almond Joy, York Peppermint Patties, Codbury chocolate.

Quaker City Chocolate & Confectionery Company, Inc.
2901 Grant Ave., Philadelphia, PA 19114. Tel.: (215) 677-6500.
Manufacturers of 5¢ and 10¢ candies: Good and Plenty, Spice Drops, Spearmint Leaves, Orange Slices and Good 'N Fruity. Exclusive distributors for Bassett's Liquorice All Sorts.

H. B. Reese Candy Company, Inc., Subsidiary of Hershey Chocolate Co.
Hershey, PA 17033. Tel.: (717) 534-4100.
Manufacturers of Peanut Butter Cups.

Rex Packaging Company—A Division of Standard International Corp.
10 Minue Street, Carteret, NJ 07008. Tel.: (201) 969-1234.
Manufacturers of noiseless paper popcorn bags and a complete line of outdoor concession bags.

Roll-A-Grill Corp. of America

645 First Ave., New York, NY 10016. Tel.: (212) CH 4-5000.

Manufacturers of Roll-A-Grill automatic frankfurter machines, Roll Warmers, Sandwich Grills, Toas-Treat Sandwich Makers, Roll-A-Grill Speed Fryer, Roll-A-Spreader, compactor, miracle freezer, Roll-A-Slicer, Pressure Fryer.

Rowe International, Inc., A Subsidiary of Triangle Industries, Inc.

75 Troy Hills Road, Whippany, NJ 07981. Tel.: (201) 887-0400.

Manufacturers of Automatic Venders, music systems and bill and coin changers.

Royal Crown Cola Co.

1000 Tenth Avenue, P.O. Box 1440, Columbus, GA 31902. Tel.: (404) 322-4431.

Branches: 108-08 Queens Blvd., Forest Hills, NY 11375. Tel.: (212) 268-3100; 4849 Scott Street, Suite LL322, Schiller Park, IL 60176. Tel.: (312) 671-2565; Suite 127, 1145 Empire Central Plaza, Dallas, Texas 75247. Tel.: (214) 631-0755; Suite 1005, 3450 Wilshire Blvd., Los Angeles, CA 90005. Tel.: (213) 386-2711.

Manufacturers of soft drinks.

Scotsman Ice Systems

505 Front St., Albert Lea, MN 56007. Tel.: 373-3961.

Manufacturers of Scotsman ice cube and flake machines, combination ice machines and drink dispensers.

The Seven-Up Company

121 South Meramec, St. Louis, MO 63105. (314) 889-7777.

7UP and Diet 7UP are available in bottles, cans, pre-mix, and post-mix from the local 7UP Bottling company. The 7UP Bottler is a source for pre-mix and post-mix dispensing equpment and bottle and can venders.

Simonin's, C. F. Sons, Inc.

Tioga & Belgrade Streets, Philadelphia, PA 19134. Tel.: (215) GA 6-2300.

Manufacturers of popcorn oils and colored and flavored seasonings.

Smithfield Ham & Products Company

Smithfield, VA 23430. Tel.: (804) 357-2121.

James River brand barbecued meats and other genuine Smithfield Foods.

Stein Industries, Inc.

22 Sprague Avenue, Amityville, NY 11701. (516) 691-2222.

Manufacturers and distributors of popcorn warmers and concession stands. Doorman stub receptacles, box offices, display frames.

Sunkist Soft Drinks, Inc.

2600 Century Parkway, Atlanta, GA 30345. (404) 321-1776; A division of General Cinema Corp.

Suppliers of Sunkist Orange Soda Fountain syrup, bottles, cans.

Vendo Company

10500 Barkley, Overland Park, KS 66212. Tel.: (913) 341-1300.

Manufacturers of automatic venders for food, beverages (hot and cold), candy and cigarettes; distributors of stereo music systems, butter dispensers, etc.

Virga's Pizza Crust Company

2236 Conner Street, New York, NY 10466, Tel.: XX 4-9100.

Frozen pizza and ingredients.

Manufacturers and Services By Product Classification

Animation Equipment
Oxberry Berkey Technical
S.O.S. Photo-Cine-Optics, Inc.

Attraction Advertising Equipment
A-Wagner Zip Change
Bevilite-Adler

Beverages and Beverage Dispensers
Canada Dry Corp.
Coca-Cola USA
Crush International
Dr Pepper Co.
Jet Spray Corp.
Manley, Inc.
Pepsi-Cola Co.
Royal Crown Cola Corp.
Seven-Up Company
Sunkist Soft Drinks
Vendo Co.

Camera Equipment
Bell & Howell Company
Camera Mart, Inc.
F&B/CECO, Inc.
Mauer, J. A., Inc.
Mitchell Camera Corp.
Oxberry Berkey Technical
S.O.S. Photo-Cine-Optics, Inc.

Candy and Candy Machines
Beich, Paul F., Co.
Heide, Henry, Inc.
Hershey Chocolate Corp.
Holloway, M. J. Co.
Hollywood Brands, Inc.
M&M/Mars
Quaker City Chocolate & Confectionery Co., Inc.
H. B. Reese Candy
Vendo Co.

Carbons, Carbon Savers & Carbon Coolers
The Marbe Co., Inc.
Union Carbide Corp.
Xetron

Coin Changing Machines
National Rejectors, Inc.

Concession Stands
Butler Fixture & Mfg. Co.

Cups & Trays
American Can Company
Continental Can Co.
Lily-Tulip Cup Corp.

Curtains and Curtain Controls and Acoustical Drapes
Automatic Devices Co.
Econo-Pleat
Novelty Scenic Studios
Soundfold, Inc.

Drive-In Admissions Control
Eprad
K-Hill Signal Corp.

Drive-In Screens and Towers
Ballantyne of Omaha
Selby Industries, Inc.
Technikote

Equipment Cases
Fiberbilt, Division of Ikelheimer-Ernst, Inc.

Film Editing
A.V.E. Corporation
S.O.S. Photo-Cine-Optics, Inc.
Westrex-Litton Industries, Inc.

Film Splicers
Prestoseal Mfg. Corp.

Floor Coverings
Gulistan Carpet
Koneta Matting
Smith, Alexander, Inc.

Food and Food Concessions Suppliers
Castleberry's Food Co.
Rowe Mfg. Co.
Smithfield Ham & Products Co.
Tri-State Refreshments, Inc.
Vendo Co.
Virga's Pizza Crust Company

Food Equipment
Greer Enterprises, Inc.

In-Car Speakers and Heaters
Ballantyne of Omaha
Eprad, Inc.
The Marble Co., Inc.
Projected Sound, Inc.

Interior Decoration
Novelty Scenic Studios

Lenses, Projection
Atlantic Audio Visual Corp.
Bausch & Lomb, Inc.
Kollmorgen Corp.
The Marble Co., Inc.
Panavision, Inc.
Schneider Corp. of America

Lighting Equipment, Studio
Kliegl Bros. Universal Electric Stage Lighting Co., Inc.
Charles Ross, Inc.

Playground Equipment
American Playground Device Co.
Herschell, Allan, Co., Inc.
Miracle Space Equipment Co.

Popcorn Machines and Supplies
Blevins Popcorn Co.
Manley, Inc.
Rex Packaging
Simonin's, C. F. Sons, Inc.
Stein Industries, Inc.

Projection Light Equipment
Ballantyne of Omaha
Canrad Hanovia, Inc.
Imperial Electric Co.
Hertner Division, General Battery Corp.
The Marble Co., Inc.
Kneisley Electric Co.
Optical Radiation Corp.
Osram Sales Corporation
RCA
Rank Organisation
Strong Electric Co.
Xetron

Projection Room Accessories
Neumade Products Corp.
Theatre Equipment Co.

Projectors and Parts
A.V.E. Corporation
Ballantyne of Omaha
Century Projector Corp.
Kinotone, Inc.
La Vezzi Machine Works
National Theatre Supply
RCA
Simplex Equipment Corp.
Edward H. Wolk

Recording Equipment
Ampex Corporation
Bach Auricon, Inc.
Magnasync Corp.
Maurer, J. A., Inc.
RCA
Reeves Equipment Corp.
S.O.S. Photo-Cine-Optics, Inc.
Westrex-Litton Industries, Inc.

Screen Frames
Stewart Filmscreen Corp.

Screens and Screen Paint
Hurley Screen Co.
Stewart Filmscreen Corp.
Technikote Corp.
Williams Screen Co.

Seating for Auditoriums
American Desk Co.
American Seating Co.
Griggs Int'l. Inc.
Heywood-Wakefield Co.
Ideal Seating Corp.
Irwin Seating Co.
Mannk Fabrics Co., Inc.
Massey Seating Co.

Sound Equipment
Altec-Lansing
Ballantyne of Omaha
Century Projector Corp.
Cinematograph International, Inc.
Kinotone, Inc.
RCA

Simplex Equipment Corp.
Westrex-Litton Industries, Inc.

Spotlights
Kneisley Electric Co.
Strong Electric Co.

Stage Lighting
Century Strand, Inc.
Kliegl Bros.

Studio Lighting
Century Strand, Inc.
Frost, Inc., Jack A.
S.O.S. Photo-Cine-Optics, Inc.
Charles Ross, Inc.

Theatre Design
Forest Bay Construction

Ticket Machines and Boxes
Eprad

Theatre Supply Dealers

IN THE UNITED STATES AND CANADA

ALABAMA
Birmingham
QUEEN FEATURE SERVICE, 2409 First Ave., North. Tel.: (205) 251-8665

ARIZONA
Phoenix
ARIZONA THEATRE EQUIPMENT, 1410 E. Washington. Tel.: (602) 437-0215

CALIFORNIA
Culver City
BUDD THEATRE SUPPLY, INC., 8537 West Washington Blvd. Tel.: (213) 870-9301

Inglewood
CARTER EQUIPMENT CO., INC., 1050 W. Florence Ave. Tel.: (213) 677-6117

Los Angeles
AUTOMATIC DEVICES CO., 553 Oak Knoll Ave., Pasadena. Tel.: 681-4338
BARRETT-ROBINSON CO., 9165 Las Tunas Dr., Temple City. Tel.: 285-1229
CONSOLIDATED SEATING, 1314 Scott Road, Bradbury, L.A. Tel.: 849-7637
CURRAN PRODUCTIONS, 1215 Bates Ave., L.A. Tel.: 662-8129
FILBERT, JOHN P., 1100 Flower, Gelendale. Tel.: 247-6550
GROSH, R. L., & Sons, 4114 Sunset Blvd. Tel.: 662-1134
NATIONAL THEATRE SUPPLY, 2001 S. La Cienega Blvd. 90034. Tel.: (213) 838-1821
OLESEN CO., 1535 Ivar Ave. L.A. Tel. 461-4631
PEMBREX THEATRE SUPPLY, 1100 Flower, Glendale. Tel.: 247-6550
THEATRE SERVICE & SUPPLY, INC., 1250 E. Walnut St., Pasadena, 91106. (213) 792-7158
THEATRE UPHOLSTERING CO., 1338 W. 24th, L.A. Tel.: 734-0740

San Francisco
PACIFIC THEATRE EQUIPMENT CO., 142 Leavenworth St. Tel.: (415) 771-2950
WESTERN THEATRICAL EQUIPMENT, 187 Golden Gate Ave. Tel.: (415) 861-7571

COLORADO
Denver
WESTERN SERVICE & SUPPLY, 2100 Stout St. Tel.: (303) 534-7611. R. K. Tankersley, mgr

DISTRICT OF COLUMBIA
Washington
BEN LUST, 623 Sligo Ave., Silver Spring, MD 20910; 589-6606. Irwin Lust, pres
R&S THEATRE SUPPLY CO., 4701 42nd St. N.W., Tel.: (202) 244-1500
WILMO CORP., 3322 M St., N.W. Tel.: (202) 337-6680

FLORIDA
Jacksonville
JACKSONVILLE FILM SERVICE, INC., 2208 West 21st. Tel.: (904) 355-5447

Miami
JOE HORNSTEIN, INC., 759 W. Flagler St. Tel.: (305) 545-5842

GEORGIA
Albany
DIXIE THEATRE SERVICE & SUPPLY, 1010 N. Slappey Dr

Atlanta
AMERICAN THEATRE SUPPLY, P.O. Box 54553. (30303) Tel.: (404) 875-3167
CAPITAL CITY SUPPLY, 2124 Jackson Parkway, N.W. Tel.: (404) 792-9424

NATIONAL THEATRE SUPPLY, 1325 Logan Circle, N.W. 30318. Tel.: (404) 351-1419
WIL-KIN THEATRE INC., 301 No. Avenue, N.E. Tel.: (404) 876-0342

Savannah
RHODES SOUND & PROJECTION SERVICE, 218 E. 56th St

ILLINOIS
Chicago
ABBOTT THEATRE EQUIPMENT, 1311 S. Wabash Ave. (312) 427-7573
NATIONAL THEATRE SUPPLY (National Screen Service), 1322 S. Wabash Ave. 60605. Tel.: (312) 427-8211

INDIANA
Indianapolis
GER-BAR, INC., 339 N. Capitol Ave. Tel.: (317) 634-1727

IOWA
Des Moines
DES MOINES THEATRE SUPPLY, 1121 High St. Tel.: (515) 243-6520

KANSAS
Kansas City
MID-CONTINENT THEATRE SUPPLY CORP., 1800 Wyandotte. Tel.: (816) 221-0480
Wichita
SOUTHWEST THEATRE EQUIPMENT, 118½ W. Douglas Ave., P.O. Box 2138

KENTUCKY
Louisville
FALLS CITY THEATRE EQUIPMENT, 427 S. Third St
HADDEN THEATRE SUPPLY, 909 Emerson Ave., P.O. Box 4151

LOUISIANA
New Orleans
NATIONAL THEATRE SUPPLY, 5624 Jefferson Hwy., Harahan, LA 70123
SOUTHERN THEATRE SUPPLY, INC., 3822 Airline Highway, Metairie, Tel.: (504) 831-1001

MARYLAND
Baltimore
ALLIED THEATRE EQUIPMENT CO., INC., 12 E. 25th St. Tel.: (301) 235-2747
DUSMAN MOTION PICTURE SUPPLIES, 12 E. 25th St. Tel.: 235-4747
NATIONAL THEATRE SUPPLY, 6707 Whitestone Rd. Tel.: (301) 944-8844

MASSACHUSETTS
Boston
MAJOR THEATRE EQUIPMENT CORP., 44 Winchester St. Tel.: (617) 542-0445
MASSACHUSETTS THEATRE EQUIPMENT, 20 Piedmont St. Tel.: (617) 542-9814
NATIONAL THEATRE SUPPLY, 95 Broadway 02116. Tel.: (617) 542-2663

MICHIGAN
Detroit
ALTEC SERVICE CO., 401 Commerce Bldg. Tel.: 963-3180
AMUSEMENT SUPPLY CO., 208 W. Montcalm. Tel.: WO 1-3440
NORTHWEST STUDIOS, INC., 16209 W. McNicholis. Tel.: BR 3-2650
Garden City
RINGOLD THEATRE EQUIPMENT, 32647 Ford Road, Tel.: (313) 522-4650

Grand Rapids
RINGOLD THEATRE EQUIPMENT, 952 Ottawa, N.W. Tel.: (616) 454-8852

MINNESOTA
Minneapolis
MINNEAPOLIS THEATRE SUPPLY CO., 51 Glenwood Ave. Tel.: (612) 335-1166

MISSOURI
Kansas City
DRIVE-IN THEATRE MANUFACTURING CO., 709 N. Sixth St.: 321-3978
MID CONTINENT THEATRE SUPPLY, 1800 Wyandotte. Tel.: 221-0480
NATIONAL THEATRE SUPPLY, 1800 Baltimore 64108. (816) 221-9858
SHREVE THEATRE SUPPLY, 709 North Sixth. Tel.: 321-3978
St. Louis
RINGOLD CINEMA EQUIPMENT CORP., 8421 Gravois Road, 63123 Tel.: (314) 352-2020

NEBRASKA
Omaha
QUALITY THEATRE SUPPLY, 1515 Davenport. Tel.: (402) 341-7253
SLIPPER THEATRE SUPPLY, INC., 1502 Davenport St. Tel.: (402) 341-3921

NEVADA
Las Vegas
PEMBREX THEATRE SUPPLY CO., 3519 Algonquin Dr. Tel.: (702) 735-5278

NEW JERSEY
Camden
MID-ATLANTIC THEATRE EQUIPMENT CO., 2600 Mt. Ephriam Ave., Tel.: (609) 962-6632
NATIONAL THEATRE SUPPLY CO., 130 Ferry Ave. 08104. Tel.: (609) 962-9200

NEW YORK
Albany
ALBANY THEATRE SUPPLY, 443 N. Pearl St. Tel.: (518) 465-8894. Jack McGrath
Kingston
SUMMIT ENTERPRISES, Gov. Clinton Hotel. Tel.: (914) 338-5095
Tarrytown
MOTION PICTURE ENTERPRISES, P.O. Box 276, 10591. (212) 245-0969. Herbert R. Pilzer, pres.
New York City
CAPITOL MOTION PICTURE SUPPLY, CORP., 630 Ninth Ave. Tel.: (212) 757-4510
JOE HORNSTEIN, INC., 341 W. 44th St. Tel.: (212) 246-6285
NATIONAL THEATRE SUPPLY, 1600 Broadway. Tel.: (212) 245-6900
STAR CINEMA SUPPLY, 217 W. 21st Street, Tel.: 675-3515
TIMES SQUARE THEATRICAL & STUDIO SUPPLY CORP., 318 W. 47th Street, Tel.: 245-4155

NORTH CAROLINA
Charlotte
AMERICAN THEATRE SUPPLY CO., 529 N. Tryar St. Tel.: 333-5076
CHARLOTTE THEATRE SUPPLY CO., 227 S. Church St. Tel.: (704) 333-9651
HARRIS THEATRE SALES, INC., 315 S. Church St.
STANDARD THEATRE SUPPLY, 1624 West Independence Blvd. Tel.: (704) 375-6008
WIL-KIN, INC., 800 S. Graham St., Tel.: (704) 333-6101

Greensboro

STANDARD THEATRE SUPPLY CO., 125 Higgins Street. Box 20660, Tel.: (919) 272-6165

OHIO
Cincinnati

NATIONAL THEATRE SUPPLY, 1105 W. 8th St., 45203. Tel.: (513) 621-8903

Cleveland

OHIO THEATRE SUPPLY CO., 7976 Broadview Rd. (216) 526-2783

Toledo

TOLEDO THEATRE SUPPLY, 3916 Secor Rd

OKLAHOMA
Oklahoma City

CAPITOL THEATRE SUPPLY, 5900 Mosteller Drive, Tel.: (405) 842-0860
OKLAHOMA THEATRE SUPPLY, 628 W. Sheridan Ave. Tel.: (405) 236-8691

OREGON
Portland

WEST COAST THEATRE SERVICE, 909 N.W. 19th St., Tel.: (503) 227-2932

PENNSYLVANIA
Philadelphia

ALLIED THEATRE EQUIPMENT CO., INC., 157 N. 12th St. Tel.: (215) 567-2047
BLUMBERG BROS., 1305 Vine St. Tel.: (215) WA 5-7240

Pittsburgh

ATLAS THEATRE SUPPLY, 1519 Forbes Ave
NATIONAL THEATRE SUPPLY, 107 6th St. (Fulton Bldg.) Tel.: (412) 471-4630
THEATRE EQUIP. & SERVICE CO., 100 Lighthill St. Tel.: (412) 322-4600

RHODE ISLAND
Providence

RHODE ISLAND SUPPLY, 357 Westminster St

TENNESSEE
Memphis

NATIONAL THEATRE SUPPLY, 412 S. Second St. Tel.: (901) 525-6616
TRI-STATE THEATRE SUPPLY, 151 Vance Ave. Tel.: 525-8249

Nashville

CAPITAL CITY SUPPLY CO, 713 Seduken Bldg. Tel.: (615) 256-0347
MID-SOUTH THEATRE SERVICE, 439 Brewer Drive. Tel.: (615) 832-5660

TEXAS
Dallas

HARDIN THEATRE SUPPLY, 714 S. Hampton Rd
HERBER BROS., 408 S. Harwood St.
MODERN SALES & SERVICE, 2200 Young St. Tel.: (214) 747-3191
NATIONAL THEATRE SUPPLY, 7138 Envoy Court, 75247. Tel.: (214) 634-7150
PINKSTON'S SALES AND SERVICE, 4207 Lawnview Ave. Tel.: (214) 388-1550
LOU WALTERS SALES & SERVICE, 4207 Lawnview Ave. Tel.: (214) 388-1550

Houston

SOUTHWESTERN THEATRE EQUIPMENT, 1702 Rusk Ave. Tel.: (713) 222-9461

San Antonio

INDEPENDENT THEATRE SUPPLY, 2750 E. Houston
TEXAS THEATRE SUPPLY, 915 S. Alamo St. 78205. Tel.: (214) 222-1002

UTAH
Salt Lake City

L&S SUPPLY CO., 214 E. First South St. Tel.: (801) 328-1641. Herb Schoenhardt, mgr
PETERSON THEATRE SUPPLY, 19 E. 2nd South, Tel.: (801) 822-3685
UNIVERSAL THEATRE SUPPLY, 264 East First South St., Tel.: (801) 328-1641

VIRGINIA
Roanoke

PERDUE MOTION PICTURES EQUIPMENT, INC., 2315 Williamson Rd., N.E. Tel.: (703) 366-0295

WASHINGTON
Seattle

ALTEC SERVICE CORP., White Henry Stuart Bldg. MA 3-8221
AMERICAN GENERAL SUPPLY CO., INC., 2300 1st Avenue. MA 4-4572
BERESFORD, CHAS. H. INC., 308 W. Republican. AT 4-6658
BROCKLIND'S INC., 901 Olive Way. MU 2-5898
BURNS, S.F. & CO., INC., 2319 2nd. (206) 624-2515
CHAMPION CRAFT & COSTUME SUPPLY, 216 Stewart. MA 3-1925
DISPLAY & STAGE LIGHTING INC., 2410 1st
FACTORY DIRECT DRAPERIES INC., 8300 Aurora N. LA 5-7932
FAIRBANKS HARLAN CO., 1405 Elliott W. 284-7420
GIBSON SOUND & LIGHT CO., 501 N. 36th
J. SCHLEIS THEATRICAL & DISPLAY SERVICES CO., 123 Belmont E. EA 2-1478
NATIONAL SCREEN SERVICE CORP., 2413 2nd Ave. (201) 265-2700
NATIONAL THEATRE SUPPLY CO., 2413 2nd Ave. 98121. (206) 624-7710
SLATER, W.A. CO., 2323 2nd. MU 2-0154
STAGECRAFT INDUSTRIES, 10237 Main, Bellevue. GL 4-3089

WEST VIRGINIA
Charleston

CHARLESTON THEATRE SUPPLY, 506 Lee St
MOORE THEATRE EQUIPMENT, 213 Delaware Ave., P.O. Box 782, Tel.: (304) 344-4413

WISCONSIN
Milwaukee

HARRY MELCHER ENTERPRISES, 3607 W. Fond Du Lac Ave. Tel.: (414) 442-5020

CANADA
Calgary

GENERAL SOUND & THEATRE EQUIPMENT, LTD., 6812-C 6th St. S.W. Calgary T2H 2K4. (403) 252-3773.

Montreal

GENERAL SOUND & THEATRE EQUIPMENT, LTD., 5887 Monkland Ave., H4A 1G6 (514) 589-5331

St. John, N.B.

GENERAL SOUND & THEATRE EQUIPMENT, LTD., 55 Bentley St., E2K 1B2 (506) 693-2819

Vancouver

GENERAL SOUND & THEATRE EQUIPMENT, LTD., 2182 W. 12th St., Vancouver B.C. V6K-2N4 (604) 736-5506

Winnipeg

GENERAL SOUND & THEATRE EQUIPMENT, LTD., 430 Kensington St., Winnipeg, Man. R3J 1J7 (204) 888-7543

British-Based Equipment/Services

ACMADE INTERNATIONAL
Oakside Oxford Road, Uxbridge, Mddx. UB9 4DX (89-36313) Telex: 8954606.

AEG-TELEFUNKEN (UK) LTD.
217 Bath Road, Slough, Berks. SL1 4AW (2-872101)

AGFA-GEVAERT LTD.
Great West Road, Brentford, Middx: (OL 560 2131)

AKG ACOUSTICS LTD.
191 The Vale, London, W3 7QS (01 749 2042)

ALLOTROPE LTD.
36/38 Lexington Street, London, W1R 3HR (01 437 1892) Telex: 21624 ALO FFD

AMPEX INTERNATIONAL
Acre Road, Reading, Berks, (0734 85200)

ANIMATION EQUIPMENT ENGINEERING LTD.
Wembley Commercial Centre, Unit 17, East Lane, Wembley, Middx. (01-904 0611)

ASCOTTS VIDEO
3 Soho Square, London, W.1. (01-734 2116)

ASTON ELECTRONIC DEVELOPMENTS LIMITED
125 Deepcut Bridge Road, Deepcut, Camberley, Surrey (02516 6221)

AUDIX LTD.
Station Road, Wenden, Saffron Walden, Essex.

AV DISTRIBUTORS (LONDON) LTD.
26 Park Road, London NW1 4SH (01-935 8161)

BALLANCROFT FILM & TV EQUIPMENT CO, LTD.
292 Worton Road, Isleworth, Middlesex, (01-560 494)

F.W.O. BAUCH LTD.
49 Theobald Street, Boreham Wood, Herts. (01-953 0091)

BELL & HOWELL LTD.
Alperton House, Bridgewater Road, Wembley, Middlesex HAO 1EG (01-902 8812)

BERKEY COLORTRAN (UK) LTD.
P.O. Box 5, Burrell Way, Thetford, Norfolk (0842-2484)

ROBERT BOSCH LTD.
PO Box 166, Rhodes Way, Watford.

BRABURY ELECTRONICS LTD.
119a Loverock Road, Reading, Berks RG3 1MS.

BOSTON INSULATED WIRE (UK) LTD.
1 Canbury Park Road, Kingston-upon-Thames, Surrey.

BRITISH FILMS LTD.
Carlyle House, 235 Vauxhall Bridge Road, London, SW1V 1EJ. (01 828 7965)

CANDA TELEVISION EQUIPMENT LTD.
5 Hanover Trading Estate, 1 North Road, London, N7 9HD. (01-607 9961) Telex: 28604 Mono Ref. 477 LDN

CINEFOCUS RENTALS
1 Pavilion Parade, Wood Lane, London, W12 0HQ. (01-743 2552)

CINTRON GROUP
Grove House, 551 London Road, Isleworth, Middlesex TW7 4DS (01-568 0131) Telex: 935054

DOEL ENGINEERING LTD.
Station Road, Hatfield Peverel, Chelmsford, Essex CM3 2DX (0245 380151) Telex: 987562 COCHAC.

DOLBY LABORATORIES INC.
346 Clapham Road, London SW9 9AP (01-720 1111).

EDRIC AUDIO VISUAL LTD.
34-36 Oak End Way, Gerrards Cross, Bucks. SL9 8BR (02813 84646 and 86521)

ELECTROSONIC LTD.
815 Woolwich Road, London, SE7 8LT (01 855 1101)

ELF AUDIO VISUAL LTD.
836 Yeovil Road, Trading Estate, Slough, Berks. (75-36123)

ENGLISH ELECTRIC VALVE COMPANY LIMITED
Chelmsford, Essex CM1 2QU, (0245 61777)

EUMIG (UK) LTD.
14 Priestley Way, Eldon Wall Trading Estate, London NW2 7TN (01-450 8070)

EVERSHED POWER-OPTICS LTD.
Bridge Wharf, Bridge Road, Chertsey, Surrey KT16 8LJ (09328-61181)

FILM FACILITIES (MAGNETIC).
3 Springbridge Mews, Springbridge Road, Ealing Broadway, London, W5 2AB (01-567 3613/4)

FUJI PHOTO FILM (UK) LTD.
99 Baker Street, London, W1R 3HR (01-487 5711)

FUTURE FILM DEVELOPMENTS
36-38 Lexington Street, London W1R 3HR. (01-437 1892) Telex: 21624 ALO FED

GEC (LAMPS AND LIGHTING) LTD.
PO Box 17, East Lane, Wembley, Middlesex HA9 7PG (01-904 4321).

GORDON AUDIO VISUAL LTD.
28 Market Place, Oxford Circus, London W1N 8PH (01-580 9191)

HARKNESS SCREENS LTD.
The Gate Studios, Station Road, Boreham Wood, Herts. (01-953 3611)

HAYDEN LABORATORIES LTD.
Hayden House, Chiltern Hill, Chalfont St. Peter Gernards Cross, Bucks. SL9 9EW. (02813-88447)

HEYDEN AND SONS LTD.
Spectrum House, Hillview Gardens, London NW4 (01 2035171)

HEYDEN-KEM ELECTRONIC MECHANISMS LTD.
24 Vivian Avenue, London NW4 3XP (01-202 0244)

INDEPENDENT CAMERA AND EQUIPMENT CO. LTD.
60 Farringdon Road, London EC1R 3BP. (01-251 3885)

INTERNATIONAL VIDEO CORPORATION (UK) LTD.
10 Portman Road, Reading, Berks., RG3 IJR, (0734 585421)

KADEK VISION
P.O. No. 21, Shepperton Studio Centre, Studios Road, Shepperton, Middx. TW17 0QD. (093 2866941)

JOHN KING FILMS, LTD.
FILM HOUSE, 71 East Street, Brighton BN1 1NZ. Brighton 202671)

KODAK LTD.
P.O. Box 66, Kodak House, Station Road, Hemel Hempstead, Herts. (0442-62331)

LEE ENTERPRISES LTD.
128 Wembley Park Drive, Wembley, Mddx. (01-969 9521)

LEE FILTERS LTD.
Walworth Industrial Estae, Andover, Hants. SP10 5AN (0264-66245)

LIPSNER-SMITH CO. LTD.
Unit 7, Cowley Mill Trading Estate, Longbridge Way, Uxbridge, Middx: (89 52191)

3M UNITED KINGDOM LTD.
3M HOUSE, P.O. Box 1, Bracknell, Berks. RG12 1JU (0344 26726)

MARCONI COMMUNICATION SYSTEMS LTD.
Marconi House, New Street, Chelmsford, Essex CM1 1PL. (0245 53221)

NEILSON-HORDELL LTD.
Central Trading Estate, Staines, Middlesex (81-56456)

NEVE ELECTRONICS INTERNATIONAL
Cambridge House Melbourn, Nr. Royston, Herts: SG8 6AU (0763 60776)

OPTICAL & TEXTILE LTD.
Barnet Trading Estate, Park Road, High Barnet, Herts. (01-442 2199) Telex: 8955869.

OSRAM (GEC) LTD.
P.O. Box 17, East Lane, Wembley, Middx. HA9 7PG. (01-904 4321)

JOHN PAGE LTD.
Wesley House, 75 Wesley Avenue, London, N.W. 10. (01 961 4181)

P.A.G. FILMS LTD., & P.A.G. POWER LTD.
565 Kingston Road, London SW20 85A (01-543 3131)

PHOTOGRAPHIC ELECTRICAL CO. LTD.
71 Dean Street, London W1V 6DE. (01-437 4633)

PHOTOMEC (LONDON) LTD.
(Humphries Group) Valley Road Industrial Estate, St. Albans, AL3 6NU, Herts. (56 50711).

PYE TVT LTD.
(The Broadcasting Company of Phillips) PO Box 41, Coldhams Lane, Cambridge, CB1 3JU, (0223 45115)

RANK AUDIO VISUAL
P.O. Box 70, Great West Road, Brentford, Middlesex TW8 9HR (01-568 9222)

RANK CINTEL
Watton Road, Ware, Hertfordshire, (0920 3939)

RANK FILM LABORATORIES LTD.
North Orbital Road, Denham, Uxbridge, Middlesex UB9 5HQ (01-332 2323)

RANK STRAND STUDIO DIVISION
P.O. Box 54, Great WEst Road, Brentford, Middx. TW8 9HR. (01-568 9222)

RANK TAYLOR HOBSON
P.O. Box 36, Guthlaxton Street, Leicester LE2 OSP (Leicester 23801)

RANK PHICOM VIDEO GROUP
Film House, 142 Wardour Street, London W1V 4BU (01-734 2235-9) Telex: 261237

RCA INTERNATIONAL LTD.
Lincoln Way, Windmill Road, Sunbury-on-Thames, Middx: (76 85511)

ROBERT RIGBY LTD.
Premier Works, Northington Street, London WC1N 2JN (01-405 2944)

SAMCINE SALES LTD.
303 Cricklewood Broadway, London NW2 6PQ (01-450-4557)

SAMUELSON FILM SERVICE LTD.
303-315 Cricklewood Broadway, London NW2 6PQ. (01-452 8090)

SAMUELSON SIGHT & SOUND LTD.
303-315 Cricklewood Broadway, London NW2 6PQ (01-452 8090)

SCREEN ELECTRONICS LTD.
19 Anson Road, Martlesham Heath, Nr. Ipswich, Suffolk. (0473 623748) Telex 988732.

SHURE ELECTRONICS LTD.
Eccleston Road, Maidstone, Kent, ME15 6AU (0622 59881)

SONY BROADCAST LTD.
City Wall House, Basing View, Basingstoke, Hants. RG21 2LA (0256 55011)

TELEVISION INTERNATIONAL OPERATIONS LTD.
9-11 Windmill Street, London W1P 1HF (01-637 2477)

THOMSON-CSF ELECTRONIC TUBES LTD.
Ringway House, Bell Road, Daneshill, Basingstoke.

THORN EMI LTD.
Thorn House, Upper St Martin's Lane, London WC2H 9ED (01-836 2444)

VALIANT ELECTRICAL WHOLESALE CO
20 Lettice Street, Fulham, London SW6 (01-736 8115)

W. VINTEN LTD.
Western Way, Bury St. Edmunds, Suffolk IP33 3TB. (0284-2121)

WESTREX COMPANY LTD.
Bilton Fairway Estate, Long Drive, Greenford, Middx. (01-578 0950)

Government Film Bureaus

DEPARTMENT OF AGRICULTURE:

Motion Picture Division, Room 1614 South Bldg., 14th & Independence Ave., S.W., Washington, DC 20250; 447-6072; V. Buddy Renfro, Chief, Motion Picture Division.

This office produces motion pictures designed to aid in dissemination of information on the needs for agricultural products, their production, distribution, utilization and research concerning them. The films demonstrate improved methods in agriculture, stress the need for conservation of soil and other resources, explain the farm credit system, forestry, marketing, and similar subjects.

DEPARTMENT OF COMMERCE:

Bureau of Domestic Commerce, Consumer Goods and Services Division, 14th and E. Streets, N.W., Washington, DC 20230; 967-3793. SOL PADWO, Director.

This division studies and reports statistics of the industry at home and abroad. The material gathered is published in department reports and is used with information from other industries to help fulfill the function of "representing business to the government and the Government to business."

DEPARTMENT OF DEFENSE

The Pentagon Building, Washington, DC 20301.

Assistant Secretary for Public Affairs, Thomas B. Ross.

Audiovisual Division. Chief, Norman T. Hatch, 2E773, OX 7-4162. This Division is responsible for dissemination to the public through radio, television, still photos, motion pictures, and magazines and books information regarding the activities, aims and accomplished purposes of the Department of Defense (includes Army, Navy, Marine Corps, and Air Force). It also is the primary point of contact in the Department of Defense for approval of assistance to the aforementioned media on Department of Defense activities.

Audio-Visual Documentary Branch. Chief, Russell Wagner, 2E773, OX 5-0168. Acts on all requests for Department of Defense assistance from any segment of the motion picture and television industry concerned with documentary productions. Also includes television commercials and participation of armed forces personnel, bands and musical groups on TV variety programs.

Audio-Visual Production Branch. Chief, Donald E. Baruch, 2E773, OX 7-4596. Acts on all requests for Department of Defense assistance from any segment of the motion picture and television industry concerned with dramatic productions.

Audio-Visual Acquisitions Branch. Chief, Maj. Peter Friend, 2E773, OX 7-6161. Obtains and releases Department of Defense still and motion picture film to news and other media outlets. Arranges technical aspects of news conferences and media coverage at Pentagon.

ARMY AND AIR FORCE EXCHANGE SERVICE MOTION PICTURE DIVISION

(Under Board of Directors, Army & Air Force Exchange Service)
Main Office: HQ Army & Air Force Exchange Service, 3911 S. Walton Walker Blvd. (mail address: Dallas, TX 75222 (214) 330-2622, R. L. Herdeman, director; W. R. Wood, Film Procurement Branch.

DEPARTMENT OF HEALTH EDUCATION AND WELFARE:

330 Independence Avenue, S.W., Washington, DC 20201. (202) 245-6296.

Information Office: 963-4568. Sanford H. Winston, director; York Onnen, asst. director; Harry Bell, dir., (Audio Visual Services), 963-5319.

Health Services & Mental Health Administration: Dr. Vernon E. Wilson, administrator: Edward J. McVeigh, Director of Information; 443-2086.

HS and MHA produces and distributes film, audio and video tape, and multi-media materials on problems of mental and physical health by a combination of contract and in-house facilities.

National Institute of Health: Dr. Robert S. Stone, Director; Storm Whaley, Associate Director for Communications, 496-4461.

NIH's Audio Visual facilities are responsible for the production and distribution of motion pictures, slides and other materials depicting biomedical research and its implications.

Environmental Protection Agency: William D. Ruckelaus, administrator, 755-2700; Thomas Hart, dir. of public affairs, 755-2700; Luke C. Hestor, films, 443-4804.

EPA produces films on the environment and information lists for the public.

SOCIAL SECURITY ADMINISTRATION:

James B. Cardwell, Commissioner; Russell R. Jalbert, asst. commr., Public Affairs (301) 594-1990; Robert Fenwick, Audio Visual Staff Chief, 944-5587.

SSA produces and distributes films for use throughout the country describing social security and its benefits.

SOCIAL AND REHABILITATION SERVICE:

James S. Dwight, Administrator; Robert A. Wilson, Director of Public Affairs, 962-4655.

SRS produces and distributes films on a wide variety of subjects, such as social welfare services, Medicaid, rehabilitation, juvenile delinquency and related topics.

OFFICE OF EDUCATION:

Terrel H. Bell, commissioner; Melinda Vpp, chief, office of public affairs, 254-5800.

Audio-Visual division: The Office of Public affairs is responsible for clearance and monitoring of all motion picture and other audiovisual materials generated by OE contracts with, or grants to companies or non-profit organizations and Institutions. Distribution of these materials is made through the National Audio-Visual Center (located at the National Archives and Records Services) or by special arrangements with producers. Public use of OE audiovisual materials is approved by the HEW Office of Public Affairs.

Caption films division: Malcolm Norwood, asst. chief, 963-5230.

This division purchases already produced films and captions them for use by the deaf.

DEPARTMENT OF THE INTERIOR

Bureau of Mines, Motion Picture Booking Section, 4800 Forbes Ave., Pittsburgh, Pa. 15213; Tel.: 412-621-4500. This is the main distributing center; however copies of some films are deposited at cooperating educational film distribution centers throughout the country.

The Bureau maintains a library of motion pictures depicting mining and metallurgical operations and related manufacturing processes. They are loaned free of charge, except for return postage (book rate) to educational institutions, industries, training workers, engineering, and scientific societies, civic and business associations, and other responsible organizations. The cost of production is paid by co-operating industrial concerns but the pictures do not carry trademarks, trade names or other direct advertising materials. Dr. A. Nicholas Vardac (202-634-1003), officer in charge Bureau of Mines Audio-Visual Programs, Washington, is in charge of production.

DEPARTMENT OF JUSTICE:

Constitution Avenue and 10th Street, N.W., Washington, DC 20530. William Smith, Attorney General; Terence B. Adamson, Director of Public Information; 739-2014.

SMITHSONIAN INSTITUTION:

Washington, DC 20560; 628-4422.
S. Dillon Ripley, secretary; Nazaret Cherkezian, Telecommunications coordinator, 381-2414.
Coordinates production on all motion picture and TV filming.

DEPARTMENT OF STATE:

21st Stret and Virginia Avenue, Washington, D.C. 20530. Alexander Haig, Secretary of State.

OFFICE OF MEDIA SERVICES:

Paul E. Auerswald, director, 632-2083. Provides State Department assistance on film and TV production. Produces an average of one film a year on foreign policy subjects and distributes them for public service TV and classroom use.

OFFICE OF INTERNATIONAL TRADE:

Dept. of State; 632-2534.
(Concerned with commercial aspects of film industry, trade treaties, quotas, restrictions etc.)

EXECUTIVE AGENCIES

FEDERAL COMMUNICATIONS COMMISSION:

1919 M St., N.W., Washington, D.C. 20554—Charles R. Ferris,

Chairman; Samuel M. Sharkey Jr., Public Information Officer. (202) 632-7260.

Charged with regulating interstate and foreign communications including radio, television, satellite, cable and wire services. Licenses all standard, FM, and television broadcasting stations and services.

FEDERAL TRADE COMMISSION:

Sixth Street and Pennsylvania Avenue, N.W., Washington, D.C. 20580—Michael Pertschuk, chairman; Theodore O. Cron, director of information. 523-3625.

Administers statutes designed to promote fair competition; institutes proceeding to prevent unfair or deceptive practices, combinations in restraint of trade, false advertising, and illegal price discrimination. Supervises associations of exporters under the Export Trade Act.

SECURITIES AND EXCHANGE COMMISSION:

500 N. Capital St., Washington, D.C. 20549; Harold M. Williams, chairman; George A. Fitzsimmons. Secretary (information), 755-1160.

Registers security offerings and supervises exchange trading in securities.

U.S. INFORMATION AGENCY:

1750 Pennsylvania Avenue, N.W., Washington, D.C. 20547—John E. Reinhardt, director. (202) 724-9042.

Motion Picture and Television Service: 376-7806. McKinney Russell, assistant director; Stanley Moss, deputy assistant director. Certifies exemption of import duties if film is educational in nature.

USIA produces and acquires about 200 film and television documentaries annually for information and cultural programs in 117 countries. In addition, close to 350 targeted, and 150 worldwide new clips are made for use on foreign television. These are seen abroad in commercial theatres, in television, in schools and community centers, and by clubs, universities, and other audiences.

LIBRARY OF CONGRESS

10 First Street, S.E., Washingtin, D.C. 20540. 202-426-5000. Daniel J. Boorstin, Librarian of Congress; Mrs. Mary C. Lethbridge, Information Officer, 202-426-5108.

This agency serves as the national library and includes the U.S. Copyright Office as one of its departments. In addition to registering films for copyright and publishing a record of copyright registrations, the Library catalogs motion pictures and filmstrips, publishes printed catalog cards, book catalogs and machine-readable tapes for such materials, collects current film selectively, maintains an extensive archive of motion pictures from 1894 to date, and provides related bibliographic services.

Copyright Office—Barbara Ringer, Register of Copyrights.

Robert D. Stevens, Chief of the Copyright Cataloging Division, 703-557-8715, supervises the preparation of the semi-annual *Catalog of copyright Entries: Motion Pictures and Filmstrips,* which is distributed by the Superintendent of Documents, Government Printing Office, Washington, D.C. 20402. This publication contains descriptive data for all theatrical and nontheatrical pictures registered for copyright during each 6-month period and includes renewal registrations.

Processing Department—Joseph H. Howard, Director.

Vivian L. Schrader, Head of the Audiovisual Section of the Descriptive Cataloging Division, 202-426-5238, supervises the cataloging of approximately 5,000 motion pictures, filmstrips, and sets of slides and transparencies a year, largely on the basis of information supplied by producers and media libraries.

Research Department—Alan Fern, Director.

Motion Picture Section in the Prints and Photographs Division, 202-426-5840, which has custody of the Library's collection of over 60,000 motion pictures. The collection is primarily an archive. It contains educational, scientific, religious, industrial, and documentary films, as well as newsreels and features. Chiefly American, it includes German, Italian, and Japanese films, and in it are historically important films preserved by the Library from the early days of the motion-picture industry. Since 1942, about 1,500 representative titles a year have been retained.

Distributors of 16mm Feature Films

Following is a listing of distributors having substantial selections of 16mm films for lease or rental. Additionally, some of the companies may have prints available for outright purchase. Inquiries for catalogs listing complete product should be made to the addresses given below.

AUDIO BRANDON FILMS, INC.
34 MacQuesten Parkway South, Mt. Vernon, NY 10550.

AVCO EMBASSY PICTURES CORP.
300 East 42nd St., New York, NY 10017.

BENCHMARK FILMS
145 Scarborough Road, Briarcliff Manor, NY 10510.

BLACKHAWK FILMS
The Eastin-Phelan Corp., Davenport, IA 52808.

BUDGET FILMS
4590 Santa Monica Boulevard, Los Angeles, CA 90029.

CAROUSEL FILMS
1501 Broadway, New York, NY 10036.

CINEMA 5
1500 Broadway, New York, NY 10036.

COLUMBIA PICTURES
711 Fifth Avenue, New York, NY 10022.

CONTINENTAL 16
241 East 34th Street, New York, NY 10016.

CORINTH FILMS
410 East 62nd St., New York, NY 10021.

DISNEY PRODUCTIONS
500 South Buena Vista St., Burbank, CA 91521.

FILM CLASSIC EXCHANGE
1914 S. Vermont Avenue, Los Angeles, CA 90007.

FILM-MAKERS COOPERATIVE
175 Lexington Avenue, New York, NY 10016.

FILMS INCORPORATED
1144 Wilmette Ave., Wilmette, IL 60091.

GROVE PRESS, INC. FILM DIVISION
196 West Houston, New York, NY 10014.

HISTORICAL FILMS
Box 46505, Hollywood, CA 90046.

HURLOCK CINE-WORLD, INC.
13 Arcadia Rd., Old Greenwich, CT 06870.

INSTITUTIONAL CINEMA, INC.
10 First, Saugerties, NY

JANUS FILMS
745 Fifth Avenue, New York, NY 10022.

LEACOCK-PENNEBAKER
56 West 45th Street, New York, NY 10036.

MOVIE WONDERLAND
6116 Glen Tower, Hollywood, CA 90028.

MUSEUM OF MODERN ART FILM LIBRARY
11 West 53rd STreet, New York, NY 10019.

NATIONAL CINEMA SERVICE
333 West 57th Street, New York, NY 10019.

NEW LINE CINEMA
853 Broadway, New York, NY 10003.

NEW YORKER FILMS
16 West 61st St., New York, NY 10023.

OPERA PRESENTATIONS, INC.
75 Maiden Lane, New York, NY 10038.

PARAMOUNT NON-THEATRICAL
5451 Marathon St., Hollywood, CA 90038.

PAULIST PRODUCTIONS
P.O. Box 1057, Pacific Palisades, CA 90272.

PYRAMID FILMS
2801 Colorado Ave., Santa Monica, CA 90404.

RADIM FILMS, INC.
1034 Lake St., Oak Park, IL 60301.

ROA'S FILMS
1696 No. Astor Street, Milwaukee, Wisc. 53202.

SELECT FILM LIBRARY
115 West 31st St., New York, NY 10001.

STANDARD FILM SERVICE
14710 W. Warren Avenue, Dearborn, MI 48120.

SWANK MOTION PICTURES
201 S. Jefferson Ave., St. Louis, MO 63166.

"THE" FILM CENTER
915 12th Street N.W., Washington, D.C. 20005.

TRANS-WORLD FILMS
332 S. Michigan Ave., Chicago, IL 60604.

TWYMAN FILMS, INC.
Box 605, Dayton, OH 45401.

UNIFILM
419 Park Avenue South, New York, NY 10016.

UNITED ARTISTS FILM RENTALS
729 Seventh Avenue, New York, NY 10019.

UNITED FILMS, INC.
1122 South Cheyenne, Tulsa, OK 74119.

WARNER BROS., INC.
Non-Theatrical Division, 75 Rockefeller Plaza, New York, NY 10019.

Corporations

* **STRUCTURE**

* **ORGANIZATION**

* **EXECUTIVE PERSONNEL**

Motion Picture Corporations

See also, Index: Distributors of 16mm Feature Films, Non-Theatrical Motion Pictures, Services. See membership of Association of Motion Picture and Television Producers, Inc. in Organization Section.

ABC Pictures International, Inc.

1330 Avenue of the Americas, New York, NY 10019. (212) 581-7777. West Coast office: 2040 Ave. of Stars, Century City, CA 90067. (213) 553-2000. (International distribution of motion pictures and films for TV). A subsidiary of American Broadcasting Companies, Inc.
VICE PRESIDENT, WORLD WIDE SALES & DISTRIBUTION
S. Arthur Schimmel (Century City)
DIRECTOR, FINANCE AND PLANNING
Robert W. Wang (New York)
DATE OF ORGANIZATION
1968

ATA Trading Corp.

505 Eighth Ave., New York, NY 10018 (212) 594-6460. (Film and video, foreign and domestic, distribution and production of features, shorts, series documentaries)
PRESIDENT
Harold G. Lewis
VICE PRESIDENT
Susan Lewis
SECRETARY
Rita Stone

Abbey Theatrical Films

9399 Wilshire Blvd., Beverly Hills, CA 90210. (213) 274-8646. (Motion picture distribution)
PRESIDENT
Nicholas Wowchuk
EXECUTIVE VICE PRESIDENT
Harry Wowchuk
FINANCIAL VICE PRESIDENT
Wallace Davidson
GENERAL MANAGER
Miles Holman
SECRETARY/TREASURER
Dorothy Ringer
SALES MANAGER
Harry Stern

Academy International Distributors, Inc.

9424 Dayton Way, Beverly Hills, CA 90210 (213) 274-4141. (Producer and Distributor)
PRESIDENT & CHIEF OPERATING OFFICER
Kenneth Hartford
CHAIRMAN OF THE BOARD
Clifford A. Jones
VICE PRESIDENT & CONTROLLER
Harold Neiman
VICE PRESIDENT IN CHARGE OF PRODUCTION
Alessandro Tasca
GENERAL SALES MANAGER, DOMESTIC
Murray Kaplan
GENERAL SALES MANAGER, FOREIGN
Maurice Braun
DIRECTOR OF MERCHANDISING
Jerry O'Farrell
PUBLICITY
Bud Testa
PUBLIC RELATIONS
Jeanette Linne

Afrasian Films

145 West 96th Street, Suite "A" New York, NY 10025. (201) 783-5934. (Producers of film & video tape productions specializing in films about India and Pakistan. Complete film crews available.)
PRODUCER
Amin Chaudhri
ASSOCIATE PRODUCER
David Hemming
PRODUCTION MANAGER
Bert Saltzman

The Aldrich Company

606 North Larchmont Blvd., Los Angeles, CA 90004. (213) 462-6511. (Motion picture producers.)
PRESIDENT
William Aldrich
DATE OF ORGANIZATION
1973

American Cinema Group

1104 Camina Del Mar, Del Mar, CA 92014. Tel.: (714) 481-1206. (Motion picture financing.)
PRESIDENT
Andrew D. T. Pfeffer
DATE OF ORGANIZATION
1976

American Cinema, Inc.

555 East Fourth South, Salt Lake City, UT 84102. (801) 521-8161. (Production and distribution.)
PRESIDENT
Jerrold R. Morgan
EXECUTIVE VICE PRESIDENT IN CHARGE OF WORLD-WIDE MARKETING
Richard Lederer

American Communications Industries

1104 Camino Del Mar, Del Mar, CA 92014 (714) 481-1206 (Motion picture production, distribution and sales) (Parent company of American Cinema Productions & American Cinema Releasing)
CHAIRMAN AND CHIEF EXECUTIVE OFFICER
Michael F. Leone
CHAIRMAN AND CHIEF OPERATING OFFICER
Joy Shelton Davis
EXECUTIVE VICE PRESIDENT
Norman B. Katz

AMERICAN CIMEMA PRODUCTIONS

1104 Camino Del Mar, Del Mar, CA 92014 (714) 481-1266. (Motion picture production.)
CHAIRMAN AND CHIEF EXECUTIVE OFFICER
Norman B. Katz

AMERICAN CINEMA RELEASING

Chesterfield Dr., Cardiff by the Sea, CA 92007 (714) 431-6622 (Motion picture distribution.)

PRESIDENT AND CHIEF EXECUTIVE OFFICER
Norman B. Katz

American-European Films, Inc.

321 West 44th Street, New York, NY 10036. (212) 582-7025. Telex: 427900 AMFILM. (Motion picture sales agents and representatives. Offices in New York, Paris, Madrid; representatives in London, Los Angeles.)

American Films, Ltd.

4265 Marina City Drive, Suite 501, West Tower North, Marina del Ray, CA 90291 (213) 822-9966. (Distributor.)
PRESIDENT
Al Landry
VICE PRESIDENT/DISTRIBUTION
Ray Axelrod

American National Enterprises, Inc.

106 West 2950 South, Salt Lake City, UT 84115. (801) 486-3155. (Motion picture production and distribution). Affiliations with other organizations: Advertising & Research International, Inc.; Rainbow Adventures, Inc.
PRESIDENT AND CHAIRMAN OF THE BOARD
R. V. Coalson
SECRETARY
Marvin Friedland
BOARD OF DIRECTORS
R. V. Coalson, Marvin Friedland, William R. Barrett
VICE PRESIDENT OF BUSINESS AFFAIRS
Beth Zimmerman
VICE PRESIDENT OF SALES & MARKETING
Charles D. King
DATE OF ORGANIZATION
1965

American Video-Cinema, Inc.

Suite 1305, Park Central III, Dallas, TX 75251. (Producer of motion pictures for theatres and television.)
PRESIDENT
Cal Habern
MARKETING VICE PRESIDENT
Allan W. Newberry, Jr.
DATE OF ORGANIZATION
1973

Analysis Film Releasing Corp.

225 West 57th St., Suite 301, New York, NY 10019. (212) 765-8734. (Motion picture distribution.)
PRESIDENT
Paul "Eagle" Cohen
VICE PRESIDENT
Robert J. Kaplan
TREASURER
Paul Leeman
DATE OF ORGANIZATION
1978

April Fools Productions, Inc.

Films Arts Bldg., 636 Northland Blvd., Cincinnati, OH 45250. (513) 851-5700. Also operates April Fools Distributing, Inc.
PRESIDENT
Phil Borack

Aquarius Releasing Inc.

Selwyn Theatre Building, Inc., 229 West 42nd St., Suite 301, New York, NY 10019 (212) 787-6208. (Distribution—U.S.A. & Canada. Foreign—exhibition, production, producers' representative, live concerts.)
CHIEF EXECUTIVE OFFICER
Terry Levene
SECRETARY-TREASURER
Ron Harvey
NEW YORK BRANCH MANAGER
Laura G. Milado
SUBSIDIARIES
Aquarius Promotions, Ltd.
Aquarius Suburban Theatres Inc.

Archive Film Productions

530 West 25th St., New York, NY 10001 (212) 620-3955. (Film production and distribution; stock shot library.)
PRESIDENT
Patrick Montgomery
DATE OF ORGANIZATION
1979

Arista Films, Inc.

9000 Sunset Blvd., Los Angeles, CA 90069 (213) 550-0780. (Motion picture distribution.)
PRESIDENT
Louis George
SECRETARY/TREASURER
Niki George
DATE OF ORGANIZATION
1974

Ark Film, Inc.

905 North St., Jacksonville, FL 32211 (904) 725-0223. (Distributor)
PRESIDENT
Harry Clark
VICE PRESIDENT
Belton Clark
NATIONAL PRINT CONTROLLER
Diane McClanahan
INTERNATIONAL SALES
Willie Tan

Army Public Affairs

Los Angeles Branch: 11000 Wilshire Blvd., Rm. 10104, Los Angeles, CA 90024 (213) 824-7621. (Technical advisors for West Coast entertainment industry; emphasis on motion picture and TV industries)
CHIEF OF PUBLIC AFFAIRS
Colonel Bruce Gard
LIEUTENANT COLONEL
Dave Wagner
SERGEANT MAJOR
Marv Sibulkin
PUBLIC INFORMATION OFFICER
Carolyn Trotter

Artists Entertainment Complex, Inc.

641 Lexington Ave., New York, NY (212) 421-3760. (Career management and motion picture production.)
EXECUTIVE VICE PRESIDENT
Gerald Delet
SECRETARY
Arnold Biegen
DATE OF ORGANIZATION
1970

Artscope, Ltd.

137 West 96th Street, New York, NY 10025 (212) 749-7400. (Producer & Distributor.)
PRESIDENT
Amin Qamar Chaudhri
ASSOCIATE PRODUCER
John Payne

PRODUCTION MANAGER
Curtis Capizzi
DATE OF ORGANIZATION
1964

Aspen Productions/Film Finance Group Ltd.

10100 Santa Monica Boulevard, Suite 1580 Los Angeles, CA 90067 (213) 552-9977. (Motion picture production.)
EXECUTIVE IN CHARGE OF PRODUCTION
John W. Hyde
ADMINISTRATOR
Kate Morris
PRODUCTION CONTROLLER
Connie Greenwood
DIRECTOR OF ADVERTISING AND PUBLICITY
Carole Keagy

Associated Advertising Productions, Inc.

627 Dumaine St., New Orleans, LA 70116 (504) 586-8444.
(Motion picture production.)
SECRETARY/TREASURER
Lee Brown
DATE OF ORGANIZATION
1967

Atlantic Releasing Corp.

Operational Headquarters: 9000 Sunset Blvd., #900, Los Angeles, CA 90069 (213) 859-8460. Sales & Distribution Office: 585 Boyleston St., Boston, MA 02116. (617) 266-5400. (Distributor.)
PRESIDENT
Thomas J. Coleman
VICE PRESIDENT
Michael S. Rosenblatt
NATIONAL SALES MANAGER
Ted Goldberg
COMPTROLLER
Linda Fields
HEAD BOOKER
June A. Cassidy
ASSISTANT TO PRESIDENT
Kathryn F. Galan

Audio Brandon Films, Inc.

34 MacQuestion Parkway South, Mt. Vernon, NY 10550 (914) 664-5051. (Distributor.)
DATE OF ORGANIZATION
1941

Audio Productions—Division of Reeves Communications, Inc.

277 East 45th St., N.Y., NY 10017 (212) 573-8656. (Producers of 16 and 35 industrials, public relations, educational, training sales, motion pictures.)
PRESIDENT
P. J. Mooney

Audubon Films, Inc.

313 East 74th St., New York, NY 10021 (212) 734-9344. (Producer-Distributor.)
PRESIDENT
Radley H. Metzger
VICE-PRESIDENT
Ava Leighton

Aurora Film Corporation

5190 N.W. 167th St., #107, Miami, FL 33014. (305) 620-5566. (Motion picture production and distribution.)
PRESISENT
Marvin J. Rappaport
EXECUTIVE VICE PRESIDENT
Lawrence B. Friedman
NATIONAL SALES MANAGER
S. M. Schermer
VICE PRESIDENT, SALES
M. A. Ripps
VICE PRESIDENT, OPERATIONS
Frank J. Reddish
MEDIA DIRECTOR
Dottie S. Pike
DATE OF ORGANIZATION
1979

Australian Films Office, Inc.

2049 Century Park East, Suite 2250, Los Angeles, CA 90067 (213) 277-6838.
PRESIDENT
Samuel W. Gelfman
ASSISTANT TO THE PRESIDENT
Patti O'Neil
ATTORNEYS
Kaplan, Livingston, Goodwin, Berkowitz and Selvin

Azteca Films, Inc.

555 No. La Brea Ave., Los Angeles, CA 90036 (213) 938-2413; Branches: 410 San Pedro Avenue, San Antonio, TX 78291; 1233 So. Wabash Ave., Chicago, IL 60605; 1500 Broadway, New York, NY 10036; 2147 Broadway, Denver, CO 80205. (Distributor of Mexican motion pictures.)
PRESIDENT
Jose Antonio Sepulveda
SECRETARY-TREASURER
Jacob Allame
BOARD OF DIRECTORS
Gonzalo Elvira, Jose Antonio Sepulveda, Enrique Pons, Manuel Aviña, Rafael Velez
DATE OF ORGANIZATION
1932

Avco Embassy Pictures Corp.

956 Seward Street, Los Angeles, CA 90038 (213) 460-7200; Cable: EMBAPIC Telex: 696320.
PRESIDENT
Frank Capra, Jr.
SR. VICE PRESIDENT, LEGAL & BUSINESS AFFAIRS
Peter Bierstedt
SR. VICE PRESIDENT, FINANCE
Roger Burlage
SR. VICE PRESIDENT, MARKETING
David Miller
VICE PRESIDENT, ADMINISTRATION
Nathan Chianta
VICE PRESIDENT OF FILM ACQUISITONS & MARKETING SERVICES
Leonard Shapiro
VICE PRESIDENT & GENERAL SALES MANAGER
William Shields
VICE PRESIDENT, ADVERTISING & PUBLICITY

VICE PRESIDENT, TELEVISION
Lois Luger
VICE PRESIDENT, INTERNATIONAL SALES
Herbert Fletcher
ASSISTANT GENERAL SALES MANAGER
James Sabo
NATIONAL DIRECTOR OF PUBLICITY
Edward Crane
EXECUTIVE IN CHARGE OF CREATIVE PROJECTS
Blossom Kahn
EXECUTIVE PROJECT DIRECTOR
Steve Segal
EXECUTIVE IN CHARGE OF TV PRODUCTION
Douglas McHenry
EXECUTIVE STORY EDITOR
Tom Leveque

446

CONTROLLER
Marvin Grossman
COUNSEL
Ronald Tropp
COUNSEL
Agnes Siedlecki
DIRECTOR OF LEGAL & BUSINESS AFFAIRS
Tina Pasternack
DIRECTOR OF PUBLICITY & ADVERTISING (EAST COAST)
Bernard Glaser
DIRECTOR OF CO-OP ADVERTISING & MEDIA
Roger Schaffner
DIRECTOR OF ADVERTISING
Ken Goodman
DIRECTOR OF PROMOTION & EXPLOITATION
Mel Richmond
DIRECTOR OF POST PRODUCTION-DOMESTIC OPERATION
Walter Keenan
DIRECTOR OF PAY T.V.
Arthur Silbur
DIRECTOR OF NON-THEATRICAL SALES
Walter Calmette
DIRECTOR OF PARTICIPATION & PRODUCER ACCOUNTING
Stuart Lisell
STORY EXECUTIVE—CREATIVE AFFAIRS
Lindsay Doran
HEAD THEATRICAL BOOKER
Jack Ledwith
PROJECT COORDINATOR—CREATIVE AFFAIRS
Avrumie Schnitzer
OFFICE MANAGER
Andy Petrow
PURCHASING MANAGER
Joan Tunney

AVCO EMBASSY PICTURES OVERSEAS CORP.

International Sales Department: 956 Seward Street, Los Angeles, CA 90038 (213) 460-7200; Telex: 696320; Cable: EMBAPIC.
VICE PRESIDENT IN CHARGE OF INTERNATIONAL SALES
Herb Fletcher
INTERNATIONAL SALES COORDINATOR
Richard Bedney
DIRECTOR OF INTERNATIONAL ADVERTISING & PUBLICITY
Guy Biondi
SALES SUPERVISOR FOR LATIN AMERICA & FAR EAST
Lawrence Garrett
DATE OF ORGANIZATION
December 29, 1964

DEPARTMENTS
Massimo Graziosi (Vice President, Continental, Middle East Manager and Sales Supervisor), Avco Embassy Pictures (ITALY) S.p.A., Via Sicilia No. 137, Scala A, Int. 5, 00187 Rome, Italy, Telephone: (011) (396) 475-9958 and (011) (396) 679-9575 Telex: 614013

AVCO EMBASSY PICTURES CORP.

DOMESTIC BRANCHES AND MANAGERS

ATLANTA: Emerson Center, 2812 New Spring Rd., Atlanta, GA 30339. (404) 434-1391 Robert Benefield, branch manager.
BOSTON: 509 Statler Office Bldg., Boston, MA 02116 (617) 482-3325. Marc Halperin, branch manager.
BUFFALO (Out of New York): 300 E. 42nd St., New York, NY 10017 (212) 949-8910. Marty Hollander, branch manager.
CHARLOTTE: Northwestern Bank Bldg., 230 South Tryon Street, Charlotte, NC 28202 (704) 375-9827. Donald Osley, branch manager.
CHICAGO: 190 N. State St., Suite 818, Chicago IL 60601 (312) 346-6122. Haywood Mitchusson, central division manager; Ed Schuerman, branch manager.
CINCINNATI: 35 East 7th St., Cincinnati, OH 45202 (513) 381-8480. Robert Rosen, branch manager.
CLEVELAND: Three Commerce Park Sq., 23200 Chagrin Blvd., Cleveland, OH 44122 (216) 292-3973. Gordon Bugie, branch manager.
DALLAS: 10300 N. Central Expwy., Dallas, TX 75231 (214) 739-0327. Robert Scarborough, southern division manager; Gene Haufler, branch manager.
DETROIT: 23300 Greenfield Rd., Oak Park, MI 48237 (313) 968-3350. Pat Woolcott, branch manager.
INDIANAPOLIS/MILWAUKEE (Out of Chicago): 190 N. State St., Suite 818, Chicago, IL 60601 (312) 346-6122. Virgil Jones, branch manager.
JACKSONVILLE: 101 Century 21 Dr., Jacksonville, FL 32216 (904) 721-8365. James Dixon, branch manager.
KANSAS CITY: Millcreek building, 4638 J. C. Nichols Prkwy.,

Kansas City, MO 64112 (816) 931-4526. bjerry Brethour, branch manager.
LOS ANGELES: 956 Seward St., Los Angeles, CA 90038 (213) 460-7200. Paul Ripps, Western division manager; Ross Merrin, branch manager; Alan Fine, salesman.
MINNEAPOLIS: 15 South 9th St., Minneapolis, MN 55402 (612) 339-2729. Dean Lutz, branch manager.
NEW YORK: 300 E. 42nd St., New York, NY 10017 (212) 949-8900. Mitchell Goldman, eastern division manager; Jerome Horowitz, branch manager; Arthur Marblestone, sales manager.
PHILADELPHIA: 42 S. 15th St., Suite 425, Philadelphia, PA 19102 (215) 563-8345. Tom Mihok, branch manager; Richard Leopold, salesman.
SALT LAKE CITY: 2095 Douglas St., Salt Lake City, UT 84015 (801) 487-4700/4709. Lyle Livsey, branch manager.
SAN FRANCISCO: 988 Market St., San Francisco, CA 94102 (415) 776-9665. Margaret Rykowski, branch manager.
WASHINGTON, D.C.: 9470 Annapolis Rd., Suite 213, Lanham, MD, 20801 (301) 577-2700. Fritz Goldschmidt, branch manager.

BCI Casting/Talent Payments

1500 Broadway, New York, NY (212) 221-1583. (Professional film and commercial casting)
CHIEF EXECUTIVE OFFICER
Paul M. Roth
PRESIDENT
Barbara Claman
EXECUTIVE VICE PRESIDENTS
Don Crossett, Larry Berkowitz
DATE OF ORGANIZATION
1977

Fred Baker Films Limited

347 West 39th St., Suite 404, New York, NY 10018 (212) 594-6100. (Motion picture distribution and production facilities rental)
PRESIDENT
Fred Baker
DATE OF ORGANIZATION
1969

Batjac Productions, Inc.

9570 Wilshire Boulevard, Suite 400, Beverly Hills, CA 90212. (213) 278-9870.
PRESIDENT
Michael A. Wayne
VICE-PRESIDENT-TREASURER & ASST. SECRETARY
Robert M. Shuman
SECRETARY & ASST. TREASURER
Thomas J. Kane

Beck, Alexander, Films, Inc.

1540 Broadway, New York, NY 10036 (212) 575-9494.
PRESIDENT
Alexander Beck
VICE PRESIDENT
S. Beck
EXECUTIVE ASSISTANT
Ellie Beck
FOREIGN
Jim Schultze
DIRECTOR OF FOREIGN OPERATIONS
Irving Weiss
CONTRACTS DEPARTMENT
Adele Schultze
LEGAL DEPARTMENT
E. J. Beck

Bedford Productions

4000 Warner Blvd, Burbank, CA 91522 (213) 954-1701. (Motion picture and TV production.)
PRESIDENT
Alan Jay Factor
VICE PRESIDENTS
David Knapp, Phyllis Factor
SECRETARY
Milton T. Raynor
TREASURER/CONTROLLER
Sid M. Lockitch
COUNSEL
Herbert Baerwitz

DATE OF ORGANIZATION
1965

Best International Films, Inc.

9200 Sunset Blvd., Los Angeles, CA 90069 (213) 550-7311. (Motion picture distribution.)
PRESIDENT
Edmond Saran
VICE PRESIDENT
Doris Rasmussen

Bless International Films

667 Madison Ave., New York, NY 10021 (212) 753-9001. (Foreign sales agent & producer's representative.)
PRESIDENT
Ivy Bless (Mrs.)
DATE OF ORGANIZATION
1977

The Blum Group

494 Tuallitan Road, Los Angeles, CA 90049, (213) 476-2229 (Production of motion pictures)
PRESIDENT
Harry N. Blum
TREASURER
Stephen L. Kadish
SECRETARY
Suzanne R. Blum
DATE OF ORGANIZATION
1973

Boardwalk Productions

5150 Wilshire Blvd., Suite 505, Los Angeles, CA 90036. (213) 938-0109. (Motion picture production.)
PRESIDENT
Robert P. Mulligan
VICE PRESIDENT
Mortimer S. Rosenthal
SECRETARY
Richard B. Kaplan
TREASURER
Joseph V. Broffman
DATE OF ORGANIZATION
1961

Nai Bonet Enterprises Ltd.

345 West 58th St., New York, NY 10019 (212) 581-8628. (Feature film producer . .)
PRESIDENT
Nai Bonet
DATE OF ORGANIZATION
1978

Bonjo Productions, Ltd.

3830 Chestnut Ave., Long Beach, CA 90807 (213) 426-3622. (Production of theatrical and TV films.)
PRESIDENT AND CHIEF EXECUTIVE OFFICER
James Bond Johnson, PHD
VICE PRESIDENT-PRODUCTION
Frank Capra, Jr.
VICE PRESIDENT-FINANCE
Joseph Price
GENERAL COUNSEL
Stuart I. Berton, Esq.
SECRETARY/TREASURER
Ruth Johnson
DATE OF ORGANIZATION
1960

Braverman Productions, Inc.

1237 Seventh St., Santa Monica, CA 90401 (213) 451-9762. (Producers of prime time specials, variety shows, commercials, documentaries, educational and corporate films, titles and special montages.)
PRESIDENT
Charles Braverman
VICE PRESIDENT & EXECUTIVE PRODUCER
Michael Roach
EDITORS
Marshall Harvey, Ted Herrmann, Dale Beldin

Joseph Brenner Associates, Inc.

570 Seventh Avenue, New York, NY 10018 (212) 354-6070. (Distributor.)
PRESIDENT
Joseph Brenner
GEN. SALES MGR.
Steven Brenner

The Brickyard Ltd., Motion Picture Arts Division

P.O. Box 1752, Salt Lake City, UT 84110. 414 West 300 North, Salt Lake City, UT 84110 (801) 363-3757. (Motion picture & television equipment sales, service, and rentals. Producers services, motion picture and television production.)
PRESIDENT & GENERAL MANAGER
Kent F. Johnson
VICE PRESIDENT
Susan D. Sandberg
VICE PRESIDENT IN CHARGE OF SALES
L. D. Johnson
DATE OF ORGANIZATION
1969

Brut Productions, Inc.

1345 Sixth Ave., New York, NY 10019. (212) 581-3114. (The entertainment arm of Faberge, Inc. engaged in production and/or financing, with distribution rights, of feature motion pictures and television-films.)
PRESIDENT
George Barrie
EXECUTIVE VICE PRESIDENTS
Stanley Federick, Alexander Yuleys
VICE PRESIDENTS
Philip Copans, Morris Lefko, Georgette Muir, Haim Eshel
SECRETARY
Stanley Frederick
TREASURER
Frederick A. Brunn
BOARD OF DIRECTORS
George Barrie, Philip Brass, Alexander Yuelys, Stanley Frederick
DATE OF ORGANIZATION
1971

The Bryna Company

141 El Camino Dr., Beverly Hills, CA 90212 (213) 274-5294.
PRESIDENT
Kirk Douglas
DATE OF ORGANIZATION
1958

Buena Vista Distribution Co., Inc.

350 South Buena Vista Street, Burbank, CA 91521 (213) 841-1000. (A subsidiary of Walt Disney Productions.)
PRESIDENT & GENERAL SALES MANAGER
Charles E. Good
ASSISTANT TO GENERAL SALES MANAGER
Richard Cook

Buena Vista International, Inc.

350 South Buena Vista Street, Burbank, CA 91521 (213) 850-5414.

PRESIDENT
Harold P. Archinal
VICE PRESIDENT/FINANCIAL ADMINISTRATION AND
TREASURER
Donald A. Escen
VICE PRESIDENTS
Barton K. Boyd, Ivan Genit, Vincent H. Jefferds, James P. Ji-
mirro, Ronald W. Miller, Roland A. Pierce, Gustave A. Zelnick
SECRETARY
Doris A. Smith
TREASURER
Donald A. Escen
DIRECTORS
Harold P. Archinal, Donald A. Escen, Vincent H. Jefferds, Don-
ald R. Sterry, Gustave A. Zelnick

Burbank International Pictures Corp.

3412 West Olive Ave., Burbank, CA 91505 (213) 846-
8441. (Motion picture distribution.)
PRESIDENT
Raphael Nussbaum
VICE PRESIDENT & TREASURER
Shirley Huetfel
SECRETARY
Jutta Nussbaum
DATE OF ORGANIZATION
1975

The Burbank Studios

4000 Warner Boulevard, Burbank, CA 91522 (213)
954-6000.
PRESIDENT
Gary M. Paster
VICE PRESIDENT—DIRECTOR OF BUSINESS AFFAIRS
Edward A. Medman
DIRECTOR OF PRODUCTION SERVICES
Ron Stein
DIRECTOR OF STUDIO SERVICES
Vince Hedges
TREASURER
Herbert Lehr
DIRECTOR OF LABOR RELATIONS
Chuck Byloos
DIRECTOR OF PERSONNEL
Caldene Wiens

Joseph Burstyn, Inc.

301 West 53rd St., New York, NY 10019 (212) 245-
1750 and 863-5741. (Motion picture distribution.)
PRESIDENT
Fae R. Miske
VICE PRESIDENT & TREASURER
Gerald N. Goldberger
SECRETARY
Arthur L. Goldberger
DATE OF ORGANIZATION
1935

CBS Theatrical Films

4024 Radford Ave., Studio City, CA 91604 (213) 760-
6134. (Producer of theatrical motion pictures)
PRESIDENT, CBS THEATRICAL FILMS GROUP
Michael I. Levy
PRESIDENT, CBS THEATRICAL FILMS DIVISION
Joe Wizan
VICE PRESIDENT & ASSISTANT TO PRESIDENT, CBS THE-
ATRICAL FILMS GROUP
Sheldon Perry
VICE PRESIDENT, FINANCE, CBS THEATRICAL FILMS
GROUP
Gary McCarthy
VICE PRESIDENT PRODUCTION (WEST COAST) CBS THE-
ATRICAL FILMS DIVISION
Nancy Hardin
VICE PRESIDENT, THEATRICAL DEVELOPMENT (EAST
COAST) CBS THEATRICAL FILMS DIVISION
Kathrin Seitz
GROUP VICE PRESIDENT—PLANNING, CBS THEATRICAL
FILMS GROUP
Joy Shelton Davis
VICE PRESIDENT, EXECUTIVE PRODUCTION MANAGER,
CBS THEATRICAL FILMS DIVISION
Lindsley Parsons, Jr.

VICE PRESIDENT, FOREIGN SALES, CBS THEATRICAL
FILMS DIVISION
Stephen A. Unger
DATE OF ORGANIZATION
1979

Canadian Film Development Corporation

800 Place Victoria, Suite 2220, Montreal, Canada,
H4Z 1A8 (514) 283-6363.
CHAIRMAN OF THE BOARD
Michel Vennat
EXECUTIVE DIRECTOR
Michael McCabe
ASSISTANT DIRECTORS
Sam Freeman, Richard Woods, Pierre Thibeault

Cannon Films, Inc.

6464 Sunset Blvd., Suite 1150, Hollywood, CA 90028.
(213) 469-8124. (Film production and distribution)
CHAIRMAN OF THE BOARD
Menahem Golan
PRESIDENT
Yoram Globus
FOREIGN SALES MANAGER
Dan Dimbort
GENERAL SALES MANAGER
Tom Berman
CORPORATE CONTROLLER
William Steinbach
DATE OF ORGANIZATION
1979

Cardinal IV TV Film Distributors

509 Madison Ave., New York, NY 10022 (212) 371-
5480. (Distribution of theatrical feature films and spe-
cialty films)
PRESIDENT
Erwin Lesser
OFFICE MANAGER
Silvana Radman

Carmen Productions Inc.

353 No. Street, Greenwich, CT 06830 (203) TO9-
6777. (Servicing, financing, producers, representa-
tion and foreign sales)
PRESIDENT, TREASURER
Jean Carmen Dillow
VICE PRESIDENT, SECRETARY
C. Connor
DATE OF ORGANIZATION
1956

Carolco Service, Inc.

8810 Melrose Ave., Suite 201, Los Angeles, CA (213)
273-0284. (Servicing and foreign sales for the motion
picture industry.)
VICE PRESIDENT
Andrew G. Vajna
DATE OF ORGANIZATION
1976

Cavalcade Pictures, Inc.

959 North Fairfax Ave., Hollywood, CA 90046; (213)
654-4144; Cable Address: Cavalpic Hollywood. (Pro-
ducer distributor/exporter.).
PRESIDENT
Harvey Pergament
VICE-PRESIDENT
Robert M. Pergament
SECRETARY-TREASURER
Esther Pergament
BOARD OF DIRECTORS
Harvey Pergament, Robert M. Pergament, Esther Pergament

Certified Reports Inc. (CRI)

Kinderhook, NY 12106. (518) 758-6403. (Theatre checking, industry research.)
CHAIRMAN OF BOARD
Jack J. Spitzer
PRESIDENT
Harold Roth

Chancellor Films, Inc.

1540 Broadway, New York, NY 10036. (212) 575-8182. (Foreign sales).
PRESIDENT
Bondi Wilson-Walters

Chartoff-Winkler Productions

10125 West Washington Blvd., Culver City, CA 90230. (213) 836-3000. (Producer)
PRINCIPALS
Robert Chartoff, Irwin Winkler

Cinar Productions, Inc.

4805 Beach Park Dr., Tampa, FL 33609 (813) 872-9925.
PRESIDENT & SALES MANAGER
Paul Rubenstein
SECRETARY
Roger M. Priede
DATE OF ORGANIZATION
1969

Cinema Arts Associated Corp.

One Village Square, Westport, CT 06880 (203) 226-4801. Telex: 964346. (Production and distribution of motion pictures, television, audiovisual and publishing.)
VICE PRESIDENT
R. B. Katz
EXECUTIVE VICE PRESIDENT
Frederick L. Hyman
DATE OF ORGANIZATION
1975

Cinema Arts Associates, Inc.

333 West 52nd St., New York, NY 10019. (212) 246-2860. (Motion picture and video tape company)
PRESIDENT
Hans R. Dudelheim
DATE OF ORGANIZATION
1961

Cinema Consultants, Ltd.

540 Madison Ave., New York, NY 10021 (212) 628-1225. (Development and production of screenplays, consultant to producers of film distribution.)
PRESIDENT & TREASURER
Howard G. Minsky
VICE PRESIDENT & SECRETARY
Sylvia Minsky
VICE PRESIDENT
Barry Minsky

Cinema 5 Ltd.

1500 Broadway, New York, NY 10036 (212) 354-5515.
VICE PRESIDENT & GENERAL MANAGER
Ralph E. Donnelly
DIRECTOR OF SALES
Ruth Robbins

Cinema International Corporation N.V.

Headquarters, Postbus 9255, Rijswijkstraat 175, 1000 A.E. Amsterdam, The Netherlands. (Distribution and exhibition of Motion Pictures)
PRESIDENT
Pano A. Alafouzo
EXECUTIVE VICE PRESIDENT
E. Paul Lipscomb
LEGAL
John R. Hurt
GROUP PERSONNEL & ADMINISTRATION
Ben Benner
INTERNATIONAL TAX
Trevor C. Rolland
TREASURY
Mike Thistle

CONSULTING COMPANY
CIC INTERNATIONAL B.V.

139 Piccadilly, London, W1V 9FH, England.
PRESIDENT
Pano A. Alafouzo
VICE PRESIDENT, INTERNATIONAL ADVERTISING & PUBLICITY
Gerry Lewis
VICE PRESIDENT, FAR EAST, S. AFRICA & AUSTRALASIA
Howard Rochlin
VICE PRESIDENT, CONTINENTAL EUROPE, NEAR AND MIDDLE EAST
Tony Themistocleous
LATIN AMERICA
Timothy Ord
16mm AND NON THEATRICAL
Mike Macclesfield

188/189, High Street, Uxbridge UB81LB, England.
EXECUTIVE VICE PRESIDENT
E. Paul Lipscomb
PLANNING INFORMATION AND CONTROL
Keith Atkinson
TREASURY SERVICES
Joe Dreier

LIAISON COMPANY (NEW YORK)

CIC Services Inc., 1 Gulf & Western Plaza, New York, NY 10023, U.S.A.
MANAGER
Donald H. Nathan

EUROPE AND MIDDLE EAST

AUSTRIA—Cinema International Corporation GesmbH, Neubaugasse 1, 1071 Vienna, Austria. Manager: Erich Schlathau.
BELGIUM—Cinema International Corporation s.n.c., 288 Rue Royale, 1030 Brussels, Belgium. Manager: Paul Delvigne.
DENMARK—Cinema International Corporation, ApS., Hauchsvej 13, 1825 Copenhagen V, Denmark. Manager: Svend Henriksen.
FINLAND—O.Y. Cinema International Corporation, A.B., Pohjoisesplanadi 33a, 00100 Helsinki 10, Finland. Manager: Olavi Virtamo.
FRANCE—Cinema International Corporation Sarl, 1 rue du Meyerbeer 75009-Paris, France. Manager: Daniel Goldman.
GERMANY—Cinema International Corporation GmbH, Postfach 16780 Kaiserstrasse 66, 6 Frankfurt/Main, Germany. Manager: Norbert Scherer.
GREECE—Cinema International Corporation E.P.E., Gambetta Street 4, Athens 142, Greece. Manager: Yanni Tacaziadis.
ISRAEL—(Distributor) Cinema International Corporation, P.O. Box 4795, 47 Hayarkon Street, Tel Aviv, Israel. Manager: Israel Freundlich.
ITALY—Cinema International Corporation s.r.l., Via Goito 52, 00185, Rome, Italy. Manager: Mario Pesucci.
LEBANON—Cinema International Corporation S.A.R.L., P.O. Box 7122, Soummakieh Building, Mme. Curie Street, Beirut, Lebanon. Manager: Kamal G. Kawar.
NETHERLANDS—Cinema International Corporation (Netherlands) B.V. Postbus 9255, Rijswijkstraat 175, Amsterdam W3, The Netherlands. Manager: Paul Silvius.
NORWAY—Cinema International Corporation, A/S, Box 1743 Vika/Oslo 1, Huitfeldtsgate 5, Vika/Oslo 2, Norway. Manager: Christian Bretteville.
PORTUGAL—(Distributor) Filmes Lusomundo S.A.R.L., Praca de Alegria 22-1, Apartado 1063, Lisbon 2, Portugal. Manager: Luis da Silva.
SPAIN—Cinema International Corporation y Cia, Plaza del Callao 4, Planta 6a, Madrid 13, Spain. Manager: Gualberto Bana.
SWEDEN—Cinema International Corporation A.B., P.O. Box 1346, Kungsgatan 26, 6&R, 24 Stockholm, Sweden. Manager: Curt Bergelin.

SWITZERLAND—Cinema International Corporation GmbH (Schweiz) Postfach 38, CH8034, Kreuzstrasse 26, CH8008, Zurich, Switzerland. Manager: Walter Hirt.

UNITED KINGDOM—Cinema International Corporation (UK), 114 Jermyn Street, London SW1Y 6HG, England. Manager: James Higgins.

AFRICA

SOUTH AFRICA—(Distributor) CIC—Warner (Pty) Limited, P.O. Box 5423, Johannesburg 2000, South Africa. Manager: Kevin Hyson.

LATIN AMERICA

ARGENTINA—Cinema International Corporation s.r.l., Ayacucho 518-20, 1026 Buenos Aires, Argentina. Manager: Juan Manuel Fascetto.

BOLIVIA—(Distributor) Peliculas Mexicanas De Bolivia S.A., Calle F. Gucochalla 359, Apartado Postal 2613, La Paz, Bolivia. CIC Manager: Walter Zalles Viana

BRAZIL—Cinema International Corporation Distribuidera de Filmes Ltda., Av. Rio Branco 245, 28th & 29th Floor, Cinelandia Caixa Postal 179-ZC-00, 20010, Rio de Janeiro, Brazil. Manager: Paulo Fucs.

CHILE—Cinema International Corporation (Films) Ltda., Casilla 3462, Huerfanos 786, Oficina 808, Santiago, Chile. Manager: Mario Cuevas.

COLOMBIA—Cinema International Corporation Ltda., Apartado Aéreo 3450, Calle 23, No. 5-58, Bogotá, Colombia. Manager: Alberto Liberoff.

DOMINICAN REPUBLIC—(Distributor) C.I.C. Coblan S.A., P.O. Box 2307, Cervantes 103-B, Zona 1, Santo Domingo, Dominican Republic. Manager: Michael Heuser.

ECUADOR—(Distributor) Peliculas Mexicana del Ecuador, S.A., Apartado 1090, 9 de Octubre 823, Guayaquil, Ecuador. Manager: Luis Valarezo Hernandez.

GUATEMALA—Cinema International Corporation y Compania Ltda., Apartado Postal 2166, 3a Avenida 13-33, Zona 1, Guatemala City, Guatemala. Manager: Mario Alvarez Echeverria.

JAMAICA—(Distributor) Worldwide Film Agency Ltd., 15 Old Hope Road, Kingston 5, Jamaica W1. Manager: Patrick Chung II.

MEXICO—Cinema International Corporation S. de R.L., Apartado Postal 70 bis, Guanajuato 215, Mexico D.F., Mexico. Manager: Alejandro Arroyo.

PANAMA—Cinema International Corporation s. de R.L., P.O. Box 5252, Via España, Altos Edificio Elga, Panama 5, Republic of Panama. Manager: Peter Dignan.

PERU—Cinema International Corporation s.r.l., Apartado 582, Jiron Augusto N. Wiese 915, Lima 1, Peru. Manager: Miguel Joseph.

TRINIDAD—Cinema International Corporation, P.O. Box 64, Film Centre, 14, Humphrey Street, St. James, Port of Spain, Trinidad. Manager: Mausley Ellis.

URUGUAY—Cinema International Corporation Limitada (Suiza), San José 1211, 1° piso, Montevideo, Uruguay. Manager: Enrique Martin.

VENEZUELA—(Distributor) C.A. Cinematogr áfica Blancica, P.O. Box 273, 4A, Avenida Las Delicias, Edificio Las Delicias—PB, Sabana Grande, Caracas, Venezuela. President: Tony Blanco.

FAR EAST

HONG KONG—Cinema International Corporation, P.O. Box 120, 205-206 Holland House, 9 Icehouse Street, Hong Kong. Manager: Robert Chen.

INDIA—Distribution Liaison Officers Paramount Films of India Ltd., Hague Building, Sprott Road, Ballard Estate, P.O. Box 623, Bombay 400038, India. Manager: C. A. Ramchandran.

Universal Films of India B.V., Hague Building, Sprott Road, Ballard Estate, P.O. Box 357, Bombay 400038, India. Manager: C. A. Ramchandran.

JAPAN—Y.K. Cinema International Corporation, P.O. Box 514, 2nd Floor, Riccar Kaikan 2-1, 6 chome Ginza, Chuo-ku, Central, Tokyo, Japan. Manager: Itsuo Araki.

PHILIPPINES—Cinema International Corp., A.B., P.O. Box 4454, 4th floor, State Theatre Bldg., Rizal Ave., Manila, Republic of Philippines. Manager: Richard Guardian.

SINGAPORE/MALAYSIA—Cinema International Corporation (PTE), Post Box No. 132, Killiney Road Post Office, Suites 709-710 Shaw House, Orchard Road, Singapore 9123, Republic of Singapore. Manager: K. S. Vaidyanatham.

THAILAND—Cinema International Corporation, P.O. Box 220, 315 Silom Road, Bangkok, Thailand. Manager: Chana Chaikijkarana.

AUSTRALASIA

AUSTRALIA—Cinema International Corporation Pty., Ltd., P.O. Box 4040, 53-57 Brisbane Street, Sydney, N.S.W. 2001, Australia. Manager: John Neal.

NEW ZEALAND—Cinema International Corporation (NZ) Ltd., P.O. Box 8850 Symonds St., P.O. 157-159, Symonds Street, Auckland, New Zealand. Manager: Reg Felton.

Cinema Shares International Distribution Corporation

450 Park Avenue, New York, NY 10022 (212) 421-3371.

CHAIRMAN OF THE BOARD
Richard Friedberg
VICE PRESIDENT/FINANCE
Eric Ablog
CINEMA SHARES INTERNATIONAL TELEVISION, LTD.
PRESIDENT
Ken Israel
VICE PRESIDENT PROGRAM SERVICES
Beverly Partridge
DATE OF ORGANIZATION
1972

The Cinema Think Tank

84 Fulton Ave., Atlantic Beach, NY 11509 (516) 239-1862. (Marketing of motion pictures.)

PRESIDENT
Robert S. Ferguson
DATE OF ORGANIZATION
1976

Cinematograph

13 Edsal Avenue, Nanuet, NY 10954 (914) 623-8609. (Motion picture and television production.)

PRESIDENT
Victor Eisenberg
DATE OF ORGANIZATION
1974.

Cinemax Marketing and Distribution Corporation

277 Park Avenue, New York, NY 10172 (212) 935-5844. (Producer's marketing and distribution consultants; creative presentation and maximization of potential for motion pictures.)

PRESIDENT
Arthur Manson
VICE PRESIDENT
Norman Delaney

Cine-Media International, Ltd.

3830 Chestnut Ave., Long Beach, CA 90807 (213) 426-3622. (Production and distribution of theatrical motion pictures and television films.)

PRESIDENT & CHIEF EXECUTIVE OFFICER
J. Bond Johnson, PHD
VICE PRESIDENT
Rudolph A. Maglin
SECRETARY
Ruth Johnson
TREASURER
Lenore Maglin
EXECUTIVE PRODUCER
Frank Capra, Jr.
CREATIVE CONSULTANT
Chester Dent
DIRECTOR OF PRODUCTION
Travis Edward Pike
DIRECTOR OF FINANCE
William A. Becker, CPA
BUSINESS MANAGER
Joe Price
GENERAL COUNSEL
Stuart I. Berton, Esq.

Cinerama, Inc.

120 North Robertson Blvd., Los Angeles, CA 90048 (213) 657-8420. Theatre operator; hotel operator. Subsidiaries include: Cinerama Hawaiian Hotels, Inc., Cinerama Theatres, Inc. of California, and RKO-Stanley-Warner Theatres, Inc.)

CHAIRMAN, CHIEF EXECUTIVE OFFICER & PRESIDENT
  Michael R. Forman
VICE PRESIDENT & TREASURER
  Charles P. Emma
SECRETARY
  Charles P. Emma
ASST. SECRETARY & ASST. TREASURER
  Constantine Hambas
BOARD OF DIRECTORS
  Michael R. Forman, Richard R. Kelley, & Roy E. Kelley

Cinetudes Film Productions, Ltd.

295 West 4th St., New York, NY 10014 (212) 966-4600. (Motion picture and television production)
PRESIDENT
  Christine Jurzykowski
VICE PRESIDENT
  Neal Marshad
PRODUCTION MANAGER
  Gale Goldberg
DATE OF ORGANIZATION
  1976

Cineworld Corporation

P.O. Box 61-276, No. Miami, FL 33161 (305) 891-1181. (Distribution, production, international co-production financing and packaging.)
PRESIDENT
  John F. Rickert
SECRETARY/TREASURER
  Ildiko M. Rickert

Circuit Films

910 Hennepin Ave., Minneapolis, MN 55403 (612) 338-7970. (Film distribution.)
PRESIDENT
  David Zimmerman
DATE OF ORGANIZATION
  1977

City Film Productions—City Film Center Inc.

64-12 65th Place, Middle Village (Queens County, N.Y.C.) NY 11379 (212) 456-5050. (Producers of, and production services for motion pictures for television, business, industry, research.)
EXECUTIVE PRODUCER
  John R. Gregory
PRODUCERS
  Clarence Schmidt
  Herbert Avvenire

Dick Clark Cinema Productions

3003 West Olive Ave., Burbank, CA 91505. (213) 841-3003. (Production of films for theatres and television)
PRESIDENT
  Dick Clark
EXECUTIVE VICE PRESIDENT IN CHARGE OF PRODUCTION
  Francis La Maina
VICE PRESIDENT OF THEATRICAL & TELEVISION PRODUCTION
  Preston Fischer
DATE OF ORGANIZATION
  1979

Columbia Pictures Industries, Inc.

711 Fifth Avenue, N.Y., NY 10022 (212) 751-4400
CHAIRMAN OF THE BOARD
  Herbert A. Allen
PRESIDENT AND CHIEF EXECUTIVE OFFICER
  Francis T. Vincent, Jr.
EXECUTIVE VICE PRESIDENT
  Robert L. Stone

SENIOR VICE PRESIDENT AND GENERAL COUNSEL
  Richard C. Gallop
SENIOR VICE PRESIDENT
  Victor A. Kaufman
SENIOR VICE PRESIDENT AND CHIEF FINANCIAL OFFICER
  Charles R. Lee
VICE PRESIDENT—FINANCE
  C. Charles Jowaiszas
VICE PRESIDENT AND TREASURER
  William R. Lewis
VICE PRESIDENT—PERSONNEL AND ADMINISTRATION
  Paul M. Cholak
CONTROLLER
  Fred Hiller
DEPUTY GENERAL COUNSEL
  Morton H. Fry
ASSOCIATE GENERAL COUNSELS
  Jared Jussim, Ellis A. Regenbogen
DIRECTOR—CORPORATE COMMUNICATIONS
  Raymond A. Boyce
DIRECTOR—INTERNAL AUDIT
  Ilana Cytto
BOARD OF DIRECTORS
  Herbert A. Allen, Dwayne O. Andreas, Edward J. Bloustein, Karl Eller, Leo Jaffe, Irwin H. Kramer, Dan W. Lufkin, John G. McMillian, Walter F. Mondale, Frank Price, Robert S. Strauss, Jack H. Vaughn, Francis T. Vincent, Jr., and Judd A. Weinberg.
DATE OF CORPORATION
  October 14, 1969 under laws of Delaware.
CAPITALIZATION
  20,000,000 shares of common authorized, 10,332,992 at March 28, 1981, $0.10 par value outstanding. 5,000,000 shares preferred issued and none outstanding, par value, $0.10.
HISTORY OF COLUMBIA PICTURES INDUSTRIES, INC.
  Columbia Pictures INDUSTRIES, Inc. is the successor to Columbia Pictures Corp. which was incorporated January 10, 1924 under New York laws. The Company's origin traces back to Harry Cohn, who was an independent producer making shorts. Jack Cohn resigned from Universal to go into the motion picture business for himself. The firm of Jack and Harry Cohn was then organized. Later Jack and Harry Cohn prevailed upon Joseph Brandt, who had been the general manager of Universal to join them. The name of the company was changed to CBC Sales Corporation. Later it was changed to Columbia and on December 28, 1968 was reorganized as Columbia Pictures Industries, Inc. with Columbia Pictures and Screen Gems (now Columbia Pictures Television) as its major divisions. In December 1969, Columbia was reorganized under Delaware law.

Columbia Pictures

Columbia Plaza, Burbank, CA 91505 (213) 954-6000.
CHAIRMAN AND PRESIDENT
  Frank Price
VICE CHAIRMAN
  Victor A. Kaufman (New York office)
EXECUTIVE VICE PRESIDENT
  Jonathan L. Dolgen
EXECUTIVE VICE PRESIDENT-BUSINESS AFFAIRS
  Eli Horowitz
SENIOR VICE PRESIDENT-FINANCE AND ADMINISTRATION (Filmed Entertainment)
  Peter C. Kells
SENIOR VICE-PRESIDENT—WORLDWIDE BUSINESS AFFAIRS
  Arnold Messer
VICE PRESIDENT-TALENT RELATIONS
  Linda Berken
VICE-PRESIDENT-MUSIC
  Richard Berres
VICE PRESIDENT AND ASSISTANT TO PRESIDENT
  David Forbes
VICE PRESIDENT-ADMINISTRATION
  Al Linton
VICE PRESIDENT-LABOR RELATIONS
  Orison Marden
DIRECTOR-EMPLOYEE RELATIONS
  Harvey Lehman

COLUMBIA PICTURES PRODUCTION

PRESIDENT
  John Veitch
VICE PRESIDENTS-PRODUCTION
  Amy Ephron
  Robert Lawrence
VICE PRESIDENT-POST PRODUCTION
  Thomas McCarthy
VICE PRESIDENT AND EXECUTIVE PRODUCTION MANAGER
  Sheldon Schrager

ADVERTISING/PUBLICITY/PROMOTION

PRESIDENT-MARKETING AND RESEARCH
Marvin Antonowsky
VICE PRESIDENT AND DIRECTOR OF RESEARCH
Stephen F. Randall
VICE PRESIDENT AND DIRECTOR OF PUBLICITY AND PROMOTION OPERATIONS
Marvin Levy
VICE PRESIDENT IN CHARGE OF ADVERTISING
Ken Blancato
VICE PRESIDENT-MEDIA ADVERTISING
Paula Garrett Kelley
VICE PRESIDENT-EAST COAST PUBLICITY (New York Office)
Robert A. Levine
DIRECTOR-NATIONAL PUBLICITY
Sue Barton-Kirkland
DIRECTOR-ADVERTISING PRODUCTION
Charles Bigbee
DIRECTOR-MEDIA ADVERTISING
Diane Charbanic
DIRECTOR-INDUSTRY RELATIONS
John Flinn
DIRECTOR-CO-OP ADVERTISING
Jack Friend
DIRECTOR-EAST COAST PUBLICITY (New York Office)
Victoria Horsford
DIRECTOR RESEARCH
Perry M. Katz
DIRECTOR-PROMOTIONAL ACTIVITIES AND FIELD OPERATIONS
Gary Shapiro
DIRECTOR OF ADMINISTRATION-ADVERTISING-PUBLICITY
John Spinka
DIRECTOR-ADVERTISING
Randy Wicks
ASSOCIATE DIRECTOR OF ADVERTISING
Scott Woodward
MANAGER-NATIONAL PUBLICITY
Peter Benoit
EXECUTIVE ART DIRECTOR
Ken Harman
EASTERN PUBLICITY COORDINATOR (New York Office)
Ira Tulipan

COLUMBIA PICTURES DOMESTIC DISTRIBUTION

PRESIDENT
Robert L. Friedman
VICE PRESIDENT AND GENERAL SALES MANAGER
James R. Spitz
VICE PRESIDENT AND EXECUTIVE ASSISTANT TO PRESIDENT
Arthur W. Standish
VICE PRESIDENT AND ASSISTANT GENERAL SALES MANAGER-WEST
Eugene Margoluis
ADMINISTRATIVE ASSISTANT TO THE VICE PRESIDENT & GENERAL SALES MANAGER
Edward Bader
DIRECTOR-BRANCH OPERATIONS
Al Cameron
MANAGER-ACCOUNTING/SYSTEMS DEVELOPMENT
Conrad Steely
MANAGER-PRINT DISTRIBUTION
Nathan Goldblatt

DOMESTIC BRANCHES & MANAGERS

VICE PRESIDENT & ASSISTANT SALES MGR.—EAST
Michael Scagluso
EASTERN DIVISION MANAGER
Franklin Osborne, 1700 Broadway, N.Y., NY 10019, (212) 751-4400.
ALBANY/NEW HAVEN/BUFFALO: Debra Finegold (see New York)
BOSTON: Gasper Urban, 20 Providence St., Boston, MA 02116 (617) 426-8980.
NEW YORK: Joseph Curtin (see New York)
PHILADELPHIA: Abe Dortheimer, 1612 Market St., Philadelphia, PA 19103 (215) 568-3889.
PITTSBURGH: Jonathan Sands (see Philadelphia)
WASHINGTON, D.C.: Martin Zeidman, 2011 I Street, N.W., Wash., D.C. 20006 (202) 466-6570.
SOUTHERN DIVISION MANAGER
John Lundin, 10830 North Central Expressway, Dallas, TX 75231 (214) 750-0100.
ATLANTA: Henry Harrell, 2600 Century Parkway, Atlanta, GA 30345 (404) 325-9525.
CHARLOTTE: Edward McLaughlin, 230 S. Tryon St., Charlotte, NC 28202 (704) 375-0705.
DALLAS/OKLAHOMA CITY: Jack Foley.
JACKSONVILLE: Terry Tharpe, 9550 Regency Square Blvd., Jacksonville, FL 32211 (904) 725-8891.

NEW ORLEANS/MEMPHIS: Gene Gibbons, 1001 Howard Ave., New Orleans, LA 70113 (504) 529-2461.
CENTRAL DIVISION MANAGER:
Jerry Jorgensen, 8550 West Bryn Mawr Ave., Chicago, IL 60631 (312) 693-3500.
CHICAGO: Evan Williams (see Chicago)
CLEVELAND/CINCINNATI: Richard Sands, One Commerce Park Square, 23200 Chagrin Blvd., Cleveland, OH 44122 (216) 292-3610.
DES MOINES: Glenn Abrams, 1501 Ingersoll Ave., Des Moines, IW 50309 (515) 243-0105.
DETROIT: Vacant, 24100 Southfield Rd., Southfield Road, Southfield, MI 48075 (313) 557-2150.
INDIANAPOLIS: Kenneth Newbert (see Chicago)
MILWAUKEE: Martin Marks
MINNEAPOLIS: Jack Ignatowicz, 711 Hennepin Ave., Minneapolis, MN 55403 (612) 333-6227.
WESTERN DIVISION MANAGER
Daniel Sapernakis, 8671 Wilshire Blvd., Beverly Hills, CA 90211 (213) 657-6410. Mailing address: P.O. Box 5253, Beverly Hills, CA 90210.
DENVER/SALT LAKE CITY: William Kreigenhafer, 1860 Lincoln St., Denver, CO 80295 (303) 861-9048.
KANSAS CITY/ST. LOUIS: James Donlon, 3130 Broadway, Kansas City, MS 64111 (816) 561-3021.
LOS ANGELES: Robert Humak
SEATTLE/PORTLAND: Bernard Livingston (see Beverly Hills)
SAN FRANCISCO: Robert Capps, Jr., 595 Market St., San Francisco, CA 94105 (415) 546-7211.
CANADIAN GENERAL MANAGER
Joseph Brown, 720 King St. West, Toronto, Ontario, Canada M5V2T3 (416) 363-5655.
TORONTO: Michael Brager (see Toronto)

COLUMBIA PICTURES HOME ENTERTAINMENT

Columbia Plaza, Burbank, CA 91505 (213) 954-6000.
VICE PRESIDENT & GENERAL MANAGER
Robert L. Blattner II

COLUMBIA PICTURES PAY TELEVISION

Columbia Plaza, Burbank, CA 91505 (213) 954-6000
VICE PRESIDENT & GENERAL MANAGER
Anthony J. Lynn
DIRECTOR-FEATURE FILM MARKETING
Richard A. Rosen
MANAGER-CLIENT SERVICES
Dana M. Douglas

COLUMBIA PICTURES INTERNATIONAL THEATRICAL, TELEVISION AND HOME ENTERTAINMENT DISTRIBUTION

711 Fifth Ave., New York, N.Y. 10022 (212) 751-4400
PRESIDENT
Patrick M. Williamson
SENIOR EXECUTIVE VICE PRESIDENT & INTERNATIONAL THEATRICAL MANAGER
David A. Matalon
SENIOR VICE PRESIDENT AND TREASURER
Peter K. J. Vadasdy
SENIOR VICE PRESIDENT-INTERNATIONAL TELEVISION
J. Brian McGrath
VICE PRESIDENT-ADVERTISING & PUBLICITY
Martin Blau
VICE PRESIDENT & THEATRICAL SALES MANAGER
Donald F. McConville
VICE PRESIDENT-VIDEO & PAY TV MARKETING
Michael R. Tarant
DIRECTOR OF ADMINISTRATION
Louis P. Mont
DIRECTOR OF FINANCE
Arthur L. Peckoff

COLUMBIA PICTURES INTERNATIONAL THEATRICAL & TELEVISION OFFICES & AGENTS

Argentina—Theatrical: Columbia Pictures of Argentina, Inc., Fox Film De La Argentina Inc., LaValle 1878, Buenos Aires, Argentina, Emilio Planchadell, Manager. *Television:* Columbia Pictures of Argentina, Inc., LaValle 1878, Buenos Aires, Argentina, Armando Cortez, General Manager.
Australia—Theatrical: Fox Columbia Film Distributors Pty., Ltd., 505-523 George St., Sydney N.S.W. Australia 2000, A. Griffin, Manager. *Television:* Columbia Pictures Television Pty., Ltd., 45 MacQuarie St., Sydney, 2000 Australia, Hugh Broun, Managing Director.
Austria—Theatrical: Warner-Columbia Film GmbH, Mondscheingasse 18, 1070 Vienna VII Austria, Rudolph Neumann, Manager.

Belgium—Theatrical: Warner Columbia Films, S.N.C., Rue Royale, 326 1030 Brussels, Belgium, Edouard Weinberg, Manager.

Bolivia—Theatrical: Distribuidores Asociados De Peliculas, Av. Montes 768, 3 er. Piso-Edifico De Col, La Paz, Bolivia, Licnio Manay, Manager.

Brazil—Theatrical: Screen Gems Columbia Pictures of Brazil, Inc., Rua Joaquim Silva, 98, Lapa, Rio de Janeiro, Brazil, Giovanni Gentili, Manager. *Television:* Screen Gems Columbia Pictures of Brazil, Inc., Rua Santa Isabel 160-7° Andar, 01221 Sao Paulo, Brazil, Helios D. Alvarez, General Representative.

Canada—Television: Columbia Pictures Television Canada, 365 Bloor Street East, Suite 1602, Toronto. Ontario M4W 3L4, David G. McLaughlin, General Manager. *Television:* Columbia Pictures Television Canada Limited, 1245 Rue Sherbrooke Quest, Montreal H3G 1G2, John Verge, Director of French Operations.

Chile—Theatrical: Columbia Pictures of Chile Inc., Asociacion Twentieth Century/Fox Chile, Inc., Huerfanos 786 Oficina 210, Santiago, Chile, Anibal Codebo, Manager.

Colombia—Theatrical: Fox/Columbia Pictures of Colombia Inc., Carrera 5 No. 22-85, Piso 5, Bogota, Colombia, Horacio Hermida, Manager.

Denmark—Theatrical: Columbia/Fox, 16, Soendermarksvej, DK-2500 Copenhagen Valby, Denmark, Jorgen Nielsen, Manager.

Ecuador—Theatrical: Prnductora Filmica Nacional Del Ecuador CIA, Ltd., Calle 9 De Octubre, 424, Guayaquil, Ecuador, Carlos Espinosa, Agent.

Egypt—Theatrical: Columbia Motion Pictures, Inc., 25 Orabi Street, Cairo, A.R.E., Egypt. *Television:* 14 Gawad Hosni Street, 4th Floor, Apt. 47, Cairo, A.R.E., Galal Rizk, Agent.

Finland—Theatrical: OY Warner-Columbia Films AB, Pohj Esplanaadikatu 33, Helsinki 10, Finland, Aune Turja, Manager.

France—Theatrical: Warner Columbia Film, 20 Rue Troyon, 75017 Paris, France, Elie Costa, Manager. *Television:* Columbia Pictures Television, 20 Rue Troyon, 75017 Paris, France, Jacques Porteret, Director of French Sales.

Germany—Theatrical: Warner Columbia Filmverleih G. m. b.H., 8 Munich Ickstrattstrasse 1 West Germany, Erich Mueller, Manager. *Television:* Columbia Television Vertriebsgesellschaft, m.b.H., Ickstattstrasse 1, 8000 Munich 5, West Germany, Max Kimental, Managing Director.

Greece—Theatrical: Columbia Pictures Hellas Sarl, 2 Capod, Athens 147, Greece, Paul N. Tsitsilianos, Manager. *Television:* Hellas Television International, 96 Akadimias Street, Athens 141, Greece, George Michaelides, Agent, Bill Protopsaltis, Agent.

Holland—Theatrical: Columbia International Films (Holland) B.V., Achter Oosteinde 9, 1017 XP Amsterdam, Holland, Edward J. Katz, Manager.

Hong Kong—Theatrical: Fox-Columbia Film Distributors, Loong San Buildino, 140-142 Connaught Road C., Hong Kong, P. Kwok, Acting Manager.

India—Theatrical: Columbia Films of India, Ltd., Metro House 1st Floor, Mahatma Gandi Road, P.O. Box 390, Bombay 400001, India, Joseph M. D'Cunha, Manager.

Israel—Theatrical & Television: Albert D. Matalon & Co. Ltd., 15 Hess Street, Tel Aviv, Israel, Amnom Matalon, Agent.

Italy—Theatrical: Cinematografica Edizione Internazionali Artistiche/Diatribuzione, S.R.L., Via Palestro N. 24, C.A.P. 00185, Rome, Italy, Paolo Ferrari, Manager. *Television:* TV Overseas S.R.L., Via Sicilia N. 50, 00187, Rome, Italy, Jimmy Manca, Agent.

Japan—Theatrical: Columbia Films, Ltd., Kanesaka Bldg. 5-4 Shimbashi, 2-chome, Minato-Ku, Tokyo 105 Japan, Kunikazu Sogabe, General Manager. *Television:* Japan International Enterprises, Inc., 4th floor, Yoneda Building, 17-20 Shimbashi 6-chome, Minato-Ku, Tokyo Pref., 105 Japan, Toru Ohnuki, General Manager.

Kuwait—Television: Scientific Instruments Trading Establishment, P.O. Box 35127, Al-Shaab, Kuwait, Arabian Gulf, Hamid Al-Nakeshly, Agent.

Lebanon-Theatrical: Les Fils de Georges Haddad & Co., Empire Cinema Bldg., Beyrouth, Lebanon, Michel G. Haddad, Agent.

Mexico—Theatrical: Columbia Pictures, S. A., Sinaloa #20, Mexico 7, D.F., Jack Jackter, Manager. *Television:* Columbia Pictures Television International, Darwin 68, Office 301, Mexico City, Mexico 5, D.F., Alvaro Mutis, General Manager.

New Zealand—Theatrical: Columbia Warner Distributors, 24/26 Nikau Street, Auckland 3, New Zealand, Lester McKellar, Manager.

Norway—Theatrical: I/S Columbia Warner, Stortingsgaten #30, Oslo 1, Norway, Jon Narvestad, Manager.

Panama—Theatrical: Columbia Pictures of Panama, Inc., Edificio Elga, Via Espana #46-50, Panama, P. Branca, Manager.

Peru-Theatrical: Columbia Pictures of Peru, Inc., Jr. Lampa 1115, Of. 1002, Lima, Peru, Tomas Rios, Manager.

Philippines—Theatrical: Columbia Pictures Industries, Inc., Rooms 307-308 Philippine, President Lines Bldg., 1000 United Nations Avenue, Manila, Philippines. Artemio Diaz, Manager. *Television:* Columbia Pictures Television International, 3rd Floor, Room 307, Philippine, President Lines Bldg., 1000 United Nations Avenue, P.O. Box 3373, Manila, Philippines, Conrado Javier, Sales Representative.

Portugal—Theatrical: Columbia Warner Filmes de Portugal LDA, Avenida Duque de Loule 90-3° Esq., Lisboa, Portugal, A. Farah, Manager.

Puerto Rico—Theatrical: Columbia Pictures, Ponce de Leon 1255, Santurce, Puerto Rico 00908, Efrain Cruz, Manager.

Santo Domingo—Theatrical: Columbia Film Trading Corp., Avendia Independencia #310, Zona-1, Santo Domingo, Dominican Republic, Mauro Lara, Manager.

Singapore/Malaysia—Theatrical: Cathay Film Distributors Private Ltd., Cathay Building, Singapore, 0922, Phillip Lau, Agent.

South Africa—Theatrical: Ster Kinekor Films (PTY) Ltd., 158 Main Street, Johannesberg 2000, South Africa, Geoffrey B. Rawsthorne, Columbia Supervisor.

Spain—Theatrical: Columbia Films, S.A., Calle Veneras, 9-6° Piso, Madrid 13, Spain, L. Sheprus, Manager. *Television:* San Lucas 21.-1, Madrid 4, Spain, Antonio Sanchez-Gijon, Agent.

Sweden—Theatrical: Warner Columbia Film A. B., Kungsgatan 24, VI, Stockholm C., Sweden, Nils Persson, Manager.

Switzerland—Theatrical: Twentieth Century-Fox Film Corporation, 2, Place Du Cirque, 1204 Geneva, Switzerland, Jean Pierre Reyren, Manager.

Taiwan—Theatrical: Columbia Films of China, Ltd., 3rd Floor, 20 Hsi-ning South Road, Taipei, 100 Republic of China, C.N. Hsia, Manager.

Thailand—Theatrical: Columbia Films of Thailand, Inc., South East Insurance Bldg., 315 Silom Road, Bangkok, Thailand, William Blamey, Manager.

Trinidad—Theatrical: Morgan Films Limited Deluxe Theatre, 9-11 Keate Street, Port of Spain, Trinidad, WI, Dr. Y. Morgan, Agent.

U.K. and Eire—Theatrical: Columbia—EMI—Warner Distributors Ltd., 135 Wardour Street, London WIV 4 AP, England, H.C. Nicholas, Managing Director. *Television:* Columbia Pictures Television, St. Margaret's House, 19/23 Wells Street, London WIP, 3 FP, England, Tim Vignoles, Managing Director.

Uruguay—Theatrical: Cinema International Corp. Ltda., San Jose 1211 p.1, Montevideo, Uruguay, Enrique Martin, Manager.

Venezuela—Theatrical: Columbia Pictures of Venezuela, Inc., Avenida Las Palmas, Edificio Teatro Las Palmas—4° Piso, Caracas, Venezuela, John J. Finder, Manager.

Kenya/Zambia—Theatrical: Cosmopolitan Film BV, P.O. Box 74244, Nairobi, Kenya, Christopher Hedges, Agent.

COLUMBIA PICTURES TELEVISION

Columbia Plaza, Burbank, CA 91505 (213) 954-6000.

PRESIDENT
Herman Rush
SENIOR VICE PRESIDENT-ADMINISTRATION
Paul B. Stager
SENIOR VICE PRESIDENT & EXECUTIVE PRODUCTION MANAGER
Seymour Friedman
VICE PRESIDENT-MUSIC
Richard Berres
VICE PRESIDENT-FINANCIAL ANALYSIS
Jim Claiborne
VICE PRESIDENT-DAYTIME
Noreen Conlin
VICE PRESIDENT-PUBLICITY & PROMOTION
Doug Duitsman
VICE PRESIDENT-SERIES PROGRAMS
Christine Foster
VICE PRESIDENT-LIVE AND TAPE PRODUCTION
Bill Fischer
VICE PRESIDENT-POST PRODUCTION
Christina Friedgen
VICE PRESIDENT-CREATIVE AFFAIRS
Stephen Girard
VICE PRESIDENT IN CHARGE OF BUSINESS AFFAIRS
Sid Kalcheim
VICE PRESIDENT-TALENT & CASTING
Meryl O'Laughlin
VICE PRESIDENT-LABOR RELATIONS
Orison Marden
VICE PRESIDENT-MOVIES & MINISERIES
Fernando Roca
DIRECTOR-TALENT & CASTING
Fran Bascom
DIRECTOR-LITERARY AFFAIRS
Devorah Cutler
DIRECTOR-BUSINESS AFFAIRS
Michael H. Lauer
DIRECTOR-EMPLOYEE RELATIONS
Harvey Lehman
DIRECTOR-CURRENT PROGRAMMING
Kathleen St. Johns
DIRECTOR-DRAMATIC DEVELOPMENT
Rachel Tabori

COLUMBIA PICTURES TELEVISION DOMESTIC DISTRIBUTION

15250 Ventura Blvd., Sherman Oaks, CA 91403 (213) 995-1300.

PRESIDENT
Henry A. Gillespie
VICE PRESIDENT-DOMESTIC SALES
Joseph Indelli

VICE PRESIDENT-ADVERTISING & PROMOTION
  Steve Astor
VICE PRESIDENT-FINANCIAL ADMINISTRATION
  Phil Cuppett
VICE PRESIDENT-FEATURE MARKETING
  Dalton Danon
VICE PRESIDENT-DOMESTIC ADMINISTRATION
  Irma Flamenco
VICE PRESIDENT-SALES AND RESEARCH DEPARTMENT
  John Walden
VICE PRESIDENT-PROGRAMMING
  Edward A. Warren
DIRECTOR-INFORMATION SERVICES
  Richard Gire
DIRECTOR-SYNDICATED PROGRAM DEVELOPMENT
  Brandy French
CREATIVE DIRECTOR-ADVERTISING & PROMOTION
  Janet Radeck

NEW YORK OFFICE

711 Fifth Ave., New York, NY 10022 (212) 751-4400.
VICE PRESIDENT-SALES, EAST
  Herbert O. Weiss
EASTERN SALES ACCOUNT EXECUTIVE
  Ken Doyle

SYNDICATION SALES FIELD REPRESENTATIVES

MIDWEST (Chicago, 312-329-1650)
DIRECTOR/SALES ACCOUNT EXECUTIVE
  Stuart Stringfellow

SOUTHWEST (Dallas, 214-967-2184/742-5060)

VICE PRESIDENT
Jack Ellison

SOUTHEAST (Atlanta, 404-256-3007)

VICE PRESIDENT
Don Bryan
PROGRAMMING EXECUTIVE
Tom Holland

WEST (Los Angeles, 213-995-1300)

VICE PRESIDENTS
Dick Campbell
Joe Abruscato

COLUMBIA PICTURES COMMUNICATIONS

P.O. Box 10612, 2402 E. Arizona Biltmore Circle, Phoenix, AZ 85016, (602)956-8940
PRESIDENT
  Karl Eller
SENIOR VICE PRESIDENT-OPERATIONS/FINANCE
  Murray H. Topham

PRESIDENT-RADIO GROUP

Edward R. Boyd, Columbia Plaza, Burbank, CA 91505, (213) 954-6000.

KCPX-AM & FM

1760 Freemont Drive, Salt Lake City, Utah 84104 (801) 972-3030.
VICE PRESIDENT & GENERAL MANAGER
  Bruce Cummings
BUSINESS MANAGER & CONTROLLER
  Randy Kimball

WWVA-AM/WCPI-FM

Capitol Music Hall, 1015 Main Street, Wheeling, WA 26003 (304) 232-1170.
VICE PRESIDENT & GENERAL MANAGER
  Ross Felton
BUSINESS MANAGER & CONTROLLER
  Robert Haggerty

WYDE

2112 Eleventh Avenue South, Birmingham, AL 35205 (205) 322-4511.
VICE PRESIDENT & GENERAL MANAGER
  Berkley Fraser
BUSINESS MANAGER & CONTROLLER
  Robert Haggert

NEW YORK SUBWAYS ADVERTISING CO.

750 Third Avenue, N.Y., NY 10017, (212) 867-4700
PRESIDENT
  Marvin Schwartz
EXECUTIVE VICE PRESIDENT
  William A. Apfelbaum

COLUMBIA PICTURES MERCHANDISING

711 Fifth Avenue, N.Y., NY 10022 (212) 751-4400
VICE PRESIDENT AND GENERAL MANAGER
  Lester Borden

COLUMBIA PICTURES PUBLICATIONS

16333 N.W. 54th Avenue, Hialeah, FL 33014 (305) 620-1500
PRESIDENT
  Frank Hackinson

EUE/SCREEN GEMS

222 East 44th Street, N.Y., NY 10017 (212) 867-4030; 3701 Oak Street, Burbank, CA 91505 (213) 954-3000
PRESIDENT
  Steve Elliot
EXECUTIVE VICE PRESIDENT AND GENERAL MANAGER
  George Cooney
VICE PRESIDENT-DIRECTOR OF OPERATIONS
  Nicholas Bavaro
VICE PRESIDENT-FINANCE
  John Clarke
VICE PRESIDENT AND SALES MANAGER
  Eli Feldman
VICE PRESIDENT
  Errol Linderman
VICE PRESIDENT
  Thomas Whitesell
SENIOR VICE PRESIDENT AND GENERAL MANAGER (West Coast)
  Jerry Bernstein
VICE PRESIDENT AND EXECUTIVE PRODUCER (West Coast)
  Larry DeLeon
VICE PRESIDENT-MIDWEST SALES REPRESENTATIVE (Chicago, 312-641-0808)
  Daniel O'Brien
DIRECTORS (East Coast)
  Bruce Dowad
  Michael Elliot
  Stephen Elliot
  Bob Forgione
  John McShane
  Mickey Trenner
DIRECTORS (West Coast)
  Richard Black
  Dick Cunha
  Stan Dragoti
  David Dryer
  Paul Herriot
  Remi Kramer
  Michael Zingale

EUE VIDEO

222 East 44th Street, N.Y. NY 10017 (212) 867-4030
EXECUTIVE VICE PRESIDENT AND GENERAL MANGER
  Dan Rosen
EXECUTIVE VICE PRESIDENT-OPERATIONS
  Shirley Danko
VICE PRESIDENT-ENGINEERING
  Steve Walsh
VICE PRESIDENT-VIDEO SYNDICATION
  Richard H. Smith
VICE PRESIDENT-VIDEO ACCOUNT EXECUTIVE
  Tim Timpanaro
VIDEO ACCOUNT EXECUTIVE-KINESCIPE
  Jerry Cantwell
DIRECTOR OF POST PRODUCTION SERVICES
  Mary Gibney
ACCOUNT EXECUTIVE-POST PRODUCTION SERVICES
  Jill Debin

ALTON FILMS

400 Madison Avenue, New York, N.Y. 10017 (212) 753-7522.
EXECUTIVE PRODUCER
Jordan Caldwell

INDEPENDENT ARTISTS

16 W. 56 Street, New York, N.Y. 10019 (212) 765-4640.
EXECUTIVE PRODUCER
Herb Sidel
SALES/PRODUCER
Paul Rosen
MIDWEST SALES REPRESENTATIVE (Chicago, 312-943-0606)
Al Gay

FRED LEVINSON & CO.

12 East 82 Street, New York, N.Y. 10028 (212) 472-8888.
PRODUCERS
Stephen Brind
Michael Sitzer

TESTPATTERNS

222 E. 44 Street, New York, N.Y. 10017 (212) 551-8480.
VICE PRESIDENT & EXECUTIVE PRODUCER
Robert Elliott

COLUMBIA PICTURES VIDEOCASSETTE SERVICES

1501 Landmeier Road, Elk Grove Village, Illinois 60007 (312) 640-2350.
EXECUTIVE VICE PRESIDENT
George Ricci
DIRECTOR-TECHNICAL SERVICES
Michael Sterling
GENERAL MANAGER
T. Martin Rennels
MANAGER-INDUSTRIAL SALES
Pamela M. Arnest
MANAGER-PAY TV SALES
Richard Oliver
OPERATIONS MANAGER
Alex Rafferty
CONTROLLER
Irene Janczkowski

EDITEL—CHICAGO

301 East Erie, Chicago, Illinois 60611 (312) 440-2360.
EXECUTIVE VICE PRESIDENT
Doyle Kaniff
GENERAL MANAGER
Lenard Pearlman
OPERATIONS MANAGER
Sarah Swiskow

EDITEL—LOS ANGELES

729 North Highland Ave., Hollywood, Calif. 90038 (213) 931-1821.
EXECUTIVE VICE PRESIDENT
Vince Lyons
GENERAL MANAGER
William Johnson
VICE PRESIDENT-ENGINEERING
Sam Holtz
CONTROLLER
Michael Vallens

D. GOTTLIEB & CO.

165 West Lake Street, Northlake, IL 60164 (312) 562-7400
CHAIRMAN OF THE BOARD
Alvin J. Gottlieb
PRESIDENT AND CHIEF EXECUTIVE OFFICER
Robert W. Bloom
VICE PRESIDENT-FINANCE & ADMINISTRATION
William J. Kwasniewski
VICE PRESIDENT-PRODUCT DEVELOPMENT
Gilbert G. Pollock

VICE PRESIDENT (MARKETING)
C. Marshall Caras
VICE PRESIDENT-PRODUCT MANAGEMENT
Howard Rubin
CONTROLLER
Daniel K. Miller

Comet International Film Associates

6200 West 3rd St., Los Angeles, CA 900436 (213) 930-0615 and 937-2460
PRESIDENT
Stanley Norman
VICE PRESIDENT
Michael Kirner
Branch Offices: Mexico 7 DF, 86, Tehuantepec, Tel.: 5-647728 and 647750; 8 Munich 2, Im Tal 18/III, Tel. 292202, West-Germany, Rome, Via di Villa Ruffo 21, Tel.: 316028.

Compass International Pictures

9229 Sunset Blvd., #818, Los Angeles, CA (213) 273-9125. (Distributor.)
PRESIDENT
Irwin Yablans
CONTROLLER
Margaret Grevich
SALES MANAGER
George Mitchell
DIRECTOR OF ADVERTISING & PUBLICITY
Barbara Javitz
DIRECTOR OF CABLE SALES
Diane Ward

The Corporation for Entertainment & Learning, Inc.

515 Madison Avenue, New York, NY 10022. (212) 421-4030. Creators of Cindex, a visual encyclopedia of American in the 20th Century on motion picture film and tape.)
PRESIDENT
Merton Y. Koplin
EXECUTIVE VICE PRESIDENT
Charles D. Grinker

Thomas Craven Film Corp.

316 East 53rd St., New York, NY 10022 (Producer featurettes and documentaries TV Programs.)
PRESIDENT
Thomas Craven
CONTROLLER
Marvin Barouch
DIRECTOR OF PRODUCTION
Willis Briley
DATE OF ORGANIZATION
1951

Crosby, Bing, Production, Inc.

6311 Romaine St., Hollywood, CA 90038 (213) 465-3114.
VICE-PRESIDENT—FINANCE & BUSINESS AFFAIRS
J. R. Rodgers
SECRETARY & TREASURER
Ray Tucker
ASSISTANT SECRETARY & ASSISTANT TREASURER
Al Chunka

Crossover Programming Company

1237 7th St., Santa Monica, CA 90401 (213) 451-9762.
Supplier of original programming for pay television; producer of variety shows, specials, commercials documentaries; titles and special montages.
PRESIDENT
Charles Braverman
VICE PRESIDENT
Michael Roach

456

DIRECTOR OF PHOTOGRAPHY
  Mark Krenzien
FIELD PRODUCER AND EDITOR
  Dale Beldin
EDITORS
  Marshall Harvey, Ted Herrmann

Crown International Pictures

292 South La Cienega Blvd., Beverly Hills, CA 90211 (213) 657-6700.
PRESIDENT & CHIEF OPERATING OFFICER
  Mark Tenser
VICE PRESIDENT/BUSINESS AFFAIRS
  Albert Giles
GENERAL SALES MANAGER
  Mitchell Blum
CONTROLLER
  Terry Myerson
DIRECTOR OF ADVERTISING & PUBLICITY
  John Calhoun
DIRECTOR OF PAY TELEVISION
  Jon Douglas
DOMESTIC COORDINATOR
  Richard Ettlinger
WESTERN DIVISION SALES MANAGER
  Don Foster
LOS ANGELES BRANCH MANAGER
  Jim Prince
DISTRICT MANAGER, SAN FRANCISCO, SEATTLE
  Andy Anderson
DATE OF ORGANIZATION
  1959

Crystal Pictures, Inc.

1560 Broadway, New York, NY 10036 (212) 757-5130; Cable: CRYSPIC NEW YORK. TELEX: 620852.
(Importers and exporters of theatrical and TV films, shorts and documentaries, film financing and specialized distribution, domestic and foreign.)
PRESIDENT
  F. Feinstein
GENERAL SALES MANAGER
  Sidney Tage

A. S. Csaky Motion Pictures, Inc.

15 Hull Avenue, Annapolis, MD 21403 (301) 439-6943 and 267-6778. (Development and production of screen properties and distribution of theatrical films; publication production; graphics, designs and photography; television and radio commercials; talent management.)
CHAIRMAN OF THE BOARD AND PRESIDENT
  A. S. Csaky
SENIOR VICE PRESIDENTS—PRODUCTION
  Prof. Thaddeus G. Csaky
  Mary C. Turpin
VICE PRESIDENT—ADVERTISING
  Robert Kriger
VICE PRESIDENT—SCREENPLAY DEVELOPMENT
  Bud Fleisher
LEGAL COUNSEL
  Goldstein, Ahalt & Bennett
RESEARCH LIBRARIAN
  Mary L. Becker
LOCATION DEVELOPMENT—EUROPE
  Massimo Silvi
LOCATION DEVELOPMENT—MIDDLE EAST
  Sirious Parsaei
LOCATION DEVELOPMENT—EAST AFRICA
  Vincent F. Cidosa
DATE OF ORGANIZATION
  1968

Cutlass Productions, Inc.

10202 W. Washington Blvd., Culver City, CA 90230 (213) 836-3000.
PRESIDENT
  Frank P. Rosenberg
VICE PRESIDENT & TREASURER
  Herbert M. Gross

SECRETARY
  Maryanne S. Rosenberg
DATE OF ORGANIZATION
  1975

Dale System, Inc., Theatre Division

200 Garden City Plaza, Garden City, NY 11530. (516) 741-2070. Nationwide system for testing honesty and efficiency of theatre personnel through use of checkers, undercover operatives and polygraph examinations. Evaluates procedures, eliminates loss.
CHAIRMAN
  Addison H. Verrill
PRESIDENT
  Harvey Yaffe
VICE PRESIDENT
  Maurice (Mickey) Gitlin
TREASURER
  Alan Lowell
THEATRE DIVISION DIRECTOR
  Helen Robin
BRANCH OFFICES
  New Haven, Boston, Cleveland, Pittsburgh, Rochester, Maplewood, Miami, New York, Los Angeles, Kansas City.

Dandrea Releasing

3412 West Olive Avenue, Burbank, CA 91505 (213) 846-8441. (Motion picture production and distribution.)
PRESIDENT
  Irvin S. Dorfman
DATE OF ORGANIZATION
  1973

D. A. D. Films, Ltd.

726 N. Cahuenga Blvd., Hollywood, CA 90038 (213) 469-6256. (Motion picture production and distribution.)
PRESIDENT
  Donald A. Davi

Curt Deckert Associates, Inc.

Koll Center, Suite 3000, 4000 MacArthur Blvd., Newport Beach, CA 92660 (714) 851-9110; (213) 488-1161; (415) 362-1579. (Technical management and marketing consultants; development of optical-photographic special effects equipment.)
PRESIDENT
  Curt Deckert
SECRETARY/TREASURER
  Janet Deckert
DATE OF ORGANIZATION
  1976

DeVecchi, Mario, Productions

℅ Stern and Fixler, 950 Third Ave., New York, NY 10022 (212) 355-7220. (Film producer and producer's representative.)
OWNER & PRESIDENT
  Mario De Vecchi
DATE OF ORGANIZATION
  1963

Dino De Laurentiis Corporation

One Gulf & Western Plaza, New York, N.Y. 10023 (212) 399-0101.
CHAIRMAN OF THE BOARD
  Dino De Laurentiis
EXECUTIVE VICE PRESIDENT AND TREASURER
  Fredric M. Sidewater
GENERAL COUNSEL AND VICE PRESIDENT
  J. Blake Lowe, Jr.

VICE PRESIDENT IN CHARGE OF PRODUCTION
Federico De Laurentiis
CONTROLLER
Gary Massimino

Disney, Walt, Productions

500 South Buena Vista Street, Burbank, CA 91521
(213) 840-1000

CHAIRMAN OF THE BOARD AND CHIEF EXECUTIVE OF-
FICER
E. Cardon Walker
CHAIRMAN OF THE EXECUTIVE COMMITTEE
Donn B. Tatum
PRESIDENT & CHIEF OPERATING OFFICER
Ronald W. Miller
SENIOR VICE PRESIDENT—FINANCE
Michael L. Bagnall
SENIOR VICE PRESIDENT—BUSINESS AND LEGAL AF-
FAIRS
Ronald J. Cayo
SENIOR VICE PRESIDENT WALT DISNEY MARKETING DI-
VISION
Vincent H. Jefferds
SENIOR VICE PRESIDENT—ADVERTISING, PUBLICITY,
PROMOTION AND PUBLIC RELATIONS
Jack B. Lindquist
VICE PRESIDENT—CONSUMER PRODUCTION AND MER-
CHANDISING
Barton K. Boyd
VICE PRESIDENT—EPCOT
Carl G. Bongirno
VICE PRESIDENT—TAX ADMINISTRATION AND COUNSEL
Jose M. Deetjen
VICE PRESIDENT—STUDIO OPERATIONS
Robert W. Gibeaut
VICE PRESIDENT—CORPORATE AND STOCKHOLDER AF-
FAIRS
Luther R. Marr
VICE PRESIDENT—GENERAL COUNSEL
Richard T. Morrow
VICE PRESIDENT—TELEVISION
Lennart Ringquist
VICE PRESIDENT—WALT DISNEY OUTDOOR RECREA-
TION DIVISION
Richard A. Nunis
VICE PRESIDENT—CONSTRUCTION AND CONTRACT
ADMINISTRATION AND PURCHASING
Howard M. Roland
SECRETARY
Doris A. Smith
TREASURER
Donald A. Escen
CONTROLLER
Bruce F. Johnson
ASSISTANT SECRETARY-TREASURER
Leland L. Kirk
ASSISTANT SECRETARY
Neal E. McClure
ASSISTANT TREASURER
Donald E. Tucker
ASSISTANT CONTROLLER
Douglas E. Houck
DIRECTORS
Philip M. Hawley, Caroline Leonetti Ahmanson, Roy E. Disney,
Ronald W. Miller, Richard T. Morrow, Donn B. Tatum, E. Cardon
Walker, Raymond L. Watson, William Anderson, Advisory direc-
tors: Ignacio E. Lozano, Richard A. Nunis.

Walt Disney Music Company

500 South Buena Vista Street, Burbank, CA 91521.

CHAIRMAN OF THE BOARD
E. Cardon Walker
VICE PRESIDENT—GENERAL MANAGER
Gary Krisel
EXECUTIVE VICE PRESIDENT
Vincent H. Jefferds
VICE PRESIDENT—MAGIC KINGDOM CLUB
Jack B. Lindquist
VICE PRESIDENT—LEGAL
Luther R. Marr
VICE PRESIDENT—DISNEY SCHOOLHOUSE
James P. Jimirro
SECRETARY
Doris A. Smith
ASSISTANT SECRETARY
Franklin Waldheim

TREASURER
Donald A. Escen
DIRECTORS
E. Cardon Walker, Gary Krisel, Vincent H. Jefferds, Luther R.
Marr, Donn B. Tatum

Dubie-Do Productions, Inc.

New York City (212) 765-4240 or 1 Laurie Drive,
Englewood Cliffs, NJ 07632 (201) 568-4214. (Produc-
tion of motion pictures for Theatres and TV.)
PRESIDENT
Richard S. Dubelman

M. Ducommun Company, Minerva Stopwatches

48 Main Street, Warwick, NY 10990 (914) 986-5757.
(Specialists in timing instruments for radio, TV, films;
headquarters for stop watch repairs and servicing—
all makes.)
PRESIDENT
M. Ducommun

EDP Films, Inc.

600 Madison Avenue, New York, NY 10022. (212)
758-4777. (Motion picture distribution.)
PRESIDENT
Eugene D. Picker
VICE PRESIDENT
Peter Kares

EMI Films, Inc.

9489 Dayton Way, Beverly Hills, CA 90210 (213) 278-
4770. (Motion picture production and distribution.)
EXECUTIVE VICE-PRESIDENT
John Kohn
VICE PRESIDENT
Norma A. Jackson
CONTROLLER
Richard West
DATE OF ORGANIZATION
1971

The E.O. Corp.

P.O. Box 184, Shelby, NC 28150 (704) 482-0611.
(Motion picture production and distribution.)
PRESIDENT
Earl Owensby
VICE PRESIDENT
Gene Blackburn
SECRETARY
Linda Comer
SALES MANAGER
Michael Putnam
DATE OF ORGANIZATION
1973

Eastman Kodak Company

343 State Street, Rochester, NY 14650, (716) 724-
4000; 1901 W. 22nd St., Oakbrook, IL 60521 (312) 654-
5300; 6706 Santa Monica Boulevard, Hollywood, CA
90038. (213) 464-6131; 1133 Ave. of the Americas, NY.,
NY 10036 (212) 262-6000. (Motion picture film offices
& laboratories.)
Also located at: 3250 Van Ness Avenue, San Francisco, CA 94109 (415) 776-6055; 6300 Cedar Springs
Road, Dallas. TX 75235 (214) 351-3221.

CHAIRMAN OF THE BOARD & CHIEF EXECUTIVE OFFI-
CER
Walter A. Fallon
PRESIDENT
Colby H. Chandler

458

VICE PRESIDENT, DIRECTOR, CORPORATE COMMERCIAL AFFAIRS
David S. Greenlaw
VICE PRESIDENT, DIRECTOR, PHOTOGRAPHIC STRATEGIC PLANNING
R. Frederick Porter
ASSISTANT VICE PRESIDENT & DIRECTOR GOVERNMENT RELATIONS
T. Hiatt
VICE PRESIDENT & DIRECTOR CORPORATE COMMUNICATIONS
D. J. Metz
DIRECTOR CORPORATE PLANNING
R. B. Murray

U.S. AND CANADIAN PHOTOGRAPHIC DIVISION

EXEC. VICE PRESIDENT, GENERAL MANAGER, U.S. & CANADIAN PHOTOGRAPHIC DIV.
Douglass C. Harvey
EXEC. VICE PRESIDENT & GENERAL MANAGER, PHOTOGRAPHIC DIVISION
K. R. Whitmore
VICE PRESIDENT, INTERNATIONAL PHOTOGRAPHIC DIVISION
Anthony Frothingham
VICE PRESIDENT, GENERAL MANAGER, MARKETING DIV.
J. Phillip Samper
VICE PRESIDENT, GENERAL MANAGER, CUSTOMER EQUIPMENT SERVICE DIV.
John H. Barnes
VICE PRESIDENT, GENERAL MANAGER, HEALTH SCIENCES DIVISION
John C. Fink
VICE PRESIDENT, GENERAL MANAGER, MOTION PICTURE AND AUDIOVISUAL MARKETS DIVISION
Kenneth M. Mason
ASSISTANT VICE PRESIDENT, DIRECTOR, ADVERTISING AND PROMOTION
William K. Pedersen
VICE PRESIDENT GENERAL MANAGER, CONSUMER MARKETS, CONSUMER/PROFESSIONAL & FINISHING MARKETS DIVISION
John R. Robertson
VICE PRESIDENT, GENERAL MANAGER, GRAPHICS MARKETS DIVISION
William E. Sherman
VICE PRESIDENT, GENERAL MANAGER, BUSINESS SYSTEMS MARKETS DIVISION
J. Raymond Sutcliffe
VICE PRESIDENT, GENERAL MANAGER, KODAK PARK DIVISION
Richard T. Kramer
VICE PRESIDENT, ASST. GENERAL MANAGER, KODAK PARK DIVISION
Wendel W. Cook
VICE PRESIDENT, GENERAL MANAGER, DISTRIBUTION DIVISION
George A. Snyder
VICE PRESIDENT, GENERAL MANAGER, KODAK APPARATUS DIVISION
J. M. Sewell
ASST. VICE PRESIDENT, ASST. GENERAL MANAGER, KODAK APPARATUS DIVISION
Richard C. Kleinhans
PRESIDENT AND GENERAL MANAGER, KODAK CANADA LTD.
Bramwell B. Coles

INTERNATIONAL PHOTOGRAPHIC DIVISION

GROUP VICE PRESIDENT, GENERAL MANAGER, INTL. PHOTOGRAPHIC DIVISION
C. J. Murphy
VICE PRESIDENT, GENERAL MANAGER, EUROPEAN REGION
David W. Hunt
CHAIRMAN & MANAGING DIRECTOR, KODAK LTD. (UNITED KINGDOM)
F. James Moorfoot
GENERAL MANAGER, KODAK A.G. (WEST GERMANY)
Helmut Nagel
PRESIDENT & GENERAL MANAGER, KODAK-PATHE S.A. (FRANCE)
Paul L. Vuillaume
VICE PRESIDENT, GENERAL MANAGER, ASIAN, AFRICAN, & AUSTRALIAN REGION
John E. Riggs
VICE PRESIDENT, GENERAL MANAGER, LATIN AMERICAN REGION
R. L. Smith

EASTERN CHEMICALS DIVISION

EXEC. VICE PRESIDENT, GENERAL MANAGER, EASTMAN CHEMICALS DIVISION
T. J. Reid
VICE PRESIDENT, ASSISTANT GENERAL MANAGER, EASTMAN CHEMICALS DIVISION
Robert C. Petrey
VICE PRESIDENT, ASSISTANT GENERAL MANAGER, EASTMAN CHEMICALS DIVISION
J. H. Sanders
VICE PRESIDENT, GENERAL MANAGER's STAFF, EASTMAN CHEMICALS DIVISION
James A. Mitchell
PRESIDENT, ARKANSAS EASTMAN CO.
Marvin L. Gemert
PRESIDENT, TENNESSEE EASTMAN CO.
R. C. Hart
PRESIDENT, CAROLINA EASTMAN CO.
E. M. Olson
PRESIDENT, TEXAS EASTMAN CO.
Jack C. Vander Woude

EASTMAN TECHNOLOGY, INC.

PRESIDENT, EASTMAN TECHNOLOGY, INC.
David S. Greenlaw
PRESIDENT, SPIN PHYSICS, INC.
James U. Lemke

KODAK RESEARCH LABORATORIES

VICE PRESIDENT, DIRECTOR, KODAK RESEARCH LABORATORIES
Leo J. Thomas

Legal

SENIOR VICE PRESIDENT & GENERAL COUNSEL
Kendall M. Cole
SECRETARY
Leonard S. Zartman
ASST. SECRETARY
James K. Robinson

Finance and Administration

SENIOR VICE PRESIDENT, DIRECTOR, FINANCE & ADMINISTRATION
Robert A. Sherman
ASSISTANT VICE PRESIDENT, DIRECTOR, ADMINISTRATIVE SERVICES
Roy N. Holmes
ASSISTANT VICE PRESIDENT, DIRECTOR, CORPORATE PHOTOGRAPHIC PRICING
Collins M. McKelvey
GENERAL COMPTROLLER
L. G. Pierce
ASSISTANT COMPTROLLERS
Wayne K. Gilman, Donald R. Whitney
TREASURER
Donald E. Snyder
ASST. TREASURER
Harold C. Passer

Corporate Relations

SENIOR VICE PRESIDENT DIRECTOR, CORPORATE RELATIONS
James S. Bruce
VICE PRESIDENT, ASSISTANT DIRECTOR, CORPORATE RELATIONS
William L. Sutton
DIRECTORS
Walter A. Fallon, Roger E. Anderson, James S. Bruce, Colby H. Chandler, Kendall M. Cole, Charles T. Duncan, Douglass C. Harvey, Robert S. Hatfield, J. Paul Lyet, T. F. Reid, Robert A. Sherman, J. C. Smale, W. Allen Wallis, Gerald B. Zornow, Juanita M. Kreps
EXECUTIVE COMMITTEE
Walter A. Fallon, James S. Bruce, Colby H. Chandler, Kendall M. Cole, Douglass C. Harvey, T. F. Reid, Robert A. Sherman

Enterprises Productions, Inc.

P.O. Box 424, Malibu, CA 90265 (213) 456-6616.
(Motion picture production and distribution.)
PRESIDENT AND TREASURER
Jack H. Harris
ADMINISTRATION
Beth Woods
DATE OF ORGANIZATION
1970

Entertainment Marketing Corporation

159 West 53rd St., New York, NY 10019 (212) 757-9706. (Motion picture marketing services and distribution.)
PRESIDENT
E. Anthony Myerberg
ASSISTANT TO PRESIDENT
Eleanor Kane
TRAFFIC MANAGER
Peri Nussbaum
HEAD BOOKKEEPER
G. Epstein
DATE OF ORGANIZATION
1977

Entertainment Ventures, Inc.

1654 Cordova St., Los Angeles, CA 90007 (213) 731-7236. (Motion picture production, distribution, exhibition.)
PRESIDENT
David F. Friedman
VICE PRESIDENT-SALES
Jerry Persell
SECRETARY-TREASURER
Dan L. Sonney
CONTROLLER
Beatric Hurwitz
DATE OF ORGANIZATION
1964

Epic Productions, Inc.

626 South Hudson Avenue, Los Angeles, CA 90005 (213) 937-5000. (Distributor of motion pictures.)
PRESIDENT
G. David Schine

Everest Cine-Metaphors, Inc.

213 East 53rd St., New York, NY 10022 (212) 838-5599. (Film and video production and distribution; features; shorts; recordings; TV series, etc.)
PRESIDENT
Prince Chandra/Niel Everest
EXECUTIVE VICE PRESIDENT
Elliott H. Knoe

FDM Productions

745 Fifth Ave., New York, NY 10151. (Film production.)
PRESIDENT
Francois de Menil
DATE OF ORGANIZATION
1970

Factor-Newland Production Corporation

1438 N. Gower Street, Suite 250, Los Angeles, CA 90028 (213) 467-1143. (Motion picture and TV production.)
CHAIRMAN OF THE BOARD
John Newland
PRESIDENT
Alan Jay Factor
EXECUTIVE VICE PRESIDENT—BUSINESS AFFAIRS
Milton T. Raynor
PRODUCTION SUPERVISOR
Hal Schaffel
CONTROLLER
Stuart Besser
COUNSEL
Herbert Baerwitz
DATE OF ORGANIZATION
1975

Fairbanks, Jerry, Productions

826 No. Cole Avenue, Hollywood, CA 90038 (213) 462-1101. (Producer of theatrical short subjects and features, commercial and television films.)
EXECUTIVE PRODUCER
Jerry Fairbanks
CREATIVE DEPARTMENT
Leo S. Rosencrans

WESTERN AUDIO VISUAL ENTERPRISES

826 No. Cole Avenue, Hollywood, CA 90038 (213) 466-8567. (Motion picture print distribution center.)
OWNER
Jerry Fairbanks

YUKON PICTURES, INC.

826 No. cole Ave., Hollywood, CA 90038 (213) 462-0701. (Theatrical feature production and distribution.)
PRESIDENT
Jerry Fairbanks

Famous Players International

1210 N. Wetherly Drive W. Hollywood, CA 90069 (213) 276-6627. (Producers.)
PRESIDENT
Albert Zugsmith
VICE-PRESIDENT & TREASURER
Susanne Zugsmith
SECRETARY
Suzan Smith
ASSISTANT SECRETARY
Leane Morgan
BOARD OF DIRECTORS
Albert Zugsmith, Susanne Zugsmith, Suzan Smith

Fasha Enterprise, Inc.

11422 Harry Hines Blvd., Dallas, TX (214) 243-5171. (Motion picture distribution.)
PRESIDENT
Charles D. King
FIRST VICE PRESIDENT
James G. Slater
SECOND VICE PRESIDENT
William Crane
SECRETARY
R. V. Coalson
DATE OF ORGANIZATION
1975

Feltner Entertainment Corporation

Box 664, Palm Beach, FL 33480; New York office: One Times Square, NY 10036 (212) 354-3966. (Produces motion pictures.)
CHAIRMAN OF THE BOARD
C. E. Feltner, Jr.
EXECUTIVE VICE PRESIDENT
Robert J. Levine

Film Investment Corp.

2055 South Saviers Road, Suite 12, Oxnard, CA 93030 (805) 486-4495. Cable: WEISSPICT (Producer-Distributor of motion pictures and TV films.)
PRESIDENT
Adrian Weiss
SECRETARY TREASURER
Steven A. Weiss
OPERATIONS MANAGER
Joleen Meibos

FilmFair, Inc.

10900 Ventura Blvd., Studio City, CA 19604 (213) 877-3191. (Film production.)

PRESIDENT
  William D. Jekel
VICE PRESIDENTS
  Gus Jekel, Theodore Geotz
DATE OF ORGANIZATION
  1959

Filmcrest International Corporation

595 Madison Ave., New York, NY 10022 (212) 371-4620. (Motion picture distributor)
PRESIDENT & CHIEF EXECUTIVE OFFICER
  Pedro Teitelbaum
DATE OF ORGANIZATION
  1980

Film/Jamel Productions, Inc.

9200 Sunset Blvd., Suite 913, Los Angeles, CA 90069 (213) 273-7773.
PRESIDENT
  Gilbert Cates

Filmlife, Incorporated, Founders of American Film Repair Institute

141 Moonachie Road, Moonachie, NJ 07074 (201) 440-8500. West Coast sales office: 1456 Aldridge Dr., Beverly Hills, CA. (Restoration, protection and preservation of damaged motion picture film including scratch removal, rehumidification of brittle film, removal of abrasions, cinch marks, curls, dirt, shrinkage, oil stains, etc.; Theatrical & television storage, shipping and distribution worldwide; Close inspection and repair of TV syndication prints prior to each station's screening. Additional services: editing, commercial insertions and deletions of shows, national and international booking.
PRESIDENT & CHIEF EXECUTIVE OFFICER
  Marvin A. Bernard
CHAIRMAN OF THE BOARD
  John Natali
EXECUTIVE VICE PRESIDENT
  Sheila N. Bernard
FIRST VICE PRESIDENT
  Milton Miller
GENERAL MANAGER
  George F. Leuck
MARKETING DIRECTOR
  Lawrence Bernard
ADMINISTRATIVE DIRECTOR
  Mary Ann Vonderosten
DIRECTOR OF TECHNICAL OPERATIONS
  Paul Delplare
CHIEF ENGINEER & DESIGNER
  Russell Dupree
CHIEF LABORATORY STAFF
  Toni Caruso
WESTERN REGIONAL DIRECTOR
  Ben Harris
ADVISORY BOARD
  Gerson Feiner, Michael Garstin, Gerald Armstrong, George Geller, Marvin Kratter, Russell Knapp.

The Film Company

1600 Broadway, Suite 701, New York, NY 10019. (212) 246-2750. (Film production for theatres and television)
OFFICERS
  Elliot Geisinger, Ronald Saland, Howard Kuperman, Marcel Broekman
DATE OF ORGANIZATION
  1980

Filmplan International

Montreal: 225 Roy St. East, Montreal, Quebec, Canada. H2W 1M5 (514) 845-5211. Toronto: 2 Elgin Ave., Toronto, Ontario, Canada. M5R 2G6 (416) 922-3168. Telex: 05-27238. (Producer)
PRINCIPALS
  Pierre David, Victor Solnicki, Claude Heroux
DATE OF ORGANIZATION
  1979

Films Around the World, Inc.

745 Fifth Avenue, New York, NY 10151. (212) 752-5050. Telex: 420572.
PRESIDENT
  Irvin Shapiro
VICE PRESIDENT
  Diana F. Shapiro
SECRETARY
  Anne Exelberth

Filmtreat International Corp.

National Headquarters: 250 W. 64th St., New York, NY 10023 (212) 799-2500. (Rejuvenation of Damaged Film, Inspection, Storage and Cleaning Facilities.)
PRESIDENT
  Y. W. Mociuk
VICE PRESIDENT
  Sam Borodinsky

Film Ventures International, Inc.

16027 Ventura Boulevard, Suite 201, Encino, CA 91436.
PRESIDENT AND CHIEF EXECUTIVE OFFICER
  Edward L. Montoro
VICE PRESIDENT AND CHIEF OPERATING OFFICER
  Robert Evans
VICE PRESIDENT-DIRECTOR OF MARKETING
  Sam Helfman
VICE PRESIDENT AND GENERAL SALES MANAGER
  Robert Steuer

Filmways, Inc.

2049 Century Park East, Suite 3500, Los Angeles, CA 90067 (213) 557-8700; 540 Madison Avenue, New York, NY 10022 (212) 758-5100.
CHAIRMAN, CHIEF EXECUTIVE OFFICER AND PRESIDENT
  Richard L. Bloch
VICE CHAIRMAN OF THE BOARD
  L. Douglas Nolan
EXECUTIVE VICE PRESIDENT & CHIEF OPERATING OFFICER
  Gerald S. Armstrong
EXECUTIVE VICE PRESIDENT
  Robert A. Grunburg
SENIOR VICE PRESIDENT & CHIEF FINANCIAL OFFICER
  Michael E. Garstin
SENIOR VICE PRESIDENTS
  Salvatore J. Iannucci, Jr., Stanley S. Sills
SENIOR VICE PRESIDENT/GENERAL COUNSEL & SECRETARY
  Alan R. Markizon
VICE PRESIDENT, CONTROLLER, CHIEF ACCOUNTING OFFICER, TREASURER, ASSISTANT SECRETARY
  Eugene Boylan
ASSISTANT SECRETARY
  David Z. Rosensweig
ASSISTANT SECRETARY
  Barbara Shapiro
DIRECTORS:
  Richard L. Bloch, Alfred di Scipio, Lawrence H. Manheimer, L. Douglas Nolan, Donald Pitt, Robert A. Grunburg, James A. Harmon, David Z. Rosensweig, Alan R. Markizon, Allan B. Goldman, Michael Garstin, Gerald Armstrong

SUBSIDIARIES

Motion Picture & Television Production:
  Filmways Pictures, Inc., 9033 Wilshire Blvd., Beverly Hills, CA 90211 (213) 278-8118
  Filmways Television, Inc., 2049 Century Park East, Los Angeles, CA 90067 (213) 557-8700
  Filmways Productions, Inc., 2049 Century Park East, Los Angeles, CA 90067 (213) 557-8700

Domestic & International Television Syndication and Theatrical and Non-Theatrical Motion Picture Distribution:
Filmways International, Ltd., 2049 Century Park East, Los Angeles, CA 90067 (213) 557-8700
Filmways Enterprises, Inc., 2049 Century Park East, Los Angeles, CA 90067 (213) 557-8700
Filmways Pictures, Inc., 9033 Wilshire Blvd., Beverly Hills, CA 90211 (213) 278-8118

Filmways Pictures, Inc.

9033 Wilshire Blvd., Beverly Hills, CA 90211 (213) 278-8118. (Distributor) (A subsidiary of Filmways, Inc.)
CHAIRMAN OF THE BOARD
  George Litto
PRESIDENT & CHIEF OPERATING OFFICER
  Robert Meyers
VICE CHAIRMAN OF THE BOARD
  Richard L. Bloch
EXECUTIVE VICE PRESIDENT—WORLDWIDE SALES AND DISTRIBUTION
  Joseph M. Sugar
EXECUTIVE VICE PRESIDENT—WORLDWIDE ADVERTISING/PUBLICITY/PROMOTION
  Jonas Rosenfield
EXECUTIVE VICE PRESIDENT
  Eugene Tunick
EXECUTIVE VICE PRESIDENT BUSINESS AFFAIRS
  Rudy Petersdorf
GENERAL SALES MANAGER & SECRETARY
  Alan R. Markizon
ASSISTANT TREASURER
  Lucille Keister
ASSISTANT SECRETARY
  M. Morton Seigel
VICE PRESIDENT—CONTROLLER
  James C. Bullard
VICE PRESIDENT OF ADVERTISING/PUBLICITY/PROMOTION
  Edward Russell
DIRECTOR OF CREATIVE ADVERTISING & AFFAIRS
  Michael Kaiser
NATIONAL DIRECTOR PUBLICITY
  Richard Delson
NEW YORK PUBLICITY—ADVERTISING FIELD REPRESENTATIVE
  Lawrence Steinfeld
VICE PRESIDENT AND FOREIGN OPERATIONS MANAGER
  Murray Cohen
SENIOR VICE PRESIDENT—PRODUCTION
  Jeff Young
SENIOR VICE PRESIDENT—PRODUCTION MANAGEMENT
  Michael S. Glick
VICE PRESIDENT—PRODUCTION
  Christopher Chesser
VICE PRESIDENT—POST PRODUCTION
  Salvatore Billitteri

Filmwest Associates Limited

10116-105 Avenue, Edmonton, Alberta, Canada T5H OK2; (403) 439-2075. (Producer-distributor of educational, documentary, industrial, historical and theatrical films. Production services.)
PRESIDENT
  Dale Phillips
VICE PRESIDENT
  Bob Reece
SECRETARY-TREASURER
  Ken Pappes
FILMMAKERS
  Allan Stein, Harvey Spak

Filmworld Export Corp.

745 Fifth Avenue, New York, NY 10151 (212) 752-5050. Telex: 420572.
PRESIDENT
  Irvin Shapiro
VICE PRESIDENT
  Diana F. Shapiro
SECRETARY
  Anne Exelberth

First American Films

4265 Marina City Dr., Suite 203, Marina del Rey, CA 90291 (213) 821-4444. (Financing, production and distribution of motion pictures.)
CHAIRMAN OF THE BOARD & PRESIDENT
  John B. Kelly
VICE PRESIDENT
  Frank McGrath
VICE PRESIDENT MARKETING & PROMOTION
  Robert A. McGree
DIRECTOR OF DISTRIBUTION
  John J. McGettican
OFFICE MANAGER
  Donna Baker

First Artists Production Company, Ltd.

14651 Ventura Blvd., Ste. 210, Sherman Oaks, CA 91403 (213) 995-4121. (Operates in the areas of developing, financing, producing and distributing theatrical motion pictures and the importing, manufacturing and sale of men's sports shirts.)
DIRECTOR & PRESIDENT
  Edwin E. Holly
DIRECTOR VICE PRESIDENTS
  Joel Schwartz
SECRETARY
  Edward Rubin
ASSISTANT SECRETARY
  Karolyn Hilker
DIRECTOR
  Philip L. Lowe
TREASURER
  Adelina Villaflor
DIRECTOR
  Edward Traubner

Franklin Media Corp.

123 East 54th St., New York, NY 10022. (212) 888-1050. (Production and distribution)
PRESIDENT
  Dan Pomerantz
EXECUTIVE VICE PRESIDENT
  Kobi Jaeger
DIRECTOR OF DISTRIBUTION
  Ed Cruea
ADMINISTRATIVE DIRECTOR
  Orly Berger
DATE OF ORGANIZATION
  1978

Frankovich Productions

9200 Sunset Blvd., Suite 920, Los Angeles, CA 90069 (213) 278-0929. (Motion picture and television production.)
PRESIDENT
  M. J. Frankovich
VICE PRESIDENT
  Binnie Barnes Frankovich
SECRETARY & TREASURER
  Alexander Tucker
ASST. SECRETARIES
  Marvin Meyer, Don Rosenfeld
DATE OF ORGANIZATION
  1968

G. G. Communications, Inc.

20 Statler Bldg., Boston, MA 02116 (617) 542-9633. (Motion picture distribution.)
PRESIDENT AND TREASURER
  Nicholas W. Russo
VICE PRESIDENT AND NATIONAL SALES MANAGER
  Rick Russo

Gades Films International, Ltd.

1350 Avenue of Americas, New York, NY 10019. (212) 582-0840. Telex: 234963. (Representation of foreign film producers, acquisition of films, co-production and packaging.)

PRESIDENT
Gabriel Desdoits
VICE PRESIDENT
France Desdoits
DATE OF ORGANIZATION
1964

Global Entertainment Media Corporation (GEM)

901 Washington St., Wilmington DL 19801 (302) 654-5511. (Motion picture and television production and related activities)
PRESIDENT/PRODUCER/DIRECTOR
Travis Johnson
SECRETARY/TREASURER
Nelson F. Mansker
DATE OF ORGANIZATION
1977

Globe Pictures, Inc.

37 West 57th St., New York, NY 10019 (212) 751-6040. (Distributor.)
PRESIDENT
Joseph Green

The Golden Harvest Group

8 Hammerhill Road, Kowloon, Hong Kong. Tel.: 3-275155. (Financer, producer and distributor of motion pictures)
PRESIDENT
Raymond Chow
EXECUTIVE VICE PRESIDENT
Leonard K. C. Hol
VICE PRESIDENT PRODUCTION
Andre Morgan
VICE PRESIDENT DISTRIBUTION
Tom Gray
VICE PRESIDENT/CHIEF FINANCIAL OFFICER
Ron Dandrea
DATE OF ORGANIZATION
1970

Goldfarb Distributors

1888 Century Park East, #1218, Los Angeles, CA 90067 (223) 553-4144. (Producer and distributor)
PRESIDENT
Howard Goldfarb
VICE PRESIDENTS
Judi Goldfarb, Katy Moraskie
DATE OF ORGANIZATION
1978

Goldstone Film Enterprises, Inc.

69-11 184th Street, Fresh Meadows, NY 11365 (212) 969-7231. (Motion picture distribution.)
PRESIDENT
Harry Goldstone
COMPTROLLER & TREASURER
Florence Goldstone
SECRETARY
Estelle Friedman
ACCOUNTANT
Sol Sobel

Samuel Goldwyn, Productions, Inc.

1041 North Formosa Ave., Los Angeles, CA 90046 (213) 650-2407. (Producer.)
PRESIDENT
Samuel Goldwyn, Jr.
VICE PRESIDENT, SECRETARY & TREASURER
Meyer Gottlieb
BOARD OF DIRECTORS
Samuel Goldwyn, Jr., Meyer Gottlieb

Goldwyn, Samuel Studios

1041 North Formosa Avenue, Los Angeles, CA 90046 (213) 650-2500.
GENERAL MANAGER
Jack Foreman
ASST. GENERAL MANAGER
Donald Daves
CONTROLLER
Leonard Johnson

Goodson-Todman Productions

375 Park Ave., New York NY 10022 (212) 751-0600; 6430 Sunset Boulevard, Hollywood, CA 90028 (213) 464-4300 (Producer.)
CHIEF OFFICER
Mark Goodson
EXECUTIVE VICE PRESIDENT
Giraud Chester
VICE PRESIDENT DIRECTOR OF BUSINESS AFFAIRS
Howard F. Todman

Bert I. Gordon Films

9640 Arby Drive, Beverly Hills, CA 90210
PRESIDENT
Bert I. Gordon

Gordon Films, Inc.

10 Columbus Circle, New York, NY 10019 (212) 757-9390. (Producers and Distributors.)
PRESIDENT
Richard Gordon
VICE PRESIDENT
Joseph R. Cattuti
TREASURER
Richard Gordon
DATE OF ORGANIZATION
1949

Grand Slam Productions Corp.

225 West 57th St., Suite 301, New York, NY 10019. (212) 765-8587. (Motion picture production.)
PRESIDENT
Robert J. Kaplan
VICE PRESIDENT
Paul "Eagle" Cohen
TREASURER
Paul Leeman
DATE OF ORGANIZATION
1977

Greshler, Abner J. Productions, Inc.

9200 Sunset Blvd., Hollywood CA 90069 (213) 278-8146; 119 West 57th St., New York, NY (Producer.)
PRESIDENT AND TREASURER
Abner J. Greshler
VICE-PRESIDENT AND SECRETARY
Violet Greshler
NEW YORK MANAGER
Camille Harris
BOARD OF DIRECTORS
Abner J. Greshler, Violet Greshler, Woodrow N. Irwin

The Jerry Gross Organization

1901 Avenue of the Stars, Suite 1401, Los Angeles, CA 90067. (213) 552-9723. (Motion picture theatrical distributors)
PRESIDENT
Jerry Gross
SENIOR VICE PRESIDENT
Mari C. Kirnan
TREASURER
Sid Macofsky
VICE PRESIDENT
Steve Ader

DATE OF ORGANIZATION
1979

The Group 1 International Distribution Organization Ltd. (Group 1 Films)

9200 Sunset Blvd., Los Angeles, CA 90069 (213) 550-8767. Cable: Groupfilm Los Angeles. Telex: 673291. (Production and distribution of feature films, TV specials and TV series)

PRESIDENT
Brandon Chase
VICE PRESIDENT, FINANCIAL AFFAIRS
Larry Ackerman
VICE-PRESIDENT, GENERAL SALES MGR.
Jack Leff
LEGAL-EAST COAST
Myron Saland (Phillips, Nizer, Benjamin, Krim and Ballon)
LEGAL-WEST COAST
Saul Rittenberg (Loeb & Loeb)
PRODUCTION MANAGER
Storey Ames
POST PRODUCTION SUPERVISORS
Terry Forbes
Marty Levenstein
DOMESTIC SALES COORDINATOR
Leonard Capp
FOREIGN SALES COORDINATORS
London, Geoff Raines; Rome, Roberto Papaleo; Tokyo, Eiko Asuame; Munich, Peggy Reindl; Paris, Claude Nouchi
EUROPEAN PRODUCTION AND SALES SUPERVISOR
Marianne Schyberg
STORY EDITOR
Stephanie Cousins
TALENT COORDINATOR (U.S.A.)
George Champlis
TALENT COORDINATOR (EUROPE)
Simon DeVrey, Paris
ART DIRECTOR
Louis Freidman, N.Y.—Gregg Painton, L.A.
ADVERTISING DIRECTOR
Sander George, L.A.
ASST. SALES MANAGER (U.S.A.)
Marshall Thomas
NEW PROJECTS DEVELOPMENT
Frank Ray
NEW PRODUCT ACQUISITION
Marianne Schyberg
MAIL ROOM MANAGER
Barry Chase
PRODUCTION UNIT MANAGER
Simmy Bow
DATE OF ORGANIZATION
1964

Guinness Film Group

10100 Santa Monica Blvd., Suite 1580 Los Angeles, CA 90067 (213) 552-9977 (Motion picture production and distribution.)

PRESIDENT
Richard R. St. Johns
VICE PRESIDENT—PRODUCTION
John W. Hyde
VICE PRESIDENT—FINANCE
Matthew Minor
DATE OF ORGANIZATION
1976

Gus Productions, Inc.

10889 Wilshire Blvd., Suite 606, Los Angeles, CA 90024 (213) 936-2280. (Motion picture and television production.)

PRESIDENT
Alan J. Pakula
VICE PRESIDENT & TREASURER
Hannah C. Pakula
DATE OF ORGANIZATION
1969

Leo Gutman, Inc.

230 Park Ave., New York, NY 10017 (212) 682-5652.

(Distributor of theatrical motion pictures and television series.)

PRESIDENT
Leo A. Gutman
SECRETARY
Georgia B. Gutman
VICE PRESIDENT
Esther Balenzano
DATE OF ORGANIZATION
1967

HG Entertainment, Ltd.

141 East 56 St., Ninth Floor, New York, NY 10022 (212) 688-5815. (Distributor.)

PRESIDENT
M. A. Nelson
U.S. REPRESENTATIVE
J. Nelson

H.W.C., Inc.

250 S. County Road, Palm Beach, FL 33480 (305) 659-1660. (Film financing/production)

PRESIDENT
James J. McNamara
DATE OF ORGANIZATION
1979

Hanover Security Reports, Inc.

17 Battery Place, Suite 1028, New York, NY 10004. (212) 943-2370. (Open and blind checking of theatre attendance for distributors, industrial security programs, and general investigations. A wholly owned subsidiary of The McRoberts Corp.)

PRESIDENT
Thomas S. Perakos
DATE OF ORGANIZATION
1966

Hemdale Leisure Corporation

375 Park Ave., New York, NY 10022 (212) 421-9022. West Coast office: 9255 Sunset Blvd., Los Angeles, CA (213) 550-6894 (Producer)

Hollywood Film Archive

8344 Melrose Ave., Hollywood, CA 90069 (213) 933-3345. (Compiles and publishes motion picture reference information; also functions as research service.)

PRESIDENT
D. Richard Baer
DATE OF ORGANIZATION
1972

Hollywood International Film Corp. of America

1044 S. Hill St., Los Angeles CA 90015 (213) 749-2067.

PRESIDENT
Carlos Tobalina
VICE-PRESIDENT
Maria P. Tobalina
IN CHARGE OF SALES
Sandy Magdaleno

Harry Hope & Inter-Associates

3122 Arrowhead Drive, Hollywood, CA 90068 (213) 469-5596. (Producer and distributor of motion pictures.)

PRESIDENT
Harry Hope

TREASURER & VICE PRESIDENT
Nancy Chu
VICE PRESIDENT
James Griffin
SECRETARY
D. Fieldman
TREASURER & VICE PRESIDENT
O. Nichols
DATE OF INCORPORATION
1957
BRANCH OFFICES & ASSOCIATES
Spectacular Trading, 59 Via Archimede, Rome, Italy; Dragon Films
International, 11F Rm6, 760 Nathan Rd., Hong Kong.

Horizon Pictures, Inc.

711 Fifth Ave., New York, NY 10022 (212) 421-6810.
(Producer.)
PRESIDENT
Sam Spiegel
SECRETARY
Albert Heit
DATE OF ORGANIZATION
1948

Sandy Howard Productions

1302 Devlin Dr., Los Angeles, CA 90069 (213) 657-
8300 (Film production)
PRESIDENT
Sandy Howard
EXECUTIVE VICE PRESIDENT/HEAD OF PRODUCTION
Derek Gibson
HEAD OF CREATIVE AFFAIRS
Sandra Bailey
HEAD OF BUSINESS AFFAIRS
Keith Rubinstein

Hurlock Cine-World, Inc.

13 Arcadia Rd., Old Greenwich, CT 06870 (203) 637-
4319. (Distributor.)
PRESIDENT & TREASURER
Roger W. Hurlock
VICE-PRESIDENT & SECRETARY
Mary L. Hurlock
VICE PRESIDENT-OPERATIONS
Ronald J. Hurlock
VICE PRES. & SALES MANAGER
John R. Hurlock
DATE OF ORGANIZATION
1969

ILRO Productions, Ltd.

9056 Santa Monica Blvd., Los Angeles, CA 90069
(213) 276-3532. (Producers for films and television.)
PRESIDENT
Curtis Roberts
VICE PRESIDENT
Ahna Lee
SECRETARY
John Woolf
TREASURER
Baxter Lehman, Jr.
DATE OF ORGANIZATION
1975

Imagery Films, Inc.

2509 N. Campbell Ave., Suite 213, Tucson, AZ 85719
(602) 745-5971. (Motion picture production.)
PRESIDENT
Ken Byrnes
VICE PRESIDENTS
J. Frank James, Ray Cardi, Marie Cardi
DATE OF ORGANIZATION
1976

The Images Film Archive, Inc.

300 Phillips Park Road, Mamaroneck, NY 10543
(914) 381-2993. (Distributor)

PRESIDENT
Robert A. Harris
VICE PRESIDENT
Steve Feltes
DATE OF ORGANIZATION
1977

ITC Entertainment, Inc.

115 East 57th Street, New York, NY 10022 (212)
371-6660. (A wholly owned subsidiary of Associated
Communications Company.)
PRESIDENT
Abe Mandell
SENIOR EXECUTIVE VICE PRESIDENT—CORPORATE
ADMINISTRATION, FINANCE & BUSINESS AFFAIRS:
TREASURER & SECRETARY
Leonard I. Kornblum
EXECUTIVE VICE PRESIDENT—U.S. SYNDICATION SALES
Pierre Weis
EXECUTIVE VICE PRESIDENT—FOREIGN SALES
Armando Nunez
VICE PRESIDENT—ADVERTISING & PUBLIC RELATIONS
(TELEVISION DIVISION)
Murray M. Horowitz
EXECUTIVE VICE PRESIDENT—PRODUCTION SERVICES
Nathan Leipziger

ITM Releasing Corporation

321 West 44th Street, New York, NY 10036 (212)
582-6946. (National distribution of features through
local sub-distributor offices.)

Inflight Services, Inc.

485 Madison Ave., New York, NY 10022 (212) 751-
1800. (Distributor of films to airlines, hotels and mo-
tels.)
PRESIDENT & CHIEF OPERATING OFFICER
Lawrence R. Miles
VICE CHAIRMAN
C. B. Newbery
VICE PRESIDENT & TREASURER
John J. Willis
SENIOR VICE PRESIDENT—OPERATIONS
Antony Latessa
VICE PRESIDENT—SALES
Peter Homegger
EXECUTIVE DIRECTOR-PROGRAMMING
John McMahon

Intermedia Financial Services, Ltd.

Suite 610, 89 Avenue Road, Toronto, Canada, M5R
2G4. (416) 961-5525. Cable: INMEDIAFIN. (Specialists
in motion picture and television financing; factoring,
short term, receivables, inventory, contract discount-
ing, mergers, consultants and professional negotia-
tors.)
PRESIDENT
S. Dean Peterson
SECRETARY
J. H. Whiteside
TREASURER
Donald J. Shier
DATE OF ORGANIZATION
1970

International Artists Pictures

3927 Sylvania Ave., Suite 4, Toledo, OH 43623 (419)
474-4408. (Production and distribution of motion pic-
tures.)
PRESIDENT
J. Edwin Baker
VICE PRESIDENT
Beverly E. Jan

TREASURER
Margaret E. Miller
SECRETARY
Marjorie R. Baker
DATE OF ORGANIZATION
1960

International Creative Management

40 West 57th St., New York, NY 10019 (212) 556-5600. 8899 Beverly Blvd., Los Angeles, CA 90048 (213) 550-4000. (Representatives of performing and creative talent in the entertainment industry.) A division of Marvin Josephson Associates, Inc., the agency is the successor by merger of Creative Management Associates and International Famous Agency.
CHAIRMAN
Ralph Mann
PRESIDENT
Jeff Berg

International Film Exchange, Ltd.

159 West 53rd Street, New York, NY 10019; (212) 582-4318; Cable: IFEXREP—New York; Telex: 420748. Paris Office: 45 Rue de Ponthieu, Paris 8e; 359-9600; Cable; FILMEXCHANGE, PARIS. (International distributors and producers of theatrical, non-theatrical, educational and television films.)
EXECUTIVE OFFICERS
Gerald J. Rappoport
Christopher Wood
Beulah Rappoport
Micheline Charest
Ron Weinberg
Christiane Kieffer (Paris)

International Film Industries

450 Main St., New Rochelle, NY 10802 (914) 576-3330. (Feature film production and distribution)
PRESIDENT
Leonard Kirtman
ASSOCIATE PRODUCERS
Robert Zaslow, Wendy S. Lidell
DATE OF ORGANIZATION
1968

International Harmony, Inc.

1697 Broadway, New York, NY 10039 (212) 582-9133. (Distributor.)
PRESIDENT
Stuart S. Shapiro
VICE PRESIDENT
Stella Shapiro

International Picture Show Co.

500 No. Omni International, Atlanta, GA 30303 (404) 522-7075.
(Production, financing, distribution of feature-length, family-oriented films.)
CHAIRMAN OF THE BOARD & CHIEF EXECUTIVE OFFICER
Lloyd N. Adams, Jr.
PRESIDENT, GENERAL SALES MANAGER & TREASURER
◆Malcolm M. Barbour
SECRETARY
A. Ronald Adams
VICE PRESIDENT/NATIONAL SALES MANAGER
Gordon Craddock
VICE PRESIDENT/OPERATIONS
Terry Hughes
DATE OF ORGANIZATION
1977

International Research & Evaluation (IRE)

21098 IRE Control Ctr., Eagan, MN 55121 (612) 888-9635. (Market research, including probes, surveys, studies and information.)
RESEARCH DIRECTOR
Randall L. Voight
DIRECTORS
Ronald D. Olson, Sharon W. King, Norman Begley
DATE OF ORGANIZATION
1972

International Television and Film Distributors, Inc.

4106 Aurora Street, Coral Gables, FL 33146 (305) 444-1159. (Distributor of feature films and television programs for TV markets of Spanish-speaking stations in U.S. and Central, South Americas and Caribbean area.)
PRESIDENT
Georgo Caputo.

Inter-Ocean Film Sales, Ltd.

2029 Century Park East, Los Angeles, CA 90067 (213) 557-1400. (Motion picture distributor in foreign market and packagers.)
CHAIRMAN
Anne Kopelson
PRESIDENT
Edward Carlin
DATE OF ORGANIZATION
1978

Isram Film Corp.

360 East 65th St., New York, NY 10021 (212) 570-9190. (Consultant to independent motion picture producers on marketing and co-production.)
PRESIDENT
Alex Massis
DATE OF ORGANIZATION
1977

JAD Films International, Inc.

1900 Avenue of Stars, Suite 1890, Century City, CA (213) 203-0288. (Motion picture packaging and distribution.)
PRESIDENT
Arthur M. Herskovitz
VICE PRESIDENT
Arthur A. Jacobs
DATE OF ORGANIZATION
1974

Jalem Productions, Inc.

141 El Camino, Suite 201, Beverly Hills, CA 90212 (213) 278-7750. (Motion picture production.)
PRESIDENT
Jack Lemmon
VICE PRESIDENT
Connie McCauley

Key International Film Distribution Co., Inc.

8000 East Girard, Denver, CO 80231 (303) 755-7666. (Distribution of films on regional, national and worldwide basis.)
PRESIDENT
Patrick H. Halloran
GENERAL SALES MANAGER
Jack C. Micheletti

DATE OF ORGANIZATION
1975

Killiam Shows, Inc.

6 East 39th St., New York, NY 10016 (212) 679-8230. (Production and distribution of documentaries and restored silent feature films; pre-1930 stock footage library.)
PRESIDENT
Paul Killiam
VICE PRESIDENT
John Rogers
DATE OF ORGANIZATION
1950

King International Corporation

(Formerly King Bros. Productions, Inc.)
124 Lasky Drive, Beverly Hills, CA 90212 (213) 274-0333.
PRESIDENT
Frank King
VICE PRESIDENT & SECRETARY
Herman King

Kings Road Productions

4000 Warner Blvd., Burbank, CA 91522 (213) 954-6000 (Producer)
PRESIDENT & CHIEF EXECUTIVE
Stephen Friedman

Kino International Corp.

250 West 57th St., Suite 314, New York, NY 10107 (212) 586-8720. (Motion picture distribution.)
PRESIDENT
Donald Krim
DIRECTOR OF OPERATIONS
David Wollos
DATE OF ORGANIZATION
1977

Kodiak Films, Inc.

11681 San Vicente Blvd., Los Angeles, CA 90049 (213) 820-7511; Cable: KODFILM; Telex: 194719. (Motion picture production, domestic distribution and foreign sales).
PRESIDENT
Wolf Schmidt
FOREIGN SALES MANAGER
Maurice Braun
EXECUTIVE ASSISTANT
Marianne Meeker

Stanley Kramer Productions Ltd.

Studio Center, 4024 Radford Ave., Studio City, CA 91604.
PRESIDENT & EXEC. PRODUCER
Stanley E. Kramer
VICE PRESIDENT
William G. Levine
SECRETARY-TREASURER
Marian Demby

Robert I. Kronenberg & Associates, Inc.

9255 Sunset Blvd., Los Angeles, CA 90069 (213) 275-4574. (Distribution, foreign sales, 35mm and 16mm and TV sales, domestic and foreign.)
PRESIDENT
Robert I. Kronenberg

The Ladd Company

4000 Warner Blvd., Burbank, CA 91522. (213) 843-6000. New York office: 75 Rockefeller Plaza, New York, NY 10019. (212) 484-8000. (Motion picture producers; films distributed through Warner Bros.)
PRESIDENT
Alan Ladd, Jr.
VICE PRESIDENT
Jay Kanter, Gareth Wigan
VICE PRESIDENT, PRODUCTION
Paula Weinstein
VICE PRESIDENT, MARKETING—DISTRIBUTION
Ashley Boone, Jr.
VICE PRESIDENT, ADVERTISING, PUBLICITY & PROMOTION
Robert Dingilian
VICE PRESIDENT, BUSINESS AFFAIRS
Joseph Graham
VICE PRESIDENT, PRODUCTION OPERATIONS
Leonard Kroll
VICE PRESIDENT, FINANCE & ADMINISTRATION
Burt Morrison
VICE PRESIDENT, EAST COAST OPERATIONS
Lois Bonfiglio
VICE PRESIDENT, INTERNATIONAL
Sanford Lieberson
DATE OF ORGANIZATION
1980

Landau, Inc., Edie and Ely

2029 Century Park East, Los Angeles, CA 90067 (213) 553-5010. (Producer)
PRINCIPALS
Edie and Ely Landau
DATE OF ORGANIZATION
1979

Lajon Productions, Inc.

2907 West Olive Ave., Burbank, CA 91505 (213) 841-1440. (Producers of feature films, theatrical trailers, television commercials, full facilities, including ¾" on line convergence editing system.)
PRESIDENT
Lawrence Appelbaum
VICE-PRESIDENT IN CHARGE OF PRODUCTION
Mark Hebdon
VICE-PRESIDENT IN CHARGE OF OPERATIONS
Harvey Genkins

Lanira Releasing Corp.

569 Chert St., Sanibel, FL 33957 (813) 472-3301. (Motion picture production and distribution; television syndication, international sales.)
PRESIDENT
Martin Grasgreen
VICE PRESIDENT/SALES
Ira Grasgreen

Lantz, Walter, Productions, Inc.

6311 Romaine St., Hollywood, CA 90038 469-2907. (Cartoon producer.)
PRESIDENT
Walter Lantz
SECRETARY AND TREASURER
Robert Lee Miller

Legion Films

204 South Beverly Dr., #115, Beverly Hills, CA 90210 (213) 274-6647.
VICE PRESIDENTS
William N. Graf, Billy Graf

Dan Leeds Productions

810 Pirates Cove, Mamaroneck NY 10543. (212) 757-2897. (Producer of theatrical & TV films.)
PRESIDENT
Dan Leeds
VICE-PRESIDENT
P. C. Leeds
SECRETARY
P. C. Leeds
TREASURER
Edward Cohen

Joseph E. Levine Presents, Inc.

277 Park Avenue, New York, NY 10017 (212) 826-0370. (Producer.)
CHAIRMAN OF THE BOARD
Joseph E. Levine
PRESIDENT
Richard P. Levine
DATE OF ORGANIZATION
1974

Levitt-Pickman Film Corporation

505 Park Avenue, New York, NY 10022 (212) 832-8842.
PRESIDENT
Jerome Pickman
SECRETARY-TREASURER
Lester Dembitzer

Levy-Gardner-Laven Productions

9570 Wilshire Blvd., Suite 400 Beverly Hills, CA 90212 (213) 278-9820.
PRINCIPALS
Jules Levy, Arthur Gardner, Arnold Laven

Liberty Studios, Inc.

238 East 26th St., New York, NY 10010. (212) 532-1865. (Complete live action and special effects production. Owns and operates fully equipped sound stages, editing/optical facilities, cameras, lighting, grip and sound equipment, equipment transfer trucks for sound stage as well as location shooting)
PRESIDENT, PRODUCER/DIRECTOR
Anthony Lover
DATE OF ORGANIZATION
1961

Libra Films Corporation

419 Park Ave., South, New York, NY 10016 (212) 686-5050. (Film distribution.)
PRESIDENT
Ben Barenholtz
VICE PRESIDENT
Bruce Trinz
DATE OF ORGANIZATION
1975

Lion's Gate Films, Inc.

1861 South Bundy Drive, Los Angeles, CA 90025 (213) 820-7751. (Motion picture production.) New York office: 128 Central Park South, Suite 4B, New York, NY 10022 (212) 582-2970.
PRESIDENT
Robert B. Altman
VICE PRESIDENT
James Quinn
SECRETARY
Robert Eggenweiler
DATE OF ORGANIZATION
1965

Lirol Productions

6335 Homewond Ave., Hollywood, CA 90028 (213) 467-8111. (Production of TV programming, commercials, educational, industrial, documentary, governmental films and videotape.) A division of the Lirol Corporation.
PRESIDENT
Frederic Rheinstein
SECRETARY-TREASURER
Yetta K. Gisser
DATE OF ORGANIZATION
1958

Lone Star Pictures International, Inc.

1347 North Cahuenga Blvd., Hollywood, CA 90028. (213) 463-3175.
PRESIDENT
Lee Thronburg
EXECUTIVE VICE PRESIDENT
Jim Bohan
GENERAL SALES MANAGER
George Roth
FOREIGN SALES MANAGER
Norbert Meisel

Lorimar Productions, Inc.

3970 Overland Ave., Culver City, CA 90230 (213) 202-2000. (Motion picture and television producer.)
PRESIDENT
Lee Rich
CHAIRMAN OF THE BOARD
Merv Adelson

Lucasfilm, Ltd.

P.O. Box 2009, San Rafael, CA 94912 (415) 457-5282. (Motion picture production.)
CHAIRMAN OF THE BOARD
George W. Lucas, Jr.
PRESIDENT & CHIEF EXECUTIVE OFFICER
George W. Lucas, Jr.
SENIOR VICE PRESIDENT/FINANCE & ADMINISTRATION
Robert M. Greber
VICE PRESIDENT/FINANCE
Chris Kalabokes
SECRETARY
Herbert Roffman
DATE OF ORGANIZATION
1971

MCA, INC.

100 Universal City Plaza, Universal City, CA 91608 (213) 985-4321; 445 Park Avenue, New York, NY 10022 (212) 759-7500.
CHAIRMAN OF THE BOARD, CHIEF EXEC. OFFICER
Lew R. Wasserman
PRESIDENT, CHIEF OPER. OFFICER
Sidney Jay Sheinberg
VICE PRESIDENTS
Bob R. Baker, J. Eugene Brog, Salvatore T. Chiantia, Albert A. Dorskind, James N. Fiedler, Louis N. Friedland, Eugene L. Froelich, Gareth Hughes, Stanley Newman, Donald Sipes, George Smith, Jay S. Stein, Ned Tanen, Thomas Wertheimer
VICE-PRESIDENT & SECTRETARY
Michael Samuel
VICE-PRESIDENT & TREASURER
Harold M. Haas
CONTROLLER
Richard E. Baker
ASSISTANT TREASURER
Joni Robbins
DIRECTORS
Mary Gardiner Jones, Thomas V. Jones, Louis B. Lundborg, Felix Rohatyn, Ned Tanen, Charles B. Thornton, Thomas Wertheimer, Lew R. Wasserman, Sidney Jay Sheinberg.

PRINCIPAL SUBSIDIARIES & DIVISIONS

Universal City Studios, Inc., Universal Theatrical Motion Pictures Division, Universal Pictures Division, Universal Television Division, Universal Film Exchanges, Inc., Universal International

Films, Inc., Universal City Studios (DISC) Inc., Universal Educational & Visual Arts, Universal City Studio Tours and Amphitheatre Div., Merchandising corp. of America, Inc., Landmark Services, Inc., MCA Records, Inc., MCA Records (Disc), Inc., MCA Distributing Corp., MCA Music Division, MCA Development Co. Division, MCA DiscoVision, Inc., MCA DiscoVison Mfg., Inc., MCA New Ventures, Inc., MCA Corporate Films, Inc., MCA Publishing Division, MCA Financial Inc., Columbia Savings & Loan Assoc. (Colorado), Spencer Gifts Inc., Yosemite Park and Curry Co., Almours Securities, Inc., G. P. Putnam's Sons, New Times Communication Corp., theatrical, television, and record prod. & distrib. companies and music companies in principal foreign countries.

Metro-Goldwyn-Mayer Film Company

10202 West Washington Blvd, Culver City, CA 90230
(213) 558-5000
CHAIRMAN OF THE BOARD AND CHIEF EXECUTIVE OFFICER
Frank E. Rosenfelt
PRESIDENT AND CHIEF OPERATING OFFICER
David Begelman
EXECUTIVE VICE PRESIDENT
Joseph A. Fischer
VICE PRESIDENT-GENERAL COUNSEL-ENTERTAINMENT
Karla Davidson
VICE PRESIDENT-BUSINESS AFFAIRS
Frank I. Davis
VICE PRESIDENT-GENERAL COUNSEL-CORPORATE AND SECRETARY
Stanley B. Feuer
VICE PRESIDENT AND CONTROLLER
Robert A. Harrison
VICE PRESIDENT-TREASURER
Walter C. Hoffer
VICE PRESIDENT-ADMINISTRATION
Roger L. Mayer
VICE PRESIDENT-FINANCE
Jason Rabinovitz
VICE PRESIDENT AND ASSISTANT TREASURER-TAXES AND PLANNING
David C. Terrasi
ASSISTANT SECRETARY
Benjamin B. Kahane
ASSISTANT CONTROLLER
Kenneth A. Wagner
BOARD OF DIRECTORS
Frank E. Rosenfelt, Chairman; James D. Alijan, David Begelman, Alvin Benedict, Fred Benninger, Barrie K. Brunet, Cary Grant, Peter M. Kennedy, Arthur G. Linkletter, Walter M. Sharp, Dr. Kenneth L. Trefftzs
DATE AND PLACE OF INCORPORATION
January 31, 1980; under the laws of Delaware
HISTORY OF METRO-GOLDWYN-MAYER FILM CO.
Metro-Goldwyn-Mayer Film Co. is the former filmed entertainment business of Metro-Goldwyn-Mayer Inc. (now known as MGM Grand Hotels, Inc.) which originated in 1919 as Loew's Inc. Under the Metro-Goldwyn-Mayer name, the Company had long been a leading producer of motion pictures and network television programs. In June 1980, the motion picture operations of Metro-Goldwyn-Mayer Inc. were spun off to stockholders, share for share, as Metro-Goldwyn-Mayer Film Co. In 1981 MGM bought United Artists (see history of that company).

MGM MOTION PICTURE DIVISION

PRESIDENT AND CHIEF OPERATING OFFICER
David Begelman
EXECUTIVE VICE PRESIDENT-WORLDWIDE THEATRICAL PRODUCTION
David Chasman
SENIOR VICE PRESIDENT-MOTION PICTURE PRODUCTION AND DEVELOPMENT
John B. Tarnoff
VICE PRESIDENT-EXECUTIVE PRODUCTION MANAGER
George Justin
VICE PRESIDENT-EAST COAST PRODUCTION
B. Boatwright
VICE PRESIDENT-POST PRODUCTION MANAGER
Gary Bell
VICE PRESIDENT-MOTION PICTURE DEVELOPMENT
Willet Hunt
VICE PRESIDENT-PRODUCTION
Madeline Warren
VICE PRESIDENT-SPECIAL ASSISTANT TO THE PRESIDENT
Albert M. Rosenhaus
VICE PRESIDENT-TALENT
Joseph D'Agosta
DIRECTOR OF MOTION PICTURE BUSINESS AFFAIRS
Mary S. Ledding
PRODUCTION EXECUTIVE
Michael G. Nathanson
EXECUTIVE ASSISTANT TO THE PRESIDENT
Constance Danielson

EXECUTIVE ASSISTANT TO DAVID CHASMAN
Sanford Climan
STORY EDITOR
Candice Lawrence
PRODUCTION MANAGER
Kevin Donnelly

MARKETING

SENIOR VICE PRESIDENT-WORLDWIDE HEAD OF MARKETING
Richard Kahn
VICE PRESIDENT-DOMESTIC DISTRIBUTION
Byron M. Shapiro
VICE PRESIDENT-WORLDWIDE PUBLICITY AND PROMOTION
Alfred S. Newman
VICE PRESIDENT-WORLDWIDE ADVERTISING/MARKETING
Gregory G. Morrison
VICE PRESIDENT-EASTERN DIRECTOR OF ADVERTISING, PUBLICITY, & PROMOTION
John Skouras
VICE PRESIDENT-INTERNATIONAL ADVERTISING & PUBLICITY
G. W. Edwards
VICE PRESIDENT-SALES MANAGER (INTERNATIONAL)
Stephen Clug
DIRECTOR OF MARKETING MANAGEMENT SERVICES
Deanna Rae Wilcox
DIRECTOR OF PUBLICITY
Phyllis Gardner
ASSISTANT TO THE VICE PRESIDENT-DOMESTIC DISTRIBUTION
George Cohn
NATIONAL ADVERTISING COORDINATOR
Ted Hatfield
NEW YORK SALES REPRESENTATIVE
Sid Eckman
DIRECTOR OF FILM SERVICES
Mel Rydell

MGM TELEVISION PRODUCTION DIVISION

PRESIDENT
Thomas D. Tannenbaum
SENIOR VICE PRESIDENT-BUSINESS AFFAIRS & ADMINISTRATION
Arthur Joel Katz
SENIOR VICE PRESIDENT-PROGRAMS
Werner Michel
VICE PRESIDENT-PROGRAM DEVELOPMENT
Dori Weiss
VICE PRESIDENT-CURRENT PROGRAMS
Jerome H. Stanley
VICE PRESIDENT-EXECUTIVE PRODUCTION MANAGER
Richard Birnie
VICE PRESIDENT-ADMINISTRATION
Leslie H. Frends
VICE PRESIDENT-TALENT
Joseph D'Agosta
DIRECTOR OF MOVIES AND MINI-SERIES
Virginia K. Hegge
DIRECTOR OF BUSINESS AFFAIRS
Steven P. Maier
DIRECTOR OF BUSINESS AFFAIRS
David G. Stanley
DIRECTOR OF COMEDY DEVELOPMENT
Phyllis A. Golden-Gottlieb
STORY EDITOR
Frederique Becker
ASSISTANT TO THE PRESIDENT
William S. Todman, Jr.

TELEVISION SALES DIVISION

EXECUTIVE VICE PRESIDENT-WORLDWIDE SYNDICATION-N.Y.
Lawrence E. Gershman
SENIOR VICE PRESIDENT-DOMESTIC SALES-N.Y.
Joseph C. Tirinato
VICE PRESIDENT-DOMESTIC SYNDICATION-N.Y.
Neil Russell
SALES MANAGER-MID-WESTERN DIVISION-CHICAGO
Robert J. Horen
SALES MANAGER-WESTERN DIVISION-L.A.
William A. Kunkel
SALES MANAGER-SOUTHERN DIVISION-ATLANTA
Virgil B. Wolff
SALES MANAGER-EASTERN DIVISION-N.Y.
Philip L. Smith
DIRECTOR OF CREATIVE MARKETING-N.Y.
Susan Swimer
DIRECTOR OF MARKETING RESEARCH-N.Y.
Jean Goldberg

DIRECTOR OF INTERNATIONAL ADMINISTRA-
TION/CLIENT RELATIONS
  Sheryl S. Hardy
MARKETING RESEARCH ANALYST-N.Y.
  Anna Greenberg
CONTRACT ADMINISTRATOR
  Stacey Valenza
MANAGER OF WORLDWIDE FILM SERVICES
  Dennis Murphy

ANCILLARY RIGHTS DIVISION
VICE PRESIDENT-ANCILLARY RIGHTS DIVISION
  Peter W. Kuyper
PAY TV SERVICES COORDINATOR
  Meyer Shwarzstein

INDUSTRIAL RELATIONS DIVISION
VICE PRESIDENT
  Benjamin B. Kahane
DIRECTOR OF LABOR RELATIONS
  Ronald M. Bruno
DIRECTOR OF PERSONNEL/E.E.O.
  Royal B. Regan
PERSONNEL ADMINISTRATION
  Karen S. Nordli

FACILITIES DIVISION
VICE PRESIDENT-FACILITIES AND STUDIO MANAGER
  Arnold Shupack
ADMINISTRATIVE ASSISTANT TO STUDIO MANAGER
  Barbara Cobb

ADMINISTRATIVE SERVICES
VICE PRESIDENT-ADMINISTRATION
  Roger L. Mayer
DIRECTOR OF ADMINISTRATIVE SERVICES
  Frank D. Bowe

METRO-GOLDWYN-MAYER INTERNA-
TIONAL   10202 West Washington Blvd., Culver City,
CA 90230 (213) 836-3000
CHAIRMAN OF THE BOARD
  Frank E. Rosenfelt
VICE CHAIRMAN OF THE BOARD
  David Begelman
PRESIDENT
  Richard Kahn
EXECUTIVE VICE PRESIDENT-DISTRIBUTION
  Jack gordon
EXECUTIVE VICE PRESIDENT
  Maccabi Attas
VICE PRESIDENT-ADVERTISING & PUBLICITY
  G. W. Edwards
VICE PRESIDENT-SALES
  Stephen Clug
VICE PRESIDENT & GENERAL COUNSEL-ENTERTAIN-
MENT
  Karla Davidson
VICE PRESIDENT & GENERAL CNUNSEL-CORPORATE &
SECRETARY
  Stanley B. Feuer
VICE PRERIDENT-FINANCE & TREASURER
  Jason Rabinovitz
CONTROLLER
  Robert A. Harriron
BOARD OF DIRECTORS
  Maccabi Attas, David Begelman, Jacj Gordnn, Richard Kahn, Jasnn
Rabinnvitz, Frank E. Rosenfelt

MGM LABORATORIES, INC. 10202 West
Washington Blvd., Culver City, CA 90230 (213) 204-
00
CHAIRMAN OF THE BOARD
  Frank E. Rosenfelt
EXECUTIVE VICE PRESIDENT
  Roger L. Mayer
SENIOR VICE PRESIDENT & GENERAL MANAGER
  Walter Eggars
VICE PRESIDENT
  Stanley b. Feuer
VICE PRESIDENT & ASSISTANT GENERAL MANAGER
  Jim George
VICE PRESIDENT & CHIEF FINANCIAL OFFICER
  Jason Rabinovitz
SECRETARY
  Stanley B. Feuer
TREASURER
  Robert A. Harrison
CONTROLLER
  Frank Juracka

BOARD OF DIRECTORS
  Stanley B. Feuer, Roger L. Mayer, Jason Rabinovitz, Frank E.
Rosenfelt

M.P.K. Omega Company
  3615 Carson, Amarillo, TX 79109. (Film producer)
PRESIDENT
  Mike Kiefer
VICE PRESIDENT
  June Kiefer
TREASURER
  Tom Davis
SECRETARY
  Secta Smith
MANAGER, WORLDWIDE PRODUCTION
  Jacques Cantrell
MANAGER, PUBLISHING
  Leon Domino

Howard Mahler Films, Inc.,
  509 Madison Ave., Suite 1206, New York, NY (212)
371-5480. (Distribution of theatrical feature films, na-
tionally.)
PRESIDENT
  Howard Mahler
TREASURER
  Joan Mahler

Majestic Film Sales Ltd.
  P.O. Box 3889, Beverly Hills, CA 90212 (213) 274-
7002. (Represents independent feature films to
worldwide distributors.)
PRESIDENT
  Christopher Wood
DATE OF ORGANIZATION
  1975

Manley Productions, Inc.
  111 West 57th St., New York, NY 10019 (212) 541-
7733. (Producer-Distributor.)
GENERAL MANAGER
  Walter Manley

Manson International
  9145 Sunset Blvd., Los Angeles, CA 90069. (213)
273-8640. Cable: MANSON, Telex: 691242.
CHAIRMAN, BOARD OF DIRECTORS
  Edmund Goldman
PRESIDENT
  Michael F. Goldman
VICE-PRESIDENT—FINANCE
  Warren Braverman
VICE PRESIDENT—ACQUISITIONS
  Peter Elson
GENERAL MANAGER
  Devon Jackson
EXPORT MANAGER
  Hal Levy
SALES MANAGER
  Michael J. Werner

Marble Arch Productions
  12711 Ventura Blvd., Studio City, CA 91604. (213)
760-2110. (Motion picture and television production)
PRESIDENT
  Martin Starger
VICE PRESIDENT, EXECUTIVE PRODUCTION MANAGER
  Howard Alston
VICE PRESIDENT, PUBLICITY & ADVERTISING
  Regina Gruss
VICE PRESIDENT, BUSINESS AFFAIRS & ADMINISTRATION
  Stuart K. Mandel
VICE PRESIDENT IN CHARGE OF PRODUCTION
  Richard L. O'Connor
VICE PRESIDENT, POST PRODUCTION
  James Potter

VICE PRESIDENT, CHIEF FINANCIAL OFFICER
Ralph Rivera
DATE OF ORGANIZATION
1978

Marine Corps Public Affairs—Los Angeles

11000 Wilshire Blvd., Suite 10117, Los Angeles, CA 90024 (213) 824-7272. (Provides technical aid and support to the motion picture and television industries, including script review, stock footage, on-base locations, equipment and Marine "extras")
OFFICER IN CHARGE
Major Pat Coulter
ASSISTANT OFFICER IN CHARGE
1st Lt. Nancy LaLuntas
PUBLIC AFFAIRS CHIEF
Gunnery Sgt. Jim Bell
ADMINISTRATION CHIEF
Sgt. Bill Stonick
DATE OF ORGANIZATION
1948

Maritime Cinema Service Corp.

1501 Broadway, Suite 1416, New York, NY 10036. (212) 840-2445. (Supplying ships, government agencies, industrial companies, with motion picture film and equipment.)
PRESIDENT
Roy A. Weiner
VICE-PRESIDENT
Jeanne Heller
ASST. SECRETARY
Jack Steinberg

Maverick Pictures International

300 East Wendover Ave., P.O. Box 22012, Greensboro, NC 27420. (919) 379-0181. International Distribution Office: One Perimeter Way, N.W., Suite 220, Atlanta, GA 30339; Acquisition & Production Office: 6253 Hollywood, CA 90028. (Distributor)
CHAIRMAN OF THE BOARD & PRESIDENT
H. V. McCoy, Sr.
VICE PRESIDENT & SECRETARY
Dennis R. Snead, Jr.
TREASURER
Robert L. Vitelli
EXECUTIVE VICE PRESIDENT, DOMESTIC & INTERNATIONAL DISTRIBUTION
E. J. Kimling
VICE PRESIDENT OF ACQUISITON
John Carr
EASTERN REGIONAL DISTRIBUTION & ADVERTISING COORDINATION
Brian Fackrell
CENTRAL DISTRIBUTION
Robin Kimling

Midwest Film Productions, Inc.

600 Madison Ave. New York, NY 10022 (212) 757-7129. (Motion picture production and distribution). A wholly owned subsidiary of Midwestern Land Development Corp.
PRESIDENT
Raphael D. Silver
VICE PRESIDENT
Joan Micklin Silver
SECRETARY
Jordan C. Band
DATE OF ORGANIZATION
1974

MIFED

Largo Domodossola 1, Milan 20145, Italy. Tel.: 495 495. Cable: MIFED MILAN. Telex: 37360. USA Information. (International Film, TV Film and Documentary Market April and October) Milan Fair Ground.
GENERAL DIRECTOR
Dr. Michele G. Franci
PUBLIC RELATIONS
Dr. Vergara Caffarelli

Minotaur Productions, Inc.

1600 Broadway, New York, NY 10019 (212) 489-8844. (Production, post production, post synch, dubbing)
PRESIDENT
George Gonneau
DATE OF ORGANIZATION
1974

Miracle Films

6311 Romaine St., Hollywood, CA 90038 (213) 468-8867. (Producer and distributor)
PRESIDENT
Stuart Segall
VICE PRESIDENT
Martin Greenwald
DATE OF ORGANIZATION
1972

The Mirisch Corporation of California

3966 Overland Ave., Culver City, CA 90230 (213) 202-0202.
CHAIRMAN OF THE BOARD & CHIEF EXECUTIVE OFFICER
Marvin E. Mirisch
PRESIDENT AND CHIEF PRODUCTION OFFICER
Walter Mirisch

Modern Talking Picture Service, Inc.

45 Rockefeller Plaza, New York, NY 10111 (212) 765-3100 (Distributor); 5000 Park St. North, St. Petersburg, FL 33709 (813) 541-7571.
PRESIDENT
Carl H. Lenz
EXECUTIVE VICE PRESIDENT
William M. Oard
VICE PRESIDENT & GENERAL MANAGER
Dan Kater
VICE PRESIDENT, OPERATIONS
James D. McPoland
VICE PRESIDENT, THEATRICAL
Don Konny
DATE OF ORGANIZATION
1937

BOOKING CENTERS

All numbers can be called collect.
St. Petersburg, FL 33709—5000 Park St. North, Outside of Florida Call Toll Free (800) 237-8913 Florida Residents Call 813-541-7571

Monarch Releasing Corp.

8831 Sunset Blvd., Suite 303, Los Angeles, CA 90069 (213) 652-9900. (Motion picture distribution.)
PRESIDENT
Ann Shackleton
DATE OF ORGANIZATION
1968

Moonlight Productions

2243 Old Middlefield Way, Mountain View, CA 94043 (415) 948-0199. (Producer and distributor of undersea environmental films—16mm, color, optical sound; undersea stock shot library.)
SOLE OWNER
Dr. Lee Tepley
DATE OF ORGANIZATION
1971

The Milton I. Moritz Company, Inc.

9601 Wilshire Boulevard, Suite 640, Beverly Hills, CA, 90210. (213) 271-6111. (Producers' sales and marketing representation.)
PRESIDENT
Milton I. Moritz

Mirik Pictures, Inc.

9255 Sunset Blvd., Los Angeles, CA 90069 (213) 278-1853. (Non-theatrical motion picture distribution; television distribution.)
PRESIDENT
Milton·J. Salzburg
SECRETARY
Gus Klein

Morningside Pictures Corporation

1370 Avenue of the Americas, New York, NY 10019 (212) 757-4000. (Affiliated with Morningside Productions, Inc. same address and staff.)
PRESIDENT
Charles H. Schneer
VICE PRESIDENT
Jerome B. Lurie
TREASURER
Charles H. Schneer
SECRETARY
Shirley S. Schneer
ASSISTANT SECRETARIES
Robert W. Partnoy, Rita Sultan
DIRECTORS
Robert W. Partnoy and Rita Sultan
DATE OF ORGANIZATION
1965

Morris, Nelson Productions

11 East 48th Street, New York, NY 10017 (212) 753-1484. (Producer of feature films.)
EXECUTIVE PRODUCER
Nelson Morris

Morris Agency, Inc., William

(See William Morris Agency under W.)

Morison Film Group Incorporated

10100 Santa Monica Blvd., Suite 1580 Los Angeles, CA 90067 (213) 552-9977. A Member of the Guinness Group of Companies. Company includes: Producers Sales Organization; General Rights Corporation; Film Finance Distributors, U.K.; Morison Finance, Ltd. and Aspen Productions. (Motion picture and television production and distribution.)
CHAIRMAN OF THE BOARD & CHIEF EXECUTIVE OFFICER
Mark Damon
PRESIDENT & CHIEF OPERATING OFFICER
John W. Hyde

Movielab, Inc.

619 West 54th St., New York, NY 10019 (212) 586-0360; Telex: 12-6785. Cable address: Movielab. (35 & 16 and Super 8 color motion picture film laboratory.)
CHAIRMAN OF THE BOARD & PRESIDENT & CHIEF EXECUTIVE OFFICER
Saul Jeffee
EXECUTIVE VICE PRESIDENT—PLANT OPERATIONS & ENGINEERING
John J. Kowalak
VICE PRESIDENT & TREASURER
Leonard P. Weg
VICE PRESIDENT—SALES ADMINISTRATION
Peter P. Cardasis

VICE PRESIDENT—SALES
Norman E. Rinehart
VICE PRESIDENT-SALES
Bernie Macklin
SECRETARY
David M. Perlmutter
ASSISTANT SECRETARY
Marjorie M. Burgess
AUDIO VISUAL DIVISIONS
DIRECTOR OF ADMINISTRATION
Tom Trudel

MOVIELAB-HOLLYWOOD, INC.

6823 Santa Monica Blvd., Hollywood, CA 90038 (213) 469-2211.
CHAIRMAN OF THE BOARD & PRESIDENT
Saul Jeffee
VICE-PRESIDENT—ADMINISTRATION
Jack Griffith
VICE PRESIDENT & TREASURER
Leonard P. Weg
VICE PRESIDENT—ENGINEERING
John J. Kowalak
VICE PRESIDENT—MARKETING
Peter P. Cardasis
VICE PRESIDENT—PLANT OPERATIONS
Robert F. Burns
LABORATORY SERVICES ADMINISTRATION
Donald R. Stearns
SALES ADMINISTRATION
Frank A. Matera
CUSTOMER SERVICES MANAGER
Courtland C. Morelock

MOVIELAB THEATRE SERVICE, INC.

619 West 54th St., New York, NY 10019 (212) 586-0360. (Complete preview screening room, cutting rooms, storage vaults.)
VICE PRESIDENTS
Peter P. Cardasis, Norman E. Rinehart
MANAGER
Harold T. Dempsey

Movies En Route Inc.

1540 Broadway, New York, NY 10036 (212) 575-8100. (Distributor.)
PRESIDENT
Richard Barnett
VICE-PRESIDENT
Irwin Dickman

Mulberry Square Productions, Inc.

10300 N. Central Expressway #120, Dallas TX 75231 (214) 369-2430. (Production of feature films) Affiliated with Mulberry Square Releasing, Inc., Mulberry Square Publishing, Inc., Mulberry Square, Inc., and Mulberry Square Merchandising, Inc.
PRESIDENT
Joe Camp
VICE PRESIDENT
Carolyn Camp
TREASURER-ASSISTANT SECRETARY
Carolyn Camp
SECRETARY
Martin Heller

Multicolor Film Laboratories, Inc.

244 West 49th Street, New York, NY 10019 (212) 247-4770. (Film Laboratories.)
PRESIDENT & TREASURER
M. W. Pomerance

Mutual General Film Co.

P.O. Box 5263, Beverly Hills, CA 90210 (213) 274-8646. (Motion picture production and distribution) Distribution through AIP branches.

PRESIDENT
Nicholas Wowchuk
EXECUTIVE VICE PRESIDENT
Harry Wowchuk
FINANCIAL VICE PRESIDENT
Wallace Davidson
GENERAL MANAGER
Miles Holman
SALES MANAGER
Harry Stern

National American Entertainment Corp.

8530 Wilshire Blvd., Suite 300, Beverly Hills, CA 90211 (213) 659-1872. (Distributor)
PRESIDENT & CHIEF EXECUTIVE OFFICER
John L. Daniel
VICE PRESIDENT
Robert I. Levy
DIRECTOR OF MARKETING
Stewart Engebretson
COMPTROLLER/DIRECTOR OF ACQUISITIONS
Harriet Robbins
DIRECTOR OF ADVERTISING & PUBLICITY
Eric Bernstein
ADMINISTRATIVE ASSISTANT
Isabel DeKoven
DATE OF ORGANIZATION
1977

National Film Carriers, Inc.

38 West 39th St., New York, NY 10018 (212) 944-1788. (Film shipping and service.)
PRESIDENT
H. R. Matthews
Benton Bros. Film Express, Atlanta, GA
VICE PRESIDENT
Paul Grunewald
Northwest Film Service, Seattle, WA
TREASURER
Jack Callahan
Exhibitors Service Company, McKees Rocks, PA
DIRECTORS
Reagin S. McAllister
Texas Tepac, San Antonio, TX
Stanley Adleman
New Jersey Messenger Service, Camden, NJ
H. J. Noel
Indiana Transit Service, Indianapolis, IN
GENERAL MANAGER
Arnold Brown
38 West 39th St. New York, NY 10018

National Film Service, Inc.

38 West 39th St., New York, NY 10018 (212) 944-1788. (Physical distribution and warehousing of motion picture film.)
PRESIDENT
William Rosen
EXECUTIVE VICE PRESIDENT/TREASURER
Arnold Brown
VICE PRESIDENT
John H. Vickers
SECRETARY
Wesley Frysztacki
ASSISTANT SECRETARY
Betty Neuer
BOARD OF DIRECTORS
Don Brandon, Bert Benton, Wesley Frysztacki, Earl E. Jameson, Jr., Meyer Kahan, Herb Matthews, Matt Molitch, William Rosen, John H. Vickers.

National Screen Service Corp.

1600 Broadway, New York, NY 10019 (212) 246-5700. (Producer and distributor of trailers, specialty and standard accessories.)
CHAIRMAN
Burton Robbins
PRESIDENT
Norman Robbins
SR. VICE PRESIDENT, FINANCE
Jules Leder

VICE PRESIDENT & TREASURER
Vassos Poupoulas
VICE PRESIDENT, SECRETARY & GENERAL COUNSEL
Frederick J. Psaki, Jr.
VICE PRESIDENT-DIRECTOR MARKETING & SALES
Paul Silliman
VICE PRESIDENT-GENERAL OPERATIONS MANAGER
Peter Koplik
VICE PRESIDENT-GENERAL OPERATIONS MANAGER, SIMPLEX PROJECTOR CO.
Richard Green
CONTROLLER
Alfred DiPreta
DIRECTOR-MANUFACTURING AFFAIRS
David Robbins
DIRECTOR-FIELD & ANCILLARY SALES
Seymour Kaplan

SIMPLEX PROJECTOR CO.

(A Division of National Screen Service Corp.) 1600 Broadway, New York, NY 10019 (212) 246-5700.
VICE PRESIDENT-GENERAL OPERATIONS MANAGER
Richard Green
REGIONAL SALES MANAGER
Howard Straight
West Coast Sales Office—2001 S. LaCienega Blvd., Los Angeles, Calif. 90034 (213) 838-1821)

ADVERTISING INDUSTRIES

(A Division of National Screen Service Corp.) E. 64 Midland Avenue, Paramus, N.J. 07652 (201) 265-7300. (Manufacture and sale of frame and display cases.)
MANAGER
John Cicinelli

CONTINENTAL LITHOGRAPH CORP

(A Subsidiary of National Screen Service) 952 E. 72nd St., Cleveland, OH 44103 (216) 361-4860.
VICE PRESIDENT & CONTROLLER
Donald Moore

DOMESTIC BRANCHES & MANAGERS

ATLANTA: 30318: 1325 Logan Circle, N.W.: Regional Sales Mgr., Robert Sedlak; Branch Mgr., Willard Kohorn
BOSTON: 02116: 95 Broadway: Regional Sales Mgr., Joseph Rossi; Branch Mgr., Paul Mueller
CHICAGO: 60605: 1322 So. Wabash Ave.: Regional Sales Mgr., Paul Ayotte; Branch Mgr., Robert Newman
CINCINNATI: 45203: 1150 W. 8th St.: Regional Sales Mgr., Dennis Carver; Branch Mgr., David Farkes
DALLAS: 75247: 7138 Envoy Court: Regional Sales Mgr., Seymour Kaplan; Branch Mgr., Henry Gatehouse
KANSAS CITY, MO: 64108: 1800 Baltimore Ave.: Regional Sales Mgr., William Lustig; Branch Mgr., Mitchell Wilen
LOS ANGELES: 90034: 2001 S. LaCienega Blvd.: Regional Sales Mgr., Richard Barnes; Branch Mgr., Martha Salido; Print Control, Mona Spicer
NEW ORLEANS, (HARAHAN, LA.) 70123: 5624 Jefferson Hwy.: Regional Sales Manager, Joseph Moll
PHILADELPHIA: (CAMDEN, N.J.) 08104: 130 Ferry Ave., Regional Sales Manager, Steve Rockabrand
SEATTLE: 98121: 2413 Second Ave.: Regional Sales Mgr., James Kehoe; Branch Mgr., Scheffer
CLEVELAND: 44108: (Distribution Center) 341 Eddy Road: Manager, Richard Massey
LOS ANGELES: 90048: 116 No. Robertson Blvd.: Director of Studio Relations, David Garland
LONDON, ENGLAND: 15 Wadsworth Road, Greenford, Middlesex UB67JN: Chairman & Managing Director, Russ Cradick

National Telefilm Associates, Inc.

12636 Beatrice Street, Los Angeles, CA 90066 (213) 306-4040; 141 East 56th Street, New York, NY 10022 (212) 752-4982.
CHAIRMAN OF THE BOARD
George C. Hatch
PRESIDENT
Aubrey W. Groskopf
VICE PRESIDENT—GENERAL SALES MANAGER
Arthur Gross
DIRECTOR—INTERNATIONAL SALES
Larry Cervantes
SECRETARY
Paul J. O'Brien
RESIDENT COUNSEL
Lawrence M. Adelman

473

The Nautilus Film Company

18445 Collins St., Suite 122, Tarzana, CA 91356.
(213) 343-6412. (Production and distribution)
PARTNERS
Steve Barkett, Lynne Margulies Barkett

New Line Cinema Corporation

853 Broadway, New York, NY (212) 674-7460. (Distribution & production of theatrical and nontheatrical motion pictures, lecture bureau, video tape distribution.)
PRESIDENT
Robert Shaye
SENIOR VICE PRESIDENT—WORLDWIDE SALES
Stan Dudelson
SENIOR VICE PRESIDENT—MARKETING
Michael Harpster
VICE PRESIDENT-PRODUCTION
Sara Risher

NEW LINE DISTRIBUTION CORP.

853 Broadway, New York, NY 10003 (212) 674-7460.
(Motion picture distribution) A subsidiary of New Line Cinema Corp.
PRESIDENT
Stanley E. Dudelson
DATE OF ORGANIZATION
1965

New World Pictures

11600 San Vicente Blvd., Los Angeles, CA 90069
(213) 820-6733. (Motion picture production and distribution.)
PRESIDENT
Roger Corman
EXECUTIVE VICE PRESIDENT, CHIEF OPERATING OFFICER
Barbara D. Boyle
VICE PRESIDENT DOMESTIC DISTRIBUTION
Frank Moreno
VICE PRESIDENT INTERNATIONAL DISTRIBUTION
Ed Carlin
VICE PRESIDENT TELEVISION & NON-THEATRICAL DISTRIBUTION
Alice Tapp
VICE PRESIDENT BUSINESS AFFAIRS
Paul S. Almond
VICE PRESIDENT OF FINANCE
Paul Connolly

New Yorker Films

16 West 61st Street, New York, NY 10023. (212) 247-6110. (Motion picture distribution.)
PRESIDENT
Daniel Talbot

Fima Noveck Productions, Inc.

1560 Broadway, New York, NY 10036 (212) 221-2695.
(Production, post production of features and other films. Script and film "doctoring.")
PRESIDENT
Fima H. Noveck
TREASURER
France Noveck
DATE OF ORGANIZATION
1958

Opera Presentations, Inc.

75 Maiden Lane, New York, NY 10038 (212) 269-3430. (Owners, distributors and producers of 16mm and 35mm films, mostly opera, ballet and biographical.)
PRESIDENT
Joseph Schlang

Orion Pictures

75 Rockefeller Plaza, New York, NY 10019 (212) 484-7000. West Coast Office: 4000 Warner Blvd., Burbank, CA 91522. (Motion picture production.)
CHAIRMAN OF THE BOARD
Arthur Krim
PRESIDENT & CHIEF EXECUTIVE OFFICER
Eric Pleskow
EXECUTIVE VICE PRESIDENTS
William Bernstein, Mike Medavoy
SENIOR VICE PRESIDENTS
Ernst Goldschmidt, International Operations; Fred Goldberg, Domestic Advertising; Floyd Leipzig, Domestic Publicity; Robert Sherman, West Coast Production
VICE PRESIDENTS
Vince Giovinco, Chief Financial Officer; Judy Feiffer, East Coast Production
EAST COAST STORY EDITOR
Joel DiTrolio
WEST COAST STORY EDITOR
Julie Kirkham
DATE OF ORGANIZATION
1978

Osmond Communications

1420 East 800 North, Orem, UT, 84059. (801) 224-4444. (Motion picture and television production; studio facilities)
PRESIDENT
Reed R. Callister
EXECUTIVE VICE PRESIDENT
Alan Osmond
SENIOR VICE PRESIDENTS
Wayne Osmond, Merrill Osmond
VICE PRESIDENT, FINANCE
John Taylor
VICE PRESIDENT, ACCOUNTING
Karen Gordon
CORPORATE SECRETARY
Gordon Bench
DIRECTORS
George V. Osmond, chairman; Reed R. Callister, G. Barton Heuler, Alan Osmond, Merrill Osmond, Paul H. Dunn
DATE OF ORGANIZATION
1978

OSMOND INTERNATIONAL

PRESIDENT
Michael Wuergler
VICE PRESIDENT
Phillip Catherall

OSMOND TELEVISION SALES

PRESIDENT
David Sifford

OSMOND TELEVISION

PRESIDENT
Toby Martin
VICE PRESIDENT
Dennis Johnson
VICE PRESIDENT/CONTROLLER
Karen Gordon
VICE PRESIDENT/FILM PRODUCTION
Jack Reddish

OSMOND COMMERCIAL PRODUCTIONS

PRESIDENT
David Anderson
SENIOR VICE PRESIDENT
Dean Proctor

OSMOND STUDIO FACILITIES

PRESIDENT
William L. Critchfield
VICE PRESIDENT/STUDIO OPERATIONS
Cal McWhorter
VICE PRESIDENT/ENGINEERING
Pat Brennan

P.J. Productions Co.

201 East 69th St., Apt. 3-K, New York, NY 10021. (Feature film production.)
PARTNERS
John M. Grissmer, Patricia Grissmer
DATE OF ORGANIZATION
1974

Pace Films, Inc.

411 East 53rd Street, New York, NY 10022 (212) 755-5486. (Consultation, scripting, and production of features & documentaries.)

Pacific International Enterprises, Inc.

1133 South Riverside, Medford, OR 97501 (503) 779-0990. (Motion picture production and distribution.)
PRESIDENT/PRODUCER
Arthur R. Dubs
SECRETARY-TREASURER
Barbara J. Brown
FINANCIAL CONTROLLER
Arn Wihtol
DIRECTOR OF MEDIA
Paul Blumer
DATE OF ORGANIZATION
1969

Palm Productions, Inc.

595 Madison Ave., New York, NY 10022 (212) 310-1520. (Feature film and television production.)
PRESIDENT
Thomas M. C. Johnston
SECRETARY
Robert H. Montgomery, Jr.
DATE OF ORGANIZATION
1974

Parade Pictures

6353 Homewood Ave., Hollywood, CA 90028 (213) 464-4708.
PRESIDENT
Riley Jackson
DATE OF ORGANIZATION
1961

Paragon Productions

3106 Sweetbrier Circle, Lafayette, CA 94549 (415) 284-75171. (Producer of theatrical shorts, television programs, industrial, educational and public relations films.)
OWNER/PRODUCER-DIRECTOR
Stephen F. Booth
DATE OF ORGANIZATION
1956

Paramount Pictures Corporation

New York (Home Office)
1 Gulf & Western Plaza, New York, NY 10023; (212) 333-7000. Cable: Gulfwestin. (Producer and distributor.)
CHAIRMAN OF THE BOARD & CHIEF EXECUTIVE OFFICER
Barry Diller
PRESIDENT AND CHIEF OPERATING OFFICER
Michael D. Eisner
EXECUTIVE VICE PRESIDENT—FINANCE & ADMINISTRATION
Arthur Barron
VICE PRESIDENT—LEGAL
Walter Josiah, Jr.
VICE PRESIDENT—CORPORATE PLANNING
Alan R. Fields

VICE PRESIDENT—CORPORATE CONTROLLER
Patrick Purcell
VICE PRESIDENT—PLANNING & ADMINISTRATION
Bradford R. Campbell
VICE PRESIDENT—MANAGEMENT INFORMATION SERVICES
Richard F. Gallagher
VICE PRESIDENT—THEATRICAL DISTRIBUTION COUNSEL
Paul D. Springer
CORPORATE SECRETARY
Thomas Lewyn
ASSISTANT SECRETARIES
Eugene H. Frank, Norman R. Forson (G&W)
BOARD OF DIRECTORS
Charles G. Bluhdorn, David N. Judelson, Martin S. Davis, Thomas M. Lewyn
DATE AND PLACE OF INCORPORATION
Incorporated under the laws of New York State, November 15, 1949.
HISTORY OF PARAMOUNT
PARAMOUNT PICTURES CORP., currently in production, as well as in distribution, may be said to have taken most of its origins from the activities of Adolph Zukor, who entered the amusement field in the dawn years with a penny arcade, with Hales's Tours, a motion picture exhibition device, and with nickelodeon theatres, including an early association with the late Marcus Loew in those undertakings. Mr. Zukor in 1912 formed the Engadine Corporation, to distribute an imported picture, which evolved into his Famous Players Film Company, which was to make famous plays with famous players in them. W. W. Hodkinson, emerging from General Film Company, the "trust" of the day, in 1914 formed Paramount Pictures Corporation, which took over distribution of the Zukor product and along with it the product of the Jesse L. Lasky Feature Play Company and others. This led to a course of mergers, with Mr. Zukor dominant.

Famous Players-Lasky Corporation was incorporated on July 19, 1916. In 1917 twelve producing companies merged with it. At the same time the corporation integrated production and distribution by acquiring a national distribution system through a merger with Artcraft Pictures Corporation and Paramount Pictures Corporation.

In 1919 the corporation started its theatre acquisition program. It acquired stock interest in Southern Enterprises, Inc., with 135 theatres in the South; in 1920 it acquired stock interest in New England Theatres, Inc., with 50 New England theatres; in the Butterfield Theatre Circuit with 70 theatres in Michigan about 1926; in Balaban & Katz with 50 theatres in Illinois at the same time. Later numerous theatres in the West and Middle West were acquired.

Paramount's first great star was Mary Pickford, around whom Mr. Zukor built his Famous Players. The roster of the organization has included a preponderance of the great names of the screen. "The Covered Wagon," and "The Ten Commandments" are landmarks of Paramount tradition.

In April, 1927, the corporate name was changed to Paramount Famous Lasky Corporation, and in April, 1930, to Paramount Publix Corporation. In 1933, Paramount Publix Corporation was adjudicated bankrupt in the Federal District Court for the Southern District of New York. In June, 1935, it was reorganized under Section 77B of the Bankruptcy Act under the name of Paramount Pictures, Inc.

In December, 1949, as a result of the reorganization required by the Consent Decree in the action of the Government against the major companies, Paramount split into two companies—Paramount Pictures Corporation, for production-distribution, and United Paramount Theatres, Inc., for theatre operation.

Paramount merged with Gulf & Western Industries Oct. 19, 1966, with Gulf & Western as the surviving corporation and Paramount as a subsidiary with its own management.

PRODUCTION

PARAMOUNT PICTURES CORPORATION— WEST COAST OFFICES (BEVERLY HILLS).
FEATURES DIVISION

202 North Cannon Drive, Beverly Hills, CA 90210 (213) 463-0100.
CHAIRMAN OF THE BOARD & CHIEF EXECUTIVE OFFICER
Barry Diller
PRESIDENT & CHIEF OPERATING OFFICER
Michael D. Eisner
EXECUTIVE VICE PRESIDENT, FINANCE & ADMINISTRATION
Arthur R. Barron
VICE PRESIDENT, WEST COAST FINANCE
Warren Larson
SENIOR VICE PRESIDENT & ASSISTANT TO THE PRESIDENT
Richard Zimbert

SENIOR VICE PRESIDENT, STUDIO OPERATIONS & ADMINISTRATION
Paul A. Birmingham
SENIOR VICE PRESIDENT, PRODUCTION
Jeff Katzenberg
VICE PRESIDENT, PRODUCTION
Dawn Steel
VICE PRESIDENT, PROGRAM EVALUATION
Grant Rosenberg
VICE PRESIDENT, STUDIO RELATIONS
Brenda G. Mutchnick
VICE PRESIDENT, LEGAL AFFAIRS
Ralph Kamon
PRESIDENT, PRODUCTION, MOTION PICTURE DIVISION
Donald C. Simpson
VICE PRESIDENT, EMPLOYEE RELATIONS
Dean S. Ferris
VICE PRESIDENT, LABOR RELATIONS
Richard P. Schonland
VICE PRESIDENT, STUDIO PRODUCTION OPERATIONS
Gordon B. Forbes
VICE PRESIDENT, POST PRODUCTION
Paul Haggar
VICE PRESIDENT, BUSINESS AFFAIRS
Leonard Kalcheim
VICE PRESIDENT, POST-THEATRICAL DISTRIBUTION
Martin S. Pollins
VICE PRESIDENT, MUSIC
Hunter Murtaugh
EXECUTIVE VICE PRESIDENT, NOW-THEATRICAL & EDUCATIONAL DISTRIBUTION DIVISION
Paul Birmingham
VICE PRESIDENT, BUSINESS AFFAIRS
Joseph A. Adelman
DIRECTOR, PRODUCTION FINANCE
Jeffrey Snetiker

MOTION PICTURE DIVISION PUBLICITY— PROMOTION

New York Office:
SENIOR VICE PRESIDENT, MARKETING
Gordon Weaver
VICE PRESIDENT—INTERNATIONAL MARKETING
David Van Houten
VICE PRESIDENT—NATIONAL ADVERTISING
Tom Campanella
VICE PRESIDENT, PUBLICITY AND PROMOTION
Kathy Jones
EXECUTIVE DIRECTOR—CREATIVE ADVERTISING
Shelly Hochron
NATIONAL DIRECTOR OF ADVERTISING
Sid Eisenberg
EXECUTIVE DIRECTOR—PUBLICITY AND PROMOTION
Howard A. Levine
DIRECTOR, FIELD PUBLICITY AND PROMOTION
Jay Goldberg
EXECUTIVE DIRECTOR—NATIONAL SALES PROMOTION
Louis D'Andre Shafir
DIRECTOR OF NATIONAL PUBLICITY
Tamara Rawitt
DIRECTOR PUBLICITY PROJECTS
Ellen David

West Coast Office:
VICE PRESIDENT—WEST COAST MARKETING
Laurence Mark
DIRECTOR, WEST COAST PUBLICITY MARKETING
Susan Pile
FOREIGN PRODUCTION OFFICES
London—Paramount British Pictures, Ltd., 162 Wardour Street, London, W.1, England: Tel: 01-437-7700; Telex: 263361; Cable: Paraserv, W.1.
Rome—Paramount Films of Italy, Inc., c/o Interserco S.R.L., Via San Basilio 41, 00187 Rome; Tel. 46-15-18; Telex: 843-615-44; Cable: Paramount, Luigi Luraschi, Continental production executive;
Paris—Marianne Productions, 1 Rue Meyerbeer, Paris 9e, France; Tel. 073-73-78; Cable: Marianneprod. Christian Ferry, continental production executive.

DISTRIBUTION
(Domestic)

PRESIDENT, PARAMOUNT DISTRIBUTION
Frank G. Mancuso
SENIOR VICE PRESIDENT, DOMESTIC DISTRIBUTION
Martin Kutner
VICE PRESIDENT—ASSISTANT SALES MANANGER
Gino Campagnola
VICE PRESIDENT, GENERAL SALES MANAGER
Barry London
DIRECTOR OF SALES OPERATIONS
Steven Rappaport

VICE PRESIDENT—WORLD WIDE TECHNICAL FACILITIES
Al LoPresti
VICE PRESIDENT—ASSISTANT TO PRESIDENT
Buffy Shutt
VICE PRESIDENT—FILM & VIDEOTAPE SECURITY
Joseph A. Moscaret
DIVISIONAL DISTRICT MANAGERS
Eastern, Ed Bader (Alexandria); Larry St. John, J. Keegan (district managers Boston); Southern, Wayne Lewellen (Dallas); Royce Brimage (district manager, Jacksonville); Central, Herb Gillis (Chicago); Jack Simmons (district manager, Detroit); Western, Jeff Blake (Beverly Hills); Mike Morrison (district manager, San Francisco)
DOMESTIC BRANCHES AND MANAGERS
ALEXANDRIA, VA. 22304—Landmark Prof. Bldg., 5249 Duke St., Claudia Unger.
ATLANTA: 30329—17 2600 Century Parkway, M.V. McAfee.
BEVERLY HILLS: 90210—9440 Santa Monica Blvd., Walter Lange.
BOSTON: 02116—31 St. James Ave., Joe Rathgeb.
BUFFALO: 14202—300 Delaware Ave., Antonio Mercurio.
CHARLOTTE: 28202—230 S. Tryon St., Joseph Cutrell.
CHICAGO: 60601—111 ED. Wacker Dr., Jeff Blake.
CINCINNATI: 45202—414 Walnut St., Mike Share.
DALLAS: 75206—8350 N. Central Expressway, Terry Kierzek.
DENVER: 80206—158 Fillmore St., Robert Box.
DES MOINES: 50309—1535 Linden St., Charles Caliguri.
DETROIT: 48237—23300 Greenfield Rd., Oak Park, MI, James Goldschlager.
JACKSONVILLE: 32211—9550 Regency Square Blvd., Al Stout.
KANSAS CITY: 66205—4220 Johnson Dr., Shawnee Mission, Kan., Mike Klein.
MIMMEAPOLIS: 55426—6950 Waysata Blvd., Forrie Myers.
NEW ORLEANS: 70002—3525 N. Causeway Blvd., Metairie, LA David Garfinkle.
NEW YORK: 10023—1 Gulf Western Plaza, Russ Topal.
PHILADELPHIA: 19103—1603 Fox Bldg., 1612 Market St. Ralph Garman.
PUERTO RICO: 00906—P.O. Box 5446, San Juan, Nestor Rivera.
SAN FRANCISCO: 94111—1700 Montgomery St., Ron Litvin.
SEATTLE: 98109—975 John St., Joe Vigil.

(Canada)

GENERAL MANAGER
Robert Lightstone
CALGARY, ALBA. T3C 0M8—1410 11th Ave., S.W., Donald Popow.
MONTREAL, QUEBEC: H4A 1G6—5887 Monkland Ave., Romeo Goudreau.
TORONTO, ONT.: M5E 1E9—1 Yonge St., Toronto Star Bldg., Wayne LaForrest.
ST. JOHN, N.B.: E2L 2E8—77 Germain St., Jean White.
VANCOUVER, B.C.: V6P 3G6—1646 West 75th Av., Chris Sullivan.
WINNIPEG, MAN.: R3B 2H6—313 Donald St., Capitol Theatre Bldg., Clyde Brazer.

DISTRIBUTION
(Foreign)

DISTRIBUTION OUTSIDE U.S. AND CANADA IS HANDLED BY CINEMA INTERNATIONAL CORPORATION. (SEE C.I.C. LISTING)

FAMOUS MUSIC CORPORATION

1 Gulf & Western Plaza, New York, NY 10023 (212) 333-7000.

FAMOUS MUSIC PUBLISHING COMPANIES

PRESIDENT AND CHIEF OPERATING OFFICER
Marvin Cane
VICE PRESIDENT & SECRETARY
Sidney Herman

FAMOUS MUSIC PUBLISHING CO.

5451 Marathon Street, Hollywood, CA 90038 (213) 463-0100.
VICE PRESIDENT IN CHARGE OF MUSIC FOR FEATURE & TELEVISION
William R. Stinson

PARAMOUNT COMMUNICATIONS & EDUCATIONAL DIVISIONS

6430 Sunset Blvd., Suite 718, Hollywood, CA 90028.
VICE PRESIDENT
Robert Peters

Paramount Television & Video Distribution

5451 Marathon St., Hollywood, CA 90038 (213) 468-5000

PRESIDENT, PARAMOUNT TELEVISION & VIDEO DISTRIBUTION
Richard Frank

PRODUCTION
PRESIDENT
Gary Nardino
SENIOR VICE PRESIDENT, BUSINESS AFFAIRS
Richard Weston
SENIOR VICE PRESIDENT, PRODUCTION
Robert Rosenbaum
VICE PRESIDENT, PROGRAM DEVELOPMENT
Jeffrey Benson
VICE PRESIDENT, CURRENT PROGRAMS
Mark Ovitz
VICE PRESIDENT, LEGAL AFFAIRS
Howard Barton
EXECUTIVE CASTING DIRECTOR
Hoyt Bowers
EXECUTIVE DIRECTOR, PUBLICITY/ADVERTISING
Richard J. Winters

DISTRIBUTION
PRESIDENT, TELEVISION DOMESTIC DISTRIBUTION
M. Randolph Reiss
PRESIDENT, PARAMOUNT INTERNATIONAL TELEVISION DISTRIBUTION
Bruce Gordon
PRESIDENT, PARAMOUNT VIDEO
Mel Harris
SENIOR VICE PRESIDENT, SALES
Robert Jacquemin
VICE PRESIDENT, OPERATIONS (NY)
Leonard J. Grossi
MANAGER, ADMINISTRATION
Helen Ricketts
DIRECTOR, ADVERTISING & PROMOTIONAL SERVICES
Rick Weidner
SENIOR VICE PRESIDENT, PROGRAMMING
John Goldhammer

Pathe News, Inc.

250 West 57th St., New York, NY 10019 (212) 582-6155. (Producer and distributor of documentaries, educational films and children's programs.)

PRESIDENT
Joseph P. Smith
VICE PRESIDENT, SECRETARY & TREASURER
Samuel A. Costello
VICE PRESIDENT & GENERAL COUNSEL
James J. Harrington
BOARD OF DIRECTORS
All of above
DATE OF ORGANIZATION
1959

Pathe Pictures, Inc.

250 West 57th St., New York, NY 10019 (212) 582-6155. (Production and distribution of feature motion pictures, shorts, documentaries and programs for TV.)

Same officers as for Pathe News

Pebble Productions, Inc.

P.O. Box 1777, Beverly Hills, CA 90213 (213) 273-4292. (Producer.)

PRESIDENT
Robert S. Levy
VICE-PRESIDENT
Jon Adam Levy
TREASURER
Marcel Akselrod
SECRETARY
Sanford Starman
DATE OF ORGANIZATION
1963

Peerless Film Processing Corporation

250 West 64th St., New York, NY 10023 (212) 799-2500. (Protective and preservative film treatments; film reconditioning, incl. Peer-Renu for shrunken originals, scratch removal, rehumidification, repairs, cleaning, distribution servicing of film libraries and TV shows on films.)

PRESIDENT
Y. W. Mociuk
VICE-PRESIDENT
Sam Borodinsky

DOMESTIC LICENSEES
Detroit, MI—Allied Film Laboratory, 7375 Woodward Ave.;
San Francisco, CA—W. A. Palmer Films, 611 Howard St.; Leo Diner Films, Inc., 332-350 Golden Gate Ave., 94102;
Washington, DC—Byron, Inc., 65 K. St. N.E.

FOREIGN LICENSEES
Australia—Colorfilm Pty. Ltd., 35 Missenden Rd., Camperdown, N.S.W. 2050;
Canada—Bonded Services Int'l, 205 Richmond St., West, Toronto;
Mexico—Cinematografica Vaporate Process, S.A., Martires Irlandeses No. 35, Churubusco 21, D.F.;
Switzerland—Schwarz-Filmtechnik, Breiteweg 36, 3072 Ostermundigen, Berne.

Peppercorn-Wormser Film Distributors

1585 Broadway, New York, NY 10019 (212) 247-8380. (Motion picture distribution.)

PRESIDENT
Carl Peppercorn
VICE PRESIDENT & TREASURER
Irving Wormser
DATE OF ORGANIZATION
1966

Persky-Bright Organization

555 Madison Avenue, New York, NY 10022 (212) 421-4141. (Finances and produces feature motion pictures.)

PARTNERS
Lester Persky, Richard Bright
DATE OF ORGANIZATION
1973

Lester Persky Productions, Inc.

555 Madison Ave., New York, NY 10022 (212) 421-4141. (Film producer)

PRESIDENT
Lester Persky

Pike Productions, Inc.

47 Galen St., Watertown, MA 02172 (617) 924-5000. (Production of trailers, radio & television campaigns for features; custom trailers & headers for theatres.)

PRESIDENT
James A. Pike
OPERATIONS MANAGER
Stephen E. Hughes
DIRECTOR OF PHOTOGRAPHY
Edward J. Searles
DIRECTOR OF RECORDING
Andrew H. Jablon
PRINT DISTRIBUTION
Polly van den Honert
DATE OF ORGANIZATION
1958

Polygram Pictures

8255 Sunset Blvd., Los Angeles, CA 90046 (213) 650-8300. 810 Seventh Avenue, New York, NY 10019 (212) 399-4011. (Production.)

CHAIRMAN OF THE BOARD
  Peter Guber
PRESIDENT
  Gordon Stulberg
EXECUTIVE VICE PRESIDENT, WORLDWIDE THEATRI-
CAL PRODUCTION
  Jere Henshaw
EXECUTIVE VICE PRESIDENT, BUSINESS AFFAIRS
  David Saunders
EXECUTIVE VICE PRESIDENT, FINANCE
  Jim Johnson
DATE OF ORGANIZATION
  1980

Producers Commercial Productions Inc.

223 Route Eighteen, East Brunswick, NJ 08816 (201) 249-8982. (Producer of feature films, TV specials, TV series.)
PRESIDENT
  Samuel M. Sherman
VICE PRESIDENT & TREASURER
Dan Q. Kennis
EXECUTIVE PRESIDENT
  Al Adamson

Producer's Distribution Company

8833 Sunset Blvd., Suite 303, Los Angeles, CA 90069 (213) 657-8620. (Motion picture production and distribution.)
CHAIRMAN
  William B. Silberkleit
DATE OF ORGANIZATION
  1975

Producers Sales Organization

10100 Santa Monica Blvd., Los Angeles, CA 90067 (213) 552-9977. (Worldwide promotion, distribution and sales representation of feature films in all media.)
PRESIDENT
  Mark Damon
SENIOR VICE PRESIDENT/ADMINISTRATION
  Janet Blair Fleming
VICE PRESIDENT/FINANCE
  Philip A. Franzel
VICE PRESIDENT/OPERATIONS
  Gregory Cascante
VICE PRESIDENT/ADVERTISING AND PUBLICITY
  Pattie Zimmerman
DATE OF ORGANIZATION
  1977

PRODUCERS SALES ORGANIZATION, UK (PSO, UK)

120 Pall Mall, 4th Floor; London SW1 England (01) 839-3292
MANAGING DIRECTOR
  Keith Turner

PRODUCERS SALES ORGANIZATION, FRANCE (PSO, Paris)

73 Champs Elysees, 75008 Paris, France (331) 225-0703
MANAGING DIRECTOR
  Pierre Kalfon

Productions Extraordinaire, Ltd.

P.O. Box 3811, Olympic Station, Beverly Hills, CA 90212 (213) 839-1397. (Feature film development)
PRINCIPALS
  Edward L. Olson, Chauncey Monroe Barrymore, Janet-Clair Barrymore

Q.E.D. Productions Inc.

21 West 46th Street, New York, NY 10036 (212) 582-4291. (Producers of television commercials, industrial films, sales training films, tourist promotion films, and theatrical motion pictures; complete video tape facilities in studio and location.)
PRESIDENT, EXECUTIVE PRODUCER, DIRECTOR
  Robert Baron
DIRECTORS
  John Whited, Bob Naud

Quartet/Films, Incorporated

60 East 42nd St., Suite 3301, New York, NY 10017 (212) 867-9780. (Motion picture distribution.)
CHAIRMAN OF THE BOARD
  Charles Benton
VICE CHAIRMAN OF THE BOARD AND EXECUTIVE VICE PRESIDENT
  Arthur M. Tolchin
PRESIDENT
  Meyer Ackerman
EXECUTIVE VICE PRESIDENT
  Allen Green
VICE PRESIDENT/SECRETARY
  Edward Schuman
VICE PRESIDENT/TREASURER
  Sanford Greenberg
NATIONAL SALES MANAGER
  Michael Gosset
ASSISTANT TO NATIONAL SALES MANAGER
  Keith Johnson
DATE OF ORGANIZATION
  1977

RKO General, Inc.

1440 Broadway, New York, NY 10018
CHAIRMAN OF THE BOARD
  Thomas F. O'Neil
VICE CHAIRMAN OF THE BOARD
  John B. Poor
PRESIDENT
  Frank Shakespeare
EXECUTIVE VICE PRESIDENT-FINANCE AND LEGAL
  Hubert J. DeLynn
SENIOR VICE PRESIDENTS
  Henry V. Greene, Jr., C. Robert Manby
VICE PRESIDENTS
  J. Howard Carter, Jr., Dwight Case, Eugene J. Caser, Hubert J. DeLynn, Kenneth R. Frankl, Robert L Glaser, Henry P. Sabatell, Arnold Kaufman, Lloyd D. Ruth, Patrick J. Winkler, Jeffrey Ruthizer, Charles A. Carrature, John B. Fitzgerald, Roger H. Shook, Shane O'Neil.
TREASURER
  Hubert J. DeLynn
SECRETARY & GENERAL COUNSEL
  Kenneth R. Frankl
ASSISTANT SECRETARIES
  Joseph J. Shortall, Patrick J. Winkler, Oliver J. Janney
ASSISTANT TREASURERS
  Charles A. Carrature, Charles J. Marshall
CONTROLLER
  John B. Fitzgerald

RKO Pictures, Inc.

(A Subsidiary of RKO General, Inc.) 1440 Broadway, New York, NY 10018 (212) 764-7000. Cable: RKOEX (National distributor).
PRESIDENT
  C. Robert Manby
EXECUTIVE VICE PRESIDENT
  Henry V. Greene, Jr.
VICE PRESIDENTS
  Shane O'Neil, Jack Brooks
TREASURER
  John B. Fitzgerald
SECRETARY
  Kenneth R. Frankl
ASSISTANT SECRETARY
  Oliver J. Janney
ASSISTANT TREASURER
  Charles A. Carrature

Radio City Music Hall Productions, Inc.

50th Street & Ave. of Americas, New York, NY 10020 (212) 246-4600.
CHAIRMAN
Alton G. Marshall
PRESIDENT, EXECUTIVE PRODUCER
Robert F. Jani
EXECUTIVE VICE PRESIDENT, CHIEF OPERATING OFFICER
Richard H. Evans
VICE PRESIDENT, BUSINESS AND FINANCIAL AFFAIRS
James McManus
VICE PRESIDENT, ENTERTAINMENT CENTER OPERATIONS
Robert Buckley
VICE PRESIDENT, MARKETING/COMMUNICATIONS
Patricia H. Robert

Robert B. Radnitz Productions, Ltd.

10182½ Culver Blvd., Culver City, CA 90230 (213) 559-9720. (Motion picture production, both theatrical and TV.)
PRESIDENT
Robert B. Radnitz
DATE OF ORGANIZATION
1970

Ragsdale, Carl, Associates, Ltd.

4725 Stillbrooke, Houston, TX 77035 (713) 729-6530. (Producers of films for industry, television and government.)
PRESIDENT
Carl V. Ragsdale
BRANCH OFFICES:
630 Ninth Ave. Suite 414, New York, NY 10036. (Production facilities) Tel: (212) PL 7-8699; 2120 "L" Street NW, Suite 200, Washington, DC 20037. Arthur Neuman, Exec. Prod. in charge. Tel: (202) 347-7095; 16036 Tupper St. Sepulveda, CA 91343, Tel: (213) 894-6291. Exec. Prod. in charge: Frank Coghlan; Piazza Cairoli, 113 Roma, Italy 00186, Tel: 654-5182, Douglas R. Fleming, Exec. Prod. in charge.

Rainbow Productions, Inc.

1900 Ave. of the Stars, Suite 2270, Los Angeles, CA 90067.
PRESIDENT
Ralph Nelson

Rank Industries America, Inc.

411 East Jarvis Ave., Des Plaines, IL 60018 (312) 297-2124. (Manufacture of theatre lighting and of precision instruments. Marketing of a wide range of Rank products in the U.S., including theatre and TV studio lighting and controls, sound systems, hi fi, TV broadcast equipment, lenses, precision measuring instruments, fibre optics, metal detectors and numbering equipment through companies listed below.)
PRESIDENT
B. A. Edney

RANK PRECISION INDUSTRIES, INC.

411 East Jarvis Ave., Des Plaines, IL 60018 (312) 297-7720, J. M. Campbell, president & general manager; 260 North Route 303, P.O. Box 332, West Nyack, NY 10094 (914) 358-4450, K. Sadhvani, contact.

RANK SCHERR-TUMICO, INC.

301 Armstrong Blvd., P.O. Box 29, St. James, MN 56081 (507) 375-3211 L. T. Smith, president.

RANK NUMBERING MACHINES, INC.

411 East Jarvis Ave., Des Plaines, IL 60018 (312) 297-7720, J. M. Campbell, contact.

STRAND CENTURY, INC.

5432 West 102nd St., Los Angeles, CA 90045 (213) 776-4600, Marvin Altman, president & general manager; 20 Bushes Elmwood Park, NJ (201) 791-7000, W. Liento, Jr., executive vice president.

CANADIAN OFFICES

RANK PRECISION INDUSTRIES (CANADA) LTD.

6520 Northam Drive, Mississauga, Ontario L4V 1H9 (416) 677-7408, Mrs. J. Martinkowski, sales administration.

STRAND CENTURY CO., LTD.

6520 Northam Drive, Mississauga, Ontario, L4V 1H9 (416) 677-7130, P. A. Bogod, president & general manager.

Rankin/Bass Productions

1 East 53rd St., New York, NY 10022 (212) 759-7721 (Producer.)
PRESIDENT
Arthur Rankin, Jr.
VICE PRESIDENT
Jules Bass

Rapid Film Technique

37-02 27th St., Long Island City, NY 11101 (212) 786-4600. (Film reconditioning, rejuvenation inspection, repair.)
PRESIDENT
Jerry Gober

RAPID FILM DISTRIBUTORS

(Film and videotape shipping, distribution, storage.)

Rastar Films, Inc.

c/o Columbia Pictures Industries, Inc., Colgems Square Burbank, CA 91505 (213) 843-6000. (Motion picture production.)
CHAIRMAN OF THE BOARD
Ray Stark
PRESIDENT & CHIEF EXECUTIVE OFFICER
Guy McElwaine
SENIOR VICE PRESIDENT
Steve Deutsch
VICE PRESIDENT—FINANCE
Richard Parness
VICE PRESIDENT—BUSINESS AFFAIRS
Robert O. Price
CASTING DIRECTOR
Jennifer Shull

The Walter Reade Organization, Inc.

Executive Offices: 241 East 34th St., NY 10016 (212) 683-6300.
DIRECTORS
Daniel Bruno, Sheldon Gunsberg, Dolly Reade Borgia, William C. MacMillen, Jr., Charles F. Simonelli, Edward L. Schuman
PRESIDENT
Sheldon Gunsberg
EXECUTIVE VICE PRESIDENT & TREASURER
Christopher W. Preuster
CONTROLLER AND ASS'T SECRETARY
Marvin Katz

ADMINISTRATIVE DIRECTOR-NON-THEATRICAL FILMS
DIVISION
  Paul Baise
CONCESSIONS DIRECTOR
  Stefan Mayer
GRAPHIC ARTS GROUP PRESIDENT
  Berton P. Couturier
TRANSFER AGENT
  Manufacturers Hanover Bank, 4 New York Plaza, New York, NY
10004.
REGISTRAR
  Manufacturers and Traders Trust Company, 654 Madison Ave.,
New York, NY 10021
GENERAL COUNSEL
  Weil, Gotshal, & Manges, 767 Fifth Ave., New York, NY 10022.

Reeves Communications Corporation

General Office: 605 Third Avenue, New York, NY
10017 (212) 573-8600

Videotape production, creative and post-production services, editing, film to tape transfers, duplication, distribution, syndication services, mobile crews and equipment, videotape studio; transfer, mixing dubbing and duping of sound tracks for film and video; television program development and acquisition; corporate television network development and programming; creation and production of specials, series and mini-series for television and motion picture feature films; meeting planning, multi-media creation and production, film and video business communications; educational film series, promotional materials and consultation for sales development; video systems engineering, installation and maintenance.

CHAIRMAN OF THE BOARD PRESIDENT & CHIEF EXECUTIVE OFFICER
  Marvin H. Green, Jr.
VICE CHAIRMAN
  Frank G. Marshall
PRESIDENT
  William A. Wetzel
CHIEF FINANCIAL OFFICER/SENIOR VICE PRESIDENT
  Meyrick Payne
TREASURER/SECRETARY
  Robert E. Trivers
CHAIRMAN, ENTERTAINMENT GROUP
  Alan Landsburg

Republic Corporation

1900 Avenue of the Stars, Los Angeles, CA 90067
(213) 553-3900.

(Diversified film processing; printing; mine roof-bolts; expanded metal; custom molding; hot rolled steel angles & flats.)

CHAIRMAN, PRESIDENT & CHIEF EXECUTIVE OFFICER
  Ralph O. Briscoe
SENIOR VICE PRESIDENTS
  Curtis F. Bourland, Rembrandt P. Lane, Raymond J. Wilcox
VICE PRESIDENT & GENERAL COUNSEL
  Norman S. Marshal
TREASURER
  Ervin J. Bolks
VICE PRESIDENT & CONTROLLER
  John L. Olson
ASST. SECRETARY
  Anita J. Cutchall
ASST. TREASURER
  Albert M. Bensusan
BOARD OF DIRECTORS
  Howard P. Allen, Curtis F. Bourland, Ralph O. Briscoe, Irving
M. Felt, Robert H. Finch, John Guerin, Jr., Rembrandt P. Lane,
Leonard M. Leiman, Richard Seaver
DIVISIONS OF REPUBLIC CORPORATION
  Binghamton Plastics, Consolidated Film Industries, Consolidated
Molded Products, Continental Graphics, Glen Glenn Sound, Harmony Industries, Kentucky Electric Steel, Niles Expanded Metals,
Tazewell Industries, Visual Information Systems, Western Metal
Lath, Lucerne Industries, Delmar Studios, Advanced Mining Systems
SUBSIDIARIES
  Dauman Displays, Inc., Delmar Printing Company, IMEC Corp.,
National Airmotive Corporation, Physicians Radio Network Inc.,
Trans-Air Supply Company

CONSOLIDATED FILM INDUSTRIES

(Division of Republic Communications, Inc.)
West Coast Laboratory, 959 Seward Street, Hollywood, CA 90038 (213) 462-3161.

PRESIDENT
  Jesse T. Ellington
CHAIRMAN, EXEC. COMM.
  Sidney P. Solow
VICE PRESIDENT & TREASURER
  W. James Lawler
VICE PRESIDENT PRODUCTION
  Theodore Fogelman
VICE PRESIDENT—FILM LABORATORY
  Burt Mills
VICE PRESIDENT ENGINEERING
  Edward H. Reichard
VICE PRESIDENT SALES & MKT.
  Jerry Virnig
VICE PRESIDENT VIDEOTAPE
  Tom Bruehl
CONTROLLER
  Jean H. Anderson

Riviera Productions

6610 Selma Ave., Hollywood, CA 90028 (213) 462-8585. Branches: 340 Westmoor, Brookfield, Wisc. SU
2-8815. (Producer-distributor.)

EXECUTIVE PRODUCER
  F. W. Zens
ASSOCIATE PRODUCERS
  Leif Rise, Jan Elblein
DATE OF ORGANIZATION
  1953

Rob-Rich Films, Inc.

% Sidney Ginsberg, 305 East 24th St., New York,
NY 10010 (212) 889-3034. (Production and distribution of motion pictures.)

PRESIDENT
  Sidney Ginsberg
VICE PRESIDENT, SECRETARY & TREASURER
  Nelly M. Ginsberg
DATE OF ORGANIZATION
  1977

Robin International Cinerama Corporation

410 Park Avenue, New York, NY 10022 (212) 752-3900. (Exhibition of Cinerama outside the U.S.A.)

PRESIDENT
  A. Darroudi
VICE-PRESIDENTS
  F. F. Ritterbusch, S. H. Murley, Jean Bouchel-Ysaye
ASSISTANT VICE-PRESIDENT
  A. Z. Landi
SECRETARY-TREASURER
  C. Lynch

Rosamond Productions, Inc.

7461 Beverly Blvd., Los Angeles, CA 90036 (Motion
picture producer.)

PRESIDENT
  David Chudnow
VICE PRESIDENT
  Rosamond Chudnow

SDP Communications, Ltd.

Suite 610, 89 Avenue Road, Toronto, Canada, M5R
2G4 (416) 961-5525. (Packaging/producing company.)

PRESIDENT
  S. Dean Peterson
DATE OF ORGANIZATION
  1972

S. J. International Pictures

1500 Broadway, New York, NY 10036 (212) 921-9855. (Film distributor in U.S. and Canada.)
PRESIDENT
Salah Jamal
DATE OF ORGANIZATION
1975

Salzburg Enterprises, Inc.

98 Cuttermill Road, Great Neck, NY 11021 (516) 487-4515. (Non-theatrical motion picture distribution; television distribution.)
PRESIDENT
Richard B. Salzburg
DATE OF ORGANIZATION
1977

Salzburg Enterprises, Inc. of California

9255 Sunset Bard, Los Angeles, CA 90069 (213) 278-1853 (Non-theatrical motion picture distribution; television distribution; cable distribution, video & discs).
PRESIDENT
Milton J. Salzburg
DATE OF ORGANIZATION
1980

Sanrio Communications, Inc.

1930 Century Park West, Suite 402, Los Angeles, CA 90067 (213) 552-0525. (Motion picture production and distribution.)
MANAGING DIRECTOR
Keiichi (Ken) Kawarai
SALES MANAGER
Vincent Petrillo
ASSISTANT SALES MANAGER
Robert Parlen
MARKETING AND ADVERTISING MANAGER
Peter Gastaldi
PRODUCTION CONSULTANT
Walt DeFaria
COMPTROLLER
Etsuo Iida
DATE OF ORGANIZATION
1977

Satra Films and Special Projects Corporation

1211 Avenue of the Americas, 31st floor, New York, NY 10036 (212) 354-3939. Cable NYSAT-RACO. Telex: 234532. (Member of the Satra Group.)
PRESIDENT
John J. Kapstein
EXECUTIVE SECRETARY
Wilma Meghoo
OFFICE MANAGER
Sonia Marron

Schine Productions

626 South Hudson Avenue, Los Angeles, CA 90005 (213) 937-5000. (Produce motion pictures for theatrical and television release.)
PRESIDENT
G. David Schine

Schoenfeld Film Distributing

241 East 34th St., New York, NY 10016 (212) 532-5210.
PRESIDENT
Lester Schoenfeld

Scotia American Productions

600 Madison Avenue, New York, NY 10022. (212) 758-4775. (Motion picture production and distribution.)
PRESIDENT
Peter J. Kares
DIRECTOR
Eugene D. Picker
GENERAL SALES MANAGER
Robert E. Ginsberg
LONDON OFFICE
51 South Audley St., London W1Y 6HB, England, Tel.: 493-7428. S. Ben Fisz, mgr. dir.
MUNICH OFFICE
8 Munchen 80 (Bogenhausen), Possart Strasse 14. Tel.: 473027. Sam Waynberg, mgr. dir.

Screenvision, Inc.

420 Lexington Ave., New York, NY 10017. (212) 661-4180. (National screen advertising.) A joint venture of Mediavision, Inc., Paris, France and Capital Cities Communications New York.
PRESIDENT
William R. James
SENIOR VICE PRESIDENT/THEATRICAL
W. Robert Rich
VICE PRESIDENT AND GENERAL SALES MANAGER
Richard North
DIRECTOR OF COMPUTER SERVICES
Richard Oras
DATE OF ORGANIZATION
1976

Sebastian International Pictures

32162 West Oakshore Dr., Westlake Village, CA 91861 (213) 889-3697. (Motion picture production and distribution.)
PRESIDENT
Ferd Sebastian
VICE PRESIDENT—SECRETARY—TREASURER
Beverly Sebastian
DATE OF ORGANIZATION
1971

Sebastian International Enterprises

P.O. Box 1425, Crystal Bay, NV 89450 (702) 831-5538 (Cable, Pay-TV, and theatrical production and distribution)
PRESIDENT
Ferd Sebastian III
VICE PRESIDENT
Tracy Loren Sebastian
DATE OF ORGANIZATION
1978

Sebastian International Pictures

32162 Oakshore, Westlake Village, CA 91361 (213) 889-3697. (Financial, film and television production)
PRESIDENT
Ferd Sebastian
VICE PRESIDENT
Beverly C. Sebastian
SECRETARY
Tracy Sebastian
TREASURER
Ferd Sebastian III

Security Pictures, Inc.

8315 Camino Del Oro, La Jolla, CA 90037 (714) 454-2363.
PRESIDENT AND TREASURER
Philip Yordan
VICE PRESIDENT-SECRETARY
Dan Yordan

Selected Pictures Corporation

Brainard Place, 29001 Cedar Ave., Rm. 451, Lyndhurst, OH 44124 (216) 461-9770.
PRESIDENT
Sam Schultz
EXECUTIVE OFFICER
Jay Schultz
BRANCH MANAGER
Morris Zryl

Edward Shaw Productions

P.O. Box 35149, Los Angeles, CA 90035. (Motion picture production.)
PRESIDENT
Edward Shaw
VICE PRESIDENT
Ronald Lopes
VICE PRESIDENT/PRODUCTION
Marci Baulsir
DATE OF ORGANIZATION
1969

Short Film Showcase

625 Broadway, New York, NY 10012. (212) 473-3400. (National film distribution of independently produced short subjects.)
PROJECT ADMINISTRATOR
Alan Mitosky
ADMINISTRATIVE ASSISTANT
Susan Linfield

Showcorporation of America

P.O. Box 1070, Stamford, CT 06904 (203) 327-9252.
PRESIDENT
C. Robert Manby
EXECUTIVE VICE PRESIDENT
Robert Manby

The Sidaris Company

1891 Carla Ridge, Beverly Hills, CA 90210 (213) 275-2682. (Television and theatrical motion picture production.)
PRESIDENT
Andrew Sidaris
OFFICERS
Arlene Sidaris, Drew Sidaris

Sigma Productions, Inc.

129 East 64th St., New York, NY 10021 (212) 535-6001.
PRESIDENT
Otto Preminger

Silverstein International Corp.

200 West 57th Street, New York, NY 10019 (212) 541-6620. (Production and distribution of motion pictures.)
PRESIDENT
Maurice Silverstein
DATE OF ORGANIZATION
1970

Melvin Simon Productions, Inc.

260 S. Beverly Drive, Beverly Hills, CA 90212 (213) 273-5450. (Motion picture production.)
CHAIRMAN OF THE BOARD & CHIEF EXECUTIVE OFFICER
Melvin Simon
PRESIDENT & CHIEF OPERATION OFFICER
Milton Goldstein
EXECUTIVE VICE PRESIDENT IN CHARGE OF WORLD-WIDE PRODUCTION
Robert E. Relyea
SENIOR VICE PRESIDENT OF BUSINESS & LEGAL AFFAIRS
Keith G. Fleer
VICE PRESIDENT IN CHARGE OF CREATIVE AFFAIRS
Linda Carwin
VICE PRESIDENT AND GENERAL SALES MANAGER
John F. Rubinich
VICE PRESIDENT IN CHARGE OF WORLDWIDE ADVERTISING AND PUBLICITY
Cheryl E. Boone
POST PRODUCTION SUPERVISOR
Joseph Dervin, Jr.
DIRECTOR OF PUBLICITY
Candiss L. Cates
TREASURER
Juan Molina

Aaron Spelling Productions, Inc.

132 South Rodeo Drive, Beverly Hills, CA 90212. (213) 858-2000. (Production of motion pictures and television.)
PRESIDENT
Aaron Spelling
DATE OF ORGANIZATION
1968

Spiegel-Bergman Productions

2029 Century Park East, Suite 1850, Los Angeles, CA 90067 (213) 552-0577. (Motion picture production.)
PARTNERS
Larry Spiegel, Melvin Bergman, Bob Greenberg

Stereovision International, Inc.

3421 West Burbank Blvd., Burbank, CA 91505 (213) 841-1127. (Producer and distributor of 3-D film; consultant in all phases of 3-D filming and equipment; supplier of 3-D cameras and projection equipment; also distributes regular films)
PRESIDENT
Chris J. Condon
DATE OF ORGANIZATION
1969

Summit Feature Distributors, Inc.

116 North Robertson Blvd., Los Angeles, CA 90048 (213) 652-7702. (Film distributor)
CHAIRMAN OF THE BOARD
C. Gregory Earls
PRESIDENT
Harvey M. Baren
DATE OF ORGANIZATION
1980

Sunset International Releasing, Inc.

8222 West 3rd Street, Los Angeles, CA (213) 653-5200. (Motion picture distribution.) Affiliated with Park Lane Pictures and H. B. Enterprises, Inc.
PRESIDENT
Herb Bromberg
VICE PRESIDENT
Jay Belitz
TREASURER
Ruth Bromberg
DATE OF ORGANIZATION
1970

482

Surrogate Releasing

3412 West Olive Avenue, Burbank, CA 91505 (213) 846-8441. (Film production and distribution.)
PRESIDENT
Irvin Dorfman
DATE OF ORGANIZATION
1975

The Taft Entertainment Company

10100 Santa Monica Blvd., Suite 2440, Los Angeles, CA 90067 (213) 557-0388.
PRESIDENT & CHIEF EXECUTIVE OFFICER
Sy Fischer
EXECUTIVE VICE PRESIDENT
Karl Honeystein
SENIOR VICE PRESIDENT, CREATIVE
Joel Cohen

Divisions

Cine Guarantors, 6311 Romaine St., Suite 7204, Hollywood, CA 90038 (213) 567-3006.
Hanna-Barbera Productions, Inc., 3400 Cahuenga Blvd., Hollywood, CA 90068 (213) 851-5000.
QM Productions, 1041 N. Formosa, Hollywood, CA 90046 (213) 650-2674.
Ruby-Spears Enterprises, 3459 Cahuenga Blvd., Hollywood, CA 90068 (213) 874-1500.
The Sy Fischer Company, Inc., 10100 Santa Monica Blvd., Suite 2440, Los Angeles, CA 90067 (213) 557-0388.
One East 57th Street, New York, NY 10022 (212) 486-0426.
Taft Merchandising Group, 660 Madison Ave., 3rd Floor, New York, NY 10021 and 1906 Highland Ave., Cincinnati, OH 45219, (513) 421-9611.
Taft Pictures International, 10100 Santa Monica Blvd., Suite 2440, Los Angeles, CA 90067 (213) 557-0388 and P.O. Box 3039, Park City, Utah 84060 (801) 649-7300.
Titus Productions, 211 East 51st St., New York, NY 10022 (212) 752-6460.

Taft International Pictures, Inc.

556 East 200 South, Salt Lake City, UT 84102. (801) 363-2040. (Production and distribution)
PRESIDENT & CHIEF OPERATING OFFICER
Charles E. Seller, Jr.
DISTRIBUTION PRESIDENT
Raylan Jensen
VICE PRESIDENT, PRODUCTION
James L. Conway
VICE PRESIDENT, ADMINISTRATION
Allan C. Pedersen
VICE PRESIDENT, DISTRIBUTION
Don Otto
DATE OF ORGANIZATION
1980

Taurus Film Co.

9145 Sunset Blvd., Los Angeles, CA 90069 (213) 273-8640. Cable: MANSON, Telex: 691242.
DIRECTOR
Michael F. Goldman
DATE OF ORGANIZATION
1964

Technicolor, Inc.

2049 Century Park East, Suite 2400, Los Angeles, CA 90067 (213) 553-5200.
CHAIRMAN OF THE BOARD & CHIEF EXEC. OFFICER
Morton Kamerman
CHAIRMAN OF THE EXECUTIVE COMMITTEE
Guy M. Bjorkman
PRESIDENT & CHIEF OPERATING OFFICER
Arthur N. Ryan
VICE PRESIDENT-FINANCE & TREASURER
R. Stevens Shean
GENERAL COUNSEL & SECRETARY
John H. Oliphant
DIRECTORS
Guy M. Bjorkman, Richard M. Blanco, William R. Frye, Jonathan T. Isham, Morton Kamerman, George Lewis, Arthur N. Ryan, Charles S. Simone, Fred R. Sullivan

TECHNICOLOR, INC. PROFESSIONAL FILM DIVISION

4050 Lankershim Blvd., N. Hollywood, CA 91608 (213) 769-8500.
PRESIDENT
Raymond A. Gaul

TECHNICOLOR, INC. EAST COAST DIVISION

321 W. 44th St., New York, NY 10036 (212) 582-7310.
VICE PRESIDENT & GENERAL MANAGER
Norman Stein

Telemated Motion Pictures

77 Bleeker St., New York, NY 10012 (212) 682-3434. (Producer of documentaries, industrial, corporate image, sales promotion, training public relations and educational films.)
PRODUCER-DIRECTOR
Saul Taffet

Televicine International Distribution Corporation

8560 Sunset Blvd., 9th floor, Los Angeles, CA 90069 (213) 657-8166. (Distributor of motion pictures to the Spanish language market, principally in the U.S. Puerto Rico, and the Dominican Republic)
PRESIDENT
Merrill Dean
VICE PRESIDENT
Mel Edelstein
CHIEF FINANCIAL OFFICER
Paul Grant
DATE OF ORGANIZATION
1980

Telic

317 West 89th St., New York, NY 10024 (212) 595-7078. (Designers, co-producers and consultants film and tape programs.)
PRESIDENT & PRODUCER-DIRECTOR
Elwood Siegel

Bob Thomas Productions

55 West 42nd St., New York, NY 10036 (212) 221-3602. Branch office: P.O. Box 1787, Wayne, NJ 07470 (201) 696-7500. (Motion picture and television producer; motion picture 3-D slides and motion pictures—Curbside Cinema.)
PRESIDENT
Robert G. Thomas
DATE OF ORGANIZATION
1968

Times Film Corporation

144 West 57th Street, New York, NY 10019 (212) 757-6980. (Motion picture distribution.)
PRESIDENT
Jean Goldwurm
VICE PRESIDENT & SECRETARY
Miriam Leeds
VICE PRESIDENT
Lotte S. Bilgrey
DATE ORGANIZATION
1951

TIMES FILM INTERNATIONAL CORP.

144 West 57th Street, New York, NY 10019 (212) 757-6980. (Production of theatrical motion pictures;

producer's representative; national distribution of theatrical motion pictures in U.S.) Affiliated with Times Film Corp., with same officers as that company.

Todd-AO Corporation, The

2545 Hempstead, East Meadow, NY 11554 (516) 466-3300. (Operator of sound recording studio.) Hollywood: 1021 N. Seward, Hollywood 38, 903-1136.
PRESIDENT
Salah Hassanein
VICE-PRESIDENTS
Fred Hynes, Gladstone T. Whitman, Buzz Knudson
SECRETARY
Morris Goldschlager, Esq.
TREASURER
Irving Palace
DATE OF ORGANIZATION
1953

Toho Co., Inc.

1501 Broadway, Suite 2005, New York, NY 10036 (212) 391-9058. 2049 Century Park East, Los Angeles, CA 90067 (213) 277-1081. (Exporters and importers of films & film distribution.)
NEW YORK REPRESENTATIVE
Kazuto Ohira
LOS ANGELES REPRESENTATIVE
Tetsuzo Ueda

Tomorrow Entertainment, Inc.

Executive Offices: 666 Third Ave., New York, NY 10017 (212) 421-2424. (Motion picture and television production). Production Officers: 4421 Riverside Dr., Burbank, CA (213) 849-3116.
CHAIRMAN OF THE BOARD
Thomas W. Moore
PRESIDENT
John R. Backe
VICE PRESIDENT, PRODUCTION
Jean Moore Edwards

Topar Films, Inc.

116 North Robertson Blvd. Los Angeles, CA 90048 (213) 271-6193. Telex: 181149.
PRESIDENT & TREASURER
Tom Parker
VICE PRESIDENT & SECRETARY
Rick Parker
VICE PRESIDENT
Richard Beaty
VICE PRESIDENT
John McLaurin
VICE PRESIDENT & ASSISTANT SECRETARY
Jacqueline Richard

TOPAR FILMS OF CANADA LIMITED
PRESIDENT
Tom Parker

Tower Productions

½ Covey & Covey, P.C., 1000 Santa Monica Blvd., Los Angeles CA 90067 (213) 203-0800. (Producer.)
PRESIDENT
Clarence Greene
VICE PRESIDENT
Robert Reed
SECRETARY
Richard D. Covey
DATE OF ORGANIZATION
1976

Trans-Lux Corporation

625 Madison Avenue, New York, NY 10022 (212) 751-3110. (Principally engaged in the business of producing and leasing of electronic equipment for the display of stock and commodity quotations, last sale transactions, financial and other news; and electronic teleprinters for Western Union's Telex and TWK network. It also operates a chain of motion picture theatres and a multimedia presentation, "The New York Experience"; Exhibitor.) (See Index: Theatre Circuits.)
CHAIRMAN EMERITUS
Percival E. Furber
PRESIDENT & CHAIRMAN OF THE BOARD
Richard Brandt
EXECUTIVE VICE-PRESIDENT
Buddy Levy
ADMIN. VICE-PRES. & SECRETARY
Raymond G. Pugh
SENIOR VICE PRESIDENTS
Louis A. Credidio, Charles Holloman
VICE PRESIDENTS
Albert Boyars, Thomas M. Waltz, Victor Liss
TREASURER & ASST. SECY.
James S. Hersh
ASST. VICE PRESIDENTS
Thomas Calello, Nicholas Curtis, Frank Daniels, David Gizer, Francis Mesko, Rsenior vice presidents
Louis A. Credidio, Charles Holloman
VICE PRESIDENTS
Albert Boyars, Thomas M. Waltz, Victor Liss
TREASURER & ASST. SECY.
James S. Hersh
ASST. VICE PRESIDENTS
Thomas Calello, Nicholas Curtis, Frank Daniels, David Gizer, Francis Mesko, Robert Maas, Mark Zonich
BOARD OF DIRECTORS
Richard Brandt, Chester Bland, Robert F. Dirkes, Allan Fromme, Phd., Percival E. Furber, Robert Greenes, William F. Hogan, Buddy Levy, Edward H. Meyer, Howard S. Modlin, Eugene Picker, Raymond G. Pugh, Melvin Starr
DATE AND PLACE OF INCORPORATION
February 5, 1920—Delaware
WHOLLY OWNED SUBSIDIARIES
Trans-Lux Corporation, Trans-Lux Yorkville Corporation, Trans-Lux News-Sign Corporation, Trans-Lux Service Corporation, Saunders Realty Corporation, District Cinema Corporation, Trans-Lux Multimedia Corporation, Trans-Lux Syndicated Programs Corporation, Canadian Trans-Lux Corporation, Ltd., Trans-Lux York Corporation, Trans-Lux New Orleans Corporation, Trans-Lux St. Louis Corporation, Trans-Lux Richmond Corporation, Trans-Lux Experience Corporation, Trans-Lux Connecticut Corporation, Trans-Lux Danbury Corporation, Trans-Lux Greenwich Corporation, Trans-Lux Ridgeway Corporation.

Transvue Pictures Corp.

14724 Ventura Blvd., Suite 909, Sherman Oaks, CA 91403. (213) 990-5600. (World-wide distribution and production of motion pictures.)
PRESIDENT
Herbert B. Schlosberg
VICE PRESIDENT
J. B. Schlosberg
VICE PRESIDENT
L. M. Uris
SECRETARY
K. Galloway
TREASURER
Herbert B. Schlosberg
DIRECTOR OF PUBLICITY AND PROMOTION
Sue Madison
YEAR OF ORGANIZATION
1970

TriStar Pictures, Inc.

5500 Interstate North Pkwy, Suite 415, Atlanta, GA 30328 (404) 231-8726. (Finances, produces and distributes motion pictures.)
PRESIDENT
Lang Elliott
VICE PRESIDENT
Wanda Dell
DATE OF ORGANIZATION
1978

Troma, Inc.

165 West 46th St., New York, NY 10036. (212) 869-1925. (Motion picture producer and distributor)
PRESIDENT
Lloyd Kaufman, Jr.
VICE PRESIDENT
Michael Herz
DIRECTOR OF MARKETING & DISTRIBUTION
Eileen Nad Castaldi

Twentieth Century-Fox Film Corporation

Box 900 Beverly Hills, CA 90213 (213) 277-2211. Cable: Centfox (Producer, Distributor and Exhibitor) New York Office: 40 West 57th St., New York, N.Y. 10019 (212) 977-5500.
OWNER
Marvin Davis
CHAIRMAN OF THE BOARD AND CHIEF EXECUTIVE OFFICER
Alan Hirschfield
PRESIDENT
C. Joseph LaBonte
SENIOR VICE PRESIDENT AND GENERAL COUNSEL
David Y. Handelman
SENIOR VICE PRESIDENT, FINANCE AND CONTROLLER
John P. Meehan
VICE PRESIDENT, CORPORATE DEVELOPMENT AND INTERNATIONAL THEATRES
Raymond A. Doig
VICE PRESIDENT, PLANNING AND INFORMATION SERVICES
Charles C. Tucker
VICE PRESIDENT, TREASURER
E. Lyle Marshall
VICE PRESIDENT, PERSONNEL
Charles F. Weiss
VICE PRESIDENT, PUBLIC AFFAIRS AND TAXES
Raymond T. Bennett
VICE PRESIDENT, CORPORATE ACCOUNTING
Arthur L. Ventrone
CORPORATE SECRETARY AND ASSISTANT GENERAL COUNSEL AND VICE PRESIDENT TELECOMMUNICATIONS LEGAL AFFAIRS
Richard Garzilli
BOARD OF DIRECTORS
Marvin Davis, Gerald R. Ford, Henry Kissinger, Alan Hirschfield, Myron Miller, Gerald Gray, Arthur Modell, Gerald Bergman, Edward Bennett Williams
DATE AND PLACE OF INCORPORATION
As Fox Film Corp., February 1, 1915; New York. Succeeded by Twentieth Century-Fox Film Corp., July 22, 1952. Delaware.
HISTORY OF TWENTIETH CENTURY-FOX
TWENTIETH CENTURY-FOX FILM CORPORATION is the end result of a business begun back in the nickelodeon days of show business by William Fox. In a 58-year span, the company has grown to a $68,000,000 corporation, operating a 63-acre studio in Los Angeles, producing annually from 15 to 20 features. The company is a leader in television production.

At the turn of the century, Mr. Fox, then in textiles, entered the arcade and nickelodeon business and became a member of the exhibition firm of Fox, Moss and Brill. His associates were B. S. Moss and Sol Brill. This association led to the establishment by Mr. Fox of a film exchange, the Greater New York Film Rental Company. In 1913 he organized the Box Office Attraction Company, later acquiring the services of Winfield Sheehan, associated with Mr. Fox for many years.

February 1, 1915, the Fox Film Corporation was founded with the intention of combining production, exhibition and distribution under one name. Film exchanges were established in a dozen cities throughout the country. Today the company has 80 domestic branches and offices located throughout the world.

In 1917, with the shift of production from the east to the west coast, Fox Films moved into its Sunset Studio in Hollywood.

When sound came to the industry, in 1926, Fox Film was able to use the pioneering efforts of Theodore Case and Earl I. Sponable, who invented Movietone, a sound-on-film process.

About 1929 there started a series of reorganizations and financial deals and involvements, principally of which was the purchase by Fox Films of control of Loew's, Inc., for approximately $44,000,000. By order of the Government, the Fox Company's ownership of Loew's was later dissolved and various banking interests acquired control of the stock in the Loew Company.

During these reorganizations, William Fox's connections with the company were discontinued. Sidney R. Kent joined the company as executive vice-president on April 1, 1932, and two weeks later became the company's president. Mr. Kent continued as president until his death, early in 1942.

In 1935, The Fox Film Corporation was merged with a major producing organization. Twentieth Century Pictures, headed by Joseph M. Schenck and the company assumed its present corporate name. This merger brought Darryl F. Zanuck into the company as vice-president in charge of production of the merged organizations. Mr. Schenck became chairman of the board and continued in that position until his resignation in June, 1942, when Wendell L. Wilkie took over the post.

Darryl F. Zanuck remained as Production Head until 1956, when he resigned to enter independent production. Buddy Adler succeeded Darryl F. Zanuck as Production Head. Upon Mr. Adler's death, Robert Goldstein and then Peter G. Levathes took over studio reins.

Following Mr. Kent's death, Spyros P. Skouras a leading theatre operator, became president. On July 25, 1962, Darryl F. Zanuck was elected president and Spyros P. Skouras was named chairman of the board, a position he held until March 1969 when he retired. Thereafter Richard D. Zanuck was named Executive Vice-President in Charge of Worldwide Production. Within a short period of time the Zanucks turned an ailing company into one of leadership and prestige in the entertainment field. In 1969, Darryl F. Zanuck was made Chairman of the Board and Chief Executive Officer, and Richard D. Zanuck was made president.

In 1971, 20th Century-Fox Film Corporation weathered a trying proxy fight which had the resounding effect of giving the company added resolve. A new managerial team was elected by the Board of Directors which saw Dennis C. Stanfill succeeding Richard D. Zanuck as President of the company, and, shortly thereafter, elevated to the position of Chairman of the Board of Directors and the studio's Chief Executive Officer.

In June, 1972, the majority of the company's East Coast personnel consolidated with that of the West Coast, thus placing the distribution, publicity, advertising, promotion and general accounting departments all under the same roof.

The company does not operate or directly own any theatres in the U.S. The company has a controlling interest in the Hoyt's group of about 50 theatres in Australia. Twentieth Century also owns Amalgamated Theatres, Ltd., comprising 21 theatres in New Zealand. It also has theatres in Egypt, Holland, Colombia, S.A., Chile and other countries.

The company also own three television stations, Pebble Beach Corp., Aspen Ski Corp., and Coca-Cola Bottling Midwest, Inc.

Fox merged with a company owned by Marvin Davis and his family—effective June 12, 1981.

TWENTIETH CENTURY-FOX PICTURES

PRESIDENT, TWENTIETH CENTURY-FOX PRODUCTIONS
Sherry Lansing
EXECUTIVE VICE PRESIDENT, WORLDWIDE PRODUCTIONS
David Field
EXECUTIVE VICE PRESIDENT
Danton Rissner
SENIOR VICE PRESIDENT, WORLDWIDE PRODUCTIONS
Richard L. Berger
SENIOR VICE PRESIDENT, PRODUCTION, NEW YORK
Henry Guettel
VICE PRESIDENT CREATIVE AFFAIRS
Susan Merzback
VICE PRESIDENT, CREATIVE AFFAIRS
Lorna Darmour

TWENTIETH CENTURY-FOX ENTERTAINMENT, INC.

PRESIDENT
Norman Levy
SENIOR VICE PRESIDENT AND GENERAL SALES MANAGER
Raymond McCafferty
VICE PRESIDENT, FINANCE
Donald Tractenberg
VICE PRESIDENT, STUDIO OPERATIONS
Bernard Barron
NON-THEATRICAL SALES MANAGER
Sam Weinstein

ADVERTISING AND PUBLICITY

EXECUTIVE VICE PRESIDENT, WORLDWIDE ADVERTISING, PUBLICITY & PROMOTION
Robert Cort
SENIOR VICE PRESIDENT, ADVERTISING, PUBLICITY & PROMOTION
Irv Ivers
VICE PRESIDENT, ADVERTISING
Kenneth Markman
VICE PRESIDENT, WORLDWIDE MARKETING ADMINISTRATION
Burt Messer
VICE PRESIDENT, MEDIA & CO-OP ADVERTISING
Richard Ingber
VICE PRESIDENT, MUSIC DEPARTMENT
Lionel Newman
VICE PRESIDENT, PRODUCTION MANAGEMENT
Herbert Wallerstein

DISTRIBUTION (Domestic) Home Office: P.O. Box 900, Beverly Hills, CA 90213 (213) 277-2211.

SENIOR VICE PRESIDENT
Peter S. Myers
VICE PRESIDENT, SALES MANAGER, EASTERN REGION
Richard Myerson
VICE PRESIDENT, SALES MANAGER, SOUTHERN REGION
Sheila De Loach
VICE PRESIDENT, SALES MANAGER, WESTERN REGION
John Peckos
VICE PRESIDENT, SALES ADMINISTRATION
Morris Stermer
VICE PRESIDENT SALES ADMINISTRATION
Harold P. Saltz

DOMESTIC BRANCHES AND MANAGERS

ATLANTA, GA 30345—Suite 901, 2200 Century Parkway, Jerry Smith
BEVERLY HILLS, CA 90210—9440 Santa Monica Blvd., Donna Littman
BOSTON, MA 02116—31 St. James Avenue, Morris Birnbaum
BUFFALO, NY 14202—in N.Y. Office, Ralph Farnham
CHARLOTTE, NC 28202—Northwestern Bank Bldg., Rm. 490, 230 South Tryon Street, Larry Jameson
CHICAGO, IL 60601—35 E. Wacker Drive, Suite 2160, Ray Russo
CINCINNATI, OH 45202—Enquirer Bldg. Room 1001–1006, 617 Vine Street, Anthony Knollman
CLEVELAND, OH 44124—Brainard Place, Suite 402, 29001 Cedar Rd., Lyndhurst, Ohio, William Anderhalt
DALLAS, TX 75215—115 51 Forest Antrol Drive, Richard King
DENVER, CO 80203—88 Steele St., Gary Erickson
DES MOINES, IA 50309—3737 Woodland Ave., Mary Ann Shaughnessy
DETROIT, MI 48075—Southfield Office Plaza, 17117 W. 9 Mile Road, Southfield, Mich., Charles Vaden
INDIANAPOLIS, IN 46220—in Chicago, Doris Payne
JACKSONVILLE, FL 32211—One Regency Place, Suite 309, 9570 Regency Square Blvd., Woodrow Townsend
KANSAS CITY, MO 64111—406 W. 34th Street, Neil Blatt
MINNEAPOLIS, MN 55403—600 So. Country Rd. #18, Suite 1490, Avron Rosen
NEW ORLEANS, LA 70002—3829 Veterans Memorial Blvd., Metairie, LA. Jeff Lee
NEW YORK, NY 10019—40 West 57th St., Leo Fisch
PHILADELPHIA, PA 19103—1429 Walnut St., Lou Korte
SALT LAKE CITY, UT 84102—515 South 700 East, Gordon Larsen
SAN FRANCISCO, CA 94105—605 Market St., Suite 500, J. Edward Shugrue
SEATTLE, WA 98119—South Tower, Suite 202, 100 West Harrison St., William Robinson
WASHINGTON, DC 20005—1156 15th Street, N.W., Francis X. Gornley

Canada

Toronto M,5V2T3, Ontario—720 King Street, Cullen (Ted) Hulse, Canadian Sales Manager

DISTRIBUTION (Foreign)

TWENTIETH CENTURY FOX INTERNATIONAL CORPORATION

P.O. Box 900, Beverly Hills, CA 90213. (213) 277-2211. Cable: CENTFOX.

HOME OFFICE EXECUTIVES

EXECUTIVE VICE PRESIDENT, INTERNATIONAL
Jean Louis Rubin
VICE PRESIDENT—INTERNATIONAL OPERATIONS
Paco Rodriquez
VICE PRESIDENT—INTERNATIONAL ADMINISTRATION
James Langshard
VICE PRESIDENT AND EXECUTIVE ASSISTANT TO JEAN-LOUIS RUBIN
Harold Mars
VICE PRESIDENT—INTERNATIONAL ADVERTISING & PUBLICITY
Joel H. Coler
ASSISTANT VICE PRESIDENT, ADMINISTRATION, FOX INTERNATIONAL
Joseph Verlezza
VICE PRESIDENT, INTERNATIONAL OPERATIONS
Francisco Rodriquez

FOREIGN BRANCHES AND MANAGERS

Great Britain and Eire

Twentieth Century-Fox Film Co., Ltd., 31-32 Soho Square, London, WIV 6AP, England. Telex: 27869 CENTFOX F. Cables: CENTFOX LONDON WI (Distribution) Telephone: 01 437 7766. TWENIFOX LONDON (Production) Night Line: 437 2755; Vice President, Supervisor for the United Kingdom and East and South Africa, Ascanio Branca; Assistant to Mr. Branca, Kevin Christie; Director of Finance and Administration, David Tarr; Director of Publicity and Advertising, Colin Hankins; Media Relations Coordinator—Gilly Hodson.
Dublin Branch
Prosperity Chambers, 5/7 Upper O'Connell Street, Dublin 1, Telephone: dublin (00017) 43068 Manager, G. F. Duffy.
Twentieth Century-Fox Productions Ltd., 31-32 Soho Square, London WIV 6AP. Managing Director, Tim Hampton; Company Secretary—David Tarr.

EUROPEAN DIVISION

Austria

Vienna—Centfox-Film Ges, M.B.H., 25 Neubaugasse, 1071 Vienna; Roman Hoerman, Manager.

Belgium

Brussels—Twentieth Century-Fox Film Belge S.A., Chaussee de Haecht 67, 1030 Brussels; George Buyse, manager.

France

Twentieth Century-Fox France Inc.
Bordeaux—6 Bis. Rue du Temple, Paul Brilli, manager.
Lyons—10 Rue de Plat, Jean Ottavi, manager.
Marseille—35 Boulevard de Longchamp, Louis Touron, manager.
Paris (Head Office)—33 Champs Elysees, 75008 Paris, Robert Balk, Managing Director, Continental Mid-East Supervisor; Andre Goudier, Administrative manager; Denise Breton, Director Adv. & Pub., Continental Europe; Marc Bernard, Publicity Manager.
Paris (Exchange)—33 Champs Elys ées, 75008 Paris, Henri Ruimy, District manager.
Strasbourg—23 Rue de la Premiere Armee; Pieree Bressange, manager.

Germany

Twentieth Century-Fox of Germany GMBH, Hainer weg 37/53, D-6000 Frankfurt/M. 70 Hellmuth P. Gattinger, General manager, Home office rep. Germany Regional Director Northern Europe, Hans Gambaro; Willi Welker, chief of administration; Sales Manager, Werner Kaspers; Publicity Director, Wolfgang Wittig.
Berlin—Kurfurstendamm 52, D-1000 Berlin 15., Gunter Grunberg, manager.
Düsseldorf—Garaf-Adolf-Strasse 108, D-4000, Dusseldorf 1., Albert-Ernst Tobias, manager.
FRANKFURT/MAIN—Taunusstrasse 40-42, D-6000, Frankfurt/M. 1, Walter Schweer, manager.
Hamburg—Klosterwall 4 (City-Hof), D-2000 Hamburg 1., Eberhard Woehlert, manager.
Munich—Lenbachplatz 3, D-8000 München 2, Kurt Schreiber, manager.

Greece

Twentieth Century-Fox Hellas Sarl (Fox) Columbia-Fox O.E. (Joint Venture) 2 Capodistria Street, Athens (147) Greece, General Manager, Paul N. Tsitsilianos, Publicity Manager, Michael Courouniotis, Sales Mgr. John Paizis.

Holland

Amsterdam—City Film Distribution, B.V., Herengracht 102, P.O. Box 3326, 1001 A. C. Amsterdam. Telephone: 2646404—267071. Telex: 15010, Cagle: City film Amsterdam. Managing Director, Bart H. Wilton; General Manager, Alfred Denker.

Italy

20th Century-Fox Italy, Inc., Via Palestro 24, 00185 Rome, Gaetano Scaffidi, general manager.
Ancona—Via Marsala 15—Enzo Porcarelli, Agent
Rome—Via dei Mille 34, Roberto Balmas, Agent
Bari—Piazza Umberto 1, 49—Francesco D'Accico, Agent
Bologna—Via Amendola 12/C—Oscar Palmirani, Agent
Cagliari—Via Barcellona 2—Ugo Sassu, Agent
Catania—Via De Felice 60—Edoardo Cumitini
Florence—Via Fiume 14—Alfredo Lasagni
Genoa—Via Fiasella 62-64/r—Mario Gavanna, Agent.
Milan—Via Spoerga 20—Lucio Umberto Vicini
Naples—Piazza Gesu Nuovo 33—Antonio Stella
Padua—Via Triesta 6—Francesco Miola
Turin—Via Pomba 20—Massimo Eieuteri

Norway

Oslo—Kommunenes Film Central A/S Nedre Vollgt 9, Oslo 1 Oddvar Hangenaes, Managing Director

Portugal

Lisbon—Filmes Castello Lopes, Lda., Praca Marques de Pombal, nno. 6-1°, Lisbon 1, Gerard Castello Lopes & Jose Manuel Castello Lopes, Directors.

Spain

Hispano Foxfilm, S.A.E., Madrid (Head Office), Plaza del Callao, 4, Madrid 13 Benjamin Benhamou, Managing Director.
Madrid—Plaza del Callao, 4, Madrid 13, Julio Ga Valdés, manager.
Barcelona—Paeso de Garcia, 77, Barcelona 8, Raimundo Bartra, manager.
Valencia—Gran Via Germanias, 53, Valencia 6., Francisco Rizo, manager.
Bilbao—Ercilla, 20, Bilbao, Heliodoro LaFuente, manager.
Sevilla—Santa Maria de Gracia, 3, Sevilla, Jose Muñoz, manager.
3La Coruna—J. L. Perez de Cepeda, 15, La Coruna, Luis Carames, agent.
Balearic Islands—Exclusivas Films Baleares, Via Roma, 3, Palma de Mallorca, Rafael Salas, agent.
Canary Islands—Doctor Juan de Padilla, 24 Las Palmas de Gran Canaria, Jesús Rodriquez Doreste, agent.

Sweden

Stockholm—Fox-Stockholm Film, Kungsgatan 18, Box 1327, S-111 83 Stockholm Conny Planborg & Ove Sjoros, joint managing directors, Bengt Bengtson, sales manager & home office representative.

Switzerland

Geneva—20th Century-Fox Film Corporation, Societe d'Exploitation pour la Suisse, 2 Place du Cirque, P.O. Box 121, 1211 Geneva 8, Jean-Pierre Reyren, manager.

NEAR EAST

Egypt

Cairo—20th Century-Fox Import Corp., 11, Sarai Saray el-Ezbekieh, P.O. Box 693, Cairo, Egypt, Saad Nessim, acting manager.

Israel

Tel Aviv—Albert D. Matalon & Co., Ltd., 15 Hess Street (P.O. Box 4388) Amnon Matalon, General Manager.

Lebanon

Beirut—20th Century-Fox Import Corp., Lyon Street (Hamra), Moussa Makki Bldg, Beirut—Abraham Havounjian, Director for Near & Middle East

AUSTRALIA AND NEW ZEALAND

Australia

Fox Columbia Film Distributors Pty Ltd., 6th Floor, 505-523 George Street, Sydney, N.S.W. 2000. G.P.O. Box 3342, Sydney, N.S.W. 2001. Telephone: 235 7877 Cable: COLUMFILM Telex: 26278 Direct: 011-61-2-235-7877; Arthur B . Griffin, Managing Director; Peter C. Wilkinson, Deputy Managing Director; Barry M. Cooper, Sales Manager; Guy Scott, Director of Advertising; Bruce Keen, Advertising Manager.
Branches

Melbourne—103 Hoddle Street, Richmond, Victoria 3121, P.O. Box 137, East Melbourne, Vic. 3002—Frank Henley., Manager
Brisbane—Cnr. Manning & Melbourne Streets, South Brisbane, Queensland 4101, P.O. Box 189, Brisbane, Old 4001—Sonny Schattling, Manager.
Adelaide—159 Helifax Street, Adlaide, S.A. 5000—Russell Anderson, Manager Perth—276 Stirling Street, Perth, W.A. 6000—Colin Garrity, Manager

New Zealand

Auckland—Twentieth Century-Fox Film Corporation (N.Z.) Ltd., 73-75 Lorne Street, P.O. Box 5147, Wellesley Street, Auckland 1., Alan L. Flyger, manager & Secretary

AFRICA

Republic of South Africa

Johannesburg—Twentieth Century-Fox Film (S.A.) (Pty) Ltd., 11th Floor, Kalhof, 112 Pritchard Street, Johannesburg 2001, Transvaal, South Africa, P.O. Box 1100 Johannesburg 2000, Geoffrey B. Rawsthorne, managing director (Also supervises the East territories).

East Africa—Anglo American Film Distributors Ltd. (Rep. Kenya, Uganda, Tanzania & Zambia) (Head Office) P.O. Box 30082, Nairobi, Kenya, Managing Director, Wim J. F. Van Ewijk.

FAR EASTERN DISTRICT

Hong Kong—Fox-Columbia Film Distributors, Loong San Bld., 6th floor, 140-42 Connaught Road Central, Hong Kong, G.P.O. Box 397, General Post Office, H. K., Charles C. F. Dean, manager.

India

20th Century-Fox Corporation (India) Pvt. Ltd., Metro House, 3rd Floor, Mahatma Gandhi Road, Bombay 400 020., G.P.O. 765, Bombay 1., Pokka V. Prabhu, managing director.
Calcutta—19 Jawaharlal Nehru Road, Calcutta 13, S. M. Karnad, manager.
Madras—1/17H Mount Road, Madras 2, T. C. Krishnan, manager.
New Delhi—Plaza Theatre Building, Connaught Circus, New Delhi, J. Noronha, manager.

Japan

Tokyo Film Building, No. 109, Ginza 3-chone, Chuo-ku Tokyo 104 Japan. Robert King, managing director, Noriyoshi Matsumoto, dir. for marketing.
Fukuoka—Fukuoka Film Building, 8-31, Tsunabamachi, Hakataku, Fukuoka 812, Fukuoka Pref., Japan, K. Nishimura, branch manager.
Osaka—Osaka Film Building, No. 1-7 Dojimahamadori 1-chome, Kita-ku, Osaka 530, K. Hiromoto, branch manager.
Sapporo—Nichigeki Building, South 1-jo, West 1-chome, Chuo-ku, Sapporo 060, Hokkaido, Japan, I. Kamada, branch manager.

Pakistan

Karachi—Twentieth Century-Fox Pakistan Inc., 207 Hotel Metropole, Club Road, Karachi 17, G.P.O. Box 3734, Karachi, M. G. D. Nayeem, general manager.
Lahore—Twentieth Century-Fox Pakistan Inc., 43 Shahran E. Quaid E Azam, Lahore G.P.O. Box 75, Lahore, Syed Wahid Shah, branch manager.

Republic of the Philippines

Manila—20th Century-Fox Films Philippines Inc., Penthouse, Avenue Theatre Bldg., Rizal Avenue, Manila, P.O. Box 423, Manila, Pedro O. Baesa, manager.
Manila—Mever Films, Inc., Penthouse, Avenue Theatre Bldg., Rizal Avenue, Manila, P.O. Box 3174, Manila Philippines, John Litton, president (agent).
Singapore—20th Century-Fox Film (East) Private Ltd., 83 Victoria Street (1st Floor) P.O. Box 141 Queen Street, Post Office, Singapore Rep. of Singapore, John Foo, Managing Director.

Taiwan

Taipei—Twentieth Century-Fox Inc. USA (Taiwan Branch), 109, G-Mei Street, 3rd Floor, Joseph D. H. Chan, manager.

Thailand

Bangkok—Twentieth Century-Fox Thailand Inc., South-East Insurance Building—6th Floor, 315 Silom Road, P.O. Box 2492, Bangkok 5, William H. Blamey, manager.

LATIN AMERICAN DIVISION

Argentina

Columbia Pictures of Argentina, Inc., Fox Film De La Argentina, S.A.—mailing address: Columbia-Fox, Lavalle 1878, Buenos Aires, Argentina, Emilio Planchadell, general manager, Jorge A. Mozuc, admin. manager.
Bahia Blanca—Disciba S.R.L., Soler 346—Bahia Blanca Pcia de Buenos Aires
Cordoba—Distribuidora Parana S.R.L., Lima 346, Cordoba.
Rosario—Distribuidora Pamama S.R.L., Maipu 973 Rosario Pcia de Santa Fe.
Sante Fe—Distribuidora Panama S.R.L., Hipolito Yrigoyen 2564 Santa Fe, Pcia de Santa Fe.
Mendoza—Mitre 1623—Mendoza, Mendoza.
Tucuman—Discinor S.R.L., Jujuy 120, San Miguel De Tucuman, Tucuman

Bolivia

La Paz—Distribuidores Asociados De Peliculas LTDA., Av. Montes 768, 3er, Piso-Edificio De Col., Mailing Address: Casilla 4709, La Paz, Bolivia, Licinio Manay, manager.

Brazil

Fox Film do Barzil (S.A.): Harry Anastassiadi, general manager; Rua Joaquin Silva 98, 6°/7° ands., Lapa ZC-06, Caixa Postal 989-ZC-00, 20.000 Rio de Janeiro, RJ. Belo Horizonte, MG.—José Dinez, branch manager., Rua Aaraõ Reis Sala 204. Caixa Postal 486, 30.000 Belo Horizonte, MG.

Botucatú—Araujo & Passos, Rua Joao Passos 702, Caixa Postal 38 and 72, 18600 Botucatù, Sao Paulo, (agent).

Curitiba—Fama Films S.A., Rua Barão do Rio Branco 370/1°, Caixa Postal 994, Curitiba, Paranà (agent).

Porto Alegre—Dist. Filmes Wermar Ltda. Rua Siqueira Campos 820, Porto Alegre, Rio Grande do Sul (agent).

Recife—União Cinematográfica Brasileira, S.A., Rua Aurora 175, Bioco A, Ed. Duarte Coelho, 3°andar, Caixa Postal 27, Recife, Pernambuco (agent).

Rubeirão Preto—Cinefilmes Distrib. Import. Cinematográfica Ltda., Rua Duque de Caxias 639/2°andar, Caixa Postal 305, Ribeirão Preto, São Paulo (agent).

São José do Rio Preto—Agência de Filmes Rio Preto Ltda., Rua Col. Spinola 3054, Caixa Postal 190, São José do Rio Preto, São Paulo (agent).

Salvador—Art Films, S.A., Rua Lopes Cardoso 41, 2°andar 40.000 Salvador, Bahia (Agent).

Brazil-Joint Operation—Columbia-Fox Servicos de Distribuição de Filmes Ltda. (For information only. Do not address mail to the service company in Rio de Janeiro.) Harry Anastassiadi Fox Rep., William E. Hummel, Columbia Rep.

Chile

Santiago—Columbia Pictures of Chile, Inc. Asociacion Twentieth Century Fox Chile, Inc., Huerfanos 786, Of. 210, Santiago, Casilla 9003 or Casilla 3770, Santiago Anibal Codebo, Manager; Arturo Parra, sales manager.

Colombia

Bogotá—Fox-Columbia Pictures of Colombia, Inc., Carrera 5 No. 22-85, 5o. Piso, Apartado Aéreo 3892, Bogotá, D.E., Colombia, S.A., Horacio Hermida, general manager.

Barranquilla—Fox Columbia Pictures of Colombia, Inc., Calle 53 No. 52-68, 2o Piso, Apartado Aéreo 380, Barranquilla, Colombia, S.A. Efrain Gomez, branch manager.

Cali—Fox Columbia Pictures of Colombia, Inc., Carrera 4 No. 14-45, Apartado Aéreo 138, Cali, Colombia, S.A., Mario Perlaza, branch manager.

Dominican Republic

Santo Domingo—Twentieth Century Fox-Dom. Rep. Inc., Avenida Independencia #310 Zona 1, Santo Domingo, D.R., P.O. Box 1459, Santo Domingo, D.R., Maurio Lara, manager.

Ecuador

Guayaquil—Productira Filmica Nacional Del Ecuador CIA, Ltda., Malexon 1006, P.O. Box 3445, Guayaquil, Carlos Espinosa, general manager.

Mexico

Twentieth Century Fox Films De Mexico, S.A.-Columbia Pictures, S.A., Sinaloa No. 20 Mexico 7, D.F., Apartado Postal 373, Mexico, D.F. (Z.P. 1)., Michel Rosenthal, manager; Federico Cavia Gonzales, sales manager.

Monterrey—Peliculas de La Sultana, S.A. Calle General Trevino No. 831 Pte. Monterrey, N.L., Zacarias Cobas, Agent.

Guadalajara—Peliculas Nacionales E. Internacionales de Guadalajara, S.A., Av. Libertad 1047, Guillermo Quezada, manager.

Merida—Agencia Distribuidora de Peliculas, Calle 60 No. 492, Merida, Yuc., Juan Gene Anay, manager.

Torreon—Distribuidora de Peliculas Jose Ignacio Maynez, J.A. de La Fuenta 244 Sur, Torreon, Coah., Jose Ignacio Maynez, manager.

Panama

Columbia Pictures of Panama, Inc., Twentieth Century-Fox Film, S.A., Via Espana Entre Calles 46 y 50 Este, Apartado 4492, Panama 5, Rep. de Panama, Francisco Rossi, managing director joint operation. Paul Branca, manager.

Costa Rica—Discine, S.A., Apartado Postal 1147, San Jose, Costa Rica, Alvaro Rovira Guido, agent.

Guatemala—Cadena Cinematográfica Guatemalteca, 7a. Ave. 19-28 Zona 1, Guatemala, Guatemala, Rodolfo Rosenberg, agent.

Nicaragua—Distribuidora de Peliculas, Cortes-Hernandez, Apartado 3941, Managua, Nicaragua, Aginadack Cortes, agent.

Honduras—Hugo R. Erazo, Apartado 299, Tegucigalpa, Honduras, agent.

El Salvador—Julio Suvillaga Z., Apartado 19 (Sucursal del Centro), San Salvador, El Salvador, agent.

Peru

Lima—Twentieth Century-Fox Peruna S.A., Jr. Lampa 1115, Of. 1002, Lima 1, Peru, Casilla Postal 2532 & 6085, Lima 1, Peru, Tomas Rios de Armero, managing director.

Puerto Rico

San Juan—Twentieth Century Fox Puerto Rico Inc., Metro Building, 1255 Ponce de Leon Ave., P.O. Box "S" 422, San Juan, Puerto Rico 00902, Luis Rodriguez, managing director.

Jamaica

Kingston—A. Russell Graham Agency, P.O. Box 320, Kingston, Jamaica, A. Russell Graham, agent.

Uruguay

Montevideo—United Artists of Uruguay, Inc., Paraguay 1472, Montevideo, Uruguay Washington Medina, manager.

Venezuela

Caracas—D.F., S.R.L., Edificio Teatro Las Palmas, piso. 4 Avenida Principal Las Palmas; Leon Nebenzahl, representatives.

SUBSIDIARIES

PRESIDENT, TELECOMMUNICATIONS
  Stephen Roberts
VICE PRESIDENT, BUSINESS AFFAIRS, TELECOMMUNICATIONS
  Larry Harris
VICE PRESIDENT, PLANNING AND ADMINISTRATION, TELECOMMUNICATIONS
  Arvin Erickson
VICE PRESIDENT, TELECOMMUNICATION SALES
  Edwin B. Michalove
VICE PRESIDENT, LICENSING CORPORATION
  Marc W. Pevers
VICE PRESIDENT, CONTROLLER, TELECOMMUNICATIONS
  Keith Lent

OTHER DIVISIONAL OFFICERS

PRESIDENT, REALITY AND DEVELOPMENT
  Judith M. Frank
VICE PRESIDENT, REALTY AND DEVELOPMENT
  Vincent G. Maher
VICE PRESIDENT, STUDIO OPERATIONS AND INDUSTRIAL RELATIONS DIVISION
  Marshall Wortman

TELEVISION DIVISION

CHAIRMAN OF THE BOARD
  Harris Katleman
GROUP EXECUTIVE VICE PRESIDENT
  Edward B. Gradinger
EXECUTIVE VICE PRESIDENT, CHARGE OF PRODUCTION
  Andrea Baynes
VICE PRESIDENT, DEVELOPMENT
  Peter Grad
VICE PRESIDENT AND EXECUTIVE PRODUCER SPECIAL PROJECTS
  Barry Lowen
VICE PRESIDENT, DAYTIME, SYNDICATED PROGRAMS & SPECIALS
  George Paris
VICE PRESIDENT, TV MOVIES & MINISERIES
  Richard Rosetti
VICE PRESIDENT, PROGRAMS
  Lea Stalmaster
VICE PRESIDENT, BUSINESS AFFAIRS
  Dayna A. Kalins
VICE PRESIDENT, NETWORK BUSINESS AFFAIRS
  Allan L. Rice
VICE PRESIDENT, FINANCE
  George Sefeotis
VICE PRESIDENT, PRODUCTION MANAGEMENT
  Mark Evans
VICE PRESIDENT, TV POST PRODUCTION
  Joseph Silver
SR. VICE PRESIDENT DOMESTIC TELEVISION
  Robert Morin
SR. VICE PRESIDENT, INTERNATIONAL SYNDICATION
  Richard Harper
VICE PRESIDENT, DOMESTIC SYNDICATION
  Steven R. Orr
VICE PRESIDENT AND GENERAL SALES MANAGER (NEW YORK)
  Joe Green
VICE PRESIDENT, ADVERTISING, PUBLIC RELATIONS, PROMOTION
  Jerry Greenberg
DIRECTOR OF PROGRAM DEVELOPMENT
  Arvin Kaufman
DIRECTOR OF CURRENT PROGRAMS
  Richard Conger
DIRECTOR, DAYTIME & SYNDICATED PROGRAM DEVELO9PMENT
  Craig Kellem
DIRECTOR OF BUSINESS AND SALES ADMINISTRATION
  Stanley DeCovnick

ASSOCIATE DIRECTOR, MOVIES & MINI SERIES
Harriet Brown
ASSOCIATE DIRECTOR, BUSINESS AFFAIRS, SYNDICATION
Michael Shapiro
WESTERN DIVISION SALES MANAGER
David Skillman
DIRECTOR OF PRODUCTION, DAYTIME AND SYNDICATED TELEVISION
Bob Braithwaite
DIRECTOR OF MARKETING, ADVERTISING AND PROMOTION
Jeffrey Schadlow
TV BUDGET AND COST ADMINISTRATOR
Ed Lahtai
RESEARCH DIRECTOR (NEW YORK)
Charles Gersh
DIRECTOR, SALES ADMINISTRATION, INTERNATIONAL SYNDICATION
Matt Barbera
DIRECTOR OF OPERATIONS, INTERNATIONAL SYNDICATION
Edwin Greenberg
DIRECTOR OF SERVICING, INTERNATIONAL SYNDICATION
Lourdes Chaves
ASSISTANT TO VICE PRESIDENT, PRODUCTION MANAGEMENT
Dick Glassman
DIRECTOR OF PLANNING AND ADMINISTRATION
Laurie Lindner

DELUXE GENERAL, INC.

PRESIDENT
Burton Stone
VICE PRESIDENT, FINANCE & ADMINISTRATION
Robert J. Aten
SENIOR VICE PRESIDENT
Fred J. Scobey
VICE PRESIDENT, MARKETING
Robert E. Klees
VICE PRESIDENT, PRODUCTION
Fred E. Austin

MUSIC COMPANY AND RECORD COMPANY

CHAIRMAN OF THE BOARD, TWENTIETH CENTURY-FOX RECORDS AND PRESIDENT FOX MUSIC PUBLISHING COMPANIES
Herbert N. Eiseman
PRESIDENT—RECORD COMPANY
Neil Portnow
VICE PRESIDENT, FINANCE ADMINISTRATION
Monty Houdeshell

21st Century Distribution Corp.

1650 Broadway, Suite 1003, New York, NY 10019 (212) 541-4722. (Film Distributor worldwide.)
PRESIDENT
Tom Ward
EXECUTIVE VICE PRESIDENT
Art Schweitzer

Twyman Films, Inc.

National headquarters: Box 605, 4700 Wadsworth Road, Dayton OH 45401 (513) 276-5941. Regional offices: Room 803, 45 W. 45th St., New York, NY 10036. (800) 543-9594; 149 N. Detroit St., Los Angeles CA 90036. (800) 543-9594. (Distributor: theatrical, nontheatrical & television.)
CHAIRMAN OF THE BOARD
Alan B. Twyman
PRESIDENT
Alan P. Twyman
VICE-PRESIDENT
M'Benenah Twyman
SECRETARY & TREASURER
John F. Heck
DATE OF ORGANIZATION
1935

UPA Pictures, Inc.

California Studios; 4440 Lakeside Drive, Burbank, CA 91505 (213) 842-7171.
PRESIDENT
Henry G. Saperstein

DATE OF INCORPORATION
1945

U.T.A., Inc.

1658 Cordova St., Los Angeles, CA 90007 (213) 734-0510.
PRESIDENT
Joan Atamian Bodin
VICE PRESIDENT
Louis Atamian
SECRETARY
Alice Casarjian
TREASURER
Zaven Atamian

United Film Distribution Co.

2545 Hempstead Turnpike, East Meadow, NY 11554 (516) 579-8400
PRESIDENT
Richard Hassanein
CONSULTANT
Al Fitter

United Film Enterprises, Inc.

37 West 57th St., New York, NY 10019 (212) 758-0870. Telex: 237851. (Representing major motion picture and television producers, studios and export companies. Also, acting as purchasing agent for motion picture distributors in various countries.)
PRESIDENT
Munio Podhorzer
VICE-PRESIDENT & SECRETARY
Nathan Podhorzer

United Artists Corporation

(A subsidiary of the MGM Film Co.)
729 Seventh Avenue, York, NY 10019 (212) 575-3000
Cable: Unartisco, (Distributor.)
PRESIDENT & CHIEF EXECUTIVE OFFICER
Norbert Auerbach
EXECUTIVE VICE PRESIDENT
Dean Stolber
SENIOR VICE PRESIDENT/DOMESTIC SALES & MARKETING
Jerry Esbin
SENIOR VICE PRESIDENT/WORLDWIDE PRODUCTION
Raphael Etkes
SENIOR VICE PRESIDENT/WORLDWIDE ADMINISTRATION
Milton Fishman
SENIOR VICE PRESIDENT/TELEVISION, VIDEO, SPECIAL MARKETS
Nathaniel Troy Kwit, Jr.
SENIOR VICE PRESIDENT/FINANCE
Mauro Sardi
SENIOR VICE PRESIDENT/FOREIGN MANAGER
Michael Williams-Jones
VICE PRESIDENT/TAXES
Benjamin P. Acker
VICE PRESIDENT & SECRETARY
Alan A. Benjamin
VICE PRESIDENT/WEST COAST ADMINISTRATION
Richard R. Bruning
VICE PRESIDENT/STRATEGIC PLANNING
Stephen Cotler
VICE PRESIDENT/EXECUTIVE ASSISTANT TO THE PRESIDENT
Mel Danheiser
VICE PRESIDENT/INFORMATION SERVICES
Peter Dawson
VICE PRESIDENT/WEST COAST BUSINESS AFFAIRS
Lawrence Erbst
VICE PRESIDENT/WORLDWIDE BUSINESS AFFAIRS
Robert French
VICE PRESIDENT/ASSISTANT GENERAL SALES MANAGER
Bernard Goldin
VICE PRESIDENT/FOREIGN ADVERTISING & PUBLICITY
Fred W. Hift
VICE PRESIDENT/DOMESTIC PUBLICITY
Joanne Horowitz
VICE PRESIDENT/DOMESTIC MARKETING
Edward Kalish

VICE PRESIDENT/PRODUCTION MANAGEMENT
Derek Kavanagh
VICE PRESIDENT/WEST COAST ADVERTISING
Bernard Korban
VICE PRESIDENT/FILM SERVICES
Sol Lomita
VICE PRESIDENT/LATIN AMERICA
S. Anthony Manne
VICE PRESIDENT/FAR EAST
Michael Murphy
VICE PRESIDENT/CONTRACTS & PLAYDATES
Arthur Reiman
VICE PRESIDENT/CREATIVE ADVERTISING
David Rosenfelt
VICE PRESIDENT & CONTROLLER
Harold E. Samboy
VICE PRESIDENT & GENERAL COUNSEL
Herbert T. Schottenfeld
VICE PRESIDENT/ADMINISTRATION
Robert P. Schwartz
VICE PRESIDENT/PRODUCTION
Lois Smith
VICE PRESIDENT/EUROPE & MIDDLE EAST
William Stuart
VICE PRESIDENTS/PRODUCTION
Anthea Sylbert, Robert J. Wunsch
ASSISTANT CONTROLLERS
Charles DeGruccio, Saul Zamost
ASSISTANT SECRETARY
Julia Kaminski
ASSISTANT TREASURES
Louis Castelli, Henry Pasniewski, Morton Scher
EXECUTIVE DIRECTOR OF PROMOTION
Carl Ferrazza
ADVERTISING DIRECTOR
Lester Littlehale
DIRECTOR OF MEDIA
Terry Steiner
EASTERN ADVERTISING MANAGER
Charles Green
EXECUTIVE DIRECTOR/BRANCH & SALES OPERATIONS
Don Silechhio
EASTERN DIVISION MANAGER
Seymour Berman (Washington, D.C.)
SOUTHERN DIVISION MANAGER
Joseph P. Kennedy (Jacksonville)
WESTERN DIVISION MANAGER
Bob Coley (Los Angeles)
CENTRAL DIVISION MANAGER
Bill Doebel (Detroit)
NEW YORK/PHILADELPHIA DIVISION MANAGER
Bob Burke (New York)
CANADIAN GENERAL MANAGER
George Heiber (Toronto)
BOARD OF DIRECTORS
Norbert Auerbach, Alan A. Benjamin, Frank C. Herringer, Blair
C. Pascoe, Herbert T. Schottenfeld, Dean Stolber, Michael Wil-
liams-Jones

HISTORY OF UNITED ARTISTS
United Artists was founded on April 17, 1919, by four of the most
colorful screen personalities of their day—stars Charles Chaplin,
Mary Pickford and Douglas Fairbanks, Sr., and director D. W.
Griffith. These four artists set up their own company "to improve
the artistic standards of the photoplay industry and to market pho-
toplays in the interests of the artists who created them."
The first film released by the company was "His Majesty, the
American," starring Douglas Fairbanks, Sr. Thereafter, throughout
the twenties, the thirties and the early forties, the company distributed many landmark films produced by its founders—Chaplin's "City
Lights," "Modern Times," "The Gold Rush," Pickford's "Pollyanna," Fairbanks' "Robin Hood," "The Three Musketeers," and
others. It also became the distribution home for such eminent film-
makers as Sam Goldwyn, David Selznick, Alexander Korda, Walt
Disney, among others.
During this period, the company did not finance or produce any
motion pictures; it distributed its films solely for the benefit of its
producers and held no ownership interest in them.
Declining fortunes began to plague the company in the mid-for-
ties. Only two of its original founders, Miss Pickford and Chaplin,
remained alive. The bursting of the bubble of war prosperity and
the advent of television made it difficult to find sufficient product
to meet the overhead of a vast domestic and international organization.
Between 1947 and 1951, a succession of management groups grap-
pled unsuccessfully with the joint problems of mounting losses and
a shortage of motion pictures. By early 1951, the total world gross
of the company had fallen to a level of only a few million dollars a
year; the losses had risen to $100,000 a week. The company had not
been able to produce a single new film for release for over twelve
months. A receivership appeared inevitable.
In February, 1951, two law partners, Arthur B. Krim, as President, and Robert S. Benjamin, as Chairman, shortly joined by a
group including Arnold Picker, Max E. Youngstein and William J.
Heineman, as Vice Presidents, took over the management of the
company under a contract with Miss Pickford and Chaplin. The

contract provided that the new management group would have complete control of the company for a three-year period and that they
would become owners of 50% of the stock of the company if they
could succeed in showing a profit in any one of the three succeeding
years.
The profit was accomplished in the first year and the stock vested.
In 1955 the company acquired the stock of Chaplin, and in 1956 the
stock of Miss Pickford, at which time the new management group
became the sole owners of the company.
Starting in a limited way in 1951, United Artists embarked on a
policy of financing motion pictures made by independent producers.
All creative talents—stars, writer, and directors—were encouraged
in their aspirations to produce pictures for themselves. By 1954,
when the credit of the company was firmly established, United Artists financed and had an ownership interest in virtually all of the
motion pictures which it distributed. By the end of the fifties, bas-
ically because of the impact of this policy on the motion picture
industry as a whole, most of the major motion picture companies
followed suit and changed their policy of concentration on studio-
owned pictures to one of financing independent producers. The
increased diversity in filmmaking in the past decade has been largely
the direct result of this basic change.
In recent years, the company enlarged its activities to the fields
of music publishing and records. Approximately 30% of the revenues
of the company are now derived from these activities.
Since 1951, pictures produced for United Artists have won more
of the top Academy Awards than those of any other major company—in the Best Picture category alone, ten of the last 19 awards
have been won by United Artists releases.
The films are: "Marty"—1955; "Around the World in 80 Days"—
1959; "The Apartment"—1960; "West Side Story"—1961; "Tom
Jones"—1963; "In The Heat of the Night"—1967; "Midnight Cowboy"—1969; "One Flew Over The Cuckoo's Nest"—1975; "Rocky"—
1976 and "Annie Hall"—1977. UA also leads in the overall total
numbers of Best Picture Oscars, with 11 including "Rebecca"—
1940.
In 1957 United Artists became a public company and in 1967 it
became a wholly-owned subsidiary of Transamerica Corporation in
a sale involving approximately 9,500,000 shares of Transamerica stock.
In 1981, after 14 years of ownership, Transamerica sold its interests in U.A. to the MGM Film Company, whose stockholders en-
dorsed the sale at a price of $380,000,000. MGM issued an addi-
tional 25,000,000 shares of $1 par value common stock, bringing its
total authorized stock to 75,000,000. Under the plan UA retained
its present executives, and the company became a wholly-owned
subsidiary of the MGM Film Company, which maintains that title
as parent company.

DOMESTIC BRANCHES AND MANAGERS

ALBANY: 12204—991 Broadway, Franklin Meadows, Sales Man-
ager.
ATLANTA: 30308—401 W. Peachtree N.E., Suite 1760, Larry
Terrell.
BOSTON: 02116—Suite 941, 31 St. James Avenue, Joseph Griffin
BUFFALO: 14202—300 Delaware Avenue, William Abrams
CHARLOTTE: 28202—230 So. Tryon Street, Philip Cutrall
CHICAGO: 60601—203 N. Wabash Avenue, Louis Aurelio
CINCINNATI: 45202—35 East 7 Street, Tom Morris
DALLAS: 75206—Suite 438, 6060 N. Central Expressway, Enoch
Stevens
DENVER: 80206—88 Steele Street, Suite 203, Edna Gallagher
DES MOINES: 50309—1213 Grand Avenue, George Bloxham
DETROIT: 48075—Suite 310, 24100 Southfield Road, Southfield,
MI Robert Kaplowitz.
INDIANAPOLIS: 46220—7002 North Graham Road, Tom Morris
JACKSONVILLE: 32211—9550 Regency Square Boulevard, Suite
203, Walter Johnson
KANSAS CITY: MO 64108—1703 Wyandotte Street, Morton Truog
LYNDHURST, OH 44124—29001 Cedar Road, Doug Buckley
LOS ANGELES: 90048—116 No. Robertson Boulevard, Robert
Wood
MEMPHIS: 38104—1437 Central Avenue, K. Keifer, Office Man-
ager
MILWAUKEE: 53203—711 W. Wisconsin Avenue, John McKenna
MINNEAPOLIS: 55403—704 Hennepin Avenue, Walter Badger
NEW ORLEANS: 70002—4900 Veterans Memorial Boulevard,
Suite 512, Metairie, Larry Greg Potash
NEW YORK: 10019—729 Seventh Avenue, Robert Shein
OKLAHOMA CITY: 73106—2000 Classen Boulevard, Toni Dyk-
sterhuis
PHILADELPHIA: 19103—1117 S. 17th St., Suite 1008, Lew O'Neil
PITTSBURGH: 15222—107 Sixth Street, David Litto
ST. LOUIS: 63103—1750 So. Brentwood Boulevard, Suite 256,
Edward Stevens
SALT LAKE CITY: 84147—Quirrh Place, 350 South 4th East,
Robert Loftis
SAN FRANCISCO: 94105—Monadnock Building, 681 Market
Street, Suite 705, Mike Muscela
SEATTLE: 98004—225 108th Avenue N.W., Suite 400, Bellevue,
Washington, S. Amato
WASHINGTON, DC 20014—7315 Wisconsin Avenue, Suite 502W,
Douglas Potash

CANADA

CANADIAN GENERAL MANAGER
George Heiber (Toronto)
CALGARY: T2R 0M4—1003 11th Ave., S.W., Barry Newstead
MONTREAL: H4B 2M7—3290 Cavendish Boulevard, Alvin Himelfarb
ST. JOHN: E2L 4S4—P.O. Box 6991, Station "A", 77 Germain Street, Isadore Davis
TORONTO: M4S 2B9—2180 Yonge Street, Suite 800, Vern Haraldson
VANCOUVER: V6J 1S5—Suite 210, 1682 West 7th Avenue, Thomas Lightburn
WINNIPEG: R3B 2K3—365 Hargrave Street, Meyer Nackimson

FOREIGN BRANCHES AND MANAGERS

Great Britain and Eire

LONDON—John Esson, Mg. Dir., United Artists Corp., Ltd. Mortimer House, 37-41 Mortimer St., London, W1A 2JL
DUBLIN, IRELAND—Harold H. Band, 53 Middle Abbey St.

CONTINENTAL EUROPE

Austria

Vienna—Erich Wania Twentieth Century for GMBH Neubaugasse 35, subdistributor Vienna, 1070. Reinhard Rumler

Belgium

George Buyse, Les Artistes Associes, S.A.B., 67 Chaussee D'Halcht, 1030. Brussels. Bruno Jamin

Denmark

Paul E. Pedersen, United Artists A/S Christinsborggade 1 1558 DK, Copenhagen V.Poul Larsen

Finland

Kurt Dahl, OY United Artists Films AB Pohj. Makasiinikatu 7 00130, Helsinki, Finland.

France

Head Office—Les Artisies Associes, S.A. 25/27 Rue d'Astorg, Paris, 75008, Mr. Andre Darmon, Mr. Bertrand Devort
Paris Exchange—Charles Bucamp, 25/27 Rue d'Astorg.
Bordeaux—Charles Spariat, 34 rue Rodrigues Pereire.
Lille—Jean Demarez, 13 rue Faidherbe.
Lyon—Georges Escudier—98 Blvd. Des Belges, Lyon, France.
Marseilles—Claude Damianthe, 55 Boulevard Longchamp.

Germany

Head Office—Alfred Sorg, United Artists Corp. GmBH Stresemannalle 13 Post Fach 16 740 6000 Frankfurt/Main. Werner Rochau
Frankfurt Exchange—Friedrich Spalek, Stresemannalle 13.
Berlin—Mrs. Karla Otto Lietzenburgerstrasse 51, Berlin.
Dusseldorf—Mrs. Karen Drekopf, Graf-Adolf-Str. 108.
Hamburg—Klaus Grundmann Spitalerstrasse 11.
Munich—Anton Herrmann, Baerstrasse 13.

Greece

Yanni Tacaziadis, United Artists of Greece, EPE, Gambetta St. #4, Athens 141, Greece. Nicholas Kalogerakis

Italy

Bologna—Mrs. Alba Tellarini, Via C. Boldrini, 14
Rome—Sandro Pierotti, United Artists Europa, Inc., Largo Ponchielli, 6, 00198, Rome. Osvaldo DeSantis
Milan—Mrs. Orsolina Ferrari, Via Sopirga, 36.

Norway

Oddvar Hagenaes, Kommunenes Filmcentral, Nedre Voligaten 9, Oslo, sub-distributor. Bjorn Jacobsen

Holland

Amsterdam—A. J. J. Duyvestbyn Nova Film Hobbemastraat 20, Post Box 5537, sub-distributor. Pim Di Miranda

Portugal

Simao Lourenco Fernandes, Rank Filmes de Portugal Ltda., Av. Da Liberdale 175B, Lisbon. 2. sub-distributor.

Spain

Casimiro Bori, C. B. Films. S.A. Av. Generalismo Franco, 407 Barcelona 8, sub-distributor.

Sweden

Mr. Kay Wall, United Artists Aktiebolag, Alstromergaton, 20, 112, 47, Stockholm. Phillip Hollström

Switzerland

Hans-Ulrich Daetwyler, Unartisco. S.A. Signaustrasse 6, Zurich Ch-8032. Andrea Hurlimann

NEAR EAST

Egypt—United Artists Corporation of Egypt, c/o Mr. Antoine Zeind, c/o 20th Century Fox, 11, Saray El Ezbekieh St. P.O.B. 693, Cairo, sub-distributor.
Israel—Amnon R. Matalon, Albert R. Matalon & Co., Ltd.,15 Hess St., P.O. Box 4383, Tel-Aviv. (Subdistributor)
Lebanon—Director for the Near and Middle East, Abraham Havounjian, U.A. of North Africa, Inc., Lyon Street, Hamra District Moussa Makki Bldg., P.O. Box 6737, Beirut-Lebanon.

AFRICA

South Africa—Mr. John Abel, United Artists Corporation (SA) (Pty) Ltd., 8th Floor, 24 Eloff St., Atkinson House, Johannesburg 2000. Helena Nossell
Nigeria—William Ramzi, American Motion Picture Export Co. (Africa) Inc., P.O. Box 244, Apapa.

FAR EAST

Australia

Head Office—Richard Guadio, United Artists (A/Asia) Pty, Ltd., Town Hall House, 456 Kent St., Sydney, NSW2000. Linda Monmouth
Adelaide—Stewart A. Handfield, Lombard House, 88 Curie Street, Adelaide, South Australia.
Brisbane—D. A. Ross, Maritime Bldgs., Circular Quay, Petries Bight, Brisbane, Queensland 4000.
Melbourne—Greg Hood, 140 Bourke St., Melbourne, Victoria 3000.
Perth—Mr. Francis F. Hackett, "Premier Film Centre," 282 Stirling Street, G.P.O. Box 876 K. East Perth.
Sydney—David Chard, KMS Bldg., 6th floor, 8/24 Kippax St., Sunny Hills 2010.
Auckland (New Zealand)—Steve Noonan U.A. Australasia Pty., Ltd., 11 Beach Road, Commerce Bldg., Auckland 1, New Zealand.

Hong Kong

Robert Chow—U.A. China Inc., Rm. 222, 2nd floor, J. Hotung House, 5/15 Hankow Road, Tsimshatsui, Kowloon, H.K.

India

Sub-distributors.
P. V. Prabhu, 20th Century Fox Corp. (India) Ltd., Metro House., 3rd floor, Mahatma Gandhi Road, Bombay 40020.

Japan

Tokyo—Head Office, Michael Murphy, United Artists of Japan, Inc. No. 15 Mori Building, 2-10 Toranomon 2-chome, Minato-ku, Tokyo 105.
Nagoya—Sadao Matsui, Mainichi Nagoya Kaikan, 7-35, Meieki 4-chomes Nakamura-Ku.
Osaka—Hiroshi Kanda, The Asahi Bldg., No. 3-chome, Nakanoshima, Kita-ku.
Fukuoka—Takashi Matsunaga, Hananoseki Building, 12-46, 4-chome, Nakasu Hakata-ku, Fukuoka.
Sapporo—Mr. Hiroyuki Imai, Dogin Bldg., No. 1, Nishi, 4-chome, Ohdori.

Philippine Islands

Manila—Policarpo Domingo. United Artists of Phillipines Inc., P.O. Box 434, Manila

Singapore

Michael Huang, United Artists Corp., 269 Orchard Road, Singapore 092:3

Malaysia

United Artists of Malaya, Inc. 140 Jalan Choo Chevy Khay, Kuala Lumpur 08-02, Selangor. Kam Thean Aun

Taiwan

Tapei—K. K. Poon, United Artists China, Inc., 109, OMei St., 3rd floor, Taipei 100, R.O.C.

Thailand

Bangkok—Benchamas Thanavet, United Artists of Thailand Inc., South East Insurance Bldg., 6th Floor, 315 Silom Road.

LATIN AMERICA

Argentina

Buenos Aires—Head Office, Jean Pigree Roy, Gen. Manager, United Artists So. American Corp. Viamonte 2146, Piso 7, Buenos Aires.
Santa Fe—A. J. Mellit; 25 de Mayo St. 2800

Uruguay

Montevideo—United Artists of Uruguay, Inc., Paraguay 1472, Washington, Medina.

Venezuela

Caracas—Antonio Blanco, Blanco y Travieso C.A., Edificio Las Delicias, 4A Avenide Las Delicias, Sabana Grande, Caracas

Dominican Republic

Leonel Mota, general manager, United Artists Dominicana, Branch of United Artists of Puerto Rico, Cinema Centro Dominicano, P.O. Box 1200.

Brazil

Rio de Janeiro—Head Office, Stuart Salter, general manager, U.A. of Brazil, Inc., Rua Senador Dantas, 74-3 Andar ZC-06, 20,000. Paulho Vasconcelos

Belo Horizonte—Olegario Moreira Guedas, mgr.; Rua Aarao Reis No. 538 S/306 (Caixa Postal 108), 30,000 Belo Horizonte, Minas Gerais.

Botucatu—Luiz Giudiee, mgr.; Rua Major Leonidas Cardoso, 136 Caixa Postal 24, 18600 Botucatu, Estado de Sao Paulo.

Porto Alegre—Dirceu Alves Pereira, mgr.; Caixa Postal 708, Rua 7 de Setembro, 661/11-15, 90,000 Porto Alegre, Rio Grande do Sul.

Recife—Mr. Chateaubriand Benicio de Salles, mgr.; Avenida Marques de Olinda 290-S/210-220, Caixa Postal 98, 50,000 Recife, Pernambuco.

Ribeirao Preto—Agnaldo Biagini, mgr.; Rua Amador Bueno No. 262, Caixa Postal 132, 14100 Ribeirao Preto, Sao Paulo.

Sao Paulo—Antonio DeNardi, Rua Dos Andradas No. 241, Caixa Postal 486, 01208 Sao Paulo, S.P.

Salvador (Bahia)—Condor Filmes, S.A. Rua Miguel Calmon, 61-2 Andar, Bahia, sub-distributor.

Chile

Santiago—Fidel Venegas Aguilera, manager; U.A. South American Corp., P.O. Box 623, San Antonio 378, Santiago, Chile.

Colombia

Bogota—Head Office, Maitland Prichett, manager; United Artists Corp. de Columbia, S.A., Calle 23 No. 5-85.

Cali—Egidio Linares C., United Artists Corp., S.A. Calle 23A Norte #2N-31

Bucaramanga—Alfonso Bernal & CIA. United Artists corporation de Colombia, S.A.,; Apartado Aereo 487, Calle 45 #16-103, Bucaramanga, sub-distributor.

Ecuador

Quito—Head Offic, Marco Aguas H., United Artists of Ecuador, Inc., Venezuela 659, Edificio Banco de Prestamos, Third Floor Office C and D.

Trinidad—Kelvin Lucky, United Artists of Trinidad Inc., Film Centre, P.O. Box 336, Port-of-Spain, Trinidad

Mexico

Mexico City—Mr. Michel Rosenthal, Columbia Fox de Mexico, Sinaloa 20, 1er Piso, Mexico 7, DF, sub-distributor.

Panama

Panama City—Head office Francisco Rossi, dir. manager, United Artists of Panama, Inc., Calle 45 #T3-106.
Sub-Distributors:
San Jose, Costa Rica—Henry Loria, Films Magaly, S.A., Apartado 8-6750, San Jose.
Guatemala City—Leonil Samayoa, Altos del Cine Reforma, Calle Mariscal Cruz 9-44 Zona 4.
Honduras—Hugo Erazo, Apartado 299, Tegucigalpa.
Nicaragua—Abinadack Cortes, Distribuidora de Peliculas Cortes, Hernandez, Apartado 3941, Managua.
El Savador—Miguel Pinto, Diario Latino, San Salvador, El Salvador.

Peru

Lima—Head Office, Sonia Repetto, manager, United Artists of Peru, Inc., Apartado 2782.

Puerto Rico

San Juan—Head Office, Jan Lambert, manager, United Artists Corp. of Puerto Rico. Garraton Bldg., P.O. Box 8455, Fernandez Juncos Station, Santuro

UNITED ARTISTS MUSIC CO., INC.

PRESIDENT
Harold Seider
VICE PRESIDENT/OPERATIONS
Steven E. Salmonsohn
VICE PRESIDENT/ASSISTANT SECRETARY
Frank E. Banyai

VICE PRESIDENT
Jimmy Gilmer
VICE PRESIDENT/TREASURER
Mauro A. Sardi
CONTROLLER/ASSISTANT TREASURER
Werner Hintzen
SECRETARY
Linda S. Wohl
ASSISTANT SECRETARY
Silvia J. Blach
ASSISTANT SECRETARY
Eve Sasko
ASSISTANT TREASURER
Benjamin Acker
ASSISTANT TREASURER
Louis F. Castelli
ASSISTANT TREASURER
Henry T. Pasniewski
GENERAL COUNSEL
Sidney Shemel

Universal Pictures

(A division of Universal City Studios, Inc., Subsidiary of MCA, Inc.)

445 Park Avenue, New York, NY 10022; PLaza 9-7500. Cable: Unifilman. (Producer and distributor.)

PRESIDENT
Ned Tanen
GENERAL SALES MANAGER
Bill Soady
EXECUTIVE VICE PRESIDENTS
Robert N. Wilkinson, David Weitzner
VICE PRESIDENTS
Gordon Armstrong, Gerald Barton, James Fiedler, Hilton Green, George Jones, Charles Morgan, Peter Ratican, Melvin Sattler, Herbert Steinberg
TREASURER
Harold M. Haas
SECRETARY
Girard A. Jacobi

HISTORY OF UNIVERSAL

Universal Pictures has a history stemming from the pioneer days of the industry. The company was formed under the title, "Universal" in 1912, when Carl Laemmle amalgamated Bison 101, Nestor, Powers and several other organizations, including his own Imp firm. Carl Laemmle had entered the picture business as an exhibitor, opening the White Front Theatre on Milwaukee Avenue, Chicago, February 24, 1906.

He founded Laemmle Film Service on October 1 of that year, quit the Patents Company in April, 1909, and released his first Independent Motion Picture (Imp) Company "Feature," "Hiawatha," length, 998 feet, on October 25, 1909.

In that experimental epoch, Universal launched the star system by hiring Florence Lawrence for $1,000 a week and billing her as "Queen of the Screen." The studio also produced the screen's initial "expos" film, "Traffic in Souls," first film to be reviewed by the drama critics of the daily press. Universal acquired a studio at Sunset Boulevard and Gower Street in 1914, and began making pictures in Hollywood. In 1915, production was moved to the present site, Universal City. Here appeared Wallace Reid, Lon Chaney, Mary Pickford, Rudolph Valentino and Boris Karloff, among many others.

"Foolish Wives," "first million-dollar feature," "The Hunchback of Notre Dame," "All Quiet On the Western Front," and screen dramas of like import, were filmed in the decades which followed.

On March 16, 1920, Carl Laemmle and R. H. Cochrane assumed complete control of the company.

On April 2, 1936, Universal passed under new management, with J. Cheever Cowdin as chairman of the board. On January 6, 1938, Nate J. Blumberg became president of the company.

Under the new management Universal embarked upon the policy of developing star values and had been most successful during the time it has operated in the establishment of such names as Deanna Durbin, Abbott & Costello, Maria Montez, Donald O'Connor and others under contract.

During 1946, the company underwent its second transformation. Production-wise, it eliminated the production of all so-called "B" pictures, Westerns and serials, following a merger and acquisition of the assets of International Pictures Corp. of Leo Spitz and William Goetz. Mr. Spitz and Mr. Goetz became the production heads and Universal-International trademark emerged.

Secondly, Universal completed a distribution deal with the J. Arthur Rank organization for the American distribution of the top British pictures produced by the Rank affiliated companies.

The year 1946 also saw the emergence of United World Pictures, a wholly-owned Universal subsidiary, to handle the production and distribution of non-theatrical films. United World acquired the Bell and Howell Filmsound Library of 6,000 subjects. It then purchased Castle Films, the largest seller of non-theatrical packaged films to the home. The year 1950 saw the resignation of J. Cheever Cowdin with Mr. Blumberg assuming full command. Alfred E. Daff, who had been foreign sales manager, assumed the top post in the foreign distribution setup and then became director of world sales with the resignation of W. A. Scully—a post without parallel in the industry. Mr. Scully was to continue until 1954 as domestic sales consultant. Charles J. Feldman was appointed domestic sales manager under Mr. Daff and Americo Aboaf foreign sales head.

In November, 1951 Decca Records acquired approximately 28 per cent of Universal's common stock to make it the largest single stockholder in the company. For this interest Decca paid $3,773,914, for the 234,900 shares involved and the right to purchase 32,500 additional warrants, according to a report made by Milton R. Rackmil, president of Decca, to the Securities and Exchange Commission.

He reported that of these shares, 78,000 were purchased on the New York Stock Exchange, while the balance, most of which formerly was owned by the Paul G. Brown estate, was bought from Gertrude Bergman. Maurice A. Bergman, Lewis Fox Blumberg, N. J. Blumberg, Vera F. Blumberg, Alfred E. Daff, Edith Mayer Goetz, William Goetz, Doris Jean Mayer and Leo Spitz.

The warrants were purchased from N. J. Blumberg and Doris Jean Mayer, at a reported price of $5 each. The purchases on the New York Stock Exchange were made at current market prices; the purchases from the individuals named were made at prices reached as a result of negotiations. Purchase of the holdings of Spitz as executive head of production and Goetz as executive in charge of production. Their block of about 15,000 shares was acquired at approximately $15 a share. Blumberg's holdings included 15,000 shares and 32,500 warrants. In announcing the purchase, Rackmil declared, "The ownership of these shares will bring about a close association between our two companies. We have kindred interests in the entertainment business. These interests can be developed for our mutual benefit. The transaction indicates the confidence that our respective companies have in the future of the motion picture and allied industries."

In the spring of 1952, Decca Records became the controlling stockholders of Universal. Its interests were acquired partly in the open market and partly through the purchase of all J. Arthur Rank's stock in the company. As a result, Milton R. Rackmil, president of Decca Records, was made a member of the Universal board and subsequently elected president of Universal in July, 1952. In June of 1962, MCA, Inc., exchanged its common and a newly-issued preferred stock for Decca capital stock leading to a consolidation of the two companies and making Universal Pictures Company the theatrical film producing division of MCA, Inc.

In the Spring of 1964 the creation of the Universal City Studios image started with the separate motion picture and television arms. On March 25, 1966, Universal Pictures became a division of Universal City Studios, Inc., a subsidiary of MCA, Inc.

PRODUCTION

UNIVERSAL THEATRICAL MOTION PICTURES

(A division of Universal City Studios, Inc., Subsidiary of MCA, Inc.) Universal City, CA 91608 (213) 985-4321.
PRESIDENT
Ned Tanen

DISTRIBUTION (Domestic)

UNIVERSAL FILM EXCHANGES, INC.

445 Park Avenue, New York, NY 10022; PLaza 9-7500.
PRESIDENT
Robert N. Wilkinson
EXECUTIVE VICE PRESIDENT & GENERAL SALES MANAGER
Bill Soady
VICE PRESIDENTS
Robert Bowers, Ben Cammack, Robert Carpenter, Thomas E. Dunn, Jerome Evans, Eugene F. Gidpuinto, Albert Quaedylieg, James Mooney, Richonx, Philip Sherman, Bill Soady
TREASURER
Harold M. Haas
REGIONAL SALES MANAGERS
Robert Bowers, Dallas, TX; D. A. Richoux, Los Angeles; Al Kolkmeyer, Chicago; Philip Sherman, NY; Tom Dunn, Atlanta.

DOMESTIC BRANCHES AND MANAGERS

ATLANTA: 30303—205 Walton Street, (404) 523-5081, Weber Howell.
BOSTON: 02116—44 Winchester Street, (617) 426-8760, Joan Corrado.
CHARLOTTE: NC 28202—705 E. Morehead Street (704) 333-5564, W. A. McClure.
CHICAGO: 60611—425 N. Michigan Avenue, (312) 822-0513, W. Gehring.
CINCINNATI: 45210—1628 Central Parkway, (513) 421-3820, D. Coons.
CLEVELAND: 44114—1721 Superior Avenue, (216) 771-0413, J. Ryan.

DALLAS: 75243—11551 Forest Central Dr., Suite 330 B. Bob Harris.
DENVER: 80205—801 21st Street, (303) 623-3281, J. Box.
DETROIT (TROY):— *48084*—59 Park Street, (313) 583-1720, D. Gonda.
JACKSONVILLE: 32211—One Regency Place, 9570 Regency Square Blvd., Suite 336, (904) 721-1250, G. F. Byrd.
KANSAS CITY: 64108—1700 Wyandotte Street, (816) 421-5624, S. Miller.
LOS ANGELES: 90048—8901 Beverly Blvd., (213) 550-7461, J. Finn.
MINNEAPOLIS: 55430—6800 Shingle Creek Parkway, (612) 566-9620, F. Zanotti.
NEW ORLEANS (METAIRIE,) 70005—734A Martin Behrman Ave., (504) 837-2631, N. Gazaway.
NEW YORK: 10022—445 Park Avenue, (212) 759-7500, A. Quaedvlieg.
PHILADELPHIA: (CHERRY HILL, NJ) 08003—1165 Marlkress Road, (609) 424-5045, P. Ciccotta.
PUERTO RICO: 00923—1606 Ponce de Leon Ave., Suite 200, Santuree, P.R. 00909. Mailing: P.O. Box 3291, San Juan, P.R. 00910. A. Lopez
SAN FRANCISCO: 94102—693 Sutter Street, (415) 776-3660, J. B. Mooney.
SEATTLE: 98301—Lake Villa Apts., 25010 106th St., Apt. 80 8-201 E Kent, WA (206) 859-1429
WASHINGTON DC: (Riverdale, MD) 20840—6801 Kenilworth Avenue, (301) 699-3200, S. Turner.
NO. HOLLYWOOD: 91609—P.O. Box 9665, (213) 985-4321, Film Exchange Acc'ting

DISTRIBUTION (Foreign)

UNIVERSAL INTERNATIONAL FILMS, INC.

445 Park Avenue, New York, NY 10022; Cable: Unfilman.
PRESIDENT
Robert N. Wilkinson
VICE PRESIDENTS
Richard Baker, Harold M. Haas, George Smith, Eugene Froelich.
TREASURER
Harold M. Haas
SECRETARY
Girard D. Jacobi

UNIVERSAL TELEVISION

(A division of Universal City Studios)
Universal City Studios, Universal City, CA (213) 985-4321. (Producer of TV films.)
PRESIDENT
Robert Harris
EXECUTIVE VICE PRESIDENT
Charles Engle
VICE PRESIDENTS
Burt AStor, Earl Bellamy, William De Cinces, Bernard Fisher, Norman Glenn, Gerry Gottlieb, Stefanie Kowal, Kerry McCluggage, Paul Miller, George Santoro, Peter Thompson, Thomas Wertheimer.
VICE PRESIDENT, PUBLICITY, PROMOTION AND ADVERTISING
Ben Halpern
SECRETARY
Michael Samuel
TREASURER
Harold M. Haas

UNITED WORLD FILMS

(A division of Universal City Studios, Inc.) 445 Park Avenue, New York, NY 10022; a subsidiary of MCA, Inc.)
PRESIDENT
Sidney J. Sheinberg
EXECUTIVE VICE PRESIDENT
Robert N. Wilkinson
VICE PRESIDENTS
E. F. Giaquinto, George Smith
SECRETARY
Michael Samuel
TREASURER
Harold M. Haas

Valentino, Thomas J., Inc.

151 West 46th Street, New York, NY 10036 (246) 4675-6. (Sound effects, theatrical and industrial film production music; video stock footage.)
PRESIDENT
Robert F. Valentino

Valiant International Pictures

4774 Melrose Ave., Hollywood, CA 90029. (213) 665-5257. Cable: Valintfilm. (Production and distribution.)
PRESIDENT
Harry Novak
VICE PRESIDENT
Carmen Novak
SECRETARY TREASURER
Louis Stein

Vanguard Film Company, Inc.

Box 664, Palm Beach FL 33480 (305) 842-1558. New York office: Suite 607, One Times Square, NY 10036 (212) 354-3966 (Owns and produces feature motion pictures, TV series, and specials)
CHAIRMAN OF THE BOARD
C. E. Feltner, Jr.
EXECUTIVE VICE PRESIDENT
R. L. Levine

Vanguard Releasing, Inc.

8831 Sunset Blvd., Los Angeles, CA 90069 (213) 652-2630. (Motion picture distribution.)
PRESIDENT
Barry Cahn
DATE OF ORGANIZATION
1976

Van Praag Productions, Inc.

135 East 55th Street, New York, NY 10022 (212) 832-2111. (Producer)
PRESIDENT AND EXECUTIVE DIRECTOR
William Van Praag
STAFF DIRECTORS
Eugene Van Praag
Jeffe Glasserow

Variety Films, Inc.

1540 Broadway, New York, NY 10036 (212) 575-8182 (Producer and distributor)
PRESIDENT
Bondi Wilson-Walters

Vatica Productions, Inc.

502 Hillcrest Road, Beverly Hills, CA 90210. (213) 272-0196. (Production and distribution of motion pictures)
PRESIDENT
Alfredo Leone
DATE OF ORGANIZATION
1979

Vavin, Inc. (Video & Visual Information Films)

235 East 46th St., New York, NY 10017 (212) 753-3923. (Production of documentary, industrial, public relations and travel films for theatrical, nontheatrical, and TV distribution.)

Veritas Productions, Inc.

New York City (212) 765-4240 or 1 Laurie Drive, Englewood Cliffs, NJ 07632 (201) 568-4214; (Production of motion pictures for Theatres and TV.)
PRESIDENT
Richard S. Dubelman

WHH Productions

Box 24844, Los Angeles, CA 90024 (213) 393-8368. (Production of motion pictures and television programming.)

Warner Bros. Inc.

(A subsidiary of Warner Communications, Inc.) 75 Rockefeller Plaza, New York, NY 10019 (212) 484-8000; 4000 Warner Blvd. Burbank, CA 91522 (213) 843-6000.
CHAIRMAN OF THE BOARD AND CO-CHIEF EXECUTIVE OFFICER
Ted Ashley
VICE CHAIRMAN
Frank Wells
PRESIDENT AND CHIEF OPERATING OFFICER
Terry Semel
PRESIDENT, THEATRICAL PRODUCTION DIVISION
Robert Shapiro
PRESIDENT, FOREIGN OPERATIONS
Myron D. Karlin
EXECUTIVE VICE PRESIDENT AND GENERAL SALES MANAGER
Barry Reardon
EXECUTIVE VICE PRESIDENT, STUDIO
Charles Greenlaw
VICE PRESIDENT, WORLDWIDE PRODUCTION MANAGEMENT
Fred Gallo
EXECUTIVE VICE PRESIDENT, WORLDWIDE ADVERTISING AND PUBLICITY
Sanford E. Reisenbach
EXECUTIVE VICE PRESIDENT
Sidney Kiwitt
SENIOR VICE PRESIDENT, PRODUCTION
Mark Rosenberg
VICE PRESIDENT PRODUCTION
Mark Canton
VICE PRESIDENT, TREASURER
Ralph Peterson
VICE PRESIDENT, PRODUCT ACQUISITION WORLDWIDE BUSINESS AFFAIRS
Jack E. Freedman
VICE PRESIDENT, CONTROLLER
Ed Romano
VICE PRESIDENT
Arthur Kananack
VICE PRESIDENT, MARKET RESEARCH
Richard del Belso
VICE PRESIDENT, EAST COAST PRODUCTION
Susan Braudy
VICE PRESIDENT, CREATIVE ADVERTISING
Joel Wayne
VICE PRESIDENT, GENERAL COUNSEL
Peter Knecht
VICE PRESIDENT, PUBLICITY
Joe Hyams
VICE PRESIDENT, PRODUCTION MANAGEMENT
Ed Morey
VICE PRESIDENT, TALENT
Marion Daugherty
VICE PRESIDENT AND ASST. GENERAL SALES MANAGER
Daniel L. Fellman
VICE PRESIDENT AND GENERAL COUNSEL
Peter Knecht
VICE PRESIDENT AND ASSOCIATE GENERAL COUNSEL
Stanley Belkin
VICE PRESIDENTS, BUSINESS AFFAIRS
Michael Donohew, Jim Miller
VICE PRESIDENT, SALES ADMINISTRATION
Phil Shonfeld
VICE PRESIDENT AND DIRECTOR OF MEDIA
Mardi Marans
VICE PRESIDENT, INDUSTRIAL RELATIONS
Alan Raphael
VICE PRESIDENT, ADMINISTRATIVE SERVICES AND OPERATIONS
Sam Pasqua

HISTORY OF WARNER BROS. PICTURES, INC.

Incorporated on January 16, 1953, in Delaware, in order to acquire the motion picture production, distribution and certain other assets of its predecessor, Warner Bros. Pictures, Inc., incorporated in 1923 (dissolved), in compliance with the divorcement provisions of a Consent Judgment entered into on January 5, 1951, in an antitrust proceeding instituted in the United States District Court for the Southern District of New York against the later corporation. The Corporation and its predecessor have conducted the Corporation's present business since 1923.

The Corporation produces feature motion pictures for exhibition in theatres and films for exhibition on television, and distributes films in the United States and throughout the world.

On July 15, 1967, a subsidiary of Seven Arts Productions Limited acquired substantially all the assets and business of Warner Bros. Pictures, Inc. The company subsequently was called Warner Bros.-Seven Arts Limited.

On July 8, 1969, substantially all the assets and business of Warner Bros.-Seven Arts were acquired by Kinney National Service, Inc., a company now known as Warner Communications Inc., of which Warner Bros. Inc. is a subsidiary.

DISTRIBUTION (Domestic)

WARNER BROS. DISTRIBUTING CORP.

4000 Warner Blvd., Burbank, CA 91522 (213) 843-6000; 75 Rockefeller Plaza, New York, NY 10019 (212) 484-8000.

PRESIDENT AND CHIEF OPERATING OFFICER
Terry Semel
VICE PRESIDENT AND GENERAL SALES MANAGER
Barry Reardon
VICE PRESIDENT AND ASSISTANT GENERAL SALES MANAGER
Daniel R. Fellman
VICE PRESIDENT, SALES ADMINISTRATION
Phil Shonfeld
SECRETARY
Bernard R. Sorkin
DIRECTOR OF BRANCH OPERATIONS
Howard Welinsky
DIRECTOR OF SALES ADMINISTRATION
Dan Rothinberg
NATIONAL PUBLICITY DIRECTOR
Fred Skidmore
NATIONAL DIRECTOR OF PROMOTION
Ernie Grossman
EASTERN DIRECTOR OF PUBLICITY/ADVERTISING
George Nelson
EASTERN DIVISION MANAGER
Robert Miller (N.Y.)
EASTERN DISTRICT MANAGER
Andy Gruenberg (N.Y.)
SOUTHERN DIVISION MANAGER
J. R. Motley (Dallas)
SOUTHERN DISTRICT MANAGER
R. E. Heffner (Jacksonville)
WESTERN DIVISION MANAGER
Richard Hill (L.A.)
WESTERN DISTRICT MANAGER
Richard Hill (Los Angeles)
MIDWESTERN DISTRICT MANAGER
Floyd Brethour (Chicago)
MIDWESTERN CANADIAN DIVISION SALES MANAGER
Irving Stern (Toronto)
CANADIAN DISTRICT MANAGER
Phil R. Carlton
NEW YORK METROPOLITAN SALES MANAGER
Herb Gaines

DOMESTIC BRANCHES AND MANAGERS

ATLANTA: 30345—2600 Century Parkway, 472, Roy Donaldson
BOSTON: 02116—31 St. James Ave., Jeff Goldstein
CHARLOTTE: 28202—330 South Tryon St., Harold Duckett
CHICAGO: 60606—550 West Jackson Blvd., Seymour Hite
CINCINNATI: 45202—414 Walnut St., 12, Bill Waynberg
CLEVELAND: 44124—29001 Cedar Rd., Lyndhurst, Andrew Silverman
DALLAS: 75231—7424 Greenville Ave., Jackie Stanley
DENVER: 80206—88 Steele ST., 302, Jay Peckos
DETROIT: 48237—20820 Greenfield Rd., Oak Park, Don E. Martin
JACKSONVILLE: 32211—9550 Regency Sq. Blvd., 1107, R. E. Heffner
KANSAS CITY: MO: 64108—2440 Pershing Rd., 150, Frank Rhodes
LOS ANGELES: 90211—8484 Wilshire Blvd., Beverly Hills, Shirley Becker
NEW ORLEANS: 70002—4539 North I-10 Road, Metairie, Daniel Chinich
NEW YORK: 10019—75 Rockefeller Plaza, Herb Gaines
PHILADELPHIA: 19106—400 Market St., Frank Carroll
SAN FRANCISCO: 94102—544 Golden Gate Ave., Mike Timko
WASHINGTON, DC: 20814—7315 Wisconsin Ave., Charles Jordan

CANADA

GALGARY: T2R-059—1147 Seventeenth Ave., S.W., Blain Covert
MONTREAL: H4A-1G2—5890 Monkland Ave., 107, Archie Cohen
TORONTO: M5B-1L7—70 Carlton St.
VANCOUVER: V6K-2N4—202-8041 Granville, Roland Rickard
WINNIPEG: R38-1Z8—583 Ellice Ave., Florent Boulet
SUPERVISORS: R. L. H. Davidson (Tokyo): Far East. G. Erikson (London): Continental Sales Manager, B. N. Nadkarni (Bombay): Bangladesh, Burma, India, Pakistan, Sri Lanka. F. Pierce (London): Europe, Middle East, Africa. A. Sanz (Burbank): Latin America.

DISTRIBUTION)Foreign)

WARNER BROS. INTERNATIONAL

4000 Warner Blvd., Burbank, CA 91522 (213) 843-6000. Cable: WARBROS Telex: 677129.

PRESIDENT
Myron Karlin
VICE PRESIDENTS
Richard Ma (Sales)
Julian G. Binstock (Administration)
John Friedkin (Advertising/Publicity)
TREASURER
William Starr
CONTROLLER
Mike Goodnight
SECRETARY
Darlene Robson

REGIONAL SUPERVISORS
EUROPE, MIDDLE EAST, AFRICA
Frank Pierce, vice president, London WIV 4AP, 135 Wardour St.
FAR EAST
R. H. Davidson, vice president, Tokyo, 2-4 Kyobashi, 3 Chome, Mchuo-Ku
LATIN AMERICA
Andrew Sanz, vice president, Burbank,CA

FOREIGN BRANCHES AND MANAGERS

Argentina

WARNER BROS. (SOUTH) INC. John Bruckman, Manager.
Buenos Aires—Tucuman 1938.

Australia

WARNER BROS. (AUSTRALIA) PTY. LTD., S. Parker, Managing Director.
Sydney—49 Market St.

Austria

WARNER COLUMBIA FILMVERLEIH GmbH, (Distributor) Rudolf Neumann, manager.
Vienna—Mondscheingasse 18.

Belgium

WARNER BROS. (TRANSATLANTIC), INC. WARNER COLUMBIA FILM S.N.C. (Distributor), Edouard Weinberg, Manager.
Brussels—326 Rue Royale.

Bolivia

DISTRIBUIDORES ASOCIADOS DE PELICULAS LTDA., Licnio Manay. Manager. Avenida Montes 768.

Brazil

WARNER BROS. (SOUTH), INC., Albert S. Salem, Manager.
Rio De Janeiro—Rua Senador Dantas, 19.
Belo Horizonte—Rua Aarao Reis, 538.
Porto Alegre—Rua General Joao Monael, 207.
Recife—Av. Barbosa Lima, 149.
Sao Paulo—Av. Sao Joao, 802.
Ribeirao Preto—Servicos de Distribuicao de Filmes, Ltda. Rua Alvares Cabral, 871

Chile

WARNER BROS. (SOUTH), INC. Bruno Frydman, Manager.
Santiago—Fanor Velasco 18-A.

Colombia

WARNER BROS. (SOUTH), INC. CINE COLOMBIA, S.A. (Distributor) Jaime Joseph, Representative.
Bogota—Apartado aereo 3455.

Denmark

WARNER BROS. (D) A/S WARNER BROS. (D) A/S WARNER & METRONOME FILM ApS (Distributor), Steen Gregers, Manager.
Copenhagen—Sondermarksvej 16.

Dominican Republic

WARNER BROS. (SOUTH) INC. Joseph Ambar, Gen. Mgr. Santo Domingo—Calle Santiago 359

East Africa
COSMOPOLITAN FILM BV, Nairobi, Kenya P.O. Box 74244

Ecuador
PRODUCTORA FILMICA NACIONAL DEL ECUADOR CIA. LTDA., (Distributor) Carlos Espinosa, Managing Director.
Guayaquil—Calle 9 de Octubre, 424.

Egypt
WARNER BROS. (F.E.), INC., M. K. Elserty, Manager.
Cairo—31/33 Orabi Street.

England
COLUMBIA-EMI-WARNER DISTRIBUTORS LTD. (Distribution) T. Nicholas, Managing Director.
London W1V 4AP—135 Wardour Street.

Finland
WARNER BROS. (FINLAND) OY WARNER-COLUMBIA FILMS AB (Distributor) Aunz Turfja, Manager.
Helsinki—P. Esplanadi 33-A.

France
WARNER BROS. (TRANSATLANTIC). INC. WARNER-COLUMBIA FILM G.I.E. (Distribution) Elie Costa, Manager.
Paris—20, rue Troyon.
Bordeaux—112, rue Sainte-Catherine.
Lyon—22, rue d'Algerie.
Marseille—42, Bd. Longchamps.
Strasbourg—4, rue de Mutzig.

Germany
WARNER BROS. FILM GmbH WARNER-COLUMBIA FILM-VERLEIH GmbH (Distribution) Erich Muller, General Manager.
Munich—Ickstattstrasse 1
Berlin—29 Schraperstrasse
Dusseldorf—Bismarckstrasse 95 1
Frankfurt—66 Kaiserstrasse
Hamburg—32 Steindamm

Greece
Victor G. Michaelides (Distributor)
Athens—96 Akadimias Street

Guyana
GANGA PRASAD & SONS LTD. (Distributor) Chandra Prasad.
Georgetown—162 Charlotte & Wellington Streets.

Holland
WARNER BROS. (HOLLAND) E. J. Katz, Manager.
Amsterdam—Achter Oosteinde 9-11.

Hong Kong
WARNER BROS. (F.E.), INC. Chen Li, Manager.
Kowloon—5, Canton Road, TST

India
WARNER BROS. (F.E.), INC. L. A. Colaco, Manager.
Bombay—42 M. Karve Road.
Calcutta—19A Jawaharlal Nehru Road.
Madras—1/17 Mount Road.
New Delhi—Plaza Theatre Bldg., Connaught Circus

Israel
E. GILAD & CO. (Distributor), Ephraim Gilad.
Tel Aviv—Hayarden St. 11.

Italy
PRODUZIONE INTERCONTINENTALE CINEMATOGRAFICA, S.p.A. (Distributor), Bernhard Weinreich, Managing Director.
Rome—Via Varese, 16/B.

Jamaica
RUSSGRAM INVESTMENTS LIMITED (Distributor), A. Russell Graham.

Kingston—12 Slipe Road.

Japan

WARNER BROS. (JAPAN), INC. Veronique Maingard, General Manager.

Tokyo—2-4 Kyobashi 3-chome, Chuo-ku.
Fukuoka—9-17 Tenjin 1-chome, Chuo-ku.
Nagoya—3-3 Sakae 1-chome, Naka-ku.
Osaka—11 Kitahama 3-chome, Higashi-ku.
Sapporo—Nishi 1-chome, Minami Ichijo, Chuo-ku.

Lebanon
WARNER BROS. (F.E.) INC. Joseph Chacra, manager.
Beirut—Makki Bldg., Mneimneh/Lyon St.-Hamra.

Mexico
WARNER BROS. (MEXICO), S.A.
Mexico 7, D.F.—Calle Acapulco 37.

New Zealand
WARNER BROS. (N.Z.) LTD. COLUMBIA-WARNER DISTRIBUTORS (Distribution) Lester McKellar, Managing Director.
Auckland—24/26 Nikau Street.

Norway
WARNER BROS. (NORWAY) A/S I/S COLUMBIA-WARNER (Distribution) Jon Narvestad, Manager.
Oslo—Stortingsgaten 30.

Pakistan
H. HUSEIN & CO. LTD. (Distributor), Humayan Baigmohamed.
Karachi—Palace Cinema Bldg.

Panama
WARNER BROS. (SOUTH), INC.
Panama City—Edificio Elga Via Espana 46-50.

Peru
WARNER BROS. (SOUTH), INC. Carlos Guzman, Manager.
Lima—Nicolas de Pierola #938.

Philippines
WARNER BROS. (F.E.), INC.
Manila—PPL Building, United Nations Avenue.

Portugal
COLUMBIA & WARNER FILMES DE PORTUGAL LIMITADA (Distribution), Veronique Maingard, Manager.
Lisbon—Avenida Duque de Loule, 90.

Puerto Rico
WARNER BROS. (SOUTH), R. Lopez de Pedro, Manager.
Santurce—1702 Fernandez Juncos Avenue, Stop 25.

Singapore
WARNER BROS. (F.E.), INC. Diane Sherman, Manager.
Singapore—112, Middle Road.
Kuala Kumpar—98 Jalan Imbi.

South Africa
WARNER BROS. (AFRICA) (PTY.) LTD. Kevin Hyson, Managing Director.
C.I.C.-WARNER (PTY.) LTD. (Distribution), Kevin Hyson, Managing Director.
Johannesburg—160 Main Street.

Spain
WARNER ESPANOLA, S.A. (Distribution), Roman Machtus, Representative.
Barcelona—Paseo de Gracia 77.

Sweden
WARNER BROS. (SWEDEN) AB, WARNER-COLUMBIA FILM AB (Distribution). Nils Persson, Manager.
Stockholm—Kungsgatan 24, VI.

Switzerland
WARNER BROS. (TRANSATLANTIC), INC. Max Berger, Manager.
Zurich—Nuschelerstrasse 31.

Taiwan (Formosa)
WARNER BROS. (F.E.), INC. Kimball P. Liang, Manager.
Taipei—24 Kai Fang Street.

Thailand
WARNER BROS. (F.E.), INC. Boon Thirakomen, Manager.
Bangkok—315 Silom Road.

Trinidad

WARNER BROS. (SOUTH) INC. CINEMA INTERNATIONAL CORP. (Distributor), Vincent C. Seerattan (Representative). *Port of Spain*—Film Center, St. James.

Uruguay

S.A.U.D.E.C. (Distributor) H. Garcia Arocena, Manager. *Montevideo*—Canelones 1238.

Venezuela

DIFRA (Distributor), Juan Falcon (Representative). *Caracas*—Edificio Las Palmas, Apartado Correos 1146.

Warner Bros. Television

TELEVISION PROGRAMMING

4000 Warner Blvd., Burbank, CA 91522 (213) 843-6000; 75 Rockefeller Plaza, New York, NY 10019 (212) 484-8000.

PRESIDENT
Alan Shayne
EXECUTIVE VICE PRESIDENT
Barry M. Meyer
SENIOR VICE PRESIDENT, CREATIVE AFFAIRS
Franklin Barton
SENIOR VICE PRESIDENT, BUSINESS AFFAIRS
Art Stolnitz
SENIOR VICE PRESIDENT IN CHARGE OF PRODUCTION
Richard Kobritz
VICE PRESIDENT, PUBLICITY, ADVERTISING & PROMOTION
David Horowitz
VICE PRESIDENT CURRENT PROGRAMMING
David Sacks
VICE PRESIDENT, MOVIES AND MINI-SERIES
Chuck McLain
VICE PRESIDENT, BUSINESS AFFAIRS
Johanna Levine
DIRECTOR PROGRAM DEVELOPMENT
Jane Auerbach
DIRECTOR OF COMEDY DEVELOPMENT
Dori Weiss
DIRECTOR, LEGAL AFFAIRS
Daniel J. Schiffer
DIRECTOR, STORY DEPARTMENT
Gus Blackmon

WORLDWIDE TELEVISION DISTRIBUTION

4000 Warner Blvd., Burbank, CA 91522 (213) 843-6000.

PRESIDENT WARNER BROS. TV DISTRIBUTION
Charles D. McGregor
VICE PRESIDENT, BUSINESS AFFAIRS AND ADMINISTRATION
Arthur Kananack
VICE PRESIDENT, DOMESTIC SALES MANAGER
George Mitchell
VICE PRESIDENT, INTERNATIONAL SALES & ADMINISTRATION
John Whitesell
VICE PRESIDENT, ADVERTISING, PROMOTION & PUBLICITY
Gordon A. Hellmann
DIRECTOR OF PRODUCT COORDINATION
Dee Eulberg

630 Ninth Avenue, New York, NY 10036: (212) 484-8000.

MANAGER, TECHNICAL SERVICES
Erwin Markisch
MANAGER, BOOKING SERVICES
Clara Falkoff
MANAGER, PROGRAM INFORMATION
Louis B. Marino

Fred Weintraub Productions, Inc.

12655 Washington Blvd., Suite 202, Los Angeles, CA 90066 (213) 390-7636.

PRESIDENT
Fred Weintraub
DATE OF ORGANIZATION
1978

Weiss Global Enterprises

333 South Beverly Drive, Beverly Hills, CA 90212 (213) 553-5806. Cable: WEISSRICT (Producer of feature films, owner-distributor of 120 full-length features; television distributor of features.)

PRESIDENT
Adrian Weiss
SECRETARY-TREASURER
Steven A. Weiss
VICE PRESIDENTS
Edith L. Weiss, Laurie Weiss
OPERATION MANAGER
Joleen Meibos

William Morris Agency, Inc.

1350 Avenue of the Americas, New York, NY 10019 (212) 586-5100. Beverly Hills Office: 151 El Camino (213) 274-7451. Nashville: 2325 Crestmoor Rd. (615) 385-0310. Overseas Offices: London, Rome & Munich. (Representatives for artists and all creative talent in the entertainment and literary worlds.)

CO-CHAIRMEN OF THE BOARD, EMERITI
Abe Lastfogel, (Beverly Hills)
Nat Lefkowitz (New York)
CHAIRMAN OF THE BOARD
Morris Stoller (Beverly Hills)
PRESIDENT
Sam Weisbord, (Beverly Hills)
EXECUTIVE VICE PRESIDENTS
(Beverly Hills)
Norman Brokaw
Roger Davis
Tony Fantozzi
Stan Kamen
Walter Zifkin
(New York)
Lee Stevens
Lou Weiss
VICE PRESIDENT, TREASURER
Larry Lewis (New York)
MOTION PICTURE DEPARTMENT
Beverly Hills—Flo Allen, Allan Badiner, Ed Bondy, Dennis Brody, Martin Caan, Roger Davis, Debra Greenfield, Annette Handley, Leonard Hirshan, Joan Hyler, Stan Kamen, Ed Limato, Gary Lucchesi, Ron Mardigian, Peter Meyer, Ed Mitchell, Mike Peretzian, John Ptak, Arnold Stiefel, Peter Turner, Irene Webb, Mike Zimring.
New York—Martin Bauer, Getrge Lane, Carmen La Via, Biff Liff, Fred Milstein, Gilbert Parker, Johnnie Planco, Ed Robbins, Janet Roberts, Katie Rothacker, Esther Sherman, Elle Shushan, Lee Stevens
TELEVISION DEPARTMENT
Beverly Hills—Larry Auerbach, Arthur Axelman, Jeralyn Badgley, Alan Berger, Norman Brokaw, Bruce Brown, Lee Cohen, Robert Crestani, Ruth Englehardt, Tony Fantozzi, Bob Goodman, Sam Haskell, Martin Hurwitz, Alan Iezman, Jerry Katzman, Steve Konow, Sol Leon, Debbie Miller, Marc Pariser, Pam Prince, Joe Rivkin, John Rosenmayer, Hal Ross, David Schiff, Michael Shaw, Steve Weiss, Fred Westheimer, Jeff Witjas, Paul Yamamoto
New York—Lucy Aceto, Leo Bookman, Art Fuhrer, Jim Griffin, Leon Memoli, Jonathan Russo, James Sarnoff, Lee Stevens, Lou Weiss, Ron Yatter

Wolper Organization, Inc.-Warner Bros.

4000 Warner Boulevard, Burbank, CA 91522 (213) 843-6000.

Worldfilm Motion Picture & TV Productions

1681 Kennedy Causeway, North Bay Village, FL (3p5) 864-7777. West Coast: MGM Studios, Culver City, CA.

PRESIDENT & CHAIRMAN OF THE BOARD
W. Ed Herder
EXECUTIVE VICE PRESIDENT/MOTION PICTURE PRODUCTION WORLDWIDE
Peter Gale
VICE PRESIDENT/TELEVISION
Thomas Conners
VICE PRESIDENT/CASTING
J. C. Courtier

VICE PRESIDENT & GENERAL COUNSEL
Edmond W. Frank

World Northal Corp.

1 Dag Hammarskjold Plaza, New York, NY 10017
(Motion Picture acquisition and distribution.)
CO-CHAIRMEN
Frank Stanton, Victor Elmaleh
PRESIDENT & CHIEF OPERATING OFFICER
Mel Maron
CHIEF FINANCIAL OFFICER
Martin Schildkraut
VICE PRESIDENT IN CHARGE OF TELEVISION
George Hankoff
IN CHARGE OF PRODUCTION
Richard Salzberg
WEST COAST PRODUCTION HEAD
Tony Elmaleh
SALES MANAGER
Ivory Harris
ADMINISTRATIVE ASSISTANT TO THE PRESIDENT
Carole Schwartz
NORTH EAST DIVISION MANAGER
Dominick Frascella
NATIONAL PRINT CONTROLLER
Richard Bonnano
NATIONAL ADVERTISING DIRECTOR
Walter Epstein
NORTH EAST ADVERTISING DIRECTOR
Wayne Weil
PUBLIC RELATIONS
Renee Furst
DATE OF ORGANIZATION
January 1, 1977

Worldwide Entertainment Corporation

22525 Pacific Coast Highway #204, Malibu, CA
90265 (213) 456-6615.
PRESIDENT & TREASURER
Jack H. Harris
ADMINISTRATION
Beth Woods
DATE OF ORGANIZATION
1974

Wrather Corporation

270 N. Canon Dr., Beverly Hills, CA 278-8521. (Pro-
ducer & Distributor.)
PRESIDENT & CHAIRMAN OF THE BOARD
J. D. Wrather, Jr.
EXECUTIVE VICE PRES.—GENERAL COUNSEL
Monte E. Livingston
SENIOR VICE PRESIDENT-MARKETING
William Shay
VICE PRESIDENTS
Donald B. Brown, William A. Mahan, Vivian Moriarty, Richard
S. Stevens, Stanley Stunell, Gerald L. Weisberger, Bonita Granville
Wrather

CHIEF FINANCIAL OFFICER
William A. Mahan
SECRETARY
Gerald L. Weisberger
ASSISTANT VICE PRESIDENTS
Stefania Moyers, Robert E. Treese, Christopher C.f Wrather
ASSISTANT SECRETARY
Stefania Moyers

Frank Yablans Presentations, Inc.

%20th Century-Fox, 10201 W. Pico Blvd., Los An-
geles, CA 90064 (Motion picture producer.)
PRESIDENT
Frank Yablans
DATE OF ORGANIZATION
1975

The Saul Zaentz Company Film Center

2600 Tenth St., Berkeley, CA 94710. (415) 549-
1528/1529. (Motion picture production and rental of
complete post-production facilities)
PRESIDENT
Saul Zaentz
PRODUCTION EXECUTIVE
Nancy Eichler
DIRECTOR, POST-PRODUCTION FACILITIES
Michael Cunningham

Zanuck/Brown Company

20th Century-Fox Studio, Box 900, Beverly Hills,
CA 90213 (213) 203-3215. (Production of motion pic-
tures, theatrical and TV.)
PRESIDENT
Richard D. Zanuck
VICE PRESIDENT
David Brown
SECRETARY-TREASURER
Haldon Harrison
DATE OF ORGANIZATION
1972

Zoetrope Studios

529 Pacific Avenue, San Francisco, CA 94133. (415)
788-7500. (Motion picture production and rental of
production facilities.)
PRESIDENT
Robert R. Spiotta
VICE PRESIDENT
Bernard Gersten

498

Theatre Circuits

* **IN THE UNITED STATES**

* **IN CANADA**

* **BUYING AND BOOKING SERVICES**

Theatre Circuits

These listings embrace companies operating three or more theatres and are arranged alphabetically by corporate names. Circuits in Canada follow the U.S. list. Buying and Booking Services follow circuits.

A

Ackerman, Greenberg, Tolchin Theatres

60 E. 42nd St., Suite 3301, New York, NY 10019. (212) 682-6091.

MEYER ACKERMAN, SANFORD GREENBERG, ARTHUR TOLCHIN, J. ROBERT TOLCHIN, chief officers; LOUIS SPRUNG, booker; JAMES PISAPIA, film buyer.
CONNECTICUT—Trumbull: U.A. Trumbull
NEW YORK—NEW YORK CITY: Amboy Twin, Greenwich Twin, Hylan Twin Cinema, Lane Theatre, 57th St. Playhouse, 68th St. Playhouse. WESTCHESTER: Scarsdale Plaza, Cinema 100 Twin, Rye Ridge Twin, Fine Arts.
VERMONT—Bennington: Bennington Twin

Alger Theatres, Inc., The

P.O. Box 31, Lakeview, OR 97630. (503) 947-2023.

DONALD R. ALGER, pres.; NORENE C. ALGER, v.p. & sec.
OREGON—LAKEVIEW: Alger, Circle J-M D.I.

Allen Theatres, Inc.

P.O. Drawer 1500, 208B West Main St., Farmington, NM 87401. Tel.: 325-9313.

LARRY F. ALLEN, pres.; LANE E. ALLEN, v.p.; BOYD F. SCOTT, sec. & gen. mgr.; HALLMARK THEATRE SERVICES, film buyer.
NEW MEXICO—FARMINGTON: Allen, Apache Twin D.I., Totah, Valley D.I., Cameo, Centennial Twin.

Almi Century Theatres

3333 New Hyde Park Road, New Hyde Park, NY 11042. (516) 627-9494.

ALBERT SCHWARTZ and MICHAEL S. LANDES, co-chmn. of bd.; SYLVAN SCHEIN, LEON GREENSBERG, and LOUIS LETTER, exec. v.p.s; ROBERT JORDAN, v.p.; ROBERT WISCO, v.p./secty.; HENRY SCHOENFELD, asst. treas.
NEW YORK—AMITYVILLE: Amityville 1 & 2; BAYSHORE: Bayshore; BROOKLYN: Brook, College, King's Plaza No., King's Plaza So., Kingsway 1, 2 & 3, Midwood, Nostrand; LONG ISLAND: Baldwin; BELLEROSE: Bellerose; FLORAL PARK: Floral; FLUSHING: Meadows 1 & 2, Prospect 1 & 2; FARMINGDALE: Farmingdale; GARDEN CITY: Roosevelt Field 1 & 2; GARDEN CITY PARK: Park East; GLEN OAKS: Glen Oaks; HUNTINGTON: Shore 1, 2 & 3, Whitman, York; LAKE GROVE: Mall, Smith-Haven; NEW HYDE PARK: Alan; PATCHOGUE: Patchogue; PORT JEFFERSON STATION: Franklin; ROCKVILLE CENTRE: Fantasy; VALLEY STREAM: Green Acres; PLAINVIEW: Morton Village, Plainview; WOODMERE: Five Towns; STATEN ISLAND: New Springville, Richmond; NEW ROCHELLE: Mall.
NEW JERSEY—PARAMUS: Paramus 1 & 2.
PENNSYLVANIA—LANCASTER: Park City East & West.

American Multi-Cinema, Inc. (A Durwood Corporation)

1700 Power and Light Bldg., Kansas City, MO 64105. (816) 474-6150.

STANLEY H. DURWOOD, pres.; JOEL RESNICK, v.p., film & real estate; RON D. LESLIE, v.p., operations & finance; EUGENE A. JACOBS, v.p., ARNOLD SHARTIN, v.p.

ALABAMA—MOBILE: Springdale 6.
ARIZONA—MESA: Fiesta Village 6; PHOENIX: Town & Country 6, Metro Village 6; TEMPE: Lakes Plaza 6.
CALIFORNIA—BAKERSFIELD: Stockdale 6; CERRITOS: Alondra 6; COLMA: Serramonte 6; HAWTHORNE: Hawthorne 6; INDUSTRY: Puente 10; LA HABRA: Fashion Square 4; MOUNTAIN VIEW: Old Mill 6; ORANGE: Orange 6; ROSEMEAD: Rosemead 4; SAN BERNARDINO: Central City 4; SAN DIEGO: Fashion Valley 4; SAN JOSE: Oakridge 6, Saratoga 6; SUNNYVALE: Sunnyvale 6.
COLORADO—DENVER: Buckingham 10, Westminster 11, Brentwood 4, Colorado 4; PUEBLO: Southside 4.
FLORIDA—ORLANDO: Interstate 6; BOCA RATON: Boca Mall 6; CLEARWATER: Clearwater 4, Countryside 6; DAYTONA BEACH: Daytona 6; GAINSVILLE: Oaks 6; LAUDERDALE LAKES: Lakes 6; MERRITT ISLAND: Merritt Square 6; MIAMI: Omni 6, Marina 8; JACKSONVILLE: Orange Park 5; PANAMA CITY: Panama City 4; PENSACOLA: Westwood 4; SARASOTA: Sarasota 6; ST. PETERSBURG: Tyrone Square 6, Crossroads 2, 9th Avenue 1; TAMPA: Horizon Park 4, Twin Bays 4, Varsity 6; W. PALM BEACH: Cross County Mall 6. SEMINOLE: Seminole 2; LEESBURG: Lake Square 6.
GEORGIA—ATLANTA: Omni 6, Tower Place 6; Franklin 3.
ILLINOIS—CARBONDALE: University 4; CHICAGO: Ogden 6, Barrington 6; DECATUR: Hickory Point 6.
KANSAS—KANSAS CITY: Indian Springs 10; OVERLAND PARK: Oak Park 6.
KENTUCKY—BOWLING GREEN: Greenwood 6; PADUCAH: Paducah 2.
LOUISIANA—SHREVEPORT: St. Vincent 6.
MARYLAND—GREENBELT: Academy 6; NEW CARROLLTON: Carrollton 6; LAVALE: Country Club 6.
MASSACHUSETTS—HADLEY: Mountain Farms 4; Hampshire 4; SWANSEA: Swansea 4.
MICHIGAN—E. LANSING: Meridian 8.
MISSOURI—KANSAS CITY: Brywood 6, Bannister Square 6, Midland Empire 7; Metro North 6, Metro Plaza 4, Independence Center 2.
NEBRASKA—GRAND ISLAND: Conestoga 4; OMAHA: Six West.
NEW JERSEY—LAWRENCEVILLE: Quaker Bridge 4; ROCKAWAY: Rockaway 12.
NEW YORK—BUFFALO: Como 8, Holiday 6.
NORTH CAROLINA—GREENSBORO: Circle 6.
OHIO—TOLEDO: Southwyck 8, North Towne 5. COLUMBUS: Westerville 6; COLUMBUS: Eastland Plaza.
PENNSYLVANIA—HARRISBURG: East 5, PHILADELPHIA: Woodhaven 4, Bucks Mall 2, Leo Mall 2, Premiere 2.
TENNESSEE—KINGSPORT: Fort Henry 5; KNOXVILLE: Cinema 6.
TEXAS—ARLINGTON: Forum 6; AUSTIN: Northcross 6, Americana 1, Aquarius 4, Southwood 2. DALLAS: Northtown 6, Northwood Hills 4, Park Cities 2, Prestonwood 5; HOUSTON: Alameda 9, Greenway 3, North Oaks 6, Northwest 4, Southway 6, Town & Country 6, Champions Village 2, Festival 6, Kingwood 2, Shamrock 6, Westchose 5, Humble 6; WICHITA FALLS: Sikes Senter 6.
VIRGINIA—BRISTOL: Bristol 6; HAMPTON: Coliseum 4, Newmarket 4; NORFOLK: Circle 10, Showcase 3; PORTSMOUTH: Tower Mall 2; VIRGINIA BEACH: Hilltop 2.
WASHINGTON—SEATTLE: SeaTac 6.
WASHINGTON, DC—Skyline 6.
WISCONSIN—MADISON: University Square 4.

Arista Theatres, Inc.

1501 Broadway, New York, NY 10023. (212) 840-0010.

NICK MARK JUSTIN, pres.; JAMES DUKE, v.p., gen. mgr.; MARC LAFFE, buyer and booker.
NEW YORK—NEW YORK CITY: D. W. Griffith, Cinema Village; QUEENS-FOREST HILLS: Cinemart; WOODHAVEN: Haven; REGO PARK: Drake.

Armstrong Circuit, Inc.

135½ N. Main Street, Box 769, Bowling Green, OH 43402. Tel: (419) 352-5195.

Fred C. Lentz, pres.; Robert Breisacher, gen. mgr. & controller; William Herring, concession mgr.
MICHIGAN—ADRIAN: Studio South Cinemas I & II, Sky DI
OHIO—ATHENS: Athena 1-2-3, Valley DI; BOWLING GREEN: Cla-Zel, Skylite DI, Stadium Cinemas I & II; DAYTON: Belmont Auto Theatre, Sunset Auto Theatre; DEFIANCE: Valentine, Holiday Cinema, Defiance DI; FINDLAY: Findlay DI; FOSTORIA: Starlite DI; MAUMEE: Maumee; MILLBURY: Eastside DI; PORT CLINTON: Ottawa DI; TOLEDO: Parkside DI.

Art Theatre Guild, Inc.

Home Office: P.O. Box 146, Scottsdale, AZ 85252. (602) 947-2426. 1034 Kearny, San Francisco, CA 94133. (415) 391-1073.

LOUIS K. SHER, pres.; ROBERT J. SHER, secty.-treas.; LES NATALI, film buyer; GENE KENT NITZ, gen. mgr.; CLARK F. CRITES, dir. of physical theatres.
ARIZONA—SCOTTSDALE: Kiva, Portofino.
CALIFORNIA—FRESNO: Fine Art; SACRAMENTO: Towne; SAN DIEGO: Academy; SAN FRANCISCO: Presidio, N. Beach Movie, Centre; SAN JOSE: Towne.
ILLINOIS—CHAMPAIGN: Art, Illini.
KENTUCKY—LOUISVILLE: Crescent.
OHIO—AKRON: Art; DAYTON: Art; CLEVELAND: Heights, Westwood; COLUMBUS: Bexley I & II, World; DAYTON: Art; TOLEDO: Westwood; YELLOW SPRINGS: Little Art; YOUNGSTOWN: Foster.
WASHINGTON—SEATTLE: Midtown.

Arthur Enterprises, Inc.

527 N. Grand Avenue, St. Louis, MO 63103.

JAMES ARTHUR, pres.
Management company for Fox Theatre and St. Louis Amusement Co., St. Louis, MO

Ashmun Theatres

Main Office, Strand Theatre Building, 101 So. State Street, Caro, MI 48723. Tel (517) 673-3033; 2440; 2214.

R. J. ASHMUN and R. D. ASHMUN, owners, R. D. ASHMUN, gen. mgr.
MICHIGAN—BAD AXE: M-53 D.I.; CARO: Caro D.I., Strand; EAST TAWAS: Tawas D.I.

Associated Theatres of Kentucky, Inc.

4050 Westport Road, Suite 106, Louisville, KY 40207 (502) 893-0221.

HENRY I. SAAG, pres.; DOLORES SHERFICK, dir. of adv.
KENTUCKY—ELIZABETHTOWN: State, Cinema, Starlite D.I., Knox D.I.; LEXINGTON: Crossroads I & II, Downtown Cinema, Kentucky; LOUISVILLE: Village 8 Theatres, J-Town Theatres, Kentucky, Preston D.I.; South Park D.I.

Auto-Cine Inc.

1400 W. 28th Street, Grand Rapids, MI 49509. (616) 532-6302.

JOHN D. LOEKS, pres.; FRANK THOMAS, gen. mgr.
MICHIGAN—MT. PLEASANT: Cinema I, Cinema II; GRAND RAPIDS: Alpine I, Alpine II; MUSKEGON: Cinema Four Theatre; KALAMAZOO: Plaza 2; ST. JOSEPH: Southtown Twin.

B

B.A.C. Theatres, Inc.

100 S. Charles St., Belleville, IL 62220.

FLORENCE BLOOMER, pres.; HARRY BLOOMER, v.p.; STEVEN J. BLOOMER, treas. & gen. mgr.; CLARK CHILDERS, film buyer and booker.
ILLINOIS—ALTON: Starlight Drive-In 1 & 2, B.A.C. Cine, Eastgate Cinema 1 & 2; BELLEVILLE: B.A.C. Cinema, Ritz III, Skyview Drive-In, Fairview Cinema 1 & 2, B.A.C. French Village Drive-In (Belleville Area); CAHOKIA: Plaza Twin Cine, Cahokia D.I.; CENTRALIA: B.A.C. Cinema, Illinois Theatre 1 & 2, Hollywood Drive-In; COLLINSVILLE: Miners.

B & B Movie Co.

Box 171, Salisbury, Mo 65281. (816) 388-5219.

ELMER BILLS, S.H. BAGBY, and BOB BAGBY.
MISSOURI—CALIFORNIA: Cinema; FULTON: Cinema I & II, King Cal D.I.; HOLT SUMMIT: Plaza I & II

Balaban, H. & E. Corp.

190 N. State Street, Chicago, IL 60601. (312) 372-2262.

ELMER BALABAN, pres. & treas.; DICK BALABAN, booker; DAVID SANDINE, maintenance.
ILLINOIS—CHICAGO: Milford; DES PLAINES: Des Plaines.

Bass & Parsley Amusement Co.

Box 392, Rockdale, TX 76567. (806) 446-3435.

H. LEE PARSLEY, JR. and GEORGE L. BASS, owners.
TEXAS—CALDWELL: Belle D.I.; ROCKDALE: Dixie, Rockdale D.I.

Benfield Theatres, Inc.

P.O. Box 218, Valdese, NC 28690 (704) 874-2721.

J. KENNETH BENFIELD, pres.
NORTH CAROLINA—HICKORY: Carolina; Hickory D.I.; LOUISBURG: Louisburg, Car View D.I.; SHELBY: Rogers, Sunset D.I.

Benitez Theatres

Weslaco, TX 78596

M. BENITEZ, SR., owner & pres.; R. BENITEZ, treas.; M. BENITEZ, JR., gen. mgr. & booking agent; H. BENITEZ, asst. booker.
TEXAS—DONNA: Rio; EDCOUCH: Texas; EDINBURG: Alameda, Roxy; ELSA: Alameda, Roxy; SANTA MARIA: Mexico; SANTA ROSA: Lux; LA VILLA: Grande; WESLACO: Iris, Nacional.

Berger Amusement Co.

922 Plymouth Bldg., Minneapolis, MN 55402. (612) 333-6481.

BENJ. BERGER, pres.
MINNESOTA—CLOQUET: Chief; DETROIT LAKES: Cinema, Skyview D.I.

Bills Theatres Inc.

Lyric Theatre, Box 171, Salisbury, MO 65281. (816) 388-5219.

ELMER E. BILLS JR., owner.
MISSOURI—BROOKFIELD: Lin-Vu D.I.; MARCELINE: Star D.I.; MOBERLY: State, Hiway 63 D.I., 4th St. Cinema; SALISBURY: Lyric; BRUNSWICK: El-Jon.

Blumenfeld Theatres

1521 Sutter St., San Francisco, CA 94109. Tel.: (415) 563-6200.

JOSEPH BLUMENFELD, chief executive, ROBERT BLUMENFELD, booker & supervision, NATHAN BLUMENFELD, purchasing agent, MAX BLUMENFELD, concessions, ALLAN BLUMENFELD, real estate & chief financial officer.

CALIFORNIA—DANVILLE: Village; NOVATO: Novato; OAKLAND: Roxie II; SACRAMENTO: Esquire I & II; SAN JOSE: Meridian 1, 2, 3, 4, 5, 6; SAN FRANCISCO: Regency I, Regency II, Royal, Royal, Alhambra I, Alhambra II, San Francisco Experience; TIBURON: Playhouse.

Gene Boggs Enterprises

P.O. Box 229, Lake Hamilton, AR 71951 (501) 624-2713 & 624-0659.

EUGENE L. BOGGS and ERNESTINE M. BOGGS, partners.

ARKANSAS—BENTON: Boggs Twin Cinema; HOT SPRINGS: Gene Boggs Twin Cinema; LITTLE ROCK: Chicot Center Cinema; OSCEOLA: Murr Theatre & Osceola Drive In; STUTTGART: Gene Boggs Twin Cinema; WEST HELENA: Gene Goggs Twin Cinema & Dixie Drive In.

Harry Brandt Booking Office Inc.

229 W. 42nd Street, New York, NY 10036. (212) 921-0011.

RICHARD BRANDT, chm. of bd.; JOE INGBER, pres. & chief buyer; RICHARD HORN, head booker

CONNECTICUT—AVON: Avon Park N & S; DERBY: Valley Cinema I & II; GROTON: Groton Cinema I & II; MYSTIC: Village Cinema I & II; NORWICH: Norwich Cinema I & II; WATERFORD: Waterford Cinema; GREENWICH: Greenwich Plaza I, III, DANBURY: Cine I, II, III, Cinema I & II, Palace I, II, III; STAMFORD: Avon I & II, Landmark Sq. I. II, III, Ridgeway; STORRS: College Twin I & II.

INDIANA—CLARKSVILLE: TransLux Gold & Blue.

NEW HAMPSHIRE—CONCORD: Concord.

NEW JERSEY—EMERSON: Town; MOUNT HOLLY: Lumberton Cinema I & II; MORRISTOWN: Community; PARLIN: Sayrewood; SAYREVILLE: Cinema 9; TENAFLY: Bergen; UNION CITY: Cinema, Summit; WESTFIELD: Westfield Cinema I & II.

NEW YORK—BUFFALO: Granada; CHAMPLAIN: Northway D.I.; COPAKE: Copake; BROOKLYN: Commodore, Regent, Williamsburg; BRONX: City Cinema I & II; QUEENS: Cross Island Cinema I & II, Whitestone; Earle, Jackson Heights; Rochdale, Jamaica; MANHATTAN: Cosmo, Empire, Essex, Liberty, Lyric, Midtown, Selwyn, Times Square, Victory, TransLux Gotham; LONG ISLAND: Hauppauge Theatre, Hauppauge, Islip I, II, III, Islip; Mayfair, Commack; Mattituck: I & II; Mattituck; Merrick, Merrick; Sayville, Sayville; Suffolk, Riverhead; Hampton Arts, Westhampton; WESTCHESTER: Cinema 22, Bedford Village; Town; New Rochelle; Town I & II, New City; Cinema 45, Spring Valley; NO. TONAWANDA: Riviera.

OKLAHOMA—MUSKOGEE: TransLux Gold & Blue

VIRGINIA—RICHMOND: TransLux Gold & Blue.

Brecher Theatres

43 West 61st St., New York, NY 10023. (212) 757-0290.

WALTER BRECHER, pres.

NEW YORK—NEW YORK; 68th St. Playhouse.

Broumas Showcase Theatres

P.O. Box 41047, Bethesda, MD 20014.

JOHN G. BROUMAS, pres.; RUTH D. BROUMAS, sectytreas.; IRVING COOPERSMITH, v.p.-buyer.

MARYLAND—CAMP SPRINGS: Andrews Manor; CUMBERLAND: Center, Light Cinema, Potomac D.I., Super 51 D.I.; GRANTSVILLE: Garrett Cinema; GREENBELT: Beltway Plaza; McCOOLE: Hi-Rock D.I.; OXON HILL: Oxon Hill; ROCKVILLE: Rockville Mall I & II, Pike; WALDORF: Waldorf I & II; WESTERNPORT: tri-Towns I & II; WHEATON: Mercado, Wheaton Plaza I, II & III.

VIRGINIA—ALEXANDRIA: Hybla Valley I & II, Beacon Mall IV; ANNANDALE: Bradlick; FAIRFAX: Fairfax Circle, Fair City Mall III, Super 29 D.I., Turnpike, University III; HERNDON: Herndon I & II, MANASSAS: Mall Cinema, Manaport, Reb Yank; McLEAN: McLean; SPRINGFIELD: Rolling Valley Mall III; VIENNA: Vienna.

WASHINGTON, DC—Embassy, Tenley Circle I, II & III.

Budco Quality Theatres, Inc.

P.O. Box 389, Doylestown, PA 18901.

CLAUDE J. SCHLANGER, pres.

DELAWARE—CLAYMONT: Naamans D.I. Theatre; NEWARK: Bronmar, Cinmea City; WILMINGTON: Cinema 141, Concord Mall Cinema, Edgemoor, Pleasant Hill D.I., Prices Corner D.I., Cinemart.

FLORIDA—NORTH PALM BEACH: Twin City Cinema I & II; MIAMI: Northside #1 and #2; POMPANO BEACH: Palm-Aire I, II & III; TAMPA: Floriland Cinema I & 2; TEQUESTA: Lighthouse Cinema; WEST PALM BEACH: Century City Theatre I & II.

NEW JERSEY—CHERRY HILL: Community Barclay Farms Theatre, Ellisburg Circle Cinema; DELRAN: Millside Twin I & II; OAKLYN: Ritz; PENNSAUKEN: Pennsauken D.I.; PRINCETON: Prince Theatre I & II; TRENTON: Ewing D.I. Theatre; VINELAND: Delsea D.I., landis., Vineland Cinema I & II.

PENNSYLVANIA—ALLENTOWN: Capri, Super Skyway D.I.; ARDMORE: Suburban-Ardmore; BRYN MAWR: Bryn Mawr; CHAMBERSBURG: Southgate; CLIFTON HEIGHTS: Family D.I.; COLUMBIA: Columbia D.I.; CONSHOHOCKEN: Plymouth Cinema, Ridge Pike D.I.; DOYLESTOWN: County, Barn Cinemas I, II, III & IV; EXTON: Exton Cinema I & II, Exton D.I.; HATBORO: Hatboro; LANCASTER: Eden Theatre; Wonderland Cinema I & II; MORRISVILLE: Morrisville D.I.; NESHAMINY: Bucks County D.I.; PHILADELPHIA: Andorra Theatre I & II, City Line Center Theatre I & II, Esquire, Goldman Theatre I & II, Midtown, Olde City Cinema II, Orleans Theatre Cinemas I & II, Regency Theatre I & II, 61st Street D.I.; QUAKERTOWN: Quakertown Theatre I & II, Starlite D.I.; ROYERSFORD: HiWay D.I.; SPRINGFIELD: Cinema 1 & 2; SPRING HOUSE: 309 Cinema I & II, 309 D.I.; SWARTHMORE: College; THOMASVILLE: Lincoln D.I.; WAYNE: Anthony Wayne Theatre, Gateway Cinema I, II & III; WEST CHESTER: 202 D.I.; YORK: Hiway Theatre, Stony Brook D.I., York Cinema I & II.

Butterfield Circuit

21311 Civic Center Drive, Southfield, MI 48037. (313) 352-4520.

Operating W. S. Butterfield Theatres, Inc., Butterfield Michigan Theatres Co., Carley Amusement Company; J. R. Denniston Theatre Company.

LYLE W. SMITH, pres.; J. W. STERLING, v.p. & secty.; W. R. BLENMAN, treas.

MICHIGAN—ALLEGAN: Regent; ALPENA: State; ANN ARBOR: Campus, State 1, 2, 3, 4, University D.I.; BATTLE CREEK: Auto D.I., West Point D.I., Bijou, Towne, Cinema 1 & 2; BAY CITY: State; BIG RAPIDS: Big Rapids; EAST LANSING: Campus I & II, State; FLINT: Cinema, Genesee Valley 1-2-3-4, Town Cinema 1, 2, 3 & 4, Northland D.I., South Dort D.I., West Side D.I.; GRAND BLANC: Bella Vista, Cinema 1 & 2; GRAND RAPIDS: Eastbrook, Vista D.I.; GREENVILLE: Silver; HILLSDALE: Dawn; HOLLAND: Holland, Park, Starlight D.I.; IONIA: Ionia; JACKSON: Plaza Cinema 1, 2 & 3, Michigan; KALAMAZOO: Beacon Cinema 1 & 2, Campus, State, Douglas D.I., Portage D.I.; LANSING: Lansing D.I., Starlite D.I., Michigan; LUDINGTON: Lyric; MANISTEE: Vogue; MONROE: Denniston Cinema 1 & 2, Dennison D.I.; NILES: Ready; OWOSSO: Capitol; PORT HURON: Huron 1 & 2; SOUTH HAVEN: Michigan; TRAVERSE CITY: Plaza Cinema 1 & 2, State 1 & 2,; YPSILANTI: Wayside.

C

CAPA, LTD.

950 Bonifant Street, Silver Spring, MD 20910. (301) 587-8450.

IRWIN R. COHEN, pres.; PAUL ROTH, v.p.; NORMON FALK and AARON SEIDLER, film buyers; WAYNE ANDERSON, gen. mgr.; PHIL RIDEJOUR, dist. mgr.

MARYLAND—CUMBERLAND: Center, Light Cinema, Super 51 D.I.; FROSTBURG: Cinemas, 1, 2, 3; WESTERNPORT: Tri-Towns 1 & 2.
PENNSYLVANIA—CARLISLE: Carlisle; GETTYSBURG: Majestic Village 1 & 2; GREENCASTLE: Stateline D.I.
VIRGINIA—WINCHESTER D.I.

Carey & Alexander

Lebanon, IN 46052. Tel.: 482-5330.

J. P. ALEXANDER
INDIANA—ATTICA: Devon; LEBANON: Avon, Sky-Vue Drive-In.

Carisch Theatres, Inc.

330 S. Walker St., Wayzata, MN 55391; (612) 473-4291.

GEORGE L. CARISCH, pres.; GERALD F. CARISCH, v.p.; JAMES ELLIS, film buyer; ROBERT H. SAARANEN, mgr. operations.
IOWA—WATERLOO: Crossroad 7.
MINNESOTA—ALBERT LEA: Broadway Twin, Starlight Drive-In; AUSTIN: Sterling Twin, Starlite Drive-In; MANKATO: Cine 2, Mall 4, Twin Star Drive-In; WAYZATA: Wayzata; WINONA: Cine 4; OWATONNA: Cameo 2; ROCHESTER: Starlight 1, 2, 3, Drive-In.
MONTANA—BILLINGS: Cine 4, Fox 1 & 2, Sage 1, 2, 3, 4 Drive-In; GREAT FALLS: Fox Holiday, Cine 4, Twilite 1 and 2, Twilite Drive-In, Village Twin; BUTTE: Fox.
NORTH DAKOTA—MINOT: Cine 5, Starlite Drive-In.
SOUTH DAKOTA—WATERTOWN: Plaza I & II, East Park Drive-In.
WISCONSIN—RICE LAKE: El Lago, Auto Vue Drive-In.

Carnahan & Hughes

Manchester, KY 40962; (502): LYric 8-5861.

J. F. CARNAHAN, purchasing agent.
KENTUCKY—CAMPTON: Wolfe; MANCHESTER: Family D.I., Manchester; McKEE: McKee, Hill Top D.I.; MOUNT VERNON: Valley D.I.; RICHMOND: Richmond D.I.; SAND GAP: Sand Gap.

Carrolls' Development Corp.

(See CinemaNational)

Central States Theatre Corp.

500 Empire Bldg., Des Moines IA 50307. (515) 243-5287.

MYRON BLANK, pres., treas.; JACQUELINE BLANK, v.p., asst. sec., E. Ray Jackson, sec., asst. tres.
IOWA—ALGONA: Algona, Starlite D.I.; ALTOONA: New Starlight D.I.; AMES: Ames, Century I & II, Mall 1 & 2, Varsity, Ranch D.I.; BURLINGTON: West 1 & 2, Palace, Drive In; CEDAR FALLS: Cinema I, II, III; Regent, Hillcrest D.I.; CEDAR RAPIDS: Cedar Rapids Twin D.I., Collins Road D.I.; COUNCIL BLUFFS: Council D.I.; DES MOINES: Capitol D.I., S.E. 14th St. D.I.; DUBUQUE: Dubuque D.I.; FORT DODGE: Cinema I & II, Fort Dodge D.I.; CENTERVILLE: Majestic; CHARLES CITY: Charles City D.I., Charles; CLINTON: Capri, Cinema 1, Drive-In; GRINNELL: Cinema, Drive-In; IOWA CITY: Astro, Englert, Iowa, Cinema I & II; MASON CITY: Palace, Park 70, Drive-In; NEWTON: Capitol, Drive-In; OELWEIN: Oelwein D.I.; OSKALOOSA: Rivola, Drive-In; OTTUMWA: Capitol, Capri, Drive-In; WATERLOO: Sky-Vue D.I., Starlite D.I.
NEBRASKA—COLUMBUS: Columbus I & II, Columbus D.I.; FREMONT: Cinema I, II & III, Empress, D.I.; HASTINGS: Rivoli, Strand, Hastings D.I.; KEARNEY: World, D.I.; NORFOLK: Cinema I, II & III, D.I.; YORK: Sun, D.I.; OMAHA: Golden Spike D.I., 76 & West Dodge D.I.

Chakeres Theatres

State Theatre Bldg., Springfield, OH 45501. Tel.: 323-6447-8-9.

M. H. CHAKERES, pres. & chairman of the board; GRANT FRAZEE, gen. mgr.; WALLEY ALLEN, film buyer; PHILIP CHAKERES, booker.
OHIO—ATHENS: Varsity Cinema; CELINA: Celina, Lake D.I.; COLUMBUS: Cinema North I & II, Cinema East, North

High D.I. I, II, III; Holiday D.I. I & II, East Main D.I.; DAYTON: Southtown Twin Cinemas, Page Manor Cinemas I & II, Mall Cinema I, II, III & IV, Southland 75 Twin D.I., Cinema North I & 2, Ketterling Cinemas 1 & 2, Cinema Center 1 & 2, Washington Sq. Cinema, Cinema South; Melody 49 D.I.; FAIRBORN: Fairborn, Twin Cinemas I & II, Skyborn D.I.; HILLSBORO: Colony: Cinema, Hocking D.I.; NEW CARLISLE: Park Layne D.I.; PIQUA: Cinema I & II, Piqua 36 D.I.; PORTSMOUTH: Scioto Breeze D.I.; SIDNEY: Sidney 1, 2 & 3; SPRINGFIELD: Regent 1 & 2, State, Melody Cruise-In 1 & 2; ST. MARY'S: St. Mary's Cinema; TROY: Troy-Dixie D.I.; URBANA: Urbana Cinema I-II, Champaign Auto; WILMINGTON: Murphy, Wilmington D.I.; XENIA: Xenia Cinema I-II, North Xenia D.I.
KENTUCKY—ASHLAND: Trail D.I.; DANVILLE: Starlite D.I.; FRANKFORT: Brighton Park Twin Cinemas, Franklin Square Cinemas I & II, Starway D.I.; HARRODSBURG: Twin Hills D.I.; MOREHEAD: University Cinema, Trail Cinema; WINCHESTER: Leeds, Sky Vue D.I.

Chertcoff, Harry, Circuit

419 E. King Street, Lancaster, PA 17602.

LEAHAD THEATRES, INC.
PENNSYLVANIA—LANCASTER: King I & II LANCASTER DRIVE-IN THEATRES, INC.
PENNSYLVANIA—LANCASTER: Sky-Vue Drive-In.

Cinema Centers Corp.

39 Church Street, Boston, MA 02116. (617) 482-3410.

(See Theatre Management Services).

Cinema Entertainment Corp.

Box 1126, St. Cloud, MN 56301. (612) 251-9131.

ROBERT A. ROSS, pres.; DAVID M. ROSS, sec.; GEORGE R. BECKER, treas.; STANLEY McCULLOCH, booker.
IOWA—WATERLOO: Crossroads I, II, III & IV.
MINNESOTA—BRECKENRIDGE: Ridge; DULUTH: Kenwood 1 & II, Skyline D.I., Cinema I & II; ST CLOUD: Cinema 1 & II, Cloud Outdoor, 10 Hi D.I., Cinema Arts; MOOREHEAD: Moonlite D.I.
NORTH DAKOTA—FARGO: Cinema I & II, Cinema 70, Starlite D.I., Gateway; WAHPETON: The Cinema, Valley D.I.

Cinema 5 Theatres

1500 Broadway, New York, NY 10036. (212) 354-5515.

RALPH E. DONNELLY, v.p. & gen. mgr.
NEW JERSEY—UNION: Fox.
NEW YORK—ALBANY: Colonie 1 & 2; MANHATTAN: Art, Beekman, Gramercy, D.W. Griffith, Sutton, Murray Hill, Cinema I, Cinema II, Cinema 3, Paris, Plaza, Manhattan I & II; BROOKLYN: Albermarle; STATEN ISLAND: Fox, Plaza I & II; LONG ISLAND: Hicksville Twin North, Hicksville Twin South, Wantagh, Hewlett, Fox, East Setauket.

CinemaNational

968 James St., Syracuse, New York 13203 (315) 424-0513. (A Division of Carrols Development Corp.)

HERBERT N. SLOTNIK, bd. chmn.; DAVID J. CONNOR, pres.; ROBERT M. RODMAN, v.p. operations; JACK CLARK, v.p., mktg. & adv.; AMERICAN THEATRE MANAGEMENT CORP., booking agent, 488 Madison Ave., New York, NY 10022, (212) 758-9588.
NEW YORK—BINGHAMTON: Cinema 1 & 2, Crest; BROCKPORT: Strand, Studio; ENDICOTT: Cinema, Towne; JOHNSON CITY: Airport D.I., Oakdale Mall, Cinemas 1, 2, 3; LATHAM: Cinema 7; LOCKPORT: Cinema 1 & 2; MIDDLETOWN: Cinema; NANUET: Mall Cinema; OSWEGO: Cinema; POUGHKEEPSIE: Dutchess Cinema, 9-G D.I.; ROME: Cinema 1 & 2; SCHENECTADY: Mohawk Mall Cinemas 1, 2, 3; SYRACUSE: Cinema East, Cinema North, Bayberry, Fayetteville Mall Cinemas 1, 2, 3, Genesee, Mini-1, Penn Can Mall Cinemas 1, 2, 3, Shop City Cinema, Shoppingtown Cinemas 1 & 2, Tri-County Mall Cinema, Westhill; UTICA: Cinema New Hartford, Marcy D.I., New Hartford D.I., Paris Cinema, Riverside Mall Cinemas 1, 2, 3, Skyler D.I. 1 & 2; VESTAL: V-D.I.

NORTH CAROLINA—DURHAM: South Square Mall Cinemas 1, 2, 3, 4.

Cinemette Corporation of America

107 Sixth St., Pittsburgh, PA 15222. Tel.: (412) 232-0042.

ERNEST A. STERN, pres. & chm. of bd.; GEORGE STERN, v.p.; FRANK FALCIONE, treas.; RICHARD STERN, secty.; PAUL SIMENDINGER, dir., adv. & operations; JOHN VENTURO, JR., dir., maintenance & purchasing; RAYMOND H. OLMO, dir., concessions; MELVIN MEYERS, KENNETH KURTZMAN, WILLIAM BROOKS, RICHARD STERN, bookers; JOANNA FORSTY, PATRICIA HODDER, media buyers.
MAINE—ELLSWORTH: Maine Coast Cinemas I & II; OLD TOWNE: University Cinemas I & II.
NEW HAMPSHIRE—CONWAY: North Conway; GORHAM: Grandview Drive-In; WEST LEBANON: Valley Cinemas I & II.
OHIO—KENT: Cinemas I & II, Plaza Cinemas I & II; NORTHFIELD: Northfield Plaza I & II, Northfield Drive-In; ST. CLAIRSVILLE: Ohio Valley Quad (under construction); SOLON: Solon Square; STEUBENVILLE: Cinemas III, Cinema, Grand; YOUNGSTOWN: Liberty Plaza, Lincoln Knolls, Uptown.
PENNSYLVANIA—ALLISON PARK: Hampton Plaza I & II; ALTOONA: Park Hills Quad; BETHEL PARK: South Park Drive-In; BUTLER: Penn Cinemas I & II, Pioneer Drive-In, Plaza; CLARION: Garby, Orpheum; CONNEAUT LAKE: Lakeside Drive-In; CRANBERRY: Ski-Hi Drive-In; EDINBORO: Village Cinemas, Drive-In; ERIE: Cinema 18, Cinema World I, II, III, & IV, Eastway I & II, Peninsula Drive-In I & II, Plaza, Strand; GREENSBURG: CINEMA World I, II, III, & IV, Westmoreland Mall Quad; GROVE CITY: Larkfield Drive-In, Guthrie; IMPERIAL: Penn Lincoln Drive-In; INDIANA: Cinema; IRWIN: Blue Dell D.I.; JEFFERSON BOROUGH: Colonial Drive-In, Echo Drive-In; LIBRARY: Fairgrounds Drive-In; McMURRAY: Crest, Mt. Lebanon Drive-In I & II; MEADVILLE: Cinemas I & II; MONACA: Movie World; MONROEVILLE: Cinema 22, Cinemette East I, II, III, & IV; MURRAYSVILLE: Miracle Mile Drive-In; NEW CASTLE: Cinema; NORTH HUNTINGDON: Maple Drive-In; NORTH VERSAILLES: Eastland I & II; OIL CITY: Drake Cinema; PITTSBURGH: Belleview Cinemas I & II, Camp Horne Drive-In, Cinemette South I & II, Denis I & II, Fiesta, Forum, Fulton, Fulton-Mini, Gateway, Hollywood, Kings Court, Manor I & II, McKnight Cinemas, North Hills, Penn Hills, Regent, Squirrel Hill, Village, Warner; PLEASANT HILLS: Cinema World I, II, III, & IV; PLEASANT UNITY: Rustic Drive-In; SHARON: Basil, Cinema World I, II, III, Columbia; SOMERSET: Cinema 219; STATE COLLEGE: Cinema I & II, Flick, State; TRANSFER: Reynolds Drive-In; WASHINGTON: Cinema 19 Twin, Midtown, Route 19 Drive-In, Washington Mall Twin.
RHODE ISLAND—WOONSOCKET: Cinema IV, Walnut Hill Cinemas I, II, III.
WEST VIRGINIA—CHARLESTON: Owens Drive-In, Virginian, Walnut Grove; MORGANTOWN: Warner I, II, & III, Mountaineer Mall I & II; WHEELING: Coronet, Court, Victoria, Warwood I & II.

Cluster Circuit

119 South Broadway, Salem, IL 62881. 548-0310.

LOREN & STEWART CLUSTER, co-managers.
ILLINOIS—SALEM: Salem, Cluster Drive-In.

Cobb Theatres

924 Montclair Road, Birmingham, AL 35213. Exec. Off. Omni International, 190 Techwood Dr. N.E. Atlanta, GA 30303: Booking Off.

R. C. COBB, owner, pres.; NORM LEVINSON, exec. v.p.; JOE LEE, v.p. & film buyer; JOSEPH MOORE, v.p., IRV RICHLAND, v.p.
ALABAMA—BIRMINGHAM: Brookwood I & II, Cinema I & II, Cinema City I, II, III, IV, V, VI, VII, & VIII, Eastwood Mall I & II, Empire, Fairpark I & II, Greensprings I, II, III, IV, V & VI, Melba, Midfield I & II, Mustang D.I., Village East I & II, Vestavia; CLANTON: Mart I & II; SELMA: Cahaba I & II; TUSCALOOSA: Cobb I & II, Tide I & II, Capri.
FLORIDA—BELLEVIEW: Belleview Square I & II; BRADENTON: Cortez I & II; ENGLEWOOD: Palm Plaza I & II; FORT MYERS: Cinema I & II, Colonial I, II & III, Cape Coral I & II, McGregor I, II, III & IV; FORT MYERS BEACH: Beach; NORTH FORT MYERS: I, II & III; FORT PIERCE: Village I & II; JUPITER: Jupiter I, II & III; KEY WEST: Cinema I & II, Plaza I & II; MELBOURNE: Sarno Plaza I

& II; NAPLES: Coastland I & II, Gulfgate I & II, Kon Tiki; NEW PORT RICHEY: Embassy I, II, III, IV, V & VI, Southgate I & II; PALM BAY: Port Malabar I & II; PENSACOLA: Showtown D.I. I & II; PORT CHARLOTTE: Prominades I & II; PUNTA GORDA: Harbor; ST. LUCIE: St. Lucie I, II & III; STUART: Mayfair I & II; Smithfield I, II & III; VENICE: Jacaranda I & II, Venice I & II; VERO: Oslo I, II & III; VERO BEACH: Plaza
GEORGIA—CARROLLTON: Village, Mall I & II.
MISSISSIPPI—OXFORD: Cinema I & II, Ritz.
TENNESSEE—MEMPHIS: Fare I, II, III & IV, Frayser I, II & III.
PUERTO RICO—SAN JUAN: New Broadway, Isla Verde I & II; CAUGUAS: Bairoa I & II; FAJARDO: Cinema I, II & III; VIRGIN ISLANDS-ST. THOMAS: Four Winds I, II, III & IV.

C.J. Collier Circuit

P.O. Box Drawer B., Cleveland, MS 38732. (601) 843-4037.

MISSISSIPPI—CLEVELAND: Ellis, Cleveland Twin Cinema; Chief D.I.

Columbia Amusement Co., Inc.

Arcade Theatre Bldg., Paducah, Ky 42001. (502) 443-2381.

JOHN W. KEILER II, Pres. and gen. mgr.; STEVE KEILER, asst. to pres.; GLENN SCHRADER, booker, buyer and purchasing agent; WILLIAM E. ROETTEIS, adv. dir.
KENTUCKY—PADUCAH: Arcade, Columbia 1 & 2, Paducah D.I., South Twin D.I.

Columbia Amusement Co., Inc.

144 Elmora Avenue, Elizabeth, NJ 07202. (201) EL 4-1555.

NEW JERSEY—ELIZABETH: Elmora; MAPLEWOOD: Maplewood; ROSELLE PARK: Park.

Columbia Basin Theatres

Box 1057, Ephrata, WA 98823. (206) 754-3982.

JACK BARBER, owner, real estate; JACK BARBER, owner-operator.
WASHINGTON—EPHRATA: Lee; ELLENBURG: Liberty, Village, Ellen D.I.; MOSES LAKE: Lake, Skyline D.I.; SOAP LAKE: Park D.I.; OTHELLO: Sunset D.I.; COULEE DAM: Village Cinema.

Commonwealth Theatres, Inc.

215 West 18th Street, Kansas City, MO 64108. (816) 474-3050.

RICHARD H. OREAR, bd. chmn.; DOUGLAS J. LIGHTNER, vice chm. of bd.; DALE N. STEWART, pres.; EARL W. DOUGLASS, v.p.; RICHARD H. SPENCER, secty.; DAVID H. KRAUSE, treas.; DARRELL MANES, eastern div. mgr.; PHIL BLAKEY, western div. mgr.
BRANCH OFFICES: 6060 N. Central Expressway, Suite 638, Dallas, TX 75206 (214) 361-9786; 88 Steele St., Denver, CO 80206 (303) 399-6900.
ARKANSAS—BATESVILLE: Melba, White River D.I.; FAYETTEVILLE: 112 D.I., 62 D.I.; HARRISON: Lyric, Mall Twin 1 & Ozark D.I.; HOT SPRINGS: Malco 1 & 2; MOUNTAIN HOME: Village Twin; PINE BLUFF: Malco, Saenger, Flick Twin, Zebra D.I., Broadmoor Cinema 1 & 2, Pines Drive-In; ROGERS: Twin City D.I.; SEARCY: Rialto, Dixie D.I.; SPRINGDALE: Grove D.I.
COLORADO—ARVADA: Arvada Plaza, Wadsworth D.I.; AURORA: East DI, Havana D.I.; BROOMFIELD: Norwest D.I.; CANON CITY: Skyline, Sunset D.I.; DENVER: Paramount, Target Village Triplex, U-Hills 1, 2 & 3, Continental, Cooper-Cameo, Flick; ENGLEWOOD: Cinderella Twin D.I.; LAKEWOOD: Colfax D.I., West D.I., LA JUNTA: Fox, La Junta D.I.; LITTLETON: Cherry Knolls 1 & 2, South D.I.; ROCKY FORD: Grand; THORNTON: North Star D.I., Thornton 1, 2 & 3; WHEATRIDGE: Lakeside Twin; BOULDER: Basemar 1 & 2, Flatirons, Village, Holiday Twin D.I.; FT. COLLINS: Aggie, Campus West, Foothills Twin; LOVELAND: Orchards Twin; GREELEY: Cooper Twin, Greeley Mall Twin, Wilshire Twin; COLORADO SPRINGS: Mail of the Bluffs Twin, Rustic Hills, Rustic Hills North Twin, Cooper 1-2-3, Ute 70; PUEBLO: Pueblo Mall Cinema 1-2-3, East D.I.,

Lake D.I., Pueblo D.I.; NORTHGLENN: Northglenn I & II; WESTMINISTER: North D.I.
IDAHO—BOISE: Fairvu Cinema 1-2-3; Overland Park Cinema 1-2-3, Fairvu D.I., Meridian D.I., Broadway D.I.
IOWA—CRESTON: Strand.
KANSAS—ARKANSAS CITY: Burford; ATCHISON: Fox, Frontier 1 & 2; BELLEVILLE: Blair, Blair D.I.; EMPORIA: Fox, Petite 1 & 2, 50-S Drive-In; GARDEN CITY: State, Garden D.I.; GOODLAND: Sherman; GREAT BEND: Village Twin 1 & 2, Crest, Great Bend D.I.; HUTCHINSON: Cinema 1, Cinema 2, Flag, Southutch D.I., Airport D.I.; JUNCTION CITY: Colonial, Junction, Kaw Midway D.I.; LAWRENCE: Cinema Twin 1 & 2, Granada, Hillcrest 1, Hillcrest 2, Hillcrest 3, Varsity, Sunset D.I.; LIBERAL: South Gate 1 & 2, Tucker, Great Western D.I.; MANHATTAN: Campus, Varsity, Wareham, West Loop 1, West Loop 2, Sky-Vue D.I.; OTTAWA: Plaza, Hillcrest D.I.; OVERLAND PARK: Ranch Mart 1, Ranch Mart 2, Ranch Mart 3, Ranch Mart 4, Valley View 1 & 2; PARSONS: Parsons, Parsons D.I.; PRATT: Barron, Trail D.I.; SHAWNEE: Trailridge 1, 2 & 3; WICHITA: Crest, Twin Lakes 1, Twin Lakes 2, Sunset, Terrace D.I., Meadowlark D.I., Twin D.I., Pawnee 1, 2, 3, 4.
MISSOURI—CHILLICOTHE: Ben Bolt; CLINTON: Crest, 52 D.I.; COLUMBIA: Cinema, Film Arts, Hall, Missouri, Uptown, Sky-Hi D.I.; JOPLIN: Crest D.I., Tri-State D.I.; KANSAS CITY: Crest D.I. 1, Crest D.I. 2; MONETT: Gillioz, Ozark D.I.; PARKVILLE: Riverside D.I.; ROLLA: Ritz, Uptown, Rolla D.I.; SEDALIA: State Fair 1 & 2; Fox, Uptown, 50 Hiway D.I.; SPRINGFIELD: Hi-M D.I.; Holiday D.I., Queen City D.I. 1, Queen City D.I. 2, Sunset D.I., TRENTON: Plaza, Grand-Vu D.I.; WARRENSBURG: Campus 1, Campus 2, Star, Starlet D.I.; WASHINGTON: Calvin, Sunset D.I.; WAYNESVILLE: Woodlane D.I.
MONTANA—MISSOULA: Village Twin.
NEBRASKA—ALLIANCE: Alliance, CHADRON: Eagle, Starlite D.I.; GRAND ISLAND: Grand, Grand Island D.I. 1, Grand Island D.I. 2; LINCOLN: Cooper, Plaza IV; NORTH PLATTE: Pawnee D.I.; OMAHA: Indian Hills, Cameo; SCOTTSBLUFF: Bluffs, Midwest, Carena D.I.; SUPERIOR: Crest.
NEW MEXICO—ALAMOGORDO: Sierra, Sands, Starlite D.I., Yucca D.I.; ALBUQUERQUE: Coronado 1, 2, 3 & 4, Cinema East 1, Cinema East 2, Eastdale, Hiland, Lobo, Los Altos 1, Los Altos 2, Montgomery Plaza 1, II, III, Winrock Twin, 66 Drive-In, Sunset D.I.; CARLSBAD: Yucca Twin, Cavern, Big Sky D.I., Fiesta D.I.; CLOVIS: La Fonda Twin D.I., State, Lyceum, Hilltop 1, Hilltop 2; GALLUP: EL Morro, Chief, Zuni D.I., Aztec Plaza I & II; HOBBS: Broadmoor, Frontier, Reel, Flamingo East D.I., Flamingo West D.I.; LOVINGTON: Lea, Wildcat D.I.; PORTALES: Tower Twin, Varsity D.I.; ROSWELL: Park Twin 1 & 2, Plains, Yucca D.I., Starlite D.I. 1, Starlite D.I. 2; SANTA FE: Coronado 1 & 2, Capital, The Movies 1 & 2, Lensic, Pueblo D.I.; TUCUMCARI: Odeon.
OKLAHOMA—MIDWEST CITY: Apollo I & II, NORMAN: Heisman 1, 2, 3, 4, Hollywood; OKLAHOMA CITY: Reding 1, 2, 3, 4, Quail Twin I & II, Sooner Drive-In I & II.
SOUTH DAKOTA—HOT SPRINGS: Hot Springs; LEAD: Homestake; RAPID CITY: Rushmore 3 Cinema, Northgate 1 & 2; Elks, Rapid Pines D.I., Sioux D.I.; YANKTON: Broadway Cinema, Dakota, Yankton D.I.
TEXAS—FT. STOCKTON: Pecos, Trail D.I.; GAINESVILLE: State, Hi-Ho D.I.; GEORGETOWN: Palace, Holiday D.I.; GONZALES: Lynn; GRAHAM: Graham D.I.; HEREFORD: Star, Texas, Tower D.I.; PECOS: State, Texan D.I.; UVALDE: El Lasso, Stardust D.I.
UTAH—SALT LAKE CITY: Elks Twin, Flick 1 & 2.
WYOMING—CASPER: America, Beverly Plaza 1, Beverly Plaza 2, Rialto, Terrace D.I., Mile-Hi D.I.; CHEYENNE: Cole Square Twin, Paramount Motor-Vu D.I.; DOUGLAS: Mesa; LARAMIE: Wyo, Skyline D.I.; NEWCASTLE: Dogie, Wyo D.I.; RIVERTON: Acme, Gem, Knight D.I.; ROCK SPRINGS: White Mt. Twin.

Community Theatres

3000 Town Center, Suite 1780, Southfield, MI 48075. (313) 358-1680.

IRVING, ADOLPH & FREDERICK S. GOLDBERG
MICHIGAN—DETROIT: Adams, Bel Air D.I. I & II, Adams; FARMINGTON: Grand River D.I.; OAKPARK: Westside D.I.; ROSEVILLE: Gratiot D.I. 1 & 2.

Connet Theatres

Box 421, Roxy Theatre, Newton, MS 39209.

MAX A. CONNETT, pres. and gen. mgr.
ALABAMA—ANDALUSIA: Martin, Fendley D.I.; ATMORE: Strand; BAY MINETTE: Rex; BREWTON: Ritz, Eagle D.I.; EVERGREEN: Pix; GREENVILLE: Ritz, Camellia D.I.; OPP: Dixieland D.I.

MISSISSIPPI—BAY SPRINGS: Lyric; FOREST: Town; KOSCIUSKO: Strand; NEWTON: Roxy; WINONA: Winona.

Consolidated Amusement Co., Ltd.

P.O. Box 3737, Honolulu, HI 96812.

HAWAII—ISLAND OF HAWAII: (Hilo) Waiakea I, II, III, (Kona) Hualalai I, II, III; ISLAND OF OAHU: Aikahi, Asian Cinema 1 & 2; Cinerama, Hawaii, Kailua D.I., Kam D.I., #I & II, Kapiolani, Kuhio I & II, Liberty, Pearlridge I, II, III & IV, Toyo, Varsity, Waikiki I, II, III; ISLAND OF MAUI: Maui Theatre.

Co-op Theatres of Michigan.

23300 Greenfield Rd., Suite 127, Oak Park, MI 48237 (313) 967-0400

ROBERT BUERMELE, pres.
MICHIGAN—AUGUSTA: Park; BAD AXE: Bad Axe; BALDWIN: Pine-Aire D.I.; BOYNE CITY: Boyne; BRONSON: Bronson; BROOKLYN: Star; CHEBOYGAN: Kingston, Cheboygan D.I.; CLARE: Ideal; CORUNNA: Skyway D.I.; DOWAGIAC: 5 Mile D.I.; EAST TAWAS: Family; GRAND RAPIDS: Alpine I & II, Studio 1-2-3-4-5-6, Beltline D.I., Plainfield D.I., Woodland D.I.; GRAYLING: Rialto; HALE: Gem; HARTFORD: Sunset D.I.; KALAMAZOO: Eastowne 1-2-3-4-5, Plaza I & II; LOWELL: Strand; MEREDITH: Meredith D.I.; MT. PLEASANT: Broadway, Cinema I & II, Ward; MUSKEGON: Cinema 1-2-3-4, Harbor, Auto D.I., Getty D.I., North D.I.; OSCODA: Lake; PETOSKEY: Gaslight, Northland D.I.; ROSCOMMON: Strand; ST. HELEN: Northwoods D.I.; ST. JOHNS: Clinton, Family D.I.; STURGS: Strand; WEST BRANCH: Midstate.

Roy Cooper Company

988 Market St. Suite 711, San Francisco, CA 94102.

GLENN COFFEY, gen. mgr.; ADELAIDE S. COOPER, bd. chmn; SUSAN GILLESPIE, adv., pub. head; BARBARA MANNHEIMER, PAULA HARRIS, AL CAMILLO, film buyer; ARNOLD LAVAGETTO, booker
CALIFORNIA—BELMONT: Belmont Triplex Cinemas; CUPERTINO: Oaks Triplex; DAVIS: Cinema II Theatre, Varsity Twin Cinemas; JACKSON: Jackson Cinemas 4; LIVERMORE: Vine Twin Cinemas; OAKLAND: Lux Theatre; SAN MATEO: Manor Twin Cinemas; SONORA: Sonora Plaza Twin Cinemas; SUNNYVALE: Cinema Hacienda Triplex; TULARE: Tower Square Cinemas; VACAVILLE: Vacaville Theatre; VISALIA: Tower Plaza Cinemas.

Cornell Theatres, Inc.

1055 West Genesee Street, Post Office Box 1093, Syracuse, NY 13201, (315) 472-6341.

WILLIAM P. BERNINSTEIN, pres.; HENRY W. BERINSTEIN, exec. v.p.
NEW YORK—DRYDEN: Dryden Drive-In; ITHACA: State I, State II, Ithaca, Cinema; BIG FLATS: Elmira Drive-In

Crown Cinema Corporation

406 West 34th St., Kansas City, MO 64111.

RICHARD M. DURWOOD, pres.; MRS. ROSALIE WISE, office mgr.; MRS. CINDY KEESLER, secty.; EVERETT HUGHES, operations supervisor.
KANSAS—LEAVENWORTH: Skylark D.I., Landing 4 Theatres; TOPEKA: Gage 4 Theatres.
MISSOURI—JEFFERSON CITY: Ramada 4 Theatres, Capital II Theatres, Bridge D.I.; ST. JOSEPH: Hillcrest 4; Belt D.I.; Skylark D.I.

D

Dalke's Theatres, Inc.

138 N. Main Woodstock, VA 22664 (703) 459-2221

WILLIAM DALKE, JR., pres.-treas.: KATHRYN S. DALKE v.p.; J. TIMOTHY DALKE, Secty & Gen. Mgr.

VIRGINIA—STEPHENS CITY; Family D.I.; STRAS-
BURG: Home; WOODSTOCK: Community; PENNSYLVA-
NIA: College Cinema.

DeWitt Theatres

P.O. Box 277, 215 S. Harrison St., Shelbyville, IN
46176 (219) 318-7318.

(A subsidiary of TGJ Amusement Corp.)
ELMER N. DeWITT, pres. & film buyer; JAMES DeWITT,
v.p.; RICHARD DELANEY, secty.
INDIANA—CONNERSVILLE: Times; GREENSBURG:
Holiday D.I.; SHELBYVILLE: Cinema A, B and C, Skyline
D.I. I and II; RUSHVILLE: Princess.

Dickinson Operating Co., Inc.

5913 Woodson Road, Mission, KA 66202. (913) 432-
2334.

GLEN W. DICKINSON, JR., bd. chm.; KENT DICKIN-
SON, pres.; WOOD DICKINSON, SCOTT DICKINSON,
GEORGIA DICKINSON, LEON HOOFNAGLE, JERRY
DICKSON, PAUL KELLY, v.p.s. EARLE LOVE, sec./treas.
ILLINOIS—QUINCY: Quincy Mall Cinema I, II, & III.
KANSAS—HAYS: Fox; HUTCHINSON: Fox; NEWTON:
Fox; OLATHE: Trail; OVERLAND PARK: Metcalf, Glen-
wood I & II, PITTSBURGH: Cinema, Fox, Pittsburg D.I.;
SALINA: Fox, Vogue, Midstates I & II, Sunset Plaza I & II,
81 D.I.; TOPEKA: Chief D.I., Cloverleaf D.I., Dickinson,
Fairlawn I & II, Fox Whitelakes I & II; WICHITA: Boulevard,
Fox Garvey I & II, Mall Cinema.
MISSOURI—BRANSON: Tablerock I & II; CARTHAGE:
66 D.I.; COLUMBIA: Biscayne I, II & III, Forum; GLAD-
STONE: Gladstone I, II, III, IV; JOPLIN: Eastgate I, II &
III, Northpark I & II; KANSAS CITY: Antioch I & II, Plaza
I & II; KIRKSVILLE: Kennedy; MACON: Macon; MONROE
CITY: Monroe; ST. JOSEPH: Fox East Hills, Trail; SPRING-
FIELD: Century 21, Fox, Fremont I, II & III, Gillioz, Tower;
WEBB CITY: Webb City D.I.
NEBRASKA—OMAHA: Fox Westroads I & II.

Dickinson Theatre Co.

15 E. Villard St., Dickinson, ND 58601. (701) 225-
9910.

F. S. HALLOWELL, pres; owner.
NORTH DAKOTA—Dix I & II, Hillcrest D.I.

Dipson Theatres, Inc.

P.O. Box 579, Batavia, NY 14020. (716) 343-2700.

NEW YORK—BATAVIA: Cinemas I & II, Mall I & II, Ba-
tavia D.I.; BUFFALO: Amherst I, II & III, Colvin, Kensing-
ton, North Park, Plaza North, Broadway D.I.; DUNKIRK: Van
Buren D.I., Cine, Regent; ELMIRA: Capitol, Colonial, Elmira
Cinemas I, II, III, Heights Roxy D.I.; FREDONIA: Cinema
I; HORNELL: Cinemas I & II; JAMESTOWN: Chautauqua
Mall Cinemas I & II, Lakewood D.I., Palace, Pic 17 D.I., Win-
tergarden; LEROY: LeRoy; NEWARK: Rose City D.I.; WEST-
FIELD: Westfield D.I.
PENNSYLVANIA—BRADFORD: Cinemas I & II.

Dubinsky Bros. Theatres

Lincoln Office: 326 Stuart Bldg., P.O. Box 82849;
Lincoln, NE 68501. Des Moines Office: 1024 Walnut,
P.O. Box 1475, Des Moines, IA 50306.

SARGE DUBINSKY, pres.; CARL HOFFMAN, film buyer
(Des Moines office); DICK GLENN, adv.-pub. director (Des
Moines office.)
ILLINOIS—Moline, Rock Island, Rockford, Collinsville,
Galesburg, Macomb.
MINNESOTA—Austin.
MISSOURI—Cape Girardeau, Springfield.
NEBRASKA—Lincoln, Omaha, Grand Island.
IOWA—Sioux City, Des Moines, Marshalltown, Cedar Rap-
ids, Ft. Madison, Davenport, Waterloo, Dubuque.

Dubuque Theatre Corp.

75 J. F. Kennedy Road, Dubuque, IA 52001. (319)
588-4639.

N. J. YIANNIAS, pres.; CAI SCHMIDT, asst.
IOWA—DUBUQUE: Cinema Center 1, 2, 3 & 4, Super 20
D.I. East, Super 20 D.I. West.

Durkee, F. H., Enterprises

Arcade Theatre Bldg., 5436 Hartford Rd., Baltimore
MD 21214

FRANK H. DURKEE, III, pres.: C. ELMERNOLTE, Jr.,
v.p. & man. dir.; AUGUST NOLTE, concession mgr.; FRED
G. SCHMUFF, exec. film buyer; SAMUEL B. TEMPLE, div.,
mgr.
MARYLAND—ANNAPOLIS: Plaza I & II, Circle, Eastport,
I & II; BALTIMORE: Boulevard I & II, Glenburnie Mall
Grand, Liberty I & II, Patterson I & II Senator, North Point
D.I.; BELAIR: Harford I & II.

E

E. & W. Management Co.

(See Wisper & Westman)

East-Towne 5 Theatre, Inc.

1400 28th St., S.W., Grand Rapids, MI 49509. (616)
532-6302.

JOHN D. LOEKS, pres.; FRANK THOMAS, gen. mgr.
MICHIGAN—KALAMAZOO: Eastowne 5 Theatres.

Eastern Federal Corp.

513 So. Tryon St., Charlotte, NC 28202 (704) 377-
3495.

IRA S. MEISELMAN, pres.; L. A. POSTON, v.p. & treas.;
P. E. LLOYD, secty; JACK DURELL, film buyer; C. H.
DEAVER, dir. of adv.-pub.
FLORIDA—JACKSONVILLE: Cedar Hills 1 & 2, Town &
Country 1 & 2, Royal Palm 1, 2 & 3, Fox D.I. 1 & 2, Midway
D.I. 1 & 2, Northside 1 & II; TALLAHASSEE: Varsity 1, 2
& 3, Miracle 1, 2 & 3; GAINESVILLE: Royal Park 1, 2, 3 &
4; ORLANDO: Orange Blossom 1 & 2, Conway 1 & 2, North-
gate, 1, 2, 3 & 4.
NORTH CAROLINA—CHARLOTTE: Regency 1, 2 & 3,
Manor; CHAPEL HILL: Varsity, Plaza 1, 2 & 3; FAYETTE-
VILLE: Miracle, Fox 1, 2 & 3; LUMBERTON: Town & Coun-
try 1, 2, 3 & 4; ROCKINGHAM: Cinema 1 & 2.
GEORGIA—ATLANTA: Baronet, Coronet, Belvedere 1 &
2, Ben Hill 1 & 2, Cobb Cinema, Miracle 1 & 2, Town &
Country 1 & 2, North Springs 1 & 2.
SOUTH CAROLINA—COLUMBIA: Atlantic 1 & 2.

Edgerton Theatres, Inc.

Warren Amusements, Inc.

205 Roanoke Ave., Roanoke Rapids, NC 27870. (919) 537-
3409.
LYLE M. WILSON, secty. and gen. mgr.
NORTH CAROLINA—ROANOKE RAPIDS: Peoples Theatre, Gaston D.I.

Ellis, A. M., Theatres Co.

1737 Chestnut St., Philadelphia, PA 19103. (215)
563-8441.

MARTIN B. ELLIS, gen. mgr.
NEW JERSEY—BORDENTOWN: Dix D.I.
PENNSYLVANIA—BALA-CYNWYD: Bala; PHILADEL-
PHIA: Benner, Castor, Crest, Erlen, Tyspn, ALLENTOWN:
Plaza; JENKINTOWN: Hiway.

Elray Theatres, Inc.

26 Main St., Springfield VT 05156. (802) 885-3131.

WALT ELLIS, pres.; RAY ELLIS, v.p.; ELEANOR ELLIS, secty.
VERMONT—SPRINGFIELD: Ellis; BELLOWS FALLS: Falls Cinema.

Esquire Theatres of America, Inc.

46 Church St., Boston, MA 02116. (617) 482-4310.

S. G. MINASIAN, pres.; P. J. SCUDERI, treas.; ROBERT P. BARSAMIAN, v.p. & clerk.
MAINE—BRUNSWICK: Cinema I, Cinema II; PORTLAND: Cinema I-II-III, Paris Cinema; AUGUSTA: Cinema I & II.
MASSACHUSETTS—BROCKTON: Colonial, Penthouse; PITTSFIELD: Paris Cinema; BOSTON: Kenmore Square Cinema, Park, Paris Cinema; WORCESTER: Paris Cinema I & II; SPRINGFIELD: Parkway D.I.; LOWELL: Cinema I-II-III-IV, Strand, Lowell D.I., Wamest D.I.; MEDFORD: Medford Irwin D.I.
NEW HAMPSHIRE—KEENE: Plaza Cinema I & II; CONCORD: Cinema 93.
NEW YORK—UTICA: 258 Cinema 1, 2 & 3, Paris Cinema; LITTLE FALLS: Valley D.I.
RHODE ISLAND—WAKEFIELD: Campus; NARRAGANSETT: Pier; SMITHFIELD: Rt. 44 D.I.; PROVIDENCE: Four Seasons I-II-III-IV; NEWPORT: Newport D.I.

Essaness Theatres Corp.

54 W. Randolph St., Chicago, IL 60601. (312) 332-7465.

JACK SILVERMAN, chmn. of bd.; ALAN SILVERMAN, pres.; EDWARD ROCKSKA, sr. v.p.; JACK BELASCO, exec. v.p.; SUSAN SILVERMAN, v.p.; JOSEPH STANCHER, v.p. construction; BILL TAN, adv. & booking; ROBERT PERSA, cont.; LARRY HANSON, v.p.
ILLINOIS—ARLINGTON HEIGHTS: Town 'n Country Six-Plex; CHICAGO: Lincoln Village, Woods, Plaza Tri-Plex; HOFFMAN ESTATES: Century Tri-Plex; HOMEWOOD: Diana Tri-Plex; MONEE: Cicero Twin Outdoor; MORTON GROVE: Morton Grove; NILES: Golf Mill; RIVERDALE: Halsted Twin; ST. CHARLES: Arcada, Foxfield Tri-Plex, St. Charles Tri-Plex; TINLEY PARK: Bremen Tri-Plex, I-80 Outdoor.
INDIANA—HAMMOND: Hammond Twin Outdoor.
WISCONSIN—BELOIT: Prairie Tri-Plex; DELEVAN: Delevan Twin; FRANKLIN: 41-Outdoor 4-Plex; GREEN BAY: Bay Tri-Plex, West, Valley Outdoor, Starlite Outdoor; JANESVILLE: 26 Outdoor, Mid-City Outdoor; KENOSHA: Lake Twin, Mid-City Kenosha Outdoor, Keno Outdoor; LAKE GENEVA: Geneva Twin; SHEBOYGAN: Stardusk Outdoor; WAUKESHA: 59-Outdoor.

F

F.L.W. Management Co.

(See Wisper & Wetman)

Fall River Theatres Corp.

214 Harvard Ave., Boston, MA 02134. (617) 232-1400.

EDWARD W. LIDER, pres.; ALFRED ODDIE, gen. mgr.
MASSACHUSETTS—ALLSTON: Allston Twin Cinema; BOSTON: Exeter St. Theatre; CAMBRIDGE: Galeria Cinema; DARTMOUTH: Dartmouth D.I.; FAIRHAVEN: Fairhaven D.I.; FALL RIVER: Center Twin Theatre; NEWTON: Academy Twin Cinema; SEEKONK: Bay State D.I.; SOMERSET: Somerset D.I.; WESTPORT: Westport D.I.
NEW HAMPSHIRE—BEDFORD: Bedford Grove D.I.; HANOVER: Nugget Twin Cinema; HOOKSET: Sky Bay D.I.; MILFORD: Milford D.I.; NASHUA: Nashua D.I.
RHODE ISLAND—TIVERTON: Ponta D.I.

Family Theatres, Inc.

2909 S. Sheridan St., Tulsa, OK 74129.

MARJORIE J. SNYDER, owner
OKLAHOMA—OKLAHOMA CITY: Shepherd Twin; TULSA: Boman Twin, Spectrum Twin, Plaza 3, Park Lane.

Fletcher Theatres of Alaska

Box 276, Seward, AK 99664. (907) 224-5418.

W. E. FLETCHER, pres.
ALASKA—KENAI: Kambe; KODIAK: Orpheum; SEWARD: Liberty.

Floyd Enterprises, Inc.

P.O. Box 367, Haines City, FL 33844.

CARL FLOYD, bd. chm. & chief exec. officer.
FLORIDA—ARCADIA: Arcadia 1 & 2 AUBURN-DALE: Dale D.I.; AVON PARK: Hilans; BRADENTON: Bradenton D.I.; BROOKSVILLE: Brooksville 1 & 2, #41 D.I.; CLEARWATER: Carib, Thunderbird D.I., Gulf Bay D.I.; DADE CITY: Pasco, Joy Lan D.I.; DAYTONA: #1 D.I., Nova Road D.I.; DELAND: Boulevard D.I.; EDGEWATER: Fun Lan D.I.; HAINES CITY: Lake Haines D.I.; LAKELAND: Filmland D.I., Silver Moon D.I., Lakeland D.I.; ORLANDO: Pine Hill D.I., Orange Ave. D.I.; Prairie Lake D.I., Rimar D.I.; PALMETTO: Skyway D.I.; SARASOTA: Teatro Theatre; SEBRING: Sevon D.I., Southgate; TAMPA: Skyway D.I., Fun Lan, 20th Century, Tower, Auto Park; TARPON SPRINGS: Mall Theatre, Midway D.I.; VENICE: Twin I, Twin II; WAUCHULA: Star Lite D.I.; WINTER GARDEN: Starlite D.I.; WINTER HAVEN: Ritz, Haven Dale D.I., Continental; LAKE WALES: Wales D.I.; PLANT CITY: Starlite D.I., Mall I & II; SANFORD: Movieland D.I., Plaza; PALATKA: Plaza, NEW PORT RICHEY: Southgate; FT. MYERS: Edison, North Side D.I., South Side D.I.
GEORGIA—HAZELHURST: Trail D.I.; STATESBORO: South Side D.I.

The Forty Second Street Company

Executive office: 229 West 42nd St., New York, NY 10036. (212) 730-0300.

NEW YORK—MANHATTAN: Empire, Liberty, Lyric, Selwyn, Times Square, Victory.

Martin Foster Enterprises

582 Market St., Suite 900, San Francisco, CA, 94104.

MARTIN M. FOSTER, SYLVIA K. FOOTE, PHILIP HARRIS, HELENA R. FOSTER, chief officers.
CALIFORNIA—ALBANY: Albany 1 & 2; BERKELEY: Act I & II, Cinema, California Cinema Center A, B, C; OAKLAND: Piedmont Cinema.

Fourth Avenue Corporation

Suite 356 Francis Bldg., Louisville, KY 40202. (502) 582-2608.

D. IRVING LONG, pres.
INDIANA—LAFAYETTE: East Side D.I., Lafayette, Mars, Cinema West; TERRE HAUTE: North D.I., Corral D.I.
KENTUCKY—LOUISVILLE: Twilite D.I.

Fox Theatres, Inc.

1700 Walnut St., Philadelphia, PA 19103. (215) 732-5252.

STEVEN FOX, pres.
NEW JERSEY—BRIDGETON: Bridgeton D.I.; BURLINGTON: Burlington D.I., Fox, High; EDGEWATER PARK: Super 130 D.I.; MAPLE SHADE: Roxy; MOORESTOWN: Criterion; MT. HOLLY: Fox, Holly; RIVERSIDE: Fox; TRENTON: Fox; VINELAND: Delsea D.I.; WILDWOOD: Wildwood Twin D.I.; WILLINGBORO: Fox I & II; PENNSAUKEN: Pennsauken D.I.
PENNSYLVANIA—BRISTOL: Grand, Lewistown, Towne, Roosevelt D.I.; PHILADELPHIA: Colonial, Devon Hill, Liberty, Mayfair, Merlin; LEVITTOWN: Fox, Towne I & II; MIDDLETOWN TOWNSHIP: Roosevelt D.I.; NORRISTOWN: Norris; CHELTENHAM: Cheltenham; LANGHORNE: Lincoln Plaza Twin.

Franklin Amusement Co., Inc.

1021 E. Franklin Ave., Minneapolis, MN 55404.

O. C. WOEMPER and L. R. FRANK.
MINNESOTA—OWATONNA: Roxy; MINNEAPOLIS: Boulevard, Avalon; WEST ST. PAUL: West.

Frels Theatres, Inc.

210 E. Constitution Street, Victoria, TX 77901. (512) 575-4748.

RUBIN S. FRELS, pres.; EDDIE REYNA, film buyer and booker, GARY DUNNAM, gen. mgr.
TEXAS—EL CAMPO: Normana; VICTORIA: Victoria, Lone Tree D.I., Playhouse, Salem Six; WHARTON: Plaza III.

Fridley Theatres

1024 Walnut St. Des Moines, IA 50309.

IOWA—BOONE: Boone, Boone D.I.; DES MOINES: Sierra 3, Riviera, River Hills Cinerama, Riviera; EMMETS-BURG: Iowa; LAKE CITY: Capri; NEVADA: Camelot; IDA GROVE: King; JEFFERSON: Sierra; NEW SHARON: Capri; PERRY: Perry; POCAHONTAS: Rialto; STORM LAKE: Vista, Corral D.I.; SPENCER: Spencer I, II & III; Corral D.I.; CHEROKEE: American, Corral D.I.; CARROLL: Carroll I & II, Carroll D.I.

Frisina Enterprises, Inc.

100 E. Market, Taylorville, IL 62568. P.O. Box 500, (217) VA 824-2295-6

ROSE MARIE BELL, pres.; WILLIAM P. HOPKINS III, secty. & gen. mgr.
ILLINOIS—CHARLESTON: Charleston D.I., Will Rogers; JACKSONVILLE: "67" D.I., Times; LAWRENCEVILLE: Midway D.I.; LITCHFIELD: Capitol, Sky-view D.I.; MATTOON: Time, Skyway D.I.; MT. OLNEY: Arcadia, Olney D.I.; ROBINSON: Gordon D.I., Lincoln; SHELBYVILLE: Kay D.I.; SPRINGFIELD: Springfield D.I., TAYLORVILLE: Capitol, Frisina D.I.; Cinema 1 & 2.
IOWA—KEOKUK: Grand, Skylark D.I.
MISSOURI—HANNIBAL: Sky-Hi D.I., Huck Finn; MEXICO: Liberty, Little Dixie D.I.

G

G.C.C. Theatres, Inc.

27 Boylston St., Chestnut Hill, MA 02167. (617) 232-6200.

(A subsidiary of General Cinema Corporation.)

MELVIN R. WINTMAN, pres.; PAUL DELROSSI, exec. v.p.; LARRY LAPIDUS, sr. v.p., film; SEYMOUR H. EVANS, v.p. public relations and publicity; HOWARD W. SPIESS, v.p. theatre operations.
ARKANSAS—in NORTH LITTLE ROCK: McCain Mall Cinema I & II.
ARIZONA—PHOENIX: Thomas Mall I & II, Metro Center Cinema I, II, & III, Paradise Mall I, II, III & IV; SCOTTSDALE: Camelback I, II & III.
CALIFORNIA—BAKERSFIELD: Valley Plaza I & II; CONCORD: Sun Valley I & II; FRESNO: Manchester Mall Cinema I & II; HAYWARD: Southland I, II & III; LOS ANGELES: Avco I, II & III; MODESTO: Vintage Fair, Cinema I, II, III, IV; MONTCLAIR: Montclair I, II III, IV, V, VI, VII, & VIII; NORTHRIDGE: Cinema I, II, & III; REDONDO BEACH: South Bay I, II, III & IV; SACRAMENTO: Sacramento Inn I, II & III, SAN BERNARDINO: Inland Cinema I & II; SAN FRANCISCO: Ghirandelli Square; SAN MATEO: Hillsdale I, II & IV; SANTA ANITA: Cinema I, II, III, IV; SHERMAN OAKS: Cinema I, II, III, IV & V; STOCKTON: Sherwood Plaza I & II; VISALIA: Sequoia Mall Cinema I, II, & III; WESTWOOD: Avco Cinema I, II & III; WOODLAND HILLS: Cinemas I, II & III.
COLORADO—AURORA: Aurora Cinema I, II, & III; COLORADO SPRINGS: Citadel I & II; DENVER: Cherry Creek Cinema I & II, Villa Italia Cinema I & II, Cinderella City Cinema I & II, Westland Cinema I & II, North Valley Cinema I & II, South Glen Cinema I, II & III.
CONNECTICUT—MILFORD: Cinema I & II; NEWINGTON: Cinema I & II; WATERBURY: Naugatuck I, II, III & IV.
DELAWARE—WILMINGTON: Christiana Mall I, II & III.
DISTRICT OF COLUMBIA—WASHINGTON: Jenifer Cinema I & II.
FLORIDA—ALTAMONTE SPRINGS: Altamonte Cinema I & II; CORAL GABLES: Riviera I & II; DAYTONA BEACH: Bellair Cinema I & II; FT. LAUDERDALE: 16th St. Cinema, Lauderhill I & II, Galleria I, II, III & IV; HIALEAH: Hialeah

Mall Cinema I, II, & III; JACKSONVILLE: Expressway Mall Cinema I, II & III; LAKELAND: Grove I & II, Imperial Mall I & II; MIAMI: Cutler Ridge Cinema I & II, Westchester I & II; MIAMI BEACH: 170th St. Cinema I & II; ORLANDO: Parkwood Cinema I & II; Seminole Cinema I & II, Fashion Square Cinema I, II, III, IV, V & VI; ORANGE PARK: Orange Park I, II, III & IV; PINELLAS PARK: Pinellas Square Cinema I, II & III; PLANTATION: Broward Mall I, II, III & IV; POMPANO: Cinema I & II; SARASOTA: Gulfgate Mall Cinema I & II; ST. PETERSBURG: 5th Avenue Cinema, I & II, Gateway Mall Cinema I & II; TAMPA: Britton Cinema, I, II & III; University Square Cinema I, II, III & IV, Tampa Bay Cinema I & II, Eastlake Square Cinema I, II, III; W. PALM BEACH: Cinema 70.
GEORGIA—ATHENS: Georgia Square I, II, III & IV; ATLANTA: Perimeter Mall Cinema I, II, III & IV; Northlake Mall Cinema I, II, III; Akers Mill Square Cinema I, II, III & IV; Southlake Cinema I, II & III; AUGUSTA: Regency Mall Cinema I, II, & III.
ILLINOIS—CARPENTERSVILLE: Meadowdale Cinema I, II, III, IV & V; CHICAGO: Ford City Cinema I, II, III, IV, V & VI; BLOOMINGTON: Eastland Mall Cinema I, II & III; CHAMPAIGN: Marketplace I, II, III & IV; DECATUR: Northgate I, II & III; DEERFIELD: Deerbrook Mall Cinema I & II; JOLIET: Jefferson Cinema I, II & III, Louis Joliet I, II, & III; LOMBARD: Yorktown Cinema I, II, III & IV; NORTH RIVERSIDE: Cinema I & II; MATTESON: Lincoln Mall Cinema I, II & III; MT. PROSPECT: Mt. Prospect Cinema I & II, Randhurst Cinema I & II; PEKIN: Pekin Mall Cinema I & II; WAUKEGAN: Belvidere Mall I & II, Lakeshurst Cinema I, II, & III; HANOVER PARK: Tradewinds I & II; SPRINGFIELD: White Oaks Cinema I, II, III, IV & V.
INDIANA—ANDERSON: Mounds Mall Cinema I & II; BLOOMINGTON: College Mall I, II & III; GARY: Ridge Plaza Cinema I & II; GRANGER: University Park Cinema I, II, & III; University Mall Cinema I, II, III & IV; INDIANAPOLIS: Glendale Cinema I & II, III, IV, V & VI. Castleton Square I, II, III, IV, V & VI, Lafayette Square Cinema I, II, III, IV, & V, Greenwood Cinema I, II, III & IV, Speedway Cinema I & II; COLUMBUS: Courthouse Square Cinema I & II; KOKOMO: Kokomo Mall Cinema I, II & III, Alpha I & II; MERRILLVILLE: Crossroads Cinema I & II, Southlake Cinema I, II, III & IV; MICHIGAN CITY: Michigan City I, II, III, IV, V & VI; MUNCIE: Northwest I, II & III; GARY: Dunes Plaza I & II; FT. WAYNE: Southtown I, II & III, Northwood Park Cinema I & II; Glenbrook Cinema I, II & III; TERRE HAUTE: Honey Creek I, II & III, Town South Cinema I, II & III.
IOWA—CEDAR RAPIDS: Westdale I, II, III & IV; DAVENPORT: Northpark Cinema I & II; BETTENDORF: Duck Creek Cinema I & II; DUBUQUE: Kennedy Mall I & II; SIOUX CITY: Southern Hills I, II, III & IV.
KANSAS—TOPEKA: Topeka Boulevard Cinema I & II; WICHITA: Towne East Cinema I, II, III, IV, V & VI; Town West I, II, III, IV, & V.
KENTUCKY—LEXINGTON: Turfland Cinema I & II, Fayette Mall Cinema I & II; NEWPORT: Cinema I & II.
LOUISIANA—ALEXANDRIA: Alexandria Mall Cinema I & II; BATON ROUGE: Contana Mall Cinema I, II & III; GRETNA: Oakwood Cinema I, II, III & IV; LAFAYETTE: Arcadiana I, II, III, IV & V; LAKE CHARLES: Prien Lake Cinema I, II & III; METAIRIE: Lakeside Cinema I, II, III, IV & V; NEW ORLEANS: Gentilly Cinema I & II; SHREVEPORT: Quail Creek Cinema I & II, Southpark Cinema I & II.
MAINE—PORTLAND: Maine Mall Cinema I, II & III.
MARYLAND—BALTIMORE: Perring Plaza Cinema I & II, York Road Cinema I & II, Security I & II; GLEN BURNIE: Harundale I & II; COLUMBIA: Columbia City Cinema I & II.
MASSACHUSETTS—BRAINTREE: South Shore Cinema I, II, III & IV; South Shore Twin D.I.; BROCKTON: Cinema Centre I, II, III, IV & V; BURLINGTON: Cinema I, II & III; CAMBRIDGE: Fresh Pond I & II; CHESTNUT HILL: Chestnut Hill Cinema I, II, III, IV & V; FRAMINGHAM: Shoppers' World Cinema I, II, III, IV & V; NORTH DARTMOUTH: Cinema I, II, III & IV; PEABODY: North Shore Cinema I, II & III; HANOVER: Cinema I, II, III & IV; SAUGUS: Cinema I & II; STONEHAM: Cinema I & II; WALTHAM: Cinema I & II; WORCESTER: Cinema I, II & III.
MICHIGAN—FLINT: Dort Mall Cinema I & II; KALAMAZOO: Maple Hill Cinema I, II & III; LIVONIA: Cinema I, II & III; PONTIAC: Cinema I, II & III; ROSEVILLE: Macomb Cinema I, II, & III; SAGINAW: Green Acres Cinema I & II; TROY: Somerset Cinema I, II & III; WARREN: Cinema I, II, III & IV.
MINNESOTA—BLAINE: Northtown Cinema I, II, III & IV; BROOKLYN CENTER: Brookdale East Cinema I, II, III & IV; BLOOMINGTON: Southtown Cinema I & II; EDINA: Southdale Cinema I, II, III, & IV; MINNEAPOLIS: Academy Cinema, Mann Cinema, Orpheum Cinema; ROSEBILLE: Har Mar Cinema I, II, III, IV, V, VI, VII, VIII, IX, X & XI; ST. LOUIS PARK: Shelard Cinema I, II & III.
MISSISSIPPI—JACKSON: Metro Center Cinema I, II, III & IV.

508

MISSOURI—CHESTERFIELD: Chesterfield I, II, III & IV; FLORISSANT: Grandview Cinema I & II, Jamestown Cinema I & II; ST. ANN: Northwest Plaza I & II; ST. LOUIS: Northland Cinema I & II, South County Cinema I & II, Sunset Hills Cinema I, II & III.

NEW HAMPSHIRE—BEDFORD: Bedford Mall Cinema I, II & III; NASHUA: Nashua Mall Cinema I, II, III & IV.

NEW JERSEY—CEDAR KNOLLS: Morris County Cinema I & II; DEPTFORD: Cinema I, II, III, IV, V, & VI; E. BRUNSWICK: Brunswick Square Cinema I & II; JERSEY CITY: Hudson Plaza I & II; LAWRENCEVILLE: Mercer Mall Cinema I, II, & III; MENLO PARK: Cinema I & II, NEW BRUNSWICK: Rutgers Plaza Cinema I & II; OCEAN CITY: Seaview Square I & II; PLAINFIELD: Blue Star I, II & III; SHREWSBURY: Shrewsbury Plaza Cinema I, II & III; TOTOWA: Totowa Cinema I & II; CHERRY HILL: Cinema I & II; W. ORANGE: Essex Green Cinema I, II & III; RARITAN: Somerville Circle Cinema I, II & III; TOMS RIVER: Ocean County Mall I, II & III; VINELAND: Cumberland Mall Cinema I & II; VORHEES TOWNSHIP: Echelon Mall I, II & III; WOODBRIDGE: Woodbridge I & II

NEW MEXICO—ALBUQUERQUE: Mall Cinema I & II, Louisiana Boulevard Cinema I, II, & III.

NEVADA—RENO: Reno—Sparks Cinema.

NEW YORK—AMHERST: University City I, II, III & IV; BUFFALO: Seneca Mall I & II, Boulevard Mall Cinema I, II, III & IV; Eastern Hills I, II & III, Thruway Plaza Cinema I, II & III; YONKERS: Central Plaza Cinema I & II; OSSINING: Arcadian Cinema I & II; ROCHESTER: Westmar Cinema I & II, Todd Mart I & II; HARTSDALE: Cinema I, II, III & IV; NIAGARA: Summit Park I & II; ELMIRA: Cinema-on-the-Mall I & II; MOHEGON LAKE: Westchester Mall Cinema I, II & II; WHITE PLAINS: Galeria I & II.

NORTH CAROLINA—CHARLOTTE: Charlottestown Cinema I, II & III, Southpark Cinema I, II & III, Eastland Mall Cinema I, II & III; FAYETVILLE: Crosscreek Cinema I, II & III; GREENSBORO: 4 Seasons Cinema I, II, III & IV; WINSTON SALEM: Hanes Mall Cinema I, II, III & IV.

OHIO—AKRON: Chapel Hill Cinema I, II & III, Rolling Acres Cinema I, II & III; CANTON: Mellett Mall Cinema I & II; CINCINNATI: Gold Circle Cinema I & II; COLUMBUS: Great Western Cinema I & II, Town & Country Cinema I & II, University City Cinema I & II, Eastland, Northland I & II; MAPLE HEIGHTS: Southgate Cinema I & II; MENTOR: Mentor Mall Cinema I, II & III; PARMA: Parmatown Cinema I, II & III; WILLOWICK: Shoregate Cinema I, II & III; CLEVELAND: Mayland I & II, Mercury I & II, Westgate I, II, III & IV; LIMA: Lima Center I, II & III; MANSFIELD: Richland Mall I, II & III; NORTH RANDALL: Randall Park I, II & III; SPRINGFIELD: Upper Valley I, II & III.

OKLAHOMA—TULSA: Admiral Twin D.I., Southroads Mall Cinema, Village I & II, Woodland Hills I, II & III.

PENNSYLVANIA—MONACO: Beaver Valley Cinema I, II, III & IV; VALLEY FORGE: Cinema I & II; PHILADELPHIA: Walnut Mall Cinema I, II & III, Northeast Cinema I, II, III & IV; SCRANTON: Viewmont Cinema I, II & IV; PLYMOUTH MEETING: Cinema I & II; WILKES BARRE: Wyoming Mall I, II, III, IV & V; ERIE: Mill Creek Cinema I, II, & III; GREENBURG: Greengate Cinema I, II & III; WHITEHALL: Lehigh Valley Cinema I, II, III, IV & V.

RHODE ISLAND—CRANSTON: Garden City Cinema I & II; LINCOLN: Lincoln Mall Cinema I, II, III & IV; WARWICK: Cinema I, II & III.

SOUTH CAROLINA—CHARLESTON: Ashley Plaza Cinema I, II & III, Charlestown Cinema I & II; COLUMBIA: Bush River Mall Cinema I, II, III & IV, Columbia Mall Cinema I, II, III & IV.

TENNESSEE—MEMPHIS: Plaza Cinema I & II, Whitehaven Cinema I & II, Raleigh Springs I & II, Mall of Memphis I, II, III, IV & V, Hickory Ridge I, II, III & IV.

TEXAS—ARLINGTON: Park Plaza Cinema I & II, Seminary South Cinema I, II, III & IV; Six Flags Cinema I, II, III, IV & V; AUSTIN: Capital Plaza Cinema I, II & III, Highland Mall Cinema I & II; DALLAS: Northpark Cinema I, II, III & IV, Treehouse Cinema I & II, Valley View Cinema I & II, Red Bird Mall Cinema I, II, III, IV, V, VI, VII, VIII, IX, X; Prestonwoods I, II, III & IV; EL PASO: Cielo Vista I, II, III, IV, V & VI; HOUSTON: Willowbrook I, II, III, IV, V, VI; Greenpoint Mall Cinema I, II, III, IV, & V, Westwood Fashion Cinema I, II & III, Galleria Cinema I, II & III, Gulfgate Cinema I & II, Meyerland Cinema I, II & III, Northline Cinema I, II & III, Baybrook Mall Cinema I, II, III & IV; MIDLAND: Midland I, II, III & IV; SAN ANTONIO: Ingram Square I, II, III & IV; Northstar Cinema I & II, McCreless Cinema I & II; WACO: Lake Air Cinema I & II; AMARILLO: Western Plaza Cinema I & II; ABILENE: Westgate I & II; BEAUMONT: Gateway I & II, Parkdale Mall Cinema I, II & III; MESQUITE: Town East Cinema I & II; Big Town I & II; IRVING: Irving Mall I, II & III; FT. WORTH: Opera House Cinema, Richland Plaza Cinema I & II; Ridgemar I, II, III, IV & V; GALVESTON: Galvez Plaza I, II & III; RICHARDSON: Richardson Square Cinema I, II & III.

VIRGINIA—LYNCHBURG: River Ridge I, II, III & IV; NORFOLK: Janaf Cinema I, II, III & IV; HAMPTON: Coliseum Mall Cinema I & II; ROANOKE: Tanglewood Mall Cinema I, II, & III; SPRINGFIELD: Springfield Mall Cinema I, II, III, IV, V & VI.

WASHINGTON—BELLEVUE: Overlake Mall Cinema I & II; EVERETT: Everett Mall Cinema I, II, III, IV, V, VI, VII, VIII, IX, X; SEATTLE: Aurora Cinema I, II & III, King Cinema; RENTON: Renton Village Cinema I, II & III; TACOMA: Villa Plaza Cinema I, II & III.

WEST VIRGINIA—PARKERSBURG: Grand Central Cinema I & II; Huntington Cinema I, II, III, IV, V & VI.

WISCONSIN—EAU CLAIRE: London Square Cinema I & II; FOND DU LAC: Forest Mall Cinema I & II; MILWAUKEE: Brookfield Square Cinema I & II, Westlane Cinema I & II; MADISON: East Towne I, II & III, West Towne I, II & III; RACINE: Westgate Cinema I & II.

General Theatre Corp.

6405 Park Avenue, West New York, NJ 07093. (201) UNion 52010.

ALBERT MARGULIES, pres.
NEW JERSEY—UNION CITY: Cinema; WEST NEW YORK: Mayfair; EMERSON: Town.

General Theatres Co.

523 Brainard Place, 29001 Cedar Road, Lyndhurst, OH, 44124.

LEONARD L. MISHKIND, pres; NORMAN BARR, gen. mgr.
OHIO—CLEVELAND: Detroit, LaSalle, Parma, Showplace; ORRVILLE: Orr Twin; BRYAN: Hub Drive In; TIFFIN: Tiffin Drive In; TALLMADGE: East Twin Drive In; CAMBRIDGE: Cruise In Drive In; BRUNSWICK: 42 Drive in.

General Theatrical Company

230 Hyde St., San Francisco, CA 94102. (415) 673-2343.

BEN LEVIN, gen. mgr.
CALIFORNIA—SAN JOSE: Jose.

Georgia Theatre Company

3445 Peachtree Road, N.E. (P.O. Drawer 18707), Atlanta, GA 30326. Telephone: (404) 261-3711.

JOHN H. STEMBLER, pres.; KIP SMILEY, exec. v.p.; DENNIS P. MERTON, sec. & treas.
ALABAMA—GADSDEN: Mall Cinema I, II & III; Gadsden Cinema I & II; Pitman; Rebel D.I.
GEORGIA—ATHENS: Classic I, II & III, Athens D.I.; ATLANTA: Belmont, Cobb Center I, II, III & IV, Greenbriar I & II, Lenox Square I, II, III & IV, South DeKalb I, II, III & IV, Suburban Plaza I & II, Parkaire Twin I & II, Village I & II, Westgate I, II & III, Bankhead D.I., Northeast Expressway D.I. I & II, Roosevelt D.I., South Expressway D.I. I & II, Twin Starlight D.I. I & II, Lithia D.I.; AUGUSTA: Daniel Village I & II, Masters 4 Cinemas 1, 2, 3 & 4, Miller, Southgate, Hilltop D.I., Skyview D.I.; U.S. 25 D.I.; BRUNSWICK: Altama Village Cinema I, II & III, Lanier I & II, Mall Cinema, Sunset D.I.; MACON: Macon Mall Quad Cinemas I, II, III & IV, Cinemas 3, 1, 2 & 3, Westgate I, II, III, IV, V & VI, 41 D.I., Riverside D.I., Southside D.I.; MOULTRIE: Colquitt, Moultrie Twin Cinema I & II, Sunset D.I.; SAVANNAH: Oglethorpe I & II; THOMASVILLE: Gateway Cinemas I & II, Hiwa D.I.; WAYCROSS: Mall Cinemas I & II, Ritz, U.S. #1 D.I.

Giddens & Rester Theatres

Box 16524, Mobile, AL 36616, (205) 476-1970.

KENNETH R. GIDDENS, T. J. RESTER ESTATE, owners; WELDON E. LIMMROTH, gen. mgr., film buyer, booker, W. E. "GENE" WILLIAMS, adv. dir.
ALABAMA—MOBILE: Downtown, Bel Air Cinema I & II, Village 4 (mobile) 6 screen indoor.
FLORIDA—PENSACOLA: Cordova Cinema I & II.
MISSISSIPPI—MERIDIAN: College Park Cinema I, II & III.

509

Glenmar Cinestate, Inc.

(formerly District Theatres Corp.)
Suite 400, One Farragut Square South, Washington, DC 20006. (202) 638-1000.

RONALD NADLER, pres.; RONALD STEFFENSEN, booker.
DISTRICT OF COLUMBIA—WASHINGTON: Lincoln
VIRGINIA—HENRICO COUNTY: Fairfield D.I.; RICHMOND: Cloverleaf Mall I & II, Broad Street Cinema I & II, Plaza Drive-In; SANDSTON: Airport, D.I.; GOOCHLAND COUNTY: Patterson D.I.; FALLS CHURCH: Loehmann's Plaza 1 & 2.
MARYLAND—LANHAM: Palmer D.I.; RANDOLPH VILLAGE: Central Ave. D.I.; RIVERDALE: Riverdale Plaza; LARGO: Hampton Mall 1 & 2; LAUREL: Towne Center 1 & 2, Laurel Twin Cinema 1 & 2; SILVER SPRING: Capri.

Glenoris Corp.

Box 2139, Falls Church, VA 22042.

C. GLENN NORRIS, pres.; BEN G. NORRIS: HARLEY W. DAVIDSON.

Golden Theatre Management Corp.

40 East 49 St., New York, NY 10017.

JEFREY W. DENEROFF, pres.; BERNARD E. GOLDBERG, v.p., film buyer.
NEW YORK—NEW YORK CITY: Brooklyn: Benson Twin, Beverly Twin, Fortway Fiveplex, Oceana Triplex, Rugby Twin; Manhattan: Quad Cinema Fourplex, Olympia Quad.

Goodrich Theaters, Inc.

3565 29th St., SE, Kentwood, MI 49508. (616) 949-8760.

ROBERT EMMETT GOODRICH, pres.; JOSEPHINE DOBROWOLSKI, gen. mgr.
MICHIGAN—ANN ARBOR: Ann Arbor 1 & 2; BATTLE CREEK: W. Columbia 1, 2 & 3; BAY CITY/SAGINAW: Quad 8 1, 2, 3, 4, 5, 6, 7 & 8; BIG RAPIDS: University Drive-In; CADILLAC: Cinema 1 & 2, Cadillac Drive-In; GRAND RAPIDS: 29th Street Quad 1, 2, 3 & 4; Northtown 1 & 2; MANISTEE: Chippewa Drive-In.

Greater Indianapolis Amusement Co., Inc.

Circle Theatre, 45 Monument Circle, Indianapolis, IN 46204.

CHARLES M. REAGAN, pres.; D. IRVING LONG, v.p. & sec.; VERA L. COCKRILL, v.p. asst. sec. & asst. treas.; ANTHONY KERN, treas.
INDIANA—INDIANAPOLIS: Circle, Indiana, Sherman D.I., Tibbs D.I., Greenwood D.I.

Greime & Fasken Theatres

17 South Mission St.; Wenatchee, WA 98801. (509) NOrmandy 2-8052.

WILL D. GREIME, manager.
WASHINGTON—OMAK: Omak; WENATCHEE: Vitaphone, Vue-Dale, Liberty.

Gross-Alaska, Inc.

12040 98th Ave., NE, Suite 102, Kirkland WA (206) 821-5588.

ROBERT W. CALLIES, gen. mgr.
ALASKA—HAINES: Coliseum; KETCHIKAN: Coliseum; JUNEAU: 20th Century; SITKA: Coliseum.

Guild Enterprises, Inc.

2089 Broadway, New York, NY 10023. (212) 873-7107.

NORMAN W. ELSON, pres. and treas.; PETER H. ELSON, exec. v.p.

NEW YORK—NEW YORK: Broadway Embassy (Broadway at 46th St.), Guild (Rockefeller Plaza), Embassy (Broadway at 72nd St.), Embassy 5 (Broadway at 46th St.), and Embassy 2, 3, 4, (7th Ave. and 47th St.).

Gulf International Cinema Corp.
Gulf States Theatres

P.O. Box 51360, New Orleans, LA 70151; Home Office: 510 O'Keefe Avenue, New Orleans, LA, (504) 581-1610.

T. G. SOLOMON, SR., chairman-of-the-board; GARY SOLOMON, pres.; GEORGE SOLOMON, v.p., gen. mgr.; J. E. ALFORD, JR., v.p.; GAYLE CHAMBERS, secty.; VICTOR TALBERT, treas.; GARY GOLDEN, film buyer; BILLY GAY, advertising director.
ALABAMA—MOBILE: Bama Drive-In, Do Drive-In.
LOUISIANA—BATON ROUGE: Cinema 8, University Cinema, Bon Marche, Showtown D.I.; BOGALUSA: Trackside Twin; CROWLEY: Rice; HAMMOND: Hammond Sq., Town & Country Twin, University Twin; HOUMA: Park, Southland Four Plex, Woolco Twin; LAFAYETTE: Nona, Northgate Triple, Westwood, Showtown D.I.; LAKE CHARLES: Oak Park Cinema 6, New Moon D.I.; MONROE: Showtown D.I.; NEW ORLEANS: Plaza Cinema Four, Sena Mall Cinema, Aurora Village Six, Airline D.I., Algiers D.I., Jeff D.I., Westgate D.I.; OPELOUSAS: Vista Village Four Plex, Yam D.I.; SHREVEPORT: Don, Shreve City Twin Cinema, Showtown D.I.; SLIDELL: Tammany Twin Cinema, Tiger D.I.
MISSISSIPPI—BILOXI: Surfside Cinema 4, Beach D.I.; BROOKHAVEN: Haven, Westbrook Twin; GREENVILLE: Cinema 1-82 Four Plex, Showtown D.I.; GREENWOOD: Highland Park Triple; HATTIESBURG: Twin Cinema; JACKSON: Meadowbrook Cinema Six, Town & Country D.I.; LAUREL: Northside Twin; MCCOMB: Camellia Cinema IV, Ren D.I.; MERIDIAN: Royal Cinema Four, Royal D.I.; NATCHEZ: Natchez Mall Cinema IV, Clarke, Tracetown Twin; PASCAGOULA: Twin Cinema, Ritz; VICKSBURG: Battlefield Twin, Joy, Showtown D.I.
TEXAS—TEXARKANA: Oaklawn, Southwest Mall Triple.

H

H. and H. Theatres

P.O. Box 187, Winters, TX 79567. (915) 754-5338.

H. J. HODGE, JR., accountant-partner; co-executor of Midland Group.
TEXAS—MIDLAND: ODESSA: Ector, Grandview Cinema.

Hager Circuit

P.O. Box 174, Madison, WV 25130.

C. D. HAGER, pres.; R. E. BELL, booker.
WEST VIRGINIA—CHAPMANSVILLE: Chapmansville D.I., Hager, Rex; CLOTHIER: Hager; YOLYN: Rum Creek; SETH: Hager; WHARTON: Hager.

Hall Industries Theatres, Inc.

Drawer 'D', Beeville, TX 78102. (512) 358-3233.

H. W. HALL, JR., pres.
TEXAS—ALICE: Rialto, Sage; BEEVILLE: Rialto, Bronco D.I. Plaza Twin; KERRVILLE: Arcadia, Plaza; KINGSVILLE: Texas; SINTON: Rialto; THREE RIVERS: Rialto.

Harris-Voeller Theatres, Inc.

Burley Theatre, Box 278, Burley, ID 83318.

I. G. HARRIS, pres. & gen. mgr.
IDAHO—BURLEY: Burley, Century Cinemas, Harris, Alfresco D.I.; RUPERT: Wilson; PAYETTE: Pay-Out D.I.

Hawk Circuit

239 Virginia St., Salt Lake City, UT 84103. (801) 355-9600.

H. F. HAWK, pres.
NEVADA—CALIENTE: Rex.
UTAH—PANGUITCH: Gem.

Holiday Amusement Co.

1600 Central Parkway, Cincinnati, OH 45210. (513) 381-1111.

JOANNE B. COHEN, pres.; SHIRLEY JONES, PAMM SANDLIN, bookers/buyers.
FLORIDA—ST. PETERSBURG: Garden.
KENTUCKY—BELLEVUE: Marianne; ERLANGER: Village; RUSSELLVILLE: Village, Jesse James D.I.
OHIO—CINCINNATI: Mt. Healthy, Mt. Lookout, Starlite, Hiway 28, Westwood Cinemas I & II, Lake, Auto D.I., Dent D.I., HAMILTON: Acme, Colonial, Court, Holiday, Valley, Village; LANCASTER: Plaza.

Holiday Theatres, Inc.

Midway Mall, 7793 W. Flagler St., Miami, FL 33144. Tel.: (305) 266-5070.

ALEX WEINSTOCK, pres.; PETE DAWSON, v.p.
FLORIDA—HOMESTEAD: New Homestead, Premier, Breezeway D.I.; LAKE WORTH: Holiday Theatre; MIAMI: Holiday, Midway Mall.

Home Theatres Co.

Brainerd Theatre Bldg., Brainerd, MN 56401

FRANK MANTZKE, pres.; PAUL LUNDQUEST, sec.-treas.
MINNESOTA—BRAINERD: Brainerd; ELY: Ely; INTERNATIONAL FALLS: Border, Grand; PARK RAPIDS: Park; THIEF RIVER FALLS: Avalon, Falls.

Hook Theatres

Broad St., Aliceville, AL 35442.

R. E. HOOK, pres.
ALABAMA—EUTAW: Hook; REFORM: Pickens.

Hunt's Theatres, Inc.

Hunt's Shore Building, 3511 Atlantic Avenue, Wildwood, NJ 08260. (609) 522-2420.

W. D. HUNT, pres.; W. L. DRY, sec.-treas.
NEW JERSEY—CAPE MAY: Beach; STONE HARBOR: Harbor, Park; WILDWOOD: Blaker, Shore, Strand, Ocean, Twins I & II.

I

Ideal Theatre, Inc.

607 McEwan Avenue, Clare, MI 48617.

WILLARD KOCH, owner.
MICHIGAN—CLARE: Ideal.

Interstate Amusement, Inc.

P.O. Box 868, Shelby, MT 59474.

LARRY FLESCH, gen. mgr.
MONTANA—CONRAD: Orpheum, Star; CUT BANK: State, Derrick; SHELBY: Roxy, North Star.

Interstate Theatres Corp.

20 Newbury Street, Boston, MA 02116

JAMES M. STONEMAN, pres. & treas.; SOL SHERMAN, v.p. film buyer & booker; CHRISTOPHER JOYCE, v.p. theatre operations; JOSEPH GOLDBERG, v.p. & asst. treas.
CONNECTICUT—CLINTON: Clinton D.I.; MADISON: Madison Cinemas 1 & 2; OLD SAYBROOK: Saybrook Cinemas 1 & 2; ROCKVILLE: Rockville Cinema; QUINEBAUG: Quinebaug D.I.
GEORGIA—ATLANTA: Roswell Mall Cinemas 1, 2, 3 & 4.
MARYLAND—FREDERICK: Frederick Cinema Centre 1, 2 & 3; Frederick Plaza Cinemas I, II & III; HAGERSTOWN: Long Meadow Cinemas I & II.
MASSACHUSETTS—AVON: Avon D.I.; BILLERICA: Billerica Cinema Centre 1, 2 & 3; BROCKTON: Westgate Cinemas I, II, III, IV & V; CHATHAM: Chatham Cinema; DENNIS: Dennis D.I.; DENNISPORT: Dennisport Cinema; GREAT BARRINGTON: Mahaiwe Cinema 1 & 2; HANOVER: Hanover Mall Cinemas I, II, III & IV; HARWICHPORT: Port Cinema; HYANNIS: Cape Cod Mall Cinemas I, II & III, Hyannis Cinema, Hyannis D.I.; MASHPEE: New Seabury Twin Cinemas; MENDON: Milford D.I.; MILFORD: Milford Cinemas I & II, Cinema Center 495, I, II & III; ORLEANS: Cinemas I & II; PLYMOUTH: Standish Plaza Cinemas I & II; STOUGHTON: Stoughton Cinema; YARMOUTH: Cinema 28, I & II, Yarmouth D.I.
NEW HAMPSHIRE—BEDFORD: Bedford Mall Cinemas I, II & III; NASHUA: Nashua Mall Cinemas I, II, III & IV; PLYMOUTH: Plymouth Cinemas 1 & 2.
NEW YORK—WATERTOWN: Stateway Plaza Cinemas I, II & III.
VERMONT—WHITE RIVER JUNCTION: White River D.I.

Irvin—Fuller Theatres

P.O. Box 79, Columbia, SC 29202.

JACK D. FULLER, pres.; SAM L. IRVIN, v.p.; JACK FULLER, JR., film buyer.
NORTH CAROLINA—ASHEVILLE: Plaza Theatre I & II; Merrimon North Theatre, Merrimon South Theatre, Asheville West 1 & 2.
SOUTH CAROLINA—COLUMBIA: Carolina Theatre, Plaza III, Fox Theatre, Jefferson Square Theatre, Dutch Square North & South Twin Theatres; Gamecock 1 & 2 Twin Theatres; Columbia East 1 & 2 Twin Theatres, Spring Valley 1, 2, 3 & 4 Quad Theatres; SPARTANBURG: Hillcrest 1 & 2 Theatres.

J

JF Theatres

733 West 40th St., Suite 102, Baltimore, MD 21211. (301) 366-6422.

JACK FRUCHTMAN, pres.; JACK FRUCHTMAN, JR., exec. v.p.
MARYLAND—BALTIMORE: Hippodrome, Mayfair, New, Northpoint Plaza Cinema, Pikes, Randallstown, Reisterstown Plaza, Rotunda Cinemas I & II, Town; BELAIR: Campus Hills Cinemas I & II; JOPPATOWN: Joppatowne Cinema; LEXINGTON PARK: Park, Plaza, 235 Drive-In.

JUR Theatre Circuit

P.O. Box 187, Parkersburg, WV 26101. (304) 422-1311.

DAVID S. JOSEPH, v.p.
OHIO—BELPRE: Belpre Open Air; CONSTITUTION: Riverside D.I.; MARIETTA: Starlite D.I.
WEST VIRGINIA—PARKERSBURG: Burwell, Smoot, Sundowner, D.I.

Joy's Theatres, Inc.

P.O. Box 785, Metairie, LA 70004; Tel.: 834-8510.

JOY N. HOUCK, pres.
LOUISIANA—KENNER: Joy's Cinema Six; METAIRIE: Panorama 4, Aereon III; MONROE: Joy's Twin Cinema, East-

gate Cinema III; BATON ROUGE: Robert E. Lee Theatre 4; Shreveport—Joy's Cinema Six, Princess Theatre, Winnsboro. **TEXAS**—DALLAS: Bruton Terrace; TEXARKANA: Joy's Twin D.I. and Cinema City 4.

K

K. B. Theatres

4818 Yuma St., N.W. Washington, DC 20016. (202) 244-7700.

MARVIN GOLDMAN, RON GOLDMAN, owners.
DISTRICT OF COLUMBIA—WASHINGTON: MacArthur, Cinema, Fine Arts, Studio 1, 2, and 3., C. Janus I, II & III, Cerberus I, II & III.
MARYLAND—ROCKVILLE: Congressional 5, Rockville D.I.; SILVER SPRING: Langley, Silver; BETHESDA: K-B Twins I & II, Baronet West I & II, Bethesda.
VIRGINIA—ARLINGTON: Rosslyn Plaza, Crystal City; FAIRFAX: Cinema 7.

Kent Theatres, Inc.

2709 Art Museum Drive; P.O. Box 10066, Jacksonville, FL 32207. (904) 733-0941.

FREDERICK H. KENT, bd. chmn.; J. CLEVELAND KENT, pres.; JOHN B. KENT, v.p. and general counsel; T. L. HYDE, v.p. in charge of operations; MRS. NORMA F. KENT, sec.; MRS. NORMA K. LOCKWOOD, treas.; MRS. JOANN GREEN, asst. secty.; ROBERT M. FULFORD, asst. treas.-comptroller.
FLORIDA—DAYTONA BEACH: Halifax I & II; SATEL-LITE BEACH: Satellite I & II; FORT PIERCE: Sunrise, Fort Pierce D.I.; JACKSONVILLE: Normandy I & II. Plaza I & II, St. Johns I & II; NEPTUNE BEACH: Neptune I, II & III; MELBOURNE: Palms 5, Brevard D.I., MERRITT ISLAND: Merritt I & II; TALLAHASSEE: Capital D.I., Northwood Mall, Cinema I & II, Parkway 5, VERO BEACH: Vero D.I., Florida.

Kerasotes Theatres

Kerasotes Building, 104 No. 6th Street, Springfield, IL 62701. (217) 788-5200.

GEORGE G. KERASOTES, pres.; NICHOLAS KERASOTES, v.p.; LOUIS G. KERASOTES, treas.; JOHN G. KERASOTES, sec.
ILLINOIS—ANNA: Rodgers, Anna Drive In; BLOOMINGTON: Castle, Irvin, College Hills, Plaza Cinema I, II, III & IV, Bloomington Drive In; CANTON: Capitol, Garden; CARBONDALE: Saluki I & II, Varsity I & II; CHAMPAIGN: Co-Ed I, II, III & IV, Rialto, Orpheum, Virginia, Twin City Drive In; CHILLICOTHE: Town; DANVILLE: Fischer, Palace, Times, Village Mall Cinema; DECATUR: Avon, Lincoln, Rogers, Decatur Drive In, Outdoor Drive In; DeKALB: Campus Cinema I, II, III & IV, DeKalb; GALESBURG: Orpheum, West I & II, Galesburg Drive In; HAVANA: Lawford, Havana Drive In; HERRIN: Egyptian Drive In; HIGHLAND: Lory I & II; JERSEYVILLE: Stadium I & II; KEWANEE: Midland Plaza Cinema, Wanee, Wanee Drive In; LA SALLE: La Salle, Majestic, La Salle Drive In; MACOMB: Illinois, Lark, Fort Drive In; MARION: Town & Country I, II, III & IV; MATTOON: Mattoon I, II & III; MONMOUTH: Rivoli; MORRIS: Morris I & II; MT. VERNON: Granada, Stadium, Times Square Cinema, Mt. Vernon Drive In; MURPHYSBORO: Liberty; NORMAL: Cinema I & II, Normal; NORRIS: Hillcrest Drive In; OREGON: Oregon, Pines Drive In; OTTAWA: Roxy I & II; PARIS: Paris, Twin Lakes Drive In; PEKIN: Starlite Drive In; PEORIA: Beverly, Metro I & II, Landmark Cinema I, II, III, IV & V, Varsity, Westlake I, II, III. IV & V, Holiday Drive In, Peoria Drive In, Pioneer Drive In; PERU: Peru, Peru Mall Cinema I & II; PONTIAC: Crescent, Eagle, Starchief Drive In; PRINCETON: Apollo, Alexander Park Drive In; QUINCY: Adams Cinema I & II, State, Washington, Quincy Drive In I & II; RANTOUL: Wings Cinema I & II, Rantoul Drive In; ROCHELLE: Hub; ROCKFORD: Coronada, Belford Indoor I & II, Belford Outdoor I & II; SPRINGFIELD: Capital City Cinema, Esquire I, II, III & IV, Senate, I & II, 66 Drive In, Twin Drive In I & II; STREATOR: Majestic I & II, Streator Drive In; SULLIVAN: Sullivan Drive In; TUSCOLA: Tuscola Drive In; URBANA: Cinema, Thunderbird, Widescreen Drive In.
INDIANA—ANDERSON: Mounds Cinema I & II, BLOOMINGTON: Indiana, Von Lee, I & II; COLUMBUS:

Columbus Center Cinema I & II; CONNERSVILLE: Connersville Drive In; INDIANAPOLIS: South Keystone Cinema I & II; LA PORTE: La Porte Cinema I, II, III, & IV; MARION: Marion-Air Drive In; Movies I, II, III & IV; PERU: Eastwood Cinema I & II; RICHMOND: Cinema I & II, Mall Cinema I & II, Sidewalk Cinema, Bel-Air Drive In, Hi-Way Drive In; VINCENNES: Vincennes Drive In; WASHINGTON: Indiana, East 50 Drive In.
MISSOURI—CAPE GIRARDEAU: Broadway, Rialto, Town Plaza Cinema I & II, Starvue Drive In; DEXTER: Town & Country I & II, FARMINGTON: Corral Drive In I & II; FLAT RIVER: Roseland; KENNETT: Kennett Cinema, Tommie's Drive In; MALDEN: Autovue Drive In; PERRYVILLE: Mercier I & II, Hilltop Drive In; POPLAR BLUFF: Rodgers, Mansion Mall Cinema I & II, Poplar Bluff Drive In.

Kindair Corporation

Kindair Building, Carmel Rancho Shopping Center, P.O. Box 221190, Carmel, CA 93922, (408) 624-5552.

D. KIRKE ERSKINE, pres.; BILL WILLIAMS, v.p., film buyer.
CALIFORNIA—MONTEREY: Cinema 70; CARMEL: Center Cinemas (Twin); CARMEL VALLEY: Valley Cinema; SALINAS: Northridge Cinemas (4); APTOS: Aptos Twin: CAPITOLA: 41ST Avenue Playhouse (Triplex); REDDING: Gateway Cinemas (4).

Kortes Theatres

Box 115, Plainwell MI 49080. Tel.: 685-6564.

STACEY KORTES, gen. mgr.
MICHIGAN—PLAINWELL: 131 D.I., Sun.

L

L&M Management Co., Inc.

35 East Wacker Drive, Suite 2322, Chicago, IL 60601.

DOROTHY BERMAN, pres.; S. J. BERMAN, v.p., gen. mgr.; GEORGE COLLONS, v.p.; ROBERT PETERSON, asst. gen. mgr.; HOWARD LUCAS, film buyer.
ILLINOIS—AURORA: West Plaza Triplex; DIXON: Dixon; JOLIET: Bel-Air D.I., Hilltop D.I., Mode; KANKAKEE: Starlite Twin D.I.; PRAIRIEVILLE: Midway D.I.; ROCKFORD: Sunset D.I., Robin D.I.
INDIANA—OSCEOLA: Starlite Twin D.I., SOUTH BEND: Western D.I.; CHIPPEWA: Twin D.I.
IOWA—KEOKUK: Plaza Cinema; MUSCATINE: Plaza 1 & 2.

Laemmle Theatres

11523 Santa Monica Blvd., Los Angeles, CA 90025. (213) 478-1041.

MAX and ROBERT LAEMMLE, chief officers. GEORGE REESE, associate.
CALIFORNIA—BEVERLY HILLS: Music Hall; ENCINO: Town & Country Cinemas 1, 2 & 3; HOLLYWOOD: Continental, Los Feliz; PASADENA: Esquire; SANTA MONICA: Monica 4-plex; WEST LOS ANGELES: Royal, Westland 1 & 2.

Laskey Bros. Amusement Corp.

23 Mont View St., Uniontown, PA 15401.

THEODORE J. LASKEY, pres.; GEORGE J. LASKEY, gen. mgr., booker & purchasing agent; THEODORE J. LASKEY, film buyer.
PENNSYLVANIA—CONNELLSVILLE: Blue Ridge D.I., Comet D.I.; UNIONTOWN: Super 51 D.I., Starlite D.I.
WEST VIRGINIA—FAIRMOUNT: Starlite D.I.; MORGANTOWN: Westover D.I.

Latchis Theatre Circuit

Hotel Bldg., 50 Main St., Brattleboro, VT 05310; (803) 254-5800.

LATCHIS BROS., owners.
NEW HAMPSHIRE—CLAREMONT: Latchis; KEENE: Colonial, Latchis; NEWPORT: Latchis.
VERMONT—BRATTLEBORO: Latchis Memorial.

Leon Theatres

Home Office: 3385 No. 3rd, Abilene, TX 79603. Tel.: (915) 673-7181.

C. D. LEON, owner; BOB HILL, gen. mgr.; DOWLEN RUSSELL, booker.
TEXAS—PASADENA: Town & Country D.I. 1 & 2; FT. WORTH: Southside Twin D.I., Mansfield Twin D.I.; DENISON: Twin City D.I.

Lightstone Theatre Enterprises, Inc.

2743 Long Beach Road, Oceanside, NY 11572. (516) 432-1950.

MORTY LIGHTSTONE, pres. and film buyer; JORDAN MARKS, buyer-booker.
CONNECTICUT—BANTAM: Cinema IV.
NEW JERSEY—BOGOTA: Queen Anne; PALISADES: Grant Lee; LAKEWOOD: Strand; ISELIN: Iselin.
NEW YORK—NEW YORK CITY: Cine 1 & 2, Olympia, Quad 1-2-3 & 4; QUEENS (Astoria): Ditmars; QUEENS (Flushing): Utopia; BROOKLYN: Benson 1 & 2; Beverly, Graham Cinema, Granada, Rugby 1 & 2, Brooklyn Heights 1 & 2, City Line: MASSAPEQUA: Jerry Lewis Cinemas 1 & 2; EAST ISLIP: East Islip; PORT WASHINGTON: Sands Point; ROOSEVELT: Nassau; EAST NORTHPORT: Larkfield; WEST BABYLON: South Bay 1, 2 & 3; NEW PALTZ: Academy; WAPPINGER FALLS: Imperial; WOODSTOCK: Tinker Street.
VIRGINIA—RICHMOND: Biograph 1 & 2.
WASHINGTON, DC—Biograph.

Robert L. Lippert Theatres

Pier 32, San Francisco, CA 94105. (415) 546-9200.

ROBERT L. LIPPERT JR., pres.; CARMEN BONACCI, vice pres., head film buyer.
CALIFORNIA—ALAMEDA: Southshore 2 Cinemas; HAYWARD: Hayward 5 Cinemas; MARYSVILLE: Marysville Drive-In; YUBA CITY: Yuba City Drive-In; LOS ANGELES: Americana 6 Cinemas; Northridge 4 Cinemas; Eagle Rock 4 Cinemas.

Loeks, Jack, Theatres

1400 28th Street, S.W., Grand Rapids, MI 49509. (616) 532-6302.

JOHN D. LOEKS, pres.; FRANK THOMAS, gen. mgr.
MICHIGAN—GRAND RAPIDS: Studio 28 Theatres, Beltline D.I., Plainfield D.I., Woodland D.I.; MUSKEGON: Auto D.I., Getty D.I., North D.I.; GRAND HAVEN: Grand Theatre.

Loew's Corporation

666 Fifth Avenue, New York, NY 10019. (212) 841-1000.

LOEWS THEATRES

BERNARD MYERSON, pres.; BERNARD DIAMOND, exec. v.p.; WILLIAM TRAMBUKIS, v.p. and gen. mgr.; FRANK PATTERSON, v.p. chief film buyer; DON BAKER, v.p. adv.; TED EARNOW, asst. v.p. and nat'l adv. dir.; GEORGE MCNEIL, v.p. construction & maintenance.
FLORIDA—CORAL SPRINGS: Loews Six; HOLLYWOOD: Loews Penbrook Pines Quad; MIAMI: Bay Harbor Twin, 167th St. Twins, Kendall Twins, Skylake Twins.
GEORGIA—ATLANTA: Twelve Oaks Twins, Tara Twin.
INDIANA—INDIANAPOLIS: Loews Twin Triplex, Loews Quad., Loews Greenwood (6 plex) Loews Washington Square (6 plex)
LOUISIANA—NEW ORLEANS: State, Triplex.
NEW JERSEY—EDGEWATER: Loews Showboat Quad; JERSEY CITY: Jersey City Triplex; EAST BRUNSWICK: Route 18 Twin; PARSIPPANY: Troy Hills Twin; SECAUCUS: Harmon Cove Quad.
NEW YORK—LONG ISLAND: Loews Nassau Quad, Stony Brook Triplex, South Shore Mall Twin; NEW ROCHELLE: Loews Twin; NEW YORK CITY: (Bronx): American Twin, Paradise Quad, Riverdale; (Brooklyn): Alpine Twin, Georgetown Twin, Metropolitan Quad, Oriental Twin; (Manhattan): Astor Plaza Cine, 83rd Street Quad, Orpheum Twin, State I, State II, Tower East, New York Twin, Loews 34th St. Showplace (3); (Queens): Bay Terrace Twin, Elmwood Twin, Parsons Twin, Trylon; ROCHESTER: Loews Triplex, Loews Twin (Greece, N.Y.).
OHIO—AKRON: State Twin; CLEVELAND: East Twins, West Twins, Yorktown Twins, Cedar Center Twins, Riverside Twin, Berea Triplex, Richmond Village Triplex; COLUMBUS: Arlington Twin, Morse Road Twin, Westerville Twin; DAYTON: Ames Twin.
TENNESSEE—NASHVILLE: Crescent, Madison, Melrose.
TEXAS—DALLAS: Loews Quad, Studio 1, 2, 3, Delman; HOUSTON: Town & Country 1, 2, 3, Saks Center Twin.

Loew's E.M., Theatres

164 Tremont St., Boston, MA 02111. (617) 482-9200.

ELIAS M. LOEW, pres.; RAY E. CANAVAN, exec. asst.; R. OWENS, buyer, booker.
CONNECTICUT—BRIDGEPORT: Candlelite-Pix D.I.; BRISTOL: Farmington D.I.; HARTFORD: Drive-In; MONTVILLE: Norwich-New London Twin D.I.
MAINE—BANGOR: Brewer D.I.; MANCHESTER: Augusta D.I.; PORTLAND: Fine Arts; WELLS BEACH: Wells Beach.
MARYLAND—GLEN BURNIE: Gov. Ritchie D.I.
MASSACHUSETTS—AUBURN: Auburn D.I.; BEVERLY: Fine Arts; BILLERICA: Pinehurst D.I.; BOSTON: Publix, West End Cinema; DORCHESTER: Park Cinema; HAVERHILL D.I.; LYNN: Capital; METHUEN: Merrimac Park D.I.; NEW BEDFORD: Center; NORTH ADAMS: Mohawk; WEST SPRINGFIELD: Riverdale D.I.; WEBSTER: Liberty State; WORCESTER: Fine Arts, Plymouth.
NEW HAMPSHIRE—PORTSMOUTH: Civic, E. M. Loew's Cinema.

Logan Luxury Theatres Corp.

(Formerly Mitchell Theatre Corp.)
209 N. Lawler St., Mitchell, SD 47301; (605) 996-5444.

JEFFREY N. LOGAN, pres. & gen. mgr.; LINDA W. LOGAN, v.p.; JIM WILSON, booker.
SOUTH DAKOTA—MITCHELL: Roxy, State, Starlite D.I.; HURON: Starlite D.I., Twin State I & II.

Long Theatres

P.O. Box 312, Safford, AZ 85546.

LOUIS F. LONG, pres.
ARIZONA—AJO: Oasis, Ajo D.I.; BENSON: Benson D.I.; BUCKEYE: Roxy; CASA GRANDE: Desert D.I., Paramount; CLIFTON: Three Way D.I.; COOLIDGE: Prince D.I., San Carlo, Studio; DUNCAN: Duncan; ELOY: Dustbowl, Y Drive-In; FLORENCE: Spur; GILA BEND: Rio; HAYDEN: Rex; MAMMOTH: Mammoth D.I.; McNARY: McNary; PIMA: Pima; SAFFORD: Drive-In, Gila, Safford; SAN MANUEL: San Manuel D.I.; SPRINGERVILLE: El Rio; SUPERIOR: Drive-In, Uptown; WILCOX: Wilcox.

Lubbock Video Theatres

P.O. Box 6036, Lubbock, TX 79413. (806) 792-0964. (Subsidiary of Video Independent Theaters, Inc.)

J. E. BROOKS, pres.; R. P. DAVIS, gen. mgr.; JIM BUCKALEW, film buyer.
TEXAS—LUBBOCK: Winchester Twin, Cinema West.

Lucas Theatre Circuit

Arlington Theatre, Arlington Heights, IL 60004. (312) CL 3-5200.

ROBERT G. RUBENS, gen. mgr.
ILLINOIS—ARLINGTON HEIGHTS: Arlington; OAK LAWN: Coral; JOLIET: Rialto.

Lust, Sidney, Theatres

Rear of 7719 Wisconsin Ave., Bethesda, MD 20014

MARYLAND—BELTSVILLE: Beltsville, D.I.

M

MCM Theatres, Ltd., Inc.

Tropic Theatre Bldg., P.O. Box 390, Leesburg, FL 32748; Tel.: (904) 787-2255.

BILL P. CUMBAA, pres.
FLORIDA—EUSTIS: Movie Gardens D.I.; HIGH SPRINGS: Priest; INVERNESS: Cinema On The Square; LEESBURG: Crest D.I., Tropic I & II, Vista; LAKE CITY: Cinema 90 Twin; Lake City D.I., PALATKA: Linda D.I., St. Johns D.I.; WILLISTON: Arcade; CLERMONT: Clervue D.I.; ST. AUGUSTINE: Plaza I & II, Cinema Plus.

Madison 20th Century Theatres

777 West Glencoe Pl., Bayside, WI 53217. (414) 351-3000.

DEAN D. FITZGERALD, pres.
WISCONSIN—MADISON: Orpheum, Strand, Hilldale, Cinema, Stage Door, Badger Outdoor; MIDDLETON: Middleton, Big Sky D.I.

Malco Theatres, Inc.

5851 Hyatt Ridgeway Parkway, P.O. Box 171809, Memphis, TN 38117 (901) 761-3480.

M. A. LIGHTMAN, bd. chmn.; RICHARD L. LIGHTMAN, pres.; HERBERT R. LEVY, v.p. & secty.; HERBERT KOHN, v.p. & treas.
ARKANSAS—BLYTHEVILLE: Malco Trio, Starvue D.I.; FAYETTEVILLE: Malco Twin, Mall Twin, Razorback Twin; FORT SMITH: Mall Trio, Malco Twin, Phoenix Village Twin, Skyvue D.I.; JONESBORO: Malco Cinema 5, Plaza Twin, Skyvue D.I., Indian D.I.; ROGERS: Malco Twin; SPRINGDALE: Springdale Twin.
KENTUCKY—OWENSBORO: Malco, Mall Twin, Plaza Twin, Owensboro Twin, Cardinal D.I., Starlight D.I.
MISSISSIPPI—COLUMBUS: Malco Twin, Mall, Varsity Twin, Princess, Fiesta D.I.; TUPELO: Lyric, Malco Twin, Mall, Tupelo Twin, 78 D.I.
MISSOURI—SIKESTON: Malco Twin, Mall, Delta D.I.
TENNESSEE—JACKSON: Malco, Mall, Malco Twin, Cabana Twin, Paramount; MEMPHIS: Memphian, Malco's Quartet, Malco's Ridgeway Four, Southwest Twin D.I., Summer Twin D.I., Bellevue D.I., Frayser D.I.

Mallers-Spirou Management Corp.

933 Northcrest Shopping Center, Fort Wayne, IN 46805.

GEORGE P. MALLERS, pres.; ARTHUR G. SPIROU, exec. vice pres. & sec.; RICHARD L. WALLS, film buyer; FRED THACKER, adv.-pub. head.
ILLINOIS—LANSING: Lans.
INDIANA—BLUFFTON: Bluffton Drive-In; FORT WAYNE: Holiday I & II, Georgetown Square I & II, Quimby Village 1 & 2, Hillcrest Drive-In; TERRE HAUTE: Meadows 1 & 2, Plaza North 1 & 2.

Mallers Theatres

1716 Wheeling Ave., Room 2, Muncie, IN 47303. (317) 288-2556.

ANTHONY G. MALLERS, pres.; MORRIS CANTOR, film buyer.
INDIANA—MUNCIE: Delaware Cinema 1 & 2; NOBLESVILLE: ABC Noblesville D.I., Diana Theatre; PORTLAND: Hines Theatre.

Mann Theatres Corporation of California

Suite 301, 9200 Sunset Blvd., Los Angeles, CA, 90069; P.O. Box 60909, Terminal Annex, Los Angeles, CA, 90060. (213) 273-3336.

TED MANN, chm. of bd.; LARRY GLEASON, pres.; BERNARD KAUFMAN, v.p. & gen. counsel; PAUL ROSENFELD, v.p. head film buyer; JIM SHEEHAN, asst. head film buyer; KEN CROWE, treas.; LYNDELL MAYBERRY, asst. treas.; WILLIAM HERTZ, dir. of oper.; EDWIN STUART, dir. of real estate & construction; JOE VLECK, dir. of adv.; WILLIAM RECTOR, dir. of concessions; BARCLAY SMITH, dir. of maintenance.
ARIZONA—GLENDALE: Thunderbird D.I.; MESA: Fiesta Fiveplex, Poca Fiesta Fourplex; PHOENIX: Christown Fiveplex; TUCSON: Buena Vista Twin, Park Mall Fourplex
CALIFORNIA—BAKERSFIELD: Crest Drive-In Twin; BEVERLY HILLS: Fine Arts; BREA: Mann Brea Fourplex; CANOGA PARK: Fallbrook Twin; COVINA: Fox Triplex; DUBLIN: Mann Sixplex; GLENDALE: Alex, Glendale Twin; HOLLYWOOOD: Chinese I, II, & III, Fox, Hollywood, Vogue; LA JOLLA: University Towne Center Sixplex; MANHATTAN BEACH: Mann Sixplex; OCEANSIDE: Mann El Camino Eightplex; OXNARD: Esplanade Triplex, Fox; NATIONAL CITY: Plaza Bonita Sixplex; PASADENA: Academy, Hastings Ranch Triplex; SACRAMENTO: Birdcage Sixplex; SAN DIEGO: Cinema 21, Loma, Rancho Bernardo Twin, Sports Arena Sixplex, Valley Circle; SAN JOSE: Town & Country; SAN LUIS OBISPO: Fremont; SAN MATEO: Mann Sixplex; SANTA MONICA: Wilshire Twin; SHERMAN OAKS: La Reina; STUDIO CITY: Studio; THOUSAND OAKS: Conejo Twin; TORRANCE: Old Towne Sixplex; UPLAND: Mountain Green Fourplex; VENTURA: Fox; VALENCIA: Mann Sixplex; VISALIA: Fox Triplex; WESTWOOD: Bruin, Mann Triplex, National, Plaza, Regent, Village.
COLORADO—BOULDER: Arapahoe Fourplex, Fox; DENVER: Aladdin, Arapahoe East Fourplex, Century 21, Tamarac Sixplex; DURANGO: Gaslight Twin, Kiva; FT. COLLINS: Fox, Century Mall Triplex; LAKEWOOD: Lakeridge Twin, Village Union Square Sixplex.
IDAHO—BOISE: Five-Mile Fourplex; IDAHO FALLS: Paramount, Yellowstone Plaza Triplex; POCATELLO: Chief, Mann Triplex.
ILLINOIS—CARBONDALE: Fox East Gate; CHAMPAIGN: Mann's Country Fair Fouplex; JACKSONVILLE: Illinois; PEORIA: Fox; SPRINGFIELD: Fox Town & Country.
LOUISIANA—NEW ORLEANS: Robert E. Lee.
MICHIGAN—ANN ARBOR: Village Fourplex; BENTON HARBOR: Starlite D.I.; LANSING: Spartan Triplex.
MISSOURI—ST. ANN: Cypress Village Twin; ST. LOUIS: Mark Twain.
MONTANA—MISSOULA: Fox, Mann's Triplex.
NEBRASKA—NORTH PLATTE: Mall Triplex.
NEVADA—LAS VEGAS: Fox, Boulevard Twin; RENO: Cinema, Mann's Old Towne Triplex.
OKLAHOMA—TULSA: Fox Twin.
TEXAS—AMARILLO: Bell Plaza Fourplex, Fox Twin; AUSTIN: Fox Triplex, Mann Westgate Triplex; CORPUS CHRISTI: National Twin; EL PASO: Fox Twin; LUBBOCK: Fox Fourplex, Mann Slideraod Fourplex.
UTAH—LOGAN: Cache Valley Mall Triplex; MURRAY: Olympus D.I.; OGDEN: City Plaza Fourplex, Riverdale Fourplex; OREM: Carillon Square Fourplex; PROVO: Academy, Central Square Fourplex, Fox Prono; SALT LAKE CITY: Fox Cottonwood Fourplex, Mann Plaza 5400 Sixplex, Villa.
WYOMING—CHEYENNE: Lincoln; LARAMIE: Fox Twin.

March Theatres

Box 151, Wayne, NB 68787. (402) 375-1280.

JACK P. MARCH, pres. & film buyer.
IOWA—IOWA FALLS: Met, Falls; LeMARS: Royal Twin I & II, Mars Under Stars D.I. (Terry March, president). MILFORD: Lakeland D.I.; SPIRIT LAKE: Royal, Spirit D.I.
NEBRASKA—WAYNE: Gay, Dude Ranch D.I.
S. DAK.—VERMILLION: Coyote, Vermillion, U-Vu D.I.

Marchesi Brothers

Amboy Theatre, Amboy, IL 61310.

AUGUST MARCHESI, gen. mgr. & film buyer.
ILLINOIS—PROPHETSTOWN: Town; SAVANNA: Times.

Marcus Theatres Corporation

212 W. Wisconsin Ave., Milwaukee, WI 53203. (414) 272-6020.

BEN MARCUS, pres.
WISCONSIN—APPLETON: Valley Fair Cinemas I II & III, Viking, Cinema I, Marc I & II, 41 Outdoor, Tower Outdoor; BEAVER DAM: Wisconsin, Beaver Outdoor; CEDARBURG: Rivoli and 57 Outdoor; GREEN BAY: Stadium Cinema I, II & III, Marc I & II, Vic; LA CROSSE: Rivoli, Marc I & II, North Star (Outdoor); MADISON: Esquire I & II, Westgate I & II; MANITOWOC: Capital, Mikadow, Lake-Vue Outdoor; MENOMINIE FALLS: Marc I & II; MENOMINIE: State I & II, Menominie Outdoor; MILWAUKEE: Bluenround Outdoor, Prospect Mall Cinemas I & II, Villa, Tosa, Times, Starlite Outdoor I & II, Centre I & II, Esquire, Southtown I, II, III, Skyway I, II & III, Capitol Court I & II, Northtown I, II & III, Neenah; OSHKOSH: Time, 44 Outdoor, Cinema I & II; NEW BERLIN: Hy, 24 Outdoor I & II; SHEBOYGAN: Sheboygan I & II, Marc I & II; RACINE: Racine Cinema I & II, Rapids Plaza, Cinema I & II; RIPON: Campus, Ripon Outdoor; TOMAH: Erwin; STEVENS POINT: Campus Cinema I & II; WAUSAU: Highway 29 D.I., Crossroads Cinema I & II, Marc I & II; WISCONSIN RAPIDS: Cinema 8.

Markoff Theatre Circuit

32 Main Street, Colchester, CT 06415. Tel.: LEhigh 7-2775.

CONNECTICUT—COLCHESTER: Colchester; EAST HAMPTON: East Hampton; MOODUS: Moodus; PORTLAND: Portland D.I.; STAFFORD SPRINGS: Palace; WILLIAMANTIC: Strand.

Marshall Movie Co.

BOX 171, Salisbury, MO 65281. (816) 388-5219.

STEVE BAGBY and ELMER BILLS, partners.
MISSOURI—CARROLLTON: Uptown, Carol D.I.; MARSHALL: Cinema I & II, Parkside D.I.

Martin Theatres, Inc.

Home Office: 1308 Broadway, P.O. Box 391, Columbus, GA 31994 (404) 323-7365. Buying and Booking Office: 2211 North Druid Hills Road, N.E., Atlanta, GA 30329 (404) 325-1772; 230 South Tryon Street, Suite 1010, Charlotte, NC 28202; 6060 North Central Expressway, Suite 729, Dallas, TX 75206.

C. L. PATRICK, bd. chm.; CHARLES H. KUERTZ, SR., pres.; RONNIE OTWELL, SR., sr. v.p.; MICHAEL W. PATRICK, v.p.; GENE J. PATTERSON, v.p.; KENNETH R. STRICKLIN, fin. v.p., treas. & asst. secty; ROBERT E. HOSSE, v.p.-film; FOSTER HOTARD, v.p.-booking; QUINTON GREEN, v.p.-concessions; JOHN McKINLEY, v.p.-technical; CHRISTOPHER L. MEACHAM, secty. & gen. counsel; ROY E. MARTIN, III, asst. secty.
ALABAMA—AUBURN: War Eagle; CULLMAN: Marbro Drive In, Martin Twin, Town Square Triple; FLORENCE: Capri Twin, Joylan Drive In, Martin; HUNTSVILLE: Alabama, Martin, Westbury Twin; MONTGOMERY: Eastdale Triple, Martin Twin; MUSCLE SHOALS: Cinema I & II; OPELIKA: Plaza Twin; PHENIX CITY: Phenix Twin; SYLACAUGA: Comet Drive In, Plaza Twin; TALLADEGA: Martin Triple.
FLORIDA—PANAMA CITY: Capri, Florida Triple, Gulf Drive In, Isle of View Drive In.
GEORGIA—ALBANY: Albany, Georgia 4, Mall Twin, Martin 4, Slappey Drive In, State; AMERICUS: Cinema I & II; ATLANTA: Rialto; BAXLEY: Marbro Drive In; CALHOUN: Martin Triple; CARTERSVILLE: Plaza Twin, Starlite Drive In; COLUMBUS: Columbus Square 4, Georgia, Peachtree Triple, Rexview Drive In; CORDELE: Cordele Drive In, Martin Triple; DALTON: Capri, Cherokee Drive In, Martin Triple, Plaza Twin; DOUGLAS: Martin Twin, Skyview Drive In; FITZGERALD: Capri Twin; FT. OGLETHORPE: Southgate Triple; MARIETTA: Marbro Twin Drive In; MILLEDGEVILLE: Campus, Martin; TIFTON: Marbro Drive In, Tift, Towne; VALDOSTA: Cinema Twin, Park Twin, Martin Drive In.
KENTUCKY—BOWLING GREEN: Martin Twin, Plaza Twin, Riverside Drive In, State; HOPKINSVILLE: Alhambra, Martin Twin; MADISONVILLE: Martin Twin; PRINCETON: Capitol.
NORTH CAROLINA—ASHEBORO: Cinema II; ASHEVILLE: Biltmore Twin; BOONE: Chalet Twin; BURLING-

TON: Park Twin; Chapel Hill; Ram Triple; DURHAM: Northgate Twin, Yorktowne Twin; ELIZABETH CITY: Gateway Twin; GASTONIA: Eastridge Twin, Village Twin; GOLDSBORO: Paramount; HIGH POINT: Capri Triple, Martin Twin, Towne Twin; KINSTON: Park; MORGANTON: Studio Twin; RALEIGH: Falls Twin, South Hills Twin, Terrace Twin, Valley Twin, Village Twin; ROCKINGHAM: Plaza Twin; WINSTON-SALEM: Parkview Twin, Parkway Plaza.
SOUTH CAROLINA—AIKEN: Mark I; CLEMSON: Astro III, Clemson; GREENVILLE: Astro Twin; LAURENS: Oaks Cinema; ORANGEBURG: Cinema Twin; SUMTER: Cinema Twin, Palmetto, Skyvue Drive In, Sumter.
TENNESSEE—ATHENS: Plaza Twin; CHATTANOOGA: Four Square Triple, Marbro Drive In, Northgate Cinema I, Northgate 2 & 3, Red Bank Drive In, Showcase Twin, 23rd St. Drive In; CLARKSVILLE: Capri Twin, Martin Twin, Roxy; CLEVELAND: Village Twin; CROSSVILLE: Capri Twin; DYERSBURG: Martin Triple; FAYETTEVILLE: Lincoln; FRANKLIN: Franklin Cinema; GREENVILLE: Ashway Drive In, Capri; HARRIMAN: Midtown Drive In, Princess; KINGSPORT: Marbro Drive In, Martin, Strand; LEBANON: Martin Triple; MORRISTOWN: Capri, Princess, Volunteer Twin; MURFREESBORO: Marbro Drive In, Martin Twin; NASHVILLE: Belcourt Twin, Belle Meade, Bellevue 4, Capri Twin, Colonial Twin Drive In, Hermitage 4, Martin Twin, Plaza, Rivergate 1 & 2, Rivergate 3 & 4, Skyway Drive In; PULASKI: Moonglo Drive In. SPRINGFIELD: Springfield Cinema.
TEXAS—BEAUMONT: Colonade 4, Gaylynn Twin, Lamar Art, Showtown Twin Drive In; CONROE: North Hills Twin; GREENVILLE: Rolling Hills Twin; JACKSONVILLE: Cinema 3; LONGVIEW: Cargill Triple, Cinema I & II, Martin Twin, River Road Triple Drive In; LUFKIN: Angelina Twin, Redland Drive In, Showtown Twin Drive In, Town Square 4; NACOGDOCHES: Northview Plaza Twin; ORANGE: MacArthur Drive In; PORT ARTHUR: Golden Triple, Don Twin Drive In, Village Triple; SILSBEE: Pines; WICHITA FALLS: Twin Falls Drive In.
VIRGINIA—BLACKSBURG: Capri Twin; HAMPTON: Riverdale Twin; NEWPORT NEWS: Beechmont Twin; WILLIAMSBURG: Martin Cinema I & II.

Martin, Ralph, Theatres

1465 Groveway, Hayward, CA 94546 (415) 886-7727.

CALIFORNIA—GRAND: Tracy; OAKLAND: Plaza; SAN LEANDRO: Bal; SOLEDAD: Soledad; SALINAS: Fox, Cinema 7, Plaza; VISILIA: Visilia.

Massie Circuit

P.O. Box 929, Waynesville, NC 28786

MARY MASSIE, owner & operator; STEWART EVERETT, buyer & booker.
NORTH CAROLINA—WAYNESVILLE: Smoky Mountain D.I., Strand.

Maxi Cinema Enterprises

42 North Strathmore St., Valley Stream, NY 11581.

MAX FRIED and SELMA FRIED, chief officers.
NEW YORK—BAYSHORE: Encore; HARRISON: Cinema East; LYNBROOK: Studio One; SAGUERTIES: Orpheum; WHITE PLAINS: Colony.
NEW JERSEY—BRADLEY BEACH: Beach Cinema; NUTLEY: Franklin; WASHINGTON TOWNSHIP: Washington Cinema.

McCormick Circuit

Skyline Theatre, P.O. Box 271, Canon City, CO 81212. (303) 275-2801 or 275-2625.

H. L. McCORMICK, owner; HARROLD McCORMICK, gen. mgr. & booker.
COLORADO—CANON CITY: Skyline, Sunset D.I.

McLendon, Fred T., Circuit

P.O. Box 352, Union Springs, AL 36089. (205) 738-2380.

FRED T. MCCLENDON, pres. & gen. mgr.
ALABAMA—ANDALUSIA: Martin, Fendley D.I.; ATMORE: Strand, Palms D.I.; BAY MINETTE: Rex; BREWTON: Ritz and Eagle D.I.; EVERGREEN: Pix; GREEN-

VILLE: Ritz and Camellia D.I.; MONROEVILLE: Monroe; OPP: Dixieland D.I., Carousel Twin; ROBERTSDALE: Hub D.I.

FLORIDA—MILTON: Milton.
GEORGIA—CORNELIA: Grand; TOCCOA: Ritz, Toccoa D.I.
NORTH CAROLINA—FRANKLIN: Macon, Franklin D.I.

Harry Melcher Enterprises

3615 W. Fond du Lac Avenue, Milwaukee, WI 53216 (414) 442-5020.

HARRY MELCHER, gen. mgr.; DICK MELCHER, equipment mgr.
WISCONSIN—PRAIRIE DU CHIEN: Metro.

Mescop, Inc.

9235 W. Capitol Drive, Milwaukee, WI 53222. (414) HO 6-1700.

FRED FLORENCE, pres. & buyer; JAMES FLORENCE, vice pres.
MICHIGAN—MARQUETTE: Delft, Nordic, Cinema; ISHPEMING: Butler, Ishpeming, Evergreen D.I.; ESCANABA: Delft, MI, Plaza, Hilltop D.I.; IRON RIVER: Delft; GLADSTONE: Rialto; MANISTIQUE: Cinema I, Cinema II O.D.; SAULT STE. MARIE: Soo I & II, Starlite D.I.; IRON MOUNTAIN: Braumart, Tri-City O.D.; MONOMINEE: Lloyd; IRONWOOD: Ironwood, Ironwood O.D.; HOUGHTON: Lode; HANCOCK: Pic; CRYSTAL FALLS: Adlo; STEVENSON: Tivoli; LAKE LINDEN: Lakes O.D.; CHASSEL: Hiawatha; NEGAUNEE: Airport D.I.
WISCONSIN—STURGEON BAY: Donna; WISCONSIN RAPIDS: Wisconsin, Hiway 13 O.D.; ANTIGO: Palace, Antigo D.I.; MERRILL: Cosmo; TOMAHAWK: Tomahawk; WOODRUFF: Lakeland Cinema; OCONTO FALLS: Grand; SPARTA: Sparta, Hiway 16 D.I.; BLACK RIVER FALLS, Falls; RICHLAND CENTER: Eskin, Hiway 14 D.I.; BARABOO: Ringling; PORTAGE: Portage, 51/16 D.I.; STOUGHTON: Badger; SPRING GREEN: Gard; FORT ATKINSON: Fort; PLATTEVILLE: Avalon, Platteville D.I.; JEFFERSON: Hiway 18 D.I.; MARINETTE: Hiway 64 D.I.; MINOCQUA: Castle D.I.; EAGLE RIVER: Eagle River D.I.; EPHRIAM: Skyway D.I.; BAILEYS HARBOR: Lake Cinema; NEILLSVILLE: Neillsville; ELROY: Elroy; BOSCOBEL: Blaine; MAUSTON: Gail; BURLINGTON: Plaza; WATERFORD: Ford.

Metropolitan Theatres Corp.

8727 West Third St., Los Angeles CA (213) 272-8281.

BRUCE C. CORWIN, pres.; IRVING FULLER, exec. v.p.; MORTON LIPPE, film buyer; WILLIAM E. COOPER, gen. mgr. theatre operations; GONZALO CHECA, mgr. Spanish Language Operations; ED GOLDSTEIN, treas.
CALIFORNIA—LOS ANGELES: Alameda, Arcade, Boulevard, Broadway, Brooklyn, California, Cinema 21, El Monte, El Portal, Globe, Golden Gate, Lankershim, Los Angeles, Million Dollar, Olympic, Palace, Panorama, Park (Los Angeles) Park (Huntington Park) Rialto, Roxie, State, Downtown, Studio, United Artists, Westlake; OXNARD: Vogue, Boulevard; PALM SPRINGS: Camelot I, II & III; Plaza I & II; Village I & II; Palms to Pines I, II & III; Palm Springs D.I.; Sunaire, D.I., Cinemart; RIVERSIDE: Fox; SANTA BARBARA: Airport D.I., Arlington Center for the Performing Arts, Cinema I & II, Fairview I & II, Fiesta I, II, III & IV, Granada I, II & III, Magic Lantern I & II, Plaza de Oro I & II, Riviera, Santa Barbara D.I. I & II; SIMI VALLEY: Simi D.I.

Mid-America Theatres

9900 Page Blvd., Overland, MO 63132. (314) 429-7550.

LOUIS JABLONOW, bd. chmn.; SCOTT JABLONOW, pres.; JULIAN JABLONOW, v.p. adv.; JACK A JABLONOW, gen. mgr.
INDIANA—BLOOMINGTON: Village.
ILLINOIS—ALTON: Cameo; EAST ST. LOUIS: Falcon D.I., Shop City D.I.; GRANITE CITY: Bel-Air I and D.I., Nameoki Cinema I & II; SPRINGFIELD: Green Meadows Twin D.I. I & II.
MISSOURI—BRENTWOOD: Brentwood; CAMDENTON: Camdenton; CHESTERFIELD: Woods Mill Cinema I & II; COLUMBIA: Campus Cinema I & II; CRESTWOOD: Crestwood; CRYSTAL CITY: Twin City Cinema I & II; FLORISSANT: Paddock Cinema I & II; HAZELWOOD: Village The-

atre I, II & III; KIRKWOOD: Kirkwood Cinema; LAKE OZARK: Lake Ozark Cinema; MANCHESTER: Manchester Cinema I & II; MEHLEVILLE: South City Cinema I & II; OVERLAND: Holiday D.I. I, II, III & IV; RICHMOND HEIGHTS: Esquire Theatre I, II, III, & IV; ST. CHARLES: Plaza D.I.; ST. PETERS: I-70 D.I. I & II, Cave Springs Cinema I & II; UNIVERSITY CITY: Fine Arts.

Midway Enterprises

Rehoboth Beach, DE 19971.

RICHARD H. DERRICKSON, pres.
DELAWARE—DAGSBORO: New Clayton; DOVER: Twin Oaks Drive-In; LAUREL: Sussex West Drive-In; REHOBOTH: Beachwood, Center, Midway Palace I & II, Midway Drive-In; SEAFORD: Layton.
MARYLAND—POCOMOKE CITY: Pocomoke Drive-In.
VIRGINIA—CHINCOTEAGUE: Chincoteague.

Mid States Theatres

120 East Fourth St., Suite 750, Cincinnati, OH 45202. Tel. (513) 579-3500.

ROY B. WHITE, president.
KENTUCKY—ASHLAND: Midtown I, II & III; LEXINGTON: Lexington Mall Cinemas 1 & 2, Chevy Chase Cinemas I & II, Bluegrass Drive In, Circle 25 Drive In, Family Drive In, North Park Cinemas 6, South Park Cinemas 6; LOUISVILLE: Oxmoor Cinemas 1-2-3-4-5; Raceland Cinemas 1-2-3-4, Westland Cinemas 1-2-3-4; FLATWOODS: Corral Drive In; FLORENCE: Florence Cinema City 9; RICHMOND: Campus Cinemas 1 & 2.
OHIO—CINCINNATI: Kenwood 1 & 2, Hollywood Cinemas I & II, Covedale 1 & 2, Princeton 1 & 2, Valley Cinemas 1 & 2, Cine' Carousel 1 & 2, Mariemont Cinemas East 1 & 2, Studio Cinemas 1 & 2, Northgate Cinemas 1-2-3-4-5, Skywalk Cinemas 1 & 2, Tri County Cinemas 1-2-3-4-5, Montclair Cinemas East 1-2-3-4-5-6; CHESAPEAKE: Tri-State Drive In; DAYTON: Dabel, Salem Mall 1-2-3-4; Beaver Valley Cinemas 1-2-3-4-5-6; COLUMBUS: Continent Cinemas 1-2-3-4-5-6-7.

Milgram Theatres Inc.

1616 Walnut St., Ste. 2000, Philadelphia, PA 19103. (215) 985-4900.

WILLIAM MILGRAM, pres.; HENRY MILGRAM, exec. vice pres.
DELAWARE—DELMAR: Delmar D.I.; DOVER: Dover Cinema, Towne Cinema, Capitol, Kent D.I.; FELTON: Highway 13; MIDDLETOWN: Everett; NEWARK: Cinema Center, State; WILMINGTON: Branmar Cinema.
MARYLAND—DENTON: Crossroads D.I.; ELKTON: Elkton D.I.; TRAPPE: Super 50 D.I.; OCEAN CITY: Sun I & II, Surf I & II; SALISBURY: Mall Cinema I & II.
NEW JERSEY—ATLANTIC CITY: Charles; AUDUBON: Coronet; BORDENTOWN: Dix D.I.; GLASSBORO: Chews Landing, Glassboro; NORTHFIELD: Tilton I & II; PITMAN: Broadway; TRENTON: Directors Chair I & II; TURNERSVILLE: Plaza Cinema; WESTMONT: Westmont.
PENNSYLVANIA—ALLENTOWN: Plaza, Rialto; BALA CYNWYD: Bala; CORNWELLS HEIGHTS: Premiere I & II; ELKINS PARK: Yorktown; FEASTERVILLE: Bucks Mall Colonial I & II; GLENSIDE: Keswick; HANOVER: Hanover, Plaza I & II; HAZLETON: Churchill I & II, Hersker; JENKINTOWN: Hiway; LANCASTER: F&M College; LEBANON: Academy, Fox I & II, Howard I & II; MANSFIELD: Twain; MT. POCONO: Casino; MT. WOLF: Mt. Wolf; NANTICOKE: State; NEW CUMBERLAND: Shore D.I., West Shore; NEW OXFORD: Cross Keys D.I.; PHILADELPHIA: Avenue, Benner, Castor, Crest, Erlen, Fox, Leo I & II, Milgram, Parkwood Manor, Ritz I, II, & III, Stage Door Cinema, Theatre 1812, Tyson, Uptown, Yeadon; POTTSTOWN: Fox I & II, Towne, Norco Mall I & II; POTTSVILLE: Capitol, Deer Lake D.I., Fox I & II; READING: Fox I, II, III, & IV, Fox Midtown I & II, Fox North, Mt. Penn D.I., Reading D.I.; SINKING SPRINGS: Sinking Springs D.I.; SOUDERTON: Broad.

Moffitt Theatres, Inc.

P.O. Box 2094, Montgomery, AL 36103.

H. M. ENGLISH, pres.
ALABAMA—MONTGOMERY: Pekin; TUSKEGEE: Lincoln D.I.

Monarch Theatres

701 Executive Park, Louisville, KY 40207. (502) 893-3695.

BRUCE D. SHINBACH, pres.
INDIANA—JEFFERSONVILLE: Grant Plaza Twin Cinemas.
KENTUCKY—LOUISVILLE: Alpha Cinemas 1, 2, 3, 4, 5, 6, 7.

Monessen Amusement Co., Inc.

40 North Pennsylvania Avenue, Greensburg, PA 15601.

KALLIOPE MANOS, pres.; T. M. MANOS, v.p.; JOSEPH BUGALA, booker; DONALD WOODWARD, gen. mgr.
MARYLAND—HAGERSTOWN: Valley Mall, I, II & III; Cinema I & II, Hager, D.I.; FREDERICK: Cinema III, Holiday Cinemas
NEW YORK—OLEAN: Cinema Four.
PENNSYLVANIA—ALTOONA: Cinema 1, 2, 3 & 4, Altoona D.I., 764 Twin D.I.; BEAVER FALLS: Super 51 D.I.; CHARLEROI: State; Hilltop D.I., Coyle; CONNELLSVILLE: Comet D.I.; DUBOIS: Cinemas Four; GREENSBURG: Laurel 30; INDIANA: Indiana, Cinema Four; LATROBE: Hi-Way D.I., MONESSEN: Manos; UNIONTOWN: Manos, Starlite, Twin 40 Cinemas, Laurel Mall, Moonlite; VANDERGRIFT: Casino, Cinema I, II, III; WARREN: Cinema III.
WEST VIRGINIA—BLUEFIELD: Cinema V; ELKINS: Twin Cinema.

Moore, Donald, Circuit

Box 782, Charleston, WV 25323. (304) 344-4413.

WEST VIRGINIA—CLENDENIN: Roxy.

Moss, B. S., Enterprises

505 Park Ave., New York, NY 10022. (212) 688-6700.

CHARLES B. MOSS, JR., pres.; HANK LIGHTSTONE, film buyer.
NEW YORK—NEW YORK (Manhattan): Criterion 1, 2, 3, 4, 5 & 6, Movieland; LONG ISLAND, CEDARHURST: Central 1, 2, & 3; WESTCHESTER, YONKERS: Movieland 1, 2, 3, 4, 5 & 6.
NEW JERSEY—PARAMUS: Bergen Mall.

Moyer Theatres

1953 N.W. Kearney, Portland, OR 97209. (503) 226-2735.

LARRY R. MOYER, pres.
OREGON—PORTLAND: Town Center Cinema at Tanasbourne (3 screens), 104 St. D.I. (2 screens), 82nd St. D.I. (2 screens), Powell D.I., Bagdad Theatre (3 screens), 5th Avenue No. 1, 5th Avenue No. 2, Rose Moyer Cinemas (6 screens); EUGENE: Valley River Twin Cinema No. 1, Valley River Twin Cinema 2, West 11th Entertainment Center (2 drive-ins, 3 walk-ins), New Eugene D.I. (3 screens).
WASHINGTON—VANCOUVER: Vancouver Mall Cinema (4 screens); OLYMPIA: Capitol Mall Cinema (4 screens).

Music Makers Theatres, Inc.

1650 Oak Street, Lakewood, NJ 08701 (201) 367-0080.

MITCH LEIGH, bd. chrm.; MILTON HERSON, pres.; DAVID R. TUCKERMAN, sr. v.p. & sr. film buyer.
NEW JERSEY—FREEHOLD: Quad 1, 2, 3 & 4; HAZLET: Plaza; RAMSEY: Interstate 1 & 2; BRICKTOWN: Circle Triplex, Brick Plaza I & II, Mall Cinema I, II, III; LAKEWOOD: Town & Country Twin; BAYVILLE: Berkeley Cinema I & II; EAST WINDSOR: Cinema I & II; LONG BRANCH: Movies I & II; OCEAN TOWNSHIP: Middlebrook Cinema I & II; RED BANK: Movies I & II; GLASSBORO: College I & II; CINNAMINSON: Cinema I & II; WEST MILFORD: Abby Cinemas 1-2-3-4; EATONTOWN: Community I & II; TOMS RIVER: Dover I & II; SAYREVILLE: Madison Twin.
DELAWARE—NEWARK: King & Queen; NEW CASTLE: Triangle Mall Cinema.
PENNSYLVANIA—STROUDSBURG: Stroud Mall Cinemas 1, 2, 3, 4, 5.

Myers Circuit

Myers Theatre, Rich Square, NC 27869.

CHARLES E. MYERS, pres.
NORTH CAROLINA—AYDEN: Myers; RICH SQUARE: Myers.

N

Harry Nace Company, The

P.O. Box 7308, Phoenix, AZ 85011. (602) 264-9981.

HARRY L. NACE, JR., pres.; JOHN V. LOUIS, gen. mgr.
ARIZONA—FLAGSTAFF: Orpheum, Flag East, University Plaza 1 & 2; HOLBROOK: Roxy; MESA: Velda Rose D.I., Mesa, Pioneer D.I. 1 & 2; PHOENIX: Bethany, Phoenix D.I., Maryvale I & II; SCOTTSDALE: Kachina, Round-Up D.I.; TEMPE: University I & II; WINSLOW: Rialto, Tonto D.I.; PRESCOTT: Marina I & II; ELKS: Senator D.I.
NEVADA—LAS VEGAS: Las Vegas Cinerama.

Nasser Bros. Theatres

988 Market Street, San Francisco, CA 94102. (415) 885-1810.

HENRY NASSER, TED NASSER, chief officers.
CALIFORNIA—SAN FRANCISCO: New Mission.

National Theatre Corp.

29001 Cedar Rd., Cleveland, OH 44124.

BLAIR MOONEY, pres.; STUART WINTNER, v.p. & sec.; RUSSELL WINTNER, gen. mgr.
OHIO—AKRON: Starlight D.I. 1 & 2; Akron Cine Six, Summit Mall 1 & 2; ALLIANCE: Park Auto D.I.; ASHTABULA: Cinema Center 1, 2, 3 & 4; CANTON: McKinley 1 & 2; CLEVELAND: Great Northern 1 & 2, Great Lakes Mall 1, 2, 3, 4 & 5, Fairview 1 & 2, Midway Mall 1 & 2, Avon Lake 1, 2, 3 & 4, Auto D.I., Memphis D.I. 1, 2 & 3, Brookgate 1-5; HARRISBURG: Mid City D.I.; MARION: Southland Mall 1, 2, 3 & 4; NILES: Howland D.I., Movie World 1-5, Eastwood Mall 1 & 2; YOUNGSTOWN: Northside D.I., Southside D.I., Westside D.I., Ski Hi D.I., Newport, Southern Park 1 & 2, Boardman, Wedgewood 1 & 2, Austintown 1, 2 & 3.

Neighborhood Theatre, Inc.

830 E. Main St., P.O. Box 3-J, Richmond, VA 23206. (804) 644-0771.

MORTON G. THALHIMER, JR., pres.; SAM BENDHEIM, III, v.p.; DAVID LEVY, secty. & treas., MICHAEL L. SOFFIN, asst. secy.; FRANK NOVAK, v.p., operations and food service, asst. treas.; R. WADE PEARSON, v.p. Northern Va.
VIRGINIA—ANNANDALE: Annandale; ARLINGTON: Arlington, Byrd, Buckingham; CHARLOTTESVILLE: Barracks Road, University, FALLS CHURCH: Jefferson, State; FARMVILLE: Farmville D.I., State; McLEAN: Tyson Cinema, Tyson Corner 4; FREDERICKSBURG: Spotsylvania Four; PETERSBURG: Bluebird, Crater Cinema I, II, III, & IV, Walnut Mall I & II; RICHMOND: Bellwood Drive-In 1 & 2, Willow Lawn, Westover, Ridge I, II, III & IV, Chesterfield 1, 2, 3, Towne, Byrd, Westhampton, Capitol, State, Colonial; WOODBRIDGE: Marumsco; DALE CITY: Dale Cinema I & II; SPRINGFIELD: Springfield Cinema I & II.
MARYLAND—MARLOW HEIGHTS: Marlow I & II; LANDOVER: Landover 6; KENSINGTON: White Flint 5; NEW CARROLLTON: New Carrollton.

Newbold-Keesling Circuit

Bramwell, WV 24315. (304) Cherry 8-6685.

J. C. NEWBOLD, pres.; HAZEL KEESLING, v.p.; DONALD ANELLO, sec.-treas.; DON KEESLING, buyer & booker; Bramwell Theatres Inc., Freeman & Newbold, Inc., Oak Hill Theatres, Inc., Hinton Theatre Corp. Skyline Drive-In Theatre, Inc., Freeman Theatres, Inc.
VIRGINIA—WAYNESBORO: Skyline D.I.
WEST VIRGINIA—CHARLESTON: Lyric; HINTON: Ritz; LOGAN: Logan; WILLIAMSON: Cinderella Theatre.

Nilman, Carl H., Theatres

Shelburne Falls, MA 01370. (617) 625-6696.

CARL H. NILMAN, owner & mgr.
MASSACHUSETTS—CHARLEMONT: Community D.I.; SHELBURNE FALLS: Memorial.

Northeast Theatre Corp.

31 James Avenue, Boston, MA 02116. (617) Hubbard 2-5400.

MICHAEL REDSTONE, bd. chmn.; SUMNER REDSTONE, pres.
CONNECTICUT—MILFORD: Milford D.I.; ORANGE: Cinema 1, 2, 3, 4 & 5; HARTFORD: Cinema 1, 2, 3, 4 & 5.
ILLINOIS—MILAN: Memr. D.I., Cinema 1, 2, 3, 4 & 6; SILVIS: Semri D.I.; MOLINE: Corral D.I.
INDIANA—NEW ALBANY: New Albany D.I.
IOWA—DAVENPORT: Oasis D.I., Bel-Air D.I.
KENTUCKY—LOUISVILLE: Kenwood D.I., Parkway D.I., Cinema 1, 2, 3, 4, 5, 6 & 7; COVINGTON: Dixie Gardens D.I.; FLORENCE: Florence D.I.; COLD SPRINGS: Pike 27 D.I.; DAYTON: Riverview D.I.; ERLANGER: Showcase Cinemas 1, 2, 3, 4 & 5.
MARYLAND—BALTIMORE: Carlin D.I.; WEST HYATTSVILLE: Queens Chapel D.I.
MASSACHUSETTS—DEDHAM: Dedham D.I.; BOSTON: VFW Parkway, Neponset; NORTH READING: Starlite D.I.; CLEVELAND CIRCLE: Circle; LAWRENCE: Showcase Cinema 1, 2, 3 & 4; WORCESTER: Cinema 1, Showcase Cinemas 1, 2, 3 & 4; REVERE: Revere D.I.; SEEKONK: Showcase Cinemas 1, 2, 3, 4 & 5; SHREWSBURY: White City Theatre; SPRINGFIELD: Cinema 1, 2, 3, 4, 5, 6, 7 & 8; WOBURN: Showcase Cinemas 1, 2, 3, 4, & 5; DEDHAM: Showcase Cinemas 1, 2, 3 & 4.
MICHIGAN—JACKSON: Bel Air D.I., Jackson D.I.; GRAND RAPIDS: Cascade D.I.; PONTIAC: Miracle Mile, Pontiac D.I., Blue Sky D.I., Showcase Cinemas 1, 2, 3, 4 & 5; WATERFORD: Waterford D.I.; FLINT: Miracle Twin D.I.; E. LANSING: M-78 D.I., SAGINAW, Auto D.I., Bel Air D.I., Twilite D.I.; STERLING HEIGHTS: Showcase Cinemas 1, 2, 3, 4 & 5; MIDLAND: Sunset Drive-In; HARPER WOODS: Beacon East Cinemas 1 & 2.
NEW JERSEY—HAZLET: Route 35 D.I.; GLOUCESTER: Starlite D.I.; CAMDEN: Atco D.I.; NEWARK: Newark D.I.; PALMYRA: Tacony-Palmyra Bridge D.I.; PERTH AMBOY: Amboys D.I.
NEW YORK—NEW YORK: Whitestone Bridge D.I.; ROCHESTER: Washington, Lake Shore; NEDROW: Salina D.I.; VALLEY STREAM: Sunrise D.I.
OHIO—CINCINNATI: Oakley D.I.; TOLEDO: Showcase Cinemas, Cinema I, II, III & IV, Franklin Park D.I., Miracle Mile D.I., Maumee D.I.; Colony Theatre, Franklin Park Cinemas 4 & 5; LOVELAND: Academy D.I.; SPRINGDALE: Showcase Cinemas 1, 2, 3, 4 & 5.
PENNSYLVANIA—KUTZTOWN: Bethlehem D.I.; EASTON: Starlite D.I.; PITTSBURGH: Showcase Cinemas 1, 2, 3 & 4.
VIRGINIA—ALEXANDRIA: Mt. Vernon D.I.; MERRIFIELD: Lee HIGHWAY D.I.

Notopulos Theatres, Inc.

1104 Eleventh Avenue, Altoona, PA 16603. (814) 943-2617.

P. A. NOTOPULOS, pres.; C. A. NOTOPULOS, v.p. & film buyer; GEORGE NOTOPULOS, sec.-treas.
PENNSYLVANIA—ALTOONA: Capitol, Olympic, Rivoli; HUNTINGTON: Grand.

B. L. Nutter Theatres

P.O. Box 44, Rt. 44, Putnam Pike, CT 06260. (401) 568-5298.

(Operating Imperial Cinema Corp. and Nutter Theatre Management Associates)
BRUCE L. NUTTER, pres. & treas.; EDNA R. NUTTER, v.p. & secty.; BRUCE L. NUTTER, gen. mgr.; CHRISTINE E. NUTTER, asst. gen. mgr.
CONNECTICUT—HARTFORD: Colonial; PUTNAM: Royale Deluxe Theatre I & II.
MASSACHUSETTS—PALMER: Imperial Cinema; SPENCER: Imperial Cinema; WINCHENDON: Capitol.
RHODE ISLAND—PROVIDENCE: New Imperial Art Cinema; WEST GLOCESTER: Cold Springs Theatre I & II.

O

Ogden-Perry Theatres, Inc.

1 Shell Square, New Orleans, LA 70139. (504) 586-0123. 9810 Florida Blvd., Baton Rouge, LA 70815. (504) 927-4820.

EARL G. PERRY, SR., pres.; GUY P. OGDEN, v.p.; J. RANDOLPH OGDEN, secty-treas.
FLORIDA—FT. WALTON: Santa Rosa Triple Cinema.
LOUISIANA—NEW ORLEANS: Kenilworth Cinema I & II, Elmwood Cinema I, II, III & IV; BATON ROUGE: Broadmoor I & II; BAKER: Baker Cinema I & II; LAFAYETTE: Center Cinema I, II, & III; LAKE CHARLES: Charles Cinema I, II & III; ALEXANDRIA: MacArthur Village Cinema I, II, III & IV; SHREVEPORT: Eastgate Plaza I, II, III & IV; NEW IBERIA: Admiral Doyle Twin Cinema; HOUMA: Plaza Cinema I, II, III & IV; THIBODAUX: Nicholls Cinema I & II.
MISSISSIPPI—JACKSON: Jackson Mall Cinema, Ellis Esle I, II, III & IV; BILOXI: Edgewater Plaza Cinema I, II, III & IV; HATTIESBURG: Broadacres Cinema I, II, III & IV.
TENNESSEE—MEMPHIS: Southaven Cinema I, II, III, IV, V, & VI.

Oklahoma Cinema Theatres

Suite 330, 50 Penn Place Bldg., Oklahoma City, OK 73118.

LINDBURGH SHANBOUR, FARRIS SHANBOUR, JERRY BENSON, PAUL TOWNSEND, chief officers.
OKLAHOMA—OKLAHOMA CITY: North Park Cinema IV, French Market Cinema I & II; West Park Cinema I & II.

Orkin Amusements Co.

335 No. Farish St., Jackson, MS 39202.

ANDREW W. ORKIN, pres.; AD ORKIN, secty.-treas., & booker.
MISSISSIPPI—JACKSON: Alamo Theatre.

Oxmoor Cinemas

(See Mid States Theatres, Inc.)

P

Pacific Theatres

120 North Robertson Boulevard, Los Angeles, CA 90048. (213) 657-8420.

MICHAEL R. FORMAN, bd. chm., pres. & chief exec., JEROME A. FORMAN, exec. v.p. & gen'l mgr., JAMES J. COTTER, exec. v.p., finance, HAROLD CITRON, v.p., theatre operations, CHARLES EMMA, v.p., finance, MEL GOLDSMITH, v.p. real estate, TED MINSKY, v.p., ROBERT W. SELIG, v.p., ART SILBER, v.p., CHAN WOOD, v.p. & head film buyer.
Drive-in Theatres
CALIFORNIA—ANAHEIM: Anaheim Triplex; BALDWIN PARK: Edgewood; BUENA PARK: Buena Park, Lincoln; BURBANK: Pickwick; CHATSWORTH: Winnetka Four; COMPTON: Compton; CULVER CITY: Studio; DUARTE: Big Sky; EL MONTE: El Monte, Starlite; FONTANA: Bel Air; FOUNTAIN VALLEY: Fountain Valley; FRESNO: Woodward Park Four, Sunnyside Twin, Sunset; GARDENA: Vermont Triplex, Twin-Vue; HIGHLAND: Baseline; HUNTINGTON BEACH: Warner; CITY OF INDUSTRY: Vineland; INGLEWOOD: Century Twin; LA HABRA: La Habra; LOMA LINDA: Tri City; LONG BEACH: Circle, Lakewood, Los Altos Triplex; MONTEREY PARK: Floral; ORANGE: Orange Twin; OXNARD: Sky-View; PICO RIVERA: Fiesta Four; PARAMOUNT: Rosecrans Triplex, Paramount Twin; RIALTO: Foothill; SANTA ANA: Harbor Blvd.; SANTA FE SPRINGS: Norwalk; SAN BERNARDINO: Mt. Vernon Twin; SAN JUAN CAPISTRANO: Mission; SAN PEDRO: San Pedro; SOUTH GATE: South Gate; THOUSAND OAKS: Thousand Oaks; TORRANCE: Torrance; VAN NUYS: Sepulveda, Van Nuys; VENTURA: 101 Triplex; WESTCHESTER: Centinela; WESTMINSTER: Hi-Way 39; WHITTIER: Sundown.

518

CALIFORNIA—CITY OF COMMERCE: Commerce Four; HOLLYWOOD: Hollywood Pacific Triplex, Pacific's Cinerama Dome, Pix, Vine, World; HUNTINGTON PARK: Warner; LAGUNA: South Coast Twin; LA JOLLA: La Jolla Village Twin; LAKEWOOD: Lakewood Center Four, Lakewood Center South; LA MESA: Grossmont; LA MIRADA: La Mirada Six; LOS ANGELES: Cameo, Tower; MONTEBELLO: Garmar; PORTERVILLE: Porter Theatre 3; SAN DIEGO: Clairemont Twin, Center Three Cinerama; SHERMAN OAKS: Galleria Four; WEST LOS ANGELES: Picwood; WHITTIER: Whittier, Whittwood; WOODLAND HILLS: Topanga Twin.

Pal Amusement Co.

P.O. Box 750, Vidalia, GA 30474. (912) 537-7902.

BARRON W. GODBEE, JR., pres.
GEORGIA—HINESVILLE: Brice Cinema City (Cinema I, Cinema II, Cinema Drive-In); VIDALIA: Brice Cinema, New Pal, Pete's Drive-In.

Parr Theatres

Box 231, Tillamook, OR 96141.

WILLIAM L. PARR and JANICE K. PARR, owners.
OREGONCOTTAGE GROVE: Corral D.I.; LINCOLN CITY: Lakeside; NEW PORT: Midway, Yaquina D.I.; TILLAMOOK: Coliseum, Tillavue D.I.; TOLEDO: Ross.

Pend Oreille Theatres

315½ Washington Avenue, Newport, WA 99156.

CHARLES and RUTH BISHOP, owners.
IDAHO—PRIEST RIVER: Roxy.
WASHINGTON—CUSICK: Cusick; GARFIELD: Family, Rita, Star; METALINE FALLS: Little Playhouse; NEWPORT: Rex; PALOUSE: Congress.

Perakos Theatres Elmwood Theatre Corp.

468 Main Street, New Britain, CT 06051. (203) 223-6486 or 224-4152

SPERIE PERAKOS, president & ass't treas.; JOHN PERAKOS, vice-pres.; PETER G. PERAKOS, JR., treasurer & ass't sct.; ATTY. STEVEN E. PERAKOS, secretary.
CONNECTICUT—BRIDGEPORT: Beverly; ELMWOOD: Elm 1 & 2; NEW BRITAIN: Palace; PLAINVILLE: Plainville D.I.; SOUTHINGTON: Southington Twin D.I.; THOMPSONVILLE: Enfield Cinema; STRATFORD: Hi-Way Cinema 1 & 2.

Piedmont Theatres

Northwestern Bank Bldg., Suite 1090, 230 S. Tryon St., Charlotte, NC 28202 (704) 375-3734

L.L. THEIMER, C.C. TALBERT and JERRY L. THEIMER, owners.
NORTH CAROLINA—AHOSKIE: Ahoskie D.I., Earl I & II; ALBEMARLE: Badin Rd. D.I., Albermarle Rd. D.I.; ASHEVILLE: Park D.I.; BOONE: Flick I & II; BURLINGTON: Circle G. D.I.; CHARLOTTE: Plaza, South 29 D.I.; CLINTON: Cinema I, II, & III; 403 D.I.; DURHAM: Forest D.I., Midway D.I., Starlite D.I.; ELKIN: Elk I & II, Valley D.I.; FAYETTEVILLE: King I, II, & III, Fort I, II, & III D.I., Towne; GREENSBORO: Star; HICKORY: Springs Road D.I., T-Bird D.I.; HIGH POINT: Tar Heel D.I.; LEXINGTON: Welcome D.I.; RALEIGH: Center D.I., Tryon; ROCKY MOUNT: Tower D.I.; SELMA: SS Cinema I & II; SHELBY: Flick I & II; SMITHFIELD: Howell I & II, County D.I.; WILMINGTON: Manor; WILSON: Wilson; WINSTON-SALEM: Flamingo D.I., Mall Cinema; ZEBULON: Wak-Art.
SOUTH CAROLINA—CHARLESTON: Fox I & II, Port D.I.; COLUMBIA: Sunset D.I.; EASLEY: Easley Mall I & II; GAFFNEY: Hub I & II; GEORGETOWN: Hub I & II; GREENVILLE: Cedar Lane D.I.; SPARTANBURG: Circle South 29 D.I., Westview D.I.
VIRGINIA—DANVILLE: 360 D.I.; LYNCHBURG: Fort Green-Gold, Fort I & II D.I.; ROANOKE: 220 D.I., Shenandoah D.I.

Plitt Theatres

175 N. State Street, Chicago, IL 60601. Tel: RA6-5300. California headquarters: 2020 Avenue of the Stars, Los Angeles, CA

HENRY G. PLITT, bd. chm. & chief operating officer; ROY H. AARON, pres.; HAROLD J. KELIN, exec. v.p.; RAYMOND C. FOX, senior v.p.; ALLAN HURWITZ, v.p.; JEROME WINSBERG, v.p. & head film buyer; JAMES A. SORENSEN, fin. v.p. & treasurer; IRWIN COHEN, v.p., midwest; EDWARD M. PLITT, v.p., west; FRANK E. NEWELL, concession head.
ARIZONA—PHOENIX: Cine Capri, Indian D.I.; SCOTTSDALE: El Camino; TUCSON: El Dorado 1 & 2, Catalina 1 & 2, Coronado, Miracle D.I.
CALIFORNIA—LOS ANGELES: Century City 1 & 2; DALY CITY: Plaza 1 & 2; ORANGE: City 1 & 2; CONCORD: Capri; SAN FRANCISCO: Northpoint, St. Francis 1 & 2; STOCKTON: Sherwood; SACRAMENTO: Capitol 1 & 2, State 1 & 2; RICHMOND: Hilltop 1, 2, 3, 4.
IDAHO—BOISE: Egyptian, 8th St. Marketplace I & II, Midway.
ILLINOIS—ALTON: Grand; AURORA: Fox Valley 1, 2, 3 & 4; BERWYN: Berwyn; BLUE ISLAND: Lyric; BOLINGBROOK: #1-2 & 3; CALUMET CITY: River Oaks 1, 2, 3 & 4; CHICAGO: Chicago, Esquire, Gateway, Nortown, Oakbrook, State-Lake, United Artists, Will Rogers, Water Tower 1, 2, 3 & 4; EDWARDSVILLE: Wildey; ELGIN: Crocker, Grove; ELMWOOD PARK: Mercury; FREEPORT: State; CREST HILL: Hillcrest; KANKAKEE: Paramount; La Grange; ORLAND: Orland Park 1, 2, 3 & 4; PEORIA: Madison; ROCKFORD: Cherryvale 1, 2, 3, Midway, Times; SCHAUMBURG: Woolfield 1, 2, 3 & 4; VERNON HILLS: Hawthorn 1-2-3-4; WAUKEGAN: Academy, Genesee.
INDIANA—HAMMOND: Paramount; SOUTH BEND: River Park, State, Scottsdale; MISHAWAKA: Town & Country 1 & 2; MICHIGAN CITY: Marquette 1 & 2.
MICHIGAN—DETROIT: Palms; LANSING: Lansing Mall; FLINT: Eastland Mall, Northwest.
MINNESOTA—BROOKLYN CENTER: Brookdale; DULUTH: Norshor; FAIRMONT: Lake; LAKE ELMO: Vali-Hi D.I.; MANKATO: Grand, State; MAPLEWOOD: Plaza; MINNEAPOLIS: Cooper, Cameo, Skyway 1, 2, 3 & 4; ROCHESTER: Chateau, Oakview; ST. CLOUD: Hays, Paramount; ST. PAUL: Norstar, Riviera.
NEVADA—LAS VEGAS: Parkway 1, 2, 3.
NORTH DAKOTA—FARGO: Fargo, Lark; GRAND FORKS: Cinema International, Empire; MINOT: Empire.
SOUTH DAKOTA—ABERDEEN: Capitol; SIOUX FALLS: State, West Mall 1 & 2.
UTAH—OGDEN: Wilshire 1, 2, 3; PROVO: Paramount, Uinta; SALT LAKE CITY: Centre, Utah 1, 2, 3, Regency, Woodland; OREM: University 1 & 2.
WISCONSIN—EAU CLAIRE: State; LA CROSSE: Hollywood; SUPERIOR: Palace.

Polk Properties, Inc.

1055 West Genesee Street, Post Office Box 1093, Syracuse, NY 13201, (315) 472-6341.

WILLIAM P. BERINSTEIN, president; HENRY W. BERINSTEIN, exec. v.p.
NEW YORK—CORTLAND: Airport Drive In; OSWEGO: Oswego I, Oswego II.

Presidio Enterprises, Inc.

7020B Village Center Drive, Ste. 103, Austin, TX 78731. (512) 346-3600.

CHARLES B. CHICK, pres.; DICK L. CHICK, v.p./film buyer; JOHN A. BIRD, v.p.; JOHN E. ATHEY, secty., treas., gen. counsel.
TEXAS—AUSTIN: Village Cinema Four, Riverside Twin Cinema, Dobie Twin Screens, Lakehills Cinema Four; LONGVIEW: North Loop Six.

Priority Theatres

1010 E. 86th Street, #46—1040 Bldg., Indianapolis, IN 46240. Tel.: 846-3426.

JOSEPH CANTOR, DANIEL CANTOR, owners.
INDIANA—INDIANAPOLIS: Georgetown, Carlyle, Regency I, Regency II, Lafayette Road Outdoor, Shadeland Outdoor, South 31 Outdoor, National Outdoor.

Q

Query Enterprises, Inc.
Marion, VA 24354.

T. D. FIELD, owner.
VIRGINIA—ABINGDON: Zephyr; MARION: Lincoln, Center; NORTON: Koltown.

R

R/C Theatres
19 West Mt. Royal Avenue, Baltimore, MD 21201. (301) 332-0222.

IRWIN R. COHEN, pres. & chief executive officer; AARON B. SEIDLER, exec. v.p.; JOHN M. HESSION, v.p. & gen. mgr.; J. WAYNE ANDERSON, v.p.; SCOTT R. COHEN and JOSEPH BERNHEIMER, booking mgrs.; MRS. SAREBA MASLOW, Baltimore office mgr.; MRS. FRANCES SIMPSON, Fredericksburg.
MARYLAND—ARBUTUS: Hollywood; CAMBRIDGE: Bay Cinemas 1 & 2; CHURCHVILLE: Bel-Air D.I.; CUMBERLAND: Light Cinema, Super 51 D.I.; FROSTBURG: Frostburg Cinema 1, 2 & 3, Palace; HANCOCK: Hancock D.I.; LAVALE: Center; REISTERTOWN: Village; SALISBURY: Boulevard, Mall Cinema 1 & 2, World Cinemas 1 & 2; SYKESVILLE: Carrolltowne Cinemas 1 & 2; TANEYTOWN: Monocacy D.I.; WESTERNPORT: Tri-Town Cinemas 1 & 2; WESTMINSTER: Carroll.
PENNSYLVANIA—CARLISLE: Carlisle; GETTYSBURG: Majestic, Village 1 & 2; STATE LINE: State Line D.I.
VIRGINIA—CLIFTON FORGE: Stonewall; CULPEPER: Regal Cinemas 1 & 2, State, Culpeper D.I.; EMPORIA: South; FRANKLIN: State; FREDERICKSBURG: Greenbriar Cinemas 1 & 2, Colonial, Victoria, Virginians Cinemas 1, 2, 3 & 4, Fredericksburg D.I.; FRONT ROYAL: Park, Front Royal D.I.; LEESBURG: Tally-Ho 1 & 2; LEXINGTON: Lyric Cinema, State; MANASSAS: Manassas D.I.; STAUNTON: Plaza Cinema; SUFFOLK: Plaza Cinema; WAYNESBORO: Wayne Cinemas 1 & 2, North 340 D.I.; WINCHESTER: Winchester D.I.
WEST VIRGINIA—CHARLESTOWN: Charles Cinemas 1 & 2; WHITE SULPHUR SPRINGS: Cinema 2, Cinema #3 D.I.

RKO-Stanley Warner Theatres, Inc.
1585 Broadway, New York, NY 10036 (212) 975-8300.

HARRY S. BUXBAUM, pres.; ROBERT N. POLSON, dir., theatre operations; RONALD POLON & NICK GUADAGNO, film buyers; JOHN DEANE, v.p. & tres.; ALAN B. WOLFER, v.p. & gen. counsel; ANDY GAROFALO, adv. & pub.
CONNECTICUT—BRIDGEPORT: Merritt Twin;
NEW JERSEY—BLOOMFIELD: Royal Twin; CRANFORD: Cranford Twin; EAST ORANGE: Hollywood; HACKENSACK: Oritani, Triplex; JERSEY CITY: Staney, live shows & special attractions; MILBURN: Milburn Twin; NEWARK: Branford, Quad; PARAMUS: Stanely Warner Rt. 4 Quad; RIDGEWOOD: Warner, Twin; WAYNE: Twin; UNION: Union Twin.
NEW YORK—BROOKLYN: Kenmore, Quad; BRONX: Fordham Quad; FLUSHING: Keith's Triplex; JAMAICA: Alden Quad; NASSAU: Triplex Lawrence, Twin Rockville Center, Twin, Plainview, Valley Stream, Mineola, Hempstead; NEW ROCHELLE: Proctor's Fiveplex; NEW YORK: Coliseum Twin, Cinerama I & II, 86th Street Twin; SUFFOLK: Twin Babylon, Twin Commack.
OHIO—CLEVELAND: Vogue.

Rappaport Theatres
222 St. Paul Place, Baltimore, MD 21202. (301) MU5-7828.

M. ROBERT RAPPAPORT, pres.
MARYLAND—BALTIMORE: Eastpoint 4 Cinemas, Ritchie Cinemas 1-2-3, Timonium Cinemas 1-2-3, Hillendale Cinema, Jumpers Cinemas 1, 2, 3, 4 & 5.
OHIO—CLEVELAND: Hillendale Cinemas 1 & 2; Severance I & II; World East and West.

The Walter Reade Organization, Inc.
241 E. 34th St., New York, NY 10016. (212) 683-6300.

SHELDON GUNSBERG, pres. and chief executive officer; CHRISTOPHER W. PREUSTER, executive vice pres. and treasurer; JOHN BALMER, asst. secty.; WILLIAM QUIGLEY, film buyer; DONNA LERNER, adv. mgr.
NEW YORK—KINGSTON: Community, Sunset D.I.; Mayfair 1 & 2; NEW YORK CITY: Bay, Baronet, Coronet, 34th St. East, Ziegfield, Little Carnegie, New Yorker 1 & 2, Waverly, Festival.

Recreation Enterprise, Inc.
P.O. Box 419, Columbia, TN 38401. (615) 388-2077.

HENRY P. VINSON, JR., pres. & gen. mgr.
KENTUCKY—MURRAY: Capri Twin, Cheri Twin, Central Cine I & II, Murray D.I.
TENNESSEE—COLUMBIA: Polk Cinema I & II, Sundown D.I.

Redstone Management
(See Northeast Theatre Corp.)

Redwood Theatres, Incorporated
544 Golden Gate Ave., San Francisco, CA 94102. Tel.: (415) 771-5900.

RICHARD MANN, pres. & gen. mgr.; GEORGE VOGAN, v.p. & asst. gen. mgr.; W. E. McLAIN, sec.-tres.; LILLIAN JOHNS, asst. sec.-treas.
CALIFORNIA—EUREKA: Eureka Theatres 3, State 1, 2, & 3, Old Town Cinemas 4; Midway D.I.; MODESTO: Briggsmore, Cinema 1 & 2; SANTA ROSA: Coddingtown Cinemas 1, 2 & 3, Park Cinema I & II, Village D.I.; UKIAH: Ukiah 4; WOODLAND: State 1, 2 & 3.
OREGON—KLAMATH FALLS: Esquire, Tower 1 & 2, Pelican Cinemas 1, 2, 3, & 4, Shasta D.I. Theatres (1, 2 & 3).

Rifkin Theatres
(See Theatre Management Services)

Rockwood Theatres, Inc.
414 Whitley Building, Nashville, TN 37212. (615) 269-4513.

MRS. IDA H. STENGEL, pres.
ALABAMA—RUSSELLVILLE: Roxy.
TENNESSEE—CLINTON: Ritz; HUNTINGTON: Court, Carroll; McKENZIE: Park; ROCKWOOD: Roane; ROGERSVILLE: Roxy.

Rogers Cinema, Inc.
P.O. Box 28, Marshfield, WI 54449. (715) 387-3437.

PAUL J. ROGERS, pres.; JOHN DIONNE, buyer and booker.
WISCONSIN—MARSHFIELD: Rogers Cinema 1-2-3, 10-13 D.I.; STEVENS POINT: Rogers 1 & 2, 51 D.I., Fox; WAUSAU: Rogers Cinema 1 & 2; WISCONSIN RAPIDS: Rogers Cinema 1 & 2.

Rome Theatres, Inc.
1514 Reisterstown Rd., Baltimore, MD 21208. (301) 484-3500.

H. PAUL ROME, pres.; LEON B. BACK, gen. mgr.
MARYLAND—BALTIMORE: Apollo, Super, 170 D.I.

Roth Theatres
950 Bonifant Street, Silver Spring, MD 20910. Tel.: (301) 587-8450.

PAUL A. ROTH, pres.; NED C. GLASER, exec. v.p. & gen. mgr.; NORMAN FALK, film buyer; MICHAEL E. ROWAN, dir. of finance.

MARYLAND—SILVER SPRING: Roth's Silver Spring, Roth's Silver Spring East; CLINTON: Ranch D.I.; WALDORF: 301 Drive-In; GAITHERSBURG: Roth's Montgomery I & II, Roth's Quince Orchard; BETHESDA-POTOMAC: Roth's Seven Locks I & II; ROCKVILLE: Roth's Parkway 1, 2, 3, Roth's Randolph 1 & 2, Roth's Manor 1 & 2.

VIRGINIA—HARRISONBURG: Virginia, Harrisonburg D.I., Roth's 1-2-3, Roth's D.I.; FAIRFAX CITY: Roth's Mt. Vernon 1 & 2; ANNANDALE: Roth's Americana; McLEAN: Roth's Tyson '5'; WOODBRIDGE: Roth's Featherstone; CHARLOTTESVILLE: Greenbrier 1 & 2.

Royal Theatres

Leisure Industries, Inc., P.O. Box 269, West Point, GA 31833. (205) 768-2050.

BARBARA ROYAL, pres.; G. MONTE ROYAL, vice pres. ALABAMA—SHAWMUT: Royal, Hiway Drive In. MISSISSIPPI—MERIDIAN: Royal Cinema 1 & 2, Royal, Royal Drive In, Meridian Drive In; PASCAGOULA: Ritz, Towne, Moss Point Cinema, Chico Twin, Super Twin Drive In, Lake Twin Drive In.

Royal Theatres

Honolulu, Hawaii 96814.

IRVING H. LEVIN, pres.; FRANK R. MILLER, v.p. & controller; LEO MILLER, buyer and booker. HAWAII—HILO: Mamo; HONOLULU: King Twin; KAHALA: Waialae D.I.; WAIKIKI BEACH: New Royal, Royal Marine Twin; WAIPAHU: Royal Sunset D.I.

S

SBC Management Corporation

Assembly Square Office Park, Somerville, MA 02145. (617) 628-6700.

DOUGLASS N. AMOS, pres.; FRANCIS LYNCH, v.p./film; RICHARD WILSON, v.p./merchandising; MAX L. YUNIK, treas. CONNECTICUT—BRIDGEPORT: Candlelite-Pix Twin D.I.; DANBURY: Danbury D.I.; EAST WINDSOR: East Winsor D.I.; HARTFORD: Cinema City; ENFIELD: Cine Enfield 1-2-3-4-5-6, Enfield Mall; TORRINGTON: SkyVue D.I., Torrington D.I.; WATERBURY: Pine Twin D.I., Plaza 1, 2, 3, 4; SOUTH WINDSOR: East Hartford D.I. MAINE—AUBURN: Auburn D.I.; FARMINGTON: State; LEWISTON: Lewiston D.I.; PORTLAND: Portland Twin D.I.; SKOWHEGAN: Skowhegan D.I.; WINSLOW: Winslow D.I.; SACO: Saco D.I.; Waterville; Cinema Center Sixplex. MASSACHUSETTS—SCITUATE: Satuit Playhouse 1 & 2. NEW HAMPSHIRE—CONCORD: Concord D.I.; BOSCAWEN: Sky-Hi D.I.; NEWINGTON: Cine 1-2-3-4-5-6. NEW YORK—ALBANY: Cine 1-2-3-4-5-6; ROCHESTER: Cine 1, 2, 3, 4. RHODE ISLAND—PROVIDENCE: Castle 1 & 2. Cinerama 1 & 2. VERMONT—BURLINGTON: Cinema 1, 2 & 3.

S.J.M. Entertainment Corporation

722 University Bldg., Syracuse, NY 13202 (315) 422-8180.

SAMUEL J. MITCHELL, pres. NEW YORK—CANTON: American; CAZENOVIA: Cazenovia; CORTLAND: Plaza I & II, Airport D.I.; DRYDEN: Dryden D.I.; ELMIRA: Elmira D.I.; ITHACA: State I & K LL II, Ithaca; MASSENA: Massena; OGDENSBURG: Mall I & II; OSWEGO: Oswego I & II; POTSDAM: Roxy I & II.

Sack Theatres

141 Tremont Street, Boston, MA 02111. (617) 542-3334.

A. ALAN FRIEDBERG, pres.; WILLIAM GLAZER, gen. mgr.; SUSAN FRAINE, dir. of adv./pub. MASSACHUSETTS—BOSTON: Beacon Hill 1, 2, & 3, Charles 1-2-3, Cheri 1-2-3, Cinema 57 1-2, Paris Cinema, Pi

Alley 1-2, Saxon; BROCKTON: Sack Cinemas 1-2-3-4; DANVERS: Sack Cinemas Liberty Tree Mall 1-2, Sack Cinemas 1-2-3-4-5-6; GARDNER: Sack Cinema 1-2; LEOMINSTER: Sack Cinemas 1-2-3-4-5-6-7; NATICK: Sack Cinemas 1-2-3-4-5-6; SOMERVILLE: Sack Cinema Assembly Square (eightplex); SPRINGFIELD: Sack Cinemas 1-2, at Eastfield Mall; WEST SPRINGFIELD: Sack Palace Cinemas 1-2.

St. Louis Amusement Co. and Associated Companies

527 N. Grand Blvd., St. Louis, MO 63153.

EDWARD B. ARTHUR, pres. ILLINOIS—GRANITE CITY: Washington. MISSOURI—CLAYTON: Shady Oak; KIRKWOOD: Kirkwood Cinemas; Avalon, Fox, Granada, Hi-Pointe, Ellisville, Lewis & Clark, Stadium Cinema I & II, St. Ann Cinema, 4-Screen D.I., Shenandoah, 270 D.I., Cross Keys Cinema, St. Andrews Cinema; WEBSTER GROVES: Webster Groves Cinema.

Sameric Corporation

1605 Chestnut Street, Philadelphia, PA 19103 (215) 561-0440.

MERTON SHAPIRO, pres.; MARTHA GERMSCHEID, secty.; IRVING LOMIS, film buyer; ROBERT ARNOLD, adv./pub. head; WILLIAM SARRIS, operations; MERTON SHAPIRO, pres., Sameric-West. DELAWARE—CLAYMONT: Eric I, II & III & IV-Tri-State Mall; NEWARK: Eric Newark D.I. I & II. NEW JERSEY—CAMDEN: Eric Black Horse Pike D.I. I & II; CHERRY HILL: Eric I & II-Rt. 38; LAWRENCEVILLE: Eric I & II; MOORESTOWN: Eric Plaza; PENNSAUKEN: Eric I, II & III; PRINCETON: Eric Garden I & II, Eric Playhouse; STRATFORD: Eric I & II; TRENTON: Eric I & II-Independence Mall; WESTMONT: Eric; WILLINGBORO: Eric I & II. PENNSYLVANIA—ALLENTOWN: Eric I, II & III; ARDMORE: Eric I & II; BROOKHAVEN: Eric I & II; BROOMALL: Eric I & II-Lawrence Park; CLIFTON HEIGHTS: Eric I & II; CONCORDVILLE: Eric I & II; DREXEL HILL: Eric-Pilgrim Gardens; EASTON: Eric I, II, III & IV; FAIRLESS HILLS: Eric I & II, Eric Penn Jersey I & II, U.S. #1 North D.I. I & II; FEASTERVILLE: Eric I, II & III; FRAZER: Eric I & II; GLENOLDEN: Eric MacDade D.I. I & II; HARRISBURG: Eric I & II-Colonial Park, Eric I & II-East Park, Eric Keystone D.I. I & II, Eric I & II-Union Deposit Mall; HOLMES: Eric I & II-MacDade Mall; HORSHAM: Eric I & II; JENKINTOWN: Eric I & II-Baderwood; KING OF PRUSSIA: Eric King I & II, Eric Plaza I & II; LANCASTER: Eric I & II, Eric Pacific I, II & III; MONTGOMERYVILLE: Eric I, II & III; PHILADELPHIA: Eric I & II-Chestnut Hill, Duke, Duchess, Eric I & II-Fernrock, Eric I & II-Ivy Ridge, Eric's Mark I, Eric's Place, Eric I & II-Rittenhouse Square, Sameric I, II & III, Sam's Place I & II, Eric on the Campus I, II & III-University City; READING: Eric I & II; SHILLINGTON: Eric I & II; UPPER DARBY: Eric I & II-Barclay Square, Eric Terminal; WEST GOSHEN: Eric I & II; WYNNEWOOD: Eric.

Savar Corporation

4605 Westfild Ave., Pennsauken, NJ 08110.

HENRIETTA V. KRAVITZ, pres.; SAMUEL KALIKMAN, sec.; SAMUEL PASSMAN, asst. treas. & asst. secty. NEW JERSEY—CAMDEN: Midway.

Schneider-Merl

4325 Glenwood Avenue, Raleigh, NC 27612.

STAN SCHNEIDER, pres.; LEONARD MERL, v.p.; HUGH SYKES, film buyer; MARGIE THOMAS, booker; J. B. BREULIEU, adv.-pub.; TONY SWEENEY, purchasing agent. NORTH CAROLINA—BOONE: Chalet; BURLINGTON: Park; DURHAM: Yorktowne; ELIZABETH city; gateway; GASTONIA: Village; HIGH POINT: Towne; RALEIGH: Colony, Valley; WINSTON-SALEM: Parkway, Parkview.

Schwaber World Fare Cinemas

910 Bldg., Pikesville, MD 21208. (301) 484-6100.

MILTON SCHWABER, pres.; HOWARD A. WAGONHEIM, v.p.; MARK D. WAGONHEIM, treas. MARYLAND—BALTIMORE: Apex, 5 West, Paramount, Playhouse; LUTHERVILLE-TIMONIUM: Cinema I & II, Yorkridge; PIKESVILLE: mini-flick 1 & 2; WHITEMARSH: Pulaski D.I.

Selected Theatres Mgmt. Co.

Brainard Place, 29001 Cedar Ave., Rm. 451, Lyndhurst, OH 44124. (216) 461-9770.

SAM SCHULTZ, gen. mgr.; JAY SCHULTZ; KEN WALTER, EARL STEIN.
OHIO—AKRON: Ascot D.I. 1, 2 & 3, Gala D.I. 1 & 2; ASHTABULA: Skyway D.I.; CANTON: E. 30 D.I. 1, 2 & 3; CLEVELAND: Euclid Ave. D.I., Pearl Road D.I., Mapleton; LIMA: American Mall Theatres 1 & 2, Springbrook D.I., Brookgate Theatres 1, 2, 3, 4 & 5; LORAIN: Lorain D.I. 1 & 2; MADISON: Skyway D.I.; MARION: North D.I., MENTOR: Mentor D.I. 1 & 2; N. KINGSVILLE: Midway D.I.; ZANESVILLE: Maple D.I.; WOOSTER: Skyline D.I. 1 & 2.

Shriver Theatres Co.

8th and Boardwalk, Ocean City, NJ 08226. (609) 399-0099.

ARTHUR W. OEHLSCHLAGER, gen. mgr.
NEW JERSEY—OCEAN CITY: Moorlyn Twin, Strand, Village.

Simons, W.A. Co.

(A Division of Sharp-Sias Enterprises)
P.O. Box 7277, Missoula, MT 59807; Salt Lake City, 555 East 2nd South.

EDWARD SHARP, pres.; ROBERT V. SIAS, v.p.; C. Barry Walker, buyer & booker.
IDAHO—COEUR D'ALENE: Wilma; KELLOGG: Rena.
MONTANA—MISSOULA: Wilma 1 & 2, Roxy, Go West D.I.

The Skirball Investment Company

3690 Orange Place, Suite 355, Cleveland, OH 44122. (216) 621-1594.

JACK H. SKIRBALL and JOSEPH LISSAUER, gen. mgrs.
OHIO—AKRON: Summit D.I.; BRYAN: Bryan; WINTERSVILLE: Winter D.I.

Slotnick Enterprises, Inc.

968 James Street, Syracuse, NY 13203. (315) 424-7700.

HERBERT N. SLOTNICK, pres.
NEW YORK—DEWITT: Dewitt D.I.; LIVERPOOL: Lakeshore D.I.; CICERO: North D.I.

Southwest Theatres, Inc.

P.O. Box 2270, Corpus Christi, TX 78403. (512) 855-0241.

O. M. RICHTER, pres.; MRS. MARTHA R. RANKIN, v.p.; LEON NEWMAN, sec.-tres.
TEXAS—EDINBURG: Century, Citrus, Capri.

Standard Theatres, Inc.

19065 North Hills Dr., P. O. Box 632, Brookfield, WI 53005 (414) 784-1450.

JOHN F. LING, pres.
WISCONSIN—Beloit: Prairie Cinema; DELAVAN: Delavan; GREEN BAY: Valley Outdoor, Bay, West; JANESVILLE: Midcity D.I.; KENOSHA: Lake, Midcity Outdoor, Kenosha; LAKE GENEVA: Geneva; MILWAUKEE: 41 Twins Outdoor; SHEBOYGAN: Star Dusk D.I.: Waukesha; Highway 59.

Statesville Theatre Corp.

Stearns Bldg., Statesville, NC 28677. (704) 873-9041.

A. F. SAMS, JR., chm.; WILLIAM T. SAMS, pres.; MRS. PHYLLIS HARRIS, treas.
NORTH CAROLINA—BOONE: Appalachian; STATESVILLE: Playhouse, Newtowne, Gateway 1 & 2, I-77 D.I.; COVINA: Capri Triplex, Covina D.I. I & II; EL CAJON: Park-

way Triplex; GLENDALE: Roxy; HOLLYWOOD: Holly, Paramount; LOS ANGELES, Crest, MONTCLAIR: Montclair Triplex; OXNARD: Carriage Square I & II; PASADENA: Colorado, Pasadena Hastings; SANTA FE SPRINGS: La Mirada D.I.; TORRANCE: Rolling Hills Twin.

Sterling Recreation Organization

P.O Box 1723, Bellevue, WA 98009 (206) 455-8100 (Sterling Theatres Co., a Division of S.R.O.)

FREDRIC A. DANZ, pres.; JERRY D. VITUS, general mgr.; TAD DANZ, v.p., admin.; ROBERT M. HAZARD, film buyer; ROB MCQUISTON, ad manager; ROBERT BOND, director of NW theatre division; GEORGE PEARN, director of California theatre division.
WASHINGTON—BELLEVUE: Bel-Vue, John Danz, Factoria Cinemas, Bel-Kirk Twin D.I.; BELLINGHAM: Viking Twin, Samish Twin D.I., Sehome III; EVERETT: Puget Park D.I. & Swap; KIRKLAND: Totem Lake Cinemas; LONGVIEW/KELSO: Columbia, Kelso, Longview, Your Twin D.I.; LYNWOOD: Grand Cinemas Alderwood, Lynn Four; TRI-CITIES: Clearwater Cinemas, Metro 4 Cinemas, Pasco, River-Vue D.I. & Swap, Columbia Center Tri-Plex, Uptown, Island View D.I.; WALLA WALLA: Liberty, Sky-Vue D.I.; SPOKANE: East Sprague D.I. & Swap, East Trent D.I., Garland, Lincoln Heights Tri-Plex, North Cedar D.I., Riverpark Square Cinemas, State, West End D.I.; TACOMA: Tacoma Mall Twin, Tacoma West Tri-Plex; SEATTLE: Admiral Twin, Cinerama, Lake City, Lewis & Clark Tri-Plex, Music Box, Northgate, Southcenter, Town, Uptown.
CALIFORNIA—Los Angeles Office, 5900 Wilshire Blvd., Los Angeles, CA 90036: Capri, Carriage Square I & II, Colorado, Covina D.I. I & II, Crest, Holly, La Mirada D.I., Montclair Tri-Plex, Pasadena Hastings, Parkway Tri-Plex, Paramount, Rolling Hills Twin, Roxy.

Sterling Theatres

310 West Kennewick Ave., P.O. Box 6045, Kennewick, WA 99336. (509) 586-1121.

JACK COBB, supvr.
WASHINGTON—KENNEWICK: Columbia Center Tri-plex Clearwater Cinemas; PASCO: Pasco, River-Vu D.I.; RICHLAND: Metro 4 Cinemas, Uptown, Island View D.I., WALLA-WALLA: Liberty, Sky-Vu D.I.

Stewart & Everett Theatres, Inc.

1514 N. Tryon St., P.O. Box 1658, Charlotte, NC 28232. (704) 334-9771.

CHARLES B. TREXLER, pres., treas.; CHARLES B. TREXLER, JR., exec. v.p.; H. M. PICKETT, JR., v.p.; LLOYD TODD, film buyer, W. W. CUNNINGHAM, CHARLES H. JONES, FLOYD NAYLOR, HOWARD GAINEY, dist. mgrs.; E. M. MARKS, dir. adv. & pub.; JOHN TREXLER, v.p. & adv. mgr.
NORTH CAROLINA—BOONE: Appalachian; CHARLOTTE: Capri I & II, Village 1 & 2; DUNN: Stewart, Plaza 1 & 2; FAYETTEVILLE: Westwood Cinema 1, 2 & 3; GOLDSBORO: Berkeley Cinema 1, 2 & 3; Eastgate Cinema; GRAHAM: Graham; GREENSBORO: Golden Gate 1 & 2, Quaker Cinema 1 & 2; GREENVILLE: Park, Plaza Cinema 1, 2 & 3; HAVELOCK: Cherry Cinema; HENDERSON: Cinema, Embassy; JACKSONVILLE: Brynn Marr, Cinema 1 & 2, Center 1 & 2, Iwo Jima, Towne Cinema, Northwoods 1 & 2, Cinema D.I.; KANNAPOLIS: Park-In; KINSTON: Mall Cinema, Paramount, Plaza Cinema 1 & 2; LAURINBURG: Cinema 1 & 2, Gibson; LENOIR: Avon, Westgate Cinema I & II; LINCOLNTON: Cinema 1 & 2, Century, Starlite D.I., MOREHEAD CITY: Morehead 1 & 2, Cinema 1, 2 & 3; MORGANTON: Mimosa Cinema 1 & 2; MOUNT AIRY: Cinema; NEW BERN: Cinema 1 & 2; NORTH WILKESBORO: West Park Cinema 1 & 2; ROANOKE RAPIDS: Peoples, Cinema 1 & 2, Gaston D.I.; ROCKY MOUNT: Englewood Cinema I & II; Oakwood Cinema 1 & 2; RUTHERFORD COUNTY: Cinema 1 & 2; SALISBURY: Center; SANFORD: Kendale Cinema 1 & 2, Wilrik; SHELBY: Cinema 1 & 2; SOUTHERN PINES: Sunrise, Town & Country Cinema 1 & 2; STATESVILLE: Newtowne, Playhouse, I-77 D.I., Gateway Cinema 1 & 2; WASHINGTON: Washington Square Cinema 1, 2 & 3; WILLIAMSTON: Cinema; WILMINGTON: Longleaf Cinema 1 & 2, Oleander 1 & 2, Skyline D.I., Starway D.I., New Centre 1, 2 & 3; Independence Mall Cinema 1, 2 & 3; WILSON: Gold Park Cinema 1 & 2, Parkwood Cinema 1 & 2; WINSTON-SALEM: Reynolda Cinema 1 & 2, University Plaza 1 & 2.
SOUTH CAROLINA—AIKEN: Cinema; BENNETTSVILLE: Cinema; CHESTER: Chester Cinema 1 & 2; CHARLESTON: Pinehaven Cinema 1 & 2, South Windermere 1 & 2, Mt. Pleasant Cinema 1-2-3; CONWAY: Holiday; FLOR-

ENCE: Cinema 5; GAFFNEY: Capri; GREENVILLE: Mall Cinema 1 & 2; HARTSVILLE: Cinema 1 & 2; MYRTLE BEACH: Cinema, Dunes Cinema 1, 2 & 3; South Myrtle Cinema 4, Rivoli 1 & 2; NORTH MYRTLE BEACH: Ocean Cinema 1, 2 & 3; ROCK HILL: Cinema, Pix.
VIRGINIA—BLACKSBURG: Studio I & II; LYNCHBURG: Boonsboro Cinema 1 & 2, Plaza 1, 2, 3 & 4; DANVILLE: Plaza Cinema 1 & 2, Riverside Cinema 1 & 2.

Storey Theatres Inc.

572 Morosgo Drive N.E. Atlanta, GA 30324

FREDERICK G. STOREY, chmn.; JAMES H. EDWARDS, pres.; MANUEL F. RODRIGUEZ, exec. v.p.; COLEY W. HAYES, v.p.; secty. treas.
GEORGIA—ATLANTA: Lakewood Twin, National Four, North Dekalb Twin, North 85 Twin D.I., Shannon Four, Glenwood D.I., Gwinnett D.I.; GAINSVILLE: Blueridge Triple, Sherwood, Lake Lanier D.I., Skyview D.I.
TENNESSEE—CHATTANOOGA: Brainerd, Plaza.

Strebe, Earle C., Theatres

207 N. Palm Canyon Drive, Palm Springs, CA 92262. (213) 325-2626.

CALIFORNIA—BIG BEAR LAKE: Lake D.I.; CRESTLINE: Crestline; LAKE ARROWHEAD: Arrowhead Village; PALM SPRINGS: Palm Springs, Plaza, Palm Springs D.I., Chi Chi Starlite.

Sunny-Mount Theatres, Inc.

988 Market St., San Francisco, CA 94102. (415) PRospect 6-4703.

WILLIAM B. DAVID, pres.; R. O. FOLKOFF, sec.-treas.
CALIFORNIA—CAMPBELL: Campbell; LOS GATOS: Los Gatos; MT. VIEW: Cinema, Mt. View, Monte Vista D.I.; SUNNYVALE: Sunnyvale; LOS ALTOS: Los Altos.
NEVADA—RENO: El Rancho.

Syndicate Theatres, Inc.

55½ E. Court Street, Franklin, IN 46131. (219) 736-7144.

TRUEMAN T. REMBUSCH, pres.; MICHAEL REMBUSCH, v.p., operations; GRACE HANDLEY, treas.
INDIANA—BATESVILLE: Gibson; COLUMBUS: Crump, Columbus D.I.; CRAWFORDSVILLE: Ben Hur D.I.; ELWOOD: Elwood, Elwood D.I.; FRANKLIN: Artcraft; HUNTINGTON: Huntington, Huntington D.I.; WABASH: Eagles, 13-24 D.I.; MADISON: Ohio I-II, Skyline D.I.

T

Talley Enterprises

Box 24, Pleasanton, TX 78064.

GIDNEY TALLEY, owner & gen. mgr.
TEXAS—DEVINE: Medina D.I.; PLEASANTON: Plestex.

Tanner Theatre Circuit

Box 189, Pana, IL 62557.

HERMAN TANNER, pres. & gen. mgr.
ILLINOIS—NOKOMIS: Palace; PANA: Roseland, Tanner D.I.; VANDALIA: Liberty, Tanner D.I.

Tentelino Enterprises, Inc.

P.O. Box 621, Alexandria, MN 56308. (612) 763-3669.

RAY VONDERHAAR, v.p. & gen. mgr.
MINNESOTA—ANDRIA 1 & 2—ALEXANDRIA: And Sunset D.I.; FERGUS FALLS: Westgate Cinema 1 & 2, Fergus, Fergus D.I.; INTERNATIONAL FALLS: Border 1 & 2, Parkway D.I.; LITTLE FALLS: Falls, Airport D.I.; BRAINERD:

Paramount, Gull D.I.; WORTHINGTON: State 1 & 2, Gay D.I.
SOUTH DAKOTA—MADISON: Madison D.I.

Tercar Theatre Company

Windsor Theatre Bldg., 5078 Richmond Ave., P.O. Box 22608, Houston, TX 77027.

ROBERT H. PARK, bd. chmn.; CHARLES F. PAINE, pres.; BRANDON DOAK, v.p. film buying; ROBERT L. PARK, JEFF WOLF, theatre operations, MARY YATES MYER, asst. to pres.
TEXAS—BAYTOWN: Brunson I & II; Bay Plaza Twin, Decker I & II; HOUSTON: Airline D.I., Gaylynn I & II, Gaylynn Terrace, King Center D.I. East and West, Memorial I & II, Telephone Road D.I. I & II, Windsor Cinerama; ROSENBERG: Cole, State, Twin City D.I.; SUGARLAND: Palms I & II.

Theater Management Services

39 Church Street, Boston, MA 02116. (617) 482-3410.

PHILIP L. LOWE, chm of board; JULIAN RIFKIN, pres.; MALCOLM C. GREEN, v.p., HARMON RIFKIN, v.p.; PHILIP M. LOWE, treas.; GEORGE ROBERTS, sec.; EARL CLANCY, gen. mgr.
INDIANA—MARION: Park Plaza Twin Cinema.
MAINE—LEWISTON: Lewiston Twin Cinema, Lisbon D.I., Northwood Plaza Twin Cinema; BANGOR: Bangor Cinema, Westgate Cinema, Bangor Twin D.I.; BREWER: Cinema Center 1-4; ORONO: Mall Cinema.
MASSACHUSETTS—BROCKTON: Skyview D.I.; FALMOUTH: Elizabeth Cinema, Cod D.I.; HOLYOKE: Holyoke Mall Cinemas 1-8; SEEKONK: Seekonk Twin, D.I.; WAREHAM: Wareham D.I.
NEW YORK—AUBURN: Auburn Mall Cinemas 1-7; PLATTSBURGH: Pyramid Mall Twin Cinema, Strand Twin Cinema, Super 87 Drive In Theater, Skyway Studio Cinema; GLENS FALLS: Aviation Mall Triple Cinema Route 9 Cinemas 1-5; SARATOGA SPRINGS: Pyramid mall Triple Cinema; ITHACA: Ithaca Mall Cinemas 1-4; UTICA: Sangertown Mall Cinemas 1-6.
RHODE ISLAND—TIVERTON: Ponta del Goda D.I.; WARWICK: Midland Cinema.
WEST VIRGINIA—CLARKSBURG: Terrace Cinema I, II & III.
BRITISH WEST INDIES—CAYMAN ISLANDS: Cayman Twin Cinema.

Thomas Theatre Co.

Iron Mountain, MI 49801. (313) 744-5404.

THOMAS R. RENN, pres. & gen. mgr.
MICHIGAN—IRON MOUNTAIN: Braumart Twin, Tri-city D.I.; IRONWOOD: Ironwood, Ironwood D.I.; MENOMINEE: Lloyd.
WISCONSIN—MARINETTE: 64 Outdoor.

Thompson Theatres Co.

P.O. Box 6 Atoka, OK 74525. (405) 889-2371.

JOHN N. THOMPSON, pres.
OKLAHOMA—ATOKA: Thompson, Watson, Choctaw D.I.

Tos Theatres

P.O. Box 638, Claxton, GA 30417; (912) 739-3013.

GIL T. MINCEY, v.p. & gen. mgr.
GEORGIA—CLAXTON: Drive-In, Tos.

Trans-Lux Corporation

110 Richards Ave., Norwalk, CT 06851 (203) 853-4321.

RICHARD BRANDT, ch. of bd.; BUDDY LEVY, pres.; LOUIS A. CREDIDIO, exec. v.p.; VICTOR LISS, v.p., finance & admin.; CHARLES HOLLOMAN, sr. v.p.; ALBERT BOYARS, v.p.; LEN SHAW, v.p.; THOMAS M. WALTZ, v.p.; JAMES S. HERSCH, treas.; THOMAS CALELLO, asst. v.p.; NICHOLAS CURTIS, asst. v.p.; ROBERT MAAR, asst. v.p.; FRANCIS MESKO, asst. v.p.; MARK ZUNICH, asst. v.p.
CONNECTICUT—DANBURY: Cine 1, 2 & 3; GREEN-

WICH: Plaza 1, 2 & 3; STAMFORD: Cinema 1 & 2, Avon 1 & 2, Ridgway.
INDIANA—CLARKSVILLE: Blue & Gold.
NEW YORK—NEW YORK CITY: Trans-Lux East, Trans-Lux 85th St., New York Experience.
OKLAHOMA—MUSKOGEE: Trans-Lux Inflight Cine Blue & Gold.
VIRGINIA—RICHMOND: Blue & Gold.

Triple S. Theatres

Box 326, Wolf Point, MT 59201.

RICHARD C. SNYDER, owner.
MONTANA—WOLF POINT: Liberty, Sundown D.I.

Trolley Theatres, Incorporated

515 South 7th East, Salt Lake City, UT 84102. (801) 364-7231.

DAVID L. GILLETTE, pres.; JERRY M. PLACE, exec. v.p.; F. M. BAY, sec.-treas., TONY RUDMAN, v.p., booker, buyer.
UTAH—SALT LAKE CITY: Trolley Square Theatres 1, 2, 3 & 4, Midtown Trolley Theatre, Family Center Trolley Theatres 1, 2, 3 & 4 Carriage Square Trolley Theatres 1 & 2; BOUNTIFUL: Trolley North Theatres 1 & 2.

Turner-Reynolds Theatres

21½ W. Poplar Street, Harrisburg, IL 62946. (618) 252-6757.

O. L. TURNER, gen. mgr.
ILLINOIS—CARMI: carmi; ELDORADO: Orpheum; HARRISBURG: Cinema 1 & 2, Orpheum, Cine 3, Starlite D.I.; SPARTA: Sparta.

U

United Amusement Co., Inc.

Albertville Shopping Center, Albertville, AL 35950.

W. W. Hammonds, JR., pres.; W. R. HAMMONDS, v.p.; BRYAN MERCER, gen. mgr.
ALABAMA—ALBERTVILLE: Martin, Mall Cinema #1 and #2, Marshall; DECATUR: Gateway, Thunderbird Drive-In, Mall Cinema 1, 2, 3; SCOTTSBORO: Tawasentha D.I., Holiday Twin Cinema.

United Artists Theatre Circuit, Inc.

UNITED ARTISTS EASTERN THEATRES, INC.

2545 Hempstead Turnpike, East Meadow NY 11554. Tel.: (212) 895-7100 and (516) 466-3300.

S. M. HASSANEIN, pres.; ALLEN PINSKER, v.p.; MILT DALY, v.p.; GLADSTONE T. WHITMAN, financial v.p.; IRVING PALACE, v.p. & treas.; MORRIS GOLDSCHLAGER, sec.; R. ZIMMERMAN, comp. & asst. treas.; JOSEPH KELLY, v.p.; T. ASSEF, v.p.
United Artists Theatre Circuit, Inc. directly and through subsidiary and affiliated corporations in the United States, operates the following:
CONNECTICUT—DARIEN: Darien Playhouse; GROTON: U.A. Groton; MANCHESTER: U.A. Theatres East 1, 2, 3; NEW CANAAN: New Canaan Playhouse; TRUMBULL: U.A. Trumbull; WEST HARTFORD: Movies 1, 2, 3 at Westfarms.
FLORIDA—BRADENTON: Desoto Square Mall Cinemas, DAYTONA BEACH: Volusia Mall Cinemas; JACKSONVILLE: Movies at Orange Park; MIAMI: Movies at The Falls; PENSACOLA: University Mall Cinemas; PLANTATION: Movies at Plantation; POMPANO BEACH: Movies at Pompano; WEST PALM BEACH: Movies at Village Green, Palm Beach Mall Cinemas.
ILLINOIS—OAKBROOK: U.A. Cinema 1 & 2; CHICAGO: Marina I, II & III; ROCKFORD: Movies at Machesney Park.
INDIANA—GREENWOOD: Greenwood D.I.; INDIANAPOLIS: Circle, Sherman Twin D.I., Tibbs Outdoor 1, 2, 3; KOKOMO: Markland Mall; LAFAYETTE: Tippicanoe Mall Cinemas, East D.I., Lafayette, U.A. cinema I & II, Lafayette

Square; LOGANSPORT: Movies at Cass Plaza; MUNCIE: Movies 1, 2, 3; SEELYVILLE: Corral D.I.; TERRE HAUTE: Indiana, North D.I.; WEST LAFAYETTE: Cinema West, Cameo I & II; KOKOMO: Markland Mall 1 & 2.
MARYLAND—BALTIMORE: Golden Ring 1, 2, 3.
MICHIGAN—ANN ARBOR: Movies at Briarwood; GRAND RAPIDS: Movies at Woodland; WARREN: Universal City 1 & 2; KALAMAZOO: West Main; NOVI: Movies at 12 Oaks 1, 2, 3, 4, 5; DEARBORN: Movies at Fairlane 1, 2, 3, 4, 5; STERLING HEIGHTS: Movies at Lakeside 1, 2, 3, 4; SOUTHFIELD: Movies at Prudential Center 1, 2; BENTON HARBOR: Fairplane Plaza 1 & 2; MUSKEGON: Plaza 1 & 2; MIDLAND: Stadium Cinemas 1 & 2; JACKSON: Westwood Cinema 1 & 2; TROY: Movies at Oakland Mall.
MINNESOTA—BURNSVILLE: The Movies 1, 2, 3, 4; MAPLEWOOD: Movies 1, 2, 3, 4, 5, 6; EDEN PRAIRIE: Movies 1, 2, 3, 4, 5; COTTAGE GROVE: Movies 1, 2, 3; DULUTH: Movies 1, 2, 3 at Miller Hill.
NEW JERSEY—BERGENFIELD: Palace; CLOSTER: Closter; EAST BRUNSWICK: Turnpike All Weather D.I., Turnpike Indoor; FORT LEE: Linwood; HACKENSACK: Fox; EDISON: Plainfield-Edison All Weather D.I.; JERSEY CITY: LIVINGSTON: Colony; MIDDLETOWN: UA Middletown 1, 2 & 3; NEW BRUNSWICK: Brunswick D.I.; SOMERVILLE: Cort, Somerville D.I.; SOUTH PLAINFIELD: Cinema I & II; TOTOWA: Cinema 46; UPPER MONTCLAIR: Bellevue; FAIRLAWN: Hyway; WESTFIELD: Rialto; HAZLET: U.A. Cinemas 1 & 2; WAYNE: Wayne; WESTWOOD: Pascack.
NEW YORK—ALBANY: Hellman, Centre, Towne; BABYLON: Babylon; BAYSIDE: Bayside; BAYSHORE: Bayshore, Bayshore Sunrise D.I. I & II Cinema; BEDFORD VILLAGE: Bedford Playhouse; BROOKLYN: Duffield, Marboro, Highway; BLAUVELT: Nyack D.I.; BRONX: Capri, Interboro Four, Vallentine; BRONXVILLE: Bronxville; BRENTWOOD: Brentwood; CARMEL: Cinema I & II; COLONIE: Mohawk D.I.; COMMACK: Commack D.I.; COPIAGUE: Johnny All Weather D.I.; CORAM: Coram D.I.; EASTHAMPTON: Easthampton; EAST MEADOW: Meadowbrook; FARMINGVILLE: College Plaza 1 & 2; FLUSHING: UA Quartet; FOREST HILLS: Forest Hills, Midway 1, 2, 3, 4; GREAT NECK: Playhouse, Squire; HICKSVILLE: Hicksville 1 & 2; LARCHMONT: Larchmont Playhouse; LATHAM: Latham D.I.; LINDENHURST: Lindenhurst; LONG ISLAND CITY: Astoria 1, 2, 3, 4; LYNBROOK: Lynbrook; MAMARONECK: Mamaroneck Playhouse; MANHASSET: Manhasset; MASSAPEQUA: Pequa, Movies at Sunrise Mall; MENANDS: Tri-City Twin D.I. I & II; MUNSEY: Rockland D.I.; NANUET: Route 59; NESCONSET: Smithtown All Weather D.I.; NEW CITY: UA Cinema; NEW YORK CITY: Gemini 1 & 2, Palladium, East Side Cinema, Rivoli, UA East; NORTHPORT: Northport; ORANGEBURG: 303 Drive-In; OZONE PARK: Crossbay 1, 2; PATCHOGUE: Patchogue, Patchogue-Sunrise All Weather D.I., Sunwave Twin; PORT JEFFERSON: Art Cinema; ROCKY POINT: Rocky Point; ROTTERDAM: Plaza 1 & 2; SHIRLEY: Shirley D.I.; SMITHTOWN: Smithtown; STATEN ISLAND: Island 1, 2; SYOSSET: Syosset, UA Cinema 150; WESTHAMPTON: Westhampton; WESTBURY: Westbury D.I. Triplex; WHITE PLAINS: U.A. Cinema.
PENNSYLVANIA—ALLENTOWN: Colonial, Boulevard D.I.; CAMP HILL: Capital City Mall, UA Theatres 1 & 2; EASTON: State; MUNCY: Movies at Lycoming Mall; TREXLERTOWN: Movies 1, 2, 3; WILLIAMSPORT: Movies at Loyal Plaza, WYOMISSING: Mall, Movies 1, 2, 3; YORK: U.A. Cinemas 1, 2, 3, 4 & 5, Movies at York Mall. CAROLINA: Movies at Plaza Carolina.
PUERTO RICO—SANTURCE: UA Cinema 150, Paramount.
WISCONSIN—BROOKFIELD: Ruby Isle; JANESVILLE: U.A. Cinemas 1, 2, 3, Jeffris; KENOSHA: UA Cinema I & II; MILWAUKEE: Modjeska, Riverside, Northridge Movies 1, 2, 3, 4, 5 & 6, Southridge Movies 1, 2, & 3; Southgate, Uptown; WAUWATOSA: Mayfair.

UNITED ARTISTS THEATRES, INC.

172 Golden Gate Avenue, San Francisco, CA 94102. (415) 928-3200.

MARSHALL NAIFY, honorary chm. of bd.; ROBERT NAIFY, pres. and chm. of bd.; S. M. HASSANEIN, exec. v.p.; JOHN ROWLEY, v.p.; A. C. CHILDHOUSE, sr. v.p.; GLADSTONE T. WHITMAN, financial v.p.; RON ZIMMERMAN, treas. & comptroller; JAMES GALLAGHER, v.p. and gen. mgr.; JOE CROTTY, film buyer.
CALIFORNIA—BAKERSFIELD: UA Movies; BERKELEY: UA Cinemas, Elmwood; BREA: UA Movies; CAMPBELL: UA Pruneyard Cinemas; CARMEL: Golden Bough Cinema; CARMICHAEL: Westerner D.I.; CERRITOS: UA Mall Cinemas, UA Twin Cinemas; CHICO: UA Cinemas, El Rey, Senator, Starlite D.I.; CITRUS HEIGHTS: UA Sunrise Cinemas, DALY CITY: Serra; EL CAJON: UA Cinemas; FRESNO: UA Cinemas, UA Movies; GLENDALE: Capitol;

GRASS VALLEY: Del Oro; HAYWARD, Hayward Auto Movies; HOLLYWOOD: Egyptian I, Egyptian II and III; LONG BEACH: UA Movies; LOS ANGELES: UA Cinema Center Westwood, UA Westwood; MARYSVILLE: State; MARINA: Marina Auto Movies; MARINA DEL REY: UA Cinemas; MERCED, UA Cinema, Merced Twin, Regency, Starlite D.I.; MILLBRAE: Millbrae Theatre; MONTEREY: Hill, Regency, State; NO. HOLLYWOOD: UA Movies; ORANGE: UA City Cinemas; OROVILLE: Mesa D.I., State; PASADENA: UA Pasadena; PHOENIX: UA Cinemas; REDDING: Cascade, UA Movies; RIVERSIDE: UA Cinemas; SACRAMENTO: Southgate Outdoor Movies; SAN BRUNO: UA Tanforan Cinemas; SANTA ANA: UA Cinemas; SAN FRANCISCO: Alexandria, Balboa, Coliseum, Coronet, Metro, Metro II, UA Twin Cinemas Stonestown, Vogue; SAN JOSE: UA Blossom Hill Cinemas; SANTA CLARA, Cinema 150; SANTA CRUZ: UA Cinemas I & II, Del Mar, Rio; SANTA MARIA: UA Movies; SANTA ROSA: UA Cinemas, Redwood I & II; SCOTTSDALE: UA Movies; THOUSAND OAKS: UA Movies; TORRANCE: UA Del Amo Cinemas, UA Torrance; VALLEJO: Crescent D.I.; WESTMINSTER: UA Westminster Twin A & B, UA Mall Cinemas; WOODLAND HILLS: UA Cinemas, YUBA CITY: Sutter.

COLORADO—BOULDER: Regency; COLORADO SPRINGS, Cinema 150; IDAHO FALLS: UA Cinemas, MURRAY, UA Fashion Place Mall Cinemas.

NEVADA—RENO: UA Cinemas I & II, Granada Twin Theatres.

WASHINGTON—SEATTLE: UA Cinema 70 & 150; SPOKANE: UA Cinema I & II.

ROWLEY UNITED DIVISION

314 S. Harwood Street, Dallas, TX 75201; (214) 747-1822.

DI DIVISIONAL OFFICERS: JOHN H. ROWLEY, v.p.; ELVIN L. SHARP, V.P.: JOHN TREADWELL, v.p.; JERRY BRAND, film buyer.
ARKANSAS—ARKADELPHIA: Cinema I, II; BENTON: Royal I, II; CLARKSVILLE: Strand, Ark-Air Drive-In; CONWAY: UA Cinema I, II, 65 Drive-In; FORT SMITH: Minitek I, II, Sky-Vue Drive-In; LITTLE ROCK: UA Cinema City, UA University Quartet, Heights, UA Cinema 150, UA Four, Asher Drive-In, Razorback Drive-In, Twin City Drive-In; MAGNOLIA: Cameo; MALVERN: Ritz, Malvern Drive-In, MORRILTON: Rialto, Rivervue Drive-In.
OKLAHOMA—MCALESTER: Okla, Cinema 69, 270 Drive-In; TULSA: UA Annex 3, Fontana 4, UA Forum Twin.
TEXAS—ABILENE: UA 6; AMARILLO: UA Cinema 6; BIG SPRING: Ritz, I, II, R-70 Drive-In; BROWNSVILLE: Cinema I, II; CORPUS CHRISTI: Ayers, Centre, Cine 6, Cine West I, II, UA Pueblo Park 4, Viking Twin Drive-In; CORCKETT: Ritz; DALLAS: Texas, UA Cine I, II, Wynnewood I, II, UA Skillman 6; DENTON: Golden Triangle 4; FORT WORTH: UA Hulen 6, Belknap Drive-In; HARKER HEIGHTS: Showplace 3; HARLINGEN: UA Commerce Cinema I, II; HURST: Northeast Mall 6; KILLEEN: Center, Northside Cinema I, II, Ritz, Sadler, Texas, Cinema Plaza I, II, 440 Drive-In, Killeen Drive-In, Rancier Drive-In; LAREDO: Cinema Del Norte, Plaza, Bordertown Drive-In; LUBBOCK: UA South Plains Cinema Four; MCALLEN: UA Mall Trio; MIDLAND: UA 4: MINERAL WELLS: UA Cinema 3; ODESSA: Winwood I, II; UA Permian Mall IV; PALESTINE: Cinema I, II, Dogwood Drive-In; PORT ARTHUR: UA Cinema 6; SAN ANGELO: Parkway, Texas, Sherwood I, II, UA Sunset Mall Four, Angelo Twin Drive-In, Twin Vue Drive-In; San Antonio: UA Cine Cinco, UA Ingram Mall 6; SHERMAN: Cinema Four, Sher-Den Twin Drive-Inn; SULPHUR SPRINGS: Mission, Hi-Vue Drive-In; TAYLOR: Howard I, II; TERRELL: Iris, Terrell Drive-In.
TENNESSEE—MEMPHIS: UA Southbrook 7.

United Theatres

c/o T. Golding, Corp. Sec., 8933 SW Leahy Rd., Portland, OR 97225. Tel.: (503) 292-1598.

MICHAEL and JERRY FORMAN, chief officers.
OREGON—PORTLAND: 82nd St. D.I., Sandy Blvd. D.I.

V

Viano Theatres Inc.

13A Medford St., Arlington, MA 02174. (617) 643-0802.

MASSACHUSETTS—ARLINGTON: Regent, Capitol; SOMERVILLE: Broadway, Somerville.

Video Independent Theatres, Inc.

11½ North Lee, P.O. Box 1334, Oklahoma City, OK 73125.

J. E. BROOKS, pres.; DALE DAVIS, v.p. theatre operations; LANNY B. GUTHRIE, sec.-treas., PAUL WEST, concessions.
NEW MEXICO—ALBUQUERQUE: Silver Dollar D.I.; LAS CRUCES: Rio Grande, Fiesta D.I., Video Fourplex Theatre; ARTESIA: Cinema Twin, Hermosa D.I.
OKLAHOMA—ADA: McSwain Mini Theatre 1 & 2, Cine Hills D.I.; ALTUS: Plaza, Cinema, Altus D.I.; ARDMORE: Video No. 1 & No. 2 Tivoli, Skyview D.I.; BARTLESVILLE: Eastland Twin, Hilltop, Penn; CHICKASHA: Washita 1 & 2, Chief D.I.; CLAREMORE: Video, Rogers D.I.; CLINTON: Redland, Clinton D.I.; CUSHING: Dunkin, Sundown D.I.; DUNCAN: Palace Twin, Duncan D.I.; ELK CITY: Westland, 66 D.I.; EL RENO: Cinema, Squaw D.I.; ENID: Esquire, Cinema 1 & 2, Enid D.I., Trail D.I., Video Twin Theatre; GUTHRIE: Melba, Beacon D.I.; LAWTON: Vaska, 82nd St. Twin D.I., Video Twin Theatre; Showcase Twin; MIAMI: Coleman, Sooner D.I.; NORMAN: Rancho D.I., Cinema East; OKMULGEE: Orpheum Twin, Tower D.I., PAWHUSKA: Kihekah, Corral D.I.; PONCA CITY: Poncan, Ponca Plaza Twin, Airline D.I.'s; SAPULPA: Tee Pee D.I., SEMINOLE: Skyway D.I.; SHAWNEE: Cinema 1 & 2, Hornbeck, Penthouse, Ritz, Starlite D.I.; STILLWATER: Leachman, Cinema 1 & 2, 177 North D.I., East 6th D.I. Satellite Twin; TULSA: 11th St. D.I., Airview D.I., VINITA: Center, Lariat D.I.
TEXAS—ABILENE: Town & Country Twin D.I., Tower Twin D.I., BORGER: Morley 1 & 2, Bunavista D.I.; BROWNWOOD: Bluffvue D.I., Camp Bowie D.I.; CLEBURNE: Esquire I & II, Chief D.I.; LUBBOCK: Winchester 1 & 2, Cinema West; MIDLAND: Hodge 1 & 2, Chief D.I., Texan D.I., Westwood; NEW BRAUNFELS: Brauntex 1 & 2, Tower, Drive-In; ODESSA: Video 1, 2 & 3; PAMPA: Capri, Top O'Texas D.I.; PLAINVIEW: Granada 1 & 2, Astro D.I.

Vinstrand Theatres, Inc.

600 So. San Vicente Blvd., Los Angeles, CA 90048.

CECIL VINNICOF, PAUL VINNICOF, JEANETTE MAHLER, chief officers.
CALIFORNIA—ANAHEIM: Brookhurst-Loge.

Virginia Amusement Co.

Box 718, 133 Main St., Hazard, KY 41701 (502) 436-2621.

ERMAN F. WIRTZ, pres.
KENTUCKY—HAZARD: Family Theatre.

Vogel Theatres

2299 East State Street, Salem, OH 44460 (419) 337-7085.

JACK K. VOGEL, pres.; AILEEN V. VOGEL, v.p.; A. FRED VOGEL, v.p.; JAN WILLEM PETERS, secty.-treas.
OHIO—ALLIANCE: College Cinema I & II; RAVENNA: Midway D.I.; SALEM: Salem D.I.; COLUMBUS: Dublin D.I.
MARYLAND—BALTIMORE: Bengies D.I., Carrollwood I & II; EDGEWOOD: Edgewater I & II.
PENNSYLVANIA—NEW KENSINGTON: Gateway D.I.

Volk Brothers Theatres

4219 Webber Parkway, Minneapolis, MN 55412; (612) 588-4655.

SIDNEY VOLK, pres.
MINNESOTA—MINNEAPOLIS: Camden, Riverview, Nile.

Vore Cinema Corp.

3143 E. Center St., Warsaw, IN 46580. (219) 267-6341.

ROGER VORE, pres.; TIM YEAGER, gen. mgr.; SHARON VORE, purchasing agent.
INDIANA—GOSHEN: Goshen Theatre; MONTICELLO: Twin Lakes Theatre; MUNCIE: Rivoli 1 & 2, Strand; NORTH WEBSTER: WaWa D.I.; PLYMOUTH: Tri-Way D.I., Rees Theatre; SYRACUSE: Pickwick Theatre; WARSAW: Center Cinema 1 & 2, Lake Theatre.
MICHIGAN—THREE RIVERS: Riviera Theatre.

W

W&K Theatres

Box 518, Oil City, LA 71061.

L. W. WATTS, pres. and gen. mgr.
LOUISIANA—NEW ORLEANS: Abalon; OIL CITY:
Strand; VIVIAN: Wakea.
TEXAS—JEFFERSON: Strand.

Wallace Theatres, Inc.

Town and Country Shopping Center, 330 University Ave., Lubbock, TX 79415. (806) 762-5222.

WESLEY B. BLANKENSHIP, pres.; RANDALL WALDRIP, gen. mgr.
TEXAS—LEVELLAND: Wallace.

The Washington Circle Theatre Corp.

1101 23rd St., N.W., Washington, DC 20037. (202) 331-7471.

THEODORE PEDAS, pres.; JAMES PEDAS, vice pres.;
CHARLES COSTOLO, gen. mgr.
WASHINGTON, DC—Dupont Circle Theatre, Circle Theatre, Inner Circle, Outer Circle 1, Outer Circle 2, West End Circle, Tenley Circle 1, Tenley Circle 3, Embassy Circle Theatre, Avalon I, Avalon II, Uptown Old Town I & II.

Wehrenberg Theatres, Inc.

1215 Des Peres Road, St. Louis, MO 63131. (314) 822-4520.

RONALD P. KRUEGER, pres.; WOODY COLE, booker and film buyer; GEORGE PHILLIPS, asst. film buyer; A. RAY PARKER, gen. mgr.; CLYDE PATTON, asst. gen. mgr.; DON CARROLL, dir. concessions.
MISSOURI—DeSOTO: Melba, Sky-Vue Dr. I.; ST. LOUIS: Crown, Creve Coeur Cinema, Westport 1 & 2, Des Peres 4 Ciné, Cinema 4 Center, Ronnie's Six Ciné, Halls Ferry Six Ciné, North Twin Dr. I.; Rock Road D.I. Shady Oak, Stadium I, Stadium II, St. Ann Ciné, Ellisville Twin, Cross Keys, St. Andrews, Airway Twin D.I., South Twin D.I., I-44 D.I., 66 D.I., St. Ann Four Screen D.I.
ILLINOIS—ALTON: Alton Ciné 1 & 2.

Western Amusement Company, Inc.

9100 Sunset Blvd., Los Angeles, CA 90069. (213) 276-2372.

JUANITA PEGGY JONES, pres. and gen. mgr.; WAYNE PATTERSON: purchasing agent; JIM HOLLIS, film buyer; SKIP KAMM, booker.
CALIFORNIA—AVALON: Avalon; BARSTOW: Barlen D.I., Barstow I & II, Skyline D.I.; CORONA DEL MAR: Port; LANCASTER: Antelope I & II, Jet D.I.; VICTORVILLE: Joshua D.I., Balsam D.I. I & II, El Rancho I & II; VISTA: Avo.
OREGON—BAKER: Eltrym; EUGENE: Oakway; LA GRANDE: Granada I & II, La Grande D.I.; SPRINGFIELD: Cascade D.I., Fine Arts.

Western Massachusetts Theatres, Inc.

265 State St., Springfield, MA 01103.

RONALD I. GOLDSTEIN, pres.
MASSACHUSETTS—AMHERST: Amherst Cinema; CHICOPEE: Rivoli; GREENFIELD GARDEN: Showplace; HOLYOKE: Victory, Strand; NORTHAMPTON: Calvin; PITTSFIELD: Capitol, Palace, Showplace; SPRINGFIELD: Bing, Paramount; WARE: Casino; WESTFIELD: Strand.
VERMONT—BRATTLEBORO: Paramount.

Westland Theatres

1827 Pacific Ave., Stockton, CA 94102. (209) 466-4943.

R. W. HARVEY, pres.; DON S. BABCOCK, v.p. and gen. mgr.; RODDA W. HARVEY, sec.; film booking office, P.O.

Box 2015, Agouro, CA 91301; CAROL BERGAMINE, film buyer & booker.
CALIFORNIA—STOCKTON: Stockton Royal 4, West Lane D.I., Hammer D.I. Motor Movies, Ritz; VISALIA: Sequoia Auto, Mooney East, Mooney West.
NEVADA—WINNEMUCCA: Sage.

Westland Theatres, Inc.

Box 1150, Colorado Springs, CO 80901.

L. A. STARSMORE, pres.; WILLIAM MITCHELL, v.p.;
C. H. BAGGS, sec.-treas.; NEAL LLOYD, buyer and booker.
COLORADO—COLORADO SPRINGS: Broadmoor, Security Cinema, Peak, Cinema 70 #1, 2 & 3, Aircadia D.I., 8th St. D.I., Vista Vue D.I., Sky Vue D.I., Falcon D.I., GRAND JUNCTION: Mesa, Cooper, Teller Arms 1 & 2, Chief D.I., Rocket D.I.; PUEBLO: Chief, Cooper, Cinema I, Cinema II, Mesa D.I.
NEBRASKA—LINCOLN: Cinema I & II, State.

West Side-Valley Theatres

(See Roy Cooper Company, Inc.)

Williams, K. Lee, Theatres, Inc.

Sevier Theatre Bldg., DeQueen, AR 71832. (501) 584-2657.

R. L. ROBISON, pres. and gen. mgr.; VANCE TAYLOR, sec.-treas.; L. R. "PETE" JUNELL, v.p.; CECIL CALLAHAN, asst. sec.
ARKANSAS—ASHDOWN: Williams; DeQUEEN: Sevier, Queen Auto Theatre; FORDYCE: Fordyce Auto Theatre; GURDON: Hoo Hoo; NASHVILLE: Elberta, Howard Auto; WALDRON: Scott.
OKLAHOMA—BROKEN BOW: Chief; WILBURTON: Latimer.

Williams Theatres, Inc.

101 West Main St., Union, MO 63084.

L. J. WILLIAMS, gen. mgr.
MISSOURI—UNION: Cinema 101.

Wineland Circuit

4165 Branch Ave., Marlow Heights, MO 20031. (301) 423-3767.

LLOYD G. WINELAND, pres.; FRED L. WINELAND, v.p. & treas.
MARYLAND—DISTRICT HEIGHTS: Jerry Lewis Cinema 3; HILLSIDE: Hillside D.I.; LAUREL: Laurel D.I.; OXON HILL: ABC D.I.; SILESIA: Super Chief D.I.

Wisconsin Amusement Corp.

13 N. Main St., Fond du Lac, WI 54935. (414) 922-3430.

N. P. FRANK, gen. mgr.
WISCONSIN—FOND DU LAC: Lake Park Outdoor, Retlaw, Fond du Lac I and II; WEST BEND: West Bend, Cinema I & II.

Wisper & Wetsman, Inc.

132 N. Woodward Ave., Birmingham, MI 48011 (313) 642-5100 or 564-6800

WM. M. WETSMAN, pres.
ARIZONA—(E & W Management Co.) PHOENIX: Big Sky D.I., Rodeo D.I., Valley D.I.; TEMPE: South Twin D.I.
INDIANA—(WLZ Amusement Co.) INDIANAPOLIS: Bel-Air D.I., Northside D.I., Twin D.I. East, West; Agent For: Meridian D.I.
MICHIGAN—ALMA: Strand; BRIGHTON: Lakes D.I.; CHARLOTTE: Eaton; COLDWATER: Main; DEARBORN: Calvin; GREENVILLE: Greenville D.I.; HILLSDALE: Hillsdale D.I.; HOWELL: Howell; IONIA: Ionia D.I.; LAPEER: Pix; MAPLE CITY: Maple City D.I.; MARYSVILLE: Marysville D.I.; PLYMOUTH: Penn; STURGIS: Sturgis D.I.; WALLED LAKE: Walake D.I.; Agent For: BRIGHTON: Brighton Cinemas 1, 2, 3; GAYLORD: Gaylord; RIVERVIEW:

Showboat Cinemas 1, 2, 3; SOUTHFIELD: Tel-Ex Cinemas 1, 2, 3, 4. (Theatre Booking Agency, Inc.) Agent for: BLOOM-FIELD HILLS: Kingswood; CLARE: Northland D.I.; DEARBORN: Ford-Wyoming D.I.; DETROIT: Civic, Eastwood; FARMINGTON: Farmington Civic; FLINT: U.S. 23 D.I.; GROSSE POINTE: Esquire; LINDEN: Silver D.I.; MENDON: M-60 D.I.; MT. CLEMENS:
Mt. Clemens D.I.; MT. PLEASANT: Pleasant D.I.; NEW BALTIMORE: Chesterfield Cinemas 1, 2, 3; ROCHESTER: Hills; ROSEBUSH: Sundown D.I.; ROSEVILLE: Roseville; ROYAL OAK: Oak D.I.; SHELBY: Shelby 1, 2; SPRING LAKE: M-104 D. I. 1, 2; TAYLOR: Pandora; WHITE CLOUD: M-37 D.I.

NEW MEXICO—Agent For: ALBUQUERQUE: First Plaza Twin 1, 2, Hoffmantown Cinema.

TEXAS—(FLW Theatre Co.) DALLAS: Apollo D.I. North, South, Astro D.I. 1, 2, 3, Casa Linda 1, 2, 3, 4, Century IV D.I. 1, 2, 3, 4, Gemini D.I. North, South, East, Park Forest, Plano D.I. 1, 2, Preston Royal; EL PASO: Cinema Park D.I. 1, 2, 3; FORT WORTH: Cherry Lane D.I. East, West; GALVESTON: Bayou D.I. 1, 2, 3; HOUSTON: Gulfway D.I. 1, 2 & 3, Triple D.I. 1, 2, 3; Agent For: ALDINE: Deauville; BROWNSVILLE: Majestic Twin 1, 2; HOUSTON: Lakewood Twin 1, 2; SAN ANTONIO: Aztec 1, 2, 3, Judson D.I. 1, 2, 3, 4.

Wometco Enterprises, Inc.

P.O. Box 01-2440, 316 No. Miami Ave., Miami FL 33128. Tel.: (305) 374-6262.

MITCHELL WOLFSON, chm. b. and pres.; VAN MYERS, exec. v.p. in charge of vending, food services and bottling; STANLEY L. STERN, sr. v.p. in charge of the entertainment div.; J. D. RICHARDS, special assistant to sr. v.p. in charge of entertainment division operations; JACK MITCHELL, v.p. and general manager, Florida theatres; WALTER SENIOR, pres., Wometco de Puerto Rico; HUGH McCAULEY, v.p. & general manager, Wometco-Lathrop Co., Alaska; ARTHUR H. HERTZ, sr. v.p., treas., & chief financial officer; EDWARD STERN, v.p. in charge of Florida motion picture film buying; WILLIAM R. BRAZZIL, v.p. in charge of WTVJ & sales agent, Broadcast Division; RALPH A. RENICK, v.p. in charge of Wometco TV news operations; MICHAEL BROWN, v.p. & controller; RICHARD J. VURA, JR., v.p. personnel; J. BRUCE IRVING, sec. & gen. counsel; HAROLD FUNT, v.p. real estate; JOE MARTINEZ, v.p. vending; CHARLES H. BEACH, v.p. bottling; GERALD WHALEY, v.p. public affairs.

FLORIDA—BOCA RATON: Boca Raton I & II; MIAMI: 163rd St. I & II & III, Parkway, Tower, 27th Ave. D.I.; MIAMI BEACH: Normandy, Surf, Byron-Carlyle Triplex; NORTH MIAMI BEACH: Boulevard D.I.; CORAL GABLES: Miracle I & II; FT. LAUDERDALE: Gateway I & II; HIALEAH: Palm Springs I & II; SOUTH DADE: Kendale Lakes Triplex, Dadeland Twin, Sunset, Miller Square 4-plex; WEST HOLLYWOOD: Plaza I & II; ORLANDO: Park East, Park West; GAINESVILLE: Plaza I & II; OCALA: Ocala Twin; HALLANDALE: Hallandale; HOMESTEAD: Campbell Square Triplex.

BAHAMAS—NASSAU: Capitol, Shirley Street, Wulff Road; FREEPORT: Columbus, Dolphin D.I.

PUERTO RICO—CAGUAS: Caguas; HATO REY: Plaza I, II, III & IV; PONCE: Santa Maria; CAYEY: Cayey Twin; RIO PIEDRAS: El Senorial I & II; SANTURCE: Cinerama, Excelsior, Puerto Rico, Radio City; MAYAGUEZ: Mayaguez I, II, III & IV; BAYAMON: Cinema Centro I & II, Bayamon Oeste I & II

VIRGIN ISLANDS—ST. CROIX: Sunny Isle Twin.

ALASKA—ANCHORAGE: 4th Ave. Theatre, Denali, Fireweed I, II & III, Polar Twin, Totem Triplex; FAIRBANKS: Goldstream I & II.

DOMINICAN REPUBLIC—Cine Triplex, Double Twin, El Portal, Plaza, Naco I & II, Max, Rialto, Olimpia, Diane, Lido, Apolo.

Wood Theatre Group

35 Washington St., Morristown, NJ 07960 (201) 539-9114.

NORMAN J. SCHONFELD, Pres.
NEW JERSEY—LINDEN: Linden Twin Cinema; RAHWAY: Old Rahway; UNION: Lost Picture Show; SUMMIT: Strand; MORRISTOWN: Morristown Triplex Cinema; MADISON: Madison.

Y

Y & W Management Corp.

503 Investor Trust Building, Indianapolis, IN 46204. (317) 635-4371-2.

Also operating Theatrical Managers, Inc.
VERN R. YOUNG, pres., treas.
INDIANA—ANDERSON: North D.I.; BLOOMINGTON: Y & W D.I., Princess; MERRILLVILLE: Y & W D.I.; MUNCIE: Muncie D.I.; Ski-Hi D.I.; NEW CASTLE: Castle, Sky-Vu D.I.; FORT WAYNE: Gateway I, II, III, Cinema South East 30 D.I.; INDIANAPOLIS: Eastwood; VINCENNES: Plaza Cinema.

Yakima Theatres, Inc.

426 Miller Bldg., P.O. Box 50, Yakima, WA 98907 (509) 248-1360.

MICHAEL M. MERCY, pres.; EARL BARDEN, v.p.
WASHINGTON—YAKIMA: Mercy Quad, Plaza 1, 2 & 3, Cinema West 1 & 2, Cascade D.I.; WENATCHEE: Columbia Cinema 1, 2 & 3.

Yavapai Amusements Corp.

Box 1071, Prescott, AZ 86301.

ARIZONA—PRESCOTT: Marina Theatres 1 & 2.

CANADA

B&L Theatres & Entertainment (Owned and operated by Stanmore Enterprises Ltd.)

P.O. Box 596, Saint John, New Brunswick, E2L 4A5. (506) 652-1900.

M. L. BERNSTEIN.
NEW BRUNSWICK—CHATHAM: Vogue.
NOVA SCOTIA—ANTIGONISH: Capitol; WINDSOR: Imperial.

Biltmore Theatres

Suite 1101, 415 Yonge St., Toronto, Ontario, Canada. M5B 2E7. (416) 977-2488.

B. C. ROTHBART, pres.; C. A. BERGMAN, sec.-treas.; M. A. FARQUHARSON, buying & booking.
ONTARIO—TORONTO: Biltmore.

Canadian Odeon Theatres Ltd.

225 Consumers Road, Willowdale, Ontario M2J 4G9. (416) 491-1660; 43 Church Street, St. Catharines, Ontario L2R 6Z9. (416) 364-5022/(416) 682-7267.

Directors: M. W. ZAHORCHAK, MRS. M. ZAHORCHAK, R. A. ZAHORCHAK, C. R. B. SALMON, R. E. MYERS, D. M. ALLEN, G. A. SUTHERLAND, J. J. MARTIN, A. KARP.
Officers: Chairman: M. W. ZAHORCHAK; President: C. R. B. SALMON; Executive Vice-Pres. & Gen. Mgr.: R. A. ZAHORCHAK; R. E. MYERS; Executive Vice-Pres.: D. M. ALLEN; Vice-Pres. & Secy.:V. MANDVERE; Treas.: J. S. BAIN, Asst.
Executive Personnel: Director Public Relations: F. LAWSON; Director Advertising: W. SNELLING; Director Confectionery Sales: C. L. SWEENEY; Director Insurance: D. A. DAVIS; Director Personnel: R. YEOMAN; Director Engineering: E. McCORMACK & R. HILDER; Director Drive-In Operations: R. P. TIBONI; Eastern Canada general manager; J. C. MOORE; Ontario District Managers: "A"-G. W. H. SPRATLEY, "B"-F. P. J. KENNEDY; Ontario Supervisor: L. MARTYN; Quebec Vice-President & General Manager: J. J. MARTIN; Quebec District Managers: J. CYR, L. BERNARD; British Columbia & Calgary General Manager: B. REGAN; British Columbia District Manager: N. REAY; Calgary District Manager: C. VAN SNELLENBERG; Edmonton District Manager: S. BINDER; Maritimes District Manager: F. C. LEAVENS; Manitoba & Saskatchewan General Manager: J. G. FUSTEY.
ALBERTA—CALGARY: North Hill, Grand 1 & 2, Uptown 1 & 2, Westbrook 1, 2 & 3, Marlborough 1, 2 & 3, Odeon 1 & 2, Brentwood, Tivoli, Stampede D.I., 17th Ave. D.I., EDMONTON: Odeon 1 & 2, Rialto 1 & 2, Meadowlark, Plaza 1 & 2, Capilano, Varscona, Roxy, Avenue, Studio 82, Twin D.I. 1 & 2.

BRITISH COLUMBIA—DUNCAN: Odeon; KAMLOOPS: Skyway D.I.; KELOWNA: Drive-In; PENTICTON: Twilight D.I.; PRINCE GEORGE: Triple, Startime D.I., Moonlight D.I.; VERNON: Drive-In; VANCOUVER: Broadway 1 & 2, Odeon, Vogue, Coronet Twin, Odeon West 1 & 2, Westminster Mall Triplex, Westminster D.I., Clova, Dolphin, Dunbar, Fraser, Hyland, Park, Varsity, Hillcrest D.I., Surrey D.I.; VICTORIA: Odeon 1 & 2, Haida, Counting House I & II.

MANITOBA—WINNIPEG: Odeon, Grant Park, Drive-In, Garrick 1 & 2, Kings, Park, Hyland, North Main D.I., Convention Centre.

NEW BRUNSWICK—MONCTON: Capitol; ST. JOHN: Odeon.

ONTARIO—TORONTO: Varsity 1 & 2, Fairlawn 1 & 2, Hyland 1 & 2, York 1 & 2, Finch 1, 2 & 3, Sheridan 1 & 2, Albion 1 & 2, Humber 1 & 2, Fairview 1 & 2, Don Mills, Elane, Weston, Dufferin D.I., Parkway D.I.; HAMILTON: Centre W., Centre E., Odeon 1 & 2, Hyland, Towne, CI D.I., Starlite D.I.; OTTAWA: St. Laurent 1 & 2, Somerset, Elmdale, Queensway; LONDON: Odeon 1 & 2, Westmount 1 & 2; Hyland, Twilite D.I.; BURLINGTON: Odeon; OAKVILLE: Plaza 1 & 2; BRAMPTON: Odeon; BRANTFORD: Odeon, Cinemas 1 & 2; OSHAWA: Odeon, Hyland; WINDSOR: Palace, Odeon, Skyway D.I., Windsor D.I.; KITCHENER: Hyland, Odeon, Parkway D.I.; ST. CATHARINES: Pendale 1 & 2, Town 1 & 2, Canadian D.I.; WELLAND: Seaway 1 & 2, Park, Welland D.I.; NIAGARA FALLS: Seneca 1 & 2, Niagara Square 1, 2 & 3, Hollywood D.I.; KINGSTON: Odeon 1 & 2, Hyland, Kingston D.I.; GUELPH: Odeon 1 & 2; PETERBORO: Odeon; SARNIA: Odeon 1 & 2; CHATHAM: Drive-In; SUDBURY: Odeon 1 & 2; NORTH BAY: Odeon, Drive-In; SOSAULT STE. MARIE: Odeon; THUNDER BAY: Victoria 1 & 2, Court; OWEN SOUND: Roxy, Centre; MIDLAND: Odeon, Drive-In; GRIMSBY: Roxy; NEWMARKET: Odeon; TIMMINS: Palace.

QUEBEC—MONTREAL: Atwater 1 & 2, Cote Des Neiges 1 & 2, Decarie 1 & 2, Bonaventure 1 & 2, Place du Canada, Champlain 1 & 2, Cremazie, Mercier, Odeon Berri, Dauphin 1 & 2, Villeray, Cinema de Paris, Laval 1 & 2, Brossard 1, 2 & 3, Longueuil, Verdun, Cine Parc Chateauguay, Cine Parc Vaudreuil, Cine Parc St. Mathieu; BOUCHERVILLE: Cine Parc 1 & 2; QUEBEC CITY: Frontenac 1 & 2, Dauphin, Canadiere; ST. JEROME: Rex, Cine Parc; ST. JEAN: Capitol; THREE RIVERS: Fleur de Lis.

NOVA SCOTIA—HALIFAX: Casino, Oxford, Hyland; NEW GLASGOW: Odeon, Drive-In; YARMOUTH: Odeon.

SASKATCHEWAN—SASKATOON: Odeon; REGINA: Odeon Coronet 1, 2, & 3.

Consolidated Theatres Ltd.

5887 Monkland Ave., Montreal, H4A 1G6, Quebec. (514) 489-8461.

Affiliated with Famous Players

G. P. DESTOUNIS, chr. of brd. & pres.; M. PHANEUF, v.p. & managing dir.; DONALD DRISDELL, scy.-treas. QUEBEC—MONTREAL: Le Parisien.

Famous Players Limited

130 Bloor Street West, Toronto, Ontario M5S 1P3, Area Code 416 Phone 964-5800.

CHARLES G. BLUHDORN, chmn. of bd.; GEORGE P. DESTOUNIS, pres.; RENARD M. MERCURIO, v.p. & treas.; J. LAWRENCE PILON, v.p., gen. counsel & secty.; WILLIAM N. MURRAY, v.p. & gen. mgr.; JACK BERNSTEIN, v.p. & dir. of programming; DOUGLAS A. GOW, v.p., western theatre operations; LESLIE E. MITCHELL, v.p., eastern theatre operations; JOHN G. BACOPULOS, v.p., real estate; WILLIAM G. COWAN, controller; ANNE P. CARROLL, asst. secty.; MICHAEL J. TAYLOR, asst. secty.; JOSEPH P. WHYTE, asst. treas.

THEATRE SUPERVISION

Alberta
Suite 1065, 808-4th Avenue S.W., Calgary. (403) 265-5236, Brian Halberton, District Supervisor.

British Columbia
1086 Park Royal, West Vancouver, B.C. V7T 1A1 (604) 926-7321. Jack Tomik, District Supervisor.

Manitoba and Saskatchewan
315 Donald Street, Winnipeg, Manitoba. (204) 942-7823. Brian Cameron, District Supervisor.

Maritime and Newfoundland
Suite 1310, Cogswell Tower, 2000 Barrington ST.,

Halifax, Nova Scotia B 3J 3K1 Alan Bell, District Supervisor. Saint John, New Brunswick, E2M 4X5. Phillip A. Traynor, District Supervisor.

Ontario
130 Bloor Street West, Toronto, Ontario. M5S 1P3. (416) 964-5800. Verd Marriott, Dudley Dumond, Mike Micelli, District Supervisors.

Quebec
5887 Monkland Avenue, Montreal, Quebec. (514) 489-8461. Don Drisdell, District Supervisor, United Theatres Ltd.

Landmark Cinemas of Canada Ltd.

14566–125 Avenue, Edmonton, Alberta T5L 3C5 (403) 455-1766.

P. H. MAY, pres.; H. H. ROSS, secty.; BRIAN McINTOSH, gen. mgr.; TERRY YUSCHCHYSHYN, dir. of operations; MAURICE KISHIUCHI, dir. of finance and accounting. Directors: P. H. MAY, C. D. K. MAY, H. H. ROSS, F. KETTNER. Film Buying & Booking Office: 522—11th Avenue, S. W., Calgary, Alberta T2R 0C8. (403) 264-4660.

BRITISH COLUMBIA—ABBOTSFORD: Towne Cinema (Twin); CRANBOOK: Armond Theatre; KELOWNA: Uptown Cinema Centre (Twin); MISSION: Mission Cinema, PENTICTON: Pen Mar Theatre (Twin); REVELSTOKE: Roxy Theatre, Revelstoke Drive In; TRAIL: Royal Theatre; VICTORIA: Towne Cinema; WESTBANK: Westbank Drive In.

ALBERTA—CALGARY: Towne Cinema (Twin); CAMROSE: Bailey Theatre; EDMONTON: Jasper Cinema Centre (Twin), Towne Cinema, Millwoods Drive In (Twin); EDSON: Nova Theatre; GRAND PRAIRIE: Gaiety Theatre, Jan Cinema, Prairie Cinema Centre (Twin), Wapiti Drive In; HINTON: Roxy Theatre; MEDICINE HAT: Towne Cinema (Twin); REDCLIFF: Gemini Drive In; RED DEER: Uptown Theatre; ST. ALBERT: St. Albert Drive In; STETTLER: Jewel Theatre; VERMILION: Columbia Theatre; WAINWRIGHT: Alma Theatre, Stardust Drive In.

SASKATCHEWAN—LLOYDMINSTER: May Cinema Centre (Twin), C & H Drive In; REGINA: Cinema 6 Drive In (Twin); SASKATOON: Towne Cinema (Twin), Skyway Drive In, Sundown Drive In; WEYBURN: Soo Theatre, Twilite Drive In; YORKTON: Tower Theatre, Crest Drive In, Parkland Cinema Centre (Twin).

MANITOBA—BRANDON: Towne Cinema; LYNN LAKE: Roxy Theatre; SELKIRK: Garry Theatre.

IDAHO—LEWISTON: Liberty Theatre, Orchards Cinema (Triple), Orchards Auto Theatre, Roxy Theatre.

WASHINGTON—CLARKSTON: Clarkson Auto Theatre.

Premier Operating Corporation, Ltd.

425 University Ave., Toronto M5G 2B9.

BARRY ALLEN, pres.; LEONARD BERNSTEIN, exec. v.p. & gen. mgr.

ONTARIO—ALLISTON: Mustang D.I.; ATIKOKAN: Park; BARRIE: Cinemas 1 & 2; BRAMPTON: Shoppers; BURLINGTON: Cinemas 1 & 2; CAMBRIDGE: Cinemas 1 & 2, Sunset D.I.; COBOURG: Park, Midway D.I.; CORNWALL: Mustang D.I.; ELLIOT LAKE: Lake; FORT ERIE: Mustang D.I.; GERALDTON: Strand; GODERICH: Park, Mustang D.I.; GUELPH: Mustang D.I.; HAILEYBURG: Strand; HAWKESBURY: Mustang D.I.; KAPUSKASING: Strand; KINGSTON: Mustang D.I.; KIRKLAND LAKE: Strand, Lasalle; KITCHENER: Frederick Mall Cinemas North & South, Capitol 1 & 2, Cinema, Fairview, Lyric, K-W D.I.; LEAMINGTON: Vogue, LINDSAY: Mustang D.I.; LONDON: Mustang D.I. 1 & 2; MALTON: Cinema; MANITOWADGE: Strand; MARKHAM: Towne; MISSASSAUGA: Dixie (five); OAKVILLE: #5 D.I.; OSHAWA: Marks; PETERBORO: Mustang D.I.; PICTON: Mustang D.I.; PORT HOPE: Capitol; SARNIA: Mustang D.I.; SIMCOE: Strand; SMITHS FALLS: Soper; STRATFORD: Vogue, Stratford D.I.; TILLSONBURG: Strand, Skylark D.I.; WATERLOO: Waterloo; WILLOWDALE: Willow.

MANITOBA—THOMPSON: Strand.

QUEBEC—CHIBOUGAMAU: Vimy; VAL D'OR: Marcel, Strand, Capitol, ROUYN, Paramount.

Twentieth Century Theatres

175 Bloor Street E., Toronto M4W 1E 1, Canada, (416) 960-8900.

Theatres operated by Twinex Century Theatres Corporation Ltd.

N. A. TAYLOR, pres. M. L. AXLER, v.p.; H. S. MANDELL, sec.-treas.

ONTARIO—LONDON: 401 Drive-In; OSHAWA: Oshawa Drive-In; OTTAWA: Airport D.I. 1, 2, & 3, Britannia Drive-In 1 & 2, Cinema 6; SUDBURY: La Salle D.I.; TORONTO: 400 D.I. 1, 2 & 3, 7 & 27 D.I. 1 & 2, TePee D.I.

Cinemas Unis. Ltd.

5887 Monkland Avenue, Montreal H4A 1G 6, Quebec. (514) 489-8461.

G. P. DESTOUNIS, pres. & man. dir.; M. PHANEUF, exec. v.p.; DON DRISDELL, vice-pres., general manager & secretary-treasurer; J. SPERDAKOS, v.p.

QUEBEC—DORVAL: Dorval; MONTREAL: La Cité, Parisien, Monkland, Papineau, Rivoli, Snowdown, Claremont, Van Horne, York, Chateau, Kent, Loews, P. V. M., Versailles; QUEBEC CITY: Capitol, Empire; ST. HYACINTHE: Maska; SHERBROOKE: Carrefour de L'Estrie; WESTMOUNT: Avenue, Westmont Square; THREE RIVERS: Capitol, Les Rivieres; GREENFIELD PARK: Greenfield Park; LAVAL: Laval; STE. FOY: Ste. Foy, Le Canadien; QUEBEC CITY: Place Quebec; POINTE CLAIRE: Fairview, Dollard Des Ormeaux, Dollard Drive-In.

BERMUDA

Bermuda General Theatres, Ltd.

Hamilton, Bermuda. (809) 295-5575.

W. SKINNER, gen. mgr.

BERMUDA—HAMILTON: Rosebank; ST. GEORGE'S: Somers Playhouse; SOMERSET: Sandys.

Buying and Booking Services

AMC Film Marketing Inc.
106 W. 14th St. Kansas City MO 64105 (816) 474-6150
JOEL RESNICK, v.p.

BRANCHES
P.O. Box 8299, Jacksonville FL 32211 (904) 721-1871.
GENE JACOBS, v.p.

139 Gaither Dr., Mount Laurel NJ 08054 (609) 778-8400.
CHARLES WESOKY, v.p.

1221 Baltimore, Kansas City MO 64105 (816) 474-5116.
ED DURWOOD, v.p.

10300 N. Central Expwy., Bldg. 5 Suite 245, Dallas TX 75231 (214) 369-4400
BERNIE PALMER, v.p.

Two Century Plaza, 2049 Century Park East, Suite 1020, Los Angeles CA 90067 (213) 552-3344.
ARNOLD SHARTIN, v.p.

Affiliated Theatres Corp.
46 Church Street, Boston MA (617) 542-2550.
ALAN C. HOCKBERG, pres. & treas.

Allied Theatres Buying and Booking Circuit
185 N. Wabash Ave., Chicago, IL 60601. 346-4731.
AARON SHLESMAN, pres.

Armstrong Circuit, Inc.
135½ N. Main St., P.O. Box 679, Bowling Green, OH 43402. (419) 352-5195. (For personnel see listing under circuits.)
Booking and buying agent in Michigan and Ohio.

Art Cinema Booking Service Inc.
1501 B'way, New York, NY 10036. (212) 840-2445.
SANFORD WEINER, pres.; JEANNE WEINER, v.p.; ROY A. WEINER, sales mgr.; JACK STEINBERG, asst. secty.
   Theatrical & Non Theatrical Distribution of 35m & 16m films.

Harry Brandt Booking Office, Inc.
229 W. 42nd Street, New York, NY 10036 (212) 921-0011.
Theatres which this circuit books are included in the list of its own houses. See: Theatre Circuits.

Carolina Booking Service, Inc.
230 S. Tryon St., Charlotte, NC 28202. (704) 377-9341.
FRANK LOWRY, pres. and owner; BILL CLINE, booker.

Cinema Booking Service of New England, Inc.
39 Church St., Boston, MA 02116
STANTON DAVIS, pres.

Clark Theatre Service
Suite 225, International Plaza, 23300 Greenfield Road, P.O. Box 37007, Oak Park, MI 48237. (313) 968-4888 or 566-4749.
WILLIAM M. CLARK, owner; CRYSTAL CLARK, cashier.

Consolidated Theatre Service, Inc.
Suite 25, 3901 N. Meridian St., Indianapolis, IN 46208. (317) 923-2331.
MORRIS CANTOR, buyer & booker; NORMA MESALAM, officer mgr. & cashier.

Co-Operative Theatres of Ohio, Inc.
29001 Cedar Rd., Cleveland, OH 44124. (216) 461-2700.
BLAIR MOONEY, pres.; DAVID BEAUPAIN, JOHN KNEEP, PHIL LAVER, bookers

Film Booking Service
837 Park Square Building, Boston, MA 02116. (617) 426-4006.
SUMNER MYERSON, pres.

Film Booking Service of California
215 South La Cienega Blvd., Suite 206, Beverly Hills, CA 90211. (213) 653-2722.
BRUCE POYNTER, owner.

Florin-Creative Film Services
231 West 47th St., New York, NY 10036. (212) 489-0850.
STEVEN FLORIN, MARC LAFFIE, representatives.

Florin Enterprises, Seymour
221 West 47th St., New York, NY 10036. (212) 489-0850.
SEYMOUR FLORIN, STEVEN FLORIN, representatives.

Guy-Con Enterprises, Inc.
Film Buying and Booking Service. 3859 West 95th St., Shawnee Mission, KA 66206.
HAROLD P. GUYETT, pres., film buyer & booker.

Torrence Hudgins Buying & Booking Service
5526 Dyer St., Suite 112, Dallas, TX 75206. (214) 363-8801.
TORRENCE HUDGINS, owner.

Independent Theatres, Inc.
5205 Leesburg Pike, Suite 203, Bailey's Crossroads, VA 22041. (703) 379-6633.
HARLEY DAVIDSON, pres.; JANE M. KLOTZ, mgr.

Ind-Ex Booking Service
500 South Ervay, 160B, Dallas, TX 75201. (741) 1974-5-0.
JUANITA WHITE, buying and booking.

Indianapolis Cooperative Theatres

617 E. 38th St., Indianapolis, IN 46205. (317) 923-7578.
PETER J. FORTUNE, owner, film buyer.

Lockwood/Friedman Film Corp.

430 Park Sq. Building, Boston, MA 02116.
ROGER LOCKWOOD, ARTHUR FRIEDMAN, chief officers.

Lovett Interstate Thea. Service

935 N.W. 19th Ave., Portland, OR 97209. (503) 222-1381.
DICK CARLSON, mgr.; LOUISE TODD, asst.

Marcus Theatres Corporations

212 W. Wisconsin Ave., Milwaukee, WI 53203. (414) 272-6020, 272-6027.
RICHARD L. KITE, pres.; HENRY B. TOLLETTE, chmn. of the bd; STEPHEN MARCUS, v.p.; BRUCE J. OLSON, v.p.; CHARLES LOWE, v.p., MICHAEL KOMINSKY, v.p. & film buyer; TRUMAN SCHROEDER, MICHEL OGRODOWSKI, asst. v.p.s & buyers & bookers; RICHARD HEINTZ, controller.

Mescop, Inc.

9235 W. Capitol Drive, Milwaukee, WI 53222. (414) HO6-1700.
FRED FLORENCE, pres. & buyer; JAMES FLORENCE, TODD SZMANIA, booking dept.

Milgram Theatres, Inc.

1616 Walnut St., Suite 2000, Philadelphia, PA 19103. (215) 985-4900.
WILLIAM MILGRAM, pres.; HENRY MILGRAM, exec. v.p.

Neighborhood Booking/Buying Service

P.O. Box 3-J, Richmond, VA 23206. (804) 644-0771.
SAM BENDHEIM, III, gen. mgr.

Northwest Diversified Entertainment

500 Wall Street—Suite 317, Seattle, WA 98121. (206) 623-5380.
BENJAMIN L. HANNAH, pres.

Northwest Theatre Service

215 Produce Bank Bldg., 100 North 7th St., Minneapolis, MN 55403, (612) 336-8660.
JOHN R. KELVIE, booking and buying; DOROTHY E. DURAY, secretary, cashier and purchasing agent.

Ornstein, E. L., Theatres

4016 Shelbyville Road, Louisville, KY 40207. (502) 896-8805-6.
E. L. ORNSTEIN, owner, buyer and booker.

Queen City Advertising

230 South Tryon Street, Suite 1020, Charlotte, NC 28202.
JIM MURPHY, pres.; ANN MURPHY, secty.-treas.; KIT HALL, media div.

R/C Theatres Booking Service

19 West Mount Royal Avenue, Baltimore, MD 21201 (301) 332-0222.
IRWIN R. COHEN, pres.; MRS. SAREBA MASLOW, office manager.

Reinhardt, Max, Enterprises, Inc.

1113 Spencer Ave., Gastonia, NC 28052. (704) 864-2274.
MAX REINHARDT, pres.

Saffle Theatre Service

209 Dayton St., Edmonds, WA, 98020. (206) 774-9111.
M. W. "BUD" SAFFLE, owner; JIM BALLANTINE, booker.

Stearn-Hanna Co-Operative Theatre Service

14 West North Ave., Pittsburgh, PA 15212. (412) 231-2123.
LOUIS E. HANNA, SR., owner.

Tanner, W. R.

P.O. Box 398, Kenbridge, VA 23944. (703) 676-2267.
W. R. TANNER, buyer and booker.

Triangle Theatre Service, Inc.

1585 Broadway, New York, NY 10036. (212) 581-0900.
IRVING DOLLINGER and RICHARD DOLLINGER, representatives.

Tri-State Theatre Service, Inc.

Film Arts Building, 636 Northland Blvd. Cincinnati, OH 45240 (513) 851-5700
PHIL BORACK, pres.; EDWARD HANDLER, v.p.

United Booking Service

Midway Mall, 7793 Flagler St., Miami FL 33144. (305) 266-5070.
PETE DAWSON, PAT DAWSON.

Vean Gregg Buying & Booking Service

5526 Dyer St., Suite 136, Dallas, TX 75206. (214) 739-6450.
VEAN GREGG, owner.

CANADA

Allied Cinema Services

648 Finch Ave. E., Suite #2, Willowdale, MZK ZE6; Ont.
JERRY STONE, gen. mgr.

Associated Booking Service, Inc.

Suite 1210, 21 Dundas Sq., Toronto, Ont. M5B 1B7. (416) 368-1139.
CURLY S. POSEN, pres.

Canfilm Screen Service Limited

16mm. distributors for Universal & Avco Embassy, I.F.D., Astral, Ambassador & others. 615-71 Avenue, S.E., Calgary, Alberta, T2H OS7 (403) 259-4444. Telex No.: 03-825741.
R. C. GIBSON, gen. mgr.

956 Richards Street, Vancouver, B.C. (604) 682-3646.
Telex: 04 507759.
DAVE GILFILLAN, br. mgr.

583 Ellice Ave., Winnipeg, Manitoba. (204) 786-6759.
Telex: 07 587678.
HAROLD JOYAL, manager

Independent Theatre Services

109 Gordon Rd., Willowdale, Ontario, (416) 225-9610.
HAROLD PFAFF.

Quebec Cinema Booking, Ltd.

1430 Bleury St. (Suite 10), Montreal H3A 2J1, Que.,
(514) 288-6336.
MORT PREVOST, pres.; JACQUES PATRY, vice pres.

Select Pictures Limited

583 Ellice Ave., Winnipeg, Canada, R3B 127. (613)
774-4451.
BARRY MYERS, manager.

Drive-In Theatres

* **NAME**

* **LOCATION**
  (Alphabetically by State & Town)

* **OWNER**

* **CAPACITY**

Drive-In Theatres

Theatre Name	Address	City & Zip	Circuit	Cars
ALABAMA				
THC Drive In		Adamsville 35005	Borders, J.	200
Rebel Drive In		Alabaster 35007	Watson, T.E.	400
Marshall Drive In	Box 429	Albertville 35950	Hammonds, W.	400
Pines Drive In	Box 181	Alexander City 35010	Legg, H.	300
Bama Drive In		Anniston 36201	Cine Media	400
Midway Drive In	Box 1243	Anniston 36202	Cine Media	200
Pineview Drive In	Box 458	Arab 35016	Word	200
Hatfield Drive In	Highway 315	Athens 35611	Martin	300
Auto Movies #1		Bessemer 35020	Engler, Jr.P.	300
Fair Park Drive In	2801 Lomb Ave.	Birmingham 35208	Cobb, R.C.	800
Mustang Drive In	1701 Center Point Rd.	Birmingham 35215	Cobb, R.C.	
Eagle Dr. In		Brewton 36426	Con-McLend	300
Southport Drive In	Box 297	Bridgeport 35740	Word	300
Clanton Drive In	P.O. Box 1166	Clanton 35045	Clark, B.	400
Marbro Drive In	Highway 31 No.	Cullman 35055	Martin	400
Thunderbird Dr. In	Box 1055	Decatur 35601	Hammonds, W.	300
Grove Dr. In		Demopolis 36732	Holloway, J.	250
Skyview Drive In	Box 1689	Dothan 36301	Davis, R.	400
Circle Drive In	Box 570	Enterprise 36331	Clark, M.	
Coffee Drive In	P.O. Box 346	Enterprise 36330	Davis, R.	300
Joylan Drive In	Cloverdale Road	Florence 35632	Martin	600
Hub Drive In		Foley 36535	Con-McLend	300
Hamilton Drive In	Box 117	Ft. Payne 35967	Hamilton, D.	300
Rebel Drive In	Box 1398	Gadsden 35902	Georgia The.	200
Neva Drive In	Rt. #1 Box 93 East	Geneva 36340	Howell, K.	300
Camellia Drive In	P.O. Box 369	Greenville 36067	McLendon	
Camellia Drive In		Greenville 36037	Con-McLend	300
Area Drive In		Grove Hill 36451	Waterfall, C.	
Gu Win Drive In		Guin 35594	Borders, J.	200
Havala Drive In		Haleyville 35565	Lakeman, J.	200
Ford Drive In	Box 280	Hamilton 35570	Bedford, W.	300
Goober Drive In		Headland 36345	Bennett, J.	225
Whitesburg D.I.	Box P	Huntsville 35804	Crute, C.	400
72 Drive In	Box P	Huntsville 35801	Crute, C.	400
78 Drive In		Jasper 35501	Kennedy, R.M.	300
Twin City Drive In	Rt. 1 Box 280	Livingston 35470	Royal Theas.	
Crenshaw Drive In		Luverne 36049	Gaylard, J.	300
Do Drive In		Mobil 36601	Gulf States	300
Air Sho Dr. In		Mobile 36601	Giddens & Res	300
Bama Dr. In	3251 Halls Mill Rd.	Mobile 36606	Gulf States	400
Jet Drive In	Box 11207	Montgomery 36111	Kennedy, R.M.	500
South Plaza D.I.	P.O. Box 11207	Montgomery 36111	Kennedy, R.M.	
Marbro Drive In	Woodward Ave.	Muscle Shoals 35660	Martin	400
Skyvue Drive In	Box 507	Oneonta 35121	Carter, W.H.	300
Skyway Drive In		Oxford 36203	Cine Media	300
Phenix Drive In	14th Street	Phenix City 36867	Martin	300
Piedmont Drive In		Piedmont 36272	Quarles, C.	200
Prattmont Drive In	P.O. Box 31	Prattville 36067	Jones, L.	200
Kings Drive In		Russellville 35653	King, A.	200
Top Drive In		Samson 36477	Howell, M.	200
Tawasentha Drive In	Box 787	Scottsboro 35768	Word	300
Sel Mont Drive In	Box 848	Selma 36701	Engler, P.	600
80 Drive In	Box 848	Selma 36701	Engler, Jr., P.	400
Hi-Way Drive In		Shawmut 36876	Royal, Jr., L.	900
Sumiton Drive In		Sumiton 35148	Borders, J.	400
Comet Drive In	Birmingham Highway	Sylacauga 35150	Martin	400
Broadway Drive In	Broadway Ave.	Talladega 35160	Martin	300
Starlight Drive In	Box 385	Troy 36081	Gaylard, J.	300
Lincoln Drive In		Tuskegee 36083	Moffitt, J.	200
ALASKA				
Sundowner Dr. In	Box 1540	Anchorage 99501	Wometco/Lat.	600
ARIZONA				
Oasis Drive In	P.O. Box 717	Avondale 85323	Howell Thea.	400
Bagdad Dr. In	P.O. Box 264	Bagdad 86321	Springwicks	108
Valley Drive In	P.O. Box 1768	Bullhead City 86430	Paradis, L.	150
Mustang Drive In	245 N. Washington	Chandler 85252	Howell Thea.	400
Ft. Cochise Drive In		Douglas 85607	Springwick	500
Thunderbird Drive In	5533 No. 59th	Glendale 85301	Mann Theas.	1,050
Mohave Dr. In	4601 Hwy. 95	Lake Havasu City 86403	Durham	
Pioneer Dr. In 1&2	2165 W. Main St.	Mesa 85201	Nace	692
Velda Rose Drive In	103 S. Recker Rd.	Mesa 85205	Nace	700
Nogales Drive In		Nogales 85621	Springwicks	400
Parker Drive In	P.O. Box AF	Parker 85344	Parker Ths.	
Acres Drive In	3720 W. Van Buren	Phoenix 85009	Pacific Dr.	1,100
Big Sky Drive In	4111 W. Indian Schl. Rd.	Phoenix 85019	E&W Mgment.	400
Indian Drive In	4141 No. 27th Ave.	Phoenix 85017	Plitt	1,360
Nu View Drive In	3150 W. Buckeye Rd.	Phoenix 85009	Pacific Dr.	
Peso Drive In	3720 W. Van Buren	Phoenix 85009		
Phoenix Drive In	3600 East Van Buren	Phoenix 85008	Nace	400

534

Theatre Name	Address	City & Zip	Circuit	Cars
Rodeo Drive In	1223 E. Buckeye Rd.	Phoenix 85034	E&W Mgment.	500
Silver Dollar Drive In	7201 So. Central	Phoenix 85040	Agosta, P.	900
Valley Drive In	Cave Creek & Sweetwater	Phoenix 85022	Wetsman, Eis	500
Senator Drive In		Prescott 86301	Nace	350
Roundup Drive In		Scottsdale 85252	Nace	700
Wagon Wheel Drive In	P.O. Box 8490	Showlow 85901	Rawlings	300
Geronimo Drive In		Sierra Vista 85635	Wetsman, Eis	304
Scottsdale 6 Dr. In #1	1625 N. Hayden Rd.	Tempe 85281	Syufy Ent.	1,800
Scottsdale 6 Dr. In #2	1625 N. Hayden Rd.	Tempe 85281	Syufy Ent.	
Scottsdale 6 Dr. In #3	1625 N. Hayden Rd.	Tempe 85281	Syufy Ent.	
Scottsdale 6 Dr. In #4	1625 N. Hayden Rd.	Tempe 85281	Syufy Ent.	
Scottsdale 6 Dr. In #5	1625 N. Hayden Rd.	Tempe 85281	Syufy Ent.	300
Scottsdale 6 Dr. In #6	1625 N. Hayden Rd.	Tempe 85281	Syufy Ent.	
South Twin Dr. In 1	56th & Elliott	Tempe 85283	E&W Managm.	
South Twin Dr. In 2	56th & Elliott	Tempe 85283	E&W Managm.	
Apache Drive In 1	1600 Benson Hway.	Tucson 85726	De Anza	220
Apache Drive In 2	1600 Benson Hway.	Tucson 85726	De Anza	
Apache Drive In 3	1600 Benson Hway.	Tucson 85726	De Anza	
De Anza Dr. In #1	P.O. Box 26886	Tucson 85726	De Anza	600
De Anza Dr. In #2	P.O. Box 26886	Tucson 85726	De Anza	
De Anza Drive In 3	P.O. Box 26886	Tucson 85726	De Anza	
Rodeo Drive In		Tucson 85726	De Anza	800
Tucson 4 Dr. In 1	1055 W. Grant Rd.	Tucson 85719	Syufy Ent.	1,570
Tucson 4 Dr. In 2	1055 W. Grant Rd.	Tucson 85719	Syufy Ent.	
Tucson 4 Dr. In 3	1055 W. Grant Rd.	Tucson 85719	Syufy Ent.	
Tucson 4 Dr. In 4	1055 W. Grant Rd.	Tucson 85719	Syufy Ent.	
22nd Street Drive In	1401 So. Belvedere Av.	Tucson 85711	Mann Theas.	500
Tonto Drive In		Winslow 86047	Nace	300
Crest Auto	254 Main Street	Yuma 85364	Sturdivant	954
Mesa Drive In	2600 Fourth Ave.	Yuma 85364	Pacific Dr.	400

ARKANSAS

Theatre Name	Address	City & Zip	Circuit	Cars
Skyvue Drive In	P.O. Box 586	Arkadelphia 71923	U.A. Theas.	300
32 Drive In		Ashdown 71822	Powell, H. Jr.	
White River Drive In		Batesville 72501	Commonwealth	300
Starvue Drive In		Blytheville 72315	Malco Theas.	400
Razorback Dr. In		Camden 71701	Fenwick, D.	
Ark Air Drive In		Clarksville 72830	U.A. Theas.	700
65 Drive In		Conway 72032	U.A. Theas.	300
Queen Auto		De Queen 71832	Silva, B.	200
Skyvue Drive In		Eldorado 71730	Riley, J.	450
62 Drive In	P.O. Box 337	Fayetteville 72701	Commonwealt	588
71 Drive In	P.O. Box 337	Fayetteville 72701	Commonwealt	400
Carousel Dr. In	P.O. Box 946	Fordyce 71742	Womble P&P	225
Starlite Drive In	Box 157	Gassville 72635	Brixey, B.	200
Glenwood Drive In		Glenwood 71943	Stasiak, S.J.	300
Sunset Drive In	Box 472	Hamburg 71646	Carpenter, R.	300
Ozark Drive In		Harrison 72601	Commonwealt	200
Crest	Box 387	Helena 72342	Debro, W.	600
Dixie Drive In		Hope 71801	Bee Amus.	
Skyvue Drive In		Jonesboro 72401	Malco Theas.	300
Lepanto Drive In	P.O. Box 397	Lepanto 72354	Shinall, R.	
Asher Drive In		Little Rock 72203	U.A. Theas.	500
Big Red Twin Dr. In		Little Rock 72201	U.A. Theas.	400
Wild Hog Twin Dr. In		Little Rock 72201	U.A. Theas.	400
Rocket Dr. In	P.O. Box 707	Magnolia 71753	U.A. Theas.	300
Malvern Dr. In	P.O. Box 40	Malvern 72104	U.A. Theas.	400
Kenda Drive In	Box 355	Marshall 72650	Sanders, K.	200
Mena Drive In		Mena 71953	Geyer	
Monticello Drive In		Monticello 71655	Williams, J.	200
Rivervue Drive In	P.O. Box 149	Morrilton 72110	U.A. Theas.	300
Stone Drive In	Box 76	Mt. View 72560	Thompson, S.	200
Twin Dr. In Front Screen		N. Little Rock 72115	U.A. Theas.	
Twin Drive In		N. Little Rock 72115	U.A. Theas.	500
Howard Auto		Nashville 71852	Johnson, J.	300
Osceola Dr. In		Osceola 72370	Boggs, G.	300
Paris Drive In	Box 449	Paris 72855	Zeiler, A.	200
Pines Drive In		Pine Bluff 71601	Commonwealt	400
Skylark Drive In		Pocahontas 72455	Novak, D.	
Twin City Dr. In	Box 519	Rogers 72756	Commonwealt	740
64 Drive In		Russellville 72801	Weber	300
Dixie Drive In		Searcy 72143	Commonwealt	300
Movie Park Dr. In	P.O. Box 598	Siloam Springs 72761	Smith, E.L.	200
Grove Drive In		Springdale 72764	Commonwealt	300
67 Drive In		Texarkana 75501	Gulf States	400
Warren Drive In		Warren 71671	Williams, J.	400
Dixie Drive In	P.O. Box 2339	West Helena 72390	Boggs Ent.	

CALIFORNIA

Theatre Name	Address	City & Zip	Circuit	Cars
Island Auto Movie	791 Thau Way	Alameda 94502	Syufy Ent.	700
Anaheim Dr. In #2	1502 N. Lemon St.	Anaheim 92805	Pacific Dr.	500
Anaheim Dr. In #3	1502 N. Lemon St.	Anaheim 92805	Pacific Dr.	500
Anaheim Drive In	1520 No. Lemon	Anaheim 92805	Pacific Dr.	1,800
Bridgehead D. I. 1 & 2	Antioch Oaklay Hwy.	Antioch 94509	Stamm Theas.	1,000
Edwards Dr. In	4469 E. Live Oak	Arcadia 91006	Edwards	700
Arcata Drive In	Gwintoli Lane & Hwy. 1	Arcata 95521	Thomas, M.	500
Magnolia Drive In	10540 Magnolia Ave.	Arlington 92503	Sero Amusem.	500
Van Buren Dr. In 1	3035 Van Buren Blvd.	Arlington 92503	Sero Amusem.	900
Van Buren Dr. In 2	3035 Van Buren Blvd.	Arlington 92503	Sero Amusem.	
Van Buren Dr. In 3	3035 Van Buren Blvd.	Arlington 92503	Sero Amusem.	
Kings Drive In	P.O. Box 785	Armona 93202	Graff, T.	500
Azusa Foothill D. I.	675 E. Foothill Blvd.	Azusa 91702	Edwards	1,600

Theatre Name	Address	City & Zip	Circuit	Cars
Crest Drive In	P.O. Box 1125	Bakersfield 93302	Mann Theas.	1,000
Edison Drive In	P.O. Box 6306	Bakersfield 93307	Sero Amusem.	500
Southchester Drive In	Hway. 99 & Chester Ave.	Bakersfield 93304	Exhib., L.A.	500
Terrace Drive In	300 W. Terrace Way	Bakersfield 93304	Exhib., L.A.	700
99 Drive In	Pierce Rd. Hwy. 99	Bakersfield 93308	Exhib., L.A.	600
Edgewood Drive In	13159 E. Bess	Baldwin Park 91706	Pacific Dr.	1,200
Skyline Drive In	Highway 91 & 58	Barstow 92311	Western Amu.	600
Lake Drive In	P.O. Box 1858	Big Bear Lake 92315	Strebe, E.	400
Oasis Drive In	Drawer BB	Blythe 92225	Folsom, D.	375
Brawley Drive In	4255 Hwy. 86	Brawley 92227	Meyer, F.	550
Buena Park Drive In	6540 Lincoln Blvd.	Buena Park 90620	Pacific Dr.	1,950
Lincoln Drive In	6612 Lincoln Ave.	Buena Park 92805	Pacific Dr.	800
Pickwick Drive In	1100 W. Alameda	Burbank 91506	Pacific Dr.	800
Burlingame Drive In #1	350 Beach Street	Burlingame 94010	Syufy Ent.	
Burlingame Drive In #2	350 Beach Street	Burlingame 94010	Syufy Ent.	
Burlingame Drive In #3	350 Beach Street	Burlingame 94010	Syufy Ent.	
Burlingame Drive In #4	350 Beach Street	Burlingame 94010	Syufy Ent.	
Mt. Burney Dr. In	P.O. Box J	Burney 96013	Frank & White	
Winchester Drive In #1	535 Westchester Dr.	Campbell 95008	Syufy Ent.	
Winchester Drive In #2	535 Westchester Dr.	Campbell 95008	Syufy Ent.	
Winchester Drive In #3	535 Westchester Dr.	Campbell 95008	Syufy Ent.	900
U.A. Westerner Drive In	4001 Manzanita Ave.	Carmichael 95608	U.A. Theas.	735
Ceres Drive In	P.O. Box 35	Ceres 94307	Maestri	350
Winnetka D. I. #1	20210 Prairie Ave.	Chatsworth 91311	Pacific	
Winnetka D. I. #2	20210 Prairie Ave.	Chatsworth 91311	Pacific	
Winnetka D. I. #3	20210 Prairie Ave.	Chatsworth 91311	Pacific	
Winnetka D. I. #4	20210 Prairie Ave.	Chatsworth 91311	Pacific	
Starlite Drive In	P.O. Box 3530	Chico 95926	U.A. Theas.	639
Big Sky Drive In	2245 Main St.	Chula Vista 92011	Sero Amusem.	2,000
Harbor Drive In	P.O. Box 1265	Chula Vista 92012	Eldorado	1,100
Vineland Drive In	443 N. Vineland	City of Industr. 91744	Pacific Dr.	1,700
Lake Drive In	P.O. Box 147	Clearlake Park 95424	Sampson, H.	350
Coalinga Drive In	P.O. Box 923	Coalinga 93210	Bell, C.	
Compton Drive In	2111 E. Rosecrans	Compton 90221	Pacific Dr.	1,200
Auto Movies	Concord Ave.	Concord 94520	Syufy Ent.	425
Solano Drive In 1	1611 Solano Way	Concord 94520	Syufy Ent.	
Solano Drive In 2	1611 Solano Way	Concord 94520	Syufy Ent.	800
Paula Drive In	3051 Newport Blvd.	Costa Mesa 92627	Pacific Dr.	800
Covina Dr. In #1	1034 E. Arrow Hwy.	Covina 91722	Sterling Th.	
Covina Dr. In #2	1034 E. Arrow Hwy.	Covina 91722	Sterling Th.	
Ocean Dr. In		Crescent City 95531	Sonomarin	400
Studio Drive In	5250 Sepulveda Blvd.	Culver City 90230	Pacific Dr.	1,000
Geneva Dr. In 1	607 Carter Street	Daly City 94014	Syufy Ent.	751
Geneva Dr. In 3	607 Carter Street	Daly City 94014	Syufy Ent.	
Mission Drive In	500 Guttenberg	Daly City 94014	Syufy Ent.	1,040
Midway Drive In	P.O. Box 215	Dinuba 93618	Harrah, J.	800
Big Sky Drive In	1044 E. Huntington	Duarte 91010	Pacific Dr.	800
San Ramon Auto Movie #1	P.O. Box 2257	Dublin 94566	Enea Bros.	850
San Ramon Auto Movie #2	P.O. Box 2257	Dublin 94566	Enea Bros.	380
Aero Drive In	1470 E. Broadway	El Cajon 92021	Sero Amusem.	500
Motor Vu Dr. In 1 & 2	P.O. Box 1933	El Centro 92243	Gran, R.	550
El Monte Drive In	9700 Lower Azusa Rd.	El Monte 91731	Pacific Dr.	900
Starlite Drive In	2559 No. Chico Blvd.	El Monte 91731	Pacific Dr.	900
Escondido Drive In	755 West Mission	Escondido 92025	Crowder, J.	300
Midway Drive In	P.O. Box 1013	Eureka 95502	Thea. Mgt.	525
Chief Auto Movie	P.O. Box 48	Fairfield 94533	Tegtmeier, H.	540
Bel Air Drive In	P.O. Box 696	Fontana 92335	Pacific Dr.	1,000
Fountain Valley Dr. In	18245 Brookhurst	Fountain Valley 92708	Pacific Dr.	
Fremont Auto Movie	Fremont Blvd.	Fremont 94538	Enea Bros.	770
Nimitz Auto Movies #1	P.O. Box 1395	Fremont 94537	Enea Bros.	
Nimitz Auto Movies #2	P.O. Box 1395	Fremont 94537	Enea Bros.	410
Starlite Dr. In So.	4888 North Fresno St.	Fresno 93726	Pacific Dr.	586
Starlite Drive In No.	4888 N. Fresno	Fresno 93726	Pacific Dr.	
Sunnyside Dr. In #1	5550 E. Olive Ave.	Fresno 93727	Pacific Dr.	1,600
Sunnyside Dr. In #2	5550 E. Olive Ave.	Fresno 93727	Pacific Dr.	1,600
Sunset Drive In	842 So. Hughes	Fresno 93726	Pacific Dr.	609
Woodward Pk. Dr. In #1	7150 No. Abby	Fresno 93710	Pacific Dr.	
Woodward Pk. Dr. In #2	7150 No. Abby	Fresno 93710	Pacific Dr.	
Woodward Pk. Dr. In #3	7150 No. Abby	Fresno 93710	Pacific Dr.	
Woodward Pk. Dr. In #4	7150 No. Abby	Fresno 93710	Pacific Dr.	
Twin Vue Drive In	15201 So. Figueroa	Gardena 90247	Pacific	500
Vermont Dr. In 1	17737 So. Vermont Ave.	Gardena 90247	Pacific Dr.	900
Vermont Dr. In 2	17737 S. Vermont	Gardena 90247	Pacific Dr.	
Vermont Dr. In 3	17737 S. Vermont	Gardena 90247	Pacific Dr.	
Hecker Pass D. I.	7588 Monterey St.	Gilroy 95020	Peters, J.	450
Airport Drive In		Goleta 93017	Metropolita	700
Santa Barbara D. I. No.	907 So. Kellogg Ave.	Goleta 93105	Metropolita	
Santa Barbara D. I. So.	907 So. Kellogg Ave.	Goleta 93105	Metropolita	
Hemacinto Drive In	1015 E. Florida Cine	Hemet 92343	Martin, H.	400
Baseline Drive In	26653 Baseline	Highland 92346	Pacific Dr.	800
Drake	7566 Melrose Ave.	Hollywood 90046	A/R	
Warner Drive In	7361 Warner Ave.	Huntington Beach 92647	Pacific Dr.	600
South Bay Drive In	2170 Coronado Ave.	Imperial Beach 92032	Sero Amusem.	1,500
Indio Drive In #1	P.O. Drawer F	Indio 92201	Lippert, R.	
Indio Drive In #2	P.O. Drawer F	Indio 92201	Lippert, R.	
Century Dr. In #1	3560 W. Century Blvd.	Inglewood 90303	Pacific Dr.	2,054
Century Dr. In #2	3560 W. Century Blvd.	Inglewood 90303	Pacific Dr.	
La Habra Drive In	1000 W. Imperial	La Habra 90631	Pacific Dr.	1,400
Alvarado Drive In	7910 E. El Cajon Blvd.	La Mesa 92043	Mann Theas.	900
Mt. Baldy Drive In	3515 White	La Verne 91750	Mann Theas.	1,200
Lakeport Auto Movies	P.O. Box 668	Lakeport 95433	Tegtmeier, H.	396
Jet Dr. In		Lancaster 93534	Western Amu.	400
Lancaster Dr. In 1	P.O. Box 526	Lancaster 93534	Lancaster, C.	850
Lancaster Dr. In 2	P.O. Box 526	Lancaster 93534	Lancaster, C.	1,958

Theatre Name	Address	City & Zip	Circuit	Cars
Lancaster Dr. In 3	P.O. Box 526	Lancaster 93534	Holiday Ths.	508
Ace Drive In	8015 Imperial Ave.	Lemon Grove 92045	Eldorado	900
Tri City Dr. In	25352 Redlands Blvd.	Loma Linda 92354	Pacific Dr.	700
Valley Drive In		Lompoc 93436	Metropolita	700
Circle Drive In	1633 Ximeno	Long Beach 90804	Pacific Dr.	1,000
Lakewood Drive In	2100 E. Carson	Long Beach 90807	Pacific Dr.	1,000
Long Beach Drive In	22120 S. Santa Fe	Long Beach 90810	Pacific Dr.	1,200
Los Altos Dr. In 1	2800 Bellflower Blv.	Long Beach 90815	Pacific Dr.	2,100
Los Altos Dr. In 2	2800 Bellflower Blvd.	Long Beach 90815	Pacific Dr.	
Los Altos Dr. In 3	2800 Bellflower Blvd.	Long Beach 90815	Pacific Dr.	
Centinela Drive In	5700 Centinela	Los Angeles 90045	Pacific Dr.	800
Park Vu Drive In	P.O. Box 241	Madera 93637	Gran R.	400
Motor In	4125 So. Highway 99	Malaga 93721	Pacific Dr.	903
Sierra Drive In	5575 Chestnut Road	Marysville 95901	Lippert, R.	500
Starlite Drive In	Box 509	Merced 95341	U.A. Theas.	640
McHenry Drive In 1&11	P.O. Box 4718	Modesto 95352	Maestri	1,000
Prescott Dr. In 1 2 3	P.O. Box 3088	Modesto 95353	Maestri	900
U/A Marina Auto Movie	P.O. Box 1030	Monterey 93940	U.A. Theas.	754
Floral Drive In	1465 Kern Ave.	Monterey Pk. L.A. 91754	Pacific Dr.	
Monte Vista Drive In	Grant Rd. & Elcamino	Mountain View 94040	Syufy Ent.	800
Mt. View Drive in	Hiway So. Junc. 89&99	Mt. Shasta 96067	Thomas	560
Mofett Drive In 3	1500 Stierlin Road	Mt. View 94041	Syufy Ent.	
Moffett Drive In 1	1500 Stierlin Road	Mt. View 94041	Syufy Ent.	1,299
Moffett Drive In 2	1500 Stierlin Road	Mt. View 94041	Syufy Ent.	
Kay Von Drive In	1127 Foster Road	Napa 94558	Blumenfeld	2,110
Thousand Oak Dr. In	1960 Newbury Rd.	Newbury Pk. 91320	Pacific Dr.	1,000
Crest Drive In	2400 Hammer Ave.	Norco 91760	Lamb, T.	
Coliseum Dr. In #1	5401 Industrial Way	Oakland 94621	Syufy Ent.	
Coliseum Dr. In #3	5401 Industrial Way	Oakland 94621	Syufy Ent.	
Coliseum Dr. In 2	5401 Industrial Way	Oakland 94621	Syufy Ent.	600
Valley Drive In 1234	3480 Mission Avenue	Oceanside 92054	Siegel Bros.	
Orange Drive In #1	291 N. State College	Orange 92666	Pacific Dr.	1,200
Orange Drive In #2	291 N. State College	Orange 92666	Pacific Dr.	
Stadium Drive In 1	1501 W. Katella	Orange 92667	Syufy Ent.	
Stadium Drive In 2	1501 W. Katella	Orange 92667	Syufy Ent.	
Stadium Drive In 3	1501 W. Katella	Orange 92667	Syufy Ent.	
Stadium Drive In 4	1501 W. Katella	Orange 92667	Syufy Ent.	
Mesa Dr. In	P.O. Box 431	Oreville 95965	U.A. Theas.	
Sky View Drive In	1250 So. Oxnard Ave.	Oxnard 93030	Pacific Dr.	1,000
Palm Springs Drive In	67607 E. Ramon Rd.	Palm Springs 92262	Metropolita	800
Palmdale Dr. In	1201 Avenue #2	Palmdale 93550	Lancaster, C.	
Smith Ranch Dr. In	P.O. Box 148	Palms 92277	Clemons, A.	400
Paramount Twin Dr. In	14711 Paramount Blvd.	Paramount 90723	Exhib., L.A.	
Rosecrans Drive In	8864 E. Century Blvd.	Paramount 90723	Pacific Dr.	1,600
Midway Drive In	5393 Redwood Hghwy	Petaluma 94952	Finlayment	600
Parkway Auto Movie	5155 Petaluma Blvd. N.	Petaluma 94953	Cinema West	760
Eldorado Dr. In	P.O. Box 961	Placerville 95667	Toler, A.	440
Motor Movies	2040 Contra Costa Bl.	Pleasant Hill 94523	Lippert	600
Mission D. I. #1	10789 Romona Ave.	Pomona 91766	Sero Amusem.	1,400
Mission D. I. #2	10789 Romona Ave.	Pomona 91766	Sero Amusem.	
Mission Dr. In #3	10798 Ramona Ave.	Pomona 91766	Sero Amusem.	
Mission Dr. In #4	10798 Ramona Ave.	Pomona 91766	Sero Amusem	
Thunderbird Dr. In	11091 Folsom Blvd.	Rancho Cordova 95670	Shu Ming	1,182
Skyvue Drive In	P.O. Box 4335	Redding 96001	Maestri	500
Starlite Drive In	P.O. Box 4335	Redding 96001	Maestri	700
Redwood Drive In 1	Bayshore Hwy. & Whipple	Redwood City 94064	Syufy Ent	
Redwood Drive In 2	Bayshore Hwy. & Whipple	Redwood City 94064	Syufy Ent.	600
Foothill Drive In	555 E. Foothill Blvd	Rialto 92376	Pacific Dr.	669
Hill Top Drive In	Hilltop Rd. & Frwy. 40	Richmond 94803	Syufy Ent.	950
Crest Drive In	P.O. Box 366	Ridgecrest 93555	Cummings, E.	
Hills Drive In	18485 South Marks	Riverdale 93656	Lasley, L.	300
Citrus Heights D. 1	Box 399	Roseville 95678	General The.	760
Rubidoux Drive In	3770 Opal	Rubidoux 92509	Sero Amusem.	700
Spruce Drive In 1	55 South Spruce	S. San Francisco 94080	Syufy Ent.	
Spruce Drive In 2	55 South Spruce	S. San Francisco 94080	Syufy Ent.	1,500
Fruitridge Dr. In	5201 Fruitridge Rd.	Sacramento 95820	Blumenfeld	848
Sacramento Dr. In 2	9616 Dates	Sacramento 95823	Syufy Ent.	
Sacramento Dr. In 3	9616 Dates	Sacramento 95823	Syufy Ent.	
Sacramento Dr. In 4	9616 Dates	Sacramento 95823	Syufy Ent.	
Sacramento Dr. In 5	9616 Dates	Sacramento 95823	Syufy Ent.	
Sacramento Drive In #1	9616 Oates	Sacramento 95823	Syufy Ent.	
Skyview Drive In 123	3100 47 Ave.	Sacramento 95823	Strawn, W.	1,800
Starlite D. I. 1&2	2200 Harvard Street	Sacramento 95815	Cinerama	975
U.A. Mather Auto Movies	9977 Folsom Blvd.	Sacramento 95827	U.A. Theas.	886
U.A. So. Gate Auto Movie	7700 Stockton Blvd.	Sacramento 95823	U.A. Theas.	
49er Dr. In #1	4450 Marysville Blvd.	Sacramento 95838	Syufy Ent.	
49er Dr. In #2	4450 Marysville Blvd.	Sacramento 95838	Syufy Ent.	450
49er Drive In 3	4450 Marysville Road	Sacramento 95838	Syufy Ent.	
49er Drive In 4	4450 Marysville Road	Sacramento 95838	Syufy Ent.	
Auto Movies #1	10 Simas St.	Salinas 93901	Syufy Ent.	
Auto Movies #2	10 Simar St.	Salinas 93901	Syufy Ent.	850
Auto Movies #3	10 Simas St.	Salinas 93901	Syufy Ent.	
Skyview Drive In	201 Harrison Rd.	Salinas 93902	Martins, N.	550
Mt. Vernon D. I. #2	632 S. Mt. Vernon Ave.	San Bernardino 92410	Pacific Dr.	1,100
Mt. Vernon Drive In #1	632 S. Mt. Vernon Ave.	San Bernardino 92410	Pacific Dr.	1,100
Campus Drive In	6147 El Cajon Blvd.	San Diego 92115	Eldorado	900
Frontier Twin Drive In	3601 Midway Drive	San Diego 92101	Sero Amusem.	1,400
Midway Drive In	3901 Midway Drive	San Diego 92110	Sero Amusem.	700
Pacific Drive In	4860 Mission Bay Drive	San Diego 92109	Eldorado	1,300
San Gabriel Drive In	140 W. Valley Blvd.	San Gabriel 91776	Edwards	1,100
Capitol Drive in #3	3630 Hillcap Ave.	San Jose 95123	Syufy Ent.	
Capitol Drive In #4	3630 Hillcap Ave.	San Jose 95123	Syufy Ent.	601
Capitol Drive In 1	3630 Hillcap Ave.	San Jose 95123	Syufy Ent.	
Capitol Drive In 2	3630 Hillcap Ave.	San Jose 95123	Syufy Ent.	

Theatre Name	Address	City & Zip	Circuit	Cars
Capitol Drive In 5	3630 Hillcap Ave.	San Jose 95123	Syufy Ent.	
Capitol Drive In 6	3630 Hillcap Ave.	San Jose 95123	Syufy Ent.	
El Rancho Drive In	1505 Almaden Road	San Jose 95125	Catalana, P.	1,000
San Jose Drive In	750 E. Gish Road	San Jose 95112	Saso, R.	750
Mission Drive In	30002 Del. Obispo St.	San Juan Cap. 92675	Pacific Dr.	
Sunset Drive In	Box 77A Route One	San Luis Obispo 93401	Gran R.	500
Rancho Drive In	1220 Connecticut Ave.	San Pablo 94806	Syufy Ent.	1,004
San Pedro Drive In	1811 No. Gaffey	San Pedro 90731	Pacific Dr.	900
101 Movies	76 Smith Road	San Rafael 94903	Blumenfeld	1,000
Harbor Blvd D. I.	3700 McFadden	Santa Ana 92704	Pacific Dr.	
U.A. Moonlite Drive In	2726 El Camino Real	Santa Clara 95051	U.A. Theas.	1,064
Skyview Dr. In 1 & 2	3240 Soquel	Santa Cruz 95062	Martins, N.	1,400
La Mirada Dr. In	13963 Alondra	Santa Fe Spring 90670	Sterling Th.	
Norwalk Blvd. Drive In	11202 Norwalk Blvd.	Santa Fe Spring 90670	Pacific Dr.	1,200
Highway Drive in	3085 Broadway	Santa Maria 93456	Metropolita	
Park Aire Drive In	295 E. Donovan Rd.	Santa Maria 93454	Gran, B.	500
U.A. Redwood Drive In	24 Millbrae Ave.	Santa Rosa 95404	U.A. Theas.	706
Village Drive In	P.O. Box 6695 Coddington	Santa Rosa 95405	Redwood	750
Santee Drive In	10990 Woodside Ave.	Santee 92071	Poynter, J.	700
Mustang Drive In	21021 Solidad Can. Rd.	Saugus 91350	Poynter, J.	900
Simi Drive In	361 Tierra Rejada R.	Simi 93065	Metropolita	500
Tahoe Drive In	P.O. Box 13902	So. Lake Tahoe 95702	T&R Theas.	200
Spruce Dr. In 3	55 South Spruce	So. San Francisco 94080	Syufy Ent.	
El Rancho Twin Dr. In	157 Hickey Blvd.	So. San Francisco 94080	Merrill, A.	850
Spruce Dr. In 4	55 South Spruce	So. San Francisco 94080	Syufy Ent.	
Southgate Dr. In	5131 E. Firestone Bvd.	Southgate 90280	Pacific Dr.	800
Crest Drive In	4100 South Hiway 99	Stockton 95206	Dye, D.	1,000
Hammer Drive In	P.O. Box 7187	Stockton 95207	Westland Th.	720
Motor Movies	P.O. Box 6187	Stockton 95206	Westland Th.	830
West Lane Drive In	P.O. Box 7187	Stockton 95207	Westland Th.	1,136
99 East Drive In	3999 N. Wilson Way	Stockton 95205	Dye, D.	
Sunland Dr. In	8010 Foothill Blvd.	Sunland 91040	Edwards	600
Sunnyvale Drive In No. 1	1035 Aster	Sunnyvale 94086	Syufy Ent.	
Sunnyvale Drive In No.2	1035 Aster	Sunnyvale 94086	Syufy Ent.	1,800
Lassen Auto Movies	P.O. Box 31	Susanville 96130	Green, H.	400
Roadium Drive In	2500 Redondo Beach B.	Torrance 90504	Pioneer	
Torrance Drive In	5501 Torrance	Torrance 90503	Pacific Dr.	1,200
Lucky Drive In	1419 Falkerth Rd.	Turlock 95380	Maestri	450
State Drive In	P.O. Box 30	Ukiah 95482	Redwood	460
Union City D/I #4	31200 Alvarado Niles	Union City 94587	Syufy Ent.	
Union City D/I #5	31200 Alvarado Niles	Union City 94587	Syufy Ent.	
Union City D/I #6	31200 Alvarado Niles	Union City 94587	Syufy Ent.	
Union Drive In #1	31200 Alvarado Niles	Union City 94587	Syufy Ent.	
Union Drive In 2	31200 Alvarado Niles	Union City 94587	Syufy Ent.	600
Union Drive In 3	31200 Alvarado Niles	Union City 94587	Syufy Ent.	
U.A. Crescent Drive In	P.O. Box 106	Vallejo 94590	U.A. Theas.	727
Vallejo Auto Movies #1	1300 Benecia	Vallejo 94590	Syufy Ent.	
Vallejo Auto Movies #2	1300 Benecia	Vallejo 94590	Syufy Ent.	
Van Nuys Drive In	15040 Roscoe Blvd.	Van Nuys 91402	Pacific Dr.	900
Sepulveda Dr. In	6127 Sepulveda Blvd.	Van Nuys 91411	Pacific Dr.	1,500
101 A Drive In	4826 E. Telephone Rd.	Ventura 93003	Pacific Dr.	900
101 B. Drive In	4826 E. Telephone Rd.	Ventura 93003	Pacific Dr.	
101 Drive In C.	4826 E. Telephone Rd.	Ventura 93003	Pacific Dr.	
Joshua Dr. In		Victorville 92392	Western Amu.	400
Mooney Drive In East	P.O. Box 3147	Visalia 93277	Westland Th.	700
Mooney Drive In West	P.O. Box 3147	Visalia 93277	Westland Th.	
Sequoia Auto Movie	P.O. Box 1184	Visalia 93278	Westland Th.	592
Starlite Drive In	P.O. Box 781	Watsonville 95077	Garcia, H.	686
Highway 39 Drive In	7901 Trask	Westminster 92683	Pacific Dr.	1,900
Sundown Dr. In	12335 E. Washington	Whittier 90606	Pacific Dr.	1,000
299 Drive In	P.O. Box 1054	Willow Creek 95573	Brander, S.	110
Sunset Drive In	Route 1 Box 216	Woodland 95695	Tomkinson	390
Auto See Drive In	935 Market Street	Yuba City 95991	R	500
Sky Drive In	Star Rt. 2 Box 1217	Yucca Valley 92284	Everett, E.C.	
Starlite D. I. #1	P.O. Box 85	29 Palms 92277	Shay, J.	500
Starlite D. I. #2	P.O. Box 85	29 Palms 92277	Shay, J.	

COLORADO

Ski Hi Drive In		Alamosa 81101	Murphy Cir.	350
Wadsworth Drive In	5100 Wadsworth Blvd.	Arvada 80002	Wolfberg Th.	475
East Drive In	12800 East Colfax Ave.	Aurora 80010	Wolfberg Th.	740
Havana Drive In	1349 South Havana	Aurora 80010	Wolfberg Th.	650
Holiday #2	P.O. Box 1619	Boulder 80302	Highland Th.	
Holiday Drive In #1	P.O. Box 1619	Boulder 80306	Highland Th.	
Kar Vu Drive In	111 Weld County Rd. 27	Brighton 80601	Prevost, A.	300
Nor West Drive In	P.O. Box 193	Broomfield 80020	Highland Th.	600
Commanche Dr. In		Buena Vista 81211	Groy, J.	210
Burlington Dr. In		Burlington 80807	Edmundson, J.	
Sunset Drive In	Box 271	Canon City 81212	Commonwealt	275
New Frontier D.		Center 81125	Bohn, E.	
Aircadia Drive In		Cold Springs 80901	Westland Th.	500
Falcon Drive In	P.O. Box 1150	Colorado Spgs. 80901	Westland Th.	500
Sky Vu Drive In	Box 1150	Colorado Spgs. 80901	Westland Th.	400
8th Street Drive In		Colorado Spgs. 80905	Westland Th.	500
Vista Vu Drive In	P.O. Box 1150	Colorado Spgs. 80901	Westland Th.	600
88th Drive In	Rt. 1 Box 206	Commerce City 80022	Holshue	450
Arroyo Drive In		Cortez 81321	Allen Ths.	350
Romantic Motor Vu D. I.		Craig 81435	Dewsnup, S.	
Big Sky Drive In		Delta 81416	Dewsnup, S.	400
Tru Vu Drive In		Delta 81416	Standewsnup	300
Evans Drive In	2705 W. Evans Ave.	Denver 80219	Deluxe	500
North Drive In		Denver 80221	Wolfberg Th.	800
North Star Drive In		Denver 80229	Wolfberg Th.	800

538

Theatre Name	Address	City & Zip	Circuit	Cars
West Drive In	601 Kipling Street	Denver 80226	Wolfberg Th.	700
Rocket Drive In		Durango 81301	Scales, J.	400
Cinderella Twin D. I. #1	3400 So. Platte River	Englewood 80110	Highland Th.	400
Cinderella Twin D. I. #2	3400 So. Platte River	Englewood 80110	Highland Th.	200
Motorena Drive In	2930 So. 11th East	Evans 80620	Wesco Theas.	390
Valley Drive In		Fort Morgan 80701	Boehm, N.	399
Holiday Twin Dr. In 1&2	2206 S. Overland Trl.	Ft. Collins 80526	Person, M.	
Sunset Drive In	Box 1070	Ft. Collins 80521	Highland Th.	520
Canyon Drive In		Glenwood Spgs. 81601	Glenn Theas.	500
Chief Drive In		Grand Junction 81501	Westland Th.	450
Rocket Drive In	Box 1397	Grand Junction 81501	Westland Th.	360
Greeley Drive In	2522 Sunset Lane	Greeley 80631	Prevost, A.	425
La Junta Drive In	Box 1080	La Junta 81050	Commonwealt	350
Lakeshore Drive In	1701 Sheridan Blvd.	Lakewood 80215	Monarch	1,000
Arrow Drive In	P.O. Box 108	Lamar 81052	Wolfenberg	400
South Drive In		Littleton 80110	Wolfberg Th.	1,000
Star Vu Drive In	P.O. Box 843	Longmont 80501	Klein, R.	300
L & L Motor Vue	841 Lincoln	Louisville 80027	Golden, H.	200
Pines Drive In		Loveland 80537	Peterson, V.	382
Star Drive In	2830 West U.S. 160	Monte Vista 81144	Kelloff, G.	360
Fox #2		Montrose 81401	Dewsnup, S.	
Star Drive In	Box 86	Montrose 81401	De Vries, G.	360
Uranium Dr. In	P.O. Box 191	Nucla 81424	Stieb, L.	225
Paonia Drive In		Paonia 81428	Linza, D.	300
East Drive In	Box 852	Pueblo 81002	Highland Th.	400
Mesa Drive In		Pueblo 81501	Westland Th.	963
Pueblo Drive In	Box 852	Pueblo 81002	Highland Th.	400
Starlight Drive In		Rocky Ford 81067	Commonwealt	300
Kar Vu Drive In		Springfield 81073	Baca Thea.	200
Starlight Drive In	Box 990	Sterling 80751	Cory Paul	350
Peak Drive In		Trinidad 81082	Sawaya, J.	350
Trail Drive In		Walsenburg 81089	Piazza, F.	160

CONNECTICUT

Theatre Name	Address	City & Zip	Circuit	Cars
Blue Hills Drive In		Bloomfield 06002	Genl. Cinema	
Summit D. I.		Branford 06405	Dr. In Theas.	
Torrington Drive In		Burrville 06790	SBC Mgt. Corp.	
Canaan Drive In	Route 7	Canaan 06018	Eisenberg, P.	
Clinton Drive In	Boston Post Road	Clinton 06413	Interst. Ths.	
Danbury Drive In	Box 590	Danbury 06818	SBC Mgt. Corp.	
Farmington Drive In		Forestville 06011	E.M. Loews	
Groton Drive In	% Ackerman	Groton 06340	Ackerman	
Middletown Drive In	Route 9 Saybrook Rd.	Middletown 06457	Schwab, H.	900
Milford Drive In		Milford 06460	Redstone	
Valley Drive In		Naugatuck 06770	Laflamme, C.	
Valley Drive In	1188 New Haven Rd.	Naugatuck 06770	Hallmark	
Hartford Drive In		Newington 06111	E.M. Loews	
Pike Drive In		Newington 06111	Menschell, B.	
New Haven D. I.		No. Haven 06473	Dr. In Theas.	
Plainville Drive In		Plainville 06072	Perakos	
Southington Drive In		Plantsville 06479	Perakos	
Rogers Corner Dr. In		Pleasant Valley 06063	Heilbron, D.	
Portland Drive In		Portland 06480	Markoff	600
Quinebaug Drive In		Quinebaug 06262	Interst. Ths.	600
East Hartford Fam. D. I.		South Windsor 06095	S.B.C. Mgt. Corp.	
Skyvue Drive In		Torrington 06790	S.B.C. Mgt. Corp.	
Pine Twin Drive In		Waterbury 06702	S.B.C. Mgt.	
Waterford Drive In		Waterford 06385	Goldberg, L.	
Watertown Dr. In		Watertown 06795	La Flamme	
Bowl Drive In	62 Orange Ave.	West Haven 06516	Cinema	666
Mansfield Drive In	R.F.D. #3	Willimantic 06226	Jungden, M.	950
Lake Drive In	1395 Waterbury	Wolcott 06716	Cinema	

DELAWARE

Theatre Name	Address	City & Zip	Circuit	Cars
Twin Oaks Dr. In	Route 42	Cheswold 19936	Derrickson	200
Naamans Corner Dr. In	Rt. 13 & Naamans Rd.	Claymont 19703	Budco	
Sussex West Drive In	Route 13	Laurel 19956	Derrickson	
Newark Drive In	300 E. Cleveland St.	Newark 19711	Sameric	450
Pleasant Hill Drive In	1317 W. Newport Pike	Newport 19804	Budco	300
Midway Dr. In	Midway Shopping Ctr.	Rehoboth Beach 19971	Derrickson	300
Prices Corner Drive In	1225 Centerville Rd.	Wilmington 19808	Budco	600

FLORIDA

Theatre Name	Address	City & Zip	Circuit	Cars
Prairie Lake Drive In	Box 278	Altamonte Sprgs. 32701	Floyd	400
#1 Drive In		Apalachicola 33321	Nichols, N.J.	200
Dale Drive In		Auburndale 33823	Floyd	200
Outdoor Drive In	490 W. Clower St.	Bartow 33830	Preston, H.	300
Lake Drive In		Belle Glades 33430	Gold Dobrow	
Blountstown Dr. In	Box 508	Bluntstown 32424	Harris, D.	200
Als Drive In	Box 217	Bonifay 32425	Brannon, D.L.	200
Bradenton Drive In	2305 9th St. West	Bradenton 33505	Floyd	200
41 Drive In	P.O. Box 428	Brooksville 33512	Floyd	200
Sumter Drive In		Bushnell 33513	Eason, B.	300
Escambia Drive In	P.O. Box X	Century 32535	Wood, P.	300
Starlight Dr. In	Box 568	Chipley 32428	Sapp, R.	150
Gulf to Bay Drive In	25 N. Belcher Rd.	Clearwater 33517	Floyd	500
Clervue Drive In	Box 97	Clermont 32711	MCM Theas.	200
Skyvue Drive In	P.O. Box 1825	Cocoa 32922	Green, G.	
Vanguard Drive In	Box 1717	Cocoa 32923	Kent	400
Dixie Drive In		Crestview 32536	Robinson, N.	200
Princess Drive In	Box AA	Cross City 32628	McKinney, N.	200

Theatre Name	Address	City & Zip	Circuit	Cars
Joy Lan Drive In		Dade City 33525	Floyd	200
Hi Way Drive In	1930 Federal Hwy.	Dania 33004	Henn, P.B.	
Gold Coast Drive In		Deerfield Beach 33441	Henn, P.B.	400
Boulevard Drive In	1492 S. Woodland Blvd.	Deland 32720	Floyd	300
Del Ray Drive In	Box 2304	Delray Beach 33444	Henn, P.B.	400
Brevard Drive In	Box 856	Eau Gallie 32925	Kent	200
Fun Lan Dr. In	P.O. Box 218	Edgewater 32032	Floyd	300
Movie Garden Drive In	P.O. Box M	Eustis 32726	MCM Theas.	400
Reef Drive In	Rte. 1 Box 55	Fernandina Beach 32034	Wingate, C.	300
Northside D. I.	Box 1629	Fort Myers 33901	Floyd	400
Southside Dr. In	Box 1629	Fort Myers 33902	Floyd	
Ft. Pierce Drive In	P.O. Box 3511	Fort Pierce 33450	Kent	400
Lauderdale Drive In	2695 W. Broward Blvd.	Ft. Lauderdale 33312	Henn, P.B.	500
Thunderbird Twin Dr. In	3121 W. Sunrise Blvd.	Ft. Lauderdale 33311	Henn, P.B.	
Showtown Twin 1&2 D. I.	Box 760	Ft. Walton 32548	Tringas, A.	
Gainesville Drive In	2400 Hawthorne Rd.	Gainesville 32602	Muma, G.	400
Suburbia Triple Dr. In	Box 722	Gainesville 32601	Gibson	488
Lake Haines Drive In	P.O. Box 958	Haines City 33844	Floyd	200
Arrow Drive In		Hollywood 33021	Henn, P.B.	400
Breezeway Drive In	Box 217	Homestead 33030	Holiday Ths.	300
Blanding Drive In	Box 7266	Jacksonville 32201	Kent	800
Fox Drive In 1&2	P.O. Box 37041	Jacksonville 32205	Eastern Fed.	800
Lake Forest Dr. In	2702 Rogero Rd.	Jacksonville 32211	Skinner, M.	300
Main Street Drive In		Jacksonville 32206	Clark Film	700
Midway Dr. In 1&2	Box 16424	Jacksonville 32216	Eastern Fed.	800
Pine Drive In	139 Easport Road	Jacksonville 32218	Clark Film	300
Playtime Drive In	6300 Blanding Blvd.	Jacksonville 32210	Accord, W.R.	
Ribault Drive In	4819 Soutel Dr.	Jacksonville 32208	Clark, H.	400
Southside Drive In		Jacksonville 32202	Clark Film	600
Islander Drive In	1214 Laird St.	Key West 33040	Sirugo, D.	600
Lake City Drive In	Box 1549	Lake City 33055	MCM Theas.	400
Lunar Outdoor	Box 1549	Lake City 33055	MCM Theas.	200
Wales Drive In	Box 591	Lake Wales 33853	Floyd	
Skydrome Drive In	Box 620	Lake Worth 33460	Henn, P.B.	600
Trail Drive In		Lake Worth 33460	McCain	
Filmland Drive In	Box 1350	Lakeland 33802	Floyd	400
Lakeland Drive In	Box 73	Lakeland 33802	Floyd	300
Silver Moon Drive In	Box 73	Lakeland 33802	Floyd	300
Thunderbird Dr. In	3701 E. Bay Dr.	Largo 33540	Floyd	800
Crest Drive In	Box 390	Leesburg 32748	MCM Theas.	300
Family Twin Drive In	811 Duval St.	Live Oak 32060	Vaughn, L.	600
Ri Mar Drive In	Box 17732	Lockhart 32810	Floyd	300
Wildcat Drive In	P.O. Box 348	Mac Clenny 32063	Johns, A.	145
Lakeshore Dr. In	1000 State Rd. 7	Margate 33063	Henn, P.B.	
Double D Drive In	P.O. Box 877	Marianna 32446	Harris	200
Melbourne Outdoor	Box 856	Melbourne 32935	Kent	200
Causeway Drive In	P.O. Box 1206	Merritt Island 32952	Kent	200
Miami Drive In	8100 N.W. 7th Ave.	Miami 33150	E.M. Loews	600
Tropicaire Drive In	7751 Red Rd.	Miami 33155	McComas, D.K.	800
27th Ave. Dr. In	2700 N.W. 87th St.	Miami 33147	Wometco	600
Naples Twin Dr. In	Route 84	Naples 33940	Cook, A.W.	700
Trail Drive In	1157 3rd St.	Naples 33940	Haynes, D.A.	300
Tropical Drive In	Box 1077	Nokomis 33555	Royston	200
North Dade Dr. In	17175 N.W. 27th Ave.	North Miami 33054	Wometco	700
Ocala Drive In	4850 South Pine St.	Ocala 32670	Quarto Corp.	500
Skylark Drive In	4850 South Pine St.	Ocala 32670	Quarto Corp.	292
Skylake Dr. In 1&2	P.O. Box 1395	Okeechobee 33472	Hales, R.	600
Golden Glades East D. I.	3401 N.W. 167 St.	Opa Locka 33054	Nareg Ent.	
Golden Glades West D. I.	3401 N.W. 167th St.	Opa Locka 33054	Nareg Ent.	1,000
Turnpike Drive In	Box 41	Opa Locka 33054	Nareg Ent.	900
Colonial Drive In	P.O. Box 20353	Orlando 32814	Floyd	500
Orange Ave. Drive In		Box 8216	Orlando 32806	Floyd
Orlando Drive In	Box 2209	Orlando 32802	Dixie Drive	300
Pine Hills Drive In	5050 W. Colonial Dr.	Orlando 32808	Floyd	300
South Trail Drive In	8621 Orange Blossom	Orlando 32809	Floyd	600
Winter Park Drive In	Box 2209	Orlando 32802	Dixie Drive	300
Nova Drive In	Box 665	Ormond Beach 32074	Floyd	
Linda Drive In	712 S. Palm Ave.	Palatka 32077	MCM Theas.	400
St. John Drive In		Palatka 32077	MCM Theas.	
Skyway Drive In		Palmetto 33561	Floyd	
Gulf Drive In	525 E. 15th St.	Panama City 32401	Martin	400
Isle of View Dr. In	No. Everette Ave.	Panama City 32401	Martin	500
Showtown 1&2 Dr. In	6600 N. Pensacola Blvd.	Pensacola 32507	Cobb, R.C.	700
Twin Air 1&2 Dr. In	P.O. Box 4387	Pensacola 32507	Cobb, R.C.	700
Graves Drive In	Box 131	Perry 32347	Graves, L.	200
Mustang Drive In	7301 Park Blvd. No.	Pinellas Park 33565	Floyd	800
Starlite Drive In	Box 1867	Plant City 33566	Floyd	200
Beach Drive In		Riviera Beach 33404	Henn, P.B.	600
Ruskin Drive In	Box 308	Ruskin 33570	Kirby, J.	200
Movieland Drive In	Box 534	Sanford 32771	Floyd	300
Bee Ridge Twin D. I.	3920 Bee Ridge Rd.	Sarasota 33580	Shapiro, Sid	
Trail Drive In	6801 N. Tamiami Trail	Sarasota 33578	Shapiro, S.	500
Sevon Drive In	Box 72	Sebring 33870	Floyd	200
Garden Dr. In	4103 Park St. N.	St. Petersburg 33709	Holiday Amu.	
28th Street Drive In	4990 28th Street	St. Petersburg 33714	Floyd	400
301 Dr. In	P.O. Box 1027	Starke 32091	Barksdale, R.	200
Capitol Drive In	Box 959	Tallahassee 32302	Kent	300
Auto Park Drive In	3612 22nd St. Causeway	Tampa 33619	Floyd	500
Fun Lan Drive In	E. Hillsboro A. 22nd S.	Tampa 33604	Floyd	400
Hillsboro Drive In	3306 W. Hillsboro Ave.	Tampa 33614	Plitt South	300
Skyway Drive In	P.O. Box 17426	Tampa 33612	Floyd	
Tower Drive In	Box 8385	Tampa 33604	Floyd	300
20th Century Drive In	Box 10512	Tampa 33611	Floyd	600
Midway Drive In	Box 1365	Tarpon Springs 33589	Floyd	200

540

Theatre Name	Address	City & Zip	Circuit	Cars
Titusville Dr. In	P.O. Box 5155	Titusville 32780	Balcierak	
Vero Drive In	Box 368	Vero Beach 32960	Kent	300
Starlite Drive In		Wauchula 33873	Floyd	200
Boulevard Dr. In	4921 Southern Blvd.	West Palm Beach 33401	McCain	500
Starlite Drive In	Box 67	Winter Garden 32787	Floyd	200
Haven Dale Drive In	Box 1032	Winter Haven 33880	Floyd	200

GEORGIA

Theatre Name	Address	City & Zip	Circuit	Cars
Slappey Drive In	3003 No. Slappy Dr.	Albany 31702	Martin	400
Alps Drive In	Box 366	Athens 30601	Morrison	400
Athens Drive In		Athens 30601	Georgia The.	400
Bankhead Drive In	3350 Bankhead Hwy.	Atlanta 30318	Georgia The.	800
No.&So. Starlight D. I.	2000 Moreland S.E.	Atlanta 30316	Georgia The.	
Thunderbird Drive In	3885 Jonesboro Rd. S.E.	Atlanta 30354	Cobb, R.C.	1,200
Weis Drive In		Augusta 30906	Weis	800
Marbro Drive In	Jesup Highway	Baxley 31513	Martin	400
Swan Drive In	P.O. Box 275	Blue Ridge 30513	Jones, J.	300
Sunset Drive In	P.O. Box 799	Brunswick 31520	Georgia The.	400
Buford Drive In		Buford 30518	J. Woodall	
300	Cairo Drive In	Box 180 Cairo 31788	Bearden, D.	300
Dunn Dr. In	P.O. Box 146	Camilla 31730	Dunn, R.	300
Canton Drive In		Canton 30114	Woodall, R.	300
Carroll Drive In	Box 846	Carrollton 30117	Jones, J.E. Sr.	300
Starlite Drive In	No. Tennessee St.	Cartersville 30120	Martin	300
North 85 Twin 1 & 2 D. I.	2781 N.E. Expressway	Chamblee 30005	Storey	1,000
Tos Drive In	Box 638	Claxton 30417	Tos	200
Cleveland Dr. In		Cleveland 30528	Woodall, K.	200
Roosevelt Dr. In	2939 Roosevelt Hwy.	College Pk. 30337	Georgia The.	700
Columbus Dr. In	Box 6406	Columbus 31907	Plitt South	600
Rexview Drive In	1121 45th Street	Columbus 31902	Martin	500
Commerce Drive In		Commerce 30529	Woodall, J.	200
Moonlit Drive In		Conyers 30207	Edwards, V.	300
Cordelle Drive In	Tremont Road	Cordele 31015	Martin	300
Cornelia Dr. In		Cornelia 30531	Woodall, D.	
Hub Drive In	P.O. Box 149	Covington 30209	Osman	300
Judean Drive In	Rte. 1	Dallas 30132	McDonald, T.	500
Cherokee Drive In	Cleveland Road	Dalton 30720	Martin	300
Glenwood Drive In	4421 Glenwood Rd.	Decatur 30032	Storey	800
N.E. Expressway 1&2 D. I.	4151 N.E. Expressway	Doraville 30040	Georgia The.	600
Skyview Drive In	Ocilla Road	Douglas 31533	Martin	200
Dublin Drive In		Dublin 31021	Theatres In	200
South Expressway 1&2	5158 Kennedy Road	Forest Park 30050	Georgia The.	900
Lake Lanier Drive In	Box 676	Gainesville 30501	Storey	400
Skyview Drive In	Box 676	Gainesville 30501	Storey	200
Forum Drive In	P.O. Box 591	Griffin 30223	Goolsby, J.	
Hart Drive In	P.O. Box 745	Hartwell 30643	Brown, B.	200
Trail Drive In	Box 565	Hazlehurst 31539	Floyd	200
Sherryl Auto Dr. In	P.O. Box 313	Hiawassee 30546	Hogsed, F.	200
Brice Cinema Dr. In	P.O. Box 557	Hinesville 31313	Pal Amuse.	240
Jackson Drive In	Box 3836	Jackson 30233	Baker, T.	200
Jesup D/I Twin 1	Box 624	Jesup 31545	Floyd	250
Jesup D/I Twin 2	Box 624	Jesup 31545	Floyd	125
La Grange Drive	P.O. Box 302	La Grange 30240	Lam	500
Blue Sky Drive In		Lafayette 30728	Waters, W.	400
Lawrenceville Dr. In	P.O. Box 503	Lawrenceville 30245	Woodall, J.	200
Lithia Drive In	4176 Bankhead Hiway	Lithia Springs 30057	Georgia The.	200
Riverside Drive In	Box 6276	Macon 31208	Georgia The.	800
Southside Drive In	Box 6276	Macon 31208	Georgia The.	250
41 Hiway Dr. In	Box 6276	Macon 31208	Georgia The	700
Georgia Drive In	Clay Street	Marietta 30060	Martin	700
Marbro Twin 1&2 Dr. In	1746 Austell Road	Marietta 30060	Martin	
Smyrna Drive In		Marietta 30060	Martin	400
Twin City Drive In		McCaysville 30555	Wheat, W.	300
Candler Drive In	P.O. Box 272	Metter 30401	Shirah, J.	300
Sunset Drive In	Box 127	Moultrie 31768	Georgia The.	400
Newnan Drive In	P.O. Box 1113	Newnan 30263	Lam	500
Gwinnett Drive In	Box 273	Norcross 30071	Storey	600
Perry Dr. In		Perry 31069	Legg, H.	400
Cedar Valley Dr. In		Rome 30161	Lam	500
North 53 Drive In		Rome 30161	Lam	500
West Rome Dr. In		Rome 30161	Lam	400
Weis Auto Cine 1&2	Box 1326	Savannah 31402	Weis	
Kings Bay Drive In	Box 710	St. Mary 31558	Hernandez W.	200
Ranch Drive In	Box 409	Summerville 30747	Smith, R.	200
Hiway 56 Drive In	Box 354	Swainsboro 30401	Bellamy, T.	200
Hiway Drive In	Box 649	Thomasville 31792	Interst. Ent.	300
Marbro Drive In	Albany Highway	Tifton 31794	Martin	300
Tiger Drive In		Tiger 30576	Wilson, W.F.	200
Toccoa Drive In	Box 789	Toccoa 30577	Con-M.C. Lend	300
Martin Drive In	Box 588	Valdosta 31601	Martin	300
Petes Drive In	P.O. Box 750	Vidalia 30474	Pal Amuse.	240
M and T Drive In	P.O. Box 877	Warner Robins 31093	Delchamps, C.	300
U.S. #1 Drive In	Box 164	Waycross 31501	Georgia The.	300

IDAHO

Theatre Name	Address	City & Zip	Circuit	Cars
Motor Vu Drive In	P.O. Box 467	Blackfoot 83221	Treasure	
Broadway Drive In	P.O. Box 4117	Boise 83701	Commonwealt	400
Fair Vu Drive In	P.O. Box 4117	Boise 83701	Commonwealt	600
Meridian Dr. In	P.O. Box 4117	Boise 83701	Commonwealt	300
Midway Drive In	Box 1427	Boise 83702	Plitt	
Alfresco Drive In		Burley 83318	Voeller, H.	350
Nampa Drive In	P.O. Box 280	Caldwell 83605	Odell, V.	350

Theatre Name	Address	City & Zip	Circuit	Cars
Terrace Drive In	P.O. Box 280	Caldwell 83605	Odell, V.	300
Coeur D. Alene Drive In	Box 848	Coeur D. Alene 83814	Moyer, T.	400
Spud Drive In		Driggs 83422	Davis, G.	170
Emmett D. I.	Box 611	Emmett 83617	Gratton, B.	200
Sunset Auto Vue		Grangeville 83530	Wagner, Jr. A.	486
Sky Vu Drive In	435 Fanning Avenue	Idaho Falls 83401	Ellis, K.	400
Orchards Auto Drive In		Lewiston 83501	Yushchyshyn	340
Main	P.O. Box #61	Mackay 83251	Ausich, J.	300
Motor Vu Drive In		Montpelier 83254	Rock Thea.	200
Motor Vu Drive In		Mountain Home 83647	Dudley, A.	250
Parma Motor Vu Dr. In	P.O. Box 338	Parma 83660	Dobbs	200
O Hadi Drive In	% Reeds Cafe Hway 95	Plummer 83851	Hall, C.	
Starlite Drive In	P.O. Box 5397	Pocatello 83201	Morris, R.M.	650
Sunset Dr. In	P.O. Box 5397	Pocatello 83201	Morris, R.M.	300
Teton Vu Drive In	119 N. Third East	Rexburg 83440	Prestwich, R.	350
Sunset Drive In	P.O. Box 240	Salmon 83467	Anderson, G.	300
Valley Ctr. Flick D/I		Smelterville 83868	Metzger, G.	300
Idanha Drive In	20 No. Third East	Soda Springs 83276	Idanha	200
Grand Vu Drive In		Twin Falls 83301	Interst. Amu.	500
Motor Vu Drive In	P.O. Box T	Twin Falls 83301	Interst. Amu.	400

ILLINOIS

Theatre Name	Address	City & Zip	Circuit	Cars
Sky Hi Drive In 1&2	800 So. Route 53	Addison 60101	M&R Amuse.	
Starlight Drive In #1		Alton 62002	BAC Ths.	450
Anna Drive In		Anna 62906	Kerasotes	500
Hi Lite 30 Drive In	Route 2 Box 126	Aurora 60507	Howaniec, A.	
Starlight Drive In		Beardstown 62618	Moran, D.	300
Skyview Drive In		Bellville 62221	BAC Ths.	700
Rendlake D. I.		Benton 62812	Strauss, B.	500
Bloomington D. I.	1720 So. Main St.	Bloomington 61701	Kerasotes	
Avon Drive In		Breese 62230	Keith, A.	300
Campus Drive In		Carbondale 62901	Mid Am. Thea.	400
Diane Drive In		Carlinville 62626	Frieda, P.	300
460 Drive In		Carmi 62821	Kerasotes	500
Centralia Drive In		Centralia 62801	BAC Ths.	492
Twin City D. I.	R.R. #4	Champaign 61823	Kerasotes	
Wide Screen D. I.	P.O.B. 2580 Sta. A	Champaign 61820	Kerasotes	
Charleston D. I.		Charleston 61920	Frisina	500
Double Drive In #1&2	2800 Columbus Drive	Chicago 60623	M&R Amuse.	
Bel Air Drive In #1&2	3100 S. Cicero Ave.	Cicero 60626	M&R Amuse.	
Clinton Outdoor		Clinton 61727	Wagner, M.	300
Crystal Drive In	Route #14	Crystal Lake 60014	Kohlberg	
Dixie 3 Screen D/I	3525 No. Vermillion	Danville 61832	Gibson, P.	
Illiana Drive In	East on Route 136	Danville 61832	Butler	
Skyway Drive In	1611 Georgetown Road	Danville 61833	Butler	
Decatur Drive In	2500 N. Jasper St.	Decatur 62522	Kerasotes	
Decatur Outdoor		Decatur 62525	Kerasotes	
Holiday Drive In		Duquoin 62832	Kerasotes	200
French Village Dr. In	Edgemont Station	E. St. Louis 62203	BAC Theas.	600
Dyas 34 Drive In	Route #4	Earlville 60518	Dyas, C.W.	
Dundale Drive In		East Dundee 60118	M&R Amuse.	
Falcon Drive In		East St. Louis 62201	Mid Am. Thea.	700
Shop City D. I.		East St. Louis 62203	Mid Am. Thea.	600
Starlight Drive In #1		Effingham 62401	Frisina	400
Starview Drive In	Route 20 at 59	Elgin 60120	Marsico, F.	600
Fairfield Dr. In		Fairfield 62837	Jones, H.	500
Rendezvous Dr. In		Flora 62839	Snyder	
Bennis Drive In		Freeport 61032	Bennis, W.	400
Galesburg Drive In	Route 34	Galesburg 61401	Kerasotes	
Harvest Moon Drive In		Gibson City 60936	Cliffordorr	350
Grays Lake Outdoor	Route 1 Box 247	Grays Lake 60030	Ryan, H.	1,000
Starlite Dr. In		Harrisburg 62930	Farrar, T.	600
Havana Drive In		Havana 62644	Kerasotes	
Egyptian Drive In		Herrin 62948	Kerasotes	600
Riviera Drive In		Herrin 62948	Mid Am. Thea.	400
Skyway Drive In	837 E. Lincoln St.	Hoopeston 60942	R&B Sanders	350
67 Drive In		Jacksonville 62651	Frisina	400
Hilltop Drive In	1800 Maple Road	Joliet 60435	L&M Mgt.	600
Starlite Drive In	Route 17 E	Kankakee 60901	L&M Mgt.	
Wanee Drive In		Kewanee 61443	Kerasotes	400
Lasalle Drive In		LaSalle 61301	Kerasotes	
Midway D. I.		Lawrenceville 62439	Frisina	300
Bennis Auto Vue		Lincoln 62656	Bennis, W.	
Skyview D. I.		Litchfield 62056	Frisina	400
Bel Air Drive In	Romeoville Rd. Rt. 53	Lockport 60435	L&M Mgt.	
Fort Drive In		Macomb 61455	Kerasotes	
Marion Dr. In	Rt. 37 No. P.O. Box 486	Marion 62959	Kerasotes	500
Skyway D. I.		Mattoon 61938	Frisina	400
McHenry Dr. In		McHenry 60050	Rhyan	
Memri Drive In		Milan 61264	Redstone	
Bel-Air Drive In		Mitchell 62040	Mid Am. Thea.	700
Corral Drive In		Moline 61265	Redstone	
Eri Lyn Dr. In	Rt. 78 So.	Morrison 61270	Kontos	
Carmel D. I.		Mount Carmel 62863	Frisina	400
Mt. Vernon D. I.		Mt. Vernon 62864	Kerasotes	400
Skylark D. I.	31 W. 460 Ogden	Naperville Twnsh. 60540	Lubnr/Stern	1,200
Fairview Drive In	R.F.D. #5	Newton 62448	Simmons, L.	300
Harlem Outdoor	4101 N. Harlem Ave.	Norridge 60634	Harlem Mgt., I.	
Hillcrest Drive In		Norris 60450	Kerasotes	
Sheridan Dr. In	79th St. S. Harlem Ave.	Oak Lawn 60648	Levin Svce.	
Sheridan Dr. In	79th St. S. Harlem Ave.	Oak Lawn 60648	Levin Svce.	
Oleny D. I.		Olney 62450	Frisina	400
Pines Drive In		Oregon 61061	Kerasotes	

542

Theatre Name	Address	City & Zip	Circuit	Cars
53 Outdoor		Palatine 60067	Kohlberg	
Tanner Drive In	Box 189	Pana 62557	Tanner, H.	400
Twin Lake Drive In	Box 124	Paris 61944	Kerasotes	400
Bellevue Drive In		Peoria 61614	Kohlberg	
Holiday Drive In	213 SW. Jefferson	Peoria 61602	Kerasotes	500
Peoria Drive In	1631 W. Glen Ave.	Peoria 61614	Kerasotes	380
Pioneer Drive In	2727 W. Laura Ave.	Peoria 61614	Kersasotes	
Starlite Dr. In	213 SW. Jefferson Ave.	Peoria 61554	Kerasotes	
Starchief Drive In		Pontiac 61764	Kerasotes	
Alexander Park Dr. In		Princeton 61356	Kerasotes	
Quincy Drive In	Box 1208	Quincy 62301	Kerasotes	700
Quincy Drive In 2	Box 1208	Quincy 62301	Kerasotes	
Rantoul Drive In	Box 397	Rantoul 61866	Kerasotes	
Halsted Drive In	139th & Halstead Str.	Riverdale 60627	Essaness	
Gordon D. I.		Robinson 62454	Frisina	400
Robin Drive In	6903 W. State St.	Rock Ford 61105	L&M Mgt.	700
Belford Drive In #1	8301 E. State RR #5	Rockford 61108	Kerasotes	
Belford Drive In #2	8301 E. State RR #5	Rockford 61108	Kerasotes	
Riverlane Outdoor	P.O. Box 866	Rockford 61105	Dubinsky	600
Sunset D. I.	1801 Samuelson Rd.	Rockford 61109	L&M Mgt.	1,000
Cluster Drive In		Salem 62881	Cluster, L.	400
Hollywood Drive In	R.F.D. #1	Sandoval 62882	BAC Theas.	400
Kay D. I.		Shelbyville 62565	Frisina	400
Sunset Drive In	7320 McCormick Blvd.	Skokie 60076	M&R Amuse.	
Saulk Trail Drive In		So. Chicago Hts. 60411	Bates, W.	
Green Meadows D. I. 1&2	Hwy. 34 & Rt. #4	Springfield 62703	Mid Am. Thea.	875
Kerasotes Twin Dr. In		Springfield 62701	Kerasotes	1,400
66-Drive In		Springfield 62707	Kerasotes	1,000
Midway Drive In	404 Locust Street	Sterling 61081	L&M Mgt.	
Streator Dr. In	Route 23 Box 371	Streator 61364	Kerasotes	
Sullivan Drive In	11 North Main St.	Sullivan 61951	Kerasotes	300
Clark Drive In		Summerhill 62372	Gates, T.	300
Frisina D. I.		Taylorville 62568	Frisina	400
I 80 Drive In	159th & Harlem	Tinley Pk. 60477	Essaness	1,200
Tuscola Drive In		Tuscola 61953	Kerasotes	
Tanner Drive In	Box 172	Vandalia 62471	Tanner, H.	300
Waukegan Dr. In	328 Fourth St.	Waukegan 60085	Brotman	900
Cascade Outdoor	28 W. 741 North Ave.	West Chicago 60185	Charukus, S.	
Twin Dr. In Theas. 123	1010 S. Milwaukee Ave.	Wheeling 60090	M&R Amuse.	
Green Drive In		Winchester 62694	Woodcock & K.	200
Capri Drive In		Woodriver 62095	Mid Am. Thea.	600

INDIANA

Theatre Name	Address	City & Zip	Circuit	Cars
Anderson North	5 Mi. No. St. RD9 R.R. 2	Anderson 46013	Sport Service	500
South Drive In	1801 W. 53Rd. St.	Anderson 46015	Turlukis, P.	500
Lakeland Drive In	P.O. Box 238	Angola 46703	Cook, C.	
Starlite Dr. In	R.R. #1 Box 231	Aurora 47001	Whisman, L.	500
Meadowbrook Drive In	R.R. 1	Bainbridge 46105	Albin, J.	450
Batesville Drive In		Batesville 47006	Glaub, J.	210
Bedford Dr. In		Bedford 47421	Bedford	450
East 50 Drive In	1416 I Street	Bedford 47421	Bedford	478
Family Drive In		Bloomfield 47424	Sipes, B.	
Starlite Drive In	1017 No. College Ave.	Bloomington 47401	Stewart	450
Y & W Drive In	R.R. #10 Box 660-A	Bloomington 47401	Y&W Mgt. Cor.	430
Bluffton Drive In		Bluffton 46714	Mallers	500
Great Oaks Dr. In		Cedar Lake 46303	Allen, F.	
Centerbrook Drive In	R.R. 6 P.O. Box 252	Centerton 46116	Terrell, R.	250
Charlestown Drive In		Charlestown 47111	Robertson	450
Clarksville Dr. In	701 North Clark Blv.	Clarksville 47130	Woehrle, J.	450
Maplecroft D. I.	Rural Route #1	Clayton 46118	Turlukis	565
Deluxe Drive In		Clermont 46119	Cantor, M.	500
Breezeway Drive In	P.O. Box 332	Clinton 47842	Marietta	350
Columbus Dr. In		Columbus 47201	Syndicate	500
Connersville Dr. In		Connersville 47331	Kerasotes	500
Ben Hur Dr. In	P.O. Box 129	Crawfordsville 47933	Syndicate	500
National Outdoor	W. S. 40 East	Cumberland 46227	Priority	700
Decatur Dr. In		Decatur 46733	Kalver, R.	500
Midway Auto Drive In		Dunlap 46526	Rochs, J.	
Dunes Drive In		East Gary 46405		
Elwood Drive In	P.O. Box 98	Elwood 46036	Syndicate	500
Evansville Drive In	4700 Morgan Avenue	Evansville 47711	Coleman, H.	500
Family Cinema 41 D. I.		Evansville 47714	Cinema Ths.	500
Sunset Dr. In	4209 Hwy. 41 N/U31614	Evansville 47711	Cobb, Doug	700
Westside Drive In	5555 Broadway Box 893	Evansville 47712	Koewler, W.J.	500
Hillcrest Drive In	949 Northcrest S. Ctr.	Fort Wayne 46825	Mallers	500
Frankfort Drive In	P.O. Box 1	Frankfort 46041	Sport Serv.	500
East 30 Drive In	P.O. Box 1111	Ft. Wayne 46803	Sport Servic.	500
Ft. Wayne Drive In	5800 Bluffton Road	Ft. Wayne 46802	Sport Servic.	500
Lincolndale Dr. In	P.O. Box 1140	Ft. Wayne 46801	Sport Servic.	500
Garrett Dr. In		Garrett 46738	Hudson Entp.	400
Georgetown Drive In		Georgetown 47122	Powell, B.	300
Cinema 40 Drive In	3143 East Ctr. St.	Greencastle 46180	Turlukis, P.	500
Holiday Drive In	R.R. 1 Box 21	Greensburg 47240	Dewitt, E.	300
Greenwood Drive In		Greenwood 46142	U.A. Theas.	450
Meridian Drive In	120 State Rd. 135 No.	Greenwood 46142	Snow, H.	375
Hammond Outdoor		Hammond 46324	Essaness	
Hammond 41 Outdoor	2500 Calumet Ave.	Hammond 46320	Kohlberg	
Blackford D. I.		Hartford City 47348	Thompson, H.	
Huntington Drive In	P.O. Box 71	Huntington 46750	Syndicate	500
Tibbs Drive In #2	480 South Tibbs St.	Indianapolis 46241	U.A. Theas.	300
Bel Air Drive In		Indianapolis 46241	W.L.Z. Amuse.	750
Lafayette Rd. Drive In	H On U.S. 52 Corw. 38th.	Indianapolis 46254	Priority	720
Northside Drive In	2463 Hoyt Avenue	Indianapolis 46240	W.L.Z. Amuse.	1,000

Theatre Name	Address	City & Zip	Circuit	Cars
Shadeland Drive In	2500 N. Shadeland	Indianapolis 46219	Priority	750
Sherman D. I. #1	2505 N. Sherman Dr.	Indianapolis 46218	U.A. Theas.	1,300
Sherman D. I. #2	2505 N. Sherman Drive	Indianapolis 46218	U.A. Theas.	625
South #31 Drive In	7800 U.S. 31 At Shelby	Indianapolis 46227	Priority	1,650
Southview Dr. In	1421 W. Thompson Road	Indianapolis 46217	Orders, C.	600
Tibbs Drive In #1	480 South Tibbs St.	Indianapolis 46221	U.A. Theas.	1,455
Tibbs Drive In #3	480 South Tibbs St.	Indianapolis 46241	U.A. Theas.	430
Twin D. I. Eastside	2463 Hoyt Ave.	Indianapolis 46303	W.L.Z. Amuse.	1,500
Twin Dr. In Westside	2463 Hoyt Ave.	Indianapolis 46303	W.L.Z. Amuse.	1,500
Westlake Dr. In	6275 W. 10th Street	Indianapolis 46224	Cantor, M.	500
Family Drive In		Jasper 47546	Midway Amus.	500
Lakewood Drive In	Rural Route #2	Jeffersonville 47130	Woehrle, J.	425
Hi Vue Dr. In		Kendallville 46755	Hudson Entp.	500
Melody Drive In	R.R. 3 Box 744	Knox 46960	Heise, E.	200
North Drive In	Rt. 31 5 Miles N. Bx.2356	Kokomo 46901	Sport Servic.	500
South Drive In	Rt. 31 4 Miles South	Kokomo 46901		400
Deluxe Drive In		La Porte 46350	Kohlberg	
Eastside Drive In		Lafayette 47905	U.A. Theas.	500
Pendelton Pike D. I.	9300 Pendelton Pike	Lawrence 46236	Westoutdoor	1,000
Sky Vue Dr. In		Lebanon 46052	Careypalex	500
Linton Dr. In	P.O. Box 68	Linton 47441	Cassida, C.	350
Skyline Drive In	Hwy. 117 1½ Miles No.	Logansport 46947	Ritchie, B.	350
Skyline Dr. In	P.O. Box 433	Madison 47250	Galvin, J.	500
Hi Way Drive In	P.O. Box 967	Marion 46952	Bove, G.	500
Marion Air Dr. In	U.S. Hwy. 21 4 Mile West	Marion 46952	Kerasotes	500
Martinsville Dr. In	439 Valley Dr.	Martinsville 46151	Scott, L.	430
Lebanon Frankfort D. I.	Route 1	Mechanicsburg 46071	Osborne, J.	250
Y&W Drive In	6600 Bway P.O.B. 8136	Merrillville 46410	Y&W Mgt. Cor.	
Y&W Open Air Dr. In	P.O. Bo. 8136	Merrillville 46410	Y&W Mgt. Cor.	
212 Outdoor		Michigan City 46360	Kohlberg	
Holiday Drive In		Mitchell 47446	Webb, G.	200
Monticello Dr. In		Monticello 47960	Brazee, M.	400
Muncie Dr. In	P.O. Box 769	Muncie 47305	Y&W Mgt. Cor.	500
Sky Hi Drive In	P.O. Box 769	Muncie 47305	Y&W Mgt. Cor.	500
Sky Vue Drive In	P.O. Box #207	New Castle 47362	Y&W Mgt. Cor.	800
A B C Drive In	P.O. Box 225	Noblesville 46060	Mallers	500
North Vernon Dr. In		North Vernon 47265	Stardust Am.	
Oakland City Drive In	P.O. Box 91	Oakland City 47660	Carnahan, R.	350
Starlite Dr. In Thea. 2	U.S. 20 & Indiana	Oscelola 46561	L&M Mgt.	
Starlite Dr. In Thea. 1	U.S. 20 & Indiana	Osceola 46561	L&M Mgt.	
Paoli Drive In		Paoli 47454	Ray, J.	400
Miami Open Air		Peru 46970	Sport Serv.	500
Tri Way Dr. In	Old Road 31 North	Plymouth 46563	Vore, R.	400
Skyvue Drive In		Portland 47371	Mallers	500
Starlite Drive In	So. U.S. Highway 41	Princeton 47670	Sport Servic.	400
Bel Air Drive In		Richmond 47374	Kerasotes	350
Hi Way Dr. In		Richmond 47374	Kerasotes	600
Holiday Drive In	P.O. Box 111	Rockport 46735	Sport Servic.	400
Family Dr. In		Rockville 47872	Marietta, G.	400
Salem Drive In		Salem 47167	Ellis, C.	400
Moonglo Dr. In		Scottsburg 47170	West, P.	450
Corral Dr. In	P.O. Box 845	Seelyville 47807	U.A. Theas.	450
Stardust Drive In		Seymour 47274	Stardust Am.	500
Skyline Drive In	P.O. Box 218	Shelbyville 46176	Dewitt, E.	800
Chippewa Twin 1	500 W. Chippewa	South Bend 46617	L&M Mgt.	
Chippewa Twin 2	500 W. Chippewa	South Bend 46617	L&M Mgt.	
Western Drive In	P.O. Box 266	South Bend 46617	L&M Mgt.	
Cinema 67 Drive In		Spencer 47460	Walker, J.	350
Starlite Drive In	R.R. 1 Box 62	Tell City 47586	Horton, E.	400
Eastside Dr. In	Route 42 East	Terre Haute 47803	Gross, R.	450
North Dr. In	3100 Lafayette Ave.	Terre Haute 47805	U.A. Theas.	650
Forty-Niner Drive In		Valparaiso 46383	Shauer, G.G.	
Veedersburg Dr. In		Veedersburg 47042	Allen, N.	300
Bel Air Dr. In	Route 1 P.O. Box 63	Versailles 47042	Holokan, J.	300
Alps Auto	P.O. Box 161	Vevay 47043	Stepp, S.	444
Vincennes Dr. In	Box 157	Vincennes 47591	Kerasotes	500
13 24 Drive In		Wabash 46992	Syndicate	500
Warsaw Drive In		Warsaw 46580	Vore, R.	425
East 50 Dr. In		Washington 47501	Kerasotes	500
Airline Drive In	P.O. Box #230	Winchester 47394	Make M.	500

IOWA

Theatre Name	Address	City & Zip	Circuit	Cars
Starlite Drive In		Algona 50511	Central Sta.	300
New Starlite Drive In	R.R.2 Box 272A	Altoona 50009	Central Sta.	450
Ranch Drive In	P.O. Box 606	Ames 50010	Central Sta.	500
Atlantic Drive In	26 W. 5th Street	Atlantic 50022	Kerr	300
Boone Drive In		Boone 50036	Fridley	300
Drive In		Burlington 52601	Central Sta.	
Carroll Drive In		Carroll 51401	Fridley Cir.	300
Hillcrest Drive In	P.O. Box 276	Cedar Falls 50613	Central Sta.	500
New Collins Road Dr. In	1566 Collin Road N.E.	Cedar Rapids 52402	Central Sta.	
Twin D. I. East	6300 6th Street S.W.	Cedar Rapids 52404	Central Sta.	
Twin Dr. In West	6300 6th Street S.W.	Cedar Rapids 52401	Central Sta.	
Town & Country Dr. In		Centerville 52544	Knode, L.	400
218 Drive In		Charles City 50616	Central Sta.	700
Corral Drive In		Cherokee 51012	Fridley Cir.	300
Clarinda Dr. In		Clarinda 51632	Frederick	300
Drive In	P.O. Box 368	Clinton 52732	Central Sta.	
Coralville Drive In	1215 5th St. Bx. 6305	Coralville 52242	Central Sta.	
Council Bluffs Dr. In	1130 W. So. Omaha Brd.	Council Bluffs 51501	Central Sta.	630
Bel Air Drive In		Davenport 52808	Redstone	700
Oasis Drive In	63rd & Brady Street	Davenport 52804	Redstone	
Decorah Drive In	P.O. Box 29	Decorah 52101	Viking	300

544

Theatre Name	Address	City & Zip	Circuit	Cars
Capitol Drive In	4646 East 14th St.	Des Moines 50313	Central Sta.	500
Pioneer Drive In	2099 S.E. 14th St.	Des Moines 50314	Dubinsky	700
Plantation Drive In		Des Moines 50311	Dubinsky	
S.E. 14th St. Drive In	6000 S.E. 14th St.	Des Moines 50309	Central Sta.	600
Westvue Drive In		Des Moines 50322	Central Sta.	800
Dubuque Drive In	John Deere Road	Dubuque 52001	Central Sta.	600
Super 20 Drive In East		Dubuque 52001	Yiannias	
Super 20 Drive In West		Dubuque 52001	Yiannias	600
Chief Drive In	17 North 6th St.	Estherville 51334	Kozak	200
Fairfield Drive In		Fairfield 52556	Central Sta.	
Fort Dodge Drive In	P.O. Box 1257	Fort Dodge 50501	Central Sta.	226
Grinnell D. I.		Grinnell 50112	Central Sta.	240
Harlan Drive In		Harlan 51537	Woodraska	300
Wigwam D/I	P.O. Box 307	Hawarden 51023	Mossengren	200
Hy. 2&65 Drive In		Humeston 50123	Knode, L.	450
Drive In		Oskaloosa 52577	Central Sta.	
Falls Drive In	P.O. Box 1104	Iowa Falls 50126	March, J.	
Skylark Drive In		Keokuk 52632	Frisina	500
Hi-Vue Drive In		Knoxville 50138	Kerr	300
Mars Under Stars Dr. In		Le Mars 51031	March Bros.	300
61 Drive In		Maquoketa 52060	Voy, D.	280
Twixt Town Dr. In	Box 216	Marion 52302	Davis, D.	625
Marshalltown D. I.	516 Friendly Dr.	Marshalltown 50158	Houtz, N.	300
Drive In		Mason City 50401	Central Sta.	
Lakeland Dr. In		Milford 51351	Travis	
Ridge Drive In		Mt. Pleasant 52641	Doughton	275
Hilltop Drive In		Muscatine 52761	Boston, C.	
Valle Drive In	1202 S. 15th Ave. West	Newton 50208	Rhodes, S.	
Drive In		Oelwein 50662	Central Sta.	
South Drive In		Ottumwa 52501	Central Sta.	
Corral Drive In	P.O. Box 446	Perry 50220	Mertz	
Red Oak Drive In		Red Oak 51566	Frederick	300
Triangle Drive In		Rockwell City 50579	Hanson, D.	300
Iowa Drive In		Shenandoah 51601	Cole, W.H.	375
Capri Dr. In	4900 Hiway 75 So.	Sioux City 51102	Dubinsky	800
Gordon Twin #1 Dr. In	411 Gordon Dr. West	Sioux City 51102	Dubinsky	700
Gordon Twin #2 Dr. In	411 Gordon Dr. West	Sioux City 51102	Dubinsky	350
75 Drive In		Sioux City 51101	Dubinsky	725
Corral Outdoor		Spencer 51301	Fridley Cir.	300
Spirit Lake Drive In		Spirit Lake 51360	March	275
Bel Air Drive In		St. Ansgar 50472	Anderson, H.	300
Corral Outdoor		Storm Lake 50588	Fridley Cir.	320
Waco Drive In		Washington 52353	Garbett	
Skyvue Drive In		Waterloo 50704	Central Sta.	
Starlite Drive In	4000 University Ave.	Waterloo 50704	Central Sta.	
Waverly D. I.	Highway 3 East	Waverly 50677	Peterson, G.	

KANSAS

Theatre Name	Address	City & Zip	Circuit	Cars
Trails End Drive In		Abilene 67410	Strowig, C.	315
Star Vue Drive In		Anthony 67003	Ash, B.	200
Ark Vue Drive In	2411 North Summit	Arkansas City 67005	Bullard, C.	300
Frontier Drive In		Atchison 66002	Commonwealt	300
Augusta Drive In		Augusta 67010	Bisagno, D.	250
Twilight Drive In		Baxter Springs 66713	Dickinson	350
Blair Drive In		Belleville 66935	Commonwealt.	300
Fiesta Drive In		Beloit 67420	Markley, J.	230
Neocha Dr. In		Chanute 66720	Walsh, R.	
Skyline Drive In		Clay Center 67432	Smith	250
Tal S Drive In		Coffeyville 67337	Richardson	360
Colby Drive In	P.O. Box 806	Colby 67701	Phillips, D.	
Columbus Dr. In		Columbus 66725	Golden, R.	275
Cloud 9 Drive In		Concordia 66901	Smith, R.	350
Ritz Drive In		Council Grove 66846	Picolet	300
Dighton Dr. In		Dighton 67839	Roy, I.	185
Boot Hill Drive In	P.O. Box 195	Dodge City 67801	Cooper, G.A.	300
South Drive In	P.O. Box 195	Dodge City 67801	Cooper, G.A.	300
Star Vu Drive In		Eldorado 67042	Schroeder	300
50-S Drive In		Emporia 66801	Commonwealt.	565
Mo Kan Drive In		Fort Scott 66701	Snitz, G.	300
Fredonia Drive In		Fredonia 66736	Stigall	300
Garden City Drive In	P.O. Box 458	Garden City 67846	Commonwealt.	300
Great Bend Drive In		Great Bend 67530	Commonwealt.	320
Hays Drive In 1	P.O. Box 195	Hays 67601	Cooper	300
Hays Drive In 2	P.O. Box 195	Hays 67601	Cooper	
Riverside Drive In	217A N. Pomeroy	Hill City 67642	Welty, L.	
Hugoton Drive In		Hugoton 67951	Harris, G.	275
Airport Drive In	P.O. Box 1206	Hutchinson 67501	Commonwealt.	508
South Hutch Dr. In	P.O. Box 1206	Hutchinson 67501	Commonwealt.	600
Sunset Drive In		Independence 67301	Buscher, B.	312
54 Drive In		Iola 66749	Buscher, B.	300
Midway Drive In	P.O. Box 429	Junction City 66441	Commonwealt.	500
Kanopolis Drive In	P.O. Box 97	Kanopolis 67454	Blazina, A.	743
Boulevard Dr. In	1051 Merriam Lane	Kansas City 66103	Potter & Lux	425
State #1 Drive In	51st & State Ave.	Kansas City 66102	Twin D.I. Ths.	
State #2 Drive In	51st & State Ave.	Kansas City 66102	Twin D.I. Ths.	750
Sunset Drive In	P.O. Box 808	Lawrence 66044	Commonwealt.	520
Fort Drive In	Box 107	Leavenworth 66048	Mid Am. Thea.	350
Skylark Drive In		Leavenworth 66048	Crown Cinem.	395
Great Western Drive In	Box 317	Liberal 67901	Commonwealt.	300
Lyons Drive In		Lyons 67554	Eveleigh	300
Sky Vue Drive In		Manhattan 66502	Commonwealt.	383
Hilltop Drive In		Marysville 66508	Smith, R.	225
Starview Drive In		McPherson 67460	McConnel	450

Theatre Name	Address	City & Zip	Circuit	Cars
Starlite Drive In	P.O. Box 667	Meade 67864	Cane, E.	
Pageant Drive In		Medicine Lodge 67104	Sill, O.	250
Star Drive In		Ness City 67560	Ricketts, P.	200
West Vue Drive In		Newton 67114	Roberson, R.	250
Sunset Drive In	P.O. Box 277	Norton 67654	Eveleigh	300
South Twin 1 D. I.	119th & I 35	Olathe 66061	Twin D. I. Ths.	
South Twin 11 D. I.	119th. & I-35	Olathe 66061	Twin D. I. Ths.	700
Hillcrest Drive In	Route 4	Osage City 66523	Ruch	250
Midway Drive In		Osawatomie 66064	Thomas, C.J.	300
Hillcrest Drive In		Ottawa 66067	Commonwealt	300
Parsons Drive In		Parsons 67357	Stein	500
Phillipsburg Drive In		Phillipsburg 67661	Bagby, S.H.	250
Pittsburg Drive In		Pittsburg 66762	Dickinson	500
Trail Drive In		Pratt 67124	Commonwealt	400
Sky-Vue Drive In	P.O. Box 591	Russell 67665	Danielson, D.	350
Nemaha Dr. In		Sabetha 66534		
Rocket Drive In		Salina 67401	Mann Theas.	550
81 Drive In		Salina 67401	Dickinson	590
Scott City Drive In		Scott City 67871	Kite, R.	235
Center D. I.		Smith Center 66967	Bagby, S.H.	300
Starlite Drive In	P.O. Box 681	St. Francis 67756	Edmundson, J.	275
Park Drive In		Stockton 67669	Bagby, S.H.	
Chief Drive In	Box 95	Topeka 66605	Dickinson	750
Cloverleaf Drive In		Topeka 66608	Dickinson	640
Community Drive In	25th & California St.	Topeka 66605	Mann Theas.	700
Ulysses Drive In		Ulysses 67880	Dudley, D.	225
Chisholm Trail Dr. In		Wellington 67152	Johnston, M.	400
K 42 Drive In	4308 Southwest Blvd.	Wichita 67210	Moore, B.A.	400
Landmark D. I. #1	3928 So. Hydraulic	Wichita 67202	McClure	
Landmark Dr. In 2	3928 So. Hydraulic	Wichita 67202	McClure & Bar	
Meadowlark Dr. In I	P.O. Box 18208	Wichita 67208	Commonwealt	
Meadowlark Dr. In II	P.O. Box 18208	Wichita 67208	Commonwealt	400
Terrace Drive In	Box 18208	Wichita 67218	Commonwealt	300
Westport Drive In	401 South West	Wichita 67213	McClure & Bar	325
Yates Center Drive In	P.O. Box 267	Yates Center 66783	McLallen, D.	225

KENTUCKY

Theatre Name	Address	City & Zip	Circuit	Cars
Al Mar Drive In		Allen 41601	Absher, J.	275
Trail Drive In	Box 1816	Ashland 41101	Chakeres	500
Knox Drive In	P.O. Box 440	Barbourville 40906	Mitchell, P.	250
Gypsy Drive In		Bardstown 40004	Lutes, G.	400
Sunset Drive In	P.O. Box 573	Beattyville 41311	Mahaffey	250
Tri City Dr. In		Beaver Dam 42320	Moseley, D.	200
Moonlite Dr. In		Booneville 41314	Cornett, O.	150
Riverside Drive In	31 West By Pass	Bowling Green 42101	Martin	
Highway 27 Dr. In		Burnside 42519	Roaden, H.	300
Lakeview Dr. In		Burnside 42519	Johnson, B.	380
Calvert Drive In	Box 245	Calvert City 42029	Harrington	200
Campbellsville Dr. In	113 W. Main St.	Campbellsville 42718	Curry, R.	450
Twilight Dr. In		Central City 42330	Moseley, D.	200
Adair Drive In		Columbia 42728	Roaden	277
Corbin Dr. In		Corbin 40701	Carn & Hughes	325
Auburn Drive In		Cumberland 40823	Roaden	
Midway Dr. In	P.O. Box 172	Cynthiana 41031	Lutes, G.	400
Star-Lite Drive In		Danville 40422	Chakeres	300
Judy Drive In		Dry Ridge 41035	May, F.	290
Starlight Dr. In	c/o State Thea. P.O. Box 388	Elizabethtown 42701	Town Amus. E.	500
Corral Drive In		Flatwoods 41139	Mid States	500
Flemingsburg D. I.	P.O. Box 267	Flemingsburg 41041	Purvis	300
Starway Drive In	Box 386	Frankfort 40601	Chakeres	433
Franklin Drive In		Franklin 42134	Holiday Amu.	
31 West Drive In	Rte. 3	Franklin 42134	Rhoton, J.C.	
Blue Grass Auto		Georgetown 40324	Mid States	450
Star Drive In	P.O. Box 445	Glasgow 42141	Aspley	500
Skyline Drive In	P.O. Box 306	Greensburg 42743	Ford, D.	300
Harlan Drive In		Harlan 40831	Roaden	400
Wayne Drive In		Harlan 40831	McClelland	400
Skyline Dr. In		Harned 40143	Ford, D.	150
Twin Hills Drive In	Box 223	Harrodsburg 40330	Chakeres	250
Starlite Drive In	2534 U.S. 60 East	Henderson 42420	Haynes, B.	
Smithfield Drive In		Hindman 41822	Smith, R.	
Twin City Drive In		Horse Cave 42749	Bales, K.	400
Hyden Drive In	Box 909	Hyden 41749	Ashner	165
Del Vue Drive In		Irvine 40336	Baker, D.	360
Irvington Drive In		Irvington 40146	Ford, D.	200
Jaxon Drive In		Jackson 41339	Tolson	230
Lebanon Drive In		Lebanon 40033	Howard, P.	350
Lakeview Drive In	724 Spring Street	Leitchfield 42754	McCoy, R.	150
Circle 25 Auto	574 Angliana Avenue	Lexington 40508	Mid States	1,060
Family Drive In		Lexington 40508	Mid States	650
Southland 68 Auto	P.O. Box 8255	Lexington 40503	Hughes	1,250
Green River Drive In		Liberty 42539	Campbell, D.	275
London Drive In	Loyall Theatre	London 40854	Roaden	300
Kenwood Dr In		Louisville 40214	Redstone	500
Parkway Drive In	2702 Millers Lane	Louisville 40216	Redstone	500
Preston Drive In	6705 Preston Highway	Louisville 40219	Saag Essane	500
South Park Drive In	9205 Nail Turnpike	Louisville 40118	Saag Essane	1,500
Twilight Drive In	4015 Crittenden Dr.	Louisville 40209	4th Ave. Amu.	500
Family Drive In	Box 276	Manchester 40962	White, C.	300
Marion Drive In	P.O. Box 310	Marion 42064	Gass, H.	200
Cardinal Drive In	P.O. Box 473	Mayfield 42066	Jones, D.	
Park Drive In		Maysville 41056	Ohio Movies	350
Hilltop Drive In		McKee 40447	Carnahan Hu.	200

546

Theatre Name	Address	City & Zip	Circuit	Cars
Rosa Drive In		Middlesboro 40965	Roaden	500
Stardust Dr. In		Monticello 42633	Mr. Carlhuff	300
Morehead Dr. In		Morehead 40351	Roaden	300
Broadview Drive In		Morganfield 42437	McElroy, J.	420
Hi Way Drive In	606 Brookmead	Mt. Sterling 40353	Baker, D.	330
Judy Drive In	P.O. Box 432	Mt. Sterling 40353	Baker, D.	275
Murray Drive In	Box 111	Murray 42071	Vinson, H.P.	350
Lexington Drive In	R.R. #1	Nicholasville 40356	Johnson, J.W.	500
Starlit Drive In	Hiway 41A South	Oak Grove 42262	Oakgrove Am.	
Cardinal Drive In		Owensboro 42301	Malco Theas.	
Starlite Drive In	Box 597	Owensboro 42301	Malco Theas.	
Paducah Drive In		Paducah 42001	Columbia	400
Paducah Southtwin D. I.		Paducah 42001	Columbia	800
Sky Vue Drive In		Paintsville 41240	Absher, J.	300
Bourbon Dr. In	P.O. Box 354	Paris 40361	Earlywine E.	320
Lakeview Drive In		Pendleton 40055	Powars W.	300
New Drive In	P.O. Box 29	Pikeville 41501	Childers	450
Prestonburg Drive In		Prestonburg 41653	Absher, J.	300
Skyway Dr. In		Princeton 41445	McDaniel, C.	297
Buccaneer Drive In		Richmond 40475	Roaden, H.	400
Richmond Drive In		Richmond 40475	Carnahan-Hu	400
Lake Trail Dr. In		Russell Springs 42642	Luttrell	300
Jesse James Dr. In	R.R. #3	Russellville 42276	Holiday Amu.	
Pollyanna Drive In	Route 2 Box 275	Shelbiana 41501	Powell	400
Hi Way 55 Drive In		Shelbyville 40065	Head, J.B.	290
Bel Vista Dr. In	Campbellsvill Rd.	Springfield 40033	Noland, S.	450
Stanford Dr. In	325 W. Main Street	Stanford 40484	Downs	300
Mountain View Dr. In		Stanton 40380	Baker, D.	200
Skyview Drive In		Tompkinsville 42167	Whiles, S.	250
Valley Dr. In	14700 Dixie Hway	Valley Sta. 40172	Holiday Amu.	
Knox Drive In	c/o State Thea. P.O. Box 388	Vine Grove Jct. 42701	Town Amus. E.	420
Lycinda Dr. In	Box 123	Viper 41774	Nease, G.	260
New Dixie Drive In	P.O. Box 179	Williamsburg 40769	Hughes	200
Sky Vue Dr. In		Winchester 40391	Chakeres	350

LOUISIANA

Theatre Name	Address	City & Zip	Circuit	Cars
Lafitte Drive In		Abbeville 70510	F&R Theat.	300
Showtown Twin Dr In	P.O. Box 4498	Alexandria 71303	Gulf States	
St. Bernard Drive In	P.O. Box 55	Arabi 70032	Bell Wiltse	500
Showtown Twin Dr. In	7200 Florida	Baton Rouge 70806	Gulf States	1,000
State		Bogalusa 70427	Gulf States	600
Jet Drive In		Cut Off 70345	Cheramie, L.	
Joy Twin Dr. In		Hammond 70401	Edwards, J.	
Houma Drive In	P.O. Box 887	Houma 70361	Breaux, V.	300
Tiger Dr. In		Jennings 70546	May, P.	300
Showtown Twin Dr. In	P.O. Box 2043	Lafayette 70501	Gulf States	750
New Moon Dr. In	P.O. Box 3007	Lake Charles 70601	Gulf States	1,000
Pines Drive In		Leesville 71446	Page Amusem.	300
De Soto Dr. In	Box 820	Mansfield 71052	Adkison, M.J.	
Do Twin Drive In	244 Focis St.	Metairie 70005	Gulf States	1,000
Joy Drive In		Minden 71055	Cobb, W.	499
Showtown Drive In		Monroe 71201	Gulf States	500
Echo Drive In		New Iberia 70560	Gulf States	300
Airline Drive In	4000 Airline Hwy.	New Orleans 70001	Gulf States	
Algiers Drive In Twin	3424 Gen. Meyer Ave.	New Orleans 70114	Gulf States	400
Jeff Dr. In	4100 Jefferson Hwy.	New Orleans 70006	Gulf States	
Skyvue Drive In	5947 Chef Menteur Hw.	New Orleans 70126	Shiell, L.	700
Yam Dr. In	Route 5 Box 103	Opelousas 70570	Gulf States	300
Ruston Drive In		Ruston 71270	Gulf States	300
Showtown Twin Drive In		Shreveport 71101	Gulf States	
Tiger Drive In		Slidell 70458	Gulf States	
Rancho Dr. In	Box 755	Springhill 71075	Adkinson, B.	290
Parkway Drive In	Hwy. 84 c/o Huey P. Long	Winnfield 71483	Smith, P.K.	300

MAINE

Theatre Name	Address	City & Zip	Circuit	Cars
Auburn Drive In		Auburn 04210	SBC Mgt. Corp.	300
St. Croix Valley Dr. In		Baring 04610	Bernard	300
Belfast Drive In		Belfast 04915	Graphic	400
E.M. Loews Drive In		Brewer 04412	E.M. Loews	700
Bridgton Drive In		Bridgton 04009	Tevanian, J.	300
Brunswick Drive In		Brunswick 04011	Dakin, R.	400
Dorseyland Drive In		Caribou 04736	Dorsey	300
Polaris Drive In		Caribou 04736	Barnard, R.	470
Midway Drive In		Detroit 04929	Brigham, H.	300
Bowdoin Drive In	U.S. Rte. #1	E. Brunswick 04011	Dakin, R.	400
Estcourt Drive In		Fort Kent 04743		
Fort Kent Drive In		Fort Kent 04743	Levesque	400
Boundary Line Drive In	P.O. Box 435	Ft. Fairfield 04742	Dodge, Lois	300
Bangor Twin Dr. In		Hermon 04401	Theatre Mgt.	300
Borderland Drive In		Houlton 04730	Webber	400
Kennebunk Drive In		Kennebunk 04043	Tevanian	400
Kittery York Drive In		Kittery 03904	Norad Enter.	400
Lewiston Dr. In		Lewiston 04240	SBC Mgt. Corp.	500
Lisbon Drive In	Lisbon Road	Lewiston 04242	Thea. Mgt. Se.	800
Madawaska Drive In		Madawaska 04756	Eldon, St. Cyr	300
Skylit Drive In	89 13th Ave.	Madawaska 04756	Pelletier	395
Augusta Drive In		Manchester 043351	E.M. Loews	900
Katahdin Drive In		Mattawamkeag 04459	Bilodeau	300
Milo Drive In		Milo 04463	Treworgy	300
Windham Drive In		No. Windham 04062	Kennedy	300
Norway Drive In		Norway 04268	Kingsley	300
Presque Isle Drive In		Presque Isle 04769	Barnard, R.	350

Theatre Name	Address	City & Zip	Circuit	Cars
Rockland Drive In	Box 46	Rockland 04856	Graphic	400
Rumford Drive In		Rumford 04276	Cinemette	300
Saco Drive In		Saco 04072	SBC Mgt. Corp.	600
Sanford Drive In		Sanford 04073	E.M. Loews	300
Portland Twin Dr. In		Scarboro 04074	SBC Mgt. Corp.	700
Skowhegan Dr. In		Skowhegan 04976	SBC Mgt. Corp.	300
Ellsworth Trenton D. I.	Route 3	Trenton 04605	Smith, H.	200
Van Buren Drive In		Van Buren 04785	Grandmaison	500
Endfield Drive In		West Endfield 04493	Nyer, S.	200
Jay Hill Drive In		Wilton 04294	Young, C.	300
Winslow Drive In		Winslow 04901	SBC Mgt. Corp.	500

MARYLAND

Theatre Name	Address	City & Zip	Circuit	Cars
Monocacy Drive In	19 W. Mt. Royal Avenue	Baltimore 21201	Cohen, M.	300
North Point Drive In	4001 North Point Bld.	Baltimore 21222	Durkee Cir.	600
Beltsville Drive In		Beltsville 20705	Gettinger, W.	600
213 Drive In		Churchill 21620	Pete Prince	300
Belaire Drive In	P.O. Box 37	Churchville 21028	Wagner, R.	400
Ranch Drive In	P.O. Box 39	Clinton 20735	Roth Theas.	600
Potomac Drive In		Cumberland 21502	Broumas	
Super 51 Drive In	818 Gephart Drive	Cumberland 21502	Broumas	400
219 Drive In	Rt. 2 Box 45	Deer Park 21527	Hoag, R.	200
Cross Roads Dr. In	Route 404	Denton 21629	Schwartz Th.	1,300
Elkridge Drive In		Elkridge 21227	Brehm	500
Elkton Drive In	Route 40	Elkton 21921	Schwartz Th.	700
Frederick Dr. In	Route 4	Frederick 21701	Weinberg	2,000
Valley Drive In	Reistertown & Valley Rd.	Garrison 21055	Schwaber	800
Gov. Ritchie Open Air	1706 Ritchie Hwy.	Glen Burnie 21061	E.M. Loews	600
Hager Drive In		Hagerstown 21740	Fruchtman, J.	500
Hiway Drive In	Box 247	Hagerstown 21740	Fruchtman, J.	500
Hancock Dr. In		Hancock 21750	Ridenour	400
Hillside Drive In	P.O. Box 4742	Hillside 20023	Wineland	725
Laurel Drive In	1110 Washington Blvd.	Laurel 20810	Wineland	825
235 Drive In	101 Coral Drive So.	Lexington Park 20653	Fruchtman, J.	300
Hi Rock Drive In		McCoole 26726	Broumas	
Bengies Drive In	3417 Eastern Blvd.	Middle River 21220	Vogel	600
Shore Drive In	P.O. Box 22	Ocean City 21842	Getjar Corp.	500
Super 170 Drive In	P.O. Box 37	Odenton 21113	Rome Theas.	700
ABC Drive In	7100 Indian Head Rd.	Oxon Hill 20022	Wineland	925
Shore Drive In		Pasadena 21122		
Pocomoke Drive In		Pocomoke City 21851	Derrickson	275
Rockville Drive In	810 N. Washington St.	Rockville 20850	K&B Theatre	400
Salisbury Bowl Dr. In		Salisbury 21801	R/C Theas.	
Super Chief Drive In	11901 Livingston Rd.	Silesia 20022	Wineland	600
Lake Drive In	P.O. Box 36	Sykesville 21784	Maskell, C.	200
Timonium Drive In	P.O. Box 277	Timonium 21093	Westoutdoor	2,200
Super 50 Drive In	P.O. Box 167	Trappe 21673	Schwartz Th.	400
301 Drive In		Waldorf 20601	Roth Theas.	500
Gen. Pulaski Drive In		Whitemarsh 21162	Schwaber	700

MASSACHUSETTS

Theatre Name	Address	City & Zip	Circuit	Cars
Hoosac Drive In	199 Howland Ave.	Adams 01220	Coury	600
Auburn Drive In		Auburn 01501	E.M. Loews	800
Avon Drive In		Avon 02322	Interst Ths.	500
Bellingham Auto		Bellingham 02019	Pirani, J.	300
Pinehurst Drive In		Billerica 01821	E.M. Loews	500
Nashoba Valley Dr. In		Boxboro 01921	Abate, F.	600
So. Shore Plaza Twin D. I.		Braintree 02184	Genl. Cinema	1,500
Skyview Drive In		Brockton 02401	Hochberg, A.	800
Blue Hills Drive In		Canton 02021	Minasian, S.	500
Chelmsford Twin D. I.	P.O. Box 147	Chelmsford 01824	Carpenter	1,300
Air Line Drive In		Chicopee Falls 01020	Schwab, H.	500
Dartmouth Open Air		Dartmouth 02714	Fall Riv. Th.	500
Dennis Drive In		Dennis 02638	Interst Ths.	700
Fairhaven Drive In		Fairhaven 02719	Fall Riv. Th.	700
Cod Drive In		Falmouth 02540	Theatre Mgt.	600
Whalom Auto	Rte. #13	Fitchburg 01420	Williams	500
Mohawk Drive In		Gardner 01440	Zerinsky	500
Cinema 95 Drive In		Georgetown 01830	De Santis, A.	500
Gloucester Drive In	Route 128 Concord St.	Gloucester 01930	Desantis, T.	800
Hadley Drive In	P.O. Box 285	Hadley 01035	Matusaw, H.	500
Riverview Drive In		Haverhill 01830	Arekelian, S.	600
Hyannis Drive In		Hyannis 02601	Interst Ths.	500
Kingston Drive In		Kingston 02360	E.M. Loews	400
Leicester Drive In		Leicester 01524	Minasian, S.	600
Lowell Drive In		Lowell 01854	Hallmark	900
Tri-Town Drive In		Lunenburg 01462	Fideli	800
Marshfield Drive In	Route 139	Marshfield 02050	Camponeschi	400
Meadow Glen Drive In		Medford 02155	Thea. Mgt. Se.	1,100
Medford Twin Drive In	100 Revere Beach Pky.	Medford 02155	Hallmark	
Milford Drive In		Mendon 01757	Interst Ths.	500
Merrimack Park Dr. In		Methuen 01844	E.M. Loews	500
Meadowbrook Drive In	Rte. 44 P.O. Box 130	Middleboro 02346	Alemian, Z.	700
Route 114 Drive In		Middleton 01949	Hallmark	1,100
Starlite Dr. In		No. Reading 01864	Redstone	500
Parkway Drive In		No. Wilbraham 01067	Schwab, H.	1,000
Courys Drive In		North Adams 01247	Coury	600
Boro Drive In		North Attleboro 02760	Stangler	700
Oxford Twin Dr. In		North Oxford 01537	Menasian	1,300
Pioneer Valley Dr. In	Rte. 2	Orange 01364	Zerinsky	500
Metro Drive In		Palmer 01069	Miceli	400
Pittsfield Drive In		Pittsfield 01201	Cate	600

Theatre Name	Address	City & Zip	Circuit	Cars
Plainville Drive In	43 Taunton St.	Plainville 02762	Neveau	500
Raynham Drive In		Raynham 02767	Alemian, Z.	400
Hi-Way Drive In		Salisbury 01950	Arekelian, S.	500
Bay State Drive In		Seekonk 02771	Fall Riv. Th.	500
Seekonk Twin Drive In		Seekonk 02771	Thea. Mgt. Se.	1,300
Community Drive In		Shelburne Falls 01370	Nelman, C.	
Edgemere Drive In		Shrewsbury 01545	Minasian, S.	1,000
Shrewsbury Drive In		Shrewsbury 01545	Minasian, S.	600
Somerset Family Dr. In		Somerset 02722	Fall Riv. Th.	800
Red Rock Drive In		Southampton 01073	Yamilkowski	500
Wamesit Drive In		Tewksbury 01876	Hallmark	700
Tyngsboro Drive In		Tyngsboro 01879	Carpenter	300
Quaker Drive In		Uxbridge 01569	Eisner	700
West Boylston Dr. In		W. Boylston 01583	E.M. Loews	1,400
Wareham Drive In		Wareham 02571	Thea. Mgt. Se.	600
Wellfleet Drive In		Wellfleet 02667	Jentz	600
Yarmouth Drive In		West Yarmouth 02673	Interst Ths.	900
Westport Drive In		Westport 02790	Fall Riv. Th.	500

MICHIGAN

Theatre Name	Address	City & Zip	Circuit	Cars
Lenawee Drive In	P.O. Box 283	Adrian 49221	Selcop	600
Sky Drive In		Adrian 49221	Jenkins, W	500
Albion Drive In		Albion 49224	Mid States	600
Seaway Drive In		Algonac 48001	Univ. Amus.	800
Alpena Drive In	9547 W. Langlake Rd.	Alpena 49707	Sweet, L.	400
Thunder Bay Drive In		Alpena 49707	Sweet, L.	400
Scio Drive In	6588 Jackson Rd.	Ann Arbor 48103	Genl. Cinema	700
University Drive In		Ann Arbor 48104	Butterfield	1,033
YPSI Ann Drive In	4675 Washtenaw	Ann Arbor 48104	Genl. Cinema	600
M 53 Drive In		Bad Axe 48413	Ashmun, R.J.	400
Pine Air Drive In		Baldwin 39203	Ghent, J.C	300
Auto Drive In	Rte #5 Box 1302	Battle Creek 49017	Butterfield	900
West Point Drive In	4060 West Mich.	Battle Creek 49017	Butterfield	500
Starlite Drive In		Bay City 48706	Ashmun, R.J.	700
Tuscola Drive In		Bay City 48706	Ashmun, R.J.	800
Starlite Drive In		Benton Harbor 49022	Mann Theas.	700
Big Rapids Univer. D. I.	18580 Northland Dr.	Big Rapids 49307	Goodrich	300
Lakes Drive In		Brighton 48116	Wetsman & Wis.	900
Burnside Drive In		Brown City 48416	Fishner, N.	500
Cadillac Drive In	9096 S. U.S. 131	Cadillac 49601	Goodrich	500
Caro Drive In		Caro 48723	Ashmun, R.J.	400
Blue Sky Drive In		Caseville 48725	Hughes, A.	300
Maple City Drive In		Charlotte 48813	Wetsman Wis.	500
Hiawatha Drive In		Chassell 49913	Gasuoda, A.J.	
Cheboygan Drive In		Cheboygan 49721	Wagner, E.	500
Northland Drive In		Clare 48617	Wetsman Wis.	500
Capri Drive In	Route #5	Coldwater 49036	Clark, Jr.	700
Skyway Drive In		Corunna 48817	Dean & Chas. W.	500
Dearborn Drive In	26500 Ford Road	Dearborn 48206	Westoutdoor	1,200
Ford Wyoming Drive In	10400 Ford Road	Dearborn 48126	Clark, H.	1,000
Bel Air Drive In #1	8600 E. 8 Mile Road	Detroit 48234	Community	1,900
Bel Air Drive in 2	8600 E. 8 Mile Rd.	Detroit 48234	Community	1,100
Five Mile North D. I.	R #6 Box 4	Dowagiac 49047	White, D.	500
Tawas Drive In		East Tawas 48730	Ashmun, R.J.	400
Hilltop Drive In	R.R. #1	Escanaba 49829	Mescop	500
Ken Mar D. I.	1631 S. 16th St.	Escanaba 49029	Pinasek, D.	500
Grand River Drive In.	30200 Grand River	Farmington 48024	Community	1,200
Silver Drive In		Fenton 48430	Sears, A.	400
Miracle Red & Blue D. I.	6383 E. Court St.	Flint 48423	Redstone	1,050
Northland Drive In		Flint 48505	Butterfield	1,200
Southdort Drive In	G 5117 S. Dort Highwy.	Flint 48507	Butterfield	1,200
U.S. 23 Drive In		Flint 48507	Warrington	1,200
West Side Dr. In	% G. 5117 So. Dort Hwy.	Flint 48507	Butterfield	1,000
Meredith Drive In	General Delivery	Gladwin 48624	Munia, G.	400
Plainfield Drive In		Grand Rapids 49505	Loeks	1,000
Vista Drive In	4500 Lake M gan D.	Grand Rapids 49504	Butterfield	1,300
Greenville Drive In		Greenville 48838	Wetsman Wis.	300
East Side Drive In	19440 Harpe Avenue	Harper Woods 48236	Westoutdoor	1,000
Sunset Drive In		Hartford 49057	White, D.	300
Hastings Drive In		Hastings 49058	Salzwedel, R.	300
Hillsdale Drive In		Hillsdale 49242	Wetsman Wis.	400
Cherry Bowl Drive In		Honor 49640	Griffin, L.J.	300
Ionia Drive In		Ionia 48846	Wetsman Wis.	300
Tri City Drive In		Iron Mountain 49801	Mescop	300
Ironwood Drive In		Ironwood 49938	Mescop	390
Airport Drive In	310 Cleveland Ave.	Ishpeming 49849	Delft. Affil.	700
Evergreen Drive In	Rte. 1 Box 599 D.	Ishpeming 49849	Matchett, J.	
Bel Air Drive In		Jackson 49202	Redstone	700
Jackson Drive In	4400 Ann Arbor Rd.	Jackson 49202	Redstone	700
Douglas Drive In	1900 Douglas Ave.	Kalamazoo 49007	Butterfield	800
Portage Drive In	5528 Portage Rd.	Kalamazoo 49002	Butterfield	700
Woodland Drive In		Kentwood 49508	Loeks	800
Lake Outdoor		Lake Linden 49945	Delft Affil.	350
Lansing Drive In	5207 Cedar	Lansing 48910	Butterfield	1,100
Northside Drive In		Lansing 48906	W.W. Bus. Mgt.	800
Starlite Drive In	3020 Snow Road	Lansing 48917	Butterfield	1,100
Sunset Drive In		Lapeer 48446	Mid States	400
Starlite Drive In	U.S. 10 At U.S. 31	Ludington 49431	Loseth, J.	500
Galaxy Drive In		Madison Heights 48071	George, N.	1,400
Chippewa Drive In	1781 E. Parkdale	Manistee 49660	Goodrich	500
Perry Circle D. I.		Marinette 54173	Perry, A.	
Marysville Drive In		Marysville 48040	Wetsman & Wis.	900
M 60 Drive In		Mendon 49072	Eisner	400

Theatre Name	Address	City & Zip	Circuit	Cars
Sunset Drive In		Midland 48640	Redstone	450
Galaxy Drive In		Mio 48647	Mohney, H.	400
Bel Aire Drive In	6231 No. Monroe	Monroe 48161	Selcop	800
Denniston Drive In		Monroe 48161	Butterfield	1,100
Mt. Clemens Drive In		Mt. Clemens 48043	Jos. Eilul	1,200
Pleasant Drive In		Mt. Pleasant 48858	Wetsman, Wis.	500
Auto Drive In		Muskegon 49441	Loeks	700
Getty Drive In		Muskegon 49440	Loeks	1,200
North Drive In		Muskegon 49445	Loeks	1,000
31 Outdoor		Niles 49120	Kohlberg	
West Side Drive In	14350 W. 8 Mile Rd.	Oak Park 48237	Westoutdoor	800
Crest Dr. In	1096W Grand River Ave.	Okemos 48864	Univ. Amuse.	800
Northland Dr. In		Petoskey 49711	Nelson	400
131 Drive In		Plainwell 49080	Kortes, S	
Miracle Mile Dr. In	2103 So. Telegraph	Pontiac 48053	Redstone	1,600
Pontiac Drive In		Pontiac 48055	Redstone	1,200
Lakeshore Drive In	5737 Lakeshore Road	Port Huron 48060	Lepa, S.	500
Sundown Drive In		Rosebush 48878	Wetsman, Wis.	500
Gratiot Drive In	31900 Gratiot	Roseville 48026	Community	1,000
Oak Drive In	2916 Normandy Rd.	Royal Oak 48073	Miskinis, J.	900
Auto Dr. In	5113 Dixie	Saginaw 48601	Redstone	750
Bel Air Dr. In	3504 Janes	Saginaw 48601	Redstone	1,000
Hi Way Drive In		Sandusky 48471	Fetting, S.	400
Starlite Drive In		Saugatuck 49453	Butterfield	300
Starlite Drive In	%Soo #1 Theatre	Sault Ste. Marie 49783	Soo Amuse.	300
Fort George Drive In		Southgate 48192	George, N.	1,300
Michigan Drive		Southgate 48192	George, N.	1,200
Northwoods D/I		St. Helen 48656	Amy, Y.	
Family Drive In		St. Johns 48879	Massey, P.	500
St. Joe Auto Drive In		St. Joseph 49085	Western	400
Skytop Drive In	1892 W. Monroe Rd.	St. Louis 48880	Epps, T.	500
Ecorse Drive In	21366 Ecorse Road	Taylor 48180	Sportsvs.	1,000
Jolly Rogers Drive In		Taylor 48180	George, N.	1,600
Traverse City Drive In		Traverse City 49684	Ringold, H.J.	500
Holiday Drive In	23000 West Road	Trenton 48183	Bzoui, D.	1,200
Troy Drive In		Troy 48084	Affiliated	1,000
Commerce Drive In	8305 Richardson Road	Walled Lake 48088	George, N.	1,000
Walake Dr. In	P.O. Box 393	Walled Lake 48088	Wetsman, Wis.	1,200
Van Dyke Drive In	32341 Van Dyke	Warren 48093	Detroit The.	1,500
Waterford Dr. In	Williams Lake Road	Waterford 48095	Redstone	700
Wayne Drive In 1		Wayne 48184	Shafer	
Wayne Drive In 2		Wayne 48184	Shafer	
Algiers Drive In		Westland 48184	Shafer	1,500
M37 Drive In		White Cloud 49349	Eisner	300
Beltline Drive In #1	1400 28th St. S.W.	Wyoming 49509	Loeks	
Beltline Drive In #2	1400 28th St. S.W.	Wyoming 49509	Loeks	
Beltline Drive In #3	1400 28th St. S.W.	Wyoming 49509	Loeks	

MINNESOTA

Theatre Name	Address	City & Zip	Circuit	Cars
Rainbow Dr. In		Aitkins 56431	Bellefeuill	
Starlite Dr. In		Albert Lea 56007	Carisch	366
Sunset Drive In		Alexandria 56308	Tentelino	350
218 Hiway D. I.		Austin 55912	Carisch	350
Bronco Dr. In		Bemidji 56601	Woodard	250
Cisco Dr. In		Bemidji 56601	Woodard	350
65 Hi Dr. In		Blaine 55414	N.W. Cinema	550
Gull Dr. In		Brainerd 56401	Tentelino, E.	500
Cine Buff Drive In		Buffalo 55313	Dupont, D.	200
Coon Rapids Dr. In		Coon Rapids 55433	N.W. Cinema	600
Sky View Drive In		Detroit Lakes 56501	Berger Amus.	350
Skyline Drive In		Duluth 55802	Cinema Ent.	200
Vons Drive In		Eveleth 55734	Deutch, D.	400
Family Dr. In		Fairmont 56031	Watters, J.P.	400
Family Drive In		Faribault 55021	Feichtinger	450
Fergus Drive In		Fergusfalls 56537	Berger Amus.	295
Hub Dr. In		Forest Lake 55025	Strubble, E.	300
100 Twin Drive In		Fridley 55432	Herringer, C.	
100 Twin Drive In West		Fridley 55432	Herringer, C.	850
Sky Blue Dr. In		Garrison 56450	Wilcox, D.	370
Pine Tree Drive In		Grand Rapids 55744	Heller, S.	350
75 Hi Drive In	Box 495	Hallock 56728	Carriere, J.	225
Garrick	501 Front Street	Hawley 56549	Floberg, V.	
Cinema 2 Dr. In		Hector 55342	Jular Theas.	300
Hibbing Dr. In	313 Mesabi Drive	Hibbing 55746	Mann Steve	350
Flying Cloud D. I.	S. Hwy. 169 & Hwy. 212	Hopkins 55343	N.W. Cinema	700
Starlite Drive In		Hutchinson 55350	Mid Contin.	250
Parkway Drive In		Intl. Falls 56649	Tentelino	450
Jordan Dr. In		Jordan 55352	Tillmans	
Kim Hi Drive In		Kimball 55353	Greeley, R.	200
Vali Hi Drive In	Post #179	Lake Elmo 55402	Plitt	500
Starlite Drive In		Litchfield 55355	Lutz, D.	300
Rex		Little Fork 56653	Thompson	200
Airport Drive In		Littlefalls 56345	Tentelino	295
Long Drive In	MPEN	Long Prairie 56347	Zastrow, J.	250
Berne Drive In	327 W. Warren	Luverne 56156	Deutsch, W.	265
Star Drive In	Rte. 1 Box 106	Mahnomen 56557	Ahmanns	200
Kato Drive In		Mankato 56001	Carisch	389
Mankato Twin Star D/I	P.O. Box 1299	Mankato 56001	Carisch	
Starlite Drive In		Marshall 56258	Hiller, W.	450
Colonial Dr. In		Medina 55340	N.W. Cinema	500
Lucky Twin Dr. In	100 E. Hwy. 13	Minneapolis 55378	Venture Ths.	3,000
Starlite Drive In		Montevideo 56265	Mid Contin.	350
Starlite D. I.		Moorhead 55650	Cinema Ent.	450

Theatre Name	Address	City & Zip	Circuit	Cars
Lake Dr. In		Moose Lake 55767	Lower, W.O.	250
Colonial Drive In		Morris 56267	Collins, B.	395
Navarre Amph. Dr. In		Navarre 55392	N.W. Cinema	399
Starlite Drive In		Newulm 56073	Mid Contin.	350
Starlite Drive In		Owatonna 55060	Carisch	380
Rapids Dr. In	P.O. Box 271	Park Rapids 56470	Olson	450
Prairie Dr. In	Box 285	Perham 56573	Quincer, D.	250
Pine Outdoor Dr. In		Pine City 55063	Gross	300
Sunset Drive In		Pipestone 56164	Schafer	400
Red Wing D/I		Red Wing 55066	Fraser, J.	450
71 Drive In		Redwood Falls 56283	Buckley, R.	380
Starlite No. Dr. In		Rochester 55901	Carisch	500
Starlite So. Drive In		Rochester 55901	Carisch	550
Skyvue Drive In		Sauk Centre 56378	Douvier	350
Green Lake Dr. In	Rt. 2	Spicer 56288	Mertens, M.	1,000
Spring Valley D. I.		Spring Valley 55975	Strain, F.	150
Cloud Outdoor Drive In.		St. Cloud 56301	Cinema Ent.	389
10 Hi Drive In		St. Cloud 56301	Cinema Ent.	400
Corral Dr. In		St. Paul 55118	Venture Ths.	500
Maple Leaf Dr. In		St. Paul 55115	Herringer, C.	630
Rose Dr. In		St. Paul 55112	Venture Ths.	600
Cottage Vue Drive In		St. Paul Park 55071	Herringer, C.	950
Satellite Dr. In	Box 337	Thief River 56701	Hickerson, J.	250
Martys Skyvue Drive In		Twin Valley 56584	Martinson, L.	150
Rand Drive In		Verndale 56481	Mrnak, D.	350
Wadena Drive In		Wadena 56482	Quincer, D.	350
Hi Y Drive In		Walker 56484	Goble, G.	250
Skyvue Drive In	R.R. #1 Bx. 1 620 E. Johnson	Warren 56762	Novak, L.	200
Chief Dr. In		Willmar 56201	Mid Contin.	450
Skyvue Drive In		Winona 55987	Berg, P.	450

MISSISSIPPI

Theatre Name	Address	City & Zip	Circuit	Cars
Sunset Drive In	Box 238	Amory 38821	Harlow	300
Trace Drive In	Box 238	Amory 38821	Harlow, A.	200
Starlite Dr. In	P.O. Box 217	Belmont 38827	Curtis, J.	200
Beach Twin Dr. I	P.O. Drawer 4439	Biloxi 39530	Gulf States	700
51 Drive In		Brookhaven 39601	Carruth, A.	300
Twilite Drive		Bruce 38915	Franklin, M.	240
Morrow Dr. In		Calhoun City 38916	Morrow, T.	270
Starliner Dr. In	606 S. Valley St.	Carthage 39051	Wallace, T.	200
Fiesta Drive In		Columbus 39701	Malco Theas.	
Skylark Drive In		Corinth 38834	Simmons, F.	200
Don Drive In		Edgewater Park 39553	Gulf States	600
Eupora Drive In		Eupora 39744	Burlson, F.	
Showtown Drive In Twin		Greenville 38701	Gulf States	200
Delta Drive In		Greenwood 38930	Gulf States	
White Haven Drive In		Grenada 38901	L.B. & Gloria, B.	300
Beverly Drive In		Hattiesburg 39402	Hargroder, J.	400
Broadway Drive In		Hattiesburg 39401	Hargroder, J.	400
8 Drive In	Box 466	Houston 38851	Lloyd, T. E.	200
Iuka Drive In		Iuka 38852	Jordan	100
Town & Country D. I. 12 & 3		Jackson 39201	Gulf States	1,350
Drive In		Laurel 39440	Jenner, C.E.	300
Northside Twin Cin.		Laurel 39440	Gulf States	
Rebel Drive In	Box 45	Laurel 39440	Gulf States	
Auto Vue Dr. In		Lorman 39096	Abraham	
Ritz Drive In		Lucedale 39452	Graham, S.	200
Camellia Twin Cinema		McComb 39648	Gulf States	206
Ren Drive In		McComb 39648	Gulf States	
Meridian Drive In		Meridian 39301	Gulf States	200
Royal Dr. In		Meridian 39301	Gulf States	200
Rebel Drive In		Oxford 38655	Cobb, R.C.	300
Super Twin Dr. I	P.O. Box 178	Pascagoula 39567	Gulf States	
Philadelphia Drive In		Philadelphia 39350	Clark, C.B.	200
Lake Drive In		Sardis 38666		
Lakeside Drive In		Starkville 39759	Rikoff	400
Lee Drive In	1604 Trace St.	Tupelo 38801	Heard, J.F.	300
Lee Drive In 2	1604 Trace St.	Tupelo 38801	Heard, J.	225
78 Drive In		Tupelo 38801	Malco Theas.	500
Battlefield Village TW	P.O. Box 687	Vicksburg 39180	Gulf States	
Showtown Drive In Twin		Vicksburg 39180	Gulf States	300
Delta Dr. In	816 Grady Avenue	Yazoo City 39194	Conn McLen	200

MISSOURI

Theatre Name	Address	City & Zip	Circuit	Cars
Killarney Drive In		Arcadia 63621	Basden, B.	300
Sunset Drive In		Aurora 65605	Marks, L.	475
Frontier Dr. In		Bethany 64424	Knode, L.	
Lucky 13 Drive In		Bolivar 65613	Hembree, M.	300
Starlight Dr. In		Boonville 65233	Long, M.B.	
Cinema 248 D. I.	1100 West Highway 76	Branson 65616	Kambeitz	250
Lin Vue Drive In		Brookfield 64628	Linvue	
Highway 65 Dr. In	Route #1	Buffalo 65622	De Jarnette	132
Sky Vue Drive In		Butler 64730	Snitz, G.	260
Starvue Drive In	Box 773	Cape Girardeau 63701	Kerasotes	700
Carol Drive In		Carrollton 64633	Commonwealt	280
66 Drive In		Carthage 64836	Dickinson	500
Green Hills Drive In	P.O. Box 431	Cassville 65625	Hall, G.	300
Stardust Dr. In		Centralia 65240	Sullivan, J.	500
65 Drive In		Chillicothe 64601	Saccaro, A.	2650
52 Drive In		Clinton 64735	Commonwealt	238
Ski Hi Drive In	P.O. Box 518	Columbia 65201	Commonwealt	610
Ozark Drive In	Rt. #1 Box 301A	Crocker 65452	Routh, M.	200

Theatre Name	Address	City & Zip	Circuit	Cars
19 Drive In	806 So. Phillips	Cuba 65453	Spreng, D.	
Sky Vue Drive In		DeSoto 63020	Wehrenberg	
Family Drive In		Dexter 63841	Kerasotes	.300
Stadium Drive In	H	Doniphan 63935	Spencer, D.	.200
Corral Drive In		Eldon 65026	Fleener, J.	.275
Eldorado Drive In		Eldorado Spring 64744	Hembree	.225
21-Drive In		Ellington 63638	Davis, C.E.	.800
Tri City Drive In		Excelsior Sprg. 64024	Foster, D.	
Corral Drive In 1&2		Farmington 63640	Kerasotes	.300
270 Drive In	2925 Dunn Rd.	Florissant 63033	Arthur Ent.	1,200
Hi-Y Drive In		Fredricktown 63645	Parmely, B.	.300
King Cal Drive In		Fulton 65251	Wehrenberg	.400
Hillcrest Dr. In		Gasaland 64118	Weary, F.	
Gravois Mills Drive In		Gravois Mills 65037	Fleener, J.	.100
Sky-Hi D. I.		Hannibal 63401	Frisina	.500
Cass County Drive In	P.O. Box 26	Harrisonville 64701	Commonwealth	.300
Hi Way 13 Drive In		Henrietta 64036	Weary, F.G.	.300
Crest Drive In 1	11400 So. 71 Hiway	Hickman Mills 64131	Commonwealth	1,550
Crest Drive In 2	11400 South 71 Hiway	Hickman Mills 64131	Commonwealth	.650
Hillcrest Drive In		Higginsville 64037	Adkins, R.L.	.190
Sunset D. I.		Houston 65483	Wyatt	.200
Twin Drive In #1	1320 No. 71 By-Pass	Independence 64050	Twin D.I. Ths.	
Twin Drive In #2	1320 No. 71 By-Pass	Independence 64050	Twin D.I. Ths.	.850
Bridge Drive In		Jefferson City 65101	Crown Cinem.	.395
Twin 50 Drive In #1	2117 Missouri Blvd.	Jefferson City 65101	Tharp Nickl.	.350
Twin 50 Drive In #2	2117 Missouri Blvd.	Jefferson City 65101	Tharp Nickl.	
Crest Drive In	P.O. Box 1077	Joplin 64801	Commonwealth	.400
Mini Drive In	Rt. 1 P.O.B. 18A	Joplin 64801	Younger, R.	.120
Tri State Drive In	P.O. Box 1077	Joplin 64801	Commonwealth	.500
Fairland #1 Dr. In	76th & Prospect	Kansas City 64132	Finkelstein	.852
Fairyland ;2 Drive In	76th & Prospect	Kansas City 64132	Finkelstein	1,506
Heart Drive In	6500 E. 40 Highway	Kansas City 64129	Wiles, R.	.900
Hi-Way 40 Drive In	14301 E. 40 Highway	Kansas City 64136	Westoutdoor	.900
I 70 Drive In	8701 East 40 Hiway	Kansas City 64129	Mid Am. Thea.	1,200
Lake Park Twin 1 Dr. In	400 South 59th Lane	Kansas City 66111	Twin D.I. Ths.	
Lake Park Twin 2 Dr. In	400 South 59th Lane	Kansas City 66111	Mid Amer.	
63rd Street Dr. In	63rd St. & 50 Hiway	Kansas City 64133	Mid Am. Thea.	1,400
Tommies Dr. In	Box 471	Kennett 63857	Kerasotes	.300
Silver Star Drive In		Kirksville 63501	Mangus, C.D.	.350
Barco Drive In		Lamar 64759	Butlerfelts	.250
Terrace Cinema		Laurie 65038	Fleener	
Mini 5 Drive In		Lebanon 65536	Burton, C.	
Ski Hi Drive In	P.O. Box 523	Lebanon 65536	Kennedy, F.	.200
Macon Drive In		Macon 63552	Arnold, O.M.	.300
Autovue Drive In		Malden 63863	Kerasotes	.300
Star Drive In		Marceline 64658	Bills, E.E.	.300
Parkside Drive In		Marshall 65340	Thomas, C.J.	.300
South Cinema Dr. In	Box 456	Maryville 64468	Cinema Entp.	
Airway Drive In		Memphis 63555	Helton, C.	.400
Little Dixie D/I		Mexico 65265	Frisina	.400
High Five Drive In	815 E. 3rd	Milan 63556	Helton, H.	.220
Hi Way 63 Drive In		Moberly 65270	Bills, E.E.	.295
Ozark Drive In		Monett 65708	Commonwealth	.230
Mountain Grove Dr. In	601 N. Carlton	Mountain Grove 65711	Agee, E.	.300
Rubles Drive In	312 East Pleasant	Mt. Vernon 65712	Ruble, C.	.200
Edgewood Drive In		Neosho 64850	Armstrong, M.	.300
Trail Drive In		Nevada 64772	Felts, B.	.309
Holiday Dr. In 1234		Overland 63132	Mid Am. Thea.	
Rock Road Dr. In	6898 St. Chas. Rock Rd.	Pagedale 63133	Wehrenberg	
Riverside Drive In	Route 25	Parkville 64150	Commonwealth	.775
Hilltop Dr. In		Perryville 63775	Kerasotes	.300
Sixty One South D		Pevely 63070	Kohler, J.	.600
Pinehill Dr. In		Piedmont 63957	Ross	.200
Poplar Bluff Dr. In		Poplar Bluff 63901	Kerasotes	.600
Southland Drive In		Poplar Bluff 63901	Kerasotes	.200
Starlite Dr. In		Potosi 63664	Mercille	.200
North Twin I Drive In	71 Highway & 51st St. No.	Riverside 64168	Twin D.I. Ths.	
North Twin II Dr. In	71 Hwy. E. 51st St. No.	Riverside 64168	Twin D.I. Ths.	.700
Rolla Drive In		Rolla 65401	Commonwealth	.400
Starlite Drive In	P.O. Box 70	Salem 65560	Count, L.	.200
50 Highway Drive In	P.O. Box 189	Sedalia 65301	Commonwealth	.350
Delta Drive In	P.O. Box 66	Sikeston 63801	Malco Theas.	400 Hi M Drive
Hi M Drive In	3630 E. Sunshine	Springfield 65804	Commonwealth	.650
Holiday Drive In	3630 E. Sunshine	Springfield 65804	Commonwealth	.529
Queen City D. I. 1	3630 East Sunshine	Springfield 65804	Commonwealth	
Queen City D. I. 2	3630 East Sunshine	Springfield 65804	Commonwealth	
Sunset Drive In	3630 E. Sunshine	Springfield 65804	Commonwealth	.520
Airway Drive In	10634 St. Charles Rock Rd.	St. Ann 63074	Wehrenberg	1,000
Plaza Drive In		St. Charles 63302	Mid Am. Thea.	.800
Belt Drive In		St. Joseph 64506	Crown Cinem.	.500
Parkview Dr. In	1526 Parkview	St. Joseph 64504	Mid Am. Thea.	.300
Skylark Drive In	137 No. Belt Hgway	St. Joseph 64506	Crown Cinem.	.500
Futura Drive In	P.O. Box 8133	St. Louis 63156	James, J.	
North Dr. In	9425 Highway 67	St. Louis 63136	Wherenberg	1,000
Ronnie S. Dr. In		St. Louis 63125	Wehrenberg	1,000
South Twin Dr. In	Buckley & Lemay Rd.	St. Louis 63125	Wehrenberg	.500
St. Ann Twin D/I	16425 St. Chas. Rock Rd.	St. Louis 63074	Wehrenberg	1,000
66 Drive In		St. Louis 63126	Wehrenberg	.800
I 70 Drive In		St. Peters 63376	Mid Am. Thea.	
39 Drive In		Stockton 65785	Hembree, M.	.250
Grande Drive In		Sullivan 63080	Grande Invs.	.300
Thayer Drive In		Thayer 65791	Mooney	.200
Grand Vue Drive In		Trenton 64683	Commonwealth	.240
Sky Vue Drive In	P.O. Box 387	Unionville 63565	Knowles, J.	.240

Theatre Name	Address	City & Zip	Circuit	Cars
I 44 Drive In		Valley Park 63088	Wehrenberg	200
Vandalia Drive In		Vandalia 63382	Stoutz, L.	200
Starlet Drive In	P.O. Box 138	Warrensburg 64093	Commonwealt	230
Sunset Dr. In		Washington 63090	Commonwealt	200
Woodlane Dr. In		Waynesville 65583	Commonwealt	200
Webb City Drive In		Webb City 64870	Dickinson	350
63-Drive In		West Plains 65775	Davis Theas.	300
Winona Drive In		Winona 65588	Counts, R.	

MONTANA

Theatre Name	Address	City & Zip	Circuit	Cars
Baker Dr. In	Box Q	Baker 59513	Flint, W.	229
Big Timber Dr. In	Box 757	Big Timber 59011	Brekke	150
Big Sky Drive In	P.O. Box 1404	Billings 59103	Thea. Opera.	440
Motor Vu Drive In	P.O. Box 20195	Billings 59102	Carisch	650
Sage Drive In		Billings 59102	Carisch	550
Starlite Dr. In	P.O. Box 1629	Bozeman 59715	Arimont	500
Motor Vu Drive In		Butte 59701	Carisch	500
Red Rock Drive In	Box 867	Chinook 59523	Eliason, L.	150
Star D. I.		Conrad 59425	Interst. Amu.	300
Derrick Drive In		Cutbank 59427	Interst. Amu.	250
Fortress D. I. Roundup	Box 234	Ekalaka 59324	Anderson, J.	125
Starlite D. I.	Box 165	Forsyth 59327	Logan, G.	200
West Drive In	P.O. Box 391	Glasgow 59230	Terry, P.	260
Skylark Drive In	P.O. Box 851	Glendive 59330	Moore, L.W.	250
Falls Motor Vu Dr. In	Box 1439	Great Falls 59401	Carisch	500
Twilite Dr. In	Box 1439	Great Falls 59401	Carisch	500
Starlite Drive In	Box 553	Hamilton 59840	Bailey, J.	300
Sky Vu Drive In	P.O. Box 242	Hardin 59034	Seder, B.	326
Sunset Drive In	P.O. Box 1829	Havre 59501	Schirusky, W.	300
Sky Hi Dr. In	P.O. Box 861	Helena 59601	Thea. Opera.	500
Sunset Dr. In	P.O. Box 5599	Helena 59601	Thea. Opera.	500
Midway Drive In		Kalispell 59901	Ryder, S.	250
Sundown Drive In	P.O. Box 977	Kalispell 59901	Ryders, S.	475
Westernaire Drive In	P.O. Box 639	Lewistown 59457	Campbell, D.	200
Libby Drive In	604 Mineral Ave.	Libby 59923	Weisbeck, D.	210
Sunset Drive In	Box 671	Miles City 59301	Thea. Opera.	400
Go West Drive In	P.O. Box 7277	Missoula 59807	Sharp Sias	650
Sunset Drive In		Plentywood 59254	Nielsen, G.	150
Sunset Drive In		Plentywood 59254	Nielsen, G.	
Wikiwow Drive In		Polson 59860	Pickerill	250
Chief Dr. In	Box 1058	Poplar 59255	Moran, N.	
Chief Drive In	P.O.B. 392	Poplar 59255	Erickson	300
Riverview Dr. In		Scobey 59263	Richardson	300
Riverview Drive In		Scobey 59263	Danielson	
N. Star Dr. In		Shelby 59474	Interst. Amu.	250
Motor Vu Drive In	Box 113	Sidney 59270	Stoops, L.	300
Sundown Dr. In		Wolfpoint 59201	Snyder	
Sundown Drive In		Wolfpoint 59201	Snyder, J.	200

NEBRASKA

Theatre Name	Address	City & Zip	Circuit	Cars
Pineview Drive In	Box 431	Ainsworth 69210	Cole, D.	300
Albion Drive In		Albion 68620	Juracek, B.	300
Starlight Dr. In	P.O. Box 642	Alliance 69301	Kirschenman	300
Crest Drive In		Beatrice 68310	Struve, H.W.	420
Sunset Drive In	Box 447	Bridgeport 69336	Meyer, K.	150
Broken Bow Drive In	1243 South D. St.	Broken Bow 68822	Agena, D.	320
Starlight Drive In		Chadron 69337	Commonwealt.	300
Columbus Drive In		Columbus 68601	Central Sta.	275
Breezy Hill Dr. In	P.O. Box 488	Falls City 68355	Johnson, H.	400
Fremont Drive In	P.O. Box 510	Fremont 68025	Central Sta.	460
Chief Drive In		Gordon 69343	Great Gord	300
Grand Island Drive In		Grand Island 68801	Commonwealt.	300
Grand Island Twin #2	316 West Third St.	Grand Island 68801	Commonwealt	425
Hi Vue Drive In		Hartington 68739	Becker, E.	250
Hastings Drive In		Hastings 68901	Central Sta.	460
Oregon Trail Drive In		Hebron 68370	Struve, H.W.	250
Tower Drive In		Holdrege 68949	Braner, E.	250
Kearney Drive In		Kearney 68847	Central Sta.	364
Panhandle Drive In		Kimball 69145	Cory, D.	250
Motor Movie Drive In		Lexington 68850	Scholz, K.	350
Starview Drive In		Lincoln 68501	Dubinsky	690
West O Drive In	925 Stuart Bldg.	Lincoln 68508	Dubinsky	490
84th & O Drive In		Lincoln 68501	Brehm, R.	600
Bison Drive In	901 Sunset Road	McCook 69001	Owens, D.	350
Trail Drive In		Nebraska City 68410	Frederick, P.	235
Starlite Drive In		Neligh 68756	Johnson, D.	300
Norfolk Drive In		Norfolk 68701	Central Sta.	390
Valley Drive In		North Loup 68862	Markowski	220
Pawnee Drive In		North Platte 69101	Commonwealt.	275
West 5th Street Dr. In		Ogallala 69153	Evergreen	300
Capri Drive In		Omaha 68102	Brehm	500
Golden Spike Drive In	114th & Dodge	Omaha 68102	Central Sta.	650
Q Twin Drive In		Omaha 68501	Brehm, R.	650
Skyview Drive In	144 South 40th St.	Omaha 68131	Benson	410
76 West Dodge Drive In	76th & West Dodge	Omaha 68114	Central Sta.	688
84th & Center Drive In		Omaha 68501	Brehm, R.	600
Sky Way Drive In		Schuyler 68661	Johnson, D.	
Carena Drive In		Scottsbluff 69361	Commonwealt.	500
Plains Drive In		Sidney 69162	Cook, D.	350
Sandhills Drive In	P.O. Box 178	Valentine 69201	Coble, A.D.	275
Dude Ranch Drive In		Wayne 68787	March Bros.	300

Theatre Name	Address	City & Zip	Circuit	Cars
Y Knot Drive In		West Point 68788	Mueller, E.	275
York Drive In		York 68467	Central Sta.	248

NEVADA

Theatre Name	Address	City & Zip	Circuit	Cars
Elko Motor Vu Drive In		Elko 89801	Westates	250
Elko Motor Vue D. I.	Box 430	Elko 89801	Westates	
Motor Vu Drive In	Box 360	Ely 89301	Assoc. Nevad.	300
Roper Drive In	71 So. Maine Street	Fallon 89406	Whitaker, W.	350
Mineralite D. I.	P.O. Box 1695	Hawthorne 89415	Knight, C.	350
Desert Dr. In #2	2606 S. Lamb	Las Vegas 89105	Syufy Ent.	
Desert Dr. In #3	2606 S. Lamb	Las Vegas 89105	Syufy Ent.	
Desert Dr. In #4	2606 S. Lamb	Las Vegas 89105	Syufy Ent.	
Desert Dr. In #5	2606 S. Lamb	Las Vegas 89105	Syufy Ent.	
Desert Drive In 1	2606 S. Lamb	Las Vegas 89105	Syufy Ent.	
Las Vegas D. I. 2	4150W. Smoke Ranch Rd.	Las Vegas 89108	Syufy Ent.	
Las Vegas D. I. #4	4150W. Smoke Ranch Rd.	Las Vegas 89108	Syufy Ent.	
Las Vegas D. I. 3	4150W. Smoke Ranch Rd.	Las Vegas 89108	Syufy Ent.	
Las Vegas Drive In #1	4150W. Smoke Ranch Rd.	Las Vegas 89108	Syufy Ent.	950
Skyway Dr. In	P.O. Box 14926	Las Vegas 89114	Tabor, F.	800
Sunset Dr. In	P.O. Box 14926	Las Vegas 89114	Sero Amusem.	
Nevada Drive In	3873 N. Salt Lake Hwy.	No. Las Vegas 89030	Tabor, F.	1,200
Midway Drive In 2	2995 So. Virginia	Reno 89502	Syufy Ent.	
Mudway Drive In 1	2995 So. Virginia St.	Reno 89502	Syufy Ent.	
El Rancho Drive	555 El Rancho Drive	Spark 89431	Syufy Ent.	
El Rancho Dr. In 1	555 El Rancho Drive	Sparks 89431	Syufy Ent.	568
El Rancho Drive In #2	555 El Rancho Drive	Sparks 89431	Syufy Ent.	
El Rancho Drive In #3	555 El Rancho Drive	Sparks 89431	Syufy Ent.	
Sage Crest Drive In	P.O. Box 428	Yerington 89447	Perry, R.	250

NEW HAMPSHIRE

Theatre Name	Address	City & Zip	Circuit	Cars
Bedford Grove Drive In		Bedford 03102	Fall Riv. Th.	800
Skyhi Drive In		Boscawen 03303	SBC Mgt. Cor.	300
Claremont Drive In		Claremont 93743	Gamache	500
Concord Drive In		Concord 03301	SBC Mgt. Corp.	500
Grand-View Drive In		Gorham 03581	Cinemette	400
Princess Drive In	Berlin Gorham Rd.	Gorham 03581	Gaudreau, B.	
Keene Drive In		Keene 03431	Shakour	400
Weirs Drive In		Laconia 03246	Baldi, L.	
Litchfield Drive In		Litchfield	Dufault	300
Midway Drive In	Box 594	Littleton 03561	Tegu, L.	275
Sky Ray Drive In		Manchester 03105	Fall Riv. Th.	400
Milford Drive In	P.O. Box 4	Milford 03055	Fall Riv.	300
Nashua Drive In		Nashua 03060	Fall Riv. Th.	400
Newington Drive In		Newginton 03801	Morrison, W.	4,000
White Mountain Dr. In		No. Conway 03860	Lowd	300
Seacoast Drive In		North Hampton 03862	Norad Entrp.	400
Starlite Drive In		Orford 03777	Hill	200
North Country D. I.		Ossipee 03864	Renner	200
Plaistow Drive In		Plaistow 03865	Arakelian	500
Rochester Drive In		Rochester 03867	Ciccotelli	400
Route 16 Drive In		Somersworth 03878	Interst. Ths.	300
Northfield Drive In		Winchester 03470	Shakour	220
Meadows Dr. In		Woodsville 03785	Tegu, L.	

NEW JERSEY

Theatre Name	Address	City & Zip	Circuit	Cars
Atco Drive In	State Hwy. 73 & 30	Atco 08004	Redstone	1,000
Super 130 Drive In	Route 130	Beverly 08010	Fox, R.	
Dix Drive In	Route #206	Bordentown 08505	Ellis	1,100
Bridgeton Drive In	North Pearl Street	Bridgeton 08302	Fox, M.	400
Black Horse Dr. In #1&2	2800 Mt. Ephraim Ave.	Camden 08104	Sameric	900
Turnpike Drive In		East Brunswick 08816	U.A. Theas.	1,700
Eastontown D. I.		Eastontown 07724	Reade, W.	
Plainfield Dr. In	1659 Oak Tree Rd.	Edison 08817	U.A. Theas.	
Plainfield Edison 1 & 2	1659 Oak Tree Rd.	Edison 08817	U.A. Theas.	
Shore Drive In		Farmingdale 08108	Arcadia Th.	
Circus Drive In	Route 30	Hammonton 08037	Frank, A.	1,000
35 Drive In		Hazlet 07730	Redstone	1,200
Roosevelt Drive In		Jersey City 07305	Smerling, R.	1,700
Laurelton Motor Vue		Laurelton 08723	Reade, W.	
Drive In		Ledgewood 07852	Smith, F.	600
Hackensack Drive In	P.O. Box 67	Little Ferry 07643	Smerling, R.	
Brunswick Drive In		New Brunswick 08902	U.A. Theas.	650
Newton Dr. In	Rt. 206 Hampton Tpk.	Newton 07860	Smith, F.	
Paramus Drive In	Rt. 4 at Garden Sta. Pl.	Paramus 07652	Tri State E.	
Pennsauken Drive In	Route 73 Rogers Blvd.	Pennsauken 08110	Budco	
Atlantic Drive In	Blkhorse Pk. & Tilton	Pleasantville 08232	Frank, A.	792
Wildwood Twin Dr. In	Delsea Drive	Rio Grande 08242	Fox, M	300
Route 3 Drive In	P.O. Box 318	Rutherford 07070	Smerling, R.	1,570
Somerville Drive In	3091 U.S. 22	Somerville 08876	U.A. Theas.	1,000
Parkway Drive In	Route 130	Thorofare 08086	Miles, R.	800
Bay Drive In		Tom River 08753	Reade, W.	
Tom River Drive In		Tom River 08753	S.W.K. Theas.	
Totowa Drive In		Totowa 07512	Genl. Cinema	1,000
Ewing Drive In	1471 Prospect St.	Trenton 08638	Budco	600
Rt. U.S. 1 Brunswick Pk.	Rt. U.S. 1 Brunswick Pk.	Trenton 08638	Hellman, N.	882
Troy Hills Drive In		Troy Hills 07054	Smerling, R.	
Union Drive In	Route 22	Union 07087	Smerling, R.	1,400
Route 17 Drive In	P.O. Box 394	Upper Saddle Ri. 07458	U.A. Theas.	
Delsea Drive In	Route 47 Delsea Dr.	Vineland 08360	Budco	500

554

Theatre Name	Address	City & Zip	Circuit	Cars

NEW MEXICO

Theatre Name	Address	City & Zip	Circuit	Cars
Starlite Drive In	P.O. Box 658	Alamogordo 88310	Commonwealt	300
Yucca Drive In	P.O. Box 658	Alamogordo 88310	Commonwealt	400
Albuquerque 6 D/I #1	4901 Pan American	Albuquerque 87107	Syufy Theas.	2,100
Albuquerque 6 D/I #2	4901 Pan American	Albuquerque 87107	Syufy Theas.	350
Albuquerque 6 D/I #3	4901 Pan American	Albuquerque 87107	Syufy Theas.	350
Albuquerque 6 D/I #4	4901 Pan American	Albuquerque 87107	Syufy Theas.	350
Albuquerque 6 D/I #5	4901 Pan American	Albuquerque 87107	Syufy Theas.	350
Albuquerque 6 D/I #6	4901 Pan American	Albuquerque 87107	Syufy Theas.	350
Cactus Drive In	P.O. Box 1315	Albuquerque 87103	Commonwealt	400
Duke City Dr. In	Box 8445	Albuquerque 87108	Video Indep.	1,000
Silver Dollar Drive In	Box 8445	Albuquerque 87108	Video Indep.	800
Terrace Drive In	9600 Central Ave. S.E.	Albuquerque 87109	Video Indep.	
Terrace Drive In	P.O. Box 8445	Albuquerque 87108	Video Indep.	630
Tesuque Drive In	Box 8325 Station C	Albuquerque 87109	Video	
Wyoming Drive In	Box 8325 Station C	Albuquerque 87108	Video	1,000
66 Drive In		Albuquerque 87103	Commonwealt	500
Hermosa Drive In		Artesia 88210	Bareleet, R.	
Big Sky Drive In		Carlsbad 88220	Commonwealt	700
Fiesta Drive In	P.O. Box 1180	Carlsbad 88220	Commonwealt	600
Trail Drive In		Clayton 88415	Murphy	220
Yucca Drive In		Clovis 88101	Franklin, L.	400
Placita Hills Dr. In		Cuba 87013	Edge, W.	200
Mimbres Drive In		Deming 88030	Dollison	
Starlighter Drive In		Espanola 87532	Dollison, L.	300
Apache Drive In		Farmington 87401	Crawford, K.	300
Valley Drive In		Farmington 87401	Allen, R.P.	330
Zuni Drive In		Gallup 87301	Commonwealt	300
Trail Drive In		Grants 87020	Thea. Opera.	200
Flamingo D. I. #1		Hobbs 88240	Commonwealt	1,000
Fiesta Drive In	P.O. Box 2279	Las Cruces 88001	Video	
Fort Union Drive In		Las Vegas 87701	Dollison, L.	350
Varsity Drive In		Portales 88130	Commonwealt	200
85 Drive In		Raton 87740	Murphy	350
Starlight D. I. 1		Roswell 88201	Commonwealt	738
Starlight D. I. 2		Rosell 88201	Commonwealt	350
Mt. Vue Drive In		Ruidoso Downs 88345	Yates, Joe	300
Pueblo Drive In		Sant Fe 87501	Commonwealt	
Yucca Drive In	P.O. Box 575	Santa Fe 87501	Winoko Corp.	500
Chief Drive In		Shiprock 87420	Allen, R.P.	200
Silver Sky Vu Drive In		Silver City 88061	Kane, U.A.	275
Sundowner Drive In	Mitchell Route	Silver City 88061	Moss, J.	400
Sierra Vista Drive In	Box 1125	Socorro 87801	Dollison	
Kit Carson Drive In		Taos 87571	Dollison, L.	

NEW YORK

Theatre Name	Address	City & Zip	Circuit	Cars
Orleans Dr. In	200 Foxpoint Dr. West	Albion 14411	Cohen, S.	1,600
Bay Drive In	Rt. 26	Alexandria Bay 13607	Beach, W.	
Allegany Drive In		Allegany 14706	Bordonaro	500
Carman Drive In	248 East Main St.	Amsterdam 12010	Barenoff, B.	
Grandview Drive In	P.O. Box 48	Angola 14006	Cohen, S.	600
East Drive In	P.O. Box 426	Auburn 13021	Fields	
Finger Lakes Dr. In	P.O. Box 426	Auburn 13021	Fields	
Hollywood Drive In	Route 66	Averill Park 12018	Fisher, F.	
Super 50 Drive In		Ballston Lake 12019	Iselin	
Malta Drive In	R.D. 3	Ballston Spa 12020	Smaldone, S.	
Batavia Drive In		Batavia 14020	Dipson	
Bath Drive In	Rt. 415 South	Bath 14810	Midway	
Bayshore Sunrise D. I. #2	1881 Sunrise Highway	Bayshore L.I. 11706	U.A. Theas.	
Bayshore Sunrise D. I. #1	1881 Sunrise Hway.	Bayshore L.I. 11706	U.A. Theas.	
Black River Drive In	Rte. 3	Black River 13612	Atko	
Star Drive In	P.O. Box 2015	Blasdell 14219	Carlson, B.	
Nyack Drive In	Route 303	Blauvelt 10913	U.A. Theas.	
Bridge Hampton Dr. In		Bridge Hampton 11932	U.A. Theas.	
Vail Mills Dr. In	Rte. 30	Broadalbin 12025	Atko	
Art	1 West Tremont	Bronx 10453	Pozin, T.	600
Boulevard Drive In	344 Delaware Ave.	Buffalo 14202	Berkson	
Wherle Outdoor	Tansit Rd. Wherle Dr.	Buffalo 14221	Jo Mor	
Parkway Dr. In	Box 125 Lakeshore Dr.	Canandaigua 14424	Cinema Natl.	500
Ideal Drive In	P.O. Box 231	Canton 13617	Gilson, D.	
Centereach		Centereach L.I. 11720	U.A. Theas.	599
Northway Drive In	Route 11	Champlain 12919	Zurlo, J.H.	
Broadway Drive In		Cheektowaga 14225	Atlas, M.	
North Drive In	8064 Brewerton Rd.	Clay 13041	Cinema Natl.	700
Cobleskill Dr. In		Cobleskill 12043	Nigro, A.	
Mohawk Drive In		Colonie 12905	U.A. Theas.	
Commack Drive In		Commack L.I. 11725	U.A. Theas.	
All Weather Dr. In 2		Copaigue L.I. 11726	U.A. Theas.	
All Weather Drive In		Copiague L.I. 11726	U.A. Theas.	
Coram Drive In		Coram L.I. 11727	U.A. Theas.	
Homer Drive In		Cortland 13045	Sorkin	
Hi Way Drive In		Coxsackie 12051	Klein, M.	
Delavan Drive In		Delevan 14042	Mendola, G.P.	400
Dewitt Drive In	Erie Blvd. East	Dewitt 13214	Cinema Natl.	800
Van Buren Drive In	Route 5	Dunkirk 14048	Cohen	
Auto Vision Drive In		East Greenbush 12061	Iselin	
Park Drive In	Orchard Park Rd.	Ebenezer 14224		
Elmira Drive In		Elmira 14903	S.J.M. Ent. Co.	
Fair Oaks Drive In		Fair Oaks 08086	Miles, R.	800
Enterprise Dr. In		Falconer 14733	Saullo	
Fishkill Drive In		Fishkill 12524	Miles, R.	
Lockport Drive In		Gasport 14067	Midway	
Aust Drive In	P.O. Box 575	Glen Fall 12801	A/R	

Theatre Name	Address	City & Zip	Circuit	Cars
Glen Drive In	R.F.D. 2	Glen Falls 12801	Gardner, J.	
Hi Way Drive In		Gouverneur 13642	Hulbert, W.	
Skyway Drive In		Greenport 11944	Coleman	
Dix Drive In	Box 388	Hudson Falls 12839	Goldstein, H.	
Hyde Park Drive In		Hyde Park 12538	Cohen, S.F.	
9G Drive In	Box 126	Hyde Park 12538	Cinema Natl.	600
Dryden Drive In		Ithaca 14850	SJM Ent. Co.	
Pic 17 Drive In	Route 17	Jamestown 14701	Dipson Cir.	
Airport Drive In	Airport Road	Johnson City 13790	Cinema Natl.	
Sunset Drive In		Kingston 12401	Reade, W.	
Sunset Drive In		Kingston 12401	Reade, W.	
Overlook Drive In		Lagrange 12540	Cohen, S.F.	
Fort George Dr. I		Lake George 12845	Miller, J.	
Lakewood Drive In		Lakewood 14750	Dipson Cir.	400
Lathams Drive In	P.O. Box 826	Latham 12110	U.A. Theas.	300
Mountain Dr. In		Liberty 12754		
Mountain Drive In	Rt. 52	Liberty 12754	Curry, K.	428
Valley Drive In		Little Falls 13365	Coffin, E.	
Lakeshore Drive In	911 Old Liverpool Rd.	Liverpool 13088	Cinema Natl.	600
Conesus Drive In		Livonia 14487	Iamon, R.	
Transit Drive In		Lockport 14094	Cohen, M.	
Valley Brook Drive In	R.F.D. 2	Lowville 13367	Matuszcak	
Mahopac Drive In		Mahopac 10541	Casagrondi	
Marcy Drive In	Box 194	Marcy 13402	Cinema Natl.	
56 Auto Drive In		Massena 13662	Leger, W.	
Hudson River Drive In	49 Dewey Avenue	Mechanicsville 12118	Carelli, D.	
Tri City Twin D. I. #1	586 Broadway	Menands 12204	U.A. Theas.	
Tri City Twin D. I. #2	586 Broadway	Menands 12204	U.A. Theas.	
Middletown Drive In		Middletown 14105	Taylor	
Midway Drive In	Rte. 48 W. River Rd.	Minetto 13115	Midway	
Rockland Drive In		Monsey 10952	U.A. Theas.	
Salina Drive In	P.O. Box 364	Nedrow 13120	Redstone	1,200
Smithtown A/W D. I.#1	Smithtown Bypass	Nesconset L.I. 11767	U.A. Theas.	
Smithtown A/W Dr. In 2	Smithtown Bypass	Nesconset L.I. 11787	U.A. Theas.	
Brookside Drive In	Route 17 K.	Newburgh 12550	Cinema Natl.	
Middlehope Drive In	M.D. 25	Newburgh 12550	Columbia	
Falls Auto View Dr. In	21 Fall Street	Niagara Falls 14303	Hayman Bros.	500
Starlight Drive In	21 Fall Street	Niagara Falls 14303	Hayman Bros.	800
Norwich Drive In		Norwich 13815	Countrywide	
C Way Drive In	Rte. 37	Ogdensburg 13669	Vernsey, R.	
Del Sego Drive In	25 Ravine Park Dr.	Oneonta 13820	Warner, Jr., W.	
Route 303 Drive In		Orangeburg 10962	U.A. Theas.	
El Rancho Drive In	Rte. #5	Palatine Brdg. 13428	Hallmark	300
A/W Sunrise Dr. In 2		Patchogue L.I. 11772	U.A. Theas.	
All Weather Sunrise D. I.		Patchogue L. I. 11772	U.A. Theas.	
Silver Lake Drive In		Perry 14530	Stefanon, J.	200
Stardust D. I.	80 Boynton Ave.	Plattsburgh 12901	Henry, L.	
Super 87 D/I	R.F.D. Box 71	Plattsburgh 12901	Thea. Mgmt.	
Essex		Port Henry 12974	Broadhead, D.	
Portville Dr. In		Portville 14770	Bordinaro	
Hollowbrook Drive In	P.O. Box 291	Putnam Valley 10579	Genl. Cinema	
Central Drive In	1700 Long Pond Road	Rochester 14606	Jo Mor	800
Starlite Drive In	2970 Henrietta Road	Rochester 14620	Schwartz, J.	
Rockhill Drive In	P.O. Box 318	Rockhill 12775	Taylor	
Rocky Point Drive In		Rocky Point L.I. 11697	U.A. Theas.	
West Rome Drive In		Rome 13440	Goldstein	
Riverview Drive In	P.O. Box 868	Rotterdam Junct. 12150	U.A. Theas.	
Shirley Drive In		Shirley L.I. 11967	U.A. Theas.	
I-290 Drive In	800 Young Street	Tonawanda 14150	Lawton, M.	
Sheriden Dr. In 1 & 2		Tonawanda 14150	Cohen Thea.	1,600
Unadilla Drive In		Unadilla 13849	Chonka	
New Hartford Drive In	Box 525	Utica 13503	Cinema Natl.	
Skyler Twin Dr. In 1		Utica 13503	Cinema Natl.	600
Skyler Twin Dr. In 2		Utica 13502	Cinema Natl.	300
V Dr. In	Vestal Parkway East	Vestal 13850	Cinema Natl.	
Indian Ladder Dr. 1		Voorheesville 12186	Hallenbeck	
Warwick Drive In	Rte. 94	Warwick 10990	Seeber, F.	
Seneca Dr. In	R.R. #1 Box #28A	Waterloo 13165	Midway	
Northside Drive In	Route 12	Watertown 13601	Midway	
Starlite Drive In		Watertown 13601	Atko	
Roxy Drive In	R.D. #1	Wellsburg 14894	Cornell	
Outdoor Dr. In		Wellsville 14895	Scoville, P.	
U.S. Military Academy 2		West Point 10996	Aafes	
Empire Drive In	P.O. Box 166	West Webster 14580	Jo Mor	900
Westbury Drive In	Box 639 Brushollow Rd.	Westbury 11590	U.A. Theas.	

NORTH CAROLINA

Theatre Name	Address	City & Zip	Circuit	Cars
Ahoskie Drive In		Ahoskie 17910	Howell Thea.	175
Badin Road Drive In		Albemarle 28001	Exhibitors	500
Albermarle Dr. In		Albemarle 28001	Exhibitors	250
N. 220 Drive In		Asheboro 27203	Consolidate	420
Dreamland Drive In	P.O. Box 5936	Asheville 28803	Pless, J.	400
Park Drive In	Hwy. 1 Swannanoa Riv.	Asheville 28805	Piedmont	
Belmont Drive In	Box 83	Belmont 28012	Consolidate	142
Star Vue Dr. In	P.O. Box 648	Benson 27504	Stephenson	175
Bessemer City Drive In	Box 664	Bessemer City 28016	Stinette, R.	600
Twilite Drive In		Beulaville 28518	Stephenson	200
Biscoe Drive In		Biscoe 27209	Exhibitors	189
Brevard Drive In		Brevard 28712	Carter, C.B.	200
Circle G Drive In		Burlington 27217	Piedmont	300
70 Twin 1 Drive In	P.O. Box 3324	Burlington 27215	Consolidate	
70 Twin 11 Drive In	P.O. Box 3324	Burlington 27215	Consolidate	479
Pines Drive In		Chadbourn 28431	Edmund	180

Theatre Name	Address	City & Zip	Circuit	Cars
Fox Drive In		Charlotte 28205	Hodges, C.	280
South 29 Drive In	P.O. Box 1262	Charlotte 28201	Theimer, L.L.	315
Thunderbird Dr. In	5448 N. Tryon St.	Charlotte 28213	Plitt South	650
Viking Twin #1 Dr. In	P.O. Box 8685	Charlotte 28208	Consolidate	310
Viking Twin #2 Dr. In	P.O. Box 8685	Charlotte 28208	Consolidate	620
Poplar Drive In		Concord 28025	Morgan, W.	250
Davidson Drive In		Davidson 28036	Morgan, W.M.	
Coes Drive In	Rte. #3	Dobson 27107	Coe, R.	150
Hi Peak Drive In	Box 1235	Drexel 28619	Glennon, D.	165
Forest Drive In	3416 Holloway St.	Durham 27704	Howell Thea.	350
Midway Drive In	Rt. 2 Box 424	Durham 27704	Howell Thea.	200
Starlite Drive In		Durham 27704	Howell Thea.	175
East Bend Drive In		East Bend 27018	Holder, M.N.	200
Eden Drive In	Box 504	Eden 27288	Consolidate	200
South 17 Drive In	Rte. 6-Box 176	Elizabeth City 27909	Sawyer, K.	400
Valley Dr. In		Elkin 28621	Piedmont	300
Boulevard Drive In	P.O. Box 3943	Fayetteville 28305	Plitt South	450
Fort Drive In 1 2 3	P.O. Box 35905	Fayetteville 28303	Piedmont	750
Fox Drive In #1	P.O. Box 5513	Fayetteville 28302	Eastern Fed.	450
Fox Drive In #2	Box 5513	Fayetteville 28302	Eastern Fed.	
Midway Drive In	Box 53476	Fayetteville 28305	Loyd, R.	525
Moonlite Drive In	Box 5092	Fayetteville 28302	Movie Exhib.	150
Midway Drive In	Box 263	Forest City 28043	Dantzic	260
Tri City Drive In		Forest City 28043	Exhibitors	178
Franklin Drive In		Franklin 28734	Con-Mc Lend	300
Ft. Bragg D. I. #5		Ft. Bragg 28303	Aafes	
Cairo Drive In		Fuquay Springs 27526	Bullock, J.M.	250
Monte Vista Drive In	705 Myrtle School Rd.	Gastonia 28052	Deaton, R.L.	460
No. 29 Diane Drive In		Gastonia 28052	Consolidate	200
So. 29 Diane Drive In	Box 12337	Gastonia 28052	Consolidate	450
Waco Drive In		Goldsboro 27530	Champion, R.	200
Skyline Drive In	P.O. Box 6013	Greensboro 27402	Consolidate	315
Meadowbrook Drive In	Box 3725	Greenville 27834	Lyles, N.T.	350
Tice Drive In	Box 3725	Greenville 27834	Lyles, N.T.	350
Havelock Drive In	Box 995	Havelock 28532	Edwards, B.	325
Raleigh Road Outdoor	P.O. Box 1412	Henderson 27536	Lyles, N.T.	300
Hendersonville Dr. In	P.O. Box 1128	Hendersonville 28739	Exhibitors	200
Hickory Dr. In	Box 2073	Hickory 28601	Colonial Th.	150
Springs Road Drive In		Hickory 28601	Rumley, A.	194
Thunderbird Drive In		Hickory 28601	Rumley, A.	500
Tar Heel Drive In	P.O. Box 4037	High Point 27263	Piedmont	300
Cinema Drive In		Jacksonville 28540	Stewart	400
Marine Drive In	Box 5051 New River Plz.	Jacksonville 28540	Plitt South	225
North 17 Drive In		Jacksonville 28540	Aragona, S.	
South 17 Drive In		Jacksonville 28540	Aragona, S.	400
Park In		Kannapolis 28081	Stewart	468
King Drive In		King 27021	Forset, E.R.	240
North 11 Drive In	P.O. Box 921	Kinston 28501	Lund, K.	175
Lake Junaluska		Lake Junaluska 28745	Fowler	
Flamingo Drive In		Laurinburg 28352	Tucker, C.	225
Laur Max Drive In		Luarinburg 28352	Whitley, L.J.	
Farm 1 Drive In		Lenoir 28645	Farmer, A.	195
Pine Tree Drive In	P.O. Box 182	Lenoir 28645	Haines, C.,	238
Lexington Dr. In	R.F.D. 16 Box 2	Lexington 27292	Callahan, J.	250
Roseland Drive In		Lincolnton 28092	Chapman, R.	184
Starlite Drive In		Lincolnton 28092	Stewart	194
Locust Drive In		Locust Level 28097	Morgan, W.	
Car View Drive In	P.O. Box 59	Louisburg 27549	Harris, G.	275
211 Drive In	2400 5th St.	Lumberton 28358	Stephen	300
Drive In	Route 3	Madison 27025	Baker, J.T.	200
Garden City Drive In		Marion 28752	Cooper, Hal	
Madison Drive In		Marshall 28753	Shaffer, C.G.	150
Monroe Drive In		Monroe 28110	Faw, C.H.	225
New Super Drive In		Monroe 28110	Bundy, D.	298
Bright Leaf Drive In		Mt. Airy 27030	Davis, E.L.	150
Murphy Drive In		Murphy 28906	Henn, P.J.	200
Midway Drive In	P.O. Drawer 1637	New Bern 28560	Parrott, P.G.	225
24 West Drive In		Newport 28570	Aragona, C.	
Brooks Drive In		Pantego 27860	Brooks, John	125
South Drive In		Pelham 27311	Donahue	
Pilot Drive In		Pilot Mountain 27041	Holder, M.N.	160
Center Drive In		Raleigh 27603	Piedmont	450
Forest Drive In	P.O. Box 11295	Raleigh 27604	Consolidate	460
Midway Drive In		Reidsville 27320	Hendrix, W.	450
Gaston Drive In		Roanoke Rapids 27870	Stewart	240
Sundown Drive In		Robersonville 27871	Highsmith, J.	150
Sky Vue Drive In		Rockingham 28379	Whitley, L.J.	
Center		Rocky Mt. 27801	Piedmont	800
Sky-Vue Drive In		Rocky Mt. 27801	Champion, R.	175
Tower Drive In	Box 2664	Rocky Mt. 27801	Piedmont	400
Carolina Drive In		Roxboro 27573	Obriant, R.M.	175
Thunderbird 601 D. I.	P.O. Box 671	Salisbury 28144	Plitt South	400
Starlite Dr. In	Rt. 7	Sanford 27331	Stephenson	
Skyvue Drive In	P.O. Box 1147	Shelby 28150	Mc Clure, B.	270
Sunset Drive In		Shelby 28150	Colonial Th.	300
Siler City Dr. In		Siler City 27344	Curtis, J.W.	190
County Drive In	Rt. 3 Box 323	Smithfield 27577	Howell	250
Star Vue Drive In		Southern Pines 28387	Huntley, C.A.	200
Twin Oaks Drive In		Sparta 28675	Atwood, C.F.	200
Tri County Dr. In		Spruce Pine 28777	Cooper, T.	
I-77 Drive In	1009 Salisbury Rd.	Statesville 28677	Statesville	480
Villa Heights Dr. In	2031 Newton Dr.	Statesville 28677	Stewart	250
Midway Drive In	P.O. Box 541	Thomasville 27360	Consolidate	468
West 74 Drive In		Wadesboro 28174	Tucker, C.	200

Theatre Name	Address	City & Zip	Circuit	Cars
Bel Air Drive In	Box 307	Walkertown 27051	McGee, P.G.	180
Park View Drive In	Rt. 5 Box 243P	Washington 27889	Bateman, T.	350
Smoky Mt. Drive In		Waynesville 28786	Massie, J.E.	270
Waynesville Drive In		Waynesville 28786	Whisenhunt	225
Welcome Drive In		Welcome 27374	Piedmont	175
Starlite Drive In		Whiteville 28472	Burney, C.	172
N. Wilkesboro D. I.	Box 255	Wilkesboro 28659	Statesville	250
Starlite Drive In	P.O. Box 255	Wilkesboro 28697	Statesville	310
Twilite Drive In	Rt. 3 Box 453	Williamston 27802	J. Mobley	205
Oleander Dr. In	P.O. Box 3925	Wilmington 28406	Stewart	175
Skyline Drive In	P.O. Box 3925	Wilmington 28406	Stewart	300
Starway Drive In	P.O. Box 3925	Wilmington 28406	Stewart	400
Starlite Drive In	P.O. Box 3483	Wilson 27893	Champion, R.	275
Flamingo Drive In		Winston Salem 27102	Piedmont	500
Thunderbird Drive In	3774 Konnoak Drive	Winston Salem 27107	Watson, D.	600
Winston Salem Drive In	400 Howell St.	Winston Salem 27106	McGee, P.G.	450

NORTH DAKOTA

Theatre Name	Address	City & Zip	Circuit	Cars
Starlite Drive In	Box 1622	Bismarck 58501	Mid Contin.	395
Sundowner D. I.		Bowman 58623	Svihovec, J.	
Starnite Dr. In		Cavalier 58220	Brandhagen	200
Starlite Drive In		Devils Lake 58301	Mid Contin.	350
Hillcrest Dr. In		Dickinson 58601	Hallwell, F.	400
Lake Vue D. I.		Dickinson 58601	Kosteleski	400
Starlite Drive In	West Acres Shp. Ctr.	Fargo 58102	Cinema Ent.	450
Stardust 17 Dr. In		Grafton 58237	Henricksen	300
Starlite Drive In	Box 208	Grand Forks 58201	Mid Contin.	450
52 Hi Drive In		Harvey 58341	Springer, A.	278
Starnite Drive In		Hatton 58240	Brandhagen	200
Hettinger Dr. In	Route 1	Hettinger 58639	Remington, J.	300
Park Drive In		Jamestown 58401	Ludwig	304
Sunset Dr. In		Langdon 58249	Taillon, L.	200
Linton Dr. In		Linton 58552	Baer, D.	350
Starlite Outdoor		Minot 58701	Carisch	450
Starnite Dr. In		New Rockford 58356	Brandhagen	75
Rugby Drive In		Rugby 53868	Massine, F.	275
Marty's Sky Vu II D. I.		Valley City 58072	Martinson, L.	
Valley Drive In		Velva 58790	Vebeto, W.	200
Valley Drive In		Wahpeton 58075	Cinema Ent.	400
Stardust Drive In	Box 333	Walhalla 58282		
Lake Park Drive In		Williston 58801	Snyder, J.W.	450

OHIO

Theatre Name	Address	City & Zip	Circuit	Cars
Riverside Dr. In	P.O. Box 351	Aberdeen 41056	Ohio Movies	400
Ascot Auto	3409 State Rd.	Akron 44201	Selected	
Ascot Auto 123	3409 State Road	Akron 44201	Selected	450
Gala Drive In	2215 East Waterloo	Akron 44312	Selected	475
Starlight Drive In	Rt. 224 & Emmit Rd.	Akron 44306	Winter & Moon	400
Summit Dr. In	3205 Manchester Rd.	Akron 44319	Skirball	800
Roselawn Auto	Box 279A	Allensburg 45142	Enright, P.	275
Park Auto		Alliance 44601	M.G.H. Mgt.	600
Pymatuning Lake Dr. In	5863 Beach St.	Andover 44003	Leonhard, E.	
Ashland Dr. In	1225 Wooster Rd.	Ashland 44805	Eckard, W.	500
Skyway Dr. In	P.O. Box 1658	Ashtabula 44004	Selected	377
Valley Dr. In	20 So. Court St.	Athens 45701	Geary, B.	400
Magic City Drive In		Barberton 44203	Selected	500
Leatherwood Dr. In	Leatherwood Road	Barnesville 43713	Hall, R.	200
New Drive In	R.R. #3 Ludlow Rd.	Belle Center 43311	Eleman, D.	400
Belpre Open Air Dr. In	P.O. Box 187	Belpre 26101	Jur Theas.	400
Portage Dr. In		Bowling Green 43402	Armstrong	596
Hub Dr. In	P.O. Box 282	Bryan 43506	General The.	400
Tri City Drive In	Box 745	Bucyrus 44820	Martin	
Cadiz Drive In	Rt. #1	Cadiz 43907	Thompson	225
Cruise In	Route #6	Cambridge 43725	General The.	300
Giant Auto		Canton 44730	Selected	600
Indian Trail Dr. I.	Route #2	Carey 43316	Compton, J.	297
Lake Drive In	P.O. Box 270	Celina 45822	Chakeres	475
Valley Drive In	8228 E. Washington	Chagrin Falls 44022	Poroznski	800
Mayfield Road Drive In	12091 Mayfield Road	Chardon 44024	Maisano	350
Tri State Dr. In	Rural Route 1	Chesapeake 45619	Mid States	500
Fiesta Drive In	R.R. 4	Chillicothe 45601	Payne, E.	600
Torch Drive In	Route #4	Chillicothe 45601	Payne, E.	450
Auto In	Anderson Ferry Road	Cincinnati 45238	Selected	500
Dent Auto	6231 Harrison Ave.	Cincinnati 45239	Selected	820
Ferguson Hills Dr. In	2310 Ferguson Road	Cincinnati 45238	Levin Svce.	1,500
Oakley Dr. In	5033 Madison Rd.	Cincinnati 45227	Redstone	950
Twin Drive In Norwood		Cincinnati 45229	Selected	1,300
Twin Drive In Reading		Cincinnati 45229	Selected	
North Auto Dr. In	Route 23 North	Circleville 45601	Bennett	375
Starlight Dr. In		Circleville 45601	Bennett	350
Auto Drive In	11395 Brookpark Road	Cleveland 44130	Sport Servic.	890
Canal Road Drive In	3420 Euclid Hgts. Blvd.	Cleveland 44118	Cinemette	1,000
Cloverleaf D. I.	Granger & Warner Rd.	Cleveland 44102	Lombardo, C.	
Memphis Drive In	3290 Warrensville Rd.	Cleveland 44122	Wintner, P.	1,000
Miles Dr. In	19001 Miles Ave.	Cleveland 44128	Sport Servic.	1,000
Pearl Road Drive In	7591 Pearl Road	Cleveland 44130	Selected	510
Town & Country Dr. In	20 So. Court St.	Coalton 45701	Geary, B.	300
Airport In Outdoor D. I.	645 N. James Rd.	Columbus 43219	Rainbow Ent.	1,000
C.C.C. Dr. In #1	1375 Harrison Pike	Columbus 43223	Rainbow Ent.	500
C.C.C. Dr. In #2	1375 Harrison Pike	Columbus 43223	Rainbow Ent.	
East Main Auto	4750 East Main St.	Columbus 43221	Chakeres	735
Eastside Dr. In	3811 East Main St.	Columbus 43213	Rainbow Ent.	225

Theatre Name	Address	City & Zip	Circuit	Cars
Holiday Auto #1	P.O. Box 28066	Columbus 43228	Chakeres	700
Holiday Auto #2	P.O. Box 28066	Columbus 43228	Chakeres	350
Linden Air Drive In	3168 Westerville Rd.	Columbus 43224	L&H Corp.	500
North Hi Auto 1	P.O. Box 575	Columbus 43085	Chakeres	1,250
North Hi Auto 2	P.O. Box 575	Columbus 43085	Chakeres	625
South Dr. In	3050 S. High St.	Columbus 43207	Rainbow Ent.	750
West Fifth Ave. Dr.	900 W. Fifth Ave.	Columbus 43227	Rainbow Ent.	500
17th Avenue Auto	1770 E. 17th Ave.	Columbus 43219	Academy Th.	800
Riverside Dr. In	P.O. Box 187	Constitution 26101	Jur. Theas.	650
Montrose Drive In	4030 W. Market St.	Copley 44313	Ratener, L.	700
Belmont Auto	2660 County Line Rd.	Dayton 45430	Belmont	868
Captain Kidd Dr. In	111 West First St.	Dayton 45402	Levin Svce.	
Dayton East Drive In	2700 Valley St.	Dayton 45404	Levin Svce.	600
Dixie Dr. In	6201 Dixie Dr.	Dayton 45414	Levin Svce.	865
North Star Dr. In	5601 North Dixie Dr.	Dayton 45414	Parker, E.	900
Salem Drive In	3607 Salem Avenue	Dayton 45406	Levin Svce.	400
Sherwood Twin No. Dr. In	5327 West Third St.	Dayton 45407	Levin Svce.	
Sherwood Twin So. Dr. In	5327 W. Third St.	Dayton 45407	Levin Svce.	500
Southland 75 Drive In	3700 Miamisburg Ctr.	Dayton 45459	Chakeres	1,279
Sunset Cruise I		Dayton 45430	Swaney, W.	400
Defiance Drive In		Defiance 43512	Armstrong	586
Kingman Drive In		Delaware 43015	Yassenoff	
Van Del Drive In	P.O. Box 105	Delphos 45891	Epps, T.	536
Dublin Drive In	4148 W. State Rt. 161	Dublin 43017	Vogel, P.	
East 30 D. I. #2	P.O. Box 1675	East Canton 44730	Auto Cinema	
East 30 Dr. In #1	P.O. Box 1675	East Canton 44730	Auto Cinema	800
Skyview Drive In	3405 Main St.	East Liverpool 26062	Anas Weir	526
Super 30 Dr. In		East Liverpool 43920	Anas Weir	400
East Lake Dr. In	34280 Vine St.	Eastlake 44094	Community	900
Cinema 35 Drive In		Eaton 45320	Turlukis, P.	400
Tower Drive In	2301 Lake Avenue	Elyria 44035	Whiting, H.	464
Melody 49 Dr. In	P.O. Box 218	Englewood 45322	Chakeres	1,280
Skyborn Drive In	P.O. B. 349	Fairborn 45501	Chakeres	480
Acme Auto	6130 Dixie Highway	Fairfield 45014	Holiday Amu.	560
Findlay Dr. In	2224 W. Sandusky Rd.	Findlay 45840	Armstrong	512
Millstream D. I.	606 So. Main Street	Findlay 45840	Stern Enter.	600
Starlight Dr. In	P.O. Box 363	Fostoria 44830	Armstrong	486
Fremont Drive In	2673 E. State St.	Fremont 43420	Sweeney Ent.	510
Galion Drive In 1		Galion 44833	Thompson, H.	
Kanauga Drive In	Box 31	Gallipolis 45631	Wheeler, H.	400
Skyway Dr. In	426 4th St.	Gibsonburg 43420	Binder, J.	300
Ranch Drive In	P.O. Box 7	Greenfield 45123	Teicher	400
Speedway Auto		Greenville 45331	Tabor, J.	325
Holiday Auto	1816 Old Oxford Rd.	Hamilton 45013	Holiday Amu.	485
Valley Drive In	2380 Hamilton Eaton	Hamilton 45015	Holiday Amu.	1,150
Mid-City Drive In	1210 Valley View Rd.	Harrisburg 44720	Alliance	636
Plaza Drive In	646 West Fair	Lancaster 43130	Holiday Amu.	
Skyview Drive In	315 Timberlane N.E.	Lancaster 43130	Crum, C.	460
Old Fort Auto	Rt. 42	Lebanon 45036	Tabor, J.	300
Gloria Drive In	2600 West Elm	Lima 45805	Selected	626
Lima Dr. In	317 W. Market St.	Lima 45805	Selected	453
Sharon Drive In	2600 West Elm Street	Lima 45805	Selected	680
Springbrook Drive In	2600 West Elm	Lima 45805	Selected	604
Hocking Dr. In	Box 509	Logan 43138	Chakeres	400
Lorain Dr. In 2	2620 Cleveland Blvd.	Lorain 44052	Selected	
Lorain Drive In	2620 Cleveland Blvd.	Lorain 44052	Selected	350
Academy Drive In	700 C.C.C. Highway	Loveland 45241	Redstone	700
Highway 28 Drive In	1451 Goshen Pike	Loveland 45140	Holiday Amu.	450
Scioto Breeze Auto	Box 706	Lucasville 45648	Chakeres	350
Skyway Drive In		Malvern	Clement, B.	600
Midway Drive In	3124 Ashland Rd. Rt. 42	Mansfield 44905	Lombardo	514
Springmill Drive In		Mansfield 44906	Sweeney Ent.	622
Sunset Drive In	1155 Laurelwood Rd.	Mansfield 44907	Nusbaum, H.	438
Starlite Drive In	Rt. #7	Marietta 26101	Jur Theas.	750
North Drive In		Marion 43302	Sport Servic.	646
South Dr. In		Marion 43302	Sport Servic.	594
Marysville Dr. I		Marysville 43040	Tabor, J.	300
Highway 42 Drive In	Rt. #42	Mason 45040	McLain, R.	450
Stark Drive In #2		Massillon 44646	Skirball	500
Stark Drive In #1		Massilon 44646	Skirball	1,000
Maumee Drive In#1	1360 North Conant	Maumee 43537	Redstone	772
Maumee Drive In #2	1360 North Canant	Maumee 43537	Redstone	
42 Drive In	2330 Pearl Road	Medina	General The.	600
Mentor Drive In	9160 Mentor Rd.	Mentor 44060	Selected	420
Cruise In Auto		Miamisburg 45342	Parker, E.D.	400
Dixie Cruise In		Middletown 45042	Cox, E.	300
Starglow Drive In		Middletown 45042	Starglow	428
Eastside Drive In		Millbury 43447	Armstrong	402
Mt. Healthy Drive In	6 Monroe Dr.	Mount Healthy 45036	Holiday Amu.	650
Lake Drive In		Mount Orab 45154	Holiday Amu.	300
Knox Auto	P.O. Box 31	Mount Vernon 43050	Strugess, R.	570
Auto Rama Dr. In #1	33395 Lorain Rd.	N. Ridgeville 44035	Sherman, G.	
Auto Rama Dr. In #2	33395 Lorain Rd.	N. Ridgeville 44035	Sherman, G.	500
Trail Dr. In	P.O. Box 147	Napoleon 43545	Armstrong	350
33 Drive In	Rt. 1	Nelsonville 45784	Ohio Movies	155
Park Layne #69 Dr. In		New Carlisle 45344	Chakeres	650
Starlite Dr. In	P.O. Box 579	New Comerstown 43832	Clement, B.	312
Skyline Dr. In		New Lexington 43764	Epifano, Jr., J.	350
Twilight Dr. In	8749 Spankle S.W.	New Phila. 44662	Reding	
Westville Dr. In		New Westville 47374	Kerasotes	450
Heath Auto	P.O. Box 790	Newark 43055	Price	500
Valley Drive In	P.O. Box 790	Newark 43055	Price	350
North Canton Drive In	P.O. Box 2202	North Canton 44720	Selected	538
Midway Drive In		North Kingsvill 44068	Selected	370

559

Theatre Name	Address	City & Zip	Circuit	Cars
Skyway Dr. In		North Madison 44057	Selected	350
Starview Drive In		Norwalk 44857	Steel, S.	520
Carlisle Drive In		Oberlin 44035	Tender	568
Little Flower Dr. In		Ottawa 45875	Martin	
Mound Drive In		Peebles 45660	Enright, P.	280
Piqua 36 Dr. In	P.O. Box 909	Piqua 45356	Chakeres	300
Plymouth Dr In	P.O. Box 181	Plymouth 44865	Martin, O.	380
Ottawa Dr. In		Port Clinton 43452	Armstrong	338
Sunset Drive In		Portsmouth 45662	Lutes, G.	275
Midway Dr. In		Ravenna 44266	Vogel, P.	598
Riverside D. I.		Rayland 43943	Gardner, J.	400
40 East D/I #2	8659 E. Main St.	Reynoldsburg 43068	Rainbow Ent.	
40 East Dr. In	8659 E. Main St.	Reynoldsburg 43068	Rainbow Ent.	400
Starlite Drive In		Saint Henry 45883	Jones, M.	300
Salem Drive In		Salem 44460	Vogel, P.	494
Sandusky D. I.	P.O. Box 550	Sandusky 44870	Seitz	584
Auto-Vue Drive In	P.O. Box 92	Sidney 45365	Negelspach	450
Skyway Drive In	U.S. Rt. #22 R.R. #7	So. Zanesville 43701	Selected	350
Starlite Auto		South Point 45680	Hyman, E.	400
Midway Drive In		Spencerville 45887	Heaton, C.	
Melody Cruise I		Springfield 45502	Chakeres	300
New Moon Drive In		Springfield 45502	Levin Svce.	350
Showboat Drive In	3950 E. National Rd.	Springfield 45501	Parker, E.	500
Stardust Drive In		Springfield 45506	Levin Svce.	300
70 40 Drive In		St. Clairsville 43950	Tally	458
Midway Dr. In		St. Marys 45887	Enright, P.	
Lynn Auto	Route #1	Strasburg 44680	Reding, R.	225
East Dr. In		Tallmadge 44278	General The	700
Tiffin Drive In		Tiffin 44883	General The	476
Jesse James Drive In		Toledo 43615	Armstrong	1,100
Miracle Mile Dr. In 1 & 2		Toledo 43612	Redstone	1,800
Parkside Drive In	4540 Navarre Ave.	Toledo 43616	Armstrong	500
Telegraph Dr. In	Telegraph & Alexis	Toledo 43612	Armstrong	692
Troy Dixie Drive In		Troy 45373	Chakeres	465
Champaign Auto		Urbana 43078	Enright, P.	410
Ridgeway Dr. In	P.O. Box 105	Van Wert 45869	Epps, T.	442
Blue Sky Drive In		Wadsworth 44281	Selected	428
Elm Road Dr. In #1	1895 Elm Road	Warren 44446	Hreno, M.	600
Elm Road Dr. In #2	1895 Elm Road	Warren 44483	Hreno, M.	
Howland Drive In		Warren 44483	Youngstown	520
Skyway Drive In	1805 N. Leavitt Road	Warren 44485	Doane, S.	350
Super 45 Drive In	974 Todd S.W.	Warren 44485	Frankie, J.	250
3 C.S. Drive In		Washington Ch. 43160	Chakeres	400
Star Auto	720 Spruce St.	Wauseon 43567	Wyse, R.	250
Atomic Dr. In	R.R. #4	Waverly 45601	Payne, E.	400
Millers Grove D. I.	11923 Frederick	West Milton 45321	Miller, D.	350
Sunset Drive In		West Union 45693	Enright, P.	250
Skyline Outdoor		Westrichfield 44109	Scheab	980
Johnda Lou Dr. In		Wheelersburg 45694	Carey, J.	500
Euclid Auto	28737 Euclid Avenue	Wickliffe 44092	Selected	800
Drive In	P.O. Box 431	Wilmington 45177	Chakeres	450
Winter Dr. In #1	Route 43	Wintersville 43952	Skirball	1,000
Winter Dr. In #2	Route 43	Wintersville 43952	Skirball	
Skyline Drive In		Wooster 44691	Selected	275
North Xenia Drive In	35 Greene St.	Xenia 45385	Chakeres	450
Northside Drive In	795 Southern Pkmall.	Youngstown 44512	Youngstown	630
Ski Hi Drive In	U.S. Rt. #422	Youngstown 44512	Youngstown	874
Southside Drive In		Youngstown Ohio 44503	Youngstown	598
Westside Drive In		Youngstown 44505	Youngstown	609
Maple Drive In	2800 Maple Ave.	Zanesville 43701	Selected	500

OKLAHOMA

Theatre Name	Address	City & Zip	Circuit	Cars
Oakhills Drive In		Ada 74820	Video Indep.	500
Altus Drive In		Altus 73521	Video Indep.	500
Stadium D. I.		Alva 73717	Jones, J.C.	300
Kiamichi Drive In		Antlers 74523	Cooper, J.N.	200
Skyview Drive In	Box 1902	Ardmore 73401	Video Indep.	300
Choctaw Drive In		Atoka 74525	Watson, C.	
Hilltop Drive In		Bartlesville 74003	Video Indep.	400
Pioneer Dr. In		Blackwell 74631	Video	
51 Drive In		Broken Arrow 74012	Stevens, B.H.	200
Sage Drive In		Broken Bow 74728	Silva, P.	
69 Drive In		Checotah 74426	Crumpler, G.	100
Chief Drive In		Chickasha 73018	Video Indep.	400
Roger Dr. In		Claremore 74017	Video	
B L B Drive In		Clayton 74536	Padgett, B.E.	200
Cleveland Dr. In	409 E. Delaware St.	Cleveland 74020	Woodall	
Clinton Drive In		Clinton 73601	Video Indep.	200
Sundown Drive In		Cushing 74023	Video Indep.	300
Duncan Drive In		Duncan 73533	Video Indep.	500
Ship Drive In	Box 711	Durant 74701	Hamm, V.	400
Woodstock Drive In		Edmond 73034	Roupe, E.	200
Squaw Drive In		El Reno 73036	Video Indep.	200
66 Drive In		Elk City 73644	Video Indep.	300
Enid Drive In		Enid 73701	Video Indep.	600
Trail Drive In		Enid 73701	Video Indep.	500
Beacon Drive In		Guthrie 73044	Video Indep.	300
Corral Drive In		Guymon 73942	Mahaney, E.	200
Derrick Drive In	407 W. Main	Healdton 73438	Thompson, R.	200
Lynn Family Dr. In	P.O. Box 427	Hollis 73550	Lynn Teeter	200
Circus Dr. In		Hugo 74743	Boucher, J.	
Rancho Drive In		Idabel 74745	Gore, J.	300
Hankins Drive In		Lawton 73501	Hamm, V.E.	300

Theatre Name	Address	City & Zip	Circuit	Cars
82nd Street D/I #1&2		Lawton 73501	Video Indep.	964
Hillcrest Dr. In		Lindsay 73052	Wolfenbarge	300
Capital Drive In	P.O. Box 641	Mangum 73554	McConnel, J.	200
Cinema 69 Drive In		McAlester 74501	U.A. Theas.	
Carlton Drive In		McAlester 74501	Weaver, C.	400
Hiway 270 Drive In		McAlester 74501	U.A. Theas.	400
Sooner Drive In		Miami 74354	Video Indep.	
Rancho Drive In		Norman 73069	Video Indep.	300
Sky Vue Drive In		Nowata 74048	Woodall, L.	240
Jewel Drive In		Okemah 74859	Banks, C.	800
Cinema 70 Drive In	P.O. Box 1341	Oklahoma City 73107	Shanbour, G.	400
Skyview Drive In	1133 No. W. 23rd. St.	Oklahoma City 73106	Caporl, C.	
Sooner Twin Drive In	S.E. 29th & Sooner	Oklahoma City 73110	Commonwealt.	900
Sooner Twin West D/I	S.E. 29th Sooner	Oklahoma City 73110	Commonwealt.	
Winchester Dr. In	6900 South Westn.	Oklahoma City 73109	Shanbour, G.	
14 Flags Drive In	9901 South Western	Oklahoma City 73139	Grube, G.	
Tower Drive In		Okmulgee 74447	Video Indep.	300
Brewer S. Drive In		Pauls Valley 73075	Brewer, L.E.	500
Corral Drive In		Pawhuska 74056	Video Indep.	300
Lakeside Drive In		Pawnee 74058	McCray, P.	
Airline Drive In		Ponca City 74601	Video Indep.	400
Pryor Drive In		Pryor 74361	Townsend, C.	
Tee Pee Drive In		Sapulpa 74066	Video Indep.	300
Skyway Drive In		Seminole 74868	Video Indep.	400
Starlite Drive In		Shawnee 74801	Video Indep.	
Sunset Drive In	Rt. 2 Box 42 A.C.	Spiro 74959	Burdick	160
Medo Drive In		Stigler 74462	Roye	200
East 6th Drive In	H.	Stillwater 74074	Video Indep.	400
North 177 Dr. In		Stillwater 74074	Video Indep.	300
Tahlequah Drive In		Tahlequah 74464	Archer, J.D.	200
Westside Drive In	131 Water Street	Tahlequah 74464	Gourley, D.	200
Admiral 1&2 Dr. In	7355 E. Easton St.	Tulsa 74115	Westoutdoor	1,200
Airview Drive In		Tulsa 74101	Video Indep.	600
Apache Drive In		Tulsa 74101	Snyder, L.E.	200
Capri Drive In	P.O. Box 2653	Tulsa 74101	Family Thea.	
Riverside Drive In		Tulsa 74101	Video Indep.	600
11th Street Drive In		Tulsa 74101	Video Indep.	500
Lariat Drive In		Vinita 74301	Video Indep.	300
Okla Drive In		Walters 73572	Hall, L.	200
Watonga Drive In		Watonga 73772	Terry, N.	200
40 West Drive In		Weatherford 73096	Sylvester, W.	
Terrytime Drive In		Woodward 73801	Terry, D.V.	300
Little River Drive In		Wright City 74766	Crosby, B.	100
Corral Drive In	Route #2	Wynnewood 73098	Smith, J.	

OREGON

Theatre Name	Address	City & Zip	Circuit	Cars
Albany Drive In	Box 579	Albany 97321	Adamson The.	350
Lithia Drive In	P.O. Box #430	Ashland 97520	Putney, J.F.	400
Old Trail Dr. In	Box 210 Rt. #1	Baker 97814	Voeller, R.	
Canyon Drive In		Beaverton 97005	Adamson, A.W.	350
Reds Drive In	Rte. 2 Box 54	Brookings 97415	Thomas, L.	167
Sundown Dr. In	68 Broadway	Burns 97720	Elliott	
Frontier Drive In	P.O. Box 331	Cave Junction 97523	Musil, L.	300
Motor Vu Drive In		Coos Bay 97420	McSwain	500
Carvue Drive In		Cornelius 97330	Moyer, T.	425
Midway Drive In	5995 N.E. Hwy. 20	Corvallis 97330	Adamson, A.W.	350
Corral Drive In	78035 So. 6th	Cottage Grove 97424	Atchley	
Motor Vue Drive In	P.O. Box 538	Dallas 97338	Wernli, D.E.	350
Eugene D/I % Valley Rv.	1077 Valley River Way	Eugene 97401	Moyer, L.	650
Eugene Drive In #3	1077 Valley River Way	Eugene 97401	Moyer, L.	
North End D/I	4720 Dove Lane	Eugene 97402	Moyer, T.	
West 11th Dr. In #1	1077 Valley River Way	Eugene 97401	Moyer, L.	785
Rhododenron Dr. In	P.O. Box 772	Florence 97439	Hick	350
Redwood Drive In	P.O. Box 110	Grants Pass 97526	Mangel	412
Trail Outdoor	Box 358	Hood River 97031	McSwain, B.	400
Grant County D. I.	Box 288	John Day 97845	Elliott, D.	300
Shasta Drive In 1 2 3	P.O. Box 1480	Klamath Falls 97601	Redwood	600
La Grande Dr. In	P.O. Box 771	La Grande 97850	Western Amu.	350
Lebanon Motor Vu Dr. In	190 Cascade Drive	Lebanon 97355	Hermanson, C.	309
Yaquina Drive In	P.O. Box 226	Lincoln City 97367	Worlein, W.	
K & D Drive In	P.O. Box I	Madras 97741	Paplia, A.	300
Starlite Drive In	P.O. Box 1067	Medford 97501	Maestri	600
M-F Drive In	225 Cherry St.	Milton Freewater 97862	Spiess, L.	375
99 West Drive In		Newburg 97132	Francis, J. &	325
Pay Ont Drive In	Box #711	Ontario 97914	Voeller, R.	500
Oregon City Dr. In	11841 So. Partlow Rd.	Oregon City 97045	Larson, J.	400
Roundup Dr. In	Box 561	Pendleton 97801	Spiess, L.	312
Amphitheatre Dr. In		Portland 97211	Moyer, T.	500
Foster Road Dr. In 1	11501 Foster Road	Portland 97206	Moyer, T.	1,800
Foster Road Dr. In 2	11501 S.E. Foster Rd.	Portland 97206	Moyer, T.	
Foster Road Dr. In 3	11501 S.E. Foster Rd.	Portland 97206	Moyer, T.	
Powell Blvd. Dr. In	112th & Powell Blvd.	Portland 97266	Moyer, L.	
Super 99 Dr. In		Portland 97222	Moyer, T.	500
104th St. Drive In		Portland 97216	Moyer, L.	
82nd St. Drive In	9600 S.E. 82nd Ave.	Portland 97266	Moyer, L.	600
Tri City Dr. In	P.O. Box 71	Riddle 97469	Love, W.E.	509
Pine Motor Dr. In	P.O. Box#1066	Roseburg 97470	Hemmilla, E.	316
Roseburg Starlite D. I.	Box 400 Grant Smith Rd.	Roseburg 97470	Bates, W.	800
North Salem Dr. In	6242 Portland Rd.	Salem 97303	Moyer, T.	
South Salem Dr. In #1	365 Lancaster Dr. S.E.	Salem 97301	Moyer, T.	
South Salem Dr. In #2	365 Lancaster Dr. S.E.	Salem 97301	Moyer, T.	
South Salem Dr. In #3	365 Lancaster Dr. S.E.	Salem 97301	Moyer, T.	
Cascade Drive In	Box 208	Springfield 97477	Western Amu.	600

Theatre Name	Address	City & Zip	Circuit	Cars
Motor Vue Drive In		Springfield 97477	Moyer, T.	
Cloverleaf Dr. In	Box 428	Sutherlin 97479	L & J Grauf	.350
Santiam Dr. In	1242 47th Ave.	Sweethome 97386	Hermansen	.200
Starlite Drive In		The Dalles 97058	Foster Brot.	.350
The Dalles Drive In	P.O. Box 886	The Dalles 97058	Sterling Th.	.308
Family Drive In #1	11626 S.W. Pacific Hwy.	Tigard 97223	Moyer, T.	.450
Family Drive In #2	11626 S.W. Pacific Hwy.	Tigard 97223	Moyer, T.	
Grove Drive In	203 Jefferson St.	Umatilla 97882	Mor Grove	
Woodburn Dr. In		Woodburn 97071	Stitt, L.	.350

PENNSYLVANIA

Theatre Name	Address	City & Zip	Circuit	Cars
Boulevard Drive In	556 Union Blvd.	Allentown 18103	U.A. Theas.	.600
Altoona D. I.		Altoona 16601	Blatt Bros.	.500
Super 220 D. I.		Altoona 16601	Neff, R.	.500
Andalusia Drive In	724 Bristol Pike	Andalusia 19020	Hellman, N.	.400
A.B.C. D. I.	Rt. 65	Baden 15005	Westoutdoor	.600
Tusca Drive In		Beaver 15009	Geibel, W.J.	.500
Spotlight 88 Dr. In		Beaver Falls 15010	Felton, Dave	.300
Super 51 Dr. In		Beaver Falls 15010	Monessen Am.	.500
Moonlite Dr. In	R.D. #1	Beford 15522	Hickes, T.	.500
Super 71 B. Dr. In		Belle Vernon 15012	Castelli	.300
Super 71 A. Dr. In		Belle Vernon 15012	Castelli, V.	.700
Motor View Dr. In		Berwick 18603	Sacco, F.	.500
Moonlight D. I.		Brookville 15825	Neff, R.	.300
Tri State Dr. In		Burgettstown 15021	Mungello	
Pioneer Dr. In		Butler 16001	Cinemette	.600
Skyway Drive In		Butler 16001	Cinemette	.300
Bethlehem Drive In	Easton Avenue	Butztown 18017	Redstone	.800
Camp Horne D. I.		Camp Horn 15202	Cinemette	.500
Skyview Drive In		Carmichaels 15320	Cinemette	.400
Hiway Drive In		Carrolton 15722	Cinemette	.500
Sunset Drive In	R.D. #2	Chambersburg 17201	Kagan, H.	.500
Chicora Drive In		Chicora 16025	Summerville	
Maple Drive In		Circleville 15642	Cinemette	.700
Midway Drive In		Clarion 16214	De Marsh	.200
Super 322 Dr. In		Clearfield 16830	Favuzza	.500
Family Drive In	713 E. Baltimore Ave.	Clifton Hgts. 19018	Budco	.700
Columbia Dr. In	Lincoln Highway	Columbia 17512	Weinstock, L.	
Lakeside Dr. In	R.E. #1	Conneaut Lk. #2 16316	Cinemette	.400
Comet Drive In		Connellsville 15425	Monessen, A.M.	
Comet Drive In		Connellsville 15425	Monessen, A.M.	.425
Ridge Pike Drive In	Ridge Pk. & Colwell Rd.	Conshohocken 19428	Budco	.500
Dependable Drive In		Coraopolis 15108	Glaus, R.	.500
Kenmawr Drive In	15 Evelyn Drive	Coraopolis 15108	Lambros, L.	.500
Corry Drive In		Corry 16407	Blatt Bros.	.300
Ski Hi Drive In		Cranberry 16319	Cinemette	.300
Dallas Drive In	Route 309	Dallas 18612	Fox, R.	.500
Haars Drive In	R.D. 3	Dillsburg 17019	Harr, V.	.500
Hazleton Drive In	Rt. 309 Butler Twsp.	Drums 18222	Morgan, J.	.550
Hiway D. I.		Dubois 15801	Stern, Hanna	
Blatt 764 #2 Drive In	R.D. #2	Duncansville 16635	Blatt Bros.	.774
Blatt 764 #1 Drive In	R.D. #2	Duncansville 16635	Blatt Bros.	
Comerford Dr. In	Route #315	Dupont 18641	Sport Servic.	.500
Greater Pgh. Dr. In		E. McKeesport 15035	Warre, E.	
East Stroudsburg Dr. In		E. Stroudsburg 18301	Hulst, J.	.800
Blue Dell D. I.		East McKeesport 15035	Cinemette	.600
Starlite Dr. In	Freemansburg Hiway	Easton 18042	Redstone	.800
Blue Sky Drive In		Ellwood City 16117	Affeltrange	.300
Shimmerville Dr. In		Emmaus 18049	Bruno, J.	
Lakeview Drive In		Erie 16501	Blatt Bros.	.400
Peninsula #1 Drive In		Erie 16505	Cinemette	.400
Peninsula #2 Drive In		Erie 16505	Cinemette	.400
Skyway Drive In		Erie 16505	Clement, B.	.500
Star Drive In		Erie 16505	Blatt Bros.	.700
Exton Drive In	Route 30 and 100	Exton 19341	Budco	.500
Midvalley Dr. In	Route #6	Eynon 18418	Sport Servic.	.900
U.S. #1&2 North Dr. In	Rt. 1 Near Old Blvd.	Fairless Hills 19030	Sameric	.900
Super 66 Drive In	Box 266	Ford City 16226	Searao, R.	
Hiway Drive In		Frackville 197970	Heinback, M.	.500
Popular Dr. In		Freeland 18224	Lazo, J.	.200
Trail Drive In	R.D. #1 Rt. #11	Glen Rock 17327	Carey, J.	.200
Skyview Drive In		Gratz 17030	Trautman, M.	.200
Rustic Drive In	R.D. #8	Greensburg 15601	Cinemette	.400
White Beauty Dr. In		Greentown 18426	Guccini, R.	.500
Larkfield Dr. In		Grove City 16127	Cinemette	.300
Halifax Drive In		Halifax 17032	Trautman, M.	.300
Harrisburg Drive In	6001 Allentown Blvd.	Harrisburg 17112	U.A. Theas.	.600
Keystone Drive In	3800 Paxton St.	Harrisburg 17110	Sameric	.700
Laurel Drive In	R.D. 1	Hazleton 18201	Sacco, F.	.500
Maple Dr. In	Route 6	Honesdale 18431	Del Fino, M.	.300
Nu Way Drive In	Rt. 11 & 15 Monroe Twp.	Hummels Wharf 17831	Sport Servic.	.600
Garden Drive In	Rt. 2	Hunlocks Creek 18621	Cragle, A.	.300
Huntingdon Drive In		Huntingdon 16652	Wilson Circ.	.300
Penn Lincoln Drive In		Imperial 15126	Cinemette	.400
Palace Dr. In		Indiana 15701	Kerzan, H.	.300
Super 422 Dr. In		Indiana 15701	Monessen, A.M.	.400
Colonial D. I.		Jefferson Twp. 15025	Cinemette	.700
Family Drive In		Kane 16735	Brown	.300
Westside Drive In	P.O. Box 1003	Kingston 18704	Sport Servic.	.700
Community D. I.		Kittanning 16201	Searao, R.	.500
Super Skyway Drive In		Kuhnsville 18104	Schlanger	
Comet Drive In	By Pass 230	Lancaster 17602	Chertcoff	.600

562

Theatre Name	Address	City & Zip	Circuit	Cars
Skyview Drive In	Lincoln Hwy. East	Lancaster 17602	Chertcoff	800
Roosevelt Drive In	Rt. U.S. 1 Middletown Tp.	Langhorne 19047	Fox, M.	500
Echo D. I.		Large 15025	Cinemette	700
Hiway Drive In		Latrobe 15650	Monessen, A.M.	600
Lawrence Park D/I		Lawrence Park 15055	Blatt Bros.	500
Key Drive In	P.O. Box 74	Lebanon 17042	Weber, J.	500
Mahoning Valley Dr.	Box 23	Lehighton 18235	Morgan, J.	
Silvermoon Dr. In	Rt. 15	Lewisburg 17837	Lewis, F.	
Midway Dr. In	P.O. Box 407	Mahoning Valley Dr. In	Royer, F.	
Burnham Dr. In	Logan Blvd.	Lewistown 17044	Royer, F.	600
Fair Grounds Drive In	Brownsville Road	Library 15236	Cinemette	600
Port Drive In	R.D. #1	Linden 17744	Sports Svce.	400
Park Drive In	232 East Main St.	Lock Haven 17745	Park Dr. In	500
222 Drive In		Maiden Creek 17055	Witmer, D.	
Strinestown Drive In	R.D.1	Manchester 17345	Witmer, R.	200
Tri State Drive In	P.O. Box 237	Matamoras 18336	Hulst, I.	300
Airway Dr. In		Meadville 16335	Sherry, J.	
Hilltop Drive In		Monongahela 15063	Monessen, A.M.	200
Morrisville Drive In	Trenton Avenue	Morrisville 19067	Budco	300
Silver Springs Dr. In		Mt. Holly Spring 17065	Jones, R.J.	
Family Drive In		Mundys Corner 15943	County Amus.	575
Miracle Mile D.		Murraysville 15146	Cinemette	600
Natalie Drive In		Natalie 17854	Trautman, M.	500
Sunset View Dr. In		Natrona Heights 15165	Cinemette	400
Bucks County Drive In	401 Easton Road	Neshaminy 18976	Budco	
Skyline Drive In	1707 Wilmington Rd.	New Castle 16105	Cinemette	400
Shore Drive In	Harrisburg Airport	New Cumberland 17070	Freistak, F.	300
Family D. I.		New Kensington 15068	Cinemette	500
Gateway Drive In	Box 483	New Kensington 15068	Vogel, A.	500
Crosskey's Drive In		New Oxford 17350	Fox, R.	300
Cumberland Drive In	Route 1	Newville 17241	Mowery, D.	300
Point Drive In	R.D. #1 Box 334G	Northumberland 17857	Sports Ser.	
Shankweiler Dr. In	R.D. #1	Orefield 18069	Malkames, R.	
Deer Lake Drive In		Orwigsburg 17961	Fox, R.	600
61st Street Drive In	3201 So. 61st Street	Philadelphia 19151	Budco	
Ardmore D. I.		Pittsburgh 15221	Cinemette	700
Northside D. I.		Pittsburgh 15212	Cinemette	700
South Hills Drive In		Pittsburgh 15216	Warren, E.	500
South Park D. I.		Pittsburgh 15102	Cinemette	400
Bar Ann Dr. In		Portage 15946	Wasko, G.	
Roulette Drive In		Roulette 16746	Brown	300
Hiway Drive In	1788 East Ridge Pike	Royersford 19468	Budco	600
Valley Drive In		Sayre 18840	Foster, J.	400
Evergreen Dr. In		Scottsdale 15683	Michael, H.	
Circle Drive In	Carbondale Highway	Scranton 18511	Delfino, M.J.	600
Brookside D. I.	R.D. #4 Box 92	Sewickley 15143	Marr, E.	300
Hickory Drive In		Sharon 16148	Lambros, L.	600
Sinking Spring Drive In		Sinking Spring 19608	Fox, N.	900
Moonlite Drive In		Smithfield 15478	Monessen, A.M.	600
309 Drive In 1 & 2	P.O. Box 255	Springhouse 19477	Budco	300
Fairvie Drive In		St. Marys 15857	Blatt Bros.	
Starlite D. I.		State College 16801	Royer, F.	500
Temple Drive In		State College 16801	Edsdiscount	500
State Line Drive In	Hagerstown Route	State Line 17263	Cohen, I.	
Valley Drive In	R.D. 2	Tamaque 18252	Petrole, J.	500
Reading Drive In	P.O. Box 408	Temple 19560	Fox, R.	800
Auto Drive In	R.D. #3	Titusville 16354	Neff, R.	400
Reynolds Drive In		Transfer 16154	Cinemette	400
Lincoln Drive In	Roosevelt & City Line	Trevose 19040	Hellman, N.	800
Starlite Drive In		Tunkhannock 18657	Sand, M.	200
Starlite Dr. In		Uniontown 15401	Monessen, A.M.	
Starlite Dr. In	23 Montview	Uniontown 15401	Laskey, M.J.	600
Woodland Drive In		Vandergrift 15690	Monessen, A.M.	400
Malden Dr. In	300 Old National Rd.	W. Brownsville 15418	Shashura, A.	
Super 18 D. I.		Wampum 16157	Fontanella	400
Whiteway Drive In		Warren 16365	Blatt	500
Mt. Lebanon #1 D.		Washington 15301	Cinemette	800
Mt. Lebanon #2 D.		Washington 15301	Cinemette	800
Route 19 D. I.		Washington 15301	Cinemette	800
Waynesburg Drive In		Waynesburg 15370	Cinemette	
Y Drive In	R.D. #3	Wellsboro 16901	Dunham, R.	200
202 Drive In	5 miles West of	West Chester 19380	Budco	300
Moonlite Dr. In	1190 Shoemaker Ave.	West Wyo. 18644	Rizzo, J.	400
Starlite D. I.		Wexford 15090	Nash, J.	500
Wilkes Barre Drive In	Ashley By Pass	Wilkes Barre 18702	Scavo, F.	516
Pike Drive In	R.D. #1 Montgomery	Williamsport 17752	Sports Svce.	600
Silver Drive In		Windber 15963	County Amus.	400
Wysox Drive In		Wysox 18854	Buffington	300
Lincoln Drive In	Route 30	York 17364	Budco	500
Stoneybrook Drive In	3690 Market St. E.	York 17402	Budco	

RHODE ISLAND

Cranston Auto	1400 Oaklawn Ave.	Cranston 02920	Erinakes, S.	700
Hilltop Drive In		East Greenwich 02818	Erinakes	500
Lonsdale Twin Dr. In		Lonsdale 02864	Erinakes, S.	1,670
Starlight Newport D. I.		Newport 02840	Erinakos	700
Rustic Drive In		No. Smithfield 02876	Hallmark	500
Ponta Del Gada Drive In		No. Tiverton 02878	Fall Riv. Th.	750
Quonset Drive In		North Kingston 02852	Stanzler, J.	700
Prov. Pawt. Dr. In	Box 6391	Providence 02904	E.M. Loews	700
Westerly Drive In	Post Road	Westerly 02891	Hochberg	500

Theatre Name	Address	City & Zip	Circuit	Cars
		SOUTH CAROLINA		
Fox Drive In	P.O. Box 408	Anderson 29621	Bolt, C.	300
Skyway Drive In	Box 408	Anderson 29622	Bolt, C.	300
Viking Outdoor Cinema	P.O. Box 408	Anderson 29621	Bolt, C.	350
South Hill Drive In	Allendale Hiway.	Barnwell 29821	Kerr, H.	225
Plaza 21 Drive In		Beaufort 29902	Trask, P.	300
By Pass Drive In		Bennettsville 29512	Coan, G.	250
Gateway Drive In	Box 10084 Riv. Annex	Charleston 29411	Consolidate	1,200
North 52 Drive In	P.O. Box 10064	Charleston 29411	Consolidate	400
Port Drive In	5300 Rivers St.	Charleston 24405	Piedmont	800
Chester Drive In		Chester 29706	Bagley, J.	240
York Clover Drive In	Route #3 Bx. 149A	Clover 29710	Cabe, T.	184
Alice Drive In		Columbia 29203	Shealy, J.C.	300
Beltline Drive In	1301 Sunset Drive	Columbia 29203	Burts, C.S.	300
North #1 Drive In	8757 Two Notch Rd.	Columbia 29206	Daghestani	450
Skyway Drive In	Box 5191	Columbia 29202	Koochagian	244
Sunset Drive In		Columbia 29201	Schrader, R.	462
Terrace D. I.		Columbia 29203	Shealy, J.	300
Twilite Drive In	3800 Two Notch Rd.	Columbia 29204	Warren, J.	300
301 Drive In	Care Post Office	Dillon 29536	Sanderson, P.	216
Palmetto Drive In		Florence 29501	Smith H.	300
Carolina Drive In		Georgetown 29440	Lowry, F.	
Augusta Rd. Drive In	Box 8223 A.	Greenville 29602	Consolidate	480
Cedar Lane Dr. In	Cedar Lane Rd.	Greenville 29611	Piedmont	400
White Horse Drive In	4131 Whitehorse Road	Greenville 29601	Exhibitors	350
Auto Drive In		Greenwood 29646	Zouras, P.	150
Greer Drive In	P.O. Box 153	Greer 29651	McManus, H.P.	175
Terrace View Drive In		Hartsville 29950	Kerr, H.	225
Moonlite Drive In	19 F Street	Inman 29349	Littlefield	
East Main Drive In	Rte. 4 Martha Law Dr.	Lake City 29560	Funk, W.S.	230
Motor In Drive In	P.O. Box 428	Lancaster 29720	Hyatt, J.S.	180
Eppron D. I.	P.O. Box 1013	Laurens 29360	Barbosa, R.	186
No. 1 Drive In		Lexington 29072	Ray, G.	220
Monetta Drive In		Monetta 29105	Warren, J.	210
Swamp Fox Dr. In	P.O. Box 937	Monks Corner 29461	Consolidate	200
Clover Leaf Drive In		Newberry 29108	Exhibitors	270
Hilltop Drive In		North Augusta 29841	Georgia The.	600
Orangeburg Drive In		Orangeburg 29115	Tarlton, F.	150
Fort Roc Drive In		Rock Hill 29731	Jeffries, R.	279
Fox Drive In		Seneca 29678	Osteen, H.	300
Camelot Dr. In	P.O. Box 4845	Spartanburg 29303	Watson, D.	300
Circle So. 29 Drive In	P.O. Box 1251	Spartanburg 29301	Piedmont	350
Pine St. Extension D. I.		Spartanburg 29302	Belmont, N.	300
Thunderbird Dr. In	P.O. Box 4565	Spartanburg 29303	Consolidate	540
West View D. I.	P.O. Box 1587	Spartanburg 29301	Piedmont	350
New Skyvue Drive In		Sumter 29150	Martin	400
Sunset Drive In		Union 29379	Coan, G.	
Walterboro Drive In		Walterboro 29488	Gibson, R.	80
		SOUTH DAKOTA		
Starlite Drive In		Aberdeen 57401	Mid Contin.	390
Kling Drive In		Belle Fourche 57717	Kling, H.	308
Sioux Drive In		Brookings 57006	Peterson, D.	400
Western Drive In		Chamberlain 57325	Sorenson, S.	
Harney		Custer 57730	Johnson, R.	350
Atomic Drive In		Edgemont 57735	Calland, C.	225
Rainbow Dr. In		Gettysburg 57442	Bowden, S.	300
Hilltop Drive In		Gregory 57533	Bradshaw, C.	300
Starlite Drive In	P.O. Box 930	Huron 57350	Logan, J.	350
Fort Randall Drive In		Lake Andes 57356	Durkam	250
Mile Hi Drive In	P.O. Box 697	Lead 57754	Steele, L.	290
Whitetail Dr. In		Lemmon 57638	Svihovec	300
Madison Drive In		Madison 57042	Tentelino	300
Defea Dr. In		Milbank 57252	De Fea, J.	125
Midway Drive In		Miller 57362	Schweigerdt	270
Starlite Outdoor		Mitchell 57301	Logan, J.	400
Pheasant Dr. In		Mobridge 57601	Maier, R.	350
Sioux Dr. In		Pierre 57501	Peterson, D.	400
Pines Drive In	P.O. Box 1460	Rapid City 57709	Commonwealt.	850
Sioux Drive In	P.O. Box 1460	Rapid City 57709	Commonwealt.	350
Starlight Drive In		Rapid City 57701	Commonwealt.	500
Pheasant Drive In	625 East Third St.	Redfield 57469	Gallup	342
East Park Dr. In		Sioux Falls 57105	Mid Contin.	400
Starlite Drive In		Sioux Falls 57105	Mid Contin.	450
Siskota Drive In		Sisseton 57262	Nathem, L.	200
Hills Drive In		Spearfish 57783	Steele, L.	350
Ski Hi Drive In	P.O. Box 11	Tyndall 57066	Metzger, F.E.	250
East Park Drive In		Watertown 57201	Carisch	400
Pix Drive In	P.O. Box 248	Winner 57580	Cmetzger, R.	275
Yankton Drive In		Yankton 57078	Commonwealt.	300
		TENNESSEE		
Lakemont Drive In	Box 5	Alcoa 37701	Lakemont	300
Beacon D. I.	P.O.B. 747	Bristol 37620	Leonard, A.	
Twin City Dr. In	2512 Volunteer Pkway.	Bristol 37620	Warden, D.	
Midway Drive In		Camden 38320	Scott, D.	230
Green Hills Drive In	Box 39	Carthage 37030	Harper, J.	
Bel Air Drive In		Centerville 37033	Warren, W.	200
Marbro Drive In	6055 Lee Highway	Chattanooga 37421	Martin	500
23rd Street Drive In	1600 East 23rd St.	Chattanooga 37404	Martin	500
Moonlit Drive In		Clarksville 37040	Oak Grove	300

Theatre Name	Address	City & Zip	Circuit	Cars
Starvue Drive In		Cleveland 37312	Benton, C.H.	.400
Sundown Drive In	Box 444	Columbia 38401	Vinson, H.P.	.500
Putnam Drive In		Cookeville 38501	Highland En.	.300
Raco Drive In		Covington 38019	Ruffin Amus.	.400
Mack	P.O. Box 77	Cumberland Gap 37724	McClanahan	
Rhea Drive In		Dayton 37321	Mid Tenn. Am.	.200
Broadway Drive In	209 Cullom Ave.	Dickson 37055	Armstrong	.240
Lebanon Drive In	2607 Lebanon Rd.	Donelson 37214	Martin	.500
Dunlap Drive In	Box 178	Dunlap 37327	Boston, L.	.200
Marbro Drive In		Dyersburg 38024	Martin	.400
Stateline Drive In	Box 466 Zip 37643	Elizabethton 37643	Glover, R.	.200
Holiday Drive In		Erwin 37650	Hendren, J.	
Midway Drive In	P.O. Box 348	Etowah 37331	Catlin, W.R.	.300
64 Drive In		Fayetteville 37334	Dyer, J.	
Sumner Drive In		Gallatin 37066	Smith, H.	.400
Ashway Drive In	Asheville Highway	Greenville 37743	Martin	.300
Sunset Drive In		Gruetli 37339	Hicks, G.	.200
Midtown Drive In	Highway 70 Rte. 1	Harriman 37748	Martin	.300
Colonial Twin D/I 1&2	Gallatin Rd. Ct. Pt. Rd.	Hendersonville 37075	Martin	.936
Highland Drive In		Hohenwald 38462	Scott, D.	.300
Skyway Drive In		Humboldt 38343	Barksdale	.200
Carroll Drive In		Huntingdon 38344	Rockwood, A.M.	.200
Jaxon Drive In	903 West Forest	Jackson 38301	Shivley, C.	.400
Twilight Drive In	Box J	Jamestown 37758	Patton, N.	
Maloy Drive In	Box 192	Jefferson City 37760	Baker	.300
Skyline Drive In	Box 158	Johnson City 37601	Wylie, P.	.300
Marbro Drive In	Rt. 1 East Stone Dr.	Kingsport 37660	Martin	.500
Chapman Hwy. Drive In	Route 9	Knoxville 37920	Simpson, C.	.200
Cinema Drive In	Box 5343	Knoxville 37901	Plitt South	.500
Family Drive In	4300 No. Broadway	Knoxville 37917	Plitt-South	.600
Knoxville Dr. In	128 Forest Pk. Blvd.	Knoxville 37919	Plitt-South	
River Breeze Drive In	Rte. 4	Knoxville 37914	Simpson, C.	.300
Twin Aire Dr. In East		Knoxville 37919	Simpson, C.	
Twin Aire Dr. In West		Knoxville 37919	Simpson, C.	.500
Macon Drive In		Lafayette 37083	Haney, B.C.	.200
Lawco Drive In	Box 165	Lawrenceburg 38464	Mid Tenn. Am.	.300
Dixie Lee Dr. In	Box A	Lenoir City 37771	Vista	.300
Hi Way 50 Drive In		Lewisburg 37091	Hawkins, C.	.400
Skyline Drive In		Livingston 38570	Allred, W.	.200
Cole Drive In	Route #3	Loudon 37774	Clark, J.	.200
Madisonville Dr. In	Hiway 411 N. Rte. 3	Madisonville 37354	Wheat, W.	.300
Manchester Dr. In		Manchester 37355	Mid Tenn. Am.	.300
Sunset Drive In		Martin 38237	Shivley	.400
Druid Hill Drive In	Box 386	Maryville 37801	Elrod, P.	.500
Parkway Drive In		Maryville 37801	Cinemette	.300
Ben Lomand Drive In	Box 562	McMinnville 37110	Mid Tenn. Am.	.300
Bellevue Drive In	2350 S. Bellevue	Memphis 38106	Malco Theas.	.600
Frayser Drive In	930 Stage Rd.	Memphis 38101	Malco Theas.	.600
Southland Dr. In		Memphis 38114	Carter, C.	.500
Southwest Twin #1 Dr. In	61 Hiway Raines Rd.	Memphis 38109	Malco Theas.	
Southwest Twin #2 Dr. In	61 Hiway Raines Rd.	Memphis 38109	Malco Theas.	
Summer Twin #1 Dr. In	5310 Summer Ave.	Memphis 38128	Malco Theas.	
Summer Twin #2 Dr. In	5310 Summer Ave.	Memphis 38102	Malco Theas.	.600
51 Twin Drive In		Millington 38053	Nicholson, H.	.400
Marbro Drive In	Russellville Highway	Morristown 37814	Martin	.300
Sunset Drive In	2348 W. A/J Hwy.	Morristown 37814	Winstead, B.	.200
Marbro Drive In	New Nashville Hwy.	Murfreesboro 37130	Martin	.400
Skyway Drive In	3207 Dickerson Rd.	Nashville 37207	Martin	.600
Newport Drive In	P.O. Box 176	Newport 37821	Smith, H.	.300
Scenic Drive In		Newport 37821	Tucker, J.	.400
Woodzo Drive In	Box 87	Newport 37821	Smith, H.	.300
Skyway Drive In	Box 142	Oak Ridge 37830	Pemberton, R.	.500
Carefree Dr. In	Box 71	Oliver Sprg. 37840	Duncan, L.	.200
Sky-Vue Drive In		Oneida 37841	Newport	.200
Skyvue Drive In	Box 747	Paris 38242	Smith, L.	.300
Midway Drive In	Box 929	Pigeon Forge 37863	Lakemont	.200
Moonglo Drive In	Lawrenceburg Hway.	Pulaski 38478	Martin	.400
Red Bank Drive In		Red Bank 37415	Martin	.500
Jolly Roger Dr. In	Box 307	Rogersville 37857	Thomas, T.	.300
Skyvue Drive In		Savannah 38372	Gooch, R.B.	.400
Sunset Drive In		Selmer 38375	Smith, L.	.400
41 Drive In	Highway 41 A East	Shelbyville 37160	Christianse	.400
Dekalb Drive In		Smithville 37166	Mid Tenn. Am.	.200
Sparta Drive In		Sparta 38583	Mid Tenn. Am.	.625
Tazewell Drive In	Box 240	Tazewell 37825	Duncan, L.	.200
Trenton Drive In	Box 336	Trenton 38382	Scott, D.	.200
Arnold Drive In	Box 1436	Tullahoma 37388	Mid Tenn. Am.	.400
Space Age Dr. In		Tullahoma 37388	Cumberland	
Valley Drive In	P.O. Box 330	Waverly 37185	Flexer, N.	
Cross Roads Drive In	No. Main Street	Whitwell 37397	Reeves, R.B.	.200
Family Drive In	Box 523	Winchester 37398	Martin, E.	.200
Lake County Drive In		Wynnburg 38077	Scott, D.	.300

TEXAS

Park Drive In		Abilene 79601	Plitt South	.300
Town & Country Dr. In		Abilene 79605	Video Indep.	.700
Buckhorn Drive In		Alice 78332	Gunter, H.	.400
Twin Drive In	P.O. Box 31344	Amarillo 79120	McDonald	.600
El Rey Drive In		Amherst 79312	Ray, E.F.	.200
Mustang Drive In		Andrews 79714	Hutte, R.	.300
Brazos Twin Dr. I.		Angelton 77515	B&B Theas.	1,000
Twilight Drive In	Box 592	Anson 79501	Ingram, E.	.300
Tarpon Drive In		Aransas Pass 78336	Davis, T.A.	.300

Theatre Name	Address	City & Zip	Circuit	Cars
Fiesta Drive In	P.O. Box 6386	Austin 78702	Flache, J.	
Showtown USA Twin D. I.	P.O. Box 2281	Austin 78767	Martin	400
Southside Dr. In Twin	P.O. Box 2281	Austin 78767	Martin	
Hillcrest Drive In		Ballinger 76821	Ofe, A.	400
Decker 1&2 Dr. In		Baytown 77520	Tercar Thea.	
Showtown USA Twin D. I.	% Jefferson Bx. 2357	Beaumont 77704	Martin	
Bonham Drive In		Bonham 75418	Princen, B.	300
Bunavista Drive In		Borger 79006	Fagan, J.	200
Mustang Drive In		Bovina 79009	Mahaney, G.	200
Trail Drive In	Box 310	Bowie 76230	Salter, H.	
Corral Drive In		Breckenridge 76024	Creagh, B.	
Rustic Drive In		Brownfield 79316	Jones, S.	400
Camp Bowie Drive In		Brownwood 76801	Watson, V.	400
Skyway Twin D. I.	P.O. Box 446	Bryan 77803	Bryan Amuse.	400
77 Drive In	P.O. Box 690	Cameron 76520	Vogelsang, F.	300
Winter Garden Drive In		Carrizo Springs 78834	Carter, K.	300
Apache Drive In		Center 75935	Adkison	400
Red River Drive In		Clarksville 75426	Commonwealt	200
Chief Drive In		Cleburne 76031	Video Indep.	300
Twin Ranch Drive In	Route 6 Box 700	Cleveland 77327	Wood, H.	300
Gulf Drive In	P.O. Box 611	Clute 77531	Gulf Dr. In	
Cole Anna Drive In	P.O. Box 911	Coleman 76834	Thompson	400
Circle Drive In	P.O. Box 67	College Station 77840	Schulman, B.	400
Joy Drive In		Copperas Cove 76522	Whatley, R.	400
Gulf Drive In		Corpus Christi 78405	Villarreal	700
Surf Drive In	4609 Ayers	Corpus Christi 78415	Kellogg, S.	
Thunderbird Drive In	4910 Leopard	Corpus Christi 78408	Benitez, M.	500
Twin Palms Dr. In		Corpus Christi 78415	Kellogg, S.	800
Viking Twin 1 Drive In		Corpus Christi 78415	U.A. Theas.	1,400
Viking Twin 2 Drive In		Corpus Christi 78415	U.A. Theas.	
Navarro Drive In		Corsicana 75111	Hagle, B.L.	300
Mimosa Drive In	P.O. Box 49	Cotulla 78014	Garcia	
Derrick Drive In		Crane 79731	Sanchez, G.	
Pioneer Drive In	P.O. Box 216	Cross Plains 76443	Wills, G.	
El Rancho Drive In		Dalhart 79022	Gilbert, D.E.	300
Kaufman Pike D. I.	7041 Hawn Freeway	Dallas 75217	Weisenberg	500
Astro I Drive In	3241 Walton Walker	Dallas 75211	FLW Theatre	
Astro II Drive In	3141 Walton Walker	Dallas 75211	FLW Theatre	
Astro III Drive In	3141 Walton Walker	Dallas 75211	FLW Theatre	
Buckner Blvd. D. I.	3333 Buckner Blvd.	Dallas 75228	Sitco	400
Gemini 1 Drive In	11990 N. Central Expy.	Dallas 75231	FLW Theatre	
Gemini II Drive In	11990 N. Central Expy.	Dallas 75231	FLW Theatre	
Gemini 3 Drive In	11990 N. Central Exp.	Dallas 75231	FLW Theatre	
Kiest Dr. In	3100 E. Kiest	Dallas 75203	Guggenheim	600
King Drive In	4601 South Lamar	Dallas 75215	Cates, D.	
Linda Kay Dr. In		Dallas 75213	Weisenburg	200
Lone Star Dr. In	4600 Lawnview	Dallas 75227	Hartstein, H.	
Starlite Drive In	5101 S. Lamar	Dallas 75215	Guggenheim	350
Weeping Oak Drive In		De Leon 76444	Brinson, E.D.	200
Sunset Drive In		Decatur 76234	Texas Cinem.	
Co. Ed. Drive In		Denton 76201	Noble, J.	
Town & Country Twin D. I.	P.O. Box 1010	Denton 76201	Texas Cinem.	700
Mustang Drive In		Denver City 79323	Schwartz, E.	120
Me Dina Valley Dr. In		Devine 78016	Talley, G.	
Rebel Drive In		Dublin 76446	Poor, D.	200
Prairie Drive In	P.O. Box 476	Dumas 79029	Wolfenbarge	300
Pan-Am Drive In #1		Edinburg 78539	Plitt South	927
Pan-Am Drive In #2		Edinburg 78539	Plitt South	452
Ascarate Drive In	P.O. Box 9704	El Paso 79987	Pierce, D.M.	
Bordertown Dr. In	9200 Montana Ave.	El Paso 79923	Sitco	800
Bronco Drive In	8410 Almeda	El Paso 79925	McLendon	
Cinema Park I Drive In	10676 Montana	El Paso 79926	FLW Theatre	
Cinema Park II Dr. In	10676 Montana	El Paso 79926	FLW Theatre	
Cinema Park III Dr. In	10676 Montana	El Paso 79926	FLW Theatre	
Fiesta 11 Drive In		El Paso 79942	Hartstein, H.	
Lomaland Dr. In	804 Lomaland Dr.	El Paso 79907	Garner, R.	400
Rocket Drive In	10405 Dyer	El Paso 79924	Sitco	500
Fiesta 1 Drive In		El Paso 79942	Hartstein, H.	
Midway Drive In	P.O. Box 416	Elsa 78543	Flores, J.	
Foxfire Drive In		Ennis 75119	Mitchell, M.	
Mid Cities Dr. In	P.O. Box N	Euless 76039	Williams	300
Capada Drive In	Box 566	Floydada 79235	U.A. Theas.	
Belknap Drive In	5709 E. Belknap	Fort Worth 76117	FLW Theatre	
Cherry Lane 1 Dr. In	1492 S. Cherry Lane	Fort Worth 76108	FLW Theatre	
Cherry Lane II Dr. In	1492 S. Cherry Lane	Fort Worth 76108	Crim, L.M.	600
Cowtown Drive In		Fort Worth 76114	Leon Theas.	1,254
Mansfield 1 & 2 Dr. In	2935 So. Seminary Dr.	Fort Worth 76119	Medrano, R.	
Meadowbrook Drive In	1701 Riverside Dr.	Fort Worth 76111	Hardy, B.J.	
Parkaire Drive In	1600 S. University	Fort Worth 76107	Leon Theas.	1,200
Southside Twin Dr. In	6200 Old Hemphill Rd.	Fort Worth 76134	Meagher	500
Twin Drive In		Fort Worth 76101	Hartstein, H.	500
Westerner Drive In		Fort Worth 76114	Fred Thea.	300
87 Drive In	P.O. Box 857	Fredericksburg 78624	McGlothlin	200
Elk Dr. In		Friona 79035	Sitco	400
Corral Dr. In	6300 Jacksboro Hwy.	Ft. Worth 76135	Hartstein, H.	600
Riverside Drive In	Box 7102 Sylvania Sta.	Ft. Worth 76111	Commonwealt	300
Hi Ho Drive In		Gainesville 76240	FLW Theatre	
Apollo I Drive In	3307 S. Garland Rd.	Garland 75040	FLW Theatre	
Apollo II Drive In	3307 S. Garland Rd.	Garland 75040	Palmer, G.	300
Town & Country Dr. In		Gatesville 76528	Commonwealt	400
Graham Drive In		Graham 76046	Johnson	200
Brazos Drive In		Granbury 76048	FLW Theatre	
Century 1 Drive In	2510 W. Main St.	Grand Prairie 75050	FLW Theatre	
Century IV Drive In	2510 W. Main St.	Grand Prairie 75050	FLW Theatre	

Theatre Name	Address	City & Zip	Circuit	Cars
Century II Drive In	2510 W. Main St.	Grand Prairie 75050	FLW Theatre	
Century III Dr. In	2510 W. Main St.	Grand Prairie 75050	FLW Theatre	
Trail Drive In		Greenville 75401	Martin	
Tower Drive In		Hereford 79045	Commonwealt.	300
Airline Drive In	4507 Airline Drive	Houston 77022	Tercar Thea.	600
Gulfway I Dr. In	9025 Wald Drive	Houston 77034	FLW Theatre	
Gulfway II Dr. In	9025 Wald Drive	Houston 77034	FLW Theatre	
Irvington Dr. In	8411 Irvington Blvd	Houston 77022	Tercar	
King Center Dr. In Twin	6400 South Pk. Bld.	Houston 77033	Tercar Ths.	400
McLendon Triple	11991 S. Main St.	Houston 77035	FLW Theatre	
McLendon Triple 1	11991 S. Main St.	Houston 77035	FLW Theatre	
McLendon Triple 3	11991 S. Main St.	Houston 77035	FLW Theatre	
Post Oak II Drive In	1255 N. Post Oak Rd.	Houston 77024	McLendon	
Telephone Rd. Twin D. I.	11020 Telephone Rd.	Houston 77001	Tercar Thea.	
Tidwell Drive In	9603 Homestead Rd.	Houston 77016	Griffith	575
Humble Drive In	Highway 59	Humble 77338	Gugenheim	
Picture Show Drive In		Huntsville 77340	Marsh, J.	400
Pines Drive In		Huntsville 77340	Schulman, B.	
Park Plaza Drive In	P.O. Box 517	Irving 75061	Meagher	600
Texas Stadium Dr. In I		Irving 75060	Meagher	
Texas Stadium II D. I.		Irving 75060	Meagher	
Texas Stadium III D. I.		Irving 75060	Meagher	
183 Drive In	P.O. Box 517	Irving 75061	Meagher	300
Mesquite Drive In		Jacksboro 76056	Leach, S.	200
Yellow Jacket Drive In		Kermit 79745	Smith, B.	300
Bolero Drive In		Kerrville 78028	Hiegel, H.	300
Killeen Drive In		Killeen 76541	U.A Theas.	400
Rancier Twin 1 Dr. In		Killeen 76541	U.A. Theas.	400
440 Drive In #1		Killeen 76541	U.A. Theas.	
440 Twin 2 Drive In		Killeen 76541	U.A. Theas.	
Kings Drive In		Kingsville 78363	Texas Cinem.	300
Bayou I Drive In	P.O. Box 696	La Marque 77568	FLW Theatre	
Bayou II Drive In	P.O. Box 696	La Marque 77568	FLW Theatre	
Bayou III Drive In	P.O. Box 696	La Marque 77568	FLW Theatre	
Sky Vue Drive In	P.O. Box 1303	Lamesa 79331	Noret Theas.	300
Circle Dr. In		Lampasas 76550	Sallas, B.	457
Bordertown 1 Dr. In		Laredo 78040	U.S. Atheas.	1,000
Bordertown 2 Drive In		Laredo 78040	U.A. Theas.	
Lobo Drive In		Levelland 79336	Blankenship	
Lewisville 121 Twin D. I.	Hwy. 121	Lewisville 75067	Weisenberg	1,000
Milentz Drive In	1816 Sam Houston	Liberty 77575	Milentz, A.	300
Picture Show D. I.	304 N. Washington	Livingston 77351	Marsh, J.	
Llano Dr. In		Llano 78643	Gage, K.	
Lone Star Drive In		Lone Star 75668	Bass, G.	300
River Road Dr. In 1 2 & 3	P.O. Box 1762	Longview 75601	Martin	400
Twin Pines Dr. In		Longview 75601	Watson, J.	400
Dona Lin Drive In		Loraine 79532	Newton, E.	400
Circle Drive In	2517 55th St.	Lubbock 79413	Boren, B.	
Corral Drive In		Lubbock 79408	Boren, B.	
Golden Horseshoe Dr. In		Lubbock 79401	Bearden, Th.	800
Red Raider Drive In		Lubbock 79408	Bearden, W.	600
Redland Drive In	Box 1408	Lufkin 75901	Martin	1,200
Showtown Twin Dr. In		Lufkin 75901	Martin	
Marfa Drive In	218 Hiland Ave.	Marfa 79843	Buren, P.	300
Circus Dr. In	P.O. Box 933	McCamey 79752	Penn, J.	300
Tower Drive In		Memphis 79245	Craven	200
Yellow Jacket Dr. In		Menard 76859	De Anda	500
Wes Mer Drive In		Mercedes 78570	Benitez	400
Bruton Road Dr. In		Mesquite 75217	Weisenburg	700
Chief Drive In		Midland 79701	Video Indep.	400
Fiesta Drive In		Midland 79701	Video Indep.	300
Texan Drive In		Midland 79701	Video Indep.	
Tek Drive In		Mineral Wells 76067	Simmons, R.	200
Lobo Drive In		Monahans 79756	Klatt, P.	
Pleasant Drive In		Mt. Pleasant 75455	U.A. Theas.	
X I T Drive In		Muleshoe 79347	Pummill, H.	200
Lumberjack Dr. In		Nacogdoches 75961	Texas Cinem.	
Longhorn Drive In	504 N. Center	New Boston 75570	Price, A.	
Tower Dr. In		New Braunfels 78130	Video	
Chief Drive In		Nocona 76255	Nunneley, E.	200
Twin Terrace Drive In		Odessa 79760	Scott, M.	1,000
Mustang Drive In		Olton 79064	Rucker, R.	200
MacArthur Dr. In		Orange 77630	Martin	
Big O Drive In	P.O. Box 1522	Ozona 76943	Collett	250
Dogwood Twin D. I. 1		Palestine 75801	U.A. Theas.	600
Dogwood Twin 2 D. I.		Palestine 75801	U.A. Theas.	
Top O Texas Drive In		Pampa 79065	Video Indep.	400
Pasadena Drive In	2221 So. Shaver	Pasadena 77502	Tercar Thea.	400
Town & Country Tw. D/I	4716 Red Bluff	Pasadena 77502	Leon Thea.	1,000
Trevino Drive In	P.O. Box 717	Pearsall 78061	Trevino, F.	300
Texan Drive In		Pecos 79772	Commonwealt.	400
Ranger Dr. In		Perryton 79070	Mahaney, E.	200
Plano Dr. In 3	Hwy. 75 Parker Rd.	Plano 75074	FIW Theas.	
Plano 1 Drive In	Hwy. 75 Parker Rd.	Plano 75074	FIW Theas.	
Plano 2 Drive In	Hwy. 75 Parker Rd.	Plano 75074	FIW Theas.	
Trail Drive In		Pleasanton 78064	Degenhardt	400
Don Drive In		Port Arthur 77641	Martin	800
Chief Drive In		Quanah 79252	Kinnaman, F.	206
Midway Drive In		Quitaque 79245	Hamm, B.	200
Ranger Drive In		Ranger 76470	Morgan, R.	200
Corral Drive In	Box 718	Raymondville 78580	Gomez	400
H & H Drive In		Rio Grande City 78582	Garza, H.	200
Reel Drive In		Rockdale 76567	Parsley, H.	200
Cove Drive In		Rockport 78382	Davis	

567

Theatre Name	Address	City & Zip	Circuit	Cars
Garzas Drive In		Roma 78584	Garza, A.	
Twin City Drive In		Rosenberg 77471	Tercar Thea.	400
Tower Drive In		Rule 79547	Wharton, E.B.	200
Angelo Twin 1 Dr. In		San Angelo 76901	U.A. Theas.	
Angelo Twin 2 Drive In		San Angelo 76901	U.A. Theas.	
Twin Vue 1 Drive In		San Angelo 76901	U.A. Theas.	
Twin Vue 2 Drive In		San Angelo 76901	U.A. Theas.	
El Capitan Drive In		San Antonio 78228	Killian	600
El Charro Dr. In	P.O. Box 7147	San Antonio 78207	Martinez	
Fredericksburg Rd. D. I.	3534 Fredericksburg	San Antonio 78201	Santikos	
Judson 4 Drive In		San Antonio 78233	Braha, M.	
Loop 13 Drive In	2335 S.W. Military Dr.	San Antonio 78224	Ruenes, R.	100
Mission D. I. Fourplex	3100 Rosevelt	San Antonio 78214	Santikos	600
San Pedro Outdoo	600 Bitters Road	San Antonio 78216	Santikos	1,050
Trail Drive In	1031 S.E. Military	San Antonio 78214	Santikos	500
Valley Hi Drive In	6300 Medina Base Rd.	San Antonio 78242	Carabaza, J.	500
Varsity Drive In	2202 Culebra	San Antonio 78223	Santikos	
Citrus Drive In	P.O. Drawer 543	San Benito 78586	Brady, T.	600
Juarez Drive In	Rt. 1 Box 389-E	San Benito 78586	Canas, B.	
Corral Drive In		San Saba 76877	Wharton, E.B.	
Starlite Dr. In	1020 F.M. 78	Schertz 78154	Farmer, R.	175
Dixie Drive In		Sequin 78155	Roscoe	
Chief Drive In		Seminole 79360	Hutte, R.	300
Brazos Drive In		Seymour 76380	Hatfield, K.	300
Sher Den Twin 1 D. I.		Sherman 75090	U.A. Theas.	700
Sher Den Twin 2 D. I.		Sherman 75090	U.A. Theas.	
Twin City Dr. In		Sherman 75090	Leon Theas.	400
Tiger Drive In	P.O. Drawer K	Snyder 79549	Noret, R.A.	500
Holiday Dr. In		Spearman 79081	Ellsworth	
Wagonwheel Drive In		Spearman 79081	Wilbanks, J.	200
H & H Drive In		Stamford 79553	Hodge, S.	400
Hi Vue Drive In		Sulphur Springs 75482	U.A. Theas.	400
Rocket Drive In		Sweetwater 79556	U.A. Theas.	325
Texas Drive In		Taylor 76574	U.A. Theas.	200
Terrell Drive In		Terrell 75160	U.A. Theas.	
Tradewind Drive In		Texas City 77590	Long	600
Tulia Drive In		Tulia 79088	Gruber, H.V.	
Apache Drive In	Route 11 Box 76	Tyler 75701	Hardy, D.	350
Rose Garden Drive In	P.O. Box 6641	Tyler 75701	Plitt South	500
Stardust Drive In		Uvalde 78801	Commonwealt.	400
El Rancho Drive In		Vernon 76384	Hamm, C.C.	400
Gemini Drive In		Victoria 77901	Prichard	800
Lone Tree Drive In		Victoria 77901	Frels Thea.	700
Joy Drive In	P.O. Box 4133	Waco 76705	Circle Dith.	600
Weatherford D. I.	111 College	Weatherford 76086	Poye, F.	500
Falls Twin Drive In		Wichita Falls 76307	Martin	
Seymour Drive In		Wichita Falls 76301	Slaughter	

UTAH

Theatre Name	Address	City & Zip	Circuit	Cars
Mesa Drive In		Blanding 84511	Howe Thea.	
Hyland Drive In		Cedar City 84720	Sawyers, J.	200
Desert Drive In	P.O. Box 515	Delta 84624	Grayson, J.	200
Starlite Drive In	P.O. Box 808	East Carbon 84520	Dickerson, T.	300
Davis Drive In		Layton 84111	Westates	400
Cache Drive In	Box 232	Logan 84321	Westates	
HCS Cache Drive In		Logan 84321	Westates	
Ute Drive In		Midvale 84047	Sero	
Grand Vu Drive In	1382 Mill Creek Dr.	Moab 84532	Victor, G.	250
Montezuma Creek D. I.		Montezuma Creek 84534	Howe	
Nu Vu Drive In	P.O. Box 683	Monticello 84535	Johnson	
Fox Olympus Drive In	P.O. Box 7005	Murray 84107	Mann Theas.	700
Redwood Dr. In 1 & 2	3688 S. Redwood Rd.	Murray 84119	Sero	
Motor Vu Drive In	5368 So. 1050 West	Ogden 84403	Mann Theas.	
North Star Drive In #2	4061 Edge Hill Drive	Ogden 84403	Webb, W.	900
North Star Drive In	4061 Edge Hill Drive	Ogden 84403	Webb, W.	500
Riverdale Drive In		Ogden 84067	Tullis, R.	800
Utah Drive In	1876 Washington Blvd.	Ogden 84401	Ellis, D.	450
Timpanagos Dr. In		Orem 94057	Sero	
Price Motor Vue		Price 84501	Dewsnup, S.	300
Hyland Dr. In	3670 S. Highland Dr.	Salt Lake City 84106	Sero	
Park Vu Dr. In	1145 E. 3900 South	Salt Lake City 84117	Sero	
Valley Vu Dr. In	3560 So. 4800 Granger	Salt Lake City 84111	Sero	
Woodland Drive In	4005 South 7th East	Salt Lake City 84115	Plitt	600
Art City Cinemotor	Box 185	Springville 84663	Lind	400
Starlite Drive In		St. George 84770	Westates	200

VERMONT

Theatre Name	Address	City & Zip	Circuit	Cars
Midway Drive In		Ascutney 05030	Gamache	400
Belmont Drive In		Bellows Falls 05101	Spaulding	300
Bennington Drive In	P.O. Box 675	Bennington 05401	Goldstein, H.	300
Randall Drive In		Bethel 05032	Osterberg	200
Burlington Drive In		Burlington 05401	Jarvis, G.	400
Malletts Bay Drive In		Burlington 05401	Jarvis, G.	400
Sunset Drive In		Burlington 05401	Jarvis, M.	500
Fort Warren Drive In		Castleton 05735	Handy, P.	
Derby Port Drive In	Box 34	Derby 05829	McNally	400
Hi Way 5 Drive In		Fairlee 05045	Drown	300
Manchester D. I.		Manchester 05254	Brothwell	
Mid Haven Drive In	P.O. Box 191	Middlebury 05753	Graphic	400
Moonlight Drive In		Montpelier 05602	Cody Enter.	400
New Twin City Drive In		Montpelier 05604	Cody Enter.	200
Morrisville Drive In		Morrisville 05661	McNally	300

Theatre Name	Address	City & Zip	Circuit	Cars
Norton Drive In		Norton 05907	Rancourt, V.	200
St. Albans Drive In		St. Albans 05478	Gamache	300
Blue Moon Drive In		St. Johnsbury 05819	Atkins	400
White River Drive In		White River Jct. 05001	Interst Ths.	500
Mt. View Drive In		Winooski 05404	Jarvis, M.	500

VIRGINIA

Theatre Name	Address	City & Zip	Circuit	Cars
Moonlite Drive In	P.O. Box 594	Abingdon 24210	Mays	300
Sunset Drive In	Baileys Cross Roads	Alexandria 22206	Hodges, W.	200
Coswell Drive In		Appomattox 24522	Matthews	100
Bedford Drive In	P.O. Box 883	Bedford 24523	Parks, J.	300
Powell Valley Dr. In	2719 2nd Ave.	Big Stone Gap 24219	Collier, A.	
Grove Drive In		Blackstone 23824	Zack Perdue	
Central Drive In		Blackwood 24222	Kiser, J.	100
Highland Drive In	Rt. 220 near Monterey	Blue Grass 24413	Rexode & Puf.	100
Buena Vista Drive In	Buena Vista 24416	R/C Theatre		200
Blue Grass Drive In	Route 3	Castlewood 24224	Robinette, T.	100
Ridge Drive In	P.O. Box 671	Charlottesville 22902	Neighborhood	295
Chase City Drive In	P.O. Box 185	Chase City 23924	McNeer, J.	100
Starlight Drive In	P.O. Box 97	Christiansburg 24073	Beasley, H.W.	300
Hiway Drive In		Covington 24426	Fleshman, N.	300
Super 17 Drive In	5108 Geo. Wash. Hiway	Craddock 23702	Price, E.	300
Pitts Culpeper Dr. In		Culpepper 22701	Cohen, I.	300
Dicks Drive In		Cumberland 23093	Robertson, R.	
Crescent Dr. In		Danville 24541	Consolidate	
360 Drive In		Danville 24541	Piedmont	
Pulaski Drive In		Dublin 24084	Mullins, L.	300
Exmore Drive In		Exmore 23350	Mears, E.B.	
Super 29 Drive In		Fairfax 22030	Aikens, H.W.	400
Farmville Dr. In		Farmville 23901	Neighborhood	1,000
Fork Union Dr. In		Fork Union 23055	White, F.	
Carrsville Drive In	Box 657	Franklin 23851	R/C Theas.	200
Fredericksburg Dr. In		Fredericksburg 22401	R/C Theas.	500
Front Royal Dr. In	P.O. Box 311	Front Royal 22630	Cohen, I.	300
Airport Drive In	Rt. 2 Box 66	Galax 24333	Jones, R.	200
Summit Drive In		Glade Springs 24340	Meek, J.L.	200
Dukes Drive In	Rt. 1 Box 401A	Glen Allen 23060	Duke, L.	
Gordonsville Drive In	P.O. Box 336	Gordonsville 22942	White, V.	100
Harrisonburg Dr. In		Harrisonburg 22801	Roth Theas.	
Roths Drive In		Harrisonburg 22801	Roth Theas.	200
Cinema X2 Dr. In	P.O. Box 198	Keyville 23947	Clark, R.	
Cavalier Drive In		Lebanon 24266	Coleman, H.	200
Hulls Drive In		Lexington 24450	Hull, S.	300
Dicks Drive In		Louisa 23093	Robertson, R.	
Luray Drive In		Luray 22835	Bowen, C.	
Amherst Drive In	Rt. 29 N. Madison Hgts.	Lynchburg 24504	Howell	1,000
Fort Drive In	7306 Timber Lake Rd.	Lynchburg 24502	Howell Thea.	
Manassas Drive In	P.O. Box 337	Manassas 22110	Cohen, I.	1,300
Skyvue Drive In	New Hwy. 11 West	Marion 24354	Shenandoah	100
Castle Drive In		Martinsville 24112	R.C. Theas.	300
Martinsville Drive In		Martinsville 24112	R.C. Theas.	300
220 Drive In		Martinsville 24112	Piedmont	460
220 Drive In		Martinsville 24112	Brown, R.	
Lynn Drive In		New Castle 24127	Abbott, J.	100
Anchor Drive In	Jefferson Ave. & Main	Newport News 23601	Martin	300
Green Acres Dr. In	2227 W. Pembrooke Ave.	Newport News 23605	Martin	300
Hampton Drive In		Newport News 23601	Sandy, J.	500
Peninsula #2 Dr. In	12073 Jefferson Ave.	Newport News 23602	Price, E.	
Pennisula Twin #1 D. I.	12073 Jefferson Ave.	Newport News 23602	Price, E.	
12073 Jefferson Ave.	Newport News 23602	Price E		
Azalea Drive In	5505 Lynn Street	Norfolk 23513	Price, E.	600
Lonesome Pine Dr. In	921 East Park Ave.	Norton 24273		
Pitts Orange Dr. In		Orange 22960	R/C Theas.	
Park Drive In	P.O. Box 484	Pearisburg 24134	Giles	300
Blue Star Drive In		Petersburg 23803	Kent Benson	300
Park Drive In	2301 Cty. Dr. Bx. 1812	Petersburg 23803	Patrick, R.	300
New Autodrome Drive In		Radford 24141	Carpenter, R.	500
Guys Drive In		Richlands 24641	Flanary, R.G.	100
Bellwood Drive In	9201 Jefferson Davis	Richmond 23234	Neighborhood	1,000
Fairfield Drive In	3101 Williamsburg Rd.	Richmond 23231	Glenmar	
Patterson Drive In	Rt. 2 P.O. Box 440	Richmond 23229	Glenmar	600
Sunset Drive In	8000 Midlothian Pike	Richmond 23235	Rainey, T.	400
Lee Hi Drive In	P.O. Box 6012	Roanoke 24017	Consolidate	300
North 11 Drive In	3325 Oakland Blvd. N.W.	Roanoke 24012	Lovell, G.G.	250
Shenandoah Drive In		Roanoke 23203	Piedmont	300
Trail Drive In	Route 1 Box 157	Roanoke 24012	Davis, F.L.	240
220 Drive In	P.O. Box 8001	Roanoke 24014	Piedmont	
220 Drive In		Roanoke 24004	Piedmont	
Starvue Drive In	Route 1	Rocky Mount 24151	Gaubatz, H.	200
Hiland Drive In		Rural Retreat 24368	Dalton, C.E.	200
Richmond Airport Dr. In	5200 Williamsburg Rd.	Sandston 23150	Glenmar	
Sinai West Dr. In	Box 923	So. Boston 24592	Logan	
South Dr. In	Campostella Road	So. Norfolk 23506	Price, E.	300
Oak Drive In		South Hill 23970	Curtis, J.	300
Staunton Drive In	P.O. Box 334	Staunton 24401	R/C Theas.	300
Plantation Dr. In	P.O. Box 188	Suffolk 23434	R/C Theas.	200
York Drive In		Tabb 23602	Sandy, J.	
Sunset Drive In		Tazewell 24651	Hughes, W.E.	300
Triangle Drive In		Triangle 22172	Triangle	
Van Sant Drive In	P.O. Box 742	Van Sant 24656	McDaniel	
Dixie Drive In	P.O. Box 157	Vinton 24179	Park, E.	200
Sand Screen Dr. In	Indep. Bl. & Holland Rd.	Virginia Beach 23513	Price, E.	
Shore Drive In	4640 Shore Drive	Virginia Beach 23455	Price, E.	500

569

Theatre Name	Address	City & Zip	Circuit	Cars
Surf Screen Dr. In	Indep. Bl. & Holland Rd.	Virginia Beach 23452	Price, E.	
Warrenton Drive In		Warrenton 22186	Cohen, J.	200
Rappahanneck Dr. In		Wash 22747	J&M Enter.	
Dream Drive In		Wattsville 23483	Justice, J.	400
North 340 Drive In		Waynesboro 22980	R/C Theatre	
Skyline Drive In	P.O. Box 1053	Waynesboro 22980	R/C Theas.	300
B & L Drive In	111 Oak Raod	Williamsburg 23185	Legume, L.	
Winchester Drive In	Route 11 North	Winchester 22601	Goldhammer	300

WASHINGTON

Theatre Name	Address	City & Zip	Circuit	Cars
Harbor Drive In 1&2	5515 Olympic Hiway.	Aberdeen 98520	Saffle, B.	385
Circus Drive In		Anacortes 98221	Bonholzer, J.	500
Valley D. I. #2	Box 1	Auburn 98002	Forman Unit	
Valley D. I #3	Box 1	Auburn 98002	Forman Unit	
Valley Dr. In 1	Box 1	Auburn 98002	Forman Unit	400
Bel Kirk Drive In 1&2	11100 33rd Place N.E.	Bellevue 98004	Sterling, Th.	500
Sunset Drive In	12600 S.E. 37th	Bellevue 98006	Sterling, Th.	800
Samish Drive In		Bellingham 98225	Sterling, Th.	575
Kenmore Dr. In	18505 68th N.E.	Bothell 98011	Forman Unit	650
Kitsap Lake Dr. In	2412 Woodland Drive	Bremerton 98310	Cascade Clin.	460
Kitsap Lake Drive In 2	2412 Woodland Dr.	Bremerton 98310	Cascade	
Mountain Vu Drive In	Route #1	Cashmere 98115	Speiss, R.	400
Twin City Dr. In 1&2	Box 428	Centralia 98531	Saffle, M.	500
Clarkston Auto Dr. In		Clarkston 99403	Yushchyshyn	225
Auto View Drive In		Colville 99114	Jest, Ths.	202
Holiday Drive In	4621 Village Circle	Custer 98366	Thibadeau	
Dayton Drive In		Dayton 99328	Otterson	340
Deer Park Drive In	P.O. B. 988	Deer Park 99006	MacKay, L.	130
Ellen Drive In		Ellensburg 98926	Barber, J.	500
Motor Movies D/I	910 75th Street	Everett 98201	Forman Unit	730
Puget Park Dr. In	13020 Meridian Ave.	Everett 98201	Sterling, Th.	703
Thunderbird Drive In		Everett 98201	Burns, S.F.	560
J & R Drive In	Rt. 2 Box 212A	Goldendale 98620	Wilken, J.	120
El Rancho Dr. In	19852 84th South	Kent 98031	Forman Unit	490
Your Drive In	P.O. Box 899	Longview 98632	Sterling, Th.	500
Sno King Drive In	17310 Highway 99	Lynnwood 98036	Forman Unit	630
Midway Drive In	P.O. Box 3068	Midway 98031	Forman Unit	465
Skyline Drive In		Moses Lake 98837	Barbar, J.	450
Skagit Drive In		Mount Vernon 98273	Babington	400
Blue Fox Drive In	1403N. Monroe Land Rd.	Oak Harbor 98277	Whidbey, Dr.	175
North Beach Dr. In	Route 4 Box 61	Ocean City 98569	Burns, S.F.	200
Lacey Drive In	800 Sleater-Kinney Rd.	Olympia 98506	Moyer, T.	450
Skyline D. I.	4621 Village Circle	Olympia 98501	Thibadeau, F.	354
Sunset Drive In	Capitol Blvd. & Israel Rd.	Olympia 98501	Moyer, T.	420
Sky Vu Drive In	P.O. Box 1847	Omak 98841	Art & Cliff	250
Oroville Drive In		Oroville 98844	Burns, S.F.	490
Sunset Drive In		Othello 99344	Barber, J.	300
River Vue Dr. In		Pasco 99301	Sterling, Th.	600
Port Angeles Dr. In #1		Port Angeles 98326	Lassila, P.	300
Port Angeles Dr. In #2		Port Angeles 98326	Lassila, P.	
Rodeo Dr. In #1	7369 State Hwy. 3 S.W.	Port Orchard 98366	Cascade Cin.	600
Wheel In Drive In	N.	Port Townsend 98368	Wiley, D.	190
Big Bear Drive In	P.O. Box 25	Poulsbo 98370	Lilquist, J.	175
Rodeo Dr. In #2	7369 State Hwy. 3 S.W.	Pt. Orchard 98366	Cascade Cin.	
Rodeo Dr. In #3	7369 State Hwy. 3 S.W.	Pt. Orchard 98366	Cascade Cin.	
Big Sky Drive In	P.O. Box 428	Pullman 99163	Kenworthy, M.	480
Island Vue D. I.	1529 Columbia Dr. S.E.	Richland 99352	Sterling, Th.	500
Aurora Dr. In	13500 Aurora Ave. N.	Seattle 98133	Forman Unit	575
Duwamish Drive In	So. 112th & Hiway 99	Seattle 98178	Forman Unit	600
Park In Dr. In		Soap Lake 98851	Barber, J.	275
Starlite Drive In	Box 9036	South Tacoma 98409	Forman Unit	490
Autovue Drive In	6800 No. Divison St.	Spokane 99218	Nimmer, M.	740
East Sprague Drive In	Box 2188	Spokane 99210	Sterling, Th.	500
East Trent Drive In	Box 2188	Spokane 99210	Sterling, Th.	500
North Cedar Drive In	Box 2188	Spokane 99210	Sterling, Th.	750
Starlite D. I.	N. 10505 Newport Hwy.	Spokane 99218	Hefner, W.	501
West End Drive In	Box 2188	Spokane 99210	Sterling, Th.	600
Y Drive In	8804 North Division	Spokane 99218	Nimmer, M.G.	400
Starlite Drive In	P.O. Box 37	Sunnyside 98944	Sites, Y.	500
Auto View Dr. In	1202 No. Pearl St.	Tacoma 98465	Forman Unit	725
Fife Drive In	1601 Goldau Rd. East	Tacoma 98424	Forman Unit	650
112th Street Drive In	112th E. D. Street	Tacoma 98445	Forman Unit	825
Hazel Dell Drive In		Vancouver 98660	Adamson, A.W.	330
Renfro		Vancouver 98660	Adamson, A.W.	300
Sky Vue Drive In		Walla Walla 99362	Sterling, Th.	400
Vu Dale Dr. In	P.O. Box 2506	Wenatchee 98801	Wenatchee	600
Rodeo Drive In		White Salmon 98675	Holtman, L.	197
Cascade Drive In	P.O. Box 1557	Yakima 98901	Mercy Theas.	580
Country Drive In	8301 Tieton Drive	Yakima 98902	Anderson, B.	750
Fruitvale Drive In		Yakima 98901	Bonholzer, J.	500

WEST VIRGINIA

Theatre Name	Address	City & Zip	Circuit	Cars
Bartow Drive In	P.O. Box 6	Bartow 24920		
Crab Orchard Drive In	317 Porter St.	Beckley 25827	Warden	400
Moonlite Drive In	Eisenhower Dr.	Beckley 25801	Warden, R.	
Raleigh Drive In		Beckley 25801	Keesling	435
Trail Dr. In		Belle 25323	Aaron	525
Skyway Drive In	403 Mountainview Ave.	Bluefield 24701	N. K.	500
Ellis Drive In	920 W. Main Street	Bridgeport 26330	Ellis, L.	500
Buckeye Drive In		Buckeye 24924	Graham, W.W.	100
West D. I.	Rt. 6 Box 546	Buckhannon 26201	West	400
Chapmansville Dr. In		Chapmansville 25508	Dillon, F.	

Theatre Name	Address	City & Zip	Circuit	Cars
Owens Drive In	P.O. Box 4137	Charleston 25304	Cinemette	500
Hilltop D. I.	N.	Chester 26034	Anas Weir	300
Skyline D. I.		Clarksburg 26301	Caputo, S.	300
Craigsville Drive In		Craigsville 26205	Hanna, J.	300
Valley Drive In		Dailey 26264	Collins, A.	100
Maple Leaf Drive In	Box 125	Dellslow 26531	Van Culp	200
Sunset Drive In		East Rainelle 25962	Nutter, J.E.	282
Elkins D. I.	1002 Coles Ave.	Elkins 26241	Talbott, H.A.	300
Elkview Drive In	P.O. Box 246	Elkview 25323	Sweeney	487
Grove Drive In		Elm Grove 26003	Gardner, J.	600
Starlite Dr. In		Fairmont 26554	Carunchio, J.	600
Twilite Drive In		Fairmont 26554	Carunchio	
Ohio Valley D. I.		Follansbee 26062	Anas Weir	500
Warner Dr. In	P.O. Box 23	Franklin 26807	Warner, M.	
Elk Drive In		Gassaway 26624	Rose Morris	250
Glendale D. I.		Glendale 26038	Anas Weir	400
Daves Drive In	P.O. Box 328	Glenville 26351	Montgomery	185
Grafton Dr. In	Rt. 5 Box 128	Grafton 26354	De Angelis	200
East Outdoor	Box 1957	Huntington 25720	Hyman, E.	650
Kermit Drive In	P.O. Box 416	Kermit 25674	Preece, B.	350
Lewisburg Drive In	Rte. 4 Box 149 N.	Lewisburg 24901	Warden, D.	194
Midway Dr. In	P.O. Box 1661	Logan 25601	Tomblin, R.	
Monitor Drive In	Box 1821	Logan 25601	Mathis, T.W.	514
Madison Dr. In		Madison 25130	Boyd & Cook	
Blackshere Dr. In	U.S. Route 250	Mannington 26582	Minicinemas	434
Pine Grove Drive In	Route 11 North	Martinsburg 25401	Goldhammer	
Skyvue Drive In		Martinsburg 24134	Goldhammer	300
Mason Drive In		Mason 25550	Smith, H.S.	400
Meadowbridge Dr. In	P.O. Box 291	Meadowbridge 25976	Thomas, L.	180
Sunset Dr. In	P.O. Box 118	Meadowbrook 26404	Deangelis, M.	500
Moorefield Dr. In		Moorefield 26836	Lambert, R.	
Blue Horizon D/I	319 Monon Gahela	Morgantown 26505	Gardner, J.	400
Westover D. I.	Box 1168	Morgantown 26505	Comuntzis, J.	500
Mt. Zion Dr. In		Mt. Zion 26151	Johnson, T.	150
Works D. I.		N. Martinsville 26155		
Jungle Dr. In		Parkersburg 26101	Westbrook, C.	308
Sundowner D/I	P.O. Box 187	Parkersburg 26101	Jur	
Fort Hill Drive In	P.O. Box 568	Petersburg 26747	Veach, T.	200
Pineville Drive In		Pineville 28474	Warden, R.	250
Richwood Drive In		Richwood 26261	Thomas	200
Airport Drive In		Short Creek 26058	Gardner, J.	200
Pipe Stem Drive In		Speedway 25873	Warden, R.	285
Valley Drive In	P.O. Box 188	St. Albans 25177	Erwin, W.	650
Belle Air D. I.		Weirton 26062	Anas Weir	500
Starland Drive In	403 Mountain View	Welch 24701	Russell	400
Blue Moon D. I.		Wellsburg 26070	Digiancinto	300
Lovett S. D. I.		Weston 26452	Baker, G.	200
Downs Auto		Wheeling 26003	Cinemette	
Cinema #3 D. I.	Box D	White Sulphur Spg. 24986	Kraft	
Cinema04 ;1	Box D	White Sulphur Spg. 24986	Kraft	
Cinema #2	Box D	White Sulphur Spg. 24986	Kraft	
Walnut Grove D. I.	P.O. Box 4137	Winfield 25304	Gunter	

WISCONSIN

Theatre Name	Address	City & Zip	Circuit	Cars
1329 Drive In		Abbotsford 54405	Hood, R.	150
Antigo Drive In		Antigo 54409	Suick	
Triad Dr. In		Ashland 54806	Bergman, A.	499
Beaver Dam Drive In		Beaver Dam 53913	Marcus	300
Blue Mound Drive In	16125 Blue Mound Rd.	Brookfield 53005	Westoutdoor	
Highway 57 Outdoor	Box 64	Cedarburg 53012	Marcus	600
Fort Tepee Outdoor		Clearwater Lake 54518	Cozzuol, J.P.	100
Lakes Outdoor	P.O. Box 422	Delavan 53115	Kohlberg	600
Eagle River Drive In	Box 225	Eagle River 54521	Lind, S.	300
Vilas		Eagle River 53521	Conway, S.	
Gemini Drive In		Eau Claire 54701	Grengs, G.	300
Stardusk Drive In		Eau Claire 54701	Grengs, G.	400
Skyway Drive In		Ephraim 54202	Voeks, D.	
Lake Park Outdoor	500 N. Main St.	Fond Du Lac 54936	Wisc. Amusem.	
Franklin-100 Outdoor	Highway 100	Franklin 53132	Kohlberg	
41 Twin North Drive In	7701 South 27th St.	Franklin 53130	Standard	
41 Twin South Drive In	7701 South 27th St.	Franklin 53130	Standard	
Starlite Outdoor	1220 Hickory Hill Dr.	Green Bay 54304	Rogers	
Valley Outdoor		Green Bay 54303	Standard	
24 Outdoor	P.O. Box 8	Hales Corners 53130	Marcus	
Hayward Drive In		Hayward 54843	Donnellan, A.	295
St. Croix Hilltop Dr. In		Houlton 55082	N.W. Cinema	350
Mid City Outdoor		Janesville 53546	Standard	600
26 Outdoor	2500 Milton Ave.	Janesville 53545	Rogers	
Hyway 18 Outdoor		Jefferson 53548	Gorski, K.	
Keno Family Drive In		Kenosha 53140	Standard	600
Mid City Outdoor Dr. In		Kenosha 53140	Standard	
North Star Drive In		Lacrosse 54601	Marcus	500
Starlite Drive In		Lacrosse 54601	Marcus	400
Tower Drive In		Little Chute 54140	Marcus	600
Badger Outdoor		Madison 53713	Capitol Ser.	600
Lake Vue Outdoor		Manitowoc 54220	Marcus	300
64 Outdoor		Marinette 54143	Mescop	400
10/13 Motor Movie D. I.		Marshfield 54449	Rogers	
Starlite Outdoor	Route 3 Box 689	Menominee Falls 53051	Marcus	1,100
Victory Drive In	N. 48 W. 15382	Menomonee Falls 53051	Kohlberg	
Menomonie Drive In	% State Theatre	Menomonie 54751	Marcus	425
Big Sky Drive In	V	Middelton 53562	Capitol Ser.	1,100
Castle Drive In	P.O. Box 403	Minocqua 54548	Delft. Affil.	

Theatre Name	Address	City & Zip	Circuit	Cars
Sky Vue Drive In		Monroe 53711	Goetz	
41 Outdoor		Neenah 59456	Marcus	.500
Hyway 15 Outdoor	14525 W. National Ave.	New Berlin 53151	Koutnik, R.	.500
16 S. Drive In		Oconomowoc 53066	Marcus	.300
44 Outdoor		Oshkosh 54902	Marcus	.500
Platteville Drive In		Platteville 53818	Steers, S.	.300
51 16 Drive In		Portage 53901	McWilliams	.300
Westgate Outdoor		Racine 53403	Standard	.600
Rouman Drive In		Rhinelander 54501	Rouman Circ.	
53 Auto Vue Dr. In		Rice Lake 54868	Carisch	.450
Highway 14 Outdoor		Richland Center 53581	Delft. Affil.	.500
Ripon Outdoor		Ripon 54971	Marcus	.500
Highway 29 Dr. In	5405 Alderson Street	Schofield 54476	Marcus	.500
Shawano Drive In	220 Main St.	Shawano 54166	Reilly, J.	
Stardusk Drive In		Sheboygan 53082	Standard	.500
Slinger Outdoor	353 Slinger Road	Slinger 53086	Melcher Ent.	
Highway 16 Outdoor		Sparta 54656	Mueller, G.	.300
51 Outdoor		Stevens Point 54481	Rogers	.400
Starlite Drive In	812 Delaware	Sturgeon Bay 54235	Norton	
Stardusk Drive In	1928 Penn Ave.	Superior 54880	Paine, R.	.395
Hiway 59 Outdoor		Waukesha 53187	Standard	
Hi Way 10 Outdoor	Box 93	Waupaca 54981	Keinert, L.	.300
Winnebago Drive In		Wisconsin Dells 53965	Melcher Ent.	.350
Highway 13 Outdoor		Wisconsin Rapid 54494	Gruetzmache	.400

WYOMING

Theatre Name	Address	City & Zip	Circuit	Cars
Cory Drive In		Basin 82410	Mercer, A.	.300
Sunset Dr. In	Box 105	Buffalo 82834	Campbell	
Mile Hi Drive In	Box 2554	Casper 82601	Commonwealt.	.823
Terrace Drive In	P.O. Box 2554	Casper 82601	Commonwealt.	.600
Motor Vu Drive In		Cheyenne 82001	Commonwealt.	.300
Starlight Drive In		Cheyenne 82001	Commonwealt.	.300
Park Drive In		Cody 82414	Schultz, J.	.300
West Drive In		Cody 82414	Ritter, F.	.300
Star Drive In	P.O. Box 274	Douglas 82633	Kaysbier, F.	
Ski Hi Drive In #4	P.O. Box B-1	Gillette 82716	Semple, W.	
Ski Hi Drive In	P.O. Drawer Bl	Gillette 82716	Semple, W.	.275
Aspen Drive In	P.O. Box 1228	Jackson 83001	Horn, J.	.300
Diane Drive In		Lander 82520	Thea. Opera	.300
Skyline Drive In		Laramie 82070	Wesco Theas.	.200
Drive In		Louell 82431	Bischoff, H.	.400
Lusk Drive In	Box 1107	Lusk 82225	Schwartz	.250
Wyo. Drive In		Newcastle 82701	Commonwealt.	.300
Vali Drive In	Box 271	Powell 82435	Mercer, A.	.200
Knight Drive In		Riverton 82501	Commonwealt.	.350
West Drive In	Box 853	Riverton 82501	Latman	.400
Motor Vue Drive In		Rock Springs 84111	Westates	.200
Skyline Dr. In	Box C	Sheridan 82801	Campbell	
Sundance Drive In		Sundance 82729	Goodwill Inc.	
Rio Drive In	904 Arapahoe	Thermopolis 82443	Hayek, J.	.300
Hilltop Karvu Dr. In		Torrington 82240	Maxfield	.307
West Drive In		Torrington 82240	Heyl, R.	.375
Upton Drive In		Upton 82730	Goodwell	.300
Seven Flags Dr. In		Wheatland 82201	Heyl, R.	.340
Lloyds Drive In		Worland 82401	Faure, F.	.360

Non-Theatrical Motion Pictures

* **PRODUCERS**

* **DISTRIBUTORS**

* **SERVICES**

* **LIBRARIES**

Producers, Distributors, Libraries of Non-Theatrical Motion Pictures

FOLLOWING is a list of producers, distributors and film libraries handling educational, entertainment and advertising pictures mainly for non-theatrical distribution to schools, clubs, civic organizations, teaching groups and other units, as well as television. Other sources of such films include most large manufacturing and public utility companies, trade associations in various industries, medical and public health societies and agencies, social service groups, educational organizations, museums, and state universities. Many of these supply films free or merely at a charge for transportation.

ARTCOM
Division of Mervin W. LaRue Films, Inc. 708 North Dearborn Street, Chicago, IL 60610; (312) 787-8657. (Producers and distributors of Art, Art History, Architectural, Religious, and general historical motion pictures, slidefilms, slide presentations, and still photography.)

A-V Corporation
2518 North Boulevard, Houston, TX 77098; 523-6701. P.O. Box 66824. Houston 77006. (Producers industrial, scientific, medical, public relations, educational and training films, black and white, color, sound, laboratory, sound stage commercials, animation.)

Academy Film Productions, Inc.
3918 West Estes Aves., Lincolnwood, IL 60645; (312) 674-2132. (Producers of motion pictures and videotapes, slide-films, slides and wide screen presentations for business, TV, conventions, meetings, audio-visual sales aids for industry.) Bernard Howard, exec. prod.

Admaster, Inc.
95 Madison Ave., New York, NY 10016; (212) 679-1134. (Creators and producers of slides, slide productions, filmstrips and limited animations.)

Alden Films
7820 20th Ave., Brooklyn, NY 11214. (212) 331-1045. (Distributors of TV and educational films.)

American Film Productions, Inc.
1540 Broadway, New York, NY 10019; (212) 582-1900. (Produces 16- and 35-mm. sponsored films & slidefilms for industrials, education, sales, public relations, TV commercials and television) (Distributes educational films, provides post production services.)

Association Films, Inc.
866 Third Ave., NY 10022; (212) 935-4210. (Free-loan educational, documentary and entertainment films for TV, cable, theatre and general audiences.)

Association Films Inc.
512 W. Burlington Ave., LaGrange, IL 60525. (312) 352-3377.

Audio Brandon Films, Inc.
34 MacQuesten Parkway So., Mount Vernon, NY 10550. (914) 664-5051. (Distributor.)

Audio & Visual Methods Co.
97–99 Edinburgh St., Rochester, NY 14608; (716) 546-6383, Rochester, NY 14619.

Automated Marketing Systems, Inc.
20300 Civic Center Drive, Southfield, MI 48076. (Marketing Services, sales promotion, and training, motion picture and collateral material.)

Bay State Film Productions, Inc.
35 Springfield Street, Agawam, MA 01001. (413) 786-4454. (Produces commercial and television motion pictures; slidefilms, video.)

Becker, Marvin-Filmmaker
2111 California St., San Francisco, CA 94115. (415) 567-2160. (Industrial, documentary, business films; TV films and commercials.)

Bransby, John, Productions, Ltd.
47 W. 57th Street, New York, NY 10019; (212) 688-6225. (Produces training, documentary, industrial, and educational films.)

Calvin Communications, Inc.
1105 Truman Road, P.O. Box 15607, Kansas City, MO 64106. (Script to screen 16mm services for TV commercials; films for business industry, government and education. Complete in-house lab facilities.)

Cameron Film Productions
222 Minor Avenue No., Seattle, WA 98108; (206) 623-4103. (16mm and 35mm sales, advertising, public relations and training motion pictures.)

Carousel Films, Inc.

1501 Broadway, Suite 1519, N.Y., NY 10036; (212) 354-0315. (Distribution educational and documentary films to schools, libraries, industry.)

Cavalcade Productions, Inc.

7360 Potter Valley Rd., Ukiah, CA 95482; (707) 743-1168. (Motion picture, sound filmstrip, and videotape production.)

Chapman/Spittler Inc.

1908 California, Omaha, NB 68102; (402) 348-1600. (16/33mm motion pictures; filmstrips; 35mm slides, slide presentations, agricultural AV specialists, multi-media, productions, sales meetings, artwork, still photography; TV films & commercials; editing & scripts.) Los Angeles: 12206 Magnolia Blvd., No. Hollywood, CA 91607. (213) 769-5900.

Charles, Henry, Motion Picture Studios

Plainfield Ave., P.O. Box 307, Edison, NJ 08817; (201) 545-5104. (Design and production of industrial and sales films, also motion pictures for television and group audiences sponsored by organizations and governmental agencies.)

Chenoweth Films, R.B.

1860 E. North Hills Dr., La Habra, CA 90631. (213) 691-1652, (213) 691-7195. (Motion Pictures and slidefilms for public relations, sales reports, training and education.)

Cinecraft, Inc.

2515 Franklin Blvd., Cleveland 13, OH; 781-2300. (Produces industrial sales and job training, civic relations motion pictures; slidefilms; TV spots & package shows, film and video tape facilities.)

Cinemakers, Inc.

200 West 57th St., New York, NY 10019; (212) 765-1168. (Motion pictures, filmstrips, TV spots, recording, film and sound editing.)

Cine-Pic Hawaii

1847 Pacific Heights Road, Honolulu, HI 96813; 533-2677. (Complete 16mm production for motion pictures and TV.)

City Film Productions, City Film Center Inc.

64-12 65th Place, Middle Village, Queens, NY 11379; (212) 456-5050. (Producers of 8mm/16mm/35mm motion pictures for the fields of business, industry, advertising, sales, science, religion, education, health, entertainment and TV. Creative, consultation and production services.)

Contempo Communications

1841 Broadway, Suite #1111, New York, NY 10023; (212) TR 3-3333. (Creative and production services for motion pictures, Super-8 and closed-circuit TV, 16mm and 35mm; multi-media productions all AV modes.)

Continental Film Productions Corp.

4220 Amnicola Highway, P.O. Box 5126, Chattanooga, TN 37406. (615) 622-1193. (Producers of 16mm, 35mm, and S-8mm live and animated motion pictures, filmstrips, and multi-media presentations for business and industry. CFPC distributes all major brands of audio visual equipment, and can thus provide complete script to screen service for its clients. Other production areas include sales promotion, training, commercial advertising, education, documentation and public relations.)

Countryman-Klang, Inc.

6154 Olson Memorial Hwy., Minneapolis, MN 55422; (612) 332-2538. (Producers of industrial, educational, sports, sales, sales training, TV commercials and filmstrips, 16mm and 35mm.)

Craven, Thomas, Film Corporation

316 E. 53 St., New York, NY 10022; (212) 688-1585. (Production of television, industrial, public information, training and educational films and programming; theatrical featurettes and promos; videotape production and editing services; programming for cable television systems.)

Custom Films/Video, Inc.

11 Cob Drive, Westport, CT 06880; (203) 226-0300. (Film and video production for sports, industry, broadcast and cable TV. Two broadcast quality mobile units. ¾″ and 1″ equipment. Complete 16mms production service.)

Dekko Film Productions, Inc.

295 Huntington Ave., Boston, MA 02115. (16mm and 35mm production services for education, science, industry and TV; slidefilms, complete sound studio.)

Disney, Walt, Non-Theatrical

500 South Buena Vista Street, Burbank, CA 91521.

Ditzel, William, Productions

933 Shroyer Rd., Dayton, OH 45419; (513) 298-5381. (Script and produce motion pictures, filmstrips, TV programs, commercials, and meetings.)

Dolphin Productions, Inc.

140 East 80th St., New York, NY 10021; (212) 628-5930. (Commercial, industrial, educational motion pictures; radio transcriptions; television commercials.)

Elms, Charles, Productions, Inc.

1260 S. 350 West, Bountiful, UT, 84010; (801) 295-2727. (Research & production of 16 & 35mm. motion pictures; 70mm Widescope presentations, sound slide films, slide presentations, training manuals & charts.)

Empire Photosound, Inc.

4444 W. 76th St., Minneapolis; Telex: 029-5317. (Films for industry, sales training & TV; animation; sound slidefilms.)

Feil, Edward, Productions
4614 Prospect Ave., Cleveland, OH 44103; (216) 771-0655. (Producers of industrial, institutional and promotion films.)

Film Effects
342 Richmond St., W., Toronto, Ont., M5V 1X2. (416) 360-1270. (Opticals, animation and special effects 35/16mm.)

Film Enterprises, Inc.
516 Fifth Ave., New York, NY 10036; (212) 840-1966. (Production of 16 and 35mm motion pictures for business and industry.)

Films Incorporated
1144 Wilmette Ave., Wilmette, IL 60091. (312) 256-4730. (Distributor). Southeast Division: 476 Plasamour Drive, N.E., Atlanta, GA 30324; (404) 873-5101. West Division: 5625 Hollywood Blvd., Hollywood, CA 90028; (213) 466-5481. Northeast Division: 440 Park Avenue South, New York, NY 10016; (212) 889-7910. Central Division: 733 Green Bay Road, Wilmette, IL 60091; (312) 256-6600.

Flagg Films Inc.
Box 1107, Studio City, CA 91604. (213) 985-5050. (Industrial films, sales films, medical films, TV commercials, TV sports shows.)

Fried, Si Productions, Inc.
250 West 57th St., New York, NY 10019 (212) PL-7-4424. (Motion pictures, filmstrips—including industrial, documentary, TV Spots, etc.)

Gemini Films, Inc.
119 West 57 St., New York, NY 10019; (212) 757-7997. (Conception, design, production of films for government, industry, TV and theater.)

Goldberger Productions, Edw. H.
1210 Tamm Ave., St. Louis, MO 63139; (314) 647-7112. (Motion pictures for documentary, custom footage filmed for inserts, newsreel & public relations; 16mm.)

Goldsholl Associates, Inc.
420 Frontage Road, Northfield, IL 60093; (312) 446-8300. (Producers of motion pictures and slidefilms for business, industry, TV and education.)

Gotham Film Productions, Inc.
11 E. 44th St., New York, NY 10017; (212) 697-6020. (Motion Pictures: 35 mm, 16mm and 8mm; video tapes; slide motion; slidefilms; flipcharts; talking manuals.)

Graphic Films Corporation
3341 Cahuenga Blvd. West, Los Angeles, CA 90068. (213) 851-4100. (Production of animated and live action films for industry and government; films and special effects for exhibits.)

Guggenheim Productions, Inc.
3121 South Street, N.W., Washington, DC 20007; (202) 337-6900. (Production of theatrical and non-theatrical motion pictures.)

Hallmark Films & Recordings, Inc.
51 New Plant Ct., Owings Mills, MD 21213; (301) 363-4500. (Motion pictures, sound slidefilms, sales, motivational training and educational.)

Hanna-Barbera Productions, Inc.
3400 Cahuenga Blvd., Hollywood, CA 90068; (213) 851-5000. (Motion picture production—live action and animation—for industry, theatre and television.)

Hardcastle Films
7319 Wise Avenue, St. Louis, MO 63117; (314) MI 7-4200. (Production of sound motion pictures, slidefilms, TV documentaries and commercials in b&w and color.)

Hartley Film Foundation, Inc.
Cat Rock Rd., Cos Cob, CT 06807; (203) 869-1818. (Produces and distributes films on parapsychology, the human potential, and Eastern philosophy.)

Harvest Films, Inc.
309 Fifth Ave., New York, NY 10016; (212) 684-7950. (Production of motion pictures and filmstrips for industry, governments, educational and social service organizations. Distribution of selected films for clients.)

Haycox Photoramic, Inc.
1531 Early Street, Norfolk, VA 23502; (804) 855-1911. (Complete motion picture production services.)

Hurlock Cine-World, Inc.
13 Arcadia Rd., Old Greenwich, CT 06870; (203) 637-4319. (Exclusive distributor in non-theatrical field of all Lorimar's Allied Artists films in current library.)

Ivy Film
165 West 46th Street, New York, NY 10036. (212) 765-3940. (Exclusive distributors worldwide of over 1500 feature films and 2000 short subjects from the libraries of National Telefilm Associates, Inc., M.&A. Alexander Inc., Crystal Pictures, Inc. Republic Pictures, and other independents. Foreign distribution handled on a country by country basis, both exclusive and non-exclusive licenses.

J P I And Associates
13001 West 29th Ave., Golden, CO 80401; (303) 278-8380. (Motion Pictures, slidefilms; TV films and commercials; live shows; meeting presentations; still photography; video tape production.)

576

Johnston, Inc., Hugh & Suzanne

16 Valley Road, Princeton, NJ 05840; (609) 924-7505. (Design and production of educational, television and sponsored motion picture films; specialized film promotion and distribution services.)

K&H Productions, Inc.

3601 Oak Grove, Dallas, TX 75204, 214/526-5268. (35mm and 16mm motion picture production for sales, training, education, and TV commercials. Multi-media audio-visual production. Producer's services in production, animation, titles and optical printing.)

Kayfetz, Victor Productions, Inc.

112 Bentwood Drive, Stamford, CT 06903, (203) 329-7795. (Motion pictures and slidefilms; combining live action & animation.)

Kim & Gifford Productions, Inc.

342 Madison Ave., New York, NY 10017; (212) YU 6-2826. (Creative service and production of animated and live-action films.)

Le Roy Motion Picture Production Studios

Studio: 213 West 35th Street, New York, NY 10001; (212) 564-6793; Office: 531 South St., Philadelphia, PA 19147; (215) X-2-L-E-R-O-Y. (Producers of industrial, educational, promotional films and television commercials and television programs.)

Lieb Productions Inc., Jack

200 E. Ontario St., Chicago, IL 60611; (312) 943-1440. (Motion picture production; industrial, theatrical, TV, sales promotion, institutional and sales training; specialists in travel promotion films, TV productions, spots and shows.)

Lilly, Lou-Films/West, Inc.

518 N. La Cienega Blvd., Hollywood, CA 90028; (213) 659-0024. (TV commercials; industrial and educational films.)

Lopatin Productions, Inc., Ralph

1728 Cherry St., Philadelphia, PA 19103; (215) 568-6400. (Live photography, recording, animation, title editing, film distribution.)

MPO Videotronics

820 Second Ave., New York, NY 10017; (212) 557-9260. (Complete production of motion pictures for sales promotion, training, public relations and product demonstrations. Filmed TV commercials. Distribution service to TV, stations, schools, etc. Film and live presentations and stage shows for industry, closed circuit and live presentations for sales force and management meetings.)

MRC Films & Video (Division of McLaughlin Research Corp.)

71 W. 23rd St., New York 10010; (212) 989-1754. (Production of motion pictures, filmstrips, recordings and multimedia presentations for TV, government, & industry.) Complete videotape production services. Also consultants "inplant" film units, providing script, editing, animation, recording and production completion services.

Madison Films, Inc.

216 East 49th St., New York, NY 10017; (212) 838-4856. (Producers of industrial, documentary, public relations, sales, education and TV films and TV commercials.)

Manbeck Pictures Corp.

3621 Wakonda Dr., Des Moines, IA 50321; 285-8345. (Distributes unusual 16mm silent and sound film classics.)

Marathon International Productions, Inc.

10 East 49th St., New York, NY 10017; (212) MU 8-1130. (Public information films, worldwide news service, company newsreels, special events coverage for industry; film editing, stock shots, etc.)

Mass Media Ministries, Inc.,

Mass Media Building, 2116 North Charles Street, Baltimore, MD 21218. (301) 727-3270.

Maysles Films, Inc.

250 West 54th St., New York, NY 10019; (212) 582-6050. (All services in connection with production of motion picture films.)

Melendez Productions, Inc., Bill

439 N. Larchmont Blvd., Los Angeles, CA 90004; (213) 463-4101. (Production of 16/35mm animated & live action motion pictures, TV programs & commercials, industrial & public relation films.) London office: 32/34 Great Marlborough Street, London W. 1, England; 01-734-0691.

Mendelson Film Productions, Inc., Lee

1408 Chapin Ave., Burlingame, CA 94010; (415) 342-8284. (Network TV specials, films for business, government and industry.)

Mode-Art Pictures, Inc.

3075 West Liberty Avenue, Pittsburgh, PA; (412) 343-8700. 1904 Preuss Road, Los Angeles, CA 90034. 870-3190. (Produces 16mm and 35mm advertising, industrial, educational films, TV.)

Modern Talking Picture Service, Inc.

5000 Park St., North, St. Petersburg, FL 33709; (813) 541-7571. (516) 437-6300. (Distributor of free-loan sponsored motion pictures for theatres, community groups, schools, television and resort circuits. Also circulates educational and entertainment films on a rental basis through its Modern Film Rentals service.)

Arthur Mokin Productions, Inc.

17 West 60th St., New York, NY 10023; (212) PL 7-4868. (Production and distribution of nontheatrical motion pictures.)

Monumental Films & Recordings, Inc.

2160 Rockrose Ave., Baltimore, MD 21211; (301) 462-1550. (Scripting, motion picture services, editorial services, narration and commercials, industrial, commercial and educational films, sound recordings.)

Byron Morgan Associates, Inc.

5309 Locust Ave., Bethesda, MD 20014; (301) 530-1770. (Motion picture writing, direction and production for government, education, industry, public relations, TV and entertainment industry.)

Moss Communications Inc.

1206 Masters Way, Kingwood, TX 77339 (713) 358-7700. (16mm motion pictures, videotaping, multi-media, slidefilms & slides for sales meetings, training, selling, commercials and television.)

Multi Media Entertainment, Inc.

165 West 46th St., New York, NY 10036. (212) 765-3940. (Licenses and sells feature films, TV shows, short subjects, video-cassettes, video cartridges throughout the world.)

Burt Munk & Co.

666 Dundee Road, Northbrook, IL 60062 (312) 564-0855. (Creation and production of motion pictures, slidefilms and related materials for business communication.)

NFL Films, Inc.

410 Park Ave., New York, NY 10022; (212) 758-8380. Sales: 230 N. 13th St., Phila., PA 19107; (215) 567-4315 (production). (Official motion picture production unit of the National Football League. Producing color films of all phases of N.F.L. Football for TV, schools, industry.)

National Television News

13691 West Eleven Mile Road, Oak Park, MI 48237; (313) 541-1440. 6016 Fallbrook Ave., Woodland Hills, CA 91367. (213) 883-6121. (Production of 16mm information films and videotape for education, TV, sales promotion, public relations. Specialists in planning, production and distribution of television newsfilm, TV sportsfilm, TV public service spots. Counselling.)

Niles Communications Centers, Inc., Fred A.

1058 W. Washington Blvd., Chicago, IL 60607; (312) 738-4181. 240 W. 60th St., New York, NY; (212) 586-2333; 8530 Wilshire Blvd., Suite 500, Beverly Hills, CA 90211; (213) 659-7392. (TV commercials; industrial films; sales training films; sales meetings; complete videotape facilities; etc.)

Nowak Associates, Inc., Amram

1776 Broadway, New York, NY 10019; (212) LT 1-3140. (Producer of documentary motion pictures and public service TV spots for health, social welfare, religious and educational agencies.)

O'Connor Company, Walter G.

Box Y, Hershey, PA 17033; (717) 534-1000. (Script to screen production of motion pictures and slidefilms, including public relations and public service, industrial training and sales, educational, reports, live action and animated TV commercials.)

Omnicom Productions, Inc.

4700 Ardmore, Okemos, MI 48864 (517) 349-6303. (Motion picture productions, filmstrips, sales meetings, training programs.)

Pace Films, Inc.

411 E. 53rd St., New York, NY 10022; (212) PL5-5486. (Consultation, scripting and production of features, shorts, documentaries and distribution.)

Panel Film Productions, Inc.

271 Madison Ave., New York, NY 10016; (212) 679-6401. (TV commercials, industrial and sales promotion films.)

Pilot Productions, Inc.

1819 Ridge Ave., Evanston, IL 60201; (312) 273-4141. (16mm motion, 35mm sound slidefilms.)

Pinn Audio Visual

114 W. Illinois St., Chicago, IL 60610; (312) 787-8432. (Creation and production of slidefilms, TV slides, slide presentations and Vista-Sell programs for industry, business and education, full inhouse sound and cassette dupe.)

Playhouse Pictures

1401 North La Brea Ave., Hollywood, CA 90028; (213) 851-2112. (Animation specialists in industrial, educational, entertainment and TV commercials.)

Portafilms Inc.

4180 Dixie Highway, Drayton Plains, MI 48020; (313) 674-0489. (Designers and producers of motion pictures for business and education.)

Producers Row, Inc.

666 Fifth Ave., New York, NY 10019; (212) 399-2755. (Motion pictures, presentations and stage shows for industry; slide-films and other audio-visual media.)

Production Center, Inc.

221 W. 26th St., New York, NY 10001; (212) OR 5-2211. (16/35mm motion pictures for theatrical and TV use. Documentaries, TV commercials & sales presentations.)

Riviera Productions
6610 Selma Ave., Hollywood, CA 90028; (213) 462-8585. (Producers of TV film series; theatrical motion pictures; TV commercials.)

Roy, Ross, Inc.
2751 East Jefferson Avenue, Detroit, MI 48207; (Produces video tapes, motion pictures, sound slide-films, sales meetings, industrial theatre presentations.)

Ken Saco/Curt Lowey, Inc.
925 Westchester Ave., White Plains, NY 10604. (914) 948-6500. (Script, design, and produce multi media programs, business meetings, and slide and filmstrip presentations.)

Science House
Szchvdglck Manor Road, Manchester, MA 01944. (617) 526-1120; (Creative science and engineering consultants to advertising agencies, industry and film producers.)

Scientificom (Division of Mervin W. LaRue Films, Inc.)
708 North Dearborn Street, Chicago, IL 60610; (312) 787-8656. (Producers and distributors of medical and scientific motion pictures, slidefilms, slide presentations, and still photography.)

Skyline Films, Inc.
P.O. Box C1012, Wykagyz Station, New Rochelle, NY 10804; (212) 490-1668. (Research, create, write, produce films and videotape for business, industry, education, government, TV, plus production of TV commercials.)

Snazelle Film/Tape Inc.
155 Fell Street, San Francisco, CA 94102; (415) 431-5490; 5609 Sunset Blvd., Hollywood, CA 90028; (213) 466-4309. 333 N. Michigan Ave., Chicago, Ill. 60601 (312) 782-4590. 122 E. 42nd Street, New York, N.Y. 10017 (212) 599-2260. 1100 17th St. N.W. Suite 1000, Washington D.C. 20036 (202) 466-2560. (TV film commercial production company)

Snyder Films, Inc., Bill
1419 First Ave. South, Fargo, ND 58103 Mailing address: Box 2784, Fargo, ND 58108; (701) 293-3600. (16mm sales promotion, public relations and educational films for business, agriculture; TV commercials; sound slidefilms; news film coverage; agricultural film stock footage library, film completion for in-plant photographers.)

Sportlite Films
20 North Wacker Dr., Chicago, IL 60606; (312) 236-8955. (Official sports color films— Major League Baseball, NBA, NITC, U.S. Open, UPI Sports Year Olympics, Famous Fights for industry, TV, education, meetings, commercials, (stock footage) how-to marketing; in-plant productions, entertainment, trade shows and Dartnell sales motivation.)

Spots Alive, Inc.
342 Madison Avenue, New York, NY 10173; (212) 953-1677. (Full service creative preparation and production of motion picture films and video tape materials; specialists in motion picture campaign promotion, industrial presentations, sales meetings.)

Sterling Educational Films
(A division of the Walter Reade Org., Inc., 241 East 34th St., New York, NY 10016. (212) 683-6300. (Distributor) Paul Baise, adm. dir.

Stokes Associates, Inc., Bill
5642 Dyer Street, Dallas, TX. (214) 363-0161. (Producer of Motion Pictures, TV commercials, sound slidefilms, animation and multi-media slide presentations. Producer service for other producers in sound, editing, equipment rental, cinematographer and stage rental.)

Swain Productions, Inc., Hack
1185 Cattleman Rd., Sarasota, FL 33578; P.O. Box 10235, Sarasota, 33578. (813) 371-2360. (Production of 16mm industrial, educational, documentary & training films; TV spots; slidefilms & stripfilms; ½" & ¾" videotape industrial production.)

Swank Motion Pictures, Inc.
National headquarters: 201 South Jefferson Ave., St. Louis, MO 63166, (314) 534-6300. Regional offices: 393 Front Street, Hempstead, NY 11550, (516) 538-6500; 7926 Jones Branch Drive, McLean, VA, 22101, (703) 821-1040; 220 Forbes Road, Braintree, MA, 02184, (617) 848-8300; 1200 Roosevelt Road, Glen Ellyn, IL 60137, (312) 629-9004; 5200 W. Kennedy Blvd., Tampa, FL 33609, (813) 870-0500; 201 S. Jefferson Ave., St. Louis, MO 63166, (314) 535-1200; 4111 Director's Row, Houston, TX 77018, (713) 683-8222; 6767 Forest Lawn Drive, Hollywood, CA 90068, (213) 851-6300.

Swartwout Productions
6736 E. Avalon Dr. Scottsdale, AZ 85251; (602) 994-4774. (Business, documentary, educational & public relations films; integrated instructional & promotional packages, including films, phonograph records & printed materials.)

TR Productions, Inc.
1031 Commonwealth Ave., Boston, MA 02215; (617) 783-0200. (Producers of motion pictures and multi-image sound/slide productions for business, government, and education; audio recording, sound tracks, and radio spots; industrial videotape.)

Take Ten Incorporated
2700 River Road, Suite 210, Des Plaines, IL 60018; (312) 297-1010. (Industrial motion pictures; live industrial shows; sound-slidefilms; slide presentations; TV films; videotape; creative consultation.)

Tel-Air Interest, Inc.

1755 N.E. 149th St., Miami, FL 33181; (305) 944-3268. (Motion picture production, cinematography, editing, sound recording, script writing, record pressing, high speed audio tape duplicating, distribution.)

Telic

317 West 89th St., New York, NY 10024; (212) 595-7078. (Consultants, co-producers and directors)

Tilton Films, Inc., Roger

241 West G. St., San Diego, CA 92101; (714) 233-6513. 6640 Sunset Blvd., Hollywood, CA 90028; (213) 467-3191. (Motion picture and filmstrip production, TV commercials; government and industrial films; live action and animation.)

Training Films, Inc.

Laurel St., Butler, NJ 07405; (201) 838-4363. (Film and slide production and distribution.)

Trans World Films, Inc.

332 S. Michigan Ave., Chicago, IL 60604; (312) 922-1530. (Non-theatrical 16mm feature film distributor.)

Twyman Films, Inc.

National headquarters: 329 Salem Avenue, Dayton, Ohio 45401. (800) 543-9594. Regional offices: 175 Fulton Avenue, Suite 306, Hempstead, New York 11550. (516) 481-4050; 2321 West Olive, Burbank, CA 91506. (213) 843-8052. (Distributor for Universal, Warner Brothers, Columbia, Disney and foreign. Features, shorts & featurettes.)

Universal Education & Visual Arts

C/O Educational Media Corporation, 6930½ Tujunga Avenue, North Hollywood, CA 91605; 985-3921. (Producer and distributor of 8mm and 16mm educational films.)

Video Films, Inc.

679 East Mandoline, Madison Heights, MI 48071. (313) 588-7171. (Television and industrial films, slides and slidefilms.)

Warner Productions, Robert

7 East 78th St., New York, NY 10021; (212) 744-7979. (Live, film and tape programs and commercials.)

Wexler Film Productions, Inc.

801 N. Seward St., Los Angeles, CA 90038;

(213) HO 2-6671. (Educational and medical-educational motion pictures. Specialized services of 16mm and 35mm production, color printing, animation and equipment design.)

Zachry Associates, Inc.

709 North Second St., Box 1739, Abilene, TX 79604; (915) 677-1342. (TV commercials, industrial, training, filmstrips.)

Canada

Bird Films Ltd.

Golden Mile Plaza, S4S 3R2, Regina, Saskatchewan. (306) 586-0311. (Motion Pictures.)

Crawley Films Ltd.

19 Fairmont Ave., Ottawa, Ontario K1Y 3B5; 728-3513. (Branches in Toronto) (Motion picture and slidefilms for Canadian and United States industry, government, education and TV.)

Film Effects

342 Richmond St., W., Toronto, Ont.; (416) 360-1270. (Opticals, animation and special effects 35/16mm.)

Graphic Films, Ltd. (A subsidiary of Crawley Films Ltd.)

19 Fairmont Ave., Ottawa, Ontario, K1Y 3B5. (Laboratory & producer's service company associated with Crawley Films Ltd. Printing & processing of 16/35mm b/w films, 16mm Ektachrome processing, 16mm b/w reversal processing; also 16mm additive color printing, internegs & color positive prints. Ektachrome masters & reversal color prints. Scene-to-scene color corrections.)

Peterson Productions, Limited

Suite 610, 89 Avenue Road, Toronto, Ontario M5R 2G4; 366-3287. (Produces commercial, industrial films, TV commercials.)

SDP Communications, Ltd.

Suite 610, 89 Avenue Rd., Toronto, Canada, M5R 2G4; (416) 961-5525. (Produces television and theatrical product for domestic and international release.)

Western Films Ltd.

695 Sargent, Winnipeg, Manitoba, Canada; (204) 786-8567. (Motion pictures, live and animated.)

Motion Picture Organizations

* **PRODUCER-DISTRIBUTOR**

* **EXHIBITOR**

* **GUILDS AND UNIONS**

* **VARIETY CLUB, FILM CLUBS AND GENERAL GROUPS**

Producer-Distributor Organizations

American Film Marketing Assn.

8281 Melrose Ave., Suite 305, Los Angeles, CA 90046; (213) 852-1777. (Trade organization formed in 1981 by 26 firms—later expanded to 38—engaged in the sale of independently-produced films to the international market. Sponsors the American Film Market in Los Angeles in the Spring.)

PRESIDENT
  Robert Meyers
SENIOR VICE PRESIDENTS
  Michael Goldman, Larry Sugar
CHIEF FINANCIAL OFFICER
  William Moraskie
VICE PRESIDENT & GENERAL MANAGER & EXECUTIVE DIRECTOR OR AMERICAN FILM MARKET
  B.H. "Buddy" Goldbert
EXECUTIVE COMMITTEE: Andy Adelson (Lorimar Distribution International), Ed Carlin (Inter-Ocean Film Sales), Mark Damon (Producers Sales Organization), Herb Fletcher (Avco Embassy Pictures Overseas Corp.), Larry Friedricks (Hemdale Leisure Corp.), Lou George (Arista Films), Howard Goldfarb (Goldfarb Distributors, Inc.), Michael Goldman (Manson International), John Rubinich (Melvin Simon Productions), Helen Sarlui (American Cinema Services), Wolf Schmidt (Kodiak Films), Jules Stein (American Cinema), Bonnie Sugar (Serendipity Productions) and Andy Vajna (Carolco Services).
MEMBERS:
ABC Motion Pictures, 2020 Avenue of Stars, Los Angeles, CA 90067
American Cinema, 6834 Hollywood Blvd., Los Angeles, CA 90028
American Cinema Services, 321 S. Beverly Drive, Beverly Hills, CA 90212
Arista Films, 9000 Sunset Blvd., Los Angeles, CA 90069
Australia Film, 9229 Sunset Blvd., Los Angeles, CA 90069
Avco Embassy Pictures Overseas Corp., 956 Seward St., Los Angeles, CA 90038
Barry & Enright Intl., Inc., 1888 Century Park East, Los Angeles, CA 90069
Carolco Service, 8810 Melrose Ave., Los Angeles, CA 90069
Filmaccord, 1110 Sherbrooke West, Montreal, Canada H3A 1G8
Filmcrest International, 595 Madison Ave., New York, NY 10022
Films Around the World, 745 Fifth Ave., New York, NY 10022
Filmways Pictures International, 9033 Wilshire Blvd., Beverly Hills, CA 90211
Goldfarb Distributors, 1888 Century Park East, Los Angeles, CA 90067
Golden Communications, c/o Pinetree Postproductions, 1041 No. Formosa, Los Angeles, CA 90046
Hemdale Leisure Corp., 375 Park Ave., New York, NY 10022
Inter-Ocean Film Sales, 2029 Century Park East, Los Angeles, CA 90067
Isram Film Corp., 360 E. 65th St., New York, NY 10021
Jad Films Internationsl, 405 Park Ave., New York, NY 10022
J&M Film Sales & P. Wachsberger, 8899 Beverly Blvd., Los Angeles, CA 90048
Kodiak Films, 11681 San Vincente Blvd., Los Angeles, CA 90049
Lorimar Distribution International, 5150 Overland Ave., Los Angeles 90230
Manson International, 9145 Sunset Blvd., Los Angeles, CA 90069
Melvin Simon Productions, 260 So. Beverly Drive, Beverly Hills, CA 90212
Miracle Films, 6311 Romaine St., Los Angeles, CA 90038
Overseas Filmgroup, 8758 Venice Blvd., Los Angeles, CA 90034
Pacific International Enterprises, 1133 So. Riverside, Medford, OR 97501
PolyGram Pictures, 8285 Sunset Blvd., Los Angeles, CA 90046
Producers Sales Organization, 10100 Santa Monica Blvd., Los Angeles CA 90046
Satori Productions, 250 West 57th St., New York, NY 10017
Serendipity Productions, 6363 Sunset Blvd., Los Angeles, CA 90028
Silverstein International, 200 West 57th St., New York, NY 10019
Taft International Pictures, 6363 Sunset Blvd., Los Angeles, CA 90028

Time Life Films, Motion Pictures Division, 1271 Ave. of Americas, New York, NY 10020
TPC Films International, 291 So. La Cienega Blvd., Beverly Hills, CA 90211

Association of Motion Picture and Television Producers, Inc.

(Organized January, 1924; Membership: Studios and Producers) 8480 Beverly Blvd., Los Angeles, CA 90048; (213) 653-2200.

CHAIRMAN OF THE BOARD
  Dennis Stanfill
PRESIDENT
  Jack Valenti
FIRST VICE PRESIDENT
  Edward P. Prelock
SECRETARY
  Robert F. Cortes
TREASURER
  Patrick D. Walters
MEMBERS
(California area code: 213).
Aaron Spelling Productions Inc. 132 So. Rodeo Dr., Beverly Hills, CA 90212. 278-6700.
A&S Productions, Inc., 7046 Hollywood Boulevard, #801, Hollywood, CA 90028. 461-3426.
The Alpha Corporation 13063 Ventura Blvd., Studio City, CA 91604. 788-5750.
American International Productions 9033 Wilshire Blvd., Beverly Hills, CA 90211. 278-8118.
Andras Enterprises, Inc. 9163 Sunset Blvd. L.A. 90069; 271-5830
Aspen Productions 10100 Santa Monica Blvd., #1580, Los Angeles, CA 90067, 552-9977.
Aubrey Schenck Enterprises, Inc., 7046 Hollywood Blvd. #801, Hollywood, CA 90028, 461-3426.
Bing Crosby Productions, Inc. 6311 Romaine St., Hollywood, CA 90038 465-3114.
Bristol Productions, Inc. c/o Nathan Golden, 9601 Wilshire Blvd., Beverly Hills, CA 90210, 278-1103.
The Burbank Studios 4000 Warner Boulevard, Burbank, CA 91522, 843-6000.
Charleston Enterprises Corp. 501 Madison Avenue, New York, NY 10022, (212) 755-0285.
Charles Fries Productions 4024 Radford Ave., Studio City, CA 91604. 763-8495.
Chrislaw Productions 1006 Cory Ave. Los Angeles, CA 90069 464-0255.
Cine Films, Inc. 11166 Gault Street, No. Hollywood, CA 91605, 764-9900.
Cine Guarantors, Inc. TV Center Studios, 6311 Romaine St. Hwyd., CA 90038, 467-3006.
Cinema Payments Inc. of California 20440 Tiara St., Woodland Hills, CA 91367. 703-1312.
Cinema Video Communications, 10202 Washington Blvd., Culver City, CA 90230, 836-3000.
Columbia Pictures Industries, Inc. Colgems Square, Burbank, CA 91522, 843-6000.
C-O-P Productions 2049 Century Park East #1550, Los Angeles, CA 90067. 879-9901.
Daisy Productions c/o William Morris Agency 151 El Camino Dr., Bev. Hills, CA 90212, 274-7451.
Danny Thomas Productions 11350 Ventura Blvd. Studio City, CA 91604, 985-2940.
Darr-Don, Inc. 4024 Radford Avenue, Studio City, CA 91604, 760-5000.
Dubie-Do Productions, Inc. 2049 Century Park East #1550, Los Angeles, CA 90067, 879-9901.
Edprod Pictures, Inc. Hollywood Taft Building, 1680 North Vine, #1210, Hollywood, CA 90028. 766-7327.
EGS International P.O. Box 28, Edmund, WA 98020 (206) 778-7926.
Filmways Feature Prod., Inc. 2049 Century Park East, Los Angeles, CA 90067, 557-8700
Filmways Pictures, Inc. 9033 Wilshire Blvd. Beverly Hills, Ca 90067, 557-8700
Filmways Productions, Inc. 2049 Century Park East, Los Angeles, CA 90067, 557-8700.
Finnegan Associates, 4225 Coldwater Cyn. Blvd., Studio City, CA 91604, 985-0430.

Four Star International, Inc. 400 South Beverly Drive, Beverly Hills, CA 90212, 277-7444.

Geoffrey Productions, Inc. (Trellis Entp. Inc.) 1888 Century Park E. #1616 Los Angeles, CA 90067 553-6741.

GJL Productions, Inc., 1041 N. Formosa Ave., Los Angeles, CA 90046, 650-2500.

Gus Productions, Inc. 10889 Wilshire Blvd., Los Angeles, CA 90027, 477-3046.

Hanna-Barbera Productions, Inc. 3400 Cahuenga Blvd., Hollywood, CA 90068, 851-5000.

Harold Hecht Co. 336 S. Spaulding "C", Bev. Hills, CA 90212, 552-9188.

Herbert Leonard Enterprises, Inc. 5300 Fulton Avenue, Van Nuys, CA 91401, 783-0457.

Jack Chertok TV, Inc. 415 S. Beverly Glen, West Los Angeles, CA 279-1934 (res).

Jack Rollins & Charles H. Joffe Productions 130 West 57th Street, New York, NY 10019, (212) 765-3957.

Joe R. Hartsfield Productions, Inc. 1220 S. Omni Int'l., Atlanta, GA 30303 (404) 525-2272, 525-2200.

John Charles Walters Prod. 5451 Marathon St. Hollywood, CA 90038 468-5000

Lance Enterprises, 12827 Kling Street, Suite #5, Studio City, CA 91604, 761-8396.

Lassie Films, Inc. 270 North Canon Drive, Beverly Hills, CA 90210. 278-8521.

Lassie Productions, Inc. and Lassie TV, Inc. 5461 Bothwell Road, Tarzana, CA 91356, 345-4682.

Leonard Films, Inc. 5300 Fulton Avenue, Van Nuys, CA 91401, 783-0457.

Levy-Gardner-Laven Productions, Inc. 9570 Wilshire Blvd., Suite 400, Beverly Hills, CA 90210. 278-9820.

Location Productions 11166 Gault Street, North Hollywood, CA 91605, 764-9900.

Lucille Ball Productions, Inc. 9601 Wilshire Blvd. #526, Beverly Hills, CA 90210. 278-6060.

The Malpaso Company c/o Gang, Tyre & Brown, 6400 Sunset Blvd., Hollywood, CA 90028, 463-4863.

Marble Arch Productions, Inc. Studio Center, 4024 Radford St., Studio City, CA 91604. 760-6200.

Max E. Youngstein Enterprises, Inc. 9220 Sunset Blvd. Suite 210, Los Angeles, CA 90069, (213) 274-0371.

McDermott Productions 250 N. Canon Drive, Beverly Hills, CA 90210. 278-8521.

Meteor Films, Inc. 706 N. Beverly Dr,. Beverly Hills, CA 90213, 271-4517.

Metromedia Producers Corp. 5746 Sunset Blvd. L.A. CA 90028 462-7111

Mirisch Corporation 100 Universal City Plaza, Universal City, CA. 91608, 508-2933

Murakami-Wolf Productions, Inc. 1463 Tamarind Avenue, Hollywood, CA 90028, 462-6474.

NGC Television Inc., #1 Carthay Plaza, Los Angeles, CA 90048, 947-4100.

Norlan Productions, Inc. 9601 Wilshire Blvd. #322, Beverly Hills, Ca 90210.

Pax Enterprises, Inc. 300 Colgems Square, Burbank, CA 91522, 843-6000.

Pax Films, Inc. 300 Colgems Square, Burbank, CA 91522, 843-6000.

Proserco of California Ltd. 7051 Santa Monica Blvd., Hollywood, CA 90038. 465-5790.

Rainbow Productions c/o Gunther Schiff, Esq., 9777 Wilshire Blvd., Beverly Hills, CA 90212, 278-1500.

Rastar Enterprises, Inc. 300 Colgems Square, Burbank, CA 91522. 843-6000.

Rastar Prod., Inc., 300 Colgems Square Burbank, CA 91522 843-6000

Rastar Television, Inc. 300 Colgems Square, Burbank, CA 91522. 843-6000.

RFB Enterprises, Inc. 501 Doheny Road, Beverly Hills, Ca 90210. 278-8777.

Robert B. Radnitz Productions, Ltd. 9336 W. Washington Blv. Culver City, CA 90230 871-0360

Ruby Spears Prods., Inc. c/o Filmways, Inc. 2049 Century Park East L.A., CA 90067 557-8700.

Samuel Goldwyn Jr. Productions, Inc. 1041 North Formosa Avenue, Hollywood, CA 90046, 650-2500.

Sheldon Leonard Productions c/o William Morris Agency, 151 El Camino Drive, Beverly Hills, CA 90212. 274-7451

Spelling-Goldberg Productions 10201 W. Pico Blv., Los Angeles, CA 90035, 277-2211.

Stanley Kramer Productions Ltd. P.O. Box 158 Bellevue, WA 98009 (206) 454-1785

Summit Films, Inc., 6363 Wilshire Blvd., Los Angeles, CA 90048. 653-7330.

Suncrest Cinema Corp. 2049 Century Park East, Suite 1920, Los Angeles, CA 90067. 552-1234.

T&L Productions, Inc. c/o William Morris Agency, 151 El Camino Dr., Beverly Hills, CA 90212, 274-7451.

Tori Productions, Inc. 5300 Fulton Avenue, Van Nuys, CA 91401. 662-3108.

Twentieth Century-Fox Film Corp. 10201 West Pico Blvd., Los Angeles, CA 90035. 277-2211

Viacom Prods., Inc. 4024 Radford Ave. Studo City, CA 91604 760-5000.

Warner Bros. Inc. 4000 Warner Boulevard, Burbank, CA 91522. 843-6000.

(The) Wolper Organization, Inc. c/o The Burbank Studios, 4000 Warner Blvd., Burbank, CA 91522. 843-6000.

Wrather Entertainment Intl. 270 N. Canon Dr., Beverly Hills, CA 90210, 278-8521.

AMPTP BOARD OF DIRECTORS
J. R. Rodgers, Bing Crosby Productions, Inc.
Orison Marden, Columbia Pictures Industries, Inc.
Salvatore Iannucci, Filmways, Inc.
David Charnay, Four Star International, Inc.
Marvin Mirisch, Mirisch Productions, Inc.
Marshall Wortman, 20th Century Fox Film Corp.
Ronald Jacobs, Danny Thomas Productions
Alan Raphael, Warner Bros. Inc.
Edward Prelock, Warner Bros. Inc.

The Canadian Film and Television Association

Suite 512, 55 York St., Toronto, Canada M5J 1S2. (416) 363-8374.

(The aim of this association, which was formed in the fall of 1949, is to promote higher standards and represent the interests of motion picture producers and laboratories and associated industries throughout Canada.

PRESIDENT
Findlay J. Quinn
VICE PRESIDENT
W. Paterson Ferns
OTHER DIRECTORS
Gunter Henning, Dov. Zimmer, Joseph Koenig, Robin Chetwynd, Garnet Graham, Donald C. McLean, Robert Kain, Gerald Keeley, Glenn Robb, Fred Stinson
GENERAL MANAGER
John A. Teeter
ACTIVE MEMBERS
Adfilms Limited, 2221 Yonge St., Suite 604, Toronto, Ont. M4S 2BY (416) 483-3551.

Airspeed Brokers (1962) Ltd., P.O. Box 4040 Terminal "A", Toronto, Ont. M5W 1L2, (416) 364-4183.

Alpha Cine Services Ltd., 916 Davie St. Vancouver. B. C. V6Z 1B8, (604) 688-7757.

Animated Cinematographics, 4064 St. Lawrence Blvd., Montreal, Que. H2W 1Y8, (514) 288-6693.

ARRI/NAGRA INC., 6467 Northam Drive, Mississauga, Ont. L4V 1J2, (416) 677-4033.

Asterisk Films & Videotape Productions Ltd. 165 Spadine Ave., Ste 7, Toronto, Ont. M5T 2C4, (416) 364-9450.

A. V. Centre., 111 Bond St., Toronto, Ont. M5V 1Y2. (416) 361-1555.

Bellevue Pathe Quebec Ltd., 175 Montpellier Blvd., Montreal, Que. H4N 2G5, (514) 748-6541.

Best Film Industries Ltd., 344 Jarvis St., Toronto. Ont. M4Y 2G6, (416) 921-2137.

James Beveridge Associates Ltd., 90 Forest Hill Road, Toronto, Ont. M4V 2L5, (416) 484-6449.

Bonded Services International Ltd., 205 Richmond St. West, Toronto, Ont. M5V 1V5, (416) 363-6414.

Robert Brooks Associates Ltd., 10 Banigan Drive, Toronto, Ont. M4H 1E9, (416) 421-8820.

Canadian Filmtronics Aid, 410 Adelaide St. West, 6th Floor, Toronto, Ont. M5V 1S8, (416) 363-5071.

Canadian Super 8 Centre, 205 Richmond St. W. Ste. 201, Toronto, Ont. M5V 1V5, (416) 363-2075.

W. Carsen Company Ltd., 25 Scarsdale Road, Don Mills, Ont. M3B 3G7, (416) 444-1155.

Century II Motion Pictures Ltd., 8540-109 St., Edmonton, Ab. T6G 1E6, (403) 432-1750.

Cherry Film Productions Ltd., 25 Bell St., Regina, Sas. S4S 4B7, (306) 586-5177.

Chetwynd Films Ltd., 10 Banigan Drive, Toronto, Ont. M4H 1E9, (416) 421-8820.

Jack Chisholm Film Productions Ltd., 277 Davenport Road, Toronto, Ont. M5R 1K4, (416) 925-2281.

Cinema Productions, A Div. of Light Images Ltd., 100 Richmond St. E. Ste. 207, Toronto, Ont. M5C 1P4, (416) 362-7530.

Cinera Productions Ltd., 439 Wellington St. West, Toronto, Ont. M5V 1E7, (416) 367-0480.

Alex L. Clark Ltd., 30 Dorchester Ave., Toronto, Ont. M8Z 4W6, (416) 255-8594.

Crawley Films Ltd., P.O. Box 3040, 19 Fairmont Ave., Ottawa, Ont. K1Y 3B5, (613) 728-3513; 409 King St. West, Toronto, Ont. M5V 1K1, (416) 366-0771.

Crone Films Ltd., 400 Walmer Road, Toronto, Ont. M5P 2X7, (416) 924-9044.

Direction Films, 2146A Queen St. East, Toronto, Ont. M4E 1E3.

Educational Film Distributors Ltd., 285 Lesmill Road, Don Mills, Ont. M3B 2V1, (416) 447-9181.

F & M. Productions Ltd., 282 Richmond St. E, Toronto. Ont. M5A 1P4, (416) 364-3034.

Film Arts Limited, 461 Church St., Toronto. Ont. M4Y 2C5, (416) 962-C181.

Film Effects, 342 Richmond St. West, Toronto, Ont. M5V 1X2, (416) 360-1270.

Film Opticals of Canada Ltd., 410 Adelaide St. West, Toronto. Ont. M5V 1S8, (416) 363-4987.

Emerson Screen Productions Ltd., P.O. Box 204, Stn. "S", Toronto. Ont. M5M 4L7, (416) 481-1965.

Wayne Finucan Productions Ltd., 697 Sargent Ave., Winnipeg, Man. R3E OA7 (204) 786-5578.

Grattan Productions Inc., 4606 rue St. Catherine West, Montreal, Que. H3Z 1S3, (514) 932-1463.

Peter Gerretsen Productions Ltd., 118 Castlefield Ave., Toronto, Ont. M4R 1G4, (416) 484-9671.

The Group Productions Ltd., 5101 De Maisonneuve Blvd. West, Montreal, Quebec H4A 1Z1, (514) 487-5616.

Ron Hastings Communications Ltd., 205 Richmond St. West, Suite 203, Toronto, Ont. M5V 1V5, (416) 367-0834.

Intercomm Films Ltd., 274 Parliament St., Toronto. Ont. M5A A4, (416) 366-7773.

Intermedia Financial Services Ltd., 89 Avenue Rd., Suite 610, Toronto, Ont. M5R 2G3, (416) 961-5525.

International Cinemedia Center Ltd., 49 Bathurst St. Ste 401, Toronto. Ont. M5V 2P2, (416) 361-0333.

Keeley Productions, 25 Scenic Millway, Willowdale, Ont., M2L 1S4, (416) 444-0949.

KEG Productions Ltd., 481 University Ave., 7th Floor, Toronto. Ont. M5W 1A7, (416) 595-1792.

Kingsway Film Equipment Ltd., 821 Kipling Ave., Toronto, Ont. M8Z 5G8, (416) 233-1101.

Kodak Canada Ltd., 3500 Eglinton Avenue West, Toronto, Ont. M6M 1V3, (416) 766-8233.

Karl H. Konnry Film Productions, 7 Clarendon Ave., Toronto. Ont. M4V 1H8, (416) 921-9849.

Laboratoire Kineco Inc., C.P. 368, Quebec City, Que. G1K 6W6, (418) 527-1742).

Lumby Productions Ltd., 306 Isabella St. West, Saskatoon, Sask. 57M OE1, (306) 652-2124.

David Mackay Ltd., 105 Davenport Rd., Toronto, Ont., M5R 1H6, (416) 924-0458.

MacKenzie Equipment Company Ltd., Saxony Building 26 Duncan St., Toronto, Ont. M5V 2B9, (416) 364-2266.

John McGreevy Productions, 14 Ross St., Toronto. Ont. M5T 1Z9 (979-1273).

Maltby Films Ltd., 2 Brighton St. Toronto., Ont. M4M 1P4, (416) 461-0670.

M. S. Art Services Ltd., 410 Adelaide St. West, Toronto. Ont. M5V 1S8, (416) 363-2621.

Medallion Film Laboratories, 559 Rogers Road, Toronto, Ont. M6M 1B4, (416) 653-6176.

Mediavision Inc., 1709 Bloor Street West, Toronto. Ont. M6P 1B2, (416) 762-8107.

Mellenco Films, Riverfalls R.R. 1, Markdale, Ont. NOC 1HO, (519) 369-2762.

Millard Film Services Ltd., 425 Adelaide St. West, Toronto, Ont. M5V 1S4, (416) 363-1076.

MLV Film Productions, 123 John St., Toronto, Ont. M5V 2E2, (416) 363-8108.

Modern Talking Picture Services, Inc., 1943 Leslie St., Don Mills, Ont. M3B 2M3, (416) 444-7359.

Mount Royal Film Corp., 1240 St. Antoine St. Ouest, Montreal, Quebec H3C 1B9,

M.R. Communication Consultants Inc., P. O. Box 369, Toronto Dominion Centre, Toronto, Ont. M5K 1K8, (416) 862-1162.

NBE Productions Canada Ltd., 15 Draper St., Toronto. M5V 2M3, (416) 368-3438.

New Communication Concepts Ltd., 210-811 Beach Ave., Vancouver. B.C. V6Z 2B5, (604) 689-9511.

Nielsen-Ferns Inc., 55 University Ave. Ste 1100, Toronto. Ont. M5J 2H7, (416) 361-0306.

Norfolk Communications Ltd., 55 University Ave Ste 1105, Toronto. Ont. M5J 1H7, (416) 862-7665.

North American Pictures, 1903-170 Hargrave St., Winnipeg, Manitoba R3C 3H4, (204) 943-1697.

Northern Motion Pictures Laboratories Ltd., 65 Granby St., Toronto. Ont. M5B 1H8, (416) 362-7631.

Owl Films Ltd., 216 Carlton St., Toronto. Ont. M5A 2L1, (416) 923-1191.

Palette Productions, 52 Edward St., Toronto. Ont. M5G 1C9, (416) 597-0415.

Panavision (Canada) Ltd., 2264 Lakeshore Blvd West, Toronto. Ont. M8V 1A9, (416) 252-5457.

P.F.A. Labs, Division of Production Film Makers Associates Ltd., 330 Adelaide St. West, Toronto. Ont. M5V 1R4, (416) 366-1556.

Photo Importing Agencies Ltd., 29 Gurney Crescent, Toronto, Ont. M6B 1S9, (416) 787-5691.

Rabko Television Productions Co. Ltd., 179 Richmond Street West, Toronto, Ont. M5V 1V3, (416) 598-3083.

Racal Zonal Magnetics Ltd., 4500 Shepherd Avenue East, Unit 37, Scarborough, Ont. M1S 3R6, (416) 292-1524.

Bruce A. Raymond Company Ltd., 63 Huntley St., Toronto. Ont. M4Y 2L2, (416) 923-9654.

Hal Roach Studios International Ltd., 185 Davenport Road, Toronto. Ont. M5R 1J1, (416) 962-9292.

J. T. Ross Associates Ltd., 38 Yorkville Ave., Toronto. Ont. M4W 1L5, (416) 925-5561.

Douglas Sinclair Productions Ltd., P. O. Box 28, St Jovite Station, Quebec JOT 2HO, (819) 425-3595.

Sonolab Inc.,1500 Rue Papineau, Montreal, Que. H2K 4L9, (514) 527-8671.

SPOT Labs Ltd., 487 Adelaide St. West, Toronto. Ont. M5V 1T4, (416) 366-8001.

Al. Stewart Enterprises Ltd., 437 Jarvis St., Suite 102, Toronto. Ont. M4Y 2H1, (416) 966-5040.

Stiliadis Productions Ltd., 73 Walker Ave., Toronto, Ont. M4V 1G3, (416) 924-1028.

Studios 523, 523 Richmond St. E, Toronto. Ont. M5A 1R4, (416) 862-0353.

Summit Film Productions Ltd., R. R. #22, Cambridge, Ont. N3C 2V4, (519) 658-2852.

Bob Schultz Productions Ltd., 78 Scollard St., Toronto. Ont. M5R 1G2, (416) 923-5752.

TDF Film Productions Ltd., 980 Yonge Street (2nd Floor), Toronto. Ont. M4W 2J9, (416) 924-3371.

The Partners Film Co. Ltd., 508 Church St., Toronto. Ont. M4Y 2C8, (416) 966-3500.

Trimension Ltd., 44 Beechwood Drive, Toronto, Ont. M4K 3H8, (416) 423-6250.

Videoart Productions Ltd., 100 Lombard St. Suite 202, Toronto. Ont. M5C 1M3, (416) 360-1456.

VTR Productions Ltd., 47 Scollard St., Toronto. Ont. M5R 1G1, (416) 921-5127.

West Coast Film Opticals Ltd., 1252 Burrard Street, Room 103, Vancouver. B.C. V6Z 1Z3, (604) 687-4491.

Western Films Ltd., 695 Sargent Ave., Winnipeg, Manitoba R3E OA8, (204) 786-8567.

Westminster Films Ltd., 259 Gerrard Street East, Toronto. Ont. M5A 2G1, (416) 929-3166.

Berkeley Studio, Division of Communication, The United Church of Canada, 315 Queen St. East, Toronto. Ont. M5A 1S7, (416) 366-9221.

Reisenauer Films Inc., 306 Spadina Road, Toronto. Ont. M5R 2V6, (416) 962-0678.

AFFILIATE MEMBERS

Heinz A. K. Drege, 174 Highbourne Road, Toronto. Ont. M5P 2J7, (416) 485-1727.

Gerald Graham, 20655 Lakeshore Road, Baie u'Urfee, Que. H9X 1R5, (514) 457-6105.

Lew Parry, 535 Stevens Dr., Vancouver. B.C., V7S 1E1.

Elvino Sauro, 11 Croydon Road, Toronto, Ont. M6C 1S6, (416) 782-5983.

The Canadian Motion Picture Distributors Association (and Canadian Film Boards)

(Organized 1920) Suite 2207, One Yonge St., Toronto, Canada, M5E 1E5. Tel.: (416) 366-9266.

PRESIDENT
William Soody
VICE PRESIDENT
Robert Lightstone
TREASURER
Irving Stern
EXECUTIVE DIRECTOR
Millard S. Roth
BOARD OF DIRECTORS
Michael Stevenson, Joe Brown, Wayne Case, Frank Young, Charles Chaplin, George Heiber.

Hollywood Center for the Audio-Visual Arts.

(A facility of the Los Angeles City Recreation and Parks Department—412 South Parkview St.—Los Angeles, CA 90057 (213) 383-7342.)

DIRECTOR
Clarence Inman.
SENIOR MUSEUM PREPARATOR
Walter J. Daugherty.

Motion Picture Association of America, Inc.

(Incorporated in 1922 under the laws of the State of New York); 522 Fifth Ave., New York, NY 10036; (212) 840-6161. 1600 Eye St., N.W., Washington, DC 10006 (202) 293-1966; 8480 Beverly Blvd., Los Angeles, CA 90048 (213) 653-2200.

OFFICERS

PRESIDENT
Jack Valenti

EXECUTIVE VICEPRESIDENTS
Kenneth W. Clark, G. Griffith Johnson
SENIOR VICE PRESIDENT
Barbara Scott
VICE PRESIDENTS
Fritz Attaway, James Bouras, Allen R. Cooper, William H. Fineshriber, Jr., John Giles, Bethlyn Hand
GENERAL COUNSEL
Louis Nizer
GENERAL ATTORNEY
Barbara Scott
SECRETARY & DEPUTY GENERAL ATTORNEY
James Bouras
TREASURER
Thomas J. McNamara
ASSISTANT TREASURER
Ralph R. Martens
ASSISTANT TREASURER—ASSISTANT SECRETARY
Robert T. Watkins (Hollywood Office)
ASSISTANT SECRETARY
Dorothy Daly

NEW YORK OFFICE

EXECUTIVE VICE-PRESIDENT
G. Griffith Johnson
VICE PRESIDENT IN CHG. OF TV
William H. Fineshriber, Jr.
SENIOR VICE PRESIDENT & GENERAL ATTORNEY
Barbara Scott
VICE PRESIDENT & DEPUTY GENERAL ATTORNEY AND SECRETARY
James Bouras
TREASURER
Thomas J. McNamara
ASSISTANT TREASURER
Ralph R. Martens
PRESS RELATIONS DIRECTOR
Charlene Soltz
DIRECTOR OF RESEARCH
Michael Linden
ASSISTANT DIRECTOR OF RESEARCH
Joseph Infantino
FOREIGN FILM ADVISORY UNIT
Charlene Soltz
TITLE REGISTRATION
Dorothy R. Beer
OFFICE MANAGER
Wilma C. Hennig

WASHINGTON OFFICE

PRESIDENT
Jack Valenti
EXECUTIVE VICEPRESIDENTS
Kenneth W. Clark, G. Griffith Johnson
VICE PRESIDENT
Fritz Attaway
VICE PRESIDENT/TECHNOLOGY EVALUATION & PLANNING
Allen R. Cooper
VICE PRESIDENT
John Giles

HOLLYWOOD OFFICE

VICE PRESIDENT WEST COAST ADMINISTRATION
Bethlyn Hand
OFFICE OF CODE ADMINISTRATION CHAIRMAN
Richard D. Heffner
ADMINISTRATIVE DIRECTOR
Alfred E. Van Schmus
STAFF
Julie Dash, Simona B. Elkin, Timothy J. Joyce, Gustav E. Landen, Richard R. Mathison
OFFICE OF CODE FOR ADVERTISING
Bethlyn J. Hand Director
BOARD OF DIRECTORS OF MPAA
Andreas Albeck, United Artists
Ted Ashley, Warner Bros. Dist.
David Begelman, MGM
Joseph L. Bos, United Artists
Peter Bierstedt, Avco Embassy
Richard Block, Filmways Pictures
Joseph L. Bos, United Artists
Barry Diller, Paramount
Michael Eisner, Paramount
Ralph Etkes, Filmways Pictures
Robert A. Grunberg, Filmways Pictures
Alan J. Hirschfield, Twentieth Century-Fox
Leo Jaffe, Columbia
G. Griffith Johnson, MPAA
Frank Price, Columbia
Jason Rabinovitz, MGM
Robert Rehme, Avco Embassy
Frank E. Rosenfelt, MGM
Terry Semel, Warner Bros. Dist.
Dennis C. Stanfill, Twentieth Century-Fox
Sidney Sheinberg, Universal

Dean C. Stolber, United Artists
Ned Tanen, Universal
Donn B. Tatum, Walt Disney
Jack J. Valenti, MPAA
Francis T. Vincent, Jr., Columbia
E. Cardon Walker, Walt Disney
Lew Wasserman, Universal
Frank G. Wells, Warner Bros. Dist.
Emanuel L. Wolf, Allied Artists
Abe Schneider, Columbia (Honorary)
MEMBERS OF MPAA
Avco Embassy Pictures Corp., 956 Seward St., Los Angeles, CA 90038
Columbia Pictures Industries, Inc., 711 Fifth Ave., New York, NY 10022
Walt Disney Productions, and Buena Vista Distribution Co., Inc., Burbank, CA 91521
Filmways Pictures, Inc., 9033 Wilshire Blvd., Beverly Hills, CA 90211
Metro-Goldwyn-Mayer, Inc., 10202 West Washington Blvd., Culver City, CA 90230
Paramount Pictures Corporation, 1 Gulf & Western Plaza, New York, NY 10023
Twentieth Century-Fox Film Corp., 40 West 57th St., New York, NY 10019
United Artists Corporation, 729 Seventh Ave., New York, NY 10102
Universal Pictures, a division of Universal City Studios, Inc., 100 Universal Plaza, Universal City, CA 91608
Warner Bros. Distributing Corporation, 4000 Warner Blvd., Burbank CA 91522.
ASSOCIATE MEMBERS OF MPAA
Eastman Kodak Company, 343 State Street, Rochester, NY 14650
Technicolor, Inc., 2049 Century Park East, Suite 2400, Los Angeles, CA 90067

Motion Picture Export Association of America, Inc.

522 Fifth Avenue, New York, NY 10036

PRESIDENT
Jack Valenti
EXECUTIVE VICEPRESIDENT
G. Griffith Johnson
VICE-PRESIDENTS
Norman Alterman, Joseph Bellfort, Kenneth W. Clark, William H. Fineshriber, S. Frederick Gronich, Robert V. Perkins, Barbara Scott, Marc Spiegel, Harry J. Stone
TREASURER
Thomas J. McNamara
SECRETARY
Norman Alterman
ASSISTANT SECRETARY
Wilma C. Hennig
ASSISTANT TREASURER
Ralph R. Martens
DIRECTOR ASIAN DIVISION
Joseph Bellfort
DIRECTOR TELEVISION EXPORT ACTIVITIES
William Fineshriber, Jr.

OVERSEAS REPRESENTATIVES
LONDON
S. Frederick Gronich, Brien Noriss
MANILA
Robert V. Perkins
NEW DELHI
Dennis Pereira
MEXICO CITY
Robert J. Corkery
RIO DE JANEIRO
Harry J. Stone
ROME
Marc Spiegel

FILM SECURITY OFFICE
Film Security Office (California)
Richard H. Bloeser, Director
Ewing G. Layhew, Executive Director
Robert U. Mann
William D. Andrews
6464 Sunset Boulevard, Suite 520, Hollywood, CA 90028, (213) 464-3117
Film Security Office (New York)
Edward J. Murphy
Frederick V. Behrends
Motion Picture Association of America, Inc., 522 Fifth Avenue, New York, NY 10036, (212) 840-6161
Continental Film Security Office (France)
Paul Pequignot, Director
Claude Barbini
Film Security Office (England)
Percy Browne

Film Security Office (East Asia)
Francis G. Knight

American Motion Picture Export Company (Africa) Inc.

P.O. Box 244, Apapa, Nigeria, West Africa

PRESIDENT
   G. Griffith Johnson
VICE-PRESIDENTS
   Joseph Bellfort
SECRETARY
   Norman Alterman
TREASURER
   Thomas J. McNamara
ASSISTANT SECRETARY
   Wilma C. Hennig
ASSISTANT TREASURER
   Ralph R. Martens
MEMBERS
   Buena Vista International Inc.; Columbia Pictures International Corp.; Metro-Goldwyn-Mayer, Paramount Pictures Corp.; 20th Century-Fox International Corp; United Artists Corp.; Universal International Films, Inc.; Warner Bros. International, a division of Warner Bros. Inc.

Afram Films, Inc.

522 Fifth Ave., New York, NY 10036

PRESIDENT
   G. Griffith Johnson

VICE PRESIDENTS
   Joseph Bellfort, Raymond Schulman
SECRETARY
   Norman Alterman
TREASURER
   Thomas J. McNamara
ASSISTANT SECRETARY
   Wilma C. Hennig
ASSISTANT TREASURER
   Ralph R. Martens
MEMBERS
   Columbia Pictures International Corp.; Metro-Goldwyn-Mayer; Paramount Pictures Corp.; 20th Century-Fox International Corp.; United Artists Corp.; Universal International Films, Inc.; Warner Bros. International a division of Warner Bros. Inc.

Non-Theatrical Film Distributors Association

Box 397, Mamaroneck, NY 10543 421-5555. (Trade association for the non-theatrical film industry.)

PRESIDENT
   Kirk Karhi
VICE PRESIDENT
   Ernie Raab
TREASURER
   Steve Feltes
DATE OF ORGANIZATION
   1973

Exhibitor Organizations

NATIONAL

National Association of Theatre Owners, Inc.

1500 Broadway, Suite 2011, New York, NY 10036 (212) 730-7420.

PRESIDENT
   Richard H. Orear, Kansas City
CHAIRMAN OF THE BOARD
   A. Alan Friedberg, Boston
PRESIDENT DESIGNATE
CHAIRMAN OF THE FINANCE COMMITTEE
   John H. Stembler, Sr., Atlanta
TREASURER
   Ben Marcus, Milwaukee
SECRETARY
   Bernard Diamond, New York
EXECUTIVE DIRECTOR AND VICE PRESIDENT
   Joseph G. Alterman, New York
BOARD OF DIRECTORS
PAST PRESIDENTS
   Myron N. Blank, A. Alan Friedberg, Marvin J. Goldman, George G. Kerasotes, Ben D. Marcus, E.D. Martin, Eugene Picker, Albert M. Pickus, Sumner M. Redstone, Julian S. Rifkin, Paul A. Roth, John H. Rowle, T.G. Solomon, Ernest G. Stellings, John H. Stembler, Sir., Roy B. White, Mitchell Wolfson

VICE PRESIDENTS
   Douglass N. Amos, Albert Boudouris, Ross Campbell, Fredric Danz, Roland Hassanein, Jack Infald, William F. Kartozian, Ronald P. Krueger, M.A. Lightman, Jr., C. Glenn Norris, Harmon Rifkin, John H. Rowley, Stanley L. Stern, B.V. Sturdivant, Charles B. Trexler.

EXECUTIVE COMMITTEE
   Charles E. Bazzell, Jr., Myron N. Blank, Gerald F. Carisch, Michael H. Chakeres, Irwin R. Cohen, Bruce C. Corwin, Irving Dollinger, Richard M. Durwood, Richard A. Fox, A. Alan Friedberg, Marvin J. Goldman, Salah M. Hassanein, John W. Keiler, II, George Kerasotes, Ben D. Marcus, William Milgram, Jack Mitchell, Bernard Myerson, Richard H. Orear, Carl

L. Patrick, Eugene Picker, Sumner M. Redstone, Joel Resnick, Julian S. Rifkin, Paul A. Roth, Richard Sloan, T.G. Solomon, John H. Stembler, Sr., Sylvia Stieber, Herman A. Stone, B.V. Sturdivant, Morton G. Thalhimer, Jr., Ray Vonderhaar, Roy B. White.

STATE AND REGIONAL

NATO OF ALABAMA
Rufus Davis, Pres.
P.O. Box 1689
Dothan, AL 36302

NATO OF ARIZONA
John V. Louis, Pres.
P.O. Box 7308
Phoenix, AZ 85011

NATO OF ARKANSAS
Joe Hosey, Pres.
P.O. Box 1329
Little Rock, AK 72203

CONNECTICUT ASSOC. OF THEATRE OWNERS
Sylvia Stieber, Pres.
P.O. Box 416
Avon, CT 06001

NATO OF NORTH AND SOUTH
CAROLINA
Herman A. Stone, Pres.
147 Brevard Court
Charlotte, NC 28202

NATO OF METROPOLITAN DC
R. Wade Pearson, Pres.
107 Park Place
Falls Church, VA 22046

NATO OF FLORIDA
Jack Mitchell, Pres.
P.O. Box 012440
Miami, FL 33101

NATO OF GEORGIA
John Stembler, Jr., Bd. Chmn.
P.O. Drawer 18707
Atlanta, GA 30326

NATO OF IDAHO
Roger Davenport, Pres.
Karcher Mall Twin Theatre
Nampa, ID 83651

NATO OF IOWA
Neal Houtz, Pres.
516 Friendly Drive
Marshalltown, IA 50158

NATO OF KENTUCKY
Paul Hollembaek, Pres.
3408 Bardstown Rd.
Louisville, KY 40218

NATO OF LOUISIANA
Randolph Ogden, Pres.
9810 Florida Blvd
Baton Rouge, LA 70815

NATO OF MARYLAND
George A. Brehm, Pres.
c/o Westview Cinema
6002 Baltimore National Pike
Baltimore, MD 21228

NATO OF MISSISSIPPI
Richard F. Heard
1906 Allyson Dr.
Tupelo, MS 38801

MONTANA ASSOC. OF THEATRE
OWNERS
Richard Snyder, Pres.
Box 326
Wolf Point, MT 59201

NATO OF NEBRASKA
Sarge S. Dubinsky, Pres.
P.O. Box 82849
Lincoln, NE 68501

THEATRE OWNERS OF NEW
ENGLAND
Anthony J. DeSantis, Pres.
141 Tremont St.
Boston, MA 02111

NATO OF NEW JERSEY
Jack Infald, Pres.
P.O. Box 124
Kearny, NJ 07032

NEW MEXICO THEATRE OWNERS
ASSOC.
Bert English, Pres.
Box 3090
Albuquerque, NM 87110

NATO OF NEW YORK STATE
Sidney J. Cohen, Pres.
688 Main St.
Buffalo, NY 14202

INDEPENDENT THEATRE OWNERS
ASSOCIATION OF NEW YORK
Sy Frank, Pres.
1600 Broadway
New York, NY 10019

NATO OF NORTH CENTRAL STATES
Harold J. Engler, Pres.
429 Excelsior Ave.
Hopkins, MN 55343

NATO OF OHIO
Russell J. Wintner, Pres.
88 East Broad Street
Columbus, OH 43215

OREGON THEATRE OWNERS ASSN.,
INC.
Larry R. Moyer
1953 N.W. Kearney
Portland, OR 97209

THEATRE OWNERS OF
PENNSYLVANIA
Richard A. Fox, Pres.
99 West Ave.
Jenkintown, PA 19042

NATO OF WESTERN PENNSYLVANIA
George Tice, Pres.
1135 Fulton Bldg.
107 Sixth Street
Pittsburgh, PA 15222

NATO OF TENNESSEE
Herbert R. Levy, Pres.
c/o Malco Theatres
P.O. Box 171809
Memphis, TN 38117

NATO OF TEXAS
John Treadwell, Pres.
1509 Main St.
Suite 1016
Dallas, TX 75201

UNITED MOTION PICTURE
ASSOCIATION
George Kieffer, Pres.
3612 Karnes Blvd.
Kansas City, MO 64111

NATO OF VIRGINIA
J. Mike Hession, Pres.
9817 Jefferson Ave.
Newport News, VA 23605

NATO OF WEST VIRGINIA
David Joseph
P.O. Box 187
Parkersburg, WV 26101
MOTION PICTURE EXHIBITORS OF
WASHINGTON, NORTHERN IDAHO &
ALASKA

M.W. "Bud" Saffle, Pres.
1644 116th St. N.E.

Bellevue, WA 98004
NATO OF WISCONSIN

Rance Mason, Pres.
212 W. Wisconsin Ave.
Milwaukee, WI 53203

NATIONAL

National Independent Theatre Exhibitors Association

P.O. Box 2770, Big Spring, TX 79720. (915) 263-8511; (915) 758-5616; (915) 523-3269.
PRESIDENT EMERITUS
Thomas Patterson
PRESIDENT
Robert E. Hutte (Big Spring, TX)
VICE PRESIDENTS
Sylvia Steiber (Avon, CT. (203) 677-0817)
Fred Florence (Milwaukee, WI. (414) 466-1700)
Roy Roper (Twin Falls, ID. (208) 734-2401)
SECRETARY-TREASURER
Arlie Crites (Dallas, TX. (214) 361-5381)
ASSISTANT TREASURER
John Galvin, (Madison, IN. (812) 265-2151)

CANADA

Motion Picture Theatre Associations of Canada

175 Bloor St. East, Toronto, Ont. M4W 1C8(416) 929-0865.
PRESIDENT
Chris Salmon
TREASURER
Frank Lawson, 225 Consumers Road, Willowdale, Ontario M2J 4G9
EXECUTIVE SECRETARY & DIRECTOR
Curly S. Posen, 21 Dundas Square, Ste. 1210, Toronto, Ontario M5B 1B7
MEMBER ORGANIZATIONS
Alberta Theatres Association: British Columbia Exhibitors Association; Atlantic Motion Picture Exhibitors Association; Manitoba Motion Picture Exhibitors Association; Motion Picture Theatres Association of Ontario; Saskatchewan Motion Picture Exhibitors Association.

Guilds and Unions

Actor's Equity Association (AAAA-AFL-CIO-CLC)

(Organized May 26, 1913; Membership 26,000) 165 West 46th St., New York, NY 10036. (212) 869-8530; Jay Moran, 465 California St., San Francisco, CA 94104; Edward Weston, 6430 Sunset Blvd., Hollywood, CA 90028; John Van Eyck, 360 N. Michigan Ave., Chicago, IL 60601.

PRESIDENT
  Theodore Bikel
FIRST VICE-PRESIDENT
  Barbara Colton
SECOND VICE-PRESIDENT
  Nancy Lynch
THIRD VICE-PRESIDENT
  Jeanna Belkin
FOURTH VICE-PRESIDENT
  Vincent Beck
RECORDING SECRETARY
  Carl Harms
EXECUTIVE SECRETARY
  Willard Swire
COUNSEL
  Cohn, Glickstein, Lurie, Ostrin & Lubell
MIDWEST REGIONAL V.P.
  Michael Lloyd
WESTERN REGIONAL V.P.
  Joseph Ruskin

American Cinema Editors

(Organized November 28, 1950; Membership: 250) 4416-1/2 Finley Avenue, Los Angeles, CA 90027 (213) 660-4425

PRESIDENT
  John A. Martinelli
VICE-PRESIDENT
  Jerrold L. Ludwig
SECRETARY
  Byron "Buzz" Brandt
TREASURER
  Ernest V. Milano
BOARD OF DIRECTORS
  Bernard Balmuth, David G. Blangsted, Robert N. (Toby) Brown, John F. Burnett, Sheldon Kahn, Frederic L. Knudtson, Rita Roland.

American Federation of Musicians (AFL-CIO)

(Organized October, 1896; Membership: 280,000) 1500 Broadway, New York, NY 10036. (212) 869-1330.

PRESIDENT
  Victor W. Fuentealba, 1500 Broadway, New York, NY 10036. (212) 869-1330.
VICE-PRESIDENT
  David Winstein, 2401 Esplanade Avenue, New Orleans, LA 70119. (504) 947-1700.
CANADA VICE-PRESIDENT
  J. Alan Wood, 83 Overlea Blvd., Toronto, Ont., Canada M4H 1C6.
SECRETARY-TREASURER
  J. Martin Emmerson, 1500 Broadway, New York, NY 10036 (212) 869-1330.
EXECUTIVE BOARD
  Above Officers and Max L. Arons, 261 West 52nd Street, New York, NY 10019; Mark Tully Massagli, 5020 Stacey Avenue, Las Vegas, NV 89108; Eugene V. Frey, 19 West Court St., Cincinnati, OH 45202; Max Herman, 817 North Vine Street, Hollywood, CA 90038; Harold (Hal) Dessent, 175 W. Washington St., Chicago, IL 60602

AFM LOCAL 47 (LOS ANGELES)

(See Musicians Mutual Protective Association.)

AFM LOCAL 10-208 (CHICAGO)

(Membership: 13,650) 175 West Washington Street, Chicago, IL 60602

PRESIDENT
  Nicholas Bliss
VICE-PRESIDENT
  Hal Dessent

American Guild of Authors & Composers

40 W. 57th St., New York, NY 10019. (212) 757-8833. CA Office: 6430 Sunset Blvd., Hollywood, CA 90028. (213) HO 2-1108.

PRESIDENT
  Ervin Drake

American Guild of Musical Artists, Inc. (AAAA-AFL)

(Organized 1936; Membership 4,000) 1841 Broadway, New York, NY 10023; COlumbus 5-3687-8-9.

PRESIDENT
  Gene Boucher
FIRST VICE PRESIDENT
  Don Yule
SECOND VICE PRESIDENT
  Henry Butler
THIRD VICE-PRESIDENT
  Eugenia Hoeflin
FOURTH VICE-PRESIDENT
  Muriel Costa-Greenspon
FIFTH VICE-PRESIDENT
  Betty Baisch
TREASURER
  Lawrence Davidson
RECORDING SECRETARY
  Elinor Harper
NATIONAL EXECUTIVE SECRETARY
  DeLloyd Tibbs
COUNSEL
  Becker & London
ASSISTANT TO THE NAT'L EXEC. SECRETARY
  Joan Greenspan, Alan Olsen
FINANCIAL SECRETARY & MEMBERSHIP DEPARTMENT
  Catherine Thomas
ADMINISTRATIVE ASSISTANT
  Annelise Kamada
DIR. OF PUBLIC RELATIONS
  Mildred Grant
CANADA: Graham Spicer, 64 Shuter Street, Toronto, Ontario M5B 2G7, (416) 869-1334; CHICAGO: Herbert Neuer, 307 N. Michigan Ave., Chicago, IL 60601, (312) 372-8081; LOS ANGELES: Dennis Moss, 1308 West Eighth St., Los Angeles, CA 90017 (213) 385-3071; NEW ENGLAND: Robert M. Segal, 11 Beacon Street, Boston, MA 02108 (617) 742-0208; NEW ORLEANS: Kay Long, 34 San Jose Ave., New Orleans, LA 70121 (504) 835-4180; NORTHWEST: Carolyn Carpp, 2253 Gilman Drive W., #202, Seattle, WA 98119; PHILADELPHIA: Mark P. Muller, Lafayette Bldg. 8th floor 5th and Chestnut Streets, Philadelphia, PA 19106 (215) 925-8400; SAN FRANCISCO: Harry Polland, Donald Tayer, 100 Bush St., Suite 1500, San Francisco, CA 94104, (415) 986-4060; TEXAS: Benny Hopper, 4745 Shands Drive, Mesquite, TX 75149 (214) 279-4720; WASHINGTON, DC: Evelyn Freyman, Suite 210, Chevy Chase Center Bldg, Washington, DC 20015 (202) 657-2560.

American Guild of Variety Artists (AAAA AFL-CIO)

(Organized July 14, 1939; Registered Membership; 78,000; Active Membership: 5,000) 1540 Broadway, New York, NY 10036 (212) 765-0800.

HONORARY PRESIDENT
  George Burns

American Society of Cinematographers, Inc.

(Organized 1919; Membership: 286) 1782 North Orange Drive, Hollywood, CA 90028 (213) 876-5080.
PRESIDENT
Harry Wolf
FIRST VICE-PRESIDENT
Stanley Cortez
SECOND VICE-PRESIDENT
Leonard South
THIRD VICE-PRESIDENT
Milton Krasner
TREASURER
Linwood Dunn
SECRETARY
George Folsey

Art Directors

LOCAL 876 (IATSE) (See IATSE)

Associated Actors and Artistes of America (AAAA)-AFL-CIO

(Organized July 18, 1919; Membership: 85,000) 165 West 46th St., New York, NY 10036 (212) 869-0358.
PRESIDENT
Frederick O'Neal
VICE PRESIDENTS
Chester L. Migden, H. O'Neil Shanks, Willard Swire, Alan Jan Nelson, DeLloyd Tibbs
TREASURER
Harold M. Hoffman
EXECUTIVE SECRETARY
Sanford I. Wolff
AFFILIATES
Actors' Equity Association, American Federation of Television and Radio Artists, American Guild of Musical Artists, American Guild of Variety Artists, Asociacion of Puertorriqueña de Artistas y Tecnicos del Espectaculo, Hebrew Actors Union, Italian Actors Union, Screen Actors Guild, Screen Extras Guild.

Associated Musicians of Greater New York

LOCAL 802 AFM (New York)
(Organized August 27, 1921; Membership: 30,000) 261 W. 52nd St., New York, NY 10019. (212) PLaza 7-7722.
PRESIDENT
Max L. Arons
VICE-PRESIDENT
Al Knopf
SECRETARY
Lou Russ Russo
TREASURER
Hy Jaffe

Association of Film Craftsmen

Local No. 531 (NABET, AFL-CIO) 1800 North Argyle, Suite 501, Hollywood, CA 90028. (213) 462-7484.
BUSINESS MANAGER
Louis J. Favara

Association of Talent Agents

(Organized July, 1937, as Artists' Managers Guild—official organization of agents in Hollywood; name changed as of Jan. 1, 1979, to conform to state of California legislation designating agents as "talent agents" rather than artists' managers). Membership: 150.
9255 Sunset Blvd., Suite 930, Los Angeles, CA 90069 (213) 274-0628.
PRESIDENT
Marvin Faris
FIRST VICE PRESIDENT
Roger Davis
VICE PRESIDENT
Sandy Bresler
VICE PRESIDENT
J. Carter Gibson
SECRETARY-TREASURER
Sandra L. Joseph

Authors' Guild, Inc.

(Membership: 6,000) 234 West 44th St., New York, NY 10036; 212-398-0838.
PRESIDENT
Anne Edwards
VICE-PRESIDENT
Madeline L'Engle
SECRETARY
Gerold Frank
TREASURER
Barbara W. Tuchman
COUNCIL
Roger Angell, Anne Beattie, Bruce Bliven, Jr., John Brooks, Susan Brownmiller, Robert A. Caro, E. L. Doctorow, Gerold Frank, Mary Gordon, Philip Hamburger, John Hersey, Daniel Hoffman, Elizabeth Janeway, Bel Kaufman, Joseph P. Lash, Madeleine L'Engle, Milton Meltzer, Nancy Milford, Herbert Mitgang, Toni Morrison, Albert Murray, Victor S. Navasky, Sidney Offit, Frederik Pohl, Peter S. Prescott, Nora Sayre, Isaac Bashevis Singer, Louis L. Snyder, Barbara W. Tuchman, Sarah E. Wright
EXECUTIVE SECRETARY
Peter Heggie
COUNSEL
Irwin Karp

The Authors League of America, Inc.

(Membership: 10,000) Authors League, 234 West 44th St., New York, NY 10036; 391-9198.
PRESIDENT
Harrison E. Salisbury
VICE PRESIDENT
Robert Anderson
SECRETARY
Toni Morrison
TREASURER
Garson Kanin
COUNCIL
Robert Anderson, Roger Angell, John Brooks, Robert A Cars, E. L. Doctorow, Gerold Frank, Frank D. Gilroy, Ruth Goodman Goetz, James Goldman, John Hersey, Israel Horowitz, John K. Hutchens, Elizabeth Janeway, James Kirkwood, Jerome Lawrence, Walter Lord, Eve Merriam, Herbert Mitgang, Mary Rodgers, Peter Stone, Barbara W. Tuckman, Maurice Valency, Jerome Weidman
COUNSEL
Irwin Karp
ADMINISTRATIVE ASSISTANT
Helen Stephenson

Broadcasting Studio Employees

LOCAL 782 (IATSE) (See IATSE)

Catholic Actors Guild of America

(Organized April, 1914; Membership: 700)
1501 Broadway, Suite 2400, New York, NY 10036 (212) 398-1868.
PRESIDENT
Jack O'Brian

VICE-PRESIDENTS
Frederick O'Neal, John J. Martin, Lisa Di Julio.
CHAIRMAN OF EXECUTIVE BOARD
William J. O'Malley
EXECUTIVE SECRETARY
Michael J. Tucci

Catholic Writers Guild of America, Inc.

(Organized December 12, 1919; 65 E. 89th St., New York, NY 10028.)
HONORARY PRESIDENT
His Eminence Terence Cardinal Cooke, Archbishop of New York.
VICE-PRESIDENT
Bernard McMahon
SPIRITUAL DIRECTOR
Most Rev. Philip J. Furlong, D.D.

Directors Guild of America, Inc. (DGA)

National Office, 7950 Sunset Blvd., Hollywood, CA 90046. (213) 656-1220; 110 West 57th St., New York NY 10019 (212) 581-0370; Chicago: 40 East Oak St., Chicago, IL 60611 (312) 787-5050.
PRESIDENT
Jud Taylor
VICE PRESIDENTS
Tom Donovan, Gilbert Cates, John Avildsen, Ira Marvin, Karl Genus
SECRETARIES
William Beaudine, Jr., Enid Roth
TREASURERS
Sheldon Leonard, Marilyn Jacobs
NATIONAL EXECUTIVE SECRETARY
Michael H. Franklin
BOARD MEMBERS
Alan Alda, John Avildsen, William Beaudine, Jr., Jerome J. Blumenthal, Paul Bogart, Mel Brooks, Gilbert Cates, Hal Cooper, Andrew M. Costikyan, Tom Donovan, Milton Felsen, Karl Genus, Arthur Hiller, Marilyn Jacobs, Norman Jewison, Elia Kazan, Sheldon Leonard, Ira Marvin, Franklin Melton, Chris Montross, Edmund Nadell, Ted Nathanson, John Rich, Enid Roth, Jonathan Sanger, George Schaefer, Franklin Schaffner, Jane Schimel, Jack Shea, Elliott Silverstein, Abby Singer, Jud Taylor

The Dramatists Guild, Inc.

(Membership: 708 Active; 2746 Associate; 284 Subscribing); 234 West 44th St., New York, NY 10036 (212) 398-9366
PRESIDENT
Stephen Sondheim
VICE PRESIDENT
Richard Lewine
SECRETARY
Sheldon Harnick
EXECUTIVE DIRECTOR
David E. LeVine
COUNSEL
Irwin Karp

East Coast Council

Motion Picture Studio Locals of the International Alliance of Theatrical Stage Employees and Moving Picture Machine Operators of the United States and Canada.
1515 Broadway, New York, NY 10036. (212) 730-1770.
CHAIRMAN
Michael W. Proscia
SECRETARY-TREASURER
Ed Callaghan
MEMBERS
Motion Picture Cameramen, Local 644; Motion Picture Studio Mechanics, Locals 52, 59, 366 and 22; Film Editors, Local 771; Motion Picture Projectionists, Locals 306, and 640; Script Supervisors, Local 161; Motion Picture Wardrobe Attendants, Local 764; Makeup Artists and Hair Stylists, Local 798; Motion Picture Laboratory Technicians, Local 702; Screen Cartoonists, Local 841, Publicists Local 818, Mixed Local 642, Stagehands Local 11, Stagehands Local 21, Stagehands Local 8, Stagehands Local 41, Stagehands Local 545.

Episcopal Actors Guild of America, Inc.

(Organized 1926, 750 members) 1 East 29th St., New York, NY 10016 (212) 685-2927.
HONORARY PRESIDENTS
PRESIDING BISHOP
The Most Reverend John Maury Allin, D.D.
BISHOP OF NEW YORK
The Right Reverend Paul Moore, Jr., S.T.D.
RETIRED BISHOP OF NEW YORK
The Right Reverend Horace W. B. Donegan, D.D.
PRESIDENT
Ray Heatherton
VICE PRESIDENTS
Rev. Norman J. Catir, Jr., Warden of the Guild
Walter Abel
Joan Fontaine
Rex Harrison
RECORDING SECRETARY
Judy Frank
TREASURER
Anthony Mercede
EXECUTIVE SECRETARY
Lon C. Clark
COUNCIL
Myrtle Ash, Dorothy Blackburn, Col. C. L. Campbell, Kathleen Claypool, Helen Coates, Elizabeth Council, John Connell, Tom Dillon, Alfred Drake, Jose Ferrer, Larry Gates, Eleanor Cody Gould, Gordon Grant, Bernard Grossman, Peter Harris, Josephine Hutchinson, Tessa Kosta, Frederick Langford, Robert Lissauer, Raymond Massey, Mike Mearian, Mildred Murray, Mildred Natwick, Louis Rachow, Anne Seymour, Jean Stapleton, Donald Sutphin, Lila Tyng, Dirck Vreeland, L. Herndon Werth.

Exhibition Employees

LOCAL 829 (IATSE) (See IATSE)

Film Exchange Employees, Back Room, Locals (IATSE)

(See IATSE)

Film Exchange Employees, Front Office

LOCAL F-45 (IATSE) (See IATSE)

First Aid Employees

LOCAL 767 (IATSE) (See IATSE)

Hollywood Film Council

(Organized September, 1947; incorporated November 1948.) 3629 Cahuenga Boulevard West, Hollywood, CA 90068. (213) 851-4301.
PRESIDENT
Wm. K. Howard
VICE PRESIDENTS
Max Herman
Chester Migden
Jerry Lennon
TREASURER
Gene Allen
SECRETARY
H. O'Neil Shanks

International Alliance of Theatrical Stage Employes & Moving Picture Machine Operators of the U.S. and Canada (AFL-CIO)

(Organized nationally, July 17, 1893; internationally, October 1, 1902.) 1515 Broadway, New York, NY 10036. (212) 730-1770.

The Alliance is comprised of approximately 900 local unions covering the United States, Canada and Hawaii. Following is a list of the New York, Chicago and Hollywood locals:

PRODUCTION

ART DIRECTORS, LOCAL 876 (IATSE) HOLLYWOOD

(Chartered January 7, 1960) 7715 Sunset Blvd., Hollywood, CA 90046 (213) 876-4330.

AFFILIATED PROPERTY CRAFTSMEN LOCAL 44 (IATSE—AFL—CIO), HOLLYWOOD

(Organized May 15, 1939) 7429 Sunset Blvd., Hollywood, CA 90046. (213) 876-2320 and 838-7788.

COSTUME DESIGNERS GUILD LOCAL 892

11286 Westminster, Hollywood, CA 90066.

FIRST AID EMPLOYEES, LOCAL 767 (IATSE), LOS ANGELES

(Chartered Oct. 30, 1942) 8736 Swinton Ave., Sepulveda, CA 91343. (213) 894-3781.

INTERNATIONAL PHOTOGRAPHERS OF THE MOTION PICTURE INDUSTRIES (Cameramen) IPMPI LOCAL 666, CHICAGO

(Chartered Jan. 1, 1929) Suite 1122, 327 S. La Salle St., Chicago, IL (312) 341-0966.

IPMPI, LOCAL 659 (IATSE), LOS ANGELES

(Organized 1928) 7715 Sunset Blvd., Hollywood, CA 90046. (213) 876-0160

IPMPI, LOCAL 644 (IATSE), NEW YORK

(Organized Nov. 15, 1926) 250 W. 57th St., New York, NY 10019. (212) Circle 7-3860.

INTERNATIONAL SOUND TECHNICIANS OF THE MOTION PICTURE BROADCAST AND AMUSEMENT INDUSTRIES, LOCAL 695 (IATSE-AFL), LOS ANGELES

(Organized Sept. 15, 1930) 15840 Ventura Blvd., Encino, CA 91436. (213) 872-0452 and 981-0452.

LABORATORY TECHNICIANS, LOCAL 780 (IATSE), CHICAGO

(Chartered Nov. 10, 1944) 327 S. La Salle St., Room 1720, Chicago, IL (312) 922-7105.

LABORATORY TECHNICIANS, LOCAL 683 (IATSE-AFL-CIO), LOS ANGELES

(Organized Sept. 29, 1919) 6721 Melrose Ave., Hollywood, CA 90038. (213) 935-1123.

LABORATORY TECHNICIANS, LOCAL 702 (IATSE-AFL), NEW YORK

(Organized September, 1937) Room 1405, 165 West 46th Street, New York, NY 10036. (212) 757-5540.

MAKE-UP ARTISTS & HAIR STYLISTS, LOCAL 706 (IATSE), HOLLYWOOD

11519 Chandler Blvd., No. Hollywood, CA 91601.

MAKE-UP ARTISTS AND HAIR STYLISTS, LOCAL 798 (I.A.T.S.E.), NEW YORK

(Chartered Feb. 18, 1949) 1790 Broadway, New York, NY 10019. (212) 354-6016.

MOTION PICTURE COSTUMERS, LOCAL 705 (IATSE-AFL), HOLLYWOOD

(Chartered Nov. 1, 1937) 1427 N. La Brea Ave., Hollywood, CA 90028. (213) 851-0220.

MOTION PICTURE EDITORS GUILD, LOCAL 776 (IATSE), LOS ANGELES

(Chartered Aug. 2, 1944) Secretary's Address: 7715 Sunset Blvd., Hollywood CA 90046. (213) 876-4770.

MOTION PICTURE FILM EDITORS, LOCAL 771 (IATSE), NEW YORK

(Chartered Aug. 18, 1943) 630 Ninth Ave., New York, NY 10036. (212) 582-3728.

MOTION PICTURE SCRIPT SUPERVISORS AND PRODUCTION OFFICE COORDINATORS LOCAL 161

140 E. 40, Suite 1B, New York, NY 10016. (212) 245-4562.

MOTION PICTURE SET PAINTERS, LOCAL 729 (IATSE), HOLLYWOOD

(Chartered Aug. 1, 1953) 12754 Ventura Blvd., No. Hollywood, CA 91604. (213) 984-3000.

MOTION PICTURE STUDIO CINETECHNICIANS, LOCAL 789 (IATSE), HOLLYWOOD

(Chartered April 16, 1945) 1635 Vista Del Mar, Hollywood, CA 90028. (213) 462-7288.

MOTION PICTURE SCREEN CARTOONISTS, LOCAL 839 (IATSE), HOLLYWOOD

(Chartered Jan. 18, 1952) 12441 Ventura Blvd., Studio City, CA 91604.

MOTION PICTURE SCREEN CARTOONISTS, LOCAL 841 (IATSE), NEW YORK

(Chartered April 16, 1952) 25 W. 43rd St., New York, NY 10036.

MOTION PICTURE STUDIO ELECTRICAL TECHNICIANS, LOCAL 728 (IATSE), AND M.P.M.O. of U.S. AND CANADA-A.F.L.-C.I.O.

(Chartered May 15, 1939) 3400 Barham Blvd., Hollywood, CA 90068.

MOTION PICTURE CRAFTS SERVICE, LOCAL 727 (IATSE), HOLLYWOOD

(Organized May 15, 1939) 12754 Ventura Blvd., Suite 205, North Hollywood, CA 91604.

MOTION PICTURE STUDIO ART CRAFTSMEN. (Illustrators and Matte Artists) LOCAL 790 (IATSE), HOLLYWOOD

(Chartered April 17, 1945) Suite 210, 7715 Sunset Blvd., Los Angeles CA 90046 (213) 876-2010

MOTION PICTURE STUDIO GRIPS, LOCAL 80 (IATSE), Hollywood

(Organized May 15, 1939) 6926 Melrose Ave., Los Angeles, CA 90038. (213) 931-1419.

MOTION PICTURE STUDIO TEACHERS AND WELFARE WORKERS, LOCAL 884 (IATSE) HOLLYWOOD

(Chartered September 1, 1960) 641 Toyopa Dr., Pacific Palisades, CA 90270. (213) 754-8419.

PRODUCTION OFFICE COORDINATORS & ACCOUNTANTS GUILD LOCAL 717

7715 Sunset Blvd., Hollywood, CA 90046. (213) 876-1600.

PUBLICISTS, LOCAL 818 (IATSE), HOLLYWOOD

(Chartered July 11, 1955) 1427 N. La Brea Ave., Hollywood, CA 90028.

RADIO AND TELEVISION SOUND EFFECTS, LOCAL 844 (IATSE), NEW YORK

(Chartered July 17, 1952), Box 637, Ansonia Station, New York, NY 10023.

SCENIC & TITLE ARTISTS, LOCAL 816 (IATSE), LOS ANGELES

(Chartered March 31, 1949) 7429 Sunset Blvd., Hollywood, CA 90046. (213) 876-1440.

SCRIPT SUPERVISORS, LOCAL 871 (IATSE), HOLLYWOOD

(Chartered January 1, 1958) 7715 Sunset Blvd., Hollywood, CA 90046. (213) 876-4433.

SET DESIGNERS AND MODEL MAKERS, LOCAL 847 (IATSE), HOLLYWOOD

(Chartered Nov. 14, 1952) Suite 210, 7715 Sunset Blvd., Los Angeles CA 90046 (213) 876-2010.

STORY ANALYSTS, LOCAL 854 (IATSE), HOLLYWOOD

(Chartered Oct. 18, 1954) 7715 Sunset Blvd., Los Angeles CA 90046.

MOTION PICTURE STUDIO MECHANICS, LOCAL 476 (IATSE), CHICAGO

(Chartered Feb. 2, 1931) Room 1743; 327 S. LaSalle St., Chicago, IL 60604 (312) 922-5215.

STUDIO MECHANICS, LOCAL 52 (IATSE-AFL), NEW YORK

(Organized 1924) 221 W. 57th St., New York, NY 10019. (212) 765-0741.

STUDIO PROJECTIONISTS, LOCAL 165 (IATSE), HOLLYWOOD

(Chartered May 15, 1939) 6640 Sunset Blvd., Suite 110, Hollywood, CA 90028 (213) 461-2985.

TELEVISION BROADCASTING STUDIO EMPLOYEES, LOCAL 794 (IATSE), NEW YORK

(Chartered June 7, 1945) 144 Astor Ave. Hawthorn, NY 10532.

DISTRIBUTION

FILM EXCHANGE EMPLOYEES, BACK ROOM, LOCAL B-45 (IATSE), CHICAGO

(Chartered May 1, 1937)

FILM EXCHANGE EMPLOYEES, BACK ROOM, LOCAL B-61 (IATSE), LOS ANGELES

(Chartered May 1, 1937) 7715 Sunset Blvd., Room 226, Hollywood, CA 90046.

FILM EXCHANGE EMPLOYEES, FRONT OFFICE, LOCAL F-45 (IATSE), CHICAGO

(Chartered Sept. 4, 1942) c/o G. R. Kuehnl, Apt. 1611, 5455 Sheridan Rd., Chicago, IL 60640.

In addition to the above, there are 34 locals of Back Room Employees and 29 locals of Front Office Employees in the other exchange cities.

MOTION PICTURE HOME OFFICE AND FILM EXCHANGE EMPLOYEES, LOCAL H-63 (IATSE), NEW YORK

(Chartered Mar. 19, 1945) 1650 Broadway, New York, NY 10019 (212) CIrcle 7-7630.

EXHIBITION

AMUSEMENT AREA EMPLOYEES, LOCAL B-192 (IATSE) LOS ANGELES

(Chartered Oct. 1, 1965) 7715 Sunset Blvd., Room 226, Los Angeles, CA 90046.

EXHIBITION EMPLOYEES, LOCAL 829 (IATSE), NEW YORK

(Chartered December 11, 1950) 150 E. 58 St., New York, NY 10022 (212) 752-4427.

PROJECTIONISTS LOCAL 110 (IATSE), CHICAGO

(Chartered Feb. 4, 1915) 875 N. Michigan Ave., Suite 4160, Chicago, IL 60611. (312) 787-0220.

PROJECTIONISTS LOCAL 150 (IATSE), LOS ANGELES

(Chartered July 16, 1908) 6255 Sunset Blvd., Los Angeles 90028, CA (213) 461-2928.

PROJECTIONISTS LOCAL 306 (IATSE), NEW YORK

(Organized July, 1913) 745 7th Ave., New York, NY 10019. (212) JUdson 6-5157, and 55 Flatbush Ave., Brooklyn NY 11210 (212) 852-2700

STAGE EMPLOYEES, LOCAL 4 (IATSE), BROOKLYN

(Chartered April 8, 1888) 2917 Glenwood Rd., Brooklyn, NY 11210 (212) 252-8777.

STAGE EMPLOYEES, LOCAL 2 (IATSE), CHICAGO

(Chartered July 17, 1893) 222 W. Adams St., Room 1345, Chicago, IL 60606.

STAGE EMPLOYEES, LOCAL 33 (IATSE), LOS ANGELES

(Chartered Mar. 1, 1896) 4605 Lankershim Blvd. Suite 833, N. Hollywood, CA 91602 (213) 985-9633-4.

STAGE EMPLOYEES, LOCAL 1 (IATSE), NEW YORK

(Chartered July 17, 1893) 1775 Broadway, New York, NY 10019 (212) 489-7710.

THEATRE EMPLOYEES, LOCAL B-46 (IATSE), CHICAGO

(Chartered May 1, 1937) 875 N. Michigan Ave. Suite 4160, Chicago, IL 60611. (312) 787-0220.

THEATRE EMPLOYEES, LOCAL B-183 (IATSE), NEW YORK

(Chartered May 6, 1942) 235 W. 46th St., Rm. 320, New York, NY 10036. (212) 245-2331, 2332.

THEATRICAL WARDROBE ATTENDANTS, LOCAL 769 (IATSE), CHICAGO

3314 Lake Shore Drive, Apt. 805, Chicago, IL 60657.

THEATRICAL WARDROBE ATTENDANTS, LOCAL 768 (IATSE), LOS ANGELES

(Chartered Dec. 3, 192) 5909 Melrose Ave. Suite 17, Los Angeles, CA 90038.

THEATRICAL WARDROBE ATTENDANTS, LOCAL 764 (IATSE), NEW YORK

(Chartered Sept. 4, 1942) 1501 Broadway, Room 1604, New York, NY (212) 582-4910-1.

TREASURERS AND TICKET SELLERS & CASHIERS, LOCAL 750 (IATSE), CHICAGO

(Chartered Aug. 1, 1941) 188 W. Randolph St., Room 1920, Chicago, IL 60601

TREASURERS AND TICKET SELLERS, LOCAL 857 (IATSE), LOS ANGELES

(Chartered June 1, 1955) 6513 Hollywood Blvd., Room 204, Hollywood, CA 90028.

TREASURERS AND TICKET SELLERS, LOCAL 751 (IATSE), NEW YORK

(Chartered Aug. 1, 1941) Hotel Piccadilly, 227 West 45th St., New York, NY 10036. (212) CIrcle 5-7186.

Outside the three cities covered by the above listings, there are over 900 IATSE locals in the exhibition field.

International Brotherhood of Electrical Workers (AFL)

(Organized November 28, 1891; Membership over 1,000,000) 1125 15th Street, N.W., Washington, DC 20005. Tel.: 833-7000.

INTERNATIONAL PRESIDENT
Charles H. Pillard, 1125 15th St., N.W., Washington, DC 20005.

INTERNATIONAL SECRETARY
Ralph A. Leigon, 1125 15th St. N.W., Washington, DC 20005.
INTERNATIONAL TREASURER
Thomas Van Arsdale, Jr., 158-11 Jewel Ave., Flushing, NY 11365.
DISTRICT OFFICES
Willowdale, Ontario: 45 Sheppard Ave. East, Suite 401; K. G. Rose.
Braintree, MA: 161 Forbes Road, Fourth Floor, John E. Flynn.
White Plains, NY 222 Mamaroneck Ave., J. J. Barry
Cincinnati, OH 7710 Reading Rd., Suite 9, B. G. Williamson.
Birmingham, AL No. 2 Metroplex Dr., Suite 113, D. H. Waters.
Carol Stream, IL: 373 Schmale Road, Suite 201, J. P. Conway
Arlington, Tx; 2701 Ave. E. East, Suite 412, R. G. Duke.
Denver, CO: 2460 West 26th Ave., Suite 264-C, L. D. Farnan.
Walnut Creek, CA: 150 N. Wiget Lane, Suite 100, S. R. McCann
Rosemont, IL: 10400 W. Higgins Rd., Suite 400, A. M. Ripp.
Springfield, MO: 300 So. Jefferson, Suite 300, J. F. Moore.
Chattanooga, TN: Franklin Bldg., Suite 515, M. A. Williams.

IBEW LOCAL 349 (FILM)

(Organized April 24, 1904) 1657 N.W. 17th Avenue, Miami FL 33135. (305) 325-1330.
BUSINESS MANAGER
Don Poppenhager

IBEW LOCAL 40 (FILM)

(Organized March 5, 1923) 5643 Vineland Ave., No. Hollywood, CA 91601. (213) 877-1171.
BUSINESS MANAGER
Russell J. Bartley

International Photographers of the Motion Picture Industries

IPMPI LOCALS (See IATSE)

International Sound Technicians of the Motion Picture Broadcast and Amusement Industries

LOCAL 695 (IATSE-AFL) (See IATSE)

Laboratory Technicians

LOCALS (IATSE) (See IATSE)

Make-Up Artists & Hair Stylists

LOCAL 706 (IATSE) (See IATSE and Local 798)

Motion Picture Assistant Directors

LOCAL 161 (IATSE) (See IATSE)

Motion Picture Costumers

LOCAL 705 (IATSE) (See IATSE)

Motion Picture Crafts Service

LOCAL 727 (IATSE) (See IATSE)

Motion Picture Film Editors

LOCALS (IATSE) (See IATSE)

Motion Picture Home Office Employes

LOCAL H-63 (IATSE) (See IATSE)

Motion Picture Screen Cartoonists

LOCALS 839, 841, 732 (IATE) (See IATSE)

Motion Picture Set Painters

LOCAL 729 (IATSE) (See IATSE)

Motion Picture Studio Electrical Technicians

LOCAL 728 (IATSE) (See IATSE)

Musicians Union, (Local 47, AFM, AFL-CIO)

(Organized October 30, 1894; Membership: 15,000) 817 Vine Street, Hollywood, CA 90038, (213) 462-2161.
PRESIDENT
Max Herman
VICE-PRESIDENT
Vince DiBari
SECRETARY
Marl Young
TREASURER
Bob Manners
TRUSTEES
Johnny Rotella, Abe Most, Lyle (Spud) Murphy
DIRECTORS
Chase Craig, Nellie Lutcher, Frank (Chico) Guerrero, Ray Siegel, Serena Williams, Tibor Zelig
TRIAL BOARD
Clint Neagley, chairman, Beverly Carmen, Bob Karp, Thomas Cortez, Joe R. Holguin, Peggy Gilbert, Anthony Horowitz

NABET/Association of Film Craftsmen

Local No. 532 (NABET, AFL-CIO, CLC) San Francisco: 860 Second St., San Francisco, CA 94107 (415) 541-0131.
PRESIDENT
Charles Rudnick
VICE PRESIDENT
Kris Samuelson
SECRETARY
Phil Perkins

Producer-Writers Guild of America Pension Plan

310 North San Vicente Boulevard, Suite 305, Los Angeles, CA 90048. (213) 659-6430.
CHAIRMAN
Donald S. Sanford
VICE CHAIRMAN
Edward Jurist
SECRETARY
Robert Key
VICE SECRETARY
Jay Ballance

Producers Guild of America

(Organized 1950; Membership: 600) 8201 Beverly Blvd., Los Angeles, CA 90048 (213) 651-0084.
PRESIDENT
David Dortort
VICE PRESIDENT
Jon Epstein
SECRETARY
David Levy
TREASURER
Carol Raskin

EXECUTIVE CHAIRPERSON
Rosalind W. Wyman

Projectionists, IATSE & MPMO Locals

(See IATSE)

Publicists Guild, Inc.

LOCAL 818 (IATSE) (See IATSE)

Radio & Television Sound Effects

LOCAL 844 (IATSE) (See IATSE)

Scenic Artists

LOCAL 816 (IATSE) (See IATSE)

Screen Actors Guild (AAAA-APL)

(Organized July, 1933; Membership: 50,000) 7750 Sunset Blvd., Hollywood, CA 90046. (213) 876-3030. Branches—New York, 1700 Broadway, New York, NY 10019, John T. McGuire; Chicago, IL 60601, 307 N. Michigan Ave., Herbert H. Neuer, 372-8081; Boston, MA 02108, 11 Beacon Street, Rm. 1100, Robert M. Segal, 742-2688; Lathrop Village, MI 48076, 28690 Southfield Rd., Barbara Honner, 559-9540; Coral Gables, FL 33134, 3226 Ponce de Leon Blvd., Melvin B. Karl, 444-7677; Dallas, TX 75204, 3220 Lemmon Ave., Ste. 102, Clinta Dayton, 522-2080; San Francisco, CA 94104, 100 Bush St., Don Tayer, 391-7510; Philadelphia, PA 19102, 1405 Locust St., #811, Glen Goldstein, 545-3150; Denver, CO 80222. 6825 E. Tennessee, #639, Jerre Hookey, 388-4287; Atlanta, GA 30305, 3110 Maple Dr., N.E., #210, Tom Even, 237-9961; Las Vegas, NV, Perry Sheehan Adair, 878-4875; Phoenix, AZ 85012, 3030 N. Central, #919, Donald Livesay, 279-9975; Santa Fe, NM, Arthur Wagner, 876-2034; Houston, TX 77057, 2620 Fountainview, Suite 215, Claire Gordon. The Guild also has offices in San Diego as well as representation in Cleveland, Minneapolis/St. Paul, St. Louis, Seattle and Washington, D.C.

PRESIDENT
William Schallert
FIRST VICE-PRESIDENT
Kent McCord
SECOND VICE-PRESIDENT
Larry Keith
THIRD VICE-PRESIDENT
Joseph Ruskin
FOURTH VICE-PRESIDENT
Lee Zimmer
FIFTH VICE PRESIDENT
Regina Waldon
SIXTH VICE-PRESIDENT
Hugh Lampman
SEVENTH-VICE PRESIDENT
Jessica Walter
EIGHTH VICE-PRESIDENT
Ralph Bell
NINTH VICE-PRESIDENT
Kathleen Freeman
TENTH VICE-PRESIDENT
Bob Kaliban
VICE PRESIDENT
Fern Parsons
RECORDING SECRETARY
Philip Sterling
TREASURER
Gilbert Perkins

NATIONAL EXECUTIVE STAFF

NATIONAL EXECUTIVE SECRETARY
Chester L. Migden

ASSISTANT NATIONAL EXECUTIVE SECRETARIES
Ken Orsatti, James L. Nissen, John T. McGuire, Melvin B. Karl, Michel DeMers, Paulyne Golden, Constance Minnett.
INFORMATION DIRECTOR
Kim Fellner
COUNSEL
Berger, Kahn, Shafton & Moss
Shea, Gould, Chmenko & Casey
CONTROLLER
Paulyne Golden

Screen Composers Of America

Suite 206, 6735 Forest Lawn Drive, Los Angeles CA 90068. (213) 876-9931.
PRESIDENT
Herschel Burke Gilbert
VICE PRESIDENT
John Parker
SECRETARY
Frank DeVol
TREASURER
Nathan Scott

Screen Extras Guild, Inc.

(Organized 1945) 3629 Cahuenga Blvd., W. Hollywood, CA 90068. (213) 851-4301.
PRESIDENT
Roy Wallack
VICE-PRESIDENTS
Len Felber, Josephine Parra
NATIONAL EXECUTIVE SECRETARY
H. O'Neil Shanks
TREASURER
Leland Sun
SECRETARY
Kathryn Janssen

Screen Writers' Guild, Inc.

(See Writers Guild of America.)

Script Supervisors

LOCAL 871 (IATSE) (See IATSE)

Service Employees International Union

LOCAL 278

(Organized March, 1944; Membership: 500) 740 South Western Avenue, Suite 212 Los Angeles, CA 90005. (213) 386-4815.
PRESIDENT
Sherman Jones
VICE-PRESIDENT
Anita Taylor
SECRETARY-TREASURER/BUSINESS MANAGER
Evans Amos

Set Designers And Model Makers

LOCAL 847 (IATSE) (See IATSE)

Society of Motion Picture Art Directors

LOCAL 876 (IATSE) (See IATSE)

Stage Employees Locals (IATSE)

(See IATSE)

Story Analysts

LOCAL 854 (IATSE) (See IATSE)

596

Studio Grips

LOCAL 80 (IATSE) (See IATSE)

Studio Mechanics, Locals (IATSE)

(See IATSE)

Studio Projectionists

LOCAL 165 (IATSE) (See IATSE)

Studio Property Craftsmen

LOCAL 44 (IATSE) (See IATSE)

Theatre Authority, Inc.

(Organized May 21, 1934) 485 Fifth Avenue, New York, NY 10017. (212) 628-4215/6.

PRESIDENT
Harold M. Hoffman
FIRST VICE-PRESIDENT
Elizabeth Morgan
SECOND VICE-PRESIDENT
Willard Swire
THIRD VICE-PRESIDENT
John T. McGuire
COUNSEL
Jacob I. Goodstein
FOURTH VICE-PRESIDENT
Alan Jan Nelson
RECORDING SECRETARY
Stanford B. Wolff
TREASURER
Delloyd Tibbs
COUNSEL
Jacob I. Goodstein
ADVISORY COMMITTEE
Julie Andrews, Fred Astaire, Pearl Bailey, Lucille Ball, Harry Belafonte, Joey Bishop, Sammy Davis, Jr., Maurice Evans, Henry Fonda, Jackie Gleason, Helen Hayes, Charlton Heston, Jerome Hines, Bob Hope, Alan King, Jerry Lewis, George London, Dean Martin, Mary Martin, Gregory Peck, Debbie Reynolds, Dinah Shore, Frank Sinatra, Kate Smith, Eleanor Steber, Barbara Streisand, Danny Thomas

Theatre Employees

LOCALS (IATSE) (See IATSE)

Theatrical Wardrobe Attendants

LOCALS (IATSE) (See IATSE)

Treasurers and Ticketsellers

LOCALS (IATSE) (See IATSE)

Western Theatre Authority

6255 Sunset Blvd., Hollywood, Ca. 90028
CHAIRMAN
Claude L. McCue
EXECUTIVE DIRECTOR
Evonne M. Fairburn

Writers Guild of America

NATIONAL CHAIRMAN
Daniel Taradash

WRITERS GUILD OF AMERICA, EAST, INC.

555 West 57th Street, New York, NY 10019 (212) 245-6180.
PRESIDENT
Allegra Branson
VICE-PRESIDENT
Edward Adler
SECRETARY-TREASURER
Ken Gaughran
EXECUTIVE DIRECTOR
Leonard Wasser

WRITERS GUILD OF AMERICA, WEST, INC.

8955 Beverly Boulevard, Los Angeles, CA 90048 (213) 550-1000.
PRESIDENT
Melville Shavelson
VICE-PRESIDENT
Frank Pierson
SECRETARY-TREASURER
William Ludwig
EXECUTIVE DIRECTOR
Leonard Chassman

Variety Clubs, Film Clubs and General Organizations

Academy of Motion Picture Arts and Sciences

(Organized June, 1927; Membership 4,300) 8949 Wilshire Blvd., Beverly Hills, CA 90211, 278-8990.
PRESIDENT
  Fay Kanin
FIRST VICE-PRESIDENT
  Marvin E. Mirisch
VICE PRESIDENTS
  Arthur Hamilton, Donald C. Rogers
TREASURER
  Gene Allen
SECRETARY
  Charles Powell
EXECUTIVE DIRECTOR
  James M. Roberts
LEGAL COUNSEL
  Gyte Van Zyl
BOARD OF GOVERNORS
  John Addison, Gene Allen, Edward Asner, Paul Bogart, John F. Burnett, James R. Cook, Norman Corwin, William Devane, Linwood G. Dunn, Hal Elias, George Folsey, June Foray, William A. Fraker, Sidney Ganis, Arthur Hamilton, T. Hee, Richard Kahn, Fay Kanin, Bronislau Kaper, Howard Koch, Jack Lemmon, Tom Mankiewicz, Mike Medavoy, Marvin E. Mirisch, Walter Mirisch, Charles M. Powell, Martin Ritt, Donald C. Rogers, Frank E. Rosenfelt, Tex Rudloff, Frederic Steinkamp, Walter M. Scott, Ralph E. Winters, Robert Wise, Richard D. Zanuck.

The American Film Institute

The John F. Kennedy Center for the Performing Arts, Washington, DC 20566; (202) 828-4044
DIRECTOR
  Jean Firstenberg
CALIFORNIA OFFICE

  2021 No. Western Ave., Los Angeles, CA 90027 (213) 856-7600.
EXECUTIVE COUNSEL
  Robert Blumofe
BOARD OF TRUSTEES
  Charlton Heston (on leave of absence) and George Stevens, Jr., co-chairman. Norbert Auerbach, Jeanine Basinger, David Begelman, Richard L. Bloch, Richard Brandt, Steve Broidy, David Brown, George Chasin, Bruce C. Corwin, Robert Daly, Michael Eisner, William Ellinghaus, Jean Firstenberg (Ex Officio), M. J. Frankovich, Ina Ginsburg, Samuel Goldwyn, Jr., Mark Goodson, Andre Guttfreund, Alan Jacobs, Leo Jaffe, Gene Jankowski, Deane F. Johnson, Fay Kanin, Sherry Lansing, Joseph E. Levine, David Lynch, Harry C. McPherson, Walter Mirisch, Mace Neufeld, Richard Orear, Ted Perry, Frederick S. Pierce, Eric Pleskow, Franklin J. Schaffner, John A. Schneider, Fred Silverman, Gordon Stulberg, Jack Valenti, Robert W. Wagner, Richard J. Whalen, Bonita Granville Wrather.

American Humane Association

(Organized 1877) Hollywood office: 8480 Beverly Blvd., Hollywood, CA 90048; (213) 653-3394; Denver: 9725 East Hampden, Denver, CO 80231. (Liaison with the television and motion picture industry as supervisors of animal action in television and motion picture production)
PRESIDENT
  Robert Hudson
VICE-PRESIDENT
  Charles Ennis
TREASURER
  Charles Ferguson
ASSISTANT SECRETARY
  Charles W. Friedrichs

SECRETARY & EXECUTIVE DIRECTOR
  Martin Passaglia, Jr.
DIRECTOR—HOLLYWOOD OFFICE
  Carmelita Pope

American Society of Composers, Authors and Publishers (ASCAP)

(Organized February 13, 1914; Membership: 17,000 Music Writers, 6,500 Publishers) One Lincoln Plaza, New York, NY 10023; (212) 595-3050.
PRESIDENT
  Hal David
VICE-PRESIDENTS
  Salvatore Chiantia, Arthur Hamilton
SECRETARY
  Morton Gould
TREASURER
  Ernest R. Farmer
ASSISTANT SECRETARY
  Gerald Marks
ASSISTANT TREASURER
  Leon J. Brettler
COUNSEL
  Bernard Korman
MANAGING DIRECTOR
  Paul Marks
WESTERN REGIONAL DIRECTOR
  Todd Braber and Michael Gorfaine, ASCAP, 6430 Sunset Boulevard, Hollywood, CA 90028
SOUTHERN REGIONAL EXECUTIVE DIRECTOR
  Connie Bradley, ASCAP, Two Music Square West, Nashville, TN 37203

Artists' Representatives Association, Inc.

1350 Avenue of Americas, New York, NY 10019. 586-5487.
PRESIDENT
  David C. Baumgarten
FIRST VICE PRESIDENT
  Howard Hausman
VICE PRESIDENTS
  Jack Russell, Herbert Cheyette, Dolores Rosaler
TREASURER
  Larry Lewis
SECRETARY
  Ken Lindner
COUNSEL EMERITUS
  Abraham Males
BOARD OF GOVERNORS
  Willard Alexander, Bert Blue, King Broder, Herbert Cheyette, Oscar Cohen, Elliott Gunty, Howard Hausman, Ken Lindner, Robert Rexer, Dolores Rosaler, Jack Russell, Charles Ryan, Lee Salomon, Joe Sully.

Association of Cinema & Video Laboratories, Inc.

(Organized 1953 to deal with technical and administrative problems of motion picture laboratories in the U.S., Canada, and other North American countries.) % Executive Secretary, Dudley Spruill, P.O. Box 34932, Bethesda, MD 20819.
PRESIDENT
  Irwin W. Young
VICE PRESIDENT
  J. Lambert Levy
TREASURER
  John Newell
SECRETARY
  Burton Stone

598

Australia Film

(Organized 1975; Promotes and develops the Australian Film industry. It is the U. S. office of the Australian Film Commission.) #720, 9229 Sunset Blvd., Los Angeles, CA 90069. (213) 275-7074.

GENERAL MANAGER
  Joe Skrzynski
DIRECTOR OF PROJECTS
  John Daniell
DIRECTOR/CREATIVE DEVELOPMENT
  Lachlan Shaw
U.S. MANAGER
  James M. Henry
U.K./EUROPE MANAGER
  Ray L. Atkinson

BMI Canada Limited
(See Performing Rights Organization of Canada Limited)

B'nai B'rith—Unit No. 6000—Cinema/Radio/TV

(Organized November 10, 1939; Membership: 800) 1600 Broadway, New York, NY 10019. Tel.: (212) 581-1721.

PRESIDENT
  Max Fried
EXECUTIVE VICE-PRESIDENTS
  Murray Horowitz, Irene Levy
VICE-PRESIDENT & TREASURER
  Pearl Levinson
VICE-PRESIDENTS
  William N. Benderman, David A. Cohn, Louise E. Dembeck, Mark Dymond, Sheldon Freund, Edward LaPidus, Martin Levinson, Robert Schwartz, Sam Silverstein
SECRETARY
  Maury Benkoil
CHAPLAIN
  Rabbi Ralph Silverstein

Broadcast Music, Inc.

320 West 57th Street, New York, NY 10019 (212) 586-2000, 6255 Sunset Boulevard, Hollywood, CA 90028 (213) 465-2111; 710 16th Ave., So., Nashville, TN (615) 259-3625; 1325 Remington Road, Schaumberg, IL 60195 (312) 843-7771; 1320 S. Dixie Highway, Coral Gables, FL 33146 (305) 666-6122; 1650 Borel Place, San Mateo, CA 94402 (213) 441-7255; Gallery Building, 3115 West Loop South, Houston, TX 77027 (713) 626-8570.

BOARD CHAIRMAN
  Robert Wells
PRESIDENT
  Edward M. Cramer
SENIOR VICE PRESIDENT, PERFORMING RIGHTS
  Theodora Zavin
VICE PRESIDENT, FINANCE, AND TREASURER
  Edward J. Molinelli
VICE PRESIDENT, NASHVILLE
  Frances W. Preston
VICE PRESIDENT, CALIFORNIA
  Ronald M. Anton
VICE PRESIDENT, LICENSING
  Alan H. Smith
COUNSEL AND SECRETARY
  Edward W. Chapin

Canadian Film Board

(See National Film Board of Canada)

Canadian Film Institute/Institut Canadien Du Film

1105-75 Albert Street, Ottawa, Canada K1P 5E7. (The Canadian Film Institute was founded in 1935 to foster and promote the study, appreciation and use of motion pictures and television in Canada. It currently operates the National Film Theatre, the National Film Library, the Publications and Research Division, the Canadian Centre for Films on Art, and the Ottawa International Animation Festival.)

EXECUTIVE DIRECTOR
  Frederik Manter

Canadian Picture Pioneers

(Membership: 700) Office: 175 Bloor St. East, Toronto, Ont. M4W 1C8, (416) 929-0865.

NATIONAL PRESIDENT
  Blain Cavert
NATIONAL VICE-PRESIDENT
  Phil May
NATIONAL SECRETARY-TREASURER
  Fred Levitt
TRUST FUND CHAIRMAN
  David Ongley, Q.C.
BOARD OF DIRECTORS
  William Murray, Morris Appleby, Zeke Sheine, Charles Chaplin, Barry Carnon, Bob Curry, Joel Samuels, Frank Price
TRUST FUND COMMITTEE
  David Ongley, Q.C., Frank Fisher
HON. SOLICITOR
  David Ongley, Q.C.
MARITIMES BRANCH
  President: Frank McGuire, Jr., 49 Alexander St., Glace Bay, N.S.
  Secretary: ed Mullis
QUEBEC BRANCH
  President: Gerry Nadeau, 1590 Mount Royal Ave. E., Montreal, P. Que.
WINNIPEG BRANCH
  President: Harold Joyal, 583 Ellis Ave., Winnipeg, Man.
  Secretary-Treasurer: Herm. Thorvaldson
CALGARY BRANCH
  President: Don Purnell, Paramount Theatre, Red Deer, Alberta
ONTARIO BRANCH
  President: Gerald R. Dillon, 175 Bloor St. E., Toronto
  Secretary-Treasurer: Alan Youngson
VANCOUVER BRANCH
  President: James Baldwin, 2114 London St., New Westminster, B.C.
  Secretary-Treasurer: John Bernard

Catholic Film Office

(See Office for Film & Broadcasting)

Communication Commission of National Council of Churches of Christ in the USA

475 Riverside Dr., New York, NY 10115; (212) 870-2567.

CHAIRPERSON
  Sonia Francis
ASSISTANT GENERAL SECRETARY FOR COMMUNICATION, NCC
  William F. Fore
EXECUTIVE DIRECTOR FOR BROADCASTING
  D. Williams McClurken
DIRECTOR FOR MEDIA RESOURCES
  David W. Pomeroy
DIRECTOR, ECUMEDIA NEWS SERVICE AND BROADCAST NEWS
  L. Franklin Devine

The Community Film Workshop Council

(Organized in 1968 to coordinate the activities, supply direction and seek financial support for community workshops throughout the U.S., functions as a vehicle to provide entry for minority and low income film-makers into the broadcast media.)

17 West 60th Street, New York, NY (212) 247-3192.

EXECUTIVE DIRECTOR
  Cliff Frazier

Composers, Authors & Publishers Association of Canada, Limited

Head Office: 1240 Bay Street, Toronto, Ontario M5R 2C2. (416) 924-4427.

Quebec office: 1245 Sherbrooke St. W., Suite 1470, Montreal, Quebec H3G 1G2. (514) 288-4755.

Vancouver office: 1 Alexander St., Suite 401, Vancouver, British Columbia V6A 1B2. (604) 689-8871.

GENERAL MANAGER
John V. Mills, OC, Q.C.

Council on International Nontheatrical Events (CINE)

1201 Sixteenth Street, N.W., Washington, DC 20036. (202) 785-1136, 785-1137.

Organized 1957, CINE (A non-profit association) selects and enters television documentaries, theatrical short subjects, educational, religious, industrial, scientific and similar classes of film and television productions in approximately 75 to 80 international film competitions held abroad each year. Professional films retained for festival entry receive the CINE Golden Eagle and amateur films, the CINE Eagle. Annually (in the Fall) diplomatic officials in Washington, DC present international honors received by CINE films at festivals and competitions held abroad.

PRESIDENT
Hartwell Sweeney
CHAIRMAN OF THE EXECUTIVE COMMITTEE
Guilford Kater
FIRST VICE PRESIDENT
Frank Kavanaugh
EXECUTIVE DIRECTOR
Shreeniwas R. Tamhane

Educational Film Library Association

(Organized in 1943 as a non-profit membership organization to serve as a national clearinghouse for information about 16mm films and other nonprint media, including their production distribution and use in education, the arts, science industry, religion) 43 West 61 St., New York, NY 10023.

EXECUTIVE DIRECTOR
Nadine Covert
BOARD OF DIRECTORS
Stephen Hess (pres.), Clifford Ehlinger (pres. elect), Angie LeClercq (sec'y), Helen Cyr, Frances Dean, Catherine Egan, Lilly Loo, Lillian Katz, Elfrieda McCauley.

Film Society of Lincoln Center

140 West 65th St., New York, NY 10023 (212) 877-1800. (An arts organization sponsoring film programs, e.g., The New York Film Festival and publisher of Film Comment magazine).

CHAIRMAN
William F. May
PRESIDENT
Alfred R. Stern
EXECUTIVE DIRECTOR
Joanne Koch
ASSOCIATE DIRECTOR
Wendy Keys

DATE OF ORGANIZATION
1969

The Foundation of the Motion Picture Pioneers, Inc.

1600 Broadway, Suite 605, New York, NY 10019 (212) 247-5588.

PRESIDENT
Bernard Myerson
CHAIRMAN OF BOARD
B. V. Sturdivant
EXECUTIVE VICE-PRESIDENT
Henry Plitt
TREASURER
Martin H. Newman
SECRETARY
Robert Sunshine

French Film Office/Unifrance Film U.S.A.

(Organized 1954; promotes French films in U.S.) 745 Fifth Avenue, New York, NY 10151 (212) 832-8860.

DIRECTOR
Catherine Verret
DATE OF ORGANIZATION
1954

Friars Club

57 E. 55th St., New York, NY 10022, (212) PLaza 1-7272.

ABBOT
Frank Sinatra
ABBOT EMERITUS
Milton Berle
DEAN
William B. Williams
TREASURER
Jack H. Klein
TREASURER EMERITUS
Dr. S. L. Meylackson
SCRIBE
Jack L. Green
SCRIBE EMERITUS
Red Buttons
EXECUTIVE DIRECTOR
Walter C. Goldstein
ASSISTANT EXECUTIVE DIRECTOR
Jean-Pierre L. Trebot
BARD
Sammy Davis, Jr.
KNIGHT
Johnny Carson
KNIGHT
Jesse Block
PROCTOR
George N. Burns
HERALD
Paul Anka
MONITOR
Alan King
HISTORIAN
Howard Cosell
MONK
Robert Merrill
SAMARITAN
Norman King
DIRECTOR OF SPECIAL EVENTS
David W. Tebet
LYRICIST
Sammy Cahn
BIOGRAPHER
Joey Adams

Friars Club of California, Inc.

(Organized 1947) 9900 Santa Monica Blvd., Beverly Hills, CA 90212. (213) 553-0850; 879-3375.

PRESIDENT OF THE BOARD
Milton Berle
ABBOT
George Jessel

PRIOR
Frank Sinatra
HERALD
Sammy Davis, Jr.
SECRETARY
William Sarnoff

Girls Friday of Show Business

(A philanthropic organization composed of women in the entertainment industry dedicated to providing funds for reconstructive surgery for children) P.O. Box 2535, North Hollywood, CA 91602. (213) 855-1010.
PRESIDENT
La Donna Webb
EXECUTIVE VICE PRESIDENT/WAYS AND MEANS
Kathy Grant
FIRST VICE PRESIDENT/PROGRAM
Marilyn Mitchell
SECOND VICE PRESIDENT/MEMBERSHIP
Bea Colgan
TREASURER
Judy Collinge
CORRESPONDING SECRETARY
Carolyn Hewett
RECORDING SECRETARY
Ann Hahn
PHILANTHROPY CHAIRMAN
Christie Palmer
PUBLICITY CHAIRMAN
Beth Naranjo
SOCIAL CHAIRMAN
Beverly Sebastian
BULLETIN CHAIRMAN
Judie Gold

The Los Angeles International Film Exposition (Filmex)

6525 Sunset Blvd., Hollywood, CA 90028. (213) 469-9400. Cable Rosebud, Hollywood. (Organized August 1971)
SPONSORS
The city of Los Angeles. The Academy of Motion Picture Arts and Sciences. The American Film Institute, Art Center College of Design, The Los Angeles County Museum of Art, and the UCLA Film Archives
BOARD OF TRUSTEES
Thomas P. Pollock, chairman; Mike Medavoy, president; Gary Abrahams, Frederick Brisson, Kathleen Brown, Philip Chamberlan, Rob Cohen, Michael D. Eisner, Gary Essert, Gary R. Familian, Phil Feldman, David Field, Peter Geiger, Wendy Goldberg, Peter Guber, Robert K. Hagel, Jeremy Kagan, Gloria Katz, Arthur Knight, Howard Krom, Gary Kurtz, Alan Ladd, Jr., Leonard Levy, W. M. Marcussen, Walter Mirisch, Franklin D. Murphy, Helen Neufeld, Jack Nicholson, Max Palevsky, Elisabeth Pollon, Frank Price, Danton Rissner, Henry Rogers, Richard S. Rosenzweig, Michael Roshkind, Daniel Selznick, Robert W. Shapiro, Sidney J. Sheinburg, Richard A. Shepherd, Charles J. Weber, Jerry Weintraub.
DIRECTOR
Gary Essert
ASSISTANT DIRECTOR
Barbara Zicka Smith

Motion Picture Associates, Inc.

(See Variety Clubs International, Tent No. 35.)

Motion Picture and Television Fund

23450 Calabasas Road, Woodland Hills, CA 91364. Hollywood Offices: 335 No. LaBrea Avenue, Los Angeles, CA 90036. (213) 937-7250.
PRESIDENT
John L. Dales
FIRST VICE-PRESIDENT
Ralph Clare
SECOND VICE-PRESIDENT
Robert Blumofe
THIRD VICE-PRESIDENT
Walter Seltzer
TREASURER
Michael Bagnall

EXECUTIVE DIRECTOR
Jack E. Staggs
COUNSEL
Robert Vallier
PRESIDENT EMERITUS
Mary Pickford
INVESTMENT FINANCE COMMITTEE
Alfred Chamie, Chairman, Jack E. Staggs, Ralph Clare, Alan Miller, Herman Herles, Larry Tryon, Chester Migden, Gene Allen, Donald Haggerty, Michael Bagnall, Joseph Youngerman, Louis Harria.
DIRECTOR OF PROFESSIONAL SERVICES
Irwinn Salkin, M.D.

Museum of Modern Art, Department of Film

(Organized May, 1935) 11 West 53rd Street, New York, NY 10019. Tel: (212) 956-6100.
ADMINISTRATOR
Mary Lea Bandy
CURATOR
Eileen Bowser
CURATOR
Adrienne Mancia

National Association of Concessionaires

(Organized 1944) 35 East Wacker Drive, Chicago, IL 60601. (312) 236-3858
EXECUTIVE DIRECTOR
Charles A. Winans
PRESIDENT
Vernon B. Ryles, Jr.
BOARD CHAIRMAN
Philip M. Lowe
VICE PRESIDENTS
Leonard Lowengrub, Shelley Feldman, Douglas E. Larson, Jim Coleman
TREASURER
Lloyd Hughes
DIRECTORS AT LARGE
Norm Chesler, Art Savard, Herb Ring, Van Myers
LIFETIME honorary members board of directors
Louis L. Abramson, Larry Blumenthal, Nat Buchman, J. J. Fitzgibbons, Jr., Bert Nathan, Melville B. Rapp, Lee Koken, Augie J. Schmitt, Sydney Spiegel.
COUNCIL OF PAST PRESIDENTS
Andrew S. Berwick, Jr., Harold F. Chesler, J. J. Fitzgibbons, Jr., Lee Koken, Alfred S. Lapidus, Julian Lefkowitz, Philip L. Lowe, Bert Nathan, Edward S. Redstone, Augie J. Schmitt, Paul Mezzy

National Board of Review of Motion Pictures, Inc.

(Organized March, 1909) P.O. Box 589, c/o Films in Review, New York, NY 10021. (212) 535-2528.
PRESIDENT
Robert Giroux
SECRETARY
John Chapin
TREASURER
Frank Kissner

National Film Board of Canada

(Organized May 2, 1939), 3155 Cote de Liesse Road, Montreal H4N 2N4, Quebec, Canada (P.O. Box 6100, Montreal, P.Q. H3C 3H5, (514) 333-3333.
MEMBERS OF THE BOARD
James de B. Domville, chairman; Mrs. Roma Franko, vice chairman; A. G. S. Griffin; Paul Fortin; Mervin I. Chertkow; Andrew Wells; A. E. Gotlieb; Marcel Masse
GOVERNMENT FILM COMMISSIONER AND CHAIRMAN OF THE BOARD
James de B. Domville
ASSISTANT GOVERNMENT FILM COMMISSIONER
François N. Macerola
ASSISTANT GOVERNMENT FILM COMMISSIONER, PLANNING, POLICY AND EXTERNAL RELATIONS
Reta Kilpatrick
DIRECTORS OF PRODUCTION
Peter Katadotis (English); Jean-Marc Garand (French)

DIRECTOR OF ADMINISTRATION
Marc Devlin
DIRECTOR OF TECHNICAL SERVICES
Michael Carriere
DIRECTOR OF DISTRIBUTION
William Litwack
DIRECTOR OF OTTAWA SERVICES
Robert Monteith
DIRECTOR OF PUBLIC RELATIONS
Roland Ladouceur
DIRECTOR OF PERSONNEL
Gilles Roy
FOREIGN OFFICES
New York: 1251 Avenue of the Americas, 16th Floor New York, NY 10020, Rep. Ken Shere
Chicago: Canadian Travel Film Library, Suite 313, 111 East Wacker Drive, Chicago, IL 60601. Rep. Ian McCutcheon
London, England: National Film Board of Canada, No. 1 Grosvenor Square, London, England W1X OAB, Rep. Jarvis Stoddart
Paris, France: Office national du film du Canada, 15 rue de Berri, Paris, France 75008, Rep. Andre Lafond
Sydney, Australia: National Film Board of Canada, 9th Floor AMP Centre, 50 Bridge Street, Sydney, N.S.W. 2000, Australia. Rep. Tom Bindon

National Music Publishers' Association, Inc.

210 East 59th Street, New York, NY 10022. (212) PLaza 1-1930.
PRESIDENT
Leonard Feist
VICE-PRESIDENTS
Wesley H. Rose, Ralph Peer II, Michael Stewart
SECRETARY
Leon J. Brettler
TREASURER
Sidney Herman

New York City Mayor's Office for Motion Pictures & Television

(Organized to promote and coordinate filmmaking in New York City) 110 West 57th St., New York, NY 10019 (212) 489-6714.
DIRECTOR
Nancy Littlefield
FILM COORDINATOR
Beverly Sammartino
DATE OF ORGANIZATION
1966

Office for Film and Broadcasting (OFB)

Suite 1300, 1011 First Avenue, New York, NY 10022 (212) 644-1880.
DIRECTOR
Rev. Patrick J. Sullivan, S.J.
Office for Film and Broadcasting (OFB) is a unit of the Department of Communication of the National Conference of Catholic Bishops and the United States Catholic Conference. It was formed in January, 1972, through a reorganization of the former National Catholic Office for Motion Pictures and the National Catholic Office for Radio and Television.
OFB provides a national service of information for diocesan communications offices throughout the country.
For the motion picture medium, OFB publishes the twice-monthly *Film & Broadcasting Review* which reviews all current nationally released 35mm films and provides information about resources for films utilization and education (16mm films, books, magazines, festivals). The critical reviews are addressed to the moral as well as artistic dimensions of motion pictures and are the result of a consensus based on the reactions of OFB's professional staff and board of consultors. All films reviewed are also classified according to the OFB rating system. Film classifications appear every month as part of the *Review*. In addition, the publication carries information and evaluative studies on trends and issues pertinent to television, with an emphasis on educational material.
The division maintains a 16mm film library of Catholic program material and a consultation service for educational and religious film program directors.
For the broadcast media, OFB is responsible for cooperating with the three major networks (ABC, CBS, and NBC) in the production of all regularly scheduled network radio and tele-

vision programs involving Catholic participation: (See Radio and Television).
For the Catholic press, OFB publishes a weekly film/broadcast service consisting of reviews, information, articles and photos. Special projects are undertaken with individual publications, religious and general.
OFB also plays a liaison role for the NCCB/USCC with the film and broadcasting industries, national media, and religious agencies and organizations. It is a member of OCIC and UNDA, the international Catholic organizations for film and broadcasting, respectively. Consultations and information services are also provided for the Pontifical Commission for Social Communications and the communications offices of national episcopal conferences throughout the world.

Permanent Charities Committee of the Entertainment Industries

Samuel Goldwyn-Permanent Charities Building, 463 N. La Cienega Blvd., Los Angeles, CA 90048. (213) 652-4680. (A donor federation within the entertainment industries supporting community wide charities)
PRESIDENT
Albert A. Dorskind
FIRST VICE-PRESIDENT
Josef Bernay
SECOND VICE-PRESIDENT
Paul Masterson
SECRETARY
Sidney P. Solow
TREASURER
George Slaff
EXECUTIVE VICE-PRESIDENT
William E. Arnold
CAMPAIGN CHAIRMAN
Barry Diller

SESAC Inc.

(One of the world's foremost music licensing organizations. A special projects department handles scoring for motion pictures, slide films, syndicated TV series and agency produced commercials; programming or background music and premium albums; and the leasing of masters.)

The Coliseum Tower, 10 Columbus Circle, New York, NY 10019 (212) 586-3450.
CHAIRMAN
A. H. Prager
PRESIDENT
Norman S. Weiser
TREASURER
R. C. Heinecke

Society of Motion Picture and Television Engineers

(Organized 1916; Membership: 7,500) 862 Scarsdale Ave., Scarsdale, NY 10583 (914) 472-6606.
PRESIDENT
Robert M. Smith
PAST PRESIDENT
William D. Hedden
EXECUTIVE VICE-PRESIDENT
Charles E. Anderson
ENGINEERING VICE-PRESIDENT
Roland J. Zavada
EDITORIAL VICE-PRESIDENT
K. Blair Benson
FINANCIAL VICE-PRESIDENT
Joseph A. Flaherty
CONFERENCE VICE-PRESIDENT
Harry Teitelbaum
SECTIONS VICE-PRESIDENT
Leonard F. Coleman
VICE-PRESIDENT PHOTO-SCIENCE AFFAIRS
Daan Zwick
VICE-PRESIDENT FOR EDUCATIONAL AFFAIRS
Raymond Fielding
VICE-PRESIDENT FOR TELEVISION AFFAIRS
Frederick M. Remley
VICE-PRESIDENT FOR PHOTO INSTRUMENTATION AFFAIRS
Lincoln L. Endelman

VICE-PRESIDENT FOR MOTION-PICTURE AFFAIRS
Fred J. Scobey
SECRETARY
Harold J. Eady
TREASURER
Charles A. Ahto
EXECUTIVE DIRECTOR
Donald F. Breidt
EDITOR
David A. Howell

Theatre Equipment Association

Office of the Executive Director: 1600 Broadway, New York, NY 10019 (212) 246-6460.
PRESIDENT
Jerry Harrah
VICE PRESIDENT
John F. Dawsey
SECRETARY
Donald Moore
EXECUTIVE DIRECTOR
Robert Sunshine

The Troupers, Inc.

(Organized June, 1948; Membership: women in show business & allied fields) Buckingham Apts., 101 West 57th St., New York, NY 10019. (212) 246-1500, 265-9778.
PRESIDENT
Ann Turkus
VICE PRESIDENTS
Sally De May, Vivian Fisch, Sylvia Levy, Dorothy Borodkin
FINANCIAL SECRETARY
Jill Roth
RECORDING SECRETARY
Rosalind Frenkel
TREASURER
Syd Peterman
CORRESPONDING SECRETARY
Muriel Zeman
SOCIAL SECRETARY
Rita Dawson

USA Film Festival

(Organized in 1971 as non-competitive film festival devoted exclusively to films directed by U.S. citzens; open to students and new film-makers as well as established ones.) P.O. Box 3105, Dallas, TX 75275.
NATIONAL BOARD OF ADVISORS
George Cukor, Martin Jurow, Stanley Marcus, Gregory Peck.
CRITICS PANEL
Judith Crist, Barbara Bryant, Hollis Alpert, Charles Champlin, Roger Ebert, Arthur Knight.

Variety Clubs International

(Organized October 10, 1927; Membership: 10,000) International Office: Tower 58, Suite 23-C, 58 West 58th St., N.Y., NY 10019 (212) 751-8600.
INTERNATIONAL OFFICERS
PRESIDENT
Robert R. Hall, Q.C.
CHAIRMAN
Burton Robbins
HONORARY CHAIRMAN
Monty Hall
PAST PRESIDENTS
Sir James Carreras, George W. Eby, Edward Emanuel, M. J. Frankovich, George C. Hoover, Eric D. Morley, Ralph W. Pries, John H. Rowley
VICE PRESIDENTS
Samuel Z. Arkoff, Peter J. Barnett, Monty Berman, Trevor E. Chinn, Fred Danz, Salah M. Hassanein, Philip Isaacs, Ben Marcus, Bernard R. Myerson, Carl L. Patrick, Henry G. Plitt, Michael Samuelson, Sam Shopsowitz, Joseph Sinay, Frank Srean
ADDITIONAL DIRECTOR
Edward Shafton
INTERNATIONAL AMBASSADORS
George Barrie, Rick Bourke, Tom Eggerdon, Tom Fenno, Cary Grant, Lou Lavinthal, Frank Mancuso, Hank Milgram,

Nat Nathanson, Edward A. Pantano, Stanley I. Reynolds, Kenneth Rive, Joe Simpkins, Jack Sparberg, E. Cardon Walker, Reg Watson
CHAIRMAN, LIFE PATRON COMMITTEE
Robert L. Bostick
INTERNATIONAL PUBLIC RELATIONS
David Jones (eastern hemisphere)
Al Dubin (western hemisphere)
EXECUTIVE DIRECTOR
Morton Sunshine
VARIETY CLUB TENTS

TENT No. 1: Variety Club of Pittsburgh, William Penn Hotel, 530 William Penn Place, Pittsburgh, PA 15230.
TENT No. 4: Variety Club of St. Louis, 7900 Natural Bridge Road, St. Louis, MO 63121.
TENT No. 5: Variety Club of Detroit, 3000 Town Center, Suite 1780, Southfield, MI
TENT No. 6: Variety Club of Northern Ohio, 3201 Carnegie Ave., Cleveland, OH 44155.
TENT No. 7: Variety Club of Buffalo, 193 Delaware Avenue, Buffalo, NY 14202.
TENT No. 8: Variety Club of Kansas City, P.O. Box 12070, Shawnee MIssion, KS 66212.
TENT NO. 10: Variety Club of Indianapolis, P.O. Box 21056, Indianapolis, IN 46221.
TENT No. 11: Variety Club of Washington, DC, 3801 Calvert St., N.W. Washington, D.C. 20007.
TENT No. 12: Variety Club of the Northwest, 500 WCCO Bldg., Minneapolis, MN 55402.
TENT No. 13: Variety Club of Philadelphia, The Warwick, 17th & Locus St., Philadelphia, PA 19103.
TENT No. 14: Variety Club of Wisconsin, P.O. Box 600, Milwaukee, WI 53201.
TENT No. 15: Variety Club of Iowa, 504 Shops Bldg., 8th & Walnut, Des Moines, IA 50309.
TENT No. 16: Variety Club of Nebraska, Concession Supply, Inc., 4808 G St., Omaha NB 68117.
TENT No. 17: Variety Club of Texas, 5518 Dyer St., Dallas, TX 75206.
TENT No. 19: Variety Club of Baltimore, 1052 Flagtree Lane, Baltimore, MD 21208.
TENT No. 20: Variety Club of Memphis, P.O. Box 1523, Memphis, TN 31801.
TENT No. 21: Variety Club of Atlanta, 4735 Roswell Road, Apt. 29-A, Atlanta, GA 30342.
TENT No. 22: Variety Club of Oklahoma, 3529 Shields Blvd., Oklahoma City, OK 73129.
TENT No. 23: Variety Club of New England, Interstate Theatres, 20 Newbury St., Boston, MA 02116.
TENT No. 25: Variety Club of Southern California, 1830 S. Robertson Blvd., Los Angeles, CA 90035
TENT No. 26: Variety Club of Illinois, 190 N. State St., Room 504, Chicago, IL 60601.
TENT No. 27: Variety Club of Grand Rapids, 202 Brown St. S.E., Grand Rapids, MI 49507.
TENT No. 28: Variety Club of Ontario, Suite 1721—Westbury Hotel, 475 Yonge St., Toronto, Ont. M4G 1X7 Canada.
TENT No. 29: Variety Club of Mexico, Hamburgo #87-A, Mexico 6 D.F.
TENT No. 32: Variety Club of Northern California, 988 Market S. Suite 304, San Francisco, CA 94102.
TENT No. 33: Variety Club of Greater Miami, 9801 Collins Ave., Bal Harbor, FL 3354.
TENT No. 35: Variety Club of New York, 1600 Broadway, Rm. 605, New York, NY 10019.
TENT No. 36: Variety Club of Great Britain, Avon House, 360 Oxford St., London W1N ODY England.
TENT No. 37: Variety Club of Colorado, 6000 E. Evans, Denver, CO 80215.
TENT No. 39: Variety Club of Southern Nevada, 130 S. Fourth St., Las Vegas, NV 89101.
TENT No. 41: Variety Club of Ireland, 52 Dame St., Dublin 2, Ireland.
TENT No. 45: Variety Club of New Orleans, 820 Howard Ave., New Orleans, LA 70113.
TENT No. 46: Variety Club of Pacific Northwest, 419 Occidental Ave., S., Seattle, WA 98104.
TENT No. 47: Variety Club of British Columbia, #1170 Bute St., Vancouver, B.C. Canada V6E 1Z6.
TENT No. 50: Variety Club of Hawaii, 710 Palekaua St., Honolulu, HI 96816.
TENT No. 51: Variety Club of Israel, 13 Ranak St., Tel Aviv, Israel.
TENT No. 52: Variety Club of Jersey C.I., Maison Variety, Five Oaks St., Saviour, Jersey, Channel Isles.
TENT No. 53: Variety Club of Puerto Rico, P.O. Box 8896, Fernandez Juncoa Station, Santurce, Puerto Rico 00910.
TENT No. 54: Variety Club of France, 179 Avenue Victor Hugo, 75116 Paris, France.
TENT No. 55: Variety Club of Guernsey C.I.: Les Ruettes Lane, St Andrews, Guernsey, Channel Islands.
TENT No. 56: Variety Club of Australia, Oakridgge Bldg., 52 Phillip St., Sydney, N.S.W. 2000, Australia 2061.
TENT No. 57: Variety Club of San Diego, 17596 Corbel Court, San Diego, CA 92128.

TENT No. 58: Variety Club of Manitoba, Marlborough Hotel, 331 Smith St., Winnipeg, Manitoba, Canada R3B 2G9.
TENT No. 59: Variety Club of Phoenix: 8514 E. Chapparal, St., Phoenix, AZ 85253.

Will Rogers Memorial Fund

785 Mamaroneck Avenue, White Plains, NY 10605: (212) 757-0270.
PRESIDENT
Bernard Myerson
CHAIRMAN OF THE BOARD
Salah M. Hassanein
CHAIRMAN OF THE BOARD (Emeritus)
Richard F. Walsh
EXECUTIVE VICE PRESIDENT
Frank Mancuso
VICE PRESIDENTS
Harry Buxbaum, Walter F. Diehl, Al Fitter, Jerome A. Forman, Robert L. Friedman, Norman Levy, Henry G. Plitt, Robert Rehme, Terry Semel, Robert N. Wilkinson, Melvin R. Wintman
TREASURER
Charles R. Hacker

SECRETARY
Seymour Smith
EXECUTIVE DIRECTOR
Martin H. Newman

WOMPI International

c/o New World Pictures, 207 Westport Rd., #201, Kansas City, MO 64111.
INTERNATIONAL OFFICERS
PRESIDENT
Miss Virginia Porter
VICE PRESIDENT
Mrs. Tillie Spadaro
CORRESPONDING SECRETARY
Mrs. Sylvia Todd
RECORDING SECRETARY
Mrs. Mary Crump
TREASURER
Ms. Florence Work
IMMEDIATE PAST INTL. PRESIDENT
Mrs. Marshal Weaver
INTERNATIONAL COMMITTEE CHAIRMEN
Mrs. Gladys Nelson (by-laws); Miss Betty Hemstook (finance); Ms. Lili Beaudin (extension); Mrs. Myrtle Parker (publicity); Mrs. Amalie Gantt (bulletin).

U.S. STATE FILM COMMISSIONS

ALABAMA

Phil Cole, Alabama Film Commission, 340 N. Hull Street, Montgomery, AL 36130, (800) 633-5898

ALASKA

Steve Smirnoff, Travel Information Officer, Division of Tourism, Department of Economic, Development, Pouch E. Juneau, AK 99811, (907) 465-2013

ARIZONA

Bill MacCallum, Director, Arizona Motion Picture Development, 1700 West Washington, 5th Floor, Phoenix, AZ 85604, (602) 255-5011

City of Phoenix

Lucy Alvarado, Motion Picture Coordinating Office, City of Phoenix, Room 901, Municipal Building, 251 W. Washington St., Phoenix, AZ 85003 (602) 262-7916 or (602) 262-4850

City of Tucson

Judy Moson, George Gray, Tucson Film Commission, P.O. Box 27210, Tucson, AZ 85726, (602) 791-4000

ARKANSAS

Arkansas Industrial Development Commission, Joe Glass, Director of the Office of Motion Picture Development, #1 State Capitol Mall, Little Rock, AR 72201, (501) 375-4506, (501) 371-1121

CALIFORNIA

Christina Gallante, Chairwoman; Kris Wagner, Director, California Motion Picture Council, 6725 Sunset Blvd. #511, Hollywood, CA 90028, (213) 736-2465

City of San Diego

Wally Schlotter, Director, San Diego Motion Picture and Television Bureau, 110 W. C St., Suite 1600, San Diego, CA 92101, (714) 232-0124 (714) 234-FILM

COLORADO

Karol Smith, Director; Sue Anderson, Asst. Director; Bob Edwards, Commercials; Colorado Motion Picture and Television Advisory Commission, 1313 Sherman St., Room 500, Denver, CO 80203, (303) 866-2205, (303) 866-2778

CONNECTICUT

Barney D. Laschever, Anthony Davenport, Tourism Division, Connecticut Economic Development, 210 Washington St., Hartford, CT 06106, (203) 566-3385

DELAWARE

Donald Mathewson, Delaware Travel Service, 630 State College Road, Dover, DE 19901, (800) 441-8846

DISTRICT OF COLUMBIA

Richard Maulsby, Director, Office of Motion Picture & Television Development, 201 District Building, Washington, D.C. 20004, (202) 727-6600

FLORIDA

Ben Harris, Director; Laura Katzmiller & Charles Poretto, Assoc., Motion Picture and Television Office Division of Economic Development, 107 West Gaines St., Tallahassee, FL 32301, (904) 487-1100

GEORGIA

Ed Spivia, Director, Motion Picture and Television Advisory Committee, Georgia Dept. of Industry and Trade, P.O. Box 1776, Atlanta, GA 30301, (404) 656-3552

HAWAII

Henry L. Wong, Director, Hawaii Film Office Dept. of Planning and Economics, Kamamalu Building, P.O. Box 2359, Honolulu, HI 96804, (808) 548-4535

IDADO

Steve Wilson, Idaho Film Bureau, Capitol Bldg. Room 108, Boise, ID 83720, (208) 334-4357

ILLINOIS

Lucy Salenger, Managing Director, Illinois Film Office and Television Services, 205 Wacker Drive, Chicago, IL 60606, (312) 793-3600

INDIANA

Guy Johnson, Communications Director, Lieutenant Governor's Office (317) 232-8814; Sue Linder, Staff Photographer, Simone Smilganic/Wesley Grant, Communications Division, Department of Commerce, Rm. 333 State House, Indianapolis, IN 46204, (317) 232-8813

IOWA

John Arends, Director of Public Information; Bill Linstrom, Asst., Iowa Development Commission, 250 Jewett Bldg., Des Moines, IA 50309, (515) 281-3185

KANSAS

Department of Economic Develtpment, 503 Kansas Ave., 6th Floor, Topeka, KS 66603, (913) 296-3481

KENTUCKY

Olivia Maggard, Director; Betty Lampkin, Assistant, Kentucky Film Commission, Capitol Plaza Tower 22nd Floor, Frankfurt, KY 40601, (502) 564-2240

LOUISIANA

Jo Beth Bolton, Director, Louisiana Film Commission, Box 44185, Baton Rouge, LA 70804, (504) 342-5403

MARYLAND

Jack K. Smith, Director of Motion Picture and Television Development, 2525 Riva Road, Annapolis, MD 21401, (301) 269-3500

MASSACHUSETTS

Mary Lou Crane, Director, Massachusetts Film Bureau Department of Commerce & Development, 100 Cambridge Street, 13th Floor, Boston, MA 02202, (617) 727-3330

MICHIGAN

Robert J. Scott, Office of Film and Television Services, Michigan Plaza Bldg., 1200 6th Street, Detroit, MI 48226, (313) 256-9098

MINNESOTA

Steve Kane, Pres., Merrill Busch, Vice Pres. Director, Minnesota Motion Picture & Development Board, Inc., 1111 West 22nd Street, Minneapolis MN 55405, (612) 377-9203

MISSISSIPPI

Ward Embling, Mississippi Film Commission, P.O. Box 849, Jackson, MS 39205, (601) 354-6715

MISSOURI

Chuck Boyd, Director, (314) 751-3051; Dean Brooks, Media Specialist, Missouri Division of Tourism, 308 East High St., P.O. Box 1055, Jefferson City, MO 65101, (314) 751-3246

MONTANA

Gary Wunderwald, State Travel Promotion Bureau, Department of Highways, Helena, MT 59620, (406) 449-2654 or Patrick Mathews, 2501 Ivanhoe Dr., Los Angeles, CA 90039, (213) 665-2429

NEBRASKA

Don Atwater, Public Information Office, 301 S. Centennial Mall, Lincoln NE 68509, (402) 471-3111

NEVADA

Walt MacKenzie, Director of the State of Nevada Economic Development, Capital Compllex, Carson City, NV (702) 885-4322

NEW HAMPSHIRE

Marty Leighton, Director of New Hampshire, Film and Television Bureau, Box 856, Concord, NH 03301, (603) 271-2598

NEW JERSEY

JP Miller, Chairman; Michele Kuhar, Executive Director, New Jersey Motion Picture and Television Development Commission, Gateway 1, Suite 510, Newark, NJ 07102, (201) 648-6279

NEW MEXICO

Larry Hamm, Director; Susan Jo Brown, Location Director, Film Division, Dept. of Development, 1050 Old Pecos Trail, Santa Fe, NM 87501, (505) 827-2880 or (800) 545-9871

NEW YORK

Elisabeth Forslinl Harris, Director of New York State Motion Picture & Television Develoment, 230 Park Ave., New York, NY 10169, (212) 949-8514

NORTH CAROLINA

William Arnold, Director, Office of Motion Picture Development, 430 N. Salisbury St., Raleigh, NC 27611, (919) 733-7651

NORTH DAKOTA

Bill McCombs, Public Information Manager, Department of Business and Industrial Development, Bismarck, ND 58505, (701) 244-2810

OHIO

Mari Barnum, Manager, Ohio Film Bureau, P.O. Box 1001, Columbus, OH 43216 (614) 466-2284 or (800) 848-1300

OKLAHOMA

Paul Davis, Coordinator, Film Industry Task Force, 500 Will Rogers Bldg., Oklahoma City, OK 73105, (405) 521-3525

OREGON

Warren Merrill, Manager of Motion Picture Services, Dept. of Economic Development, 155 Cottage Street, N.E., Salem, OR 97310, (503) 378-4735

PENNSYLVANIA

Amy Woods, Interim Director, Bureau of Film Promotion, 461 Forum Bldg., Harrisburg, PA 17120 (717) 787-5333

RHODE ISLAND

Leonard Panaggio, Tourist Promotion Division, Dept. of Economic Development, #7 Jackson Walkway, Providence, RI 02903, (401) 277-2601

SOUTH CAROLINA

Debra Rosen, South Carolina Film Location Contact, South Carolina Education TV Network, Drawer L, Columbia, SC 29250, (803) 758-3091

SOUTH DAKOTA

William Gipp, Industrial Development Expansion Agency, 221 S. Central, Pierre, SD 57501, (605) 773-3375

TENNESSEE

Patricia Ladford, Coordinator of Film Tape and Music Industry, 1021 Andrew Jackson Building, Nashville, TN 37219, (615) 741-1888 or (800) 8594

TEXAS

Ms. Pat Wolf, Texas Film Commission, Office of the Governor, P.O. Box 12428, Austin, TX 78711, (512) 475-3785

City of El Paso

Dale Lockett, Film Liaison, El Paso Convention & Visitors Bureau, 5 Civic Center Plaza, El Paso, TX 79901 (915) 544-3650

City of Houston

Fred Kuehnert, Director, Motion Picture Council of Houston, 3000 S. Post Oak Road, Suite 1480, Houston, TX 77056

UTAH

John Earle, Utah Film Development, #2 Arrow Press Square, Ste. 200, Salt Lake City, UT 84101, (800) 453-8824 or (801) 533-5325

VERMONT

J. Gregory Gerdel, Agency of Development and Community Affairs, 61 Elm St., Montpelier, VT 05602, (802) 828-3236

VIRGINIA

Mike Wallace, Director of Film Assistance, Virginia State Travel Service, 6 N. Sixth St., Richmond, VA 23219, (804) 786-4346

WASHINGTON,

Art Kulman, Dept. of Commerce and Economic Development, Motion Picture Bureau, 312 First Ave. North, Seattle, WA 98109, (206) 464-7148

WEST VIRGINIA

Sherry O'Dell, Director of Communications, Government Office of Economic & Community Development, State Capitol Bldg., Charleston, WV 25305, (304) 348-0410

WISCONSIN

Stanley Solheim, Film Liaison, Division of Tourism & Department of Development, 123 West Washington Ave., Madison, WI 53702, (608) 266-7018/(608) 266-7621

WYOMING

Randall Wagner, Director, Wyoming Travel Commission, Interstate 25 at College Drive, Cheyenne, WY 82002, (307) 777-7777

PUERTO RICO

Tito Bonilla, Exec. Director, Institute Film and Television, G.P.O. Box 2350, San Juan, PR 99036, (809) 754-8580 (809) 754-8414

VIRGIN ISLANDS

Win DeLugo, P.O. Box 6400, Charlotte Amalie, St. Thomas VI 00801, (809) 774-8784

The Press

* **TRADE PUBLICATIONS**

* **NEWSPAPER LISTING**

Trade Publications

Quigley Publishing Company

Publishers of Motion Picture Product Digest (25 times a year), Motion Picture Almanac (Annual), Television Almanac (Annual). + Fame. 159 West 53rd St., New York, NY 10019; (212) 247-3100; Cable: Quigpubco, New York.

PRESIDENT AND PUBLISHER
Martin Quigley, Jr.
EDITOR-IN-CHIEF
Richard Gertner
SECRETARY
Michael Mayer
GENERAL MANAGER
Robert McDonald

LONDON BUREAU

William Pay, Manager and London Editor; 15 Samuel Road, Langdon Hills, Basildon, Essex, England. Tel.: 0268-42824.

FOREIGN BUREAUS

ARGENTINA: Natalio Bruski, Calle Paso 240 (8°-C), Buenos Aires.
BELGIUM: Marc Turfkruyer, Van Maerlantstraat, 71 Antwerp.
CEYLON: Chandra Perera, 437 Pethiyagoda, Kelanuja, Sri Lanka, Ceylon.
EGYPT: Ahmed Sami, 4 El Ommara St., Apt. 13, Abbassia, Cairo.
FINLAND: Mrs. Hellevi Rinkihainen, Finnish Film Foundation, Kaisaniemenkatu 3 B 25 SF-00100 Helsinki 10.
GREECE: Rena Velissariou, 32, Kolokotroni Str., Agia Paraskevi, Attikis, Athens.
HOLLAND: Philip de Schaap, 9 Henriette Bosmansstrant, Amsterdam (Zuid).
INDIA: B. D. Garga, D-11 Commerce Centre, Tardeo Road, Bombay 34.
JAPAN: A. C. Pinder, Whaley-Eaton Service, Central P.O. Box 190, Tokyo, Japan.
NEW ZEALAND: Mark R. Galloway, N. Z. Film Services Ltd., P.O. Box 9340, Courteneay Pl., Wellington, C.3.
PAKISTAN: A. R. Slote, P.O. Box 7426, Karachi. 1-3.
SPAIN: Mariano del Pozo, Conde de Penalver 36, Madrid 6.
SWITZERLAND: Gerda Goepfert-Klimisch, Film Beld Agentur 6911, Barbengo, Ticino.

QUIGLEY PUBLICATIONS

Motion Picture Product Digest

(Published 25 times a year) 159 West 53rd St., New York, NY 10019; 247-3100; Cable: Quigpubco, New York.

PRESIDENT AND PUBLISHER
Martin Quigley, Jr.
EDITOR-IN-CHIEF
Richard Gertner
OPERATIONS MANAGER
Robert McDonald

Motion Picture Almanac

(Annually) 159 West 53rd St., New York, NY 10019; 247-3100; Cable: Quigpubco, New York.

EDITOR
Richard Gertner
ASSOCIATE EDITOR
William Pay
ADVERTISING AND DISTRIBUTION
Robert McDonald

Television Almanac

(Annually) 159 West 53rd St., New York, NY 10019; 247-3100; Cable: Quigpubco, New York.

EDITOR
Richard Gertner
ASSOCIATE EDITOR
William Pay
ADVERTISING AND DISTRIBUTION
Robert McDonald

Fame

159 West 53rd St., New York, NY 10019; 247-3100; Cable: Quigpubco, New York.

EDITOR
Richard Gertner
ASSOCIATE EDITOR
William Pay

The American Cinematographer

(Monthly on the 1st—Semi-technical) Published by American Society of Cinematographers, Inc., 1782 North Orange Drive, Hollywood, CA 90028; 876-5080.

EDITOR
Herb A. Lightman
ASSISTANT EDITOR
Lyla Dusing
ACCOUNTING
Barbara Prevedel
RESEARCH
Patty Armacost
EDITORIAL ADVISORY COMMITTEE
Milton Krasner, Chairman; Lester Shorr, Stanley Cortez, Linwood Dunn, Ernest Laszlo.

AV Guide: The Learning Media Newsletter

(Comprehensive coverage of trends, materials, equipment across the learning media field, for anyone involved in learning processes.) 380 Northwest Highway, Des Plaines, IL 60016 (312) 298-6622

PUBLISHER
H. S. Gillette
EDITORS
Sherry A. Guariglia, Laura Stepanek
CIRCULATION MANAGER
Evelyn Duff

Back Stage

(Weekly dealing with entertainment communications industry and non-theatrical films, television shows and commercials, cassettes, cable, and theater, published Friday), 330 W. 42nd St., New York, NY 10036, (212) 947-0020; 5670 Wilshire Blvd., L.A. CA 90036, (213) 936-5201; 841 North Addison Ave., Elmhurst IL 60126 (312) 843-7533

MANAGING EDITOR & PUBLISHER
Allen Zwerdling
ADVERTISING DIRECTOR & PUBLISHER
Ira Eaker
EDITOR
Tom Tolnay

Back Stage Television, Film, Tape & Syndication Directory

(Annually, January), 330 W. 42nd St., New York, NY 10036, (212) 947-0020.
EDITOR
Allen Zwerdling

Billboard

(International music/record tape/video cassette/video disc newsweekly with readership comprising retailers/wholesalers of recording/playback equipment, record programmers for radio, discotheques, jukeboxes, music publishers, record producers/manufacturers; buyers/sellers of performing talent, artists, song writers/composers.) 9000 Sunset Blvd., Los Angeles, CA 90069; 273-7040; 1 Astor Plaza, New York, NY 10036, 764-7300; 150 N. Wacker Drive, Chicago, IL 60606; Central 6-9818; 2160 Patterson Street, Cincinnati, OH 45214; 733 15 St., N.W., Washington 5, DC; 393-2580.
PUBLISHER
Lee Zhito
CHAIRMAN
William D. Littleford
EXECUTIVE VICE PRESIDENT
Jules Perel
SECRETARY
Ernest Lorch
MANAGING EDITOR
Adam White
DIRECTOR OF SALES
Tom Noonan

Boxoffice

(Film Monthly), 1800 N. Highland, Suite 316, P.O. Box 226, Hollywood, CA. 90028 (213) 465-1186.
PUBLISHING DIRECTOR
Robert L. Oietmeiler
EDITOR & PUBLISHER
Alexander Auerbach
ADVERTISING DIRECTOR
Morris Schlozman
NATIONAL AD MANAGER
Michael Feinberg
BUREAUS
WEST: 1800 N. Highland, Suite 316, P.O. Box 226, Hollywood, CA. 90028, (213) 465-1185, Alexander Auerbach
MIDWEST: 7950 College Blvd., P.O. Box 2939, Shawnee Mission, KA. 66201 (913) 381-6310, John Berry
Published by RLO Communications, Inc., 203 N. Wabash Ave., Chicago, IL 60605

Canadian Film Digest Yearbook

Film Publications of Canada Ltd., 175 Bloor Street East, Toronto, Ontario M4W 1E1, (416) 960-8900.
PUBLISHER
N. A. Taylor
EDITOR
Patricia Thompson
DIRECTOR OF ADVERTISING
Ben Silver
EDITORIAL ASSISTANT
Cathleen Ryan

CinéMag

(24 times per year.) Publication office & Subscriptions: Box 398, Outremont Station, Montreal, P.Q. H2V 4N3.
EDITOR/PUBLISHER
Jean-Pierre and Connie Tadros

Daily Variety

(Motion picture, television, radio, theatre, night clubs daily) 1400 N. Cahuenga Blvd., Hollywood, CA 90028; (213) 469-1141.
EDITOR
Thomas M. Pryor
MANAGING EDITOR
Peter P. Pryor
ADVERTISING MANAGER
Ned Diamant
MARKETING DIRECTOR
Michael Malak
GENERAL MANAGER
F. Phil Turner
PRODUCTION MANAGER
Bob Butler

Editor & Publisher

(Weekly) 575 Lexington Ave., New York, NY 10022; Phone: PLaza 2-7050.
PRESIDENT & EDITOR
Robert U. Brown
MANAGING EDITOR
Jerome H. Walker, Jr.

Film Bulletin

(Monthly). Publication Business Offices: 1239 Vine Street, Philadelphia, PA; (215) 568-0950. Branches: New York (212) MO1-8563; West Coast (213) 839-8685.
EDITOR AND PUBLISHER
Mo Wax
ASSOCIATE PUBLISHER
Paul N. Lazarus
DEPUTY PUBLISHER/EDITOR
Philip R. Ward
MANAGING EDITOR
Daniel Silk
PUBLICATION MANAGER
Frances P. Sacks
CIRCULATION DIRECTOR
Robert Heath, Jr.
WEST COAST EDITOR
Dale Munroe

Films in Review

(Published by National Board of Review) P.O. Box 589, New York, NY 10021; (212) 535-2528.
EDITOR
Ronald Bowers

Film Quarterly

(Quarterly; published Fall, Winter, Spring and Summer. A critical journal of motion pictures and their related arts; successor to *The Quarterly of Film, Radio, and Television and the Hollywood Quarterly*.) Editorial, Sales, and Advertising office: University of California Press, Berkeley, CA 94720; (415) 642-6333.
EDITOR
Ernest Callenbach
Published by University of California Press

Filmworld

Daisons Publications, Ltd., 1000 Lawrence Ave., West, Toronto, Ontario, Canada M6A 1P2. (Monthly newspaper for film, television, and cable affairs)
PRESIDENT & PUBLISHER
Paul Iannuzzi

EDITOR
Margo Raport
MANAGING EDITOR
Stephanie MacKendrick
MARKETING AND SALES DIRECTOR
Earl D. Weiner
ADVERTING SALES
Marie Hewak

The Hollywood Reporter

(Film, TV, Entertainment, Daily) 6715 Sunset Boulevard, Hollywood, CA 90028; (213) 464-7411; and 1501 Broadway, N.Y., NY 10036; (212) 354-1858.

PUBLISHER & EDITOR IN CHIEF
Tichi Wilkerson
MANAGING EDITOR
Cynthia Wilkerson
BUREAUS
  NEW YORK: Martin Gould, 1501 Broadway, New York, NY 10036, Tel.: (212) 354-1858.
  WASHINGTON, DC: Theresa McMasters, 1234 National Press Bldg., Washington, DC 20045 (202) 224-3121.
  ATLANTA: Barbara Thomas, 5100 Peachtree and Dunwoody, 30342, Tel.: (404) 572-5384.
  LAS VEGAS: Mark Tan, 1859 Helm Drive, Las Vegas, Nevada 89119, Tel.: (702) 361-2518.
  ITALY: Francesca Steinman, Viale Giotto, 25/1 00153 Rome. Tel.: 571-824.
  FRANCE: Anne Head, 6 Rue de Lille, Paris 7, Tel.: 260-74-79.
  ISRAEL: Itour Gelbitz, 38 Khovevei Tzion, Tel Aviv, Tel.: 282-336.
  USSR: Natalie Yakovleva, Novosti Press Agency, Moscow.
  MEXICO: Martha Naranjo, Ave. Nuevo Leon 139-1, Mexico City 11 DF. Tel.: (905) 511-6281.
  BELGIUM: Joe van Cottom, Avenue Marechal Foch 7, 1030 Brussels. Tel.: 215-62-21 or 216-32-57.
  ARGENTINA: Leo Balter, Casilla 2573 Correo Central, 1000 Buenos Aires.
  WEST GERMANY: Joseph Hermann, Pfundmayerstrasse 21, 8000 Munich 70, Tel.: (089) 714-2511.
  AUSTRALIA: Matt White, Sydney Daily Mirror, Sydney.
  POLAND: Andrzej Kolodynski, Grojecka 19/25 Flat 96 02-021 Warsaw.
  ENGLAND: George Waldo and Kenelm Jenour, 57 Duke St., Grosevnor Sq., London W1M 5DH, Tel.: 01-493-5015-8.
  SWEDEN: Lars Olof Lothwall, P.O. Box 27 126, S-102 52 Stockholm, Tel.: (08) 63 05 10.
  INDIA: Hameeduddin Mahmood, 11835/7 Satnagar, New Delhi 110005.
  SPAIN: Javier Moro, c/o Nervion No. 25, Madrid 2, Tel.: (341) 411-11-10.

I.A.T.S.E. Official Bulletin

(Quarterly) 1515 Broadway, New York, NY 10036. Tel.: 730-1770.

EDITOR
James J. Riley

The Film Journal

(Bi-monthly) 1600 Broadway, Suite 605, New York, NY 10019; (212) 246-6460.

PUBLISHER-EDITOR
Robert H. Sunshine
MANAGING EDITOR
Jimmy Sunshine
CIRCULATION MANAGER
Patricia DiPiazza

Journal of the Society of Motion Picture and Television Engineers

(Technical monthly) Editorial office: SMPTE Headquarters, 862 Scarsdale Ave., Scarsdale, NY 10583; (914) 472-6606.

EDITOR
Jack F. Christensen
ADVERTISING MANAGER
Jeffrey B. Friedman

Screen World

(Annual) Published by Crown Publishers, Inc., 1 Park Avenue, New York, NY 10016 (212) 532-9200. (An illustrated listing of film releases in the U.S. each year, Academy Award winners, promising personalities, and other data)

EDITOR
John Willis

Seven Arts Press, Inc.

6253 Hollywood Blvd., Hollywood, CA. Tel.: (213) 469-1095. (Publishes books on entertainment industry—The Record Industry Book, The Movie Industry Book, Film Superlist: 20,000 films in U.S. public domain, © Copyright, Motion Picture Distribution.)

PRESIDENT
Walter E. Hurst
VICE PRESIDENT
Joseph Yore
SECRETARY
Sharon Marshall

Variety

(General amusements and professional weekly, published Wednesdays) 154 West 46th Street, New York, NY 10036; (212) 582-2700; 1400 N. Cahuenga Blvd., Hollywood, CA 90028; (213) 469-1141; 1050 Potomac St., N.W., Washington, DC 20005 (202) 965-4301; 400 North Michigan Ave., Chicago, IL 60611; (312) 337-4984; PARIS: 33 Champs Elysees, Paris 75008; Phone 225-08-07; ROME: VARIETY, Via Bissolati, 20, Rome, 00187 Italy; 463-290. LONDON: VARIETY, 49 St. James's St., London SW1A 1JX, England; 493-4561; MADRID, Spain, Calle Lagasca, 104; Phone 276-4262; SYDNEY N.S.W. 2000 1-7 Albion Place, Phone 267-3124.

PUBLISHER AND EXECUTIVE EDITOR
Syd Silverman
ADVERTISING DIRECTOR
Mort Bryer

Newspapers in Principal Markets of the U.S.

Arranged alphabetically by states, this list gives the names and addresses of newspapers in cities and market areas of over 100,000 population which maintain regular motion picture and entertainment departments.

Alabama

Birmingham, The News, 2200 North 4th Ave., 35202.
Birmingham, Post-Herald, 2200 North 4th Ave., 35202.
Huntsville, Times, 2317 Memorial Pkway., 35807.
Mobile, Mobile Press Register., 304 Government St., 36602.
Montgomery, Advertiser, 107 South Lawrence, 36104.

Arizona

Phoenix, Republic, 120 East Van Buren St., 85004.
Tucson, Arizona Star, 208 North Stone., 87501.

Arkansas

Little Rock, Democrat, Capitol Ave. & Scott., 72203.
Little Rock, Arkansas Gazette, 112 West Third St., 72203.

California

Anaheim, Bulletin, 232 South Lemon St., 92805.
Berkeley, Berkeley Gazette, 2048 Center St., 94704.
Burbank, Daily Review, 220 E. Orange Grove Ave., 91502.
Culver City, Evening Star News, 4043 Irving Place., 90230.
Fresno, Bee, 1559 Van Ness Ave., 93721.
Glendale, News Press. 111 North Isabel, 91209.
Long Beach, Independent Press-Telegram, 604 Pine Ave., 90801.
Huntington Park, Daily Signal, 6414 Rugby Ave., 90255.
Los Angeles, Herald-Examiner, 1111 S. Broadway., 90054.
Los Angeles, Times Mirror Co., Times Mirror Sq., 90053.
Oakland, The Tribune Publishing Co., 401-13th St., 94612.
Pasadena, Star News, 525 East Colorado St., 91109.
Riverside, Press-Enterprise Co., 3512-14th St., 92502.
Sacramento, Bee, 21st & Q Streets, 95813.
Sacramento, Sacramento Union Inc., 301 Capitol Mall., 95812.
San Bernardino, Sun, 399 "D" St., 92401.
San Diego, DBA Union-Tribune, 940 Third Ave., 92112.
San Francisco, Chronicle, 901 Mission St., 94119.
San Francisco, The Examiner, 110 5th Ave., 94119.
San Gabriel Valley, The Tribune, 2037 W. San Bernardino Rd., 91790.
San Jose, Mercury-News, 750 Ridder Park Dr., 95131.
San Pedro, News Pilot, 356 W. 7th Street., 90733.
Santa Ana, Register, 625 North Grand Ave., 92711.
Santa Monica, Evening Outlook, 1540 Third., 90406.
Stockton, Stockton Daily Record, 530 E. Market St., 95202.
Torrance, South Bay Breeze, 5215 Torrance Blvd., 90503.
Van Nuys, Van Nuys News & Valley News & Green Sheet, 14539 Sylvan St., 91408.

Colorado

Denver, The Post, 650 15th St., 80202.
Denver, Rocky Mt. News, 400 West Colfax Ave., 80204.

Connecticut

Bridgeport, Post, 410 State St., 06602.
Hartford, Courant, 285 Broad St., 06101.
Hartford, The Times, 10 Prospect St., 06101.
New Haven, The Journal-Courier, 367 Orange St., 06503.
New Haven, Register, 367 Orange St., 06503.
Waterbury, American-Republican, Inc., 389 Meadow St., 06702.

Delaware

Wilmington, News-Journal Co., 831 Orange St., 19899.

District of Columbia

Washington, Post, 1515 "L" St., N.W., 20005.

Florida

Fort Lauderdale, News, 101 North New River Drive East., 33302.

Jacksonville, Florida Times-Union, One Riverside Ave., 32201.
Miami, Herald, 1 Herald Plaza, 33101.
Miami, The News, 1 Herald Plaza, 33101.
St. Petersburg, Times, P.O. Box 1121, 33731.
Tampa, Tribune, 505 East J. F. Kennedy Blvd., 33602.

Georgia

Atlanta, Journal-Constitution, 10 Forsyth St. N.W., 30302.
Columbus, Ledger-Enquirer Newspapers, 17 West 12th St., 31902.
Macon, Telegraph, 120 Broadway, 31201.
Savannah, Savannah News-Press, 105-111 West Bay St., 31402.

Hawaii

Honolulu, Advertiser, P.O. Box 3110., 96802.
Honolulu, Honolulu Star-Bulletin, Inc. 605 Kapiolani Blvd., 96813.
Honolulu, Hawaii Hochi, 917 Kokea St., 96817.
Honolulu, Hawaii Times, 916 Nuuana Ave., 96807.

Illinois

Chicago, Chicago Today, 445 N. Michigan Ave., 60611.
Chicago, Daily Calumet, 9120 Baltimore., 60617.
Chicago, The News, 401 North Wabash, 60611.
Chicago, The Sun-Times, Field Enterprises, Inc., Newspaper Div., 401 North Wabash, 60611.
Chicago, Tribune, 435 North Michigan Ave., 60611.
Joliet, Herald News, 78 No. Scott St., 60431.
Moline, Daily Dispatch, 1720-5th Ave., 61265.
Peoria, Peoria Journal Star Inc., 1 News Plaza, 61601.
Rock Island, Argus, 1724-4th Ave., 61202.
Rockford, Register-Star, 99 East State St., 61105.
Waukegan, News-Sun, 100 W. Madison St., 60085.

Indiana

Evansville, Courier & Press, 201 N.W. 2nd St., 47701.
Fort Wayne, Journal-Gazette, 701 S. Clinton St., 46802.
Fort Wayne, News Sentinel, 600 West Main St., 46802.
Gary, Post-Tribune, 1065 Broadway, 46402.
Hammond, Times, 417 Fayette St., 46320.
Indianapolis, Star & News, 307 North Pennsylvania St., 46206.
South Bend, Tribune, 225 West Colfax, 46626.

Iowa

Cedar Rapids, Gazette, 500-3rd Ave. S.E., 52401.
Davenport, Times Democrat, 124 E. 2nd St., 52808.
Des Moines, Register & Tribune, 715 Locust St., 50304.
Sioux City, Journal, 5th & Douglas St., 51102.
Waterloo, Courier, 501 Commercial St., 50704.

Kansas

Kansas City, Kansan, 901 North 8th St., 66101.
Topeka, Capital-Journal, 6th & Jefferson, 66607.
Wichita, The Eagle and Beacon, 825 E. Douglas St., 67201.

Kentucky

Louisville, The Courier-Journal & Times, 525 West Broadway, 40202.

Louisiana

Baton Rouge, Advocate, 525 Lafayette St., 70821.
New Orleans, The Times-Pacayune, 3800 Howard Ave., 70140.
Shreveport, Journal-Times, 222 Lake St., 71102.

Maryland

Baltimore, News American, Lombard & South Sts., 21203.
Baltimore, Sun, Calvert & Center Sts., 21203.

Massachusetts

Boston, Christian Science Monitor, One Norway St., 02115.
Boston, Globe, 135 Morrissey Blvd., 02107.
Boston, Boston-Herald Traveler, 300 Harrison Ave., 02106.
Boston, Record American, 5 Winthrop Square, 02106.
New Bedford, Standard-Times, 555 Pleasant St., 02742.
Springfield, Republican, 1860 Main St., 01101.
Worcester, Worcester Telegram & Gazette, 20 Franklin St., 01601.

Michigan

Ann Arbor, News, 340 E. Huron St., 48106.
Detroit, Free Press, 321 West Lafayette Blvd., 48231.
Detroit, Evening News, 615 Lafayette Blvd., 48231.
Flint, The Journal, 200 East 1st St., 48502.
Grand Rapids, The Press, Press Plaza, Vandenberg Center, 49502.
Kalamazoo, Kalamazoo Gazette, 401 S. Burdick St., 49003.
Lansing, State Journal, 120 East Lenawee St., 48919.
Muskegon, Chronicle, 981 Third St., 49443.
Pontiac, Press, 48 W. Huron St., 48056.
Royal Oak, Tribune, 210 E. Third St., 48068.
Saginaw, News, 203 South Washington Ave., 48605.

Minnesota

Duluth, Herald, 424 West 1st., 55801.
Minneapolis, Star & Tribune, Fifth and Portland Ave., 55415.
St. Paul, Dispatch, 55 East 4th St., 55101.

Mississippi

Biloxi-Gulfport, Herald, De Buys Rd., 39501.
Jackson, Clarion Ledger-News, Box 40, 39205.

Missouri

Kansas City, Star, 1729 Grand Ave., 64108.
St. Louis, Globe-Democrat, 12th Blvd. at Delmar, 63101.
St. Louis, The Post-Dispatch, 1133 Franklin Ave., 63101.
Springfield, Springfield News & Leader, 651 Boonville, 65801.

Nebraska

Lincoln, Journal-Star, 926 "P" Street, 68501.
Omaha, World-Herald, 14th & Dodge Sts., 68102.

Nevada

Las Vegas, Review-Journal, 737 North Main St., 89101.
Las Vegas, Sun, 121 S. Highland Ave., 89104.

New Hampshire

Manchester, Union Leader, 35 Amherst St., 03105.

New Jersey

Camden, Courier-Post, 08101.
Elizabeth, Journal, 295-299 North Broad St., 07207.
Jersey City, Journal, 30 Journal Square, 07306.
Newark, Evening News, 215-221 Market St., 07101.
Newark, Newark Morning Ledger, 1 Star Ledger Plaza, 07101.
Passaic-Clifton, Herald-News, 988 Main Ave., 07055.
Paterson, News, News Plaza & Straight St., 07509.
Trenton, Times, 500 Perry St., 08605.

New Mexico

Albuquerque, Journal, 7th & Silver, S.W., 87101.

New York

Albany, Times-Union, 645 Albany-Shaker Road, 12201.
Buffalo, The Evening News, 218 Main St., 14240.
Buffalo, Courier-Express, 787 Main St., 14240.
Long Island, Newday, 500 Stewart Ave., Garden City, 11530.
New York City:
Brooklyn Daily, Inc., 2427 Surf Ave., Brooklyn, 11224.
The News, 220 East 42nd St., 10017.
The Post, 210 South St., 10002.
The Times, 229 West 43rd St., 10036.
Wall St. Journal, 30 Broad St., 10004.
Niagara Falls, Gazette, 310 Niagara St., 14302.
Rochester, Times-Union, 55 Exchange St., 14614.
Syracuse, The Post-Standard, Clinton Square, 13202.
Utica, Observer-Dispatch, 221 Oriskany Plaza, 13503.
Yonkers, The Herald Statesman, Larkin Plaza, 10702.

North Carolina

Charlotte, Observer & News, 600 South Tryon St., 28201.
Durham, Herald, 115-19 Market St., 27702.
Greensboro, The News, 200-04 North Davie St., 27402.
Raleigh, News & Observer, 215 S. McDowell St., 27601.
Winston-Salem, Journal-Sentinel, 416-20 North Marshall 27102.

North Dakota

Fargo, Forum, 101-5th St., 58102.

Ohio

Akron, The Beacon Journal, 44 East Exchange St., 44309.
Canton, The Repository, 500 Market Ave., South, 44702.
Cincinnati, The Enquirer, 617 Vine St., 45201.
Cincinnati, Post & Times-Star, 800 Broadway St., 45202.
Cleveland, The Plain Dealer, 1801 Superior Ave., 44114.
Cleveland, The Press, 901 Lakeside Ave., 44114.
Columbus, The Citizen-Journal, 34 South Third St., 43216.
Columbus, The Dispatch, 34 South Third St., 43216.
Dayton, Journal-Herald, 4th & Ludlow Sts., 45401.
Toledo, The Toledo Blade, 541 Superior St., 43604.
Youngstown, The Vindicator, Vindicator Square, 44501.

Oklahoma

Oklahoma City, Oklahoma Journal, 7430 S.E. 15 St., 73110.
Oklahoma City, Oklahoman, 500 North Broadway, 73125.
Tulsa, The World & Tribune, 315 South Boulder Ave., 74102.

Oregon

Portland, The Oregon Journal, 1320 Southwest Broadway, 97201.
Portland, The Oregonian, 1320 Southwest Broadway, 97201.

Pennsylvania

Allentown, The Call, 6th & Linden Sts., 18105.
Erie, The Times, 20 East 12th St., 16501.
Philadelphia, The Bulletin, 30th & Market Sts., 19101.
Philadelphia, The Inquirer, 400 North Broad St., 19101.
Philadelphia, The News, 400 N. Broad St., 19101.
Pittsburgh, Post Gazette, 50 Blvd. of Allies, 15222.
Pittsburgh, Pittsburgh Press Co., 34 Blvd. of Allies., 15222.
Reading, The Eagle, 345 Penn St., 19601.
Scranton, Tribune, 338 North Washington Ave., 18501.
Scranton, The Times, Penn & Spruce, 18501.

Rhode Island

Providence, The Journal, 75 Fountain St., 02902.

South Carolina

Columbia, The State-Record, P.O. Box 1333, 29202.

Tennessee

Chattanooga, The News-Free Press, 400 E. 11th St., 37401.
Chattanooga, Times, 117 E. 11th St., 37401.
Knoxville, The Journal, 210 W. Church Ave., 37901.
Knoxville, The News-Sentinel, 204 West Church Ave., 37901.
Memphis Press-Scimitar, 495 Union Ave., 38101.
Nashville, The Banner, 1100 Broadway, 37203.
Nashville, The Tennessean, 1100 Broadway, 37203.

Texas

Abilene, Reporter News, North 2nd & Cypress Sts., 79604.
Amarillo, The Globe-Times, 900 Harrison St., 79105.
Austin, American-Statesman, 308 Guadalupe, 78767.
Beaumont, The Enterprise, 380 Walnut St., 77704.
Corpus Christi, The Caller-Times, 820 Lower Broadway, 78401.
Dallas, The News, Communications Center, 75222.
Dallas, The Times Herald, 1101 Pacific, 75202.
El Paso, News, 401 Mills St., 79999.
Fort Worth, The Press, 507 Jones, 76102.
Fort Worth, The Star-Telegram, 400 West 7th St., 76101.
Houston, The Chronicle, 512-20 Travis St., 77002.
Houston, The Post, 4747 Southwest Freeway, 77001.
Lubbock, The Avalanche-Journal, 8th St. & Avenue "J", 79408.
San Antonio, The Express, Avenue "E" & 3rd St., 78205.
San Antonio, The Light, McCullough & Broadway, 78206.

614

Waco, Tribune-Herald, 900 Franklin, 76703.
Wichita Falls, The Times, 1301 Lamar St., 76307.

Utah

Salt Lake City, Desert News, 34 East 1st St. South, 84110.
Salt Lake City, The Tribune, 143 South Main St., 84101.

Virginia

Alexandria, Gazette, 717 No. St. Asaph St., 22313.
Arlington, Northern Va. Sun, 3409 Wilson Blvd., 22210.
Newport News-Hampton, The Daily Press, 7505 Warwick Blvd., 23607.
Norfolk, Virginian-Pilot, 150 West Brambleton Ave., 23501.

Richmond, Times-Dispatch, 333 East Grace St., 23213.
Roanoke, Times-World, 201-09 W. Campbell Ave., 24010.

Washington

Seattle, The Post-Intelligencer, 6th & Wall, 98121.
Seattle, The Times, Fairview Ave. N & John, 98111.
Seattle, Daily Journal of Commerce, 83 Columbia St., 98104.
Spokane, Chronicle, W. 927 Riverside, 99210.
Tacoma, The Tribune, 711 Helens Ave., 98401.

Wisconsin

Madison, Capital-Times, 115 South Carroll St., 53701.
Milwaukee, The Journal, 333 West State, 53201.
Milwaukee, Sentinel, 918 N. 4th St., 53201.

Rules and Regulations of the Classification and Rating Administration

Rules and Regulations of the Classification and Rating Administration

Plagued from its earliest days by numerous varieties of social reformers and would-be censors, the organized motion picture industry in the U.S. made several attempts at formalized self-regulation, none of which proved effective until the adoption of the document known as The Motion Picture Production Code in 1930. The Code, which was drafted by Martin Quigley, Catholic layman and trade paper publisher, and Daniel A. Lord, a Jesuit priest, was divided into two parts: Part One, a preamble with general principles and particular applications; Part Two, the philosophical rationale for each of the sections of the first part. (For complete text of The Code, see previous editions of the International Motion Picture Almanac.)

Toward the end of the 1950s violations of the Code had become rampant, and several modifications were made. Finally, in 1968, the Code was scrapped completely and replaced with a film rating system under the direction of the Classification and Rating Administration (CARA). The Administration is governed by its three founders: The Motion Picture Association of America. The National Association of Theatre Owners, and The International Film Importers and Distributors of America.

In the beginning films submitted to CARA were classified into one of four designations: G (suggested for general audiences); M (suggested for mature audiences—adults and mature young people); R (restricted, persons under 16 not admitted unless accompanied by parent or adult guardian; X (persons under 16 not admitted). In 1970 the M rating was changed to GP (general audience—parental guidance suggested), and the age limits for R and X were increased to 17. In 1972 GP was changed to the current designation, PG (parental guidance suggested—some material may not be suitable for pre-teenagers).

Text of the Rules and Regulations of the Classification and Rating Administration follows:

ARTICLE I POLICY REVIEW COMMITTEE

Section I. Organization

A. A policy Review Committee is established to be comprised of representatives of the National Association of Theatre Owners ("NATO"), International Film Importers and Distributors of America ("IFIDA") and Motion Picture Association of America, Inc. ("MPAA").

B. Each organization shall have four representatives on the Policy Review Committee.

(1) The Chairman of CARA shall participate in all meetings as an *ex officio* member of the Policy Review Committee.

(2) Each organization shall have the right to have an additional person attend for secretarial purposes.

C. Attendance by eight members, exclusive of *ex officio* members, shall constitute a quorum, provided that at least two members are present from each organization.

D. The Chairmanship of the Policy Review Committee shall rotate among the President of NATO, a member of the Board of Governors of IFIDA and the President of MPAA.

E. The Policy Review Committee shall meet at least twice a year at times scheduled through consultation among the President of NATO, a member of the Board of Governors of IFIDA and the President of MPAA. Special meetings may be called as circumstances require through the same procedure.

F. Minutes shall be kept and distributed to the members of the Policy Review Committee. Such minutes shall in all respects be confidential.

G. MPAA counsel, in cooperation with the Executive Director of NATO, shall serve as Secretary to the Policy Review Committee and shall be responsible for circulating minutes of the meetings and such other materials as the Policy Review Committee determines should be circulated.

Section II. Duties

A. The Policy Review Committee shall determine the policies, rules and procedures to be followed by the Classification and Rating Administration in the conduct of its duties.

B. The Policy Review Committee shall determine the policies, rules and procedures to be followed by the Classification and Rating Appeals Board and its subcommittees in the conduct of Appeals and other proceedings.

C. The Policy Review Committee shall have the authority to make changes in the Rating System and the policies, rules and/or procedures necessary for implementation. Such changes may be made on the Policy Review Committee's own initiative or on the basis of proposals from members of the Appeals Board, the Chairman of CARA or other appropriate sources.

ARTICLE II CLASSIFICATION AND RATING ADMINISTRATION

Section I. Organization

A. A Classification and Rating Administration (CARA) is established.

B. It shall be comprised of a Chairman and staff members, one of whom, shall be designated Administrative Director.

Section II. CARA's Duties

A. All motion pictures produced or distributed by members of the MPAA and their subsidiaries shall be submitted to CARA for rating.

B. All motion pictures produced or distributed by non-members of the MPAA may be submitted to CARA in the same manner and under the same conditions as members of MPAA.

C. The actual rating of a motion picture shall be made only upon the viewing by CARA of the completed motion picture. Solely at the request of the producer or the distributor of a motion picture, CARA may consult with them on rating criteria at any time before completion of the motion picture.

Section III. Rating and Re-rating by CARA

A. CARA will rate or re-rate any motion picture at any time before it is exhibited in any theatre in the United States.

B. CARA will rate or re-rate any motion picture if that motion picture has not been exhibited in more than four theatres for a period not exceeding thirty days. The thirty-day period shall commence with the first date of exhibition in any one theatre and run continuously therefrom.

C. CARA will re-rate any motion picture that has been exhibited and does not qualify under subsection B above, only if any and all versions of the motion picture are permanently withdrawn from exhibition and all such versions are not exhibited or advertised anywhere in the United States for a period of 90 days prior to the date the re-rated version is re-released in exhibition. The 90-day time period may be changed in exceptional cases by the Waiver Committee as prescribed in Section III-H below.

D. CARA will rate a motion picture released without previously being submitted to CARA at any time after release, provided it is submitted for a rating in exactly the same form in which it is in release. If the producer or distributor seeking the rating chooses to edit or otherwise revise the picture, CARA will rate the picture in accordance to Section III-C above.

E. CARA will rate any motion picture previously released with a self-applied X rating (or without a self-applied X rating, but under similar admissions policy) under the rules set out in Sections III B-C, except that if upon review CARA issues the motion picture an X rating, the producer or distributor submitting need not remove the motion picture nor certify that it has been removed from exhibition for the time period specified in Section III-C above.

F. CARA shall issue the Rating Certificate containing the rating or re-rating only after the producer or distributor who submitted the motion picture certifies that:

(1) All prints conform identically to the version rated or re-rated by CARA and only such conforming prints shall be exhibited in the United States; and

(2) The time period for which the motion picture must be withdrawn, if any, has been completed.

G. Motion pictures submitted for rating or rerating shall be subject to the advertising approval procedures provided in the rules for the Advertising Code.

H. A Waiver Committee is established to be comprised of three members each from NATO, IFIDA and the MPAA. Upon the initiative of CARA or the producer or distributor of the motion picture, the Committee shall have the authority to hold a hearing and to decide either to lengthen or shorten the 90-day time period prescribed in Section III-C above.

(1) Five members shall constitute a quorum, provided that at least one member is present from each organization. Each member shall have one vote and a majority vote of those voting shall govern.

(2) The Waiver Committee shall have the final authority to set a time period of 90 days or less. If the Waiver Committee imposes a time period in excess of 90 days, the producer or distributor may appeal the decision to the Appeals Board.

(3) The Appeals Board has the authority to reduce the time period set by the Waiver Committee down to 90 days exactly, affirm the time period set by the Waiver Committee or modify the decision of the Waiver Committee to a time period of greater than 90 days but less than that imposed by the Waiver Committee. The procedures for such appeals are prescribed in Article III, Sections II and III.

I. For the purposes of determining the applicability of Section III A-F hereof, CARA or the Waiver Committee may require applicants to supply, in writing, all necessary and pertinent information.

Section IV. Rating Procedures

A. When the producer or distributor of a completed motion picture elects to release the motion picture with a CARA rating, it shall be submitted to CARA and rated either:

(1) G—General Audiences. All ages admitted.

(2) PG—Parental Guidance Suggested. Some material may not be suitable for children.

(3) R—Restricted. Under 17 requires accompanying parent or adult guardian. (Age may vary in some jurisdictions.)

(4) X—No one under 17 admitted. (Age may vary in some jurisdictions.)

B. The G, PG and R ratings set out above are Certification Marks registered by the MPAA with the United States Patent and Trademark Office.

(1) The G, PG, or R ratings may not be self-applied.

(2) The X rating may be self-applied by producers and distributors who are non-members of the MPAA.

C. In issuing the ratings provided in Section IV-A above, CARA shall consider as criteria among others as deemed appropriate the treatment of the theme, language, violence, nudity and sex.

D. A producer or distributor shall pay CARA a fee in accordance with the uniform schedule of fees.

Section V. Use of the Ratings

A. A rating is issued by CARA on the condition that all prints of a picture to be distributed for exhibition in the United States shall be identical to the print rated by CARA. The agents, assignees and other persons acting under the actual or apparent authority of the applicant are bound by this requirement.

B. A rating is issued by CARA on the condition that all the terms and conditions stated in the Rating Certificate are binding on the producer or distributor who submits the motion picture, as well as his agents, assignees and other persons acting under his actual or apparent authority.

C. Motion pictures of MPAA member companies rated G, PG, or R by CARA shall bear upon a prominent frame of every print distributed in the United States the number of Rating Certificate and the official Seal of the Association with the words "Certificate Number," followed by the number of the Rating Certificate and the symbol of the rating assigned to it. So far as possible, the Seal of the Association, the rating and number shall be displayed in uniform type, size and prominence.

D. Motion pictures of non-MPAA member companies rated G, PG, or R by CARA may bear upon a prominent frame of every print distributed in the

United States the words "Certificate Number," followed by the number of the Rating Certificate and shall bear the symbol of the rating assigned to it. Prints of such pictures may also display the official Seal of the Association. So far as possible, the Seal of the Association and the number, if displayed and the rating shall be displayed in uniform type, size and prominence.

E. Motion pictures submitted for rating which are rated X, shall display the symbol X on all prints of the motion picture distributed in the United States in uniform type, size and prominence. The Seal of the Association shall not be displayed on a motion picture rated X.

Section VI. Unauthorized Use and Revocation

A. The use of CARA ratings without a duly issued CARA Rating Certificate is not permitted. In addition to the remedies provided in these rules, legal action may be instituted to prevent unauthorized use of the ratings.

B. Any producer or distributor issued a Rating Certificate who distributes the motion picture in violation of the terms and conditions specified in these rules or the Rating Certificate may have the rating revoked.

C. An action for revocation other than for a violation of the Advertising Code shall be commenced by CARA.

(1) CARA shall file a letter with the President of the MPAA stating the relevant facts on which the revocation is sought.

(2) A copy of the letter shall be sent to the producer or distributor and, where possible, be accompanied by telephone notice.

(3) In consultation with the President of the MPAA and the Chairman of CARA, a date and a time for a hearing shall be set to provide the producer or distributor an opportunity to be heard.

D. Hearings on revocation shall be heard by a representative designated by the President of the MPAA, a representative designated by the Board of Governors of IFIDA, and a representative designated by NATO, if, by majority vote, the three representatives of MPAA, IFIDA and NATO determine that the violation did occur, they may order the rating revoked and the Rating Certificate voided.

a) Only one request for a re-hearing shall be entertained and that must be filed within fifteen business days after the date of the original appeal.

b) The producer or distributor may submit new information in support of the request for a re-hearing.

c) A majority vote of the members shall be required for a re-hearing to be granted and the decision shall be final. In the event of a tie vote, the Chairman of the Appeals Board shall decide whether to grant the re-hearing.

d) The re-hearing of an appeal shall be conducted under the same procedures as prescribed for appeals generally.

B. (1) After a motion picture has been initially rated or re-rated by CARA and such rating or re-rating sustained by the Appeals Board in the appeal provided for in Section II-A above, the producer or distributor may resubmit the motion picture to CARA for a subsequent re-rating one or more times, subject only to the fee schedule and rule requirements provided in Article II, Section III.

(2) The Appeals Board shall hear and determine appeals from decisions by CARA issuing a subsequent re-rating in accordance with the same rules and procedures provided in this article for appeals generally, except that

a) The producer or distributor shall be granted only one appeal on a subsequent re-rating as a matter of right. This appeal of right may be taken after the first or after any subsequent re-submission to CARA at the option of the producer or distributor.

b) The producer or distributor shall be granted additional appeals, after the appeal of right provided for in sub-section (a) above, only in exceptional cases and only with the express consent of the Chairman of the Appeals Board. The approval of the Chairman shall be granted only where the producer or distributor demonstrates that there is a substantial change in the motion picture giving the reasons why such changes were not made prior to the last appeal of right.

ARTICLE III CLASSIFICATION AND RATING APPEALS BOARD

Section I. Organization

A. A Classification and Rating Appeals Board is established, to be composed as follows:

(1) The President of the MPAA and ten representatives designated one each by the member companies of the MPAA.

(2) Nine exhibitors designated by NATO.

(3) Four distributors designated by IFIDA.

B. A substitute member for any appeal, to replace a regular member unable to attend, may be designated in accordance with the same procedures for selecting regular members.

C. The President of the MPAA shall be Chairman of the Appeals Board, and the MPAA shall provide its Secretariat.

D. The presence of twelve members is necessary to constitute a quorum of the Appeals Board for the hearing of the appeal, provided that at least five members each, designated by MPAA and NATO, respectively, and one member designated by IFIDA are present. Upon the unanimous concurrence of the Chairman of the Appeals Board, the representative of CARA and the representative of the producer or distributor taking the appeal, the quorum requirements may be waived.

Section II. Duties

A. (1) The Appeals Board shall hear and determine appeals taken by producers or distributors from an initial decision by CARA. Appeals may only be taken where a less restrictive rating is sought by the producer or distributor. The Appeals Board may affirm the decision of CARA or apply a different rating as it deems appropriate.

(2) Upon the request of the producer or distributor whose appeal received a majority vote, but less than a two-thirds vote and therefore did not overturn CARA's rating, the Chairman of the Appeals Board shall poll the members of the Appeals Board who voted on the appeal on whether a re-hearing of the appeal should be granted.

c) When an appeal is sought pursuant to subsection (b) above, by a non-member of MPAA, the Chairman shall, at the request of the producer or distributor, consult with a member of the Governing Board of IFIDA in determining whether to grant the appeal.

(3) If a producer or distributor seeking an appeal pursuant to Section II-B-2 (b and c) is denied the right to take an appeal, such producer or distributor may have that decision reviewed by the President of NATO, the Chairman of the Board of Governors of IFIDA and the President of MPAA. A majority vote shall decide whether an appeal shall be granted and such decision shall be final.

(4) In determining the appeal rights of a producer or distributor under Section II-B, the grant or denial of a re-hearing of any prior appeal, as provided for in section II-A-2, shall be of no effect.

C. The Appeals Board shall hear and determine appeals from a waiting-time period in excess of 90 days imposed by the Waiver Committee pursuant to Article II Section III-C.

D. The Appeals Board or any member may offer proposals to the Policy Review Committee regarding the policies, rules or procedures of the Appeals Board, CARA, the Waiver Committee, or any other matter involving the Rating System. The final decision to adopt such proposals shall be made by the Policy Review Committee.

E. (1) No member of the Appeals Board shall participate in an appeal involving a motion picture in which the member or any company with which he or she is associated has a financial interest.

(2) Except as allowed in these rules, it shall be grounds for dismissal of the appeal or other appropriate sanction for the producer or distributor taking an appeal to discuss the subject of the appeal with one or more members of the Appeals Board, other than the Chairman of the Appeals Board, prior to the hearing of the Appeal. It shall be the duty of the member or members contacted to inform the Chairman who shall rule on the sanction to be imposed.

Section III. Appeals–Time for Filing

A. An appeal from a decision of the Waiver Committee on the time-period requirement provided for in Article II Section III-C may be made to the Appeals Board at any time during the time period originally established by the Waiver Committee.

B. An appeal from a decision by CARA may be filed at any time until the motion picture in question has opened at any theatre in the United States.

C. When the appeal from a decision by CARA involves a motion picture in exhibition, an appeal may be filed only with approval of the Waiver Committee. The producer or distributor seeking the appeal shall submit a letter, stating the reasons why the appeal was filed after the date of exhibition with a rating and providing the information required in Subsection D below. The decision of the Waiver Committee shall be final.

D. The Waiver Committee's consideration shall in part be based on:

(1) The date upon which the motion picture was rated by CARA;

(2) The date upon which the motion picture was first exhibited;

(3) The number of theatres in which the motion picture has been exhibited, is being exhibited and is booked to be exhibited as of the dates upon which the appeal is filed and is to be heard, and

(4) The nature of the advertising and extent to which the motion picture has been advertised.

Section IV. Conduct of Appeals

A. An appeal from a decision by CARA or the Waiver Committee shall be instituted by the filing of a notice of appeal.

(1) The notice shall state the intention to appeal, the running time of the motion picture and certify that the print to be shown at the appeal conforms identically to the version rated by CARA.

(2) The information required in Article III, Section III-D.

(3) A check in the amount of $100 made out to the MPAA.

(4) The letter should be sent to the Chairman of the Appeals Board as follows: President Motion Picture Association of America, Inc. 1600 Eye Street Washington, D.C. 20006

B. With the filing of an appeal, the producer or distributor taking the appeal shall be required to pay a uniform fee in the amount of $100, said amount to be used exclusively towards the cost involved in scheduling and hearing of the appeals.

C. Appeals shall be scheduled no less than seven days after the filing of the notice of the appeal. In exceptional cases the executives of NATO, IFIDA and MPAA may modify this rule.

D. Provision shall be made for the screening by the members of the Appeals Board at the hearing or prior thereto of a print of the motion pictue identical to the one rated by CARA.

(1) The hearing of an appeal from a rating by CARA shall commence with the screening of the motion picture involved.

(2) The hearing of an appeal from a time period decision by the Waiver Committee shall commence with the screening of the motion picture involved at the discretion of the Chairman of the Appeals Board.

E. The producer or distributor taking the appeal, CARA or the Waiver Committee may present written statements to the Appeals Board.

(1) If either the producer or distributor taking the appeal, CARA or the Waiver Committee desires to present such written statements to the Appeals Board, any such written statement should be furnished to the Secretary at least seven days before the date fixed for the hearing of the appeal. The Secretary will distribute such statements to the Executive Secretaries of IFIDA, NATO and MPAA for circulation to their respective members of the Appeals Board. If prior submission is not possible, the written statement shall be distributed at the hearing of the appeal.

(2) Submission of written statements shall not diminish or alter the right to present oral statements or arguments on behalf of the producer or distributor taking the appeal and CARA or the Waiver Committee.

F. The producer or distributor taking the appeal, CARA or the Waiver Committee may present oral statements to the Appeals Board at the hearing.

(1) The Appeals Board will hear oral statements on behalf of the producer or distributor by not more than two persons, except by special permission. Oral statements or arguments on behalf of CARA shall be made only by the Chairman of CARA or his designated representative

and on behalf of the Waiver Committee by a member or a designated representative.

(2) On appeals of decisions by the Waiver Committee, the producer or distributor taking the appeal and the representative of the Waiver Committee may offer the oral testimony of two witnesses. Such witnesses shall be subject to questioning by the Appeals Board.

(3) The producer or distributor taking the appeal, the representative of CARA or the Waiver Committee shall be afforded the opportunity for rebuttal.

(4) Normally no more than a half hour will be allowed for oral arguments to the party taking the appeal, and a like time to CARA or the Waiver Committee. If a producer or distributor taking an appeal, CARA or the Waiver Committee is of the opinion that additional statements or additional time are necessary for the adequate presentation of the appeal, the producer or distributor, CARA or the Waiver Committee may make such request by letter addressed to the Secretary stating the reasons why such statements or time is required for the adequate presentation of the appeal.

(5) When such request is made by a non-member of MPAA, the Secretary shall consult with a member of the Governing Board of IFIDA in determining whether and to what extent the request may be granted.

(6) A request for the participation of additional persons or for the allowance of additional time, to the extent that it is not granted, may be renewed to the Appeals Board at the commence-ment of the hearing of the appeal for disposition by the Appeals Board.

(7) In no circumstances shall the time allowed to any producer or distributor, the Waiver Committee or CARA, for the hearing of an appeal, extend beyond one hour.

G. The members of the Appeals Board shall have the opportunity to question the producer or distributor taking the appeal and/or the representative of CARA or the Waiver Committee.

(1) The time for questioning shall not run against the prescribed time allocations.

(2) At the conclusion of the questioning the producer or distributor taking the appeal and the representative of CARA or the Waiver Committee shall leave the room in which the hearing is being conducted.

H. After a reasonable time for discussion, the designated members of the Appeals Board shall vote to either sustain or to overrule the decision of CARA or the Waiver Committee.

(1) No decision of CARA shall be overruled upon appeal unless two-thirds of those present and voting shall vote to overrule. Upon an overruling of its decision, CARA shall rate the picture involved in conformity with the decision of the Appeals Board.

(2) No decision of the Waiver Committee shall be overruled unless a majority of those present and voting shall vote to overrule. Upon the overruling of its decision, the Waiver Committee shall implement the time requirement set by the Appeals Board in accordance with the provisions in Article II, Section III.

Advertising Code Regulations

*T*he MPAA Code for Advertising is administered
through the California Office of the MPAA. All
advertisements for films that are rated by the
Classification and Rating Administration (CARA)
must meet the following requirements of the MPAA
Code for Advertising. They must be submitted for
approval in advance of their public use.

The MPAA Code for Advertising is designed to
ensure that all advertisements for films rated by
CARA carry the correct rating designation and to
ensure that these advertisements are not offensive.
Every advertisement must be suitable for all audiences except theatrical trailers, which are rated either G (suitable for all audiences) or R (suitable
only for audiences viewing R or X rated features).

I. ADVERTISING CODE REGULATIONS

1. These regulations are applicable to all
members of the Motion Picture Association of
America, to all other producers and distributors of
motion pictures with respect to each picture for
which a Classification and Rating Administration
rating is sought and to all other producers and distributors who self-apply the X rating to their motion pictures and voluntarily submit their advertising.

2. The term "advertising" as used herein shall
be deemed to mean all forms of motion picture advertising and exploitation including but not limited
to the following: pressbooks; still photographs;
newspaper, magazine and trade paper advertising;
publicity copy and art intended for use in pressbooks or otherwise intended for general distribution in printed form or for theatre use; trailers;
posters, lobby displays and other outdoor displays;
advertising accessories, including heralds and
throwaways; novelties; copy for exploitation tieups;
and all radio and television copy and spots.

3. All advertising for motion pictures which
have been submitted to the Classification and Rating Administration for rating shall be submitted to
the Director of Advertising for approval and shall
not be used in any way until so submitted and
approved. All print advertising with the exception
of stills shall be submitted in duplicate, particularly
pressbooks.

4. In reviewing advertising submitted to the
Advertising Code office, the Director shall consider:

(1) Whether the advertising material misrep-
resents the character of the motion picture.

(2) Whether the advertising material depicts
graphic displays of nudity or sexual activity.

(3) Whether the advertising material depicts
graphic displays of violence or brutality.

(4) Whether the advertising material exploits
or capitalizes upon censorship disputes or the
designated rating.

(5) Whether the advertising material demeans
religions, race or national origin.

5. Acting as promptly as feasible, the Director
of Advertising shall stamp "Approved" on one copy
of all advertising approved and return the stamped
copy to the producer or distributor who submitted
it. If the Director disapproves any advertising, the
Director shall stamp the word "Disapproved" on
one copy and return it to the producer or distributor who submitted it, together with the reasons for
such disapproval.

6. The Director of the Code for Advertising
shall require all approved advertising for pictures
submitted to the Classification and Rating Administration by members of the Motion Picture Association of America and their subsidiaries to carry the
official Association seal and a designation of the rating assigned to the picture by the Classification and
Rating Administration. Uniform standards as to
type, size and prominence of the display of the seal
and rating will be set forth by the Advertising Code
Administrator.

7. Approved advertising for pictures submitted
for rating to the Classification and Rating Administration by companies other than members of the
Motion Picture Association of America and their
subsidiaries may bear the official Association seal at
the distributor's option, but all such advertising
shall bear the assigned rating.

8. Approved advertising for motion pictures
rated X by the Classification and Rating Administration shall bear the X rating but may not bear the
official Association seal.

9. All pressbooks approved by the Director of
the Code for Advertising shall bear in a prominent
place the rating and its definition assigned to the
picture by the Classification and Rating Administration. Pressbooks shall also carry the following
notice:

All advertising in this pressbook, as well as all
other advertising and publicity materials referred to herein, have been approved under the
standards for Advertising of the Motion Picture
Association of America. All inquiries on this procedure may be addressed to:

Director of the Code for Advertising
Motion Picture Association of America
8480 Beverly Boulevard
Los Angeles, CA 90048

10. The Director of Advertising shall have the
authority to promulgate supplementary regulations
for the purpose of implementing the objectives of
the Advertising Code.

11. Appeals. Any producer or distributor whose
advertising has been disapproved may appeal the
decision of the Director of the Code for Advertising
as follows:

A producer or distributor shall serve notice of
such appeal on the Director of the Code for Advertising and on the President of the Association.
The President, or in his absence a Vice President
designated by him, shall within a week hold a
hearing to pass upon the appeal. Oral and written evidence may be introduced by the producer
or distributor and by the Director of the Code for
Advertising, or their representatives. The appeal
shall be decided as expeditiously as possible and
the decision shall be final.

On appeals by companies other than members
of the Motion Picture Association of America and
their subsidiaries, the President shall, if requested, decide the appeal in consultation with a

representative of Int'l Film Importers and Distributors of America, as designated by its Governing Board.

12. Any producer or distributor issued a Rating Certificate by the Classification and Rating Administration must use approved advertising in accordance with the rules and supplemental regulations of the Advertising Code. Noncompliance shall be a violation of the terms and conditions upon which the rating was issued and shall constitute grounds for revocation of the rating.

An action for revocation shall be commenced by the Director of Advertising.

(1) The Director shall file a letter with the President of the Motion Picture Association of America stating the relevant facts on which the revocation is sought.

(2) A copy of the latter shall be sent to the producer or distributor and where possible be accompanied by telephone notice.

(3) In consultation with the President of the Motion Picture Association and the Director of Advertising a date and time for a hearing shall be set to provide the producer or distributor an opportunity to be heard.

Hearings on revocation shall be heard by the President of the Motion Picture Association or, in his absence, a designated Vice President of the Association. If the President determines that the violation did occur, he may order the Rating Certificate revoked and voided.

On hearings by producers or distributors other than members of the Motion Picture Association of America and their subsidiaries, the President shall, if requested, make the determination of whether a violation did occur in consultation with a representative of the Int'l Film Importers and Distributors of America, Inc., as designated by its Governing Board.

13. Each company shall be responsible for compliance by its employees and agents with these regulations.

HOW TO WORK MOST EFFECTIVELY WITH THE CODE FOR ADVERTISING

The main function of the Advertising Code is to make certain that all advertising with the exception of restricted trailers is suitable for general audiences and that such advertising contains nothing that most parents would find offensive for their children to see or hear. Experience has shown that advertising approved by the Advertising Code office is more readily accepted by the various media—newspapers, radio and TV—and oftentimes without such approval is totally rejected by the media. Therefore, it is in your best interest to submit your advertising in its earliest stages to prevent costly changes later on.

The following paragraphs are a few guidelines that will be beneficial to you concerning the submission of advertising material.

THE MPAA RATING MUST BE USED IN ALL ADVERTISING

II. PRINT ADVERTISING

This includes everything but theatre trailers and radio and TV spots.

A. *STILLS* Any and all stills being contemplated for use as print advertising or exhibition of any kind—and this includes the trade papers and magazines—must be submitted for approval.

B. *NEWSPAPER ADS.* All newspaper ads must carry the designated rating and those ads 150 lines and over must carry the definition of the rating. Such rating definitions must be large enough to be legible in print and must be placed in a prominent position in the ad—preferably at the bottom but not buried in the credits.

C. *TEASER ADS.* No mention of the rating need be in a teaser ad UNLESS the theatre where the film will be playing is mentioned. If the theatre is noted in the ad, it must show a rating. However, all teaser ads as well as other advertising must be approved by the Advertising Code prior to release.

D. *POSTERS AND BILLBOARDS.* Submit art work and layouts for posters and billboards well in advance, even before the final rating of the picture. You can always add the correct rating symbol later. Use of rating symbol and full definition is required on all posters and billboards.

E. *MAGAZINE AND TRADE ADS* Ads to appear in magazines or in the trades must be approved prior to their use.

F. *PRESSBOOKS.* Never go to final pressbook print unless all of the advertising elements and publicity stills used have been given earlier Advertising Code approval. Once everything in your pressbook is submitted and approved, please add the following notice for all films rated either "G," "PG" or "R" (not "X") in a prominent place: **APPROVED**—All advertising in this pressbook, as well as all other advertising and publicity materials referred to herein, have been approved under the standards for Advertising of the Motion Picture Association of America. All inquiries on this procedure may be addressed to: Director of the Code for Advertising, Motion Picture Association of America, 8480 Beverly Blvd., Los Angeles, CA 90048.

III. THEATRICAL TRAILERS

The theatrical trailer is the key element in every motion picture distribution campaign. We are aware of the importance of the theatrical trailer to every distributor and exhibitor. We also know—all too well—that it is one of the most sensitive areas in the industry's film rating program. Use of the official MPAA rating tags are required to be shown on all trailers for rated films. There are no audio requirements for theatrical trailers.

We examine trailers and approve them for TWO audiences only—"G" Unrestricted or General Audiences—and "R" Restricted (Under 17 must be accompanied by parent or adult guardian). Trailers for "PG" films should be suitable for "G" audiences, regardless of the content of the "PG" film. Remember, a patron selects a "PG" film after having been warned concerning the content. This *does not* mean that all of the material in the film can play to a "G" General Audience. Please note that in general, scenes approved for a "PG," "R" or "X" feature when spread out over a 90 minute film have a much stronger impact when reduced to a two minute trailer. It is important to keep this fact in mind when preparing trailers—and this applies particularly to those who may be working on their first feature release.

G—General Audience

A family audience viewing a "G-rated" film may object to a trailer they feel is unsuitable for their children who may be with them. Parents can be very protective about what they didn't select, and resent material that may be thrust upon them because they happen to be in the audience.

A trailer for General Audiences and television spots have the same standards. Oftentimes the 60-second television spot is used as a "teaser" or "crossplug" trailer for General Audiences. Because a G trailer must be suitable for all audiences and must not contain any scenes which most parents would find objectionable to their young children, the following are some of the guidelines to be mindful of when preparing a G trailer:

No blood
No victim/weapon in the same frame
No exposed breasts or nudity of any kind
No bed scenes with any action
No use of blasphemous language (allowing only "hell" and "damn")

R—Restricted Audience

It should be clearly understood that Restricted trailers cannot carry the same scenes of sex, violence and language that may be approved in the R-rated feature. The advertising must necessarily eliminate all strong sex or excessive violence in theatre trailers. Again, the impact of those scenes is heightened when compacted in a short trailer. Some of the scenes unacceptable in R trailers are:

Excessive sex violence
Dismemberment
Genitals
Pubic hair
Use of sexually connotative words
Humping, lesbianism, fondling or masturbation

We suggest you use the following procedure; let us look at your rough cut before going to a composite. And even before we see it, you should eliminate excessive violence—close-up shootings, stabbings, hacking with axes, etc. Show the weapon, not the meeting against the flesh. Eliminate all blood in general audience trailers and as much as possible in R trailers. If guns are fired in a G trailer, do not use close-up shots where the bullet hits body, but cut to body on the ground or just before body hits the ground.

Where making a "G" audience trailer is not possible with an "R"-rated feature, we suggest accepting a restricted audience trailer and using a one-minute TV spot for the "G"-rated general audience trailer. Many companies do this successfully.

IV. TEASER TRAILERS

Since a regular trailer cannot be released before the feature has been rated, many companies use a shorter teaser trailer. Any teaser trailer for a film not yet rated must be suitable for general audiences and must carry the front tag once it has been approved by the Director of the Code for Advertising. A teaser need not carry the end tag *unless* the feature has been rated.

V. TRAILER TAGS

There are two head tags which indicate for which audience the trailer is intended—either "All Audiences" or "Restricted Audiences."

ALL TAGS ARE TO REMAIN ON THE SCREEN FOR FIVE (5) SECONDS.

Trailer negatives have been supplied to most of the major labs in New York, Los Angeles and Miami. Contact the Code for Advertising office if you have trouble locating the trailer tag you need.

All trailers must carry the proper MPAA tags. Failure to attach the proper tag is cause for disapproval. Also, unless the trailer carries the tags, many exhibitors will refuse to run it.

VI. TELEVISION SPOTS

All television trailers should be made with a general audience in mind. TV spots containing sexual references, violence, blood or profanity are not acceptable. It is suggested that when possible, several spots be made of varying degree as stronger spots may be acceptable for late night viewing. TV standards are different for prime time viewing as opposed to late night viewing.

The MPAA Advertising Regulations which follow give specific information on the use of the rating symbols in TV spots both *visually* and *verbally* in 60-30-20 and 10-second spots. This arrangement was worked out in cooperation with the National Association of Broadcasters and must be carefully adhered to.

TV spots should carry rating and definition large enough to be legible on a home viewer's screen and can appear in the same frame with the film title and credits, but must remain on the screen for four (4) seconds.

NOTE: IN PAST EXPERIENCES WHEN THE STATIONS FELT THAT THE RATING AND DEFINITION WERE NOT LARGE ENOUGH, THEY WOULD FLASH ON AN ADDITIONAL COPY OF THE RATING AND DEFINITION, USUALLY IN LARGE WHITE LETTERS, OVER SCENES IN THE SPOT.

VII. RADIO SPOTS

There is little difference in acceptable content between TV and radio spots. Most radio spots are acceptable provided there is no profanity, use of the Lord's name or sexually-oriented language. Many stations in the middle west will not accept vulgar references to racial or national groups. These should be avoided. In general, advertisers should be guided by good taste and use language in radio spots that is acceptable to family audiences.

MPAA REGULATIONS FOR TELEVISION AND RADIO SPOTS

(Worked out in cooperation with the National Association of Broadcasters)

I. Television Spots

60-30-20-10 second spots

A. Visual
Show the MPAA Seal (except when rating is X)
Show the *Rating Symbol Letter* (G, PG, R or X)
Show the *Full Definition* of the Symbol
(See page 9 for samples.)

Full Definition:

G—GENERAL AUDIENCES
All Ages Admitted
PG—PARENTAL GUIDANCE SUGGESTED
Some Material May Not Be Suitable for Children
R—RESTRICTED
Under 17 Requires Accompanying Parent or Adult Guardian
X—NO ONE UNDER 17 ADMITTED
(Age limit may vary in certain areas)

624

B. Audible—State the **Rating Symbol Letter**
"*RATED G*"
"*RATED PG*"
"*RATED R*"
"*RATED X*"

Note: The visual code information (MPAA Seal, Rating Symbol and Full Definition) should be included when the title of the film comes on the screen and remain for *four* seconds.

II. Radio Spots

60-30-20 second spots

A. State the *Rating Symbol* (G, PG, R or X) and also state the *Abbreviated Definition*

"RATED G—GENERAL AUDIENCES"
"RATED PG—PARENTAL GUIDANCE SUGGESTED"
"RATED R—UNDER 17 NOT ADMITTED WITHOUT PARENT"
"RATED X—UNDER 17 NOT ADMITTED"

10 seconds spots

"RATED G"	"RATED R"
"RATED PG"	"RATED X"

VIII. GENERAL INFORMATION ON RATED FILMS

A. Sneak Previews:

When a film is sneaked, for everyone's protection, the rating must be in the ads. All advertising for a sneak preview must carry the rating.

B. Re-issues:

ALL ADVERTISING FOR A RE-ISSUE MUST BE RE-SUBMITTED
If a film is a re-issue, it is suggested that it be mentioned directly or inferred in the advertising to avoid confusion, i.e., "now you can see again," "brought back by popular demand," "a (company name) re-release."

C. Title Changes:

ALL ADVERTISING FOR A TITLE CHANGE MUST BE RE-SUBMITTED
It is suggested that the former title be mentioned in all advertising, such as "formerly released as . . ."

D. Kiddie Shows:

The only trailers that should be shown during a kiddie matinee are trailers for *future kiddie matinee* features.

E. Double Bills:

On a double bill where each feature has a different rating, *only the more restricted of the two ratings can be used in the advertising*. The more restricted rating governs box office admittance.

F. Foreign Language Films:

In the state of New York, if a foreign language film is released with sub-titles, it must so state in *ALL ADVERTISING*, i.e., (French film-English sub-titles).
If a foreign language film is released in two versions, English and foreign, it must differentiate in the advertising which version is playing.

G. Rating Changes:

If your film has been *re-rated* by the Classification and Rating Administration, all advertising must reflect the change in rating.
It is advised that words such as "original," "uncut," not be used in the ad campaign. The change in rating cannot be exploited.

H. Distributor Changes:

If you have recently acquired a film carrying an MPAA rating, please notify us so that we can adjust our records accordingly. Also, if you change your name, address or telephone number, we would appreciate your advising us for future correspondence.

I. Posting ("wild" etc.):

Posters seen in public places other than theatres are subjected to great criticism. Therefore, it is most important that these posters are approved before use and are inoffensive (see "AREAS IN ADVERTISING MOST SENSITIVE TO CRITICISM")

J. "G"-rated films:

Phrases such as, "for the whole family" or "family entertainment" cannot be used in any advertising unless the film has received a "G" rating.

K. New Campaigns:

If an ad campaign that has already been approved is revised or changed or a second campaign substituted, any new advertising must be submitted.

IX. AREAS IN ADVERTISING MOST SENSITIVE TO CRITICISM:

(1) SEX
(2) VIOLENCE, WEAPONS (i.e. gunsites)
(3) LANGUAGE AND GESTURES
(4) NUDITY
(5) DRUGS AND PARAPHERNALIA (i.e. needles)
(6) DEFAMATION
(7) ETHNIC OR MINORITY GROUPS
(8) SACRILEGE
(9) CHILD ABUSE
(10) CRUELTY TO ANIMALS
(11) BODY FUNCTIONS
(12) ASSASSINATION
(13) VENEREAL DISEASES
(14) MUTATIONS
(15) PHYSICAL HANDICAPS (i.e. amputations)
(16) CADAVERS (i.e. eyes opened, abuse)
(17) RAPE AND MOLESTATIONS
(18) LAVATORY OR LAVATORY JOKES

The Industry in
Great Britain and Ireland

* **INDUSTRY DEVELOPMENTS OF YEAR**

* **COMPANIES AND PERSONNEL**

* **TRADE ORGANIZATIONS**

* **GOVERNMENT FILM DEPARTMENTS**

* **STUDIOS AND LABORATORIES**

* **CHIEF THEATRE CIRCUITS**

BRITISH YEAR IN REVIEW

DESPITE the continued decline in cinema admissions by mid-1981 there were signs of stabilization with average weekly attendances of around 2 million and weekly box-office takings of $5 million. It is an indication that regardless of the opposition of home video and "free" television, there is still a business, if not such a lucrative one, in persuading people to visit British cinemas.

Rationalization by the major circuits in recent years has meant the closure of many larger houses and the conversion of others into "twins" and "triples." In fact the number of licensed screens in the UK has recently increased to over 1600.

Films of the calibre of "For Your Eyes Only," "Raiders of the Lost Ark," "Time Bandits' and "Excalibur" were also helping to rejuvenate British boxoffices during 1981.

It is on the home production front, however, that there have been depressing signs of inactivity. So much so that the government was forced to cut the quota—the minimum percentage of UK and EEC feature films required by law to be shown in British cinemas—by half, from 30 to 15 per cent.

There is every indication that British quota films registered in 1982 will be less than half those registered in the 1981 quota period and there could be fewer than 20 quota films in all. In 1980, 22 per cent of all cinemas failed to reach quota levels.

Overseas expenditure of UK film companies in 1979 was $104 million. As table 4 shows, a large part of the overseas expenditure by UK film companies, 64 per cent in 1979, is by UK subsidiaries of the major United States film companies. The proportion of total expenditure accounted for by such businesses has in recent years fluctuated between just under 60 per cent to just over 70 per cent, but is now lower than in the early '70s when they were responsible for around 80 per cent of overseas expenditure of UK film companies. Most of the overseas payments by these subsidiaries are for performances in cinemas or on television.

With the country going through an economic depression, there is little liklihood of government financial support for the British film production industry. Only the Eady Levy remains as a regular source of subsidy for producers of British films. Basis of this is that a proportion of the boxoffice takings on all films, British or foreign, that are shown in British cinemas, is paid into a fund and later paid out so as to ensure that a percentage of the revenue earned by British films goes to the makers of those films.

An eligible film is a British quota film which is produced by a person ordinarily resident in, or a company registered in, and the central management of whose business is exercised in, the UK. It also reqires that no more than 7½% of the playing time consists of scenes made in studios outside the UK.

Exhibitors here have maintained their ban on theatrical films being made available to the local TV networks within three years of their trade-show. It is a vital stand, for the opposition to the cinema boxoffice mounts daily with home video reaching boom proportions, the expansion of the commercial television channels, the introduction of subscription television and sales to "free" television of blockbusting films.

Countries of origin of foreign and community films registered in 1980

	Playing time					
	Over 72 minutes		33⅓–72 minutes		Under 33⅓ minutes	
Countries of origin	Foreign	EC	Foreign	EC	Foreign	EC
Brazil	1					
Bulgaria					1	
France	1	12	1	1		
Germany (Fed Rep)	6	9				
Greece	2					
Hungary	1					
Italy	4	11	1	2		
Japan	1					
Netherlands			1		1	
Netherlands Antilles	1					
South Africa					1	
Spain	1					
Sweden	1					
Switzerland	3		1			
United States	122		7		8	
USSR	4					
Yugoslavia	1					
Joint productions						
Cyprus/Greece	1					
France/Belgium		1		1		
France/Italy/ Germany (Fed Rep)		1				
France/Switzerland	2	1				
Germany (Fed Rep)/ France		1				
Germany (Fed Rep)/ Spain	1					
Italy/France	1	2				
Italy/Hong Kong	1					
South Africa/ Germany (Fed Rep)	1					
United States/ Germany (Fed Rep)	1					
Others	21[1]		1[2]		5[3]	
Totals	178	38	12	4	16	

For instance, "Gone With The Wind" was included in a $9 million deal with the BBC and a similar arrangement with the commercial networks made "Jaws" available.

Nevertheless, given a supply of good product, the exhibition industry here firmly believes it will survive to help provide the greatly increased and improved leisure facilities which must be a feature of any future society.

Table 1 Overseas transactions in respect of film and television material £ million

	1968	1969	1970	1971	1972	1973	1974	1975	1976	1977	1978	1979
Receipts[1]												
Film companies[2]	44.5	40.7	27.6	36.2	31.5	27.4	29.5	45.9	51.1	60.5	85.2	86.1
Television companies[3]	5.1	6.9	5.7	10.6	9.1	10.1	10.4	12.6	18.4	35.7	37.0	41.9
Total	49.6	47.6	33.3	.46.8	40.6	37.5	39.9	58.5	69.5	96.2	122.2	128.0
Expenditure[4]												
Film companies[2]	21.4	26.8	15.4	19.6	20.3	21.5	23.0	29.5	31.6	30.1	42.7	51.5
Television companies[3]	4.1	5.2	4.8	4.9	5.0	7.7	9.1	10.8	17.6	16.9	21.7	28.0
Total	25.5	32.0	20.2	24.5	25.3	29.2	32.1	40.3	49.2	47.0	64.4	79.5
Receipts less expenditure												
Film companies[2]	23.1	13.9	12.2	16.6	11.2	5.9	6.5	16.4	19.5	30.4	42.5	34.6
Television companies[3]	1.0	1.7	0.9	5.7	4.1	2.4	1.3	1.8	0.8	18.8	15.3	13.9
Total	24.1	15.6	13.1	22.3	15.3	8.3	7.8	18.2	20.3	49.2	57.8	48.5

[1] Sums receivable from overseas residents. [2] Includes transactions by film companies in respect of rights restricted to television. [3] Includes transactions in respect of BBC sound broadcasting and independent Television News. [4] Sums payable to overseas residents.

Table 2 Overseas transactions in respect of film companies[2]; analysis by area £ million

	1974	1975	1976	1977[5]	1977[5]	1978	1979
Receipts[1]							
EC	4.8	6.2	8.5	9.6	9.6	9.7	11.7
Other western Europe	2.3	2.1	2.6	4.2	4.2	4.7	4.3
North America	14.3	27.7	26.9	29.7	29.7	52.1	47.8
Other developed countries[5]	—	—	—	—	5.6	6.7	7.2
Overseas sterling countries[5]	5.4	7.1	7.2	9.6	—	—	—
Rest of the world[5]	2.7	2.8	5.9	7.4	11.4	12.0	15.1
Total	29.5	45.9	51.1	60.5	60.5	85.2	86.1
Of which receipts in respect of rights restricted to television	1.7	1.6	3.0	3.6	3.6	2.4	3.2
Expenditure[4]							
EC	5.9	5.4	9.0	6.9	6.9	7.7	12.1
Other western Europe	1.0	1.6	3.0	2.1	2.1	1.0	2.0
North America	14.4	18.3	16.5	19.4	19.4	32.5	33.2
Other developed countries[5]	—	—	—	—	0.5	0.3	0.6
Overseas sterling countries[5]	0.9	2.4	1.1	1.0	—	—	—
Rest of the world[5]	0.8	1.8	2.0	0.7	1.2	1.2	3.6
Total	23.0	29.5	31.6	30.1	30.1	42.7	51.5

[1][2][3] see table 1. [4][5] Other developed countries are Australia, Japan, New Zealand and South Africa. Prior to 1977 Japan was included with rest of the world while the other countries were included with overseas sterling countries. In 1977 figures were collected on both bases—means nil or less than half of final digit shown.

Table 3 **Overseas transactions in respect of film companies[2]; analysis by area and type of transaction** £ million

| | 1978 | | | | | | 1979 | | | | | |
	Total	EC	Other western Europe	North America	Other developed countries[5]	Rest of the world[5]	Total	EC	Other western Europe	North America	Other developed countries[5]	Rest of the world[5]
Receipts[1]												
Performances in cinemas or on television	46.0	8.1	4.1	18.7	5.9	9.2	45.2	8.7	3.6	15.9	6.0	11.0
Production of films	39.2	1.6	0.6	33.4	0.8	2.8	40.9	3.0	0.7	31.9	1.2	4.1
Total	85.2	9.7	4.7	52.1	6.7	12.0	86.1	11.7	4.3	47.8	7.2	15.1
Expenditure[4]												
Performances in cinemas or on television	32.6	6.9	0.1	25.1	0.1	0.4	36.7	10.9	0.1	25.4	0.2	0.1
Production of films	10.1	0.8	0.9	7.4	0.2	0.8	14.8	1.2	1.9	7.8	0.4	3.5
Total	42.7	7.7	1.0	32.5	0.3	1.2	51.5	12.1	2.0	33.2	0.6	3.6

[1][4][5] see tables 1 and 2.

Table 4   **Overseas transactions in respect of film companies[2]; analysis by type of transaction and category of company**   £ million

	1974	1975	1976	1977	1978	1979
Total receipts[1]	29.5	45.9	51.1	60.5	85.2	86.1
United Kingdom subsidiaries of the major						
United States film companies	8.5	10.1	12.0	10.5	13.4	10.4
Other	21.0	35.8	39.1	50.0	71.8	75.7
Total expenditure[4]	23.0	29.5	31.6	30.1	42.7	51.5
United Kingdom subsidiaries of the major						
United States film companies	15.3	17.2	18.8	20.1	30.8	33.1
Other	7.7	12.3	12.8	10.0	11.9	18.4

[1][2][3]see table 1.
Source: British business.

The Industry in Britain and Ireland
Companies, Structure, Personnel

Abbey Films Ltd.

Film House, 35 Upper Abbey Street, Dublin 1; Tel: Dublin 741238 and 71 Middle Abbey Street, Dublin 1, Ireland. Tel. Dublin 746735. Telegraphic Address: Filmwards, Dublin.
DIRECTORS
K. Anderson, L. Ward, A. Ryan

Ace Distributors Ltd.

(Ace Film Productions)
14 Broadwick Street, London, W1V 1FH. Tel. 01-437 3165.
DIRECTORS
John S. Green, E. L. Sarvis

Acmade International

(Division of Oakside Industries Ltd.) Oakside, Oxford Road, Uxbridge, Middx. Tel. Uxbridge 36313. Telex: 8954606
DIRECTORS
B. J. Drinkwater, G. R. Ireland

A.C.T. Films, Ltd.

2 Soho Square, London W. 1, Tel. Gerrard 8506.
HON. CONSULTANT
Ralph Bond
SECRETARY
Anton Bates
DATE OF INCORPORATION
April, 1957
CAPITAL
Limited by guarantee

Aegis Productions Ltd.

Thames House, 117 Albert Bridge Road, London, SW11. Tel. 01-228 7766.
DIRECTORS
John Hanson, Primrosse Hanson

Agfa-Gevaert Ltd.

Great West Road, Brentford, Middlesex: Tel. 01-560 2131.
SALES DIRECTOR, Motion Picture Division
E. J. Drew, F.B.K.S

Algonquin Films Ltd.

Pinewood Studios, Iver Heath, Bucks. Tel: 0753651700

Alpha Films Ltd.

13-14 Archer Street, London, W1V 7HG. Tel. 01-437 0516

Allied Film Makers Ltd.

c/o Wilding Hudson & Co. 24-30 Holborn, London, ECIN 2H5

DIRECTORS
Michael Relph, Sir Richard Attenborough, Bryan Forbes, Guy Green
SECRETARY
Kewferry Management (Films) Ltd.
DATE OF INCORPORATION
September 30, 1959
CAPITAL
Authorised £5,000 (Ord. Shares)
Issued: 400 Ord. shares of £1 each

Allied Stars

Pinewood Studios, Pinewood Road, Iver, Bucks, SLO ONH. Tel.: 0753 651 700.
DIRECTORS
E. Brown, J. G. Hadjioannov, N. Hudson.

Almanak Film Productions, Ltd.

17 Pembridge Place, London, W.2. Tel: Bayswater 0497.
DIRECTORS
K. W. Beckett, Otto Kreisler, C. H. Bonner
DATE OF INCORPORATION
May 8, 1948
CAPITAL
£100

Ambro Distributing Corp.

Twentieth Century House, 31 Soho Square, London, W1V 6AP. Tel: 01-439 8083-4. Telex: 266541 Cables: Ambrotel, London.
DIRECTOR, THEATRICAL SALES
Douglas F. Brunger.

Gerry Anderson Productions Ltd.

Pinewood Studios, Iver Heath, Bucks, SL0 0NH; Tel. 0753 652344.
DIRECTORS
Gerry Anderson, Keith Shackleton

Andor Films Ltd.

8 Ilchester Place, London W14 8AA. Tel: 01-602-2382. Cables: Andorfilm, London.
DIRECTORS
R. M. Fletcher, M. J. Farrer-Brown, Charles H. Schneer (U.S.A.) Managing
DATE OF INCORPORATION
1975

Angle Films Limited

25 Blenheim Crescent, London W11 2EF; Tel.: 229 9762; Telex: 8953396 REXPYK G

Animated Motion Pictures Ltd.

72 Wardour Street, London, W.1. Tel: 01-437-8282.
DIRECTORS
Nat Miller (Managing), D. Siebenmann

Anvil Film and Recording Group Ltd.

Denham Studios, Denham, Bucks: Tel: Denham 83522.
DIRECTORS
Ken Cameron, O.B.E., B.Sc., (chairman), R.I.C.H. Warren (Managing), R. W. Keen, R. K. T. Scrivener, Ken Somerville, C. Eng. M.I.E.R.E.

James Archibald

35 Morpeth Mansions, Morpeth Terrace, London, SW1P-1EU Tel: 01-828-9691.

Autocue Ltd.

Autocue House, 265 Merton Road, London, SW. 18 5JS. Tel: 01-870 0104.

Avco Embassy Pictures (UK) Ltd.

113-117, Wardour Street, London. W1V 3TD Tel: 01-734 9561. Cables: Embapic London Telex 28527.
DIRECTORS
R. Rehme (USA), H. Fletcher (USA), T. L. Kirby, C. J. Davis

Avton Film Productions Ltd.

9 Clifford Street, London, WIX IRB Tel: 01-439 7321. Cables: Klingfilm, London W1; Telex: 261828.

A.W.M. Productions Ltd.

32 The Rise, Elstree, Herts WD6 3JU: Tel: 01-953 7070.
DIRECTORS
Alfred W. Marcus, E. M. Marcus
DATE OF INCORPORATION
June 24, 1953
CAPITAL
£100

AZ Productions Ltd.

Lorrimer House, 47 Dean Street, London, W.1. Tel.: 01-437 7349.

Bamore Film Productions Ltd.

EMI Elstree Studios, Shenley Rd., Borehamwood, Herts. Tel: 01-953 1600.
DIRECTORS
Robert S. Baker, Roger G. Moore
DATE OF INCORPORATION
1966

Barber International Films Ltd.

113-117 Wardour Street, London, W1V 3TD Tel: 01-437 0068. Telex: 299856.
DIRECTORS
Arnold Barber (Managing), David Barber, Peter Frolich (Chairman), Danny O'Donovan, John Velasco

Basic Films, Ltd.

68 Lebanon Park, Twickenham. TW1 3DQ. Tel: 01-891 0338.
DIRECTORS
J. B. Napier-Bell, H. W. Palk
SECRETARY
M. Napier-Bell

Beaconsfield Films, Ltd.

52 Queen Anne Street, London, W1M 9LA. Tel: 01-935 1186.
DIRECTORS
Ralph P. Thomas, Joy Thomas, Denis G. Truscott
DATE OF INCORPORATION
March 21, 1951

Beaver Films Ltd.

Beaver Lodge, The Green, Richmond, Surrey. Tel: 01-940 7234.
DIRECTORS
Sir Richard Attenborough C.B.E., Bryan Forbes

Berkey Colortran U.K.

P.O. Box No. 5, Burrell Way, Thetford, Norfolk. IP243RB Tel.: Thetford 2484. Telex: 81294.
MANAGING DIRECTOR
M. R. Waterland
MARKETING DIRECTOR
J. Thornley
SALES DIRECTOR
T. Cowie

Bermans and Nathans Ltd.

Head Office: 18 Irving Street, Leicester Square, London, W.C.2H 7AX Tel: 01-839 1651. Main Store: 40 Camden Street, London NW1 OEN Tel: 01-387 0999.
DIRECTORS
Louis Benjamin (Chairman), Monty M. Berman, MBE (Managing), Lindsay Jamieson (Jnt. Dep. Man.), John Gudenian (Jnt. Dep. Man.), Noel Howard, Phillip Linke, D. Honey.

B-H-P Films Ltd.

36 Park Lane, London, W1Y 3LE. Tel. 01-493 7741
DIRECTORS
Sir John Woolf, Ralph S. Bromhead, Brian Sandelson

Border Film Productions London Ltd.

84 Wardour Street, London, W.1. Tel: 01-437 3945.

Box, Sydney, Associates, Ltd.

52 Queen Anne Street, London, W1M 9LA. Tel 01-935 1186.
DIRECTORS
Mrs. B. E. Rogers, D. G. Truscott

Brent Walker Film Distributors Ltd.

147-9 Wardour Street, London, W1V 3TB. Tel: 01-434 1961. Telex: 23639.
CHAIRMAN
Edward D. Simons
DIRECTOR OF SALES
K. G. Dowling

Britannia Film Distributors, Ltd.

10 Green Street, London, W.1. Tel. 01-629 6863/5.
DIRECTORS
David Henley (Chairman), Steven Pallos, Claude Pascoe.
SECRETARY
F. Kelly

British Films, Ltd.

Carlyle House, 235 Vauxhall Bridge Road, London, S.W.1. Tel.: 01-828 7965. Telex 947165.

British Movietonews, Ltd.

North Orbital Road, Denham, Nr. Uxbridge, Middx: Tel. 0895 832323.
DIRECTORS
Mary, Lady Rothermere, G. F. Sanger, C.B.E., J. P., P. Livingstone, J. P. Meehan, E. Buyse, D. Tarr, E. A. Candy
GENERAL MANAGER
E. A. Candy
EDITOR
P. Hampton
FILM LIBRARY
P. Holder

British Transport Films

Melbury House, Melbury Terrace, London, NW1 6LP. Tel: 01-262 3232.

Brocket Productions Ltd.

27-29 Berwick Street, London W1V 3RF. Tel: 01-437 0136.
DIRECTORS
Matt McCarthy, John Black

Bryanston Films Ltd.

Stratton House, Picadilly, London, W1X 6AS. Tel. 01-629 8886.
DIRECTORS
John T. Davey, F.C.A., Colin S. Wills, MA, FCA.

Burnup Service, Ltd.

15 Samuel Road, Langdon Hills, Basildon, Essex, England, Tel: 0268-42824.
DIRECTORS
William C. A. Pay (Managing), G. H. P. Laban
DATE OF INCORPORATION
January 3, 1951

Butcher's Film Distributors, Ltd.

Kingscreen House, 6-7 Great Chapel Street, London, W1V 3AG
DIRECTORS
J. I. Phillips (Man), G. F. Roberts, L. E. Manuel

Camera Location Services

(Bill Moxley) Studio 16, St. James' Close, St. Johns, Woking, Surrey. Tel. 0486 2 4645.

Campbell Connelly & Co. Ltd.

(Music Publishers) 37 Soho Square, London, W1V 5DG Tel: 01-439 9181

Capitol Film Distributors, Ltd.

193 Wardour St., London, W.1. Tel. Gerrard 8196
DIRECTOR
M. Crook

Allan Carr Enterprises Ltd.

2 Berkeley Square, London, W.1. Tel: 01-408 0222.

Cassius Film Productions Ltd.

8A, Glebe Place, Chelsea, London, S.W.3. Tel: 01-352 6838.
DIRECTORS
Henry de Pinna Weil, John Gorst, M.P., Roy Boulting, John Boulting

Cattermoul Film Service

(Cecil Cattermoul Ltd.)
Registered Office: Colquhoun House, Broadwick Street, London, W.1. Tel. 01-437 3592. Telegrams: Scanofil, London, W1V 2ER.
DIRECTORS
Marina Cattermoul (Mrs.). R. H. Marshall, L. A. Thomas

Cavalier Films Ltd.

34 Deacons Hill Road, Elstree, Herts: Tel. 01-953 1403.
DIRECTORS
J. E. Rogers, F.R.P.S., M.B.K.S., M. A. Rogers, D. T. Rogers

Charter Film Productions, Ltd.

8a Glebe Place, London, S.W.3. Tel: 01-352 6838.
DIRECTORS
The Lord Goodman, C.H. LL.D., (Chairman), Lord Rayne, Roy Boulting, John Boulting

Chrysalis Visual Programming Division

12 Stratford Place, London, W1N 9AF. Tel.: 01-408 2355. Telex: 21753.

Roger Cherrill Ltd.

65-66 Dean Street, London, W1V 5HD. Tel.: 01-437 7972.

Cinecenta Ltd.

147/9 Wardour Street, London, W1V 3TB. Tel: 01-734 521.

Cine-Lingual Ltd.

27-29 Berwick Street, London, W1V 3RF. Tel. 01-437 0136.
DIRECTORS
Matt McCarthy, John Black.

Cine-Lingual Sound Studios Ltd.

27/29 Berwick Street, London, W1V 3RF. Tel: 01-437 0136.
DIRECTORS
Tony Anscombe, Edwin Quainton, John Black.

Cinema International Corporation (UK)

114 Jermyn Street, London, SW1Y 6HG. Tel: 01-734 8222
MANAGING DIRECTOR
James Higgins

Cinesound Effects Library Ltd.

Imperial Studios, Maxwell Road, Elstree Way, Boreham Wood, Herts: Tel. Elstree 5837, 5545, 4904, 1587.

Herman Cohen Productions

13 Wigmore Street, London, W.1. Tel.: 01-636 2355.

Columbia Pictures Corporation, Ltd.

19 Wells Street, London, W1P 3FP. Tel.: 01-580 2090.
SECRETARY
Arthur Leese

Columbia (British) Productions

(A Division of Columbia Pictures Corp., Ltd.)
19 Wells Street, London, W1P 3FP. Tel: 01-580 2090.

Columbia-E.M.I.-Warner Distributors Ltd.

135 Wardour Street, London, W1V 4AP. Tel: 01-734 6352.
MANAGING DIRECTOR
Tom Nicholas

Connaught-UK Films Ltd.

25 Dover Street, London, W.1. Tel.: 01-491 7621.
CHAIRMAN
Andrew Holcombe
INT. MAN. DIRECTORS
Ken Paul, Donald Langdon

Connaught International Films Ltd.

83 High Street, Marlow, Bucks. Tel.: Marlow 73815.
MANAGING DIRECTOR
J. A. Holcombe

Constellation Films, Ltd.

The Coach House, Estate House, High Road, Chigwell, Essex. Tel: 01-500 0936.
CHAIRMAN
Anthony Havelock-Allan
DIRECTORS
Robert Garrett, Stanley Gorrie.

Control Systems Ltd.

The Island, Uxbridge, Middx. UB8 2UT. Tel: Uxbridge 51255.
MANAGING DIRECTOR
E. H. Mude

Crawford Films Ltd.

15-17, Old Compton Street, London, W.1. Tel. 01-734 5298.
DIRECTORS
N. A. Weekes, B. G. Sammes

Cresswell Productions Ltd.

Pinewood Studios, Iver Heath, Bucks. Tel.: Iver 652485.
DIRECTORS
John Dark, Gregory Dark, Malcolm Cockran

Cupid Productions Ltd.

13 Quarry Street, Guildford, Surrey GU1 3UY. Tel.: 0483 38552.
DIRECTORS
Oliver Stanley, A. H. Westropp

Curzon Film Distributors Ltd.

38 Curzon Street, London, W1Y 8EY. Tel.: 01-629 8961.
DIRECTORS
E. Erdman, R. C. Wingate, T. J. Bowen

Cygnet Guild Communications Ltd.

Guild House: Upper St. Martin's Lane, London, WC2H 9EL Tel. 01-836 5420 and Bushey Studios, Melbourne Road, Bushey, Herts. Tel.: 01-950 1621.
DIRECTORS
R. Evans (Man.), P. Ferguson, W. Partington, R. Price, J. Wiles

C.Z. Scientific Instruments Ltd.

(Elmo Projectors)
2, Elstree Way, Borehamwood, Hertfordshire.

Darnborough, Antony, Productions Ltd.

43 Bury Walk, Chelsea, London, S.W.3. Tel. 01-589 2096.
DIRECTORS
Antony C. Darnborough, M.C., D. Hall.

Data Film Distributors, Ltd.

20 Great Chapel Street, London, W1V 3AQ. Tel. 01-734 9987.
DIRECTORS
W. Goodman, B. V. Goodman, N. Aphale (Secretary)

De Lane Lea Ltd.

75 Dean Street, London, W.1. Tel.: 01-439 1721.
Cables: Delpros, London.
DIRECTORS
J. C. Jeffrey, C. S. Wills, R. J. Paynter

Diamond Films, Ltd.

34 South Molton Street, London, W.1.
DIRECTORS
Stanley Baker, E. R. Baker, Cy Endfield (U.S.A.), H. B. Endfield

Disney, Walt, Productions Ltd.

68 Pall Mall, London, S.W.1. Tel. 01-839 8010. Cables: Waltdisney, London. Telex: London 21532.
MANAGING DIRECTOR
Gus A. Zelnick

Dolphin International Film Distributors Ltd.

81 Piccadilly, London, W.1. Tel. 01-493 8811.

Domino Productions Ltd.

36 Park Lane, London W1Y 3LE. Tel. 01-493 7741.
DIRECTORS
Sir John Woolf (Chairman), Brian Sandelson, Ralph S. Bromhead

Drummer Films Ltd.

14 Haywood Close, Pinner HA5 3LQ.
PRODUCER
Martin M. Harris (Man. Dir.)

Duck Lane Film Productions Ltd.

8 Duck Lane, London, W1V 1FL. Tel.: 01-734 0853.
DIRECTORS
D. R. Andrews, A. O'Aguiar

Eagle Films, Ltd.

15-17 Old Compton Street, London, W1V 6JR. Tel.
01-437 9541. Cables: Eaglepix, London, W.1.
DIRECTORS
Barry Jacobs, A. Jacobs

Educational and Television Films, Ltd.

247a Upper Street, London, N1 1RU Tel: 01-226 2298.
GENERAL MANAGER
Stanley Forman

Electronic Publishing Co. Ltd.

71 Dean Street, London, W1V 6DE. Tel. 01-734 1874.
Telex. PEC/LON 25554.
DIRECTORS
Jack Le Vien (Chrm.) (USA), Nicholas de Rothschild (Man.), Jan Kaplan

EMI Cinemas Ltd.

30-31 Golden Square, London W1R 4AA. Tel. 01-437 9234.
CHIEF EXECUTIVE
Robert Webster

EMI Films Ltd.

(A Member of the Thorn EMI Group of Companies)
142 Wardour Street, London, W1A 3BY. Tel. 01-437 0444. Telex: 22760.
CHAIRMAN AND CHIEF EXECUTIVE
Barry Spikings
DIRECTORS
Lord Delfont, Nat Cohen, Alan Goatman, Michael Bromhead (Dir. Overseas Sales), John Chambers (Fin. Dir.), E. A. Maxwell (non-Exec.), A. Mitchell, R. A. Webster, Frank Leach, David Jones, R. A. Mercer

EMI Elstree Studios, Ltd.

Boreham Woods, Herts. Tel.: 01-953 1600. Telegrams: EMI-FILMS, BOREHAM WOOD. Telex: 922436 E. FILMS G.
DIRECTORS
Barry Spikings, chairman; Andrew Mitchell, managing director; Lord Delfont; E. A. Maxwell; R. A. Webster.

EMI Pathe

50-54 Beak Street, London, W.1. Tel: 01-437 1544.
Telex: 22760. Telegrams: PATHEQUIP—LONDON.

English Film Company Ltd.

Suite 4, 60-62 Old Compton Street, London, W.1.
Tel: 01-734 6197.
DIRECTORS
B. Sen, P. Sen

Enterprise Pictures Ltd.

27 Soho Square, London W1V 6BH. Tel: 01-734 3372. Telex: 298713.
DIRECTORS
John Hogarth (Managing), Michael Samuelson, Anthony Arden, Anne Boyle.

Entertainment Film Distributors Ltd.

60-66 Wardour Street, London, W.1. Tel: 01-734 4678. Telex: 27950.
DIRECTORS
Michael L. Green, Peter L. Andrews, J. F. Andrews, J. Green.

Eon Productions, Ltd.

2 South Audley Street, London. W1Y 5DQ. Tel.: 01-493 7953. Cables: Brocfilm, London, W1.
DIRECTORS
M. G. Wilson, F. B. Coote, R. A. Barkshire

Europa Films, Ltd.

Registered Office: Park House 158/160, Arthur Road, Wimbledon Park, London, S.W.19.
DIRECTORS
Hugh Stewart, Frances H. Stewart.

Euston Films

365 Euston Road, London, NW1 3AR.
CHIEF EXECUTIVE
Verity Lambert
EXECUTIVE-IN-CHARGE, PRODUCTION
Johnny Goodman

Evershed Power-Optics Ltd.

Bridge Wharf, Bridge Road. Chertsey, Surrey KT16 8LJ Tel.: 093-28 61181 Telex: 929945 Epochy G. Cables: Lenservo Chertsey.

Excelsior Film Productions, Ltd.

Registered Office: 2 Acacia Road, London, N.W.8.
Tel. 01-722 2648.
DIRECTORS
Marcel Hellman, H. Alan Hawes, F.C.A., Renee Hellman, J. Fenton
SECRETARY
H. Alan Hawes, F.C.A.

Eyeline Films Ltd.

77 Dean Street, London, W.1. Tel. 01-734 3391.
DIRECTORS
Harold Orton, George H. Brown, Jacki Roblin, Kenneth More, Alfred Shaughnessy, Gordon Grimward

Fancey, E. J., Productions, Ltd.

84 Wardour Street, London, W.1. Tel. 437 3945/6.
DIRECTORS
J. Mellis-Smith, O'Negus Fancey
DATE OF INCORPORATION
November 30, 1954.

Falcon Visual Services Ltd.

Twickenham Film Studios, St. Margarets, Twickenham, Middx. Tel.: 01-892 4477.

Fantale Films Ltd.

Twickenham Studios, St. Margarets, Middlesex Tel.: 01-892 4477.
MANAGING DIRECTOR
Harry Fine.

Far International Films, S.r.l.

(British prod. subsidiary: Almerline Ltd.) 44 Viale Parioli, Rome, Italy. Tel.: 806050. London office: c/o

Jade Film Marketing Ltd., 91 Highfield Avenue, London, N.W. 11. Tel: 01-455 0240.

Film and General Productions Ltd.

74 Kensington Park Road; London. W11 2PL. Tel.: 01-221 1141.

DIRECTORS
Clive Parsons, Davina Belling.

Film and Television Marketing Services Ltd.

4 Tilney Street, London, W.1. Tel. 01-499 2446.

DIRECTORS
Richard Blayney, Sheila Brewster, Barbara Norris

Film Distributors Associated (16mm)

(A division of Twentieth Century Fox Film Co. Ltd.)
Building 9, GEC Estate, East Lane, Wembley, Middx.
Tel.: 01 908 2366.

CHAIRMAN
A. Branca

Film Finances, Ltd.

34 South Molton Street, London, W1Y 1HA. Tel.: 01-629 6557/9. Telex: 298060 (filfin).

DIRECTORS
Robert E. F. Garrett (Chairman); William A. Croft, R. M. Soames (Man. Dir.), R. S. Aikin, M. L. Carr
SECRETARY
Wm. A. Croft, F.C.A.
DATE OF INCORPORATION
February 24, 1950

Filmarketeers Ltd.

81 Piccadilly Square, London, W1V 9HB. Tel.: 01-499 7419.

Filmtext Ltd.

Twickenham Film Studios, St. Margarets, Middx:
Tel. Pohesgrove 4477.

Filmverhuurkantoor De Dam B.V.

4 Red Lion Yard, Waverton Street, London, W.1.
Tel.: 01-493 1687. Telex: 917801. Cables: DEDAM
London W1.

Fisz, S. Benjamin, Productions Ltd.

51 South Audley Street, London, W.1. Tel: 01-493 7428.

DIRECTORS
Benjamin Fisz, Maude Spector, Sue Carrington-Green, Irving Mitchell Felt, S. Simmons.

Flamingo Film Productions

P.O. Box 324, London, SW1X 8LG. Tel.: 01-235 8243.

DIRECTORS
J. S. Kruger, R. Kruger, H. R. Kruger

Mark Forstater Productions Ltd.

19 Court Hope Road, London, N.W.3. Tel: 01-267 6178.

DIRECTORS
Mark Forstater (USA), Mitsuko Forstater (USA), M. Hatton, R. I. Harris, G. C. Wheatley.

Four Star Films, Ltd.

52 Queen Anne Street, London, W1M 9LA. Tel: 01-935 1186.

DIRECTORS
E. J. Edwards, D. Truscott.
DATE OF INCORPORATION
October, 1958.

Fowler-Chapman Co. Ltd.

(Assoc. company: CraneZoom Ltd.)
14a, Albert Court, Kensington Grore, London, SW7 2BG. Tel.: 01-589 0204.

Foxwell Film Productions Ltd.

99 Aldwych, London, W.C.2.

DIRECTORS
Ivan Foxwell, A. G. Cotterell, Richard Foxwell, CBE.
DATE OF INCORPORATION
January 13, 1949.

F.T.S. (Freight Forwarders), Ltd.

Registered & Head Office: Fairfield House, Court Farm Estate, Northumberland Close, Stanwell, Middx. Tel. 69-43901

DIRECTORS
I. D. Whittington, D. G. Larby, J. C. Mangan, I. A. Whittington, I. M. F. Whittington
DATE OF INCORPORATION
1976
CAPITAL
£100,000

Fuji Photo Film(UK) Ltd.

99 Baker Street, London, W1M 1FB. Tel.: 01-487 5711.

Gala Film Distributors, Ltd.

(Associated Company. Galaworldfilm Productions Ltd.).
Gala House, 15-17 Old Compton Street, London, W1V 6JR Tel. 01-734 3701.

DIRECTORS
Kenneth Rive (Managing), A. Rive.
DATE OF INCORPORATION
February 9, 1953

Gannet Films Ltd.

EMI Elstree Studios, Borehamwood, Herts, Tel.: 01-953 1600.

DIRECTORS
Bob Kellett, Anne Kellett
SECRETARY
B. C. Stebbings

Garrett, James, & Partners, Ltd.

5 Queen Street, London, W.1. Tel.: 01-499 6452.
Telex: 261163.

DIRECTORS
J. L. M. P. Garrett (Chmn. & Man. Dir.), D. T. Peers (Dep'y Chmn.), M. Garrett, G. A. Forster

General Film Distributors Ltd. (16mm dist.)

34 Lower Abbey Street, Dublin 1, Ireland. Tel. Dublin 744774 and 743842.

DIRECTORS
C. M. Anderson, K. Anderson, L. Ward, M. O'Brien

General Screen Enterprises Ltd.

97 Oxford Road, Uxbridge, Middx, Tel. Uxbridge 31931. Telex: 934883.
DIRECTORS
Peter Rogers, Gerald Thomas, Fred Chandler (Managing).

G.H.W. Productions, Ltd.

52 Queen Anne Street, London, W1M 9LA. Tel. 01-935 1186.
DIRECTORS
Peter Rogers, Betty E. Box, O.B.E., D. G. Truscott

Glendale Music Ltd.

37 Soho Square, London, W1V 5DG Tel.: 01-439 9181
DIRECTORS
R. Berry, P. A. Newbrook, A. Fisher

Golden Era Film Distributors

(Prop. Ranworth Film Services, Ltd.), 138 Wardour Street, London, W.1. Tel. LO1-437 1407.
DIRECTORS
L. G. Greenspan (Chairman and Managing), Peter Gordon Greenspan, Denis Young Wyser, L. Greenspan

Golden Harvest Films Limited

27 Soho Square, London, W1V 5FL.
CHAIRMAN
Raymond Chow (Hong Kong)
DEPUTY CHAIRMAN
Leonard K. C. Ho (Hong Kong)
MANAGING DIRECTOR
David A. E. Shepperd

Gordon Film Productions Ltd.

8 Connaught Square, London, W.2. Tel. 01-723 6287/8.
DIRECTORS
Melvin Frank, W. P. Robinson, R. M. F. Fletcher

Granada Group, Ltd.

36, Golden Square, London, W.1. Tel. 01-734 8080.
DIRECTORS
Alex Bernstein, (Chairman): W. Robert Carr, Sir Denis Forman, Mark Littman, QC., Quentin Morris, Bryan Quilter, C. G. Stanton, F.C.A., C. Stringer, Joseph Warton, F.C.C.A.
SECRETARY
D. James, F.C.I.S.

Grand National Film Distributors, Ltd.

13/14 Dean Street, London, W.1. Tel. 01-437 5792/6. Telegrams: Granapic, London W1.
MANAGING DIRECTOR
Ronald Wilson.

GTO Films (Distributions) Ltd.

115-123 Bayham Street, London, NW1 0AL Tel.: 01-485 5622. Telex 25584 GTO GEM G.
CHIEF EXECUTIVE
Laurence Myers

Guest, Val, Productions, Ltd.

Registered Office: 9 Cavendish Square, London, W.1. Tel. 01-286 5766.
DIRECTORS
Val Guest, John A. Maeer

Guild Sound & Vision Ltd.

Woodston House, Oundle Road, Peterborough PE2 9PZ. Tel.: 0733 63122.
CHAIRMAN
J. Gratwick
MANAGING DIRECTOR
I. D. Muspratt

G.W. Films, Ltd.

41 Montpelier Walk, London, S.W.7. IJH. Tel. 01-589 8829. Cables: BRAPICS London SW7.
DIRECTORS
Lord Brabourne, Richard Goodwin.

Halas and Batchelor Animation Ltd.

3/7 Kean Street, London, W.C.2. Tel: 240 3888.
DIRECTORS
John Halas, Joy Batchelor, Jack King, Harold Whitaker, Rolf Deyhle

Hammer Film Productions, Ltd.

EMI Elstree Studios, Boreham Wood, Herts. Tel.: 01-953 1600.
DIRECTORS
Brian Lawrence, Roy Skeggs
DATE OF INCORPORATION
February 12, 1949

Hampden Gurney Studios Ltd.

Hampden Gurney Street, London W1H 5AL. Tel.: 01-402 6255. Cables: Jaksonfilm, London. W1. Telex: 896559 GECOMS-G.
DIRECTORS
Brian Jackson, John Elford

Hand Made Films Distributors Ltd.

26 Cadogan Square, London, SW1X OJP. Tel.: 01-581 1265. Telex: 8951338 URODO.
DIRECTORS
Denis O'Brien, Alfred Jarratt, Derek Taylor, Mark Vere Nicoll

Harlequin Productions, Ltd.

2 Lower James Street, London W1R 3PN. Tel. 01-437 7015.
DIRECTORS
Leon Clore, John Arnold, Anthony Simmons
SECRETARY
Cyril Solomons

Harkness Screens Ltd.

Gate Studios, Station Road, Boreham Wood, Herts: WD6 1DQ. Tel.: 01-953 3611. Cables: Screens, London. Telex: 21792, Ref: 1319.

Hawk Films Ltd.

Box 123, Boreham Wood, Herts. Tel. 01-953 1600.

Hemdale International Films Ltd.

3 Audley Square, South Audley Street, London W1Y 5DR. Tel. 01-491 7491.
DIRECTORS
J. Daly, D. J. Dawson, G. E. Miller

Hemisphere Productions Ltd.

105 Mount Street, London, W.1. Tel.: 01-493 5041

Historical Research Unit

Stone House, Kings Sulton, Nr. Banbury, Oxon. Tel. 0295 810952.

Holdsworth, Gerard, Productions Ltd.

31 Palace Street, London, SW1E 5HW. Tel. 01-828 1671.

DIRECTORS
Gerard A. Holdsworth, Mary V. Holdsworth, P. H. Filmer-Sankey, Don Kelly

Horizon Pictures (G.B.) Ltd.

31 Dover Street, London, W1X 3RA. Tel. 01-493 8292. Cables: Horizonpic, London, W1.

DIRECTORS
S. Spiegel, Lord Herschell
DATE OF INCORPORATION
March, 1952.
CAPITAL
£5,000

Howell Optical Printers Ltd.

36 Berwick Street, London, W1V 3RS. Tel.: 01-734 2323.

Humphries Film Laboratories Ltd.

(Film processors.)

P.O. Box 2HL, 71-81, Whitfield Street, London, W1A 2HL. Tel.: 01-636 3636; also at Ralli Building, Stanley Street, Salford 3, Manchester, and Croydon House, Croydon Street, Domestic Street, Leeds II.

DIRECTORS
J. C. Jeffrey (managing), R. G. Ellis, G. F. Bridge

Image International Video & Film Productions Ltd.

5 Kendrick Mews, London, S.W.7. Tel.: 01 0 584 6048

Independent Film Distributors Ltd.

106-107 Middle Abbey Street, Dublin 1, Ireland. Tel.: 01-786700. Telegrams: Filmhouse, Dublin.

DIRECTORS
Michael D. Collins, P.C. (Managing), Mrs. Vourneen Collins

IFA (Scotland) Ltd.

I North Claremont Street, Glasgow, C3 7NR, Scotland, Tel. 041-332 3620.

ITC Entertainment Ltd.

17 Great Cumberland Place, London, W1H 1AG. Tel.: 01-262 8040.

DIRECTORS
Lord Grade, Jack Gill, B. J. Kingham, E. S. Birk, Ian R. Jessel, David C. Withers, A. D. Brook

ITC Film Distributors Ltd.

14-15 Carlisle Street, London, W.1. Tel.: 01-493 6611. Telex: 291004 ITCFDG.

MANAGING DIRECTOR
Alan Kean
DIRECTOR OF SALES
Roy Graham

Jade Film Marketing Ltd.

91 Highfield Avenue, London, NW11 9 Tel.: 01-455 0240.

MANAGING DIRECTOR
Frank E. Hildebrand
SALES DIRECTOR
Penny Karlin, Jr.

J. S. Associates Ltd.

92 Fulham Road, Chelsea, London, SW3. Tel.: 01-584 3734.

Jaras Entertainments Ltd.

21 Cavendish Place, London, W1M 9DL. Tel.: 01-580 5927.

J & M Film Sales Ltd.

9 Clifford Street, London, W.1. Tel.: 01-734 2181.

Kay Laboratories, Ltd.

(Film Laboratories.) 91/95 Gillespie Road, Highbury, London, N.5 Tel.: 01-226 4422. Telex: 28463. (Sound Studio) 22 Soho Square, London, W.1. Tel.: 01-437 7811. Video Division, 22 Soho Square, London. W.1. Tel.: 01-437 7811.

DIRECTORS
David Martineau (chmn.), F. Alan Martineau (vice-chmn.), Marshal D. Kochman (mng. dir.), G. R. Hawkes, N. J. Simpson, B. E. Compton, L. T. Allen, E. G. West, R. J. Venis, D. A. Clipsham.

Keep Films Ltd.

5 Eaton Place, London, S.W.1. Tel. 01-235 6552. Cables: Keepfilm, London.

DIRECTORS
Jules Buck, J. G. Buck, Peter O'Toole, S. Phillips

Kenilworth Film Productions Ltd.

41 Montpelier Walk, London, S.W.7 IJH. Tel. 01-589 8829. Cables: BRAPICS London SW7.

DIRECTOR
Lord Brabourne, Richard Goodwin

Kensington Film Co., LTD.

A Rodway Road, Roehampton, London, SW15 5DS. Tel. 01-789 1532.

DIRECTORS
E. A. Humphriss, B.Sc. (Eng.), M.I.E.E. Monica Ross.

Kendon Films Ltd.

8 Berwick Street, London, W1V SRG. Tel.: 01-734 1888.

Kenwood Films Ltd.

6 Goodwins Court, London, W.C.2. Tel. 01-235 9238.

DIRECTORS
Kenneth Harper, Arthur Davey

Kettledrum Films Ltd.

37 Connaught Square, London, W.2. Tel. 01-262 0077.

Kodak, Ltd.

Motion Picture Sales, P.O. Box 66, Kodak House, Station Road, Hemel Hempstead, Herts: HP1 1JU. Tel. Hemel Hempstead 62331.

SALES MANAGER
D. J. Kimbley
DATE OF INCORPORATION
November 15, 1898.

Michael Klinger Ltd.

9 Clifford Street, London, W1X 1RB. Tel.: 01-439 7321. Cables: Klingfilm, London, W.1. Telex: 261828.

Kruger Organisation (Film & TV Distribution) Ltd.

P.O. Box 324, London, SW1X 8LG. Tel.: 01-235 8243. Telex: 896795.

DIRECTORS
J. S. Kruger, R. Kruger, H. R. Kruger

K-Tel Motion Pictures

(K-Tel International (UK) Ltd.)
620 Western Avenue, London, W.3. Tel.: 01-992 8000.

Lee International Film Studios Ltd.

128 Wembley Park Drive, Wembley, Middx. 01-902 1262.

Leevers-Rich Equipment Ltd.

319 Trinity Road, London, SW 18 3SL. Tel. 01-874 9054. Telex: 923455.

Legion Film Productions

16 Bloomfield Terrace, London, SW1W 8PG. Tel: 01-730 9581.

Leisure Seating Ltd.

34 Shuna Place, Glasgow G209ED, Scotland. Tel.: 041-946 0211/3.

Lesslie, Colin, Productions, Ltd.

Registered Office: 99 Aldwych, London, WC 2B 4JY
DIRECTORS
D. E. Ryland, E. E. Leslie.
DATE OF INCORPORATION
October 17, 1949

Le Vien Films, Ltd.

15 Chesterfield Hill, London, W Tel.: 01-629 4545. Cable: Vienfilms London W.1.

CHAIRMAN AND PRODUCER
Jack Le Vien

Lion Television Services Ltd.

Shepperton Studios, Squires Bridge Road, Shepperton, Middx: Tel: 09328 60241.

GENERAL MANAGER
Alan J. Mashford.

Lloyd, Euan, Productions Ltd.

% Nicholas and Co., 81, Piccadilly, London, W.1. Tel. 01-493 8811.

London Film Productions Ltd.

37 Bedford Street, London, WC2 9EN Tel: 01-379 3366. Telex: 896805.

London & Overseas Film Services, Ltd.

Tennyson House, 159-165 GRT. Portland Street, London, W1N LNR.Tel. 01-637 1164. Telex: 263953. Cables: Helpful, London.

DIRECTORS
Ian R. Warren; I. L. Donald, T. L. Donald
DATE OF INCORPORATION
October 23, 1944.
CAPITAL
£2,000.

London Independent Producers Ltd.

52 Queen Anne Street, London, W1M 9LA. Tel. 01-935-1186.

DIRECTORS
Sydney Box, M. V. Box, William MacQuitty, Ralph Thomas, Betty Box, D. G. Truscott
SECRETARY
F. J. Esnouf
DATE OF INCORPORATION
February 3, 1950

Lorimar Television

16 Berkeley Street, London, W1X 5AE. Tel.: 01 493 1566.

MANAGING DIRECTOR
Ray Lewis

Mallicon Film Productions Ltd.

190 Fleet Street, London, E.C.4. Tel. 01-262 0638. Cables and telegrams: Janetbenet London EC4.

CHAIRMAN & MANAGING DIRECTOR
Umesh Mallik, B.A. (India)
SECRETARY
J. R. F. Williamson, M.B.E., F.C.A.

I.R. Maxwell (Film Distributors) Ltd.

Headington Hill Hall, Oxford OX3 OBW. Tel. Oxford 64881.

Meadway Productions Ltd.

70 Wardour Street, London, W.1. Tel. 01-439 4351.

Mersham Productions Ltd.

41 Montpelier Walk, London, S.W.7. IJH. Tel.: 01-589 8829. Cables: Brapics, London, S.W.7.

DIRECTORS
Lord Brabourne, Countess Mountbatten of Burma, Richard Goodwin

Metro-Goldwyn-Mayer

11 Hamilton Place, London, W.1. Tel: 01-493 5994.

Miracle Films, Ltd.

(Miracle International Films Ltd) 92-94 Wardour Street, London, W1V 4JH. Tel. 01-437 0507 (4 lines).
DIRECTORS
P. Kutner, M. Myers

Mirisch Films Ltd.

Pinewood Studios, Iver Heath, Bucks: Tel. 0753 651700.
DIRECTORS
R. M. F. Fletcher, M. J. Farrer-Brown

MLG Film Agency Ltd.

15-17 Old Compton Street, London, W1V 6JR. Tel. 01-437 9541. Cables: Eaglepix, London, W.1.
DIRECTORS
Barry Jacobs, A. Jacobs

Molliko Films (London) Ltd.

16-18 New Bridge Street, London, E.C.4 Tel. 01-262 0638. Cables: Umeshmalik, London, E.C.4.
CHAIRMAN AND MAN. DIR.
Umesh Mallik, B.A., India
SECRETARY
J. R. F. Williamson, M.B.E., F.C.A.
DIRECTOR-PRODUCTION
Bina Chatterjee (Miss)

Moore-British Film Productions, Ltd.

73, Delamere Road, Ealing, London, W.5. Tel. Ealing 4347. Cables: Mauriford, London.
DIRECTORS
Maurice Ford, G. A. Ford, Bert Ford

Anthony Morris London Ltd.

6 Goodwins Court, St. Martins Lane, London WC2N 4LL. Tel. 01-836 0576.
DIRECTORS
Anthony Morris, J. K. Morrow

Moving Picture Company

25 Noel Street, London, W.1. Tel: 01-734 9151. Telex: 27256.

National Film Studios of Ireland

Ardmore House, Bray, Co. Wicklow, Ireland. Tel.: Dublin 862971. Telex: 30418.

National Screen Service, Ltd.

Studios: 15 Wadsworth Road, Greenford, Middx. Tel: 01-998 2851. London Office: Nascreno House, Soho Square, London, W1V6BH. Tel: 01-437 4851.
DIRECTORS
Burton E. Robbins (U.S.A.), Norman Robbins (U.S.A.), Robert Gruen (U.S.A.), Sir James Carreras, M.B.E. (U.K.), Esther Harris, F.B.K.S. (U.K.)
CHAIRMAN AND CHIEF EXECUTIVE
Russell Cradick (U.K.)

National Telefilm Associates Inc. (UK) Ltd.

28 Berkeley Square, London, W1X 5NA. Tel.: 01-499 5945. Telex: 881 2226 NTA LDN.
FOREIGN MANAGER
Art Jacobs

Norfolk International Pictures Ltd.

107-115 Long Acre, London, WC2E 9NT. Tel.: 01-240 0863.

Ronald Neame Productions Ltd.

Registered Address: 99 Aldwych, London, W.C.2. Tel.: 01-242 0211.

New Realm Distributors Ltd.

22-25 Dean Street, London, W1. Tel.: 01-437 9143.
DIRECTORS
Mrs. B. C. C. Fancey, Miss A. M. B. Fancey, M. J. G. Fancey, Jack Gray

Ogam Films Ltd.

4 Park Circus, Glasgow G3 6AX. Tel.: 041 337 9335.

Omandry International Ltd.

1 Fernsleigh Close, Chalfont St. Peter Gerards Cross, Bocks SL9 OHR. Tel.: 02-407 4149
DIRECTORS
F. S. Poole, F. C. Poole

On-The-Spot Equipment Ltd.

208 Kensal Road, Westbourne Park, London, W.10. Tel. 01-969 6496.

Open Road Films, Ltd.

25 Jermyn Street, London, S.W.1. Tel. 437 4534 & 434 3671. Cables: Carlform London. S.W1.

Orb Productions Ltd.

72 Wardour Street, London, W.1. Tel. 01-437 8282. Cables: Orbilm, London.
DIRECTORS
Nat Miller, Louise Miller.

Original Electric Picture Company

15 Pembroke Gardens London, W.8. Tel.: 01-603 8192.
PRODUCTION
Stanley Dubens
ACCOUNT EXECUTIVE
Roger Moss

Orion Pictures Company

135 Wardour Street, London, W.1. Tel.: 01-434 3893.

Osprey Film Ltd.

120 Pall Mall, London, S.W.1. Tel.: 01-839 3292. Telex: 8951569.

Overseas Film and Television Centre Ltd.

Overseas House, 19-23 Ironmonger Row, London, EC1.

Pacesetter Productions Ltd.

82 Wardour street, London. W1V 3LF, Tel.: 01-437 3907.

DIRECTORS
Lord Brabourne (chmn.), Ronald C. Spencer (managing), Robert Angell

Palomar Pictures International (U.K.) Ltd.

3 Gray's Inn Place, London, W.C.1. Tel. 01-242 1212 and 7485.

Paramount British Pictures, Ltd.

162-170 Wardour Street, London, W.1. Tel. 01-437 7700.

Paramount Pictures (UK) Ltd.

162-170 Wardour Street, London, W.1. Tel.: 01-437 7700.

DIRECTORS
W. E. Marshall, A. Barron (U.S.A.), A. J. Buck.

The Pearl & Dean Group Ltd.

Broadwick House, Broadwick Street, London, W1V 1FP. Tel.: 01-434 2200.

DIRECTORS
C. R. Hollick (Chairman), J. Simmonds (Man.), J. G. Adley, L. R. Parker.

Pendennis Pictures Corporation, Ltd.

10 Green Street, London, W.1. Cables: Pendennis, London. Tel. 629-6863.

DIRECTORS
S. Pallos, Sir Percy Rugg
SECRETARY
F. Kelly

Perforated Front Projection Screen Co. Ltd.

182, High Street, Cottenham, Cambs. CB4 4RX. Tel.: Cottenham 50139.

DIRECTOR
F. E. J. Witchalls
DATE OF INCORPORATION
January, 1931.

Phoenix Films Ltd.

2 Manor Road, Goring-on-Thames, RG8 9DP: Tel. 04914-2365.

DIRECTORS
B. G. Hanson, M. E. Hanson

Plato Films Ltd.

247a Upper Street, London N1 IRU. Tel.: 01-226 2298.

Stanley Forman

Polytel Film Ltd.

1 Rockley Road, London, W14 ODL. Tel.: 01-743 3474. Telex: 298816

S. Presbury & Co. Ltd.

Gloucester House, 19 Charing Cross Road, London, W.C.2. Tel. 01-930 3601.

DIRECTORS
P. S. Presbury, J. G. Presbury, R. Salisbury

DATE OF INCORPORATION
1930
CAPITAL
£10,000

Python (Monty) Pictures Ltd.

26 Cadogan Square, London, SW1X OJP. Tel.: 01-581 1265.

DIRECTORS
Graham Chapman, John Cleese, Terry Gilliam, Eric Idle, Terry Jones, Michael Palin

Platypus Films, Ltd.

9 Grape Street London WC2H 8DR Tel. 01-240-0351. Telex 885738.

MANAGING DIRECTOR
Andrew Lee

Q Film Productions Ltd.

Rosehill House, Rose Hill, Nr. Burnham, Bucks. Tel.: Burnham 5129.

Qwertyuiop Productions Ltd.

118-120 Wardour Street, London, W.1. Tel. 01-437 3225.

MANAGING DIRECTOR
David Land.

The Rank Organisation Ltd.

38 South Street, London, W1A 4QU. Tel: 01-629 7454. Telex: 263549.

DIRECTORS
Harry Smith (Chairman), Russell W. Evans MC LL.B. (Managing Director), Sir Robert Bellinger GBE D.Sc, L. H. Bond, J. B. Smith (Dep. Man. Dir.), P. H. Courtney, R. F. H. Cowen MBE, J. C. Duckworth, Sir Arnold France GCB, Sir Reay Geddes KBE, Sir Patrick Meany, Sir Denis Mountain, Bt, The Hon Angus Ogilvy, K. S. Russell, Sir Richard Trehane D.Sc.
DATE OF INCORPORATION
February 20th, 1937

RANK ADVERTISING FILMS LTD.

127 Wardour Street, London, W1V 4AD. Tel. 01-439 9531.

MANAGING DIRECTOR
D. R. Thomas

RANK FILM LABORATORIES LTD.

Denham, Uxbridge, Middlesex UB9 5HQ. Tel. Denham 832323. Telex: 934704 and 142 Wardour Street London, W.1. Tel.: 01-734 2511.

MANAGING DIRECTOR
J. W. Downer
DIRECTOR OF OPERATIONS
R. W. Login
SALES CONTROLLER
M. A. Levy

PINEWOOD STUDIOS LTD.

Iver Heath, Bucks. Tel.: Iver 651700. Telex: 847505.

MANAGING DIRECTOR
C. R. Howard

RANK AUDIO VISUAL LTD.

(Motion Picture and Television Studio Equipment, Lighting, Seating, Furnishings)
P.O. Box 70, Great West Road, Brentford, Middx. W8 9HR. Tel: 01-568 9222. Telex: 27976

MANAGING DIRECTOR
D. N. James

RANK LEISURE SERVICES LTD.

7 Great Russell Street, London, WC 1B 3NL. Tel.: 01-580 2010. Telex: 22356
MANAGING DIRECTOR
H. A. Crichton-Miller

RANK CINTEL

(Broadcast television equipment)
Watton, Ware, Herts. SG1Z OAE. Tel.: 0920 3939. Telex: 81415.
GENERAL MANAGER
J. Etheridge

RANK PHICOM VIDEO GROUP

142 Wardour Street, London, W1V 4BU. Tel.: 01-734 2235. Telex: 261237. Cables: Vidipost, London, W.1.
MANAGING DIRECTOR
G. Sadler
MANAGING DIRECTOR (TVI)
I. Reed
MANAGING DIRECTOR (A&V)
R. Osborne

RANK HOTELS LTD.

51 Holland Street, London, W8. Tel. 01-937 8022.
MANAGING DIRECTOR
S. A. May

RANK FILM DISTRIBUTORS LTD.

127 Wardour Street, London, W1V 4AD. Tel: 01-437 9020.
MANAGING DIRECTOR
Frederick P. Turner

RANK TAYLOR HOBSON

(Cooke Cine Lenses)
P.O. Box 36, Guthlaxton Street, Leicester LE2 OSP. Tel.: 0533 23801. Telex: 34411.
GENERAL MANAGER
W. Ramsden

RANK CITY WALL LTD.

Sloane Avenue House, 74 Sloane Avenue, London, S.W.3. Tel: 01-584 6225.
CHAIRMAN
R. W. Evans, M.C.
JOINT GENERAL MANAGERS
B. T. Penfold, T. Thomas

Ranworth Film Services Ltd.

138 Wardour Street, London, W.1. Tel. 01-437 1407/6628. Telegraphic Address: Goldra, London, W.1.
DIRECTORS
Leslie G. Greenspan (Chairman & Managing), Peter Gordon Greenspan, Denis Young-Wyser, L. Greenspan.

Rayant Pictures

(Division of Cygnet Guild Communications Ltd.)
Bushey Studios, Melbourne Road, Bushey, Herts. Tel.: 01-950 5791.
MANAGING DIRECTOR
Rae Evans

RCA Ltd.

(Subsidiary of RCA Corporation)
Lincoln Way, Windmill Road, Sunbury-on-Thames, Middlesex. Tel. Sunbury 85511. Telegraphic Address: Foreign: RCA London, U.K.: RCA London Telex.
MANAGING DIRECTOR, SERVICE DIVISION
G. G. Gray

COMMERCIAL COMMUNICATIONS, SYSTEMS DIVISION
K. G. Johnson
DATE OF INCORPORATION
September 10, 1929.
CAPITAL
Authorized £200,000

Renaissance Film Sales

16 Broadwick Street, London, W1V 1FH. Tel.: 01-734 1787.

Renown Pictures International, Ltd.

(Associated companies: Alderdale Films Ltd.; Fernwood Films Ltd.; George Minter Productions Ltd.; Hyde Film Management Ltd.; Oakland Films, Ltd.; Renown British Pictures Ltd.; Renown Film Productions Ltd.; Screen Administration Ltd.; Talisman Films Ltd.), 197a, Shenley Road, Boreham Wood, Herts.
DIRECTORS
B. R. Parker, B. J. Shaw, J. E. Powell
DATE OF INCORPORATION
August 29, 1950
BANKER
Bank of America

Rigby, Robert, Ltd.

Premier Works, Northington Street, London, W.C.1N 2JH Tel.: 01-405 2944. Telegrams: Precinemat London, W.C.1. Telex.: 28604. Ref. 2359.
DIRECTORS
P. J. Rigby, J. J. Rigby, P. P. Rigby

Romulus Films, Ltd.

36, Park Lane, London, W1Y 3LE. Tel.: 01-493 7741. Cables: Romulus, London, W.1.
DIRECTORS
Sir John Woolf (Chairman), R. S. Bromhead, M.V.O., Lady Woolf

Safir Films Ltd.

22-25 Dean Street, London, W1V 5AL. Tel.: 01-734 5085. Telex.: 25572

Salamander Film Productions Ltd.

Seven Pines, Wentworth, Surrey.
DIRECTORS
Bryan Forbes, Nanette Forbes, John L. Hargreaves

Samuelson Film Service Ltd.

303-315, Cricklewood Broadway, London, N.W.2. 6PQ. Tel.: 01-452 8090. Samcine, London, Telex. 21430.
DIRECTORS
Sydney Samuelson C.B.E. (Chairman and Chief Executive), Michael Samuelson (Man. Dir.), David Samuelson (Tech. Dir.), Anthony Samuelson (Finance Director)

Santor Film Productions Ltd.

c/o Wilding Hudson & Co. 24-30 Holborn, London, EC1N 2HS.
DIRECTORS
Leslie F. Baker, F.C.A., Maureen Anderson

Satori Films Ltd.

Thames House, 117 Albert Bridge Road, London, SW11. Tel.: 01-228 7766.
DIRECTORS
John Hanson, Philip Saville

Schulman, Richard, Entertainments Ltd.

87 Wardour Street, London, W.1. Tel.: Regent 4591.
DIRECTORS
Richard S. Schulman

Scimitar Films Ltd.

6-8 Sackville Street, London, W1X 1DD. Tel.: 01-734 8385.
DIRECTORS
Michael Winner, M.A. (Cantab), John Fraser, M.A. (Oxon)

Seven Pines Productions Ltd.

Seven Pines, Wentworth, Surrey.
DIRECTORS
Bryan Forbes, Nanette Forbes, Ronald Shedlo (USA), Michael S. Laughlin (USA), Richard Gregson
SECRETARY
John L. Hargreaves

Shand Pictures Ltd.

Rosehill House, Rose Hill Nr. Burnham, Bucks. Tel.: Burnham 5129.
DIRECTORS
I. E. L. Shand, D. J. Bennett

Shepperton Studio Centre

Studios Road, Shepperton, Middlesex, TW17 0QD. Tel.: 09328. 62611. Telex.: 929416 Movies G.

Shipman, Kenneth, Productions Ltd.

c/o Twickenham Film Studios, St. Margarets, Twickenham, Middx: Tel.: 01-892 4477.
DIRECTORS
Kenneth Shipman (Managing), Dee Shipman

Siege Productions Ltd.

17 Adam's Row, London W.1. Tel.: 01-493 4441-2.
MANAGING DIRECTOR
Peter Fetterman

Signal Films Ltd.

13 Hobury Street, London, SW10. Tel.: 01-352 0218.
DIRECTORS
D. M. Rankin (Managing), D. S. K. Rankin

Silverpine Studios Ltd.

Bray Co. Wicklow, Ireland. Tel.: Dublin 867691/2 and 867073.
CHAIRMAN
P. O'Toole
MANAGING DIRECTOR
W. Stapleton

Sintel International Ltd.

51 South Audley Street, London W1Y 6HB. Tel.: 01-493 7428.

Sound & Scene Services (London) Ltd.

57-60 Compton Street, London, EC1V OEU. Tel.: 01-251 3601. Telex: 267928.

DIRECTORS
S. J. Lambert, F.C.A. (chrm.), A. M. Goldwater, F. T. A. Tinker, M. H. Tippett, E. T. Tucker, T. V. Ross, M. J. Wingrove

Southern Pictures Ltd.

58 Frith Street, London, W1V 5TA. Tel.: 01-439 2367. Telex.: Southtel 261 682.
CREATIVE DIRECTOR
Mark Shivas

Sovexport Film

10 Kensington Palace Gardens. London, W8. Tel.: 01-229 3216.

The Robert Stigwood Organisation Ltd.

67 Brook Street, London, W1Y IYE Tel. 01-629 9121. Cables: Stigwood, London, W1. Telex.: 264267.
DIRECTORS
Robert Stigwood, Beryl Vertue, Rod Gunner, David Land, Roger Forrester, David Herring

Superground Ltd.

Suite 4, 60/62 Old Compton Street, London, W.1. Tel.: 01-734 6197.
DIRECTORS
P. A. Sen, K. S. Sen, S. L. Sen

Sword and Sorcery Productions Ltd.

20 Stradella Road, London, SE24 9HA. Tel.: 01-274 3205
DIRECTORS
Milton Subotsky (USA) Angela M. Lebus, David J. Norris

Target International Pictures

National House, 60-66 Wardour Street, London, W.1. Tel. 01-439 4451-4.
DIRECTORS
Neil Agran, Montague Barber

Technicolor Ltd.

(Subsidiary of Technicolor Inc.)
Bath Road, P.O. Box No. 7, West Drayton, Middlesex. UB7 0DB. Tel: 01-759 5432; Telegraphic and Cable Address: Technicolor, West Drayton.
DIRECTORS
R. J. Dutfield (Chairman & Chief Executive Officer) A. N. Ryan (Deputy Chairman) (U.S.A.) R. Gaul (U.S.A.) P. I. Hayman R. Jarvis (U.S.A.) M. Kamerman (U.S.A.) A. Mitchell L. U. Ostinelli R. S. Shean (U.S.A.) R. A. Webster
DATE AND PLACE OF INCORPORATION
July 22, 1935, London
CAPITAL
Authorized G £1,000,000
ISSUED
£1,000,000 in shares of 25 p each

Tempean Films, Ltd.

EMI-MGM Elstree Studios, Boreham Wood, Herts. Tel. 01-953 1600.
DIRECTORS
Robert S. Baker, N. M. Berman
DATE OF INCORPORATION
1948.

Theatrical Agency (South Africa) LTD.

15-17 Old Compton Street, London, W.1. Tel.: 01-439 9919.

Tigon Film Distributors Ltd.

14-15 Carlisle Street, London, W.1.V. 5RE. Tel.: 01-439 6611. Telex.: 291004 ITCFDG
MANAGING DIRECTOR
Alan Kean

Titan Film Distributors Ltd.

9 Harebell Hill, Cobham, Surrey. Tel.: 093 26 2316.
DIRECTORS
P. Newbrook, B.S.C., D. Newbrook

Tonav Film Productions Ltd.

9 Clifford Street, London, W1X IRB. Tel.: 01-439 7321/4. Cables: Klingfilm, London, W1. Telex: 261828.

Trans World Films, Ltd.

130 Wardour Street, London, W.1. Tel.: 01-437 3400.
DIRECTORS
K. A. Collinson, N. Collinson

Triangle Film Productions, Ltd.

15 Oslo Court, Prince Albert Road, London, N.W.8. Tel.: 01-722 5656.
DIRECTORS
Theodora Olembert

Troy Films, Ltd.

c/o Film Rights Ltd., Hammer House, 113 Wardour Street, London, W1V 4EH. Tel.: 01-437 7151.
DIRECTORS
Michael Anderson, Maurice Lambert

Twentieth Century-Fox Film Co., Ltd.

20th Century House, 31-32 Soho Square, London, W1V 6AP. Tel.: 01-437 7766; Telex No. 27869. Telegrams: Centfox, London, Telex. Cables: Centfox, London, W.1.
CHAIRMAN
P. Livingstone
MANAGING DIRECTOR
A. Branca
DIRECTORS
P. Livingstone, A. Branca, (USA) D. E. Tarr, E. L. Marshall (USA), J. P. Meehan (USA), J. L. Rubin
SECRETARY
D. E. Tarr
DATE OF INCORPORATION
March 29, 1916.
SHARES
100,000 Ordinary of £1 each. Fully paid

Twentieth Century-Fox Productions, Ltd.

Registered Office: 31/32 Soho Square, London, W1V 6AP. Tel.: 01-437 7766. Telex No. 27869. Telegrams: Centfox London Telex. Cables: Centfox London, W.1.
DIRECTORS
P. Livingstone, (Chairman), T. Hampton (Managing), A. Branca, D. E. Tarr, Miss H. Dixon

Twickenham Film Studios Ltd.

(Owns Twickenham Studios)
St. Margarets, Twickenham, Middlesex. Tel.: 01-892 4477. Telex.: 8814497.
DIRECTORS
G. Coen, G. Humphreys, John T. Davey, FCA T. L. Kirby, M. Landsberger, S. J. Mullins
SECRETARY
A. Miller
CAPITAL
£251650

Tyburn Productions Ltd.

(Associated Company: Tyburn Productions Inc.)
Pinewood Studios, Iver Heath, Bucks. Tel.: Iver 651700. Telex.: 847505.
DIRECTORS
Kevin Francis, F. H. Toby, J. W. Malins, F.C.A.
EXECUTIVE PRODUCER
Kevin Francis
STORY & RESEARCH EDITOR
Gillian Garrow
MUSIC SUPERVISOR
Philip Martell

United Artists Corporation, Ltd.

Mortimer House, 37-41 Mortimer Street, London, W1A 2JL Tel.: 01-636 1655.
DIRECTORS
N. Auerbach, (USA) (Chairman), John Esson (New Zealand) (Mananaging), Brian C. Yell, J. B. Horgan (Secretary)
DATE AND PLACE OF INCORPORATION
March 15, 1921; London
CAPITAL
17,500 ordinary shares of £1 each

Universal Pictures Ltd.

139 Piccadilly, London, W.1. Tel.: 01-629 7211.

Variety Film Distributors Ltd.

60-66 Wardour Street, London, W.1. Tel.: 01-439 4451.

Vaughan Rogosin Films Ltd.

28a, North Audley Street, London, W.1. Tel. 01-629 2470.
MANAGING DIRECTOR
Jimmy Vaughan

Viking Films, Ltd.

6A Rodway Road, Roehampton, London, SW15 5DS. Tel.: 01-789 1532.
DIRECTORS
Eric Humphriss, B.Sc. (Eng.), M.I.E.E.; Monica Ross

Vinten, W., Ltd.

Western Way, Bury St. Edmunds, Suffolk IP33 3TB. Tel. Bury St. Edmunds 2121. Cables: Vintacinni. Telex 81176.

Viscom Production Ltd.

25-27 Farringdon Road, London, EC1M 3HA. Tel.: 01-404 5041. Telegraphic Address: Agavision London W1 Telex: 24474 Viscom G.
DIRECTORS
D. Kingsley (Chmn.), Patrick F. Friesner, Geoffrey J. Reeve, I. P. M. Phillips

Visnews Ltd.

Cumberland Avenue, London, N.W. 10 7EH. Tel.: 01-965 7733.
MANAGING DIRECTOR
Brian Quinn
GENERAL MANAGER
Peter Marshall
COMPANY SECRETARY/FIN. CONTROLLER
Norman Bull
News Division
EDITOR-IN-CHIEF
Robert Kearsley
DEP. EDITOR-IN-CHIEF
Nichol Hutton
Broadcast Facilities
CHIEF ENGINEER
Roy Vilty
Production Services Division
GENERAL MANAGER
Julian Dinsell

Vista Films Ltd.

56 Berkeley House, 15 Hay Hill, London, W.1. Tel.: 01-493 2225.

Viewsport Ltd.

21 Cavendish Place, London, WIM 9DL. Tel.: 01-580 5927.
DIRECTORS
Jarvis Astaire, H. W. Abbey, S. Burns

Visual Programme Systems Ltd.

16 Broadwick Street, London, W1V 1FH. Tel.: 01-734 1787. Cables: Visprogram. Telex: 21879.

Wallace Productions Ltd.

8 Berwick Street, London, W.1. Tel.: 01-734 1888.
DIRECTORS
The Hon. A. G. Samuel (Chairman), D. M. Rankin (Managing), M. J. Samuel, D. S. K. Rankin, W. G. Bayley

Walport Ltd.

(Subsidiary of Rediffusion (Holdings) Ltd.)
Walport House, 62/66 Whitfield Street, London, W1P 6JH. Tel.: 01-631 4373. Cables: Sewalport, London, W.1. Telex 261567
DIRECTORS
J. T. Davey, John Hay (Managing), C. Wills, R. M. I. Denny, G. D. Nugus, G. Binns

Warfield Productions Ltd.

2 South Audley Street, London, W1Y 5DQ. Tel.: 01-493 7953. Cables: Brocfilm London W.1.

Warner Bros. Distributors, Ltd.

135-141 Wardour Street, London W1V 4AP. Tel.: 01-437 5600.
DIRECTORS
Myron D. Karlin (USA) (Chmn.), A. R. Parsons, T. C. Lima, J. Cook, D. J. Harrup

Warner Bros. Productions Ltd.

Warner House, Pinewood Studios, Iver Heath, Bucks. SLO ONH. Tel.: 0753 654545.
DIRECTORS
P. Hitchcock (Managing), T. L. Kirby, E. H. Senat

Welbeck Film Distributors, Ltd.

52 Queen Anne Street, London, W1M 9LA. Tel.: 01-935-1186.
DIRECTORS
Mrs. B. E. Rogers, R. P. Thomas, D. G. Truscott

Westchester Productions Ltd.

Unit N.22, Cricklewood Trading Estate, Claremont Road, London, NW2 1TU. Cables: Westquip London NW2. Tel.: 01-450 2584./5.
DIRECTORS
Michael Leaver, Sidney Leaver

West One Film Producers Ltd.

2 Lower James Street, London W1R 3PN. Tel.: 01-437 7015.
DIRECTOR
Anthony Simmons
SECRETARY
Cyril Solomons
DATE AND PLACE OF INCORPORATION
London, January 30, 1964

Richard Williams Animation Ltd.

London Studio: 13 Soho Square, London, W1V 5FB. Tel.: 01-437 4455. Cables: Animfilm, London, W.1.V.5FB. Telex: 299556 Anfilm G. Hollywood Studio: 3193 Boulevard, Hollywood, CA 90068, USA. Tel.: (213) 851 8060.
DIRECTORS
Richard Williams, Carl Gover

Willis World Wide Productions Ltd.

21-25 St. Anne's Court, glondon, W1V 3AW. Tel.: 01-434 1121.
DIRECTORS
Lord Willis (Chairman), C. T. Parris, P. Gilpin, A. R. English

Willoughby Film Productions, Ltd.

26, Bryanston Square, London, W.1. Tel. 01-262 0883. Cables: Medivac, London.
DIRECTORS
George W. Willoughby, E. G. G. S. Willoughby
DATE OF INCORPORATION
October 29, 1948

Winkast Programming Ltd.

Pinewood Studios, Iver Heath, Bucks.
DIRECTORS
Elliott Kastner, D. Holt, R. M. F. Fletcher

Woodfall Limited

23 Albemarle Street, London. W.1.
DIRECTORS
Tony Richardson, Neil Hartley (USA)

World Film Services Ltd.

(World Film Sales Ltd.)
4 Claridge House, 32 Davies Street, London, W.1. Tel. 01-493 3045.
CONSULTANT
John Heyman
DIRECTORS
Murray Inglis (Managing), Norma Heyman, Edward Oldman, Henry Thomas (USA)

Worldmark Productions Ltd.

303-315 Cricklenwood Broadway, London, NW2 6PQ. Tel.: 01-452 8090. Telex: 21430.
DIRECTORS
Tony Maylam, Michael Samuelson

World Wide Pictures, Ltd.

21-25, St. Anne's Court, London, W1V3AW. Tel. 01-434 1121.

DIRECTORS
C. T. Parris (Chrmn.), P. Gilpin (Man.), R. Aylott, F.C.A., C. Hope, Lord Willis of Chislehurst, R. King, R. Townsend

Saul Zaentz Production Co.

113-117 Wardour Street, London, W.1. Tel.: 01-437 3902.

British Trade Organization, & Government Units

Association of Cinematograph, Television and Allied Technicians

(Affiliated to Trades Union Congress and Labour Party)
2 Soho Square, London, W.1. Tel.: 01-437 8506.
GENERAL SECRETARY
Alan Sapper
TREASURER
Fred Varley
DEPUTY GENERAL SECRETARY
Roy Lockett, B.A.
TRUSTEES
Basil Wright, A. Jeakins.
The Association is the recognized Trade Union for film, television and radio technicians and negotiates salaries and working conditions; publishes "Film and TV Technician," formerly "The Cine-Technician," eleven times a year. It also controls an Employment Bureau as an agency exclusively for film and television technicians.

Association of Independent Cinemas, Ltd.

National House, 93 Wardour Street, London, W1V 4JB. Tel. 01-734-0919.
Registered March 25, 1953, as a company limited by guarantee, without share capital. The original number of members is 1,000, each being liable for £1 in the event of winding up.
Objects: To safeguard and promote the interests, financial and otherwise, of all members of the association and to conduct and undertake advertising campaigns; to arrange and promote the adoption of equitable forms of contracts and other documents in cinematograph trade, etc.
PRESIDENT
P. McRae, 5-7 Brewer Street, London, W.1
VICE-PRESIDENT AND HON. SECRETARY
Aubrey R. Partner

Association of Independent Producers

17 Great Pulteney Street, London, W1R 3DG. Tel.: 01-437 3549.

Association of Professional Recording Studios Ltd.

23 Chestnut Avenue, Chorleywood, Herts, WD3 4HA. Tel.: Rickmansworth 72907.
SECRETARY
E. L. Masek

British Academy of Film and Television Arts

195 Piccadilly, London, W1V 9LG. Tel.: 01-734 0022.
PRESIDENT
H. R. H. The Princess Anne
VICE PRESIDENT
Sir Richard Attenborough, C.B.E.
CHAIRMAN
Timothy Burrill
DIRECTOR
Reginald Collin
HON. TREASURER
Martin Schute
The British Academy of Film and Television Arts exists in order to promote, improve and advance original and creative work amongst people engaged in film and television production.

British Actors' Equity Association

(Incorporating the Variety Artistes' Federation)
8 Harley Street, London, WIN 2AB. Tel.: 01-6379311.
Cable Address: Britequity, London, W.1.
PRESIDENT
John Barron
GENERAL SECRETARY
Peter Plouviez

British Board of Film Censors

3, Soho Square, London, W1V 5DE Tel.: 01-437 2677-8. Telegrams: Censofilm, London.
PRESIDENT
The Rt. Hon. The Lord Harlech, P.C., K.C.M.G.
SECRETARY
James Ferman, M.A.

Britih Federation of Film Societies

81 Dean Street, London, W1V 6AA. Tel.: 01-437 4355.

British Film Producers Assn. Ltd.

162-170 Wardour Street, London, W.1. Tel: 01-734 2142.
PRESIDENT
Ken Maidment
ASSISTANT SECRETARY
Andrew Patrick

British Industrial and Scientific Film Association

26 D'Arblay Street, London W1V 3FH. Tel.: 01-439 8441.
DIRECTOR
Colonel K. A. M. Bennett, M.C.

British Kinematograph, Sound, and Television Society

110/112 Victoria House, Vernon Place, London, WC1B 4DJ. Tel.: 01-242 8400.

PRESIDENT
J. Alfred
SECRETARY
William Pay

Founded in 1931, the Society was incorporated in 1946 to service the industries of its title encouraging technical and scientific progress. To further these aims, the Society disseminates to its Members information on technical developments within these industries, arranges technical lectures and demonstrations, and encourages the exchange of ideas. The broad nature of its purpose is made possible by the subscriptions of its Members and by its freedom from political or commercial bias. The *BKSTS Journal* is published monthly and is sent free to all members.

British Music Information Centre

(Reference library of works by 20th century British composers.)

10 Stratford Place, London, W1N 9AE. Tel.: 01-499 8567.

LIBRARIAN
Roger W. Wright

British Society of Cinematographers, Ltd.

(To promote and encourage the pursuit of the highest standards in the craft of motion picture photography)

c/o Technicolor Ltd., Bath Road, Harmondsworth, West Drayton, Middx. Tel.: 01-759 5432.

SECRETARY & TREASURER
Francis Coffey

Central Casting, Ltd.

Licensed annually by the Dept. of Employment.

2 Lexington Street, London W1R 3HS. Tel.: 01-437 1881.

DIRECTORS
O. Benselinck, B. J. Kingham, K. L. Maidment
GENERAL MANAGER
F. T. Kennedy

Children's Film Foundation, Ltd.

6-10A, Great Portland Street, London, W1N 6JN. Tel.: 01-580 4796. Cables: Chififo, London, W.1.

SECRETARY/ADMINISTRATOR
S. T. Taylor, FCIS
UK DISTRIBUTION MANAGER
J. E. Woodin
DATE OF INCORPORATION
July 18, 1951

(Non-profit company set up by the six trade associations for the purpose of ensuring the production, distribution and exhibition of entertainment films specially suited for children.)

Cinema Advertising Association, Ltd.

127 Wardour Street, London, W1V 4AD. Tel.: 01-439 9531.

PRESIDENT
Douglas Thomas
SECRETARY
Bob Wittenbach
PRINCIPAL OBJECTS

The association represents the contractors in cinema and theatre screen space for advertising. The Association is also responsible for the Code of Standards of Advertising practice relating to cinema advertising which was issued in 1960, revised in 1967, with the cooperation and support of the C.E.A., the Incorporated Society of British Advertisers, the Institute of Incorporated Practitioners in Advertising.

Membership is confined to firms and companies engaged in the buying and selling of screen space for advertising purposes.

Cinema and Television Benevolent Fund

(Founded 1924) Royalty House, 72 Dean Street, London, W1V 6LT Tel. 01-437 6567. (The Fund gives relief by financial grants and allowances to needy members or ex-members of the Film Industry or Independent Television, and their widows; maintenance and education of orphans and relief in sickness, unemployment or old age and generally to assist those in distress. Convalescence is available to assist in recovery after illness or operations at "Glebelands," Wokingham, Berkshire, Admission to Convalescent Home free upon application to the Secretary.

EXECUTIVE DIRECTOR:
Maj. Gen. C. M. Griggs, CBE, MC
SECRETARY
H. V. Hughes
ADMINISTRATION CONTROLLER AND APPEALS EXECUTIVE
K. Matthews

Cinematograph Exhibitors' Association of Great Britain & Ireland

22/25 Dean Street, London W1V 6HQ. Tel: 01-734 9551.

PRESIDENT
R. J. Dowdeswell, "Fairfields", 16 North Park, Iver, Bucks SLO 9DJ. (0753 653179)
VICE-PRESIDENT
G. W. Rhodes, 38 Marlborough Mansions, Cannon Hill, London NW6. (01-435 0355)
HON. TREASURER
T. W. Clarke, Victoria Playhouse Group, Quality House, 41 High Street, Sutton Coldfield, West Midlands. (021-355 2330)
IMMEDIATE PAST PRESIDENT
D. M. Cameron, Dominion Cinema, Newbattle Terrace, Morningside, Edinburgh. (031-447 2660)
GENERAL SECRETARY
E. J. Lee, B.Sc. (Econ.), 22/25 Dean Street, London W1V 6HQ. (01-734 9551)
DELEGATES

Birmingham, Midlands & North Staffordshire Branch—M. P. Jervis, Kings Cinema Screens 1, 2, 3, Kings Square, West Bromwich, Staffs. (021-553 0030) W. B. Williamson, Theatre Administration Ltd., Regional Buildings, Augusta Place, Leamington Spa CV32 5EP. (0926 22157) Deputy: K. F. S. West, FCA, Prudential Buildings, Colmore Row, Birmingham B3 2PZ. (021-236 6646)

Devon, Cornwall & West of England Branch—D. G. Arthur, Cine Enterprises (Cornwell) Ltd., The Grand Cinema, Market Street, Falmouth, Cornwall TR11 3AS. (0326 312412) C. W. A. Painter, Torbay Cinema, Paignton, Devon. (0803 55944) Deputy: N. Prince, Riviera Cinema (Teignmouth) Ltd., Riviera Cinema, Teignmouth, Devon.

London Regional Branch—J. W. Davies, OBE., 9-11 Richmond Buildings, Dean Street, London W1. (01-437 1454) E. A. Rhodes, Curzon Cinemas 1, 2, 3, Langney Road, Eastbourne, Sussex. (0323 31441) S. Shurman, Coronet Cinema, Notting Hill Gate, London W11 3LB. (01-221 0123) M. G. Wright, Regal Theatre, Eastleigh, Hants. SO5 5RL. (0703 612029) L. P. Huddleston, Palace Cinema, 31 Market Square, Witney, Oxon, (0993 3147) Deputy: R. Chuter, Regent Leisure Group, 68 Salusbury Road, London N.W.6. (01-328 4230)

Manchester & Northern Counties Branch—R. I. Godfrey, Cheshire County Cinemas Ltd., 13-15 Winnington street, Northwich, Cheshire C8 1AQ. (0606 76415/6) J. S. Stansby, Rex Cinema, Alderly Road, Wilmslow, Cheshire. (0625 522266) G. B. Henshaw, Bonanza Bingo Clubs, Tudor Buildings, Elm Grove, Didsbury, Manchester. (061-445 1753) Deputy: P. W. Higginbotham, Majestic Picture House, High Street, Macclesfield, Cheshire.

Northern Ireland Branch—W. Dowds, 100 Great Patrick Street, Belfast 1. (Belfast 28011) Deputy: J. A. Gaston, Curzon Cinema, 300 Ormeau Road, Belfast 7. (Belfast 641373)

Scottish Branch—B. Kemp, Hamilton Street, Saltcoats, Ayrshire. (02946 3345) J. H. McLaughlin, 31 Lothian Road, Edinburgh EH1 2DJ. (031-229 7670) Deputies: J. K. S. Poole, 34 Home Street, Tollcross, Edinburgh EH3 9LZ. (031-229 1211)B. Kirke, Messrs. Fyfe & Fyfe Ltd., Dumbarton Road, Glasgow G1. (041-339 1225) A. Shaw, Regal Cinema, Murray Place, Leslie, Fife.

South Wales & Monmouthshire Branch—G. R. Isaacs, The Embassy, Bridgend, Glam. (0656 3429) Wyndham Lewis, OBE., JP., 18 Park Grove, Cardiff. (0222 20354) Deputies: B. H. Snowball, Screens 1-2-3, The Mall, Cumbran, Gwent, D. J. Cooper, Dene Cinema Enterprises, 51 Cuthbert Street, Wells, Somerset BA5 2AW. (0749 72036)

CIRCUIT DELEGATES

Rank Leisure Services Ltd.—7 Great Russell Street, London WC1B 3NL. (01-580 2010) A. Crichton-Miller, C. D. Spruce, (08832 3355) S. Fishman, A. B. O'Ferrall, D. Geary, J. Maynard (08832 3355) J. Gaukrodger (01-554 2500) Deputy: D. G. Cole

EMI Cinemas Ltd—30-31 Golden Square, London W1R 4QX. (01-437 9234) R. A. Webster, G. Lennox, R. C. Warbey, I. N. Riches, G. A. Coombes, D. J. Walters, L. H. T. Hodson, L. Dodkin

The Classic Cinemas Ltd.—The Classic Cinema, 63/65 Haymarket, London SW1Y 4RQ. (01-839 2525/6) B. J. Kingham, ACC House, 17 Great Cumberland Place, London W1A 1AG. (01-262 8040) B. T. Yeoman, D. C. Pratt

Granada Theatres Ltd.—36 Golden Square, London W1R 4AH. (01-734 8080) R. M. Morgan, Deputy: I. Cluley

Caledonian Associated Cinemas.—P.O. Box 21, 4 Academy Street, Inverness IV1 1LA. (0463 36611) F. M. Irons, CA., C. K. Mackenzie (041-248 6109)

Hutchinson Leisure Group of Companies Ltd.—1/3 Grimshaw Street, Burnley, Lancs. (0282 22057) A. R. Hutchinson. Deputy: C. L. Flitcroft.

Unit Four Cinemas Ltd.—56 Bank Parade, Burnely, Lancs. (0282 28221) R. Cryer, D. Tattersall.

Composers' Guild of Great Britain

10 Stratford Place, London, W1N 9AE. Tel. 01-499 8567. (Objects: to further artistic and professional interests of its members.)

GENERAL SECRETARY
Miss Elizabeth Yeoman.

Critics' Circle

(Film Section)

CHAIRMAN
Tom Hutchinson, 64 Southwood Lane, London, N.6.
HON. SECRETARY
Virginia Dignam, Oxgate Farm, London, N.W.2.

Electrical, Electronic Telecommunication and plumbing Union

Hayes Court, West Common Road, Bromley, BR2 7AU. Tel. 01-462 7755. (Representing electrical operatives engaged in studio production.)

GENERAL SECRETARY
F. J. Chapple.

Film Artistes' Association

(Registered Trade Union No. 1990 T) F. A. A. House, 61 Marloes Road, London, W.8. Tel. 01-937 4567-8.

GENERAL SECRETARY
Sean Brannigan.

Film Industry Defence Organisation, Ltd.

19 New Bridge Street, London, EC4. Tel.: 01-353 0211.

OBJECTS
To promote, further and protect the interests, financial welfare and success of the cinematograph film industry in the United Kingdom in every possible way and to promote, support and encourage co-operation amongst those engaged in the film industry for the protection of their mutual interest. To make and enter into with producers, renters, exhibitors, and other, upon any terms which may be considered expedient in the interests of the Film Industry, arrangements and agreements relating to television rights, to hold television rights to films, and to release upon any terms which may be considered expedient to the aforesaid any rights which may be so acquired.

Guild of British Camera Technicians

303-315 Cricklewood Broadway, London, NW2 6PQ. Tel.: 01-450 3821.

SECRETARY
Brian M. Rose

Guild of British Film Editors

Travair, Spurlands End Road, Great Kingshill, High Wycombe, Bucks. HP15 6HY. Tel.: 0494 712313. (Objects: To ensure that the true value of film and sound editing is recognized not only by those engaged in it but by the whole of the film industry as an important part of the creative and artistic aspect of film production.)

HON. SECRETARY
Alfred E. Cox
HON. TREASURER
Chris Barnes

Guild of Film Art Directors

12 Quick Road, Chiswick, London, W.4. Tel: 01-994 2731.

SECRETARY
Martin Atkinson

Guild of Film Production Executives

Pinewood Studios, Iver. Bucks. Tel: Iver 651700.

PRESIDENT
Johnny Goodman
HON. SECRETARY
Hugh Attwooll

Guild of Film Production Accountants and Financial Administrators

Pinewood Studios, Iver. Bucks. SLO ONH. Tel.: Iver 651700.

CHAIRMAN
Cyril Howard
HON. SECRETARY
Robin Busby

Mechanical-Copyright Protection Society, Ltd.

Elgar House, 41 Streatham High Road, London, SW16 1ER Tel. 01-769 4400. Cables & Telegrams: Mecolico, London, S.W.16.

OBJECTS
The Society has the authority of some ten thousand music copyright owners in the U.K. and Commonwealth, U.S.A., Germany, Italy and other countries to license the use of their works for all forms of mechanical reproduction, including sound synchronisation in cinematograph, television and advertising films.
MANAGING DIRECTOR
R. W. Montgomery
COMPANY SECRETARY & FINANCIAL CONTROLLER
K. R. D. Lowde
COMMERCIAL OPERATIONS CONTROLLER
G. J. Churchill.

Motion Picture Export Association of America, Inc.

162-170 Wardour Street, London, W1V 4AB. Tel.: 01-437 7700.

Musicians' Union

60-62 Clapham Road, London, SW9 OJJ. Tel.: 01-582 5566. Cables: Amuse, London SW9
GENERAL SECRETARY
John Morton

The National Association of Executives Managers and Staffs

337 Grays Inn Road, London, WC1X 8PX. Tel.: 01-837 6789. (To represent the interests of Managers and Executives and Staffs and to negotiate salaries and conditions of employment.)
GEN. SECRETARY
Ivor Gayus, M.I.E.M.

National Association of Theatrical, Television and Kine Employees

Registered Office: 155 Kennington Park Rd., London, SE11 4JU. Tel.: 01-735 9068.
GENERAL SECRETARY
J. L. Wilson

The Performing Right Society Ltd.

29/33 Berners Street, London, W1P 4AA. Tel.: 01-580 5544.

The Performing Right Society (PRS) is an Association of Composers, Authors and Publishers of musical works established in 1914 to administer on behalf of its members certain of the rights granted to them under copyright legislation. The Society is limited by guarantee, has no share capital and is non-profit making. No fees or subscriptions are required from Members.
CHIEF EXECUTIVE
M. J. Freegard FCIS

The Personal Managers' Association Ltd.

c/o Jill Foster Ltd. 35 Brompton Road, London, SW3 1DE. (An association of the principal Personal managers who represent stars, feature players, writers, producers, directors and technicians).

Royal Photographic Society of Great Britain

The Octagon, Milsom Street, Bath BAI IDN. Tel.: 0225 62841.
SECRETARY
Kenneth R. Warr, B.A., F.S.A.E., F.B.I.M.
MOTION PICTURE GROUP CHAIRMAN
Alan Schofield, F.R.P.S.

St. Paul Book and Media Centre

5A-7 Royal Exchange Square, Glasgow, G1 3AH, Scotland. Tel.: 041 226 3391.
E 1 cational and religious 35mm filmstrips/audio-visual materials.

Screen Advertising World Association Ltd.

205 Wardour Street, London, W1V 3FA. Tel.: 01-734 7621.
SECRETARY GENERAL
Simon I. Dalgleish.

Society of Film Distributors Ltd

Royalty House, 72 Dean Street, London, W.1. Tel.: 01-437 4383.
PRESIDENT
P. Livingstone
COUNCIL
Barber International Films Ltd., Brent Walker Film Distributors Ltd., Cinema International Corp. UK, Columbia-EMI-Warner Film Distributors Ltd., Crawford Films Ltd., Eagle Films Ltd., Enterprise Pictures Ltd., Gala Film Distributors Ltd., Grand National Film Distributors Ltd., GTO Films Ltd., HandMade Film Distributors Ltd., ITC Film Distributors Ltd., Rank Film Distributors Ltd., Twentieth Century Fox Film Co. Ltd., United Artists Corp. Ltd., Walt Disney Productions Ltd.

Variety Club of Gt. Britain (Tent No. 36)

Avon House, 3rd Floor, 360 Oxford Street, London, W.1.
CHIEF BARKER
Robert Webster
PRESS GUY
David Jones, C.B.E.
Purposes: The purpose of association is to provide a means by which persons of good moral character and reputation engaged in the motion picture, theatrical, amusement, sports and allied industries, wherever situated, may associate in friendly relationship, and by such association support worthy children's charitable projects, foster high ideals and ethics in the motion picture, theatrical, amusement, sports and allied industries.

The Writers' Guild of Great Britain

(In 1959 the British Screen and Television Writers Association and the Radio and Television Writers Association were amalgamated to form this Guild. Its object to further and protect the interests of its members and to obtain for screen theatre and book writers terms comparable of those long accepted in other fields.)
430 Edgware Road, London, W2 1EH Tel. 01-723 8074-6.
PRESIDENT
Eric Paice
JOINT CHAIRMAN
Donald Bull, Jack Gratus
HON. TREASURER
Alice Robinson
GENERAL SECRETARY
Ian Rowland Hill, M.A.

Government Divisions On Film Affairs

Australian Film Commission (Film Australia)

Canberra House, 10-16 Maltravers Street, Strand, London, WC2R 3EH. Tel: 01-438 8376 and 438 8000. Telex: 27565.

British Film Institute

127 Charing Cross Road, London, WC2H 0EA. Tel. 01-437 4355.

Founded 1933. Principal object to encourage the development of the art of the film, to promote its use as a record of contemporary life and manners and to foster public appreciation and study of it from these points of view. The Institute has a similar role in relation to television. The Board of Governors is appointed by the Secretary of State for Education and Science. The National Film Archive and the National Film Theatre are departments of the Institute which publishes Sight and Sound, a quarterly film magazine and the Monthly Film Bulletin.

CHAIRMAN
Sir Basil Engholm, KCB
DIRECTOR
Anthony Smith
DEPUTY DIRECTOR & SECRETARY
Gerry Rawlinson

British Film Fund Agency
7 Portland Place, London, W1N 4HS
Tel. 01-323 2741.

(The Agency was established on July 1, 1957, in accordance with regulations made by the Department of Trade under powers conferred on them by the Cinematograph Films Act, 1957, to distribute to British film makers the proceeds of the levy imposed on exhibitors by the Act.)

MEMBERS
P. E. Heywood, F.C.A. (chairman), E. S. Jackson, C.B., J. K. Oldale
SECRETARY
R. M. McCleery, F.C.A., Messrs. Champness, Cowper & Co.

Central Office of Information

Hercules Road, London, SE1 7DU. Tel. 01-928 2345.
FILMS AND TELEVISION DIVISION DIRECTOR
A. C. White

Cinematograph Films Council

Films Branch, Department of Trade, Sanctuary Buildings, 20 Great Smith Street, London, SW1P 3DB. Tel: 01-215 3685.
CHAIRMAN
Dame Elizabeth Ackroyd, DBE
INDEPENDENT MEMBERS
D. Gordon, C. Drury, OBE, Vincent Porter, Maj. Gen. Norman Wheeler, C.B., C.B.E., K. Whitehorn.
REPRESENTING MAKERS OF BRITISH FILMS
Lord Brabourne, K. L. Maidment, Timothy Burrill, K. Trodd
REPRESENTING FILM RENTER
P. Livingstone, C. Cooper
REPRESENTING EXHIBITORS
C. G. Bernstein, J. K. S. Poole, T. W. Clarke, R. A. Webster, Clare Holtham
REPRESENTING PERSONS EMPLOYED BY MAKERS, RENTERS OR EXHIBITORS OF BRITISH FILMS
J. Morton, P. Plouviez, A. Sapper, J. Wilson
SECRETARY
D. N. Hill

Department of Trade, Films Branch

Sanctuary Blgs., 16-20 Great. Smith Street, London, SW1P 3DB. Tel: 01-215 3685.
(The Films Branch has general responsibility for the commercial and industrial aspects of the British film industry. One of its main tasks is the administration of the Films Acts 1960 to 1981; this involves enforcement of the quota and other regulations in relation to the distribution and exhibition of films and the negotiation of co-production agreements with other countries and the application of those agreements. The Branch deals with general questions about the production, distribution and exhibition of films in the U.K., particularly matters which concern the promotion of British film production. It is responsible for questions relating to the British film levy under the Film Levy Finance Act, 1981 for the British Film Fund Agency. It also provides the Secretariat for the Cinematograph Films Council.)

Films of Scotland

32A Rutland Square, Edinburgh EH1 2BW, Scotland. Tel: 031 229 3456
HON. PRESIDENT
George Singleton, C.B.E., J.P.
CHAIRMAN
Andrew Stewart, C.B.E., LL.D.
HON. TREASURER
William Wallace, C.A.
DIRECTOR
James Wilson
(Objects: Films of Scotland was set up in 1955 to encourage the production of Scottish films in the national interest. Productions are undertaken for public and private sponsors—for cinemas, for television, for video outlets and for non-theatrical purposes. There is a 16 mm lending library with more than a hundred titles—Scottish life as seen by the camera, literally from A to Z.)

National Film Finance Corporation

Established under Cinematograph Film Production (Special Loans) Act, 1949. 22 Southampton Place, London, WC1A 2BP. Tel.: 01-831 7561. Telex: 888694.
CHAIRMAN
Geoffrey Williams
MANAGING DIRECTOR
Mamoun Hassan
DIRECTORS
The Lord Remnant, Barry Norman, David Puttnam, Felicity Green, Colin Young, Romaine Hart
SECRETARY
Ian Smyth

National Film School

Beaconsfield Film Studios, Station Road, Beaconsfield, Bucks HP9 ILG Tel.: 04946 71234.
DIRECTOR
Colin Young

National Panel for Film Festivals

British Council, Films Dept. 65 Davies Street, London, W1Y 2AA. Tel.: 01-499 8011, Cables: Britcoun, London, Telex 916522.
FESTIVALS OFFICER
Christian Routh

The Services Kinema Corporation

Chalfont Grove, Narcot Lane, Gerrards Cross, Buckinghamshire SL9 8TN. Tel. 02407 4461. Telegrams: Serkincor, Gerrards Cross. Telex: 837254.
PATRON
H.R.H. The Princess Margaret
BOARD OF MANAGEMENT CHAIRMAN
Group Captain G. H. Pirie, CBE, DL.
ACTING MANAGING DIRECTOR
Air Vice-Marshal D. G. Bailey, CB, CBE.
DIRECTOR OF OPERATIONS
G. D. Wilson
BOOKING MANAGER
S. E. Pound
BUYER
D. J. Stapleton
(All film matters for the Army, Royal Air Force and UK Shore Establishments of the Royal Navy are handled by the civilian Services Kinema Corporation. The Corporation produces training films and film strips for the Army, and distributes and exhibits training and entertainment films to the Forces throughout the world. Under the terms of its charter the facilities and services of the Corporation may also be used for the production or exhibition of training or educational films for any Government department.)

British and Irish Studio Facilities & Processing Laboratories

Studio Facilities

ATV ELSTREE STUDIO CENTRE. Borehamwood, Herts. Telephone: 01-953 6100. Owned by ATV Network Limited. Four electronic studios. Two 116′ × 80′ one with permanent audience seating for over 300, Two 84′ × 80′. Q File lighting, 12 colour cameras and 7 quadruplex video tape machines for 625 PAL or 525 NTSC operation, 16mm and 35mm telecine computerised CDL editing facilities and Digital standards convertor for international exchange of programmes.

BRAY STUDIOS. Windsor Road, Windsor, Berks. Telephone: Maidenhead 22111. 3 Stages total 13,300 square feet. All depts, theatre, sound recording effects workshops bar and catering. Studio Manager: David Goodenough. Contact: Fiona Latto.

BUSHEY, Melbourne Road, Bushey, Herts. Telephone: 01-950 1621; Cygnet Guild Communications Ltd. 2 Stages, 70′ × 40′, 30′ × 20′.

CTVC Hillside, Merry Hill Road, Bushey, Watford WD2 IDR. Tel.: 01-950 4426.

DE LANE LEA SOUND CENTRE, 75 Dean Street, London, W.1. Telephone: 01-439 1721. Bookings: Louise Charter.

EMI ELSTREE STUDIOS, Boreham Wood, Herts. Telephone: 01-953 1600. 9 stages (1-30,000 sq. ft., 4-15,000 sq. ft., 1-15,750 sq. ft., 2-8,000 sq. ft., 1-5,200 sq. ft.) Theatres: Three viewing, one dubbing, one looping. Exterior lot. Dolby installation in transfers, looping, dubbing and viewing for producing Dolby encoded optical sound tracks. Andrew Mitchell, managing director.

HALLIFORD FILM STUDIOS. Manygate Lane, Shepperton, Middlesex. Telephone: Walton-on-Thames 26341. 2 stages (60 × 60; 60 × 40) totalling 6,000 square feet. Studio Manager: Eugene Andrews.

HAMPDEN GURNEY STUDIOS. Hampden Gurney Street, London, WIH 5AL. Telephone: 01-402 6255. Cables: Jaksonfilm, London. W1. Telex: 896559 GECOMS-G.

KAY LABORATORIES SOUND STUDIOS. 22 Soho Square, London, W.1. Telephone: 01-437 7811. Telex: 28463. Managing Director: Marshall D. Kochman, Studio Manager: G. Latter.

KAY LABORATORIES VIDEO DIVISION. 22 Soho Square, London, W.1. Telephone: 01-437 7811. Manager: R. J. Venis.

LEE INTERNATIONAL FILM STUDIOS LTD. 128 Wembley Park Drive, Wembley, Middx. Telephone: 01-902 1262.

NATIONAL FILM STUDIOS OF IRELAND. Ardmore House, Bray, Co. Wicklow, Ireland. Telephone: Dublin 862971. Telex: 30418.

PINEWOOD STUDIOS, Iver Heath, Bucks. Telephone: Iver 651700; Cables: Pinewood, Iver Heath. Telex: 847505 Pinew G. Managing Director: C. R. Howard, Pinewood Studios Ltd.
A. 165 ft. × 110 ft. × 35 ft. (with tank 40 ft. × 30 ft. × 8 ft.) B.110 ft. × 80 ft. × 35 ft. C. 110 ft. × 80 ft. × 35 ft. D. 165 ft. × 110 ft. × 35 ft. (with tank 40 ft. × 30 ft. × 8 ft.) E. 165 ft. × 110 ft. × 35 ft. (with tank 40 ft. × 30 ft. × 8 ft.) F. 100 ft. × 75 ft. × 35 ft. (with tank 20 ft. × 20 ft. × 8 ft.) G. 55 ft. × 49 ft. × 23 ft. H. 90 ft. × 37 ft. × 28 ft. North Tunnel: 175 ft. × 28 ft. including West Wing 68 ft. × 33 ft. Special effects stage (silent)—89 ft. × 80 ft. × 20 ft. J. 110 ft. × 80 ft. × 30 ft. (dual-purpose, film and TV). K. 110 ft. × 80 ft. × 30 ft. (dual-purpose, film and TV). L. 105 ft. × 90 ft. × 31 ft. (dual-purpose, film and TV). M. 105 ft. × 90 ft. × 31 ft. (dual-purpose, film and TV). 007 Stage. World's Largest Silent Stage, 374 ft. × 160 ft. × 53 ft. 7 theatres for viewing, dubbing, and post-sync, effects. Any ratio, 16mm, 35mm, 70mm, viewing available, with sync separate sound. Up to 115 seats. Dubbing in multitrack, stereo, Dolby up to 6 tracks. 50 cutting rooms. Cameras: Fully equipped camera department. Special effects: Matte stage. Vis 35mm. back projection. Fully equipped process projection dept. including front projection and 70m rear and foreground projection. Triple head process system. Models of all kinds. Beam splitting cameras for monochrome, color and scope traveling matte. Stills: Stills studio. Still cameras to cover all re-

quirements. Dressing rooms. Production and Unit Offices: Many available. Exterior Lot: 72 acres with formal gardens, lake, woods, and concrete service roads. Multi-Purpose Catering Dept. Paddock tank 230 ft. wide narrowing to 110 ft. Backing 240 ft. × 60 ft. Another tank 75 ft. × 225 ft. Both tanks contain approximately 800,000 gallons. Props available and world's largest scene dock.

PRODUCTION VILLAGE. (Samuelson Film Service) 100 Cricklewood Lane, London, NW2 2DS. Tel.: 01-450 8969.

ST. JOHN'S WOOD STUDIOS LTD., St. John's Wood Terrace, London, N.W. 8. Telephone 01-722 9255. (4 lines). Two sound stages: "A" (63 × 32 × 25). "B" (45 × 25 × 23). Infinity Cycloramas, each stage 16 ft. high. Managing Directors: Michael Silverman

SHEPPERTON STUDIO CENTRE. (owned by Shepperton Studios Ltd.) Shepperton, Middlesex, TW170QD. Telephone: Chertsey 62611—Stages: 9 (two 150 × 230, two 120 × 100, one 80 × 36, one 40 × 40). Two silent stages (250 × 20, 123 × 56); E stage (100 70).

TWICKENHAM, St. Margarets, Twickenham. Telephone: 01-892 4477, owned by Twickenham Film Studios, Ltd.—Three stages. RCA sound. Recording and dubbing theatre with 36 in-put 6 track stereo rock and roll. Directors: G. Coen, G. Humphreys, John T. Davey, FCA., T. L. Kirby, M. Landsberger.

Film & Video Laboratories

BRENT LABORATORIES, LTD., North Circular Road, Cricklewood, London, NW2 7AT. Telephone: 01-452 4271.

BUCK FILM LABORATORIES LTD., 714 Banbury Avenue, Slough, Berks SL1 4LH. Telex.: 848393 BUCLAB G. Tel.: 0753 76611.

COLOUR FILM SERVICES LTD., 22/25 Portman Close, Baker Street, London, W1A 4BE. Telephone: 01-486 2881.

FILMATIC LABORATORIES LTD., 16 Colville Road, London, W.11. 2BS. Telephone: 01-229 9347.

HUMPHRIES FILM LABORATORIES LIMITED (Film Processors), P.O. Box 2HL, 71-81 Whitfield Street, London, W1A 2HL. Telephone 01-636 3636; Cables Humphrilab London W.1. Telegrams: Humphrilab London W.1. Also at Ralli Building, Stanley Street, Salford 3, Manchester, and Croydon House Croydon Street. Domestic Street, Leeds 11.

KAY LABORATORIES, LTD. 91/95 Gillespie Road, Highbury, London N.5. Telephone: 01-226 4422; Telex 28463; Managing Director: Marshall D. Kochman.

KAY LABORATORIES, LTD., 22 Soho Square, London, W.1. Telephone: 01-437 7811. Telex 28463. Marshall D. Kochman (Managing Director)

KAY LABORATORIES VIDEO DIVISION, 22 Soho Square, London, W.1. Telephone: 01-437 7811. Manager: R. J. Venis.

NATIONAL SCREEN SERVICE, 15 Wadsworth Road, Greenford, Middx. Telephone: 01-998 2851. Telex: 934522.

RANK FILM LABORATORIES. Denham. Uxbridge. Middlesex. UB9 5HQ. Telex: 934704. Telephone: 0895 832323. Managing Director: J. W. Downer, Director of Operations: R. W. Login. Sales Controller: M. A. Levy

RANK PHICOM VIDEO GROUP, 142 Wardour Street, London, W1V 4BV. Tel.: 01-734 2235. Telex: 261237.

REEDS COLOUR FILM LABORATORIES, LTD., 89/91 Wardour Street, London W1V 4EP. Telephone: 01-437 5548.

STUDIO FILM & VIDEO LABORATORIES, LTD., 8-14 Meard Street, London, W1V 3HR. Tel.: 01-437 0831.

TECHNICOLOR LTD., P.O. Box 7 Bath Road, West Drayton, Middlesex, UB7 ODB. Telephone: 01-759 5432.

UNIVERSAL FILM LABORATORY LTD., Braintree Road, Ruislip, Middx. Tel.: 01-841 5101.

Chief Theatre Circuits

ASSOCIATED G.P. CINEMAS, 90 Mitchell Street, Glasgow G1, Scotland.

BRENT WALKER FOCUS CINEMAS, 5-7 Brewer Street, London, W.1. Tel.: 01-437 7377.

CALEDONIAN ASSOCIATED CINEMAS LTD., 109 Hope Street, Glasgow, G2 6LW, Scotland.

CINECENTA LTD., 147/9 Wardour Street, London, W1V 3TB. Telephone: 01-734 7521.

CLASSIC CINEMAS LTD., 63/65 Haymarket, London, SW1Y 4RQ.

EMI CINEMAS LTD., 30/31 Golden Square, London, W1A 4QX. Telephone: 01-437 9234.

FOCUS CINEMAS LTD. 147-149 Wardour Street, London, W1V 3TB. Tel.: 01-434 1961.

GRANADA THEATRES, LTD., 36 Golden Square, London, W.1. Telephone 01-734-8080.

HUTCHINSON LEISURE GROUP OF COMPANIES LTD., 1-3 Grimshaw Street, Burnley, Lancs. Telephone: 0282 22057.

KINGSWAY ENTERTAINMENTS LTD., 110/112 Rosslyn Street, Kirkcaldy, Scotland. Telephone: Kirkcaldy 52627.

ODEON IRELAND, Savoy Building, 16/17 Upper O'Connell Street, Dublin 1, Ireland. Tel.: Dublin 747911.

PARAMOUNT THEATRES (Holdings) LTD. and Associated Companies, Clive Buildings, Welshpool, Powys. SY21 7DH. Telephone: Welshpool 2772.

RANK LEISURE LTD., 7 Great Russell Street, London, WC1B 3NL. Telephone: 01-580 2010.

SNAPE GROUP OF ASSOCIATED CINEMA COMPANIES, "Electric House," Barton Road, Swinton, Manchester. Telephone: 061-794 0411.

STAR GROUP OF COMPANIES LTD., Cavendish House, The Headrow, Leeds 1. Telephone: Leeds 38561.

SUPREME CINEMAS LTD. and ASSOC. COMPANIES, 133 Royal Avenue, Belfast, N. Ireland.

THEATRE ADMINISTRATION LTD., Regal Buildings, Augusta Place, Leamington Spa, CV32 52P. Tel.: 0926 22157.

THOMPSON'S ENTERPRISES (1977) LTD., 251 Acklam Road, Middlesbrough. Telephone: Middlesbrough 88156.

UNIT FOUR CINEMAS LTD., 56 Bank Parade, Burnley, Lancs. Telephone: 0282 28221.

WARD CINEMA CIRCUIT, Princess Parade, Princess Road, Fallowfield, Manchester 14. Telephone: Moss Side.

Public Relations, Publicity Marketing Services

BILL BATCHELOR (PUBLICITY) LTD., Flat 47, Six Hall Road, London, N.W.8. Telephone: 01-286-6900.

BURNUP SERVICE LTD., 15 Samuel Road, Langdon Hills, Basildon, Essex, England. Telephone: 0268-42824.

CITADEL MOVIE PUBLICITY LTD., 33 Highfield Avenue, Kingsbury, London, N.W. Telephone: Telephone 01-204 5846.

COWAN BELLEN ASSOCIATES, 45 Poland Street, London W1V 4AV. Telephone: 01-434 3871. Cables: Cowboy, London W.1.

DENNIS DAVIDSON ASSOCIATES LTD., 61-65 Conduit Street, London, WIR9FD Telephone: 01-439 6391. Telex: 24148 DADASS G. Cables: DADASS, W.1.

EUROPEAN PUBLIC RELATIONS LTD., 109/110 Bolsover Street, London, W.1. Telephone: 01-636 8862.

RICHARD LAVER PUBLICITY, 3 Troy Court, High Street Kensington, London, W.8. Telephone: 01-937 7322.

PFEIFFER-BURRY LTD., Flat 2, 10 Connaught Place, London, W.2. Telephone: 01-723 6215.

PIC PUBLICITY LTD., 92-94 Wardour Street, London, W.1. Tel.: 01-734 0243.

RAINBOW, FRANK ASSOCIATES, 32 Hyde Gardens, Eastbourne, Sussex.

ROGERS & COWAN, INC., 27 Albemarle Street, London, W.1. Telephone: 01-499 0691. Telex. 25571 Rocolo G.

UK INTERNATIONAL, Aspen House, 25 Dover Street, London, W1X 3PA. Tel.: 01-491 7621.

URQUHART PUBLIC RELATIONS, 35 Curzon Street, London, W.1. Tel.: 01-629 1666.

The World Market

* **MARKET ANALYSES**
  Producers and Product
  Distributors

The World Market

ARGENTINA

Number of 35 mm Theatres in Operation: 1,600
Number of Clubs, Entities, etc. (16mm) in Operation: 120 (Estimated)

Censorship: A special committee from the Culture Ministry judges films before they are exhibited and determines on moral grounds if they are fit to be shown to minors under 14 or 18 years. This entity can suppress scenes or ban films entirely.

Customs: Printed positive costs pay for duties U$S. 4.95 each 100 meters, plus added value tax 16% on CIF, plus duties, plus statistics. Negative temporary imports for making local cities pay for duties: none. Temporary importation on one print for censorship purposes. Duties: none; statistical tax: U$S.0.30 per each 100 meters; added value tax: 20%.

Financial Exchange Regulations: Film distributors are free to effect the remittance of a company's earnings, the type of monetary exchange being the one prevailing at the time of the transference. The exchange rate is actually of pesos 6.500 per dollar.

Film Releases: In 1980, 339 feature films were released, according to the following origins: Argentina, 34; American, 136; Italian, 47; French, 35; Taiwan, 1; Japan, 4; Australia, 7; German, 4; Mexican, 3; Brazil, 5; Poland, 2; Czechoslovakia, 2; URSS, 5; China, 6; Israel, 1; Denmark, 1. To these must be added 15 co-productions of diverse origins.

Trade Publications: Only one trade paper is edited in Buenos Aires: "Heraldo del Cine" who also turn out a Year Book under the name of "Guia Heraldo". Address is Moreno 1215, Buenos Aires. (TLX 17387 TRAFI AR).

Principal Industry Organizations in Buenos Aires: Asociación Argentina de Actores (Viamonte 1443); Asociación Argentina de Distribuidores de Peliculas (Ayacuhci 457); Asociación Cinematográfica de Mutualidad (Calleo 341); Asociación Cinematográfica de Exhibidores Independientes (Ayacucho 457); Asociación de Cronistas Cinematográficos de la Argentina (Maipu 621); Asociación de Empresarios Cinematográficos de la Provincia de Buenos Aires (Ayacucho 457); Asociación de Empresarios de Cinematográfos (Lavalle 1934); Asociación General de Productores Cinemtográficos de la Argentina (Av. R.S. Peña 547); Asociación Productores de Peliculas Argentinas (Tucuman 929); Asociación Productoras de Peliculas Independientes (Lavalle 710); Camara Argentina-Norte Americana de Distribuidores de Films (American Film Board) (Alsina 1360); Directores Argentinos Cinematográficos (Lavalle 1934); Federación Cinematográfica Argentina (Viamonte 2045); Fondo Nacional de las Artes (Alsina 673); Fundación Cinemateca Argentina (Lavalle 2168); Museo del Cine (Sarmiento 1551); Sindicato Empleados de Distribuidoras de Cine (Ayacucho 580); Sindicato Industria Cinematográfica Argentina (Juncal 2029); Sindicato de Operadores Cinematográfico de la República Argentina (Viamonte 2045); Sindicato Unico de Trabajadores del Espectaculo Público (Pasco 148); Sociedad Argentina de Escenógrafos Cinematográficos (Cangallo 1671); Sociedad Cinematográfica de la Provincia de Buenos Aires (Ayacucho 457).
—NAT BRUSKI

AUSTRALIA

Number of Theatres: There are some 518 indoor theatres in Australia, 251 of which are located in and around the principal cities. There are approximately 295 driveins.

Exhibition: Three major chains control most of the city-located theatres: Hoyts Theatres, Ltd. (owned and controlled by 20th Century-Fox which also distributes that company's films here); The Greater Union Organisation (50 per cent owned by the Rank Organisation and the rest by Australians); and Village Theatres Pty. Ltd. (30 per cent owned by Greater Union). Both Greater Union and Village also have distribution arms.

Film Production: Australian film production continued to increase with the total for calendar 1981 expected to reach from 22 to 25 projects. This compares with only 12 films completed in the whole of 1980.

Principal Production Companies: APA Leisuretime International Ltd., 43 Yeo Street, Neutral Bay, NSW, 2089; Aquataurus Film Productions, 42 Hartnett Towers, 42 New Beach Road, Darling Point, NSW, 2027; Australian Film Institute, 79-81 Cardigan Street, Carlton, VIC, 3053; B.C. Productions, 26 Glebe Point Road, Broadway, NSW, 2007; Bilcock & Copping Film Productions Pty., Ltd., 48 High Street, St. Kilda, VIC, 3182.; Richard Brennan, 161 Victoria Street, Potts Point, NSW, 2011; Anthony Buckley Productions Pty. Ltd., 7/530 Mowbray Road, Lane Cove, NSW, 2066; Tim Burstall & Associates Pty. Ltd., 48 High Street, St. Kilda, VIC, 3182; Cash Harmon Television Pty. Ltd., 35 Grosvenor Street, Neutral Bay, NSW, 2089; Crawford Productions Pty. Ltd., 1 Southampton Crescent, Abbotsford, VIC, 3067; Vega Film Productions Pty. Ltd., 558 Drummond Street, North Carlton, VIC 3054; Edgecliff Films Pty. Ltd., 21 Pier Street, Sydney, NSW, 2000; Film Australia, Eaton Road, Lindfield, NSW, 2070; The Film House Pty,. Ltd., Fred Schepisi (d), 272 George Street, Fitzroy, VIC, 3065; Hedon Productions, 41 Bent Street, Sydney, NSW, 2060; Hexagon Pty. Ltd., 46-48 High Street, St. Kilda, VIC, 3182; Island Films Pty. Ltd., 122 Whale Beach Road, Whale Beach, NSW, 2107; Tom Jeffrey, 44 Liverpool Street, Paddington, NSW, 2021; Kavanagh Productions Pty. Ltd., 27 Arthur Street, Eltham, VIC, 3095; John Lamond Motion Picture Enterprises Pty. Ltd., 4 Fairfield Avenue, Camberwell, VIC, 3124; Limelight Productions, 81 Bent Street, Lindfield, NSW, 2070; Chris Lofven, 13/262 Barkly Street, North Fitzroy, VIC, 3068; Longford Productions Pty. Ltd., 578 St. Kilda Road, Melbourne, VIC, 3004; John McCallum, 1740 Pittwater Road, Bayview, NSW, 2104; McElroy & McElroy, 34 Neridah Street, Chatswood, NSW, 2067; Margaret Fink Productions, 71 Wallaroy Road, Woollahra, NSW, 2025; The Movie Company Pty. Ltd., 49 Market Street, Sydney, NSW, 2000; Quest Films, 53 Glencairn Avenue, East Brighton, VIC, 3187; Roger Whittaker Films, The Stonehouse, Clavering Road, Seaforth, NSW, 2092; Romac Productions Pty. Ltd., 76 Hersey Street, Jolimont, WA, 6014; Smart Street Films, 467 Old South Head Road, Rose Bay, NSW, 2029; Spectrum Film Producers Pty. Ltd., 137 Penshurst Street, Willoughby, NSW, 2068; South Australian Film Corporation, P.O. 263, Norwood, SA., 5067; Stoney Creek Films, Cnr Glynns Road & Research Road, Warrandyte North, VIC, 3113; Terryrod Productions, 3 Barcoo Place, St. Ives, NSW, 2075; Timon Productions, 8 March Street, Bellevue Hill, NSW, 2023; TLN Film Productions, P.O. Box 348, North Melbourne, VIC, 3051; David Waddington, 273 Alfred Street, North Sydney, NSW, 2060; Peter Weir, 89 Prince Alfred Avenue, Newport, NSW, 2106; Voyager Films Pty. Limited, Post Office, Palm Beach, NSW, 2018.

Principal Distributors and Exhibitors: BEF (Film Distributors) Aust. Pty. Ltd., 49 Market Street, Sydney, NSW, 2000; Blake Films (d/e), S. Blake, 155 Castlereagh Street, Sydney, NSW, 2000; Cinema Centre Group (d/e), Reg McLean, P.O. Box 413, Canberra City, ACT, 2601; C.I.C. Pty. Ltd. (d), (Incorporating Paramount, Universal, M.G.M.), 53 Brisbane Street, Surry Hills, NSW, 2010; Consolidated Exhibitors Pty. Ltd., Richard Waldberg (d/e), 628 George Street, Sydney, NSW, 2000; Columbia Pictures Pty. Ltd. (d), 49 Market Street, Sydney, NSW, 2000; Dendy Cinemas (e), 360 Pacific Highway, Crows Nest, NSW, 2065; Filmways Australasia Distributors Pty. Ltd. (d/e), Mark Josem, 243 Glenferrie Road, Melbourne, VIC, 3144; Garland Productions Pty. Ltd. (d), Eric Dare, 8 Peaker Lane, Woollahra, NSW, 2025; The Greater Union Organisation Pty. Ltd. (e), 49 Market Street, Sydney, NSW, 2000; Hoyts Theatres Ltd. (e), 600 George Street, Sydney, NSW, 2000; Robert Kapferer (d), 4 Norwich Road, Rose Bay, NSW, 2029; Quality Films (d), Edmund Allison, 405 Sussex Street, Sydney, NSW, 2000; Regent Investments Pty. Ltd. (e), Ron Brown, 164 Castlereagh Street, Sydney, NSW, 2000; Regent Trading Enterprises Pty. Ltd. (d), Errol Heath, 280 Pitt Street, Sydney, NSW, 2000; Roadshow Distributors Pty. Ltd., Grahame Burke, c/o Village Theatres, P.O. Box 1411M GPO, Melbourne, VIC, 3001; Seven Keys Films Pty. Ltd. (d/e), Andrew Gaty, 68 Alfred Street, Milsons Point, NSW, 2061; Twentieth Century Fox Corp. Aust. Pty. Ltd. (d), 4351 Brisbane Street, Surry Hills, NSW, 2010; United Artists (A/asia) Pty. Ltd. (d), 8 Kippax Street, Surry Hills, NSW, 2010; Village Theatres Pty. Ltd. (e), P.O. Box 1411M GPO, Melbourne, VIC, 3000.

AUSTRIA

Number of Theatres in Operation: 507, 72 of which are in Vienna.

Total Attendance: About 17,865,964 million in 1979; population approximately 7 million.

Films Released: 254 in 1979 (from 19 countries) compared with 287 in 1978. Only 8 films were made in Austria in 1979. Breakdown of foreign films: 98 from U.S.; 46, West Germany; 33, France; 25, Italy; 14, Great Britain; 8, Hong Kong; 5, Sweden; 3 each from Canada, Denmark, Japan and Switzerland; 2 each from Israel and the U.S.S.R.; and 1 each from Australia, Czechoslovakia, the German Democratic Republic, the Phillipines and South Africa.

Censorship: There is no official censorship, except for matters "dangerous to the State." A commission determines the fitness of pictures for young age-groups, permitting general attendance or barring films to persons under the age of sixteen (in some districts eighteen years).

Subsidies: No direct subsidies are paid for film production but in certain cases the government may guarantee the repayment of 80% of loans extended by private banks to film producers.

Newsreels: Austria Wochenschau, Wiener-Str. 100-106, Vienna 23; Fox Toenende Wochenschau (distributed by MGM) and Weltjournal, Wiener-Str. 100, Vienna 23.

Government Department: Bundesministerium für Handel und Wiederaufbau (Federal Ministry for Commerce and Reconstruction), Abteilung Filmwesen (filmsection), Vienna, Ministerialrat Robert Steyskal.

Principal Producers (All in Vienna): Comopol-Film-GmbH, Mariahilfer Strasse 99. Cosmos-Film-Produktions-GmbH, Karl-Schweighofergasse 5. Donau-Film, Neubaugasse 38, Erma-Film, Blechturmgasse 10. Hope Film, Karl-Schweighofergasse 6. Neusser-Film-GmbH, Parkring 18. Oesterreichische-Film-GmbH, Strauchgasse 1. Projektograph-Film-Verleih-GmbH. Neubaugasse 25. Ring-Film-Produktions-und Vertdiebs-GmbH, Neubaugasse 11. Rondo-Film-produktion, Rennweg 33. Sascha-Film-Produktion, Siebensterngasse 31. Schönbrunn-Film, Neubaugasse 1. Vindobona-Film-GmbH, Wallneerstrasse 2, Paula Wessely Filmproduktion-GmbH, Neubaugasse 2. Wiener Kunstfilm, Habsburgergasse 1. Wiener Mundus-Film, Opernring 17. Zenith Filmproduktion, Schöonbrunnerstrasse 282.

Principal Distributors: (all in Vienna): Atlantic Filmverleih, Siebensterngasse 19; Austria Film GmbH, Neubaugasse 25; Constantin-Film GmbH, Siebensterngasse 37; Czerny Film, Neubaugasse 1; FZ Stadthalle Wien, Neubaugasse 35; Iris Film GmbH, Mariahilferstrasse 88a; Jupiter-Film, Neubaugasse 25; Oefram Film GmbH, Neubaugasse 36; Universal Film, Neubaugasse 38.

BELGIUM

Population: 9,950,000.
Number of Cinemas:6022 (35mm, 644; 70mm, 8)
Total Annual Admissions: 27,000,000.
Average Annual Attendance per Person: 2.9.
Average Seat Price: Fr 120 & 130.
Censorship: No direct censorship, but a government department decides which films are suitable for children aged under 16. Import duties of Fr 1.66 per metre for positive films and Fr 1.33 per metre for negative films are payable. Exchange remittances can be exported freely, common market free. A subsidy is paid to domestic producers equal to 80% of admissions tax collected from showing domestic feature films, 25% for shorts and 5% for the newsreels. The subsidy is worth 150 million Belgian francs per year. An admissions tax of between 6% and 24% of gross box office taking is collected.

Industry Legislation: There is no definite legislation on the motion picture industry in Belgium, which works independently from government instances. In very extraordinary cases, such as those in which the whole national economy is concerned and of which resulted the agreement about import and export of the dollar zone products, the Belgian Government will act as an advisor in order to serve as well as possible the interest of everybody concerned, including those of the motion picture people.

Government Departments: As far as necessary, the Ministry of Economical Affairs and the Ministry of Finance are concerned with films.

Industry Organizations: The Belgium film trade consists, from this year on, of two basic organizations; They are: "Chambre Syndicale Belge du Cinema" and the "Association des Directeurs de Théatres Cinématographiques de Belgique," which groups most of the exhibitors. As a rule, the films are distributed on a percentage basis. This amounts to 30¢ to 70¢ for the so-called exceptional films.

Chambre Syndicale Belge du Cinema: avenue de l'Astronomie 22, Brussels. President: d. Balatchoff.

Association des Directeurs de théatres Cinematographiques de Belgique: (Exhibitors) rue Royale 300, Brussels. President: R. Anneez.

Union Nationale des Producteurs Belges de films: Presidents: R. Jauniaux and De Roisy.

—MARC TURFKRUYER

BRAZIL

Statistics for 1979—latest available
Number of Theatres in Operation: 3200 with 35 mm., 102 with 16 mm.

Attendance: Dropped 17 per cent in 1979.

Production: Local production runs about 80 film per year. In 1979 the figure was 98. Some 300 films were imported, with 152 from MPEA members.

Censorship: Approval of all films for the entire Brazilian territory must be obtained from the Departamento de Divertimentos Públicos (Divisao de Censura). There are four classes of censorship: films for all ages; unsuitable for children under 10 years; unsuitable for youngsters under 14 years; unsuitable for youngsters under 18 years.

Admission Taxes: Taxes on admissions are in Rio de Janeiro 10% municipal tax, 10% "statistics." In Sao Paulo, there is no "popular stamp," however, municipal tax is 15%, 10% statistics, Cr. $1.00 social assistance.

Industry Legislation: All theatres are required to show one full-length Brazilian feature for each 8 foreign programs, besides of locally produced news reels or shorts which must be played in every bill.

Subsidies: The Bank of Brazil finances national producers up to an amount of 30,000 new cruzeiros per film and the Bank of the State of Guanabara up to 18,000 cruzeiros. The State of Guanabara and the Municipality of Sao Paulo impose cinema admission taxes which go into film production subsidy funds for producers in those areas.

In addition, the Federal government requires the withholding of 40% of the basic income tax levied on the producer's share of income derived from the exhibition of imported films, to be set aside in a special account to be used for the production of Brazilian films, subject to certain conditions specified by the Government Film Office. This is in lieu of payment of the amount to the tax collector.

A Brazilian film, for this purpose, is defined as one produced by a Brazilian company in the Portuguese language, with a cast and technical staff two-thirds of whom are Brazilian or persons resident in Brazil for two years, with all studio scenes shot in Brazil, and with prints and soundtrack made in Brazil.

Industry Organizations: Sindicato Nacional da Industria Cin ématogr áfica—President Mario Sombra—Av. Catogeras 15—4°—Rio de Janeiro. Associaçao Brasileira Cinematográfica—Pres. Rudy Gottschalk—Praca Mahatma Gandhi 2—Rio de Janeiro. APICESP (Professional Association of the Motion Picture Industry of the State of Sao Paulo)—Pres. Abilio Pereira de Almeida—Rua Major Diogo 307—°—Sao Paulo. ATACESP (Association of Motion Picture Technicians and Artists of the State of Sao Paulo) Pres. Paulo Cotrim—Rua Major Diogo 307—2°—Sao Paulo. Associaçao Brasileira Cinématográfica—Pres. Oswaldo Sampaio—Rua do Arouche 15—Sao Paulo. Centro de Estudos Cinématográficos—Pres. Paulo Emilio de Salles Gomes—Museu de Arte Moderna—Rua 7 de Abril 230—Sao Paulo. Seminário de Cinema—Mangr. Plinio Garcia Sanches—Museu de Arte de Sao Paulo—Rua 7 de Abril 230—Sao Paulo.

Exhibitor Organizations: Sindicato de Emprésas Exibidoras Teatrais e Cinematográficas—Pres. Gilberto Ferrer—Praca Mahatma Gandhi 2—Rio de Janeiro. Sindicato de Empresas Exhibidoras Cinematográficas de Sao Paulo—Pres. Dr. Lucidio Calio Ceravolo, Rua 15 Novembro 137, 6°, Sao Paulo.

CANADA

Film production in Canada in 1980 hit a record $170 million and it was hoped that this would at least be matched in 1981 although at mid-year the number of films produced was running behind.

Figures for 1980 released by the Canadian Film Development Corporation showed that 36 English-language films with total budgets of over $140 million and 14 French-language productions with budgets over $23 million were produced, breaking the record $150 million for 55 pictures set in film production here in 1979.

Of the 50 films the CFDC provided financial assistance of $6 million to 27 projects. This includes $4.6 million in interim loans or equity investments in 19 English films and $1.4 million in loans or equity investments in eight French films or co-productions.

Total feature film box office was estimated at $300,000,000 for the calendar year 1980. Some 80 per cent of this represents income from U.S. product. (Canada is Hollywood's second best foreign customer, ranking after Japan.)

American distributors continued to pick up Canadian films in 1980 and 1981 for U.S. handling although none to date has come anywhere near matching the $40 million gross racked up by "Meatballs" in the U.S. in 1979. Avco Embassy distributed "Prom Night" in 1980 and its gross of $14,000,000 in the U.S. was the highest of any Canadian film in the American market that year.

During 1981 Canadian productions released in the U.S. included "Atlantic City" (Paramount), "Scanners" and "Dirty Tricks," (Avco Embassy), "Nothing Personal" (Filmways), and "Happy Birthday To Me" and "Heavy Metal" (Columbia).

Statistics below, supplied by Statistics Canada, are for 1979, the latest available:

Number of theatres: 1,362, of which 1,070 are regular and 292 drive-ins. This compares with a total of 1,374 in 1978, of which 1,079 were regular and 295 drive-ins.

Admission receipts: Total receipts from admissions (excluding taxes) amounted to $277,500,000 in 1979, an increase of 10.2% over the $251,900,000 reported the year before. Receipts from regular threatres accounted for 86.2% of this amount, or $239,349,000. Drive-ins took in $38,175,000.

Attendance: The number of paid admissions for 1979 was 98,200,000, an increase of 5.4% over the 93,231,000 in 1978. In 1979 regular theatres had 86,010,000 (81,597,000 in 1978) and drive-ins 12,151,000 (11,634,000 in 1978).

Per capita expenditure for motion picture entertainment: $12.16 in 1979, up from the $11.20 recorded in 1978. Per capita expenditure is calculated by dividing the total admission receipts (including amusement taxes) of regular theatres and drive-ins by the population estimates as of June, 1979. Per capita expenditure by province was as follows: Newfoundland, $6.62; Prince Edward Island, $13.75; Nova Scotia, $9.77; New Brunswick, $8.08; Quebec, $10.32; Ontario, $13.19; Manitoba, $10.66; Saskatchewan, $10.98; Alberta, $16.29; British Colombia, $14.09; Yukon and Northwest Territories: $15.15.

CEYLON

(See Sri Lanka)

CHILE

Trends: Censorship has loosened considerably in this country with films shown uncut in recent times including "La Cage Aux Folles," "Mad Max," "Coming Home," and "The Tin Drum." This improvement was sorely needed to help bolster audience attendance, which has been diminishing severely in recent years. The market recouped somewhat in 1980 after a 20 per cent drop the year before.

Films Released: A total of 223 films—43 less than in 1979—opened in 1980. Of these, 37.5 per cent were distributed by the U.S. major companies and the rest by independents. Reissues, however, increased from 29 in 1979 to 50.

Ticket Prices: First-run admissions in downtown Santiago (which represents approximately 60 per cent of the country's film revenue) were $2.50 in 1980. Helping theatre owners was a drop in the value added tax (VAT) from 22 to 20 per cent.

Number of Theatres: There are 49 theatres in Santiago, compared with 48 in 1940, 66 in 1950, 95 in 1960, and 75 in 1970. Some 20 per cent of Santiago's cinemas hold over 1,000 spectators.

Attendance: In Santiago it has gradually dropped over the years from 201,635 in 1974 to 137,832 in 1980.

CHINA (Communist)

Annual movie attendance for the past year is given as 24.3 billion with admissions averaging 16¢. Of the 11 main studios producing full length features, the most important of these, Shanghai Film Studio, raised annual production from 12 to 52 films. Average cost of making a black-and-white film averages about $192,000 with color features estimated at $384,000.

Communist China now boasts over 2,000 regular cinemas but these are augmented by 4,000 clubs in both cities and countryside at which films are shown, and 75,000 film projection units which bring periodic cinema shows to peasants and workers in far places.

In the past 15 years a total of 540 feature films has been produced which averages less than 36 per year but of late production each year has exceeded 40. In addition, over the past 14 years 190 full-length documentaries, 2,900 short documentaries, 3,000 newsreels, 1,400 scientific films and 200 cartoons have been produced. Over 1,400 foreign films from Asia, Africa, Latin America, America and Europe have been dubbed for Chinese audiences.

Of Red China's estimated 80 film studios only 11 make full length feature films including the Sian Studio, Chukiang Studio in Canton, August 1st Studio in Peking, Changchun Studio, and the Haiven, Tienma, Shanghai Film and Kiangnan Studios in Shanghai.

Four cinemas are equipped for showing stereoscopic film produced in China or imported. Distributor is China Film Distribution and Exhibition Corp., Peking.

After 6 months of delays on the Chinese side, the first American Film Festival was held in 1981 with only five features being shown: "Singing in the Rain," "Snow White & the 7 Dwarfs," "Guess Who's Coming to Dinner," "Shane," and "The Black Stallion." Packed houses resulted in extra showings in Peking, Shanghai, Tianjin, Xian and Wuhan with 20 cent tickets at the box office bringing $1.33 from scalpers. Few American imports had been shown before because the Chinese refused to pay more than $10,000 for filming rights, and several American distributors asked for a percentage of box office receipts as they do in other foreign countries. While the Chinese authorities requested additional films, they refused to pay what American companies feel is a reasonable fee. The Chinese still uncertainty in picking films which "would develop Western material desires and strain the social fabric or economic health of the country." Thus certain films were judged "inappropriate." for showing in China. The Chinese now want to mount their own film festival in the U.S.

CHINA (Taiwan)

Number of Theatres: 460.
Number of Features Produced: 166.
Number of Imported Features: 226.
Movie Attendance: 138.3 million.

The government provides encouragement to film production with annual awards to the best ones, plus import quotas to studious producing laudable films, rebates on customs duties for imports of overseas Chinese-language films, and reductions in entertainment taxes.

There are 9 studios and 20 sound stages with annual production of 125 feature films and 60 documentaries. Some 400 distribution companies service domestic and imported films. Average annual attendance 10 times per person. However, theatre owners complain that an average of three imported feature films televised weekly are hurting their box offices.

The sum of $70,000 is allocated for the average feature film for which a 30% profit is envisaged. Average admission price is about 40 cents. Theatre-operators and movie producers took concerted (and successful) action to stop local TV from showing Chinese-language feature films, imported from Hong Kong, claiming that such showings, especially on Sundays and holidays, made a 40% difference in boxoffice. This may be relaxed later by government action to allow showing of such Chinese-language films at times which would not have so much effect on the boxoffice. The government is not concerned with the closure of movie theatres since it feels that one theatre for every 30,000 of the population (total population is 16 million) is sufficient and speaks of turning closed theatres into "cultural and recreation centers." The Cultural Bureau has been mulling plans to raise production standards of domestic films, assist producers, distributors and exhibitors, etc. but had done nothing tangible except to cut the 40% admission tax to 30% for domestic films.

Producers: Central Motion Picture Corp., Taipei; China Film Studio, Taipei; Taiwan Film Studio, Taipei. All three KMT Party owned; there are 64 independents, including Kuo Lien Film Co.

Distributors (All in Taipei): China Film Enterprises, Columbia Films of China, Far East Film, Italfilm, Hansing Films Ltd., Hua Shing Film Co., Kaidar Pictures, M-G-M of China, Ming Hwa Motion Picture Co., Cinema International Corp., Peace Film Service, Shin Sheng Movie Co., South East Motion Picture Co., Ta Tung Motion Picture Co., Tai Shing Film Co., United Artists of China, Warner Bros. Pictures, Washington Development Co., and Yung Cheong Film Film Co., New Star Film, 20th Century-Fox and Tung Tai Films.

Agencies: Taipei Motion Picture Guild, Taipei Motion Picture Censorship Dept., Taipei.

DENMARK

Number of theatres in Operation: First-run, Copenhagen: 15. Subsequent-run, Copenhagen and surrounding districts: 39. Provinces: 326 (approx. 30% of these are solo situations); 10 mobile cinemas; 2 Drive-in.

Censorship: There is no adult censorship, however films can still be banned for showing to children under the ages of 12 or 16.

Import Duties, etc.: Negatives and positive prints (35 mm and 16 mm) are subject to a 15% added value tax based on the invoiced value of the print/negative. There is also a customs duty of D. Kr.

7.80 (approx. $1.00) per kilogram. This customs duty does not apply for material imported from the EFTA countries.

Industry Organizations: Association of Danish Film Producers, Montergade 22, 1116-Copenhagen-K (telephone PA-2592); Association of Danish Film Directors, Legal advisor: Jorgen Hoffmeyer, Norregade 13, Copenhagen-K (telephone 12-14-32); Danish Film Fund, St. Sondervoldstraede, 1419 Copenhagen K, (telephone AS-6500); Association of Danish Film Distributors, Bredgade 73,1260 Copenhagen K (telephone (01) 14-88-611; Legal Advisor, Advokat E. Toft; (The majority of American distributors have recently joined this association instead of operating separately as members of the MPEA); Cinema Owners' Association, Nygade 3, 1164 Copenhagen K, (telephone 12-34-80); (There are three associations covering Copenhagen and the provinces, however, these are being combined into the above).

Main Independent Distributors: A/S ASA Filmudlejning, Hauchsevej 13, 1825 Copenhagen V (telephone 31-32-30); A/S Constantin Films, Radhuspladsen 16, 1550 Copenhagen V (telephone 12-87-67); Dansk-Svent A/S, Reventlowsgade 28, 1651 Copenhagen V (telephone 31-00-93, or -94); A/S Nordisk Films Kompagni; Bernstorffgade 21, 1577 Copenhagen V (telephone 14-76-06); A/S Palladium Filmudlejning, Vestersohus, Sogade 78, 1601 Copenhagen V (telephone 14-18-18); Panorama Film A/S, H. C. Andersens Blvd. 49, 1553 Copenhagen V (telephone 14-36-20); Regina Film A/S, Frederiksberggade 1a, 1459 Copenhagen K (telephone PA 975); Most of the major American companies have their own offices.

There are three principal studios:

Danish Film Studios: Asavaenget, 2800 Kgs. Lyngby, (87-27-00); Laterna Film Studio: Klampenborgvej 50, Klampenborg, (OR 10,888); Nordisk Films Kompagni: Mosedalvej, Valby, (30-10-33); Risby Studio A/S: Ledojevej 1,2620 Albertslund, (64-96-46);

There are approximately twenty-five feature films produced each year. Costs in Denmark are relatively lower than in most other countries due mostly to the fact that there are no prohibiting union rules and regulations.

All the studios are well equipped with modern equipment and are also used extensively by producers from other countries.

ECUADOR

Number of Theatres in Operation: Approximately 260 35 mm houses and 70 16 mm houses.

Ticket Prices: Box office prices at premiere houses are about $1.35 currently. Only two cities—Quito (capital) and Guayaquil (port city) account for almost 80 per cent of all film revenue.

Censorship: Censorship in the country is divided by provinces. Each province has its own Censorship Board formed by local representatives. In Guayaquil Censorship Board must approve all films before release. Films fall into four classes: "A" excellent, for general audience. "B" rejected for children. "C" pictures to be exhibited separately for women and men; and "D" banned. The companies must ask for censorship within three days in advance. Also pictures released more than six months need to be reviewed. In Quito the Censorship Board is controlled by the Municipality and also must approve all films before release but the same pictures released in Guayaquil are banned in Quito, especially Mexican pictures.

Government Departments: Comisaria de Espectaculos which controls all film business and where all the managers must be registered: chief Enrique Castro Barreiro. Direccion General de Aduanas (Customs House Direction) chief: General Ricardo Astudillo.

EGYPT

Number of Theatres in Operation: About 161. Some 51 belong to the government and the remaining are privately owned.

Production in 1981: About 55 films.

Customs and Other Duties: Black and white imported films must pay 13 Egyptian pounds a Kilo including many taxes, colored films must pay 15 Egyptian pounds a Kilo. And every imported picture must pay 150 E. P. to be released for 3 years. After that period every new copy imported of the same film must pay 75 E.P.

Legislation: Theatres pay about 40 or 45 per cent of their take at the box office. Under an arrangement with the government. Motion Picture Association of America members can withdraw 35 per cent in sterling.

Government Department: Ministry of Culture is under the guidance of Mr. Mansour Hassan, Minister of State. Attached to the Ministry are (1) The Censorship Dept. headed by Mr. Sami Zakzouk (2) The Visual Images Technical Center headed by Mr. Ahmed El Hadary (3) Supreme Council of Culture, attached to this council. a) The National Center of Documentary Films; b) National Center for Experimental Films, directed by Mr. Sadi Abdel Salam. 4) Misr Company for distribution and theatres, headed by Mr. Abbas Ragheb. This company supervises distribution of local films and also runs all governmental theatres. 5) Misr Company for film productions and Studios—headed by Mr. Hassan El Touni (supervise all governmental production and studios.)

Free Film Centers: Catholic Film Center, 9 Adly Street, Cairo. General Secretary Mr. Farid El Mazzawi. Film Society, 18 Youssef El Guindi Street, Cairo, Chairman of board Mr. Ahmed El Hadary. The American Center (Part of the US Embassy) and the British Film Center (part of the British Embassy) also have a film library.

Studios: (These are government controlled): Misr Studios, (five stages) Al Ahram Street, Giza; Al Ahram Studios (four stages) Al Ahram St., Giza; El Nil Studios (one stage) Gamal El Din Afghani Street off the Al Ahram Street); Galal Studio, (two stages) Hadaek El Koba (rented recently to the film director, Yousef Chahine); Sound Center (three labs) headed by Mr. Nasry Abdel Nour.

The Ministry of Culture also controls The Academy of Arts, (attached to the academy is (1) The High Cinema Institute (2) Theatrical Arts Institute (3) Conservatory for Music (4) Ballet and Dance Institute. The Academy is headed by Dr. Rashad Roushdi.

Private Sector Studio: Nassibian Studio, (one stage) Ramses Circus Faggala.

Producers: There are about 85 fully registered producers. They all have the right to produce and distribute their own local productions either alone or in some cases co-producing with others. Cairo Cinema Production Society, 31 Oraby St., Cairo. Halmi Rafla, 87 Ramses Street, Gamal El Leissy, 14 Saray El Ezbakia. Aflam El Ittehad, 45 Kasr El Nil Street, El Cinmayine El Mottahidin, Ramses Street. Misr International Films, 35 Champollion St., Cairo (owned by Youssef Chahine, Director); El Ithad Films, 43 Kasr El Nil St., Cairo, Mr. Abas Helmi; AFLAM Misr Al Gadida, 36 Sherif Street, Cairo; A. Films, 14 El Montazah St., Zamalek, Cairo; Mr. Shadi Abdel Salam, Director; Haiman Films, 16 Adly Street, Cairo; Al Aflam El Motahida, 17 Soliman El Halaby Street, Cairo; Salah Abu Seif Productions, 16 Boursat El Tewfikia Street, Cairo; Soat El Faan Films, 16 Adly Street, Cairo; Aflam Magda, 26 Sherif Street, Cairo; Lotus Films, 26 Sherif Street, Cairo; Aflam El Ashree, 33 Orabi Street, Cairo; Morad Films, 83 Ramses Street, Cairo; Aflam Galal, 82 Ramses Street, Cairo; N.B. Films, 37 Emad El Din Street, Cairo; El Lessey Films, 37 Kasr El Nil St., Cairo; Arab Producers, 1 26 of July Street, Cairo; Aflam Riad El Erian, 16 Hoda Shawarey Street, Cairo; Polla Films, 5 Kamel El Shenawi Street, Garden City, Cairo; El Saudia Cinema Company, 6 El Shawarby St., Cairo; Aflam Mahmoud Yaseen & Co., 17 Soliman El Halaby St., Cairo.

Distributors: Producers listed above are also distributors. Others: Government Dept. for interior and exterior film distribution (controlled by the Cinema Organisation); Columbia Pictures (Near East) Ltd. 25 Orabi St., Cairo; Films Nasr El Hadissa, 17 Doubreh St., Cairo; Lotus Films, 26 Sherif Street, Cairo; Magda Films, 26 Sherif Street, Cairo; Films Masr El Gadida (Abdel Rahman Mohamed) 36 Sherif Street, Cairo; M-G-M of Eypt, 35 Talaat Harb Street, Cairo; Paramount Films of Egypt, 17 Doubreh St., Cairo; 20th Century Fox, 11 Saraya El Ezbekieh Street, Cairo; United Artists Corp. of Egypt, 45 Abdel Khalek Sarwat St., Cairo; Warner Bros., 33 Orabi Street, Cairo; Barakat Films, 36 Sherif Street, Cairo; Ramses Naguib, 83 Ramses Street, Cairo; Cine-Media Productions, Mr. Ahmed Sami, 4 El Ommara Street, Abassia, Cairo (handling foreign productions in Egypt).

Exhibitors: Cinema Miami, Talaat Harb St., (Governmental Cine Organisation); Cinema Radio, Talaat Harb St., (Governmental Cine O^rganisation); Cinema Kasr El Nil, Kasr El Nil St., Cairo (Goverment Cine Organisation); Cinema Metro, Talaat Harb St., Cairo (M-G-M); Cinema Rivoli, 26 July Street, Cairo (Govern. Cinema Organisation); Cinema Diana, El Alfy Street, Cairo (Govern. Cinema Organisation); Cinema Ramses, Ramses Street, Cairo (Govern. Cinema Organisation); Cinema Opera, Opera Sq., Cairo (Govern. Cinema Organisation); Cairo Palace, Saray Ezbekia St., Cairo (20th Century Fox). These are the major cinemas. There are many others which would be listed as "neighborhood" houses.

The following cinemas are in Alexandria: Cinema Rio, Cinema Radio, Cinema Rex, Cinema Ritz, Cinema Star, Cinema Rialto, Cinema Cosmo, Cinema Strand, and all belong to Governmental Cine Organisation.

—AHMED SAMI

FINLAND

Number of theatres in operation: 352 commercial houses at the end of 1980, compared with 336 the year before.

Censorship: All films intended for public showing in Finland are viewed by the State Board of Film Censorship, which a) classifies each film (banned to children under 18 years of age, banned to children under 16, banned to children under 12, banned to children under 8, no age restrictions, approved for public exhibition after specified cuts, banned altogether) and b) decides what class of admission tax, if any, should be imposed.

Customs and Other Duties: imported films are not subject to duty, but an equalization tax amounting to 4.1% of the value of the prints must be paid in addition to the 16.28% turnover (sales) tax. Film advertising material is correspondingly subject to a 2.5% equalization tax, 12.5 customs duty and 16.28 turnover tax.

Admission Taxes: There are three classes of taxes on films. The most usual tax amounts to 10% of the price of admission. Films dealing with sex and violence are subject to a 30% admission tax, whereas children's movies and pictures with a notable educational content are tax-free.

In practice, the film tax is compensated by a 4% payment to the Finnish Film Foundation. The system works out this way: all the motion picture theatres pay the foundation this percentage from their proceeds on tax-free films; and in the case of films in the 30% tax class, 25% goes to the State and 4% to the foundation, the balance being retained by the theatres. As for picture houses seating over 250, or if cinemas are located in a community of over 4,000 inhabitants, they pay in lieu of the 10% admission tax the 4% owing to the foundation, whereas the rest of the cinemas in practice pay hardly any admission taxes on films in the 10% tax class—and these small houses are further exempt from the foundation fee in the case of such films. Since July 1979, the film tours have been released from paying the foundation fee, if the film is in the 10% tax class.

Financial Exchange Regulations: There are no quotas limiting the number of films that can be imported into Finland. The number, content and quality of the films imported are determined in practice by the interest of the film-going public. In 1980 theatres in Finland showed a total of 236 new full-length feature films. These came from 21 different countries of origin, 113.8 films having been made in the United States, 22.3 in England, 21.3 in Italy, 11 in Finland, 10.1 in France, 8.6 in Canada and 8.5 in the Soviet Union.

Suomen Elokuvasäätiö—The Finnish Film Foundation: The Finnish Film Foundation was set up in 1969 by the Ministry of Education and the three central organizations of the motion-picture industry. The Board of the foundation is appointed by the Council of State since the beginning of the year 1977, and so that the Board represent the different social schools of thought in proportion to their parliamentary strength, as divided between non-socialists and socialist political parties. The aim of the foundation is to promote and support, in the main, domestic film production and art, cinema operations and other cultural activities connected with motion pictures. The foundation also seeks to make Finnish films and conditions in the Finnish motion-picture industry known abroad. Starting in 1980, a film catalogue titled Finnish Films/Films Finlandais has been given out annually by the foundations.

Government Departments: Taideteollinen korkeakoulu, Kuvallisen viestinnän laitos, Elokuva-ja tv-linja of Industrial Arts, Faculty of Visual Communication, Film and TV Studies), Ilmalantori 1 D, SF-00240 Helsinki 24. Director: Juha Rosma. Valtion elokuvatarkastamo (State Board of Film Censorship), Jaakonkatu 5 B, SF-00100 Helsinki 10. Chairman: Jerker A. Eriksson. Valtion elokuvataidetoimikunta (State Motion-Picture Art Commission), Mariankatu 14 D 27, SF-00170 Helsinki 17. Chairman: Erkki Seiro.

Organizations: ELOKUVA-JA TELEVISIOKASVATUKSEN KESKUS ry (Centre of Film and TV Education in Finland). Chairman: Riika Tuomari. Yrjönkatu 11 D 10, SF—00120 Helsinki 12. Tel.: +358—0—602 052. MAINOSELOKUVATUOTTAJAIN LIITTO ry (Advertising Film Producers' Association of Finland). Chairman: Matti Mantynen. Kaisaniemenkatu 3 B 29, SF—00100 Helsinki 10. Tel: +358—0—636 305. SUOMEN ELOKUVAARKISTO (Finnish Film Archive). Chairman: Juhani Saarivuo. Director: Olli Alho. P.O. Box 216, SF—00181 Helsinki 18 (Lönnrotinkatu 30 C, SF-00180 Helsinki 18). Tel.: +358—0—643 416. SUOMEN ELOKUVAK-ERHOJEN LIITTO ry (The Federation of Finnish Film Societies). Chairman: Tarja Laine. Yrjönkatu 11 A 5a, SF-00100 Helsinki 12. Tel.: +358—0—648 354. SUOMEN ELOKUVAKONTAKTI ry (The Finnish Film Contact). Chairman Jukka Mannerkorpi. Yrjönkatu 11 E 10, SF-00120 Helsinki 12. Tel.: +358—0—607 380. SUOMEN ELOKUVASÄÄTIÖ The Finnish Film Foundation). Chairman: Jorn Dorner. General Secretary: Kari Uusitalo. Salomonkatu 17 B 6, SF—00100 Helsinki 10. Tel.: +358—0—69 41 255. SUOMEN ELOKUVATEATTERINOMISTAJAIN LIITTO ry (Finnish Cinmea Owners' Association). Chairman: Ilmo Mäkelä. Kaisaniemenkatu 3 B 29, SF-00100 Helsinki 10. Tel.: +358—0—636 305. SUOMEN ELOKUVATIOMISTOJEN LIITTO ry (The Finnish Film Distributors' Association. Chairman: Kurt Dahl. Kaisaniemenkatu 3 B 24, SF—00100 Helsinki 10. Tel: +358—0—630 010. SUOMEN ELOKUVATUOTTAJAT ry (Finnish Film Producers). Chairman: Pekka Lehto. C/o Seiro, Iso Roobertinkatu 3—5 A 25, SF—00120 Helsinki 12. Tel.: +358—0—179 099. SUOMEN ELOKU-VATYÖNTEKIJÄT ry (The Association of Finnish Film Workers). Chairman:— Timo Linnsasalo, Maneesikatu 4 c, SF—00170 Helsinki 17. Tel: +358—0—607 975. SUOMEN FILMIKAMARI ry (Finnish Film Chamber, the central organization). Chairman: Lars Åberg. Managing Director: Leo Nordberg. Kaisaniemenkatu 3 B

29, SF-00100 Helsinki 10. Tel.: +358—0—636 305. SUOMEN FIL-MIVALMISTAJIEN LIITTO ry (The Finnish Film Producers' Association). Chairman: Tuure A. Korhonen. Kaisaniemenkatu 3 B 29, SF—00100 Helsinki 10. Tel.: +358—0—636 305 c/o Walhalla, Mannerheimintie 18 A, SF—00100 Helsinki 10. Tel: +358—0—643 852. THE NORDIC FILM FESTIVAL Chairman: Ari Tolppanen. VALTION AUDIOVISUAALINEN KESKUS (State AV-Centre) Chairman: Kalevi Pihanurmi. Manager: Ms. Aino Toivonen. Hakaniemenk. 2, SF—00530 Helsinki 53. Tel: +358—0—7061.

Principal Producers: ARCTIC-FILMI OY, Siltak. 12 A 5, SF-33100 Tampere 10; ATELJE SEPPO PUTKINEN & KNI, Risukallio, SF-83100 Liperi; OY EPIDEM AB, Kalevank. 34 D 9, SF-00180 Helsinki 18; CINE-ART OY, Höyläämönt. 5, SF-00380 Helsinki 38; CURLY-PRODUKTION, Iso Uusik. 10 B, SF-28000 Pori 10; FEN-NADA-FILMI OY, Kulosaarent, 27, SF-00570 Helsinki 57; FIL-MIAUER Oy, Korkeavuorenk. 2 b G, SF-00140 Helsinki 14; FILMI-JATTA OY, Eerikink. 5, SF-00100 Helsinki 10; FILMINOR OY, Laivastok. 8—10 D 33, SF-00160 Helsinki 16; FILMITUOTANTO SPEDE PASANEN OY, Veneentekijänt. 14, SF-00210 Helsinki 21; FILMITYÖ OY, Luotsik. 3 C 19, SF-00160 Helsinki 16; FINN CO-PRODUCERS OY, c/o Filmi-Jatta Oy, Eerikink. 5, SF-00100 Helsinki 10; JÖRN DONNER PRODUCTIONS OY, Pohjoisranta 12, SF-00170 Helsinki 17; KARI KEKKONEN & PEKKA PAJUVIRTA Jaakkimant. 24 D, SF-02140 Espoo 14; KINOTUOTANTO OY, Katajanokank. 6, SF-00160 Helsinki 16; KÄPY-FILMI OY & NA-TIONAL-FILMI OY, Iso Roobertink. 35—37 G 88, SF-00120 Helsinki 12; LÄHIKUVA OY, Jämeräntaival 11 C, SF-02150 Espoo 15; MARKKU LEHMUSKALLIO, Forselleksent. 5—7 C 23, SF-02700 Kauniainen; PARTANEN & RAUTOMA, Kasarmik. 4 C, SF-00140 Helsinki 14; P-KINO OY, Katajanokank. 6, SF-00160 Helsinki 16; REPPUFILMI OY, Korkeavuorenk. 2 b G, SF-00140 Helsinki 14; RIITTA NELIMARKKA & JAAKKO SEECK, Niittyranta 22, SF-00930 Helsinki 93; SATEENKAARIFILMI OY, Albertink. 27 A 8, SF-00180 Helsinki 18; SUOMI-FILMI OY, Bulevardi 12, SF-00120 Helsinki 12; OY SYDÄNFILMI AB, Vänrikki Stoolink. 9 A 22, SF-00100 Helsinki 10.

Principal Distributors: ADAMS FILMI Oy, Mikonkatu 13, SF-00100 HELSINKI 10; Oy CINEMA INTERNATIONAL CORPO-RATION Ab, P. Esplanadi 33 a, SF-00100 HELSINKI 10; CINE-STUDIO Oy, Mannerheimintie 6, SF-00100 HELSINKI 10; DIANA-FILMI Oy, Kruunuvuorenkatu 5 F, SF-00160 HELSINKI 16; EINI CARLSTEDT, Hakakuja 2 C, SF-02120 ESPOO 12; FILMARI Ky, Ari Tolppanen, Itäranta 11 A 4, SF-02100 ESPOO 10; Oy FOX FILMS Ab, P. Makasiinikatu 7 A 4, SF-00130 HELSINKI 13; KAM-RAS FILM AGENCY, Albertinkatu 36 D, SF-00180 HELSINKI 18; KASETTI-TV Oy, PL 284, SF-00101 HELSINKI 10; KINO-FILMI Oy, Itäinen teatterikuja 5 A 1, SF-00100 HELSINKI 10; O.Y. KINOSTO, Kaisaniemenkatu 2 B, SF-00100 HELSINKI 10; KOSMOS-FILMI Oy, Annankatu 41 G SF-00100 HELSINKI 10; LII-FILMI Oy, Kaisaniemenkatu 1 B, SF-00100 HELSINKI 10; LUNARIS Oy, PL 284, SF-00101 HELSINKI 10; Oy MAGNA-FILMI Ab, Fredrikinkatu 55, SF-00100 HELSINKI 10; Ky MÅRTEN KIHLMAN, Laivurinkatu 33 C 69, SF-00150 HELSINKI 15; RE-PUBLIC-FILMI Oy, Kaisaniemenkatu 1 B, SF-00100 HELSINKI 10; RUUSUJEN AIKA Oy, Yrjönkatu 11 D, SF-00120 HELSINKI 12; SUOMI-FILMI Oy, Bulevardi 12, SF-00120 HELSINKI 12; Oy UNITED ARTISTS FILMS Ab, P. Makasiinikatu 7 A 4, SF-00130 HELSINKI 13; Oy VALIO-FILMI AB, Kasarmikatu 48 B, SF-00130 HELSINKI 13; Oy WARNER-COLUMBIA FILMS Ab, P. Esplanadi 33, SF-00100 HELSINKI 10.

—HELLEVI REINIKAINEN

FRANCE

Number of Theaters in Operation: 4,464.

France produced 189 feature films in 1980 compared with 174 in 1979. The 8.62 per cent rise was credited to increased co-production with television, which resulted in 43 pictures in 1980. Total investment in production was $180,000,000, of which $143,500,000 was French funds, according to the National Cinema Centre.

The number of purely French feature films was 144, compared with 126 in 1979 and 116 in 1978. Investment in these pictures was $112,250,000 in 1980, compared with $96,130,000 in 1979 and $82,000,000 in 1978. (U.S. $1 equals Frs. 4.20)

French films cost an average of $780,000 and co-productions an average of $1,500,000.

Receipts at the box offices in 1980 were up 7.5%, hitting $284,828,000. This rise was aided by a hike in admission prices—a result of a slackening of government control over them.

Total entries for 1980 recorded by the Cinema Center were 173,739,000—1.49% less than in 1979 when attendance dropped 0.5 per cent from 1978.

An exception to this downward trend was recorded by American films which drew over 61,200,000 people—18.36 per cent more than in 1979. U.S. features amassed 35.23 per cent of the total ticket sales and 36.31 per cent of the national box office gross. The American total was $212,730,000.

Ticket sales for French pictures fell off in 1980 to 81,570,000 which was down 7.37 per cent from 1979. Native productions attracted less than 47 per cent of the total audience and grossed $279,400,000, which was only 0.35 per cent higher than the previous year's aggregate income figure.

Industry Organizations: The industry is divided into the following professional organizations: Production A.F.P.F. Ass. Franc. des Producteurs de Films 79 Champs Elysées, Paris 8. Chambre Syndicale des Producteurs et Exportateurs de Films Francais Anatole Daunan) Federation des Producteurs Francais Gerard Oeytoot (Francis Cose); Chambre Syndicale des Producteurs Francais de Films de Court Metrage et video Production (Pres. M. Brunsvig); Chambre Syndicale Francaise de la Presse Filmee (Pres. Marcel Lathiere); Distribution: Chambre Syndicale des Distributeurs de Films d'Art de Repertoire et d'Essai (Pres. Pierre Braunberger); Federation Nationale des Distributeurs de Films (Pres. D. Roscan Du Plantier Lorali) The Federation Nationale des DISTRIBUTEURS DI Films in grouping the three following syndicates: Francais des Distributeurs de Films (Pres. Bernard Harispuru), Syndicat Franco-Americain de la Cinematographic (Pres. R. Schwartz; Exploitation: Federation Nationale des Cinemas Francais (Pres. J. C. Eveline); The Federation Nationale des Cinemas Francais is grouping the three following syndicates; Chambre Syndicale des Theatres Cinematographiques (Pres. Brocard), Syndicat Francais des Directeurs de Theatres Cinematographiques (Pres. M. G. Douvin), Union de la Petite Exploitation Cinematographique et du Syndicat National Substandard (Pres. M. Galandrin); Industries Techniques; Federation Nationale des Industries Techniques (Pres. J. G. Noel); The Federation Nationale du film Cinema et Television des Industries Techniques du Cinema in grouping the four following syndicates: Chambre Syndicale des Constructeurs de Materiel Cinematographique et Industries Annexes (Pres. Roger Mathio), Chambre Syndicale des Laboratoires Cinematographiques⟨Pres. M. Passy), Chambre Syndicale de la Pellicule Vierge Cinematographique (Pres. M. Mery), Chambre Syndicale des Studios Cinematographiques (Pres. M. Dormoy); Material Substandard; Syndicat National des Industries du Cinema Substandard (Pres. M. Burgeot); Syndical Organizations; Syndicat National des Cadres et Syndicat Francais du Cinema, de ia Radio et de la Television F.O. (Pres H. Lesage); Federation Nationale du Spectacle G.G.T. (Pres. R. Jammeve), Syndicat National des Techniciens de la Production Cinematographique et de la Television (Pres. Philippe Lefebvre); Syndicat National des Ingenieurs et Techniciens de la Reproduction Cinematographique (Pres. Marcel Metzler); Syndicat General des Operateurs et Techniciens e l'Exploitation Cinematographique C.G.T. (General secretary Pierre Ehret); Syndicat National des Operateurs Projectionnistes F.O. (General secretary Raoul Rossi); Syndicat "Force Ouvriere" de Personnel de Placement et des Employes des Theatres Cinematographiques (General secretary Rene Tainon). Syndicat de video communication 13 rue Beethoven Paris 16 (J. d'Aroy) 524 43-13.

Principal Producers: Action Films, 97 Avenue Hoche 75008 Paris (256.04.04); Adel Productions, 4 rue Chambiges 75008 Paris (225.20.63); Albina Productions, 39 Rue Marboeur 75008 (256.21.19); Ariane Films, 44 Champs Elysées 75008 Paris (225.05.63); Argos Films, 4 Rue Edouard Mortier 92200 Neuilly (722.91.26); Camera One, 6 Rue Georgaud Paris 17 (754.89.04) Paris (758.12.21); Dimage, 6 rue de Monsigny 75.002 Paris (266.36.89); Daber Films, 1 Rue Lord Byron 75008 Paris (225,93.50); Elysée Films, 37 Rue d'Hauteville 75010 Paris (770.31.47); F.F.C.M., 126 rue de la Bo ëtie 75008 Paris (359.59.65); Filmoblic, 22 rue de Cambacérés 75008 Paris (266.08.87); Films Armorial, 223, Boulevard Péreire 75017 Paris (755.72.72); Films L'Arquebuse, 8 rue du Colonel Moll, 75017 Paris (755.68.16); Films de l'Equinoxe, 18 Galerie Vero Dodart 75001 Paris (231.73.12); Films 2001 Films du Jeudi, 95 Champs Elysées 75008 Paris (723.51.49); Films du Losange, 26 Av. Pierre 1er de Serbie 75016 Paris (720.54.12); Films La Boëtie, 50 Champs Elysées 75008 Paris (225.95.98); Films de la Marquise, 17 rue de l'Arc de Triomphe 75017 Paris (380.06.50); Films 13, 15 Avenue Hoche 75008 Paris (227.00.89); Gaumont, 30 Ave Ch. de Gaulle 92200 Neuilly (758.11.40); Hamster Films, 37 rue Marbeuf 75008 Paris (359.90.90); Iskra, 74 rue Albert 75013 Paris (583.94.63); Kortho Production, 34, rue de Penthievre 75008 Paris (266.11.58); Leitienne (les films Jacques), 52 Champs Elysées 75008 Paris (225.96.54); Marianne Production, 1 rue Meyerbeer 75008 Paris (073.34.30); Number One, 16 Avenue Hoche 75008 Paris (455.25.27); Pierson Productions, 59 Rue des Trois Freres 75008 Paris (076.02.42); Productions Artistes Associés, 25/27 rue d'Astorg 75008 Paris 260.40.36; Productions et Editions Cin ématographiques Francaises (P.E.C.F.), 20 Rue Troyon 75017 Paris (380.70.00); Promocinéma, 78 Rue Denfert Rochereau 92100 Boulogne (604.46.11); Reganne Films, 14 Rue de Chateaula Garenne Colombes, 2.250 (780.71.00); Renn Production, 10 rue Lincoln 75008 Paris (256.25.90); S.N.D. 27 rue Desportes 93400 Saint-Ouen (255.53.00); Stephen Films, 18 rue de la Boëtie 75008 Paris (265.94.51); Trinacra Films, 42 Avenue Ste-Foy 92200 Neuilly

(745.49.50); Walt Disney Production, 52 Champs Elys ées 75008 Paris (359.05.45); Warner Bros., 20 Rue Troyon 75017 Paris (380.70.00).

Principal Distributors: Alpha France, 126 rue de la Boetie 75008 Paris (359.59.65); A.M.L.F. 11 rue Lincoln 75008 Paris (359.82.15); (256.25.90); Argos Films, 4 rue Edouard Nortier 92200 Neuilly Seine (722.91.26); Artistes Associes, 25/27 rue d'Astorg 75008 Paris (266.40.36; Capital Films, 20 rue du Temple 75004 Paris (277.93.62); Cinemas Associes, 52 rue de Ponthieu 75008 Paris (359.94.73); C.I.C., 1 rue Meyerbeer 75009 Paris (073.34.30); Marceau Cocinor, 44 avenue des Champsélysées 75008 Paris (359.64.31); C.C.F.C., 93 avenue des Champs-élysées 75008 Paris (723.71.52); C.F.D.C., 5 avenue Vélesquez 75008 Paris (563.11.11); C.F.F.P., V rue la Boetie 75008 Paris (265.01.69); Dimage, 6 rue de Monsigny 75002 Paris (266.36.89); Films Moliere, 71 rue de Monceau 75008 Paris (522.22.57); Films 13, 15 avenue Hoche 75008 Paris (227.00.89); Films Y.D., 34 Quai de Béthune 75004 Paris (033.79.74); Framo, 11 rue Vernier 75017 Paris (766.19.37); Galba Films, 11 rue St. Augustin 75002 Paris (742.76.50); Gaumont, 30 avenue Charles de Gaulle 92200 Neuilly (758.11.40); Grands Films Classiques, 49 avenue Théophile Gautier 75016 Paris (524.43.24); Hustaix, 29 avenue de Wagram 75008 Paris (380.31.30); Imperia Distribution, 6 rue Lincoln 75008 Paris (359.66.01); Impex Films, 72 avenue des Champs-Elysées 75008 Paris (225.73.71); Leitienne Films, 52 avenue des Champs-Elysées 75008 Paris (225.96.54); Lugio Films, 52 avenue des Champs-Elysées 75008 Paris (225.96.54); Lugio Films, 4 rue Paul Baudry 75008 Paris (359.10.02/256.21.61); MKZ N.E.F. Diffusion, ave d'Océanie-Zone d'activité de Courtaboeuf-91402 Orsay (590.80.31); Olympic, 10 rue Boyer Barret 75014 Paris (783.67.42); Parafrance, 93 avenue des Champs-Elysées 75008 Paris (723.72.81); Planfilm, 30 avenue de Messine 75008 Paris (292.23.39); Pleiade Distribution, 95 avenue des Champs-Elys ées 75008 Paris (225.68.82); Prodis, 3 rue de Téhéran 75008 Paris (924.55.69); Sofradis, 11 rue Lincoln 75008 Paris (256.05.22); U.Z. Diffusion, 25 rue Clisson 75013 Paris (359.75.59); Walt Disney, 52 avenue des Champs-Elys ées 75008 Paris (225.17.66); Warner Columbia, 20 rue Troyon 75017 Paris (380.70.00).

GREECE

Number of Theatres in Operation: The number of indoor theatres in operation is still around 500 while the number of outdoor theatres is 600. Some of the indoor theatres have moveable roofs and operate all year round.

Seating Capacity: Nearly 500,000.

Annual Attendance: There was a slight increase in attendance in 1980 especially in the first run theatres of Athens, but the summer season of 1980 was not as good as in 1979.

Censorship: Every feature, short, trailer as well as their publicity material are subject to censorship. A government censorship board judges all films as to whether they are fit to be shown for minors or general release. The films and trailers fall into three classifications: 1) Suitable for youths under 13, 2) Suitable for youths under 17 and 3) For youths over 17. The minimum age at which children are not allowed to attend movies is set at five. In case a film is banned by the first board its distributor may apply to the second grade board, which may approve or reject the first board's decision. In case of a second rejection only the Minister has the right to grant a release license. Local productions must have their scripts approved by a similar censorship board to get a license. Hardcore porno films are entirely banned and others with explicit sex scenes are suffering severe cuts.

Censorship Fee: Drachmas 600 ($20.00) per feature, 100 per trailer and 100200 per short subject. The fee for an appeal to the second grade committee is drachmas 2,000 ($66.00).

Customs and Other Duties: The calculation of duty is so complicated that it is almost impossible to determine its exact percentage to the print cost. It is approximately 25 per cent on the print cost and royalty not acceding $1,500. In cases where a royalty is not included in the respective invoice an approximate royalty of $1,335. is taken as a base for the calculation of the duty.

Admission Prices: Film Exhibitors and distributors are urging the Government to reconsider its freezing of admission prices as of August, 1978, due to soaring inflation. Present prices are drachmas 50–80 ($1,10–1,81), but it is certain that they will be increased within the year.

Admission Taxes: There was further tax relief in 1979, but the people in the trade are continuing their efforts to effect a further decrease of the tax.

Number of pictures imported: The number of pictures imported during 1980 was between 500 and 550 (exact data not available).

Local Production: There was a revival of local film production not only in the number of films which totalled 30 but in box-office results as well.

Foreign Production: Foreign production and co-production deals are in great demand and the State grants many facilities to lure foreign producers, at this end, the most important of which are: Low interest loans covering all the production cost locally and 25 per cent of all the above-the-line expenses repayable within three years. Also duty free importation of equipment, raw stock, etc.— Free use of the Archeological sites and the Greek Army etc.—The Motion Picture Directorate by the Ministry of Industry assists all foreign producers in obtaining the above facilities.

Financial Exchange Regulations: A foreign exchange permit and the approval of the Currency Committee are necessary. The Committee approves and controls the allocations to foreign producers three times a year.

Industry Organizations: Union of Film Importers and Distributors: President, Savvas Pylarinos; Greek Film Producers Association: President, Michael Lefakis; Greek Film Exhibitors Association: President, Takis Karavias; Union of Film Exhibitors of Northern Greece: President, Basile Papadopoulos; Union of Greek Motion Picture Directors, Union of Motion Picture Technicians, Union of Motion Picture Employees: President, Antony Oztentzos.

Principal Producers: K. Karayannis-A. Karatzopoulos, Greca Films-Michael Lefakis, Klearhis Konitsiotis, Dinos Katsourides, Telecolor Films, James Botsis.

Government Departments: Directorate of the Motion Picture Industry by the Ministry of Industry and Directorate of Audio-Visual Means by the Ministry of Presidency.

Principal Distributors: Th. Damaskinos & V. Michaelides A. E. and Victor Michaeides A.E. distributors of Warner Bros., Emi, Avco Embassy, Arthur Rank, and many European films, head office 96 Academias Str. Athens, Manager Victor Michaelides. Columbia-Fox Hellas, distributing Columbia, Twentieth Century Fox films, Walt Disney and some European films, head office, 2 Kapodistrion Str. Athens, manager Paul Tsitsilianos. C.I.C.-U.A. joined operations releasing films of United Artists, Metro Goldwyn Mayer, Universal and Paramount, manager John Takaziades, head office 4, Gamvetta Str. Athens. K. Karayannis-A. Karatzopoulos distributing Greek and European films, head office 13, Gravias Str. Athens, Spentzos Films, releasing films of EMI, Lorimar, ITC, Carolco, Melvin Simon, Shaw Bros., head office 13, Gravias Str. Athens; manager, George Spentzos; Nicos Papadopoulos, releasing Greek and European films, 31 Themistocleous Street Athens. Acropolis Films releasing several independent films head office 7 Klisovis Str. Athens; Kinimatografili EPE; President George Skouras; Rex Films, 7 Klissovis Str., Manager N. Karpanos; G. Krezias-G. Sarris, 23–25 Themistocleous Str. Athens, and some minor distribution offices.

First Run Theatres: Victor Michaelides Company releases films at Pallas, Orpheus, Opera Aello, Danaos, Nirvana, Pigalle, Petit Palais, Metropolitan, Ellie, Callithia, Odeon, Alma, Trianon, Marguarita.

Columbia-Fox releases at the Attikon, Embassy, and Granada (covering half of their program) and at the Achilleus, Argentina, Ilyssia, Alexandra.

C.I.C.-UA is covering the other half of the program at the Apollon, Embassy, Granada and Astron, Plaza Tropical.

Spentzos Films is releasing films at the Athineon, Attica, Embassy, Granada Angela, ABC, Ideal, Oscar, Rida, Leto.

—RENA VELISSARIOU

HOLLAND

Number of Theatres in Operation: 523, with 155,504 seating capacity. (1 drive in theatre included)

Number of Visitors: 27,934,000, 1980. In 1979 28,403,000, 1978, 30,522,000, 1977 26,285,000, 1976 26,521,000, 1975 28,331,000, 1974 28,100,000.

Gross receipts: 1980 213,000,000 Dutch florins, 1979 200,300,000. (one dollar = Dutch florins 2.70 now). In percentages per country: USA 49.22, Italy 14.61, England 9.32, France 7.82, Holland 7.06, West Germany 5.64, Hong Kong 1.84, other countries 4.49.

Number of Features Imported in 1980: USA 141, France 55, West Germany 27, Italy 26, Hong Kong 21, England 20, Soviet Union 6, Canada 5, Japan 5, Switzerland 5, Denmark 4, Australia 3, Spain 3, Sweden 3, Belgium 2, Greece 1, Thailand 1, Czechoslovakia 1, a total of 329 features. Total number of features released: 336, included 7 Dutch productions.

Feature Production (domestic) 1980: 7, included 1 film for youth. Most successful: Spetters (also released in the United States).

Studios: The main studios are Cinetone at Duivendrecht, Amsterdam, and Cinecentrum, Hilversum. There are 8 film laboratoria and 34 film production companies.

Censorship: Three classes: for those over 12, for those over 16, for all classes. Censorship is moderate. Hard porno pictures and censored for those over 18.

Customs, Fees and Other Duties: No import duties for negatives and positives for pictures made in European Common Market countries. For all other countries hfl. 11.48 for 70 mm prints per 100 meter, hfl. 11.58 per 100 meter for 35mm, all for positive prints. For other countries no duties for negatives.

Admission Taxes: There is no entertainment tax, but a value-added tax of 18%.

Government Department: Ministry of Culture, Recreation and Social Work. (C.R.M.)

Industry Organizations: Nederlandse Bioscoopbond (Federation of distributors, exhibitors, producers, etc.), 2 Jan Luijkenstraat, 1071 CM Amsterdam. President: J. Nijland, Manager J.Th, van Taalingen. President of the distributors department of the trade organization: A.J.J. Duyvesteyn, President of the exhibitors department: J. van Dommelen.

Number of Distributors: 34.

Most Successful Films in 1980: 1. Spetters (Dutch) 2. Kramer vs. Kramer, 3. Caligula, 4. I am with the hippopotamus (italy), 5. "10".

Average Film Rental: 1980, 37%. In 1979, 38.3%.

Current and Future Problems: Piracy and video.

—PHILIP DE SCHAAP

INDIA

Number of Theatres in Operation: 10,830 permanent and touring theatres with an estimated weekly attendance; 70 million. Hindi films are shown in the country through 11 major distribution circuits. English language films are shown in most of the major urban towns. There are over a hundred theatres showing these films all the year round.

Production: India continues to produce the largest number of feature films in the world, with 742 feature films produced in 1980 at its three major centres of film production—Bombay, Madras and Calcutta—in 16 languages.

Export: India earned an estimated Rs. 151 million from the export of feature films during 1980–81 as against Rs. 120 million earned during 1979–80. Indian films are exported to U.K., Singapore, Dubai, Indonesia, Mauritius, Fiji and Kenya, all of which have strong ties with India, besides some countries of Eastern & Western Europe, Africa and Latin America.

Censorship: Films can only be exhibited in India after having been certified by the Central Board of Film Censors. The board has headquarters in Bombay, and regional Offices in Bombay, Madras and Calcutta. All members of the board are appointed by the government.

The Board grants "A" certificates for exhibition restricted to adults above 18 years and "U" certificates for unrestricted exhibition. The board can refuse or ask for modifications before issuing a certificate.

The government of India has prescribed the guidelines to the Central Board of Film Censors and has directed that only such films as satisfy the following conditions are certified for public exhibition:

Anti-social activities such as violence are not glorified or justified; the *modus operandi* of criminals or other visuals or words likely to incite the commission of any offence are not depicted; pointless or avoidable scenes of violence, cruelty and horror are not shown; human sensibilities are not offended by vulgarity; obscenity and depravity; visuals or words contemptuous or racial, religious or other groups are not presented; the sovereignity and integrity of India is not called in question, the security of the State is not jeopardised or endangered; friendly relations with foreign states are not strained; public order is not endangered and visuals or words involving defamation or contempt of court are not presented.

It is learnt that the Information & Broadcasting Ministry is considering amending the Cinematograph Act in an effort to grant autonomy to the Film Censor Board as the final authority to decide on all matters relating to the grant of certificate of exhibition to films.

Principal Importers: The two most important importers of foreign films are the Government controlled Film Finance Corporation, which is the canalising agency for importing feature films and the Motion Picture Export Association of America. Principal distributors of American films are: Allied Arts of India Inc., Metro House, M. G. Road, Bombay 400020; Columbia Films of India Ltd., Metro House, M. G. Road, Bombay 400020; Metro-Goldwyn-Mayer India Ltd., Metro House, M. G. Road, Bombay 400020; Paramount Films of India Ltd., Hague Building, Sprott Road, Bombay 400202; 20th Century Fox Corporation (India) Pvt. Ltd., Metro House, M. G. Road, Bombay 400020; United Artists Corporation, Metro House, M. G. Road, Bombay 4000020; Universal Pictures India Pvt. Ltd., Hague Building, Sprott Road, Bombay 4000020; Warner Bros (F.D.) Inc., Eros Theatre Building, 42 M. Karve Road, Churchgate, Bombay 400020. Besides, the Russian Sovexportfilm released 52 feature films in India last year.

Principal Exporters: (Name & Address followed by Cablegram) Asian Film Corporation, Alankar Cinema Building, Room No. 9, 4th floor, S.V.P. Road, Bombay 400004 (GODSON); A. G. Enterprise, Lotia Palace, 373, Linding Road, Khar, Bombay 400052 (AGFILCO); AASIA Films, 315-G, New Charni Road, Bombay 400004 (HANDRILL); Bombay United Traders, 25/26, Kailash Darshan, Kennedy Bridge, Bombay 400007 (GOLDCOINS); Bajaj Bros. (Pvt.) Ltd., Round Building, 3rd floor, Kalbadevi, Bombay 400002 (PRITPAL); C.A. Corporation, Hanuman Building, 3rd floor, Picket Road, Bombay 400002 (CHANDUFILM); Chhabria Enterprises, 301, Grand Canyon, 87 Pali Hill, Bandra, Bombay 400050 (TRESSA); Chandra Brothers, Owners Court, A, Road, Churchgate, Bombay (CEE CHANDRA); Damubhai M. Thakker, Alankar Cinema Building, Sardar V.P. Road, Bombay 400004 (SURYATEJ); Delhi Iron & Steel Co. P. Ltd., Warden House, 1st floor, Sir P.M. Road, Fort, Bombay 400001 (WORKERS); Ellora Films, 4-E, Naaz Building, Lamington Road, Bombay 400004 (SHOWARTS); International Film Distributors, 5, Feltham House, 2nd floor, 10, Graham Road, Ballard Estate, Bombay 400038 (SAVANIBROS); Krishna Films, 5-A Naaz Cinama Building, Lamington Road, Bombay 400004 (KIFILS); Kishore Film Distributors, 5/41, Tardeo Air Conditioned Market, Tardeo Road, Bombay 400004 (KISORJAY); Mini Movies, Hanuman Building, 3rd floor, Picket Road, Bombay 400002; Rajshri Productions (P) Ltd., Bhavana, 422, Veer Savarkar Road, Prabhadevi, Bombay 400004 (RAVIPIC); Sippy Films P. Ltd., 3-G,. Naaz Building, Lamington Road, Bombay 400004 (ARCADIA) Tiger Films Pvt. Ltd., 213/15, Jolly Bhavan 1, 10, New Marine Lines, Bombay 400020 (ENGIBROS); Trimurti Films Pvt. Ltd., 8–11, Commerce Centre, Tardeo Road, Bombay 400034 (DEEWAAR)

Trade Associations: Film Federation of India, 91 Walkeshwar Road, Bombay 400006; Indian Motion Picture Producers' Association, Cutch Castle, S.V.P. Road, Bombay 400004; Eastern India Motion Picture Association; 98-E Chowranghee Square, Calcutta 0013; South India's Film Chamber of Commerce 122 Mount Road, Madras 600002; All India Film Producers Council, Shantshree, Rajkamal Kala Mandir, Parel, Bombay 400012; The Indian Motion Picture Distributors' Association, 33 Vijay Chambers, Tribhuvan Road, Bombay 400004; Federation of Film Societies of India, C-7 Bharat Bhavan, 3 Chittaranjan Avenue, Calcutta 0072; Indian Film Exporters Association, c/o. 4-E Naaz Building, Dr B. Bhadmamkar Marg, Bombay 400004; Indian Documentary Producers' Association, National House, Tulloch Road, Bombay 400039; Kinematograph Renter's Society Pvt. Ltd., Haroon House, Perin Nariman Street, Bombay 400001; Cinematograph Exhibitors' Association of India, Flat No 22/23 B1st floor "Vellard View", Tardeo Road, Bombay 400034.

—B. D. GARGA

INDONESIA

Number of Theatres: 422.
Number of Features produced: 74.
Number of Features imported: 520.
Annual Admissions: 24.3 million.
Distribution Gross: $10,000,000.

American films are making a comeback after a boycott by the former government-in-power which allowed the import of features only from Communist or so-called neutral countries. However, a shortage of foreign exchange limits quality and quantity and most American films shown are not of recent vintage.

All film imports must be effected by Indonesian nationals recognized by the Government and new cinemas can be established jointly by private and regional government funds. To accelerate and control film distribution cooperation among producers, importers and cinemas are "regulated" by the government. The Indonesian Government is subsidizing and controlling film production. Plans call for an increase in features produced locally each year. Other plans call for the building of cinemas in populated areas to bring them up to one theatre for every 50,000 people.

Basic entertainment tax is around 50% with government pressure keeping admission prices to low levels. Studios are Gema Masa Film, Indonesian Film Corp., Penas Film Studio, Olympiad Film, all in Jakarta.

ISRAEL

Number of Theatres Operating: 227
Seating Capacity: approximately 157,000.
In addition to above data there are about 600 localities for releases of 16mm prints, mostly Kibutzim and smaller settlements.

Production: Average number of films produced locally each year is 16, in addition to co-productions and foreign productions handled by some 50 local producers.

Ticket Sales: In 1980 theatre attendance showed an overall drop of 23 per cent. Sales of tickets for domestically produced films fell more than 31 per cent, from 31,000,000 tickets in 1979 to 2,100,000 in 1980.

Production Companies: April Films Ltd., 237 Dizengoff St., Tel Aviv; Golan-Globus Productions Ltd., 32 Allenby St., Tel Aviv; Golan, Moshe, 24 Haneslim St., Petach-Tikva; Idan Film & TV Productions Ltd., 6 Shamgar St., Jerusalem; Israfilm Motion Pictures, Production Services Ltd., 61 Pinsker St., Tel Aviv; Jerusalem Capital Studios Ltd., Binyanei Hauma, Jerusalem; J.C.C. Jerusalem, Communication Centre, 4 Shamgar St., Jerusalem; Kastel Enterprises Ltd., 18 Hashmonaim St., Jerusalem; Omri Maron—Filron Ltd., 2 Tamar St., Neve Monoson, Tel Aviv; RazFilms Ltd., 11 Frug St., Tel Aviv; Rimon Communications Ltd., 24 Harav Berlin St., Jerusalem; Roll Film Productions, Ltd., 43 Shimon Hatarsi St., Tel Aviv; Tel-Ad Jerusalem Studios Ltd., Jerusalem Theatre Bldg., Jerusalem; Thirtieth Century Film, 125 Arlozorov St., Tel Aviv; United Studios of Israel Hakessem St., Herzilya; Rony Yacov, 20 Neve Raim St., Neve Magen, Ramat, Hasharon.

ITALY

Number of Theatres in Operation: Approximately 11,000, some 3,800 of which are commercial year-round houses while 3,600 are church-owned and parochial theatres. The rest operate less than 21 days per month, among them outdoor theatres which are open only during the summer.

Attendance: From 454,000,000 admissions in 1976, attendance dropped to 374,000,000 the following year, then to 318,000,000 in 1978 and under 300,000,000 for 1979. The 1980 figure was 280,000,000.

Box Office Receipts: Dropped from 213-billion, 505,000,000 lire (roughly $250,000,000 at a three-year average of 800 lire equals $1) in 1976 to 178-billion, 305,000,000 lire in 1977 and 149-billion in 1978. This is a three-year loss of approximately $75,000,000.

Film Production: Number of Italian films, including co-productions with other countries, totalled 163 in 1980, of which 130 were all-Italian. This compares with 141 and 115 respectively, in 1979 and 123 and 98 in 1978.

Imported pictures: Box office revenue for foreign films increased to 197 billion lire in 1978 from 161 billion 313,000,000 lire in 1976. U.S. share was 43% in 1978–79, compared to 36% for Italian product.

Studios: Italy has more than 70 sound stages operated by 16 companies, 15 private and one State-operated. The leading studios are: Dear Film TV Center (5 stages); Centro Sperimentale (3 stages); Cinecitta (14 stages); De Paolis (9 stages); Istituto Nazionale Luce (2 stages); Titanus Appia (6 stages); ATC Grottaferrata (2 stages); Elios (2 stages); Vides (2 stages).

The above listed studios are located in Rome. Cosmopolitan (4 stages) in Tirrenia. ICET-De Paolis (4 stages in Milan. Fert (3 stages) in Turin. Bertolazzi (2 stages) in Peschiera on Lake Garda. There are other numerous studios of minor importance for the production of documentaries and advertising material.

JAPAN

Number of Theatres in Operation 2,364.
Number of Domestic Features released: 320.
Number of Features Imported: 209.
Annual attendance: 165,918,000.
Box Office Admissions: $730 million.
Distributor Revenues: $282.2 million.
Japanese Export Earnings: $6.8 million.
Admission Tax: From April 1975 tickets under $7.50 are tax-free, 10% over that figure.

Censorship: Japan's voluntary censorship board, EIREN, consisting of local and foreign distributors, reviews both imported and domestic films in a liberal and enlightened manner, and very rarely bars a film though it may suggest slight cuts.

Import Rules: Japan became a free market for film imports from abroad in 1964 and there were fears that a glut of imports would have an adverse effect on the already ailing local industry. Rather than face legislation imposing a quota of film imports or a law controlling showings of imported films, the industry decided to voluntarily adhere to a suggested screen quota system which includes stipulations that all movie theatres devote a certain number of days

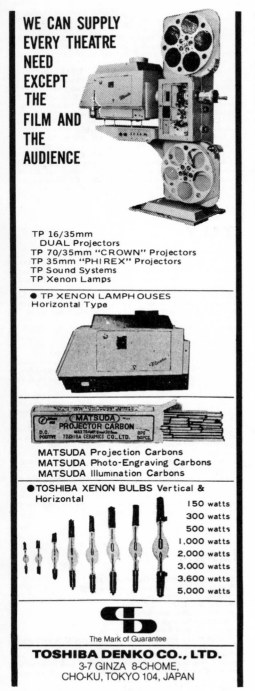
each year to the screening of domestic features. This system resembles similar ones already in force in France, Britain, Italy, Brazil and certain other countries. In Japan's case it was decided that certain theatres devoted to showing only imported films would devote 40 days a year to showing domestic films of high quality.

Trends: Unofficial figures on "film rentals" gave last year's total as $282.2 million, with imported films registering $127.1 million and domestic films $155.1 million, shares of about 45% and 55% respectively. Toho-Towa led distributors of imports with $25.7 million, followed by Nippon Herald $24.4 million aided by the hits "Apocalypse Now," "Caligula," and "Miracle Worker." Columbia with "Kramer vs. Kramer," "1941" and "Blue Lagoon" racked up $19.1 million, while 20th-Century Fox chalked up $15.1 million of which most was contributed by the block-buster of the year "The Empire Strikes Back."

In the domestic film field Toho took in $58.6 million of which some $12 million came from their "Shadow General" and $10.6 million came from distributing the independent Kadokawa production "Virus," two box office champions. Shochiku film rentals were $24.4 million, Toei $32.2 million and Nikkatsu $15.1 million, with the rest going to independents.

Of the 2,364 theatres in operation (down 10 from last year), 1,085 showed domestic films, 701 imports and 578 mixed bills. Domestic feature films released dropped from 355 to 320 of which 119 were produced by the Big Four studios and 201 by independent producers (which used Big Four distribution networks). Imported features were up from 196 to 209 of which 141 came from U.S.A., followed by France, Italy, etc. Theatre box offices admission rose by over 200,000 people and by $10 million for the year. Receipts from film rentals were up 5.9% for domestic pictures and down .4% for imports, compared with the previous year.

Regular admission price to a first run film in Tokyo is $6.65 or $9.75 for a reserved seat, with road shows running slightly higher, and the national average is estimated at about $4.95 for a first-run seat, usually in a somewhat run-down not-too-clean theatre without even paper towels in the lavatories. There is no restraint on admissions, so popular shows have standees in the aisles and blocking emergency exits. Second-run admissions run about $2.25 and the national admission average is between $4.60 and $5.10.

The Big Four Studios, while restricting the showing of their movies on TV, cooperate with television studios in the production of many shows since they can do it cheaper and usually better due to lower wages (different unions) and better-equipped studios. In addition, various TV studios import large number of motion pictures from overseas which are dubbed into Japanese and broadcast.

To improve the quality of Japanese films, the Ministry of Education offers up to 15 annual grants totalling some $500,000 to the producers of finished films which are picked for their high quality. However, this does not help solve financing problems and since banks and large corporations are loathe to loan funds for making films, the role of the independents is hard. Kadokawa Productions, backed by a publishing empire with ample funds, has thus become the chief independent producer and, though its pictures meant to please the public rather than to win praise from critics or prizes, they mount the most fervent advertising campaigns by TV, radio and printed word and attract film-goers.

In 1958 with some 7,500 theatres in operation, attendance was 1.127 billion but by 1972 only half this number of theatres were operating and attendance was down to 187.39 million, a decrease of over 83%, followed by more decreases until annual attendance levelled off between 165 million and 170 million.

Import Duty: Exposed 70 mm is 18¢ per meter, 35 mm is 5.3¢ per meter, and 16 mm is 4.4¢ per meter. There is no restriction on imports of foreign films unless they are judged inimical to public morals. Though there is no official censor, a non-official organ of the movie industry, may suggest removal of scenes or "masking" of certain physical features after review by the Motion Picture Code of Ethics Administration Commission (EIREN).

Principal Theatre Circuits: Toho, Shochiku, Nikkatsu, Toei, Tokyo Recreation Co., Subaru Kogyo, Tokyo Teatro, Tokyo Rakutenchi, Musashino Eiga Gekijo, Kinki Eiga Gekijo, and O-S Company (Osaka).

Principal Producing Companies: Shochiku Co., Toho Co., Tokyo Eiga, Sho Taguchi, Toei Motion Picture Co., Nihon Eiga Shinsha Ltd., International Motion Picture Co., Dentsu Motion Picture Co., Nikkatsu Co., Shin Riken Motion Picture Co., Yomiuri Motion Picture Co., Educational Film Co., Iwanami Productions, Miki Motion Pictures, Mitsui Geijutsu Productions, Premier Motion Picture Co., Kadokawa Productions, Sanrio Productions, Nippon Animation, Gendei, Eiken.

Principal Industry Organizations: Association for Diffusion of Japanese Films Abroad (UniJapan Film), Nakamura Bldg., 5-9-13, Ginza, Tokyo; Motion Picture Producers Association of Japan, Sankei Kaikan, 1-7-2 Ote-machi, Tokyo, Federation of Japanese Film Industry, Sankei Kaikan, 1-7-2 Otemachi, Tokyo; Foreign Film Importers-Distributors Association, Mori Bldg., 7-5-4 Ginza, Chuo-Ku, Tokyo, Educational Films Producers Association of Japan. Eikyo Kaikan, 26 Shiba Nishikubo Sakurogawa-Cho, Minato-Ku, Tokyo, Motion

Picture Engineering Society of Japan, Sankei Kaikan Building, Tokyo; Union of Motion Picture Exhibitors Associations of Japan, 3-19-18 Higashi Ginza, Tokyo; Photo-Sensitized Materials Manufacturers Association, Kyodo Bldg., 2-2 Kanda Nishiki-cho Chiyoda-Ku, Tokyo; Japan Motion Picture Equipment Industrial Association, 3-5-8 Shiba Koen, Tokyo; Screen Writers Association, 12 Azabu Kasumicho, Tokyo; Commission of Motion Picture Code of Ethics, 3-4 Ginza Higashi, Tokyo; Nippon Screen Directors Association, Tsukada Building, 1-2 Sakaedori, Shibuya, Tokyo; Japan Audio-Visual Education Association, 1-17-1 Toranomon, Minato-Ku, Tokyo 105.

Principal Distribution Companies: Nikkatsu, Shochiku, Toei, Toho, Tokyo-First Films, Towa, Avco Embassy Pictures, Cinerama, Columbia, M-G-M, Cinema International Corporation, 20th Century Fox, United Artists, Warner Bros. Pictures, Walt Disney Productions (Japan) Ltd., Sovexportfilm, Nippon Herald, Shochiku-Eihai, Dainichi-Eihai, New Cinema Corp. and Toho International.

Exporters of Theatre Supplies: Toshiba Denko Co., Ltd., 10, 8-chome Nishi Ginza, Tokyo; Sansha Electric Manufacturing Co., Ltd., 7-5 Uchikanda 1-chome, Chiyoda-ku, Tokyo, or 14-3, 2-chome, Awaji, Higashi Yodogawa-ku, Osaka.

—A. C. PINDER

MEXICO

Number of Theatres in Operation: about 2,200 for 35mm pictures, about 1,000 for 16mm; and about 30 70mm.

Production: Close to 100 features were completed in Mexico in 1980, the majority of which were made by private producers without government aid. These films receive wide distribution in the Spanish-speaking market in the U.S. Pelimex, the offshore sales arm of the government, reported that film sales in 1980 were excellent, not only in the U.S., but in Central America, Colombia and Venezuela. It is estimated that the U.S. market represents 60 per cent of Pelimex's foreign sales. Billings are reported at $11,000,000 for 1980 in the U.S., of which some 65–70 per cent came from California. Pelimex released 60 features last year through its U.S. subsidiary, Aztec Films.

Admissions and Grosses: Admissions throughout Mexico were down in 1979 to a total of 222,000,000, according to estimates made by the Department of Information and Statistics of the Camara Nacional de la Industria Cinematografica. In 1978 totals were 228,000,000 compared to 236,000,000 in 1977; 265,000,000 in 1976 and 257,000,000 tickets sold in 1975. Countrywide grosses for 1979 were estimated at $179,000,000 compared to $135,000,000 the previous year. The U.S. topped the countries supplying films with 154 premieres, followed by 79 from Italy, 78 from Mexico, 23 from England, 18 from Spain and 16 from France.

Motion picture production and exhibition and broadcast facilities are under the jurisdiction of the Dirección General de Radio, Television & Cine. General head of this Direction is Srita. Margarita Lopez Portillo. Director General of the Dirección de Cinematografia (General Cinema Office) is Lic. Jose Maria Sbert. Government contact with the film industry is centralized through this office, which not only issues permits for exhibition, but also permits which must be obtained for all productions, whether intended for domestic exhibition or export. Moya Palencia has established a policy of offering all possible facilities for foreign producers. Scripts for productions must be approved before a shooting permit is issued. The National Cinema Bank is part of the Office, finances productions and encourages coproduction with other countries. It is headed by Lic. Hiram Garcia Borja.

Censorship: Commercial exhibition authorization is for all Mexico; supervision is guaranteed within three working days after supervision application is filed and all pictures, unless with special permission, must be offered for examination. The censor must render his ruling within 24 hours after examining a picture and if approved the Chief Censor must immediately advise the owner. All pictures produced in Mexico must obtain an export permit if intended to be shipped abroad for commercial purposes. Head of the Supervision Department is Lic. Fernando Macotela.

Customs Duties: $4.40 per 2/14 lbs., plus 20% ad valorem.

Censorship Fees: $200.00 Mx. Cy. per reel (US $8.80-at the actual rate of $22.70 per 1.00 US Dlr.).

Admission Taxes: Range from 15 to 30 per cent, varying in different communities.

Industry Organizations: The federal government owns and operates the Cia. Operadora de Teatros and the Cadena de Oro, controlling approximately 330 of the best movie houses in the country and possibly 100 more through a system of "affiliation." The two strongest independent chains are the Longoria group in the North (about 40 houses) and the Mortez circuit in the Central states (about 40 houses). President, and manager, is Juan Pellicer; Exhibidores Metropolitanos, S.A.; Impulsora de Cines Independientes, S.A. de

C.V.; Asociacion de Productores de Peliculas Mexicanas, Fernando de Fuentes, Pres.; Federacion Nacional de la Industria Cinematografica; Sindicato de Autores y Adaptores Cinematograficos; Sindicato de Trabajadores de la Industria Cinematografica. Rodolfo Landa, General Secretary; Sindicato Nacional de Directores Cinematograficos; Camara Nacional de la Industria Cinematografica, Lic. Cesar Santos Galindo, Pres.: Distribuidora de Peliculas Nacionales; Calderon Films, S. de R.L.; Cinematografica Mexicana Exportadora, S. de R.L. de I.P. y C.V.; Distribuidora Central de 16mm; Distribuidora Independiente, S.A.; Pereda Films, Ramon Pereda, Pres.: Posa Films, S.A., Santiago Reachi, Pres.; Producciones Raul de Anda; Producciones Sotomayor, S.A.; Productores Unidos, S.A.; Producciones Zacarias, S.A.; Peliculas Internacionales, S.A.; Noticiarios y Documentales, S.A.; Filmadora Mexicana, S.A.; Exportadora de Peliculas, S.A.

U.S. Firms with Distributors in Mexico: Cinema International Corporation (Distributors for: M.G.M., Paramount and Universal); Warner Brothers; Columbia; 20th Century Fox, United Artists (through 20th Century-Fox).

Independent Distributors: Tele Films International. SA., Arte-Cinema de México. SA; Cinematografia Anahuac. SA; Distribuidora Rivero. SA; Organización Apolo. SA; Cine Producciones Tauro. SA; Ulyses Films. SA; Poli Films Mundiales. SA; Films Scorpio. SA; Cinematografica Independiente de Peliculas, SA; Distribuidora Rozil. SA.

Theatre circuits: Major film exhibition circuits in Mexico are (1) the government-owned Compania Operadora de Teatros, with 408 locations, totalling 675,000 seats with an average admission price of 78¢; (2) Organizacion Ramirez, 83 cinemas totalling 46,000 seats charging $1.21 for the average ticket; (3) Circuito Montes, 55 theatres, 84,000 seats, 73¢ admissions; (4) Circuito Colonial, 52 situations, 15,000 seats, 24¢ per ticket; (5) Cine Club de Arte, 35 situations, 20,000 seats, $1.21 average ticket.

MONGOLIA

This tiny Communist country in Asia at last reports boasts 59 theatres and 410 touring film projection teams. An average of about 10 feature pictures a year are produced in addition to newsreels. Most imported films are from Communist countries. First reported sale of an American feature was in 1968 when Mongol Film Procot purchased UI's "Spartacus," a 1960 release starring Kirk Douglas.

NEW ZEALAND

Number of Theatres in Operation: 177.

Number of Features Imported: 298 (35mm), 214 (16mm).

Origin of Feature Films: (35mm first, 16mm second); Australia 9, 7; Austria 1, 0; Belgium 2, 0; Burma 0, 1; Canada 5, 5; China 3, 1; Cuba 1, 0; Czeck 0, 1; Denmark 3, 0; France 23, 34; E. Germany 1, 0; Greece 7, 0; W. Germany 8, 21; Hong Kong 17, 0; Hungary 2, 0; Indonesia 1, 0; Iran 1, 0; Israel 1, 0; Italy 16, 4; Japan 7, 6; Mexico 1, 0; Netherlands 1, 2; New Zealand 2, 5; Norway 1, 0; Philippines 1, 0; Poland 3, 2; South Africa 1, 1; Spain 1, 1; Sweden 1, 0; United Kingdom 40, 25; United States 127, 93; U.S.S.R. 7, 0; Yugoslavia 1, 0.

Censorship: All films must be submitted to the Censor for examination. The number of 35 mm feature films approved for general exhibition (35mm first 16mm second) 152, 139; of this 47, 41; were "G" certificate (general certificate without qualification) 37, 37; "GY" certificate (recommended for persons aged 13 or over); 68, 61; "GA" certificate (recommended as more suitable for adults); The number of 35mm feature films carrying restrictions are (35mm first 16mm second) 137, 73; Restricted to 13 years and above, 10, 5; Restricted to 16 years and above 67, 40; Restricted to 18 years and above 46, 25; Restricted to 20 years and above 4, 0; restricted for use in Film Societies 10, 3. The balance of films were those rejected by the censor.

Film Censorship Board of Review: On four occasions the applicant's "right of review" was exercised for "The Fruit Is Ripe" (which had the previous cuts replaced) with "The Magic Garden of Stanley Sweetheart" the original censor's decision to ban it was upheld. "I'm not Feeling Myself Tonight": censor's decision to ban was upheld. "Mad Max": censor's decision to ban was upheld.

Administration: The Department of Internal Affairs, Private Bag, Wellington, administers the Cinematograph Films Act 1976. The Films Licensing Authority deals with exhibitor and distributor licences. The Film Censorship Board of Review, on request from distributors who are dissatisfied with the censor's decision, re-examines films without regard to the previous decision, to determine whether they are injurious to the public good. The Film Trade Board is a statutory body comprising exhibitor and distributor interests under an independent chairman. It was established to maintain high standards of film exhibition to the public and to act as a forum for the film industry. It also makes recommendations to the Minister of Internal Affairs on industry matters, initiates and supervises the development of training schemes for employees of the industry. A committee of the Board deals with disputes that arise within the film industry.

Industry Organisations: N.Z. Motion Picture Exhibitor's Association Inc., Secretary: A. B. Cunningham, P.O. Box 363, Wellington. Motion Picture Distributors of N.Z.; Secretary: A. J. Crisp, 1 Tui Glen Road, Birkenhead, Auckland 10. The Northern Motion Picture Projectionists Union; Secretary: D. A. Lee, P.O. Box 6575, Wellesley Street, Auckland. The N.Z. Federated Motion Picture Projectionists Industrial Association of Workers; Secretary: Sir Leonard Hadley, P.O. Box 6093, Wellington. N.Z. Federation of Film Soc. Inc. Bill Gosden, Secretary; Programme Director, Box 9544, Wellington.

General: The Cinematograph Films Act 1976, which came into effect on 1 April, 1977, consolidates and amends the 1961 Act and reflects changing attitudes in the field of censorship. The N.Z. Film Commission was established by the Government in October 1977 to advise on the establishment of a permanent agency and on policies which will lead to the development of a sound motion picture production industry. The full Commission was established in the second half of 1978, and will receive $6,000,000 per year for 3 years from lottery profits. Five films currently in production have already been given support by the Commission, 20 films have received support for script development. The Government is currently considering delicensing both exhibitors and distributors with a view to allowing a more open market situation. This move will be preceded by a tribunal who will be charged with taking submissions from all interested parties and reporting to the Government.

Statutory Organisations: The Film Trade Board, P.O. Box 12-339, Wellington. Films Licensing Authority, P.O. Box 12065, Wellington. The Films Censorship Board of Review, P.O. Box 12065, Wellington, N.Z. Film Commission, Box 11-546 Wellington. All these departments come under the auspices of the Internal Affairs, Private Bag, Wellington.

—MARK R. GALLOWAY

NORWAY

Number of Theatres in Operation: 452 equipped for 35mm, of which there are 223 municipal cinemas and 229 other. Total number of seats is 140,000.

Industry Trends: The number of cinemas in Norway has remained quite stable over the past few years. Half of the theatres, which account for 82% of the box office, are owned or operated by municipalities. Up to 75% of these cinemas are running at a deficit because of heavy expenses—especially in wages and freight. They can continue in business because the cities make up the losses. Municipalities are willing to keep financially lagging theatres going because film is regarded as an important part of the culture, along with theatre, opera, TV, etc. Cinema managers in return are expected to draw up a diversified program consisting of films for children and for those interested in film as an art, along with those for the large audience seeking popular entertainment.

One reason for the relatively high attendance at theatres is the restriction placed on feature films shown over the only Norwegian TV channel (state-owned and non-commercial). Only about 65 feature films are shown on TV each year. Some 26% of the population of Norway can also tune in the two Swedish channels as well.

Censorship: All films must be approved by the Statens Filmkontroll (Government Censorship Board). Six kinds of certificates are issued: Yellow: for adults (over 16); Green: for all audiences over 12 years; Red: for all audiences over 7 years; White: banned; red: with special age limit for all audiences over 5 years; yellow: special certificates for adults above 18 years. In 1976 some 263 features were approved by the board as follows: American, 105; British, 37; French 29; Italian, 18; Swedish 13; Norwegian, 12; Russian, 10; Other, 39.

Censorship Fee: For features, shorts and trailers, kr. 41-per 100 meters of film. For second and further prints of all subjects: Fee reduced by one half, provided they are submitted within half a year.

Custom fees: Films originating from EFTA countries furnished with EFTA stamped invoices are duty free; other countries: kr. 8.00 per kilogram.

Government Departments: Klingenberggaten 5, Oslo. Statens Filmkontroll (Government Censorship Board), Klingenberggaten 5, Oslo; Mrs. Karen Boe Skaug 1st Censor. Statens Filmsentral (The Government Film Rental Office, Documentary and Educational Films Only), Schwensensgate 6, Oslo; Editor Magnus Sandberg, chairman. Statens Filmtekniske Nemnd (Government Film Technical Board), Klingenberggaten 5, Oslo; Paul Dag Poppe, President, Statens Film-produksjonsutvalg (The Government Film Production Board), KU-dep., Oslo dep., Jon Stenklev, chairman. Statens Skolefilmnemnd (Government School & Educational Film Center), Schwenzengate. 6, Oslo; Kjell Wiik, chairman. Norsk Barnefilmnemnd (Norwegian Children's-Film Board), Ministry of Church and Education, KU-dep., Oslo dep. Elsa Brita Marcussen, Chairman; Norsk Filmrad (Norwegian Film Council), Tor Erling Staff, chairman; Statens Velferdskontor for Handelsflaten (Norwegian States Welfare Office for Merchant Marines), Gunnar Sand, chairman.

Principal Industry Organizations: Kommunale Kinematografers Landsforbund (Municipal Cinemas National Association), Nedre Voll Gate 9, Oslo 1, Gunnar Germeten, President. Norske Filmbyraers Sammenslutning (Norwegian Filmrenters Association), Stortingsgt, 12, Oslo 1; Frie Norske Filmutleiebyraers Forening, Stortingsgt. 30, Oslo 1; Stein Saelen, President. Norske Kinoleverandorers Landsforbund Bankplassen la, Oslo 1, (Norwegian Cinema Suppliers Association) Dronningensgt. 22, Oslo 1; Leif Wigaard, President. Norske Filmkomponistforening (Norwegian Film-composers Association). Klingenberggaten 5, Oslo 1; J. Kramer-Johansen. President, Norske Filmprodusenters Forening (Norwegian Filmproducers Association), Drammensvlien 30, Oslo 2; Oyvind Vennerod, President. Norke Kinosjefers Forbund (Norwegian Cinema Managers Society; Tor Klovstad, President, Norsk Filmforbund (Norwegian Film Society—technical), Postboks 2725, St. Haunshaugen, Oslo, Olav Solum, President; Norsk Filminstitutt (Norwegian Film Institute—Members of Federation Internationale des Archives du Film), Aslakveien 14B, Oslo 7, Oyvin Semmingsen, chairman.

PAKISTAN

Number of Theatres in Operation: 692, including 15 equipped with Todd/AO and touring talkies. (Population of country is about 83.7 millions). Attendence is at 47.7 million and receipts after taxes are approximately 149 million rupees. Pakistan's biggest city, Karachi (population over 7 million) has 86 cinemas, including three drive-ins with a capacity of 500, 700 and 1000 cars, about 400 chairs and a playground attached to the cafeteria (canteen). Besides admission tickets, these cinemas charge Rs. 2/-per car.

Attendance: An average of 5.3 per cent people in village visit cinemas, while in cities/towns 31.4 per cent go to movies. 52.6 per cent of those who attend movies once a week are in the age group of 11 to 29 and 33% are between 30 to 50 years of age. About 60% in cities and hardly 7% in villages visit cinemas once a month or less.

Plans investment: The capital investment was estimated at the end of 1980 as: Film studios-Rs. 176,500,000-00; Production, distribution-Rs. 160,000,000-00; Cinemas-Rs. 203,150,000-00 for a total of Rs. 540,000,000-00. Number of full and part time employees in Pakistan cinemas is estimated to be 14,625. Average monthly salary of these employees is Rs. 511,875,000-00. Average capacity of a city and village cinema is estimated at 600 and 300, respectively. Foreign films (excluding Indian) are imported on rental and outright purchases basis. Rental basis is on three conditions: a) titles are approved by the National Film Development Corporation (NRFDEC), b) 70% from the distributors share is allowed to be remitted, of the 30% remaining in Pakistan 20% is alllowed to distributors for local expenses and 10% goes to the NAFDEC as service charges, c) MPEA will have to supply the same number of films to NAFDEC on the same conditions. Pakistani agents of MPEA also get the same facilities. Private parties are also allowed (since 1979) to import films from non-MPEA companies on two conditions: 1. Titles are approved by the NAFDEC, which also have their physical distribution, 2. without any investment NAFDEC charges 30% as its service commission on the gross. Under the new scheme, the private importer can sell the movies (if NAFDEC approves the price), on which the importer will have to pay 30% to NAFDEC.

During the year under review NAFDEC imported about 66 films, but due to long runs of films could release hardly 41 films. UA's "Live And Let Die" proved the biggest boxoffice hit of 1980/81, by collecting a sum of Rs. 821,903 (excluding ent. tax) during its 22 weeks run.

Production: Due to higher cost of production, strict censorship, telecasts twice a week of Indian films from Amritsar (India) TV and once a week on Oman TV, exhibition of new Indian and foreign films on VCRs and shy finances, the number of films, as predicted on this page last year, has gone down considerably in 1980/81 and is expected to go down further because of the new censor code. Up to June 30, 1981, (in 6 months) only 21 new films were released as compared to 25 last year. Chances of lifting the ban on old Indian films (with Islamic background) have brightened after the extraordinary success of the Indian film "Noorjehan" and decertification of about 150 Pakistani films. However, the Government has made it clear that new films with Indian artists will not be allowed to be exhibited in Pakistan.

There are about 700 old Indian films in Pakistan that were decertified after the 1965 conflict between the two countries. The new Indian film, "Kashish," which was released on May 30, 1981 under special permission, broke all previous records for flops throughout the country, by losing a sum of Rs. 10 millions of those third parties and cinemas.

Taxes: Like most other countries, the Pakistan film industry is a heavily taxed trade. The rate of entertainment tax remained 150% in Punjab and NWFP on admission, 100% on Sind and fixed capacity system (from 15 to 60%) in Baluchistan. The highest rate of admission, including entertainment tax, was raised to Rs.12.00 and Rs. 7.50 in the cinemas situated in Cantonmene and Provincial areas, respectively. The fee for granting new theatre licenses remained at Rs. 25,000. Fees for renewal of licenses also remained the same at Rs. 3000 and Rs. 2,000 for urban and rural areas respectively. Under the new Film Censorship Rules, 1980, also, cinemas licensed as "foreign houses" have to allot a minimum 15% of their playing time to Pakistani films. Similarly, those showing Pakistani pictures can screen foreign films (other than Indian) in their 15% playing time. But hardly an exhibitor abides by this rule. The Sind Government has abolished the fixed tax of Rs. 1000/- per year on cinemas from July 1, 1981.

Censorship: With the formation of the latest censor code, 1981, framed under Islamic laws and levying heavier punishment and fines, problems for inexperienced producers have increased. Importers, who used to bring "sexy" and "lawless" thrillers, will also be affected. Once again the Pakistan film industry has reiterated use of the same yardstick for domestic as well as foreign films. The Central Board of Film Censors has decertified hundreds of imported and domestic films for "violence and vulgarity." The board at Islamabad examines foreign and objectionable Pakistani films. Lahore and Karachi continued to censor films made at their stations for exhibition throughout the country. Certificates are, however, issued from Islamabad. The screening and censorship fees, which were Rs. 300 and Rs. 40 per 1,000 feet feature film, were doubled in early 1980.

Future: The Pakistan film industry is coming out of the worst ever crisis during the year under review of strict censorship and increase in the cost of production, shortage of cinemas, high taxes and the dictates of NAFDEC. The PICIC, IDBP and commercial banks do not finance film makers. Lahore studios have come to life with production activities. Activities on the front of Urdu films are likely to increase in Karachi with the shifting of top producers, artistes, directors and technicians. Lahore may remain the centre of production for Punjabi films, if censorship rules are liberalised. The Ministry of Culture is expected to take over the control of the entire film business, including licenses, foreign film festival participations, holding the festivals of Pakistani films in foreign lands, scrutiny of film scripts, registration of producers, etc. The position of import may not be improved in spite of a liberalised policy for non-availability of cinemas and strict terms of NAFDEC.f

The MPEA offices in Pakistan and their agents here are not happy with the present system of rental for various reasons, including the conditions of the NAFDEC. The conditions on the domestic front can be improved only if the film makers are given incentives, like state awards, loans, tax holidays, facilities for co-productions, training institutes, etc.

Film Industry Organisations: Pakistan Film Producers' Association is supposed to be the prime body of the industry. The other Associations are: Pakistan Film Distributions' Association, Pakistan Film Exhibitors' Association, Pakistan Film Importers' Group, Pakistan Film Writers' Association, Pakistan Film Directors' Association, Pakistan Film Artistes' Association and Film Journalists' Association. Most of these Associations have their office at Lahore and Karachi. Head offices of all are supposed to be shifted between Karachi and Lahore on alternate years but very little attention is paid to the regulations. Producers' Association is situated at Regal Cinema Building, The Mall, Lahore; Distributors' Association at Rattan Cinema Building, McLeod Road, Lahore; Exhibitors' Association at Lyric Cinema Building, Garden Road, Karachi. Importers' at Dayal Singh Mansion, The Mall, Lahore, while the office of the Film Journalists' Association is situated at Lyric Cinema Building Karachi.

—A. R. SLOTE

PHILIPPINES

Number of Theatres in Operation: 919.
Number of Features Produced: 137.
Number of Features Imported: 385.

Higher production costs, increasing imports and taxes have seriously jeopardized movie-producing in the Philippines and several studios have closed or turned into rental properties, but several new studios have sprung up. Box office gross, on the whole, seems to have picked up somewhat.

Average admission tax is 28%–30%. The Board of Censors is strict and extend supervision to posters and stills which must bear censor's stamp. Movie censorship in the Philippines, in response to the objectives of the "New Society," has assumed, in addition to its basic function of elevating the moral quality of human life, a new and unique role: that of promoting the artistic standards of Filipino films. Some 62 producing companies now engaged in making domestic features. Customs duty is 29 centavos per linear meter in 35mm film and 58 centavos for 70mm. Earnings are no longer blocked and may be remitted but the change in the exchange rates has raised prices of imports 45%–50% in local currency.

Local producers operate on a shoestring budget, about 1/10 of a picture produced in the West. The longest shooting time is from three to four months. Quickies are made in a fortnight, shooting night and day. Local movie industry is one of the most heavily taxed. Roughly 26% of its earnings go to privilege, custom, censorship, municipal and footage taxes. Theatres screen on the average of 650 features yearly. Local films accounted for 28%, foreign 32%. Theatres charge one of the lowest admission fees in the world: 20¢ without air conditioning; 40¢ with air conditioning; blockbusters, $1.25.

The Filipino Academy of Movie Arts and Sciences (FAMAS), Philippine Movie Producers Association and the Philippine Movie Press Club (PMPC) are active.

Principal Cinema Producers: Am Productions, FPJ Productions, Hemisphere Pictures, HPS Productions, Juver-Junar, JE Productions, Crown Seven Film Productions, Lea, NV Productions, RVQ, Roma, Tagalog Ilang-Ilang, Cubao Cinema, Imus, Regal Films Inc., Emperor Films, Alaminos, Luis San Juan, MBM, MVN, Pacific Films, Sampaguita-VP Pictures, GPS, Metropolitan Films, Rosas Productions, El Oro, JPM, Seven Star, Film Entertainment, Liliw, King Richard, Rive Gauche, Associates & Celso Ad Castillo, PPI, Alleluia, Wonder Films, Pera Films, Margarita, Robert Films, RPM Film Productions, S.Q. Film Prod., R. L. Castañeda, Festival YLY, Vera-Cruz, DSF, Maglinao Enterprises, Diamond, Villa Films and Dynamic Films.

Distributors, Importers: Columbia Film Exchange, Mever Films, UDIA, United Artists and Warner Bros.

POLAND

Number of Theatres in Operation: 3,232, including film theatres and halls. All are state-owned and operated. They comprise 460,200 urban and 162,700 rural seats.

Box Office Attendance: Ticket sales annually exceed 125,000,000. (Population of Poland is 34,000,000.)

Production: Film Polski, which comes under the Supreme Cinematography Authority, as set up by the Ministry of Culture and The Arts, makes about 35 features a year. Studios are at Lodz, Wroclaw and Warsaw.

Film Imports: Most of the foreign features shown here come from other Socialist Republics. Only a small number of American movies is acquired.

PUERTO RICO

Number of Theatres in Operation: 146.
Number of Distributors: 20.

Film Imports: An increase of 20 percent in imports from the United States mainland, principal market and source of supply for the motion picture industry, was registered due to great number of movies used by television stations. Features from Mexico, Spain, Argentina, England, Italy also increased slightly, in the importation registers.

Several of the United States distributors operating in San Juan also ship some of the features and newsreels to U.S. Virgin Islands, Dominican Republic and other adjacent islands where they operate branch offices.

Censorship: None on imports from the United States. The Custom House officials require the screening of foreign films before exhibition. A bill has been introduced in the Puerto Rican legislature to establish a movies censorship board. Customs fees and other duties: U.S. imports pay 2 cents per linear foot. Imports from foreign countries pay the same tax, plus the U.S. tariff duty of one-half cent per linear foot.

Admission Taxes: 20% tax in admission if charge exceeds 20 cents; if less than 20 cents no admission tax is paid, according to legislation enacted this year. Principal Industry organizations: Film Board of Trade; Cobian Film Center, Puerta de Tierra, San Juan, P.R.; MP Operators Union (AFL-CIO) has collective bargaining pact with all exhibitors.

SINGAPORE

Number of Theatres in Operation: 75.
Annual Admissions: 40 million.
Singapore's population of 2.2 million people each averaged an astounding 19 visits a year to the cinema for an estimated 40 million total. Tickets run from 69¢ to $1.61.

SOUTH KOREA

Number of Theatres: 491.
Seating Capacity: 312,000.
Commercial Features Produced: 116.
Cultural Features Produced: 30.
Imported Features: 30.
Annual Film Attendance: 75,000,000.
Trends: In the Republic of Korea admission prices are decided by national laws based on the production cost of each feature film, though theatre owners are now petitioning for the right to decide their own admission charges. Average ticket runs about $1.70 for domestic films, or $2.55 for imports. There is an admission tax of 10% and a cultural tax levy of 17¢ per ticket which brings tax to an average 17%.

Booking is not controlled by the government and contracts between producer and theatre owner are private, averaging 55% to the former and 45% of receipts to the theatre. Since ROK has a population of some 40 million, this means each visits a movie theatre 2.3 times a year.

There are now 20 film producers in ROK and no free lance or independents are allowed by the government, and these make up the Korean Motion Picture Association. Formation of studios requires government consent. Average cost of a domestic feature is $240,000 to $300,000, double that of four years ago. Only film producers are allowed to import pictures from abroad, and imports are kept to about a third of domestic production with the government allocating import permits and foreign exchange for payment. Of 31 films imported last year, 17 were American. In 1978 ROK exported 28 of its films, mostly to Asia. All films shown are subject to censorship by the Ministry of Culture & Information. Inquiries should be addressed to the Motion Picture Promotion Corporation of Korea, Seoul. The ROK Government is itself a cultural film producers with its Korea Film Unit with an annual budget of $3.2 million. Imported films are distributed in their original language with Korean subtitles. Korean television depends on imports almost entirely since domestic commercial films are rarely shown on TV.

SPAIN

Number of Theatres in Operation: 4,288, compared with 4,430 in 1978.
Attendance in 1979: 200,485,325, compared with 220,110,077 in 1978.
Picture Grosses in 1979: 22,418 million pesetas (Spanish films: 3,651 million), compared with 20,825 million in 1978 (Spanish films: 4,520). American films grosses are about one third of foreign films grosses.
Private Theatres in Operation: Near 6,500 (16 or 35 mm.) in youth clubs, schools, colleges, parishes, etc.
Features Produced in 1980: 118. In 1979 were produced 89 features, and 107 in 1978.
Features Released in 1980: 419, compared with 570 in 1979, and with 401 in 1978. The number of Spanish releases was 114.
Current Situation: It is a fact that foreign quality films arrive now in Spain sooner than before, thanks to the disappearance of former censorship strictures. For instance, almost all the films with Oscar nominations in 1981 were on the screens prior to the Academy gala night, from "Ordinary Peple," "Raging Bull" and "Coal Miner's Daughter" to "Tess," "Kagemusha" and "Le Dernier Métro." Besides, the year 1980 saw two major breakthroughs in cinema restrictions: the releases of Oshima's "The Empire of the Senses" and Pasolini's "Salo or The 120 Days of Sodoma." Information and receptivity of Spanish audiences is now at European level. There is also a steady flow of soft-core porn films, classified "S" (similar to "X" abroad), national and foreign, catering to the low tastes of "dirty old" and not-so-old Spaniards.

Among the 114 Spanish films released in 1980, only a handful were box office hits, and some of them got awards at international Festivals (Montreal, Berlin, Venice) and even Academy nominations. Of these films 36 were co-produced: 18 with Italy, 6 with France, 7 with Mexico, 2 with the United States, and the rest with

other countries. All the released Spanish films get a subsidy of 15 per cent of their box office receipts, with double subsidy for "special" films, and cash awards to "quality" product. More help comes from the exhibition and distribution quotas: a) One Spanish film exhibited for each four foreign ones, in a quarterly basis; b) An one-to-three quota for distributors.

The dubbing licenses to import foreign fare are granted to the producers of Spanish films according to budgets. Many small production companies are making quick product just for the licenses, for if a major film can get five licenses, five films at lower budgets can be granted 15 permits. The "quickies" are usually so lacking in quality that many remain on the shelves, and others even turn off audiences. Another serious competition comes from Spanish TV, which programmes about 200 film features a year, mainly on weekends.

Admission Prices: "Frozen" for years due to an official policy promoting cheap popular entertainment, the rate for first-run houses was 75 pesetas in 1971, raised to 100 pesetas in 1974, to 125 in 1977, to 150 in 1978, to 180 in 1979 and to 200 in 1980 ($2.10 at the Summer '81 exchange rate). Most first-run houses give separate performances twice daily, with matinees in Saturdays and holidays.
Government Departments: Director General of Film and Book Promotion, Matias Vallés, Ministry of Culture, Paseo de la Castellana 109, Madrid 16.
Junta de Clasificación (Classification Board).—This official body reviews all imported and domestic films, sorting them under four lines: "apt for all people," "apt for people over 14," "apt for people over 16," "apt for people over 18." As it was said above, films that could hurt sensitive audiences in matters of sex or violence are rated "S." In certain films children and young people are admitted to the next age level if accompanied by an adult.
Consejo Nacional de Cinematografia.—This reorganized body assumes the activities of the former "Consejo Coordinador de la Cinematografia" and the "Instituto Nacional de Cinematografia." It has an advisory function in all matters of the film industry. It must be heard preceptively on general governing conditions for Spanish film production and exhibition. The Consejo Nacional has taken an important part in the redaction of current film laws. Secretariat: Paseo de la Castellana 109, Madrid 16.
Cinespaña S.A.—This revitalized agency deals with the sales of Spanish film produce. Offices in Gran Via 42, Madrid 13.
Escuela Oficial de Cinematografia.—This institution taught the theory and practice of filmmaking. Its task has been absorbed by the Facultad de Ciencias de la Informaciń (College of Information Sciences) at the University of Madrid.

—MARIANO DEL POZO

SRI LANKA (Ceylon)

Number of Theatres: 385 are permanent cinemas; 8 are touring tents.
Number of Feature Films Produced in 1980: 70 Sinhalese and 5 Tamils.
Number of Locally Produced Features Released in 1980: Sinhalese 30; Tamil 4.
Number of Features Imported: 84 English, 8 Tamil-(Indian); 1 Hindhi (Indian).
Total Number of Tickets Sold: 80,000,000.
Total Gross Collection (State Film Corporation and others): Rs. 240,000,000 (US $12,631,584).
Number of people Seeing Films Daily: 127,880 Sinhalese; 43,235 Tamils; 45,345 others. An average of 76½ of the population see films in Sri Lanka.
Average Cost to Produce a Sinhalese Feature Film: Rs. 650,000 ($34,210) for a black and white film and Rs. 1,200,000 ($63,157) for a colour film.
Average Receipts for a Sinhalese Film: Rs. 3,000,000 ($157,894).
The Government has recognised the film industry in Sri Lanka. The Presidential awards of 1980 were the greatest honour bestowed on the national cinema. The continuation of the National Film Festival and awards yearly gave evidence of this recognition.

The State Film Corporation Act of 1972 is to be amended to set up a National Film Corporation. The colour film era has commenced in Sri Lanka. Producing colour films for local screening is not satisfactory, as the cost of production is exorbitant; therefore a foreign market for local Sinhala colour films has to be found if it is to be profitable. State Film Corporation did not suffer any loss, and, in fact, Rs. 7.3 million profits were made in 1979. A number of film seminars were held to find ways and means of increasing the standards of Sinhala films and to improve the tastes of audiences while providing entertainment and to provide better facilities for filmgoers.

All foreign film companies obtain clearances from the Ministry of State and Ministry of Foreign Affairs and the main requirement is that the producers provide a bank guarantee that they will take back the equipment they brought into the country. While a lot of useful publicity for the country as been obtained as a result of such television productions, there have been instances when some damage has been done. The Government is concerned about a skilled and effective campaign launched in Europe and America to suggest that the Tamils here are subject to various disabilities.

At present many foreign film companies are making films on location in Sri Lanka, including a film on the mass suicides in Georgetown. An Italian film company made three films on location here, which turned out to be top box office pictures: "The Mountain in the Jungle", "The Bridge at River Cayne" and "George Town Suicide" film. A Sinhala film titled "Beddegama", or "The Village in the Jungle", based on the story written by the British Civil Servant, Leonard Wolf, produced in colour and directed by Srilankan Lester James Peiris, was sold to many European countries recently, including the U.K. and Germany.

Board of Directors of the State Film Corporation: Anton Wickramasinghe (Chairman and Chief Executive); D. H. Abeyasinghe, Dr. P. L. Peiris, Dr. D. L. Abeyawardhena, D. T. L. Guruge, R. D. K. Jayawardhena, Mrs. Iranganie Serasinghe, Joe Abeyawickrema, Anura Gunasekera (Director of Information), Mrs. Savithri Samasundera (Secretary), W. B. Ratnayake (General Manager), Piyasiri Gunaratne, Mgr. (Film Studios and Laboratories "Sarasavi Studios" owned by the State Film Corporation) Wijeratne Warakagoda, Manager Film Production.

Producers of Local Films: Government Film Unit, Department of Information, Kirillapone, Colombo 6. Produce Documentary and News reels. Studios and Laboratories at Kirillapone, Colombo 6. Director in Charge of Film Unit: Mrs. Manel Abeyaratne, Director Consultant to the Film Unit: George Wickramasinghe.

Cinemas Ltd, Ceylon Theatres Ltd, Cine Lanka Ltd., DNFC Films, Globe International Films, Sena Samarasinghe Films, Cinetra- Telecinex. Kelaniya

Ministry of State (Films, Information and Broadcasting); Minister: Anandatissa de Alwis; Secretary Ministry of State: Sarath Amunugama; Director of Information: Anura Gunasekera. Address: Sir Baron Jayatileke Mawatha, Colombo 1. State Film Corporation is directly under the President H.E.J.R. Jayawardhena.

Film Equipment Hirers: Vijay Studios, Hendala, Wattala, Sri Lanka, Ceylon Studios Ltd., Kirula Road, Comobo 5—(Studio facilities, & equipment hire) Government films division, Kirllapone, Colombo 5 (Laboratory and camera hire); Sampan Film Equipment Services, Kundasale, Kandy, (lights and cranes, dolly, etc); Sumitta Enterprises, 12/1, 5th Lane, Kotte, Sri Lanka (lights and equipment).

Liasoning, Services for Foreign Production in Sri Lanka, Producers of Films for Foreign Exhibition and Television: News, documentary, television, commercial and feature films) photo safaris, tours, liaisoning, financing, location scouting for foreign films. All film production services and facilities, joint venture finance for foreign co-production, promotion for foreign producers. Chandra S. Perera, Cinetratelecinex, 437 Pethiyagoda, Kelaniya, Sri Lanka. Cables: "TELECINEX"—Colombo or "TF 7285 KELANIYA", PHONE: 075-7285.

—CHANDRA S. PERERA

SWEDEN

Attendance: Following a brief recovery in 1978–79 attendance at Sweden's 1,200 film theatres declined in the year to June 1980 by 159,000 to a total of 24,900,000 admissions.

Ticket Prices: Up from $3.61 average in 1978–79 to $3.95 in 1979–80.

Box Office Receipts: In 1979–80 up 6.6 per cent from year before to $98,316,000.

Local Production: Number took a big jump: from 14 to 21 pictures released. Market share, however, dropped from 16.4 to 12 per cent for local product. Total number of films released in the country was up from 250 in 1978–79 to 284.

SWITZERLAND

Number of the Theatres in Operation: 483.
Number of the Features Imported: 440.

Censorship: In peace time there is no national censorship. Authorities of the cantons, or of the towns or communities, censor, but almost only when action is brought against the film by some citizens or local associations or religious authorities. There is a Catholic and

a Protestant Organization with a central film bureau which classifies the films like the old American Legion of Decency and which has great influence on a large number of exhibitors. Censorship is practiced on moral and religious grounds, but seldom on a political basis. Censorship has been completely abolished in some parts of Switzerland (the cantons of Bern, Aargau, Basel-Stadt, Luzern, Solothurn, Zug and Zürich, St. Gallen, Basel-Land).

Customs and Other Duties: Duty on all imported films is charged by length, but there are some additional taxes.

Admission Taxes: 12 per cent generally, in many cantons or communities 20 per cent.

Legislation: There is a national law concerning motion pictures since January 1, 1963. The cantonal authorities rule over admission of children to the theatres; generally the limit is 16 years, in some cantons, 18. There are other laws which are concerned with theatres safety.

Government Departments: The national Commission for Films, a branch of the cultural ministry. Although the Commission is not a legislative body, it acts in a consultative capacity, deciding questions of a general nature (preparation of the national film law, arbitration committee in controversies between the theatres owners and distributors etc.). The Commission consists of 25 representatives of the industry (production, distribution and exhibition).

Industry Organization: Association Suisse des Techniciens du Film; Josefstr. 106, 8031 Zürich, President: Madeleine Fonjallaz; Association des Producteurs Suisses de Films et d'AV, Löwenstrasse 53, 8023 Zürich, Schweiz. Filmverleiher-Verband (distributors-Associat.), Schwarztorstrasse 7, Postfach 2485, 3001 Bern, President: Marc Wehrlin; Schweiz. Lichtspieltheater-Verband (Exhibitors of German and Italian Switzerland), Postfach 2674, 3001 Bern, President: Manfred Fink; Association Cinématographique Suisse Romande (French-Swiss Exhibitors), 5, Place de la Riponne, 1000 Lausanne, President: W.-P. Wachtl.

—GERDA GOEPFERT-KLIMISCH

SYRIA

Number of Theatres in Operation: 70.

Local Exchange Regulations: Syria is still controlling the foreign Currencies. U.S. Dollars and Sterling Pounds are consequently under the complete control of the Government. For importing Pictures, applications should be submitted to the competent authorities to obtain the necessary License and the Foreign currencies.

Local Censorship: Is based on a decree issued in 1934 which provides conditions for exhibition of pictures. Censorship Visa is usually granted for sympathize crime against the law, religion, etc.

Local Production: In spite of the Government effort for encouraging local production, this industry remains very limited. Only documentaries and some agricultural subjected pictures are released. Pictures exploited are imported from USA, Egypt, France, England, India and Italy.

Taxes on Pictures: Importers pay LS.25.—(about $.10.) per kilogram as censor charges and similar amount as Customs duty.

Admissions Are as Follows: First class theaters' admissions are limited from 50 to 100 piasters; for 2nd-class theatres, it is from 35 to 50.

Taxes on Admissions: Finance Ministry collects 15 pts. per seat and Municipality collects 200 Pounds as entertainment tax.

Associations: Theatre owners have two associations, one in Damascus and the other in Aleppo. Workers associations are three, located in Damascus, Aleppo and Lattaquieh.

WEST GERMANY

Number of Theatres in Operation: 3,422 in the Federal Republic and West Berlin in 1980, according to SPIO (Spitzenorganisation der Filmwirtschaft, see: Principal industry organizations). This compares to 1,150 theatres in 1945. In addition 23 drive-ins were operating.

Breakdown of Theatre Capacity: 1,945 seating under 300; 875 in the 301-500 category; 289 with 501 to 750 and another 71 with 751 to 1,000 seats. Only 6 cinemas seat more than 1,000, all of them in the major cities.

Admission Prices: Average ticket in 1980 cost about $3.15, up from $2.98 in 1979.

Attendance: Some 143,777,000 tickets were sold in 1980, an increase of about 1.3 percent from the amount sold in 1980. (Population of West Germany is 60,000,000.) Box office gross for 1980 was $452,585,000, up 6.7 percent over 1979.

Production Costs: The average German film costs about $1,000,000 to make, up from about $900,000 in 1979 and $600,000 six years ago. In practice, budgets for individual projects vary widely. R.W. Fassbinder's latest, "Lili Marleen" cost about $5,000,000 to make, and Wolfgang Petersen's "The Boat" cost $10,000,000, and is said to be the highest single post-war picture budget.

Principal Studios: Ammersee-Filmatelier GmbH, Herrschinger Str. 12, Inning/Obb.; Arnold & Richter KG, Turkenstr. 89, Munchen 13; Ateher Betriebsges. Bendestorf mbH, Bendestorf b. Hamburg; Bavaria Atelier Gesellschaft mbH, Bavaria-Film-Platz 7, Geiselgasteig b. Munchen; Berliner Union-Film GmbH & Co. Studio KG, Oberlandstr 26-35, Berlin 42; Carlton Film GmbH & Co. Atelier KG, Wurzerstr. 17, Munchen 22; CCC-Film-Studio GmbH, Verl. Daumstr. 16, Berlin 20; Filmstudio Wiesbaden, Unter den Eichen. Wiesbaden; Grundstucksgesellschaft Pichelsberg Reitman KG, Knesebeckstr. 30, Berlin 12; Riva film-und lichttechnische Betriebe GmbH, Unterfoehring b. Munchen; Studio Hamburg Atelierbetriebs GmbH, Tonndorfer Hauptstr. 90, Hamburg 70.

Government Departments: Bundesministerium des Innern Ministerialrat Guenter Fuchs. Auswaertiges Amt, Dr. Reichelt, Bonn. Bundesministerium der Wirtschaft Regierungsdirektor Hans Schuessler, Bonn. Bundesministerium für gesamtdeutsche Fragen, Ministerialrat Guenter Zaluskowski, Bonn. Deutscher Bundestag, Auschuss fuer Kulturpolitik und Publizistik, Ulrich Lohmar, Bundeshaus. Bonn: Filmfoerderunsanstalt; Berlin 301, P.B87. Tel. 136006, Chairman J. Raffert.

Principal Industry Organizations: Spitzenorganisation der Filmwirtschaft e. V. (SPIO) (the central representation of Western German motion picture industry, producer, distributor, theatre and supply organizations) Verband Deutscher Spielfilmproduzenten e. V., Arbes'ts gerne usdraft nene dentsiles Spiel film produfenber. Verband Deutscher Dokumentarund Kurzfilm-produzenten e.V., Verband Deutscher Werbefilmproduzenten e.V., Vereinigung der Industriefilmproduzenten e.V. (producers); Verband der Filmverlieher e.V. (distributors); Hauptverband Duetscher Filmtheater e.V., (theatres); Alle: Wiesbaden, Langenbeckstr. 9-Verband Technischer Betriebe für Film und Fernsehen e.V., Berlin 15, Kurfurstendamm 179-Deutsche Kinotechnische Gesellschaft für Film and Fernsehen e.V., Berlin 15, Schaperstr. 15-Arbeitsgemeinschaft neuer deutscher Spiel-filmproduzenten e.V., Munchen-Berlin, Munchen-Berlin, Munchen 13, Ainmillerstr. 6-Deutsches Institut f ur Filmkunde e.V., Wiesbaden-Biebrich. Schloss-Deutsche Union der Filmschaffenden, Munchen 22, Schwanthalerstr. 64-66-Export-Union der Deutschen Filmindustrie e.V., Wiesbaden, Langenbeckstr. 9-Filmbewertungsstelle Wiesbaden (FBW), Wiesbaden-Biebrich, Schloss-Freiwillige Selbstkontrolle der Filmwirtschaft (FLK), Wiesbaden-Biebrich, Schloss-Friedrich Wilhelm-Murnau-Stiftung, Wiesbaden, Langenbeckstr. 9- GEMA (corresponding to ACAP in USA), Berlin 30, Bayreuther Str. 37/38- Internationale Filfestspiele Berlin, Berlin 15, Bundesalle 1-12-Verband der Deutschen Film-Clubs e.V., Frankfurt (Main), Jim Sachsenlager 13.